ANNOTATED LEADING CASES OF

INTERNATIONAL CRIMINAL TRIBUNALS

VOLUME LXIX

INTERNATIONAL CRIMINAL TRIBUNAL
FOR THE FORMER YUGOSLAVIA /
INTERNATIONAL RESIDUAL MECHANISM
FOR CRIMINAL TRIBUNALS

30 June 2016 – 29 November 2017

ANNOTATED LEADING CASES OF

INTERNATIONAL CRIMINAL TRIBUNALS

VOLUME LXIX

INTERNATIONAL CRIMINAL TRIBUNAL FOR THE FORMER YUGOSLAVIA / INTERNATIONAL RESIDUAL MECHANISM FOR CRIMINAL TRIBUNALS

30 June 2016 – 29 November 2017

André KLIP/ Steven FREELAND (editors)

Enikő Deák (assistant-editor)

INTERSENTIA

Cambridge – Antwerp – Chicago

Intersentia Ltd
8 Wellington Mews | Wellington Street
Cambridge | CB1 1HW | United Kingdom
Tel.: +44 1223 736 170
Email: mail@intersentia.co.uk
www.intersentia.com | www.intersentia.co.uk

Distribution for the UK and the rest of the world (incl. Eastern Europe):
NBN International
1 Deltic Avenue, Rooksley
Milton Keynes MK13 8LD
United Kingdom
Tel.: +44 1752 202 301 | Fax: +44 1752 202 331
Email: orders@nbninternational.com

Distribution for Europe:
Lefebvre Sarrut Belgium NV
Hoogstraat 139/6
1000 Brussels
Belgium
Tel.: +32 (0)2 548 07 13
Email: mail@intersentia.be

Distribution for the USA and Canada
Independent Publishers Group
Order Department
814 North Franklin Street
Chicago, IL 60610
USA
Tel.: +1 800 888 4741 (toll free) | Fax: + 1312 337 5985
Email: orders@ipgbook.com

Please cite as: Decision on Defence Motion for a Fair Trial and the Presumption of Innocence or, in the alternative, a Mistrial, *Prosecutor v. Mladić*, Case No. IT-09–92-T, T. Ch. I, 4 July 2016 in Klip/Freeland ALC-LXIX-9.

International Criminal Tribunal for the Former Yugoslavia / International Residual Mechanism for Criminal Tribunals 30 June 2016 – 29 November 2017
© The editors and contributors severally 2022

Cover design: Grafische Vormgeving bv

ISBN 978-1-83970-216-7
D/2023/7849/22
NUR 828

British Library Cataloguing in Publication Data. A catalogue record for this book is available from the British Library.

TABLE OF CONTENTS

Fair Trial Matters and Disqualification of Judges

Provisional Release / Early Release / Sentence Remission

Judgement I – Stanišić and Župljanin

Judgement II – Prlić et al. (part one)

PREFACE

This is the sixty-ninth volume in the series 'Annotated Leading Cases of International Criminal Tribunals' and contains the most important decisions of the International Criminal Tribunal for the Former Yugoslavia (ICTY) / International Residual Mechanism for Criminal Tribunals (MICT) handed down in the period 30 June 2016 – 29 November 2017. It is the twenty-seventh volume in the series containing decisions of the ICTY/MICT. Given the ongoing jurisprudential output of that institution, a number of further volumes on ICTY/MICT case law will be published in the series.

This volume is in its approach and structure similar to previous volumes when we slightly changed our process. Thus, the book contains the full text of all the annotated decisions and judgements, including any separate, concurring and dissenting opinions, as well as annexes to the decisions. As with previous volumes, the Editors have ensured that the decisions are identical to the *written* original text, as issued by the ICTY/ MICT Press and Information Office, and which bears the signatures of the Judges, as only these can be considered as authoritative versions. In the course of our editorial work on this and previous volumes, we have occasionally discovered inconsistencies between the written original version of the decision and any available internet versions.

Although we are only able to include the full text of the decisions by reducing their original format, we wanted the reader to be able to identify the page number of the original text, which is placed in brackets [ ].

We are very pleased that a number of distinguished international law scholars were prepared to write interesting and stimulating commentaries regarding these decisions and believe that their contributions will add to the breadth of knowledge and understanding about the work of the ICTY/MICT.

A few words regarding the selection of decisions in the ALC volumes are appropriate given the fact that we have decided to change the policy concerning the publication of judgements. In earlier volumes for other courts and tribunals, we selected all final judgements, rendered by both the Trial Chamber as well as by the Appeals Chamber in the same case. In view of the fact that more and more judgements deal with established case law, and in light of the space all the judgements cover in the series, we have decided no longer to select judgements at the Trial Chamber stage in cases in which there is already an existing Appeals Chamber judgement. The commentator to the latter judgement is invited to include a comparison of the Trial and Appeals Chamber judgements in his or her contribution. In doing so, we expect to be able to focus more on the key issues that are at stake in the case at hand. In addition, we expect to be able to publish the volumes sooner following the handing down of the relevant Appeals Chamber judgement.

With regard to other decisions, the existing policy will be maintained. This means that, additionally, we will continue to publish decisions taken at any stage of the proceedings that are important for other reasons: because they deal with a specific legal question, because they are representative of a specific type of decision, or because they enter new legal waters. As a result, we may not publish decisions in which issues have been decided in a way similar or identical to a decision that has already been selected.

The decisions annotated in this volume cover a range of considerations arising from proceedings before the ICTY/MICT. A number of these address issues related to fair trial rights and the disqualification of Judges, as well as matters pertaining to provisional release, sentence remission and early release. It also includes the Appeals Chamber Judgement in the *Stanišić and Župljanin* case, as well as the first part of the very lengthy Appeals Chamber Judgement in the *Prlić et al.*, case (the second part of that judgement and the commentary will appear in Volume 70 of this series).

Once again, we gratefully acknowledge the assistance of many people without whom we could not have completed this volume. These include the Press and Information Office of the ICTY/MICT, which offered generous assistance in obtaining all the necessary copies of decisions, our publisher Intersentia, in particular Margit Bal and Isabelle van Dongen, and also our excellent former Assistant Editor, Victoria Häberle, who recently left us to pursue her studies and career. We certainly wish Victoria well and thank her for her excellent assistance. We have also welcomed Enikő Deák as our new Assistant Editor and are enjoying working with her.

Of course, we would again like to thank the distinguished authors for their commentaries on the decisions, and their cooperation throughout the process.

We hope that this volume will contribute to the further dissemination of the important work of the ICTY/ MICT, and that it will provide access to its decisions to practitioners, academics and students.

We continue to make every effort to maintain the high standard of previous volumes, and the Editors welcome feedback and suggestions as to how the ALC series can be continuously improved, so as to maximise its value to readers. The ALC is the largest case law series on international criminal jurisprudence in the world, and it is our on-going aim to make it as useful as possible to all persons interested in the work of the various institutions.

We therefore hope that you will find this volume to be a significant addition to your research resources in this ever more important area of international law.

André Klip and Steven Freeland

Maastricht/Sydney, December 2021

andre.klip@maastrichtuniversity.nl

s.freeland@westernsydney.edu.au

UNITED
NATIONS

International Tribunal for the Prosecution of Persons Responsible for Serious Violations of International Humanitarian Law Committed in the Territory of the former Yugoslavia since 1991	Case No. IT-09-92-T Date: 4 July 2016 Original: English

IN TRIAL CHAMBER I

Before: **Judge Alphons Orie, Presiding**
                 Judge Bakone Justice Moioto
                 Judge Christoph Flügge

Registrar: **Mr. John Hocking**

Decision of: **4 July 2016**

PROSECUTOR

v.

RATKO MLADIĆ

PUBLIC

DECISION ON DEFENCE MOTION FOR A FAIR TRIAL AND THE PRESUMPTION OF INNOCENCE OR, IN THE ALTERNATIVE, A MISTRIAL

Office of the Prosecutor
Mr Peter McCloskey
Mr Alan Tieger

Counsel for Ratko Mladić
Mr Branko Lukić
Mr Miodrag Stojanović

[page 1]I. PROCEDURAL HISTORY

1.   On 19 May 2016, the Defence filed a motion ("Motion") alleging that the fair-trial rights of Ratko Mladić ("Accused") have been violated by the integration of chamber staff who previously worked for the trial chamber seised of the case of *Prosecutor v. Radovan Karadžić ("Karadžić* case") into the present case, and requesting certain information or, in the alternative, that the Chamber declare a mistrial[1] On 31 May 2016, the Prosecution responded ("Response"), opposing the Motion.[2] On 7 June 2016, the Defence requested leave to reply ("Request to Reply"),[3] attaching its reply as an annex ("Reply").[4]

II. SUBMISSIONS OF THE PARTIES

2.   The Defence submits that most of the chamber staff who drafted the trial judgement in the *Karadžić* case ("Impugned Staff") are currently assisting the judges in the present case by providing substantive legal support upon which the judges' work is based[5]. The Defence argues that because the two cases are so closely related and have virtually identical indictments, and because findings were made in the *Karadžić* judgement which "for all intents and purposes convicted" the Accused, the Impugned Staff are no longer impartial towards the Accused.[6] The Defence submits that for these reasons, the influence of the Impugned Staff on the judges in the present case is an association that might affect the judges' impartiality under Rule IS(A) of the Tribunal's Rules of Procedure and Evidence ("Rules"), creating either actual bias or an objective appearance of bias against the Accused.[7] The Defence argues, therefore, that the Accused's fundamental fair trial rights have been violated.[8]

3.   To address these concerns, the Defence seeks confirmation from the Chamber that the Impugned Staff neither have worked, nor will work, on the judgement in the present case, nor discussed case-related matters with anyone who has.[9] Alternatively, the Defence seeks copies of any written undertakings that the Impugned Staff have signed prior to taking up their duties on the **[page 2]** present case, and a detailed description of all other efforts that the Chamber has taken to protect the Accused's rights ' in relation to this issue.[10] If the above requests are not granted, and if the judges in the present case might have already relied on the work of the Impugned Staff, the Defence requests that the Chamber declare a mistrial.[11] The Defence also seeks leave to exceed the word limit for motions given the "complex and subtle" issues at hand.[12]

4.   The Prosecution submits that a judge's decision-making authority is solely within the judge's purview and is not diminished or infringed upon by the assistance of personnel such as legal officers or consultants.[13] The Prosecution argues that because the presumption of impartiality is not rebutted when judges work on overlapping cases, it cannot be rebutted when those assisting the judges work on overlapping cases, in particular when the Tribunal's judges are required to provide well-reasoned opinions in writing that identify the evidentiary basis for their findings.[14] The Prosecution submits that the jurisprudence cited as support in the Motion is unpersuasive because the cases relied, upon concern chamber personnel having a direct link

---

[1]   Motion for a Fair Trial and the Presumption of Innocence or, in the Alternative, a Mistrial, 19 May 2016, paras 2831.
[2]   Prosecution Response to Defence Motion for a Fair Trial and the Presumption of Innocence, or in the Alternative, a Mistrial, 31 May 2016, para. 5.
[3]   Defence Request for Leave to Reply in Support of Motion for a Fair Trial and the Presumption of Innocence or, in the Alternative, a Mistrial, 7 June 2016, para. 6.
[4]   Defence Request for Leave to Reply in Support of Motion for a Fair Trial and the Presumption of Innocence or, in the Alternative, a Mistrial, 7 June 2016, Annex A: Reply in Support- of Motion for a Fair Trial and the Presumption of Innocence or, in the Alternative, a Mistrial.
[5]   Motion, paras 1-2, 10-12.
[6]   Motion, paras 2, 14,18, 24-26.
[7]   Motion, paras 17-28.
[8]   Motion, paras 8-9, 28.
[9]   Motion, para. 29.
[10]   Motion, para. 30.
[11]   Motion, para. 31.
[12]   Motion, para. 3.
[13]   Response, para. 2.
[14]   Response, para. 3.

to one of the parties in a case rather than the issue raised in the Motion.[15] The Prosecution submits that Defence's arguments are negated by the Tribunal's relevant jurisprudence and the Motion therefore should be dismissed.[16]

5.   The Defence submits that it should be allowed to reply in order to address certain submissions of the Prosecution concerning the critical issue of the Accused's fair trial rights.[17] In its Reply, the Defence submits that the jurisprudence cited by the Prosecution supports the Defence arguments concerning impartiality and that activities of chamber staff can violate the fairtrial rights of the Accused.[18] The Defence further submits that Prosecution's argument that judicial decisionmaking is solely within the purview of the judge is not applicable to the Chamber in the present case, which has issued decisions by emails sent by staff and interns.[19] Lastly, the Defence submits that the Prosecution has ignored its main argument about the impact of alleged staff bias on the Accused's presumption of innocence.[20] **[page 3]**

III.   APPLICABLE LAW

6.   Article 13 of the Statute of the Tribunal ("Statute") states that the Tribunal's judges shall be persons of high moral character, impartiality, and integrity. Article 21 of the Statute guarantees an accused's right to a fair trial.

7.   Rule lS(A) of the Rules . provides that:

> A Judge may not sit on a trial or appeal in any case in which the Judge has a personal interest or concerning which the judge has or has had any association which might affect his or her impartiality. The Judge shall in any such circumstance withdraw, and the President shall assign another Judge to the case.

8.   Rule lS(B) of the Rules governs the procedure for determining disqualification:

> (i)   Any party may apply to the Presiding Judge of a Chamber for the disqualification and withdrawal of a judge of that Chamber from a trial or appeal upon the above grounds. The Presiding Judge shall confer with the judge in question and report to the President.
>
> (ii) Following the report of the Presiding Judge, the President shall, if necessary, appoint a panel of three Judges drawn from other Chambers to report to him its decision on the merits of the application. If the decision is to uphold the application, the President shall assign another Judge to sit in the place of the Judge in question.
>
> (iii) The decision of the panel of three Judges shall not be subject to. interlocutory appeal.
>
> (iv) If the Judge in question is the President, the responsibility of the President in accordance with this paragraph shall be assumed by the Vice-President or, if he or she is not able to act in the application, by the permanent Judge most senior in precedence who is able to act.

9.   The Tribunal's Appeals Chamber, in considering an allegation of judicial bias in *Prosecutor v. Furundžija ("Furundžija* case"), found that an integral component of the right to a fair trial is the right of an accused to be tried before an independent and impartial tribunal.[21] The Appeals Chamber ultimately dismissed the complaint however, finding a presumption of impartiality that attaches to judges which is well-established in international and domestic jurisprudence.[22] To rebut this presumption of impartiality, such as in an application to disqualify a judge, a high threshold must be reached, showing the existence of a reasonable and firmly established apprehension of bias.[23] Accordingly, judges should not only be subjectively free from bias, but there should . be nothing which objectively gives rise to an appearance of bias.[24] Any

---

[15]   Response, para. 4.
[16]   Response, para. 5.
[17]   Request to Reply, paras 2-5.
[18]   Reply, paras 2-3.
[19]   Reply, para . 5 .
[20]   Reply, paras 6-7.
[21]   *Prosecutor v. Furundžija*, para. 177.
[22]   *Furundžija* Appeal Judgement, para. 196. *See e.g., Prosecutor v. Kordić et al.,* Case No. IT-95-14/2-PT, Decision of the Bureau, 4 May 1998, p. 2.
[23]   *Furundžija* Appeal Judgement, para. 197.
[24]   *Furundžija* Appeal Judgement, para. 189.

questions of potential bias must be considered in the context of the presumption of impartiality.[25] On this basis, the Appeals Chamber **[page 4]** considered in assessing potential bias that: (1) a judge is not impartial if it is shown that actual bias exists; and (2) there is an unacceptable appearance of bias if either:

(a) a judge is a party to the case, or has a financial or proprietary interest in the outcome of a case, or if the judge's decision will lead to the promotion of a cause in which he or she is involved, together with one of the parties, under which circumstances, a judge's disqualification from the case is automatic, or

(b) the circumstances would lead a reasonable observer,[26] properly informed, to reasonably apprehend bias.[27]

10. In *Prosecutor v. Reenzaho ("Renzaho* case"), the Appeals Chamber of the International Criminal Tribunal for Rwanda ("ICTR") dismissed an allegation that a judge was influenced by hearing evidence in a related case, and confirmed its earlier findings that a properly informed and reasonable observer would expect frequent and considerable overlap between cases at the ICTR which would not affect the impartiality of judges.[28] In dismissing similar allegations of bias stemming from judges hearing related cases, the Trial and Appeals Chambers of the Tribunal and the ICTR have clearly established that judges cannot be disqualified simply by sitting in multiple criminal trials arising out of the same series of events, even when hearing evidence relating to those events across multiple cases because, absent evidence to the contrary, a reasonable observer would presume that judges rule fairly on the issues before them by virtue of their training and experience, relying exclusively on the evidence adduced in the relevant case.[29] Not only does the training and **[page 5]** professional experience of judges give them the ability to disregard evidence from related trials, the Tribunal's requirement that they ' render well-reasoned opinions in writing explaining the basis of their findings means that they are necessarily confined to considering only the evidence in the relevant case.[30]

---

[25] *Furundžija* Appeal Judgement, para. 197.
[26] *Furundžija* Appeal Judgement, para. 190. A "reasonable person must be an informed person, with knowledge of all the relevant circumstances, including the traditions of integrity and impartiality that form a part of the background and apprised also of the fact that impartiality is one of the duties that Judges swear to uphold."
[27] *Furundžija* Appeal Judgement, para. 189. With regard to the appearance of bias, the test is "whether the reaction of the hypothetical fair-minded observer (with sufficient knowledge of the circumstances to make a reasonable judgment) would be that the judge in question might not bring an impartial and unprejudiced mind to the issues arising in the case." *Prosecutor v. Delalić et al.,* Case No. IT-96-21-A, Judgement, 20 February 2001 *("Delalić* Appeal Judgement"), para. 683. *See also Prosecutor v. Brđanin and Talić,* Case No. IT-99-36-T, Decision on Joint Motion to Disqualify, 3 May 2002, para. 26. For the requirement that such an apprehension of bias must be a reasonable one, see *Delalić* Appeal Judgement, para. 697. *See also Prosecutor v. Akayesu,* Case No. ICTR-96-4-A, Judgement 1 June 2001, para. 91; *Prosecutor v. Karemera et al.,* The Bureau, Decision on Motion by Nzirorera for Disqualification of Trial Judges of 17 May 2004, paras 8-11.
[28] *Prosecutor v. Renzaho,* Case No. ICTR-97-31-A, Judgement, 1 April 20 II, para. 22.
[29] *Prosecutor v. Šešelj,* Case No. IT-03-67-PT, Decision on Motion for Disqualification, 16 February 2007, para. 25; *Prosecutor v. Nahimana* et al.,Case No. ICTR-99-52-A, Judgement, 27 November 2008, para. 78. The ICTY Bureau had found that two judges in the *Prosecutor v. Kordić and Čerkez* case, who at the time were hearing related witnesses and evidence in the *Prosecutor v. Blaškić* case, were not precluded from hearing the case against Kordić and Čerkez. *See Prosecutor v. Kordić and Čerkez,* Case No. IT-95-14-T, Decision of the Bureau of 5 May 1998; *Prosecutor v. Kordić and Čerkez,* Case No. IT-95-14/2-PT, Decision on the Application of the Accused for Disqualification of Judges Jorda and Riad of 21 May 1998. *See also Prosecutor v. Popović et al.,* Case No. IT-05-88-A, Decision on Drago Nikolić Motion to Disqualify Judge Liu Daqun, 20 January 2011, paras 3, 7-8, 10, 12. Tribunal decisions regularly refer to the professional capacity of judges to put out of their mind evidence other than that presented in the trial before them in rendering a verdict. For example, in *Prosecutor v. Kupreškić et al.,* the Trial Chamber ruled that whatever evidence was adduced in *Furundžija* would not be regarded as evidence in the *Kupreškić et al.* case, see *Prosecutor v. Kupreškić et al.,* Case No. IT-95-16-T, Order on Emergency Motion to Limit Prosecutor's Inquiry Relating to Accused Anto Furundžija, 26 August 1998. *See also Prosecutor v. Krajišnik,* Case No. IT-00-39-PT, Decision on the Defence Application for Withdrawal of a Judge from the Trial, 22 January 2003, paras 15, 17. The Presiding Judge in *Prosecutor v. Krajišnik* considered that the reasonable observer would know that the Tribunal is established to hear a number of cases related to the same overall conflict, *i.e.* the violations of international humanitarian law committed in the territory of the former Yugoslavia since 1991. 'The judges of the Tribunal will therefore be frequently faced with oral and material evidence relating to the same facts which, as highly qualified professional judges, will not affect their impartiality.
[30] *Prosecutor v. Galić,* IT-98-29-T, Decision on Galić's Application Pursuant to Rule 15(B), 28 March 2003, para. 16. "'Judges' training and professional experience engrain in them the capacity to put out of their mind evidence other than that presented at trial in rendering a verdict. Judges who serve as fact-finders may often be exposed to information about the cases before them either in the media or, in some instances, from connected prosecutions. The Bureau is not of the view that Judges should be disqualified simply because of such exposure. [...] The need to present a reasoned judgement explaining the basis of their findings means that Judges at the Tribunal are forced to confine themselves to the evidence in the record in reaching their conclusions."

12

11.   In examining the issue of maintaining impartiality while adjudicating overlapping cases involving alleged co-perpetrators, the European Court of Human Rights ("ECHR") in *Poppe v. The Netherlands ("Poppe* case") considered that the work of criminal courts frequently involves judges sitting on separate trials in which a number of co-accused are charged, and that it would render the work of the criminal courts impossible, if by that fact alone, a judge's impartiality could be called into question.[31] In the *Poppe* case, the ECHR applied the objective test and held that:

> [T]he mere fact that a judge has already ruled on similar but unrelated criminal charges or that he or she has already tried a co-accused in separate criminal proceedings is not, in itself, sufficient to cast doubt on that judge's impartiality in a subsequent case. It -is, however, a different matter if the earlier judgments contain findings that actually prejudge the question of the guilt of an accused in such sub sequent proceedings.[32]

12.   In finding that the applicant's fear of bias was not objectively justified, the court further held that in determining such a "question of the guilt" the court had to take into account:

> Whether the applicant's involvement with [other co-perpetrators mentioned in the earlier judgements] fulfilled all the relevant criteria necessary to constitute a criminal offence and, if so, whether the applicant was guilty, beyond reasonable doubt, of having committed such an offence was [...] addressed, determined or assessed by the trial judges whose impartiality the applicant now wishes to challenge.[33]

13.   In *Miminoshvili v. Russia ("Miminoshvili* case"), the ECHR confirmed the standard it had set in the *Poppe* case, finding that mere references to co-accused in overlapping cases did not determine an applicant's guilt in the subsequent proceedings.[34] In concluding that the trial chamber **[page 6]** had been impartial, the court also noted that a professional judge is *a priori* better prepared to disengage from their experience in previous proceedings when compared to a lay judge or juror, which supported their ability to examine overlapping cases without bias.[35] Similarly, in *Khodorkovskiy and Lebedev* v. *Russisa ("Khodorkovskiy* case"), the ECHR found that a judge sitting in overlapping cases did not prejudge an applicant's guilt in subsequent proceedings because the judgement in the former case did not analyze or establish the constituent elements of the crimes alleged in the latter case.[36] As in the *Mimino'shvili* case, the court also found that a professional judge was able to disengage herself from her previous experience and was in no way bound by her earlier legal findings in an overlapping case because she had to consider the subsequent case on its own merits.[37]

14.   With respect to the influence chamber personnel might have on the judicial process, the ICTR Appeals Chamber has rejected allegations of conflicts of interests and bias on the part of chamber staff in *Prosecutor v. Bizimungu et al. ("Bizimungu* case") and *Prosecutor v. Nyiramasuhuko et at. ("Nyiramasuhuko* case"), finding that those assisting judges are not subject to the same standards of impartiality, and that decision-making is solely within the purview of judges to whom legal officers and consultants merely provide assistance in conformity with the judges' instructions.[38] *In the Case against Florence Hartmann ("Hartmann* case"), a Tribunal Panel dismissed a request for recusal of a chambers staff member, finding that -neither Rule 15 of the Rules nor the Tribunal's jurisprudence envisage the disqualification of chamber personnel, whose conduct it considered irrelevant to the impartiality of judges.[39]

---

[31]   *Poppe* v. *The Netherlands,* Judgement on Application No. 32271/04 *("Poppe* Judgement"), 24 March 2009, paras 22-23.
[32]   *Poppe* Judgement, para. 26.
[33]   *Poppe* Judgement, para. 28. The ECHR therefore examined the judgements handed down by the national court in relation to Poppe's co-accused, in order to determine whether these included any finding that in fact prejudged Poppe's guilt. It found that in these judgements, the judges had not addressed the issue of whether the applicant's involvement fulfilled all the relevant criteria necessary to constitute a criminal offence and, if so, whether the applicant was guilty beyond reasonable doubt.[33] The ECHR therefore found that the applicant's fear of bias on the part of the two judges was not objectively justified.
[34]   *Miminoshvili* v. *Russia,* Judgement on Application No. 20197/03 *("Miminoshvili* Judgement"), 28 June 2011, paras 116, 118.
[35]   *Miminoshvili* Judgement, para. 120.
[36]   *Khodorkovskiy and Lebedev* v. *Russia,* Judgement on Application Nos. 11082/06 and 13772/05 *("Khodorkovskiy* Judgement"), 25 July 2013, paras 549-554, 557.
[37]   *Khodorkovskiy* Judgement, paras 548, 554, 556.
[38]   *Prosecutor* v. *Bizimungu et al.,* Case No. ICTR-99-50-AR73.8, Decision on Appeals Concerning the Engagement of a Chambers Consultant or Legal Officer, 17 December 2009, paras 5, 9; *Prosecutor* v. *Nyiramasuhuko,* Case No. ICTR-98-42-A, Judgement, 17 December 2015, para. 273.
[39]   *In the Case against Florence Hartmann,* Case No. IT-02-54-R77.5, Report of Decision on Defence Motion for Disqualification of Two Members of the Trial Chamber and of Senior Legal Officer, 27 March 2009, para. 54.

15.   With regard to the request for the declaration of a mistrial, the Chamber notes that although neither the Statute nor the Rules explicitly regulate motions for a declaration of mistrial, a chamber may issue pursuant to Rule 54 of the Rules such orders as necessary for the conduct of proceedings.[40] Finally, in relation to the request to exceed the word limit for motions, the Chamber notes that the Practice Direction on the Length of Briefs and Motions states that motions shall not exceed 3,000 words and that a party must seek authorization from the relevant chamber to exceed **[page 7]** this word limit, providing an explanation of the exceptional circumstances that necessitate the oversized filing.[41]

IV. DISCUSSION

A. Preliminary Matters

16.   The Chamber will grant the Defence's request for an extension of the Motion's word limit due to the importance of the subject matter and because the limit was not significantly exceeded.[42] Moreover, in light of the submissions in the Response, the Chamber finds that the Defence has shown good cause for its request to reply.

17.   The Chamber notes that the Defence's substantive arguments appear to be based in the requirements set out in Rule 15(A) of the Rules and related jurisprudence, alleging actual or at least possible bias on the part of the judges in the present case, as well as an appearance of bias resulting from allegedly prejudiced staff assisting those judges. The Chamber notes however that the Motion contains no related applications for disqualification of the judges or the Impugned Staff, and none of the relief requested is provided for in Rule 15 or elsewhere in the Rules, or in the related jurisprudence. Under these circumstances, the Chamber will first consider the role of the Impugned Staff and whether they influence the judges, and then consider the allegations of judicial bias pursuant to the principles formulated in Rule 15(A), in order to determine whether there is cause to issue a decision as requested by the Defence pursuant to Rule 54 of the Rules as necessary for the conduct of the trial and the protection of the Accused's fair trial rights.

B. Role of the Impugned Staff

18.   With regard to the Defence's submissions alleging bias on the part of the Impugned Staff because of their role in the *Karadžić* case trial judgment, the Chamber notes at the outset the Defence's erroneous assumption that most of the Impugned Staff are assisting judges in the present case, and that it was the Impugned Staff rather than the judges in the *Karadžić* case who made findings in that case. The Chamber notes, however, that to date only two Impugned Staff have worked on the present case and considers that in accordance with the *Bizimungu* and *Nyiramasuhuko* cases, the role of the Impugned Staff in both cases has been and continues to be only that of providing assistance to the judges, while the decision-making remains entirely within the judges' purview. Moreover, the Chamber considers that just as in the *Hartmann* case, the conduct of the Impugned Staff in the present case is, therefore, irrelevant to the impartiality of the **[page 8]** judges, and neither the Tribunal's Rules nor the related jurisprudence provide for the disqualification of the Impugned Staff.

19.   As for the Defence's argument that chambers staff in the present case do more than only provide assistance, but instead perform tasks within the purview of judges when emailing decisions to the parties, the Chamber notes that such decisions, like all chamber decisions, are nonetheless made exclusively by the judges. Although as a courtesy to the parties, some decisions are communicated informally by chamber personnel to provide guidance to the parties on timesensitive matters until formal decisions can be placed on the record, this is only ever done pursuant to explicit instructions by the judges.

20.   For these reasons, the Chamber finds that although Impugned Staff assist the judges in the present case with tasks like legal research, drafting, and even communicating with the parties, this assistance does

---

[40]   *See Prosecutor v. Stanišić and Župljanin*, Case No. IT-08-91-A, Decision on Mićo Stanišić's Motion Requesting a Declaration of Mistrial and Stojan Župljanin's Motion to Vacate Trial Judgement, 2 April 2014, para. 20.
[41]   Practice Direction on the Length of Briefs and Motions, IT/184 Rev. 2, 16 September 2005, paras 5, 7.
[42]   According to the Defence, the Motion exceeds the 3,000 word limit by 518 words.

not influence the decision-making ability of the judges, nor is the previous work of the Impugned Staff on the *Karadžić* case relevant to the judges' impartiality.

C. Bias of the Judges in the Present Case

21.   With regard to the general allegations of bias on the part of the judges in the present case, the Chamber first considers, in accordance with the *Furundžija* case, whether the Defence has shown that actual bias exists on the part of the judges. The Chamber notes in this respect that although the Motion contains some ambiguous references to the possibility of actual bias of the judges, the Defence presents no facts or arguments demonstrating any indication of actual bias. The Chamber therefore finds that no actual bias has been shown to exist on the part of the judges in the present case.

22.   Similarly, with respect to the Defence allegation of an appearance of bias on the part of the judges in the . present case, the Chamber has considered, as set out in the *Furundžija* case, whether the circumstances described in the Motion would lead a properly informed observer to reasonably apprehend such bias. The Chamber notes in this regard that there is a considerable degree of overlap between the *Karadžić* case and the present case in that the indictments and evidentiary record for each case share similarities. The Chamber considers, however, that just as in the *Furundžija* case, a properly informed and reasonable observer would not consider, on the basis of the circumstances described in the Defence submissions, that the judges in the present case had failed to maintain the high degree of integrity and impartiality to which they are sworn, even if they or the Impugned Staff had worked on both cases. **[page 9]**

23.   Moreover, as established in the *Renzaho* case, the Chamber considers that a properly informed and reasonable observer would expect frequent and considerable overlap between cases at the Tribunal just as at the ICTR, which would not affect the impartiality of judges, regardless of whether the judges had actually adjudicated such cases or their staff had assisted them in doing so. Just as with the reasonable observer in the *Renzaho* case, the Chamber considers that a properly informed and reasonable observer in the present case would not expect, on the basis of the circumstances described in the Defence submissions, that the judges would do anything other than rule fairly on the issues before them by virtue of their professional training and experience, relying exclusively on the evidence adduced in the present case, even if they or their staff had been ' exposed to relevant evidence in both cases.

24.   Furthermore, in accordance with the *Poppe, Miminoshvili,* and *Khodorkovskiy* cases, the Chamber considers that even if a legal finding had been made in the *Karadžić* case related to the Accused, this would not be sufficient to cast doubt on a judge's impartiality unless the judge had found that the Accused's participation fulfilled all the relevant criteria necessary to constitute a criminal offence, and then had found the Accused guilty beyond a reasonable doubt of having committed that offence. The Chamber notes in this respect that not only did the Impugned Staff and judges in the present case not make any findings in the *Karadžić* case, the findings referenced by the Defence as having "convicted" the Accused neither establish the criteria to constitute a criminal offence, nor make findings on the criminal responsibility of the Accused.

25.   Additionally, the Chamber notes that the jurisprudence cited by the Defence is comprised of cases in which alleged bias stems from associations with parties to the proceedings rather than with another chamber in a related case and, therefore, do not support the arguments raised in .the Motion.[43] Lastly, the Chamber notes that the International Criminal Court decision cited by the Defence only mentions the possibility that legal officer bias might raise an issue with regard to the disqualification of judges, but does not make any legal findings in this regard. [44]

26.   For all of the above reasons, the Chamber considers that the presumption of impartiality attached to the judges in the present case has not been rebutted on the basis that the Impugned Staff worked on the overlapping *Karadžić* case in which factual findings were made in relation to the Accused. For this reason, the Chamber finds that there exists neither actual bias nor an objective appearance of bias with respect to the Impugned Staff or judges in the present case. The Chamber finds, therefore, that there have been no violations

---

43   *See, e.g., Hamidv. Price Waterhouse,* 51 F.3d 1411 (9th Cir. 1995).
44   *The Prosecutor v. Thomas Lubanga Dyilo,* Case No. ICC-01/04-01-06, Decision on the Prosecutor's Application to Separate the Senior Legal Adviser to the Pre-Trial Division from Rendering Legal Advice regarding the Case, 27 October 2006, p. 2.

of the Accused's fair trial or other rights, and **[page 10]** finds no merit in the requests for information or materials related to chamber personnel, nor in the request for a declaration of a mistrial.

V. DISPOSITION

27.   For the foregoing reasons, pursuant to Rule 54 of the Rules, the Chamber

GRANTS the Defence request to exceed the word limit in the Motion;

GRANTS the Defence Request to Reply; and

DENIES the remainder of the Motion.

Done in English and in French, the English version being authoritative.

Judge Alphons Orie
Presiding Judge

Dated this fourth day of July 2016

At The Hague

The Netherlands

[Seal of the Tribunal]

UNITED
NATIONS

International Tribunal for the Prosecution of Persons Responsible for Serious Violations of International Humanitarian Law Committed in the Territory of the former Yugoslavia since 1991		Case No.	IT-09-92-AR73.6 IT-09-92-AR73.7
		Date:	26 October 2016
		Original:	English

THE PRESIDENT OF THE TRIBUNAL

Before: Judge Liu Daqun, Acting President

Registrar: Mr. John Hocking

Decision of: 26 October 2016

PROSECUTOR

v.

RATKO MLADIĆ

PUBLIC

DECISION ON RATKO MLADIĆ'S MOTION FOR DISQUALIFICATION OF JUDGE CARMEL AGIUS

Counsel for Ratko Mladić:

Mr. Branko Lukić
Mr. Miodrag Stojanović

The Office of the Prosecutor:

Mr. Peter McCloskey
Mr. Alan Tieger

[page 1] 1. **I, Liu Daqun,** Acting President of the International Tribunal for the Prosecution of Persons Responsible for Serious Violations of International Humanitarian Law Committed in the Territory of the former Yugoslavia since 1991 ("Tribunal"), am seised of the "Appellant's Motion Pursuant to Rule 15(B) Seeking Disqualification of Judge Carmel Agius from the Appeals Chamber", filed by Ratko Mladić ("Mladić") in Cases Nos. IT-09-92-AR73.6 & IT-09-92-AR73.7, on 10 October 2016 ("Motion").

I. BACKGROUND

2. On 4 July 2016, Trial Chamber I of the Tribunal ("Trial Chamber"), issued a decision rejecting Mladić's allegations that his fair trial rights have been violated by the integration of Chambers staff who previously worked for the trial chamber seized of the case of *Prosecutor v. Radovan Karadžić,* Case No. IT-95-5/18-T *("Karadžić case")*, and denying his request for information or materials related to Chambers personnel or, alternatively, for a declaration of mistrial.[1]

3. On 9 September 2016, the Trial Chamber issued a scheduling order setting 25 October 2016 as the date for the filing of final trial briefs by Mladić and the Office of the Prosecutor ("Prosecution").[2]

4. The Trial Chamber granted certification to appeal the Decision of 4 July 2016 and the Scheduling Order on 27 September 2016[3] and 28 September 2016,[4] respectively. On October 2016, Mladić filed the "Interlocutory Appeal Brief Challenging the Decision of the Trial Chamber on the Defence Motion for a Fair Trial and Presumption of Innocence", and on October 2016, Mladić filed the "Interlocutory Appeal Brief Challenging the Decision of the Trial Chamber on the Defence Motion Regarding Scheduling Order" (together, "Mladić's Interlocutory Appeals").[5] **[page 2]**

5. On 6 October 2016, Judge Carmel Agius ("Judge Agius"), the President of the Tribunal assigned a bench of the Appeals Chamber of the Tribunal ("Appeals Chamber") to hear each of Mladić's Interlocutory Appeals, both benches including himself.[6]

6. On 13 October 2016, following the filing of the Motion, Judge Agius, the President of the Tribunal assigned me pursuant to Rule 15(B)(iv) of the Rules to consider the Motion in his place both as Presiding Judge and President of the Tribunal for the purpose of Rule 15(B) of the Rules.[7]

7. The Motion seeks the voluntary withdrawal or the disqualification of Judge Agius from Mladić's Interlocutory Appeals on the grounds of an alleged appearance of bias by reason of prejudgement.[8] On 11 October 2016, the Prosecution filed a response arguing that the Motion should be dismissed.[9] On 17 October 2016, Mladić requested leave to file a reply and attached his reply to the request.[10]

---

[1]   *Prosecutor v. Ratko Mladić,* Case No. IT-09-92-T, Decision on Defence Motion for a Fair Trial and the Presumption of Innocence or, in the Alternative, a Mistrial, 4 July 2016 ("Decision of 4 July 2016"), paras 1, 26-27.

[2]   *Prosecutor v. Ratko Mladić,* Case No. IT-09-92-T, Scheduling Order, 9 September 2016 ("Scheduling Order"), p. 4.

[3]   *Prosecutor v. Ratko Mladić,* Case No. IT-09-92-T, Decision on Defence Motion for Reconsideration or Certification to Appeal Decision on Motion for a Fair Trial or a Mistrial, 27 September 2016, para. 16.

[4]   *Prosecutor v. Ratko Mladić,* Case No. IT-09-92-T, Decision on Defence Motion Seeking Reconsideration of or Certification to Appeal Scheduling Order, 28 September 2016, para. 13.

[5]   *Prosecutor v. Ratko Mladić,* Case No. IT-09-92-AR73.6, Interlocutory Appeal Brief Challenging the Decision of the Trial Chamber on the Defense Motion for a Fair Trial and Presumption of Innocence, 4 October 2016 ("Interlocutory Appeal Brief on the Trial Chamber's Decision on Motion for a Fair Trial and Presumption of Innocence"); *Prosecutor v. Ratko Mladić,* Case No. IT-09-92-AR73.7, Interlocutory Appeal Brief Challenging the Decision of the Trial Chamber on the Defense Motion Regarding Scheduling Order, 5 October 2016 ("Interlocutory Appeal Brief on Scheduling Order").

[6]   *Prosecutor v. Ratko Mladić,* Case No. IT-09-92-AR73.6, Order Assigning Judges to a Case before the Appeals Chamber, 6 October 2016, p.1; *Prosecutor v. Ratko Mladić,* Case No. IT-09-92-AR73.7, Order Assigning Judges to a Case before the Appeals Chamber, 6 October 2016, p. 1.

[7]   *Prosecutor v. Ratko Mladić,* Case No. IT-09-92-AR73.6, Order Assigning Motions to a Judge, 13 October 2016, p. 2; *Prosecutor v. Ratko Mladić,* Case No. IT-09-92-AR73.7, Order Assigning Motions to a Judge, 13 October 2016, p. 2.

[8]   Motion, paras 1, 17-24.

[9]   *Prosecutor v. Ratko Mladić,* Case Nos. IT-09-92-AR73.6 & IT-09-92-AR73.7, Consolidated Prosecution Response to Mladić's Motions pursuant to Rule15(B) Seeking disqualification of Judges Carmel Agius, Theoder Meron and Fausto Pocar, 11 October 2016 ("Response"), paras 1, 7.

[10]   *Prosecutor v. Ratko Mladić,* Case Nos. IT-09-92-AR73.6 & IT-09-92-AR73.7, Appellant's Motion for Leave to Reply in Support of Motions Pursuant to Rule 15(B) seeking disqualification of Judges Carmel Agius, Theodor Meron, and Fausto Pocar,

II. APPLICABLE LAW

8.   Article 21(3) of the Statute of the Tribunal ("Statute") guarantees that an accused shall be presumed innocent until proven guilty. In addition, the Statute and the Rules guarantee an accused's right to be tried by impartial judges.[11] Rule 15(A) of the Rules specifically provides that:

> A Judge may not sit on a trial or appeal in any case in which the Judge has a personal interest or concerning which the Judge has or has had any association which might affect his or her impartiality. The Judge shall in any such circumstance withdraw, and the President shall assign another Judge to the case.

9.   The Appeals Chamber has held that "there is a general rule that a Judge should not only be subjectively free from bias, but also that there should be nothing in the surrounding circumstances **[page 3]** which objectively gives rise to an appearance of bias."[12] On this basis, the Appeals Chamber has considered that the following principles should direct it in interpreting and applying the impartiality requirement of the Statute:

> A. A Judge is not impartial if it is shown that actual bias exists.
>
> B. There is an unacceptable appearance of bias if:
>
> i) a Judge is a party to the case, or has a financial or proprietary interest in the outcome of a case, or if the Judge's decision will lead to the promotion of a cause in which he or she is involved, together with one of the parties. Under these circumstances, a Judge's disqualification from the case is automatic; or
>
> ii) the circumstances would lead a reasonable observer, properly informed, to reasonably apprehend bias.[13]

10.   With respect to the reasonable observer prong of this test, the Appeals Chamber has held that the "reasonable person must be an informed person, with knowledge of all the relevant circumstances, including the traditions of integrity and impartiality that form a part of the background and apprised also of the fact that impartiality is one of the duties that Judges swear to uphold."[14]

11.   The Appeals Chamber has also emphasised that there is a presumption of impartiality that attaches to any judge of the Tribunal and considered that, in the absence of evidence to the contrary, it must be assumed that the judges of the Tribunal "can disabuse their minds of any irrelevant personal beliefs or predispositions."[15] Accordingly, the party who seeks the disqualification of a judge bears the burden of adducing sufficient evidence that the judge is not impartial.[16] In this respect, the Appeals Chamber has consistently held that there is a high threshold to reach to rebut the presumption of impartiality.[17] The party must demonstrate that "there is a reasonable apprehension of bias by reason of prejudgement" that is "firmly established".[18] The

---

17 October 2016 ("Motion for Leave to Reply"); Annex A, Appellant's Reply in Support of Motions Pursuant to Rule 15(B) Seeking Disqualification of Judges Carmel Agius, Theodor Meron, and Fausto Pocar, 17 October 2016 ("Reply").

[11]   See Article 13 of the Statute; Rule 14(A) of the Rules. See also *Ferdinand Nahimana et al. v. The Prosecutor*, Case No. ICTR-99-52-A, Judgement, 16 May 2008 (original French version filed on 28 November 2007) ("*Nahimana et al.* Appeal Judgement"), para. 47; *Édouard Karemera et al.*, Case No. ICTR-98-44-AR75.15, Decision on Joseph Nzirorera's Appeal Against a Decision of Trial Chamber III Denying the Disclosure of a Copy of the Presiding Judge's Written Assessment of a Member of the Prosecution Team, 5 May 2009 ("*Karemera et al.* Appeal Decision"), para. 9; *Ildephonse Hategekimana v. The Prosecutor*, Case No. ICTR-00-55B-A, Judgement, 8 May 2012 ("*Hategekimana* Appeal Judgement"), para. 16.

[12]   *Prosecutor v. Anto Furundžija*, Case No. IT-95-17/1-A, Judgement, 21 July 2000 *("Furundžija* Appeal Judgement"), para. 189.

[13]   *Furundžija* Appeal Judgement, para. 189. See also, *e.g., Prosecutor v. Zejnil Delalić et al.*, Case No. IT-96-21-A, Judgement, 20 February 2001 *("Čelebići* Appeal Judgement"), paras 682-683; *The Prosecutor v. Jean-Paul Akayesu*, Case No. ICTR-96-4-A, Judgment, 23 November 2001 (original French version filed on 1 June 2001) ("*Akayesu* Appeal Judgement"), para. 203; *Prosecutor v. Stanislav Galić*, Case No. IT-98-29-A, Judgement, 30 November 2006 ("*Galić* Appeal Judgement"), para. 39; *Nahimana et al.* Appeal Judgement, para. 49.

[14]   *Furundžija* Appeal Judgement, para. 190. See also, *e.g., Čelebići* Appeal Judgement, para. 683; *Galić* Appeal Judgement, para. 40; *Nahimana et al.* Appeal Judgement, para. 50.

[15]   *Furundžija* Appeal Judgement, paras 196-197. See also, *e.g., Akayesu* Appeal Judgement, paras. 91, 269; *Galić* Appeal Judgement, para. 41; *Nahimana et al.* Appeal Judgement, para. 48; *Karemera et al.* Appeal Decision, para. 11; *Hategekimana* Appeal Judgement, para. 16.

[16]   *Furundžija* Appeal Judgement, para. 197. See also, *e.g., Akayesu* Appeal Judgement, para. 91; *Galić* Appeal Judgement, para. 41; *Nahimana et al.* Appeal Judgement, para. 48; *Hategekimana* Appeal Judgement, para. 16.

[17]   *Furundžija* Appeal Judgement, para. 197. See also, *e.g., Čelebići* Appeal Judgement, para. 707; *Galić* Appeal Judgement, para. 41.

[18]   *Furundžija* Appeal Judgement, para. 197. See also, *e.g., Čelebići* Appeal Judgement, para. 707.

Appeals Chamber has explained that this high threshold is required because, "just as any real appearance of **[page 4]** bias o[n] the part of a judge undermines confidence in the administration of justice, it would be as much of a potential threat to the interests of the impartial and fair administration of justice if judges were to disqualify themselves on the basis of unfounded and unsupported allegations of apparent bias".[19]

12.   Furthermore, Rule 15(B)(i) of the Rules provides that:

> Any party may apply to the Presiding Judge of a Chamber for the disqualification and withdrawal of a Judge of that Chamber from a trial or appeal upon the above grounds. The Presiding Judge shall confer with the Judge in question and prepare a report which shall include any comments or material provided by the challenged Judge. The Presiding Judge shall present this report to the President.

13.   In addition, Rule 15(B)(iv) of the Rules provides that:

> If the Judge in question is the President, the responsibility of the President in accordance with this paragraph shall be assumed by the Vice-President or, if he or she is not able to act in the application, by the permanent Judge most senior in precedence who is able to act.

III. DISCUSSION

A. Submissions of the parties

14.   Mladić submits that Judge Agius should withdraw or be disqualified from the benches appointed to determine Mladić's Interlocutory Appeals since a reasonable observer would conclude that Judge Agius has pre-judged the merits of this case and that this reasonable apprehension of bias has been firmly established.[20] Mladić contends that, as a member of the bench in the trial chamber seised of the *Prosecutor v. Vujadin Popović et al.*, Case No. IT-05-88-T (*"Popović et al.* Trial Chamber"), Judge Agius made prejudicial statements and findings about Mladić which individually and together demonstrate prejudgement on his guilt.[21] In Mladić's submissions, the statements and findings made by Judge Agius as a member of the bench in the *Popović et al.* Trial Judgement were inessential to the findings of guilt of the accused in trial in this case and indicates that Judge Agius has already determined Mladić's guilt affecting his impartiality in determining issues related to his fair trial rights in Mladić's Interlocutory Appeals.[22]

15.   To support his claim, Mladić points to findings from the *Popović et al.* Trial Judgement stating that: (i) statements by Mladić were "deliberate lies"; (ii) it was "inconceivable" that Mladić was not involved in a joint criminal enterprise to murder and was a "central, driving force" behind **[page 5]** it; (iii) Mladić issued "patently illegal" orders to commit genocide; and (iv) the position of one of the accused "cloaked with the authority of Mladić" was an aggravating factor in sentencing.[23] Mladić further argues that in the *Popović et al.* Trial Judgement, Judge Agius made findings in relation to all the Srebrenica's incidents charged in his indictment on issues that are contested in his case.[24] He adds that Judge Agius frequently reference Maldić's involvement or order, assuming his membership in the joint criminal enterprise, to prove his subordinates' membership therein.[25] Finally, Mladić submits that Judge Agius has already made findings about his criminal intent in relation to Srebenica.[26]

16.   As relief, Mladić requests the voluntarily withdrawal or the disqualification of Judge Agius and the appointment of another Judge to hear Mladić's Interlocutory Appeals, or in the alternative the assignment of the Motion to the Bureau for resolution under Rule 15(B) of the Rules.[27]

---

[19]   *Čelebići* Appeal Judgement, para. 707.
[20]   Motion, paras 17, 24.
[21]   Motion, paras. 19, 24, referring to *Prosecutor v. Vujadin Popović et al.*, Case No. IT-05-88-T, Judgement, 10 June 2010 (*"Popović et al.* Trial Judgement").
[22]   Motion, para. 19.
[23]   Motion, para. 20, referring to *Popović et al.* Trial Judgement, paras 1071, 1259, 1412, 2165.
[24]   Motion, para. 21
[25]   Motion, paras 22, referring to *Popović et al.* Trial Judgement, paras 1300, 1641.
[26]   Motion, para. 23, referring to *Popović et al.* Trial Judgement, paras 1004, 1641.
[27]   Motion, p. 10.

17.   The Prosecution responds that the Motion should be dismissed since Mladić does not demonstrate that a reasonable observer would reasonably apprehend bias in Judge Agius's involvement in the *Popović et al.* case.[28] According to the Prosecution, it is well established that in criminal trials arising out of the same series of events, a reasonable observer would presume that judges decide each case exclusively on the basis of the evidence heard by the chamber in relation to each particular case.[29] In the Prosecution's view, Mladić has not raised any indication that Judge Agius is unable to act in a manner consistent with this expectation and has failed to rebut the presumption of impartiality.[30] The Prosecution contends that the fact that Judge Agius was involved in making findings on the criminal responsibility of Mladić in the *Popović et al.* Trial Judgement on the basis of the evidence adduced in that case does not indicate that Judge Agius would bring a partial or prejudiced mind to Mladić's Interlocutory Appeals.[31] **[page 6]**

18.   Mladić replies that the Prosecution provides no support for its assertion that the factual and legal findings made by Judge Agius in the *Popović et al.* case relating to Mladić's guilt would not continue to influence the judge's decision-making.[32]

B.   Analysis

19.   On 17 October 2016, pursuant to Rule 15(B) of the Rules, I conferred with Judge Agius regarding the Motion.[33] Judge Agius considers that the Motion is without merit. Judge Agius firmly rejects any allegation of actual bias and does not believe that the circumstances would lead a reasonable observer properly informed, to reasonably apprehend bias against him. He considers that the Tribunal's established jurisprudence supports the conclusion that the fact that the *Popović et al.* Trial Judgement contains findings regarding Mladić does not rebut the strong presumption of impartiality attached to judges. Judge Agius adds that none of the specific findings in the *Popović et al.* Trial Judgement to which Mladić refers would lead a reasonable observer, properly informed, to reasonably apprehend bias on his part.

20.   At the outset, I observe that the request for disqualification of Judge Agius is directed to his participation in the benches appointed by the President of the Tribunal to determine Mladić's Interlocutory Appeals.[34] I recall that the Appeals Chamber has held that determinations of actual bias or unacceptable appearance of bias under Rule 15 of the Rules should be made on a case-by-case basis.[35] The issue I must therefore address in this case, is whether the involvement of Judge Agius in another case, the *Popović et al.* case on trial, and in particular the findings pointed out by Mladić, would lead a reasonable observer, properly informed, to reasonably apprehend bias on the part of Judge Agius when adjudicating Mladić's Interlocutory Appeals. I consider that any apprehension of bias by reason of prejudgement must not only be firmly established,[36] but also **[page 7]** cannot be assessed in the abstract as it will depend on the issues that require adjudication in the particular case.

---

28   Response, paras. 1, 7.
29   Response, para. 2 *referring to Prosecutor v. Vojislav Šešelj*, Case No. IT-03-67-PT, Decision on Motion for Disqualification, 16 February 2007, para. 24; *The Prosecutor v. Ferdinand Nahimana et al*, Case No. ICTR-99-52-A, Appeal Judgement, 28 November 2008, para. 78.
30   Response, para. 2.
31   Response, para. 3.
32   Reply, para. 4. See also Reply, para. 3. I consider that I would benefit from submissions in reply on the issue to adjudicate the Motion. Therefore, pursuant to Rule 126*bis* of the Rules, I grant the Motion for Leave to Reply and accept the Reply attached as an annex to the Motion for Leave to Reply as validly filed.
33   I recall that when the Presiding Judge and the President of the Tribunal is the same person, the requirement of Rule 15(B)(i) of the Rules that the Presiding Judge report to the President of the Tribunal becomes inapplicable. See *Prosecutor v. Mićo Stanišić and Stojan Župljanin*, IT-08-91-A, Decision on Motion Requesting Recusal, 3 December 2013, para. 21; *Prosecutor v. Vojislav Šešelj*, Case No. IT-03-67-R77.2-A, Decision on Motion for Disqualification of Judges Fausto Pocar and Theodor Meron from the Appeals Proceedings, 2 December 2009, para. 3; *Prosecutor v. Vojislav Šešelj*, IT-03-67-R77.2-A, Decision on Motion for Disqualification, 6 November 2009 ("Decision of 6 November 2009"), para. 5.
34   See Motion, paras 1, 19, 24-25.
35   *Prosecutor v. Mićo Stanišić & Stojan Župljanin*, Case No. IT-08-91-A, Judgement, 30 June 2016 ("*Stanišić and Župljanin* Appeal Judgement"), para. 32 and references cited therein. In the *Stanišić and Župljanin* Appeal Judgement, the Appeals Chamber also noted that a Judge who has not met the requirements of this Rule in a specific case has otherwise been entitled to continue to exercise the functions of a Judge of the Tribunal and sit in other cases when he fulfils the requirements of Rule 15 of the Rules in those other cases. See *Stanišić and Župljanin* Appeal Judgement, para. 32, fn. 126.
36   See *supra*, para. 11.

21.   Accordingly, in order to determine whether a reasonable observer, properly informed, would reasonably apprehend bias on the part of Judge Agius when adjudicating Mladić's Interlocutory Appeals, I consider that in this case, it is necessary for Mladić to abduct sufficient evidence showing that the substantive issues arising from the *Popović et al.* Trial Judgement pointed out by Mladić are so closely linked to the substantive issues in Mladić's Interlocutory Appeals so as to cast doubt on the impartiality of Judge Agius.[37]

22.   As evidence of an appearance of bias by prejudgment on his guilt, Mladić points to findings from the *Popović et al.* Trial Judgement that overlap with his case or expressly mention Mladić. These findings or statements relate to: (i) specific Srebrenica incidents that are also charged in the Mladić's indictment; (ii) an assessment of evidence where Mladić is mentioned; (iii) the role and involvement of Mladić in the "plan to murder and its implementation"; (iii) the role and involvement of Mladić in certain incidents or operation; and (iv) the discriminatory intent of Mladić for persecution as a crime against humanity.[38]

23.   In Mladić's Interlocutory Appeals, however, the Appeals Chamber will have to address allegations of violations of Mladić's fair trial rights and presumption of innocence related to: (i) the integration in his case of Chambers staff who previously worked for the trial chamber seised of the *Karadžic* case; and (ii) the date of the filing of Mladić's final trial brief.[39] Having carefully reviewed Mladić's Interlocutory Appeals, I observe that the issues raised therein will not require any consideration by the Appeals Chamber of Mladić's individual criminal responsibility. Rather, the subject matter of the Mladić's Interlocutory Appeals is procedural and Mladić's Interlocutory **[page 8]** Appeals only requires rulings on some specific allegations of violations of fair trial rights in the ongoing Mladić's trial proceedings.

24.   Based on these considerations, I find that the substantive issues arising from the *Popović et al.* Trial Judgement to which Mladić points to cannot be said to be so closely related to the fair trial issues at the centre of Mladić's Interlocutory Appeals so as to cast doubt on the impartiality of Judge Agius. I am therefore not convinced that any of the relevant findings from the *Popović et al.* Trial Judgement would lead a reasonable observer, properly informed, to reasonably apprehend bias on the part of Judge Agius when adjudicating Mladić's Interlocutory Appeals. I consider that Mladić's argument that the findings from the *Popović et al.* Appeal Judgement which in his view show a prejudgement on Mladić's guilt, is insufficient to rebut the presumption of impartiality of Judge Pocar to adjudicate Mladić's Interlocutory Appeals.

25.   In light of the foregoing, I consider that Mladić has not rebutted the strong presumption of impartiality of Judge Agius and that the Motion is without merit. For the reasons explained above, I also consider that it is not necessary to appoint a panel of three judges pursuant to Rule 15(B) of the Rules to consider the Motion.

---

[37]   *See* Decision of 6 November 2009, para. 6. I observe that such approach finds support in the jurisprudence of the European Court of Human Rights ("ECtHR"). The ECtHR has found that it is not *"prima facie* incompatible with the requirements of impartiality if the same judge is involved, first, in a decision on the merits of a case and, subsequently, in proceedings in which the admissibility of an appeal against that decision is examined." See *Warsicka v. Poland*, ECtHR, No. 2065/03, Judgment, 16 January 2007 (*"Warsicka* ECtHR Judgement"), para. 40. It also found that "the assessment of whether the participation of the same judge in different stages of a civil case complies with the requirement of impartiality laid down by Article 6 § 1 is to be made on a case-to-case basis, regard being had to the circumstances of the individual case and, importantly, to the characteristics of the relevant rules of civil procedure applied to the case. In particular, it is necessary to consider whether the link between substantive issues determined in a decision on the merits and the admissibility of an appeal against that decision is so close as to cast doubt on the impartiality of the judge." See *Warsicka* ECtHR Judgement, para. 40. See also *Case of Central Mediterranean Development Corporation Limited v. Malta*, ECtHR, No. 18544/08, Judgment, 22 November 2011, paras 33-37. I observe that the above-mentioned ECHR cases relates to situations where the judges exercised judicial functions in two successive stages of the same proceedings. The same principles should *a fortiori*, hold true when the question, like in this case, is not related to two successive stages of the same proceedings but between two distinct proceedings.

[38]   See Motion, paras 20-23.

[39]   Interlocutory Appeal Brief on the Trial Chamber's Decision on Motion for a Fair Trial and Presumption of Innocence, paras. 1, 16, 43; Interlocutory Appeal Brief on Scheduling Order, paras. 1, 25, 55.

IV.   DISPOSITION

26.   For the foregoing reasons and pursuant to Rule 15 of the Rules, I hereby **DENY** the Motion.

Done in English and French, the English text being authoritative.

Dated this twenty sixth day of October 2016,

_____

Judge Liu Daqun

at The Hague, The Netherlands.

[Seal of the Tribunal]

UNITED
NATIONS

International Tribunal for the
Prosecution of Persons
Responsible for Serious Violations of
International Humanitarian Law
Committed in the Territory of the
former Yugoslavia since 1991

Case No.   IT-09-92-AR73.6

Date: 27 February 2017

Original: English

IN THE APPEALS CHAMBER

Before: **Judge Carmel Agius, Presiding**
                    Judge Liu Daqun
                    Judge Fausto Pocar
                    Judge Theodor Meron
                    Judge Burton Hall

Registrar: **Mr. John Hocking**

Decision of: **27 February 2017**

PROSECUTOR

v.

RATKO MLADIĆ

PUBLIC

DECISION ON INTERLOCUTORY APPEAL AGAINST DECISION ON DEFENCE MOTION FOR A FAIR TRIAL AND THE PRESUMPTION OF INNOCENCE

The Office of the Prosecutor:

Mr. Peter McCloskey
Mr. Alan Tieger

Counsel for the Accused:

Mr. Branko Lukić
Mr. Dragan Ivetić

[page 1] 1.   The Appeals Chamber of the International Tribunal for the Prosecution of Persons Responsible for Serious Violations of International Humanitarian Law Committed in the Territory of the former Yugoslavia since 1991 ("Appeals Chamber" and "Tribunal", respectively) is seised of an appeal filed by Ratko Mladić ("Mladić") on 4 October 2016[1] against the "Decision on Defence Motion for a Fair Trial and the Presumption of Innocence or, in the Alternative, a Mistrial" issued by Trial Chamber I of the Tribunal ("Trial Chamber") on 4 July 2016.[2] The Office of the Prosecutor ("Prosecution") filed a response on 11 October 2016.[3] Mladić filed a reply on 17 October 2016.[4]

I. BACKGROUND

2.   On 24 March 2016, Trial Chamber III of the Tribunal, composed of Judges O-Gon Kwon, Presiding, Howard Morrison, Melville Baird, and Flavia Lattanzi, Reserve Judge, issued the Trial Judgement in the case of *Prosecutor v. Radovan Karadžić,* Case No. IT-95-5/18-T *("Karadžić* case").[5]

3.   On 19 May 2016, Mladić filed a motion before the Trial Chamber submitting that his rights to a fair trial and the presumption of innocence had been compromised by the engagement in his case of staff members who had previously worked on the *Karadžić* case and participated in the drafting of the *Karadžić* Trial Judgement ("Impugned Staff").[6]

4.   On 4 July 2016, the Trial Chamber issued the Impugned Decision, whereby it: (i) rejected Mladić's allegation that his rights had been violated by the Trial Chamber's engagement of the Impugned Staff; and (ii) denied his request for certain information and material related to Trial Chamber personnel or, in the alternative, for a declaration of mistrial.[7]

5.   In particular, the Trial Chamber first addressed Mladić's allegations of bias on the part of the Impugned Staff because of their role in the *Karadžić* case and found that the assistance provided by the Impugned Staff did not influence the decision-making ability of the Judges and that their **[page 2]** previous work on the *Karadžić* case was irrelevant to the Judges' impartiality.[8] The Trial Chamber then turned to Mladić's allegations of bias on the part of the Judges in this case and found that their presumption of impartiality had not been rebutted on the basis that the Impugned Staff had worked on the overlapping *Karadžić* case in which factual findings were made in relation to Mladić.[9] It concluded that since there was "neither actual bias nor an objective appearance of bias with respect to the Impugned Staff or judges in the present case", there had been no violations of Mladić's "fair trial or other rights".[10]

6.   On 27 September 2016, the Trial Chamber denied Mladić's request for reconsideration of the Impugned Decision but granted his request for certification to appeal it.[11] Mladić filed the present Appeal on 4 October 2016.[12]

7.   On 10 October 2016, Mladić filed motions seeking the respective disqualification of Judges Carmel Agius, Fausto Pocar, and Theodor Meron in relation to two interlocutory appeals, including the present

---

[1]   Interlocutory Appeal Brief Challenging the Decision of the Trial Chamber on the Defence Motion for a Fair Trial and Presumption of Innocence, 4 October 2016 ("Appeal").
[2]   *Prosecutor v. Ratko Mladić,* Case No. IT-09-92-T, Decision on Defence Motion for a Fair Trial and the Presumption of Innocence or, in the Alternative, a Mistrial, 4 July 2016 ("Impugned Decision").
[3]   Prosecution Response to Interlocutory Appeal Brief Challenging the Decision of the Trial Chamber on the Defence Motion for a Fair Trial and Presumption of Innocence, 11 October 2016 ("Response").
[4]   Reply in Support of the Interlocutory Appeal Brief Challenging the Decision of the Trial Chamber on the Defence Motion for a Fair Trial and Presumption of Innocence, 17 October 2016 ("Reply").
[5]   *Prosecutor v. Radovan Karadžić,* Case No. IT-95-5/18-T, Public Redacted Version of Judgement Issued on 24 March 2016, 24 March 2016 *("Karadžić* Trial Judgement").
[6]   *Prosecutor v. Ratko Mladić,* Case No. IT-09-92-T, Motion for a Fair Trial and the Presumption of Innocence or, in the Alternative, a Mistrial, 19 May 2016 ("19 May 2016 Motion"), paras 1-2, 7, 28.
[7]   Impugned Decision, paras 26-27.
[8]   Impugned Decision, para. 20. See also Impugned Decision, paras 18-19.
[9]   Impugned Decision, para. 26. See also Impugned Decision, paras 21-25.
[10]   Impugned Decision, para. 26.
[11]   *Prosecutor v. Ratko Mladić,* Case No. IT-09-92-T, Decision on Defence Motion for Reconsideration or Certification to Appeal Decision on Motion for a Fair Trial or a Mistrial, 27 September 2016 ("Certification Decision"), paras 11, 14-16.
[12]   See *supra,* para. 1.

Appeal.[13] On 13 October 2016, the President of the Tribunal, Judge Carmel Agius, assigned Vice-President Liu Daqun to consider the Disqualification Motions in place of himself.[14] On 26 October 2016, Judge Liu Daqun denied Mladić's Disqualification Motions.[15]

II. STANDARD OF REVIEW

8.   The Trial Chamber's determination of whether the engagement of certain staff would lead to actual bias or the appearance of bias is a discretionary decision to which the Appeals Chamber must accord deference.[16] In order to successfully challenge a discretionary decision, a party must demonstrate that the trial chamber has committed a discernible error resulting in prejudice to that party.[17] The Appeals Chamber will only overturn a trial chamber's discretionary decision where it **[page 3]** is found to be: (i) based on an incorrect interpretation of governing law; (ii) based on a patently incorrect conclusion of fact; or (iii) so unfair or unreasonable as to constitute an abuse of the trial chamber's discretion.[18] The Appeals Chamber will consider whether the trial chamber has given weight to extraneous or irrelevant considerations or has failed to give weight or sufficient weight to relevant considerations in reaching its decision.[19]

III. APPLICABLE LAW

9.   The Appeals Chamber recalls that legal officers assisting Judges at the Tribunal are not subject to the same standards of impartiality as the Judges of the Tribunal, and that judicial decision-making is the sole purview of the Judges.[20] Legal officers merely provide assistance to the Judges in legal research and preparing draft decisions, judgements, opinions, and orders in conformity with the instructions given to them by the Judges.[21]

10.   Notwithstanding the above, in some cases, a prospective staff member's statements or activities may be so problematic as to either impugn the perceived impartiality of the Judges or the appearance thereof, or, even if this were not the case, the Tribunal's fundamental guarantees of fair trial.[22] In this respect, the Appeals Chamber recalls in particular, that an unacceptable appearance of bias exists, *inter alia*, where the circumstances would lead a reasonable observer, properly informed, to reasonably apprehend bias.[23] The Appeals Chamber further recalls that there is a presumption of impartiality which attaches to the Judges of the Tribunal and which cannot be easily rebutted.[24] **[page 4]**

---

[13]   Appellant's Motion Pursuant to Rule 15(B) Seeking Disqualification of Judge Carmel Agius from the Appeals Chamber, 10 October 2016; Appellant's Motion Pursuant to Rule 15(B) Seeking Disqualification of Judge Fausto Pocar from the Appeals Chamber, 10 October 2016; Appellant's Motion Pursuant to Rule 15(B) Seeking Disqualification of Judge Theodor Meron from the Appeals Chamber, 10 October 2016 (collectively, "Disqualification Motions").

[14]   Order Assigning Motions to a Judge, 13 October 2016, p. 2.

[15]   Decision on Ratko Mladić's Motion for Disqualification of Judge Carmel Agius, 26 October 2016, para. 26; Decision on Ratko Mladić's Motion for Disqualification of Judge Fausto Pocar, 26 October 2016, para. 25; Decision on Ratko Mladić's Motion for Disqualification of Judge Theodor Meron, 26 October 2016, para. 24.

[16]   *The Prosecutor v. Casimir Bizimungu et al.*, Case No. ICTR-99-50-AR-73.8, Decision on Appeals Concerning the Engagement of a Chambers Consultant or Legal Officer, 17 December 2009 ("*Bizimungu et al.* Appeal Decision"), para. 4.

[17]   *Prosecutor v. Ratko Mladić*, Case No. IT-09-92-AR73.7, Decision on Interlocutory Appeal Against Scheduling Order, 2 December 2016 (confidential) ("*Mladić* Appeal Decision of 2 December 2016"), para. 14; *Prosecutor v. Goran Hadžić*, Case No. IT-04-75-AR73.1, Decision on Prosecution's Urgent Interlocutory Appeal from Consolidated Decision on the Continuation of Proceedings, 4 March 2016 ("*Hadžić* Appeal Decision"), para. 6; *Prosecutor v. Ratko Mladić*, Case No. IT-09-92-AR73.5, Decision on Interlocutory Appeal Against the 27 March 2015 Trial Chamber Decision on Modality for Prosecution Re-Opening, 22 May 2015 ("*Mladić* Appeal Decision of 22 May 2015"), para. 6.

[18]   *Mladić* Appeal Decision of 2 December 2016, para. 15; *Hadžić* Appeal Decision, para. 6; *Mladić* Appeal Decision of 22 May 2015, para. 6.

[19]   *Mladić* Appeal Decision of 2 December 2016, para. 15; *Hadžić* Appeal Decision, para. 6; *Mladić* Appeal Decision of 22 May 2015, para. 6.

[20]   *The Prosecutor v. Pauline Nyiramasuhuko et al.*, Case No. ICTR-98-42-A, Judgement, 14 December 2015 ("*Nyiramasuhuko et al.* Appeal Judgement"), para. 273, referring to, *inter alia*, *Bizimungu et al.* Appeal Decision, para. 9, *Ildephonse Hategekimana v. The Prosecutor*, Case No. ICTR-00-55B-A, Judgement, 8 May 2012 ("*Hategekimana* Appeal Judgement"), para. 20.

[21]   *Nyiramasuhuko et al.* Appeal Judgement, para. 273; *Bizimungu et al.* Appeal Decision, para. 9.

[22]   *Bizimungu et al.* Appeal Decision, para. 11.

[23]   See, *e.g.*, *Prosecutor v. Mićo Stanišić and Stojan Župljanin*, Case No. IT-08-91-A, Judgement, 30 June 2016 ("*Stanišić and Župljanin* Appeal Judgement"), para. 43 and references cited therein.

[24]   See, *e.g.*, *Stanišić and Župljanin* Appeal Judgement, para. 44 and references cited therein; *Nyiramasuhuko et al.* Appeal Judgement, para. 273; *Hategekimana* Appeal Judgement, para. 16.

IV. SUBMISSIONS

11.   As a preliminary matter, Mladić submits that the Appeal is "closely related to other outstanding matters" and that it would be more efficient to consider it together with his interlocutory appeal on the scheduling order for the filing of the parties' final trial briefs and closing arguments,[25] and another potential appeal against the Trial Chamber's decision regarding allegations of systemic bias,[26] for which a request for certification to appeal was pending before the Trial Chamber at the time the Appeal was filed.[27]

12.   In relation to the standard of review applicable to the present Appeal, Mladić asserts that the denial of a motion relating to the presumption of innocence is a non-discretionary decision since the right to the presumption of innocence is absolute.[28] He argues that the applicable standard of review is "whether the Trial Chamber committed an error of law invalidating the decision, or an error of fact occasioning a miscarriage of justice."[29]

13.   On the merits, Mladić submits that the Trial Chamber committed errors of fact and law in the Impugned Decision that individually and cumulatively result in a violation of his right to a fair trial and to the presumption of innocence.[30] He requests the Appeals Chamber to indicate the "proper test for judicial impartiality" and to grant him the relief sought before the Trial Chamber in the 19 May 2016 Motion.[31]
[page 5]

14.   Mladić submits that, despite his extensive submissions, the Trial Chamber failed to address and to provide a reasoned decision on his primary concern that allowing the Impugned Staff to work on his case violates his right to be presumed innocent.[32] He contends that the Trial Chamber did not examine the presumption of innocence in its analysis.[33] Mladić adds that, instead, the Trial Chamber focused on the presumption of impartiality attached to Judges, although his reason to raise this issue was to show that the "presumption of innocence could be engaged at a level below the standard [...] for judicial impartiality".[34]

15.   Mladić further argues that the Trial Chamber erred in determining "that the biases of the Impugned Staff did not affect his right to be presumed innocent."[35] Mladić asserts that by merely denying that the Judges' impartiality was affected, the Trial Chamber implicitly acknowledged that its staff members may

---

[25]   Appeal, para. 3, referring to *Prosecutor v. Ratko Mladić*, Case No. IT-09-92-T, Decision on Defence Motion Seeking Reconsideration of or Certification to Appeal Scheduling Order, 28 September 2016; Reply, para. 3. The Trial Chamber issued its scheduling order for the filing of the parties' final trial briefs and closing arguments on 9 September 2016 (*Prosecutor v. Ratko Mladić*, Case No. IT-09-92-T, Scheduling Order, 9 September 2016 ("Scheduling Order")). On 5 October 2016, Mladić filed his appeal against the Scheduling Order (*Prosecutor v. Ratko Mladić*, Case No. IT-09-92-AR73.7, Interlocutory Appeal Brief Challenging the Decision of the Trial Chamber on the Defence Motion Regarding Scheduling Order, 5 October 2016 (public with confidential and public redacted annexes) ("Scheduling Order Appeal")).

[26]   *Prosecutor v. Ratko Mladić*, Case No. IT-09-92-T, Decision on Defence Motion for Stay of Proceedings for Systemic Bias or, in the Alternative, a Mistrial, 22 September 2016 ("Systemic Bias Decision").

[27]   Appeal, para. 3, referring to *Prosecutor v. Ratko Mladić*, Case No. IT-09-92-T, Defence Motion for Certification to Appeal Decision on Defence Motion for Stay of Proceedings for Systemic Bias or, in the Alternative, a Mistrial (a Protest Against Trial Chamber I's "Insert Defence Acknowledgment Here" Decision-Making Process), 29 September 2016; Reply, para. 3.

[28]   Appeal, para. 14. Mladić adds that the "imperative language" in Article 21(3) of the Statute of the Tribunal ("Statute") that the accused "shall" be presumed innocent until proven guilty means that the right to the presumption of innocence is absolute and that "it would violate all precepts of justice if a trial could be found to be unfair but continue anyway" (Appeal, paras 13-14).

[29]   Appeal, para. 14.

[30]   Appeal, paras 16, 43.

[31]   Appeal, para. 43, referring to the 19 May 2016 Motion, paras 30-31. In his 19 May 2016 Motion, Mladić requested *inter alia*: (i) copies of any written undertakings that the Impugned Staff signed prior to taking up their duties on his case; and (ii) a detailed description of all other efforts that the Trial Chamber had undertaken to protect his rights to a fair trial and to be presumed innocent (19 May 2016 Motion, para. 30). In the alternative, Mladić requested a mistrial on the basis that all three Judges in his case may have already relied on the Impugned Staff's work (19 May 2016 Motion, para. 31).

[32]   Appeal, paras 16(a), 17-18. See also Appeal, para. 19.

[33]   Appeal, para. 18.

[34]   Appeal, para. 19.

[35]   Appeal, para. 23.

short of demonstrating any error in the Trial Chamber's conclusion that Mladić's fair trial rights were not violated.[78]

31.   In light of the above, the Appeals Chamber finds that Mladić has failed to demonstrate an error in the Trial Chamber's assessment of the Impugned Staff's role.

D.   Whether the Trial Chamber Erred by Introducing and Applying an Incorrect Standard for Judicial Impartiality

32.   When addressing the "Bias of the Judges in the Present Case",[79] the Trial Chamber found:

> [I]n accordance with the *Poppe*, *Miminoshvili*, and *Khodorkovskiy* cases, the Chamber considers that even if a legal finding had been made in the *Karadžić* case related to the Accused, this would not be sufficient to cast doubt on a judge's impartiality unless the judge had found that the Accused's participation fulfilled all the relevant criteria necessary to constitute a criminal offence, and then had found the Accused guilty beyond a reasonable doubt of having committed that offence. The Chamber notes in this respect that not only did the Impugned Staff and judges in the present case not make any findings in the *Karadžić* case, the findings referenced by the Defence as having "convicted" the Accused neither establish the criteria to constitute a criminal offence, nor make findings on the criminal responsibility of the Accused.[80]

33.   Regarding Mladić's argument that the Trial Chamber erred by introducing and applying an incorrect legal standard for judicial impartiality,[81] the Appeals Chamber observes that the ECtHR jurisprudence relied upon by the Trial Chamber relates to the impartiality of Judges sitting in overlapping criminal proceedings involving co-accused.[82] However, none of the Judges in this case were members of the bench that delivered the *Karadžić* Trial Judgement. Accordingly, even if the Appeals Chamber were to consider this ECtHR jurisprudence authoritative, it would be of no relevance when assessing the impartiality of the Judges in the present case. Furthermore, since legal officers assisting Judges are not subject to the same standards of impartiality as the Judges of the Tribunal and that judicial decision-making is the sole purview of the Judges,[83] the jurisprudence at issue is not applicable to the Impugned Staff. **[page 12]**

34.   Nevertheless, the Trial Chamber effectively applied the ECtHR jurisprudence to findings made in the *Karadžić* Trial Judgement. Indeed, the Trial Chamber found that "the findings referenced by the Defence as having 'convicted' [Mladić] neither establish the criteria to constitute a criminal offence, nor make findings on [his] criminal responsibility".[84] The Appeals Chamber considers that the Trial Chamber's application of this jurisprudence was unnecessary to address the question whether the engagement of the Impugned Staff impacted on the impartiality of the Judges in this case and whether Mladić's fair trial rights were violated. Whether the Trial Chamber was correct in its interpretation and application of the ECtHR jurisprudence would therefore have no impact on the outcome of the Impugned Decision. Accordingly, given that the question whether or not the ECtHR jurisprudence is applicable at the Tribunal and has been correctly applied by the Trial Chamber does not have the potential to cause the Impugned Decision to be reversed or revised,[85] the Appeals Chamber finds it unnecessary to address the merits of this argument.

35.   For the same reasons, the Appeals Chamber finds it unnecessary to address on the merits Mladić's submissions aimed at demonstrating that, even if the standard for judicial impartiality derived from the

---

[78]   See Impugned Decision, para. 26.
[79]   Impugned Decision, p. 8.
[80]   Impugned Decision, para. 24.
[81]   See *supra*, para. 16.
[82]   See Impugned Decision, paras 11, 13.
[83]   See *supra*, para. 9.
[84]   Impugned Decision, para. 24.
[85]   See, *e.g.*, *Stanišić and Župljanin* Appeal Judgement, para. 24; *Prosecutor v. Zdravko Tolimir*, Case No. IT-05-88/2-A, Judgement, 8 April 2015, para. 13; *Nyiramasuhuko et al.* Appeal Judgement, para. 34.

ECtHR jurisprudence would be applicable, the Trial Chamber erred in its application to the facts of this case.[86]

36.   In light of the foregoing, the Appeals Chamber finds that Mladić fails to demonstrate an error of the Trial Chamber, warranting the Appeals Chamber's intervention, in relation to the legal standard for impartiality applied by the Trial Chamber.

E.   Whether the Trial Chamber Erred in its Application of the Reasonable Observer Test

37.   When addressing whether the impartiality of the Judges in this case could be affected by the Impugned Staff's involvement in the *Karadžić* case, the Trial Chamber found that, even though "there is a considerable degree of overlap between the *Karadžić* case and the present case", "a properly informed and reasonable observer would not consider [...] that the judges in the present case ha[ve] failed to maintain the high degree of integrity and impartiality to which they are sworn, even if they or the Impugned Staff had worked on both cases."[87] It added that a properly informed and reasonable observer would not expect that the Judges in this case would do anything other than rule fairly on the issues before them, relying exclusively on the evidence adduced in the present case, even if they or their staff had been exposed to evidence in both cases.[88] The Trial Chamber [page 13] concluded that the presumption of impartiality attached to the Judges in this case had not been rebutted on the basis that the Impugned Staff had worked on an overlapping case in which factual findings were made in relation to Mladić.[89]

38.   With respect to Mladić's argument that the Trial Chamber failed to sufficiently reason its conclusions relating to the application of the reasonable observer test,[90] the Appeals Chamber considers that Mladić's arguments effectively amount to a challenge to how the reasonable observer test has been interpreted in the case law. The Appeals Chamber is of the view that Mladić's argument reflects his disagreement with the jurisprudence relied upon by the Trial Chamber and set out in detail in the applicable law section of the Impugned Decision,[91] as well as with the Trial Chamber's reliance on this jurisprudence when assessing whether the Impugned Staff's involvement in the *Karadžić* case could lead to an appearance of bias of the Judges in this case[92] without explaining how the Trial Chamber erred in following this case law. The Appeals Chamber finds that Mladić fails to demonstrate an error in the Trial Chamber's reasoning.

39.   Moreover, the Appeals Chamber recalls that "'mere assertions to the effect that a staff member may influence a Judge during deliberations or the adjudication process are not a sufficient basis, in and of themselves', to create in the mind of a reasonable observer, properly informed, an appearance of bias or to rebut the presumption of impartiality of judges."[93] Accordingly, the Appeals Chamber does not consider that a staff's previous work on an overlapping case is, in and of itself, sufficient to impugn the Judges' impartiality or the appearance thereof. The Appeals Chamber therefore finds no merit to Mladić's argument that a reasonable observer would consider that the fact that the Impugned Staff previously worked on the closely-related *Karadžić* case, is sufficient to rebut the impartiality of the Judges in this case.

40.   In light of the above, the Appeals Chamber finds no merit to Mladić's argument that the Trial Chamber insufficiently reasoned and erred in its application of the reasonable observer test for judicial [page 14]

---

[86]   See *supra*, para. 16.
[87]   Impugned Decision, para. 22.
[88]   Impugned Decision, para. 23.
[89]   Impugned Decision, para. 26.
[90]   See *supra*, para. 17.
[91]   Impugned Decision, paras 9-10.
[92]   Impugned Decision, paras 22-23.
[93]   *Hategekimana* Appeal Judgement, para. 20, quoting *Bizimungu et al.* Appeal Decision, para. 10.

VI. DISPOSITION

41.   For the foregoing reasons, the Appeals Chamber:

DISMISSES the Appeal.

Done in English and French, the English text being authoritative.

Dated this twenty-seventh day of February 2017,
At The Hague,
The Netherlands.

_____

Judge Carmel Agius
Presiding Judge

[Seal of the Tribunal]

ANNEX

Modalities for Trial

1.   The Registry shall make the appropriate arrangements to ensure that, upon Stanišić's arrival at the United Nations Detention Unit in The Hague ("UNDU"), a multi-disciplinary team of medical specialists is available to examine Stanišić. At least three days before the start of the trial, the UNDU Medical Service shall submit a written report informing the Trial Chamber of the current state of Stanišić's health and the medical services being made available to him at the UNDU, taking into account the views of the multi-disciplinary team of medical specialists. The UNDU Medical Service shall continue to submit written reports on Stanišić's medical condition every three weeks or more frequently if there is a significant change in Stanišić's condition. In addition, Stanišić shall be examined regularly by relevant independent medical experts who will report in writing to the Trial Chamber on his medical condition at least once every eight weeks or more frequently if there is a significant change in his condition.

2.   The Trial Chamber will hold hearings three days a week, on consecutive days from Tuesday to Thursday, unless reasons of effective court management require otherwise. The hearings will be scheduled as follows:

> 11:30-13:00 (90 min)
>
> 13:00-15:00 break (120 min)
>
> 15:00-16:30 (90 min)

In addition to the scheduled breaks, Stanišić may address the Trial Chamber at any point to request additional breaks.

3.   While at the holding cell at the Mechanism's premises, Stanišić will have the possibility to use a sofa and will have access to adjacent toilet facilities.

4.   Stanišić shall, ordinarily, be present in the courtroom during the hearings. He may, however, waive his right to be present in court. If Stanišić decides to waive his right to be present in court he shall inform the Trial Chamber as soon as possible. If Stanišić waives his right due to illness, he is to follow the procedure set out by the Registry, including completion of the "Absence from court due to illness" form for waiving the right as will be provided to him by UNDU staff.

5.   A remote participation room, with toilet facilities, shall be made available to Stanišić if he chooses not to be present in the courtroom and, instead, participate in the proceedings from the UNDU. The remote participation room shall have: (i) a video-conference link, to allow Stanišić to follow the proceedings, see the witnesses as they testify, and address the court; (ii) a telephone link,

to allow Stanišić to communicate with his counsel in the courtroom; and (iii) the necessary equipment to enable Stanišić to access eCourt and the Livenote transcript. The Trial Chamber and the parties in the courtroom will also be able to see Stanišić continuously through the videoconference link. A member of the Defence team may be present with Stanišić in the remote participation room. Stanišić shall inform UNDU staff of his decision to participate in the proceedings from the UNDU as early as possible. The UNDU staff shall inform the Trial Chamber, through the Court Officer, before the start of that day's hearings.

6.   On court days, the Commanding Officer, Deputy Commanding Officer, or any other authorized officer of the UNDU shall remind Stanišić of the court schedule for the day and that the normal arrangements are in place for his transport to the court. If Stanišić indicates that he is too unwell to attend court in person, the Commanding Officer is to remind him of his right to be present in court, ask him if he waives his right to attend and offer him the opportunity to communicate with counsel. The Commanding Officer shall also inform Stanišić that he may participate in the proceedings from the UNDU using the facilities available in the remote participation room, including the video-conference link.

7.   If Stanišić asserts that he is too unwell to be physically present in the courtroom or to participate in the proceedings using the facilities available in the remote participation room and does not waive his right to

be present in court, he shall undergo a medical examination before the hearing. The UNDU Medical Service shall inform the Trial Chamber, through the Court Officer, of Stanišić's health condition and submit an "Absence from court due to illness" form. An authorized officer of the UNDU shall inform the Trial Chamber, through the Court Officer, of Stanišić's decision, including whether Stanišić has undergone a medical examination, as soon as possible. At the beginning of the hearing, Stanišić's Counsel shall confirm to the Trial Chamber that Stanišić has not waived his right to be present. The Trial Chamber shall then, if it deems necessary and with Stanišić's informed consent, hear the UNDU Medical Officer or his/her deputy via the video-conference link in the remote participation room. The Trial Chamber may also seek further information about Stanišić's health condition.

8.   Upon hearing the UNDU Medical Officer or his/her deputy, the Trial Chamber shall determine whether to: (i) adjourn proceedings until the next scheduled hearing, having found that Stanišić is too unwell to participate in the proceedings; or (ii) continue the trial, having found that by voluntarily absenting himself from the courtroom without medical justification, Stanišić has forfeited his right to be tried in his presence under Article 19(4)(d) of the Statute.

9.   The present schedule and reporting regime will be valid until decided otherwise.

Commentary

Fair Trial Matters and Disqualification of Judges

This commentary relates to general fair trial matters and motions for the disqualification of judges. Specifically, it discusses:

(1) the question of bias or apparent bias of judges based on:

(a) their involvement in earlier trials involving closely linked substantive issues;[1] or

(b) potential influence from legal officers working on trials involving closely linked substantive issues;[2] and

(2) the question of exceptions to the right of physical presence during trial and the issue of remote participation by video-link for reasons of ill health, particularly where an accused cannot stay in The Hague due to their medical condition.[3]

1.   Presumption of Innocence and Impartiality of Judges

An accused's fair trial rights include the presumption of innocence[4] and, relatedly, the right to be tried before an independent and impartial tribunal.[5]

The starting point is that judges are presumed to be impartial;[6] a presumption that is not intended to be easily rebutted.[7] In other words, judges are trusted to perform their judicial functions appropriately. Any challenge to a judge's impartiality would need to demonstrate subjective bias or an objective apprehension of bias.

Regarding subjective bias, Rule 15A of the ICTY Rules of Procedure and Evidence (ICTY RPE) prohibits a judge from sitting on a trial or appeal bench where there is a personal interest or association which might affect their impartiality (for example, where the judge has a stake in the case, or a connection with the accused or with legal counsel).[8]

Regarding objective appearance of bias, the Appeals Chamber in Mladić recalled that "an unacceptable appearance of bias exists, *inter alia*, where the circumstances would lead a reasonable observer, properly

---

[1]   ICTY, Decision on Ratko Mladić's Motion for Disqualification of Judge Carmel Agius, *Prosecutor v. Mladić*, Case Nos. IT-09-92-AR73.6 and IT-09-92-AR73.7, A. Ch., 26 October 2016, in this volume, PAGINA.

[2]   ICTY, Decision on Defence Motion for a Fair Trial and the Presumption of Innocence or, in the alternative, a Mistrial, *Prosecutor v. Mladić*, Case No. IT-09-92-T, T. Ch. I, 4 July 2016, in this volume, PAGINA; ICTY, Decision on Interlocutory Appeal against Decision on Defence Motion for a Fair Trial and the Presumption of Innocence, *Prosecutor v. Mladić*, Case No. IT-09-92-AR73.6, A. Ch., 27 February 2017, in this volume, PAGINA.

[3]   MICT, Decision on Modalities for Trial, *Prosecutor v. Stanišić and Simatović*, Case No. MICT-15-96-PT, T. Ch., 13 April 2017, in this volume, PAGINA.

[4]   Art. 21(3) ICTY Statute, as amended by Resolution 1877, 7 July 2009.

[5]   The ICTY Statute does not explicitly require this, but Art. 13 requires that the "judges shall be persons of high moral character, impartiality and integrity" and Art. 20(1) provides that the Trial Chambers "shall ensure that a trial is fair and expeditious and that proceedings are conducted in accordance with the rules of procedure and evidence, with full respect for the rights of the accused ...". See also International Covenant on Civil and Political Rights (ICCPR), Art. 14(1); ICTY, Judgment, *Prosecutor v. Furundžija*, Case No. IT-95-17/1-A, A. Ch., 21 July 2000, in Klip/Sluiter ALC-V-291, par. 177.

[6]   ICTY, Judgment, *Prosecutor v. Furundžija*, Case No. IT-95-17/1-A, A. Ch., 21 July 2000, par. 196-197, relied upon, for example, in ICTY, Judgment, *Prosecutor v. Galić*, Case No. IT-98-29-A, A. Ch., 30 November 2006, par. 41 and ICTR, Decision on Chambers Consultant or Legal Officer, *Prosecutor v. Bizimungu et al*, ICTR-99-50-AR73.8, A. Ch., 17 December 2009, par. 10.

[7]   See, for example, Decision on Defence Motion for a Fair Trial and the Presumption of Innocence, *supra* n. 2, par. 9-10 (citations omitted); Decision on Ratko Mladić's Motion for Disqualification of Judge Carmel Agius, *supra* n. 1, par. 11; Decision on Interlocutory Appeal against Decision on Defence Motion for a Fair Trial and the Presumption of Innocence, *supra* n. 2, par. 10. See also G. Boas, J. L. Bischoff, N. L. Reid and B. D. Taylor III, International Criminal Law Practitioner Library: Vol. III International Criminal Procedure, Cambridge University Press, Cambridge 2011, p. 256-257 (citations omitted). See also generally M. El Zeidy, Commentary, in Klip/Sluiter ALC-XIX-280, p. 281-283.

[8]   ICTY, Rules of Procedure and Evidence, U.N. Doc. IT/32 Rev.50, 8 July 2015, Rule 14(A), 15(A) (ICTY RPE). See also UN Basic Principles on the Independence of the Judiciary, adopted by the Seventh UN Congress on the Prevention of Crime and the Treatment of Offenders, 26 August-6 September 1985, endorsed by UN General Assembly Resolution A/RES/40/32 29 November 1985 and A/RES/40/146 13 December 1985, Principle 2. See also MICT, Code of Professional Conduct for the Judges of the Mechanism, MICT/14, 11 May 2015, Art. 2.1.

informed, to reasonably apprehend bias".[9] Being "properly informed" means that the hypothetical observer is not any fair-minded person, but someone with knowledge of the "traditions of integrity and impartiality" within the judiciary.[10]

a.   Judicial Involvement in Closely Linked Substantive Issues

During the Mladić trial, the Defence submitted a motion for the disqualification of Judge Agius on the grounds of an alleged appearance of bias by reason of prejudgment made during the Popović trial.[11] Acting President Judge Daqun decided that there would need to be evidence that the substantive issues arising from the Popović trial were sufficiently linked to those of Mladić's case such that they would cast doubt on Judge Agius' impartiality.[12] Since Judge Agius was sitting on Mladić's interlocutory appeals only, it was held that issues of individual criminal responsibility were not being considered by Judge Agius. The presumption of impartiality was therefore not rebutted.[13]

This left open the possibility that, in other circumstances, the substantive issues in two trials might have sufficient overlap to cast such a doubt.

Logically, for specially established tribunals such as the ICTY or ICTR, one could expect overlap in factual allegations.[14] Regarding the Mladić trial in particular, because it was one of the last cases heard, there were a significant number of adjudicated facts submitted and accepted by the Chamber. Nevertheless, such facts cannot concern the alleged acts and conduct of the accused, nor legal qualifications – i.e. they remain part of the proceedings and cannot be pre-decided as such.[15]

In this light, it is also relevant to consider that, at the ICTY, the fact that a judge has been involved in a case during the pre-trial/confirmation of charges phase does not rule them out from acting as a trial or appeal judge in the same case.[16] Although perhaps based on resource practicalities, this more permissive stance relies heavily on the strong presumption of impartiality:

> a fair-minded observer would know that Judges' training and professional experience engrain in them the capacity to put out of their mind evidence other than that presented at trial in rendering a verdict.[17]

In contrast, the ICC Statute, with the aim of ensuring 'effective and fair functioning',[18] does not allow this.[19] Indeed, the ICTY Rule is a 1999 amendment from the original Rule which, like at the ICC, prevented a confirming judge from participating in later stages of a case.[20] As such, some scholars have suggested that

---

9   Decision on Interlocutory Appeal against Decision on Defence Motion for a Fair Trial and the Presumption of Innocence, *supra* n. 2, par. 10. See also Boas *et al.*, *supra* n. 7, 256, citing Judge Hunt in ICTY, Decision on Application by Momir Talić for the Disqualification and Withdrawal of a Judge, *Prosecutor v. Brđanin and Talić*, Case No. IT-99-36-PT, 18 May 2000, par. 15. See also ICTY, Judgment, *Prosecutor v. Delalić, Mucić, Delić, and Landžo*, Case No. IT-96-21-A, 20 February 2001, in Klip/Sluiter ALC-V-369, par. 697; ICTY, Judgment, *Prosecutor v. Hadžihasanović and Kubura*, Case No. IT-01-47-A, 22 April 2008, par. 78; Decision on Ratko Mladić's Motion for Disqualification of Judge Carmel Agius, *supra* n. 1, par. 9-10.
10   Decision on Ratko Mladić's Motion for Disqualification of Judge Carmel Agius, *supra* n. 1, par. 10, citing ICTY, Appeal Judgment, *Prosecutor v. Furundžija*, Case No. IT-95-17/1-A, A. Ch., 21 July 2000, in Klip/Sluiter ALC-V-291, par. 190.
11   *Ibid.*, par. 14, referring to ICTY, Judgment, *Prosecutor v. Popović et al.*, Case No. IT-05-88-T, T. Ch. II, 10 June 2010.
12   *Ibid.*, par. 21.
13   *Ibid.*, par. 23-26.
14   See, for example, ICTY, Judgment, *Renzaho v. Prosecutor*, Case No. ICTR-97-31-A, A. Ch., 1 April 2011, in Klip/Freeland ALC-LII-211, par. 22, cited in Decision on Interlocutory Appeal against Decision on Defence Motion for a Fair Trial and the Presumption of Innocence, *supra* n. 2, par. 10.
15   J. Nilsson, The Mladić Trial: An Insider's View, Lecture, TMC Asser Instituut, 31 January 2018, www.internationalcrimesdatabase.org/Commentary/VideoAndAudio2018.
16   Rule 15(C) ICTY RPE. See also ICTY, Prosecution Response to Defence Motion for a Fair Trial and the Presumption of Innocence or, in the alternative, a Mistrial, *Prosecutor v. Mladić*, Case No. IT-09-92-T, T. Ch. I, 31 May 2016, par. 3, citing *Prosecutor v. Galić*, Judgment, *supra* n. 6, par. 44.
17   *Prosecutor v. Galić*, Judgment, *supra* n. 6, par. 44.
18   See Art. 64(4) ICC Statute.
19   Art. 39(4), 41(2)(a) ICC Statute. See the general discussion in Boas *et al.*, *supra* n. 7, 257-258. See also Art. 17(2) International Court of Justice Statute.
20   Discussed in S. Zappalà, Human Rights in International Criminal Proceedings, Oxford University Press, Oxford 2003, p. 105-106, 108.

There are three things to note by way of background. First, this implies physical presence.[56] The underlying purpose, however, is to ensure that the accused can understand, follow and participate in the trial, rather than merely securing physical presence *per se*. Large parts (but not all) of such participation can therefore also be achieved via remote video participation where required and proportionate.[57] Nevertheless, because physical presence is provided for, participation via remote video-link is not expressly contemplated in the ICTY Statute or ICTY RPE. Rather, remote participation is considered constructive presence only.[58]

Secondly, the right to be present is not absolute and can be waived where the accused is represented by counsel.[59] Such a waiver of the right can be implied where the accused refuses to attend trial[60] or asks not to attend the trial on a particular day.[61]

Thirdly, an accused who has been granted provisional release during trial may be physically absent and represented by counsel, and is considered to have voluntarily and unequivocally waived their right to be present.[62]

b.   Remote participation via video-conference link?

Where serious health conditions of an accused have impacted on trial proceedings, accommodation has been made to help ensure an accused's effective participation in the trial, such as reducing the amount of weekly sitting time and including longer breaks.[63] In the Stanišić trial, modalities proposed by the Trial Chamber to accommodate Stanišić's chronic health conditions also included the possibility for remote participation via video-conference link, assuming he waived his right to be physically present at trial. This link was set up at the United Nations Detention Unit in The Hague.[64]

Stanišić suggested, however, that he remain on provisional release for the duration of the trial, waiving his right to be present at least for the presentation of the prosecution case. This would allow the trial to proceed in a timelier manner. The co-accused Simatović, in contrast, was not waiving his right to follow the trial proceedings but requested to remain on provisional release and therefore to follow the trial via conference-link from Belgrade.[65] Similarly, Stanišić argued that, if he were required to participate in the trial, particularly in the presentation of the case for the Defence, it should likewise be by way of video-conference link set up in Belgrade, with the necessary modalities limiting trial sitting hours and providing for breaks.[66]

---

[56]   See, for example, ICTY, Decision on Defence Appeal of the Decision on Future Course of Proceedings, *Prosecutor v. Stanišić and Simatović*, Case No. IT-03-69-AR73.2, A. Ch., 16 May 2008, in Klip/Sluiter ALC-XXXV-185, par. 6; ICTR, Decision on Interlocutory Appeal, *Prosecutor v. Zigiranyirazo*, Case No. ICTR-01-73-AR73, A. Ch., 30 October 2006, par. 11-13.

[57]   C. H. Wheeler, The Right to Be Present at Trial in International Criminal Law, Brill Nijhoff, Leiden/Boston 2019, p. 200-201, 226. Regarding aspects that cannot be satisfied remotely, see, for example, G. Kyakuwa, Commentary, in: Klip/Sluiter, ALC-XXV-244.

[58]   Decision on Interlocutory Appeal, *supra* n. 56, par. 12, citing ICTY RPE, Rule 65*bis* as illustrating that participation via video-link is not considered presence. Note also, regarding the weight to be given to physical presence, Boas *et al*, *supra* n. 7, p. 274-276, citing Decision on Defence Appeal of the Decision on Future Course of Proceedings, *supra* n. 56, par. 12-22 and Decision on Interlocutory Appeal, *supra* n. 56, par. 3-7.

[59]   MICT RPE, Rule 98; Decision on Defence Appeal of the Decision on Future Course of Proceedings, *supra* n. 56, par. 6. See also on the waiver of the right to presence, Boas *et al*, *supra* n. 7, p. 273.

[60]   Boas *et al*, *supra* n. 7, p. 273 and note 125; MICT RPE, Rule 98. See also ICTR RPE, Rule 82*bis* and the discussion in ICTR, Appeal Judgment, *Prosecutor v. Nahimana et al*, Case No. ICTR-99-52-A, A. Ch., 28 November 2007, in Klip/Sluiter ALC-XXXI-257, par. 97-99.

[61]   Sometimes by providing written consent for the trial to proceed in their absence: Boas *et al*, *supra* n. 7, 273. There is also the possibility that a trial continue without an accused being present without their waiver/consent where the accused has been disrupting the trial and continues to do so following a warning (Rule 80(B) ICTY RPE). In such a situation, the disruptive accused may be excluded from the courtroom, although only for as short a time as is required. The excluded accused should nevertheless be given the opportunity to continue to follow the proceedings remotely, for example via video-link. See discussion in Boas *et al*, *supra* n. 7, p. 273-273.

[62]   Rule 68(B) MICT RPE. See also Decision on Modalities for Trial, *supra* n. 3, par. 16.

[63]   See, for example, Decision on Modalities for Trial, *supra* n. 3, par. 2, 4.

[64]   *Ibid.*, par. 3. The modalities established for the accused Simić provide another example. Simić was able to view the trial through video-link from The Hague detention centre: ICTY, Sentencing Judgment, *Prosecutor v. Simić*, Case No. IT-95-9/2-S, T. Ch. II, 17 October 2002, in Klip/Sluiter ALC-XI-905, par. 8, 110, discussed in Boas *et al*, *supra* n. 7, p. 273 and note 128.

[65]   *Ibid.*, par. 14.

[66]   *Ibid.*, par. 5, 6; see also par. 14.

Underlying the two accused's submissions on modalities were their wishes to remain in Belgrade on provisional release rather than returning to detention in The Hague. The situation was exceptional given that Stanišić and Simatović were facing a retrial on all counts after nearly 14 years of proceedings, albeit a length of trial significantly affected by delays and extended scheduling to accommodate Stanišić's medical condition.[67]

In its Decision on Modalities for Trial, the Trial Chamber therefore had to consider whether the two accused could remain in Belgrade, waiving their right to be physically present during the trial and, if so, what modalities would be required so that a wish to participate in certain portions of the trial could be accommodated.[68]

Importantly, requests for provisional release were treated as an entirely distinct matter from the question of effective participation. As mentioned above, they were considered to involve a waiver of the accused's right to be present. In other words, where an accused requests and is granted provisional release, they were advised to "bear in mind" that the Mechanism is under no obligation to ensure their remote participation from another location, although it remains open for it to do so.[69]

The Trial Chamber found that its:

> obligation to ensure an accused's right to be present extends only to ensuring meaningful physical presence in the courtroom. Once that right has been voluntarily and unequivocally waived, no additional responsibility exists on the part of the Trial Chamber to facilitate remote participation via video-conference link.[70]

This pragmatic position risks giving insufficient weight to the complicating factor of the non-participation of an accused being undesired or unintentional. This may occur, for example, where an accused cannot be detained or remain in The Hague for medical reasons, yet still wishes to participate in the proceedings.[71] In a simple case, delaying trial for a reasonable time to allow medical treatment is a straightforward modality to adopt. Grappling with the required modalities becomes more difficult when the health issues are long-term, and/or where the situation of one co-accused is affecting a co-accused's right to an expeditious trial, as occurred with the Stanišić and Simatović case.[72]

Specifically, illustrative here was the situation of Simatović, who argued that his health problems precluded his detention and, therefore, that he required provisional release, but that he still wished to follow the trial proceedings.[73] In such a situation, the notion outlined above – that a request for provisional release entails the necessary waiver of a right to participation in the trial – cannot be assumed. Indeed, the accused is expressly negating any such waiver. Even where the motives underlying a request for provisional release may be mixed, where serious medical reasons exist, the challenge is how to ensure that a trial is fair and expeditious – i.e. that it can progress while also respecting the accused's right to be effective participation.[74] Reflecting this, while the underlying position treating provisional release as a waiver was kept in mind, the Trial Chamber nevertheless considered the technical and practical feasibility of participation through video-link from Belgrade.

Although protected witnesses were sometimes heard from the Belgrade Field Office, and participation via video-link from the UN Detention Unit facility was contemplated, this was considered to be quite different from establishing a facility in Belgrade for day-to-day remote participation in a trial.[75] Part of the reasoning

---

[67]   *Ibid.*, par. 13.
[68]   *Ibid.*, par. 15.
[69]   *Ibid.*, par. 16, 20.
[70]   *Ibid.*, par. 17.
[71]   Where the inability to effectively participate in the trial involves mental health issues or an impaired mental state, including where mental health or stamina is impaired by physical health issues, the Trial Chamber may ultimately find an accused unfit to stand trial. See Boas *et al*, *supra* n. 7, p. 276, note 141. On fitness to stand trial generally, see K. Clark, Commentary, in: Klip/Sluiter, ALC-XXIX-206, and on mental fitness, see Wheeler, *supra* n. 57, p. 215.
[72]   Boas *et al*, *supra* n. 7, p. 274-75, citing Decision on Defence Appeal of the Decision on Future Course of Proceedings, *supra* n. 56, par. 12-22.
[73]   Decision on Modalities for Trial, *supra* n. 3, par. 7, 31.
[74]   See Boas *et al*, *supra* n. 7, p. 274, 276 (citations omitted).
[75]   Decision on Modalities for Trial, *supra* n. 3, par. 18, 19. On testimony by video-link, see also Boas *et al*, *supra* n. 7, p. 271.

concerned the potential reluctance of witnesses to testify with the accused in the same facility.[76] The Prosecution had submitted concerns that allowing the accused to participate via video-link from Belgrade would "compromise the integrity of the proceedings, expose witnesses to risk, and cause delays".[77] The Mechanism's Belgrade Field Office would also need technical and human resource adaptations.[78]

In its decision, the Trial Chamber found that, at this stage of the proceedings, these factors argued against Stanišić and Simatović participating remotely from the Belgrade office on a day-to-day basis should their provisional release be extended; that it would not be in the interests of justice to provide for this.[79] Importantly, the Trial Chamber did not rule out that the balance of the considerations might change in favour of such remote participation in future stages of the trial, notably the presentation of the Defence cases, since the concerns about witnesses would not apply with equal force.[80] This kept open the possibility of the interests of justice in other situations requiring reasonable efforts to adapt such remote participation possibilities in the location of the accused's provisional release/medical treatment.

Marnie Lloydd

---

[76]   *Ibid.,* par. 19 and note 58.
[77]   *Ibid.,* par. 8 (citation omitted).
[78]   *Ibid.,* par. 12.
[79]   *Ibid.,* par. 19.
[80]   *Ibid.,* par. 19 and note 58.

International Tribunal for the Prosecution of Persons Responsible for Serious Violations of International Humanitarian Law Committed in the Territory of the former Yugoslavia since 1991	Case No.	IT-04-74-A
	Date:	1 December 2016
	Original:	English

IN THE APPEALS CHAMBER

Before: **Judge Carmel Agius, Presiding**
                    Judge Liu Daqun
                    Judge Fausto Pocar
                    Judge Theodor Meron
                    Judge Bakone Justice Moloto

Registrar: **Mr. John Hocking**

Decision of: **1 December 2016**

PROSECUTOR

v.

JADRANKO PRLIĆ
BRUNO STOJIĆ
SLOBODAN PRALJAK
MILIVOJ PETKOVIĆ
VALENTIN ĆORIĆ
BERISLA V PUŠIĆ

PUBLIC

PUBLIC REDACTED VERSION OF THE "DECISION ON VALENTIN ĆORIĆ'S REQUEST FOR PROVISIONAL RELEASE" ISSUED ON 15 AUGUST 2016

The Office of the Prosecutor:
Mr. Douglas Stringer
Ms. Barbara Goy
Ms. Laurel Baig

Counsel for the Accused:
Ms. Dijana Tomašegović-Tomić and Mr. Dražen Plavec for Mr. Valentin Ćorić

[page 1]THE APPEALS CHAMBER of the International Tribunal for the Prosecution of Persons Responsible for Serious Violations of International Humanitarian Law Committed in the Territory of the former Yugoslavia since 1991 ("Appeals Chamber" and "Tribunal", respectively);

RECALLING that, on 29 May 2013, Trial Chamber III of the Tribunal convicted Ćorić of 22 counts of war crimes and crimes against humanity and sentenced him to 16 years of I mpri sonment;[1]

BEING SEISED of "Valentin Ćorić's Request for Provisional Release", filed confidentially and **ex parte** with a confidential and *ex parte* annex by Valentin Ćorić ("Ćorić") on 12 May 2016 ("Motion"), in which Ćorić requests to be provisionally released "during the upcoming period, 2 pending the Appeals [*sic*] Judgement";[2]

NOTING that, in support of his request, Ćorić submits that "special circumstances" warrant his provisional release, namely that he has spent a significant amount of time in custody exceeding two-thirds of his sentence and that this determination should include the periods that he spent on provisional release, which qualify as periods of detention;[3]

NOTING that Ćorić further asserts that: (i) the judicial proceedings in his case started in 2006;[4] (ii) the appellate proceedings against him will last for at least another year or longer and, by the time the appeal judgement is rendered, he will have been in custody for a period much longer than two-thirds of his sentence;[5] and (iii) he has always exhibited good behaviour while in detention, has complied with all terms of prior custodial release, and returned voluntarily to the United Nations Detention Unit ("UNDU");[6]

NOTING that Ćorić argues that he is not a flight risk and he will not pose a danger to any victim, witness, or other person if provisionally released;[7]

NOTING the "Prosecution Response to Valentin Ćorić's Request for Provisional Release" filed confidentially and *ex parte* by the Office of the Prosecutor ("Prosecution") on 23 May 2016 ("Response"), in which the Prosecution opposes the Motion on the basis, *inter alia*, that Ćorić fails to establish special circumstances warranting provisional release because he has not served **[page 2]** two-thirds but only 52% of his sentence at the time of the filing of his Motion[8] and that the time spent on provisional release cannot be considered as "time served";[9]

[REDACTED],[10] [REDACTED];[11]

NOTING that Ćorić did not file a reply;

NOTING the guarantees provided by the Government of Croatia[12] and the correspondence received from The Netherlands;[13]

RECALLING that, pursuant to Rule 65(1) of the Tribunal's Rules of Procedure and Evidence ("Rules"), the Appeals Chamber may grant provisional release to convicted persons pending an appeal or for a fixed period, if it is satisfied that: (i) the appellant, if released, will either appear at the hearing of the appeal or will surrender into detention at the conclusion of the fixed period, as the case may be; (ii) the appellant, if

---

[1]   *Prosecutor v. ladranko Prlić et al.*, Case No. IT-04-74-T, Judgement, 6 June 2014 (French original filed on 29 May 2013), Vol. 4, p. 431.

[2]   Motion, p. 2. See also Motion, paras 2-3, 23, 32-34, p. 10,

[3]   Motion, paras 23-28. See also Motion, paras 1, 5.

[4]   Motion, para. 29.

[5]   Motion, para. 30. See also Motion, para. 4.

[6]   Motion, para. 31. See also Motion, paras 4, 6, 8.

[7]   Motion, paras 11-22. See also Motion, para. 7.

[8]   Response, paras 1-3, 6.

[9]   Response, para. 4. See also Response, para. 1. The Prosecution also contends that Ćorić has failed to establish that. if released, he would surrender into detention at the end of the release period. It further argues that flight risk is greater after a sentence of sixteen years of imprisonment has been imposed than during trial, especially when a prosecution sentencing appeal is pending. See Response, paras 1,5-6.

[10]   [REDACTED].

[11]   [REDACTED].

[12]   Motion, Annex A.

[13]   Correspondence from the Ministry of Foreign Affairs of the Kingdom of the Netherlands, "Protocol Department

released, will not pose a danger to any victim, witness, or other person; and (iii) special circumstances exist warranting such release;

RECALLING that the requirements under Rule 65(1) of the Rules must be considered cumulatively and "[w]hether an applicant satisfies these requirements is to be determined on a balance of probabilities, and the fact that an individual has already been sentenced is a matter to be taken into account by the Appeals Chamber when balancing the probabilities";[14]

RECALLING that, while detention for a substantial period of time may amount to a special circumstance within the meaning of Rule 65(I)(iii) of the Rules, a determination must be made on a case-by-case basis;[15]

RECALLING the "Decision on Valentin doric's Motion Seeking Provisional Release" issued confidentially and *ex parte* by the Appeals Chamber on 12 March 2015 ("Decision of March 2015"), in which it dismissed a similar motion filed by Corie contending, *inter alia,* that **[page 3]** the periods he spent on provisional release should be included in the computation of his time served;[16]

CONSIDERING, Judge Poear partially dissenting, that by renewing his request for provisional release under the present circumstances, Ćorić is in effect seeking a reconsideration of the Decision of 12 March 2015 without showing a clear error of reasoning or that particular circumstances, which can be new facts or new arguments, justify its reconsideration to prevent an injustice in this regard;[17]

CONSIDERING, Judge Pocar partially dissenting, that the passage of 17 months since the issuance of the Decision of 12 March 2015 does not constitute a material change in the factors considered by the Appeals Chamber in the decision thereof because, excluding the time spent on provisional release, Ćorić's period of detention at the UNDU is still shorter than two-thirds of his 16 year sentence, which[18] the Appeals Chamber found in the past to be "sufficiently substantial to constitute a special circumstance warranting" provisional release, under certal n cond'tions;[19]

FINDING, therefore, that Ćorić has failed to demonstrate the existence of special circumstances required by Rule 65(I)(iii) of the Rules;

CONSIDERING that as the requirements of Rule 65(1) of the Rules are cumulative, there is no need to consider whether the requirements of Rules 65(I)(i) and (ii) of the Rules are met;[20]

---

[14]   *See, e.g.,* Decision on Jadranko Prlić's Renewed Request for Provisional Release on Compassionate Grounds, 10 May 2016 (confidential) ("Decision of 10 May 2016"), p. 2; Decision on Jadranko Prlić's Request for Provisional Release on Compassionate Grounds, 6 April 2016 (confidential) ("Decision of 6 April 2016"), p. 2.

[15]   *See, e.g.,* Decision on Valentin Corikis Motion Seeking Provisional Release Until Translation of the Judgement, 19 December 2013 (confidential and ex parte) p. 2 and references cited therein.

[16]   Decision of 12 March 2015, para. 11. See also Decision of 12 March 2015, para. 4.

[17]   See Decision on Prosecution Urgent Motion for Reconsideration and Stay of Decision on Petković's Motion for Provisional Release, 21 September 2015 (confidential and *ex parte),* p. 2; *Prosecutor v. Mićo Stanišić and Stojan Župljanin,* Case No. IT-08-91-A, Decision on *Mićo* Stanišić's Motion Seeking Reconsideration of Decision on Stanišić 's Motion for Declaration of Mistrial and Župljanin's Motion to Vacate Trial Judgement, 24 July 2014, para. 11. *Cf. Prosecutor v. Vujadin Popović et al,,* Case No. IT-05-88-A, Decision on Vinko Pandurevid's Renewed Motion for Provisional Release. 12 December 2014, p. 2.

[18]   See Decision of 12 March 2015, para. 11 and references cited therein.

[19]   Decision of 12 March 2015, para. 11; *Prosecutor v. Enver Hadžihasanović and Amir Kubura,* Case No. IT-01-47-A, Decision on Motion on behalf of Enver Hadžihasanović for Provisional Release, 20 June 2007, para. 13.

[20]   Decision of 10 May 2016, p. 3; Decision of 6 April 2016, p. 3.

FOR THE FOREGOING REASONS,

HEREBY DENIES, Judge Pocar partially dissenting, the Motion in its entirety.

Judge Pocar appends a partially dissenting opinion. **[page 4]**

Done in English and French, the English version being authoritative.

Done this first day of December 2016,
At The Hague,
The Netherlands.

_____
Judge Carmel Agius
Presiding

[Seal of the Tribunal]

[page 1] I. PARTIALLY DISSENTING OPINION OF JUDGE POCAR

1.   In this decision ("Decision"), the Appeals Chamber treats "Valentin Ćorić's Request for Provisional Release" filed confidentially and **ex parte** with a confidential and *ex parte* annex by Valentin Ćorić ("Ćorić") on 12 May 2016 ("Motion") as a request for reconsideration of the "Decision on Valentin Ćorić's Motion Seeking Provisional Release" issued confidentially and *ex parte* by the Appeals Chamber on 12 March 2015 ("Decision of 12 March 2015") and denies the Motion on the basis that Ćorić has failed to show "a clear error of reasoning or that particular circumstances, which can be new facts or new arguments, justify its reconsideration to prevent an injustice in this regard".[1] For the reasons mentioned below, while I agree to deny the Motion, I dissent with the majority's decision to the extent that it treats Ćorić's Motion as a request for reconsideration without properly assessing Ćorić's arguments. I also dissent with the majority's decision to re-affirm the general ruling contained in the Decision of 12 March 2015 that any time spent on provisional release should not be included in the computation of time served in detention, despite this issue being raised on appeal by several of the co-appellants in this case.

2.   In my view, and contrary to the Decision[2]? the majority follows an incorrect approach in interpreting Ćorić's Motion as a request for reconsideration of the Decision of 12 March 2015 and denying it without properly assessing Ćorić's arguments. In this respect, I first note that 14 months have elapsed between the Decision of 12 March 2015 and the filing of Ćorić's Motion, which in light of the crux of the matter at stake – i.e. whether two-thirds of the sentence imposed has been served – is an important element especially given that the Appeals Chamber never clarified the exact number of days Ćorić has spent at the United Nations Detention Unit ("UNDU") thus far.[3]

3.   More importantly, the majority brushes aside Ćorić's new arguments, stating that he has not "show[n] a clear error of reasoning or that particular circumstances, which can be new facts or new arguments, justify its reconsideration to prevent an injustice in this regard", but in so doing fails to even mention or assess his new arguments[4] I find it perplexing that the majority determines that Ćorić fails to present new arguments justifying reconsideration without itself assessing those arguments. In this respect, I note that, in his motion for provision release which led to the Decision **[page 2]** of 12 March 2015, Ćorić simply alleged that "the restricted custodial release periods do not interrupt the computation of time spent in custody, since he was in the custody of the authorities [of the] Republic of Croatia during those periods."[5] However, in his current Motion, Ćorić advances new arguments, including that: (i) "he was in the custody of the Croatian Police during those periods [of provisional release.]";[6] (ii) the periods of provisional release were undertaken pursuant to conditions which "were akin to detention, rather than bail or some other form of less restrictive provisional release, insofar as liberties and freedoms were abridged"[7] (iii) jurisprudence from the Tribunal and of the Special Court for Sierra Leone "support the position that provisional release under conditions akin to detention counts the same as time spent in actual detention by a convicted person';[8] (iv) the laws of Croatia similarly support this position;[9] (v) some of his provisional release periods "essentially involved house arrest, where the accused was guarded by police officials while at his home residence";[10] and (vi) he was released for medical treatment for a substantial period of time during which he was subject to police monitoring and surveillance at the hospital, which constitutes detention.[11] None of these arguments are

---

[1]   Decision, p. 3.
[2]   Decision, p. 3.
[3]   With respect to this issue, I note that the Appeals Chamber never established the number of days spent at the UNDU and on provisional release, simply noting that Ćorić was detained at the UNDU during the periods between 5 April 2004 and 9 September 2004 and between 24 April 2006 and 21 December 2011, except for short periods of provisional release, and that he has also been detained there since 21 May 2013", without clarifying how many days these "short periods of provisional release" amount to. See Decision of 12 March 2015, p. 5. See also Decision on Valentin Ćorić's Motion Seeking Provisional Release Until Translation of the Judgement, 19 December 2013 (confidential and *ex parte)*, p. 3.
[4]   See Decision, pp. 1-4.
[5]   Valentin Ćorić's Request for Provisional Release, 5 December 2014, para. 21.
[6]   Motion, para. 24.
[7]   Motion, para. 25.
[8]   Motion, para. 26.
[9]   Motion, para. 26.
[10]   Motion, para. 26.
[11]   Motion, para. 27.

summarised or addressyd in the Decision, although the majority surprisingly states that Ćorić has not "show[n] a clear error of reasoning or that particular circumstances, which can be new facts or new arguments, justify its reconsideration to prevent an injustice in this regard". hi order to arrive to such a conclusion, the Appeals Chamber has a duty to provide a reasoned opinion as to why these arguments should be dismissed. The majority, unfortunately, fails to do so.

4.   For all these reasons, I dissent with the majority's decision to the extent that it treats Ćorić's Motion as a request for reconsideration without properly assessing Ćorić's arguments.

5.   In addition, I also dissent with the majority's decision to re-affirm the general ruling contained in the Decision of 12 March 2015 that any time spent on provisional release should not be included in the computation of time served in detention, despite this issue being raised on appeal not only by Ćorić but also by four other co-appellants in this case[12] By doing so, the majority **[page 3]** decides upon an alleged error of law and fact raised by several co-appellants without assessing their arguments.

6.   While I recognise that the Appeals Chamber already enounced this general ruling in its Decision of 12 March 2015, I recall that the Appeals Chamber has an inherent discretionary power to reconsider its own non-final decisions if a clear error of reasoning has been demonstrated or if it is necessary to do so in order to prevent an injustice.[13] In my view, Ćorić's Motion provides the Appeals Chamber with the opportunity to reconsider *proprio motu* its Decision of 12 March 2015 and to rule that the issue of whether any time spent on provisional release should be included in the computation of time served in detention will be decided in its appeal judgement, thereby giving due consideration to the submissions of all the co-appellants raising similar arguments. To do so is, in my view, necessary to prevent an injustice and is in line with the Appeals Chamber's previous approach when confronted with a similar request concerning Pusie"s time spent in detention[14] as well as with its jurisprudence that "a request for provisional release is not the appropriate forum to argue the substance of the appeal."[15]

---

[12]   Ćorić: Re-Filed Notice of Appeal Filed on Behalf of Mr. Valentin Ćorić, 23 December 2014, paras 96-98; Corrigendum to Appellant's Brief of Valentin Ćorić, 23 March 2016, paras 333-339; Pušić: Notice of Appeal on Behalf of Berislav Pusie, 13 March 2014, para. 37.3; Notice of Re-Filing of Redacted Appeal Brief of Berislav Pušić, 28 July 2015, paras 253-254; Stojić: Bruno Stojić's Notice of Appeal, 4 August 2014, para. 64; Notice of Filing the Corrigendum to the Public Redacted Version of Bruno Stojić 's Appellant Brief, 28 July 2015, paras 434-439; Petković: Milivoj Petković's Notice of Appeal, 5 August 2014, para. 144; Notice of Re-Filing of Redacted Versions of Milivoj Petković Appeal Brief and Book of Authorities, 29 July 2015, paras 459-469; Prlić: Jadranko Prlić's Notice of Appeal, 5 August 2014, para. 21.3.

[13]   See, *e.g., Prosecutor v. Momčilo Krajišnik,* Case No. 1T-00-39-A, Decision on "Motion by Momcilo Krajisnik for Reconsideration of the Appellate Chamber's Decision of September 11, 2007", 27 September 2007, p. 1; *Juvenal Kajelijeli* v. *The Prosecutor,* Case No. ICTR-98-44A-A, Judgement, 23 May 2005, para. 203; *Ferdinand Nahimana et al. v. The Prosecutor,* Case No. ICTR-99-52-A, Decision on Jean-Bosco Barayagwiza's Request for Reconsideration of Appeals Chamber Decision of 19 January 2005 , 4 February 2005, p. 2. In this respect, I note that the standard for reconsideration does not require – as erroneously enunciated in the Decision – that the party seeking reconsideration bears the burden of proof, since a decision to reconsider its own non-final decision may also be adopted *proprio motu* by the Appeals Chamber. See also Dissenting Opinion of Judge Pocar, 21 September 2015 ("Dissenting Opinion of 21 September 2015"), para. 2, appended to Decision on Prosecution Urgent Motion for Reconsideration and Stay of Decision on Petkovics Motion for Provisional Release, 21 September 2015 (confidential and *ex parte); Corrigendum* to Decision on Prosecution Urgent Motion for Reconsideration and Stay of Decision on Petković's Motion for Provisional Release, 22 September 2015 (confidential and *ex parte).*

[14]   Decision on Deputy Registrar's Rule 33(B) Submission and Prosecution's Motion for Leave to File a Submission Regardjng Calculation of Time Served by Berislav Pušić, 17 April 2014 (confidential), pp. 1-2.

[15]   *The Prosecutor* v. *Théoneste Bagosora et al.,* Case No. ICTR-98-41-A, Decision on Aloys Ntabakuze's Motions for Provisional Release and Leave to File *Corrigendum,* 2 September 2009, para. 22 ("The Appeals Chamber first emphasizes that a request for provisional release is not the appropriate forum to argue the substance of the appeal. The Appeals Chamber will determine the issues raised in the appeal in its judgement at the conclusion of the appeal proceedings. At this stage, the outcome of Ntabakuze's appeal cannot be foreseen and thus the merits of the case cannot amount to factors that could be taken into account in determining whether provisional release should be granted. Ntabakuze's reliance on arguments from his Appeal Brief therefore constitutes an improper basis for his application for provisional release.") (internal references omitted). See also *Prosecutor v. Mićo Stanišić and Stojan Zupljanin,* Case No. 1T-08-91-A, Decision on Motion on Behalf of Mićo Stanišić Seeking Provisional Release, 19 December 2013, paras 18-19; *Prosecutor v. Stanislav Galić,* Case No. 1T-98-29-A, Decision on Second Defence Request for Provisional Release of Stanislav Galić, 31 October 2005 *("Galić* Decision of 31 October 2005"), para. 16 ("the outcome of the appeal is unforeseeable and thus is not a factor that can be relied upon in determining whether provisional release should be granted."); *Prosecutor v. Dario Kordić and Mario Čerkez,* Case No. IT-95-14/2-A, Decision on Mario Čerkez's Request for Provisional Release, 12 December 2003 *("Kordić and Čerkez* Decision of 12 December 2003"), para. 8 ("The outcome of the case is unforeseeable, and thus is not a factor that can be relied upon in determining whether provisional release should be granted.").

7.   In light of the above, I dissent with the majority decision. That being said, I would also deny the Motion because, regardless of whether or not Ćorić has already served two-thirds of his sentence, "the ultimate decision of whether or not to grant provisional release is subject to the **[page 4]** Appeals Chamber's discretion"[16] and the fact that an appellant has already served two-thirds of a sentence *may,* in certain cases, be "sufficiently substantial to constitute a special circumstance warranting" provisional release but cannot be considered as an entitlement per se.[17] In my view, other relevant factors, such as the fact that the Prosecution appealed Ćorić's acquittals and sentence and requested that Ćorić's sentence be increased to 35 years of imprisonment,[18] weigh against granting Ćorić provisional release.[19]

Done in English and French, the English text being authoritative.

Judge Fausto Pocar

Dated this first day of December 2016,
at The Hague,
The Netherlands.

[Seal of the Tribunal]

---

[16]   See, *e.g., Prosecutor v. Vujadin Popović et al.,* Case No. IT-05-88-A, Decision on Vinko Pandurević's Motion for Provisional Release, 14 March 2014 *("Popović et al.* Decision of 14 March 2014"), para. 19; *The Prosecutor v. Pauline Nyiramasuhuko et al.,* Case No. ICTR-98-42-A, Decision on Nsabimana's Motion for Provisional Release, 10 September 2014 (confidential) *("Nyiramasuhuko et al.* Decision of 10 September 2014"), p. 4.

[17]   *Prosecutor v. Enver Hadžihasanović and Amir Kuhura,* Case No. IT-01-47-A, Decision on Motion on behalf of Enver Hadžihasanović for Provisional Release, 20 June 2007, para. 13. See also Decision of 12 March 2015, para. 11; *Popović et al.* Decision of 14 March 2014, para. 19; *Nyiramasuhuko et al.* Decision of 10 September 2014, pp. 3-4.

[18]   Prosecution's Notice of Appeal, 27 August 2013, paras 17-19; Prosecution Revised Public Redacted Appeal Brief, 12 January 2015, paras 338; 401-408, 419, 424 (the Prosecution requests the Appeals Chamber to increase Ćorić's sentence to 35 years of imprisonment).

[19]   See, *e.g., Popović et al.* Decision of 14 March 2014, para. 19; *Prosecutor v. Vujadin Popović et al.,* Case No. IT-05- 88-A, Decision on Vinko Pandurević's Renewed Motion for Provisional Release, 12 December 2014, pp. 1-2. See also *Galić* Decision of 31 October 2005, para. 16; *Kordić and Čerkez* Decision of 12 December 2003, para. 8.

	Case No.	MICT-15-96-PT
Mechanism for International Criminal Tribunals	Date:	19 May 2017
	Original:	English

IN THE TRIAL CHAMBER

Before: **Judge Burton Hall, Presiding
Judge Joseph E. Chiondo Masanche
Judge Seon Ki Park**

Registrar: **Mr. Olufemi Elias**

Decision of: **19 May 2017**

PROSECUTOR

v.

JOVICA STANIŠIĆ
FRANKO SIMATOVIĆ

PUBLIC

DECISION ON STANIŠIĆ'S MOTION FOR EXTENSION OF PROVISIONAL RELEASE

The Office of the Prosecutor:

Mr. Serge Brammertz
Mr. Douglas Stringer

Counsel for the Defence:

Mr. Wayne Jordash and Mr. Iain Edwards for Mr. Jovica Stanišić
Mr. Mihajlo Bakrać and Mr. Vladimir Petrović for Mr. Franko Simatović

[page 1] 1.   The Trial Chamber of the International Residual Mechanism for Criminal Tribunals ("Trial Chamber" and "Mechanism", respectively)[1] is seised of "Stanišić Defence Motion for Extension of Provisional Release" filed confidentially with confidential annex A by Jovica Stanišić on 5 May 2017 ("Motion"). The Prosecution filed a response on 12 May 2017,[2] and Stanišić filed a reply on 17 May 2017.[3]

I. BACKGROUND

2.   On 30 May 2013, Trial Chamber I of the International Criminal Tribunal for the Former Yugoslavia ("ICTY") acquitted Stanišić on all counts of the Indictment and ordered his immediate release from the United Nations Detention Unit ("UNDU") in The Hague.[4] On 9 December 2015, the ICTY Appeals Chamber granted, in part, the ICTY Prosecution's appeal and quashed Stanišić's acquittals of aiding and abetting and committing, through participation in a joint criminal enterprise, murder as a violation of the laws and customs of war and murder, deportation, other inhumane acts (forcible transfer), and persecution as crimes against humanity.[5] Further, the ICTY Appeals Chamber ordered that Stanišić be retried on all counts of the Indictment.[6]

3.   On 9 December 2015, the ICTY Appeal Chamber ordered the arrest and detention on remand of Stanišić and, on 15 December 2015, he was transferred to the UNDU in The Hague.[7] In accordance with Article 1(4) of the Transitional Arrangements annexed to the Statute of the Mechanism ("Statute"),[8] the President of the Mechanism assigned the case to the Trial Chamber on 17 December 2015.[9] The Pre-Trial fudge held Stanišić's initial appearance, in accordance with Rule 64 of the Mechanism's Rules of Procedure and Evidence ("Rules"), on 18 December 2015, and Stanišić entered a plea of "not guilty" on all counts in the Indictment.[10] **[page 2]**

4.   On 22 December 2015, the Trial Chamber granted Stanišić's urgent request for provisional release to the Republic of Serbia.[11] In its decision, the Trial Chamber instructed the UNDU Medical Service to: (i) put questions to Stanišić by telephone once every three weeks during Stanišić's provisional release, with a view to identifying in particular any symptoms which might suggest a deterioration or potential deterioration in Stanišić's condition and/or his ability to travel; (ii) report to the Trial Chamber on Stanišić's medical condition within two days of the aforementioned interviews; and (iii) remain available, to the extent possible, for consultation regarding the treatment Stanišić should receive, if contacted by an institution treating Stanišić during the period of his provisional release.[12]

5.   On 24 June 2016, the Trial Chamber varied the conditions of Stanišić's provisional release by instructing the UNDU Medical Service to put questions to Stanišić's treating physician and, if necessary, to Stanišić by telephone at least once every three weeks during Stanišić's provisional release, with a view to

---

[1]   *See* Order Replacing a Judge in a Case Before a Trial Chamber, 21 February 2017, p. 1.

[2]   Prosecution Response to Stanišić Defence Motion for Extension of Provisional Release, 12 May 2017 (confidential with confidential and *ex parte* Annex)("Response").

[3]   Stanišić Reply to Prosecution Response to Defence Motion for Extension of Provisional Release, 17 May 2017 (confidential with confidential and *ex parte* annex) ("Reply").

[4]   *Prosecutor v. Jovica Stanišić and Franko Simatović,* Case No. IT-03-69-T, Judgement, 30 May 2013 (public with confidential Appendix C), para. 2363. *See also The Prosecutor v. Jovica Stanišić and Franko Simatovid,* Case No. IT-03-69-PT, Prosecution Notice of Filing of Third Amended Indictment, 10 July 2008 ("Indictment").

[5]   *Prosecutor v. Jovica Stanišić and Franko Simatović,* Case No. IT-03-69-A, Judgement, filed in writing on 9 December 2015 and pronounced in public on 15 December 2015 ("Appeal Judgement"), para. 131. *See also Prosecutor v. Jovica Stanišić and Franko Simatović,* Case No. IT-03-69-A, T. 15 December 2015, pp. 103-116.

[6]   Appeal Judgement, paras. 129, 131.

[7]   *Prosecutor v. Jovica Stanišić and Franko Simatović,* Case No. IT-O3-69-A, Warrant of Arrest and Order for Surrender of Jovica Stanišić, 9 December 2015, p.2; Appeal Judgement, para. 131; T. 18 December 2015, p. 2.

[8]   U.N. Security Council Resolution 1966, U.N. Doc. S/Res/1966, 22 December 2010, Annex 2 ("Transitional Arrangements").

[9]   Order Assigning Judges to a Case Before a Trial Chamber, 17 December 2015, p.1.

[10]   T. 18 December 2015, p. 6. *See also* Order Designating a Pre-Trial Judge, 17 December 2015.

[11]   Decision on Stanišić's Urgent Motion for Provisional Release, 22 December 2015 ("Provisional Release Decision"), para. 16.

[12]   Provisional Release Decision, p. 9.

identifying in particular any symptoms which might suggest a deterioration or potential deterioration in Stanišić's condition and/or his ability to travel.[13]

6.   That same day, in order to determine the trial schedule and bearing in mind Stanišić's history of chronic health conditions,[14] the Trial Chamber requested the Registrar to appoint independent medical experts to examine Stanišić and to submit detailed written reports.[15] The Trial Chamber received the reports of Dr. Eric Vermetten and Dr. Peter Siersema on 26 and 27 September 2016, respectively.[16] On 12 December 2016 and 2 February 2017, Dr. Vermetten and Dr. Siersema appeared before the Trial Chamber and were questioned in relation to their reports.[17]

7.   On 10 February 2017, the Trial Chamber proposed modalities for the trial, which included: (i) a preliminary examination and health monitoring regime for Stanišić on his return to the UNDU; (ii) a trial schedule limited to three consecutive days a week, each day composed of two sessions of 90 minutes with a two hour break; and (iii) in the event that Stanišić waived his right to be present **[page 3]** at trial, the possibility for remote participation via video-conference link in a pre-existing facility set up for that purpose at the UNDU.[18]

8.   The Trial Chamber requested the parties and the Registrar to comment on the proposed modalities and to make any other proposals that may facilitate Stanišić's effective participation in the trial proceedings and the efficient use of court time.[19] In response, Stanišić submitted, *inter alia,* that, in view of the exceptional circumstances present in this case, he should be permitted to remain on provisional release throughout the duration of the trial and that, if he is required to participate in certain parts of the trial and during the presentation of the Defence case, his participation should be via video-conference link from Belgrade.[20] On 13 April 2017, the Trial Chamber set the modalities for trial, holding that any motion requesting extension of provisional release, pursuant to Rule 68 of the Rules, should be filed separately and be accompanied by a signed, voluntary and unequivocal waiver of Stanišić's right to be present.[21] It further held that, if such a request were to be granted, Stanišić must bear in mind that, at this stage, the Trial Chamber will not ensure his participation in the proceedings via video-conference link from Belgrade.[22]

9.   On 17 May 2017, the Trial Chamber held a Pre-Trial Conference in accordance with Rule 81 of the Rules.[23] It is anticipated that the trial will commence on 13 June 2017, subject to the outcome of any pending litigation.[24]

II. SUBMISSIONS

10.   Stanišić requests that his provisional release be extended for the duration of the Prosecution case.[25] In support of his request, Stanišić submits that he continues to satisfy the requirements of Rule 68(B) of the

---

[13]   Decision Amending Decision on Stanišić's Urgent Motion for Provisional Release, 24 June 2016 (public redacted version), para. 21.

[14]   *See* Decision on the Prosecution's Request for an Independent Medical Examination of Jovica Stanišić, 24 June 2016 ("Medical Examination Decision"), paras. 3, 4.

[15]   Medical Examination Decision, paras. 10, 13(i). *See also* Decision on Registrar's Request for Extension of Time, 17 August 2016, p. 1; Decision on Registrar's Request for Extension of Time, 20 September 2016, p. 1.

[16]   Registrar's Submission of the Written Report of the Independent [Medical Expert], 26 September 2016 (confidential and *ex parte)'*, Registrar's Submission of the Written Report of the Independent [Medical Expert], 27 September 2016 (confidential and *ex parte).*

[17]   Witness Eric Vermetten, T. 12 December 2016 pp. 75-154 (confidential and *ex parte); *Witness Peter Siersema, T. 2 February 2017 pp. 175-234 (confidential and *ex parte).*

[18]   Order for Submissions on Modalities for Trial, 10 February 2017 (confidential) ("Order on Modalities"), Annex.

[19]   Order on Modalities, p. 2.

[20]   Submissions on Modalities for Trial, 24 February 2017 *(ex parte* with confidential annex; confidential redacted version filed on 27 February 2017) ("Stanišić Submissions"), paras. 7-14, 17, 25, 38, 40-62, 65; Stanišić Consolidated Response to Prosecution and Registrar Submissions on Mod ah ties for Trial, 13 March 2017 (confidential), para. 14.

[21]   Decision on Modalities for Trial, 13 April 2017 ("Modalities Decision"), para. 20.

[22]   Modalities Decision, para. 20.

[23]   Scheduling Order, 3 May 2017, p. 1.

[24]   Pre-Trial Conference, T.17 May 2017 p. 269.

[25]   Motion, paras. 8, 20.

Rules and has, without exception, complied with the conditions of his provisional release.[26] Stanišić appends a signed, voluntary, and unequivocal waiver of his right to be present during the presentation of the Prosecution case, acknowledging that the Trial Chamber **[page 4]** will not ensure his participation in the proceedings via video-conference link from Belgrade,[27] He asserts that, if allowed to remain on provisional release, he will continue to be represented by counsel in court, follow the proceedings by reviewing daily transcripts and watching the live stream of the public broadcast of the trial over the internet, and instruct counsel on an ongoing basis.[28] Stanišić also appends a personal guarantee and waiver of doctor-patient privilege for the duration of his provisional release.[29]

11. In response, the Prosecution opposes Stanišić's request for the extension of his provisional release.[30] The Prosecution contends that Stanišić fails to meet one of the main criteria for provisional release, namely that he will appear for trial.[31] The Prosecution further notes that Stanišić's waiver is not unequivocal as he reserves the right to revoke it at any point, which may result in trial disruptions, in particular if revoked after he becomes too sick to travel while on provisional release.[32] In addition, the Prosecution argues that the original guarantees offered by Serbia are insufficient to ensure Stanišić's presence if ordered by the Trial Chamber.[33] The Prosecution also highlights the heightened risk for protected witnesses because communication between counsel and Stanišić in Serbia increases the risk of disclosure of confidential information.[34] Finally, the Prosecution argues that Stanišić's health and the impact that provisional release would have on the Mechanism's integrity militate against provisional release given that he has not shown that he cannot obtain adequate treatment in The Hague and that witnesses may question why they should endure the inconvenience and stress of testifying while Stanišić is allowed to remain at home.[35]

III. APPLICABLE LAW

12. Under Rule 68(B) of the Rules, the Trial Chamber may grant provisional release only if it is satisfied that, if released, the accused will appear for trial and will not pose a danger to any victim, witness, or other person; and after having given both the host country and the State to which the accused seeks to be released the opportunity to be heard. Provisional release may be ordered at any stage of the trial proceedings prior to the rendering of the final judgement, and a trial chamber in **[page 5]** granting such a release may consider the existence of sufficiently compelling humanitarian grounds.[36] When considering whether or not to grant the provisional release of an accused, a trial chamber is required to assess whether the conditions of Rule 68(B) of the Rules are fulfilled not only as they exist at the time it reaches its decision on provisional release, but also, as much as can be foreseen, at the time the accused is expected to return to the Mechanism.[37]

---

[26] Motion, paras. 9-14; Reply, paras. 4, 10, 11, Annex *See also* Reply, paras. 8, 9, 12, 13.
[27] Motion, para. 17, Annex, paras. 1, 2. Stanišić reserves his right to withdraw his waiver and seek a revision of the matter of his participation in proceedings via video-conference link from Belgrade at the end of the Prosecution case. *See* Motion, para. 18; Reply, paras. 6, 7.
[28] Motion, paras. 16,19.
[29] Motion, Annex, paras. 3-5.
[30] Response, paras. 1, 12.
[31] Response, para. 3.
[32] Response, paras. 4, 5.
[33] Response, para. 6.
[34] Response, para. 7.
[35] Response, paras. 8, 10, 11.
[36] *See* Rule 68(B) of the Rules; *Prosecutor v. Jadranko Prlić et al.* Case No. IT-04-74-AR65.35, Decision on the Prosecution's Appeal of the Decision on Further Extension of Milivoj Petković's Provisional Release, 12 June 2012 *("Prlić* Decision of 12 June 2012")*, para. 5.
[37] See *Prosecutor v. Vojislav Šešelj,* Case No. IT-03-67-AR65.1, Decision on Prosecution Appeal against the Decision on the Prosecution Motion to Revoke the Provisional Release of the Accused, 30 March 2015 *("Šešelj* Decision of 30 March 2015"), para. 14, *referring, inter alia, to Prosecutor* v. *Jadranko Prlić et al.* Case No. IT-04-74-AR65.24, Decision on Jadranko Prlić's Appeal of the Trial Chamber Decision on his Motion for Provisional Release, 8 June 2011, para. 6; *Prosecutor* v. *Ramush Haradinaj et al.,* Case No. IT-04-84*bis*-AR65.1, Decision on Prosecution Appeal of the Trial Chamber's Decision on Ramush Haradinaj's Motion for Provisional Release, 16 December 2010, para. 7; *Prosecutor* v. *Jadranko Prlić et al.,* Case No. IT-04-74-AR65.14, Decision on Jadranko Prlić's Appeal Against the *Décision relative à la demande de mise en liberté provisoire de l'accusé Prlić,* 9 April 2009, 5 June 2009, para. 8; *Prosecutor* v. *Vujadin Popović et al.,* Case Nos. IT-05-88-AR65.4, IT-05-88-AR65.5 & IT-05-88-AR65.6,

13.   In deciding whether the requirements of Rule 68(B) of the Rules have been met, a trial chamber must consider all relevant factors that a reasonable trial chamber would have been expected to take into account before coming to a decision.[38] What these relevant factors are, as well as the weight to be accorded to them, depends upon the particular circumstances of each case.[39] This is because decisions on motions for provisional release are fact-intensive, and cases are considered on an individual basis in light of the particular circumstances of the individual accused.[40] The same legal principles applicable to a motion for provisional release apply *mutatis mutandis* to a motion for extension of provisional release.[41]

14.   In accordance with Article 19(4)(d) of the Statute, an accused has a fundamental right to be tried in his presence. The right to be present, however, may be waived under Rule 98 of the Rules, provided that: (i) the accused has made an initial appearance pursuant to Rule 64 of the Rules; (ii) the Registrar has duly notified the accused that he is required to be present at trial; (iii) the accused is physically and mentally fit to be present for trial; (iv) the accused has voluntarily and unequivocally waived, or has forfeited, his right to be tried in his presence; and (v) the interests of the accused are represented by counsel. **[page 6]**

IV.   DISCUSSION

15.   As a general rule and in practice, provisional release ends when trial begins.[42] While the Trial Chamber did not fix the duration of Stanišić's provisional release, with the impending commencement of trial,[43] it could be reasonably expected that his provisional release would be terminated imminently, and as such giving rise to the present request for extension of provisional release.

16.   As noted in the Modalities Decision, Rule 68(B) of the Rules clearly envisions that "[r]elease may be ordered at any stage of the trial proceedings prior to the rendering of the final judgement". This could include stages involving hearings and the presentation of evidence to the extent that the accused continues to satisfy the conditions for provisional release, is represented by counsel, and has voluntarily and unequivocally waived his right to be present in the courtroom during that stage of the ongoing trial.[44] Normally, an accused person should be present at his trial, and authorizing provisional release during the course of ongoing proceedings, especially the presentation of evidence, should be the exception.

17.   This case, however, is exceptional amongst those that have been tried before the *ad hoc* Tribunals: a full retrial on all counts following the acquittal of accused who have been in proceedings for nearly 14 years, including one whose health conditions profoundly impacted the length and pace of the original proceedings.[45] As recognized in the Modalities Decision, Stanišić - although fit to attend trial - continues to have health conditions that limit the duration of court time to a maximum of nine hours per week.[46] Against this backdrop, it is understandable why Stanišić would seek to waive his presence during the presentation of the

---

Decision on Consolidated Appeal Against Decision on Borovčanin's Motion for a Custodial Visit and Decisions on Gvero's and Miletic's Motions for Provisional Release during the Break in Proceedings, 15 May 2008, para. 6.

[38]   See *Prosecutor* v. *Goran Hadžić*, Case No. IT-04-75-AR65.1, Decision on Urgent Interlocutory Appeal from Decision Denying Provisional Release, 13 April 2015 (public with confidential annex) *("Hadžić* Decision of 13 April 2015"), para. 7, *referring to Šešelj* Decision of 30 March 2015, para. 13.

[39]   *Hadžić* Decision of 13 April 2015, para. 7 *referring to Šešelj* Decision of 30 March 2015, para. 13.

[40]   *Prlić* Decision of 12 June 2012, para. 6, *referring to Prosecutor* v. *Jadranko Prlić et al.*, Case No. IT-04-74-AR65.26, Decision on Prosecution Appeal of Decision on Provisional Release of Jadranko Prlić, 15 December 2011, para. 6.

[41]   *Prlić* Decision of 12 June 2012, para. 11, *referring to Prosecutor v. Nikola Šainović et al*, Case No. IT-05-87-A, Decision on the Third Urgent Defence Motion Requesting Prolongation of Provisional Release of Vladimir Lazarevic, 4 August 2009 (public redacted version), para. 5.

[42]   See Rule 68(B) of the Rules ("Release may be ordered at any stage of the trial proceedings prior to the rendering of the final judgement by the Trial Chamber only after giving the host country and the State to which the accused seeks to be released the opportunity to be heard and *only if it is satisfied that the accused will appear for trial* [...].")(emphasis added); Rule 68 (C) of the Rules ("The Trial Chamber may impose such conditions upon the release of the accused as it may determine appropriate, including the execution of a bail bond and the observance of such conditions *as are necessary to ensure the presence of the accused for trial* and the protection of others.") (emphasis added).

[43]   See *supra* para. 9.

[44]   Modalities Decision, para. 16.

[45]   See Modalities Decision, para. 27; Medical Examination Decision, para. 3, and references cited therein.

[46]   Modalities Decision, paras. 26, 27, Annex, para. 2.

Prosecution case and to remain on provisional release. It would appreciably reduce the length of his proceedings by allowing the Trial Chamber to maximize sitting times and expedite his case.

18.   The Trial Chamber notes that "the judicial activity calendar may be a relevant factor when assessing a request for provisional release, notably to avoid unwarranted disruptions or undue **[page 7]** delays in the proceedings".[47] Authorizing Stanišić's provisional release during the Prosecution case would in fact have an appreciable impact on the expeditious conduct of these proceedings, in particular in view of the background of this case. This factor, however, is not the touchstone of the Trial Chamber's analysis or consideration, but simply one which highlights the exceptional nature of Stanišić's situation and placing it into a narrow category of cases where provisional release may be considered appropriate during a portion of the ongoing trial.

19.   In granting Stanišić provisional release, the Trial Chamber noted that Stanišić was provisionally released for extended periods during the pre-trial stage of the original trial and on several occasions during the original trial proceedings and that, on each occasion, he appeared for trial and did not pose any danger to any victim, witness, or other person.[48] In relation to his current provisional release, the Trial Chamber has received regular reports from the Government of the Republic of Serbia confirming Stanišić's compliance with the conditions of his provisional release. The Trial Chamber has no reason to believe that Stanišić would cease to abide by these conditions should his request to remain on provisional release be granted.

20.   When the Provisional Release Decision was issued, the Trial Chamber was also satisfied that Stanišić would not pose any danger to any victim, witness, or other person.[49] There is no information before the Trial Chamber that the circumstances in this regard have changed, even if there are increased exchanges of information between Stanišić and his counsel. In this respect, the Trial Chamber notes that, for much of the 14 years of proceedings, Stanišić has either been on provisional release or released following his acquittal without incident, while having full access to all confidential information in his original trial and to the identity of nearly all witnesses in this trial. It is assumed that Stanišić has been in regular contact with his counsel during this current period of provisional release which has lasted for the duration of the pre-trial phase.

21.   The Trial Chamber considers that other factors are also relevant to Stanišić's request to remain on provisional release for the initial stage of the trial. The Trial Chamber is cognizant that allowing Stanišić to remain on provisional release after the trial's commencement may affect the confidence of the victims and witnesses in the proper administration of justice by the Mechanism. However, having carefully considered the specific circumstances of this case, the Trial Chamber finds that such a factor must also be viewed in the context of Stanišić's history of compliance, the exceptional nature of this case, and the lack of any concrete information before the Trial Chamber **[page 8]** that Stanišić remaining on provisional release will in fact impact the Prosecution's ability to secure witnesses.

22.   Moreover, as noted above, nearly 14 years have passed since Stanišić's arrest and initial transfer to the UNDU, of which Stanišić has spent nearly five years in detention.[50] In circumstances where Stanišić continues to satisfy the conditions of Rule 68(B) of the Rules, the period that he has already spent in detention warrants consideration when deciding whether Stanišić should be allowed to remain on provisional release.

23.   Further, the Trial Chamber notes that the expeditious conduct of the proceedings is contingent upon Stanišić's health.[51] The Trial Chamber has received reports from the UNDU Medical Service on Stanišić's health and several submissions by the Government of the Republic of Serbia in relation to Stanišić's treatment at the Military Medical Academy in Belgrade. In the Motion, Stanišić has renewed his waiver of doctor-patient privilege.[52] The Trial Chamber considers that the monitoring and reporting regime currently in place in connection with his provisional release mitigates against a risk of serious disruption to the trial proceedings

---

[47]   *Prosecutor* v. *Jadranko Prlić et al.*, Case No. IT-04-74-AR65.15, Decision on Prosecution's Appeal Against the Trial Chamber's Decision on Slobodan Praljak's Motion for Provisional Release, 8 July 2009, para. 10.
[48]   Provisional Release Decision, para. 9, and references cited therein.
[49]   Provisional Release Decision, para. 10.
[50]   Decision on Stanišić's Request for Stay of Proceedings, 2 February 2017, para. 19, and reference cited therein.
[51]   *See supra* paras. 6, 7, 17.
[52]   Motion, Annex A, para. 4.

should Stanišić's health deteriorate if he were to remain on provisional release. The Trial Chamber is mindful, however, that Stanišić has not been examined by independent experts since September 2016 and that it was anticipated that the Trial Chamber would receive updated independent medical information immediately prior to and during the course of the trial.[53]

24.   The Trial Chamber turns next to Stanišić's waiver of his right to be present during the presentation of the Prosecution case. The Trial Chamber notes that Stanišić has made an initial appearance under Rule 64 of the Rules, is physically and mentally fit to be present for trial, and has voluntarily waived his right to be present for the presentation of the Prosecution case.[54] The fact that he may revoke this waiver does not undermine its validity since Stanišić has the right to be present at trial. The Trial Chamber further notes that Stanišić is represented by counsel who has an in-depth familiarity with the case as he represented Stanišić during the original trial, and Stanišić has confirmed that he will continue to instruct counsel remotely, if allowed to remain on provisional release.[55]

25.   This case is exceptional and the balance of the above factors indicates that it may be appropriate to allow Stanišić to remain on provisional release during some parts of the Prosecution **[page 9]** case. In the Trial Chamber's view, however, the trial's commencement and its first trial session are among the most important stages of these proceedings.[56] Although this retrial will be similar in scope to the original proceedings, this is a new trial with a differently composed Bench and Prosecution team. The initial phase will set the tone for how this case will be conducted. Accordingly, it would not be appropriate or in the interests of justice to allow Stanišić to remain on provisional release during the initial stage of the Prosecution case.

26.   Moreover, the Trial Chamber notes that its Modalities Decision provides for a renewed assessment of Stanišić's health condition by relevant medical professionals in advance of the trial.[57] This updated information will ensure that the Trial Chamber continues to have accurate and independent information on the state of Stanišić's health, which would give greater meaning to the periodic medical monitoring of his provisional release regime should he be granted provisional release at a later stage of the Prosecution case. It will also provide a key safeguard against any trial disruptions due to a deterioration of his medical condition or ability to travel.

27.   In sum, the Trial Chamber decides not to extend Stanišić's provisional release during the opening session of this case. A separate order terminating provisional release in anticipation of the start of the trial will follow. Before the judicial recess, the Trial Chamber will revisit the question of whether it is appropriate to allow Stanišić to be provisionally released during subsequent sessions of the Prosecution case should Stanišić wish to waive his right to be present and subject to the most recent independent medical reporting indicating that he remains fit to travel.

---

[53]   *See supra* n. 16. *See also* Modalities Decision, Annex, para. 1.
[54]   Motion, Annex A, para. 1.
[55]   *See* Motion, para. 16.
[56]   The Trial Chamber further recalls that, in initially proposing to remain on provisional release during the Prosecution case, Stanišić noted that he "would [...] comply with any order of the Trial Chamber that he participate in certain parts of the retrial [...], if required, at the seat of the [Mechanism] including, for example, opening statements [...] and any other hearing as directed by the Trial Chamber." *See* Stanišić Submissions, para. 16.
[57]   Modalities Decision, Annex, para. 1.

V. DISPOSITION

28.   For the foregoing reasons, pursuant to Rule 68(B) of the Rules, the Trial Chamber **DENIES** the Motion without prejudice.

Done in English and French, the English version being authoritative.

Done this 19th day of May 2017,
At The Hague,
The Netherlands

_____

Judge Burton Hall, Presiding

[Seal of the Mechanism]

UNITED
NATIONS

Mechanism for International Criminal Tribunals	Case No.	MICT-14-63-ES
	Date:	11 August 2017
	Original:	English

THE PRESIDENT OF THE MECHANISM

Before:	Judge Theodor Meron, President
Registrar:	Mr. Olufemi Elias
Decision of:	11 August 2017

PROSECUTOR

v.

GORAN JELISIĆ

PUBLIC

PUBLIC REDACTED VERSION OF 22 MAY 2017 DECISION OF THE PRESIDENT ON RECOGNITION OF COMMUTATION OF SENTENCE, REMISSION OF SENTENCE, AND EARLY RELEASE OF GORAN JELISIĆ

The Office of the Prosecutor

Mr. Serge Brammertz

The Applicant

Mr. Goran Jelisić

The Italian Republic

[page 1] 1.   I, Theodor Meron, President of the International Residual Mechanism for Criminal Tribunals ("President" and "Mechanism", respectively), am seised of an application for recognition of commutation, remission of sentence, and early release from Mr. Goran Jelisić ("Jelisić") dated 28 December 2015 ("Application") and received on 13 January 2016.[1] I consider the Application pursuant to Article 26 of the Statute of the Mechanism ("Statute"), Rules 150 and 151 of the Rules of Procedure and Evidence of the Mechanism ("Rules"), and paragraph 3 of the Practice Direction on the Procedure for the Determination of Applications for Pardon, Commutation of Sentence, and Early Release of Persons Convicted by the ICTR, the ICTY or the Mechanism ("Practice Direction").[2]

I. BACKGROUND

2.   Jelisić was arrested on 22 January 1998 and was immediately transferred to the United Nations Detention Unit in The Hague, The Netherlands.[3] On 29 October 1998, Jelisić entered a plea of not guilty to the count of genocide and pleaded guilty to 31 counts comprising violations of the laws or customs of war and crimes against humanity of the second amended indictment filed against him.[4] Trial Chamber I of the International Criminal Tribunal for the Former Yugoslavia ("Trial Chamber" and "ICTY", respectively) was satisfied that the guilty plea entered by Jelisić was voluntary, informed, and unequivocal, and declared Jelisić guilty of the crimes he admitted to in his guilty plea.[5] The proceedings before the Trial Chamber were accordingly limited to the single count of genocide.[6]

3.   On 14 December 1999, the Trial Chamber entered convictions against Jelisić on 16 violations of the laws or customs of war, 12 for murder, three for cruel treatment, and one for plunder, as well as 15 counts of crimes against humanity, including 12 counts of murder and three counts of inhumane acts.[7] Pursuant to Rule *98bis* of the ICTY Rules of Procedure and Evidence, the Trial Chamber acquitted Jelisić of the count of genocide.[8] The Trial Chamber sentenced Jelisić to a single sentence of 40 years of imprisonment.[9] On 5 July 2001, the Appeals Chamber of the ICTY **[page 2]** unanimously affirmed the sentence of 40 years of imprisonment.[10] Jelisić was transferred to the Italian Republic ("Italy") on 29 May 2003 to serve the remainder of his sentence.[11]

II. THE APPLICATION

4.   On 18 February 2016, I conveyed to the Registry of the Mechanism ("Registry") the Application,[12] which includes: (i) a request for early release addressed to the Massa Supervising Magistrate, dated 5 August 2015; (ii) a letter from the Director of the Penitentiary Administration Department, Massa Penitentiary Facility, dated 27 August 2014, attaching a report of the Vice Commander for observation and treatment during Jelisić's detention, dated 18 July 2014; (iii) a general report of Jelisić's time in detention, dated 26 August 2014, and (iv) a letter from the Deputy Commander of the Prison Administration Department, Prison Police Department Command, to the Department Commander, dated 26 August 2014.[13] On 28 April 2016,

---

[1]   Letter from Jelisid to Judge Theodor Meron, President, dated 28 December 2015 (with annexes), received on 13 January 2016 and filed on 28 April 2016. All references herein are to the English translation of the Application.
[2]   MICT/3, 5 July 2012.
[3]   *The Prosecutor v. Goran Jelisić,* Case No. IT-95-10-T, Judgement, 14 December 1999 ("Trial Judgement"), paras. 5, 123, 135.
[4]   Trial Judgement, paras. 8, 11,24. *See also Prosecutor v. Goran Jelisić,* Case No. IT-95-10-A, Judgement, 5 July 2001 ("Appeal Judgement"), para. 2.
[5]   Trial Judgement, paras. 11, 24, 26-27, 58.
[6]   See Trial Judgement, paras. 11-15.
[7]   Trial Judgement, paras. 58, 109, 138.
[8]   Trial Judgement, paras. 16, 108.
[9]   Trial Judgement, para. 139.
[10]   Appeal Judgement, p. 41, para. 7.
[11]   *See* Press Release, Goran Jelisić Transferred to Italy to Serve Prison Sentence, dated 29 May 2003, *available at* http://www.ictv.org/en/press/goran-ielisic-transferred-italy-serve-prison-sentence.
[12]   Internal Memorandum from Judge Theodor Meron, President, to Mr. John Hocking, Registrar, dated 18 February 2016 *transmitting* the Application.
[13]   1 note that the dates on the English translations of these documents do not accord with the Italian versions of the documents. The original dates, contained in the Italian versions, are authoritative.

I filed the Application on the record. On the same day, having determined to deal with the Application as a request for early release on the basis that Jelisić asserted early release in the context of recognition of commutation of his sentence in the national courts, taken together with the contended cumulative effects of remission(s) of sentence, I requested the Registry to undertake the steps prescribed in the Practice Direction.[14]

5. On 22 June 2016, I received a memorandum from the Registry conveying information collected in accordance with paragraphs 3, 4, and 5 of the Practice Direction,[15] including: (i) a letter from the Director of the Department of Penitentiary Administration, Penitentiary Facility in Massa, to the Italian Ministry of Justice, dated 31 May 2016, conveying, first, Jelisić's behavioural report dated 31 May 2016 ("Behavioural Report"), and, second, [REDACTED] and (ii) a letter from the Director, Judicial Affairs Department of the Ministry of Justice, Directorate General of Penal Justice, Office II - International Judicial Cooperation, to the Italian Embassy in The Hague, dated 27 May 2016 ("27 May 2016 Letter"), conveying a letter from the Office of the Prosecutor of the Republic Attached to the Court of Appeals of Rome to the Ministry of Justice and the Management **[page 3]** of the Massa Penitentiary Facility Education Centre, dated 23 May 2016 ("23 May 2016 Letter"), transmitting a certificate of updated status of enforcement, dated 19 May 2016 ("Certificate of Enforcement").

6. On 1 June 2016, the Registry conveyed to me a memorandum from the Office of the Prosecutor of the Mechanism ("Prosecution"), dated 30 May 2016 ("Prosecution" and "Prosecution Memorandum", respectively).[16] The Registry informed me that in accordance with paragraphs 5 and 6 of the Practice Direction, the collated documents were transmitted to Jelisić on 4 July 2016.[17]

7. On 14 July 2016, Jelisić sent me a letter informing me that he had received the collated documents on 12 July 2016, and submitted his response thereto ("Observations").[18] In his Observations, Jelisić raised that the 22 June 2016 Memorandum was missing a report concerning [REDACTED] dated 30 May 2016 ("Missing Report").[19] On 15 August 2016, having not received further information about the Missing Report, I informed Jelisić that on 11 August 2016, I had instructed the Registrar of the Mechanism to inquire with the Italian authorities about this matter and to request a copy of the Missing Report.[20]

8. On 20 August 2016, I received a further letter from Jelisić clarifying, *inter alia,* that he was seeking a 180 days sentence remission for the period of 22 July 2013 to 22 July 2015, and that he had sent a new request for a further 90 days sentence remission for the period from 22 July 2015 to **[page 4]** 22 July 2016 to the

---

[14]   Internal Memorandum from Judge Theodor Meron, President, to Mr. John Hocking, then Registrar, dated 28 April 2016. On 2 May 2016, via letter, I informed Jelisid that 1 was considering his Application as a request for early release, Letter from Judge Theodor Meron, President, to Mr. Goran Jelisić, 2 May 2016 (confidential)("Letter of Notification").

[15]   Internal Memorandum from Mr. Gus de Witt, Officer-in-Charge, Registry, Hague Branch, to Judge Theodor Meron, President, dated 22 June 2016 ("22 June 2016 Memorandum"). All references to the attachments are to the English translations thereof.

[16]   Internal Memorandum from Mr. Gus de Witt, Officer-in-Charge, Registry, Hague branch, to Judge Theodor Meron, President, dated 1 June 2016 ("Registry Memorandum").

[17]   Registry Memorandum.

[18]   Letter from Mr. Goran Jelisii to the President, dated 14 July 2016 and received by me on 27 July 2016. The English translation of the letter was received on 3 August 2016. All references to the letter and the attachments are to the English translations thereof. As part of his Observations, Jelisit attaches 14 separate documents, including: (i) a letter from NULIFE srl. to Mr. Goran Jelisić, dated January 2016 ("Employment Letter"); (ii) Certificate of Acquired Knowledge for training course, dated 7 June 2013 ("Certificate for Training"); (iii) Two Reports of Grades from Institution of Vocational Education "Fermo Solari", dated 2011/2012 ("Reports of Grades"); (iv) Diploma of completion of first cycle of education, dated 22 June 2010 ("Diploma"); (v) Certificates of Competence for Italian Language levels A2 and Bl, dated 4 June 2010 and 24 September 2010 ("Language Certificates"); (vi) Certificate of Attendance on the course of "General Culture", dated 6 June 2008 ("Certificate of Attendance"); (vii) two Letters from the Office of the Prosecutor of Bosnia and Herzegovina to Mr. Goran Jelisid, entitled "Witness Interview", dated 18 June 2014 ("Letters from the Prosecutor of Bosnia and Herzegovina"); (viii) Judgement of Judge for Preliminary Investigations, Court of Padua, dated 29 October 2010 ("Judgement of Padua Court"); (ix) Record of the unsolicited statement given by the detainee, issued by the Penitentiary Facility Massa, dated 24 June 2014 ("Unsolicited Statement"); (x) Letter from Counsel Alessandro Maneschi to The Honourable Preliminary Investigation Judge of the Court in Massa, dated 14 April 2015 ("Letter from Counsel").

[19]   Observations, p. 1. *See also,* Letter from Mr. Goran Jelisid to Judge Theodor Meron, President, 20 August 2016 (confidential) ("Letter of 20 August 2016").

[20]   Letter from Judge Theodor Meron, President, to Mr. Goran Jelisić, 15 August 2016.

relevant Italian authorities.[21] On 16 September 2016, I informed Jelisić that I was still awaiting receipt of a Missing Report from the Italian authorities.[22]

9.   On 6 October 2016, I received from the Registry a report on [REDACTED], dated 6 September 2016, provided by the Italian authorities.[23]

10.   On 1 November 2016, Jelisić notified me that the Missing Report I was not provided with was a report from [REDACTED], asserted to have been compiled on 30 May 2016.[24] Jelisić also renewed his request for 180 days sentence remission for the period from 22 July 2013 to 22 July 2015, and for a further 90 days for the period 22 July 2015 to 22 July 2016.[25]

11.   On 17 February 2017, the Registry conveyed to me a *note verbale* from the Italian authorities, dated 27 January 2017, informing the Mechanism that only two expert reports in fact existed: (i) a [REDACTED] report dated 31 May 2016 prepared by [REDACTED], referred to as the Behavioural Report; and (ii) a report dated 6 September 2016, prepared by [REDACTED], which was previously incorrectly dated 30 May 2015 and which the Italian authorities informed was due to a computer error [REDACTED].[26]

12.   Noting the above described circumstances, essential aspects of the process under the Practice Direction, notably the follow up on materials being sought from the Italian authorities, and the need for confirmation as to the existence and correct dating of certain materials, while undertaken in the most efficient manner possible, have lengthened the period of time necessary to render this decision.

III.   APPLICABLE LAW

13.   Under Article 26 of the Statute, if, pursuant to the applicable law of the State in which the convicted person is imprisoned, he or she is eligible for pardon or commutation of sentence, the State concerned shall notify the Mechanism accordingly. Article 26 of the Statute further provides **[page 5]** that there shall only be pardon or commutation of sentence if the President so decides on the basis of the interests of justice and the general principles of law.

14.   Rule 149 of the Rules echoes Article 26 of the Statute and provides that the enforcing State shall notify the Mechanism of a convicted person's eligibility for pardon, commutation of sentence, or early release under the enforcing State's laws. Rule 150 of the Rules provides that the President shall, upon such notice, determine, in consultation with any Judges of the sentencing Chamber who are Judges of the Mechanism, whether pardon, commutation of sentence, or early release is appropriate. Pursuant to Rule 151 of the Rules, in making a determination on pardon, commutation of sentence, or early release, the President shall take into account, *inter alia,* the gravity of the crime or crimes for which the prisoner was convicted, the treatment of similarly-situated prisoners, the prisoner's demonstration of rehabilitation, and any substantial cooperation of the prisoner with the Prosecution.

15.   Paragraph 2 of the Practice Direction provides that upon a convicted person becoming eligible for pardon, commutation of sentence, or early release under the law of the enforcing State, the enforcing State shall, in accordance with Article 26 of the Statute and with its agreement with the United Nations on the enforcement of sentences and, where practicable, at least 45 days prior to the date of eligibility, notify the Mechanism accordingly.

---

[21]   Letter of 20 August 2016 (confidential).

[22]   Letter to Mr. Goran Jelisid from Judge Theodor Meron, President, 16 September 2016 (confidential).

[23]   Internal Memorandum from Ms. Kate Mackintosh, Deputy Registrar, ICTY, to Judge Theodor Meron, President, dated 6 October 2016.

[24]   Letter from Mr. Goran Jelisid to Judge Theodor Meron, President, 1 November 2016 (confidential)("Letter of 1 November 2016"). While Jelisii contends that there is a [REDACTED] compiled on 30 May 2016, upon my request for clarification as to the medical reports available, the Italian authorities confirmed that only two expert reports existed, one prepared by [REDACTED] and the other by [REDACTED], Internal Memorandum from Ms. Asa Rydberg van der Sluis, Acting Officer in Charge, Registry, to Judge Theodor Meron, President, dated 17 February 2017, conveying a *note verbale* from the Italian authorities, dated 27 January 2017.

[25]   Letter of 1 November 2016.

[26]   [REDACTED].

16.   The above provisions also apply to a request for sentence remission, as a reduction of a detainee's sentence while in detention amounts, in essence, to a commutation of sentence.[27]

17.   Article 3(1) of the Agreement between the Government of the Italian Republic and the United Nations on the Enforcement of Sentences of the International Criminal Tribunal for the Former Yugoslavia, dated 6 February 1997 ("Enforcement Agreement"), provides that the Italian authorities shall be bound by the duration of the sentence imposed by the ICTY.[28] Article 3(2) of **[page 6]** the Enforcement Agreement provides that the conditions of imprisonment shall be governed by the law of Italy, subject to the supervision of the Mechanism.[29] According to Article 3(3) of the Enforcement Agreement, if a detainee becomes eligible for non-custodial measures or working activities outside the prison, or is entitled to benefit from conditional release under Italian law, the relevant Italian authorities are to notify the President.[30] Article 8 of the Enforcement Agreement provides, *inter alia,* that, following notification from the Italian authorities of a detainee's eligibility for pardon or commutation under Italian law, the President shall determine, in consultation with Judges of the Mechanism, whether pardon or commutation is appropriate, and the Registrar shall inform the Italian authorities of the President's determination, who shall act accordingly.[31]

IV. DISCUSSION

18.   None of the Judges of the sentencing Chamber are Judges of the Mechanism. In light thereof, no consultations with other Judges of the Mechanism are required under Rule 150 of the Rules in connection with determining Jelisić's eligibility for pardon, commutation of sentence, or early release.

19.   On 2 May 2016, I informed Jelisić that his Application was being considered as a request for early release, arising from his request for recognition of the commutation of sentence from 40 years to 30 years of imprisonment granted by a decision of the exequatur Appeals Judgement of the Italian Supreme Court of 9 December 2002 ("Commutation Decision"), in conjunction with recognition of any and all remissions of sentence that had been granted by the Italian authorities for the purposes of considering his eligibility for early release.[32]

20.   Accordingly, in order to consider Jelisić's early release, there are three matters that need to be considered: (ii) Jelisić's request for recognition of the Commutation Decision; (ii) Jelisić's Sentence Remission Requests; and (iii), in light of the conclusions on these matters, the consequential impact in terms of Jelisić's request for early release.

A. Recognition of the Commutation Decision

21.   Jelisić contends that if the 30 year sentence handed down by the Italian authorities in the Commutation Decision, rather than the 40 years of imprisonment imposed by the ICTY, is accepted **[page 7]** by the

---

[27]   *Prosecutor* v. *Goran Jelisić,* Case No. M1CT-14-63-ES, Decision of the President on the Sentence Remission of Goran Jelisić, 1 June 2015 (confidential)("*Jelisić* 2015 Remission Decision"), para. 9; *Prosecutor* v. *Milomir Stakić,* Case No. MICT-13-60-ES, Decision of the President on Sentence Remission of Milomir Stakić, 19 December 2013 (confidential)("Stakić Remission Decision"), para. 11, *citing Prosecutor v. Goran Jelisić,* Case No. IT-95-10-ES, Decision of the President on Sentence Remission of Goran Jelisić, 28 May 2013 (public redacted version)*(" Jelisić* 2013 Remission Decision"), para. 13.

[28]   Security Council Resolution 1966 (2010) provides that all existing agreements still in force as of the commencement date of the Mechanism shall apply *mutatis mutandis* to the Mechanism. Accordingly, the Enforcement Agreement applies to the Mechanism. *See* U.N. Security Council Resolution 1966, U.N. Doc. S/RES/1966 (2010), 22 December 2010, para. 4 ("[T]he Mechanism shall continue the jurisdiction, rights and obligations and essential functions of the ICTY and the ICTR, respectively, subject to the provisions of this resolution and the Statute of the Mechanism, and all contracts and international agreements concluded by the United Nations in relation to the ICTY and the ICTR, and still in force as of the relevant commencement date, shall continue in force *mutatis mutandis* in relation to the Mechanism."). According to Article 25(2) of the Statute, "[t]he Mechanism shall have the power to supervise the enforcement of sentences pronounced by the ICTY, the ICTR or the Mechanism, including the implementation of sentence enforcement agreements entered into by the United Nations with Member States".

[29]   *See supra,* fn. 28.

[30]   *See supra,* fn. 28.

[31]   *See supra,* fn. 28.

[32]   Letter of Notification.

Mechanism, then he has currently served two-thirds of his sentence and therefore would be eligible for early release.[33]

22.   I have previously considered the Commutation Decision, and observed that, pursuant to Article 3(1) of the Enforcement Agreement, "[i]n enforcing the sentence pronounced by the [ICTY], the competent national authorities of the requested State shall be bound by the duration of the sentence". I went on formally to reserve the right to terminate the enforcement of Jelisić's sentence in Italy, and to continue enforcement in another State, in accordance with the sentence pronounced in the Appeal Judgement of 40 years of imprisonment.[34]

23.   Accordingly, I emphasise that Jelisić's sentence, for the purpose of considering his present Application, and any such application in the future, shall therefore be construed as 40 years of imprisonment.

B.   Provisional recognition of remission of sentence

24.   Under both settled ICTY and Mechanism precedents, sentence remission claimed or granted

under the domestic systems of the enforcing States may be recognized "provisionally" at the time claimed so long as the other criteria of Rule 151 of the Rules weigh in favour of said recognition; however, such remission remain subject to the supervision of the Mechanism and "may be withdraw[n] at a subsequent time" when the convicted person's eligibility for early release is at issue.[35]

25.   I have, on previous occasion, twice provisionally recognised remission of sentence granted to Jelisić by the Italian authorities.[36] Jelisić now requests the provisional recognition of a further 180 days sentence remission for the period from 22 July 2013 to 22 July 2015, and for a further 90 days for the period from 22 July 2015 to 22 July 2016.[37] **[page 8]**

1.   Eligibility under Italian Law and Treatment of Similarly-Situated Prisoners

26.   I have been informed by the relevant Italian authorities that under Italian law, up until 22 July 2014, Jelisić has been granted a total of 1440 days of sentence remission by the Italian authorities.[38] Any sentence remission granted by the relevant State authorities is not final and is subject to the final approval of the Mechanism. However, in provisionally recognising periods of sentence remissions, I must necessarily be guided by the information provided by the relevant State authorities as to the number of days that have been in fact granted.

27.   Turning to the period of time included in Jelisić's Sentence Remission Request encompassing 22 July 2014 until the present, based on inquiries by the Registry with the Italian authorities and as I have informed Jelisić, I have to date received no indication of the disposition by the requisite Italian authorities of Jelisić's request for additional days of sentence remission following 22 July 2014. Nevertheless, upon receipt of further information as to any decision by the Italian authorities of additional period(s) of sentence remission, I would be in a position, in application of the usual criteria, to further consider such additional provisional remission in accordance with the Practice Direction.

28.   In the present case, Jelisić is therefore eligible under Italian law for the recognition of a sentence remission of 1440 days in total, up until 22 July 2014, for which I have been formally notified of by the Italian authorities, provided that the other criteria of Rule 151 of the Rules militate in favour of such recognition.[39]

---

[33]   Observations, p. 3.

[34]   *The Prosecutor v. Goran Jelisić*, Case No. IT-95- 10-ES, Amended Order Designating the State in which Goran Jelisić is to Serve his Sentence, 2 April 2003 (confidential)("2003 Amended Order"), p. 2. *See also,* Behavioural Report, p. 2 (Registry pagination); 23 May 2016 Letter, p. 6 (Registry pagination); Certificate of Enforcement, pp. 8-9 (Registry pagination).

[35]   *Jelisić* 2015 Remission Decision, para. 14; *Stakić* Remission Decision, paras. 16-17; *Jelisić* 2013 Remission Decision, para. 19; *Prosecutor v. Haradin Bala,* Case No. IT-03-66-ES, Decision on Application of Haradin Bala for Sentence Remission, 15 October 2010 *("Bala* Decision"), para. 15.

[36]   *See Jelisić* 2013 Remission Decision, paras. 34, 36. *See also Jelisić* 2015 Remission Decision, paras. 28-29.

[37]   Application; Letter of 20 August 2016; Letter of 1 November 2016.

[38]   Certificate; Behavioural Report.

[39]   *See Jelisić* 2013 Remission Decision, para. 21. *See also Bala* Decision, para. 16.

Such recognition, however, is without prejudice to the President's full discretion to count this sentence remission in calculating the amount of time served for other purposes, including in determining whether Jelisić has completed two-thirds of his sentence.[40]

29.   In terms of provisional recognition of sentence remission, I recall that sentence remission is generally regarded as an effective tool of prisoner management in domestic systems and that nonMechanism prisoners in these domestic prisons largely benefit from it. If the Mechanism did not recognise any sentence remission to which a convicted person was entitled under the laws of the enforcing State, it would result in discriminatory treatment of Mechanism prisoners vis-a-vis other prisoners in the same prison and, consequently, could render their management more difficult.[41] **[page 9]**

30.   While the sentence remission of 1440 days granted under Italian law is subject to final approval of the President, I would provisionally recognise the sentence remission for which Jelisid has become eligible, provided that the other factors set out in Rule 151 of the Rules, discussed below, taken together, also on balance militate in favour of this recognition.

2.   Gravity of Crimes

31.   Under Rule 151 of the Rules, for present purposes of recognition of remission of sentence, the President shall take into account the gravity of the crime or crimes for which the prisoner was convicted.

32.   The crimes for which Jelisić has been convicted are of a high gravity. Jelisić pleaded guilty to, and was convicted for, crimes related to his participation in attacks against the non-Serbian civilian population of Brčko.[42] In this regard, the Trial Chamber noted the "repugnant, bestial and sadistic nature" of Jelisić's behaviour in committing these crimes, and concluded that "[h]is coldblooded commission of murders and mistreatment of people attest to a profound contempt for mankind and the right to life".[43] As established by witness testimony and Jelisić's own presentations at his initial hearing before the Trial Chamber, Jelisić fashioned himself to be a "Serbian Adolf [Hitler]", motivated by the goal of killing Muslims.[44] The Trial Chamber further stated that Jelisić abused his power to decide which of his "defenceless victims" would live or die, which had far-reaching consequences on both his victims and the witnesses to these crimes.[45] In this regard, the Trial Chamber also ultimately recommended that Jelisić receive psychological and psychiatric follow-up treatment.[46]

In these circumstances, I am of the view that the high gravity of the crimes for which Jelisić pleaded guilty, and was convicted of, weighs strongly against recognising remissions of sentence.

3.   Demonstration of Rehabilitation

33.   Rule 151 of the Rules provides that the President shall take into account a "prisoner's demonstration of rehabilitation" in determining whether, for present purposes, recognition of remission of sentence is appropriate. In addressing the convicted person's rehabilitation, paragraph 4(b) of the Practice Direction states that the Registrar shall: **[page 10]**

> [r]equest reports and observations from the relevant authorities in the enforcing State as to the behavior of the convicted person during his or her period of incarceration and the general conditions under which he or she was imprisoned, and request from such authorities any psychiatric or psychological evaluations prepared on the mental condition of the convicted person during the period of incarceration[...]

34.   According to the Behavioural Report, since his arrival at the Massa prison, Jelisić has fully complied with the rules of detention of the facility, which resulted in him being granted the sentence remissions

---

[40]   *Jelisić* 2013 Remission Decision, paras. 34, 36.
[41]   *Jelisić* 2015 Remission Decision, para. 15; *Jelisić* 2013 Remission Decision, para. 20; *Stakić* Remission Decision, para. 18.
[42]   Trial Judgement, paras. 24, 57, 109, 128.
[43]   Trial Judgement, para. 130.
[44]   Trial Judgement, para. 102.
[45]   Trial Judgement, paras. 131-132.
[46]   Trial Judgement, para. 140.

totalling to a period of 1440 days currently at issue.[47] The Behavioural Report states that Jelisić was previously employed in a tailor's establishment, and thereafter was employed at a company manufacturing coffee pod machines, where he received positive feedback from his employer and showed an aptitude for teamwork, and this work was described as "central" to his reintegration into society.[48] The Behavioural Report and [REDACTED] state that Jelisić finds his employment "profitable and personally highly rewarding", [REDACTED].[49]

35.   The Behavioural Report states that his employment is the central component of Jelisić's resocialisation course, that he is "shy" and "reserved" and that he participates only occasionally in "treatment activities of cultural, sporting or recreational nature", preferring to "dedicate his leisure time to reading, reflection and rest".[50] Jelisić has participated in a photography workshop, where he demonstrated "considerable artistic sensitivity".[51] Jelisić submits that it is not feasible for him to always participate in such activities because he works up to 14 hours a day and the activities end at 5:00 p.m.,[52] and that he has taken part in various training courses.[53]

36.   According to the Behavioural Report, Jelisić has maintained frequent telephone contact with his immediate family, [REDACTED].[54]

37.   [REDACTED].[55] [REDACTED].[56] [REDACTED].[57] [REDACTED].[58]

38.   The Behavioural Report [REDACTED].[59] [REDACTED].[60] [REDACTED].[61] **[page 11]**

39.   [REDACTED].[62]

40.   Jelisić submits that because he actively cooperated with [REDACTED].[63] [REDACTED].[64]

41.   Jelisić states that he has been cooperating with [REDACTED] because it is his "moral and human obligation to tell the truth", in order to ensure that those who committed crimes are accordingly punished.[65] He asserts that the victims and their families "deserve respect and homage" and that, therefore, he would do all he can for them to "learn the truth and find the mortal remains of their family members".[66] He further contends that "[t]here is no justification for what [he] did in the period between 7 May and 17 May 1992", that he is "filled with sorrow, regret and shame" and that his actions were "repulsive and disgusting".[67]

42.   Based on the above, and in this context, noting the fact that Jelisić's behaviour in detention has been appropriate and has not given rise to any disciplinary complaints, and that he expresses regret and shame for the crimes he committed, his current signs of rehabilitation weighs in favour of provisionally recognising the sentence remission for which he is eligible under Italian law.

47	Behavioural Report, p. 2 (Registry pagination),
48	Behavioural Report, p. 2 (Registry pagination).
49	Behavioural Report, p. 3 (Registry pagination); [REDACTED],
50	Behavioural Report, p. 2 (Registry pagination).
51	Behavioural Report, p. 2 (Registry pagination).
52	Observations, p. 1; Employment Letter.
53	Observations, p. 1; Certificate for Training; Reports of Grades; Diploma; Language Certificates; Certificate of Attendance.
54	Behavioural Report, pp. 2-3 (Registry pagination).
55	Behavioural Report, p. 3 (Registry pagination); [REDACTED],
56	Behavioural Report, p. 3 (Registry pagination); [REDACTED],
57	Behavioural Report, p. 3 (Registry pagination); [REDACTED],
58	Behavioural Report, p. 3 (Registry pagination); [REDACTED],
59	Behavioural Report, p. 3 (Registry pagination).
60	Behavioural Report, p. 3 (Registry pagination).
61	[REDACTED],
62	Observations, p. 2.
63	Observations, p. 2; Letters from the Prosecutor of Bosnia and Herzegovina; Judgement of Padua Court; Unsolicited Statement; Letter from Counsel.
64	Observations, p. 2; Unsolicited Statement.
65	Observations, p. 2.
66	Observations, p. 2.
67	Observations, p. 2.

4. Substantial Cooperation with the Prosecution

43.   Rule 151 of the Rules states that the President shall take into account any "substantial cooperation" of the prisoner with the Prosecution. Paragraph 4(c) of the Practice Direction states that the Registrar shall request the Prosecution "to submit a detailed report of any co-operation that the convicted person has provided to the Office of the Prosecutor and the significance thereof".

44.   According to the Prosecution, Jelisić did not substantially cooperate with the Prosecution and/or the Prosecutor of the ICTY ("ICTY Prosecution") in the course of his trial, appeal, or at any point while serving his sentence.[68]

45.   Jelisić submits that he agrees with my assessment of his cooperation with the Prosecution in the *Jelisić* 2015 Remission Decision, that his guilty pleas beneficially impacted the efficient administration of justice.[69] **[page 12]**

46.   I recall that Jelisić pleaded guilty to a majority of the crimes for which he was indicted, and that the entry of such a guilty plea by an accused constitutes a degree of cooperation with the Prosecution, as said plea beneficially impacts the efficient administration of justice.[70] I therefore consider that Jelisić's cooperation, in this regard, is a factor that provides some support in favour of provisional recognition of Jelisić's sentence remission for which he is eligible under Italian law.

5. Conclusion on remission of sentence

47.   Consistent with the Mechanism's practice on sentence remission, and taking into consideration the factors identified in Rule 151 of the Rules, as well as all the relevant information on the record, specifically his behaviour while being incarcerated and his guilty plea at the ICTY, I am of the view that the 1440 days of sentence remission, granted up until the 22 July 2014 by the Italian authorities further to Jelisić's eligibility under Italian law, should be provisionally recognized by the Mechanism. I stress that this recognition is provisional and without prejudice to the discretion of the President not to count this provisionally-recognised remission of sentence, or additional future remissions granted or claimed under Italian law, in calculating the amount of time served for other purposes, including in determining Jelisić's eligibility for early release pursuant to the practice of the Mechanism.[71]

C. **Early Release**

48.   Having reached the above conclusions with respect to recognition of commutation sentence and of remission of sentence, it falls to consider the matter within the context of early release. Jelisić asserts that he is eligible for early release in the context of commutation of his sentence in the national courts taken together with the contended cumulative effect of remission of sentence.

49.   I will now, in turn, address the customary factors that shall be taken into account, as provided for in Rule 151 of the Rules, in making a determination as to the early release of a convicted person. **[page 13]**

1. Gravity of Crimes

50.   Rule 151 of the Rules provides that, in making a determination on early release, the President shall take into account the gravity of the crime or crimes for which the prisoner was convicted.

51.   As I concluded in my discussion of this element in the context of provisional recognition of remission of sentence, the crimes for which Jelisić has been convicted are of a high gravity and weigh strongly against early release.

---

68   Prosecution Memorandum, para. 2.
69   Observations, p. 3. *See Jelisić* 2015 Remission Decision, paras. 25-27.
70   *Jelisić* 2015 Remission Decision, para. 26.
71   *Jelisić* 2013 Remission Decision, paras. 19, 34, 36; *Bala* Decision, para. 15.

2. Treatment of Similarly-Situated Prisoners

52.   Pursuant to Rule 151 of the Rules I am required to consider, as a separate factor, the need for equal treatment of similarly-situated prisoners when deciding early release applications. In this respect, I recall that ICTY convicts, like Jelisić, are considered "similarly-situated" to all other prisoners under the Mechanism's supervision and that all convicts supervised by the Mechanism are to be considered eligible for early release upon the completion of two-thirds of their sentences, irrespective of the tribunal that convicted them.[72] I also note that a convicted person may apply for early release even before the completion of the two-thirds of his or her sentence. In such circumstances, the President would consider a convicted person's application or eligibility for early release, in exceptional cases, such as cases involving extraordinary cooperation with the Prosecution or humanitarian emergencies, and where other factors have also weighed in favour of early release.[73]

53.   However, I note that a convicted person having served two-thirds of his or her sentence shall be merely eligible to apply for early release and not entitled to such release, which may only be granted by the President as a matter of discretion, after considering the totality of the circumstances in each case.[74] In the present case, recalling that Jelisić has been granted 1440 days of sentence remission under Italian law which have been provisionally recognised, I note that Jelisić has not **[page 14]** completed two-thirds of his 40 year sentence of imprisonment imposed by the ICTY, given that all the remissions he is entitled to receive under Italian law counted towards his sentence would result in a release date of 13 October 2020.

54.   In the context of the early release analysis, therefore, the treatment of similarly situated persons weighs against his early release.

3. Demonstration of Rehabilitation

55.   Rule 151 of the Rules provides that the President shall take into account a "prisoner's demonstration of rehabilitation" in determining whether early release is appropriate. I refer to the detailed description of the record above with respect to the demonstration in this case. For the same reasons set out above, specifically that Jelisić's behaviour in detention has been appropriate and has not given rise to any disciplinary complaints, and that he expresses regret and shame for the crimes he committed, his current signs of rehabilitation likewise weighs in favour of early release.

4. Substantial Cooperation with the Prosecution

56.   Rule 151 of the Rules states that the President shall take into account any "substantial cooperation" of the prisoner with the Prosecution. Paragraph 4(c) of the Practice Direction states that the Registrar shall request the Prosecution "to submit a detailed report of any co-operation that the convicted person has provided to the Office of the Prosecutor and the significance thereof".

57.   As I noted in my discussion of this element in the context of recognition of remission of sentence, and for the same reasons there set out, I therefore consider that Jelisić's cooperation, in this regard, is a factor that provides some support in favour of his early release.

---

[72]   *See Prosecutor* v. *Dragoljub Kunarac,* Case No. MICT-15-88-ES.1, Decision of the President on the Early Release of Dragoljub Kunarac, 2 February 2017 (public redacted version), para. 22. *See also Prosecutor v. Paul Bisengimana,* Case No. MICT-12-07, Decision of the President on Early Release of Paul Bisengimana and on Motion to File a Public Redacted Application, 11 December 2012 (public redacted version), paras. 17, 20.
[73]   *See, e.g., Prosecutor* v. *Aloys Simba,* Case No. MICT-14-62-ES.1, Decision of the President on the Early Release of Aloys Simba, 2 February 2016 (public redacted version), para. 17; *Prosecutor v. Drago Nikolić,* Case No. MICT-15-85- ES.4, Public Redacted Version of the 20 July 2015 Decision of the President on the Application for Early Release or Other Relief of Drago Nikolić, 13 October 2015, para. 21; *Prosecutor v. Mladen Naletilić,* Case No. IT-98-34-ES, Public Redacted Version of the 29 November 2012 Decision of the President on Early Release of Mladen Naletilić, 26 March 2013, paras. 32-35; *Prosecutor v. Dragan Obrenović,* Case No. IT-02-60/2-ES, Decision of President on Early Release of Dragan Obrenovid (public redacted version), 29 February 2012, paras. 25-28.
[74]   *See Prosecutor v. Alphonse Nteziryayo,* Case No. MICT-15-90, Decision of the President on the Early Release of Alphonse Nteziryayo, 9 March 2016 (public redacted version), para. 16; *Bisengimana* Decision, paras. 21, 35.

5.   Conclusion on early release

58.   In light of the above, and having carefully considered the factors identified in Rule 151 of the Rules, as well as all the relevant information on the record, I am inclined to deny Jelisić's Application in so far as it constitutes a request for early release. While his guilty plea and cooperation with the Prosecution weighs in favour of his early release, as does, his progress towards rehabilitation, the crimes for which Jelisić was convicted are very grave. Recalling further, that Jelisić has not yet served two-thirds of his sentence imposed by the ICTY, even taking into account the recognition of the cumulative remission of sentence that has been provisionally granted to date, **[page 15]**

I am therefore not persuaded that Jelisić has demonstrated that exceptional circumstances exist warranting his early release at this time.

V.   DISPOSITION

59.   For the foregoing reasons and pursuant to Article 26 of the Statute, Rules 150 and 151 of the Rules, paragraph 9 of the Practice Direction, and Article 8 of the Enforcement Agreement, I hereby provisionally recognize the sentence remission of 1440 days, up until 22 July 2014, for which Jelisić has become eligible under Italian law, without prejudice to consideration of further periods of remission as may be notified by the Italian authorities. The remainder of Jelisić's Application is **DENIED.**

60.   The Registrar is hereby **DIRECTED** to inform the authorities of Italy of this decision as soon as practicable, as prescribed in paragraph 13 of the Practice Direction.

Done in English and French, the English version being authoritative.

Done this 11th day of August 2017,
At The Hague,
The Netherlands.

Judge Theodor Meron
President

[Seal of the Mechanism]

	Case No.	MICT-13-60-ES
Mechanism for International Criminal Tribunals	Date:	6 October 2017
	Original:	English

THE PRESIDENT OF THE MECHANISM

Before: **Judge Theodor Meron, President**

Registrar: **Mr. Olufemi Elias**

Decision of: **6 October 2017**

PROSECUTOR

v.

MILOMIR STAKIĆ

PUBLIC

DECISION OF THE PRESIDENT
ON SENTENCE REMISSION OF MILOMIR STAKIĆ

The Office of the Prosecutor:

Mr. Mathias Marcussen

Mr. Milomir Stakić

The Republic of France

[page 1] 1.   I, Theodor Meron, President of the International Residual Mechanism for Criminal Tribunals ("President" and "Mechanism", respectively), have been advised by the authorities of the Republic of France ("France"), pursuant to Article 26 of the Statute of the Mechanism ("Statute"), Rules 149 of the Rules of Procedure and Evidence of the Mechanism ("Rules"), and paragraph 2 of the Practice Direction on the Procedure for the Determination of Applications for Pardon, Commutation of Sentence, and Early Release of Persons Convicted by the ICTR, the ICTY or the Mechanism ("Practice Direction"),[1] that Mr. Milomir Stakić ("Stakić") is eligible for further remission of his sentence under French law.[2] I consider Stakić's eligibility for further sentence remission pursuant to Article 26 of the Statue, Rules 150 and 151 of the Rules, and paragraph 2 of the Practice Direction.

I. BACKGROUND

2.   Stakić was arrested in Belgrade, Serbia, on 23 March 2001 and was immediately transferred to the United Nations Detention Unit in The Hague.[3] Stakić was charged with 8 counts of genocide, crimes against humanity, and violations of the laws of customs of war, all in relation to crimes that occurred in the Prijedor municipality between 30 April and 30 September 1992.[4]

3.   On 31 July 2003, Trial Chamber II of the International Criminal Tribunal for the Former Yugoslavia ("Trial Chamber" and "ICTY", respectively) found Stakić guilty of extermination and persecution as crimes against humanity, as well as murder as a violation of the laws or customs of war, for his role in a campaign aimed at ethnically cleansing the non-Serb population of the Prijedor municipality.[5] The Trial Chamber sentenced Stakić to life imprisonment, with credit for time served.[6] On 22 March 2006, the Appeals Chamber of the ICTY affirmed Stakić's convictions, **[page 2]** entered new convictions for deportation and inhumane acts (forcible transfer) as crimes against humanity, and substituted Stakić's life imprisonment with a term of 40 years of imprisonment.[7]

4.   On 31 August 2006, France was designated as the enforcing State,[8] and on 12 January 2007, Stakić was transferred to France to serve the remainder of his sentence.[9]

II. NOTIFICATION

5.   On 11 July 2017, I was notified by the French authorities that Stakić is eligible, under French law, for a reduction of his sentence by a total of fifteen (15) months.[10] On 19 September 2017, the Registry informed

---

1   MICT/3, 5 July 2012.

2   Note Verbale from the Embassy of the Republic of France to the Netherlands, dated 6 July 2017 ("Note Verbale"), and received on 11 July 2017, *transmitting, inter alia,* (i) Report from the Department of Criminal Affairs and Pardons, dated 2 June 2017 ("Sentence Remission Report 2017"); (ii) a conduct report dated 23 January 2017 ("Conduct Report"), (iii) a yearly monitoring report from the prison rehabilitation and probation service, dated 24 January 2017 ("Prison Report"); (iii) an annual report, dated August 2015 ("Annual Report"); and (iv) Submission from the District Prosecutor, dated 8 September 2015 ("District Prosecutor Submission 2015"). The English translation of the Note Verbale was received on 14 July 2017. While the Note Verbale was originally submitted to me in French, all references herein are to the Mechanism's certified English translation of the Note Verbale, also annexed to the Internal Memorandum from Judge Theodor Meron, President, to Mr. Olufemi Elias, Registrar, dated 21 July 2017 ("July 2017 Memorandum"), *transmitting, inter alia,* the Note Verbale. The same is true for references to other materials received from the French authorities. The page numbers referenced in this Decision are as provided for on the document, *see also* July 2017 Memorandum, *transmitting, inter alia,* the Note Verbale.

3   *Prosecutor* v. *Milomir Stakić,* Case No. IT-97-24-T, Judgement, 31 July 2003 ("Trial Judgement"), para. 10.

4   *Prosecutor* v. *Milomir Stakić,* Case No. 1T-97-24-PT, Fourth Amended Indictment, 10 April 2002, paras. 39-59.

5   Trial Judgement, paras. 336-408, 882.

6   Trial Judgement, Disposition, p. 253.

7   *Prosecutor* v. *Milomir* Stakid, Case No. IT-97-24-A, Judgement ("Appeal Judgement"), Disposition, pp. 141-142.

8   *Prosecutor* v. *Milomir Stakić,* Case No. IT-97-24-ES, Order Designating the State in Which Milomir Stakid is to Serve his Prison Sentence, 31 August 2006 (issued confidentially, but made public pursuant to the Order Withdrawing the Confidential Status of Order Designating the State in Which Milomir Stakid is to Serve his Prison Sentence, 29 October 2008, p. 2)

9   *See* Press Release, CT/MOW/PR1140e, Milomir Stakid Transferred to Serve Sentence in France, 12 January 2007, *available at* http://www.icty.org/sid/8907.

10   Sentence Remission Report 2017, p. 4.

me that on 7 September 2017 Stakić had been notified of his eligibility for sentence remission and provided with copies of the information received from the French authorities and the Prosecution.[11]

6.   On 19 September 2017, the Registrar of the Mechanism ("Registrar"), in accordance with paragraphs 4 and 5 of the Practice Direction, provided me with: (i) Stakić's response to the copies of the information received from the French authorities and the Prosecution, dated 17 September 2017 ("Stakić's Response"); and (ii) the Prosecution Memorandum.[12]

III.   APPLICABLE LAW

7.   Under Article 26 of the Statute, if, pursuant to the applicable law of the State in which the convicted person is imprisoned, he or she is eligible for pardon or commutation of sentence, the State concerned shall notify the Mechanism accordingly. Article 26 of the Statute further provides that there shall only be pardon or commutation of sentence if the President so decides on the basis of the interests of justice and the general principles of law.

8.   Rule 149 of the Rules echoes Article 26 of the Statute and provides that the enforcing State shall notify the Mechanism of a convicted person's eligibility for pardon, commutation of sentence, **[page 3]** or early release under the enforcing State's laws. Rule 150 of the Rules provides that the President shall, upon such notice, determine, in consultation with any Judges of the sentencing Chamber who are Judges of the Mechanism, whether pardon, commutation of sentence, or early release is appropriate. Pursuant to Rule 151 of the Rules, in making a determination on pardon, commutation of sentence, or early release, the President shall take into account, *inter alia,* the gravity of the crime or crimes for which the prisoner was convicted, the treatment of similarly-situated prisoners, the prisoner's demonstration of rehabilitation, and any substantial cooperation of the prisoner with the Prosecution.

9.   Paragraph 2 of the Practice Direction provides that upon a convicted person becoming eligible for pardon, commutation of sentence, or early release under the law of the enforcing State, the enforcing State shall, in accordance with Article 26 of the Statute and its agreement with the United Nations on the enforcement of sentences and, where practicable, at least forty-five days prior to the date of eligibility, notify the Mechanism accordingly.

10.   The above provisions also apply to a request for sentence remission, as reductions of a prisoner's sentence while in detention amounts, in essence, to a commutation of sentence.[13]

11.   Article 3(1) of the Agreement between the United Nations and the Government of the French Republic on the Enforcement of Sentences of the International Criminal Tribunal for the Former Yugoslavia, dated 25 February 2000 ("Enforcement Agreement"), provides that the French authorities shall be bound by the duration of the sentence imposed by the ICTY.[14] Article 3(2) of the Enforcement Agreement provides that the

[11]   Memorandum from Ms. Esther Halm, Legal Officer to Judge Theodor Meron, President, dated 19 September 2017 ("Registry Memorandum"). The Registry reported that the following documents, *inter alia,* were provided to Stakid: (i) Note Verbale; (ii) Conduct Report; (iii) Prison Report; and (iv) Annual Report; and (v) Memorandum from the Office of the Prosecutor, dated 10 August 2017 ("Prosecution Memorandum").
[12]   *See* Registry Memorandum.
[13]   *See Prosecutor* v. *Goran Jelisić,* Case No. MICT-14-63-ES, Public Redacted Version of 22 May 2017 Decision of the President on Reocgnition of Commutation of Sentence, Remission of Sentence, and Early Release of Goran Jelisid, 11 August 2017 *("Jelisić* 2017 Remission Decision"), para. 16; *Prosecutor* v. *Milomir Stakić,* Case No. MICT-13-60-ES, Decision of the President on Sentence Remission of Milomir Stakid, 19 December 2013 (confidential), para. 11; *Prosecutor* v. *Milomir Stakić,* Case No. MICT-13-60-ES, Decision of the President on Sentence Remission of Milomir Stakid, 17 March 2014 (Public Redacted Version) *("Stakić* Remission Decision"), para. 11, *citing Prosecutor* v. *Goran Jelisić,* Case No. IT-95-10-ES, Decision of the President on Sentence Remission of Goran Jelisić, 28 May 2013 (public redacted version) *("Jelisić* 2013 Remission Decision"), para. 13.
[14]   The Enforcement Agreement, concluded between France and the ICTY, applies to the Mechanism pursuant to Security Council Resolution 1966 (2010), which provides that all existing agreements still in force as of the commencement date of the Mechanism shall apply *mutatis mutandis* to the Mechanism. *See* U.N. Security Council Resolution 1966, U.N. Doc. S/RES/1966 (2010), 22 December 2010, para. 4 ("[TJhe Mechanism shall continue the jurisdiction, rights and obligations and essential functions of the ICTY and the ICTR, respectively, subject to the provisions of this resolution and the Statute of the Mechanism, and all contracts and international agreements concluded by the United Nations in relation to the ICTY and the ICTR, and still in force as of the relevant commencement date, shall continue in force *mutatis mutandis* in relation to the Mechanism."). According to Article 25(2) of the Statute, "[t]he Mechanism shall have the power to supervise the enforcement of sentences pronounced by the ICTY, the

conditions of imprisonment shall be governed by the **[page 4]** law of France, subject to the supervision of the Mechanism.[15] According to Article 3(3) of the Enforcement Agreement, if a detainee becomes eligible for release on parole or any other measure altering the conditions or length of detention under French law, the competent French authorities are to notify the Mechanism.[16] Article 8 of the Enforcement Agreement provides, *inter alia,* that, following notification from the French authorities of a detainee's eligibility for pardon or commutation under French law, the President shall determine, in consultation with Judges of the Mechanism, whether pardon or commutation is appropriate, and the Registrar shall inform the French authorities of the President's determination, who shall act accordingly.[17]

IV. DISCUSSION

12.   None of the Judges of the sentencing Chambers are Judges of the Mechanism. In light of this, no consultations with other Judges of the Mechanism are required under Rule 150 of the Rules in determining Stakić's eligibility for remission of his sentence.

13.   Under both settled ICTY and Mechanism precedents, sentence remission claimed or granted under the domestic systems of the enforcing States may be recognized "provisionally" at the time claimed, so long as the other criteria of Rule 151 of the Rules weigh in favour of said recognition. However, such remission remain subject to the supervision of the Mechanism and "may be withdraw[n] at a subsequent time" when the convicted person's eligibility for early release is at issue.[18]

14.   I have, on one previous occasion, provisionally recognised remission of sentence of thirty (30) months for which Stakić had become eligible under French law.[19] Stakić now requests the provisional recognition of a further fifteen (15) months for the period from 31 January 2014 to 31 January 2017.[20]

A.   Eligibility under French Law and Treatment of Similarly-Situated Prisoners

15.   Pursuant to the Note Verbale, for the period from 31 January 2014 to 31 January 2017, Stakić has become eligible for a reduction of his sentence by: (i) six months, to which he is entitled **[page 5]** as-of-right under French law; and (ii) an additional reduction of nine months due to "the efforts made by Mr[...] Stakić to integrate and to invest his time in prison".[21]

16.   I note that according to Article 3 of the Enforcement Agreement, France is bound to respect the duration of the sentence of persons convicted by the ICTY, as imposed by the ICTY. Pursuant to this Article, as well as Article 26 of the Statute, Rules 150 and 151 of the Rules, and Article 8 of the Enforcement Agreement, the reduction of sentences of persons convicted by the ICTY falls exclusively within the discretion of the President. Therefore, the French authorities may not approve any measures, such as sentence remissions, which would affect the duration of a sentence imposed by the ICTY without first informing the President. The President retains the discretion to determine, in consultation with the Judges of the Mechanism (as applicable), whether the suggested measures are appropriate, in light of the Mechanism's Statute, Rules, and practice.[22] However, in provisionally recognising periods of sentence remissions, I must necessarily be guided by the information provided by the relevant State authorities as to the number of days and/or months that have been in fact granted.

17.   In terms of the provisional recognition of sentence remission, I recall that sentence remission is generally regarded as an effective tool of prisoner management in domestic systems and that non-Mechanism

---

ICTR or the Mechanism, including the implementation of sentence enforcement agreements entered into by the United Nations with Member States".

[15]   *See supra,* fn. 14.

[16]   *See supra,* fn. 14.

[17]   *See supra,* fn. 14, Article 3(4).

[18]   *Jelisić* 2017 Remission Decision, para. 24; *Stakić* Remission Decision, paras. 16-17; *Prosecutor* v. *Haradin Bala,* Case No. 1T-03-66-ES, Decision on Application of Haradin Bala for Sentence Remission, 15 October 2010 *("Bala* Decision"), para. 15.

[19]   *Stakić* Remission Decision, paras. 29-32.

[20]   Sentence Remission Report 2017, p. 4.

[21]   Sentence Remission Report 2017, p. 4.

[22]   *See* Enforcement Agreement, Articles 3(3), 3(4), and 8.

prisoners in these domestic prisons largely benefit from it. If the Mechanism did not recognize any sentence remission to which a convicted person was entitled under the laws of the enforcing State, it would result in discriminatory treatment of Mechanism prisoners vis-a-vis other prisoners in the same prison and, consequently, could render their management more difficult.[23]

18.   Furthermore, sentence remissions granted or claimed under national law to convicts supervised by the Mechanism may only be recognised provisionally, if the other criteria of Rule 151 of the Rules militate for such recognition, and may be reconsidered or withdrawn when the convict's eligibility for early release is at issue.[24] In the present case, Stakić is eligible under French law for the recognition of a sentence remission of fifteen (15) months, for the period of 31 January 2014 to 31 January 2017.[25] It is not claimed that Stakić will have completed two-thirds of his sentence even if all remissions he is eligible to receive under French law are counted towards his sentence. As explained above, these remissions are in any case not final and are subject to the final **[page 6]** approval of the President when Stakić's eligibility for early release is at issue. Therefore, I will provisionally recognize the sentence remissions for which Stakić has become eligible under French law, provided that the other criteria of Rule 151 of the Rules militate in favour of such recognition.

B.   Gravity of Crimes

19.   Under Rule 151 of the Rules, for present purposes of recognition of remission of sentence, the President shall take into account the gravity of the crime or crimes for which the prisoner was convicted.

20.   Stakić was convicted of crimes of very high gravity, *i.e.,* extermination, persecution, deportation, and inhumane acts as crimes against humanity and murder as a violation of the laws and customs of war.[26] These crimes were part of a campaign to persecute the non-Serb population of Prijedor, with the final goal of creating an ethnically clean Serbian municipality.[27] In sentencing Stakić, the Trial Chamber emphasized that Stakić "played a unique pivotal role in co-ordinating the persecutory campaign carried out by the military, police and civilian government in Prijedor" and that "[s]uch a wide-scale, complex and brutal persecutory campaign could never have been achieved without the essential contribution of leading politicians such as Dr. Stakić".[28] The Trial Chamber went on to state that it

> [...] regards the acts of persecution and extermination as the heart of the criminal conduct of Dr. Stakić. Persecutions constitutes [*sic*] inherently a very grave crime because of its distinctive feature of discriminatory intent. All the constitutive acts of the persecutorial campaign are serious in themselves and the Trial Chamber has taken into account their scale and cumulative effect within the Municipality of Prijedor where, more than 1,500 people were killed and tens of thousands deported.[29]

The Trial Chamber also pointed out that "[t]he gravity of the crimes committed by Dr. Stakić is reflected in the tragic extent of the harm and suffering caused to the victims of the criminal campaign."[30]

21.   The Appeals Chamber affirmed Stakić's convictions, entered new convictions for deportation and inhumane acts (forcible transfer) as crimes against humanity, and substituted Stakić's life imprisonment handed down by the Trial Chamber with a term of 40 years of imprisonment.[31] **[page 7]**

22.   I am therefore of the view that the very high gravity of the crimes of which Stakić was convicted weighs against recognizing the remission of his sentence.

---

[23]   *Jelisić* 2017 Remission Decision, para. 29; *Stakić* Remission Decision, para. 18.
[24]   *Jelisić* 2017 Remission Decision, para. 28; *Stakić* Remission Decision, para. 17.
[25]   Sentence Remission Report 2017, p. 4.
[26]   See Appeal Judgement, Disposition, pp. 141-142.
[27]   See Appeal Judgement, paras. 68-98; Trial Judgement, paras. 475, 498, 593, 818-819, 823, 826.
[28]   Trial Judgement, para. 906.
[29]   Trial Judgement, para. 907 (citations omitted).
[30]   Trial Judgement, para. 910.
[31]   See Appeals Judgment, Disposition, pp. 141-142.

C. Demonstration of Rehabilitation

23.   The Sentence Remission Report states that the recommendation to grant Stakić's sentence remission is based notably on the activities undertaken by Stakić, his diligence in the prison workshops, his commitment to the regular psychiatric treatment and his overall good conduct towards his fellow prisoners and inmates.[32] The prison administration notes that he continues to use his time in incarceration positively, and does so with exemplary regularity.[33] The Conduct Report states that "[h]is continuous efforts are remarkable and demonstrate serious signs of social rehabilitation".[34]

24.   Notably, Stakić continues to maintain the proactive approach he adopted upon his arrival to prison and he remains respectful of the prison staff, his fellow prisoners, and the rules, while remaining discreet and very independent—no incidents involving Stakić have been reported.[35] Stakić continues to work in the Brennensthul workshop, where his employer is satisfied with the quality of his work and it is reported that "Stakić is involved, motivated, available, punctual and diligent, and is a driving force in the work process and shows a satisfactory level of adaptation and comprehension".[36] Stakić continues to attend his educational courses and has obtained an "access to university degree" ("DAEU"), is continuing to learn English, has shown tremendous progress in French, and is "becoming increasingly better at expressing himself thanks to his diligent approach to the assignments given to him" and, so the Conduct Report states, "his efforts should be praised".[37] Further, Stakić keeps in regular telephone and written communication with his family and friends, and where possible, they come to visit him in prison.[38] Stakić asserts that his behaviour in prison is a reflection of how he has "been brought up: to work, to improve myself, [and] to respect other people, whether they be prison staff or inmates".[39] **[page 8]**

25.   Stakić has been undergoing regular psychiatric treatment within the prison from the beginning of his incarceration;[40] however, the French authorities did not provide a professional psychiatric or psychological evaluation of Stakić. Nevertheless, I am of the view that the lack of provision of such an evaluation, over which Stakić has no control, should not of itself negatively affect Stakić's eligibility for sentence remission.[41]

26.   The Prison Report notes that "Stakić does not acknowledge the crimes for which he has been incarcerated [and]... [he claims] that he did not order the commission of any crimes or issue a single order, but because of his position he was held responsible for the crimes that were committed".[42] However, in Stakić's Response he wished to explain a "misunderstanding" during his conversation in preparation of the Prison Report,[43] asserting a limited oral capacity in French and the ensuing possibility of miscommunication.[44] Stakić asserts that he would request a meeting to clarify the misunderstanding, and if necessary, will also request a translator for the meeting.[45] Stakić went on in his Response to detail his own position, stating that he regrets that many crimes were committed and that people were unnecessarily persecuted and killed and that he is "deeply shaken and...sorry for all the people who have suffered and are

---

[32]   Sentence Remission Report, p. 4.
[33]   Conduct Report, p. 12.
[34]   Conduct Report, p. 12.
[35]   Conduct Report, p. 12; Prison Report, p 18; District Prosecutor Submission 2015, pp. 24-25, 28; *Stakić* Remission Decision, paras. 22-26 (provides an overview of the demonstration of Stakić's rehabilitation since he arrived in prison on 12 January 2007).
[36]   Conduct Report, p. 12; Prision Report, p. 16; District Prosecutor Submission 2015, p. 27.
[37]   Conduct Report, p. 12; Prison Report, p17; District Prosecutor Submission 2015, p. 27.
[38]   Conduct Report, p. 12; Prison Report, p. 15.
[39]   Stakić's Response, p. 2.
[40]   Prison Report, p. 17; District Prosecutor Submission 2015, p. 28.
[41]   *Stakić* Remission Decision, para. 24; *Prosecutor v. Omar Serushago*, Case No. MICT-12-28, Public Redacted Version of Decision of the President on the Early Release of Omar Serushago, 13 December 2012, paras. 16-17; *Prosecutor v. Paul Bisengimana*, Case No. MICT-12-07, Decision of the President on Early Release of Paul Bisengimana and on Motion to File a Public Redacted Application, 11 December 2012 (public redacted version), para. 26.
[42]   Prison Report, p. 17. *See also* District Prosecutor Submission 2015, p. 28.
[43]   Stakić's Response, p. 1.
[44]   Stakić's Response, p. 1.
[45]   Stakić's Response, p. 1.

still suffering because of what happened in Prijedor".[46] He further asserts that "I am sorry I did not do more to stop things, but I did not have the power to do it".[47]

27.   Based on the above, and in this context, noting the fact that Stakić's behaviour in detention has been appropriate and has not given rise to any disciplinary complaints, and that in response to the Prison Report he expresses certain regret for the crimes in Prijedor and the inadequacy of his own conduct, his current signs of rehabilitation weigh in favour of provisionally recognising a measure of the sentence remission for which he is eligible under French law. **[page 9]**

D.   Substantial Cooperation with the Prosecution

28.   The Prosecution asserts that Stakić did not cooperate with ICTY Office of the Prosecutor in the course of his trial or appeal, nor at any point while serving his sentence.[48]

29.   I note that the Prosecution does not indicate whether the Office of the Prosecutor of the ICTY or the Mechanism sought Stakić's cooperation at any point during his trial or after he was convicted. I also note that an accused person is under no obligation, in the absence of a plea agreement, to cooperate with the Prosecution.[49] I therefore consider that Stakić's lack of cooperation with the Office of the Prosecutor of the ICTY or the Mechanism is a neutral factor in my determination of whether to recognize the sentence remission for which he is eligible under French law.

E.   Conclusion

30.   In my previous Decision in 2013, I held that it would be fair for the Mechanism to recognize the as-of-right remissions corresponding to the seven years that Stakić had been imprisoned in France - *i.e.,* fifteen (15) months in total (three months for the first year and two months for each of the other six years that Stakić has been detained in France) and that the as-of-right 15-month remission should be added the remission of fifteen (15) months for which Stakić has qualified because of his good conduct while in prison.[50] I did not at the time accept the advance recognition of the additional months that Stakić may have been entitled to as-of-right for the total years of his sentence because of "the meager evidence of Stakić's rehabilitation and the gravity of his crimes".[51] I only accepted the sentence remission for the period for which Stakić had been serving his sentence in France.

31.   I have now been notified by the French authorities that Stakić is further eligible, under French law, for a reduction of his sentence by a total of fifteen (15) months for the period from 31 January 2014 to 31 January 2017, including: (i) six months, to which he is entitled as-of-right under French law; and (ii) an additional reduction of nine months due to "the efforts made by Mr[...] Stakić to integrate and to invest his time in prison".[52] Consistent with past practice on sentence remissions, **[page 10]** including my first decision on recognition of remission of sentence in this case, and taking into consideration the factors identified in Rule 151 of the Rules, as well as all the relevant information on the record, I am of the view that, while the gravity of the crimes for which Stakić was convicted are very high and that there continues to be a paucity of evidence as to the degree of his rehabilitation, taking into account the totality of the circumstances in this case, the sentence remissions for which Stakić is now eligible under French law should be recognized by the Mechanism on a provisional basis. The provisional recognition of these fifteen (15) months of sentence

---

[46]   Stakić's Response, p. 2.
[47]   Stakić's Response, p. 2.
[48]   Prosecution Memorandum, para. 2.
[49]   *See, e.g., Stakić* Remission Decision, para. 28; *Prosecutor* v. *Ljube Boškoski and Johan Tarčulovski,* Case No. IT-04- 82-ES, Decision of President on Early Release of Johan Tarčulovski, 8 April 2013, para. 25; *Prosecutor v. Mladen Naletilić,* Case No. IT-98-34-ES, Public Redacted Version of the 29 November 2012 Decision of the President on Early Release of Mladen Naletilić, 26 March 2013, para. 30.
[50]   *Stakić* Remission Decision, para. 30.
[51]   *Stakić* Remission Decision, para. 30.
[52]   Sentence Remission Report 2017, p. 4.

remission is considered consistent with fundamental fairness and justice, which must guide any decision under Article 26 of the Statute.[53]

32.   I stress that recognition of these fifteen (15) months of sentence remission is provisional and without prejudice to the discretion of the President of the Mechanism not to count this provisionally recognized remission, or additional future remissions granted or claimed under French law, in calculating the amount of time served for other purposes, including in determining Stakić's eligibility for early release pursuant to the practice of the Mechanism.[54]

V. DISPOSITION

33.   For the foregoing reasons and pursuant to Article 26 of the Statute, Rules 150 and 151 of the Rules, paragraph 9 of the Practice Direction, and Article 8 of the Enforcement Agreement, I hereby provisionally recognize the sentence remission of fifteen (15) months for which Stakić has become eligible under French law.

34.   The Registrar is hereby **DIRECTED** to inform the French authorities of this decision as soon as practicable, as prescribed in paragraph 13 of the Practice Direction.

Done in English and French, the English version being authoritative.

Done this 6th day of October 2017,
At The Hague,
The Netherlands.

Judge Theodor Meron
President

[Seal of the Mechanism]

---

[53]   Article 26 of the Statute provides that "[t]here shall only be pardon or commutation of sentence if the President of the Mechanism so decides on the basis of the interests of justice and the general principles of law".
[54]   *Stakić* Remission Decision, para. 31; *Bala* Decision, para. 15.

Commentary

Introduction

This commentary explores the criteria for sentence remissions and 'release' at the International Criminal Tribunal for the former Yugoslavia (ICTY) and, as it is now, the International Residual Mechanism for International Criminal Tribunals (IRMCT).

It considers the application of the Rules 150 and 151 of the Rules of Procedure and Evidence (RPE)[1] criteria through the lens of the Jelisić and Stakić decisions,[2] as well as the interpretation of early release provisions in recent decisions rendered in both cases.[3] From these, it appears that convicted persons are falling through the cracks of the enforcement state's sentencing regime and into the void of the Mechanism's.

Further, in the context of requests for provisional release, this commentary analyses both the requirement that two-thirds of a sentence be served before it can be constitute a special circumstance, and the weight given to the optics of release.[4]

As the majority of the decisions are from the IRMCT (or the Mechanism for International Criminal Tribunals (MICT) as it was), the IRMCT Statute and RPE will be cited to ensure consistency between the decisions.

The Legal Framework

Early release

When the ICTY was established, the United Nations Security Council was clear that it would contribute to peace, security, and reconciliation, as well as contributing to the historical record of the crimes committed.[5] Unlike in domestic courts, there are no formal sentencing guidelines that judges must have regard to when imposing a sentence on a convicted person. Article 24(2) ICTY Statute simply states that 'Trial Chambers should take into account such factors as the gravity of the offence and individual circumstances of the convicted person'.[6] In practice, the Tribunal's jurisprudence establishes that the primary consideration when determining the appropriate sentence is, in fact, gravity.[7]

Holá, van Wijk, and Kelder conducted an empirical study on the aims of sentencing referred to by the Tribunal and found that those most frequently cited in judgements were retribution, deterrence, rehabilitation, and reconciliation.[8] However, the judgements remain silent on precisely how these can be achieved through

---

[1]   IRMCT, Rules of Procedure and Evidence, MICT/1/Rev.7, 4 December 2020.

[2]   MICT, Public Redacted Version of 22 May 2017 Decision of the President on Recognition of Commutation of Sentence, Remission of Sentence, and Early Release of Goran Jelisić, *Prosecutor v. Jelisić*, Case No. MICT-14-63-ES, The President of the Mechanism, 11 August 2017 (*Jelisić* 2017 Decision), in this volume, PAGINA; MICT, Decision of the President on Sentence Remission of Milomir Stakić, *Prosecutor v. Stakić*, Case No. MICT-13-60-ES, The President of the Mechanism, 6 October 2017 (*Stakić* 2017 Decision) in this volume, PAGINA.

[3]   IRMCT, Decision on Sentence Remission and Early Release on Goran Jelisić, *Prosecutor v. Jelisić*, Case No. MICT-14-63-ES, The President of the Mechanism, 11 March 2021 (*Jelisić* 2021 Decision); IRMCT, Decision on Sentence Remission and Early Release of Milomir Stakić, *Prosecutor v. Stakić*, Case No. MICT-13-60-ES, The President of the Mechanism, 31 December 2020 (*Stakić* 2020 Decision).

[4]   ICTY, Public Redacted Version of the "Decision on Valentin Ćorić's Request for Provisional Release" Issued on 15 August 2016, *Prosecutor v. Ćorić*, Case No. IT-04-74-A, A. Ch., 1 December 2016 (*Ćorić* Provisional Release Decision), in this volume, PAGINA; MICT, Decision on Stanišić's Motion For Extension of Provisional Release, *Prosecutor v. Stanišić and Simatović*, Case No. MICT-15-96-PT, T. Ch. I, 19 May 2017 (*Stanišić* Provisional Release Decision), in this volume, PAGINA.

[5]   United Nations Security Council, Resolution 827 (1993) S/Res/827; United Nations Security Council, Resolution 955 (1994) S/Res/955.

[6]   This provision appears at Art. 22(3) IRMCT Statute (UN Doc. S/1966).

[7]   ICTY, Public Redacted Version of Judgement issued on 24 March 2016, *Prosecutor v. Karadžić*, Case No. IT-95-5/18-T, T. Ch. III, 24 March 2016, par. 6030, fn 20592.

[8]   B. Holá, J. van Wijk and J. Kelder, Effectiveness of International Criminal Tribunals: Empirical Assessment of Rehabilitation as Sentencing Goal, in: Nobuo Hayashi and Cecilia M. Baillet (eds.), The Legitimacy of International Criminal Tribunals: Studies on International Courts and Tribunals, Cambridge University Press, Cambridge 2017, p. 351-375.

the imposition of a criminal sentence.[9] For some commentators, the early release regime significantly undermines these objectives and replaces it with leniency.[10]

The enforcement agreements between states and the Mechanism provide that the former is bound by the duration of the sentence imposed by the ICTR, ICTY, and IRMCT.[11] However, conditions of imprisonment are governed by the law of the state within which the convicted person is serving their sentence. Pursuant to Art. 26 of the Statute, the state is under an obligation to notify the President of the Mechanism if a detainee becomes eligible for non-custodial measures or working activities outside of the prison or is entitled to benefit from conditional release under domestic laws.[12]

Rule 150 RPE requires the President, upon notice from the enforcement state, to determine, in consultation with any judges of the sentencing Chambers who were judges of the Mechanism, whether pardon, commutation of sentence, or early release are appropriate. The President must decide whether it is in the interests of justice and in accordance with the general principles of law to do so.

In making this determination, Rule 151 provides that the President shall take into account *inter alia* the gravity of the crime or crimes for which the prisoner was convicted, the treatment of similarly situated prisoners, the prisoner's demonstration of rehabilitation, and any substantial cooperation of the prisoner with the Prosecution.

Convicted persons serving a sentence under the supervision of the Mechanism will generally be eligible to be considered for early release upon having served two-thirds of their sentence as imposed by the ICTR, ICTY or the Mechanism.[13] This applies irrespective of where a convicted person serves their sentence, and whether an early release matter is brought before the President through a direct petition by the convicted person, or a notification from the relevant enforcement state.[14]

However, this eligibility threshold does not entitle a convicted person to early release, as this may only be granted by the President as a matter of discretion after considering the totality of the circumstances in each case (as required by Rule 151).[15]

Provisional release

Rule 68(B) RPE provides that release may be ordered at any stage of the trial proceedings prior to the rendering of the final judgement by the Trial Chamber only after giving the host country and the state to which the accused seeks to be released the opportunity to be heard and only if it is satisfied that the accused will appear for trial and, if released, will not pose a danger to any victims, witness, or any other person. The existence of sufficiently compelling humanitarian grounds may be considered in granting such release. The Trial Chamber may impose appropriate conditions upon the release of the accused.[16]

Further, pursuant to Rule 65(I), the Appeals Chamber may grant provisional release to a convicted person pending an appeal or for a fixed period, if it is satisfied that: (i) the appellant, if released, will either appear at the hearing of the appeal or will surrender into detention at the conclusion of the fixed period, as the case may be; (ii) the appellant, if released, will not pose a danger to any victim, witness, or other person; and (iii)

---

9   See A. Hole, The sentencing provisions of the International criminal Court, 1 International Journal of Philosophical Studies 2005, p. 37-69.
10   See A. Merrylees, 2016, Two-Thirds and You're Out? The Practice of Early Release at the ICTY and ICC, in: Light of the Goals of International Criminal Justice, 8 Amsterdam Law Forum, p. 69-76, p. 71; J. H. Choi, Early release in international criminal law, 123 Yale Law Journal 2014, p. 1784-1828. E. Riegler, 2020, Rehabilitating Enemies of Mankind: An Exploration of the Concept of Rehabilitation as a Sentencing Aim at the ICTY and ICC, 20 International Criminal Law Review, p. 701-727.
11   See, for example, *Jelisić* 2017 Decision, par. 22; *Stakić* 2017 Decision, par. 16.
12   See further, Rule 149 RPE.
13   IRMCT, Practice Direction on the Procedure for the Determination of Applications for Pardon, Commutation of Sentence, or Early Release of Persons Convicted by the ICTR, the ICTY, or the Mechanism, MICT/3/Rev.3, 15 March 2020, par. 7-8.
14   *Stakić* 2020 Decision, par. 42, fn 87.
15   *Stakić* 2020 Decision, par. 43; Practice Direction, par.10.
16   Rule 68(c) RPE.

special circumstances exist warranting such release. Importantly, this is a cumulative test and one that must be satisfied on the balance of probabilities.[17]

Davidson argues that the objectives of the Tribunal shape the way in which the provisional release regime is used.[18] She notes that the "release-unfriendly precedent of the ad hoc tribunals may be justifiable in the particular circumstances of international criminal tribunals" for this reason.[19] While the rules permit the provisional release of accused or convicted persons, the key question has become whether or not so doing would be seen to undermine the aims of the Tribunal.[20]

Sentence Remissions

Sentence remissions are reductions in sentence given to prisoners for good behaviour under the domestic laws. In both the Jelisić 2017 and Stakić 2018 decisions, the President applied Rules 150 and 151 to requests to provisionally recognise the sentence remissions afforded by the enforcement states. Both motions were considered by Judge Meron, acting in his capacity as the President of the Mechanism.

Jelisić was sentenced to 40 years imprisonment on 14 December 1999. This was affirmed on appeal, and on 29 May 2003 he was transferred to Italy to serve the remainder of his sentence. Stakić was sentenced to life imprisonment on 31 July 2003, which was upheld on appeal on 22 March 2006. He was transferred to France to serve his sentence.

In both cases, the President's starting point was whether Jelisić and Stakić were eligible for sentence remission under the relevant enforcement state's law.[21] Based on the information provided by the state authorities, he concluded that both were.[22] In justifying the Mechanism's power to provisionally recognise sentence remissions, the President explained that "it would result in discriminatory treatment of Mechanism prisoners vis-à-vis other prisoners in the same prison and, consequently, could render their management more difficult" if it did not.[23]

With regards to the gravity of the crimes, the decision cited the key facets of the judgements against Jelisić and Stakić to support the conclusion that the gravity of crimes weighed against recognition.[24]

Rehabilitation is arguably the most subjective of the Rule 151 criteria.[25] Rehabilitation is not defined by the Statute, Rules, or in the case law. The Mechanism does not require the completion of a rehabilitation programme tailored to international crimes. Rehabilitation becomes a matter for the convicted person to persuade the Mechanism of. There is, however, no further guidance on what form this must take or objective criteria by which to measure whether a convicted person has demonstrated that they have in fact be rehabilitated.

With regards to rehabilitation, material from the authorities in the enforcement state relating to convicted person's conduct, as well as any medical evidence, proved fundamental to the President decision.[26] In both cases, he highlighted evidence of compliance with the prison rules, education, employment, integration within the prison community, as well as references from staff.[27]

---

[17]   *Ćorić* Provisional Release Decision, p. 3, fn 14.
[18]   C. Davidson, No Shortcuts on Human Rights: Bail and the International Criminal Trial, 60 American University Law Review 2010, p. 12.
[19]   *Ibid.*
[20]   See further, R. Sznajder, Provisional Release at the ICTY: Rights of the Accused and the Debate that Amended a Rule, 11 Northwestern Journal of International Human Rights 2013; A. Trotter, Innocence, Liberty and Provisional Release at the ICTY: A Post-Mortem of 'Compelling Humanitarian Grounds' in Context, 12 Human Rights Law Review 2012, p. 353; M. Fairlie, The Precedent of Pretrial Release at the ICTY: A Road Better Left Less Traveled, 33 Fordham International Law Journal 2010, p. 1101. M. DeFrank, Provisional Release: Current Practice, a Dissenting Voice, and the Case for a Rule Change, 80 Texas Law Review 2002, p. 1429.
[21]   *Jelisić* 2017 Decision, par. 26; *Stakić* 2017 Decision, par. 18.
[22]   *Jelisić* 2017 Decision, par. 30; *Stakić* 2017 Decision, par. 18.
[23]   *Jelisić* 2017 Decision, par. 29; *Stakić* 2017 Decision, par. 17.
[24]   *Jelisić* 2017 Decision, par. 31-32; *Stakić* 2017 Decision, par. 19-23.
[25]   *Jelisić* 2017 Decision, par. 33-42; *Stakić* 2017 Decision, par. 23-27.
[26]   *Jelisić* 2017 Decision, par. 33.
[27]   *Jelisić* 2017 Decision, par. 34-40; *Stakić* 2017 Decision, par. 24-25.

Moreover, in both decisions, the President considered whether Jelisić and Stakić had demonstrated insight into, and remorse for, the crimes they were convicted of.[28] Acceptance of the verdict, the sentence imposed, an understanding of the impact of the crimes, and any active steps towards reconciliation, were underscored. The focus of this assessment appears to be whether they continue to pose a danger to the public. While there was sufficient evidence that both had behaved appropriately in detention and expressed regret and shame for the crimes,[29] it is easy to see how a lack of cooperation and remorse could easily weigh against the provisional recognition of any sentence remission in the interests of justice. Coupled with this, the President focused on factors that are relevant to their reintegration into society.

Jelisić's guilty plea was recognised by the President as a "degree of cooperation" that could be taken into account.[30] However, in Stakić, it was recalled that "an accused person is under no obligation" to cooperate with the Prosecution.[31] In light of this, the President considered Jelisić's cooperation to provide "some support" in favour of provisional recognition of his sentence remission, while treating Stakić's lack of cooperation as a "neutral factor".[32] From this, it is clear that cooperation with the Prosecution is not, in and of itself, a determinative factor.

After considering all the Rule 151 criteria, the President of the Mechanism provisionally recognised the sentence remissions requests from both Jelisić and Stakić.[33]

Although Rule 151 does not suggest the existence of a hierarchy within the criteria, to satisfy the President that any sentence remission is consistent with fundamental fairness and justice, the gravity of the crimes and demonstration of rehabilitation are the core competing interests that the Mechanism must balance. Evidence of rehabilitation appears to be the gateway to shifting the balance in favour of provisionally recognising any sentence remission. The practical effect of this on a convicted person's sentence is considered in the next section.

Early release

Jelisić 2017 Decision

Jelisić argued that, on the basis of a decision of the exequatur Appeals Judgement of the Italian Supreme Court of 9 December 2002 to substitute his 40-year sentence from the ICTY with one of 30 years, he would have served two-thirds of his sentence and would be eligible for early release.[34] He asserted that this was a commutation of sentence in accordance with Rule 150.

This was rejected. Article 3(1) of the Enforcement Agreement between the Mechanism and Italy expressly states that "the competent national authorities of the requested State shall be bound by the duration of the sentence" pronounced by the ICTY.[35] For this reason, the President held that a commutation of sentence at the domestic level could not alter the length of the sentence imposed by the Tribunal.

It is clear from the enforcement agreements that the Mechanism's authority on the duration of the sentence takes primacy. While the agreement allows a state to deal with the day-to-day management of the convicted person,[36] they are a separate and distinct class of detained person over whose sentence the domestic courts have no power to amend. The President's interpretation and application of the enforcement agreement in *Jelisić* can be seen to send a clear reminder that international sentences are immune from domestic challenge. Considering the divergent sentencing practices in enforcing states, this approach arguably maintains the integrity of an international sentence.

28	*Jelisić* 2017 Decision, par. 41; *Stakić* 2017 Decision, par. 26.
29	*Jelisić* 2017 Decision, par. 42; *Stakić* 2017 Decision, par. 27.
30	*Jelisić* 2017 Decision, par. 46.
31	*Stakić* 2018 Decision, par. 29.
32	*Stakić* 2018 Decision, par. 29.
33	*Jelisić* 2017 Decision, par. 59; *Stakić* 2017 Decision, par. 33.
34	*Jelisić* 2017 Decision, par. 19-20.
35	*Jelisić* 2017 Decision, par. 22; *Stakić* 2017 Decision, par. 16.
36	*Jelisić* 2017 Decision, par. 22; *Stakić* 2017 Decision, par. 16.

Is the Mechanism's willingness to provisionally accept sentence remissions an exception to this? The President in both the Jelisić 2017 and Stakić 2018 decisions, confirmed the settled precedent that sentence remission claimed or granted under the domestic systems of the enforcing states may be provisionally recognised at the time of the motion, provided the criteria in Rule 151 weighed in favour of this.[37] However, there is an important caveat to this: any remission remains subject to the supervision of Mechanism and "may be withdraw[n] at a subsequent time" when a convicted person's eligibility for early release is at issue.[38]

Therefore, any sentence remission granted by the relevant state authorities, even if provisionally recognised, can be ignored at a later stage. What remained unanswered was whether sentence remissions could in fact influence the length of sentence under the Mechanism's framework. Recent developments in this regard have put any ambiguity in this regard to bed.

Recent developments

Both Jelisić and Stakić recently requested early release on the basis that, with the sentence remissions provisionally recognised, they had each served two-thirds of their sentence.[39] The Jelisić 2021 and Stakić 2020 decisions provide further guidance on the impact of sentence remissions on a convicted person's sentence. Judge Agius, in his capacity as the President of the Mechanism, ruled on their requests.

With regards sentence remissions, he emphasised that persons convicted by the ICTY, the ICTR and the Mechanism, "will always be in a different position vis-à-vis other prisoners serving in enforcement states".[40] He went on to say that "any comparison of their status with that of the domestic prison population" was "counterproductive".[41] Judge Agius concluded that sentence remissions "introduce an element of inequality when viewed in relation to similarly-situated convicted persons in other enforcement states".[42] Therefore, in practical terms, sentence remission decisions "may be used to evidence good behaviour and progress with regard to rehabilitation".[43]

He made abundantly clear that, "sentence remissions cannot influence the length of sentence under the Mechanism's framework".[44] As such, any ambiguity as to whether sentence remissions can impact on the Mechanism's calculation of two-thirds of the end date of a convicted person's sentence has now been resolved.

The Jelisić 2021 Decision and the Stakić 2020 Decision make it plain that the Mechanism has little interest in considering any applications under Rule 150 unless a convicted person has served two-thirds of the sentence imposed, or that exceptional circumstances exist.[45] This begs the question: is there any point in a convicted person applying for provisional recognition of sentence remissions when it has no bearing on the Mechanism's approach to release? Save for in the run up to the two-thirds mark, there is no incentive or benefit to them. This line of authorities could result in convicted persons disengaging from, or failing to cooperate with, enforcement states.

Perhaps an alternative to this lies in the creation of a system of sentence remissions specifically for convicted persons under the supervision of the Mechanism. This would ensure consistency as between those serving sentences from the ICTR, ICTY and Mechanism, while allowing convicted persons to benefit from remissions that, in one form or another, exist in enforcing states. If the President's concern is about equality as between convicted persons at the Tribunal, surely this would be an appropriate solution to the problem. It would ensure convicted people remain engaged, which would in turn encourage compliance and rehabilitation.

---

[37] *Jelisić* 2017 Decision, par. 28; *Stakić* 2017 Decision, par. 18.
[38] *Jelisić* 2017 Decision, par. 24; *Stakić* 2017 Decision, par. 13.
[39] *Jelisić* 2021 Decision; *Stakić* 2020 Decision.
[40] *Jelisić* 2021 Decision, par. 25; *Stakić* 2020 Decision, par. 27.
[41] *Jelisić* 2021 Decision, par. 25; *Stakić* 2020 Decision, par. 27.
[42] *Jelisić* 2021 Decision, par. 25; *Stakić* 2020 Decision, par. 27.
[43] *Jelisić* 2021 Decision, par. 31; *Stakić* 2020 Decision, par. 33.
[44] *Jelisić* 2021 Decision, par. 35; *Stakić* 2020 Decision, par. 37.
[45] *Jelisić* 2021 Decision, par. 35; *Stakić* 2020 Decision, par. 37.

The danger is that, without any incentive to engage with the enforcing state's programmes, convicted persons will become alienated. However, the absence of any proposals in this vein is perhaps indicative of the Mechanism's focus on the sentencing objectives of retribution and deterrence.

Provisional release

Time served

The Appeals Chamber's decision on Ćorić's request for provisional release demonstrates the way in which time served impacts on the provisional release criteria.[46]

Ćorić was convicted of 22 counts of war crimes and crimes against humanity by a Trial Chamber on 29 May 2013. He was sentenced to 16 years imprisonment. He requested to be provisionally released pending the Appeals judgement.[47] Ćorić argued that the fact that he had served a significant amount of time in custody and on provisional release, which he said cumulatively exceeded two-thirds of his sentence, amounted to a special circumstance that weighed in favour of his release.[48]

In response, the Prosecution asserted that he had only served 52% of his sentence at the time of filing his motion and that any time spent on provisional release could be considered as time served.[49]

The Appeals Chamber held that the time spent on provisional release did not constitute time served, and for that reason Ćorić's period of detention at the UN Detention Unit was shorter than two-thirds of his 16-year sentence.[50] However, it did accept that there was case law which supported the proposition that, under certain conditions, serving a "sufficiently substantial" part of a sentence could "constitute a special circumstance" warranting provisional release.[51]

The decision in this case shows how the two-thirds point of a convicted person's sentence is the benchmark for both early and provisional release. Consistency between the two prevents remissions and/or provisional release from undermining the integrity of the sentence imposed. However, it does leave open the possibility that serving two-thirds of a sentence can in some cases tip the scales in favour of granting a request for provisional release.

Optics

The Trial Chamber's decision on Stanišić's motion for an extension of provisional release reveals an extra-legal consideration: the optics of an accused not being present in court.[52]

On 30 May 2013, following a trial, Stanišić was acquitted on all counts of the indictment and his immediate release from the UN Detention Unit was ordered. The Appeals Chamber ordered that Stanišić be retried on all counts of the Indictment on 9 December 2015.

The Trial Chamber granted Stanišić provisional release to Serbia on 22 December 2015 on health grounds. There were a number of expert reports provided to the Court in this regard over a 3-year period. His chronic health conditions were such that the Trial Chamber amended the sitting schedule to ensure that he could effectively participate.[53] This included *inter alia* Stanišić appearing remotely via video-conference link.

Stanišić requested that his provisional release be extended for the duration of the Prosecution's case.[54] He signed a waiver of his right to be present during the presentation of the Prosecution's case. The Prosecution

---

[46]   *Ćorić* Provisional Release Decision.
[47]   *Ćorić* Provisional Release Decision, p. 2.
[48]   *Ćorić* Provisional Release Decision, p. 2.
[49]   *Ćorić* Provisional Release Decision, p. 3.
[50]   *Ćorić* Provisional Release Decision, p. 4.
[51]   *Ćorić* Provisional Release Decision, p.4; ICTY, Decision on Motion on Behalf of Enver Hadžihasanović for Provisional Release, *Prosecutor v. Hadžihasanović and Kubura*, Case No. IT-01-47-A, A. Ch., 20 June 2007, par. 13.
[52]   *Stanišić* Provisional Release Decision.
[53]   *Stanišić* Provisional Release Decision, par. 7.
[54]   *Stanišić* Provisional Release Decision, par. 10.

argued in response that he would fail to appear for trial, that there was a heightened risk for protected witnesses because communications between counsel and Stanišić in Serbia increased the risk of disclosure of confidential information, and that he had failed to show that he could not obtain adequate medical treatment in The Hague.[55] It also pointed to the unfairness arising from Stanišić being absent and at home, while witnesses had to ensure the "inconvenience and stress of testifying".[56]

The Trial Chamber highlighted the "exceptional nature" of Stanišić's situation, namely his acquittal and chronic health conditions, and concluded that it placed him "into a narrow category of cases where provisional release may be considered appropriate during a portion of the ongoing trial".[57] It rejected the Prosecution's contention that he was a flight risk or posed a danger to any victim, witness, or other person.[58] It held that "for much of the 14 years of proceedings, Stanišić's has either been on provisional release or released following his acquittal without incident, while having full access to all confidential information in his original trial and to the identity of nearly all witnesses in this trial".[59]

For that reason, it rejected the Prosecution's suggestion that cross-border communications presented a danger. The Trial Chamber accepted that Stanišić had voluntarily waived his right to be present, but that he was represented and could continue to instruct counsel remotely.[60]

Despite the test in Rule 68(B) for provisional release being met, the Trial Chamber refused Stanišić's request for release on the basis that his absence from the opening stages would not set the appropriate "tone" for the case.[61] For this reason, it held that it would not be appropriate or in the interests of justice to allow Stanišić to remain on provisional release at that time.[62]

Given that the Trial Chamber itself accepted that the requirements for release under the rules had been satisfied, the decision shows how the optics of his absence were, in fact, determinative. The approach taken, and the decision made, reveals a deep-rooted commitment to the objective aims of the process and the Chamber's willingness to frame its decision-making on release around these.

Conclusion

Releasing an accused or convicted person is inherently controversial. While the existing provisions are consistent with human rights norms, acceding to a request for early or provisional release of a person could be interpreted as diminishing the gravity of the offences.

Additionally, allowing the balance to fall in favour of an accused or convicted person risks defeating the objectives of the Tribunal. While these decisions illustrate how the Tribunal has sought to weigh up the competing interests, it is clear that those accused of crimes and convicted persons are treated as a special class of offender to which extra-legal considerations also apply.

Peta-Louise Baggott

---

[55]   *Stanišić* Provisional Release Decision, par. 11.
[56]   *Stanišić* Provisional Release Decision, par. 11.
[57]   *Stanišić* Provisional Release Decision, par. 18.
[58]   *Stanišić* Provisional Release Decision, par. 19-20.
[59]   *Stanišić* Provisional Release Decision, par. 20.
[60]   *Stanišić* Provisional Release Decision, par. 24.
[61]   *Stanišić* Provisional Release Decision, par. 26.
[62]   *Stanišić* Provisional Release Decision, par. 26.

UNITED
NATIONS

International Tribunal for the
Prosecution of Persons
Responsible for Serious Violations of
International Humanitarian Law
Committed in the Territory of the
former Yugoslavia since 1991

Case No.   IT-08-91-A

Date: 30 June 2016

Original: English

IN THE APPEALS CHAMBER

Before: **Judge Carmel Agius, Presiding**
                     Judge Liu Daqun
                     Judge Christoph Flügge
                     Judge Fausto Pocar
                     Judge Koffi Kumelio A. Afanđe

Registrar: **Mr. John Hocking**

Decision of: **30 June 2016**

PROSECUTOR

v.

MIĆO STANIŠIĆ

STOJAN ŽUPLJANIN

PUBLIC WITH CONFIDENTIAL ANNEX C

JUDGEMENT

The Office of the Prosecutor:

Ms. Laurel Baig
Mr. Aditya Menon
Mr. Todd Schneider
Ms. Grace Harbour
Ms. Sarah Finnin

Counsel for Mićo Stanišic:

Mr. Slobodan Zečević
Mr. Stéphane Bourgon

Counsel for Stojan Župljanin:

Mr. Dragan Krgović
Ms. Tatjana Čmerić
Mr. Christopher Gosnell

[page 1|1. INTRODUCTION

1.   The Appeals Chamber of the International Tribunal for the Prosecution of Persons Responsible for Serious Violations of International Humanitarian Law Committed in the Territory of the former Yugoslavia since 1991 ("Appeals Chamber" and "Tribunal" or "ICTY", respectively) is seised of the appeals filed by Mićo Stanišić,[1] Stojan Župljanin,[2] and the Office of the Prosecutor of the Tribunal[3] ("Stanišić", "Župljanin", and "Prosecution", respectively) against the judgement rendered by Trial Chamber II on 27 March 2013 in the case of *Prosecutor v. Mićo Stanišić and Stojan Župljanin*, Case No. IT-08-91-T ("Trial Judgement" and "Trial Chamber", respectively).

A. Background

2.   Stanišić was born on 30 June 1954 in Ponor, a village in the municipality of Pale in Bosnia and Herzegovina ("BiH").[4] From 21 December 1991, he was a Minister without Portfolio in the Council of Ministers, and an *ex officio* member of the National Security Council ("NSC"), the first *de facto* executive body of the *Republika Srpska*, the Serb Republic in BiH ("RS").[5] He was appointed the first Minister of the Ministry of Interior of the RS ("Minister of Interior" and "RS MUP", respectively) on 31 March 1992,[6] by virtue of which he was also a member of the Government of the RS ("RS Government"), until his resignation at the end of 1992.[7]

3.   Župljanin was born on 22 September 1951 in Maslovare, a village in the municipality of Kotor Varoš in BiH.[8] On 6 May 1991, he became Chief of the Regional Security Services Centre ("CSB") of Banja Luka and, from at least 5 May 1992 until July 1992, he was a member of the Autonomous Region of Krajina ("ARK") Crisis Staff.[9] **[page 2]**

4.   The events giving rise to these appeals occurred in BiH from at least 1 April 1992 to at least 31 December 1992.[10] The Prosecution charged Stanišić and Župljanin with the following crimes against humanity under Article 5 of the Statute of the Tribunal ("Statute") committed during that period: (i) persecutions on political, racial, and religious grounds (Count 1); (ii) extermination (Count 2); (iii) murder (Count 3); (iv) torture (Count 5); (v) inhumane acts (Count 8); (vi) deportation (Count 9); and (vii) other inhumane acts (forcible transfer) (Count 10).[11] The Prosecution also charged Stanišić and Župljanin with the following violations of the laws or customs of war under Article 3 of the Statute: (i) murder (Count 4); (ii) torture (Count 6); and (iii) cruel treatment (Count 7).[12] The Indictment alleged Stanišić and Župljanin to be responsible for these crimes pursuant to both Article 7(1) (instigating, aiding and abetting, and committing, through participation in a joint criminal enterprise)[13] and Article 7(3) of the Statute (superior responsibility).[14]

---

[1]   See Notice of Appeal on behalf of Mićo Stanišić, 13 May 2013; Appellant's Brief on behalf of Mićo Stanišić, 19 August 2013 ("Stanišić Appeal Brief"); Amended Notice of Appeal on behalf of Mićo Stanišić, 23 April 2014 ("Stanišić Notice of Appeal"); Additional Appellant's Brief on behalf of Mićo Stanišić, 26 June 2014 ("Stanišić Additional Appeal Brief").

[2]   See Notice of Appeal on behalf of Stojan [Ž]upljanin, 13 May 2013; Stojan [Ž]upljanin's Appeal Brief, 19 August 2013 (confidential; public redacted version filed on 23 August 2013, re-filed on 21 April 2016) ("Župljanin Appeal Brief"); [Ž]upljanin's Submission of Corrected Notice of Appeal, 22 August 2013; [Ž]upljanin's Submission of Amended Notice of Appeal, 9 October 2013; Župljanin's Submission of Second Amended Notice of Appeal, 22 April 2014 ("Župljanin Notice of Appeal"); Stojan Župljanin's Supplement to Appeal Brief (Ground Six), 26 June 2014 ("Župljanin Additional Appeal Brief").

[3]   See Prosecution Notice of Appeal, 13 May 2013 ("Prosecution Notice of Appeal"); Prosecution Appeal Brief, 19 August 2013 ("Prosecution Appeal Brief").

[4]   Trial Judgement, vol. 1, para. 2; Trial Judgement, vol. 2, para. 537.

[5]   Trial Judgement, vol. 1, para. 2; Trial Judgement, vol. 2, paras 144, 549.

[6]   Trial Judgement, vol. 2, paras 542-543, 558. See Trial Judgement, vol. 1, para. 2.

[7]   Trial Judgement, vol. 1, para. 2; Trial Judgement, vol. 2, para. 543.

[8]   Trial Judgement, vol. 1, para. 3; Trial Judgement, vol. 2, para. 348.

[9]   Trial Judgement, vol. 1, para. 3; Trial Judgement, vol. 2, paras 349, 353.

[10]   Trial Judgement, vol. 1, para. 6. See Trial Judgement, vol. 2, paras 518-530, 729-798.

[11]   *Prosecutor v. Mićo Stanišić and Stojan Župljanin*, Case No. IT-08-91-T, Second Amended Consolidated Indictment, 23 November 2009 ("Indictment"), paras 24-41.

[12]   Indictment, paras 29-36.

[13]   Indictment, paras 4-5. See Indictment, paras 6-16.

[14]   Indictment, para. 23. See Indictment, paras 17-23.

The Indictment further alleged Župljanin to be responsible for these crimes pursuant to Article 7(1) of the Statute (planning and ordering).[15]

5.   The Trial Chamber concluded that many of the crimes alleged in the Indictment were committed[16] in the 20 municipalities listed in the Indictment ("Municipalities"),[17] including the municipalities in the ARK ("ARK Municipalities").[18] It found that a joint criminal enterprise came into existence no later than 24 October 1991 and remained in existence throughout the Indictment period, with the objective "to permanently remove Bosnian Muslims and Bosnian Croats from the territory of the planned Serbian state" ("JCE").[19] It also found that this objective was implemented through the crimes of deportation, other inhumane acts (forcible transfer), and persecutions through underlying acts of forcible transfer and deportation as crimes against humanity (collectively, "JCE I Crimes"), but that there was insufficient evidence to demonstrate that other crimes alleged in the Indictment were part of the JCE.[20] **[page 3]**

6.   The Trial Chamber found Stanišić responsible for crimes committed in each of the Municipalities,[21] while Župljanin was found responsible for crimes committed in the ARK Municipalities.[22] They were both convicted under Article 7(1) of the Statute for committing, through participation in the JCE, persecutions as a crime against humanity (through the underlying acts of killings; torture, cruel treatment, and inhumane acts; unlawful detention; establishment and perpetuation of inhumane living conditions; forcible transfer and deportation; plunder of property; wanton destruction of towns and villages including destruction or wilful damage done to institutions dedicated to religion and other cultural buildings; and imposition and maintenance of restrictive and discriminatory measures), and murder and torture as violations of the laws or customs of war.[23] In addition, Župljanin was convicted for committing, through participation in the JCE, extermination as a crime against humanity,[24] and for ordering persecutions through plunder of property.[25] On the basis of the principles relating to cumulative convictions, the Trial Chamber did not enter convictions against Stanišić and Župljanin for murder, torture, inhumane acts, deportation, and inhumane acts (forcible transfer) as crimes against humanity, or cruel treatment as a violation of the laws or customs of war.[26] Stanišić and Župljanin were both sentenced to 22 years of imprisonment.[27]

---

15   Indictment, paras 5, 16.
16   Trial Judgement, vol. 1, paras 212-228, 275-285, 340-350, 481-494, 685-703, 805-817, 873-883, 931-938, 974-986, 1034-1044, 1111-1122, 1185-1193, 1240-1251, 1281-1289, 1349-1359, 1408-1417, 1491-1501, 1548-1556, 1672-1691.
17   Namely, Banja Luka, Bijeljina, Bileća, Bosanski Šamac, Brčko, Doboj, Donji Vakuf, Gacko, Ilijaš, Ključ, Kotor Varoš, Pale, Prijedor, Sanski Most, Skender Vakuf, Teslić, Vlasenica, Višegrad, Vogošća, and Zvornik (see Indictment, Schedules A-G; Trial Judgement, vol. 2, para. 927).
18   Namely, Banja Luka, Donji Vakuf, Ključ, Kotor Varoš, Prijedor, Sanski Most, Skender Vakuf, and Teslić (see Indictment, Schedules A-E; Trial Judgement, vol. 2, para. 946).
19   Trial Judgement, vol. 2, para. 313.
20   Trial Judgement, vol. 2, para. 313.
21   Trial Judgement, vol. 2, paras 804, 809, 813, 818, 822, 827, 831, 836, 840, 844, 849, 854, 858, 863, 868, 873, 877, 881, 885. See Trial Judgement, vol. 1, para. 8.
22   Trial Judgement, vol. 2, paras 805, 832, 845, 850, 859, 864, 869. See Trial Judgement, vol. 1, para. 9.
23   Trial Judgement, vol. 2, paras 955-956. Stanišić and Župljanin were found guilty under the first and third categories of joint criminal enterprise, more specifically, the first category of joint criminal enterprise with regard to persecutions through deportation and forcible transfer and the third category of joint criminal enterprise with regard to the remaining underlying acts of the crime of persecutions and the crimes of murder and torture (see Trial Judgement, vol. 2, paras 804-805, 809, 813, 818, 822, 827, 831-832, 836, 840, 844-845, 849-850, 854, 858-859, 863-864, 868-869, 873, 877, 881, 885).
24   Trial Judgement, vol. 2, para. 956. Župljanin was convicted of extermination pursuant to the third category of joint criminal enterprise (see Trial Judgement, vol. 2, paras 805, 845, 850, 859).
25   Trial Judgement, vol. 2, para. 805. See Trial Judgement, vol. 2, paras 526, 956.
26   Trial Judgement, vol. 2, paras 912-917, 955-956. See Trial Judgement, vol. 2, paras 800, 804-805, 809, 813, 818, 822, 827, 831-832, 836, 840, 844-845, 849-850, 854, 858-859, 863-864, 868-869, 873, 877, 881, 885.
27   Trial Judgement, vol. 2, paras 955-956.

B. **Appeals**

1. Stanišić's appeal

7.   Stanišić challenges the Trial Judgement on 16 grounds.[28] Stanišić's first ground of appeal alleges that the Trial Chamber erred in law by failing to provide a reasoned opinion in support of its findings on the first and third categories of joint criminal enterprise.[29] Under his second through seventh grounds of appeal, Stanišić advances arguments challenging the Trial Chamber's findings relating to his liability through participation in the JCE. In particular, he alleges errors in relation to: **[page 4]** (i) his membership (Ground 2);[30] (ii) the common criminal purpose (Ground 3, in part);[31] (iii) his intent to further the JCE (Ground 3, in part, and Ground 4);[32] (iv) the legal standard for contribution to a joint criminal enterprise through failure to act (Ground 5);[33] (v) his contribution to the JCE (Ground 6);[34] and (vi) the Trial Chamber's evaluation of his interview with the Prosecution, conducted between 16 and 21 July 2007 ("Interview") (Ground 7).[35] Grounds of appeal eight through eleven relate to Stanišić's convictions pursuant to the third category of joint criminal enterprise.[36] Under his twelfth through fifteenth grounds of appeal, Stanišić alleges a number of errors of law and fact in relation to his sentence.[37] Under his ground of appeal 1*bis*, he argues that the Trial Chamber violated his right to a fair hearing by an independent and impartial tribunal, thereby invalidating the Trial Judgement.[38]

8.   In response, the Prosecution argues, *inter alia*, that the Appeals Chamber should dismiss Stanišić's appeal because he received a fair trial from an impartial panel of judges, and fails to demonstrate any error in the Trial Judgement.[39]

9.   In reply, Stanišić submits, *inter alia*, that the Prosecution repeats the Trial Chamber's findings but fails to respond to most of his arguments on appeal.[40]

2. Župljanin's appeal

10.   Župljanin challenges the Trial Judgement on six grounds.[41] Under his first ground of appeal, he advances a number of sub-grounds with respect to his conviction pursuant to first category of joint criminal enterprise.[42] Under his second and third grounds of appeal, Župljanin challenges his convictions pursuant to the third category of joint criminal enterprise,[43] and alleges errors of law and fact in relation to the Trial Chamber's findings on his responsibility for the crime of **[page 5]** extermination.[44] Under his fourth ground of appeal, Župljanin alleges multiple errors of law and fact in relation to his sentence,[45] and under his fifth ground of appeal, he claims that the Trial Chamber erred in law and fact in finding that he ordered persecutions

---

[28]   Stanišić Notice of Appeal, para. 19.
[29]   Stanišić Notice of Appeal, paras 23-25; Stanišić Appeal Brief, paras 22-54.
[30]   Stanišić Notice of Appeal, paras 26-28; Stanišić Appeal Brief, paras 55-74.
[31]   Stanišić Notice of Appeal, paras 29-31. Stanišić Appeal Brief, paras 76-86.
[32]   Stanišić Notice of Appeal, paras 29-36; Stanišić Appeal Brief, paras 75, 87-187.
[33]   Stanišić Notice of Appeal, paras 37-39; Stanišić Appeal Brief, paras 188-234.
[34]   Stanišić Notice of Appeal, paras 40-44; Stanišić Appeal Brief, paras 235-301.
[35]   Stanišić Notice of Appeal, paras 45-48; Stanišić Appeal Brief, paras 302-332.
[36]   Stanišić Notice of Appeal, paras 49-69; Stanišić Appeal Brief, paras 333-476.
[37]   Stanišić Notice of Appeal, paras 70-82; Stanišić Appeal Brief, paras 477-550.
[38]   Stanišić Notice of Appeal, paras 20-22; Stanišić Additional Appeal Brief, paras 2-131, p. 30. See Stanišić Appeal Brief, para. 21.
[39]   Prosecution Response to Appeal of Mićo Stanišić, 21 October 2013 (confidential, public redacted version filed on 15 November 2013) ("Prosecution Response Brief (Stanišić)"), paras 5-8; Prosecution's Consolidated Supplemental Response Brief, 18 July 2014 ("Prosecution Consolidated Supplemental Response Brief"), para. 1.
[40]   Brief in Reply on behalf of Mićo Stanišić, 11 November 2013 ("Stanišić Reply Brief"), paras 1, 5; Additional Brief in Reply on behalf of Mićo Stanišić, 29 July 2014 ("Stanišić Additional Reply Brief"), paras 1, 3.
[41]   Župljanin Notice of Appeal, paras 7-49.
[42]   Župljanin Notice of Appeal, paras 8-23; Župljanin Appeal Brief, paras 7-181.
[43]   Župljanin Notice of Appeal, paras 24-37; Župljanin Appeal Brief, paras 182-242.
[44]   Župljanin Notice of Appeal, paras 30-37; Župljanin Appeal Brief, paras 227-242.
[45]   Župljanin Notice of Appeal, paras 38-46; Župljanin Appeal Brief, paras 243-277.

through the "appropriation of property".[46] Under his sixth ground of appeal, Župljanin argues that the Trial Chamber violated his right to a fair trial "by an impartial, independent and competent court".[47]

11.   The Prosecution responds that the Appeals Chamber should dismiss Župljanin's appeal because he fails to establish an error of law invalidating the Judgement or an error of fact occasioning a miscarriage of justice.[48] It further submits that Župljanin "received a fair trial from an impartial panel of Judges".[49]

12.   In reply, Župljanin argues that the Prosecution fails to rebut any of his arguments on appeal.[50]

3. Prosecution's appeal

13.   The Prosecution challenges the Trial Judgement on two grounds.[51] Under its first ground of appeal, the Prosecution asserts that the Trial Chamber erred by imposing inadequate sentences on Stanišić and Župljanin.[52] Under its second ground of appeal, it alleges that the Trial Chamber erred in law by only convicting Stanišić and Župljanin for the crime against humanity of persecutions and failing to enter cumulative convictions for other crimes against humanity for which they were found criminally responsible: (i) murder (Count 3); (ii) torture (Count 5); (iii) deportation (Count 9); and (iv) inhumane acts (forcible transfer) (Count 10).[53] The Prosecution requests that the Appeals Chamber enter convictions for these crimes in order to fully reflect Stanišić's and Župljanin's criminal responsibility.[54] **[page 6]**

14.   In response, Stanišić and Župljanin submit that the Appeals Chamber should dismiss the Prosecution's appeal,[55] In particular, they respond that the Prosecution fails to show that the Trial Chamber abused its sentencing discretion or committed an error[56] and submit that the Trial Chamber's decision not to enter cumulative convictions should be upheld.[57]

15.   The Prosecution replies that neither Stanišić nor Župljanin demonstrate that the imposed sentences were reasonable.[58] Furthermore, it replies that Stanišić and Župljanin fail to show the existence of cogent reasons justifying the departure from the Tribunal's well-settled jurisprudence on cumulative convictions.[59]

C. **Appeal hearing**

16.   The Appeals Chamber heard oral submissions from the parties regarding these appeals on 16 December 2015.[60] Having considered the written and oral submissions of Stanišić, Župljanin, and the Prosecution, the Appeals Chamber hereby renders its Judgement. **[page 7]**

---

[46]   Župljanin Notice of Appeal, paras 47-48; Župljanin Appeal Brief, paras 278-282.

[47]   Župljanin Notice of Appeal, para. 49; Župljanin Additional Appeal Brief, paras 1-35.

[48]   Prosecution Response to Stojan Župljanin's Appeal Brief, 21 October 2013 (confidential; public redacted version filed on 25 June 2014) ("Prosecution Response Brief (Župljanin)"), paras 3, 245.

[49]   Prosecution Consolidated Supplemental Response Brief, para. 1.

[50]   See generally Stojan [Z]upljanin's Reply to Prosecution's Response Brief, 11 November 2013 (confidential; public redacted version filed on 13 November 2013) ("Župljanin Reply Brief"), paras 1-86; Stojan Župljanin's Reply to Prosecution's Consolidated Supplemental Response Brief Concerning Additional Ground, 25 July 2014 ("Župljanin Additional Reply Brief"), paras 1-23.

[51]   See Prosecution Notice of Appeal, paras 2-5, Prosecution Appeal Brief, paras 1-61.

[52]   Prosecution Notice of Appeal, paras 2-3; Prosecution Appeal Brief, paras 1, 3-53, 61.

[53]   Prosecution Notice of Appeal, paras 4-5; Prosecution Appeal Brief, paras 2, 54-61.

[54]   Prosecution Notice of Appeal, para. 5; Prosecution Appeal Brief, paras 2, 54, 60-61.

[55]   Respondent's Brief on behalf of Mićo Stanišić, 21 October 2013 ("Stanišić Response Brief"), paras 3, 110, 182; Stojan [Ž]upljanin's Response to Prosecution Appeal Brief, 21 October 2013 ("Župljanin Response Brief"), para. 26. *Cf.* Stanišić Response Brief, para. 180.

[56]   Stanišić Response Brief, paras 3, 110; Župljanin Response Brief, paras 2, 16.

[57]   See Stanišić Response Brief, paras 115, 118, 179-180; Župljanin Response Brief, paras 17-21, 23.

[58]   Consolidated Prosecution Reply to Mićo Stanišić's Respondent's Brief and Stojan Župljanin's Response to Prosecution Appeal, 11 November 2013 ("Prosecution Consolidated Reply Brief"), paras 1-17.

[59]   Prosecution Consolidated Reply Brief, paras 1, 18-25.

[60]   Appeal Hearing, 16 Dec 2015, AT. 61-244.

II. STANDARD OF APPELLATE REVIEW

17.   Article 25 of the Statute stipulates that the Appeals Chamber may affirm, reverse, or revise the decisions taken by a trial chamber. The Appeals Chamber recalls that an appeal is not a trial *de novo*.[61] On appeal, parties must limit their arguments to legal errors that invalidate the decision of the trial chamber and to factual errors that result in a miscarriage of justice.[62] These criteria are set forth in Article 25 of the Statute and are well-established in the jurisprudence of both the Tribunal and the International Criminal Tribunal for Rwanda ("ICTR").[63] In exceptional circumstances, the Appeals Chamber will also hear appeals in which a party has raised a legal issue that would not invalidate the trial judgement but it is nevertheless of general significance to the Tribunal's jurisprudence.[64]

18.   A party alleging an error of law must identify the alleged error, present arguments in support of its claim, and explain how the error invalidates the decision.[65] An allegation of an error of law that has no chance of changing the outcome of a decision may be rejected on that ground.[66] However, even if the party's arguments are insufficient to support the contention of an error, the Appeals Chamber may find for other reasons that there is an error of law.[67] It is necessary for any appellant claiming an error of law on the basis of the lack of a reasoned opinion to identify the specific issues, factual findings, or arguments that the appellant submits the trial chamber omitted to address and to explain why this omission invalidates the decision.[68]

19.   The Appeals Chamber reviews the trial chamber's findings of law to determine whether or not they are correct.[69] Where the Appeals Chamber finds an error of law in the trial judgement arising from the application of the wrong legal standard, the Appeals Chamber will articulate **[page 8]** the correct legal standard and review the relevant factual findings of the trial chamber accordingly.[70] In so doing, the Appeals Chamber not only corrects the legal error, but when necessary, applies the correct legal standard to the evidence contained in the trial record and determines whether it is itself convinced beyond reasonable doubt of the factual finding challenged by an appellant before the finding is confirmed on appeal.[71] The Appeals Chamber will not review the entire trial record *de novo*. Rather, it will in principle only take into account evidence referred to by the trial chamber in the body of the judgement or in a related footnote, evidence contained in the trial record and referred to by the parties, and, where applicable, additional evidence admitted on appeal.[72]

20.   When considering alleged errors of fact, the Appeals Chamber will apply a standard of reasonableness.[73] In reviewing the findings of the trial chamber, the Appeals Chamber will only substitute its own finding for

---

[61]   *Stanišić and Simatović* Appeal Judgement, para. 15; *Đorđević* Appeal Judgement, para. 13; *Kordić and Čerkez* Appeal Judgement, para. 13.

[62]   *Tolimir* Appeal Judgement, para. 8; *Popović et al.* Appeal Judgement, para. 16; *Đorđević* Appeal Judgement, para. 13.

[63]   *Stanišić and Simatović* Appeal Judgement, para. 15; *Popović et al.* Appeal Judgement, para. 16; *Đorđević* Appeal Judgement, para. 13; *Nyiramasuhuko et al.* Appeal Judgement, para. 29.

[64]   *Stanišić and Simatović* Appeal Judgement, para. 15; *Tolimir* Appeal Judgement, para. 8; *Popović et al.* Appeal Judgement, para. 16. *Cf. Ndahimana* Appeal Judgement, para. 8; *Mugenzi and Mugiraneza* Appeal Judgement, para. 12; *Gatete* Appeal Judgement, para. 8.

[65]   *Stanišić and Simatović* Appeal Judgement, para. 16; *Tolimir* Appeal Judgement, para. 9; *Popović et al.* Appeal Judgement, para. 17; *Nyiramasuhuko et al.* Appeal Judgement, para. 30; *Ngirabatware* Appeal Judgement, para. 8.

[66]   *Stanišić and Simatović* Appeal Judgement, para. 16; *Tolimir* Appeal Judgement, para. 9; *Popović et al.* Appeal Judgement, para. 17. See *Ndahimana* Appeal Judgement, para. 8; *Ngirabatware* Appeal Judgement, para. 8.

[67]   *Stanišić and Simatović* Appeal Judgement, para. 16; *Tolimir* Appeal Judgement, para. 9; *Popović et al.* Appeal Judgement, para. 17.

[68]   *Stanišić and Simatović* Appeal Judgement, para. 16; *Tolimir* Appeal Judgement, para. 9; *Popović et al.* Appeal Judgement, para. 17.

[69]   *Stanišić and Simatović* Appeal Judgement, para. 17; *Tolimir* Appeal Judgement, para. 10; *Popović et al.* Appeal Judgement, para. 18.

[70]   *Stanišić and Simatović* Appeal Judgement, para. 17; *Tolimir* Appeal Judgement, para. 10; *Popović et al.* Appeal Judgement, para. 18.

[71]   *Stanišić and Simatović* Appeal Judgement, para. 17; *Tolimir* Appeal Judgement, para. 10; *Popović et al.* Appeal Judgement, para. 18.

[72]   *Stanišić and Simatović* Appeal Judgement, para. 17; *Tolimir* Appeal Judgement, para. 10; *Popović et al.* Appeal Judgement, para. 18.

[73]   *Stanišić and Simatović* Appeal Judgement, para. 18; *Tolimir* Appeal Judgement, para. 11; *Popović et al.* Appeal Judgement, para. 19. See *Ngirabatware* Appeal Judgement, para. 10.

that of the trial chamber when no reasonable trier of fact could have reached the original decision.[74] The Appeals Chamber applies the same reasonableness standard to alleged errors of fact regardless of whether the finding of fact was based on direct or circumstantial evidence.[75] It is not any error of fact that will cause the Appeals Chamber to overturn a decision by a trial chamber, but only one that has caused a miscarriage of justice.[76]

21.   In determining whether or not a trial chamber's finding was reasonable, the Appeals Chamber will not lightly disturb findings of fact by the trial chamber.[77] The Appeals Chamber recalls, as a general principle, the approach adopted by the Appeals Chamber in *Kupreškić et al.*, wherein it was stated that:

> [p]ursuant to the jurisprudence of the Tribunal, the task of hearing, assessing and weighing the evidence presented at trial is left primarily to the Trial Chamber. Thus, the Appeals Chamber must give a margin of deference to a finding of fact reached by a Trial Chamber. Only where the evidence relied on by the Trial Chamber could not have been accepted by any reasonable tribunal **[page 9]** of fact or where the evaluation of the evidence is "wholly erroneous" may the Appeals Chamber substitute its own finding for that of the Trial Chamber.[78]

22.   When considering an appeal by the Prosecution, the same standard of reasonableness and the deference to factual findings applies. The Appeals Chamber will only hold that an error of fact was committed when it determines that no reasonable trier of fact could have made the impugned finding.[79] Considering that it is the Prosecution that bears the burden at trial of proving the guilt of an accused beyond reasonable doubt, the significance of an error of fact occasioning a miscarriage of justice is somewhat different for a Prosecution appeal against acquittal than for a defence appeal against conviction.[80] An accused must show that the trial chamber's factual errors create reasonable doubt as to his or her guilt.[81] The Prosecution must show that, when account is taken of the errors of fact committed by the trial chamber, all reasonable doubt of the accused's guilt has been eliminated.[82]

23.   The Appeals Chamber recalls that, where additional evidence has been admitted on appeal and an alleged error of fact is raised, but there is no error in the legal standard applied in relation to the factual finding, the following two-step standard will apply:

> (i) The Appeals Chamber will first determine, on the basis of the trial record alone, whether no reasonable trier of fact could have reached the conclusion of guilt beyond reasonable doubt. If that is the case, then no further examination of the matter is necessary as a matter of law.

> (ii) If, however, the Appeals Chamber determines that a reasonable trier of fact could have reached a conclusion of guilt beyond reasonable doubt, then the Appeals Chamber will determine whether, in light of the trial evidence and additional evidence admitted on appeal, it is itself convinced beyond reasonable doubt as to the finding of guilt.[83]

---

[74]   *Stanišić and Simatović* Appeal Judgement, para. 18; *Tolimir* Appeal Judgement, para. 11; *Popović et al.* Appeal Judgement, para. 19.

[75]   *Stanišić and Simatović* Appeal Judgement, para. 18; *Tolimir* Appeal Judgement, para. 11; *Popović et al.* Appeal Judgement, para. 19.

[76]   *Stanišić and Simatović* Appeal Judgement, para. 18; *Tolimir* Appeal Judgement, para. 11; *Popović et al.* Appeal Judgement, para. 19.

[77]   *Stanišić and Simatović* Appeal Judgement, para. 19; *Tolimir* Appeal Judgement, para. 12; *Popović et al.* Appeal Judgement, para. 20.

[78]   *Kupreškić et al.* Appeal Judgement, para. 30. See *Stanišić and Simatović* Appeal Judgement, para. 19; *Tolimir* Appeal Judgement, para. 12; *Popović et al.* Appeal Judgement, para. 20.

[79]   *Popović et al.* Appeal Judgement, para. 21; *Đorđević* Appeal Judgement, para. 18; *Šainović et al.* Appeal Judgement, para. 24.

[80]   *Popović et al.* Appeal Judgement, para. 21; *Đorđević* Appeal Judgement, para. 18; *Šainović et al.* Appeal Judgement, para. 24.

[81]   *Popović et al.* Appeal Judgement, para. 21; *Đorđević* Appeal Judgement, para. 18; *Šainović et al.* Appeal Judgement, para. 24.

[82]   *Popović et al.* Appeal Judgement, para. 21; *Đorđević* Appeal Judgement, para. 18; *Šainović et al.* Appeal Judgement, para. 24.

[83]   *Lukić and Lukić* Appeal Judgement, para. 14; *Krajišnik* Appeal Judgement, para. 15; *Kvočka et al.* Appeal Judgement, para. 426.

24.   The Appeals Chamber recalls that it has inherent discretion in selecting which submissions merit a detailed reasoned opinion in writing, and may dismiss arguments which are evidently unfounded without providing detailed reasoning.[84] Indeed, the Appeals Chamber's mandate cannot be effectively and efficiently carried out without focused contributions by the parties.[85] In order for **[page 10]** the Appeals Chamber to assess a party's arguments on appeal, the party is expected to present its case clearly, logically, and exhaustively.[86] The appealing party is also expected to provide precise references to relevant transcript pages or paragraphs in the decision or judgement to which the challenges are being made.[87] The Appeals Chamber will not consider a party's submissions in detail when they are obscure, contradictory, vague, or suffer from other formal and obvious insufficiencies.[88] Arguments which do not have the potential to cause the impugned decision to be reversed or revised may be immediately dismissed by the Appeals Chamber and need not be considered on the merits.[89]

25.   When applying these basic principles, the Appeals Chamber recalls that in previous cases it has identified the general types of deficient submissions on appeal which may be dismissed without detailed analysis.[90] In particular, the Appeals Chamber will generally dismiss: (i) arguments that fail to identify the challenged factual findings, that misrepresent the factual findings or the evidence, or that ignore other relevant factual findings; (ii) mere assertions that the trial chamber must have failed to consider relevant evidence without showing that no reasonable trier of fact, based on the evidence, could have reached the same conclusion as the trial chamber did; (iii) challenges to factual findings on which a conviction does not rely and arguments that are clearly irrelevant, that lend support to, or that are not inconsistent with the challenged finding; (iv) arguments that challenge a trial chamber's reliance or failure to rely on one piece of evidence without explaining why the conviction should not stand on the basis of the remaining evidence; (v) arguments contrary to common sense; (vi) challenges to factual findings where the relevance of the factual finding is unclear and has not been explained by the appealing party; (vii) mere repetition of arguments that were unsuccessful at trial without any demonstration that their rejection by the trial chamber constituted an error warranting the intervention of the Appeals Chamber; (viii) allegations based on material not on the trial record; (ix) mere assertions unsupported by any evidence, undeveloped **[page 11]** assertions, or failure to articulate errors; and (x) mere assertions that the trial chamber failed to give sufficient weight to evidence or failed to interpret evidence in a particular manner.[91]

26.   Finally, where the Appeals Chamber finds that a ground of appeal, presented as relating to an alleged error of law, formulates no clear legal challenge but challenges the trial chamber's factual findings in terms of its assessment of evidence, it will either analyse these allegations to determine the reasonableness of the impugned conclusions or refer to the relevant analysis under other grounds of appeal.[92] **[page 12]**

---

[84]   *Stanišić and Simatović* Appeal Judgement, para. 21; *Tolimir* Appeal Judgement, para. 13; *Popović et al.* Appeal Judgement, para. 22.
[85]   *Stanišić and Simatović* Appeal Judgement, para. 21; *Popović et al.* Appeal Judgement, para. 22; *Đorđević* Appeal Judgement, para. 19.
[86]   *Stanišić and Simatović* Appeal Judgement, para. 21; *Tolimir* Appeal Judgement, para. 13; *Popović et al.* Appeal Judgement, para. 22.
[87]   Practice Direction on Formal Requirements for Appeals from Judgement, IT/201, 7 March 2002, paras 1(c)(iii)-(iv), 4(b)(ii). See *Stanišić and Simatović* Appeal Judgement, para. 21; *Tolimir* Appeal Judgement, para. 13; *Popović et al.* Appeal Judgement, para. 22.
[88]   *Tolimir* Appeal Judgement, para. 13; *Popović et al.* Appeal Judgement, para. 22; *Šainović et al.* Appeal Judgement, para. 26.
[89]   *Tolimir* Appeal Judgement, para. 13; *Perišić* Appeal Judgement, para. 11; *Gotovina and Markač* Appeal Judgement, para. 14; *Nyiramasuhuko et al.* Appeal Judgement, para. 34; *Karemera and Ngirumpatse* Appeal Judgement, para. 17; *Ngirabatware* Appeal Judgement, para. 11.
[90]   *Stanišić and Simatović* Appeal Judgement, para. 22; *Tolimir* Appeal Judgement, para. 14; *Popović et al.* Appeal Judgement, para. 23.

10
[91]   *Stanišić and Simatović* Appeal Judgement, para. 22; *Tolimir* Appeal Judgement, para. 14; *Popović et al.* Appeal Judgement, para. 23.
[92]   *Tolimir* Appeal Judgement, para. 15; *Popović et al.* Appeal Judgement, para. 24; *Đorđević* Appeal Judgement, para. 21. See *Strugar* Appeal Judgement, paras 252, 269.

III.   ALLEGED DENIAL OF THE RIGHT TO A FAIR TRIAL BY AN INDEPENDENT AND IMPARTIAL TRIBUNAL (STANIŠIĆ'S GROUND OF APPEAL *1BIS* AND ŽUPLJANIN'S SIXTH GROUND OF APPEAL)

A.   Introduction

27.   On 27 March 2013, the Trial Chamber, composed of Judges Burton Hall, Guy Delvoie, and Frederik Harhoff ("Judge Harhoff"), unanimously convicted Stanišić and Župljanin pursuant to joint criminal enterprise liability.[93] Following the delivery of the Trial Judgement, a Danish newspaper published a letter written by Judge Harhoff and addressed to 56 recipients, dated 6 June 2013 ("Letter").[94] On 9 July 2013, Vojislav Šešelj, an accused on trial before a chamber of which Judge Harhoff was a member, requested that Judge Harhoff be disqualified from his case on the basis of the Letter.[95] On 28 August 2013, a chamber convened in the *Šešelj* case by the Acting President of the Tribunal ("Special Chamber") found, by majority, that in the Letter, Judge Harhoff "demonstrated a bias in favour of conviction such that a reasonable observer properly informed would reasonably apprehend bias".[96] Judge Harhoff was subsequently disqualified from the *Šešelj* proceedings.[97] On 14 April 2014, the Appeals Chamber admitted the Letter in its entirety as additional evidence on appeal in this case[98] and allowed Stanišić and Župljanin to supplement their respective appeals to include submissions on the Letter.[99] The Appeals Chamber also admitted three documents in rebuttal, namely two media articles ("Media Articles"),[100] as well as a memorandum **[page 13]** dated 8 July 2013 from Judge Harhoff to Judge Jean-Claude Antonetti, Presiding Judge in the *Šešelj* case, in relation to the Letter ("Memorandum") (collectively, "Rebuttal Material").[101]

28.   Stanišić and Župljanin submit that their right to a fair trial by an independent and impartial court was violated as a result of the participation of Judge Harhoff in the trial proceedings,[102] which invalidates their convictions.[103] They argue that: (i) Judge Harhoff's disqualification from the *Šešelj* proceedings must lead to the same result in the proceedings against them;[104] and (ii) the Letter reveals an unacceptable appearance of bias on the part of Judge Harhoff in favour of convicting accused persons, which rebuts the presumption of

---

[93]   Trial Judgement, vol. 2, paras 955-956. See Trial Judgement, vol. 2, paras 313-315, 489-530, 729-798, 912, 916, 918. In addition, Župljanin was convicted for ordering persecutions through plunder of property (see *supra*, para. 6).
[94]   See Exhibit 1DA1.
[95]   *Prosecutor v. Vojislav Šešelj*, Case No. IT-03-67-T, Professor Vojislav Šešelj's Motion for Disqualification of Judge Frederik Harhoff, 9 July 2013.
[96]   *Prosecutor v. Vojislav Šešelj*, Case No. IT-03-67-T, Decision on Defence Motion for Disqualification of Judge Frederik Harhoff and Report to the Vice-President, 28 August 2013 ("*Šešelj* Decision on Disqualification"), para. 14. The Special Chamber, by majority, denied a request by the Prosecution for reconsideration and Stanišić and Župljanin's request to make submissions in that case (*Prosecutor v. Vojislav Šešelj*, Case No. IT-03-67-T, Decision on Prosecution Motion for Reconsideration of Decision on Disqualification, Requests for Clarification, and Motion on Behalf of Stanišić and Župljanin, 7 October 2013 ("*Šešelj* Reconsideration Decision"), para. 22). The Appeals Chamber will refer to the *Šešelj* Decision on Disqualification and the *Šešelj* Reconsideration Decision together as the "*Šešelj* Decisions".
[97]   *Šešelj* Decision on Disqualification, paras 14-15; *Prosecutor v. Vojislav Šešelj*, Case No. IT-03-67-T, Order Assigning a Judge Pursuant to Rule 15, 31 October 2013 ("*Šešelj* Order Replacing Judge Harhoff"), p. 2.
[98]   Decision on Mićo Stanišić's Motion Seeking Admission of Additional Evidence Pursuant to Rule 115, 14 April 2014, paras 22-24, 27. See *infra*, Annex A, para. 5. The Letter was admitted into evidence on appeal as Exhibit 1DA1.
[99]   Decision on Mićo Stanišić's Motion Seeking Leave to Amend Notice of Appeal, 14 April 2014 ("Decision on Stanišić's Motion to Amend Notice of Appeal"), paras 23-24; Decision on Župljanin's Second Request to Amend His Notice of Appeal and Supplement His Appeal Brief, 14 April 2014, paras 16-19. See Župljanin Notice of Appeal; Stanišić Notice of Appeal, 23 April 2013; [Z]upljanin's Second Request to Amend His Notice of Appeal and Supplement His Appeal Brief, 9 September 2013; Supplemental Submission in Support of Mićo Stanišić's Motion to Amend Notice of Appeal, 9 September 2013. Stanišić's ground of appeal *1bis* and Župljanin's ground of appeal 6 were subsequently added to the appeal proceedings.
[100]   Exhibit PA2 (entitled "Two Puzzling Judgments in The Hague" dated 1 June 2013 and published by *The Economist*); Exhibit PA3 (entitled "What Happened to the Hague Tribunal?" dated 2 June 2013 and published by *The New York Times*).
[101]   Exhibit PA1.
[102]   See Stanišić Additional Appeal Brief, paras 2-10. See also Stanišić Additional Appeal Brief, p. 30; Župljanin Additional Appeal Brief, paras 1, 34-35; *infra*, Annex A, para. 5.
[103]   Stanišić Additional Appeal Brief, paras 4, 9-10, 106-131; Župljanin Additional Appeal Brief, paras 2-3, 30-34. See Appeal Hearing, 16 Dec 2015, AT. 70, 160.
[104]   Stanišić Additional Appeal Brief, paras 33-52; Župljanin Additional Appeal Brief, paras 4-12, 28-29; Stanišić Additional Reply Brief, paras 28-30.

impartiality in this case.[105] Stanišić and Župljanin request that the Appeals Chamber quash the Trial Chamber's findings, vacate the Trial Judgement, and conduct a *de novo* assessment of all findings or order a re-trial before a new trial chamber.[106] Alternatively, they request that a full acquittal be pronounced.[107]

29.   The Prosecution responds that Stanišić and Župljanin received a fair trial from an impartial panel of judges[108] and that their appeals in this regard should be dismissed.[109] It argues that Stanišić and Župljanin have: (i) incorrectly focused on Judge Harhoff's disqualification from the *Šešelj* case, which it submits, was erroneous and not binding in this case;[110] and (ii) neither rebutted the presumption of Judge Harhoff's impartiality nor demonstrated that a reasonable apprehension of bias is firmly established.[111] **[page 14]**

B.   Whether Judge Harhoff's disqualification in the *Šešelj* proceedings must lead to the same result in this case

1.   Submissions of the parties

30.   Stanišić and Župljanin submit that the disqualification of Judge Harhoff from the *Šešelj* proceedings, although not legally binding, must lead to the same result in the proceedings against them.[112] Stanišić argues that Judge Harhoff's disqualification in the *Šešelj* case attaches to him in his capacity as a Judge of the Tribunal and is not limited to a particular case.[113] Similarly, Župljanin asserts that the bias found in the *Šešelj* Decisions was not directed against Šešelj in particular but arose from Judge Harhoff's predisposition to convict accused persons.[114] Stanišić and Župljanin also argue that the *Šešelj* Decision on Disqualification is final and the Appeals Chamber cannot invalidate it by arriving at a different conclusion in the present case.[115] In this respect, Stanišić and Župljanin submit that the *Šešelj* case and the present proceedings are essentially "identical" as the *Šešelj* Decisions address the same issue (*i.e.* Judge Harhoff's impartiality in light of views expressed in the Letter), are based on the same material (*i.e.* the Letter), are not limited to a specific accused, and concern the same subject matter (*i.e.* Judge Harhoff's interpretation of joint criminal enterprise liability).[116] Stanišić contends that the Appeals Chamber is not empowered to render a decision contrary to the *Šešelj* Decisions since the *Šešelj* Decisions were referred to by the Acting President of the Tribunal as

---

[105]   Stanišić Additional Appeal Brief, paras 53-105; Župljanin Additional Appeal Brief, paras 13-27. See Appeal Hearing, 16 Dec 2015, AT. 69-70, 72-73, 144-145.
[106]   Stanišić Additional Appeal Brief, para. 10, p. 30; Župljanin Additional Appeal Brief, paras 1, 3, 30-35. See Appeal Hearing, 16 Dec 2015, AT. 92-93, 160-161.
[107]   Stanišić Additional Appeal Brief, para. 10, p. 30; Župljanin Additional Appeal Brief, paras 1, 3, 30-35. See Appeal Hearing, 16 Dec 2015, AT. 92-93.
[108]   Prosecution Consolidated Supplemental Response Brief, para. 1.
[109]   Prosecution Consolidated Supplemental Response Brief, para. 4. See Appeal Hearing, 16 Dec 2015, AT. 129, 134-135, 183, 204.
[110]   Prosecution Consolidated Supplemental Response Brief, para. 3.
[111]   Prosecution Consolidated Supplemental Response Brief, para. 3. See Prosecution Consolidated Supplemental Response Brief, paras 1, 4.
[112]   See Stanišić Additional Appeal Brief, paras 33-52; Župljanin Additional Appeal Brief, paras 4-12, 28-29; Stanišić Additional Reply Brief, paras 28-30.
[113]   Stanišić Additional Appeal Brief, paras 6, 35-41. See Župljanin Additional Appeal Brief, paras 12, 28-29. See also Appeal Hearing, 16 Dec 2015, AT. 73-75. Stanišić argues further that "[a] judge who expressed views which gave rise to an apprehension that he was predisposed to convict persons accused in one case – while sitting simultaneously on a second case – cannot be disqualified from the former and found *not* to have exhibited an appearance of bias in the latter." (Stanišić Additional Appeal Brief, para. 30). See Stanišić Additional Appeal Brief, paras 49-52 (arguing that the disqualification of Judge Harhoff in the *Šešelj* proceedings is inseparable from the determination of whether he should be disqualified in this case); Stanišić Additional Reply Brief, para. 32; Appeal Hearing, 16 Dec 2015, AT. 90-91.
[114]   Župljanin Additional Appeal Brief, paras 9-10. See Stanišić Additional Appeal Brief, para. 43.
[115]   Stanišić Additional Appeal Brief, para. 41. See Župljanin Additional Appeal Brief, paras 1, 9-12. See also Appeal Hearing, 16 Dec 2015, AT. 90. Stanišić also argues that "[w]ere the Appeals Chamber to come to a different conclusion regarding the impact of the Letter in this case, it would have the effect of indirectly invalidating the [*Šešelj* Decisions] based on the indistinguishable features underlying both cases" (Stanišić Additional Appeal Brief, para. 46). See Stanišić Additional Appeal Brief, paras 35, 41-42.
[116]   Stanišić Additional Appeal Brief, paras 42-44, 57; Župljanin Additional Appeal Brief, paras 10, 12. Stanišić identifies two differences between this case and that of *Šešelj* but argues that the finding of apparent bias in the *Šešelj* proceedings is applicable in this case. Specifically, he notes that: (i) the Trial Judgement was already issued when the Letter was published, which only has an effect on the remedy available; and (ii) the Special Chamber did not consider the Rebuttal Material (Appeal Hearing, 16 Dec 2015, AT. 91; Stanišić Additional Appeal Brief, para. 45). See Stanišić Additional Reply Brief, paras 27-31).

121

"now final"[117] and no clear error of reasoning or change of **[page 15]** circumstances has been established or raised to justify overturning the *Šešelj* Decisions.[118] According to Stanišić, the apparent bias of Judge Harhoff undermines confidence in the administration of justice, is contrary to Article 13 of the Statute, and thus disqualifies him from acting in a judicial capacity.[119]

31. The Prosecution responds that the *Šešelj* Decisions are neither binding nor equally applicable to this case.[120] It argues that prior judicial disqualifications are case-specific, and "[t]he Appeals Chamber must therefore reach its own determination as to Judge Harhoff's impartiality in this case."[121] In particular, the Prosecution refers to the differences between the *Šešelj* case and the present case, namely, the arguments, evidence, and the fact that the Trial Judgement had already been rendered at the date of the publication of the Letter.[122] It submits further that the *Šešelj* Decisions are erroneous and not persuasive regarding Judge Harhoff's impartiality in this case.[123]

2. Analysis

32. On the issue of disqualification of Judges, Rule 15(A) of the Rules of Procedure and Evidence of the Tribunal ("Rules") provides that "[a] Judge may not sit on a trial or appeal in any case in which the Judge has a personal interest or concerning which the Judge has or has had any **[page 16]** association which might affect his or her impartiality."[124] In light of Article 13 of the Statute – which requires Judges to be, *inter alia*, impartial – Rule 15(A) of the Rules has been interpreted and applied in accordance with the principle that a Judge is not impartial if actual bias or an unacceptable appearance of bias exists.[125] The Appeals Chamber also notes that a Judge who has not met the requirements of this Rule in a specific case has otherwise been entitled to continue to exercise the functions of a Judge of the Tribunal and sit in other cases when he fulfils

---

[117]   See Stanišić Additional Appeal Brief, para. 41, referring to *Šešelj* Order Replacing Judge Harhoff. See Appeal Hearing, 16 Dec 2015, AT. 90. Stanišić asserts that the *Šešelj* Decision on Disqualification was subject to an unsuccessful appeal, and that *Šešelj* Decisions have been implemented. Stanišić Additional Appeal Brief, para. 47.

[118]   Stanišić Additional Appeal Brief, paras 41, 47-48. See Stanišić Additional Reply Brief, paras 23-24, 26. See Župljanin Additional Reply Brief, para. 2. See also Appeal Hearing, 16 Dec 2015, AT. 143.

[119]   Stanišić Additional Appeal Brief, paras 49-52, referring to *The Prosecutor v. Edouard Karemera et al.*, Case No. ICTR-98-44-T, Decision on Joseph Nzirorera's Motion for Disqualification of Judge Byron and Stay of the Proceedings, 20 February 2009 ("*Karemera et al.* Disqualification Decision"), para. 6, *Prosecutor v. Radovan Karadžić*, Case No. IT-95-05/18-PT, Decision on Motion to Disqualify Judge Picard and Report to the Vice-President Pursuant to Rule 15(B)(ii), 22 July 2009 ("*Karadžić* Disqualification Decision"), para. 17.

[120]   Prosecution Consolidated Supplemental Response Brief, para. 28; Appeal Hearing, 16 Dec 2015, AT. 132.

[121]   Prosecution Consolidated Supplemental Response Brief, para. 31. See Prosecution Consolidated Supplemental Response Brief, paras 28-30. The Prosecution contends that the "case-specific nature of judicial bias claims is further confirmed by how prior judicial disqualifications at international criminal tribunals have only applied to particular cases, and have not impacted the challenged Judges' ability to sit on other cases" (Prosecution Consolidated Supplemental Response Brief, para. 30, referring to *Prosecutor v. Zejnil Delalić et al.*, Case No. IT-96-21-T, Decision of the Bureau on Motion to Disqualify Judges Pursuant to Rule 15 or in the Alternative that Certain Judges Recuse Themselves, 25 October 1999 ("*Delalić et al.* Disqualification and Recusal Decision"), para. 9, *Prosecutor v. Issa Hassan Sesay*, Case No. SCSL-2004-15-AR15, Decision on Defence Motion Seeking the Disqualification of Justice Robertson from the Appeals Chamber, 13 March 2004 ("*RUF* Decision"), paras 1, 18, *Edouard Karemera et al. v. The Prosecutor*, Case No. ICTR-98-44-AR15bis.2, Reasons for Decision on Interlocutory Appeals Regarding the Continuation of Proceedings with a Substitute Judge and on Nzirorera's Motion for Leave to Consider New Material, 22 October 2004, paras 68-69).

[122]   Prosecution Consolidated Supplemental Response Brief, para. 31; Appeal Hearing, 16 Dec 2015, AT. 133-134. The Prosecution argues that the unanimous Trial Judgement shows that the Special Chamber's majority interpretation of the Letter was incorrect and that the Memorandum was erroneously considered to be immaterial. See Appeal Hearing, 16 Dec 2015, AT. 133-134. The Prosecution also argues that a conclusion contrary to the *Šešelj* Decisions would be consistent with prior instances where different chambers reached different conclusions based on different arguments and evidence. Prosecution Consolidated Supplemental Response Brief, para. 31.

[123]   Prosecution Consolidated Supplemental Response Brief, paras 21-26. See Appeal Hearing, 16 Dec 2015, AT. 132-133. The Prosecution asserts that "[t]o the extent that any language in the Decisions could be construed as having a broader impact, any such conclusions would be beyond the competence of the *Šešelj* special panel." Prosecution Consolidated Supplemental Response Brief, para. 28.

[124]   See *Šainović et al.* Appeal Judgement, para. 179.

[125]   *Furundžija* Appeal Judgement, paras 189-191; *Šainović et al.* Appeal Judgement, paras 179-181. See *Furundžija* Appeal Judgement, para. 175 (noting that Rule 15(A) of the Rules calls for a Judge to withdraw from a particular case if he or she believes that his or her impartiality is in question).

the requirements of Rule 15 of the Rules in those other cases.[126] The Appeals Chamber therefore considers that determinations of actual bias or unacceptable appearance of bias under Rule 15 of the Rules should be made on a case-by-case basis.[127] Accordingly, the Appeals Chamber finds that Judge Harhoff's disqualification in the *Šešelj* case, which was determined pursuant to Rule 15 of the Rules, does not automatically disqualify him from other cases. Stanišić and Župljanin therefore cannot rely on a finding of apparent bias made in another case and must instead show that those actions of Judge Harhoff which allegedly demonstrate an unacceptable appearance of bias, impacted on his impartiality in their trial proceedings.[128]

33.   Additionally, as held by the Appeals Chamber, there has been no general finding or final determination on Judge Harhoff's partiality with regard to the present case,[129] and the factual findings in the *Šešelj* Decisions were limited to the particular circumstances of that case.[130] The Appeals Chamber emphasises in this respect that, as a rule, factual findings made by one chamber are not binding upon subsequent chambers.[131] The Appeals Chamber also does not find **[page 17]** Stanišić and Župljanin's argument that the *Šešelj* case and the current proceedings are "identical" to be persuasive.[132] Recalling that it is the burden of the party seeking disqualification of a Judge to demonstrate a reasonable apprehension of bias,[133] the Appeals Chamber notes that the arguments presented in the *Šešelj* case, as well as the evidence considered, differ from those in this case, and that in the *Šešelj* case, the Letter was sent by Judge Harhoff while the case was ongoing.[134] Thus, Stanišić and Župljanin's reliance on the findings in the *Šešelj* case is insufficient to meet their burden of proof. Furthermore, the Appeals Chamber considers that Stanišić takes out of context the Acting President's Order Replacing Judge Harhoff in the *Šešelj* proceedings.[135] It is clear that the relevant statement in the order, *i.e.* that Judge Harhoff's disqualification was "therefore now final", concerned the finality of the disqualification pursuant to Rule 15 of the Rules in the *Šešelj* proceedings and related only to that case.[136] Similarly, Stanišić and Župljanin's argument that a different conclusion on Judge Harhoff's impartiality in this case would invalidate the *Šešelj* Decisions is without merit and is dismissed.

34.   In light of the foregoing, the Appeals Chamber dismisses Stanišić and Župljanin's arguments that the *Šešelj* Decisions must automatically lead to the same result in the present case.

---

[126]   See *Čelebići* Appeal Judgement, para. 683 (stating that the "relevant question to be determined by the Appeals Chamber is whether the reaction of the hypothetical fair-minded observer (with sufficient knowledge of the circumstances to make a reasonable judgement) would be that [the Judge] might not bring an impartial and unprejudiced mind to the issues arising in *the* case" (emphasis added)). See also *Delalić et al.* Disqualification and Recusal Decision, para. 9 ("If the Judge does not fulfil the requirements referred to in Rule 15(B), he or she is disqualified from hearing that particular case, although he or she is fully entitled to continue to exercise the functions of a Judge of the Tribunal and sit in other cases").

[127]   See *Delalić et al.* Disqualification and Recusal Decision, paras 9-10. See also *Prosecutor v. Chea Nuon et al.*, Case No. 002/19-09-2007/ECCC/TC, Decision on Ieng Sary's Application to Disqualify Judge Nil Nonn and Related Requests, 28 January 2011, para. 7 ("It follows that a finding of bias in a case does not by itself require the judge's disqualification from other, unrelated cases.").

[128]   See *Furundžija* Appeal Judgement, paras 197 ("It is for the Appellant to adduce sufficient evidence to satisfy the Appeals Chamber that Judge Mumba was not impartial in his case"), 200 ("even if it were established that Judge Mumba expressly shared the goals and objectives [...] in promoting and protecting the human rights of women, that inclination, being of a general nature, is distinguishable from an inclination to implement those goals and objectives as a Judge in a particular case").

[129]   See Decision on Mićo Stanišić's Motion requesting a Declaration of Mistrial and Stojan Župljanin's Motion to Vacate Trial Judgement, 2 April 2014 ("Mistrial Decision"), para. 25.

[130]   Decision on Mićo Stanišić's Motion Seeking Reconsideration of Decision on Stanišić's Motion for Declaration of Mistrial and Župljanin's Motion to Vacate Trial Judgement, 24 July 2014, para. 15, referring to Mistrial Decision, para. 25.

[131]   See Mistrial Decision, para. 25 (with references cited therein).

[132]   See *supra*, para. 30.

[133]   See *Furundžija* Appeal Judgement, para. 197; *supra*, para. 44.

[134]   See *e.g.* *Šešelj* Decision on Disqualification, paras 2 (the Šešelj Defence argued that Judge Harhoff had a strong inclination to convict accused persons of Serbian ethnicity, and contended that contempt proceedings should be initiated), 8-14 (no consideration in the *Šešelj* case of the Rebuttal Material); *Šešelj* Reconsideration Decision, paras 12-20 (no consideration in the *Šešelj* case of the Media Articles, but the Special Chamber found that the Memorandum was immaterial and not probative).

[135]   See *supra*, para. 30; *Šešelj* Order Replacing Judge Harhoff.

[136]   *Šešelj* Order Replacing Judge Harhoff, p. 1.

C. **Whether the Letter rebuts the presumption of impartiality of Judge Harhoff in this case**

1. Submissions of the parties

35.   Stanišić and Župljanin submit that the presumption of impartiality is rebutted in this case and that a reasonable apprehension of bias is firmly established.[137] They argue that the contents of the Letter demonstrate an appearance of bias in favour of convicting accused persons.[138] Stanišić submits that a number of statements in the Letter, in and of themselves, justify a finding of apparent bias and that the contents "'*when read as a whole*' rebut the presumption of impartiality afforded to Judge Harhoff".[139] In Stanišić's view, even though the *Gotovina and Markač* Appeal Judgement, **[page 18]** the *Perišić* Appeal Judgement, and the *Stanišić and Simatović* Trial Judgement, to which Judge Harhoff refers in the Letter, did not alter the parameters of JCE, "it is through his critique of these judgements that Judge Harhoff reveals his own views on JCE liability and how he has applied it as a Judge of the International Tribunal".[140] Stanišić and Župljanin assert that the statements made by Judge Harhoff in the Letter are more than mere disagreement with the law.[141] According to Župljanin, the reasonable apprehension of bias test should be applied with "reference to a reasonable observer properly informed from any of the ethnic groups affected by Judgements of the Tribunal".[142]

36.   Stanišić submits that, when taken into account with his legal and academic background, Judge Harhoff's statements are "particularly shocking".[143] He also argues that Judge Harhoff's statement that "he had always 'presumed that it was right to convict leaders for the crime committed with their knowledge'" under joint criminal enterprise liability is particularly relevant to the assessment of whether an unacceptable appearance of bias exists in this case.[144] Stanišić and Župljanin submit that: (i) they are specifically included in the category of persons likely to be convicted as a result of Judge Harhoff's predisposition;[145] and (ii) Judge Harhoff's views demonstrate that he considers that accused persons may be convicted under joint criminal enterprise liability without proving the requisite legal elements.[146]

37.   Further, Stanišić and Župljanin submit that the "deep professional and moral dilemma" expressed by Judge Harhoff shortly after the delivery of the Trial Judgement demonstrates his difficulty in applying the jurisprudence at the time in which he was deliberating their guilt or otherwise.[147] In Župljanin's submission, bias may be established on the basis of remarks or comments made after a judge's participation in the case for which bias is alleged,[148] including on **[page 19]** the basis of predisposition against the faithful application of the law.[149] Stanišić and Župljanin also assert that Judge Harhoff's allegation that the then President of the

---

[137]   Stanišić Additional Appeal Brief, para. 98. See Appeal Hearing, 16 Dec 2015, AT. 69-70, 72-73. See also Stanišić Additional Appeal Brief, paras 61-97; Župljanin Additional Appeal Brief, paras 13-26. See Stanišić Additional Reply Brief, paras 3-4, 9, 18-19; Župljanin Additional Reply Brief, para. 4.
[138]   See Stanišić Additional Appeal Brief, paras 61-76; Župljanin Additional Appeal Brief, paras 10-11, 13-17, 22-27. See also Appeal Hearing, 16 Dec 2015, AT. 77-85, 144-153.
[139]   Stanišić Additional Appeal Brief, para. 62, referring to the *Šešelj* Disqualification Decision, para. 13 (emphasis in original).
[140]   Stanišić Additional Appeal Brief, para. 68.
[141]   Stanišić Additional Appeal Brief, paras 65-71; Župljanin Additional Appeal Brief, paras 11, 13; Stanišić Additional Reply Brief, para. 34. See Appeal Hearing, 16 Dec 2015, AT. 212-213. Župljanin also asserts that Judge Harhoff should have expressed any reservations on the jurisprudence openly and judicially in a dissenting opinion. Župljanin Additional Reply Brief, paras 17-21. See Stanišić Additional Reply Brief, para. 36.
[142]   Župljanin Additional Appeal Brief, paras 16-17, referring to *Piersack v. Belgium*, Application No. 8692/79, ECtHR, Judgement, 1 October 1982 ("*Piersack v. Belgium*"), para. 30, *Hoekstra v. HM Advocate (No. 2)* (Scottish High Court of Justiciary), 2000 J.C. 391 ("*Hoekstra v. HM Advocate*"), paras 18, 22. See Appeal Hearing, 16 Dec 2015, AT. 160.
[143]   Stanišić Additional Appeal Brief, para. 72.
[144]   Stanišić Additional Appeal Brief, para. 79 (emphasis omitted).
[145]   Appeal Hearing, 16 Dec 2015, AT. 79, 84. See also Appeal Hearing, 16 Dec 2015, AT. 152.
[146]   Stanišić Additional Appeal Brief, paras 65-71, 73, 78-79 (referring to Letter, pp 3-4); Župljanin Additional Appeal Brief, paras 4, 10-13. See Appeal Hearing, 16 Dec 2015, AT. 149-154; Stanišić Additional Reply Brief, paras 12, 34-35.
[147]   Stanišić Additional Appeal Brief, paras 66, 74; Župljanin Additional Appeal Brief, paras 4, 13. See Appeal Hearing, 16 Dec 2015, AT. 84-85, 144, 147, 152, 158. Župljanin further submits that the "retrospective and deep-seated nature of the views expressed" demonstrates an apprehension of bias in relation to Judge Harhoff's evaluation of the evidence and law in this case (Župljanin Additional Appeal Brief, para. 13). See Stanišić Additional Reply Brief, para. 18.
[148]   Župljanin Additional Appeal Brief, para. 14, referring to *Hatchcock v. Navistar Intern. Transp. Corp.*, 53 F. 3d 36, 39 (4th Cir. 1995) ("*Hatchcock v. Navistar*").
[149]   Župljanin Additional Appeal Brief, para. 15, referring to *Hoekstra v. HM Advocate*, paras 18, 20, 22.

Tribunal and other Judges were influenced to change the law by outside forces underscores the appearance of bias.[150]

38.   Stanišić and Župljanin further submit that the Rebuttal Material is irrelevant and does not diminish the appearance of bias but, instead, compounds it.[151] In particular, Stanišić and Župljanin contend that the Memorandum is a self-serving and improper *ex post facto* attempt to justify abandoning the requirements of joint criminal enterprise liability.[152] Stanišić and Župljanin further argue that the Rebuttal Material: (i) fails to explain Judge Harhoff's views that there was a "set practice" of convicting accused persons until autumn 2012;[153] and (ii) focuses almost exclusively on aiding and abetting liability.[154] According to Stanišić, the allegations in the Media Articles regarding the potential political influence distract from the real issue at hand, namely Judge Harhoff's views that there was a set practice of convicting accused persons.[155]

39.   The Prosecution responds that Stanišić and Župljanin have failed to rebut the strong presumption of impartiality attached to Judge Harhoff or to satisfy the high threshold of demonstrating that a reasonable apprehension of bias is firmly established.[156] It argues that the Letter was private, informal, and addressed to a group of "personal friends", and therefore Judge Harhoff's failure to use technical legal language is unsurprising.[157] The Prosecution contends that the relevant circumstances informing a "hypothetical, fair-minded observer" include the Letter's silence regarding this case, Judge Harhoff's explanations in the Memorandum, and the public controversy surrounding the cases discussed in the Letter.[158] It argues that the Letter reveals Judge **[page 20]** Harhoff's disagreement on a legal issue on which reasonable minds can disagree,[159] and thus "falls squarely within those categories of judicial comments that do not give rise to a reasonable apprehension of bias".[160] The Prosecution also submits that Judge Harhoff's opinion that war criminals should be punished is not a basis for disqualification[161] and does not reveal any prejudice since he did not discuss the merits of this case, or any other case on which he served as a Judge.[162] It asserts that Judge Harhoff's remarks concerning improper influence on judges do not show bias.[163]

40.   The Prosecution also responds that Judge Harhoff's lack of bias in favour of conviction is demonstrated by the Trial Judgement, which contains both convictions and acquittals,[164] and his numerous rulings against

---

[150]   Stanišić Additional Appeal Brief, para. 63; Župljanin Additional Appeal Brief, paras 22-27. See Župljanin Additional Appeal Brief, para. 23. According to Župljanin, "Judge Harhoff had other, legally and ethically acceptable avenues at his disposal through which to address his 'professional and moral dilemma'" but that he instead "opted for speculations and insinuations" (Župljanin Additional Appeal Brief, para. 26).

[151]   See Stanišić Additional Appeal Brief, paras 81-105; Župljanin Additional Appeal Brief, para. 21; Appeal Hearing, 16 Dec 2015, AT. 86-87, 153-154, 157-158. Stanišić and Župljanin argue that the Appeals Chamber should adopt the approach of the Special Chamber and find that the Rebuttal Material is immaterial to the issue of whether a reasonable, informed observer would apprehend bias on the part of Judge Harhoff (Stanišić Additional Appeal Brief, para. 96; Župljanin Additional Appeal Brief, paras 18-19). See also Stanišić Additional Appeal Brief, paras 100-102.

[152]   Stanišić Additional Appeal Brief, paras 83-98; Župljanin Additional Appeal Brief, para. 20. See Appeal Hearing, 16 Dec 2015, AT. 87-89, 158.

[153]   Stanišić Additional Appeal Brief, para. 100. See Stanišić Additional Reply Brief, para. 34.

[154]   Stanišić Additional Appeal Brief, paras 100-102, 104-105; Župljanin Additional Appeal Brief, paras 20-21.

[155]   Stanišić Additional Appeal Brief, paras 104-105.

[156]   Prosecution Consolidated Supplemental Response Brief, paras 3, 19 (citations omitted).

[157]   Prosecution Consolidated Supplemental Response Brief, para. 6, quoting Exhibit PA1, p. 1; Appeal Hearing, 16 Dec 2015, AT. 130, 204.

[158]   Prosecution Consolidated Supplemental Response Brief, para. 2 (citations omitted). See Prosecution Consolidated Supplemental Response Brief, para. 1, quoting *Furundžija* Appeal Judgement, para. 197. See also Prosecution Consolidated Supplemental Response Brief, para. 6, referring to Exhibit PA1.

[159]   Prosecution Consolidated Supplemental Response Brief, paras 2, 14-16; Appeal Hearing, 16 Dec 2015, AT. 130-131, 205.

[160]   Prosecution Consolidated Supplemental Response Brief, paras 2, 18.

[161]   Prosecution Consolidated Supplemental Response Brief, paras 16-17, referring to *Furundžija* Appeal Judgement, para. 202, *RUF* Decision, paras 2, 14-18.

[162]   Prosecution Consolidated Supplemental Response Brief, paras 8, 17. See Appeal Hearing, 16 Dec 2015, AT. 131.

[163]   Prosecution Consolidated Supplemental Response Brief, paras 34-35. The Prosecution argues that the issue of bias is a separate matter from any inappropriateness or impropriety as to his concerns that Judges might be improperly influenced (Prosecution Consolidated Supplemental Response Brief, para. 34, referring to, *inter alia*, *Delalić et al.* Disqualification and Recusal Decision, para. 9).

[164]   Prosecution Consolidated Supplemental Response Brief, para. 10. See Appeal Hearing, 16 Dec 2015, AT. 131. The Prosecution argues that the Trial Chamber found that the scope of joint criminal enterprise was narrower than what was alleged. It further argues that Judge Harhoff would have supported full conviction on all allegations had he been biased (Prosecution

125

the interests of the Prosecution in the present case.[165] The Prosecution argues that neither Stanišić nor Župljanin point to any matter in the trial record or the Trial Judgement showing that Judge Harhoff was predisposed in favour of conviction.[166] It adds that Judge Harhoff's commitment and ability to fairly decide this case is reflected in the solemn declaration he took to perform his duties and his experience as a professor of law and as a judge in Denmark.[167] The Prosecution further responds that the Memorandum provides context to the Letter,[168] and that Judge Harhoff clarifies various issues therein.[169]

41.   Stanišić and Župljanin reply that the Prosecution fails to address the main issues raised by the Letter, misunderstands both the jurisprudence and the nature of the bias revealed by the Letter,[170] and refers to immaterial circumstances,[171] including the informal nature of the Letter.[172] **[page 21]** Stanišić also replies that the assertion that Judge Harhoff's remarks merely propose that "war criminals should be punished" and are only his personal opinion, is disingenuous.[173]

2.   Analysis

42.   The right to be tried before an independent and impartial tribunal is an integral component of the right to fair trial, as guaranteed by Article 21 of the Statute. Article 13 of the Statute provides that the Judges of the Tribunal shall be persons of high moral character, impartiality, and integrity.[174] As noted above,[175] a Judge must withdraw from a case if it is shown that actual bias exists or there is an unacceptable appearance of bias on his part.[176] In the present case, Stanišić and Župljanin have made no allegations of actual bias on the part of Judge Harhoff.[177]

43.   An unacceptable appearance of bias exists where: (i) a Judge is a party to the case, or has a financial or proprietary interest in the outcome of a case, or if the Judge's decision will lead to the promotion of a cause in which he or she is involved, together with one of the parties; or (ii) the circumstances would lead a reasonable observer, properly informed, to reasonably apprehend bias.[178] Stanišić and Župljanin have made no allegations against Judge Harhoff concerning the first part of this principle, and therefore the relevant

---

Consolidated Supplemental Response Brief, para. 10). The Prosecution also points to Judge Harhoff's judicial history at the Tribunal, which includes both convictions and acquittals. Prosecution Consolidated Supplemental Response Brief, para. 12, referring to *Delić* Trial Judgement, paras 337-355, 518-535, *D. Milošević* Trial Judgement, paras 406, 414, 579. See Appeal Hearing, 16 Dec 2015, AT. 131.

[165]   Prosecution Consolidated Supplemental Response Brief, para. 11.
[166]   Prosecution Consolidated Supplemental Response Brief, para. 1.
[167]   Prosecution Consolidated Supplemental Response Brief, para. 13.
[168]   Prosecution Consolidated Supplemental Response Brief, para. 9, referring to Exhibit PA1, p. 2. See Appeal Hearing, 16 Dec 2015, AT. 131.
[169]   Prosecution Consolidated Supplemental Response Brief, para. 9. The Prosecution asserts that Stanišić and Župljanin fail to undermine the Memorandum's reliability (Prosecution Consolidated Supplemental Response Brief, para. 20).
[170]   Stanišić Additional Reply Brief, paras 3-4, 9, 18-19; Župljanin Additional Reply Brief, para. 4.
[171]   Stanišić Additional Reply Brief, paras 10, 15-19. See Stanišić Additional Reply Brief, paras 12-13, 19-22. See Appeal Hearing, 16 Dec 2015, AT. 142. Župljanin asserts that the Trial Chamber correctly set out the applicable law since bias is seldom established through judicial error (Župljanin Additional Reply Brief, paras 9-10, referring to, *inter alia*, *Karemera et al.* Disqualification Decision, para. 67; *Prosecutor v. Vojislav Šešelj*, Case No. IT-03-67-T, Decision on Appeal Against Decision on Continuation of Proceedings, 6 June 2014, Dissenting Opinion of Judge Koffi Kumelio A. Afande, para. 14). Župljanin also asserts that Judge Harhoff's judicial rulings are irrelevant. Župljanin Additional Reply Brief, paras 5-10, referring to *Liteky v. United States*, 510 U.S. 540, 555 (1994), *Prosecutor v. Vidoje Blagojević et al.*, Case No. IT-02-60-PT, Decision on Blagojević's Application Pursuant to Rule 15(B), 19 March 2003, para. 14.
[172]   Stanišić Additional Reply Brief, paras 13, 18. See Appeal Hearing, 16 Dec 2015, AT. 142.
[173]   Stanišić Additional Reply Brief, paras 12, 34. See Appeal Hearing, 16 Dec 2015, AT. 142. Stanišić contends that the assertion that the Letter "'falls squarely within those categories of judicial comments'" is also disingenuous (Stanišić Additional Reply Brief, para. 36 (emphasis omitted)). See also Župljanin Additional Reply Brief, paras 14-16 (arguing that the Prosecution presumes that Judge Harhoff considered all accused to be "war criminals").
[174]   *Šainović et al.* Appeal Judgement, para. 179.
[175]   See *supra*, para. 32.
[176]   See *Šainović et al.* Appeal Judgement, para. 180; *Prosecutor v. Vojislav Šešelj*, Case No. IT-03-67-R77.4-A, Decision on Vojislav Šešelj's Motion to Disqualify Judges Arlette Ramaroson, Mehmet Güney and Andresia Vaz, 10 January 2013, para. 10. As held by the Appeals Chamber, "a Judge should not only be subjectively free from bias, but also that there should be nothing in the surrounding circumstances which objectively gives rise to an appearance of bias" (*Furundžija* Appeal Judgement, para. 189).
[177]   See Stanišić Additional Reply Brief, para. 39.
[178]   *Šainović et al.* Appeal Judgement, para. 180; *Furundžija* Appeal Judgement, para. 189.

issue in this case is whether a reasonable observer, properly informed, would reasonably apprehend bias on the part of Judge Harhoff based on the Letter and its surrounding material circumstances. The Appeals Chamber further recalls that the apprehension of bias test reflects the maxim that "justice should not only be done, **[page 22]** but should manifestly and undoubtedly be seen to be done"[179] and is founded on the need to ensure public confidence in the judiciary.[180]

44. The Appeals Chamber stresses that there is a strong presumption of impartiality attached to a Judge which cannot be easily rebutted.[181] It is for the party alleging bias to adduce reliable and sufficient evidence to rebut that presumption.[182] No Judge may be disqualified on the basis of sweeping or abstract allegations that are neither substantiated nor detailed.[183] The reason for this high threshold is that, just as any real appearance of bias on the part of a Judge undermines confidence in the administration of justice, it is equally important that judicial officers "do not, by acceding too readily to suggestions of apparent bias, encourage parties to believe that, by seeking the disqualification of a judge, they will have their case tried by someone thought to be more likely to decide the case in their favour".[184] Before a Judge can be disqualified, a reasonable apprehension of bias must be "firmly established".[185]

45. As a preliminary matter, insofar as Župljanin argues that the reasonable apprehension of bias test should be applied with "reference to a reasonable observer properly informed from any of the ethnic groups affected by Judgements of the Tribunal",[186] the Appeals Chamber first observes that the references cited by Župljanin do not support his assertion.[187] Second, the Appeals Chamber recalls that the "reasonable person must be an informed person, with knowledge of all the relevant circumstances, including the traditions of integrity and impartiality that form a part of the background and apprised also of the fact that impartiality is one of the duties that Judges swear to **[page 23]** uphold".[188] Župljanin's argument, suggesting a departure from this principle and asserting that the reasonable observer must come from the region, is thus dismissed.

46. As a further preliminary matter, Stanišić and Župljanin argue that the Memorandum is an *ex post facto* attempt to justify Judge Harhoff's statement and is irrelevant.[189] The Appeals Chamber recalls that the Memorandum was admitted in rebuttal because it was relevant and clearly addressed the Letter and its contents, thus providing additional context and meaning in order to assess the Letter's evidentiary value.[190] As far as Stanišić and Župljanin argue that the Memorandum should be accorded little weight, the Appeals Chamber considers that it may be taken into account and assessed together with all the evidence from the perspective of the reasonable observer. The Appeals Chamber will therefore consider the Memorandum and the Media Articles to which it refers.

---

[179] *Furundžija* Appeal Judgement, para. 195. See *The Prosecutor v. Athanase Seromba*, Case No. ICTR-2001-66-T, Decision on Motion for Disqualification of Judges, 25 April 2006, para. 9 (with references cited therein).

[180] *Čelebići* Appeal Judgement, para. 707; *Karemera et al.* Disqualification Decision, para. 6.

[181] *Furundžija* Appeal Judgement, paras 196-197. See *Šainović et al.* Appeal Judgement, para. 181; *Prosecutor v. Vujadin Popović et al.*, Case No. IT-05-88-A, Decision on Drago Nikolić Motion to Disqualify Judge Liu Daqun, 20 January 2011 ("*Popović et al.* Decision"), para. 5.

[182] *Šainović et al.* Appeal Judgement, para. 181; *Popović et al.* Decision, para. 5.

[183] See *Šešelj* Decision on Disqualification, para. 7. See also *Renzaho* Appeal Judgement, para. 21; *Rutaganda* Appeal Judgement, para. 43; *Ntagerura et al.* Appeal Judgement, para. 135.

[184] *Čelebići* Appeal Judgement, para. 707. See *Furundžija* Appeal Judgement, para. 197; *Prosecutor v. Vojislav Šešelj*, Case No. IT-03-67-R77.3, Decision on Motion by Professor Vojislav Šešelj for the Disqualification of Judges O-Gon Kwon and Kevin Parker, 19 November 2010, para. 17 (holding that "[disqualifying judges based upon unfounded allegations of bias is as much a threat to justice as a judge who is not impartial").

[185] *Šainović et al.* Appeal Judgement, para. 181; *Furundžija* Appeal Judgement, para. 196. See *Galić* Appeal Judgement, para. 44. See also *Popović et al.* Decision, para. 5.

[186] Župljanin Additional Appeal Brief, paras 16-17, referring to *Piersack v. Belgium*, para. 30, *Hoekstra v. HM Advocate*, paras 18, 22.

[187] See Župljanin Additional Appeal Brief, para. 16, referring to *Piersack v. Belgium*, para. 30 (discussing generally the objective test but not the attributes of the reasonable observer); *Hoekstra v. HM Advocate*, paras 18, 22 (considering that the Judge in question could not be seen to have been impartial, especially on the part of the Dutch appellants).

[188] *Šainović et al.* Appeal Judgement, para. 181; *Furundžija* Appeal Judgement, para. 190. See *Karadžić'* Disqualification Decision, para. 18 (referring to the perception of the hypothetical fair-minded observer with sufficient knowledge of the circumstances to make a reasonable judgement), fn. 55.

[189] See Stanišić Additional Appeal Brief, paras 83-98; Župljanin Additional Appeal Brief, para. 32.

[190] Decision on Prosecution Motion to Admit Rebuttal Material, 11 June 2014, para. 13. See Prosecution Motion to Admit Rebuttal Material, 1 May 2014.

47.   Another preliminary issue concerns the Prosecution's submission that Judge Harhoff's numerous rulings against it in this case demonstrate a lack of bias. The Appeals Chamber observes that, although Judge Harhoff took decisions that resulted favourably for Stanišić and Župljanin, his judicial record in this case is not instructive as to whether a reasonable observer properly informed could apprehend bias.[191] The Appeals Chamber notes, in particular, that Judge Harhoff's judicial record does not take into account that procedural decisions have limited impact on the substantive issues to be decided in a final trial judgement.

48.   The Appeals Chamber will now turn to Stanišić's and Župljanin's submissions that the presumption of impartiality is rebutted and that a reasonable apprehension of bias on the part of Judge Harhoff is firmly established. In considering whether a reasonable apprehension of bias has been firmly established, the Appeals Chamber bears in mind that a reasonable observer is a hypothetical fair-minded person, acting in good faith, with sufficient knowledge of the relevant circumstances to make a reasonable judgement of whether a Judge might not bring an impartial and 192 unprejudiced mind to the issues arising in the case.[192] **[page 24]**

49.   Judge Harhoff, as a result of what he perceived to be a change in the jurisprudence concerning joint criminal enterprise liability after the acquittals in the *Gotovina and Markač* Appeal Judgement, the *Perišić* Appeal Judgement, and the *Stanišić and Simatović* Trial Judgement,[193] made the following statements in the Letter:

> [i]n brief: Right up until autumn 2012, it has been a more or less set practice at the court that military commanders were held responsible for war crimes that their subordinates committed during the war in the former Yugoslavia [...].[194]

> [...]

> However, this is no longer the case. Now apparently the commanders must have had a direct intention to commit crimes – and not just knowledge or suspicion that the crimes were or would be committed.[195]

> [...]

> The result is now that not only has the court taken a significant step back from the lesson that commanding military leaders have to take responsibility for their subordinates' crimes (unless it can be proven that they knew nothing about it) – but also that the theory of responsibility under the specific 'joint criminal enterprise' has now been reduced from contribution to crimes (in some way or another) to demanding a direct intention to commit crime (and so not just acceptance of the crimes being committed). Most of the cases will lead to commanding officers walking free from here on [...].[196]

50.   Judge Harhoff further remarked in the Letter:

> [i]n all the courts I have worked in here, I have always presumed that it was right to convict leaders for the crimes committed with their knowledge within a framework of a common goal. It all boils down to the difference between knowing on the one hand that the crimes actually were committed or that they were going to be committed, and on the other hand planning to commit them. [...]

> How do we now explain to the 1000s of victims that the court is no longer able to convict the participants of the joint criminal enterprise, unless the judges can justify that the participants in their common goal actively and with direct intent contributed to the crimes? Until now, we have convicted these participants who in one way or another had showed that they agreed with the common goal (= to eradicate the non Serbian population from areas the Serbians had deemed 'clean') as well as, in one way or another, had contributed to achieving the common goal – without having to specifically prove that they had a direct intention to commit every single crime to achieve it. It is almost impossible to prove..[197]

---

[191]   See *Karemera et al.* Disqualification Decision, para. 15 (considering that a comparison of decisions to detect a pattern "is troublesome" as all decisions are made on an individual basis as a result of particular request, and also that the decisions in question were decided by a three Judge panel and not by a particular Judge).
[192]   *Šainović et al.* Appeal Judgement, para. 181; *Celebiai* Appeal Judgement, para. 683; *Nahimana et al.* Appeal Judgement, para. 50.
[193]   See Exhibit 1DA1, p. 3. See also Exhibit 1DA1, pp 1-2.
[194]   Exhibit 1DA1, p. 1.
[195]   Exhibit 1DA1, p. 2.
[196]   Exhibit 1DA1, p. 3.
[197]   Exhibit 1DA1, p. 3.

51. The Appeals Chamber particularly notes that a reasonable observer properly informed would be aware that: (i) Judge Harhoff's comments only generally concern the mode of liability of joint criminal enterprise;[198] (ii) none of the cases referred to by Judge Harhoff altered the scope of **[page 25]** joint criminal enterprise liability, contrary to his assertions;[199] and (iii) it has never been the law or practice, contrary to Judge Harhoff's statement, to "convict leaders for the crimes committed with their knowledge within a framework of a common goal".[200] Further, it is the Appeals Chamber's view that a reasonable observer properly informed of all relevant circumstances would be aware of the relevant jurisprudence of the Tribunal.[201] A reasonable observer would therefore be aware that knowledge on the part of an accused that crimes were committed is insufficient to find an accused responsible under either the first or the third category of joint criminal enterprise.

52. The Appeals Chamber notes that a reasonable observer would also consider the fact that Judge Harhoff neither distinguished the facts nor the respective modes of liability relevant to the *Gotovina and Markač* Appeal Judgement, the *Perišić* Appeal Judgement, and the *Stanišić and Simatovic* Trial Judgement.[202] Based on his views on the law and practice, which do not align with the Tribunal's jurisprudence, coupled with his sweeping generalisations of the judgements in question, Judge Harhoff expressed deep dissatisfaction with what he considered a change in "set practice"[203] at the Tribunal. However, the Appeals Chamber recalls that personal convictions and opinions of Judges are not in themselves a basis for inferring a lack of impartiality.[204] Additionally, a reasonable observer, properly informed, would take into account that at no time did Judge Harhoff direct his comments to Stanišić and Župljanin. Thus, the Appeals Chamber is not convinced by Stanišić's submission that Judge Harhoff was predisposed to convicting Stanišić and Župljanin.[205]

53. Regarding Župljanin's argument that sections of the Trial Judgement indicate that the wrong *mens rea* standard was applied,[206] the Appeals Chamber is not convinced that a reasonable observer would consider that these cited sections reflect, or were influenced by, the same opinions that Judge Harhoff expressed in the Letter.[207] In this regard, the Appeals Chamber notes that the Trial Chamber applied the correct legal standard for JCE liability[208] to the circumstances of the case and not the views expressed in the Letter. Further, a reasonable observer would also take into account **[page 26]** Judge Harhoff's statement that he did not set out in the Letter all of the applicable principles necessary to assess criminal liability, including proof beyond a reasonable doubt.[209] The Appeals Chamber also finds that a reasonable observer would consider the Media Articles as providing some background information concerning the public controversy surrounding cases mentioned in the Letter. The Appeals Chamber observes that the statements contained in the Letter must therefore be viewed in the context provided by the Rebuttal Material.

54. The Appeals Chamber is of the view that when considering the statements contained in the Letter, a reasonable observer would bear in mind that it was addressed to 56 individuals, written in an informal style

---

[198]   The Appeals Chamber is cognisant that this is the mode of liability through which Stanišić and Župljanin were convicted. See Trial Judgement, vol. 2, paras 955-956.
[199]   The Appeals Chamber considers that Judge Harhoff confuses the *Perišić* Appeal Judgement which addressed the elements for aiding and abetting.
[200]   See Exhibit 1DA1, p. 3. See also *infra*, paras 109-110 , 375, 386, 595, fn. 2463.
[201]   See *Tolimir* Appeal Judgement, paras 431, 514; *Popović et al.* Appeal Judgement, paras 1369, 1431; *Đorđević* Appeal Judgement, paras 468, 906; *Brđanin* Appeal Judgement, para. 365.
[202]   See Exhibit 1DA1. See also Exhibit PA1, p. 2. For instance, while Judge Harhoff's remarks concern the so-called change in joint criminal enterprise liability, the Appeals Chamber notes his reference to the *Perišić* Appeal Judgement. The Appeals Chamber observes in this regard that Momčilo Perišić was acquitted of his conviction for aiding and abetting pursuant to Article 7(1) of the Statute.
[203]   Exhibit 1DA1, p. 1.
[204]   *Čelebići* Appeal Judgement, para. 699, referring to *Furundžija* Appeal Judgement, para. 203. See also *Hoekstra v. HMAdvocate*, p. 401(E-G); *Newcastle City Council v. Lindsay* [2004] NSWCA 198, paras 35-36.
[205]   See Stanišić Additional Appeal Brief, paras 68-71. See also *supra*, para. 36.
[206]   Appeal Hearing, 16 Dec 2015, AT. 154-157.
[207]   See *infra*, paras 906-944. See also *infra*, 366-585.
[208]   Trial Judgement, vol. 1, paras 99-106.
[209]   See Exhibit PA1, pp 1-3.

and not "as a legal intervention",[210] and was intended to be private.[211] These contextual circumstances could be considered by a reasonable observer as operating against a finding of apparent bias. The Appeals Chamber is of the view that the reasonable observer would also take into account the fact that – in contrast with the *Šešelj case* – the Letter was published several months after the Trial Judgement was issued.

55.   The Appeals Chamber further considers that the Letter contains no language which would suggest to a reasonable observer that Judge Harhoff believed that a finding of guilt could be made without reviewing the particular evidence of a case or that he had difficulty applying the Tribunal's jurisprudence. A reasonable observer properly informed of all the circumstances would have regard for the fact that Judges are presumed to be impartial, and that before taking up his duties, Judge Harhoff made a solemn declaration to perform his duties "honourably, faithfully, *impartially* and conscientiously".[212] The Appeals Chamber considers that a fair-minded and informed observer would regard this judicial oath as an important protection against the appearance of bias. Additionally, the reasonable observer would consider Judge Harhoff's role as a Judge of the Tribunal and his professional experience. While Judge Harhoff's views on the law as expressed in the Letter do not align with the current case law of the Tribunal, Judge Harhoff was (at the time of writing the Letter) a Judge of the Tribunal and a legal professional who was to be relied upon to **[page 27]** bring an impartial mind to the evidence and issues before him.[213] The Appeals Chamber considers that, in the absence of evidence to the contrary, a reasonable observer properly informed of these circumstances would presume that Judge Harhoff as a Judge of the Tribunal could disabuse his mind of any irrelevant personal beliefs or predispositions.[214]

56.   Further, Judge Harhoff postulates in the Letter that the "change" in the jurisprudence may have been as a result of external pressure being exerted on the President of the Tribunal at the time, and that Judges in turn may have been influenced to change the law by outside forces.[215] While inappropriate and unsubstantiated, a reasonable observer, properly informed would not apprehend bias on the part of Judge Harhoff against Stanišić and Župljanin on the basis of these comments. On this issue, the Appeals Chamber observes that although Judge Harhoff stated in the Letter that he was faced with "deep professional and moral dilemma",[216] he explained that this reference related to his concern, if he were to discover improper influence by external forces on fellow Judges.[217] The Appeals Chamber finds that the reasonable observer would consider that this explanation weighed against finding that a reasonable apprehension of bias exists. Turning to Judge Harhoff's remarks that it "has been more or less set practice at the court that military commanders were held responsible for war crimes that their subordinates committed during the war",[218] the Appeals Chamber is of the view that this personal opinion must be considered in the context of the remaining parts of the Letter as well as in light of Judge Harhoff's explanations indicating that the crimes and responsibility for the crimes must be proven.[219] Thus, the Appeals Chamber is not convinced that Judge Harhoff's remark would lead a reasonable observer properly informed to conclude that he was predisposed to convicting accused persons before the Tribunal.

---

[210]   Exhibit PA1, p. 2 (emphasis omitted).

[211]   The Appeals Chamber observes that the cases cited by Župljanin in support of his contention that bias may be established on the basis of remarks made after a judge's participation in a case are distinguishable from the present case. First, the *Hatchcock* case concerned a public speech made by a judge while a jury trial on the issue of damages in that case was pending (*Hatchcock v. Navistar*, p. 39). Second, the *Hoekstra* case concerned a comment published by a judge just over a week after the appeal presided over by this judge was dismissed (*Hoekstra v. HM Advocate*, para. 11). In that case, the High Court of Justiciary of Scotland took into account the close time between the decision and the judge's comments in deciding the claim of bias (*Hoekstra v. HM Advocate*, para. 22). *Cf. Gaudie v. Local Court of New South Wales and Anor* [2013] NSWSC 1425, para. 183 ("[t]he fact that the Magistrate made his comments in a letter and an interview, and not in a court judgment, would not be an especially significant factor in the mind of the bystander"); *Hoekstra v. HM Advocate*, p. 401(D) (the court considered that their conclusion that apparent bias existed would have been different if the Judge had published his views, in moderate language, in a legal journal instead of hostile language in a newspaper article).

[212]   Rule 14(A) of the Rules (emphasis added).

[213]   See Article 13 of the Statute (Judges are required to be "persons of high moral character, impartiality and integrity"); Rule 14 of the Rules (Judges are required to take an oath to exercise their powers "honourably, faithfully, impartially and conscientiously").

[214]   See *Šainović et al.* Appeal Judgement, para. 181; *Furundžija* Appeal Judgement, paras 196-197.

[215]   Exhibit 1DA1, pp 2-3.

[216]   Exhibit 1DA1, p. 3.

[217]   Exhibit PA1, p. 3.

[218]   Exhibit 1DA1, p. 1.

[219]   See *supra*, para. 54.

57.   Based on the foregoing, the Appeals Chamber finds that Stanišić and Župljanin have failed to demonstrate that a reasonable observer, properly informed of all the relevant circumstances, would reasonably apprehend bias on the part of Judge Harhoff in this case. Stanišić and Župljanin have therefore failed to rebut the presumption of impartiality and failed to firmly establish a reasonable appearance of bias. The Appeals Chamber accordingly dismisses Stanišić's and Župljanin's arguments. Thus, Stanišić's and Župljanin's arguments on the impact of any alleged bias are moot and need not be addressed.**[page 28]**

D. Conclusion

58.   In light of the foregoing, the Appeals Chamber dismisses Stanišić's ground of appeal 1*bis* and Župljanin's sixth ground of appeal in their entirety. **[page 29]**

IV. JOINT CRIMINAL ENTERPRISE

A. Introduction

59.   The Trial Chamber found that from no later than 24 October 1991 and throughout the Indictment period, a joint criminal enterprise existed, with the objective of permanently removing Bosnian Muslims and Bosnian Croats from the territory of the planned Serbian state through the commission of the JCE I Crimes, namely the crimes of persecutions (through underlying acts of forcible transfer and deportation) (Count 1), deportation (Count 9), and inhumane acts (forcible transfer) (Count 10) as crimes against humanity.[220]

60.   The Trial Chamber found both Stanišić and Župljanin responsible pursuant to the first category of joint criminal enterprise liability for the JCE I Crimes.[221]

61.   The Trial Chamber also found Stanišić responsible pursuant to the third category of joint criminal enterprise for crimes that fell outside the common purpose, namely, persecutions (through the underlying acts of killings, torture, cruel treatment, inhumane acts, unlawful detention, establishment and perpetuation of inhumane living conditions, plunder of property, wanton destruction of towns and villages, including destruction or wilful damage done to institutions dedicated to religion and other cultural buildings, and imposition and maintenance of restrictive and discriminatory measures) as a crime against humanity (Count 1), murder, torture, and cruel treatment as violations of the laws or customs of war (Counts 4, 6, and 7, respectively)[222] as well as murder, torture, and inhumane acts as crimes against humanity (Counts 3, 5, and 8, respectively) (collectively, "Stanišić's JCE III Crimes").[223] Further, the Trial Chamber found Župljanin responsible pursuant to the third category of joint criminal enterprise for the aforementioned crimes that fell outside the common purpose (Counts 1 and 3 to 8) as well as extermination as a crime against humanity (Count 2) (collectively, "Župljanin's JCE III Crimes").[224] **[page 30]**

62.   In this section, the Appeals Chamber considers the appeals of Stanišić and Župljanin with respect to the Trial Chamber's findings on their responsibility, under Article 7(1) of the Statute, for participation in a joint criminal enterprise.[225]

---

[220]   Trial Judgement, vol. 2, para. 313.
[221]   Trial Judgement, vol. 2, paras 804-805, 809, 813, 818, 822, 827, 831-832, 836, 840, 844-845, 849-850, 854, 858-859, 863-864, 868-869, 873, 877, 881, 885, 955-956.
[222]   Trial Judgement, vol. 2, paras 804, 809, 813, 818, 822, 827, 831, 836, 840, 844, 849, 854, 858, 863, 868, 873, 877, 881, 885, 955.
[223]   Trial Judgement, vol. 2, paras 804, 813, 818, 822, 827, 831, 836, 840, 844, 849, 854, 858, 863, 868, 873, 877, 881, 885, 955.
[224]   Trial Judgement, vol. 2, paras 805, 832, 845, 850, 859, 864, 869, 956.
[225]   Namely, Stanišić's first through eleventh grounds of appeal, sub-grounds (A)-(F) of Župljanin's first ground of appeal, and Župljanin's second and third grounds of appeal.

B. **Alleged errors in relation to defining the common criminal purpose (Stanišić's third ground of appeal in part and sub-ground 1(F) in part of Župljanin's first ground of appeal)**

63.   The Trial Chamber found that as of 1991, the aim of the Bosnian Serb leadership was for "Serbs to live in one state with other Serbs in the former Yugoslavia".[226] It found further that, following the adoption of the declaration of independence in the Assembly of the Socialist Republic of BiH ("BiH Assembly") on 15 October 1991, the Bosnian Serb leadership intensified the process of territorial demarcation, an important part of which was "the forceful assumption of control over territories".[227] The Trial Chamber found that this was done through the setting up of separate and parallel Bosnian Serb institutions and establishing Serb municipalities.[228] It found further that "violent takeovers" of the municipalities and a "widespread *and* systematic campaign of terror and violence resulting in crimes" against Muslims and Croats followed.[229] The Trial Chamber was satisfied that the Bosnian Serb leadership was in charge of these events taking place in the Municipalities through its control over the Serb forces, Serbian Democratic Party ("SDS") structure, crisis staffs, and the RS Government.[230] This, in combination with the "numerous statements of the Bosnian Serb leadership at the time", led the Trial Chamber to find that "the goal of these actions was the establishment of a Serb state, as ethnically 'pure' as possible, through the permanent removal of the Bosnian Muslims and Bosnian Croats".[231] The Trial Chamber concluded that, from no later than 24 October 1991 and throughout the Indictment period, "a common plan did exist, the objective of which was to permanently remove Bosnian Muslims and Bosnian Croats from the territory of the planned Serbian state through the commission of the [JCE I Crimes]".[232]

1.   Submissions of the parties

64.   Stanišić submits that the Trial Chamber erred in law by conflating the legitimate political goal for Serbs to live in one state with other Serbs in the former Yugoslavia with the criminal **[page 31]** objective of the JCE.[233] He argues that the Trial Chamber's findings on the aim of the Bosnian Serb leadership for Serbs to live in one state,[234] on its intensification of the processes of territorial demarcation, and on its initiation of the process of establishing Serb municipalities in late 1991,[235] "either individually or collectively, do not amount to anything other than a legitimate political goal, in line with the Cutileiro plan designed by the international community".[236]

65.   Župljanin submits that the Trial Chamber erred in law by failing to precisely define "a common purpose that, in and of itself, 'amounts to or involves the commission of a crime provided for in the Statute'".[237] He contends that the Trial Chamber inconsistently defined the intended common purpose as either the "'permanent removal' of non-Serbs" or "the creation of a 'Serb state, as ethnically pure as

---

[226]   Trial Judgement, vol. 2, para. 309.
[227]   Trial Judgement, vol. 2, para. 310.
[228]   Trial Judgement, vol. 2, para. 310.
[229]   Trial Judgement, vol. 2, para. 311. See Trial Judgement, vol. 2, paras 290-298.
[230]   Trial Judgement, vol. 2, para. 311.
[231]   Trial Judgement, vol. 2, para. 311.
[232]   Trial Judgement, vol. 2, para. 313.
[233]   Stanišić Appeal Brief, paras 76-86. See Appeal Hearing, 16 Dec 2015, AT. 101. Stanišić argues, *inter alia*, that any individual "reading a newspaper or watching television and finding themselves agreeing with the espousal of the objective to create a separate Serbian entity would, by the [Trial Chamber's] flawed reasoning, be considered to have shared the intent to deport and forcibly transfer Bosnian Muslims and Bosnian Croats" (Stanišić Appeal Brief, para. 85).
[234]   Stanišić Appeal Brief, para. 78, quoting Trial Judgement, vol. 2, para. 309.
[235]   Stanišić Appeal Brief, para. 78, referring to Trial Judgement, vol. 2, para. 310.
[236]   Stanišić Appeal Brief, para. 78, referring to Exhibit P2200. See Stanišić Appeal Brief, para. 82. See also Stanišić Reply Brief, para. 29. In support to his argument, Stanišić further argues that the Trial Chamber failed to explain how the pursuit of a legitimate political goal which "occasioned crimes", meant that the commission of those crimes was "an intended aim of this political goal" (Stanišić Appeal Brief, para. 79) and thus failed to consider whether one could have supported the goal for Serbs to live in one state with other Serbs without intending this to occur by the commission of crimes (Stanišić Appeal Brief, para. 77. See Stanišić Appeal Brief, paras 81, 83-84).
[237]   Župljanin Appeal Brief, para. 27 (emphasis omitted), referring to *Brđanin* Appeal Judgement, para. 364. See Župljanin Appeal Brief, paras 13, 26, 28-34, 39, 53.

possible'",[238] and that neither of these objectives in and of themselves involve criminal acts and therefore cannot amount to a common purpose within the meaning of the law on joint criminal enterprise.[239] He argues that the standard can be easily subverted through "loose definitions of the common purpose that merely involve an objective where it is probable that a crime will be committed in pursuit of the objective".[240] Župljanin further submits that, although the Trial Chamber included a criminal component to the common purpose by stating that it was to be achieved *through* the commission of crimes, the common purpose, as found by the Trial Chamber, was bifurcated, as follows: "(i) an overall 'objective' that is not inherently criminal (the creation of an ethnically homogenous state); and (ii) using means that are inherently criminal (the crime of forcible transfer)".[241] **[page 32]**

66.   The Prosecution responds that the Trial Chamber correctly found that the JCE members pursued the ethnic cleansing campaign to realise their objective of creating an ethnically pure Serb state through the commission of forcible displacement crimes.[242] It submits that Stanišić seeks to disassociate "the goal of achieving a separate Serb state from the means through which it was to be achieved", *i.e.* through the commission of JCE I Crimes.[243] With respect to Župljanin, the Prosecution responds that: (i) the Trial Chamber correctly concluded, on the basis of extensive evidence, that the "Bosnian Serb leadership, and others, shared a precisely-defined common *criminal* purpose which amounted to and involved the commission of crimes in the Statute";[244] and (ii) Župljanin takes the words of the Trial Chamber out of their natural context and wrongly attempts to sever the "goal" and "means" of the common purpose, when in fact, they are indivisible and together formed the common criminal purpose.[245]

2. Analysis

67.   The Appeals Chamber recalls that under joint criminal enterprise liability, a trial chamber is required to determine whether a common plan, design, or purpose existed "which amounts to or involves the commission of a crime provided for in the Statute".[246]

68.   Contrary to Stanišić's argument, the Trial Chamber did not conflate the political goal to create a separate Serb entity with the common criminal purpose of the JCE. The Trial Chamber's findings on the political aim of the Bosnian Serb leadership for Serbs to live in one state and the subsequent intensification of the process of territorial demarcation are merely factors that the Trial Chamber took into account, together with other factors,[247] in reaching its conclusion on the common criminal purpose of the JCE.[248] **[page 33]**

---

[238]   Župljanin Appeal Brief, para. 28. See Župljanin Appeal Brief, para. 15.

[239]   Župljanin Appeal Brief, paras 28-29, referring to *Martić* Trial Judgement, para. 442. See Župljanin Appeal Brief, para. 30.

[240]   Župljanin Appeal Brief, para. 32. Župljanin also argues that this has an effect of reducing the requisite subjective standard to a foreseeability or "*dolus eventualis*" standard (Župljanin Appeal Brief, paras 32-33). The Appeals Chamber has addressed this argument elsewhere in this Judgement (see *infra*, para. 920. See Župljanin Appeal Brief, paras 31, 39. See also Appeal Hearing, 16 Dec 2015, AT. 146-147).

[241]   Župljanin Appeal Brief, para. 37. Župljanin further argues that the Trial Chamber failed to "define the 'goal' and the 'means' of the common criminal objective in precisely identical terms" (Župljanin Appeal Brief, para. 16. See Župljanin Appeal Brief, para. 28).

[242]   Prosecution Response Brief (Stanišić), para. 30. See Prosecution Response Brief (Stanišić), para. 31.

[243]   Prosecution Response Brief (Stanišić), para. 31. Further, the Prosecution submits that Stanišić's argument that the Trial Chamber accepted that any form of support for the alleged legitimate "political goal" of achieving a separate Serb entity would have been sufficient to establish an individual's membership in the JCE, misconstrues the Trial Chamber's findings (Prosecution Response Brief (Stanišić), para. 32).

[244]   Prosecution Response Brief (Župljanin), para. 9. See Prosecution Response Brief (Župljanin), paras 10, 12-13, 15.

[245]   Prosecution Response Brief (Župljanin), para. 11, referring to Župljanin Appeal Brief, paras 16, 19, 37. See Prosecution Response Brief (Župljanin), paras 8, 12.

[246]   *Tadić* Appeal Judgement, para. 227 (emphasis omitted). See *Brđanin* Appeal Judgement, para. 364; *Stakić* Appeal Judgement, para. 64; *Kvočka et al.* Appeal Judgement, para. 117.

[247]   See *e.g.* the Trial Chamber's findings set out in paragraphs 309 to 311 of volume two of the Trial Judgement, listing *inter alia*: (i) the violent takeovers of the Municipalities and the widespread and systematic campaign of terror and violence resulting in the commission of crimes against Muslims and Croats; (ii) the fact that the Bosnian Serb leadership was in charge of these events taking place in the Municipalities through its control over the Serb forces, SDS party structure, crisis staffs, and the RS Government; and (iii) numerous statements of the Bosnian Serb leadership at the time (Trial Judgement, vol. 2, para. 311). See also *supra*, para. 63.

[248]   Moreover, the Appeals Chamber notes that the Trial Chamber's consideration of the above mentioned factors and its ultimate conclusion that the purpose of the JCE was to be reached through the commission of crimes clearly indicate that it did not find that the aim of the Bosnian Serb leadership for Serbs to live in one state and the ensuing process merely "occasioned crimes" (see Stanišić

69.   The Appeals Chamber is also not persuaded by Župljanin's contentions that the Trial Chamber inconsistently defined the common purpose, or that it erroneously divided the goal and means of the common criminal purpose and failed to define the two in identical terms. The Appeals Chamber notes that the Trial Chamber found that the common criminal purpose of the JCE was the permanent removal of Bosnian Muslims and Bosnian Croats *through* the commission of crimes provided for in the Statute.[249] The Trial Chamber thus correctly applied the legal standard and found that there existed a common purpose amounting to or involving the commission of crimes provided for in the Statute.[250] Thus, having clearly identified the crimes that were part of the JCE, the Trial Chamber did not define the common criminal purpose to "merely involve an objective where it is probable that a crime will be committed", as Župljanin argues.[251] The Trial Chamber's finding also shows that it clearly determined that the common criminal purpose of the JCE was more than the mere aspiration of an ethnically-homogeneous, planned Serb state. Župljanin's argument in this regard is therefore without merit.

70.   Similarly, contrary to Stanišić's submission, the Appeals Chamber considers that the question of whether the aim of the Bosnian Serb leadership to have a separate Serb entity was in line with the legitimate purposes of the peace plan enunciated at the conclusion of a the International Commission convened in Lisbon, in February 1992 ("Cutileiro Plan")[252] has no bearing on the Trial Chamber's finding, given that the Trial Chamber unequivocally found that the common criminal purpose of the JCE involved the commission of crimes provided for in the Statute. **[page 34]**

3.   Conclusion

71.   For the foregoing reasons, the Appeals Chamber finds that Stanišić and Župljanin have failed to demonstrate that the Trial Chamber erred in defining the common criminal purpose of the JCE. The Appeals Chamber therefore dismisses Stanišić's third ground of appeal in part and sub-ground (F) in part of Župljanin's first ground of appeal.

C.   **Alleged errors in relation to the membership of the JCE (Stanišić's second ground of appeal and sub-ground (F) in part of Župljanin's first ground of appeal)**

72.   The Trial Chamber found that the "aim of the Bosnian Serb leadership as of 1991 was for Serbs to live in one state with other Serbs in the former Yugoslavia",[253] and defined the Bosnian Serb leadership as consisting of "leading members of the SDS and those who occupied important posts in the RS [...]. The most important organs of the RS were the Presidency, the Government, the NSC, and the BSA".[254]

Appeal Brief, para. 79). With regard to Stanišić's related argument that the Trial Chamber failed to consider whether one could have supported the goal for Serbs to live in one state with other Serbs without intending this to occur through the commission of JCE I Crimes, the Appeals Chamber has dismissed this argument elsewhere, finding that the Trial Chamber was cognisant that some members of the Bosnian Serb leadership may not have shared the goal of the majority, which was the establishment of "a Serb state, as ethnically 'pure' as possible, through the permanent removal of the Bosnian Muslims and Bosnian Croats" (see *infra*, paras 81-82).

[249]   Trial Judgement, vol. 2, para. 313. The Trial Chamber found that the permanent removal of Bosnian Muslims and Bosnian Croats was to be achieved through the commission of the JCE I Crimes, namely, the crimes of persecutions (through underlying acts of forcible transfer and deportation) (Count 1), deportation (Count 9), and inhumane acts (forcible transfer) (Count 10) as crimes against humanity, which are all provided for in the Statute (Trial Judgement, vol. 2, para. 313).

[250]   In this regard, the Appeals Chamber recalls that it has affirmed the *Martić* Trial Judgement which held that, while: "the objective of uniting with other ethnically similar areas did not in and of itself amount to a common criminal purpose within the meaning of the law on JCE pursuant to Article 7(1) of the Statute, [...] 'where the creation of such territories is intended to be implemented through the commission of crimes within the Statute this may be sufficient to amount to a common criminal purpose'" (*Martić* Appeal Judgement, para. 123, quoting *Martić* Trial Judgement, para. 442. See *Martić* Appeal Judgement, para. 112. See also *Đorđević* Appeal Judgement, paras 116-119; *Krajišnik* Appeal Judgement, paras 699-704. See also *Šainović et al.* Appeal Judgement, para. 664, confirming *Milutinović et al.* Trial Judgement, vol. 3, paras 95-96.

[251]   See Župljanin Appeal Brief, para. 32. For the same reasons, the Appeals Chamber is not persuaded by Župljanin's argument that the Trial Chamber's frequent reference to forcible takeover of the Municipalities, which does not constitute a crime, indicates that the Trial Chamber defined a common purpose that was not criminal (see Župljanin Appeal Brief, para. 35).

[252]   See Trial Judgement, vol. 2, para. 553.

[253]   Trial Judgement, vol. 2, para. 309.

[254]   Trial Judgement, vol. 2, para. 131.

73.   Having considered, among other factors, how the Bosnian Serb leadership acted in furtherance of its goal and the statements it made,[255] the Trial Chamber further found that the following persons were members of the JCE: Radovan Karadžić, Momčilo Krajišnik, Biljana Plavšić, Nikola Koljević, Ratko Mladić, Momčilo Mandić, Velibor Ostojić, Momir Talić, Radoslav Brđanin, Milomir Stakić, Simo Drljača, Vojislav Kuprešanin, Vlado Vrkeš, Mirko Vručinić, Jovan Tintor, Nedeljko Dekanović, Savo Tepić, Stevan Todorović, Blagoje Simić, Vinko Kondić, Malko Koroman, Dorie Ristanić, Predrag Radić, Andrija Bjelošević, Ljubiša Savić, a.k.a. "Mauzer", Predrag Ješurić, and Branko Grujić.[256] The Trial Chamber further stated that it would "determine whether [Stanišić and Župljanin] were members of the JCE in the sections [...] dedicated to their individual criminal responsibility".[257]

74.   Stanišić and Župljanin raise several challenges to the Trial Chamber's findings in relation to the membership of the JCE.[258] The Prosecution responds that Stanišić's and Župljanin's arguments should be dismissed.[259] The Appeals Chamber will address these arguments in turn. **[page 35]**

1.   Alleged error in arbitrarily constructing the term Bosnian Serb leadership without an evidentiary basis

75.   Stanišić submits that the Trial Chamber arbitrarily constructed a definition of the term Bosnian Serb leadership "without any evidential basis or justification".[260] He argues that the Trial Chamber put together a "vaguely identified" group of people by virtue only of their posts or their membership in a political party while "[s]uch an amalgamate of individuals" as the Bosnian Serb leadership "never existed as an identifiable group in reality".[261]

76.   The Prosecution responds that the Trial Chamber did not arbitrarily define the term Bosnian Serb leadership without any evidentiary basis.[262]

77.   The Appeals Chamber recalls that the Trial Chamber found that the Bosnian Serb leadership "consisted of leading members of the SDS and those who occupied important posts in the RS".[263] The Trial Chamber described, in detail, the positions and roles of the RS institutions, their members,[264] as well as their respective powers and interrelationships.[265] In this respect, it scrutinised and explained the role of: (i) the President and the Presidency of the RS; (ii) the RS Government; and (iii) the NSC.[266] The Trial Chamber also found that "[t]he political influence within the SDS was wielded by Radovan Karadžić, Momčilo Krajišnik, Biljana Plavšić, and Nikola Koljević."[267] As a basis for the above findings, the Trial Chamber analysed and referred to documentary evidence, as well as witness testimonies and adjudicated facts.[268] The Trial Chamber used the term Bosnian Serb leadership to describe the connections and interrelationships between key political and military leaders and political institutions.[269] The Appeals Chamber has confirmed the correctness of this approach in earlier judgements.[270] **[page 36]**

---

[255]   Trial Judgement, vol. 2, paras 309-312.

[256]   Trial Judgement, vol. 2, para. 314.

[257]   Trial Judgement, vol. 2, para. 314.

[258]   Stanišić Appeal Brief, para. 55; Župljanin Appeal Brief, para. 15. See Stanišić Appeal Brief, paras 56-74.

[259]   Prosecution Response Brief (Stanišić), para. 23; Prosecution Response Brief (Župljanin), para. 8. See Prosecution Response Brief (Stanišić), paras 24-29; Prosecution Response Brief (Župljanin), fn. 9.

[260]   Stanišić Appeal Brief, para. 57. See Stanišić Appeal Brief, paras 56, 58-59. See also Appeal Hearing, 16 Dec 2015, AT. 100.

[261]   Stanišić Appeal Brief, para. 58.

[262]   Prosecution Response Brief (Stanišić), para. 24.

[263]   Trial Judgement, vol. 2, para. 131.

[264]   See Trial Judgement, vol. 2, paras 131-134, in particular, describing the positions and roles of Radovan Karadžić ("Karadžić"), Momčilo Krajišnik ("Krajišnik"), Biljana Plavšić ("Plavšić"), and Nikola Koljević ("Koljević").

[265]   Trial Judgement, vol. 2, paras 131-149. The Trial Chamber further discussed other Serb leaders, such as: Ratko Mladić ("Mladić"), Rajko Dukic, and Radoslav Brđanin ("Brđanin") (Trial Judgement, vol. 2, paras 145-147).

[266]   Trial Judgement, vol. 2, paras 136-149.

[267]   Trial Judgement, vol. 2, para. 131.

[268]   Trial Judgement, vol. 2, fns 428-495.

[269]   See Trial Judgement, vol. 2, paras 131-149.

[270]   See *Brđanin* Appeal Judgement, paras 127, 216, 234, 236; *Tolimir* Appeal Judgement, para. 388; *Deronjić* Sentencing Appeal Judgement, para. 69. The Appeals Chamber notes that in *Brđanin*, *Tolimir*, and *Deronjić*, the Appeals Chamber relied on the concept of Bosnian Serb leadership as defined by the trial chambers without questioning its existence or definition. See also *Brđanin* Trial Judgement, para. 65; *Tolimir* Trial Judgement, para. 1040; *Deronjić* Sentencing Judgement, paras 56-58, 66, 190.

78.   Consequently, the Appeals Chamber finds that Stanišić has failed to show that the Trial Chamber arbitrarily constructed a definition of the Bosnian Serb leadership without an evidentiary basis or justification. His submissions in this regard are therefore dismissed.

2. Alleged errors in equating being part of the Bosnian Serb leadership with membership in the JCE and failing to identify those within the Bosnian Serb leadership who were not JCE members

79.   Stanišić submits that the Trial Chamber erroneously equated being part of the Bosnian Serb leadership with membership in the JCE.[271] In particular, he argues that the Trial Chamber erred in law by imposing collective responsibility upon all those considered to be members of the Bosnian Serb leadership and by criminalising membership in the Bosnian Serb leadership.[272] Stanišić contends that the Trial Chamber erroneously concluded that the JCE was proved for the whole Bosnian Serb leadership by reference solely "to the aims of the 'majority'"[273] and considered "the minority" of the Bosnian Serb leadership to have the intent to commit crimes "despite acknowledging evidence to the contrary".[274] Stanišić further submits that by erroneously finding that the aims of the Bosnian Serb leadership were the commission of crimes, the Trial Chamber failed to make an assessment of each individual's responsibility.[275] In a similar vein, Župljanin submits that the Trial Chamber failed to identify those within the Bosnian Serb leadership whom it did not consider to be members of the JCE, as implied by the word "majority".[276]

80.   The Prosecution responds that Stanišić and Župljanin fail to demonstrate any error in the Trial Chamber's approach.[277] In particular, the Prosecution submits that Stanišić misconstrues the Trial Chamber's findings.[278]

81.   Contrary to Stanišić's argument, the Trial Chamber did not impose collective responsibility on all members of the Bosnian Serb leadership, nor did it criminalise membership therein. The Appeals Chamber notes that while the Trial Chamber acknowledged that "at times there were **[page 37]** conflicts" between the Serb forces,[279] SDS party structure, crisis staffs, and the RS Government,[280] it found that they "all shared and worked towards the same goal under the Bosnian Serb leadership".[281] In addition, it also considered evidence that "on some occasions Serb leaders made statements that their aim was not an ethnically pure state or that international humanitarian law should be respected"[282] but concluded that, in light of all the evidence, "these statements [did] not reflect the true aims of the *majority* of the Bosnian Serb leadership",[283] which was the establishment of "a Serb state, as ethnically 'pure' as possible, through the permanent removal of the Bosnian Muslims and Bosnian Croats".[284] It is thus clear that the Trial Chamber was cognisant that some members of the Bosnian Serb leadership may not have shared the goal of the majority.[285]

---

[271]   Stanišić Appeal Brief, paras 56, 60-69. In support, Stanišić submits that the Trial Chamber also erroneously established the elements of the JCE, including the common purpose and its implementation, by reference to the acts and statements of the Bosnian Serb leadership as a group (Stanišić Appeal Brief, paras 60-61).
[272]   Stanišić Appeal Brief, paras 67, 69. See Stanišić Appeal Brief, paras 64-65, 68. See also Stanišić Reply Brief, paras 25-26; Appeal Hearing, 16 Dec 2015, AT 101-102.
[273]   Stanišić Appeal Brief, para. 64 (emphasis omitted). See Appeal Hearing, 16 Dec 2015, AT. 101-102. According to Stanišić, the Trial Chamber found that the "'true aims of the majority of the Bosnian Serb leadership' were not reflected in the statements of certain Bosnian Serb leaders that were contrary to the desire for an ethnically pure state, or which called for respect of provisions of international humanitarian law" (Stanišić Appeal Brief, para. 63, referring to Trial Judgement, vol. 2, para. 312 (emphasis omitted). See Stanišić Appeal Brief, para. 64).
[274]   Stanišić Appeal Brief, para. 64 (emphasis omitted). See Stanišić Reply Brief, para. 23.
[275]   Stanišić Appeal Brief, para. 67. See Stanišić Appeal Brief, paras 64-65, 68-69, referring to *Tadić* Appeal Judgement, para. 186. See also Stanišić Reply Brief, paras 25-26.
[276]   Župljanin Appeal Brief, para. 15.
[277]   Prosecution Response Brief (Stanišić), paras 24-26; Prosecution Response Brief (Župljanin), fn. 9.
[278]   Prosecution Response Brief (Stanišić), para. 25.
[279]   See *infra*, Annex B.
[280]   Trial Judgement, vol. 2, para. 311.
[281]   Trial Judgement, vol. 2, para. 311.
[282]   Trial Judgement, vol. 2, para. 312.
[283]   Trial Judgement, vol. 2, para. 312 (emphasis added).
[284]   Trial Judgement, vol. 2, para. 311.
[285]   Trial Judgement, vol. 2, para. 312.

82.   Moreover, the Trial Chamber assessed and made findings on the criminal responsibility of Stanišić and Župljanin only, and did so on the basis of their individual acts and conduct.[286] Since the Trial Chamber assessed their criminal responsibility pursuant to joint criminal enterprise liability, it analysed the requisite elements of this mode of liability, including whether a plurality of persons acted together.[287] While the Trial Chamber was required to establish that the persons belonging to the joint criminal enterprise shared the common criminal purpose, it was not required to make an "assessment of each individual's responsibility"[288] in the Trial Judgement.[289] Having identified members of the JCE, the Trial Chamber concluded that they formed a plurality of persons who participated in the realisation of the common criminal plan.[290] In so doing, the Trial Chamber identified members of the JCE by name.[291] Accordingly, the Trial Chamber's findings demonstrate that it considered that some of the members of the Bosnian Serb leadership were also members of the JCE.[292] However, as described above,[293] the Trial Chamber was aware that certain members of the Bosnian Serb leadership may not have shared the goal of the majority, and did not find that **[page 38]** every member of the Bosnian Serb leadership was also a member of the JCE.[293][294] Consequently, there is no basis for the argument that the Trial Chamber criminalised the Bosnian Serb leadership as such. Finally, and contrary to Župljanin's argument, there was no need for the Trial Chamber to identify those within the Bosnian Serb leadership whom it did not consider to be members of the JCE as it is irrelevant to his criminal responsibility. The Appeals Chamber finds that Župljanin has failed to articulate an error, his argument is unsupported by jurisprudence of the Tribunal, and he ignores the relevant findings of the Trial Chamber.[295] The Appeals Chamber therefore dismisses both Stanišić's and Župljanin's arguments.

3.   Alleged error in finding that Stanišić was a member of the JCE on the sole basis of his association with the Bosnian Serb leadership as Minister of Interior

83.   Stanišić submits that the Trial Chamber placed him within the Bosnian Serb leadership "solely by virtue of his ministerial position".[296] According to Stanišić, by finding that the Bosnian Serb leadership was part of the JCE and that he belonged to the Bosnian Serb leadership, the Trial Chamber impermissibly presumed that he contributed to the common plan and shared the intent to commit persecutory crimes.[297] Stanišić further submits that this represents a "presumption of guilt" and an "unacceptable reversal of [his] right to be presumed innocent".[298] As such, he argues that the Trial Chamber failed to determine whether he was a member of the JCE on the basis of his individual acts and conduct.[299]

[286]   See for Stanišić's criminal responsibility, Trial Judgement, vol. 2, paras 531-781. See for Župljanin's criminal responsibility, Trial Judgement, vol. 2, paras 343-530.
[287]   Trial Judgement, vol. 2, paras 314-315. In this regard, the Appeals Chamber recalls that "[t]he crimes contemplated in the Statute mostly constitute the manifestations of collective criminality and are often carried out by groups of individuals acting in pursuance of a common criminal design or purpose" (*Martić* Appeal Judgement, para. 82, referring to *Tadić* Appeal Judgement, para. 191). However, the mode of criminal liability of joint criminal enterprise is not a form of collective responsibility and its contours, described in the jurisprudence of the Tribunal, contain sufficient safeguards to avoid this (*Martić* Appeal Judgement, para. 82, referring to *Brđanin* Appeal Judgement, paras 427-431). See *Krajišnik* Appeal Judgement, fn. 418.
[288]   Stanišić Appeal Brief, para. 67.
[289]   See *Đorđević* Appeal Judgement, paras 141, 158.
[290]   Trial Judgement, vol. 2, paras 314-315.
[291]   Trial Judgement, vol. 2, para. 314.
[292]   See Trial Judgement, vol. 2, paras 136-149, 314.
[293]   See *supra*, para. 81.
[294]   See Trial Judgement, vol. 2, paras 136-149, 314. For example, the Trial Chamber found that Witness Branko Deric (RS Prime Minister) ("Witness Deric"), Milan Trbojevic (RS Deputy Prime Minister), and Bogdan Subotic (RS Minister of Defence) were members of the Bosnian Serb leadership, but did not find them to be members of the JCE (see Trial Judgement, vol. 2, paras 137, 139-141, 144, 314).
[295]   See Trial Judgement, vol. 2, paras 136-149, 144, 314. See also *supra*, para. 81.
[296]   Stanišić Appeal Brief, para. 70. See Stanišić Appeal Brief, para. 55.
[297]   Stanišić Appeal Brief, para. 71.
[298]   Stanišić Appeal Brief, para. 71. See Stanišić Appeal Brief, para. 72.
[299]   Stanišić Appeal Brief, para. 73.

84.   The Prosecution responds that the Trial Chamber properly determined Stanišić's membership in the JCE on the basis of its findings concerning his contributions and shared intent, rather than merely relying on Stanišić's affiliation with the Bosnian Serb leadership as Minister of Interior.[300]

85.   At the outset, the Appeals Chamber notes that while the Trial Chamber made no explicit statement that Stanišić was a member of the JCE and did not specify a date in this regard, **[page 39]** the Appeals Chamber considers that it is clear from the Trial Judgement, when read as a whole, that the Trial Chamber was satisfied that Stanišić was a member of the JCE during the Indictment period.[301]

86.   The Trial Chamber found that Stanišić was the Minister of Interior within the RS Government.[302] The Trial Chamber also found that the RS Government was one of the most important organs in the RS and that the Bosnian Serb leadership consisted of, *inter alios*, those who occupied important posts of the RS.[303] In light of the foregoing, the Appeals Chamber understands that the Trial Chamber identified Stanišić to be a member of the Bosnian Serb leadership. This consideration is, however, irrelevant since the Trial Chamber convicted him on the basis of his membership in the JCE, not his membership in the Bosnian Serb leadership.[304] Indeed, the Trial Chamber considered his position as Minister of Interior in combination with other factors – including his acts and conduct – to find that he contributed to the JCE[305] and shared the requisite intent.[306] It thus did not "presume" that he contributed to the common plan and shared the persecutorial intent on the basis of his membership in the Bosnian Serb leadership. The Appeals Chamber therefore finds that Stanišić has failed to show that the Trial Chamber found that he was a member of the JCE only by virtue of his association with the Bosnian Serb leadership as Minister of Interior. His arguments in this respect are therefore dismissed.

4. Conclusion

87.   In light of the foregoing, the Appeals Chamber finds that Stanišić and Župljanin have failed to show that the Trial Chamber erred in its findings in relation to the membership of the JCE. The Appeals Chamber thus dismisses Stanišić's second ground of appeal in its entirety and sub-ground (F) in part of Župljanin's first ground of appeal. **[page 40]**

D. **Alleged errors regarding Stanišić's participation in the JCE**

1. Introduction

88.   Stanišić was elected Minister of Interior on 24 March 1992 and officially appointed to the position on 31 March 1992.[307] The Trial Chamber convicted Stanišić pursuant to Article 7(1) of the Statute for committing, through participation in the JCE, the crimes of persecutions as a crime against humanity as well as murder and torture as violations of the laws or customs of war.[308] The Trial Chamber also found Stanišić responsible, but did not enter convictions on the basis of the principles relating to cumulative convictions, for committing, through participation in the JCE, the crimes of: murder, torture, inhumane acts, deportation, and inhumane acts (forcible transfer) as crimes against humanity, and cruel treatment as a violation of the

---

[300]   Prosecution Response Brief (Stanišić), para. 28, quoting Stanišić Appeal Brief, paras 70-72. See Prosecution Response Brief (Stanišić), para. 24. See also Appeal Hearing, 16 Dec 2015, AT. 124. *Cf.* Stanišić Reply Brief, para. 22.

[301]   See Trial Judgement, vol. 2, paras 342, 781-782, 799. See also Trial Judgement, vol. 2, paras 804, 809, 813, 818, 822, 827, 831, 836, 840, 844, 849, 854, 858, 863, 868, 873, 877, 881, 885.

[302]   Trial Judgement, vol. 2, para. 141.

[303]   Trial Judgement, vol. 2, para. 131. See *supra*, para. 72.

[304]   See Trial Judgement, vol. 2, paras 804, 809, 813, 818, 822, 827, 831, 836, 840, 844, 849, 854, 858, 863, 868, 873, 877, 881, 885, 955.

[305]   See Trial Judgement, vol. 2, paras 729-765. See also *infra*, paras 143-365.

[306]   Trial Judgement, vol. 2, para. 769. See Trial Judgement, vol. 2, paras 766-768. The question of whether the Trial Chamber committed errors in its findings on Stanišić's intent will be dealt with elsewhere in this Judgement (see *infra*, paras 573-595).

[307]   Trial Judgement, vol. 2, para. 542.

[308]   Trial Judgement, vol. 2, paras 804, 809, 813, 818, 822, 827, 831, 836, 840, 844, 849, 854, 858, 863, 868, 873, 877, 881, 885, 955.

laws or customs of war.[309] The Trial Chamber further found Stanišić not guilty pursuant to Articles 7(1) and 7(3) of the Statute for the crime of extermination as a crime against humanity.[310]

89.   In the section of the Trial Judgement addressing Stanišić's responsibility, the Trial Chamber presented the evidence relating to his "acts prior to and following his appointment as Minister of Interior".[311] Under the heading entitled "Findings on Mićo Stanišić's membership in JCE",[312] the Trial Chamber then set out its findings on his "contribution to JCE",[313] followed by a conclusion on his intent,[314] and ended with a discussion of his "responsibility for crimes outside scope of JCE".[315] The Appeals Chamber notes that in the section of the Trial Judgement dedicated to the conclusions on Stanišić's responsibility (*i.e.* the section entitled "Findings on Mićo Stanišić's membership in JCE"[316]) the Trial Chamber provided no cross-references to earlier findings or citations to evidence on the record.[317] **[page 41]**

90.   It is regrettable that the Trial Chamber adopted such an approach, as the exercise of identifying underlying findings and analysis has been greatly convoluted as a result.[318]

91.   Stanišić asserts that the Trial Chamber failed to provide a reasoned opinion for several findings in relation to the elements of joint criminal enterprise liability.[319] Stanišić also raises a number of other legal and factual challenges regarding the Trial Chamber's findings relating to his contribution to the JCE and his intent to further the JCE, as well as his responsibility under the third category of joint criminal enterprise liability.[320] The Appeals Chamber will address his submissions in turn.

    2.   Alleged errors in the evaluation of Stanišić's Interview (Stanišić's seventh ground of appeal)

92.   From 16 to 21 July 2007, before trial proceedings had commenced, Stanišić voluntarily gave an interview to the Prosecution (*i.e.* the Interview), the transcripts of which were admitted into evidence at trial as Prosecution exhibits. The Trial Chamber noted that Stanišić relied on the Interview for the truth of its content in support of his defence case. It emphasised that it "considered [the Interview] in the course of its analysis of the evidence pertaining to Mićo Stanišić's responsibility".[321]

(a) Submissions of the parties

93.   First, Stanišić submits that the Trial Chamber erred in law by not according full probative value to his Interview.[322] According to him, full probative value must be attributed to the evidence of an accused which is admitted into evidence at the Prosecution's request and not rebutted by any reliable evidence.[323] He argues that the Trial Chamber failed to consider the fact that his Interview was adduced into evidence by the

---

[309]   Trial Judgement, vol. 2, paras 804, 809, 813, 818, 822, 827, 831, 836, 840, 844, 849, 854, 858, 863, 868, 873, 877, 881, 885, 955.
[310]   Trial Judgement, vol. 2, paras 804, 822, 844, 849, 858, 873, 877, 885, 955.
[311]   Trial Judgement, vol. 2, paras 544-728.
[312]   Trial Judgement, vol. 2, paras 729-769.
[313]   Trial Judgement, vol. 2, paras 729-765.
[314]   Trial Judgement, vol. 2, paras 766-769.
[315]   Trial Judgement, vol. 2, paras 770-781.
[316]   Trial Judgement, vol. 2, paras 729-769.
[317]   Trial Judgement, vol. 2, paras 729-769. *Cf.* Trial Judgement, vol. 2, para. 767, fn. 1870.
[318]   See *infra*, paras 138, 378. See also *infra*, paras 131, 142, 367, 376-377, 422, 433, 440, 456, 478, 484, 491, 507, 517, 669, 689. The Appeals Chamber acknowledges that the effects of this regrettable approach also permeate sections other than Stanišić's responsibility, see *e.g. infra*, paras 710, 843, 999, 1115, 1148.
[319]   Stanišić Appeal Brief, paras 22-54 (Stanišić's first ground of appeal). See Stanišić Appeal Brief, paras 120, 235, 239-242, 370-387, 429-431.
[320]   Stanišić Appeal Brief, paras 87-476 (Stanišić's third ground of appeal in part and Stanišić's fourth, fifth, sixth, seventh, eighth, ninth, tenth, and eleventh grounds of appeal). Stanišić also advances related arguments in paragraphs 55 to 86 of his appeal brief (Stanišić's second ground of appeal and Stanišić's third ground of appeal in part), which have been addressed in the previous sections in this Judgement (see *supra*, paras 63-87).
[321]   Trial Judgement, vol. 2, para. 536.
[322]   Stanišić Appeal Brief, paras 310, 315, 318.
[323]   Stanišić Appeal Brief, paras 303, 310, 315, 318. See Stanišić Appeal Brief, paras 312-313.

Prosecution for the truth of its contents.[324] Furthermore, Stanišić argues that in adducing the Interview *via* a bar table motion, the Prosecution acknowledged the **[page 42]** reliability, relevance, and probative value of this evidence and extensively relied on its contents in its pre-trial brief, its opening statement, and during the trial.[325]

94.   Second, Stanišić submits that the Trial Chamber erred in law by not addressing the parties' arguments on the weight to be attributed to the Interview.[326] Stanišić submits that the Prosecution's contention at trial – that his "numerous self-serving statements" should be rejected unless corroborated by other credible evidence – is unfounded, unspecified, and should be disregarded.[327]

95.   Third, Stanišić submits that the Trial Chamber erred in law and fact by failing to "grasp the thrust of the information provided" in his Interview and to "attribute the correct probative value to this evidence".[328] He refers in this respect to specific aspects of his acts and conduct which, he argues, were clearly revealed by his Interview, including that: (i) he did not participate in the creation of the SDS and his ability to influence SDS decisions was at best minimal; (ii) he supported the Cutileiro Plan; (iii) he was not involved in the politics of the conflict; (iv) he was not close to Radovan Karadžić ("Karadžić") and did not share his views; (v) his ability to communicate with the various CSBs and Public Security Stations ("SJBs") and other persons was extremely limited; (vi) he had no jurisdiction over the creation and/or operation of prisons, camps and other detention facilities, and the information available to him was very limited; (vii) he was opposed to the presence and actions of paramilitary groups in BiH and took multiple measures to prevent and report crimes committed by such groups; and (viii) he took every possible measure with a view to investigating, reporting, and arresting perpetrators regardless of their ethnicity.[329] Stanišić argues that he consented to the Interview without the benefit of having heard any of the witnesses at trial[330] and voluntarily responded to topics in good faith.[331] He also points out that the Interview is overwhelmingly corroborated by credible evidence in the form of witness testimony and documentary evidence – mostly adduced by the Prosecution[332] – as well as by numerous orders he **[page 43]** issued.[333] He contends that the "clear lack of criminal intent demonstrated throughout the [I]nterview was not accorded appropriate probative value" by the Trial Chamber.[334]

96.   According to Stanišić, had his Interview been properly assessed, no reasonable trial chamber could have found that he was a member of the JCE.[335] Consequently, he requests that his convictions for Counts 1, 4, and 6 be quashed.[336]

97.   With respect to Stanišić's first argument, the Prosecution responds that the weight accorded to an accused's statement, like any other evidence, is determined at the close of a case with regard to the record as

---

[324]   Stanišić Appeal Brief, paras 303, 305-306, 311, 318. See Stanišić Appeal Brief, paras 312-313. Stanišić also contends that the weight to be attributed to the contents of Stanišić's Interview was extensively debated during final oral arguments (see Stanišić Appeal Brief, para. 305).

[325]   Stanišić Appeal Brief, paras 311-313. See Stanišić Appeal Brief, para. 318.

[326]   Stanišić Appeal Brief, paras 316, 322. See Stanišić Appeal Brief, para. 305.

[327]   Stanišić Appeal Brief, para. 317. See Stanišić Appeal Brief, paras 318-319, 322-324. Stanišić submits that the Prosecution: (i) failed to raise any argument at trial that justified discarding specific parts of the information he provided; and (ii) inaccurately argued at trial that he did not answer all questions during Stanišić's Interview, although he admits that there were documents he preferred not to comment on so as to avoid revealing aspects of his defence case (see Stanišić Appeal Brief, paras 323-324).

[328]   Stanišić Appeal Brief, para. 329. See Stanišić Appeal Brief, para. 330. Stanišić also argues that his defence case "matched in every point" his Interview and that, had his evidence been correctly evaluated, the Trial Chamber could not have found that he was aware of and shared the persecutory intent of the perpetrators and that he contributed to the JCE (see Stanišić Appeal Brief, paras 325-326, 328). See Stanišić Reply Brief, para. 85.

[329]   Stanišić Appeal Brief, para. 330. See Stanišić Appeal Brief, para. 329; Stanišić Reply Brief, para. 85.

[330]   Stanišić Appeal Brief, paras 308, 327; Stanišić Reply Brief, para. 83.

[331]   Stanišić Appeal Brief, paras 307-309.

[332]   Stanišić Appeal Brief, paras 317, 321. See Stanišić Appeal Brief, para. 319; Stanišić Reply Brief, para. 83.

[333]   Stanišić Appeal Brief, paras 319-320. Stanišić provides a table highlighting the orders that he submits corroborate his Interview (see Stanišić Appeal Brief, para. 320).

[334]   Stanišić Reply Brief, para. 83. See Stanišić Appeal Brief, para. 329; Stanišić Reply Brief, para. 85.

[335]   Stanišić Appeal Brief, paras 302, 304, 331; Stanišić Reply Brief, para. 85.

[336]   Stanišić Appeal Brief, para. 332.

a whole and that Stanišić's "newly-created legal test" is unsupported by the jurisprudence.[337] Second, the Prosecution responds that the Trial Chamber did refer to Stanišić's arguments concerning the weight to be attributed to the Interview[338] and that the Trial Chamber "reasonably found that Stanišić lied during his [I] nterview on several critical issues".[339]

98.   Third, the Prosecution responds that Stanišić merely seeks to substitute his interpretation of his Interview for that of the Trial Chamber and thus his submissions warrant summary dismissal.[340] It argues that the Trial Chamber properly weighed the Interview in light of the totality of the evidence on the record and that it does not undermine the reasonableness of the finding that Stanišić was a member of the JCE.[341] The Prosecution submits that the Trial Chamber discussed Stanišić's Interview at length, repeatedly cited portions of it crediting Stanišić's evidence on some issues,[342] but also finding that several of Stanišić's statements in the Interview were inconsistent with the remainder of the evidence and, therefore, not credible.[343] The Prosecution also argues that Stanišić focuses on irrelevant considerations, such as how the Interview was conducted.[344] Finally, according to the Prosecution, Stanišić reiterates arguments contained in his final trial brief by citing **[page 44]** the same exhibits whilst ignoring that the Trial Chamber addressed most of these exhibits in the Trial Judgement.[345]

(b) Analysis

99.   The Appeals Chamber considers that all evidence adduced at trial, irrespective of which party tendered it, should be analysed according to the same legal standard. Once a trial chamber satisfies itself that the tendered piece of evidence meets the admissibility requirements, *i.e.* is relevant and has probative value, it may admit that evidence into the trial record.[346] The Appeals Chamber however recalls that the decision to admit a document has no bearing on the weight a trial chamber will ultimately accord it, and that the weight to be accorded is determined at the close of the case, having regard to the evidence as a whole.[347] The Appeals Chamber recalls that it is well established in the Tribunal's jurisprudence that a trial chamber has broad discretion in determining the weight to attach to evidence,[348] and that it is within its discretion to evaluate whether evidence taken as a whole is reliable and credible and to accept or reject the fundamental features of the evidence.[349]

100.   With regard to Stanišić's argument that his Interview should be accorded full weight because it was adduced into evidence by the Prosecution and was not rebutted by reliable evidence, the Appeals Chamber considers that it was within the discretion of the Trial Chamber to decide what weight to afford to a piece of evidence even if this evidence was not rebutted by other evidence.[350] The fact that the Prosecution acknowledged the probative value of the Interview when tendering it into evidence cannot be seen as limiting the Trial Chamber's discretion to evaluate its weight in light of the entire trial record. The Appeals Chamber,

---

[337]   Prosecution Response Brief (Stanišić), paras 155, 157, referring to Stanišić Appeal Brief, para. 310. See Prosecution Response Brief (Stanišić), paras 154, 156.
[338]   Prosecution Response Brief (Stanišić), para. 159, referring to Trial Judgement, vol. 2, para. 536.
[339]   Prosecution Response Brief (Stanišić), para. 154. See Prosecution Response Brief (Stanišić), paras 158, 160, 162.
[340]   Prosecution Response Brief (Stanišić), paras 154, 160.
[341]   Prosecution Response Brief (Stanišić), paras 154, 166.
[342]   Prosecution Response Brief (Stanišić), para. 161, referring to Trial Judgement, vol. 2, paras 6, 341, 537-543, 545-546, 549, 551-552, 557-559, 561-562, 573, 576, 595, 616, 618, 624-625, 637, 708.
[343]   Prosecution Response Brief (Stanišić), paras 162, 166, referring to Trial Judgement, vol. 2, paras 6, 542-543, 545, 548, 554-555, 558, 564, 581, 588, 620, 633, 654, 656, 693, 729, 731, 735-736, 739, 753, 759, 761-762; Exhibit 1D135, p. 1. See Prosecution Response Brief (Stanišić), paras 155-156, 158, 161, 166; Exhibits P198, pp 6-9, P1999, p. 59.
[344]   Prosecution Response Brief (Stanišić), para. 163.
[345]   Prosecution Response Brief (Stanišić), para. 165.
[346]   Rule 89(C) of the Rules.
[347]   *Boškoski and Tarčulovski* Appeal Judgement, para. 196. See *Popović et al.* Appeal Judgement, para. 90; *Rutaganda* Appeal Judgement, para. 266, fn. 63.
[348]   *Popović et al.* Appeal Judgement, paras 131, 952, 1131, 1215; *Đorđević* Appeal Judgement, paras 319, 483, 797; *Lukić and Lukić* Appeal Judgement, para. 112.
[349]   *Popović et al.* Appeal Judgement, para. 1358; *Munyakazi* Appeal Judgement, para. 51. See *Hategekimana* Appeal Judgement, para. 282; *Bagosora and Nsengiyumva* Appeal Judgement, para. 253.
[350]   *Cf. Bikindi* Appeal Judgement, para. 115.

therefore, finds that Stanišić has failed to demonstrate an error in the Trial Chamber's exercise of its discretion in assessing evidence by according to his Interview the weight it deemed fit.

101. Insofar as Stanišić argues that the Trial Chamber erred in law by not addressing the parties' arguments on the weight to be attributed to the Interview, the Appeals Chamber recalls that "the Trial Chamber is not under the obligation to justify its findings in relation to every submission made during the trial" and "it is in the discretion of the Trial Chamber as to which legal arguments **[page 45]** to address".[351] In any event, the Appeals Chamber notes that, although the Trial Chamber did not expressly refer to all of the parties' arguments concerning the weight to be attributed to Stanišić's Interview, it considered the issue in detail and made a case-by-case assessment on the weight it would attribute to the Interview. Indeed, the Trial Chamber stated that it had considered Stanišić's Interview in the course of its analysis of the evidence pertaining to Stanišić's responsibility,[352] and referred extensively and continuously to Stanišić's Interview during its discussion on Stanišić's acts and conduct – thereby accepting portions of the Interview whilst explaining why it rejected other parts.[353] Based on the foregoing, the Appeals Chamber finds that Stanišić has failed to demonstrate an error in the Trial Chamber's exercise of its discretion.

102. Finally, with regard to Stanišić's submission that the Trial Chamber erred in law and fact by failing to "grasp the thrust of the information" in the Interview and to attribute the correct probative value to it,[354] the Appeals Chamber notes that the specific portions of the Interview to which Stanišić refers concern issues that the Trial Chamber assessed and discussed.[355] Moreover, the Trial Chamber was cognisant of the fact that Stanišić consented to being interviewed without having heard witnesses and voluntarily gave evidence to the Prosecution.[356] The Appeals Chamber considers that Stanišić seeks to substitute his interpretation of the Interview for that of the Trial Chamber as he merely challenges the weight attributed to some portions of his Interview without showing that the Trial Chamber improperly exercised its discretion in weighing them against the rest of the trial record.

103. To the extent that Stanišić argues that his Interview was overwhelmingly corroborated and, therefore, should have been afforded full weight, the Appeals Chamber recalls that "corroboration of testimonies, even by many witnesses, does not establish automatically the credibility, reliability or weight of those testimonies" and that it is "neither a condition nor a guarantee of reliability of a single piece of evidence".[357] Other than stating that the listed exhibits corroborate his Interview,[358] **[page 46]** Stanišić does not present any arguments demonstrating how the Trial Chamber erred in its assessment of the Interview in light of the entire trial record. The Appeals Chamber emphasises that, regardless of whether these exhibits corroborate the contents of Stanišić's Interview, the Trial Chamber had full discretion in weighing and assessing the evidence in light of the entire trial record.[358][359] Stanišić has failed to demonstrate that the Trial Chamber ventured outside the scope of its discretion.

---

[351] *Kvočka et al.* Appeal Judgement, para. 23; *Čelebići* Appeal Judgement, para. 498.
[352] Trial Judgement, vol. 2, para. 536.
[353] See *e.g.* Trial Judgement, vol. 2, paras 555, 562-564. See also Trial Judgement, vol. 2, paras 536-554, 556-561, 565-728.
[354] See *supra*, para. 95.
[355] See Trial Judgement, vol. 2, paras 545-546, 552-568, 577-580, 585, 588, 594, 617, 620, 624, 633, 637, 640, 644, 647, 675, 677-688, 695-708, 709-730, 732-733, 744-759, 761-762, 764-765, 769.
[356] See Trial Judgement, vol. 2, para. 536, in which the Trial Chamber referred to the dates of the Interview (*i.e.* from 16 to 21 July 2007) and noted that Stanišić "was read his rights pursuant to the Rules at the start of each interview session and affirmed that he understood them".
[357] *D. Milošević* Appeal Judgement, para. 248, referring to *Limaj et al.* Appeal Judgement, para. 203. See also *Čelebići* Appeal Judgement, paras 492, 506; *Gacumbitsi* Appeal Judgement, para. 72; *Musema* Appeal Judgement, paras 37-38; *Karera* Appeal Judgement, para. 45. The Appeals Chamber further recalls that a "trial chamber has full discretion to assess the credibility of a witness and determine the appropriate weight to be accorded to his or her testimony; corroboration is one of many potential factors relevant to this assessment" (see *Gatete* Appeal Judgement, para. 138). See *Popović et al.* Appeal Judgement, paras 132, 243, 1009.
[358] See Stanišić Appeal Brief, para. 320. The table, provided by Stanišić, lists Exhibits 1D56, 1D73, P1420, P1013, P1472, 1D48, P564, 1D52, P192, 1D563, 1D77, 1D57, 1D634, P1004, P173, P581, P582, 1D55, 1D640, 1D64, 1D651, 1D61, P792, P1252, P553, P57, 1D62, P856, 1D91, P190, 1D58, 1D59, 1D176, 1D94, P2349, P2348, 1D572, P543, P545, P534, P580, 1D76. *Cf.* Prosecution Response Brief (Stanišić), fns 646-647. Stanišić does not identify any further testimonial or documentary evidence which allegedly corroborates the Interview (see Stanišić Appeal Brief, paras 317, 321).
[359] See *supra*, para. 99. See also *Gatete* Appeal Judgement, para. 138; *Popović et al.* Appeal Judgement, paras 132, 243, 1009.

(c) Conclusion

104.   Based on the foregoing, the Appeals Chamber finds that Stanišić has failed to show that the Trial Chamber erred in its assessment of Stanišić's Interview. The Appeals Chamber therefore dismisses Stanišić's seventh ground of appeal.

3.   Alleged error regarding the legal standard for contribution to a joint criminal enterprise through failure to act (Stanišić's first ground of appeal in part and fifth ground of appeal in part)

105.   In concluding that Stanišic contributed to the JCE, the Trial Chamber considered, *inter alia*, "his role in prevention, investigation, and documentation of crimes",[360] and its finding that despite his knowledge of the crimes that were being committed, Stanišić "took insufficient action to put an end to [these crimes] and instead permitted RS MUP forces under his overall control to continue to participate in joint operations with other Serb forces involved in the commission of crimes".[361] The Trial Chamber also considered Stanišić's "role in unlawful arrest and detentions"[362] and its finding that he "contributed to [the] continued existence and operation [of detention and penitentiary facilities] by failing to take decisive action to close these facilities or, at the very least, by failing to withdraw the RS MUP forces from their involvement in these detention centres".[363] **[page 47]**

(a) Submissions of the parties

106.   Stanišić submits that the Trial Chamber erred in law by failing to set out and apply the correct legal standard for contribution to a joint criminal enterprise "by omission".[364] He contends that it is well established in the jurisprudence of the Tribunal that responsibility for participating in a joint criminal enterprise falls within the ambit of Article 7(1) of the Statute, under the heading "committing", which covers the "culpable omission of an act [...] mandated by a rule of criminal law".[365] Stanišic argues that, consequently, participation in a joint criminal enterprise by way of omission can only be established when the omission arises from a "legal duty to act mandated by a rule of criminal law" and if the accused had the ability to act.[366]

107.   Stanišic further submits that the Trial Chamber erred by finding that he contributed to the JCE on the basis of omissions which do not meet the requirements for incurring joint criminal enterprise liability by omission under Article 7(1) of the Statute.[367] Accordingly, Stanišić requests that his convictions under Counts 1, 4, and 6 be quashed.[368]

108.   The Prosecution responds that the Trial Chamber correctly articulated and applied the law relating to joint criminal enterprise liability and that Stanišić's arguments should be dismissed.[369] In particular, the Prosecution submits that Stanišic's argument that contribution to a joint criminal enterprise by omission must be based "on a duty mandated by a rule of criminal law" should be dismissed considering that, as the

---

[360]   Trial Judgement, vol. 2, paras 745-759.
[361]   Trial Judgement, vol. 2, para. 759.
[362]   Trial Judgement, vol. 2, paras 760-765.
[363]   Trial Judgement, vol. 2, para. 761.
[364]   Stanišić Appeal Brief, paras 43, 189, 191-194, referring to *Prosecutor v. Mićo Stanišić and Stojan Župljanin*, Case No. IT-08-91-PT, Decision on Mićo Stanišić's and Stojan Župljanin's Motions on Form of the Indictment, 19 March 2009 ("Decision on Form of the Indictment"), para. 39, Trial Judgement, vol. 1, para. 103. See Stanišić Appeal Brief, paras 195-205.
[365]   Stanišić Appeal Brief, paras 195-196. See Stanišić Appeal Brief, para. 195. Stanišić adds that recent jurisprudence of the Tribunal has confirmed in the context of joint criminal enterprise that responsibility for omission can only be established where the requirements for a culpable omission under Article 7(1) are met. Stanišić Appeal Brief, para. 198, referring to *Tolimir* Trial Judgement, para. 894, fn. 3528).
[366]   Stanišić Appeal Brief, para. 199. See Stanišić Appeal Brief, paras 202-205). See also Stanišić Reply Brief, paras 56, 60.
[367]   Stanišić Appeal Brief, paras 188-190, 206-209, 212-214, 216, 218-220, 223-228, 230-232. Stanišić submits in this regard that the Trial Chamber erred because it relied on his "purported omissions [which] do not arise from a duty mandated by a rule of criminal law" and/or because he did not have the ability to act (Stanišić Appeal Brief, para. 207).
[368]   Stanišić Appeal Brief, para. 234.
[369]   Prosecution Response Brief (Stanišić), paras 17, 85-87, 91.

Trial Chamber correctly observed, such contribution need neither be criminal nor form part of the *actus reus* of the crime.[370] **[page 48]**

(b) Analysis

109.   The Appeals Chamber considers that Stanišic's argument that the Trial Chamber failed to apply the correct legal standard to his "purported omissions"[371] is based on the premise that each failure to act assessed in the context of joint criminal enterprise liability must, *per se*, meet the legal conditions set out in the Tribunal's case law in relation to commission by omission. In this respect, the Appeals Chamber recalls that although participation in a joint criminal enterprise – which is based on an accused's significant contribution to the common criminal purpose – is a form of "commission" under Article 7(1) of the Statute, this is a mode of liability distinct from commission by omission and is characterised by different objective and subjective elements.[372]

110.   In this respect, the Trial Chamber properly held that for an accused to be found criminally liable on the basis of joint criminal enterprise liability, it is sufficient that he acted in furtherance of the common purpose of a joint criminal enterprise in the sense that he significantly contributed to the commission of the crimes involved in the common purpose.[373] Beyond that, the law does not foresee specific types of conduct which *per se* could not be considered a contribution to a joint criminal enterprise.[374] Within these legal confines, the question of whether a failure to act could be taken into account to establish that the accused significantly contributed to a joint criminal enterprise is a question of fact to be determined on a case-by-case basis.[375] Furthermore, the Appeals Chamber recalls that the relevant failures to act or acts carried out in furtherance of a joint criminal enterprise need not involve carrying out any part of the *actus reus* of a crime forming part of the common purpose, or indeed any crime at all.[376] That is, one's contribution to a joint criminal enterprise need not be in and of itself criminal, as long as the accused performs acts (or fails to perform acts) that in some way contribute significantly to the furtherance of the common purpose.[377] In light of the above, contrary to Stanišic's assertion, when establishing an accused's participation in a joint criminal enterprise through his failure to act, the existence of a legal duty to **[page 49]** act deriving from a rule of criminal law is not required.[378] The nature of the accused's duty and the extent of his ability to act are simply questions of evidence and not determinative of joint criminal enterprise liability.[379]

111.   In the present case, as part of its factual determination of Stanišic's contribution to the JCE, the Trial Chamber considered, together with his other actions,[380] his failure to discipline the RS MUP personnel who

---

[370]   Prosecution Response Brief (Stanišić), para. 86. The Prosecution argues in this regard that Stanišić unpersuasively relies on the *Tolimir* Trial Judgement as, contrary to Stanišić's assertion, this judgement does not specifically address the issue of the limits of joint criminal enterprise through omission liability (Prosecution Response Brief (Stanišić), para. 87).
[371]   Stanišić Appeal Brief, paras 190, 207.
[372]   See *Tadić* Appeal Judgement, paras 188, 227-228. See also *Krajišnik* Appeal Judgement, para. 662. As for the elements of joint criminal enterprise liability, see further *Brđanin* Appeal Judgement, paras 364-365, 429-430; *Stakić* Appeal Judgement, paras 64-65. As for the elements of commission by omission, see further *Orić* Appeal Judgement, para. 43, *Brđanin* Appeal Judgement, para. 274, *Galić* Appeal Judgement, para. 175, *Ntagerura et al.* Appeal Judgement, para. 334, *Blaškić* Appeal Judgement, para. 663.
[373]   Trial Judgement, vol. 1, para. 103, referring to *Brđanin* Appeal Judgement, para. 430. See *Krajišnik* Appeal Judgement, paras 215, 696. See also *Popović et al.* Appeal Judgement, para. 1378.
[374]   *Krajišnik* Appeal Judgement, para. 696.
[375]   See *Šainović et al.* Appeal Judgement, paras 1233, 1242. *Cf. Krajišnik* Appeal Judgement, para. 696.
[376]   *Krajišnik* Appeal Judgement, para. 215; *Brđanin* Appeal Judgement, para. 427; *Stakić* Appeal Judgement, para. 64; *Kvočka et al.* Appeal Judgement, para. 99; *Tadić* Appeal Judgement, para. 227. The Appeals Chamber observes that the Trial Chamber correctly recalled the jurisprudence in this regard (see Trial Judgement, vol. 1, para. 103).
[377]   *Popović et al.* Appeal Judgement, para. 1653; *Šainović et al.* Appeal Judgement, para. 985; *Krajišnik* Appeal Judgement, paras 215, 695-696. See *Šainović et al.* Appeal Judgement, paras 1233, 1242.
[378]   The Appeals Chamber considers Stanišić's reliance on the *Tolimir* Trial Judgement inapposite as, in the reference cited by Stanišic, the *Tolimir* Trial Chamber recalled in general terms the well-established jurisprudence on liability by omission pursuant to Article 7(1) of the Statute, which does require proof of a legal duty to act, without addressing the specific issue at stake in the present case (see *Tolimir* Trial Judgement, para. 894, fn. 3528).
[379]   See *Šainović et al.* Appeal Judgement, para. 1233, 1242. See also *Šainović et al.* Appeal Judgement, para. 1045; *Martić* Appeal Judgement, para. 28; *Krajišnik* Appeal Judgement, paras 193-194, 204.
[380]   See, *e.g.* Trial Judgement, vol. 2, para. 734, 737-744. See also Trial Judgement, vol. 2, paras 58, 588, 591-595, 729-736.

had committed crimes and to protect the civilian population,[381] despite his duties to do so, together with his ability, as the highest authority, to investigate and punish those who had committed crimes.[382] The Appeals Chamber observes that in the jurisprudence of the Tribunal, a failure to intervene to prevent recurrence of crimes or to halt abuses has been taken into account in assessing an accused's contribution to a joint criminal enterprise and his intent where the accused had some power and influence or authority over the perpetrators sufficient to prevent or halt the abuses but failed to exercise such power.[383] Therefore, Stanišić has not shown that the Trial Chamber applied an erroneous legal standard when it considered instances of his failures to act in assessing whether he contributed to the JCE.

112.   In light of the above, the Appeals Chamber dismisses Stanišic's argument that the Trial Chamber erred in law by failing to set out and apply the correct legal standard for joint criminal enterprise liability through failure to act. The Appeals Chamber therefore need not address Stanišić's further arguments that his failures to act considered by the Trial Chamber do not meet the **[page 50]** purported requirements of contribution to a joint criminal enterprise "by omission"[384] and that, as such, the Trial Chamber erred in considering his failures to act when finding that he contributed to the JCE. His arguments in this regard are therefore dismissed as moot.[385]

(c) Conclusion

113.   Based on the foregoing, the Appeals Chamber dismisses Stanišić's first ground of appeal in part and fifth ground of appeal in part.

4.   Alleged error in failing to pronounce on the issue of re-subordination (Stanišić's first, fifth, and sixth grounds of appeal in part)

(a) Introduction

114.   In its discussion on the "issue of the re-subordination of police to the military",[386] the Trial Chamber noted that "[t]he central question was whether [Stanišić and Župljanin] could be held criminally responsible for the actions of the members of the police who committed crimes while they may have been re-subordinated to the JNA or VRS".[387] Having analysed the evidence relating to this issue,[388] the Trial Chamber concluded that it was "unable to find whether it was the military or the civilian authorities which may have been responsible for the investigation and prosecution of crimes against Muslims and Croats which may have been

---

381   Trial Judgement, vol. 2, paras 695, 698, 754. See Trial Judgement, vol. 2, paras 18, 37-43.
382   Trial Judgement, vol. 2, para. 755.
383   See *Šainović et al.* Appeal Judgement, paras 1233, 1242 (The Appeals Chamber found that the accused's duty to prevent or punish his subordinates' crimes and failure to do so was "not determinative of his criminal responsibility" for joint criminal enterprise liability but "was part of the circumstantial evidence from which his intent and contribution to the JCE could be inferred" (*Šainović et al.* Appeal Judgement, para. 1242)); *Krajišnik* Appeal Judgement, para. 194 (the Appeals Chamber found that the accused had "some power and influence" and "the power to intervene" and that the *Krajišnik* Trial Chamber could rightfully consider his failure to intervene "as one of the elements tending to prove [his] acceptance of certain crimes" (*Krajišnik* Appeal Judgement, para. 194)); *Kvočka et al.* Appeal Judgement, paras 195196 (The Appeals Chamber observed that in concluding that the accused's participation in the functioning of the camp had furthered the criminal purpose, the Trial Chamber had considered *inter alia* its findings "that he held a high-ranking position in the camp and had some degree of authority over the guards; that he had sufficient influence to prevent or halt some of the abuses but that he made use of that influence only very rarely" (*Kvočka et al.* Appeal Judgement, para. 195 (internal citations omitted)). See also *Krajišnik* Appeal Judgement, paras 216(e), 217. For further factual background of the jurisprudence cited in the current footnote, see *Milutinović et al.* Trial Judgement, paras 773, 777, 782; *Krajišnik* Trial Judgement, paras 1118-1119, 1121(e), 1121(j); *Kvočka et al.* Trial Judgement, paras 372, 395-396. See further *infra*, para. 734.
384   Stanišić Appeal Brief, paras 43, 189, 191-194, referring to Decision on Form of the Indictment, para. 39, Trial Judgement, vol. 1, para. 103. See Stanišić Appeal Brief, paras 195-205.
385   To the extent that Stanisić raises factual challenges to the Trial Chamber's findings on his authority and failure to act, the Appeals Chamber will address these arguments, developed in his fifth ground of appeal, under the sub-section dealing with the factual errors he alleges with regard to his contribution to the JCE (see *infra*, paras 246, 303-305, 309, 310, 353).
386   Trial Judgement, vol. 2, para. 317. See Trial Judgement, vol. 2, paras 318-342.
387   Trial Judgement, vol. 2, para. 317.
388   Trial Judgement, vol. 2, paras 320-341. See Trial Judgement, vol. 2, paras 317-319.

committed by policemen re-subordinated to the military".[389] It noted, however, that "criminal responsibility for actions of re-subordinated policemen is primarily of importance for [...] responsibility pursuant to Article 7(3) of the Statute".[390] It further referred to its finding that the JCE existed and that members of the police, the Yugoslav People's Army ("JNA"), and the Army of *Republika Srpska* ("VRS") were all used as tools in the furtherance of the JCE, of which Stanišić and Župljanin were members.[391] On this basis, the Trial Chamber stated that it would consider "whether the actions of policemen which the Defence claims were re-subordinated to the military at the time of the commission of the crimes, can be imputed to a member of the JCE and ultimately to [Stanišić and Župljanin]".[392] Accordingly, **[page 51]** the Trial Chamber concluded that it was "not necessary to make any further findings on the issue of re-subordination".[393]

(b) Submissions of the parties

115.   Stanišić contends that the Trial Chamber erred by failing to pronounce on whether military or civilian authorities were responsible for the investigation and prosecution of crimes against non-Serbs committed by policemen re-subordinated to the military, thereby failing to provide a reasoned opinion.[394] He contends that this failure "gravely impeded" his ability to effectively exercise his right of appeal and "fatally hinders" the Appeals Chamber's capacity to understand and review the Trial Judgement.[395]

116.   More specifically, Stanišić contends that the Trial Chamber's failure to pronounce on the issue of re-subordination "goes to the heart of" his criminal responsibility as "most of the underlying crimes in this case" can be attributed to policemen re-subordinated to the military.[396] In this context, he also argues that the Trial Chamber erred by: (i) relying on his purported failure to investigate or prosecute crimes committed by policemen re-subordinated to the military to find implicitly that he contributed to the JCE;[397] and (ii) attributing the actions of the re-subordinated police to him for the purposes of establishing his JCE membership.[398] Stanišić further argues that the Trial Chamber failed to provide reasons for the contradiction between its finding that he possessed "overall command and control over the RS MUP police forces and all other internal affairs organs" and its inability to pronounce on the issue of re-subordination.[399] In addition, he contends that the Trial Chamber erred by finding that he permitted RS MUP forces under his control to continue to participate in joint operations with other Serb forces, while it made an inconclusive finding on re-subordination and whether Stanišić retained control over such forces.[400]

117.   The Prosecution responds that, in determining Stanišić's responsibility, the Trial Chamber reasonably relied upon his command and control over the RS MUP on the basis of its exhaustive **[page 52]** analysis of evidence and that, by seizing "on the absence of a general finding on resubordination", Stanišić "miscasts" the Trial Judgement.[401] It contends that Stanišić's argument is based on the sweeping yet unsupported assertion that most underlying crimes can be attributed to police who were re-subordinated to the military.[402] The Prosecution further submits that it was "entirely reasonable" for the Trial Chamber to determine

---

[389]   Trial Judgement, vol. 2, para. 342.

[390]   Trial Judgement, vol. 2, para. 342.

[391]   Trial Judgement, vol. 2, para. 342.

[392]   Trial Judgement, vol. 2, para. 342 (citations omitted).

[393]   Trial Judgement, vol. 2, para. 342.

[394]   Stanišić Appeal Brief, paras 22-23, 27-35. See Stanišić Reply Brief, para. 9.

[395]   Stanišić Appeal Brief, para. 28, referring to *Naletilić and Martinović* Appeal Judgement, para. 603. See Stanišić Appeal Brief, para. 27; Stanišić Reply Brief, para. 12, referring to Trial Judgement, vol. 2, paras 321-342; Appeal Hearing, 16 Dec 2015, AT. 95.

[396]   Stanišić Appeal Brief, para. 29. See Appeal Hearing, 16 Dec 2015, AT. 95-96.

[397]   Stanišić Appeal Brief, para. 31. See Stanišić Appeal Brief, paras 29, 227. See also Appeal Hearing, 15 Dec 2015, AT. 94-95, where Stanišić referred to, *inter alia*, the Trial Chamber's findings at paragraphs 737, 740, 743, 745, and 757 of volume two of the Trial Judgement in support of his arguments that the Trial Chamber relied upon the action of police who may have been re-subordinated to the military.

[398]   Stanišić Appeal Brief, para. 34. See Stanišić Appeal Brief, para. 33; Appeal Hearing, 16 Dec 2015, AT. 96. See also Stanišić Appeal Brief, paras 32, 35; Stanišić Reply Brief, para. 13.

[399]   Stanišić Appeal Brief, para. 30, quoting Trial Judgement, vol. 2, para. 736. See Stanišić Appeal Brief, para. 259; Stanišić Reply Brief, para. 10.

[400]   Stanišić Appeal Brief, para. 287.

[401]   Prosecution Response Brief (Stanišić), para. 11.

[402]   Prosecution Response Brief (Stanišić), para. 12, quoting Stanišić Appeal Brief, para. 29.

Stanišić's responsibility on the basis of his failure to investigate and punish subordinates for their crimes against non-Serbs.[403]

(c) Analysis

118.   The Appeals Chamber observes that Stanišić's assertion that the Trial Chamber erred in failing to pronounce on the issue of re-subordination of policemen is based on the premise that "most of the underlying crimes in this case" can be attributed to policemen re-subordinated to the military.[404] The Appeals Chamber notes that this assertion is unsupported by any reference to the Trial Judgement or to evidence on the record and thus may be dismissed without detailed analysis. However, in view of the nature of Stanišić's challenges under this subsection, the Appeals Chamber will further consider this argument.

119.   The Appeals Chamber recalls that "an accused who participated in a [joint criminal enterprise] with the requisite *mens rea* may be held responsible for crimes committed by principal perpetrators who were not [members of the joint criminal enterprise], so long as those crimes were linked with, and therefore can be imputed to, one of the [joint criminal enterprise] members" acting in accordance with the common plan, even if that member is someone other than the accused.[405] Moreover, the link between the principal perpetrators and the joint criminal enterprise member is to be assessed on a case-by-case basis.[406] Whether a joint criminal enterprise member had a duty and ability to investigate and prosecute crimes committed by the principal perpetrators is merely one of **[page 53]** the factors that may be taken into account by a chamber when determining whether crimes can be imputed to that member.[407]

120.   In this regard, the Appeals Chamber notes that the Trial Chamber recalled its findings that the JCE existed and that members of the police, the JNA, and the VRS were all used as tools in the furtherance of the JCE, of which Stanišić and Župljanin were members.[408] It then held, on this basis, that it would consider "whether the actions of policemen which the Defence claims were re-subordinated to the military at the time of the commission of the crimes, can be imputed to a member of the JCE and ultimately to [Stanišić and Župljanin]".[409] This consideration led the Trial Chamber to conclude that it was "not necessary to make any further findings on the issue of re-subordination",[410] even though it was "unable to find whether it was the military or the civilian authorities which may have been responsible for the *investigation and prosecution* of crimes against Muslims and Croats which may have been committed by policemen re-subordinated to the military".[411] Accordingly, the Appeals Chamber discerns no error on the part of the Trial Chamber insofar as it found that there is no legal requirement to make "any further findings on the issue of re-subordination" for the assessment of joint criminal enterprise liability.[412]

121.   However, the Appeals Chamber understands that Stanišić also supports his contention by asserting that the Trial Chamber erred in relying on his purported failure to investigate or prosecute crimes committed by re-subordinated police to find that he contributed to the JCE, and in turn, to establish his membership in

[403]   Prosecution Response Brief (Stanišić), para. 13, referring to Prosecution Response Brief (Stanišić), paras 69-75, 79-84, 133-134, 144-146. In this respect the Prosecution relies upon: (i) the orders Stanišić issued; (ii) Stanišić's role in the operation of detention facilities; and (iii) the breadth of Stanišić's duty to protect the civilian population (Prosecution Response Brief (Stanišić), para. 13). See Appeal Hearing, 16 Dec 2015, AT. 127-128.
[404]   See *supra*, para. 116.
[405]   *Šainović et al.* Appeal Judgement, para. 1520, referring to *Krajišnik* Appeal Judgement, para. 225, *Martić* Appeal Judgement, para. 168, *Brđanin* Appeal Judgement, para. 413. See *Tolimir* Appeal Judgement, para. 432; *Popović et al.* Appeal Judgement, para. 1065.
[406]   *Popović et al.* Appeal Judgement, para. 1053. See *Tolimir* Appeal Judgement, para. 432; *Đorđević* Appeal Judgement, para. 165; *Šainović et al.* Appeal Judgement, para. 1256; *Krajišnik* Appeal Judgement, para. 226.
[407]   See *Šainović et al.* Appeal Judgement, para. 1520. See also *Šainović et al.* Appeal Judgement, paras 1045, 1233, 1242.
[408]   Trial Judgement, vol. 2, para. 342. See Trial Judgement, vol. 2, paras 313, 801-802, 806-807, 810-811, 815-816, 819-820, 824-825, 833-834, 837-838, 846-847, 851-852, 860-861, 865-866, 870-871, 874-876, 878-879, 882-883.
[409]   Trial Judgement, vol. 2, para. 342.
[410]   Trial Judgement, vol. 2, para. 342. Indeed, the Trial Chamber made no such findings and did not specify whether perpetrators of crimes in the Municipalities (that it identified as police, JNA, or VRS) may have been police who were re-subordinated to the military at the time of the commission of the offences.
[411]   Trial Judgement, vol. 2, para. 342 (emphasis added).
[412]   Trial Judgement, vol. 2, para. 342.

the JCE.[413] The Appeals Chamber will therefore now examine whether, as a factual consideration in assessing his contribution to the JCE and intent, the Trial Chamber relied upon his failure to investigate or prosecute crimes of re-subordinated police.

122.   In assessing Stanišić's contribution to the JCE, the Trial Chamber made, *inter alia*, findings in a section entitled "[r]ole in prevention, investigation, and documentation of crimes".[414] In this regard, the Trial Chamber first considered that the civilian law enforcement apparatus failed to function in an impartial manner with respect to the investigation and prosecution of crimes.[415] The **[page 54]** Trial Chamber further found that this "discriminatory failure to properly investigate crimes against non-Serbs contributed to the prevailing culture of impunity and thereby facilitated the perpetration of further crimes [...] in furtherance of the common objective" and considered Stanišić's specific acts and failures to act against this contextual background.[416] This consideration of the contextual background, however, does not mean that the Trial Chamber attributed to Stanišić, personally, a failure to investigate or prosecute crimes of policemen who may have been re-subordinated to the military when it assessed his contribution to the JCE.[417]

123.   With regard to Stanišić's specific acts and failures to act relevant to measures for suppression of crimes, the Appeals Chamber notes that the Trial Chamber specifically considered: (i) that some of the orders Stanišić issued to curb crimes by RS MUP personnel were not carried out to the extent possible, given that the reserve police – among whom the problem of "unprincipled conduct" was most pronounced – were able to continue to serve within the RS MUP until the end of 1992;[418] (ii) Stanišić's failure to fulfil his duty "to discipline and dismiss [RS MUP personnel] who had committed crimes", in violation of his professional obligation to protect and safeguard the civilian population;[419] (iii) Stanišić's "ability as the highest authority to investigate and punish those found to be involved [in the theft of vehicles], even when faced by opposition from others in the Bosnian Serb leadership";[420] (iv) his actions against paramilitaries in relation only to "acts of theft, looting, and trespasses against the local RS leaders";[421] and, finally (v) his failure to take the same "decisive" action (as he took with regard to the aforementioned paramilitaries) *vis-a-vis* other crimes, such as unlawful detention, forcible displacement, killings, and inhumane treatment, **[page 55]** committed against non-Serbs, which were brought to his attention.[422] In addition, the Trial Chamber considered that Stanišić's instructions to the chiefs of CSBs regarding documentation of war crimes were limited to cases involving Serb victims.[423] Having considered Stanišić's specific acts and failures to act as described above,

[413]   Stanišić Appeal Brief, para. 31, read together with Stanišić Appeal Brief, paras 29, 34. See also *supra*, para. 116.
[414]   Trial Judgement, vol. 2, paras 745-759.
[415]   Trial Judgement, vol. 2, para. 745.
[416]   Trial Judgement, vol. 2, para. 745. See Trial Judgement, vol. 2, paras 746-759.
[417]   In the Appeals Chamber's view, this approach is confirmed by the fact that the specific findings set out in paragraphs 745-759 of volume two of the Trial Judgement are based on evidence addressed elsewhere in the Trial Judgement. In this regard, the Appeals Chamber notes that the Trial Chamber's finding on the failure of the civilian law enforcement apparatus is based on its analysis of the evidence in the section on the general description of the judiciary in the region at the relevant time (see Trial Judgement, vol. 2, paras 85-94), while the Trial Chamber's findings on his specific acts and omissions are based on the analysis of the evidence in the section specifically examining his personal acts and conduct (see *e.g.* Trial Judgement, vol. 2, paras 610-614 (Stanišić's orders to subordinates), 636 (Stanišić's letter to Witness Đerić), 640-641, 644, (Stanišić's orders of 23, 24, and 27 July 1992, 646 (reports of 5 and 6 August 1992), 651-663 (response to international outcry), 687 (placement of suspended RS MUP personnel under the VRS), 664-670 (Stanišić's orders of 8, 10, and 17 August), 675 (Stanišić's order of 24 August), 695-720 (disciplinary measures and actions against paramilitaries)).
[418]   Trial Judgement, vol. 2, para. 746. See Trial Judgement, vol. 2, paras 748-749, 752-753.
[419]   Trial Judgement, vol. 2, para. 754. See Trial Judgement, vol. 2, para. 755.
[420]   Trial Judgement, vol. 2, para. 755. The Trial Chamber also found that this ability is demonstrated by Stanišić's efforts to quell the theft of vehicles "by issuing orders to monitor and protect the facilities, requiring immediate inspection and reporting by chiefs of CSBs, instituting disciplinary action leading to dismissal from service of police officers involved in the crime, and his relentless airing of the issue as a matter of personal concern" (Trial Judgement, vol. 2, para. 755).
[421]   Trial Judgement, vol. 2, para. 756. In relation to such actions, the Trial Chamber found that Stanišić "raised the issue of the problems these [paramilitary] forces caused with the Prime Minister Branko Đerić" and alluded to evidence it had considered elsewhere regarding the operations instantiated by Stanišić aimed at the arrest and disarmament of the Yellow Wasps and other paramilitary groups (Trial Judgement, vol. 2, para. 756. See Trial Judgement, vol. 2, paras 713-720).
[422]   Trial Judgement, vol. 2, para. 757. With regard to unlawful detention, the Trial Chamber further found that he "contributed to [the] continued existence and operation [of detention and penitentiary facilities] by failing to take decisive action to close these facilities or, at the very least, by failing to withdraw the RS MUP forces from their involvement in these detention centres" (Trial Judgement, vol. 2, para. 761).
[423]   Trial Judgement, vol. 2, para. 758.

the Trial Chamber concluded that Stanišić "permitted RS MUP forces under his overall control to continue to participate in joint operations in the Municipalities with other Serb forces involved in the commission of crimes" and took insufficient action to put an end to crimes, despite his knowledge thereof.[424]

124.   In the view of the Appeals Chamber, the foregoing shows that the Trial Chamber assessed Stanišić's role in the prevention, investigation, and documentation of crimes by reference to factors that are distinct from, and do not relate to a failure by civilian or military authorities to investigate or prosecute crimes that may have been committed by re-subordinated police.[425] It follows that the Trial Chamber did not attribute to Stanišić, personally, a failure to investigate or prosecute crimes of re-subordinated policemen when it assessed his contribution to the JCE. Not only is Stanišić's implication that the Trial Chamber relied upon such a failure unsubstantiated by any reference to the Trial Judgement, but it is also not borne out by the Trial Chamber's reasoning.[426] The Appeals Chamber further finds that, to the extent the Trial Chamber relied upon Stanišić's contribution to the JCE in assessing his intent required for joint criminal enterprise liability,[427] Stanišić has failed to demonstrate that the Trial Chamber, either explicitly or implicitly, attributed to him a failure to investigate or prosecute policemen who may have been re-subordinated to the military.[428]

125.   The Appeals Chamber therefore finds that Stanišić has not demonstrated that the pronouncement on whether military or civilian authorities were responsible for the investigation and prosecution of crimes committed by re-subordinated policemen is a factual finding that was **[page 56]** essential to the determination of his guilt, the lack of which would result in a failure to provide a reasoned opinion.[429]

126.   The Appeals Chamber now moves to Stanišić's argument that the Trial Chamber's finding that he had "overall command and control over the RS MUP police forces" is contradicted by the Trial Chamber's stated inability to determine whether civilian or military apparatuses were responsible for the investigation and prosecution of crimes allegedly committed by re-subordinated police.[430] In this regard, the Appeals Chamber notes that the Trial Chamber's finding concerning Stanišić's command and control over the RS MUP was based upon his: (i) assignment of trusted members of the Ministry of Interior of the Socialist Republic of BiH ("SRBiH MUP" and "SRBiH", respectively) to important positions; (ii) appointment of SJB chiefs in accordance with recommendations of regional authorities; (iii) assignment of SJBs to newly established CSBs; (iv) orders requiring personnel from headquarters to inspect and visit municipalities; (v) orders regarding the investigation of crimes allegedly committed by RS MUP members; and (vi) actions in reassigning criminal elements from the police to the army.[431] In light of this, the Appeals Chamber considers that Stanišić has failed to demonstrate how the Trial Chamber's conclusion is undermined by its inability to determine whether civilian or military authorities were responsible for the investigation or prosecution of certain crimes which may have been committed by policemen re-subordinated to the military.

127.   Insofar as Stanišić's argues that he did not have command and control over police forces re-subordinated to the military, the Appeals Chamber recalls the Trial Chamber's finding that, pursuant to an order issued by Stanišić on 15 May 1992, organising RS MUP forces into war units ("Stanišić's 15 May 1992 Order"), RS MUP units re-subordinated to the armed forces were to act in compliance with military regulations, "but would remain 'under the command' of designated Ministry officials".[432] Stanišić has

---

[424]   Trial Judgement, vol. 2, para. 759.

[425]   For instance, the Trial Chamber found that Stanišić failed to fulfil his duty to discipline and dismiss "personnel of his Ministry who had committed crimes" and his failed attempts to take actions in this respect against Malko Koroman, Stevan Todorović, Witness Petrović, Borislav Maksimović, and Simo Drljača, resulted in a violation of his "professional obligation to protect and safeguard the civilian population in the territories under their control" (Trial Judgement, vol. 2, para. 754). The Appeals Chamber notes that Stanišić's challenges to the Trial Chamber's findings in this respect are dismissed elsewhere in this Judgement (see *supra*, paras 203-208).

[426]   See Stanišić Appeal Brief, para. 31. See also *supra*, para. 116.

[427]   See Trial Judgement, vol. 2, paras 766-769.

[428]   With respect to the Trial Chamber's assessment of the subjective element of the first category of joint criminal enterprise, see Trial Judgement, vol. 2, paras 766-769; *infra*, paras 366-585.

[429]   *Stanišić and Simatović* Appeal Judgement, para. 78; *Popović et al.* Appeal Judgement, para. 1906; *Haradinaj et al.* Appeal Judgement, paras 77, 128.

[430]   See *supra*, para. 116. See also Trial Judgement, vol. 2, paras 342, 736.

[431]   Trial Judgement, vol. 2, para. 736.

[432]   Trial Judgement, vol. 2, para. 588, referring to Alexander Krulj, 27 Oct 2009, T. 2079-2082, Sreto Gajić, 15 Jul 2010, T. 12856-12858, Drago Borovčanin, 23 Feb 2010, T. 6678-6679, Andrija Bjelošević, 15 Apr 2011, T. 19651-19652, Vidosav Kovačević, 8 Sep 2011, T. 23809-23811, Exhibit 1D46, pp 1-2. See Trial Judgement, vol. 2, para. 330. See also *supra*, para. 242.

therefore failed to show a contradiction in the relevant findings of the Trial Chamber. In the same vein, the Appeals Chamber is not persuaded by Stanišić's assertion that the Trial Chamber's inconclusive finding on the issue of re-subordination undermines **[page 57]** its finding that he permitted RS MUP forces under his control to continue to participate in joint operations with other Serb forces.[433]

128.   The Appeals Chamber notes that Stanišić does not advance any further specific arguments demonstrating that in assessing his contribution to the JCE and intent to establish his membership in the JCE, the Trial Chamber relied on its findings that would be contradictory to its finding that it was unable to determine whether civilian or military authorities were responsible for the investigation and prosecution of crimes allegedly committed by re-subordinated policemen. Therefore, the Appeals Chamber finds no merit in Stanišić's unreferenced, general contention that the Trial Chamber erred in relying upon and attributing actions of the re-subordinated police to Stanišić for the purposes of establishing his JCE membership despite the aforementioned inconclusive finding.[434]

129.   Consequently, the Appeals Chamber finds that Stanišić has failed to demonstrate that the Trial Chamber erred in failing to pronounce on whether military or civilian authorities were responsible for the investigation and prosecution of crimes against non-Serbs which may have been committed by policemen re-subordinated to the military.

(d) Conclusion

130.   In light of the foregoing, the Appeals Chamber dismisses Stanišić's first, fifth, and sixth grounds of appeal in part.

5.   Alleged errors in finding that Stanišić contributed to the JCE

(a) Introduction

131.   Under the subheading "Stanišić's contribution to JCE", the Trial Chamber made a number of findings concerning the following several factors: (i) Stanišić's role in the creation of Bosnian Serb bodies and policies;[435] (ii) the role of RS MUP forces in combat activities and takeovers of the Municipalities;[436] (iii) his role in the prevention, investigation, and documentation of crimes;[437] and (iv) his role in unlawful arrests and detentions.[438] The Appeals Chamber notes that the Trial Chamber's findings under this subheading lack cross-references to earlier underlying findings in the Trial Judgement or citations to evidence on the record. Moreover, the Trial Chamber did not enter **[page 58]** any express finding as to whether Stanišić's acts and conduct furthered the common purpose of the JCE or whether his contribution to the JCE was significant.

132.   Stanišić submits that the Trial Chamber erred by failing to provide a reasoned opinion with respect to his contribution to the JCE.[439] Further, Stanišić argues that the Trial Chamber committed numerous errors of fact in its assessment of his contribution to the JCE.[440] As a result of these errors, Stanišić avers that the Appeals Chamber must quash the convictions under Counts 1, 4, and 6.[441]

133.   The Prosecution responds that Stanišić fails to demonstrate the absence of a reasoned opinion.[442] It also avers that the Trial Chamber reasonably found that Stanišić contributed to the JCE in numerous ways, and submits that Stanišić's arguments challenging the Trial Chamber's findings in this respect should be rejected.[443]

---

[433]   See *supra*, para. 116. See also Trial Judgement, vol. 2, para. 759.
[434]   See Stanišić Appeal Brief, para. 34. See also *supra*, para. 116.
[435]   Trial Judgement, vol. 2, paras 729-736.
[436]   Trial Judgement, vol. 2, paras 737-744.
[437]   Trial Judgement, vol. 2, paras 745-759.
[438]   Trial Judgement, vol. 2, paras 760-765.
[439]   Stanišić Appeal Brief, paras 25, 42, 44-46, 235, 239-242. See Stanišić Appeal Brief, para. 22.
[440]   Stanišić Appeal Brief, paras 236-238, 243-300.
[441]   Stanišić Appeal Brief, paras 53, 301.
[442]   Prosecution Response Brief (Stanišić), paras 14-18, 93.
[443]   Prosecution Response Brief (Stanišić), paras 92-93, 153. See Prosecution Response Brief (Stanišić), paras 94-152.

(b) Alleged error in failing to provide a reasoned opinion on Stanišić's contribution to the JCE (Stanišić's first ground of appeal in part and subsection (A) of Stanišić's sixth ground of appeal)

(i) Submissions of the parties

134.   Stanišić argues that the Trial Chamber did not "make any specific findings as to whether and how [he] contributed, let alone significantly contributed, to furthering the JCE",[444] and thereby erred by failing to provide a reasoned opinion.[445] Stanišić asserts that the section of the Trial Judgement devoted to his contribution to the JCE outlines a series of findings "without any conclusion that those findings furthered the common purpose of the JCE".[446] In this respect, he submits that the Trial Chamber did not provide any indication of the evidence relied upon or excluded.[447] According to Stanišić, even a detailed review of the paragraphs concerning his responsibility does not allow him to understand the Trial Chamber's rationale for finding that he contributed to the JCE.[448] He avers, finally, that the Trial Chamber's failure to refer to other **[page 59]** findings supporting its conclusions regarding Stanišić's contribution, and its failure to enter an explicit finding on such essential elements as his contribution and its significance, hindered his ability to appeal his conviction,[449] as he has had to challenge "every single finding possibly linked to his contribution".[450]

135.   The Prosecution responds that Stanišić's mere assertion that he was unable to understand the Trial Chamber's reasoning with respect to his contributions to the JCE fails to show an absence of a reasoned opinion.[451] According to the Prosecution, despite the absence of an express finding, it is clear that the Trial Chamber was satisfied that Stanišić made a significant contribution to the JCE, given: (i) its correct recitation of the law;[452] (ii) the numerous contributions which it found Stanišić to have made;[453] and (iii) the finding that Stanišić was a member of the JCE.[454] The Prosecution asserts that Stanišić focuses on the Trial Chamber's findings in isolation without showing that, "based on the totality of his many contributions, no reasonable finder of fact could have concluded that he made a significant contribution to the JCE".[455] Finally, the Prosecution submits that Stanišić fails to demonstrate that the alleged deficiencies in the Trial Chamber's analysis of his contributions to the JCE have impaired his right of appeal.[456]

(ii) Analysis

136.   The Appeals Chamber recalls that in order to find an accused criminally responsible pursuant to joint criminal enterprise liability, a trial chamber must be satisfied that the accused "participated in furthering the

---

[444]   Stanišić Appeal Brief, para. 235.
[445]   Stanišić Appeal Brief, paras 25, 42. See Appeal Hearing, 16 Dec 2015, AT. 104, 106-107. Stanišić submits that the Prosecution acknowledges the Trial Chamber's failure to enter a finding that he significantly contributed to the furtherance of the purported JCE (Stanišić Reply Brief, para. 68).
[446]   Stanišić Appeal Brief, para. 239. Stanišić, in this context, also submits that the Trial Chamber merely summarised the evidence and "in the majority of instances incorrectly" (Stanišić Appeal Brief, para. 240). The Appeals Chamber notes that Stanišić does not provide any specific references to Trial Chamber findings or evidence on the record. His factual challenges relating to specific findings are set out elsewhere in this Judgement. See *infra*, paras 143-355.
[447]   Stanišić Appeal Brief, para. 241.
[448]   Stanišić Appeal Brief, para. 45. See Stanišić Appeal Brief, para. 241.
[449]   Stanišić Appeal Brief, paras 42, 44 (referring to the lack of references in the findings contained in paragraphs 729-765 of volume two of the Trial Judgement).
[450]   Stanišić Appeal Brief, paras 46, 242.
[451]   Prosecution Response Brief (Stanišić), paras 14, 17. See Prosecution Response Brief (Stanišić), paras 18, 93.
[452]   Prosecution Response Brief (Stanišić), para. 93, referring to Trial Judgement, vol. 1, para. 103. See Prosecution Response Brief (Stanišić), para. 17.
[453]   Prosecution Response Brief (Stanišić), para. 93, referring to Prosecution Response Brief (Stanišić), para. 92. See Prosecution Response Brief (Stanišić), para. 17, referring to Trial Judgement, vol. 2, paras 729-765, 928.
[454]   Prosecution Response Brief (Stanišić), para. 93, referring to Trial Judgement, vol. 1, para. 103, Trial Judgement, vol. 2, para. 928. See Prosecution Response Brief (Stanišić), para. 17, referring to Trial Judgement, vol. 1, para. 103, Trial Judgement, vol. 2, paras 729-765, 928; Prosecution Response Brief (Stanišić), para. 928.
[455]   Prosecution Response Brief (Stanišić), para. 93. See Prosecution Response Brief (Stanišić), para. 17.
[456]   Prosecution Response Brief (Stanišić), paras 14, 17.

common purpose at the core of the JCE"[457] and must characterise the accused's contribution in this common plan.[458] Although an accused's contribution need not be necessary or substantial, it should at least be a significant contribution to the crimes for which the accused is held responsible.[459] Not every type of conduct would amount to a significant enough **[page 60]** contribution to the crimes encompassed in the common purpose, thus giving rise to joint criminal enterprise liability.[460] The Appeals Chamber observes that the Trial Chamber correctly set out the applicable law in this respect.[461]

137.   The Appeals Chamber further recalls that pursuant to Article 23(2) of the Statute and Rule 98*ter*(C) of the Rules, trial chambers are required to give a reasoned opinion.[462] The factual and legal findings on which a trial chamber relied upon to convict or acquit an accused should be set out in a clear and articulate manner.[463] In particular, a trial chamber is required to make findings on those facts which are essential to the determination of guilt on a particular count.[464] The absence of any relevant legal findings in a trial judgement also constitutes a manifest failure to provide a reasoned opinion.[465] A reasoned opinion in the trial judgement is essential, *inter alia*, for allowing a meaningful exercise of the right of appeal by the parties and enabling the Appeals Chamber to understand and review the trial chamber's findings and its evaluation of the evidence.[466] An appellant claiming an error of law because of the lack of a reasoned opinion needs to identify the specific issues, factual findings, or arguments, which he submits the trial chamber omitted to address and to explain why this omission invalidated the decision.[467]

138.   The Appeals Chamber first turns to Stanišić's submission that the Trial Chamber failed to indicate the evidence relied upon or excluded in the section of the Trial Judgement addressing Stanišić's contribution and as such failed to provide a reasoned opinion. The Appeals Chamber notes that the section of the Trial Judgement on Stanišić's contribution to the JCE indeed does not refer to the evidence relied upon by the Trial Chamber to support its findings. Neither does it include any cross-references to its earlier findings where the Trial Chamber analysed the evidence.[468] The Appeals Chamber, however, recalls that a trial judgement must be read as a **[page 61]** whole.[469] Furthermore, there is a presumption that a trial chamber has evaluated all the evidence presented to it, as long as there is no indication that the trial chamber completely disregarded any particular piece of evidence.[470] As Stanišić acknowledges in his own submission,[471] in the section of the Trial Judgement addressing his contribution to the JCE, the Trial Chamber summarised the evidence that it had relied on in other sections of the Trial Judgement. While the Appeals Chamber considers the Trial

---

[457]   *Brđanin* Appeal Judgement, para. 427. See *Popović et al.* Appeal Judgement, para. 1378; *Šainović et al.* Appeal Judgement, paras 954, 987, 1177, 1445; *Krajišnik* Appeal Judgement, paras 218, 695.

[458]   *Brđanin* Appeal Judgement, para. 430.

[459]   *Popović et al.* Appeal Judgement, para. 1378; *Krajišnik* Appeal Judgement, paras 215, 695; *Brđanin* Appeal Judgement, para. 430, referring to *Kvočka et al.* Appeal Judgement, paras 97-98. See *Šainović et al.* Appeal Judgement, paras 954, 987.

[460]   *Šainović et al.* Appeal Judgement, para. 988. See *Brđanin* Appeal Judgement, para. 427.

[461]   The Trial Chamber found that "an accused must have participated in furthering the common purpose at the core of the joint criminal enterprise" and that "[although the contribution need not be necessary or substantial, it should at least be a significant contribution to the crimes for which the accused is to be found responsible" (Trial Judgement, vol. 1, para. 103, referring to *Brđanin* Appeal Judgement, para. 430).

[462]   *Stanišić and Simatović* Appeal Judgement, para. 78; *Popović et al.* Appeal Judgement, paras 1123, 1367, 1771; *Haradinaj et al.* Appeal Judgement, para. 128. See *Nyiramasuhuko et al.* Appeal Judgement, paras 729, 1954; *Bizimungu* Appeal Judgement, para. 18; *Ndindiliyimana et al.* Appeal Judgement, para. 293.

[463]   *Stanišić and Simatović* Appeal Judgement, para. 78; *Popović et al.* Appeal Judgement, para. 1906; *Haradinaj et al.* Appeal Judgement, paras 77, 128; *Hadžihasanović and Kubura* Appeal Judgement, para. 13. See *Bizimungu* Appeal Judgement, paras 18-19; *Ndindiliyimana et al.* Appeal Judgement, para. 293.

[464]   *Stanišić and Simatović* Appeal Judgement, para. 78; *Popović et al.* Appeal Judgement, paras 1771,1906, referring to *Haradinaj et al.* Appeal Judgement, para. 128; *Hadžihasanovićand Kubura* Appeal Judgement, para. 13.

[465]   *Stanišić and Simatović* Appeal Judgement, para. 78; *Bizimungu* Appeal Judgement, para. 19.

[466]   *Stanišić and Simatović* Appeal Judgement, para. 78; *Popović et al.* Appeal Judgement, paras 1123, 1367, 1771; *Haradinaj et al.* Appeal Judgement, para. 128; *Nyiramasuhuko et al.* Appeal Judgement, para. 729; *Bizimungu* Appeal Judgement, para. 18.

[467]   *Popović et al.* Appeal Judgement, paras 1367, 1771; *Kvočka et al.* Appeal Judgement, para. 25.

[468]   See Trial Judgement, vol. 2, paras 729-765.

[469]   *Šainović et al.* Appeal Judgement, paras 306, 321; *Boškoski and Tarčulovski* Appeal Judgement, para. 67; *Orić* Appeal Judgement, para. 38.

[470]   *Popović et al.* Appeal Judgement, para. 306; *Đorđević* Appeal Judgement, fn. 2527; *Haradinaj et al.* Appeal Judgement, para. 129; *Kvočka et al.* Appeal Judgement, para. 23.

[471]   See Stanišić Appeal Brief, paras 46, 240.

Chamber's approach regrettable,[472] it does not, in its view, amount to a failure to provide a reasoned opinion in and of itself. The Appeals Chamber therefore dismisses Stanišić's argument.

139.   In relation to Stanišić's submission that the Trial Chamber failed to provide a reasoned opinion as to whether and how his acts and conduct furthered the JCE, and whether his alleged contribution to the JCE was significant, the Appeals Chamber notes that the Trial Chamber indeed did not enter express findings in this regard. The Appeals Chamber recalls that these are legal requirements in order for joint criminal enterprise liability to be incurred[473] and that not every type of conduct will amount to a significant enough contribution to the crime to give rise to criminal liability.[474] A trial chamber's determination of whether and to what extent an accused's acts and conduct furthered the joint criminal enterprise, and whether the requisite threshold of significance is met, are therefore relevant legal findings essential to the determination of an accused's guilt, and must be set out in a clear and articulate manner.[475] The lack of explicit findings in this regard falls short of what is required under Article 23(2) of the Statute and Rule 98*ter*(C) of the Rules.[476] Neither Stanišić nor the Appeals Chamber should be expected to engage in a speculative exercise to discern the Trial Chamber's findings in this regard.[477] **[page 62]**

140.   In this context, the Appeals Chamber further considers that the absence of these essential legal findings and the accompanying reasoning have necessarily hindered Stanišić's ability to appeal his conviction, as he would have been unable to identify exactly which underlying factual findings the Trial Chamber relied upon in its ultimate conclusion that he contributed significantly to the furtherance of the JCE. The Appeals Chamber therefore finds that the Trial Chamber's failure to enter express findings as to whether and how Stanišić's acts and conduct furthered the JCE, and whether his contribution was significant constitutes a failure to provide a reasoned opinion.

(iii) Conclusion

141.   The Appeals Chamber finds that the Trial Chamber's failure to indicate the evidence relied upon or excluded in the section of the Trial Judgement addressing Stanišić's contribution to the JCE does not amount to a failure to provide a reasoned opinion and dismisses Stanišić's argument in this respect. The Appeals Chamber concludes, however, that the Trial Chamber failed to provide a reasoned opinion by failing to make express findings as to whether Stanišić's acts and conduct furthered the JCE, and whether his contribution was significant. Accordingly, the Appeals Chamber grants Stanišić's arguments in this regard.

142.   The Trial Chamber's failure to provide a reasoned opinion constitutes an error of law which allows the Appeals Chamber to consider the Trial Chamber's factual findings and evidence relied upon by the Trial Chamber and identified by the parties in order to determine whether a reasonable trier of fact could have concluded beyond reasonable doubt that the requisite element of contribution was established in relation to

---

[472]   See *supra*, para. 90.

[473]   *Popović et al.* Appeal Judgement, para. 1378; *Krajišnik* Appeal Judgement, paras 215, 218, 695; *Brđanin* Appeal Judgement, paras 427, 430. See *supra*, para. 136.

[474]   *Šainović et al.* Appeal Judgement, para. 988; *Brđanin* Appeal Judgement, para. 427.

[475]   *Stanišić and Simatović* Appeal Judgement, para. 78; *Popović et al.* Appeal Judgement, para. 1906; *Bizimungu* Appeal Judgement, paras 18-19.

[476]   See *Kordić and Čerkez* Appeal Judgement, paras 384-385; *Bizimungu* Appeal Judgement, paras 18-19.

[477]   *Cf. Orić* Appeal Judgement, para. 56. The Trial Judgement must enable the Appeals Chamber to discharge its task pursuant to Article 25 of the Statute based on a sufficient determination as to what evidence has been accepted as proof of all elements of the mode of liability charged (*Cf. Kordić and Čerkez* Appeal Judgement, para. 385). The Appeals Chamber notes that, by contrast, after analysing Župljanin's conduct, the Trial Chamber concluded that "during the Indictment period, Stojan Župljanin significantly contributed to the common objective to permanently remove Bosnian Muslims and Bosnian Croats from the territory of the planned Serbian state" (Trial Judgement, vol. 2, para. 518. See Trial Judgement, vol. 2, para. 510 (holding that Župljanin's "omission to take adequate measures to stop the mass arrest of non-Serbs and his policemen's involvement therein constituted at least a significant contribution to the unlawful arrests, if not a substantial one")). The Appeals Chamber considers that the different approach taken with respect to Župljanin further highlights the Trial Chamber's failure to enter the requisite findings with respect to Stanišić (see *Bizimungu* Appeal Judgement, para. 19 and fn. 52 (wherein the Appeals Chamber noted that "[b]y contrast, the Trial Chamber did enter relevant legal findings with respect to other convictions", specifying that the trial chamber made "legal findings on the crime of genocide in relation to Ndindiliyamana")).

Stanišić's joint criminal enterprise liability.[478] Consequently, the Appeals Chamber will assess below the Trial Chamber's findings and relevant evidence concerning Stanišić's acts and conduct to determine whether a reasonable trier of fact could have concluded beyond reasonable doubt that his acts and conduct furthered the common criminal purpose of the JCE and, ultimately, that his contribution to the JCE was significant.[479] As Stanišić raises further arguments challenging specific factual findings of the Trial Chamber related to his acts and conduct, the Appeals Chamber shall conduct this assessment after addressing these remaining challenges.[480] **[page 63]**

(c) Alleged errors of fact with regard to Stanišić's contribution to the JCE (Stanišić's fifth ground of appeal in part and subsection (B) of Stanišić's sixth ground of appeal)

143.   As recalled above, in assessing Stanišić's contribution to the JCE, the Trial Chamber made findings concerning: (i) his role in the creation of Bosnian Serb bodies and policies;[481] (ii) the role of RS MUP forces in combat activities and takeovers of RS municipalities;[482] (iii) Stanišić's role in the prevention, investigation, and documentation of crimes;[483] and (iv) his role in unlawful arrests and detentions.[484]

144.   Stanišić presents a number of challenges in relation to the Trial Chamber's consideration of each of these factors in its assessment of his contribution to the JCE.[485] The Prosecution responds that Stanišić fails to show any error in the Trial Chamber's findings and that his arguments should therefore be dismissed.[486] The Appeals Chamber will address Stanišić's challenges in turn.

(i) Alleged errors in relation to Stanišić's role in the creation of Bosnian Serb bodies and policies (subsection (B)(i) of Stanišić's sixth ground of appeal)

145.   In its discussion of Stanišić's role in the creation of Bosnian Serb bodies and policies,[487] the Trial Chamber referred to, *inter alia*, his: (i) involvement in establishing Bosnian Serb institutions in BiH, including the SDS and the RS MUP;[488] (ii) close relationship with Karadžić and direct communication with an institution that consisted of the President of the RS and senior members of SDS ("RS Presidency");[489] (iii) knowledge of the Instructions for the Organisation and Activities of the Organs of the Serb People in BiH in a State of Emergency adopted by the SDS Main Board on 19 December 1991 ("Variant A and B Instructions" or "Instructions");[490] (iv) key-role in the decision-making authorities from early 1992 onwards;[491] (v) authority with respect to the RS MUP;[492] and (vi) overall command and control over the RS MUP police forces and of all other internal affairs organs.[493] The Trial Chamber found that, "[b]y his participation in the Bosnian Serb **[page 64]** institutions, [Stanišić] participated in the enunciation and implementation of the Bosnian Serb policy, as it evolved."[494] The Trial Chamber concluded that his conduct, presence at key meetings, attendance at sessions of the Bosnian Serb Assembly ("BSA"), acceptance of the position of

---

[478]   *Cf. Kordić and Čerkez* Appeal Judgement, paras 383-388; *Nyiramasuhuko et al.* Appeal Judgement, para. 977; *Bizimungu* Appeal Judgement, para. 23; *Ndindiliyimana et al.* Appeal Judgement, para. 293. See *supra*, para. 19.
[479]   See *infra*, paras 143-355.
[480]   See *infra*, paras 356-364.
[481]   Trial Judgement, vol. 2, paras 729-736.
[482]   Trial Judgement, vol. 2, paras 737-744.
[483]   Trial Judgement, vol. 2, paras 745-759.
[484]   Trial Judgement, vol. 2, paras 760-765.
[485]   Stanišić Appeal Brief, para. 238. See Stanišić Appeal Brief, paras 243-301.
[486]   Prosecution Response Brief (Stanišić), paras 92-93, 153. See Prosecution Response Brief (Stanišić), paras 92-153.
[487]   Trial Judgement, vol. 2, paras 729-736.
[488]   Trial Judgement, vol. 2, paras 729, 734.
[489]   Trial Judgement, vol. 2, para. 730. The Trial Chamber found that the RS Presidency was a small institution that consisted of the President of the RS and senior members of the SDS, namely Koljević and Plavšić, which was expanded at some point to include more members, such as Witness Deric, former Prime Minister of the RS, who was not a member of the SDS (Trial Judgement, vol. 2, para. 137).
[490]   Trial Judgement, vol. 2, para. 731.
[491]   Trial Judgement, vol. 2, para. 732.
[492]   Trial Judgement, vol. 2, para. 733.
[493]   Trial Judgement, vol. 2, para. 736.
[494]   Trial Judgement, vol. 2, para. 734.

Minister of Interior—all indicate "his voluntary participation in the creation of a separate Serb entity within BiH by the ethnic division of the territory".[495]

146.   Stanišić challenges the Trial Chamber's findings with regard to the six factors set out above.[496] In addition, he contends that the errors in relation to these factors cumulatively led the Trial Chamber to erroneously find that he participated in the enunciation and implementation of the Bosnian Serb policy as it evolved.[497] The Prosecution responds that Stanišić was involved in all stages of the creation of the Bosnian Serb institutions and that, through his participation in such institutions, he also participated in the enunciation and implementation of Bosnian Serb policy.[498] The Appeals Chamber will address Stanišić's challenges in turn.

> a. Alleged errors in the Trial Chamber's findings regarding Stanišić's involvement in establishing Bosnian Serb institutions in BiH

147.   The Trial Chamber found that Stanišić was involved in the establishment of the SDS, displayed discontentment with the representation of Serbs within the SRBiH MUP, and attempted to intervene to retain and recruit Serbs within the SRBiH MUP.[499] The Trial Chamber also found that Stanišić worked to promote the interests, and implement the decisions, of the SDS in the SRBiH MUP and was involved in all the stages of the creation of the Bosnian Serb institutions in BiH, in particular the RS MUP.[500]

> i. Submissions of the parties

148.   Stanišić submits that the Trial Chamber erred by finding that he was involved in establishing the SDS. Referring to the transcript of the 36th session of the BSA in December 1993 ("December 1993 BSA Transcript" and "December 1993 BSA Session", respectively) and the testimonies of Witness Slobodan Škipina ("Witness Škipina"), Witness Vitomir Žepinić ("Witness Žepinić"), and Witness Radomir Njeguš ("Witness Njeguš"),[501] he asserts that the **[page 65]** evidence shows that he "was a member of the preparatory committee of the Democratic Party of BiH and not of the Serbian Democratic Party".[502] With respect to the Trial Chamber's finding that he was involved "in all stages" of the creation of "Bosnian Serb institutions", Stanišić contends that it only refers to the RS MUP – the creation of which was in line with the Cutileiro Plan – and that his involvement was "precisely the duty of the Minister of the Interior".[503] With respect to the Trial Chamber's conclusion that Stanišić showed discontentment regarding Serb representation in the SRBiH MUP and attempted to intervene,[504] he argues that this conclusion is erroneous and that he instead sought to have the agreement on the distribution of personnel that the SDS, the Party of Democratic Action ("SDA"), and the Croatian Democratic Union ("HDZ") had reached, upheld and followed.[505]

149.   The Prosecution responds that Stanišić's argument should be dismissed.[506] It submits that Stanišić repeats his trial argument concerning his involvement in establishing the SDS without showing that the Trial Chamber erred.[507] It also asserts that the December 1993 BSA Transcript, which refers to Stanišić having been part of the first SDS Main Board and a member of the Preparatory Committee for establishing the

---

[495]   Trial Judgement, vol. 2, para. 734.
[496]   Stanišić Appeal Brief, paras 243-259.
[497]   Stanišić Appeal Brief, para. 260.
[498]   Prosecution Response Brief (Stanišić), para. 94; Appeal Hearing, 16 Dec 2015, AT. 111-112.
[499]   Trial Judgement, vol. 2, para. 729.
[500]   Trial Judgement, vol. 2, para. 734.
[501]   Stanišić Appeal Brief, para. 243, referring to Exhibit P1999, pp 56-57, Slobodan Škipina, 30 Mar 2010, T. 8295, Slobodan Škipina, 1 Apr 2010, T. 8453, Vitomir Žepinić, 28 Jan 2010, T. 5707-5708, Radomir Njeguš, 7 Jun 2010, T. 11308.
[502]   Stanišić Appeal Brief, para. 243. See Stanišić Reply Brief, para. 69.
[503]   Stanišić Reply Brief, para. 69. See Stanišić Reply Brief, para. 68.
[504]   Stanišić Appeal Brief, para. 243, referring to Trial Judgement, vol. 2, para. 729.
[505]   Stanišić Appeal Brief, para. 243, referring to Exhibit 1D115.
[506]   Prosecution Response Brief (Stanišić), para. 97.
[507]   Prosecution Response Brief (Stanišić), para. 97, contrasting Stanišić Appeal Brief, para. 243 with *Prosecutor v. Mićo Stanišić and Stojan Župljanin*, Case No. IT-08-91-T, Mr. Mico Stanišić's Final Written Submissions Pursuant to Rule 86, 14 May 2012 (confidential with confidential annex A) ("Stanišić Final Trial Brief"), paras 32-37.

Party,[508] and the testimonies of Witness Škipina, Witness Žepinić, and Witness Njeguš, which confirm Stanišić's close ties with the SDS,[509] support the Trial Chamber's finding.[510] The Prosecution also contends that it was reasonable for the Trial Chamber to conclude, based on Stanišić's efforts to undermine the SRBiH MUP's authority in early 1992, that while working in the SRBiH MUP Stanišić promoted SDS interests and implemented SDS decisions.[511] **[page 66]**

ii. Analysis

150.   The Trial Chamber concluded that Stanišić was involved in establishing the SDS.[512] In the section of the Trial Judgement addressing Stanišić's participation in the formation of Bosnian Serb organs and policy,[513] the Trial Chamber noted that Stanišić: (i) "was involved in early activities of Serb intellectuals concerning the establishment of a Serb political party";[514] (ii) explained, in his Interview, "how the party name 'SDS' was adopted and how Radovan Karadžić became its President";[515] (iii) "was in regular contact with other members of the Bosnian Serb leadership";[516] (iv) "was a member of the Preparatory Committee for establishing the SDS";[517] and, on the other hand, (v) gave evidence that "he was neither an important figure in the SDS, nor was he interested in politics".[518]

151.   With respect to Stanišić's assertion that he was a member of the preparatory committee of the Democratic Party of BiH and not of the SDS, having reviewed the cited evidence, the Appeals Chamber does not find that the December 1993 BSA Transcript or the testimonies of Witness Škipina, Witness Žepinić, or Witness Njeguš support Stanišić's assertion.[519] The Appeals Chamber further notes that although the Trial Chamber did not cite the evidence it relied upon to conclude that Stanišić was involved in establishing the SDS,[520] when making findings about his participation in the formation of Bosnian Serb organs and policy,[521] the Trial Chamber referred to Stanišić's Interview,[522] and the testimonies of Witness Škipina, Witness

[508]   Prosecution Response Brief (Stanišić), para. 97, referring to Exhibit P1999, pp 56-57.
[509]   Prosecution Response Brief (Stanišić), para. 97, referring to, *inter alia*, Slobodan Škipina, 30 Mar 2010, T. 8294-8295, Vitomir Žepinić, 28 Jan 2010, T. 5707, Radomir Njeguš, 7 Jun 2010, T. 11307-11308.
[510]   Prosecution Response Brief (Stanišić), para. 97.
[511]   Prosecution Response Brief (Stanišić), paras 98 (referring to Trial Judgement, vol. 2, para. 734), 99 (arguing that Stanišić opposed the appointment of a Croat in place of a Serb as the deputy commander at a Sarajevo police stations; and held the view – shared by Karadžić as well as others in the SDS – that Serbs were being sidelined in the SUP and other institutions), 100 (arguing that: (i) at a meeting held by Serb officials of SRBiH MUP in Banja Luka on 11 February 1992, where a Serb collegium was created to prepare for establishing a Serb Ministry of Interior ("11 February 1992 Meeting"), Stanišić: (a) "blamed the Muslims for dividing the joint MUP"; (b) "stressed that Serbian personnel 'must provide the means to strengthen and supply the Serbian MUP, ensuring that resources will be distributed equally'"; and (c) "stressed the position adopted by the RS Council of Ministers at its meeting of 11 January which was that 'in the territories in [the SRBiH] which are under Serbian control, that control must be felt'" (referring to Trial Judgement, vol. 2, paras 554-555); (ii) "[i]n early 1992, he reported to SDS members on the progress in creating the RS Government (referring to Trial Judgement, vol. 2, para. 556); (iii) "[w]hen Stanišić was subsequently appointed as the RS MUP Minister, he was still employed by the SRBiH MUP and denounced its work" (referring to Trial Judgement, vol. 2, paras 558, 560-561); and (iv) "Stanišić [made] consistent efforts to promote SDS interests within the SRBiH earned high praise from Karadžić, who spoke of Stanišić having 'fought to prevail [...] for a balance of Serbian cadres' in the SRBiH MUP and then doing 'the best he could for establishing and separating the MUP at the beginning of April 1992'" (referring to Exhibit P1999, p. 57 as cited in Trial Judgement, vol. 2, para. 596). See Appeal Hearing, 16 Dec 2015, AT. 112-113.
[512]   Trial Judgement, vol. 2, para. 729.
[513]   Trial Judgement, vol. 2, paras 544-575.
[514]   Trial Judgement, vol. 2, para. 545, referring to Exhibits P2300, pp 53-54, 58, P1999, p. 57, P883.
[515]   Trial Judgement, vol. 2, para. 545, referring to, *inter alia*, Exhibit P2300, pp 53-54, 58.
[516]   Trial Judgement, vol. 2, para. 567.
[517]   Trial Judgement, vol. 2, para. 545, referring to, *inter alia*, Exhibits P2300, pp 53-54, 58, P1999, p. 57. See Trial Judgement, vol. 2, para. 564, referring to Exhibit P1999, pp 56-57 (finding that Stanišić "was a member of the Preparatory Committee for establishing the party").
[518]   Trial Judgement, vol. 2, para. 564, referring to Exhibit P2300, pp 54-58, Radomir Kezunović, 22 Jun 2010, T. 12096-12097, Vitomir Žepinić, 28 Jan 2010, T. 5707, 5721-5722, Slobodan Škipina, 30 Mar 2010, T. 8289-8295, Slobodan Škipina, 1 Apr 2010, T. 8452-8453, Radomir Njeguš, 7 Jun 2010, T. 11308.
[519]   Stanišić Appeal Brief, para. 243, referring to Exhibit P1999, pp 56-57, Slobodan Škipina, 30 Mar 2010, T. 8295, Slobodan Škipina, 1 Apr 2010, T. 8453, Vitomir Žepinić, 28 Jan 2010, T. 5707-5708, Radomir Njeguš, 7 Jun 2010, T. 11308.
[520]   Trial Judgement, vol. 2, para. 729.
[521]   Trial Judgement, vol. 2, paras 545, 564.
[522]   Trial Judgement, vol. 2, fns 1406, 1455, referring to Exhibit P2300.

Žepinić, and Witness Njeguš.[523] In this section, the Trial Chamber also relied on the December 1993 BSA Transcript,[524] **[page 67]** and on a series of intercepted conversations between Stanišić and other members of the Bosnian Serb leadership in April and May 1992.[524][525] The Appeals Chamber recalls that a trial chamber is best placed to weigh and assess the evidence[526] and for this reason will only substitute its own finding for that of the Trial Chamber when no reasonable trier of fact could have reached the original decision.[527] The Appeals Chamber is satisfied that, based on this evidence, it was reasonable for the Trial Chamber to conclude that Stanišić was involved in establishing the SDS. The Appeals Chamber considers that Stanišić seeks to substitute his own evaluation of the December 1993 BSA Transcript and the testimonies of Witness Škipina, Witness Žepinić, and Witness Njeguš for that of the Trial Chamber, without showing that, when considered in light of the entirety of the evidence, a reasonable trier of fact could not have reached the same conclusion.

152. Turning to Stanišić's challenge to the Trial Chamber's finding that he "was involved in all the stages of the creation of the Bosnian Serb institutions in BiH, in particular the MUP",[528] the Appeals Chamber recalls the Trial Chamber's findings that Stanišić: (i) worked to promote SDS interests, and implement SDS decisions, in the SRBiH MUP; (ii) was involved in all the stages of the creation of the Bosnian Serb institutions in BiH, in particular the RS MUP; and (iii) participated in the enunciation and implementation of the Bosnian Serb policy, as it evolved through his participation in these institutions.[529]

153. Insofar as Stanišić argues that the only institution he was found to have been involved in setting up was the RS MUP, the Appeals Chamber considers that Stanišić misrepresents the Trial Chamber's finding. It is clear from a plain reading of the finding that the Trial Chamber considered that, in addition to being involved in the creation of the RS MUP in particular, Stanišić was also involved in the creation of other Bosnian Serb institutions in BiH.[530] The Appeals Chamber further notes that, in the same paragraph, the Trial Chamber referred to Stanišić's conduct, presence at key meetings, attendance at BSA sessions, and acceptance of the position of Minister of Interior to conclude that he voluntarily participated in creating a separate Serb entity within BiH by the ethnic division of the territory.[531] The Appeals Chamber recalls that it has confirmed the Trial Chamber's finding that Stanišić was involved in establishing the SDS.[532] It also notes, as will be discussed in **[page 68]** more detail below,[533] that Stanišić: (i) attended the 11 February 1992 Meeting, where a Serb collegium was created to prepare for establishing a Serb Ministry of Interior;[534] (ii) accepted the position of advisor on state security matters to the SRBiH Minister of Interior in February 1992;[535] (iii) was elected the first Minister of Interior in the RS at a session of the BSA held on 24 March 1992 ("24 March 1992 BSA Session");[536] (iv) attended a majority of RS Government sessions following his appointment as Minister of Interior;[537] and (v) attended the first joint session of the NSC and RS Government held on 15 April 1992, as an NSC member.[538] In light of the above, the Appeals Chamber finds that Stanišić has failed to demonstrate that no reasonable trier of fact could have concluded that he was involved in various stages of creation of Bosnian Serb institutions in BiH, in addition to the RS MUP.

---

[523] Trial Judgement, vol. 2, fn. 1455, referring to, *inter alia*, Radomir Kezunović, 22 Jun 2010, T. 12096-12097, Vitomir Žepinić, 28 Jan 2010, T. 5707, 5721-5722, Slobodan Škipina, 30 Mar 2010, T. 8289-8295, Slobodan Škipina, 1 Apr 2010, T. 8452-8453, Radomir Njeguš, 7 Jun 2010, T. 11308.

[524] Trial Judgement, vol. 2, fns 1406, 1456, 1561, referring to, *inter alia*, Exhibit P1999.

[525] Trial Judgement, vol. 2, fns 1465 referring to Exhibits P1162, pp 9-10, P1133, P202, P203, P114. See Trial Judgement, vol. 2, fn. 1561, referring to Exhibit P1123.

[526] *Popović et al.* Appeal Judgement, para. 513; *Lukić and Lukić* Appeal Judgement, para. 384; *Limaj et al.* Appeal Judgement, para. 88; *Kupreškić et al.* Appeal Judgement, para. 32.

[527] See *supra*, para. 20.

[528] Trial Judgement, vol. 2, para. 734.

[529] Trial Judgement, vol. 2, para. 734.

[530] Trial Judgement, vol. 2, para. 734.

[531] Trial Judgement, vol. 2, para. 734.

[532] See *supra*, para. 151.

[533] See *infra*, paras 176-183.

[534] Trial Judgement, vol. 2, paras 554, 599. See Trial Judgement, vol. 1, para. 4.

[535] Trial Judgement, vol. 2, paras 540-541.

[536] Trial Judgement, vol. 2, paras 542, 558.

[537] Trial Judgement, vol. 2, para. 572.

[538] Trial Judgement, vol. 2, para. 573.

154. With respect to Stanišić's assertion that the RS MUP was created in line with the Cutileiro Plan, and that as the Minister of Interior he had a duty to be involved, the Appeals Chamber recalls that contribution to a joint criminal enterprise need not be in and of itself criminal, as long as the accused performs acts that in some way contribute significantly to the furtherance of the common purpose.[539] Moreover, the Appeals Chamber has previously held that "the fact that [the participation of an accused] amounted to no more than his or her 'routine duties' will not exculpate the accused".[540] What matters is whether the act in question furthered the common criminal purpose and whether it was carried out with the requisite intent. Therefore, the Trial Chamber did not err in considering this evidence when assessing Stanišić's contribution to the JCE. Accordingly, his argument fails.

155. Turning to Stanišić's challenge to the Trial Chamber's finding that, at the time the SDS was being created, Stanišić "displayed discontentment with the representation of Serbs within the SRBiH MUP and attempted to intervene to retain and recruit Serbs within the Ministry",[541] the Appeals Chamber notes that the Trial Chamber referred to Witness Žepinić's testimony that Stanišić "felt that the Serbs were being sidelined by the Muslims and Croats in the SRBiH MUP and other institutions".[542] The Trial Chamber also relied on Stanišić's statement, made at the 24 March 1992 BSA Session when accepting the position of Minister of Interior, "that the SRBiH **[page 69]** MUP had been used as an instrument of the SDA and the HDZ for achieving their political goals, including the creation of an army from the reserve forces comprised of only one ethnicity and the dismissal of Serbs from their positions".[543] Witness Žepinić's testimony and Stanišić's statement are both consistent with the Trial Chamber's conclusion that Stanišić displayed discontentment with the representation of Serbs within the SRBiH MUP.

156. With regard to the Trial Chamber's finding that he "attempted to intervene to retain and recruit Serbs within the Ministry",[544] the Appeals Chamber notes that, in reaching this finding, the Trial Chamber relied on the December 1993 BSA Transcript, wherein Karadžić praised Stanišić for having fought for a balance of Serb cadres in the SRBiH MUP and for his efforts "establishing and separating the MUP at the beginning of April 1992",[545] and the minutes of the 11 February 1992 Meeting at which attendees, including Stanišić and Serbs working for the SRBiH MUP, reached several conclusions concerning Serbs in the SRBiH MUP.[546] More specifically, it was decided that intensive work would be done to train and arm Serb police personnel,[547] a task which fell to the RS MUP under the Law on Internal Affairs of the RS ("LIA"),[548] and that the Serb Collegium created at the 11 February 1992 Meeting would carry out all necessary preparations for the functioning of a Serb MUP, after the promulgation of the RS Constitution.[549] Further, the Appeals Chamber notes the Trial Chamber's findings that, after the RS MUP started functioning on 1 April 1992, Stanišić exercised his powers as Minister of Interior to appoint Serbs to key positions in RS municipalities.[550]

157. Stanišić asserts that, instead of showing discontent or attempting to intervene, he sought to have an agreement among the SDS, the SDA, and the HDZ on the distribution of personnel upheld and followed.[551] The Appeals Chamber notes that in support of his argument, Stanišić refers to Exhibit 1D115, which he claims to be an inter-party agreement.[552] Having examined Exhibit 1D115, the Appeals Chamber observes that it is not dated and is not, on its face, capable of undermining the Trial Chamber's finding that he displayed

---

[539] *Popović et al.* Appeal Judgement, para. 1653; *Šainović et al.* Appeal Judgement, para. 985; *Krajišnik* Appeal Judgement, paras 215, 695-696. See *Šainović et al.* Appeal Judgement, paras 1233, 1242. See also *supra*, para. 110.

[540] *Popović et al.* Appeal Judgement, para. 1653, quoting *Blagojević and Jokić* Appeal Judgement, para. 189.

[541] Trial Judgement, vol. 2, para. 729.

[542] Trial Judgement, vol. 2, para. 540, referring to, *inter alia*, Vitomir Žepinić, 28 Jan 2010, T. 5707-5708, Vitomir Žepinić, 29 Jan 2010, T. 5808.

[543] Trial Judgement, vol. 2, para. 558; Exhibit P198, p. 8.

[544] Trial Judgement, vol. 2, para. 729.

[545] Trial Judgement, vol. 2, para. 596, referring to Exhibits P1999, p. 57, P1123, pp 14-17.

[546] Trial Judgement, vol. 2, paras 4, 554, 599.

[547] Trial Judgement, vol. 2, para. 4.

[548] Trial Judgement, vol. 2, para. 599, referring to Neǀo Vlaški, 15 Feb 2010, T. 6349-6351, Exhibits 1D135, p. 5, P530, Article 33. See Trial Judgement, vol. 2, paras 4-5.

[549] Trial Judgement, vol. 2, para. 554, referring to 1D135, p. 4, para. 3.

[550] Trial Judgement, vol. 2, para. 578, referring to ST121, 24 Nov 2009, T. 3723-3724 (private session).

[551] Stanišić Appeal Brief, para. 243.

[552] Stanišić Appeal Brief, para. 243, referring to Exhibit 1D115.

discontentment with the representation **[page 70]** of Serbs within the SRBiH MUP and attempted to intervene to retain and recruit Serbs within the SRBiH MUP. Stanišić's argument is thus dismissed.

158. For the foregoing reasons, the Appeals Chamber concludes that Stanišić has not shown any error in the Trial Chamber's findings regarding Stanišić's involvement in establishing Bosnian Serb institutions in BiH.

   b. Alleged errors in the Trial Chamber's findings regarding Stanišić's relationship with Karadžić and his direct communication with the RS Presidency

159. The Trial Chamber found that Stanišić and Karadžić, a leading member of the JCE, shared a close relationship from at least June 1991 and in the months preceding the establishment of RS.[553]

The Trial Chamber further found that "[a]s a result of his relationship with Karadžić, Stanišić often did not report through the designated channels of the RS Government but communicated directly with the Presidency."[554]

   i. Submissions of the parties

160. Stanišić challenges the Trial Chamber's findings that he and Karadžić "shared a close relationship" and that he did not report through designated RS Government channels.[555] With respect to the latter, Stanišić asserts that: (i) the RS MUP compiled and sent to the RS President and the Prime Minister 150 daily bulletins about its activities in 1992 and, in addition, 90 reports on security issues;[556] and (ii) in May 1992 the RS Government tasked the RS MUP with preparing a complete report on the security situation in the RS[557] and that the RS MUP prepared several such reports.[558] Stanišić further asserts that Witness Đerić's evidence that he did not attend government meetings is contradicted by the Trial Chamber's finding that he attended a majority of RS Government sessions.[559]

161. The Prosecution responds that Stanišić fails to show that the Trial Chamber erred in finding that he had a close relationship with Karadžić and that his arguments should be summarily **[page 71]** dismissed.[560] It argues that neither the reports sent to the RS Government nor Stanišić's attendance at RS Government sessions undermine the Trial Chamber's conclusion that he communicated directly with the RS Presidency, instead of using the designated RS Government channels.[561] The Prosecution asserts that Stanišić also ignores the testimonies of Witness Žepinić and Witness Milan Trbojević ("Witness Trbojević"), that he had "direct ties with Karadžić and often bypassed the RS Government".[562] It argues that Witness Đerić's complaints about Stanišić's meetings with Karadžić and Krajišnik, voiced during a session of the BSA held on 23 and 24 November 1992 ("November 1992 BSA Session"), are consistent with the testimonies of Witness Žepinić and Witness Trbojević on this point.[563]

   ii. Analysis

162. The Trial Chamber concluded that Stanišić and Karadžić "shared a close relationship" and that as a result, Stanišić "often did not report through the designated channels of the RS Government but communicated

---

[553]   Trial Judgement, vol. 2, para. 730. See Trial Judgement, vol. 2, para. 565.
[554]   Trial Judgement, vol. 2, para. 730. See Trial Judgement, vol. 2, paras 568, 570.
[555]   Stanišić Appeal Brief, para. 244, referring to Trial Judgement, vol. 2, para. 730 (emphasis omitted). See Stanišić Reply Brief, para. 69, referring to Prosecution Response Brief (Stanišić), paras 94, 102, 107.
[556]   Stanišić Appeal Brief, para. 244, referring to Trial Judgement, vol. 2, paras 66, 568, Exhibit P625, p. 23. Stanišić contends that the Trial Chamber "inexplicably omitted" the information about the 90 reports on security issues from Trial Judgement, vol. 2, para. 568 (Stanišić Appeal Brief, fn. 294, contrasting Trial Judgement, vol. 2, para. 66, with Trial Judgement, vol. 2, para. 568).
[557]   Stanišić Appeal Brief, para. 244, referring to Trial Judgement, vol. 2, para. 47.
[558]   Stanišić Appeal Brief, para. 244, referring to Exhibit P427.05, pp 11752-11754.
[559]   Stanišić Appeal Brief, para. 244, referring to Trial Judgement, vol. 2, paras 570, 572, Exhibit P400, pp 10-12.
[560]   Prosecution Response Brief (Stanišić), paras 107 (referring to *Krajišnik* Appeal Judgement, para. 27), 108.
[561]   Prosecution Response Brief (Stanišić), para. 107, referring to Trial Judgement, vol. 2, paras 568, 730.
[562]   Prosecution Response Brief (Stanišić), para. 107, referring to Trial Judgement, vol. 2, para. 568.
[563]   Prosecution Response Brief (Stanišić), para. 107, referring to Trial Judgement, vol. 2, para. 570.

directly with the Presidency."[564] In the section of the Trial Judgement addressing Stanišić's interactions with the Bosnian Serb leadership,[565] the Trial Chamber found that they "spoke frequently, at times calling each other at home".[566] It found that Stanišić communicated directly with Karadžić on 2 March 1992, "following the negotiations between the Muslims and Serbs on the removal of the barricades in Sarajevo",[567] and again concerning "attacks, manpower, and *materiel* for combat activities".[568]

163.   With regard to Stanišić's argument that the Trial Chamber erred in finding that he and Karadžić shared a close relationship, the Appeals Chamber notes that Stanišić merely repeats an argument that he has developed under the subsection (E) of his fourth ground of appeal.[569] The Appeals Chamber recalls that it has dismissed this argument elsewhere in the Judgement.[570]

164.   Insofar as Stanišić argues that the Trial Chamber erred by finding that he did not report through designated RS Government channels, the Appeals Chamber finds that Stanišić misrepresents the Trial Chamber's findings. The Appeals Chamber notes that the Trial Chamber **[page 72]** found that Stanišić "*often did not report through the designated channels of the RS Government but communicated directly with the Presidency*".[571] Stanišić's use of designated RS Government channels, by having the RS MUP send reports to the RS President and Prime Minister[572] and by attending RS Government sessions,[573] does not undermine the Trial Chamber's finding that he often did not report through these channels. The Appeals Chamber further notes the Trial Chamber's findings that Stanišić and Karadžić spoke frequently and that at times they called each other at home,[574] and that, in particular, they communicated directly: (i) after negotiations between the Muslims and Serbs on the removal of barricades in Sarajevo;[575] and (ii) concerning "attacks, manpower, and *materiel* for combat activities".[576] In light of these Trial Chamber's findings, Stanišić has failed to show that no reasonable trier of fact could have concluded that he often did not report through designated RS Government channels but communicated directly with the RS Presidency.

       c. Alleged errors in the Trial Chamber's findings relating to Stanišić's knowledge of the Variant A and B Instructions

165.   The Trial Chamber found that on 19 December 1991 the SDS Main Board adopted the Variant A and B Instructions[577] which: (i) "were to be implemented in 'all municipalities where the Serb people live', completely in municipalities where Serbs were in the majority (Variant A) and partially in municipalities where Serbs were not a majority (Variant B)";[578] (ii) were the "main tool" used by the Bosnian Serb leadership when initiating the process of establishing Serb municipalities;[579] and (iii) had as their main purpose, besides the demarcation of Serb territory, "to prepare the local Serb communities and their leaders to take over

---

[564]   Trial Judgement, vol. 2, para. 730. See Trial Judgement, vol. 2, paras 565, 568, 570.
[565]   Trial Judgement, vol. 2, paras 564-571.
[566]   Trial Judgement, vol. 2, para. 565.
[567]   Trial Judgement, vol. 2, para. 566.
[568]   Trial Judgement, vol. 2, para. 567.
[569]   Stanišić Appeal Brief, para. 244, referring to subsection (E) of his fourth ground of appeal. See Stanišić Appeal Brief, paras 158-164.
[570]   See *infra*, para. 514.
[571]   Trial Judgement, vol. 2, para. 730 (emphasis added).
[572]   Trial Judgement, vol. 2, paras 66, 568.
[573]   Trial Judgement, vol. 2, paras 570, 572.
[574]   Trial Judgement, vol. 2, para. 565.
[575]   Trial Judgement, vol. 2, para. 566.
[576]   Trial Judgement, vol. 2, para. 567.
[577]   Trial Judgement, vol. 1, para. 501, referring to *Prosecutor v. Mićo Stanišić and Stojan Župljanin*, Case No. IT-08-91-T, Decision Granting in Part Prosecution's Motions for Judicial Notice of Adjudicated Facts Pursuant to Rule 94(B), 1 April 2010 ("Adjudicated Facts Decision"), Adjudicated Fact 200, Simo Mišković, 1 Oct 2010, T. 1517615178, Exhibits P15, P435, pp 1-2, P1610, pp 103-107. See Trial Judgement, vol. 2, para. 228, referring to Adjudicated Fact 100, Exhibit P15. See also Trial Judgement, vol. 2, paras 548, 731.
[578]   Trial Judgement, vol. 2, para. 548, referring to Adjudicated Facts Decision, Adjudicated Fact 100, Exhibit P15, para. I.3, p. 2, Exhibit P434.
[579]   Trial Judgement, vol. 2, para. 310.

power in the municipalities".[580] **[page 73]** The Trial Chamber found that Stanišić was aware of the Instructions since the police were assigned to, and did in fact play a central role in, their implementation.[581]

i. Submissions of the parties

166.   Stanišić submits that the Trial Chamber erred by finding that he was aware of the Variant A and B Instructions because the police played a central role in their implementation.[582] He argues that it was clear from his Interview that, at the time in question, he was not aware of the Instructions and that no evidence to the contrary was adduced.[583]

167.   Stanišić asserts that the purpose, issuance, and implementation of the Instructions were "inextricably bound to the SDS".[584] In this regard, he refers to the Trial Chamber's conclusions that: (i) the SDS Main Board issued the Instructions and that they were the result of the SDS Main Committee's concern that BiH was seceding;[585] (ii) according to the Instructions, SDS municipal committees were to form crisis staffs which would be comprised of, *inter alios*, SDS nominees;[586] and (iii) "an order of the President of SDS in BiH according to a secret procedure" was required for the activities entailed in the Instructions to be applied.[587] According to Stanišić, it is telling that the Trial Chamber referred to the SDS in all of its findings on "the contemporaneous implementation of the Instructions".[588] Stanišić submits that the Trial Chamber failed to consider that he did not play a role in the SDS and "was not present at any meetings at which the Instructions were discussed".[589]

168.   Stanišić further submits that "the Crisis Staffs were a conflicting authority that usurped the powers of the RS Government" and that implementation of the Instructions at the crisis staff level did not mean that he was aware of them.[590] In relation to the Trial Chamber's finding that establishing crisis staffs was the main instrument used to implement the Instructions,[591] Stanišić refers to Witness Đerić's testimony that "the Crisis Staffs had nothing to do with the RS Government because they were formed and worked on behalf of the SDS".[592] He also asserts that Witness Đerić's testimony was corroborated by evidence that "in some instances Crisis Staffs **[page 74]** became the *de facto* superior body of SJBs, and SJBs did not inform CSBs or the [RS MUP] of the situation on the ground".[593] To this end, Stanišić cites the Trial Chamber's finding that in these cases the RS MUP did not exert its own influence until August or September 1992.[594]

169.   The Prosecution responds that Stanišić fails to show any error[595] and that his arguments that crisis staffs disrupted his authority over the RS MUP, his reliance on his Interview to deny knowledge of the Instructions, and his denial of an association with the SDS were raised at trial and failed.[596] It submits that it was reasonable for the Trial Chamber to have found that Stanišić was aware of the Instructions since the

---

[580]   Trial Judgement, vol. 2, para. 310.
[581]   Trial Judgement, vol. 2, para. 731. See Trial Judgement, vol. 2, para. 548, referring to Exhibit P15, para. II.5, pp 3-6 (under first level for Variant A), paras II.2 and II.6, p. 4 (under second level for Variant A), para. II.5, p. 5 (under first level for Variant B), and II.2, p. 6 (under second level for Variant B).
[582]   Stanišić Appeal Brief, para. 245, referring to Trial Judgement, vol. 2, para. 731.
[583]   Stanišić Appeal Brief, para. 249, referring to Exhibit P2306, pp 1-7, 13-14.
[584]   Stanišić Appeal Brief, para. 246, referring to Trial Judgement, vol. 2, paras 227-244.
[585]   Stanišić Appeal Brief, para. 246, referring to Trial Judgement, vol. 2, para. 228.
[586]   Stanišić Appeal Brief, para. 246, referring to Trial Judgement, vol. 2, para. 229.
[587]   Stanišić Appeal Brief, para. 246, referring to Trial Judgement, vol. 2, para. 231.
[588]   Stanišić Appeal Brief, para. 246, referring to Trial Judgement, vol. 2, paras 234-241.
[589]   Stanišić Appeal Brief, para. 247, referring to Exhibit P2306, pp 1-2, 6.
[590]   Stanišić Appeal Brief, para. 248, referring to Branko Đerić, 2 Nov 2009, T. 2417, 2436.
[591]   Stanišić Appeal Brief, para. 248, referring to Trial Judgement, vol. 2, para. 244.
[592]   Stanišić Appeal Brief, para. 248.
[593]   Stanišić Appeal Brief, para. 248, referring to Trial Judgement, vol. 2, para. 251 (citing Goran Mačar, 11 Jul 2011, T. 23102, 22289-22900).
[594]   Stanišić Appeal Brief, para. 248, referring to Trial Judgement, vol. 2, para. 251 (citing Goran Mačar, 11 Jul 2011, T. 23102, 22896-22898).
[595]   Prosecution Response Brief (Stanišić), para. 104, referring to Trial Judgement, vol. 2, paras 548, 731, 737, Exhibits P69, p. 12 (a copy of the Variant A and B Instructions identifying Stanišić as a recipient), P522 (naming Stanišić as a member of the Sarajevo Crisis Staff and allocating tasks to him per the Variant A and B Instructions).
[596]   Prosecution Response Brief (Stanišić), para. 106, referring to, *inter alia*, Stanišić Final Trial Brief, paras 37, 595-599, 612-613, Stanišić Appeal Brief, para. 248, *Krajišnik* Appeal Judgement, para. 24.

police were assigned to, and in fact played a central role in, their implementation.[597] In this regard, the Prosecution refers to the Trial Chamber's findings that the Instructions were the "main tool" in establishing Serb municipalities in BiH and that they "prepared local Serb communities and their leaders to take over power in municipalities across BiH".[598]

170. The Prosecution further submits that although the Trial Chamber found that crisis staffs were the main instrument used to implement the Instructions, it also found that Stanišić was closely associated with the SDS and that the SDS largely retained control over the crisis staffs.[599] The Prosecution also contends that the Trial Chamber found that Serb forces, SDS structures, crisis staffs, and the RS Government "shared and worked towards the same goal", despite the conflicts that arose between them at times.[600] According to the Prosecution, these findings demonstrate that the Trial Chamber considered, but rejected Stanišić's denial of any knowledge of the Instructions.[601]

ii. Analysis

171. At the outset, the Appeals Chamber notes that, in the absence of direct evidence, the Trial Chamber inferred Stanišić's awareness of the Variant A and B Instructions from the central role played by the police in the implementation of these Instructions.[602] **[page 75]**

172. The Appeals Chamber recalls that trial chambers may rely on either direct or circumstantial evidence to underpin their findings.[603] The Appeals Chamber observes that the Trial Chamber considered Stanišić's evidence that he had never been informed of the Instructions,[604] but rejected it in light of the central role that was assigned to – and indeed played by – the police in the implementation of the Instructions.[605] In this regard, the Appeals Chamber notes that the Trial Chamber relied on provisions in the Instructions to conclude that the police were assigned a central role in their implementation.[606] With respect to this conclusion, the Appeals Chamber notes further the Trial Chamber's findings that 19 municipalities were taken over in April and June 1992 "in accordance with the Variant A and B Instructions through the joint action of the RS MUP and other Serb forces, sometimes by advance hostile occupation of the main features in town by police forces".[607] The Appeals Chamber also notes that the Trial Chamber found that "[a]s the highest commander of the RS MUP forces and the administrative head of the organs of the RS MUP, Stanišić received reports of the involvement of the police forces in combat activities."[608] Therefore, contrary to Stanišić's contention that no evidence contradicting his statement was adduced at trial, the Appeals Chamber observes that the Trial Chamber in fact relied on a body of circumstantial evidence to reach this conclusion.

173. Turning to Stanišić's argument that the purpose, issuance, and implementation of the Instructions were "inextricably bound to the SDS" and that the Trial Chamber failed to consider that he did not play a role in the SDS,[609] the Appeals Chamber recalls that it has upheld the Trial Chamber's finding that Stanišić was involved in the establishment of the SDS.[610] The Trial Chamber also found that he worked to promote SDS

---

[597] Prosecution Response Brief (Stanišić), para. 104, referring to Trial Judgement, vol. 2, paras 548, 731, 737, Exhibits P69, p. 12 (a copy of the Instructions which identifies Stanišić as one of the recipients of the Instructions), P522 (naming Stanišić as a member of the Sarajevo Crisis Staff and allocating tasks to him per Instructions).

[598] Prosecution Response Brief (Stanišić), para. 104, referring to Trial Judgement, vol. 2, paras 227-244, 310.

[599] Prosecution Response Brief (Stanišić), para. 105, referring to Trial Judgement, vol. 2, para. 244.

[600] Prosecution Response Brief (Stanišić), para. 105, referring to Exhibit P163, p. 8.

[601] Prosecution Response Brief (Stanišić), para. 105, referring to Trial Judgement, vol. 2, paras 548, 731.

[602] Trial Judgement, vol. 2, para. 731. See Trial Judgement, vol. 2, paras 548, 737.

[603] See *Popović et al.* Appeal Judgement, para. 971; *Đorđević* Appeal Judgement, para. 348.

[604] Trial Judgement, vol. 2, para. 548, referring to Exhibit P2306, pp 1-7, 13-14. See Trial Judgement, vol. 2, para. 731.

[605] Trial Judgement, vol. 2, para. 548.

[606] Trial Judgement, vol. 2, para. 548, referring to Exhibit P15, para. II.5, p. 3 (under first level for Variant A), paras II.2, II.6, p. 4 (under second level for Variant A), para. II.5, p. 5 (under first level for Variant B), II.2, p. 6 (under second level for Variant B).

[607] Trial Judgement, vol. 2, para. 737, referring to the municipalities of Banja Luka, Bijeljina, Bileća, Bosanski Šamac, Brčko, Doboj, Donji Vakuf, Gacko, Ilijaš, Ključ, Kotor Varoš, Pale, Prijedor, Sanski Most, Teslić, Vlasenica, Višegrad, Vogošća, and Zvornik.

[608] Trial Judgement, vol. 2, para. 741. See *infra*, paras 256-257. See also Trial Judgement, vol. 2, para. 581, referring to Exhibit P741.

[609] See *supra*, para. 167.

[610] See *supra*, para. 151. See also *supra*, para. 152.

interests and implement SDS decisions in the SRBiH MUP.[611] The Appeals Chamber therefore dismisses Stanišić's argument in this regard. With respect to his submission that the Trial Chamber failed to consider that he was not present at any meetings at which the Instructions were discussed,[612] the Appeals Chamber notes that the Trial Chamber considered his assertion, in his Interview, that "he had never in fact seen these Instructions **[page 76]** nor was he ever informed of them".[613] The Appeal Chamber is satisfied that the Trial Chamber considered that Stanišić may not have had direct knowledge of the Instructions but inferred that the only reasonable conclusion was that he was nevertheless aware of the Instructions based on circumstantial evidence including his involvement in the SDS, as set out above, and the central role assigned to, and played by, the police in their implementation.[614] Stanišić's argument thus fails.

174.   With respect to Stanišić's argument concerning the effect of the crisis staffs on the RS Government's power and his assertion that the Instructions' implementation at the crisis staff level did not mean that he was aware of them, the Appeals Chamber notes that the Trial Chamber concluded "that even though at times there were conflicts between [Serb forces, SDS party structure, Crisis Staffs, and the RS Government], they all shared and worked towards the same goal under the Bosnian Serb leadership".[615] The Appeals Chamber also notes that the Trial Chamber found that the RS MUP was able to gradually restore its own influence after the autonomous regions and that the crisis staffs were abolished in August and September 1992.[616] In light of these findings, the Appeals Chamber considers that Stanišić's assertion of conflicts between the RS MUP and some crisis staffs is insufficient to demonstrate that no reasonable trial chamber could have found that he was aware of the Instructions.

175.   In light of the foregoing, and given the Trial Chamber's findings on the police involvement in the widespread implementation of the Instructions between April and June 1992 and on Stanišić's authority over the police, the Appeals Chamber considers that Stanišić has failed to demonstrate that no reasonable trier of fact could have inferred that the only reasonable conclusion was that Stanišić was aware of the Instructions.

   d. Alleged errors in the Trial Chamber's findings regarding Stanišić's role in the decision-making authorities from early 1992 onwards

176.   The Trial Chamber found that Stanišić: (i) attended the 11 February 1992 Meeting where a Serb collegium was created to prepare for establishing a Serb MUP;[617] (ii) accepted the position of advisor on state security matters to the SRBiH Minister of Interior in February 1992;[618] (iii) was elected the first Minister of Interior "in the Serb entity, RS, of the disintegrating SRBiH MUP", at the 24 March 1992 BSA Session;[619] and (iv) proclaimed, at a Serb police unit inspection on **[page 77]** 30 March 1992, that "from that day the RS had its own police force".[620] The Trial Chamber also found that after Stanišić's 31 March 1992 appointment as Minister of Interior, he attended a majority of RS Government sessions "along with the Prime Minister, Deputy Prime Minister, other ministers, and at times their delegated representatives".[621] Further, it found that as an NSC member, Stanišić attended the first NSC and RS Government joint session, held on 15 April 1992, and continued to participate in these joint sessions in April and May 1992 during which "decisions pertaining to military and security activities were taken and reports of the combat and political situation were presented".[622] The Trial Chamber concluded that "based on the minutes and agenda

---

[611]   Trial Judgement, vol. 2, para. 734.
[612]   Stanišić Appeal Brief, para. 247, referring to Exhibit P2306, pp 1-2, 6.
[613]   Trial Judgement, vol. 2, para. 548, fn. Exhibit P2306, pp 1-7, 13-14.
[614]   See *supra*, para. 172. See also Trial Judgement, vol. 2, paras 548, 731.
[615]   Trial Judgement, vol. 2, para. 735.
[616]   Trial Judgement, vol. 2, para. 251.
[617]   Trial Judgement, vol. 2, paras 554, 599, 732.
[618]   Trial Judgement, vol. 2, paras 540-541, 732.
[619]   Trial Judgement, vol. 2, para. 732. See Trial Judgement, vol. 2, paras 542, 558.
[620]   Trial Judgement, vol. 2, paras 7, 560, 732.
[621]   Trial Judgement, vol. 2, para. 572, referring to Exhibits P237, P240, P241, P247, P200, P242, P244, P248, P254, P253, P256, P429. See Trial Judgement, vol. 2, para. 732.
[622]   Trial Judgement, vol. 2, para. 573, referring to Exhibits P1318.03, p. 8743, P1318.07, pp 9124-9125, P204, P205, P206, P711, P207, P208, P209, P210, P211, P212, P213, P214. See Trial Judgement, vol. 2, para. 732.

of these entities, [...] Stanišić was a key member of the decision-making authorities from early 1992 onwards".[623]

i. Submissions of the parties

177.   Stanišić disputes the Trial Chamber's finding that he was "a key member of the decision-making authorities from early 1992 onwards".[624] He asserts that he only participated in BSA sessions twice in the Indictment period, namely the 24 March 1992 BSA Session where he was elected by the BSA as Minister of Interior and the November 1992 BSA Session,[625] and that his presence at the NSC and the RS Government meetings was "mandated by his official function and capacity as Minister".[626] He contends that the Trial Chamber did not: (i) "cite a single specific reference" for minutes of the NSC and RS Government joint sessions, RS Government regular sessions or BSA sessions;[627] or (ii) analyse "the minutes or agendas of any of these meetings or how Stanišić's attendance was sufficient to justify the extremely prejudicial and erroneous conclusion that he was a key decision maker."[628]

178.   The Prosecution responds that Stanišić's challenges to the Trial Chamber's finding that he was "a key member of the decision-making authorities from early 1992 onwards" should be summarily dismissed because he merely claims the Trial Chamber failed to consider relevant evidence without showing an error.[629] It submits that the Trial Chamber "carefully considered" **[page 78]** evidence regarding NSC and RS Government joint sessions.[630] Citing the leadership roles Stanišić held within the RS,[631] his participation in sessions of the RS Government, the NSC and the BSA,[632] and his close ties to the SDS and its leader Karadžić, the Prosecution asserts that the Trial Chamber's finding was reasonable.[633]

179.   Stanišić replies that when discussing NSC and RS Government joint sessions, RS Government sessions and BSA sessions, the Trial Chamber made it clear that he participated in his capacity as the Minister of Interior and that he attended "when matters and tasks pertaining to his Ministry were discussed".[634] He contends that his role was "limited to his ministry and did not extend to shaping Bosnian Serb policy" and is not a basis to find that he was a "key decision maker".[635] Finally, he submits that the Trial Chamber erred by relying on BSA sessions at which he was not even present.[636]

ii. Analysis

180.   Turning first to Stanišić's argument that the Trial Chamber failed to cite or analyse the relevant minutes of the NSC and RS Government joint sessions, RS Government regular sessions, or BSA sessions, the Appeals Chamber notes that the Trial Chamber did not cite the specific "minutes and agenda" it considered when concluding that Stanišić was a key member of the decision-making authorities from early 1992 onwards.[637] However, the Trial Chamber did cite them in the section of the Trial Judgement addressing Stanišić's participation in the formation of Bosnian Serb organs and policy.[638] Specifically, the Trial Chamber relied on:

[623]   Trial Judgement, vol. 2, para. 732.
[624]   Stanišić Appeal Brief, para. 251, referring to Trial Judgement, vol. 2, para. 732.
[625]   Stanišić Appeal Brief, paras 128, 251, fn. 124, referring to Trial Judgement, vol. 2, para. 558. See *infra*, para. 419.
[626]   Stanišić Appeal Brief, para. 252.
[627]   Stanišić Appeal Brief, para. 252, referring to Trial Judgement, vol. 2, para. 732.
[628]   Stanišić Appeal Brief, para. 252, referring to Trial Judgement, vol. 2, para. 732; Stanišić Reply Brief, para. 70.
[629]   Prosecution Response Brief (Stanišić), para. 103, referring to *Krajišnik* Appeal Judgement, para. 19.
[630]   Prosecution Response Brief (Stanišić), para. 103, referring to Trial Judgement, vol. 2, paras 558, 570, 572-575, 595, 600, 623, 625, 627, 639, 642, 650, 652, 663, 708, 721.
[631]   Prosecution Response Brief (Stanišić), para. 102, referring to Trial Judgement, vol. 2, paras 542, 549, 551, 554-555, 558, 560, 571, 720, 732.
[632]   Prosecution Response Brief (Stanišić), para. 102, referring to Trial Judgement, vol. 2, paras 558, 570, 572-575, 595, 600, 623, 625, 627, 639, 642, 650, 652, 663, 708, 721, 732.
[633]   Prosecution Response Brief (Stanišić), para. 102.
[634]   Stanišić Reply Brief, para. 70, referring to Trial Judgement, vol. 2, para. 732.
[635]   Stanišić Reply Brief, para. 70.
[636]   Stanišić Reply Brief, paras 70-71.
[637]   Trial Judgement, vol. 2, para. 732.
[638]   Trial Judgement, vol. 2, paras 544-575.

(i) minutes of the NSC and RS Government joint sessions held in April and May 1992 to support the conclusion that Stanišić participated in NSC and RS Government joint sessions;[639] (ii) minutes of RS Government sessions between July and December 1992 to support the conclusion that Stanišić attended a majority of the RS Government sessions after he was appointed Minister of Interior;[640] and (iii) minutes of the **[page 79]** 24 March 1992 BSA Session[641] and the November 1992 BSA Session[642] to conclude that he participated in these BSA sessions. In light of the above, the Appeals Chamber considers that Stanišić's assertions that the Trial Chamber failed to cite the relevant minutes or analyse the minutes or agendas of any of these meetings are unfounded.

181. Turning to Stanišić's argument that he only participated in BSA sessions twice in the Indictment period, the Appeal Chamber first notes that only the November 1992 BSA Session falls within this period. Nevertheless, Stanišić has failed to demonstrate why the Trial Chamber's conclusion that he was a key member of decision-making authorities should not stand based on the other evidence that he attended a number of meetings of decision-making authorities during the Indictment period.

182. Finally, with respect to Stanišić's argument that his presence at these meetings was "mandated by his official function and capacity as Minister", the Appeals Chamber recalls that contribution to a joint criminal enterprise need not be in and of itself criminal as long as the accused performs acts that in some way contribute to the furtherance of the common purpose of the JCE[643] and that the fact that his contribution amounted to no more than his routine duties will not exculpate him.[644] Therefore, even if Stanišić's presence at these meetings was mandated by his official function, the Trial Chamber did not err in relying on this evidence when entering findings with respect to his contribution. Stanišić's argument therefore fails.

183. For the reasons set out above, the Appeals Chamber finds that Stanišić has failed to show that no reasonable trier of fact could have concluded that he was a key member of the decision-making authorities from early 1992 onwards.

e. Alleged errors in the Trial Chamber's findings regarding Stanišić's authority in the RS MUP

184. The Trial Chamber found that Stanišić: (i) made a majority of key appointments in the RS MUP from 1 April 1992 onward; (ii) had the sole authority to appoint, discipline, and dismiss the chiefs of CSBs and SJBs; and (iii) under the law, also had the sole authority for establishing special police units and the authority to decide when and how a special unit could be used.[645] The Trial Chamber, however, noted that police chiefs in several municipalities were appointed by local crisis **[page 80]** staffs and that the RS MUP was not informed of the establishment of some special police units by local organs.[646]

i. Submissions of the parties

185. Stanišić raises several challenges to the Trial Chamber's findings regarding his authority in the RS MUP.

186. Stanišić challenges the Trial Chamber's finding that he "made a majority of key appointments in the RS MUP".[647] He submits that as Minister of Interior, he had a duty to appoint people to posts in the RS MUP as it was being set up, but contends that Alija Delimustafić ("Delimustafić"), Minister of the SRBiH MUP,[648]

---

[639] Trial Judgement, vol. 2, para. 573, referring to Exhibits P204, P205, P206, P711, P207, P208, P209, P210, P211, P212, P213, P214.
[640] Trial Judgement, vol. 2, para. 572, referring to Exhibits P237, P240, P241, P247, P200, P242, P244, P248, P253, P256, P429. The Trial Chamber also relies on Exhibit P254 to conclude that Stanišić was in attendance but the Appeals Chamber considers this to be an error as the exhibit reads in relevant part: "Pero Vujičić in place of Mićo Stanišić".
[641] Trial Judgement, vol. 2, para. 558; Exhibit P198.
[642] Trial Judgement, vol. 2, para. 570; Exhibit P400.
[643] *Popović et al.* Appeal Judgement, para. 1653; *Šainović et al.* Appeal Judgement, para. 985; *Krajišnik* Appeal Judgement, paras 215, 695-696. See *Šainović et al.* Appeal Judgement, paras 1233, 1242. See also *supra*, para. 110,
[644] *Popović et al.* Appeal Judgement, para. 1653, quoting *Blagojević and Jokić* Appeal Judgement, para. 189. See *supra*, para. 154.
[645] Trial Judgement, vol. 2, para. 733.
[646] Trial Judgement, vol. 2, para. 733.
[647] Stanišić Appeal Brief, para. 253, referring to Trial Judgement, vol. 2, para. 733.
[648] The Appeals Chamber notes that Stanišić refers to Delimustafić as the "Minister of the BiH MUP" (Stanišić Appeal Brief, para. 253) but also notes that Delimustafić made appointments in his capacity as the "SRBiH Minister of Interior" (Trial Judgement, vol. 2, paras 349, 538).

had already appointed the chiefs of the CSBs that existed in BiH and that these CSB chiefs "retained their positions".[649] Stanišić asserts that he only nominated the chiefs of the newly formed CSBs in Bijeljina and Sarajevo,[650] and argues that even then, in Bijeljina, Delimustafić had appointed Predrag Ješurić ("Ješurić") as the SJB Chief and that he, Stanišić, only promoted Ješurić to CSB Chief.[651] Stanišić further submits that the appointments were all temporary and made based on a policy agreed upon at a collegium of BiH Ministry of Interior officials on 1 April 1992, following the split of the Ministry of Interior ("1 April 1992 BiH-MUP Collegium").[652] According to Stanišić, although the Trial Chamber accepted that appointments of the SJB chiefs were made upon the recommendation of regional authorities,[653] it failed to take into account that municipal organs appointed a number of SJB chiefs without the approval, or sometimes even the knowledge, of Stanišić and the RS MUP.[654]

187.   Stanišić also submits that the Trial Chamber "erred by relying on the finding that he 'had the sole authority for establishing special police units and the authority to decide when and how a special unit could be used.'"[655] Referring to an order he issued on 27 July 1992 ("Stanišić's **[page 81]** 27 July 1992 Order"), Stanišić asserts that he addressed the problem of the unauthorised creation of special police units by ordering their disbandment.[656] He contends that the Trial Chamber "omitt[ed] this evidence" while accepting that he and the RS MUP were not informed that local organs had established some special police units.[657] Stanišić argues that the Trial Chamber "erred by accepting evidence but not factoring this evidence into its ultimately flawed findings".[658]

188.   Stanišić further argues that the Trial Chamber erred by finding that he had "'the sole authority' to discipline and dismiss the chiefs of CSBs and SJBs".[659] He asserts that the Trial Chamber's finding is contradicted by: (i) the relevant applicable law at the time;[660] and (ii) the Trial Chamber's own finding that "the statutory duty to initiate disciplinary proceedings lay with the SJB or CSB chief and the Minister was vested with appellate authority".[661] Stanišić contends that he had no basis to wield appellate authority unless disciplinary proceedings were initiated and that where he did have authority to act, "the severest sanction was imposed in the majority of proceedings".[662]

189.   The Prosecution responds that Stanišić's arguments should be summarily dismissed as he repeats failed arguments from trial and has not shown that the Trial Chamber erred in making the impugned finding.[663] With respect to Stanišić's first challenge, it argues that, irrespective of their positions in the SRBiH MUP, the evidence on which the Trial Chamber relied shows that on 1 April 1992, Stanišić appointed CSB chiefs to the newly-formed RS MUP.[664] The Prosecution asserts that in a decision Stanišić issued on 25 April 1992, he allowed CSB chiefs to take over the former SRBiH MUP and immediately inform him

---

[649]   Stanišić Appeal Brief, para. 253, referring to ST214, 19 Jul 2010, T. 12952-12953, ST214, 20 Jul 2010, T. 13050-13052, ST155, 5 Jul 2010, T. 12582-12584, 12574-12575; Stanišić Reply Brief, para. 72. Stanišić adds that all of these persons would have still been appointed, regardless of whether he "did anything or not" (Appeal Hearing, 16 Dec 2015, AT. 105).
[650]   Stanišić Appeal Brief, para. 253.
[651]   Stanišić Appeal Brief, para. 253, referring to Goran Mačar, 11 Jul 2011, T. 23119-23120.
[652]   Stanišić Appeal Brief, para. 253, referring to SZ007, 5 Dec 2011, T. 26105, Exhibits P1408, P1410, P1414, P1416, P384, P2320; Stanišić Reply Brief, para. 72.
[653]   Stanišić Appeal Brief, para. 253, referring to Trial Judgement, vol. 2, para. 736.
[654]   Stanišić Appeal Brief, para. 253, referring to Goran Mačar, 6 Jul 2011, T. 22884-22885, Goran Mačar, 12 Jul 2011, T. 23192-23194; Stanišić Reply Brief, para. 72.
[655]   Stanišić Appeal Brief, para. 255, referring to Trial Judgement, vol. 2, para. 733 (emphasis omitted).
[656]   Stanišić Appeal Brief, para. 255, referring to Exhibit 1D176.
[657]   Stanišić Appeal Brief, para. 255, referring to Trial Judgement, vol. 2, para. 733.
[658]   Stanišić Appeal Brief, para. 255, referring to Trial Judgement, vol. 2, paras 729-765.
[659]   Stanišić Appeal Brief, para. 254, referring to Trial Judgement, vol. 2, para. 733 (emphasis omitted).
[660]   Stanišić Appeal Brief, para. 254, referring to Exhibit P510. Stanišić argues that the legal reasoning according to which he had the sole authority to discipline and dismiss chiefs of the CSB and SJB is applicable for events only after September 1992 as the Trial Chamber accepted that the Rules on Disciplinary Responsibility of Employees within the RS MUP ("Disciplinary Rules") were adopted in September 1992 (Appeal Hearing, 16 Dec 2015, AT. 105, referring to Trial Judgement, vol. 2, paras 14, 695, Tomislav Kovač, 9 Mar 2012, T. 27238, Exhibit 1D54).
[661]   Stanišić Appeal Brief, para. 254, referring to Trial Judgement, vol. 2, para. 695. See Stanišić Reply Brief, para. 73.
[662]   Stanišić Appeal Brief, para. 254, referring to Exhibits P1288, 1D796; Stanišić Reply Brief, para. 73.
[663]   Prosecution Response Brief (Stanišić), para. 112, comparing Stanišić Appeal Brief, para. 253 with Stanišić Final Trial Brief, paras 291, 569-571, 597-598; Prosecution Response Brief (Stanišić), para. 115, referring to *Krajišnik* Appeal Judgement, paras 24, 26.
[664]   Prosecution Response Brief (Stanišić), para. 113, referring to Trial Judgement, vol. 2, para. 579.

when distributing former employees in their CSBs and SJBs ("Stanišić's 25 April 1992 Decision"),[665] and that on 15 May 1992, Stanišić confirmed a number of the temporary appointments that he had made on 1 April 1992.[666] In response to Stanišić's submission that appointments were made on the basis of the policy agreed at the 1 April 1992 BiH-MUP Collegium, the Prosecution argues that in early April 1992 Stanišić **[page 82]** worked to undermine the SRBiH MUP's authority.[667] According to the Prosecution, the Trial Chamber reasonably found that Stanišić made a majority of key appointments in the RS MUP after having considered evidence that Stanišić appointed Serbs to key positions in RS municipalities, upon the proposal of the SDS and crisis staffs, and across the ranks of the RS MUP.[668]

190.   With respect to Stanišić's challenge to the Trial Chamber's findings regarding his authority to establish special police units, the Prosecution responds that Stanišić's argument warrants summary dismissal as he misrepresents the Trial Chamber's factual finding.[669] It contends that the Trial Chamber acknowledged that the RS MUP was not informed that local organs had established some special police units,[670] and that the Trial Chamber gave little weight to the legal authority Stanišić exercised over special police units when determining the overall authority he exercised over the RS MUP.[671]

191.   With regard to Stanišić's challenges to the Trial Chamber's findings regarding his disciplinary powers, the Prosecution responds that Stanišić concedes that he had authority to act in disciplinary cases,[672] and that he removed Borislav Maksimović ("Maksimović"), the Vogošća SJB Chief.[673] It argues that Stanišić had "extensive authority under the RS MUP's disciplinary regime"[674] and that when he acted, the dismissals were for matters not connected to the crimes charged in the Indictment.[675]

192.   Stanišić replies that he did not possess "the unbridled disciplinary power" that the Prosecution attributes to him.[676] He counters that his power to amend the applicable rules was circumscribed but that he worked to reform the RS MUP "as much as his authority allowed".[677] **[page 83]** Stanišić further asserts that the Prosecution fails to address how initiating disciplinary action against individuals found to be JCE members contributed to furthering the JCE.[678]

ii. Analysis

a. Whether the Trial Chamber erred in finding that Stanišić made a majority of key appointments in the RS MUP

193.   The Trial Chamber found that from 1 April 1992, Stanišić made a majority of key appointments in the RS MUP, "rang[ing] from the chief of the SNB, commanders of police, chiefs of the CSBs and SJBs, and the

---

[665]   Prosecution Response Brief (Stanišić), para. 113, referring to Trial Judgement, vol. 2, para. 580.

[666]   Prosecution Response Brief (Stanišić), para. 113, referring to Trial Judgement, vol. 2, para. 579.

[667]   Prosecution Response Brief (Stanišić), para. 113, referring to Trial Judgement, vol. 2, paras 576-577, referring also to Trial Judgement, vol. 2, paras 558, 560.

[668]   Prosecution Response Brief (Stanišić), para. 114, referring to Trial Judgement, vol. 2, paras 578-580. See Appeal Hearing, 16 Dec 2015, AT. 112.

[669]   Prosecution Response Brief (Stanišić), para. 117, referring to *Krajišnik* Appeal Judgement, para. 18.

[670]   Prosecution Response Brief (Stanišić), para. 117, referring to Trial Judgement, vol. 2, para. 733.

[671]   Prosecution Response Brief (Stanišić), para. 117, referring to Trial Judgement, vol. 2, para. 736.

[672]   Prosecution Response Brief (Stanišić), para. 116, referring to Stanišić Appeal Brief, para. 254. The Prosecution contends that Stanišić's authority over the disciplinary regime is also "apparent from his concession that it was he who had the authority to amend and reform the disciplinary system" (Prosecution Response Brief (Stanišić), para. 116, referring to Stanišić Appeal Brief, paras 173, 221-222).

[673]   Prosecution Response Brief (Stanišić), para. 116, referring to Stanišić Appeal Brief, para. 297, Trial Judgement, vol. 2, paras 51, 707-708, 754.

[674]   Prosecution Response Brief (Stanišić), para. 116, referring to Trial Judgement, vol. 2, paras 37, 42, Tomislav Kovač, 7 Mar 2012, T. 27076, Radomir Rodic, 15 Apr 2010, T. 8778.

[675]   Prosecution Response Brief (Stanišić), para. 116, referring to Trial Judgement, vol. 2, paras 51, 698-704, 706-708, 754-755.

[676]   Stanišić Reply Brief, para. 73, referring to Prosecution Response Brief (Stanišić), para. 116.

[677]   Stanišić Reply Brief, para. 73, referring to Stanišić Appeal Brief, paras 173, 221-222, 502(i).

[678]   Stanišić Reply Brief, para. 74, referring to Prosecution Response Brief (Stanišić), para. 116; also referring to Trial Judgement, vol. 2, paras 422, 470, 816, 852, 879.

heads of the various administrations, including personnel, legal, crime prevention, and analysis".[679] It found that Stanišić issued decisions on: (i) 1 April 1992 temporarily appointing Ješurić as the Chief of the Bijeljina CSB, Krsto Savić as the Chief of the Trebinje CSB, Milenko Karišik ("Karišik") as the Commander of the MUP Special Police Detachment ("SPD"), Witness Andrija Bjelošević ("Witness Bjelošević") as the Chief of the Doboj CSB, Župljanin as the Chief of the Banja Luka CSB, and Vojin Popović ("Popović") as the Chief of the Gacko SJB;[680] (ii) 15 May 1992 confirming the appointments of Ješurić, Krsto Savić, Karišik, Witness Bjelošević, and Župljanin;[681] and (iii) 6 August 1992 appointing Dragiša Mihić as the Deputy Under-Secretary of the National Security Sevice ("SNB") of the MUP and Vlastimir Kušmuk as an advisor on duties and tasks at the SJB at the MUP.[682] The Trial Chamber also found that on 6 May 1991, Delimustafić appointed Župljanin as the Chief of the Banja Luka CSB.[683] Further, the Trial Chamber found that Stanišić's 25 April 1992 Decision authorised CSB chiefs to take over former SRBiH MUP staff and that, according to this decision, CSB chiefs were to immediately inform Stanišić when distributing former employees in their CSBs and SJBs, and to obtain his prior agreement when redistributing former high-level SRBiH MUP employees, such as heads of SNB, Public Security, SJB, and police station commanders.[684]

194.   The Trial Chamber also noted that, "in several municipalities", local crisis staffs appointed police chiefs, and local organs established some special police units, without informing the RS MUP.[685] It found that in these municipalities, crisis staffs "influenced the appointments of all **[page 84]** leading positions in the police stations and crime squads".[686] For the most part, SJB heads did not inform the CSBs or the RS MUP of situations – even when required – but instead informed the crisis staffs.[687]

195.   With respect to Stanišić's argument that Delimustafić had appointed the chiefs of the CSBs that existed in BiH and that they "retained their positions",[688] the Appeals Chamber first notes the Trial Chamber's finding that Delimustafić appointed Župljanin as the Chief of the Banja Luka CSB on 6 May 1991[689] but it did not enter similar findings with respect to any other CSB chiefs. Further, the Appeals Chamber is not satisfied that the evidence upon which Stanišić relies supports his argument as there are no references in this evidence that Delimustafić appointed any CSB chiefs.[690] The Appeals Chamber also notes the Trial Chamber's finding that on 1 April 1992, Stanišić temporarily appointed Karišik as the Commander of MUP SPD, and Ješurić, Krsto Savić, Witness Bjelošević, and Župljanin, as the chiefs of their respective CSBs, and that on 15 May 1992, he confirmed the appointments of Karišik, Ješurić, Krsto Savić, Witness Bjelošević, and Župljanin as the CSB chiefs.[691] Even if Delimustafić had appointed CSB chiefs other than Župljanin, in light of Stanišić's decision temporarily appointing and then confirming the appointments of these CSB chiefs, Stanišić has not established that Delimustafić's earlier involvement undermines the Trial Chamber's findings that from 1 April 1992 Stanišić made a majority of key appointments in the RS MUP. Stanišić concedes that he "had a duty as Minister to appoint people to posts in the Ministry as it was being set up".[692] The mere fact that some individuals retained the positions held before 1 April 1992 is not sufficient to demonstrate that no reasonable trier of fact could have concluded that Stanišić made these key appointments.

---

[679]   Trial Judgement, vol. 2, para. 733.
[680]   Trial Judgement, vol. 2, para. 579, referring to Exhibits P1000, P1411, P1409, P1416, P1414, P1413, P1410, P1408, P2016.
[681]   Trial Judgement, vol. 2, para. 579, referring to Christian Nielsen, 14 Dec 2009, T. 4752, Andrija Bjelošević, 20 May 2011, T. 21072-21073, Exhibits P456, P170, P457, P455, P458.
[682]   Trial Judgement, vol. 2, para. 579, referring to Exhibits P2022, P2021.
[683]   Trial Judgement, vol. 2, para. 349, referring to ST213, 4 Mar 2010, T. 7204 (private session), Exhibit P2043.
[684]   Trial Judgement, vol. 2, para. 580, referring to Petko Panić, 12 Nov 2009, T. 3001-3002, Exhibit 1D73.
[685]   Trial Judgement, vol. 2, para. 733.
[686]   Trial Judgement, vol. 2, para. 251, referring to Goran Mačar, 6 Jul 2011, T. 22897, 22906, 22909.
[687]   Trial Judgement, vol. 2, para. 251, referring to Goran Mačar, 6 Jul 2011, T. 22896-22898.
[688]   See *supra*, para. 186.
[689]   Trial Judgement, vol. 2, para. 349 referring to ST213, 4 Mar 2010, T. 7204 (private session), Exhibit P2043.
[690]   Stanišić Appeal Brief, para. 253 referring to ST214, 19 Jul 2010, T. 12952-12953, ST214, 20 Jul 2010, T. 13050-13052, ST155, 5 Jul 2010, T. 12582-12584, 12574-12575, Goran Mačar, 11 Jul 2011, T. 23119-23120.
[691]   Trial Judgement, vol. 2, para. 579, referring to Exhibits P1409, P1414, P1410, P1408, Christian Nielsen, 14 Dec 2009, T. 4752, Andrija Bjelošević, 20 May 2011, T. 21072-21073, P455, P456, P458, P170, P457.
[692]   Stanišić Appeal Brief, para. 253.

196.   Turning to Stanišić's argument that all the appointments were temporary and made based on a policy agreed upon at the 1 April BiH-MUP 1992 Collegium,[693] the Appeals Chamber observes that Stanišić ignores the Trial Chamber's findings that on 15 May 1992, he confirmed the appointments of Ješurić, Krsto Savić, Karišik, Witness Bjelošević, and Župljanin who had previously been appointed temporarily.[694] Further, the Appeals Chamber observes that the order **[page 85]** upon which Stanišić seeks to rely to support his contention is general in nature.[695] While this order states that "some personnel decisions were discussed as well", a clear policy concerning appointments is notably absent.[696] Therefore, by advancing his argument only on the basis of this evidence, Stanišić has failed to demonstrate that the Trial Chamber erred in its findings on his power to make key appointments.

197.   Insofar as Stanišić argues that the Trial Chamber failed to take into account that municipal organs appointed a number of SJB chiefs without the approval, or sometimes even the knowledge, of Stanišić and the RS MUP, the Appeals Chamber notes that the Trial Chamber explicitly considered the role that local crisis staffs played in the appointment of police chiefs in several municipalities.[697] In this regard, the Trial Chamber found that the crisis staffs "influenced the appointments of all leading positions in the police stations and crime squads"[698] and that Stanišić took into account the proposals of the SDS and crisis staffs when appointing Serbs to key positions in RS municipalities.[699] The Appeals Chamber therefore finds no merit in Stanišić's argument.

198.   Moreover, the Appeals Chamber observes that, in finding that Stanišić made a majority of key appointments in the RS MUP, the Trial Chamber indicated that these positions ranged from the SNB chief, to police commanders, to chiefs of the CSBs and SJBs, and finally to the heads of the various administrations, including personnel, legal, crime prevention, and analysis.[700] Stanišić only challenges the Trial Chamber's findings on the appointment of CSB chiefs and some SJB chiefs without addressing the other key appointments, and has not explained why the Trial Chamber's finding that he made a majority of key appointments in the RS MUP should not stand on the basis of the remaining evidence.

199.   For the reasons set out above, the Appeals Chamber finds that Stanišić has failed to show that no reasonable trier of fact could have concluded that he made a majority of key appointments in the RS MUP. **[page 86]**

<u>b. Whether the Trial Chamber erred in finding that Stanišić had the sole authority to establish and decide on the use of special police units</u>

200.   The Trial Chamber found that Stanišić "had the sole authority for establishing special police units and the authority to decide when and how a special unit could be used" but noted "that the RS MUP was not informed of the establishment of some special police units by local organs".[701] It also found that Stanišić's 27 July 1992 Order called for "the immediate disbandment and the placement of all special units formed during the war in the areas of the CSBs under the command of the VRS"[702]

---

[693]   Stanišić Appeal Brief, para. 253, referring to SZ007, 5 Dec 2011, T. 26105, Exhibits P1408, P1410, P1414, P1416, P384, P2320; Stanišić Reply Brief, para. 72. See *supra*, para. 186.

[694]   Trial Judgement, vol. 2, para. 579, referring to Exhibits P1409, P1414, P1410, P1408, Christian Nielsen, 14 Dec 2009, T. 4752, Andrija Bjelošević, 20 May 2011, T. 21072-21073, P455, P456, P458, P170, P457.

[695]   Stanišić Appeal Brief, para. 253, referring to Exhibit P2320; Stanišić Reply Brief, para. 72.

[696]   Exhibit P2320.

[697]   Trial Judgement, vol. 2, para. 733.

[698]   Trial Judgement, vol. 2, para. 251, referring to Goran Mačar, 6 Jul 2011, T. 22897, 22906, 22909.

[699]   Trial Judgement, vol. 2, para. 578, referring to ST121, 24 Nov 2009, T. 3723-3724 (private session).

[700]   Trial Judgement, vol. 2, paras 579 (finding that on 1 April 1992 Stanišić temporarily appointed Maksimović as Commander of the RS MUP, Nedeljko Kesić as Chief of the SNB, Malko Koroman as Inspector at the Sarajevo CSB, Popović as Chief of the Gacko SJB; on 4 May 1992 Stanišić temporarily appointed Branko Stanković to cryptographic data protection in Ilijaš; on 6 August 1992 Stanišić appointed Dragiša Mihić as Deputy Under-Secretary of the SNB of the MUP and Vlastimir Kušmuk to the position of Advisor on duties and tasks at the SJB at the MUP), 733.

[701]   Trial Judgement, vol. 2, para. 733. See Trial Judgement, vol. 2, para. 604.

[702]   Trial Judgement, vol. 2, para. 605, referring to Exhibit 1D176.

201.   The Appeals Chamber notes that although the Trial Chamber did not cite the evidence that it considered when making the impugned finding[703] about the scope of Stanišić's authority to establish and use special police units,[704] the Trial Chamber did provide citations in the section concerning "Special Police Units".[705] In this section, which included discussions of both special police units under Stanišić and special police units in municipalities,[706] the Trial Chamber considered, *inter alia*, the testimonies of: (i) Witness Obren Petrović ("Witness Petrović"), "that under the law, only the Minister, Mićo Stanišić, had the power to establish special police units";[707] (ii) Witness Drago Borovčanin ("Witness Borovčanin") that "during the initial period when the RS MUP was still organising itself, local active and reserve policemen had organised themselves into special units to defend their towns" and that before Witness Borovčanin's inspection of the Ilijaš SJB in May 1992 "neither [Borovčanin] nor the RS MUP knew that a special police unit had been set up there";[708] (iii) Witness Dobrislav Planojević ("Witness Planojević") that "Stanišić had the authority to decide when and how these special units could be used";[709] and (iv) Witness Planojević and Witness Bjelošević that they were required to seek Stanišić's approval when they wished to use the special police units.[710] In support of its finding that Stanišić disbanded all special police units **[page 87]** formed during the war in the areas of the CSBs and placed their members under the command of the VRS, the Trial Chamber relied on Stanišić's 27 July 1992 Order.[711]

202.   Recalling that a trial judgement should be read as a whole,[712] the Appeals Chamber finds no merit in Stanišić's submission that the Trial Chamber omitted evidence that he disbanded special police units. Further, in light of the body of evidence set out above and the Trial Chamber's discussion thereof,[713] the Appeals Chamber is satisfied that a reasonable trier of fact could have concluded that Stanišić had the sole authority for establishing special police units and the authority to decide when and how a special police unit could be used. Therefore, the Appeals Chamber finds that Stanišić has failed to demonstrate that the Trial Chamber erred.

c. Whether the Trial Chamber erred in finding that Stanišić had the sole authority to discipline and dismiss the chiefs of CSBs and SJBs

203.   The Trial Chamber concluded that Stanišić had the sole authority to appoint, discipline, and dismiss the chiefs of CSBs and SJBs.[714] It found that the RS MUP's disciplinary regime was set out in two documents: the LIA, which was adopted on 28 February 1992 and entered into force on 31 March 1992,[715] and the Rules on Disciplinary Responsibility of Employees of the RS MUP ("Disciplinary Rules") that Stanišić adopted on 19 September 1992.[716] The Trial Chamber found that "the statutory duty to initiate proceedings [...] lay with the SJB or CSB chief in the first instance and the Minister of Interior was vested with the final appellate authority over sanctions imposed".[717] However, "[i]n the case of a SJB or CSB chief being the subject of misconduct or violations of the LIA, the Minister was directly responsible for his discipline and dismissal."[718]

---

[703]   See *supra*, para. 187.

[704]   Trial Judgement, vol. 2, para. 733.

[705]   Trial Judgement, vol. 2, paras 601-609.

[706]   Trial Judgement, vol. 2, paras 601-603 (discussing special police units under Stanišić), 604-609 (discussing special police units in municipalities).

[707]   Trial Judgement, vol. 2, para. 604, referring to Obren Petrović, 12 May 2010, T. 10005-10006.

[708]   Trial Judgement, vol. 2, para. 604, fns 1579-1580, referring to Drago Borovčanin, 22 Feb 2010, T. 6651-6655. See Trial Judgement, vol. 2, fn. 1575, referring to Exhibit P989, p. 4.

[709]   Trial Judgement, vol. 2, para. 602, referring to Dobrislav Planojević, 22 Oct 2010, T. 16404.

[710]   Trial Judgement, vol. 2, para. 602, fns 1574 (referring to Dobrislav Planojević, 22 Oct 2010, T. 16404), 1575 (referring to Andrija Bjelošević, 20 Apr 2011, T. 19883-19884). See Trial Judgement, vol. 2, fn. 1575, referring to Exhibit 1D520.

[711]   Trial Judgement, vol. 2, para. 605, referring to Exhibit 1D176, p. 1.

[712]   *Šainović et al.* Appeal Judgement, paras 306, 321; *Boškoski and Tarčulovski* Appeal Judgement, para. 67; *Orić* Appeal Judgement, para. 38.

[713]   See *supra*, para. 201; Trial Judgement, vol. 2, paras 602, 604-605.

[714]   Trial Judgement, vol. 2, para. 733.

[715]   Exhibit P530; Trial Judgement, vol. 2, paras 5-6, 8.

[716]   Trial Judgement, vol. 2, para. 42, referring to Tomislav Kovač, 9 Mar 2012, T. 27238-27239, Exhibit 1D54. See Trial Judgement, vol. 2, para. 695.

[717]   Trial Judgement, vol. 2, para. 695.

[718]   Trial Judgement, vol. 2, para. 695, referring to "RS MUP section". See Trial Judgement, vol. 2, para. 40, referring to Tomislav Kovač, 8 Mar 2012, T. 27092.

204.   The Trial Chamber further found that "[a]s the Minister, Stanišić was under a duty, both under the law applicable in the RS at the relevant time and under international law, to discipline and dismiss the personnel of his Ministry who had committed crimes."[719] It found that Stanišić exercised these powers when, through Witness Tomislav Kovač ("Witness Kovač"), Assistant **[page 88]** Minister of Interior,[720] he initiated action against: Malko Koroman ("Koroman"), Chief of the Pale SJB; Witness Stevan Todorović ("Witness Todorović"), Chief of the Bosanski Šamac SJB; Witness Petrović, Chief of the Doboj SJB; Maksimović, Chief of the Vogošća SJB, and Simo Drljača ("Drljača"), Chief of the Prijedor SJB.[721]

205.   The Appeals Chamber notes that, to support his assertion that the Trial Chamber's finding on his authority to appoint, discipline, and dismiss the chiefs of the CSBs and SJBs is contradicted by "the relevant applicable law at the time",[722] Stanišić cites Exhibit P510, the Law on Internal Affairs of the former SRBiH which was published on 29 June 1990 ("Law of 1990").[723] The Appeals Chamber observes however that the LIA, which entered into force on 31 March 1992, was the operative law at the time of the Indictment – not the Law of 1990.[724] The Appeals Chamber observes in any case that the differences between the LIA and the Law of 1990 are minor and considers that Stanišić's reference to Exhibit P510 was an oversight. Even if Stanišić intended to rely on the LIA as the operative law, he has not provided any clear indication of what provision in LIA (or in Exhibit P510) contradicts the impugned finding. The Appeals Chamber therefore finds that this undeveloped assertion is incapable of undermining the Trial Chamber's finding.

206.   Turning to Stanišić assertion that the Trial Chamber's finding that "the statutory duty to initiate disciplinary proceedings lay with the SJB or CSB chief and the Minister was vested with appellate authority" contradicts its finding that he had the sole authority to appoint, discipline, and dismiss the chiefs of CSBs and SJBs,[725] the Appeals Chamber observes that a plain reading of these findings does not disclose a contradiction. Stanišić does not identify any evidence that the Trial Chamber failed to consider or explain why the Trial Chamber's conclusion was unreasonable. His argument in this regard thus fails.

207.   Insofar as Stanišić's contention that he had no basis to wield appellate authority unless disciplinary proceedings were initiated can be understood to mean that his ability to act was restricted,[726] the Appeals Chamber notes that, under the LIA, the Minister of Interior had to make decisions about dismissing people from service[727] and was authorised to initiate disciplinary proceedings against CSB chiefs.[728] After Stanišić adopted the Disciplinary Rules in **[page 89]** September 1992, the disciplinary regime was "expanded to heads of departments within the MUP, commanders of police detachments, and CSB chiefs" and that appeals were dealt with by the Minister of Interior.[729] There is nothing to suggest that either the LIA or the Disciplinary Rules restricted Stanišić's authority to initiate proceedings against CSB chiefs. Further, in October 1992, Stanišić exercised his authority and had actions initiated against several SJB chiefs including: Koroman, Witness Todorović, Witness Petrović, Maksimović, and Drljača.[730] The Appeals Chamber notes that Stanišić relies on disciplinary decisions that he issued in December 1992, confirming the termination of employment of the Doboj CSB Chief[731] and a Banja Luka SJB police officer,[732] but does not find that these decisions support the contention that his authority was limited to appeals of disciplinary proceedings. Accordingly, Stanišić has failed to demonstrate that no reasonable trier of fact could have found he had the sole authority to discipline and dismiss the chiefs of CSBs and SJBs.

---

[719]   Trial Judgement, vol. 2, para. 754.
[720]   Trial Judgement, vol. 2, paras 39, 256.
[721]   Trial Judgement, vol. 2, para. 754. See Trial Judgement, vol. 2, para. 698. See also Trial Judgement, vol. 2, para. 604 (Witness Petrović was the Chief of the Doboj SJB).
[722]   See *supra*, para. 188.
[723]   Stanišić Appeal Brief, para. 254, referring to Exhibit P510.
[724]   Exhibit P530; Trial Judgement, vol. 2, paras 5-6, 8.
[725]   See *supra*, para. 188.
[726]   See *supra*, para. 188.
[727]   Trial Judgement, vol. 2, para. 40, referring to Tomislav Kovač, 7 Mar 2012, T. 27076.
[728]   Trial Judgement, vol. 2, para. 40, referring to Tomislav Kovač, 8 Mar 2012, T. 27092.
[729]   Trial Judgement, vol. 2, para. 695, referring to ST161, 19 Nov 2009, T. 3477-3478 (closed session), Vladimir Tutuš, 19 Mar 2010, T. 7876-7877, Radomir Rodić, 16 Apr 2010, T. 8806, Mladen Bajagić, 4 May 2011, T. 20221-20223, Exhibit 1D54.
[730]   Trial Judgement, vol. 2, paras 707, 754.
[731]   Exhibit 1D796.
[732]   Exhibit P1288.

iii. Conclusion

208.   For the foregoing reasons, the Appeals Chamber finds that Stanišić has failed to demonstrate any error in the Trial Chamber's findings, concerning his authority with respect to the RS MUP, that he: (i) made a majority of key appointments in the RS MUP from 1 April 1992; (ii) had the sole authority for establishing special police units and the authority to decide when and how a special unit could be used; and (iii) had the sole authority to appoint, discipline, and dismiss the chiefs of CSBs and SJBs.

f. Alleged errors in the Trial Chamber's findings regarding Stanišić's overall command and control over the RS MUP police forces and of all other internal affairs organs

209.   The Trial Chamber considered "the evidence adduced by the Defence to show that the local municipal bodies, particularly the local Crisis Staffs, interfered with the appointments of police at the SJB level".[733] However, recalling "its finding that, throughout the Indictment period, the Bosnian Serb leadership was in charge of the events taking place in the municipalities through its control over the Serb Forces, SDS party structure, Crisis Staffs, and the RS Government",[734] the Trial Chamber concluded that "the local police leadership was [...] part of the formulation and **[page 90]** implementation of the decisions taken by the Crisis Staffs, which were in accordance with instruction from the RS Presidency, MUP, and the SDS".[735]

210.   The Trial Chamber found that "taking into account the role played by municipal bodies, Stanišić had overall command and control over the RS MUP police forces and of all other internal affairs organs in accordance with the policies and decisions adopted by the Presidency, NSC, and the BSA".[736] The Trial Chamber referred to several factors concerning Stanišić's specific acts and conduct that it considered bore out this conclusion.[737]

i. Submissions of the parties

211.   Stanišić submits that when analysing his alleged contribution, the Trial Chamber erred by "supplementing" evidence about his acts and conduct with "its findings on the [Bosnian Serb leadership], of which Stanišić was found to be a member".[738]

212.   In particular, Stanišić challenges the Trial Chamber's finding that he had overall command and control over the RS MUP police forces.[739] He argues that this finding was made despite the Trial Chamber's: (i) inability to make a conclusive finding regarding authority over policemen who were re-subordinated to the military;[740] and (ii) implicit acknowledgement that the municipal bodies interfered in the work of the RS MUP.[741] According to him, as a result, irrespective of the lack of his *de facto* authority over re-subordinated forces or due to the interference by other organs, the Trial Chamber found that he had overall command and control over all RS MUP forces "by virtue of the overarching control of the [Bosnian Serb leadership], of which he was found to be a part".[742]

213.   Stanišić also challenges the Trial Chamber's conclusion that "the local police leadership was [...] part of the formulation and implementation of the decisions taken by the Crisis Staffs, which were in accordance with instruction from the RS Presidency, MUP, and the SDS".[743] He asserts that the Trial Chamber did not

---

[733]   Trial Judgement, vol. 2, para. 735.
[734]   Trial Judgement, vol. 2, para. 735. See Trial Judgement, vol. 2, para. 311.
[735]   Trial Judgement, vol. 2, para. 735
[736]   Trial Judgement, vol. 2, para. 736.
[737]   Trial Judgement, vol. 2, para. 736.
[738]   Stanišić Appeal Brief, para. 256.
[739]   Stanišić Appeal Brief, para. 259, referring to Trial Judgement, vol. 2, para. 736.
[740]   Stanišić Appeal Brief, para. 259, referring to Trial Judgement, vol. 2, para. 342. See Stanišić Appeal Brief, para. 250, referring to Trial Judgement, vol. 2, paras 729-765. Stanišić argues that there could be no "legally correct assessment" of whether he had command and control over RS MUP forces without a conclusive finding on re-subordination (Stanišić Appeal Brief, para. 250, referring to Trial Judgement, vol. 2, para. 342). See also Stanišić Reply Brief, para. 75.
[741]   Stanišić Appeal Brief, para. 259, referring to Trial Judgement, vol. 2, para. 736.
[742]   Stanišić Appeal Brief, para. 259, referring to Trial Judgement, vol. 2, para. 736.
[743]   Stanišić Appeal Brief, para. 257, referring to Trial Judgement, vol. 2, para. 735.

analyse, "through the prism of Stanišić's personal acts and conduct", evidence that local crisis staffs and other entities or organs interfered in police **[page 91]** appointments.[744] Rather, he contends, the Trial Chamber's evaluation of the evidence was tainted by its findings that the Bosnian Serb leadership was in charge of the events taking place in the Municipalities through its control over crisis staffs, and that the crisis staffs' decisions accorded with instruction from the RS Presidency, RS MUP, and the SDS.[745] Stanišić submits that the Trial Chamber's "logic is circular and is patently incorrect".[746] He argues that the finding that the Bosnian Serb leadership, of which Stanišić was found to be a member, wielded authority throughout the Municipalities erroneously superseded evidence that he did not have authority.[747]

214. The Prosecution responds that it was reasonable for the Trial Chamber to conclude that Stanišić exercised overall command and control over the RS MUP based on, *inter alia*, his: (i) appointments of RS MUP personnel; (ii) orders that headquarters personnel inspect and visit municipalities; (iii) orders to investigate crimes allegedly committed by RS MUP members; and (iv) reassignment of criminal elements from the police to the army.[748] It further responds that the Trial Chamber considered evidence of interference by local crisis staffs in police appointments but found that, in light of all the evidence before it, it did not diminish Stanišić's authority because he and the crisis staffs pursued the same goal.[749] The Prosecution further argues that Stanišić merely repeats his failed trial argument[750] and that the absence of a general finding on the issue of re-subordination does not show that the Trial Chamber was wrong to rely on the factors noted above in concluding that Stanišić exercised command and control over the RS MUP.[751]

ii. Analysis

215. The Appeals Chamber notes that, in reaching its conclusion that "Stanišić had overall command and control over the RS MUP police forces and of all other internal affairs organs", the Trial Chamber considered Stanišić's following acts and conduct: (i) the assignment of trusted SRBiH MUP members to important positions; (ii) the appointment of SJB chiefs upon the recommendation of the regional authorities; (iii) the assignment of SJBs to newly established CSBs; (iv) the ordering of personnel from headquarters to conduct inspections and visits of municipalities; (v) orders to investigate crimes allegedly committed by RS MUP members; and (vi) the **[page 92]** reassignment of criminal elements from the police to the army.[752] Thus, contrary to Stanišić's assertion, rather than reaching the impugned finding "by virtue of the overarching control of the [Bosnian Serb leadership]" in the Municipalities,[753] the Trial Chamber took into account these six factors concerning his individual acts and conduct to reach its conclusion on his overall command and control.[754] Stanišić has not explained why the Trial Chamber's finding should not otherwise stand on the basis of these factors and thus, he has also failed to demonstrate that the Trial Chamber's analysis was "impermissibly tainted"[755] by its findings on the Bosnian Serb leadership.

216. With respect to Stanišić's argument that the Trial Chamber did not make a conclusive finding regarding authority over police who were re-subordinated to the military, and erroneously found his command and control irrespective of the lack of his *de facto* authority over re-subordinated police forces, the Appeals Chamber recalls that it has dismissed this argument elsewhere in this Judgement.[756]

---

[744] Stanišić Appeal Brief, para. 257, referring to Trial Judgement, vol. 2, para. 735.
[745] Stanišić Appeal Brief, para. 257 referring to Trial Judgement, vol. 2, para. 735.
[746] Stanišić Appeal Brief, para. 258.
[747] Stanišić Appeal Brief, para. 258.
[748] Prosecution Response Brief (Stanišić), para. 109, referring to Trial Judgement, vol. 2, paras 48-51, 53, 576-580, 588, 591-594, 596, 600, 613, 627, 637, 640-641, 643-646, 649, 655-656, 664-670, 675-678, 682, 684-685, 687, 698, 701-704, 706-708, 714-718, 721-725, 727-728, 736.
[749] Prosecution Response Brief (Stanišić), para. 110, referring to Trial Judgement, vol. 2, paras 735-736.
[750] Prosecution Response Brief (Stanišić), para. 110, comparing Stanišić Appeal Brief, paras 257-259 with Stanišić Final Trial Brief, paras 571, 597-598.
[751] Prosecution Response Brief (Stanišić), para. 110.
[752] Trial Judgement, vol. 2, para. 736.
[753] Stanišić Appeal Brief, para. 259.
[754] Trial Judgement, vol. 2, para. 736.
[755] Stanišić Appeal Brief, para. 257.
[756] See *supra*, paras 126-127.

217.   Turning to Stanišić's assertion that the Trial Chamber failed to analyse the Defence evidence of interference by local crisis staffs and other entities or organs in police appointments through the prism of Stanišić's personal acts and conduct, the Appeals Chamber notes that the Trial Chamber explicitly considered "the evidence adduced by the Defence to show that the local municipal bodies, particularly the local Crisis Staffs, interfered with the appointments of police at the SJB level"[757] but concluded that "the Variant A and B Instructions envisaged the creation and involvement of local bodies, including the local Crisis Staffs, at the municipal level".[758] After considering the aforementioned, alongside "evidence that the local SDS largely retained control over the Crisis Staffs in municipalities", the Trial Chamber was "satisfied that the local police leadership was in fact part of the formulation and implementation of the decisions taken by the Crisis Staffs, which were in accordance with instruction from the RS Presidency, MUP, and the SDS".[759] The Trial Chamber further concluded that the RS MUP was able to gradually restore its **[page 93]** own influence after the autonomous regions and the crisis staffs were abolished in August and September 1992[760] and that even though at times there were conflicts between the various entities, including the crisis staffs, "they all shared and worked towards the same goal under the Bosnian Serb leadership".[761] As stated above, having regard to these contextual factors combined with the factors relating to Stanišić's personal acts and conduct,[762] the Trial Chamber arrived at its conclusion that he had "overall command and control over the RS MUP police forces and of all other internal affairs organs".[763]

218.   Moreover, the Appeals Chamber recalls that a trial chamber has discretion in weighing and assessing the evidence[764] and that it is within the discretion of a trial chamber to evaluate discrepancies and to consider the credibility of the evidence as a whole, without explaining its decision in every detail.[765] In light of the above,[766] the Appeals Chamber finds that Stanišić has failed to demonstrate that the Trial Chamber erred in its evaluation of the evidence.

219.   For the foregoing reasons, the Appeals Chamber concludes that Stanišić has failed to demonstrate that the Trial Chamber erred in its assessment of the evidence about his acts and conduct or of the evidence about the Bosnian Serb leadership's authority in reaching its finding that he had overall command and control over the RS MUP forces.

g. Conclusion

220.   For the reasons set out above, the Appeals Chamber finds that Stanišić has not demonstrated that the Trial Chamber erred in its findings with respect to his: (i) involvement in establishing Bosnian Serb institutions in BiH, including the SDS and the RS MUP;[767] (ii) close relationship with Karadžić and direct communication with the RS Presidency;[768] (iii) knowledge of the Variant A and B Instructions;[769] (iv) key-

---

[757]   Trial Judgement, vol. 2, para. 735. Indeed, in the section concerning "Municipal Crisis Staffs", the Trial Chamber provided citations to evidence showing that the crisis staffs "influenced the appointments of all leading positions in the police stations and crime squads" (Trial Judgement, vol. 2, para. 251, referring to Goran Mačar, 6 Jul 2011, T. 22897, 22906, 22909).

[758]   Trial Judgement, vol. 2, para. 735 (noting that "municipal executive bodies were established with the local SDS representative as its president" and "Crisis Staffs were composed of the local Bosnian Serb leaders, including the chief of the relevant SJB or CSB" and recalling that, "throughout the Indictment period, the Bosnian Serb leadership was in charge of the events taking place in the municipalities through its control over the Serb Forces, SDS party structure, Crisis Staffs, and the RS Government, and that even though at times there were conflicts between these various entities, they all shared and worked towards the same goal under the Bosnian Serb leadership").

[759]   Trial Judgement, vol. 2, para. 735.

[760]   Trial Judgement, vol. 2, para. 251.

[761]   Trial Judgement, vol. 2, para. 735. See Trial Judgement, vol. 2, para. 311.

[762]   See *supra*, para. 215.

[763]   Trial Judgement, vol. 2, para. 736.

[764]   *Đorđević* Appeal Judgement, para. 483, referring to *Boškoski and Tarčulovski* Appeal Judgement, para. 14, *Kupreškić et al.* Appeal Judgement, paras 30-32, *Nchamihigo* Appeal Judgement, para. 47.

[765]   *Đorđević* Appeal Judgement, para. 797; *Kvočka et al.* Appeal Judgement, para. 23, referring to *Čelebići* Appeal Judgement, paras 481, 498, *Kupreškić et al.* Appeal Judgement, para. 31.

[766]   See *supra*, paras 215-217.

[767]   Trial Judgement, vol. 2, para. 729.

[768]   Trial Judgement, vol. 2, para. 730.

[769]   Trial Judgement, vol. 2, para. 731.

role in the decision-making authorities from early 1992 onwards;[770] (v) authority with respect to the RS MUP;[771] and (vi) overall command and control over the RS **[page 94]** MUP police forces and of all other internal affairs organs.[772] Consequently, Stanišić' assertion that the cumulative effect of these errors is "the total contradiction" of the Trial Chamber's finding that he participated in the enunciation and implementation of the Bosnian Serb policy as it evolved,[773] also fails. Stanišić's arguments with respect to his role in the creation of Bosnian Serb bodies and policies are therefore dismissed in their entirety.

(ii) Alleged errors in relation to RS MUP forces' role in combat activities and in the takeover of RS municipalities (subsection (B)(ii) of Stanišić's sixth ground of appeal)

221.   The Trial Chamber found that the municipalities of Banja Luka, Bijeljina, Bileća, Bosanski Šamac, Brčko, Doboj, Donji Vakuf, Gacko, Ilijaš, Ključ, Kotor Varoš, Pale, Prijedor, Sanski Most, Teslić, Vlasenica, Višegrad, Vogošća, and Zvornik were taken over in the months of April and June 1992, in accordance with the Variant A and B Instructions through the joint action of the RS MUP and other Serb forces.[774] The Trial Chamber made a number of specific findings regarding the role of RS MUP forces in combat activities and takeovers of the aforementioned municipalities and Stanišić's actions in this respect.

222.   First, the Trial Chamber found that, within the context of an ethnically motivated armed conflict, the intent behind the RS MUP's ostensibly legitimate requirement that all of its employees sign solemn declarations, was to provide a pretext to dismiss and disarm non-Serbs from the RS MUP.[775] Second, the Trial Chamber found that, following the call for mobilisation of all reserves, Stanišić's 15 May 1992 Order instructed RS MUP forces to be organised into "wartime units" by the chiefs of the CSBs and SJBs.[776] The Trial Chamber indicated that, in light of this order and Karadžić's order to Stanišić of 1 July 1992 to transfer 60 specially trained policemen, deployed in Crepoljsko, and "place them under the military command of the SRK" ("Karadžić's 1 July 1992 Order"),[777] it attached little weight to Stanišić's statement that the RS MUP was not consulted with regard to the reassignment of RS MUP forces to the army for combat tasks.[778] Third, the Trial Chamber found that the RS Government, and eventually the VRS, relied to a large extent on the RS MUP forces for combat activities.[779] The Trial Chamber found specifically that Stanišić issued orders for police forces, both regular and reserve units, to participate in "coordinated action with the **[page 95]** armed forces" and facilitated the arming of the RS MUP forces.[780] Fourth, the Trial Chamber found that, as the highest commander of the RS MUP forces and the administrative head of the organs of the RS MUP, Stanišić received reports of the involvement of the police forces in combat activities.[781] Fifth, the Trial Chamber found that the evidence of Stanišić seeking recognition from other Bosnian Serb leaders for the contributions and achievements of the RS MUP in combat activities supports a finding that Stanišić deployed the police in furtherance of the decisions of the Bosnian Serb authorities.[782] The Trial Chamber found that, despite being aware of the commission of crimes, Stanišić consistently approved the deployment of the RS MUP forces to combat activities along with the other Serb forces and only sought to withdraw regular policemen from combat activities towards the end of 1992, when most of the territory of RS had been consolidated.[783] Finally, the Trial Chamber listed several JCE members who were directly appointed by Stanišić, and who, as part of the police hierarchy and their subordinate forces, were involved in the widespread and systematic takeovers of municipalities.[784]

770   Trial Judgement, vol. 2, para. 732.
771   Trial Judgement, vol. 2, para. 733.
772   Trial Judgement, vol. 2, para. 736.
773   Stanišić Appeal Brief, para. 260.
774   Trial Judgement, vol. 2, para. 737.
775   Trial Judgement, vol. 2, para. 738.
776   Trial Judgement, vol. 2, para. 739.
777   Trial Judgement, vol. 2, para. 591.
778   Trial Judgement, vol. 2, para. 739.
779   Trial Judgement, vol. 2, para. 739.
780   Trial Judgement, vol. 2, para. 740.
781   Trial Judgement, vol. 2, para. 741.
782   Trial Judgement, vol. 2, para. 742.
783   Trial Judgement, vol. 2, para. 743.
784   Trial Judgement, vol. 2, para. 744.

a. Submissions of the parties

223.   Stanišić raises six general challenges to the Trial Chamber's findings on the role of RS MUP forces in combat activities and takeovers of the municipalities of Banja Luka, Bijeljina, Bileća, Bosanski Šamac, Brčko, Doboj, Donji Vakuf, Gacko, Ilijaš, Ključ, Kotor Varoš, Pale, Prijedor, Sanski Most, Teslić, Vlasenica, Višegrad, Vogošća, and Zvornik.[785]

224.   First, he challenges the Trial Chamber's finding on the intent behind the requirement for all RS MUP employees to sign solemn declarations.[786] He submits that the Trial Chamber improperly imputed a persecutory intention despite having acknowledged that it is common to require solemn declarations when assuming duties in a law enforcement agency.[787] Stanišić contends that the Trial Chamber failed to consider that the solemn declaration was mandatory for all authorised RS MUP officials, irrespective of ethnicity, and that it was itself non-discriminatory.[788]

225.   Second, Stanišić challenges the Trial Chamber's findings relating to the reassignment and the deployment of RS MUP forces. He submits that the Trial Chamber improperly dismissed his **[page 96]** statement that the RS MUP was not consulted about the reassignment of police forces and contends that it incorrectly assessed: (i) Stanišić's 15 May 1992 Order which required chiefs of the CSBs and SJBs to organise RS MUP forces into "wartime units"; and (ii) Karadžić's 1 July 1992 Order which instructed Stanišić to transfer 60 specially trained policemen, deployed in Crepoljsko, and place them "under the military command of the SRK".[789] Stanišić asserts that the Trial Chamber failed to take into account that Stanišić's 15 May 1992 Order "was made pursuant to and was required by the Law on All People's Defence".[790] Noting that Karadžić was the "Supreme Commander of the Armed Forces", Stanišić also argues that the Trial Chamber incorrectly referred to Karadžić's communication as a "request" when dismissing this statement – whereas it had previously found that he was "ordered" by Karadžić to transfer the 60 specially trained policemen.[791] Stanišić also disputes the Trial Chamber's finding that he consistently approved the deployment of RS MUP forces to combat activities,[792] and asserts that it failed to consider that the VRS was legally entitled to call up and re-subordinate active or reserve RS MUP members.[793] Stanišić further challenges the Trial Chamber's finding that he only sought to withdraw regular policemen from combat activities towards the end of 1992.[794] He argues that it was "clear" that he consistently raised the effects of re-subordination on the RS MUP's ability to fulfil its duties at least from the beginning of July 1992 to the highest RS authorities.[795] Stanišić further submits that he did not have the ability to withdraw the RS MUP forces re-subordinated to the army for combat activities.[796] Stanišić also submits that the Trial Chamber erroneously interpreted his request of 6 July 1992 to Karadžić that 60 RS MUP members provided to the military be replaced by members of the army due to operational needs ("Stanišić's 6 July 1992 Request") as he had requested the return of 60 RS MUP members so they could perform their duties and

---

[785]   Stanišić Appeal Brief, paras 261-272.
[786]   Stanišić Appeal Brief, para. 261.
[787]   Stanišić Appeal Brief, para. 261, referring to Trial Judgement, vol. 2, para. 738.
[788]   Stanišić Appeal Brief, para. 261. Stanišić argues that the declaration mandated that duties be executed "in a conscientious manner, to adhere to the Constitution and the Law" (Stanišić Appeal Brief, para. 261, referring to Exhibit P530, Article 41).
[789]   Stanišić Appeal Brief, paras 262-263 (emphasis omitted). See Appeal Hearing, 16 Dec 2015, AT. 105-106.
[790]   Stanišić Appeal Brief, para. 263, referring to Exhibits L1, Article 207, P1977, p. 2, 1D662, paras 233-245, Milan Trbojević, 3 Dec 2009, T. 4175-4176, Vitomir Žepinić, 1 Feb 2010, T. 5933, Milan Šćekić, 18 Feb 2010, T. 6567-6568, Radomir Njeguš, 8 Jun 2010, T. 11422-11426, Sreto Gajić, 15 Jul 2010, T. 12799-12800, 12849-12850, Mladen Bajagić, 4 May 2011, T. 20182-20184.
[791]   Stanišić Appeal Brief, para. 263, referring to Trial Judgement, vol. 2, paras 591, 739.
[792]   Stanišić Appeal Brief, para. 269, referring to Trial Judgement, vol. 2, para. 743.
[793]   Stanišić Appeal Brief, para. 269, referring to Exhibits L1, Article 104, 1D390, 1D405, 1D406, 1D409, 1D410, 1D411, 1D264, 1D266, 1D267, 1D390, 1D543, 1D468, 1D472, 1D641, 1D723, 1D729, 1D765, 1D800, 2D119, 2D120, P411.13, P1787, P1802, P1813, P1887, Vidosav Kovačević, 14 Sep 2011, T. 23647-23648, 23681, 23684-23685, 23714-23715, 23759, 23806, 23811-23812, 24124-24125, 23719-23720, 24203, Slavko Lisica, 1 Mar 2012, T. 26969-26970.
[794]   Stanišić Appeal Brief, para. 269.
[795]   Stanišić Appeal Brief, para. 269, referring to Exhibits P160, pp 4, 14-15, P427.8, pp 2, 4-5.
[796]   Stanišić Appeal Brief, para. 229, referring to Trial Judgement, vol. 2, para. 320, Vidosav Kovačević, 6 Sep 2011, T. 23720-23723, Vidosav Kovačević, 7 Sep 2011, T. 23739-23740, Vidosav Kovačević, 16 Sep 2011, T. 24316, Exhibits P411.13, P1787, P1802, P1887.

tasks, and not their replacement.[797] Stanišić argues that if he had the **[page 97]** authority to withdraw RS MUP members from their re-subordination, it would have been unnecessary to make such requests to the RS hierarchy.[798]

226.   Third, Stanišić challenges the Trial Chamber's finding regarding the reliance on RS MUP forces for combat activities and submits that it incorrectly assessed the evidence.[799] Stanišić submits that the Trial Chamber improperly found that he issued orders for police forces to participate in coordinated action with the armed forces.[800] Referring to Stanišić's 15 May 1992 Order, he argues that the use of RS MUP units in coordinated action with the armed forces *may* be ordered by, *inter alios*, the Minister of Interior, and that RS MUP units engaged in such coordinated action "shall be subordinated to the command of the armed forces".[801] Stanišić also submits that the Trial Chamber erred in finding that he facilitated the arming of RS MUP forces.[802] He asserts that, to the contrary, the evidence shows that the Federal Secretariat of Internal Affairs of Serbia ("Federal SUP") had a surplus of uniforms and weapons which were sent to the RS MUP in Pale, and that it ordered the unit of Witness Milorad Davidović ("Witness Davidović") to leave their equipment, among other things, with the RS MUP before returning to Belgrade.[803] He avers that only the weapons of 17 Federal SUP unit members and three all-terrain vehicles were left.[804] Stanišić also argues that it was within the Minister of Interior's purview to seek assistance as the RS MUP was only in the formation phase and the police needed to be equipped.[805] Regarding the Federal SUP's assistance in training a unit, Stanišić argues that this special police unit was engaged in crime prevention and detection and that, on his request, the Federal SUP unit arrived in the RS to assist the RS MUP to fight crime.[806]

227.   Fourth, Stanišić submits that the Trial Chamber erred in finding that he received reports on the police forces' involvement in combat activities as there is "nothing conclusive in the evidence" suggesting that the reports he received contained anything other than statistical information.[807]

228.   Fifth, Stanišić denies that he sought recognition for RS MUP contributions and achievements in combat activities.[808] To support his argument, Stanišić points to: (i) his statements **[page 98]** at a BSA session where he "merely 'noted'" the percentage of RS MUP forces involved in operations;[809] (ii) his statements at the first collegium meeting of senior officials of the RS MUP on 11 July 1992 ("11 July 1992 Collegium"), where he referred to the RS MUP's "immediate cooperation" with the army; and (iii) the thirteenth conclusion of the 11 July 1992 Collegium that the army and the RS MUP would coordinate action on crime prevention.[810]

229.   Sixth, Stanišić challenges the Trial Chamber's finding that he directly appointed Witness Todorović, Koroman, Drljača, Witness Bjelošević, Krsto Savić, and Župljanin.[811] He contends that the evidence "clearly shows" that: (i) Witness Todorović was appointed as the Chief of Bosanski Šamac SJB by the Municipal Assembly;[812] (ii) Koroman was appointed as the Chief of Pale SJB by Delimustafić;[813] and (iii) Drljača was

---

[797]   Stanišić Appeal Brief, para. 270, referring to Exhibit 1D100.
[798]   Stanišić Appeal Brief, para. 271.
[799]   Stanišić Appeal Brief, para. 264.
[800]   Stanišić Appeal Brief, para. 265.
[801]   Stanišić Appeal Brief, para. 265, referring to Exhibit 1D46, para. 7.
[802]   Stanišić Appeal Brief, para. 266.
[803]   Stanišić Appeal Brief, para. 266; Stanišić Reply Brief, para. 81.
[804]   Stanišić Appeal Brief, para. 266, referring to Exhibit 1D646, p. 2. See Stanišić Reply Brief, para. 81.
[805]   Stanišić Reply Brief, para. 81.
[806]   Stanišić Appeal Brief, para. 266, referring to Trial Judgement, vol. 2, para. 602, Exhibit 1D646, p. 1; Stanišić Reply Brief, para. 82. Stanišić also contends that his request for assistance cannot be considered as a contribution to the furtherance of crimes (Stanišić Reply Brief, para. 82).
[807]   Stanišić Appeal Brief, para. 267, referring to Exhibits 1D571, P158, P169, P621, P669, P731, P1888, P1928. Stanišić gives the example of statistics on the number of police that were re-subordinated to the army (Stanišić Appeal Brief, para. 267).
[808]   Stanišić Appeal Brief, para. 268.
[809]   Stanišić also notes that during this BSA session, he was "sacked" (Stanišić Appeal Brief, para. 268).
[810]   Stanišić Appeal Brief, para. 268.
[811]   Stanišić Appeal Brief, para. 272.
[812]   Stanišić Appeal Brief, para. 272, referring to Exhibits 1D606, pp 9005-9006, 9009-9010, P2159, pp 1611-1612.
[813]   Stanišić Appeal Brief, para. 272, referring to Goran Mačar, 12 Jul 2011, T. 23119-23120.

appointed as the Chief of the Prijedor SJB by the Prijedor Crisis Staff.[814] Stanišić submits that Delimustafić appointed Witness Bjelošević,[815] Krsto Savić,[816] and Župljanin[817] before the RS MUP was formed and asserts that the Trial Chamber "erroneously omitted" that the appointments he had made were only temporary.[818]

230. The Prosecution responds that all of Stanišić's arguments challenging the Trial Chamber's findings on the role of RS MUP forces in combat activities and takeovers of the municipalities of Banja Luka, Bijeljina, Bileća, Bosanski Šamac, Brčko, Doboj, Donji Vakuf, Gacko, Ilijaš, Ključ, Kotor Varoš, Pale, Prijedor, Sanski Most, Teslić, Vlasenica, Višegrad, Vogošća, and Zvornik and his related acts and conduct should be dismissed.[819]

231. With respect to the Trial Chamber's findings regarding the requirement for all RS MUP employees to sign solemn declarations, the Prosecution submits that it was reasonable for the Trial Chamber to have found that, while a solemn declaration was an "ostensibly legitimate requirement", it was designed to discriminate against non-Serbs.[820] It asserts that the requirement resulted in the dismissal of non-Serbs, which further supports the reasonableness of the impugned **[page 99]** finding.[821] The Prosecution submits that Stanišić merely seeks to substitute his evaluation of the evidence for that of the Trial Chamber without showing how it erred.[822]

232. With respect to the Trial Chamber's dismissal of Stanišić's statement that the RS MUP was not consulted about the reassignment of police forces, the Prosecution responds that the Trial Chamber reasonably relied on Stanišić's 15 May 1992 Order and Karadžić's 1 July 1992 Order, and submits that Stanišić's argument should be dismissed as he fails to show an error.[823] It argues that the assertion that Stanišić's 15 May 1992 Order was required by law is not supported on the face of the order, and that Stanišić merely repeats his trial arguments.[824] It also submits that Stanišić fails to show how the Trial Chamber's incorrect labelling of Karadžić's 1 July 1992 Order impacts the Trial Judgement.[825]

233. Regarding Stanišić's arguments disputing that he consistently approved the deployment of RS MUP forces into combat, the Prosecution responds that these arguments should be summarily dismissed as they are undeveloped and fail to articulate an error.[826] It submits that Stanišić's 15 May 1992 Order "envisaged the participation of RS MUP forces in 'coordinated action with the armed forces' upon the authorisation of a MUP official",[827] and that Karadžić's 1 July 1992 Order and Stanišić's 6 July 1992 Request demonstrate Stanišić's involvement in deploying RS MUP forces into combat.[828] The Prosecution submits further that Stanišić's prioritisation of the continued deployment of MUP forces in combat is confirmed by, *inter alia*, the Pale police having participated in an operation in Vrace based on his order,[829] and his comments in July,

---

[814]   Stanišić Appeal Brief, para. 272, referring to Exhibit P2462, ST161, 19 Nov 2009, T. 3439-3443 (closed session), Tomislav Kovač, 9 Mar 2012, T. 27240-27241, 27251-27252, Goran Mačar, 7 Jul 2011, T. 22977-22978, *Stakić* Trial Judgement, para. 64.
[815]   Stanišić Appeal Brief, para. 272, referring to Exhibit P1410.
[816]   Stanišić Appeal Brief, para. 272, referring to Exhibit P1414.
[817]   Stanišić Appeal Brief, para. 272, referring to Exhibit P1408.
[818]   Stanišić Appeal Brief, para. 272, referring to Exhibits P1408, P1410, P1414.
[819]   Prosecution Response Brief (Stanišić'), paras 120, 123-124, 126, 129, 130-132.
[820]   Prosecution Response Brief (Stanišić), para. 121.
[821]   Prosecution Response Brief (Stanišić), para. 121, referring to Trial Judgement, vol. 1, paras 298, 331, 515, 657, 722, 794, 826, 832, 867.
[822]   Prosecution Response Brief (Stanišić), para. 120.
[823]   Prosecution Response Brief (Stanišić), para. 126, referring to Trial Judgement, vol. 2, paras 588, 591, 739.
[824]   Prosecution Response Brief (Stanišić), para. 126, contrasting Stanišić Appeal Brief, para. 263 with Stanišić Final Trial Brief, paras 205-206.
[825]   Prosecution Response Brief (Stanišić), para. 126.
[826]   Prosecution Response Brief (Stanišić), para. 129, referring to *Krajišnik* Appeal Judgement, paras 24, 26-27. The Prosecution also responds that Stanišić contradicts his concessions at trial (Prosecution Response Brief (Stanišić), para. 129, contrasting Stanišić Appeal Brief, para. 270 with Stanišić Final Trial Brief, para. 226). The Prosecution also argues that Stanišić repeats his failed trial arguments. (Prosecution Response Brief (Stanišić), para. 129, contrasting Stanišić Appeal Brief, para. 269 with Stanišić Final Trial Brief, para. 208).
[827]   Prosecution Response Brief (Stanišić), para. 127, referring to Trial Judgement, vol. 2, para. 588. See Appeal Hearing, 16 Dec 2015, AT. 114.
[828]   Prosecution Response Brief (Stanišić), para. 127, referring to Trial Judgement, vol. 2, para. 591.
[829]   Prosecution Response Brief (Stanišić), para. 128, fn. 479, referring to Exhibit P1455, p. 3.

August, and October 1992 regarding the RS MUP's cooperation with, and assistance to, the army.[830] The Prosecution also responds that Stanišić's arguments concerning the withdrawal of regular policemen from combat towards the end of 1992 should be summarily dismissed as he repeats trial **[page 100]** arguments and fails to articulate an error.[831] It asserts that the Trial Chamber properly relied on Stanišić's order of 23 October 1992 to "all CSBs and SJBs that all SJBs in municipalities not directly affected by combat activities" to withdraw their active-duty police force members from the frontlines and make the reserve police available for the wartime assignment to the VRS, and to inform military commands that it was not the duty of the CSBs and SJBs to send policemen to the frontline ("Stanišić's 23 October 1992 Order"), which demonstrates Stanišić's authority to control and withdraw the MUP's deployment. It also contends that the evidence Stanišić relies on does not undermine the Trial Chamber's finding.[832]

234. Turning to Stanišić's arguments concerning the RS MUP forces' involvement in combat activities, the Prosecution asserts that they should be dismissed as they challenge the Trial Chamber's interpretation of the evidence and are undeveloped.[833] It also argues that Stanišić's challenges to the Trial Chamber's finding that he facilitated the arming of RS MUP forces should be dismissed as he fails to articulate an error.[834] Regarding the quantity of equipment provided by Witness Davidović's Federal SUP unit, the Prosecution responds that Stanišić fails to show that the Trial Chamber erred. It also contends that Stanišić's argument that he sought this Federal SUP unit's assistance to train the special police unit under his control demonstrates Stanišić's authority.[835]

235. The Prosecution further responds that the Trial Chamber reasonably relied on Stanišić's position to conclude that he received reports concerning the RS MUP forces' involvement in combat, and that Stanišić's argument should be dismissed as he seeks to give his own evaluation of the evidence.[836]

236. With respect to the Trial Chamber's conclusion concerning the recognition Stanišić sought for RS MUP contributions and achievements in combat activities, the Prosecution responds that the Trial Chamber reasonably reached the impugned conclusion.[837] It also submits that Stanišić's argument should be dismissed as he merely challenges the Trial Chamber's interpretation of his **[page 101]** comments at the BSA session and does not demonstrate how his comments at the 11 July 1992 Collegium undermine the Trial Chamber's conclusion.[838]

237. Finally, regarding the Trial Chamber's findings that Stanišić was involved in appointing JCE members to the RS MUP, the Prosecution responds that Stanišić repeats his failed trial argument concerning the temporary nature of the appointments and ignores that, on 15 May 1992, he confirmed the appointments of Witness Bjelošević, Krsto Savić, and Župljanin.[839] It also submits that Stanišić ignores evidence showing that he initially appointed Koroman as an inspector within the RS MUP's Sarajevo CSB,[840] and that Župljanin acted on his approval when retroactively appointing Drljača as the Prijedor SJB Chief on 30 July

---

[830] Prosecution Response Brief (Stanišić), para. 128, fns 480-484, referring to Exhibits P853, p. 2, P160, p. 14, P427.08, p. 4, P163, p. 3, P737, pp 3, 7, Trial Judgement, vol. 2, para. 592.

[831] Prosecution Response Brief (Stanišić), para. 130, contrasting Stanišić Appeal Brief, para. 269 with Stanišić Final Trial Brief, paras 227-228.

[832] Prosecution Response Brief (Stanišić), para. 130, referring to Stanišić Appeal Brief, fn. 371. The Prosecution submits that page 4 of Exhibit P427.08 records Stanišić as having stated that "we had [...] to replenish front-line units where the forces of the Serbian Republic were weaker" and "[a]s early as mid-May we issued a special order on organizing police and other MUP forces into war-time units for the defence of the territory of the Serbian Republic, [...]." The exhibit then records Stanišić saying that "co-operation was immediately achieved with other parts of the Serb defence forces, i.e. with the Army. Even though we were forced into this kind of behaviour, internal affairs organs must continue to help out on the front lines" (Prosecution Response Brief (Stanišić), fn. 494, quoting Exhibit P427.08, p. 4).

[833] Prosecution Response Brief (Stanišić), para. 129.

[834] Prosecution Response Brief (Stanišić), para. 124. See Appeal Hearing, 16 Dec 2015, AT. 114.

[835] Prosecution Response Brief (Stanišić), para. 125.

[836] Prosecution Response Brief (Stanišić), para. 131.

[837] Prosecution Response Brief (Stanišić), para. 132.

[838] Prosecution Response Brief (Stanišić), para. 132.

[839] Prosecution Response Brief (Stanišić), para. 122, referring to Trial Judgement, vol. 2, para. 744.

[840] Prosecution Response Brief (Stanišić), para. 123, referring to Trial Judgement, vol. 2, para. 579, Exhibit P1448 (submitting that Stanišić appointed Koroman's subordinate Stjepan Mićić on 1 April 1992 as the Head of the Group for the Prevention and Eradication of General Crime in the Pale SJB).

179

1992.[841] The Prosecution concedes that the evidence does not establish Stanišić's involvement in Witness Todorović's appointment, but argues that Stanišić fails to show that this error has any impact on the Trial Judgement.[842]

b. Analysis

i. Alleged errors concerning the intent behind the requirement to sign solemn declarations

238. The Trial Chamber found that between April and May 1992, the RS MUP required all of its employees to sign solemn declarations pledging loyalty to the Bosnian Serb authorities and imposed the sanction of dismissal on those who failed or refused to sign.[843] It concluded that "within the context of an ethnically motivated armed conflict, [...] the intent behind the ostensibly legitimate requirement was to provide a pretext to dismiss and disarm non-Serbs from the RS MUP".[844]

239. The Appeals Chamber first notes that the Trial Chamber took into account the fact that requiring persons in governmental employment to sign solemn declarations would not ordinarily merit consideration.[845] The Trial Chamber also took into account several instances where the RS **[page 102]** MUP dismissed employees who failed or refused to sign the solemn declarations[846] and that across RS territory Muslims, Croats, and other non-Serbs were dismissed from their places of employment and disarmed.[847] In the view of the Appeals Chamber, the Trial Chamber reasonably considered the combined effect of the occurrence of these events within the context of an ethnically motivated armed conflict, to infer that the intent behind the ostensibly legitimate requirement to sign solemn declarations was to provide a pretext to dismiss and disarm non-Serbs from the RS MUP.[848] Stanišić does not challenge the findings on the dismissal of RS MUP employees and non-Serbs throughout the RS or the ethnic nature of the conflict in this subground of appeal nor does he address the combined effect of this circumstantial evidence in his submissions. The Appeals Chamber therefore finds that Stanišić has failed to demonstrate that no reasonable trier of fact could have inferred that the only reasonable conclusion was that the intent behind the requirement to sign solemn declarations was to provide a pretext to dismiss and disarm non-Serbs from the RS MUP. Stanišić's arguments in this regard are thus dismissed.

ii. Alleged errors in the Trial Chamber's findings regarding the reassignment of RS MUP forces to the army for combat activities and Stanišić's approval of their redeployment

240. In reaching its conclusions regarding the reassignment and the deployment of RS MUP forces the Trial Chamber considered: (i) Stanišić's 15 May 1992 Order;[849] (ii) that on 15 June 1992, with a view to implementing the mobilisation order in the area of Novo Sarajevo, Stanišić ordered a special police unit to

---

[841] Prosecution Response Brief (Stanišić), para. 123, referring to Exhibit P2463, Trial Judgement, vol. 2, paras 580, 486. The Prosecution also contends that Župljanin was also acting on Stanišić's approval when retroactively appointing another JCE member, Mirko Vručinić, as the Sanski Most SJB Chief on 13 June 1992. Prosecution Response Brief (Stanišić), para. 123, referring to ST161, 19 Nov 2009, T. 3439-3440 (closed session), Exhibits P366 (confidential), P384 (confidential), Trial Judgement, vol. 2, para. 314.

[842] Prosecution Response Brief (Stanišić), para. 123.

[843] Trial Judgement, vol. 2, para. 738. See Trial Judgement, vol. 1, paras 331, 515, 657, 722, 794, 867; Trial Judgement, vol. 2, paras 44, 378-380, 382-383, 737.

[844] Trial Judgement, vol. 2, para. 738.

[845] Trial Judgement, vol. 2, para. 738.

[846] See Trial Judgement, vol. 1, paras 298, 331, 515, 657, 722, 794, 826, 832, 867; Trial Judgement, vol. 2, paras 379, 383.

[847] Trial Judgement, vol. 2, para. 738. See Trial Judgement, vol. 1, paras 794, 815, 949, 1138, 1204, 1258, 1278, 1428, 1490; Trial Judgement, vol. 2, paras 266, 279, 282, 379.

[848] See Trial Judgement, vol. 2, para. 738.

[849] Trial Judgement, vol. 2, para. 739. See Trial Judgement, vol. 2, paras 58, 330, 588, referring to Exhibit 1D46, pp 1-2.

hand over conscripts to the Lukavica barracks;[850] (iii) Karadžić's 1 July 1992 Order;[851] (iv) Stanišić's 6 July 1992 Request;[852] and (v) Stanišić's 23 October 1992 Order.[853]

241.   Having considered Stanišić's 15 May 1992 Order that RS MUP forces be organised into wartime units by the chiefs of CSBs and SJBs and "Karadžić's request of 1 July 1992",[854] the Trial Chamber attached little weight to the statement in Stanišić's Interview "that the RS MUP was not consulted with regard to the reassignment of RS MUP forces to the army for combat tasks".[855] It **[page 103]** found that Stanišić consistently approved the deployment of RS MUP forces to combat activities along with the other Serb forces, "[d]espite being aware of the commission of crimes by the joint Serb Forces in the Municipalities".[856] The Trial Chamber also found that Stanišić "only sought to withdraw regular policemen from combat activities towards the end of 1992, when most of the territory of RS had been consolidated, while permitting the continued use of reserve forces by the army, primarily for the purpose of guarding prisons and detention camps".[857]

242.   The Appeals Chamber first turns to Stanišić's challenge to the Trial Chamber's assessment of his statement that the RS MUP was not consulted about the reassignment of police forces. The Appeals Chamber observes that, before it dismissed this impugned statement, the Trial Chamber considered, in an earlier discussion, that Stanišić's 15 May 1992 Order stated that "MUP units would be re-subordinated to the armed forces and were to act in compliance with military regulations, but would remain 'under the command' of designated Ministry officials".[858] While Stanišić argues that the Trial Chamber failed to take into account that Stanišić's 15 May 1992 Order was in accordance with the Law On All People's Defence,[859] the Appeals Chamber notes that the Trial Chamber expressly referred to testimony that this order "was issued in accordance with the law and that the order was followed in practice".[860] Apart from pointing to the Trial Chamber's purported failure in this regard, Stanišić does not substantiate why the fact that this order was issued in accordance with the law suggests that the RS MUP was not consulted about the reassignment. Thus, Stanišić has not shown how Stanišić's 15 May 1992 Order undermines the Trial Chamber's assessment of the impugned statement. Stanišić's argument is thus dismissed.

243.   With respect to Stanišić's challenge to the Trial Chamber's assessment of Karadžić's 1 July 1992 Order,[861] the Appeals Chamber notes that Stanišić does not develop his assertion beyond alleging a contradiction between its description in the Trial Judgement as a request and as an order, and highlighting that Karadžić was the "Supreme Commander of the Armed Forces".[862] The Appeals Chamber therefore dismisses Stanišić's argument that the Trial Chamber incorrectly assessed Karadžić's 1 July 1992 Order as undeveloped and vague. Furthermore, insofar as his argument can be understood to mean that since the "Supreme Commander of the Armed Forces" ordered the re-subordination of the 60 RS MUP police, the RS MUP was obligated to **[page 104]** follow this order,[863] the Appeals Chamber considers that the mere fact that Karadžić issued an order on the re-subordination of MUP forces does not in itself mean that the RS MUP was not consulted. Without any further support for this assertion, the Appeals Chamber does not find that Karadžić's 1 July 1992 Order undermines the Trial Chamber's assessment of the impugned statement. Having concluded that Stanišić has failed to show that the Trial Chamber erred regarding either Stanišić's

---

[850]   Trial Judgement, vol. 2, para. 591, referring to Exhibit P1422.
[851]   Trial Judgement, vol. 2, para. 591, referring to Exhibit 1D99.
[852]   Trial Judgement, vol. 2, para. 591, referring to Drago Borovčanin, 24 Feb 2010, T. 6757-6758, Exhibit 1D100.
[853]   Trial Judgement, vol. 2, para. 594, referring to Exhibit 1D49, p. 1.
[854]   Trial Judgement, vol. 2, para. 739.
[855]   Trial Judgement, vol. 2, para. 739. See Trial Judgement, vol. 2, para. 588, referring to Exhibit P2302, p. 30 ("Stanišić stated that the President did not consult with the MUP but rather with the MOD and army in taking a decision to reassign police forces to combat tasks").
[856]   Trial Judgement, vol. 2, para. 743. See Trial Judgement, vol. 2, paras 766-781.
[857]   Trial Judgement, vol. 2, para. 743.
[858]   Trial Judgement, vol. 2, para. 588. See Trial Judgement, vol. 2, para. 330.
[859]   See *supra*, para. 225.
[860]   Trial Judgement, vol. 2, para. 333. See Andrija Bjelošević, 15 Apr 2011, T. 19651-19656.
[861]   See *supra*, para. 225.
[862]   Stanišić Appeal Brief, para. 263.
[863]   Stanišić Appeal Brief, para. 263.

15 May 1992 Order or Karadžić's 1 July 1992 Order, the Appeals Chamber finds that his argument that the Trial Chamber improperly dismissed the impugned statement also fails.

244.   In support of his challenge to the Trial Chamber's finding that he consistently approved the deployment of RS MUP forces to combat activities,[864] Stanišić only argues that the VRS was entitled by law to call up and re-subordinate active or reserve RS MUP members. The Appeals Chamber recalls however that contribution to a joint criminal enterprise need not be in and of itself criminal; what is important is whether the accused performs acts that furthered the common criminal purpose.[865] Moreover, the fact that his contribution amounted to no more than his routine duties will not exculpate him.[866] Stanišić has therefore failed to demonstrate that the Trial Chamber erred.

245.   Turning to Stanišić's argument on the withdrawal of policemen from combat activities, insofar as it can be interpreted to mean that by alerting the RS authorities in July 1992 of the difficulties arising from re-subordination he sought to withdraw RS MUP forces,[867] Stanišić fails to support his argument. The evidence Stanišić cites shows that the RS MUP had difficulties fulfilling its regular police duties and tasks during combat, but does not contradict the Trial Chamber's conclusion that he only sought to withdraw the regular policemen from combat activities towards the end of 1992.[868] The references in the cited evidence to removing obstacles to enhance the efficiency of internal affairs organs and to exemptions from combat duty except in emergencies[869] are insufficient to demonstrate that the Trial Chamber's conclusion was one that no reasonable trier of fact could have reached. The Appeals Chamber therefore dismisses Stanišić's argument that his attempts to alert RS authorities in July 1992 that re-subordination made it difficult for the RS MUP to fulfil its duties undermines the Trial Chamber's finding that he only sought to withdraw the regular policemen from combat activities towards the end of 1992. **[page 105]**

246.   With respect to Stanišić's argument that he did not have the ability to withdraw personnel who had been re-subordinated to the army to engage in combat activities, the Appeals Chamber 870 notes that Stanišić only cites several pieces of evidence without further developing his argument.[870] Thus, Stanišić has not shown how the alleged lack of his authority to withdraw the re-subordinated RS MUP forces from combat activities undermines the Trial Chamber's findings that he: (i) consistently "approved" the deployment of the RS MUP forces to combat activities despite being aware of the commission of crimes;[871] and (ii) only sought to withdraw regular policemen from combat activities towards the end of 1992, when most of the territory of RS had been consolidated, while "permitting" the continued use of reserve forces by the army, primarily for the purpose of guarding prisons and detention camps.[872] Stanišić's argument thus fails.

247.   Regarding the challenge to the Trial Chamber's interpretation of Stanišić's 6 July 1992 Request, the Appeals Chamber finds that Stanišić has failed to show how requesting the return of the 60 RS MUP members so that they could perform their duties and tasks differs substantively from the Trial Chamber's conclusion that he sought to have the 60 RS MUP members replaced by members of the army due to operational needs.[873] Additionally, the Appeals Chamber considers speculative and unsupported Stanišić's assertion that had he possessed the authority to withdraw RS MUP forces from their re-subordination, these requests to the RS hierarchy would be unnecessary. Thus, Stanišić's arguments are dismissed.

---

[864]   See *supra*, para. 225.
[865]   *Popović et al.* Appeal Judgement, para. 1653; *Šainović et al.* Appeal Judgement, para. 985; *Krajišnik* Appeal Judgement, paras 215, 695-696. See *Šainović et al.* Appeal Judgement, paras 1233, 1242. See also *supra*, para. 110.
[866]   *Popović et al.* Appeal Judgement, para. 1653, quoting *Blagojević and Jokić* Appeal Judgement, para. 189. See *supra*, para. 154.
[867]   See *supra*, para. 225.
[868]   Exhibits P160, pp 4, 14-15; P427.08, pp 2, 4-5. See Trial Judgement, vol. 2, para. 743.
[869]   Exhibits P160, p. 14; P427.08, p. 4.
[870]   See *supra*, para. 225.
[871]   Trial Judgement, vol. 2, para. 743.
[872]   Trial Judgement, vol. 2, para. 743.
[873]   Trial Judgement, vol. 2, para. 591. See Drago Borovčanin, 24 Feb 2010, T. 6758 ("He proposes that they be replaced by regular army troops so that they could continue with their regular police work"); Exhibit 1D100 ("[I]t is necessary to exchange these police members with members of the Serbian army so that the police members may perform the above described duties and tasks").

248.   In light of the above, the Appeals Chamber finds that Stanišić fails to demonstrate that no reasonable trier of fact could have arrived at the Trial Chamber's conclusions regarding the reassignment of RS MUP forces to the army for combat activities.

iii. Alleged errors in the Trial Chamber's findings concerning the reliance by the RS Government and the VRS on RS MUP forces for combat activities and Stanišić' s actions for the deployment and arming of the RS MUP

249.   The Trial Chamber found that the RS Government, and eventually the VRS, relied to a large extent on the RS MUP forces for combat activities, "along with other armed forces of the territory".[874] It found that Stanišić issued orders for police forces, both regular and reserve units, to participate in "coordinated action with the armed forces" and that he "facilitated the arming of the **[page 106]** RS MUP forces by seeking – and receiving – the assistance of the Federal SUP of Serbia for supplying equipment, weapons, and training for a special unit under his direct control at the Ministry level".[874][875]

250.   The only evidence that Stanišić relies on to support his challenge to the Trial Chamber's findings concerning his orders for the police forces' participation in coordinated action with the armed forces is Stanišić's 15 May 1992 Order,[876] which in relevant part reads:

> [t]he use of the Ministry units in coordinated action with the armed forces of the Serbian Republic of BH may be ordered by the [M]inister of the [I]nterior, commander of the police detachment of the Ministry [...] and chief of the CSB of the Ministry [...].
>
> [...]
>
> While participating in combat operations, the units of the Ministry shall be subordinated to the command of the armed forces; however, the Ministry units shall be under the direct command of certain Ministry officials.[877]

251.   The Appeals Chamber first observes that the use of the word "may" does not negate the Minister of Interior's authority to order the use of RS MUP units "in coordinated action with the armed forces" of the RS. The Appeals Chamber also notes that while pursuant to Stanišić's 15 May 1992 Order, MUP forces were subordinated to the command of the armed forces while participating in combat, the order explicitly provided that these units remained under the direct command of MUP officials.[878] In light of the foregoing, Stanišić has failed to demonstrate how the cited provisions from Stanišić's 15 May 1992 Order undermine the Trial Chamber's finding that he issued orders for the police forces to participate in coordinated action with the armed forces or, ultimately, the Trial Chamber's finding that "[t]he RS Government, and eventually the VRS, relied to a large extent on the RS MUP forces for combat activities, along with other armed forces of the territory."[879] Stanišić's argument is thus dismissed.

252.   The Appeals Chamber now turns to the question of whether the Trial Chamber erred in finding that Stanišić facilitated the arming of the RS MUP forces by seeking support from the Federal SUP of Serbia.[880] The Appeals Chamber notes that in reaching this conclusion,[881] the Trial Chamber considered the evidence of Witness Davidović, former Federal SUP inspector, that: (i) the Federal SUP shipped a surplus of uniforms and "high quality weapons" for approximately 500 men **[page 107]** to the RS MUP in Pale under the control of Stanišić and Witness Momčilo Mandić ("Witness Mandić"); and (ii) Petar Gračanin, of the Federal SUP in Belgrade, ordered Witness Davidović's unit to leave all of their weapons, ammunition, equipment, and vehicles with the new RS MUP special police unit headed by Karišik before returning to Belgrade,[882] as well

---

[874]   Trial Judgement, vol. 2, para. 740.
[875]   Trial Judgement, vol. 2, para. 740.
[876]   See *supra*, para. 226.
[877]   Exhibit 1D46, para. 7.
[878]   Exhibit 1D46, para. 7.
[879]   Trial Judgement, vol. 2, para. 740.
[880]   See *supra*, para. 226.
[881]   Trial Judgement, vol. 2, para. 587, referring to Exhibit P541, p. 2.
[882]   Trial Judgement, vol. 2, para. 587.

as the evidence on the agreement between the Federal SUP and the RS MUP.[883] The Appeals Chamber also notes that the relevant part of Exhibit 1D646, to which Stanišić refers, reads: "[t]he Federal Secretary accepted the request from the SR BH MUP and sent a group of 17 members of the SSUP unit with the necessary weapons and three all-terrain vehicles to the Brjeljina CSB [...] on 27 June 1992.[884]

253.   Insofar as Stanišić argues that the Federal SUP had a surplus of uniforms and weapons which it left behind, and that only the weapons of 17 Federal SUP unit members and three all-terrain vehicles were left,[885] the Appeals Chamber considers that Stanišić fails to show how the quantity of weapons and equipment supplied, even if limited,[886] undermines the Trial Chamber's finding that by seeking and receiving assistance from the Federal SUP of Serbia, he facilitated the arming of the RS MUP forces. Furthermore, as far as Stanišić implies that the uniforms and equipments supplied were not requested but were given as they were surplus items, the Appeals Chamber finds that he fails to support or develop this assertion. For reasons given earlier, the Appeals Chamber also finds no merit in Stanišić's contention that it was within the Minister of Interior's purview to seek assistance as the RS MUP was in formation phase and equipment was needed.[887] The Appeals Chamber reiterates that participation in a joint criminal enterprise that amounts to no more than his or her "routine duties" will not exculpate the accused.[888] Therefore, whether or not it was within Stanišić's purview or his legal obligation to seek assistance does not demonstrate that the Trial Chamber erred.

254.   With respect to Stanišić's arguments that the special police unit – trained with the assistance of the Federal SUP of Serbia and under his command – was engaged in crime prevention and detection,[889] the Trial Chamber noted Witness Davidović's testimony that, as a member of the Federal SUP, he assisted in forming and training Stanišić's own RS MUP special police unit – composed of approximately 170 members and led by Karišik – in Vrace at the beginning of **[page 108]** April 1992.[890] It also noted Witness Planojević's testimony that Stanišić had the authority to decide on the use of these special units, and that he had to ask Stanišić to use the special police unit led by Karišik in crime prevention and detection – a request Stanišić approved without further query.[891] The Appeals Chamber does not find that either the type of engagement undertaken by the special police unit or Stanišić's assertion that the unit arrived at his request undermines the Trial Chamber's finding that, by seeking and receiving assistance from the Federal SUP of Serbia for the training of a special police unit under his direct control, Stanišić facilitated the arming of the RS MUP forces. The Appeals Chamber therefore finds no merit in Stanišić's argument.

255.   In light of the above, the Appeals Chamber concludes that Stanišić has failed to demonstrate that the Trial Chamber erred in finding that: (i) he issued orders for police forces to participate in coordinated action with the armed forces; (ii) he facilitated the arming of the RS MUP forces by seeking the Federal SUP of Serbia's support; and (iii) the RS Government and the VRS relied on RS MUP forces for combat activities.

>   iv.   Alleged errors in the Trial Chamber's findings that Stanišić received reports on the involvement of police forces in combat activities

256.   The Trial Chamber found that Stanišić issued an order on 16 May 1992 directing "all five CSBs to send daily fax reports on combat activities, terrorist activities, implementation of tasks under the LIA, and war crimes and other serious crimes committed against Serbs" ("Stanišić's 16 May 1992 Order").[892] It also found

---

[883]   Exhibit P541, p. 2 ("According to the agreement with the Serbian SSUP and the Serbian MUP, we should request the equipment they can give us").
[884]   Exhibit 1D646, pp 1-2.
[885]   See *supra*, para. 226.
[886]   See Exhibit P1557.01, para. 39 (evidence that uniforms, flak jackets, and high quality weapons for approximately 500 men was delivered to a football field in Pale).
[887]   See *supra*, para. 244.
[888]   *Popović et al.* Appeal Judgement, para. 1653, quoting *Blagojević and Jokić* Appeal Judgement, para. 189. See *supra*, para. 154.
[889]   See *supra*, para. 226.
[890]   Trial Judgement, vol. 2, para. 601, referring to, *inter alia*, Milorad Davidović, 23 Aug 2010, T. 13532-13533; Exhibit P1557.01, p. 12.
[891]   Trial Judgement, vol. 2, para. 602.
[892]   Trial Judgement, vol. 2, para. 723. See Exhibit P173, p. 1.

that "[a]s the highest commander of the RS MUP forces and the administrative head of the organs of the RS MUP, Stanišić received reports of the involvement of the police forces in combat activities."[893]

257.   The Appeals Chamber notes that Stanišić's 16 May 1992 Order directed the CSBs to send daily fax reports on combat activities,[894] and that these daily reports were to be submitted to the RS MUP with one of their purposes being to monitor combat operations.[895] With respect to combat activities, Stanišić's 16 May 1992 Order required the reports to contain information on: (i) the type, duration, and location of combat operations; (ii) coordination with "the Serbian Army"; (iii) movement of Serb forces to new positions; (iv) any RS MUP losses; (v) assessments or exact information on the opposing side's losses; and (vi) other important observations regarding combat **[page 109]** activities.[896] Furthermore, the Trial Chamber noted the requirement that reports had to be as broad and detailed as possible.[897] Considering Stanišić's position as the RS MUP forces' highest commander and the RS MUP organs' administrative head, as well as Stanišić's 16 May 1992 Order, the Appeals Chamber does not find Stanišić's argument[898] convincing. The Appeals Chamber therefore finds that Stanišić has failed to demonstrate that no reasonable trier of fact could have concluded that he received reports of the involvement of the police forces in combat activities.

v. Alleged errors concerning the Trial Chamber's finding that Stanišić sought recognition for the contributions and achievements of the RS MUP in combat activities

258.   The Trial Chamber relied on "the evidence of Stanišić seeking recognition from other Bosnian Serb leaders for the contributions and achievements of the RS MUP in combat activities" to support its finding that he "deployed the police in furtherance of the decisions of the Bosnian Serb authorities, of which his Ministry was considered an instrumental organ".[899] In this regard, the Trial Chamber considered that at the November 1992 BSA Session, Stanišić "noted that '50% of the daily number of police officers' took part in combat and 'fought and defended' the territories 'to create a legal state to at least some degree'".[900] It also noted that Stanišić opened the 11 July 1992 Collegium with remarks concerning the political and security situation in RS,[901] and remarked on the "immediate cooperation" RS MUP forces had provided to the army.[902] He added that, in order to establish full constitutionality and legality, it was decided not only to prevent criminal activities committed by citizens but also those committed by soldiers, army officers, active duty and reserve police, and members of the internal affairs organs and their officers.[903]

259.   In light of these findings of the Trial Chamber, the Appeals Chamber does not find persuasive Stanišić's argument that he merely "noted"[904] the percentage of the RS MUP forces involved in military operations. Furthermore, Stanišić does not show the relevance of the fact that a conclusion from the 11 July 1992 Collegium was similar to his own comment. The Appeals Chamber is satisfied that Stanišić has failed to demonstrate an error on the part of the Trial Chamber in considering that he sought recognition for the RS MUP contributions and achievements in combat activities. In the view of the Appeals Chamber, Stanišić merely disagrees with the Trial **[page 110]**Chamber's evaluation of the evidence and offers his own interpretation without demonstrating that no reasonable trier of fact could have reached the same conclusion. Stanišić's argument is therefore dismissed.

---

893   Trial Judgement, vol. 2, para. 741.
894   Trial Judgement, vol. 2, para. 723.
895   Exhibit P173, p. 1.
896   Exhibit P173, p. 1.
897   Trial Judgement, vol. 2, para. 723.
898   See *supra*, para. 227.
899   Trial Judgement, vol. 2, para. 742.
900   Trial Judgement, vol. 2, para. 595, referring to Exhibit P400, pp 16-17.
901   Trial Judgement, vol. 2, para. 630, referring to Andrija Bjelošević, 15 Apr 2011, T. 19703-19705, Exhibits 1D476, P160, pp 15-16.
902   Trial Judgement, vol. 2, para. 630, referring to Exhibit P160, pp 14-15.
903   Trial Judgement, vol. 2, para. 630, referring to Exhibit P160, pp 14-15.
904   See *supra*, para. 228.

vi. Alleged errors concerning the appointment of JCE members to the RS MUP

260. The Trial Chamber found that JCE members Witness Todorović, Koroman, Drljača, Witness Bjelošević, Krsto Savić, and Župljanin were "directly appointed by Stanišić" to their posts as SJB or CSB chiefs.[905] It found that: (i) on 6 May 1991, Delimustafić appointed Župljanin as the Chief of the Banja Luka CSB;[906] (ii) on 1 April 1992, Stanišić issued decisions "temporarily appointing" Koroman as the Inspector at the Sarajevo CSB,[907] Witness Bjelošević as the Chief of the Doboj CSB,[908] Krsto Savić as the Chief of the Trebinje CSB,[909] and Župljanin as the Chief of the Banja Luka CSB;[910] and (iii) on 15 May 1992, Stanišić issued a series of orders confirming the appointments of Witness Bjelošević, Krsto Savić, and Župljanin.[911] With respect to Witness Todorović, the Trial Chamber found that, in a 25 November 1992 letter sent to Stanišić, Witness Bjelošević proposed replacing Witness Todorović, Chief of the Bosanski Šamac SJB, due to "frequent and grave violations of duty".[912] It also referred to Witness Bjelošević's statement in this letter that Witness Todorović had never received an official letter of appointment to his post.[913]

261. With respect to Stanišić's argument on Koroman's appointment,[914] the Appeals Chamber notes evidence that Delimustafić had appointed Koroman as the Chief of Pale SJB in 1991.[915] Given Stanišić's 1 April 1992 decision appointing Koroman as Inspector at the Sarajevo CSB, the Appeals Chamber is not persuaded that Delimustafić's involvement in Koroman's earlier **[page 111]** appointment undermines the Trial Chamber's finding that Koroman was "directly appointed by Stanišić"[916] as Inspector at the Sarajevo CSB.

262. Regarding Drljača's appointment, the Appeals Chamber notes that the Trial Chamber found that he was originally appointed as the Chief of the Prijedor SJB by the Prijedor Crisis Staff,[917] and that on 30 July 1992 Župljanin formally appointed him, with retroactive effect as of 29 April 1992.[918] It found that Drljača's appointment was in accordance with Stanišić's 25 April 1992 Decision, which gave Župljanin the power to appoint SJB chiefs provided he had Stanišić's prior agreement.[919] The Trial Chamber also found that Drljača was directly subordinated to Župljanin "who in turn was directly subordinated to Stanišić as the Minister of RS MUP who exercised overall command and control of the Ministry".[920] Given Župljanin's 30 July 1992 decision and Stanišić's 25 April 1992 Decision, the Appeals Chamber is not persuaded that the Prijedor Crisis Staff's involvement in Drljača's earlier appointment undermines the Trial Chamber's finding that Stanišić appointed Drljača. Furthermore, although it would have been more accurate for the Trial Chamber

---

[905] Trial Judgement, vol. 2, para. 744.
[906] Trial Judgement, vol. 2, para. 349, referring to ST213, 4 Mar 2010, T. 7204 (private session), Exhibit P2043.
[907] Trial Judgement, vol. 2, para. 579, referring to Exhibit P1416. The Appeals Chamber notes that the Trial Chamber also found that Koroman was appointed Chief of the Pale SJB by Stanišić on 1 April 1992 (Trial Judgement, vol. 2, para. 700, referring to Tomislav Kovač, 9 Mar 2012, T. 27224, Exhibit P1416). However, the evidence referred to by the Trial Chamber does not support this conclusion as Exhibit P1416 states that Koroman was appointed Inspector at the Sarajevo CSB by Stanišić on 1 April 1992 while the testimony of Witness Kovač is that Koroman: (i) was the Chief of the Pale SJB, pursuant to a decision issued by the minister, Delimustafić, in 1991; and (ii) was appointed Inspector at the Sarajevo CSB in April 1992 (Tomislav Kovač, 9 Mar 2012, T. 27220-27221, 27224-27225).
[908] Trial Judgement, vol. 2, para. 579, referring to Exhibit P1410.
[909] Trial Judgement, vol. 2, para. 579, referring to Exhibit P1414.
[910] Trial Judgement, vol. 2, para. 579, referring to Exhibit P1408.
[911] Trial Judgement, vol. 2, para. 579, referring to Christian Nielsen, 14 Dec 2009, T. 4752, Andrija Bjelošević, 20 May 2011, T. 21072-21073, Exhibits P455, P458, P170.
[912] Trial Judgement, vol. 2, para. 699, referring to Tomislav Kovač, 9 Mar 2012, T. 27220, Exhibit P2086.
[913] Trial Judgement, vol. 2, para. 699, referring to Exhibit P2086.
[914] See *supra*, para. 229.
[915] Tomislav Kovač, 9 Mar 2012, T. 27220-27221, 27224-27225. See *supra*, fn. 902.
[916] Trial Judgement, vol. 2, para. 744.
[917] Trial Judgement, vol. 2, para. 856. See Trial Judgement, vol. 2, para. 350.
[918] Trial Judgement, vol. 2, para. 486, referring to Exhibit P2463. See Trial Judgement, vol. 1, para. 507, referring to Tomislav Kovač, 8 Mar 2012, T. 27184-27186, Exhibit P2463. See also Trial Judgement, vol. 2, paras 791, 856.
[919] Trial Judgement, vol. 2, para. 791. See Trial Judgement, vol. 1, para. 507; Trial Judgement, vol. 2, para. 356, referring to Exhibit 1D73.
[920] Trial Judgement, vol. 2, para. 791.

to have found that Stanišić authorised Drljača's appointment, as Stanišić was involved in the appointment, the Appeals Chamber is satisfied that a reasonable trier of fact could have made the impugned finding.[921]

263. Before addressing the merits of Stanišić's challenges to the Trial Chamber's findings regarding the appointments of Witness Bjelošević, Krsto Savić, and Župljanin,[922] the Appeals Chamber notes that the Trial Chamber refers to the named individuals as "JCE members"[923] but did not find that Krsto Savić was a member of the JCE.[924] The Appeals Chamber also notes that Ljubisa Savic, who the Trial Chamber specified also went by the name of "Mauzer", was found to have been a JCE member.[925] The Appeals Chamber considers that Krsto Savić's inclusion in the list of JCE members was an inadvertent error as the Trial Chamber had not previously made an explicit finding that he was indeed a member. The impact of this error, if any, will be considered below. **[page 112]**

264. Turning to the merits of Stanišić's challenges to the Trial Chamber's findings regarding the appointments of Witness Bjelošević, Krsto Savić, and Župljanin,[926] the Appeals Chamber notes that the Trial Chamber found that Stanišić issued decisions "temporarily appointing" Witness Bjelošević, Krsto Savić, and Župljanin on 1 April 1992,[927] and that on 15 May 1992 he issued a series of orders confirming their appointments.[928] It is clear from the Trial Judgement that the Trial Chamber considered that the appointments were temporary but that this did not prevent it from arriving at its finding.[929] The Appeals Chamber therefore finds no merit in Stanišić's argument that the Trial Chamber "erroneously omitted" that the appointments he had made were only temporary. With respect to Stanišić's argument that Delimustafić appointed Witness Bjelošević, Krsto Savić, and Župljanin before the RS MUP was formed, the Appeals Chamber recalls the Trial Chamber's finding that Delimustafić appointed Župljanin as the Chief of the Banja Luka CSB on 6 May 1991,[930] but it did not enter similar findings with respect to any other CSB chiefs.[931] Neither the evidence that Stanišić cites, nor the Trial Judgement, identifies who appointed Witness Bjelošević and Krsto Savić prior to their 1 April 1992 appointment.[932] Nevertheless, even if Delimustafić had previously appointed Witness Bjelošević and Krsto Savić, given the decisions Stanišić issued on 1 April 1992 appointing Witness Bjelošević, Krsto Savić, and Župljanin, the Appeals Chamber is not persuaded that Delimustafić's involvement in prior appointments undermines the Trial Chamber's finding that they were "directly appointed by Stanišić".[933] Accordingly, the Appeals Chamber finds that Stanišić has failed to demonstrate that the Trial Chamber erred.

265. With respect to Stanišić's argument on Witness Todorović's appointment,[934] the Appeals Chamber notes that the Trial Chamber did not cite any evidence to support its finding that Witness Todorović was "directly appointed by Stanišić"[935] – and in fact referred to evidence that Witness Todorović never received an official letter of appointment.[936] In light of the above, having reviewed the evidence to which Stanišić refers,[937] and noting the Prosecution's submissions,[938] the Appeals **[page 113]** Chamber considers that the

---

[921] See *supra*, para. 260.
[922] See *supra*, para. 229.
[923] Trial Judgement, vol. 2, para. 744.
[924] Trial Judgement, vol. 2, para. 314.
[925] Trial Judgement, vol. 2, para. 314.
[926] See *supra*, para. 229.
[927] Trial Judgement, vol. 2, para. 579, referring to Exhibits P1410, P1414, P1408.
[928] Trial Judgement, vol. 2, para. 579, referring to Christian Nielsen, 14 Dec 2009, T. 4752, Andrija Bjelošević, 20 May 2011, T. 21072-21073, Exhibits P455, P458, P170.
[929] See *Popović et al.* Appeal Judgement, para. 1257. See also *Haradinaj et al.* Appeal Judgement, para. 129; *Krajišnik* Appeal Judgement, para. 353; *Kvočka et al.* Appeal Judgement, para. 23.
[930] Trial Judgement, vol. 2, para. 349, referring to ST213, 4 Mar 2010, T. 7204 (private session), Exhibit P2043.
[931] See *supra*, para. 195.
[932] Stanišić Appeal Brief, para. 272, referring to Exhibits P1410, P1414.
[933] See Trial Judgement, vol. 2, para. 744. See *supra*, para. 195.
[934] See *supra*, para. 229.
[935] Trial Judgement, vol. 2, para. 744.
[936] Trial Judgement, vol. 2, para. 699.
[937] ST121, 24 Nov 2009, T. 3728, 3731; ST121, 25 Nov 2009, T. 3806 (private session); Exhibits 1D606, pp 9005-9006, 9009-9010, P2159, pp 1611-1612.
[938] See *supra*, para. 237.

Trial Chamber erred in finding that Witness Todorović was directly appointed by Stanišić. The impact of this error, if any, will be considered below.

266. The Appeals Chamber recalls that in the impugned finding, the Trial Chamber identified six individuals who it indicated were found to be JCE members and who "were directly appointed by Stanišić and [...] used the police force as physical perpetrators to implement the common plan".[939] The Appeals Chamber has found that the Trial Chamber's finding that Witness Todorović was directly appointed by Stanišić was erroneous,[940] and that although the Trial Chamber found that Krsto Savić was directly appointed by Stanišić, it did not find that he was a JCE member.[941] Therefore, the Trial Chamber erred in considering the appointments of Witness Todorović and Krsto Savić as evidence of Stanišić's direct appointments of JCE members to the RS MUP. However, Stanišić has failed to show that the Trial Chamber's conclusion that he appointed JCE members to the RS MUP would not stand on the basis of the Trial Chamber's findings on his involvement in the appointments of Koroman, Drljača, Witness Bjelošević, and Župljanin – which the Appeals Chamber has confirmed.

267. In light of the errors identified above with regard to the appointments of Witness Todorović and Krsto Savić,[942] the Appeals Chamber will consider the Trial Chamber's findings on Stanišić's direct appointments of JCE members to the RS MUP with the exception of the appointments of these two individuals, when assessing whether a reasonable trier of fact could have concluded beyond reasonable doubt that Stanišić's relevant acts and conduct significantly contributed to the JCE.[943]

c. Conclusion

268. Based on the foregoing, the Appeals Chamber finds that Stanišić has failed to show that the Trial Chamber erred in its conclusions regarding the RS MUP forces' role in combat activities and in the takeovers of the municipalities of Banja Luka, Bijeljina, Bileća, Bosanski Šamac, Brčko, Doboj, Donji Vakuf, Gacko, Ilijaš, Ključ, Kotor Varoš, Pale, Prijedor, Sanski Most, Teslić, Vlasenica, Višegrad, Vogošća, and Zvornik as well as his actions in this regard, with the exception **[page 114]** of the appointments of Witness Todorović and Krsto Savić,[944] the impact of which will further be assessed below.[945]

(iii) Alleged errors in relation to Stanišić's role in preventing, investigating, and documenting crimes (Stanišić's fifth ground of appeal in part and subsection (B)(iii) of Stanišić's sixth ground of appeal)

269. In its discussion on Stanišić's role in preventing, investigating, and documenting crimes,[946] the Trial Chamber found that: (i) the police and civilian prosecutors failed to function in an impartial manner;[947] (ii) Stanišić's orders of 8, 10, 17, and 24 August 1992 – instructing all CSB and SJB chiefs to obtain information concerning the treatment of detainees and requiring CSB chiefs to initiate criminal reports against perpetrators of crimes – were prompted by international attention;[948] (iii) Stanišić had the authority to take measures against crimes and failed to do so sufficiently;[949] (iv) Stanišić's actions against paramilitaries were only undertaken due to their refusal to submit to the command of the army and their commission of crimes against Serbs;[950] and (v) Stanišić focused primarily on crimes committed against Serbs.[951] Taking into account, *inter alia*, these factors, the Trial Chamber concluded that, despite his knowledge of the crimes that were being committed, Stanišić "took insufficient action to put an end to them and instead permitted RS

---

[939] Trial Judgement, vol. 2, para. 744.
[940] See *supra*, para. 265.
[941] See *supra*, para. 263. See also *supra*. para. 260.
[942] See *supra*, paras 263, 265-266.
[943] See *infra*, paras 356-364.
[944] See *supra*, paras 263, 265-266.
[945] See *infra*, paras 356-364. See also *supra*, para. 267.
[946] Trial Judgement, vol. 2, paras 745-759.
[947] Trial Judgement, vol. 2, para. 745.
[948] Trial Judgement, vol. 2, paras 752-753.
[949] Trial Judgement, vol. 2, paras 754-757.
[950] Trial Judgement, vol. 2, para. 756.
[951] Trial Judgement, vol. 2, para. 758.

MUP forces under his overall control to continue to participate in joint operations in the Municipalities with other Serb Forces involved in the commission of crimes, particularly the JNA/VRS and the TO".[952]

270.   Stanišić challenges the Trial Chamber's above findings on his role in preventing, investigating, and documenting crimes committed by Serb perpetrators against non-Serbs.[953] The Prosecution responds that the Trial Chamber reasonably concluded that Stanišic took insufficient action to protect non-Serbs, considering his ability and failure to punish his subordinates for their crimes against non-Serbs and that Stanišić's arguments should be dismissed.[954] The Appeals Chamber will address Stanišić's challenges in turn. **[page 115]**

a. Preliminary matter

271.   Before turning to Stanišić's challenges, the Appeals Chamber will address a preliminary matter.

272.   In challenging the Trial Chamber's analysis on his role in preventing, investigating, and documenting crimes, Stanišić also disputes its finding, on the basis of an intercepted conversation between himself and Witness Kovač on 21 June 1992 ("21 June 1992 Intercept"), that he "specifically directed that numbers on losses suffered by the Serb side be inflated in order to create a record".[955] He submits that the Trial Chamber's finding is not supported by any reasonable interpretation of the 21 June 1992 Intercept.[956] In his view, a "correct interpretation" of the underlying evidence would undermine any notion that he contributed to the JCE and that he had the "*mens rea*" to commit discriminatory crimes.[957] However, the Appeals Chamber observes that, contrary to Stanišić's assertion, the Trial Chamber did not rely on this factual finding to establish his contribution to the JCE or his intent for joint criminal enterprise liability. His arguments are thus dismissed.

b. Alleged errors in the Trial Chamber's finding that the police and civilian prosecutors failed to function in an impartial manner

273.   The Trial Chamber found that the civilian law enforcement apparatus failed to function in an impartial manner and that between April and December 1992, the police and civilian prosecutors either did not report or under-reported "the vast number of serious crimes committed by Serb perpetrators against non-Serbs".[958] Ultimately, the Trial Chamber concluded that "the discriminatory failure to properly investigate crimes against non-Serbs contributed to the prevailing culture of impunity and thereby facilitated the perpetration of further crimes committed in furtherance of the common objective".[959]

274.   The Trial Chamber found in particular that:

> [i]n the municipalities of Bileća, Ilijas, Gacko, Višegrad, Pale, Vlasenica, Vogošća, and Bosanski Šamac, no serious crimes alleged to have been committed by Serbs against non-Serbs during the Indictment period were reported to the prosecutor's offices. In addition, one crime was reported in each of the following municipalities: Doboj, Kotor Varoš, Prijedor, and Ključ. Approximately two were reported in Zvornik, nine in Teslić, four in Sanski Most, three in Brčko, and four in Bijeljina. Based on the review of the Banja Luka Basic Prosecutor's office, there were a total of 21 serious **[page 116]** crimes by Serb perpetrators committed against non-Serb victims reported in Banja Luka, Skender Vakuf, and Donji Vakuf between 1 April and 31 December 1992.[960]

The Trial Chamber reached this conclusion after considering the evidence of Witness Staka Gojković ("Witness Gojković") – a judge of the Basic Court in Sarajevo between 20 June and 19 December 1992 – and

---

[952]   Trial Judgement, vol. 2, para. 759.
[953]   Stanišić Appeal Brief, paras 273-288.
[954]   Prosecution Response Brief (Stanišić), paras 65, 68-84, 133-149.
[955]   Stanišić Appeal Brief, para. 274, referring to Trial Judgement, vol. 2, para. 724.
[956]   Stanišić Appeal Brief, para. 274, *contra* Prosecution Response Brief (Stanišić), para. 139.
[957]   Stanišić Appeal Brief, para. 274, *contra* Prosecution Response Brief (Stanišić), para. 139.
[958]   Trial Judgement, vol. 2, para. 745. See Trial Judgement, vol. 2, paras 90, 104, referring to Staka Gojković, 15 Jun 2010, T. 11752.
[959]   Trial Judgement, vol. 2, para. 745.
[960]   Trial Judgement, vol. 2, para. 94 (citations omitted).

Witness Slobodanka Gaćinović ("Witness Gaćinović") – Higher Prosecutor for Trebinje from August 1992 – and relying upon information contained in the "logbooks from 1992 to 1995 in relation to crimes that occurred during the Indictment period".[961]

i. Submissions of the parties

275. Stanišić challenges the Trial Chamber's finding that the police and civilian prosecutors failed to function in an impartial manner.[962] He submits that the Trial Chamber improperly relied on the evidence of Witness Gaćinović concerning the 1992 logbooks of the Basic Public Prosecutor's Offices in Sarajevo, Sokolac, Vlasenica, and Višegrad including criminal offences against *known* and *unknown* perpetrators ("KT Logbooks" and "KTN Logbooks", respectively),[963] despite noting that in reviewing the KTN Logbooks and the KT Logbooks, the witness adopted a methodology which "could obfuscate the data".[964] Stanišić also contends that the Trial Chamber disregarded Witness Gaćinović's evidence "about the number of criminal complaints for serious crimes committed against Muslims and Croats by unknown perpetrators".[965] He submits further that in analysing the reporting of crimes during the Indictment period, the Trial Chamber erred by relying solely on information contained in the police registers of criminal cases reported to and investigated by the police in the RS in 1992 ("KU Registers").[966] He argues that, according to Witness Gojko Vasić ("Witness Vasić"), a crime investigator at Laktaši SJB in 1992, in order to get a complete picture of the reporting of crimes it would be necessary to also consider the police logbook of daily events and the register of on-site investigations.[967]

276. The Prosecution responds that Stanišić's arguments with respect to Witness Gaćinović should be summarily dismissed because he fails to articulate an error[968] and mischaracterises the Trial Chamber's findings regarding that witness.[969] The Prosecution also submits that Stanišić's **[page 117]** argument based on the KU Registers should be summarily dismissed, as Stanišić misrepresents the basis of the Trial Chamber's finding and seeks to substitute his evaluation of the evidence for that of the Trial Chamber without showing an error.[970] It argues that, in light of Witness Vasić's evidence, it was not wrong for the Trial Chamber to rely on the KU Registers.[971]

ii. Analysis

277. With regard to Stanišić's argument that the Trial Chamber improperly relied on the evidence of Witness Gaćinović despite noting that the witness adopted a methodology which could obfuscate the data,[972] the Appeals Chamber observes that the Trial Chamber indeed acknowledged that this witness "did not focus on transfers from [the] KTN [Log]books to [the] KT [Log]books when the suspect was finally identified" and that this "could mean a crime was listed twice and which could obfuscate the data".[973] However, the Trial

---

[961] Trial Judgement, vol. 2, para. 93. See Trial Judgement, vol. 2, paras 90-92.
[962] Stanišić Appeal Brief, para. 273, referring to Trial Judgement, vol. 2, para. 745.
[963] See Trial Judgement, vol. 2, para. 90.
[964] Stanišić Appeal Brief, para. 273, referring to Trial Judgement, vol. 2, fn. 313.
[965] Stanišić Appeal Brief, para. 273, referring to Trial Judgement, vol. 2, fn. 320, Exhibit P1609.01, p. 18.
[966] Stanišić Appeal Brief, para. 273, referring to Trial Judgement, vol. 2, para. 93.
[967] Stanišić Appeal Brief, para. 273, referring to Gojko Vasić, 25 Aug 2010, T. 13678-13679, Gojko Vasić, 26 Aug 2010, T. 13730.
[968] Prosecution Response Brief (Stanišić), para. 141, referring to *Krajišnik* Appeal Judgement, paras 19, 26.
[969] Prosecution Response Brief (Stanišić), para. 141, referring to Stanišic Appeal Brief, para. 273, Trial Judgement, vol. 2, fn. 313. The Prosecution contends further the Trial Chamber did not "disregard" the evidence of Witness Gaćinović as the "15 entries concerning crimes against non-Serbs by unknown perpetrators" referred to in her evidence do not undermine the Trial Chamber's finding that the vast number of serious crimes against non-Serbs went unreported across the Municipalities (Prosecution Response Brief (Stanišić), para. 141, referring to Exhibit P1609.1, para. 113, Trial Judgement, vol. 2, para. 745). The Prosecution further argues that Stanišić ignores Witness Gaćinović's evidence that neither the KT Logbooks nor the KTN Logbooks contained entries that corresponded to the 15 entries in the Ključ KTA Logbook, which led Witness Gaćinović to conclude that, between 1992 and 1995, the police had not filed criminal reports with the civilian prosecutor's office in relation to these incidents (Prosecution Response Brief (Stanišić), paras 113, 141 (referring to Exhibit P1609.1)).
[970] Prosecution Response Brief (Stanišić), para. 141, referring to *Krajišnik* Appeal Judgement, paras 18, 27.
[971] Prosecution Response Brief (Stanišić), para. 141, referring to Exhibit P1558.02, para. 2(c) (confidential).
[972] See *supra*, para. 275.
[973] Trial Judgement, vol. 2, fn. 313.

Chamber reached its conclusion that between April and December 1992, the police and civilian prosecutors failed to report or under-reported serious crimes committed by Serb perpetrators against non-Serbs after having analysed itself the KTN Logbooks, the KT Logbooks, and the evidence of Witness Gojković and Witness Gaćinović in light of the methodology used.[974] The Appeals Chamber therefore finds that Stanišić merely asserts that the Trial Chamber failed to interpret the evidence in a particular manner without showing any error in its approach.

278.   Insofar as Stanišić argues that the Trial Chamber disregarded Witness Gaćinović's evidence regarding the number of criminal complaints for serious crimes against Muslims and Croats *by unknown perpetrators*,[975] the Appeals Chamber notes that the Trial Chamber in fact explicitly took this evidence into account in concluding on the number of crimes committed *by Serbs perpetrators* against non-Serbs that had been reported to the prosecutor's offices during the Indictment period.[976] Moreover, the Appeals Chamber observes that the portion of Witness Gaćinović's evidence concerning crimes committed against non-Serbs by *unknown perpetrators* is irrelevant to the Trial **[page 118]** Chamber's conclusion that between April and December 1992, the police and civilian prosecutors failed to report or under-reported serious crimes committed *by Serb perpetrators* against non-Serbs.[977] Stanišić has therefore failed to show that the Trial Chamber erred in disregarding the said portion of Witness Gaćinović's evidence.[978]

279.   With respect to Stanišić's argument that the Trial Chamber failed to consider the logbook of daily events and the register of on-site investigations and relied solely on the KU Registers,[979] the Appeals Chamber notes Witness Vasić's evidence that: (i) KU Registers should contain all criminal cases reported to and investigated by the police;[980] (ii) a comprehensive analysis, such as a police station audit, would include a review of the logbook of daily events, the register of on-site investigations as well as the KU Registers;[981] and (iii) as crimes could be reported to either the police or the public prosecutor's office, the logbook of daily events plus the logbook of the public prosecutor's office were "the place where you could get a complete picture of what was reported to the police and the public prosecutor's office".[982] The Appeals Chamber also notes that although Witness Vasić's review and analysis was limited to the KU Registers,[983] the Trial Chamber's conclusions relating to the reporting of crimes do not only rely on the KU Registers. As discussed above, in addition to Witness Vasić's evidence, the Trial Chamber also reviewed and analysed the "logbooks from 1992 to 1995 in relation to crimes that occurred during the Indictment period".[984] The Appeals Chamber therefore finds that Stanišić has failed to demonstrate an error.

280.   In light of the above, the Appeals Chamber finds that Stanišić has failed to show that the Trial Chamber erred in finding that the police and civilian prosecutors failed to function in an impartial manner.

　　　　　　c. Alleged errors in the Trial Chamber's finding that Stanišić's orders of 8, 10, 17, and 24 August 1992 were prompted by international attention

281.   The Trial Chamber found that Stanišić's orders of 8, 10, 17, and 24 August 1992, by which he requested that all CSB and SJB chiefs obtain information concerning the treatment of war **[page 119]** prisoners and the conditions of life of detainees and that chiefs of CSBs initiate criminal reports against perpetrators of crimes such as mistreatment of detainees, were prompted by the international attention given to the detention camps

---

[974]　　Trial Judgement, vol. 2, paras 90-94, 104.
[975]　　See *supra*, para. 275.
[976]　　Trial Judgement, vol. 2, para. 94. See Stanišić Appeal Brief, para. 273, referring to Trial Judgement, vol. 2, fn. 320, Exhibit P1609.01, p. 18.
[977]　　Trial Judgement, vol. 2, para. 94, referring to P1609.01, pp 6-9, 12, 18, P1609.04, pp 2-6, 8, Staka Gojkovic, 15 Jun 2010, T. 11766-11768, Lazar Draško, 28 Jun 2010, T. 12299.
[978]　　See *Tolimir* Appeal Judgement, para. 161; *Popović et al.* Appeal Judgement, para. 306; *Đorđević* Appeal Judgement, para. 864; *Haradinaj et al.* Appeal Judgement, para. 129; *Kvočka et al.* Appeal Judgement, para. 23.
[979]　　See *supra*, para. 275.
[980]　　Exhibit P1558.02, para. 2(c) (confidential).
[981]　　Gojko Vasić, 25 Aug 2010, T. 13678-13679.
[982]　　Gojko Vasić, 25 Aug 2010, T. 13679-13680.
[983]　　Gojko Vasić, 25 Aug 2010, T. 13679.
[984]　　Trial Judgement, vol. 2, para. 93.

in BiH by June 1992.[985] The Trial Chamber found that these orders were a result of an instruction of 6 August 1992 by the RS Presidency, "which was concerned about its image in the eyes of the world".[986]

i. Submissions of the parties

282. Stanišić submits that the Trial Chamber erred by finding that his orders of 8, 10, 17, and 24 August 1992 were prompted by "international attention", as his motivation to issue these orders is plainly irrelevant.[987] He further submits that the Trial Chamber did not properly assess the totality of the evidence on the trial record.[988] Stanišić argues that the Trial Chamber failed to take into account Exhibit P427.08, a report on the 11 July 1992 Collegium to the President and the Prime Minster of RS, dated 17 July 1992 ("17 July 1992 Report").[989] According to him, this exhibit demonstrates that he had reported to the highest authorities of the RS and requested a meeting with the Ministry of Justice of the RS ("MOJ") and VRS to resolve the issue of detention camps, before the International Committee of the Red Cross ("ICRC") released a report on 25 July 1992 criticising the conditions at Manjača and Bileća detention camps and before the BiH President Alija Izetbegović informed the Chairman of the European Community Conference on Yugoslavia of the existence of concentration camps.[990] Stanišić also refers to an order he issued on 19 July 1992 to the chiefs of the CSBs "requesting information on procedures for arrest, treatment of prisoners, conditions of collection camps, and Muslim prisoners detained by the army at 'undefined camps' without proper documentation" ("19 July 1992 Order").[991] He argues that the 19 July 1992 Order "was a result of Stanišić becoming aware of detention camps at the 11 July 1992 Collegium, and not in response to international attention".[992] He contends that the Trial Chamber: (i) made no reference to the 17 July 1992 Report;[993] and (ii) made "only cursory reference" to the letter he sent to Witness Đerić, Prime Minister of the RS on 18 July 1992 ("Đerić Letter"), Exhibit P190, in which Stanišić, *inter alia*, reiterated a request for regulations to be issued to prevent breaches of **[page 120]** international law, and informed Witness Đerić that he had instructed the RS MUP to record war crimes regardless of the ethnicity of perpetrators.[994]

283. Stanišić further contends that the Trial Chamber erred by noting that the mistreatment in the camps continued and by imputing it to Stanišić.[995] He asserts that there is clear evidence that the RS MUP did not have authority or jurisdiction over the camps or detainees.[996] Stanišić argues that despite this lack of authority or jurisdiction, he ordered that information be gathered about the camps, expressing the need for conditions to comply with international law.[997] He further submits that although the Trial Chamber referred to some of the orders he issued "which ran contrary to the furtherance of the common purpose",[998] it failed to assess their significance and failed to consider or even refer to numerous other similar orders he issued.[999]

284. The Prosecution responds that Stanišic only issued orders concerning the protection of non-Serb detainees because of international attention on the detention camps in BiH, and misconstrues the Trial Chamber's finding that the detention camps had already attracted international attention by June 1992.[1000] It

---

[985]   Trial Judgement, vol. 2, paras 752-753.
[986]   Trial Judgement, vol. 2, para. 753.
[987]   Stanišic Appeal Brief, para. 210. See Stanišic Appeal Brief, para. 275.
[988]   Stanišić Appeal Brief, para. 279.
[989]   Stanišić Appeal Brief, para. 275, referring to Exhibit P427.08, pp 3, 6.
[990]   Stanišić Appeal Brief, para. 275, referring to Exhibit P427.08, pp 3, 6.
[991]   Stanišić Appeal Brief, para. 276, referring to Exhibit 1D76.
[992]   Stanišić Appeal Brief, para. 276, referring to Exhibit P2309, pp 18-19.
[993]   Stanišić Appeal Brief, para. 279, referring to Exhibit P427.08.
[994]   Stanišić Appeal Brief, para. 279, referring to Exhibit P190.
[995]   Stanišić Appeal Brief, para. 276, referring to Trial Judgement, vol. 2, para. 753.
[996]   Stanišić Appeal Brief, para. 276, referring to Momčilo Mandić, 4 May 2010, T. 9481-9482, 9554, Goran Mačar, 19 Jul 2011, T. 23534-23537, Milan Trbojević, 2 Dec 2009, T. 4095, Exhibit P2310, p. 9.
[997]   Stanišić Appeal Brief, para. 277, referring to Exhibits 1D563, 1D55, 1D56, 1D57.
[998]   Stanišić Appeal Brief, para. 278, referring to Trial Judgement, vol. 2, paras 747-750.
[999]   Stanišić Appeal Brief, para. 278.
[1000] Prosecution Response Brief (Stanišic), paras 71 (referring to Trial Judgement, vol. 2, paras 34-36, 39-42, 87, 90-94, 97-98, 101, 104, 600, 613-614, 637-638, 640-641, 643-646, 648, 651-673, 675-676, 684, 687, 698-704, 706-708, 743, 745-746, 748-749, 752-755, 763, 765), 142 (referring to Trial Judgement, vol. 2, paras 614, 753). See Prosecution Response Brief (Stanišić), para. 82. The Prosecution points out that Stanišic ignored reports concerning mistreatment within detention facilities in the ARK and willingly accepted false reports from his subordinates which covered up crimes against non-Serbs (Prosecution Response Brief (Stanišic),

further submits that despite issuing these orders, Stanišić was uninterested in genuinely trying to put a stop to crimes against non-Serbs, as evident from his efforts to shift the blame for these crimes to others, his continued transfers of known police offenders to the army, his willingness to accept false reports concerning the conditions within detention facilities, and his failure to secure full compliance with his orders concerning the protection of non-Serb detainees.[1001]

ii. Analysis

285. With regard to Stanišic's argument that the Trial Chamber erred in finding that his orders of 8, 10, 17, and 24 August 1992 were prompted by international attention given that his motivation for issuing these orders is irrelevant, the Appeals Chamber finds that the Trial Chamber was not legally barred from considering Stanišic's motivation for issuing these orders as it constituted a **[page 121]** relevant factual inquiry for assessing the elements of the joint criminal enterprise mode of liability. Stanišic's argument is therefore without merit.

286. With respect to Stanišic's argument that he took measures regarding the detention camps before the issue was raised by the international community at the end of July 1992, the Appeals Chamber notes that Stanišić seeks to support his argument with a reference to the 17 July 1992 Report, which he argues the Trial Chamber disregarded, and his 19 July 1992 Order.[1001][1002] The Appeals Chamber first observes that, contrary to Stanišić's contention, the Trial Chamber found that the issue of detention camps in BiH had already been raised by the international community by June 1992,[1003] before Stanišić's 17 July 1992 Report and 19 July 1992 Order. The Appeals Chamber further notes that the Trial Chamber established that in July 1992, Stanišić had already issued orders in relation to the detention camps.[1004] In this regard, the Appeals Chamber observes that the Trial Chamber specifically considered Stanišić's 17 July 1992 Report[1005] and his 19 July 1992 Order.[1006] In light of this, the Appeals Chamber finds that Stanišić has failed to show that the Trial Chamber disregarded his 17 July 1992 Report or erred in its consideration of his 19 July 1992 Order. The Appeals Chamber notes further, to the extent that Stanišić seeks to rely on the Đerić Letter of 18 July 1992, that the Trial Chamber considered it explicitly and in detail in assessing Stanišić's role in prevention, investigation, and documentation of crimes,[1007] and on this basis dismisses his argument.

287. Insofar as Stanišić submits that the Trial Chamber erred by failing to consider evidence that the RS MUP did not have authority or jurisdiction over the detention camps or detainees,[1008] the Appeals Chamber recalls that it has addressed and dismissed this argument elsewhere in this Judgement.[1009]

288. Turning to Stanišić's submission that the Trial Chamber failed to assess the significance of the orders he issued which ran contrary to the furtherance of the common purpose, and therefore failed to properly assess the totality of the evidence on the trial record,[1010] the Appeals Chamber observes that the Trial Chamber made specific findings in relation to these orders and assessed their **[page 122]** significance.[1011] The Appeals Chamber recalls the Trial Chamber's conclusion that these orders were prompted by international attention, that the conditions of detention did not improve, and that the mistreatment in the detention camps continued.[1012] The Trial Chamber further concluded that Stanišić failed to use the powers available to him under the law to ensure the full implementation of these orders despite being aware of the limited action

paras 72-73, referring to Trial Judgement, vol. 1, paras 591-635, 679-683, Trial Judgement, vol. 2, paras 631, 636, 646, 654, 659, 671-672, 676, 692, 750, 757).
[1001] Prosecution Response Brief (Stanišić), para. 143, referring to Trial Judgement, vol. 2, paras 636, 747, 757, 759.
[1002] See *supra*, para. 282.
[1003] Trial Judgement, vol. 2, paras 614, 753.
[1004] Trial Judgement, vol. 2, para. 748.
[1005] Trial Judgement, vol. 2, paras 632-633.
[1006] Trial Judgement, vol. 2, para. 748.
[1007] See *infra*, fn. 1813.
[1008] See *supra*, para. 283.
[1009] *See infra*, paras 344-355.
[1010] See *supra*, paras 282-283.
[1011] Trial Judgement, vol. 2, paras 746-753.
[1012] Trial Judgement, vol. 2, para. 753.

taken subsequent to his orders.[1013] The Appeals Chamber considers that Stanišić has therefore failed to show that the Trial Chamber erred in this regard.

289.   With regard to Stanišić's submission that the Trial Chamber failed to consider or even refer to numerous other similar orders he issued, the Appeals Chamber observes that Stanišić does not specify the evidence which he alleges the Trial Chamber failed to consider. His argument is therefore dismissed.

290.   In light of the above, the Appeals Chamber finds that Stanišić has failed to show that no reasonable trier of fact could have concluded that his orders of 8, 10, 17, and 24 August 1992 were prompted by international attention.

        d. Alleged errors in the Trial Chamber's finding that Stanišić had the authority to take measures against crimes and failed to take sufficient action to put an end to them

291.   The Trial Chamber found that as the Minister of Interior, Stanišić was under a duty, both under the law applicable in the RS at the relevant time and under international law, to discipline and dismiss the personnel of his RS MUP who had committed crimes.[1014] In this regard, the Trial Chamber held that in the exercise of these powers, Stanišić, through Witness Kovač, initiated action against Koroman, Witness Todorović, Witness Petrović, Maksimović, and Drljača, but that none of these persons were successfully removed from the RS MUP in the course of 1992.[1015] The Trial Chamber moreover held that the proceedings launched against these persons did not pertain to the crimes charged in the Indictment but instead concerned crimes such as theft and professional misconduct.[1016] The Trial Chamber found that, "given the above, Stanišić violated his professional obligation to protect and safeguard the civilian population in the territories under their control".[1017]

292.   The Trial Chamber further found that "[a]ctions by Mićo Stanišić against [Witness Dragomir Andan ("Witness Andan")], Nenad Simić, [Witness Petrović], Vladimir Petrov, and **[page 123]** Veljko [olaja resulted in dismissals [but that] these persons were only pursued for their involvement in the theft and smuggling of vehicles or persons".[1017][1018] It found that:

> the evidence on the efforts made by Stanišić to quell the theft of vehicles—by issuing orders to monitor and protect the facilities, requiring immediate inspection and reporting by chiefs of CSBs, instituting disciplinary action leading to dismissal from service of police officers involved in the crime, and his relentless airing of the issue as a matter of personal concern—demonstrates his ability as the highest authority to investigate and punish those found to be involved, even when faced by opposition from others in the Bosnian Serb leadership.[1019]

293.   In addition, the Trial Chamber found that the action taken by Stanišić against paramilitaries was only pursued following their refusal to submit to the command of the army and their continued commission of acts of theft, looting, and trespasses against the local RS leaders.[1020] The Trial Chamber further found that the primary motivation for these actions was the theft of Golf vehicles and harassment of the Serbs.[1021]

294.   Furthermore, the Trial Chamber found that Stanišić failed to act in the same decisive manner with regard to the other crimes, such as unlawful detention, displacement and removal of non-Serb civilians – and the ensuing crimes of killing and inhumane treatment of detainees.[1022]

295.   Finally, the Trial Chamber concluded that, despite his knowledge of the crimes that were being committed, Stanišić "took insufficient action to put an end to them and instead permitted RS MUP forces

---

[1013]   Trial Judgement, vol. 2, para. 753.
[1014]   Trial Judgement, vol. 2, para. 754.
[1015]   Trial Judgement, vol. 2, para. 754.
[1016]   Trial Judgement, vol. 2, para. 754.
[1017]   Trial Judgement, vol. 2, para. 754.
[1018]   Trial Judgement, vol. 2, para. 755.
[1019]   Trial Judgement, vol. 2, para. 755.
[1020]   Trial Judgement, vol. 2, para. 756.
[1021]   Trial Judgement, vol. 2, para. 756.
[1022]   Trial Judgement, vol. 2, para. 757.

under his overall control to continue to participate in joint operations in the Municipalities with other Serb Forces involved in the commission of crimes, particularly the JNA/VRS and the TO".[1023]

i. Alleged errors relating to Stanišić's authority to take measures against crimes

a. Submissions of the parties

296.   Stanišić submits that the Trial Chamber erroneously interpreted evidence of his dismissal of Witness Andan, Nenad Simic, Witness Petrovic, Vladimir Petrov, and Veljko [olaja as demonstrating his ability as the highest authority to investigate and punish.[1024] He submits that the instances the Trial Chamber referred to were ones in which disciplinary proceedings had already **[page 124]** begun and that he was therefore able to exercise his appellate power to dismiss the individuals in question.[1025] Moreover, Stanišić asserts that these dismissals "occurred despite opposition from others in the Bosnian Serb leadership", which he argues shows that he used his disciplinary powers irrespective of opposition from individuals found to be members of the JCE.[1026]

297.   Stanišic further submits that the Trial Chamber erred in considering that the measures he took to quell the theft of vehicles, to curb looting and misappropriation of property, and against paramilitaries, demonstrated his ability to act.[1027] Stanišic argues that there are practical differences between the ability to counteract thefts and other more serious crimes, often taking place near the frontline, "where the perpetrators are more likely to shoot back rather than be arrested".[1028] Stanišic further argues that: (i) the Trial Chamber's finding that his orders were not carried out to the extent possible fails to take into account that his orders for arrests and prosecutions were passed down the chain of command to the relevant RS MUP members, a fact that the Trial Chamber acknowledged;[1029] and (ii) the fact that these orders were not carried out to the extent possible shows lack of *de facto* ability to do more rather than an omission.[1030] He argues further that the Trial Chamber failed to take into account the "severe difficulties" he encountered and therefore his objective inability to do more than he actually did.[1031]

298.   The Prosecution responds that Stanišić's arguments should be summarily dismissed.[1032] It submits that Stanišić's argument ignores the full extent of his role in the actions against RS MUP officials Nenad Simić,[1033] Witness Andan,[1034] Vladimir Srebov,[1035] and Witness Petrović.[1036] The **[page 125]** Prosecution further submits that the Trial Chamber's finding that Stanišić pursued the theft of vehicles despite opposition

---

[1023]   Trial Judgement, vol. 2, para. 759.
[1024]   Stanišić Appeal Brief, para. 280, referring to Trial Judgement, vol. 2, para. 755.
[1025]   Stanišić Appeal Brief, para. 280.
[1026]   Stanišić Appeal Brief, para. 281, referring to Trial Judgement, vol. 2, para. 755.
[1027]   Stanišic Appeal Brief, paras 223-225.
[1028]   Stanišic Appeal Brief, para. 224.
[1029]   Stanišic Appeal Brief, para. 230, referring to Trial Judgement, vol. 2, paras 746, 752.
[1030]   Stanišic Appeal Brief, para. 230.
[1031]   Stanišic Appeal Brief, para. 211.
[1032]   Prosecution Response Brief (Stanišić), para. 145, referring to *Krajišnik* Appeal Judgement, para. 18 ("submissions which either misrepresent the Trial Chamber's factual findings or the evidence on which the Trial Chamber relies [...] will not be considered in detail").
[1033]   Prosecution Response Brief (Stanišić), para. 145, referring to Trial Judgement, vol. 2, para. 702 ("As a result of an investigation conducted by Dragomir Andan and others in Bijeljina, Brčko and Zvornik, Stanišić stated that a decision would be issued for the dismissal of officers for their reported involvement in criminal activities. On 29 July 1992, the Bijeljina SJB issued a ruling on the detention of Nenad Simić on the 'suspicion' that he was illegally commandeering vehicles and goods and using weapons to check drivers and vehicles at illegal checkpoints in Zvornik between 28 June and 29 July 1992").
[1034]   Prosecution Response Brief (Stanišić), para. 145, referring to Trial Judgement, vol. 2, para. 703 ("On 11 September 1992, Stanišić initiated disciplinary proceedings against Dragomir Andan for illegally confiscating a gambling machine for private purposes").
[1035]   Prosecution Response Brief (Stanišić), para. 145, referring to Trial Judgement, vol. 2, para. 704 ("Stanišić signed the initial remand order in August 1992 to detain Vladimir Srebrov, a Serb who was charged with persuading people to join the 'enemy army'").
[1036]   Prosecution Response Brief (Stanišić), para. 145, referring to Trial Judgement, vol. 2, para. 706 ("[Witness] Petrović testified that he was summarily dismissed, based upon a proposal of Andrija Bjelošević, in January 1993 pursuant to a dispatch directly from Mićo Stanišić").

from the Bosnian Serb leadership is irrelevant to the Trial Chamber's conclusion that Stanišić shared the common criminal purpose and contributed to it.[1037]

299.   The Prosecution also responds that the Trial Chamber reasonably found that Stanišic "had the 'ability as the highest authority to investigate and punish those found to be involved'" in the crimes, in light of the measures he took for matters such as theft, professional misconduct, and the smuggling of vehicles or persons.[1038] It contends that Stanišic misrepresents the Trial Chamber's factual findings when arguing that the Trial Chamber failed to take into account differences between counteracting thefts and other more serious crimes since, contrary to his submission, the crimes were not a sporadic consequence of combat.[1039]

b. Analysis

300.   With respect to Stanišić's argument that the dismissals of the five individuals referred to by the Trial Chamber were incidents in which disciplinary proceedings had already begun and that he therefore was able to exercise his appellate power to dismiss,[1040] the Appeals Chamber first notes that Stanišić does not advance any evidence to support his factual claim that the proceedings had already been initiated. The Appeals Chamber further notes that, contrary to Stanišić's contention, in relation to some of the instances to which the Trial Chamber referred, it established that Stanišić initiated the disciplinary proceedings.[1041] For example, the Trial Chamber found that Stanišić initiated internal disciplinary proceedings, including an investigative commission established to look into allegations of corruption at the Bijeljina SJB in August 1992.[1042] The Trial Chamber further found that on 11 September 1992, Stanišić initiated disciplinary proceedings against Witness Andan, a RS MUP police inspector who informally acted as chief of the Bijeljina SJB in July and August 1992,[1043] for illegally confiscating a gambling machine for private purposes.[1044] In this respect, the Appeals Chamber recalls the Trial Chamber's finding that under the RS MUP **[page 126]** regulations, the Minister of Interior had the authority to initiate appropriate disciplinary proceedings against SJB or CSB chiefs.[1045]

301.   Moreover, as far as Stanišić seeks to challenge the Trial Chamber's overall conclusion that he had authority to investigate and punish members of the RS MUP involved in crime,[1046] the Appeals Chamber recalls that the Trial Chamber relied not only on the actions he took with respect to the five individuals mentioned above but also on the evidence about the efforts Stanišić made to quell the theft of vehicles.[1047] This evidence included "issuing orders to monitor and protect the facilities, requiring immediate inspection and reporting by chiefs of CSBs, instituting disciplinary action leading to dismissal from service of police officers involved in the crime, and his relentless airing of the issue as a matter of personal concern".[1048] In light of these findings, the Appeals Chamber dismisses Stanišić's argument.

302.   Insofar as Stanišić argues that he used his disciplinary powers despite opposition from individuals found to be members of the JCE,[1049] the Appeals Chamber recalls the Trial Chamber's finding that Stanišić

[1037]   Prosecution Response Brief (Stanišić), para. 146.
[1038]   Prosecution Response Brief (Stanišic), para. 75, quoting Trial Judgement, vol. 2, para. 755. See Prosecution Response Brief (Stanišic), para. 75, referring to Trial Judgement, vol. 2, paras 707-708, 714-175, 755. See also Prosecution Response Brief (Stanišic), para. 77.
[1039]   Prosecution Response Brief (Stanišić), para. 76, referring to *Krajišnik* Appeal Judgement, para. 18, Stanišić Appeal Brief, para. 224, Trial Judgement, vol. 1, paras 201, 204-206, 211, 222, 262, 265, 269, 281-282, 332, 338, 346-347, 467, 474-476, 480, 482, 490-491, 659, 669, 671, 676-679, 681-683, 686, 699-700, 709, 755-757, 785, 798-799, 801, 803, 811, 868, 870-872, 879-880, 919, 967, 970-972, 982, 1003, 1021, 1030, 1032-1033, 1041, 1099, 1101-1106, 1110, 1118-1119, 1177, 1179, 1182, 1189-1190, 1229, 1232, 1234-1235, 1236, 1239, 1247, 1248, 1280, 1338-1339, 1342-1343, 1348, 1355-1356, 1403, 1413, 1423, 1442, 1444, 1446, 1477-1478, 1480, 1483-1485, 1490, 1497-1498, 1532, 1545, 1547, 1633, 1652-1653, 1657-1659, 1663, 1665-1668, 1670-1671, 1687.
[1040]   See *supra*, para. 296.
[1041]   Trial Judgement, vol. 2, paras 697, 703-704. See Trial Judgement, vol. 2, paras 695-696.
[1042]   Trial Judgement, vol. 2, para. 697.
[1043]   Trial Judgement, vol. 1, para. 894.
[1044]   Trial Judgement, vol. 2, para. 703.
[1045]   Trial Judgement, vol. 2, paras 40, 695, 698.
[1046]   See *supra*, para. 296.
[1047]   Trial Judgement, vol. 2, para. 755.
[1048]   Trial Judgement, vol. 2, para. 755. See Trial Judgement, vol. 2, para. 708.
[1049]   See *supra*, para. 296.

used his disciplinary powers with respect to persons involved in the theft and smuggling of vehicles or professional misconduct, but not with respect to those involved in the crimes charged in the Indictment.[1050] The Appeals Chamber considers that the fact that individuals within the Bosnian Serb leadership opposed Stanišić's efforts to investigate and punish crimes not charged in the Indictment does not demonstrate that the Trial Chamber erred in concluding that Stanišić had the ability to investigate and punish members of the RS MUP. Stanišić's argument is therefore dismissed.

303. The Appeals Chamber now turns to Stanišic's contention that the Trial Chamber erred in considering that the measures he took to curb looting and misappropriation of property, and against paramilitaries, demonstrated his ability to act as there are practical differences between the ability to counteract thefts and other more serious crimes, often taking place near the frontline.[1051] In this regard, the Appeals Chamber observes that the vast majority of crimes against the civilian **[page 127]** population which the Trial Chamber took into account were committed across areas of the Municipalities where no combat activity was taking place.[1052] The Appeals Chamber therefore considers that Stanišic's argument misrepresents the Trial Chamber's findings and dismisses it.

304. With regard to Stanišic's argument that the Trial Chamber's finding that his orders were not carried out to the extent possible fails to take into account that his orders for arrests and prosecutions were passed down the chain of command and that the fact that his orders were not carried out to the extent possible shows lack of *de facto* ability to do more, the Appeals Chamber finds that it is inapposite. The Trial Chamber acknowledged that Stanišic's orders were passed down the chain of command,[1053] but found that: (i) his orders from May 1992 to arrest and prosecute or dismiss and hand over to the VRS, members of the reserve police – among whom the problem of "unprincipled conduct" was most pronounced – were not carried out to the extent possible since the reserve police continued to serve within the RS MUP until the end of 1992;[1054] and (ii) "despite being aware of the limited action taken subsequent to his orders" to obtain information concerning the treatment of war prisoners and requiring chiefs of CSBs to initiate criminal reports against perpetrators of crimes, "Stanišic failed to use the powers available to him under the law to ensure the full implementation of these orders".[1055] Considering these findings, Stanišić has failed to explain how the mere fact that these orders were not carried out by his subordinates demonstrates the lack of his *de facto* ability to take further action to ensure the full implementation of his orders. The Appeals Chamber therefore dismisses Stanišic's argument.

305. With regard to Stanišic's contention that the Trial Chamber failed to take into account the "severe difficulties" he encountered while carrying out his duties and, therefore, his objective inability to do more than he actually did,[1056] the Appeals Chamber notes that to support his argument, Stanišic exclusively relies on Trial Chamber's findings based on evidence regarding the difficulties he encountered.[1057] The Appeals Chamber therefore finds that, contrary to Stanišic's contention, the Trial Chamber did not fail to take into account the "severe difficulties" he encountered while carrying out his duties.[1058] To the extent that Stanišic argues that the Trial Chamber failed to give sufficient weight to the evidence it considered, the Appeals Chamber considers that he merely asserts that the evidence should have been interpreted in a particular **[page 128]** manner without further showing any error on the part of the Trial Chamber. The Appeals Chamber consequently dismisses Stanišic's argument.

[1050] Trial Judgement, vol. 2, paras 754-755. The Appeals Chamber recalls that the Indictment charged Stanišić with the following crimes against humanity under Article 5 of the Statute: (i) persecutions on political, racial, and religious grounds; (ii) extermination; (iii) murder; (iv) torture; (v) inhumane acts; (vi) deportation; and (vii) other inhumane acts (forcible transfer). The Indictment also charged Stanišić with the following violations of the laws or customs of war under Article 3 of the Statute: (i) murder; (ii) torture; and (iii) cruel treatment (Indictment paras 24, 26, 28-29, 31-32, 34, 36-38, 41). See *supra*, para. 4.

[1051] See *supra*, para. 297.

[1052] See Trial Judgement, vol. 1, paras 200-211, 260-274, 331-339, 453-480, 655-684, 782-804, 867-872, 915-930, 967-973, 1028-1033, 1099-1110, 1174-1184, 1228-1239, 1278-1280, 1337-1348, 1397-1407, 1476-1490, 1539-1547, 1633-1671.

[1053] Trial Judgement, vol. 2, paras 746, 752.

[1054] Trial Judgement, vol. 2, para. 746.

[1055] Trial Judgement, vol. 2, para. 753. See Trial Judgement, vol. 2, para. 752.

[1056] See *supra*, para. 297.

[1057] See Stanišic Appeal Brief, para. 211, referring to Trial Judgement, vol. 2, paras 581-583, 697.

[1058] See *e.g.* Trial Judgement, vol. 2, para. 735.

ii. Alleged errors in relation to Stanišić's failure to take sufficient action to put an end
to crimes

a. Submissions of the parties

306.   Stanišic argues that the Trial Chamber erred in finding that placing reserve policemen at the disposal of the army was not sufficient to fulfil his duties, considering that it acknowledged that this was the only applicable disciplinary procedure available at that time for reserve policemen.[1059] He contends further that the Trial Chamber failed to take into account actions he took, to the extent of his ability, to reform the disciplinary system, including dismissing a large number of personnel, and the time required for the disciplinary measures and reforms to be completed.[1060] Stanišić argues that the Trial Chamber failed to give appropriate weight to the measures he took against named individuals, regardless of his purported motivation for doing so.[1061]

307.   The Prosecution responds that, while Stanišić argues that the transfer of reserve policemen to the army was the only sanction available to him to deal with delinquent reserve policemen, he repeatedly transferred such personnel to the army, sometimes even before disciplinary proceedings against them had concluded.[1062] It argues that Stanišić should have ensured that criminal reports were filed against offenders who committed serious crimes and that the VRS was duly informed of these crimes upon transfer.[1063] In this regard, the Prosecution adds that, as he concedes that he had authority to reform the disciplinary system, Stanišic could have ensured that the system did not facilitate further contact between civilians and known offenders within his ranks.[1064]

308.   Stanišic replies that the Prosecution's assertion that he failed to inform the VRS about the crimes committed by the reserve policemen when they were being transferred is unfounded, as the **[page 129]** documentation detailing their behaviour and disciplinary record accompanied them upon their transfer to the army.[1065]

b. Analysis

309.   With regard to Stanišic's argument that the Trial Chamber erred in finding that placing errant reserve policemen at the disposal of the army was not sufficient to fulfil his duties,[1066] the Appeals Chamber notes that the Trial Chamber acknowledged that such a placement was in accordance with the applicable disciplinary procedures.[1067] The Trial Chamber nonetheless found that this measure was not sufficient to fulfil Stanišić's duty to protect the Muslim and Croat population, considering that the transfer of known offenders in the reserve police to the army in fact further facilitated their continued interaction with civilians.[1068] In light of the Trial Chamber's findings regarding the involvement of the VRS in takeovers of municipalities and in guarding the detention facilities,[1069] the Appeals Chamber considers that the transfer

---

[1059]   Stanišic Appeal Brief, paras 213-215, 217 (referring to Trial Judgement, vol. 2, paras 43, 342, 696-697, Vladimir Tutuš, 18 Mar 2010, T. 7750), 218.
[1060]   Stanišic Appeal Brief, paras 221-222, 225, referring to Exhibits P1252, P553, P1013, P571, P427.08, P855, 1D58, 1D59, P592, 1D64, 1D662, Trial Judgement, vol. 2, paras 42, 582, 647, 694, 698, 700-702, 755, 756, 768.
[1061]   Stanišic Appeal Brief, para. 221.
[1062]   Prosecution Response Brief (Stanišic), para. 74.
[1063]   Prosecution Response Brief (Stanišic), paras 73-74, referring to Sreto Gajic, 15 Jul 2010, T. 12838-12839, 12845-12846, Exhibits 1D666, 1D58, 1D59, 1D176, 1D60, P855, P1013, Trial Judgement, vol. 1, para. 1413, Trial Judgement, vol. 2, paras 18, 25, 34-36, 39-42, 48-51, 53, 87, 90-94, 97-98, 101, 104, 354, 578-580, 588, 591-596, 605-609, 613-621, 623-625, 629, 631-633, 636-641, 644-646, 651-652, 654-657, 659-673, 675, 677-680, 684, 687, 689692, 698, 701-704, 706-708, 714-715, 717-718, 733, 736, 743, 745-746, 748-752, 754, 756-759, 761-765.
[1064]   Prosecution Response Brief (Stanišic), para. 74, referring to Stanišić Appeal Brief, paras 173, 221-222, Trial Judgement, vol. 2, para. 42.
[1065]   Stanišic Reply Brief, para. 66, referring to Radomir Rodić, 16 Apr 2010, T. 8805.
[1066]   See *supra*, para. 306.
[1067]   Trial Judgement, vol. 2, para. 751.
[1068]   Trial Judgement, vol. 2, para. 751.
[1069]   See *e.g.* Trial Judgement, vol. 1, paras 235-248, 254, 258, 261, 263, 268, 274, 333, 337, 343, 378, 504, 735-747, 827, 1055, 1139, 1204, 1314.

of known offenders from the reserve police to the army may have exposed the civilians to a greater risk of abuses. The Appeals Chamber therefore finds that a reasonable trier of fact could have concluded that this measure was not enough to fulfil Stanišić's duty to protect civilians. Stanišic's argument is dismissed.

310.   With respect to Stanišic's argument that the Trial Chamber failed to take into account evidence establishing actions he took, to the extent of his ability, to reform the disciplinary system, including firing a large number of personnel,[1070] the Appeals Chamber first recalls that it is not necessary for a trial chamber to refer to every piece of evidence on the record, as long as there is no indication that the trial chamber completely disregarded evidence which is clearly relevant.[1071] It is presumed that the trial chamber evaluated all evidence presented before it.[1072] In the present instance, the Trial Chamber duly considered evidence and made findings in relation to the measures he took for the errant reserve policemen to be placed at the disposal of the army and to curb looting and misappropriation of property.[1073] Furthermore, insofar as Stanišic argues that the Trial Chamber **[page 130]** failed to give appropriate weight to the measures he took against named individuals and to the time required to implement the reforms,[1074] the Appeals Chamber observes that he merely asserts that the Trial Chamber failed to give sufficient weight to certain evidence without articulating any further error. The Appeals Chamber therefore dismisses Stanišic's argument.

iii. Conclusion

311.   In light of the above, the Appeals Chamber finds that Stanišić has failed to show any error in the Trial Chamber's findings with regard to his authority to take measures against crimes and his failure to take sufficient action to put an end to them.

e. Alleged error in the Trial Chamber's finding that Stanišić's actions against paramilitaries were only undertaken due to their refusal to submit to the command of the army and their commission of crimes against Serbs

312.   With regard to actions taken against paramilitaries, the Trial Chamber referred to evidence that Stanišić was "opposed to the use of paramilitaries from outside BiH to forward the Serb cause, primarily at the behest of Biljana Plavšić, and that he raised the issue of the problems these forces caused with the Prime Minister Branko Đerić".[1075] The Trial Chamber, however, found that "the action against the Yellow Wasps in Zvornik and other paramilitaries in Bijeljina, Brčko, and other municipalities was only pursued by Stanišić following their refusal to submit to the command of the army and their continued commission of acts of theft, looting, and trespasses against the local RS leaders".[1076] It found that "[t]he primary motivation for these actions was the theft of Golf vehicles and harassment of the Serbs, an issue that concerned the RS authorities since the start of hostilities".[1077]

i. Submissions of the parties

313.   Stanišić submits that the Trial Chamber erred in finding that his actions against paramilitaries from outside BiH were only undertaken due to the paramilitaries' refusal to submit to the command of the army and their commission of crimes against Serbs.[1078] He contends that the Trial Chamber's finding is "a selective

---

[1070]   See *supra*, para. 306.

[1071]   *Tolimir* Appeal Judgement, para. 56; *Popović et al.* Appeal Judgement, paras 306, 340, 359, 375, 830, 847, 925, 1024, 1123, 1136, 1171, 1213, 1257, 1521, 1541, 1895, 1971; *Đorđević* Appeal Judgement, fn. 2527.

[1072]   *Tolimir* Appeal Judgement, paras 54, 56; *Popović et al.* Appeal Judgement, paras 306, 340, 359, 375, 830, 847, 925, 1094, 1123, 1136, 1171, 1213, 1257, 1521, 1541, 1895, 1971; *Đorđević* Appeal Judgement, fn. 2527.

[1073]   See Trial Judgement, vol. 2, paras 433, 640-641, 687, 746, 751, 754-755. See also Stanišić Appeal Brief, paras 221222, fns 267, 272, referring to Exhibits P1252, P553, P1013, P571, P427.08, P855, 1D58, 1D59, P592, 1D64, 1D662. The Appeals Chamber notes that the evidence cited by Stanišic is related to the measures he took for the errant reserve policemen to be placed at the disposal of the army, to quell the theft of vehicles, and to curb looting and misappropriation of property.

[1074]   Stanišić Appeal Brief, para. 221.

[1075]   Trial Judgement, vol. 2, para. 756.

[1076]   Trial Judgement, vol. 2, para. 756.

[1077]   Trial Judgement, vol. 2, para. 756.

[1078]   Stanišić Appeal Brief, para. 282, referring to Trial Judgement, vol. 2, para. 756.

misreading of the evidence".[1079] Stanišić submits that as **[page 131]** early as May 1992, he sought the assistance of the Federal SUP to tackle "the worsening security situation including the issue of paramilitaries".[1080] Stanišić argues that he appointed "Davidović from the [Federal SUP] to act 'as a police chief in the [RS MUP] with all powers while he was in the BH area'"[1081] and that Witness Davidović and his unit used this power to disarm and suppress "criminal and in some cases inhumane activities" by: (i) a paramilitary group led by Željko Ražnatović, alias Arkan ("Arkan"), known as the Serbian Volunteer Guard or Arkan's Men ("Arkan's Men"); (ii) the Red Berets, an armed formation of the SDS, also known as the Serb Defence Forces ("SOS" or "Red Berets"); and (iii) the Yellow Wasps, a Serbian paramilitary group also known as Žućo or Repic's men ("Yellow Wasps").[1082] Stanišić submits in particular that: (i) he initially sent Witness Davidović and Witness Andan to Bijeljina "to restore law and order";[1083] (ii) in Brčko, the unit under their command took part in actions to arrest and eliminate paramilitaries;[1084] and (iii) he gave them full authority to "uncover any kind of criminal acts" and they "took such actions in Bijeljina and Zvornik".[1085] Stanišić contends that contemporaneous notes of Witness Andan detail the steps Stanišić took against paramilitaries in Brčko, Zvornik, Foča, Rudo, Višegrad, and Trebinje.[1086]

314. The Prosecution responds that Stanišić merely repeats a failed trial argument without articulating an error[1087] and that therefore his argument should be summarily dismissed.[1088]

315. Stanišić replies that his actions against paramilitaries from outside BiH, which resulted in the reduction of the commission of crimes, even regardless of their motivation, cannot be considered a contribution to the common purpose to commit crimes.[1089]

ii. Analysis

316. With regard to Stanišić's submission that the Trial Chamber erred in finding that his actions against paramilitaries from outside BiH were only undertaken due to the paramilitaries' refusal to submit to the command of the army and their commission of crimes against Serbs,[1090] the Appeals **[page 132]** Chamber notes that Stanišić repeats arguments from his final trial brief.[1091] The Trial Chamber implicitly rejected Stanišić's arguments by concluding that the action he took against some paramilitaries was only pursued following their refusal to submit to the command of the army and their continued commission of acts of theft, looting, and trespasses against the local RS leaders.[1092] The Appeals Chamber will determine if the rejection of Stanišić's arguments by the Trial Chamber constitutes an error warranting its intervention.

317. The Appeals Chamber observes that the evidence advanced by Stanišić to support his argument that as early as May 1992, he sought the Federal SUP's assistance to tackle the issue of paramilitaries, does not support his factual claim.[1093] The Appeals Chamber further observes that Stanišić's submission ignores relevant findings of the Trial Chamber, namely that: (i) the position of the RS MUP was that, once the VRS had been established, all armed forces had to be under the command of the Ministry of Defence of the RS ("MOD"), however the paramilitaries did not come under the command of the MOD and continued to cause security problems;[1094] (ii) between June and the beginning of July 1992, Stanišić was informed by several

---

[1079] Stanišić Appeal Brief, para. 285, referring to Trial Judgement, vol. 2, para. 756.
[1080] Stanišić Appeal Brief, para. 283, referring to Milorad Davidović, 23 Aug 2010, T. 13563-13567.
[1081] Stanišić Appeal Brief, para. 283, referring to Exhibit 1D646, p. 1 (emphasis omitted).
[1082] Stanišić Appeal Brief, para. 283, referring to Exhibit 1D646, p. 6.
[1083] Stanišić Appeal Brief, para. 284, referring to Exhibits 1D97, p. 3, 1D646, p. 9.
[1084] Stanišić Appeal Brief, para. 284, referring to Dragomir Andan, 27 May 2011, T. 21456-21466, 21472-21473, 21666-21674.
[1085] Stanišić Appeal Brief, para. 284, referring to Milorad Davidović, 23 Aug 2010, T. 13565-13566, 13614-13615, Dragomir Andan, 27 May 2011, T. 21687-21688, Exhibit P317.22.
[1086] Stanišić Appeal Brief, para. 284, referring to Exhibits 1D557, 1D539, 1D650, 1D651.
[1087] Prosecution Response Brief (Stanišić), para. 147, contrasting Stanišić Appeal Brief, paras 283-284 with Stanišic Final Trial Brief, paras 334-338, 348, 357.
[1088] Prosecution Response Brief (Stanišić), para. 147, referring to *Krajišnik* Appeal Judgement, paras 24, 26.
[1089] Stanišic Reply Brief, para. 80.
[1090] See *supra*, para. 313.
[1091] See Stanišić Final Trial Brief, paras 334-377.
[1092] Trial Judgement, vol. 2, para. 756.
[1093] See Stanišić Appeal Brief, para. 283, referring to Milorad Davidović, 23 Aug 2010, T. 13563-13567.
[1094] Trial Judgement, vol. 2, para. 719.

sources of the activities of the paramilitary groups in Zvornik, including war crimes;[1095] (iii) Witness Davidović received instructions from Stanišić and Čedo Kljajić to take action with respect to the Yellow Wasps "to do whatever was necessary, as even Karadžić and Krajišnik insisted that this formation needed to be disbanded";[1096] (iv) on 29 and 30 July 1992 the RS MUP, in coordination with the army, arrested members of the Yellow Wasps in Zvornik;[1097] (v) the police questioning of the Yellow Wasps members focused primarily on their involvement in thefts and a criminal report was filed against members of this group for aggravated theft, principally of Volkswagen Golf vehicles;[1098] (vi) Stanišić only intervened against paramilitaries in Zvornik after Velibor Ostojić, the RS Minister for Information, was stopped and forced to eat grass at a checkpoint by members of the Yellow Wasps;[1099] (vii) Witness Andan and Witness Davidović led actions against the paramilitary groups in Bijeljina and against the Red Berets in Brčko but these paramilitary groups resisted and refused to fall under the command of the army;[1100] and (viii) at a 20 December 1992 meeting of the Supreme Command Stanišić raised the issue of paramilitary groups that needed to be resolved and **[page 133]** stated that such groups "had to be placed under one command".[1101] In light of the above, the Appeals Chamber dismisses Stanišić's submission.

318.   With respect to Stanišić's submission that his actions against paramilitaries which resulted in the reduction of the commission of crimes, even regardless of their motivation, cannot be considered a contribution to the common purpose to commit crimes,[1102] the Appeals Chamber notes that the Trial Chamber did not take into account these actions in relation to his contribution to the common purpose of the JCE, as it found that Stanišić took these actions only with respect to crimes of theft, looting, and trespasses as well as harassment, and only when these crimes were committed against Serbs, including local RS leaders.[1103] The Appeals Chamber further notes the Trial Chamber's finding that Stanišić failed to act in the same decisive manner with regard to other crimes, "such as unlawful detention and displacement and removal of non-Serb civilians".[1104] The Appeals Chamber therefore understands the Trial Chamber's reference to Stanišić's actions against paramilitaries as a factual element taken into account in relation to his ability to act and not as his contribution to the common purpose of the JCE, as such. The Appeals Chamber therefore dismisses Stanišić's argument.

319.   In light of the above, the Appeals Chamber considers that Stanišić has failed to demonstrate that no reasonable trier of fact could have concluded that his actions against paramilitaries from outside BiH were only undertaken due to the paramilitaries' refusal to submit to the command of the army and their commission of crimes against Serbs.

   f. Alleged errors in the Trial Chamber's finding that Stanišić focused primarily on crimes committed against Serbs

320.   The Trial Chamber noted, when dealing with war crimes, that "Stanišić focused primarily on crimes committed against Serbs".[1105] The Trial Chamber found that "[f]ollowing the 22 April 1992 instruction from the Federal SUP in Belgrade, Stanišić directed the chiefs of the CSBs to forward detailed documentation and investigation of war crimes and other serious crimes committed against Serbs for its use by the 'war crimes commission'."[1106] It further found that Stanišić's instruction to the CSBs on documenting war crimes and other mass atrocities was specifically limited to instances where Serbs were the victims, and not all civilians.[1107] In reaching **[page 134]** this finding, the Trial Chamber took into account "the language of the

---

1095	Trial Judgement, vol. 2, para. 713.
1096	Trial Judgement, vol. 2, para. 714.
1097	Trial Judgement, vol. 2, para. 714.
1098	Trial Judgement, vol. 2, para. 715. See *infra*, paras 692-693.
1099	Trial Judgement, vol. 2, para. 715.
1100	Trial Judgement, vol. 2, para. 717.
1101	Trial Judgement, vol. 2, para. 720.
1102	See *supra*, para. 315.
1103	See Trial Judgement, vol. 2, para. 756.
1104	Trial Judgement, vol. 2, paras 755-757.
1105	Trial Judgement, vol. 2, para. 758.
1106	Trial Judgement, vol. 2, para. 758.
1107	Trial Judgement, vol. 2, para. 758.

orders of 16 May, 26 May, 17 June, 11 July, and 17 July 1992", which it considered together with the testimonies of Witness ST174, Witness Goran Mačar ("Witness Mačar"), Witness Gojković, and the 22 April 1992 instruction from the Socialist Federal Republic of Yugoslavia ("22 April 1992 Instruction" and "SFRY", respectively).[1108]

i. Submissions of the parties

321. Stanišić submits that the Trial Chamber erred by finding that he "focused primarily on war crimes committed against Serbs".[1109] He contends that the Trial Chamber's conclusion "ignores the voluminous evidence that Stanišić continuously reiterated that investigations into crimes, including war crimes, was to be on a non-discriminatory basis".[1110]

322. The Prosecution responds that Stanišić's arguments warrant summary dismissal as he merely claims that the Trial Chamber failed to consider relevant evidence[1111] and repeats an argument which failed at trial.[1112] The Prosecution further submits that Stanišić fails to show that no reasonable trier of fact could have reached the conclusions of the Trial Chamber.[1113]

ii. Analysis

323. With respect to Stanišić's argument that the Trial Chamber ignored the voluminous evidence that he had continuously reiterated that investigations into crimes were to be conducted on a non-discriminatory basis,[1114] the Appeals Chamber notes that the Trial Chamber took into account the portion of the 17 July 1992 Report Stanišić refers to in his appeal brief.[1115] On the basis of this portion of the report, the Trial Chamber found that, *inter alia*, during the 11 July 1992 Collegium, the detection and documentation of war crimes, including those committed by Serbs, was listed as a **[page 135]** priority for both the SNB and the Crime Investigation Service.[1116] The Appeals Chamber further notes that, contrary to Stanišić's submission, the Trial Chamber also took into account Exhibit 1D572, an order issued by Stanišić on 5 October 1992, by which he reiterated a request to all the CSBs to submit completed questionnaires on any criminal reports filed against persons suspected of having committed war crimes ("5 October 1992 Order").[1117] With regard to Exhibit 1D63, an order issued by Stanišić on 19 July 1992, the Appeals Chamber notes that although the Trial Chamber did not explicitly refer to the order in the Trial Judgement, it did not ignore this evidence. Indeed, the 5 October 1992 Order is a reiteration of the original request contained in Exhibit 1D63 to complete the questionnaire on any criminal reports filed against persons suspected of having committed war crimes. The Appeals Chamber observes in this regard that the 5 October 1992 Order explicitly refers to Exhibit 1D63.[1118] With respect to Exhibit 1D328, a report from a meeting in Sokolac of heads of departments for criminology in the area of the Romanija-Birač CSB dated 28 July 1992 ("Sokolac Report"), the Appeals

[1108] Trial Judgement, vol. 2, para. 758.
[1109] Stanišić Appeal Brief, para. 286, referring to Trial Judgement, vol. 2, para. 758.
[1110] Stanišić Appeal Brief, para. 286, referring to Exhibits P427.08, pp 5-7, 1D63, 1D572, 1D328.
[1111] Prosecution Response Brief (Stanišić), para. 136, contrasting Stanišić Appeal Brief, para. 286 with Stanišić Final Trial Brief, paras 378-379. With respect to Exhibit 1D328 on which Stanišić relies, the Prosecution contends that at the meeting referred to in this exhibit, concern was expressed about the looting of non-Serb property because the MUP's position was "that all the movable and immovable property on liberated Serbian territories [...] belongs to the Serbian state" (Prosecution Response Brief (Stanišić), para. 138, referring to Exhibit 1D328, p. 3).
[1112] Prosecution Response Brief (Stanišić), para. 136, referring to *Krajišnik* Appeal Judgement, paras 19, 24.
[1113] Prosecution Response Brief (Stanišić), para. 138. The Prosecution argues that the Trial Chamber reasonably relied on: (i) "[e] xpress language in his orders of 15 May, 16 May, 26 May and 17 July 1992 directing that measures be taken to document crimes committed against Serbs which were in accordance with the dictates of the RS Presidency"; (ii) "[e]vidence that the RS MUP followed through on Stanišić's order and compiled such information"; and (iii) "[t]he RS MUP's failure to report or its under-reporting of crimes against non- Serbs" (Prosecution Response Brief (Stanišić), para. 137, referring to Trial Judgement, vol. 2, paras 104, 723-727, 745; also referring to Trial Judgement, vol. 2, paras 34-36, 87, 90-94, 96-98, 101).
[1114] See *supra*, para. 321.
[1115] Trial Judgement, vol. 2, para. 632. See Stanišić Appeal Brief, para. 286, referring to Exhibits P427.08, pp 5-7, 1D63, 1D572, 1D328.
[1116] Trial Judgement, vol. 2, para. 632.
[1117] Trial Judgement, vol. 2, para. 682.
[1118] Exhibit 1D572, p. 1.

Chamber notes that this report concerns the difficulties encountered by these departments in the area of Romanija-Birač CSB in dealing with offences against movable and immovable property in "liberated Serbian territories".[1119] The Appeals Chamber therefore considers that the Trial Chamber did not err in not relying on the Sokolac Report as it is irrelevant to the issue at stake.

324.   The Appeals Chamber moreover recalls the Trial Chamber's findings that following the 22 April 1992 Instruction, Stanišić directed the chiefs of the CSBs to forward detailed documentation and investigation of war crimes and other serious crimes committed against Serbs for use by the state commission in Serbia mandated to collect and verify data in relation to war crimes, genocide, and crimes against humanity in Croatia and other areas.[1120] The Trial Chamber found that the instruction did not include the investigation of all crimes irrespective of the ethnicity of the victims.[1121] The Trial Chamber further found that, in view of the language of the orders of 16 May 1992, 26 May 1992, 17 June 1992, 11 July 1992, and 17 July 1992,[1122] the instruction from Stanišić to the CSBs on documenting war crimes and other mass atrocities was specifically limited to instances where Serbs were the victims, and not all civilians.[1123] **[page 136]**

325.   In light of the above, the Appeals Chamber finds that Stanišić has failed to demonstrate that no reasonable trier of fact could have found that he focused primarily on war crimes committed against Serbs, and therefore dismisses his argument.

> g. Alleged error in the Trial Chamber's finding that Stanišić permitted RS MUP forces under his control to participate in joint operations in the Municipalities

326.   Having considered various factors in relation to Stanišić's role in preventing, investigating, and documenting crimes, including those discussed above, the Trial Chamber concluded that Stanišić "took insufficient action to put an end to [crimes that were being committed] and instead permitted RS MUP forces under his overall control to continue to participate in joint operations in the Municipalities with other Serb Forces involved in the commission of crimes, particularly the JNA/VRS and the TO".[1124]

327.   Stanišić asserts that the Trial Chamber disregarded its own inconclusive finding on the issue of re-subordination of police forces and, on this basis, disputes its finding that he permitted RS MUP forces under his overall control to continue to participate in joint operations in the Municipalities with other Serb forces.[1125] The Appeals Chamber recalls that it has addressed and dismissed this argument elsewhere in this Judgement.[1126]

> h. Conclusion

328.   For the reasons set out above, the Appeals Chamber finds that Stanišić has failed to demonstrate that the Trial Chamber erred in finding that: (i) the police and civilian prosecutors failed to function in an impartial manner;[1127] (ii) Stanišić's orders of 8, 10, 17, and 24 August 1992 were prompted by international attention;[1128] (iii) Stanišić had the authority to take measures against crimes and failed to take sufficient action to put an end to them;[1129] (iv) Stanišić's actions against paramilitaries were only undertaken due to their refusal to submit to the command of the army and their commission of crimes against Serbs;[1130] and (v)

[1119]   Exhibit 1D328, pp 1-5.
[1120]   Trial Judgement, vol. 2, paras 722, 758.
[1121]   Trial Judgement, vol. 2, para. 758.
[1122]   See Trial Judgement, vol. 2, paras 723-727. The Appeals Chamber observes that the orders of 16 May 1992, 26 May 1992, 17 June 1992, 11 July 1992, and 17 July 1992 were issued by Stanišić and the RS Presidency to organise the gathering of information on war crimes and mass atrocities committed against Serbs during the armed conflict (see Trial Judgement, vol. 2, paras 723-727).
[1123]   Trial Judgement, vol. 2, para. 758.
[1124]   Trial Judgement, vol. 2, para. 759.
[1125]   Stanišić Appeal Brief, para. 287, referring to Trial Judgement, vol. 2, paras 342, 759.
[1126]   See *supra*, paras 126-127.
[1127]   Trial Judgement, vol. 2, para. 745.
[1128]   Trial Judgement, vol. 2, paras 752-753.
[1129]   Trial Judgement, vol. 2, paras 746-756.
[1130]   Trial Judgement, vol. 2, para. 756.

Stanišić focused primarily on crimes committed against Serbs.[1131] Neither has he demonstrated any error in the Trial Chamber's conclusion that he took insufficient action to put an end to the crimes and instead permitted RS MUP forces under his overall control to continue to participate in joint operations in the **[page 137]** Municipalities with other Serb forces.[1132] Stanišić's arguments with regard to his role in preventing, investigating, and documenting crimes are therefore dismissed in their entirety.

(iv) Alleged errors in relation to Stanišić's role in unlawful arrest and detentions (subsection (B)(iv) of Stanišić's sixth ground of appeal)

329. In considering Stanišić's role in the unlawful arrest and detentions of non-Serbs as a factor in its assessment of his contribution to the JCE, the Trial Chamber first found that in addition to detention centres at the SJBs or police stations, members of the police were involved in guarding detainees at the following detention centres at which crimes were found to have been committed: Bileća; Luka detention camp in Brčko; the Power Station Hotel in Gacko; the Nikola Mačkić School in Ključ; the detention facility at the gymnasium in Pale ("Gymnasium"); Omarska and Keraterm detention camps in Prijedor; the Territorial Defence ("TO") building in Teslić; Sušica detention camp in Vlasenica; and the Bunker in Vogošća.[1133] Further, the Trial Chamber found that the RS MUP shared responsibility for the detention centres with the MOJ and the VRS during the time relevant to the Indictment, either by establishing, managing, or guarding these facilities, or otherwise assisting in their functioning.[1134] The Trial Chamber also concluded that Stanišić contributed to their continued existence and operation by failing to take decisive action to close these facilities or, at the very least, by failing to withdraw the RS MUP forces from their involvement in these detention centres.[1135]

a.   Submissions of the parties

330. Stanišić submits that in its assessment of the objective element of the first category of joint criminal enterprise, the Trial Chamber "improperly relied on findings in relation to detention camps, many of which are manifestly incorrect"[1136] and that no reasonable trier of fact could have been satisfied "on the basis of these incorrect findings that he contributed to the 'continued existence and operation' of the detention camps".[1137]

331. Stanišić submits that the Trial Chamber failed to make a conclusive finding as to whether the Luka detention camp in Brčko was controlled by either the SDS in Bijeljina or Brčko police.[1138] **[page 138]**

332. Further, Stanišić submits that the Trial Chamber failed to make specific findings to support its conclusion that the RS MUP had "joint authority" over the Sušica camp.[1139] Stanišić submits that the Trial Chamber erred in finding that the RS MUP had "joint authority" with the crisis staff over the Sušica camp in the municipality of Vlasenica as the RS MUP headquarters had no influence over the crisis staff in Vlasenica in mid-1992, which "prompted] efforts by the Serb leadership to end [the crisis staff's] 'apparent independence and autonomy'".[1140] He submits that "[t]his failed, however, with [Witness] Đokanović testifying that nothing changed except the name of the Crisis Staff."[1141]

333. Stanišić also argues that the Trial Chamber erred in relation to the Gymnasium in Pale by failing to make findings supporting its conclusion that the RS MUP "guarded" the Gymnasium.[1142] Stanišić also

---

[1131]   Trial Judgement, vol. 2, para. 758.
[1132]   Trial Judgement, vol. 2, para. 759.
[1133]   Trial Judgement, vol. 2, para. 760.
[1134]   Trial Judgement, vol. 2, para. 761.
[1135]   Trial Judgement, vol. 2, para. 761.
[1136]   Stanišić Appeal Brief, para. 289.
[1137]   Stanišić Appeal Brief, para. 300.
[1138]   Stanišić Appeal Brief, para. 290, referring to Trial Judgement, vol. 2, para. 760.
[1139]   Stanišić Appeal Brief, para. 291, referring to Trial Judgement, vol. 2, para. 760.
[1140]   Stanišić Appeal Brief, para. 292, referring to Trial Judgement, vol. 2, paras 54, 260.
[1141]   Stanišić Appeal Brief, para. 292, referring to Trial Judgement, vol. 2, para. 262, Exhibit P397.02, pp 10576, P397.04, pp 10773-10774.
[1142]   Stanišić Appeal Brief, para. 291, referring to Trial Judgement, vol. 2, para. 760.

argues that the Trial Chamber erred by failing to consider that the SDS controlled the Pale Crisis Staff,[1143] and that he took measures to remove Koroman, the Chief of the Pale SJB and head of the police guarding the Gymnasium, "but was unsuccessful due to the strong support Koroman received locally".[1144] Stanišić further points to the testimony of Witness Slobodan Marković ("Witness Marković"), a member of the Commission for Exchange of Prisoners set up on 8 May 1992,[1145] that while working on prisoner exchanges in Pale, Stanišić told him that prisoners should be treated in accordance with the Geneva Conventions I-IV of 12 August 1949 ("Geneva Conventions"), even though the exchanges were under the authority of the MOJ and the VRS and that Stanišić had no power in this regard.[1146]

334.   With regard to Gacko municipality, Stanišić submits that the Trial Chamber erred by: (i) failing to make findings supporting its conclusions that the RS MUP "controlled" the Power Station Hotel in Gacko;[1147] and (ii) failing to consider its earlier finding regarding the difficulties with communications,[1148] and that SJB Chief Popović told the commission for detention facilities in **[page 139]** the municipalities of Trebinje, Gacko, and Bileća[1149] ("Second Commission for Detention Facilities") that there were no prisoners in Gacko.[1150]

335.   Stanišić also submits that the Trial Chamber failed to consider that Ključ was taken over in late July 1992 by "cooperated action" between a police detachment and the VRS through re-subordination of the police under the army command.[1151] He submits that the evidence further shows that in August 1992, it was reported to the RS MUP that there were no camps in the municipality.[1152]

336.   With regard to Omarska detention camp, Stanišić submits that the Trial Chamber erred by failing to consider that it was established by a decision of Drljača, Chief of the Prijedor SJB, as ordered by the Prijedor Crisis Staff, "in clear contravention of his competence and authority".[1153]

337.   With regard to the Bunker, the detention centre in Vogošća, Stanišić submits that the Trial Chamber failed to refer to the evidence that it was run by Branko Vlačo, who had been appointed by the military authorities,[1154] and that the MOJ was *de facto* and *de jure* in charge of the detention centre.[1155] He also argues that the Trial Chamber failed to consider that the problem of autonomous local authorities disregarding the RS MUP was particularly pronounced in Vogošća.[1156] In this regard, Stanišić asserts that the failure of Maksimović, Chief of the Vogošća SJB, to follow orders and the fact that he took instruction from the crisis staff alone led to his removal by Stanišić and the filing of a criminal complaint against him by the RS MUP.[1157]

338.   Stanišić also argues that the Trial Chamber erred in failing to refer to the testimony of Witness Predrag Radulović ("Witness Radulović") concerning contemporary reports indicating that **[page 140]**

[1143]   Stanišić Appeal Brief, para. 293, referring to Trial Judgement, vol. 2, para. 852.
[1144]   Stanišic Appeal Brief, para. 293, referring to Trial Judgement, vol. 2, paras 698, 700, 852, Tomislav Kovač, 9 Mar 2012, T. 27226-27227, ST127, 17 Jun 2010, T. 11924-11925, Exhibit P2461.
[1145]   See Trial Judgement, vol. 2, para. 616.
[1146]   Stanišić Appeal Brief, para. 293, referring to Trial Judgement, vol. 2, para. 617, Witness Marković, 12 Jul 2010, T. 12674-12675, 12690, Witness Marković, 13 Jul 2010, T. 12730.
[1147]   Stanišic Appeal Brief, para. 291, referring to Trial Judgement, vol. 2, para. 760.
[1148]   Stanišic Appeal Brief, para. 294, referring to Trial Judgement, vol. 2, para. 74, Aleksander Krulj, 26 Oct 2009, T. 1992.
[1149]   Trial Judgement, vol. 2, para. 673.
[1150]   Stanišić Appeal Brief, para. 294, referring to Trial Judgement, vol. 2, para. 673, Exhibit P165.
[1151]   Stanišić Appeal Brief, para. 295, referring to Trial Judgement, vol. 2, paras 405, 502, Vidosav Kovačević, 15 Sep 2011, T. 24316, Slavko Lisica, 1 Mar 2012, T. 26933-26934, 26999.
[1152]   Stanišić Appeal Brief, para. 295, referring to Trial Judgement, vol. 2, para. 426, Exhibit P972.
[1153]   Stanišić Appeal Brief, para. 296, referring to Trial Judgement, vol. 2, paras 422, 856, Exhibits P1560, 1D166. In this regard, Stanišić asserts that Drljača was appointed by the Prijedor Crisis Staff (Stanišić Appeal Brief, para. 296 referring to Exhibit P2462, ST161, 19 Nov 2009, T. 3439-3443, Tomislav Kovač, 9 Mar 2012, T. 27240-27241, 27251-27252).
[1154]   Stanišić Appeal Brief, para. 297, referring to Momčilo Mandić, 4 May 2010, T. 9535-9536. Stanišić further asserts that in spite of Momčilo Mandić's testimony, the Trial Chamber was "unable to make a conclusive finding whether Vlačo was a member of the police or a MOJ official" (Stanišić Appeal Brief, fn. 438, referring to Trial Judgement, vol. 2, para. 879).
[1155]   Stanišić Appeal Brief, para. 297, referring to Exhibits P1318.30, P1318.31, P1318.33, P1872, P1308, P1475, Witness Marković, 12 Jul 2010, T. 12673-12675.
[1156]   Stanišić Appeal Brief, para. 297, referring to Drago Borovčanin, 24 Feb 2010, T. 6772.
[1157]   Stanišić Appeal Brief, para. 297, referring to Exhibits 1D106, 1D182, 1D184, 1D186.

Stanišić had not been informed in 1992 about the events that occurred in the municipalities of Prijedor and Teslić.[1158]

339.   Stanišić further submits that the Trial Chamber's finding that he had authority over RS MUP forces who were involved in detention centres is "tainted" by the Trial Chamber's improper reliance on its findings in relation to the Bosnian Serb leadership.[1159] Stanišić also argues that the Trial Chamber erred in finding that he failed to take decisive action to withdraw RS MUP forces from their involvement in detention facilities which were the shared responsibility of the MOJ, VRS, and RS MUP.[1160] In this regard, Stanišić refers to arguments made earlier in his appeal brief that he "did not have the power to withdraw RS MUP forces from their re-subordination", and that the Trial Chamber attributed to him the criminal conduct of these re-subordinated forces without making an express finding that he had authority over these forces.[1161] Stanišić submits that the Trial Chamber thereby incorrectly based its conclusion that he had authority over these forces on the underlying finding that the Bosnian Serb leadership was in control over events taking place in the municipalities.[1162]

340.   Ultimately, Stanišić submits that no reasonable trial chamber could have been satisfied on the basis of these incorrect findings that Stanišić contributed to the "continued existence and operation" of the detention camps.[1163]

341.   The Prosecution responds that the Trial Chamber reasonably found that Stanišić contributed to the continued existence and operation of the detention facilities by failing to take action to close these detention facilities, or at the very least, by failing to withdraw RS MUP personnel working within these facilities.[1164] It submits that even though Stanišić knew of the unlawful detentions of non-Serbs at the latest by the beginning of June 1992,[1165] he did not withdraw his personnel from these facilities and, quite the opposite, informed his subordinates that if necessary, reserve **[page 141]** personnel could be deployed to assist them.[1166] The Prosecution contends that Stanišić's argument that police forces in detention facilities were re-subordinated to the army "ignores that he expressly signalled to his subordinates that they could continue to deploy reserve personnel to work within these facilities".[1167] Further, the Prosecution contends that Stanišić's orders to his subordinates regulating the treatment of the detainees demonstrate that he could have withdrawn RS MUP personnel from detention facilities.[1168] It submits that Stanišić's argument that he issued

---

[1158]   Stanišić Appeal Brief, para. 298, referring to Predrag Radulović, 2 Jun 2010, T. 11205-11209.

[1159]   Stanišić Appeal Brief, para. 299, referring to Trial Judgement, vol. 2, para. 761. More specifically, Stanišić argues that the Trial Chamber incorrectly based its conclusion that he had authority over re-subordinated RS MUP forces on its finding that the Bosnian Serb leadership was in control over events taking place in the Municipalities (Stanišić Appeal Brief, para. 299).

[1160]   Stanišić Appeal Brief, paras 228-229, referring to Trial Judgement, vol. 2, para. 761.

[1161]   Stanišić Appeal Brief, para. 299, referring to Stanišić Appeal Brief, para. 269 and to his first ground of appeal, in general. See Stanišić Appeal Brief, paras 228-229.

[1162]   Stanišić Appeal Brief, para. 299.

[1163]   Stanišić Appeal Brief, para. 300, referring to Trial Judgement, vol. 2, para. 761.

[1164]   Prosecution Response Brief (Stanišić), para. 150, referring to Trial Judgement, vol. 2, para. 761. See Appeal Hearing, 16 Dec 2015, AT. 115-116.

[1165]   Prosecution Response Brief (Stanišić), para. 150, referring to Trial Judgement, vol. 2, para. 762; also referring to Trial Judgement, vol. 2, paras 614-621, 623-625, 763-764. In this regard, the Prosecution argues that by July 1992, Stanišić knew that in the ARK "several thousands" Muslims and Croats were being held at different locations and that the RS MUP was securing detention camps where conditions were bad and the international norms not observed (Prosecution Response Brief (Stanišić), para. 150, referring to Trial Judgement, vol. 2, paras 631, 638).

[1166]   Prosecution Response Brief (Stanišić), para. 150, referring to Trial Judgement, vol. 2, para. 667. The Prosecution also argues that Stanišić knew that the reserve personnel included "thieves and criminals" (Prosecution Response Brief (Stanišić), para. 150, referring to Trial Judgement, vol. 2, paras 600, 643, 743).

[1167]   Prosecution Response Brief (Stanišić), para. 151, referring to Stanišić Appeal Brief, para. 299. According to the Prosecution, while Stanišić challenges the Trial Chamber's conclusion that the RS MUP exercised responsibility over detention facilities on the premise that the police working in these facilities were re-subordinated to the military, this challenge fails because: (i) his duty to protect the civilian population imposed upon him the obligation to conduct investigations to determine the identity of perpetrators, irrespective of their affiliation; (ii) the RS MUP shared the responsibility for detention facilities along with the MOJ and the VRS, and many police stations operated as detention facilities; and (iii) a wealth of evidence demonstrates Stanišić's deep involvement in the detention of non-Serbs (Prosecution Response Brief (Stanišić), paras 78-80).

[1168]   Prosecution Response Brief (Stanišić), para. 151, referring to Prosecution Response Brief (Stanišić), paras 11-13, 79-83.

such orders but did not exercise jurisdiction or authority over the personnel in detention facilities defies common sense[1169] and should be summarily dismissed.[1170]

342. The Prosecution also submits that Stanišić's challenges to the Trial Chamber's findings concerning his authority over "individual" detention facilities should be summarily dismissed.[1171] In particular, it argues that Stanišić: (i) ignores the Trial Chamber's findings in volume one of the Trial Judgement regarding Sušica detention camp, the Gymnasium in Pale, and the Power Station Hotel in Gacko;[1172] (ii) misrepresents the evidence he claims the Trial Chamber ignored,[1173] repeats his **[page 142]** failed arguments from trial,[1174] and refers to evidence without demonstrating an error;[1175] (iii) fails to identify an error in the Trial Chamber's finding that Luka detention camp in Brčko was "controlled by either the SDS in Bijeljina or Brčko police" given that RS MUP personnel were involved in the operation of the camp;[1176] and (iv) seeks to substitute his own evaluation of the evidence pertaining to the RS MUP's authority over Sušica detention camp without showing an error.[1177]

343. In reply, Stanišić argues that the Prosecution's arguments regarding detention-related crimes do not address issues of jurisdiction and authority, and that he did not exercise any authority over detention camps or over the forces entrusted with guarding the facilities.[1178] He also submits that the lack of a conclusive finding as to the authority exercised over re-subordinated forces prevents the Prosecution from attributing actions by RS MUP forces guarding detention camps to him.[1179]

    b.   Analysis

344. With regard to Stanišić's argument that the Trial Chamber erred by failing to make a conclusive finding whether Luka detention camp in Brčko was "controlled by either the SDS in Bijeljina or Brčko police",[1180] the Appeals Chamber observes that the Trial Chamber did not make an explicit finding as to which authority exercised control over Luka detention camp. The Trial Chamber found that Goran Jelisić

[1169] Prosecution Response Brief (Stanišić), para. 151, referring to Stanišić Appeal Brief, paras 276-277.

[1170] Prosecution Response Brief (Stanišić), para. 151, referring to *Krajišnik* Appeal Judgement, para. 22.

[1171] Prosecution Response Brief (Stanišić), para. 152, referring to *Krajišnik* Appeal Judgement, paras 18-19, 23-24, 26-27.

[1172] Prosecution Response Brief (Stanišić), para. 152, referring to Stanišić Appeal Brief, para. 291. Regarding Sušica detention camp, the Prosecution points to the Trial Chamber's findings that: (i) decisions concerning the camp and its detainees were made by the crisis staff and the RS MUP; (ii) RS MUP personnel were among the guards at the camp; (iii) RS MUP received reports concerning the camp; and (iv) detainees were removed from the camp under the authority of the Vlasenica SJB Chief (Prosecution Response Brief (Stanišić), para. 152, referring to Trial Judgement, vol. 1, paras 1452, 1456, 1471). Regarding the Gymnasium in Pale, the Prosecution refers to the Trial Chamber's reliance on testimonies of detainees that the facility was guarded by members of the Pale police as well as reserve police (Prosecution Response Brief (Stanišić), para. 152, referring to Trial Judgement, vol. 1, paras 1319, 1323, 1326, 1330). With regard to the Power Station Hotel in Gacko, the Prosecution refers to the Trial Chamber's finding that the facility was commanded by Radinko Joric and Ranko Ignjatovic, both RS MUP employees, and that the orders at the facility came from Popović, as well as Bo'idar Vucurevic, President of the SAO Herzegovina (Prosecution Response Brief (Stanišić), para. 152, referring to Trial Judgement, vol. 1, para. 1220).

[1173] Prosecution Response Brief (Stanišić), para. 152, referring to, *inter alia*, Stanišić Appeal Brief, paras 293 (according to the Prosecution the evidence Stanišić cites merely confirms that he appointed Koroman to posts within the RS MUP in 1994, Exhibit P2461, pp 3-4), 298 (submitting that in fact: (i) Witness Radulović testified that during a conversation in 2000, Stanišić "said that most of the things that we talked about [Stanišić] had not been informed about"; (ii) it was Witness Radulović's "impression" that Stanišić "was really insufficiently informed"; (iii) Stanišić "knew about the events in Prijedor and Teslić and Doboj because these were well known cases and events which anyone who lived in Republika Srpska could have known about"; and (iv) it was Witness Radulović's general understanding that Stanišić "was not informed in a timely manner about those events"), referring to Predrag Radulović, 2 Jun 2010, T. 11206-11209).

[1174] Prosecution Response Brief (Stanišić), para. 152, comparing Stanišic Appeal Brief, para. 293 with Stanišić Final Trial Brief, paras 498, 501, 574, Stanišić Appeal Brief, para. 296 with Stanišić Final Trial Brief, paras 571, 610, and Stanišic Appeal Brief, para. 297 with Stanišić Final Trial Brief, paras 509, 572.

[1175] Prosecution Response Brief (Stanišić), para. 152.

[1176] Prosecution Response Brief (Stanišić), para. 152, referring to Stanišic Appeal Brief, para. 290, Trial Judgement, vol. 1, para. 1101.

[1177] Prosecution Response Brief (Stanišić), para. 152, referring to Stanišic Appeal Brief, para. 292.

[1178] Stanišić Reply Brief, para. 79, referring to Prosecution Response Brief (Stanišić), paras 133, 142-143, 150-152.

[1179] Stanišić Reply Brief, para. 79, referring to Prosecution Response Brief (Stanišić), paras 133, 143, 150-152.

[1180] See *supra*, para. 331.

("Jelisić"), who was in charge of the camp, was seen at times in a blue uniform like the one worn by the police in the former Yugoslavia and at times in a military camouflage uniform.[1181] The Trial Chamber cited evidence indicating that Jelisić was a member of the reserve police, but also referred to evidence that he "appeared to follow the orders of Vojkan Đurković, a member of the SDS".[1182] However, it then also referred to evidence that Jelisić was a member of a paramilitary organisation.[1183] The Trial Chamber further cited evidence that the Brčko SJB had no authority over Luka detention camp and that the camp was controlled by the army.[1184] In addition, the Trial Chamber cited evidence that members of the Brčko RS MUP visited the camp **[page 143]** and that police officers questioned and occasionally mistreated detainees.[1184][1185] The Trial Chamber also cited evidence that the guards at the camp were Serb soldiers from Serbia, Bijeljina, and Brčko and that members of the Red Berets detained Muslims at the camp.[1186] In light of the contradictory evidence the Trial Chamber referred to, and considering the Trial Chamber's failure to enter a finding as to which authority exercised control over Luka detention camp, the Appeals Chamber considers the Trial Chamber's finding that Stanišić failed to take decisive action to close Luka detention camp or to withdraw the RS MUP forces from it and its reliance on this finding in the assessment of Stanišić's contribution to the JCE,[1187] to be unreasonable and therefore an error. The impact of this error will be assessed later in this Judgement.[1188]

345. With respect to Stanišić's arguments pertaining to the Sušica detention camp in Vlasenica,[1189] the Appeals Chamber considers that the Trial Chamber's conclusion must be read in conjunction with the factual findings made earlier in the Trial Judgement. In particular, the Appeals Chamber notes the Trial Chamber's findings that: (i) decisions concerning Sušica detention camp and detainees were made by the crisis staff and the RS MUP, which received reports on the situation in the camp;[1190] and (ii) members of the police were involved in guarding, beating, and mistreating detainees at the camp.[1191] Insofar as Stanišić argues that the RS MUP headquarters had no influence over the crisis staff in Vlasenica, the Appeals Chamber notes that the Trial Chamber has indeed made findings suggesting that the crisis staff had certain autonomy in Vlasenica.[1192] However, Stanišić merely points to the Trial Chamber's findings and evidence suggesting that the crisis staff had certain autonomy in Vlasenica,[1193] without substantiating how such alleged autonomy of the crisis staff undermines the Trial Chamber's conclusion that the RS MUP had "joint authority"[1194] with the crisis staff over the Sušica camp in the municipality of Vlasenica. In light of these findings, the Appeals Chamber finds that Stanišić has failed to show that the Trial Chamber **[page 144]** erred by failing to make findings to support its conclusion that the RS MUP and the crisis staff in Vlasenica had joint authority over Sušica detention camp.

346. Turning to Stanišić's argument that the Trial Chamber erred in its finding in relation to the Gymnasium in Pale,[1195] the Appeals Chamber first recalls that the Trial Chamber found that members of the Pale SJB, the reserve police, and a special police unit were involved in the beatings that took place at the Gymnasium,[1196] that police units of Pale guarded the detainees,[1197] and that "[t]he local police, through Koroman, were

---

[1181]   Trial Judgement, vol. 1, para. 1079.
[1182]   Trial Judgement, vol. 1, para. 1079.
[1183]   Trial Judgement, vol. 1, para. 1079.
[1184]   Trial Judgement, vol. 1, para. 1080.
[1185]   Trial Judgement, vol. 1, para. 1080.
[1186]   Trial Judgement, vol. 1, para. 1080.
[1187]   See Trial Judgement, vol. 2, para. 761.
[1188]   See *infra*, paras 354-355.
[1189]   See *supra*, para. 332.
[1190]   Trial Judgement, vol. 1, para. 1452.
[1191]   Trial Judgement, vol. 1, paras 1453-1460, 1477-1478, 1485, 1487, 1490.
[1192]   The Trial Chamber found that the RS MUP headquarters had no influence over some SJBs, including the SJB in Vlasenica, between May and July 1992 (Trial Judgement, vol. 2, para. 54) and that Dragan Đokanović ("Witness Đokanović") – appointed on 9 June 1992 by Karadžić to the position of Republican Commissioner tasked with forming municipal war commissions and the restoration of power to the elected local civilian authorities – travelled to several municipalities, including Vlasenica, and that despite their apparent independence and autonomy, the crisis staffs in these municipalities reorganised themselves according to Witness Đokanović's directions without opposition (Trial Judgement, vol. 2, para. 260).
[1193]   See *supra*, para. 332.
[1194]   Trial Judgement, vol. 2, para. 760.
[1195]   See *supra*, para. 333.
[1196]   Trial Judgement, vol. 1, paras 1325, 1330-1331, 1338-1339, 1342; Trial Judgement, vol. 2, para. 851.
[1197]   Trial Judgement, vol. 1, paras 1319, 1339, 1341.

subordinated to the RS MUP, which was under the control of Mico Stanišić".[1198] Consequently, the Appeals Chamber considers that Stanišić has failed to demonstrate that the Trial Chamber erred by failing to make findings supporting its conclusion that the police subordinated to the RS MUP guarded the Gymnasium. Insofar as Stanišić argues that the Trial Chamber erred in failing to consider its own finding that the Pale Crisis Staff was controlled by the SDS,[1199] the Appeals Chamber observes that Stanišić has failed to substantiate how this alleged error had an effect on the Trial Chamber's conclusion that the police subordinated to the RS MUP, which was under Stanišić's control, guarded the Gymnasium. Stanišić's arguments are therefore dismissed.

347. With regard to Stanišić's argument that the Trial Chamber erred by failing to consider its own finding that he took measures to remove Koroman, the Chief of the Pale SJB and head of the police guarding the Gymnasium, but was unsuccessful due to the strong support Koroman received locally,[1200] the Appeals Chamber recalls the Trial Chamber's finding that the proceedings were launched against him towards the end of 1992 and did not pertain to the crimes charged in the Indictment but instead concerned crimes such as theft and professional misconduct.[1201] Stanišić's argument thus falls short of demonstrating an error in the Trial Chamber's finding that he failed to take decisive action against crimes committed in detention centres for which the RS MUP shared responsibility.[1202] With respect to Stanišić's argument based on the evidence of Witness Marković,[1203] the Appeals Chamber notes the Trial Chamber's assessment of evidence that members of the Pale police and of the reserve police were guarding the facility, which included an **[page 145]** assessment of Witness Marković's evidence in this regard.[1204] In light of these findings, the Appeals Chamber finds that Stanišić has not demonstrated that the Trial Chamber failed to consider the testimony of Witness Marković. Consequently, the Appeals Chamber finds that Stanišić has failed to show that the Trial Chamber erred in relying on his failure with respect to the Gymnasium in Pale when assessing his contribution to the JCE. Stanišić's arguments are therefore dismissed.

348. Stanišić further argues that the Trial Chamber erred in its findings relating to the Power Station Hotel in Gacko.[1205] The Appeals Chamber first notes the Trial Chamber's findings that: (i) the Power Station Hotel was commanded by members of the police; (ii) orders at the facility came from SJB Chief Popović; and (iii) members of the police guarded and mistreated detainees.[1206] Consequently, the Appeals Chamber considers that Stanišić has failed to demonstrate that the Trial Chamber erred by failing to make findings supporting its conclusion that the RS MUP "controlled" the Power Station Hotel in Gacko. As to Stanišić's argument that the Trial Chamber erred by failing to consider earlier findings,[1207] the Appeals Chamber finds that Stanišić has failed to demonstrate how the lack of communication in the municipality of Trebinje to which he refers, invalidates the Trial Chamber's conclusion regarding the RS MUP control over the Power Station Hotel in Gacko. Further, the Appeals Chamber observes that the report Stanišić refers to when arguing that Popović told the Second Commission for Detention Facilities that there were no prisoners in Gacko, concerns the period between the middle to the end of August 1992,[1208] whereas the crimes for which Stanišić was found responsible occurred from June 1992 onwards.[1209] Moreover, in light of the evidence cited by the Trial Chamber pertaining to, *inter alia*, the detention of Witness Osman Music and other individuals during the month of June 1992,[1210] the Appeals Chamber finds that the Trial Chamber reasonably concluded that prisoners were present at the Power Station Hotel during the relevant period. Consequently, the Appeals

---

[1198] Trial Judgement, vol. 2, para. 852.
[1199] Stanišić Appeal Brief, para. 293, referring to Trial Judgement, vol. 2, para. 852. See *supra*, para. 334. See also Trial Judgement, vol. 1, paras 1298, 1343.
[1200] Stanišić Appeal Brief, para. 293, referring to Trial Judgement, vol. 2, paras 698, 700, 852, Exhibit P2461, ST127, 17 Jun 2010, T. 11924-11925, Tomislav Kovač, 9 Mar 2012, T. 27226-27227.
[1201] Trial Judgement, vol. 2, para. 754.
[1202] Trial Judgement, vol. 2, para. 761. See Trial Judgement, vol. 2, paras 754, 757, 760.
[1203] See *supra*, para. 333.
[1204] See Trial Judgement, vol. 1, paras 1319, 1323, 1330.
[1205] Stanišić Appeal Brief, paras 291, 294. See *supra*, para. 334.
[1206] Trial Judgement, vol. 1, paras 1220, 1221, 1222, 1229, 1230, 1232, 1239.
[1207] Stanišić Appeal Brief, para. 294, referring to Trial Judgement, vol. 2, para. 74, Witness Krjul, 26 Oct 2009, T. 1992.
[1208] Exhibit P165.
[1209] Trial Judgement, vol. 1, paras 1220-1227.
[1210] Trial Judgement, vol. 1, paras 1220-1227.

Chamber finds that Stanišić has failed to show an error in the Trial Chamber's reliance on his failure to act with regard to the Power Station Hotel in Gacko municipality. Stanišić's arguments in this respect are therefore dismissed.

349. With regard to Stanišić's argument that the municipality of Ključ was taken over in late July 1992 by a joint action between the police and the VRS,[1211] the Appeals Chamber considers that the cooperation between members of the Banja Luka CSB SPD and the VRS, as established by the **[page 146]** Trial Chamber,[12111212] does not undermine the Trial Chamber's findings that members of the police were involved in guarding detainees at the Nikola Mačkić School. The Appeals Chamber notes in this respect the Trial Chamber's findings that members of the police in Ključ, of the Banja Luka CSB SPD, and of the reserve police were involved in bringing in, interrogating, and mistreating detainees at the Nikola Mačkić School.[1213] The Appeals Chamber also considers that Exhibit P972 is dated 27 August 1992, whereas the crimes for which Stanišić was found responsible occurred from May 1992 onwards.[1214] In consequence, the Appeals Chamber finds that Stanišić has failed to show that the Trial Chamber erred in relation to the municipality of Ključ.

350. With regard to Stanišić's argument that the Trial Chamber erred in failing to consider that Omarska detention camp was established by Drljača pursuant to an order of the Prijedor Crisis Staff, "in clear contravention of his competence and authority",[1215] the Appeals Chamber notes the Trial Chamber's finding that the Prijedor SJB was in charge of the Omarska detention camp.[1216] The Appeals Chamber therefore finds that Stanišić has failed to demonstrate an error on the part of the Trial Chamber and his arguments are dismissed.

351. Turning to Stanišić's arguments regarding the Bunker in the municipality of Vogošća, the Appeals Chamber notes the Trial Chamber's findings that Branko Vlaćo, the warden of the Bunker, was either a member of the police or an official of the MOJ.[1217] Therefore, contrary to Stanišić's submission,[1218] the Trial Chamber considered the possibility that the MOJ may have been in charge of the detention centre when assessing Stanišić's responsibility. With regard to Stanišić's argument that local authorities were acting autonomously from the RS MUP in the municipality of Vogosea, the Appeals Chamber recalls the Trial Chamber's finding that in May and June 1992, some CSB chiefs were unable to control the situation and cope with the SJB chiefs in their areas and that this problem was "particularly pronounced in Vogošća and Zvornik".[1219] The Trial Chamber found, however, that Maksimović, Chief of the Vogošća SJB, was found guilty of dereliction of duty and official misconduct and was temporarily relieved of his duties by Stanišić,[1220] which shows that even if members of the SJBs refused to follow orders, Stanišić had the power to remove them. Stanišić therefore has failed to demonstrate that no reasonable trier of fact could have found that the **[page 147]** police were involved in guarding detainees at the Bunker in Vogošća. Stanišić's arguments in this regard are dismissed.

352. With respect to Stanišić's argument that the Trial Chamber failed to consider the evidence of Witness Radulović regarding reports indicating that Stanišić lacked knowledge of the crimes committed against non-Serbs in the municipalities of Prijedor and Teslić in 1992,[1221] the Appeals Chamber notes that the Trial Chamber considered Witness Radulović's testimony. The Trial Chamber found that the information contained in the reports that were not submitted to Stanišić was nevertheless relayed to him "through the leadership of Banja Luka".[1222] The Trial Chamber further found that despite difficulties between April and

---

[1211] See *supra*, para. 335.
[1212] Trial Judgement, vol. 2, paras 405, 502.
[1213] Trial Judgement, vol. 1, para. 308.
[1214] Trial Judgement, vol. 1, paras 331-339.
[1215] See *supra*, para. 336.
[1216] Trial Judgement, vol. 2, paras 422, 486. See *infra*, para. 806.
[1217] Trial Judgement, vol. 1, para. 1543.
[1218] Stanišić Appeal Brief, para. 297.
[1219] See Trial Judgement, vol. 2, para. 583.
[1220] Trial Judgement, vol. 2, para. 707.
[1221] Stanišić Appeal Brief, para. 298. See *supra*, para. 338.
[1222] Trial Judgement, vol. 2, para. 689.

August 1992, the communication system within the RS MUP did function.[1223] In light of these findings, the Appeals Chamber finds that Stanišić has failed to demonstrate that the Trial Chamber erred in its consideration of the evidence when assessing his role in the arrest and detentions of non-Serbs in the municipalities of Prijedor and Teslić. Stanišić's argument is therefore dismissed.

353.   Finally, insofar as Stanišić argues that he did not have the power to withdraw re-subordinated RS MUP forces from detention facilities,[1224] the Appeals Chamber notes that, in support, he only submits that he had no authority to withdraw personnel who had been re-subordinated to the army to engage in combat activities. In so doing, Stanišić has failed to show how the alleged lack of his authority to withdraw the re-subordinated RS MUP forces from the combat activities impacts the Trial Chamber's findings with regard to his failure to take decisive action to withdraw RS MUP forces from their involvement in detention facilities which were the shared responsibility of the MOJ, VRS, and RS MUP.[1225] Moreover, Stanišić's argument that the Trial Chamber improperly found his authority over re-subordinated RS MUP forces on the basis of its finding that the Bosnian Serb leadership was in control of events taking place in the Municipalities, ignores the Trial Chamber's findings based on a plethora of evidence specifically related to Stanišić's authority over various detention facilities.[1226] His arguments are therefore dismissed.

c. Conclusion

354.   The Appeals Chamber has found that the Trial Chamber erred by finding that Stanišić failed to take decisive action to close the Luka detention camp in Brčko or to withdraw the RS MUP **[page 148]** forces from it and by relying on this failure to act when assessing his contribution to the JCE.[1227] However, the Appeals Chamber recalls that it has confirmed the Trial Chamber's findings regarding Sušica detention camp in Vlasenica, the Gymnasium in Pale, the Power Station Hotel in Gacko, the Nikola Mačkić School in Ključ, the Omarska camp in Prijedor, the TO building in Teslić, and the Bunker in Vogošća.[1228] On the basis of these upheld findings, the Appeals Chamber is satisfied that a reasonable trial chamber could have reached the conclusion that Stanišić "contributed to [the] continued existence and operation [of the detention and penitentiary facilities for which the RS MUP shared responsibility with the MOJ and VRS] by failing to take decisive action to close these facilities or, at the very least, by failing to withdraw the RS MUP forces from their involvement in these detention centres".[1229]

355.   Nonetheless, when assessing whether a reasonable trier of fact could have reached beyond reasonable doubt the conclusion that Stanišić's relevant acts and conduct significantly contributed to the JCE, the Appeals Chamber will consider his role in the unlawful arrest and detentions of non-Serbs – *i.e.* Stanišić's contribution to the continued existence and operation of the detention and penitentiary facilities for which the RS MUP shared responsibility with the MOJ and VRS – with the exception of the Trial Chamber's overturned finding on his role in the Luka detention camp in Brčko.

(d) Conclusion

356.   The Appeals Chamber has found that the Trial Chamber erred in law by failing to make findings on whether Stanišić's acts and conduct furthered the JCE and whether his contribution was significant, thereby failing to provide a reasoned opinion.[1230] The Appeals Chamber recalls that a trial chamber's failure to provide a reasoned opinion constitutes an error of law which allows the Appeals Chamber to consider the relevant evidence and factual findings in order to determine whether a reasonable trier of fact could have established beyond reasonable doubt the findings challenged by the appellant.[1231] The Appeals Chamber

---

[1223]   Trial Judgement, vol. 2, para. 690.
[1224]   See *supra*, para. 338.
[1225]   See *supra*, para. 245.
[1226]   See *supra*, paras 344-352. See also Trial Judgement, vol. 2, paras 760-761.
[1227]   See *supra*, para. 344.
[1228]   Trial Judgement, vol. 2, para. 760.
[1229]   Trial Judgement, vol. 2, para. 761.
[1230]   See *supra*, paras 136-142.
[1231]   *Cf. Kordić and Čerkez* Appeal Judgement, paras 383-388; *Nyiramasuhuko et al.* Appeal Judgement, para. 977; *Bizimungu* Appeal Judgement, para. 23; *Ndindiliyimana et al.* Appeal Judgement, para. 293. See *supra*, paras 19, 142.

shall therefore assess, on the basis of the Trial Chamber's findings and evidence relied upon by the Trial Chamber and identified by the parties whether a reasonable trier of fact could have concluded beyond reasonable doubt that Stanišić significantly contributed to the JCE. **[page 149]**

357.   With regard to the common criminal purpose of the JCE, the Appeals Chamber has upheld the Trial Chamber's conclusion that, from no later than 24 October 1991 throughout the Indictment period, "a common plan did exist, the objective of which was to permanently remove Bosnian Muslims and Bosnian Croats from the territory of the planned Serb state through the commission of the [JCE I Crimes]".[1232]

358.   The Trial Chamber further found that in the months of April and June 1992, the municipalities of Banja Luka, Bijeljina, Bileća, Bosanski Šamac, Brčko, Doboj, Donji Vakuf, Gacko, Ilijaš, Ključ, Kotor Varoš, Pale, Prijedor, Sanski Most, Teslić, Vlasenica, Višegrad, Vogošća, and Zvornik were taken over, in accordance with the Variant A and B Instructions through the joint action of the RS MUP and other Serb forces, sometimes by advance hostile occupation of the main features in town by police forces.[1233] According to the Trial Chamber, what followed was the mass exodus and involuntary departure of Muslims, Croats, and other non-Serbs from their homes, communities, villages, and towns either provoked by violent means that entailed unlawful detention at the local SJBs and improvised camps and centres or by the imposition of harsh, unliveable conditions and discriminatory measures by Serb forces, including members of the RS MUP.[1234]

359.   With regard to Stanišić's contribution to the JCE, the Appeals Chamber recalls that Stanišić has not demonstrated any error in the Trial Chamber's findings, made under the subheading "Stanišić's contribution to JCE", on the following factors: (i) Stanišić's role in the creation of Bosnian Serb bodies and policies;[1235] (ii) the role of RS MUP forces in combat activities and takeovers of RS municipalities and Stanišić's actions in this regard, with the exception of the appointments of Witness Todorović and Krsto Savić considered as evidence of Stanišić's direct appointments of JCE members to the RS MUP, which were overturned by the Appeals Chamber;[1236] (iii) Stanišić's role in the prevention, investigation, and documentation of crimes;[1237] and (iv) Stanišić's role in unlawful arrests and detentions, with the exception of his role in the Luka detention camp in Brčko, which was overturned by the Appeals Chamber.[1238]

360.   With regard to the first factor, the Trial Chamber found that, *inter alia*, Stanišić: (i) was involved in establishing Bosnian Serb institutions in BiH, including the SDS and the RS MUP;[1239] **[page 150]** (ii) had a close relationship with Karadžić, "a leading member of the JCE", from at least June 1991 and in the months preceding the establishment of the RS;[1240] (iii) was a key member of the decision-making authorities from early 1992 onwards;[1241] (iv) was aware of the Variant A and B Instructions, since the police were assigned, and played a central role in the implementation of the Instructions;[1242] (v) made the majority of key appointments in the RS MUP from 1 April 1992 onwards;[1243] and (vi) by his participation in the Bosnian Serb institutions, participated in the enunciation and implementation of the Bosnian Serb policy, as it evolved.[1244] The Trial Chamber concluded that his "conduct, presence at key meetings, attendance at sessions of the BSA, acceptance of the position of Minister of Interior—all indicate his voluntary participation in the creation of a separate Serb entity within BiH by the ethnic division of the territory".[1245] The Trial Chamber also found that Stanišić had overall command and control over the RS MUP police forces and over all other internal affairs organs.[1246]

[1232]   Trial Judgement, vol. 2, para. 313. See *supra*, paras 63-71.
[1233]   Trial Judgement, vol. 2, para. 737. See Trial Judgement, vol. 1, paras 133-1691.
[1234]   Trial Judgement, vol. 2, para. 737. See Trial Judgement, vol. 1, paras 133-1691.
[1235]   See *supra*, paras 145-220.
[1236]   See *supra*, paras 221-268.
[1237]   See *supra*, paras 269-328.
[1238]   See supra, paras 329-355.
[1239]   Trial Judgement, vol. 2, paras 729, 734.
[1240]   Trial Judgement, vol. 2, para. 730.
[1241]   Trial Judgement, vol. 2, para. 732.
[1242]   Trial Judgement, vol. 2, para. 731.
[1243]   Trial Judgement, vol. 2, para. 733.
[1244]   Trial Judgement, vol. 2, para. 734.
[1245]   Trial Judgement, vol. 2, para. 734.
[1246]   Trial Judgement, vol. 2, para. 736.

361. With respect to the second factor, the Trial Chamber found that Stanišić: (i) ordered RS MUP forces, on 15 May 1992, to be organised into "wartime units" by the chiefs of the CSBs and SJBs;[1247] (ii) issued orders for police forces, both regular and reserve units, to participate in "coordinated action with the armed forces" and facilitated the arming of the RS MUP forces;[1248] (iii) deployed police forces in joint combat operations with the military in furtherance of the decisions of the Bosnian Serb authorities;[1249] and (iv) consistently approved the deployment of the RS MUP forces to combat activities along with the other Serb forces despite being aware of the commission of crimes.[1250] The Trial Chamber also found that in the police hierarchy, Stanišić directly appointed Koroman, Chief of Pale SJB, Drljača, Chief of Prijedor SJB, Witness Bjelošević, Chief of Doboj CSB, and Župljanin, Chief of Banja Luka CSB, who the Trial Chamber established were JCE members and were involved in the widespread and systematic takeovers of municipalities.[1251] The Trial Chamber found that they used the police forces as physical perpetrators to implement the common plan.[1252] The Trial Chamber also considered the appointments of Witness Todorović, Chief of Bosanski Šamac SJB, and Krsto Savić, Chief of the Trebinje CSB, as evidence **[page 151]** of Stanišić's direct appointments of JCE members to the RS MUP,[1253] however, the Appeals Chamber recalls its finding that the Trial Chamber erred in so doing.[1254] Nonetheless, the Appeals Chamber has found that Stanišić has failed to show that the Trial Chamber's conclusion that he appointed JCE members to the RS MUP would not stand on the basis of the Trial Chamber's findings on his involvement in the appointments of JCE members Koroman, Drljača, Witness Bjelošević, and Župljanin – which the Appeals Chamber has upheld.[1255]

362. As regards the third factor, the Trial Chamber found that Stanišić: (i) had the authority to investigate and punish members of the RS MUP involved in crimes but failed to comply with his professional obligation to protect and safeguard the civilian population in the territories under his control;[1256] (ii) took action against paramilitaries but only because of their refusal to submit to the command of the army and their commission of crimes against Serbs;[1257] (iii) failed to act in the same decisive manner with respect to crimes charged in the Indictment;[1258] and (iv) focused primarily on the investigation of crimes against Serbs.[1259] The Trial Chamber concluded that Stanišić took insufficient action to put an end to crimes and instead permitted RS MUP forces under his overall control to continue to participate in joint operations in the Municipalities with other Serb forces involved in the commission of crimes – particularly the JNA/VRS and TO – with the knowledge that crimes were being committed.[1260]

363. Finally, regarding the fourth factor, the Trial Chamber considered that, *inter alia*, the RS MUP shared responsibility for the detention centres with the MOJ and the VRS during the time relevant to the Indictment, either by establishing, managing, or guarding these facilities, or otherwise assisting in their functioning.[1261] It then concluded that Stanišić contributed to the continued existence and operation of detention and penitentiary facilities "by failing to take decisive action to close these facilities or, at the very least, by failing to withdraw the RS MUP forces from their involvement in these detention centres".[1262] The Appeals Chamber recalls in this regard that it **[page 152]** has found that the Trial Chamber erred by finding that

---

[1247] Trial Judgement, vol. 2, para. 739.
[1248] Trial Judgement, vol. 2, para. 740.
[1249] Trial Judgement, vol. 2, para. 742.
[1250] Trial Judgement, vol. 2, para. 743.
[1251] Trial Judgement, vol. 2, para. 744. See Trial Judgement, vol. 2, paras 314, 520.
[1252] Trial Judgement, vol. 2, para. 744.
[1253] Trial Judgement, vol. 2, para. 744.
[1254] See *supra*, paras 263, 265-266.
[1255] See *supra*, para. 266.
[1256] Trial Judgement, vol. 2, paras 754-755. See Trial Judgement, vol. 2, paras 695, 698. In particular, the Trial Chamber noted Stanišić's insufficient actions against the personnel of the RS MUP who it found were JCE members and had committed crimes, such as Koroman, Todorović, and Drljača (Trial Judgement, vol. 2, para. 754, read together with Trial Judgement, vol. 2, para. 314). The Trial Chamber also found that Stanišić issued orders that all members of the RS MUP who had committed crimes or against whom official criminal proceedings had been launched be placed at the disposal of the VRS, which was insufficient to fulfil his duty to protect the Muslim and Croat population (Trial Judgement, vol. 2, paras 749, 751).
[1257] Trial Judgement, vol. 2, para. 756.
[1258] Trial Judgement, vol. 2, para. 757. See *supra*, paras 293-294, 318.
[1259] Trial Judgement, vol. 2, para. 758.
[1260] Trial Judgement, vol. 2, para. 759.
[1261] Trial Judgement, vol. 2, para. 761.
[1262] Trial Judgement, vol. 2, para. 761.

Stanišić failed to take decisive action to close the Luka detention camp in Brčko or to withdraw the RS MUP forces from it.[1263] However, the Appeals Chamber has found that, on the basis of the upheld findings in relation to Stanišić's role in unlawful arrest and detentions, a reasonable trial chamber could have reached the conclusion that Stanišić contributed to the continued existence and operation of the detention and penitentiary facilities for which the RS MUP shared responsibility with the MOJ and VRS by failing to take decisive action to close these facilities or, at the very least, by failing to withdraw the RS MUP forces from their involvement in these detention centres.[1264]

364.   Based on the Trial Chamber's findings as recalled above as well as the evidence the Trial Chamber relied upon in this regard, with the exception of the overturned findings, the Appeals Chamber finds that a reasonable trier of fact could have concluded beyond reasonable doubt that Stanišić significantly contributed to the JCE. Therefore, the Appeals Chamber finds that the Trial Chamber's error of law of failing to provide a reasoned opinion by failing to make findings on whether Stanišić's acts and conduct furthered the JCE and whether his contribution to the JCE was significant does not invalidate the Trial Chamber's conclusion on Stanišić's responsibility through participation in the JCE.

365.   Based on the foregoing, the Appeals Chamber dismisses Stanišić's first, fifth, and sixth grounds of appeal in part. However, given that the Appeals Chamber has found that the Trial Chamber erred in considering the appointments of Witness Todorović and Krsto Savić as Stanišić's direct appointments of JCE members to the RS MUP and in finding that Stanišić failed to take decisive action to close the Luka detention camp in Brčko or to withdraw the RS MUP forces from it,[1265] the Appeals Chamber will consider the impact of these errors, if any, on Stanišić's sentence below.[1266]

6.   Alleged errors in finding that Stanišić shared the intent to further the JCE

(a) Introduction

366.   The section of the Trial Judgement dedicated to Stanišić's intent pursuant to the first category of joint criminal enterprise ("*Mens Rea* Section") reads as follows:

> [t]o assess Stanišić's state of mind in relation to the conduct examined above, the Trial Chamber first considered evidence on Stanišić's knowledge of the commission of crimes against Muslims and Croats in the geographic area and during the time period covered by the Indictment. **[page 153]**

> Aside from evidence on Mićo Stanišić's knowledge, the Trial Chamber, in assessing Stanišić's alleged *mens rea*, also reviewed evidence on the political stances of the SDS and the BSA in the period preceding the Indictment and Stanišić's conduct and statements in relation to these policies. The Trial Chamber recalls that the views of the Bosnian Serb leadership—that there be an ethnic division of the territory, that 'a war would lead to a forcible and bloody transfer of minorities' from one region to another, and that joint life with Muslims and Croats was impossible—were expressed during the sessions of the BSA of which Stanišić was a member and during the meetings of the SDS in late 1991 and early 1992. The Trial Chamber further recalls that the six strategic objectives, which had been set by, among others, the RS Government, were issued on 12 May 1992 and presented to the BSA. The first goal called for the separation of Serb people from Muslims and Croats. Stanišić also attended the first meeting of the Council of Ministers of the BSA, where the boundaries of ethnic territory and the establishment of government organs in the territory were determined to be priorities.

> In this regard, the Trial Chamber has considered the evidence that Stanišić, albeit opposed to the presence of some paramilitary groups in BiH, approved of the operation of Arkan's Men in Bijeljina and Zvornik and allowed Arkan to remove whatever property in exchange for 'liberating' the territories. Moreover, Stanišić was present at sessions of the RS Government where the RS MUP was tasked with gathering information about Muslims moving out of the RS and the needs of refugees and displaced persons. He was also present at the 11 July Collegium meeting, where the relocation of citizens and entire villages was discussed. Finally, on 13 July 1992, the Višegrad SJB Chief Risto Perišic reported to the RS MUP that certain police

[1263] See *supra*, para. 354.
[1264] See *supra*, para. 354.
[1265] See *supra*, paras 263, 265-266, 354.
[1266] See *infra*, para. 1191.

214

officers were exhibiting a lack of professionalism while over 2,000 Muslims moved out of the municipality in an organised manner.

Considering his position at the time, his close relationship with Radovan Karadžić, and his continued support of and participation in the implementation of the policies of the Bosnian Serb leadership and the SDS, the Trial Chamber finds that the only reasonable inference is that Stanišić was aware of the persecutorial intentions of the Bosnian Serb leadership to forcibly transfer and deport Muslims and Croats from territories of BiH and that Stanišić shared the same intent.[1267]

367. The Appeals Chamber notes that in the *Mens Rea* Section, the Trial Chamber provided no cross-references to earlier findings or citations to evidence on the record.[1268]

368. Stanišić submits that the Trial Chamber failed to provide a reasoned opinion for concluding that he had the requisite *mens rea* pursuant to the first category of joint criminal enterprise.[1269] Stanišić also submits that the Trial Chamber erred in finding that he was "aware of the persecutorial intentions of the Bosnian Serb leadership to forcibly transfer and deport Muslims and Croats from territories of BiH and that Stanišić shared the same intent", since this finding is based on circumstantial evidence, and is not the sole reasonable inference available on the evidence.[1270]

369. In particular, he alleges that the Trial Chamber erred in: (i) finding that his support for a legitimate political goal and his participation in the Bosnian Serb leadership was sufficient to prove his intent to further the JCE;[1271] (ii) relying on his purported knowledge of the crimes in assessing **[page 154]** his intent to further the JCE;[1272] (iii) relying on the factors set out in paragraph 767, volume two of the Trial Judgement in finding that Stanišić had the intent to further the JCE;[1273] (iv) relying on the factors listed in paragraph 768, volume two of the Trial Judgement in finding that Stanišić had the intent to further the JCE;[1274] (v) relying on the factors listed in paragraph 769, volume two of the Trial Judgement in finding that Stanišić had the intent to further the JCE;[1275] and (vi) failing to consider "the considerable exculpatory" evidence demonstrating that he did not intend to commit crimes.[1276]

370. Stanišić requests that the Appeals Chamber reverse the Trial Chamber's finding that he possessed the requisite *mens rea* pursuant to the first category of joint criminal enterprise, and quash the findings of guilt for Counts 1, 4, and 6.[1277]

371. The Prosecution responds that Stanišić fails to demonstrate the absence of a reasoned opinion.[1278] It also submits that the Trial Chamber reasonably concluded that Stanišić shared the common criminal purpose of the JCE.[1279]

(b) Alleged error in failing to provide a reasoned opinion for finding that Stanišić shared the intent to further the JCE (Stanišić's first ground of appeal in part and fourth ground of appeal in part)

(i) Submissions of the parties

372. Stanišić submits that while the Trial Chamber summarised a large quantity of evidence, it subsequently failed to provide a reasoned opinion for drawing the inference that he possessed the requisite *mens rea*

[1267] Trial Judgement, vol. 2, paras 766-769 (internal citations omitted).
[1268] Trial Judgement, vol. 2, paras 766-769. *Cf.* Trial Judgement, vol. 2, para. 767, fn. 1870.
[1269] Stanišić Appeal Brief, paras 36-41.
[1270] Stanišić Appeal Brief, paras 96, 98, 111, 187. See Stanišić Appeal Brief, paras 101-103; Appeal Hearing, 16 Dec 2015, AT. 97.
[1271] Stanišić Appeal Brief, paras 99-100, 112-116. See Stanišić Appeal Brief, paras 168-170. See also Stanišić Appeal Brief, paras 75-76, 87-94.
[1272] Stanišić Appeal Brief, paras 104, 117-124.
[1273] Stanišić Appeal Brief, paras 105-107, 125-138.
[1274] Stanišić Appeal Brief, paras 108, 139-155.
[1275] Stanišić Appeal Brief, paras 109, 156-170.
[1276] Stanišić Appeal Brief, para. 110. See Stanišić Appeal Brief, paras 39, 171-186.
[1277] Stanišić Appeal Brief, paras 95, 187. See Stanišić Appeal Brief, para. 53.
[1278] Prosecution Response Brief (Stanišić), paras 14-15.
[1279] Prosecution Response Brief (Stanišić), para. 36.

pursuant to the first category of joint criminal enterprise.[1280] He argues that the Trial Chamber reached its conclusion on his *mens rea* "in no more than 4 paragraphs that fail to refer specifically to other findings",[1281] and contends that even a thorough examination of the paragraphs where the Trial Chamber discusses his individual criminal responsibility does not make it possible to understand the reasoning in the *Mens Rea* Section,[1282] including the date as of when he formed the requisite *mens rea*.[1283] He asserts, moreover, that the Trial Chamber "provided no **[page 155]** reasons for failing to consider voluminous exculpatory evidence", demonstrating that other reasonable inferences compatible with Stanišić's innocence could have been drawn.[1284] He contends, in this context, that in certain circumstances, insufficient analysis of evidence on the record can amount to a failure to provide a reasoned opinion.[1285] Finally, he argues that on the "sole occurrence" where the Trial Chamber examined his acts and conduct to draw inferences about his *mens rea* "it failed to address serious inconsistencies" in the evidence of Witness Davidović without providing a reasoned opinion.[1286]

373. The Prosecution responds that Stanišić fails to show the absence of a reasoned opinion.[1287] It contends that neither the length of the "section in the Judgement summarising the Chamber's conclusion regarding Stanišić's shared intent" nor the absence of citations in that section, demonstrate a lack of a reasoned opinion.[1288] It contends, further, that Stanišić's challenges to the Trial Chamber's consideration of Witness Davidović's evidence repeat arguments under his fourth and fifth grounds of appeal and that he fails to show any error.[1289] The Prosecution submits, finally, that the Trial Chamber's findings show that Stanišić shared the requisite intent with other JCE members "from the JCE's beginning", *i.e.* from no later than 24 October 1991.[1290]

374. Stanišić replies that the Prosecution does not address the Trial Chamber's failure to explain how the evidence it summarised "sustained its erroneous inferences".[1291] He argues that the Prosecution wrongly asserts that the Trial Chamber considered the exculpatory evidence he identifies, and fails to consider that the Trial Chamber "missed the important contradictions" in Witness Davidović's testimony in this case.[1292]
[page 156]

(ii) <u>Analysis</u>

375. The Appeals Chamber recalls that in order to establish a failure to provide a reasoned opinion, an appellant must show that the trial chamber failed to indicate clearly the legal and factual findings underpinning its decision to convict or acquit.[1293] In particular, a trial chamber is required to provide clear, reasoned

---

[1280] Stanišić Appeal Brief, para. 38. See Stanišić Appeal Brief, paras 40-41.

[1281] Stanišić Appeal Brief, para. 37, referring to Trial Judgement, vol. 2, paras 766-769 (and pointing out that these paragraphs of the Trial Judgement do not contain any footnotes); Appeal Hearing, 16 Dec 2015, AT. 96-97.

[1282] Stanišić Appeal Brief, para. 38, referring to Trial Judgement, vol. 2, paras 532-728.

[1283] See Appeal Hearing, 16 Dec 2015, AT. 104.

[1284] Stanišić Appeal Brief, para. 39, referring to his arguments set out with respect to subsection (F) of his fourth ground of appeal. See Appeal Hearing, 16 Dec 2015, AT. 96-97, where he submits that the Trial Chamber failed to consider the totality of the evidence on the record, and in some cases, failed to even refer to relevant evidence.

[1285] Stanišić Appeal Brief, para. 36, referring to *Perišić* Appeal Judgement, para. 92.

[1286] Stanišić Appeal Brief, para. 40. See Stanišić Appeal Brief, para. 41, referring to Trial Judgement, vol. 2, para. 768, Milorad Davidović, 24 Aug 2010, T. 13625-13626. See also Stanišić Reply Brief, para. 19.

[1287] Prosecution Response Brief (Stanišić), para. 14. The Prosecution adds that in concluding that Stanišić shared the common criminal purpose, the Trial Chamber drew upon its exhaustive analysis of the evidence, its findings concerning Stanišić's various contributions, his knowledge of crimes, and his persistence in implementing the JCE (Prosecution Response Brief (Stanišić), para. 15. See Prosecution Response Brief (Stanišić), fn. 15 (and citations therein); Appeal Hearing, 16 Dec 2015, AT. 119).

[1288] Prosecution Response Brief (Stanišić), para. 15.

[1289] Prosecution Response Brief (Stanišić), para. 18, referring to Prosecution Response Brief (Stanišić), paras 51-53, 65-91. See *infra*, paras 451-473.

[1290] Appeal Hearing, 16 Dec 2015, AT. 126, referring to Trial Judgement, vol. 2, paras 313, 769. See Appeal Hearing, 16 Dec 2015, AT. 121-124, 126-127.

[1291] Stanišić Reply Brief, para. 17. Stanišić contends that, other than for its "erroneous application of a knowledge standard", the Trial Judgement is devoid of any reasoning (Stanišić Reply Brief, para. 17, referring to Stanišić Appeal Brief, paras 96-187).

[1292] Stanišić Reply Brief, para. 19. See Stanišić Reply Brief, para. 18.

[1293] *Stanišić and Simatović* Appeal Judgement, para. 78; *Popović et al.* Appeal Judgement, para. 1906; *Haradinaj et al.* Appeal Judgement, paras 77, 128; *Hadžihasanović and Kubura* Appeal Judgement, para. 13. See *Bizimungu* Appeal Judgement, paras 18-19; *Ndindiliyimana et al.* Appeal Judgement, para. 293. See *supra*, para. 137.

findings of fact as to each element of the crime or mode of liability charged.[1294] In the circumstances of this case, in order to demonstrate that the subjective element of the first category of joint criminal enterprise was met in relation to Stanišić, the Trial Chamber was required to establish that he shared with the other JCE members the intent to commit the JCE I Crimes and the intent to participate in a common plan aimed at their commission.[1295] While such intent can be inferred from circumstantial evidence, it must be the only reasonable inference.[1296]

376. The Trial Chamber concluded that "Stanišić was aware of the persecutorial intentions of the Bosnian Serb leadership to forcibly transfer and deport Muslims and Croats from territories of the BiH and that [he] shared the same intent".[1297] In reaching this conclusion the Trial Chamber did not make an express determination as of when Stanišić shared the intent with other members of the JCE,[1298] nor did the Trial Chamber, at the very least, set out when it considered Stanišić first contributed to the JCE with the requisite intent.[1299] In the circumstances of this case, the absence of such determinations complicates the task of understanding the Trial Chamber's reasoning. Nonetheless, recalling that a trial judgement must be read as a whole,[1300] and in light of the Trial Chamber's analysis elsewhere in the Trial Judgement, the Appeals Chamber understands that it found that Stanišić possessed the requisite intent throughout the Indictment period (*i.e.* at the latest from 1 April 1992 until 31 December 1992).[1301] **[page 157]**

377. Insofar as Stanišić contends that a thorough examination of the *Mens Rea* Section does not make it possible to understand the Trial Chamber's reasoning, the Appeals Chamber notes that, in addition to the absence of the aforementioned findings, the *Mens Rea* Section lacks cross-references to the Trial Chamber's analysis or findings elsewhere in the Trial Judgement or references to evidence in support of the factors listed therein.[1302] Moreover, with regard to a number of factors listed in the *Mens Rea* Section the Trial Chamber adopted vague, generic, and nondescript terms to refer to factual findings contained in the section of the Trial Judgement dedicated to Stanišić's contributions to the JCE or in other portions of the Trial Judgement.[1303]

378. This approach of the Trial Chamber is problematic, and has complicated the Appeals Chamber's review of the reasoning in the Trial Judgement. Nonetheless, through a careful and thorough examination of the Trial Judgement as a whole, as is demonstrated below,[1304] the Trial Chamber's reasoning in the *Mens Rea* Section is discernable. In this respect, the Appeals Chamber considers that the factors identified in the *Mens*

[1294]   *Cf. Kordić and Čerkez* Appeal Judgement, para. 383; *Ndindiliyimana et al.* Appeal Judgement, para. 293; *Renzaho* Appeal Judgement, para. 320. See *Orić* Appeal Judgement, para. 56.

[1295]   *Popović et al.* Appeal Judgement, para. 1369. See *Đorđević* Appeal Judgement, para. 468; *Brđanin* Appeal Judgement, para. 365.

[1296]   *Popović et al.* Appeal Judgement, para. 1369; *Šainović et al.* Appeal Judgement, para. 995; *Krajišnik* Appeal Judgement, para. 202.

[1297]   Trial Judgement, vol. 2, para. 769. See *infra*, para. 386.

[1298]   Trial Judgement, vol. 2, para. 769.

[1299]   The Appeals Chamber notes that, in contrast, with regard to Župljanin's intent, the Trial Chamber made a clearer finding stating that "he intended, with other members of the JCE, to achieve the permanent removal of Bosnian Muslims and Bosnian Croats from the territory of the planned Serbian state through the commission of [JCE I Crimes] against Muslims and Croats in the ARK Municipalities" and that "Župljanin was a member of the JCE starting at least in April 1992 and throughout the rest of 1992" (Trial Judgement, vol. 2, para. 520).

[1300]   *Šainović et al.* Appeal Judgement, paras 306, 321; *Boškoski and Tarčulovski* Appeal Judgement, para. 67; *Orić* Appeal Judgement, para. 38.

[1301]   *Cf.* Trial Judgement, vol. 2, paras 531-532, 766, 927-928, 955. The Appeals Chamber notes that the Trial Chamber convicted Stanišić for his responsibility for crimes occurring throughout the Indictment period, which it identified as "from no later than 1 April 1992" until 31 December 1992 (Trial Judgement, vol. 2, para. 532. See Trial Judgement, vol. 2, paras 531, 955) and expressly identified that Stanišić had committed these crimes through his participation in a joint criminal enterprise (Trial Judgement, vol. 2, para. 928). Moreover, in its assessment of his intent, the Trial Chamber "considered evidence on Stanišić's knowledge of the commission of crimes against Muslims and Croats in the geographic area and during the time period covered by the Indictment" (Trial Judgement, vol. 2, para. 766) and stated that it reviewed other evidence in the context of "assessing Stanišić's *alleged mens rea*" (which the Indictment alleges he possessed throughout the duration of the Indictment period) (Trial Judgement, vol. 2, para. 767 (emphasis added). See Trial Judgement, vol. 2, para. 532).

[1302]   See Trial Judgement, vol. 2, paras 766-769.

[1303]   See generally, Trial Judgement, vol. 2, paras 766-769. For example, the Trial Chamber referred to Stanišić's: (i) "knowledge of the commission of crimes" (Trial Judgement, vol. 2, para. 766); (ii) "position at the time" (Trial Judgement, vol. 2, para. 769); (iii) "close relationship with Radovan Karadžić" (Trial Judgement, vol. 2, para. 769); and (iv) "continued support of and participation in the implementation of the policies of the Bosnian Serb leadership and SDS" (Trial Judgement, vol. 2, para. 769).

[1304]   See generally *infra*, paras 389-529.

Rea Section must be understood as a summary of the conclusions, findings, and analysis of evidence set out elsewhere in the Trial Judgement. The Appeals Chamber recalls in this regard that a reasoned opinion does not require a trial chamber to articulate every step of its reasoning.[1305] When viewed in the context of the Trial Chamber's analysis and findings contained elsewhere in the Trial Judgement, the Appeals Chamber considers that the *Mens Rea* Section is sufficiently clear to enable the understanding of the Trial Chamber's reasoning. Stanišić's argument that it is not possible to understand the Trial Chamber's reasoning in the *Mens Rea* Section, when read in the context of the Trial Judgement as a whole, is therefore without merit.

379. Insofar as Stanišić contends that the Trial Chamber erred by failing to consider "voluminous exculpatory evidence",[1306] the Appeals Chamber has dismissed these arguments for reasons set out **[page 158]** below.[1307] Similarly, Stanišić's assertion that the Trial Chamber failed to address inconsistencies in Witness Davidović's evidence is dismissed for reasons given elsewhere in this Judgement.[1308] The Appeals Chamber thus finds that Stanišić has not demonstrated that the Trial Chamber's analysis of the evidence was so "insufficient" that it amounts to a failure to provide a reasoned opinion.[1309]

380. In light of the above, the Appeals Chamber considers that Stanišić has not demonstrated that the Trial Chamber failed to provide a reasoned opinion for concluding that he possessed the requisite intent pursuant to the first category of joint criminal enterprise. His arguments in this respect are accordingly dismissed.

(c) Alleged error in finding that Stanišić' s support for a legitimate political goal was determinative of his intent pursuant to the first category of joint criminal enterprise (Stanišić's third ground of appeal in part and fourth ground of appeal in part)

381. In the conclusion of the *Mens Rea* Section, considering, *inter alia*, "his continued support of and participation in the implementation of the policies of the Bosnian Serb leadership and the SDS", the Trial Chamber found that "Stanišić was aware of the persecutorial intentions of the Bosnian Serb leadership to forcibly transfer and deport Muslims and Croats from the territories of the BiH and that Stanišić shared the same intent".[1310]

(i) Submissions of the parties

382. Stanišić submits that the Trial Chamber erred in law by finding that his support for a legitimate political goal (*i.e.* the Bosnian Serb leadership's aim for Serbs to live in one state with other Serbs) was sufficient to prove that he possessed the requisite intent.[1311] In support, Stanišić argues that the Trial Chamber failed to make the requisite finding that the criminal purpose it identified (*i.e.* the permanent removal of non-Serbs through the commission of JCE I Crimes) was common to all the persons acting together within the JCE.[1312] Reiterating his submission under his second ground of appeal, Stanišić argues that the Trial Chamber instead considered that a group it termed as the "Bosnian Serb leadership", including him, necessarily shared the same criminal purpose "by virtue of their grouping", without properly assessing whether he (as well as other individuals within this leadership) personally possessed the requisite intent to commit the **[page 159]** crimes.[1313] He avers that the Trial Chamber therefore impermissibly inferred that he shared the intent of the Bosnian Serb leadership to commit crimes, merely having found him to be part of this leadership.[1314]

[1305] See *supra*, paras 137, 375.
[1306] See *supra*, para. 372.
[1307] See *infra*, paras 530-571.
[1308] See *infra*, paras 456-473.
[1309] See *Perišić* Appeal Judgement, para. 92.
[1310] Trial Judgement, vol. 2, para. 769.
[1311] Stanišić Appeal Brief, paras 75-76, 87-94.
[1312] Stanišić Appeal Brief, para. 87, referring to *Brđanin* Appeal Judgement, para. 430, *Stakić* Appeal Judgement, para. 69. See Stanišić Appeal Brief, para. 88.
[1313] Stanišić Appeal Brief, para. 88. See Stanišić Appeal Brief, paras 89, 109, 112, 168, referring to Stanišić Appeal Brief, paras 57-59, 70-73. See also Stanišić Appeal Brief, paras 75-76.
[1314] Stanišić Appeal Brief, paras 168-169, referring to Stanišić Appeal Brief, paras 70-73. See Stanišić Appeal Brief, paras 75-76, 88, 109, 170; Appeal Hearing, 16 Dec 2015, AT. 101.

383.   Stanišić further contends that a "minority" within the Bosnian Serb leadership existed that did not share the requisite intent to be considered part of the JCE, but rather intended to achieve their aim without committing crimes.[1315] He argues that a proper analysis of the evidence with regard to his acts and conduct leads to the reasonable inference that he shared the aim of this "minority" within the Bosnian Serb leadership and therefore did not intend to commit any "persecutory act".[1316]

384.   The Prosecution responds that Stanišić's argument is based on the "mistaken assumption that his JCE membership was determined by reference to his status as a Bosnian Serb leader" and ignores the Trial Chamber's analysis of his criminal responsibility.[1317] It requests that the Appeals Chamber summarily dismiss Stanišić's arguments.[1318]

(ii) Analysis

385.   The Appeals Chamber observes that Stanišić essentially repeats arguments raised under his second ground of appeal, while shifting the focus to the question of his intent and directly referring to the Trial Chamber's conclusion in this respect.[1319] Insofar as these arguments can be understood to assert that, in reaching this conclusion, the Trial Chamber failed to find that he *shared the intent with the other JCE members* to further the common purpose of the JCE, the Appeals Chamber finds that Stanišić misconstrues the Trial Judgement.

386.   In this regard, the Appeals Chamber recalls that, in order for the subjective element of the first category of joint criminal enterprise to be met, the accused must share, with the other participants, the intent to commit the crimes that form part of the common purpose of the joint**[page 160]** criminal enterprise and the intent to participate in a common plan aimed at their commission.[1320] The Appeals Chamber notes that the Trial Chamber found that "Stanišić was aware of the *persecutorial intentions of the Bosnian Serb leadership* to forcibly transfer and deport Muslims and Croats from territories of BiH and that Stanišić shared *the same intent*".[1321] Thus, the Trial Chamber did not explicitly find that Stanišić shared the intent with the JCE members but rather that he shared the persecutorial intentions with the Bosnian Serb leadership. However, the Appeals Chamber also notes that the Trial Chamber found that the goal of the *majority* of the Bosnian Serb leadership was the "establishment of a Serb state, as ethnically 'pure' as possible, through the permanent removal of Bosnian Muslims and Bosnian Croats".[1322] The Trial Chamber further found that a joint criminal enterprise existed which had the common purpose of permanently removing Bosnian Muslims and Bosnian Croats from the territory of the planned Serbian state through the commission of JCE I Crimes.[1323] The Trial Chamber also identified members of this JCE by specifically naming them, and found that they formed a plurality of persons.[1324] Therefore, although an explicit finding would have been preferable,[1325] the Appeals Chamber is satisfied that the Trial Chamber did find that Stanišić shared with the JCE members the intent to participate in the common criminal purpose and the intent to commit the JCE I Crimes.

[1315]   Stanišić Appeal Brief, paras 99-100, 113-114. See Stanišić Appeal Brief, para. 112.
[1316]   Stanišić Appeal Brief, paras 100, 115-116. See Stanišić Appeal Brief, paras 112-113. See also Appeal Hearing, 16 Dec 2015, AT. 101. In support of this argument, Stanišić makes some specific references to evidence on the trial record (Stanišić Appeal Brief, paras 90-94, 116, fn. 100; Stanišić Reply Brief, paras 31-32).
[1317]   Prosecution Response Brief (Stanišić), paras 32-33. See Prosecution Response Brief (Stanišić), paras 28, 36-37. See also Appeal Hearing, 16 Dec 2015, AT. 124. See further Prosecution Response Brief (Stanišić), paras 30, 34, responding to Stanišić's specific references to evidence in the trial record which purportedly shows that he did not share the requisite intent.
[1318]   Prosecution Response Brief (Stanišić), para. 30.
[1319]   See in particular, Stanišić Appeal Brief, paras 88, 168.
[1320]   *Popović et al.* Appeal Judgement, para. 1369. See *Đorđević* Appeal Judgement, para. 468; *Brđanin* Appeal Judgement, para. 365.
[1321]   Trial Judgement, vol. 2, para. 769 (emphasis added).
[1322]   Trial Judgement, vol. 2, para. 311.
[1323]   Trial Judgement, vol. 2, para. 313.
[1324]   Trial Judgement, vol. 2, para. 314. See *supra*, paras 73, 82.
[1325]   The Appeals Chamber notes that, in contrast, with regard to Župljanin's intent, the Trial Chamber made a clearer finding stating that: "he intended, with other members of the JCE, to achieve the permanent removal of Bosnian Muslims and Bosnian Croats from the territory of the planned Serbian state through the commission of [JCE I Crimes] against Muslims and Croats in the ARK Municipalities" (Trial Judgement, vol. 2, para. 520).

387. Turning to Stanišić's argument that the Trial Chamber presupposed that all Bosnian Serb leaders, including Stanišić, shared the criminal purpose by virtue of their grouping without examining their individual intent,[1326] the Appeals Chamber recalls that it has already dismissed his argument to this effect elsewhere.[1327] In this regard, the Appeals Chamber recalls its conclusion that the Trial Chamber neither equated being part of the Bosnian Serb leadership with membership in the JCE nor found that Stanišić was a member of the JCE solely by virtue of his association with the Bosnian Serb leadership.[1328] Rather, the Trial Chamber examined Stanišić's criminal responsibility on the basis of his individual acts and conduct.[1329] In particular, as regards Stanišić's individual intent, the Appeals Chamber notes that the Trial Chamber specifically relied on a number of factors **[page 161]** concerning Stanišić's individual knowledge and actions,[1330] and found that Stanišić had the intent to forcibly transfer and deport Muslims and Croats from the territories of the BiH,[1331] thereby finding that he shared the intent of the other members of the JCE.[1332]

388. In light of the foregoing, the Appeals Chamber finds no merit in Stanišić's argument that the Trial Chamber reached the conclusion that he possessed the requisite intent solely by virtue of his participation in the Bosnian Serb leadership or his support for its legitimate political goal. Thus, his arguments in this respect are dismissed. The question of whether a reasonable trial chamber could have reached this conclusion, as well as the specific challenges raised by Stanišić with regard to the Trial Chamber's assessment of evidence, are addressed elsewhere in this Judgement.[1333]

(d) Alleged errors in relying on Stanišić's purported knowledge of the crimes in finding that he had the intent to further the JCE (Stanišić's fourth ground of appeal in part and first ground of appeal in part)

389. In the first paragraph of the *Mens Rea* Section, the Trial Chamber stated that "[t]o assess Stanišić's state of mind in relation to the conduct examined above, [it] first considered evidence on Stanišić's knowledge of the commission of crimes against Muslims and Croats in the geographic area and during the time period covered by the Indictment."[1334] Apart from evidence on Stanišić's knowledge, the Trial Chamber also reviewed evidence on a number of different factors[1335] and subsequently found that he shared the intent to forcibly transfer and deport Muslims and Croats from the territories of BiH.[1336]

(i) Submissions of the parties

390. Stanišić submits that the Trial Chamber erred in law by impermissibly applying a "'knowledge' standard" when determining his *mens rea* rather than assessing whether he intended to commit the crimes.[1337] According to Stanišić, the Trial Chamber's approach, in first considering evidence on his knowledge of the commission of crimes, demonstrates that it assessed his **[page 162]** knowledge of the commission of crimes rather than assessing whether he intended the commission of crimes.[1337][1338] He submits that, while the Trial Chamber's reliance on factors such as the meetings he attended or the reports of ill-discipline within the RS

[1326] Stanišić Appeal Brief, paras 87-88.
[1327] See *supra*, paras 79-87.
[1328] See *supra*, paras 82, 86.
[1329] See Trial Judgement, vol. 2, paras 531-781.
[1330] Trial Judgement, vol. 2, paras 766-769.
[1331] Trial Judgement, vol. 2, para. 769. See Trial Judgement, vol. 2, paras 313-314.
[1332] Trial Judgement, vol. 2, paras 313-314. See *supra*, para. 376.
[1333] See *supra*, paras 83-86. In particular, in the section "Alleged errors in equating being part of the Bosnian Serb leadership with membership in the JCE and failing to identify those within the Bosnian Serb leadership who were not JCE members", the Appeals Chamber will address Stanišić's arguments referring to specific evidence which allegedly demonstrates that he shared the aim of the "minority" within the Bosnian Serb leadership rather than intending to commit any persecutory act (Stanišić Appeal Brief, paras 90-94, 116, fn. 100; Stanišić Reply Brief, paras 31-32. See *infra*, paras 530-571).
[1334] Trial Judgement, vol. 2, para. 766.
[1335] Trial Judgement, vol. 2, paras 767-769.
[1336] Trial Judgement, vol. 2, para. 769.
[1337] Stanišić Appeal Brief, para. 104. See Stanišić Appeal Brief, paras 40, 117-118, 124. See also Appeal Hearing, 16 Dec 2015, AT. 102-103, 108.
[1338] Stanišić Appeal Brief, paras 40, 117-118.

MUP[1339] could be relevant to assessing his knowledge of crimes, they cannot "go to assessing whether [he] possessed and shared the intent to commit crimes".[1340]

391.   Stanišić further submits that the Trial Chamber committed an error of law by relying on his knowledge of crimes without making "conclusive findings" as to the extent of his knowledge about "the Indictment crimes" and when he should be considered to have had knowledge about these crimes.[1341] He argues, moreover, that the Trial Chamber committed an error of fact in relying solely on the communications logbook of the RS MUP Headquarters and Sarajevo CSB from 22 April 1992 to 2 January 1993 ("Communications Logbook") when finding that he "was regularly informed throughout 1992 about crimes and actions being taken to investigate them", since the evidence cited by the Trial Chamber in support of its conclusion shows that the earliest relevant report was sent to the RS MUP on 19 July 1992.[1342] According to Stanišić, the Trial Chamber also committed an error of fact when "referring to" the "daily, weekly and quarterly reports", as the earliest of such reports relevant to the crimes alleged in the Indictment is dated 17 July 1992.[1343] Finally, Stanišić submits that, when referring to the reports prepared by the "Miloš Group" prior to July 1992, the Trial Chamber failed to consider the testimony of Witness Radulović, head of the Miloš Group, who testified that Stanišić did not receive reports in 1992.[1344]

392.   The Prosecution responds that the Trial Chamber reasonably inferred Stanišić's intent from a number of factors, including his knowledge of and reaction to crimes committed against **[page 163]** non-Serbs, as well as his persistence in implementing the JCE.[1345] The Prosecution further submits that the Trial Chamber did not err by failing to make conclusive findings with regard to his knowledge of the crimes.[1346] The Prosecution contends, specifically, that Stanišić: (i) had knowledge of crimes that "formed part of the violent means of forcing non-Serbs out", such as lootings and beatings, starting in April 1992; (ii) was aware of unlawful detention of non-Serbs by early June 1992, at the latest; and (iii) was aware of the displacement of non-Serbs from at least July 1992.[1347] It argues that Stanišić only refers to a fragment of the evidence on which the Trial Chamber relied in this regard and mischaracterises it.[1348] It submits that throughout the conflict, he received a steady stream of information concerning the crimes being committed against non-Serbs from sources within the RS MUP, as well as the RS Presidency, the RS Government, international organisations and media.[1349]

   (ii) Analysis

393.   The Appeals Chamber recalls that the requisite intent for the first category of joint criminal enterprise can be inferred from factors such as a person's knowledge of the common criminal purpose or the crime(s) it involves, combined with his or her continuing participation in the crimes or in the implementation of the

---

[1339]   Stanišić's specific challenges to the Trial Chamber's findings in this respect are dealt with below in Stanišić's fourth ground of appeal, subsections C, D, E, and F (see *infra*, paras 414-571).
[1340]   Stanišić Appeal Brief, para. 119 (emphasis omitted). See Stanišić Reply Brief, para. 34. See also Stanišić Reply Brief, paras 35-36.
[1341]   Stanišić Appeal Brief, paras 120, 123. See Appeal Hearing, 16 Dec 2015, AT. 103, where Stanišić reiterates that, considering that the Trial Chamber relied on Stanišić's knowledge to infer his *mens rea*, a determination as of when Stanišić knew of which crimes is fundamental.
[1342]   Stanišić Appeal Brief, para. 121, referring to Trial Judgement, vol. 2, para. 690, fn. 1771, Exhibit P1428. See Appeal Hearing, 16 Dec 2015, AT. 137-138, where Stanišić adds that the number of dispatches decreased significantly during the first nine months of the war.
[1343]   Stanišić Appeal Brief, para. 121, referring to Trial Judgement, vol. 2, para. 690, Exhibit P427.08.
[1344]   Stanišić Appeal Brief, para. 122, referring to Trial Judgement, vol. 2, para. 689, fn. 1768, Predrag Radulović, 2 Jun 2010, T. 11205-11209. See Appeal Hearing, 16 Dec 2015, AT. 137 (during the Appeal Hearing, Stanišić referred to other transcript pages of Witness Radulović's testimony than the ones he refers to in his appeal brief (see Appeal Hearing, 16 Dec 2015, AT. 137, referring to Predrag Radulović, 28 May 2010, T. 11014, Predrag Radulović, 31 May 2010, T. 11073, Predrag Radulović, 1 Jun 2010, T. 11188, Predrag Radulović, 2 Jun 2010, T. 11199)). The Appeals Chamber notes that the Trial Chamber found that the Miloš Group was a unit collecting intelligence for the SNB (Trial Judgement, vol. 2, para. 372).
[1345]   Prosecution Response Brief (Stanišić), para. 49. See Appeal Hearing, 16 Dec 2015, AT. 119, where the Prosecution reiterates that the Trial Chamber's finding on Stanišić's *mens rea* did not rest on his knowledge alone.
[1346]   Prosecution Response Brief (Stanišić), para. 50.
[1347]   Appeal Hearing, 16 Dec 2015, AT. 126-127, referring to Trial Judgement, vol. 2, paras 603, 610-612, 627, 632, 634, 762.
[1348]   Prosecution Response Brief (Stanišić), para. 49.
[1349]   Prosecution Response Brief (Stanišić), para. 49. See Appeal Hearing, 16 Dec 2015, AT. 121-124.

221

common criminal purpose.[1350] While such intent can be inferred from circumstantial evidence, this inference must be the only reasonable inference.[1351]

394. The Appeals Chamber observes that in its assessment of Stanišić's intent, the Trial Chamber considered, first, "evidence on [his] knowledge of the commission of crimes against Muslims and Croats in the geographic area and during the time period covered by the Indictment".[1352] Aside from the evidence on his knowledge, it also considered, *inter alia*: (i) the political stances of the SDS and the BSA during the period preceding the Indictment and Stanišić's conduct and statements in **[page 164]** relation to these policies;[1353] (ii) Stanišić's close relationship with Karadžić;[1354] and (iii) Stanišić's "continued support of and participation in the implementation of the policies of the Bosnian Serb leadership and the SDS".[1355] Stanišić's assertion that the Trial Chamber relied exclusively on his knowledge when inferring his intent and that this shows that it applied a "'knowledge' standard"[1356] is thus without merit. Accordingly, the Appeals Chamber considers that Stanišić has failed to demonstrate that the Trial Chamber erred in law in its application of the standard for the subjective element of the first category of joint criminal enterprise.

395. In relation to Stanišić's argument that the Trial Chamber erred by failing to make conclusive findings on the extent of his knowledge about "the Indictment crimes" and when he should be considered to have had knowledge about these crimes,[1357] the Appeals Chamber understands him to refer to his knowledge of crimes committed by Serb forces against Muslims and Croats in the area and at the time relevant to the Indictment.[1358] The Appeals Chamber, upon a careful reading of the Trial Judgement as a whole,[1359] is able to identify several findings of the Trial Chamber related to Stanišić's knowledge of such crimes. The Appeals Chamber understands that the Trial Chamber's reference to consideration of evidence on Stanišić's knowledge of the crimes as set out in paragraph 766 of volume two of the Trial Judgement – *i.e.* "evidence on Stanišić's knowledge of the commission of crimes against Muslims and Croats in the geographic area and during the time period covered by the Indictment" – must be understood in the context of the Trial Chamber's below-mentioned analysis of the evidence[1360] and findings elsewhere in the Trial Judgement.

396. The Appeals Chamber considers the clearest finding in this regard to be the following: Stanišić "learned of the unlawful detention of Muslims [and] Croats, at the latest, by the beginning of June 1992".[1361]
[page 165]

[1350] *Stanišić and Simatović* Appeal Judgement, para. 81. See *Popović et al.* Appeal Judgement, para. 1369; *Dorlevic* Appeal Judgement, para. 512. See also *Krajišnik* Appeal Judgement, paras 202, 697; *Kvočka et al.* Appeal Judgement, para. 243.

[1351] *Popović et al.* Appeal Judgement, para. 1369; *Šainović et al.* Appeal Judgement, para. 995; *Krajišnik* Appeal Judgement, para. 202.

[1352] Trial Judgement, vol. 2, para. 766. The Appeals Chamber notes that the geographic area of the Indictment covers the municipalities of Banja Luka, Bijeljina, Bileća, Bosanski Šamac, Brčko, Doboj, Donji Vakuf, Gacko, Ilijaš, Ključ, Kotor Varoš, Pale, Prijedor, Sanski Most, Skender Vakuf, Teslić, Vlasenica, Višegrad, Vogošća and Zvornik and that the Indictment period is from 1 April 1992 to 31 December 1992 (see Indictment, para. 11). See Trial Judgement, vol. 2, paras 762-765. See also *infra*, paras 395-409.

[1353] Trial Judgement, vol. 2, paras 767-768. See Trial Judgement, vol. 2, paras 729-736. See also *infra*, paras 422-428.

[1354] Trial Judgement, vol. 2, para. 769. See Trial Judgement, vol. 2, para. 730. See also *infra*, paras 507-514.

[1355] Trial Judgement, vol. 2, para. 769. See Trial Judgement, vol. 2, paras 729-765. See also *infra*, paras 517-528.

[1356] Stanišić Appeal Brief, para. 104. See Stanišić Appeal Brief, paras 40, 117-118, 124.

[1357] See *supra*, para. 391.

[1358] See Stanišić Appeal Brief, para. 120, read in the context of Stanišić Appeal Brief, paras 121-123. See also *supra*, para. 391.

[1359] See *Šainović et al.* Appeal Judgement, paras 306, 321; *Boškoski and Tarčulovski* Appeal Judgement, para. 67; *Orić* Appeal Judgement, para. 38.

[1360] See *infra*, paras 396-404.

[1361] Trial Judgement, vol. 2, para. 762. See Trial Judgement, vol. 2, paras 763-765. See also Trial Judgement, vol. 2, paras 617, 623, 631-633, 639, 646, 660-663. In making this finding, the Trial Chamber relied upon evidence regarding: (i) Stanišić's attendance at a Government meeting on 10 June 1992, where it was decided that the MOJ would prepare a report, focusing on, *inter alia*, matters such as the treatment of the civilian population, POWs, accommodation, and food (Trial Judgement, vol. 2, paras 623, 763); (ii) Stanišić's discussion with Witness Marković, a member of the Central Commission for the Exchange of Prisoners which was set up by a decision on 8 May 1992, on the treatment of women and children in the context of prisoner exchanges (Trial Judgement, vol. 2, paras 617, 764. See *supra*, para. 700); (iii) the fact that the information gathered by the SNB inspectors, who the Trial Chamber found to have played a significant role in the interrogation of Muslims and Croats in detention camps, such as in Prijedor and Manjača, was available to Stanišić (Trial Judgement, vol. 2, paras 26, 689, 764. See *supra*, paras 400-401); (iv) Stanišić's attendance at the 11 July 1992 Collegium, where Župljanin stated that "the army and Crisis Staffs were requesting that as many Muslims as possible be 'gathered' and that the security of 'undefined camps', where international norms were not respected, was left to RS MUP organs" (Trial Judgement, vol. 2, paras 631-632, 765. See *infra*, paras 484-487); (v) Stanišić's attendance at an RS Government session on

397. With respect to Stanišić's knowledge of other incidents of crimes committed against Croats and Muslims, the Trial Chamber noted relevant evidence in different sections of the Trial Judgement. More specifically, concerning his knowledge of unlawful arrests, the Trial Chamber considered evidence that: (i) on 18 April 1992, Stanišić was informed by Radomir Kojić that a certain "Zoka" had arrested Muslims in Sokolac for "messing up with the weapons" and wanted to bring them to Vrace, telling Stanišić that "there '[t]hey can beat them, they can do whatever they fucking want', to which Stanišić responded: '[f]ine'";[1362] and (ii) on 20 July 1992, "Župljanin informed Stanišić that the VRS and the police had arrested 'several thousands' of Muslims and Croats, including persons of no security interest, whom Župljanin proposed to use as hostages for prisoner exchanges".[1363]

398. With regard to Stanišić's knowledge of looting, the Trial Chamber considered evidence that in late April 1992, Stanišić was informed about the looting of Muslim property by reserve police in Vrace and about the unit of Duško Malović ("Malović") stealing cars from the TAS factory in Vogošća to which Stanišić responded that the former was "normal" in times of war and that for the latter "'we' should work on preventing such issues".[1364] In addition, the Trial Chamber also considered evidence that at the 11 July 1992 Collegium attended by Stanišić, "looting, mainly perpetrated during 'mopping-up operations' was considered to be a serious problem", and "war crimes" committed by Serbs was also discussed.[1365] The Trial Chamber also found that between June and the beginning of July 1992, Stanišić was informed by several sources of the activities of the paramilitary groups in Zvornik, "including [committing] war crimes".[1366]

399. With respect to Stanišić's knowledge of killings, the Appeals Chamber notes the Trial Chamber's finding that on 21 August 1992 at Korićanske Stijene, Prijedor policemen killed **[page 166]** approximately 150-200 Muslim men from Trnopolje detention facility who were taking no active part in hostilities,[1367] and its consideration of Stanišić's Interview where he stated that he first "learned of the incident at Korićanske Stijene two or three days after the incident" (*i.e.* 23 or 24 August 1992).[1368]

400. Recalling the Trial Chamber's finding that "[e]vidence on the various channels of reporting and information demonstrate Stanišić's knowledge of the crimes that were being committed",[1369] the Appeals Chamber further notes the Trial Chamber's analysis of the channels of reporting and general information Stanišić received. The Trial Chamber considered evidence concerning the channel of information reaching Stanišić from the SNB. It found that Witness Škipina – appointed on 6 August 1992 as Advisor on matters relating to the SNB – reported directly to the Minister of the RS MUP on events that were brought to his attention.[1370] The Trial Chamber also considered reports from the SNBs to the RS MUP.[1371] In this context, the Trial Chamber noted that: (i) members of the SNB visited various locations from the outbreak of the conflict and kept the RS MUP "abreast of the developments in the municipalities";[1372] (ii) members of the

---

22 July 1992 where "instances of unlawful treatment of war prisoners were discussed" (Trial Judgement, vol. 2, paras 639, 765) ; (vi) the fact that on 5 August 1992, Witness Sreto Gajić ("Witness Gajić"), Head of the Defence Preparations of the Police section in the RS MUP, reported to Stanišić that camps still existed in Prijedor and that 300 policemen were engaged in securing them (Trial Judgement, vol. 2, paras 644, 646, 750, 765); and (vii) the fact that in October 1992, Slobodan Avlijaš, Deputy Minister of Justice and Inspector for Penitentiary Institutions under the MOJ, reported to Stanišić that the police in Zvornik were detaining people "without any justification in law" (Trial Judgement, vol. 2, paras 652, 660-663, 765).

[1362] Trial Judgement, vol. 2, para. 612. The Appeals Chamber notes that this finding is challenged by Stanišić in his eleventh ground of appeal and that the Appeals Chamber has found that the Trial Chamber erred in fact in finding that the arrests in Sokolac involved Muslims (see *supra*, paras 664-665).

[1363] Trial Judgement, vol. 2, para. 765. See Trial Judgement, vol. 2, para. 638.

[1364] Trial Judgement, vol. 2, para. 603.

[1365] Trial Judgement, vol. 2, para. 632. See Trial Judgement, vol. 2, para. 631.

[1366] Trial Judgement, vol. 2, para. 713, referring to the testimony of Dragan Dokanovic, 20 Nov 2009, T. 3586-3588; ST222, 9 Nov 2010, T. 17101-17104 (confidential). For crimes committed by paramilitaries in Zvornik, see *e.g.* Trial Judgement, vol. 1, paras 1652, 1663, 1666, 1670.

[1367] Trial Judgement, vol. 1, para. 696.

[1368] Trial Judgement, vol. 2, para. 677.

[1369] See Trial Judgement, vol. 2, para. 759.

[1370] Trial Judgement, vol. 2, para. 689, referring to Slobodan Škipina, 30 Mar 2010, T. 8308-8312, 8316-8317, 8323; Exhibits P1254, P1267, P1268. With respect to Stanišić's argument in relation to Witness Škipina's testimony on the reports, see *infra*, para. 638.

[1371] Trial Judgement, vol. 2, para. 689.

[1372] Trial Judgement, vol. 2, para. 689.

secret service branch of the RS MUP prepared reports on "rising ethnic tensions, the outbreak of hostilities, the death toll on both sides following the takeovers of towns and municipalities, crimes against Muslim and Croat civilians and the arrest and detention of civilians by the army and SJBs";[1373] and (iii) while not all the reports prepared by the "Miloš Group" intelligence team – which collected intelligence for the SNB[1374] – were directly submitted to the RS MUP, the information contained in these report was relayed "through the leadership of Banja Luka to the upper echelons of decision makers".[1375] In light of the above, the Trial Chamber found that "information gathered by the SNB was available to the decision makers of the RS, which included Stanišić".[1376]

401. The specific Milos Group reports cited by the Trial Chamber in this context are Exhibits P1368, P1375, P1376, P1377, and P1387.[1377] The Appeals Chamber notes, first, that **[page 167]** Exhibits P1368 and P1375 do not mention crimes against Muslims and Croats. Exhibits P1376 and P1377, Miloš Group reports dated 28 May 1992 and 30 May 1992 respectively, when read together, indicate that a large number of Muslims, including civilians, were arrested and detained (it is not specified by whom) and that municipal authorities had difficulties providing them with food and accommodation.[1378] Exhibit P1387, a Miloš Group report dated 3 June 1992, states that "in the areas of Prijedor, Sanski Most, Doboj and other towns [...] individuals and groups among our forces are behaving wilfully. We have information that persons of Muslim and Croatian nationality, mostly civilians, have been victims of crimes."[1379] The Appeals Chamber notes that the report does not mention the type of crime suffered by these civilians, but specifies the perpetrators as "individuals and groups among our forces".[1380]

402. The Trial Chamber further noted that "according to the communications logbook of the RS MUP headquarters, Stanišić was regularly informed throughout 1992 about crimes and actions being taken to investigate them".[1381]

403. In addition, the Trial Chamber also made general findings on the communication system within the RS MUP and found that: (i) from April to the summer of 1992, the communications system (through fax machines, teleprinters, telephone and couriers) did function, albeit with disruptions; and (ii) by the second half of 1992, the communications system was well established.[1382] It also found that "[d]aily, weekly, and quarterly reports were compiled, in addition to security situation reports on a periodic basis",[1383] and referenced witness testimony to the effect that these reports were prepared in order for "the Minister" to know what was going on in the territory of the RS.[1384] In addition, the Trial Chamber noted that "reports

---

[1373]   Trial Judgement, vol. 2, para. 689.
[1374]   Trial Judgement, vol. 2, para. 372.
[1375]   Trial Judgement, vol. 2, para. 689.
[1376]   Trial Judgement, vol. 2, para. 764. With respect to Stanišić's specific challenges relating to the Trial Chamber's reliance on the testimony of the head of the Miloš Group, Witness Radulović, see *infra*, para. 409.
[1377]   Trial Judgement, vol. 2, para. 689, fn. 1768, referring to, *inter alia*, Exhibits P1368 (Report of the Miloš Group Regarding the Inter-Ethnic Division in the SJBs in Prijedor, Sanski Most, Kotor Varoš, Bosanski Novi, and Ključ, 9 Apr 1992), P1375 (Report of the Miloš Group Regarding Prijedor Takeover, 30 Apr 1992), P1376 (Miloš Group Report 28 May 1992), P1377 (Miloš Group Report, 30 May 1992), P1387 (Miloš Group Report, 3 Jun 1992).
[1378]   The Appeals Chamber notes that Exhibit P1376 is a Miloš Group report dated 28 May 1992 and mentions that following fighting in the area of Kozarac in the Municipality of Prijedor a "huge number of persons", including "many children, women and old people", were arrested or surrendered, and that the municipal authorities encountered "great difficulty in providing them with food and shelter" (Exhibit P1376). Exhibit P1377 is a Miloš Group report dated 30 May 1992 stating that "[t]he problem of detained and captured persons of Muslim background is still present, and one of the greatest problems is that of food and accommodation" (Exhibit P1377).
[1379]   Exhibit P1387.
[1380]   Exhibit P1377.
[1381]   Trial Judgement, vol. 2, para. 690. The Communications Logbook, relied on by the Trial Chamber in reaching this finding, contains a number of entries referring to crimes in general terms, mostly without articulating ethnicity of perpetrators or victims (Trial Judgement, vol. 2, para. 690, fn. 1771, referring to multiple entries in Exhibit P1428). With respect to Stanišić's specific challenges relating to the Trial Chamber's reliance on the Communications Logbook, see *infra*, para. 407.
[1382]   Trial Judgement, vol. 2, paras 103, 690.
[1383]   Trial Judgement, vol. 2, para. 690, fn. 1772, referring to, *inter alia*, Exhibits P155, P427.08, P432.12, P595, P633, P748, P866, 2D25, 1D334. The Appeals Chamber notes that Stanišić's argument relating to this finding will be addressed later in this section.
[1384]   Trial Judgement, vol. 2, para. 690.

made public by the ICRC, **[page 168]** ECMM, and CSCE, as well as open media reports, were the subject of discussion and negotiation with the RS Presidency and Government".[1385]

404. Having examined the Trial Chamber's analysis of the evidence and findings as recalled above, the Appeals Chamber is of the view that it is discernible that the Trial Chamber considered that Stanišić acquired knowledge: (i) on 18 April 1992, that a certain "Zoka" had arrested Muslims in Sokolac for "messing up with the weapons", in relation to which it was suggested to Stanišić that "[t]hey can beat them, they can do whatever they fucking want", to which Stanišić responded "fine";[1386] (ii) in late April 1992, that reserve police in Vrace were looting Muslim property;[1387] (iii) at the end of May 1992, that Muslim civilians were arrested and detained in the municipality of Prijedor;[1388] (iv) on 3 June 1992, that Muslim and Croat civilians were victims of unspecified crimes, the perpetrators of which were identified as "individuals and groups among our forces";[1389] (v) at the latest by the beginning of June 1992 (and then again in July, August, and October 1992), of the unlawful detention of Muslims and Croats;[1390] (vi) at some point between June and the beginning of July 1992, of the activities of the paramilitary groups in Zvornik, "including [committing] war crimes";[1391] (vii) on 11 July 1992, of "looting, mainly perpetrated during 'mopping-up operations'" and "war crimes" committed by Serbs;[1392] (viii) on 20 July 1992, "that the VRS and the police had arrested 'several thousands' of Muslims and Croats, including persons of no security interest [...]";[1393] and (ix) by around 23 or 24 August 1992, that Pryedor policemen killed approximately 150-200 Muslim men from Trnopolje detention camp at Korićanske Stijene.[1394]

405. It is also apparent from the Trial Judgement that, while the Trial Chamber considered its analysis of evidence and findings concerning the communication system and the channels of **[page 169]** reporting and information in general,[1395] it did not place substantial weight on this evidence given that it is not specific enough as to types of crimes or ethnicity of victims and perpetrators contained in the information Stanišić received, or whether, and if so, when Stanišić received the information in question.[1396]

406. In light of the above, the Appeals Chamber considers that Stanišić's argument that the Trial Chamber failed to enter "conclusive findings" with respect to the extent of his knowledge of crimes committed against

---

[1385] Trial Judgement, vol. 2, para. 692.
[1386] See *supra*, para. 397. The Appeals Chamber notes that this finding is challenged by Stanišić in his eleventh ground of appeal and that the Appeals Chamber has found that the Trial Chamber erred in fact in finding that the arrests in Sokolac involved Muslims (see *supra*, paras 664-665).
[1387] See *supra*, para. 398. While the looting of Muslim property in Vrace is not charged in the Indictment, the Appeals Chamber notes that the Trial Chamber was entitled to consider the evidence concerning the information Stanišić received with respect to this looting in assessing his knowledge of crimes against Muslims and Croats (*cf. Šainović et al.* Appeal Judgement, paras 1193-1196, 1199). However, with regard to the looting of cars from the TAS factory in Vogošća, given that the Trial Judgement does not elucidate whether Stanišić was informed of this looting as an offence committed against non-Serbs (see Trial Judgement, vol. 2, para. 603; Trial Judgement, vol. 1, para. 1553, fn. 3591), the Appeals Chamber understands the Trial Chamber to have not considered this as part of the "evidence on Stanišić's knowledge of the commission of crimes against Muslims and Croats in the geographic area and during the time period covered by the Indictment" (Trial Judgement, vol. 2, para. 766).
[1388] See *supra*, para. 401.
[1389] See *supra*, para. 401.
[1390] See *supra*, para. 396, fn. 1361.
[1391] See *supra*, para. 398.
[1392] Trial Judgement, vol. 2, para. 632. See Trial Judgement, vol. 2, para. 631. See *supra*, para. 398.
[1393] See *supra*, para. 397.
[1394] See *supra*, para. 399; Trial Judgement, vol. 2, para. 677. See also Trial Judgement, vol. 1, para. 696.
[1395] This includes: (i) the Trial Chamber's finding on the basis of the Communications Logbook that "[a]ccording to the communications logbook of the RS MUP headquarters" he was regularly informed throughout 1992 about crimes and actions being taken to investigate them (Trial Judgement, vol. 2, para. 690. See *supra*, para. 402); (ii) its analysis of evidence concerning the communication system and the channel of information reaching Stanišić from some of the SNB and the Miloš Group reports, which do not include specific information concerning crimes against non-Serbs (Trial Judgement, vol. 2, para. 689. See *supra*, para. 401); and (iii) reports made public by the ICRC, ECMM, and CSCE, as well as open media reports, which were the subject of discussion and negotiation with the RS Presidency and RS Government (Trial Judgement, vol. 2, para. 692. See *supra*, para. 403).
[1396] For instance, this is shown by the fact that, in finding that Stanišić learned of the unlawful detention of Muslims and Croats by the beginning of June 1992 (see Trial Judgement, vol. 2, para. 762), the Trial Chamber did not rely on the Communications Logbook which contained entries with relatively general information, such as "gathering data on camps" and "treatment of war prisoners" (see Trial Judgement, vol. 2, paras 763-765, in comparison with Trial Judgement, vol. 2, para. 690, fn. 1771, referring to, *inter alia*, Exhibit P1428, log 311, p. 44, log 362, p. 53).

Muslims and Croats in the area and at the time relevant to the Indictment, and when he should be considered to have had knowledge of these crimes,[1397] is without merit.

407. Turning to Stanišić's specific challenge to the Trial Chamber's finding that he was "regularly informed throughout 1992 about crimes", the Appeals Chamber notes the Trial Chamber's finding that "*[a]ccording to the communications logbook of the RS MUP headquarters,* Stanišić was regularly informed throughout 1992 about crimes and action being taken to investigate them."[1398] The Communications Logbook referred to by the Trial Chamber is a logbook of dispatches sent and received by the RS MUP headquarters from 22 April 1992 to 2 January 1993.[1399] Thus, it does not cover the period from 1 January to 21 April 1992. In addition, the Appeals Chamber observes that the Communications Logbook suggests that the earliest report referring to crimes in general (without articulating ethnicity of perpetrators or victims) was sent by the RS MUP on 23 April 1992 to, *inter alia*, the RS Government.[1400] The Appeals Chamber therefore finds that, based on the Communications Logbook alone, no reasonable trier of fact could have found that Stanišić was "regularly informed throughout 1992 about crimes".[1401] The impact of **[page 170]** this error on the Trial Chamber's finding regarding Stanišić's knowledge of crimes against Muslims and Croats will be assessed below.[1402]

408. With regard to Stanišić's argument concerning the Trial Chamber's purported reliance on "[d]aily, weekly and quarterly reports" to establish his knowledge of crimes during the Indictment period,[1403] the Appeals Chamber recalls that the Trial Chamber found that such reports were compiled, in addition to security situation reports, on a periodic basis.[1404] It then referred to the testimony of Witness Aleksander Krulj ("Witness Krulj") who stated that these reports were prepared in order for "the Minister" to "know what happened in the territory of the republic".[1405] The Appeals Chamber notes that while the Trial Chamber, in its discussion of these reports, may have placed some reliance on them to the extent Witness Krulj testified they were produced for the purposes of informing Stanišić of what was going on in the RS, it is clear that it was only one of the factors it considered in assessing his knowledge of events on the ground in general. Moreover, the Trial Chamber does not specify the types of crimes, or draw a conclusion as to whether Stanišić had knowledge of crimes through these reports.[1406] Therefore, the Appeals Chamber is of the view that Stanišić misinterprets the scope of this particular finding, and his argument is thus without merit.

409. Finally, with regard to Stanišić's argument that the Trial Chamber failed to consider Witness Radulović's testimony concerning the Miloš Group reports,[1407] the Appeals Chamber first notes that the passages relied on by Stanišić in his appeal brief are specifically referred to by the Trial Chamber in support

---

[1397] See *supra*, para. 391.
[1398] Trial Judgement, vol. 2, para. 690 (emphasis added). See Trial Judgement, vol. 2, para. 690, fn. 1771, referring to multiple entries in Exhibit P1428.
[1399] Exhibit P1428. See Trial Judgement, vol. 2, para. 690, referring to Exhibit P1428.
[1400] See Exhibit P1428, log 3, p. 1, referring to "massacre of Predrag Mocević".
[1401] Trial Judgement, vol. 2, para. 690.
[1402] See *infra*, paras 411-413.
[1403] Stanišić Appeal Brief, paras 120-121. The Appeals Chamber notes that in footnote 1772 of volume two of the Trial Judgement, the Trial Chamber referred to several reports sent by or to the RS MUP, CSBs and SJBs in support of its finding (Trial Judgement, vol. 2, fn. 1172, referring to Exhibits P155, P423.12, p. 3, P427.08, p. 3, P432.12, P595, P663, P748, p. 2, P866, 2D25, 1D334). However, not all of these exhibits refer to crimes (see *e.g.* Exhibits P155, P432.12) or mention that Stanišić was informed of their content (see *e.g.* Exhibits P866, P748). Additionally, some of these reports were relied on by the Trial Chamber to make specific findings on his knowledge of crimes and will be discussed in that context.
[1404] See Trial Judgement, vol. 2, para. 690. See also *supra*, para. 403.
[1405] See Trial Judgement, vol. 2, para. 690.
[1406] The Appeals Chamber notes that some of the information contained in these reports has been relied on by the Trial Chamber to make specific findings on Stanišić's knowledge of specific crimes and are dealt with elsewhere in this Judgement. See *e.g.* Exhibit P427.08, which is a report of the RS MUP to the President of the Presidency and the Prime Minister on 17 July 1992. This report relates to the 11 July 1992 Collegium attended by Stanišić. The Appeals Chamber notes that this exhibit was not specifically referred to by the Trial Chamber when making its findings on Stanišić's knowledge of crimes, however, the information contained in this report was relied on by the Trial Chamber elsewhere (see Trial Judgement, vol. 2, paras 630-631, 765). See also *infra*, paras 484-487. See also Exhibit P633, a dispatch from the chief of the SJB Višegrad, Risto Perišić, to the Ministry of Interior, providing a brief overview of the military and security situation in Višegrad, dated 13 July 1992. According to Risto Perišić, "[w]ith the help of the Red Cross, over 2,000 Muslims moved out the municipality in an organised manner. There is a continued interest in moving out, so that this process should be continued in a coordinated way on some higher level". This information about the Muslims moving out is set out in paragraph 634 of volume two of the Trial Judgement. See also *infra*, paras 491-495.
[1407] See *supra*, para. 391

of its finding that "[w]hile not every report prepared by the 'Miloš Group' intelligence team, headed by Predrag Radulović, was directly submitted to the RS MUP, the **[page 171]** information in these reports was relayed through the leadership of Banja Luka to the upper echelons of decision makers."[1408] Second, the Appeals Chamber considers that Stanišić's submissions, interpreting Witness Radulović's evidence as showing "that Stanišić did not receive reports in 1992",[1409] are not supported by the witness's testimony.[1410] Third, the Trial Chamber referred to a number of transcript pages of the testimony of Witness Radulović, which lasted for more than four days, in addition to the pages referred to by Stanišić.[1411] Stanišić's argument thus amounts to a mere assertion that the Trial Chamber failed to interpret Witness Radulović's evidence in a particular manner and falls short of establishing an error by the Trial Chamber. Stanišić's argument is, therefore, dismissed.

(iii) Conclusion

410. The Appeals Chamber has found that Stanišić has failed to demonstrate that the Trial Chamber erred: (i) in law by applying an incorrect standard when assessing his intent;[1412] (ii) by failing to make conclusive findings as to the extent of his knowledge about the crimes alleged in the Indictment and as of when he should be considered to have had knowledge about these crimes;[1413] (iii) by relying on the "[d]aily, weekly and quarterly reports" as a factor demonstrating his knowledge of crimes during the Indictment period;[1414] and (iv) by failing to consider Witness Radulović's evidence in relation to the Miloš Group reports.[1415]

411. However, the Appeals Chamber has found that the Trial Chamber erred in finding, based on the Communications Logbook, that Stanišić was "regularly informed throughout 1992 about crimes".[1416] Further, the Appeals Chamber recalls its finding, elsewhere, that the Trial Chamber **[page 172]** erred in finding that, on 18 April 1992, Stanišić was informed that a certain "Zoka" had arrested Muslims in Sokolac.[1417] The Appeals Chamber will now assess the impact of these factual errors, if any, on the Trial Chamber's finding concerning Stanišić's knowledge of the commission of crimes against Muslims and Croats.

412. The Appeals Chamber is of the view that, given the limited weight attached to the Communications Logbook in assessing Stanišić's knowledge of crimes committed against Muslims and Croats,[1418] the Trial Chamber's error in relation to this evidence on its own has no impact on the Trial Chamber's findings concerning Stanišić's knowledge of crimes against Muslims and Croats as set out above.[1419] However, given that the Trial Chamber's finding on Stanišić's knowledge of the arrest of Muslims in Sokolac on 18 April

---

[1408] Trial Judgement, vol. 2, para. 689. Stanišić argues that the Trial Chamber failed to consider Witness Radulović's testimony and, in support of his argument, refers to Predrag Radulović, 2 Jun 2010, T. 11205-11209. However, the Trial Chamber explicitly referred to Predrag Radulović, 2 Jun 2010, T. 11206-11209 (Trial Judgement, vol. 2, para. 689, fn. 1769), and the Appeals Chamber notes that T. 11205 (the only transcript page not referred to by the Trial Chamber) does not contain any information relevant to the present issue.

[1409] Stanišić Appeal Brief, para. 122.

[1410] Indeed, Witness Radulović testified about an encounter he had with Stanišić in 2000 when: (i) Stanišić told him that he did not know about "the majority or most of the [crimes against non-Serbs] that [they] talked about" (Predrag Radulović, 2 Jun 2010, T. 11206. See Predrag Radulović, 2 Jun 2010, T. 11207-11208), but that he knew about the "events" in Prijedor, Teslić, and Doboj because they were "well known cases and events which anyone who lived in Republika Srpska could have known about" (Predrag Radulović, 2 Jun 2010, T. 11208); (ii) his "impression" was that Stanišić was insufficiently informed (Predrag Radulović, 2 Jun 2010, T. 11207); and (iii) Witness Radulović's "general understanding" was that Stanišić was not informed "in a timely manner" about the "events" in Prijedor, Teslić, and Doboj (Predrag Radulović, 2 Jun 2010, T. 11208-11209).

[1411] See Trial Judgement, vol. 2, para. 689, fn. 1769. The Appeals Chamber notes that the additional pages referred to by Stanišić during the Appeal Hearing (see Appeal Hearing, 16 Dec 2015, AT. 137, referring to Predrag Radulović, 28 May 2010, T. 11014, Predrag Radulović, 31 May 2010, T. 11073, Predrag Radulović, 1 Jun 2010, T. 11188, Predrag Radulović, 2 Jun 2010, T. 11199) do not present a substantive addition to the submission at hand.

[1412] See *supra*, para. 394.

[1413] See *supra*, para. 406.

[1414] See *supra*, para. 408.

[1415] See *supra*, para. 409.

[1416] Trial Judgement, vol. 2, para. 690. See *supra*, para. 407.

[1417] See *supra*, para. 397; *infra*, para. 665. See also Trial Judgement, vol. 2, para. 612, referring to Exhibit P1115, pp 1-2.

[1418] See *supra*, para. 405.

[1419] See *supra*, para. 404.

1992 has also been overturned, the Appeals Chamber finds that on the basis of the Trial Chamber's remaining findings, a reasonable trier of fact could have found that the earliest time at which he acquired knowledge of crimes committed against Muslims and Croats in the area relevant to the Indictment was late April 1992, when he was informed that reserve police in Vrace were looting Muslim property.[1420]

413.   The Appeals Chamber therefore grants, in part, Stanišić's challenge to the Trial Chamber's finding on his knowledge of crimes committed against Muslims and Croats. The Appeals Chamber will further assess the impact of this finding, if any, on the Trial Chamber's ultimate conclusion on Stanišić's intent in a section below.[1421]

(e) Alleged errors in relying on factors set out in paragraph 767 of volume two of the Trial Judgement in finding that Stanišić had the intent to further the JCE (subsection (C) of Stanišić's fourth ground of appeal)

414.   The Trial Chamber held that:

> [a]side from evidence on Mico Stanišić's knowledge, [...] in assessing Stanišić's alleged *mens rea*, [it] also reviewed evidence on the political stances of the SDS and the BSA in the period preceding the Indictment and Stanišić's conduct and statements in relation to these policies. The Trial Chamber recalls that the views of the Bosnian Serb leadership—that there be an ethnic division of the territory, that 'a war would lead to a forcible and bloody transfer of minorities' from one region to another, and that joint life with Muslims and Croats was impossible—were expressed during the sessions of the BSA of which Stanišić was a member and during the meetings of the SDS in late 1991 and early 1992. The Trial Chamber further recalls that the six strategic objectives, which had been set by, among others, the RS Government, were issued on 12 May 1992 and presented to the BSA. The first goal called for the separation of Serb people **[page 173]** from Muslims and Croats. Stanišić also attended the first meeting of the Council of Ministers of the BSA, where the boundaries of ethnic territory and the establishment of government organs in the territory were determined to be priorities.[1422]

415.   Stanišić advances three groups of arguments challenging these findings. First, he argues that his conduct and statements regarding the political stances of the BSA and SDS do not demonstrate that he possessed the requisite intent.[1423] Second, he submits that the Trial Chamber erroneously relied on the six strategic objectives presented to the session of the BSA on 12 May 1992 ("Strategic Objectives") by incorrectly imputing knowledge of these objectives to him.[1424] Finally, he asserts that no reasonable trial chamber could have found participation in the work of the Council of Ministers as demonstrative of his intent.[1425] These arguments will be discussed in turn below.

(i) Alleged errors in finding that Stanišić's conduct and statements regarding the political stances of the BSA and SDS demonstrate intent to further the JCE

416.   As recalled above, in assessing Stanišić's intent, the Trial Chamber considered, *inter alia*, "Stanišić's conduct and statements in relation to" the policies of the SDS and the BSA in the period preceding the Indictment.[1426] In this context, the Trial Chamber recalled that:

> the views of the Bosnian Serb leadership – that there be an ethnic division of the territory, that 'a war would lead to a forcible and bloody transfer of minorities' from one region to another, and that joint life with Muslims and Croats was impossible – were expressed during the sessions of the BSA of which Stanišić was a member and during the meetings of the SDS in late 1991 and early 1992.[1427]

[1420]   With regard to the information on crimes against Muslims and Croats that Stanišić received after this date, see *supra*, para. 404. See also *supra*, para. 398.

[1421]   See *infra*, paras 573-585.

[1422]   Trial Judgement, vol. 2, para. 767 (citations omitted).

[1423]   Stanišić Appeal Brief, paras 125-132.

[1424]   Stanišić Appeal Brief, paras 133-135.

[1425]   Stanišić Appeal Brief, paras 136-138.

[1426]   Trial Judgement, vol. 2, para. 767.

[1427]   Trial Judgement, vol. 2, para. 767.

a. Alleged error in finding that Stanišić was a member of the BSA

417.   Stanišić submits that the Trial Chamber erred by finding that he was a member of the BSA.[1428] He contends that: (i) he "could not [...] have been a member both of the legislature and the executive"; (ii) the BSA consisted of directly elected representatives; and (iii) it is "patently evident" from the Trial Chamber's findings that he was not an elected representative.[1429] The Prosecution concedes "that there is insufficient evidence to establish Stanišić's membership in the **[page 174]** BSA",[1430] but contends that Stanišić's argument should be summarily dismissed, as he fails to show how this error impacts the Trial Judgement.[1431]

418.   The Appeals Chamber notes that Stanišić has failed to identify any evidence capable of supporting his assertion that he could not have simultaneously occupied roles in the legislative and executive. The Appeals Chamber recalls that mere assertions unsupported by any evidence are generally liable to dismissal.[1432] Nonetheless, considering that the Trial Chamber's only mentioning of Stanišić's membership in the BSA is unreferenced and that there is no finding in the Trial Judgement to substantiate this conclusion, the Appeals Chamber finds that the Trial Chamber erred in fact in finding that Stanišić was a member of the BSA. Since the Trial Chamber relied on this finding in support of its conclusion that Stanišić had the intent to forcibly transfer and deport Bosnian Muslims and Croats from the territories of the BiH, the Appeals Chamber will consider the impact of the Trial Chamber's error, if any, below.[1433]

b. Alleged error concerning the Trial Chamber's reliance upon statements made at meetings of the BSA and SDS

i. Submissions of the parties

419.   Stanišić submits that when assessing his intent the Trial Chamber erred by relying on statements made at meetings of the BSA and SDS.[1434] Stanišić submits that the Trial Chamber erred in relying on a statement by Karadžić at a session of the BSA on 18 March 1992 ("18 March 1992 BSA Session")[1435] "that the occurrence of war would include the 'forcible and bloody transfer of minorities'",[1436] as there is no evidence that Stanišić was present.[1437] He also contends that "there are only two references to [him] in the context of the BSA during the Indictment period": (i) when he was elected as Minister of Interior on 24 March 1992;[1438] and (ii) his participation in the November 1992 BSA Session.[1439] Stanišić argues that the Trial Chamber "improperly and prejudicially" cited his speech to the BSA at the November 1992 BSA Session, mischaracterising **[page 175]** his words as an admission of his involvement in the acceptance of criminal elements into the reserve police, as a result of a translation error.[1440]

420.   With regard to the SDS meetings, Stanišić contends that the Trial Chamber improperly referred to a statement by Todor Dutina ("Dutina"), that "joint life with Muslims and Croats was impossible",[1441] made at

---

[1428]   Stanišić Appeal Brief, paras 125-126. See Stanišić Reply Brief, paras 47-48. See also, Appeal Hearing, 16 Dec 2015, AT. 99.
[1429]   Stanišić Appeal Brief, para. 125, referring to Trial Judgement, vol. 2, para. 165. See Appeal Hearing, 16 Dec 2015, AT. 134-135.
[1430]   Prosecution Response Brief (Stanišić), para. 47, referring to Trial Judgement, vol. 2, para. 767. See Appeal Hearing, 16 Dec 2015, AT. 99.
[1431]   See Prosecution Response Brief (Stanišić), para. 47.
[1432]   *Krajišnik* Appeal Judgement, para. 26 (with references cited therein). See *Stanišić and Simatović* Appeal Judgement, para. 22; *Tolimir* Appeal Judgement, para. 14; *Popović et al.* Appeal Judgement, para. 23.
[1433]   See *infra*, paras 573-585.
[1434]   Stanišić Appeal Brief, paras 127-132; Stanišić Reply Brief, para. 48.
[1435]   Stanišić argues that the Trial Chamber improperly attributed Karadžić's statement to the Bosnian Serb leadership as a whole (Stanišić Appeal Brief, fn. 123). This argument is addressed above in relation to Stanišić's second ground of appeal (see *supra*, paras 83-86).
[1436]   Stanišić Appeal Brief, para. 127, referring to Trial Judgement, vol. 2, para. 767.
[1437]   Stanišić Appeal Brief, para. 127.
[1438]   Stanišić Appeal Brief, para. 128, referring to Trial Judgement, vol. 2, paras 531, 549, 558.
[1439]   Stanišić Appeal Brief, para. 128. He further submits that "[t]he sole other reference is to a session of the BSA in 1993, outside the Indictment period" (Stanišić Appeal Brief, para. 128, referring to Trial Judgement, vol. 2, para. 596).
[1440]   Stanišić Appeal Brief, para. 129, referring to Hearing, 5 May 2010, T. 9566.
[1441]   Stanišić Appeal Brief, para. 131 (emphasis omitted).

a meeting of the SDS held on 15 October 1991 ("15 October 1991 SDS Meeting"),[1442] as he was neither present at this meeting nor a member of the SDS.[1443]

421.   The Prosecution responds that in concluding that Stanišić was aware of the view that ethnic separation would be achieved through violence, the Trial Chamber appropriately relied on his close relationship with Karadžić and high-level position within the RS leadership.[1444] It submits that the Trial Chamber's conclusion "did not turn on" evidence of Stanišić's physical presence at specific meetings.[1445] According to the Prosecution, Stanišić attempts to undermine the Trial Chamber's finding "by denying an association with the SDS".[1446] The Prosecution also submits that Stanišić "wrongly asserts" that the Trial Chamber "improperly and prejudicially" cited his speech at the November 1992 BSA Session.[1447]

ii. Analysis

422.   As stated above, in assessing Stanišić's intent, the Trial Chamber considered "Stanišić's conduct and statements" in relation to the "political stances of the SDS and the BSA".[1448] In this context, the Trial Chamber referred to the "views of the Bosnian Serb leadership [...] expressed during the sessions of the BSA [...] and during the meetings of the SDS in late 1991 and early 1992".[1449] More specifically, the Trial Chamber recalled the views of the Bosnian Serb leadership "that there be an ethnic division of the territory, that 'a war would lead to a forcible and bloody transfer of minorities' from one region to another, and that joint life with Muslims and Croats was impossible".[1450] **[page 176]**

423.   The Appeals Chamber notes that although the Trial Chamber did not include any citations to evidence or cross-references to findings elsewhere,[1451] through a careful reading of the Trial Judgement as a whole, it is nonetheless able to identify several findings substantiating the Trial Chamber's conclusion regarding the views of the Bosnian Serb leadership expressed in sessions of the BSA and meetings of the SDS in late 1991 and early 1992. Specifically, elsewhere in the Trial Judgement, the Trial Chamber considered statements of: (i) Karadžić, at the 18 March 1992 BSA Session, that any war would lead to an ethnic division and "include the forcible and bloody transfer of minorities from one region to another and the creation of three ethnically homogenous regions within BiH";[1452] (ii) Dutina, at the 15 October 1991 SDS Meeting, that "an end must be put to the illusion that a joint existence with Muslims and Croats was possible";[1453] and (iii) Vojislav Kuprešanin ("Kuprešanin"), at the 25 February 1992 session of the BSA ("25 February 1992 BSA Session"), that "I am against any kind of joint institution with the Muslims and Croats of BiH. I personally consider them to be our natural enemies. You already know what natural enemies are, and that we can never again live together. We can never again do anything together."[1454] Accordingly, the Appeals Chamber considers that it is these statements of Karadžić, Dutina, and Kuprešanin that the Trial Chamber referred to as the views

---

[1442]   Stanišić Appeal Brief, para. 131, referring to Trial Judgement, vol. 2, para. 162.

[1443]   Stanišić Appeal Brief, para. 131, referring to Trial Judgement, vol. 2, para. 162, Exhibit P14. See Stanišić Reply Brief, para. 49, referring to Prosecution Response Brief (Stanišić), para. 46. See also Stanišić Appeal Brief, para. 132.

[1444]   Prosecution Response Brief (Stanišić), para. 46, referring to Trial Judgement, vol. 2, paras 156-157, 161-162, 167-170, 174, 178-179, 188, 199, 769.

[1445]   Prosecution Response Brief (Stanišić), para. 46, referring to Stanišić Appeal Brief, paras 127-128, 130-132.

[1446]   Prosecution Response Brief (Stanišić), para. 46, referring to Stanišić Appeal Brief, para. 131.

[1447]   Prosecution Response Brief (Stanišić), fn. 107, referring to Stanišić Appeal Brief, para. 129.

[1448]   Trial Judgement, vol. 2, para. 767.

[1449]   Trial Judgement, vol. 2, para. 767.

[1450]   See Trial Judgement, vol. 2, para. 767.

[1451]   *Cf. supra*, paras 377-380.

[1452]   Trial Judgement, vol. 2, para. 179, referring to Exhibits P397.02, pp 10554-10555, P707, p. 4. *Cf.* Stanišić Appeal Brief, para. 127. The Trial Chamber also considered evidence that Karadžić was the President of the SDS, President of the RS Presidency, and President of the NSC, (Trial Judgement, vol. 2, para. 132, referring to Branko Đerić, 29 Oct 2009, T. 2279, Christian Nielsen, 14 Dec 2009, T. 4708, Momčilo Mandić, 3 May 2010, T. 9432, 9442, Exhibits P257, L327) and was a member of the JCE (Trial Judgement, vol. 2, para. 314).

[1453]   Trial Judgement, vol. 2, para. 162, referring to Exhibit P14, p. 1. *Cf.* Stanišić Appeal Brief, paras 131-132. The Trial Chamber also considered evidence that Dutina was present at the 15 October 1991 SDS Meeting and later became the Director of the Serbian News Agency, SRNA (Trial Judgement, vol. 2, para. 162, referring to Exhibits P14, p. 1, P204, pp 1-2).

[1454]   Trial Judgement, vol. 2, para. 174, quoting Momčilo Mandić, 3 May 2010, T. 9443, Exhibit P427.09, p. 59. The Trial Chamber also considered evidence that Kuprešanin attended various sessions of the BSA (Trial Judgement, vol. 2, paras 174, 224), was President of the ARK Assembly and a prominent member of the SDS (Trial Judgement, vol. 2, para. 350, referring to Exhibit

expressed during the 15 October 1991 SDS Meeting, the 25 February 1992 BSA Session, or the 18 March 1992 BSA Session (collectively, "BSA and SDS Meetings") when assessing Stanišić's intent.[1455]

424.   In this regard, the Appeals Chamber notes that, as rightly pointed out by Stanišić, at no point in the Trial Judgement did the Trial Chamber make any findings on, or refer to evidence of, Stanišić's physical presence at the abovementioned BSA and SDS Meetings, or his awareness of their content. In addition, the Trial Chamber cited no evidence that Stanišić was aware of these particular statements. However, a plain reading of the Trial Judgement indicates that the Trial **[page 177]** Chamber merely referred to these statements as contextual evidence demonstrating the "political stances" or "policies" of the BSA and the SDS, when it examined "Stanišić's conduct and statements in relation to these policies".[1456]

425.   In this respect, the Appeals Chamber recalls that it has found that the Trial Chamber erred in finding that Stanišić was a member of the BSA.[1457] However, the Trial Chamber also noted the evidence that: (i) at the 24 March 1992 BSA Session, Stanišić was elected the first Minister of Interior of the RS Government and remarked that "the SRBiH MUP had been used as an instrument of the SDA and the HDZ for achieving their political goals, including the creation of an army from the reserve forces comprised of only one ethnicity and the dismissal of Serbs from their positions"[1458] and that he hoped that "in the future, the Serbian MUP [would] become a professional organisation, an organ of state administration which [would] actually protect property, life, body and other values";[1459] and (ii) at the November 1992 BSA Session, Stanišić "acknowledged in his speech to the BSA that 'in the beginning', 'thieves and criminals' were accepted into the reserve police forces because 'we wanted the country defended'",[1460] and stated, "I as a man have followed policies of the SDS Presidency and our Deputies in the former state, I have always followed these policies."[1461]

426.   With regard to his conduct in relation to the political stances of the SDS, the Trial Chamber further found that Stanišić was involved in the establishment of the SDS, displayed discontentment with the representation of Serbs within the SRBiH MUP, and attempted to intervene to retain and recruit Serbs within the SRBiH MUP.[1462] The Trial Chamber also found that Stanišić worked to promote the interests, and implement the decisions, of the SDS in the SRBiH MUP and was involved in all the stages of the creation of the Bosnian Serb institutions in BiH, in particular the RS MUP.[1463]

427.   As contextual information relevant to Stanišić's conduct and statements as described above, when assessing his intent, the Trial Chamber was entitled to rely on the statements of Karadžić, Dutina, and Kurešanin at the BSA and SDS Meetings, which are indicative of the policies adopted by the BSA and the SDS. The Appeals Chamber therefore discerns no error. **[page 178]**

428.   Regarding Stanišić's argument that the Trial Chamber mischaracterised his speech at the November 1992 BSA Session,[1464] the Appeals Chamber first recalls the Trial Chamber's finding on the basis of, *inter alia*, Exhibit P400, that in this speech, Stanišić "acknowledged that 'in the beginning', 'thieves and criminals' were accepted into the reserve police forces because 'we wanted the country defended'".[1465] The Appeals Chamber further notes that at trial, Stanišić raised the issue of a translation error in Exhibit P400 which, in his submission, had the effect of implying that Stanišić had personal involvement in the acceptance of thieves

---

P1098.03 (confidential), p. 4051, ST174, 23 Mar 2010, T. 8087 (closed session)), and was a member of the JCE (Trial Judgement, vol. 2, para. 314).

[1455]   While the Trial Chamber did not make any express findings at to whether Karadžić, Dutina, and/or Kurešanin were members of the Bosnian Serb leadership, it found that the Bosnian Serb leadership "consisted of leading members of the SDS and those who occupied important posts in the RS" (Trial Judgement, vol. 2, para. 131, referring to Adjudicated Facts Decision, Adjudicated Fact 109).

[1456]   Trial Judgement, vol. 2, para. 767.

[1457]   See *supra*, para. 418.

[1458]   Trial Judgement, vol. 2, para. 558. See Trial Judgement, vol. 2, para. 542.

[1459]   Trial Judgement, vol. 2, para. 558, referring to Exhibit P198, pp 7-8.

[1460]   Trial Judgement, vol. 2, para. 600, also quoting Stanišić's further statement that "[o]ur priority, our intentions were good and maybe that is where we went wrong, maybe that is where I went wrong, agreed."

[1461]   Trial Judgement, vol. 2, para. 570.

[1462]   Trial Judgement, vol. 2, para. 729.

[1463]   Trial Judgement, vol. 2, para. 734.

[1464]   Stanišić Appeal Brief, para. 129.

[1465]   Trial Judgement, vol. 2, para. 600, referring to, *inter alia*, Exhibit P400, p. 17.

and criminals into the reserve police, where he was in fact speaking in general terms.[1466] It is, however, clear that the corrected English translation of Exhibit P400 on the trial record does not contain the error raised in Stanišić's objection, as this exhibit quotes Stanišić as stating that "there were reserves in the police, we wanted the country defended, so *they* took on thieves and criminals".[1467] The Appeals Chamber further notes that nowhere in the Trial Judgement did the Trial Chamber refer to any alternate wording of Exhibit P400 from before the correction was made to the English translation of Exhibit P400.[1468] Stanišić has therefore failed to demonstrate that the Trial Chamber erred in its assessment of his speech to the BSA.

429.   In light of the above, the Appeals Chamber finds that Stanišić has failed to show that the Trial Chamber erred in relying upon statements made at meetings of the BSA and SDS, among other factors, when assessing his intent.

(ii) Alleged error concerning the Trial Chamber's reliance upon the Strategic Objectives

430.   In assessing Stanišić's intent, the Trial Chamber recalled that the Strategic Objectives, which had been set by the RS Government, among others, were issued on 12 May 1992 and presented to the BSA.[1469] It also noted that the first goal of the Strategic Objectives called for the separation of Serb people from Muslims and Croats.[1470] Among other factors, the Trial Chamber relied on Stanišić's continued support of and participation in the implementation of policies of the Bosnian Serb leadership and the SDS, including the Strategic Objectives, in inferring that he was aware of and shared the persecutory intentions of the Bosnian Serb leadership.[1471] **[page 179]**

a. Submissions of the parties

431.   Stanišić submits that the Trial Chamber erred by relying on the Strategic Objectives in the assessment of his intent.[1472] He argues that: (i) there is no evidence of his attendance at, or knowledge of a session of the BSA held on 12 May 1992 ("12 May 1992 BSA Session"),[1473] or a meeting prior to the 12 May 1992 BSA Session at which the Strategic Objectives were discussed by, *inter alios*, Mladić, Krajišnik, and Karadžić;[1474] (ii) the Strategic Objectives were not published until 26 November 1993;[1475] and (iii) the Trial Chamber erred by relying on Karadžić's speech rather than on the minutes of RS Government sessions, to find that the Strategic Objectives were set by, among others, the RS Government.[1476]

432.   The Prosecution responds that Stanišić fails to show that no reasonable trier of fact could have found that he was aware of the Strategic Objectives given Karadžić's statement at the 12 May 1992 BSA Session.[1477] It submits that Stanišić merely seeks to supplant his evaluation of the evidence for that of the Trial Chamber and that his argument should be summarily dismissed.[1478]

b. Analysis

433.   The Appeals Chamber observes that despite the deficiencies discussed above in relation to the lack of citations or cross-references to findings when referring to the Strategic Objectives in the *Mens Rea*

[1466]   Stanišić argued that "instead of putting it in the first -- in the -- first person like it is in the translation, it should be -it should be '*they*'" (Hearing, 5 May 2010, T. 9566 (emphasis added). See Hearing, 4 May 2010, T. 9560-9563).
[1467]   Exhibit P400, p. 17 (emphasis added).
[1468]   See Trial Judgement, vol. 2, paras 600, 743. See also Hearing, 4 May 2010, T. 9560-9563; Hearing, 5 May 2010, T. 9566.
[1469]   Trial Judgement, vol. 2, para. 767.
[1470]   Trial Judgement, vol. 2, para. 767, referring to "JCE section".
[1471]   Trial Judgement, vol. 2, paras 767, 769.
[1472]   Stanišić Appeal Brief, para. 135.
[1473]   Stanišić Appeal Brief, para. 133, referring to Trial Judgement, vol. 2, paras 190, 767, Exhibits P2304, p. 42, P2310, p. 30, P2311, p. 10.
[1474]   Stanišić Appeal Brief, para. 133, referring to Trial Judgement, vol. 2, para. 189.
[1475]   Stanišić Appeal Brief, para. 133, referring to Trial Judgement, vol. 2, para. 189.
[1476]   Stanišić Appeal Brief, para. 134, referring to Trial Judgement, vol. 2, para. 767.
[1477]   Prosecution Response Brief (Stanišić), para. 48.
[1478]   Prosecution Response Brief (Stanišić), para. 48.

Section,[1479] reading the Trial Judgement as a whole reveals that the Trial Chamber entered several relevant findings in this regard. In particular, it discussed the nature of the Strategic Objectives, their formation, and implementation, including establishing who was involved in drawing-up the Strategic Objectives, and as of when.[1480] Specifically, the Trial Chamber found that: (i) Krajišnik issued the Strategic Objectives at the 12 May 1992 BSA Session and specified their contents;[1481] (ii) the goals had already been discussed on 7 May 1992, at a meeting attended by, among others, Mladić, Krajišnik, and Karadžić;[1482] (iii) Krajišnik wanted to make the Strategic Objectives public immediately, "while Karadžić and others felt that they gave away too much of the **[page 180]** actual intent of the Bosnian Serb leadership";[1483] (iv) the War Presidency of the RS adopted the decision to publish the Strategic Objectives and a corresponding map of RS on 9 June 1992;[1484] and (v) the Strategic Objectives were published on 26 November 1993.[1485] The Appeals Chamber notes that the Trial Chamber also held that at the 12 May 1992 BSA Session, Karadžić stated that the goals were set by the Bosnian Serb Presidency, Government, and the NSC.[1486]

434. Insofar as Stanišić argues that the Trial Chamber erroneously found that he knew of the Strategic Objectives on the basis of the 12 May 1992 BSA Session or the 7 May 1992 meeting of, among others, Mladić, Krajišnik, and Karadžić,[1487] he misconstrues the Trial Judgement. The Trial Chamber did not make a finding on whether Stanišić became aware of the Strategic Objectives through this BSA session or this meeting. Rather, in assessing his intent, the Trial Chamber took into account, *inter alia*, Stanišić's continued support of and participation in the implementation of policies of the Bosnian Serb leadership and the SDS and considered the Strategic Objectives as part of these policies.[1488] In this context, the Trial Chamber found that Stanišić was a member of the RS Government and participated in meetings of the NSC,[1489] and that the Strategic Objectives were set by, among others, the RS Government.[1490] In these circumstances, the Appeals Chamber discerns no error in the Trial Chamber's consideration of the Strategic Objectives when assessing Stanišić's intent.[1491]

435. Turning to Stanišić's argument that the Trial Chamber erroneously found that the Strategic Objectives were set by, *inter alia*, the RS Government on the basis of Karadžić's speech at the 12 May 1992 BSA Session rather than on the minutes of RS Government sessions,[1492] the Appeals Chamber observes that Stanišić makes a general unreferenced assertion that "the minutes of the 1992 RS government sessions, which are all in the trial record" do not refer to any discussion on the **[page 181]** Strategic Objectives.[1493] Accordingly, Stanišić has failed to provide the Appeals Chamber with guidance as to the veracity of this undeveloped submission. Moreover, it was not only on Karadžić's speech at the 12 May 1992 BSA that the Trial Chamber relied to reach its conclusion that the Strategic Objectives were set by, *inter alia*, the RS Government. It also

---

[1479]   *Cf. supra*, paras 377-380.

[1480]   See generally, Trial Judgement, vol. 2, paras 188-199.

[1481]   Trial Judgement, vol. 2, paras 188, 190.

[1482]   Trial Judgement, vol. 2, para. 189, referring to Exhibit P1753, pp 262-263.

[1483]   Trial Judgement, vol. 2, para. 189, referring to Robert Donia, 16 Sep 2009, T. 412-413.

[1484]   Trial Judgement, vol. 2, para. 189, referring to Exhibit P260.

[1485]   Trial Judgement, vol. 2, para. 189, referring to Exhibit P24.

[1486]   Trial Judgement, vol. 2, para. 190.

[1487]   Stanišić Appeal Brief, para. 133.

[1488]   Trial Judgement, vol. 2, paras 767, 769.

[1489]   See Trial Judgement, vol. 2, paras 20, 572-575. The Trial Chamber found that, on 24 March 1992, Stanišić was elected the first Minister of Interior and officially appointed to the position on 31 March 1992 (Trial Judgement, vol. 2, para. 542, referring to Branko Đerić, 29 Oct 2009, T. 2281-2282, Christian Nielsen, 16 Dec 2009, T. 4890, Exhibits P198, pp 6-9, P353, P508, para. 83, P2301, pp 30-35, P2307, pp 9-11, 15. See Trial Judgement, vol. 2, para. 558) and considered that he was a member of the RS Government by virtue of his position as Minister of Interior (see Trial Judgement, vol. 2, paras 20, 558). The Trial Chamber also found that: (i) Stanišić attended a majority of the RS Government sessions; (ii) on the occasions that Stanišić did not attend RS Government sessions, Petar Bujičić or Tomislav Kovač attended as his delegated representative (Trial Judgement, vol. 2, para. 572); and (iii) Stanišić participated in joint meetings of the RS Government and NSC from April through May 1992 (Trial Judgement, vol. 2, para. 573. See Trial Judgement, vol. 2, paras 574-575). The Appeals Chamber recalls that it has found that the Trial Chamber erred in fact by finding that Stanišić was a member of the BSA (see *supra*, para. 418).

[1490]   Trial Judgement, vol. 2, para. 767.

[1491]   See Trial Judgement, vol. 2, paras 767, 769 (referring to, *inter alia*, the Strategic Objectives and Stanišić's position during the Indictment period).

[1492]   Stanišić Appeal Brief, para. 134.

[1493]   See Stanišić Appeal Brief, para. 134.

considered other evidence, as set out above.[1494] The Appeals Chamber recalls that the task of assessing and weighing the evidence presented at trial is left primarily to trial chambers and only where the evidence relied on by the trial chamber could not have been accepted by any reasonable tribunal of fact or where the evaluation of the evidence is "wholly erroneous" may the Appeals Chamber substitute its own finding for that of the trial chamber.[1495] Consequently, Stanišić has failed to show that the Trial Chamber erred in its reliance on Karadžić's speech at the 12 May 1992 BSA, among other evidence, in determining who set the Strategic Objectives.

436. In light of the above, the Appeals Chamber finds that Stanišić has not demonstrated that the Trial Chamber erred by relying on the Strategic Objectives, among other factors, when assessing his intent. Stanišić's arguments in this respect are therefore dismissed.

(iii) Alleged error concerning the Trial Chamber's reliance upon Stanišić's participation in the work of the Council of Ministers

437. In assessing Stanišić's intent the Trial Chamber relied on, *inter alia*, his attendance at "the first meeting of the Council of Ministers of the BSA, where the boundaries of ethnic territory and the establishment of government organs in the territory were determined to be priorities", and his conduct in relation to this policy.[1496]

a. Submissions of the parties

438. Stanišić submits that the Trial Chamber erred in relying on his participation at the first meeting of the Council of Ministers of the BSA on 11 January 1992 ("1st Council Meeting") in assessing his intent.[1497] He asserts that "presence at a meeting is not indicative of intent to commit persecutory crimes"[1498] and that the legitimate priorities propagated thereat (including the "defining of ethnic territory" and formation of government organs) do not demonstrate an intent to commit **[page 182]** crimes.[1499] He submits that the Trial Chamber "failed to refer to Stanišić's evidence that he viewed the creation of the Council of Ministers as a centrally organized authority for the RS by the Serbs as fulfilling the conditions for the Cutileiro plan to deal with the problem in BiH".[1500] Finally, Stanišić contends that the Trial Chamber failed to refer to evidence that he refused to take part in or contribute to work of the Council of Ministers because it was incompatible with his work as Secretary of the Sarajevo SUP.[1501]

439. The Prosecution responds that the Trial Chamber reasonably relied on the 1st Council Meeting when inferring Stanišić's intent.[1502] It contends that Stanišić fails to show that no reasonable trier of fact could have found that Stanišić's efforts to promote the demarcation of ethnic Serb territory "were connected to the ethnic cleansing campaign which the Bosnian Serbs unleashed in the spring of 1992".[1503] The Prosecution submits that, contrary to Stanišić's submission, the Trial Chamber considered evidence concerning Stanišić's view of the creation of the Council of Ministers, his presence at the 1st Council Meeting, as well as his emphatic support for the priorities set thereat.[1504] It recalls that subsequently, at the 11 February 1992 Meeting involving Serb employees of the SRBiH MUP, Stanišić provided active support to these priorities.[1505]

[1494]   Trial Judgement, vol. 2, paras 188-199.
[1495]   See *supra*, para. 21.
[1496]   Trial Judgement, vol. 2, para. 767.
[1497]   Stanišić Appeal Brief, para. 136.
[1498]   Stanišić Appeal Brief, para. 138, referring to *Stanišić and Simatović* Trial Judgement, paras 2312, 2315, 2340, 2354, *Perišić* Trial Judgement, Dissenting Opinion of Judge Moloto on Counts 1 to 4 and 9 to 12, paras 61-75.
[1499]   Stanišić Appeal Brief, para. 138. See Stanišić Appeal Brief, para. 136.
[1500]   Stanišić Appeal Brief, para. 137, referring to Exhibit P2301, pp 5-6.
[1501]   Stanišić Appeal Brief, para. 137, referring to Exhibit P2301, pp 17-20.
[1502]   Prosecution Response Brief (Stanišić), para. 42, referring to Trial Judgement, vol. 2, paras 549, 551, 554-556, 767.
[1503]   Prosecution Response Brief (Stanišić), para. 43, referring to Trial Judgement, vol. 2, paras 308-313.
[1504]   Prosecution Response Brief (Stanišić), para. 44, referring to Trial Judgement, vol. 2, para. 563. See Prosecution Response Brief (Stanišić), para. 45. The Prosecution contends that "[t]his finding is consistent with the [Trial] Chamber's determination that the effort to demarcate ethnic Serb territory was a component of the common criminal purpose" (Prosecution Response Brief (Stanišić), para. 44, referring to Trial Judgement, vol. 2, paras 308-313).
[1505]   Prosecution Response Brief (Stanišić), para. 45, referring to Trial Judgement, vol. 2, paras 554-555.

The Prosecution argues that the minutes of this meeting belie Stanišić's statements in his Interview that he refused to take part in or contribute to the work of the Council of Ministers, statements which the Trial Chamber considered and appropriately rejected.[1506]

b. Analysis

440. Although the Trial Chamber provided no cross-references or citations to evidence on the record when relying upon Stanišić's attendance at the 1st Council Meeting in the *Mens Rea* Section,[1507] reading the Trial Judgement as a whole reveals several relevant findings in this respect. Specifically, the Trial Chamber found that on 11 January 1992, Stanišić attended the 1st Council Meeting, where it was decided that the "'defining of ethnic territory' and the 'establishment of government organs in the territory' were priorities emanating from the Declaration of the RS on **[page 183]** 9 January".[1508] The Trial Chamber found further that at this meeting, Stanišić was appointed to a working group to deal with issues regarding the organisation and scope of national security and was given responsibility for the work of this group. The Trial Chamber also found that during their first two meetings, the members of the Council of Ministers of the BSA decided to establish new ethnically divided government organs.[1509]

441. Insofar as Stanišić argues that the Trial Chamber erred in law as "presence at a meeting is not indicative of intent to commit persecutory crimes", the Appeals Chamber notes that he seeks to rely on the *Stanišić and Simatović* Trial Judgement and Judge Bakone Justice Moloto's dissenting opinion in the *Perišić* case, where the accused's attendance at meetings was found not to be indicative of intent. In the view of the Appeals Chamber, however, Stanišić's reliance upon these authorities is misplaced as they do not give rise to any principle of law that "[p]resence at a meeting is not indicative of intent to commit persecutory crimes."[1510] To the contrary, the determinations made by the *Stanišić and Simatović* Trial Chamber and Judge Moloto in his dissenting opinion in the *Perišić* case turn upon the factual considerations unique to those cases.[1511]

442. With respect to Stanišić's argument that the priorities propagated at the 1st Council Meeting were legitimate, the Appeals Chamber recalls that contribution to a joint criminal enterprise need not be in and of itself criminal,[1512] and that the requisite intent for a conviction under joint criminal enterprise can be inferred from circumstantial evidence.[1513] The Trial Chamber therefore did not err in law in relying on Stanišić's participation in the 1st Council Meeting in its assessment of his intent.

443. As far as Stanišić argues that the Trial Chamber erred in fact in its assessment of the 1st Council Meeting, the Appeals Chamber considers that the Trial Chamber's findings regarding the 1st Council Meeting should be viewed in the context of its findings concerning the formation of the plan to establish a Serb state as ethnically "pure" as possible.[1514] The Appeals Chamber notes in this respect the Trial Chamber's findings that following the declaration of independence in the BiH Assembly on 15 October 1991, "the SDS and the Bosnian Serb leadership intensified the process of territorial demarcation, an important part of which was the forceful assumption of control over **[page 184]** territories".[1515] According to the Trial Chamber's conclusions, even prior to the negotiations in Lisbon in February 1992 regarding the Cutileiro Plan, "Serbs had already coalesced around the idea of a separate Serb entity carved out of the territory of the SRBiH" and this agenda came to coincide with the proposals discussed at the Lisbon negotiations.[1516] The Trial Chamber

---

[1506] Prosecution Response Brief (Stanišić), para. 45.
[1507] *Cf. supra*, paras 377-380.
[1508] Trial Judgement, vol. 2, para. 551.
[1509] Trial Judgement, vol. 2, para. 551.
[1510] See Stanišić Appeal Brief, para. 138.
[1511] See *Stanišić and Simatović* Trial Judgement, paras 2312, 2315, 2340, 2354; *Perišić* Trial Judgement, Dissenting Opinion of Judge Moloto on Counts 1 to 4 and 9 to 12, paras 61-75.
[1512] *Popović et al.* Appeal Judgement, para. 1653; *Šainović et al.* Appeal Judgement, para. 985; *Krajišnik* Appeal Judgement, para. 215, 695-696. See *Šainović et al.* Appeal Judgement, paras 1233, 1242. See *supra*, para. 110.
[1513] See *Popović et al.* Appeal Judgement, para. 1369; *Šainović et al.* Appeal Judgement, para. 995; *Krajišnik* Appeal Judgement, para. 202.
[1514] Trial Judgement, vol. 2, para. 311.
[1515] Trial Judgement, vol. 2, para. 310.
[1516] Trial Judgement, vol. 2, para. 563.

found that Bosnian Serb control over the territories was achieved "through the setting up of separate and parallel Bosnian Serb institutions" including eventually, the RS and its separate government.[1517] It also considered that the Bosnian Serb leadership initiated a "process of establishing Serb municipalities" through the Variant A and B Instructions, which led to the violent takeovers of the Municipalities.[1518]

444. Moreover, the Appeals Chamber notes that contrary to Stanišić's submissions, the Trial Chamber expressly referred to his evidence that "he refused to take part in or contribute to the work of the Council [...] because it was incompatible with his work as a Secretary of the Sarajevo SUP".[1519] At the same time, however, the Trial Chamber referred to evidence that Stanišić worked to promote the priorities set at the 1st Council Meeting.[1520] His argument that the Trial Chamber disregarded his evidence is therefore without merit.

445. The Trial Chamber found that the establishment of Bosnian Serb bodies, policies, and parallel institutions,[1521] the creation of a separate Serb entity within BiH,[1522] and the implementation of the Variant A and B Instructions,[1523] were all actions that preceded the violent takeovers of the Municipalities,[1524] to which Stanišić contributed.[1525] Moreover, these actions were undertaken at a time that the Bosnian Serb leadership espoused inflammatory and ethnically charged views about **[page 185]** the future of the BiH,[1526] which the Trial Chamber considered as evidence that the goal of the violent takeover of the Municipalities was to establish an ethnically "pure" Serb state through the permanent removal of Bosnian Muslims and Bosnian Croats.[1527]

446. Taking stock of these findings, the Appeals Chamber therefore considers that even though there was nothing criminal, *per se*, in either the conclusions reached at the 1st Council Meeting or Stanišić's subsequent promotion of the priorities spelled out thereat, Stanišić has failed to demonstrate that the Trial Chamber erred in fact in relying on his participation in the 1st Council Meeting and his conduct in relation to the policy determined thereat in its assessment of his intent.

(iv) Conclusion

447. In light of the above, the Appeals Chamber finds that the Trial Chamber erred in fact by relying upon Stanišić's membership in the BSA when assessing his intent. The Appeals Chamber will discuss the potential impact of this error below.[1528] The Appeals Chamber further finds that Stanišić has failed to show that the Trial Chamber erred in relying upon the following factors when assessing his intent: (i) statements made at meetings of the BSA and SDS; (ii) the Strategic Objectives; and (iii) his participation in the 1st Council Meeting and his conduct in relation to the policy determined thereat. Therefore, it dismisses the remainder of Stanišić's arguments with respect to paragraph 767 of volume two of the Trial Judgement.

[1517] Trial Judgement, vol. 2, para. 310.
[1518] Trial Judgement, vol. 2, para. 310. See Trial Judgement, vol. 2, para. 311.
[1519] Trial Judgement, vol. 2, para. 551, referring to Exhibit P2301, pp 17-20.
[1520] See generally, Trial Judgement, vol. 2, paras 554-556. In particular, the Trial Chamber considered Stanišić's attendance, in his capacity as a member of the Council of Ministers, at a meeting of Serbs working in the SRBiH MUP in Banja Luka on 11 February 1992, during the negotiations of the Cutileiro Plan (see Trial Judgement, vol. 2, paras 554-555). Specifically, the Trial Chamber referred to the minutes of this meeting, at which Stanišić stated:

> '[t]he position of the Council of Ministers at the last session was that the territories in [SRBiH] which are under Serbian control, that control must be felt'; that the joint MUP was 'being divided by the Muslims'; and that Serbian personnel in the MUP 'must provide the means to strengthen and supply the Serbian MUP, ensuring that resources will be distributed equally' (Trial Judgement, vol. 2, para. 555, referring to Exhibit 1D135, p. 1).

The Appeals Chamber further notes that the Trial Chamber expressly considered and rejected Stanišić's challenge as to the reliability of the minutes of this 11 February 1992 Meeting (Trial Judgement, vol. 2, para. 555).
[1521] See Trial Judgement, vol. 2, paras 151-206.
[1522] See Trial Judgement vol. 2, paras 207-226.
[1523] See Trial Judgement, vol. 2, paras 227-244. See also Trial Judgement, vol. 2, paras 245-262.
[1524] Trial Judgement, vol. 2, paras 309-311. See Trial Judgement, vol. 2, paras 281-298.
[1525] With respect to Stanišić's participation in the JCE, see generally, Trial Judgement, vol. 2, paras 544-765.
[1526] See Trial Judgement, vol. 2, para. 311. See also Trial Judgement, vol. 2, paras 156-157, 159, 161-162, 167-170, 172, 174, 176, 178-181, 184, 194-195, 199, 201-202, 208, 215, 241.
[1527] See Trial Judgement, vol. 2, para. 311.
[1528] See *infra*, paras 573-585.

(f) Alleged errors in relying on the factors set out in paragraph 768 of volume two of the Trial Judgement in finding that Stanišić had the intent to further the JCE (subsection (D) of Stanišić's fourth ground of appeal)

448. In assessing Stanišić's intent, the Trial Chamber further stated that:

> [it] has considered the evidence that Stanišić, albeit opposed to the presence of some paramilitary groups in BiH, approved of the operation of Arkan's Men in Bijeljina and Zvornik and allowed Arkan to remove whatever property in exchange for "liberating" the territories. Moreover, Stanišić was present at sessions of the RS Government where the RS MUP was tasked with gathering information about Muslims moving out of the RS and the needs of refugees and displaced persons. He was also present at the 11 July Collegium meeting, where the relocation of citizens and entire villages was discussed. Finally, on 13 July 1992, the Višegrad SJB Chief Risto Perišić reported to the RS MUP that certain police officers were exhibiting a lack of professionalism while over 2,000 Muslims moved out of the municipality in an organised manner.[1529]

[page 186]

449. Stanišić challenges the Trial Chamber's reliance on the factors referred to in this paragraph of the Trial Judgement in assessing his intent.[1530] He argues that no reasonable trial chamber could have found that he approved of Arkan's operations.[1531] Stanišić also argues that the Trial Chamber erred by relying upon: (i) his presence at the 36th and 42nd sessions of the RS Government held on 4 and 29 July 1992 ("4 July 1992 Session" and "29 July 1992 Session", respectively; "July 1992 Sessions", collectively);[1532] (ii) his presence at the meeting of senior officials of the RS MUP on 11 July 1992;[1533] and (iii) the report by the Chief of the Višegrad SJB, Risto Perišić, dated 13 July 1992 ("Perišić Report").[1534]

(i) Alleged error in finding that Stanišić approved of Arkan's operations in the municipalities of Bijeljina and Zvornik

450. As noted above, in assessing Stanišić's intent, the Trial Chamber considered "the evidence that Stanišić, albeit opposed to the presence of some paramilitary groups in BiH, approved of the operation of Arkan's Men in Bijeljina and Zvornik and allowed Arkan to remove whatever property in exchange for 'liberating' the territories".[1535]

a. Submissions of the parties

451. Stanišić submits that the Trial Chamber erred by finding that he approved of "Arkan's operations in Bijeljina and Zvornik and allowed Arkan to remove any property [...] he wished".[1536] He contends that the Trial Chamber erred by relying on Witness Davidović's testimony in *Krajišnik* as the sole basis for this finding and in ultimately concluding that he intended to commit persecutory crimes.[1537]

452. Stanišić submits that the Trial Chamber "ignored" Witness Davidović's *viva voce* testimony in the present case showing that his statement about Stanišić making a "deal" with Arkan is unreliable and uncorroborated hearsay.[1538] Stanišić points out that Witness Davidović's testimony **[page 187]** in the present case that he heard about the "deal" between Stanišić and Arkan from Mladić is directly contradicted both by his testimony in *Krajišnik* and his witness statement.[1539]

[1529] Trial Judgement, vol. 2, para. 768.
[1530] See Stanišić Appeal Brief, paras 139-155.
[1531] Stanišić Appeal Brief, paras 139-146.
[1532] Stanišić Appeal Brief, paras 147-149.
[1533] Stanišić Appeal Brief, paras 150-152.
[1534] Stanišić Appeal Brief, paras 153-155.
[1535] Trial Judgement, vol. 2, para. 768. See Trial Judgement, vol. 2, para. 710.
[1536] Stanišić Appeal Brief, para. 139. See Appeal Hearing, 16 Dec 2015, AT. 99.
[1537] Stanišić Appeal Brief, paras 139-146. See Stanišić Reply Brief, para. 42; Appeal Hearing, 16 Dec 2015, AT. 140.
[1538] Stanišić Appeal Brief, paras 139-140, 145.
[1539] Stanišić Appeal Brief, para. 140, referring to Exhibits P1557.04, pp 14253-14254, P1557.01, pp 31-32; Stanišić Reply Brief, para. 42. See Stanišić Reply Brief, para. 45.

453.   Stanišić also submits that the Trial Chamber failed to explain why it chose to rely on certain aspects of Witness Davidović's testimony in *Krajišnik* and to omit any reference to contradictory statements made in the present case.[1540] He alleges that Witness Davidović made inconsistent and contradictory statements in relation to: (i) whether he had informed Stanišić about Arkan's takeover of Bijeljina SUP;[1541] (ii) Stanišić's attendance at a meeting at Bosanska Vila with, *inter alios*, Karadžić, Krajišnik, and Arkan in April or May 1992 ("Bosanska Vila Meeting"), at which "certain tasks were distributed";[1542] and (iii) Stanišić's statement that Arkan's Men could not be opposed.[1543] According to Stanišić, these inconsistencies serve to undermine the reliability of Witness Davidović's testimony regarding Stanišić's dealings with Arkan.[1544]

454.   Finally, Stanišić submits that the Trial Chamber's finding regarding his "deal" with Arkan is contradicted by direct evidence that he attempted to deal with the paramilitaries responsible for committing crimes,[1545] and was publicly criticised by Plavšić for doing so.[1546]

455.   The Prosecution responds that Stanišić fails to show that no reasonable trier of fact could have relied on Witness Davidović's evidence in *Krajišnik*, as that evidence is not inconsistent with Witness Davidović's testimony in this case.[1547] The Prosecution further submits that Stanišić's arguments with regard to the specific inconsistencies in Witness Davidović's evidence should be summarily dismissed as he merely disagrees with the Trial Chamber's interpretation of evidence **[page 188]** and fails to demonstrate any inconsistencies.[1548] Finally, the Prosecution points out that Stanišić initiated measures against paramilitaries only after they refused to submit to the army's command and committed crimes against local RS leaders.[1549]

b. Analysis

456.   In assessing Stanišić's intent, the Trial Chamber stated that it "considered the evidence" that Stanišić "approved of the operation of Arkan's Men in Bijeljina and Zvornik and allowed Arkan to remove whatever property in exchange for 'liberating' the territories".[1550] In doing so, the Trial Chamber provided no references to earlier findings or citations to evidence on the record.[1551] Nonetheless, a reading of the Trial Judgement as a whole reveals that it did discuss evidence concerning Stanišić's actions with respect to paramilitaries suspected of committing crimes, including Arkan's Men.[1552] Specifically, the Trial Chamber relied exclusively upon evidence of Witness Davidović in *Krajišnik* when stating that:

> Davidović testified that Arkan's forces participated in 'liberating' territories in Zvornik and Bijeljina with Stanišić's knowledge and approval. Stanišić, who had met with Arkan in Bijeljina on several occasions, had

---

[1540]   Stanišić Appeal Brief, para. 141. See Stanišić Appeal Brief, paras 40-41, referring to Trial Judgement, vol. 2, para. 768, Milorad Davidović, 24 Aug 2010, T. 13625-13626. See also Stanišić Reply Brief, para. 19.

[1541]   Stanišić Appeal Brief, para. 142. Stanišić argues that in *Krajišnik*, Witness Davidović testified that he informed Stanišić about the takeover of Bijeljina SUP by Arkan's Men, later to testify in the present case that he did not have any conversation with Stanišić about the presence of Arkan and his men in Bijeljina and what they were doing there and he only assumed that Stanišić knew about it (Stanišić Appeal Brief, para. 142, referring to Milorad Davidović, 23 Aug 2010, T. 13544, Exhibit P1557.03, pp 14220-14221).

[1542]   Stanišić Appeal Brief, para. 144, referring to, Trial Judgement, vol. 2, para. 711, Exhibit P1557.05, p. 14362, Milorad Davidović, 24 Aug 2010, T. 13624.

[1543]   Stanišić Appeal Brief, para. 143, referring to Milorad Davidović, 23 Aug 2010, T. 13545-13546, Milorad Davidović, 24 Aug 2010, T. 13625-13626, Exhibit 1D646, p. 1.

[1544]   Stanišić Appeal Brief, para. 145. See Stanišić Reply Brief, para. 42.

[1545]   Stanišić Appeal Brief, para. 146, referring to Andrija Bjelošević, 15 Apr 2011, T. 19711-19712, ST161, 19 Nov 2009, T. 3456 (confidential), Radovan Pejić, 25 Jun 2010, T. 12202-12204, Dragomir Andan, 27 May 2011, T. 21421, 21460-21464, Dragomir Andan, 30 May 2011, T. 21503-21505, 21538-21541, 21545-21546, Dragomir Andan, 1 Jun 2011, T. 21697-21698, 21701-21702, ST215, 28 Sep 2010, T. 15002-15003, Milorad Davidović, 23 Aug 2010, T. 13531-13533, 13564-13566, 13590, Milorad Davidović, 24 Aug 2010, T. 13613-13616, 13623-13630, Exhibits P1557.04, pp 14292-14293, 1D76, P2309, P1476, 1D567, 1D557, 1D558, 1D173, 1D646, 1D97, 1D554, P339, P591, P1557.01, pp 26-27. See Appeal Hearing, 16 Dec 2015, AT. 99.

[1546]   Stanišić Appeal Brief, para. 146, referring to Exhibit P400, p. 20, Momčilo Mandić, 6 May 2010, T. 9274-9276.

[1547]   Prosecution Response Brief (Stanišić), para. 51.

[1548]   Prosecution Response Brief (Stanišić), paras 52 (referring to Exhibit P1557.03, pp 74-75, Milorad Davidović, 23 Aug 2010, T. 13544-13545), 53.

[1549]   Prosecution Response Brief (Stanišić), para. 52, referring to Trial Judgement, vol. 2, paras 714-720, 756, Milorad Davidović, 24 Aug 2010, T. 13623-13624, Exhibit P1557.01, paras 51-82.

[1550]   Trial Judgement, vol. 2, para. 768.

[1551]   Trial Judgement, vol. 2, para. 768. *Cf. supra*, paras 377-380.

[1552]   See Trial Judgement, vol. 2, paras 709-712.

agreed that, in exchange for their engagement in the area, Arkan's forces could take any property they wanted from the territories they liberated.[1553]

457. The Appeals Chamber notes that the Trial Chamber relied extensively on the evidence of Witness Davidović throughout the Trial Judgement.[1554] In particular it relied upon Witness Davidović's *viva voce* testimony and evidence in *Krajišnik* in stating that "Stanišić told Davidović that Karadžić, too, was aware of Arkan's engagement in the area."[1555] It also relied exclusively upon Witness Davidović's evidence in *Krajišnik* when stating that he "assumed that Stanišić was aware of the crimes of Arkan's men in Bijeljina, Brčko, and other territories, because these crimes were well-known, and Stanišić received information from a number of different sources", and [page 189] Arkan acted with full freedom and consent of the MUP of Serbia.[1556] Further, the Trial Chamber relied exclusively on Witness Davidović's testimony in *Krajišnik* regarding the Bosanska Vila Meeting, when finding that:

> Davidović also testified that, in April or May of 1992, after Arkan's Men had entered Bijeljina, he attended a meeting at Bosanska Vila with Radovan Karadžić, Momčilo Krajišnik, [Mićo Stanišić, Pero Mihajlović, Frenki Simatović, and Arkan. Davidović attended at the invitation of Stanišić to discuss the transport of ammunition. At this meeting, certain tasks were distributed to the units of the Federal SUP. Arkan was told to stay out of certain matters, while permitted to participate in other tasks as assigned by Karadžić, Krajišnik, and Stanišić.[1557]

The Trial Chamber also recalled Witness Davidović's *viva voce* testimony "that Stanišić neither ordered nor prohibited him to arrest Arkan or members of his forces".[1558] As is discussed further in the following paragraphs, the Trial Chamber did not note any inconsistencies regarding Witness Davidović's *viva voce* testimony and his evidence in *Krajišnik*.

458. Failure to discuss inconsistent or contradictory evidence is, however, not necessarily indicative of disregard.[1559] The Appeals Chamber reiterates in this respect that "[c]onsidering the fact that minor inconsistencies commonly occur in witness testimony without rendering it unreliable, it is within the discretion of the Trial Chamber to evaluate it and to consider whether the evidence as a whole is credible, without explaining its decision in every detail".[1560]

459. With respect to Stanišić's argument that the Trial Chamber erred by relying on Witness Davidović's testimony in *Krajišnik* as the sole basis for finding that he approved of "Arkan's operations in Bijeljina and Zvornik and allowed Arkan to remove any property [...] he wished",[1561] the Appeals Chamber notes that Witness Davidović gave evidence about the interactions between Stanišić and Arkan, both in *Krajišnik* and in the present case.[1562] Specifically, the Appeals Chamber notes that in his witness statement in *Krajišnik*, Witness Davidović stated that:

> [Arkan] had a training camp at Erdut for which he had received the consent of the Serbian MUP. Mićo Stanišić had been invited to the training camp and when he went there he was amazed to see how well it was run and the respect Arkan received from his men. Mićo Stanišić met him several times in Bijeljina where Arkan had total control. Although Mićo Stanišić knew what Arkan and his staff were doing in Bijeljina he dared not interfere because of Arkan's links with the Serbian MUP. [...] Mićo Stanišić whilst at Lukavica with Ratko Mladić had seen some of Arkan's men there. [...] Stanišić had made a deal with Arkan for him to come into Sarajevo and occupy any territory he wanted and that he could take whatever he wanted and

---

[1553] Trial Judgement, vol. 2, para. 710.

[1554] See Trial Judgement, vol. 1, paras 887, 891, 894-897, 899-900, 1052, 1057-1058, 1079-1080, 1092, 1098, 1562, 1568, 1577, 1596, fns 2028, 2036, 2038, 2045-2046, 2049-2051, 2055-2056, 2058, 2060-2066, 2068-2073, 2078, 2084, 2406, 2426-2427, 2517, 2525, 2586, 3711, 3742, 3758-3788, 3869; Trial Judgement, vol. 2, paras 122-123, 126, 185, 288, 587, 601, 603, 709-715, 717, fns 390, 406, 408, 420, 579-580, 834, 1539-1540, 1570-1572, 1576-1577, 1820-1824, 1826-1829, 1832, 1836, 1839. See also Trial Judgement, vol. 1, paras 918, 920, 923, 925. But see Trial Judgement, vol. 1, paras 1079, 1101, fn. 2518.

[1555] Trial Judgement, vol. 2, para. 710, referring to Milorad Davidović, 23 Aug 2010, T. 13544-13545, Exhibit P1557.01, p. 31.

[1556] Trial Judgement, vol. 2, para. 710, referring to Exhibits P1557.04, pp 14251-14254, P1557.01, p. 31, P1557.03, pp 14220-1121.

[1557] Trial Judgement, vol. 2, para. 711, referring to Exhibits P1557.04, pp 14255-14258, P1557.05, pp 14362-14363, P1557.07, pp 15280-15281.

[1558] Trial Judgement, vol. 2, para. 712, referring to Milorad Davidović, 24 Aug 2010, T. 13625-13626.

[1559] *Popović et al.* Appeal Judgement, para. 1151.

[1560] *Popović et al.* Appeal Judgement, para. 1151; *Kvočka et al.* Appeal Judgement, para. 23 (internal citations omitted).

[1561] Stanišić Appeal Brief, paras 140, 145.

[1562] Milorad Davidović, 24 Aug 2010, T. 13625-13626; Exhibits P1557.01, para. 125, P1557.04, pp 14253-14254.

take it to Serbia. He was **[page 190]** allowed to take the territory right down to the Baščaršija where there were some 50 jewellery shops.[1563]

460.   According to Witness Davidović's in-court testimony in *Krajišnik*, Stanišić had informed Witness Davidović of Arkan's activities in the territory of Bijeljina, stating that "Arkan's forces were in Bijeljina and Zvornik".[1564] Witness Davidović testified that when he was in the Lukavica barracks, Stanišić had told him that "Arkan's forces were helping them to liberate territory that they believed should become part of Republika Srpska".[1565] When questioned as to whether Stanišić had told him anything else about Arkan's presence in the RS, Witness Davidović responded "[n]othing special, except that they were engaged there and they had his approval to help out in the area and that there was agreement amongst themselves that whatever they liberated and took would be an area in which they could do as they liked with any property."[1566]

461.   In the present case, Witness Davidović testified that Stanišić's "deal" with Arkan existed "in the sense of Mićo Stanišić calling [Arkan's Men] to Sarajevo and giving them the possibility [to loot]".[1567] Specifically, Witness Davidović recalled that, while he was at the garrison at Lukavica, Mladić told him:

> that there was lootings going on, and so on, and that [Stanišić] had called to Sarajevo, allegedly, the members of Arkan's Guard and gave them certain rights, I think they were talking about Baščaršija and said, Look you can take whatever you want, whatever you liberate, whatever you take in that sense, all of that is yours. That's what General Ratko Mladić said to me then when he was telling me how these paramilitaries were not coming spontaneously or by accident, but rather that they were enjoying somebody's support.[1568]

462.   The Appeals Chamber notes that the Trial Chamber did not refer to this evidence in relation to its findings about the existence of a "deal" between Stanišić and Arkan.[1569] As for Stanišić's argument that the Trial Chamber "ignored" this portion of Witness Davidović's testimony in the present case, the Appeals Chamber recalls that it is to be presumed that the Trial Chamber evaluated all the evidence presented to it, provided that there is no indication that the Trial Chamber completely disregarded any particular piece of evidence.[1570] Such disregard is shown when **[page 191]** evidence which is clearly relevant to the findings is not addressed in the Trial Chamber's reasoning.[1571]

463.   The Appeals Chamber notes that throughout his evidence in *Krajišnik* and the present case, Witness Davidović was consistent that there was a "deal" between Arkan and Stanišić, in the sense of Stanišić giving Arkan and his men the opportunity to occupy any territory they wanted and to loot such areas of whatever property they wished.[1572] Therefore, the only notable discrepancy in Witness Davidović's evidence concerns the person from whom Witness Davidović heard about Stanišić's "deal" with Arkan. The Trial Chamber did not make any specific finding as to how Witness Davidović became aware of Stanišić's deal with Arkan and hence did not discuss this potential inconsistency.[1573] The Appeals Chamber therefore considers that even if Witness Davidović's knowledge about the "deal" was in fact hearsay, and even if it was uncorroborated,[1574]

[1563]   Exhibit P1557.01, para. 125.
[1564]   Exhibit P1557.04, p. 14253.
[1565]   Exhibit P1557.04, p. 14253.
[1566]   Exhibit P1557.04, pp 14253-14254.
[1567]   Milorad Davidović, 24 Aug 2010, T. 13625-13626.
[1568]   Milorad Davidović, 24 Aug 2010, T. 13626.
[1569]   See Trial Judgement, vol. 2, fn. 1821.
[1570]   *Popović et al.* Appeal Judgement, para. 306; *Dorlevic* Appeal Judgement, fn. 2527; *Haradinaj et al.* Appeal Judgement, para. 129; *Kvočka et al.* Appeal Judgement, para. 23.
[1571]   *Tolimir* Appeal Judgement, para. 161; *Popović et al.* Appeal Judgement, para. 306; *Dorlevic* Appeal Judgement, para. 864; *Haradinaj et al.* Appeal Judgement, para. 129; *Kvočka et al.* Appeal Judgement, para. 23.
[1572]   See *supra*, paras 459-461. Indeed, Witness Davidović confirmed in his testimony in the present case that this was the meaning of his earlier statement that a "deal" existed between Stanišić and Arkan to this effect (see Milorad Davidović, 24 Aug 2010, T. 13625-12626). See also Exhibits P1557.01, para. 125, P1557.04, pp 14253-14254. Further, his evidence appears to be compatible in relation to the location at which Witness Davidović heard about Stanišić's "deal" with Arkan (see Milorad Davidović, 24 Aug 2010, T. 13626, Exhibit P1557.04, pp 14253-14254).
[1573]   See Trial Judgement, vol. 2, paras 709-712, 768.
[1574]   The Appeals Chamber recalls that "nothing prohibits a Trial Chamber from relying on uncorroborated evidence; it has the discretion to decide in the circumstances of each case whether corroboration is necessary or whether to rely on uncorroborated, but otherwise credible, witness testimony" (*Popović et al.* Appeal Judgement, para. 1009). The Appeals Chamber further recalls that a trial chamber may rely on hearsay evidence, provided it is reliable and credible (*Popović et al.* Appeal Judgement, para. 1276. See

it was still within the Trial Chamber's discretion to rely on it if it considered such evidence credible as a whole.

464.   Consequently, and given that the potential inconsistency in Witness Davidović's evidence has no direct impact on the Trial Chamber's ultimate finding on the *existence* of the "deal" between Stanišić and Arkan, which his testimony in both *Krajišnik* and the present case fully supports, the Appeals Chamber finds that Stanišić has failed to show that the Trial Chamber erred by not explicitly addressing Witness Davidović's testimony as to *how* he became informed about this arrangement. Moreover, Stanišić has failed to demonstrate that this potential inconsistency renders the Trial Chamber's finding regarding his "deal" with Arkan unsafe.

465.   The Appeals Chamber now turns to Stanišić's argument that the Trial Chamber failed to explain Witness Davidović's alleged inconsistent and contradictory statements in relation to whether Witness Davidović informed Stanišić about Arkan's takeover of Bijeljina SUP.[1575] The Appeals Chamber notes that, in setting out the evidence in respect of Stanišić's deal with Arkan and **[page 192]** his awareness of the participation of Arkan's forces in the operations in Bijeljina and Zvornik, the Trial Chamber referred to Witness Davidović's testimony in *Krajišnik* that "Stanišić told Davidović that Karadžić too, was aware of Arkan's engagement in the area".[1575][1576] Witness Davidović also testified in *Krajišnik* that he had reported the takeover of Bijeljina to Stanišić.[1577] In the present case, when questioned as to whether he had discussed with Stanišić "the presence of Arkan and his men and what they were doing in Bijeljina, Brčko, and the other territories where they had been seen in action",[1578] Witness Davidović testified that he "did not elaborate" on this issue with Stanišić as "[t]here was no need",[1579] but that he assumed Stanišić was aware that Arkan had come to Bijeljina and committed a series of crimes including murders and robberies.[1580]

466.   The Appeals Chamber notes that the Trial Chamber did not make any specific finding as to whether Witness Davidović informed Stanišić about Arkan's presence in the area of Bijeljina and hence did not discuss this potential inconsistency.[1581] It notes, however, that Witness Davidović was consistent in his evidence that Stanišić was aware of Arkan's engagement in the area of Bijeljina.[1582] In the Appeals Chamber's view, the potential inconsistency in Witness Davidović's evidence concerning whether he informed Stanišić about Arkan's presence in the area of Bijeljina is therefore not such that the Trial Chamber ventured outside of its discretion in finding, on the basis of Witness Davidović's evidence, that Stanišić was aware of, and approved of, the operation of Arkan's Men in Bijlejina and Zvornik.[1583]

467.   Regarding the challenge to the Trial Chamber's finding that Stanišić attended the Bosanska Vila Meeting, at which he, Karadžić, and Krajišnik, assigned certain tasks to Arkan, and the Trial Chamber's reliance on Witness Davidović's testimony in *Krajišnik* in this respect,[1584] Stanišić's argues that this evidence is unreliable as the witness never mentioned the Bosanska Vila Meeting during his interview with the Prosecution.[1585] The Appeals Chamber notes that this issue was **[page 193]** addressed thoroughly in cross-examination in *Krajišnik*.[1586] The Appeals Chamber recalls that the Trial Chamber should be afforded

---

[1575]   *Bizimungu* Appeal Judgement, paras 180, 236; *Šainović et al.* Appeal Judgement, para. 846. See also *Nizeyimana* Appeal Judgement, para. 95; *Đorđević* Appeal Judgement, paras 229, 397; *Lukić and Lukić* Appeal Judgement, para. 577).

[1575]   Stanišić Appeal Brief, para. 142.

[1576]   Trial Judgement, vol. 2, para. 710.

[1577]   Exhibit P1557.03, p. 14220.

[1578]   Milorad Davidović, 23 Aug 2010, T. 13544. The Appeals Chamber further notes that on the basis of this testimony the Trial Chamber concluded that "Davidović assumed that Stanišić was aware of the crimes of Arkan's men in Bijeljina, Brčko, and other territories" (see Trial Judgement, vol. 2, para. 710, referring to Milorad Davidović, 23 Aug 2010, T. 13544-13545).

[1579]   Milorad Davidović, 23 Aug 2010, T. 13544.

[1580]   Milorad Davidović, 23 Aug 2010, T. 13544-13545.

[1581]   See Trial Judgement, vol. 2, paras 709-712, 768.

[1582]   See Milorad Davidović, 23 Aug 2010, T. 13544-13545; Exhibit P1557.03, p. 14220.

[1583]   See Trial Judgement, vol. 2, paras 710, 768.

[1584]   Stanišić Appeal Brief, para. 144. See Trial Judgement, vol. 2, para. 711.

[1585]   Stanišić Appeal Brief, para. 144, referring to Trial Judgement, vol. 2, para. 711, Exhibit P1557.05, p. 14362, Milorad Davidović, 24 Aug 2010, T. 13624.

[1586]   The Appeals Chamber notes that the Trial Chamber referred to Witness Davidović's evidence-in-chief, cross-examination, and re-examination in relation to the issue of the Bosanska Vila Meeting (see Trial Judgement, vol. 2, fn. 1823). The Appeals Chamber notes, in particular, that when cross-examined as to why he had not mentioned "this very significant event" in his interview with the Prosecution, Witness Davidović replied "I don't know why it is supposed to be significant. I answered to questions put to

deference in assessing various factors that affect a witness's credibility.[1587] It finds that by simply repeating the lack of reference to the Bosanska Vila Meeting in Witness Davidović's interview with the Prosecution, Stanišić has failed to demonstrate any error in the Trial Chamber's assessment of the witness's evidence in finding that Stanišić attended the Bosanska Vila Meeting.

468.   As to Stanišić's argument that Witness Davidović's testimony in *Krajišnik* concerning the Bosanska Vila Meeting is inconsistent with Witness Davidović's testimony in the present case, the Appeals Chamber notes that Stanišić points to Witness Davidović's evidence in the present case that, upon arriving in Bijeljina, Stanišić told him that, if needed, he could arrest paramilitaries regardless of their "name, gender, everything that had happened".[1588] However, Stanišić has not demonstrated how this statement contradicts Witness Davidović's testimony in *Krajišnik*, or the Trial Chamber's finding based thereon, that Stanišić attended the Bosanska Vila Meeting, at which he, among others, assigned certain tasks to Arkan.[1589] Stanišić's argument in this respect is therefore dismissed.

469.   Regarding Witness Davidović's alleged inconsistent and contradictory statements in relation to whether Stanišić told him that Arkan's Men could not be opposed,[1590] the Appeals Chamber notes that in the present case Witness Davidović first testified that a deal had existed between Stanišić and Arkan "in the sense of Mićo Stanišić calling [Arkan's Men] to Sarajevo and giving them [the] possibility" to allow Arkan to loot whatever he wanted.[1591] He testified that "when I came with the intention of disarming the paramilitaries, I was told [by Stanišić] that quite simply they could not have opposed them".[1592] Witness Davidović further explained that "[a]fter all, they came under the guise of some kind of patriots [...]. However, very soon, they turned into their very contradiction".[1593] Subsequently, he clarified that: **[page 194]**

> [h]owever, in later procedures that I undertook in order to disarm paramilitaries, [Stanišić] never said, [d]o not arrest Arkan or whoever. I actually have to say that, had I had an opportunity to arrest him, I would have done it with pleasure. [...] There was no hindrance in that sense. It's not that [Stanišić] said, Do not arrest Arkan or Arkan's forces, no.[1594]

The Appeals Chamber notes, however, that the Trial Chamber resolved this inconsistency and accepted Witness Davidović's clarification by finding that "Davidović testified that Stanišić neither ordered nor prohibited him to arrest Arkan or members of his forces."[1595] Other than alleging that this inconsistency has a negative impact on the credibility of Witness Davidović's evidence regarding Arkan, Stanišić does not demonstrate that the Trial Chamber erred in its approach.

470.   Turning to Stanišić's argument that the alleged inconsistencies discussed above "fundamentally undermine the reliability of Davidović's testimony regarding Arkan",[1596] the Appeals Chamber recalls that a trial chamber is best placed to assess the credibility of a witness and reliability of the evidence adduced,[1597] and therefore has broad discretion in assessing the appropriate weight and credibility to be accorded to the testimony of a witness.[1598] As with other discretionary decisions, the question before the Appeals Chamber is not whether it "agrees with that decision" but "whether the trial chamber has correctly exercised its

---

me. There's a whole range of issues in which I did not provide details or did not answer questions that were not put to be me by the investigator" (Exhibit P1557.05, p. 14363).

[1587]   *Tolimir* Appeal Judgement, para. 469; *Popović et al.* Appeal Judgement, para. 1142. See *Šainović et al.* Appeal Judgement, para. 658; *Lukić and Lukić* Appeal Judgement, para. 112.

[1588]   Stanišić Appeal Brief, para. 144, referring to Milorad Davidović, 24 Aug 2010, T. 13624.

[1589]   Trial Judgement, vol. 2, para. 711.

[1590]   Stanišić Appeal Brief, paras 143, 145.

[1591]   Milorad Davidović, 24 Aug 2010, T. 13625-13626.

[1592]   Milorad Davidović, 23 Aug 2010, T. 13545.

[1593]   Milorad Davidović, 23 Aug 2010, T. 13545.

[1594]   Milorad Davidović, 24 Aug 2010, T. 13626. See Milorad Davidović, 23 Aug 2010, T. 13590.

[1595]   Trial Judgement, vol. 2, para. 712.

[1596]   Stanišić Appeal Brief, para. 145.

[1597]   *Tolimir* Appeal Judgement, para. 469; *Popović et al.* Appeal Judgement, para. 131; *Šainović et al.* Appeal Judgement, paras 437, 464, 1296; *Lukić and Lukić* Appeal Judgement, para. 296. See *Đorđević* Appeal Judgement, para. 395.

[1598]   *Tolimir* Appeal Judgement, para. 76; *Popović et al.* Appeal Judgement, para. 131; *Đorđević* Appeal Judgement, paras 781, 797, 819; *Ndahimana* Appeal Judgement, paras 43, 93; *Lukić and Lukić* Appeal Judgement, paras 86, 235, 363, 375.

discretion in reaching that decision".[1599] The party challenging a discretionary decision by the trial chamber must demonstrate that the trial chamber has committed a discernible error.[1600]

471. In light of the above, the Appeals Chamber is of the view that the inconsistencies within Witness Davidović's account identified by Stanišić concern either relatively minor issues on which the Trial Chamber did not enter any findings,[1601] or were resolved to the benefit of Stanišić.[1602] Further, the Appeals Chamber stresses that Witness Davidović was consistent in his evidence **[page 195]** regarding the existence of Stanišić's "deal" with Arkan, which is the evidence relied on by the Trial Chamber in its assessment of Stanišić's intent. The Appeals Chamber finds that Stanišić has failed to demonstrate that the Trial Chamber committed a discernible error in its assessment of the credibility of Witness Davidović on this issue. Stanišić's arguments in this respect are therefore dismissed.

472. As to Stanišić's argument that the Trial Chamber's conclusion concerning his arrangement with Arkan is contradicted by "direct evidence" relating to his efforts to deal with paramilitaries, for which he was publicly criticised by Plavšić,[1603] the Appeals Chamber notes that, with the exception of portions of Witness Davidović's testimony in the present case, the evidence Stanišić relies upon does not specifically address the issue of Arkan's Men.[1604] With respect to Witness Davidović's evidence, the Appeals Chamber has already dismissed Stanišić's arguments regarding alleged contradictions in this witness's testimony in the present case and his evidence in the *Krajišnik* case.[1605] Moreover, the Appeals Chamber considers that Stanišić ignores the context of the Trial Chamber's findings regarding his deal with Arkan and actions against paramilitary groups in general. The Trial Chamber did consider evidence that Stanišić's action directed at breaking up paramilitary groups put him in conflict with Plavšić, including evidence on which Stanišić relies,[1606] and concluded nonetheless that the action taken against these groups:

> was only pursued by Stanišić following their refusal to submit to the command of the army and their continued commission of acts of theft, looting, and trespasses against the local RS leaders. The primary motivation for these actions was the theft of Golf vehicles and harassment of the Serbs, an issue that concerned the RS authorities since the start of hostilities.[1607]

Moreover, the Trial Chamber found that Stanišić failed to act in the same decisive manner with regard to the other crimes, including the displacement and removal of non-Serb civilians.[1608] Accordingly, the Appeals Chamber considers that Stanišić has failed to demonstrate any contradiction between the Trial Chamber's reliance upon his deal with Arkan and its finding regarding the limited action he took against some paramilitary groups. Stanišić's arguments in this respect are therefore dismissed. **[page 196]**

[1599] *Popović et al.* Appeal Judgement, para. 131; *Prosecutor v. Ante Gotovina et al.*, Case No. IT-06-90-AR73.1, Decision on Miroslav Šeparović Interlocutory Appeal Against Trial Chamber's Decisions on Conflict of Interest and Finding of Misconduct, 4 May 2007, para. 11; *Prosecutor v. Milan Lukić and Sredoje Lukić*, Case No. IT-98-32/1-AR65.1, Decision on Defence Appeal Against Trial Chamber's Decision on Sredoje Lukić's Motion for Provisional Release, 16 April 2007, para. 4; *Prosecutor v. Mićo Stanišić*, Case No. IT-04-79-AR65.1, Decision on Prosecution's Interlocutory Appeal of Mićo Stanišić's Provisional Release, 17 October 2005, para. 6.
[1600] *Popović et al.* Appeal Judgement, para. 131. The Appeals Chamber will only overturn a trial chamber's discretionary decision where it is found to be: (i) based on an incorrect interpretation of governing law; (ii) based on a patently incorrect conclusion of fact; or (iii) so unfair or unreasonable as to constitute an abuse of discretion (*Popović et al.* Appeal Judgement, para. 74; *Šainović et al.* Appeal Judgement, para. 29; *Lukić and Lukić* Appeal Judgement, para. 17; *Krajišnik* Appeal Judgement, para. 81).
[1601] See *supra*, para. 466. See also *supra*, para. 463.
[1602] See *supra*, para. 469.
[1603] See *supra*, para. 454.
[1604] See Andrija Bjelošević, 15 Apr 2011, T. 19711-19712, ST161, 19 Nov 2009, T. 3456 (confidential), Radovan Pejić, 25 Jun 2010, T. 12202-12204, Dragomir Andan, 27 May 2011, T. 21421, 21460-21464, Dragomir Andan, 30 May 2011, T. 21505, 21538-21541, Dragomir Andan, 1 Jun 2011, T. 21697-21698, 21701-21702, ST215, 28 Sep 2010, T. 15002-15003, Milorad Davidović, 23 Aug 2010, T. 13531-13533, 13564-13566, 13590, Milorad Davidović, 24 Aug 2010, T. 13613-13616, 13623-13630, Exhibits P1557.04, pp 14292-14293, 1D76, P2309, P1476, 1D567, 1D558, 1D173, 1D646, 1D97, 1D554, P339, P591, P1557.01, p 26-27. See also *supra*, fn. 1545.
[1605] See *supra*, paras 469-471.
[1606] Trial Judgement, vol. 2, paras 717-720. See *supra*, fn. 1546.
[1607] Trial Judgement, vol. 2, para. 756. See Trial Judgement, vol. 2, para. 717. See also Trial Judgement, vol. 2, fn. 1843, referring to Momčilo Mandić, 6 May 2010, T. 9723-9276.
[1608] Trial Judgement, vol. 2, para. 757.

473.   In light of the above, the Appeals Chamber finds that Stanišić has not demonstrated that no reasonable trier of fact could have relied on Witness Davidović's evidence to conclude that he: (i) approved of the operations of Arkan's Men in Bijeljina and Zvornik; and (ii) allowed Arkan to remove property in exchange for liberating the territories. Consequently, the Appeals Chamber finds that Stanišić has failed to demonstrate that the Trial Chamber erred in relying upon his arrangement with Arkan, among other factors, when assessing his intent.

(ii) Alleged error in relying upon Stanišić' s presence at RS Government sessions

474.   As noted above, in its assessment of Stanišić's intent, the Trial Chamber considered that "Stanišić was present at sessions of the RS Government where the RS MUP was tasked with gathering information about Muslims moving out of the RS and the needs of refugees and displaced persons".[1609]

a. Submissions of the parties

475.   Stanišić submits that the Trial Chamber erred by relying on minutes of the July 1992 Sessions – *i.e.* the 4 July 1992 Session and the 29 July 1992 Session of the RS Government – to infer his intent.[1610] He argues that the Trial Chamber erred by relying on the minutes of the 4 July 1992 Session as the "bare tasking of the RSMUP with gathering information on the movement of Muslims from the territory of the RS does not provide any basis upon which the [Trial Chamber] could infer Stanišić's *mens rea*".[1611] Stanišić emphasises the testimony of Witness Ðerić, that the issue was related to either "voluntary movement for security reasons" or "movement due to fear",[1612] and the fact that the RS Government did not have "a point of view on this matter" and therefore required information.[1613]

476.   Stanišić also contends that the Trial Chamber erred by relying on the minutes of the 29 July 1992 Session and wrongly attributed, to the RS MUP, a greater role in the assessment of the needs of displaced persons than suggested on the face of the exhibit.[1614] He argues in this respect that the minutes of the session only note that "effort should be invested to gather true information, [...] using the information from the Interior and Defence Ministries".[1615] Stanišić asserts that the minutes are therefore inconclusive regarding the role and tasks of the RS MUP,[1616] and that no **[page 197]** reasonable trial chamber could have inferred his intent to further the JCE from the tasks assigned to the RS MUP.[1617]

477.   The Prosecution responds that the Trial Chamber reasonably relied on the assignments given to the RS MUP at the July 1992 Sessions when inferring Stanišić's intent.[1618]

b. Analysis

478.   The Appeals Chamber notes that the Trial Chamber provided no cross-references to earlier findings or citations to evidence on the record in support of its finding that "Stanišić was present at sessions of the RS Government where the RS MUP was tasked with gathering information about Muslims moving out of the RS and the needs of refugees and displaced persons".[1619] Nonetheless, the Appeals Chamber is able to identify the Trial Chamber's discussion of the evidence related to the July 1992 Sessions elsewhere in the Trial Judgement.[1620]

[1609]   Trial Judgement, vol. 2, para. 768.
[1610]   Stanišić Appeal Brief, para. 147.
[1611]   Stanišić Appeal Brief, para. 147.
[1612]   Stanišić Appeal Brief, para. 147, referring to Branko Ðerić, 30 Oct 2009, T. 2361-2363.
[1613]   Stanišić Appeal Brief, para. 147, quoting Exhibit P236, p. 4 (emphasis omitted).
[1614]   Stanišić Appeal Brief, para. 148.
[1615]   Stanišić Appeal Brief, para. 148, quoting Exhibit P242, p. 6.
[1616]   Stanišić Appeal Brief, para. 148.
[1617]   Stanišić Appeal Brief, para. 149.
[1618]   Prosecution Response Brief (Stanišić), para. 54. See Prosecution Response Brief (Stanišić), paras 55-56.
[1619]   Trial Judgement, vol. 2, para. 768. *Cf. supra*, paras 377-380.
[1620]   See Trial Judgement, vol. 2, paras 627, 650.

479.   Specifically, the Trial Chamber found that Stanišić attended the 4 July 1992 Session, where "the issue of Muslims moving out of RS was raised, on which the Government decided it had no 'point of view' and asked the RS MUP to present information that could be considered before taking an appropriate position".[1621] The Trial Chamber noted Witness Đerić's testimony that the task given to the RS MUP "related to 'some kind of moving out voluntarily' for security reasons or 'forced ones due to fear'".[1622] The Trial Chamber also found that the 29 July 1992 Session was attended by Stanišić, and that the RS MUP and MOJ "were designated to assess the needs of refugees, displaced persons, and large numbers of socially deprived persons by gathering 'true information'".[1623]

480.   Thus, the Trial Chamber was fully aware that the RS Government decided that it had no "point of view" on the issue of Muslims moving out of the RS. It nevertheless still considered Stanišić's presence at the July 1992 Sessions in assessing his intent, as his presence and the discussions at these sessions are relevant to his knowledge of the movements of Bosnian Muslims out of the territory of the RS as well as the possibility that the movements were forced due to fear.[1624] In this context, the Appeals Chamber also recalls that the Trial Chamber found that **[page 198]** insecurity, violence, unlivable conditions, discriminatory measures, and fear led to the mass exodus of non-Serbs from the Municipalities, in finding that this departure was *involuntary* in nature.[1625] As stated above, the requisite intent for a conviction under the first category of joint criminal enterprise can be inferred from circumstantial evidence.[1626] Therefore, the Appeals Chamber discerns no error in the Trial Chamber's reliance on the evidence concerning Stanišić's presence at the July 1992 Sessions, as circumstantial evidence among other factors, when assessing his intent. His arguments in this respect are dismissed.

(iii) Alleged error in relying upon Stanišić's presence at the 11 July 1992 Collegium

481.   As noted above, in its assessment of Stanišić's intent, the Trial Chamber considered that Stanišić was present at the 11 July 1992 Collegium, "where the relocation of citizens and entire villages was discussed".[1627]

a. Submissions of the parties

482.   Stanišić submits that the Trial Chamber erred by relying on his presence at the 11 July 1992 Collegium when assessing his intent.[1628] He argues that the Trial Chamber's "selective summary of the evidence improperly represents the minutes of [this meeting] in a prejudicial manner".[1629] He contends that the conclusions reached at the 11 July 1992 Collegium show that the focus was on "resolving the issue of the moving out of some inhabitants, villages, etc., for which the MUP [was] not responsible, but for which the MUP [was] being blamed".[1630] Stanišić emphasises that he subsequently provided information to the

---

[1621]   Trial Judgement, vol. 2, para. 627, referring to Exhibits P236, pp 4-5, P237, pp 1, 3.
[1622]   Trial Judgement, vol. 2, para. 627, quoting Branko Đerić, 30 Oct 2009, T. 2361-2363.
[1623]   Trial Judgement, vol. 2, para. 650, referring to Exhibit P242, pp 2, 6-7.
[1624]   In this regard, the Appeals Chamber observes that the Trial Chamber correctly noted that Witness Đerić testified that the task given to the RS MUP in the 4 July 1992 Session "related to 'some kind of moving out voluntarily' for security reasons or 'forced ones due to fear'" (Trial Judgement, vol. 2, para. 627). Stanišić misrepresents Witness Đerić's evidence by describing it as stating that the issue discussed at this session was related to either "voluntary movement for security reasons" or "movement due to fear", while omitting his evidence describing the latter as "forced" movement. (See Stanišić Appeal Brief, para. 147, referring to Branko Đerić, 30 Oct 2009, T. 2361-2363).
[1625]   Trial Judgement, vol. 2, para. 737. See Trial Judgement, vol. 1, paras 196, 210, 246, 273, 281, 338, 389-396, 477, 654, 684, 699, 778-781, 803-804, 810, 859-864, 872, 879, 890-896, 917-919, 922, 934, 953, 972, 981, 1023-1025, 1032, 1040, 1060, 1107, 1118, 1173, 1178-1179, 1189, 1206, 1236, 1247, 1257, 1285, 1335, 1343-1345, 1355, 1364, 1403, 1413, 1436-1437, 1454, 1487, 1497, 1506, 1542, 1552, 1563, 1571, 1581, 1588, 1590, 1670-1671, 1686.
[1626]   *Popović et al.* Appeal Judgement, para. 1369; *Šainović et al.* Appeal Judgement, para. 995; *Krajišnik* Appeal Judgement, para. 202. See *supra*, para. 375.
[1627]   Trial Judgement, vol. 2, para. 768.
[1628]   Stanišić Appeal Brief, para. 150. See *infra*, fn. 1783.
[1629]   Stanišić Appeal Brief, para. 151. See Stanišić Appeal Brief, para. 150.
[1630]   Stanišić Appeal Brief, para. 150. Stanišić points out in this respect that the 11 July 1992 Collegium minutes reveal that the information about relocation of citizens and entire villages was raised as a problem having a direct impact on the activities of the internal affairs organs "with the army and crisis staffs gathering Muslims and thereafter trying to place responsibility on the RSMUP for them" (Stanišić Appeal Brief, para. 150).

President and the Prime Minister on this problem suggesting that a meeting be held between the MUP and the army as this issue did not fall within the MUP's competencies.[1631] Finally, Stanišić submits that the Trial Chamber failed to make any reference to the rest of the contents of the 11 July 1992 Collegium "in which numerous and **[page 199]** repeated reference is made to the prevention, documentation and detecting of crimes and the protection of citizens, irrespective of ethnicity".[1632]

483. The Prosecution responds that it was reasonable for the Trial Chamber to rely on the record of the 11 July 1992 Collegium,[1633] which provides direct evidence of Stanišić's knowledge of the forcible displacement of non-Serbs.[1634] The Prosecution also contends that the meeting that Stanišić contends he arranged with the VRS to address the issue of the forcible displacement of non-Serbs instead "focused on improving co-operation, not on protecting non-Serbs".[1635]

b. Analysis

484. The Appeals Chamber notes that in finding that Stanišić was "present at the 11 July [1992] Collegium meeting, where the relocation of citizens and entire villages was discussed" when assessing Stanišić's intent,[1636] the Trial Chamber neither provided cross-references to earlier findings nor citations to evidence on record.[1637] While this would have been preferable, the Appeals Chamber has been able to identify the Trial Chamber's discussion of the 11 July 1992 Collegium elsewhere in the Trial Judgement.[1638]

485. Specifically, the Trial Chamber considered that at the 11 July 1992 Collegium: (i) Stanišić stated that the RS MUP forces provided immediate cooperation to the armed forces;[1639] (ii) Stanišić also stated that the RS MUP had decided to prevent criminal activities irrespective of the affiliation of the perpetrators;[1640] and (iii) Župljanin reported that "army and Crisis Staffs or War Presidencies" requested as many Muslims as possible be "gathered".[1641] The Trial Chamber found that the discussion during the 11 July 1992 Collegium also focussed on achieving "more effective cooperation and coordinated action between the RS MUP and the VRS" and that a joint meeting of the two organs subsequently took place on 27 July 1992.[1642] At the same time, the Trial Chamber noted that while the discussions gave rise to a decision to call a joint meeting with the MOJ to address problems relating to extended periods of pre-trial detention, there was no evidence of such a meeting being organised.[1643] Finally, the Trial Chamber found that it was emphasised at the **[page 200]** 11 July 1992 Collegium that it was not the task of the RS MUP to relocate certain citizens, despite efforts to assign this task to it.[1644]

486. In the view of the Appeals Chamber, there is nothing in the section of the Trial Judgement dedicated to discussion of the 11 July 1992 Collegium that suggests that the Trial Chamber "improperly" or "prejudicially" relied upon evidence related to that meeting. The Trial Chamber merely summarised the contents of the discussions and noted Stanišić's own evidence that he was informed at the 11 July 1992 Collegium of the "fact that the army was bringing in captives, including to police stations".[1645] Notably, although the Trial Chamber considered that the relocation of "certain citizens, villages" was discussed at the 11 July 1992 Collegium, it did not attribute any role to Stanišić in this respect.[1646] Moreover, there is nothing in the Trial Judgement to suggest that this evidence was used by the Trial Chamber in any way other than to

---

[1631] Stanišić Appeal Brief, para. 150, referring to Exhibit P427.08, pp 2-3, 6. See Appeal Hearing, 16 Dec 2015, AT. 97.
[1632] Stanišić Appeal Brief, para. 152.
[1633] Prosecution Response Brief (Stanišić), para. 57.
[1634] Prosecution Response Brief (Stanišić), para. 57.
[1635] Prosecution Response Brief (Stanišić), para. 58.
[1636] Trial Judgement, vol. 2, para. 768.
[1637] *Cf. supra*, paras 377-380.
[1638] See Trial Judgement, vol. 2, paras 629-633.
[1639] Trial Judgement, vol. 2, para. 630.
[1640] Trial Judgement, vol. 2, para. 630. See Trial Judgement, vol. 2, para. 632, referring to Exhibit P427.08, pp 5-7.
[1641] Trial Judgement, vol. 2, para. 631, referring to Exhibit P160, pp 7-8.
[1642] Trial Judgement, vol. 2, para. 632.
[1643] Trial Judgement, vol. 2, para. 632.
[1644] Trial Judgement, vol. 2, para. 632.
[1645] See Trial Judgement, vol. 2, paras 629-633.
[1646] See Trial Judgement, vol. 2, para. 632.

show Stanišić's knowledge of these events. As recalled above, the requisite intent for the first category of joint criminal enterprise may be inferred from circumstantial evidence, including knowledge, combined with continuous contribution to crimes within the common criminal purpose.[1647] The Appeals Chamber therefore finds that Stanišić has failed to demonstrate that the Trial Chamber erred by "improperly representing" the minutes of the 11 July 1992 Collegium in a "prejudicial manner" or by relying on the discussion thereat, among other factors, in assessing his intent.

487. With regard to Stanišić's submissions that the Trial Chamber failed to make any reference to the rest of the contents of the 11 July 1992 Collegium when discussing his intent, the Appeals Chamber notes that the Trial Chamber did expressly acknowledge the conclusions of that meeting, including that senior officers were tasked to take legal and other measures to remove employees who had committed crimes.[1648] In addition, throughout the Trial Judgement, and in its discussion on Stanišić's contribution to the JCE in particular, the Trial Chamber acknowledged the existence of numerous orders issued by Stanišić that accorded with the conclusions reached at the 11 July 1992 Collegium, concerning the prevention and investigation of crimes committed in the RS.[1649] The Appeals Chamber considers that Stanišić has failed to show how the Trial Chamber erred by not explicitly referring to portions of the minutes of the 11 July 1992 Collegium in its discussion on his intent. Accordingly, Stanišić argument is dismissed. **[page 201]**

(iv) Alleged error in relying on the Perišić Report

488. As noted above, in its assessment of Stanišić's intent, the Trial Chamber considered the Perišić Report dated 13 July 1992, in which Perišić reported to the RS MUP that in the municipality of Višegrad, certain police officers were exhibiting "a lack of professionalism while over 2,000 Muslims moved out of the municipality in an organised manner".[1650]

a. Submissions of the parties

489. Stanišić submits that the Trial Chamber erred by relying on the Perišić Report to infer his intent.[1651] He argues that the Perišić Report was "erroneously characterized" as reporting that "certain police officers were exhibiting a lack of professionalism while over 2,000 Muslims moved out of the municipality".[1652] Stanišić submits that the Trial Chamber erred by linking the lack of professionalism of certain police officers to the movement of 2,000 Muslims out of the municipality of Višegrad.[1653] He also submits that the Trial Chamber failed to consider that the Perišić Report indicates that the movement of the 2,000 Muslims out of the municipality occurred "with the help of the Red Cross".[1654] According to Stanišić, the main thrust of the Perišić Report instead deals with "fierce fighting" in Višegrad municipality between paramilitaries and other factions resulting in the "consequent organized movement of civilians out of the area with international assistance".[1655]

490. The Prosecution responds that Stanišić's argument should be summarily dismissed as the Trial Chamber reasonably relied on the Perišić Report and Stanišić merely suggests an alternative interpretation.[1656] It argues that the report "confirms the RS MUP's involvement in the expulsions of non-Serbs and Stanišić's willingness to condone its participation".[1657] The Prosecution submits that it is irrelevant that the Perišić

[1647]   *Popović et al.* Appeal Judgement, para. 1369; *Đorđević* Appeal Judgement, para. 512; *Šainović et al.* Appeal Judgement, para. 995; *Krajišnik* Appeal Judgement, para. 202. See *Stanišić and Simatović* Appeal Judgement, para. 81. See also *supra*, para. 375.

[1648]   Trial Judgement, vol. 2, para. 632. *Cf.* Stanišić Appeal Brief, fn. 186; Trial Judgement, vol. 2, para. 631.

[1649]   See Trial Judgement, vol. 2, paras 635-638, 640-649. Nevertheless, on the basis of other evidence, the Trial Chamber found that Stanišić "took insufficient action to put an end to [the crimes]" (Trial Judgement, vol. 2, para. 759. See *supra*, paras 269-328).

[1650]   Trial Judgement, vol. 2, para. 768. See Trial Judgement, vol. 2, para. 634.

[1651]   Stanišić Appeal Brief, para. 153.

[1652]   Stanišić Appeal Brief, paras 153, 155.

[1653]   Stanišić Appeal Brief, para. 153. Stanišić contends that the Trial Chamber improperly suggested a persecutory disposition on the part of certain policemen "where none is evident from the report relied upon" (Stanišić Appeal Brief, para. 153).

[1654]   Stanišić Appeal Brief, para. 154.

[1655]   Stanišić Appeal Brief, para. 155.

[1656]   Prosecution Response Brief (Stanišić), para. 59.

[1657]   Prosecution Response Brief (Stanišić), para. 59.

Report refers to the assistance provided by the ICRC with regard to the departure of over 2,000 Muslims from Višegrad, as this departure occurred in the context of **[page 202]** "a lack of discipline and professionalism" and an "inclination to various abuses" of the local police, not in the context of "fierce fighting" as Stanišić argues.[1658]

b. Analysis

491. The Appeals Chamber notes that when referring to the Perišić Report in assessing Stanišić's intent,[1659] the Trial Chamber provided no cross-references to earlier relevant findings or citations to relevant evidence on record.[1660] Nonetheless, the Appeals Chamber has identified the Trial Chamber's discussion of the Perišić Report elsewhere in the Trial Judgement. Specifically, the Trial Chamber found that "Višegrad SJB Chief Risto Perišic [...] reported to the RS MUP that certain police officers were exhibiting a lack of professionalism, 'an inclination to various abuses, acquiring material gain and other deficiencies', while 'over 2,000 Muslims moved out of the municipality in an organised manner'".[1661]

492. Contrary to Stanišić's submission,[1662] the Appeals Chamber does not consider that the Trial Chamber mischaracterised the Perišić Report in this finding. The Appeals Chamber notes that the Perišić Report refers to the "[f]ierce fighting" along ethnic lines that took place on the "border area between the liberated territory of the Serbian municipality of Višegrad and the part of this former local community which has not been liberated".[1663] It also describes the situation of lawlessness that prevailed at the same time on "liberated" areas under the control of the Bosnian Serbs.[1664] Additionally, the Perišić Report identifies "[w]idespread looting and burglaries" that "create[d] a negative mood among the residents" in the Bosnian Serb controlled areas.[1665] The Perišić Report further refers to the "strong tendency" among the reserve police "not to antagonise anybody, characteristic of local circumstances and of those who are not doing their work professionally",[1666] including regarding the criminal behaviour of local residents and various paramilitary units committing crimes that were unrelated to fighting on the outskirts of Bosnian Serb controlled areas.[1667] It states that members of the police "demonstrated a particular lack of readiness" to deal with these crimes, and that the reduction in the number of police officers "in view of the former national composition of the Višegrad Public Security Station" is aggravated by a "lack of discipline and professionalism, an inclination to various abuses, acquiring material gain and other **[page 203]** deficiencies".[1668] Finally, the Appeals Chamber notes that the Perišić Report refers to the mass departure of Bosnian Muslims from the municipality, stressing that "over 2,000 Muslims moved out of the municipality" and that "[t]here is continued interest in moving out".[1669]

493. By arguing that the main thrust of the Perišić Report deals with fierce fighting in Višegrad municipality between paramilitaries and other factions resulting in the organised movement of civilians out of the area, and that the report indicates no link between a lack of professionalism on the part of police officers and the movement of Muslims, Stanišić merely presents his own interpretation of the Perišić Report without showing any error on the part of the Trial Chamber.

494. As to Stanišić's submission that the Trial Chamber erred by failing to consider that the Perišić Report indicates that the movement of Bosnian Muslims "occurred 'with the help of the Red Cross'",[1670] the Appeals Chamber recalls that it is to be presumed that the Trial Chamber evaluated all the evidence presented to it as long as there is no indication that the Trial Chamber completely disregarded any particular piece of

---

[1658] Prosecution Response Brief (Stanišić), para. 60.
[1659] Trial Judgement, vol. 2, para. 768.
[1660] See Trial Judgement, vol. 2, para. 768. *Cf. supra*, paras 377-380.
[1661] Trial Judgement, vol. 2, para. 634.
[1662] Stanišić Appeal Brief, paras 153, 155.
[1663] Exhibit P633, p. 1.
[1664] See Exhibit P633, pp 2-3.
[1665] Exhibit P633, p. 2.
[1666] Exhibit P633, pp 2-3.
[1667] See Exhibit P633, p. 3.
[1668] Exhibit P633, pp 2-3.
[1669] Exhibit P633, p. 3.
[1670] Stanišić Appeal Brief, para. 154, quoting Exhibit P633, p. 3.

evidence.[1671] The Appeals Chamber also recalls that there may be an indication of disregard when evidence which is clearly relevant to the findings is not addressed in the Trial Chamber's reasoning.[1672] In the view of the Appeals Chamber, the fact that the ICRC provided logistical support to those seeking to leave is irrelevant to the question of what caused the departure of over 2,000 Muslims. The Appeals Chamber therefore considers that Stanišić has not demonstrated that the Trial Chamber erred by disregarding the reference to the role of the ICRC when assessing the Perišić Report.

495.   Accordingly, the Appeals Chamber finds that Stanišić has failed to demonstrate any error in the Trial Chamber's reliance on the Perišic Report, among other factors, in assessing his intent.[1673]

(v) Conclusion

496.   In light of the foregoing, the Appeals Chamber considers that Stanišić has failed to show that the Trial Chamber erred by relying on the following factors when assessing his intent: (i) Stanišić's approval of Arkan's operations in Bijeljina and Zvornik; (ii) Stanišić's presence at RS Government sessions; (iii) Stanišić's presence at the 11 July 1992 Collegium; and (iv) the Perišić **[page 204]** Report. Accordingly, the Appeals Chamber dismisses the arguments raised in relation to paragraph 768 of volume two of the Trial Judgement.

(g) Alleged errors in relying on the factors set out in paragraph 769 of volume two of the Trial Judgement in finding that Stanišić had the intent to further the JCE (subsection (E) of Stanišić's fourth ground of appeal)

497.   The Trial Chamber held:

[considering his position at the time, his close relationship with Radovan Karadžić, and his continued support of and participation in the implementation of the policies of the Bosnian Serb leadership and the SDS, [...] the only reasonable inference is that Stanišić was aware of the persecutorial intentions of the Bosnian Serb leadership to forcibly transfer and deport Muslims and Croats from territories of BiH and that Stanišić shared the same intent.[1674]

498.   Stanišić challenges the Trial Chamber's reliance on the factors referred to in this paragraph of the Trial Judgement in assessing his intent.[1675] Stanišić asserts that no reasonable trial chamber could have found that: (i) his position at the time was demonstrative of his intent to commit persecutory crimes;[1676] (ii) he had a close relationship with Karadžić;[1677] and (iii) he supported and participated in the implementation of policies of the Bosnian Serb leadership and the SDS.[1678]

(i) Alleged errors in finding that Stanišić's position was demonstrative of his intent

a. Submissions of the parties

499.   Stanišić submits that the Trial Chamber erred by considering his position at the time in finding that the only reasonable inference was that he shared the intent to commit crimes.[1679] He argues that "[t]he fact alone that [he] occupied a position in the Government as Minister of the Interior does not and cannot, in and of itself, serve as a basis to infer intent to commit persecutory crimes."[1680] Referring to arguments raised under his second ground of appeal, Stanišić contends that the Trial Chamber's "flawed reasoning is

[1671]   *Popović et al.* Appeal Judgement, para. 306; *Dorlevic* Appeal Judgement, fn. 2527; *Haradinaj et al.* Appeal Judgement, para. 129.
[1672]   *Tolimir* Appeal Judgement, para. 161; *Popović et al.* Appeal Judgement, para. 306; *Đorđević* Appeal Judgement, para. 864.
[1673]   Trial Judgement, vol. 2, para. 768. See Trial Judgement, vol. 2, para. 634.
[1674]   Trial Judgement, vol. 2, para. 769.
[1675]   Stanišić Appeal Brief, paras 156-167.
[1676]   Stanišić Appeal Brief, paras 156-157. See Stanišić Appeal Brief, para. 109.
[1677]   Stanišić Appeal Brief, paras 158-164. See Stanišić Appeal Brief, para. 109. See Appeal Hearing, 16 Dec 2015, AT. 139-140.
[1678]   Stanišić Appeal Brief, paras 165-167. See Stanišić Appeal Brief, para. 109.
[1679]   Stanišić Appeal Brief, para. 156.
[1680]   Stanišić Appeal Brief, para. 156.

impermissibly based on Stanišić's purported association with those found to have been members of the JCE".[1681]

500. The Prosecution responds that the Trial Chamber appropriately relied upon Stanišić's high-level position within the RS leadership in concluding that he was aware of the view that ethnic **[page 205]** separation would be achieved through violence.[1681][1682] It contends that Stanišić challenges the Trial Chamber's findings in isolation and fails to show that no reasonable trier of fact could have concluded that he shared the common criminal purpose on the basis of all the evidence.[1683]

b. Analysis

501. At the outset, the Appeals Chamber notes that in referring to Stanišić's position at the relevant time when assessing his intent, the Trial Chamber neither provided references to its findings in other parts of the Trial Judgement nor did it include any citations to evidence on the record.[1684] Nonetheless, the Appeals Chamber has been able to identify several findings concerning Stanišić's position elsewhere in the Trial Judgement. Specifically, the Trial Chamber found that: (i) from his appointment on 31 March 1992 until the end of 1992, Stanišić was the Minister of Interior within the RS Government;[1685] (ii) the RS Government was one of the most important organs in the RS;[1686] and (iii) the Bosnian Serb leadership, of which Stanišić was a member, consisted of, *inter alios*, those who occupied important posts in the RS.[1687] The Appeals Chamber recalls that it has already dismissed Stanišić's challenges advanced under his second ground of appeal, including the allegation that the Trial Chamber incorrectly: (i) equated being part of the Bosnian Serb leadership with membership in the JCE; and (ii) found that he was a member of the JCE by virtue only of his association with the Bosnian Serb leadership.[1688]

502. The Appeals Chamber recalls, further, that in addition to Stanišić's position, the Trial Chamber also took into account a number of other factors, as set out in the *Mens Rea* Section.[1689] The Appeals Chamber considers that the component pieces of circumstantial evidence on the issue of Stanišić's intent are to be considered in relation to all other pieces of circumstantial evidence bearing on the issue, and not in isolation.[1690] Whereas the assessment of an evidentiary factor in a vacuum might fail to establish an essential matter, the weight of all relevant evidence taken together can conclusively prove the same matter beyond reasonable doubt.[1691] Accordingly, even if Stanišić's position at the time was not, in and of itself, sufficient to prove his intent beyond **[page 206]** reasonable doubt, he has failed to demonstrate that the Trial Chamber erred in considering it, among other factors, in reaching its ultimate conclusion.

503. In light of the above, the Appeals Chamber dismisses Stanišić's argument that the Trial Chamber erred by relying upon his position at the time when assessing his intent.

(ii) Alleged error in relying upon Stanišić's close relationship with Karadžić when assessing his intent

a. Submissions of the parties

504. Stanišić submits that the Trial Chamber erred by holding that he and Karadžić shared a close relationship and by relying on this finding when assessing his intent.[1692] He contends that the Trial Chamber

---

[1681] Stanišić Appeal Brief, para. 157, referring to Stanišić Appeal Brief, paras 60-73.
[1682] Prosecution Response Brief (Stanišić), para. 46, referring to Trial Judgement, vol. 2, paras 156-157, 161-162, 167-170, 174, 178-179, 188, 199, 769. See Prosecution Response Brief (Stanišić), para. 36.
[1683] Prosecution Response Brief (Stanišić), para. 37.
[1684] See Trial Judgement, vol. 2, para. 769. *Cf. supra*, paras 377-380.
[1685] See Trial Judgement, vol. 2, para. 141. See also Trial Judgement, vol. 2, para. 6.
[1686] See Trial Judgement, vol. 2, para. 131.
[1687] See Trial Judgement, vol. 2, para. 131. See also Trial Judgement, vol. 2, para. 144; *supra*, para. 86.
[1688] See *supra*, paras 79-82.
[1689] See Trial Judgement, vol. 2, paras 766-769.
[1690] *Popović et al.* Appeal Judgement, paras 1103, 1150. See *Tolimir* Appeal Judgement, para. 495, referring to *Vasiljević* Appeal Judgement, para. 120.
[1691] *Popović et al.* Appeal Judgement, paras 1103, 1150.
[1692] Stanišić Appeal Brief, paras 158-164. See Stanišić Appeal Brief, paras 109, 244; Appeal Hearing, 16 Dec 2015, AT. 139-140. See also *supra*, paras 160-164.

"arbitrarily" considered the fact that he was a Minister in the RS Government – and therefore obliged and required to interact with Karadžić – as the basis for its finding.[1693] He argues that the Trial Chamber's finding was based on a total of nine intercepted conversations[1694] only two of which relate to conversations initiated by him[1695] and four of which occurred between June and August 1991, *i.e.* outside the Indictment period.[1696]

505.   The Prosecution responds that the Trial Chamber reasonably concluded that Stanišić and Karadžić shared a close relationship from at least June 1991.[1697] It argues that Stanišić misrepresents the Trial Chamber's finding by failing to address all of the evidence on which the Trial Chamber relied,[1698] and that as such, his arguments should be summarily dismissed.[1699] Specifically, the Prosecution submits that, in addition to the intercepted conversations, the Trial Chamber also relied upon: (i) "insider evidence" of former Deputy SRBiH MUP Minister Witness Žepinić and Witness Mandić, RS MOJ Minister, who both "confirmed that Stanišić was among the people close to Karadžić";[1700] (ii) Stanišić's presence at the November 1992 BSA Session, "where he proclaimed his allegiance to Karadžić and the SDS", and stated that he always followed the **[page 207]** policies of the SDS Presidency and Deputies in the former state;[1701] (iii) evidence that Karadžić insisted upon Stanišić's appointment and rejected calls for his removal;[1702] (iv) the fact that Stanišić often communicated directly with the RS Presidency, which Karadžić governed, rather than through designated channels of the RS Government;[1703] and (v) evidence of the "lofty praise" that Karadžić gave to Stanišić at the December 1993 BSA Session "for having 'fought to prevail' for a balance of Serbian cadres in the SRBiH MUP", for his role in establishing and separating the RS MUP at the beginning of April 1992, and for having exercised authority among the police.[1704]

506.   In reply, Stanišić submits that the Prosecution "incorrectly" points to hearsay evidence of Witness Žepinić and Witness Mandić in support of the finding concerning his relationship with Karadžić.[1705] He argues that "Žepinić did not confirm a close relationship between Stanišić and Karadžić",[1706] and contends that the Prosecution overemphasises "this supposedly close relationship" despite being "unable to elicit any information in this regard when Mandić testified in this case".[1707] Stanišić also contends that the "claim that [he] was bypassing designated channels is wholly erroneous".[1708] He further asserts that the Prosecution's references to Karadžić's "praise for Minister Stanišić and rejecting calls for his removal do not prove closeness in their relationship",[1709] and argues that the Prosecution's arguments are inapposite as he was dismissed from his second term as Minister by Karadžić.[1710]

[1693]   Stanišić Appeal Brief, para. 158.
[1694]   Stanišić Appeal Brief, para. 161, referring to Exhibits P1108, P1110, P1120, P1135, P1147, P1149, P1152, P1155, P1162. See Stanišić Appeal Brief, paras 162-163.
[1695]   Stanišić Appeal Brief, para. 161, referring to Exhibits P1135, P1152.
[1696]   Stanišić Appeal Brief, para. 161, referring to Exhibits P1108, P1135, P1149, P1152. See Stanišić Appeal Brief, paras 162 (referring to Exhibit P1110, P1120, P1147, P1155, P1162), 163.
[1697]   Prosecution Response Brief (Stanišić), para. 39, referring to Trial Judgement, vol. 2, paras 564-568, 570, 596, 730, 769. See Prosecution Response Brief (Stanišić), para. 41.
[1698]   Prosecution Response Brief (Stanišić), para. 39, referring to Stanišić Appeal Brief, paras 158, 160-164.
[1699]   Prosecution Response Brief (Stanišić), para. 39.
[1700]   Prosecution Response Brief (Stanišić), para. 39, referring to Trial Judgement, vol. 2, paras 2, 141, 565.
[1701]   Prosecution Response Brief (Stanišić), para. 40, referring to Trial Judgement, vol. 2, para. 570.
[1702]   Prosecution Response Brief (Stanišić), para. 40, referring to Trial Judgement, vol. 2, paras 139, 568, Branko Đerić, 30 Oct 2009, T. 2374.
[1703]   Prosecution Response Brief (Stanišić), para. 40, referring to Trial Judgement, vol. 2, paras 137, 568, 570, 730.
[1704]   Prosecution Response Brief (Stanišić), para. 40, referring to Trial Judgement, vol. 2, para. 596.
[1705]   Stanišić Reply Brief, para. 39.
[1706]   Stanišić Reply Brief, para. 39 (emphasis omitted), referring to Vitomir Žepinić, 29 Jan 2010, T. 5774-5775.
[1707]   Stanišić Reply Brief, para. 39, referring to Momčilo Mandić, 3 May 2010, T. 9395-9471, Momčilo Mandić, 4 May 2010, T. 9473-9563, Momčilo Mandić, 5 May 2010, T. 9565-9643, Momčilo Mandić, 6 May 2010, T. 9645-9732, Momčilo Mandić, 7 May 2010, T. 9734-9821, Exhibit P1318.01, p. 8634.
[1708]   Stanišić Reply Brief, para. 41, referring to Stanišić Appeal Brief, para. 244. See Stanišić Reply Brief, para. 41, referring to Prosecution Response Brief (Stanišić), para. 40; *supra*, paras 160-164.
[1709]   Stanišić Reply Brief, para. 40.
[1710]   Stanišić Reply Brief, para. 40, referring to Exhibits P400, P2305, pp 26-27.

b. Analysis

507.   As stated above, the Trial Chamber considered Stanišić's "close relationship with Radovan Karadžić" to be a relevant factor when assessing his intent.[1711] However, in doing so the Trial Chamber neither provided references to its findings on their relationship in other parts of the Trial Judgement nor did it include any citations to evidence on the record.[1712] Nonetheless, a reading of the Trial Judgement as a whole reveals that it contains several findings underlying the Trial Chamber's conclusion that Stanišić shared a close relationship with Karadžić. Specifically, the Trial **[page 208]** Chamber found that the close relationship between Stanišić and Karadžić – a "leading member of the JCE" – was shared from at least June 1991 and in the months preceding the establishment of the RS.[17121713] It also found that: (i) the two spoke frequently, at times calling each other at home;[1714] (ii) both "Mandić and Žepinić confirmed that Stanišić was among the people close to Karadžić";[1715] (iii) Stanišić had discussed attacks, manpower, and *materiel* for combat activities with Karadžić and noted that they should exercise caution in what they said as they were being tapped;[1716] (iv) testimonial evidence from Witness Trbojević and Witness Žepinić indicated that, "although Stanišić was answerable to Branko Deric, the Prime Minister, he had direct ties with Karadžić and often bypassed the Government";[1717] and (v) Karadžić was opposed to Stanišić's removal from office.[1718] It is thus clear that, contrary to Stanišić's assertion, the Trial Chamber did not only rely on intercepted conversations and its findings in relation to these conversations but also on other factors to find that he had a close relationship with Karadžić.

508.   Turning to Stanišić's challenge to the Trial Chamber's reliance upon Witness Žepinić's testimony, the Appeals Chamber observes that Stanišić selectively refers to, and therefore mischaracterises, the evidence upon which the Trial Chamber relied. To this end, the Appeals Chamber notes that, in finding that Witness Žepinić confirmed that Stanišić and Karadžić shared a close relationship, the Trial Chamber referred to an excerpt of his testimony where he stated, *inter alia*, "I can only say that, yes, they had a quite close relationship".[1719] Contrary to Stanišić's submission,[1720] therefore, Witness Žepinić did in fact confirm a close relationship between Stanišić and Karadžić. **[page 209]**

509.   Regarding Stanišić's argument that the Prosecution did not elicit any relevant information from Witness Mandić's testimony "*in this case*",[1721] the Appeals Chamber considers that the Trial Chamber was entitled to rely upon Witness Mandić's testimony in *Krajišnik* as that testimony was part of the trial record in the present case.[1722] Stanišić has not shown why this evidence could not be relied on to find that Stanišić shared a close relationship with Karadžić, and as a consequence, has failed to demonstrate that the Trial Chamber erred by doing so.

[1711]   Trial Judgement, vol. 2, para. 769.
[1712]   Trial Judgement, vol. 2, para. 769. *Cf. supra*, paras 377-380.
[1713]   Trial Judgement, vol. 2, para. 730. See Trial Judgement, vol. 2, para. 565,
[1714]   Trial Judgement, vol. 2, para. 565, referring to Exhibits P1135, P1149. The Appeals Chamber notes that Exhibit P1135 is the transcript of a phone call made by Stanišić to Karadžić, at his home, on 20 July 1991, while Exhibit P1149 is the transcript of a phone call made by Karadžić to Stanišić, at his apartment, on 12 June 1991. The Trial Chamber noted that in June 1991, "Karadžić called Stanišić to complain angrily about Serbs in the SRBiH government being followed and tracked by the SUP and the ransacking of a warehouse in search of hidden weapons where the Serbs were stocking food" in response to which Stanišić offered to assign Mandić to look into the issue (Trial Judgement, vol. 2, para. 565, referring to Exhibit P1108, pp 2-3). It also referred to an intercept of a conversation on 31 August 1991, when Stanišić spoke to Karadžić from Bileća to inform him that nothing had been done in relation to this incident, and promised to take the matter up with Mandić and another person (Trial Judgement, vol. 2, para. 565, referring to Exhibit P1152, pp 2-3). In addition, the Trial Chamber noted direct communication between Karadžić and Stanišić following the removal of barricades in Sarajevo (Trial Judgement, vol. 2, para. 566, referring to Nе|o Vlaški, 15 Feb 2010, T. 6352-6353, 6358-6359, Exhibits P643, p. 4, P910, p. 3, P1110, pp 7-8).
[1715]   Trial Judgement, vol. 2, para. 565, referring to Exhibit P1318.01, p. 8634, Vitomir Žepinić, 29 Jan 2010, T. 5774-5775.
[1716]   Trial Judgement, vol. 2, para. 567, referring to Exhibits P2300, p. 32, P1120, pp 2-3, P1147, pp 2-3, P1155, pp 1-3.
[1717]   Trial Judgement, vol. 2, para. 568, referring to Milan Trbojević, 3 Dec 2009, T. 4145, Vitomir Žepinić, 29 Jan 2010, T. 5775, Exhibits P427.02, p. 11498, P427.04, p. 11689. See Trial Judgement, vol. 2, para. 730.
[1718]   Trial Judgement, vol. 2, para. 568, referring to Exhibits P427.01, pp 11456-11459, P427.02, p. 11498.
[1719]   Vitomir Žepinić, 29 Jan 2010, T. 5775. See Trial Judgement, vol. 2, para. 565, fn. 1458.
[1720]   Stanišić Reply Brief, para. 39.
[1721]   Stanišić Reply Brief, para. 39 (emphasis added).
[1722]   See Exhibit P1318.01, p. 8634; Trial Judgement, vol. 2, fn. 1458.

510.   The Appeals Chamber now turns to Stanišić's argument that the Trial Chamber erred by relying upon hearsay evidence. Insofar as the portion of Witness Žepinić's evidence on which the Trial Chamber relied relates to his own "observation, with regard to their relationship",[1723] the Appeals Chamber is not persuaded that this constitutes hearsay evidence. The Appeals Chamber notes, however, that the portion of Witness Mandić's evidence upon which the Trial Chamber relied does have the character of hearsay, insofar as it concerns his testimony that Stanišić was among the people who enjoyed Karadžić's trust.[1724] Nonetheless, the Appeals Chamber recalls that a trial chamber may rely on evidence, including hearsay evidence, provided it is reliable and credible.[1725] Accordingly, and given the fact that the Trial Chamber's conclusion on the basis of this evidence is supported by the other sources identified by the Trial Chamber – and referred to above[1726] – the Appeals Chamber considers that Stanišić has failed to demonstrate any error in this respect.

511.   With respect to Stanišić's argument that the Trial Chamber erred by finding that he did not report through the designated channels of the RS Government,[1727] the Appeals Chamber recalls that it has dismissed this challenge elsewhere in this Judgement.[1728]

512.   Regarding Stanišić's challenge to the Trial Chamber's reliance on the fact that Karadžić rejected calls for his removal and praised him at the December 1993 BSA Session,[1729] and his submission that it was in fact Karadžić who ultimately dismissed him,[1730] the Appeals Chamber notes that the evidence Stanišić refers to suggests that Karadžić only removed Stanišić from office **[page 210]** in July 1994,[1731] one and a half years after the end of the Indictment period. This event, therefore, does not have any direct impact on the Trial Chamber's finding that the two shared a close relationship since at least June 1991[1732] and the Trial Chamber's reliance on this close relationship in assessing Stanišić's intent during the Indictment period. Stanišić has therefore failed to demonstrate any error in this respect.

513.   Finally, the Appeals Chamber considers that other than challenging the finding about his close relationship with Karadžić, Stanišić does not present any argument showing that, if established, his close relationship with Karadžić could not be considered as a factor relevant in the assessment of his intent.

514.   In light of the foregoing, the Appeals Chamber finds that Stanišić has failed to demonstrate that the Trial Chamber erred in concluding that he shared a close relationship with Karadžić and by taking this finding into account, among other factors, in assessing his intent.[1733]

(iii) Alleged error in finding that Stanišić supported and participated in the implementation of policies of the Bosnian Serb leadership and the SDS

a. Submissions of the parties

515.   Stanišić submits that the Trial Chamber erred by failing to identify which policies of the Bosnian Serb leadership and the SDS it considered he supported, and participated in the implementation of.[1734] He argues that the Trial Chamber did not provide any information as to what this support and participation amounted to, how it was manifested, or for how long it occurred, but instead "made a bare and unreferenced assertion which no reasonable trial chamber could have considered" as a basis for inferring his intent.[1735] Stanišić also

---

[1723]   Vitomir Žepinić, 29 Jan 2010, T. 5775. See Vitomir Žepinić, 29 Jan 2010, T. 5774; Trial Judgement, vol. 2, para. 565.
[1724]   Exhibit P1318.01, p. 8634.
[1725]   *Popović et al.* Appeal Judgement, para. 1276. *See Bizimungu* Appeal Judgement, paras 180, 236; *Šainović et al.* Appeal Judgement, para. 846. See also *Nizeyimana* Appeal Judgement, para. 95; *Đorđević* Appeal Judgement, paras 229, 397; *Lukić and Lukić* Appeal Judgement, para. 577.
[1726]   See *supra*, para. 507.
[1727]   See *supra*, para. 506.
[1728]   See *supra*, paras 160-164.
[1729]   Trial Judgement, vol. 2, para. 596. See Stanišić Reply Brief, para. 40; Prosecution Response Brief (Stanišić), para. 40.
[1730]   Stanišić Reply Brief, para. 40. See Prosecution Response Brief (Stanišić), para. 40.
[1731]   See Exhibit P2305, pp 26-27.
[1732]   Trial Judgement, vol. 2, para. 730. See Trial Judgement, vol. 2, para. 565.
[1733]   See Trial Judgement, vol. 2, para. 769.
[1734]   Stanišić Appeal Brief, para. 165.
[1735]   Stanišić Appeal Brief, para. 165, referring to Trial Judgement, vol. 2, para. 769.

contends that, if the policies mentioned by the Trial Chamber were intended as references to the deportation and forcible transfer of Muslims and Croats, the Trial Chamber erred by finding that he "supported and participated in such policies".[1736] In this respect, Stanišić submits that: (i) "each and every one of the points relied on by the [Trial Chamber] regarding [his] involvement and interaction with the BSA and the RS Government failed to demonstrate support or implementation of persecutory policies";[1737] and (ii) the Trial Chamber failed to refer to the evidence showing that his acts, conduct, and statements **[page 211]** were "directly contrary to the common purpose of the JCE".[1738] Additionally, Stanišić argues that the Trial Chamber failed to consider that his conduct, presence at meetings, attendance at sessions of the BSA, and acceptance of the position of Minister of Interior, demonstrate that he supported the creation of a separate Serb entity in line with the Cutileiro Plan rather than intending the commission of crime.[1739]

516. The Prosecution responds that Stanišić's continuous support for, and participation in the implementation of, the policies of the Bosnian Serb leadership and the SDS is evidenced through his various contributions to the JCE.[1740] The Prosecution also contends that the Trial Chamber properly considered all the evidence before it and reasonably concluded that Stanišić's measures did not demonstrate that he acted decisively to stop crimes against non-Serbs.[1741] The Prosecution further avers that Stanišić's conduct, presence at meetings and BSA sessions, and his acceptance of the position as Minister of Interior support the Trial Chamber's conclusion concerning his membership in the JCE.[1742]

b. Analysis

517. The Appeals Chamber observes that, in paragraph 769 of volume two of the Trial Judgement, the Trial Chamber referred to Stanišić's support for, and participation in the implementation of, the policies of the Bosnian Serb leadership and the SDS as a factor relevant to the assessment of his intent, without identifying the specific policies or the factors it considered to constitute Stanišić's support for, or participation in the implementation of, these policies.[1743] Additionally, the Trial Chamber provided no references to its findings in other parts of the Trial **[page 212]** Judgement or citations to evidence on the record. However, paragraph 769 of volume two of the Trial Judgement should not be read in isolation. In paragraph 767 of volume two of the Trial Judgement – *i.e.* in the same *Mens Rea* Section – the Trial Chamber at least referred to the views of the Bosnian Serb leadership "expressed during the sessions of the BSA" and "meetings of the SDS" in late 1991 and early 1992 as well as the Strategic Objectives "set by, among others, the RS Government". While paragraph 767 suffers from the same deficiencies – *i.e.* the lack of references to earlier relevant findings or citations to relevant evidence – the somewhat more detailed description of the factors in this paragraph has enabled the Appeals Chamber to locate relevant underlying findings in the Trial Judgement.[1744] Moreover, a

---

[1736] Stanišić Appeal Brief, para. 166, referring to Trial Judgement, vol. 2, para. 769.
[1737] Stanišić Appeal Brief, para. 166, referring to Stanišić Appeal Brief, paras 125-164.
[1738] Stanišić Appeal Brief, para. 167. See Stanišić Appeal Brief, paras 171-186; Stanišić Reply Brief, paras 37-38.
[1739] Stanišić Appeal Brief, para. 93, referring to Trial Judgement, vol. 2, paras 734, 766-769.
[1740] Prosecution Response Brief (Stanišić), paras 49 (referring to Trial Judgement, vol. 2, para. 769), 92. Specifically, the Prosecution points to Stanišić's: (i) involvement in all stages of the creation of the Bosnian Serb institutions in BiH, and the RS MUP in particular (Prosecution Response Brief (Stanišić), paras 92 (referring to Trial Judgement, vol. 2, para. 734), 94-117); (ii) participation in the enunciation and implementation of Bosnian Serb policy through his involvement in the highest institutions of the RS leadership (Prosecution Response Brief (Stanišić), paras 92 (referring to Trial Judgement, vol. 2, paras 732, 734), 94-117); (iii) involvement in the removal of non-Serb MUP personnel, who could have otherwise impeded the JCE (Prosecution Response Brief (Stanišić), paras 92 (referring to Trial Judgement, vol. 2, paras 576-577, 738), 118, 120-121); (iv) appointment of JCE members as leaders within the RS MUP and filling the ranks of the reserve police with "thieves and criminals" (Prosecution Response Brief (Stanišić), paras 92 (referring to Trial Judgement, vol. 2, paras 579, 600, 643, 743-744), 118, 122-123); (v) facilitation of the arming of RS MUP forces (Prosecution Response Brief (Stanišić), paras 92 (referring to Trial Judgement, vol. 2, para. 740), 118, 124-125); (vi) deployment of the RS MUP forces in operations that were in furtherance of the decisions of the Bosnian Serb authorities, despite being aware of the commission of crimes by the joint Serb forces (Prosecution Response Brief (Stanišić), paras 92 (referring to Trial Judgement, vol. 2, paras 737, 740-743), 118, 126-132); and (vii) contribution to the culture of impunity within the RS by focusing on crimes against Serbs and taking insufficient action to stop crimes against non-Serbs (Prosecution Response Brief (Stanišić), paras 65-91, 92 (referring to Trial Judgement, vol. 2, paras 745, 765), 133-149, 211, 214-217, 220-223).
[1741] Prosecution Response Brief (Stanišić), paras 61-63. See *infra*, para. 533.
[1742] Prosecution Response Brief (Stanišić), para. 34.
[1743] See Trial Judgement, vol. 2, para. 769.
[1744] See *supra*, paras 414-447.

reading of the Trial Judgement as a whole – including the section on Stanišić's contribution to the JCE and preceding sections analysing the evidence in this regard – reveals that it contains numerous findings underlying the Trial Chamber's references in paragraph 769 to the policies of the Bosnian Serb leadership and the SDS, as well as Stanišić's support for, or participation in the implementation of, these policies.[1745]

518. The Appeals Chamber recalls in this respect that, at paragraph 767 of volume two of the Trial Judgement, the Trial Chamber referred to: (i) the specific views of the Bosnian Serb leadership, espoused by Karadžić, Dutina, and Kuprešanin and expressed at the BSA and SDS Meetings in late 1991 and early 1992, "that there be an ethnic division of the territory, that 'a war would lead to a forcible and bloody transfer of minorities' from one region to another, and that joint life with Muslims and Croats was impossible";[1746] (ii) the Strategic Objectives "set by, among others, the RS Government", which called for, *inter alia*, the separation of the Serb people from Muslims and Croats;[1747] and (iii) the 1st Council Meeting attended by Stanišić, "where the boundaries of ethnic territory and the establishment of government organs in the territory were determined to be priorities".[1748]

519. Further, the Trial Chamber also entered specific findings with regard to the policies of the Bosnian Serb leadership elsewhere in the Trial Judgement. Specifically, the Trial Chamber found that: (i) the SDS and Bosnian Serb leadership intensified a process of territorial demarcation following the declaration of independence in the BiH Assembly on 15 October 1991 and that the forceful assumption of control over territories was an important part of this process;[1749] (ii) prior to February 1992, Serbs had coalesced around the idea of a separate Serb entity "carved out of the **[page 213]** territory of [the] SRBiH";[1750] (iii) Bosnian Serb control over the territories was to be achieved through the establishment of separate and parallel Bosnian Serb institutions, including the RS and RS Government;[1751] and (iv) the process of establishing Serb municipalities was initiated through the Variant A and B Instructions, which led to the violent takeovers of the Municipalities, the aim of which was the establishment of an ethnically "pure" Serb state through the permanent removal of the Bosnian Muslims and Bosnian Croats.[1752] The Appeals Chamber therefore finds that the Trial Chamber did identify which policies it relied upon in assessing Stanišić's intent, albeit in portions other than paragraph 769 of volume two of the Trial Judgement.

520. The Appeals Chamber now turns to Stanišić's argument that the Trial Chamber "did not provide any information" as to what constituted his support for, and involvement in the implementation of, policies of the Bosnian Serb leadership. In this respect, the Trial Chamber noted Stanišić's statement at the November 1992 BSA Session, made in response to the assertion of Witness Đerić[1753] that Stanišić did not attend government meetings, that:

> I as a man have followed policies of the SDS Presidency and our Deputies in the former state, I have always followed these policies. Those who want to separate me from them, I will always be with them until it is shown that their wishes and intentions differ from those of their people, those who want to separate me from that are making a big mistake, I will not allow that even if it costs me my life, let alone a ministerial post.[1754]

521. The Trial Chamber also made a number of specific findings in the section of the Trial Judgement dedicated to Stanišić's contribution to the JCE, which indicate his support for, and involvement in the

---

[1745]   *Cf. supra*, paras 377-380.
[1746]   Trial Judgement, vol. 2, para. 767. See Trial Judgement, vol. 2, paras 162, 174, 179; *supra*, paras 422-429.
[1747]   Trial Judgement, vol. 2, para. 767. See Trial Judgement, vol. 2, paras 188-199; *supra*, paras 433-436.
[1748]   Trial Judgement, vol. 2, para. 767. See Trial Judgement, vol. 2, para. 551; *supra*, paras 440-446.
[1749]   Trial Judgement, vol. 2, para. 310.
[1750]   Trial Judgement, vol. 2, para. 563. See Trial Judgement, vol. 2, paras 169, 174, 551.
[1751]   Trial Judgement, vol. 2, para. 310. See Trial Judgement, vol. 2, paras 176-184, 554-559, 576-583. The Trial Chamber considered, for instance, that Stanišić had attended the 11 February 1992 Meeting in Banja Luka where a Serb collegium was created for the establishment of a Serb MUP, one of the conclusions of which was for a reserve police force of Serb ethnicity to be armed and trained by the RS MUP, in accordance with Article 33 of the LIA (Trial Judgement, vol. 2, paras 4, 554-555, 599. See Trial Judgement, vol. 2, para. 376).
[1752]   Trial Judgement, vol. 2, para. 311. See Trial Judgement, vol. 2, paras 179-180, 184, 186, 227-244, 285-307, 310.
[1753]   Witness Đerić was a member of the Government of SRBiH, a member of the Ministerial Council of the RS, and subsequently Prime Minister of the Government of the RS until his resignation at the November 1992 BSA Session (see Trial Judgement, vol. 2, paras 20, 139), and part of the expanded Presidency of the RS (Trial Judgement, vol. 2, para. 137).
[1754]   See Trial Judgement, vol. 2, para. 570, quoting Exhibit P400, p. 15.

implementation of, the policies outlined above.[1755] For example, the Appeals Chamber first notes that the Trial Chamber concluded that "Stanišić worked to promote the interests, and implement the decisions, of the SDS in the SRBiH MUP and was involved in all the stages of the creation of the Bosnian Serb institutions in BiH, in particular the [RS] MUP".[1756] This included his involvement in the establishment of the SDS,[1757] as well as the creation of the RS **[page 214]** MUP,[1758] including the dismissal of non-Serbs from the RS MUP,[1759] and the arming of the RS MUP forces.[1760]

522.   According to the Trial Chamber, "by his participation in [the Bosnian Serb] institutions, [Stanišić] participated in the enunciation and implementation of the Bosnian Serb policy, as it evolved".[1761] The Trial Chamber considered that, from 1 April 1992, Stanišić "made a majority of key appointments in the RS MUP",[1762] which included JCE members who "were involved in the widespread and systematic takeovers of municipalities" as leaders within the RS MUP.[1763] Further, the Trial Chamber found that Stanišić's "participation in the creation of a separate Serb entity within BiH by the ethnic division of the territory" was voluntary, as indicated by his "conduct, presence at key meetings, attendance at sessions of the BSA, acceptance of the position of Minister of Interior".[1764] The Appeals Chamber recalls that it has dismissed Stanišić's challenges to these findings elsewhere in this Judgement.[1765]

523.   Second, the Trial Chamber considered Stanišić's role in the deployment of RS MUP forces in joint combat activities with the military.[1766] It found, in particular, that Stanišić approved the deployment of RS MUP forces to joint combat activities with other Serb forces, despite his awareness of crimes committed by joint Serb forces.[1767] The Trial Chamber also considered that RS **[page 215]** MUP forces were deployed in joint action with other Serb forces, in accordance with the Variant A and B Instructions,[1768] and in fact

---

[1755]   See *supra*, paras 518-519.

[1756]   Trial Judgement, vol. 2, para. 734. See generally, Trial Judgement, vol. 2, paras 729-736.

[1757]   Trial Judgement, vol. 2, para. 729. See Trial Judgement, vol. 2, paras 544-575; *supra*, para. 151.

[1758]   Trial Judgement, vol. 2, paras 732-734. The Trial Chamber found that Stanišić was present at a Serb police unit inspection on 30 March 1992, where he proclaimed that from that day, the RS had its own police force (Trial Judgement, vol. 2, para. 732. See Trial Judgement, vol. 2, para. 560, referring to Goran Mačar, 5 Jul 2011, T. 22838-22845, Goran Mačar, 12 Jul 2011, T. 23163, Exhibit 1D633, p. 1).

[1759]   Trial Judgement, vol. 2, paras 576-577, 738. The Trial Chamber referred to Stanišić's dispatch to all CSBs and SJBs, dated 3 April 1992, compelling compliance with an earlier dispatch of Witness Mandić (Trial Judgement, vol. 2, para. 577, referring to, *inter alia*, Exhibit P534), which in turn informed all CSBs and SJBs of the requirement in the new RS Constitution and the LIA that RS MUP officials make a "solemn declaration" before the Minister or authorised official (Trial Judgement, vol. 2, para. 576, referring to, *inter alia*, Exhibit P353, p. 1). The Trial Chamber found that the requirement to sign solemn declarations with the sanction of dismissal on failure to do so was a "pretext to dismiss and disarm non-Serbs from the RS MUP" (Trial Judgement, vol. 2, para. 738).

[1760]   Trial Judgement, vol. 2, para. 740. The Trial Chamber concluded that Stanišić facilitated the arming of the RS MUP forces by seeking and receiving assistance of the Federal SUP of Serbia for equipment, weapons, and training for a special unit under his direct control at the level of the RS MUP (Trial Judgement, vol. 2, para. 740). It referred elsewhere in the Trial Judgement to evidence of agreement between the RS MUP and the Federal SUP regarding: (i) the provision of equipment (Trial Judgement, vol. 2, para. 587); (ii) the supply of weapons and uniforms to Stanišić and Witness Mandić (Trial Judgement, vol. 2, para. 587); and (iii) Witness Davidović's role, as a member of the Federal SUP, in assisting Stanišić to form and train his own special unit in the RS MUP at Vrace (Trial Judgement, vol. 2, para. 601).

[1761]   Trial Judgement, vol. 2, para. 734.

[1762]   Trial Judgement, vol. 2, para. 733. See Trial Judgement, vol. 2, paras 579, 744.

[1763]   Trial Judgement, vol. 2, para. 744. See Trial Judgement, vol. 2, para. 579.

[1764]   Trial Judgement, vol. 2, para. 734.

[1765]   See *supra*, paras 148-158, 193-199, 260-267. The Appeals Chamber notes that Stanišić's argument that the Trial Chamber failed to consider that his conduct, presence at key meetings, attendance at sessions of the BSA, acceptance of the position of Minister of Interior demonstrated that he supported the creation of a separate Serb entity in line with the Cutileiro Plan rather than intending the commission of crimes, is addressed below (see *infra*, paras 527, 541, fn. 1815).

[1766]   See generally, Trial Judgement, vol. 2, paras 737-744.

[1767]   Trial Judgement, vol. 2, para. 743. See Trial Judgement, vol. 2, para. 766. The Trial Chamber found elsewhere in this respect that Stanišić: (i) organised the RS MUP forces into war units on 15 May 1992 (Trial Judgement, vol. 2, para. 588); (ii) issued three orders between 15 June and 6 July 1992 relating to the deployment of police to the military (Trial Judgement, vol. 2, paras 587, 601); (iii) attended the 11 July 1992 Collegium where he stated that the RS MUP forces had provided "immediate cooperation" to the army (Trial Judgement, vol. 2, para. 630), and where the issue of effective cooperation and coordinated action between the RS MUP and VRS was discussed (see Trial Judgement, vol. 2, para. 632); and (iv) met with Bosnian Serb generals Mladić, Witness Manojlo Milovanović, and Zdravko Tolimir and deputy prime minister of the RS Government Milan Trbojević, on 27 July 1992, to discuss joint operations and increased cooperation between the RS MUP and VRS (Trial Judgement, vol. 2, para. 592. See Trial Judgement, vol. 2, paras 56, 137, 139-140).

[1768]   Trial Judgement, vol. 2, para. 737. See Trial Judgement, vol. 2, paras 740-742.

played "a central role" with respect to their implementation.[1769] It concluded that Stanišić must therefore have been aware of the Instructions.[1770] The Appeals Chamber has dismissed Stanišić's challenges with regard to these findings elsewhere.[1771]

524. Third, the Trial Chamber also concluded that, despite being aware of the infiltration of the reserve police by criminal elements, "Stanišić only sought to withdraw regular policemen from combat activities towards the end of 1992, when most of the territory of RS had been consolidated, while permitting the continued use of reserve forces by the army, primarily for the purpose of guarding prisons and detention camps."[1772]

525. Moreover, Stanišić's argument that the Trial Chamber erred by failing to refer to evidence showing that his acts, conduct, and statements were contrary to the common purpose of the JCE is dismissed for reasons set out below.[1773] Contrary to Stanišić's submission, therefore, the Trial Chamber, despite the lack of clarity in this regard, did enter sufficiently identifiable findings with respect to the conduct it relied upon as a basis for inferring his intent.

526. Finally, insofar as Stanišić contends that the "each and every one of the points relied upon by the [Trial Chamber]" concerning his interaction with the BSA and the RS Government in the *Mens Rea* Section do not demonstrate his support for the "persecutorial" policies relating to forcible transfer and deportation, the Appeals Chamber recalls its finding that the Trial Chamber did not equate the policies of the Bosnian Serb leadership, as such, with the objective of the JCE.[1774] Moreover, the Appeals Chamber recalls that the component pieces of circumstantial evidence on the issue of Stanišić's intent are to be considered in relation to all other pieces of circumstantial **[page 216]** evidence bearing on the issue, and not in isolation.[1775] The Trial Chamber did not rely upon his support for the policies of the Bosnian Serb leadership, in isolation, when inferring that he had the requisite intent for participation in the JCE. It rather examined this factor in the context of other factors summarised in the *Mens Rea* Section.[1776] His arguments in this respect are therefore inapposite.

527. In the same vein, the Appeals Chamber is not persuaded by Stanišić's argument that his conduct, presence at meetings, attendance at sessions of the BSA, and acceptance of the position of Minister of Interior, demonstrate that he supported the creation of a separate Serb entity in line with the Cutileiro Plan rather than intending the commission of crimes. The Trial Chamber was fully aware of the enunciation of the Cutileiro Plan around late February 1992 and the political developments in the SRBiH resulting from this plan.[1777] However, on the basis of other evidence, it also found that prior to February 1992, Serbs had "coalesced around the idea of a separate Serb entity carved out of the territory of the SRBiH".[1778] This consideration, as well as other factors summarised in the *Mens Rea* Section, led the Trial Chamber to find that Stanišić shared the intent to further the JCE.[1779] His argument – merely asserting the legitimacy of a separate Serb entity by ethnic division in light of the Cutileiro Plan – therefore does not demonstrate any error on the part of the Trial Chamber.

528. In light of the above, the Appeals Chamber finds that Stanišić has failed to demonstrate that the Trial Chamber erred by failing to identify which policies of the Bosnian Serb leadership and the SDS it considered

---

[1769] Trial Judgement, vol. 2, para. 731.
[1770] Trial Judgement, vol. 2, para. 731.
[1771] See *supra*, paras 165-175.
[1772] Trial Judgement, vol. 2, para. 743. See Trial Judgement, vol. 2, paras 594, 600, 643. The Trial Chamber considered that: (i) Stanišić complained at the November 1992 BSA Session "that the infiltration of criminal reserve police had hindered 'the cooperation of the army, the police, and the civilian authorities'" (Trial Judgement, vol. 2, para. 600, quoting P400, pp 16-17); (ii) Stanišić ordered all CSBs and SJBs to withdraw active police from frontlines and make reserve police available for wartime assignment to the VRS on 23 October 1992 (Trial Judgement, vol. 2, para. 594).
[1773] See *infra*, paras 530-571.
[1774] See *supra*, paras 63-71.
[1775] *Popović et al.* Appeal Judgement, paras 1103, 1150. See *Tolimir* Appeal Judgement, para. 495, referring to *Vasiljević* Appeal Judgement, para. 120.
[1776] See *supra*, para. 378.
[1777] See Trial Judgement, vol. 2, paras 552-562.
[1778] Trial Judgement, vol. 2, para. 563. See Trial Judgement, vol. 2, paras 169, 174, 551.
[1779] See generally, Trial Judgement, vol. 2, paras 766-769.

he supported and participated in the implementation of. He has also failed to show that the Trial Chamber erred in considering his support for, and participation in the implementation of, such policies, in assessing his intent.

(iv) Conclusion

529.	In light of the foregoing, the Appeals Chamber considers that Stanišić has failed to show that the Trial Chamber erred by relying on the following factors when assessing his intent: (i) his position at the time; (ii) his close relationship with Karadžić; and (iii) his support for, and participation in, the implementation of the policies of the Bosnian Serb leadership. Stanišić's arguments in this respect are therefore dismissed. **[page 217]**

(h) Alleged errors in failing to consider exculpatory evidence demonstrating that Stanišić did not intend the commission of crimes (subsection (F) of Stanišić's fourth ground of appeal)

(i) Submissions of the parties

530.	Stanišić argues that the Trial Chamber failed to consider relevant evidence in arriving at its conclusion that he shared the intent to further the JCE.[1780] He submits that evidence "omitted by the [Trial Chamber] in its findings on his *mens rea*" goes to show that his "acts, conduct and statements do not demonstrate either a general intent to commit crimes or a specific intent that those crimes be committed with a discriminatory intent".[1781]

531.	Stanišić contends that the Trial Chamber failed to refer to "numerous and repeated measures" he took in order to ensure that the RS MUP worked in accordance with the law.[1782] Specifically, he contends that the Trial Chamber failed to consider that he: (i) issued numerous orders relating to the prevention, detection, and investigation of crimes;[1783] (ii) established the **[page 218]** Crime Prevention Administration to prevent and

---

[1780]	Stanišić Appeal Brief, paras 171-186. See Appeals Hearing, 16 Dec 2015, AT. 96-99, 103-104; Stanišić Reply Brief, para. 18.
[1781]	Stanišić Appeal Brief, para. 186. See Stanišić Appeal Brief, para. 39.
[1782]	Stanišić Appeal Brief, para. 171. See Stanišić Appeal Brief, paras 115-116, 172-181; Stanišić Reply Brief, para. 37. See also Stanišić Appeal Brief, paras 100, 112-113; Appeal Hearing, 16 Dec 2015, AT. 101.
[1783]	Stanišić Appeal Brief, paras 172, 174-176, 180-181. Stanišić contends that: (i) he issued orders from the beginning of the Indictment period seeking to ensure public safety and the prevention and detection of crimes (Stanišić Appeal Brief, para. 172, referring to Exhibits 1D61, P792, 1D634, P1252, Milomir Orašanin, 7 Jun 2011, T. 21(9)63-21(9)65, Goran Mačar, 5 Jul 2011, T. 22862-22863, Momčilo Mandić, 6 May 2010, T. 9728-9729). With respect to the testimony of Witness Milomir Orašanin ("Witness Orašanin"), the Appeals Chamber notes that Stanišić refers specifically to Witness Orašanin's testimony at pages 2163-2165 of the trial transcript (Stanišić Appeal Brief, fn. 213). However, no such pages of the trial transcript corresponds with Witness Orašanin's testimony. Having reviewed the transcript of Witness Orašanin's testimony, the Appeals Chamber understands Stanišić's reference as a typographical error intended to refer to Milomir Orašanin, 7 Jun 2011, T. 21963-21965); (ii) he repeated "several times throughout the Indictment period" orders emphasising the imperative of preventing criminal activities of citizens, soldiers, active and reserve police, and "members of the internal affairs organs" (Stanišić Appeal Brief, para. 174, referring to Trial Judgement, vol. 2, paras 640-641, 644, 674, 680, Exhibits 1D58, 1D59, 1D176, P163, p. 8, P1269, pp 1, 3, P160, p. 15, P1252, Slobodan Škipina, 30 Mar 2010, T. 8315-8317, Goran Mačar, 5 Jul 2011, T. 22865-22866, Vladimir Tutuš, 19 Mar 2010, T. 7865, Milomir Orašanin, 6 Jun 2011, T. 21908-21913, Milomir Orašanin, 7 Jun 2011, T. 21915-21920, Milomir Orašanin, 9 Jun 2011, T. 22118-22123, Exhibits P553, 1D356, 1D357. See Appeal Hearing, 16 Dec 2015, AT. 98); (iii) he insisted on the investigation of war crimes, regardless of the ethnicity of the perpetrator or victims (Stanišić Appeal Brief, para. 175, referring to Radomir Njeguš, 9 Jun 2010, T. 11475-11477, Exhibits 1D63, P160, p. 22, P427.08, pp 3, 6. See Stanišić Appeal Brief, para. 180, referring to Trial Judgement, vol. 2, para. 621, Exhibit 1D63, Vladimir Tutuš, 22 Mar 2010, T. 7914-7915, Dobrislav Planojević, 29 Oct 2010, T. 16569, Simo Tuševljak, 16 Jun 2011, T. 22276-22278. See also Appeal Hearing, 16 Dec 2015, AT. 98); (iv) he insisted on the indiscriminate investigation and filing of reports on crimes, including war crimes, as reflected in the conclusions of the 11 July 1992 Collegium (Stanišić Appeal Brief, para. 181, referring to Exhibit P160, pp 22-23, Vladimir Tutuš, 22 Mar 2010, T. 7914-7915, Dobrislav Planojević, 29 Oct 2010, T. 16569, Simo Tuševljak, 16 Jun 2011, T. 22276-22278, Exhibits 1D328, p. 5, 1D189, 1D63); (v) he responded promptly and unequivocally upon becoming aware of the commission of crimes (Stanišić Appeal Brief, para. 176, referring to Radomir Njeguš, 9 Jun 2010, T. 11475-11476, Slobodan Škipina, 30 Mar 2010, T. 8339-8361, Slobodan Škipina, 31 Mar 2010, T. 8362-8364, Dobrislav Planojević, 22 Oct 2010, T. 16411-16412, Dobrislav Planojević, 28 Oct 2010, T. 16537-16539, Goran Mačar, 18 Jul 2011, T. 23473-23474, Vladimir Tutuš, 16 Mar 2010, T. 7707-7712, Exhibits P628, P847); and (vi) the RS MUP gathered substantial and reliable material during the investigation of crimes which involved victims and alleged perpetrators of all ethnicities, which formed the basis of subsequent prosecutions of both Serb and non-Serb individuals (Stanišić Appeal Brief, para. 176, referring to Exhibits 1D595, 1D596, 1D597, 1D598, 1D599, 1D600, 1D601, Simo Tuševljak, 20 Jun 2011, T. 22434-22451). Stanišić also relies on his order of 17 August to CSB

detect crimes and monitor the work of crime prevention services at CSBs and SJBs;[1784] (iii) took various actions in relation to disciplining members of the RS MUP suspected of misconduct, including criminal activity;[1785] (iv) sent inspectors into the field to gather information and provide guidance to CSBs and SJBs;[1786] (v) sought federal assistance in light of the gravity of the security situation to help in taking action 1787 to arrest, detain, and interrogate criminal elements in the RS, including paramilitaries;[1787] (vi) issued orders requesting information on detention camps and prisoners, as well as orders requiring the free movement of civilians and the immediate release of all persons not detained in accordance with existing laws;[1788] (vii) "insisted on resolving issues of jurisdiction with the army in relation to combating crime and the criminal activity of paramilitaries";[1789] and (viii) "encountered fierce opposition at the municipal level when he ordered the dismissal of illegally formed 'special police units'".[1790]

532. Stanišić also submits that the Trial Chamber erred by failing to refer to the direct evidence that he "frequently made statements contrary to the idea of a common purpose to commit **[page 219]** persecutory crimes".[1791] Specifically, Stanišić contends that: (i) his public speeches throughout the Indictment period were non-discriminatory and aimed at the promotion of the rule of law, the professionalism of the police, and the protection of life and property of all citizens;[1792] and (ii) the Đerić Letter reiterated "his request for the adoption of a legislative instrument to prevent breaches of international law", stated that he had ordered RS MUP members to "abide by international law and the criminal code", and informed Witness Đerić that the RS MUP was working to indiscriminately document evidence of war crimes.[1793]

[^] chiefs, requiring them to abide by the laws of war and international conventions (Appeal Hearing, 16 Dec 2015, AT. 98, referring to, *inter alia*, Trial Judgement, vol. 2, para. 668).

[1784] Stanišić Appeal Brief, para. 174, referring to Trial Judgement, vol. 2, para. 46.

[1785] Stanišić contends that he: (i) introduced "disciplinary offences of 'discrimination on religious or national grounds' and 'failure to file disciplinary complaint against fellow officer', as well as simplifying the disciplinary process and extending the statute of limitations so that disciplinary offences were not left unpunished" (Stanišić Appeal Brief, para. 173, referring to Exhibit 1D54); (ii) "purged" the ranks of the RS MUP, issuing orders for the dismissal of all members who had either committed crimes or had proceedings commenced against them (Stanišić Appeal Brief, para. 178, referring to Trial Judgement, vol. 2, para. 749); and (iii) requested background checks for all RS MUP personnel and the removal of employees with criminal records (Stanišić Appeal Brief, para. 178, referring to Trial Judgement, vol. 2, paras 687-688, 698-708).

[1786] Stanišić Appeal Brief, para. 172, referring to Exhibits 1D328, pp 2, (5), P427.08, p. 3, Dragomir Andan, 31 May 2011, T. 21573-21576, Exhibit P993, Simo Tuševljak, 16 Jun 2011, T. 22314-22315, Goran Mačar, 7 Jul 2011, T. 22968-22974, Goran Mačar, 15 Jul 2011, T. 23352-23354. With respect to Exhibit 1D328 (the Sokolac Report), the Appeals Chamber notes that Stanišić refers to pages 2 and 8 of that exhibit although the exhibit itself only contains five pages. Having reviewed the exhibit, the Appeals Chamber understands Stanišić's reference thereto relates to Exhibit 1D328, pp 2, 5.

[1787] Stanišić Appeal Brief, para. 172, referring to Exhibits 1D646, P1557.0(1), para. 46, P1557.03, pp 14189, 14211-14212, Milorad Davidović, 23 Aug 2010, T. 13532-13534, 13586-13591, Milorad Davidović, 24 Aug 2010, T 13623-13630, Exhibits P1557.01, paras 84-85, P1557.04, p. 14260. The Appeals Chamber notes that Stanišić refers to paragraph 46 of Exhibit P1557.02 in support of this argument. However, on reviewing Exhibit P1557.02, it is apparent that this exhibit, a corrigendum to Exhibit P1557.01, contains no paragraph 46. The Appeals Chamber will therefore treat Stanišić's reference as relating to Exhibit P1557.01, para. 46.

[1788] Stanišić Appeal Brief, para. 177, referring to Trial Judgement, vol. 2, paras 664, 667, 673, 748. See Appeal Hearing, 16 Dec 2015, AT. 98.

[1789] See Stanišić Appeal Brief, para. 179, referring to Trial Judgement, vol. 2, paras 592, 594, 637, 642, 720, Exhibits 1D76, P160, pp 24-25.

[1790] Stanišić Appeal Brief, para. 179, referring to Trial Judgement, vol. 2, paras 606-607. Stanišić contends that he was "put [...] in confrontation with individuals such as Plavšić" as a result of orders he issues against paramilitary formations throughout the territory (Stanišić Appeal Brief, para. 179, referring to Trial Judgement, vol. 2, para. 719). He submits that Plavšić was "considered by the [Trial Chamber] to be a leading member of the JCE" (Stanišić Appeal Brief, para. 179, referring to Trial Judgement, vol. 2, para. 314). He also argues that the evidence demonstrates that he clashed with crisis staffs over the appointment of RS MUP personnel "without the consent and knowledge of the RS MUP" (Stanišić Appeal Brief, para. 179, referring to Trial Judgement, vol. 2, paras 681, 684, 733).

[1791] Stanišić Appeal Brief, para. 182. See Stanišić Appeal Brief, paras 183-186; Stanišić Reply Brief, para. 37.

[1792] Stanišić Appeal Brief, para. 183, referring to Trial Judgement, vol. 2, paras 558, 560, 609, Exhibit P160, p. 4. Stanišić also argues that he made his unequivocal support for a peaceful solution in BiH, in accordance with the Cutileiro Plan, publicly known (Stanišić Appeal Brief, para. 183, referring to Trial Judgement, vol. 2, paras 557, 560, 562).

[1793] Stanišić Appeal Brief, para. 184, referring to Exhibit P190. Stanišić contends that the Đerić Letter constitutes direct evidence that he did not intent to commit crimes (Stanišić Appeal Brief, paras 90-92, referring to Exhibit P190). He submits that: (i) the Đerić Letter was sent to "the highest authorities in the RS Government, individuals who were deemed by the [Trial Chamber] to be part of the so-called [Bosnian Serb leadership] and therefore members of the JCE" (Stanišić Appeal Brief, para. 185, referring to Trial Judgement, vol. 2, para. 769); (ii) in the Đerić Letter, he criticised the RS Prime Minister for failing to disassociate the RS Government from all groups and individuals whose intentions differed "from the legitimate political goals of the Serbian people" (Stanišić Appeal Brief, para. 185, referring to Exhibit P190); and (iii) the Đerić Letter demonstrates that he opposed the commission

533.   The Prosecution responds that Stanišić merely repeats failed arguments raised at trial without demonstrating any error and as such his submissions should be summarily dismissed.[1794] It argues that the Trial Chamber properly considered all of the evidence before it,[1795] including exculpatory evidence,[1796] and was not required to refer to the testimony of every witness or every piece of evidence on the trial record.[1797]

534.   The Prosecution submits, further, that the Trial Chamber reasonably concluded that Stanišić's measures did not demonstrate that he acted decisively to stop crimes against non-Serbs.[1798] It points out in this respect that: (i) Stanišić failed to use the powers available to him under the law to ensure the full implementation of his orders, despite his awareness of the limited action taken pursuant to them;[1799] (ii) Stanišić's subordinates followed his lead by failing to report or under-reporting serious crimes by Serbs against non-Serbs;[1800] (iii) Stanišić only punished **[page 220]** subordinates for theft and professional misconduct, rather than for Indictment-related crimes,[1801] and only pursued paramilitaries when they refused to submit to the command of the army and continued to commit crimes against RS leaders;[1802] and (iv) Stanišić facilitated the continued interaction with civilians of delinquent personnel by placing them at the disposal of the army.[1803]

535.   Additionally, the Prosecution submits that Trial Chamber considered the Đerić Letter but "nonetheless found, on the basis of all the evidence before it, that Stanišić shared the common criminal purpose".[1804]

(ii) Analysis

536.   At the outset, the Appeals Chamber recalls that there is a presumption that a trial chamber has evaluated all the evidence presented to it, as long as there is no indication that it completely disregarded any particular piece of evidence.[1805] This presumption may be rebutted when evidence which is clearly relevant to the trial chamber's findings is not addressed in its reasoning.[1806]

537.   The Appeals Chamber recalls that a trial chamber's failure to explicitly refer to particular evidence will not often amount to an error of law, especially where there is significant contrary evidence on the

---

of crimes and sought the attainment of legitimate political goals through lawful means (Stanišić Appeal Brief, paras 90-92. See Stanišić Reply Brief, paras 31-32).

[1794]   Prosecution Response Brief (Stanišić), para. 61, referring to *Krajišnik* Appeal Judgement, para. 24. See Prosecution Response Brief (Stanišić), fn. 193. See also Prosecution Response Brief (Stanišić), para. 16.

[1795]   Prosecution Response Brief (Stanišić), para. 62. See Prosecution Response Brief (Stanišić), paras 34, 36-37.

[1796]   Prosecution Response Brief (Stanišić), para. 16.

[1797]   Prosecution Response Brief (Stanišić), para. 61, referring to Prosecution Response Brief (Stanišić), para. 16. The Prosecution further points out that Stanišić alleges that the Trial Chamber did not consider evidence, yet cites paragraphs of the Trial Judgement where the evidence is expressly cited and discussed (Prosecution Response Brief (Stanišić), para. 61, fn. 194).

[1798]   Prosecution Response Brief (Stanišić), para. 62.

[1799]   Prosecution Response Brief (Stanišić), paras 62 (referring to Trial Judgement, vol. 2, paras 748, 752-753), 71, 133, 142-143. See Prosecution Response Brief (Stanišić), para. 62, referring to Trial Judgement, vol. 2, paras 757-759.

[1800]   Prosecution Response Brief (Stanišić), para. 62, referring to Trial Judgement, vol. 2, paras 104, 745, 758.

[1801]   Prosecution Response Brief (Stanišić), paras 63 (referring to Trial Judgement, vol. 2, paras 754-755), 70, 75, 116, 134, 144-146, 211, 214-217, 220-223.

[1802]   Prosecution Response Brief (Stanišić), paras 52, 63, referring to Trial Judgement, vol. 2, para. 756.

[1803]   Prosecution Response Brief (Stanišić), para. 63, referring to, *inter alia*, Trial Judgement, vol. 2, para. 751. According to the Prosecution, had Stanišić genuinely intended to protect the non-Serb population, he would have used his authority to amend the disciplinary regime (Prosecution Response Brief (Stanišić), para. 63, referring to Trial Judgement, vol. 2, para. 42). The Prosecution also contends that Stanišić concedes that he had the authority to make such amendments (Prosecution Response Brief (Stanišić), para. 63, referring to Stanišić Appeal Brief, paras 173, 221-222).

[1804]   Prosecution Response Brief (Stanišić), para. 34. According to the Prosecution, Stanišić's interpretation of the contents of the Đerić Letter is insufficient to demonstrate an error (Prosecution Response Brief (Stanišić), para. 34). In addition, it argues that Stanišić merely repeats arguments he already made at trial in relation to the Đerić Letter (Prosecution Response Brief (Stanišić), paras 30, 34, referring to Stanišić Appeal Brief, paras 90-92, Stanišić Final Trial Brief, para. 401).

[1805]   *Popović et al.* Appeal Judgement, para. 306; *Dorlevic* Appeal Judgement, fn. 2527; *Haradinaj et al.* Appeal Judgement, para. 129.

[1806]   *Tolimir* Appeal Judgement, para. 161; *Popović et al.* Appeal Judgement, para. 306; *Đorđević* Appeal Judgement, para. 864. The failure to address evidence on the record that is clearly relevant to a finding may amount to an error of law by failing to provide a reasoned opinion (*Dorlević* Appeal Judgement, para. 864; *Perišić* Appeal Judgement, para. 92; *Kvočka et al.* Appeal Judgement, para. 23). However, what constitutes a reasoned opinion depends on the specific facts of a case (*Perišić* Appeal Judgement, para. 92, referring to *Kvočka et al.* Appeal Judgement, para. 24).

record.[1807] This is because a trial chamber cannot be presumed to have ignored a particular piece of evidence simply because it did not mention it in its judgement.[1808] Rather, it could be presumed, in the absence of particular circumstances suggesting otherwise, that a trial chamber chose not to rely on an unmentioned piece of evidence, meaning that it considered the evidence but was of the view that it was either not reliable or otherwise not worth citing in its **[page 221]** judgement.[18081809] In the Appeals Chamber's view, this reflects a corollary of the overarching principle of deference to the discretion of a trial chamber. The Appeals Chamber therefore concludes that only where it is shown within the substance of a trial chamber's reasoning that clearly relevant evidence has been disregarded, should the Appeals Chamber intervene in order to assess whether that evidence would have changed the factual basis supporting the trial chamber's conclusion.

538.   The Appeals Chamber considers that in arguing that evidence was disregarded in the assessment of his intent, Stanišić has failed to appreciate, as noted above,[1810] that the *Mens Rea* Section is a summary of the factors the Trial Chamber considered clearly relevant to reaching its conclusion regarding Stanišić's intent. While it would have been preferable for the Trial Chamber to expressly indicate the evidence upon which it relied in reaching its findings listed in the *Mens Rea* Section, that it did not do so does not amount, in and of itself, to a failure to provide a reasoned opinion,[1811] and is not necessarily indicative of "disregard" for particular evidence.[1812]

539.   Stanišić's submissions that the Trial Chamber disregarded "evidence" are premised on references to allegedly supportive material that falls into three broad categories: (i) evidence that is expressly referred to in the Trial Judgement; (ii) findings in sections of the Trial Judgement other than the *Mens Rea* Section; and (iii) evidence not expressly referred to in the Trial Judgement.

540.   Regarding the evidence Stanišić identifies that is expressly referred to in the Trial Judgement, the Appeals Chamber notes that in many instances the Trial Chamber has explicitly discussed the very portions of the exhibits, including the Đerić Letter, that Stanišić relies upon.[1813] **[page 222]**

[1807]   *Tolimir* Appeal Judgement, para. 53; *Perišić Appeal Judgement*, para. 95, referring to *Kvočka et al.* Appeal Judgement, paras 23, 483-484, 487, 582-583, *Simba* Appeal Judgement, paras 143, 152, 155.

[1808]   *Kamuhanda* Appeal Judgement, para. 32, referring to *Musema* Appeal Judgement, para. 118.

[1809]   *Kamuhanda* Appeal Judgement, para. 32, referring to *Musema* Appeal Judgement, para. 118.

[1810]   See *supra*, para. 378.

[1811]   The Appeals Chamber recalls that Stanišić's argument that the Trial Chamber failed to provide a reasoned opinion for finding that he shared the intent of the JCE members has been dismissed elsewhere in this Judgement (see *supra*, para. 380).

[1812]   See *supra*, para. 536.

[1813]   First, with regard to Stanišić's argument on his "numerous orders for the prevention and investigation of crimes" and his "repeated statements that the RS MUP were to respect domestic and international law in their duties", the Appeals Chamber notes that Stanišić lists 115 exhibits (see Stanišić Appeal Brief, para. 116, fn. 100), all referred to in the Trial Judgement (see Trial Judgement, vol. 2, paras 46, 386, 488, 542, 557-558, 560-562, 564, 566, 570, 572-573, 578-579, 581, 588, 594, 598, 601, 605-610, 613, 621, 628, 630-631, 637, 640-648, 655, 664, 667-670, 673-675, 679-682, 684, 687-688, 690, 692, 695, 698-703, 705-708, 711, 713-714, 716-720) without designating the relevant parts of these exhibits or explaining how they support his argument. As such, his submission in paragraph 116 of his appeal brief is clearly undeveloped and has failed to show that no reasonable trier of fact, based on the evidence, could reach the same conclusion as the Trial Chamber did. Second, the Appeals Chamber notes that the Trial Chamber considered Exhibit P993 in finding that Witness Orašanin, an inspector at the Crime Prevention Administration, and his inspection team "visited Karakaj and then went to Brčko, Bijeljina, and the new Skelani SJB" (Trial Judgement, vol. 2, para. 50, referring to, *inter alia*, Exhibit P993 (undated RS MUP report concerning the supervision of the state of the RS MUP and work of the Bratunac and Skelani Police Stations performed between 1-3 August 1992)). Having considered Exhibit P993, the Trial Chamber nonetheless concluded that the civilian law enforcement apparatus failed to function in an impartial manner and that police had failed to report or under-reported crimes against non-Serb victims by Serb perpetrators during the Indictment period (see Trial Judgement, vol. 2, paras 104, 745). Third, the Appeals Chamber notes that the Trial Chamber referred to Exhibit 1D54 in finding that Stanišić had adopted new rules on the disciplinary responsibility of RS MUP employees, in order to adapt the work of the RS MUP to "wartime conditions" (Trial Judgement, vol. 2, para. 42, referring to, *inter alia*, Exhibit 1D54 (Rules on the Disciplinary Responsibility of RS MUP Employees Under Wartime Regime). See Trial Judgement, vol. 2, paras 14, 695, 706). The Trial Chamber also referred to Exhibit 1D58 in finding that, on 23 July 1992, Stanišić ordered that legal measures be taken against all members of the RS MUP who had committed crimes since the establishment of the RS MUP, with the exception of "political and verbal offences" (see Trial Judgement, vol. 2, para. 640, referring to, *inter alia*, Exhibit 1D58. See also Trial Judgement, vol. 2, para. 684). The Trial Chamber referred further to Exhibit 1D59 in finding that on 24 July 1992, Stanišić ordered the chiefs of CSBs to dismiss all members of the RS MUP who had been criminally prosecuted or against whom criminal proceedings were being conducted before competent courts and place them at the disposal of the VRS (Trial Judgement, vol. 2, paras 641, 727, referring to, *inter alia*, Exhibit 1D59). It also referred to Exhibit P163, being a summary of a working group meeting in Trebinje on 20 August 1992, in finding that in his opening remarks at that meeting, Stanišić pointed out the need to implement the order to remove from the RS MUP those individuals not worthy of belonging to the service as well as the need to

261

In the Appeals Chamber's view it is thus clear that the Trial Chamber took this evidence into account but considered that, after assessing it in light of other evidence, it was not precluded from reaching the factual findings upon which it based its conclusions regarding Stanišić's intent.[1814] **[page 223]**

541.   Insofar as Stanišić relies on the Trial Chamber's findings in other sections of the Trial Judgement in support of his argument that it disregarded relevant evidence,[1815] his arguments are equally incongruous. While Stanišić clearly disagrees with the Trial Chamber's evaluation of the evidence and its conclusions, he has advanced no argument showing that no reasonable trier of fact, based on all the evidence, could have reached the same conclusions as the Trial Chamber did. To the contrary, Stanišić has merely identified evidence he submits supports his proposition that he did not possess the requisite intent, without indicating how this evidence demonstrates that the Trial Chamber's conclusions were unreasonable. Stanišić has therefore failed to demonstrate any error and his arguments in this respect are dismissed.

542.   The Appeals Chamber now turns to Stanišić's arguments relating to evidence allegedly disregarded by the Trial Chamber that is not expressly referred to in the Trial Judgement. Noting that there is some overlap between the evidence underlying Stanišić's various submissions, the Appeals Chamber will proceed to address related evidence together, where possible.

---

disband special units due to abuses being committed by them (see Trial Judgement, vol. 2, paras 609, 674, referring to, *inter alia*, Exhibit P163, pp 3, 8-9). Moreover, the Trial Chamber referred to pages 1 and 3 of Exhibit P1269 in finding that Stanišić chaired a meeting of RS MUP officials in Jahorina on 9 September 1992, where he stressed the need to fully implement an earlier order of 6 September 1992 and to release from service all persons who fail to meet the criteria for employment in the RS MUP (Trial Judgement, vol. 2, para. 680, referring to Exhibit P1269, pp 1, 3). Having considered Exhibits 1D54, 1D58, 1D59, P163, and P1269, the Trial Chamber nonetheless concluded that Stanišić violated his professional obligation to protect and safeguard the civilian population in the territories under the control of the RS, by only instituting disciplinary proceedings for RS MUP personnel in relation to theft and professional misconduct and not for crimes charged in the Indictment (see Trial Judgement, vol. 2, paras 755-756). Fourth, the Appeals Chamber notes that the Trial Chamber referred to Exhibit 1D176, an order of 27 July 1992, in finding that Stanišić: (i) ordered the immediate disbandment and the placement of all special units formed during the war in the areas of the CSBs under the command of the VRS; (ii) Stanišić reiterated instructions encompassed in his order of 23 July 1992 for the removal of individuals found criminally responsible for crimes and those who had committed crimes but had not yet been prosecuted, and the placement of these persons at the disposal of the VRS; and (iii) reiterated the need for professional conduct of RS MUP employees (Trial Judgement, vol. 2, paras 605, 644-645, 647, referring to, *inter alia*, Exhibit 1D176, pp 1-2). The Appeals Chamber notes in this respect that the Trial Chamber also considered Stanišić's actions in relation to the "special units and detachments in municipalities" in some detail (see Trial Judgement, vol. 2, paras 604-609) and found that the placing of errant reserve policemen at the disposal of the army, despite being in accordance with the applicable disciplinary procedures, was not sufficient to satisfy Stanišić's duty to protect the Muslim and Croat population (see Trial Judgement, vol. 2, para. 751). Fifth, the Appeals Chamber observes that the Trial Chamber referred to Exhibit 1D76 in relation to its finding concerning action taken by Stanišić pursuant to the conclusions reached at the 11 July 1992 Collegium (Trial Judgement, vol. 2, para. 637, referring to, *inter alia*, Exhibit 1D76. See Trial Judgement, vol. 2, para. 748). The Trial Chamber however also noted other evidence and ultimately concluded that he took insufficient action to put an end to crimes (Trial Judgement, vol. 2, para. 759. See Trial Judgement, vol. 2, paras 749, 751, 753). Sixth, the Appeals Chamber notes that the Trial Chamber referred to Exhibit P847 in finding that on 31 August 1992, 10 days after the killing of approximately 150-200 Muslim men by Prijedor policemen, including members of the Prijedor Intervention Platoon ("PIP"), at Korićanske Stijene in Skender Vakuf municipality on 21 August 1992, Stanišić reinforced the obligation on part of the crime service to undertake everything that was necessary and ordered investigations into the deaths of 150 Muslim victims (Trial Judgement, vol. 2, para. 677, referring to, *inter alia*, Exhibit P847). Having considered Exhibit P847, the Trial Chamber nonetheless concluded that the civilian law enforcement apparatus failed to function in an impartial manner and that Stanišić focused primarily on crimes committed against Serbs (Trial Judgement, vol. 2, paras 745, 758). Finally, the Appeals Chamber notes that the Trial Chamber explicitly considered the Đerić Letter in finding that "Stanišić sent a letter to Branko Đerić that regulations be issued directing the activities of the army, groups, and individuals in order to prevent breaches of international law that could have led to 'genocide or war crimes'. The letter was also sent to Karadžić and the Federal [Secretariat of Internal Affairs ("SUP")]." (Trial Judgement, vol. 2, para. 747. See Trial Judgement, vol. 2, para. 636, referring to, *inter alia*, Exhibit P190). Having considered the Đerić Letter, the Trial Chamber nonetheless concluded that the Trial Chamber was not satisfied that Stanišić took sufficient action to put an end to the crimes and found that instead he permitted the RS MUP forces under his control to continue to participate in joint operations with other Serb forces involved in the commission of crimes" (Trial Judgement, vol. 2, para. 759).

[1814]   *Cf. Popović et al.* Appeal Judgement, vol. 2, paras 1541-1542.

[1815]   See Stanišić Appeal Brief, paras 174 (referring to, *inter alia*, Trial Judgement, vol. 2, paras 46, 640-641, 644, 674, 680), 177 (referring to Trial Judgement, vol. 2, paras 664, 667, 673, 748), 178 (referring to Trial Judgement, vol. 2, paras 687-688, 698-708, 749), 179 (referring to, *inter alia*, Trial Judgement, vol. 2, paras 314, 592, 594, 606-607, 637, 642, 681, 684, 719-720, 733), 180 (referring to, *inter alia*, Trial Judgement, vol. 2, para. 621), 183 (referring to, *inter alia*, Trial Judgement, vol. 2, paras 557-558, 560, 562, 609).

543. The Appeals Chamber notes that the Trial Chamber referred to, and relied extensively on, the testimony of Witness Orašanin throughout the Trial Judgement,[1816] including portions of the extract of Witness Orašanin's testimony on which Stanišić relies in support of his contention that he issued orders, from the beginning of the Indictment period, seeking to ensure public safety and the prevention and detection of crimes.[1817] In the view of the Appeals Chamber, the remainder of the excerpts of Witness Orašanin's testimony that Stanišić cites, but the Trial Chamber did not, concerns a document Witness Orašanin referred to in relation to jurisdictional issues between the RS MUP "border department and military police".[1818] Nothing in the excerpts Stanišić cites, which the Trial Chamber did not, supports the contention that the Trial Chamber disregarded clearly relevant evidence when assessing Stanišić's intent. His arguments in this respect are therefore dismissed. **[page 224]**

544. The Trial Chamber referred extensively to the testimony of Witness Mačar[1819] and Witness Mandić[1820] throughout the Trial Judgement. However, it did not refer to the extracts of Witness Mačar's testimony on which Stanišić relies,[1821] in which Witness Mačar explains the nature of Exhibits 1D61 and 1D634, namely, Stanišić's order of 15 April 1992 ("Order of 15 April 1992") and his order of 16 April 1992 concerning the sanctioning of persons involved in criminal activities and protecting the civilian population (collectively, "Orders of 15 and 16 April 1992").[1822] Nor did it refer to the specific extracts of Witness Mandić's testimony on which Stanišić relies in support of his contention that he issued orders from the beginning of the Indictment period seeking to ensure public safety and the prevention and detection of crimes.[1823] The Appeals Chamber notes that this portion of Witness Mandić's testimony relates to his evidence that Exhibit 1D61 reflected the position taken by the RS MUP, to protect "law and order, and life and property".[1824] However, the Appeals Chamber also notes that the Trial Chamber referred to the existence and nature of the Orders of 15 and 16 April 1992 in the Trial Judgement,[1825] yet on the basis of other evidence, found that Stanišić took "insufficient action" to put an end to crimes.[1826] Accordingly, Stanišić has not demonstrated that the Trial Chamber disregarded the aforementioned extracts of the testimonies of Witness Mačar and Witness Mandić, and his arguments in this respect are therefore dismissed.

545. Nonetheless, the Appeals Chamber notes that the Trial Chamber did not address other orders that Stanišić identifies in support of his contention that he sought to ensure public safety and the prevention and detection of crimes throughout the Indictment period, namely: (i) Exhibit P792, Stanišić's order of 15 April 1992, requiring the return and itemisation of misappropriated material and technical property from the barracks in Faletići;[1827] and (ii) Exhibit P1252, a dispatch from Stanišić to the CSBs of Banja Luka, Bijeljina, Doboj, and Sarajevo, calling for the prosecution of perpetrators of the appropriation and plunder of real estate and public and private property committed by members in the service of the RS MUP ("17 April 1992 Dispatch").[1828] The Appeals Chamber also notes that Stanišić relies on evidence relating to the dissemination of the **[page 225]** 17 April 1992 Dispatch in support of his argument that, throughout the Indictment period,

---

[1816]   See *e.g.* Trial Judgement, vol. 2, paras 46-51, 53-55, 71, 73, 682, 686, 728, fns 142-148, 150-168, 173, 175-181, 245, 253, 686, 1756, 1763, 1867.
[1817]   See Stanišić Appeal Brief, fn. 213, referring to, *inter alia*, Milomir Orašanin, 7 Jun 2011, T. 21963-21965. These portions of Witness Orašanin's testimony relate to Stanišić's request of 5 October 1992 to the CSBs, concerning the submission of reports on persons suspected of committing war crimes (Trial Judgement, vol. 2, para. 682, referring to Exhibit 1D572, Milomir Orašanin, 7 Jun 2011, T. 21962, 21964).
[1818]   See Milomir Orašanin, 7 Jun 2011, T. 21965.
[1819]   See *e.g.* Trial Judgement, vol. 2, paras 1, 48, 56, 63, 67-68, 70, 251, 361, 560, 569, 581, 583, 611, 719, 726, fns 1, 57, 151, 214, 223, 229-230, 232, 238, 240, 747, 991, 1446, 1473, 1521, 1529, 1596, 1772, 1845, 1859-1860.
[1820]   See *e.g.* Trial Judgement, vol. 2, paras 4, 8, 576, 719, fns 20, 31, 1490, 1494, 1660, 1843-1844.
[1821]   See Stanišić Appeal Brief, fn. 213, referring to, *inter alia*, Goran Mačar, 5 Jul 2011, T. 22862-22863.
[1822]   See Goran Mačar, 5 Jul 2011, T. 22862-22863, discussing Exhibits 1D61, 1D634.
[1823]   See Stanišić Appeal Brief, para. 172, referring to, *inter alia*, Momčilo Mandić, 6 May 2010, T. 9728-9729.
[1824]   Momčilo Mandić, 6 May 2010, T. 9729. See Momčilo Mandić, 6 May 2010, T. 9728.
[1825]   Specifically, the Trial Chamber found that on 15 and 16 April 1992, respectively, Stanišić ordered: (i) "his subordinates to sanction persons seising, looting, and appropriating property and carrying out other unauthorised acts for personal gain with the 'most rigorous responsibility measures, including arrest and detention'"; and (ii) "all CSB chiefs to step up measures for the protection of the population, the prevention of crimes, and the apprehension of the perpetrators" (Trial Judgement, vol. 2, para. 610, referring to Exhibits 1D61, 1D634).
[1826]   Trial Judgement, vol. 2, para. 759. See Trial Judgement, vol. 2, paras 746, 751-758.
[1827]   See Exhibit P792, p. 1.
[1828]   See Exhibit P1252.

he repeated orders emphasising the imperative of preventing criminal activities. Specifically, Stanišić refers in this regard to Exhibit P553, a telegram sent by Župljanin to chiefs of SJBs on 29 April 1992, requiring SJB employees to be informed of Stanišić's request for action to be taken against RS MUP members involved in, *inter alia*, appropriation of moveable goods, as well as to the extracts of the testimonies of Witness Mačar, Witness Škipina, and Witness Vladimir Tutuš ("Witness Tutuš").[1829] Although the Trial Chamber referred to Witness Mačar's testimony,[1830] Witness Škipina's testimony,[1831] and Witness Tutuš's testimony[1832] throughout the Trial Judgement, the Appeals Chamber notes that it did not refer to the specific extracts cited by Stanišić, or to Exhibit P553.

546.   As to the question of whether the Trial Chamber disregarded this evidence, the Appeals Chamber first notes that Exhibit P792 does not concern crimes committed against non-Serbs and as such is not relevant to the discussion on Stanišić's intent.[1833] Second, it is clear from the Trial Judgement that the Trial Chamber was cognisant of the Orders of 15 and 16 April 1992 requiring action to be taken in relation to the prevention of crimes.[1834] With respect to Exhibits P553, P1252, and related excerpts of Witness Mačar's testimony, Witness Škipina's testimony, and Witness Tutuš's testimony, attesting to the dissemination of the Order of 15 April 1992, the Appeals Chamber notes that the Trial Chamber considered the testimony of Witness Krulj, Chief of the Ljubinje SJB, that the Order of 15 April 1992 was implemented in the Ljubinje SJB to the extent possible.[1835] However, it also found that Stanišić's follow-up orders from May 1992 with respect to the reserve police, among whom the problem of "unprincipled conduct" was most pronounced, were not carried out to the extent possible since the reserve police continued to serve within the RS MUP until the end of 1992.[1836] This and other evidence led the Trial Chamber to conclude that despite his knowledge of the crimes being committed, Stanišić took insufficient action to put an end **[page 226]** to them.[1837] Given that the evidence explicitly discussed by the Trial Chamber is similar in nature to Exhibits P553, P1252, and related excerpts of the testimonies of Witness Mačar, Witness Škipina, and Witness Tutuš, Stanišić has failed to demonstrate that the Trial Chamber disregarded this evidence. His arguments are therefore dismissed.

547.   The Appeals Chamber notes that the Trial Chamber referred to the evidence of Witness Njeguš[1838] and Witness Simo Tuševljak ("Witness Tuševljak")[1839] throughout the Trial Judgement, although not to the specific extracts upon which Stanišić relies.[1840] Nonetheless, the Trial Chamber considered that Witness Tuševljak, Witness Mačar, Witness Orasanin, and Witness Njeguš "testified that the policy at the time was to investigate all crimes equally",[1841] but concluded that this evidence was not reliable.[1842] In the Appeal's

[1829]   See Stanišić Appeal Brief, para. 174, referring to, *inter alia*, Exhibit P553, Slobodan Škipina, 30 Mar 2010, T. 8315-8317, Goran Mačar, 6 Jul 2011, T. 22865-22866, Vladimir Tutuš, 19 Mar 2010, T. 7865.
[1830]   See *e.g.* Trial Judgement, vol. 2, paras 1, 48, 56, 63, 67-68, 70, 251, 361, 560, 569, 581, 583, 611, 719, 726, fns 1, 57, 151, 214, 223, 229-230, 232, 238, 240, 747, 991, 1446, 1473, 1521, 1529, 1596, 1772, 1845, 1859-1860.
[1831]   See *e.g.* Trial Judgement, vol. 2, paras 17, 26-29, 66, 557, 564, 578, 601, 619, 689, fns 58, 83-84, 86-92, 220-221, 1140, 1455, 1499, 1573, 1623, 1767. The Appeals Chamber notes that the Trial Chamber referred to portions of the extract of Witness Škipina's testimony, on which Stanišić relies, at paragraph 689 of volume two of the Trial Judgement, in finding that Witness Škipina "was appointed Advisor on matters relating to the SNB on 6 August 1992 after having served as Head of the SNB until 3 July 1992, reported directly to the Minister of the RS MUP on events that were brought to his attention, some of which were included in daily bulletin reports for other leading members of the RS" (see Trial Judgement, vol. 2, para. 689, referring to Slobodan Škipina, 30 Mar 2010, T. 8308-8312, 8316-8317, 8323, Exhibits P1267, P1268, P1254).
[1832]   See *e.g.* Trial Judgement, vol. 2, paras 80, 396, 398, 415, 470, 488, 576, 695, fns 281, 1365-1370, 1494, 1783.
[1833]   *Cf.* Trial Judgement, vol. 2, para. 766.
[1834]   The Appeals Chamber recalls that the Trial Chamber did consider evidence regarding the existence the Orders of 15 and 16 April 1992 (see Trial Judgement, vol. 2, para. 610).
[1835]   Trial Judgement, vol. 2, para. 610, referring to, *inter alia*, Aleksandar Krulj, 28 Oct 2009, T. 2163-2165.
[1836]   Trial Judgement, vol. 2, para. 746.
[1837]   Trial Judgement, vol. 2, para. 759. See Trial Judgement, vol. 2, paras 751-758.
[1838]   See Trial Judgement, vol. 2, paras 14, 17, 355, 564, 601, 728, 936, fns 49-52, 58-59, 929, 1455, 1572, 1867.
[1839]   See *e.g.* Trial Judgement, vol. 2, paras 70-71, 708, fns 240, 244, 248, 1815.
[1840]   See Stanišić Appeal Brief, paras 175 (referring to, *inter alia*, Radomir Njeguš, 9 Jun 2010, T. 11475-11477), 180 (referring to, *inter alia*, Simo Tuševljak, 16 Jun 2011, T. 22276-22278). The Appeals Chamber notes that Stanišić also relies on this evidence in support of his contention that he responded promptly and unequivocally upon becoming aware of the commission of crimes (see Stanišić Appeal Brief, para. 181).
[1841]   Trial Judgement, vol. 2, para. 728, referring to Simo Tuševljak, 23 Jun 2011, T. 22694-22696, Goran Mačar, 13 Jul 2011, T. 23234-23241, Goran Mačar, 19 Jul 2011, T. 23528-23530, Radomir Njeguš, 9 Jun 2010, T. 11477-11479.
[1842]   The Trial Chamber found that this evidence did not represent "a true reflection of the practice of investigation and prosecution followed by the RS authorities in 1992" (Trial Judgement, vol. 2, para. 728).

Chamber's view, Stanišić has therefore failed to demonstrate the Trial Chamber's disregard of Witness Njeguš's testimony and Witness Tuševljak's testimony in this respect. His arguments in this regard are therefore dismissed.

548.   Although the Trial Chamber referred to the testimony of Witness Andan,[1843] Witness Mačar,[1844] and Witness Tuševljak,[1845] it did not refer to the portions of their testimony on which Stanišić relies with respect to inspection teams from the RS MUP conducting tours and audits of CSBs and SJBs throughout municipalities of the RS.[1846] The Appeals Chamber notes, however, that throughout the Trial Judgement, the Trial Chamber extensively referred to evidence relating to the engagement of the RS MUP's inspectors sent to SJBs and CSBs.[1847] In the Appeal's Chamber's view, the aforementioned testimonial evidence does not materially add any new argument to the Trial Chamber's discussion and as such is not of a character that its absence from the Trial Judgement shows its disregard. Stanišić's arguments in this respect are therefore dismissed. **[page 227]**

549.   Stanišić contends that the Trial Chamber failed to consider portions of Witness Davidović's *viva voce* testimony as well as Exhibits 1D646, P1557.01, P1557.03, and P1557.04 which demonstrate that he sought federal assistance to help in taking action against criminal elements.[1848] The Appeals Chamber notes that: (i) Exhibit 1D646 is a report by Witness Davidović, dated 8 August 1992;[1849] (ii) Exhibit P1557.01 is the witness statement of Witness Davidović;[1850] and (iii) Exhibits P1557.03 and P1557.04 contain Witness Davidović's testimony of 9 and 10 June 2005 in *Krajišnik*, respectively.[1851]

550.   The Appeals Chamber notes that the Trial Chamber relied on Witness Davidović's evidence, including portions of the extracts of *viva voce* testimony to which Stanišić refers, throughout the Trial Judgement. Specifically, the Trial Chamber relied on such evidence in discussing Stanišić's "deal" with Arkan,[1852] and in finding that: (i) in April or May 1992, Witness Davidović was "the chief police inspector in the federal SUP";[1853] (ii) the presence, in the RS, of paramilitary forces, who were initially invited and supported by the crisis staffs, was tolerated only until such forces "compromised the war-profiteering plans of the Crisis Staffs or harmed local Serbs";[1854] (iii) as a member of "the federal SUP", Witness Davidović had assisted Stanišić in the training of a "Special Police Unit, composed of approximately 170 members" in Vrace;[1855] (iv) Stanišić specifically gave Witness Davidović and Witness Andan full authority to deal with paramilitaries;[1856] (v) Witness Davidović met with Stanišić in Vrace to discuss arresting paramilitary formations and the Yellow Wasps in particular;[1857] (vi) Stanišić neither ordered, nor prohibited Davidović to arrest Arkan or members of his paramilitary force;[1858] and (vii) "Dragomir Andan and Milorad Davidović led actions against the paramilitary groups in Bijeljina and against the Red Berets in Brčko with assistance from Malović's Unit."[1859] The Trial Chamber found that these paramilitary groups resisted the action by Witness Andan and Witness

---

[1843]   See *e.g.* Trial Judgement, vol. 2, paras 17, 122, 537-540, 648, 665, 702-703, 714, 716-717, fns 58, 393, 396-397, 1386, 1388, 1390, 1391, 1687, 1717, 1800, 1803, 1827, 1837-1838, 1839, 1840.

[1844]   See *e.g.* Trial Judgement, vol. 2, paras 1, 48, 56, 63, 67-68, 70, 251, 361, 560, 569, 581, 583, 611, 719, 726; Trial Judgement, vol. 2, fns 1, 57, 151, 214, 223, 229-230, 232, 238, 240, 747, 991, 1446, 1473, 1521, 1529, 1596, 1772, 1845, 1859-1860.

[1845]   See *e.g.* Trial Judgement, vol. 2, paras 70-71, 708, fns 240, 244, 248, 1815.

[1846]   See Stanišić Appeal Brief, para. 172, referring to, *inter alia*, Dragomir Andan, 31 May 2011, T. 21573-21576, Exhibit P993, Simo Tuševljak, 16 Jun 2011, T. 22314-22315, Goran Mačar, 7 Jul 2011, T. 22968-22974, Goran Mačar, 15 Jul 2011, T. 23352-23354.

[1847]   See *e.g.* Trial Judgement, vol. 2, paras 48-54, 361, 392, 604.

[1848]   See Stanišić Appeal Brief, para. 172, referring to Exhibits 1D646, P1557.01, para. 46, P1557.03, pp 14189, 14211-14212, Milorad Davidović, 23 Aug 2010, T. 13586-13591, Milorad Davidović, 24 Aug 2010, T. 13623-13630, Exhibits P1557.01, paras 84-85, P1557.04, p. 14260. See also *supra*, para. 531.

[1849]   See Exhibit 1D646.

[1850]   See Exhibit P1557.01.

[1851]   See Exhibits P1557.03, P1557.04.

[1852]   See Trial Judgement, vol. 2, paras 710-711.

[1853]   Trial Judgement, vol. 2, para. 185, referring to, *inter alia*, Exhibit P1557.03, p. 14172.

[1854]   Trial Judgement, vol. 2, para. 126, referring to, *inter alia*, Exhibits P1557.01, p. 19, P1557.04, pp 14247-14250.

[1855]   Trial Judgement, vol. 2, para. 601, referring to, *inter alia*, Milorad Davidović, 23 Aug 2010, T. 13532-13533, Exhibits P1557.01, p. 12, P1127, p. 4.

[1856]   See Trial Judgement, vol. 2, para. 714, referring to, *inter alia*, Milorad Davidović, 23 Aug 2010, T. 13590, Milorad Davidović, 24 Aug 2010, T. 13613-13615, 13623-13624, Exhibit P1557.04, pp 14292-14293.

[1857]   Trial Judgement, vol. 2, para. 714, referring to Milorad Davidović, 23 Aug 2010, T. 13531-13533, 13564-13566.

[1858]   Trial Judgement, vol. 2, para. 712, referring to Milorad Davidović, 24 Aug 2010, T. 13625-13626.

[1859]   Trial Judgement, vol. 2, para. 717.

Davidović and "refused to fall under the command of the army."[1860] The Appeals Chamber considers that other **[page 228]** extracts of Witness Davidović's evidence to which Stanišić refers, but the Trial Chamber did not, merely lend further support to the Trial Chamber's finding that Stanišić authorised Witness Davidović to investigate, arrest, and institute proceedings against paramilitaries, and to train a special police unit in Vrace.[1861] Accordingly, Stanišić has failed to demonstrate that the Trial Chamber disregarded these portions of Witness Davidović's evidence. His arguments in this respect are therefore dismissed.

551.   Regarding Exhibit 1D646, a report of Witness Davidović to Stanišić dated 8 August 1992, detailing actions taken by a group of 17 members of the Federal SUP who were sent to the Bijeljina CSB on 27 June 1992 at the request of the RS MUP and were under Witness Davidović's command,[1862] the Appeals Chamber notes that the Trial Chamber *did* refer to it in the context of actions undertaken by Witness Andan and Witness Davidović against the paramilitary groups.[1863] Stanišić's argument that the Trial Chamber disregarded this evidence is therefore dismissed.

552.   The Trial Chamber did not address Exhibit 1D328 in the Trial Judgement. Stanišić relies on this exhibit in support of his contentions that he: (i) sent inspectors into the field with a view to taking measures to prevent and detect crimes, and to locate and apprehend perpetrators, irrespective of their ethnicity;[1864] and (ii) insisted on the investigation and filing of "reports on crimes, including war crimes, without any distinction being made on the basis of the ethnicity of the perpetrator or victim".[1865]

553.   The Appeals Chamber recalls that Exhibit 1D328 (the Sokolac Report) concerns a meeting on 27 July 1992 in Sokolac of leading personnel of criminology departments from the area of the Romanija-Birač CSB ("27 July 1992 Meeting").[1866] The Appeals Chamber notes that, according to the Sokolac Report, the 27 July 1992 Meeting was also attended by members of the RS MUP, Sarajevo CSB, and representatives of SJBs from various municipalities, including municipalities falling within the geographic area covered by the Indictment.[1867] The Appeals Chamber observes that Stanišić cites extracts of the Sokolac Report that detail: (i) difficulties faced by attendees, including Witness Mačar and members of the RS MUP, in performing their duties; and (ii) conclusions reached as to proceeding in the circumstances.[1868] He also relies, in particular, on the sixth conclusion reached at the 27 July 1992 Meeting, which states that "[m]aximal engagement **[page 229]** of all the operational workers is requested for the tasks of documenting war crimes and submitting criminal reports against unidentified perpetrators; to this end maximum cooperation is required with all the authorities in any particular area".[1869] The Appeals Chamber notes that the portions of the Sokolac Report referred to by Stanišić do not attest to his assertion that he "sent inspectors into the field with a view to taking measures to prevent and detect crimes, and to locate and apprehend perpetrators, irrespective of their ethnicity".[1870] In any event, as stated above, the Trial Chamber extensively referred to evidence relating to the engagement of the RS MUP's inspectors sent to SJBs and CSBs.[1871] Moreover, the Trial Chamber also referred to a number of Stanišić's orders to investigate and document crimes.[1872] In light of the foregoing, the Appeals Chamber considers that the Trial Chamber did not err by not specifically addressing the Sokolac Report. Stanišić's argument is therefore dismissed.

[1860]   Trial Judgement, vol. 2, para. 717, referring to, *inter alia*, Milorad Davidović, 24 Aug 2010, T. 13623-13630, Exhibits P1557.01, pp 26-27, 1D646, pp 6-12, 1D97, pp 2-5, 1D554, P591.
[1861]   See Trial Judgement, vol. 2, para. 714.
[1862]   Exhibit 1D646, pp 1-2.
[1863]   Trial Judgement, vol. 2, para. 717, referring to, *inter alia*, Exhibit 1D646. See Trial Judgement, vol. 2, para. 714.
[1864]   Stanišić Appeal Brief, para. 172, fn. 214.
[1865]   Stanišić Appeal Brief, para. 181, fn. 238.
[1866]   Exhibit 1D328.
[1867]   See Exhibit 1D328, p. 1.
[1868]   Exhibit 1D328, pp 2, 5.
[1869]   Exhibit 1D328, p. 5. See Stanišić Appeal Brief, fn. 238.
[1870]   See Stanišić Appeal Brief, para. 172, referring to, *inter alia*, Exhibit 1D328, pp 2, 5.
[1871]   See *e.g.* Trial Judgement, vol. 2, paras 48-54, 361, 392, 604.
[1872]   Trial Judgement, vol. 2, paras 748, 752-753. See *supra*, fn. 1813. The Appeals Chamber further notes that nothing in the Sokolac Report suggests that Stanišić insisted on the investigation and reporting of crimes *without any distinction being made on the basis of ethnicity of the perpetrator or victim*, as Stanišić argues (Exhibit 1D328, pp 1-5. See Stanišić Appeal Brief, para. 181, fn. 238).

554.   The Appeals Chamber notes that the Trial Chamber did not refer to Exhibit 1D63 an instruction to the SJB chiefs of Banja Luka, Bijeljina, Doboj, Sarajevo, and Trebinje, dated 19 July 1992 and originated by Stanišić.[1873] The exhibit pertains to the conclusion reached at the 11 July 1992 Collegium[1874] and contains questionnaires and instructions requiring SJB personnel to complete the questionnaire for all persons, regardless of ethnicity, against whom criminal reports had been submitted on reasonable grounds, as well as questionnaires for victims "regardless of whether a criminal report has been submitted or the procedure of gathering evidence for the submission of a criminal report against a perpetrator is still in progress".[1875] Exhibit 1D63 therefore relates to actions taken by Stanišić further to the conclusions reached at the 11 July 1992 Collegium. The Appeals Chamber notes, however, that the Trial Chamber considered evidence as to actions that Stanišić took further to the conclusions reached at the 11 July 1992 Collegium. For example, the Trial Chamber found that:

> [fallowing the 11 July Collegium, Stanišić sent an order on 19 July 1992 to the chiefs of all CSBs requesting information on [...] problems related to paramilitary units, procedures in taking custody, the treatment of prisoners, conditions of collection camps, and prisoners of Muslim ethnicity who were deposited without papers by the army at "undefined camps".[1876] **[page 230]**

However, the Trial Chamber found that despite this and other orders, mistreatment of detainees at the camps continued, and that Stanišić "failed to use the powers available to him under the law to ensure the full implementation of" his orders, despite being aware of the only limited action taken by his subordinates.[1877]

555.   Accordingly, the Appeals Chamber considers it apparent that the Trial Chamber expressly considered that action Stanišić took was insufficient to put an end to crimes.[1878] Given that Exhibit 1D63 is demonstrative only of limited action Stanišić took pursuant to the conclusions reached at the 11 July 1992 Collegium, the Appeals Chamber is of the view that Stanišić has failed to demonstrate that this evidence undermines the Trial Chamber's ultimate conclusion concerning Stanišić's failure to take sufficient action against crimes.[1879] As such, the Trial Chamber did not err in not explicitly addressing Exhibit 1D63 and Stanišić's argument is therefore dismissed.

556.   Stanišić refers to Exhibit P160, namely, minutes of the 11 July 1992 Collegium,[1880] in support of his arguments that the Trial Chamber failed to consider evidence that: (i) he repeated, throughout the Indictment period, orders emphasising the imperative of preventing criminal activities;[1881] (ii) he insisted on the non-discriminatory investigation of war crimes,[1882] which was reflected in the conclusions reached at the 11 July 1992 Collegium;[1883] (iii) he insisted on resolving issues of jurisdiction within the army in relation to combating crime and the criminal activity of paramilitaries;[1884] and (iv) his public speeches throughout the Indictment period were non-discriminatory and aimed at the promotion of the rule of law, the professionalism of the police, and the protection of life and property.[1885] **[page 231]**

[1873]   Exhibit 1D63, pp 1-2.
[1874]   Exhibit 1D63, p. 1.
[1875]   Exhibit 1D63, pp 1, 3-4.
[1876]   Trial Judgement, vol. 2, para. 637, referring to, *inter alia*, Exhibit 1D76. See Trial Judgement, vol. 2, para. 748.
[1877]   Trial Judgement, vol. 2, para. 753. See Trial Judgement, vol. 2, paras 748, 752. See Trial Judgement, vol. 2, para. 761. In addition, the Trial Chamber considered Stanišić's orders in the latter half of July, that all members of the MUP who had committed crimes or against whom official criminal proceedings had been launched should be relieved of duty and placed at the disposal of the VRS (Trial Judgement, vol. 2, para. 749). The Trial Chamber found, however, that the placing of errant reserve policemen at the disposal of the army "was not sufficient to fulfil his duty to protect the Muslim and Croat population, considering the fact that transferring known offenders in the reserve police to the army in fact further facilitated their continued interaction with civilians" (Trial Judgement, vol. 2, para. 751). Finally, the Appeals Chamber also notes that considering the language of the orders of, *inter alia*, 11 and 17 July 1992, the Trial Chamber found that "the instruction from Stanišić to the CSBs on documenting war crimes and other mass atrocities was specifically limited to where Serbs were the victims, and not all civilians" (Trial Judgement, vol. 2, para. 758).
[1878]   See Trial Judgement, vol. 2, para. 759.
[1879]   See Trial Judgement, vol. 2, para. 759.
[1880]   Exhibit P160, pp 1-2.
[1881]   Stanišić Appeal Brief, para. 174, referring to, *inter alia*, Exhibit P160, p. 15.
[1882]   Stanišić Appeal Brief, para. 175, referring to, *inter alia*, Exhibit P160, p. 22.
[1883]   Stanišić Appeal Brief, para. 181, referring to, *inter alia*, Exhibit P160, pp 22-23.
[1884]   Stanišić Appeal Brief, para. 179, referring to, *inter alia*, Exhibit P160, pp 24-25.
[1885]   Stanišić Appeal Brief, para. 183, referring to, *inter alia*, Exhibit P160, p. 4.

557. The Appeals Chamber notes that the Trial Chamber *did* refer to some of the portions of Exhibit P160, including to some portions that Stanišić identifies.[1886] The Appeals Chamber also recalls that elsewhere in the Trial Judgement, it has already dismissed Stanišić's argument that the Trial Chamber erred by not explicitly referring to the rest of Exhibit P160 in its discussion of his intent.[1887]

558. The Appeals Chamber now turns to: (i) Exhibits 1D595 to 1D601, and portions of the testimony of Witness Tuševljak, which Stanišić contends demonstrate that the RS MUP "gathered substantial and reliable material during the investigation of crimes which involved victims and alleged perpetrators of all ethnicities" and that this evidence "subsequently formed the basis of prosecutions of accused Serb and non-Serb individuals";[1888] (ii) Exhibits 1D356 and 1D357, and portions of the testimony of Witness Orašanin, which Stanišić argues demonstrate that he repeatedly emphasised the imperative of preventing criminal activities; and (iii) Exhibit 1D189 which Stanišić argues demonstrate that he insisted on the indiscriminate investigation and filing of reports on crimes.[1889]

559. The Appeals Chamber notes that the Trial Chamber did not refer to Exhibits 1D595 to 1D601, or the portion of Witness Tuševljak's testimony on which Stanišić relies, in the Trial Judgement.[1890] Having reviewed Exhibits 1D595 to 1D601, it is apparent to the Appeals Chamber that these exhibits relate to the subsequent prosecutions of individuals, *i.e.* outside of the Indictment period, for crimes committed in BiH during the Indictment period.[1891] The Appeals Chamber also notes that Witness Tuševljak testified that the public prosecutors in the RS and BiH continue to rely heavily upon documentary evidence gathered by the RS MUP during the Indictment period in order to establish convictions for perpetrators of crimes perpetrated at that time.[1892] The Appeals Chamber observes, specifically, Witness Tuševljak's testimony that Exhibit 1D595, a document of the Zvornik public prosecutor's office enclosing a criminal report of the Bratunac SJB, was indicative of a prosecution arising, at least in part, from evidence gathered by the RS MUP during **[page 232]** the Indictment period,[1893] while Exhibits 1D596 to 1D601 were admitted on the basis that they were demonstrative of similar prosecutions.[1894]

560. Further, the Trial Chamber did not refer at any point in the Trial Judgement to Exhibits 1D356 and 1D357, namely, reports submitted to the public prosecutor's office by Witness Bjelošević, Chief of the Doboj CSB, dated 1 August 1992 concerning, respectively, the death of Sejfudin Hadžimujić and the suspected murder of Derviš and Nejra Begović, all non-Serbs. The Appeals Chamber also notes that the Trial Chamber did not refer to Witness Orašanin's testimony in relation to these exhibits,[1895] or to Exhibit 1D189, a criminal report of 12 December 1992 to the public prosecutor's office in Sarajevo concerning the killing of nine prisoners in Vogošća municipality,[1896] in the broader context of his evidence concerning the role of the police, prosecutors, and the judiciary in conducting investigations of crimes.[1897]

561. The Appeals Chamber considers that Stanišić has not demonstrated that the Trial Chamber's failure to address Exhibits 1D356, 1D357, 1D189, 1D595 to 1D601 as well as the portions of Witness Orašanin's testimony and Witness Tuševljak's testimony that he cites, was indicative of any error, when viewed in the full context of the Trial Chamber's findings and analysis. In this respect, the Appeals Chamber observes that

---

[1886] See Trial Judgement, vol. 2, paras 81, 510, 630-631, fns 284, 1194, 1210, 1650-1653, referring to, *inter alia*, Exhibit P160, pp 7-9, 12, 14-17.
[1887] See *supra*, para. 485.
[1888] Stanišić Appeal Brief, para. 176, referring to Exhibits 1D595, 1D596, 1D597, 1D598, 1D599, 1D600, 1D601, Simo Tuševljak, 20 Jun 2011, T. 22434-22451.
[1889] See Stanišić Appeal Brief, para. 174, referring to, *inter alia*, Milomir Orašanin, 6 Jun 2011, T. 21908-21913, Milomir Orašanin, 7 Jun 2011, T. 21915-21920, Milomir Orašanin, 9 Jun 2011, T. 22118-22123, Exhibits 1D356, 1D357.
[1890] The Appeals Chamber, however, notes that the Trial Chamber did refer to Witness Tuševljak's testimony throughout the Trial Judgement (see *e.g.* Trial Judgement, vol. 2, paras 70-71, 708, fns 240, 244, 248).
[1891] See Exhibits 1D595, 1D596, 1D597, 1D598, 1D599, 1D600, 1D601.
[1892] Simo Tuševljak, 20 Jun 2011, T. 22437.
[1893] See Simo Tuševljak, 20 Jun 2011, T. 22434-22438.
[1894] Hearing, 20 Jun 2011, T. 22449-22451.
[1895] See Stanišić Appeal Brief, para. 174, referring to, *inter alia*, Milomir Orašanin, 7 Jun 2011, T. 21915-21920.
[1896] The Appeals Chamber notes that although the Trial Chamber did refer to this exhibit, it did so to establish that the crime mentioned in this report occurred, and hence not in the context relevant to the discussion on Stanišić's *mens rea* (see Trial Judgement, vol. 1, para. 1537, referring to, *inter alia*, Exhibit 1D189).
[1897] See Milomir Orašanin, 7 Jun 2011, T. 21915-21920. See also Milomir Orašanin, 9 Jun 2011, T. 22118-22123.

the Trial Chamber specifically noted that it had analysed: (i) the KT Logbooks and KTN Logbooks;[1898] (ii) the 1993 entries in the logbook from the "Sarajevo Basic Prosecutor's Office II";[1899] and (iii) prosecutor logbooks for the period 1992 to 1995, covering the Municipalities charged in the Indictment (collectively, "Prosecutor's Logbooks").[1900] On this basis, the Trial Chamber found that:

> [i]n the municipalities of Bileća, Ilijas, Gacko, Višegrad, Pale, Vlasenica, Vogošća, and Bosanski Šamac, no serious crimes alleged to have been committed by Serbs against non-Serbs during the Indictment period were reported to the prosecutor's offices. In addition, one crime was reported in each of the following municipalities: Doboj, Kotor Varoš, Prijedor, and Ključ. Approximately two were reported in Zvornik, nine in Teslić, four in Sanski Most, three in Brčko, and four in Bijeljina. Based on the review of the Banja Luka Basic Prosecutor's office, there were a total of 21 serious crimes by Serb perpetrators committed against non-Serb victims reported in Banja Luka, Skender Vakuf, and Donji Vakuf between 1 April and 31 December 1992.[1901] **[page 233]**

562. Moreover, the Trial Chamber also considered the testimonial evidence of Witness Gojković, a judge of the Basic Court in Sarajevo between 20 June and 19 December 1992, and Witness Gaćinović, the higher prosecutor for Trebinje in August of 1992, regarding their respective analyses of the Prosecutor's Logbooks, that supported the Trial Chamber's conclusion that "the police and civilian prosecutors failed to report or under-reported serious crimes committed by Serb perpetrators against non-Serbs".[1902] The Appeals Chamber notes that Stanišić's challenges to the Trial Chamber's reliance on the evidence relating to the KT Logbooks and KTN Logbooks are dismissed elsewhere in this Judgement.[1903]

563. The Appeals Chamber accepts that Exhibits 1D356, 1D357, 1D189, 1D595 to 1D601, as well as the portions of Witness Orašanin's testimony and Witness Tuševljak's testimony cited by Stanišić, suggest that *some* reports of the crimes committed against non-Serbs were filed with the RS Prosecution's office and that *some* information gathered by the RS MUP during the Indictment period was utilised in subsequent investigations and prosecutions of perpetrators of crimes, including against non-Serbs.[1904] However, it is unknown from this evidence whether subsequent prosecutions were based solely, or even to any significant extent, on reports and investigations conducted by the RS MUP during the Indictment period. Furthermore, the Trial Chamber did consider evidence of the reporting of serious crimes within the RS MUP and by the RS MUP to the judiciary during the Indictment period.[1905] Nonetheless, in light of other evidence on the record, the Trial Chamber rejected evidence, including that of Witness Tuševljak, that it was the policy of the RS MUP to investigate all crimes equally.[1906] The Appeals Chamber therefore considers that Stanišić has failed to demonstrate that these exhibits and portions of witness testimony are so clearly relevant that the absence of references to them in the Trial Judgement shows the Trial Chamber's disregard. Stanišić's arguments in relation to this evidence are therefore dismissed.

564. The Appeals Chamber now turns to Stanišić's assertion that he insisted on the indiscriminate investigation and filing of reports on crimes, including war crimes, as reflected in the conclusions reached at the 11 July 1992 Collegium.[1907] Although the Trial Chamber referred to portions of the testimony of Witness Planojević and Witness Tutuš throughout the Trial **[page 234]** Judgement,[1908] it did not refer to the specific extracts upon which Stanišić relies.[1909] The Appeals Chamber notes that Witness Planojević's testimony and

---

[1898] Trial Judgement, vol. 2, para. 90. See Trial Judgement, vol. 2, para. 93.
[1899] Trial Judgement, vol. 2, para. 90. See Trial Judgement, vol. 2, para. 93.
[1900] Trial Judgement, vol. 2, para. 91. See Trial Judgement, vol. 2, para. 93.
[1901] Trial Judgement, vol. 2, para. 94 (citations omitted).
[1902] Trial Judgement, vol. 2, paras 104, 745. See Trial Judgement, vol. 2, para. 462.
[1903] See *supra*, paras 273-280.
[1904] See Exhibits 1D595, 1D596, 1D597, 1D598, 1D599, 1D600, 1D601.
[1905] Trial Judgement, vol. 2, paras 104, 745. See *e.g.* Trial Judgement, vol. 2, paras 66-94, 462.
[1906] See Trial Judgement, vol. 2, para. 728, referring to Staka Gojković, 15 Jun 2010, T. 11738, 11740-11741, 11572-11573, 11769, Exhibits P1609.01, p. 5, P1284.55, p. 28. See also Trial Judgement, vol. 2, para. 745.
[1907] See *supra*, fn. 1783.
[1908] With respect to Witness Planojević, see Trial Judgement, vol. 2, paras 537, 601-602, 708, fns 1386-1387, 1572, 1574, 1813, referring to Dobrislav Planojević, 22 Oct 2010, T. 16395, 16404, 16432. With respect to Witness Tutuš, see *e.g.* Trial Judgement, vol. 2, paras 80, 396, 398, 415, 470, 488, 576, 695, fns 281, 1365-1370, 1494, 1783.
[1909] See Stanišić Appeal Brief, para. 181, referring to, *inter alia*, Vladimir Tutuš, 22 Mar 2010, T. 7914-7915, Dobrislav Planojević, 29 Oct 2010, T. 16569, Simo Tuševljak, 16 Jun 2011, T. 22276-22278. Insofar as Stanišić also relies upon the pages 22276-22278 of Witness Tuševljak's testimony in support of this argument, the Appeals Chamber recalls its finding above that Stanišić has

Witness Tutuš's testimony corroborate evidence in Exhibits P160 and P427.08 as to the conclusions reached at the 11 July 1992 Collegium, following discussions led by Stanišić.[1910] As noted above,[1911] the Trial Chamber considered the 11 July 1992 Collegium, including Exhibit P160.[1912] Accordingly, the Appeals Chamber is of the view that Stanišić has failed to demonstrate that the Trial Chamber disregarded the portions of Witness Planojević's testimony and Witness Tutuš's testimony that he cites, and his arguments are therefore dismissed.

565.   Stanišić contends that Exhibit P628 and portions of the testimonies of Witness Mačar, Witness Škipina, Witness Planojević, and Witness Tutuš demonstrate that he responded promptly and unequivocally upon becoming aware of the commission of crimes.[1913] The Appeals Chamber notes that the Trial Chamber only referred to portions of Exhibit P628, a report of Witness Tutuš concerning "registered illegal activities" of the members of the former Banja Luka CSB SPD, dated 5 May 1993,[1914] in the section of the Trial Judgement dedicated to Župljanin's responsibility.[1915] The Appeals Chamber further notes that Stanišić does not explain how Exhibit P628 is demonstrative of his prompt or unequivocal response to crimes, and is liable to be dismissed on those grounds alone.[1916] Nonetheless, the Appeals Chamber notes that Exhibit P628 details various crimes committed by members of the Banja Luka CSB SPD in both 1992 and 1993. The Appeals Chamber notes, further, that the crimes referred to in Exhibit P628 were predominantly directed **[page 235]** against Serb victims,[1917] many of whom were policemen in the RS MUP.[1918] While the exhibit does mention isolated instances of crimes committed against non-Serbs,[1919] it does not contain evidence going to the issue of what, if any, follow up action was taken in relation to these incidents.[1920] Further, the Appeals Chamber notes that Stanišić does not contend that any of the incidents referred to in Exhibit P628 are demonstrative of action taken by the RS MUP in relation to the crimes charged in the Indictment.[1921] Finally, the Appeals Chamber notes that the Trial Chamber addressed Stanišić's actions in relation to the Banja Luka CSB SPD in some detail in the Trial Judgement.[1922] In light of the above, the Appeals Chamber is not persuaded that the absence of the Trial Chamber's explicit references to certain portions of Exhibit P628 shows its disregard of this evidence. His argument that the Trial Chamber erred by disregarding this evidence is therefore dismissed.

566.   While the Trial Chamber referred to Witness Mačar's testimony,[1923] Witness Škipina's testimony,[1924] and Witness Planojević's testimony,[1925] throughout the Trial Judgement, it did not refer to the particular

---

failed to demonstrate that the Trial Chamber erred by disregarding this evidence (see *supra*, para. 547). Moreover, Stanišić also relies upon these portions of Witness Tutuš's testimony, Witness Planojević's testimony, and Witness Tuševljak's testimony, in support of his argument that conclusions reached at the 11 July 1992 Collegium "reflected [his] insistence to investigate and file criminal reports on crimes, including war crimes, without any distinction being made on the basis of the ethnicity or perpetrator of the victim" (see Stanišić Appeal Brief, para. 181, referring to, *inter alia*, Vladimir Tutuš, 22 Mar 2010, T. 7914-7915, Dobrislav Planojević, 29 Oct 2010, T. 16569).

[1910]   Vladimir Tutuš, 22 Mar 2010, T. 7914-7915; Dobrislav Planojević, 29 Oct 2010, T. 16569. See Trial Judgement, vol. 2, para. 637; Exhibits P160; P427.08.
[1911]   See Trial Judgement, vol. 2, paras 629-633.
[1912]   The Trial Chamber also expressly rejected the suggestion that the policy of the RS MUP was to investigate all crimes equally and in an impartial manner (see Trial Judgement, vol. 2, para. 728).
[1913]   Stanišić Appeal Brief, para. 176, referring to, *inter alia*, Slobodan Škipina, 30 Mar 2010, T. 8339-8361, Slobodan Škipina, 31 Mar 2010, T. 8362-8364, Dobrislav Planojević, 22 Oct 2010, T. 16411-16412, Dobrislav Planojević, 28 Oct 2010, T. 16537-16539, Goran Mačar, 18 Jul 2011, T. 23473-23474, Vladimir Tutuš, 16 Mar 2010, T. 7707-7712, Exhibit P628. See *supra*, fn. 1813.
[1914]   Exhibit P628, p. 1.
[1915]   Trial Judgement, vol. 2, para. 438, referring to, *inter alia*, Exhibit P628, p. 10. See Trial Judgement, vol. 2, para. 488, referring to, *inter alia*, Exhibit P628.
[1916]   See Stanišić Appeal Brief, para. 176, fn. 223.
[1917]   See Exhibit P628, pp 2-20.
[1918]   See *e.g.* Exhibit P628, pp 2-8, 10, 13.
[1919]   See Exhibit P628, pp 2, 6, 12.
[1920]   See Exhibit P628, pp 2-20.
[1921]   See Stanišić Appeal Brief, para. 176.
[1922]   See Trial Judgement, vol. 2, paras 606-609.
[1923]   See *e.g.* Trial Judgement, vol. 2, paras 1, 48, 56, 63, 67-68, 70, 251, 361, 560, 569, 581, 583, 611, 719, 726; Trial Judgement, vol. 2, fns 1, 57, 151, 214, 223, 229-230, 232, 238, 240, 747, 991, 1446, 1473, 1521, 1529, 1596, 1772, 1845, 1859-1860.
[1924]   See *e.g.* Trial Judgement, vol. 2, paras 17, 26-29, 66, 557, 564, 578, 601, 619, 689; Trial Judgement, vol. 2, fns 58, 83-84, 86-92, 220-221, 1140, 1455, 1499, 1573, 1623, 1767.
[1925]   See Trial Judgement, vol. 2, paras 537, 601-602, 708, fns 1386-1387, 1572, 1574, 1813.

extracts upon which Stanišić relies in this respect. The Appeals Chamber notes that aforementioned portions of testimonies relate to, *inter alia*, the RS MUP's efforts to arrest the paramilitary Veselin "Batko" Vlahović ("Vlahović") in or around May 1992, who was considered responsible for crimes, including rape, killings, and armed robberies, against "Bosniaks" in parts of Sarajevo.[1926]

567.   In this respect, the Appeals Chamber notes that Stanišić refers to a large extract of the testimony of Witness Škipina,[1927] who was the chief of the SNB in the RS from early April 1992 to 3 July 1992.[1928] This portion of Witness Škipina's testimony includes his evidence that allegations against Vlahović were an example of the evidence he received about crimes from his inspectors.[1929] **[page 236]** Witness Škipina testified that he did not know what ultimately happened to Vlahović, and was unaware if any further action was taken against him.[1930] Witness Mačar recalled that the RS MUP received information about Vlahović's criminal activities, and that he remembered that "pursuant to [Witness Planojević's] orders, and after consultations with the minister, attempts were made to arrest him, but a short while before that, the military police arrested him and launched the relevant procedure".[1931]

568.   The Appeals Chamber notes that Witness Škipina also gave evidence in relation to an informal meeting between himself, Witness Đerić, and Witness Planojević, where the high incidence of crimes was one of the topics discussed.[1932] Witness Planojević testified in more detail in relation to this meeting, which occurred in about May 1992,[1933] stating that he had mentioned Vlahović to Witness Đerić, and that Witness Đerić, in his presence, then made a phone call requesting that the issue of Vlahović be resolved.[1934] Witness Planojević testified that "soon after that" Vlahović was arrested by the armed forces.[1935] The Appeals Chamber further notes Witness Planojević's testimony that he had previously spoken to Stanišić about Vlahović, and that Stanišić: (i) stated that he would call the Main Staff of the armed forces; and (ii) requested Witness Planojević to "please follow this and see whether anything will really be done about that".[1936] Nonetheless, Witness Planojević also testified that he was unaware if Stanišić ever contacted the Main Staff about Vlahović.[1937]

569.   The Appeals Chamber accepts that the testimonies of Witness Mačar, Witness Škipina, and Witness Planojević suggest that the RS MUP and Stanišić took some action in relation to Vlahović. However, this evidence is inconclusive as to whether Stanišić personally made any efforts to resolve the issue. Moreover, even if accepted as evidence of Stanišić's intention to resolve this issue, the Appeals Chamber considers that this isolated example of action taken in relation to one paramilitary member alleged to be a perpetrator of crimes against non-Serbs on territory outside of the geographical scope of the Indictment, is insufficient, when considered in the context of the evidence as a whole, to undermine the Trial Chamber's finding that: (i) action against paramilitaries was "only pursued by Stanišić following their refusal to submit to the command of the army and **[page 237]** their continued commission of acts of theft, looting, and trespasses against the local RS leaders";[1938] and (ii) "when dealing with war crimes, Mićo Stanišić focused *primarily* on crimes

[1926]   See Slobodan Škipina, 30 Mar 2010, T. 8339-8341; Slobodan Škipina, 31 Mar 2010, T. 8362-8364; Dobrislav Planojević, 22 Oct 2010, T. 16411-16412; Dobrislav Planojević, 28 Oct 2010, T. 16537-16539; Goran Mačar, 18 Jul 2011, T. 23473-23474. See also Slobodan Škipina, 30 Mar 2010, T. 8342-8361.
[1927]   Stanišić Appeal Brief, para. 176, referring to, *inter alia*, Slobodan Škipina, 30 Mar 2010, 8339-8361, Slobodan Škipina, 31 Mar 2010, T. 8362-8364.
[1928]   Trial Judgement, vol. 2, para. 17.
[1929]   Slobodan Škipina, 30 Mar 2010, T. 8339-8340. The Appeals Chamber notes that Witness Škipina also testified that, *inter alia*: (i) the only information he received about crimes was from his inspector (Slobodan Škipina, 30 Mar 2010, T. 8339-8840); (ii) he did not receive information about crimes through informal channels other than Radio Sarajevo (Slobodan Škipina, 30 Mar 2010, T. 8340-8341); (iii) the RS MUP may have received information from other sources, but that the SNB did not, in part due to communications issues (Slobodan Škipina, 30 Mar 2010, T. 8344-8345); and (iv) he attended two cabinet meetings in lieu of Stanišić, at the Minister of Interior's request (Slobodan Škipina, 30 Mar 2010, T. 8347-8348. See Slobodan Škipina, 30 Mar 2010, T. 8349-8352).
[1930]   Slobodan Škipina, 31 Mar 2010, T. 8364.
[1931]   Goran Mačar, 18 Jul 2011, T. 23474.
[1932]   See Slobodan Škipina, 30 Mar 2010, T. 8353-8555.
[1933]   Dobrislav Planojević, 22 Oct 2010, T. 16411.
[1934]   Dobrislav Planojević, 22 Oct 2010, T. 16412.
[1935]   Dobrislav Planojević, 22 Oct 2010, T. 16408, 16412.
[1936]   Dobrislav Planojević, 22 Oct 2010, T. 16407. See Dobrislav Planojević, 22 Oct 2010, T. 16412.
[1937]   Dobrislav Planojević, 22 Oct 2010, T. 16408.
[1938]   Trial Judgement, vol. 2, para. 756.

committed against Serbs".[1939] Accordingly, the Appeals Chamber is of the view that Stanišić has failed to demonstrate that the Trial Chamber erred by not explicitly addressing this evidence in the Trial Judgement. His arguments in this respect are therefore dismissed.

570. Finally, the Appeals Chamber notes that the Trial Chamber in fact considered the portion of Witness Tutuš's testimony upon which Stanišić relies, which relates to an incident on 21 July 1992, when 30 armed members of the Banja Luka CSB SPD freed two members of the detachment from the Tunjice prison in Banja Luka.[1940] Accordingly, Stanišić has failed to demonstrate that the Trial Chamber disregarded this evidence and his arguments in this respect are dismissed.

(iii) Conclusion

571. In light of the above, the Appeals Chamber finds that Stanišić has failed to demonstrate that the Trial Chamber erroneously disregarded evidence demonstrating that he did not intend the commission of crimes. Accordingly, the Appeals Chamber dismisses Stanišić's arguments in this respect.

(i) Whether the Trial Chamber erred in concluding that Stanišić possessed the requisite intent pursuant to the first category of joint criminal enterprise (Stanišić's first ground of appeal in part and fourth ground of appeal in part)

(i) Submissions of the parties

572. As set out above,[1941] Stanišić contends that the Trial Chamber erred in finding that the only reasonable inference on the basis of the evidence was that he was aware of the persecutorial intentions of the Bosnian Serb leadership to forcibly transfer and deport non-Serbs from BiH and shared that intent.[1942] The Prosecution responds that the Trial Chamber reasonably concluded that Stanišić shared the common criminal purpose of the JCE.[1943] **[page 238]**

(ii) Analysis

573. The Appeals Chamber recalls its previous finding that the Trial Chamber found that, Stanišić possessed the requisite intent throughout the Indictment period (*i.e.* from at least 1 April 1992 until 31 December 1992),[1944] when it concluded that he shared the "persecutorial intentions of the Bosnian Serb leadership to forcibly transfer and deport Muslims and Croats from territories of BiH".[1945] In the preceding sections of this Judgement, the Appeals Chamber has addressed Stanišić's arguments concerning the factors referred to by the Trial Chamber in the *Mens Rea* Section – namely, at paragraphs 766 to 769 of volume two of the Trial Judgement – in reaching its conclusion that he shared this requisite intent. As indicated above, the Appeals Chamber considers that the factors referred to by the Trial Chamber in the *Mens Rea* Section must be understood as a summary of findings contained throughout the Trial Judgement and must be read in the context of the Trial Judgement as a whole.[1946] The Appeals Chamber will now proceed to assess the effect of the findings in the preceding sections concerning the factors listed in the *Mens Rea* Section on the Trial Chamber's ultimate conclusion regarding Stanišić's intent.

[1939] Trial Judgement, vol. 2, para. 758 (emphasis added).
[1940] See Trial Judgement, vol. 2, para. 488, referring to, *inter alia*, Vladimir Tutuš, 16 Mar 2010, T. 7708-7712. While Stanišić also refers to Vladimir Tutuš, 16 Mar 2010, T. 7707, the Appeals Chamber considers that the testimony of Witness Tutuš therein is not such that it impacts upon the testimony at pages 7708-7712 of the transcript.
[1941] See *supra*, para. 368.
[1942] Stanišić Appeal Brief, para. 96, referring to Trial Judgement, vol. 2, para. 769. See Stanišić Appeal Brief, paras 98, 111, 187, Appeal Hearing, 15 Dec 2015, AT. 97, where Stanišić reiterates that the Trial Chamber erred in drawing the inference that he shared the *mens rea*. See also Stanišić Appeal Brief, paras 101-102, Appeal Hearing, 15 Dec 2015, AT. 98-99, 103-104.
[1943] Prosecution Response Brief (Stanišić), para. 36.
[1944] See *supra*, para. 376.
[1945] Trial Judgement, vol. 2, para. 769.
[1946] See *supra*, para. 378. See generally *supra*, paras 389-571.

574. In assessing Stanišić's intent, the Trial Chamber "first considered evidence on Stanišić's knowledge of the commission of crimes against Muslims and Croats in the geographic area and during the time period covered by the Indictment".[1947] In this respect, the Appeals Chamber has found that the Trial Chamber erred in finding: (i) on the basis of the Communications Logbook, that Stanišić was "regularly informed throughout 1992 about crimes";[1948] and (ii) that on 18 April 1992, Stanišić was informed that a certain "Zoka" had arrested Muslims in Sokolac.[1949]

575. Nonetheless, the Appeals Chamber has found that in light of the remaining findings of the Trial Chamber, a reasonable trier of fact could have found that Stanišić acquired knowledge of crimes committed against Muslims and Croats in the area relevant to the Indictment as of late April 1992.[1950] More specifically, the Appeals Chamber has upheld the Trial Chamber's findings that Stanišić became aware: (i) in late April 1992, of the looting of Muslim property by reserve police in Vrace, to which Stanišić responded that it was "normal" in times of war;[1951] (ii) at the end of May 1992, that a large number of Muslims, including civilians, were arrested and detained in the **[page 239]** municipality of Prijedor;[1952] (iii) on 3 June 1992, that Muslim and Croat civilians were victims of unspecified crimes, the perpetrators of which were identified as "individuals and groups among our forces";[1953] (iv) "at the latest, by the beginning of June 1992" (and again in July, August, and October 1992), of the unlawful detention of Muslims and Croats;[1954] (v) at some point between June and the beginning of July 1992, of the activities of the paramilitary groups in Zvornik, "including [committing] war crimes";[1955] (vi) on 11 July 1992, of "looting, mainly perpetrated during 'mopping-up operations'" and "war crimes" committed by Serbs;[1956] (vii) on 20 July 1992, that "the VRS and the police had arrested 'several thousands' of Muslims and Croats, including persons of no security interest, whom Župljanin proposed to use as hostages for prisoner exchanges";[1957] and (viii) by around 23 or 24 August 1992, of the killing of approximately 150-200 Muslim men from Trnopolje detention camp by Prijedor policemen at Korićanske Stijene.[1958]

576. Further, the Trial Chamber considered various other factors in assessing Stanišić's intent. Among those was Stanišić's "position at the time".[1959] In this regard, the Appeals Chamber recalls that it has found that the Trial Chamber erred in finding that Stanišić was a member of the BSA.[1960] Regardless of whether he was a member of the BSA, the Trial Chamber further considered that from 31 March 1992 until the end of 1992, he held the position of Minister of Interior within the RS Government,[1961] which was one of the most important organs in the RS.[1962]

577. The Trial Chamber further considered evidence of Stanišić's conduct and statements in relation to policies of the BSA and SDS.[1963] As regards these policies, the Trial Chamber noted, in particular: (i) views expressed by Karadžić, Dutina, and Kuprešanin at the BSA and SDS Meetings in late 1991 and early 1992, "that there be an ethnic division of the territory, that 'a war would lead to a forcible and bloody transfer of minorities' from one region to another, and that joint life with Muslims and Croats was impossible";[1964] (ii) Stanišić's attendance at the 1st Council Meeting on 11 January 1992, where the boundaries of ethnic territory

---

[1947] Trial Judgement, vol. 2, para. 766.
[1948] See *supra*, para. 411.
[1949] See *infra*, paras 664-665. Trial Judgement, vol. 2, para. 612.
[1950] See *supra*, para. 412.
[1951] Trial Judgement, vol. 2, para. 603.
[1952] Trial Judgement, vol. 2, para. 689, referring to, *inter alia*, Exhibits P1376, P1377. See Trial Judgement, vol. 2, paras 420, 764.
[1953] Trial Judgement, vol. 2, para. 689, referring to, *inter alia*, Exhibit P1387. See Trial Judgement, vol. 2, para. 764.
[1954] Trial Judgement, vol. 2, para. 762. See Trial Judgement, vol. 2, paras 617, 623, 631-633, 639, 646, 660-663, 763-765.
[1955] Trial Judgement, vol. 2, para. 713, referring to Dragan Dokanovic, 20 Nov 2009, T. 3586-3588, ST222, 9 Nov 2010, T. 17101-17104 (confidential). For crimes committed by paramilitaries in Zvornik, see *e.g.* Trial Judgement, vol. 1, paras 1652, 1663, 1666, 1670.
[1956] Trial Judgement, vol. 2, para. 632. See Trial Judgement, vol. 2, para. 631.
[1957] Trial Judgement, vol. 2, para. 765. See Trial Judgement, vol. 2, para. 638.
[1958] Trial Judgement, vol. 2, para. 677. See Trial Judgement, vol. 1, para. 696.
[1959] Trial Judgement, vol. 2, para. 769.
[1960] See *supra*, para. 418.
[1961] Trial Judgement, vol. 2, paras 141, 542. See Trial Judgement, vol. 2, paras 6, 797.
[1962] Trial Judgement, vol. 2, para. 131.
[1963] Trial Judgement, vol. 2, para. 767.
[1964] Trial Judgement, vol. 2, para. 767. See Trial Judgement, vol. 2, paras 162, 174, 179.

and the establishment of government **[page 240]** organs in the RS were determined to be priorities;[1964][1965] and (iii) the Strategic Objectives, presented to the BSA on 12 May 1992, which called for the separation of Serb people from Muslims and Croats.[1966]

578. The Appeals Chamber observes that, with respect to Stanišić's statements in relation to these policies, the Trial Chamber found that: (i) on 24 March 1992, when he was elected the Minister of Interior by the BSA, Stanišić remarked that "the SRBiH MUP had been used as an instrument of the SDA and the HDZ for achieving their political goals, including the creation of an army from the reserve forces comprised of only one ethnicity and the dismissal of Serbs from their positions";[1967] (ii) upon his election as the Minister of Interior, Stanišić also stated that he hoped that "in the future, the Serbian MUP [would] become a professional organisation, an organ of state administration which [would] actually protect property, life, body and other values";[1968] (iii) at the November 1992 BSA Session, Stanišić "acknowledged that 'in the beginning', 'thieves and criminals' were accepted into the reserve police forces because 'we wanted the country defended'";[1969] and (iv) at the same BSA session, Stanišić stated that he had always followed "policies of the SDS Presidency and our Deputies in the former state".[1970]

579. In this context, the Trial Chamber also considered Stanišić's "close relationship with Karadžić" from at least June 1991.[1971]

580. Further, the Trial Chamber took into account evidence of Stanišić's deal with Arkan's Men, in the sense that he approved of the operations of Arkan's Men in Bijeljina and Zvornik, and allowed Arkan to remove property in exchange for liberating the territories.[1972] While the Trial Chamber did not specify precisely when it considered Stanišić had approved of these operations, the Appeals Chamber notes the Trial Chamber's finding that the attacks by, *inter alios*, Arkan's Men on Bijeljina and Zvornik took place in early April 1992.[1973] The Trial Chamber further considered that while Stanišić took action against some paramilitary groups, this action:

> was only pursued by Stanišić following their refusal to submit to the command of the army and their continued commission of acts of theft, looting, and trespasses against the local RS leaders. **[page 241]** The primary motivation for these actions was the theft of Golf vehicles and harassment of the Serbs, an issue that concerned the RS authorities since the start of hostilities.[1974]

581. Moreover, the Trial Chamber considered: (i) Stanišić's presence at the sessions of the RS Government on 4 and 29 July 1992 when the issue of Muslims moving out of the RS was raised and the RS MUP was tasked with gathering information about Muslims moving out of the RS and the needs of displaced persons and refugees;[1975] (ii) Stanišić's presence at the 11 July 1992 Collegium, "where the relocation of citizens and entire villages was discussed";[1976] and (iii) the Perišić Report of 13 July 1992, which detailed that in the municipality of Višegrad, "certain police officers were exhibiting a lack of professionalism while over 2,000 Muslims moved out of the municipality" of Višegrad "in an organised manner".[1977]

582. Further, the Trial Chamber considered Stanišić's "continued support for and participation in the implementation of the polices of the Bosnian Serb leadership and the SDS".[1978] In addition to the views of Karadžić, Dutina, and Kuprešanin, the Strategic Objectives, and Stanišić's attendance at the 1st Council Meeting, referred to above,[1979] the Trial Chamber also considered that: (i) SDS and Bosnian Serb leadership

---

1965	Trial Judgement, vol. 2, para. 767. See Trial Judgement, vol. 2, para. 551.
1966	Trial Judgement, vol. 2, para. 767. See Trial Judgement, vol. 2, paras 188-199.
1967	Trial Judgement, vol. 2, para. 558.
1968	Trial Judgement, vol. 2, para. 558. See Trial Judgement, vol. 2, paras 542, 732.
1969	Trial Judgement, vol. 2, para. 600.
1970	Trial Judgement, vol. 2, para. 570.
1971	Trial Judgement, vol. 2, paras 730, 769. See Trial Judgement, vol. 2, paras 565, 567-568.
1972	Trial Judgement, vol. 2, para. 768. See Trial Judgement, vol. 2, para. 710.
1973	Trial Judgement, vol. 1, paras 888, 915 (Bijeljina), 1571-1572 (Zvornik).
1974	Trial Judgement, vol. 2, para. 756. See Trial Judgement, vol. 2, paras 708, 715, 717.
1975	Trial Judgement, vol. 2, para. 768. See Trial Judgement, vol. 2, paras 627, 650.
1976	Trial Judgement, vol. 2, para. 768. See Trial Judgement, vol. 2, paras 629-633.
1977	Trial Judgement, vol. 2, para. 768. See Trial Judgement, vol. 2, para. 634.
1978	Trial Judgement, vol. 2, para. 769.
1979	See *supra*, para. 577.

intensified a process of territorial demarcation following the declaration of independence in the BiH Assembly on 15 October 1991 and that the forceful assumption of control over territories was an important part of this process;[1980] (ii) prior to February 1992, Serbs had coalesced around the idea of a separate Serb entity "carved out of the territory of the SRBiH";[1981] (iii) Bosnian Serb control over the territories was to be achieved through the establishment of separate and parallel Bosnian Serb institutions, including the RS and RS Government;[1982] and (iv) the process of establishing Serb municipalities was initiated through the Variant A and B Instructions issued on 19 December 1991, which led to the violent takeovers of the Municipalities, the aim of which was the establishment of an ethnically "pure" Serb state through the permanent removal of the Bosnian Muslims and Bosnian Croats.[1983]

583.   With respect to Stanišić's continued support for and participation in the implementation of these policies, the Trial Chamber found that Stanišić: (i) "worked to promote the interests, and implement the decisions, of the SDS in the SRBiH MUP and was involved in all the stages of the **[page 242]** creation of the Bosnian Serb institutions in BiH, in particular the [RS] MUP",[1984] which included his involvement in the establishment of the SDS,[1985] as well as the creation of the RS MUP,[1986] including through the dismissal of non-Serbs,[1987] and arming of RS MUP forces;[1988] (ii) "made a majority of key appointments in the RS MUP",[1989] which included JCE members involved in the takeover of municipalities;[1990] (iii) participated voluntarily in the creation of a separate Serb entity, as indicated by his conduct, presence at key meetings, attendance at sessions of the BSA, and acceptance of the position of Minister of Interior;[1991] (iv) consistently approved the deployment of RS MUP forces to joint combat activities with other Serb forces, despite his awareness of crimes committed by joint Serb forces;[1992] (v) was aware of the Variant A and B Instructions since the "police were assigned" and played a "central" role in their implementation;[1993] (vi) only sought to withdraw regular policemen from combat activities towards the end of 1992, when most of the territory of RS had been consolidated, while permitting the continued use of reserve forces by the army, primarily for the purpose of guarding prisons and detention camps, despite being aware that reserve police had been infiltrated by criminal elements;[1994] and (vii) despite his knowledge of crimes that were being committed, took insufficient action to put an end to them and instead permitted RS MUP forces under his overall control to continue to participate in joint operations in the Municipalities with other Serb forces involved in the commission of crimes, particularly the JNA/VRS and the TO.[1995]

584.   In light of the foregoing, despite the Trial Chamber's errors set out above,[1996] and in spite of the Appeals Chamber's conclusion that a reasonable trier of fact could have found that Stanišić first became aware of the commission of crimes against Muslims and Croats in the area relevant to the Indictment only as of late April 1992, the Appeals Chamber is not convinced that these errors have an impact on the Trial Chamber's ultimate conclusion on Stanišić's intent. On the basis of the remaining findings of the Trial Chamber set out in the preceding paragraphs,[1997] including those concerning: (i) Stanišić's position from 31 March 1992 until the end of that year, as Minister of the **[page 243]** Interior within the RS Government, which was one of the most important organs in the RS;[1998] (ii) Stanišić's deal with Arkan's Men, whereby he

---

[1980]   Trial Judgement, vol. 2, para. 310.
[1981]   Trial Judgement, vol. 2, para. 563.
[1982]   Trial Judgement, vol. 2, para. 310.
[1983]   Trial Judgement, vol. 2, paras 310-311. See Trial Judgement, vol. 2, paras 228-233.
[1984]   Trial Judgement, vol. 2, para. 734. See generally, Trial Judgement, vol. 2, paras 729-736.
[1985]   Trial Judgement, vol. 2, para. 729. See Trial Judgement, vol. 2, paras 544-575.
[1986]   Trial Judgement, vol. 2, paras 732-733. See Trial Judgement, vol. 2, para. 57.
[1987]   Trial Judgement, vol. 2, paras 576-577, 738.
[1988]   Trial Judgement, vol. 2, para. 740.
[1989]   Trial Judgement, vol. 2, para. 733. See Trial Judgement, vol. 2, para. 579.
[1990]   Trial Judgement, vol. 2, para. 744.
[1991]   Trial Judgement, vol. 2, para. 734.
[1992]   Trial Judgement, vol. 2, para. 743. See Trial Judgement, vol. 2, paras 587-588, 601, 630, 632, 592.
[1993]   Trial Judgement, vol. 2, para. 731.
[1994]   Trial Judgement, vol. 2, para. 743. See Trial Judgement, vol. 2, paras 594, 600, 643.
[1995]   Trial Judgement, vol. 2, para. 759. See Trial Judgement, vol. 2, paras 746, 751-758.
[1996]   See *supra*, paras 574-576.
[1997]   See *supra*, paras 575-583.
[1998]   Trial Judgement, vol. 2, paras 131, 141, 542. See Trial Judgement, vol. 2, paras 6, 797.

approved of the operations of Arkan's Men in Bijeljina and Zvornik in early April 1992 and allowed Arkan to remove property in exchange for liberating the territories;[1999] (iii) Stanišić's acknowledgement at the November 1992 BSA Session that "'in the beginning', 'thieves and criminals' were accepted into the reserve police forces because 'we wanted the country defended'";[2000] (iv) Stanišić's close relationship, from at least June 1991, with Karadžić, who made an inflammatory speech on 11 March 1992 at the BSA that "a war would lead to a forcible and bloody transfer of minorities from one region to another and the creation of three ethnically homogenous regions within BiH";[2001] (v) the displacement of large numbers of non-Serbs and their movement out of the RS, as discussed both at sessions of the RS Government sessions and the 11 July 1992 Collegium, when Stanišić was present, and also referred to in the Perišić Report;[2002] (vi) Stanišić's continued support for participation in the implementation of the policies of the SDS and BSA;[2003] (vii) Stanišić's consistent approval of the deployment of RS MUP forces to joint combat activities with other Serb forces, despite his awareness of crimes committed by joint Serb forces;[2004] (viii) Stanišić's statement that he had always followed the policies of the SDS Presidency and of its deputies in the former state;[2005] and (ix) Stanišić's involvement in all the stages of the creation of the Bosnian Serb institutions in BiH, and the RS MUP in particular,[2006] the Appeals Chamber concludes that a reasonable trier of fact could have concluded that the only reasonable inference is that Stanišić possessed the requisite intent throughout the Indictment period (*i.e.* from at least 1 April 1992 until 31 December 1992).

(j) Conclusion

585.   For the foregoing reasons, the Appeals Chamber finds that Stanišić has failed to demonstrate that the Trial Chamber erred in finding that he possessed the requisite intent for the first category of joint criminal enterprise liability throughout the Indictment period (*i.e.* from at least 1 April 1992 until 31 December 1992). The Appeals Chamber therefore dismisses Stanišić's first and third grounds of appeal in part and his fourth ground of appeal in its entirety. **[page 244]**

7.   Alleged errors in relation to Stanišić's responsibility pursuant to the third category of joint criminal enterprise

(a) Introduction

586.   The Trial Chamber convicted Stanišić for the following crimes falling outside the common purpose: persecutions as a crime against humanity (through the underlying acts of killings, torture, cruel treatment, inhumane acts, unlawful detention, establishment and perpetuation of inhumane living conditions, plunder of property, wanton destruction of towns and villages, including destruction or wilful damage done to institutions dedicated to religion and other cultural buildings, and imposition and maintenance of restrictive and discriminatory measures) (Count 1), murder as a violation of the laws or customs of war (Count 4) and torture as a violation of the laws or customs of war (Count 6).[2007] The Trial Chamber also found Stanišić responsible for murder, torture, and inhumane acts as crimes against humanity (Counts 3, 5, and 8, respectively) and for cruel treatment as a violation of the laws or customs of war (Count 7) pursuant to the third category of joint criminal enterprise but did not enter a conviction for these crimes on the basis of the principles relating to cumulative convictions.[2008]

[1999]   Trial Judgement, vol. 2, paras 710-711, 768.
[2000]   Trial Judgement, vol. 2, para. 600.
[2001]   Trial Judgement, vol. 2, para. 179. See Trial Judgement, vol. 2, para. 767.
[2002]   Trial Judgement, vol. 2, para. 768. See Trial Judgement, vol. 2, paras 627, 629-634, 650.
[2003]   Trial Judgement, vol. 2, para. 769. See *supra*, paras 582-583.
[2004]   Trial Judgement, vol. 2, para. 743.
[2005]   Trial Judgement, vol. 2, para. 570.
[2006]   Trial Judgement, vol. 2, para. 734.
[2007]   Trial Judgement, vol. 2, paras 804, 809, 813, 818, 822, 827, 831, 836, 840, 844, 849, 854, 858, 863, 868, 873, 877, 881, 885, 955.
[2008]   Trial Judgement, vol. 2, paras 804, 813, 818, 822, 827, 831, 836, 840, 844, 849, 854, 858, 863, 868, 873, 877, 881, 885, 955.

587. Stanišić challenges the Trial Chamber's findings on his responsibility pursuant to the third category of joint criminal enterprise and his conviction on this basis in his eighth through eleventh grounds of appeal. In particular, he submits that the Trial Chamber erred in law by: (i) entering convictions for the specific intent crime of persecutions as a crime against humanity pursuant to the third category of joint criminal enterprise;[2009] and (ii) failing to enter the required findings that the crimes charged under Counts 3 to 8 were foreseeable to Stanišić and that he willingly took that risk.[2010] Stanišić submits further that the Trial Chamber erred in fact by implicitly finding that it was foreseeable to him and that he willingly took the risk that the crimes charged under Counts 3 to 8[2011] and persecutions through underlying acts as charged under Count 1[2012] could be committed. The Prosecution responds that Stanišić's challenges in his eighth through eleventh grounds of appeal should be dismissed.[2013] **[page 245]**

(b) Alleged errors in relation to Stanišić's convictions for persecutions as a crime against humanity (Stanišić's eighth ground of appeal)

(i) Submission of the parties

588. Stanišić submits that the Trial Chamber erred in law by entering convictions for persecutions as a crime against humanity pursuant to the third category of joint criminal enterprise.[2014] He acknowledges that the Tribunal's jurisprudence allows for convictions for specific intent crimes on the basis of the third category of joint criminal enterprise but argues that cogent reasons exist to depart from this jurisprudence.[2015]

589. More specifically, Stanišić contends that the case law of the Tribunal gives rise to cogent reasons to depart from the *Brđanin* Appeal Decision of 19 March 2004 and subsequent consistent jurisprudence.[2016] He submits that in order to be convicted as a perpetrator of a specific intent crime, specific intent must be established,[2017] and that, therefore, the necessary requirements to prove the *mens rea* for persecutions are "the intent to commit the underlying act (general intent) and the intent to discriminate on political, racial or religious grounds (*dolus specialis*)".[2018] He submits that accordingly, an accused cannot be convicted for committing a specific intent crime (as a perpetrator) pursuant to the third category of joint criminal enterprise because this mode of liability only requires *dolus eventualis*.[2019] Stanišić contends that the *Stakić* Trial Judgement,[2020] *Stakić* Appeal Judgement,[2021] and Judge Shahabuddeen's "partially dissenting" opinion in the *Brđanin* Appeal Decision of 19 March 2004 provide support for the proposition that *dolus specialis* is "an

---

[2009] Stanišić Appeal Brief, paras 333-369.
[2010] Stanišić Appeal Brief, paras 370-387.
[2011] Stanišić Appeal Brief, paras 388-423.
[2012] Stanišić Appeal Brief, paras 424-476.
[2013] Prosecution Response Brief (Stanišić), paras 178, 185, 225.
[2014] Stanišić Appeal Brief, para. 333. See Stanišić Appeal Brief, paras 368-369.
[2015] Stanišić Appeal Brief, paras 334-368. The Appeals Chamber notes that Stanišić uses the terms "specific intent", "special intent", and *"dolus specialis"* interchangeably to refer to the *mens rea* elements for the crimes of persecutions and genocide, as well as for crimes in Article 2 of the International Convention for the Suppression of Terrorist Bombing, U.N. Doc. A/RES/52/164; 37 ILM 249 (1998); 2149 UNTS 284, adopted 15 December 1997, entered into force 23 May 2001 ("Convention for the Suppression of Terrorist Bombings") (see Stanišić Appeal Brief, paras 334, 336-340, 345-349, 351-353, 355-357, 359, 361-363, 365-367). Similarly, the Prosecution uses the terms "special intent crimes" and "specific intent crimes" interchangeably to refer collectively to the crimes of persecutions and genocide (see Prosecution Response Brief (Stanišić), paras 168-170, 172, 174-176) and refers to the *mens rea* requirement of the crime of persecutions as *"dolus specialis"* (see Prosecution Response Brief (Stanišić), para. 170). The Appeals Chamber will adopt the terms "discriminatory intent" or "specific intent" to refer to the *mens rea* of persecutions, and "specific intent crimes" to refer collectively to the crimes of persecutions and genocide, as well as crimes in Article 2 of the Convention for the Suppression of Terrorist Bombings.
[2016] Stanišić Appeal Brief, para. 350, referring to *Prosecutor v. Radoslav Brđanin*, Case No. IT-99-36-AR73.10, Decision on Interlocutory Appeal, 19 March 2004 (*"Brđanin* Appeal Decision of 19 March 2004"). See Stanišić Appeal Brief, paras 336-349.
[2017] Stanišić Appeal Brief, para. 336, referring to *Stakić* Appeal Judgement, para. 328. See Stanišić Appeal Brief, paras 337-339, referring to, *inter alia, Krstić* Appeal Judgement, para. 134, *Krnojelac* Appeal Judgement, para. 111, *Kvočka et al.* Appeal Judgement, para. 110, *Jelisić* Appeal Judgement, para. 49.
[2018] Stanišić Appeal Brief, para. 340 (emphasis omitted).
[2019] Stanišić Appeal Brief, para. 346. See Stanišić Appeal Brief, paras 341-344, 347.
[2020] Stanišić Appeal Brief, para. 348, referring to *Stakić* Trial Judgement, para. 530.
[2021] Stanišić Appeal Brief, para. 348, referring to *Stakić* Appeal Judgement, para. 328.

[page 246] inherent requirement and therefore a constituent part of the crime [and] cannot be varied by a mode of liability".[2022]

590.   Furthermore, Stanišić argues that recent jurisprudence of the Special Tribunal for Lebanon ("STL")[2023] and Special Court for Sierra Leone ("SCSL")[2024] demonstrates that "it would be a serious legal anomaly to allow convictions under JCE III [...] for crimes which require proof of a specific intent"[2025] and therefore provides cogent reasons to depart from the *Brđanin* Appeal Decision of 19 March 2004 and subsequent jurisprudence.[2026] In addition, relying on Article 2 of the Convention for the Suppression of Terrorist Bombings,[2027] the ICC Statute,[2028] and post-World War II cases,[2029] Stanišić submits that "no support can be found" in customary international law allowing for convictions for specific intent crimes on the basis of the third category of joint criminal enterprise.[2030]

591.   Stanišić requests that the Appeals Chamber: (i) hold that a departure from the Tribunal's case law is warranted and that no convictions for specific intent crimes may be entered under the third category of joint criminal enterprise; and (ii) quash Stanišić's convictions pursuant to the third category of joint criminal enterprise for the crime of persecutions as a crime against humanity under Count 1.[2031] **[page 247]**

592.   The Prosecution responds that there are no cogent reasons to depart from the existing jurisprudence and that Stanišić's arguments should be dismissed.[2032] Specifically, it submits that Stanišić's arguments with respect to the Tribunal's jurisprudence were each considered and rejected by the Appeals Chamber in the *Brđanin* Appeal Decision of 19 March 2004,[2033] and that contrary to Stanišić's argument, the Trial Chamber did not convict Stanišić for persecutions on the basis of *dolus eventualis*.[2034] It contends that the Trial Chamber correctly convicted Stanišić for persecutions through deportation and forcible transfer pursuant to the first category of joint criminal enterprise on the basis that he had discriminatory intent,[2035] and that "[t]here is therefore no logical reason why Stanišić should not also be found guilty under JCE III of persecution on the basis of other underlying crimes".[2036]

593.   The Prosecution further contends that recent jurisprudence of the STL and SCSL "do[es] not provide cogent reasons for the Appeals Chamber to revisit and depart from its previous and consistent jurisprudence regarding the application of JCE III to specific intent crimes".[2037] In addition, the Prosecution asserts that the

---

[2022]   Stanišić Appeal Brief, para. 349, referring to *Brđanin* Appeal Decision of 19 March 2004, Separate Opinion of Judge Shahabuddeen, para. 4. See Stanišić Reply Brief, paras 88-89.

[2023]   Stanišić Appeal Brief, paras 351-352, referring to *The Prosecutor. v. Salim Jamil Ayyash et al.*, Case No. STL-11-01/I/AC/R176bis, Interlocutory Decision on the Applicable Law: Terrorism, Conspiracy, Homicide, Perpetration, Cumulative Charging, 16 February 2011 ("STL Decision of 16 February 2011"), paras 248-249.

[2024]   Stanišić Appeal Brief, para. 353, referring to *Prosecutor v. Charles Ghankay Taylor*, Case No. SCSL-03-01-T, Judgement, 18 May 2012 ("*Taylor* Trial Judgement"), para. 468.

[2025]   Stanišić Appeal Brief, para. 352. See Stanišić Appeal Brief, para. 353.

[2026]   Stanišić Appeal Brief, para. 354. See Stanišić Appeal Brief, paras 352-353. See also Stanišić Appeal Brief, para. 334.

[2027]   Stanišić Appeal Brief, para. 356, referring to Convention for the Suppression of Terrorist Bombings, art. 2(1). See Stanišić Appeal Brief, paras 357-358.

[2028]   Stanišić Appeal Brief, para. 363, referring to Statute of the International Criminal Court, adopted by a Diplomatic Conference in Rome on 17 July 1998 ("ICC Statute"). See Stanišić Appeal Brief, paras 361-362.

[2029]   Stanišić Appeal Brief, para. 364, referring to *The United States of America, the French Republic, the United Kingdom of Great Britain and Northern Ireland, and the Union of Soviet Socialist Republics against Hermann Wilhelm Goring et al.*, Judgement, 1 October 1946, Trial of Major War Criminals Before the International Military Tribunal Under Control Council Law No. 10, Vol. 1 (1947), *The United States of America v. Altstoetter et al.*, U.S. Military Tribunal, Judgement, 3-4 December 1947, Trials of War Criminals Before the Nuernberg Military Tribunals Under Control Council Law No. 10 (1951), Vol. III ("*Justice* case"), *The United States of America v. Greifelt et al.*, U.S. Military Tribunal, Judgement, 10 March 1948, Trials of War Criminals Before the Nuernberg Military Tribunals Under Control Council Law No. 10 (1951), Vol. V.

[2030]   Stanišić Appeal Brief, para. 367. See Stanišić Appeal Brief, paras 355, 364-366.

[2031]   See Stanišić Notice of Appeal, para. 51; Stanišić Appeal Brief, paras 368-369. In his notice of appeal, Stanišić also requests the Appeals Chamber to "impose a new and appropriate, lower sentence" (Stanišić Notice of Appeal, para. 51).

[2032]   Prosecution Response Brief (Stanišić), paras 168-169, 175, 178. See Prosecution Response Brief (Stanišić), paras 170-173.

[2033]   Prosecution Response Brief (Stanišić), para. 170. See Prosecution Response Brief (Stanišić), paras 169-173.

[2034]   Prosecution Response Brief (Stanišić), para. 177, referring to Stanišić Appeal Brief, paras 344-347.

[2035]   Prosecution Response Brief (Stanišić), paras 168, 177.

[2036]   Prosecution Response Brief (Stanišić), para. 177. See Prosecution Response Brief (Stanišić), para. 168.

[2037]   Prosecution Response Brief (Stanišić), para. 175. It argues further that Stanišić's reliance on the jurisprudence of other internationalised tribunals is selective and that he ignores jurisprudence of the ICTR Appeals Chamber confirming that all three

absence of the third category of joint criminal enterprise from the Convention for the Suppression of Terrorist Bombings and the ICC Statute cannot "undermine settled jurisprudence of the Tribunal".[2038] It also submits that the post-World War II cases relied upon by Stanišić: (i) support the recognition of the third category of joint criminal enterprise under customary international law;[2039] and (ii) do not exclude a conviction of an accused for specific intent crimes pursuant to the third category of joint criminal enterprise.[2040]

(ii) Analysis

594. The Appeals Chamber recalls that the crime of persecutions consists of an act or omission that discriminates in fact and denies or infringes upon a fundamental right laid down in customary **[page 248]** international law or treaty law (*actus reus*).[2041] The *mens rea* element is satisfied when the underlying act or omission is carried out deliberately (general intent) and with the intent to discriminate on the basis of race, religion, or politics (discriminatory or specific intent).[2042]

595. The Appeals Chamber also recalls that under the third category of joint criminal enterprise, an accused can be held responsible for a crime outside the common purpose if, under the circumstances of the case: (i) it was foreseeable to the accused that such a crime might be perpetrated by one or more of the persons used by him (or by any other member of the joint criminal enterprise) in order to carry out the *actus reus* of the crimes forming part of the common purpose; and (ii) the accused willingly took the risk that such a crime might occur by joining or continuing to participate in the enterprise.[2043]

596. It is well established in the case law of the Tribunal that the Appeals Chamber may, exceptionally, depart from its previous decisions if there are cogent reasons to do so,[2044] *i.e.* if the previous decision was made "'on the basis of a wrong legal principle' or given *per incuriam*, that is, 'wrongly decided, usually because the judge or judges were ill-informed about the applicable law'".[2045] It is for the party advocating a departure to demonstrate that there are cogent reasons in the interests of justice that justify such departure.[2046]

597. With respect to Stanišić's argument that the Tribunal's case law gives rise to cogent reasons to depart from the Tribunal's case law, the Appeals Chamber considers that Stanišić conflates the *mens rea* requirement for the crime of persecutions with the subjective element of a mode of liability by which criminal responsibility may attach to an accused. It recalls that for a conviction for persecutions pursuant to the third category of joint criminal enterprise, it is sufficient that it was foreseeable to the accused that an act of persecutions could be committed and that it could be committed with discriminatory intent.[2047] This is well established in the Tribunal's jurisprudence,[2048] and Stanišić fails to show that this jurisprudence is based on

---

forms of joint criminal enterprise liability may be applied to the specific intent crime of genocide (Prosecution Response Brief (Stanišić), para. 176, referring to *Andre Rwamakuba v. The Prosecutor*, Case No. ICTR-98-44-AR72.4, Decision on Interlocutory Appeal Regarding Application of Joint Criminal Enterprise to the Crime of Genocide, 22 October 2004 ("*Rwamakuba* Appeal Decision on Joint Criminal Enterprise of 22 October 2004"), paras 10, 13, 24, 31, *Prosecutor v. Radovan Karadžić*, Case No. IT-95-5/18-PT, Decision on Six Preliminary Motions Challenging Jurisdiction, 28 April 2009, para. 32).

[2038]   Prosecution Response Brief (Stanišić), para. 174.

[2039]   Prosecution Response Brief (Stanišić), para. 174, referring to *Rwamakuba* Appeal Decision on Joint Criminal Enterprise of 22 October 2004, para. 24, *Brđanin* Appeal Judgement, paras 393-404.

[2040]   Prosecution Response Brief (Stanišić), para. 174.

[2041]   *Popović et al.* Appeal Judgement, paras 737, 761; *Đorđević* Appeal Judgement, para. 693.

[2042]   *Popović et al.* Appeal Judgement, paras 737-738; *Đorđević* Appeal Judgement, para. 558; *Šainović et al.* Appeal Judgement, para. 579.

[2043]   *Tolimir* Appeal Judgement, para. 514; *Đorđević* Appeal Judgement, para. 906; *Šainović et al.* Appeal Judgement, paras 1061, 1557; *Brđanin* Appeal Judgement, paras 365, 411.

[2044]   *Đorđević* Appeal Judgement, para. 23; *Galić* Appeal Judgement, para. 117; *Aleksovski* Appeal Judgement, para. 107.

[2045]   *Đorđević* Appeal Judgement, para. 24, quoting *Aleksovski* Appeal Judgement, para. 108.

[2046]   *Đorđević* Appeal Judgement, para. 24. See *Popović et al.* Appeal Judgement, para. 1674.

[2047]   *Đorđević* Appeal Judgement, para. 919; *Brđanin* Appeal Decision of 19 March 2004, para. 6. It must further be shown that the accused willingly took the risk that the crime might be committed (see *supra*, para. 595).

[2048]   See *Popović et al.* Appeal Judgement, paras 1440, 1707-1708; *Đorđević* Appeal Judgement, para. 83, referring to *Krstić* Appeal Judgement, para. 150, *Martić* Appeal Judgement, paras 194-195, 202-205. See also *Đorđević* Appeal Judgement, paras 84, 929. With regard to the *Stakić* Appeal Judgement and *Krstić* Appeal Judgement to which Stanišić refers, the Appeals Chamber notes that in fact these cases confirm that convictions for specific intent crimes may be entered pursuant to the third category of joint criminal enterprise (*Stakić* Appeal Judgement, para. 38; *Krstić* Appeal Judgement, paras 150-151, p. 87). In addition, the Appeals Chamber notes that in the *Brđanin* Appeal Decision of 19 March 2004, Judge Shahabuddeen did not dissent from the majority's

incorrect legal **[page 249]** principles or given *per incuriam*. In light of the above, the Appeals Chamber is of the view that Stanišić has failed to demonstrate that the Tribunal's case law provides cogent reasons to depart from the existing jurisprudence.

598. Insofar as Stanišić relies upon the jurisprudence of the STL and SCSL, the Appeals Chamber recalls that it is not bound by the findings of other courts – domestic, international, or hybrid – and that, even though it will consider such jurisprudence, it may nonetheless come to a different conclusion on a matter than that reached by another judicial body.[2049] The Appeals Chamber considers that in order to constitute a cogent reason for departing from its established jurisprudence on a matter, the party advocating a departure would need to show that a non-binding opinion of another court is the correct law and demonstrate that there is a clear mistake in the Appeals Chamber's approach.[2050] Accordingly, and on review of the STL Decision of 16 February 2011 and the *Taylor* Trial Judgement,[2051] the Appeals Chamber finds that Stanišić has not demonstrated any error in the Appeals Chamber's well-established jurisprudence.

599. With respect to Stanišić's argument that customary international law does not permit convictions for specific intent crimes pursuant to the third category of joint criminal enterprise, the Appeals Chamber observes that in its analysis of customary international law in the *Tadić* case, it specifically considered the provisions of the Convention for the Suppression of Terrorist Bombings and the ICC Statute cited by Stanišić.[2052] It found, on the basis on numerous sources from both civil and common law jurisdictions, including post-World War II cases, that the third category of joint criminal enterprise has existed as a mode of liability in customary international law since at least 1992 and that it applies to all crimes.[2053] While Stanišić asserts that the Convention for the Suppression of Terrorist Bombings, the ICC Statute, and the post-World War II cases on which he relies do not expressly provide for convictions for specific intent crimes on the basis of the third **[page 250]** category of joint criminal enterprise or even the third category of joint criminal enterprise itself,[2054] this does not undermine the Appeals Chamber's analysis of customary international law and conclusion in the *Tadić* case, which has been consistently confirmed in the Tribunal's subsequent jurisprudence.[2055] In the Appeals Chamber's view, Stanišić merely relies upon the absence of express support in the sources he identifies, without showing that they give rise to cogent reasons to depart from the Tribunal's existing jurisprudence.

(iii) Conclusion

600. In light of the above, the Appeals Chamber finds that Stanišić has failed to demonstrate that cogent reasons exist to depart from the Tribunal's well-established case law and dismisses Stanišić's eighth ground of appeal.

---

decision to reverse the acquittal of Brđanin of genocide with respect to the third category of joint criminal enterprise, but appended a separate opinion, and stated that the third category of joint criminal enterprise "does not dispense with the need to prove intent [but] provides a mode of proving intent in particular circumstances, namely, by proof of foresight in those circumstances" (*Brđanin* Appeal Decision of 19 March 2004, Separate Opinion of Judge Shahabuddeen, para. 2).

[2049] *Đorđević* Appeal Judgement, para. 83, referring to *Celebia* Appeal Judgement, para. 24. See *Tolimir* Appeal Judgement, para. 226; *Popović et al.* Appeal Judgement, para. 1674.

[2050] See *Popović et al* Appeal Judgement, para. 1674, referring to *Đorđević* Appeal Judgement, para. 24, *Aleksovski* Appeal Judgement, para. 108.

[2051] See, in particular, STL Decision of 16 February 2011, paras 248-249; *Taylor* Trial Judgement, para. 468. *Cf. Đorđević* Appeal Judgement, para. 83.

[2052] *Tadić* Appeal Judgement, paras 221-223, referring to Convention for the Suppression of Terrorist Bombings, art. 2(3)(c), ICC Statute, art. 25(3). See Stanišić Appeal Brief, paras 355-363.

[2053] *Tadić* Appeal Judgement, paras 194-226. See *Đorđević* Appeal Judgement, para. 81; *Rwamakuba* Appeal Decision on Joint Criminal Enterprise of 22 October 2004, paras 10, 17, referring to *Tadić* Appeal Judgement, paras 188, 193.

[2054] See Stanišić Appeal Brief, paras 356-358, 361-366.

[2055] *Popović et al.* Appeal Judgement, para. 1672, referring to *Đorđević* Appeal Judgement, para. 81; *Martić* Appeal Judgement, para. 80; *Brđanin* Appeal Judgement, para. 405. See *Rwamakuba* Appeal Decision on Joint Criminal Enterprise of 22 October 2004, paras 14-25. In this regard, the Appeals Chamber also recalls that "it is not required to demonstrate that every possible combination between crime and mode of liability be explicitly allowed by, or have precedents in, customary international law" (*Đorđević* Appeal Judgement, para. 81 (emphasis omitted)).

(c) Alleged errors of law by failing to make the required third category of joint criminal enterprise subjective element findings in relation to Counts 3 to 8 (Stanišić's first ground of appeal in part and ninth ground of appeal)

601.   In assessing Stanišić's responsibility for crimes outside the scope of the JCE, the Trial Chamber first considered that Stanišić intended to permanently remove Bosnian Muslims and Bosnian Croats from the territory of the planned Serbian state through the commission of JCE I Crimes.[2056] Further, it considered that Stanišić was "aware of the criminal background and propensity of members of the Bosnian Serb Forces to commit crimes, and particularly the RS reserve police force, which were mobilised in the early months of the conflict to effect this removal".[2057]

602.   The Trial Chamber found that "the forcible removal of Bosnian Muslims and Bosnian Croats from BiH was engineered by enforcing unbearable living conditions following the takeover of identified towns and villages".[2058] It concluded that the possibility of the imposition and maintenance of restrictive and discriminatory measures against the non-Serbs in these towns and **[page 251]** villages, with a discriminatory intent, in the execution of the common plan was sufficiently substantial so as to be foreseeable to Stanišić, and that he willingly took that risk.[2059]

603.   The Trial Chamber also found that, in the execution of the common plan, the possibility of the unlawful detention of Bosnian Muslims and Bosnian Croats at SJBs, prisons, and improvised detention centres and camps, with a discriminatory intent, was sufficiently substantial so as to be foreseeable to Stanišić, and that he willingly took that risk.[2060]

604.   The Trial Chamber further found that, "in the ethnically charged atmosphere during the 'reorganisation' of the internal organs of the municipalities", the possibility that killings, both during the attacks and takeover of municipalities and in the prisons, detention centres, and camps, could be committed with a discriminatory intent in the execution of the common plan, was sufficiently substantial as to be foreseeable to Stanišić and that he willingly took that risk.[2061]

605.   The Trial Chamber found that, given Stanišić's knowledge of the large-scale detention of the non-Serb civilians in prisons, SJBs, detention centres, and camps, which were guarded by the armed forces of the RS with the support by both active and reserve forces of the SJBs in individual municipalities approved by his direct orders, it was foreseeable to him that the torture, cruel treatment, and other inhumane acts, including beatings and rape, and inhumane conditions of detention, such as provision of starvation rations, and unhygienic and insufficient amenities, could be committed subsequently in the course of unlawful detentions.[2062] The Trial Chamber further found that the possibility that these crimes could be committed with a discriminatory intent in the execution of the common plan was sufficiently substantial as to be foreseeable to Stanišić, and that he willingly took that risk.[2063]

606.   In addition, considering the evidence on the numerous reports and meetings that addressed the increased level of looting, search and seizure, appropriation, and plunder of the moveable and immoveable property of the Bosnian Muslims, Bosnian Croats, and other non-Serbs in the Municipalities (during the takeover of the Municipalities, during their transportation to detention centres and camps and while in detention, and in the course of their escorted removal from Serb-held territory), the Trial Chamber was satisfied that the possibility that these crimes could be **[page 252]** committed with a discriminatory intent in the execution of the common plan was sufficiently substantial so as to be foreseeable to Stanišić, and that he willingly took that risk.[2064]

[2056]   Trial Judgement, vol. 2, para. 771.
[2057]   Trial Judgement, vol. 2, para. 771.
[2058]   Trial Judgement, vol. 2, para. 772.
[2059]   Trial Judgement, vol. 2, para. 772.
[2060]   Trial Judgement, vol. 2, para. 773.
[2061]   Trial Judgement, vol. 2, para. 774.
[2062]   Trial Judgement, vol. 2, para. 776.
[2063]   Trial Judgement, vol. 2, para. 776.
[2064]   Trial Judgement, vol. 2, para. 777.

607.   The Trial Chamber further found that, in light of its finding that the wanton destruction and damage of religious and cultural property was "carried out in a concerted effort to eliminate the historical moorings of the Bosnian Muslims and Bosnian Croats during and following the takeover of the Municipalities was foreseeable to Mićo Stanišić in the course of the execution of the common plan",[2065] the possibility that these crimes could be committed with a discriminatory intent in the execution of the common plan was sufficiently substantial as to be foreseeable to Stanišić, and that he willingly took that risk.[2066]

608.   Finally, considering its finding that the crimes of unlawful detention; imposition and maintenance of restrictive and discriminatory measures; killings; torture, cruel treatment, and inhumane acts; establishment and perpetuation of inhumane living conditions in the detention facilities; appropriation of property and plunder; and wanton destruction and damage of religious and cultural property were all committed with a discriminatory intent, the Trial Chamber was satisfied that they comprised underlying acts of persecutions, the possibility of which was sufficiently substantial as to be foreseeable to Stanišić, and that he willingly took that risk.[2067]

(i) Submissions of the parties

609.   Stanišić argues that the Trial Chamber erred in law by failing to expressly make the required findings on the subjective element of the third category of joint criminal enterprise liability in relation to the crimes under Counts 3 to 8.[2068] He contends that the Trial Chamber, when recalling its foreseeability findings in the section addressing Stanišić's responsibility for each municipality, "in fact recalled findings that do not exist".[2069] According to Stanišić, the Trial Chamber's findings on the third category of joint criminal enterprise liability refer "solely and expressly" to his responsibility for persecutory acts included under Count 1.[2070] He submits that the Trial Chamber **[page 253]** thus failed to provide reasons as to why the crimes under Counts 3 through 8 were foreseeable to him and how he willingly took the risk that they could be committed.[2071]

610.   In addition, Stanišić argues that the crimes against humanity charged under Counts 3, 5, 7, and 8 and the violations of the laws or customs of war charged under Counts 4 and 6 "are distinct offences each comprising specific and essential elements that must be examined independently".[2072] Therefore, he submits that the Trial Chamber's findings regarding the foreseeability of "persecutory acts included under Count 1 cannot make up for the absence of findings for Counts 3-8".[2073] Stanišić claims that in the absence of these essential findings, his convictions for Counts 4 and 6 and the findings that he was responsible for Counts 3,

---

[2065]   Trial Judgement, vol. 2, para. 778.

[2066]   Trial Judgement, vol. 2, para. 778.

[2067]   Trial Judgement, vol. 2, para. 779.

[2068]   Stanišić Appeal Brief, paras 49, 51, 370-372. The Appeals Chamber recalls that the crimes under Counts 3 to 8 are the following: (i) murder as a crime against humanity and as a violation of the laws or customs of war (Counts 3 and 4, respectively); (ii) torture as a crime against humanity and as a violation of the laws or customs of war (Counts 5 and 6, respectively); (iii) cruel treatment as a violation of the laws or customs of war (Count 7); and (iv) inhumane acts as a crime against humanity (Count 8) (Stanišić Appeal Brief, paras 49, 51, 370. See Trial Judgement, vol. 2, paras 313, 772-774, 776, 955).

[2069]   Stanišić Appeal Brief, para. 374 (emphasis omitted). See Stanišić Reply Brief, para. 29.

[2070]   Stanišić Appeal Brief, para. 373, referring to Trial Judgement, vol. 2, paras 770-774, 776-779. The Appeals Chamber recalls that the persecutory acts charged under Count 1 (other than forcible transfer and deportation) are the following: killings, torture, cruel treatment, inhumane acts, unlawful detention, establishment and perpetuation of inhumane living conditions, plunder of property, wanton destruction of towns and villages, including destruction or wilful damage done to institutions dedicated to religion and other cultural buildings, and imposition and maintenance of restrictive and discriminatory measures (Trial Judgement, vol. 2, paras 313, 772-774, 776-779, 955).

[2071]   Stanišić Appeal Brief, paras 49, 51, 375. See Stanišić Appeal Brief, paras 376-378.

[2072]   Stanišić Appeal Brief, para. 380. See Stanišić Reply Brief, para. 91. Stanišić illustrates his argument with reference to murder as a violation of the laws or customs of war, for which it must be proven that the victim took "no active part in the hostilities", an element which he argues does not exist for killings as a crime against humanity (Stanišić Appeal Brief, para. 381 (emphasis omitted)). He argues that, when assessing the foreseeability of a crime, all the essential elements of that crime must be taken into consideration and thus a finding that killings as a crime against humanity is foreseeable to an accused is "evidently distinct" from a finding that murder as a violation of the laws or customs of war was foreseeable (Stanišić Appeal Brief, para. 382 (emphasis omitted)). See Stanišić Appeal Brief, para. 382. Further, Stanišić stresses the necessity of finding that each of the specific elements of joint criminal enterprise are satisfied for each crime (Stanišić Appeal Brief, paras 384-385, referring to *Brđanin* Appeal Judgement, paras 428-429, *Tadić* Appeal Judgement, para. 220).

[2073]   Stanišić Appeal Brief, para. 379. See Stanišić Appeal Brief, para. 386.

5, 7, and 8 have been entered without any legal basis.[2074] As such, he requests the Appeals Chamber to quash his convictions under Counts 4 and 6, and the findings of responsibility under Counts 3, 5, 7, and 8.[2075]

611. The Prosecution responds that Stanišić fails to show any legal error and that his arguments should be dismissed.[2076] It contends that the Trial Chamber applied the correct subjective standard for third category joint criminal enterprise liability and made the required findings.[2077] It argues that when the Trial Judgement is read as a whole, it is clear that the Trial Chamber appropriately assessed the foreseeability of the crimes under Count 1 and crimes under Counts 3 to 8 "at the same time".[2078] The Prosecution submits that the crimes of murder, torture, cruel treatment, and inhumane acts were also charged as underlying acts of persecutions under Count 1.[2079] It argues that, therefore, when the Trial Chamber found that the commission of killings, torture, cruel treatment, and other inhumane acts with discriminatory intent was foreseeable to Stanišić, it made findings that were sufficient to also establish his responsibility for the crimes in Counts 3 to 8 pursuant to the **[page 254]** third category of joint criminal enterprise.[2080] According to the Prosecution, this reading of the Trial Judgement is consistent with the Trial Chamber's conclusions on Stanišić's responsibility with respect to each municipality, where it "recalled its earlier findings" on the foreseeability of Stanišić's JCE III Crimes.[2081]

612. The Prosecution further argues that since the Trial Chamber did not enter convictions for the crimes charged under Counts 7 and 8, "[a]ny alleged failure to enter JCE III liability findings relating to the crimes charged under those counts would have no impact on his convictions."[2082]

(ii) Analysis

613. At the outset, the Appeals Chamber notes that while Stanišić was not convicted for the crimes charged under Counts 3, 5, 7, and 8, the Trial Chamber entered findings of responsibility in relation to these crimes.[2083] Moreover, the Appeals Chamber recalls its finding elsewhere in the Judgement that the Trial Chamber erred in law by failing to enter convictions of Stanišić for these crimes.[2084] In light of this, the Appeals Chamber finds it appropriate to address Stanišić's submissions with respect to the crimes under Counts 3, 5, 7, and 8.

614. The Appeals Chamber recalls that, as correctly set out by the Trial Chamber, an accused can only be held responsible for a crime outside the common purpose if, under the circumstances of the case: (i) it was foreseeable to the accused that such a crime might be perpetrated by one or more of the persons used by him (or by any other member of the joint criminal enterprise) in order to carry out the *actus reus* of the crimes forming part of the common purpose; and (ii) the accused willingly took the risk that such a crime might occur by joining or continuing to participate in the enterprise.[2085] In this regard, the Appeals Chamber recalls further that the foreseeability requirement applies to the *crime* with all its legal elements.[2086]
[page 255]

[2074]   Stanišić Appeal Brief, para. 378. See Stanišić Reply Brief, para. 21.

[2075]   Stanišić Appeal Brief, paras 53, 387.

[2076]   Prosecution Response Brief (Stanišić), paras 19-20, 179, 185. See Prosecution Response Brief (Stanišić), paras 180-184.

[2077]   Prosecution Response Brief (Stanišić), para. 179.

[2078]   Prosecution Response Brief (Stanišić), para. 180. See Prosecution Response Brief (Stanišić), para. 20.

[2079]   Prosecution Response Brief (Stanišić), para. 180. See Prosecution Response Brief (Stanišić), para. 20.

[2080]   Prosecution Response Brief (Stanišić), para. 180. The Prosecution submits that therefore the Trial Chamber did not need to repeat its earlier findings that the elements of each of these crimes were met (Prosecution Response Brief (Stanišić), para. 180).

[2081]   Prosecution Response Brief (Stanišić), para. 181.

[2082]   Prosecution Response Brief (Stanišić), para. 184.

[2083]   Trial Judgement, vol. 2, paras 804, 818, 822, 827, 831, 836, 840, 844, 849, 854, 858, 863, 868, 873, 877, 881, 885, 955.

[2084]   See *infra*, para. 1097. The Appeals Chamber recalls that it refrained from entering new convictions (see *infra*, para. 1096).

[2085]   85 *Tolimir* Appeal Judgement, para. 514; *Đorđević* Appeal Judgement, para. 906; *Šainović et al.* Appeal Judgement, paras 1061, 1557; *Brđanin* Appeal Judgement, paras 365, 411. See Trial Judgement, vol. 1, para. 106.

[2086]   See *e.g. Šainović et al.* Appeal Judgement, paras 1073, 1075, 1081, where the Appeals Chamber found that, *inter alia*, in finding that murder as a war crime was foreseeable, the *Šainović et al.* Trial Chamber erroneously relied on certain reports on the basis that it was unclear as to whether the killings reported therein constituted murder or were the result of legitimate combat activity (*Šainović et al.* Appeal Judgement, paras 1073, 1075). The Appeals Chamber examined whether the remaining factual findings were sufficient to establish that murder was foreseeable to the accused. The Appeals Chamber listed the remaining findings on the accused's awareness of crimes prior to 7 May 1999 against the civilian population. It concluded that the evidence did not establish

615. The Appeals Chamber notes that the Indictment charged Stanišić with killings during and after attacks on villages and towns, in detention facilities, and during transfer to and from detention facilities as: (i) persecutions as a crime against humanity through the underlying act of killings; (ii) murder as a crime against humanity; and (iii) murder as a violation of the laws or customs of war.[2087] The Appeals Chamber recalls in this regard that persecutions through the underlying act of killings, murder as a crime against humanity, and murder as a violation of the laws or customs of war are distinct crimes with distinct elements.[2088] In order to find Stanišić responsible for these crimes pursuant to the third category of joint criminal enterprise, the Trial Chamber had to be satisfied, in relation to each of these crimes, that it was foreseeable to Stanišić that they might be committed and that he willingly took that risk.[2089]

616. The Appeals Chamber observes that the Trial Chamber did not make an explicit finding that murder as a crime against humanity and murder as a violation of the laws or customs of war were foreseeable to Stanišić. Rather, the Trial Chamber found that it was foreseeable to Stanišić, that in the course of the attacks and takeover of the municipalities and in the context of detention, killings could be committed with a discriminatory intent and that he willingly took this risk.[2090] The Appeals Chamber considers that the absence of explicit findings on such an important issue is unfortunate. The Appeals Chamber observes, however, that the Trial Chamber found elsewhere in the Trial Judgement that these killings satisfied the elements of murder as a crime against humanity and murder as a violation of the laws or customs of war.[2091] In these circumstances, the Appeals Chamber understands that by finding that killings with discriminatory intent were foreseeable to Stanišić and he willingly took the risk that they could be committed, the Trial Chamber considered that the crimes of murder as a crime against humanity and murder as a violation of the laws or customs of war were foreseeable to Stanišić and that he willingly took that risk. Stanišić's argument that the Trial Chamber erred in law by failing to make the required findings on the subjective element of the third category of joint criminal enterprise liability in relation to the crimes under Counts 3 to 4 is therefore dismissed. **[page 256]**

617. The Appeals Chamber notes that the same reasoning applies to torture, cruel treatment, and other inhumane acts, which were all charged as underlying acts of persecutions as a crime against humanity (Count 1) while also charged as: (i) torture and inhumane acts as crimes against humanity (Counts 5 and 8, respectively); and (ii) torture and cruel treatment as violations of the laws or customs of war (Counts 6 and 7, respectively).[2092] The Trial Chamber found that it was foreseeable to Stanišić that torture, cruel treatment, and other inhumane acts could be committed,[2093] and that it was foreseeable to him, and he willingly took the risk, that these crimes might be committed with discriminatory intent.[2094] The Trial Chamber also found elsewhere in the Trial Judgement that these acts satisfied the elements of torture as a crime against humanity, torture as a violation of the laws or customs of war, cruel treatment as a violation of the laws or customs of war, and inhumane acts as a crime against humanity.[2095] In these circumstances, the Appeals Chamber understands that by finding that acts of torture, cruel treatment, and other inhumane acts were foreseeable to Stanišić and that he willingly took the risk that such acts might be committed with discriminatory intent, the Trial Chamber considered that the subjective element of the third category of joint criminal enterprise liability was met in relation to Stanišić with respect to the crimes charged under Counts 5 to 8. Therefore, Stanišić's argument in this regard is dismissed.

---

that prior to 7 May 1999, the accused was aware "of acts of violence to *civilians* of such gravity as to make murders, in particular, foreseeable to him" (*Šainović' et al.* Appeal Judgement, para. 1081 (emphasis added)).

[2087]   Indictment, paras 24, 26(a)-(b), 28-29, 31.

[2088]   See *Đorđević* Appeal Judgement, para. 548; *Kvočka et al.* Appeal Judgement, para. 261; *Kordić and Čerkez* Appeal Judgement, paras 37, 113. See also *Popović et al.* Appeal Judgement, para. 1714; *Đorđević* Appeal Judgement, para. 840; *Kordić and Čerkez* Appeal Judgement, para. 1036.

[2089]   See *infra*, para. 621.

[2090]   Trial Judgement, vol. 2, para. 774.

[2091]   See Trial Judgement, vol. 1, paras 215-218, 278, 343, 484-487, 688-689, 691, 693-694, 696, 876, 977, 1037, 1114-1115, 1243-1244, 1352, 1411, 1494, 1675-1677.

[2092]   Indictment, paras 26(c)-(d), 32, 34, 36.

[2093]   The Appeals Chamber notes that the Trial Chamber did not make a separate finding that Stanišić willingly took the risk that torture, cruel treatment, and other inhumane acts could be committed (see Trial Judgement, vol. 2, para. 776).

[2094]   Trial Judgement, vol. 2, para. 776.

[2095]   See Trial Judgement, vol. 1, paras 220, 280, 345, 489, 698, 808-809, 878, 979-980, 1039, 1117, 1188, 1246, 1284, 1354, 1496, 1551, 1685.

(iii) Conclusion

618.   In light of the foregoing, the Appeals Chamber finds that Stanišić has failed to demonstrate that the Trial Chamber erred in law by failing to make the required findings on the subjective element of third category of joint criminal enterprise liability in relation to Counts 3 to 8, thereby failing to provide a reasoned opinion for its findings on the third category of joint criminal enterprise. Therefore, the Appeals Chamber dismisses Stanišić's first ground of appeal in part and ninth ground of appeal in its entirety.

(d) Alleged errors of law in relation to whether Stanišić's JCE III Crimes were natural and foreseeable consequences of the common purpose (Stanišić's first ground of appeal in part and eleventh ground of appeal in part)

619.   Stanišić avers that the Trial Chamber erred in law by failing to enter findings that Stanišić's JCE III Crimes were natural and foreseeable consequences of the common purpose of the JCE, **[page 257]** thereby failing to provide a reasoned opinion.[2096] He submits that in order for liability under the third category of joint criminal enterprise to attach, it must be shown that the crimes outside of the scope of the joint criminal enterprise were "natural and foreseeable consequences of that enterprise", which he refers to as "objectively foreseeable".[2097] He argues that the "objective foreseeability" does not depend upon the accused's state of mind.[2098] In light of the Trial Chamber's alleged error in failing to conduct this assessment, Stanišić requests the Appeals Chamber to quash his convictions for Counts 1 (through underlying acts other than forcible transfer and deportation), 4, and 6.[2099]

620.   The Prosecution responds that Stanišić's challenges should be dismissed since the "objective foreseeability" is only "the first step" in the analysis concerning responsibility for crimes pursuant to the third category of joint criminal enterprise.[2100] It argues that, ultimately, a trial chamber must find that these crimes were foreseeable "to a particular accused", which is what the Trial Chamber found in relation to Stanišić.[2101]

621.   The Appeals Chamber recalls that, as correctly set out by the Trial Chamber:[2102]

> an accused may be responsible for crimes committed beyond the common purpose of the [...] joint criminal enterprise, if they were a natural and foreseeable consequence thereof. However, it is to be emphasized that this question must be assessed in relation to the knowledge of a particular accused. [...] What is natural and foreseeable to one person [...] might not be natural and foreseeable to another, depending on the information available to them. Thus, participation in a [...] joint criminal enterprise does not necessarily entail criminal responsibility for *all* crimes which, though not within the common purpose of the enterprise, were a natural or foreseeable consequence of the enterprise. A participant may be responsible for such crimes only if the Prosecution proves that the accused had sufficient knowledge such that the additional crimes were a natural and foreseeable consequence to him.[2103]

622.   Accordingly, the Appeals Chamber considers that Stanišić's argument creates and rests upon an artificial distinction – that the subjective element of the third category of joint criminal enterprise contains distinct objective and subjective elements – in direct contravention of the **[page 258]** law.[2104] Stanišić's unfounded argument, which departs from well-established jurisprudence, therefore has no merit. As such,

---

[2096]   Stanišić Appeal Brief, paras 48 (relating to the crime of persecutions under Count 1 (through underlying acts other than forcible transfer and deportation)), 51 (relating to crimes under Counts 3 to 8). See Stanišić Appeal Brief, paras 429-431.
[2097]   Stanišić Appeal Brief, para. 429, referring to *Prosecutor v. Radoslav Brđanin and Momir Talić*, Case No. IT-99-36-PT, Decision on Form of Further Amended Indictment and Prosecution Application to Amend, 26 June 2001, para. 30.
[2098]   Stanišić Appeal Brief, para. 429, in which Stanišić also avers that the "objective foreseeability" must be examined on the basis of the prevailing circumstances at the time, assessed from the point of view of a reasonable person (see Stanišić Appeal Brief, paras 430-431).
[2099]   Stanišić Appeal Brief, paras 53, 476.
[2100]   Prosecution Response Brief (Stanišić), paras 22, 194.
[2101]   Prosecution Response Brief (Stanišić), para. 194. See Prosecution Response Brief (Stanišić), para. 187.
[2102]   Trial Judgement, vol. 1, para. 99.
[2103]   *Kvočka et al.* Appeal Judgement, para. 86.
[2104]   *Popović et al.* Appeal Judgement, paras 1690, 1696-1698, 1713-1717; *Šainović et al.* Appeal Judgement, paras 1575-1604; *Kvočka et al.* Appeal Judgement, paras 83-86.

the Appeals Chamber dismisses Stanišić's first ground of appeal in part and eleventh ground of appeal in part concerning this issue.[2105]

(e) Alleged errors in finding that Stanišić' s JCE III Crimes were foreseeable to Stanišić and that he willingly took the risk that they might be committed (Stanišić's first ground of appeal in part, tenth ground of appeal, and eleventh ground of appeal in part)

623.   Stanišić submits that the Trial Chamber erred: (i) in law by failing to provide a reasoned opinion for: (a) its implicit findings that the possibility that crimes under Counts 3 to 8 could be committed was sufficiently substantial as to be foreseeable to him;[2106] and (b) its findings that the possibility that the crime of persecutions charged in Count 1 (through underlying acts other than forcible transfer and deportation) could be committed was sufficiently substantial as to be foreseeable to him;[2107] (ii) in fact by finding that Stanišić's JCE III Crimes were foreseeable to him;[2108] and (iii) in fact by finding that he willingly took the risk that Stanišić's JCE III Crimes could be committed.[2109] In light of these errors, Stanišić requests the Appeals Chamber to quash his convictions for Counts 1 (for underlying acts other than forcible transfer and deportation), 4, and 6 and the Trial Chamber's findings of responsibility for Counts 3, 5, 7, and 8.[2110] The Prosecution responds that Stanišić's challenges should be dismissed.[2111] **[page 259]**

(i) Alleged errors in failing to provide a reasoned opinion for finding that Stanšić's JCE III Crimes were foreseeable to Stanišić (Stanišić's first ground of appeal in part)

624.   Stanišić submits that the Trial Chamber has failed to provide any reasons in support of its implicit findings that the possibility that the crimes under Counts 3 through 8 could be committed was sufficiently substantial so as to be foreseeable to him.[2112] In addition, Stanišić avers that the Trial Chamber failed to provide any reasons in support of its findings that the possibility that the crime of persecutions charged under Count 1 (through underlying acts other than forcible transfer and deportation) could be committed was sufficiently substantial as to be foreseeable to him.[2113] Stanišić argues that these errors amount to failures to provide a reasoned opinion, errors of law.[2114]

625.   The Prosecution responds that the Trial Chamber provided a reasoned opinion for its findings on the foreseeability of Stanišić's JCE III Crimes.[2115]

626.   Given that, as found above,[2116] the Trial Chamber's third category of joint criminal enterprise findings for the crimes in Counts 3 to 8 are encompassed in the Trial Chamber's findings on the crimes in Count 1,

---

[2105]   The Appeals Chamber notes that Stanišić also submits that the Trial Chamber erred in fact by (implicitly) finding that Stanišić's JCE III Crimes were natural and foreseeable consequences of the JCE (see Stanišić Appeal Brief, paras 391, 395-399, 426, 431). In light of its conclusion that under the third category of joint criminal enterprise, the accused may be responsible for crimes beyond the common purpose of a joint criminal enterprise if they were natural and foreseeable consequences of the common purpose *to him*, the Appeals Chamber will address these arguments to the extent that they are relevant to the Trial Chamber's consideration in this regard. These arguments will be addressed in the next section together with Stanišić's factual challenges raised with respect to the Trial Chamber's findings that Stanišić's JCE III Crimes were foreseeable to him (see *infra*, paras 635-671).

[2106]   Stanišić Appeal Brief, paras 50-51. See Stanišić Appeal Brief, paras 49, 375-377.

[2107]   Stanišić Appeal Brief, para. 48.

[2108]   Stanišić Appeal Brief, paras 388, 392, 400-410 (relating to crimes under Counts 3 to 8), 424, 427, 432-448 (relating to the crime of persecution under Count 1 (through underlying acts other than forcible transfer and deportation)). The Appeals Chamber notes that in his notice of appeal, Stanišić only challenges his convictions for Counts 4 and 6 under his tenth ground of appeal. However, the Appeals Chamber recalls that after leave was granted, Stanišić filed an amended notice of appeal on 23 April 2014 adding Counts 3, 5, 7, and 8 to the counts targeted by the alleged error of fact in his tenth ground of appeal (Decision on Stanišić's Motion to Amend Notice of Appeal. See Stanišić Notice of Appeal, paras 55-58).

[2109]   Stanišić Appeal Brief, paras 388, 393, 411-422 (relating to crimes under Counts 3 to 8), Stanišić Appeal Brief, paras 428, 449-475 (relating to the crime of persecution under Count 1 (through underlying acts other than forcible transfer and deportation)).

[2110]   Stanišić Appeal Brief, paras 53, 423, 476.

[2111]   Prosecution Response Brief (Stanišić), paras 22, 187, 225.

[2112]   Stanišić Appeal Brief, paras 50-51.

[2113]   See Stanišić Appeal Brief, para. 48.

[2114]   Stanišić Appeal Brief, paras 48, 50-51.

[2115]   Prosecution Response Brief (Stanišić), para. 19.

[2116]   See *supra*, paras 616-617.

the Appeals Chamber will assess whether the Trial Chamber provided a reasoned opinion for its findings that crimes were foreseeable to Stanišić in relation to all Stanišić's JCE III Crimes together.[2117]

627.　The Appeals Chamber recalls that it is not necessary for the purposes of the third category of joint criminal enterprise that an accused be aware of the past occurrence of a crime for the same crime to be foreseeable to him.[2118] Knowledge of factors such as the nature of the conflict, the means by which a joint criminal enterprise is to be achieved, and how the joint criminal enterprise is implemented on the ground may make the possibility that such a crime might occur sufficiently substantial as to be foreseeable to members of the joint criminal enterprise.[2119]

628.　The Appeals Chamber notes that the trial Chamber found that Stanišić's JCE III Crimes occurred in the context of the JCE, which had the common plan to permanently remove Bosnian Muslims and Bosnian Croats from the territory of the planned Serbian state through the commission of the crimes of deportation, inhumane acts (forcible transfer), and persecutions through forcible **[page 260]** transfer and deportation, as crimes against humanity.[2120] The Appeals Chamber observes in this regard the Trial Chamber's findings elsewhere in the Trial Judgement that in implementing the JCE, violent takeovers of the Municipalities occurred together with an ensuing widespread and systematic campaign of terror and violence,[2121] aimed at establishing a Serb state as ethnically "pure" as possible.[2122] Furthermore, in finding that Stanišić's JCE III Crimes were foreseeable to him and he willingly took the risk that they might be committed, the Trial Chamber relied on its findings, which have not been overturned on appeal, that Stanišić: (i) shared the intent to forcibly remove non-Serbs from the territory of the planned Serb state through the commission of the crimes of deportation, inhumane acts (forcible transfer), and persecutions through deportation and forcible transfer as crimes against humanity;[2123] and (ii) was aware of the criminal background and propensity of members of the Bosnian Serb forces to commit crimes, particularly the RS reserve police force, which were mobilised from the early months of the conflict.[2124] In addition to these factors, the Trial Chamber relied on certain other factors in assessing the foreseeability of individual crimes.

629.　Specifically, in finding that it was foreseeable to Stanišić and he willingly took the risk that the imposition and maintenance of restrictive and discriminatory measures against non-Serbs in towns and villages after their takeover might be committed, with a discriminatory intent, in the execution of the common plan, the Trial Chamber also relied on the fact that the forcible removal of the Bosnian Muslims and Bosnian Croats from BiH was "engineered by enforcing unbearable living conditions following the takeover of identified towns and villages".[2125]

630.　In finding that it was foreseeable to Stanišić and he willingly took the risk that in the execution of the common plan killings might be committed, the Trial Chamber, in addition, relied on the "ethnically charged atmosphere during the 'reorganisation' of the internal organs of the municipalities".[2126]

631.　In finding that it was foreseeable to Stanišić and he willingly took the risk that torture, cruel treatment, and other inhumane acts might be committed, with discriminatory intent, in the course of unlawful detentions and in the execution of the common plan, the Trial Chamber relied, in addition, on Stanišić's knowledge of the large-scale detention of non-Serb civilians in prisons, SJBs, **[page 261]** detention centres, and camps which were guarded by the armed forces of the RS with the support of both active and reserve forces of the SJBs in individual municipalities approved by his direct orders.[2127]

[2117]　See *supra*, para. 609.

[2118]　*Šainović et al.* Appeal Judgement, para. 1081.

[2119]　See *Šainović et al.* Appeal Judgement, para. 1089.

[2120]　Trial Judgement, vol. 2, paras 770-774, 776-779. See Trial Judgement, vol. 2, para. 313.

[2121]　Trial Judgement, vol. 2, paras 310-311.

[2122]　Trial Judgement, vol. 2, para. 311. See Trial Judgement, vol. 2, paras 310, 738. See also Trial Judgement, vol. 2, para. 292.

[2123]　Trial Judgement, vol. 2, paras 770-771. See Trial Judgement, vol. 2, paras 766-769. See also Trial Judgement, vol. 2, paras 313, 770, 955.

[2124]　Trial Judgement, vol. 2, para. 771. See Trial Judgement, vol. 2, paras 526, 598, 613, 746-747, 749.

[2125]　Trial Judgement, vol. 2, para. 772. See Trial Judgement, vol. 2, paras 292, 294, 300, 522, 737.

[2126]　Trial Judgement, vol. 2, para. 774. See Trial Judgement, vol. 2, paras 310, 548, 551, 731, 734, 738.

[2127]　rial Judgement, vol. 2, para. 774. See Trial Judgement, vol. 2, paras 310, 548, 551, 731, 734, 738. Trial Judgement, vol. 2, para. 776. See Trial Judgement, vol. 2, paras 748, 750, 752, 757, 759, 762-765.

632. Furthermore, the Trial Chamber relied on evidence on "numerous reports and meetings" that addressed the increased level of looting, search and seizure, appropriation, and plunder of the moveable and immoveable property of non-Serbs during the takeover of Municipalities, in the course of transporting them to detention centres and camps, while in detention, and in the course of their escorted removal from Serb-held territory, to find that it was foreseeable to Stanišić and he willingly took the risk that these property crimes could be committed with discriminatory intent in the execution of the common plan.[2128]

633. Finally, in finding that it was foreseeable to Stanišić and he willingly took the risk that the wanton destruction and damage of religious and cultural property could be committed, with discriminatory intent, in the execution of the common plan, the Trial Chamber in addition relied on its finding that such destruction was "carried out in a concerted effort to eliminate the historical moorings of the Bosnian Muslims and Bosnian Croats during and following the takeover of the Municipalities".[2129]

634. The Trial Chamber thus relied on a combination of factors, including both specific reports of crimes as well as more generally, Stanišić's intent for the JCE I Crimes, the context in which Stanišić's JCE III Crimes were committed, and his knowledge of events. The Appeals Chamber sees no error in this approach. The Appeals Chamber is further satisfied that by doing so, the Trial Chamber provided a reasoned opinion for its findings that Stanišić's JCE III Crimes were foreseeable to him. Stanišić's submissions in this respect are thus dismissed.

(ii) Alleged errors of fact in finding that Stanišić's JCE III Crimes were foreseeable to Stanišić (Stanišić's tenth ground of appeal in part and eleventh ground of appeal in part)

a. Submissions of the parties

635. Stanišić argues that the Trial Chamber erred in fact by: (i) implicitly concluding that the crimes under Counts 3 to 8 were foreseeable to him;[2130] and (ii) finding that the crime of **[page 262]** persecutions under Count 1 (through underlying acts other than forcible transfer and deportation)[2131] were foreseeable to him.[2132]

636. With regard to the crimes under Counts 3 to 8, Stanišić argues first that the Trial Chamber failed to take into account the prevailing circumstances at the time, namely that the Cutileiro Plan had been signed by all parties to the conflict, which provided the prospect of a peaceful resolution.[2133] Stanišić further avers that the situation, along with the crimes that occurred, was completely unprecedented since World War II.[2134] Stanišić submits that instead of taking these circumstances into account, the Trial Chamber found that an "'ethnically charged atmosphere' existed", which according to him does not make the possibility of killings sufficiently substantial as to be foreseeable.[2135] Referring to the *Popović et al.* Trial Judgement, Stanišić also contends that the forcible transfer of a population does not make "opportunistic killings" necessarily foreseeable to an accused.[2136]

[2128] Trial Judgement, vol. 2, para. 777. See Trial Judgement, vol. 2, paras 631-632, 746.

[2129] Trial Judgement, vol. 2, para. 778. See Trial Judgement, vol. 2, paras 292, 294, 451.

[2130] Stanišić Appeal Brief, paras 388, 391-392, 394-395, 399-400, 410. See Stanišić Reply Brief, para. 97; Stanišić Appeal Brief, para. 388.

[2131] See *supra*, fn. 2070.

[2132] Stanišić Appeal Brief, paras 424, 426-427, 431, 448 (the Appeals Chamber notes that in paragraph 430 of his appeal brief, Stanišić refers to crimes under Count 3 to 8. However, given that the section in which these arguments are made concerns the crime of persecutions under Count 1 (through underlying acts other than forcible transfer and deportation), the Appeals Chamber understands this to be a typographical error).

[2133] Stanišić Appeal Brief, para. 397, referring to Exhibits P2200, P2203, 1D134. In this regard, Stanišić also refers to his Interview in which he indicated that at the time, both sides of the conflict expected that the situation would improve rather than get worse (Stanišić Appeal Brief, para. 397, referring to Exhibit P2301, p. 54. The Appeals Chambers understands Stanišić's reference to "P2301, P54" (see Stanišić Appeal Brief, para. 397, fn. 535) to be a reference to Exhibit P2301, p. 54 since Exhibit P54 is not relevant to the issue at hand, while page 54 of Exhibit P2301 is the relevant portion of Stanišić's Interview (see Exhibit P2301, p. 54)).

[2134] Stanišić Appeal Brief, paras 397-398. See Stanišić Appeal Brief, para. 430. See also Stanišić Reply Brief, para. 97.

[2135] Stanišić Appeal Brief, para. 398 referring to Trial Judgement, vol. 2, para. 774. See Stanišić Appeal Brief, para. 431.

[2136] Stanišić Appeal Brief, para. 399, referring to *Popović et al.* Trial Judgement, vol. 2, para. 1830.

637.   Stanišić further submits that the Trial Chamber erred by failing to properly consider the evidence of Witness Mačar that SJBs chiefs frequently did not inform the CSBs or the RS MUP of "situations", despite their obligation to do so.[2137] Stanišić argues that this evidence was corroborated by Prosecution witnesses, Witness Mandić,[2138] Radovan Pejić ("Witness Pejić"),[2139] and Dragan Kezunović ("Witness Kezunović")[2140] who also testified about the critical breakdown and lack of **[page 263]** communications between the central government and the municipalities.[2141] Moreover, Stanišić submits that the Trial Chamber erred in its assessment of the evidence of Witness Davidović, given that his testimony directly contradicts the Trial Chamber's findings on Stanišić's knowledge of the killing of several families in Bijeljina by Malović and his unit.[2142] In addition, Stanišić argues that there are "numerous additional examples [...] in the Judgement where evidence directly related to [his] lack of knowledge and/or information [...] was obviously not considered" by the Trial Chamber.[2143]

638.   Next Stanišić submits that the Trial Chamber heavily relied on the evidence of Witness Radulović, head of the Miloš Group, when finding that he was informed of the commission of crimes[2144] in spite of his testimony[2145] and Witness Goran Sajinović's ("Witness Sajinović") evidence,[2146] that the Miloš Group reports were neither sent to the RS MUP nor to Stanišić but were sent directly to Belgrade.[2147] He also refers to the evidence of Witness Škipina that, as the chief of SNB, he did not receive any reports or information from Witness Radulović and that the Miloš Group was operating outside the rules of service.[2148] Stanišić submits that their testimonies show that he was not privy to the information produced by the Miloš Group.[2149] Thus, according to Stanišić, the Trial Chamber disregarded parts of their evidence, since on the basis of the testimonies of Witness Radulović, Witness Sajinović, and Witness Škipina, "no reasonable trier of fact could have held that the only reasonable conclusion [...] was that this information [contained in the Miloš Group reports] was available to [him]".[2150]

639.   In addition, Stanišić argues that the Trial Chamber erred in relying on Exhibit P1428, the Communications Logbook,[2151] and daily reports to find that he had knowledge of crimes.[2152] Stanišić submits that the Communications Logbook does not show that he was personally informed about the crimes and the actions taken to investigate them.[2153] He contends that the entries cited by the Trial Judgement mainly concern requests for information on crimes sent by either Sarajevo CSB **[page 264]** or the RS MUP headquarters and "did not receive a response".[2154] Stanišić submits that the drastic decline in the number of

---

[2137]   Stanišić Appeal Brief, para. 403, quoting Trial Judgement, vol. 2, para. 251. See Stanišić Appeal Brief, para. 402.

[2138]   Stanišić Appeal Brief, paras 402, 404-405. Stanišić argues that Witness Mandić testified that "in some places", individuals "ran out of control completely" and that communications broke down (Stanišić Appeal Brief, para. 404, referring to Momčilo Mandić, 5 May 2010, T. 9588, Trial Judgement, vol. 2, para. 253).

[2139]   Stanišić Appeal Brief, para. 405. Stanišić argues that Witness Pejić testified that "there were no appropriate means of communications that the MUP of the RS could use" (Stanišić Appeal Brief, para. 405 (emphasis omitted), referring to Radovan Pejić, 25 Jun 2010, T. 12192).

[2140]   Stanišić Appeal Brief, para. 405. Stanišic argues that Witness Kezunović testified at length as to the severity of the communications breakdown, including the fact that there was "a complete disruption, breakdown in communications from the source of events to the seats of organisational units" (Stanišić Appeal Brief, para. 405 (emphasis omitted), referring to Dragan Kezunović, 10 Jun 2010, T. 11538, 11540, 11542, 11544, Dragan Kezunović, 14 Jun 2010, T. 11692-11693). See Stanišić Appeal Brief, para. 402.

[2141]   Stanišić Appeal Brief, paras 402, 404-405. See Stanišić Reply Brief, para. 99.

[2142]   Stanišić Appeal Brief, paras 406-408. See Stanišić Appeal Brief, para. 402.

[2143]   Stanišić Appeal Brief, para. 409, referring to Trial Judgement, vol. 2, paras 581, 583, 588-589, 604, 617, 637.

[2144]   Stanišić Appeal Brief, para. 435.

[2145]   Stanišić Appeal Brief, para. 436, referring to, *inter alia*, Predrag Radulović, 28 May 2010, T. 11016-11017.

[2146]   Stanišić Appeal Brief, para. 437, referring to, *inter alia*, Goran Sajinović, 17 Oct 2011, T. 25120, Goran Sajinović, 18 Oct 2011, T. 25220.

[2147]   Stanišić Appeal Brief, paras 436-437.

[2148]   Stanišić Appeal Brief, para. 438, referring to Slobodan Škipina, 31 Mar 2010, T. 8413-8415. See Stanišić Reply Brief, para. 99.

[2149]   Stanišić Appeal Brief, para. 439.

[2150]   Stanišić Appeal Brief, para. 439. See Stanišić Appeal Brief, paras 435-438.

[2151]   Stanišić Appeal Brief, para. 440.

[2152]   Stanišić Appeal Brief, para. 440, referring to Trial Judgement, vol. 2, para. 690; Stanišić Reply Brief, para. 99.

[2153]   Stanišić Appeal Brief, para. 441.

[2154]   Stanišić Appeal Brief, para. 441. Stanišić also contends that the entries in the Communications Logbook do not contain sufficient detail and information and that therefore they "cannot [...] be relied on to describe what was happening in any detail" (Stanišić Appeal Brief, para. 442).

dispatches from April to December 1992 resulting from the "chronic breakdown in communications" must also be taken into account.[2155] Furthermore, Stanišić asserts that the Trial Chamber erroneously relied on evidence from Witness Krulj that Stanišić was regularly informed via reports since he also testified that he "could not verify who actually received such reports".[2156]

640. Finally, Stanišić submits that the Trial Chamber's finding that he was informed of crimes committed against Muslims who were arrested in Sokolac is based on an erroneous interpretation of the evidence.[2157] He argues that the intercepted conversation on which the Trial Chamber relied does not mention that the arrested persons were Muslims.[2158] Moreover, he contends that since Sokolac was a predominantly Serb town[2159] and Serbs were selling weapons on the black market, it is more likely that the persons arrested "for messing up with the weapons" were in fact Serbs.[2160]

641. The Prosecution responds that the Trial Chamber reasonably found that Stanišić's JCE III Crimes were foreseeable to him.[2161] It submits that Stanišić's arguments should be summarily dismissed since he ignores that the Trial Chamber's findings were "based primarily on the nature of the common criminal purpose that [he] intended and the context in which he knew it was implemented".[2162]

642. The Prosecution first submits that: (i) the Trial Chamber's analysis was properly based in part on the prevailing circumstances at the time; (ii) while the crimes may have been unprecedented since World War II, they were not unexpected once the campaign of terror and violence started across the RS; and (iii) the Cutileiro Plan did not lessen the likelihood of the commission of crimes.[2163] The Prosecution argues that Stanišić "artificially isolates" the Trial Chamber's finding regarding the ethnically charged atmosphere, as it was the totality of factors **[page 265]** on the basis of which the Trial Chamber found that Stanišić's JCE III Crimes were foreseeable.[2164] It also submits that the finding of a different trial chamber based on a different crime base does not undermine the Trial Chamber's findings.[2165]

643. The Prosecution further responds that Stanišić's "one-sided presentation of the evidence" regarding the alleged breakdown of communication within the RS MUP should be summarily dismissed.[2166] Moreover, the Prosecution submits that Stanišić shows no contradiction in the Trial Chamber's "treatment" of Witness Davidović's testimony on the killings in Bijeljina by Malović and his unit.[2167] The Prosecution also avers that Stanišić's citations to numerous paragraphs of the Trial Judgement where the Trial Chamber discussed evidence of his purported lack of knowledge prove that the Trial Chamber explicitly considered and reasonably rejected such evidence in light of other evidence concerning Stanišić's knowledge of crimes.[2168]

644. In response to Stanišić's arguments concerning the Miloš Group reports, the Prosecution submits that he ignores the Trial Chamber's broader finding that he received information from various sources in the SNB, to which the Miloš Group belonged, including from Witness Škipina, who was the head of the SNB and reported directly to him.[2169] The Prosecution further argues that: (i) Witness Radulović testified that

[2155] Stanišić Appeal Brief, para. 443.
[2156] Stanišić Appeal Brief, para. 444, referring to Aleksander Krulj, 26 Oct 2009, T. 1986.
[2157] Stanišić Appeal Brief, paras 445-446, referring to Trial Judgement, vol. 2, para. 612.
[2158] Stanišić Appeal Brief, paras 445-446, referring to Exhibit P1115, pp 1-2.
[2159] Stanišić Appeal Brief, para. 446, referring to Exhibit 1D541, p. 219.
[2160] Stanišić Appeal Brief, paras 446-447.
[2161] Prosecution Response Brief (Stanišić), para. 189.
[2162] Prosecution Response Brief (Stanišić), para. 187. See Prosecution Response Brief (Stanišić), para. 199. The Appeals Chamber notes that the Prosecution responds to Stanišić's tenth and eleventh grounds of appeal in one consolidated section (Prosecution Response Brief (Stanišić), para. 188).
[2163] Prosecution Response Brief (Stanišić), para. 196. The Prosecution also submits that "Stanišić allegedly originally thinking in April 1992 that 'armed incidents' might soon end [...] is a separate issue from the objective foreseeability" of crimes (Prosecution Response Brief (Stanišić), para. 196).
[2164] Prosecution Response Brief (Stanišić), para. 197, referring to Trial Judgement, vol. 2, paras 738, 774.
[2165] Prosecution Response Brief (Stanišić), para. 198. The Prosecution adds that numerous judgements have found that "killings were natural and foreseeable consequences of a [joint criminal enterprise] aimed at forcibly displacing civilians" (Prosecution Response Brief (Stanišić), para. 198 (and references cited therein).
[2166] Prosecution Response Brief (Stanišić), para. 201.
[2167] Prosecution Response Brief (Stanišić), para. 202.
[2168] Prosecution Response Brief (Stanišić), para. 203.
[2169] Prosecution Response Brief (Stanišić), para. 204, referring to, *inter alia*, Trial Judgement, vol. 2, para. 689.

Stanišić received some reports from the Miloš Group; and (ii) Witness Sajinović testified that information contained in those reports was also sent up the RS MUP chain of command.[2170] The Prosecution argues that it was reasonable for the Trial Chamber to rely on such evidence, even if Witness Škipina gave contrary evidence.[2171]

645.   The Prosecution further responds that the information in the Communications Logbook was "detailed enough to alert"[2172] and that the absence of responses confirms the Trial Chamber's findings on the "inadequacy of RS MUP efforts to combat these crimes".[2173] According to the Prosecution, the fact that the Communications Logbook does not specify that Stanišić was notified and that it was "shared between the RS MUP headquarters and the CSB Sarajevo" does not weaken **[page 266]** the Trial Chamber's finding.[2174] The Prosecution argues that the number of dispatches is irrelevant to Stanišić's knowledge about crimes.[2175] Further, according to the Prosecution, Witness Krulj gave evidence that Stanišić received regular reports on the situation within the RS and that the information Witness Krulj compiled was "sent up the chain of command until it reached Stanišić".[2176]

646.   Finally, the Prosecution submits that, while the evidence does not specify the ethnicity of the persons arrested in Sokolac, the Trial Chamber reasonably found that they were Muslims in light of the ongoing and widespread campaign to disarm the non-Serb population.[2177]

b. Analysis

647.   As discussed elsewhere in this Judgement,[2178] in finding that Stanišić's JCE III Crimes were foreseeable to Stanišić, the Trial Chamber relied on a number of factors, such as that Stanišić: (i) shared the intent to forcibly remove non-Serbs from the territory of the planned Serb state through the commission of the crimes of deportation, inhumane acts (forcible transfer), and persecutions through deportation and forcible transfer as crimes against humanity;[2179] and (ii) was aware of the criminal background and propensity of members of the Bosnian Serb forces to commit crimes, particularly the RS reserve police force, which were mobilised from the early months of the conflict.[2180] Further, in relation to some of Stanišić's JCE III Crimes, the Trial Chamber relied also on: (i) Stanišić's knowledge of the large scale detention of non-Serb civilians in prisons, SJBs, detention centres, and camps which were guarded by the armed forces of the RS with the support of both active and reserve forces of the SJBs approved by his direct orders;[2181] and (ii) evidence on "numerous reports and meetings" that addressed the increased level of looting, search and seizure, appropriation, and plunder of the moveable and immoveable property of non-Serbs during the takeover of Municipalities, in the course of transporting them to detention centres and camps, while in detention, and in the course of their escorted removal from Serb-held territory.[2182] Considering that the Trial Chamber thus relied to some extent on Stanišić's knowledge of crimes to find that **[page 267]** Stanišić's JCE III Crimes were foreseeable to him, the Appeals Chamber will address his arguments on knowledge, insofar as they relate to one or more of the factors listed above. The Appeals Chamber recalls that the foreseeability of crimes outside the scope of the

---

[2170]   Prosecution Response Brief (Stanišić), para. 205.

[2171]   Prosecution Response Brief (Stanišić), para. 205.

[2172]   Prosecution Response Brief (Stanišić), para. 206.

[2173]   Prosecution Response Brief (Stanišić), para. 206.

[2174]   Prosecution Response Brief (Stanišić), para. 206. The Prosecution adds that the fact that the Communications Logbook was shared between the RS MUP and the Sarajevo CSB was acknowledged by the Trial Chamber (Prosecution Response Brief (Stanišić), para. 206, referring to Trial Judgement, vol. 2, para. 63).

[2175]   Prosecution Response Brief (Stanišić), para. 209.

[2176]   Prosecution Response Brief (Stanišić), para. 207.

[2177]   Prosecution Response Brief (Stanišić), para. 208, referring to Trial Judgement, vol. 1, paras 265, 454, 658, 785, 1179, Trial Judgement, vol. 2, paras 274-278.

[2178]   See *supra*, para. 628.

[2179]   Trial Judgement, vol. 2, paras 770-771.

[2180]   Trial Judgement, vol. 2, para. 771.

[2181]   Trial Judgement, vol. 2, para. 776 (in relation to specifically the foreseeabilty of torture, cruel treatment, and other inhumane acts). See Trial Judgement, vol. 2, paras 748, 750, 752, 757, 759, 762-765.

[2182]   Trial Judgement, vol. 2, para. 777 (in relation to specifically the foreseeability of looting, search and seizure, appropriation, and plunder of property). See Trial Judgement, vol. 2, paras 631-632, 691, 746.

joint criminal enterprise must be assessed in relation to the individual knowledge of each accused.[2183] As recalled in the *Šainović et al.* Appeal Judgement, "[depending on the information available, what may be foreseeable to one member of a JCE, might not be foreseeable to another."[2184]

648.   As another preliminary matter, the Appeals Chamber understands that the Trial Chamber was satisfied that the subjective element of the third category of joint criminal enterprise was met in relation to Stanišić throughout the Indictment period, *i.e.* at least from 1 April 1992, and in any event, when Stanišić's JCE III Crimes were committed.[2185]

649.   With respect to Stanišić's argument that, in assessing the foreseeability of the crimes under Counts 3-8, the Trial Chamber failed to consider the prevailing circumstances at the time, namely that the Cutileiro Plan had been signed and that the crimes were unprecedented since World War II, the Appeals Chamber notes that the Trial Chamber considered the Cutileiro Plan at length in the context of assessing Stanišić's responsibility.[2186] After examining the events surrounding the negotiation of the Cutileiro Plan and the conduct of the Bosnian Serb leadership, the Trial Chamber accepted that the withdrawal of assent by Alija Izetbegović was one of the reasons for the failure of the Cutileiro Plan.[2187] However, it also found that "prior to the negotiations in Lisbon, the Serbs had already coalesced around the idea of a separate Serb entity carved out of the territory of SRBiH in order to remain within a rump state of Yugoslavia—an agenda that came to coincide with the proposals of the Cutileiro Plan—and eventually in a greater Serbian state".[2188] In light of these findings, while the Trial Chamber did not explicitly consider the Cutileiro Plan in the context of the foreseeability of the crimes, it did consider it in the broader context of his responsibility, and therefore, the Appeals Chamber finds that Stanišić's submission that the Trial Chamber failed to **[page 268]** consider the Cutileiro Plan fails. Moreover, considering the Trial Chamber's findings on the context in which the crimes occurred,[2189] the Appeals Chamber finds that Stanišić has failed to show that no reasonable trier of fact could have reached the findings on the foreseeability of the crimes under Counts 3 to 8, as the Trial Chamber did, in light of the Cutileiro Plan.

650.   The Appeals Chamber also considers that, given the factors relied upon by the Trial Chamber in its foreseeability assessment, as well as its findings elsewhere in the Trial Judgement that a widespread and systematic campaign of terror and violence against non-Serbs was implemented by Serb forces with the ultimate aim to permanently remove them from the planned Serbian state,[2190] the fact that the nature of crimes may have been unprecedented since World War II does not undermine the Trial Chamber's findings on the foreseeability of the crimes under Counts 3 to 8.

651.   With respect to Stanišić's argument that the "ethnically charged atmosphere" was insufficient to make killings foreseeable,[2191] the Appeals Chamber considers that he ignores relevant findings. As set out above,[2192] the Trial Chamber's findings on the foreseeability of killings were based on several factors, including, but not limited to, the ethnically charged atmosphere. His argument is therefore dismissed.

2183   *Šainović et al.* Appeal Judgement, para. 1575. See *Tolimir* Appeal Judgement, para. 514.
2184   *Šainović et al.* Appeal Judgement, para. 1575. See *Tolimir* Appeal Judgement, para. 514.
2185   The Appeals Chamber notes that for the assessment of the foreseeability of all of Stanišić's JCE III Crimes, the Trial Chamber relied on, *inter alia*, the common purpose of the JCE as well as Stanišić's awareness of "the criminal background and propensity of members of the Bosnian Serb Forces to commit crimes, and particularly the RS reserve police force, which were mobilised in *the early months of the conflict*" (Trial Judgement, vol. 2, para. 771 (emphasis added). See Trial Judgement, vol. 2, para. 770). Moreover, Stanišić was convicted pursuant to the third category of joint criminal enterprise for crimes occurring throughout the Indictment period (see *e.g.* Trial Judgement, vol. 2, paras 801, 804, 806, 809-810, 813, 815, 818-819, 822, 824, 827-828, 831, 833, 836-837, 840-841, 844, 846, 850-851, 854-855, 858, 860, 863, 865, 868, 870, 873-874, 877-878, 881-882, 885, 955). The Appeals Chamber notes that the Trial Chamber identified the Indictment period as "from no later than 1 April 1992" until 31 December 1992 (Trial Judgement, vol. 2, para. 532. See Trial Judgement, vol. 2, para. 531).
2186   Trial Judgement, vol. 2, paras 552-563. See Trial Judgement, vol. 1, para. 131.
2187   Trial Judgement, vol. 2, para. 563.
2188   Trial Judgement, vol. 2, para. 563. In light of these Trial Chamber findings, the Appeals Chamber finds Stanišić's submission that there was a general expectation that things would get better unconvincing.
2189   See *supra*, para. 628.
2190   Trial Judgement, vol. 2, para. 313. See Trial Judgement, vol. 2, paras 737-738.
2191   Stanišić Appeal Brief, para. 398, referring to Trial Judgement, vol. 2, para. 774. See Stanišić Appeal Brief, para. 431.
2192   See *supra*, paras 628, 630.

652.   Considering that the Trial Chamber's findings were based on the trial record in this specific case, the Appeals Chamber further finds no merit in Stanišić's argument that other trial chambers have found that killings were not a foreseeable consequence of a joint criminal enterprise aimed at forcibly displacing a population. Moreover, the Appeals Chamber recalls that an error cannot be established by merely pointing to the fact that another trial chamber has reached a different conclusion.[2193]

653.   As regards Stanišić's argument that the Trial Chamber failed to properly assess the evidence of Witness Mačar, Witness Mandić, Witness Pejić, and Witness Kezunović concerning problems with communications between the RS MUP and the Municipalities during the conflict, the Appeals Chamber notes that the Trial Chamber explicitly considered their evidence in relation to communication problems,[2194] as well as other evidence concerning communication difficulties, in **[page 269]** its assessment of communication within the RS MUP.[2195] The Trial Chamber also considered ample evidence, both on the overall communications within the RS MUP as well as on the communication systems in the Sarajevo CSB,[2196] Bijeljina and Trebinje CSBs,[2197] Doboj CSB,[2198] and Banja Luka CSB,[2199] indicating that despite the difficulties, communications remained possible.[2200] Among other things, it took into account that in April 1992, in the absence of a communication system within the police, most communications between the RS MUP and the CSBs occurred through existing fax and telephone lines.[2201] Furthermore, in Bijeljina and Trebinje CSBs, couriers were used almost daily.[2202] The Trial Chamber also took into account that at the Banja Luka CSB, telephone and telegraph exchanges had remained operational, thus helping communications with all SJBs in the region to be linked to the telephone or telegraph lines.[2203] The Trial Chamber also took into account Witness ST219's testimony that the communication centre in Pale was able to use teleprinters, radio communication, and other types of communications, despite the difficulties caused by the outbreak of hostilities.[2204] After assessing all the evidence, the Trial Chamber acknowledged that there were indeed many difficulties in the communications within the RS MUP, especially in the period from April to the summer of 1992.[2205] However, it was satisfied that during this period, "the system of communications through fax machines, teleprinters, telephone, and couriers did function, albeit with disruptions".[2206] The Trial Chamber also found that the communication system was well established in the second half of 1992.[2207]

654.   The Appeals Chamber recalls that "it is the trier of fact who is best placed to assess the evidence in its entirety"[2208] and that trial chambers enjoy broad discretion in doing so.[2209] The Appeals Chamber considers that Stanišić merely prefers a different interpretation of the evidence but has failed to show that no reasonable trier of fact could have concluded as the Trial Chamber did. His arguments in this regard are therefore dismissed. **[page 270]**

655.   Turning to Stanišić's argument regarding the killings in Bijeljina,[2210] the Appeals Chamber notes that, contrary to Stanišić's submission, the Trial Chamber did not make a finding that he knew about these killings.[2211] Stanišić therefore misrepresents the Trial Chamber's findings and consequently, his argument is dismissed.

[2193]   See *Đorđević* Appeal Judgement, para. 257; *Krnojelac* Appeal Judgement, para. 12.
[2194]   Trial Judgement, vol. 2, paras 56, 60-65, 67-6, 74, 76, 83, 251, 253.
[2195]   Trial Judgement, vol. 2, paras 61, 65, 67-71, 73-74, 76, 78-80, 82-83.
[2196]   Trial Judgement, vol. 2, paras 70-72 (and references cited therein).
[2197]   Trial Judgement, vol. 2, paras 73-74 (and references cited therein).
[2198]   Trial Judgement, vol. 2, paras 75-76 (and references cited therein).
[2199]   Trial Judgement, vol. 2, paras 77-84 (and references cited therein).
[2200]   See Trial Judgement, vol. 2, paras 61-67, 69, 72-73, 75, 77, 79.
[2201]   Trial Judgement, vol. 2, para. 68. See Trial Judgement, vol. 2, para. 73.
[2202]   Trial Judgement, vol. 2, para. 74.
[2203]   Trial Judgement, vol. 2, para. 77. See Trial Judgement, vol. 2, para. 81.
[2204]   Trial Judgement, vol. 2, para. 72.
[2205]   Trial Judgement, vol. 2, para. 103.
[2206]   Trial Judgement, vol. 2, para. 103.
[2207]   Trial Judgement, vol. 2, para. 103.
[2208]   *Dorlević* Appeal Judgement, para. 395 (and references cited therein).
[2209]   See *e.g. Đorđević* Appeal Judgement, para. 856; *Boškoski and Tarčulovski* Appeal Judgement, para. 14; *Kupreškić et al.* Appeal Judgement, paras 30-32.
[2210]   See Stanišić Appeal Brief, paras 406-408.
[2211]   See Trial Judgement, vol. 2, para. 603.

293

656.   As regards Stanišić's argument that there are "numerous additional examples" in the Trial Judgement where the Trial Chamber failed to consider evidence relating to his lack of knowledge,[2212] the Appeals Chamber considers that he has failed to identify an error, and merely 2213 points to paragraphs of the Trial Judgement without explaining how the Trial Chamber erred.[2213] Stanišić's argument in this respect is thus dismissed.

657.   The Appeals Chamber now moves to Stanišić's argument that the Trial Chamber erred in relying on the Miloš Group reports in finding that he had knowledge of crimes. The Appeals Chamber observes that the Trial Chamber found that the Miloš Group was collecting intelligence for the SNB[2214] and, on the basis of Witness Radulović's evidence, found that "[w]hile not every report prepared by the 'Miloš Group' intelligence team, [...] was directly submitted to the RS MUP, the information in these reports was relayed through the leadership of Banja Luka to the upper echelons of decision makers."[2215] Based on the foregoing, the Trial Chamber ultimately concluded that the "information gathered by the SNB was available to the decision makers of the RS, which included Stanišić".[2216]

658.   The Appeals Chamber recalls that it has already dismissed Stanišić's argument elsewhere in this Judgement that the Trial Chamber failed to consider Witness Radulović's evidence that Stanišić did not receive the Miloš Group reports.[2217]

659.   Turning to Stanišić's argument that the Trial Chamber disregarded parts of Witness Sajinović's evidence that the Miloš Group reports were neither sent to the RS MUP nor to Stanišić, but directly to Belgrade,[2218] the Appeals Chamber observes that Stanišić ignores the part of Witness Sajinović's testimony, considered by the Trial Chamber, that the Miloš Group reports were also **[page 271]** sent to "Sajinović and Radulović's superiors in the Banja Luka SNB".[2219] Regarding Stanišić's argument that Witness Škipina did not receive any reports or information from Witness Radulović,[2220] the Appeals Chamber notes that indeed, the Trial Chamber did not rely on his evidence to find that the information gathered by the SNB was available to Stanišić.[2221] The Appeals Chamber recalls that "it is within the discretion of the Trial Chamber to evaluate [witnesses' testimony] and to consider whether the evidence as a whole is credible, without explaining its decision in every detail".[2222] In view of the consistent evidence of Witness Radulović and Witness Sajinović on this issue, the Appeals Chamber finds that Stanišić has failed to show that, in light of Witness Škipina's testimony, no reasonable trier of fact could have found that the "information gathered by the SNB was available to the decision makers of the RS, which included Stanišić".[2223]

660.   Turning to Stanišić's arguments regarding the Trial Chamber's analysis of and reliance on the Communications Logbook, the decline in the number of dispatches from April to December 1992, and Witness Krulj's evidence, the Appeals Chamber notes that the Trial Chamber found that:

> [a]ccording to the communications logbook of the RS MUP headquarters, Stanišić was regularly informed throughout 1992 about crimes and action being taken to investigate them.[2224] Daily, weekly, and quarterly

---

[2212]   Stanišić Appeal Brief, para. 409.

[2213]   See Stanišić Appeal Brief, para. 409, referring to Trial Judgement, vol. 2, paras 581, 583, 588-589, 604, 617, 637.

[2214]   Trial Judgement, vol. 2, para. 372.

[2215]   Trial Judgement, vol. 2, para. 689, referring to Predrag Radulović, 25 May 2010, T. 1072010721, 10722-10723 (private session), 10728-10731, Predrag Radulović, 27 May 2010, T. 10894-10897, 10898 (private session), 10950-10951 (private session), Predrag Radulović, 28 May 2010, T. 10997, Predrag Radulović, 1 Jun 2010, T. 11119-11121, Predrag Radulović, 2 Jun 2010, T. 11206-11209, 11213-11214.

[2216]   Trial Judgement, vol. 2, para. 764.

[2217]   See *supra*, para. 409.

[2218]   See *supra*, para. 638.

[2219]   Trial Judgement vol. 2, para. 372.

[2220]   See *supra*, para. 638.

[2221]   Trial Judgement, vol. 2, para. 689, referring to Predrag Radulović, 25 May 2010, T. 10720-10721, 10722-10723 (private session), 10728-10731, Predrag Radulović, 27 May 2010, T. 10894-10897, 10898 (private session), 10950-10951 (private session), Predrag Radulović, 28 May 2010, T. 10997, Predrag Radulović, 1 Jun 2010, T. 11119-11121, Predrag Radulović, 2 Jun 2010, T. 11206-11209, 11213-11214.

[2222]   *Popović et al.* Appeal Judgement, para. 1151, quoting *Kvočka et al.* Appeal Judgement, para. 23.

[2223]   Trial Judgement, vol. 2, para. 764.

[2224]   Trial Judgement, vol. 2, para. 690, referring to Exhibit P1428, pp 5, 33-34, 43-44, 49, 53, 63, 74, 114, 129, 132, 143-144, 218, 231, 235, 247, 294.

reports were compiled, in addition to security situation reports on a periodic basis.[2225] Aleksander Krulj testified that these reports were prepared in order for the Minister to 'know what happened in the territory of the republic'.[2226]

661. Insofar as Stanišić argues that the Trial Chamber erred in relying on the Communications Logbook to find that he had knowledge of crimes, the Appeals Chamber recalls its finding that no reasonable trier of fact could have found, based on this evidence, that Stanišić was informed about the crimes "throughout 1992".[2227] The Appeals Chamber recalls its findings earlier in this Judgement that this error has no impact on the Trial Chamber's findings concerning Stanišić's knowledge of crimes committed against Muslims and Croats.[2228] **[page 272]**

662. With respect to Stanišić's argument regarding the decline in the number of dispatches between April and December 1992,[2229] the Appeals Chamber observes that the Trial Chamber considered this argument in its analysis of the communications systems in the RS, noting that "on average, 15 dispatches a day were sent to the centres and other organs from the RS MUP headquarters (a total of 4,170 in all lines of work) and on average 16 dispatches per day were received (a total of 4,400)".[2230] The Trial Chamber also considered Witness Kezunović's testimony that the number of dispatches for the "first nine months in 1992 amounted to less than 10% of the number of dispatches for the same period in 1991".[2231] The Trial Chamber further considered Witness Dragan Raljić's ("Witness Raljić") testimony that "there was a significant drop in the number of incoming and outcoming [*sic*] dispatches in the period from 11 June 1992 until the end of the year".[2232] Based on, *inter alia*, the evidence listed above, the Trial Chamber found that "there were indeed many difficulties in the communications within the RS MUP, especially in the period from April to the summer of 1992".[2233] However, the Trial Chamber ultimately found that "the system of communications through fax machines, teleprinters, telephone, and couriers did function, albeit with disruptions" and that "[i]n the second half of 1992, the communications system was well established."[2234] In light of these findings, Stanišić has not shown that no reasonable trier of fact could have concluded as the Trial Chamber did.

663. The Appeals Chamber now turns to Stanišić's argument that the Trial Chamber erroneously disregarded Witness Krulj's evidence that he "could not verify who actually received such reports" and yet relied on his testimony to support its findings that Stanišić was kept regularly informed through reports.[2235] Witness Krulj testified that "these reports were prepared in order for the Minister to 'know what happened in the territory of the republic'"[2236] and the Appeals Chamber therefore considers that Stanišić misrepresents Witness Krulj's testimony. Moreover, the Appeals Chamber recalls the Trial Chamber's finding that from April to the summer of 1992 the system of communication did function, albeit with interruptions, and that in the second half of 1992, communication was well established.[2237] Consequently, the Appeals Chamber finds that Stanišić has failed to show that the Trial Chamber erred in relying on Witness Krulj's evidence in assessing the general sources of information available to Stanišić at that time. **[page 273]**

664. Turning to Stanišić's argument regarding the arrests in Sokolac, the Appeals Chamber notes that the Trial Chamber found that:

> on 18 April 1992, Radomir Kojić informed Stanišić that a certain 'Zoka' had arrested Muslims in Sokolac for 'messing up with the weapons'. Kojić agreed with 'Zoka' that the arrested people would be brought to

---

[2225] Trial Judgement, vol. 2, para. 690, referring to, *inter alia*, Exhibits P155, P595, P427.08, p. 3, P432.12, p. 3, P633, p. 3, 2D25, P866, P748, p. 2, 1D334.
[2226] Trial Judgement, vol. 2, para. 690, referring to Aleksander Krulj, 26 Oct 2009, T. 1983-1987.
[2227] See *supra*, para. 407.
[2228] See *supra*, para. 412.
[2229] Stanišić Appeal Brief, para. 443.
[2230] Trial Judgement, vol. 2, para. 61, referring to Exhibit P625, p. 23.
[2231] Trial Judgement, vol. 2, para. 83, referring to, *inter alia*, Dragan Kezunović, 14 Jun 2010, T. 11690-11692, 11694-11695, Exhibits 2D52, p. 11, P621, p. 31, P595, p. 12.
[2232] Trial Judgement, vol. 2, para. 83, referring to, *inter alia*, Dragan Raljić, 30 Jun 2010, T. 12450-12451, Dragan Kezunović, 14 Jun 2010, T. 11691-11692, Exhibits P595, p. 12, P621, p. 31, P1486.
[2233] Trial Judgement, vol. 2, para. 103.
[2234] Trial Judgement, vol. 2, para. 103.
[2235] Stanišić Appeal Brief, para. 444.
[2236] Trial Judgement, vol. 2, para. 690, referring to Aleksander Krulj, 26 Oct 2009, T. 1983-1987.
[2237] Trial Judgement, vol. 2, paras 103, 690.

Vrace, telling Stanišić that there '[t]hey can beat them, they can do whatever they fucking want', to which Stanišić responded: '[f]ine'.[2238]

665. The Appeals Chamber notes that this finding is based on Exhibit P1115, which is an intercepted conversation between Stanišić and Radomir Kojić dated 18 April 1992.[2239] The Appeals Chamber further notes that the exhibit in fact does not mention whether the people arrested were Muslims or provide any information from which their ethnicity could be inferred.[2240] Further, the incident is not discussed elsewhere in the Trial Judgement. Additionally, the fact that the arrested people "would be brought to Vrace" does not provide any further information since there is no indication anywhere in the Trial Judgement as to the ethnicity of those detained in Vrace. Therefore, the Appeals Chamber finds that the Trial Chamber erred in its analysis of this evidence and in finding that the arrests in Sokolac involved Muslims. The Appeals Chamber recalls its findings elsewhere in this Judgement that this error has an impact on the Trial Chamber's findings concerning Stanišić's knowledge of crimes committed against Muslims and Croats, and that a reasonable trial chamber could have found that Stanišić acquired such knowledge only as of late April 1992.[2241]

c. Conclusion

666. The Appeals Chamber will now assess the impact, on the Trial Chamber's findings on the foreseeability of Stanišić's JCE III Crimes, of the abovementioned error in relation to the arrests in Sokolac, and the Appeals Chamber's finding elsewhere in this Judgement that, in light of this error, a reasonable trial chamber could have found that Stanišić acquired knowledge of crimes committed against Muslims and Croats only as of late April 1992.[2242] [page 274]

667. The Appeals Chamber recalls that in finding that Stanišić's JCE III Crimes were foreseeable to him, the Trial Chamber relied on the fact that they occurred in the context of the JCE.[2243] The Trial Chamber further relied on Stanišić's intent to permanently remove Bosnian Muslims and Bosnian Croats from the territory of the planned Serbian state through the commission of crimes,[2244] and his awareness of the criminal background and propensity of members of the Bosnian Serb forces to commit crimes and particularly the RS reserve police force which were mobilised in the early months of the conflict to effect this removal.[2245]

668. The Appeals Chamber notes that it has upheld the Trial Chamber's finding on the existence of the JCE.[2246] The Appeals Chamber further recalls that, despite its finding that a reasonable trier of fact could have found that Stanišić acquired knowledge of crimes committed against Muslims and Croats only as of late April 1992,[2247] it has upheld the Trial Chamber's finding that Stanišić possessed the intent to permanently remove Bosnian Muslims and Bosnian Croats from the territory of the planned Serbian state through the commission of JCE I Crimes during the Indictment period (*i.e.* from 1 April 1992 to 31 December 1992).[2248]

669. With regard to Stanišić's awareness of the criminal background and propensity of members of the Bosnian Serb forces to commit crimes, while the section in the Trial Judgement on Stanišić's responsibility

---

[2238] Trial Judgement, vol. 2, para. 612, referring to Exhibit P1115, pp 1-2.
[2239] Trial Judgement, vol. 2, para. 612, referring to Exhibit P1115.
[2240] See Exhibit P1115, pp 1-2.
[2241] See *supra*, para. 412.
[2242] See *supra*, para. 412. The Appeals Chamber recalls that while it has also found an error in relation to the Communications Logbook, it has concluded that this error has no impact on the Trial Chamber's findings concerning Stanišić's knowledge of crimes committed against Muslims and Croats (see *supra*, paras 411-412). In light of this, coupled with the fact that the Trial Chamber did not rely directly on the Communications Logbook in its foreseeability assessment (see *supra*, paras 629-633), the Appeals Chamber finds that the error in relation to the Communications Logbook does not have any impact on the Trial Chamber's foreseeability findings. As such, the Appeals Chamber will not address this error further in this section.
[2243] Trial Judgement, vol. 2, paras 770-774, 776-779. See Trial Judgement, vol. 2, para. 313.
[2244] Trial Judgement, vol. 2, paras 770-771. See Trial Judgement, vol. 2, paras 766-769. See also Trial Judgement, vol. 2, paras 313, 770, 955.
[2245] Trial Judgement, vol. 2, para. 771. See Trial Judgement, vol. 2, paras 600, 746-747, 749, 751.
[2246] Trial Judgement, vol. 2, paras 313-314. See *supra*, paras 71, 87.
[2247] See *supra*, para. 412.
[2248] See *supra*, para. 584.

for Stanišić's JCE III Crimes lacks references, the Appeals Chamber understands the Trial Chamber to have relied on its findings regarding Stanišić's: (i) knowledge of crimes committed by these forces against Muslims and Croats;[2249] (ii) acknowledgement at the November 1992 BSA Session that "'in the beginning', 'thieves and criminals' were accepted into the reserve police forces because 'we wanted the country defended'";[2250] and (iii) orders from 15 April 1992 that measures be taken against his subordinates who engaged in looting and misappropriation or other "unprincipled conduct", which the Trial Chamber found were not carried out to the extent possible.[2251] As regards Stanišić's knowledge of crimes committed against Muslims and Croats, as recalled above,[2252] the Appeals Chamber has found that due to the error in **[page 275]** the Trial Chamber's finding on Stanišić's knowledge of the arrests in Sokolac,[2253] a reasonable trier of fact could have found that Stanišić acquired knowledge of crimes committed against Muslims and Croats only as of late April 1992.[2254] However, the Appeals Chamber considers that this has no impact on the Trial Chamber's finding that he was aware of the criminal background and propensity of members of the Bosnian Serb forces to commit crimes, in light of his knowledge of crimes against Muslims and Croats from late April,[2255] as well as the remaining factors considered by the Trial Chamber.

670. In addition to taking into account that Stanišić's JCE III Crimes occurred in the context of the JCE, that Stanišić had the intent to permanently remove Bosnian Muslims and Bosnian Croats from the territory of the planned Serbian state through the commission of JCE I Crimes, and that he was aware of the criminal background and propensity of members of the Bosnian Serb forces to commit crimes, the Trial Chamber also relied on other varying factors in relation to assessing the foreseeability to Stanišić of specific crimes for which he was found responsible for pursuant to the third category of joint criminal enterprise.[2256] However, there is no indication that the Trial Chamber relied specifically on Stanišić's knowledge of the Sokolac arrests.[2257]

671. For the foregoing reasons, the Appeals Chamber finds that the error in the Trial Chamber's finding on Stanišić's knowledge of the Sokolac arrests has no impact on the Trial Chamber's finding that it was foreseeable to Stanišić that Stanišić's JCE III Crimes could be committed in the execution of the common plan of the JCE. In the absence of any further submissions, Stanišić has failed to demonstrate that the Trial Chamber erred in fact in reaching this conclusion. His arguments in this regard are therefore dismissed. **[page 276]**

[2249] Trial Judgement, vol. 2, paras 420, 603, 612, 617, 623, 631-633, 638-639, 646, 660-663, 677, 689, 713, 762-765. See *supra*, para. 404.

[2250] Trial Judgement, vol. 2, para. 600.

[2251] Trial Judgement, vol. 2, paras 746-747, 749, 751, 759. See Trial Judgement, vol. 2, paras 605, 610, 613, 636, 640-641, 644.

[2252] See *supra*, para. 666.

[2253] Trial Judgement, vol. 2, para. 612. See *supra*, para. 665.

[2254] See *supra*, para. 412.

[2255] Trial Judgement, vol. 2, paras 420, 603, 617, 623, 631-633, 638-639, 646, 660-663, 677, 689, 713, 762-765. See *supra*, para. 575.

[2256] See *supra*, paras 629-633.

[2257] With respect to the foreseeability of inhumane acts and persecutions through torture, cruel treatment, and inhumane acts as crimes against humanity; torture as a crime against humanity and a violation of the laws or customs of war; and cruel treatment as a violation of the laws or customs of war, the Appeals Chamber notes that the Trial Chamber relied on Stanišić's knowledge of the large-scale detention of the non-Serbs civilians (Trial Judgement, vol. 2, para. 776). In this respect, the Appeals Chamber observes that the Trial Chamber found elsewhere that he learned of the unlawful detentions of Muslims and Croats, at the latest, by the beginning of June 1992 (Trial Judgement, vol. 2, para. 762. See Trial Judgement, vol. 2, paras 617, 623, 631-633, 639, 646, 660-663, 763-765. See also Trial Judgement, vol. 2, paras 637, 646, 664, 667-668, 675, 748, 750, 752, 757, 759, 763-765). In reaching this conclusion, the Trial Chamber however did not rely on his knowledge of the Sokolac arrests (see Trial Judgement, vol. 2, paras 762-765. See also Trial Judgement, vol. 2, paras 617, 623, 631-633, 639, 646, 660-663; *supra*, paras 404-405). With respect to the foreseeabilty of the plunder of property as an underlying act of persecutions as a crime against humanity, the Trial Chamber additionally considered evidence on numerous reports and meetings that addressed the increased level of looting, search and seizure, and plunder of the moveable and immoveable property of the Bosnian Muslims and Bosnian Croats, and other non-Serbs in the Municipalities (Trial Judgement, vol. 2, para. 777. See Trial Judgement, vol. 2, paras 603, 631-632, 746). However, it is evident that the Trial Chamber did not rely on Stanišić knowledge of the Sokolac arrests in reaching its conclusion on the information he received concerning property crimes (see Trial Judgement, vol. 2, paras 762-765. See also Trial Judgement, vol. 2, paras 617, 623, 631-633, 639, 646, 660-663; *supra*, paras 404-405).

(iii) Alleged errors in finding that Stanišić willingly took the risk that Stanišić's JCE III Crimes could be committed (Stanišić's tenth ground of appeal in part and eleventh ground of appeal in part)

a. Submissions of the parties

672.   Stanišić argues that the Trial Chamber erred in fact by finding that he willingly took the risk that the crimes under Counts 3 to 8 and the crime of persecutions under Count 1 (through underlying acts other than forcible transfer and deportation)[2258] could be committed.[2259] In particular, Stanišić submits that the Trial Chamber failed to provide references in finding him responsible for crimes in the Municipalities outside the scope of the JCE and "simply follow[ed] its incorrect reasoning from paragraphs 771-774 and 776-779" of volume two of the Trial Judgement.[2260]

673.   Stanišić further submits that the evidence demonstrates that he took numerous positive measures against those who committed crimes, but that the Trial Chamber mischaracterised this evidence.[2261] In particular, Stanišić contends that the Trial Chamber mischaracterised efforts to bring the Yellow Wasps to justice by focussing on the charges of vehicle theft and by finding that "[m]embers of the Yellow Wasps were released from detention on 28 August 1992 and an indictment against them was only issued in 1999."[2262] Stanišić refers to Witness Andan's evidence that on the basis of the information provided by him to the Serbian authorities, the leaders of the Yellow Wasps were indicted in Serbia in 1993 and convicted and sentenced in 1994,[2263] and that other paramilitaries were also arrested and prosecuted.[2264] Stanišić further argues that in finding that operations similar to those against the Yellow Wasps never occurred "because Davidović 'returned to Serbia' and Andan was removed from RS MUP", the Trial Chamber mischaracterised Witness Andan's evidence.[2265] According to Stanišić, Exhibits 1D75, a report from the Crime Police Directorate within the RS MUP on criminal activity of the Yellow Wasps, and 1D557, the diary of **[page 277]** Witness Andan from July-August 1992, also demonstrate that measures were taken against paramilitaries in relation to their involvement in serious crimes and not only thefts.[2266]

674.   Stanišić submits that the Trial Chamber acknowledged many examples where he took measures to counter crimes.[2267] Further, he argues that it accepted that Witness Dokanović and Stanišić "were the only people in the RS Government who were interested in addressing the issue of war crimes",[2268] but disregarded this evidence when concluding that he willingly took the risk that such crimes could be committed.[2269] In addition, Stanišić argues that the Trial Chamber ignored several exhibits showing that he did not willingly take the risk that crimes under Counts 3 to 8 be committed.[2270]

675.   Stanišić further refers to the Trial Chamber's finding that he issued strict instructions "for the purpose of safeguarding the lives of people in the detention centres"[2271] and to his orders to counter serious crimes as soon as he was informed of such crimes.[2272] He submits that the Trial Chamber erred in finding that he

---

[2258]   See *supra*, fn. 2070.
[2259]   Stanišić Appeal Brief, paras 393-394, 411, 425, 451. See Stanišić Appeal Brief, paras 454, 461, 466, 470, 472, 475.
[2260]   Stanišić Appeal Brief, para. 450.
[2261]   Stanišić Appeal Brief, para. 417. See Stanišić Appeal Brief, paras 412-416. See also Stanišić Reply Brief, para. 99.
[2262]   Stanišić Appeal Brief, para. 412 (emphasis omitted), quoting Trial Judgement, vol. 2, para. 715.
[2263]   Stanišić Appeal Brief, para. 413, referring to Dragomir Andan, 1 Jun 2011, T. 21688, 21690-21692, Exhibit P1979.
[2264]   Stanišić Appeal Brief, para. 414, referring to Dragomir Andan, 1 Jun 2011, T. 21690-21692, 21700-21702.
[2265]   Stanišić Appeal Brief, para. 415, referring to Trial Judgement, vol. 2, para. 716. Stanišić refers to Trial Chamber findings and Witness Andan's evidence that the operation to counter paramilitaries in Foča was cancelled due to the MUP of Serbia and Montenegro's refusal to "allow them to cross onto their territory" (Stanišić Appeal Brief, para. 415, referring to Trial Judgement, vol. 2, paras 716, 718, Dragomir Andan, 30 May 2011, T. 21547-21548).
[2266]   Stanišić Appeal Brief, paras 414, 416, referring to, *inter alia*, Exhibits 1D75, p. 3, 1D557, pp 6-8.
[2267]   Stanišić Appeal Brief, paras 418-419, referring to Trial Judgement, vol. 2, paras 635-637, 640-641, 644-645, 647-648, 698.
[2268]   Stanišić Appeal Brief, para. 451 (emphasis omitted), quoting Trial Judgement, vol. 2, para. 694.
[2269]   Stanišić Appeal Brief, paras 419, 451. See Stanišić Reply Brief, para. 98; Stanišić Appeal Brief, para. 421.
[2270]   Stanišić Appeal Brief, para. 422, referring to Exhibits 1D61, P792, P1252, P1323, P847, 1D94, 1D62, P553, P571, 1D58, 1D59, 1D49, P855. See Stanišić Appeal Brief, para. 420; Stanišić Reply Brief, para. 99. In support of his argument, Stanišić also refers to his submissions in his fourth ground of appeal (see Stanišić Appeal Brief, fn. 566, referring to Stanišić Appeal Brief, para. 116).
[2271]   Stanišić Appeal Brief, para. 452, referring to Trial Judgement, vol. 2, para. 667, Exhibit 1D55.
[2272]   Stanišić Appeal Brief, para. 453, referring to Trial Judgement, vol. 2, para. 649.

willingly took the risk that killings in detention centres and the Municipalities, as underlying acts of persecutions under Count 1, could be committed.[2273]

676. With respect to the Trial Chamber's finding that he willingly took the risk that imposition and maintenance of restrictive and discriminatory measures as an underlying act of persecutions could be committed,[2274] Stanišić refers to the Trial Chamber's findings that he took action when informed of these acts.[2275] He further argues that the Trial Chamber erred when finding that the civilian law enforcement apparatus did not function impartially.[2276] **[page 278]**

677. Stanišić also contends that the Trial Chamber erred in finding that he willingly took the risk that unlawful detentions could be committed,[2277] arguing that the Trial Chamber acknowledged that he issued orders requesting information on the condition of detention but failed to take them into account.[2278] He further submits that the Trial Chamber erroneously relied on his conversations with Witness Marković[2279] to find that he willingly took that risk.[2280]

678. Furthermore, Stanišić submits that the Trial Chamber erred in finding that he willingly took the risk that torture, cruel treatment, and other inhumane acts could be committed since it disregarded that he: (i) ordered CSB chiefs to abide by the relevant laws on the treatment of POWs and civilians, and SJBs to release and allow free movement to the civilian population;[2281] (ii) requested to be informed where "treatment violated internal and international standards", and ordered that criminal reports be filed against perpetrators;[2282] (iii) forwarded to CSBs and SJBs requests from the Ministry of Health, Work, and Social Security regarding the collection of data on detention centres;[2283] and (iv) requested CSBs to submit "questionnaires on criminal reports filed in cases of war crimes" and that such reports be processed irrespective of ethnicity.[2284]

679. Stanišić also submits that the Trial Chamber erred in finding that he willingly took the risk that looting, search and seizure, appropriation, and plunder of moveable and immoveable property could be committed, considering that: (i) following complaints raised by RS MUP members at the 11 July 1992 Collegium about "[a]rmy looting", the RS MUP took positive actions within several **[page 279]** weeks;[2285]

[2273]   Stanišić Appeal Brief, para. 454.
[2274]   Stanišić Appeal Brief, para. 461.
[2275]   Stanišić Appeal Brief, para. 455, referring to Trial Judgement, vol. 2, paras 610, 635, 682, 746. Stanišić refers to orders that legal measures be taken against RS MUP members who committed crimes and that CSB chiefs dismiss RS MUP members subjected to criminal proceedings (Stanišić Appeal Brief, para. 455, referring to Trial Judgement, vol. 2, paras 640-641).
[2276]   Stanišić Appeal Brief, para. 457, referring to Trial Judgement, vol. 2, paras 91-94. See Stanišić Appeal Brief, para. 456, referring to Trial Judgement, vol. 2, para. 745. Stanišić submits that the Trial Chamber: (i) did not take into account that the success of police investigations was dependent on government bodies over which he had no control (Stanišić Appeal Brief, para. 456, referring to Trial Judgement, vol. 2, paras 87-89); (ii) found that only one crime committed by Serbs against non-Serbs was reported in Doboj while six additional reports were entered into the Doboj logbook (Stanišić Appeal Brief, para. 458, referring to Trial Judgement, vol. 2, para. 94, Hearing, 23 May 2011, T. 21087); (iii) disregarded "highly significant material" in its assessment of the prosecutor's logbooks regarding the reporting of crimes against non-Serbs (Stanišić Appeal Brief, para. 459, referring to Trial Judgement, vol. 2, paras 91-94); and (iv) ignored relevant evidence of Witness Gaćinović that investigations of crimes against non-Serbs were being conducted (Stanišić Appeal Brief, para. 460, referring to Trial Judgement, vol. 2, para. 94, fn. 320, Exhibit P1609.01, p. 18. Stanišić argues that the fact that the perpetrators could not be identified does not show that crimes were going unreported, as the Trial Chamber erroneously found (Stanišić Appeal Brief, para. 460)).
[2277]   Stanišić Appeal Brief, para. 466.
[2278]   Stanišić Appeal Brief, para. 462, referring to Trial Judgement, vol. 2, para. 748. Stanišić submits that following his orders, commissions were set up in each CSB leading to inspections and reports that there were no detention centres in certain municipalities (Stanišić Appeal Brief, para. 462, referring to Trial Judgement, vol. 2, paras 673, 676, 752, Exhibits 1D57, P165, 2D95, P671, P679).
[2279]   Stanišić Appeal Brief, para. 464, referring to Trial Judgement, vol. 2, para. 764.
[2280]   Stanišić submits that: (i) he and Witness Marković discussed the exchange of prisoners conducted under supervision of the ICRC and United Nations Protection Force ("UNPROFOR"); and (ii) his general statement to ensure proper treatment cannot be used to infer that he willingly took that risk (Stanišić Appeal Brief, paras 465-466, referring to Slobodan Marković, 12 Jul 2010, T. 12674-12675, Exhibit P179.18).
[2281]   Stanišić Appeal Brief, para. 467, referring to Trial Judgement, vol. 2, para. 445, Exhibit 1D563.
[2282]   Stanišić Appeal Brief, para. 467, referring to Trial Judgement, vol. 2, para. 668, Exhibit 1D56.
[2283]   Stanišić Appeal Brief, para. 468, referring to Trial Judgement, vol. 2, para. 675, Exhibit 1D57.
[2284]   Stanišić Appeal Brief, para. 469, referring to Trial Judgement, vol. 2, paras 48, 682, Exhibits 1D572, 1D63, 1D84, 1D328, P568, P989, Simo Tuševljak, 24 Jun 2011, T. 22771-22773, 22754-22755.
[2285]   Stanišić Appeal Brief, para. 471, referring to Trial Judgement, vol. 2, para. 631, fn. 1653, Exhibit P160. See Stanišić Appeal Brief, para. 472.

and (ii) the Trial Chamber found that as early as 15 April 1992, Stanišić issued an order to curb looting and misappropriation of property.[2286]

680.   Finally, with regard to wanton destruction and damage of religious and cultural property, Stanišić submits that the Trial Chamber "failed to mention any evidential basis" on which to conclude that the subjective element of the third category of joint criminal enterprise was met in relation to him for these crimes.[2287] Furthermore, he argues that in light of all the orders he issued to prevent crimes, including property crimes,[2288] the Trial Chamber could not have found that these crimes were foreseeable to him and that he willingly took that risk.[2289]

681.   The Prosecution responds that Stanišić's argument that the Trial Chamber failed to provide references to relevant evidence in its finding on the third category of joint criminal enterprise should be summarily dismissed as undeveloped.[2290] The Prosecution also contends that many of Stanišić's references to the Trial Judgement or exhibits do not support his submissions and that the orders he refers to were directly addressed by the Trial Chamber, proving that it did not disregard them.[2291]

682.   The Prosecution submits that the Trial Chamber reasonably found that: (i) the RS MUP investigations against the Yellow Wasps primarily focused on the thefts of cars despite their involvement in serious crimes;[2292] (ii) they were released shortly after being arrested;[2293] and (iii) they were not indicted within the RS until 1999.[2294] The Prosecution further responds that the operation in Foca to which Stanišić refers was never carried out and that in any case, it was to focus **[page 280]** on property crimes and the harassment of Serbs.[2295] With respect to Exhibits 1D75 and 1D557, the Prosecution argues that they support the Trial Chamber's findings on selective prosecutions.[2296]

683.   The Prosecution also submits that Stanišić misreads the Trial Judgement when claiming that the Trial Chamber "accepted" the evidence of Witness Dokanović regarding Stanišić's efforts to combat war crimes,[2297] as the Trial Chamber specifically rejected it in light of the totality of the evidence.[2298]

684.   In response to Stanišić's arguments concerning the imposition and maintenance of restrictive and discriminatory measures, the Prosecution contends that the Trial Chamber was aware of the distinction between the roles of the police and that of the prosecutor and thus properly focused on Stanišić's orders aimed only at documenting crimes against Serbs.[2299]

[2286]   Stanišić Appeal Brief, para. 471, referring to Trial Judgement, vol. 2, para. 746. See Stanišić Appeal Brief, para. 472.
[2287]   Stanišić Appeal Brief, para. 473.
[2288]   Stanišić Appeal Brief, para. 474, referring to Exhibits 1D61, P792, 1D634, P1252, P1323, 1D84. See Stanišić Reply Brief, para. 98.
[2289]   Stanišić Appeal Brief, paras 474-475.
[2290]   Prosecution Response Brief (Stanišić), para. 219.
[2291]   Prosecution Response Brief (Stanišić), para. 213, referring to, *inter alia*, Stanišić Appeal Brief, paras 418-419, 422, 452-453, 455, 462, 467-469, 471, 474.
[2292]   Prosecution Response Brief (Stanišić), para. 214.
[2293]   Prosecution Response Brief (Stanišić), paras 214-215. The Prosecution argues that, contrary to Stanišic's submission, Witness Andan did not testify that the Yellow Wasps were handed over to or prosecuted in Serbia on the basis of information he provided. Rather, according to the Prosecution, Witness Andan confirmed that they were released shortly after their arrest (Prosecution Response Brief (Stanišić), para. 215, referring to Dragomir Andan, 30 May 2011, T. 21526, Dragomir Andan, 1 Jun 2011, T. 21688).
[2294]   Prosecution Response Brief (Stanišić), para. 215. The Prosecution adds that Stanišic ignores Witness Andan's testimony that "a deliberate choice had been made to expel paramilitaries to Serbia rather than prosecute them in the RS" (Prosecution Response Brief (Stanišić), para. 216).
[2295]   Prosecution Response Brief (Stanišić), para. 216.
[2296]   Prosecution Response Brief (Stanišić), para. 217.
[2297]   Prosecution Response Brief (Stanišić), para. 220.
[2298]   Prosecution Response Brief (Stanišić), para. 220.
[2299]   Prosecution Response Brief (Stanišić), para. 221, referring to Trial Judgement, vol. 2, paras 87-89, 723-728, 758. In addition, it submits that Stanišić's arguments concerning the Doboj prosecutor's logbook ignore that the Trial Chamber also relied on logbooks from 19 other municipalities to find that very few serious crimes against non-Serb victims had been recorded (Prosecution Response Brief (Stanišić), para. 221, referring to Trial Judgement, vol. 2, paras 91-94). The Prosecution further submits that it has already addressed Stanišić's arguments regarding Witness Gaćinović as part of its response to Stanišić's fourth ground of appeal (Prosecution Response Brief (Stanišić), para. 221, referring to Prosecution Response Brief (Stanišić), para. 141).

685. With regard to Stanišić's arguments concerning Witness Marković's evidence, the Prosecution submits that this evidence together with the remainder of the trial record, supports the Trial Chamber's finding that he was liable for unlawful detentions under the third category of joint criminal enterprise.[2300]

686. The Prosecution contends that Stanišić takes a selective approach to the evidence in his arguments regarding looting, search and seizure, appropriation, and plunder of the moveable and immoveable property, as the evidence shows that the police also engaged in stealing.[2301]

687. Finally, the Prosecution responds that, in arguing that the Trial Chamber failed to explain the evidentiary basis for finding him liable for wanton destruction and damage of religious and cultural property, Stanišić ignores the Trial Chamber's findings that these crimes were foreseeable to him because "they were carried out to pressure non-Serbs to leave and to wipe out traces of their **[page 281]** existence in the RS".[2302] According to the Prosecution, this argument should be summarily dismissed.[2303]

b. Analysis

688. The Appeals Chamber recalls that for a conviction for a crime under the third category of joint criminal enterprise, it must be shown that it was foreseeable to the accused that such a crime might be committed in order to carry out the *actus reus* of the crimes forming part of the common purpose.[2304] In addition, it must be shown that the accused willingly took the risk that such a crime might be committed, *i.e.* that the accused joined or continued to participate in the joint criminal enterprise with the awareness that the crime was a possible consequence thereof.[2305]

689. At the outset, the Appeals Chamber notes that Stanišić is correct in stating that the Trial Chamber provided no references for its findings on his responsibility for Stanišić's JCE III Crimes in the Municipalities.[2306] However, as also noted by Stanišić, earlier in the Trial Judgement, the Trial Chamber found that it was foreseeable to Stanišić that Stanišić's JCE III Crimes could be committed and that he willingly took that risk.[2307] These findings, together with the Trial Chamber's findings that Stanišić's JCE III Crimes were committed by members of the JCE or persons used by members of the JCE,[2308] were sufficient for the Trial Chamber to conclude that Stanišić was responsible for these crimes pursuant to the third category of joint criminal enterprise. The Appeals Chamber will address below whether the Trial Chamber reasonably found that Stanišić willingly took the risk that Stanišić's JCE III Crimes could be committed.

690. The Appeals Chamber understands that the Trial Chamber based its conclusion that Stanišić willingly took the risk that Stanišić's JCE III Crimes could be committed, on its findings that these crimes were foreseeable to him in the implementation of the JCE,[2309] and that Stanišić was a **[page 282]** member of the JCE and continued to support and participate in the JCE throughout the Indictment period.[2310] These findings have been upheld on appeal.[2311]

[2300] Prosecution Response Brief (Stanišić), para. 222, referring to Slobodan Marković, 12 Jul 2010, T. 12674-12675, Trial Judgement, vol. 2, paras 620, 764, 772, 776. The Prosecution points in particular to Stanišić's own admission that "he learned about [the] conditions of detention and treatment of prisoners from the Commission's reports" (Prosecution Response Brief (Stanišić), para. 222).

[2301] Prosecution Response Brief (Stanišić), para. 223, referring to, *inter alia*, Exhibit P160, p. 17.

[2302] Prosecution Response Brief (Stanišić), para. 224, referring to Trial Judgement, vol. 2, paras 292, 294, 778.

[2303] Prosecution Response Brief (Stanišić), para. 224.

[2304] *Tolimir* Appeal Judgement, para. 514; *Đorđević* Appeal Judgement, para. 906; *Šainović et al.* Appeal Judgement, paras 1061, 1557; *Brđanin* Appeal Judgement, paras 365, 411.

[2305] *Tolimir* Appeal Judgement, para. 514; *Đorđević* Appeal Judgement, para. 906; *Šainović et al.* Appeal Judgement, paras 1061, 1557; *Brđanin* Appeal Judgement, paras 365, 411.

[2306] See Trial Judgement, vol. 2, paras 804, 809, 813, 818, 822, 827, 831, 836, 840, 844, 849, 854, 858, 863, 868, 873, 877, 881, 885.

[2307] Trial Judgement, vol. 2, paras 772-774, 776-779.

[2308] Trial Judgement, vol. 2, paras 799, 801-802, 806-807, 810-811, 815-816, 819-820, 824-825, 828-829, 833-834, 837-838, 841-842, 846-847, 851-852, 855-856, 860-861, 865-866, 870-871, 874-875, 878-879, 882-883.

[2309] See Trial Judgement, vol. 2, paras 772-774, 776-779.

[2310] See Trial Judgement, vol. 2, paras 769-770. See also Trial Judgement, vol. 2, paras 801, 804, 806, 809-810, 813, 815, 818-819, 822, 824, 827-828, 831, 833, 836-837, 840-841, 844, 846, 849, 851, 854-855, 858, 860, 863, 865, 868,870, 873-874, 877-878, 881-882, 885.

[2311] See *supra*, paras 87, 356-364, 573-585, 669.

691.   The Appeals Chamber now turns to Stanišić's specific challenges to the Trial Chamber's assessment of evidence with regard to his willingly taking the risk.

i. Alleged errors in mischaracterising Witness Andan's evidence

692.   As regards Stanišić's arguments that the Trial Chamber mischaracterised Witness Andan's evidence regarding the Yellow Wasps,[2312] the Appeals Chamber notes the following Trial Chamber findings:

> [according to an RS MUP report, on 29 and 30 July 1992 the RS MUP, in cooperation with the army, 'disarmed and arrested 100 members of paramilitary formations' in Zvornik.[2313] [...]

> The police questioning of the Yellow Wasps, however, focused primarily on their involvement in thefts [...].[2314] Members of the Yellow Wasps were released from detention on 28 August 1992 and an indictment against them was only issued in 1999.[2315] [...]

> Andan testified that he understood from conversations he had with Stanišić [...] that he would be involved in similar operations to deal with paramilitaries [...]. However, this never occurred because Davidović 'returned to Serbia' and Andan was removed from the RS MUP.[2316]

693.   The Appeals Chamber sees no inconsistency between Witness Andan's evidence and these findings, which the Trial Chamber based, in part, on the evidence Stanišić refers to in his submissions.[2317] The Appeals Chamber further observes that Witness Andan did not testify that members of the Yellow Wasps were prosecuted in Serbia on the basis of information he provided. Rather, he testified that some paramilitaries were handed over to Serbia with a "brief description of the crimes they had committed and their names".[2318] The Appeals Chamber is unable to see how **[page 283]** this testimony undermines the Trial Chamber's finding that in the RS, members of the Yellow Wasps were released shortly after their arrest in 1992 and only indicted in 1999.

694.   Insofar as Stanišić argues that the Trial Chamber mischaracterised Witness Andan's evidence regarding the operation in Foča,[2319] the Appeals Chamber notes that the Trial Chamber explicitly noted this evidence and found, on the basis of it, that the operation was cancelled for lack of authorisation from the MUPs of Serbia and Montenegro for the necessary passage through their territory.[2320] However, the Trial Chamber also noted that Witness Andan confirmed that, although he had understood from Stanišić that he would be involved in further operations like those in Zvornik, this never occurred as he was removed from the RS MUP.[2321] The Appeals Chamber sees no inconsistency in the Trial Chamber's findings on the reasons why operations similar to those against the Yellow Wasps never occurred again and Witness Andan's evidence, and finds that Stanišić has failed to show an error.

ii. Alleged errors in disregarding evidence that Stanišić took measures to combat crimes

695.   The Appeals Chamber now turns to Stanišić's argument that the Trial Chamber acknowledged evidence that he took a number of measures to combat crimes and yet disregarded this evidence when finding

---

[2312]   See *supra*, para. 673.

[2313]   Trial Judgement, vol. 2, para. 714. See Trial Judgement, vol. 2, fn. 1831, referring to Exhibit 1D558, Witness ST121, 23 Nov 2009, T. 3678.

[2314]   Trial Judgement, vol. 2, para. 715. See Trial Judgement, vol. 2, fn. 1834, referring to, *inter alia*, Exhibits P403 (confidential), 1D75, P1533, P2002, P2003, P322.

[2315]   Trial Judgement, vol. 2, para. 715. See Trial Judgement, vol. 2, fn. 1835, referring to Witness ST215, 28 Sep 2010, T. 15003, Exhibits P317.21, P317.19.

[2316]   Trial Judgement, vol. 2, para. 716. See Trial Judgement, vol. 2, fn. 1837, referring to Dragomir Andan, 1 Jun 2011, T. 21700-21702, Exhibit 1D557, p. 14.

[2317]   See Trial Judgement, vol. 2, fns 1831, 1834-1835, 1837, referring to, *inter alia*, Exhibits 1D75, 1D557, p. 14, Dragomir Andan, 1 Jun 2011, T. 21700-21702. See also Stanišić Appeal Brief, paras 414-417, referring to Dragomir Andan, 30 May 2011, T. 21547-21548, Dragomir Andan, 1 Jun 2011, 21683-21695, 21700-21702, Exhibits 1D557, pp 6-8, 1D75, p. 3. The Appeals Chamber further notes that Witness Andan confirmed that members of the Yellow Wasps were released shortly after their arrest by the RS MUP 1992 (Dragomir Andan, 1 Jun 2011, T. 21688. See Dragomir Andan, 30 May 2011, T. 21526).

[2318]   Dragomir Andan, 1 Jun 2011, T. 21688.

[2319]   See *supra*, para. 673.

[2320]   Trial Judgement, vol. 2, para. 718, referring to Dragomir Andan, 30 May 2011, T. 21548. See Dragomir Andan, 1 Jun 2011, T. 21698.

[2321]   Trial Judgement, vol. 2, para. 716, referring to, *inter alia*, Dragomir Andan, 1 Jun 2011, T. 21700-21702.

that he willingly took the risk that Stanišić's JCE III Crimes could be committed.[2322] The Appeals Chamber notes that in the paragraphs of the Trial Judgement referred to 2323 by Stanišić, the Trial Chamber considered evidence on measures he took to combat crimes.[2323] However, Stanišić ignores that the Trial Chamber ultimately concluded, in light of the trial record, that: (i) his orders on actions to be taken against the reserve police force were not carried out to the extent possible;[2324] (ii) placing errant policemen at the disposal of the VRS was not sufficient to fulfil his duty to protect the Muslim and Croat population since transferring known offenders to the army further facilitated their continued interaction with civilians;[2325] (iii) Stanišić failed to use his **[page 284]** powers to ensure the full implementation of his orders regarding detentions despite being aware of the limited action taken subsequent to his orders;[2326] (iv) by failing to remove the personnel of the RS MUP who had committed crimes, Stanišić violated his professional obligation to protect and safeguard the civilian population in the territories under his control;[2327] (v) although Stanišić had the ability to investigate and punish "those found to be involved" in crimes, he failed to act when learning of serious crimes such as unlawful detention, forcible displacement, cruel treatments or killings;[2328] and (vi) Stanišić took "insufficient action" to put an end to the crimes and instead "permitted RS MUP forces under his overall control to continue to participate in joint operations in the Municipalities with other Serb Forces involved in the commission of crimes".[2329] In light of these findings, which have been upheld on appeal,[2330] the Appeals Chamber considers that Stanišić has failed to show that no reasonable trier of fact could have concluded as the Trial Chamber did. Stanišić's argument that the Trial Chamber disregarded that he took a number of measures to combat crimes in assessing whether he willingly took the risk is therefore dismissed.[2331]

696.   With respect to the exhibits Stanišić argues the Trial Chamber ignored, and which allegedly demonstrate that he did "everything he could" to counter crimes,[2332] the Appeals Chamber considers that he has failed to identify any error. Stanišić merely lists the exhibits, most of which are explicitly referred to in the Trial Judgement,[2333] without explaining how they render the Trial Chamber's finding unsafe. Stanišić's argument in this respect is therefore dismissed.

       iii. Alleged errors in finding that Stanišić willingly took the risk that underlying acts of persecutions could be committed

697.   With respect to Stanišić's challenge to the Trial Chamber's finding that he willingly took the risk that killings in detention centres and the Municipalities could be committed,[2334] the Appeals Chamber notes the Trial Chamber's finding that, in the course of July and August 1992, Stanišić **[page 285]** issued a number of

---

[2322]   See *supra*, para. 674.

[2323]   See, *inter alia*, Trial Judgement, vol. 2, paras 635, 637, 640-641, 644-645, 647-648 (on Stanišić's orders of 17, 19, 23, 24 and 27 July 1992 concerning, *inter alia*, information to be provided on the commission of crimes, the involvement of police therein, issues related to detention and treatment of detainees, and legal and administrative measures to be taken against MUP members engaged in criminal activities); Trial Judgement, vol. 2, para. 636 (on the Đerić Letter); Trial Judgement, vol. 2, para. 694 (on the evidence of Witness Đokanović that he and Stanišić "were the only people in the RS Government who were interested in addressing the issue of war crimes"); Trial Judgement, vol. 2, para. 698 (on Stanišić's instructions of 23 October 1992 to take action against errant staff). See also Stanišić Appeal Brief, paras 418-419, referring to Trial Judgement, vol. 2, paras 635-637, 640-641, 644-645, 647-648, 698.

[2324]   Trial Judgement, vol. 2, para. 746.

[2325]   Trial Judgement, vol. 2, para. 751.

[2326]   Trial Judgement, vol. 2, para. 753.

[2327]   Trial Judgement, vol. 2, para. 754.

[2328]   Trial Judgement, vol. 2, para. 757. See Trial Judgement, vol. 2, para. 755.

[2329]   Trial Judgement, vol. 2, para. 759.

[2330]   See *supra*, paras 240-255, 288, 300-305, 309-311.

[2331]   The Appeals Chamber further notes that Stanišić's related submission on burden of proof falls short of articulating an error. The Appeals Chamber finds that this argument is clearly underdeveloped and thus dismisses it.

[2332]   See *supra*, para. 674.

[2333]   See Trial Judgement, vol. 2, paras 510 (Exhibit P1013), 594 (Exhibit 1D49), 610 (Exhibit 1D61), 640 (Exhibit 1D58), 641 (Exhibit 1D59), 677 (Exhibit P847), 687 (Exhibit P855), 708 (Exhibit 1D94), 724 (Exhibit 1D62). See also Stanišić Appeal Brief, para. 422, referring to Exhibits 1D61, P792, P1252, P1323, P847, 1D94, 1D62, P553, P1013, P571, 1D58, 1D59, 1D49, P855.

[2334]   See *supra*, para. 675.

orders and instructions relating to detention.[2335] The Trial Chamber also noted actions that followed these orders, such as the inspections between 18 and 20 August 1992 and the reports sent to Stanišić.[2336] However, Stanišić ignores that the Trial Chamber found that his orders of 8, 10, 17, and 24 August 1992 on detention related matters, were "prompted by the international attention given to the detention camps in BiH by June 1992" and "a result of an instruction of 6 August by the RS Presidency, which was concerned about its image in the eyes of the world".[2337] The Trial Chamber further noted that the conditions and mistreatment continued and ultimately found that "Stanišić failed to use the powers available to him under the law to ensure the full implementation of these orders despite being aware of the limited action taken subsequent to his orders".[2338] In light of these findings, which have been upheld on appeal,[2339] the Appeals Chamber considers that Stanišić merely disagrees with the Trial Chamber's conclusion that he willingly took the risk and has failed to show that no reasonable trier of fact could have reached this conclusion.

698.   Further, in support of his argument that he issued orders to counter serious crimes as soon as he was informed thereof, Stanišić refers to paragraph 649 of volume two of the Trial Judgement.[2340] In this paragraph, the Trial Chamber considered evidence that, after being informed in July 1992 "that 'criminal gangs' (often wearing RS MUP and army uniforms) were committing serious crimes against all citizens', Stanišić demanded vigorous action by the SJBs and the CSBs to fight these kinds of activities, jointly with the military".[2341] The Appeals Chamber notes that the Trial Chamber later found that Stanišić issued a number of orders in the course of July and August 1992 relating to, *inter alia*, "criminal elements in the police".[2342] In response to the orders he issued in July 1992, the Trial Chamber found that Stanišić was informed that "disciplinary measures were instituted against 35 policemen at the Vlasenica SJB and that a number of policemen in Doboj and in the ARK were transferred to the VRS".[2343] However, the Trial Chamber ultimately concluded that Stanišić's placing of errant reserve policemen at the disposal of the army "was not sufficient to fulfil his duty to protect the Muslim and Croat population",[2344] which has been upheld on appeal.[2345] In light of **[page 286]** these findings, the Appeals Chamber finds that Stanišić has failed to show that no reasonable trier of fact could have found that he willingly took the risk and his argument is dismissed.

699.   With respect to Stanišić's arguments that the Trial Chamber erred in finding that he willingly took the risk that the underlying act of unlawful detention could be committed,[2346] the Appeals Chamber first observes that insofar as he refers to his orders requesting information on the conditions of detention, resulting in the setting up of commissions,[2347] it has already dismissed his arguments[2348] and thus will not address these orders again here.

700.   Stanišić also argues that the Trial Chamber erred in relying on Witness Marković's evidence to find that he knew about unlawful detentions and willingly took the risk that these could be committed.[2349] The Appeals Chamber notes in this regard that the Trial Chamber found that Witness Marković, as a member of the Commission for Exchange of Prisoners on behalf of the RS MUP, was not obliged to file reports with the

---

[2335]   See Trial Judgement, vol. 2, paras 445 (on Stanišić's order of 8 August 1992), 637 (on Stanišić's request for information of 19 July 1992), 667 (on Stanišić's order of 10 August 1992), 675 (on Stanišić's order of 24 August 1992). See also Trial Judgement, vol. 2, paras 664, 668, 748; *supra*, paras 281-290.

[2336]   Trial Judgement, vol. 2, paras 673, 676, referring to Exhibits P165, 2D95, P972, Tomislav Kovač, 7 Mar 2012, T. 27067-27068, Andrija Bjelošević, 19 Apr 2011, T. 19809-19810. See Trial Judgement, vol. 2, para. 752.

[2337]   Trial Judgement, vol. 2, para. 753. See Trial Judgement, vol. 2, para. 752. See also Trial Judgement, vol. 2, paras 651-668.

[2338]   Trial Judgement, vol. 2, para. 753. The Appeals Chamber further notes the Trial Chamber's finding that Stanišić failed to act in a decisive matter with regard to, *inter alia*, killings and inhumane treatment of detainees (see Trial Judgement, vol. 2, para. 757).

[2339]   See *supra*, paras 281-290, 304.

[2340]   See *supra*, para. 675.

[2341]   Trial Judgement, vol. 2, para. 649, referring to Goran Mačar, 11 Jul 2011, T. 23109, Exhibit P595, pp 7-8.

[2342]   Trial Judgement, vol. 2, para. 748. See *supra*, para. 697.

[2343]   Trial Judgement, vol. 2, para. 749.

[2344]   Trial Judgement, vol. 2, para. 751.

[2345]   See *supra*, para. 309.

[2346]   See *supra*, para. 677.

[2347]   See *supra*, para. 677.

[2348]   See *supra*, para. 697.

[2349]   See *supra*, para. 677.

RS MUP on his work on prisoners exchanges[2350] but spoke twice to Stanišić about it.[2351] The Trial Chamber considered that Stanišić told him that "the prisoners should be treated in line with the Geneva Conventions [and] that especially women and young children were not to be maltreated".[2352] Given the reference to women and young children in the context of prisoner exchanges,[2353] the Appeals Chamber considers that this evidence supports the Trial Chamber's finding that Stanišić knew of unlawful detentions.[2354] Stanišić has failed to show that the Trial Chamber erred in its assessment and his arguments are dismissed.

701.   Regarding Stanišić's submission that the Trial Chamber erred in finding that he willingly took the risk that torture, cruel treatment, and other inhumane acts could be committed,[2355] the Appeals Chamber notes that it has already dismissed his argument elsewhere in this Judgement.[2356]

702.   The Appeals Chamber now turns to Stanišić's challenge to the Trial Chamber's finding that he willingly took the risk that imposition and maintenance of restrictive and discriminatory **[page 287]** measures could be committed.[2357] It notes that the paragraphs of the Trial Judgement he refers to in support do not refer to actions Stanišić took against the imposition and maintenance of restrictive and discriminatory measures.[2358] Rather, they concern looting and appropriation or more generally "other severe crimes"[2359] or "war crimes".[2360] Since the Trial Chamber's findings in these paragraphs are considered elsewhere in this Judgement,[2361] the Appeals Chamber will not address them here. Furthermore, as regards Stanišić's argument that the Trial Chamber could not have found that he willingly took the risk that imposition and maintenance of restrictive and discriminatory measures could be committed in light of his orders of 23 and 24 July 1992, the Appeals Chamber notes that it has already addressed and dismissed his arguments on these orders above.[2362] Regarding Stanišić's argument on the civilian law enforcement apparatus, the Appeals Chamber recalls its earlier findings that he has failed to show that no reasonable trier of fact could have found that the civilian law enforcement apparatus failed to function in an impartial manner.[2363]

703.   Turning now to Stanišić's submission that the Trial Chamber erred in finding that he willingly took the risk that looting, appropriation, and plunder of moveable and immoveable property could be committed,[2364] the Appeals Chamber notes that Stanišić fails to provide support for his submission that "positive action was taken by the [RS] MUP within several weeks" after the report of looting during the 11 July 1992 Collegium.[2365] However, the Appeals Chamber notes the Trial Chamber's finding that after the 11 July 1992 Collegium,

---

[2350]   Trial Judgement, vol. 2, paras 616-617, referring to, *inter alia*, Slobodan Marković, 12 Jul 2010, T. 12689-12690; Exhibit P2310, p. 10.

[2351]   Trial Judgement, vol. 2, para. 617, fn. 1612, referring to Slobodan Marković, 12 Jul 2010, T. 12640-12641, 12643, 12674, 12764.

[2352]   Trial Judgement, vol. 2, para. 617, fn. 1613, referring to Slobodan Marković, 12 Jul 2010, T. 12674-12675, 12690.

[2353]   See Trial Judgement, vol. 2, para. 764.

[2354]   The Appeals Chamber also notes that Stanišić stated that his knowledge on the detention conditions and treatment of detainees came from the Commission for Exchange of Prisoners (see Trial Judgement, vol. 2, para. 620, referring to Exhibit P2308, pp 36-38. See also Trial Judgement, vol. 2, para. 764).

[2355]   See *supra*, para. 678.

[2356]   See *supra*, paras 320-325, 697.

[2357]   See *supra*, para. 676.

[2358]   See Stanišić Appeal Brief, para. 455, referring to Trial Judgement, vol. 2, paras 610, 635, 682, 746.

[2359]   Trial Judgement, vol. 2, para. 635. See Trial Judgement, vol. 2, paras 610, 746.

[2360]   Trial Judgement, vol. 2, para. 682.

[2361]   See *supra*, paras 320-325 (concerning Trial Judgement, vol. 2, para. 682), 695 (concerning Trial Judgement, vol. 2, para. 635); *infra*, para. 704 (concerning Trial Judgement, vol. 2, paras 610, 746).

[2362]   See *supra*, paras 695-696.

[2363]   See *supra*, paras 277-280.

[2364]   See *supra*, para. 679.

[2365]   See Stanišić Appeal Brief, para. 471, referring to Trial Judgement, vol. 2, para. 631, fn. 1653, Exhibit P160. The Appeals Chamber notes that Stanišić only refers to Exhibit P160, which are the minutes of the 11 July 1992 Collegium when the issue was reported. The Appeals Chamber further notes that Stanišić refers to "[a]rmy looting". However, Witness Planojević stated at the meeting that police was also involved in such activity (see Exhibit P160, p. 17, where it reads that he stated that "looting [...] is most frequently committed in the so-called mopping up of territory, when paramilitary and military formations and police engage in stealing". See also Trial Judgement, vol. 2, para. 630, where the Trial Chamber noted Stanišić's statement at the 11 July 1992 Collegium that there was a need "to prevent criminal activities committed not only by citizens but also soldiers and [a]rmy officers, active duty and reserve police and members of the internal affairs organs and their officers who are found to have committed crimes of any kind").

Stanišić issued several orders, including on the involvement of the police in criminal activities. These orders have been addressed above and his argument in relation to them has already been dismissed.[2366]

704. Further, Stanišić is correct in noting that the Trial Chamber found that "[a]s early as 15 April 1992, Stanišić issued an order to curb looting and misappropriation of property by his **[page 288]** subordinates".[2367] The Trial Chamber found that Stanišić was under a duty to discipline and dismiss the personnel of the RS MUP who had committed crimes.[2368] The Trial Chamber further found that Stanišić did initiate proceedings pertaining to theft and concluded that this demonstrated his ability "as the highest authority to investigate and punish".[2369] Stanišić, however, ignores the Trial Chamber's finding, which has been upheld on appeal,[2370] that "he took insufficient action to put an end" to the crimes.[2371] Other than disagreeing with it, he has failed to show that no reasonable trier of fact could have reached this conclusion. Accordingly, his argument that the Trial Chamber erred in finding that he willingly took the risk that persecutory looting, appropriation, plunder, and other similar acts could be committed fails.

705. The Appeal Chamber now turns to Stanišić's arguments concerning the Trial Chamber's finding on wanton destruction and damage of religious and cultural property.[2372] To the extent that he argues that the Trial Chamber failed to explain on what basis it concluded that these underlying acts of persecutions were foreseeable to him,[2373] the Appeals Chamber notes that it has already addressed elsewhere in this Judgement whether the Trial Chamber provided sufficient reasons for its findings concerning the foreseeability of underlying acts of persecutions, including wanton destruction and damage to religious and cultural property.[2374] Insofar as Stanišić argues that the Trial Chamber failed to provide reasons for its conclusion that he willingly took the risk that wanton destruction and damage of religious and cultural property could be committed,[2375] the Appeals Chamber recalls, as set out above, that an inference that an accused "willingly took the risk" may be drawn from the fact that the accused was aware that the crime was a possible consequence of the joint criminal enterprise but nevertheless decided to join or continues to participate in that enterprise.[2376] The Appeals Chamber further recalls that a trial judgement must be read as a whole.[2377] The Appeals Chamber notes that the Trial Chamber found that it was foreseeable to Stanišić that persecutory wanton destruction and damage of religious and cultural property could be committed.[2378] Furthermore, the Trial Chamber found that Stanišić participated in **[page 289]** the JCE and continued to do so until the end of 1992.[2379] The Appeals Chamber understands that it is on this basis that the Trial Chamber found that Stanišić willingly took the risk that these crimes could be committed. Stanišić has thus failed to show an error.

706. Regarding Stanišić's argument that the Trial Chamber could not have found that he willingly took the risk that persecutory wanton destruction and damage of religious and cultural property could be committed in light of the orders he issued to prevent crimes, including these crimes,[2380] Stanišić merely lists exhibits, some of which were explicitly considered by the Trial Chamber,[2381] but has failed to explain how they render

---

[2366] See *supra*, para. 695.

[2367] Trial Judgement, vol. 2, para. 746. See Trial Judgement, vol. 2, para. 610.

[2368] Trial Judgement, vol. 2, para. 754.

[2369] Trial Judgement, vol. 2, para. 755. See Trial Judgement, vol. 2, para. 754. See also Trial Judgement, vol. 2, paras 698-706. The Appeals Chamber further notes the Trial Chamber's finding that Stanišić focused on crimes committed against Serbs (See Trial Judgement, vol. 2, para. 758).

[2370] See *supra*, para. 312.

[2371] Trial Judgement, vol. 2, para. 759. See Trial Judgement, vol. 2, paras 698-708.

[2372] See *supra*, para. 680.

[2373] See *supra*, para. 680.

[2374] See *supra*, para. 628. The Appeals Chamber notes that the reasonableness of the Trial Chamber's findings on foreseeability has been addressed in the previous section of this Chapter (see *supra*, paras 647-671).

[2375] Stanišić Appeal Brief, paras 473-474.

[2376] See *supra*, para. 688.

[2377] *Šainović et al.* Appeal Judgement, paras 306, 321; *Boškoski and Tarčulovski* Appeal Judgement, para. 67; *Orić* Appeal Judgement, para. 38.

[2378] Trial Judgement, vol. 2, paras 778-779.

[2379] See Trial Judgement, vol. 2, paras 769-770. See also Trial Judgement, vol. 2, paras 801, 804, 806, 809-810, 813, 815, 818-819, 822, 824, 827-828, 831, 833, 836-837, 840-841, 844, 846, 849, 851, 854-855, 858, 860, 863, 865, 868, 870, 873-874, 877-878, 881-882, 885.

[2380] See *supra*, para. 680.

[2381] See Trial Judgement, vol. 2, paras 74 (Exhibit 1D84), 610 (Exhibits 1D61, 1D634).

the Trial Chamber's finding unsafe. Therefore, the Appeals Chamber dismisses this argument. Moreover, the Appeals Chamber notes that the orders Stanišić refers to do not address the destruction or damage of religious property,[2382] and that he has not shown why they are relevant to the Trial Chamber's finding in question.

c. Conclusion

707. In light of all the foregoing, the Appeals Chamber finds that Stanišić has failed to show that the Trial Chamber erred in finding that he willingly took the risk that the crimes underlying his convictions pursuant to the third category of joint criminal enterprise could be committed.

(iv) Conclusion

708. The Appeals Chamber has found that Stanišić has failed to show that the Trial Chamber erred in law by failing to provide a reasoned opinion for its finding that the crimes under Counts 3 to 8 were foreseeable to Stanišić and for its finding that the persecutory acts charged under Count 1 (other than forcible transfer and deportation) were foreseeable to Stanišić.[2383] The Appeals Chamber has further found that Stanišić has failed to show that the Trial Chamber erred in fact by finding that Stanišić's JCE III Crimes were foreseeable to him[2384] and that he willingly took the risk that **[page 290]** they might be committed.[2385] Therefore, the Appeals Chamber dismisses Stanišić's first ground of appeal in part, tenth ground of appeal, and eleventh ground of appeal in part.

E. Alleged errors regarding Župljanin's participation in the JCE

1. Introduction

709. Župljanin became Chief of the Banja Luka CSB on 6 May 1991 and, from at least 5 May 1992 until July 1992, was a member of the ARK Crisis Staff.[2386] The Trial Chamber found Župljanin responsible for crimes committed in the ARK Municipalities. Specifically, he was convicted pursuant to Article 7(1) of the Statute for committing, through participation in the JCE, the crimes of persecutions and extermination as crimes against humanity, murder, and torture as violations of the laws or customs of war.[2387] The Trial Chamber found Župljanin responsible, but did not enter convictions on the basis of the principles relating to cumulative convictions, for committing, through participation in the JCE, the crimes of: murder, torture, inhumane acts, deportation, and inhumane acts (forcible transfer) as crimes against humanity, and cruel treatment as a violation of the laws or customs of war.[2388]

710. In the section of the Trial Judgement addressing Župljanin's responsibility, the Trial Chamber considered evidence relating to his "role and authority",[2389] "sources of knowledge",[2390] and "alleged conduct

---

[2382]   See Exhibits P792 (an order issued by Stanišić on misappropriation of VRS materials and technical equipment, dated 15 April 1992); P1252 (an order issued by Stanišić on appropriation of private property, dated 17 April 1992); P1323 (an order issued by Mandić, Deputy to the Minister of Interior concerning the need for patrols in Sarajevo in light of escalation of terrorism, violence, and robberies dated 19 April 1992); 1D61 (an order issued by Stanišić concerning identification and measures to be taken against people involved in looting, appropriation, and other property crimes, dated 15 April 1992); 1D84 (instructions signed by Witness Planojević, then Assistant Minister for Prevention and Detention of Crime, on measures to be taken against perpetrators of property crimes and war crimes, dated 5 June 1992); 1D634 (an order issued by the Ministry of Interior to increase measures of protection, not signed, dated 16 January 1992).
[2383]   See *supra*, para. 634.
[2384]   See *supra*, para. 671.
[2385]   See *supra*, para. 707.
[2386]   Trial Judgement, vol. 2, paras 542-543, 558. See Trial Judgement, vol. 1, para. 2.
[2387]   Trial Judgement, vol. 2, paras 805, 832, 845, 850, 859, 864, 869, 956.
[2388]   Trial Judgement, vol. 2, paras 805, 832, 845, 850, 859, 864, 869, 956.
[2389]   Trial Judgement, vol. 2, p. 110. See Trial Judgement, vol. 2, paras 348-368.
[2390]   Trial Judgement, vol. 2, p. 119. See Trial Judgement, vol. 2, paras 369-374.

in furtherance of JCE".[2391] Under the heading "Findings on Stojan Župljanin's membership in JCE",[2392] the Trial Chamber then set out its findings on his "duties, authority, and powers",[2393] followed by "Findings on Župljanin's contribution to JCE".[2394] The latter section includes the Trial Chamber's conclusions regarding Župljanin's significant contribution to the JCE,[2395] his intent pursuant to the first category of joint criminal enterprise,[2396] his membership in the JCE,[2397] and his responsibility "in the context of the third category of joint criminal enterprise".[2398] The Appeals Chamber notes that in the section of the Trial Judgement dedicated to the conclusions on Župljanin's responsibility, *i.e.* the section entitled "Findings on Stojan **[page 291]** Župljanin's membership in JCE",[2399] the Trial Chamber provided no cross-references to earlier findings or citations to evidence on the record.[2400] It is regrettable that the Trial Chamber adopted such an approach, as the exercise of identifying underlying findings and analysis has been unnecessarily convoluted as a result.

711. Župljanin asserts that the Trial Chamber erred in finding him responsible pursuant to the first category of joint criminal enterprise.[2401] He also raises a number of other legal and factual challenges regarding the Trial Chamber's findings concerning his responsibility for crimes pursuant to the third category of joint criminal enterprise,[2402] including challenges to the Trial Chamber's findings regarding his liability for the crime of extermination.[2403] The Appeals Chamber will address his submissions in turn.

2. Alleged errors regarding Župljanin's responsibility under the first category of joint criminal enterprise (sub-grounds (A) to (E) and sub-ground (F) in part of Župljanin's first ground of appeal)

(a) Introduction

712. In the section of the Trial Judgement dedicated to its conclusions on Župljanin's responsibility pursuant to the first category of joint criminal enterprise, the Trial Chamber found that Župljanin was a member of the JCE starting from at least in April 1992 and throughout the rest of 1992 and was responsible for committing, through participation in the JCE, the JCE I Crimes, *i.e.* deportation, other inhumane acts (forcible transfer), and persecutions through underlying acts of deportation and forcible transfer, as crimes against humanity.[2404]

713. With respect to Župljanin's contribution to the JCE, the Trial Chamber found that:

> starting on 1 April 1992 and continuing throughout the rest of the year, Stojan Župljanin ordered and coordinated the disarming of the non-Serb population in the ARK Municipalities. He created a unit, the Banja Luka CSB Special Police Detachment, which he used to assist other Serb Forces in the takeovers of the ARK Municipalities. He was fully aware of and took part in the unlawful arrest of non-Serbs and their forcible removal. He failed to launch criminal investigations and discipline his subordinates who had committed crimes against non-Serbs, thus creating a climate of impunity which only increased the commission of crimes against non-Serbs. He failed to protect the non-Serb population even when they pleaded with him for protection, thereby exacerbating their feeling of insecurity and strongly contributing to their flight out of the ARK Municipalities. **[page 292]** Therefore, during the Indictment period, Stojan

---

[2391] Trial Judgement, vol. 2, p. 121. See Trial Judgement, vol. 2, paras 375-488.
[2392] Trial Judgement, vol. 2, p. 167. See Trial Judgement, vol. 2, paras 448-530.
[2393] Trial Judgement, vol. 2, p. 167. See Trial Judgement, vol. 2, paras 488-493.
[2394] Trial Judgement, vol. 2, p. 168. See Trial Judgement, vol. 2, paras 494-530.
[2395] Trial Judgement, vol. 2, para. 518.
[2396] Trial Judgement, vol. 2, paras 519-520.
[2397] Trial Judgement, vol. 2, para. 520.
[2398] Trial Judgement, vol. 2, para. 521. See Trial Judgement, vol. 2, paras 522-528.
[2399] Trial Judgement, vol. 2, paras 448-530.
[2400] Trial Judgement, vol. 2, paras 448-530. *Cf.* Trial Judgement, vol. 2, paras 490, 494, 516-517, 526, fns 1371-1375.
[2401] Župljanin Appeal Brief, paras 8-181 (sub-grounds (A) to (E) and sub-ground (F) in part of Župljanin's first ground of appeal). Under sub-ground (F) of his first ground of appeal, Župljanin also raises arguments related to the common criminal purpose (see Župljanin Appeal Brief, paras 15-16, 27-33, 35, 37, 39). The Appeals Chamber recalls that it has already addressed and dismissed Župljanin's arguments in this respect (see *supra*, paras 67-71).
[2402] Župljanin Appeal Brief, paras 182-242 (Župljanin's second and third grounds of appeal).
[2403] Župljanin Appeal Brief, paras 227-242 (Župljanin's third ground of appeal).
[2404] Trial Judgement, vol. 2, para. 520. See Trial Judgement, vol. 2, paras 805, 832, 845, 850, 859, 864, 869.

Župljanin significantly contributed to the common objective to permanently remove Bosnian Muslims and Bosnian Croats from the territory of the planned Serbian state.[2405]

714. With respect to Župljanin's intent under the first category of joint criminal enterprise, the Trial Chamber stated that it had:

> primarily considered Župljanin's role in the blockade of Banja Luka; his ties to the SDS, demonstrated by the unreserved support given by top SDS leaders in the ARK to his appointment as Chief of the CSB and by his interactions with other SDS members; his attendance at the 14 February 1992 SDS Main Board meeting at the Holiday Inn in Sarajevo; and his contribution to the implementation of SDS policies in Banja Luka and in other ARK municipalities. The Trial Chamber has also considered Župljanin's failure to protect the non-Serb population in conjunction with his enrollment of the SOS in the [Banja Luka CSB SPD], his inaction in relation to the crimes committed by this unit, and his statements and actions taken in response to requests for protection by the Muslims of Banja Luka. In this context, the Trial Chamber has considered that Župljanin issued orders to protect the non-Serb population in the ARK and filed some criminal reports for crimes committed against non-Serbs. However, even though he continued to receive information that crimes, including unlawful detention, were being committed on a large scale, he did not take steps to ensure that these orders were in fact carried out. It has also considered that Župljanin did successfully take action against the Mićé Group, the members of which committed crimes against non-Serbs in Teslić, but having considered all the instances in which Župljanin neglected to protect the non-Serb population, the Trial Chamber finds that he did so only because the Mićé Group had become a nuisance to Serb municipal authorities. Based on this evidence, the Trial Chamber finds that Župljanin's failure to protect the Muslims and Croatian population formed part of the decision to discriminate against them and force them to leave the ARK Municipalities, and was not merely the consequence of simple negligence. With regard to the unlawful arrests, the evidence clearly shows that Župljanin was aware of the arrests, of their unlawfulness, and that in spite of this he actively contributed to the operation. Through the formation of a feigned commission and by providing false information to the judicial authorities, he endeavoured, and successfully managed, to shield his subordinates from criminal prosecution for the murder, unlawful arrests, looting, and cruel treatment of non-Serb prisoners, thus creating a climate of impunity that encouraged the perpetration of crimes against non-Serbs and made non-Serbs decide to leave the ARK Municipalities. The Trial Chamber finds that all of Župljanin's actions described above were voluntary.[2406]

On this basis, the Trial Chamber found that:

> Župljanin's acts and omissions demonstrate beyond reasonable doubt that he intended, with other members of the JCE, to achieve the permanent removal of Bosnian Muslims and Bosnian Croats from the territory of the planned Serbian state through the commission of [the JCE I Crimes] against Muslims and Croats in the ARK Municipalities.[2407]

715. Župljanin contends that the Trial Chamber erred in law and fact in concluding that he significantly contributed to the JCE and that he possessed the intent to further the JCE.[2408] In support, Župljanin alleges errors in relation to the Trial Chamber's reliance on the following factors: (i) his failure to launch criminal investigations, to discipline his subordinates, and to protect the non-Serb population;[2409] (ii) his knowledge of, and role in, unlawful arrests and detentions of **[page 293]** non-Serbs in the ARK Municipalities;[2410] and (iii) his other positive acts, in particular, his attendance at the SDS Main Board meeting at the Holiday Inn in Sarajevo on 14 February 1992 ("Holiday Inn Meeting"), his role in the takeovers of the ARK Municipalities and the blockade of Banja Luka, and his close ties with SDS political leaders.[2411] In addition, Župljanin contends that, even assuming that there is no error in its assessment of these factors, the Trial Chamber erred in concluding on the basis of these factors that he significantly contributed to the JCE[2412] and possessed the intent to further the JCE.[2413]

[2405] Trial Judgement, vol. 2, para. 518.
[2406] Trial Judgement, vol. 2, para. 519.
[2407] Trial Judgement, vol. 2, para. 520.
[2408] Župljanin Appeal Brief, paras 7-11.
[2409] Župljanin Appeal Brief, paras 55-111, 127-135, 139-151, 155-156, 162-177.
[2410] Župljanin Appeal Brief, paras 112-125. See Župljanin Appeal Brief, paras 153, 161.
[2411] Župljanin Appeal Brief, paras 139, 152, 154-155, 157-160.
[2412] Župljanin Appeal Brief, paras 126, 136.
[2413] Župljanin Appeal Brief, paras 12-13, 17-25, 31-32, 35-39, 40-53, 102-104, 155-156, 178-179.

716.   In response, the Prosecution submits that Župljanin fails to show any error in the Trial Chamber's reasoning establishing his intentional participation in the common criminal purpose to forcibly and permanently remove non-Serbs from BiH, and that his arguments should be dismissed.[2414]

717.   The Appeals Chamber will address Župljanin's challenges in turn.[2415]

(b) Alleged errors in relying on Župljanin's failure to launch criminal investigations, to discipline his subordinates, and to protect the non-Serb population

718.   When assessing Župljanin's contribution to the JCE, the Trial Chamber considered, in combination with his positive acts, Župljanin's omissions in relation to his failure to: (i) launch criminal investigations;[2416] (ii) discipline subordinates who had committed crimes against non-Serbs;[2417] and (iii) to protect the non-Serb population, even when they pleaded for his protection.[2418] Moreover, in finding that Župljanin intended to further the JCE, the Trial Chamber also relied on his inactions in relation to the crimes committed by the Banja Luka CSB SPD, and on **[page 294]** his failure to protect the non-Serb population.[2419] Specifically, the Trial Chamber noted that despite continuing to receive information regarding the commission of crimes, Župljanin did not take steps to ensure that the orders he issued to protect the non-Serb population were actually carried out.[2420] It found, in particular, that Župljanin: (i) issued orders to protect the non-Serb population and filed reports for some crimes committed against non-Serbs,[2421] but did not take steps to ensure such orders were carried out,[2422] even though he continued to receive information that crimes, including unlawful detention, were being committed on a large scale;[2423] and (ii) successfully took action against the Mićе Group, who had committed crimes against non-Serbs in Teslić, only because the Mićе Group had become a nuisance to Serb municipal authorities.[2424] Finally, the Trial Chamber referred to the fact that Župljanin formed a "feigned commission" and provided false information to judicial authorities.[2425]

719.   In support of its conclusion that Župljanin failed to discipline subordinates who had committed crimes against non-Serbs, the Trial Chamber relied upon findings elsewhere in the Trial Judgement that he: (i) did nothing to rein in the behaviour and to effectively discipline members of the Banja Luka CSB SPD,

---

[2414]   Prosecution Response Brief (Župljanin), paras 4-137.

[2415]   The Appeals Chamber observes that the factors relied upon by the Trial Chamber in concluding that Župljanin significantly contributed to the JCE and that he possessed the intent to further the JCE are largely overlapping (compare Trial Judgement, vol. 2, para. 518 with Trial Judgement, vol. 2, para. 519). As a result, many of Župljanin's arguments challenging the Trial Chamber's findings and/or reliance on these underlying factors pertain to both his contribution and intent. Therefore, the Appeals Chamber will first address his challenges concerning the underlying factors and the Trial Chamber's reliance thereon in the context of both his contribution and intent. Subsequently, the Appeals Chamber will address his overall arguments that, even assuming that there is no error in its assessment of these factors, the Trial Chamber erred in concluding on the basis of these factors that he significantly contributed to the JCE and possessed the intent to further the JCE.

[2416]   See Trial Judgement, vol. 2, para. 518. See Trial Judgement, vol. 2, paras 499, 506-510, 513. See also Trial Judgement, vol. 2, paras 368, 415-440, 457-482.

[2417]   See Trial Judgement, vol. 2, para. 518. See Trial Judgement, vol. 2, paras 501-505, 510, 515. See also Trial Judgement, vol. 2, paras 438-440, 483-488. *Cf.* Trial Judgement, vol. 2, paras 368, 384-398, 405-406, 415-440, 506-512.

[2418]   Trial Judgement, vol. 2, para. 518. See Trial Judgement, vol. 2, paras 506-509, 513-514. See also Trial Judgement, vol. 2, paras 415-456.

[2419]   Trial Judgement, vol. 2, para. 519.

[2420]   Trial Judgement, vol. 2, para. 519. See Trial Judgement, vol. 2, paras 506-513, 515. See also Trial Judgement, vol. 2, paras 407-440, 415-449, 453-464.

[2421]   Trial Judgement, vol. 2, para. 519. See Trial Judgement, vol. 2, para. 510. See also Trial Judgement, vol. 2, paras 357, 432-437.

[2422]   Trial Judgement, vol. 2, para. 519. See Trial Judgement, vol. 2, paras 510, 514. See also Trial Judgement, vol. 2, paras 457-464.

[2423]   Trial Judgement, vol. 2, para. 519. See Trial Judgement, vol. 2, paras 506-513. See also Trial Judgement, vol. 2, paras 407-440.

[2424]   Trial Judgement, vol. 2, para. 519. See Trial Judgement, vol. 2, para. 515. See also Trial Judgement, vol. 2, paras 453-454. According to the Trial Chamber, Župljanin's failure to protect the Muslim and Croat populations formed part of the decision to discriminate against them and force them to leave the ARK Municipalities (Trial Judgement, vol. 2, para. 519).

[2425]   Trial Judgement, vol. 2, para. 519. According to the Trial Chamber, by doing so, Župljanin "endeavoured, and successfully managed to shield his subordinates from criminal prosecution for the murder, unlawful arrests, looting, and cruel treatment of non-Serb prisoners, thus creating a climate of impunity that encouraged the perpetration of crimes against non-Serbs" (Trial Judgement, vol. 2, para. 519). See Trial Judgement, vol. 2, paras 514, 516-517. See also Trial Judgement, vol. 2, paras 446-447, 465-482.

notwithstanding his extensive knowledge of crimes committed by them;[2426] (ii) never attempted to remove Simo Drljača, the Chief of the Prijedor SJB ("Drljača"), from Prijedor despite his knowledge of the atrocities committed in the detention camps in Prijedor municipality and Witness Radulović's warning about Drljača;[2427] and (iii) failed to take adequate measures to stop the mass arrest of non-Serbs and the involvement of policemen therein, regardless of his knowledge of crimes against non-Serbs and in particular of their unlawful detention.[2428] **[page 295]**

720.   In reaching its conclusions that Župljanin failed to launch criminal investigations, the Trial Chamber relied upon its findings that he: (i) failed to take adequate measures to stop the mass arrest of non-Serbs and his policemen's involvement therein;[2429] (ii) did nothing to rein in the behaviour and to effectively investigate members of the Banja Luka CSB SPD;[2430] and (iii) failed to ensure that his police duly investigated crimes committed against non-Serbs in the ARK Municipalities, notwithstanding his extensive knowledge of the crimes committed in the ARK by Serb forces against non-Serbs.[2431]

721.   Based on the foregoing findings, the Trial Chamber also reached the conclusion that Župljanin did not do anything to reassure and protect the non-Serb population,[2432] even when they pleaded with him for protection, aside from issuing ineffective and general orders exhorting the ARK SJBs to respect the law that were not genuinely meant to be implemented.[2433]

722.   Župljanin submits that the Trial Chamber erred in finding that he failed to launch criminal investigations, to discipline his subordinates, and to protect the non-Serb population, and in relying on these findings to convict him under the first category of joint criminal enterprise.[2434] Specifically, Župljanin alleges that the Trial Chamber: (i) erred regarding the legal standard for contribution to a joint criminal enterprise though failure to act;[2435] (ii) failed to make the required findings in relation to his failure to act over policemen re-subordinated or otherwise not under his control;[2436] (iii) failed to establish that Župljanin acted with knowledge of his duties;[2437] (iv) erred in reaching its findings that Župljanin failed to investigate and discipline members of the Banja Luka CSB SPD;[2438] and (v) erred in finding that Župljanin failed to protect the non-Serb population by issuing general and ineffective orders which were not genuinely meant to be effectuated.[2439] **[page 296]**

723.   The Prosecution responds that the Trial Chamber correctly applied the law of joint criminal enterprise and did not err in its rejection of Župljanin's argument at trial on the issue of re-subordination of the police to the military.[2440]

[2426]   Trial Judgement, vol. 2, paras 504-505. See Trial Judgement, vol. 2, paras 501-503. See also Trial Judgement, vol. 2, paras 368, 384-398, 405-406, 438-440, 483-488.
[2427]   Trial Judgement, vol. 2, para. 515. See Trial Judgement, vol. 2, para. 508. See also Trial Judgement, vol. 2, paras 420-424.
[2428]   Trial Judgement, vol. 2, para. 510. See Trial Judgement, vol. 2, paras 506-509. See also Trial Judgement, vol. 2, paras 368, 415-440.
[2429]   Trial Judgement, vol. 2, paras 510-511. See Trial Judgement, vol. 2, paras 506-507. See also Trial Judgement, vol. 2, paras 432-437.
[2430]   Trial Judgement, vol. 2, paras 504-505. See Trial Judgement, vol. 2, paras 501-503. See also Trial Judgement, vol. 2, paras 368, 384-398, 405-406, 438-440, 483-488.
[2431]   Trial Judgement, vol. 2, para. 513. See Trial Judgement, vol. 2, paras 506-509. See also Trial Judgement, vol. 2, paras 368, 415-440.
[2432]   Trial Judgement, vol. 2, para. 514. See *e.g.* Trial Judgement, vol. 2, paras 451-452. See also Trial Judgement, vol. 2, paras 513-514.
[2433]   Trial Judgement, vol. 2, paras 514, 518. See Trial Judgement, vol. 2, paras 441-456. *Cf.* Trial Judgement, vol. 2, paras 415-449.
[2434]   See generally, Župljanin Appeal Brief, paras 30, 55-57, 60-125, 127, 130-134, 139-154.
[2435]   See Župljanin Appeal Brief, paras 70, 107-111, 127, 130-134.
[2436]   See Župljanin Appeal Brief, paras 30, 55-57, 60-101.
[2437]   See Župljanin Appeal Brief, paras 102-104.
[2438]   See Župljanin Appeal Brief, paras 112-125.
[2439]   See Župljanin Appeal Brief, paras 139-154.
[2440]   Prosecution Response Brief (Župljanin), paras 33-76.

(i) Alleged errors regarding the legal standard for contribution to a joint criminal enterprise through failure to act (sub-ground (A) in part, sub-ground (B), and sub-ground (C) in part of Župljanin's first ground of appeal)

a. Submissions of the parties

724.   Župljanin submits that the Trial Chamber erred in law in relying on his omissions to convict him pursuant to the first category of joint criminal enterprise since it did not apply the correct legal standard for omissions.[2441] Župljanin submits in particular that in order for the Trial Chamber to rely on his omissions in relation to his contribution and intent for the first category of joint criminal enterprise, the Trial Chamber was required to establish that the threshold conditions for an omission were satisfied, namely: (i) the existence of a legal duty; (ii) the capacity to fulfil the duty; (iii) the knowledge of the duty and capacity to act; and (iv) the failure to fulfil the duty.[2442]

725.   In relation to his legal duty to act, Župljanin argues that the Trial Chamber erred in referring to Article 10 of the RS Constitution and Article 42 of the LIA since reliance on a failure to fulfil domestic legal obligations constitutes a "radical and unprecedented extension of omission liability in international criminal law".[2443] **[page 297]**

726.   In relation to his capacity or ability to act, Župljanin asserts that the *actus reus* of commission through omission requires an accused to exercise at least "concrete influence" over subordinate physical perpetrators[2444] and that this threshold should apply *mutatis mutandis* to all forms of commission, including through joint criminal enterprise.[2445] Župljanin further argues that the Trial Chamber assessed his omissions

---

[2441]   Župljanin Appeal Brief, paras 70, 107-111, 127, 130-134. See Appeal Hearing, 16 Dec 2015, AT. 165. Župljanin contends that the Trial Chamber's error in this respect renders the Trial Chamber's findings on the *actus reus* and *mens rea* of joint criminal enterprise liability unsafe and invalidates his conviction for all the crimes committed pursuant to the first category of joint criminal enterprise (Župljanin Appeal Brief, paras 111, 128).

[2442]   Župljanin Appeal Brief, para. 70, referring to *Galić* Appeal Judgement, para. 175; *Orić* Appeal Judgement, para. 43; *Brđanin* Appeal Judgement, para. 274; *Ntagerura et al.* Appeal Judgement, para. 334. See Župljanin Appeal Brief, para. 71. See also Župljanin Reply Brief, paras 42, 46; Appeal Hearing, 16 Dec 2015, AT. 165, 167.

[2443]   Župljanin Appeal Brief, paras 107, 109-110. See Župljanin Reply Brief, para. 47. Appeal Hearing, 16 Dec 2015, AT. 207-208. In support of his contention, Župljanin argues that: (i) a criminal prohibition of acts or conduct does not imply a general obligation to prevent the criminalised conduct (Župljanin Appeal Brief, para. 107. See Župljanin Appeal Brief, para. 110); (ii) by relying on a domestic legal obligation, the Trial Chamber exceeded the subject matter jurisdiction of the Tribunal pursuant to Articles 2 to 5 of the Statute, which restricts the Tribunal's jurisdiction to crimes in international criminal law (Župljanin Appeal Brief, para. 110); and (iii) the Trial Chamber's reference to a duty to protect "the entire civilian population" is contrary to the Appeals Chamber's jurisprudence that the duties giving rise to liability in international criminal law are narrowly defined (Župljanin Appeal Brief, para. 110). With respect to his argument that a criminal prohibition of acts or conduct does not imply a general obligation to prevent the criminalised conduct, Župljanin puts forward that in domestic law, even when a duty to prevent certain types of harm gives rise to a statutory breach it does not give rise to liability for the relevant criminal conduct (Župljanin Appeal Brief, para. 107). He further argues that there is no general principle of law supporting the view that breaches of a police officer's law enforcement obligations render him liable for the crime facilitated or permitted due to the breaches of his obligations (Župljanin Reply Brief, para. 48). With respect to his argument that duties giving rise to liability in international criminal law are narrowly defined, Župljanin underlines that the Appeals Chamber has only recognised two legal duties to act that may give rise to criminal liability, namely superior responsibility and failure to fulfil obligations concerning prisoners of war as provided for by the Geneva Conventions and that no other duties have been recognized as giving rise to criminal responsibility (Župljanin Appeal Brief, para. 108, referring to Hadžihasanović and Kubura Appeal Judgement, para. 39; Blaškić Appeal Judgement, para. 663; Mrksic and Sljivancanin Appeal Judgement, paras 70-71, 73). Finally, he submits that the Trial Chamber failed to provide reasons for its extension of omission liability, which impaired the exercise of his right to appeal (Župljanin Appeal Brief, para. 110).

[2444]   Župljanin Appeal Brief, para. 130, quoting *Orić* Appeal Judgement, para. 41. See Župljanin Appeal Brief, paras 127, 131-134, 137. He points out that this is a higher level of control or influence than that required for superior responsibility or aiding and abetting by omission (Župljanin Appeal Brief, paras 130, 133, referring to *Orić* Appeal Judgement, para. 41; *Blaškić* Appeal Judgement, para. 664; *Mrkšić and Šljivančanin* Appeal Judgement, para. 156). Župljanin adds that the jurisprudence for aiding and abetting by omission requires that the accused "had the ability to act but failed to do so" and that the same logic must apply when relying on an omission as a contribution to the JCE (Župljanin Appeal Brief, para. 70, referring to *Mrkšić and Šljivančanin* Appeal Judgement, paras 82, 99). See also Župljanin Appeal Brief, para. 137.

[2445]   Župljanin Appeal Brief, para. 131, referring to *Milutinović et al.* Appeal Decision on Joint Criminal Enterprise of 21 May 2003, paras 20, 31. Župljanin relies upon statements of the Appeals Chamber in that decision to the effect that joint criminal enterprise is a form of commission under Article 7(1) of the Statute (Župljanin Appeal Brief, fn. 187, referring to *Milutinović et al.* Appeal Decision on Joint Criminal Enterprise of 21 May 2003, paras 20, 31). Župljanin argues that, "[t]he authority of an accused

without first establishing in each case whether Župljanin had authority over the perpetrators.[2446] He submits that the Trial Chamber made no attempt to "make particularized findings" as to in which events "he had such a high degree of control that his 'omission' could count as part of the *actus reus* of commission".[2447]

727.   The Prosecution responds that the Trial Chamber correctly found that Župljanin's omissions formed part of his significant contribution to the JCE.[2448] The Prosecution contends that Župljanin's **[page 298]** arguments in this respect rest on a misunderstanding of the applicable law and the Trial Judgement, and should therefore be rejected.[2449]

728.   The Prosecution rejects Župljanin's argument that the Trial Chamber expanded the scope of omission liability and submits that Župljanin seeks to import elements not required to establish a significant contribution to a joint criminal enterprise.[2450] It argues that, contrary to Župljanin's contention, a contribution to a joint criminal enterprise by omission can be based on a duty derived from national law, as the nature of the duty is not relevant for the *actus reus* of joint criminal enterprise.[2451]

729.   The Prosecution further responds that there is no basis for Župljanin's argument that the Trial Chamber should have applied any standard of "concrete influence" over subordinates.[2452] It submits that: (i) an "elevated degree of concrete influence" is not an element of the *actus reus* of joint criminal enterprise, even when an accused's contribution includes omissions;[2453] and (ii) a position of authority is not an element of joint criminal enterprise but rather only a contextual factor that may be relevant to an assessment of an accused's contribution to a joint criminal enterprise.[2454] The Prosecution argues that Župljanin erroneously

---

[...] is relevant to the assessment of *actus reus*" (Župljanin Appeal Brief, para. 132, referring to *Kvočka et al.* Appeal Judgement, paras 101 103), especially in respect of omissions in order to avoid that any failure to prevent crimes can be found to satisfy the objective element of joint criminal enterprise (Župljanin Appeal Brief, para. 132, referring to *Milutinović et al.* Appeal Decision on Joint Criminal Enterprise of 21 May 2003, paras 25-26. See Appeal Hearing, 16 Dec 2015, AT. 208).

[2446]   Župljanin Appeal Brief, para. 135. See Župljanin Appeal Brief, para. 73. In this respect, he underlines that the Trial Chamber assessed his "every inaction, his every deficient performance of his duties, [and] every crime against non-Serbs committed in the seven ARK municipalities, as amongst the omissions constituting the *actus reus* of committing forcible transfers through JCE" (Župljanin Appeal Brief, para. 135). Župljanin argues that the Trial Chamber's findings concerning his omissions relate to "sub-findings referring to a wide range of different situations", and that the Trial Chamber failed to differentiate between "gradations" in the level of control he exercised over the physical perpetrators in each of these situations (Župljanin Appeal Brief, para. 129. See Župljanin Appeal Brief, para. 130).

[2447]   Župljanin Appeal Brief, para. 135. See Župljanin Appeal Brief, paras 127, 138. See also Appeal Hearing, 16 Dec 2015, AT. 167, 169. In this respect he contends that the Trial Chamber erred by occasionally stating that he could have taken certain measures against subordinates, "without ever making any finding of who was subordinate to him, with the possible exception of the Special Police Detachment" (Župljanin Appeal Brief, para. 135). Župljanin further contends that the Trial Chamber failed to make findings resembling those made in the *Blaškić* Appeal Judgement or the *Mrkšić and Šljivančanin* Appeal Judgement "concerning the extent of control necessary for an omission to be categorized as part of the *actus reus* of the crime" (Župljanin Appeal Brief, para. 135. See Župljanin Appeal Brief, para. 130, 133).

[2448]   Prosecution Response Brief (Župljanin), paras 79, 85. See Appeal Hearing, 16 Dec 2015, AT. 185, 190-191.

[2449]   Prosecution Response Brief (Župljanin), paras 77, 86. See Appeal Hearing, 16 Dec 2015, AT. 195.

[2450]   Prosecution Response Brief (Župljanin), paras 77-78.

[2451]   Prosecution Response Brief (Župljanin), paras 77, 80. See Appeal Hearing, 16 Dec 2015, AT. 194-195, referring to *Nyiramasuhuko et al.* Appeal Judgement, para. 2194. The Prosecution emphasises that nothing in the Tribunal's jurisprudence establishes that there is a "closed" list of duties, the breach of which may establish contributions to a joint criminal enterprise (Prosecution Response Brief (Župljanin), para. 82), and rejects Župljanin's argument that the Trial Chamber exceeded the subject-matter jurisdiction conferred by the Statute (Prosecution Response Brief (Župljanin), para. 81, referring to Župljanin Appeal Brief, paras 108, 110). In this respect, the Prosecution submits in particular that there is a "clear practice" in the Tribunal that omissions may be punished as a war crime, crime against humanity, or genocide provided that they meet the elements of a mode of liability under Article 7(1) of the Statute (Prosecution Response Brief (Župljanin), para. 81). The Prosecution specifies that in the case of commission by omission – where the omission itself satisfies the *actus reus* of the crime – it may be appropriate to require that the nature of the duty be derived from international law in order "to ensure uniformity of norms" (Prosecution Response Brief (Župljanin), para. 80). The Prosecution submits that, in any event, Župljanin's duty as a police officer is recognised by national and international law (Prosecution Response Brief (Župljanin), paras 77, 83-84, fn. 331, referring to Exhibit P119, pp 97, 118, 123. See Appeal Hearing, 16 Dec 2015, AT. 195).

[2452]   Prosecution Response Brief (Župljanin), para. 94, referring to Župljanin Appeal Brief, paras 127, 133. The Prosecution also submits that Župljanin's claim that there were "gradations" of control over his subordinates is irrelevant, provided that the threshold of effective control was passed "as it was in this case" (Prosecution Response Brief (Župljanin), para. 94).

[2453]   Prosecution Response Brief (Župljanin), para. 88.

[2454]   Prosecution Response Brief (Župljanin), para. 90, referring to *Kvočka et al.* Appeal Judgement, paras 101, 192, 238.

313

conflates references in the jurisprudence to "concrete influence" over the *crimes* with the superior responsibility concept of control over *subordinates*.[2455]

730. In response to Župljanin's argument that the Trial Chamber failed to make particularised findings regarding his control over perpetrators, the Prosecution submits that the Trial Chamber **[page 299]** properly established that he was both under a legal duty as a police officer to protect the civilian population, and that he maintained the ability to execute this duty.[2456] Furthermore, the Prosecution submits that the Trial Chamber only relied on Župljanin's failure to discipline particular subordinates when it made the requisite factual finding that the subordinates in question were under his control.[2457]

b. Analysis

731. Recalling the applicable law set out above in relation to Stanišić's similar arguments,[2458] the Appeals Chamber considers that Župljanin's challenges are based on the incorrect premise that each failure to act assessed in the context of joint criminal enterprise liability must, *per se*, meet the legal conditions set out in the Tribunal's case law for commission by omission.[2459]

732. Contrary to Župljanin's assertion, the demonstration of a duty to act that would meet the legal conditions set out in the Tribunal's case law for commission by omission is not required when relying on an accused's failure to act in the context of assessing his participation in a joint criminal enterprise.[2460] The Appeals Chamber emphasises that nothing in the law prevented the Trial Chamber from considering Župljanin's failure to fulfil his domestic duty in its factual assessment of his contribution to the JCE and when inferring his intent. Consequently, the Appeals Chamber finds no error of law in the Trial Chamber's reliance on Župljanin's failure to fulfil his domestic obligation under article 10 of the RS Constitution and article 42 of the LIA as part of its factual analysis of his contribution to the JCE and to infer his intent. Since the remainder of Župljanin's arguments in relation to a duty to act are based on the incorrect premise that the Trial Chamber's reliance on a failure to fulfil domestic legal obligations constitutes an extension of omission liability, the Appeals Chamber dismisses them without further discussion.[2461]

733. Turning to Župljanin's arguments in relation to his capacity or ability to act, based on the same reasoning, the Appeals Chamber finds no merit in Župljanin's attempt to conflate the Appeals **[page 300]** Chamber's statement that the objective element of commission by omission requires, at a minimum, an "elevated degree of 'concrete influence'",[2462] with the significant contribution requirement of joint criminal enterprise liability.[2463] For the same reason, the Appeals Chamber dismisses Župljanin's argument that the

---

[2455] Prosecution Response Brief (Župljanin), para. 89, referring to Župljanin Appeal Brief, paras 127, 132-135, *Mrkšić and Šljivančanin* Appeal Judgement, fn. 554, *Blaškić* Appeal Judgement, para. 664.

[2456] Prosecution Response Brief (Župljanin), para. 93. The Prosecution also submits that since Župljanin's duty depended on his status as a police officer and not on his position as a superior, the Trial Chamber was not required to determine that he exercised "control" or "influence" over any perpetrators (Prosecution Response Brief (Župljanin), para. 93. See Appeal Hearing, 16 Dec 2015, AT. 196). The Prosecution further submits that Župljanin makes "no attempt" to show that the Trial Chamber was unreasonable in its findings (Prosecution Response Brief (Župljanin), para. 93).

[2457] Prosecution Response Brief (Župljanin), para. 94. The Prosecution submits that Župljanin fails to show any error in the Trial Chamber's assessment of his failure to prevent the crimes of certain subordinates since the Trial Chamber adequately established Župljanin's duty to control the acts of his subordinates, his ability to act, and his failure to do so (Prosecution Response Brief (Župljanin), para. 94).

[2458] See *supra*, paras 109-110.

[2459] The Appeals Chamber notes that Stanišić raises similar arguments with respect to his contribution to the JCE (see *supra*, paras 106-107).

[2460] See *supra*, para. 110.

[2461] See *supra*, paras 724-725.

[2462] *Mrkšić and Šljivančanin* Appeal Judgement, para. 156; *Orić* Appeal Judgement, para. 41; *Blaškić* Appeal Judgement, para. 664.

[2463] *Cf. Mrkšić and Šljivančanin* Appeal Judgement, para. 156, where the Appeals Chamber rejected Veselin Sljivancanin's attempt to conflate the substantial contribution requirement of the objective element of aiding and abetting with the elevated degree of concrete influence. The Appeals Chamber further considers inapposite Župljanin's contention that "anyone's failure to prevent crimes" would satisfy the objective element of joint criminal enterprise in the absence of a threshold of concrete influence over subordinates (Župljanin Appeal Brief, para. 132). His argument in this respect once more ignores the requirements for joint criminal enterprise liability, that an accused must make at least a significant contribution to the execution of the common plan (*Popović et al.*

Trial Chamber failed to make findings or particularised findings as to whether "he had such a high degree of control over his subordinates that his 'omission' could count as part of the *actus reus* of commission".[2464]

734. Finally, the Appeals Chamber observes that in the jurisprudence of the Tribunal a failure to intervene to prevent recurrence of crimes or to halt abuses has been taken into account in assessing an accused's contribution to a joint criminal enterprise and his intent, where the accused had some power and influence or authority over the perpetrators sufficient to prevent or halt the abuses but failed to exercise such power.[2465] In the present case, the Trial Chamber considered Župljanin's failure to protect the non-Serb population, launch criminal investigations, and discipline his subordinates who committed crimes against non-Serbs, together with his other actions, as part of its factual determination of Župljanin's contribution to the JCE and in inferring his intent.[2466] In this context, the Trial Chamber made detailed findings on Župljanin's authority over perpetrators and his power to prevent or halt abuses.[2467] The Appeals Chamber therefore finds that Župljanin has not **[page 301]** shown that the Trial Chamber applied an erroneous legal standard when it considered instances of his failures to act in determining whether he contributed to the common purpose and had the requisite intent.[2468]

c. Conclusion

735. In view of the above, the Appeals Chamber rejects Župljanin's argument that the Trial Chamber erred in law by relying on his failures to act to find that he significantly contributed to the JCE and possessed the requisite intent and to convict him pursuant to the first category of joint criminal enterprise.

(ii) Alleged errors regarding Župljanin's failure to act over policemen re-subordinated to the military or otherwise not under his control (sub-ground (A) in part of Župljanin's first ground of appeal)

736. Župljanin contends that the Trial Chamber erred in relying on his omissions to infer his contribution to the JCE and criminal intent, as it failed to make findings that he had sufficient control or authority over the police by failing to pronounce on issues of re-subordination of the police to the military.[2469] He also points to three specific examples that he asserts demonstrate the pervasive consequence of the Trial Chamber's failure to address the re-subordination issues.[2470] The Appeals Chamber will address these contentions in turn.

Appeal Judgement, para. 1378; *Kvočka et al.* Appeal Judgement, paras 97-98; *supra*, para. 110. See *Šainović et al.* Appeal Judgement, paras 954, 987).

[2464] Župljanin Appeal Brief, para. 135._The Appeals Chamber further notes that_Župljanin's submissions that the Trial Chamber failed to make particularised findings regarding his control and authority over his subordinates is based on the unsupported statement that the Trial Chamber relied upon his failure to fulfil his duties with respect to every Indictment crime it evaluated, and considered his every inaction in assessing his contribution to the JCE. As explained below, the Appeals Chamber considers that Župljanin's assertion misinterprets the Trial Judgement (see Župljanin Appeal Brief, para. 135. See *infra*, paras 736-813).

[2465] See *Šainović et al.* Appeal Judgement, paras 1233, 1242; *Krajišnik* Appeal Judgement, para. 194; *Kvočka et al.* Appeal Judgement, paras 195-196. See *supra*, para. 111. The Appeals Chamber also recalls that although a *de jure* or *de facto* position of authority is not a material condition required by law under the theory of joint criminal enterprise, it is a relevant factor in determining the scope of the accused's participation in the common purpose (see *Kvočka et al.* Appeal Judgement, para. 192. See also *Kvočka et al.* Appeal Judgement, para. 104).

[2466] Trial Judgement, vol. 2, paras 518-519.

[2467] In particular, in assessing his failure to act, the Trial Chamber considered that Župljanin was the highest police authority in the ARK (Trial Judgement, vol. 2, para. 493) and found that, pursuant to Article 10 of the RS Constitution and Article 42 of the LIA, he had a duty to protect the civilian population regardless of religion, ethnicity, race, or political beliefs, even when the execution of such activities and tasks placed his life in danger (Trial Judgement, vol. 2, para. 489. See Trial Judgement, vol. 2, para. 354, referring to Exhibits P181, art. 10; P530, art. 42). The Trial Chamber also found that Župljanin had legal authority over police in the ARK (Trial Judgement, vol. 2, para. 355) and by 11 May 1992, the Banja Luka CSB had "'total control' of 25 police stations in the ARK" (Trial Judgement, vol. 2, para. 351). The Trial Chamber further found that Župljanin had *de jure* and *de facto* authority over the SJBs of the ARK Municipalities, which included the power to appoint and remove RS MUP staff, including SJB chiefs, to order the 300 police to perform specific tasks, and to take disciplinary measures against his subordinates (Trial Judgement, vol. 2, para. 493).

[2468] The Appeals Chamber will address in detail below Župljanin's specific challenges that the Trial Chamber failed to make findings pertaining to his authority and his capacity to act to prevent or halt abuses (see *infra*, paras 737-760, 821-869).

[2469] Župljanin Appeal Brief, paras 55-75, 105-106.

[2470] Župljanin Appeal Brief, paras 76-104. Župljanin alleges the Trial Chamber failed to make sufficient findings with respect to: (i) the municipalities of Donji Vakuf, Kotor Varoš, and Ključ (Župljanin Appeal Brief, paras 77-87); (ii) re-subordinated police

a. Failure to make findings in relation to policemen re-subordinated to the military or otherwise not under his control

737.   In its discussion of the "issue of the re-subordination of police to the military",[2471] the Trial Chamber noted that "[t]he central question was whether [Stanišić and Župljanin] could be held criminally responsible for the actions of members of the police who committed crimes while they may have been re-subordinated to the JNA or VRS".[2472] Having analysed the evidence relating to **[page 302]** this issue,[2473] the Trial Chamber concluded that it was "unable to find whether it was the military or the civilian authorities which may have been responsible for the investigation and prosecution of crimes against Muslims and Croats which may have been committed by policemen re-subordinated to the military".[2474] It noted, however, that "criminal responsibility for actions of re-subordinated policemen is primarily of importance for [...] responsibility pursuant to Article 7(3) of the Statute".[2475] It further referred to its finding that the JCE existed and that members of the police, the JNA, and the VRS were all used as tools in furtherance of the JCE, of which Stanišić and Župljanin were members.[2476] On this basis, the Trial Chamber stated that it would consider "whether the actions of policemen, which the Defence claims were re-subordinated to the military at the time of the commission of the crimes, can be imputed to a member of the JCE and ultimately to [Stanišić and Župljanin]".[2477] Accordingly, the Trial Chamber concluded that it was "not necessary to make any further findings on the issue of re-subordination".[2478]

i. Submissions of the parties

738.   Župljanin submits that the Trial Chamber erred by relying heavily on his failures to discharge two inter-related duties, derived from his position as regional police commander in the ARK, to infer his contribution to the JCE and his criminal intent.[2479] He contends that the Trial Chamber relied upon his omissions "in coming to the view that he committed forcible transfer through a JCE and, in particular, inferring his criminal intent".[2480] He asserts that the Trial Chamber's error arises from its failure to make findings on the extent to which policemen: (i) were periodically re-subordinated to the military;[2481] or (ii) were under the control of municipal crisis staffs,[2482] to the exclusion of his own authority.

739.   Župljanin argues that the Trial Chamber deliberately declined to make findings on whether he had a duty to prevent or punish specific crimes committed by policemen by failing to determine **[page 303]** the scope of re-subordination of the police forces.[2483] He asserts that since the Trial Chamber found that it was unable to determine whether it was the military or the civilian authorities which may have been responsible for the investigation and prosecution of crimes committed by re-subordinated policemen, it was also unable to determine whether he exercised *de jure* or *de facto* control over the re-subordinated policemen to an extent

serving in military-run detention facilities (Župljanin Appeal Brief, paras 88-89); and (iii) the extent to which he exercised control over the Prijedor SJB, including the Keraterm and Omarska detention facilities (Župljanin Appeal Brief, paras 90-101).
[2471]   Trial Judgement, vol. 2, para. 317. See Trial Judgement, vol. 2, paras 318-342.
[2472]   Trial Judgement, vol. 2, para. 317.
[2473]   Trial Judgement, vol. 2, paras 320-341.
[2474]   Trial Judgement, vol. 2, para. 342.
[2475]   Trial Judgement, vol. 2, para. 342.
[2476]   Trial Judgement, vol. 2, para. 342.
[2477]   Trial Judgement, vol. 2, para. 342 (citations omitted).
[2478]   Trial Judgement, vol. 2, para. 342.
[2479]   Župljanin Appeal Brief, paras 55, 63-64. See Župljanin Appeal Brief, paras 61-62 (referring to, *inter alia*, Trial Judgement, vol. 2, paras 518-519); Župljanin Reply Brief, para. 21. See also Appeal Hearing, 16 Dec 2015, AT. 163-164. Župljanin characterises these duties as a duty of a commander to prevent or punish crimes committed by subordinates (the "authority duty") and the duty of a policeman to protect the civilian population regardless of the identity of the perpetrator (the "jurisdictional duty") (Župljanin Appeal Brief, paras 55 (referring to Trial Judgement, vol. 2, paras 441, 499, 510, 513, 518-519), 64 (referring to Trial Judgement, vol. 2, paras 354, 441-455, 483-489, 496, 505, 513, 518-519).
[2480]   Župljanin Appeal Brief, para. 60. See Župljanin Appeal Brief, paras 61-62, referring to Trial Judgement, vol. 2, paras 518-519.
[2481]   Župljanin Appeal Brief, paras 56, 65.
[2482]   Župljanin Appeal Brief, para. 57.
[2483]   Župljanin Appeal Brief, paras 56, 68. See Župljanin Appeal Brief, paras 55, 65-67, 71-75. See also Župljanin Reply Brief, paras 22 (referring to, *inter alia*, Trial Judgement, vol. 2, para. 342), 23.

that would create a duty to "protect or punish crimes" committed by them.[2484] In his submissions, the Trial Chamber's findings therefore meant that he had no authority or duty to prevent or punish his subordinate policemen's crimes "unless the policemen committing the crime were not re-subordinated".[2485]

740. Moreover, Župljanin underlines that the Trial Chamber found that he was the highest police authority in the ARK and that he had *de facto* and *de jure* authority over SJBs in the ARK Municipalities without any temporal or geographic limitation.[2486] He submits that he, however, had presented the Trial Chamber with considerable evidence regarding re-subordination of police force,[2487] and that the Trial Chamber acknowledged that the JNA and the VRS periodically exercised control over policemen "for certain periods or in the performance of certain tasks".[2488] He argues that, nonetheless, the Trial Chamber deliberately declined to make "findings about the scope of re-subordination or to determine whether particular crimes were committed by re-subordinated policemen".[2489] Župljanin contends that "[t]he least that was required of the [Trial] Chamber [...] was a determination as to which crimes were committed by re-subordinated, as opposed to non-re-subordinated, policemen".[2490] In his view, to rely on his omissions to infer his participation in the JCE, the Trial Chamber was required to determine if he had a duty to act, and he only had **[page 304]** such duty with respect to police that were not re-subordinated, which, in turn, required a determination of the re-subordination issue.[2491]

741. According to Župljanin, the Trial Chamber then incoherently proceeded to infer his participation in the JCE based on his alleged failures to exercise authority over these same policemen.[2492] He contends that as a consequence, the Trial Chamber attributed "a host of 'omissions'" to him without having determined whether he had a duty, or the practical capacity, to act.[2493] Finally, according to Župljanin, the issue of re-subordination is also "determinative of whether there was any civilian police jurisdiction over the crime[s]" since crimes committed by soldiers, reservists, TO, or re-subordinated police were subject to the exclusive military jurisdiction.[2494]

742. Župljanin further contends that the Trial Chamber also attributed several omissions to him without having considered the extent to which local police stations were influenced or commanded by municipal crisis groups or the VRS to the exclusion of his own authority.[2495] He points in particular to the fact that the Trial Chamber failed to take into account its own finding that the Prijedor police were under the influence of the municipal authorities and were not under his effective control or authority.[2496] He also argues that the

---

[2484] Župljanin Appeal Brief, para. 67.

[2485] Župljanin Appeal Brief, para. 67 (emphasis omitted), referring to Trial Judgement, vol. 2, paras 317-342.

[2486] Župljanin Appeal Brief, para. 65, referring to Trial Judgement, vol. 2, para. 493. The Appeals Chamber notes Župljanin refers to paragraph 350 of volume two of the Trial Judgement, but that the relevant paragraph is 351. He also points to the Trial Chamber's findings that Banja Luka CSB was "reportedly" in "total control" of 25 local police stations, that by virtue of his position as the head of CSB he "had authority over and coordinated the activities of the ARK SJBs (see Župljanin Appeal Brief, para. 65, referring to Trial Judgement, vol. 2, paras 35(1), 355, 356, 368).

[2487] Župljanin Appeal Brief, paras 73-74, referring to, *inter alia*, Exhibit P621, p. 7 (Report dated October 1992); *Prosecutor v. Mićo Stanišić and Stojan Župljanin*, Case No. IT-08-91-T, Župljanin Defence Final Trial Brief, 14 May 2012 (confidential) ("Župljanin Final Trial Brief"), paras 233-239, 255-277, 284, 289-291, 300-315, 331, 393 (arguing that evidence was presented at trial indicating that in some municipalities, the VRS went as far as declaring military rule and subordinated police commanders to perform certain tasks, encompassing arresting non-Serbs in combat areas where they would pose a security threat, guarding detainees, and transporting detainees from one detention facility to another). See Župljanin Reply Brief, para. 22.

[2488] Župljanin Appeal Brief, para. 66, referring to Trial Judgement, vol. 1, para. 637, Trial Judgement, vol. 2, paras 58, 311. See Župljanin Appeal Brief, para. 73.

[2489] Župljanin Appeal Brief, paras 56, 68. See Župljanin Appeal Brief, paras 65-67, 70-75. See also Župljanin Reply Brief, paras 22 (referring to, *inter alia*, Trial Judgement, vol. 2, para. 342), 23. Župljanin also underlines that the Trial Chamber declined to make findings because he would still be liable for those crimes as long as he was a member of the JCE (see Župljanin Appeal Brief, para. 69).

[2490] Župljanin Appeal Brief, para. 75. According to Župljanin "that would have been the only way, logically, to avoid imputing omissions to [him] where he had no duty to act" (Župljanin Appeal Brief, para. 75).

[2491] Župljanin Appeal Brief, paras 70-71, 73.

[2492] Župljanin Appeal Brief, para. 56.

[2493] Župljanin Appeal Brief, paras 56, 71, 73. In this respect, he contends that he did not have "plenary jurisdiction" over crimes in the ARK since he did not have authority over VRS soldiers present in the BiH by July 1992 and no jurisdiction to punish crimes committed by TO soldiers or re-subordinated police officers (see Župljanin Appeal Brief, para. 105).

[2494] Župljanin Appeal Brief, para. 72.

[2495] Župljanin Appeal Brief, para. 57.

[2496] Župljanin Appeal Brief, para. 57.

Trial Chamber acknowledged that there were other governmental institutions exercising authority in the ARK Municipalities in 1992, including the Serb forces, the SDS party structure, and crisis staffs.[2497]

743.   According to Župljanin, the Trial Chamber's failure to enter findings about the scope of his duties "affects all findings on which the [Trial] Chamber relied to impose JCE liability".[2498] Župljanin asserts that the aforementioned errors invalidate the Trial Chamber's conclusions regarding his joint criminal enterprise liability.[2499] He requests that the Appeals Chamber "reverse the conclusion that [he] committed forcible transfer through a JCE".[2500]

744.   The Prosecution responds that Župljanin fails to show that the Trial Chamber erred in its analysis of re-subordination or in its analysis of his acts and omissions in reaching its finding that [page 305] he contributed to the JCE.[2501] The Prosecution submits that the Trial Chamber correctly applied the law on joint criminal enterprise, relying on the Trial Chamber's rejection of Župljanin's re-subordination argument to establish his participation in the JCE.[2502] It argues that, in order for Župljanin to investigate and prosecute crimes committed against non-Serbs, he did not need to possess control over the perpetrators of those crimes.[2503] It argues that the Trial Chamber found that Župljanin exercised authority over those subordinates whose actions it took into account when concluding on his failure to prevent crimes or punish the perpetrators.[2504]

745.   The Prosecution further submits that the Trial Chamber's findings pertaining to Župljanin's conduct establish that he had power and authority over the police forces.[2505] It argues in particular that as the "highest police authority in the ARK", Župljanin was able to "set and enforce the pattern for the symbiotic relationship between regional and local crisis staffs and the police" and that his police subordinates were used to carry out crimes.[2506]

746.   In reply, Župljanin argues that the Trial Chamber purposefully renounced determining the issue of re-subordination, in light of evidence confirming that the crimes, committed by his subordinates while being re-subordinated to the military, were within exclusive military jurisdiction.[2507] [page 306]

ii. Analysis

747.   Župljanin's contention regarding the Trial Chamber's alleged errors in failing to determine the scope of re-subordination of police, fails to appreciate both the Trial Chamber's reasoning and the basis for his conviction.

[2497]   Župljanin Appeal Brief, para. 66, referring to Trial Judgement, vol. 2, para. 311.

[2498]   Župljanin Appeal Brief, para. 106.

[2499]   Župljanin Appeal Brief, paras 60, 105-106.

[2500]   Župljanin Appeal Brief, para. 106.

[2501]   Prosecution Response Brief (Župljanin), para. 33.

[2502]   Prosecution Response Brief (Župljanin), paras 33-38. The Prosecution submits in this respect that: (i) the Trial Chamber properly addressed the "extensive" arguments made by the parties during the course of the trial (Prosecution Response Brief (Župljanin), para. 34, referring to Trial Judgement, vol. 2, paras 317, 319-341); (ii) the Trial Chamber found that the military, the police, and the civil authorities worked closely together, but that "[cooperation cannot [...] be equated, with resubordination" (Prosecution Response Brief (Župljanin), para. 34, referring to Trial Judgement, vol. 2, paras 493, 761); (iii) Župljanin exaggerates the scope of re-subordination (Prosecution Response Brief (Župljanin), para. 34, comparing Župljanin Appeal Brief, para. 73, fn. 93 with Exhibits P621, P624, p. 5); (iv) the Trial Chamber did make findings pertaining to the issue of subordination of specific individuals or groups as were necessary to determine Župljanin's liability (Prosecution Response Brief (Župljanin), para. 35, referring to Župljanin Appeal Brief, para. 69, Trial Judgement, vol. 2, para. 342. See Prosecution Response Brief (Župljanin), para. 37); and (v) the issue of re-subordination was irrelevant to the two elements at the core of the Trial Chamber's reasoning regarding Župljanin's JCE responsibility (Prosecution Response Brief (Župljanin), para. 36. See Prosecution Response Brief (Župljanin), paras 37, 40-42).

[2503]   Prosecution Response Brief (Župljanin), para. 36. See Prosecution Response Brief (Župljanin), para. 94. See also Prosecution Response Brief (Župljanin), paras 37, 40-42.

[2504]   Prosecution Response Brief (Župljanin), para. 37, referring to Trial Judgement, vol. 2, paras 505, 515, 791, 802.

[2505]   Prosecution Response Brief (Župljanin), paras 39-42.

[2506]   Prosecution Response Brief (Župljanin), para. 39, referring to Trial Judgement, vol. 2, paras 491-493, 500, 510, 735. See Prosecution Response Brief (Župljanin), para. 93. The Prosecution also submits that the Trial Chamber reasonably concluded that "Župljanin had *de jure* and *de facto* authority over the SJBs of the ARK Municipalities" and could "take disciplinary measures, [...] against his subordinates" (Prosecution Response Brief (Župljanin), para. 39, referring to, *inter alia*, Trial Judgement, vol. 2, para. 493).

[2507]   Župljanin Reply Brief, para. 22.

748. Župljanin's unreferenced assertion that the Trial Chamber found that he had no *de jure* or *de facto* control "unless the policemen committing the crime were not re-subordinated",[2508] is not borne out by the Trial Judgement. Rather, the Trial Chamber held that it was "unable to find whether it was the military or the civilian authorities which may have been responsible for the *investigation and prosecution* of crimes against Muslims and Croats which may have been committed by policemen re-subordinated to the military".[2509] Although this finding could be an indication that Župljanin's capacity to act may have been somewhat limited when policemen were re-subordinated to the military, in the view of the Appeals Chamber, it does not imply that the Trial Chamber found that Župljanin had no control over policemen whatsoever, unless such policemen were not re-subordinated.[2510]

749. Moreover, the Appeals Chamber considers that Župljanin's assertion that the Trial Chamber deliberately declined to make findings about the scope of re-subordination misrepresents the Trial Judgement.[2511] The Trial Chamber stated that it was unable to ascertain whether civilian or military authorities were responsible for the investigation and prosecution of crimes that may have been committed by re-subordinated police.[2512] However, it further found that members of the police, JNA, and VRS were used as tools in furtherance of the common criminal purpose and stated that it would consider, in the sections of the Trial Judgement related to Stanišić and Župljanin's individual responsibility, "whether the actions of policemen, which the Defence claims were re-subordinated to the military at the time of the commission of the crimes, can be imputed to a member of the JCE and ultimately to [Stanišić and Župljanin]".[2513] The Trial Chamber concluded that it was "not necessary to make any further findings on the issue of re-subordination".[2514] Therefore, the Trial Chamber did not decline to make findings about the scope of re-subordination but rather found that it was unnecessary to make any further findings on this issue, since it was to address elsewhere whether the actions of policemen "which the Defence claims were re-subordinated to the military at **[page 307]** the time of the commission of the crimes" could be imputed to Stanišić, Župljanin, or another JCE member.

750. Recalling the applicable law set out above in relation to Stanišić's similar arguments,[2515] the Appeals Chamber discerns no error in the Trial Chamber's finding that, with regard to the question of whether crimes can be attributable to Župljanin under joint criminal enterprise liability, no further findings were necessary in relation to the issue of re-subordination. The Appeals Chamber recalls that, so long as it is established that Župljanin participated in the JCE and that the subjective element is met, he can be held responsible for crimes committed by perpetrators who were not members of the JCE provided that those crimes are linked to a member of the JCE who used the perpetrator in furtherance of the common criminal purpose.[2516]

751. To the extent that Župljanin argues that the Trial Chamber was required to address the issue of re-subordination when assessing his contribution to the JCE by his failure to act, the Appeals Chamber, as a preliminary matter, observes that he does not support his premise that the Trial Chamber attributed him a host of "omissions"[2517] by any reference to the Trial Judgement and has failed to appreciate the basis for his conviction. As set out above, the Trial Chamber clearly identified several specific failures to act that it attributed to Župljanin in assessing his significant contribution to, and intent to further the JCE – namely: (i) his failure to launch criminal investigations; (ii) his failure to discipline subordinates who had committed crimes against non-Serbs; and (iii) ultimately, his failure to protect the non-Serb population.[2518]

[2508] See *supra*, para. 739.
[2509] Trial Judgement, vol. 2, para. 342 (emphasis added).
[2510] See Župljanin Appeal Brief, para. 67, referring to Trial Judgement, vol. 2, paras 317-342. See also Župljanin Reply Brief, para. 22.
[2511] See *supra*, paras 740, 746.
[2512] See Trial Judgement, vol. 2, para. 342.
[2513] Trial Judgement, vol. 2, para. 342 (citations omitted).
[2514] Trial Judgement, vol. 2, para. 342.
[2515] See *supra*, para. 119.
[2516] See *Šainović et al.* Appeal Judgement, para. 1520, referring to *Krajišnik* Appeal Judgement, para. 225, *Martić* Appeal Judgement, para. 168, *Brđanin* Appeal Judgement, para. 413. See *Tolimir* Appeal Judgement, para. 432; *Popović et al.* Appeal Judgement, para. 1065.
[2517] See *supra*, para. 741.
[2518] See *supra*, para. 718.

752.   In this regard, the Appeals Chamber observes that in the jurisprudence of the Tribunal, a failure to intervene to prevent recurrence of crimes or to halt abuses has been taken into account in assessing an accused's contribution to a joint criminal enterprise and intent, where the accused had some power and influence or authority over the perpetrators to prevent or halt the abuses, but failed to exercise such powers.[2519] The existence of such influence or authority is a factual matter to be determined on a case-by-case basis.[2520] Therefore, in order to rely on Župljanin's failures to act as a **[page 308]** contribution to the JCE, the Trial Chamber indeed had to be satisfied that he had sufficient powers, influence, or authority to prevent or carry out such tasks. In light of the foregoing, and of the Trial Chamber's findings in relation to Župljanin's failures to act, the Appeals Chamber considers that Župljanin's argument that the Trial Chamber failed to make findings about the scope of the re-subordination of the police in assessing his failure to act is only relevant to the Trial Chamber's finding that he failed to discipline subordinates who had committed crimes against non-Serbs. Indeed, that is the sole finding of the Trial Chamber on Župljanin's failure to act where his capacity to prevent or halt abuses could have been affected by the re-subordination of policemen to the military.[2521]

753.   However, having reviewed the Trial Chamber's findings – and having addressed below Župljanin's specific arguments on the matter[2522] – the Appeals Chamber considers that there is no indication that the Trial Chamber attributed to Župljanin a failure to discipline policemen re-subordinated to the military when it assessed his contribution to the JCE and inferred his intent. Moreover, the Trial Judgement contains sufficient findings regarding Župljanin's relationship to, and authority over, subordinate policemen where such findings were necessitated by the Trial Chamber's reliance upon Župljanin's failures to act in assessing his contribution to the JCE and his intent.

754.   In this respect, the Appeals Chamber observes that when the Trial Chamber relied upon Župljanin's failures to "discipline his subordinates" in its assessment of his contribution to the JCE,[2523] it considered specific findings that it made elsewhere. Namely, the Trial Chamber relied upon findings that Župljanin: (i) failed to rein in the behaviour and effectively discipline members of the Banja Luka CSB SPD, despite his knowledge of their involvement in crimes;[2524] (ii) never attempted to remove Drljača, the Chief of the Prijedor SJB, from Prijedor, notwithstanding Župljanin's knowledge of the atrocities committed in the detention camps and Witness Radulović's **[page 309]** warning about Drljača;[2525] and (iii) failed to take adequate measures to stop, and in particular to discipline, policemen involved in the unlawful arrests.[2526]

755.   The Appeals Chamber notes that Župljanin's specific challenges to the Trial Chamber's findings regarding his authority over the Banja Luka CSB SPD, including whether the Banja Luka CSB SPD may have been re-subordinated to the military and that the Trial Chamber was required to further address the issue of re-subordination, are addressed and dismissed elsewhere in this Judgement.[2527] Moreover, the

---

[2519]   See *Šainović et al.* Appeal Judgement, paras 1233, 1242; *Krajišnik* Appeal Judgement, para. 194; *Kvočka et al.* Appeal Judgement, paras 194-196. See also *supra*, para. 111.

[2520]   See *Šainović et al.* Appeal Judgement, paras 1233, 1242. See also *Šainović et al.* Appeal Judgement, para. 1045; *Martić* Appeal Judgement, para. 28; *Krajišnik* Appeal Judgement, paras 193-194, 204. *Cf. Krajišnik* Appeal Judgement, para. 696, where the Appeals Chamber held that "[w]hat matters in terms of law is that the accused lends a significant contribution to the commission of the crimes involved in the JCE" and that, beyond that, "the question of whether the accused contributed to a JCE is a question of fact to be determined on a case-by-case basis".

[2521]   The Appeals Chamber considers that the issue of re-subordination of policemen to the military is irrelevant to the Trial Chamber's conclusion that Župljanin failed to launch criminal investigations, including for crimes committed by policemen, since it is based on his duty as a police officer to protect the civilian population and to investigate crimes, in particular to file criminal reports to the public prosecutor for crimes committed in the Banja Luka CSB's area of responsibility (see Trial Judgement, vol. 2, paras 354-356, 489, 518). The Appeals Chamber considers that the same holds true for the Trial Chamber's finding that Župljanin failed to ensure that his police duly investigated crimes committed against non-Serbs in the ARK Municipalities since it is not based on his failure to act against his subordinates but on his duty as a police officer to protect the civilian population and in failing to ensure that crimes were duly investigated (see Trial Judgement, vol. 2, para. 513).

[2522]   See *infra*, paras 761-812.

[2523]   Trial Judgement, vol. 2, para. 518. See *supra*, paras 718-720.

[2524]   Trial Judgement, vol. 2, paras 504-505.

[2525]   Trial Judgement, vol. 2, para. 515. See Trial Judgement, vol. 2, paras 360-362. See also Trial Judgement, vol. 2, paras 453-456.

[2526]   Trial Judgement, vol. 2, paras 510, 518. See Trial Judgement, vol. 2, paras 368, 483-485.

[2527]   See *infra*, paras 821-836.

Appeals Chamber has dismissed, in the following section, the specific examples that Župljanin asserts are demonstrative of the Trial Chamber's failure to address the issue of the re-subordination of the police to the military.[2528] As for the remaining events in the ARK Municipalities, the Appeals Chamber notes that the Trial Chamber made express findings that the police involved in the commission of crimes charged in the Indictment – including unlawful arrest – in these municipalities were under the authority of Župljanin as the highest police authority in the ARK[2529] and that he had *de jure* and *de facto* authority over the SJBs of the ARK Municipalities, including the capacity to take disciplinary measures against his subordinates.[2530] Župljanin does not advance any further argument suggesting that the Trial Chamber attributed to him a failure to discipline policemen re-subordinated to the military when it assessed his contribution to the JCE and inferred his intent in relation to the remaining events in the ARK Municipalities. **[page 310]**

756.   With respect to his failure to launch criminal investigations and, in particular to ensure that his police duly investigated crimes committed against non-Serbs in the ARK Municipalities,[2531] Župljanin has again failed to appreciate the basis of his conviction. Contrary to his submission,[2532] whether the crimes committed were subject to military jurisdiction is irrelevant to the Trial Chamber's findings on Župljanin's contribution to the JCE and his intent. Indeed, the Trial Chamber's conclusion that Župljanin failed to launch criminal investigations, was based on his general failure to fulfil his duty as a police officer to protect the civilian population and to investigate crimes, in particular to ensure the filing of criminal reports to the public prosecutor for crimes committed in the Banja Luka CSB's area of responsibility.[2533]

757.   Finally, insofar as Župljanin contends that the Trial Chamber attributed failures to act to him, without having considered the extent to which local police stations were influenced or commanded by municipal crisis groups,[2534] he points to no evidence or findings in support of this general argument.[2535] Accordingly, Župljanin has provided the Appeals Chamber with no basis upon which to assess his unsupported claims. Thus, the Appeals Chamber dismisses this argument.

758.   Moreover, to the extent that Župljanin's argument rests upon his assertion that the Trial Chamber failed to take into account its own finding that the police in Prijedor were under the influence of the municipal authorities, Župljanin mischaracterises the Trial Chamber's findings. The Appeals Chamber notes in this respect that the Trial Chamber did not find that the police in Prijedor were under the influence of the municipal authorities to the exclusion of Župljanin's authority,[2536] but rather "that certain SJBs, like Prijedor and Sanski Most, received and implemented instructions of municipal Crisis Staff to guard and transport

---

[2528]   See *infra*, paras 761-812.

[2529]   See Trial Judgement, vol. 2, paras 801-802 (Banja Luka: perpetrators included members of the police and the Banja Luka CSB SPD, Banja Luka CSB, SNB Prijedor, Sanski Most, Ključ, and other ARK Municipalities, members of the crew of the red van were police under the authority of Župljanin, the highest police authority in the ARK), 828-829 (Donji Vakuf: perpetrators included members of the police force, including personnel from the Donji Vakuf SJB and the regular and reserve police in Donji Vakuf reported through the Banja Luka CSB, which was under the command of Župljanin); 841-842 (Ključ: perpetrators included members of the Ključ SJB and the Sanica sub-station, under Chief Vinko Kondić ("Kondić"), and Župljanin was the highest police authority in the ARK); 846-847 (Kotor Varoš: perpetrators included members of the SJB; members of the police force under the command of Savo Tepic; members of the Banja Luka CSB SPD, which was under the authority of Župljanin. The SJB in Kotor Varoš came under the Banja Luka CSB, with Župljanin as the Chief of CSB Banja Luka and the highest police authority in the ARK); 855-856 (Prijedor and Skender Vakuf: perpetrators included members of the Prijedor SJB; the PIP, and the perpetrators in Skender Vakuf were Prijedor policemen, including members of the Prijedor Intervention Platoon. Župljanin was the highest police authority in the ARK) 860-861 (Sanski Most: perpetrators included the Sanski Most SJB, under Chief Mirko Vručinić. Župljanin was the highest police authority in the ARK); 865-866 (Teslić: perpetrators included members of the police, including personnel from the Doboj CSB, the Teslić SJB, reserve police officers, and members of the Banja Luka CSB SPD, and a group known as the Red Berets or the Mice Group which was composed of both police and VRS personnel. The local police in Teslić and members of the Banja Luka CSB SPD were under the authority of Stojan Župljanin).

[2530]   See Trial Judgement, vol. 2, paras 355-356, 368, 493.

[2531]   See Trial Judgement, vol. 2, paras 513, 518.

[2532]   See Župljanin Appeal Brief, para. 72.

[2533]   See Trial Judgement, vol. 2, para. 513. See also Trial Judgement, vol. 2, paras 354, 356, 489, 516-517, 518; *supra*, paras 720-721; *supra*, fn. 2521.

[2534]   See *supra*, para. 742.

[2535]   To the extent that Župljanin's argument could be understood as referring to the alleged control of the Prijedor Crisis Staff over the Prijedor SJB, the Appeals Chamber has addressed this argument below (see *infra*, paras 758, 795 805-811).

[2536]   See Župljanin Appeal Brief, para. 57.

non-Serb detainees".[2537] It further stated "that several exhibits [...] show that the Prijedor SJB kept the Banja Luka CSB informed of the events in the municipality and requested its assistance in a number of matters, including the transport of prisoners from Prijedor to the Manjača camp, throughout the summer of 1992".[2538] On the basis of this and other evidence, the Trial Chamber concluded that:

> [w]hile some SJBs in his area of responsibility performed tasks assigned by local Crisis Staffs, the evidence shows that the ARK Crisis Staff, municipal Crisis Staffs, and the Banja Luka CSB were **[page 311]** *cooperating closely* in matters such as the takeover of the ARK Municipalities by Serb Forces, the imprisonment of non-Serbs, and their resettlement in other areas of BiH or in other countries.[2539]

It found, moreover, that Župljanin exercised *de jure* and *de facto* control over the ARK SJBs, *i.e.* irrespective of the fact that some SJBs performed tasks assigned by local crisis staffs.[2540] Furthermore, the Appeals Chamber has dismissed Župljanin's arguments regarding the Trial Chamber's alleged error in failing to address whether, or to what extent, he exercised authority over the Prijedor SJB and in relation to his alleged failure to order police to disregard the orders of the local crisis staffs elsewhere in this Judgement.[2541]

759.   Turning to Župljanin's argument that the Trial Chamber acknowledged that there were other governmental institutions exercising authority in the ARK Municipalities in 1992, the Appeals Chamber fails to see how this fact would undermine the Trial Chamber's findings regarding his own specific authority over the police and his failure to act.[2542]

760.   In light of the above, the Appeals Chamber dismisses Župljanin's arguments that the Trial Chamber generally failed to make sufficient findings on the extent to which civilian policemen were periodically re-subordinated to the military or under the control of municipal crisis staffs, and thus erred in relying on his failures to launch criminal investigations, discipline his subordinates, and protect the non-Serb population, in assessing his contribution to the JCE and his intent.

b. Failure to make findings regarding re-subordinated police in specific instances

761.   Župljanin advances three "examples" he contends demonstrate the "pervasive consequence" of the Trial Chamber's alleged failure to address the issue of his jurisdiction and control over re-subordinated police in respect of his participation in the JCE and "show the manifest unreasonableness" of the Trial Chamber's reliance on his omissions.[2543] He contends that the Trial Chamber failed to: (i) address the issue of VRS town commands in the municipalities of Donji Vakuf, Kotor Varoš, and Ključ;[2544] (ii) make findings as to whether police serving in the Manjača and Trnopolje detention facilities were re-subordinated;[2545] and (iii) address the extent to which he **[page 312]** exercised authority over the Prijedor SJB, including the Keraterm and Omarska detention facilities.[2546]

762.   The Prosecution responds that Župljanin fails to show any error in the Trial Chamber's reasoning as the Trial Chamber made the necessary findings.[2547]

[2537]   Trial Judgement, vol. 2, para. 491.
[2538]   Trial Judgement, vol. 2, para. 491.
[2539]   Trial Judgement, vol. 2, para. 493. See Trial Judgement, vol. 2, paras 491-492.
[2540]   Trial Judgement, vol. 2, para. 493.
[2541]   See *infra*, para. 811.
[2542]   The Appeals Chamber also notes that to support his contention, Župljanin points to a finding in relation to the common purpose (see Župljanin Appeal Brief, para. 66, referring to Trial Judgement, vol. 2, para. 311). In paragraph 311 of volume two of the Trial Judgement, the Trial Chamber only found that the Serb Forces, SDS party structure, crisis staffs, and the RS Government were exercising authority in the municipalities but that even though at times there were conflicts between these various entities, they all shared and worked towards the same goal under the Bosnian Serb leadership (see Trial Judgement, vol. 2, para. 311).
[2543]   Župljanin Appeal Brief, para. 76. See Župljanin Appeal Brief, paras 77-101.
[2544]   Župljanin Appeal Brief, paras 77-87.
[2545]   Župljanin Appeal Brief, paras 88-89.
[2546]   Župljanin Appeal Brief, paras 90-101.
[2547]   Prosecution Response Brief (Župljanin), para. 43.

i. <u>Re-subordination of police in the municipalities of Donji Vakuf, Kotor Varoš, and</u>
<u>Ključ</u>

763.   In assessing Župljanin's participation in the JCE, the Trial Chamber found that Župljanin "had *de jure* and *de facto* authority over the SJBs of the ARK Municipalities".[2548] On the basis of this and other findings, the Trial Chamber found that Župljanin failed to launch criminal investigations, to discipline his subordinates, and to protect the non-Serb population.[2549] In addition to these general findings, the Trial Chamber also made specific findings in relation to the municipalities of Donji Vakuf, Kotor Varoš, and Ključ.[2550] It ultimately found that Župljanin failed to: (i) take adequate measures to stop the mass arrest of non-Serbs and the involvement of policemen therein, regardless of his knowledge of crimes against non-Serbs and in particular of their unlawful detention;[2551] and (ii) investigate crimes committed by the Banja Luka CSB SPD, or impose disciplinary sanctions against its members.[2552]

764.   With respect to the municipality of Donji Vakuf, the Trial Chamber considered, in particular, that Župljanin knew by 5 August 1992 that there was a prison for Muslims and Croats in Donji Vakuf and that the police had arrested, and were responsible for guarding, 60 prisoners.[2553] **[page 313]**

765.   As for the municipality of Kotor Varoš, the Trial Chamber found that Župljanin dispatched the Banja Luka CSB SPD to the municipality in the summer of 1992.[2554] It found that at the end of June 1992, Župljanin was informed of the Banja Luka CSB SPD's involvement in serious crimes against the non-Serb population during their deployment in Kotor Varoš,[2555] and that there was limited evidence of efforts to investigate serious crimes against non-Serbs in Kotor Varoš.[2556]

766.   The Trial Chamber also found that Župljanin dispatched the Banja Luka CSB SPD to the municipality of Ključ in the summer of 1992.[2557] It found that Župljanin knew: (i) by July 1992, of police involvement in the mass arrests and detentions in Ključ municipality during May and June 1992; (ii) on 29 August 1992, that the Ključ SJB had sent persons detained in the municipality to the Manjača camp; and (iii) in November 1992, of cases of murder, rape, theft, and arson in which the victims were Muslims and that the Chief of the Ključ SJB Chief requested instructions from the Banja Luka CSB "on whether he should make the crimes public by filing reports against unknown perpetrators".[2558]

[2548]   Trial Judgement, vol. 2, para. 493. According to the Trial Chamber, Župljanin's authority "included the power to appoint and remove RS MUP staff, including SJB chiefs, and to order the police to perform specific tasks, including […] the transport of non-Serb detainees", and "Župljanin could also take disciplinary measures, including termination of employment, against his subordinates" (Trial Judgement, vol. 2, para. 493). The Appeals Chamber notes that in reaching these findings, the Trial Chamber considered, *inter alia*, Župljanin's arguments that "municipal Crisis Staffs had usurped [his] authority over the police, […] that local police were following the orders of municipal authorities" (Trial Judgement, vol. 2, para. 490, referring to Župljanin Final Trial Brief, pp 70-76), and that he lacked "effective control over municipal police forces" (Trial Judgement, vol. 2, para. 490). It found, nonetheless, that "Župljanin himself had, until at least 30 July 1992, *de facto* legitimised the municipal police to follow the orders of the municipal Crisis Staffs" (Trial Judgement, vol. 2, para. 492). The Trial Chamber further found, on the basis of this and other evidence, that "[w]hile some SJBs in his area of responsibility performed tasks assigned by local Crisis Staffs, the evidence shows that the ARK Crisis Staff, municipal Crisis Staffs, and the Banja Luka CSB were cooperating closely" (Trial Judgement, vol. 2, para. 493). With respect to Župljanin's duties and responsibilities as Chief of the Banja Luka CSB, see Trial Judgement, vol. 2, paras 354-356. With respect to the role of ARK municipal crisis staffs during the Indictment period, see Trial Judgement, vol. 2, paras 357-367.
[2549]   See *supra*, paras 718-721. See also Trial Judgement, vol. 2, paras 518-520.
[2550]   See *infra*, paras 764-766.
[2551]   Trial Judgement, vol. 2, para. 510. See Trial Judgement, vol. 2, para. 518 (failure to discipline his subordinates).
[2552]   Trial Judgement, vol. 2, para. 505.
[2553]   Trial Judgement, vol. 2, para. 509. See Trial Judgement, vol. 2, para. 427.
[2554]   Trial Judgement, vol. 2, para. 502. The Trial Chamber found that, during the summer of 1992, Župljanin dispatched the Banja Luka CSB SPD to participate, with other Serb forces, in the takeovers of various municipalities including Kotor Varoš, Prijedor, and Ključ (Trial Judgement, vol. 2, para. 502. *Cf.* Trial Judgement, vol. 2, para. 405).
[2555]   Trial Judgement, vol. 2, para. 503. See Trial Judgement, vol. 2, para. 425.
[2556]   Trial Judgement, vol. 2, para. 504. See Trial Judgement, vol. 2, para. 425. The Trial Chamber found that the only evidence of an investigation against members of the Banja Luka CSB SPD was the filing of a report against Danko Kajkut for a "double rape" allegedly committed in Kotor Varoš but that a criminal report in relation to the incident was never filed with the public prosecutor (Trial Judgement, vol. 2, para. 504. See Trial Judgement, vol. 2, para. 462).
[2557]   Trial Judgement, vol. 2, para. 502. See *supra*, fn. 2554.
[2558]   Trial Judgement, vol. 2, para. 509. See Trial Judgement, vol. 2, para. 426.

a. Submissions of the parties

767.   Župljanin argues that the Trial Chamber's finding that the crimes committed in the municipalities of Donji Vakuf, Ključ, and Kotor Varoš were not addressed by him "is predicated on a finding that the [Trial] Chamber never makes: that he had jurisdiction over those crimes".[2559] He submits that the "general finding of *de facto* and *de jure* control was inapplicable in respect of these three municipalities" and that the Trial Chamber was "duty-bound to address the issue".[2560]

768.   He argues that the Trial Chamber failed to acknowledge, or reject, documentary[2561] and testimonial[2562] evidence showing that the police in the town of Donji Vakuf were continuously **[page 314]** re-subordinated to a VRS town command,[2563] and that "the [Trial] Chamber's own findings contradict, or at least limit, its sweeping finding that [he] exercised *de jure* and *de facto* control over all police stations in the ARK".[2564] Župljanin contends that nevertheless, the alleged unlawful detention in Donji Vakuf and his alleged failure to intervene were mentioned amongst the matters from which the Trial Chamber inferred his involvement in the JCE.[2565]

769.   Župljanin also asserts that, having found that he knew of and failed to act in relation to crimes committed in Kotor Varoš,[2566] the Trial Chamber could not have drawn the inference that he intended to commit, and did commit, forcible transfer, without first determining that police who committed serious crimes in Kotor Varoš were not re-subordinated to the VRS.[2567] Župljanin points to evidence which he submits demonstrates that a town command existed in Kotor Varoš on or about 25 June 1992,[2568] and argues that the Trial Chamber "had ample evidence that required it to consider whether the crimes of [local policemen and the Banja Luka CSB SPD] were committed while subordinated to the VRS".[2569] Župljanin underlines that the Trial Chamber did not even refer to the evidence establishing that military command was in effect in Kotor Varoš at the time of the crimes.[2570]

770.   Župljanin further argues that the Trial Chamber erred by relying on "the default peacetime statutory framework" to conclude that Župljanin had *de jure* and *de facto* control over the activities of joint combat operations in Ključ municipality or over the perpetrators of crimes committed during such operations despite evidence to the contrary.[2571] He adds that the Trial Chamber itself acknowledged an abundance of

---

[2559]   Župljanin Appeal Brief, para. 87. See Župljanin Reply Brief, para. 24. With respect to Donji Vakuf, see Župljanin Appeal Brief, paras 77-79, 87. With respect to Kotor Varoš, see Župljanin Appeal Brief, paras 80-82, 87. With respect to Ključ, see Župljanin Appeal Brief, paras 83-87.

[2560]   Župljanin Appeal Brief, para. 87. See Župljanin Appeal Brief, paras 77, 82, 85.

[2561]   See Župljanin Appeal Brief, para. 78, referring to Exhibit P1928, pp 2, 4. See also Župljanin Appeal Brief, para. 77, referring to Exhibits 1D403, 1D473.

[2562]   See Župljanin Appeal Brief, para. 79, referring to Andrija Bjelošević, 15 Apr 2011, T. 19663-19664, Vidosav Kovačević, 6 Sep 2011, T. 23684-23685, Vidosav Kovačević, 7 Sep 2011, T. 23766-23767.

[2563]   Župljanin Appeal Brief, para. 77.

[2564]   Župljanin Appeal Brief, para. 77, referring to Trial Judgement, vol. 1, para. 241, Trial Judgement, vol. 2, paras 356, 358, 493. See Župljanin Reply Brief, paras 25-28.

[2565]   Župljanin Appeal Brief, para. 77, referring to Trial Judgement, vol. 2, paras 247, 509.

[2566]   Župljanin Appeal Brief, para. 82, referring to Trial Judgement, vol. 2, paras 42(5), 503. The Appeals Chamber notes that Župljanin refers to paragraph 426 of volume two of the Trial Judgement, but understands that this is intended as a reference to paragraph 425, instead.

[2567]   Župljanin Appeal Brief, para. 82. See Župljanin Reply Brief, paras 29-33. Župljanin contends that the "[r]esolving the issue" of re-subordination was a pre-requisite to inferring his intent and contribution from his omissions (Župljanin Appeal Brief, para. 82).

[2568]   Župljanin Appeal Brief, para. 80. Župljanin points specifically to: (i) Exhibit 2D132, an excerpt of minutes of a meeting of the Kotor Varoš Crisis Staff held on 25 June 1992, and the testimony of Witness Ewan Brown, which in his submission, show that the town command in Kotor Varoš was set up on the basis of direct communication between the local VRS unit and the local crisis staff (Župljanin Appeal Brief, para. 80, referring to Exhibit 2D132, Ewan Brown, 20 Jan 2011, T. 19058-19062, Exhibit P1787, p. 6); and (ii) Exhibit P1787, an order issued by the town commander in July 1992, prescribing complete control over the movement of the population (Župljanin Appeal Brief, para. 80).

[2569]   Župljanin Appeal Brief, para. 81.

[2570]   Župljanin Appeal Brief, para. 82.

[2571]   Župljanin Appeal Brief, para. 85. See Župljanin Reply Brief, paras 34-35. Župljanin points to documentary evidence showing that a military town command was set up from 31 May 1992 onwards (Župljanin Appeal Brief, para. 83, referring to Exhibit P1783, p. 1) and that a close relationship between military and SJB forces existed at the end of May 1992 (Župljanin Appeal Brief, paras 84-85, referring to Exhibit P960.24, pp 3-4, 8).

evidence suggesting the reasonable possibility that some, if not **[page 315]** many, of the crimes were committed by soldiers, with or without the involvement of policemen.[2572] In Župljanin's submission, the combination of crimes committed by soldiers, the collaboration of the police and the military, as well as, the existence of a town command, suggests that the police were substantially or continuously re-subordinated to the military.[2573] According to Župljanin, moreover, the Trial Chamber failed to address this evidence let alone make "any finding whatsoever as to the contours of re-subordination or which crimes were committed by whom".[2574]

771. The Prosecution responds that the Trial Chamber did not have to address the issue of town commands, given that it was not a significant issue in the case.[2575] It submits that the evidence indicates cooperation between the military and the police, rather than re-subordination.[2576]

772. Regarding Donji Vakuf, the Prosecution asserts that Župljanin merely repeats submissions made at trial and fails to show any error in the Trial Chamber's reasoning.[2577] According to the Prosecution, Župljanin's submissions misstate or omit relevant evidence considered by the Trial Chamber which shows that Župljanin continued to exercise authority over the Donji Vakuf SJB, uninterrupted by the existence of a "defence command", and that there was no need for the Trial Chamber to make an express finding about the "defence command" in Donji Vakuf.[2578] It further argues the Trial Chamber's findings regarding his role in coordinated action between the RS MUP, crisis staffs, and the VRS forces are consistent with the Trial Chamber's findings regarding his authority.[2579]

773. The Prosecution responds that the Trial Chamber reasonably relied on evidence pertaining to the municipalities of Kotor Varoš in assessing Župljanin's participation in the JCE.[2580] The Prosecution contends that again, Župljanin merely repeats submissions made during trial and ignores the distinction between cooperation and re-subordination.[2581] It asserts that the evidence on **[page 316]** the record shows that to the extent that any town command existed, it did not disturb Župljanin's authority over the police in Kotor Varoš and that therefore the Trial Chamber was not obliged to make an express finding concerning the existence of a town command.[2582]

774. With regard to Ključ, the Prosecution responds that Župljanin selectively refers to evidence which the Trial Chamber reasonably considered to be insignificant in the context of the evidence read as a whole.[2583] According to the Prosecution, Župljanin also overlooks evidence showing that the "military town command" was a measure agreed upon by the Ključ Crisis Staff and was not inconsistent with Župljanin's continuing authority over the Ključ police.[2584] The Prosecution submits that it was reasonable for the Trial Chamber to

---

[2572] Župljanin Appeal Brief, para. 85, referring to Trial Judgement, vol. 1, paras 304, 311-314, 318-319, 323, 331-332, 338.

[2573] Župljanin Appeal Brief, para. 85.

[2574] Župljanin Appeal Brief, para. 86.

[2575] Prosecution Response Brief (Župljanin), para. 44. See Prosecution Response Brief (Župljanin), paras 46, 48, 52. Specifically, the Prosecution contends that the Trial Chamber did not need to make findings regarding: (i) the "defence command" in Donji Vakuf (Prosecution Response Brief (Župljanin), para. 46); (ii) the "command for the defence of Kotor Varoš" (Prosecution Response Brief (Župljanin), para. 48); and (iii) the "Ključ defence command" (Prosecution Response Brief (Župljanin), para. 52). The Prosecution contends that a trial chamber, while obliged to provide reasons for its findings of fact on each element of the crimes charged, is not obliged to articulate every step of its reasoning, cite every piece of evidence it considered, or to provide reasons for rejecting evidence that is contradicted by substantial and credible evidence to the contrary (Prosecution Response Brief (Župljanin), para. 44, referring to *Renzaho* Appeal Judgement, para. 320, *Krajišnik* Appeal Judgement, para. 139, *Perišić* Appeal Judgement, para. 92).

[2576] Prosecution Response Brief (Župljanin), para. 54.

[2577] Prosecution Response Brief (Župljanin), para. 45.

[2578] Prosecution Response Brief (Župljanin), paras 45-46.

[2579] See Prosecution Response Brief (Župljanin), para. 46.

[2580] Prosecution Response Brief (Župljanin), para. 47.

[2581] Prosecution Response Brief (Župljanin), para. 47.

[2582] See Prosecution Response Brief (Župljanin), paras 47-50, fns 151-167. In particular, the Prosecution contends that Župljanin overlooks findings on his personal involvement in deploying a Banja Luka CSB SPD platoon to Kotor Varoš, which is consistent with the Trial Chamber's finding that he exercised complete authority over the Banja Luka CSB SPD (Prosecution Response Brief (Župljanin), para. 49).

[2583] Prosecution Response Brief (Župljanin), para. 51.

[2584] Prosecution Response Brief (Župljanin), paras 51-52.

conclude that Župljanin retained control over the Ključ police, and that nothing shows that the crimes committed in Ključ or the conduct of the police were outside Župljanin's jurisdiction.[2585]

b. Analysis

775.   The Appeals Chamber recalls that there is a presumption that a trial chamber has evaluated all the evidence presented to it, as long as there is no indication that the trial chamber completely disregarded any particular piece of evidence.[2586] The Appeals Chamber also recalls that there may be an indication of disregard when evidence which is clearly relevant to the findings is not addressed in the Trial Chamber's reasoning.[2587]

776.   The Appeals Chamber is not convinced by Župljanin's contention that the Trial Chamber's findings in relation to Donji Vakuf contradict or limit its finding that he exercised *de jure* and *de facto* control over the SJBs of the ARK Municipalities, including Donji Vakuf SJB.[2588] As noted by Župljanin,[2589] the Trial Chamber found that "[o]n 13 June 1992, a military order of the 19th Partisan Division established a defence command for the town of Donji Vakuf."[2590] The Appeals Chamber is however not convinced that Exhibit 1D473 – which concerns the town of **[page 317]** Bosanski Brod and does not specifically mention the police[2591] – supports Župljanin's assertion that whenever a town command existed, the police fell directly and exclusively under the control of the military.[2592] The Appeals Chamber further observes that the Trial Chamber expressly considered, and therefore did not disregard, the order of 13 June 1992, which designated Boško Savković ("Savković") as Chief of the Donji Vakuf SJB and appointed Sufulo Šišić ("Šišić"), a military captain, as Commander of the Donji Vakuf SJB.[2593] The Appeals Chamber is also not convinced that Savković's appointment as Chief of the Donji Vakuf SJB by a military order, or the appointment of Šišić, a military captain, as Commander of the Donji Vakuf SJB is sufficient to show that no reasonable trier of fact could have found that Župljanin exercised *de jure* and *de facto* control over the Donji Vakuf SJB, even after 13 June 1992.[2594] In the Appeals Chamber's view, Župljanin merely points to evidence regarding the appointments of SJB officials to Donji Vakuf SJB, without demonstrating any error in the Trial Chamber's findings concerning Župljanin's authority over the police in the municipality. Accordingly, the Appeals Chamber finds that Župljanin has not shown that Trial Chamber's findings in relation to Donji Vakuf contradict or limit the finding that he exercised *de jure* and *de facto* control over the SJBs of the ARK Municipalities.

777.   Contrary to Župljanin's argument, the Trial Chamber expressly addressed and relied on Exhibit P1928 – a report on the work of the Donji Vakuf SJB between 1 April 1992 and 25 December 1992, dated January 1993 – in the section of the Trial Judgement dedicated to its findings in relation to Donji Vakuf municipality.[2595] The Appeals Chamber is equally unconvinced by Župljanin's reliance upon extracts of the testimonies of Witness Bjelošević and Witness Vidosav Kovačević ("Witness V. Kovačević"). The Appeals Chamber notes

---

[2585]   Prosecution Response Brief (Župljanin), para. 54.

[2586]   *Popović et al.* Appeal Judgement, para. 306; *Dorlevic* Appeal Judgement, fn. 2527; *Haradinaj et al.* Appeal Judgement, para. 129; *Kvočka et al.* Appeal Judgement, para. 23.

[2587]   *Popović et al.* Appeal Judgement, para. 306; *Đorđević* Appeal Judgement, para. 864; *Haradinaj et al.* Appeal Judgement, para. 129; *Kvočka et al.* Appeal Judgement, para. 23.

[2588]   See Trial Judgement, vol. 2, paras 493, 829. The Appeals Chamber notes in this respect the Trial Chamber's finding that "regular and reserve police in Donji Vakuf reported through the Banja Luka CSB, which was under the command of Stojan Župljanin, to the RS MUP under the control of Mićo Stanišić" (Trial Judgement, vol. 2, para. 829).

[2589]   Župljanin Appeal Brief, para. 77.

[2590]   Trial Judgement, vol. 1, para. 240 (internal references omitted).

[2591]   Exhibit 1D473.

[2592]   See Župljanin Appeal Brief, para. 77, referring to Exhibit 1D473.

[2593]   See Trial Judgement, vol. 1, para. 241. See also Trial Judgement, vol. 2, para. 829.

[2594]   The Appeals Chamber observes that the Trial Chamber's findings show that Savković was reporting to Župljanin after 13 June 1992. See Trial Judgement, vol. 2, para. 427.

[2595]   See in particular, Trial Judgement, vol. 1, para. 245, referring to Exhibit P1928. Župljanin selectively quotes this exhibit and points to extracts which do not establish that the police in the town of Donji Vakuf were continuously re-subordinated to a VRS town command (see Župljanin Appeal Brief, para. 78, referring to Exhibit P1928, pp 2, 4). Having reviewed Exhibit P1928, the Appeals Chamber notes that it evidences: (i) cooperation between the VRS and the police; (ii) joint check points established by the Donji Vakuf SJB and the military police; and (iii) the frequent participation of police in "war operations" (see Exhibit P1928).

that the portions of Witness Bjelošević's testimony on which Župljanin relies relate to a town command in Derventa, and thus are irrelevant to the issue of whether or not police in Donji Vakuf were under military control.[2596] The portions of Witness V. Kovačević's evidence on which Župljanin relies, meanwhile, only address the relationship between police units re-subordinated to the military, generally, without demonstrating that police in Donji Vakuf were in fact re-subordinated to the **[page 318]** military.[2597] Accordingly, Župljanin has failed to show that the Trial Chamber disregarded clearly relevant evidence. His arguments in this respect are dismissed.

778.   With respect to Župljanin's submissions concerning the municipality of Kotor Varoš, the Appeals Chamber considers that Župljanin has failed to demonstrate that the Trial Chamber was required to make findings, or failed to consider evidence of, re-subordination or the effect of town commands on his capacity to discipline members of the police. Having reviewed the only evidence Župljanin identifies to support his contention,[2598] the Appeals Chamber considers that it merely shows that a town command existed as of 25 June 1992, that the military units in Kotor Varoš were tasked with exercising control over the movement of population, and that the prisoners of war should be taken to the brigade command for interrogation before being sent to a prison camp.[2599] Župljanin does not explain or demonstrate how the existence of the town command impacted his ability to discipline the policemen of the Kotor Varoš SJB.

779.   Further, to the extent that Župljanin argues that the Banja Luka CSB SPD would not have been under his control because of the existence of a town command in Kotor Varoš, Župljanin has failed to substantiate his claim that the Banja Luka CSB SPD was re-subordinated to the VRS.[2600] The Appeals Chamber also recalls its finding that the Trial Chamber adequately addressed whether Župljanin had sufficient power or authority over the members of the Banja Luka CSB SPD to impose disciplinary sanctions irrespective of whether they were involved in combat operations with the army.[2601] The Appeals Chamber therefore finds that Župljanin has not shown that the Trial Chamber was required to further address the issue of re-subordination of the Banja Luka CSB SPD when deployed in Kotor Varoš or that the Trial Chamber erroneously relied on Župljanin's failure to investigate crimes committed by the Banja Luka CSB SPD there and to impose disciplinary sanctions against its members.[2602] **[page 319]**

780.   With respect to the municipality of Ključ, Župljanin has failed to show that no reasonable trier of fact could have found that he maintained *de facto* and *de jure* control over the Ključ SJB.[2603] Insofar as Župljanin relies on portions of Exhibits P1783 and P960.24 as evidence that the Trial Chamber allegedly failed to consider,[2604] the Appeals Chamber notes that the Trial Chamber expressly referred to the extracts of Exhibit P960.24 to which Župljanin refers.[2605] Župljanin merely presents an alternate interpretation of this evidence expressly considered by the Trial Chamber without showing an error. The Appeals Chamber further notes

---

[2596]   See Andrija Bjelošević, 15 Apr 2011, T. 19663-19664.

[2597]   See Vidosav Kovačević, 6 Sep 2011, T. 23684-23685; Vidosav Kovačević, 7 Sep 2011, T. 23766-23767.

[2598]   Župljanin points specifically to Exhibit 2D132, an excerpt of a meeting of the Kotor Varoš Crisis Staff held on 25 June 1992, which in his submission, shows that the town command was set upon on the basis of direct communication between the local VRS unit and the local crisis staff, and to Exhibit P1787, an order issued by the town commander in July 1992, prescribing a complete control over the movement of the population and that such evidence "was not contested by the Prosecution expert" (Župljanin Appeal Brief, para. 80, referring to Exhibit 2D132, Ewan Brown, 20 Jan 2011, T. 19058-19062, Exhibit P1787, p. 6).

[2599]   See Exhibits 2D132, P1787.

[2600]   See Župljanin Appeal Brief, para. 81.

[2601]   See *infra*, paras 827-836. The Appeals Chamber also notes the Trial Chamber's findings that, as the official exercising authority over the Banja Luka CSB SPD, Župljanin was kept informed of the crimes committed by its members, including in the municipality of Kotor Varoš (Trial Judgement, vol. 1, para. 435, referring to Predrag Radulović, 27 May 2010, T. 10911-10914. See Trial Judgement, vol. 2, para. 374) and that he acted with such authority when in turn informing the RS MUP of these crimes (Trial Judgement, vol. 2, para. 425).

[2602]   Trial Judgement, vol. 2, para. 505.

[2603]   See Trial Judgement, vol. 2, para. 493. See also Trial Judgement, vol. 2, para. 842.

[2604]   See *supra*, fn. 2571.

[2605]   Trial Judgement, vol. 2, para. 426. Specifically, the Trial Chamber found that, in July 1992, the Chief of the Ključ SJB, Vinko Kondić ("Kondić"), reported to the Banja Luka CSB that "police in cooperation with the army had processed 2,000 people and sent to detention camps 1,278 persons suspected of having been involved in armed rebellion, in the 'so called Muslim TO', or in smuggling of weapons, but also people who owned weapons without a permit, even though they were not members of any armed formation" (Trial Judgement, vol. 2, para. 426). The Trial Chamber further found that Kondić reported that "during this process, 'things happened that are not in the nature and are against the moral code of the Serbian people'" (Trial Judgement, vol. 2, para. 426). The Trial Chamber also refereed to Exhibit P960.24 in finding that "[o]n 27 March 1992, on the occasion of the adoption of the

that while the Trial Chamber did not refer to Exhibit P1783, this document only evidences the membership of the Chief of the Ključ SJB in – and the establishment of – a town command in Kotor Varoš, along with military officials and others.[2606] Thus, Exhibit P1783 was not clearly relevant to the Trial Chamber's findings regarding Župljanin's *de jure* and *de facto* control over the police, including in the municipality of Ključ.

781. Further, and contrary to Župljanin's submission,[2607] the evidence that he points to, does not show that the Trial Chamber simply relied upon "the default peacetime statutory framework" to conclude that he had the authority to discipline police from the Ključ SJB.[2608] In fact, the Trial Chamber addressed the issue of cooperation between the police and the military in finding that "the evidence shows that the ARK Crisis Staff, municipal Crisis Staffs, and the Banja Luka CSB were cooperating closely in matters such as the takeover of the ARK Municipalities by Serb Forces, the imprisonment of non-Serbs, and their resettlement in other areas of BiH or in other countries".[2609] The Appeals Chamber notes that the evidence on which Župljanin relies is not inconsistent with these findings.[2610] In the Appeals Chamber's view, Župljanin merely presents a different interpretation of the evidence on the record, without demonstrating that the Trial Chamber disregarded clearly relevant evidence.[2611] **[page 320]**

782. Finally, insofar as Župljanin argues that the Trial Chamber itself acknowledged an abundance of evidence suggesting the reasonable possibility that some, if not many, of the crimes were committed by soldiers, with or without the involvement of policemen,[2612] the Appeals Chamber considers that he again misunderstands the law of joint criminal enterprise liability. Župljanin fails to appreciate that under joint criminal enterprise liability, he can be held responsible for those crimes forming part of the common criminal purpose, so long as they are linked either to him or another JCE member.[2613] In addition, there is no indication in the relevant findings of the Trial Chamber[2614] that, in assessing Župljanin's intent and contribution, the Trial Chamber considered that he failed to discipline soldiers over whom he did not have authority.

783. The Appeals Chamber also fails to see how the fact that crimes were committed by soldiers with or without the involvement of the police would indicate that the police were re-subordinated to the military. Even if considered in combination with the collaboration of the police and the military, as well as the existence of a town command, Župljanin does not demonstrate how the commission of crimes by soldiers suggests that the police were substantially or continuously re-subordinated to the military. Accordingly, the Appeals Chamber is not convinced that soldiers' involvement in the commission of crimes renders the Trial Chamber's findings regarding Župljanin's *de jure* and *de facto* control over the police in the municipality of Ključ unsafe. Likewise the Appeals Chamber is not persuaded that Župljanin has shown that the Trial Chamber was required to further address the contours of the re-subordination of the police in relation to the existence of a town command in Ključ.

784. In conclusion, the Appeals Chamber finds that Župljanin has failed to demonstrate that the Trial Chamber erred by failing to make findings on the issue of re-subordination of policemen to the military or by failing to consider evidence relating to military commands set up in the municipalities of Donji Vakuf, Kotor Varoš, and Ključ. His arguments in this respect are therefore dismissed.

Constitution by the BSA, the Banja Luka CSB was assigned the territory of the ARK as its area of responsibility" (Trial Judgement, vol. 2, para. 351, referring to, *inter alia*, Exhibit P960.24, pp 3-4).

[2606]   Exhibit P1783, p. 1.
[2607]   See *supra*, para. 770.
[2608]   Župljanin Appeal Brief, para. 85.
[2609]   Trial Judgement, vol. 2, para. 493.
[2610]   See Exhibits P1783, p. 1, P960.24, pp 3-4, 8.
[2611]   *Cf. supra*, para. 536.
[2612]   See Župljanin Appeal Brief, para. 85.
[2613]   *Šainović et al.* Appeal Judgement, para. 1520, referring to *Krajišnik* Appeal Judgement, para. 225, *Martić* Appeal Judgement, para. 168, *Brđanin* Appeal Judgement, para. 413. See *Tolimir* Appeal Judgement, para. 432; *Popović et al.* Appeal Judgement, para. 1065. See also *supra*, para. 119.
[2614]   See *supra*, paras 747-760.

ii. Re-subordination of police forces serving in the military-run Manjača and Trnopolje detention camps

785. In assessing Župljanin's participation in the JCE, the Trial Chamber found that, *inter alia*, Župljanin "was aware that thousands of non-Serbs were detained under harsh conditions at the **[page 321]** Manjača camp, a military detention facility in the municipality of Banja Luka, where the police transported prisoners previously detained in police-run detention facilities in other ARK municipalities".[2615] The Trial Chamber also found that "Predrag Radulović informed Župljanin on more than one occasion that Serb Forces in Prijedor razed villages, destroyed mosques, and arrested large numbers of non-Serbs, including women, children, and the elderly, and detained them at Omarska, Keraterm, and Trnopolje."[2616] It further noted that on 5 August 1992, international media began to report about detainees being held at Omarska and Trnopolje detention facilities in inhumane conditions and subjected to physical abuse.[2617] Based on these findings and other evidence of Župljanin's knowledge of crimes committed against non-Serbs and of their unlawful detention in particular,[2618] the Trial Chamber found that Župljanin's failures to take adequate measures to stop the mass arrest of non-Serbs and the involvement of policemen therein, regardless of his knowledge of crimes against non-Serbs, and in particular, of their unlawful detention, constituted at least a significant contribution to the unlawful arrests, if not a substantial one.[2619]

a. Submissions of the parties

786. Župljanin submits that the Trial Chamber failed to make findings as to whether the police forces serving in the Manjača and Trnopolje detention facilities were re-subordinated to the military.[2620] To this end, he argues that: (i) the commander of the Trnopolje detention camp was the TO commander of Prijedor;[2621] (ii) the guards in the Trnopolje detention camp were dressed in military uniforms as opposed to police uniforms;[2622] (iii) the Manjača detention camp was a VRS **[page 322]** facility and was commanded by a VRS commander;[2623] and (iv) policemen were apparently present at both facilities from time to time.[2624] According to Župljanin, the Trial Chamber imputed "failures" to him in respect of crimes committed at both Manjača and Trnopolje detention facilities, "without conducting any inquiry at all as to whether policemen, in any role, were re-subordinated to the military in the course of their activities there".[2625]

[2615]   Trial Judgement, vol. 2, para. 506. In this respect, the Trial Chamber found, specifically, that: (i) on 2 July 1992, Župljanin was informed that the Sanski Most SJB had transported 250 Croats and Muslims to Manjača (Trial Judgement, vol. 2, paras 418, 506); (ii) at the end of July or the beginning of August 1992, Župljanin visited the Manjača detention facility "including the stables where the prisoners were held" (Trial Judgement, vol. 2, para. 417. See Trial Judgement, vol. 2, para. 506); (iii) on 5 August 1992, Drljača requested Župljanin to ensure safe passage for a convoy of 1,466 detainees scheduled to travel from Prijedor to Manjača on 6 August 1992 (Trial Judgement, vol. 2, paras 465, 506); and (iv) Župljanin knew of the death of approximately 20 non-Serb detainees, who suffocated whilst being transported in a truck between Sanski Most and the Manjača detention facility by Sanski Most police (Trial Judgement, vol. 2, paras 419, 506). The Trial Chamber also found that Župljanin knew that on 29 August 1992, the Ključ SJB had sent all of the persons detained in that municipality to the Manjača detention facility (Trial Judgement, vol. 2, paras 426, 509).

[2616]   Trial Judgement, vol. 2, para. 508. See Trial Judgement, vol. 2, para. 420.

[2617]   See Trial Judgement, vol. 2, para. 509. See also Trial Judgement, vol. 2, para. 444.

[2618]   See Trial Judgement, vol. 2, paras 506-510. See also Trial Judgement, vol. 2, paras 415-440, 499, 503-504, 511-519.

[2619]   Trial Judgement, vol. 2, para. 510. With respect to Župljanin's failure to discipline his subordinates, see Trial Judgement, vol. 2, para. 518.

[2620]   See Župljanin Appeal Brief, paras 88-89.

[2621]   Župljanin Appeal Brief, para. 88, referring to Trial Judgement, vol. 2, para. 638, Witness ST249, 26 Nov 2010, T. 17859-17860, Witness ST24, 18 Oct 2010, T. 16140. See Župljanin Reply Brief, para. 37.

[2622]   Župljanin Appeal Brief, para. 88, referring to Trial Judgement, vol. 1, para. 619, Witness ST249, 26 Nov 2010, T. 17859-17860, Witness ST67, 9 Dec 2010, T. 18404, Exhibit P671.

[2623]   Župljanin Appeal Brief, para. 88, referring to Trial Judgement, vol. 2, paras 337, 506, 802, *Prosecutor v. Mićo Stanišić and Stojan Župljanin*, Case No. IT-08-91-T, Prosecution's Final Trial Brief, 14 May 2012 (confidential with confidential annexes) ("Prosecution Final Trial Brief"), paras 136-137. See Župljanin Reply Brief, para. 37.

[2624]   Župljanin Appeal Brief, para. 88, referring to Trial Judgement, vol. 1, para. 172.

[2625]   Župljanin Appeal Brief, para. 89, referring to Trial Judgement, vol. 2, paras 465, 524. According to Župljanin this "presumption of plenary authority, and the corollary attribution of omissions contributing to the JCE, was based on a failure to make adequate findings" (Župljanin Appeal Brief, para. 89). See also Župljanin Reply Brief, paras 38-39.

787. The Prosecution responds that Župljanin misunderstands the Trial Chamber's findings.[2626] It contends that the Trial Chamber limited its analysis of Župljanin's intent and contribution to the JCE to the "'external' involvement" of the police in operations in the two detention camps, and that the evidence does not indicate a re-subordination of the police forces for these purposes.[2627] The Prosecution argues, specifically, that: (i) Župljanin fails to show any error in the Trial Chamber's findings on the role of the police in the Manjača detention camp or in its analysis of Župljanin's intent and contributions to the JCE based on its authority over the Banja Luka and other SJBs which supported the camp;[2628] (ii) the Trial Chamber reasonably found that Župljanin knew of the detention of thousands of non-Serbs under harsh conditions;[2629] and (iii) all of the factors taken into account by the Trial Chamber are consistent with its conclusion on his position of authority over the police forces transporting detainees to and from the camp.[2630] The Prosecution further argues that the conduct of the police at Trnopolje detention camp indicates that they were independent from the military.[2631]

b. Analysis

788. The Appeals Chamber observes that although the Trial Chamber relied on Župljanin's knowledge of the conditions of detention in the Manjača and Trnopolje detention facilities when assessing his contribution to the JCE and his intent,[2632] it did not rely on failures to discipline police forces serving in the Manjača and Trnopolje detention facilities, which were under the authority of **[page 323]** the military.[2633] In this regard, the Appeals Chamber recalls that in its assessment of his contribution and intent, the Trial Chamber relied upon Župljanin's failures to "discipline his subordinates",[2634] and that its conclusions on these failures were based on specific findings, including that he failed to take adequate measures to stop policemen's involvement in the unlawful arrest of non-Serbs.[2635] Therefore, the Appeals Chamber is of the view, that the Trial Chamber found that despite his knowledge of unlawful detention and in particular of the conditions in the Manjača and Trnopolje detention facilities, Župljanin failed to take adequate measures to stop policemen's involvement in the unlawful *arrest* of non-Serbs.[2636] This finding, in the view of the Appeals Chamber, clearly excludes that the Trial Chamber relied upon Župljanin's failure to discipline police forces serving in the Manjača and Trnopolje detention facilities. Accordingly, the issue of whether police serving at the Manjača and Trnopolje detention facilities were re-subordinated was irrelevant to the Trial Chamber's assessment of Župljanin's participation in the JCE.[2637]

789. In light of the above, the Appeals Chamber dismisses Župljanin's arguments with respect to the Trial Chamber's alleged failures to make findings on whether the police serving at the Manjača and Trnopolje detention facilities were re-subordinated to the military.

[2626]   Prosecution Response Brief (Župljanin), para. 55, referring to Župljanin Appeal Brief, para. 89.
[2627]   Prosecution Response Brief (Župljanin), para. 55.
[2628]   Prosecution Response Brief (Župljanin), para. 56, referring to Trial Judgement, vol. 1, paras 171-173, 191-193, 202, 204-206, 215-220, 223.
[2629]   Prosecution Response Brief (Župljanin), para. 57, referring to Trial Judgement, vol. 2, paras 417, 506.
[2630]   Prosecution Response Brief (Župljanin), para. 58, referring to Trial Judgement, vol. 1, paras 174-176, 223, 633, Trial Judgement, vol. 2, paras 418-419, 426-427, 447-448, 465, 487, 493, 506, 509, 511, 514, 516, 524.
[2631]   Prosecution Response Brief (Župljanin), paras 59-60, referring to Trial Judgement, vol. 1, paras 619, 622, 625-630, 680-684, Trial Judgement, vol. 2, paras 447, 791.
[2632]   See *supra*, para. 785.
[2633]   See Trial Judgement, vol. 2, paras 802 ("the Trial Chamber recalls that the [Manjača] camp was under the authority of the 1st KK, with Božidar Popović acting as the camp warden"), 856 ("[t]he Chamber further recalls that the Trnopolje camp was under the charge of the TO and guarded by Serb soldiers and that the camp commander was Slobodan Kurzunović"). See also Trial Judgement, vol. 1, paras 171-172, 619.
[2634]   See *supra*, para. 754. See also Trial Judgement, vol. 2, paras 518, 519.
[2635]   See *supra*, para. 754. See also Trial Judgement, vol. 2, paras 510, 518.
[2636]   Trial Judgement, vol. 2, para. 510 (emphasis added). See Trial Judgement, vol. 2, paras 518-519.
[2637]   The Appeals Chamber also recalls its finding that the issue of re-subordination of policemen to the military is irrelevant to the Trial Chamber's conclusion that Župljanin failed launch criminal investigations, including for crimes committed by policemen and for the Trial Chamber's finding that Župljanin failed to ensure that police under his authority duly investigated crimes committed against non-Serbs (see *supra*, fn. 2521).

iii. Župljanin's authority over the Prijedor SJB

790.   In assessing Župljanin's participation in the JCE, the Trial Chamber found that Župljanin exercised *de jure* and *de facto* control over the SJBs in the ARK (*i.e.* including the Prijedor SJB).[2638] In reaching this finding, the Trial Chamber considered, *inter alia*, that: (i) the Prijedor SJB, despite implementing some instructions of municipal crisis staffs, "kept the Banja Luka CSB informed of events in the municipality and requested its assistance in a number of matters";[2639] and (ii) a "relationship based on cooperation" existed between the War Presidency of the Prijedor **[page 324]** Municipal Assembly ("Prijedor War Presidency"), Drljača (the Chief of the Prijedor SJB), and Župljanin, "in which Župljanin played a leadership role".[2640]

791.   With respect to the Keraterm and Omarska detention facilities in particular, the Trial Chamber found that: (i) Župljanin was informed by Witness Radulović and Witness Sajinović, at some point in June 1992, "of the horrible conditions in which prisoners were held and the abuses perpetrated against them" in these camps, "including by members of the police" to which he "responded dismissively [...] and left hurriedly";[2641] (ii) on 16 July 1992, Župljanin visited Omarska detention facility with other ARK leaders "where detainees showed signs of mistreatment and were forced to give the delegation the three finger salute" while members of the delegation laughed at the scene;[2642] (iii) Župljanin was informed on more than one occasion that Serb Forces in Prijedor razed villages, destroyed mosques, and arrested a large number of non-Serbs and detained them at detention facilities in Omarska, Keraterm, and Trnopolje;[2643] and (iv) international media began reporting about detainees in the Omarska and Trnopolje detention facilities who were held in inhumane conditions and subjected to physical abuse, by 5 August 1992.[2644] The Trial Chamber further considered that "Župljanin never attempted to remove Simo Drljača from Prijedor, notwithstanding Župljanin's knowledge of the atrocities committed in the detention camps and Radulović's warning about Drljača", while Župljanin successfully took action "to arrest members of **[page 325]** the powerful Mićo Group", and "successfully prevented an attempt by paramilitary forces to kill between 300 and 600 Muslims and Roma between Doboj and Banja Luka in mid-May 1992".[2645]

[2638]   Trial Judgement, vol. 2, para. 493. See Trial Judgement, vol. 2, para. 856 ("Stojan Župljanin was the highest police authority in the ARK, and the police in Prijedor and Skender Vakuf were under the RS MUP, which was under the overall control of Mićo Stanišić").
[2639]   Trial Judgement, vol. 2, para. 491. See Trial Judgement, vol. 2, paras 359-362.
[2640]   Trial Judgement, vol. 2, para. 492. See Trial Judgement, vol. 2, para. 360. See also *e.g.* Trial Judgement, vol. 2, paras 422-423, 475-476, 479-480. The Appeals Chamber further notes that, in assessing Župljanin's participation in the JCE, the Trial Chamber also found in relation to the municipality of Prijedor that: (i) Župljanin dispatched platoons of the Banja Luka CSB SPD to the municipality during the summer of 1992, upon the request of municipal authorities (Trial Judgement, vol. 2, para. 502. See Trial Judgement, vol. 2, para. 405); (ii) on 5 August 1992, Drljača requested Župljanin to ensure safe passage for a convoy of approximately 1,466 prisoners from Prijedor to Manjača (Trial Judgement, vol. 2, paras 506, 516. See Trial Judgement, vol. 2, para. 465), and that Župljanin obliged on 6 August 1992 (Trial Judgement, vol. 2, para. 511. See Trial Judgement, vol. 2, para. 465); (iii) on 29 September 1992, Župljanin, notwithstanding his knowledge of the Prijedor police's involvement in the murder of non-Serbs, ordered the Prijedor police to escort buses transporting more than 1,500 persons from Trnopolje detention facility, in Prijedor municipality, to Croatia (Trial Judgement, vol. 2, para. 511. See Trial Judgement, vol. 2, para. 478); and (iv) Župljanin withheld information from the public prosecutor about the involvement of Prijedor police in the murder of about 150-200 Muslims at Korićanske Stijene (Trial Judgement, vol. 2, para. 517. See Trial Judgement, vol. 2, paras 466-482).
[2641]   Trial Judgement, vol. 2, para. 508. See Trial Judgement, vol. 2, para. 423.
[2642]   Trial Judgement, vol. 2, para. 508. See Trial Judgement, vol. 2, para. 424, referring to Exhibit P2096, pp 7436-7437, Predrag Radulović, 27 May 2010, T. 10879-10881, Nusret Sivac, 16 Aug 2010, T. 13196-13200, Simo Misković, 4 Oct 2010, T. 15247-15250, Exhibit P1378. The Appeals Chamber notes that, at paragraph 508 of volume two of the Trial Judgement, the Trial Chamber refers to this visit as having occurred on 17 July 1992. In light of the Trial Chamber's finding at paragraph 424 of volume two of the Trial Judgement that this visit occurred on 16 July 1992, and considering the evidence relied upon thereat, the Trial Chamber considers that the subsequent reference to 17 July 1992 is merely a typographical error (see *e.g.* Exhibit P1378, being a newspaper article referring to the visit, which was published on 17 July 1992. See also Predrag Radulović, 27 May 2010, T. 10880-10881).
[2643]   Trial Judgement, vol. 2, para. 508. See Trial Judgement, vol. 2, para. 423.
[2644]   Trial Judgement, vol. 2, para. 509. See Trial Judgement, vol. 2, para. 444. The Trial Chamber also found that the report of the commission that Župljanin established to investigate the conditions of detention facilities, "was simply a collage of previously drafted reports on Omarska, Keraterm, and Trnopolje" (Trial Judgement, vol. 2, para. 514. See Trial Judgement, vol. 2, paras 446-447).
[2645]   Trial Judgement, vol. 2, para. 515. See Trial Judgement, vol. 2, para. 453-456.

a. Submissions of the parties

792.   Župljanin submits that the Trial Chamber failed to address whether, or to what extent, he exercised authority over the Prijedor SJB, including over the Keraterm and Omarska detention camps.[2646] Župljanin submits further that when inferring his intent and contribution to the JCE, the Trial Chamber erred in relying upon his "failure to intercede to prevent mistreatment" of non-Serb detainees in Prijedor municipality.[2647]

793.   Specifically, he argues that the Trial Chamber's conclusions about the Keraterm and Omarska detention facilities being run by Serb policemen or operated jointly by the Bosnian Serb police and military personnel fall short of finding that the camps were not within the jurisdiction of the VRS and that the police there were not re-subordinated to the VRS.[2648] In this regard, he argues that there were indicia that the two detention camps were under VRS jurisdiction, namely that: (i) in the Manjača detention camp, the police on duty were considered to be re-subordinated to the military;[2649] (ii) in August 1992, Mladić, the commander of the VRS issued an order allowing journalists to visit the Omarska detention camp;[2650] (iii) the Trnopolje and Manjača detention camps were military facilities subject to military jurisdiction;[2651] and (iv) the stated purpose of the Keraterm and Omarska detention camps, to detain persons captured during combat, is relevant to military functions and is not a police-related activity.[2652] Župljanin submits that no reasonable trier of fact could have rejected evidence showing that the camps were under VRS jurisdiction and that the police serving there were re-subordinated.[2653] He adds that the Appeals Chamber is not required **[page 326]** to analyse whether that was the case since the Trial Chamber made no findings on the issue, but instead simply assumed that the camps were subject to police jurisdiction.[2654]

794.   Župljanin also argues that, even assuming that the police serving at the Keraterm and Omarska detention camps were not re-subordinated to the military, the Trial Chamber erred by failing to determine when he was "sufficiently informed" of abuses being committed against detainees.[2655] He points in this respect to the absence of findings as to whether: (i) he was informed of killings and beatings during his visit to the Omarska detention facility on 16 July 1992, or that he refrained from punishing the perpetrators of those killings;[2656] and (ii) Drljača reported any mistreatment of detainees to Župljanin.[2657]

[2646]   Župljanin Appeal Brief, paras 90-94. He refers to the Trial Chamber's findings that: (i) Keraterm and Omarska detention camps were set up by Drljača, acting on orders of the Prijedor Crisis Staff (Župljanin Appeal Brief, para. 91, referring to Trial Judgement, vol. 1, paras 563-564, Exhibit 2D90, p. 1, Adjudicated Fact Decision, Adjudicated Fact 378); (ii) at Omarska detention camp a large number of military men were security guards (Župljanin Appeal Brief, para. 91, referring to Trial Judgement, vol. 1, para. 593); (iii) the Keraterm detention camp was to be "'under the supervision of employees of the Prijedor Public Security Section and the Prijedor Military Police'" (Župljanin Appeal Brief, para. 91, referring to Exhibit 2D90, p. 28); (iv) both civilian and military personnel conducted the interrogations at the two detention camps (Župljanin Appeal Brief, para. 91); and (v) the worst incident of mistreatment at the Keraterm detention camp was "'committed by Bosnian Serb army personnel'" (Župljanin Appeal Brief, para. 91, referring to Trial Judgement, vol. 1, paras 589, 668).

[2647]   The Appeals Chamber notes that Župljanin also challenges the Trial Chamber's findings that the detentions were unlawful by cross-referencing to his arguments under sub-ground 1(G) of his appeal (Župljanin Appeal Brief, para. 90).

[2648]   Župljanin Appeal Brief, para. 92, referring to Trial Judgement, vol. 1, paras 678-679. See Župljanin Reply Brief, para. 44.

[2649]   Župljanin Appeal Brief, para. 93, referring to Trial Judgement, vol. 2, para. 337.

[2650]   Župljanin Appeal Brief, para. 93, referring to Exhibit P1683.

[2651]   Župljanin Appeal Brief, para. 93.

[2652]   Župljanin Appeal Brief, para. 93. See Župljanin Appeal Brief, para. 91, referring to Exhibits P1560, 2D90, p. 28.

[2653]   Župljanin Appeal Brief, para. 94. See Župljanin Appeal Brief, para. 93.

[2654]   Župljanin Appeal Brief, para. 94. In this respect, Župljanin notes that the Trial Chamber's finding that the Keraterm and Omarska detention facilities were run to some degree by policemen (see Župljanin Appeal Brief, para. 94). He contends that the Trial Chamber simply assumed that these detention facilities were under police jurisdiction, arguing that they could have been run to some degree by some policemen and yet remain subject to military jurisdiction (see Župljanin Appeal Brief, para. 94).

[2655]   Župljanin Appeal Brief, para. 95. See Župljanin Appeal Brief, para. 96.

[2656]   Župljanin Appeal Brief, para. 96, referring to Exhibit P1560. According to Župljanin, the Trial Chamber found instead "that [Ž]upljanin was informed orally '[a]t some point in summer 1992' of bad conditions at the camps and abuse of prisoners" (Župljanin Appeal Brief, para. 96, referring to Trial Judgement, vol. [2], paras 423, 508 (the Appeals Chamber understands that Župljanin erroneously refers to volume one of the Trial Judgement and intends to refer to volume two, instead)).

[2657]   Župljanin Appeal Brief, para. 96. He also contends that the Trial Chamber did not hear any evidence in this respect, and that "[n]o such information was included in Drljača's Work Report of the Prijedor SJB for the first half of 1992" (Župljanin Appeal Brief, para. 96, referring to Exhibit P657).

795. Župljanin further contends that the Trial Chamber erred by "unreasonably" finding that he had effective control over the Prijedor SJB and its commander Drljača.[2658] In this respect, he points to: (i) the Trial Chamber's acknowledgement that Drljača "operated with a certain degree of independence" and provided security in the detention camps, following orders from the Prijedor Crisis Staff;[2659] (ii) Exhibit P621, an October 1992 report from the Banja Luka CSB in which Župljanin "protested" the "functional 'detachment' of a number of SJBs" from his authority;[2660] and (iii) Exhibit 2D25, which demonstrates that in July 1992, he "directly upbraid[ed] the SJB chiefs for their 'benevolent attitude towards escalating criminal activities of some individuals and groups'".[2661] Župljanin contends that the Trial Chamber erred in relying upon his failure to remove **[page 327]** Drljača as "indicative of commission of forcible transfer through a JCE", despite Župljanin having no *de jure* authority to do so.[2662] He asserts that the basis for this finding was the fact that he had previously ordered the police to arrest members a paramilitary group committing crimes in Teslić.[2663] He also submits that no reasonable trier of fact could have relied upon the suggestion that he "was legally obliged to disregard the legal limitations on his power [...] against the will of local political leaders" in order to infer his effective control over Drljača.[2664]

796. Finally, Župljanin also contends that the Trial Chamber erred in finding that he was responsible "for the crimes in Omarska and Keraterm detention facilities because he failed to order the police to disregard the orders of the local crisis staffs, and because he was himself a member of the regional crisis staff, which ostensibly had some authority over the local crisis staffs".[2665]

797. The Prosecution responds that Župljanin fails to show any error in the Trial Chamber's reasoning concerning his control over the Prijedor SJB and that he repeats arguments made at trial which were rejected by the Trial Chamber.[2666]

798. The Prosecution submits that Župljanin fails to show any error and instead misrepresents or misinterprets the Trial Chamber's findings in relation to the Prijedor SJB's authority over the Keraterm and Omarska detention camps.[2667] It argues that the Trial Chamber made clear findings establishing the police authority over the Omarska and Keraterm detention camps, namely that: (i) the two detention camps were commanded by police officers;[2668] (ii) the army refused to take over responsibilities with regard to, *inter alia*,

---

[2658] Župljanin Appeal Brief, para. 95. See Župljanin Appeal Brief, paras 96-101.

[2659] Župljanin Appeal Brief, para. 97, quoting Trial Judgement, vol. 2, para. 359. According to Župljanin, the Trial Chamber recognised that Drljača "set up two prison camps on the authority of local crisis staff; ordered that the camps be kept secret; and openly obstructed or declined to follow [Župljanin's] orders" (Župljanin Appeal Brief para. 97). In this respect, Župljanin contends that the Trial Chamber made findings concerning Drljača's "political ambitions" and that Drljača obstructed his efforts to investigate the Korićanske Stijene killings (Župljanin Appeal Brief, fn. 137, referring to Trial Judgement, vol. 2, paras 358, 360).

[2660] Župljanin Appeal Brief, para. 98, referring to Exhibit P621, p. 43. See Župljanin Appeal Brief, para. 99, referring to Exhibit 2D25, pp 2-3.

[2661] Župljanin Appeal Brief, para. 99, quoting Exhibit 2D25, pp 2-3. Župljanin also contends that he complained of the unprofessional attitude of some SJB chiefs who were seeking to "deal with issues beyond the scope of their jobs" and seeking approval for certain actions from political organs (Župljanin Appeal Brief, para. 99, referring to Exhibit 2D25, pp 2-3).

[2662] Župljanin Appeal Brief, para. 100 (citations omitted).

[2663] Župljanin Appeal Brief, para. 100, referring to Trial Judgement, vol. 2, para. 515. See Župljanin Reply Brief, para. 43. He argues further in this respect, that "[m]ilitary superiority of Group A over Group B does not imply effective control by Group A over Group B" (Župljanin Appeal Brief, para. 100).

[2664] Župljanin Appeal Brief, para. 100.

[2665] Župljanin Appeal Brief, para. 101. According to Župljanin, the Trial Chamber: (i) made no "sufficient findings" on the hierarchy between the ARK Crisis Staff and the local crisis staffs; and (ii) had to acknowledge that he ordered the police to disregard the local crisis staffs instructions as of July 1992, which he contends was not untimely or delayed in order to facilitate the commission of crimes on the instructions of local authorities (Župljanin Appeal Brief, para. 101, referring to Trial Judgement, vol. 2, para. 367).

[2666] Prosecution Response Brief (Župljanin), para. 62, comparing Župljanin Appeal Brief, para. 90 with Župljanin Final Trial Brief, paras 157-163, 269-270, 297-313.

[2667] Prosecution Response Brief (Župljanin), para. 68. It points, specifically, to the Trial Chamber's findings that: (i) both detention camps were established by Župljanin's subordinate, Drljača (Prosecution Response Brief (Župljanin), para. 69, referring to Trial Judgement, vol. 1, paras 580, 593, Trial Judgement, vol. 2, para. 856, Župljanin Appeal Brief, para. 91); (ii) Serb forces arrested Muslims and Croats in Prijedor without legitimate grounds and on discriminatory basis, and then unlawfully held them in inhumane living conditions (Prosecution Response Brief (Župljanin), para. 69, referring to Trial Judgement, vol. 1, para. 700); and (iii) "even though Drljača's order to set up the Omarska detention camp was issued 'in accordance with the Decision from the [Prijedor] Crisis Staff'", he required that its implementation be done "'in collaboration with the Banja Luka [CSB]'" (Prosecution Response Brief (Župljanin), para. 69, referring to Exhibit P1560, p. 3).

[2668] Prosecution Response Brief (Župljanin), para. 70, referring to Trial Judgement, vol. 1, para. 580.

security tasks at the Keraterm detention camp;[2669] (iii) civilian and military investigators played a role in the operation of the Omarska detention **[page 328]** camp;[2670] and (iv) the army refused to assume responsibility over Omarska when asked to do so.[2671] The Prosecution further submits that there is no requirement for the Trial Chamber to "disprove hypothetical and speculative claims",[2672] and that given the evidence that the Keraterm and Omarska detention camps were police facilities, there was no need for the Trial Chamber to find that they were not military facilities.[2673] The Prosecution contends that Župljanin misrepresents the Trial Chamber's analysis of his conduct and the crimes committed in Prijedor, since "[h]e did not merely fail 'to order the police to disregard the orders of local crisis staffs' or fail 'to intercede to prevent mistreatment'" but "took positive action to shield perpetrators from investigation or punishment" and had ample knowledge of the crimes committed in the Prijedor camps.[2674]

799. The Prosecution also submits that the Trial Chamber reasonably relied on Župljanin's failure to remove Drljača despite knowing of his criminal conduct.[2675] It contends that Župljanin fails to show that the Trial Chamber erred in failing to consider evidence since the evidence was considered by the Trial Chamber and does not undermine the finding that he exercised authority over Drljača.[2676] Likewise, the Trial Chamber expressly considered that "'decisions of the ARK Crisis Staff were binding for all municipal Crisis Staffs in the region'".[2677] Further, the Prosecution argues that Župljanin fails to show an error in the Trial Chamber's reasoning regarding his ability to take action as a police officer,[2678] referring in particular to Župljanin's "decisive action" against the **[page 329]** Miće Group.[2679] Finally, the Prosecution argues that extensive evidence pertaining to the close working relationship between Župljanin and Drljača confirms the Trial Chamber's finding that the former exercised authority over the latter.[2680]

800. In reply, Župljanin argues that the findings referred to by the Prosecution in relation to his authority over Drljača only show "anecdotal cooperation" between the two and do not amount to a degree of control

---

[2669] Prosecution Response Brief (Župljanin), para. 70.

[2670] Prosecution Response Brief (Župljanin), para. 70, referring to Trial Judgement, vol. 1, para. 580.

[2671] Prosecution Response Brief (Župljanin), para. 70, referring to, *inter alia*, Trial Judgement, vol. 1, para. 593.

[2672] Prosecution Response Brief (Župljanin), para. 71.

[2673] Prosecution Response Brief (Župljanin), para. 71. The Prosecution further argues that "Župljanin's claim that the Trial Chamber's findings 'fall short of finding that Omarska and Keraterm did not fall within the VRS's jurisdiction' is untenable" given the evidence contradicting the examples pointed out by Župljanin (Prosecution Response Brief (Župljanin), para. 71, referring to Župljanin Appeal Brief, paras 92-94). In this respect, the Prosecution contends that: (i) Omarska and Keraterm differed from Manjača and Trnopolje in their command and in the circumstances of their establishment and therefore there is no inconsistency in treating Omarska and Keraterm differently from Manjača and Trnopolje; (ii) the order issued by Mladić does not imply a military jurisdiction over the detention camps; and (iii) the Trial Chamber found that the two camps were used for the unlawful and discriminatory detention of non-Serbs and not for an activity "'directly relevant to the core functions of the military'" (Prosecution Response Brief (Župljanin), para. 71).

[2674] Prosecution Response Brief (Župljanin), para. 72, referring to Župljanin Appeal Brief, paras 90, 101, Trial Judgement, vol. 2, paras 514-515, 517-518. The Prosecution submits that these actions included maintaining Drljača in his position as Chief of the Prijedor SJB, issuing non-assertive orders to SJBs to comply with the law, establishing a fake commission to investigate detention facilities in the ARK, and obstructing investigation into the Korićanske Stijene killings (Prosecution Response Brief (Župljanin), para. 72, referring to Trial Judgement, vol. 2, paras 514-515). The Prosecution also points to the Trial Chamber's finding that Župljanin had "ample knowledge of the crimes committed in Prijedor camps" (Prosecution Response Brief (Župljanin), para. 72, referring to Trial Judgement, vol. 2, para. 506).

[2675] Prosecution Response Brief (Župljanin), para. 63. It argues that the Trial Chamber's finding that "Drljača 'operated with a certain degree of independence' does not show that Župljanin lacked authority to remove him" and that the Trial Chamber specifically found that "'there was a relationship based on cooperation'" between Župljanin, Drljača, and the Prijedor War Presidency in which Župljanin played a leading role (Prosecution Response Brief (Župljanin), para. 63, referring to Trial Judgement, vol. 2, paras 360, 364-367, 492, 791. Župljanin Appeal Brief, para. 97).

[2676] Prosecution Response Brief (Župljanin), para. 64.

[2677] Prosecution Response Brief (Župljanin), para. 64, referring to Trial Judgement, vol. 2, paras 357-358, 364.

[2678] Prosecution Response Brief (Župljanin), para. 65, referring to Župljanin Appeal Brief, para. 100. See Prosecution Response Brief (Župljanin), para. 66, referring to Trial Judgement, vol. 2, para. 515.

[2679] Prosecution Response Brief (Župljanin), para. 65, referring to Trial Judgement, vol. 2, para. 515. See Župljanin Reply Brief, para. 43.

[2680] Prosecution Response Brief (Župljanin), para. 67, referring to Trial Judgement, vol. 1, paras 505, 509, 511-513, 521, 527, 564, 580-582, 592-593, 595-597, 615, 623, 636, 649, Trial Judgement, vol. 2, paras 79, 422, 447, 478, 491, 676, Exhibits P1902, P652, P656, P1005, P659, P668, P669, P671, P672, P657, P684, P689.

that would allow the Trial Chamber to infer that Župljanin failed to prevent the crimes for which Drljača is allegedly responsible.[2681]

b. Analysis

801. With regard to Župljanin's argument that the Trial Chamber failed to address whether the police serving in Keraterm and Omarska detention camps were re-subordinated to the VRS, the Appeals Chamber recalls the Trial Chamber's findings that the commander of the Keraterm detention camp was Dusko Sikirica, a police officer, and that the camp was guarded by the police (as the army declined to do so) under orders from Drljača, the Chief of the Prijedor SJB.[2682] The Trial Chamber further found that the Omarska camp was established by an order of Drljača and operated jointly by police and military personnel, including members of the Banja Luka Corps who acted as interrogators, and was commanded by Zeljko Mejakić, commander of the police sub-station in Omarska.[2683] The Appeals Chamber notes that Župljanin does not challenge these findings but rather submits that this analysis falls short of finding that the camps were not within the jurisdiction of the VRS and that the police there were not re-subordinated to the VRS.[2684]

802. The Appeals Chamber is not convinced that the evidence Župljanin points to indicates that the Trial Chamber was required to further address whether police were re-subordinated to the military at the Keraterm and Omarska detention camps. Insofar as Župljanin alleges that police on **[page 330]** duty in the Manjača detention facility were considered to be re-subordinated to the military,[2685] the Appeals Chamber fails to see how the fact that Manjača detention camp was under the authority of the military,[2686] would show that the police operating at Keraterm and Omarska detention camps – both of which were commanded by policemen – were re-subordinated to the military. The same holds true for his reliance on the Trnopolje detention facility which was also under the control of the military and guarded by Serb soldiers.[2687]

803. Similarly, the Appeals Chamber is not persuaded by Župljanin's reliance on the order issued by Mladić in August 1992, allowing journalists to visit the Omarska detention camp,[2688] given that the exhibit, on its face, does not suggest that the Omarska detention camp was under the exclusive authority of the military or that the police at the Omarska detention camp were re-subordinated to the military. By merely pointing to this exhibit, Župljanin has failed to demonstrate how it undermines the Trial Chamber's conclusions that: (i) police and military personnel jointly operated Omarska detention camp; and (ii) the facility was commanded by Mejakić, a police commander.[2689] Moreover, the Appeals Chamber observes that Župljanin's assertion that the fact that the purpose of the Keraterm and Omarska detention camps was to "detain 'persons captured in combat'" and therefore relevant to military functions, not police-related activity,[2690] ignores the Trial Chamber's findings which show that the detainees in Keraterm and Omarska detention camps were not necessarily involved in combat.[2691]

[2681] Župljanin Reply Brief, para. 41, referring to Prosecution Response Brief (Župljanin), paras 63, 67. Župljanin adds that the only finding establishing his *de facto* authority over Drljača is located in the findings regarding Stanišić's responsibility (Župljanin Reply Brief, para. 41, referring to Prosecution Response Brief (Župljanin), fn. 240).

[2682] Trial Judgement, vol. 1, para. 580; Trial Judgement, vol. 2, para. 856. See Trial Judgement, vol. 1, para. 678. The Trial Chamber also noted that teams representing both military and civilian authorities screened detainees in Keraterm to determine their involvement in the conflict (see Trial Judgement, vol. 1, para. 580).

[2683] Trial Judgement, vol. 2, para. 856. See Trial Judgement, vol. 1, paras 593, 679. The Trial Chamber also noted in Omarska, while "[a] large number of military men were security guards who manned machine gun nests", there were uniformed police officers from Prijedor SJB at the gate and the reception desk of the detention camp (Trial Judgement, vol. 1, para. 593).

[2684] See Župljanin Appeal Brief, para. 92, referring to Trial Judgement, vol. 1, paras 678-679.

[2685] See Župljanin Appeal Brief, para. 93, referring to Trial Judgement, vol. 2, para. 337.

[2686] See Trial Judgement vol. 1, para. 619; Trial Judgement, vol. 2, paras 802, 856.

[2687] See Trial Judgement, vol. 2, para. 856. See also Trial Judgement, vol. 1, paras 619, 680. The Appeals Chamber notes in this respect, the Trial Chamber's finding that "the Trnopolje camp was under the charge of the TO and guarded by Serb soldiers and that the camp commander was Slobodan Kurzunović" (Trial Judgement, vol. 2, para. 856).

[2688] See Exhibit P1683.

[2689] Trial Judgement, vol. 2, para. 856. See Trial Judgement, vol. 1, paras 593, 679.

[2690] See Župljanin Appeal Brief, para. 91, referring to Exhibits P1560, 2D90, p. 28.

[2691] See Trial Judgement, vol. 1, paras 596-597, 603, 613.

804. Consequently, the Appeals Chamber finds that Župljanin has failed to show that the Trial Chamber was required to make further findings as to whether police forces serving in the Keraterm and the Omarska detention camps were under the VRS jurisdiction.

805. With respect to Župljanin's contention that the Trial Chamber erred in failing to determine as of when he became sufficiently informed of the abuses that had been committed against the detainees in the Keraterm and Omarska detention camps, the Appeals Chamber notes the Trial Chamber's findings that: (i) at some point in June 1992, Župljanin was informed of the conditions in the Keraterm and Omarska detention camps;[2692] and (ii) on 16 July 1992, Župljanin visited the **[page 331]** Omarska detention facility, where detainees showed signs of mistreatment.[2693] In light of these findings, Župljanin's assertion is without merit. Regarding Župljanin's contention that the Trial Chamber erred by failing to make findings on whether he was informed and failed to punish perpetrators of killings and beatings at Omarska, or that Drljača reported the mistreatment of detainees to him directly,[2694] Župljanin has developed no arguments as to why such findings would be necessary to infer his responsibility through participation in the JCE.

806. With respect to Župljanin's challenges to the Trial Chamber's findings that he had effective control over the Prijedor SJB and its commander Drljača,[2695] the Appeals Chamber recalls the Trial Chamber: (i) found that Drljača's order creating the Omarska detention camp had been implemented in collaboration with the Banja Luka CSB (of which Župljanin was Chief);[2696] and (ii) considered multiple examples between May and August 1992 of instances where Drljača reported to Župljanin on matters pertaining to the Keraterm and Omarska detention camps.[2697] In the Appeals Chamber's view, neither Župljanin's reliance upon Exhibits P261 and 2D25 – both expressly considered by the Trial Chamber[2698] – nor his reliance on the Trial Chamber's finding that Drljača operated with a "certain degree of independence",[2699] is sufficient to demonstrate that no reasonable trier of fact could have concluded that: (i) there existed a relationship of cooperation between Župljanin, Drljača, and Prijedor War Presidency, in which Župljanin played a leadership role;[2700] (ii) Župljanin exercised *de jure* and *de facto* control over the SJBs in the ARK Municipalities (including the Prijedor SJB);[2701] and (iii) Drljača was "directly subordinated to" Župljanin.[2702] Župljanin merely disagrees with the Trial Chamber's assessment of the evidence without showing any error.

807. Insofar as Župljanin contends that he had no capacity to remove Drljača,[2703] the Appeals Chamber notes the Trial Chamber found that "Župljanin never attempted to remove Simo Drljača from Prijedor" notwithstanding his knowledge of the atrocities committed in the detention camps and Witness Radulović's warnings about Drljača.[2704] The Trial Chamber further found that "had **[page 332]** Župljanin wanted to remove Drljača, he could have done it".[2705] The Trial Chamber reached this conclusion by considering that Župljanin was the highest police officer in the ARK and he took action "to arrest members of the powerful Miće Group" and that "his forces successfully prevented an attempt by paramilitary forces to kill between 300 and 600 Muslims and Roma between Doboj and Banja Luka in mid-May 1992".[2706]

808. In relation to Župljanin's position as the highest police officer in the ARK, the Appeals Chamber further notes the Trial Chamber's findings that Župljanin's *de jure* and *de facto* control over the SJBs of the ARK Municipalities "included the ability to appoint and remove RS MUP staff, including SJB chiefs".[2707]

[2692] Trial Judgement, vol. 2, para. 508. See Trial Judgement, vol. 2, para. 423.
[2693] Trial Judgement, vol. 2, para. 508. See Trial Judgement, vol. 2, para. 424.
[2694] See *supra*, para. 794.
[2695] See *supra*, para. 795.
[2696] Trial Judgement, vol. 2, para. 422. See Trial Judgement, vol. 2, para. 493.
[2697] Trial Judgement, vol. 2, paras 421-422.
[2698] See Trial Judgement, vol. 2, paras 357 (referring to, *inter alia*, Exhibit 2D25, pp 2-4), 358 (referring to, *inter alia*, Exhibit P261, p. 43). See also *supra*, para. 536.
[2699] Trial Judgement, vol. 2, para. 359. See *supra*, para. 795.
[2700] See *supra*, para. 790.
[2701] See *supra*, para. 790.
[2702] Trial Judgement, vol. 2, para. 791.
[2703] See *supra*, para. 795.
[2704] Trial Judgement, vol. 2, para. 515.
[2705] Trial Judgement, vol. 2, para. 515.
[2706] Trial Judgement, vol. 2, para. 515.
[2707] Trial Judgement, vol. 2, para. 493. See Trial Judgement, vol. 2, paras 355-356.

While the Trial Chamber did not refer to any evidence regarding Župljanin's authority to remove SJB chiefs,[2708] it did expressly refer to evidence that Župljanin had the authority to appoint SJB chiefs and staff.[2709] Moreover, the Trial Chamber made a number of other findings regarding Župljanin's *de jure* and *de facto* control over the SJBs of the ARK Municipalities. In particular, it considered other evidence indicating Župljanin's powers as Chief of the Banja Luka CSB, namely that: (i) Župljanin had authority over, and coordinated the activities of, the ARK SJBs (which included Prijedor SJB);[2710] (ii) the Banja Luka CSB was duty-bound to assist the police stations in their areas of responsibility and Župljanin was responsible for police activities in the territories of the police stations in the ARK;[2711] and (iii) the SJB chiefs were obliged to follow orders coming from the Banja Luka CSB.[2712] In the view of the Appeals Chambers, these findings are sufficient to demonstrate that a reasonable trier of fact could have found that Župljanin had the ability to remove Drljača, if he wanted.[2713]

809. In addition, the Appeals Chamber considers that the Trial Chamber's conclusion in this respect must be read in the context of its findings that "Župljanin formally appointed Drljača as **[page 333]** Chief of the Prijedor SJB on 30 July 1992, *with retroactive effect* as of 29 April 1992",[2714] and did so despite reports (sent by Witness Radulović to the Banja Luka CSB in May 1992) concerning the crimes committed in Prijedor and recommending Drljača's removal.[2715]

810. Moreover, insofar as Župljanin contends that the Trial Chamber erred by "inferring effective" control over Drljača on the basis of its finding that he previously ordered his police to arrest members of the Miće Group,[2716] Župljanin has failed to demonstrate how the finding that he had the ability to remove Drljača could not be upheld on the basis of the remaining evidence that he was the highest police officer in the ARK Municipalities.[2717]

811. Finally, the Appeals Chamber turns to Župljanin's argument that the Trial Chamber erred by finding him responsible "for the crimes in the Omarska and Keraterm detention facilities because he failed to order the police to disregard the orders of the local crisis staffs, and because he was himself a member of the regional crisis staff, which ostensibly had some authority over the local crisis staffs".[2718] The Appeals Chamber considers that Župljanin has failed to substantiate his assumption that the Trial Chamber relied upon his authority over the local crisis staff in attributing responsibility to him for the crimes in the Keraterm and Omarska detention facilities.[2719] Rather than demonstrating any error in the Trial Chamber's findings, Župljanin merely disagrees with the Trial Chamber's assessment and presents his own alternative interpretation of the evidence.

812. Consequently, the Appeals Chamber finds that Župljanin has failed to demonstrate that the Trial Chamber erred in concluding that he had authority over the Prijedor SJB, including the power to remove

---

[2708] *Cf.* Trial Judgement, vol. 2, para. 493, where the Trial Chamber found that Župljanin's *de jure* and *de facto* authority over the SJBs in the ARK included the "power to appoint and remove RS MUP staff, including SJB chiefs" without referring to any evidence. However, elsewhere in the Trial Judgement, the Trial Chamber considered evidence that Župljanin had the authority to appoint SJB chiefs, with Stanišić's prior approval (Trial Judgement, vol. 2, para. 356), yet referred to no evidence indicating that Župljanin had a similar power to *remove* SJB chiefs from office. The Appeals Chamber notes, however, that Župljanin does not contend that the Trial Chamber erred by relying upon this finding (see Župljanin Appeal Brief, paras 95, 97-100). In the absence of challenges from Župljanin in this respect, and noting that the Trial Chamber's findings otherwise recalled in this paragraph support the Trial Chamber's conclusion that had Župljanin wanted to remove Drljača, he could have done it, the Appeals Chamber declines to address the issue further.
[2709] Trial Judgement, vol. 2, para. 356. The Trial Chamber found that, in order to appoint chiefs and commanders, Stanišić's prior approval was necessary (Trial Judgement, vol. 2, para. 356). *Cf.* Trial Judgement, vol. 2, para. 507.
[2710] Trial Judgement, vol. 2, para. 355.
[2711] Trial Judgement, vol. 2, para. 355.
[2712] Trial Judgement, vol. 2, para. 355.
[2713] See Trial Judgement, vol. 2, para. 515.
[2714] Trial Judgement, vol. 2, para. 486 (emphasis added). Trial Judgement, vol. 1, para. 507.
[2715] Trial Judgement, vol. 2, para. 486. See Trial Judgement, vol. 2, para. 515.
[2716] See *supra*, para. 795.
[2717] See *supra*, paras 807-809; Trial Judgement, vol. 2, para. 515.
[2718] See *supra*, para. 796.
[2719] Trial Judgement, vol. 2, para. 492. See Trial Judgement, vol. 2, para. 360. See also *e.g.* Trial Judgement, vol. 2, paras 422-423, 475-476, 479-480; *supra*, para. 796.

337

Drljača, or by failing to make sufficient findings as to his authority over the Keraterm and Omarska detention facilities when inferring his intent and contribution to the JCE.

c. Conclusion

813.   In light of the above, the Appeals Chamber considers that Župljanin has not demonstrated that the Trial Chamber erred by failing to make findings that he had sufficient control or authority over the police as a result of declining to pronounce on issues of re-subordination of the police to the military, and as a result, erred in relying on his failures to act to infer his contribution to the JCE and his intent. **[page 334]**

(iii) Alleged error in the Trial Chamber's failure to establish that Župljanin acted with knowledge of his duty (sub-ground (A) in part of Župljanin's first ground of appeal)

a. Submissions of the parties

814.   Župljanin submits that the Trial Chamber was required to establish that he had knowledge of his legal obligation to intervene and to enter findings excluding the possibility that he could have misjudged the scope of his duty or ability to act.[2720] He contends that the Trial Chamber failed to analyse whether "he may have been genuinely mistaken" about the scope of his duty and thus failed to substantiate its inferences that he significantly contributed to the JCE and possessed the requisite intent.[2721] To support his contention, Župljanin relies on evidence of an address he made on 11 July 1992 showing, in his submission, that his knowledge concerning the conditions in the Omarska and Keraterm detention camps was only general.[2722] Župljanin also refers to his decision to set up a commission to inspect the conditions of detention camps on 14 August 1992 and argues that he did bring information he had in his possession to his superiors' attention.[2723]

815.   The Prosecution responds that the Trial Chamber did address the issue of Župljanin's awareness of his legal obligations, which were stated in the RS Constitution.[2724] It further submits that the Trial Judgement established Župljanin's ability to act as the Chief of the Banja Luka CSB, and that he could not have been mistaken about his authority to prevent and punish his subordinates such as Drljača and the Banja Luka CSB SPD.[2725] Finally, the Prosecution argues that Župljanin ignores the Trial Chamber's findings "that he had 'ample knowledge of the unlawful detention, mistreatment, and murder of non-Serb detainees in detention facilities and camps in the ARK Municipalities'" and that the commission was a "feigned commission", as he himself acknowledged.[2726]

b. Analysis

816.   The Appeals Chamber recalls the Trial Chamber's finding that, as Chief of the Banja Luka CSB, Župljanin was the highest police authority in the ARK.[2727] As such, he had a duty to protect **[page 335]** the civilian population pursuant to Article 10 of the RS Constitution and Article 42 of the LIA, as well as the duty and the authority to discipline his subordinates, including permanently removing them from service and filing criminal reports on crimes his policemen committed.[2728] The Trial Chamber relied on these

---

[2720]   Župljanin Appeal Brief, paras 58, 102-103. Župljanin submits that he could have been uninformed or mistaken about the scope of his authority and duty, as well as with regard to the means at his disposal to inquire into the situation and to take remedial measures (Župljanin Appeal Brief, paras 102-103).

[2721]   Župljanin Appeal Brief, para. 104. See Župljanin Appeal Brief, paras 58, 102-103, 106.

[2722]   Župljanin Appeal Brief, para. 103, referring to Exhibit P160, p. 7.

[2723]   Župljanin Appeal Brief, para. 103, referring to Exhibit P601.

[2724]   Prosecution Response Brief (Župljanin), para. 74, referring to Trial Judgement, vol. 2, para. 354.

[2725]   Prosecution Response Brief (Župljanin), para. 75, referring to, *inter alia*, Prosecution Response Brief (Župljanin), paras 39-42, Trial Judgement, vol. 2, paras 486, 492, 500-502, 511, 514-519, 526.

[2726]   Prosecution Response Brief (Župljanin), para. 76, referring to Trial Judgement, vol. 2, paras 506, 514, 519, Župljanin Appeal Brief, paras 103, 166.

[2727]   Trial Judgement, vol. 2, para. 493.

[2728]   Trial Judgement, vol. 2, paras 489, 493. See Trial Judgement, vol. 2, paras 354-356, 501.

findings in reaching its conclusion that Župljanin failed to protect the non-Serb population, launch criminal investigations, and discipline his subordinates.[2729] It then concluded, *inter alia* on the basis of these factors, that he significantly contributed to the JCE and possessed the requisite intent.[2730]

817. The Appeals Chamber turns first to Župljanin's submissions that his knowledge of crimes was limited and the Trial Chamber erred with respect to his knowledge of his duties. Regarding his alleged lack of knowledge of the commission of crimes, Župljanin refers to his address of 11 July 1992.[2731] In light of the significant evidence of his knowledge of crimes against non-Serbs, which the Trial Chamber considered,[2732] and in particular his knowledge about the conditions at the Omarska and Keraterm detention camps,[2733] the Appeals Chamber finds that Župljanin has failed to demonstrate that his address of 11 July 1992 undermines the Trial Chamber's conclusion that he had extensive knowledge of the crimes committed against non-Serbs, including by his own police.[2734] Regarding the Trial Chamber's alleged failure to establish that Župljanin had knowledge of his legal obligation to intervene, the Appeals Chamber notes that the Trial Chamber relied on Župljanin's duties as a police officer pursuant to Article 10 of the RS Constitution and Article 42 of **[page 336]** the LIA of the RS and the fact that he was the highest police authority in the ARK.[2735] As such, the Appeals Chamber finds his unsubstantiated argument that he did not know about his legal duty to intervene unconvincing and that Župljanin has therefore failed to demonstrate any error of the Trial Chamber in this respect.

818. With respect to Župljanin's contention that he may have been mistaken about the scope of his duty or ability to act, the Appeals Chamber finds that the mere fact that Župljanin had taken some action in accordance with his duties is insufficient to establish that the Trial Chamber erred. The Appeals Chamber notes that to substantiate his claim that he brought information to his superiors' attention, Župljanin merely points to his decision to set up a commission.[2736] Relying on this evidence, the Trial Chamber found that, on 14 August 1992, Župljanin decided to form a commission to inspect the condition of detention camps.[2737] However, the Trial Chamber also found that: (i) Župljanin appointed as commissioners the "very people who were in charge of interrogating detainees" and thus, were involved or informed of their mistreatment; (ii) he gave the commission only three days to complete its work; (iii) the commission's report was simply a collage of previous reports, which did not shed any light on abuses of detainees and their perpetrators; and (iv) Župljanin did not request further investigations into mistreatments of detainees.[2738] On the basis of, *inter alia*, these findings, the Trial Chamber concluded that Župljanin's orders to apparently protect the non-Serb

---

[2729] Trial Judgement, vol. 2, paras 518-519. See Trial Judgement, vol. 2, paras 503-517.
[2730] Trial Judgement, vol. 2, paras 518-520.
[2731] The Appeals Chamber notes that Župljanin refers to p. 7 of Exhibit P160 in his submission (Župljanin Appeal Brief, para. 103, referring to Exhibit P160, p. 7). Exhibit P160 is a summary of a MUP senior officials meeting on 11 July 1992 (Exhibit P160, p. 1). Župljanin spoke at this meeting as the Chief of the Banja Luka CSB outlining problems "which are directly linked to and have an impact on the activities of internal affairs organs" (Exhibit P160, p. 7. See Exhibit P160, p. 6). He stated, *inter alia*, that "the army and crisis staffs, or war presidencies" were gathering "as many Muslims as possible" in "undefined camps" and that they left these camps "up to the internal affairs organs" (Exhibit P160, p. 7). He further stated that "[c]onditions in these camps are bad – there is no food, some individuals do not observe international norms because, among other things, such collection centres are not adequate or there are other reasons" (Exhibit P160, p. 7). The Trial Chamber relied on this evidence to conclude that, "by 11 July 1992, [Župljanin] knew of the mass arrest of Muslims by municipal authorities, of their detention and abuse in 'undefined camps', and of police involvement in the guarding of these facilities" (Trial Judgement, vol. 2, para. 510).
[2732] See *infra*, para. 934.
[2733] Trial Judgement, vol. 2, paras 503-517. With respect to the Keraterm and Omarska detention facilities in particular, the Trial Chamber found that: (i) Župljanin was informed by Witness Radulović and Witness Sajinović, at some point in June 1992, "of the horrible conditions in which the prisoners were held and of the abuses perpetrated against them" in these camps, "including by members of the police", to which he "responded dismissively [...] and left hurriedly"; (Trial Judgement, vol. 2, para. 508) (ii) on 17 July 1992, Župljanin visited Omarska detention facility with other ARK leaders "where detainees showed signs of mistreatment and were forced to give the delegation the three finger salute" while members of the delegation laughed at the scene (Trial Judgement, vol. 2, para. 508);and (iii) international media began reporting about detainees in the Omarska and Trnopolje detention facilities who were held in inhumane conditions and subjected to physical abuse by 5 August 1992 (Trial Judgement, vol. 2, para. 509). See *supra*, paras 801-805.
[2734] See Trial Judgement, vol. 2, para. 513. See also Trial Judgement, vol. 2, paras 510, 518-519.
[2735] Trial Judgement, vol. 2, paras 489, 493. See Trial Judgement, vol. 2, paras 354-356, 501.
[2736] Župljanin Appeal Brief, para. 103, referring to Exhibit P601.
[2737] Trial Judgement, vol. 2, paras 446, 514.
[2738] Trial Judgement, vol. 2, para. 514. See Trial Judgement, vol. 2, paras 446-447.

population were not genuinely meant to be effectuated.[2739] Furthermore, the Trial Chamber more broadly discussed evidence on Župljanin's efforts to investigate crimes and take disciplinary actions against subordinates but ultimately concluded that he did not take steps to ensure that his orders were carried out and successfully managed to shield his subordinates from criminal prosecution.[2740] The Appeals Chamber also notes that Župljanin does not point to any other evidence supporting his contention that he may have been mistaken about the scope of his duty or ability to act. The Appeals Chamber therefore, finds that Župljanin has failed to show that no reasonable trier of fact could have concluded that the only reasonable inference from the evidence was that he failed to protect the non-Serb population, to launch criminal investigations, and to take disciplinary actions against subordinates.

819.   Turning to Župljanin's argument that the Trial Chamber should have made findings excluding the possibility that he may have misjudged the scope of his duty or ability to act, the Appeals Chamber recalls that where the challenge on appeal is to an inference drawn to establish a **[page 337]** fact on which a conviction relies, the standard is only satisfied if the inference was the *only* reasonable one that could be drawn from the evidence presented.[2741] As set out above, the Trial Chamber relied upon a comprehensive body of circumstantial evidence to reach its conclusion that Župljanin failed to fulfil his duties to protect the non-Serb population, to launch criminal investigations, and to take disciplinary actions against subordinates. The Appeals Chamber considers that a plain reading of the Trial Judgement reflects that the Trial Chamber was satisfied that these conclusions were the only reasonable inference from the evidence. In the absence of any attempt by Župljanin to substantiate his argument, the Appeals Chamber considers that he has failed to show that the Trial Chamber erred.

c. Conclusion

820.   The Appeals Chamber therefore finds that Župljanin has failed to show that the Trial Chamber erred in failing to enter findings on his knowledge of his legal obligation to act. Župljanin's arguments are dismissed.

(iv) Alleged errors in relation to Župljanin's failure to investigate and discipline members of the Banja Luka CSB SPD (sub-ground (D) in part of Župljanin's first ground of appeal)

821.   The Trial Chamber found that in May 1992, Župljanin created the Banja Luka CSB SPD.[2742] The Trial Chamber determined that Župljanin exercised "complete authority" over this unit and could impose on its members disciplinary sanctions, including permanent removal from service.[2743] It further found that "[notwithstanding his extensive knowledge of the crimes of [the Banja Luka CSB SPD], Župljanin did nothing to rein in their behaviour and to effectively investigate and discipline its members."[2744] The Trial Chamber concluded, *inter alia*, that by failing to launch criminal investigations and to discipline his subordinates who had committed crimes against non-Serbs, Župljanin significantly contributed to the JCE.[2745] **[page 338]**

a. Submissions of the parties

822.   Župljanin submits that no reasonable trier of fact could have found that he contributed to the JCE through his role in relation to the Banja Luka CSB SPD and that the Trial Chamber erroneously characterised

---

[2739]   Trial Judgement, vol. 2, para. 514. See *infra*, paras 837-869.
[2740]   Trial Judgement, vol. 2, paras 457-488, 514-517, 519. See *infra*, paras 847-868.
[2741]   *Đorđević* Appeal Judgement, para. 700; *Stakić* Appeal Judgement, paras 219-220; *Nyiramasuhuko et al.* Appeal Judgement, paras 650, 1509.
[2742]   Trial Judgement, vol. 2, para. 518. See Trial Judgement, vol. 2, paras 384-385, 501-502, 514.
[2743]   Trial Judgement, vol. 2, para. 501. The Trial Chamber found that: (i) on 27 April 1992, the ARK Assembly decided to form a special purpose police detachment at the Banja Luka CSB of around 160 members, *i.e.* Banja Luka CSB SPD, and designated Župljanin to implement the decision (Trial Judgement, vol. 2, para. 384); (ii) on 6 May 1992, Župljanin informed the chiefs of the ARK SJBs that he had established a counter-sabotage and counter-terrorism police unit of about 150 members (Trial Judgement, vol. 2, para. 385); and (iii) the authority for appointing the commander of the Banja Luka CSB SPD rested with Župljanin (Trial Judgement, vol. 2, para. 386). The Trial Chamber also found that the Banja Luka CSB SPD was subordinated to Župljanin, who authorised payments to its members (Trial Judgement, vol. 2, para. 392).
[2744]   Trial Judgement, vol. 2, para. 504.
[2745]   Trial Judgement, vol. 2, para. 518.

his failure to punish, prevent, or otherwise discipline specific members of the Banja Luka CSB SPD as an omission amounting to a contribution to the JCE.[2746]

823. He submits in particular that the Trial Chamber erred in finding that he "exercised complete authority" over the Banja Luka CSB SPD.[2747] According to Župljanin, the Trial Chamber failed to: (i) discuss "any element of elevated control" between him and the alleged perpetrators of crimes;[2748] and (ii) make specific findings as to whether the Banja Luka CSB SPD was re-subordinated to the VRS during the commission of crimes which he was found to have failed to prevent.[2749] In this respect, Župljanin argues that: (i) the evidence clearly shows that the Banja Luka CSB SPD was re-subordinated to the VRS during the events in Kotor Varoš;[2750] (ii) there is a "real **[page 339]** possibility" that it was also re-subordinated for intervals during its engagements in Prijedor and Banja Luka;[2751] and (iii) the crimes in Doboj were committed while the Banja Luka CSB SPD was not subordinated to him, given that Doboj was outside the ARK Municipalities and therefore outside his jurisdiction.[2752] Furthermore, he contends that "no reasonable trier of fact could have ignored that by its leadership, its composition, purpose and direct evidence, the [Banja Luka CSB SPD] was intermittently and easily subordinated to the VRS throughout 1992".[2753]

824. Regarding the Trial Chamber's finding that he failed to investigate and discipline members of the Banja Luka CSB SPD, Župljanin submits that: (i) members of the Banja Luka CSB SPD were suspended and criminal proceedings were initiated in relation to their suspected involvement in crimes, specifically in Kotor Varoš as shown in Exhibit P631;[2754] and (ii) the Trial Chamber had no evidence indicating that he

---

[2746]   Župljanin Appeal Brief, paras 139-140, 150-151. Župljanin raises the factual challenges pertaining to the Trial Chamber's findings on his failure to investigate and discipline subordinates as a challenge to the Trial Chamber's findings on his contribution to the JCE (Župljanin Appeal Brief, paras 139, 151, 154). The Appeals Chamber notes that the Trial Chamber relied on these findings in reaching its conclusions on both his contribution to the JCE and his intent (Trial Judgement, vol. 2, paras 518-519). In this section, the Appeals Chamber will examine whether the Trial Chamber erred in finding that Župljanin failed to investigate and discipline his subordinates and whether the Trial Chamber erred in relying on these findings to conclude that Župljanin contributed to the JCE and had the requisite intent. Župljanin's argument as to whether it was reasonable for the Trial Chamber to ultimately conclude that he significantly contributed to the JCE and possessed the requisite intent on the basis of, *inter alia*, these factors will be addressed in other sections (see *infra*, paras 901-944). The Appeals Chamber notes that Župljanin's challenges pertaining to the Trial Chamber's finding that by enrolling SOS members into the Banja Luka CSB SPD, he created a unit comprised of Serb nationalists with criminal records, have been addressed elsewhere (see *infra*, paras 840-846).

[2747]   Župljanin Appeal Brief, paras 140 (referring to Trial Judgement, vol. 2, para. 511), 144. The Appeals Chamber notes that the reference to paragraph 511 of the Trial Judgement is incorrect and understands Župljanin to refer to paragraph 501. Referring to the Trial Chamber's finding that his contribution to the JCE included that he "failed to launch criminal investigations and discipline his subordinates [...] thus creating a climate of impunity which only increased the commission of crimes against non-Serbs", Župljanin asserts that the only express finding of his authority over the perpetrators of crimes is the Trial Chamber's finding with respect to the Banja Luka CSB SPD (Župljanin Appeal Brief, para. 140, referring to Trial Judgement, vol. 2, para. 518).

[2748]   Župljanin Appeal Brief, para. 150. See Župljanin Appeal Brief, para. 144. Župljanin submits that "[his] acquiescing in the secondment of the [Banja Luka CSB SPD] to the VRS certainly does not establish his 'effective' control for the duration of that operation" (Župljanin Appeal Brief, para. 144). Župljanin submits that the Trial Chamber's finding that he "dispatched platoons of the Detachment to participate in the takeovers is in no way determinative that he was exercising operational control over them and that the Trial Chamber failed to provide reasons "expressing any awareness that the only burden on the Defence was to raise reasonable doubt" (Župljanin Appeal Brief, fn. 215, referring to Trial Judgement, vol. 2, para. 502).

[2749]   Župljanin Appeal Brief, para. 143. See Župljanin Appeal Brief, paras 141-143. See also Župljanin Reply Brief, para. 58; Appeal Hearing, 16 Dec 2015, AT. 167, 172. Župljanin asserts that the Trial Chamber's finding rejecting the assertion that the Banja Luka CSB SPD was a military unit is not "dispositive" as it does not address the re-subordination issue (Župljanin Appeal Brief, para. 141, referring to Trial Judgement, vol. 2, para. 501). He further submits that the Trial Chamber acknowledged evidence that the Banja Luka CSB SPD took part in combat operations with VRS units (Župljanin Appeal Brief, para. 143, referring to Trial Judgement, vol. 2, para. 405).

[2750]   Župljanin Appeal Brief, para. 142. Župljanin refers in this respect to evidence that: (i) there were large numbers of men in regular uniforms and carrying long-barrelled rifles at the Kotor Varoš police station (Župljanin Appeal Brief, para. 142, referring to Trial Judgement, vol. 1, para. 406); and (ii) a VRS town command was set up in Kotor Varoš. He also submits that the Trial Chamber failed to address Witness SZ002's evidence that the Banja Luka CSB SPD's deployment in Kotor Varoš was determined in coordination with the VRS town commander, Colonel Peulić (Župljanin Appeal Brief, para. 142, referring to Trial Judgement, vol. 1, paras 351-494, Trial Judgement, vol. 2, paras 393, 501, Exhibit 2D132).

[2751]   Župljanin Appeal Brief, para. 143. Župljanin submits in particular that the commander and the deputy-commander were both military commanders, that "a certain Colonel Stevilovi[c] had a major role in the functioning of the unit", and that the unit was based in a military facility (Župljanin Appeal Brief, para. 143).

[2752]   Župljanin Appeal Brief, para. 150, referring to Trial Judgement, vol. 2, para. 440.

[2753]   Župljanin Appeal Brief, para. 143. See Župljanin Appeal Brief, para. 141.

[2754]   Župljanin Appeal Brief, para. 150, referring to Exhibit P631, p. 2. The Appeals Chamber notes that Exhibit P631 is a report on the CSB and the SJBs in the ARK Municipalities, dated 5 August 1992, which mentions with regard to "negativities" faced by the

341

resisted the disbandment of the Banja Luka CSB SPD in early August 1992 and its placement under the command of the VRS for disciplinary reasons; rather, it had evidence to the contrary.[2755]

825.   The Prosecution responds that the Trial Chamber reasonably found that Župljanin controlled the Banja Luka CSB SPD and relied upon his use of the Banja Luka CSB SPD and his failure to prevent or punish its members' crimes as part of his contribution to the JCE.[2756] The Prosecution further contends that the law does not require an "element of elevated control" in order to establish joint criminal enterprise liability.[2757] In addition, it submits that the Trial Chamber relied on Župljanin's knowledge of the crimes committed by Banja Luka CSB SPD members in Doboj in **[page 340]** order to find that he had knowledge of "undisciplined behaviour" of Banja Luka CSB SPD members, but did not consider this incident as a failure to punish the crimes of subordinates.[2758]

826.   The Prosecution further argues that Exhibit P631 does not assist Župljanin as the Trial Chamber considered evidence that no criminal reports were submitted with the public prosecutor with respect to Banja Luka CSB SPD members suspected of crimes, and that such members continued to be engaged in actions of the Banja Luka CSB SPD.[2759] Finally, the Prosecution submits that Župljanin misstates the Trial Judgement when claiming that the Trial Chamber concluded that he resisted disbanding the Banja Luka CSB SPD in August 1992, as the Trial Chamber only found that there was "reluctance by the Banja Luka officials to disband the [Banja Luka CSB SPD]".[2760]

b. Analysis

827.   The Appeals Chamber recalls that in the jurisprudence of the Tribunal a failure to intervene to prevent recurrence of crimes or to halt abuses has been taken into account in assessing an accused's contribution to a joint criminal enterprise and his intent, where the accused had sufficient power and influence or authority over the perpetrators to prevent or halt the abuses, but failed to exercise these powers.[2761]

Banja Luka CSB SPD at the time of deployment of the unit in Kotor Varoš, that "a number of employees" had been suspended and criminal proceedings initiated.

[2755]   Župljanin Appeal Brief, para. 150. Župljanin argues that even though the Trial Chamber relied on Exhibit P631, it erred in its consideration of it, particularly in light of Witness SZ002's testimony, which, in his submission, contradicts Exhibit P631 (Župljanin Appeal Brief, para. 150, referring to Exhibit P631, Witness SZ002, 9 Nov 2011, T. 25468).
[2756]   Prosecution Response Brief (Župljanin), paras 111-112. See Appeal Hearing, 16 Dec 2015, AT. 197. The Prosecution also argues that the Trial Chamber correctly and reasonably concluded that re-subordination was irrelevant to Župljanin's liability (Response Brief (Župljanin), para. 114, referring to Prosecution Response Brief (Župljanin), paras 33-76). The Prosecution further submits that contrary to Župljanin's contention, the Trial Chamber did not find that the commander and the deputy commander of the Banja Luka CSB SPD were military commanders (Prosecution Response Brief (Župljanin), para. 115, referring to Župljanin Appeal Brief, para. 143). In addition, the Prosecution submits that the Trial Chamber rejected Witness SZ002's evidence as not credible (Prosecution Response Brief (Župljanin), para. 115, referring to Trial Judgement, vol. 2, paras 386, 393).
[2757]   Prosecution Response Brief (Župljanin), para. 121, referring to Prosecution Response Brief (Župljanin), paras 87-94.
[2758]   Prosecution Response Brief (Župljanin), para. 121, comparing Trial Judgement, vol. 2, para. 440 with Trial Judgement, vol. 2, p. 144, sub-title (x). The Prosecution adds that in any event, Župljanin retained the duty to punish SDS members for crimes in Doboj (Prosecution Response Brief (Župljanin), para. 121). Furthermore, according to the Prosecution, Župljanin deployed the Banja Luka CSB SPD to Doboj, continued to deploy the commanders of the Banja Luka CSB SPD to Doboj in later operations, and subsequently even appointed them to senior positions (Prosecution Response Brief (Župljanin), para. 121, referring to Trial Judgement, vol. 2, paras 398, 405, 440, 502, 505).
[2759]   Prosecution Response Brief (Župljanin), para. 121. The Prosecution specifically refers to the Trial Chamber's finding based on Exhibit P631, that Župljanin informed Witness Gajic of crimes committed by the Banja Luka CSB SPD during its deployment in Kotor Varoš (Prosecution Response Brief (Župljanin), para. 121, referring to Trial Judgement, vol. 2, para. 425). It also refers to the Trial Chamber's findings that Župljanin knew of the crimes committed by the SPD member Danko Kajkut and continued to engage him in actions of the Banja Luka CSB SPD (Prosecution Response Brief (Župljanin), para. 121, referring to Trial Judgement, vol. 2, paras 504-505).
[2760]   Prosecution Response Brief (Župljanin), para. 121, referring to Župljanin Appeal Brief, para. 150, Trial Judgement, vol. 2, paras 395, 606. The Prosecution further argues that in any case, Župljanin's argument has no impact given that the disbandment of the Banja Luka CSB SPD would not have been an adequate measure in order to punish crimes (Prosecution Response Brief (Župljanin), para. 121, referring to Župljanin Appeal Brief, para. 150, Trial Judgement, vol. 2, paras 395, 606).
[2761]   See *Šainović et al.* Appeal Judgement, paras 1233, 1242; *Krajišnik* Appeal Judgement, para. 194; *Kvočka et al.* Appeal Judgement, paras 195-196. See also *supra*, para. 111. The Appeals Chamber also recalls that although a *de jure* or *de facto* position of authority is not a material condition required by law under the theory of joint criminal enterprise, it is a relevant factor in determining the scope of the accused's participation in the common purpose (see *Kvočka et al.* Appeal Judgement, para. 192. See also *Kvočka et al.* Appeal Judgement, para. 104).

828.   Turning to Župljanin's argument that the Trial Chamber erred in finding that he exercised complete authority over the Banja Luka CSB SPD, the Appeals Chamber first recalls that it has already dismissed Župljanin's argument that an elevated degree of control over subordinates is **[page 341]** required for failures to act in the context of joint criminal enterprise.[2762] As such, the Appeals Chamber rejects Župljanin's arguments based on this incorrect premise.

829.   Moreover, the Appeals Chamber notes that Župljanin exercised complete authority over the Banja Luka CSB SPD and could impose disciplinary sanctions against its members.[2763] The Appeals Chamber is not convinced that the Trial Chamber was required to further address the issue of re-subordination in relation to the Banja Luka CSB SPD, since the Trial Chamber adequately addressed the question of whether Župljanin had sufficient power or authority over the members of the Banja Luka CSB SPD to take measures against them. In light of the Trial Chamber's findings that: (i) Župljanin had the authority to appoint the commander of the Banja Luka CSB SPD;[2764] (ii) the SPD members were on the payroll of the Banja Luka CSB;[2765] and (iii) an officer within the Banja Luka CSB was in charge of liaising with the Banja Luka CSB SPD when it was deployed in the field,[2766] the Appeals Chamber is of the view that the Trial Chamber considered that the Banja Luka CSB SPD remained part of the CSB structure, even when its members were involved in combat operations with the army. The Trial Chamber also expressly concluded that the evidence that the Banja Luka CSB SPD was a military unit was not credible and that even though a number of Banja Luka CSB SPD members had a military background, that was not determinative of who had authority over them once they became part of the Banja Luka CSB SPD.[2767] Župljanin simply puts forth a contradictory interpretation of the evidence without showing that the Trial Chamber erred in its assessment of the relevant evidence.[2768] In addition, the Appeals Chamber is not convinced that Župljanin's statement that if "it is necessary for the detachment to fight together with the army, it will be made available" shows that the Banja Luka CSB SPD was re-subordinated to the VRS for the duration of combat-related assignments or, in any event, that Župljanin did not have sufficient power or authority over Banja Luka CSB SPD members to impose disciplinary **[page 342]** sanctions.[2769] Accordingly, Župljanin has failed to show that no reasonable trier of fact could have found that he exercised control over the Banja Luka CSB SPD to the extent that he had sufficient authority to impose disciplinary sanctions on its members irrespective of whether they were involved in combat operations with the army.

830.   Further, insofar as Župljanin argues that "no reasonable trier of fact could have ignored that by its leadership, its composition, purpose and direct evidence, the [Banja Luka CSB SPD] was intermittently and easily subordinated to the VRS throughout 1992",[2770] the Appeals Chamber considers that Župljanin ignores the Trial Chamber's relevant findings. The Trial Chamber found that the commander of the Banja Luka CSB SPD, Captain Mirko Lukić, was a serviceman, and that 2771 Ljuban Ečim ("Ečim"), the deputy commander, was a member of the Banja Luka SNB.[2771] However, the Trial Chamber also specifically considered Witness ST258's statement that what mattered with respect to the Banja Luka CSB SPD's civilian or military nature

---

[2762]   See *supra*, para. 733.
[2763]   Trial Judgement, vol. 2, para. 501. See Trial Judgement, vol. 2, paras 384-386, 392.
[2764]   Trial Judgement, vol. 2, para. 386.
[2765]   Trial Judgement, vol. 2, para. 392. See Trial Judgement, vol. 2, para. 484.
[2766]   Trial Judgement, vol. 2, para. 393.
[2767]   Trial Judgement, vol. 2, para. 501. See Trial Judgement, vol. 2, paras 386, 393.
[2768]   In this respect, the Appeals Chamber notes that, contrary to Župljanin's submission, the Trial Chamber expressly addressed the testimony of Witness SZ002 that the Banja Luka CSB SPD was a military unit under the control of Colonel Stevilović but found it not credible (Trial Judgement, vol. 2, para. 501. See Trial Judgement, vol. 2, para. 393; Župljanin Appeal Brief, para. 142). The Appeals Chamber therefore finds no merit in Župljanin's submission, on the basis of the testimony of Witness SZ002, that the fact that "a certain Colonel Stevilovi[c] had a major role in the functioning of the unit" and that the unit was based in a military facility would show re-subordination of the Banja Luka CSB SPD to the VRS (Župljanin Appeal Brief, para. 142). Župljanin's argument is a mere disagreement with the Trial Chamber's conclusion, without showing any error. In addition, the Appeals Chamber is not convinced that the fact that there were large numbers of men in regular uniforms and carrying long-barrelled rifles at the Kotor Varoš police station or Witness SZ002's evidence that the Banja Luka CSB SPD deployment in Kotor Varoš was determined in coordination with the VRS town commander would show that the members of the Banja Luka CSB SPD were not under the control of Župljanin.
[2769]   See Župljanin Appeal Brief, para. 141, referring to Trial Judgement, vol. 2, para. 385.
[2770]   Župljanin Appeal Brief, para. 143. See Župljanin Appeal Brief, para. 141.
[2771]   Trial Judgement, vol. 2, para. 386.

was not the members' origin or training, but rather the service they actually performed during the war.[2772] It then found that the background of the members of the Banja Luka CSB SPD was not determinative of who had authority over them.[2773] In this respect the Trial Chamber noted that Banja Luka CSB SPD members wore blue and grey camouflage uniforms, like those worn by the police, and blue or red berets, that the armoured personnel carriers had the word "Milicija" painted on them, and that Župljanin provided the members of the Banja Luka CSB SPD with ID cards, which authorised them to arrest people, search premises without a warrant, and to carry and use fire arms.[2774] These considerations, together with the factors described above,[2775] led the Trial Chamber to conclude that it was Župljanin who exercised complete authority over the Banja Luka CSB SPD and could impose disciplinary sanctions against its members.[2776]

831.   In light of the foregoing, the Appeals Chamber dismisses Župljanin's argument that the Trial Chamber was required to enter specific findings regarding the re-subordination of the Banja Luka CSB SPD to the VRS in the municipalities of Kotor Varoš, Prijedor, and Banja Luka.

832.   With regard to Župljanin's argument that the crimes in Doboj were committed while the Banja Luka CSB SPD was not subordinated to him as it was outside the ARK Municipalities, and thus outside his jurisdiction, the Appeals Chamber observes that the portion of the Trial Judgement, **[page 343]** on which Župljanin relies, does not support his assertion.[2777] To the contrary, the Appeals Chamber observes that the Trial Chamber's findings clearly show that Župljanin had authority over Ečim and Zdravko Samardžija ("Samardžija") who led the Banja Luka CSB SPD in Doboj,[2778] and that Župljanin was aware of the crimes committed by the Banja Luka CSB SPD in Doboj.[2779] The Trial Chamber also found that, despite this knowledge, Župljanin did not impose disciplinary measures against members of the Banja Luka CSB SPD, but instead continued to engage them in actions and that in May 1993 Ečim and Samardžija were still employed at the Banja Luka CSB.[2780] In light of these findings, the Appeals Chamber is not persuaded that the fact that Doboj was not part of the ARK Municipalities is sufficient to demonstrate that Župljanin had no authority to take action against the Banja Luka CSB SPD for the crimes committed there.[2781]

833.   The Appeals Chamber is of the view that Župljanin has failed to demonstrate an error in the Trial Chamber's reasoning and has failed to show that no reasonable trier of fact could have found that he exercised complete authority over the Banja Luka CSB SPD.

834.   The Appeals Chamber now turns to Župljanin's challenge to the Trial Chamber's finding that he failed to investigate and discipline members of the Banja Luka CSB SPD. In support of his argument that members of the Banja Luka CSB SPD were suspended and criminal proceedings initiated against them with regard to crimes committed in Kotor Varoš,[2782] Župljanin seeks to rely on Exhibit P631. Exhibit P631 is a report on the CSB and the SJBs in the ARK Municipalities, dated 5 August 1992, which mentions with regard to "negativities" faced by the Banja Luka CSB SPD at the time of deployment of the unit in Kotor Varoš, that

---

2772   Trial Judgement, vol. 2, para. 389.
2773   Trial Judgement, vol. 2, para. 501.
2774   Trial Judgement, vol. 2, para. 390.
2775   See *supra*, para. 829.
2776   Trial Judgement, vol. 2, para. 501.
2777   See Župljanin Appeal Brief, para. 150, referring to Trial Judgement, vol. 2, para. 440.
2778   Trial Judgement, vol. 1, para. 1149; Trial Judgement, vol. 2, paras 386, 440, 501.
2779   Trial Judgement, vol. 2, paras 440, 503.
2780   Trial Judgement, vol. 2, paras 398, 505. The Appeals Chamber notes that the month in which Ečim and Samardžija were still employed at the Banja Luka CSB differs in these two paragraphs of the Trial Judgement (Trial Judgement, vol. 2, paras 398, 505). In view of the evidence referred to in Trial Judgement, vol. 2, para. 398, the correct date of this finding appears to be 5 May 1993 (Trial Judgement, vol. 2, para. 398).
2781   The Appeals Chamber observes that Župljanin was not charged and convicted for the crimes committed in Doboj (see Trial Judgement, vol. 2, fn. 1208, paras 824-827). However, the Appeals Chamber observes that it is not clear from the Trial Chamber's ultimate conclusions that the Trial Chamber did not rely on his failures to launch criminal investigations and discipline members of the Banja Luka CSB SPD for the crimes they committed outside of the ARK Municipalities in finding that Župljanin significantly contributed to the JCE and had the required intent for the first category of joint criminal enterprise in the ARK Municipalities. See Trial Judgement, vol. 2, paras 518 (finding that Župljanin failed to launch criminal investigations and discipline his subordinates who had committed crimes against non-Serbs without geographical limitation), 519 (relying on Župljanin's inaction in relation to the crimes committed by the Banja Luka CSB SPD without geographical limitation).
2782   Župljanin Appeal Brief, para. 150, referring to Exhibit P631, p. 2.

"a number of employees" had been suspended and criminal proceedings initiated.[2783] Župljanin merely refers to this evidence without substantiating how it would undermine the Trial Chamber's conclusion that he failed to investigate and discipline members of Banja Luka CSB SPD. In any event, the Trial Chamber expressly **[page 344]** addressed action taken in relation to the crimes committed by Banja Luka CSB SPD members in Kotor Varoš.[2784] It noted however that the only evidence of an investigation against members of this unit for a serious crime is an entry in the Kotor Varoš "Open Cases Logbook" for 29 July 1992, which records the filing of a criminal report against Danko Kajkut ("Kajkut") for a double rape allegedly committed in Kotor Varoš.[2785] The Trial Chamber specifically referred to Exhibit P631 in reaching this conclusion,[2786] which suggests that it placed only limited or no weight on this exhibit. The Trial Chamber further found that: (i) a criminal report against Kajkut was not submitted to the public prosecutor; (ii) the charges were eventually dropped; (iii) Župljanin continued to engage him in actions of the Banja Luka CSB SPD; and (iv) in May 1993 Kajkut was still employed at the Banja Luka CSB.[2787] Accordingly, the Appeals Chamber dismisses his argument.

835.   Finally, the Appeals Chamber turns to Župljanin's contention that the Banja Luka CSB SPD was disbanded and placed under the command of the VRS in part for disciplinary reasons, a measure with which he agreed.[2788] The Appeals Chamber considers that Župljanin has failed to explain and demonstrate how the disbandment of the unit and his agreement to it would show an error in the Trial Chamber's conclusion that he failed to punish members of the Banja Luka CSB SPD during its existence.[2789] Moreover, the Trial Chamber found that following the disbandment of the Banja Luka CSB SPD, several prominent members of the Banja Luka CSB SPD who Župljanin knew had committed crimes were appointed to commanding positions within the Banja Luka CSB.[2790] The Trial Chamber's reliance on the continued employment of these members at the Banja Luka CSB in concluding that Župljanin failed to rein in the behaviour of members of the Banja Luka CSB SPD[2791] suggests that it did not consider the disbandment of the Banja Luka CSB SPD to be an effective or sufficient measure to suppress their criminal behaviour. Thus, Župljanin's mere reference to the disbandment and his agreement thereto falls short of showing that the Trial Chamber erred.

c. Conclusion

836.   In light of the foregoing, the Appeals Chamber finds that Župljanin has failed to show that no reasonable trier of fact could have found that he contributed to the JCE through his failure to investigate and discipline Banja Luka CSB SPD members. **[page 345]**

(v) Alleged errors in finding that Župljanin failed to protect the non-Serb population by issuing general and ineffective orders which were not genuinely meant to be effectuated (sub-ground (E) in part of Župljanin's first ground of appeal)

837.   In reaching its conclusion that Župljanin failed to "protect the non-Serb population",[2792] the Trial Chamber considered that Župljanin issued general and ineffective orders to the ARK SJBs "exhorting them to respect the law", which "were not genuinely meant to be effectuated".[2793]

838.   Župljanin asserts that the Trial Chamber unreasonably dismissed evidence of his efforts to suppress crimes when it concluded that his orders to protect the non-Serb population "were not genuinely meant to be

---

[2783]   Exhibit P631, p. 2.
[2784]   Trial Judgement, vol. 2, para. 425. See Trial Judgement, vol. 2, para. 503.
[2785]   Trial Judgement, vol. 2, para. 504. See Trial Judgement, vol. 2, para. 425, fn. 1176, referring to, *inter alia*, Exhibit P1558.06.
[2786]   Trial Judgement, vol. 2, para. 425, fn. 1176, referring to, *inter alia*, Exhibit P631, p. 2.
[2787]   Trial Judgement, vol. 2, para. 504.
[2788]   Župljanin Appeal Brief, para. 150.
[2789]   Trial Judgement, vol. 2, para. 505.
[2790]   Trial Judgement, vol. 2, para. 398. See Trial Judgement, vol. 2, paras 503-505.
[2791]   Trial Judgement, vol. 2, para. 505. See Trial Judgement, vol. 2, para. 504.
[2792]   Trial Judgement, vol. 2, para. 519. See Trial Judgement, vol. 2, para. 518.
[2793]   Trial Judgement, vol. 2, para. 514.

effectuated".[2794] Specifically, Župljanin challenges the Trial Chamber's factual findings that he: (i) hired criminal members of the SOS to the Banja Luka CSB SPD just a few days before issuing an order prohibiting hiring individuals with criminal records; (ii) appointed a feigned commission to investigate crimes at prisons in Prijedor, appointed the former warden of prisons in Sanski Most to be the crime inspector for white-collar crimes, and failed to remove Drljača as Chief of the Prijedor SJB; and (iii) filed reports identifying the perpetrators as unknown in respect of two important crimes.[2795]

839. The Prosecution responds that Župljanin fails to demonstrate that the Trial Chamber unreasonably concluded that certain "'ineffective and general orders' to SJBs were 'not genuinely **[page 346]** meant to be effectuated'".[2796] It adds that to the contrary, the Trial Chamber's findings demonstrate that Župljanin "tolerated and approved the commission of crimes against non-Serbs".[2797]

a. Alleged error in finding that Župljanin hired members of the SOS with criminal records

840. The Trial Chamber found that Župljanin enrolled criminal members of the SOS in the Banja Luka CSB SPD only a few days before issuing an order prohibiting hiring of persons with criminal records.[2798] In reaching this conclusion, the Trial Chamber relied on its previous findings that following the formulation of the operative work plan of the Banja Luka CSB on 25 May 1992 ("25 May 1992 Work Plan") to tackle crimes in Banja Luka committed by, *inter alios*, SOS members against non-Serbs, Župljanin filed a few criminal reports with the public prosecutor's office.[2799] It further found that Župljanin absorbed SOS's members into the newly created Banja Luka CSB SPD, notwithstanding their role in the "illegal blockade of Banja Luka and the warnings received [...] that they were dangerous criminals".[2800] The Trial Chamber also found that Župljanin, as Chief of the Banja Luka CSB, knew about the "widespread and systematic" crimes committed against non-Serbs by the SOS during and in the aftermath of the blockade in Banja Luka in the beginning of April 1992.[2801] The Trial Chamber concluded that by enrolling members of the SOS in the Banja Luka CSB SPD, "including to commanding positions, Župljanin created a unit comprised of Serb nationalists with criminal records".[2802]

i. Submissions of the parties

841. Župljanin submits that the Trial Chamber erred in finding that he hired members of the SOS with criminal records.[2803] According to Župljanin, the Trial Chamber misstates the evidence and its lack of clarity

---

[2794] Župljanin Appeal Brief, para. 163, referring to Trial Judgement, vol. 2, para. 514. See Appeal Hearing, 16 Dec 2015, AT. 180-181. Župljanin's factual challenges pertaining to the Trial Chamber's findings on his failure to protect the non-Serb population are raised as challenges to the Trial Chamber's finding of intent (Župljanin Appeal Brief, paras 156). The Appeals Chamber notes that the Trial Chamber relied on these findings in reaching its conclusions on both his contribution to the JCE and his intent (Trial Judgement, vol. 2, paras 518-519). In this section, the Appeals Chamber will examine whether the Trial Chamber erred in finding that Župljanin failed to protect the non-Serb population and whether the Trial Chamber erred in relying on these findings to conclude that Župljanin contributed to the JCE and had the requisite intent. Župljanin's argument as to whether it was reasonable for the Trial Chamber to ultimately conclude that he significantly contributed to the JCE and possessed the requisite intent on the basis of, *inter alia*, these factors will be addressed in other sections (see *infra*, paras 901-944). Under sub-ground (E) of his first ground of appeal, Župljanin also submits that the Trial Chamber erred in inferring his intent from his failure to prevent or punish the crimes charged in the Indictment because this finding resulted from the Trial Chamber's failure to address the re-subordination of police, which he raises as a separate error in sub-ground (A) of his first ground of appeal (Župljanin Appeal Brief, para. 162, referring to sub-ground (A) of his first ground of appeal). The Appeals Chamber has therefore dismissed this argument in connection with sub-ground (A) of Župljanin's first ground of appeal (see *supra*, paras 736-813).
[2795] Župljanin Appeal Brief, para. 163. See Župljanin Appeal Brief, paras 164-171. See also Župljanin Appeal Brief, paras 270-271.
[2796] Prosecution Response Brief (Župljanin), para. 127.
[2797] Prosecution Response Brief (Župljanin), para. 127.
[2798] Trial Judgement, vol. 2, paras 514, 519. See Trial Judgement, vol. 2, paras 387-391, 499, 501, 861.
[2799] Trial Judgement, vol. 2, paras 498-499. See Trial Judgement, vol. 2, para. 519.
[2800] Trial Judgement, vol. 2, para. 499. See Trial Judgement, vol. 2, para. 387.
[2801] Trial Judgement, vol. 2, paras 496, 499. See Trial Judgement, vol. 1, paras 144, 147, 157.
[2802] Trial Judgement, vol. 2, para. 499. The Trial Chamber reached this conclusion after considering that Župljanin enrolled criminal members of the SOS in his Banja Luka CSB SPD notwithstanding an order he forwarded to his SJB chiefs that persons with criminal records could not be part of the Banja Luka CSB SPD (Trial Judgement, vol. 2, paras 514, 519). See Trial Judgement, vol. 2, paras 387-391, 499, 502, 861.
[2803] Župljanin Appeal Brief, paras 145, 148, 164.

in the assessment of the evidence results from the absence of footnotes in the section containing the findings on his responsibility.[2804] He argues in particular that the Trial Chamber **[page 347]** neither found nor does the evidence support that persons with criminal records or criminal suspects were permitted to join the Banja Luka CSB SPD or that he knew anything about it.[2805] Župljanin asserts that he tried to prevent suspected criminals from joining the Banja Luka CSB SPD.[2806] In support of his submission, Župljanin refers to his interview with the *Glas* newspaper in which he stated that those claiming to be members of the SOS but engaged in "unlawful measures and activities" were not welcome in the Banja Luka CSB SPD.[2807] Župljanin further refers to the 25 May 1992 Work Plan he issued, ordering the arrest of SOS members suspected of crimes and others involved in harassment of non-Serbs in Banja Luka, and the investigation of the murder of a Muslim man and the bombing of the Arnaudija Mosque.[2808]

842.   The Prosecution responds that the Trial Chamber reasonably relied upon Župljanin's recruitment of "seasoned criminals" and nationalists to the Banja Luka CSB SPD.[2809] According to the Prosecution, the Trial Chamber clearly set out the evidence it relied on and Župljanin fails to show how the Trial Chamber erred in its assessment thereof.[2810] The Prosecution contends that the Trial Chamber's finding that Župljanin sought to enrol members of the SOS with criminal records into the Banja Luka CSB SPD and that he neither took action to exclude them nor did he punish them for their crimes was amply supported by the evidence.[2811] The Prosecution submits in **[page 348]** particular that Župljanin fails to show that the Trial Chamber was unreasonable in its approach to the *Glas* Article and the 25 May 1992 Work Plan.[2812] Finally, the Prosecution

---

[2804]   Župljanin Appeal Brief, para. 149. Župljanin submits that the absence of footnotes sets the Trial Judgement apart from most other judgements "which are usually assiduously footnoted to ensure the conformity between the ultimate findings and the rest of the Judgement" (Župljanin Appeal Brief, para. 149, referring to *Popović et al.* Trial Judgement, paras 1929-1979, *Orić* Trial Judgement, paras 677-716, *Haradinaj et al.* Retrial Judgement, paras 628-668). In support of his argument that the Trial Chamber misdirected itself in relation to important factual matters, Župljanin, *inter alia*, points to the Trial Chamber's conclusion that the Banja Luka CSB SPD included criminals from the SOS, while "earlier in the Judgement", the Trial Chamber found that only a few members of the SOS had been enrolled in the Banja Luka CSB SPD, without making a finding as to whether any of them had a criminal record (Župljanin Reply Brief, para. 57, comparing Trial Judgement, vol. 2, para. 499 with Trial Judgement, vol. 2, paras 387-388).

[2805]   Župljanin Appeal Brief, para. 164. Župljanin argues that the "mere fact that some members of the SOS were accepted into the [Banja Luka CSB SPD] and that some members of the SOS were suspected to have committed crimes during the blockade of Banja Luka in no way establishes" that members of the SOS who had criminal records were permitted to join the SPD or that "Župljanin knew that anyone permitted to join the [Banja Luka CSB SPD] was suspected of having committed a crime or was a person with a criminal record" (Župljanin Appeal Brief, para. 164).

[2806]   Župljanin Appeal Brief, paras 145, 148, 164.

[2807]   Župljanin Appeal Brief, para. 145, referring to Trial Judgement, vol. 2, para. 404, referring in turn to Exhibit P560 ("*Glas* Article").

[2808]   Župljanin Appeal Brief, para. 146, referring to Exhibit 1D198. See Appeal Hearing, 16 Dec 2015, AT. 180-181, 210-211. Župljanin also contends that the Trial Chamber's findings regarding the 25 May 1992 Work Plan are unclear and that the Trial Chamber seems to suggest that the absence of evidence concerning the release of one of the arrested persons undermines the "sincerity or robustness of the plan" (Župljanin Appeal Brief, para. 148). He also emphasises that the 25 May 1992 Work Plan was secret and argues that it was therefore genuinely meant to be implemented (see Župljanin Appeal Brief, paras 147-148, referring to Trial Judgement, vol. 2, paras 457, 498).

[2809]   Prosecution Response Brief (Župljanin), para. 128.

[2810]   Prosecution Response Brief (Župljanin), paras 117-118, referring to Trial Judgement, vol. 1, paras 143, 146, 157-158, 209, 213, Trial Judgement, vol. 2, paras 384, 386-388, 503. The Prosecution in particular argues that the Trial Chamber accepted and relied on evidence pertaining to: (i) the attack by SOS members against non-Serbs and their property after the 3 April 1992 blockade of Banja Luka; (ii) the formation of the Banja Luka CSB SPD with members of the SOS, after Župljanin expressly asked the Banja Luka SJB Chief, Witness Tutuš, in August 1992 to reconsider his initial refusal to use these members to form the special police unit; (iii) the recruitment of the SOS members Ljuban Ečim, Zdravko Samardžija, and Slobodan Dubocanin into the Banja Luka CSB SPD; (iv) the testimony of Witness Radulović concerning the recruitment of SOS members into the police; and (v) the fact that Župljanin was informed by Witness Radulović and Witness Tutuš that Banja Luka CSB SPD members continued to commit crimes after the unit was created (Prosecution Response Brief (Župljanin), para. 117).

[2811]   Prosecution Response Brief (Župljanin), para. 128. The Prosecution refers specifically to the testimonies of Witness Tutuš, Witness Radulović, Witness Radic, and Witness Sajinovic and a report prepared by VRS security chief Zdravko Tolimir (Prosecution Response Brief (Župljanin), para. 128).

[2812]   Prosecution Response Brief (Župljanin), paras 118-119. The Prosecution submits that the *Glas* Article does not assist Župljanin as the Trial Chamber considered evidence that no criminal reports were submitted with the public prosecutor with respect to Banja Luka CSB SPD members suspected of crimes, and that such members continued to be engaged in actions of the Banja Luka CSB SPD (Prosecution Response Brief (Župljanin), para. 121. See Prosecution Response Brief (Župljanin), para. 118)). The Prosecution specifically refers to the Trial Chamber's finding based on Exhibit P631, that Župljanin informed Witness Gajic of crimes committed by the Banja Luka CSB SPD during its deployment in Kotor Varoš (Prosecution Response Brief (Župljanin), para.

submits that Župljanin's argument regarding the absence of footnotes ignores the previous 116 footnoted paragraphs summarising and analysing the evidence upon which the Trial Chamber based its conclusions.[2813]

ii. Analysis

843.   Although the Trial Chamber provided no cross-references or citations to evidence on the record in the section containing the findings on Župljanin's responsibility, the Appeals Chamber considers that the Trial Chamber's conclusion that Župljanin enrolled criminal SOS members in the Banja Luka CSB SPD, must be read in conjunction with its previous findings on Župljanin's conduct in furtherance of the JCE. The Trial Chamber made a number of relevant factual findings in this respect. It found that Witness Tutuš, Chief of the Banja Luka CSB SPD, refused repeatedly to use members of the SOS for the Banja Luka CSB SPD, in part because some of them were convicted criminals.[2814] The Trial Chamber further noted that it understood that Župljanin asked him to reconsider his position and found that Witness Tutuš agreed to have SOS members accepted into the reserve police force upon preliminary background checks.[2815] Eventually, some members of the SOS were incorporated in the Banja Luka CSB SPD, others were incorporated in military units.[2816] The Trial Chamber also found that Witness Radulović expressed his concerns that the transfer of some SOS members to the active-duty police was "incomprehensible and unnecessary" as they were criminals who by becoming policemen were given a basis to continue their activities in a more "rampant" fashion.[2817] According to the Trial Chamber, Župljanin dismissed these concerns by saying that the SOS were "Serbian knights".[2818] In light of these detailed findings, the Appeals **[page 349]** Chamber finds that the Trial Chamber sufficiently identified the basis for its conclusion.[2819] Accordingly, the Appeals Chamber dismisses Župljanin's contention that the Trial Chamber never found that persons with criminal records or criminal suspects were permitted to join the Banja Luka CSB SPD or that he knew anything about it.

844.   Insofar as Župljanin seeks to rely on the *Glas* Article, the Appeals Chamber observes that the Trial Chamber expressly considered the portions of the article to which he refers.[2820] The Appeals Chamber notes that this article referred to Župljanin's statement that the SOS were "quality people, above all in terms of character" and that "the bad reputation of the unit was due to some rogue members from whom the SOS had distanced itself".[2821] As the *Glas* Article does not negate the evidence concerning Župljanin's knowledge of the criminal background of some SOS members, the Appeals Chamber considers that it is not inconsistent with the Trial Chamber's conclusions. In addition, in light of the testimony of Witness Radulović recalled above in relation to Župljanin's reaction when warned about the possible enrolment of criminal SOS members into the Banja Luka CSB SPD,[2822] the Appeals Chamber is not convinced that the *Glas* Article undermines the Trial Chamber's findings or demonstrates that Župljanin tried to prevent suspected criminals from joining the Banja Luka CSB SPD. Župljanin has failed to show that the Trial Chamber erred in its assessment of the *Glas* Article.

845.   Finally, with regard to the 25 May 1992 Work Plan, the Appeals Chamber is unconvinced that it demonstrates that Župljanin tried to prevent suspected criminals of the SOS from joining the Banja Luka CSB SPD. Indeed, the Trial Chamber expressly took into account the 25 May 1992 Work Plan, and found that it was adopted to tackle crimes that had affected Banja Luka starting in April 1992 and included crimes

---

121, referring to Trial Judgement, vol. 2, para. 425). It also refers to the Trial Chamber's findings that Župljanin knew of the crimes committed by the Banja Luka CSB SPD member Danko Kajkut and continued to engage him in actions of the Banja Luka CSB SPD (Prosecution Response Brief (Župljanin), para. 121, referring to Trial Judgement, vol. 2, paras 504-505). Furthermore, the Prosecution submits that the assertion in the 25 May 1992 Work Plan that SOS members who committed crimes should be arrested, does not alter the established fact that SOS members who committed crimes and were recruited to the Banja Luka CSB SPD were not arrested (Prosecution Response Brief (Župljanin), para. 119).

[2813]   Prosecution Response Brief (Župljanin), para. 120, referring to Trial Judgement, vol. 2, paras 375-490.
[2814]   Trial Judgement, vol. 2, para. 387.
[2815]   Trial Judgement, vol. 2, para. 387.
[2816]   Trial Judgement, vol. 2, para. 387.
[2817]   Trial Judgement, vol. 2, para. 388.
[2818]   Trial Judgement, vol. 2, para. 388.
[2819]   See *supra*, para. 840.
[2820]   See Trial Judgement, vol. 2, para. 404. See also Trial Judgement, vol. 2, para. 387.
[2821]   Trial Judgement, vol. 2, para. 404, referring to Exhibit P560, pp 3-4.
[2822]   See *supra*, para. 843.

committed by SOS members.[2823] The Trial Chamber also found that following the 25 May 1992 Work Plan, Župljanin filed only "few criminal reports" and that the commission of crimes continued throughout 1992 and in fact increased after 16 August 1992.[2824] The Trial Chamber further found that despite the fact that the Banja Luka CSB had drawn up the 25 May 1992 Work Plan to investigate some of the SOS crimes, Župljanin enrolled SOS members in the Banja Luka CSB SPD, including to commanding positions, "creat[ing] a unit comprised of Serb nationalists with criminal records".[2825] The Appeals Chamber considers that Župljanin ignores the Trial Chamber's reasoning and merely disagrees with the Trial Chamber's conclusion without **[page 350]** showing any error. Thus, Župljanin has failed to show that the Trial Chamber erred in its assessment of the 25 May 1992 Work Plan.

846.   Based on the foregoing, the Appeals Chamber finds that Župljanin has not demonstrated that no reasonable trier of fact could have found that Župljanin enrolled criminal SOS members in the Banja Luka CSB SPD only a few days before issuing an order prohibiting hiring of persons with criminal records. He has also failed to show that the Trial Chamber erred in relying on this finding to conclude that Župljanin's orders were not genuinely meant to be effectuated.

> b. Alleged error in relation to Župljanin's decisions to form a commission to inspect the conditions of detention camps, to appoint Vujanić, and not to dismiss Drljača

847.   In finding that Župljanin's orders to protect the civilian population were not "genuinely meant to be effectuated",[2826] the Trial Chamber considered that Župljanin formed a "feigned commission",[2827] appointed as commissioners individuals who were "involved, or however informed of" the mistreatment of detainees,[2828] and gave them only three days to complete their work.[2829] The Trial Chamber added that when the commissioners filed their report it did not shed any light on the abuses suffered by non-Serb detainees and on the people who were responsible.[2830] The Trial Chamber found that Župljanin did not request further investigation into mistreatments in the detention centres or take any further step to uncover those responsible for the mistreatments of which he knew.[2831] The Trial Chamber stated that, to the contrary, Župljanin appointed Drago Vujanić ("Vujanić"), warden of the detention facilities in Sanski Most, as crime inspector for white-collar crime, notwithstanding his knowledge of the implication of the Sanski Most police in the unlawful detentions and in the death of 20 detainees who suffocated while being transported between Sanski Most and the Manjača detention camp.[2832] The Trial Chamber further considered that Župljanin never attempted to remove Drljača as Chief of the Prijedor SJB "notwithstanding Župljanin's knowledge of the atrocities committed in the detention camps".[2833] **[page 351]**

i. Submissions of the parties

848.   Župljanin submits that the Trial Chamber erred in finding that his orders were not genuinely meant to be effectuated because he appointed a commission to investigate crimes at prisons in Prijedor of the very people who were in charge of interrogating the detainees.[2834] He asserts that he appointed officers to the

---

2823   Trial Judgement, vol. 2, para. 498.
2824   Trial Judgement, vol. 2, para. 499. See Trial Judgement, vol. 2, paras 459, 498.
2825   Trial Judgement, vol. 2, para. 499.
2826   Trial Judgement, vol. 2, para. 514.
2827   Trial Judgement, vol. 2, para. 519.
2828   Trial Judgement, vol. 2, para. 514.
2829   Trial Judgement, vol. 2, paras 514, 519. See Trial Judgement, vol. 2, para. 446.
2830   Trial Judgement, vol. 2, para. 514. See Trial Judgement, vol. 2, para. 447.
2831   Trial Judgement, vol. 2, para. 514.
2832   Trial Judgement, vol. 2, para. 514. See Trial Judgement, vol. 2, para. 487.
2833   Trial Judgement, vol. 2, para. 515. See Trial Judgement, vol. 2, para. 486. See also Trial Judgement, vol. 1, para. 507.
2834   Župljanin Appeal Brief, para. 163. Župljanin submits that the Trial Chamber failed to determine beyond a reasonable doubt whether he "possessed jurisdiction over any crimes that may have been committed [in Trnopolje, Omarska, and Keraterm] by police officers" who may have been subordinated to the VRS (Župljanin Appeal Brief, para. 165). This argument has already been addressed and dismissed in a different section (see *supra*, paras 785-812).

commission to "report on crimes that may have been committed at those locations" and that "rather obviously, individuals were appointed who had some knowledge of the prisons".[2835]

849. Župljanin also submits that the Trial Chamber erred in finding that his orders were not genuinely meant to be effectuated based on evidence that he: (i) appointed the former warden of prisons in Sanski Most, whose officers may have committed crimes, to be the crime inspector for white-collar crimes; and (ii) failed to remove Drljača as head of the Prijedor SJB.[2836] He argues that although Vujanić was the warden of Sanski Most detention camp when 20 detainees died of asphyxia, the Trial Chamber accepted the possibility that the killings may have resulted from negligence, but later incorrectly stated that the 20 detainees were murdered.[2837] In addition, Župljanin submits that the Trial Chamber failed to make findings that investigations had not been pursued or that Vujanić improperly handled the matter.[2838] Župljanin further challenges the relevance of this appointment "made three months after the events in question and after almost all Indictment crimes had been committed".[2839] Finally, Župljanin challenges the Trial Chamber's reliance on his failure to remove Drljača, which he argues, "is similarly not indicative of any concealed criminal intent on [his] part".[2840]

850. The Prosecution responds that the Trial Chamber reasonably relied upon Župljanin's cover-up of crimes committed in detention camps.[2841] It asserts that the Trial Chamber correctly found that the function of the commission Župljanin formed was "feigned" based on evidence that he: (i) appointed as commissioners the very persons who interrogated detainees and who were at **[page 352]** least informed of the mistreatment of prisoners; and (ii) "only gave the commissioners three days to complete their work".[2842] The Prosecution further responds that the Trial Chamber "reasonably relied upon Župljanin's actions to shield and reward criminal MUP officials".[2843] It argues that Vujanić is one example of such action and notes that the murder of at least 20 non-Serbs was not "mere negligence".[2844] The Prosecution notes that "the only consequence for Vujanić was his promotion by Župljanin to inspector for white-collar crimes".[2845] It argues that the Trial Chamber also reasonably found that Župljanin failed to remove Drljača as Chief of the Prijedor SJB, notwithstanding his knowledge of crimes committed against non-Serbs in Prijedor.[2846]

ii. Analysis

851. The Appeals Chamber notes that the Trial Chamber found that, in August 1992, Župljanin set up a commission in response to requests from the ICRC to the Bosnian Serb leadership for the improvement of the unsatisfying conditions at the Manjača detention camp as well as to foreign journalist reports that detainees at Omarska and Trnopolje were held in inhumane conditions and subject to physical abuse.[2847] The Trial Chamber considered that, *inter alia*, Župljanin "appointed as commissioners the very people who were in charge of interrogating detainees in these camps, and therefore were involved, *or however informed of,*

[2835] Župljanin Appeal Brief, para. 166. Župljanin further submits that his agreement at trial that the "report was a self-serving whitewash" does not substantiate the Trial Chamber's unsupported conclusion that he acted with ulterior motives or criminally (Župljanin Appeal Brief, para. 166).

[2836] Župljanin Appeal Brief, para. 163.

[2837] Župljanin Appeal Brief, para. 167, referring to Trial Judgement, vol. 2, para. 215, Trial Judgement, vol. 2, para. 419.

[2838] Župljanin Appeal Brief, para. 168.

[2839] Župljanin Appeal Brief, para. 168.

[2840] Župljanin Appeal Brief, para. 169. The Appeals Chamber understands Župljanin's reference to the argument he makes in sub-ground (E) of his first ground of appeal as a reference to the arguments he raises in sub-ground (A) of his first ground of appeal.

[2841] Prosecution Response Brief (Župljanin), para. 129.

[2842] Prosecution Response Brief (Župljanin), para. 129.

[2843] Prosecution Response Brief (Župljanin), para. 130. See Prosecution Response Brief (Župljanin), para. 72.

[2844] Prosecution Response Brief (Župljanin), para. 130.

[2845] Prosecution Response Brief (Župljanin), para. 130.

[2846] Prosecution Response Brief (Župljanin), para. 131.

[2847] Trial Judgement, vol. 2, paras 444, 446. The Trial Chamber found that the commission was established to: (i) determine "whether any POW camp, reception centre, investigation centre, or other facilities for the 'reception' of citizens had been established in these municipalities; the reasons for their establishment; the number of people arrested, processed, and released; and the ethnicity, gender, and age of the persons and the conditions in which they lived"; and (ii) "[ascertain] if in these municipalities there had been instances of citizens being moved out, and if so, their ethnicity, their number, and whether they had moved out voluntarily or under coercion" (Trial Judgement, vol. 2, para. 446).

their mistreatment".²⁸⁴⁸ The Trial Chamber, therefore, did not consider that Župljanin merely appointed individuals who had "*some knowledge* of the prisons" as submitted by Župljanin,²⁸⁴⁹ but that he appointed those with direct knowledge who were either involved in or informed of the mistreatment of detainees.²⁸⁵⁰ Further, Župljanin's appointment of those with knowledge of mistreatment of detainees must also be viewed in the context of the Trial Chamber's other considerations in relation to his establishment of the commission.²⁸⁵¹ In particular, the Appeals Chamber notes the Trial Chamber's findings that Župljanin "gave [the commissioners] only three days to complete their work" and that "when the **[page 353]** commissioners filed their report, it was simply a collage of previously drafted reports [...] which did not shed any light on the abuses suffered by non-Serb detainees and on the people who were responsible".²⁸⁵² In light of these findings, the Appeals Chamber finds that Župljanin has failed to demonstrate that no reasonable trier of fact could have relied on Župljanin's role in the formation of the commission to find that his orders to protect the civilian population were not genuinely meant to be effectuated.

852.   Concerning Vujanić, the Appeals Chamber notes that the Trial Chamber found that Župljanin appointed Vujanić, a police officer and warden in charge of the Betonirka detention camp in Sanski Most from June 1992, to the position of inspector for white-collar crimes.²⁸⁵³ The Trial Chamber further considered that while Vujanić was warden, non-Serbs were unlawfully detained and subjected to regular beatings at the camp.²⁸⁵⁴ In particular, the Trial Chamber found that while Vujanić was in charge, 20 detainees had been murdered by suffocation whilst being transported "packed like sardines" by police officers from the Sanski Most SJB.²⁸⁵⁵ The Trial Chamber further considered that following these murders, Župljanin appointed Vujanić "notwithstanding [Župljanin's] knowledge of the implication of the Sanski Most police in unlawful detentions and in the death of 20 detainees".²⁸⁵⁶ The Appeals Chamber finds that, contrary to Župljanin's submission,²⁸⁵⁷ the Trial Chamber was not required to establish that investigations had not been pursued or that Vujanić improperly handled the matter. It was within the Trial Chamber's discretion to consider, among other evidence, Vujanić's appointment, which occurred notwithstanding Župljanin's knowledge of the mistreatment and deaths of detainees while Vujanić was warden, when concluding that Župljanin's orders to protect the civilian population were not genuinely meant to be effectuated. The Appeals Chamber further considers that the fact that this appointment was made three months after the events in question, and after almost all Indictment crimes had been committed, is incapable of undermining the Trial Chamber's reasoning. **[page 354]**

853.   Concerning Župljanin's lack of efforts to remove Drljača,²⁸⁵⁸ Župljanin has failed to substantiate his contention that his failure to remove Drljača is "not indicative of any concealed criminal intent on [his]

---

²⁸⁴⁸   Trial Judgement, vol. 2, para. 514 (emphasis added). In particular the Trial Chamber considered that two of the four commissioners appointed to the team were involved in interrogating prisoners at the Omarska detention camp (Trial Judgement, vol. 2, para. 446. See Trial Judgement, vol. 2, para. 447). The Trial Chamber also found that at least one of the commissioners, Vojin Bera, was an officer of the Banja Luka SNB (Trial Judgement, vol. 2, para. 372).
²⁸⁴⁹   Župljanin Appeal Brief, para. 166 (emphasis added).
²⁸⁵⁰   See Trial Judgement, vol. 2, para. 514.
²⁸⁵¹   See Trial Judgement, vol. 2, para. 519.
²⁸⁵²   Trial Judgement, vol. 2, para. 514. The Trial Chamber considered that the report did not contain information concerning the mistreatment of prisoners or the inadequacy of the detention facilities (Trial Judgement, vol. 2, para. 447). Moreover, the findings of the commission appeared to be based on reports provided to the commission by the Prijedor, Sanski Most, and Bosanski Novi SJBs, rather than on first hand information obtained by the commissioners (Trial Judgement, vol. 2, para. 447).
²⁸⁵³   Trial Judgement, vol. 2, para. 514. See Trial Judgement, vol. 1, paras 769, 800-801. See also Trial Judgement, vol. 1, paras 184, 798.
²⁸⁵⁴   Trial Judgement, vol. 1, paras 184, 800-801, 808-809, 811. See Trial Judgement, vol. 1, para. 798. In particular, between 120 and 150 Bosnian Muslims and Bosnian Croats were detained in three garages of the Betonirka factory from the end of May or beginning of June 1992 until the end of June 1992 in crowded and unsanitary conditions where they were subject to beatings on a regular basis, causing serious injury (Trial Judgement, vol. 1, paras 800-801).
²⁸⁵⁵   Trial Judgement, vol. 1, paras 189, 215. See Trial Judgement, vol. 1, para. 190. The Appeals Chamber notes that it has dismissed Župljanin's submission that the Trial Chamber suggested a standard of negligence when it indicated that the police officers "knew or should have known" that transporting detainees in locked refrigerator trucks with insufficient airflow in the summer could result in their death elsewhere in this Judgement (see *infra*, fn. 3448).
²⁸⁵⁶   Trial Judgement, vol. 2, para. 514. See Trial Judgement, vol. 2, para. 487.
²⁸⁵⁷   Župljanin Appeal Brief, para. 168.
²⁸⁵⁸   The Appeals Chamber notes that the Trial Chamber considered that Župljanin appointed Drljača as Prijedor SJB Chief on 30 July 1992, with retroactive effect as of 29 April 1992, and that he did not remove Drljača from that role despite having knowledge of the crimes committed in Prijedor (see Trial Judgement, vol. 2, para. 486. See Trial Judgement, vol. 1, para. 507).

part".[2859] The Appeals Chamber considers that through his undeveloped argument Župljanin has failed to identify an error in the Trial Chamber's reasoning.[2860] His argument is therefore dismissed.

854.   Based on the foregoing, the Appeals Chamber finds that Župljanin has not demonstrated that the Trial Chamber erred in its conclusions on Župljanin's decisions to form a commission to inspect the conditions of detention camps, to appoint Vujanić, and not to dismiss Drljača.

c. Alleged errors in considering Župljanin's obstruction of criminal investigations

855.   In finding that his orders were not genuinely meant to be effectuated, the Trial Chamber further considered that Župljanin, "at least on two occasions, knowingly misled the public prosecutor in investigations concerning the murder of non-Serbs perpetrated by the Prijedor police".[2861] In particular, it took into account that Župljanin filed criminal reports against unknown perpetrators to the public prosecutor in relation to two incidents of killings at the Manjača detention camp and Korićanske Stijene, without adding any other available details regarding the first incident and without any indication on the possible implication of the Prijedor police in the second incident.[2862] The Trial Chamber also considered that the public prosecutor was "unable to proceed immediately with the prosecution"[2863] since he "needed this information in order to be able to open a criminal investigation".[2864] Regarding Korićanske Stijene, the Trial Chamber added that in an interview with *ABC Nightline* in November 1992, Župljanin stated that there were no survivors to shed light on that incident, when in fact, he was informed since 24 August 1992 that there was a survivor of the incident.[2865] The Trial Chamber also found that while the responsibility for the **[page 355]** failure of this inquiry did not rest exclusively with Župljanin, he "did what he could to ensure impunity for the perpetrators".[2866]

i. Submissions of the parties

856.   Župljanin challenges the Trial Chamber's "heavy reliance" on evidence that he submitted two reports to the public prosecutor's office in relation to the killings at the Manjača detention camp and Korićanske Stijene which concealed the names of persons suspected of perpetrating crimes.[2867] He argues that the two reports provided to the public prosecution outlined the suspected involvement of policemen in those incidents, and appended witnesses' statements, which included the names of all the suspected perpetrators and their probable affiliation with the Prijedor police.[2868] He contends further that the reports ought to be considered along with the many others in which he "identifies crimes and recommends or directs immediate action to address the crimes".[2869]

857.   Regarding the Trial Chamber's finding that Župljanin "did what he could to ensure impunity for the perpetrators" of the Korićanske Stijene killings, Župljanin argues that it reflects disregard for the evidence.[2870] He asserts that the Trial Chamber erred in relying on his: (i) failure to indicate in his criminal report to the prosecutor's office that he had grounds to believe that the perpetrators were members of the Prijedor police; and (ii) denial in a media interview that there were survivors of the incident and that it was under investigation.[2871] According to Župljanin, the Trial Chamber "fails to mention that the report to the

---

2859   Župljanin Appeal Brief, para. 169.
2860   The Appeals Chamber recalls that it has upheld the Trial Chamber's finding that Župljanin exercised authority over Drljača (see *supra*, para. 812).
2861   Trial Judgement, vol. 2, para. 516. See Trial Judgement, vol. 2, para. 517.
2862   Trial Judgement, vol. 2, para. 516. See Trial Judgement, vol. 2, para. 517.
2863   Trial Judgement, vol. 2, para. 474.
2864   See Trial Judgement, vol. 2, para. 465.
2865   See Trial Judgement, vol. 2, para. 517. See also Trial Judgement, vol. 2, para. 481.
2866   Trial Judgement, vol. 2, para. 517.
2867   Župljanin Appeal Brief, paras 170 (referring to Trial Judgement, vol. 2, paras 516-517), 176.
2868   Župljanin Appeal Brief, para. 171. See Župljanin Appeal Brief, para. 176. See also Župljanin Reply Brief, para. 60.
2869   Župljanin Appeal Brief, para. 171. See Appeal Hearing, 16 Dec 2015, AT. 180-182, 210-211.
2870   Župljanin Appeal Brief, paras 172-177, quoting Trial Judgement, vol. 2, para. 517. Župljanin contends that no reasonable trier of fact would have "committed such a serious error in appreciating the evidence", particularly where that "evidence is relied on to make such a damning and wide-ranging inference" (Župljanin Appeal Brief, para. 176).
2871   Župljanin Appeal Brief, para. 175.

Prosecutor's Office included the statements of all witnesses to the event, identifying every single suspected perpetrator and their probable affiliation with the Prijedor Police".[2872] Župljanin further submits that failure to disclose details of the investigation on international television is in no way probative that he was obstructing, or intended to obstruct, the investigation.[2873] Finally, he avers that he promptly initiated investigations into the Korićanske Stijene killings.[2874] **[page 356]**

858.   Župljanin finally asserts that "[i]n order to infer that [he] handled his duties *with the intention* of furthering" the crimes of deportation, other inhumane acts (forcible transfer), and persecutions through the same underlying acts, the Trial Chamber "would have had to eliminate the possibility that": (i) he genuinely believed (albeit mistakenly) that the police officers were re-subordinated to the military, which may have affected the extent of his efforts; (ii) he did the best he felt he could do in all the circumstances; (iii) he was grossly negligent; (iv) he was reckless in respect of the potential impact on future crimes; or (v) his acts, such as not announcing the Korićanske Stijene killings on *ABC Nightline*, were in pursuit of non-criminal goals (*i.e.* "avoiding a public relations disaster or avoiding fear among the non-Serb population in the ARK").[2875]

859.   The Prosecution responds that the Trial Chamber reasonably relied upon Župljanin's obstruction of criminal investigations and that Župljanin fails to show an "error of fact undermining these findings".[2876] It argues that the criminal report regarding the murder of eight non-Serbs at Manjača detention camp was submitted with "an unexplained delay" and contained no information on the identity of the victims, the involvement of the Prijedor police, or the fact that the victims had died more than a month before.[2877] In relation to the Korićanske Stijene killings, the Prosecution responds that at no time did Župljanin initiate investigations into the incident "promptly" but "[r]ather, he did all he could to delay, divert and obstruct justice".[2878] The Prosecution provides a number of examples of his delay, diversion, and obstruction of justice, including Župljanin's *ABC Nightline* interview, which allegedly "demonstrates his effort to conceal what he knew of Korićanske Stijene and obstruct further investigation by other interested parties".[2879]

860.   In relation to the report concerning the Manjača detention camp, Župljanin replies that the Trial Chamber did not make a finding that the report was submitted after "an unexplained delay" or that it was deficient as a whole.[2880] Župljanin further replies in relation to the Korićanske Stijene killings that the Prosecution "tries to invoke other evidence" that he obstructed the investigation and claims that he "'connived' with Drlja[č]a" which was not the Trial Chamber's finding.[2881] **[page 357]**

ii. Analysis

861.   Turning first to the killings near the Manjača detention camp, the Appeals Chamber observes that, contrary to Župljanin's submission, the annexes to the criminal report filed by Župljanin – an exhibit that the Trial Chamber considered extensively[2882] – did not name the suspected perpetrators.[2883] Instead, as noted by

---

[2872]   Župljanin Appeal Brief, para. 176, referring to Exhibit P1567, pp 4-13.
[2873]   Župljanin Appeal Brief, para. 176.
[2874]   Župljanin Appeal Brief, para. 174. Župljanin further submits in this respect that he: (i) attended the crime scene "almost immediately"; (ii) "discovered what he could" about the identity of the perpetrators; (iii) convened a meeting of the police chiefs with jurisdiction over the crime and the suspects and insisted on the prosecution of the perpetrators; (iv) demanded that a survivor of the massacre be brought to him for an interview and handed over safely to the ICRC; (v) submitted a criminal report on the incident to the Banja Luka public prosecutor's office on 8 September 1992 against unidentified perpetrators; (vi) ordered on 11 September 1992 the Prijedor police to take statements from all those escorting the convoy; and (vii) repeated his request on 7 October 1992 after the Prijedor police chief obstructed the investigation (Župljanin Appeal Brief, para. 174).
[2875]   Župljanin Appeal Brief, para. 177.
[2876]   Prosecution Response Brief (Župljanin), para. 132.
[2877]   Prosecution Response Brief (Župljanin), para. 133.
[2878]   Prosecution Response Brief (Župljanin), para. 134.
[2879]   Prosecution Response Brief (Župljanin), para. 134.
[2880]   Župljanin Reply Brief, para. 60. Župljanin submits that the Prosecution makes speculative arguments "which the Appeals Chamber would have to assess on a *de novo* basis" (Župljanin Reply Brief, para. 60).
[2881]   Župljanin Reply Brief, para. 61. According to Župljanin, "[t]he Prosecution's imputations to [him] are unfair and disregard the clear evidence of [his] genuine disgust at this event and his vigorous efforts – obstructed by Drlja[č]a with the assistance of the military – to bring the perpetrators to justice" (Župljanin Reply Brief, para. 61).
[2882]   See Trial Judgement, vol. 2, para. 465.
[2883]   Exhibit 2D71, pp 13-14.

the Trial Chamber, the annexes contain statements of two policemen who had escorted a convoy of several buses transporting detainees from Omarska detention camp to Manjača detention camp.[2884] The Trial Chamber further noted that, according to these two policemen's statements, the detainees spent the night in the buses, waiting to be admitted into the Manjača detention camp, but during the night several prisoners died.[2885]

862.   In addition, Župljanin's argument ignores the Trial Chamber's reasoning, which he does not otherwise challenge, that when a criminal report was filed against unknown perpetrators the investigation could not proceed.[2886] In this respect, the Appeals Chamber notes that the Trial Chamber considered that Župljanin filed a criminal report on 28 August 1992 to the public prosecutor Marinko Kovačević ("Witness M. Kovačević") concerning this incident.[2887] The Trial Chamber noted that the criminal report stated that there "were reasonable grounds for suspicions that unknown perpetrators had killed eight so far unidentified persons".[2888] The Trial Chamber further considered the testimony of Witness M. Kovačević that the report contained no information on: (i) the identity of the victims or that they had died at Manjača in the night of 6 to 7 of August 1992; or (ii) the involvement of the Prijedor police.[2889] The Trial Chamber also noted Witness M. Kovačević's testimony that he sent back the file to the police for further investigation to uncover the identity of the perpetrators since he needed that information to be able to open a criminal investigation.[2890] Accordingly, Župljanin has not shown that no reasonable trier of fact could have found that the criminal report he submitted on 26 August 1992 to the public prosecutor of Banja Luka was against unknown perpetrators.[2891] He has also not shown that the Trial Chamber **[page 358]** erred in relying on this report to reach the conclusion that he knowingly misled the public prosecutor in investigations concerning the murder of non-Serbs perpetrated by the Prijedor police.[2892]

863.   Turning to the Korićanske Stijene killings, the Appeals Chamber observes that, contrary to Župljanin's assertion, the annexes to the report – an exhibit that the Trial Chamber considered[2893] – neither identify the perpetrators nor provide detailed accounts of this incident.[2894] In particular, the Appeals Chamber observes that the annexes contain the statements of seven witnesses, of whom five were Bosnian Muslims survivors of the Korićanske Stijene killings and two were reserve policemen.[2895] The statements of the victims do not identify any of the perpetrators, beyond indicating that they were from the police.[2896] The Appeals Chamber notes that the statements of the two reserve policemen identify the perpetrators as a "group of six or seven policemen in blue police uniforms", commanded by a police officer with a red baseball cap.[2897] Accordingly, Župljanin's assertion that the "report to the Prosecutor's Office included the statements of all witnesses to the event, identifying every single suspected perpetrator and their probable affiliation with the Prijedor Police", has no support in the evidence.

864.   In addition, the Appeals Chamber notes that with respect to the Korićanske Stijene killings, Župljanin ignores once more the Trial Chamber's reasoning that when a criminal report was filed against unknown perpetrators the prosecution could not proceed.[2898] The Appeals Chamber notes that the Trial Chamber considered that Župljanin submitted a criminal report regarding the Korićanske Stijene killings to the Banja

---

[2884]   Trial Judgement, vol. 2, para. 465, referring to Exhibit 2D71, pp 13-14.
[2885]   Trial Judgement, vol. 2, para. 465, referring to Exhibit 2D71, pp 13-14. The Trial Chamber also noted the policemen's statement that a lieutenant colonel told them that the bodies should be dumped into the Vrbas river (Trial Judgement, vol. 2, para. 465, referring to Exhibit 2D71, pp 13-14).
[2886]   See Trial Judgement, vol. 2, para. 465.
[2887]   Trial Judgement, vol. 2, paras 465 (referring to Marinko Kovačević, 2 Sep 2010, T. 14143-14145, Exhibits 2D71, P1574), 516.
[2888]   Trial Judgement, vol. 2, para. 465, referring to Marinko Kovačević, 2 Sep 2010, T. 14142, Exhibits 2D71, pp 1-2.
[2889]   Trial Judgement, vol. 2, para. 465. See Trial Judgement, vol. 2, para. 516.
[2890]   Trial Judgement, vol. 2, para. 465, referring to Marinko Kovačević, 2 Sep 2010, T. 14156-14158, Exhibits 2D71, p. 22.
[2891]   In addition, Župljanin's argument that the report ought to be considered along with the many others in which he "identifies crimes and recommends or directs immediate action to address the crimes" is unsupported by any reference to the evidence on the records or to the Trial Chamber's findings (see Župljanin Appeal Brief, para. 171).
[2892]   Trial Judgement, vol. 2, para. 516.
[2893]   See Trial Judgement, vol. 2, para. 474.
[2894]   Exhibit P1567, pp 5-13.
[2895]   Exhibit P1567, pp 5-13.
[2896]   See Exhibit P1567, pp 6-9, 11-12.
[2897]   Exhibit P1567, p. 5. See Exhibit P1567, p. 10.
[2898]   Trial Judgement, vol. 2, para. 474.

Luka Public Prosecutor Office on 8 September 1992 but that it was filed against "unidentified perpetrators",[2899] notwithstanding his knowledge of the identity of the perpetrators and detailed information regarding the killings.[2900] The Trial Chamber **[page 359]** also noted that the deputy basic prosecutor in Banja Luka testified that he received the criminal report but was unable to proceed immediately with the prosecution since the perpetrators were unknown.[2901]

865.   The Appeals Chamber also finds no merit in Župljanin's assertion that he promptly initiated investigations into the Korićanske Stijene killings.[2902] In addition to the filing of a criminal report against unknown perpetrators, the Trial Chamber considered evidence that Župljanin and others met the day following the incident with the "policemen involved in the incident",[2903] that no statements were taken from them, and that they were not questioned about the events.[2904] Further, it considered that Župljanin issued orders to take written statements from members of the Prijedor police who had escorted the convoy only 20 days after the incident and that no such statements were taken.[2905] The Trial Chamber also considered that Župljanin and Drljača went to Korićanske Stijene along with a unit in an unsuccessful attempt to remove the bodies from the gorge and noted the evidence of one witness who did not see an investigating judge or other representative of an investigative organ at the site.[2906] Accordingly, the Appeals Chamber is of the view that Župljanin selectively quotes the Trial Judgement and merely disagrees with the Trial Chamber's conclusion that he obstructed the Korićanske Stijene investigation, without demonstrating any error.

866.   Regarding the Trial Chamber's alleged error in relation to Župljanin's television interview, the Appeals Chamber notes that, in concluding that Župljanin did what he could to ensure impunity for the perpetrators of the Korićanske Stijene killings, the Trial Chamber considered, *inter alia*, Župljanin's interview with *ABC Nightline* which aired on an unspecified date in November 1992.[2907] The Trial Chamber observed that in the interview Župljanin "stated that there were no living witnesses to confirm or deny the killing incident at Korićanske Stijene" and that the investigations were ongoing.[2908] The Trial Chamber also considered that contrary to what he stated in this interview, Župljanin was informed on 24 August 1992 that there was a survivor from the incident.[2909] In light of these findings that show that he publicly denied the existence of a survivor who could have shed light on the incident, the Appeals Chamber finds no merit in Župljanin's **[page 360]** argument that this interview is in no way probative that he was obstructing, or intended to obstruct, the investigation. His arguments in this respect are dismissed.

867.   Insofar as Župljanin alleges that the Trial Chamber "would have had to eliminate" a number of alternative inferences in order to infer that he handled his duties with the intention of furthering the JCE,[2910] the Appeals Chamber considers that Župljanin misunderstands the standard of proof for circumstantial evidence. The Appeals Chamber recalls that a trial chamber does not have to discuss other inferences it may

---

[2899]   Trial Judgement, vol. 2, para. 474. See Trial Judgement, vol. 2, para. 517 (where the Trial Chamber incorrectly mentions the date of this report as 8 October 1992).

[2900]   Trial Judgement, vol. 2, paras 469, 517. See Trial Judgement, vol. 2, para. 466. See also Trial Judgement, vol. 1, para. 674. In particular, the Trial Chamber considered that within two days of the incident, Chief of the Skender Vakuf SJB, Witness Nenad Krejić, informed Župljanin of the incident and that Prijedor police officers had admitted to the killings (see Trial Judgement, vol. 2, paras 469, 478). It further considered that at the meeting chaired by Župljanin on 24 August 1992, "there was open acknowledgment [...] that policemen from Prijedor had committed the killings" (Trial Judgement, vol. 2, para. 470). The Appeals Chamber notes Župljanin's challenge to the Trial Chamber's finding on the basis that the Skender Vakuf police were resubordinated to the military (see Župljanin Appeal Brief, para. 172). The Appeals Chamber however finds this point to be immaterial to the issue at hand since the Trial Chamber's finding that Župljanin knowingly misled the public prosecutor regarding the Korićanske Stijene killings was not based on his authority over the Skender Vakuf police, but on the finding that he withheld information (Trial Judgement, vol. 2, para. 517).

[2901]   Trial Judgement, vol. 2, para. 474.

[2902]   See *supra*, para. 857.

[2903]   Trial Judgement, vol. 2, para. 468.

[2904]   Trial Judgement, vol. 2, para. 468, referring to Exhibit P1569.

[2905]   See Trial Judgement, vol. 2, paras 475-476.

[2906]   Trial Judgement, vol. 2, para. 470.

[2907]   See Trial Judgement, vol. 2, paras 481, 517.

[2908]   Trial Judgement, vol. 2, para. 481.

[2909]   See Trial Judgement, vol. 2, paras 481, 517. The Trial Chamber considered that "Nenad Krejić testified that he was unaware of when the *ABC* interview actually took place, but that, having turned over a survivor to Župljanin, he knew that Župljanin was aware that there were survivors" (Trial Judgement, vol. 2, para. 481, referring to Nenad Krejic, 1 Sep 2010, T. 14070-14071).

[2910]   Župljanin Appeal Brief, para. 177.

have considered, as long as it is satisfied that the inference it retained was the only reasonable one.[2911] The Appeals Chamber also observes in this regard that Župljanin simply refers to the existence of alternative inferences but has failed to point to evidence or Trial Chamber findings to support his contention.

868.   In light of the above, the Appeals Chamber finds that Župljanin has failed to demonstrate that no reasonable trier of fact could have found that on at least two occasions, Župljanin knowingly misled the public prosecutor in investigations concerning the murder of non-Serbs perpetrated by the Prijedor police.

d. Conclusion

869.   For the foregoing reasons, the Appeals Chamber finds that Župljanin has failed to demonstrate that no reasonable trier of fact could have found that he issued general and ineffective orders that were not genuinely meant to be effectuated. Similarly, he has failed to show that the Trial Chamber erred in relying on this finding to conclude that Župljanin failed to protect the non-Serb population.

(vi) Conclusion

870.   Based on the foregoing, the Appeals Chamber finds that Župljanin has failed to demonstrate that no reasonable trier of fact could have found that he failed to launch criminal investigations, to discipline subordinates who had committed crimes against non-Serbs, and to protect the non-Serb population. Accordingly, Župljanin has failed to demonstrate that the Trial Chamber erred in relying on these findings to conclude that Župljanin significantly contributed to the JCE and possessed the requisite intent. **[page 361]**

(c) Alleged errors in relying on Župljanin's knowledge of and role in the unlawful arrests and detentions of non-Serbs in the ARK Municipalities (sub-ground (G), sub-ground (D) in part, and sub-ground (E) in part of Župljanin's first ground of appeal)

871.   In determining that Župljanin significantly contributed to the JCE, the Trial Chamber relied on, *inter alia*, its finding that Župljanin was fully aware of, and took part in, the unlawful arrest of non-Serbs and their forcible removal.[2912] In concluding that Župljanin intended to further the JCE, the Trial Chamber also considered that although Župljanin was informed that crimes, including unlawful detention, were being committed on a large scale and issued orders to protect the non-Serb population, he did not take steps to ensure that these orders were in fact carried out.[2913] The Trial Chamber further considered that "Župljanin was aware of the arrests, of their unlawfulness, and that in spite of this he actively contributed to the operation".[2914]

872.   In particular, the Trial Chamber found that "Župljanin [...] played a proactive role in the mass arrest operation of non-Serbs in the ARK."[2915] To reach this conclusion, the Trial Chamber relied, together with other evidence,[2916] on Exhibit P583, a letter dated 20 July 1992 ("20 July 1992 Dispatch") whereby Župljanin informed Stanišić that:

> between April and July 1992 the army and the police in the ARK had arrested several thousand citizens of Muslim and Croat nationality as a consequence of combat operations, that for some of them there was no information of involvement in combat or combat-related activities, and that they could be treated as 'hostages' and exchanged for Serb prisoners.[2917]

The Trial Chamber concluded that "Župljanin not only failed to stop the unlawful detention of non-Serbs, but also agreed with it, actively participated in it, and even proposed to use unlawfully detained non-Serbs in prisoners exchanges."[2918]

[2911]   *Đorđević* Appeal Judgement, para. 157, referring to *Krajišnik* Appeal Judgement, para. 192.
[2912]   Trial Judgement, vol. 2, para. 518. See Trial Judgement, vol. 2, paras 415-437, 506-512.
[2913]   Trial Judgement, vol. 2, para. 519. See Trial Judgement, vol. 2, paras 415-437, 506-512.
[2914]   Trial Judgement, vol. 2, para. 519.
[2915]   Trial Judgement, vol. 2, para. 511.
[2916]   See Trial Judgement, vol. 2, para. 511.
[2917]   Trial Judgement, vol. 2, para. 511.
[2918]   Trial Judgement, vol. 2, para. 511.

(i) Submissions of the parties

873.   Župljanin submits that the Trial Chamber erred in relying on his acts and omissions in relation to the unlawful arrests and detentions of non-Serbs in the ARK Municipalities to establish that he contributed to the JCE and had the requisite intent as: (i) the arrests and detentions were not unlawful under international law given the circumstances prevailing in the ARK Municipalities between April and August 1992;[2919] and (ii) the 20 July 1992 Dispatch does not support the Trial **[page 362]** Chamber's conclusion that he agreed with and actively participated in the unlawful detentions.[2920] Župljanin asserts that the Trial Chamber's error, viewed individually or cumulatively with other errors, invalidates its finding of commission through a joint criminal enterprise and occasions a miscarriage of justice.[2921]

874.   In particular, Župljanin argues that the Trial Chamber erred in law by relying on the "unanalyzed" premise that the arrests and detentions of non-Serbs in the ARK were unlawful.[2922] Župljanin submits that in an international armed conflict, international law permits the detention of combatants or direct participants in hostilities and the temporary internment of civilians for imperative security reasons.[2923] Župljanin contends that the arrests and detentions in the ARK Municipalities between April and August 1992 were lawful given the prevailing circumstances.[2924] In this respect, he submits that the arrests and detentions in the ARK area were lawful due to the "large numbers of Muslim combatants nestled in the midst of the territory of the ARK [Municipalities" between April and August 1992.[2925] He argues that not only was there an armed conflict in the ARK and a declared imminent threat of war in the RS, "but the very survival of the ARK and its inhabitants was in serious doubt during this period".[2926] Župljanin contends that Serb forces were therefore entitled to detain anyone suspected of being a combatant, and in certain areas, acted well within their discretion in arresting any and all Muslim military-aged men both on suspicion of having participated in the armed conflict or because of the likelihood that they may 2927 participate in the armed conflict in the future.[2927] **[page 363]**

875.   Župljanin further submits that the Trial Chamber erred by inferring from the 20 July 1992 Dispatch that "he was in favour of holding detainees as 'hostages'".[2928] Župljanin contends that this exhibit reveals to the contrary that he "was very concerned about the detention of individuals on insufficient grounds and the continued detention of all detainees to be adequately reviewed".[2929] Župljanin asserts that the Trial Chamber misread the 20 July 1992 Dispatch, as he did not urge the continued detention of adult men who were not of security interest but was instead alerting his superiors of the need to release them even if a negotiating

---

[2919]   Župljanin Appeal Brief, paras 112-121, 125. See Župljanin Appeal Brief, paras 153, 161.
[2920]   Župljanin Appeal Brief, paras 122-125.
[2921]   Župljanin Appeal Brief, para. 125.
[2922]   Župljanin Appeal Brief, paras 113, 121, 125. See Župljanin Reply Brief, para. 51.
[2923]   Župljanin Appeal Brief, para. 114, referring to Geneva Convention IV, arts 42 and 78, ICRC Commentary on Geneva Convention IV, art. 42. Župljanin further argues that: (i) individual determinations are not a precondition of internment; (ii) the purpose of internment is "to prevent future danger to the security of the state or the public safety"; (iii) the detention can continue for as long as "the detainee endangers or may be a danger to security"; (iv) a review of such internment is to be made "as soon as possible" and, thereafter, at least "twice yearly" but no exact definition of the requirement of a review as soon as possible has been prescribed; and (v) "[n]o full-blown criminal procedure is required" to review any such internment of civilians (see Župljanin Appeal Brief, paras 115-117, referring to, *inter alia, Louie Salama et al. v. Israel Defence Force (IDF) Commander in Judea and Samaria and Judge of the Military Appeals Court*, Case Nos HCJ 5784/03, HCJ 6024/03, HCJ 6025/03, Petition to the Supreme Court Sitting as the High Court of Justice, 11 August 2003, para. 6, *Iad Ashak Mahmud Marab et al. v. IDF Commander in the West Bank and Judea and Samaria Brigade Headquarters*, Case No. HCJ 3239/02, The Supreme Court Sitting as the High Court of Justice, Judgement, 2 May 2003 (*sic*), para. 23, ICRC Commentary on Geneva Convention IV, arts 41 and 43. See also Župljanin Reply Brief, paras 53-54). Finally, Župljanin submits that even assuming at some point the RS breached its obligations under the Geneva Conventions by failing to institute adequate judicial procedures, this failure cannot be attributed to him personally or used as a basis to impute his criminal responsibility (see Župljanin Appeal Brief, paras 113, 117).
[2924]   Župljanin Appeal Brief, paras 113, 118-121.
[2925]   Župljanin Appeal Brief, para. 119. See Župljanin Appeal Brief, para. 118.
[2926]   Župljanin Appeal Brief, para. 119. See Župljanin Appeal Brief, paras 118, 120.
[2927]   Župljanin Appeal Brief, para. 120. See Župljanin Reply Brief, paras 50, 55.
[2928]   Župljanin Appeal Brief, para. 122.
[2929]   Župljanin Appeal Brief, para. 122, referring to Exhibit P583, pp 1-2.

advantage could not be secured, "lest they be viewed as 'hostages'".[2930] He finally submits that within weeks of the 20 July 1992 Dispatch, a large number of detainees were released.[2931]

876.   The Prosecution responds that the Trial Chamber reasonably relied on Župljanin's "proactive role" in the mass arrest of non-Serbs in the ARK in concluding that he significantly contributed to the JCE and shared the intent to further its common criminal purpose.[2932] The Prosecution submits that the Trial Chamber: (i) correctly analysed unlawful arrest and detention under international law;[2933] (ii) reasonably found that the Serb forces arrested and detained non-Serbs in the ARK Municipalities without legitimate grounds, without due process of law, and on a discriminatory basis;[2934] (iii) reasonably concluded that these detentions were unlawful;[2935] and (iv) reasonably concluded that Župljanin knew of, and contributed to, the unlawful arrest and detention of non-Serbs.[2936] **[page 364]**

877.   Regarding the 20 July 1992 Dispatch, the Prosecution responds that Župljanin's interpretation of the exhibit is "nonsensical", and that none of his proposals made in the 20 July 1992 Dispatch suggested that detainees should be released or that their detention be adequately reviewed.[2937] The Prosecution also submits that Župljanin fails to cite any evidence in support of his submission that a large number of detainees were released following the 20 July 1992 Dispatch and that the Trial Chamber made no such findings.[2938]

878.   Župljanin replies that the Prosecution's characterisation of the 20 July 1992 Dispatch is false and that no reasonable trial chamber could have adopted "the highly prejudicial interpretation" of the 20 July 1992 Dispatch given the other reasonable interpretations available, particularly "without relying on any testimonial confirmation of its own interpretation".[2939]

(ii)   Analysis

879.   The Appeals Chamber observes that a plain reading of the Trial Judgement shows that when assessing Župljanin's contribution to the JCE and his intent, the Trial Chamber relied on his knowledge of, and his role in, the unlawful arrests and subsequent detentions of non-Serbs in the ARK Municipalities,[2940] which the Trial Chamber found constituted the crime of persecutions through unlawful detention as a crime against humanity pursuant to Article 5(h) of the Statute.[2941] In this respect, the Trial Chamber stated that it

---

[2930]   Župljanin Appeal Brief, para. 123. Župljanin Appeal Brief, paras 122, 124.
[2931]   Župljanin Appeal Brief, para. 123.
[2932]   Prosecution Response Brief (Župljanin), para. 110, referring to Trial Judgement, vol. 2, paras 510-511.
[2933]   Prosecution Response Brief (Župljanin), para. 101. In particular, the Prosecution submits that: (i) the detention of civilians is an exceptionally severe measure and that there must be a serious and legitimate reason for detainment based on an assessment that the person poses a particular risk to the security of the state; (ii) the mere fact that a man is of military age or a person is a national of, or aligned with, an enemy party cannot be considered a threat to security; (iii) the detention of civilians for security reasons is only justified if security cannot be safeguarded by other less severe means, and lawful detention becomes unlawful if the basic procedural rights of detained civilians are not respected; and (iv) under Article 43 of Geneva Convention IV detained persons are entitled to have their detention reviewed at the earliest possible moment by an administrative board offering the necessary guarantees of independence and impartiality (Prosecution Response Brief (Župljanin), paras 96-99, referring to, *inter alia*, *Čelebići* Appeal Judgement, paras 327-328, ICRC Commentary to Geneva Convention IV, art. 43).
[2934]   Prosecution Response Brief (Župljanin), para. 102.
[2935]   Prosecution Response Brief (Župljanin), para. 102. See Prosecution Response Brief (Župljanin), para. 103. In support of this submission, the Prosecution highlights various findings of the Trial Chamber, including: (i) with a few exceptions, the detainees were Muslims or Croats; (ii) arrests were accompanied with ethnic slurs and derogatory terms and detainees were forced to make Serb greeting signs or sign Serb songs; (iii) the majority of detainees were not informed of the reason for their arrest, or formally processed or charged with any offence; (iv) the majority of detainees were unarmed at the time of arrest and there was no indication of involvement in armed rebelling or subversive activities; and (v) detainees included women, children, elderly, the mentally impaired, and persons too sick or weak to take part in combat activities as well as prominent members of the local Muslim and Croat communities (Prosecution Response Brief (Župljanin), para. 102).
[2936]   Prosecution Response Brief (Župljanin), para. 104, referring to Trial Judgement, vol. 2, paras 415, 417, 424, 435, 506, 508, 511. See Prosecution Response Brief (Župljanin), para. 110.
[2937]   Prosecution Response Brief (Župljanin), para. 106. The Prosecution argues that Župljanin made similar submissions regarding this exhibit at trial, which the Trial Chamber reasonably rejected (Prosecution Response Brief (Župljanin), para. 107).
[2938]   Prosecution Response Brief (Župljanin), para. 109.
[2939]   Župljanin Reply Brief, para. 56.
[2940]   Trial Judgement, vol. 2, paras 506-512, 518-519.
[2941]   See Trial Judgement, vol. 1, paras 222-223, 227, 347-349, 700-702, 811, 816.

"construe[d] the charges of unlawful detention in the Indictment as charges of the crime of imprisonment",[2942] a crime against humanity under Article 5(e) of the Statute.[2943] The Trial Chamber further held that:

> [i]n order to prove the crime of imprisonment as persecution, as a crime against humanity, the Prosecution must prove the general requirements of a crime against humanity, the specific requirements of persecution, and the following elements of the underlying offence: (a) an individual is deprived of his or her liberty; (b) the deprivation of liberty is carried out arbitrarily, that is, there is no legal basis for it; and, (c) the perpetrator acted with the intent to deprive the individual arbitrarily of his or her liberty.[2944] **[page 365]**

880. Moreover, the Appeals Chamber notes that in the legal findings sections concerning the alleged crimes in each of the ARK Municipalities, the Trial Chamber found that non-Serbs were arbitrarily arrested and detained by Serb forces in the ARK Municipalities, *i.e.* without any legal ground for such detentions, and on a discriminatory basis, and concluded that they were unlawfully detained.[2945] The Appeals Chamber further notes that the Trial Chamber conducted detailed factual analyses of evidence in this respect in relation to all ARK Municipalities.[2946] In light of the above, the Appeals Chamber dismisses Župljanin's argument that the Trial Chamber's conclusions with regard to the lawfulness of the detentions of non-Serbs were "unanalyzed".[2947]

881. Turning to Župljanin's argument that the arrests and detentions of non-Serbs in the ARK Municipalities were lawful under the Geneva Conventions, the Appeals Chamber observes that Župljanin merely refers to the provisions of the Geneva Conventions containing the law on international armed conflict,[2948] without explaining why the Trial Chamber's reliance on the law applicable to the crime of imprisonment as a crime against humanity under Article 5(e) of the Statute to establish the unlawfulness of the detentions was erroneous.

882. In any event, and to the extent that Župljanin's argument can be understood to assert that because of the existence of an international armed conflict,[2949] the Geneva Conventions are the applicable law for determining the lawfulness of the detention, the Appeals Chamber finds it unnecessary to address the issue. The Appeals Chamber notes in this regard that while Župljanin refers to the provisions of the Geneva Conventions applicable to international armed conflict, he does not explain why he believes that the armed conflict in this case was of an international character. Even if the Appeals Chamber were to consider that these provisions of the Geneva Conventions are applicable in the circumstances of this case, Župljanin's assertion that the detentions were lawful given the prevailing circumstances in the ARK Municipalities is undeveloped and he has failed to identify the Trial Chamber's findings he challenges or any relevant evidence in support of his contention. **[page 366]**

883. Specifically, Župljanin has failed to identify any relevant evidence supporting his claim that there were a large number of non-Serb combatants engaged in hostilities in the ARK area.[2950] He also does not

---

[2942] Trial Judgement, vol. 1, para. 77.

[2943] Trial Judgement, vol. 1, para. 80. See Trial Judgement, vol. 1, para. 79.

[2944] Trial Judgement, vol. 1, para. 78, referring to *Gotovina et al.* Trial Judgement, para. 1815, *Krajišnik* Trial Judgement, para. 752. See also Trial Judgement, vol. 1, para. 79, referring to *Kordić and Čerkez* Appeal Judgement, para. 116, where the Trial Chamber noted that "[t]he Appeals Chamber ha[d] held that imprisonment, in the context of Article 5(e), should be understood as 'arbitrary imprisonment, that is to say, the deprivation of liberty of the individual without due process of law'".

[2945] Trial Judgement, vol. 1, paras 222-223 (Banja Luka municipality), 282 (Donji Vakuf municipality), 347 (Ključ municipality), 491 (Kotor Varoš municipality), 700 (Prijedor municipality), 811 (Sanski Most municipality), 880 (Teslić municipality).

[2946] For the factual findings, see Trial Judgement, vol. 1, paras 201-202 (Banja Luka municipality), 262 (Donji Vakuf municipality), 332 (Ključ municipality), 455, 474-476, 480 (Kotor Varoš municipality), 659-660 (Prijedor municipality), 785-786, 796 (Sanski Most municipality), 868, 870 (Teslić municipality).

[2947] Župljanin Appeal Brief, para. 113.

[2948] Župljanin Appeal Brief, paras 114-117, referring to Geneva Convention IV, arts 42, 78, ICRC Commentary on Geneva Convention IV, arts 41-43.

[2949] Župljanin Appeal Brief, para. 119. See Župljanin Appeal Brief, para. 114. In this regard, the Appeals Chamber notes that Župljanin points to the Trial Chamber's finding that an armed conflict existed on the territory of the BiH during the Indictment period (Župljanin Appeal Brief, para. 119, referring to Trial Judgement, vol. 1, para. 132).

[2950] The Appeals Chamber notes that Župljanin solely refers to paragraph 300 of volume 1 of the Trial Judgement to support his argument that a large number of non-Serbs combatants engaged in hostilities in the ARK area (Župljanin Appeal Brief, para. 118). However, the Appeals Chamber fails to see how the fact that Witness Nikola Vracar testified that he saw 30 armed Muslim wearing TO uniforms on 27 May 1992 in front of the cultural centre of the village Pudin Han would be sufficient to establish that a large number of non-Serbs combatants engaged in hostilities in the ARK area.

point to any Trial Chamber findings or evidence on the record that would support his assertion that the majority of these detainees could reasonably be perceived as a threat, or a future threat, to security.[2951] Finally, his unsubstantiated submission that arresting any and all Muslim military-aged men on the basis of a general suspicion of having participated in the armed conflict or because of the likelihood that they may participate in the armed conflict was lawful,[2952] is based on a misunderstanding of the provisions of the Geneva Conventions[2953] and misrepresents the Trial Chamber's findings. In this regard, the Appeals Chamber notes the Trial Chamber's findings that: (i) the vast majority of the persons detained were not involved in military activities or in armed rebellion;[2954] (ii) a large number of detainees were deprived of liberty without any legal basis, were not formally charged or notified of the reason for their arrest and detention;[2955] and (iii) the detainees included women, children, the elderly, and infirm.[2956]

884. In light of the foregoing, the Appeals Chamber finds that Župljanin has not demonstrated that the Trial Chamber erred in finding that, in the circumstances of this case, the detentions of non-Serbs in the ARK Municipalities were unlawful and dismisses all his arguments in relation to the application of the Geneva Conventions to the facts prevailing in the ARK Municipalities between April and August 1992.[2957]

885. With respect to Župljanin's submission that the Trial Chamber erred by inferring from the 20 July 1992 Dispatch that "he was in favour of holding detainees as 'hostages'",[2958] the Appeals Chamber observes that Župljanin merely seeks to offer another interpretation of the words "so they can be treated as hostages"[2959] as meaning "lest they be viewed as 'hostages'".[2960] The Appeals **[page 367]** Chamber notes that a plain reading of the 20 July 1992 Dispatch does not support Župljanin's interpretation.[2961] The Appeals Chamber is satisfied that a reasonable trier of fact could have concluded, based on this evidence, that Župljanin proposed to treat non-Serb detainees as hostages and to use them in prisoner exchanges.[2962] Moreover, the Appeals Chamber notes that Župljanin does not refer to any evidence to support his factual claim that within weeks of the 20 July 1992 Dispatch a large number of detainees were released.[2963] Finally, with regard to the alleged absence of "testimonial confirmation",[2964] the Appeals Chamber recalls that a trial chamber has the discretion to rely on uncorroborated evidence and to decide in the circumstances of each case whether corroboration is necessary.[2965] Accordingly, the Appeals Chamber dismisses Župljanin's arguments in relation to the 20 July 1992 Dispatch.

[2951] See Župljanin Appeal Brief, paras 118-120.

[2952] Župljanin Appeal Brief, paras 114-120.

[2953] Compare Župljanin Appeal Brief, paras 119-120 with *Čelebići* Appeal Judgement, para. 327 where the Appeals Chamber held that it is perfectly clear from the provisions of Geneva Convention IV that there is no blanket power to detain the entire civilian population of an enemy party to a conflict on the assumption that this entire civilian population necessarily constitutes a threat to security, but that there must be an assessment that each civilian taken into detention poses a particular risk to the security of the State. See *Čelebići* Appeal Judgement, para. 330.

[2954] See *e.g.* Trial Judgement, vol. 1, paras 177-179, 223, 332.

[2955] See *e.g.* Trial Judgement, vol. 1, paras 179, 223, 262, 303, 332, 407, 474, 476, 659, 765, 796, 811.

[2956] See *e.g.* Trial Judgement, vol. 1, paras 178, 223, 428, 523, 659, 786.

[2957] For Župljanin's arguments in relation to the application of the Geneva Conventions to the facts prevailing in the ARK Municipalities between April and August 1992, see *supra*, para. 874.

[2958] Župljanin Appeal Brief, para. 122.

[2959] Župljanin Appeal Brief, para. 122, referring to Exhibit P583, pp 1-2.

[2960] Župljanin Appeal Brief, para. 123.

[2961] The Appeals Chamber observes that in the 20 July 1992 Dispatch, Župljanin expressly outlined that there were three categories of mostly military aged men detained, with "the third category [being] made of adult men on which, so far, the Service doesn't have any information of security interest for us, so they can be treated as hostages" (Exhibit P583, p. 1). Župljanin then expressly proposed "to exchange military aged [men] of no security interest to [them], who can be treated only as hostages, for citizens of Serbian nationality who have been detained in camps held by Muslim-Croatian forces, according to the same criteria" (Exhibit P583, p. 2).

[2962] Trial Judgement, vol. 2, paras 435, 511. The Appeals Chamber also observes that the 20 July 1992 Dispatch constitutes direct evidence and not circumstantial evidence and that consequently, the Trial Chamber was not required to determine that its conclusion was the only reasonable inference available from the evidence (*Čelebići* Appeal Judgement, para. 458). In light of the above, the Appeals Chamber dismisses Župljanin's submission that the Trial Chamber was required but failed to eliminate all other reasonable interpretations of the 20 July 1992 Dispatch (see Župljanin Reply Brief, para. 56).

[2963] See Župljanin Appeal Brief, para. 123.

[2964] Župljanin Reply Brief, para. 56.

[2965] *Đorđević* Appeal Judgement, para. 858, fn. 2505; *Gatete* Appeal Judgement, para. 138.

(iii) Conclusion

886. In light of the foregoing, the Appeals Chamber finds that Župljanin has failed to demonstrate that the Trial Chamber erred in concluding that the arrests and detentions of non-Serbs in the ARK Municipalities were unlawful and in its assessment of the 20 July 1992 Dispatch. Župljanin does not put forth any other argument supporting his general allegation that the Trial Chamber erred in relying on his knowledge of and role in the unlawful arrests and detentions to establish his contribution to the JCE and his intent. Accordingly, the Appeals Chamber finds that Župljanin has failed to demonstrate that the Trial Chamber erred in this respect. **[page 368]**

(d) Alleged errors in relying on Župljanin's attendance at the Holiday Inn Meeting, his role in the takeovers of the ARK Municipalities and the blockade of Banja Luka, and his close ties with SDS political leaders (sub-ground (D) in part and sub-ground (E) in part of Župljanin's first ground of appeal)

887. In concluding that Župljanin significantly contributed to the JCE, the Trial Chamber considered, together with other factors, that Župljanin created a unit, the Banja Luka CSB SPD, which he used to assist other Serb forces in the takeovers of the ARK Municipalities.[2966] In finding that Župljanin intended to further the JCE, the Trial Chamber "primarily" considered Župljanin's acts in relation to, *inter alia*, his: (i) attendance at the Holiday Inn Meeting where he was scheduled to meet Karadžić;[2967] (ii) ties to the SDS;[2968] and (iii) key role in the blockade of Banja Luka by the SOS on 3 April 1992.[2969] of the parties

(i) Submissions of the parties

888. Župljanin disputes the Trial Chamber's reliance on the above-mentioned positive acts to conclude that he significantly contributed to the common criminal purpose and/or to infer that he had the requisite intent pursuant to the first category of joint criminal enterprise.[2970] In particular, Župljanin argues that the Trial Chamber erred in relying on his: (i) attendance at the Holiday Inn Meeting;[2971] (ii) participation in the takeovers of the ARK Municipalities and his role in the blockade of Banja Luka;[2972] and (iii) close ties with SDS political leaders.[2973] Župljanin argues that **[page 369]** these positive acts are not probative of anything more than the lawful objective of "setting up and defending a separate political entity in the ARK" and "did not require recourse to any criminal means to be carried out".[2974]

[2966] Trial Judgement, vol. 2, para. 518. See Trial Judgement, vol. 2, paras 501-505. See also Trial Judgement, vol. 2, paras 384-398, 405-406.

[2967] Trial Judgement, vol. 2, para. 519. See Trial Judgement, vol. 2, paras 352, 495.

[2968] Trial Judgement, vol. 2, para. 519. According to the Trial Chamber, Župljanin's ties to the SDS were demonstrated by "the unreserved support" he received from SDS leaders in the ARK to his appointment as Chief of the Banja Luka CSB and interactions with other SDS members (Trial Judgement, vol. 2, para. 519. See Trial Judgement, vol. 2, paras 349-353 (with respect to support Župljanin received from SDS leaders), 399, 452, 454, 495 (referring to Župljanin's interaction with SDS members). The Trial Chamber also referred to Župljanin's role in ensuring the implementation of the orders of the ARK Crisis Staff, of which he was a member (see Trial Judgement, vol. 1, paras 147-148, 200; Trial Judgement, vol. 2, paras 276-278, 353, 495, 500) and noted that "top leaders [of the ARK Crisis Staff] included prominent SDS members Radoslav Brđanin and Vojislav Kuprešanin, both found by the Trial Chamber to have been members of the JCE" (Trial Judgement, vol. 2, para. 500).

[2969] Trial Judgement, vol. 2, para. 519. See Trial Judgement, vol. 2, paras 495-499. See also Trial Judgement, vol. 1, paras 147-156, 200, Trial Judgement, vol. 2, paras 399-404.

[2970] Župljanin Appeal Brief, paras 139, 152, 154-155, 157-160. In connection with Župljanin's involvement in the creation of the Banja Luka CSB SPD and his use of this unit in the takeovers of the ARK Municipalities, the Appeals Chamber recalls that it has already rejected Župljanin's submissions that the Trial Chamber erred in finding that he exercised complete authority over the Banja Luka CSB SPD (see *supra*, paras 821-836. See also Župljanin Appeal Brief, paras 140-151). Furthermore, although Župljanin appears to challenge the Trial Chamber's reliance on his role in the disarming of the non-Serb population in the ARK Municipalities, he does not develop this argument anywhere in his appeal brief (see Župljanin Appeal Brief, para. 139, p. 76 (the title of sub-section (iv) within the section on sub-ground (D) of Župljanin's first ground of appeal)). Therefore, the Appeals Chamber does not consider that this argument warrants any further discussion.

[2971] Župljanin Appeal Brief, paras 157-158.

[2972] Župljanin Appeal Brief, paras 152, 157, 159.

[2973] Župljanin Appeal Brief, paras 157, 160.

[2974] Župljanin Appeal Brief, paras 157-158. See Župljanin Appeal Brief, paras 155, 159-161.

889. Župljanin challenges the Trial Chamber's reliance on his alleged attendance at the Holiday Inn Meeting in inferring his intent.[2975] Župljanin contends that the Trial Chamber made no findings, and no evidence was presented, about the content of any conversations between himself and Karadžić.[2976] According to Župljanin, even if the Trial Chamber correctly determined that he had a conversation with Karadžić, "[i]t would be a gross fallacy to infer that the content of that [*sic*] any discussion involving [him] – which could have been quite brief, according to the available evidence – included discussing the adoption of criminal methods merely because crimes were committed during the intense military conflict that ensued."[2977]

890. Župljanin also challenges the Trial Chamber's findings on his role in the blockade of Banja Luka and the takeovers of the ARK Municipalities,[2978] arguing that the blockade and the takeovers were neither unlawful nor criminal under international law and therefore, not probative of any contribution to the JCE or criminal intent.[2979] In relation to the Trial Chamber's finding that Župljanin had close ties with the SDS, he argues that it is likewise not probative of criminal intent since most leading Bosnian Serb politicians in the ARK or RS had contacts and were affiliated with the SDS and that "it would have been simply impossible to function as a police chief [...] without having extensive contacts with SDS leaders".[2980] He further argues that the Trial Chamber's reliance on this factor to prove criminal intent is "misguided" as it "comes dangerously close to attributing guilt by association".[2981]

891. The Prosecution responds that the Trial Chamber reasonably considered Župljanin's positive conduct when finding that he significantly contributed to the JCE and intended to further the JCE.[2982] The Prosecution argues that the Trial Chamber reasonably established that Župljanin **[page 370]** participated in the Holiday Inn Meeting.[2983] It contends that Župljanin's argument that the Trial Chamber failed to ascertain the content of a private conversation between himself and Karadžić during the Holiday Inn Meeting "misses the point" since it is uncontested that "during the meeting, 'Karadžić called for the formation of municipal executive boards and other municipal organs, followed by mobilisation of Serb Forces to takeover Variant A municipalities and monitor Variant B municipalities'".[2984] It contends that therefore, Župljanin's attendance at the meeting shows his knowledge of and agreement with the SDS policy of violent takeovers which were a "crucial component of the JCE".[2985]

892. The Prosecution further responds that a contribution to a joint criminal enterprise need not be criminal in and of itself,[2986] and that consequently, the question as to whether the blockade of Banja Luka and the takeovers of the ARK Municipalities were illegal under international law is immaterial.[2987] It submits that the Trial Chamber reasonably relied on Župljanin's participation in the Banja Luka blockade to determine his intent, since it demonstrates his "agreement and satisfaction with SOS activities" and "his resolve [...] to use his power to promote and/or to perpetuate crimes against non-Serbs".[2988] Moreover, according to the

---

[2975] Župljanin Appeal Brief, paras 155, 158.
[2976] Župljanin Appeal Brief, para. 158. See Appeal Hearing, 16 Dec 2015, AT. 161.
[2977] Župljanin Appeal Brief, para. 158; Appeal Hearing, 16 Dec 2015, AT. 161-162.
[2978] Župljanin Appeal Brief, paras 152, 157, 159. Župljanin also reiterates his arguments under sub-ground (D) of his first ground of appeal that he undertook efforts to ensure that crimes committed in the context of the blockade were investigated and prosecuted (Župljanin Appeal Brief, para. 159). See *supra*, paras 821-836.
[2979] Župljanin Appeal Brief, paras 152, 159. Župljanin notes that "[t]he blockade may have been unlawful under the law of Bosnia and Herzegovina (as were most actions of the Bosnian government under SFRY law)" (see Župljanin Appeal Brief, para. 159).
[2980] Župljanin Appeal Brief, para. 160. See Župljanin Appeal Brief, para. 157.
[2981] Župljanin Appeal Brief, para. 160, referring to *Stanišić and Simatović* Trial Judgement, Separate Opinion of Judge Alphons Orie, para. 2415.
[2982] Prosecution Response Brief (Župljanin), paras 111, 125. The Prosecution asserts that Župljanin's contention that "specific incidents, taken out of context, were not probative of his criminal intent" ignores that "[t]he object of the common criminal purpose was indivisible from the agreed criminal means by which it would be achieved" (Prosecution Response Brief (Župljanin), para. 125). According to the Prosecution, Župljanin focuses on irrelevant details and fails to consider the purpose for which the Trial Chamber referred to the incidents (Prosecution Response Brief (Župljanin), para. 126).
[2983] Appeal Hearing, 16 Dec 2015, AT. 199-200.
[2984] Prosecution Response Brief (Župljanin), para. 126, quoting Trial Judgement, vol. 2, para. 495.
[2985] Prosecution Response Brief (Župljanin), para. 126, referring to Trial Judgement, vol. 2, paras 310-311, 313.
[2986] Prosecution Response Brief (Župljanin), paras 122-123. The Prosecution further points out that Župljanin repeats his argument raised under sub-ground (G) of his first ground of appeal that the arrest and detention of non-Serbs in the ARK was lawful (Prosecution Response Brief (Župljanin), para. 123, referring to Župljanin Appeal Brief, para. 153).
[2987] Prosecution Response Brief (Župljanin), paras 122-123.
[2988] Prosecution Response Brief (Župljanin), para. 126, referring to Prosecution Response Brief (Župljanin), paras 29, 122.

Prosecution, Župljanin fails to show that the Trial Chamber unreasonably concluded that his assistance to the Serb forces in carrying out the takeovers, taken together with his other conduct, constituted a significant contribution to the common criminal purpose.[2989] It also submits that, contrary to Župljanin's argument that the Trial Chamber relied decisively on his close ties with the SDS leadership, the Trial Chamber reached its conclusion based on extensive evidence and that there was therefore "no danger of 'guilt by association'".[2990]

893.   Župljanin replies that even accepting as truthful the evidence of the receipt from the Holiday Inn hotel purporting to show that he stayed there on the night of 14 February 1992 as well as the **[page 371]** intercept where Karadžić indicates that he might be able to meet with Župljanin "during breaks", it does not demonstrate that Župljanin was present at the meeting.[2991] He contends that the reasonable inference remains that he was present in Sarajevo to meet Karadžić at the breaks but did not attend the Holiday Inn Meeting of the SDS, of which he was not a member.[2992]

(ii) Analysis

894.   Regarding Župljanin's argument in relation to his attendance at the Holiday Inn Meeting, the Appeals Chamber observes that the Trial Chamber found that Župljanin was present at the Holiday Inn Meeting where he was scheduled to meet with Karadžić.[2993] In reaching this conclusion, the Trial Chamber considered evidence of a phone conversation of 13 February 1992 between Karadžić and Jovan Cizmović ("Cizmović"), a Serb ARK politician, in which Cizmović asked Karadžić to meet the following day and informed him that "'Stojan' would have liked to come too".[2994] Karadžić replied that they could meet during "breaks".[2995] The Trial Chamber was satisfied that the "Stojan" referred to in the conversation was Župljanin after further considering evidence of a receipt for the stay of members of the SDS assembly at the Holiday Inn hotel for 14 and 15 February 1992.[2996] In particular, the Trial Chamber considered that according to the receipt a number of prominent SDS leaders and a guest named "Župljanin" arrived at the Holiday Inn hotel on 14 February 1992 and departed on the following day.[2997]

895.   The Appeals Chamber considers that no reasonable trier of fact could have concluded that the only reasonable inference from the evidence is that Župljanin was present at the Holiday Inn Meeting. In this respect, the Appeals Chamber notes that the Holiday Inn Meeting was a meeting of the Main and Executive Boards of the SDS, to which only SDS members appear to have been invited.[2998] The Trial Chamber made no findings that Župljanin was a member of these boards or of the SDS. In light of this, while it may have been reasonable for the Trial Chamber to conclude on the basis of the phone conversation between Karadžić and Cizmović and the hotel receipt that Župljanin was present at the Holiday Inn hotel on that day, his presence at the hotel does not exclude other reasonable inferences, including for instance, that he met with Karadžić during breaks but did not attend the Holiday Inn Meeting. The Appeals Chamber therefore concludes that the Trial Chamber erred in finding beyond reasonable doubt that Župljanin was present at the Holiday **[page 372]** Inn Meeting. It follows that the Trial Chamber erred in relying on this factor when assessing his intent to further the JCE.[2999] The impact of this error will be assessed below.[3000]

[2989]   Prosecution Response Brief (Župljanin), para. 122, referring to Trial Judgement, vol. 2, para. 518. It asserts that, in any event, the Trial Chamber's conclusion was "eminently reasonable, especially given its findings 'that the takeovers preceded the mass arrest campaign, imposition of discriminatory measures, forcible transfer, deportation, and the commission of other crimes against the non-Serb population'" (Prosecution Response Brief (Župljanin), para. 122, quoting Trial Judgement, vol. 2, para. 502).
[2990]   Prosecution Response Brief (Župljanin), para. 126.
[2991]   Župljanin Reply Brief, para. 59.
[2992]   Župljanin Reply Brief, para. 59.
[2993]   Trial Judgement, vol. 2, para. 352.
[2994]   Trial Judgement, vol. 2, para. 352.
[2995]   Trial Judgement, vol. 2, para. 352.
[2996]   Trial Judgement, vol. 2, para. 352.
[2997]   Trial Judgement, vol. 2, para. 352.
[2998]   Trial Judgement, vol. 2, paras 237 (referring to, *inter alia*, Exhibit P1841), 352. See Exhibit P1841, p. 1.
[2999]   See Trial Judgement, vol. 2, para. 519.
[3000]   See *infra*, para. 942. In light of the foregoing, the Appeals Chamber dismisses as moot the remainder of Župljanin's submissions in relation to his attendance at the Holiday Inn Meeting (see Župljanin Appeal Brief, paras 157-158).

896.   The Appeals Chamber now turns to Župljanin's challenges with regard to the Trial Chamber's reliance on its findings that he played a key role in the blockade of Banja Luka and assisted other Serb forces in the takeovers of the ARK Municipalities by using the Banja Luka CSB SPD. He argues that these actions were neither illegal nor criminal.[3001] The Appeals Chamber recalls that a contribution to a joint criminal enterprise need not be in and of itself criminal, as long as the accused performs acts that in some way contribute significantly to the furtherance of the common purpose.[3002] In addition, the Appeals Chamber recalls that intent can be proven through inference from circumstantial evidence, as long as it is the only reasonable inference based on the evidence.[3003]

897.   In light of this, the lawfulness of the blockade of Banja Luka and of the takeovers of ARK Municipalities is of no relevance to the determination as to whether the Trial Chamber erred in relying on Župljanin's role in these events to establish his contribution to the JCE and his intent. The Appeals Chamber observes that Župljanin does not raise any further challenges to the Trial Chamber's findings that he played a key role in the blockade of Banja Luka and assisted other Serb forces in the takeovers of the ARK Municipalities by using the Banja Luka CSB SPD. Therefore, the Appeals Chamber finds that Župljanin has not demonstrated that the Trial Chamber erred in relying on these findings to establish that he contributed to the JCE and had the requisite intent.

898.   The Appeals Chamber next turns to Župljanin's challenge in relation to the Trial Chamber's finding that he had "[c]lose ties with the SDS political leaders".[3004] The Appeals Chamber observes that in inferring Župljanin's intent, the Trial Chamber considered his "ties to the SDS, demonstrated by the unreserved support given by top SDS leaders in the ARK to his appointment as Chief of the CSB and by his interactions with other SDS members".[3005] The Appeals Chamber finds no merit in Župljanin's contention that his ties with the SDS were not probative of criminal intent since most **[page 373]** leading Bosnian Serb politicians in the ARK or RS had contacts and were affiliated with the SDS.[3006] The Appeals Chamber considers that Župljanin misrepresents the Trial Chamber's findings. The Trial Chamber did not rely on his general contact and ties with SDS members to infer his intent, but rather on specific interactions he had with some SDS political leaders as well as the "unreserved support" he received from top SDS leaders in the ARK for his appointment as Chief of the CSB.[3007]

899.   The Appeals Chamber also considers that the Trial Chamber's finding that Župljanin received unreserved support from top SDS leaders for his appointment as Chief of the CSB and interacted with other SDS members[3008] must be read in conjunction with the fact that the vast majority of the SDS political leaders he was found to have close ties with were also found to be members of the JCE.[3009] In addition, the Appeals Chamber does not agree with Župljanin that the Trial Chamber's reliance on this factor "comes dangerously close to attributing 'guilt by association'".[3010] Župljanin's submission ignores that the Trial Chamber did not solely rely on his close ties with the SDS, but that it was merely one of numerous factors relied upon by the

[3001]   Župljanin Appeal Brief, paras 152, 159. See also Župljanin Appeal Brief, para. 157.
[3002]   *Popović et al.* Appeal Judgement, para. 1653; *Šainović et al.* Appeal Judgement, para. 985; *Krajišnik* Appeal Judgement, paras 215, 695-696. See *Šainović et al.* Appeal Judgement, paras 1233, 1242. See also *supra*, para. 110.
[3003]   *Popović et al.* Appeal Judgement, para. 1369; *Šainović et al.* Appeal Judgement, para. 995; *Krajišnik* Appeal Judgement, para. 202.
[3004]   Župljanin Appeal Brief, para. 160. See Župljanin Appeal Brief, para. 157.
[3005]   Trial Judgement, vol. 2, para. 519. The Trial Chamber also considered that Župljanin contributed to the implementation of SDS policies in Banja Luka and other ARK Municipalities, among other factors, when inferring his intent (see Trial Judgement, vol. 2, para. 519).
[3006]   Župljanin Appeal Brief, para. 160. See Župljanin Appeal Brief, para. 157.
[3007]   Trial Judgement, vol. 2, para. 519. See Trial Judgement, vol. 2, paras 349-353 (referring to support Župljanin received from SDS leaders), 399, 452, 454, 495 (referring to Župljanin's interaction with SDS members). See also Trial Judgement, vol. 1, paras 147, 148; Trial Judgement, vol. 2, paras 276-278, 495, 500 (referring to Župljanin's role in ensuring the implementation of the orders of the ARK Crisis Staff (of which he was a member), "whose top leaders included prominent SDS members Radoslav Brđanin and Vojislav Kupresanin, both found by the Trial Chamber to have been members of the JCE").
[3008]   See Trial Judgement, vol. 2, para. 519.
[3009]   Compare Trial Judgement, vol. 2, para. 314 (see *supra*, para. 73) with Trial Judgement, vol. 2, paras 349 (Brđanin), 350 (Kupresanin), 352, 452 (Brđanin, Kupresanin, Karadžić, and Krajišnik), 495 (Karadžić), 500 (Brđanin and Kupresanin).
[3010]   See Župljanin Appeal Brief, para. 160.

Trial Chamber to infer that he intended to further the JCE.[3011] Accordingly, Župljanin has not shown that the Trial Chamber erred in relying on his close ties with SDS political leaders in assessing his intent for joint criminal enterprise liability.

(iii) Conclusion

900. In light of the foregoing, the Appeals Chamber finds that the Trial Chamber erred in finding beyond reasonable doubt that Župljanin was present at the Holiday Inn Meeting and in relying on **[page 374]** this factor when assessing his intent to further the JCE. The impact of this error will be assessed below.[3012] The Appeals Chamber further finds that Župljanin has failed to demonstrate any error in the Trial Chamber's reliance on his: (i) participation in the takeovers of the ARK Municipalities and his role in the blockade of Banja Luka; and (ii) close ties with SDS political leaders to conclude that he significantly contributed to the common criminal purpose and/or to infer that he had the requisite intent pursuant to the first category of joint criminal enterprise.

(e) Whether the Trial Chamber erred in concluding that Župljanin significantly contributed to the JCE (sub-ground (C) in part of Župljanin's first ground of appeal)

901. As recalled above, the Trial Chamber assessed Župljanin's contribution to the JCE on the basis of its findings that he: (i) ordered and coordinated the disarming of the non-Serb population in ARK Municipalities; (ii) created the Banja Luka CSB SPD, which he used to assist other Serb forces in the takeovers of the ARK Municipalities; (iii) knew of and took part in the unlawful arrest of non-Serbs and their forcible removal; (iv) failed to launch criminal investigations and to discipline his subordinates who had committed crimes against non-Serbs, creating a climate of impunity which only increased the commission of crimes against non-Serbs; and (v) failed to protect the non-Serb population even when they pleaded with him for protection.[3013] In light of these acts and failures to act, the Trial Chamber concluded that, during the Indictment period, Župljanin significantly contributed to the common objective of the JCE to permanently remove Bosnian Muslims and Bosnian Croats from the territory of the planned Serb state.[3014]

(i) Submissions of the parties

902. Župljanin submits that the Trial Chamber placed "heavy reliance on omissions" to find that he significantly contributed to the JCE,[3015] and that the Trial Chamber's errors in failing to apply the correct legal standard for omissions and make necessary findings in this regard is not remedied by the fact that the Trial Chamber relied on a mixture of acts and omissions.[3016] He argues that "the MUP in the ARK was not found to constitute a 'criminal enterprise' so as to convert general actions in support of that organ as constituting the *actus reus*".[3017] **[page 375]**

[3011]   The Appeals Chamber notes that in reaching this conclusion, the Trial Chamber considered that Župljanin: (i) played a role in the blockade of Banja Luka; (ii) had ties to the SDS; (iii) contributed to the implementation of SDS policies in Banja Luka and in other municipalities in the ARK; (iv) failed to protect the non-Serb population; (v) enrolment of the SOS in the Banja Luka CSB SPD; (vi) inaction in relation to the crimes committed by this unit; (vii) "statements and actions taken in response to requests for protection by the Muslims of Banja Luka"; (viii) was aware and actively contributed to unlawful arrest operations; and (ix) created a "climate of impunity that encouraged the perpetration of crimes against non-Serbs and made non-Serbs decide to leave the ARK Municipalities" by shielding his subordinates from criminal prosecution (Trial Judgement, vol. 2, para. 519. See *supra*, para. 906). The Appeals Chamber notes that the Trial Chamber also considered that Župljanin attended the Holiday Inn Meeting but recalls its finding that the Trial Chamber erred in relying on this factor when assessing Župljanin's intent to further the JCE (see Trial Judgement, vol. 2, para. 519. See also *supra*, para. 895).
[3012]   See *infra*, para. 942.
[3013]   Trial Judgement, vol. 2, para. 518.
[3014]   Trial Judgement, vol. 2, para. 518.
[3015]   Župljanin Appeal Brief, para. 126.
[3016]   Župljanin Appeal Brief, para. 136.
[3017]   Župljanin Appeal Brief, para. 136. Župljanin also submits that the Trial Chamber relied solely on his position as an official of the RS MUP and the fact that RS MUP organs "committed crimes or failed to prevent crimes" in order to conclude that he "committed the *actus reus* of the crime committed or not prevented by [RS] MUP organs" (Župljanin Appeal Brief, para. 126).

903.   The Prosecution responds that the Trial Chamber correctly convicted Župljanin as a JCE member on the basis of its conclusion that he made a significant contribution to the common criminal purpose.[3018] The Prosecution adds that the Trial Chamber was only required to find that "the totality of Župljanin's conduct (including both actions and omissions) – as opposed to each of his contributions considered separately – constituted a significant contribution to the implementation of the common criminal purpose",[3019] and that Župljanin fails to show any error in the Trial Chamber's assessment.[3020] Finally, the Prosecution contends that the fact that the RS MUP "was not a 'criminal enterprise' is irrelevant to Župljanin's culpability".[3021] It argues that Župljanin was convicted for his "significant and intentional contribution to a common criminal purpose", not for providing support to a broad organisation or for his "mere membership in the MUP".[3022]

(ii) Analysis

904.   At the outset, the Appeals Chamber recalls its finding that Župljanin has not shown that the Trial Chamber applied an erroneous legal standard when it considered instances of his failures to act or erred in failing to make necessary findings in this regard.[3023] The Appeals Chamber has also found that none of Župljanin's arguments demonstrate that the Trial Chamber erred in finding that he failed to launch criminal investigations, to discipline his subordinates, and ultimately, to protect the non-Serb population.[3024] Therefore, Župljanin's argument that the Trial Chamber's alleged errors in this respect are not remedied by the fact that the Trial Chamber "relied on a mixture of acts and omissions"[3025] is moot. However, to the extent that his argument can be understood to challenge the Trial Chamber's overall reasoning for its finding that he significantly contributed to the JCE, the Appeals Chamber will address his argument.

905.   In this respect, the Appeals Chamber recalls that, in addition to dismissing Župljanin's above-mentioned arguments in relation to his failures to act, it has found that he has not demonstrated that the Trial Chamber erred in its assessment of other factors, namely: (i) his knowledge of and role in unlawful arrest and detention of non-Serbs in the ARK Municipalities;[3026] and (ii) his use of the Banja Luka CSB SPD to assist other Serb forces in the takeovers of the ARK **[page 376]** Municipalities,[3027], on which it relied to conclude that he significantly contributed to the JCE.[3028] Further, Župljanin has not challenged the Trial Chamber's reliance on his order and coordination of the disarming of the non-Serb population in ARK Municipalities to conclude that he significantly contributed to the JCE.[3029] Župljanin's argument that "the MUP in the ARK was not found to constitute a 'criminal enterprise' so as to convert general actions in support of that organ as constituting the *actus reus*"[3030] is unsupported by a plain reading of the Trial Judgement. The Trial Chamber specifically identified Župljanin's conduct it considered to be demonstrative of his significant contribution to the JCE, which was not based on his mere support to the MUP.[3031] Noting that Župljanin does not advance any other allegations of error, the Appeals Chamber finds that he has not shown that no reasonable trier of fact could have found that Župljanin significantly contributed to the JCE.

[3018]   Prosecution Response Brief (Župljanin), para. 85.
[3019]   Prosecution Response Brief (Župljanin), para. 92.
[3020]   Prosecution Response Brief (Župljanin), para. 93.
[3021]   Prosecution Response Brief (Župljanin), para. 91, referring to Župljanin Appeal Brief, paras 134, 136.
[3022]   Prosecution Response Brief (Župljanin), para. 91.
[3023]   See *supra*, paras 734-735.
[3024]   See *supra*, para. 870.
[3025]   Župljanin Appeal Brief, para. 136.
[3026]   See *supra*, para. 886.
[3027]   See *supra*, para. 900.
[3028]   See Trial Judgement, vol. 2, para. 518.
[3029]   See *supra*, fn. 2970.
[3030]   Župljanin Appeal Brief, para. 136. See Župljanin Appeal Brief, para. 126.
[3031]   See Trial Judgement, vol. 2, para. 518; *supra*, para. 901.

(f) Whether the Trial Chamber erred in concluding that Župljanin possessed the requisite intent pursuant to the first category of joint criminal enterprise (sub-ground (E) in part and sub-ground (F) in part of Župljanin's first ground of appeal)

(i) Introduction

906.   The Trial Chamber concluded that Župljanin, who was found to be a member of the JCE starting at least in April 1992 and throughout the rest of 1992, intended through his acts and omissions, with other members of the JCE, to achieve the permanent removal of Bosnian Muslims and Bosnian Croats from the territory of the planned Serbian state through the commission of the JCE I Crimes.[3032] In reaching this conclusion, the Trial Chamber "primarily considered" that Župljanin: (i) played a role in the blockade of Banja Luka; (ii) had ties to the SDS; (iii) attended the Holiday Inn Meeting; and (iv) contributed to the implementation of SDS policies in Banja Luka and in other municipalities in the ARK.[3033] The Trial Chamber also considered Župljanin's failure to protect the non-Serb population, which it found "formed part of the decision to discriminate against them and force them to leave the ARK Municipalities, and was not merely the consequence of simple negligence".[3034] It considered this factor in conjunction with his: (i) enrolment of the SOS in the Banja Luka CSB SPD; (ii) inaction in relation to the crimes committed by this unit; and **[page 377]** (iii)   "statements and actions taken in response to requests for protection by the Muslims of Banja Luka".[3035] The Trial Chamber further found that Župljanin was aware and actively contributed to unlawful arrest operations, and created a "climate of impunity that encouraged the perpetration of crimes against non-Serbs and made non-Serbs decide to leave the ARK Municipalities" by shielding his subordinates from criminal prosecution.[3036]

907.   Župljanin submits that the Trial Chamber erred when concluding that he shared the intent to commit the crimes forming part of the common criminal purpose of the JCE by: (i) applying an erroneous *mens rea* standard;[3037] (ii) failing to make a finding that he shared the intent with the other JCE members;[3038] (iii) finding that he shared the intent from April 1992;[3039] and (iv) concluding that the only reasonable inference was that he possessed the requisite intent.[3040] Župljanin asserts that these errors invalidate the Trial Chamber's conclusion that he had the requisite intent for the first category of joint criminal enterprise and that all his convictions based on the first category of joint criminal enterprise should be reversed.[3041] The Prosecution responds that the Trial Chamber correctly and reasonably found that Župljanin intended to participate in and to further the JCE from April 1992, based on the proper application of the law.[3042]

(ii) Alleged errors related to the subjective element pursuant to the first category of joint criminal enterprise

a. Submissions of the parties

908.   Župljanin submits that the Trial Chamber committed several errors in relation to the applicable standard for the subjective element which is required for a conviction under the first category of joint

---

[3032]   Trial Judgement, vol. 2, para. 520. The Trial Chamber also considered that Župljanin's acts were voluntary (Trial Judgement, vol. 2, para. 519). See Trial Judgement, vol. 2, para. 518 (finding that Župljanin's contributions to the JCE started on 1 April 1992 and continued "throughout the rest of the year" and concluding that "during the Indictment period" Župljanin significantly contributed to the common purpose of the JCE).
[3033]   Trial Judgement, vol. 2, para. 519.
[3034]   Trial Judgement, vol. 2, para. 519.
[3035]   Trial Judgement, vol. 2, para. 519.
[3036]   Trial Judgement, vol. 2, para. 519.
[3037]   Župljanin Appeal Brief, paras 12-15, 17-25, 31-32, 35-44, 53.
[3038]   Župljanin Appeal Brief, paras 50-52.
[3039]   Župljanin Appeal Brief, paras 45-49.
[3040]   Župljanin Appeal Brief, paras 102-104, 155-156, 178-179.
[3041]   Župljanin Appeal Brief, para. 54. See Župljanin Appeal Brief, para. 179.
[3042]   See Prosecution Response Brief (Župljanin), paras 5, 8, 124.

criminal enterprise.[3043] He contends that these errors invalidate the Trial Chamber's finding that he "intended forcible transfer as the common criminal purpose".[3044]

909. Župljanin first submits that the Trial Chamber was required to find that he intended coercive acts to find that he shared the requisite intent pursuant to the first category of joint criminal **[page 378]** enterprise[3045] since: (i) the common purpose was to be achieved through JCE I Crimes;[3046] and (ii) the *actus reus* of JCE I Crimes requires "either physical compulsion or coercive acts against the expellee".[3047] According to Župljanin, this implies that the act inducing the departure must itself be criminal.[3048] Župljanin contends that the Trial Chamber failed to find that he intended any of the coercive acts through which the common purpose was implemented.[3049] According to Župljanin, the only "coercive acts" by which the non-Serbs were induced to flee were considered by the Trial Chamber in the context of the third category of joint criminal enterprise and found only to be foreseeable to him.[3050] Župljanin submits that the Trial Chamber's finding that he intended to further the JCE is therefore contradicted by, and incompatible with, the "finding that he did not intend any of the coercive acts by which the forcible transfer was effectuated".[3051]

910. Župljanin adds that the contradiction in the Trial Chamber's findings arises from its analysis of his intent on the basis of its "loose definitions of the common purpose that merely involve an objective where it is probable that a crime will be committed in pursuit of the objective", thereby reducing the requisite *mens rea* standard for first category of joint criminal enterprise from direct intent to *dolus eventualis*.[3052] He contends that the Trial Chamber's findings incorrectly suggest that intending to create an ethnically homogenous state, which is not inherently criminal and is rather a **[page 379]** "pursuit of lawful objectives", is sufficient to establish the subjective element of the first category of joint criminal enterprise.[3053]

[3043]   Župljanin Appeal Brief, paras 12-15, 17-25, 31-32, 35-44, 53.
[3044]   Župljanin Appeal Brief, para. 14.
[3045]   See Župljanin Appeal Brief, paras 3, 35.
[3046]   Župljanin Appeal Brief, para. 15.
[3047]   Župljanin Appeal Brief, para. 17, referring to *Stakić* Appeal Judgement, para. 279, *Popović et al.* Trial Judgement, para. 891, *Krnojelac* Trial Judgement, para. 474. See Župljanin Appeal Brief, para. 12.
[3048]   Župljanin Appeal Brief, para. 18. He further argues that measures authorised or permitted under the law of armed conflict, such as a lawful and legitimate attack on a village, do not satisfy the *actus reus* of forcible transfer. According to Župljanin, a contrary approach would "unjustifiably limit the conduct of hostilities, and overthrow the fundamental principle that 'humanitarian law is the *lex specialis* which applies in cases of armed conflict'" (Župljanin Appeal Brief, para. 18).
[3049]   Župljanin Appeal Brief, para. 53.
[3050]   Župljanin Appeal Brief, paras 8, 19. See Župljanin Appeal Brief, para. 12; Župljanin Reply Brief, paras 5, 9. Župljanin argues that the Trial Chamber "exhaustively" analysed in the context of the third category of joint criminal enterprise the coercive acts by which non-Serbs were forced to flee but found that these crimes were merely foreseeable to him (Župljanin Appeal Brief, para. 20. See Župljanin Appeal Brief, para. 23. See also Župljanin Reply Brief, para. 13).
[3051]   Župljanin Appeal Brief, para. 25. See Župljanin Appeal Brief, para. 12. Quoting the *Krajišnik* Appeal Judgement, Župljanin further submits that the parties should not be "placed in the position of having to guess [...] what may have been intended by the Chamber" in relation to elements central to his individual criminal responsibility, especially where the Trial Chamber's findings are contradictory (Župljanin Appeal Brief, para. 24 quoting *Krajišnik* Appeal Judgement, para. 176. See Župljanin Appeal Brief, para. 25).
[3052]   Župljanin Appeal Brief, para. 32. See Župljanin Appeal Brief, paras 31, 33; Appeal Hearing, 16 Dec 2015, AT. 146-147. Župljanin also contends that the Trial Chamber defined the common purpose "in such a way as to encompass goals that merely involve a possibility of crimes" (Župljanin Appeal Brief, para. 39. See Župljanin Appeal Brief, para. 38, referring to *Prosecutor v. Issa Hassan Sesay et al.*, Case No. SCSL-04-15-A, Judgement, 26 October 2009 ("*RUF* Appeal Judgement"), para. 305, Partially Dissenting and Concurring Opinion of Judge Shireen Avis Fisher, paras 17-19, 25).
[3053]   Župljanin Appeal Brief, paras 33, 37. In support of his submission, Župljanin adds that: (i) the Trial Chamber refers to "'forcible takeovers' of municipalities as if to imply that this is criminal in a legally relevant sense" and that since forcible takeover does not constitute a crime, the Trial Chamber's reference indicates that it defined a common purpose that was not, in itself, criminal and therefore erroneously assessed his intent in relation to a non-criminal purpose (Župljanin Appeal Brief, para. 35, referring to Trial Judgement, vol. 1, paras 331, 1006, 1028, Trial Judgement, vol. 2, para. 375)); (ii) the Trial Chamber failed to find that he intended acts of coercion which indicates that it had a non-criminal purpose in mind (Župljanin Appeal Brief, para. 35. See Appeal Hearing, 16 Dec 2015, AT. 155-157; Župljanin Appeal Brief, paras 19-23); and (iii) the Letter sent by Judge Harhoff suggests that a joint criminal enterprise "can be established merely on the basis of foresight and 'acceptance' of the commission of crimes, rather than a criminal intent to commit such crimes" (Župljanin Appeal Brief, para. 35. See Appeals Hearing, 16 Dec 2015, AT. 155157. See Župljanin Appeal Brief, paras 19-23). He adds that the Trial Chamber "would not have refrained from entering findings of direct intent on the basis of judicial economy" and that it had the "duty to make findings in relation to the charges on the standard of proof beyond a reasonable doubt" (Župljanin Reply Brief, para. 9).

911.   Župljanin further submits that the Trial Chamber's finding that his failure to protect the non-Serb population formed part of the decision to force non-Serbs to leave the ARK Municipalities and was not merely the consequence of "simple negligence" suggests that it applied an erroneous *mens rea* standard as the absence of "simple negligence" does not establish direct intent.[3054] He further contends that the Trial Chamber's statement that his conduct "encouraged the perpetration of crimes" implies that the Trial Chamber applied "a *mens rea* consistent with aiding and abetting, not commission".[3055]

912.   The Prosecution responds that the Trial Chamber's conclusion as to Župljanin's intent demonstrates that it correctly articulated and applied the requisite intent standard pursuant to the first category of joint criminal enterprise.[3056] The Prosecution argues that the Trial Chamber's definition of the common criminal purpose is consistent with its findings on the third category of joint criminal enterprise.[3057] It contends that there is no legal requirement that "the crime of forced displacement" be achieved through the commission of specific violent crimes, such as those for which Župljanin was convicted for under the third category of joint criminal enterprise.[3058] The Prosecution also submits that Župljanin's proposition that the act inducing the displacement of individuals must itself be criminal is "unsupported and inconsistent with the jurisprudence establishing that it suffices to employ 'mere' threats or to take advantage of a coercive environment".[3059] The Prosecution adds that nothing in the law requires the joint criminal enterprise **[page 380]** members to agree, or the Trial Chamber to make findings upon the particular form by which the coercion of non-Serbs might take place.[3060] According to the Prosecution, there is therefore no basis upon which to consider that the Trial Chamber's reference to Župljanin's JCE III Crimes was intended to be an exhaustive review of the coercive acts by which the common criminal purpose would be implemented.[3061] It further submits that Župljanin incorrectly asserts that Župljanin's JCE III Crimes "were the only 'coercive acts' relevant to the forced displacement crimes".[3062] It argues that there is no inconsistency between the Trial Chamber's conclusion that he shared the intent to further the JCE and its findings on Župljanin's JCE III Crimes since the Trial Chamber made no findings excluding Župljanin's direct (or indirect) intent for the JCE III Crimes.[3063] The Prosecution also asserts that the Trial Chamber was not required to find that Župljanin intended Župljanin's JCE III Crimes.[3064]

[3054]   Župljanin Appeal Brief, para. 42. See Župljanin Appeal Brief, paras 13, 40, referring to Trial Judgement, vol. 2, para. 519. Župljanin Reply Brief, paras 14-15. Župljanin argues that in the spectrum between "simple negligence" and direct intent, "are the mental states of recklessness, *dolus eventualis*, gross negligence, and knowledge" (Župljanin Appeal Brief, para. 42).

[3055]   Župljanin Appeal Brief, para. 42.

[3056]   Prosecution Response Brief (Župljanin), paras 12, 23.

[3057]   Prosecution Response Brief (Župljanin), p. 7 (title of section 2). See Prosecution Response Brief (Župljanin), paras 16-21.

[3058]   Prosecution Response Brief (Župljanin), para. 17.

[3059]   Prosecution Response Brief (Župljanin), fn. 36. It further responds that Župljanin's proposition is inconsistent with the principle that underlying acts of persecutions need not themselves constitute crimes under international law (Prosecution Response Brief (Župljanin), fn. 36, referring to *Brđanin* Appeal Judgement, para. 296, *Kvočka et al.* Appeal Judgement, para. 323). The Prosecution also notes that "the Appeals Chamber specifically left open the question 'whether attacks on lawful military targets could ever constitute a basis for ascribing criminal liability'" (see Prosecution Response Brief (Župljanin), fn. 36, referring to *Gotovina and Markač* Appeal Judgement, para. 114, fn. 330).

[3060]   Prosecution Response Brief (Župljanin), para. 18. The Prosecution adds that, "[i]n other words, once the JCE members had agreed to forcibly remove the non-Serbs, they did not also have to agree on the precise manner or methods by which this was to be carried out" (Prosecution Response Brief (Župljanin), para. 18).

[3061]   Prosecution Response Brief (Župljanin), para. 18.

[3062]   Prosecution Response Brief (Župljanin), para. 16. The Prosecution underlines that, to the contrary, it is clear from the Trial Chamber's findings concerning the crimes committed in the ARK Municipalities that Serb forces forced non-Serbs to leave through a range of coercive acts which were not strictly limited to Župljanin's JCE III Crimes. The Prosecution argues that, although these acts also included particular crimes, they also entailed the "use of threats, fear, and the exploitation of the general coercive environment created by the JCE members and their tools" (Prosecution Response Brief (Župljanin), para. 16).

[3063]   Prosecution Response Brief (Župljanin), para. 19. According to the Prosecution, rather, the Trial Chamber made only those findings which were necessary, and thus acted consistently with the principle of judicial economy (see Prosecution Response Brief (Župljanin), para. 19).

[3064]   Prosecution Response Brief (Župljanin), para. 21. The Prosecution notes that the Trial Chamber was not required to make this finding "except for the purpose of ascertaining – in the exercise of its direction as to appropriate modes – whether Župljanin had ordered persecution through the appropriation of property" (Prosecution Response Brief (Župljanin), para. 21 (citations omitted)).

913.   The Prosecution further argues that the Trial Chamber did not, therefore, apply a standard of *dolus eventualis* or mere intent for an "overall 'objective'" that is not criminal, as suggested by Župljanin.[3065]
[page 381]

914.   The Prosecution finally responds that while Župljanin does not challenge the intent standard for the first category of joint criminal enterprise, he "challenges the Chamber's reasoning based on a semantic argument".[3066] It argues that there is nothing in the Trial Chamber's analysis suggesting that it inferred Župljanin's intent on the basis of "simple negligence".[3067] It further argues that the Trial Chamber's reference to "negligence" was made in the context of ascertaining the intentional nature of Župljanin's omission.[3068] It finally argues that the Trial Chamber was not obliged to refute other intent standards known to law but inapposite to the facts of this case and that the Trial Chamber's conclusion "is more than adequately reasoned".[3069]

        b. Analysis

915.   The Appeals Chamber recalls that in order for the subjective element of the first category of joint criminal enterprise to be met, the accused must share, with the other participants, the intent to commit the crimes that form part of the common purpose of the joint criminal enterprise and the intent to participate in a common plan aimed at their commission.[3070]

916.   The Appeals Chamber observes that the Trial Chamber defined the common purpose of the JCE as the permanent removal of Bosnian Muslims and Bosnian Croats from the territory of the planned Serbian state, which was to be achieved through the crimes of other inhumane acts (forcible transfer), deportation, and persecutions through underlying acts of forcible transfer and deportation.[3071] The Trial Chamber then found, relying on a number of factors as set out above,[3072] that Župljanin shared the intent with other members of the JCE to further the JCE.[3073] The Trial Chamber then considered Župljanin's liability for all other charged crimes pursuant to the third category of joint criminal enterprise.[3074] In doing so, the Trial Chamber found that the possibility that Župljanin's JCE III Crimes could be committed in the execution of the common criminal **[page 382]** purpose was sufficiently substantial so as to be foreseeable to him and that he willingly took the risk that such crimes might be committed.[3075] Župljanin has failed to show any error in this reasoning.

917.   Župljanin's argument that the Trial Chamber was required to find that he intended coercive acts to find that he possessed the requisite intent pursuant to the first category of joint criminal enterprise is based on a

---

[3065]   Prosecution Response Brief (Župljanin), para. 12, referring to Župljanin Appeal Brief, paras 32-33, 36. In addition, the Prosecution avers that "forcible takeovers" were correctly considered by the Trial Chamber, along with other factual circumstances, when inferring Župljanin's intent (Prosecution Response Brief (Župljanin), para. 14). It asserts that although forcible takeover does not constitute a crime under the Statute, "a person's willingness to use force and violence as the means of securing ethnic dominance in a municipality, and the subsequent and repeated exploitation of power gained from that takeover to commit crimes, is a factor material to an intent analysis" (Prosecution Response Brief (Župljanin), para. 14). The Prosecution also submits that the comparison to the *RUF* Appeal Judgement is inapposite since: (i) the majority concluded that a common purpose existed to secure control over Sierra Leone through the commission of the charged crimes; and (ii) "Judge Fisher's Separate Opinion turned on a difference of opinion as to the proper interpretation of the Trial Judgement" (Prosecution Response Brief (Župljanin), para. 15, referring to *RUF* Appeal Judgement, paras 300, 302, 305, Partially Dissenting and Concurring Opinion of Judge Shireen Avis Fisher, para. 12).
[3066]   Prosecution Response Brief (Župljanin), para. 23.
[3067]   Prosecution Response Brief (Župljanin), para. 23, quoting Župljanin Appeal Brief, paras 40, 42.
[3068]   Prosecution Response Brief (Župljanin), para. 24. According to the Prosecution, Župljanin confuses the Trial Chamber's discussion of his failure to carry out his duty as a police officer to protect the civilian population with its "reasoning establishing his intent to further the common purpose" (Prosecution Response Brief (Župljanin), para. 24).
[3069]   Prosecution Response Brief (Župljanin), para. 27. See Prosecution Response Brief (Župljanin), para. 26.
[3070]   *Popović et al.* Appeal Judgement, para. 1369. See *Đorđević* Appeal Judgement, para. 468; *Brđanin* Appeal Judgement, para. 365.
[3071]   See Trial Judgement, vol. 2, para. 313.
[3072]   See *supra*, para. 906.
[3073]   Trial Judgement, vol. 2, para. 520. See Trial Judgement, vol. 2, para. 519.
[3074]   Trial Judgement, vol. 2, para. 521. See Trial Judgement, vol. 2, paras 522-528. Župljanin was also convicted of ordering persecutions, through appropriation of property, as a crime against humanity through plunder of property (see Trial Judgement, vol. 2, para. 805. See also Trial Judgement, vol. 2, paras 526, 956).
[3075]   See Trial Judgement, vol. 2, paras 522-528.

misunderstanding of the applicable law. The Trial Chamber was not required to establish that Župljanin intended the specific coercive acts by which the JCE I Crimes were to be achieved. The Appeals Chamber recalls that the Trial Chamber was required to find that Župljanin shared with the other members of the JCE the intent to commit the JCE I Crimes and the intent to participate in a common plan aimed at their commission.[3076] Therefore, it was necessary for the Trial Chamber to find that Župljanin shared the intent for the JCE I Crimes, and especially that he intended to forcibly displace, permanently or otherwise, the victims across the relevant *de facto* or *de jure* border to another country (as in deportation) or within a relevant border (as in forcible transfer).[3077] In the view of the Appeals Chamber, it is not required that members of the JCE agreed upon a particular form through which the forcible displacement of non-Serbs was to be effectuated or that Župljanin intended specific acts of coercion causing the displacement of individuals, so long as it is established that Župljanin intended to forcibly displace the victims.

918. In addition, Župljanin's argument that the Trial Chamber was required to find that he intended coercive acts under the first category of joint criminal enterprise because the *actus reus* of the JCE I Crimes requires that the act inducing the departure be criminal, finds no support in the jurisprudence of the Tribunal. The Appeals Chamber observes that the common purpose of the JCE was to be achieved through the JCE I Crimes, namely, the crimes of other inhumane acts (forcible transfer), deportation, and persecutions through acts of forcible transfer and deportation.[3078] In order to establish these crimes, the Trial Chamber was required to find, *inter alia*, that the displacement of persons was forced.[3079] The Appeals Chamber recalls that the requirement that the displacement be forced is not limited to physical force but can be met through the threat of force or coercion, such as that caused by fear of violence, duress, detention, psychological oppression or abuse of power, or taking advantage of a coercive environment.[3080] It is the absence of genuine choice that makes the **[page 383]** displacement unlawful.[3081] While fear of violence, use of force, or other such circumstances may create an environment where there is no choice but to leave, the determination as to whether a transferred person had a genuine choice is one to be made within the context of the particular case being considered.[3082] Contrary to Župljanin's unreferenced assertion, the jurisprudence of the Tribunal does not require that persons be displaced as a result of criminal acts.[3083]

919. Finally, and based on his incorrect statement of the law, Župljanin takes the view that the Trial Chamber exclusively relied on Župljanin's JCE III Crimes to establish the coercive acts through which the forcible displacements in question were effectuated.[3084] The Appeals Chamber finds no support in the Trial Judgement for Župljanin's assertion. A review of the Trial Chamber's findings reveals that the Trial Chamber found that non-Serbs were forced to flee through a range of coercive acts not limited to the factual basis relied upon by the Trial Chamber to find that Župljanin's JCE III Crimes were established. These coercive acts not only included particular crimes, but also entailed harassment, threats, fear, and the creation of a general coercive environment.[3085] The Appeals Chamber therefore finds no merit in Župljanin's argument that the Trial Chamber's finding that he intended to further the JCE is contradicted by, or incompatible with,

---

[3076]   *Popović et al.* Appeal Judgement, para. 1369. See *Đorđević* Appeal Judgement, para. 468; *Brđanin* Appeal Judgement, para. 365. It is noted that Župljanin does not contest this standard (see Župljanin Reply Brief, para. 12).

[3077]   See Trial Judgement, vol. 1, paras 61, 105. See also *Stakić* Appeal Judgement, paras 278, 307, 317. In this regard, the Appeals Chamber notes that the Trial Chamber correctly recounted the *mens rea* required for the JCE I Crimes (see Trial Judgement, vol. 1, para. 61).

[3078]   Trial Judgement, vol. 2, para. 313.

[3079]   *Đorđević* Appeal Judgement, paras 705, (referring to *Krajišnik* Appeal Judgement, para. 304, *Stakić* Appeal Judgement, paras 278, 307), 727. See also Trial Judgement, vol. 1, para. 63.

[3080]   *Đorđević* Appeal Judgement, para. 727, referring to *Stakić* Appeal Judgement, para. 281, *Krnojelac* Appeal Judgement, paras 229-233.

[3081]   *Đorđević* Appeal Judgement, para. 727; *Krnojelac* Appeal Judgement, para. 229.

[3082]   *Đorđević* Appeal Judgement, para. 727; *Stakić* Appeal Judgement, paras 281-282.

[3083]   In relation to Župljanin's argument that measures authorised or permitted under the law of armed conflict, such as a lawful and legitimate attack on a village, do not satisfy the *actus reus* of forcible transfer (Župljanin Appeal Brief, para. 8.), the Appeals Chamber observes that Župljanin does not point to any evidence to suggest that the displacements in this case were justified under international humanitarian law. The Appeals Chamber therefore dismisses Župljanin's argument as undeveloped and demonstrating no error.

[3084]   See Župljanin Appeal Brief, paras 19-23.

[3085]   See Trial Judgement, vol. 1, paras 208-211, 221, 273-274, 281, 338, 346, 477, 490, 684, 699, 803-804, 810, 872, 879; Trial Judgement, vol. 2, para. 522.

the Trial Chamber's finding that Župljanin's JCE III Crimes were only foreseeable to him. It follows that Župljanin has not shown that the Trial Chamber erred in this regard.

920.   Turning to Župljanin's argument that the Trial Chamber analysed his intent on the basis of its "loose definitions of the common purpose that merely involve an objective where it is probable that a crime will be committed",[3086] the Appeals Chamber recalls that it has dismissed Župljanin's argument that the Trial Chamber incorrectly defined the common purpose.[3087] It has also found that the Trial Chamber clearly determined that the common purpose of the JCE involved the commission of crimes within the Statute.[3088] Accordingly, the Appeals Chamber finds no merit in Župljanin's contentions that the Trial Chamber reduced the requisite subjective element of the first category of joint criminal enterprise from direct intent to *dolus eventualis* and that the Trial Chamber's findings suggest that intending the pursuit of a lawful objective is sufficient to establish **[page 384]** the intent required for the first category of joint criminal enterprise.[3089] The Appeals Chamber also finds no merit in the remainder of Župljanin's arguments in support of his submission that the Trial Chamber analysed his intent based on a common purpose which was not criminal.[3090]

921.   The Appeals Chamber now turns to Župljanin's argument that the Trial Chamber's findings show that it applied a standard which was inconsistent with the requisite standard of direct intent. In this respect, the Appeals Chamber underlines that the Trial Chamber expressly found that Župljanin "*intended*, with other members of the JCE" to achieve the goal of the JCE through the commission of the JCE I Crimes.[3091]

922.   In concluding that Župljanin possessed the requisite intent, the Trial Chamber considered that Župljanin's failure to protect the non-Serb population "formed part of the decision to discriminate against them and force them to leave the ARK Municipalities, and was not merely the consequence of *simple negligence*".[3092] The Appeals Chambers finds that Župljanin takes out of context and misrepresents the Trial Judgement when arguing that this finding suggests that the Trial Chamber applied an incorrect standard for the subjective element of the first category of joint criminal enterprise. A plain reading of the Trial Judgement shows that this finding was made in the context of the Trial Chamber's assessment of the intentional nature of Župljanin's failure to carry **[page 385]** out his duty as a police officer to protect the civilian population.[3093] Accordingly, the Appeals Chamber dismisses this argument.

923.   The Appeals Chamber now turns to Župljanin's submission that the Trial Chamber's statement that his conduct "encouraged the perpetration of crimes" implies that it applied a standard consistent with aiding

---

[3086]   Župljanin Appeal Brief, para. 32. See Župljanin Appeal Brief, paras 31, 33.
[3087]   See *supra*, para. 69.
[3088]   See *supra*, para. 69.
[3089]   Insofar as Župljanin seeks to rely on the *RUF* Appeal Judgement before the SCSL, the Appeals Chamber observes that the majority of the appeals chamber in the *RUF* case concluded that the trial chamber determined that a common purpose existed to secure control over Sierra Leone through the commission of crimes charged in the indictment (*RUF* Appeal Judgement, paras 300, 302, 305). Judge Shireen Avis Fisher ("Judge Fisher"), however, dissented in relation to one of the accused, noting the trial chamber's express finding that the accused did not intend a number of crimes under the first category of joint criminal enterprise (see *RUF* Appeal Judgement, Partially Dissenting and Concurring Opinion of Judge Shireen Avis Fisher, paras 14-16). According to Judge Fisher, this express finding contradicted the finding that the accused had participated in a joint criminal enterprise (see *RUF* Appeal Judgement, Partially Dissenting and Concurring Opinion of Judge Shireen Avis Fisher, paras 14-16). The Appeals Chamber notes in this regard that Judge Fisher's remarks were made in the context of the facts and findings in that case, and considers that they do not apply to the present case. In the present case, the Trial Chamber did not find that Župljanin did not intend the crimes through which the common purpose was to be implemented. Instead, it expressly found that Župljanin intended, with other members of the JCE, to achieve the common purpose through the commission of the crimes of other inhumane acts (forcible transfer), deportation, and persecutions through the same underlying acts (see Trial Judgement, vol. 2, para. 520). The reasoning of Judge Fisher's dissenting opinion is therefore inapplicable to the present case, since the Trial Judgement is neither ambiguous nor contradictory in this respect. Župljanin has therefore failed to demonstrate an error in this regard.
[3090]   As for Župljanin's submissions concerning forcible takeovers, the Appeals Chamber recalls that it has rejected Župljanin's argument that the Trial Chamber's reference to the forcible takeover of the Municipalities, which does not constitute a crime, indicates that the Trial Chamber defined a common purpose which was not criminal (see *supra*, fn. 251). The Appeals Chamber further recalls that it has rejected, above, Župljanin's argument in relation to coercive acts (see *supra*, paras 917-919). The Appeals Chamber also recalls that it has dismissed Župljanin's arguments regarding Judge Harhoff's misstatement of the subjective standard for joint criminal enterprise liability in the Letter (see *supra*, paras 52-53).
[3091]   Trial Judgement, vol. 2, para. 520 (emphasis added).
[3092]   Trial Judgement, vol. 2, para. 519 (emphasis added).
[3093]   See Trial Judgement, vol. 2, paras 519-520.

and abetting, not commission.[3094] The Appeals Chamber notes that the Trial Chamber made this statement in the context of Župljanin's participation in the JCE through his formation of a "feigned commission" that resulted in the creation of a climate of impunity.[3095] The Appeals Chamber considers that Župljanin takes the Trial Chamber's words out of context and ignores the Trial Chamber's conclusion that he *intended* with other members of the JCE to further the JCE in light of all the factors considered, including his specific role in the formation a "feigned commission".[3096] The Appeals Chamber considers that, contrary to Župljanin's assertion, there is no indication that the Trial Chamber applied the standard for the subjective element of aiding and abetting liability and not commission through participation in a joint criminal enterprise.[3097] The Appeals Chamber therefore dismisses Župljanin's argument.

924. Based on the foregoing, the Appeals Chamber finds that Župljanin has failed to demonstrate that the Trial Chamber applied an incorrect standard for the subjective element when finding that Župljanin possessed the requisite intent pursuant to the first category of joint criminal enterprise.

(iii) Alleged error in failing to find that Župljanin shared the intent to further the JCE with other JCE members

a. Submissions of the parties

925. Župljanin submits that the Trial Chamber failed to make the required findings to establish that he shared the criminal purpose common to all JCE members and not merely had the same criminal purpose.[3098] Relying on the *Brđanin* Appeal Judgement, he avers that "a coinciding *mens rea*, and even a substantial overlap in the crimes actually committed" does not suffice to **[page 386]** establish that he possessed the requisite intent.[3099] Župljanin further contends that the reasonable inference remains that his "supposedly permissive attitude towards the commission of crimes was attributable to 'a shared motive'" (rather than a common criminal purpose or shared criminal intent) and that the Trial Chamber simply presumed that his "coincident intent" meant that he became a member of the pre-existing JCE.[3100]

926. The Prosecution responds that the Trial Chamber's findings establish that "Župljanin had more than a 'shared motive' with his fellow JCE members".[3101] The Prosecution submits that the Trial Chamber did not presume his membership in the JCE based on the coincidence of his intent with that of other JCE members but rather expressly found that he intended with other members of the JCE to further the JCE.[3102] It contends that Župljanin's reference to the *Brđanin* Appeal Judgement does not assist him since the risk of mere coincidence between the acts of remote physicals perpetrators and the common criminal purpose does not arise in this case where the nexus between Župljanin and the common criminal purpose is clear.[3103]

[3094] Župljanin Appeal Brief, para. 42. See Župljanin Appeal Brief, para. 41.

[3095] Trial Judgement, vol. 2, para. 519.

[3096] Trial Judgement, vol. 2, para. 520. The Appeals Chamber also recalls that it has already dismissed Župljanin's submission that the Trial Chamber erred in relying on his formation of a feigned commission when assessing his participation in the JCE (see *supra*, para. 851).

[3097] The Appeals Chamber also fails to see how the fact that "encouragement" can constitute the objective element of aiding abetting would suggest that the Trial Chamber applied the standard for the subjective element of aiding and abetting in this case when addressing Župljanin's intent pursuant to the first category of joint criminal enterprise (*cf. Šainović et al.* Appeal Judgement, para. 1649).

[3098] Župljanin Appeal Brief, paras 50-53. Župljanin also points out that he was not found to have been a founding member of the JCE, but that he joined it in April 1992 (Župljanin Appeal Brief, para. 51).

[3099] Župljanin Appeal Brief, para. 50, referring to *Brđanin* Appeal Judgement, paras 447-448. See Župljanin Appeal Brief, paras 51-52, 54. Župljanin contends that the Trial Chamber was required to find that the criminal purpose was "not merely the same, but also common to all of the persons acting together within a joint criminal enterprise" (Župljanin Appeal Brief, para. 50, quoting *Brđanin* Appeal Judgement, paras 430, 447-448. See Župljanin Appeal Brief, paras 51-52, 54).

[3100] Župljanin Appeal Brief, para. 52. See Župljanin Appeal Brief, paras 51, 54.

[3101] Prosecution Response Brief (Župljanin), para. 31. See Prosecution Response Brief (Župljanin), para. 32.

[3102] Prosecution Response Brief (Župljanin), para. 31, quoting Trial Judgement, vol. 2, para. 520. The Prosecution adds that, reading the Trial Judgement as a whole and in particular the passages establishing his links with the SDS and other JCE members, it is clear that the Trial Chamber found that he intended to participate with other JCE members to achieve the common criminal purpose (see Prosecution Response Brief (Župljanin), para. 32).

[3103] Prosecution Response Brief (Župljanin), para. 32.

b. Analysis

927.   The Appeals Chamber recalls that in order for the subjective element of the first category of joint criminal enterprise to be met, the accused must share, with the other participants, the intent to commit the crimes that form part of the common purpose of the joint criminal enterprise and the intent to participate in a common plan aimed at their commission.[3104] The Appeals Chamber further recalls that a trial chamber must "make a finding that th[e] criminal purpose is not merely the same, but also common to all the persons acting together within a joint criminal enterprise".[3105]

928.   The Appeals Chamber observes that a plain reading of the Trial Judgement shows that the Trial Chamber found that Župljanin shared the intent with the other JCE members to further the JCE. Indeed, it found that "Župljanin's acts and omissions demonstrate beyond reasonable doubt that *he intended, with other members of the JCE, to achieve* the permanent removal of Bosnian [page 387] Muslims and Bosnian Croats from the territory of the planned Serbian state through the commission of [the JCE I Crimes]".[3106] It then concluded that "Župljanin was a member of the JCE starting at least in April 1992 and throughout the rest of 1992".[3107]

929.   Contrary to Župljanin's submission, the Trial Chamber's conclusion was not based on the presumption that his "coincident intent meant that he became a member of the pre-existing JCE".[3108] The Appeals Chamber notes that unlike in the *Brđanin* case,[3109] other reasonable inferences, including that Župljanin might have shared a motive to further the commission of the JCE I Crimes but was not a member of the JCE, did not remain in the present case. In this regard, the Trial Chamber reached its conclusion on the basis of findings establishing a clear link between Župljanin's knowledge of the crimes, his conduct that supported the commission of crimes, and his ties with other members of the JCE, notwithstanding that he was not found to have been a founding member of the JCE.[3110] The Appeals Chamber therefore considers Župljanin's reference to the finding in the *Brđanin* Appeal Judgement to be inapposite.

930.   In light of the foregoing, Župljanin has not demonstrated that the Trial Chamber failed to make findings required for establishing that he shared the intent with the other JCE members to further the JCE. His arguments are therefore dismissed.

(iv) Alleged errors in finding that Župljanin shared the intent from April 1992

a. Submissions of the parties

931.   Župljanin submits that the Trial Chamber erroneously relied on evidence of his conduct from August to November 1992 to infer that he was a member of the JCE and had the requisite intent from at least April 1992.[3111] While recognising that the Trial Chamber was "not disentitled" [page 388] to rely on evidence of

---

[3104]   *Popović et al.* Appeal Judgement, para. 1369. See *Đorđević* Appeal Judgement, para. 468; *Brđanin* Appeal Judgement, para. 365.

[3105]   *Brđanin* Appeal Judgement, para. 430, referring to *Stakić* Appeal Judgement, para. 69.

[3106]   Trial Judgement, vol. 2, para. 520 (emphasis added).

[3107]   Trial Judgement, vol. 2, para. 520.

[3108]   Župljanin Appeal Brief, para. 52.

[3109]   See *Brđanin* Appeal Judgement, para. 448. In the *Brđanin* case, the Appeals Chamber found that other reasonable inferences remained, including that those found by the *Brđanin* Trial Chamber to be members of the joint criminal enterprise "might have shared a motive in furthering the commission of the same crime but were not members of the same [joint criminal enterprise]" (*Brđanin* Appeal Judgement, para. 448).

[3110]   See Trial Judgement, vol. 2, para. 520. See also Trial Judgement, vol. 2, paras 489-519; *supra*, fn. 3009 (Župljanin's ties with the other JCE members).

[3111]   Župljanin Appeal Brief, para. 45, referring to Trial Judgement, vol. 2, paras 474, 514, 517, 519-520. See Župljanin Reply Brief, paras 16-18. See also Župljanin Reply Brief, para. 19. According to Župljanin, "[a] person cannot be liable pursuant to JCE I unless and until it is established that the crime was committed at a time when it was part of the common [...] purpose" (Župljanin Appeal Brief, para. 46, referring to *Krajišnik* Appeal Judgement, para. 173). In particular, he argues that, in order to draw inferences about his *mens rea* as of April 1992, the Trial Chamber relied "heavily" on, and made "special mention" of, evidence concerning events which occurred on 14 August 1992, 26 August 1992, and 8 September 1992 (Župljanin Appeal Brief, paras 45, 47. See Župljanin Reply Brief, paras 17-18). Župljanin refers to evidence concerning his establishment of a feigned commission to inspect

events which occurred after April 1992, Župljanin argues that the Trial Chamber was required to provide reasons as to why his alleged conduct from August and September 1992 were probative of his intent in April 1992.[3112] He argues that the Trial Chamber did not indicate that it could have found that he had the required intent since April 1992 without relying on evidence from August to November 1992.[3113] According to Župljanin, the implication is that the evidence of his conduct "through the month of July 1992 was not sufficient to reveal his criminal intent as the only reasonable inference as of that date".[3114] Župljanin finally argues that the Trial Chamber failed to identify the date upon which he allegedly joined the JCE "or what conduct, event, or statement gave rise to the inference" that his intent "crystallized" in April 1992.[3115]

932.   The Prosecution responds that the Trial Chamber's finding that Župljanin was a member of the JCE from at least April 1992 is well-grounded in evidence and not impermissibly vague.[3116] It further responds that Župljanin inaccurately interprets the Trial Judgement when arguing that the Trial Chamber should not have relied on conduct from August and September 1992 since the Trial Chamber did not rely exclusively on evidence from that period but reasonably took into account the totality of the evidence.[3117]

b. Analysis

933.   The Trial Chamber found that Župljanin possessed the requisite intent for the first category of joint criminal enterprise starting from at least April 1992 and continuing throughout the rest of the year.[3118] The Appeals Chamber considers that Župljanin's arguments are based on the premise that the Trial Chamber exclusively or mainly relied on evidence from August to November 1992 to infer that Župljanin was a member of the JCE and had the requisite intent from "at least April 1992".[3119] Župljanin merely refers to three paragraphs of the Trial Judgement without explaining why he considers them to be the only relevant paragraphs relied upon by the Trial **[page 389]** Chamber to infer that he had the requisite intent.[3120] To the contrary, in reaching its conclusion that Župljanin was a member of the JCE and had the requisite intent, the Trial Chamber, as explained below, expressly considered ample evidence which demonstrated his membership and intent from at least April 1992.[3121]

934.   The Appeals Chamber recalls that the subjective element of the first category of joint criminal enterprise may be inferred from circumstantial evidence, including a person's knowledge, combined with continuous contribution to crimes within the common criminal purpose.[3122] The Appeals Chamber observes that in assessing Župljanin's intent, the Trial Chamber considered evidence that Župljanin had extensive knowledge of crimes being committed against the non-Serb population, was well aware that the non-Serb

---

detention camps as well as the concealment of the names of perpetrators of the killings in front of the Manjača Camps and of Prijedor police officers who murdered approximately 150-200 Muslims in Korićanske Stijene (Župljanin Appeal Brief, para. 45, fn. 56, referring to Trial Judgement, vol. 2, paras 474, 514, 517).

[3112]   Župljanin Appeal Brief, para. 47. See Župljanin Appeal Brief, para. 48. See also Župljanin Reply Brief, paras 16-18.

[3113]   Župljanin Appeal Brief, para. 47. See Župljanin Reply Brief, paras 17-18. Župljanin asserts that the Appeals Chamber would need to determine whether the post-April events supported a finding of *mens rea* beyond reasonable doubt before August 1992 (Župljanin Reply Brief, para. 18).

[3114]   Župljanin Appeal Brief, para. 47.

[3115]   Župljanin Appeal Brief, para. 48.

[3116]   See Prosecution Response Brief (Župljanin), paras 29-30.

[3117]   Prosecution Response Brief (Župljanin), para. 29, referring to Župljanin Appeal Brief, paras 45-47, Trial Judgement, vol. 2, paras 349-350, 352, 378, 399-404, 495, 500-505, 519. See Prosecution Response Brief (Župljanin), para. 30.

[3118]   Trial Judgement, vol. 2, para. 520.

[3119]   See Trial Judgement, vol. 2, para. 520.

[3120]   See Župljanin Appeal Brief, para. 45, fn. 56, referring to Trial Judgement, vol. 2, paras 474, 514, 517. The Appeals Chamber also observes that the evidence Župljanin points to concerns events which occurred after Župljanin was found to have formed the requisite intent in April 1992. Župljanin particularly points to the Trial Chamber's findings that he: (i) formed a "feigned commission" to inspect detention camps on 14 August 1992 (Trial Judgement, vol. 2, para. 514. See Trial Judgement, vol. 2, para. 519); (ii) filed a criminal report on 26 August 1992 concealing the names of the perpetrators of the killings in front of the Manjača detention camp (Trial Judgement, vol. 2, paras 516, 519); and (iii) concealed the names of the Prijedor police officers who murdered approximately 150-200 Muslims at Korićanske Stijene from 23 August through November 1992 (see Trial Judgement, vol. 2, para. 517). Although this evidence does not support a finding of intent as of April 1992, this evidence, together with the remainder of the evidence relied upon by the Trial Chamber, is demonstrative of Župljanin's continued intent throughout the Indictment period.

[3121]   See *infra*, para. 928.

[3122]   *Popović et al.* Appeal Judgement, para. 1369; *Đorđević* Appeal Judgement, para. 512; *Šainović et al.* Appeal Judgement, para. 995; *Krajišnik* Appeal Judgement, para. 202. See *Stanišić and Simatović* Appeal Judgement, para. 81. See also *supra*, para. 375.

population left *en masse* out of fear for their lives, and continued to acquire information on the commission of crimes including displacements from April 1992 and continuing throughout the Indictment period.[3123]

935.   The Appeals Chamber further observes that the Trial Chamber found that Župljanin significantly contributed to the JCE from 1 April 1992 and continuing throughout the rest of the year[3124] and extensively relied on his conduct to find that he shared the requisite intent. In particular, the Trial Chamber considered Župljanin's conduct prior to April 1992[3125] and notably that he had ties to the SDS from 1991 to 1992.[3126] The Trial Chamber also considered Župljanin's role as early as 3 April 1992 in the blockade of Banja Luka and the takeover of the town, which he **[page 390]** had began planning from at least March 1992.[3127] It also took into account that Župljanin contributed to the implementation of SDS policies in the ARK Municipalities by, *inter alia*, ordering the police under his command to carry out the disarmament of the non-Serb population in May and June 1992, and deploying members of the Banja Luka CSB SPD to ARK Municipalities to participate in takeovers despite having knowledge of crimes committed by its members since April 1992.[3128] Accordingly, the Appeals Chamber considers that there is no merit in Župljanin's submission that the Trial Chamber failed to identify "what conduct, event, or statement gave rise to the inference" that his intent "crystallized" in April 1992.

936.   In light of the totality of the evidence, the Appeals Chamber finds that Župljanin has failed to show that the Trial Chamber erred in finding that he was a member of the JCE and had the requisite intent from at least April 1992. The Appeals Chamber therefore dismisses Župljanin's submission in this respect.

(v) Alleged error in finding that Župljanin possessed the requisite intent beyond reasonable doubt

a. Submissions of the parties

937.   Župljanin submits that the factors relied upon by the Trial Chamber to infer his intent, viewed cumulatively or individually, were insufficient to conclude that he possessed the requisite intent.[3129] He argues that even assuming that every finding made by the Trial Chamber was correct, it still should have established that he possessed the requisite *mens rea*.[3130] He avers that other reasonable explanations remained for his alleged lack of action, including: (i) his genuine belief, albeit mistaken, that crimes being perpetrated were beyond his authority or control; (ii) gross negligence; (iii) "reckless disregard of the potential consequences"; (iv) "being overwhelmed by the scale of events"; and (v) his belief that he "did the most he could to curb" violence.[3131] He adds that the Trial Chamber's reasoning does not eliminate the reasonable

---

[3123]   See Trial Judgement, vol. 2, paras 494-519. See also Trial Judgement, vol. 2, paras 369-374 (regarding the reporting system), 415-440 (regarding knowledge of crimes). In particular, the Appeals Chamber observes that the Trial Chamber found that Župljanin had knowledge of: (i) the commission of crimes against non-Serbs by members of the Banja Luka CSB SPD after 3 April 1992 (Trial Judgement, vol. 2, paras 415, 431, 499); (ii) unlawful detentions, mistreatment, and murder of non-Serb detainees in detention facilities and camps in the ARK Municipalities by the end of April and also in May through the end of August, and in November 1992 (Trial Judgement, vol. 2, paras 416-437, 506-511); and (iii) undisciplined behaviour of members of the Banja Luka CSB SPD in May and June 1992 (Trial Judgement, vol. 2, paras 438-440).

[3124]   Trial Judgement, vol. 2, para. 518.

[3125]   The Appeals Chamber recalls that it has overturned the Trial Chamber's finding in relation to Župljanin's attendance at the Holiday Inn Meeting on 14 February 1992. However, as discussed in more detail below, it finds that Župljanin has failed to show that the Trial Chamber's conclusion that he possessed the requisite intent would not stand on the basis of the Trial Chamber's other findings (see *infra*, para. 942).

[3126]   Trial Judgement, vol. 2, paras 349-350, 519.

[3127]   Trial Judgement, vol. 2, paras 378, 399-404, 495, 519. In particular, the Trial Chamber considered that on 2 March 1992, Župljanin told Stanišić that "he was waiting for instructions and that, if a total blockade [of Banja Luka] was needed, it would be done" (Trial Judgement, vol. 2, para. 495. See Trial Judgement, vol. 2, para. 519). The Trial Chamber found that: "[i]n light of the events that followed this conversation, the Trial Chamber has no doubt that Župljanin was referring to a possible future blockade of Banja Luka" (Trial Judgement, vol. 2, para. 495). It further considered that Župljanin immediately joined the Banja Luka Crisis Staff formed in response to the blockade, implemented the demands of the SOS who carried out the blockade, and expressed his satisfaction in May 1992 with the work of the SOS by stating that "[t]hey have finally taken power up here" (Trial Judgement, vol. 2, paras 399-404, 495, 519).

[3128]   Trial Judgement, vol. 2, paras 496, 499-505, 519.

[3129]   Župljanin Appeal Brief, para. 155.

[3130]   Župljanin Appeal Brief, para. 178.

[3131]   Župljanin Appeal Brief, para. 178, referring to Exhibit P621 (a report of Banja Luka CSB from October 1992), pp 7, 43.

inference that his mental state was **[page 391]** gross negligence, recklessness, *dolus eventualis*, or knowledge.[3132] According to Župljanin, the Trial Chamber's "inquiry was not to examine in retrospect whether [he] met the Nelson Mandela standard of public service; its inquiry was to determine whether the only possible explanation for his conduct was an intent to commit forcible transfer".[3133] He argues that the Trial Chamber failed to adequately consider these "alternative possibilities" thereby failing to provide a reasoned opinion, and simply assumed that his alleged omissions reflected his intention thereby yielding a "manifestly unreasonable outcome".[3134]

938.   The Prosecution responds that the Trial Chamber expressly concluded that Župljanin's acts and omissions demonstrate that he possessed the necessary intent beyond reasonable doubt.[3135] It submits that Župljanin's assertion that the Trial Chamber failed to establish his "'*mens rea* to the requisite standard' of proof ignores the Judgement's clear wording and repeats meritless arguments raised elsewhere in his brief".[3136] According to the Prosecution, the Trial Chamber was not required to determine "'the only possible explanation' for Župljanin's conduct but, rather, whether the findings necessary for his conviction were established beyond a reasonable doubt".[3137] It finally submits that the Trial Chamber "was not obliged to refute other intent standards known to law but inapposite to the facts of this case"[3138] and that the Trial Chamber's conclusion "is more than adequately reasoned".[3139]

b. Analysis

939.   The Appeals Chamber observes that the Trial Chamber explicitly found that "Župljanin's acts and omissions demonstrate *beyond reasonable doubt* that he intended, with other members of the JCE", to further the JCE.[3140] The Trial Chamber reached this conclusion after having considered that Župljanin: (i) played a role in the blockade of Banja Luka; (ii) had ties to the SDS; (iii) attended the Holiday Inn Meeting; (iv) contributed to the implementation of SDS policies in **[page 392]** Banja Luka and in other municipalities in the ARK; (v) failed to protect the non-Serb population; (vi) enrolled the SOS in the Banja Luka CSB SPD; (vii) failed to act in relation to the crimes committed by this unit; (viii) made statements and acted in response to requests for protection by the Muslims of Banja Luka; (ix) was aware and actively contributed to unlawful arrest operations; and (x) created a "climate of impunity that encouraged the perpetration of crimes against non-Serbs and made non-Serbs decide to leave the ARK Municipalities" by shielding his subordinates from criminal prosecution.[3141]

940.   To substantiate his claim that a number of reasonable inferences remained, Župljanin points to an October 1992 report of Banja Luka CSB where he "wrote at the time that 'it appears that the situation is increasingly getting out of control of the organs of legal authority' and specifically noted that a large percentage of police resources were being co-opted by the military in the form of re-subordinated police".[3142] The Appeals Chamber does not agree with Župljanin that this evidence shows that there are other reasonable inferences to be drawn aside from his intent to further the JCE.[3143] In particular, the evidence considered by the Trial Chamber does not demonstrate that Župljanin was mistaken as to the scope of his obligations, his ability to execute his duties, or authority, as suggested by Župljanin. The Appeals Chamber recalls in this

---

[3132]   Župljanin Appeal Brief, para. 43, referring to *Brđanin* Appeal Judgement, para. 429. He contends that the Trial Chamber's failure to eliminate the reasonable inference that his mental state was gross negligence, recklessness, *dolus eventualis*, or knowledge is "particularly significant in light of the Chamber's [...] findings in paragraphs 521 through 528, determining that all of the crimes constituting coercive acts were merely foreseeable" (Župljanin Appeal Brief, para. 43).

[3133]   Župljanin Appeal Brief, para. 179.

[3134]   Župljanin Appeal Brief, para. 179. See Župljanin Appeal Brief, para. 178. See also Župljanin Appeal Brief, para. 44, referring to *Brđanin* Appeal Judgement, para. 9, *Zigiranyirazo* Appeal Judgement, para. 46.

[3135]   Prosecution Response Brief (Župljanin), para. 135, referring to Trial Judgement, vol. 2, para. 520 (citations omitted).

[3136]   Prosecution Response Brief (Župljanin), para. 135.

[3137]   Prosecution Response Brief (Župljanin), para. 136 (citations omitted).

[3138]   Prosecution Response Brief (Župljanin), para. 26.

[3139]   Prosecution Response Brief (Župljanin), para. 27.

[3140]   Trial Judgement, vol. 2, para. 520 (emphasis added).

[3141]   See Trial Judgement, vol. 2, para. 519.

[3142]   Župljanin Appeal Brief, para. 178, referring to Exhibit P621, pp 7, 43.

[3143]   See Župljanin Appeal Brief, para. 178.

regard that it has upheld the Trial Chamber's finding that Župljanin reasonably knew of his duty and ability to repress crimes as Banja Luka CSB Chief.[3144]

941. With the exception of this specific example, Župljanin merely refers to the existence of alternative inferences or states of mind such as recklessness, gross negligence, or knowledge but has failed to point to evidence or Trial Chamber's findings to support his contention that the Trial Chamber failed to consider any alternative inferences that would show a different state of mind. In addition, Župljanin's argument that the Trial Chamber's failure to adequately consider these "alternative possibilities"[3145] amounts to a failure to provide a reasoned opinion is without merit. A trial chamber does not have to discuss other inferences it may have considered, as long as it is satisfied that the inference it retained was the only reasonable one.[3146] In view of the Trial Chamber's reasoning which expressly lists the factors it relied upon as the basis of its conclusion that Župljanin shared the intent to further the JCE,[3147] and its express finding of intent,[3148] the Appeals Chamber considers that the Trial Chamber's conclusion that he possessed the requisite **[page 393]** intent for the first category of joint criminal enterprise beyond reasonable doubt was more than adequately reasoned.

942. The Appeals Chamber now turns to Župljanin's submission that the factors relied upon by the Trial Chamber were insufficient to infer that he possessed the requisite intent.[3149] In this regard, the Appeals Chamber recalls its finding that the Trial Chamber erred in finding that Župljanin attended the Holiday Inn Meeting on 14 February 1992 and in relying on this meeting in assessing his intent.[3150] The Appeals Chamber is not persuaded, however, that this error has caused a miscarriage of justice. The Appeals Chamber observes that Župljanin's attendance of the Holiday Inn Meeting is only one among a number of factors that the Trial Chamber relied upon in order to establish that he possessed the intent to further the JCE.[3151] In addition, the Appeals Chamber has dismissed all of Župljanin's other arguments relating to the remaining factors and found that he has failed to demonstrate any error in the Trial Chamber's reliance on these factors when inferring his intent.[3152] In light of the foregoing, and noting that the Holiday Inn Meeting occurred in February 1992, two months before Župljanin was found to have become a member of the JCE, the Appeals Chamber finds that Župljanin has failed to show that the Trial Chamber's conclusion that he possessed the requisite intent would not stand without the Trial Chamber's reliance on his attendance at the Holiday Inn Meeting.

943. Thus, Župljanin has failed to demonstrate that the Trial Chamber erred in concluding that the only reasonable inference to be drawn from the evidence was that Župljanin intended to further the JCE in order to achieve the common criminal purpose.[3153] His arguments in this regard are therefore dismissed.

(vi) Conclusion

944. For the foregoing reasons, the Appeals Chamber finds that Župljanin has failed to demonstrate that no reasonable trier of fact could have found that he possessed the requisite intent pursuant to the first category for joint criminal enterprise.

(g) Conclusion

945. For the reasons set out above, Župljanin has not demonstrated that the Trial Chamber erred in concluding that he significantly contributed to the JCE and shared the intent to further the JCE. **[page 394]** Consequently, the Appeals Chamber dismisses sub-grounds (A) to (E) of Župljanin's first ground of appeal in their entirety and sub-ground (F) in part of Župljanin's first ground of appeal.

[3144] See *supra*, paras 814-820.
[3145] Župljanin Appeal Brief, paras 178-179.
[3146] *Đorđević* Appeal Judgement, para. 157, referring to *Krajišnik* Appeal Judgement, para. 192.
[3147] See Trial Judgement, vol. 2, para. 519.
[3148] See Trial Judgement, vol. 2, para. 520.
[3149] See Župljanin Appeal Brief, para. 155.
[3150] See *supra*, para. 895.
[3151] See *supra*, para. 906.
[3152] See *supra*, paras 718-900.
[3153] See Trial Judgement, vol. 2, paras 519-520.

3. Alleged errors with respect to Župljanin's responsibility pursuant to the third category of joint criminal enterprise

946.   The Trial Chamber convicted Župljanin for the following crimes pursuant to the third category of joint criminal enterprise: persecutions (through the underlying acts of killings, torture, cruel treatment, inhumane acts, unlawful detentions, establishment and perpetuation of inhumane living conditions, plunder of property, wanton destruction of towns and villages, including destruction or wilful damage done to institutions dedicated to religious and other cultural buildings, and imposition and maintenance of restrictive and discriminatory measures) and extermination as crimes against humanity (Counts 1 and 2, respectively), and murder and torture as violations of the laws or customs of war (Counts 4 and 6, respectively).[3154] The Trial Chamber also found Župljanin responsible for murder, torture, and inhumane acts as crimes against humanity (Counts 3, 5, and 8, respectively), and for cruel treatment as a violation of the laws or customs of war (Count 7) pursuant to the third category of joint criminal enterprise, but did not enter convictions on the basis of the principles relating to cumulative convictions.[3155]

947.   Župljanin alleges a number of legal and factual errors with respect to the Trial Chamber's findings on his responsibility for Župljanin's JCE III Crimes in general.[3156] He further raises specific challenges in relation to his conviction pursuant to the third category of joint criminal enterprise for extermination as a crime against humanity.[3157] The Prosecution responds that Župljanin's arguments should be dismissed.[3158]

(a) Alleged errors of law and fact in relation to the third category of joint criminal enterprise in general (Župljanin's second ground of appeal)

948.   In assessing Župljanin's responsibility for crimes outside the scope of the JCE, the Trial Chamber recalled its finding that Serb forces carried out the forcible removal of Bosnian Muslims and Bosnian Croats from the ARK Municipalities by committing crimes against them and by enforcing unbearable living conditions following the takeover of towns and villages.[3159] It also **[page 395]** recalled that Župljanin was a member of both the ARK and Banja Luka crisis staff, which issued orders restricting the rights of non-Serbs to perform certain jobs or impacting on their property rights.[3160] On this basis, the Trial Chamber concluded that the possibility that, in the execution of the common plan, Serb forces could impose and maintain restrictive and discriminatory measures against non-Serbs in the ARK Municipalities was sufficiently substantial as to be foreseeable to Župljanin, and that he willingly took that risk.[3161]

949.   The Trial Chamber further found that, in light of Župljanin's degree of knowledge and involvement in the transport and guarding of detained non-Serbs in the ARK Municipalities, the possibility that, in the execution of the common plan, Serb forces not only could, but would unlawfully detain large numbers of Bosnian Muslims and Bosnian Croats at SJB's prisons and improvised detention centres and camps was sufficiently substantial as to be foreseeable to Župljanin and that he willingly took that risk.[3162]

950.   The Trial Chamber also considered that Župljanin: (i) enrolled in the Banja Luka CSB SPD seasoned criminals of the SOS who distinguished themselves for their nationalistic stance and the commission of crimes against non-Serbs, of which he was aware;[3163] (ii) dispatched the Banja Luka CSB SPD for operations notwithstanding frequent reports on their lack of discipline and criminal activities;[3164] (iii) was present in Banja Luka after the 3 April 1992 blockade of the town, when the non-Serb community started being

---

[3154]   Trial Judgement, vol. 2, paras 805, 832, 845, 850, 859, 864, 869, 956.
[3155]   Trial Judgement, vol. 2, paras 805, 832, 845, 850, 859, 864, 869, 956.
[3156]   Župljanin Appeal Brief, paras 182-226.
[3157]   Župljanin Appeal Brief, paras 227-242.
[3158]   Prosecution Response Brief (Župljanin), paras 138, 179-180, 207. See Prosecution Response Brief (Župljanin), paras 139-178, 181-206.
[3159]   Trial Judgement, vol. 2, para. 522.
[3160]   Trial Judgement, vol. 2, para. 522. See Trial Judgement, vol. 2, paras 279-284, 353, 401, 492-493.
[3161]   Trial Judgement, vol. 2, para. 522.
[3162]   Trial Judgement, vol. 2, para. 523. See Trial Judgement, vol. 2, paras 415-437, 506-511, 516.
[3163]   Trial Judgement, vol. 2, para. 524. See Trial Judgement, vol. 2, paras 385, 499, 504.
[3164]   Trial Judgement, vol. 2, para. 524. See Trial Judgement, vol. 2, paras 405, 415, 425, 438-440, 501-505.

targeted by, *inter alia*, the SOS and the Banja Luka CSB SPD, and was informed, in the first half of April, and then again in August and September 1992, of crimes against non-Serbs committed there;[3165] (iv) knew, already on 30 April 1992, that members of ARK police were committing crimes;[3166] (v) left the Sanski Most police in charge of transporting detainees despite knowing of the incident in which 20 detainees died during their transportation from Betonirka detention camp in Sanski Most to Manjača detention camp in Banja Luka municipality by Sanski Most police officers on 7 July 1992 ("Sanski Most Incident");[3167] and (vi) knew or had strong reason to know of the involvement of the Prijedor police in the death of eight non-Serbs at the Manjača detention camp between 6 and 7 August 1992 and the killing of approximately 150-200 Muslims at Korićanske Stijene in Skender Vakuf municipality on **[page 396]** 21 August 1992, but nonetheless continued to task the Prijedor police with escorting detainees.[3168] On the basis of these findings, the Trial Chamber concluded that the possibility that Serb forces could commit murders and extermination in the execution of the common plan was sufficiently substantial as to be foreseeable to Župljanin and that he willingly took that risk.[3169]

951. Furthermore, considering that Župljanin received reports on the conditions of detention camps and that he knew of the ethnic tensions in the region,[3170] the Trial Chamber found that the possibility that Serb forces, in the execution of the common plan, could establish and perpetuate inhumane living conditions and commit torture, cruel treatment, and inhumane acts against non-Serbs was sufficiently substantial as to be foreseeable to Župljanin and that he willingly took that risk.[3171]

952. Considering the presence of criminals in the units that Župljanin dispatched in various ARK Municipalities, the weak position in which non-Serbs found themselves in relation to Serb forces arresting them and expelling them from their municipalities, and the strong ethnic tensions and resentments,[3172] the Trial Chamber also concluded that the possibility that, in the execution of the common plan, Serb forces could commit plunder and looting of non-Serb property was sufficiently substantial as to be foreseeable to Župljanin and that he willingly took that risk.[3173]

953. The Trial Chamber found that the possibility that Serb forces could carry out the wanton destruction and damage of religious and cultural property of Muslims and Croats in a "concerted effort to eliminate their historical moorings during and following the takeover of the ARK Municipalities" was sufficiently substantial as to be foreseeable to Župljanin and that he willingly took that risk.[3174]

954. In addition, the Trial Chamber recalled its finding that the imposition and maintenance of restrictive and discriminatory measures, the unlawful detentions, the killings, the establishment and perpetuation of inhumane living conditions, torture, cruel treatment, inhumane acts, plunder of property, and wanton destruction and damage of religious and cultural property in the ARK Municipalities were committed with a discriminatory intent.[3175] "Considering the ethnically charged character of the armed conflict, the existence of a widespread and systematic attack against [non-Serbs], and Župljanin's knowledge of such an attack", the Trial Chamber was satisfied that the **[page 397]** possibility that Serb forces could commit these crimes with a discriminatory intent, thereby committing the crime of persecution, was sufficiently substantial as to be foreseeable to him and that he willingly took that risk.[3176]

955. Župljanin submits that the Trial Chamber erred: (i) in law by failing to make a finding that he possessed the intent to participate in and further the criminal purpose of the JCE;[3177] (ii) in law by imposing on him

[3165] Trial Judgement, vol. 2, para. 524. See Trial Judgement, vol. 2, paras 399-404, 450-452, 495-497.
[3166] Trial Judgement, vol. 2, para. 524. See Trial Judgement, vol. 2, paras 433, 510.
[3167] Trial Judgement, vol. 2, para. 524. See Trial Judgement, vol. 2, paras 418-419, 506-507, 511; Trial Judgement, vol. 1, paras 189-190, 215.
[3168] Trial Judgement, vol. 2, para. 524. See Trial Judgement, vol. 2, paras 465-482, 511, 516-517.
[3169] Trial Judgement, vol. 2, para. 524.
[3170] Trial Judgement, vol. 2, para. 525. See Trial Judgement, vol. 2, paras 415-437, 506-511.
[3171] Trial Judgement, vol. 2, para. 525.
[3172] Trial Judgement, vol. 2, para. 526. See Trial Judgement, vol. 2, paras 405-406, 415, 425, 438-440, 501-505.
[3173] Trial Judgement, vol. 2, para. 526.
[3174] Trial Judgement, vol. 2, para. 527.
[3175] Trial Judgement, vol. 2, para. 528.
[3176] Trial Judgement, vol. 2, para. 528.
[3177] Župljanin Appeal Brief, paras 189-192; Župljanin Reply Brief, paras 62-65.

criminal liability pursuant to the third category of joint criminal enterprise for crimes of "more serious gravity" than the intended crimes;[3178] (iii) in law and fact in relation to whether Župljanin's JCE III Crimes were natural and foreseeable consequences of the JCE;[3179] and (iv) in fact by finding that Župljanin's JCE III Crimes were foreseeable to him and that he willingly took that risk.[3180] Župljanin requests the Appeals Chamber to overturn his convictions for Župljanin's JCE III Crimes.[3181] The Prosecution responds that the Trial Chamber applied the correct legal standard and properly convicted Župljanin on the basis of the third category of joint criminal enterprise.[3182]

(i) Alleged error of law in failing to make specific findings that Župljanin possessed the intent to participate in and further the criminal purpose of the JCE (sub-ground (C) of Župljanin's second ground of appeal)

956.   Župljanin submits that the Trial Chamber erred in law by failing to make specific findings with regard to his intent to participate in and further the criminal purpose of the JCE as required under the third category of joint criminal enterprise.[3183] Župljanin suggests that "the similarity between the language of JCE I *mens rea* regarding the voluntary participation and the language of JCE III *mens rea* regarding intent to participate in the JCE" may mean that the Trial Chamber **[page 398]** equated its finding that he shared the intent with other members of the JCE to achieve the permanent removal of Bosnian Muslims and Bosnian Croats,[3184] with the intent to participate in the JCE as part of its analysis on the third category of joint criminal enterprise.[3185] He argues that the "additional requirement of proof of intent to contribute, however, necessitates an independent analysis", which the Trial Chamber failed to undertake.[3186]

957.   The Prosecution responds that the Trial Chamber made the necessary specific findings to conclude that the possibility that Serb forces could commit Župljanin's JCE III crimes in executing the JCE was sufficiently substantial as to be foreseeable to Župljanin and that he willingly accepted that risk.[3187] The Prosecution further responds that the Tribunal's jurisprudence does not require "a second finding of intent in relation to the JCE I crimes to establish JCE III liability".[3188]

958.   The Appeals Chamber recalls that an accused can only be held responsible for crimes pursuant to the third category of joint criminal enterprise, when the elements of the first category of joint criminal enterprise have been satisfied.[3189] Thus, the extended form of joint criminal enterprise attaches only where a trial chamber is satisfied that an accused *already possessed* the intent to participate in and further the common

---

[3178]   Župljanin Notice of Appeal, paras 24-25; Župljanin Appeal Brief, paras 219-226; Župljanin Reply Brief, para. 73.

[3179]   Župljanin Appeal Brief, paras 193-200; Župljanin Reply Brief, paras 66-67.

[3180]   Župljanin Appeal Brief, paras 201-218; Župljanin Reply Brief, paras 68-72.

[3181]   Župljanin Appeal Brief, paras 192, 195, 218.

[3182]   Prosecution Response Brief (Župljanin), para. 138.

[3183]   Župljanin Appeal Brief, para. 190; Župljanin Reply Brief, para. 64. In this regard, he argues that the paragraphs in the Trial Judgement dealing with his *mens rea* and his criminal responsibility under the third category of joint criminal enterprise liability "make no mention of his intent as required by JCE III" but rather only deal with his foresight of crimes outside of the common criminal purpose (see Župljanin Appeal Brief, paras 189-190). Župljanin further submits that "[i]n order to establish an accused's *mens rea* for JCE III, a Trial Chamber must first establish that all of the elements of JCE I have been met" and that "it must also be established [...]: (a) that the accused possessed the intent to participate in and contribute to the common criminal purpose, and (b) (i) that the crimes were a natural and foreseeable consequence of the JCE ('the Objective Element'), and (ii) that the accused was aware that such crime was a possible consequence of the execution of that enterprise and with that awareness, willingly took the risk" (Župljanin Appeal Brief, para. 184). He also submits that he has already "raised a number of challenges to the Chamber's findings regarding Župljanin's *mens rea* in the JCE I section" under his first ground of appeal and that many of those "principles and challenges" are equally applicable here (see Župljanin Appeal Brief, fn. 272 referring to sub-grounds (A), (E), and (F) of his first ground of appeal).

[3184]   Župljanin Appeal Brief, para. 191, referring to Trial Judgement, vol. 2, para. 520.

[3185]   Župljanin Appeal Brief, para. 191.

[3186]   Župljanin Appeal Brief, para. 191, referring to *Tadić* Appeal Judgement, para. 228. Župljanin submits that the Appeals Chamber in the *Tadić* case set out three *mens rea* elements "apparently unique to JCE III" (Župljanin Appeal Brief, para. 191).

[3187]   Prosecution Response Brief (Župljanin), para. 139.

[3188]   Prosecution Response Brief (Župljanin), para. 140. See Prosecution Response Brief (Župljanin), paras 141-143. The Prosecution further submits that the Appeals Chamber has "consistently relied on the finding that the accused was a JCE member who possessed the requisite *mens rea* for JCE I" (Prosecution Response Brief (Župljanin), para. 142).

[3189]   See *Blaškić* Appeal Judgement, para. 33; *Vasiljević* Appeal Judgement, para. 99; *Tadić* Appeal Judgement, para. 228.

criminal purpose of a group.[3190] The Appeals Chamber recalls further that the subjective element of the first category of joint criminal enterprise is that an accused had the intent to commit the crimes that form part of the common purpose of the joint criminal enterprise and the intent to participate in a common plan aimed at their commission.[3191] For liability pursuant to the third category of joint criminal enterprise, a trial chamber must be satisfied in addition that: (i) it was foreseeable to the accused that a crime outside the common purpose might be perpetrated by one or more of the persons used by him (or by any other member of the joint criminal enterprise) in order to carry out the *actus reus* of the crimes forming part of the common purpose; and (ii) the accused willingly took the risk that the crime might occur by joining **[page 399]** or continuing to participate in the enterprise.[3192] The Appeals Chamber thus finds that Župljanin misconstrues the jurisprudence of the Tribunal, and in particular the *Tadić* Appeal Judgement to which he refers,[3193] when suggesting that there exists an additional requirement of proof of intent to contribute to and further the common criminal purpose as part of the assessment under the third category of joint criminal enterprise liability.

959. As noted earlier, the Trial Chamber found that Župljanin significantly contributed to the common objective to permanently remove Bosnian Muslims and Croats from the territory of the planned Serb state.[3194] Based on Župljanin's acts and failures to act, the Trial Chamber concluded that he *intended* the JCE I Crimes.[3195] The Trial Chamber then found that specific evidence supported the conclusion that the possibility that Župljanin's JCE III Crimes could be committed was sufficiently substantial as to be foreseeable to Župljanin and that he willingly took the risk that they might be committed.[3196]

960. The Appeals Chamber therefore is satisfied that the Trial Chamber made the necessary findings regarding Župljanin's responsibility under the third category of joint criminal enterprise and his arguments in this respect are dismissed.

961. In light of the foregoing, the Appeals Chamber dismisses sub-ground (C) of Župljanin's second ground of appeal.

(ii) Alleged errors in finding Župljanin liable pursuant to the third category of joint criminal enterprise for crimes of "greater gravity" than the JCE I Crimes (sub-ground (A) of Župljanin's second ground of appeal)

a. Submissions of the parties

962. Župljanin submits that the Trial Chamber erred in law by convicting him pursuant to the third category of joint criminal enterprise for crimes of extreme violence, namely "extermination, murder, torture and cruel treatment"[3197] when his intent was limited to non-violent crimes.[3198] He **[page 400]** argues that as a matter of law, liability pursuant to the third category of joint criminal enterprise should not be imposed where the foreseeable crime is of "substantially greater gravity and seriousness" than the intended crime.[3199]

[3190] See *e.g. Blaškić* Appeal Judgement, para. 33, referring to *Vasiljević* Appeal Judgement, para. 101 (quoting *Tadić* Appeal Judgement, para. 228); *Brđanin* Appeal Judgement, para. 411; *Stakić* Appeal Judgement, para. 65; *Kvočka et al.* Appeal Judgement, para. 83.
[3191] *Popović et al.* Appeal Judgement, para. 1369. See *Đorđević* Appeal Judgement, para. 468.
[3192] *Tolimir* Appeal Judgement, para. 514; *Đorđević* Appeal Judgement, para. 906; *Šainović et al.* Appeal Judgement, paras 1061, 1557; *Brđanin* Appeal Judgement, paras 365, 411.
[3193] Župljanin Appeal Brief, para. 191, referring to *Tadić* Appeal Judgement, para. 228.
[3194] Trial Judgement, vol. 2, para. 518. See *supra*, para. 901.
[3195] Trial Judgement, vol. 2, para. 520. See *supra*, para. 906.
[3196] Trial Judgement, vol. 2, paras 522-528. See *supra*, para. 916.
[3197] Župljanin Appeal Brief, para. 219. The Appeals Chamber understands Župljanin to argue that the Trial Chamber erred by convicting him of persecutions through killings, torture, and cruel treatment (Count 1); extermination as a crime against humanity (Count 2); murder as a violation of the laws or customs of war (Count 4); and torture as a violation of the laws or customs of war (Counts 6). While Župljanin was not convicted for murder as a crime against humanity (Count 3); torture as crime against humanity (Count 5); and cruel treatment as a violation of the laws or customs of war (Count 7), the Trial Chamber did find him responsible for these crimes (see Trial Judgement, vol. 2, paras 805, 845, 850, 859, 956). The Appeals Chamber therefore understands Župljanin to challenge these findings as well and, recalling its conclusion that the Trial Chamber erred in law by failing to enter convictions for Župljanin for these crimes, the Appeals Chamber finds it appropriate to also address his submissions in this regard.
[3198] Župljanin Appeal Brief, para. 219. See Župljanin Appeal Brief, para. 226.
[3199] Župljanin Appeal Brief, para. 219.

963.   Župljanin further avers that the Appeals Chamber should adopt an additional condition for imposition of third category of joint criminal enterprise liability, namely that liability for foreseeable violent crimes may only arise when the accused intended the adoption of violent means to implement the common purpose.[3200] He argues that adoption of such an additional condition would respond to "many of the concerns that have [been] expressed about the potential untrammelled breadth of JCE III".[3201] In support of this argument, he further asserts that: (i) according to the Appeals Chamber jurisprudence, including the *Tadić* and *Stakić* cases, liability pursuant to the third category of joint criminal enterprise for a violent crime is always predicated on some element of violence or the likelihood of violence;[3202] (ii) Judge Cassese has noted in extrajudicial writings that "liability should not be extended by way of JCE III to special intent crimes unless the intended crime includes the requisite intent";[3203] and (iii) many "felony-murders" statutes in common law jurisdictions similarly restrict the "distance between the intended and the foreseeable crime".[3204] Župljanin submits that the Trial Chamber made no findings that he intended to adopt any violent means to effectuate the common purpose and asserts that the Trial Chamber's "failure to consider the absence of any connection between the intended and the foreseeable crimes **[page 401]** was an error of law" thus invalidating his convictions pursuant to the third category of joint criminal enterprise.[3205]

964.   The Prosecution responds that it is not a legal error to convict an accused pursuant to the third category of joint criminal enterprise for crimes which may be viewed as "more serious" or "more violent" than the crimes intended in the common plan.[3206] The Prosecution submits that: (i) the *Stakić* and *Tadić* cases, as well as other Tribunal cases, show that an accused may be convicted pursuant to the third category of joint criminal enterprise for crimes perceived as "more serious or violent" than the intended crimes;[3207] (ii) the Appeals Chamber has rejected Judge Cassese's view on "the impossibility of a conviction for a specific intent crime through JCE III";[3208] (iii) Župljanin's references to concerns expressed by commentators do not demonstrate cogent reasons for departing from the established practice;[3209] and (iv) Župljanin's references to common law jurisdictions are unconvincing and, in any event, national jurisprudence is not binding on the Tribunal.[3210]

965.   The Prosecution further submits that the Trial Chamber reasonably convicted Župljanin for Župljanin's JCE III Crimes.[3211] It argues that Župljanin's argument rests on his repeated mistaken premise that "his intent was limited to non-violent crimes" and that Župljanin ignores the abundant evidence upon which the

---

[3200]   Župljanin Appeal Brief, paras 223, 225.

[3201]   Župljanin Appeal Brief, para. 225, referring to *Brđanin* Trial Judgement, para. 355, *Brđanin* Appeal Judgement, Partially Dissenting Opinion of Judge Shahabuddeen, paras 1-20, *Martić* Appeal Judgement, Separate Opinion of Judge Schomburg on the Individual Criminal Responsibility of Milan Martić, para. 3, *Prosecutor v. Ieng Thirith et al.*, Case File No. 002/19-09-2007-ECCC/OCIJ (PTC38), Decision on the Appeals Against the Co-Investigative Judges Orders on Joint Criminal Enterprise (JCE), 20 May 2010, ("ECCC Decision on JCE"), para. 83. Župljanin argues that his suggestion of adopting this additional condition is a more modest approach to addressing the concerns raised than those suggested by different commentators (Župljanin Appeal Brief, para. 225, referring to K. Ambos *Amicus Curiae* Concerning Criminal Case File NO. 001/18-07-2007-ECCC/OCIJ (PTC 02), 27 October 2008 ("Kai Ambos *Amicus Curiae* Application"); J.D. Ohlin, "*Joint Intentions to Commit International Crimes*", Cornell Law Faculty Publications, 169 (2011) ("Ohlin Article"); A. Cassese, "Proper Limits of Individual Responsibility Under the Doctrine of JCE", *International Criminal Justice Journal*, 5 (2007) ("Judge Cassese Article on JCE"), pp 118-120).

[3202]   Župljanin Appeal Brief, para. 220. Župljanin submits that in *Tadić*, the Appeals Chamber "contemplated the possibility of JCE III for murder in respect of expulsions intentionally carried out 'at gunpoint' or by 'burning their houses'" (Župljanin Appeal Brief, para. 220, referring to *Tadić* Appeal Judgement, para. 214). He further submits that in *Stakić*, the accused was found guilty of "extermination JCE III [*sic*] in part based on the Trial Chamber's findings that he had 'intent to kill' required for murder" (Župljanin Appeal Brief, para. 220, referring to *Stakić* Trial Judgement, para. 656, *Stakić* Appeal Judgement, para. 96).

[3203]   Župljanin Appeal Brief, para. 221, referring to Judge Cassese Article on JCE, pp 121-122.

[3204]   Župljanin Appeal Brief, para. 222, referring to G. Binder, "Felony Murder and Mens Rea Default Rules: A study in Statutory Interpretation", *Buffalo Criminal Law Review*, vol. 4:399 (2000-2001) ("Binder Article"), p. 406, S.H. Pillsbury, *Judging Evil: Rethinking the Law of Murder and Manslaughter* (1998) ("Pillsbury Article"), p. 106, 108, Homicide Act 1957, 5 & 6 Eliz.2, Ch. 11 (United Kingdom) ("UK Homicide Act"), section 1(1).

[3205]   Župljanin Appeal Brief, para. 226; Župljanin Reply Brief, para. 73.

[3206]   Prosecution Response Brief (Župljanin), para. 171.

[3207]   Prosecution Response Brief (Župljanin), para. 174.

[3208]   Prosecution Response Brief (Župljanin), para. 175.

[3209]   Prosecution Response Brief (Župljanin), para. 175.

[3210]   Prosecution Response Brief (Župljanin), paras 176-177.

[3211]   Prosecution Response Brief (Župljanin), paras 172, 178.

383

Trial Chamber relied to infer that crimes were foreseeable to him.[3212] The Prosecution contends that Župljanin intended to use violent means to implement the common criminal purpose, namely forcible transfer, deportation, and persecution through forcible displacement.[3213]

b. Analysis

966.   The Appeals Chamber understands Župljanin to argue that the Trial Chamber erred by convicting him pursuant to the third category of joint criminal enterprise for Župljanin's JCE III Crimes because these crimes are more serious than the JCE I Crimes.[3214] The Appeals Chamber, however, observes that this contention is essentially premised on his suggestion to depart from the **[page 402]** existing jurisprudence on the basis of his misconstruction of the law. More specifically, Župljanin argues that the Appeals Chamber should depart from its jurisprudence and establish an additional requirement within the subjective element of the third category of joint criminal enterprise, namely that in cases involving "violent foreseeable crimes" the accused must have "intended recourse to violent means" to implement the joint criminal enterprise.[3215] However, the Appeals Chamber is not persuaded by this contention for the following reasons.

967.   The Appeals Chamber first recalls the law on the subjective elements for the first and third categories of joint criminal enterprise liability as set out above.[3216] In addition, the Appeals Chamber recalls that criminal liability pursuant to the third category of joint criminal enterprise can attach for *any* crime that falls outside of an agreed upon joint criminal enterprise so long as that crime is foreseeable to the accused and he willingly took that risk.[3217]

968.   The Appeals Chamber further recalls that in the interests of certainty and predictability, it should follow its previous decisions.[3218] The Appeals Chamber may depart from them only where cogent reasons in the interests of justice exist,[3219] *i.e.* where the previous decision has been decided on the basis of a wrong legal principle or has been given *per incuriam*, that is, a judicial decision that has been "wrongly decided, usually because the judge or judges were ill-informed about the applicable law".[3220] It is for the party submitting that the Appeals Chamber should depart from a previous decision to demonstrate that there are cogent reasons in the interest of justice that justify such departure.[3221]

969.   The Appeals Chamber is not convinced by Župljanin's argument that the Tribunal's case law, including the *Tadić* Appeal Judgement and *Stakić* Appeal Judgement, constitutes cogent reasons to depart from its jurisprudence.[3222]

970.   The Appeals Chamber notes that the paragraph of the *Tadić* Appeal Judgement to which Župljanin refers generally describes examples of the third category of joint criminal enterprise.[3223] It states that if the common purpose or shared intent of a joint criminal enterprise was to remove members of one ethnicity from their region, the foreseeability of the crime of murder may be **[page 403]** inferred from the forcible removal of civilians "at gunpoint" or "by burning their houses".[3224] However, these are mere examples of factors from which the foreseeability of crimes outside the common purpose can be inferred. They do not imply that certain violent forms of acts must be perpetrated or intended in the execution of the common purpose in order for a trier of fact to conclude that the crime of murder is foreseeable pursuant to the third

---

[3212]   Prosecution Response Brief (Župljanin), paras 172, 178. The Prosecution submits that given the means used to implement the JCE, it was entirely reasonable for the Trial Chamber to conclude that the Župljanin's JCE III Crimes were foreseeable to him and that he willingly accepted that risk (Prosecution Response Brief (Župljanin), para. 178).
[3213]   Prosecution Response Brief (Župljanin), para. 178.
[3214]   Župljanin Appeal Brief, para. 219.
[3215]   Župljanin Appeal Brief, paras 223, 225.
[3216]   See *supra*, para. 958.
[3217]   See *Đorđević* Appeal Judgement, paras 77, 906; *Brđanin* Appeal Decision of 19 March 2004, paras 5-9.
[3218]   See *Đorđević* Appeal Judgement, para. 23; *Aleksovski* Appeal Judgement, para. 107.
[3219]   *Đorđević* Appeal Judgement, para. 23; *Galić* Appeal Judgement, para. 117; *Aleksovski* Appeal Judgement, para. 107.
[3220]   *Đorđević* Appeal Judgement, para. 24, quoting *Aleksovski* Appeal Judgement, para. 108.
[3221]   *Đorđević* Appeal Judgement, para. 24. See *Popović et al.* Appeal Judgement, para. 1674.
[3222]   Župljanin Appeal Brief, para. 220. See Župljanin Appeal Brief, para. 224.
[3223]   *Tadić* Appeal Judgement, para. 204. See Župljanin Appeal Brief, para. 220.
[3224]   *Tadić* Appeal Judgement, para. 204.

category of joint criminal enterprise. With respect to the case specifically, the *Tadić* Appeals Chamber found that Duško Tadić had the "intention to further the criminal purpose to rid the Prijedor region of the non-Serb population, by committing inhumane acts against them".[3225] It then found that in the context of that case, it was foreseeable that killings might be committed.[3226]

971.   In the paragraph of the *Stakić* Appeal Judgement that Župljanin cites, the *Stakić* Appeals Chamber referred to, *inter alia*, the *Stakić* Trial Chamber's finding that Stakić possessed "the requisite intent to kill, including the intent to cause serious bodily harm in the reasonable knowledge that it was likely to result in death".[3227] The *Stakić* Appeals Chamber considered this finding to fulfil the subjective element of the third category of joint criminal enterprise.[3228] With respect to the subjective element of the first category of joint criminal enterprise, the *Stakić* Appeals Chamber found that Stakić shared the intent to further the common purpose that was to ethnically cleanse the municipality of Prijedor by deporting and persecuting Bosnian Muslims and Bosnian Croats.[3229] It then found, as regards the third category of joint criminal enterprise, that the crimes of murder and extermination were foreseeable.[3230]

972.   The Appeals Chamber fails to see how the *Tadić* Appeal Judgement and *Stakić* Appeal Judgement differ from the present case, where the Trial Chamber found that: (i) Župljanin intended to achieve the permanent removal of Bosnian Muslims and Bosnian Croats from the territory of the planned Serb state through the commission of the JCE I Crimes, *i.e.* the crimes of deportation, inhumane acts (forcible transfer), and persecutions through forcible transfer and deportation as crimes against humanity in the ARK Municipalities;[3231] and (ii) the possibility that Župljanin's JCE III Crimes, including murder and extermination, could be committed in the execution of the **[page 404]** common purpose was sufficiently substantial so as to be foreseeable to him and that he willingly took that risk.[3232]

973.   Both the *Tadić* Appeal Judgement and the *Stakić* Appeal Judgement as well as the Trial Judgement in the present case are in line with the Tribunal's jurisprudence, which consistently set out the subjective element of the third category of joint criminal enterprise as recalled above.[3233]

974.   In support of his assertion that the "distance" between the intended and the foreseeable crimes must be restricted, Župljanin also refers to national laws and practice in common law jurisdictions[3234] as well as the extrajudicial writings of Judge Cassese.[3235] However, the Appeals Chamber recalls that the Tribunal is not bound by decisions from national jurisdictions[3236] or extrajudicial writings of a judge.[3237]

975.   With regard to Župljanin's argument that his suggested approach of imposing the additional condition of violent crimes would respond to concerns that have been raised as to the "potential untrammelled breadth" of the third category of joint criminal enterprise,[3238] the Appeals Chamber first notes that, while Župljanin relies on (i) the *Brđanin* Trial Judgement and Judge Shahabuddeen's dissenting opinion in the *Brđanin*

[3225]   *Tadić* Appeal Judgement, para. 232.
[3226]   *Tadić* Appeal Judgement, para. 232.
[3227]   *Stakić* Appeal Judgement, para. 96, quoting *Stakić* Trial Judgement, para. 656. See Župljanin Appeal Brief, para. 220.
[3228]   *Stakić* Appeal Judgement, para. 97.
[3229]   *Stakić* Appeal Judgement, paras 73, 84. See *Stakić* Appeal Judgement, para. 83.
[3230]   *Stakić* Appeal Judgement, para. 98.
[3231]   Trial Judgement, vol. 2, para. 520.
[3232]   See Trial Judgement, vol. 2, paras 522-528.
[3233]   *Tolimir* Appeal Judgement, para. 514; *Đorđević* Appeal Judgement, para. 906; *Šainović et al.* Appeal Judgement, paras 1078, 1081; *Brđanin* Appeal Judgement, paras 365, 411; *Stakić* Appeal Judgement, para. 65; *Tadić* Appeal Judgement, para. 228. See *supra*, para. 958.
[3234]   See Župljanin Appeal Brief, para. 222, referring to Binder Article, p. 406; Pillsbury Article, p. 106, 108; UK Homicide Act, section 1(1).
[3235]   See Župljanin Appeal Brief, para. 221.
[3236]   See *Krajišnik* Appeal Judgement, para. 600.
[3237]   *Đorđević* Appeal Judgement, para. 83. Moreover, the Appeals Chamber observes that in the extrajudicial writing cited by Župljanin, Judge Cassese noted that resorting to the third category of joint criminal enterprise for specific intent crimes is intrinsically ill-founded (Judge Cassese Article on JCE, p. 121. See Judge Cassese Article on JCE, p. 122). However, the Appeals Chamber has considered that this position expressed in extrajudicial writings of Judge Cassese does not justify departure from its established case law on the third category of joint criminal enterprise in relation to specific intent crimes (*Đorđević* Appeal Judgement, para. 83. See *Popović et al.* Appeal Judgement, paras 1437-1443).
[3238]   Župljanin Appeal Brief, para. 225.

Appeal Judgement; and (ii) Judge Schomburg's separate opinion in the *Martić* Appeal Judgement, these do not constitute cogent reasons to depart from the Tribunal's jurisprudence as they do not concern the issue at hand.[3239] Second, with respect to Župljanin's reliance of the ECCC Decision on JCE, the Appeals Chamber recalls its earlier conclusion that this decision does not constitute a cogent reason for the Appeals Chamber to depart **[page 405]** from its consistent jurisprudence on liability pursuant to the third category of joint criminal enterprise.[3240]

976. For the foregoing reasons, the Appeals Chamber finds that Župljanin has failed to demonstrate that there are cogent reasons warranting departure from the Tribunal's jurisprudence on the third category of joint criminal enterprise. Accordingly, the Appeals Chamber also finds no merit in Župljanin's additional argument that the Trial Chamber erred in law in failing to find that he "intended the adoption of any violent means" to effectuate the common purpose.[3241]

c. Conclusion

977. For the above reasons, the Appeals Chamber finds that Župljanin has failed to demonstrate that the Trial Chamber erred in law in convicting him of persecutions through killings, torture, and cruel treatment; extermination as a crime against humanity; murder as a violation of the laws or customs of war; and torture as a violation of the laws or customs of war and finding him responsible for murder as a crime against humanity; torture as crime against humanity; and cruel treatment as a violation of the laws or customs of war pursuant to the third category of joint criminal enterprise. The Appeals Chamber therefore dismisses sub-ground (A) of Župljanin's second ground of appeal.

(iii) Alleged errors of law in relation to whether Župljanin's JCE III Crimes were natural and foreseeable consequences of the common purpose (sub-ground (B) in part of Župljanin's second ground of appeal)

978. Župljanin submits that the Trial Chamber erred in law by failing to make a finding that Župljanin's JCE III Crimes were "objectively" natural and foreseeable consequences of the common purpose.[3242] He contends that the lack of a finding on such an essential element of the third **[page 406]** category of joint criminal enterprise liability invalidates his conviction pursuant to this form of liability.[3243]

979. The Prosecution responds that the Trial Chamber's findings on Župljanin's "'subjective foreseeability' implicitly assume that the Trial Chamber also found the crimes to have been 'objectively foreseeable'".[3244]

[3239]   The Appeals Chamber observes that: (i) Judge Shahabuddeen's dissenting opinion relates to the issue of whether the principal perpetrators of a crime must be proved to be members of the joint criminal enterprise in order for their crimes to be attributed to the members of the enterprise (*Brđanin* Trial Judgement, paras 354-355; *Brđanin* Appeal Judgement, Partially Dissenting Opinion of Judge Shahabuddeen, paras 1-20); (ii) Judge Schomburg's separate opinion in the *Martić* Appeal Judgement addresses the question of whether Martić's conduct had to be qualified as that of a "(co)- perpetrator" under the mode of liability of commission pursuant to Article 7(1) of the Statute as opposed to contribution to a joint criminal enterprise (*Martić* Appeal Judgement, Separate Opinion of Judge Schomburg on Individual Criminal Responsibility of Milan Martić, paras 2, 7).

[3240]   *Đorđević* Appeal Judgement, para. 53. See *Đorđević* Appeal Judgement, paras 50-52. See also *Martić* Appeal Judgement, paras 76, 84. With regard to Župljanin's contention that other commentators have proposed quite radically that third category of joint criminal enterprise should be abolished in favour of the concept of aiding and abetting (Župljanin Appeal Brief, para. 225, referring to Kai Ambos *Amicus Curiae* Application, pp 8-13, Ohlin Article, p. 9), the Appeals Chamber recalls that while writings of highly respected academics may be considered in determining the law, their subsidiary nature is well-established and the Appeals Chamber is not bound by them (*Đorđević* Appeal Judgement, para. 33).

[3241]   Župljanin Appeal Brief, para. 224. See Župljanin Appeal Brief, para. 226.

[3242]   Župljanin Appeal Brief, paras 193-194; Župljanin Reply Brief, para. 66. Župljanin submits that none of the paragraphs of the Trial Judgement devoted to the third category of joint criminal enterprise make a determination on whether these crimes were a natural and foreseeable consequence of the JCE. He submits that the Trial Chamber "later" makes a reference to "a finding" that the Župljanin's JCE III Crimes were "foreseeable consequences" of the execution of the common plan, but it fails to indicate where in the Trial Judgement this finding was made. According to Župljanin, the Trial Chamber might have confused its findings in paragraphs 521-528 of volume two of the Trial Judgement on "subjective foreseeability" with "objective foreseeability" with respect to which it did not make a finding (Župljanin Appeal Brief, para. 193).

[3243]   Župljanin Appeal Brief, para. 194.

[3244]   Prosecution Response Brief (Župljanin), para. 145. The Prosecution adds that the Trial Chamber confirmed this when it "recall[ed] its findings that all of the remaining crimes were foreseeable consequences of the execution of the common plan" (Prosecution Response Brief (Župljanin), para. 145).

The Prosecution submits that in these circumstances, the Trial Chamber was not required to make any additional findings on whether Župljanin's JCE III Crimes were natural and foreseeable consequences of the JCE.[3245] The Prosecution further submits that, even if the Trial Chamber should have entered a more specific finding, Župljanin fails to show that any alleged oversight by the Trial Chamber would have any impact since the only reasonable conclusion is that Župljanin's JCE III Crimes were natural and foreseeable consequences of the JCE.[3246]

980. The Appeals Chamber reiterates, as correctly set out by the Trial Chamber,[3247] that an accused may be responsible for crimes committed beyond the common purpose of the joint criminal enterprise, if they were a natural and foreseeable consequence thereof.[3248] However, this "must be assessed in relation to the knowledge of a particular accused".[3249]

981. Accordingly, the Appeals Chamber considers that Župljanin's argument creates and rests upon an artificial distinction – that the subjective element of the third category of joint criminal enterprise contains distinct objective and subjective elements – in direct contravention of the law.[3250] Župljanin's unfounded argument, which departs from well-established jurisprudence, therefore has no merit. As such, the Appeals Chamber dismisses sub-ground (B) of Župljanin's second ground of appeal in part concerning this issue.[3251][page 407]

(iv) Alleged errors in finding that Župljanin's JCE III Crimes were foreseeable to Župljanin and that he willingly took the risk that they might be committed (sub-ground (B) in part and sub-ground (D) of Župljanin's second ground of appeal)

a. Submissions of the parties

982. Župljanin submits that the Trial Chamber erred in finding that Župljanin's JCE III Crimes were foreseeable to him and that he willingly took the risk that they might be committed.[3252] He argues that the Trial Chamber "impermissibly generalized and distorted factual findings" regarding his individual criminal responsibility pursuant to the third category joint criminal enterprise.[3253] Specifically, he submits that the Trial Chamber erred in its approach by making unsupported generalisations about the ARK Municipalities as a whole, which it then used to make further findings on each municipality.[3254] In this context, Župljanin further submits that: (i) the lack of internal references makes it "impossible" to understand the Trial Chamber's findings;[3255] (ii) each of the ARK Municipalities required an independent analysis as they had different ethnic compositions, sequences of events, decision-makers, and perpetrators;[3256] and (iii) the foreseeable actions of one group of perpetrators cannot be said to be equally foreseeable in relation to

---

[3245]   Prosecution Response Brief (Župljanin), para. 145.
[3246]   Prosecution Response Brief (Župljanin), paras 144-145.
[3247]   Trial Judgement, vol. 1, para. 99.
[3248]   *Kvočka et al.* Appeal Judgement, para. 86.
[3249]   *Kvočka et al.* Appeal Judgement, para. 86. See *supra*, para. 621.
[3250]   *Popović et al.* Appeal Judgement, paras 1690, 1696-1698, 1713-1717; *Šainović et al.* Appeal Judgement, paras 1575-1604; *Kvočka et al.* Appeal Judgement, paras 83-86.
[3251]   The Appeals Chamber notes that Župljanin also submits that the Trial Chamber erred in fact by (implicitly) finding that Župljanin's JCE III Crimes were natural and foreseeable consequences of the JCE (see Župljanin Appeal Brief, paras 196-200). In light of its conclusion that under the third category of joint criminal enterprise, the accused may be responsible for crimes beyond the common purpose of a joint criminal enterprise if they were natural and foreseeable consequences of the common purpose *to him*, the Appeals Chamber will address these arguments to the extent that they are relevant to the Trial Chamber's considerations in this regard. These arguments will be addressed in the next section together with Župljanin's factual challenges raised with respect to the Trial Chamber's findings that Župljanin's JCE III Crimes were foreseeable to him (see *infra*, paras 982-1010).
[3252]   Župljanin Appeal Brief, paras 201-218.
[3253]   Župljanin Appeal Brief, paras 201-213.
[3254]   Župljanin Appeal Brief, paras 203-204, 206.
[3255]   Župljanin Appeal Brief, para. 204. See Župljanin Appeal Brief, paras 202-203. See also Župljanin Reply Brief, para. 68. Župljanin argues that the Trial Chamber's conclusions were not sufficiently referenced on a central element and that the parties and the Appeals Chamber are left to speculate on or surmise how the Trial Chamber arrived at these findings. He adds that this violates his right to a reasoned opinion (Župljanin Appeal Brief, paras 202-203, referring to, *inter alia*, *Krajišnik* Appeal Judgement, paras 23, 176; Župljanin Reply Brief, para. 68).
[3256]   Župljanin Appeal Brief, paras 203-206. See Župljanin Reply Brief, para. 69.

another group in a different municipality.[3257] According to Župljanin, the Trial Chamber's failure to make findings on the foreseeability of specific crimes in specific municipalities means that an unspecified crime at an unspecified location was a foreseeable and natural consequence of the JCE, a conclusion that "substantially and dangerously" diminishes the threshold of joint criminal enterprise liability.[3258]

983.　Župljanin also argues that no reasonable trier of fact could have found that Župljanin's JCE III Crimes were natural and foreseeable consequences of the JCE since the Trial Chamber expressly excluded from the common criminal purpose all violent crimes and acts of unlawful coercion charged in the Indictment.[3259] Župljanin argues in this regard that the violent crimes were not natural and foreseeable *consequences* of the objective to see the permanent departures of **[page 408]** non-Serbs from the ARK as many other factors contributed to these crimes.[3260] Župljanin contends further that in the absence of any meaningful definition in the Trial Judgement of what was intended within the common purpose, even non-violent crimes cannot be considered natural and foreseeable consequences of the JCE.[3261]

984.　Župljanin also contends that the Trial Chamber's findings – particularly as they relate to murder and extermination – were unreasonable, inconsistent, or insufficiently reasoned, and do not demonstrate that he had the requisite *mens rea*.[3262] Specifically, Župljanin submits that the Trial Chamber erred by relying on: (i) the enrolment of "seasoned criminals" in the Banja Luka CSB SPD and his receipt of reports on the Banja Luka CSB SPD's lack of discipline and criminal activities;[3263] (ii) "unspecified 'crimes'" committed against non-Serbs in Banja Luka;[3264] (iii) the death of 20 detainees in the Sanski Most Incident during their transportation on 7 July 1992 even though it accepted the possibility that this may not have been intentional;[3265] (iv) the death of eight non-Serbs at the Manjača detention camp between 6 and 7 August 1992 and the Korićanske Stijene killings on 21 August 1992;[3266] and (v) his tasking of the Prijedor police to escort buses of non-Serb detainees to Croatia in September 1992.[3267]

985.　Župljanin further argues that the Trial Chamber failed to properly link the principal perpetrators to members of the JCE, which affects any foreseeability imputed to him.[3268] He submits that there is neither evidence nor preliminary findings explaining how the JCE members **[page 409]** used the principal perpetrators to commit Župljanin's JCE III Crimes, and that this is not the only reasonable inference available.[3269]

[3257]　Župljanin Appeal Brief, para. 205.

[3258]　Župljanin Appeal Brief, para. 199. See Župljanin Appeal Brief, para. 200.

[3259]　Župljanin Appeal Brief, paras 196, 198.

[3260]　Župljanin Appeal Brief, para. 197. Župljanin submits that many factors contributed to the occurrence of crimes, including opportunism driven by ethnic hatred, a desire to revenge perceived atrocities by the other side, and a lack of adequate command and control in military operations. He adds that many of the crimes appear to have been committed "without the perpetrators having the slightest interest in inducing the victims to flee" (Župljanin Appeal Brief, para. 197).

[3261]　Župljanin Appeal Brief, para. 198.

[3262]　Župljanin Appeal Brief, paras 207-213.

[3263]　Župljanin Appeal Brief, para. 208. Župljanin contends that the Trial Chamber's reasoning on these matters is so vague that it fails to demonstrate his "foresight, much less that he undertook the risk that crimes would be committed" (Župljanin Appeal Brief, para. 208). Župljanin also refers to his argument under sub-ground (D)(ii) of his first ground of appeal regarding the enrolment of "seasoned criminals" into the Banja Luka CSB SPD (Župljanin Appeal Brief, para. 208, fn. 296).

[3264]　Župljanin Appeal Brief, para. 209.

[3265]　Župljanin Appeal Brief, para. 210. Župljanin submits that the Trial Chamber did not imply that these specific deaths were foreseeable and that it accepted the possibility that they were unintentional (Župljanin Appeal Brief, para. 210, referring to Trial Judgement, vol. 1, para. 215). He also submits that the Trial Chamber failed to identify any criminal behaviour, specifically murder or extermination, after 7 July 1992 involving the Sanski Most police (Župljanin Appeal Brief, para. 210).

[3266]　Župljanin Appeal Brief, para. 211. Župljanin argues that his foresight cannot be inferred on the basis of these incidents since: (i) no crimes were found to have been committed by the Prijedor police after 21 August 1992; (ii) all police involved in the Korićanske Stijene killings were transferred out of the Prijedor police force; and (iii) the preliminary report on the incident at the Manjača detention camp on 6 and 7 August 1992 was not finalised until 26 August 1992, *i.e.* after the Korićanske Stijene killings (Župljanin Appeal Brief, para. 211).

[3267]　Župljanin Appeal Brief, para. 212. Župljanin submits that no crimes, specifically violent crimes, are alleged to have occurred during the transportation (Župljanin Appeal Brief, para. 212).

[3268]　Župljanin Appeal Brief, paras 214-215, 217. See Župljanin Reply Brief, para. 72.

[3269]　Župljanin Appeal Brief, para. 216, referring to Trial Judgement, vol. 2, para. 316. Župljanin argues that how the JCE members used the physical perpetrators is an important aspect of any potential foreseeability on his part as the perpetrators in each municipality differed (Župljanin Appeal Brief, para. 217).

986. The Prosecution responds that the Trial Chamber's findings were sufficiently referenced,[3270] and that it was not required to conduct an "independent analysis" for each of the ARK Municipalities since all crimes were committed in the implementation of the JCE and followed the same pattern.[3271] Moreover, the Prosecution argues that it was not required under the third form of joint criminal enterprise liability that Župljanin foresaw "the possibility that a specific unit could commit a specific crime in a specific municipality",[3272] and that he fails to show that the Trial Chamber's approach was incorrect.[3273]

987. The Prosecution also contends that the Trial Chamber found that violent and coercive means were involved in the implementation of the JCE and that Župljanin's contrary argument rests on an incorrect premise.[3274] The Prosecution further submits that the Trial Chamber considered the factors listed by Župljanin, among others, as contributing to the occurrence of Župljanin's JCE III Crimes, when it assessed foreseeability.[3275]

988. The Prosecution further responds that Župljanin had extensive knowledge of the context of the crimes and consistently contributed to the JCE, thus the crimes were foreseeable to him and he **[page 410]** willingly took the risk of their commission.[3276] It submits that Župljanin: (i) was aware of and intended the massive forcible displacement campaign conducted against non-Serbs; (ii) knew of the widespread and systematic attack against non-Serbs and their weaker position; and (iii) was aware of the ethnically charged character of the armed conflict and shared the discriminatory intent with other JCE members.[3277] The Prosecution argues that Župljanin continuously received specific and repeated information that Serb forces, including forces under his command, committed widespread and systematic crimes against non-Serbs, both in general and regarding specific incidents.[3278] It also contends that the Trial Chamber reasonably relied on Župljanin's knowledge of the Sanski Most Incident and the Korićanske Stijene killings as they were "clear warnings" of the risk of additional murders being committed during the transport of detainees by police.[3279] The Prosecution asserts that Župljanin misunderstands the role of some factors considered by the Trial Chamber as they show that he willingly took the risk of, and encouraged, the continuation of crimes.[3280]

[3270] Prosecution Response Brief (Župljanin), para. 151. The Prosecution submits that the Trial Chamber was not obliged in its summary of conclusions on Župljanin's individual criminal responsibility to cross-reference "each of its many previous findings" considering that a judgement must be read as a whole (Prosecution Response Brief (Župljanin), para. 151, referring to *Krajišnik* Appeal Judgement, para. 237; *Mrkšić and Šljivančanin* Appeal Judgement, para. 379).

[3271] Prosecution Response Brief (Župljanin), paras 152, 154. The Prosecution submits that the JCE implementation across all the ARK Municipalities involved, *inter alia*: (i) the arming of Serbs and the disarming of non-Serbs; (ii) the forcible takeover of the ARK Municipalities; (iii) a recurring pattern of ethnic cleansing which resulted in a widespread and systematic campaign of terror; (iv) the same targeted victim group; and (v) physical perpetrators who belonged to groups used by JCE members, and who closely cooperated with each other, to further the common plan (Prosecution Response Brief (Župljanin), paras 154-155).

[3272] Prosecution Response Brief (Župljanin), para. 156.

[3273] Prosecution Response Brief (Župljanin), para. 156. See Prosecution Response Brief (Župljanin), para. 150.

[3274] Prosecution Response Brief (Župljanin), para. 146. The Prosecution submits that the furtherance of the criminal objective of the JCE involved using violent and coercive means (Prosecution Response Brief (Župljanin), para. 146, referring to Prosecution Appeal Brief (Župljanin), paras 9-12).

[3275] Prosecution Response Brief (Župljanin), para. 147. The Prosecution submits that the Trial Chamber, in particular, took into account the ethnically charged character of the armed conflict, the ethnic tensions existing in the region, the weak position in which non-Serbs found themselves in relation to the Serb forces arresting them and expelling them from their municipalities, and the strong ethnic tensions and resentments. It adds that the Trial Chamber was aware of the lack of discipline and extreme actions of certain members of the Serb forces (Prosecution Response Brief (Župljanin), para. 147). It further responds that Župljanin's assertion that "many of the crimes appear to have been committed without the perpetrators having the slightest interest in inducing the victims to flee" is not only unsupported, but is also contradicted by the evidence and the Trial Chamber's findings and that it is well established that the persons used as tools to carry out the *actus reus* of the crime need not share the *mens rea* for the joint criminal enterprise (Prosecution Response Brief (Župljanin), para. 148).

[3276] Prosecution Response Brief (Župljanin), para. 157. See Prosecution Response Brief (Župljanin), paras 158-161.

[3277] Prosecution Response Brief (Župljanin), para. 158.

[3278] Prosecution Response Brief (Župljanin), paras 159-161.

[3279] Prosecution Response Brief (Župljanin), para. 162. The Prosecution also responds that it is irrelevant that Župljanin did not finalise his report before 26 August 1992 and, given the efficient reporting system set up by Župljanin, there can be no doubt that he was informed of the murders and the likely involvement of the Prijedor police on, or soon after, the day of the incident (Prosecution Response Brief (Župljanin), para. 163).

[3280] Prosecution Response Brief (Župljanin), para. 164. The Prosecution argues that the factors considered by the Trial Chamber demonstrated that: (i) Župljanin's JCE III Crimes continued to be committed by the Banja Luka CSB SPD and other units under Župljanin's authority; (ii) Župljanin continued to redeploy and use these units with the knowledge of their crimes; and (iii) Župljanin failed to take any measures to punish them (Prosecution Response Brief (Župljanin), para. 164).

989. The Prosecution finally contends that Župljanin fails to show that the Trial Chamber erred in concluding that the JCE members used Serb forces to carry out Župljanin's JCE III Crimes in the ARK Municipalities.[3281] It argues that Župljanin's arguments in this regard warrant dismissal as they go beyond his notice of appeal.[3282] The Prosecution also submits that there is "no requirement 'of some proof of an *act* by the JCE member in order to use the non-JCE members as tools to further the JCE'".[3283] It asserts that the existence of the requisite link may be inferred from various circumstances,[3284] and that the Trial Chamber reasonably established the requisite links.[3285] **[page 411]**

990. Župljanin replies that his arguments regarding the failure to link the physical perpetrators to the JCE members do not go beyond the scope of his notice of appeal since the issue is "part and parcel" of the alleged foreseeability of the crimes and he only alleges errors of fact.[3286]

b. Analysis

991. In light of the nature of Župljanin's submissions, the Appeals Chamber will consider, first, Župljanin's arguments on the link between the principal perpetrators of Župljanin's JCE III Crimes and the JCE members and, second, his arguments on the alleged errors concerning the foreseeability of Župljanin's JCE III Crimes.

i. Alleged errors on the link between the principal perpetrators of Župljanin's JCE III Crimes and the JCE members

992. The Appeals Chamber will first determine whether Župljanin's argument concerning the link between the principal perpetrators of Župljanin's JCE III Crimes and the JCE members should be considered on the merits. The Appeals Chamber recalls that a notice of appeal shall contain, *inter alia*, the grounds of appeal, clearly specifying in respect of each ground of appeal any alleged error of law and any alleged error of fact.[3287] The Appeals Chamber notes that in Župljanin's notice of appeal, sub-ground (D) of the second ground of appeal alleges that "[n]o reasonable trier of fact could have found that the JCE III crimes were foreseeable to Mr Župljanin",[3288] and therefore gives notice of an error of fact. In his appeal brief, however, Župljanin argues that the Trial Chamber failed to properly link the principal perpetrators to JCE members, a failure which affects its findings on the foreseeability of crimes.[3289] The Appeals Chamber considers that, in so arguing, Župljanin alleges a failure of the Trial Chamber to correctly apply the jurisprudence on joint criminal enterprise to the evidence and provide a reasoned opinion, thus an error of law.[3290] Therefore, contrary to Župljanin's assertion,[3291] his argument is not correctly characterised as an error of fact and is thus not covered by paragraphs 28 and 29 of his notice of appeal. However, recalling that the purpose of listing all the grounds of appeal in a notice of appeal is to focus the mind of the respondent on the arguments which

---

[3281] Prosecution Response Brief (Župljanin), paras 165, 167.

[3282] Prosecution Response Brief (Župljanin), para. 166. The Prosecution submits that Župljanin's notice of appeal does not indicate that he intended to challenge the link between the principal perpetrators and the JCE members and alleges an error of fact while his arguments concern an error of law (Prosecution Response Brief (Župljanin), para. 166).

[3283] Prosecution Response Brief (Župljanin), para. 168.

[3284] Prosecution Response Brief (Župljanin), para. 169.

[3285] Prosecution Response Brief (Župljanin), para. 170. The Prosecution refers to findings: (i) that the JCE members, including Župljanin, had control over the hierarchically structured forces whose members committed crimes in the ARK Municipalities; (ii) that some JCE members, by virtue of their leadership over the SDS and/or their important posts in the RS, were in charge of events taking place in the municipalities through their control over the SDS structure and Crisis Staffs; (iii) that all ARK Municipalities were under the authority of the ARK Crisis Staff, whose leading members were also members of the JCE; and (iv) that the JCE members in each municipality acted in concert and with the other principal perpetrators when they committed the crimes (Prosecution Response Brief (Župljanin), para. 170).

[3286] Župljanin Reply Brief, paras 70-71.

[3287] *Popović et al.* Appeal Judgement, para. 500; *Boškoski and Tarčulovski* Appeal Judgement, para. 246. See *Prosecutor v. Momčilo Krajišnik*, Case No. IT-00-39-A, Decision on Prosecution's Motion for Clarification and Reconsideration of the Decision of 28 February 2008, 11 March 2008, para. 10 ("[a] notice of appeal need not enumerate the precise contours that an argument will take [...] however, [...] the arguments [...] advance[d] must be within the ambit of issues [...]set forth in [the] notice of appeal").

[3288] Župljanin Notice of Appeal, para. 28. See Župljanin Notice of Appeal, para. 29.

[3289] Župljanin Appeal Brief, paras 214-218.

[3290] See *Popović et al.* Appeal Judgement, para. 502.

[3291] See Župljanin Reply Brief, paras 70-71 (reiterating that the Trial Chamber's errors are errors of fact).

will be developed subsequently in the appeal brief,[3292] the **[page 412]** Appeals Chamber finds that the Prosecution will not suffer any prejudice if Župljanin's argument is considered on the merits as it had the opportunity to respond to this argument and the matter is fully litigated in the briefs.[3293] Thus, in these circumstances, the Appeals Chamber will consider Župljanin's argument.

993. The Trial Chamber found that Serb forces committed the crimes underlying Župljanin's convictions pursuant to the third form of joint criminal enterprise in the ARK Municipalities, and for each municipality, it identified the specific group or unit of the Serb forces – belonging to various police forces, paramilitary groups, or military forces – who were involved in the perpetration of these crimes in the course of implementing the JCE.[3294] The Appeals Chamber also notes that the Trial Chamber did not identify the Serb forces, or any group or unit thereof, as members of the JCE.[3295] Župljanin does not challenge the Trial Chamber's findings on the principal perpetrators of the relevant crimes or the JCE members in this sub-ground of appeal, but disputes whether the link between them was properly established.

994. The Appeals Chamber recalls that, under the third category of joint criminal enterprise, an accused may incur criminal responsibility for crimes committed by non-members of the JCE "provided that it had been shown that the crimes could be imputed to at least one member of the JCE and that this member, when using a principal perpetrator, acted in accordance with the common plan".[3296] The Appeals Chamber notes that, for each of the ARK Municipalities, the Trial Chamber identified a link between the specific group or unit of the Serb forces involved in crimes and at least one JCE member, and at times, Župljanin himself.[3297] As examples, the Appeals Chamber notes that the Trial Chamber found that the principal perpetrators of Župljanin's JCE III Crimes in Banja Luka, Ključ, Kotor Varoš, Donji Vakuf, Sanski Most, Prijedor, Skender Vakuf, and Teslić included members of forces who were under the authority of Župljanin himself and/or other JCE members, such as, Vinko Kondić, Witness Nedeljko Đekanović, Momir Talić, Mirko **[page 413]** Vručinić, Drljača, and Mladić.[3298] The Trial Chamber then concluded that the named JCE members "when using these Serb Forces" to commit crimes, acted in accordance with the common plan.[3299]

995. The Appeals Chamber recalls that the existence of the link between the principal perpetrator of a crime and a member of the joint criminal enterprise is to be assessed on a case-by-case basis.[3300] This link can be inferred from various factors, including "evidence that the JCE member explicitly or implicitly requested the non-JCE member to commit such a crime or instigated, ordered, encouraged, or otherwise availed himself of the non-JCE member to commit the crime".[3301] Insofar as Župljanin asserts that "there must be some proof of an act by the JCE member in order to use the non-JCE members as tools to further the

---

[3292] *Popović et al.* Appeal Judgement, para. 500, referring to *Boškoski and Tarčulovski* Appeal Judgement, para. 246.

[3293] *Cf. Popović et al.* Appeal Judgement, para. 489; *Nizeyimana* Appeal Judgement, paras 352-354.

[3294] Trial Judgement, vol. 2, paras 801, 828, 841, 846, 855, 860, 865. See Trial Judgement, vol. 2, paras 522-528.

[3295] See Trial Judgement, vol. 2, para. 314 (finding that the JCE members were Karadžić, Krajišnik, Plavšić, Koljević, Mladić, Mandić, Velibor Ostojić, Momir Talić, Brđanin, Stakić, Drljača, Kuprešanin, Vlado Vrkes, Mirko Vručinić, Jovan Tintor, Nedeljko Đekanović, Savo Tepić, Stevan Todorović, Blagoje Simić, Vinko Kondić, Malko Koroman, Dorde Ristanić, Predrag Radić, Andrija Bjelošević, Ljubiša Savić, a.k.a. "Mauzer", Predrag Ješurić, and Branko Grujić).

[3296] *Popović et al.* Appeal Judgement, para. 1679; *Dorlevic* Appeal Judgement, para. 911.

[3297] Trial Judgement, vol. 2, paras 314, 801-802 (Banja Luka), 828-829 (Donji Vakuf), 841-842 (Ključ), 846-847 (Kotor Varoš), 855-856 (Prijedor and Skender Vakuf), 860-861 (Sanski Most), 865-866 (Teslić). See *e.g.* Trial Judgement, vol. 1, paras 142-147, 163-164, 200, 240, 716; Trial Judgement, vol. 2, paras 311, 350-356, 384-397, 495-499, 502-503, 710, 721-727.

[3298] Trial Judgement, vol. 2, paras 801-802 (see Trial Judgement, vol. 1, paras 200-211) (Banja Luka); Trial Judgement, vol. 2, paras 314, 841-842 (see Trial Judgement, vol. 1, paras 331-339) (Ključ); Trial Judgement, vol. 2, paras 314, 846-847 (see Trial Judgement, vol. 2, paras 384-397; Trial Judgement, vol. 1, paras 453-480) (Kotor Varoš); Trial Judgement, vol. 2, paras 314, 828-832 (see Trial Judgement, vol. 1, paras 260-274) (Donji Vakuf); Trial Judgement, vol. 2, paras 314, 860-861 (see Trial Judgement, vol. 1, paras 782-804) (Sanski Most); Trial Judgement, vol. 2, paras 314, 854-856 (see Trial Judgement, vol. 1, paras 655-684) (Prijedor and Skender Vakuf); Trial Judgement, vol. 2, paras 314, 865-866 (see Trial Judgement, vol. 1, paras 867-872; Trial Judgement, vol. 2, paras 405, 418-419, 421-422, 432-433, 435, 437-448) (Teslid).

[3299] Trial Judgement, vol. 2, paras 802, 829, 842, 847, 856, 861, 866.

[3300] *Popović et al.* Appeal Judgement, para. 1053. See *Tolimir* Appeal Judgement, para. 432; *Đorđević* Appeal Judgement, para. 165; *Šainović et al.* Appeal Judgement, para. 1256; *Krajišnik* Appeal Judgement, para. 226.

[3301] *Popović et al.* Appeal Judgement, para. 1050, quoting *Krajišnik* Appeal Judgement, para. 226. See *Šainović et al.* Appeal Judgement, paras 1257, 1259.

JCE",[3302] the Appeals Chamber considers that there is no requirement that there must be "an act" by the JCE member in order to establish the necessary link.[3303]

996. The Appeals Chamber also considers Župljanin's argument on *how* the JCE members used the principal perpetrators to commit crimes to be unpersuasive and unsupported. The Appeals Chamber recalls that there is "no requirement that a trial chamber demonstrate 'how each physical perpetrator was *used* to commit the crimes' in order to establish such link", provided that the trial chamber identifies how one or more members of the joint criminal enterprise used the forces to which these physical perpetrators belonged in furtherance of the common plan.[3304] The Appeals Chamber notes that, in arriving at its conclusions on the required link, the Trial Chamber considered: (i) the hierarchical structure, which included at least one JCE member exercising command or control over the relevant Serb forces involved in the commission of the crimes; (ii) the knowledge possessed by at least one JCE member on the involvement of the identified Serb forces in the criminal activities, including the unlawful detentions, the imposition of inhumane conditions, and the crimes committed in detention facilities; and (iii) that the various units or groups of the Serb **[page 414]** forces acted in concert with each other in accordance with the common plan.[3305] In the view of the Appeals Chamber, Župljanin has failed to show an error in the Trial Chamber's consideration of these factors or that the Trial Chamber misapplied the law. The Appeals Chamber thus considers that the Trial Chamber correctly applied the jurisprudence on joint criminal enterprise. The Appeals Chamber also finds that Župljanin has not demonstrated that no reasonable trier of fact could have concluded that the only reasonable inference available is that Župljanin's JCE III Crimes can be imputed to at least one JCE member and that this member – when using the principal perpetrators – acted in accordance with the common plan. Župljanin's arguments on the link between the principal perpetrators and the JCE members are accordingly dismissed.

ii. Alleged errors on the foreseeability of Župljanin's JCE III Crimes

997. The Appeals Chamber recalls that the Trial Chamber, in its foreseeability assessment of Župljanin's JCE III Crimes committed in the ARK Municipalities, considered the overall context in which these crimes occurred as well as specific evidence which it found supported the conclusion that: (i) the possibility that, in the execution of the common plan, these crimes could be committed was sufficiently substantial as to be foreseeable to Župljanin; and (ii) he willingly took that risk.[3306] The Appeals Chamber understands that the Trial Chamber was satisfied that the subjective element pursuant to the third category of joint criminal enterprise was met in relation to Župljanin throughout the Indictment period, *i.e.* at least from 1 April 1992 and, in any event when Župljanin's JCE III Crimes were committed.[3307]

998. Insofar as Župljanin argues that the Trial Chamber erred by making unsupported generalisations about the ARK Municipalities as a whole, the Appeals Chamber finds that he ignores the Trial Chamber's

---

[3302] Župljanin Appeal Brief, para. 215.
[3303] See *e.g. Popović et al.* Appeal Judgement, para. 1057, fn. 3081; *Šainović et al.* Appeal Judgement, paras 1259, 1263; *Martić* Appeal Judgement, paras 181, 187-189, 205-206.
[3304] *Đorđević* Appeal Judgement, para. 165.
[3305] Trial Judgement, vol. 2, paras 802 (Banja Luka), 829 (Donji Vakuf), 842 (Ključ), 847 (Kotor Varoš), 856 (Prijedor and Skender Vakuf), 861 (Sanski Most), 866 (Teslić). See Trial Judgement, vol. 2, paras 405, 418-419, 421-422, 432-433, 435, 437-448 (Banja Luka), 507 (Sanski Most), 508 (Prijedor), 509 (Ključ and Donji Vakuf), 510-517.
[3306] Trial Judgement, vol. 2, paras 522-528.
[3307] The Appeals Chamber notes that for the assessment of the foreseeability of all of Župljanin's JCE III Crimes, the Trial Chamber relied on, *inter alia*, the common purpose of the JCE (Trial Judgement, vol. 2, para. 521). With regard to foreseeability of unlawful detentions, the Trial Chamber additionally relied on the "information available to Župljanin during the *Indictment period*" (emphasis added) (Trial Judgement, vol. 2, para. 523). With respect to the foreseeability of murders and extermination, it further relied on his presence in Banja Luka after the 3 April 1992 blockade of the town as well as his receipt of information about crimes against non-Serbs in Banja Luka from "the first half of April 1992" (Trial Judgement, vol. 2, para. 524). The Trial Chamber also relied on the ethnic tensions in the regions in relation to the foreseeability of plunder and looting, and his knowledge of ethnic tensions in relation to torture, cruel treatment, and inhumane acts (Trial Judgement, vol. 2, paras 525-526). Moreover, Župljanin was convicted pursuant to the third category of joint criminal enterprise for crimes occurring throughout the Indictment period (see *e.g.* Trial Judgement, vol. 2, paras 801, 805, 828, 832, 841, 845-846, 850, 855, 859-860, 864-865, 869, 956). The Appeals Chamber notes that the Trial Chamber identified the Indictment period as "from no later than 1 April 1992" until 31 December 1992 (Trial Judgement, vol. 2, para. 344. See Trial Judgement, vol. 2, para. 520).

relevant findings. In this regard, the Appeals Chamber notes that, for each of the ARK Municipalities, the Trial Chamber reviewed the evidence and made findings on **[page 415]** the sequence of events and the crimes committed,[3308] the principal perpetrators of the crimes,[3309] and Župljanin's involvement in and knowledge of the events and crimes committed.[3310] Similarly, in concluding that it was foreseeable to Župljanin that Župljanin's JCE III Crimes might be committed, the Trial Chamber considered the relevant findings for each crime.[3311] For example, as set out in detail above,[3312] the Trial Chamber's finding that it was foreseeable to Župljanin that Serb forces might impose and maintain restrictive and discriminatory measures against non-Serbs was based on, *inter alia*, his membership in "both the ARK and Banja Luka crisis staffs, which issued orders restricting the rights of Muslims and Croats to perform certain jobs or impacting on their property rights".[3313] Likewise, its finding that it was foreseeable to Župljanin that Serb forces might establish and perpetuate inhumane living conditions and commit torture, cruel treatment, and inhumane acts against Muslims and Croats was based on "the reports that Župljanin received on the conditions of detention camps and his knowledge of ethnic tensions existing in the region".[3314] It is on the basis of an analysis of all of the above findings that the Trial Chamber concluded that it was foreseeable to Župljanin, and he willingly took the risk, that restrictive and discriminatory measures might be imposed, large numbers of non-Serbs might be unlawfully detained, and that other serious crimes, including murder and extermination, could be committed.[3315] Contrary to Župljanin's argument,[3316] the Trial Chamber was not required to establish whether it was foreseeable that a *specific* group would commit the *specific* crime, as long as it found that it was foreseeable to Župljanin that a crime outside the common purpose might be perpetrated by one or more of the persons used by him (or by another member of the JCE) in order to carry out the *actus reus* of the crimes forming part of the common purpose and he willingly took the risk that the crime might be committed by joining or continuing to participate in the JCE.[3317]

999. Furthermore, for each of the ARK Municipalities, the Trial Chamber considered the principal perpetrators of the crimes and their link to JCE members before concluding that Župljanin's JCE III Crimes were foreseeable to him and that he willingly took the risk that the **[page 416]** crimes might be committed by participating in the JCE.[3318] As Župljanin argues, the portion of the Trial Judgement concerning legal findings on his individual criminal responsibility pursuant to the third category of joint criminal enterprise does not contain internal references to these and other relevant underlying findings.[3319] However, as stated above, while the Appeals Chamber considers the Trial Chamber's approach regrettable,[3320] it does not amount to a failure to provide a reasoned opinion in and of itself.[3321] The Appeals Chamber therefore considers that Župljanin has failed to show an error in the Trial Chamber's approach in its assessment of the subjective element of the third category of joint criminal enterprise. Thus, his arguments on the use of general or broad findings concerning the foreseeability of crimes and the need for individual analysis for each municipality are dismissed.

1000. Insofar as Župljanin argues that the Trial Chamber should not have concluded that JCE III Crimes were natural and foreseeable consequences of the common purpose of the JCE because it excluded violent

---

[3308] Trial Judgement, vol. 1, paras 200-228 (Banja Luka), 260-285 (Donji Vakuf), 331-350 (Ključ), 453-494 (Kotor Varoš), 655-703 (Prijedor and Skender Vakuf), 782-817 (Sanski Most), 867-883 (Teslić').

[3309] Trial Judgement, vol. 1, paras 200-211 (Banja Luka), 260-274 (Donji Vakuf), 331-339 (Ključ), 453-480 (Kotor Varoš), 655-684 (Prijedor and Skender Vakuf), 782-804 (Sanski Most), 867-872 (Teslić).

[3310] See *e.g.* Trial Judgement, vol. 2, paras 415-430, 432-437, 495-499, 506 (Banja Luka), 507 (Sanski Most), 508 (Prijedor), 509 (Ključ and Donji Vakuf), 510-517.

[3311] Trial Judgement, vol. 2, paras 522-527.

[3312] See *supra*, paras 948-954.

[3313] Trial Judgement, vol. 2, para. 522. See Trial Judgement, vol. 2, paras 279-284, 353, 401, 492-493.

[3314] Trial Judgement, vol. 2, para. 525. See Trial Judgement, vol. 2, paras 415-437, 506-511.

[3315] Trial Judgement, vol. 2, paras 522-528.

[3316] Župljanin Appeal Brief, para. 205.

[3317] See *Tolimir* Appeal Judgement, para. 514; *Đorđević* Appeal Judgement, para. 906; *Šainović et al.* Appeal Judgement, paras 1061, 1557; *Brđanin* Appeal Judgement, paras 365, 411.

[3318] Trial Judgement, vol. 2, paras 801-803, 805 (Banja Luka), 828-830, 832 (Donji Vakuf), 841-843, 845 (Ključ), 846-848, 850 (Kotor Varoš), 855-857, 859 (Prijedor and Skender Vakuf), 860-862, 864 (Sanski Most), 865-867, 869 (Teslid).

[3319] Trial Judgement, vol. 2, paras 521-528.

[3320] See *supra*, para. 90.

[3321] See *supra*, para. 138.

crimes and acts of unlawful coercion from the common purpose, he does not substantiate why the Trial Chamber's finding on the common purpose can be understood that way.[3322] To the extent that he means that the Trial Chamber found that the common purpose was not criminal or that the JCE I Crimes through which the common purpose was implemented did not involve coercive acts, the Appeals Chamber has dismissed these arguments elsewhere in this Judgement.[3323] Consequently, the Appeals Chamber finds no merit in Župljanin's assertion.

1001. The Appeals Chamber finds equally unconvincing Župljanin's argument that no reasonable trier of fact could have found that Župljanin's JCE III Crimes were natural and foreseeable consequences of the common purpose since "many factors contributed to the occurrence of crimes".[3324] While he enumerates several factors, he refers to no evidence or findings of the Trial Chamber in support.[3325]

1002. In this respect, the Appeals Chamber notes that in considering whether the crimes were natural and foreseeable consequences of the common purpose to Župljanin, the Trial Chamber rightly took into account the overall context in which crimes occurred.[3326] In particular, the Trial Chamber found that Župljanin's JCE III Crimes occurred in the context of the JCE, the common **[page 417]** purpose of which was to permanently remove the Bosnian Muslims and Bosnian Croats from the territory of the planned Serbian state through the commission of the JCE I Crimes, *i.e.* crimes of deportation, inhumane acts (forcible transfer), and persecutions through forcible transfer and deportation as crimes against humanity.[3327] The Appeals Chamber also notes the Trial Chamber's findings that in implementing the JCE, violent takeovers of the Municipalities occurred together with an ensuing widespread and systematic campaign of terror and violence,[3328] aimed at establishing a Serb state as ethnically "pure" as possible.[3329] In its foreseeability assessment, the Trial Chamber further referred to factors such as: (i) the fact that Serb forces carried out the forcible removal of Bosnian Muslims and Bosnian Croats from the ARK Municipalities by enforcing unbearable living conditions on them following the takeovers of towns and villages;[3330] (ii) the weak position in which non-Serbs found themselves in relation to Serb forces arresting and expelling them;[3331] (iii) the strong ethnic tensions and resentment in the ARK Municipalities;[3332] and (iv) the presence of criminals in units that were dispatched to carry out operations in the ARK Municipalities in close contact with non-Serbs civilians.[3333] His unsupported assertion ignores the Trial Chamber's reasoning and fails to identify an error in the Trial Chamber's consideration of these factors. The Appeals Chamber therefore finds that Župljanin has failed to show that no reasonable trier of fact could have found, while taking into account the overall context in which crimes occurred, that Župljanin's JCE III Crimes were natural and foreseeable consequences of the common purpose to him.

1003. Turning to Župljanin's challenges to specific findings on which the Trial Chamber relied in reaching its conclusion that the crimes of murder and extermination were foreseeable to him,[3334] the Appeals Chamber first recalls that it has elsewhere dismissed Župljanin's argument regarding the enrolment and deployment of seasoned criminals in the Banja Luka CSB SPD.[3335] The Appeals Chamber further notes that the Trial Chamber: (i) found that Župljanin was one of the key actors behind the organisation of the blockade of Banja Luka on 3 April 1992 and the takeover of that town, which he began planning from at least March 1992;[3336]

[3322]   Župljanin Appeal Brief, paras 196, 198. See Trial Judgement, vol. 2, para. 313.
[3323]   See *supra*, paras 69, 919.
[3324]   Župljanin Appeal Brief, para. 197.
[3325]   See *supra*, fn. 3260.
[3326]   See *Đorđević* Appeal Judgement, para. 920.
[3327]   Trial Judgement, vol. 2, para. 521. See Trial Judgement, vol. 2, para. 522.
[3328]   Trial Judgement, vol. 2, paras 310-311.
[3329]   Trial Judgement, vol. 2, para. 311. See Trial Judgement, vol. 2, para. 310. See also Trial Judgement, vol. 2, paras 292, 738.
[3330]   Trial Judgement, vol. 2, para. 522.
[3331]   Trial Judgement, vol. 2, para. 526.
[3332]   Trial Judgement, vol. 2, para. 525. See Trial Judgement, vol. 2, para. 528.
[3333]   Trial Judgement, vol. 2, para. 524. See Trial Judgement, vol. 2, paras 415-440, 456, 518.
[3334]   See *supra*, para. 984.
[3335]   See *supra*, paras 843-845.
[3336]   Trial Judgement, vol. 2, para. 495. The Trial Chamber found that during the 3 April 1992 blockade of Banja Luka, members of the SOS were armed and that, together with the Banja Luka CSB SPD, they carried out attacks against non-Serbs and their property (Trial Judgement, vol. 1, paras 144, 157, 201; Trial Judgement, vol. 2, paras 415, 496).

(ii) noted evidence that SOS members **[page 418]** who were mostly thugs or from local criminal gangs were enrolled in the Banja Luka CSB SPD;[3337] and (iii) found that the crimes and undisciplined behaviour of the Banja Luka CSB SPD were reported to Župljanin.[3338] The Appeals Chamber thus considers that in light of the Trial Chamber's findings, which – contrary to Župljanin's argument[3339] – are sufficiently clear, a reasonable trier of fact could have relied on Župljanin's knowledge of the criminal elements in the Banja Luka CSB SPD and his continued use of them in concluding that it was foreseeable to him that crimes might be committed.

1004. With respect to Župljanin's claim that the Trial Chamber erred in relying on "unspecified 'crimes'" committed against non-Serbs in Banja Luka, the Appeals Chamber notes that the Trial Chamber found that "[i]n the first half of April 1992, and then again in August and September of the same year, representatives of the non-Serb community informed Župljanin about the crimes committed against non-Serbs in Banja Luka."[3340] In assessing the foreseeability of murder and extermination, the Trial Chamber relied on this finding.[3341] While this finding is not accompanied by internal references, a reading of the Trial Judgement as a whole reveals that the Trial Chamber based this finding on the evidence described elsewhere in the Trial Judgement, evincing that: (i) by 15 April 1992 Župljanin made a statement that he could not guarantee the physical security and the safety of property of non-Serb citizens in Banja Luka;[3342] and (ii) representatives of the non-Serb community informed him of, *inter alia*, murders, attacks against property, destruction of mosques, unlawful arrests, and the situation in detention camps in August and September 1992.[3343] This shows that the Trial Chamber indeed considered Župljanin's knowledge of specific crimes committed against non-Serbs in Banja Luka. Župljanin's argument, which misconstrues the Trial Judgement, is thus dismissed.

1005. Regarding Župljanin's argument that the Trial Chamber erred in relying on the Sanski Most Incident even though it accepted the possibility that this may not have been intentional, the Appeals Chamber notes that in support of his argument, he refers to the Trial Chamber's finding that police officers who transported these detainees: (i) "intended to inflict serious bodily harm upon these detainees"; and (ii) "knew or should have known that [the way they were transported] could result in their death".[3344] The Appeals Chamber understands that, in so arguing, he repeats the argument that the Trial Chamber found that the deaths of the victims in the Sanski Most Incident "may have **[page 419]** resulted from mere negligence, rather than intent to kill",[3345] which the Appeals Chamber has dismissed elsewhere.[3346]

1006. Further, insofar as Župljanin argues that while the Trial Chamber found that the Sanski Most police were involved in the Sanski Most Incident on 7 July 1992, it failed to identify any criminal behaviour, specifically murder or extermination, after 7 July 1992 involving the Sanski Most police,[3347] the Appeals Chamber considers that his argument is premised on the misunderstanding that any subsequent acts of murder and extermination must involve the same perpetrators, *i.e.* the Sanski Most police, in order for those subsequent crimes to be foreseeable.[3348] The propensity of the police in general – not only of Sanski Most police – under Župljanin's authority to commit crimes, including murder and extermination, is relevant to the Trial Chamber's determination as to whether the occurrence of such crimes were foreseeable to him in the course of the execution of the common purpose of the JCE. Therefore, the Appeals Chamber discerns no error in the Trial Chamber's reliance on the Sanski Most Incident and Župljanin's knowledge thereof, among other evidence, in assessing the foreseeability of murder and extermination to him.[3349]

[3337]   Trial Judgement, vol. 1, para. 143. See Trial Judgement, vol. 2, para. 388.
[3338]   Trial Judgement, vol. 2, para. 503.
[3339]   Župljanin Appeal Brief, para. 208.
[3340]   Trial Judgement, vol. 2, para. 524.
[3341]   Trial Judgement, vol. 2, para. 524.
[3342]   Trial Judgement, vol. 2, para. 450.
[3343]   Trial Judgement, vol. 2, paras 451-452.
[3344]   Župljanin Appeal Brief, para. 210, referring to Trial Judgement, vol. 1, para. 215.
[3345]   Župljanin Appeal Brief, para. 234, referring to Trial Judgement, vol. 1, para. 215.
[3346]   See *infra*, fn. 3448.
[3347]   Župljanin Appeal Brief, para. 210.
[3348]   *Cf. infra*, paras 1064-1065.
[3349]   Elsewhere in his brief, Župljanin also raises an argument with regard to the question of whether, and if so when, Župljanin was informed of the Sanski Most Incident (see *infra*, paras 1050, 1054). The Appeals Chamber has addressed this argument and found an error in the Trial Chamber's reliance on one exhibit, but has found that "a reasonable trier of fact could have concluded that

1007. Turning to Župljanin's argument on the incident in the Manjača detention camp, the Appeals Chamber notes that he argues that the preliminary report on the incident at the Manjača detention camp on 6 and 7 August 1992 was not finalised until 26 August 1992, *i.e.* after the Korićanske Stijene killings on 21 August 1992.[3350] However, Župljanin does not point to any evidence or findings of the Trial Chamber to support this argument. The Appeals Chamber therefore dismisses his argument as unsubstantiated.[3351]

1008. Furthermore, the Appeals Chamber considers that, even if no crimes were committed after the Korićanske Stijene killings on 21 August 1992,[3352] the Trial Chamber reasonably relied on Župljanin's tasking of the Prijedor police to escort non-Serb detainees to Croatia in September 1992, while knowing of their prior involvement in crimes, to find that he willingly took the risk that murders and extermination of Muslims and Croats might be committed in the execution **[page 420]** of the common plan.[3353] Moreover, in arguing that all the police officers involved in the Korićanske Stijene killings were transferred out of the Prijedor police force after 21 August 1992, he does not refer to any evidence or findings of the Trial Chamber in support, thereby failing to substantiate his argument.[3354] Župljanin's arguments with regard to the Korićanske Stijene killings and his tasking of the Prijedor police to escort non-Serb detainees are thus dismissed.[3355]

1009. The Appeals Chamber is therefore satisfied that Župljanin has failed to demonstrate that no reasonable trier of fact could have concluded that the requisite subjective element of the third category of joint criminal enterprise was met in relation to Župljanin with respect to Župljanin's JCE III Crimes.

c. Conclusion

1010. In light of the foregoing, the Appeals Chamber dismisses sub-ground (B) in part and sub-ground (D) of Župljanin's second ground of appeal.

(v) Conclusion

1011. In light of the foregoing, the Appeals Chamber dismisses Župljanin's second ground of appeal in its entirety.

(b) Alleged errors of law and fact in finding Župljanin responsible for extermination as a crime against humanity (Župljanin's third ground of appeal)

1012. The Trial Chamber found Župljanin responsible for extermination as a crime against humanity (Count 2) with respect to acts committed in the municipalities of Banja Luka,[3356] Ključ,[3357] Kotor Varoš,[3358]

Župljanin was informed of the Sanski Most Incident shortly after it occurred, but in any case not later than 18 August 1992" (see *infra*, paras 1061-1062). Consequently, there is no impact of this error on the Trial Chamber's findings of the foreseeability of Župljanin's JCE III Crimes to Župljanin.

[3350] Župljanin Appeal Brief, para. 211.
[3351] See *supra*, para. 25.
[3352] See Župljanin Appeal Brief, para. 211. See also Župljanin Appeal Brief, para. 212.
[3353] See Trial Judgement, vol. 2, paras 524, 528. See also *infra*, para. 1066.
[3354] Župljanin Appeal Brief, para. 211.
[3355] See Župljanin Appeal Brief, paras 211-212.
[3356] Trial Judgement, vol. 2, para. 805. The Trial Chamber found that the Sanski Most Incident – *i.e.* the incident in which 20 detainees died during their transportation from Betonirka detention camp in Sanski Most to Manjača detention camp in Banja Luka municipality by Sanski Most police officers on 7 July 1992 – amounted to extermination (Trial Judgement, vol. 1, para. 219). See Trial Judgement, vol. 1, paras 189-190, 215, 218.
[3357] Trial Judgement, vol. 2, para. 845. The Trial Chamber found that extermination was established in relation to the combined killing of 76 victims on 1 June 1992 at Velagići and 144 victims on 10 July 1992 at Biljani (Trial Judgement, vol. 1, para. 344). See Trial Judgement, vol. 1, paras 310-321, 336-337, 343-344.
[3358] Trial Judgement, vol. 2, para. 850. The Trial Chamber found that the killing of 26 men on the way to and in front of the Kotor Varoš medical centre on 25 June 1992 amounted to extermination (Trial Judgement, vol. 1, para. 488). See Trial Judgement, vol. 1, paras 436-452, 457-464, 484-485.

Prijedor,[3359] and Skender Vakuf.[3360] The Trial Chamber found that it was **[page 421]** foreseeable to Župljanin that extermination could be committed in the implementation of the JCE and that he willingly took that risk.[3361] It therefore concluded that Župljanin was criminally responsible for extermination as a crime against humanity pursuant to the third category of joint criminal enterprise.[3362]

1013. Župljanin raises three sub-grounds of appeal against his conviction for extermination.[3363] Specifically, he alleges that the Trial Chamber erred in law and fact by finding that: (i) the *actus reus* requirement for extermination was met in relation to the Sanski Most Incident and the killing of approximately 95 victims at Omarska detention camp in Prijedor municipality in July 1992;[3364] (ii) the physical perpetrators had the required *mens rea* for extermination in relation to the Sanski Most Incident;[3365] and (iii) "it was foreseeable to [him] or that he was aware, that the extermination would be committed" in the implementation of the JCE.[3366] Župljanin argues that these errors occasion a miscarriage of justice and invalidate his conviction under Count 2.[3367] The Prosecution responds that Župljanin fails to show that the Trial Chamber erred in convicting him of extermination and requests that this ground of appeal be dismissed.[3368]

    (i) Alleged errors of law and fact in relation to the large scale requirement in the *actus reus* of extermination (sub-ground (A) of Župljanin's third ground of appeal)

1014. With regard to the Sanski Most Incident, the Trial Chamber found that on 7 July 1992, a large number of detainees were transported by Sanski Most SJB police officers from Betonirka **[page 422]** detention camp in Sanski Most to Manjača detention camp.[3369] The Trial Chamber found that about 20 of the detainees died of asphyxia during the transportation and that these deaths constituted murder.[3370] The Trial Chamber further found that, having taken into account the circumstances of the incident, the killing of 20 detainees in the Sanski Most Incident was sufficiently large as to satisfy the requirements of extermination.[3371]

1015. With regard to Omarska detention camp, the Trial Chamber found that "approximately 28 prominent members of the Prijedor Muslim community detained at Omarska, including lawyers, doctors, and police officers, were killed in an organised manner between 25 and 27 July 1992".[3372] It also found that "in an incident in July 1992, 18 persons were executed at night by camp guards based on a list provided by Rade

---

[3359]   Trial Judgement, vol. 2, para. 859. The Trial Chamber found that extermination was established in relation to the killing of: (i) approximately 800 people during the attack on Kozarac between 24 and 26 May 1992 (Trial Judgement, vol. 1, para. 688. See Trial Judgement, vol. 1, paras 529-541, 661, 686); (ii) 74 victims in the villages of Biščani and Čarakovo on 20 and 23 July 1992 (Trial Judgement, vol. 1, para. 690. See Trial Judgement, vol. 1, paras 550-554, 557-560, 664-665, 689); (iii) approximately 68 persons in Briševo on 24 July 1992 (Trial Judgement, vol. 1, para. 690. See Trial Judgement, vol. 1, paras 555, 663, 689. The Appeals Chamber observes that in the factual and legal findings sections, the Trial Chamber referred to the killings in Briševo as having occurred on 27 May 1992, which is the day on which the attack first started (see Trial Judgement, vol. 1, paras 555, 663, 689-690). In light of the Trial Chamber's analysis of the evidence and of the adjudicated facts on which it relied, the Appeals Chamber considers the reference to 27 May 1992 to be a typographical error and understands this to be a reference to 24 July 1992 (see Trial Judgement, vol. 1, paras 555, 663, referring to, Adjudicated Facts Decision, Adjudicated Facts 840, 842)); (iv) a minimum of 15 persons at Ljubija football stadium combined with a further 45 persons at Kipe mine near the stadium on the same day in July 1992 (Trial Judgement, vol. 1, paras 692, 697. See Trial Judgement, vol. 1, paras 572-578, 667, 691); (v) approximately 128 persons in Room 3 at Keraterm detention camp around 24 to 26 July 1992 (Trial Judgement, vol. 1, paras 693, 697. See Trial Judgement, vol. 1, paras 579-590, 668); and (vi) approximately 95 victims at Omarska detention camp in Prijedor municipality in July 1992 (Trial Judgement, vol. 1, paras 695, 697. See Trial Judgement, vol. 1, paras 591-617, 669-672, 694).

[3360]   Trial Judgement, vol. 2, para. 859. The Trial Chamber found that extermination was established in relation to the killing of approximately 150-200 Muslim men at Korićanske Stijene in Skender Vakuf municipality on 21 August 1992 – *i.e.* the Korićanske Stijene killings (Trial Judgement, vol. 1, paras 696-697. See Trial Judgement, vol. 1, paras 637-648, 674).

[3361]   Trial Judgement, vol. 2, paras 524, 805, 845, 850, 859.

[3362]   Trial Judgement, vol. 2, paras 805 (Banja Luka), 845 (Ključ), 850 (Kotor Varoš), 859 (Prijedor and Skender Vakuf), 956.

[3363]   Župljanin Appeal Brief, paras 227-242; Župljanin Reply Brief, paras 74-78.

[3364]   Župljanin Appeal Brief, paras 227-230; Župljanin Reply Brief, paras 74-76.

[3365]   Župljanin Appeal Brief, paras 231-234; Župljanin Reply Brief, para. 77.

[3366]   Župljanin Appeal Brief, para. 235. See Župljanin Appeal Brief, paras 236-242; Župljanin Reply Brief, para. 78.

[3367]   Župljanin Appeal Brief, para. 242.

[3368]   Prosecution Response Brief (Župljanin), para. 180.

[3369]   Trial Judgement, vol. 1, paras 189, 205, 215.

[3370]   Trial Judgement, vol. 1, paras 205, 215.

[3371]   Trial Judgement, vol. 1, para. 219.

[3372]   Trial Judgement, vol. 1, para. 694. See Trial Judgement, vol. 1, paras 669-672.

Knežević, one of the Prijedor SJB inspectors who visited the camp"[3373] and that an additional 50 persons were killed at Omarska detention camp.[3374] The Trial Chamber then found that all these killings were part of the same operation and concluded that the total number of victims, amounting to approximately 95 victims, was sufficiently large scale to satisfy the requirements for extermination.[3375]

a. Submissions of the parties

1016. Župljanin submits that the Trial Chamber "applied an incorrect legal standard for extermination and/ or relied on factual determinations that could have been made by no reasonable trier of fact, and on the basis of a failure to give reasons".[3376] More specifically, he argues that the Trial Chamber found that extermination was established with regard to incidents ranging between 20 and 800 victims, but failed to provide a reasoned opinion for "set[ting] the threshold of large-scale killing at 20 victims".[3377] He contends that the threshold of 20 victims, which is the number of victims who died in the Sanski Most Incident,[3378] appears arbitrary considering that "some events with just slightly fewer victims" were found not to meet the large scale **[page 423]** requirement.[3379] Župljanin alleges that the absence of explanation for setting this threshold is "a failure to give reasons".[3380]

1017. Župljanin further submits that the Trial Chamber erred in failing to offer any explanation for connecting various killings at or from Omarska, considering that they occurred over a period of approximately one month and did not involve "any single 'mass killing' event".[3381]

1018. The Prosecution responds that the "large scale" requirement does not imply a "numerical minimum of victims" but must be assessed on a case-by-case basis, taking into account the circumstances in which the killings occurred.[3382] The Prosecution additionally responds that the Trial Chamber "did not 'set the threshold of large scale killings at 20 victims'", but rather assessed each extermination incident on a case-by-case basis.[3383] With regard to the Sanski Most Incident, the Prosecution argues that the Trial Chamber gave reasons as to what combination of factors it considered as it specifically stated that it had "'taken into account the circumstances of this incident', thereby clearly referring to its previous findings".[3384] Moreover, it submits that Župljanin's argument that "events with just slightly fewer victims" were not categorised as extermination, does not undermine the Trial Chamber's findings as the first three incidents Župljanin refers to involve significantly less victims, and his reliance on the fourth incident, involving the killing of 18 persons, is misleading.[3385]

1019. The Prosecution also argues that an "amalgamated" number of killings can amount to extermination, regardless of whether any of the individual incidents amounts in itself to extermination[3386] and avers that the

---

[3373]   Trial Judgement, vol. 1, para. 671. See Trial Judgement, vol. 1, para. 694.
[3374]   Trial Judgement, vol. 1, para. 695. See Trial Judgement, vol. 1, paras 672, 694.
[3375]   Trial Judgement, vol. 1, para. 695.
[3376]   Župljanin Appeal Brief, para. 227.
[3377]   Župljanin Appeal Brief, para. 228. See Župljanin Appeal Brief, paras 227, 230. See also Župljanin Appeal Brief, fn. 311. Župljanin submits that extermination has "a more destructive connotation meaning the annihilation of a mass of people" and "must be collective in nature rather than directed towards singled out individuals" (Župljanin Appeal Brief, para. 229, referring to, *inter alia*, *Krstić* Trial Judgement, para. 496, *Stakić* Trial Judgement, para. 639).
[3378]   See *supra*, fn. 3356.
[3379]   Župljanin Appeal Brief, para. 230. Župljanin refers to the following incidents in support of his argument: (i) the killing of a number of men in front of Manjača detention camp on 6 August 1992; (ii) the death of a number of men resulting from beatings at Vrbas Promet factory; (iii) the death of a number of men resulting from beatings at the TO warehouse; and (iv) the killing of 18 persons in Omarska detention camp in July 1992 (see Župljanin Appeal Brief, fn. 316). See Župljanin Reply Brief, para. 75.
[3380]   Župljanin Appeal Brief, para. 230.
[3381]   Župljanin Appeal Brief, para. 228. See Župljanin Appeal Brief, para. 227.
[3382]   Prosecution Response Brief (Župljanin), para. 182. The Prosecution refers to factors relevant in the assessment of the large scale requirement but submits that they do not constitute material elements of the crime of extermination (Prosecution Response Brief (Župljanin), para. 184 (and references cited therein)).
[3383]   Prosecution Response Brief (Župljanin), para. 185.
[3384]   Prosecution Response Brief (Župljanin), para. 186, referring to Trial Judgement, vol. 1, para. 219.
[3385]   Prosecution Response Brief (Župljanin), para. 187, referring to Župljanin Appeal Brief, para. 230, fns 313, 316, Trial Judgement, vol. 1, paras 206, 216-217, 266, 278, 871, 876-877. See *supra*, fn. 3379.
[3386]   Prosecution Response Brief (Župljanin), para. 188. See Prosecution Response Brief (Župljanin), paras 189-191. The Prosecution submits that relevant factors to consider in determining whether to amalgamate killings are "whether the killings

Trial Chamber reasonably found and sufficiently justified its findings that the killings at Omarska detention camp collectively constituted extermination.[3387] **[page 424]**

1020. Župljanin replies that his reference to an incident involving 18 victims is not misleading.[3388] He argues that the Trial Chamber's finding that this incident was "'part of the same operation' with two other killings that *collectively* constituted extermination", shows that the Trial Chamber considered the killing of 18 persons, in itself, to be insufficient to constitute extermination.[3389]

      b. Analysis

1021. The Appeals Chamber recalls that the *actus reus* of extermination is "the act of killing on a large scale".[3390] It is this element of "massiveness" that distinguishes the crime of extermination from the crime of murder.[3391] However, the expression "on a large scale" does not suggest a strict numerical approach with a minimum number of victims.[3392] While extermination as a crime against humanity has been found in relation to the killing of thousands, it has also been found in relation to far fewer killings.[3393]

1022. The assessment of "large scale" is made on a case-by-case basis, taking into account the circumstances in which the killings occurred.[3394] The Appeals Chamber has found that relevant factors include but are not limited to: (i) the time and place of the killings;[3395] (ii) the selection of the victims and the manner in which they were targeted;[3396] (iii) the type of victims;[3397] (iv) whether [3398] the killings were aimed at the collective group rather than victims in their individual capacity;[3398] and (v) the population density of the victims' area of origin.[3399] These factors do not constitute elements of the crime of extermination as a crime against humanity, but rather are factors which a **[page 425]** trier of facts may take into account when assessing whether or not the "large scale" element is satisfied.[3400] Moreover, separate killing incidents may be aggregated for the purpose of meeting the "large scale requirement" if the killings are considered to be part of one and the same operation.[3401] Whether killings are part of the same operation must be assessed on a case-by-case basis taking into account the circumstances in which they occurred.[3402] As held by the ICTR Appeals Chamber, collective consideration of distinct events committed in different locations, in different

---

constitute 'one and the same incident' or operation, and whether they present similar features, *i.e.* whether they were committed within a relatively short time period, in the same or connected locations, in similar circumstances or following similar patterns, against similar victim groups by the same perpetrator groups" (Prosecution Response Brief (Župljanin), para. 189, referring to *Bagosora and Nsengiyumva* Appeal Judgement, paras 395-396, *Popović et al.* Trial Judgement, paras 803-806).
[3387] Prosecution Response Brief (Župljanin), paras 187, 190-191.
[3388] Župljanin Reply Brief, para. 76.
[3389] Župljanin Reply Brief, para. 76, referring to Trial Judgement, vol. 1, para. 695.
[3390] *Tolimir* Appeal Judgement, para. 146; *Lukić and Lukić* Appeal Judgement, para. 536, referring to *Stakić* Appeal Judgement, para. 259, *Ntakirutimana and Ntakirutimana* Appeal Judgement, para. 516; *Karemera and Ngirumpatse* Appeal Judgement, para. 660. See Trial Judgement, vol. 1, para. 44.
[3391] *Tolimir* Appeal Judgement, para. 146; *Lukić and Lukić* Appeal Judgement, para. 536; *Stakić* Appeal Judgement, para. 260; *Ntakirutimana and Ntakirutimana* Appeal Judgement, para. 516. See Trial Judgement, vol. 1, para. 44.
[3392] *Lukić and Lukić* Appeal Judgement, para. 537; *Stakić* Appeal Judgement, para. 260; *Ntakirutimana and Ntakirutimana* Appeal Judgement, para. 516.
[3393] *Lukić and Lukić* Appeal Judgement, para. 537. In the *Lukić and Lukić* case, the Appeals Chamber found that the killing of 59 persons was sufficiently large so as to constitute extermination (*Lukić and Lukić* Appeal Judgement, para. 543). In the *Akayesu* case, the ICTR Appeals Chamber upheld the finding that the killing of 16 persons constituted extermination (see *Akayesu* Appeal Judgement, paras 423-424; *Akayesu* Trial Judgement, paras 737-744).
[3394] *Lukić and Lukić* Appeal Judgement, para. 538, referring to *Martić* Trial Judgement, para. 63, *Stakić* Trial Judgement, para. 640, *Brđanin* Trial Judgement, para. 391, *Blagojević and Jokić* Trial Judgement, para. 57; *Krajišnik* Trial Judgement, para. 716, *Nahimana et al.* Trial Judgement, para. 1061. See *Brđanin* Appeal Judgement, para. 472, finding "that the scale of the killings, in *light of the circumstances in which they occurred*, meets the required threshold of massiveness for the purposes of extermination" (emphasis added).
[3395] *Lukić and Lukić* Appeal Judgement, para. 538.
[3396] *Lukić and Lukić* Appeal Judgement, para. 538.
[3397] *Lukić and Lukić* Appeal Judgement, para. 542.
[3398] *Lukić and Lukić* Appeal Judgement, para. 538.
[3399] *Lukić and Lukić* Appeal Judgement, paras 539, 542-543.
[3400] *Lukić and Lukić* Appeal Judgement, para. 542.
[3401] *Tolimir* Appeal Judgement, para. 147; *Karemera and Ngirumpatse* Appeal Judgement, paras 661-662; *Bagosora and Nsengiyumva* Appeal Judgement, para. 396.
[3402] *Cf. Tolimir* Appeal Judgement, para. 149.

circumstances, by different perpetrators, over an extended period of time cannot satisfy the requirement of killing on a large scale.[3403]

1023. Turning to Župljanin's argument that the Trial Chamber erred by failing to provide reasons for setting the threshold at 20 victims with respect to the requirement of massiveness, the Appeals Chamber first observes that the Trial Chamber correctly pointed out in the Trial Judgement that there is no numerical minimum of victims to satisfy the "large scale" requirement, and that this requirement should be assessed on a case-by-case basis.[3404] In accordance with this, in its factual and legal findings, the Trial Chamber assessed the circumstances of each incident to determine whether it met the "large scale" or "massiveness" requirement.[3405] Thus, contrary to Župljanin's argument, the Trial Chamber did not set any numerical threshold for the large scale requirement for extermination.

1024. Insofar as Župljanin argues that the Trial Chamber erred by failing to give reasons for finding that extermination was established in relation to the Sanski Most Incident while incidents with "just slightly fewer victims [were not] categorized as extermination",[3406] the Appeals Chamber notes that, when determining whether the Sanski Most Incident amounted to extermination, the Trial Chamber concluded, "*having taken into account the circumstances of this incident*", that the killing of 20 detainees in this incident was sufficiently large as to satisfy the requirements of **[page 426]** extermination.[3407] While the Trial Chamber did not explicitly mention the circumstances it took into account in reaching this finding,[3408] the Appeals Chamber considers that it is apparent from the Trial Chamber's factual findings made several paragraphs earlier, what these circumstances are.[3409] Specifically, the Appeals Chamber observes that the Trial Chamber found that the victims were killed the same day, at the same location, and in the same manner, namely by being transported inhumanely – "packed like sardines" in locked refrigerator trucks without sufficient air flow – and that the victims were detainees, some of whom were already weak and infirm.[3410] The Trial Chamber also found that at the relevant time only Muslims and Croats were detained in Betonirka detention camp and thus concluded that the victims were targeted collectively on the basis of their ethnicity rather than in their individual capacity.[3411] The Appeals Chamber recalls that these are factors that the Trial Chamber was entitled to take into account when assessing the large scale requirement.[3412] In light of the foregoing, the Appeals Chamber is satisfied that the Trial Chamber sufficiently explained the basis on which it found that the large scale requirement for the Sanski Most Incident was met. Further and in light of the above, the Appeals Chamber is satisfied that the Trial Chamber's conclusion was one that a reasonable trier of fact could have made.

1025. With respect to Župljanin's argument that the threshold of 20 victims appears arbitrary, considering that "some events with just slightly fewer victims" were found not to meet the large scale requirement,[3413] the Appeals Chamber notes that three of these incidents concern significantly fewer victims than the Sanski Most Incident and that Župljanin ignores the specific circumstances in which these killings occurred.[3414]

[3403]   *Karemera and Ngirumpatse* Appeal Judgement, para. 661; *Bagosora and Nsengiyumva* Appeal Judgement, para. 396.

[3404]   Trial Judgement, vol. 1, para. 44. See *supra*, para. 1021-1022. Insofar as Župljanin alleges that extermination has "a more destructive connotation meaning the annihilation of a mass of people" (Župljanin Appeal Brief, para. 229), the Appeals Chamber notes that this phrase has only been used in the *Krstić* Trial Judgement (see *Krstić* Trial Judgement, para. 496). As such, the Appeals Chamber is not bound by it (see *e.g Lukić and Lukić* Appeal Judgement, para. 260, fn. 195; *Aleksovski* Appeal Judgement, para. 114). Moreover, the Appeals Chamber understands that the statement of the *Krstić* Trial Chamber was merely intended to describe the *actus reus* of extermination, *i.e.* killing on a large scale, using different words and thus does not introduce a different legal standard. This interpretation is consistent with the *Krstić* Trial Chamber's own finding that extermination can be established in relation to a limited number of victims (see *Krstić* Trial Judgement, para. 501). Župljanin's argument is therefore dismissed.

[3405]   See Trial Judgement, vol. 1, paras 205, 215, 219, 336-337, 343-344, 484-485, 488, 661-665, 667-672, 674, 688-697. See also Trial Judgement, vol. 1, paras 189-190, 310-321, 436-452, 457-466, 529-561, 572-617, 637-648.

[3406]   Župljanin Appeal Brief, para. 230.

[3407]   Trial Judgement, vol. 1, para. 219 (emphasis added).

[3408]   See Trial Judgement, vol. 1, para. 219.

[3409]   See Trial Judgement, vol. 1, paras 205, 215.

[3410]   Trial Judgement, vol. 1, paras 205, 215. See *supra*, para. 1022.

[3411]   Trial Judgement, vol. 1, para. 205.

[3412]   See *supra*, para. 1022.

[3413]   See *supra*, para. 1016.

[3414]   See Trial Judgement, vol. 1, paras 216-217, 219 (eight victims at Manjača detention camp), 266, 278-279 (two victims at the Vrbas Promet factory; one victim at the TO warehouse in Donji Vakuf), 871, 876-877 (three men at the TO warehouse in Teslić). See

With respect to the fourth incident, *i.e.* the killing of 18 persons in Omarska detention camp in July 1992, the Appeals Chamber notes that the Trial Chamber found that this incident, considered together with other incidents, amounted to extermination.[3415] As set out above, killing incidents may be aggregated if they are considered to be part of one and the same operation,[3416] which the Trial Chamber found was the case for the killings at Omarska detention camp.[3417] The Appeals Chamber finds Župljanin's argument that the Trial Chamber aggregated these killings because it was not convinced that the individual incidents at Omarska detention camp **[page 427]** satisfied the large scale requirement, speculative and unconvincing. Župljanin's argument is therefore dismissed.

1026. Based on the foregoing, the Appeals Chamber finds that Župljanin has failed to show that the Trial Chamber erred in law or fact in finding that the Sanski Most Incident amounted to extermination.

1027. The Appeals Chamber now moves to Župljanin's submission that the Trial Chamber erred in law by failing to explain why it connected various killings at or from Omarska detention camp, considering that these killings occurred over a period "spanning from late June to the end of July 1992" and did not include "any single 'mass killing' event".[3418] It notes that the Trial Chamber did not consider the time frame during which the killings occurred in finding that they formed part of the same operation.[3419] However, the Appeals Chamber considers that while a trial chamber may take into consideration the time frame when assessing whether killings are part of the same operation,[3420] the jurisprudence does not establish specific time limits as a requirement for extermination.[3421] Rather, as set out above, it is the collective consideration of factors, including the time frame, which should be taken into account in determining whether the killings formed part of the same operation and thus whether they may be aggregated.[3422] In the present case, the Trial Chamber found that the killings at Omarska detention camp were part of the same operation on the basis that they all were committed in an organised manner, by the same perpetrators, and at the same location.[3423] The Appeals Chamber therefore finds no merit in Župljanin's submission that the Trial Chamber failed to set out the reasons for aggregating the killings at Omarska detention camp.

1028. Further, the Appeals Chamber notes that Župljanin offers no support for his statement that killings may only be aggregated when at least one of the incidents in itself is considered large scale,[3424] and it finds no support for this proposition in the Tribunal's case law.[3425] Župljanin has thus failed to show an error in this respect. **[page 428]**

1029. In light of the foregoing, the Appeals Chamber finds that Župljanin has failed to show that the Trial Chamber erred in law or fact by finding that the killings at Omarska detention camp satisfied the large scale requirement and collectively amounted to extermination.

Župljanin Appeal Brief, fn. 316. The Appeals Chamber notes that it is unclear whether Župljanin's submissions relate to the murders at the TO warehouse in Donji Vakuf or at the TO warehouse in Teslić.

[3415]   See Trial Judgement, vol. 1, paras 694-695.

[3416]   See *supra*, para. 1022. The Appeals Chamber notes that the question of whether the Trial Chamber erred by aggregating these killings will be addressed below (see *infra*, paras 1021-1029).

[3417]   Trial Judgement, vol. 1, para. 695.

[3418]   See Župljanin Appeal Brief, para. 228.

[3419]   See Trial Judgement, vol. 1, para. 695. See Župljanin Appeal Brief, paras 227-228.

[3420]   See *supra*, para. 1022.

[3421]   See *Tolimir* Appeal Judgement, para. 147, stating that "[i]t is not required that that the killings be on a vast scale in a concentrated location over a short period of time." See also *Karemera and Ngirumpatse* Appeal Judgement, para. 661; *Bagosora and Nsengiyumva* Appeal Judgement, para. 396.

[3422]   *Tolimir* Appeal Judgement, para. 147; *Karemera and Ngirumpatse* Appeal Judgement, para. 661; *Bagosora and Nsengiyumva* Appeal Judgement, para. 396. See *supra*, para. 1022.

[3423]   See Trial Judgement, vol. 1, para. 695.

[3424]   See Župljanin Appeal Brief, para. 228.

[3425]   The Appeals Chamber notes that in the *Brđanin* case, the Trial Chamber found killings occurring in separate incidents between 22 April 1992 and 18 December 1992 to collectively amount to extermination (10 victims at Manjača detention camp, 94 victims at Omarska detention camp, 20 victims at Trnopolje detention camp, 20 victims in the Sanski Most Incident, 4 victims in front of Manjača Camp, 190 victims at Room 3 Keraterm detention camp, 200 victims at Korićanske Stijene, 11 victims at Petar Kočić elementary school, 144 victims at Biljani, 45 victims at Teslić TO). It however did not convict Brđanin for extermination, and this finding was not challenged on appeal (see *Brđanin* Trial Judgement, paras 436-465, 467, 478-479).

401

c. Conclusion

1030. The Appeals Chamber finds that Župljanin has failed to show that the Trial Chamber erred in its findings on the large scale requirement for the *actus reus* of extermination as a crime against humanity. Therefore, the Appeals Chamber dismisses sub-ground (A) of Župljanin's third ground of appeal.

(ii) Alleged errors of law and fact in relation to the *mens rea* of extermination (sub-ground (B) of Župljanin's third ground of appeal)

1031. With regard to the Sanski Most Incident, the Trial Chamber found that police officers from the Sanski Most SJB who, on 7 July 1992, transported a large number of detainees from Betonirka detention camp to Manjača detention camp: (i) intended to inflict serious bodily harm upon the detainees; and (ii) knew or should have known that the way they were transported could result in their deaths.[3426] The Trial Chamber concluded that these deaths constituted murder.[3427] The Trial Chamber further found that the number of killings satisfied the large scale requirement of extermination.[3428] After recalling that the general requirements of Article 5 of the Statute had been satisfied, the Trial Chamber concluded that the perpetrators committed extermination as a crime against humanity.[3429]

a. Submissions of the parties

1032. Župljanin argues that the Prosecution has failed to prove beyond reasonable doubt that the principal perpetrators possessed the required *mens rea* for extermination.[3430] In particular, Župljanin submits that when concluding on the *mens rea* for extermination of the principal perpetrators of the Sanski Most Incident, the Trial Chamber found that the deaths of the victims "may have resulted **[page 429]** from mere negligence, rather than intent to kill".[3431] He avers that the Trial Chamber therefore erred in law in finding that the principal perpetrators of this incident possessed the required intent since the *mens rea* standard for extermination is not satisfied by "[recklessness or gross negligence".[3432]

1033. Župljanin further contends that the evidence of Witness ST161 – that the Sanski Most police heading the column of trucks and buses filled with detainees were not aware of the transport conditions[3433] – when considered in conjunction with Exhibits P486 and P487, shows that the Sanski Most police acted, at most, with negligence and as such did not possess the required intent for extermination.[3434] Therefore, he argues that the Sanski Most Incident cannot be characterised as extermination, or "imputed as such to the JCE even if it was foreseeable".[3435]

1034. The Prosecution responds that the Trial Chamber recalled the correct law on *mens rea* for extermination as requiring either "direct or indirect intent"[3436] and correctly found that the Sanski Most Incident could be

---

[3426]   Trial Judgement, vol. 1, para. 215. See Trial Judgement, vol. 1, para. 189.
[3427]   Trial Judgement, vol. 1, para. 215.
[3428]   Trial Judgement, vol. 1, para. 219.
[3429]   Trial Judgement, vol. 1, para. 219.
[3430]   Župljanin Appeal Brief, para. 231, referring to Trial Judgement, vol. 1, paras 200-228 (Banja Luka), 331-350, (Ključ) 453-494 (Kotor Varoš), 655-703 (Prijedor and Skender Vakuf); Trial Judgement, vol. 2, paras 801-803, 805, 841-843, 845-848, 850, 855-857, 859. See Appeal Hearing, 16 Dec 2015, AT. 176.
[3431]   Župljanin Appeal Brief, para. 234, referring to Trial Judgement, vol. 1, para. 215. See Appeal Hearing, 16 Dec 2015, AT. 173, 177. See also Župljanin Reply Brief, para. 77.
[3432]   Župljanin Appeal Brief, para. 233 and references cited therein; Appeal Hearing, 16 Dec 2015, AT. 176. Župljanin also contends that the *mens rea* standard of extermination cannot be "lower than that required for committing murder – *i.e.*, *dolus directus*" (Župljanin Appeal Brief, para. 233).
[3433]   Appeal Hearing, 16 Dec 2015, AT. 174-175 (private session), 176.
[3434]   Appeal Hearing, 16 Dec 2015, AT. 175-176 (private session), referring to Exhibits P486 (confidential) (a daily report from the operative team of the Manjača detention camp to the 1st Krajina Corps ("1st KK") Command, dated 8 July 1992 ("Daily Report of 8 July 1992")), P487 (confidential) (a daily report from the operative team of the Manjača detention camp to the 1st KK Command, dated 9 July 1992) ("Daily Report of 9 July 1992", collectively, "Daily Reports of 8 and 9 July 1992").
[3435]   Župljanin Appeal Brief, para. 234; Appeal Hearing, 16 Dec 2015, AT. 177. Župljanin argues specifically in relation to Exhibit P486 (confidential) that it criticises the "Sanski Most organs" and not the Sanski Most police (Appeal Hearing, 16 Dec 2015, AT. 176). Furthermore, he argues that both Exhibits P486 (confidential) and P487 (confidential) were sent to the 1st KK and not to the Sanski Most police or Banja Luka police or to Župljanin (Appeal Hearing, 16 Dec 2015, AT. 176).
[3436]   Prosecution Response Brief (Župljanin), para. 193; Appeal Hearing, 16 Dec 2015, AT 202.

established based on indirect intent.[3437] It further contends that, contrary to Župljanin's assertion, the Trial Chamber did not find that the deaths in this incident resulted from "mere negligence", but rather that Sanski Most police officers "'intended to inflict serious bodily harm' on the 20 non-Serb detainees and 'knew or should have known that this way of transporting the detainees could result in their death [and] accepted that risk'".[3438] The Prosecution argues that, therefore, the Trial Chamber applied the correct legal standard for murder.[3439]

1035. The Prosecution further responds that Župljanin fails to show that no reasonable trial chamber could have found that Sanski Most police officers "had the required (indirect) intent for murder" as the actions of the police officers show that they clearly intended to inflict serious bodily **[page 430]** harm on the victims, knowing that this could result in their deaths or had the intention to subject a large number of people to living conditions that would lead to their death.[3440] Moreover, the Prosecution argues that "any alleged oversight by the Chamber has no impact upon its conclusion that the Sanski Most police officers had the required intent for extermination, as it is the only reasonable conclusion on the evidence".[3441]

b. Analysis

1036. The Appeals Chamber recalls that the *mens rea* for extermination has been defined as the intention of the perpetrator to: (i) kill on a large scale; or (ii) systematically subject a large number of people to conditions of living that would lead to their deaths.[3442] In this regard, the Appeals Chamber recalls that it has consistently held that the elements of the crime of extermination are the same as those required for murder as a crime against humanity, with the difference that extermination is killing on a large scale.[3443] As such, the Appeals Chamber considers that the *mens rea* for extermination to "(i) kill on a large scale" can be met by establishing the *mens rea* for murder as a crime against humanity – *i.e.* the intent to: (i) kill the victim; or (ii) wilfully cause serious bodily harm which the perpetrator should reasonably have known might lead to death[3444] – plus the additional intention to do so on a large scale.[3445]

1037. Turning now to the Sanski Most Incident,[3446] the Appeals Chamber notes that the Trial Chamber first found that the Sanski Most police officers possessed the *mens rea* for murder by finding that they intended to inflict serious bodily harm upon the detainees who died in the Sanski Most Incident by transporting them "packed like sardines", and that the police officers knew or should have known that transporting detainees in such a manner could result in their death.[3447] The **[page 431]** Trial Chamber thus applied the correct *mens*

[3437]   Prosecution Response Brief (Župljanin), para. 195. The Prosecution contends that Župljanin incorrectly claims that extermination can only be constituted if the physical perpetrators have direct intent (*dolus directus*) (Prosecution Response Brief (Župljanin), para. 193. See Prosecution Response Brief (Župljanin), para. 195).

[3438]   Prosecution Response Brief (Župljanin), para. 195, referring to Trial Judgement, vol. 1, para. 215.

[3439]   Prosecution Response Brief (Župljanin), para. 195.

[3440]   Prosecution Response Brief (Župljanin), paras 196-197, referring to Trial Judgement, vol. 1, paras 189, 205, 215, 219. The Prosecution submits that "[t]hese considerations are implicit in the Chamber's findings" (Prosecution Response Brief (Župljanin), para. 197). See Appeal Hearing, 16 Dec 2015, AT. 201-202. The Prosecution further avers that the evidence cited by Župljanin during the Appeal Hearing does not show an error in the Trial Chamber's findings that the police played a central role in the event (Appeal Hearing, 16 Dec 2015, AT. 202-203).

[3441]   Prosecution Response Brief (Župljanin), para. 197 and references cited therein; Appeal Hearing, 16 Dec 2015, AT. 201-202. The Prosecution also argues that even if the Appeals Chamber comes to the conclusion that the Trial Chamber applied the wrong *mens rea* standard, this has no impact since the only reasonable conclusion is that the perpetrators had the required intent for extermination (Appeal Hearing, 16 Dec 2015, AT. 202).

[3442]   *Lukić and Lukić* Appeal Judgement, para. 536; *Stakić* Appeal Judgement, paras 259-260. See Trial Judgement, vol. 1, para. 45.

[3443]   *Lukić and Lukić* Appeal Judgement, para. 536; *Stakić* Appeal Judgement, para. 260. See *Popović et al.* Appeal Judgement, para. 701.

[3444]   *Kvočka et al.* Appeal Judgement, para. 261.

[3445]   In this regard, the Appeals Chamber also recalls that "[t]he principle of individual guilt requires that an accused can only be convicted for a crime if his *mens rea* comprises the *actus reus* of the crime" (*Boškoski and Tarčulovski* Appeal Judgement, para. 66, quoting *Naletilić and Martinović* Appeal Judgement, para. 114). Thus, for a conviction of extermination, not only the *actus reus* but also the *mens rea* must encompass the large scale element.

[3446]   Župljanin Appeal Brief, para. 234, referring to Trial Judgement, vol. 1, para. 215; Župljanin Reply Brief, para. 77.

[3447]   Trial Judgement, vol. 1, para. 215.

rea standard for murder.[3448] The Appeals Chamber further notes that, in assessing whether the incident amounted to extermination, in a subsequent paragraph, the Trial Chamber found that the number of victims was sufficiently large "so as to satisfy the requirements for extermination".[3449] It concluded that, therefore, "through their acts, the perpetrators committed extermination, as a crime against humanity".[3450]

1038. The Appeals Chamber considers that it is clear from the Trial Chamber's finding that it was satisfied that in the circumstances of this case, the number of 20 victims in the Sanski Most Incident is sufficiently large to meet the requirement of "large scale killing" for the *actus reus* of extermination. However, the Appeals Chamber finds that there is no such clear finding with respect to the *mens rea* of extermination, *i.e.* it is unclear whether the Trial Chamber was satisfied that the Sanski Most police officers wilfully caused serious bodily harm which they should reasonably have known might lead to the death of *a large number of detainees*. The Appeals Chamber recalls in this regard that a trial chamber is required to provide clear, reasoned findings of fact as to each element of the crime charged.[3451] In the absence of a clear finding on whether the principal perpetrators possessed the *mens rea* of extermination, which was a requirement in this case, the Appeals Chamber considers *proprio motu* that the Trial Chamber failed to provide a reasoned opinion, an error of law, which allows the Appeals Chamber to consider relevant evidence and factual findings in order to determine whether a reasonable trier of fact could have found beyond reasonable doubt that the requisite *mens rea* for extermination in relation to the Sanski Most Incident was established.[3452]

1039. In this regard, the Appeals Chamber notes that the Trial Chamber found that Serb civilian police from the Prijedor, Sanski Most, Ključ, and other ARK municipalities transported thousands of detainees to Manjača detention camp starting from mid-May 1992 to November or December 1992.[3453] The detention camp itself was under the authority of the 1st KK and detainees in the camp were guarded by the 1st KK military police.[3454] The Trial Chamber also found that in June 1992, only Muslims and Croats were detained in Betonirka detention camp in Sanski Most.[3455] It further considered that on 7 July 1992, police officers from the Sanski Most SJB transported **[page 432]** about 560 prisoners from Sanski Most to Manjača, approximately 64 of whom were Muslims and Croats from Betonirka detention camp.[3456] The Trial Chamber found that the detainees from Betonirka detention camp were transported under harsh conditions, namely "packed like sardines" in locked refrigerator trucks with insufficient airflow in the summer, while some of the detainees were already weak or infirm, and that during the transportation, about 20 of them died as a result of asphyxia.[3457] It was further satisfied that by transporting the detainees in the manner they did, the Sanski Most police officers intended to inflict serious bodily harm upon the detainees while they knew or should have known that transporting detainees in such a manner could result in their deaths and as such possessed the required intent for murder.[3458]

1040. Insofar as Župljanin argues that no reasonable trier of fact could have reached this latter finding in light of Witness ST161's evidence that the Sanski Most police officers were not aware of the transport conditions, and the Daily Reports of 8 and 9 July 1992,[3459] the Appeals Chamber notes that in reaching its finding, the Trial Chamber relied on the evidence of Witness SZ007 that police officers were present when the detainees were loaded onto trucks and escorted them to Manjača detention camp.[3460] In addition, the

---

[3448] See *supra*, para. 1036. Accordingly, the Appeals Chamber considers that Župljanin's argument that the Trial Chamber found that the deaths of the victims "may have resulted from mere negligence" clearly misrepresents the Trial Judgement (see Župljanin Appeal Brief, para. 234). Thus, his argument in this respect is dismissed.

[3449] Trial Judgement, vol. 1, para. 219.

[3450] Trial Judgement, vol. 1, para. 219.

[3451] *Cf. Kordić and Čerkez* Appeal Judgement, para. 383; *Ndindiliyimana et al.* Appeal Judgement, para. 293; *Renzaho* Appeal Judgement, para. 320. See *Orić* Appeal Judgement, para. 56.

[3452] *Cf. Kordić and Čerkez* Appeal Judgement, paras 383-388; *Ndindiliyimana et al.* Appeal Judgement, para. 977; *Bizimungu* Appeal Judgement, para. 23; *Ndindiliyimana et al.* Appeal Judgement, para. 293. See *supra*, paras 19, 142.

[3453] Trial Judgement, vol. 1, para. 202.

[3454] Trial Judgement, vol. 1, para. 202.

[3455] Trial Judgement, vol. 1, paras 189, 205.

[3456] Trial Judgement, vol. 1, paras 189, 205.

[3457] Trial Judgement, vol. 1, para. 215. See Trial Judgement, vol. 1, paras 189, 205.

[3458] Trial Judgement, vol. 1, para. 215.

[3459] See *supra*, para. 1033.

[3460] Trial Judgement, vol. 1, para. 189, referring to, *inter alia*, SZ007, 7 Dec 2011, T. 26280-26284, 26287 (closed session).

Trial Chamber relied on Witness ST172's evidence that he personally witnessed that the detainees were brought in by the Sanski Most police.[3461]

1041. The Appeals Chamber recalls that a trial chamber has broad discretion in its assessment of the evidence,[3462] and has the main responsibility for resolving inconsistencies which may arise within or among witnesses' testimony.[3463] It further recalls that the Appeals Chamber will only disturb a trial chamber's finding of fact when it considers that no reasonable trier of fact could have concluded as the trial chamber did.[3464] The Appeals Chamber considers that while Župljanin disagrees with the Trial Chamber's assessment of the evidence, he has failed to show that it was an abuse of the Trial Chamber's discretion to prefer the direct evidence of Witness SZ007 and Witness ST172 over that of Witness ST161. **[page 433]**

1042. The Appeals Chamber is further of the view that the fact that the operative team of the Manjača detention camp sent daily reports to the 1st KK, which had the authority over the camp,[3465] is incapable of undermining the Trial Chamber's finding that the Sanski Most police office, who carried out the transportation, had the required intent for murder. In addition, the Appeals Chamber considers it irrelevant that the Daily Report of 8 July 1992 does not specifically mention the Sanski Most police, and only refers to "extremely inhumane and unprofessional" behaviour on the part of the Sanski Most organs in relation to the Sanski Most Incident.[3466]

1043. In light of the foregoing the Appeals Chamber finds that Župljanin has failed to show that no reasonable trier of fact could have found that the Sanski Most police officers had the required intent for murder.

1044. Moreover, the Appeals Chamber is of the view that in light of this and the Trial Chamber's findings on the general circumstances of this incident – *i.e.* that all the approximately 64 detainees from Betornika detention camp, some of whom were weak or infirm, were transported together in one and the same truck, "packed like sardines" with insufficient airflow in the summer – as well as the modality of the Sanski Most police officers' involvement,[3467] a reasonable trier of fact could have found that the only reasonable inference is that the Sanski Most police officers wilfully caused serious bodily harm to a large number of detainees which they reasonably should have known could lead to the death of detainees, on a large scale. Therefore, the Appeals Chamber finds that a reasonable trier of fact could have concluded beyond reasonable doubt that the perpetrators of the Sanski Most Incident acted with the required *mens rea* for extermination.

c. Conclusion

1045. The Appeals Chamber finds that the Trial Chamber erred in law by failing to make the requisite *mens rea* findings for extermination with respect to the principal perpetrators of the Sanski Most Incident. Having reviewed the Trial Chamber's findings and evidence on record, the Appeals Chamber finds, however, that a reasonable trier of fact could have found beyond reasonable doubt that the principal perpetrators of the Sanski Most Incident had the requisite *mens rea* for extermination. Therefore, the Appeals Chamber finds that the Trial Chamber's error does not invalidate the Trial Judgement. On the basis of the foregoing, and in light of the fact that Župljanin has failed to show any other error in the Trial Chamber findings on the *mens rea* for extermination, the Appeals Chamber dismisses sub-ground (B) of Župljanin's third ground of appeal. **[page 434]**

[3461] Trial Judgement, vol. 1, para. 189, referring to, *inter alia*, ST172, 21 Jan 2010, T 5293-5294.
[3462] *Tolimir* Appeal Judgement, para. 76; *Popović et al.* Appeal Judgement, paras 74, 131; *Đorđević* Appeal Judgement, para. 856; *Boškoski and Tarčulovski* Appeal Judgement, para. 14.
[3463] *Đorđević* Appeal Judgement, para. 422; *Munyakazi* Appeal Judgement, para. 71.
[3464] *Tolimir* Appeal Judgement, para. 12; *Popović et al.* Appeal Judgement, paras 20, 1154; *Đorđević* Appeal Judgement, para. 856.
[3465] Trial Judgement, vol. 1, para. 202.
[3466] Exhibit P486 (confidential), p. 1.
[3467] Trial Judgement, vol. 1, para. 215. See Trial Judgement, vol. 1, paras 189, 205.

(iii) Alleged errors of law and fact in finding that extermination was foreseeable to Župljanin (sub-ground (C) of Župljanin's third ground of appeal)

1046. In setting out the subjective element of the third category of joint criminal enterprise, the Trial Chamber stated, *inter alia*, that an accused can be held responsible for a crime falling outside of the common purpose if: (i) it was foreseeable to the accused that such a crime might be committed; and (ii) the accused willingly took that risk.[3468]

1047. In assessing whether the subjective element of the third category of joint criminal enterprise liability was met in relation to Župljanin with respect to extermination, the Trial Chamber found that:

> the possibility that in the execution of the plan Serb Forces, including forces under Župljanin's control, could commit other serious crimes was sufficiently substantial as to be foreseeable to Župljanin. First, Župljanin enrolled in the Detachment seasoned criminals of the SOS who had distinguished themselves for their nationalistic stance and the commission of crimes against non-Serbs, of which he was aware. He dispatched platoons of the Detachment to carry out operations in close contact with non-Serb civilians, notwithstanding frequent reports on the lack of discipline and criminal activities carried out by this special unit. Second, Župljanin was in Banja Luka after the 3 April 1992 blockade of the town, when the non-Serb community began being targeted by the SOS, the group of people in the red van, and the Detachment. In the first half of April 1992, and then again in August and September of the same year, representatives of the non-Serb community informed Župljanin about the crimes committed against non-Serbs in Banja Luka. Exhibit P1002 shows that, already on 30 April 1992, Župljanin knew that members of the ARK police were committing crimes. With regard to police involvement in the arrest and transport of non-Serb prisoners, he knew that on 7 July 1992 20 non-Serb detainees had died in a truck while being transported by the Sanski Most police. Nevertheless, Župljanin left the Sanski Most police in charge of the transport of detainees. Although Župljanin had strong reasons to know that the Prijedor police were involved in the murder of eight non-Serbs at the Manjača camp between 6 and 7 August 1992, he not only misled the investigation into these murders, but also allowed the Prijedor police to continue escorting detainees between detention camps. On 21 August 1992 Prijedor policemen killed about 150 Muslims at Korićanske Stijene. Furthermore, notwithstanding these murders and Župljanin's knowledge of the Prijedor police's involvement, in September 1992 Župljanin tasked the Prijedor police with escorting buses of non-Serb detainees to Croatia. On this basis, the Trial Chamber finds that the possibility that Serb Forces could commit murders and extermination of Muslims and Croats in the execution of the common plan was sufficiently substantial as to be foreseeable to Župljanin and that he willingly took that risk.[3469]

a. Submissions of the parties

1048. Župljanin asserts that the Trial Chamber erred in law and fact by finding that it was foreseeable to him that extermination "would be committed" in the ARK Municipalities.[3470] Župljanin argues that it is required that participants in the plan "would know from the outset that the execution of [the] plan might foreseeably involve the commission of crimes by other members of **[page 435]** the JCE".[3471] He argues that the Trial Chamber therefore erred when it failed to provide a specific date on when he became aware of "the foreseeability of extermination" or "when he undertook the risk of extermination".[3472]

1049. Župljanin also submits that no reasonable trier of fact would have concluded that extermination was foreseeable to him as other inferences were available on the evidence.[3473] Specifically, he contends that the

---

[3468] See Trial Judgement, vol. 1, para. 106, referring to, *inter alia*, *Brđanin* Appeal Judgement, paras 365, 411, *Stakić* Appeal Judgement, paras 65, 87, *Kvočka et al.* Appeal Judgement, para. 83, *Blaškić* Appeal Judgement, para. 33, *Vasiljević* Appeal Judgement, para. 101, *Ntakirutimana and Ntakirutimana* Appeal Judgement, para. 467.

[3469] Trial Judgement, vol. 2, para. 524.

[3470] Župljanin Appeal Brief, para. 235. Župljanin submits that regardless of the exact characterisation of the error, either as an error of law and/or error of fact, it occasions a miscarriage of justice and invalidates his convictions under Count 2 (see Župljanin Appeal Brief, para. 242).

[3471] Župljanin Appeal Brief, para. 236.

[3472] Župljanin Appeal Brief, para. 241. See Župljanin Reply Brief, para. 78.

[3473] Župljanin Appeal Brief, paras 235-240, referring to Trial Judgement, vol. 2, para. 524. See Appeal Hearing, 16 Dec 2015, AT. 173.

police criminal activities referred to in his dispatch of 30 April 1992 ("30 April 1992 Dispatch") "cannot be characterized as a proper sign [...] that the ARK police would commit extermination against non-Serbs".[3474]

1050. Župljanin further argues that he was not in charge of designating policemen to transport the detainees and there is no evidence that he knew of the conditions in which detainees were being transported.[3475] He raises several arguments in this regard. First, in relation to the Sanski Most Incident, he argues that: (i) he could only have had possible knowledge of it from "a semi-annual report that most likely did not reach him until sometime in January 1993";[3476] and (ii) the complaint sent to the SNB of the Banja Luka CSB on 18 August 1992 is vague, and there is no evidence it ever reached him in person.[3477] Second, concerning the Korićanske Stijene killings, Župljanin submits that his conduct towards the murder investigations as well as the information he had and the steps he took show that the Trial Chamber's conclusion "was not the only reasonable inference a trier of fact could have made".[3478] Third, Župljanin contends that it is "entirely erroneous" to infer his *mens rea* from the dispatch of September 1992, tasking the Prijedor police with escorting buses of non-Serb detainees to Croatia ("September 1992 Dispatch"), since: (i) the decision came as a result of an agreement between the RS Government and the ICRC;[3479] (ii) he did not sign the September 1992 Dispatch in person;[3480] and (iii) there is no evidence that any incidents occurred **[page 436]** during this escort or that those involved in the Korićanske Stijene killings were assigned to this escort.[3481]

1051. The Prosecution responds that Župljanin fails to show that the Trial Chamber erred in finding that it was foreseeable to him that extermination might be committed.[3482] It argues that Župljanin's "unsupported assertion" does not show that it is required that extermination was foreseeable to him "from the outset".[3483] According to the Prosecution, the Trial Chamber found that extermination was foreseeable to Župljanin prior to its commission, which is sufficient.[3484]

1052. The Prosecution further responds that none of Župljanin's challenges to the evidence or factual findings show that the Trial Chamber's finding on his *mens rea* for extermination was unreasonable.[3485] It argues that Župljanin ignores the Trial Chamber's findings on his extensive knowledge of the widespread commission of serious crimes across the ARK Municipalities by police officers and other Serb forces, including murder, and of the context of their commission.[3486] According to the Prosecution, the Trial Chamber reasonably considered that Župljanin's specific knowledge that his subordinates were murdering non-Serbs and his continued tasking of the Banja Luka CSB SPD in operations in close contact with the vulnerable population were strong indicators that extermination was foreseeable to him.[3487]

1053. More specifically, the Prosecution argues that: (i) Župljanin fails to show that the Trial Chamber incorrectly relied on the 30 April 1992 Dispatch "in addition to many other pieces of evidence showing his

---

[3474]   Župljanin Appeal Brief, para. 238, referring to Exhibit P1002. Župljanin submits that the "one serious crime" mentioned in the 30 April 1992 Dispatch – the murder of a Serb – was committed by two members of the Banja Luka police, and that their services were ultimately terminated (Župljanin Appeal Brief, para. 238, referring to Radomir Rodić, 16 Apr 2010, T. 8814).

[3475]   Župljanin Appeal Brief, para. 239; Appeal Hearing, 16 Dec 2015, AT. 175-176 (private session). See Župljanin Reply Brief, para. 78.

[3476]   Župljanin Appeal Brief, para. 240.

[3477]   Župljanin Appeal Brief, para. 240.

[3478]   Župljnain Appeal Brief, para. 240.

[3479]   Župljanin Appeal Brief, para. 240, referring to Exhibit P1905, Trial Judgement, vol. 2, para. 636.

[3480]   Župljanin Appeal Brief, para. 240.

[3481]   Župljanin Appeal Brief, para. 240.

[3482]   Prosecution Response Brief (Župljanin), para. 198.

[3483]   Prosecution Response Brief (Župljanin), para. 199.

[3484]   Prosecution Response Brief (Župljanin), para. 199, referring to Trial Judgement, vol. 2, paras 524, 805, 845, 850, 859. The Prosecution submits that the first extermination incidents occurred at the end of May 1992 (Prosecution Response Brief (Župljanin), fn. 810, referring to Trial Judgement, vol. 2, paras 688, 690).

[3485]   Prosecution Response Brief (Župljanin), paras 200-201. See Prosecution Response Brief (Župljanin), para. 198.

[3486]   Prosecution Response Brief (Župljanin), para. 200, referring to Trial Judgement, vol. 2, paras 415-416, 418, 420-421, 425, 428, 431, 433, 438, 440, 450-453, 455-459, 465-470, 496-497, 503, 506, 509-510, 514-517, 524, Trial Judgement, vol. 1, paras 157-159, 849.

[3487]   Prosecution Response Brief (Župljanin), para. 200. The Prosecution submits that by mid-May, following Župljanin's intervention in the Doboj incident, he "had *specific* knowledge of the risk of mass killings by Serb Forces but nevertheless continued to contribute to the JCE" (Prosecution Response Brief (Župljanin), para. 200).

foresight";[3488] (ii) Župljanin's unsupported assertion that he was not aware of the conditions in which the detainees were transported is contradicted by the evidence and the Trial Chamber's findings and, in any event, he did not need to foresee the exact circumstances of each **[page 437]** extermination incident;[3489] (iii) Župljanin fails to show that on 18 August 1992, the day of the Korićanske Stijene killings, he was unaware of the Sanski Most Incident and the police's involvement therein;[3490] (iv) contrary to Župljanin's submissions, his "'conduct towards murder investigations' [...] only served to increase his awareness of the possibility of further extermination incidents" and the Trial Chamber did not err in relying on this as an indicator of his *mens rea*;[3491] (v) Župljanin "chose and ordered the Prijedor SJB to escort" the detainees from Trnopolje detention camp despite his knowledge of its involvement in the Korićanske Stijene killings and therefore it is irrelevant whether the decision to escort the prisoners originated from an agreement between the RS Government and the ICRC;[3492] and (vi) it is irrelevant whether the same persons involved in the Korićanske Stijene killings were used to escort the convoy to Croatia or whether incidents occurred, considering that "Drljača was still the Chief of Prijedor SJB" and that Župljanin knew that for Drljača "the killing of 150-200 Muslim prisoners by Serb police officers 'was normal' [...], and [...] that 'the best way of dealing with [the mass killing] would be to conceal it'".[3493]

1054. Župljanin replies that the Prosecution does not dispute that the Trial Chamber failed to provide a specific date as of when murders and extermination became foreseeable to him and when **[page 438]** he took that risk.[3494] He further submits that the Prosecution's reliance on the Korićanske Stijene killings is misplaced as it occurred well after many of the killings for which he was convicted pursuant to the third category of joint criminal enterprise.[3495]

[3488]   Prosecution Response Brief (Župljanin), para. 201. The Prosecution submits that "[w]hile the 30 April 1992 Dispatch may have referred to the killing of a Serb, it shows that, by April, [Župljanin] knew that his subordinate police officers were committing murder rather than protecting the civilian population" (Prosecution Response Brief (Župljanin), para. 201). It adds that the purported disciplinary measures taken against those involved, serve as evidence of Župljanin's ability to suppress and punish crimes (Prosecution Response Brief (Župljanin), para. 201).

[3489]   Prosecution Response Brief (Župljanin), para. 202. The Prosecution argues Župljanin "had detailed knowledge of the appalling conditions in which non-Serbs were detained and of the fact that many prisoners were killed" (Prosecution Response Brief (Župljanin), para. 202). It submits that it was thus easily foreseeable to Župljanin when he ordered or approved his subordinates to escort and/or transport non-Serb detainees that the conditions of their transport "would be no better", especially considering his knowledge that "specific mass killings" occurred on several of such transports (Prosecution Response Brief (Župljanin), para. 202).

[3490]   Prosecution Response Brief (Župljanin), para. 203. The Prosecution argues that Župljanin was sent directly a report dated 18 August 1992 mentioning the death of 21 persons "while they were in the assembly centres of being transported to Manjaća Army Camp" (Prosecution Response Brief (Župljanin), para. 203, referring to Exhibit P602, pp 1, 6, 12). Furthermore, it argues that on 18 August 1992, a report from the Sanski Most SJB Chief was sent to the SNB of the Banja Luka CSB stating that "20 persons 'perished during transportation' to Manjača Camp during which members of the Sanski Most SJB 'provided security for captives'" (Prosecution Response Brief (Župljanin), para. 203, referring to Exhibit P391, p. 3). It submits that Župljanin had an efficient system informing him in detail of criminal activities through daily reports compiling information from SJB reports and the Banja Luka SNB and that it is therefore irrelevant when he received Witness ST161's half-yearly report (Prosecution Response Brief (Župljanin), para. 203, referring to Trial Judgement, vol. 2, paras 370-372, 419).

[3491]   Prosecution Response Brief (Župljanin), para. 204, referring to Trial Judgement, vol. 2, paras 516-517, 519. In particular, the Prosecution refers to the steps Župljanin took concerning the Korićanske Stijene killings which consisted of "obstructing the investigation and shielding his subordinates from criminal prosecution" (Prosecution Response Brief (Župljanin), para. 204).

[3492]   Prosecution Response Brief (Župljanin), para. 205. The Prosecution submits that Župljanin's argument that he did not issue the order warrants summary dismissal as it merely repeats his trial submissions without showing an error (Prosecution Response Brief (Župljanin), para. 205, referring to Župljanin Final Trial Brief, paras 99-101). Moreover, it argues that even if Župljanin did not sign the order in person, he does not show that he did not approve it considering that he had authority over and coordinated the activities of the ARK SJBs, and even declared that his orders, be they oral or by dispatches, were law for the chiefs of the ARK SJBs (Prosecution Response Brief (Župljanin), para. 205, referring to Trial Judgement, vol. 2, para. 355).

[3493]   Prosecution Response Brief (Župljanin), para. 206, referring to Trial Judgement, vol. 2, para. 470. The Prosecution submits that the Trial Chamber "reasonably relied upon Župljanin having tasked the Prijedor police with escorting non-Serb prisoners, despite knowing of their involvement in extermination, to establish he was willing to accept the risk of additional crimes, including additional large killings" (Prosecution Response Brief (Župljanin), para. 206, referring to Trial Judgement, vol. 2, para. 234. See Prosecution Response Brief (Župljanin), paras 62-67, 72, 164).

[3494]   Župljanin Reply Brief, para. 78.

[3495]   Župljanin Reply Brief, para. 78, referring to Prosecution Response Brief (Župljanin), para. 203. Župljanin also replies that killings in Doboj by a "renegade paramilitary group" would not have made it foreseeable that detainees or others targeted for expulsion would be killed in the process (Župljanin Reply Brief, para. 78, referring to Prosecution Response Brief (Župljanin), para. 200).

b. Analysis

1055. The Appeals Chamber recalls that pursuant to the third category of joint criminal enterprise, an accused can only be held responsible for a crime falling outside the common purpose if: (i) it was foreseeable to the accused that such a crime might be perpetrated by one or more of the persons used by him (or by any other member of the joint criminal enterprise) in order to carry out the *actus reus* of the crimes forming part of the common purpose; and (ii) the accused willingly took the risk that such a crime might occur by joining or continuing to participate in the enterprise.[3496] Thus, liability under this category of joint criminal enterprise may attach where an accused, with the awareness that such a crime was a *possible* consequence of the implementation of the joint criminal enterprise, decided to participate in it.[3497] The subjective element of the third category joint criminal enterprise is, however, not satisfied by implausibly remote scenarios; it requires that the possibility "that a crime could be committed is sufficiently substantial as to be foreseeable to the accused".[3498]

1056. Insofar as Župljanin argues that the Trial Chamber erred in law in failing to determine whether extermination was foreseeable to the participants in the plan "from the outset",[3499] the Appeals Chamber recalls that the foreseeability standard does not include an express time frame.[3500] Accordingly, a trial chamber is not required to make a finding with respect to precisely when the crimes first became foreseeable to an accused as long as it is clear that prior to their commission, these crimes were foreseeable to the accused and he willingly took the risk that they might occur by **[page 439]** joining or continuing to participate in the joint criminal enterprise.[3501] Župljanin therefore has failed to show an error.

1057. The Appeals Chamber now turns to Župljanin's arguments concerning alleged errors of fact. In this regard, the Appeals Chamber recalls its observation that in the circumstances of the present case, while the Trial Chamber did not articulate as of when Župljanin's JCE III Crimes became foreseeable to him, it is discernible that it was satisfied that the subjective element pursuant to the third category of joint criminal enterprise was met in relation to Župljanin throughout the Indictment period, *i.e.* at least from 1 April 1992, and in any event when Župljanin's JCE III Crimes were committed.[3502] The Appeals Chamber also notes that the first extermination incident for which Župljanin was convicted pursuant to the third category of joint criminal enterprise occurred between 24 and 26 May 1992.[3503] Therefore, it understands that the Trial Chamber relied on the factors relating to a later date as mentioned in its assessment in order to further support its findings that extermination was foreseeable to Župljanin and that he willingly took, and continued to take, the risk that extermination could be committed. It is in this context that the Appeals Chamber will address Župljanin's arguments.

1058. In finding that extermination was foreseeable to Župljanin and he willingly took the risk that extermination could be committed, the Trial Chamber relied, *inter alia*, on the 30 April 1992 Dispatch,[3504] sent by Župljanin, as chief of the Banja Luka CSB, to the SJB chiefs of the ARK Municipalities concerning

---

[3496]   *Tolimir* Appeal Judgement, para. 514; *Đorđević* Appeal Judgement, para. 906; *Šainović et al.* Appeal Judgement, paras 1061, 1557; *Brđanin* Appeal Judgement, paras 365, 411. See Trial Judgement, vol. 1, para. 106.

[3497]   *Šainović et al.* Appeal Judgement, para. 1557; *Đorđević* Appeal Judgement, para. 907, referring to *Brđanin* Appeal Judgement, paras 365, 411, *Kvočka et al.* Appeal Judgement, para. 83, *Blaškić* Appeal Judgement, para. 33, *Vasiljević* Appeal Judgement, para. 101, *Tadić* Appeal Judgement, para. 228. In this regard, the Appeals Chamber observes that the Trial Chamber correctly set out the foreseeability standard (Trial Judgement, vol. 1, para. 106). The Appeals Chamber also notes that the Trial Chamber found that "the possibility that Serb Forces *could* commit murders and extermination of Muslims and Croats in the execution of the common plan was sufficiently substantial as to be foreseeable to Župljanin and that he willingly took that risk" (Trial Judgement, vol. 2, para. 524 (emphasis added)). The Appeals Chamber notes that Župljanin thus misstates the Trial Judgement when he submits that the Trial Chamber found that it was foreseeable to him that extermination *would* be committed (see Župljanin Appeal Brief, para. 235. See Župljanin Appeal Brief, para. 236).

[3498]   *Đorđević* Appeal Judgement, para. 907, quoting *Karadžić* JCE III Decision, para. 18; *Šainović et al.* Appeal Judgement, paras 1081, 1538, 1557. See *Popović et al.* Appeal Judgement, para. 1432.

[3499]   See *supra*, para. 1048; Župljanin Appeal Brief, para. 236.

[3500]   *Popović et al.* Appeal Judgement, para. 1696, referring to *Šainović et al.* Appeal Judgement, paras 1061, 1557.

[3501]   See *Šainović et al.* Appeal Judgement, paras 1061, 1557.

[3502]   See *supra*, para. 997.

[3503]   Trial Judgement, vol. 1, para. 688; Trial Judgement, vol. 2, para. 859. See Trial Judgement, vol. 1, paras 529-541, 661, 686.

[3504]   Trial Judgement, vol. 2, para. 524.

unprofessional and criminal behaviour of SJB personnel.[3505] The Trial Chamber found that this document showed that from that date, Župljanin knew that members of the ARK police were committing crimes.[3506] The Appeals Chamber observes that Župljanin is correct in arguing that the 30 April 1992 Dispatch only refers specifically to one serious crime, namely an incident of murder by two Banja Luka SJB policemen who were subsequently disciplined for their behaviour.[3507] However, the Appeals Chamber notes that in the 30 April 1992 Dispatch, Župljanin referred more generally to the occurrence of "criminal activities" by SJB employees and emphasised the need for such behaviour to be addressed.[3508] The Appeals Chamber finds that the content of the 30 April 1992 Dispatch is therefore consistent with the Trial Chamber's finding that **[page 440]** Župljanin knew that the ARK police were committing crimes. Moreover, Župljanin ignores the fact that the Trial Chamber did not rely on this document in isolation but also relied on other evidence to support its finding that Župljanin knew that his subordinates were committing crimes from 30 April and continuing in May 1992.[3509] In light of the foregoing, the Appeals Chamber finds that Župljanin has not shown that no reasonable trier of fact could have relied on the 30 April 1992 Dispatch, among other evidence, in assessing whether extermination was foreseeable to Župljanin. His argument in this regard is therefore dismissed.

1059. In finding that extermination was foreseeable to Župljanin and that he willingly took the risk that this crime could be committed, the Trial Chamber also relied on his role in and knowledge of the arrest and transportation of non-Serb detainees.[3510] Župljanin argues that he was not in charge of these transportations or aware of their conditions.[3511] He also raises distinct challenges in relation to specific transportations and incidents upon which the Trial Chamber relied in its assessment.[3512] The Appeals Chamber will address these arguments in turn.

1060. First, with respect to Župljanin's submission that he was not in charge of designating policemen to transport detainees and not aware of the conditions of these transports,[3513] the Appeals Chamber observes that the Trial Chamber found that Župljanin was the highest police officer in the ARK and that he had *de jure* and *de facto* authority over the SJBs of the ARK Municipalities, which included the power to order the police to perform specific tasks, including the transport of non-Serb prisoners to Manjača detention camp.[3514] The Appeals Chamber further observes that the Trial Chamber found that the Banja Luka CSB was constantly apprised by the Sanski Most SJB of mass arrests of non-Serbs and of its involvement in the guarding and transportation of detainees.[3515] Furthermore, the Trial Chamber found that the Prijedor SJB informed the Banja Luka CSB of events in the municipality and requested its assistance in the transportation of detainees from **[page 441]** Prijedor to Manjača.[3516] Moreover, the Trial Chamber found that Župljanin had ample knowledge of the unlawful detention, mistreatment, and murder of non-Serb detainees in detention facilities and camps in the ARK Municipalities, on the basis of reports he received but also on the basis of personal visits he made to detention camps.[3517] The Appeals Chamber considers that these findings stand in stark

---

[3505]   See Exhibit P1002, pp 1-2.
[3506]   See Trial Judgement, vol. 2, para. 524.
[3507]   See Exhibit P1002, p. 2. See also Župljanin Appeal Brief, para. 238. The Appeals Chamber further notes the evidence to which Župljanin refers indicating that the victim may have been Serb (see Župljanin Appeal Brief, para. 238, referring to Radomir Rodić, 16 Apr 2010, T. 8814).
[3508]   Exhibit P1002. See Trial Judgement, vol. 2, para. 433.
[3509]   Trial Judgement, vol. 2, para. 510, referring to Exhibits 1D666 (dispatch from Župljanin, quoting to the ARK SJB chiefs a document dated 11 May 1992 from the MUP concerning measures to be taken against members of police reserves involved in unprincipled behaviour, dated 15 May 1922), P1013 (dispatch from Župljanin quoting to the ARK SJB chiefs a document dated 11 May 1992 from the MUP concerning measures to be taken against members of police reserves involved in unprincipled behaviour, dated 15 May 1922). The Trial Chamber considered that "[e]xhibits P1002, 1D666, and P1013, for instance, show that by 30 April 1992, and continuing in May 1992, Stojan Župljanin knew that members of the ARK police were involved in criminal activities" (Trial Judgement, vol. 2, para. 510. See Trial Judgement, vol. 2, para. 433).
[3510]   See Trial Judgement, vol. 2, para. 524.
[3511]   See Župljanin Appeal Brief, para. 239.
[3512]   See Župljanin Appeal Brief, paras 238-240.
[3513]   See Župljanin Appeal Brief, para. 239.
[3514]   Trial Judgement, vol. 2, para. 493. See Trial Judgement, vol. 2, paras 350-351, 353-357, 363-368, 409, 426-427, 435, 448, 456, 478, 511.
[3515]   Trial Judgement, vol. 2, para. 491. See Trial Judgement, vol. 2, paras 418-419, 506-507, 511. See also *infra*, para. 1062.
[3516]   Trial Judgement, vol. 2, para. 491. See Trial Judgement, vol. 2, paras 420-424, 465, 506, 508, 511-512.
[3517]   Trial Judgement, vol. 2, paras 506-512. See Trial Judgement, vol. 2, paras 415-437.

contrast with Župljanin's submissions that he was not in charge of assigning police to transport detainees and not aware of the conditions of these transportations. Župljanin's arguments are therefore dismissed.

1061. Second, with respect to the Sanski Most Incident,[3518] the Trial Chamber found that Župljanin was informed of this incident and relied on this knowledge in support of its finding that extermination was foreseeable to him and he willingly took, and continued to take, the risk that extermination could be committed.[3519] The Appeals Chamber observes that when assessing Župljanin's knowledge of the Sanski Most Incident, the Trial Chamber considered Witness ST161's evidence that he informed Župljanin of the incident in one of his "half-yearly" reports.[3520] The Appeals Chamber observes that the Trial Chamber made no findings on and did not refer to evidence indicating when Witness ST161's report was circulated or when Župljanin received it. [See Annex C – Confidential Annex] .[3521] There is no report in evidence concerning July-December 1992. However, the Appeals Chamber notes that even if the incident was included in the July-December 1992 report, this could only have reached Župljanin months after the Sanski Most Incident. In light of this, the Appeals Chamber finds that no reasonable trier of fact could have relied on this evidence to find that Župljanin knew of the Sanski Most Incident at a time prior to the extermination incidents for which Žulpjanin was convicted.[3522]

1062. The Appeals Chamber notes, however, that in considering Župljanin's knowledge of crimes in Sanski Most, the Trial Chamber also considered the evidence of Witness Dragan Majkić ("Witness Majkić"), Chief of the Sanski Most SJB, and Witness ST161 that Župljanin was informed on a daily basis of crimes committed by paramilitaries in Sanski Most.[3523] In addition, the Appeals Chamber notes that in the section containing findings on Župljanin's membership in the JCE, the Trial Chamber concluded on the basis of Exhibits P117, P123, P390, and P391, and the testimonies of Witness Majkić and Witness ST161, "that the Sanski Most SJB kept the Banja Luka **[page 442]** CSB constantly apprised of the mass arrests of non-Serbs and its involvement in the guarding and transport of prisoners".[3524] In particular, the Appeals Chamber observes that Exhibit P391 is a report from the Sanski Most SJB to the SNB of the Banja Luka CSB dated 18 August 1992 which provides information, *inter alia*, on the establishment of and conditions at the "collection and investigation" centres in Sanski Most municipality and the role of the SJB in processing, guarding, and transporting detainees from these centres to Manjača detention camp.[3525] The report includes an overview of the total number of persons transferred to Manjača detention camp, persons processed and waiting to be processed, persons deceased at the camp, and those who escaped or perished during transport to Manjača.[3526] The Appeals Chamber observes that the report specifically mentions the death of 20 persons during their transportation to Manjača detention camp.[3527] The Appeals Chamber therefore disagrees with Župljanin that Exhibit P391 is "vague".[3528] Furthermore, the document was specifically addressed to the CSB[3529] and Župljanin was its chief.[3530] The Appeals Chamber thus finds that Župljanin has failed to show that no reasonable trier of fact could have relied on this evidence by merely suggesting, without any basis, that the document never reached him. Based on the foregoing, the Appeals Chamber considers that despite its error

[3518]   See *supra*, para. 1050.

[3519]   Trial Judgement, vol. 2, paras 418-419, 506, 524.

[3520]   Trial Judgement, vol. 2, para. 419, referring to ST161, 20 Nov 2009, T. 3557-3558 (closed session).

[3521]   See Annex C – Confidential Annex.

[3522]   The Appeals Chamber notes that the extermination incidents for which Župljanin was convicted occurred between 24 May and 21 August 1992 (see *supra*, para. 1012).

[3523]   Trial Judgement, vol. 2, paras 419, 507.

[3524]   Trial Judgement, vol. 2, para. 491, referring to Exhibits P117 (dispatch from Mirko Vručinić, Chief of Sanski Most SJB, to Banja Luka CSB regarding mass arrests of Muslims and Croats, dated 2 July 1992), P123 (dispatch from Mirko Vručinić, Chief of Sanski Most SJB, to Župljanin/Banja Luka CSB concerning escalation of violence against Muslims and Croats and request for assistance, dated 10 November 1992), P390 (dispatch from Mirko Vručinić, Chief of Sanski Most SJB, to Banja Luka CSB concerning, *inter alia*, violence against Muslims and Croats by paramilitary groups and responsibility of SJB concerning detainees, dated 5 August 1992), P391 (report from Mirko Vručinić, Chief of Sanski Most SJB, to the SNB of the Banja Luka CSB concerning detention facilities, departure of Muslims and Croats from municipality, and role of SJB in relation to transporting and guarding prisoners, dated 18 August 1992). See Trial Judgement, vol. 2, para. 507. See also Trial Judgement, vol. 2, paras 418-419.

[3525]   Exhibit P391, pp 1-3.

[3526]   Exhibit P391, p. 3.

[3527]   See Exhibit P391, p. 3.

[3528]   *Cf.* Župljanin Appeal Brief, para. 240.

[3529]   See Exhibit P391, p. 1.

[3530]   Trial Judgement, vol. 2, paras 350, 493.

in relying on Witness ST161's evidence about the half-yearly reports, a reasonable trier of fact could have concluded that Župljanin was informed of the Sanski Most Incident shortly after it occurred, but in any case not later than 18 August 1992, and could have relied on this knowledge in support of its finding that it was foreseeable to him that extermination could be committed and he willingly took, and continued to take, that risk in relation to incidents that occurred after this date.

1063. Third, turning to Župljanin's challenges in relation to the Prijedor police escorting non-Serb detainees to Croatia,[3531] the Appeals Chamber notes that the Trial Chamber found that it was Župljanin who ordered this task to the Prijedor police in the September 1992 Dispatch.[3532] As **[page 443]** regards Župljanin's submission that he did not personally sign the September 1992 Dispatch, the Appeals Chamber finds that he merely repeats an argument already made at trial without showing an error.[3533] While the Trial Chamber did not explicitly address this argument in the Trial Judgement, the Appeals Chamber recalls that a trial chamber need not set out each step of its reasoning.[3534] The Appeals Chamber considers that by relying on the September 1992 Dispatch to find that he ordered the Prijedor police to secure buses to transport non-Serbs to Croatia,[3535] the Trial Chamber implicitly rejected Župljanin's argument. Župljanin has failed to show that the Trial Chamber erred by so doing.

1064. The Appeals Chamber further notes that the Trial Chamber relied on the fact that Župljanin assigned the Prijedor police to this transport, despite his knowledge of their involvement in the Korićanske Stijene killings.[3536] The Appeals Chamber observes that the Trial Chamber found that he not only knew of the involvement of the Prijedor police in this incident, but also that he did what he could to ensure impunity for the perpetrators.[3537] Moreover, the Trial Chamber found that Drljača was still the chief of the Prijedor SJB.[3538] The Trial Chamber also found that Župljanin was aware of the atrocities occurring in Prijedor's detention camps and received many warnings about Drljača but never attempted to remove him.[3539] In these circumstances, the Appeals Chamber finds that it is immaterial whether the decision to escort the detainees came as a result of an agreement between the RS and the ICRC or whether any accidents occurred during the journey or that police officers involved in the Korićanske Stijene killings were assigned to this escort.[3540] The Appeals Chamber considers that on the basis of the fact that Župljanin assigned the Prijedor police to escort detainees while knowing of their prior involvement in the killing of a large number of detainees in similar circumstances, a reasonable trier of fact could have considered that Župljanin was aware of and accepted the possibility of similar incidents occurring. Therefore, the Appeals Chamber finds that Župljanin has not shown that the Trial Chamber erred in relying on the fact that he tasked the **[page 444]** Prijedor police with escorting non-Serb detainees to Croatia, despite his knowledge of their involvement in the Korićanske Stijene killings, in finding that extermination was foreseeable to Župljanin and that he willingly took the risk that such crimes might be committed.

[3531] Župljanin Appeal Brief, para. 240, referring to Exhibit P1905 (dispatch from Župljanin to the chiefs of the Prijedor and Bosanski Novi SJBs with instructions on organising the transport of 1,561 persons from Trnopolje in Prijedor, through Bosanski Novi, to Croatia, dated 29 September 1992). See *supra*, para. 1050.

[3532] Trial Judgement, vol. 2, para. 478.

[3533] See Župljanin Final Trial Brief, paras 99-101, submitting, in general, that he did not personally sign all dispatches sent by the Banja Luka CSB, as some of them bore his typed name only. See *supra*, para. 25.

[3534] *Popović et al.* Appeal Judgement, para. 972; *Đorđević* Appeal Judgement, fn. 940; *Šainović et al.* Appeal Judgement, paras 325, 378, 392, 461, 490; *Krajišnik* Appeal Judgement, para. 27; *Martić* Appeal Judgement, para. 19; *Strugar* Appeal Judgement, para. 21.

[3535] See Trial Judgement, vol. 2, para. 478.

[3536] Trial Judgement, vol. 2, paras 478, 524.

[3537] Trial Judgement, vol. 2, para. 517. See Trial Judgement, vol. 2, paras 466-482. The Appeals Chamber also notes Župljanin's sweeping statement that his "conduct toward the murder investigations, as well as the information he had and the steps he took concerning the killing incident at Korićanske Stijene [...], show that it was not the only reasonable inference a trier of fact could have made" (see Župljanin Appeal Brief, para. 240). However, the Appeals Chamber observes that Župljanin's assertion is unsupported and therefore dismisses it without further analysis.

[3538] Trial Judgement, vol. 2, para. 515.

[3539] Trial Judgement, vol. 2, para. 515. See Trial Judgement, vol. 2, paras 362, 420-424, 444, 465, 468, 470, 486, 491. See *supra*, paras 806-812.

[3540] The Appeals Chamber also notes the Trial Chamber's consideration elsewhere in the Trial Judgement of evidence that the Bosnian Serb authorities used international relief organisations to legitimise the expulsion of non-Serbs in July 1992 (see Trial Judgement, vol. 2, paras 299-307).

1065. For these reasons, the Appeals Chamber finds that Župljanin has failed to show that no reasonable trier of fact could have relied on his involvement in and knowledge of the transport conditions of non-Serb detainees in support of its finding that it was foreseeable to him that extermination could be committed and he willingly took, and continued to take, the risk.

1066. Finally, as regards Župljanin's argument that the Trial Chamber erred in relying on the Korićanske Stijene killings as they only occurred "well after many of the killings for which [he] was convicted by way of JCE III",[3541] the Appeals Chamber finds that he misreads and misrepresents the Trial Chamber's analysis. Contrary to Župljanin's assertion, the Trial Chamber did not find that Župljanin's knowledge of the Korićanske Stijene killings made it foreseeable to him that extermination could be committed prior to that date. The Trial Chamber found that Župljanin knew as early as April 1992, and thus prior to the first extermination incident, that violent crimes were being committed against non-Serbs during the implementation of the JCE.[3542] It further found that throughout the Indictment period, Župljanin received information that violent crimes, including extermination, had been committed.[3543] The Trial Chamber further considered that, regardless of this knowledge, Župljanin continued to task units which he knew were involved in the commission of such crimes to carry out tasks in close contact with the non-Serb population, and that as such, he took the risk that violent crimes – including extermination – could be committed.[3544] The Appeals Chamber understands that the Trial Chamber's reliance on the Korićanske Stijene killings must be read in this context, and it finds that Župljanin has failed to show any error in the Trial Chamber's assessment of and reliance on this evidence. **[page 445]**

1067. For the foregoing reasons, the Appeals Chamber finds that Župljanin has failed to demonstrate that no reasonable trier of fact could have concluded that it was foreseeable to him that extermination could be committed and that he willingly took that risk.

c. Conclusion

1068. The Appeals Chamber therefore finds that Župljanin has failed to demonstrate that the Trial Chamber erred in law or fact in concluding that extermination was foreseeable to him and that he willingly took the risk that it might be committed. Therefore, the Appeals Chamber dismisses sub-ground (C) of Župljanin's third ground of appeal.

(iv) Conclusion

1069. In light of the foregoing, the Appeals Chamber dismisses Župljanin's third ground of appeal in its entirety. **[page 446]**

V. ALLEGED ERRORS IN RELATION TO ŽUPLJANIN'S CONVICTION FOR ORDERING PERSECUTIONS THROUGH THE APPROPRIATION OF PROPERTY (ŽUPLJANIN'S FIFTH GROUND OF APPEAL)

1070. The Trial Chamber found that on 31 July 1992, Župljanin requested the chiefs of the ARK SJBs to: (i) implement the ARK Crisis Staff decision that individuals leaving the ARK could take with them a maximum of 300 Deutsche Mark ("DM"); (ii) issue certificates of temporary seizure when amounts in excess of 300

[3541]   Župljanin Reply Brief, para. 78. The Appeals Chamber notes that the Trial Chamber convicted Župljanin for extermination in relation to incidents which occurred between 24 May 1992 and 21 August 1992 (see *supra*, para. 1012).

[3542]   See Trial Judgement, vol. 2, para. 524. See also Trial Judgement, vol. 2, paras 370-374, 387-388, 415, 419, 431, 433, 440, 450, 456, 457, 495-496, 498-499, 510, 512. The Appeals Chamber notes the Trial Chamber's finding that owing to Župljanin's intervention, the killings of 300-600 Muslims and Roma in the Doboj incident was averted (see Trial Judgement, vol. 2, paras 456, 515).

[3543]   See Trial Judgement, vol. 2, para. 524. See also Trial Judgement, vol. 2, paras 374, 387-388, 397, 404, 415-426, 431-433, 436-440, 443, 451-455, 456-471, 474, 479-481, 487, 491, 495-499, 503-517.

[3544]   See Trial Judgement, vol. 2, para. 524. See also Trial Judgement, vol. 2, paras 385, 404-405, 415, 418, 421, 425, 438-440, 448, 465, 478, 486, 488, 497, 499-505, 507-508, 511-512, 514-515, 518-519. The Appeals Chamber notes in particular that Župljanin tasked the Prijedor police to escort the buses transporting the detainees to Croatia in September 1992 despite his knowledge of their involvement in the Korićanske Stijene killings on 21 August 1992 (see Trial Judgement, vol. 2, paras 478, 524; *supra*, para. 1064).

DM were taken; and (iii) deposit seised amounts at the Banja Luka CSB cash office ("31 July 1992 Order").[3545] On this basis, it found Župljanin responsible for ordering persecutions through the "crime of appropriation of property",[3546] and convicted him under Article 7(1) of the Statute for persecutions as a crime against humanity through the underlying act of plunder.[3547]

A. Submissions of the parties

1071. Župljanin contends that the Trial Chamber erred in law and fact by determining that he "ordered the crime of 'appropriation of property' as a form of persecution by conveying an order to chiefs of police stations that individuals were not allowed to leave the ARK with more than 300DM in cash".[3548] Specifically, he argues that the Trial Chamber erred in its definition of appropriation of **[page 447]** property, as appropriation "implies permanence",[3549] and that the Trial Chamber did not find "that the seizure of money by police constituted permanent forfeiture".[3550] Župljanin argues that in fact, the seizure was temporary given that in the 31 July 1992 Order, he "specified that the police should 'issue certificates of temporary seizure' in respect of any amounts confiscated".[3551] As such, he submits that the Trial Chamber erred by finding that temporary seizure qualified as appropriation.[3552]

1072. In addition, Župljanin asserts that, even assuming that temporary confiscation of currency could constitute appropriation, it does not meet the threshold of being "of gravity equal to the crimes listed in Article 5 of the Statute".[3553] He argues that the Trial Chamber failed to make findings concerning: (i) other options available to civilians to preserve their assets, such as depositing their savings in a bank or leaving money with friends, while still complying with the cap on currency that could be transported; (ii) the sum of money confiscated; or (iii) how many victims were affected.[3554] Župljanin further submits that the gravity of

---

[3545] Trial Judgement, vol. 2, para. 409, referring to Exhibit P594. See Trial Judgement, vol.2, paras 512, 526.

[3546] Trial Judgement, vol. 2, para. 526.

[3547] Trial Judgement, vol. 2, para. 956. See Trial Judgement, vol. 2, para. 805. The Appeals Chamber observes that Župljanin was not convicted for "appropriation of property" as a distinct and separate underlying act of persecutions as a crime against humanity. The Trial Chamber considered that the charge described as "appropriation or plunder of property" in paragraphs 26(h) and 27(h) of the Indictment "is properly construed as 'plunder of property', because the word 'appropriation' has been used by the Appeals Chamber in the definition of the crime of plunder" (Trial Judgement, vol. 1, fn. 147, referring to Indictment, paras 26(h), 27(h), *Kordić and Čerkez* Appeal Judgement, para. 84). Accordingly, it convicted Župljanin for persecutions through plunder (Trial Judgement, vol. 2, para. 956). In so doing, the Trial Chamber used the terms "appropriation", "plunder" and "appropriation and plunder" interchangeably throughout the Trial Judgement (see *e.g.* Trial Judgement, vol. 1, paras 224-226, 263, 282-283, 341, 347-348, 491-492, 545, 572, 649-650, 655, 700-701, 792, 813, 815, 874, 879-880, 982, 984, 988, 1006, 1035, 1041, 1046, 1058, 1119-1120, 1190-1191, 1195, 1248-1249, 1286, 1356-1357, 1414-1415, 1498-1499, 1553, 1636, 1689), together with other terms such as "looting" as well as references to the confiscation, relinquishing, removal, stealing, taking, or theft of property (see *e.g.* Trial Judgement, vol. 1, paras 83, 154, 201, 221, 230, 243, 248, 263, 274, 281-282, 287, 308, 311, 323, 335, 341, 352, 378, 380, 390, 435, 476-478, 490-491, 509, 518, 521, 527, 532, 546, 555, 557-558, 649-650, 655, 684, 700, 727, 737, 740, 746-747, 793, 806, 813, 831, 844-845, 865, 869, 890, 896-897, 916, 919, 953, 972, 975, 981, 988, 1006, 1029, 1046, 1058, 1061, 1081, 1107-1108, 1118-1119, 1124, 1150, 1171, 1178-1179, 1189-1190, 1195, 1203, 1208, 1236-1237, 1247-1248, 1346, 1376, 1402, 1419, 1448, 1458, 1473, 1483, 1487-1488, 1572, 1577, 1597, 1609, 1636-1637, 1639-1640, 1642, 1673). While a more consistent approach would have been preferable, the Appeals Chamber is of the view that the Trial Chamber's approach – which is not challenged by Župljanin – was not inherently erroneous since the legal definition of the underlying act, if any, is not determinative. As a result of the Trial Chamber's approach, the Appeals Chamber in this Judgement will refer to both plunder and appropriation in relation to the same acts of seizure of currency from fleeing non-Serbs.

[3548] Župljanin Appeal Brief, para. 278. See Župljanin Appeal Brief, paras 279-282. The Appeals Chamber notes that in the heading of the section on this ground of appeal, Župljanin describes his ground as addressing the argument that "[t]he Trial Chamber erred in law and fact in determining that [he] *committed* persecution by way of appropriation of property through a JCE" (Župljanin Appeal Brief, p. 125 (emphasis added)). However, in his submissions, Župljanin actually challenges the Trial Chamber's finding that he *ordered* appropriation of property (see Župljanin Appeal Brief, paras 278-282). The Appeals Chamber therefore considers Župljanin's reference to commission liability to be an inadvertent error.

[3549] Župljanin Appeal Brief, para. 279.

[3550] Župljanin Appeal Brief, para. 279.

[3551] Župljanin Appeal Brief, para. 279, referring to Trial Judgement, vol. 2, para. 409.

[3552] Župljanin Appeal Brief, para. 279.

[3553] Župljanin Appeal Brief, para. 280, referring to *Blaškić* Appeal Judgement, para. 135. Župljanin argues, by way of example, that "[t]he outright destruction of a car or personal belongings have been found of insufficient gravity to constitute the crime of persecution" (Župljanin Appeal Brief, para. 280, referring to *Kupreškić et al.* Trial Judgement, para. 631, *Blagojević and Jokić* Trial Judgement, para. 620).

[3554] Župljanin Appeal Brief, paras 279-280.

the impact must "be assessed against pre-existing legal regulations".[3555] He argues that SFRY law had previously imposed a similar cap and it would thus have been anticipated by those leaving the ARK.[3556]

1073. The Prosecution responds that Župljanin's arguments should be dismissed as the Trial Chamber correctly convicted him of ordering persecutions through appropriation of property, and he fails to show that the Trial Chamber erred in applying the law on persecutions or reached an unreasonable conclusion of fact.[3557]

B. Analysis

1074. The Trial Chamber found that by way of the 31 July 1992 Order, Župljanin ordered his subordinates to carry out the removal of currency in excess of 300 DM from non-Serbs leaving the **[page 448]** ARK Municipalities.[3558] Elsewhere in the Trial Judgement, it considered, with respect to Banja Luka municipality,[3559] that "Muslims and Croats [...] could not take more than 200 or 300 DM with them" and that "thousands had left the municipality" by September 1992.[3560] The Trial Chamber concluded that "by limiting to 200 or 300 DM the amount of money that Muslims and Croats fleeing Banja Luka could take with them [...] the ARK and Banja Luka municipal authorities committed appropriation of property".[3561]

1075. The Appeals Chamber recalls that for an act to satisfy the *actus reus* elements of the crime against humanity of persecutions, it must be established that the underlying act discriminated in fact and denied or infringed upon a fundamental right laid down in international customary or treaty law.[3562] The Appeals Chamber also reiterates that the acts underlying the crime of persecutions, whether considered in isolation or in conjunction with other acts, must be of equal gravity to the crimes listed in Article 5 of the Statute.[3563]

1076. Insofar as Župljanin argues that appropriation of property must be permanent in order to amount to an underlying act of persecutions, the Appeals Chamber notes that his arguments are not substantiated by any authority.[3564] Moreover, he has failed to demonstrate why the appropriation of personal property in accordance with the 31 July 1992 Order could not satisfy the aforementioned *actus reus* elements of persecutions as a crime against humanity regardless of its duration. The Appeals Chamber notes that, in any event, the Trial Chamber's findings indicate that the appropriation in question occurred in the context of forcible transfer and deportations, and that the victims were removed without guarantees of their future return.[3565] The Appeals Chamber is therefore of the view that Župljanin's argument that the appropriation of property occurring in this **[page 449]** context was temporary, is without basis. In the Appeals Chamber's view, Župljanin's undeveloped arguments in this respect do not warrant further consideration.

[3555] Župljanin Appeal Brief, para. 281.

[3556] Župljanin Appeal Brief, para. 281, referring to Exhibit P594, p. 1.

[3557] Prosecution Response Brief (Župljanin), para. 238, referring to Trial Judgement, vol. 1, paras 225-227, 491-493. See Prosecution Response Brief (Župljanin), paras 239-244.

[3558] Trial Judgement, vol. 2, para. 526. See Trial Judgement, vol. 2, paras 409, 512.

[3559] The Appeals Chamber notes that while the Trial Chamber also discussed the seizure of currency in excess of 300 DM in relation to non-Serbs leaving Kotor Varoš municipality (Trial Judgement, vol. 1, paras 390, 478), it did not make any findings suggesting that seizure of currency occurred after 31 July 1992, *i.e.* after the date Župljanin issued the order on the basis of which he was found responsible for ordering persecutions. Moreover, the Trial Chamber entered findings on Župljanin's responsibility for ordering persecutions through appropriation only in relation to Banja Luka municipality (Trial Judgement, vol. 2, para. 805). Therefore the Appeals Chamber understands the Trial Chamber's reference to "the imposition of this limit on non-Serbs who were being forcibly removed from the ARK Municipalities" to refer only to the appropriation in Banja Luka municipality (Trial Judgement, vol. 2, para. 526). Accordingly, Župljanin's conviction for ordering persecutions through appropriation only relates to Banja Luka municipality.

[3560] Trial Judgement, vol. 1, para. 211. See Trial Judgement, vol. 1, paras 196-197, 199; Trial Judgement, vol. 2, paras 409, 512, 526.

[3561] Trial Judgement, vol. 1, para. 225. See Trial Judgement, vol. 2, para. 512.

[3562] *Popović et al.* Appeal Judgement, paras 737, 761; *Dorlević* Appeal Judgement, para. 693. *Cf. Popović et al.* Appeal Judgement, para. 762, referring to *Nahimana et al.* Appeal Judgement, para. 985.

[3563] *Popović et al.* Appeal Judgement, para. 762, referring to, *inter alia, Nahimana et al.* Appeal Judgement, paras 985-988, *Simic* Appeal Judgement, para. 177, *Blaškić* Appeal Judgement, paras 135, 139, 154-155, 160. *Cf. Brđanin* Appeal Judgement, para. 296.

[3564] See Župljanin Appeal Brief, para. 279. See also Župljanin Appeal Brief, para. 280.

[3565] See Trial Judgement, vol. 1, para. 221; Trial Judgement, vol. 2, paras 512, 526. See also Trial Judgement, vol. 2, para. 313.

1077. The Appeals Chamber further observes that Župljanin merely asserts that the Trial Chamber was required, when assessing the gravity of the appropriation in question, to enter findings on alternate options available to civilians to preserve their assets, the sum of money confiscated, or how many victims were affected, but he has failed to point to any authority or principle of law requiring the Trial Chamber to do so. Moreover, Župljanin ignores the Trial Chamber's findings on the context in which this appropriation took place and the significance of its impact upon victims,[3566] without showing any error therein. In addition, in support of his argument that the equal gravity requirement must be assessed against pre-existing legal regulations and that SFRY law previously imposed a similar restriction, Župljanin refers only to the 31 July 1992 Order itself, which does not support his contention.[3567] The Appeals Chamber considers that he has thus failed to show any error in the Trial Chamber's conclusion. Considering that Župljanin does not further substantiate his arguments with respect to the equal gravity requirements, these arguments are also dismissed.

1078. In light of the above, the Appeals Chamber dismisses Župljanin's fifth ground of appeal in its entirety.
[page 450]

VI. CUMULATIVE CONVICTIONS (PROSECUTION'S SECOND GROUND OF APPEAL)

A. Introduction

1079. The Trial Chamber found that Stanišić and Župljanin were responsible, as members of the JCE for, *inter alia*, the crimes of murder (Count 3), torture (Count 5), deportation (Count 9), and other inhumane acts (forcible transfer) (Count 10) as crimes against humanity under Article 5 of the Statute.[3568] It also found Stanišić and Župljanin responsible for the crime of persecutions (Count 1) as a crime against humanity through underlying acts including killings, torture, inhumane acts, forcible transfer, and deportation.[3569]

1080. Having made these findings, the Trial Chamber then considered whether it was permissible to enter *intra*-Article 5 cumulative convictions.[3570] The Trial Chamber referred to the test established by the *Čelebići* Appeals Chamber, whereby cumulative convictions are permissible only if each crime has a "materially distinct element" ("*Čelebići* test").[3571] It found that the *Čelebići* test was not met in relation to the crimes of murder, torture, deportation, and other inhumane acts (forcible transfer) as crimes against humanity *vis-a-vis* the crime of persecutions as a crime against humanity through the same crimes as underlying acts,[3572] and consequently entered convictions for the crime of persecutions only.[3573]

B. Submissions of the parties

1081. The Prosecution submits that the Trial Chamber erred by failing to enter convictions under Article 5 of the Statute for the crimes of murder, torture, deportation, and other inhumane acts (forcible transfer) as crimes against humanity in addition to the convictions it entered for the crime of persecutions through the same underlying acts.[3574] It contends that the Trial Chamber failed to correctly apply the *Čelebići* test which

---

[3566]   See *supra*, paras 1074, 1076.

[3567]   Župljanin Appeal Brief, para. 281, referring to Exhibit P594, p. 1. Župljanin's 31 July 1992 Order refers to the SFRY Law on Foreign Currency Transactions and its provision providing that "the amount of foreign currency that may be taken out of the country shall be decided by the Federal Executive Council" (Exhibit P594, p. 1). However, it is unclear from this order whether a restriction similar to the one in this order was previously imposed (see Exhibit P594).

[3568]   Trial Judgement, vol. 2, paras 804-805, 809, 813, 818, 822, 827, 831-832, 836, 840, 844-845, 849-850, 854, 858-859, 863-864, 868-869, 873, 877, 881, 885, 955-956. See Trial Judgement, vol. 1, paras 228, 285, 350, 494, 703, 817, 883, 938, 986, 1044, 1122, 1193, 1251, 1289, 1359, 1417, 1501, 1556, 1691.

[3569]   Trial Judgement, vol. 2, paras 804-805, 809, 813, 818, 822, 827, 831-832, 836, 840, 844-845, 849-850, 854, 858-859, 863-864, 868-869, 873, 877, 881, 885. See Trial Judgement, vol. 1, paras 222-228, 282-285, 347-350, 491-494, 700-703, 811-817, 880-883, 935-938, 982-986, 1041-1044, 1119-1122, 1190-1193, 1248-1251, 1286-1289, 1356-1359, 1414-1417, 1498-1501, 1553-1556, 1687-1691.

[3570]   See Trial Judgement, vol. 2, paras 905-918.

[3571]   See Trial Judgement, vol. 2, paras 905-918, referring to, *inter alia*, *Čelebići* Appeal Judgement, para. 412.

[3572]   Trial Judgement, vol. 2, paras 911-913, 916, 918.

[3573]   Trial Judgement, vol. 2, paras 955-956. See Trial Judgement, vol. 2, paras 912, 916, 918.

[3574]   Prosecution Appeal Brief, paras 2, 54-58.

establishes that cumulative convictions must be entered **[page 451]** where each offence has a materially distinct element.[3575] The Prosecution further argues that pursuant to the *Čelebići* test "[a] conviction for persecutions must be cumulated with a conviction for another crime against humanity, even when based on the same conduct."[3576] According to the Prosecution, the Trial Chamber had no discretion in this matter and was required to enter convictions for each distinct crime for which Stanišić and Župljanin were found guilty in order to fully reflect their criminal responsibility.[3577] It submits that the Appeals Chamber should therefore correct the legal error and enter convictions against Stanišić and Župljanin for the crimes of murder, torture, deportation, and inhumane acts (forcible transfer) as crimes against humanity pursuant to Article 5 of the Statute.[3578]

1082. Stanišić and Župljanin respond that the Appeals Chamber should uphold the Trial Chamber's decision not to enter cumulative convictions.[3579] They argue that the Appeals Chamber should adopt the approach of a number of judgements rendered prior to the *Kordić and Čerkez* Appeal Judgement that regarded *intra*-Article 5 cumulative convictions as impermissible.[3580] In addition, Stanišić and Župljanin respond that, even if the Appeals Chamber finds that cumulative convictions are permissible for these crimes, there are cogent reasons to depart from the Tribunal's jurisprudence.[3581] In particular, Stanišić argues that there are cogent reasons based on: (i) the "correct application" of the *Čelebići* test which "does not regard convictions as permissibly 3582 cumulative where one crime includes, but goes beyond the legal elements of another crime";[3582] (ii) the case law of the Tribunal predating the *Kordić and Čerkez* Appeal Judgement and dissenting **[page 452]** opinions which found *intra*-Article 5 convictions impermissible;[3583] (iii) the case law of national jurisdictions, including "the case law upon which the '*Čelebići* test' is based";[3584] and (iv) other *supra*-national legal sources.[3585] Župljanin further argues that cumulative convictions for the same underlying

---

[3575] Prosecution Appeal Brief, paras 2, 56-59, referring to, *inter alia*, *Čelebići* Appeal Judgement, para. 412. See Prosecution Appeal Brief, para. 55.

[3576] Prosecution Appeal Brief, para. 2. See Prosecution Appeal Brief, paras 54, 56-57. It also argues that, contrary to what the Trial Chamber stated, the crime of persecutions is not always committed through another crime and that "[a]ll that is required is that the act of persecution discriminates in fact, infringes upon a fundamental right, and is deliberately carried out with the intent to discriminate on prohibited grounds" (Prosecution Appeal Brief, paras 58-59, referring to Trial Judgement, vol. 2, para. 910).

[3577] Prosecution Appeal Brief, paras 2, 54-57, 60.

[3578] Prosecution Appeal Brief, paras 2, 54, 60-61; Prosecution Reply Brief, para. 26.

[3579] See Stanišić Response Brief, paras 115, 118, 179-180; Župljanin Response Brief, paras 17-21, 23. Stanišić contends that since "there is no materially distinct element within the underlying crime that is not reciprocated in persecutions", Article 5 convictions based on the same conduct are impermissible. In particular, Stanišić argues that the crime of persecutions is an "'empty hull' that can only be established once the elements of the underlying act are proven" and that the "materially distinct element principle is offended as persecutory intent merely supplements the underlying crimes" (Stanišić Response Brief, paras 111-113, 156. See Stanišić Response Brief, paras 113, 116, 123-142, 144-149, 153-158, 176. See also Stanišić Response Brief, para. 174). Župljanin argues that the issues raised in this ground of appeal were raised before the *Đorđević* Appeals Chamber and that he therefore "adopts the submissions of the [Đorđević] Appeals Brief" as his own (Župljanin Response Brief, para. 25, referring to *the Prosecutor v. Vlastimir Đorđević*, Case No IT-05-87/1-A, Vlastimir Đorđević's Appeal Brief, 23 January 2012 (redacted public version), paras 399-406).

[3580] Stanišić Response Brief, paras 111, 114, 121, 142-143, 158, 176, 178, referring to *Krnojelac* Appeal Judgement, *Vasiljević* Appeal Judgement, *Krstić* Appeal Judgement, *Kunarac et al.* Appeal Judgement, *Stakić* Trial Judgement; Župljanin Response Brief, paras 19, 21-22, 25; Appeal Hearing, 16 Dec 2015, AT. 234. See Stanišić Response Brief, paras 112-113, 116, 123-141, 146-149, 156, 174.

[3581] Stanišić Response Brief, paras 115-116, 122-141, 143-167, 172-175, 177, 179; Appeal Hearing, 16 Dec 2015, AT. 229. See Župljanin Response Brief, para. 25. See also Župljanin Response Brief, paras 21-22.

[3582] Stanišić Response Brief, para. 140. See Stanišić Response Brief, paras 111-116, 123-142, 154.

[3583] Stanišić Response Brief, paras 116, 143-158, referring to *Krnojelac* Appeal Judgement, *Vasiljević* Appeal Judgement, *Krstić* Appeal Judgement, *Kunarac et al.* Appeal Judgement, *Stakić* Trial Judgement, *Kordić and Čerkez* Appeal Judgement, Joint Dissenting Opinion of Judge Schomburg and Judge Güney on Cumulative Convictions, *Naletilić and Martinović* Appeal Judgement, Opinion Dissidente Conjointe des Juges Güney et Schomburg sur le Cumul de Declarations de Culpabilite, *Krajišnik* Appeal Judgement, Opinion Dissidente du Juge Güney sur le Cumul de Declarations de Culpabilite, *Stakić* Appeal Judgement, Opinion Dissidente de Juge Güney sur le Cumul de Declarations de Culpabilite, *Nahimana et al.* Appeal Judgement, Partly Dissenting Opinion of Judge Güney. See Stanišić Response Brief, paras 123-141, 144-157.

[3584] Stanišić Response Brief, paras 116, 127-129, 159-164, referring to *Blockburger v. United States*, 284 U.S. 299, (1932) ("*Blockburger v. United States*") p. 304, *Rutledge v. United States*, 517, U.S. 292, (1996) ("*Rutledge v. United States*"), p. 297, *Whalen v. United States*, 445 U.S. 684 (1980) ("*Whalen v. United States*"), pp 693-694, *Ex parte Lange*, 85 U.S. 163 (1873) ("*Ex parte Lange*"), p. 168, *Kienapple v. The Queen*, [1975] 1 S.C.R. 7829 ("*Kienapple v. The Queen*"), p. 634. See Stanišić Response Brief, para. 166.

[3585] Stanišić Response Brief, paras 116, 165-167, referring to International Covenant on Civil and Political Rights, G.A. res. 2200A (XXI), 21 U.N. GAOR Supp. (No. 16) at 52, U.N. Doc. A/6316 (1966), 999 UNTS 171, entered into force 23 March 1976

417

crimes should be prohibited as they could have an "inappropriate impact" on sentencing because they might create an impression that trial chambers should "give higher sentences".[3586]

1083. Moreover, Župljanin argues that, should the Appeals Chamber increase his sentence on appeal on the basis of additional convictions, it would amount to entering new charges on appeal and therefore violate his right to appeal.[3587] He submits that, if the Appeals Chamber were to correct the Trial Chamber's reasoning and findings, it should pronounce the error but decline to enter new convictions.[3588]

1084. The Prosecution replies that the Tribunal's jurisprudence has been settled since the *Kordić and Čerkez* Appeal Judgement[3589] and that Stanišić and Župljanin fail to demonstrate cogent reasons to depart from the Tribunal's well-settled jurisprudence that has developed since then.[3590] **[page 453]**

C. Analysis

1085. The Trial Chamber referred to the *Čelebići* test, stating that it is permissible to enter convictions under more than one statutory provision for the same conduct "only if each has a materially distinct element".[3591] The Trial Chamber then noted that in the *Kordić and Čerkez* case the Appeals Chamber, in applying the *Čelebići* test, found that "*intra*-Article 5 convictions for the crime of persecutions as a crime against humanity are permissibly cumulative with other crimes against humanity because they each have a materially distinct element not contained in the other".[3592] The Trial Chamber observed that the Appeals Chamber in *Kordić and Čerkez* found that the crime of persecutions contains a materially distinct element from the other Article 5 crimes.[3593]

1086. Despite these observations, the Trial Chamber argued that the Appeals Chamber in the *Kordić and Čerkez* case improperly applied the *Čelebići* test.[3594] The Trial Chamber reasoned that:

> the Appeals Chamber [in *Kordić and Čerkez*] has looked at the elements of persecution in the abstract and divorced its analysis from persecution's nature as an 'empty hull' that must be filled with the additional elements of an underlying act [...]. This gives rise to difficulty because the *Čelebići* test provides that the issue of cumulative convictions only arises in relation to crimes which are based on the same conduct; and, in the view of the Trial Chamber, the *Kordić and Čerkez* majority failed to do this when it treated persecution in isolation from the underlying act [...]. In the Trial Chamber's view, it would appear that the Appeals Chamber did not fully appreciate the fact that persecution is always committed *through* some other crime

---

("ICCPR"), art. 14(7), Protocol No. 7 to the European Convention for the Protection of Human Rights and Fundamental Freedoms signed in Rome on 4 November 1950 ("European Convention on Human Rights"), art. 4, *Sergey Zolotukhin v. Russia*, European Court of Human Rights, no. 14939/03, Judgement, 10 February 2009 ("*Zolotukhin v. Russia*"), paras 44, 97, 122, *Ruotsalainen v. Finland*, European Court of Human Rights, no. 13079/03, Judgement, 16 June 2009 ("*Ruotsalainen v. Finland*"). In addition, Župljanin notes that the ECCC continues to apply the "pre-*Kordić* case law" (Župljanin Response Brief, para. 22, referring to *Co-Prosecutors v. Guek Eav Kaing alias "Duch"*, Case File: 001/18-17-2007/ECCC/TC, Trial Judgement, 26 July 2010 ("*Duch* Trial Judgement"), paras 563565).

[3586] Župljanin Response Brief, para. 25. See Župljanin Response Brief, para. 19. Župljanin however notes that "[t]he Chamber gives no indication, and the Prosecution does not suggest, that the formal manner of entering convictions had any effect on sentencing" (Župljanin Response Brief, para. 19).

[3587] Appeal Hearing, 16 Dec 2015, AT. 234. Župljanin emphasises that the Prosecution does not seek an increase of his sentence on the basis of the additional convictions (Appeal Hearing, 16 Dec 2015, AT. 234, referring to Prosecution Appeal Brief, fn. 2).

[3588] Appeal Hearing, 16 Dec 2015, AT. 234-235. Župljanin adds that this approach would meet the balance between fairness to the accused and the interests in convictions (Appeal Hearing, 16 Dec 2015, AT. 235).

[3589] Prosecution Reply Brief, paras 18-20. See Prosecution Reply Brief, para. 22 (internal citations omitted).

[3590] Prosecution Reply Brief, paras 18, 21-24.

[3591] Trial Judgement, vol. 2, para. 905, referring to *Semanza* Appeal Judgement, para. 315, *Kordić and Čerkez* Appeal Judgement, paras 1032-1033, *Krstić* Appeal Judgement, para. 218, *Kunarac et al.* Appeal Judgement, para. 173, *Čelebići* Appeal Judgement, para. 412, *Limaj et al.* Trial Judgement, para. 717, *Strugar* Trial Judgement, para. 447, *Blagojević and Jokić* Trial Judgement, para. 799. See Trial Judgement, vol. 2, paras 906-907.

[3592] See Trial Judgement, vol. 2, para. 909. The Appeals Chamber notes that in *Kordić and Čerkez*, the Appeals Chamber considered whether it was permissible to enter cumulative convictions for the crime of persecutions and the crimes of deportation, other inhumane acts (forcible transfer), and murder as crimes against humanity (see *Kordić and Čerkez* Appeal Judgement, paras 1041-1043).

[3593] See Trial Judgement, vol. 2, para. 909, referring to *Kordić and Čerkez* Appeal Judgement, para. 1041.

[3594] Trial Judgement, vol. 2, para. 910. See Trial Judgement, vol. 2, paras 916, 918.

[...] whose elements must still be proved in addition to the discriminatory element required for persecution. To classify a crime as 'persecution' is to add a discriminatory intent to that crime.[3595]

1087. The Trial Chamber then considered that the elements of the crimes of murder, torture, deportation, and other inhumane acts (forcible transfer) as crimes against humanity are subsumed within the crime of persecutions through underlying acts of killing, torture, deportation, and forcible transfer.[3596] It was on this basis that the Trial Chamber concluded that these other crimes against humanity do not contain any element that is materially distinct from the crime of persecutions through the same underlying acts.[3597] It therefore held that the relevant crimes are impermissibly cumulative[3598] and only entered a conviction for the crime of persecutions.[3599] **[page 454]**

1088. The Appeals Chamber recalls that the well-established jurisprudence on cumulative convictions is the *Čelebići* test, pursuant to which:

> multiple criminal convictions entered under different statutory provisions but based on the same conduct are permissible only if each statutory provision involved has a materially distinct element not contained in the other. An element is materially distinct from another if it requires proof of a fact not required by the other.[3600]

1089. The Appeals Chamber further recalls that since the *Kordić and Čerkez* Appeal Judgement, it is well-established jurisprudence that under the *Čelebići* test, *intra*-Article 5 convictions for the crime of persecutions as a crime against humanity are permissibly cumulative with convictions for other crimes against humanity, based on the same conduct, because they each have a materially distinct element not contained in the other.[3601] That is, the crime of persecutions requires proof that an act or omission discriminates in fact and proof that it was committed with specific intent to discriminate.[3602]

1090. The *Kordić and Čerkez* Appeal Judgement and subsequent appeal judgements have repeatedly rejected an interpretation of the *Čelebići* test that prohibits cumulative convictions for the crime of persecutions as a crime against humanity and other crimes against humanity.[3603] Accordingly, cumulative convictions have been found to be permissible under Article 5 of the Statute on the basis of the same conduct in relation to the crimes of deportation, other inhumane acts, murder, torture, and extermination, on one hand, and the crime of persecutions, on the other.[3604] Although prior jurisprudence adopted a different approach, the Appeals Chamber in the *Kordić and Čerkez* case considered that cogent reasons warranted a departure from its previous jurisprudence.[3605] Subsequent appeal judgements have repeatedly confirmed the approach adopted in the *Kordić and Čerkez* case[3606] and the ICTR Appeals Chamber has taken the same approach.[3607] Moreover, the Trial Chamber's reasoning that the Appeals Chamber in the *Kordić and Čerkez* case **[page 455]** improperly applied the *Čelebići* test has been previously considered and expressly rejected

---

[3595]   Trial Judgement, vol. 2, para. 910 (internal citations omitted).
[3596]   Trial Judgement vol. 2, paras 911-913, 916-918.
[3597]   Trial Judgement, vol. 2, paras 911-913, 916-918.
[3598]   Trial Judgement, vol. 2, paras 912-913, 916, 918.
[3599]   Trial Judgement, vol. 2, pp 311-313.
[3600]   *Čelebići* Appeal Judgement, para. 412.
[3601]   *Kordić and Čerkez* Appeal Judgement, paras 1040-1043.
[3602]   *Kordić and Čerkez* Appeal Judgement, para. 1041. See *Đorđević* Appeal Judgement, para. 840; *Krajišnik* Appeal Judgement, paras 390-391; *Stakić* Appeal Judgement, paras 359-362.
[3603]   *Đorđević* Appeal Judgement, para. 840 (deportation, other inhumane acts (forcible transfer), and murder); *Krajišnik* Appeal Judgement, paras 386-391 (murder, extermination, deportation, and other inhumane acts (forcible transfer)); *Stakić* Appeal Judgement, paras 359-367 (murder, deportation, other inhumane acts (forcible transfer), and extermination); *Naletilić and Martinović* Appeal Judgement, paras 589-590 (torture); *Kordić and Čerkez* Appeal Judgement, paras 1039-1043 (deportation, other inhumane acts (forcible transfer), and murder).
[3604]   See *Đorđević* Appeal Judgement, paras 839-842; *Krajišnik* Appeal Judgement, paras 388-391; *Naletilić and Martinović* Appeal Judgement, paras 587-591; *Stakić* Appeal Judgement, paras 355-367; *Nahimana et al.* Appeal Judgement, paras 1026-1027.
[3605]   *Kordić and Čerkez* Appeal Judgement, para. 1040. See *Đorđević* Appeal Judgement, paras 840-841; *Krajišnik* Appeal Judgement, para. 389.
[3606]   *Đorđević* Appeal Judgement, para. 840; *Naletilić and Martinović* Appeal Judgement, paras 587-591; *Stakić* Appeal Judgement, paras 355-367.
[3607]   *Nahimana et al.* Appeal Judgement, paras 1026-1027. See *Bagosora and Nsengiyumva* Appeal Judgement, paras 414, 735.

by the Appeals Chamber.[3608] The Appeals Chamber further observes that the Trial Chamber provided no persuasive explanation for departing from the Tribunal's well-established jurisprudence.

1091. The Appeals Chamber also observes that, although the Trial Chamber referred to the *Čelebići* test,[3609] when applying the test it incorrectly characterised the crime of persecutions as "an empty hull".[3610] The Appeals Chamber recalls that such a characterisation has been expressly rejected as it incorrectly focuses on the acts of the accused rather than the elements of the crime of persecutions.[3611] In addition, the Appeals Chamber notes that the Trial Chamber incorrectly stated that the crime of persecutions "is always committed *through* some other crime".[3612] Contrary to the Trial Chamber's assertion, the crime of persecutions does not require that underlying acts are crimes under international law.[3613]

1092. In light of the above-recalled, well-established jurisprudence, the Appeals Chamber finds that the Trial Chamber committed an error of law when it found that convictions for the crime of persecutions as a crime against humanity are impermissibly cumulative with convictions for murder, torture, deportation, and other inhumane acts (forcible transfer) as crimes against humanity based on the same conduct. In this context, the Appeals Chamber is not persuaded by the submissions of Stanišić and Župljanin that there are cogent reasons to depart from this settled jurisprudence of the Tribunal.[3614] The dissenting opinions of Judge Schomburg and Judge Güney cited by Stanišić[3615] neither bind the Appeals Chamber nor constitute cogent reasons to revisit that jurisprudence.[3616] Similarly, neither the national[3617] nor the *supra*-national legal sources[3618] cited **[page 456]** demonstrate that the Appeals Chamber has adopted its approach "on the basis of a wrong legal principle" nor provide "clear and compelling"[3619] considerations which constitute cogent reasons to depart from the Tribunal's jurisprudence. The Appeals Chamber recalls in this regard that the Tribunal's jurisprudence is not to be lightly disturbed even where another court has taken a different approach.[3620] Moreover, the Appeals Chamber observes that the Appeals Chamber of the Extraordinary Chambers in the Courts of Cambodia ("ECCC") reversed the *Duch* Trial Judgement, on which Župljanin relies,[3621] and applied the approach in the *Kordić and Čerkez* Appeal Judgement.[3622]

1093. The Appeals Chamber therefore finds no cogent reasons in the interest of justice to depart from its well-established jurisprudence that convictions, under Article 5 of the Statute, for the crime of persecutions and other crimes against humanity based on the same conduct are permissibly cumulative.

[3608] *Đorđević* Appeal Judgement, para. 840; *Krajišnik* Appeal Judgement, para. 389. See Trial Judgement, vol. 2, paras 910-912.

[3609] See Trial Judgement, vol. 2, para. 905, referring to, *inter alia*, *Čelebići* Appeal Judgement, para. 412.

[3610] Trial Judgement, vol. 2, para. 910. See *Kordić and Čerkez* Appeal Judgement, paras 1039-1041; *Krajišnik* Appeal Judgement, paras 383, 389.

[3611] See *Kordić and Čerkez* Appeal Judgement, paras 1039-1040; *Krajišnik* Appeal Judgement, paras 383, 389.

[3612] See Trial Judgement, vol. 2, para. 910.

[3613] *Popović et al.* Appeal Judgement, para. 738; *Brđanin* Appeal Judgement, para. 296; *Kvočka et al.* Appeal Judgement, para. 323; *Nahimana et al.* Appeal Judgement, para. 985.

[3614] See *supra*, para. 596. See also Stanišić Response Brief, paras 115-116, 122-158, 165-167, 172-175, 177, 179; Župljanin Response Brief, para. 25.

[3615] See Stanišić Response Brief, paras 114, 119.

[3616] See *e.g. Đorđević* Appeal Judgement, para. 841. In particular, Judge Schomburg and Judge Güney are the same judges who dissented on *intra*-Article 5 convictions for persecutions in the *Kordić and Čerkez* Appeal Judgement. Their dissenting opinions proffer a different view from the Tribunal's jurisprudence in relation to the crime of persecutions as a crime against humanity but do not provide "clear and compelling" reasons to revisit that jurisprudence (see *e.g. Đorđević* Appeal Judgement, paras 24, 841).

[3617] See *Blockburger v. United States*, p. 304; *Rutledge v. United States*, p. 297; *Whalen v. United States*, pp 693-695; *Ex parte Lange*, p. 168; *Kienapple v. The Queen*, pp 634, 751. See also Stanišić Response Brief, paras 159-164.

[3618] See ICCPR, art. 14(7), Protocol No. 7 to the European Convention on Human Rights, art. 4; *Zolotukhin v. Russia*, paras 44, 73-77, 82-84, 97, 120, 122; *Ruotsalainen v. Finland*, paras 48-50; *Duch* Trial Judgement. See also Stanišić Response Brief, paras 116, 165-167; Župljanin Response Brief, para. 22.

[3619] See *Đorđević* Appeal Judgement, para. 24, referring to *Aleksovski* Appeal Judgement, para. 108.

[3620] See *Đorđević* Appeal Judgement, para. 83.

[3621] See Župljanin Response Brief, para. 22.

[3622] *Co-Prosecutors v. Guek Eav Kaing alias "Duch"*, Case File: 001/18-17-2007/ECCC/SC, Appeal Judgement, 3 February 2012, paras 316-336; *Duch* Trial Judgement. The Appeals Chamber also notes that the *Đorđević* Appeal Chamber considered the *Duch* Trial Judgement but found that it did not constitute a cogent reason to revisit the Tribunal's jurisprudence on cumulative convictions (see *Đorđević* Appeal Judgement, para. 841).

1094. The Appeals Chamber also recalls that:

> [w]hen the evidence supports convictions under multiple counts for the same underlying acts, the test as set forth in *Čelebići* and *Kordić* does not permit the Trial Chamber discretion to enter one or more of the appropriate convictions, unless the two crimes do not possess materially distinct elements.[3623]

The Trial Chamber therefore further erred in law when it failed to enter convictions for the crimes of murder, torture, deportation, and other inhumane acts (forcible transfer) as crimes against humanity.

1095. The Appeals Chamber notes that the Prosecution requests that the Appeals Chamber correct this error by entering convictions for the crimes of murder (Count 3), torture (Count 5), deportation (Count 9), and other inhumane acts (forcible transfer) (Count 10).[3624]

1096. The Appeals Chamber recalls that the choice of remedy lies within its discretion, in light of Article 25 of the Statute.[3625] Accordingly, in the interests of fairness to Stanišić and Župljanin, **[page 457]** balanced with considerations of public interest and the administration of justice, and taking into account the nature of the offences and the circumstances of the case at hand, the Appeals Chamber finds it appropriate to refrain from entering new convictions on appeal for these crimes.[3626]

D. Conclusion

1097. In light of the foregoing, the Appeals Chamber finds that the Trial Chamber erred in law by: (i) finding that convictions for the crime of persecutions as a crime against humanity under Article 5 of the Statute are impermissibly cumulative with convictions for other crimes against humanity based on the same conduct; and (ii) failing to enter convictions for Stanišić and Župljanin pursuant to Article 7(1) of the Statute for the crimes of murder (Count 3), torture (Count 5), deportation (Count 9), and other inhumane acts (forcible transfer) (Count 10) as crimes against humanity. Consequently, the Appeals Chamber grants the Prosecution's second ground of appeal. However, it declines to enter new convictions against Stanišić and Župljanin on appeal under these counts. **[page 458]**

VII. SENTENCING

1098. The Trial Chamber convicted Stanišić and Župljanin under Article 7(1) of the Statute for persecutions as a crime against humanity, murder as a violation of the laws or customs of war, and torture as a violation of the laws or customs of war.[3627] Župljanin was, in addition, convicted for extermination as a crime against humanity.[3628] The Trial Chamber sentenced Stanišić and Župljanin each to a single sentence of 22 years of imprisonment.[3629] Stanišić, Župljanin, and the Prosecution have each appealed the sentences.[3630]

[3623] *Strugar* Appeal Judgement, para. 324, quoting *Stakić* Appeal Judgement, para. 358. See *Gatete* Appeal Judgement, paras 160-261.

[3624] Prosecution Appeal Brief, paras 2, 54, 60.

[3625] See *Jelisić* Appeal Judgement, para. 73. Article 25(2) of the Statute provides that "[t]he Appeals Chamber may affirm, reverse or revise the decisions taken by the Trial Chambers". See also *Šainović et al.* Appeal Judgement, para. 1604, fn. 5269 (with references).

[3626] See *Jelisić* Appeal Judgement, paras 73, 77; *Aleksovski* Appeal Judgement, paras 153-154, 192; *Krstić* Appeal Judgement, paras 220-227, 229, p. 87; *Stakić* Appeal Judgement, paras 359-367, pp 141-142; *Naletilić and Martinović* Appeal Judgement, paras 588-591, p. 207. See also *Šainović et al.* Appeal Judgement, paras 1604, 1766.

[3627] Trial Judgement, vol. 2, paras 955-956. The Appeals Chamber notes that the Trial Chamber also found both Stanišić and Župljanin guilty, but on the basis of the principles relating to cumulative convictions, did not enter convictions for: murder as a crime against humanity (Count 3); torture as a crime against humanity (Count 5); cruel treatment as a violation of the laws or customs of war (Count 7); inhumane acts as a crime against humanity (Count 8); deportation as a crime against humanity (Count 9); and inhumane acts (forcible transfer) as a crime against humanity (Count 10) (Trial Judgement, vol. 2, paras 955-956).

[3628] Trial Judgement, vol. 2, para. 956.

[3629] Trial Judgement, vol. 2, paras 955-956.

[3630] See Stanišić Appeal Brief, paras 477-550; Župljanin Appeal Brief, paras 243-277, 283; Prosecution Appeal Brief, paras 1, 3-53, 61.

A. Applicable law and standard of review

1099. Pursuant to Article 24 of the Statute and Rules 87(C) and 101 of the Rules, a trial chamber must take into account the following factors in determining the appropriate sentence: (i) the gravity of the offence or the totality of the culpable conduct; (ii) the individual circumstances of the convicted person; (iii) the general practice regarding prison sentences in the courts of the former Yugoslavia; and (iv) aggravating and mitigating circumstances.

1100. An appeal against sentencing is an appeal *stricto sensu*; it is corrective in nature and not a trial *de novo*.[3631] Trial chambers are vested with a broad discretion in determining an appropriate sentence, due to their obligation to individualise the penalties to fit the circumstances of the accused and the gravity of the crime.[3632] As a rule, the Appeals Chamber will not substitute its own sentence for that imposed by a trial chamber unless the appealing party demonstrates that the trial chamber committed a "discernible error" in exercising its discretion or has failed to follow the applicable law.[3633] It is for the party challenging the sentence to demonstrate how the trial chamber ventured outside its discretionary framework in imposing the sentence.[3634] In doing so, an appellant must demonstrate that the trial chamber: (i) gave weight to extraneous or irrelevant considerations; **[page 459]** (ii) failed to give weight or sufficient weight to relevant considerations; (iii) made a clear error as to the facts upon which it exercised its discretion; or (iv) made a decision that was so unreasonable or plainly unjust that the Appeals Chamber is able to infer that the trial chamber failed to properly exercise its discretion.[3635]

B. Stanišić

1101. Stanišić raises four grounds of appeal in relation to his sentence and requests that his sentence be reduced.[3636] He submits that the Trial Chamber erred by: (i) failing to adequately assess the gravity of his conduct;[3637] (ii) failing to properly consider aggravating factors;[3638] (iii) failing to properly assess mitigating factors;[3639] and (iv) considering his abuse of his official position of Minister of Interior on multiple occasions.[3640] The Prosecution submits that these grounds of appeal should be dismissed.[3641]

1. Alleged errors in assessing the gravity of Stanišić's conduct and his role in the JCE (Stanišić's twelfth ground of appeal)

1102. In its assessment of the sentence, the Trial Chamber stated that it was "guided by the principle that the sentence should reflect the gravity of the offences and the individual circumstances of the accused".[3642] In determining Stanišić's sentence, the Trial Chamber assessed the gravity of the offence and considered that:

> Stanišić [was found] responsible for massive crimes in all of the 20 municipalities alleged in the Indictment, including murder, torture, forcible displacement, and persecution. The victims number in the thousands. The effect of the crimes upon these victims and the fact that many of them were particularly vulnerable persons—such as children, women, the elderly, and persons who had been deprived of their liberty in detention centres—has also been taken into account. These crimes were not isolated instances, but rather

---

[3631] *Tolimir* Appeal Judgement, para. 627; *Popović et al.* Appeal Judgement, para. 1961.

[3632] *Tolimir* Appeal Judgement, para. 626; *Popović et al.* Appeal Judgement, para. 1961; *Đorđević* Appeal Judgement, para. 931; *Šainović et al.* Appeal Judgement, para. 1837; *Nyiramasuhuko et al.* Appeal Judgement, para. 3349.

[3633] *Tolimir* Appeal Judgement, para. 627; *Popović et al.* Appeal Judgement, para. 1961; *Đorđević* Appeal Judgement, para. 932; *Nyiramasuhuko et al.* Appeal Judgement, para. 3349.

[3634] *Tolimir* Appeal Judgement, para. 627; *Popović et al.* Appeal Judgement, para. 1961; *Đorđević* Appeal Judgement, para. 932.

[3635] *Tolimir* Appeal Judgement, para. 627; *Popović et al.* Appeal Judgement, para. 1962; *Dorlevic* Appeal Judgement, para. 932.

[3636] Stanišić Appeal Brief, paras 477, 506, 523, 549, 550. See Appeal Hearing, 16 Dec 2015, AT. 108-109.

[3637] See Stanišić Appeal Brief, paras 478, 482-506.

[3638] See Stanišić Appeal Brief, paras 507-523.

[3639] See Stanišić Appeal Brief, paras 524-539.

[3640] See Stanišić Appeal Brief, paras 540-549.

[3641] Prosecution Response Brief (Stanišić), paras 226, 231-232, 240-241, 253-254, 257. The Prosecution argues that the seriousness of the crimes to which Stanišić contributed and the nature, scope, and degree of participation in these crimes warrant an increase in his sentence, not a decrease (Prosecution Response Brief (Stanišić), paras 226, 231. See Prosecution Response Brief (Stanišić), paras 227-230).

[3642] Trial Judgement, vol. 2, para. 888.

part of a widespread and systematic campaign of terror and violence. Stanišić was a high level police official at the time of the commission of the crimes. The Trial Chamber therefore finds that the crimes for which Stanišić has been found to incur criminal liability are of a high level of gravity.[3643] **[page 460]**

The Trial Chamber also stated that the "fact that Stanišić has been found to have committed these crimes through his participation in a JCE has been taken into account in the determination of his sentence".[3644]

(a) Submissions of the parties

1103. Stanišić submits that by improperly focusing "almost exclusively" on the objective gravity of the crimes,[3645] the Trial Chamber failed to individualise his sentence based on a proper assessment of the form and degree of his participation in the JCE.[3646] He argues that the contributions of those convicted for participation in a joint criminal enterprise can vary widely[3647] and that the "mere listing" of the fact that he was a high-level police official when the crimes were committed and that he was found to have committed these crimes through his participation in a JCE "without any explanation whatsoever" is not sufficient to address the form and degree of his participation in the JCE.[3648] According to Stanišić, moreover, the Trial Chamber failed to consider extensive findings and evidence showing that: (i) he only made a limited contribution to the JCE;[3649] and (ii) his acts and conduct impeded the furtherance of the JCE.[3650]

1104. The Prosecution responds that the Trial Chamber did not focus "almost exclusively" on the objective gravity of the crimes nor did it base Stanišić's conviction solely on his position or participation in the JCE.[3651] It acknowledges that the Trial Chamber did not explicitly reiterate its findings on Stanišić's conduct in its sentencing analysis but submits that the Trial Judgement should be read as a whole.[3652] According to the Prosecution, Stanišić's participation in the JCE was **[page 461]** "extensive and enduring".[3653] It avers that Stanišić refers selectively to passages of the Trial Judgement while ignoring the Trial Chamber's ultimate findings.[3654] For instance, the Prosecution submits that the Trial Chamber did not conclude that Stanišić's conduct served to impede or hinder the common purpose, but found that he was a key member of the JCE and significantly contributed to it.[3655] It contends that the matters Stanišić raises "effectively amount to a collateral challenge on the [Trial] Chamber's findings regarding his participation in the JCE", which it argues is dealt with under other grounds of his appeal.[3656]

[3643]   Trial Judgement, vol. 2, para. 927.
[3644]   Trial Judgement, vol. 2, para. 928.
[3645]   Stanišić Appeal Brief, para. 483 (emphasis omitted). See Stanišić Appeal Brief, para. 478; Stanišić Reply Brief, para. 106.
[3646]   Stanišić Appeal Brief, paras 479, 486.
[3647]   Stanišić Appeal Brief, para. 492, referring to *Tadić* Sentencing Appeal Judgement, paras 56-58. Stanišić argues that "an individual's contribution could be absolutely pivotal to the furtherance of a common purpose, or indeed, an individual's contribution could be found to just meet the threshold of significant contribution" (Stanišić Appeal Brief, para. 492).
[3648]   Stanišić Appeal Brief, para. 485. See Stanišić Appeal Brief, paras 484, 487-488, 491-493; Stanišić Reply Brief, paras 106-107. In this respect, Stanišić submits that in international criminal law sentences are imposed on the basis of an accused's individual conduct and not on the basis of their official position (Stanišić Appeal Brief, para. 489). Stanišić submits, in addition, that his "harsh sentence" is not related to his individual conduct but stems from his affiliation to the Bosnian Serb leadership (Stanišić Appeal Brief, para. 490).
[3649]   Stanišić Appeal Brief, paras 480, 494, 499. See Stanišić Appeal Brief, para. 505. See also Appeal Hearing, 16 Dec 2015, AT. 109. Stanišić lists a series of findings in the Trial Judgement that he contends "clearly" demonstrate the limited nature of his participation in the JCE (Stanišić Appeal Brief, paras 499-500). Stanišić also asserts that the Trial Chamber did not find that he issued orders either directly aimed at the commission of crimes or related to the RS MUP's military activities (Stanišić Appeal Brief, paras 495-497).
[3650]   Stanišić Appeal Brief, paras 481, 500-503. See Stanišić Reply Brief, para. 104. Stanišić argues that the cumulative effect of all this evidence was the "substantial minimalizing" of his contribution to the JCE (Stanišić Appeal Brief, para. 503).
[3651]   Prosecution Response Brief (Stanišić), para. 227. See Prosecution Response Brief (Stanišić), paras 228-230.
[3652]   Prosecution Response Brief (Stanišić), para. 227. See Prosecution Response Brief (Stanišić), para. 228, where the Prosecution points out that the sentencing section follows an extensive analysis of Stanišić's individual criminal responsibility in which the Trial Chamber details his role and the nature, scope, and degree of his participation in the crimes. See also Prosecution Response Brief (Stanišić), para. 230, where the Prosecution argues that is clear from the Trial Chamber's findings in this regard that Stanišić's sentence was not imposed on the basis of "his affiliation to the [Bosnian Serb leadership]".
[3653]   Prosecution Response Brief (Stanišić), para. 228.
[3654]   Prosecution Response Brief (Stanišić), para. 229, referring to Stanišić Appeal Brief, paras 500, 502.
[3655]   Prosecution Response Brief (Stanišić), para. 229, referring to Trial Judgement, vol. 2, paras 740-743, 588-596.
[3656]   Prosecution Response Brief (Stanišić), para. 229, referring to Stanišić's fourth, fifth, and sixth grounds of appeal.

1105. In reply, Stanišić argues that contrary to the Prosecution's submission, there is no finding in the Trial Judgement that he was a key member of the JCE.[3657] Stanišić also submits that he did not suggest that the Trial Chamber had found that his conduct had served to impede or hinder the common purpose, but that he had "demonstrated how the [Trial Chamber's] findings can actually only lead a reasonable [trier] of fact to such a conclusion".[3658]

(b) Analysis

1106. The Appeals Chamber recalls that trial chambers have an "overriding obligation to tailor a penalty to fit the individual circumstances of the accused *and* the gravity of the crime, with due regard to the entirety of the case".[3659] To this end, they are vested with a broad discretion to determine the appropriate sentence.[3660] The determination of the gravity of the crime requires a consideration of the particular circumstances of the case, as well as the form and degree of the accused's participation in the crime.[3661] Factors to be considered include the cruelty, nature, and circumstances of the crimes; the position of authority; the number of victims; the vulnerability of the victims; and the consequences, effect or impact of the crimes upon the broader targeted group.[3662] **[page 462]**

1107. While the Trial Chamber did not explicitly reiterate its findings on Stanišić's conduct and the form and degree of his participation in the JCE in the sentencing section of the Trial Judgement, the Appeals Chamber recalls that the Trial Chamber, in its determination of sentence, stated that it took into account that Stanišić was found to have committed the crimes he was convicted for through his participation in the JCE.[3663] The Appeals Chamber notes that with respect to Stanišić's participation in the JCE, the Trial Chamber made a wide range of findings throughout the Trial Judgement, including on his official position,[3664] his acts and conduct,[3665] his contribution to the JCE,[3666] and his intent.[3667] It recalls, further, that a trial judgement should be read as a whole.[3668]

1108. Therefore, despite the brevity of the Trial Chamber's reasoning in the sentencing section with respect to the gravity of Stanišić's conduct, the Appeals Chamber finds no merit in Stanišić's assertion that the Trial Chamber failed to adequately assess the form and degree of his participation in the JCE in determining his sentence. As a result, the Appeals Chamber finds that the related submission that the Trial Chamber failed to individualise his sentence also fails. Moreover, to the extent that Stanišić argues that his sentence is based solely on his affiliation with the Bosnian Serb leadership, the Appeals Chamber recalls that it has previously addressed and dismissed similar arguments raised by Stanišić under other grounds of his appeal.[3669]

[3657]   Stanišić Reply Brief, para. 102. See Stanišić Reply Brief, para. 103.
[3658]   Stanišić Reply Brief, para. 104. See Stanišić Reply Brief, para. 105, arguing that the Prosecution cannot refute the Trial Chamber's various findings demonstrating that his acts and conduct served to impede the JCE.
[3659]   *Šainović et al.* Appeal Judgement, para. 1837, quoting *D. Nikolić* Sentencing Appeal Judgement, para. 19.
[3660]   *Tolimir* Appeal Judgement, para. 626; *Popović et al.* Appeal Judgement, para. 1961; *Đorđević* Appeal Judgement, para. 931; *Nyiramasuhuko et al.* Appeal Judgement, para. 3349.
[3661]   *Stakić* Appeal Judgement, para. 380; *Furundžija* Appeal Judgement, para. 249; *Aleksovski* Appeal Judgement, para. 182. See Trial Judgement, vol. 2, para. 892.
[3662]   See *Đorđević* Appeal Judgement, para. 972; *Mrkšić and Šljivančanin* Appeal Judgement, para. 400; *Strugar* Appeal Judgement, paras 353-354; *Galić* Appeal Judgement, paras 409-410; *Naletilić and Martinović* Appeal Judgement, paras 609, 613, 626; *Stakić* Appeal Judgement, para. 380; *Blaškić* Appeal Judgement, para. 683; *Musema* Appeal Judgement, paras 382-383. See also Trial Judgement, vol. 2, para. 892.
[3663]   Trial Judgement, vol. 2, para. 928. The Appeals Chamber also notes that the Trial Chamber stated that it was "guided by the principle that the sentence should reflect the gravity of the offences and the individual circumstances of the accused" (Trial Judgement, vol. 2, para. 888).
[3664]   Trial Judgement, vol. 2, para. 542.
[3665]   Trial Judgement, vol. 2, paras 544-728 (concerning Stanišić's acts prior to and following his appointment as Minister of Interior). The Trial Judgement includes findings on Stanišić's participation in the formation of Bosnian Serb organs and policy (Trial Judgement, vol. 2, paras 544-575), his participation in formation and deployment of RS MUP forces (Trial Judgement, vol. 2, paras 576-609), and his acts and conduct in relation to crimes (Trial Judgement, vol. 2, paras 610-728).
[3666]   Trial Judgement, vol. 2, paras 729-765 (within the section entitled "Findings on Mićo Stanišić's membership in the JCE").
[3667]   Trial Judgement, vol. 2, paras 766-769. In addition, the Trial Chamber made findings on his responsibility for crimes outside the scope of the JCE (Trial Judgement, vol. 2, paras 770-781).
[3668]   *Popović et al.* Appeal Judgement, para. 2006; *Mrkšić and Šljivančanin* Appeal Judgement, para. 379.
[3669]   See *supra*, paras 81-82.

1109. Further, with regard to Stanišić's characterisation of his participation in the JCE as "limited", the Appeals Chamber notes that it is inconsistent with the Trial Chamber's conclusions. Having considered the extent of Stanišić's participation in the section of the Trial Judgement dealing with his contribution, it was unnecessary for the Trial Chamber to reconsider the issue in the specific context of sentencing. For the same reasons, the Appeals Chamber finds that Stanišić's assertion that the Trial Chamber failed to give weight or sufficient weight to evidence that his acts and conduct impeded the furtherance of the JCE is devoid of merit. Moreover, the Trial Chamber **[page 463]** considered the evidence to which Stanišić refers,[3670] but nonetheless convicted him for the commission of crimes through participation in the JCE.[3671] In the Appeals Chamber's view, Stanišić provides his own interpretation of the evidence without showing that the Trial Chamber erred in its assessment of the weight to be attached to relevant considerations and thus he has failed to show a discernible error in the exercise of its sentencing discretion.

(c) Conclusion

1110. The Appeals Chamber finds that Stanišić has failed to show that the Trial Chamber committed a discernible error in assessing the gravity of his conduct and individualising his sentence. Therefore, the Appeals Chamber dismisses Stanišić's twelfth ground of appeal.

2. Alleged errors in assessing aggravating factors (Stanišić's thirteenth ground of appeal)

1111. In determining Stanišić's sentence, the Trial Chamber considered as aggravating circumstances: (i) Stanišić's abuse of his superior position as RS MUP Minister; (ii) the length of time over which the crimes were committed; and (iii) his education and political background.[3672]

(a) Alleged error of law in considering Stanišić's official position as an aggravating factor

1112. Stanišić submits that the Trial Chamber erred in finding that his official position as Minister of Interior "in and of itself" constituted an aggravating factor,[3673] without demonstrating how he allegedly abused his position in order to further the JCE.[3674]

1113. The Prosecution responds that the Trial Chamber did not find that it was Stanišić's official position which was, in and of itself, an aggravating factor, but rather his abuse of that position.[3675]

1114. The Appeals Chamber recalls that it is not the superior position in itself which constitutes an aggravating factor, but rather the abuse of such position which may be considered as an aggravating factor.[3676]
[page 464]

1115. The Trial Chamber considered that Stanišić's participation in the JCE was undertaken in his official capacity as Minister of Interior and found that this constituted an abuse of his superior position and as such aggravated his culpability.[3677] The Appeals Chamber observes that the Trial Chamber did not articulate how Stanišić abused his position to further the JCE as part of its analysis of aggravating circumstances.[3678] While it would have been preferable for the Trial Chamber to provide such analysis in the sentencing section, or at

---

[3670]   Trial Judgement, vol. 2, paras 42, 46, 488, 568-569, 605-607, 609, 613, 621, 632, 664, 667, 681, 684, 687-688, 694-695, 698-704, 706-708, 714, 717-719, 733, 749, 755. See Stanišić Appeal Brief, para. 502.
[3671]   Trial Judgement, vol. 2, paras 928, 955.
[3672]   Trial Judgement, vol. 2, paras 929-931.
[3673]   Stanišić Appeal Brief, para. 508. See Stanišić Appeal Brief, paras 507, 510.
[3674]   Stanišić Appeal Brief, paras 510-512, referring to, *inter alia*, *Babić* Sentencing Appeal Judgement, para. 80. See Stanišić Reply Brief, para. 111.
[3675]   Prosecution Response Brief (Stanišić), paras 232-233. The Prosecution points to a number of the Trial Chamber's findings to demonstrate that Stanišić abused his superior position and contends that Stanišić fails to demonstrate any error in the Trial Chamber's assessment related to the abuse of his official position as an aggravating factor (Prosecution Response Brief (Stanišić), paras 233-234).
[3676]   *Đorđević* Appeal Judgement, para. 939; *Hadžihasanović and Kubura* Appeal Judgement, para. 320; *Stakić* Appeal Judgement, para. 411; *Simba* Appeal Judgement, para. 285. See Trial Judgement, vol. 2, para. 896.
[3677]   Trial Judgement, vol. 2, para. 929.
[3678]   See Trial Judgement, vol. 2, para. 929.

least refer to relevant earlier findings, the Appeals Chamber recalls that a trial judgement should be read as a whole.[3679] The Appeals Chamber notes that the Trial Chamber considered in detail the manner in which Stanišić exercised his authority elsewhere in the Trial Judgement.[3680] In light of the foregoing, and irrespective of the brevity of the Trial Chamber's reasoning, the Appeals Chamber finds no merit in Stanišić's assertion that the Trial Chamber relied upon his official status as Minister of Interior *per se*, rather than his abuse of that position in assessing aggravating factors.

1116. The Appeals Chamber therefore finds that Stanišić has failed to demonstrate that the Trial Chamber committed a discernible error.

(b) Alleged error in considering the duration of the crimes as an aggravating factor

1117. Stanišić submits that the Trial Chamber erroneously considered as an aggravating factor that the crimes were committed during a period of nine months.[3681] He argues that a trial chamber should consider the length of time during which the crimes "lasted", as opposed to the length of time in which the crimes "occurred".[3682] Stanišić contends that the Trial Chamber should have considered a period of three months as the time period during which the crimes lasted given that the vast majority of crimes occurred from April to September 1992 and he was aware of the crimes only as of June 1992.[3683]

1118. The Prosecution responds that the Trial Chamber reasonably found that the nine-month period during which the crimes were committed constitutes an aggravating factor.[3684] According to the Prosecution, Stanišić's distinction between the length of time a crime "lasted" and the length of **[page 465]** time during which criminal conduct "occurred" has no basis in the Tribunal's jurisprudence.[3685] In addition, it contends that Stanišić's attempt to limit the period during which the crimes were committed to three months is baseless considering that: (i) he shared the intent for JCE I Crimes and foresaw but nonetheless took the risk that Stanišić's JCE III Crimes might be committed throughout the nine-month period (*i.e.* between April and December 1992);[3686] and (ii) the Trial Chamber found him liable for crimes after September 1992.[3687]

1119. The Appeals Chamber reiterates that the length of the period during which crimes were committed may be considered by a trial chamber as an aggravating factor in sentencing.[3688] The Appeals Chamber recalls in this regard that Stanišić was found to be responsible for "massive" crimes committed in all of the 20 Municipalities listed in the Indictment, from April to December 1992.[3689] It also found that these crimes were not isolated instances but part of a widespread and systematic campaign of terror and violence[3690] and that the commission of many of these crimes continued until December 1992.[3691] Therefore, the Appeals Chamber finds no merit in Stanišić's argument that the Trial Chamber committed a discernible error in considering the length of the commission of the crimes as an aggravating factor.

[3679] *Popović et al.* Appeal Judgement, para. 2006; *Mrkšić and Šljivančanin* Appeal Judgement, para. 379.

[3680] See *e.g.* Trial Judgement, vol. 2, paras 609, 611, 617, 620, 623-625, 631-633, 636-645, 651-652, 654-657, 659-663, 667-668, 671-673, 684, 687-692, 698-704, 706-708, 742-743, 745-748, 751-756, 759-765.

[3681] Stanišić Appeal Brief, paras 507, 508, 513. See Stanišić Appeal Brief, paras 514-518.

[3682] Stanišić Appeal Brief, para. 514 (emphasis omitted). See Stanišić Appeal Brief, para. 513.

[3683] Stanišić Appeal Brief, paras 515-517. See Stanišić Reply Brief, paras 108-109.

[3684] Prosecution Response Brief (Stanišić), paras 235, 238.

[3685] Prosecution Response Brief (Stanišić), para. 235. The Prosecution adds that Stanišić's argument is premised on a situation where crimes are sporadic and isolated, which was not the situation in the case at hand (Prosecution Response Brief (Stanišić), para. 235).

[3686] Prosecution Response Brief (Stanišić), para. 236, referring to Trial Judgement, vol. 2, paras 767-779.

[3687] Prosecution Response Brief (Stanišić), para. 237.

[3688] See *Martić* Appeal Judgement, para. 340; *Blaškić* Appeal Judgement, para. 686. See also *Hadžihasanović and Kubura* Appeal Judgement, para. 317.

[3689] Trial Judgement, vol. 2, para. 927. See Trial Judgement, vol. 2, paras 801-802, 804, 809-811, 813, 815, 818-819, 822, 824, 827-828, 831, 833, 836-837, 840-841, 844, 846, 849, 851, 854-855, 858, 860, 863, 865, 868, 870, 873-874, 877-878, 881-882, 885.

[3690] Trial Judgement, vol. 2, para. 927. See Trial Judgement, vol. 1, paras 213-214, 276-277, 341-342, 482-483, 686-687, 806-807, 874-875, 932-933, 975-976, 1035-1036, 1112-1113, 1186-1187, 1241-1242, 1282-1283, 1350-1351, 1409-1410, 1492-1493, 1549-1550, 1673-1674.

[3691] See *e.g.* Trial Judgement, vol. 1, paras 221, 223, 228, 346, 490, 494, 699, 810-811, 816-817, 938, 981, 1040, 1044, 1118, 1122, 1193, 1251, 1359, 1413, 1417, 1497, 1501, 1556.

1120. To the extent that Stanišić argues that he was aware of the crimes only as of June 1992 and, as a result, incurs criminal responsibility only from June 1992, the Appeals Chamber recalls that elsewhere in this Judgement, it has dealt with this argument and found that a reasonable trier of fact could have found that Stanišić acquired the knowledge of crimes committed against Muslims and Croats only as of late April 1992.[3692] The Appeals Chamber nonetheless found that a reasonable trier of fact could have concluded that Stanišić possessed the requisite intent for joint criminal enterprise liability during the Indictment period, *i.e.* from 1 April to 31 December 1992.[3693] Therefore, his criminal responsibility for the crimes committed during this period has been **[page 466]** affirmed. Consequently, the Trial Chamber's consideration of the duration of crimes for nine months as an aggravating factor will be unaffected.

(c) Alleged error in considering Stanišić's education and political experience as an aggravating factor

1121. Stanišić submits that the Trial Chamber erred in considering his education and political background as an aggravating factor, arguing that aggravating factors may only include "circumstances 'directly related to the crime or crimes' for which the accused has been convicted".[3694] He further argues that the Trial Chamber failed to provide a reasoned opinion as to the appropriateness of using factors outside of the Indictment period[3695] and that it should have considered his good education as a mitigating factor and not as an aggravating factor.[3696]

1122. The Prosecution responds that the Trial Chamber's finding that Stanišić's education and political background constituted an aggravating factor is consistent with the settled jurisprudence and that Stanišić fails to demonstrate an error.[3697] Furthermore, the Prosecution submits that Stanišić argues for the first time on appeal that his prior education and political experience should have been considered as a mitigating factor.[3698]

1123. Regarding Stanišić's submission that the Trial Chamber erred in considering, or failed to give a reasoned opinion as to why it considered, education and previous political experience in aggravation, the Appeals Chamber observes that the Trial Chamber correctly noted that intelligence and good education may be considered as possible aggravating factors.[3699] The Trial Chamber further found that, as a result of his legal education and political experience prior to the Indictment period, Stanišić was able to have "full insight into the context in which the crimes were committed and a thorough legal understanding of the nature of the crimes".[3700] The Appeals Chamber notes, moreover, that the two trial judgements cited by Stanišić in support of his submission that **[page 467]** aggravating circumstances must be "directly related to the crime or crimes" for which the accused has been convicted, are neither binding nor conclusive on the matter.[3701]

[3692] See *supra*, para. 412.

[3693] See *supra*, para. 584.

[3694] Stanišić Appeal Brief, para. 519 (emphasis omitted). See Stanišić Appeal Brief, paras 507, 508, 520-522. See Stanišić Reply Brief, para. 110. Stanišić argues, in this context, that the Trial Chamber erroneously considered that his domestic law degree and previous political experience during peace time was "directly related to the commission of the persecutory crimes of deportation and forcible transfer in the context of an armed conflict" (Stanišić Appeal Brief, para. 519. See Stanišić Reply Brief, para. 110).

[3695] 95 Stanišić Appeal Brief, para. 520, referring to *Stakić* Appeal Judgement, para. 423.

[3696] Stanišić Appeal Brief, paras 521-522, referring to *Hadžihasanović and Kubura* Appeal Judgement, para. 328, *Hadžihasanović and Kubura* Trial Judgement, para. 2080.

[3697] Prosecution Response Brief (Stanišić), para. 239, quoting Trial Judgement, vol. 2, para. 931 and referring to *Hadžihasanović and Kubura* Appeal Judgement, para. 328.

[3698] Prosecution Response Brief (Stanišić), para. 239.

[3699] Trial Judgement, vol. 2, para. 931. See *Hadžihasanović and Kubura* Appeal Judgement, para. 328.

[3700] Trial Judgement, vol. 2, para. 931. See Trial Judgement, vol. 2, paras 537-551.

[3701] See Stanišić Appeal Brief, para. 519 (referring to *Kunarac et al.* Trial Judgement, para. 850, *Hadžihasanović and Kubura* Trial Judgement, para. 2069). The Appeals Chamber notes that, on the contrary, the Appeals Chamber has upheld trial chamber findings of aggravating circumstances that were not directly related to the crime or crimes for which an accused was convicted. See *Popović et al.* Appeal Judgement, para. 2046 (upholding the *Popović et al.* Trial Chamber's finding (*Popović et al.* Trial Judgement, para. 2199) that one of the defendant's requests to attendees at two meetings in 1999 and 2000 not to provide any information related to the events in Srebrenica to the Tribunal, constituted an aggravating factor); *Čelebići* Appeal Judgement, para. 786 (upholding the *Čelebići* Trial Chamber finding (*Čelebići* Trial Judgement, para. 1244) that the defendant's conduct during the trial in terms of his attitude and demeanour constitute aggravating factors). See also *Čelebići* Appeal Judgement, paras 787-788. See further *Hadžihasanović and Kubura* Appeal Judgement, para. 328.

1124. Turning to Stanišić's argument that the Trial Chamber should have considered his education and political experience as a mitigating factor instead of an aggravating factor, the Appeals Chamber first recalls that, as was noted by the Trial Chamber, Stanišić did not make any direct submissions in relation to mitigating circumstances.[3702] Second, Stanišić did not raise any objections to the Prosecution's submissions concerning Stanišić's education and political experience as an aggravating factor at trial.[3703] The Appeals Chamber emphasises that appeal proceedings are not the appropriate forum to raise such matters for the first time.[3704] In any event, the Appeals Chamber recalls that whether factors going to a convicted person's character constitute mitigating or aggravating factors depends largely on the particular circumstances of the case and is within the discretion of a trial chamber.[3705] The Trial Chamber acknowledged that intelligence and good education "should [not] only be considered as aggravating"[3706] but concluded that in Stanišić's case, they constituted an aggravating factor and attributed appropriate weight to it within its discretion.[3707]

1125. In light of the foregoing, the Appeals Chamber finds that Stanišić has failed to show any error in the Trial Chamber's assessment of his education and prior political experience as aggravating factors and not in mitigation.

(d) Conclusion

1126. For the reasons set out above, the Appeals Chamber finds that Stanišić has failed to show that the Trial Chamber erred in its assessment of aggravating factors. Therefore, the Appeals Chamber dismisses Stanišić's thirteenth ground of appeal. **[page 468]**

3.   Alleged errors in relation to mitigating factors (Stanišić's fourteenth ground of appeal)

1127. In determining Stanišić's sentence, the Trial Chamber noted that he had not made any direct submissions regarding mitigating circumstances.[3708] However, it *proprio motu* considered Stanišić's voluntary surrender to the Tribunal and his cooperation in relation to provisional release as mitigating factors.[3709] The Trial Chamber also considered but attached little weight in mitigation to evidence of Stanišić's good and professional character and no weight to Stanišić's Interview.[3710] Further, while the Trial Chamber recalled in this context Stanišić's orders issued for the protection of the civilian population, it noted that he failed to use the powers available to him under the law to ensure the full implementation of these orders.[3711]

(a) Submissions of the parties

1128. Stanišić submits that the Trial Chamber erred in its assessment of mitigating factors by affording no weight to his Interview and insufficient weight to his good personal and professional character.[3712] He argues that the Trial Chamber erred in finding that Stanišić's Interview did not amount to substantial cooperation with the Prosecution,[3713] and contends that even if it did not amount to substantial cooperation, the Trial

---

[3702]   See Trial Judgement, vol. 2, para. 932.

[3703]   Trial Judgement, vol. 2, para. 920, referring to Prosecution Final Trial Brief, para. 1012.

[3704]   *Tolimir* Appeal Judgement, para. 644; *Popović et al.* Appeal Judgement, para. 2060; *Đorđević* Appeal Judgement, para. 945. See *Šainović et al.* Appeal Judgement, para. 1816.

[3705]   See *Hadžihasanović and Kubura* Appeal Judgement, para. 328; *Babić* Sentencing Appeal Judgement, para. 49.

[3706]   Trial Judgement, vol. 2, para. 931.

[3707]   See Trial Judgement, vol. 2, para. 931, referring to *Hadžihasanović and Kubura* Appeal Judgement, para. 328.

[3708]   Trial Judgement, vol. 2, para. 932.

[3709]   Trial Judgement, vol. 2, paras 933-934.

[3710]   Trial Judgement, vol. 2, paras 935-936.

[3711]   Trial Judgement, vol. 2, para. 936.

[3712]   Stanišić Appeal Brief, paras 524-525, 532-534, 539. Stanišić argues that the extensive evidence of his good character coupled with the evidence of his professional approach in carrying out his duties deserved maximum weight in mitigation (Stanišić Appeal Brief, paras 533-534).

[3713]   Stanišić Appeal Brief, paras 526-532. In this respect, Stanišić submits that the Interview was: (i) voluntary (Stanišić Appeal Brief, para. 526); (ii) beneficial to the Prosecution's case which relied upon it throughout the proceedings (Stanišić Appeal Brief, paras 528, 530, 532); and (iii) used in the case against Župljanin (Stanišić Appeal Brief, para. 530).

Chamber should have nonetheless accorded it some weight in mitigation.[3714] In addition, he submits that the Trial Chamber erred by failing to consider the orders he issued to "uphold the law" and investigate, prevent, deter, and punish the commission of crimes, as well as the fact that he did not actively facilitate, enable, or engage in deportation or forcible transfer, was never present when these crimes occurred, and never encouraged the commission of crimes.[3715]

1129. The Prosecution responds that the Trial Chamber reasonably assessed mitigating circumstances, notwithstanding that Stanišić failed to make any direct submissions at trial.[3716] In particular, the Prosecution submits that the Trial Chamber properly assessed Stanišić's Interview **[page 469]** and found that it did not reveal any substantial cooperation.[3717] The Prosecution further submits that the Trial Chamber gave appropriate weight to evidence of Stanišić's character in light of the crimes for which he was found guilty,[3718] and did not err in rejecting Stanišić's orders as mitigating factors.[3719]

(b) Analysis

1130. The Appeals Chamber recalls that trial chambers shall take into account any mitigating circumstances, including substantial cooperation with the Prosecution.[3720] The Appeals Chamber further recalls that a trial chamber enjoys a considerable degree of discretion in determining what constitutes a mitigating circumstance and the weight, if any, to be accorded to factors in mitigation.[3721]

1131. The Appeals Chamber observes that the Trial Chamber considered Stanišić's Interview but found that it did not reveal substantial cooperation with the Prosecution in light of the quality and quantity of the information given.[3722] The Appeals Chamber recalls that whether cooperation was substantial and should be afforded weight in mitigation is within the discretion of a trial chamber.[3723] It is also within a trial chamber's discretion to take into account, and accord weight to, cooperation which is less than substantial.[3724] Stanišić merely contests the Trial Chamber's evaluation of Stanišić's Interview but has failed to show that the Trial Chamber committed a discernible error by not attaching weight to it in mitigation.[3725]

1132. As regards Stanišić's argument that the Trial Chamber should have given more weight in mitigation to his good character, the Appeals Chamber recalls that this is often afforded only limited weight in mitigation.[3726] Moreover, the weight afforded to mitigating factors is weighed against the gravity of the crimes.[3727] The Appeals Chamber notes that the Trial Chamber found **[page 470]** Stanišić responsible for crimes which were of a high level of gravity.[3728] Therefore, taking into account a trial chamber's considerable discretion in weighing mitigating factors, the Appeals Chamber finds that Stanišić has failed to show a discernible error.

1133. Stanišić also argues that the Trial Chamber abused its sentencing discretion by failing to take into account as a mitigating factor his orders aimed at preventing and deterring crimes and upholding the law.

[3714]   Stanišić Appeal Brief, paras 531-532.
[3715]   Stanišić Appeal Brief, paras 525, 535, 537-538.
[3716]   Prosecution Response Brief (Stanišić), paras 241-253, referring to, *inter alia*, Trial Judgement, vol. 2, para. 932.
[3717]   Prosecution Response Brief (Stanišić), paras 242, 244-248.
[3718]   Prosecution Response Brief (Stanišić), para. 249.
[3719]   Prosecution Response Brief (Stanišić), paras 250-251.
[3720]   Rule 101(B)(ii) of the Rules.
[3721]   *Tolimir* Appeal Judgement, para. 644; *Popović et al.* Appeal Judgement, para. 2053; *Dorlevic* Appeal Judgement, para. 944; *Čelebići* Appeal Judgement, paras, 777, 780.
[3722]   Trial Judgement, vol. 2, para. 935.
[3723]   *Bralo* Sentencing Appeal Judgement, para. 51; *M. Nikolić* Sentencing Appeal Judgement, para. 91; *D. Nikolić* Sentencing Appeal Judgement, para. 66; *Jelisić* Appeal Judgement, para. 126.
[3724]   See *Bralo* Sentencing Appeal Judgement, para. 51; *D. Nikolić* Sentencing Appeal Judgement, fn. 155; *Vasiljević* Appeal Judgement, para. 180.
[3725]   The Appeals Chamber also recalls that it has dismissed Stanišić's challenges to the Trial Chamber's evaluation and weight given to Stanišić's Interview elsewhere in the Judgement (see *supra*, para. 104).
[3726]   *Babić* Sentencing Appeal Judgement, paras 48-50; *Ntabakuze* Appeal Judgement, para. 296; *Seromba* Appeal Judgement, para. 235; *Semanza* Appeal Judgement, para. 398.
[3727]   Rule 101(B) of the Rules; Article 24(2) of the Statute. See *Popović et al.* Appeal Judgement, para. 2053; *Kupreškić et al.* Appeal Judgement, para. 442; *Čelebići* Appeal Judgement, para. 731; *Aleksovski* Appeal Judgement, para. 182; *Niyitegeka* Appeal Judgement, para. 267.
[3728]   Trial Judgement, vol. 2, para. 927.

The Appeals Chamber notes, however, that Stanišić ignores that, in its assessment of mitigating factors for sentencing, the Trial Chamber expressly considered its earlier finding that he failed to use the powers available to him under the law to ensure the implementation of the orders he issued for the protection of the civilian population, despite being aware of the limited action taken in relation to them.[3729] The Trial Chamber considered this in the context of the limited weight to be attached to the evidence on his professionalism.[3730] The Trial Chamber was therefore cognisant of his issuance of the orders to suppress crimes and for the protection the civilian population, but did not accord substantial weight to it as a mitigating factor. Stanišić has shown no discernible error on the part of the Trial Chamber in this respect. With regard to Stanišić's argument that the Trial Chamber failed to take into account that he did not actively facilitate, enable, or engage in deportation or forcible transfer, was never present when these crimes occurred, and never encouraged the commission of crimes,[3731] the Appeals Chamber notes that he did not raise, and the Trial Chamber did not address, these factors as mitigating circumstances. The Appeals Chamber recalls in this regard that appeal proceedings are not the appropriate forum to raise mitigating circumstances for the first time.[3732] In any event, the Appeals Chamber observes that in referring to these factors, Stanišić ignores a number of relevant findings of the Trial Chamber concerning his participation in the JCE.[3733] In these circumstances, the Appeals Chamber finds that Stanišić has not demonstrated that the Trial Chamber abused its sentencing discretion by failing to consider these factors in mitigation.[3734]

(c) Conclusion

1134. In light of the foregoing, the Appeals Chamber considers that Stanišić has not shown that the Trial Chamber erred in its assessment of mitigating factors. Therefore, the Appeals Chamber dismisses Stanišić's fourteenth ground of appeal. **[page 471]**

4. Alleged errors in relation to double counting Stanišić's abuse of his official position (Stanišić's fifteenth ground of appeal)

1135. In its assessment of the gravity of the offences, the Trial Chamber noted that Stanišić was a high-level police official at the time of the commission of the crimes.[3735] In its assessment of aggravating circumstances, the Trial Chamber noted that he participated in the JCE in his official capacity as Minister of Interior and found that this constituted an abuse of his superior position and thus aggravated his culpability.[3736] Further, in its assessment of mitigating circumstances, the Trial Chamber recalled its finding that Stanišić failed to use the powers available to him under the law to ensure the full implementation of orders he issued for the protection of the civilian population despite being aware of the limited action taken in relation to them.[3737]

(a) Submissions of the parties

1136. Stanišić submits that the Trial Chamber erred in law by impermissibly double-counting the purported abuse of his official position in determining the gravity of the offences, and as an aggravating circumstance.[3738] He asserts that it is impermissible to rely on different aspects of the same fact,[3739] noting that the Trial Chamber referred to two different aspects of his position (*i.e.* high-level police official and Minister of

---

[3729] Trial Judgement, vol. 2, para. 936. See Trial Judgement, vol. 2, paras 745-759.
[3730] Trial Judgement, vol. 2, para. 936.
[3731] Stanišić Appeal Brief, para. 537.
[3732] *Tolimir* Appeal Judgement, para. 644; *Popović et al.* Appeal Judgement, para. 2060; *Đorđević* Appeal Judgement, para. 945. See *Šainović et al.* Appeal Judgement, para. 1816.
[3733] See *e.g.* Trial Judgement, vol. 2, paras 39-42, 609, 613-621, 623-625, 631-633, 636-641, 644-645, 652, 654-657, 659-663, 667-668, 671-673, 684, 687, 689-692, 698-704, 706-708, 742-743, 745-746, 748-749, 751-765.
[3734] See *supra*, para. 1100.
[3735] Trial Judgement, vol. 2, para. 927.
[3736] Trial Judgement, vol. 2, para. 929.
[3737] Trial Judgement, vol. 2, para. 936.
[3738] Stanišić Appeal Brief, para. 540. See Stanišić Appeal Brief, paras 541-545; Stanišić Reply Brief, para. 117.
[3739] Stanišić Appeal Brief, para. 545, referring to *D. Milošević* Appeal Judgement, para. 309.

Interior).[3740] Stanišić argues that in addition, the Trial Chamber "improperly" considered this purported abuse of his official position on a third occasion, as a factor minimising the weight to be given to mitigating circumstances.[3741] Specifically, he submits that the Trial Chamber afforded "little weight" to evidence of his good character on the basis that he "'failed to use the powers available to him under the law' for the protection of the civilian population".[3742]

1137. The Prosecution responds that the Trial Chamber only considered Stanišić's abuse of his superior position as an aggravating factor, whereas in its assessment of the gravity of the offences it **[page 472]** took into account Stanišić's actions and omissions as a high-level police official.[3743] It argues that, in assessing aggravating factors, the Trial Chamber was free to consider how Stanišić abused his position in order to carry out these acts and omissions.[3744] The Prosecution further responds that the Trial Chamber's finding that Stanišić failed to ensure "the full implementation of his orders for the protection of non-Serb civilians" was relevant to its assessment of the weight to be given to the testimony regarding Stanišić's character.[3745] In addition, it submits, the Trial Chamber did not only rely on Stanišić's failure to ensure the implementation of his orders to assess the weight of his character evidence, but also considered the crimes for which he had been found guilty.[3746]

(b) Analysis

1138. The Appeals Chamber recalls that double-counting for sentencing purposes is impermissible.[3747] In this regard, factors taken into account by a trial chamber in its assessment of the gravity of a crime cannot additionally be taken into account as separate aggravating circumstances, and *vice versa*.[3748] In weighing a fact, either as an aspect of the gravity of the crime or as an aggravating circumstance, a trial chamber is required to consider and account all of its aspects and implications on the sentence in order to ensure that no double-counting occurs.[3749]

1139. In assessing the gravity of the crimes, the Trial Chamber noted that Stanišić was "a high level police official at the time of the commission of the crimes" and concluded that the crimes were "of a high level of gravity".[3750] The Appeals Chamber finds that nothing in the Trial Judgement's language suggests that, in assessing the gravity of the offences, the Trial Chamber considered that Stanišić had abused his position at the time of the commission of the crimes.[3751] Rather, by referring to his position as a "high level police official", the Appeals Chamber understands that the Trial Chamber described his role in the crimes, which was, in turn, necessary to assess the degree of his participation in the JCE and to establish his joint criminal enterprise liability.[3752] In so doing, the Trial Chamber never suggested that a crime was graver because he

---

[3740]   Stanišić Appeal Brief, para. 544. See Stanišić Appeal Brief, paras 543, 545.
[3741]   Stanišić Appeal Brief, paras 540. See Stanišić Appeal Brief, paras 546-548; Stanišić Reply Brief, para. 118.
[3742]   Stanišić Appeal Brief, para. 547 (emphasis omitted) Stanišić argues that this aspect is "intrinsically related" to his purported abuse of his official position and that the Trial Chamber therefore "allow[ed] one aspect of the facts to have a prejudicial and wholly unjustified influence on the assessment of the appropriate sentence" (Stanišić Appeal Brief, para. 548).
[3743]   Prosecution Response Brief (Stanišić), paras 254-255.
[3744]   Prosecution Response Brief (Stanišić), para. 255.
[3745]   Prosecution Response Brief (Stanišić), para. 256, referring to Trial Judgement, vol. 2, para. 936. The Prosecution argues that the Trial Chamber's findings on Stanišić's failure to ensure full implementation of his orders showed that the evidence on his character was unreliable (Prosecution Response Brief (Stanišić), para. 256).
[3746]   Prosecution Response Brief (Stanišić), para. 256, referring to Trial Judgement, vol. 2, para. 936.
[3747]   *Đorđević* Appeal Judgement, para. 936; *Limaj et al.* Appeal Judgement, para. 143; *Deronjic* Sentencing Appeal Judgement, para. 107. See *D. Milošević* Appeal Judgement, paras 306, 309.
[3748]   *Popović et al.* Appeal Judgement, paras 2019, 2026; *Đorđević* Appeal Judgement, para. 936; *M. Nikolić* Sentencing Appeal Judgement, para. 58. See *D. Milošević* Appeal Judgement, para. 306; *Limaj et al.* Appeal Judgement, para. 143.
[3749]   *D. Milošević* Appeal Judgement, para. 309.
[3750]   Trial Judgement, vol. 2, para. 927.
[3751]   See Trial Judgement, vol. 2, para. 927. See also Trial Judgement, vol. 2, para. 928.
[3752]   See Trial Judgement, vol. 2, paras 927-928. See also Trial Judgement, vol. 2, para. 542 (with regard to his official position as the Minister of Interior), read together with Trial Judgement, vol. 2, paras 544-728 ("Mićo Stanišić's acts prior to and following his appointment as Minister of Interior"), 729-769 (the Trial Chamber's assessment of Stanišić's contribution to the JCE and his intent within the section entitled "Findings on Mićo Stanišić's membership in the JCE").

[page 473] abused his position.[3753] In this regard, the Appeals Chamber also recalls that a position of authority is a factor that may be considered in determining the gravity of the offences.[3754] By contrast, when assessing aggravating circumstances, the Trial Chamber considered that Stanišić's participation in the JCE was undertaken in his official capacity as Minister of Interior, and found this to constitute an "abuse of his superior position" which aggravated his culpability.[3755] The Trial Chamber thus only considered Stanišić's abuse of position in the context of aggravating circumstances.

1140. The Appeals Chamber now turns to Stanišić's argument concerning the Trial Chamber's alleged "improper" consideration of his abuse of his official position as a factor minimising the weight to be given to mitigating circumstances.[3756] The Appeals Chamber notes that in determining the weight to be accorded to evidence of Stanišić's good character and professionalism, the Trial Chamber concluded that this evidence had little weight as a mitigating factor in light of the crimes for which he had been found guilty.[3757] The Trial Chamber then recalled its earlier finding that Stanišić failed to use the powers available to him under the law to ensure the full implementation of the orders issued for the protection of the civilian population.[3758] It is thus apparent that while the Trial Chamber considered Stanišić's failure to ensure the implementation of his orders as a factor that would have an impact on the weight to be given to evidence on his professionalism, it did not consider this failure as an abuse of his official position in this context. Moreover, even if the Appeals Chamber were to find that the Trial Chamber erred in relying on Stanišić's failure to implement his orders, it would not be clear that such an error had any impact on the sentence imposed given that the Trial Chamber already concluded that the character evidence had little weight in light of the crimes for which Stanišić was convicted.[3759] The argument is therefore rejected.

(c) Conclusion

1141. The Appeals Chamber finds that Stanišić has failed to demonstrate that the Trial Chamber committed a discernible error and abused its sentencing discretion in relation to Stanišić's abuse of his official position. Therefore, it dismisses Stanišić's fifteenth ground of appeal. **[page 474]**

C. **Župljanin**

1. Alleged errors in relation to sentencing (Župljanin's fourth ground of appeal)

1142. Župljanin submits that the Trial Chamber erred by imposing a manifestly excessive sentence as it: (i) failed to adequately consider the nature and form of his participation in the crimes; (ii) double-counted the same factors under both the gravity of the crimes and aggravating circumstances; and (iii) failed in its assessment of mitigating circumstances.[3760] According to Župljanin, these errors, viewed separately or jointly, "caused irreparable damage to the sentencing part of the judgement".[3761] The Prosecution responds that Župljanin's appeal against his sentence should be dismissed and that he fails to demonstrate that his sentence is excessive.[3762]

[3753]   *Cf. Šainović et al.* Appeal Judgement, para. 1823; *Stakić* Appeal Judgement, para. 411; *D. Milošević* Appeal Judgement, para. 302.

[3754]   See *supra*, para. 1106.

[3755]   Trial Judgement, vol. 2, para. 929.

[3756]   See Stanišić Appeal Brief, paras 540. See also Stanišić Appeal Brief, paras 546-548; Stanišić Reply Brief, para. 118.

[3757]   Trial Judgement, vol. 2, para. 936.

[3758]   Trial Judgement, vol. 2, para. 936.

[3759]   *Cf. Krajišnik* Appeal Judgement, para. 795.

[3760]   Župljanin Appeal Brief, paras 243-277.

[3761]   Appeal Hearing, 16 Dec 2015, AT. 178.

[3762]   Prosecution Response Brief (Župljanin), paras 208-209, 232, 237. The Prosecution contends that Župljanin's sentence is "manifestly too low" (Prosecution Response Brief (Župljanin), para. 232).

(a) Alleged errors in assessing the gravity of offences (sub-ground (B) of Župljanin's fourth ground of appeal)

(i) Submissions of the parties

1143. Župljanin submits that the Trial Chamber failed to adequately consider the nature, form, and degree of his participation in the commission of crimes.[3763] He asserts that liability pursuant to the third category of joint criminal enterprise – which is applicable to the majority of the crimes for which he was found responsible – is generally less culpable than liability under the first category of joint criminal enterprise as it requires less than direct intent.[3764] He also contends that he "was not the key mover in the campaign of persecutions" and that his JCE participation, if any, was limited.[3765] Župljanin submits that he "used neither his authority nor his power to *commit* a crime".[3766]

1144. The Prosecution responds that Župljanin fails to demonstrate an error and merely disagrees with the Trial Chamber's assessment.[3767] It further submits that crimes committed under the third category of joint criminal enterprise do not necessarily entail lesser culpability.[3768] According to the **[page 475]** Prosecution, the Trial Chamber reasonably considered Župljanin's conduct and role in the crimes as a whole for sentencing purposes.[3769] The Prosecution adds that he committed, intended, and played a crucial role in the commission of crimes of the utmost gravity.[3770]

(ii) Analysis

1145. The Appeals Chamber notes that in assessing the sentence the Trial Chamber stated that it was "guided by the principle that the sentence should reflect the gravity of the offences and the individual circumstances of the accused".[3771] In considering the gravity of the offences of which Župljanin was found guilty, the Trial Chamber concluded that:

> Župljanin [was found] responsible for massive crimes throughout the ARK, including murder, extermination, torture, forcible displacement, and persecution. The victims number in the thousands. The effect of the crimes upon these victims and the fact that many of them were particularly vulnerable persons—such as children, women, the elderly, and persons who had been deprived of their liberty in detention centres—has also been taken into account. These crimes were not isolated instances, but rather part of a widespread and systematic campaign of terror and violence. Župljanin was a high-level police official at the time of the commission of the crimes. The Trial Chamber therefore finds that the crimes for which Župljanin has been found to incur criminal liability are of a high level of gravity.[3772]

The Trial Chamber also stated that the "fact that Župljanin has been found to have committed the majority of these crimes through his participation in a JCE has been taken into account in the determination of his sentence".[3773]

1146. At the outset, the Appeals Chamber notes that the jurisprudence referred to by Župljanin does not support his assertion that the commission of crimes through the third category of joint criminal enterprise

---

[3763] Župljanin Appeal Brief, para. 268; Župljanin Reply Brief, para. 85. See Appeal Hearing, 16 Dec 2015, AT. 181. Župljanin also submits that the Trial Chamber failed to "offer meaningful reasons as to how [it] weighed" the consideration of the nature and form of his participation, and that this failure deprived him of his "right to appeal effectively" (Župljanin Reply Brief, para. 85).

[3764] Župljanin Appeal Brief, paras 267-268, referring to, *inter alia*, Trial Judgement, vol. 2, para. 947, *Kajelijeli* Trial Judgement, para. 963, *Krstić* Appeal Judgement, para. 268, *Martić* Appeal Judgement, para. 350.

[3765] Župljanin Appeal Brief, para. 269.

[3766] Župljanin Appeal Brief, para. 269.

[3767] Prosecution Response Brief (Župljanin), para. 226. See Prosecution Response Brief (Župljanin), paras 227-228.

[3768] Prosecution Response Brief (Župljanin), para. 228, referring to *Babić* Sentencing Appeal Judgement, paras 26-28.

[3769] Prosecution Response Brief (Župljanin), para. 228, referring to Trial Judgement, vol. 2, para. 947.

[3770] Prosecution Response Brief (Župljanin), paras 229-230. According to the Prosecution, "Župljanin's participation in the JCE was extensive and enduring" and this warrants an increase in his sentence (see Prosecution Response Brief (Župljanin), para. 226).

[3771] Trial Judgement, vol. 2, para. 888, referring to *Galić* Appeal Judgement, para. 442, *Čelebići* Appeal Judgement, paras 429, 717.

[3772] Trial Judgement, vol. 2, para. 946.

[3773] Trial Judgement, vol. 2, para. 947.

generally entails lesser culpability than the commission of crimes through the first category of joint criminal enterprise.[3774] Župljanin has thus failed to show that, in determining his sentence, the Trial Chamber was required to distinguish between crimes committed pursuant to **[page 476]** the first and third categories of joint criminal enterprise. Župljanin's arguments in this respect are dismissed.

1147. The Appeals Chamber now turns to Župljanin's submissions that the Trial Chamber failed to adequately consider the nature, form, and degree of his participation in the commission of crimes.[3775] The Appeals Chamber notes that in addressing the gravity of the offences, the Trial Chamber explicitly considered: (i) the seriousness of the crimes, namely their scale, nature, and circumstances; (ii) the number and vulnerability of the victims, and the effect of the crimes upon them; (iii) the fact that at the time of the commission of the crimes, Župljanin was a high-level police official; and (iv) that Župljanin was found to have committed the crimes through his participation in the JCE.[3776]

1148. While the Trial Chamber did not explicitly reiterate its findings on Župljanin's form or degree of participation in the commission of crimes in the sentencing section of the Trial Judgement, the Appeals Chamber recalls first that the Trial Chamber, in its determination of sentence, explicitly stated that it took into account that Župljanin was found to have committed the crimes he was convicted for through his participation in the JCE.[3777] Furthermore, the Appeals Chamber recalls that a trial judgement should be read as a whole.[3778] The Trial Chamber's references to Župljanin's position as a high-level police official and his participation in the JCE must therefore be read in conjunction with the Trial Chamber's findings elsewhere in the Trial Judgement such as its findings on his contribution to the JCE, detailing the nature of his participation.[3779]

1149. Therefore, despite the brevity of the Trial Chamber's reasoning with respect to the gravity of Župljanin's conduct in the sentencing section, the Appeals Chamber finds no merit in his assertion that the Trial Chamber failed to adequately consider the nature, form, and degree of his participation in the commission of crimes in the determination of his sentence.[3780]**[page 477]**

1150. Based on the foregoing, the Appeals Chamber finds that Župljanin has failed to demonstrate that the Trial Chamber erred in assessing the gravity of the offences. Therefore, it dismisses sub-ground (B) of Župljanin's fourth ground of appeal.

(b) <u>Alleged errors in relation to double-counting (sub-ground (D) of Župljanin's fourth ground of appeal)</u>

(i) <u>Submissions of the parties</u>

1151. Župljanin submits that the Trial Chamber impermissibly took into account his participation in the JCE and his position of authority in assessing the gravity of the crimes, and then again as aggravating circumstances.[3781]

[3774] See Župljanin Appeal Brief, para. 268, referring to *Kajelijeli* Trial Judgement, para. 963, *Krstić* Appeal Judgement, para. 268, *Martić* Appeal Judgement, para. 350. The Appeals Chamber notes that in the relevant paragraph of the *Kajelijeli* Trial Judgement, which is not a binding precedent, the *Kajelijeli* Trial Chamber merely referred to the fact that "[s]econdary or indirect forms of participation" such as for instance incitement to commit genocide or aiding and abetting genocide, "have generally resulted in a lower sentence" (*Kajelijeli* Trial Judgement, para. 963). In the relevant paragraph of the *Krstić* Appeal Judgement, the *Krstić* Appeal Chamber only stated that "aiding and abetting is a form of responsibility which generally warrants lower sentences than responsibility as a co-perpetrator" (*Krstić* Appeal Judgement, para. 268). The paragraph cited by Župljanin from *Martić* Appeal Judgement likewise makes no specific reference to the third category of joint criminal enterprise liability, and merely recalls that "the inherent gravity of a crime must be determined by reference to the particular circumstances of the case and the form and degree of the accused's participation in the crime" (*Martić* Appeal Judgement, para. 350).
[3775] See Župljanin Appeal Brief, paras 267-269.
[3776] Trial Judgement, vol. 2, paras 946-947.
[3777] Trial Judgement, vol. 2, para. 947.
[3778] *Popović et al.* Appeal Judgement, para. 2006; *Mrkšić and Šljivančanin* Appeal Judgement, para. 379.
[3779] See Trial Judgement, vol. 2, paras 495-520. With regard to Župljanin's positions, see Trial Judgement, vol. 2, paras 492-493.
[3780] See Župljanin Appeal Brief, paras 267-269. To the extent that Župljanin asserts that he did not use his authority to commit crimes and that his involvement in the JCE was limited, the Appeals Chamber recalls that these arguments have been dealt with and dismissed in the section addressing sub-ground (A) and (D) in part of Župljanin's first ground of appeal (*supra*, paras 736-813, 821-833).
[3781] Župljanin Appeal Brief, paras 274-275. See Appeal Hearing, 16 Dec 2015, AT. 178.

1152. The Prosecution responds that Župljanin's contentions on double-counting should be summarily dismissed as they fall outside the scope of his notice of appeal.[3782] According to the Prosecution, the Trial Chamber properly took into account Župljanin's participation in the JCE and his position of authority as relevant factors in the analysis of the gravity of his offence,[3783] and the abuse of his position of authority as aggravating circumstances.[3784]

    (ii) Analysis

1153. The Appeals Chamber notes that, in the Župljanin Notice of Appeal, sub-ground (D) of his fourth ground of appeal states that "[g]iven the nature of Župljanin's involvement, the nature, number and relation of aggravating and mitigating factors, no reasonable trier of fact could have imposed a sentence of twenty-two years",[3785] and therefore alleges an error of fact. A challenge concerning the principle of double-counting, however, amounts to an allegation of an error of law. Thus, Župljanin's arguments on double-counting are not covered by his notice of appeal. Nonetheless, the Appeals Chamber finds that as the Prosecution has responded to the arguments it will not be materially prejudiced if the Appeals Chamber considers them on their merits.[3786] Therefore, the Appeals Chamber will proceed to analyse the arguments on the merits, recalling that double-counting is impermissible for sentencing purposes, and that factors considered in **[page 478]** establishing the gravity of the crimes cannot be considered again as separate aggravating circumstances.[3787]

1154. The Appeals Chamber first notes that Župljanin was convicted for his participation in the JCE pursuant to Article 7(1) of the Statute.[3788] In assessing the gravity of the offences, the Trial Chamber considered that Župljanin was responsible for "massive"[3789] crimes throughout the ARK, the majority of which he was found to have committed through his participation in the JCE.[3790] The Trial Chamber therefore considered his participation in the JCE in the gravity of the offences.[3791] Subsequently, in assessing the aggravating circumstances, the Trial Chamber considered that Župljanin's active and direct participation in the JCE was undertaken in his official capacity as chief of the Banja Luka CSB and that this constituted an abuse of his superior position.[3792] The Appeals Chamber is of the view that the latter reference to Župljanin's participation in the JCE was only intended as a preliminary and contextual statement leading to the Trial Chamber's conclusion that the abuse of his position aggravated his culpability. Thus, Župljanin has failed to demonstrate that the Trial Chamber considered his participation in the JCE *per se* as an aggravating factor.

1155. Regarding Župljanin's argument that the Trial Chamber double-counted his position of authority, the Appeals Chamber notes that in assessing the gravity of the offences, the Trial Chamber referred to the fact that Župljanin was a "high-level police official" at the time of the commission of the crimes,[3793] but reasoned that it was his abuse of this position that was an aggravating factor.[3794] The Appeals Chamber understands that, in the context of assessing the gravity of the offences, the Trial Chamber referred to Župljanin's position to describe his role in the crimes and never suggested that the crime was graver simply because he was in a

---

[3782]   Prosecution Response Brief (Župljanin), paras 234, 236.

[3783]   Prosecution Response Brief (Župljanin), paras 235-236.

[3784]   Prosecution Response Brief (Župljanin), para. 235. The Prosecution contends that, with respect to aggravating circumstances, the Trial Chamber: (i) recalled his participation in the JCE only to establish that he abused his superior position; and (ii) considered the abuse of his position of authority, not his position itself (Prosecution Response Brief (Župljanin), paras 235-236).

[3785]   Župljanin Notice of Appeal, para. 45.

[3786]   See *Krajišnik* Appeal Judgement, para. 748. *Cf. Popović et al.* Appeal Judgement, para. 489; *Nizeyimana* Appeal Judgement, paras 352-354.

[3787]   *Popović et al.* Appeal Judgement, paras 2019, 2026; *Đorđević* Appeal Judgement, para. 936; *D. Milošević* Appeal Judgement, paras 306, 309. See *supra*, para. 1138.

[3788]   Trial Judgement, vol. 2, para. 956.

[3789]   Trial Judgement, vol. 2, para. 946.

[3790]   Trial Judgement, vol. 2, paras 946-947.

[3791]   See *supra*, para. 1148.

[3792]   Trial Judgement, vol. 2, para. 948.

[3793]   Trial Judgement, vol. 2, para. 946.

[3794]   See *supra*, para. 1154.

position of authority.[3795] Moreover, in relation to the abuse of his position as an aggravating factor, while it would have been preferable for the Trial Chamber to articulate how Župljanin abused his official position, or at least refer to relevant earlier findings, the Appeals Chamber recalls that a trial judgement should be read as a whole.[3796] The Appeals Chamber notes in this respect that the Trial Chamber considered in detail both the nature of Župljanin's duty, authorities, and powers,[3797] and **[page 479]** the manner in which Župljanin exercised his authority in contributing to the JCE.[3798] The Appeals Chamber therefore finds that the Trial Chamber, when considering Župljanin's position under gravity of offences and then his abuse of this position as an aggravating factor, did not double-count his position of authority.

1156. Based on the foregoing, the Appeals Chamber finds that Župljanin has failed to demonstrate that the Trial Chamber committed a discernible error by double-counting Župljanin's position and his participation in the JCE. Therefore, it dismisses sub-ground (D) of Župljanin's fourth ground of appeal.

(c) Alleged errors in the Trial Chamber's assessment of mitigating circumstances (sub-grounds (A) and (C) of Župljanin's fourth ground of appeal)

1157. In its discussion on mitigating factors, the Trial Chamber considered Župljanin's expression of regret and sympathy for the victims and their suffering in his closing argument.[3799] It, however, accorded little weight to this factor in light of Župljanin's "crucial role in the commission of crimes".[3800] In reaching this conclusion the Trial Chamber also recalled its finding that Župljanin did nothing to protect and reassure the non-Serb population, "aside from issuing ineffective and general orders, which were not genuinely meant to be effectuated" and considered that he failed to "take steps to ensure that these orders were in fact carried out".[3801] The Trial Chamber also considered evidence of Župljanin's good character, particularly, testimony that "he always tried to help people in trouble regardless of their backgrounds" but found that while this may have been the case in "specific and isolated instances", in light of the crimes for which he was found guilty, such testimony carries little weight.[3802]

(i) Alleged failure to consider Župljanin's efforts to suppress violence

1158. Župljanin submits that the Trial Chamber failed to properly consider in mitigation his efforts to suppress violence committed against non-Serbs.[3803] Župljanin submits, in particular, that the Trial Chamber failed to consider its finding that he intervened and prevented the massacre of **[page 480]** 300-600 non-Serbs in Doboj,[3804] which, given the substantial harm prevented, warranted direct consideration as a mitigating factor.[3805]

[3795]   *Cf. Šainović et al.* Appeal Judgement, para. 1823; *Stakić* Appeal Judgement, para. 411; *D. Milošević* Appeal Judgement, para. 302. See also *Babić* Sentencing Appeal Judgement, para. 80.

[3796]   *Popović et al.* Appeal Judgement, para. 2006; *Mrkšić and Šljivančanin* Appeal Judgement, para. 379.

[3797]   Trial Judgement, vol. 2, paras 489-493.

[3798]   See Trial Judgement, vol. 2, paras 495-520.

[3799]   Trial Judgement, vol. 2, para. 953.

[3800]   Trial Judgement, vol. 2, para. 953.

[3801]   Trial Judgement, vol. 2, para. 953.

[3802]   Trial Judgement, vol. 2, para. 952.

[3803]   Župljanin Appeal Brief, paras 243, 246-260.

[3804]   Župljanin Appeal Brief, paras 243, 247 (referring to, *inter alia*, Trial Judgement, vol. 2, para. 456), 248-249. See Župljanin Reply Brief, para. 80. At the Appeal Hearing, Župljanin added that he was also actively involved in the release of hundreds of non-Serb detainees in Teslić (Appeal Hearing, 16 Dec 2015, AT. 179, referring to Hearing, 1 Jun 2012, T. 27630-27631. Considering Hearing 1 June 2012, T. 27630-27631 is not on point, but Hearing, 1 June 2012, T. 27629-27630 is, the Appeals Chamber understands that Župljanin intended to refer to the Hearing, 1 June 2012, T. 27629-27630).

[3805]   Župljanin Appeal Brief, para. 249, referring to, *inter alia*, *Blagojević and Jokić* Appeal Judgement, para. 342, *Popović et al.* Trial Judgement, paras 2194, 2220. Župljanin submits that the Trial Chamber's failure to expressly consider the Doboj incident in mitigation can only reflect a failure to have given it adequate or any consideration (Župljanin Reply Brief, para. 80). Župljanin contends that the Appeals Chamber has accepted as mitigating factors: (i) attempts to release certain non-Serb individuals from detention and the distribution of humanitarian aid; and (ii) the saving of lives even if motivated by military considerations (Appeal Hearing, 16 Dec 2015, AT. 179-180, referring to *Krajišnik* Appeal Judgement, paras 816-817, *Popović et al.* Appeal Judgement, paras 2076-2077. See Župljanin Appeal Brief, fn. 340).

1159. Župljanin also submits that the Trial Chamber disregarded evidence of his statements, orders, and reports, as well as the investigative and disciplinary measures taken to prevent crimes and protect the non-Serb population.[3806] Župljanin argues that the Trial Chamber "swept" aside this evidence by relying on its finding that he "did not do anything to reassure and protect the non-Serb population, aside from issuing ineffective and general orders, which were not genuinely meant to be effectuated"[3807] on the basis of an "unexamined presumption" that this finding applied to all his orders to suppress violence.[3808] Župljanin further submits that the Trial Chamber erred in considering in sentencing its finding that his orders to suppress violence were "not genuinely meant to be effectuated", which, in his view, was not proven beyond a reasonable doubt.[3809]

1160. The Prosecution responds that the Trial Chamber reasonably attributed minimal weight to the instances where Župljanin carried out his duties to protect non-Serbs in light of his "crucial **[page 481]** role" in the crimes.[3810] It submits that, although the Doboj incident was not expressly referred to in mitigation, this was not required as the Trial Judgement must be read as a whole.[3811]

1161. The Prosecution also submits that the Trial Chamber: (i) considered the evidence to which Župljanin refers, including evidence of the few measures he undertook and of those he consistently failed to undertake;[3812] (ii) expressly considered Župljanin's arguments in sentencing and did not need to repeat its earlier findings;[3813] and (iii) reasonably discounted his purported efforts to address crimes in light of his extensive and enduring participation in the JCE.[3814] The Prosecution further avers that Župljanin impermissibly challenges substantive liability findings in sentencing and that, in weighing mitigating factors, the Trial Chamber properly considered its reasonable finding that his orders were not genuinely meant to be implemented.[3815]

1162. The Appeals Chamber notes that the Trial Chamber correctly considered that Župljanin's purported good character may constitute a mitigating circumstance,[3816] but concluded that testimony that he "tried to help people in trouble regardless of their backgrounds" carried little weight.[3817] The Appeals Chamber further notes that the Trial Chamber correctly recalled that consideration must be given to mitigating factors

---

[3806]   Župljanin Appeal Brief, paras 250-256, 258-260. Župljanin argues that the Trial Chamber systematically disregarded, *inter alia*: (i) dispatches he issued; (ii) his media interview of 12 May 1992; (iii) an operative work plan he issued "aimed at arresting and punishing persons accused of committing crimes"; (iv) his report at the 11 July 1992 Collegium on the incidence of crime and lack of cooperation by members of the police; (v) a report of 30 July 1992 condemning violations of the law and subsequent orders issued; (vi) an October 1992 summary report of crimes committed; (vii) evidence of criminal investigations undertaken by Župljanin and orders to ensure that crimes were investigated, including the investigation into the Koričanske Stijene killings and the death of prisoners in front of the Manjača detention camp; (viii) testimony which indicated that he was opposed to any efforts to conceal murders; (ix) criminal reports filed by Župljanin; and (x) his "frequent inquiries to the SJBs to obtain more information about violent crimes" (Župljanin Appeal Brief, paras 251-256, 258-259, referring to, *inter alia*, Exhibits P355, P1002, P367, p. 2, P560, p. 3, 1D198, P860, 1D201, 1D202, 2D71, pp 18-19, P160, 1D63, 2D25, pp 1, 3, P621, 2D139, P1380, P607, P608, P595, 1D63, 2D71, 1D371, 1D372, 1D373. See Appeal Hearing, 16 Dec 2015, AT. 180-181, referring to, *inter alia*, Exhibits 1D198, P601, P624, 2D57, 2D58, 2D59 as examples of his efforts to protect the non-Serb population.
[3807]   Župljanin Appeal Brief, para. 256.
[3808]   Župljanin Appeal Brief, para. 257.
[3809]   Župljanin Appeal Brief, para. 270. See Župljanin Appeal Brief, paras 271-272. In particular, Župljanin challenges the Trial Chamber's reliance on findings that he: (i) hired criminal members of the SOS to be part of the Banja Luka CSB SPD notwithstanding a previous order to the reserve police not to hire persons with criminal records; and (ii) appointed a commission to investigate crimes in detention camps in Prijedor, which comprised individuals who were in charge of interrogating detainees in these camps (Župljanin Appeal Brief, paras 270-271).
[3810]   Prosecution Response Brief (Župljanin), paras 208, 210, referring, *inter alia*, to Trial Judgement, vol. 2, paras 354, 942-945, 952-953.
[3811]   Prosecution Response Brief (Župljanin), para. 211, referring to, *inter alia*, Trial Judgement, vol. 2, para. 456, *Mrkšić and Šljivančanin* Appeal Judgement, para. 379. It contends that even if the Doboj incident warranted specific discussion in sentencing, this would not invalidate the Trial Chamber's conclusion that such an "isolated episode" had limited weight as a mitigating factor (Prosecution Response Brief (Župljanin), para. 212. See Prosecution Response Brief (Župljanin), para. 213).
[3812]   Prosecution Response Brief (Župljanin), paras 214-215, referring to Trial Judgement, vol. 2, paras 358-359, 377, 387, 394, 404, 433-437, 442-443, 445-448, 453-488, 498-499, 510, 514-517, 519, 524.
[3813]   Prosecution Response Brief (Župljanin), para. 215. See Prosecution Response Brief (Župljanin), paras 214, 219.
[3814]   Prosecution Response Brief (Župljanin), para. 216. See Prosecution Response Brief (Župljanin), para. 217.
[3815]   Prosecution Response Brief (Župljanin), paras 208, 231.
[3816]   See Trial Judgement, vol. 2, para. 952.
[3817]   Trial Judgement, vol. 2, para. 952.

and noted that assistance to detainees or victims can be taken into account in this context.[3818] In this regard, the Trial Chamber made a finding elsewhere in the Trial Judgement that Župljanin intervened in the Doboj incident and that "owing to this intervention the massacre [of 300-600 people primarily of Roma and Muslim ethnicity] was prevented".[3819] Although the Trial Chamber did not expressly mention the Doboj incident in the context of sentencing, the Appeals Chamber recalls that a trial judgement should be read as a whole.[3820] The Trial Chamber was thus aware of its obligation to consider the mitigating factors pointed out by the parties in determining the appropriate sentence.[3821] Župljanin has therefore not **[page 482]** demonstrated that the Trial Chamber failed to consider the Doboj incident in determining the appropriate sentence or that its failure to expressly refer to the Doboj incident as a unique mitigating factor amounts to a discernible error in the exercise of its sentencing discretion.

1163. Turning to Župljanin's submission that the Trial Chamber disregarded evidence of his statements, orders, and reports, as well as the measures taken to prevent crimes,[3822] the Appeals Chamber observes that the Trial Chamber recalled, in the consideration of mitigating factors, its finding on Župljanin's lack of action other than issuing general and ineffective orders which were "not genuinely meant to be effectuated".[3823] While Župljanin challenges this finding to assert that his orders and other actions should have been considered as mitigating factors, the Appeals Chamber recalls that in earlier sections of this Judgement, it has dismissed his same challenge with regard to this finding.[3824] Thus, his submissions in this respect do not warrant further discussion. Moreover, the Appeals Chamber recalls that the weight to be given to a particular factor, if any, is a matter for the Trial Chamber to determine in the exercise of its discretion.[3825] It was therefore within the Trial Chamber's discretion to consider its earlier finding that Župljanin's orders were ineffective and not meant to be implemented as a factor affecting mitigation. Given that the Trial Chamber noted in the context of sentencing Župljanin's arguments on his actions to prevent and punish crimes,[3826] and yet considered that his orders were ineffective and not genuine, the Appeals Chamber considers that Župljanin merely disagrees with the Trial Chamber's conclusion. The Appeals Chamber therefore finds that Župljanin has failed to demonstrate that the Trial Chamber committed a discernible error regarding his purported efforts to prevent, investigate, and punish crimes in determining the appropriate sentence.

(ii) Alleged failure to consider exigent and chaotic conditions faced in Župljanin's exercise of his duties

1164. Župljanin submits that the Trial Chamber erroneously rejected, as a mitigating factor, the exigent circumstances he faced which made fulfilling his duties difficult or dangerous.[3827] He **[page 483]** argues that the Trial Chamber failed to address: (i) the death threats he received; (ii) the chaotic circumstances of war, including the influx of refugees and the lack of a proper communication system; and (iii) the inadequate operation of the local courts and prosecutor's office.[3828] Župljanin further contends that he was only a police

---

[3818]   Trial Judgement, vol. 2, paras 893, 897.

[3819]   Trial Judgement, vol. 2, para. 456.

[3820]   *Popović et al.* Appeal Judgement, para. 2006; *Mrkšić and Šljivančanin* Appeal Judgement, para. 379.

[3821]   The Appeals Chamber notes that, in his closing arguments, Župljanin specifically referred to "the incident along the Stanari-Teslić road where [he] prevented the killing of 600 non-Serbs" as shedding light on his personality (Hearing, 1 Jun 2012, T. 27629-27630).

[3822]   See *supra*, para. 1159.

[3823]   Trial Judgement, vol. 2, para. 953. See Trial Judgement, vol. 2, para. 514. See also Trial Judgement, vol. 2, para. 519. The Appeals Chamber notes that the Trial Chamber's finding was based on various findings along with evidence relating to: (i) the criminal activities of the members of the SOS (see Trial Judgement, vol. 2, paras 387-388, 404, 419, 499, 514, 519); (ii) the "feigned" commission that Župljanin had appointed (see Trial Judgement, vol. 2, paras 514, 519); and (iii) Župljanin's provision of false information to the judicial authorities in order to shield his subordinates from criminal prosecution – including in relation to the Korićanske Stijene killings and the death of prisoners in front of the Manjača detention camp (see Trial Judgement, vol. 2, paras 516-517, 519).

[3824]   See *supra*, paras 837-869.

[3825]   *Tolimir* Appeal Judgement, para. 644; *Popović et al.* Appeal Judgement, para. 2053; *Đorđević* Appeal Judgement, para. 944; *Čelebići* Appeal Judgement, paras, 777, 780.

[3826]   Trial Judgement, vol. 2, paras 943, 945.

[3827]   Župljanin Appeal Brief, paras 246, 261-264. See Župljanin Reply Brief, para. 84; Appeal Hearing, 16 Dec 2015, AT. 182-183.

[3828]   Župljanin Appeal Brief, paras 261-262. See Appeal Hearing, 16 Dec 2015, AT. 180, referring to SD166, SD167, SD182, SD172 (the Appeals Chamber understands this to be references to the testimonies of Witness Drago Raković, Witness Raljić, Witness Radulović, and Witness ST172, Exhibits 2D52, P595, P621, P160, 2D50, 2D91, 2D25, and P560).

officer and not a political figure.[3829] He also argues that the difficulty in enforcing orders in wartime has previously been taken into account as a factor in sentencing.[3830]

1165. The Prosecution responds that Župljanin repeats his trial arguments without showing that the Trial Chamber committed a discernible error.[3831]

1166. The Appeals Chamber notes that although Župljanin raised the chaotic context of war at trial, and in particular, the breakdown in communications and the operation of civilian courts,[3832] the Trial Chamber did not expressly consider it as a mitigating circumstance.[3833] In this regard, the Appeals Chamber recalls that "the chaotic context of a conflict cannot be taken into account in mitigation".[3834] By raising these matters again on appeal, Župljanin merely repeats his trial arguments without showing how the Trial Chamber committed a discernible error. The Appeals Chamber also finds Župljanin's argument that he was not a political figure to be irrelevant and undeveloped as he has failed to show how this could be considered as a mitigating factor.

1167. Turning to Župljanin's argument that he received death threats, the Appeals Chamber notes that, as part of his case at trial, he referred to death threats issued against him as well as threats to remove him from his post,[3835] but did not expressly raise this as a mitigating factor.[3836] The Appeals Chamber further notes that the Trial Chamber considered elsewhere in the Trial Judgement that **[page 484]** Župljanin was required under national law to carry out activities and tasks concerning national and public security even when this placed his life in danger.[3837] The Appeals Chamber considers that it was within the discretion of the Trial Chamber not to consider in mitigation the circumstances surrounding the exercise of a duty which is required by law. Furthermore, Župljanin's submission regarding death threats is unconvincing as he cites: (i) Witness Dragan Majkić's testimony that Župljanin himself told the witness that he received threats without citing any further corroborating evidence;[3838] and (ii) testimony on threats to remove persons from their posts but this evidence does not speak to death threats made against Župljanin.[3839] It was consequently within the Trial Chamber's discretion not to consider this factor in mitigation, and Župljanin has failed to show that a discernible error was committed.

(iii) Alleged failure to consider Župljanin's age and the country where he will serve his sentence

1168. Župljanin submits that the Trial Chamber failed to consider his age even though, in other cases, age has been routinely recognised as a mitigating factor.[3840] Župljanin also submits that the Trial Chamber failed to consider, in mitigation, that he will serve his sentence in a foreign country.[3841]

[3829] Župljanin Appeal Brief, para. 262.

[3830] Župljanin Appeal Brief, para. 261, referring to *Blaškić* Appeal Judgement, para. 711. See Župljanin Reply Brief, para. 84.

[3831] Prosecution Response Brief (Župljanin), para. 220, referring to Župljanin Final Trial Brief, paras 15(g), 22, 43, 51, 277, 377-382, 433. See Prosecution Response Brief (Župljanin), paras 221-222. The Prosecution also argues that Župljanin cannot benefit from this chaotic circumstance given that he significantly contributed to its creation and maintenance (Prosecution Response Brief (Župljanin), para. 222).

[3832] See Župljanin Final Trial Brief, paras 15(g), 22, 43, 47, 50-51, 277, 377-382, 433; Hearing, 31 May 2012, T. 27553-27555.

[3833] See Trial Judgement, vol. 2, paras 952-953. See also Trial Judgement, vol. 2, paras 941-945.

[3834] *Bralo* Sentencing Appeal Judgement, para. 13. See *Blaškić* Appeal Judgement, para. 711 ("a finding that a 'chaotic' context might be considered as a mitigating factor in circumstances of combat operations risks mitigating the criminal conduct of all personnel in a war zone. Conflict is by its nature chaotic, and it is incumbent on the participants to reduce that chaos").

[3835] Župljanin Final Trial Brief, paras 50(e), 62-63. *Cf.* Hearing, 31 May 2012, T. 27553-27595; Hearing, 1 Jun 2012, T. 27596-27640.

[3836] In this regard, the Appeals Chamber recalls that appeal proceedings are not the appropriate forum to raise mitigating circumstances for the first time (*Tolimir* Appeal Judgement, para. 644; *Popović et al.* Appeal Judgement, para. 2060; *Đorđević* Appeal Judgement, para. 945. See *Šainović et al.* Appeal Judgement, para. 1816).

[3837] Trial Judgement, vol. 2, para. 354, referring to Exhibit P530, Article 42.

[3838] See Dragan Majkić, 16 Nov 2009, T. 3200-3201.

[3839] Predrag Radulović, 1 Jun 2010, T. 11161-11162, referring to Exhibit 2D91. See ST172, 21 Jan 2010, T. 5320-5327; ST172, 22 Jan 2010, T. 5328-5405.

[3840] Župljanin Appeal Brief, para. 265, referring to *Krnojelac* Trial Judgement, para. 533, *Plavšić* Sentencing Judgement, paras 105-106, *Erdemović* Sentencing Judgement, para. 16, *Simić et al.* Trial Judgement, para. 1099. Župljanin argues that if he were to serve his sentence of 22 years of imprisonment he would be "nearly 80 years old when released" (Župljanin Appeal Brief, para. 265).

[3841] Župljanin Appeal Brief, para. 266, referring to *Prosecutor v. Issa Hassan Sesay et al.*, Case No SCSL-04-15-T, Sentencing Judgement, 8 April 2009, para. 206.

1169. The Prosecution responds that Župljanin's arguments should be dismissed as he raises these mitigating factors for the first time on appeal and they fall outside his notice of appeal.[3842] It further submits that "only limited weight can be attached to advanced age"[3843] and with regard to Župljanin serving his sentence in a foreign country, argues that although trial chambers have noted that it "may constitute an additional hardship, they have never considered it a mitigating factor".[3844]

1170. The Appeals Chamber notes that Župljanin did not put forward at trial, his age or the fact that his sentence would be served in another country as mitigating factors, and the Trial Chamber **[page 485]** did not consider these factors.[3845] The Appeals Chamber recalls in this regard that appeal proceedings are not the appropriate forum to raise mitigating circumstances for the first time.[3846] In any event, the Appeals Chamber considers that in light of the limited weight given to advanced age as mitigating factor in the jurisprudence of the Tribunal,[3847] Župljanin has not demonstrated that the Trial Chamber erred in failing to consider that his age warrants mitigation, if any at all.[3848] Further, the Appeals Chamber finds that Župljanin has failed to demonstrate why, in his particular case, the Trial Chamber should have considered the fact that he will serve his sentence in a foreign country as a mitigating factor.[3849]

(iv) Conclusion

1171. Based on the foregoing, the Appeals Chamber considers that Župljanin has failed to demonstrate any error in the Trial Chamber's assessment of mitigating circumstances. Therefore, the Appeals Chamber dismisses sub-grounds (A) and (C) of Župljanin's fourth ground of appeal.

(d) Conclusion

1172. For the foregoing reasons, the Appeals Chamber dismisses Župljanin's fourth ground of appeal in its entirety.

D. Prosecution

1. Alleged errors in relation to Stanišić and Župljanin's sentences (Prosecution's first ground of appeal)

1173. The Prosecution submits that the Trial Chamber erred by imposing manifestly inadequate sentences on Stanišić and Župljanin.[3850] It argues that the Trial Chamber: (i) failed to give **[page 486]** appropriate

---

[3842]   Prosecution Response Brief (Župljanin), para. 223.
[3843]   Prosecution Response Brief (Župljanin), para. 224, referring to *Jokić* Sentencing Judgement (with references), *Krnojelac* Trial Judgement, para. 533, *Krnojelac* Appeal Judgement, para. 251.
[3844]   Prosecution Response Brief (Župljanin), para. 225, referring to *Tadić* Sentencing Appeal Judgement, paras 18, 22-23; *Mrđa* Sentencing Judgement, para. 109; *RUF* Appeal Judgement, para. 1246.
[3845]   See Trial Judgement, vol. 2, paras 941-945, 952-953. See generally Župljanin Final Trial Brief; Hearing, 31 May 2012, T. 27553-27595; Hearing, 1 Jun 2012, T. 27596-27640.
[3846]   *Tolimir* Appeal Judgement, para. 644; *Popović et al.* Appeal Judgement, para. 2060; *Đorđević* Appeal Judgement, para. 945. See *Šainović et al.* Appeal Judgement, para. 1816.
[3847]   See *e.g. Babić* Sentencing Appeal Judgement, para. 43; *Blaškić* Appeal Judgement, para. 696; *Jokić* Sentencing Judgement, para. 100; *Plavšić* Sentencing Judgement, para. 106. See also *Tolimir* Appeal Judgement, para. 644; *Popović et al.* Appeal Judgement, para. 2052.
[3848]   See *e.g. Jokić* Sentencing Judgement, paras 100-102; *Kordić and Čerkez* Trial Judgement, para. 848.
[3849]   In this respect, the Appeals Chamber notes that in certain cases of the Tribunal, given that the serving of a sentence in a foreign country is a common aspect of prison sentences imposed by the Tribunal, it was not recognised as a mitigating factor. See *Mrđa* Sentencing Judgement, para. 109; *Tadić* Sentencing Appeal Judgement, paras 18(iii), 22-23. See also *RUF* Appeal Judgement, para. 1246 (recalling the common practice that convicted persons from international criminal tribunals serve their sentences in foreign countries, the *RUF* Appeals Chamber concluded that the appellant had "not referred to any case in which serving the sentence in a foreign country has been considered as a mitigating factor for sentencing purposes"). The Appeals Chamber considers that it is unnecessary to address the Prosecution's argument that these mitigating factors raised by Župljanin fall outside the scope of his notice of appeal.
[3850]   Prosecution Appeal Brief, paras 1, 53; Prosecution Consolidated Reply Brief, para. 2. See Appeal Hearing, 16 Dec 2015, AT. 214-227.

weight to the seriousness of the crimes;[3851] (ii) failed to give appropriate weight to Stanišić's and Župljanin's leadership positions within the JCE and the degree of their participation in the commission of crimes;[3852] and (iii) imposed a sentence outside the range imposed in similar cases.[3853] According to the Prosecution, in order to properly reflect the gravity of their crimes, the Appeals Chamber should substitute the sentences of 22 years imposed on Stanišić and Župljanin by the Trial Chamber with sentences in the range of 30 to 40 years.[3854] Stanišić and Župljanin respond that the Prosecution's arguments should be dismissed as it has failed to show that the Trial Chamber abused its sentencing discretion and committed an error.[3855]

(a) Alleged error in relation to the weight given to the seriousness of the crimes

(i)Submissions of the parties

1174. The Prosecution submits that the sentences imposed on Stanišić and Župljanin by the Trial Chamber do not adequately reflect the seriousness of the crimes for which they were convicted.[3856] It argues that the Trial Chamber failed to give adequate weight to: (i) the broad geographic and temporal scope of the crimes and their discriminatory and systematic nature;[3857] (ii) the use of arbitrary arrests, prolonged detention, brutal violence, sexual violence, and killings;[3858] and (iii) the devastating and lasting effect of the crimes on more than 100,000 victims.[3859]

1175. Stanišić and Župljanin respond that the Prosecution fails to demonstrate that the Trial Chamber erroneously considered the factors the Prosecution enumerates.[3860] Stanišić further submits that in any event, the Prosecution's submissions in support of its request for the imposition of a higher sentence are "fundamentally erroneous" as they are based on inconclusive Trial Chamber's findings.[3861] Župljanin submits that the Prosecution mischaracterises the Trial **[page 487]** Chamber's findings.[3862] According to Župljanin, if anything, the Trial Chamber afforded too much weight to the factors cited by the Prosecution, thereby failing to individualise his sentence.[3863]

(ii) Analysis

1176. The Appeals Chamber notes that, in assessing the gravity of the crimes for the purposes of determination of sentence, the Trial Chamber considered that Stanišić and Župljanin were found responsible

---

[3851]   Prosecution Appeal Brief, paras 4, 7-26.
[3852]   Prosecution Appeal Brief, paras 5, 27-48.
[3853]   Prosecution Appeal Brief, paras 49-52.
[3854]   Prosecution Appeal Brief, paras 1, 3, 49, 53.
[3855]   Stanišić Response Brief, paras 3, 110; Župljanin Response Brief, paras 2, 16.
[3856]   Prosecution Appeal Brief, paras 4, 7, 26. See Prosecution Appeal Brief, paras 8-25; Appeal Hearing, 16 Dec 2015, AT. 219-224.
[3857]   Prosecution Appeal Brief, paras 7-9. The Prosecution asserts that Stanišić's and Župljanin's crimes "continued over a nine-month period, across multiple municipalities in BiH, and harmed well over 100,000 victims" (Prosecution Appeal Brief, para. 8). It further submits that Stanišić and Župljanin were ultimately responsible for the expulsion of "well over" 130,000 and 100,000 non-Serbs from their homes, respectively (Prosecution Appeal Brief, para. 9). See Appeal Hearing, 16 Dec 2015, AT. 219-224, 227.
[3858]   See Prosecution Appeal Brief, paras 7-8, 10-25. The Prosecution notes, in particular, the incidents at the Omarska detention camp (Prosecution Appeal Brief, paras 15-17), Manjača detention camp (Prosecution Appeal Brief, paras 18-20), SJB building (Prosecution Appeal Brief, paras 21-22), and Celopek Dom (Prosecution Appeal Brief, paras 23-24). See also Appeal Hearing, 16 Dec 2015, AT. 220-224 (referring to the gravity of the crimes).
[3859]   Prosecution Appeal Brief, paras 7, 25-26. The Prosecution submits that both Stanišić and Župljanin were convicted for forcibly displacing non-Serbs from Serb-claimed territory and, relying on paragraph 813 of the *Krajišnik* Appeal Judgement, argues that persecutory deportation and forcible transfer are among the most severe crimes known to humankind (See Appeal Hearing, 16 Dec 2015, AT. 219-220).
[3860]   Stanišić Response Brief, paras 7, 15-30, 33-34, 39-41; Župljanin Response Brief, para. 3. See Stanišić Response Brief, paras 12-13.
[3861]   Stanišić Response Brief, paras 8, 42-43. In particular, Stanišić contends that the Prosecution's submissions are based on the Trial Chamber's failure to determine the extent to which: (i) RS MUP policemen were re-subordinated to the military; and (ii) municipal crisis staffs were acting independently (Stanišić Response Brief, paras 44-56). See Stanišić Appeal Brief, paras 33-39. See also Appeal Hearing, 16 Dec 2015, AT. 230-231.
[3862]   Župljanin Response Brief, paras 4-7.
[3863]   Župljanin Response Brief, paras 8-9.

441

for "massive" crimes in 20 and eight municipalities, respectively.[3864] The Trial Chamber also considered that these crimes were committed as part of a widespread and systematic campaign of violence and terror.[3865] It further considered that the victims numbered in the thousands, and took into account the effect of the crimes on these victims and that many of them were vulnerable persons such as children, women, the elderly, and those deprived of their liberty in detention centres.[3866] In addition, the Trial Chamber took into account the length of time during which crimes that Stanišić and Župljanin were found guilty of were committed, namely, a period of nine months.[3867] The Trial Chamber thus clearly took into account and gave weight to these factors when determining the sentences to be imposed upon Stanišić and Župljanin. The Appeals Chamber emphasises in this context that the appropriate weight to be accorded to a particular factor is within the broad discretion of a trial chamber.[3868] Other than repeating the Trial Chamber's findings, the Prosecution has failed to demonstrate that the Trial Chamber gave insufficient weight to these factors in its determination of sentence. The Appeals Chamber therefore finds that the Prosecution has failed to demonstrate any error in the Trial Chamber's exercise of discretion. **[page 488]**

(b) Alleged error in weight attributed to Stanišić and Župljanin's roles and the degree of their participation in the crimes

(i) Submissions of the parties

1177. The Prosecution submits that the Trial Chamber failed to give adequate weight to Stanišić's and Župljanin's precise leadership roles and the degree of their participation in the crimes through the implementation of the JCE.[3869] With regard to Stanišić, the Prosecution submits that he was among the most senior figures within the leadership of the JCE, that "there were few who were more senior" to him by his own account,[3870] and argues that his participation in the JCE was extensive and enduring.[3871] In relation to Župljanin, the Prosecution submits that he was "zealous" in furthering the common criminal purpose of the JCE,[3872] and that, moreover, the Trial Chamber failed to give adequate weight to its finding that Župljanin ordered the appropriation of property of non-Serbs despite recognising this factor in its assessment of the gravity of the crimes.[3873] According to the Prosecution, Stanišić's and Župljanin's actions to further the JCE created the situation in which the crimes of the low-level perpetrators were allowed to take place on a massive scale.[3874] It further submits that the Trial Chamber, while properly identifying aggravating factors, failed to give adequate weight to Stanišić's and Župljanin's betrayal of the trust vested in them as police officials by "neutralizing the police as a force for law and order, and its subversion into a unit of destruction and terror".[3875]

1178. Stanišić responds that he was neither "intimately involved" in the implementation of the JCE nor "highly important" to its success[3876] and that the Prosecution fails to demonstrate that his purported position within the JCE warrants an increase of his "manifestly excessive sentence".[3877] He submits that the

---

[3864] Trial Judgement, vol. 2, paras 927, 946. See also Trial Judgement, vol. 2, paras 919, 948.
[3865] Trial Judgement, vol. 2, paras 927, 946.
[3866] Trial Judgement, vol. 2, paras 927, 946.
[3867] Trial Judgement, vol. 2, paras 930, 949.
[3868] *Tolimir* Appeal Judgement, para. 644; *Popović et al.* Appeal Judgement, para. 2053; *Đorđević* Appeal Judgement, para. 944; *Čelebići* Appeal Judgement, paras, 777, 780. See *supra*, para. 1100.
[3869] Prosecution Appeal Brief, paras 5, 27-29, 47. See Appeal Hearing, 16 Dec 2015, AT. 220-221.
[3870] Prosecution Appeal Brief, para. 30. See Prosecution Appeal Brief, paras 5-6, 31; Prosecution Consolidated Reply Brief, para. 6.
[3871] Prosecution Appeal Brief, paras 6, 30-31, 47. See Prosecution Appeal Brief, paras 5, 32-38; Prosecution Consolidated Reply Brief, para. 6.
[3872] Prosecution Appeal Brief, para. 41. For further submissions concerning Župljanin's participation in the JCE, see Prosecution Appeal Brief, paras 6, 39-40, 42-45.
[3873] Prosecution Appeal Brief, para. 44.
[3874] Appeal Hearing, 16 Dec 2015, AT. 224. See Appeal Hearing, 16 Dec 2015, AT. 225-226.
[3875] Prosecution Appeal Brief, para. 46. See Prosecution Appeal Brief, paras 47-48. See also Appeal Hearing, 16 Dec 2015, AT. 224-225.
[3876] Stanišić Response Brief, para. 57; Appeal Hearing, 16 Dec 2015, AT. 232.
[3877] Stanišić Response Brief, para. 65; Appeal Hearing, 16 Dec 2015, AT. 232.

Prosecution fails to demonstrate that: (i) he was among the most senior JCE leaders, arguing that he was not a key member of the Bosnian Serb decision-making authorities;[3878] **[page 489]** and (ii) his participation in the JCE was extensive and enduring.[3879] Stanišić contends that his purported role in the JCE was "very limited", with his acts and conduct aimed at impeding the JCE rather than furthering it.[3880]

1179. Župljanin responds that the Prosecution's characterisation of his "zealous" participation in the JCE[3881] does not accord with the Trial Chamber's findings.[3882] He submits, moreover, that contrary to the Prosecution's submission, the Trial Chamber considered his involvement in ordering the appropriation of property of non-Serbs within the context of his participation in the JCE and that there was no need for the Trial Chamber to address this crime separately from his contribution to the JCE, given its relative insignificance and the lack of evidence about its impact.[3883] Župljanin submits that even if, *arguendo*, the Trial Chamber should have given weight to this particular conduct separately from his participation in the JCE, the crime in question was not of such severity as to render the imposed sentence unreasonable.[3884]

(ii) Analysis

1180. In assessing the gravity of the crimes for the purposes of determination of sentence,[3885] the Trial Chamber considered that Stanišić and Župljanin were high-level police officials at the time of the commission of the crimes[3886] and took into account that they were found to have committed the crimes through their participation in the JCE.[3887] The Trial Chamber also considered in aggravation that in undertaking their participation in the JCE in their respective capacities as Minister of Interior and Chief of the CSB Banja Luka, Stanišić and Župljanin abused their respective positions.[3888] **[page 490]**

1181. The Appeals Chamber observes that in its determination of sentence, the Trial Chamber did not explicitly reiterate its findings on Stanišić's or Župljanin's conduct and the form and degree of their participation in the crimes. However, the Appeals Chamber recalls that a trial judgement should be read as a whole.[3889] The considerations of the Trial Chamber in the context of sentencing must thus be read in conjunction with the rest of the Trial Judgement, including the Trial Chamber's findings on Stanišić's and Župljanin's roles and the degree of their participation in the crimes.[3890] In light of these findings, the Appeals Chamber is satisfied that the Trial Chamber took into account and gave weight to these factors when determining the sentences to be imposed.[3891] Further, the Appeals Chamber again emphasises that the weight

---

[3878] Stanišić Response Brief, paras 58-63.

[3879] Stanišić Response Brief, paras 9, 66-72, 85. Stanišić submits that the Prosecution bases its submissions regarding his role and responsibility on inconclusive and fundamentally flawed findings of the Trial Chamber in relation to, *inter alia*, the issue of re-subordination of the RS MUP forces to the military, and the conflicting authority between the RS MUP and municipal authorities (Stanišić Response Brief, paras 8, 33-39, 42-56, 72-74, 79. See Appeal Hearing, 16 Dec 2015, AT. 230-231). Stanišić also argues that the Trial Chamber's findings are inconclusive in relation to his knowledge of the commission of crimes by joint Serb forces (Stanišić Response Brief, paras 75-77).

[3880] Stanišić Response Brief, paras 87, 93 (emphasis omitted). See Stanišić Response Brief, para. 68. In this respect, Stanišić points to, *inter alia*, the fact that he: (i) aimed to fulfil his duties as an RS MUP official in accordance with the law (Stanišić Response Brief, para. 92. See Stanišić Response Brief, paras 82-83); (ii) initiated disciplinary proceedings against several individuals who were found to have been members of the JCE, as acknowledged by the Trial Chamber (Stanišić Response Brief, paras 80-81, 84, 88, 90); and (iii) had clashes with high-ranking individuals within the JCE due to actions he took to prevent criminal actions of paramilitaries (Stanišić Response Brief, paras 5, 91). See also Appeal Hearing, 16 Dec 2015, AT. 231.

[3881] Župljanin Response Brief, para. 4.

[3882] Župljanin Response Brief, paras 4-7, 9.

[3883] Župljanin Response Brief, paras 13-15.

[3884] Župljanin Response Brief, para. 15.

[3885] Trial Judgement, vol. 2, paras 927-928, 946-947.

[3886] Trial Judgement, vol. 2, paras 927, 946.

[3887] Trial Judgement, vol. 2, paras 928, 947. The Appeals Chamber notes that in relation to Župljanin, the Trial Chamber took into account that he was found to have committed "the majority" of the crimes through his participation in the JCE (Trial Judgement, vol. 2, para. 947).

[3888] Trial Judgement, vol. 2, paras 929, 931, 948, 950.

[3889] *Popović et al.* Appeal Judgement, para. 2006; *Mrkšić and Šljivančanin* Appeal Judgement, para. 379.

[3890] See, *inter alia*, Trial Judgement, vol. 2, paras 492-493, 518, 522, 524 (concerning Župljanin); Trial Judgement, vol. 2, paras 729, 731-734, 736, 740-759, 761-765 (concerning Stanišić). See also *supra*, para. 1107.

[3891] See *supra*, paras 1107-1108, 1110, 1147-1150.

to be accorded to a particular factor in sentencing is within the broad discretion of a trial chamber.[3892] Aside from repeating the Trial Chamber's findings, the Prosecution has failed to demonstrate that the Trial Chamber erred in its discretion when according weight to these factors.

1182. Further, as regards the Prosecution's argument that the Trial Chamber failed to give adequate weight to its finding that Župljanin ordered the appropriation of property of non-Serbs, the Appeals Chamber observes that, as acknowledged by the Prosecution,[3893] the Trial Chamber recognised in its assessment of the gravity of the crimes that Župljanin was found to have committed crimes beyond his participation in the JCE.[3894] The Appeals Chamber considers that, aside from disagreeing with the weight given to this factor by the Trial Chamber, the Prosecution has failed to demonstrate that the Trial Chamber committed a discernible error in the exercise of its broad sentencing discretion.

(c) Alleged error in imposing a sentence outside the range of sentences imposed in similar cases

(i) Submissions of the parties

1183. The Prosecution submits that it is evident from the sentencing practice of the Tribunal in other, similar cases that the Trial Chamber manifestly failed to give adequate weight to the seriousness of the crimes, the roles of Stanišić and Župljanin, and their degree of participation in the **[page 491]** crimes.[3895] According to the Prosecution, the *Brđanin* and *Stakić* cases are particularly relevant to the assessment of the sentences in the present case and demonstrate that the Trial Chamber should have imposed sentences "at least within the range of 30-40 years".[3896] The Prosecution additionally relies on a number of other cases which, in its view, demonstrate that a sentence of 22 years is erroneous for an accused convicted as a member of a joint criminal enterprise for crimes committed in eight or more municipalities.[3897] Finally, the Prosecution submits that the mitigating factors recognised by the Trial Chamber do not justify the manifestly inadequate sentences imposed, especially when viewed together with the aggravating factors found by the Trial Chamber – namely, Stanišić's and Župljanin's abuse of their superior positions, the extensive duration of the crimes, and "their insight into the context and legal nature of the crimes resulting from their careers and education".[3898]

1184. In response, Stanišić and Župljanin submit that the *Brđanin* and *Stakić* cases can be distinguished from the present case on a number of bases.[3899] Stanišić contends that the other cases cited by the

---

[3892] *Tolimir* Appeal Judgement, para. 644; *Popović et al.* Appeal Judgement, para. 2053; *Đorđević* Appeal Judgement, para. 944; *Čelebići* Appeal Judgement, paras, 777, 780. See *supra*, para. 1100.

[3893] Prosecution Appeal Brief, para. 44.

[3894] Trial Judgement, vol. 2, para. 947, where the Trial Chamber stated that in determining Župljanin's sentence, it had taken into account that Župljanin was found to have committed "the majority" of the crimes through his participation in the JCE.

[3895] Prosecution Appeal Brief, para. 49. The Prosecution argues that the sentence of 22 years imposed by the Trial Chamber places Stanišić and Župljanin's criminal responsibility in the same range as the "low-level" perpetrators who committed one or more of the "well over 100.000 crimes for which they were convicted", which sends out the wrong message (see Appeal Hearing, 16 Dec 2015, AT. 227-228).

[3896] Prosecution Appeal Brief, para. 50. The Prosecution further argues that the appropriate sentence for leadership perpetration through a joint criminal enterprise must not be less than those imposed in equivalent leadership cases (Appeal Hearing, 16 Dec 2015, AT. 228-229). It notes, in particular, that in the *Brđanin* case and *Stakić* case higher sentences (30 years and 40 years of imprisonment, respectively) were imposed in relation to convictions for fewer municipalities and/or for a less grave form of responsibility than Stanišić and Župljanin (Prosecution Appeal Brief, para. 50, referring to *Brđanin* Appeal Judgement, paras 229, 241, 290, 304, 321, 506, *Stakić* Appeal Judgement, paras 73, 83-84, 89, 428. See Prosecution Consolidated Reply Brief, paras 15-16).

[3897] See Prosecution Appeal Brief, para. 51, fns 185-188. The Prosecution refers specifically to: (i) *Kvočka et al.* Appeal Judgement, in which accused Zigic was sentenced to 25 years for "crimes at the camps in Prijedor alone" (Prosecution Appeal Brief, para. 51, fn. 186); (ii) the *Krajišnik* Appeal Judgement, where the Appeals Chamber "reduced *Krajišnik's* responsibility as a JCE member to crimes in just seven Bosnian municipalities" and "reduced his sentence from 27 years to 20 years accordingly" (Prosecution Appeal Brief, fn. 185); and (iii) the *Plavsic* Sentencing Judgement, where the Trial Chamber "gave weight to 'the age of the accused and the significant mitigating factors connected with her plea of guilty and post-conflict conduct'" and "so imposed a sentence of 11 years" (Prosecution Appeal Brief, fn. 185). It also refers to the *Zelenović, Banović, Mrđa, D. Nikolić*, and *Jelisić* cases, where the accused were sentenced to between 8 and 40 years' imprisonment (Prosecution Appeal Brief, para. 51, fns 187-188). See also Appeal Hearing, 16 Dec 2015, AT. 214-219.

[3898] Prosecution Appeal Brief, para. 52.

[3899] Stanišić Response Brief, paras 96-97; Župljanin Response Brief, paras 10-12. See Stanišić Response Brief, para. 95.

Prosecution[3900] may also be distinguished from the case at hand, because "in these cases [...] each of the accused was personally and directly involved in the commission of crimes".[3901] Stanišić further submits that the Trial Chamber failed to give sufficient weight to a number of mitigating factors.[3902] Župljanin submits that the Prosecution suggests that his sentence **[page 492]** should not be any less than for other leadership cases arising from similar circumstances without according any value to intent in assessing culpability and deciding upon sentencing.[3903]

(ii) <u>Analysis</u>

1185. The Appeals Chamber recalls that previous sentencing decisions of the Tribunal may be of assistance if they involve the commission of the same offences in substantially similar circumstances.[3904] It also recalls that a sentence should not be "capricious or excessive, and that, in principle, it may be thought to be capricious or excessive if it is out of reasonable proportion with a line of sentences passed in similar circumstances for the same offences".[3905] This does not, however, override a trial chamber's obligation to tailor a penalty to fit the individual circumstances of an accused and the gravity of the crime.[3906] Thus, comparisons with the sentences imposed in other cases are, as a general rule, "of limited assistance" as "often the differences [between cases] are more significant than the similarities, and the mitigating and aggravating factors dictate different results".[3907]

1186. Turning to the cases relied upon by the Prosecution, the Appeals Chamber notes that the *Brđanin* case – like the present case, in part – relates to crimes committed by Bosnian Serb forces in the ARK during 1992.[3908] However, while there may be some overlap between the relevant offences and circumstances of the two cases, the Appeals Chamber does not consider that the fact that Brđanin received a sentence of 30 years, reflecting the particular circumstances of that case and his role, demonstrates that the Trial Chamber erred in sentencing Stanišić and Župljanin each to 22 years of imprisonment.[3909] Similarly, the Appeals Chamber does not consider that the sentence of 40 years imposed on Stakić, which reflects the particular circumstances of that case and his role, **[page 493]** demonstrates that the Trial Chamber in the present case committed an error in imposing sentences of 22 years.[3910]

[3900]   See Stanišić Response Brief, paras 98-102; Appeal Hearing, 16 Dec 2015, AT. 214-219.
[3901]   Stanišić Response Brief, para.102. See Stanišić Response Brief, paras 98-101, Appeal Hearing, 16 Dec 2015, AT. 214-219; Stanišić Response Brief, paras 99-101. See also Appeal Hearing, 16 Dec 2015, AT. 231-232.
[3902]   Stanišić Response Brief, paras 104-107.
[3903]   Appeal Hearing, 16 Dec 2015, AT. 235-236.
[3904]   *Babić* Sentencing Appeal Judgement, para. 32; *Čelebići* Appeal Judgement, para. 720. See *Popović et al.* Appeal Judgement, para. 2093, quoting *Strugar* Appeal Judgement, para. 348; *Đorđević* Appeal Judgement, para. 949.
[3905]   *Jelisić* Appeal Judgement, para. 96. See *Đorđević* Appeal Judgement, para. 949. See also *Popović et al.* Appeal Judgement, para. 2093, quoting *Strugar* Appeal Judgement, para. 348.
[3906]   *Babić* Sentencing Appeal Judgement, para. 32. See *Tolimir* Appeal Judgement, para. 626; *Popović et al.* Appeal Judgement, para. 1961; *Đorđević* Appeal Judgement, para. 931; *Šainović et al.* Appeal Judgement, para. 1837; *Nyiramasuhuko et al.* Appeal Judgement, para. 3349.
[3907]   *Čelebići* Appeal Judgement, para. 719. See *Babić* Sentencing Appeal Judgement, para. 32, quoting *D. Nikolić* Sentencing Appeal Judgement, para. 19.
[3908]   See *Brđanin* Trial Judgement, paras 1-19.
[3909]   See *Brđanin* Trial Judgement, paras 1093-1140; *Brđanin* Appeal Judgement, paras 498-501, 506, p. 157. The Appeals Chamber notes that Brđanin was convicted of crimes under eight counts of the indictment, having been found guilty on the basis of aiding and abetting liability, as well as on the basis of having instigated and ordered crimes (see *Brđanin* Trial Judgement, paras 475-476, 534-538, 577-583, 669-670, 677-678, 1054, 1061, 1071, 1075. See also *Brđanin* Trial Judgement, para. 1067). The Appeals Chamber further observes that in sentencing Brđanin, the *Brđanin* Trial Chamber took into account numerous aggravating and mitigating circumstances which are specific to him, as well as the gravity of his offences (*Brđanin* Trial Judgement, paras 1093-1140. See *Brđanin* Appeal Judgement, paras 498-501, 506).
[3910]   See *Stakić* Appeal Judgement, p. 142. The Appeals Chamber notes that Stakić was convicted of crimes under five counts of the indictment, having been found guilty on the basis of "co-perpetratorship", and in relation to deportation also found him liable on the basis of having planned and ordered the crime (see *Stakić* Trial Judgement, paras 468, 616, 661, 712, 826, 914, p. 253). On appeal, the Appeals Chamber set aside, *proprio motu*, the *Stakić* Trial Chamber's finding that Stakić was responsible as a co-perpetrator and instead found him responsible on the basis of joint criminal enterprise liability (see *Stakić* Appeal Judgement, p. 141). In addition, the *Stakić* Appeals Chamber vacated Stakić's legal responsibility for certain acts of deportation (*Stakić* Appeal Judgement, p. 141. See also *Stakić* Trial Judgement, paras 654, 906, 912, 916). The *Stakić* Trial Chamber also took into account a number of aggravating and mitigating circumstances which are specific to him, as well as the gravity of his offences (*Stakić* Trial Judgement, paras 910, 912-915, 917-919, 921-924).

445

1187. The Appeals Chamber is also of the view that the other cases referred to by the Prosecution are inapposite, as the specific circumstances in these cases differ significantly from those in the present case.[3911] As such, these cases do not demonstrate that the Trial Chamber erred in the exercise of its discretion when sentencing Stanišić and Župljanin each to 22 years of imprisonment. For these reasons, and emphasising the Trial Chamber's considerable discretion in sentencing matters, the Appeals Chamber considers that the Prosecution has failed to demonstrate any discernible error on the part of the Trial Chamber by pointing to other allegedly similar cases.

1188. The Appeals Chamber now turns to the Prosecution's argument that the Trial Chamber erred by imposing a manifestly inadequate sentence which is not justified by the mitigating circumstances set out in the Trial Judgement. It recalls that "the Statute and the Rules do not define exhaustively the factors which may be taken into account by a Trial Chamber in mitigation or aggravation of sentence, and Trial Chambers are therefore endowed with a considerable degree of discretion in deciding on the factors which may be taken into account",[3912] as well as the weight to be given to each factor.[3913]

1189. The Appeals Chamber notes that the Trial Chamber took into account several factors in mitigation, including voluntary surrender,[3914] cooperation in relation to provisional release,[3915] good **[page 494]** character prior to commission of the crimes,[3916] and expression of regret or sympathy.[3917] As the Prosecution itself notes, however, the Trial Chamber expressly afforded little weight to these mitigating factors.[3918] In contrast, the Trial Chamber did give weight to the aggravating factors that it found, including abuse of superior position[3919] and the length of time during which the crimes took place,[3920] in the case of both Stanišić and Župljanin. Therefore, the Appeals Chamber rejects the Prosecution's argument that the mitigating circumstances were determinative of the sentences it imposed in this case. Moreover, the Appeals Chamber emphasises that mitigating circumstances are merely factors to be taken into account, among others, by a trial chamber in the exercise of its discretion, and do not alone justify a sentence.[3921] In these circumstances, the Prosecution has failed to identify any error on the part of the Trial Chamber.

(d) Conclusion

1190. The Appeals Chamber concludes that the Prosecution has failed to demonstrate that the Trial Chamber: (i) failed to give appropriate weight to the seriousness of the crimes; (ii) failed to give appropriate weight to Stanišić and Župljanin's leadership positions within the JCE and the degree of their participation in the commission of crimes; and (iii) imposed a sentence outside the range imposed in similar cases. Therefore, the Appeals Chamber dismisses the Prosecution's first ground of appeal in its entirety.

[3911] See *D. Nikolić* Sentencing Judgement, paras 117, 119, p. 73; *D. Nikolić* Sentencing Appeal Judgement, p. 44; *Plavsic* Sentencing Judgement, paras 5, 134 (cases where the accused pleaded guilty); *Banović* Sentencing Judgement, paras 90, 93, 95; *Mrđa* Sentencing Judgement, paras 10, 123, 125, 129; *Zelenović* Sentencing Judgement, paras 36, 38-40, 43, 71; *Zelenović* Sentencing Appeal Judgement, p. 13; *Jelisić* Trial Judgement, paras 138-139; *Jelisić* Appeal Judgement, p. 41 (cases involving principal perpetrators who pleaded guilty); *Kvočka et al.* Trial Judgement, paras 747, 764, 766; *Kvočka et al.* Appeal Judgement, paras 594-600, 716, p. 243 (involving the accused's key role in maintaining and functioning of a detention camp pursuant to the second category of joint criminal enterprise liability). See also *Krajišnik* Trial Judgement, para. 1126, p. 421; *Krajišnik* Appeal Judgement, para. 820 (involving an accused who had a senior role in the political sector of the Bosnian Serb leadership).
[3912] *Čelebići* Appeal Judgement, para. 780.
[3913] *Čelebići* Appeal Judgement, para. 777. See *Tolimir* Appeal Judgement, para. 644; *Popović et al.* Appeal Judgement, para. 2053; *Đorđević* Appeal Judgement, para. 944.
[3914] Trial Judgement, vol. 2, para. 933.
[3915] Trial Judgement, vol. 2, para. 934.
[3916] Trial Judgement, vol. 2, paras 936, 952.
[3917] Trial Judgement, vol. 2, para. 953.
[3918] Prosecution Appeal Brief, para. 52. The Appeals Chamber notes that the Trial Chamber afforded "little weight" to the character evidence put forward by Stanišić, in light of the crimes for which he was found guilty (Trial Judgement, vol. 2, para. 936). Similarly, the Trial Chamber gave little weight to the testimony received as to Župljanin's good character, in light of the crimes for which he was found guilty (Trial Judgement, vol. 2, para. 952), and considered that Župljanin's expression of regret and sympathy also carried little weight as a mitigating factor in view of those crimes (Trial Judgement, vol. 2, para. 953).
[3919] Trial Judgement, vol. 2, paras 929, 948.
[3920] Trial Judgement, vol. 2, paras 930, 949.
[3921] *Babić* Sentencing Appeal Judgement, para. 44, quoting *Niyitegeka* Appeal Judgement, para. 267.

E. Impact of the Appeals Chamber's Findings on Sentences

1191. With respect to Stanišić, the Appeals Chamber has affirmed all of his convictions. In so doing, the Appeals Chamber has upheld the Trial Chamber's conclusion on his responsibility for participation in the JCE.[3922] However, the Appeals Chamber recalls that it has reversed several findings of the Trial Chamber on his acts and failures to act considered as his contribution to the JCE. More specifically, the Appeals Chamber has found that the Trial Chamber erred in: (i) considering the appointments of Witness Todorović and Krsto Savić as Stanišić's direct **[page 495]** appointments of JCE members to the RS MUP;[3923] and (ii) finding that Stanišić failed to take decisive action to close Luka detention camp or to withdraw the RS MUP forces from it.[3924] The Appeals Chamber does not consider that these reversals affect Stanišic's overall criminal culpability for the serious crimes of which he has been convicted. The Appeals Chamber therefore affirms Stanišić's sentence of 22 years of imprisonment.

1192. With respect to Župljanin, the Appeals Chamber has affirmed all of his convictions. In so doing, the Appeals Chamber has upheld the Trial Chamber's conclusions on his responsibility for participation in the JCE – including all of its findings on his acts and failures to act considered as his contribution to the JCE[3925] – and on his responsibility for ordering the crime of persecutions through the underlying act of plunder of property.[3926] The Appeals Chamber thus affirms his sentence of 22 years of imprisonment. **[page 496]**

VIII. DISPOSITION

1193. For the foregoing reasons, **THE APPEALS CHAMBER**,

PURSUANT TO Article 25 of the Statute and Rules 117 and 118 of the Rules;

NOTING the respective written submissions of the parties and the arguments they presented at the Appeal Hearing on 16 December 2015;

SITTING in open session;

DISMISSES Mićo Stanišić's appeal in its entirety;

DISMISSES Stojan Župljanin's appeal in its entirety;

AFFIRMS Mićo Stanišić's convictions under Counts 1, 4, and 6 and Stojan Župljanin's convictions under Counts 1, 2, 4, and 6;

GRANTS the Prosecution's second ground of appeal and **FINDS** that the Trial Chamber erred by: (i) finding that convictions for the crime of persecutions as a crime against humanity under Article 5 of the Statute are impermissibly cumulative with convictions for other crimes against humanity based on the same conduct; and (ii) failing to enter convictions for Mićo Stanišić and Stojan Župljanin pursuant to Article 7(1) of the Statute under Counts 3, 5, 9, and 10, but **DECLINES** to enter new convictions against Mićo Stanišić and Stojan Župljanin on appeal under these counts;

DISMISSES the Prosecution's appeal in all other respects;

AFFIRMS the sentences of 22 years of imprisonment imposed by the Trial Chamber against Mićo Stanišić and Stojan Župljanin, respectively, subject to credit being given under Rule 101(C) of the Rules for the periods they have already spent in detention;

RULES that this Judgement shall be enforced immediately pursuant to Rule 118 of the Rules; and

---

[3922] See *supra*, paras 71, 87, 364, 585, 708.
[3923] See *supra*, paras 263, 266, 267. See also *supra*, paras 355, 359, 361, 363, 365.
[3924] See *supra*, paras 344, 354. See also *supra*, paras 268, 359, 361, 363, 365.
[3925] See *supra*, paras 71, 87, 905, 944-945, 1011, 1069.
[3926] See *supra*, para. 1078.

ORDERS in accordance with Rule 103(C) and Rule 107 of the Rules, that Mićo Stanišić and Stojan Župljanin are to remain in the custody of the Tribunal pending the finalisation of arrangements for their transfer to the State where their sentence will be served. **[page 497]**

Done in English and French, the English text being authoritative.

_____   _____
   Judge Carmel Agius, Presiding   Judge Liu Daqun

_____   _____   _____
   Judge Christoph Flügge   Judge Fausto Pocar   Judge Koffi Kumelio A. Afande

Judge Liu Daqun appends a declaration.

Judge Koffi Kumelio A. Afande appends a separate opinion.

Dated this thirtieth day of June 2016,
At The Hague,
The Netherlands.

[Seal of the Tribunal] [page 498]

IX.   DECLARATION OF JUDGE LIU

1.   In this Judgement the Appeals Chamber upholds the convictions of Stanišić and Župljanin for persecution as a crime against humanity pursuant to the third category of joint criminal enterprise ("JCE III").[1] While I am in agreement with the findings and the disposition of this Judgement, I find it apposite to append a declaration to share my views regarding perpetrators' culpability pursuant to JCE III liability for specific intent crimes.[2]

2.   Although I acknowledge that the Tribunal's jurisprudence provides for convictions for specific intent crimes on the basis of JCE III mode of liability,[3] I find myself unable to adhere to this interpretation of the law.[4] In my opinion, it defies reason to find an accused guilty of *committing* specific intent crimes while accepting at the same time that the specific intent of that accused was not proven in court. Specific intent crimes require a particular high standard of intent (*dolus specialis*), which cannot be satisfied, via the subjective element of JCE III, by *dolus eventualis*.

3.   This does not mean that the contribution of an accused, who is lacking the specific intent, to the execution of a specific intent crime shall go unpunished. This criminal behaviour could be criminalized under other modes of liability, such as aiding and abetting, provided that all other elements are fulfilled.

4.   It is not necessary to reiterate here all the reasons for my disagreement with this jurisprudence as I have already explained at length my point of view in the *Šainović et al.* case.[5] I note that similar concerns regarding this issue have also been raised by others.[6] **[page 499]**

---

[1]   Appeal Judgement, paras 600, 1011, 1193.

[2]   See Appeal Judgement, fn. 2015.

[3]   Appeal Judgement, paras 594-599 (with references cited therein).

[4]   While Stanišić and Župljanin were only found guilty for the specific intent crime of persecution, my views in this declaration, however, are relevant to all crimes within the jurisdiction of the Tribunal that require specific intent.

[5]   *Šainović et al.* Appeal Judgement, Partially Dissenting Opinion and Declaration of Judge Liu, paras 11-20.

[6]   See Special Tribunal for Lebanon, Case No. STL-11-01/I, "Interlocutory Decision on the Applicable Law: Terrorism, Conspiracy, Homicide, Perpetration, Cumulative Charging", 16 February 2011, paras 248-249 ("A problem arises from the fact that for a conviction under JCE III, the accused need not share the intent of the primary offender. This leads to a serious legal anomaly: if JCE III liability were to apply, a person could be convicted as a (co)perpetrator for a *dolus specialis* crime without possessing the requisite *dolus specialis* [...] the better approach under international criminal law is not to allow convictions under JCE III for special intent crimes like terrorism."); Special Court for Sierra Leone, *Prosecutor v. Charles Ghankay Taylor*, SCSL-03-01-T, Judgement, 18 May 2012, para. 468 ("The Trial Chamber concurs with the reasoning of the STL Appeals Chamber and accordingly finds that the Accused may not be held liable under the third form of JCE for specific intent crimes such as terrorism."); Report of the International Law Commission on the work of its forty-eight session, U.N. Doc. A/51/10 (1996), p. 44 ("[A] general intent to commit one of the enumerated acts combined with a general awareness of the probable consequences of such an act with respect to the immediate victim or victims is not sufficient for the crime of genocide. The definition of this crime requires a particular state of mind or a specific intent with respect to the overall consequences of the prohibited act. As indicated in the opening clause of article 17, an individual incurs responsibility for the crime of genocide only when one of the prohibited acts is 'committed with intent to destroy, in whole or in part, a national, ethnic, racial or religious group, as such'."). I note that the latter is considered "an authoritative instrument, parts of which may constitute evidence of customary international law, clarify customary rules, or, at the very least, 'be indicative of the legal views of eminently qualified publicists representing the major legal systems of the world.'" See *Šainović et al.* Appeal Judgement, para. 1647 (with references cited therein). See also *Prosecutor v. Radoslav Brđanin*, Case No. IT-99-36-T, Decision on Motion for Acquittal Pursuant to Rule 98 *BIS*, 28 November 2003, paras 30, 55-57 ("This specific intent cannot be reconciled with the *mens rea* required for a conviction pursuant to the third category of JCE. The latter consists of the Accused's awareness of the risk that genocide would be committed by other members of the JCE. This is a different *mens rea* and falls short of the threshold needed to satisfy the specific intent required for a conviction for genocide under Article 4(3)(a)"); *Stakić* Trial Judgement, para. 530 ("Conflating the third variant of joint criminal enterprise and the crime of genocide would result in the *dolus specialis* being so watered down that it is extinguished. Thus, the Trial Chamber finds that in order to "commit" genocide, the elements of that crime, including the *dolus specialis* must be met."); A. Cassese, "The Proper Limits of Individual Criminal Responsibility under the Doctrine of Joint Criminal Enterprise", *Journal of International Criminal Justice*, vol. 5(1) (2007), pp 109-133, 121-122 ("Resorting to [the third class of JCE] would be intrinsically ill-founded when the crime committed by the 'primary offender' requires a special or specific intent (*dolus specialis*)... In these cases the 'secondary offender' may not share – by definition – that special intent (otherwise one would fall under the first and second class of JCE), even though entertaining such intent is a *sine qua non* condition for being charged with the crime."). I note that Judge Shahabuddeen also addressed the issue of specific intent crimes and found that while it is necessary to show specific intent "that intent is shown by the particular circumstances of the third category of joint criminal enterprise" and that "the Appeals Chamber in *Tadić* was not of the view that intent did not have to be shown; what it considered was that intent was shown by the particular circumstances of the third category of joint criminal enterprise". See, *Brđanin* Appeal Decision of 19 March 2004, Separate Opinion of Judge Shahabuddeen, paras 5, 8.

5.   Nevertheless, I concede that the law in this Judgement regarding the application of the JCE III to specific intent crimes is part of the Tribunal's jurisprudence and is applied correctly in this Judgement. Moreover, I take note of the Trial Chamber's findings that the Appellants had persecutory intent towards Bosnian Muslims and Bosnian Croats in the execution of the JCE I Crimes, which remain unaffected by this Judgement.[7] In the circumstances of this case, I am satisfied that the Trial Chamber's findings would also lead to the conclusion that Stanišić and Župljanin possessed the discriminatory intent for other underlying acts of persecution, for which they were convicted pursuant to JCE III liability. Consequently, I do not dissent from the upholding of Stanišić's and Župljanin's convictions on the basis of the JCE III for persecution as a crime against humanity.

Done in English and French, the English text being authoritative.

_____

Judge Liu Daqun

Dated this thirtieth day of June 2016,
At The Hague,
The Netherlands.

[Seal of the Tribunal] [page 500]

---

[7]   See, *e.g.*, Trial Judgement, vol. 2, paras 311, 313, 520, 769. See also Trial Judgement, vol. 2, paras 507-512, 518, 804, 805, 809, 813, 818, 822, 831-832, 836, 840, 845, 849-850, 854, 859, 863, 864, 868-869, 873, 877, 881, 885, 955-956.

X.   SEPARATE OPINION OF JUDGE AFANĐE

A.   Introduction

1.   In principle, I should have started this separate opinion by stating that "I agree with the Majority's conclusion...but not with the reasoning". However, upon reflection and out of precaution, I have decided to take a calculated distance from the Majority's conclusions and refrain from automatically endorsing them, despite the fact that I will ultimately arrive at the same outcome. The binary reason for this precaution is that I profoundly believe that any conclusion must be the result of reasoning and that the magnetic force which any conclusion needs to attract supporters derives absolutely from the persuasive power of the reasoning that leads to it. Whilst more than one line of reasoning may properly lead to the same conclusion, that conclusion can be said to have been convincingly deduced from a specific line of reasoning only if a backward thinking process, starting from the said conclusion, enables one to recompose that particular reasoning. I am of the view that in the present case, none of the conclusions challenged here enables the supporting reasoning to be rebuilt backwards.

2.   According to a theorem attributed to the Greek philosopher and mathematician Thales of Miletus,[1] if a triangle is located in a semi-circle with its hypotenuse being equal to the radian of the full circle, then the angle of the adjacent and opposite sides is always a right angle. Clearly, many triangles can be located within one semi-circle with some of them being symmetrically inverse to one another, however, they all will have a "right angle". The conclusion therefore, that within a semi-circle there will exist a triangle with a right angle is superficial, because it does not enable us to know the precise parameters of the triangle itself. One may wonder what relevance this theorem, sometimes regarded as an axiom, has in the case before this Appeals Chamber however, by reflecting it is clear that it can be used to clearly illuminate the deficiencies in the Majority's logic. This is because the conclusion that there is a triangle (conviction) with a right angle (the liability accused/convicted) in a semi-circle (among many other persons) is only <u>convincing</u> if one is able to determine the size and weight of the triangle (sentence), based on a demonstration of both (i) the exact point where the right angle (liability of the accused/convicted) is situated on the circumference of the circle (*actus reus* and *mens rea*) and (ii) the length of the adjacent side (gravity of the crimes), in addition to the length of the opposite side (aggravating and mitigating factors) of the triangle, without which the right angle (liability of the accused/convicted) does not even exist. **[page 501]** This issue touches upon the obligation of the Appeals Chamber to provide a reasoned opinion in order to prevent judicial arbitrariness and preserve unfairness toward the accused/convicted person.

3.   The Majority's approach in the present case seems to be analogous to concluding on the existence of convictions (triangle) and of the liability of the accused (right angle) without convincingly determining the parameters of the sentencing (seize/weight of the triangle) through a clear demonstration of the liability (position of the right angle on the circle) and the gravity of the crimes (adjacent site of the triangle), as well as the aggravating and mitigating factors (opposite side of the triangle).

4.   I therefore unfortunately find it difficult to join the Majority's conclusions, since the laconism of the reasoning on each point discussed below does not convince me that it could genuinely lead to that conclusion. Hence, my arguments as developed in this "separate opinion" can perhaps rather be considered as a "dissenting opinion on the reasoning".

5.   Therefore, whilst I would have ultimately upheld Mićo Stanišić's and Stojan Župljanin's convictions, I strongly express my disagreement with the Majority's reasoning with respect to six main issues which go to the very core of the Appeal Judgement in the present case. They are namely: (i) the analysis of whether the participation in this case of Judge Harhoff, who was disqualified from the *Šešelj* case, has affected Stanišić's and Župljanin's fair trial rights; (ii) the failure to crystallise the distinction between the non criminal political goal and the common criminal purpose of the JCE; (iii) the failure to distinguish between the membership of the Bosnian Serb leadership and the membership of the JCE; (iv) the appraisal of the forseeability of the

---

[1]   Cheikh Anta Diop. Anteriorite des civilisations negres: mythes ou realite, Presence Africaine, 1967, pp. 100-101; https://belafrikamedia.com/belafrika/2014/02/07/histoire-africaine-les-longs-sejours-de-thales-et-pythagore-en-afrique-noire-www-belafrika-be-webtv/(accessed June 07, 2016).

crimes considered to be "JCE III crimes"; (v) the elevation of the "appropriation of property" as a crime *per se* and; (vi) the approach to Stanišić's and Župljanin's sentencing appeal.

B.   Whether the Disqualification of Judge Harhoff in the Šešelj Case has Rebutted his Impartiality and Affected Stanišić's and Župljanin's Right to a Fair Trial in Their Case

6.   For the purpose of the following demonstration, it imports to recall that, under grounds 1*bis* and 6 of their respective appeals, Stanišić and Župljanin submit that their right to a fair trial by an independent and impartial court has been violated as a result of the participation of Judge Harhoff in the trial proceedings,[2] which invalidates their convictions.[3] Stanišić and Župljanin argue that the letter dated 6 June 2013 written by Judge Harhoff ("Letter") and published after the rendering of the Trial Judgement in their case on 27 March 2013, reveals an unacceptable appearance of bias on **[page 502]** the part of Judge Harhoff in favour of convicting accused persons. According to them therefore, the Letter rebuts the presumption of impartiality ordinarily afforded to a Judge in their case.[4] Stanišić and Župljanin recognize that the decision by the Special Chamber disqualifying Judge Harhoff in the Šešelj case on the ground that the Letter displayed an apprehension of bias ("Šešelj Special Chamber Decision") is not binding *per se* on the Appeals Chamber. However, they request that the Appeals Chamber quash the Trial Chamber's findings, vacate the Trial Judgement and conduct a *de novo* assessment of all findings or, order a re-trial before a new trial chamber.[5] Alternatively, they request that a full acquittal be pronounced.[6]

7.   The Prosecution responds that Stanišić and Župljanin received a fair trial from an impartial panel of judges.[7] The Prosecution also contends that Stanišić and Župljanin fail to substantiate their claim that Judge Harhoff was predisposed in favour of conviction.[8] The Prosecution further argues that Stanišić and Župljanin have neither rebutted the presumption of Judge Harhoff's impartiality, nor demonstrated that a reasonable apprehension of bias is firmly established.[9]

8.   I am of the view that the Letter does not rebut the impartiality of Judge Harhoff, and that Stanišić and Župljanin have been tried by a Trial Chamber composed of independent judges. However, I feel the pressing need to dissociate myself from the Majority's line of reasoning. In particular, I find the Majority's approach to be insufficient: (i) in explaining why the finding of the Special Chamber in the Šešelj case is not automatically binding on this Chamber; and (ii) in discussing the fair trial rights of the appellants. In essence, the Majority's argument is that the disqualification of Judge Harhoff by the Special Chamber in the [eselj case is a disqualification of a judge pursuant to Rule 15 of the Rules and consequently must be considered on a case-by-case basis, and that the finding made by the Special Chamber is not of a general nature and is not binding on the Appeals Chamber in this case. Already, it is redundant on the part of the Majority to make findings on the non-binding character of the Šešelj Special Chamber Decision on this Appeals Chamber, because Stanišić and Župljanin recognise this themselves.[10] This approach is therefore unconvincing as the arguments are proclaimed just as postulates, without any elaboration as to why the Šešelj Special Chamber Decision is not transposable to this case by the ordinary Appeals Chamber. By doing so, the Majority regrettably not only fails to examine the time factors and the sequence of the procedural events which are decisive and different in both cases. It also misses the **[page 503]** opportunity to genuinely develop the central issue, which is whether or not the content of the Letter, that I will refer to as the "Harhoff Standard", shows any apprehension of bias which would have impacted on the Trial Judgement so as to affect Stanišić's and Župljanin's fair trial rights. Since, to my knowledge, this Tribunal has never determined issues similar to these ones, and given the importance which should be properly attributed to the concept of judicial bias, it is my firm view that it was the duty of the Appeals Chamber to consider the matter in as precise and

---

2   *See* Stanišić Additional Appeal Brief, paras 2-10. *See also* Stanišić Additional Appeal Brief, p. 30; Župljanin Additional Appeal Brief, paras 1, 34; *infra*, Annex A, para. 5.
3   Stanišić Additional Appeal Brief, paras 4, 9-10, 106-131; Župljanin Additional Appeal Brief, paras 2-3, 30-33.
4   Stanišić Additional Appeal Brief, paras 53-105; Župljanin Additional Appeal Brief, paras 13-27.
5   Stanišić Additional Appeal Brief, para. 10, p. 30; Župljanin Additional Appeal Brief, paras 1, 3, 30-35.
6   Stanišić Additional Appeal Brief, para. 10, p. 30; Župljanin Additional Appeal Brief, paras 1, 3, 30-35.
7   Prosecution Consolidated Supplemental Response Brief, para. 1.
8   Prosecution Consolidated Supplemental Response Brief, paras 1, 4.
9   Prosecution Consolidated Supplemental Response Brief, para. 3.
10   Stanišić Additional Appeal Brief, para. 10, p. 30; Župljanin Additional Appeal Brief, paras 1, 3, 30-35.

elaborate detail as possible. Unfortunately, I find the Majority's approach laconic in nature, and I therefore consider it necessary to proffer my position, which goes above and beyond the Majority's approach, in order to raise the discussion up to the standard of analysis expected at the appellate level.

9.   In determining if Judge Harhoff's participation in the trial proceedings violates Stanišić's and Župljanin's right to be tried by an independent and impartial trial chamber, the Majority should have assessed whether the Trial Chamber applied the correct JCE standard, as set out by the Tribunal in a number of previous judgements or opted for the "Harhoff Standard". In my view, the correct approach to make this assessment would have been for the Appeals Chamber to undertake a three-step demonstration. Specifically, it should have: (i) explained how the "reasonable observer" standard shall apply; (ii) discussed the Letter in the light of the correct standard of JCE in the Tribunal's jurisprudence in order to ascertain whether it demonstrated a bias towards conviction; and (iii) analysed the Trial Judgement, to determine whether the JCE standard applied has been influenced by the contents of the Letter.

1.   The Modalities of the Standard of the "Reasonable Observer" Relating to the Appearance of Bias

10.   I consider that the Majority should have first answered the question of whether the impartiality of Judge Harhoff is rebutted in the present case. The response to this interrogation however, is intrinsically linked to addressing the related questions of whether or not the assessment of impartiality should be based either on the Šešelj Special Chamber Decision, which found an "apprehension of bias" on the part of Judge Harhoff in the Šešelj case, or on a *de novo* assessment of the content of the Harhoff Letter? Or, whether this assessment should be based on a combination of both?

11.   Concerning the applicability of the Šešelj Special Chamber Decision in the present case, it is worth recalling that as a matter of principle, a determination made by one chamber is not binding on another. As a result, the finding of "apprehension of bias" on the part of Judge Harhoff by the **[page 504]** Special Chamber in the Šešelj case is not binding on the Appeals Chamber in the present case, as conceded by Stanišić and Župljanin.[11] However this principle does not mean, as the Majority considers, the reasoning ends, as it is only tangential to the question before this Appeals Chamber. Indeed, that principle only relates to, but does not resolve, the issue of the applicability of the Šešelj Special Chamber's Decision by the ordinary Appeals Chamber in the present case. There are two reasons for this. First, the principle that a finding by one chamber does not bind another chamber applies among the ordinary trial chambers of the Tribunal, and does not take into account the "special" nature of the chamber which made findings in the Šešelj case.[12] Second, this principle is also valid among the different ordinarily constituted benches of the Appeals Chamber, bearing in mind however that a determination of a bench of the ordinary Appeals Chamber is in theory binding on trial chambers.[13] Hence this principle does not fully address the question in the present case, which is whether or not a determination made by the "Special Chamber", convened for the Šešelj case and therefore not an "ordinary chamber", may bind an ordinarily constituted Appeals Chamber. It may well be that the "special" character of the Chamber in the Šešelj case makes its findings binding on the ordinary chambers at trial or appellate stage. This question is of a unique importance given the fact that the issue of the "appearance of bias" on the part of Judge Harhoff, which the Šešelj Special Chamber has decided upon, is of interest not only to the Tribunal, but also to the international community in its perception of justice. In this regard, the Šešelj Special Chamber's determination that a reasonable observer confronted with the Letter "would reasonably apprehend bias on the part of Judge Harhoff in favour of conviction", is a finding which is general in nature, as opposed to the Majority's view, and arguably goes beyond the Šešelj case that the Special Chamber cited *only* as an example.[14]

12.   However, contrary to the Majority's position, the approach to the question of whether or not the Šešelj Special Chamber Decision is binding or not on ordinary chambers, including the Appeals Chamber, requires that the matter be assessed with regard to the specific contexts of the Šešelj case and the Stanišić and Župljanin case. Indeed, these two cases are so different that they call for entirely separate methodological

---

11   *See* Stanišić Additional Appeal Brief, para. 10, p. 30; Župljanin Additional Appeal Brief, paras 1, 3, 30-35.
12   *See e.g. Lukić and Lukić* Appeal Judgement, para. 260.
13   *See e.g. Aleksovski* Appeal Judgement, para. 113.
14   *See* Šešelj Special Chamber Decision, para. 13.

lines in interpreting the standard of "appearance of bias". For the following series of reasons, I consider that it would be erroneous to treat them the same and to apply the Šešelj Special Chamber's approach to the Stanišić and Župljanin case. Specifically, whereas the trial proceedings in the Šešelj case were still ongoing and a judgement was expected to be delivered after the Letter was published, the trial proceedings in the Stanišić and Župljanin case were completed and a judgement had been handed down, 71 days before the Harhoff Letter came to **[page 505]** light.[15] As such, the apt approach to interpret the standard of "appearance of bias" in the Šešelj case was "prospective"[16], i.e. on the basis of a *projection* into the future of the case, under the assumption that during the upcoming deliberations and judgement Judge Harhoff *may* apply the standard which he set out in his Letter. However, projection and assumption are logically incompatible with the Stanišić and Župljanin case, since the trial had already been completed and the judgement delivered. Therefore, the Majority should have considered that it can only be logical to *retrospectively* apply the standard of the "appearance of bias" in the present case. This proper retrospective application would require this Appeals Chamber to examine *ex post facto* whether the standard in the Letter which gave rise to "apprehension of bias" for a future judgement in the Šešelj case, was already applied in the Stanišić and Župljanin case that was completed before the publication of the said Letter.

13.   It is worth mentioning that the retrospective application of the standard of the "appearance of bias" is also based on the "reasonable observer" test and should not be conflated with the standard of "actual bias" which requires a higher threshold of evidence.[17]

14.   In summary, my position is that it is not the Šešelj Special Chamber Decision *per se* that should be directly transposed to the current Stanišić and Župljanin case. The solution should rather be found in the content of the Letter, in which the Šešelj Special Chamber found that "Judge Harhoff has demonstrated a bias in favour of conviction such that a reasonable observer properly informed would reasonably apprehend bias".[18]

15.   To this end, it should also be noted that Stanišić's and Župljanin's convictions relate solely to the mode of liability of Joint Criminal Enterprise (JCE) as a form of committing.[19] Given that no party challenges which mode of liability Judge Harhoff was referring to in his Letter, the present **[page 506]** analysis will also proceed on this basis.[20] Therefore, the retrospective analysis should stem from the contents of the Letter, in order to determine whether it has tainted the Tribunal's standard of JCE that the Trial Chamber should ordinarily have applied in Stanišić's and Župljanin's Trial Judgement.

2.   The Reasonable Observer's Test as to the Conformity of the Harhoff Letter with the Standard of JCE in the Tribunal's Jurisprudence

16.   Whether a reasonable observer would conclude that the "Harhoff Standard" of JCE incorrectly deviates from the Tribunal's jurisprudence in the matter is not sufficient on its own, but it is necessary in assessing if Judge Harhoff's participation in their case has affected Stanišić's and Župljanin's fair trial rights or not. The Majority's analysis is not understandable when it seems in paragraphs 52 and 55 to insinuate that, regardless of the non-conformity of the content of the Letter to the Tribunal's case law, a reasonable observer would not apprehend bias, as it displays: (i) Judge Harhoff's "personal conviction" which is "intended to be

---

[15]   The Trial Judgement was rendered on 27 March 2013. The Letter is dated 6 June 2013. *See* Appeal Judgement para. 27.

[16]   Šešelj Special Chamber Decision, para. 14 in which the Special Chamber uses the prospective term "would reasonably apprehend" bias.

[17]   Neither Stanišić nor Župljanin makes allegations that Judge Harhoff was actually biased. *See e.g.* Stanišić Additional Reply Brief, para. 39 where Stanišić expressly contends that, he does not allege nor is he required to prove the existence of actual bias on the part of Judge Harhoff.

[18]   Šešelj Special Chamber Decision, para. 14.

[19]   I note that the Trial Chamber specifically stated that having made findings on JCE "it is not necessary for the Trial Chamber to make findings on the other forms of responsibility alleged in the Indictment" for *Stanišić. See* Trial Judgement, vol. 2 para. 529. With regards Župljanin the Trial Chamber again stated that having made findings on JCE "it is not necessary for the Trial Chamber to make findings on the other forms of responsibility alleged in the Indictment". See Trial Judgement, para. 780. For extermination which the Trial Chamber found could not be included under JCE III, other modes of liability were assessed and rejected. See Trial Judgement, paras 782-786. *See also* Trial Judgement paras 520, 521, 529, 928, 929, 948.

[20]   *See* Stanišić Supplemental Appeal Brief, paras 2-52 and Župljanin Supplemental Appeal Brief, paras 2-12 both of which consider Judge Harhoff to be discussing JCE.

private"; (ii) is written in an informal style and not "as a legal intervention"; and (iii) is published several months after the judgement. In my view, the most appropriate method at this stage for the reasonable observer test should have been to limit the analysis solely and strictly to a discussion of Judge Harhoff's Letter in the light the Tribunal's case law as to whether or not the former is correct and genuinely reflects the latter.

17.   According to the jurisprudence of the Tribunal on JCE:

   a -   the objective element for the first and third categories of JCE liability consists of: (i) a plurality of persons; (ii) the existence of a common plan, design, or purpose which amounts to or involves the commission of a crime provided for in the Statute; and (iii) the participation of the accused in the common design 21 involving the perpetration of one of the crimes provided for in the Statute.[21]

   b -   The subjective element for the first category of JCE liability is the intent to perpetrate a certain crime (this being the shared intent on the part of all co- perpetrators).[22] The third category requires that it was foreseeable to the accused that such a crime might be committed by a member of the JCE or one **[page 507]** or more of the persons used by the accused (or by any other member of the JCE) in order to carry out the objective element of the crimes forming part of the common purpose and the accused willingly took the risk that such a crime might occur by joining or continuing to participate in the enterprise.[23]

18.   It is unquestionable that the above case law on JCE offers the legal standard from which to assess whether the "Harhoff Standard" presents any deviation that is more than a mere disagreement with the law[24] as alleged by Stanišić and Župljanin and could have lead a reasonable observer to apprehend of a bias that could rebut the impartiality of Judge Harhoff.

19.   In the Letter, Judge Harhoff explained what he perceived to be a change in the Tribunal's JCE jurisprudence following the acquittals in the *Gotovina and Markač* Appeal Judgement, the *Perišić* Appeal Judgement and the *Stanišić and Simatović* Trial Judgement.[25] He further states that it has been a "set practice" at the Tribunal that military commanders were held responsible for war crimes that their subordinates committed during the war in the former Yugoslavia from 1992 to 1995.[26] He later added however, that the commanders must have had a direct *intention* to commit crimes and not just have had knowledge or suspicion that the crimes were or would be committed.[27] He continued that, the Tribunal has taken a significant step back from its position of making commanders responsible for their subordinates' crimes without proving that they knew nothing about them. According to him, that change has reduced the theory of JCE from contribution to crimes, to demanding a direct intention to commit crimes and that the acceptance of the crimes being committed is no longer sufficient. In his view, most of the commanding officers would walk free from the Tribunal. Judge Harhoff asserted that he has always presumed that it was right to convict leaders for the crimes committed with their knowledge within a framework of a common goal. He added that "we have convicted these participants who ... had showed *(sic!)* that they agreed with the common goal" and "had contributed to achieving the common goal without having to specifically prove that they had a direct intention to commit every single crime to achieve it." He wondered how to explain to the victims that the Tribunal can no longer convict the participants of a JCE, unless the judges can justify that the participants in their common goal actively and with direct intent, contributed to the crimes. **[page 508]**

---

21   *Stanišić and Simatović* Appeal Judgement, para. 77; *Tadić* Appeal Judgement, para. 227. *See also Stakić* Appeal Judgement, para. 64; *Brđanin* Appeal Judgement, para. 364.
22   *Stanišić and Simatović* Appeal Judgement, para. 77; *Tadić* Appeal Judgement, para. 228. *See also Stakić* Appeal Judgement, para. 65; *Brđanin* Appeal Judgement, para. 365; *Krajišnik* Appeal Judgement, paras 200-208, 707.
23   *See e.g. Šainović et al.* Appeal Judgement, para. 1061. *See also Brđanin* Appeal Judgement, paras 365, 411 and *Kvočka et al.* Appeal Judgement, para. 83, *referring to Tadić* Appeal Judgement, paras 204, 220, 228; *Vasiljević* Appeal Judgement, para. 99.
24   Stanišić Additional Appeal Brief, paras 65-71; Župljanin Additional Appeal Brief, paras 11, 13; Stanišić Additional Reply Brief, para. 34. *See also* Appeal Hearing, 16 Dec 2015, pp. 212-213. Župljanin also asserts that Judge Harhoff should have expressed any reservations on the jurisprudence openly and judicially in a dissenting opinion. *See* Župljanin Additional Reply Brief, paras 17-21. *See also* Stanišić Additional Reply Brief, para. 36.
25   *See* Exhibit 1DA1, p. 3. *See also* Exhibit 1DA1, pp 1-2.
26   Exhibit 1DA1, p. 1.
27   Exhibit 1DA1, p. 2.

20.   I note that as they are presented in the Harhoff Letter, the requirements for conviction under JCE do not accurately reflect the elements of JCE, as developed by the Tribunal and recalled above. In particular, the emphasis put on the "just knowledge or suspicion that the crimes were or would be committed" ostensibly deviates from the requirement of "shared intent" of the subjective element for JCE I.[2628] The Letter also seems to discuss the "contribution" which is part of the objective element and the "intent" which is rather characteristic of the subjective element, as if they were interchangeable. This approach again misrepresents the Tribunal's jurisprudence on JCE. Moreover, the assertion in the Letter according to which JCE is reduced from "contribution to crimes" to "demanding a direct intention to commit crime and not just acceptance of the crimes being committed", the former of which being the objective element and the latter suggesting the subjective element, is not clear. This statement is also misleading in the sense that it could allow the reader to wrongly believe that before autumn 2012, contribution was enough to convict an accused person for JCE, without having to prove the subjective element. The Letter also gives the incorrect impression that, regarding the subjective element of the JCE, a lower standard of a mere "acceptance" by an accused person of the crime committed", can be used instead of the higher standard of the "shared intent" as properly required. Furthermore, Judge Harhoff's reference to "direct intention" seems to imply that as a result of what he perceives to be a change, the jurisprudence of the Tribunal henceforth requires proof that the accused intends to commit "every single crime", whereas such a requirement has never formed part of either the objective or the subjective elements of a JCE even in the Tribunal's recent jurisprudence.[29]

21.   Based on the above analysis, I am of the view that Judge Harhoff's comments in the Letter substantially deviate from the Tribunal's jurisprudence on JCE and can be seen to nurture unfairness towards accused persons. If it is found that the unfair "Harhoff Standard" in the Letter was applied by the Trial Chamber, the right of Stanišić and Župljanin to a fair trial would indeed have been violated.

3.   The Reasonable Observer Test to the Standard of JCE in Stanišić and Župljanin Trial Judgement

22.   The issue of Judge Harhoff's impartiality at stake in this case, is certainly not one of a theoretical nature and resolving it requires going far beyond a mere recitation and recollection of **[page 509]** relevant legal provisions such as Article 13 and 21 of the Statute of the Tribunal. As the Majority rightly recalls in paragraph 43, the apprehension of bias test reflects the maxim that "justice should not only be done, but should manifestly and undoubtedly be seen to be done" and is founded on the need to ensure public confidence in the judiciary. However, the Majority stops its analysis of that maxim here, which, in my view, is rather the point where the discussion should have started in order to demonstrate whether justice could be seen to have been manifestly and undoubtedly done in the Stanišić and Župljanin Trial Judgement. In this case where the Trial judgement was already delivered, the best way to see whether justice has been done is to assess if it is the "Harhoff Standard" found to be erroneously deviating from the Tribunal's jurisprudence and promoting unfairness that has been applied in the Stanišić and Župljanin Trial judgement.

23.   I observe that when considering how the Trial Chamber undertook its assessment of JCE, it set out the correct standard for JCE in its summary of the applicable law.[30] I further note that in applying that correct JCE standard to the facts before it, the Trial Chamber first made initial legal findings on the crimes alleged to have been committed in the 20 municipalities, before considering the mode of liability.[31] The Majority should have assessed the Trial Chamber's findings on these crimes, and then considered whether a reasonable

---

[28]   *See above*, para. 4.
[29]   *See e.g. Popović et al.* Appeals Judgement, para. 1615 in which the Appeals Chamber reiterated that participation of an accused in a JCE need not involve the commission of a crime, but that it may take the form of assistance in, or contribution to, the execution of the common objective or purpose.
[30]   *See* Trial Judgement, vol. 1, paras 99-106.
[31]   *See* Trial Judgement, vol. 1, paras 212-228 (Banja Luka), Trial Judgement, vol. 1, paras 275-285 (Donji Vakuf), Trial Judgement, vol. 1, paras 340-350 (Ključ), Trial Judgement, vol. 1, paras 481-494 (Koto Varoš), Trial Judgement, vol. 1, paras 685-703 (Prijedor), Trial Judgement, vol. 1, paras 805-817 (Sanski Most), Trial Judgement, vol. 1, paras 873-883 (Teslić), Trial Judgement, vol. 1, paras 931-938 (Bijeljina), Trial Judgement, vol. 1, paras 974-986 (Bileća), Trial Judgement, vol. 1, paras 1034-1044 EB (Bosanski Šamac), Trial Judgement, vol. 1, paras 1111-1122 (Brčko), Trial Judgement, vol. 1, paras 1185-1193 (Doboj), Trial Judgement, vol. 1, paras 1240-1251 (Gacko), Trial Judgement, vol. 1, paras 1281-1289 (Ilijas), Trial Judgement, vol. 1, paras 1349-1359 (Pale), Trial Judgement, vol. 1, paras 1408-1417 (Vissegrad), Trial Judgement, vol. 1, paras 1491-1501 (Vlasenica), Trial Judgement, vol. 1, paras 1548-1556 (Vogošća), and Trial Judgement, vol. 1, paras 1672-1691 (Zvronik).

observer would find that the "Harhoff Standard" as presented in the Letter was applied in the Trial Judgement, which would necessarily lead to the violation of Stanišić's and Župljanin's fair trial rights.

24.   With regard to the Trial Chamber's second stage of considering JCE as a mode of liability, it examined in detail the existence of a common plan or design,[32] and the individual criminal responsibility of Stanišić and Župljanin. A careful review of the JCE standard utilized, and in particular both the objective and subjective elements used in its analysis, reveals that in convicting Stanišić and Župljanin through participation in a JCE, the Trial Chamber did not use the lower and unfair "Harhoff Standard" of the subjective element. Instead, the Trial Chamber applied the correct higher JCE standard throughout its assessment of the evidence, specifically in its analysis of Župljanin's conduct in furtherance of the JCE,[33] his membership of the JCE,[34] and his JCE **[page 510]** liability.[35] Similarly, for Stanišić, the Trial Chamber deployed the correct higher JCE standard with regard to his alleged participation in the JCE,[36] and his membership of the JCE.[37] Only after having made findings on crimes committed in each municipality, and having assessed Stanišić's and Župljanin's JCE liability, did the Trial Chamber conclude whether those crimes could be imputed to Stanišić, Župljanin or other members of the JCE.[38] I therefore conclude that in itself, this approach demonstrates to a reasonable observer that the Trial Chamber did not in fact employ the unfair "Harhoff Standard" for conviction. The Trial Chamber instead, looked in detail at every element of JCE based on the Tribunal's correct standard of the objective and subjective elements before reaching its final conclusion. Accordingly, I find that a reasonable observer would retrospectively not apprehend any bias in the Trial Chamber's approach in the Stanišić and Župljanin case.

25.   Lastly, it appears that none of the Trial Chamber judges, including Judge Harhoff himself, expressed or appended any individual view in favour of a lower standard as found in the Letter. Therefore, on the basis of the above analysis, the correct and higher standard of JCE as identified in the Trial Judgement has been applied unanimously and uniformly by all three Judges of the Trial Chamber in Stanišić's and Župljanin's case. This means that, even if it is assumed that at the time of the conviction of Stanišić and Župljanin, Judge Harhoff was already incubating views based on the lower threshold of JCE which he disclosed in the Letter, he did not apply them and did not sway the other Judges in anyway towards that position in the present case. My argument demonstrates that, contrary to what Judge Harhoff asserted in the Letter, the reasonable observer could be satisfied that there is no merit in the argument that the Tribunal were predisposed to convict accused persons. Consequently, the observation made by the Appeals Chamber, as invoked by Stanišić and Župljanin,[39] that there is a realistic possibility that they may not have been tried by three impartial judges[40] is not established. Likewise, the allegations made by Stanišić and Župljanin **[page 511]** that the Letter rebuts the impartiality of Judge Harhoff and that they have not been tried by a Trial composed of independent judges[41] are unfounded.

26.   In conclusion, based on the above analysis on the modalities of the reasonable observer's standard, the discussion of the Harhoff Letter in light of the Tribunal's jurisprudence and the JCE standard applied in the

---

[32]   *See* Trial Judgement, vol. 2, paras 128-316.
[33]   *See* Trial Judgement, vol. 2, paras 375-488.
[34]   *See* Trial Judgement, vol. 2, paras 489-517.
[35]   *See* Trial Judgement, vol. 2, paras 518-530.
[36]   *See* Trial Judgement, vol. 2, paras 532-534.
[37]   *See* Trial Judgement, vol. 2, paras 729-781.
[38]   *See* Trial Judgement, vol. 2, paras 801-805 (Banja Luka), Trial Judgement, vol. 2, paras 806-809 (Bijeljina), Trial Judgement, vol. 2, paras 810-814 (Bileća), Trial Judgement, vol. 2 815-818 (Bosanski Šamac), Trial Judgement, vol. 2, paras 819-823 (Brčko), Trial Judgement, vol. 2, paras 824-827 (Doboj), Trial Judgement, vol. 2, paras 828-832 (Donji Vakuf), Trial Judgement, vol. 2, paras 833-836 (Gacko), Trial Judgement, vol. 2, paras 837-840 (Ilijas), Trial Judgement, vol. 2, paras 841-845 (Ključ), Trial Judgement, vol. 2, paras 846-850 (Koto Varoš), Trial Judgement, vol. 2, paras 851-854 (Pale), Trial Judgement, vol. 2, paras 855-859 (Prijedor and Skender Vakuf), Trial Judgement, vol. 2, paras 860-864 (Sanski Most), Trial Judgement, vol. 2, paras 865-869 (Teslić), Trial Judgement, vol. 2, paras 870-873 (Vissegrad), Trial Judgement, vol. 2, paras 874-877 (Vlasenica), Trial Judgement, vol. 2, paras 878-881 (Vogošća), Trial Judgement, vol. 2, paras 882-885 (Zvronik).
[39]   Joint Motion on Behalf of Mićo Stanišić and Stojan Župljanin Seeking Expedited Adjudication of Their Respective Grounds of Appeal 1Bis and 6, 25 August 2014, para. 3. *See also* Stanišić Additional Appeal Brief, paras 2-10 and Župljanin Additional Appeal Brief, paras 1, 34.
[40]   Decision on Mićo Stanišić's Motion Seeking Admission of Additional Evidence Pursuant to Rule 115, 14 April 2014, para. 22.
[41]   *See* Stanišić Additional Appeal Brief, paras 2-10, 53-105 106-131 and Župljanin Additional Appeal Brief, paras 1-12, 28-34.

Trial Judgement by the Trial Chamber, including Judge Harhoff, the participation of the latter in the Trial judgement cannot be said to have violated Stanišić's and Župljanin's fair trial rights.

C. Failure to Crystallise the Distinction Between the Political Goal and Common Criminal Purpose of the JCE

27.   I consider that the Majority has regrettably missed the opportunity in this Judgement to set out clearly the distinction between the legitimate non-criminal political goal in existence at the time of the Indictment and the common criminal purpose of the JCE. Given that this issue has never been addressed by the Tribunal, this Judgement was a unique opportunity to consider this important matter. Discussion on this distinction would have been instructive in clarifying and revisiting the Appeals Chamber's approach to a number of complex issues surrounding Joint Criminal Enterprise, in the interest of a well reasoned development of international criminal law and justice. Given the Majority's failure to seize this opportunity, I feel it incumbent upon myself to do so and express my position.

28.   As the Trial Judgement made plain, the aim of the Bosnian Serb leadership in 1991 was for Serbs to live in one state with other Serbs from the former Yugoslavia.[42] Such a goal is political and not criminal by nature. Of course, one may question this goal, but this does not mean that is criminal in and of itself. Separate from this political goal, a programme was devised to *ethnically cleanse* regions of the former Yugoslavia by permanently removing non-Serb peoples, meaning Bosnian Muslims and Bosnian Croats. This plan by some members of the Bosnian Serb leadership to ethnically cleanse regions was undoubtedly criminal *per se* and not merely political. It alone embodied the "common criminal purpose" to be achieved through the commission of crimes found in the ICTY Statute. Curiously however, the Trial Judgement seems to imply that because crimes were committed as a means to achieve the common criminal purpose beside the political goal, then the latter was also criminal.[43] The Majority now upholds the Trial Chamber's line of thought, from which I strongly differ. Logically, I am of the view that the crimes were committed to further the **[page 512]** "common criminal purpose" of cleansing the said populations from the relevant regions, as a means to achieve the non-criminal political goal of Serbs living on one territory. In other words, the "common criminal purpose" is rather the operative link between the crimes committed and the noncriminal political goal of having Serbs living on one territory. Hence, whilst both the common criminal purpose and the political plan may share certain elements, it is a patent error to treat them as one and the same. In my view, the Bosnian Serb leadership's aim for all Serbs to live in one territory remained a non-criminal, political goal throughout the entirety of the conflict in the former Yugoslavia. Indeed, that political goal could have been achieved by having all Serbs living in one territory alongside other non-Serb populations or ethnic groups such as the Bosnian Muslims and Bosnian Croats. However, among other things, the speeches of Dutina (SDS meeting on 15 October 1991), of Kupresanin (25 February 1992 session of the BSA) and of Karadžić (BSA meeting on 18 March 1992) consistently illustrate that such cohabitation was not envisaged and their creation of a plan to ethnically cleanse areas of these non-Serbs as summarised by the Trial Chamber in paragraph 767 of Volume 2 of the Trial Judgement, was patently criminal. As the political goal and the common criminal purpose ran parallel to each other, the Majority fails to take the necessary precaution to use language which always draws a clear distinction between the two. If the Majority had established such a difference between both, it would have corrected the confusion already created by the language in the Trial Judgement itself, according to which because crimes were committed in furtherance to the common criminal purpose beside the political goal, then the latter was also criminal. As ambiguous as its analysis may be, the Trial Chamber at paragraph 313 of Volume 2 of the Trial Judgement, still seems to define the common criminal purpose as the plan to "permanently remove Bosnian Muslims and Bosnian Croats from the territory of the planned Serbian State". The approach of the Majority in paragraph 69 seems to confirm this definition of the common criminal purpose, which is manifestly distinguishable from the non-criminal political objective.

29.   Additional difficulties arise from the Trial Chamber's language, which as opposed to referring solely to the "common criminal purpose" where appropriate, repeatedly refers interchangeably to a "common

---

42   Trial Judgement, vol. 2, para 309 as stated in Appeal Judgement, para. 63.
43   *See e.g.* Trial Judgement, vol.2, paras 311, 313.

plan" without the adjective "criminal".[44] This unfortunate language bears the risk of conflating the non-criminal, political goal (all Serbs living in one territory) with the common criminal purpose (ethnically cleansing non-Serbs). This confusion is compounded at paragraph 63 of the Majority analysis, in its attempt to summarise the Trial Chamber's findings at paragraph 313 of Volume 2 of the Trial Judgement. Here the Majority appears to aggregate the non-**[page 513]**criminal political goal and the crimes committed to conclude on the existence of a JCE, thus not capturing this necessary distinction.

30.   Instead of directly quoting paragraph 313 of Volume 2 of the Trial Judgement, where the Trial Chamber found that the objective of the JCE was to "permanently remove Bosnian Muslims and Bosnian Croats from the territory of the planned Serbian state through the commission of crimes", paragraph 63 of the Majority's reasoning speaks of the removal of non-Serbs through the commission of "*[JCE I crimes]*". The Majority hence inserts this language of "*JCE I crimes*" *at a* place where the Trial Chamber itself had not used it and has only referred to "crimes".

31.   As will be explained below, the use of terms such as "objective of the JCE" in paragraph 526 of the Majority Judgement adds to this ambiguity. By not differentiating between both, the Majority's approach may bear the risk of supporting Stanišić's Second Ground of Appeal, as well as his Third and Fourth Ground of Appeal in part, through the equation of all members of the Bosnian Serb leadership, with members of the JCE. In addition to this point, I have some issue with the Majority's position that the Trial Chamber did not equate the policies of the Bosnian Serb leadership, as such, with the "objective of the JCE".[45] To my mind, the "objective of the JCE" is not at issue here. The issue here is the existence, or not, of a *common criminal purpose* which amounts to or involves the commission of crimes under the Tribunal's Statute as correctly recalled at paragraph 70 of the Majority Judgement. The term "objective of the JCE" is therefore misleading, especially, considering that similar language is used for the "aim" or "objective" of the noncriminal political goal. The Majority should therefore have used more precise terminology in line with the settled terms such as the "existence of a common plan." Also, given my position that the non-criminal political goal and common criminal plan should be clearly separated, paragraph 69 of the Majority reasoning should not have relied on the political goal as a factor used by the Trial Chamber to determine the existence of a common criminal plan, but should instead spell out in clear terms what "other factors" the Trial Chamber relied upon. For not having done so, the Majority continues to entertain the vexing confusion already made by the Trial Chamber between the "noncriminal political goal" and the "common criminal purpose".

32.   Taken individually or in conjunction, I consider that the Majority's approach does not contain a reasoned opinion which would have unequivocally distinguished between the "noncriminal political goal" and the "common criminal purpose", as demonstrated above. This failure, in my view, taints the Majority's analysis and amounts to a discernable error of law. **[page 514]**

D.   Failure to Distinguish Between Membership of the Bosnian Serb Leadership and Membership of the JCE

33.   Stanišić argues that the Trial Chamber failed to adequately differentiate between membership of the Bosnian Serb leadership, and membership of a joint criminal enterprise with the common criminal purpose of removing non-Serbs from areas of Bosnia and Herzegovina through the commission of crimes contained within the Tribunal's Statute.[46]

34.   Instead of finding that the Trial Chamber did make that confusion and rectify it, the Majority rather takes the position that the Trial Chamber did in fact make this distinction and applied it throughout its assessment of the evidence.[47] But the references to the Trial Chamber findings which the Majority resorts to are in and of themselves ambiguous and confirm that the confusion does exist. In particular, I note that paragraph 81 of the Majority Judgement cites paragraphs 311 and 312 of Volume 2 of the Trial Judgement as support for the position that the Trial Chamber did make the distinction between members of the Bosnian

---

[44]   *See, inter alia,* Trial Judgement, vol. 2, paras 313, 314, 494, 522, 523.
[45]   Judgement, para. 526 *referring to* Appeal Judgement, paras 63-71.
[46]   Appeal Judgement, para. 79.
[47]   Appeal Judgement, paras 81-82.

Serb leadership and members of the JCE. The Majority relies on the Trial Chamber's use of the term "majority" of the Bosnian Serb leadership to demonstrate that "not all" members of that Bosnian Serb leadership were necessarily considered members of the JCE. However, reviewing these paragraphs of the Trial Judgement, I struggle to see where this distinction is made and these paragraphs even appear to contradict this suggestion. Paragraph 311, for example, suggests that whilst there were conflicts and disagreements between different levels of the Serb authorities "**they all shared** and worked towards the same goal under the Bosnian Serb leadership". This finding by the Trial Chamber that "they all shared" the same goal appears to *oppose* the conclusion by the Majority that the Trial Chamber was of the view that at least *some* members of the leadership did not share that goal and that culpability was therefore not attributed to "all" Bosnian Serb leadership. This contradiction can only be rectified if the two following issues, which the Majority unfortunately failed to address, were clarified: (i) the "Serb authorities" that the Trial Chamber referred to as "all sharing the same goal" are distinct from the "Bosnian Serb leadership; and (ii) the "goal under the Bosnian Serb leadership referred to by the Trial Chamber as having been shared by "all those Serb authorities" is the noncriminal political one and not the "common criminal purpose". Furthermore, paragraph 312 of Volume 2 of the Trial Judgement relied on, in paragraph 81 of the Majority analysis, could be read to allude to the fact that the Trial Chamber acknowledges that on some occasions certain Serb leaders stated that "their aim was not an ethnically pure state or that international humanitarian law should be respected" However, the Trial Chamber does not subsequently recognize that these Serb **[page 515]** leaders, taking distance from the common criminal purpose, should be absolved of criminal culpability. Instead, the Trial Chamber suggests that because these diverging statements did "not reflect the true aims of the majority of the Bosnian Serb leadership", the Serb leaders expressing them shall also be liable of JCE, on the same footing as the members of the JCE.

35.   Based on these contradictions and weaknesses in paragraphs 311 and 312 of Volume 2 of the Trial Judgement, the Majority should have relied solely on references to the Trial Judgement where the drawing of the distinction between "members of the Bosnian Serb leadership" and "members of the JCE" is clearer. Namely, in paragraph 314 of Volume 2 of its Judgement the Trial Chamber found that Branko Derić (RS Prime Minister), Milan Trbojević (RS Deputy Prime Minister), and Bogdan Subotić (RS Minister of Defence) were members of the Bosnian Serb leadership, but did not find them to be members of the JCE.[48] These findings, in my view, unequivocally refute Stanišić's argument that collective responsibility was attributed to all solely by virtue of membership of the Bosnian Serb leadership.

36.   At paragraph 217 of its analysis, the Majority also entertains a similar contradiction by trying to distinguish the membership of the Bosnian Serb leadership from that of the JCE, but at the same time conflating them with each other. An illustration is that the Majority cites paragraph 311 of Volume 2 of the Trial Judgement, to support the distinction, while it invokes the same paragraph by recalling that even though at times there were conflicts between the various entities, including the crisis staffs, "they all shared and worked towards the same goal under the Bosnian Serb leadership".[49] Obviously there are serious contradictions and inconsistency in the Majority's approach to use paragraph 311 of Volume 2 of the Trial Judgement to attempt to establish that the Trial Chamber differentiated between the "Bosnian Serb leadership" and the members of the JCE, but to resort to the same paragraph 311 of Volume 2 of the Trial Judgement to support the assimilation of both.

37.   That contradiction not only vitiates the Majority's reasoning, but makes it legally nonexistent. I am therefore of the view that the Majority has committed a failure to provide a reasoned opinion, which amounts to a discernable error of law.

E.   Foreseeability of the Crimes Referred to by the Majority as "JCE III Crimes"

38.   Concerning the foreseeability of the crimes it refers to generally as "JCE III crimes", the Majority have missed the opportunity to fully engage with Stanišić's "cogent reasons to depart" **[page 516]** submissions and to uphold the necessary standard of review, when considering the Trial Chamber's approach.

---

48   *See* Trial Judgement, vol. 2, para. 314.
49   Referring to Trial Judgement, vol. 2, paras. 311, 735.

Furthermore, the Majority's finding is troubling when it characterises merely as "artificial" Stanišić's distinction on whether the foreseeability of JCE III crimes should be "objectively" or "subjectively" assessed.

39.   With respect to Stanišić's "cogent reasons to depart" submissions examined at paragraph 598 in the Majority's analysis, I find the dismissal of the submissions to be superficial. The Majority is correct when it recalls that "[i]nsofar as Stanišić relies upon the jurisprudence of the STL and SCSL.it is not bound by the findings of other courts – domestic, international, or hybrid". However, the Majority seems to be on the defensive when it adds that "… even though it will consider such jurisprudence, it may nonetheless come to a different conclusion on a matter than that reached by another judicial body". I have unsuccessfully struggled to convince myself of this reasoning by the Majority. I believe that the arguments raised by Stanišić should have been entertained to allow a full discussion on the point, as it affords the Appeals Chamber the opportunity to re-examine its stance on this issue and explain its position. In my view, it is incumbent on the Appeals Chamber to examine the nature of the common criminal purpose which forms the JCE. In the case where the common criminal purpose for JCE I is substantially different from a *dolus specialis* required for an ensuing JCE III crime, I may have some difficulty in imputing those specific intent JCE III crimes to members of a JCE, without any further convincing demonstration. But in this case, the "common criminal purpose" to ethnically cleanse parts of Bosnia and Herzegovina of non-Serbs is at its heart "discriminatory". Therefore, the specific intent of "discrimination" required for persecutions as a crime against humanity, which Stanišić is charged with under JCE III, is already ostensibly encompassed in the common criminal purpose of the JCE I. Consequently, it is not necessary to make a separate explicit finding as to whether Stanišić possessed the specific discriminatory intent concerning the persecution crimes before attaching the JCE III liability to him. If this line of reasoning was followed by the Majority, then there will absolutely be no need to examine the STL and SCSL findings on JCE III or the Rome Statue of the ICC. This approach will obviate recourse to the cursory and doubtful arguments used by the Majority to dismiss the case law and provisions of those jurisdictions.

40.   In addition, the approach at paragraphs 616 and 617 of the Majority Judgement is questionable in law. Specifically, it concludes that, despite not making explicit findings on murder, as a crime against humanity and murder, as a war crime, the Trial Chamber "considered" that these crimes were foreseeable and that Stanišić willingly took the risk. In my view the term "considered" shows clearly that the Trial Chamber did not make a "finding" of this issue. The Majority's approach therefore blatantly falls below and even violates the standard of review on appeal. This line of conclusion appears to be a dangerous attempt on the part of the Majority to read the mind of **[page 517]** the Trial Chamber instead of reviewing its reasoning as per the law, and therefore amounts to an error of law.

41.   Furthermore, the Majority's approach is laconic in dismissing Stanišić submissions on whether the natural and foreseeable consequence for JCE III emanates from the common criminal purpose (objective) or from the individual member of the JCE (subjective). I consider that the obviously defensive dismissal of this argument merely as "artificial" by the Majority at paragraph 622 truncates this Tribunal's jurisprudential evolution and is ultimately an inadequate approach to deal with the matter at hand. Regardless of the time when Stanišić is meant to have possessed the intent of the JCE crimes or to have acquired knowledge of the crimes being committed against Muslims and Croats, a finding on the foreseeability of the crimes charges under JCE III is flawed if it is not based on a well defined distinction between the various crimes. In my view, the answer may vary between "objective" and "subjective" foreseeability depending on the specific crimes to which the Trial Chamber attaches the JCE III liability. The fact that the JCE III crimes are not differentiated in the Majority's reasoning, but instead are referred to collectively as "JCE III crimes" is therefore inapposite and confusing.[50] For the purpose of demonstration, it should be recalled that according to the Majority in paragraphs 6 and 61 of the Judgement, the Trial Chamber attached liability under JCE III for the following three categories of crimes:

  a. persecution as a crime against humanity through the underlying acts of killings, torture, cruel treatment, and inhumane acts, unlawful detention, establishment and perpetuation of inhumane living conditions, plunder of property, wanton destruction of towns and villages, including destruction or wilful damage done to institutions dedicated to religion and other cultural buildings,

---

50   Examples could be found at paragraphs 626, 628 and 634 of the Majority Judgement.

and imposition and maintenance of restrictive and discriminatory measures as a crime against humanity (Count 1),

b. murder, torture, and cruel treatment as violations of the laws or customs of war (Counts 4, 6 and 7) and

c. murder, torture, and inhumane acts as crimes against humanity (Counts 3, 5 and 8).

42.   As explained at paragraph 39 above in this document, the crime of persecutions (Count 1) is based on the *dolus specialis* of discrimination, whilst discrimination is also and already an integral element of the JCE common criminal purpose. As a result, there exists a clear objective link between the common criminal purpose based on "discrimination", and the crime of persecution, which also entails "discrimination". The latter is then the objectively natural and foreseeable **[page 518]** consequence of the former. Because the JCE members necessarily share this common criminal purpose based on "discrimination", each of them, including Stanišić, is individually liable under JCE III for persecution as a crime against humanity involving the same "discrimination" as *dolus specialis*. Therefore, it is superfluous to seek to establish whether for Stanišić, as an individual, but member of the JCE, persecution based on the specific intent of "discrimination" is subjectively a natural and foreseeable consequence of that discrimination-based criminal purpose which he shares. However, this element of discrimination, and therefore the objective link with the discrimination-related common criminal purpose, does not exist for the non-discrimination based crimes of murder, torture, and cruel treatment as violations of the laws or customs of war (Counts 4, 6, and 7) and of murder, torture, and inhumane acts as crimes against humanity (Counts 3, 5, and 8). In the absence of this objective element of natural and foreseeable consequence between these crimes and the discrimination-based common criminal purpose, and failing any Trial Chamber's finding, it is incumbent on the Appeals Chamber to move to a "subjective level" in order to examine whether the acts or conduct of Stanišić demonstrate that such crimes were a natural and foreseeable consequence *for him*, as an individual. It is only if it is demonstrated that these crimes were naturally foreseeable for him, that the Appeals Chamber could uphold convictions based on liability under JCE III for those crimes. In my view, the Trial Chamber's findings on Stanišić's acts and conduct such as the deployment of police units to participate in operations, the involvement of police officers into the managements of detention camps, where the police had the proclivity to commit crimes, could be demonstrative enough to ground a finding that those crimes were also natural and foreseeable consequences of the common criminal purpose for him.

43.   By amalgamating all crimes under an arbitrary category named "JCE III crimes" and attaching a blanket liability of JCE III to all of them together, without demonstrating to what extent each of the crimes has a nexus with that mode of liability, the Majority fails to provide a reasoned opinion and thus commits a discernable error of law.

F. Appropriation of Property as an Underlying Act of Persecution

44.   I would have dismissed Župljanin's fifth ground of appeal relating to the crime of persecution[51] and upheld his conviction. I cannot however, agree with the Majority's approach to the "appropriation of property" as an underlying act of persecution which I find to be inconsistent both with the Tribunal's jurisprudence and international humanitarian law such that it amounts to a discernable error of law on the part of the Majority. **[page 519]**

45.   First, at paragraph 526 of Volume 2 of the Trial Judgement, the Trial Chamber found that the imposition of a currency limit of 300 DM on non-Serbs constitutes "the crime of appropriation of property, as an underlying act of persecution, as a crime against humanity". However, reviewing paragraph 528, footnotes 1876 and 1877 of Volume 2 of the Trial Judgement and then the disposition at paragraph 956 of Volume 2 of the Trial Judgement it appears that Župljanin was rather convicted of "plunder" (and not for the "appropriation of property") as an underlying act of persecution. The definition of plunder which has been established in the jurisprudence of the Tribunal, is the "extensive, unlawful, and wanton appropriation of property".[52] It has therefore been established that the "appropriation of property" is just one element of plunder, and whilst the

---

51   Župljanin Additional Appeal Brief, paras 278-282.
52   *Blaškić* Appeal Judgement, para. 144.

Trial Chamber entered findings for this element, it failed to enter findings for the "wanton", "unlawful" and "extensive" elements. As per the jurisprudence of the Tribunal, the Trial Chamber is required to make findings on those facts which are essential to the determination of guilt on a particular count.[53] As a result, the Trial Chamber has committed a discernable error of law for not having provided a reasoned opinion or making finding on these essential elements of the crime of persecution.

46.   This discernable error of law, of which the Appeals Chamber should have seized itself *proprio motu*, does not emerge in the Majority's analysis. Instead, the Majority uses the term "appropriation of property" interchangeably with "plunder" and at times in addition to it.[54] The jurisprudence of this Tribunal does not provide a basis for making the "appropriation of property" an underlying act of persecution in and of itself. Even the recognition of the "extensive destruction and appropriation of property" as a crime under international humanitarian law requires that the "destruction and appropriation of property" be "extensive".[55] Therefore, without that element of "extensiveness", there is no legal basis in international humanitarian law for elevating the "appropriation of property" *per se* to a crime. Furthermore, absent any findings, not only on that element of "extensiveness", but also on the "wanton" and the "unlawful" elements, the Tribunal's jurisprudence does not support raising the "appropriation of property" as found by the Trial Chamber to a crime and also not to an underlying act of persecution *per se*. This is particularly not permissible in this case, since as mentioned above, the Trial Chamber actually convicted Župljanin of *plunder* as a crime against humanity,[56] and not of "appropriation of property", without having assessed the existence of the other remaining elements which together with the "appropriation of **[page 520]** property" would have established the crime of "plunder" as per its definition in the Tribunal's jurisprudence.

47.   An examination of the evidence on record reveals however, that the remaining elements of "wanton", "unlawful" and "extensive" are indeed made out. The "unlawful" element of the plunder stems from the 31 July 1992 Order itself, since its content can be said to violate international law on the rights of property[57] and is therefore clearly "unlawful". "Wanton" is defined as "deliberate and unprovoked"[58] whilst "extensive" is referred to as "covering or affecting a large area".[59] Using these two definitions, I believe the "wanton" element can be evidenced through the fact that the appropriation of property in these circumstances was intentional and carried out without provocation by the victims. The "extensive" nature of the appropriation of property as an element of the plunder can be established through the large number of non-Serbs who were the victims of the unlawful Order and the number of municipalities that were affected, as evidenced by the trial record.

48.   Second, whilst I agree in the context of this case that the facts demonstrate that the crime of plunder is of equal gravity to other Article 5 crimes, I firmly disagree with the Majority's approach to the "equal gravity" test. Once the *actus reus* and *mens rea* elements for the crime of persecutions are fulfilled,[60] it falls to be determined on a case-by-case basis whether the act in question can be said to be of equal gravity to the other crimes listed under article 5 of the ICTY statute.[61] A number of factors can be taken into account when undertaking this analysis, however, it is my view that there is a dangerous risk of double-counting if

---

[53]   *Stanišić and Simatovic* Appeal Judgement, para. 311 *referring to Popović et al.* Appeal Judgement, para. 1906.
[54]   *See* Appeal Appeal Judgement para. 545; para. 1070 "...such as appropriation *or* plunder of property", footnote 3547.
[55]   *See e.g.* Article 50 of the 1949 Geneva convention I, Article 51 of the 1949 Geneva Convention II and Article 147 of the 1949 Geneva Convention IV recognize the "extensive destruction and appropriation of property" as grave breaches.
[56]   *See* Trial Judgement, vol. 2, p. 312.
[57]   The right to property is enshrined in several international and regional human rights instruments, *see* for example Universal Declaration of Human Rights (1948), Art. 17(1) and (2); Convention relating to the Status of Refugees (1951), Art. 13, 18, 19, 29 and 30: Convention relating to the Status of Stateless Persons (1954), Art. 13, 18, 19, 29 and 30; Convention on the Elimination of All Forms of Racial Discrimination (1965) Art. 5; European Convention on Human Rights (1952) Art. 1 Protocol 1; The American Convention on Human rights (1969) Art. 21; The African Charter on Human and Peoples' Rights (1981) Art. 14.
[58]   Wanton, adj. and n.". OED Online. March 2016. Oxford University Press. http://www.oed.com/view/Entry/225544?rskey=A yheYO&result=1 (accessed June 07, 2016).
[59]   Extensive, adj.". OED Online. March 2016. Oxford University Press. http://www.oed.com/view/Entry/66943?redirectedFro m=extensive (accessed June 07, 2016).
[60]   To establish the *actus reus* of persecution in the present case, the Trial Chamber was required to establish that the underlying acts discriminated in fact, denied or infringed upon a fundamental right laid down in international customary or treaty law. For *mens rea*, what is required is establishing that the underlying act was deliberately carried out with discriminatory intent. *See e.g. Popović et al.* Appeal Judgement, paras 738, 762.
[61]   *Blaškić* Appeal Judgement, para. 146.

caution is not exercised. This may occur through the use of *crimes themselves*, already charged under the various modes of liabilities (in this case JCE I, JCE III and Ordering) to determine the equal gravity of the plunder. Neither do I feel it is correct to use the *elements of crimes* already determined in this case to assess the equal gravity of the plunder, as such approach could also lead to double-counting. The Majority allude to "the context in which **[page 521]** this appropriation of property took place and the significance of its impact upon victims"[62] to demonstrate that the plunder in question was of equal gravity to the other Article 5 crimes, however this approach is flawed. To begin with paragraph 1074, the Majority simply recalls that a currency limit was put in place by Župljanin and cannot be classed as clarifying the "context" in which that plunder of property took place. At paragraph 1076 the Majority details that "...the appropriation in question took place in the context of forcible transfers and deportations." however it is clear that, at least in the case of forcible transfers, this is a crime which has already been used to convict Župljanin under JCE.[63] Deportation can be said to be an element of a crime which also already forms the basis of a charge against Župljanin under JCE.[64] It is my view that the use of such crimes and elements of crimes to determine the equal gravity of the plunder exposes the Majority at best, to criticism based on incongruity and at worse, to serious reproach for double-counting.

49.   Instead, the Majority should have relied solely on the *acts* surrounding the crime of plunder and their likely consequences to assess the equal gravity requirement. In order to do this, the equal gravity test as set out in *Kupreškić* and approved in *Blaškić* is most appropriate. Here, the Appeals Chamber determined that an act,[65] is of equal gravity to those listed under Article 5 of the ICTY Statute if it "constitutes an indispensable and vital asset to the owner" and if the removal of it "constitutes a destruction of the livelihood of a certain population".[66]

50.   Using the *Kupreškić* test as the basis for a finding on the equal gravity in this case, it is indubitable in my mind that the crime of plunder with value above 300 DM constitutes the removal of "vital assets" and is therefore of equal gravity to other Article 5 crimes. The assets in the present case were vital because during the war financial resources, perhaps more than any other ,were essential to the very survival of the targeted non-Serbs. They allowed people to acquire food, clothes, shelter and if possible, to move away from zones and regions where violent conflagrations are occurring. As such, the plunder of financial resources could even be viewed as a callous manoeuvre to bring about the death of victims as without them it would have been clear that they would have struggled to eat, clothe themselves, find shelter and move away from the fighting. These factors, or a combination thereof, would have been likely to bring about their deaths.

51.   Third, I dissociate myself from the Majority's determination of Župljanin's claim that the appropriation was not "permanent" but rather temporary in nature. The Majority is correct when it **[page 522]** finds in paragraph 1076 of the Judgement that the issue of permanence is "without basis".[67] However, there is an obvious inconsistency due to the fact that despite this finding, the Majority then proceeds to address the issue in the same paragraph. Not only does this approach appear to present a contradiction with the Majority's assertion that this argument is without basis, but it also gives the impression that Župljanin's position on the required permanence is in fact correct, as the Majority's choice to subsequently address his argument tacitly lends weight to it.

52.   It can be reasonably inferred from the above analysis that the Majority has unfortunately entertained a regrettable error of law committed by the Trial Chamber. It should have instead, seized itself *proprio motu* and corrected this error, especially so given the seriousness of the crime of persecution as considered in the appraisal of the "gravity of the crimes" as an element of the sentencing.[68]

---

[62]   Appeal Judgement, para 1077.
[63]   *See* Trial Judgement, vol. 2, para. 956. The Trial Chamber convicted Župljanin of Persecutions through the underlying acts of *inter alia* "Forcible transfer and deportation". *See also* Judgement, para. 6.
[64]   *Ibid.*
[65]   I note that in *Blaškić* the "act" was "destruction of property" *see Blaškić* Appeal Judgement, para. 149. In *Kupreškić* the "act" was "attacks on property" *see Kupreškić* Trial Judgement, para. 631.
[66]   *Blaškić* Appeal Judgement, para. 146, *citing Kupreškić* Trial Judgement, para. 631.
[67]   Appeal Judgement, para 1076.
[68]   *See* Trial Judgement, vol. 2, para. 946.

G. <u>Sentencing</u>

53.   I do wish to express my humble disagreement with the Majority's approach to the alleged errors in assessing (i) the gravity of Stanišić's conduct (Stanišić's twelfth Ground of Appeal) and (ii) the aggravating factors (Stanišić's thirteenth Ground of Appeal) as well as (iii) the gravity of Župljanin's conduct (Sub-ground B of Župljanin's fourth Ground of Appeal) and (iv) the doublecounting submissions (Sub-ground D of Župljanin's fourth Ground of Appeal).

54.   Considering first the assessment of Stanišić conduct, the Majority correctly sets out that the Trial Chamber failed to explicitly reiterate in the sentencing section its findings on his conduct.[69] It also identifies this failure in relation to the form and degree of Stanišić's, participation in the JCE in the sentencing section of the Trial Judgement concerning the gravity of crimes.[70] In an attempt to address this lacuna, the Majority seeks, through the principle of reading the Trial Judgement "as a whole", to mine the Trial Chamber's findings on Stanišić's contribution to the JCE in order to fill out the brevity of the Trial Chamber's findings on the gravity of the offences, and in particular at paragraph 1107 the Majority relies on a number of general findings.

55.   In paragraph 1107, the Majority concludes its "reasoning" as follows:

> The Appeals Chamber notes that with respect to Stanišić's participation in the JCE, the Trial Chamber made a wide range of findings throughout the Trial Judgement, including on his official **[page 523]** position, his acts and conduct, his contribution to the JCE, and his *mens rea*. It recalls, further, that a trial judgement should be read as a whole. [Footnotes omitted].

56.   By considering general findings from four random sections of the Trial Judgement, the Majority arguably oversteps the deference afforded to the Trial Chamber in the sense that it creates a patchwork of findings or, worse still, speculates on the Trial Chamber's opinion in order to compensate for its deficiencies. Paraphrasing the American architect Frank Lloyd Wright, according to whom an architectural mistake can be covered by "planting vines", the Majority has planted a doubtful invocation of the need to "read the Trial Judgement as a whole" in order to cover the Trial Chambers legal errors. Reading the Trial Judgement "as a whole" seems to be used by the Majority in this case to exonerate itself from strictly abiding by the principle of deference to the Trial Chamber, which is only aimed at admitting a finding or affirming a pattern of reasoning of the Trial Chamber. This principle cannot apply where there is no finding or reasoning of the Trial Chamber's to defer to. Instead, the Majority's approach goes beyond merely "reading" the Trial Judgement and enters into the realm of re-writing by linking sections of the Trial Judgement where the Trial Chamber itself did not make any explicit connection. Even on a generous reading of the impugned sections, there appears to be no inkling that the Trial Chamber intended to use the findings relied upon by the Majority in assessing the gravity of offences or aggravating circumstances.

57.   It can be admitted that despite the lack of any explicit link made by the Trial Chamber between sections and the "gravity of offences" section, the Appeals Chamber can use the former to bolster the latter. The reasons for this approach should nevertheless have been markedly explained, as this method appears to use findings that could be deemed to be unrelated to the issue at hand or worse, can lead to the possibility of double-counting. Curiously, in support of its claim that the Trial Chamber considered "acts and conduct" in relation to gravity of offences the Majority relies upon paragraphs 544 to 728 of the Trial Judgement.[71] This reference suggests that *all* 184 paragraphs are relevant to this issue. However, reviewing just a few of these paragraphs for demonstration purposes, I fail to see the relevance of paragraphs 553 and 554 of the Trial Judgement in this context. In addition, several paragraphs within this same range (paragraphs 544 to 728), of the Trial Judgement are also used to bolster the aggravating circumstances section.[72] This approach of resorting to the same findings to establish the gravity of the offences and the aggravating circumstances

---

[69]   Appeal Judgement, para. 1107.

[70]   Appeal Judgement, paras 1107, 1108.

[71]   *See* Appeal Judgement, fn. 3665.

[72]   *Compare* fn.3665 Appeal Judgement *referring to* paras 544 to 828, *and* fn. 3680, Appeal Judgement, which refers to, *inter alia*, paras 609, 611, 617, 620, 623-625, 631-633, 636-645, 651-652, 654-657, 659-663, 667-668, 671-673, 684, 687-692, 698-704, 706-708

seriously violates the principle prohibiting double-counting and should have been avoided. As it stands, this is undoubtedly an error of law on the part of the Majority. **[page 524]**

58.   Similarly, with regard to Župljanin, I note that at paragraph 1148 of the Judgement, in the "gravity of offences section", the Majority takes a similar path of referring to previous Trial Chamber findings on contribution to the JCE and detailing the nature of his participation,[72][73] to support the sentencing section. This approach is repeated on the matter of "aggravating factors" at paragraph 1155 of the Judgement, where the Majority states that the Trial Chamber considered Župljanin's duty, authorities and powers,[74] and the manner in which Župljanin exercised his authority in contributing to the JCE.[75] Accordingly, the Majority relies on paragraphs 495 to 520 of volume 2 of the Trial Judgement to support its findings on both the gravity of offences and the aggravating factors.[76] In my view, this approach again leads to the distinct possibility of the Majority engaging in impermissible double-counting, which constitutes an error of law.

H.   Conclusion

59.   In overall conclusion, based on the Majority's findings, which I have not challenged, but combined with my methodology contained in this reasoned separate (dissenting) opinion on some core issues of the case, I am of the view that Stanišić and Župljanin have failed to demonstrate errors on the part of the Trial Chamber and that the alleged errors are ultimately compensated for by the reading of the Trial Judgement as a whole.

Done in English and French, the English version being authoritative.

Done this thirtieth day of June 2016,
At The Hague,   Judge Koffi Kumelio A. Afande
The Netherlands

[Seal of the Tribunal] [page 525]

---

[73]   *See* Appeal Judgement, para. 1148, fn. 3779 *referring to* Trial Judgement, vol. 2, paras. 495-520.
[74]   Appeal Judgement, para. 1155 *referring to* Trial Judgement, vol. 2, paras 489-493.
[75]   Appeal Judgement, para. 1155 *referring to* Trial Judgement, vol. 2, paras. 495-520.
[76]   *Compare* Appeal Judgement, fn. 3779 (gravity of offences) *and* fn. 3798 (aggravating factors).

XI.   ANNEX A – PROCEDURAL HISTORY

A.   Composition of the Appeals Chamber

1.   On 8 April 2013, Judge Theodor Meron ("Judge Meron"), the then President of the International Tribunal for the Prosecution of Persons Responsible for Serious Violations of International Humanitarian Law Committed in the Territory of the former Yugoslavia since 1991 ("Tribunal"), designated himself, Judge Carmel Agius ("Judge Agius"), Judge Patrick Robinson ("Judge Robinson"), Judge Liu Daqun ("Judge Liu"), and Judge Arlette Ramaroson ("Judge Ramaroson") to the Bench in this case.[1] On 15 April 2013, Judge Meron, as presiding Judge in this case pursuant to Rule 22(B) of the Rules of Procedure and Evidence of the Tribunal ("Rules"), designated himself as Pre-Appeal Judge.[2] On 15 April 2014, Judge Meron appointed Judge William Hussein Sekule ("Judge Sekule") to replace him on the Bench, for reasons pertaining to appeal management and the Tribunal's needs in terms of distribution of cases.[3]

2.   On 2 May 2014, Judge Agius, having been elected as Presiding Judge, designated himself as the Pre-Appeal Judge.[4] On 27 June 2014, Judge Meron appointed Judge Koffi Kumelio A. Afanđe to replace Judge Liu on the Bench.[5] On 22 September 2014, Judge Meron appointed Judge Khalida Rachid Khan ("Judge Khan") to replace Judge Sekule on the Bench.[6] On 11 February 2015, Judge Meron appointed Judge Bakhtiyar Tuzmukhamedov ("Judge Tuzmukhamedov") to replace Judge Robinson on the Bench following his election as judge of the International Court of Justice.[7] On 22 April 2015, Judge Meron appointed Judge Christoph Flügge ("Judge Flügge"), Judge Fausto Pocar, and Judge Liu to replace Judge Ramaroson, Judge Khan, and Judge Tuzmukhamedov on the Bench in light of the expiration of their mandates as Judges of the International Criminal Tribunal for Rwanda.[8]

B.   Notices of appeal

3.   On 16 April 2013, the Pre-Appeal Judge extended the time limit for filing notices of appeal by 15 days.[9] The Office of the Prosecutor of the Tribunal ("Prosecution"), Mićo Stanišić **[page 526]** ("Stanišić"), and Stojan Župljanin ("Župljanin") filed their initial notices of appeal against the Trial Judgement on 13 May 2013.[10]

4.   On 19 August 2013, the Pre-Appeal Judge granted Župljanin's request to correct his notice of appeal with respect to three typographical errors.[11] Župljanin subsequently filed a corrected notice of appeal on 22 August 2013.[12] On 8 October 2013, the Appeals Chamber granted Župljanin's request to amend his notice of appeal to insert sub-ground (G) in his first ground of appeal as well as a fifth ground of appeal.[13] Župljanin filed his amended notice of appeal on 9 October 2013.[14]

5.   On 14 April 2014, the Appeals Chamber granted Župljanin's second request to amend his notice of appeal.[15] Consequently, Župljanin filed an amended notice of appeal to include an additional sixth ground of appeal alleging that his right to a fair trial by an independent and impartial Tribunal was violated by the

---

[1]   Order Assigning Judges to a Case Before the Appeals Chamber, 8 April 2013.
[2]   Order Designating a Pre-Appeal Judge, 15 April 2013.
[3]   Order Replacing a Judge in a Case Before the Appeals Chamber, 15 April 2014, p. 1.
[4]   Order Designating a Pre-Appeal Judge, 2 May 2014.
[5]   Order Replacing a Judge in a Case Before the Appeals Chamber, 27 June 2014.
[6]   Order Replacing a Judge in a Case Before the Appeals Chamber, 22 September 2014. See Corrigendum to Order Replacing a Judge in a Case Before the Appeals Chamber, 23 September 2014.
[7]   Order Replacing a Judge in a Case Before the Appeals Chamber, 11 February 2015.
[8]   Order Replacing Judges in a Case Before the Appeals Chamber, 22 April 2015.
[9]   Decision on Joint Defence Motion Seeking Extension of Time to File Notice of Appeal, 16 April 2013.
[10]   Prosecution Notice of Appeal, 13 May 2013; Notice of Appeal on Behalf of Mićo Stanišić, 13 May 2013; Notice of Appeal on Behalf of Stojan [Ž]upljanin, 13 May 2013.
[11]   Decision on Župljanin's Request to Correct his Notice of Appeal, 19 August 2013.
[12]   [Ž]upljanin's Submission of Corrected Notice of Appeal, 22 August 2013.
[13]   Decision on Stojan Župljanin's Request to Amend Notice of Appeal, 8 October 2013, p. 6.
[14]   [Ž]upljanin's Submission of Amended Notice of Appeal, 9 October 2013.
[15]   Decision on Župljanin's Second Request to Amend his Notice of Appeal and Supplement his Appeal Brief, 14 April 2014.

participation of Judge Frederik Harhoff ("Judge Harhoff").[16] On 14 April 2014, the Appeals Chamber also granted Stanišić's request to amend his notice of appeal.[17] Stanišić filed an amended notice of appeal on 23 April 2014, modifying his fourth and tenth grounds of appeal, and including an additional ground of appeal 1*bis* concerning the participation of Judge Harhoff in the trial proceedings.[18]

C. **Appeal briefs**

10.   On 21 May 2013, Stanišić filed a motion seeking an extension of 40 days to submit his appeal brief and an extension of the word limit for a total of 10,000 words.[19] On 21 May 2013, Župljanin also filed a motion seeking an extension of time for filing of his appeal brief and a request to exceed the word limit.[20] Pursuant to the Pre-Appeal Judge's decision of 4 June 2013, the deadline for filing the appellants' briefs was extended by 21 days and Stanišić and Župljanin were each granted an extension of the word limit to 10,000 words for their respective briefs.[21] The **[page 527]** Prosecution was granted a corresponding extension of the word limit for its briefs in response.[22] Stanišić and Župljanin were also each granted an extension of time by five days to submit their briefs in reply.[23] The Prosecution was granted a corresponding extension of 21 days to file its appeal brief, Stanišić and Župljanin were granted an extension of 21 days to file their respective response briefs, and the Prosecution was granted an extension of five days to file its brief in reply.[24]

11.   The Prosecution filed its appeal brief on 19 August 2013.[25] On 21 October 2013, Stanišić and Župljanin filed their respective respondent briefs.[26] The Prosecution replied on 11 November 2013.[27] Stanišić and Župljanin filed their respective appeal briefs on 19 August 2013.[28] The Prosecution responded on 21 October 2013,[29] and Stanišić and Župljanin replied on 11 November 2013.[30]

12.   On 2 May 2014, the Pre-Appeal Judge varied the deadline for filing an addition to Stanišić's and Župljanin's appeal briefs.[31] Stanisić and Župljanin subsequently filed additions to their appeal briefs on 26 June 2014[32] and the Prosecution filed a consolidated response on 18 July 2014.[33] Stanisić and Župljanin replied on 25 July 2014.[34]

---

[16]   Župljanin Notice of Appeal, 22 April 2014, p. 12.

[17]   Decision on Mićo Stanišić's Motion Seeking Leave to Amend Notice of Appeal, 14 April 2014.

[18]   Stanišić Notice of Appeal, 23 April 2014, pp 5, 7-8, 12-13.

[19]   Expedited Motion on Behalf of Mićo Stanišić Seeking a Variation of Time and Word Limits to File Appellant's Brief, 21 May 2013, p. 1.

[20]   [Ž]upljanin Request for Extension of Time to File Appeal Brief, 21 May 2013, pp 2, 5.

[21]   Decision on Mićo Stanišić's and Stojan Župljanin's Motions Seeking Variation of Time and Word Limits to File Appeal Briefs, 4 June 2013, ("4 June 2013 Decision"), p. 5.

[22]   4 June 2013 Decision, p. 5. On 21 June 2013, the Pre-Appeal Judge denied Stanišić's motion of 6 June 2013 seeking reconsideration of the 4 June 2013 Decision and requesting a reduction of the Prosecution's word limit to no more than 53,333 words (Decision on Mićo Stanišić's Motion Seeking Reconsideration of Decision on Variation of Time and Word Limits to File Appellant's Brief, 21 June 2013).

[23]   4 June 2013 Decision, p. 5.

[24]   4 June 2013 Decision, p. 5.

[25]   Prosecution Appeal Brief, 19 August 2013.

[26]   Župljanin Response Brief, 21 October 2013; Stanišić Response Brief, 21 October 2013.

[27]   Prosecution Consolidated Reply Brief, 11 November 2013.

[28]   Stanišić Appeal Brief, 19 August 2013; Župljanin Appeal Brief, 19 August 2013 (confidential). On 23 August 2013 Župljanin filed a public redacted version of his appeal brief.

[29]   Prosecution Response Brief (Stanišić), 21 October 2013 (confidential; public redacted version filed on 15 November 2013); Prosecution Response Brief (Župljanin), 21 October 2013 (confidential; public redacted version filed on 15 November 2013).

[30]   Stanišić Reply Brief, 11 November 2013; Župljanin Reply Brief, 11 November 2013.

[31]   Decision on Urgent Prosecution Motion for Variation of Supplemental Briefing Schedule, 2 May 2014.

[32]   Stanišić Additional Appeal Brief, 26 June 2014; Župljanin Additional Appeal Brief, 26 June 2014.

[33]   Prosecution Consolidated Supplemental Response Brief, 18 July 2014.

[34]   Stanišić Additional Reply Brief, 25 July 2014; Župljanin Additional Reply Brief, 25 July 2014. On 30 October 2014, the Appeals Chamber dismissed the Prosecution's motion for leave to file a sur-reply to answer Župljanin's new argument in reply concerning the late filing of the Prosecution Consolidated Supplemental Response Brief as moot (Decision on Prosecution Motion for Leave to File Sur-reply and Sur-reply to Župljanin's Reply to Prosecution's Consolidated Supplemental Response Brief Concerning Additional Appeal Ground, 30 October 2014).

13.   On 14 April 2016, the Presiding Judge ordered Župljanin to make certain redactions to the public redacted version of his appeal brief and file a further public redacted version of his appeal brief within seven days.[35] On 21 April 2016, Župljanin filed an amended public redacted version of his appeal brief.[36] **[page 528]**

D.   Decisions relating to Judge Harhoff

14.   As discussed in the paragraphs below, the parties filed nine motions relating to the allegation of bias on the part of Judge Harhoff following a letter he had written on 6 June 2013 and that was published in a Danish newspaper on 13 June 2013 ("Letter"). Considering that the references to Judge Meron in the Letter gave rise to a "conflict of interest",[37] Judge Meron issued an order replacing himself on the Bench with Judge Sekule for the purposes of considering these motions.[38]

15.   On 2 July 2013, Stanišić filed a motion seeking the admission of additional evidence on appeal consisting of excerpts from the Letter.[39] On 14 April 2014, the Appeals Chamber granted the motion and admitted the Letter as additional evidence on appeal.[40] On 11 June 2014, the Appeals Chamber granted the Prosecution's motion to admit three documents as rebuttal material.[41]

16.   On 21 October 2013, Župljanin filed a motion to vacate the Trial Judgement on the basis that the Trial Chamber was not a properly constituted trial chamber consisting of three impartial judges.[42] For the same reasons, on 23 October 2013 Stanišić filed a motion to declare a mistrial and to vacate the Trial Judgement.[43] Župljanin also filed a motion requesting that Judge Liu be recused from considering the motion to vacate,[44] which was denied on 3 December 2013 by Judge Agius in his capacity as acting President.[45] On 13 December 2013, Župljanin filed a request, joined by Stanišić, for the appointment of a panel to adjudicate the request for disqualification of Judge Liu.[46] **[page 529]** The appointed panel composed of Judge Flügge, Judge Howard Morrison, and Judge Melville Baird[47] denied the request on 24 February 2014.[48]

17.   On 2 April 2014, the Appeals Chamber denied Stanišić's Motion for Declaration of Mistrial and Župljanin's Motion to Vacate Trial Judgement.[49] On 10 April 2014, Stanišić filed a motion seeking

35   Order for Redaction of Stojan Župljanin's Appeal Brief, 14 April 2016 (confidential).
36   Stojan [Ž]upljanin's Appeal Brief, 21 April 2016.
37   Order Assigning a Motion to a Judge, 23 July 2013, p. 1.
38   Order Replacing a Judge in Respect of a Motion Before the Appeals Chamber, 24 July 2013; Order Assigning a Motion to a Judge, 10 September 2013; Order Replacing a Judge in Respect of Motions Before the Appeals Chamber, 28 November 2013; Order Replacing a Judge in Respect of a Motion Before the Appeals Chamber, 28 November 2013; Order Replacing a Judge in Respect of a Motion Before the Appeals Chamber, 28 November 2013; Order Replacing a Judge in Respect of a Motion Before the Appeals Chamber, 28 November 2013; Order Replacing a Judge in Respect of a Motion Before the Appeals Chamber, 28 November 2013. See Order Assigning a Motion to a Judge, 23 July 2013; Order Assigning a Motion to a Judge, 23 July 2013; Order Replacing a Judge in Respect of a Rule 115 Motion Before the Appeals Chamber, 24 July 2013; Order Assigning Motions to a Judge, 22 October 2013; Order Assigning Motions [*sic*] to a Judge, 23 October 2013; Order Assigning a Motion to a Judge, 25 October 2013.
39   Rule 115 Motion on Behalf of Mićo Stanišić Seeking Admission of Additional Evidence with Annex, 2 July 2013 ("Stanišić 2 July 2013 Rule 115 Motion"). Župljanin joined the Stanišić 2 July 2013 Rule 115 Motion through the Župljanin Second Request to Amend Notice of Appeal, 14 April 2014.
40   Decision on Mićo Stanišić's Motion Seeking Admission of Additional Evidence Pursuant to Rule 115, 14 April 2014 ("Rule 115 Decision"), pp 7-8. See Rule 115 Decision, para. 24.
41   Decision on Prosecution Motion to Admit Rebuttal Material, 11 June 2014.
42   Stojan [Ž]upljanin's Motion to Vacate Trial Judgement, 21 October 2013.
43   Motion on Behalf of Mićo Stanišić Requesting a Declaration of Mistrial, 23 October 2013 ("Stanišić Motion for Declaration of Mistrial").
44   Stojan [Ž]upljanin's Motion Requesting Recusal of Judge Liu Daqun from Adjudication of Motion to Vacate Trial Judgement, 21 October 2013 ("Župljanin's Motion to Vacate Trial Judgement").
45   Decision on Motion Requesting Recusal, 3 December 2013.
46   Župljanin Defence Request for Appointment of a Panel to Adjudicate the Request for Disqualification of Judge Liu Daqun, 13 December 2013; Motion on Behalf of Mićo Stanišić joining Župljanin Defence Request for Appointment of a Panel to Adjudicate the Request for Disqualification of Judge Liu Daqun, 23 December 2013.
47   See Decision on Župljanin Defence Request for Appointment of a Panel to Adjudicate the Request for Disqualification of Judge Liu Daqun, 7 February 2014.
48   Decision on Motion Requesting Recusal of Judge Liu from Adjudication of Motion to Vacate Trial Judgement, 24 February 2014.
49   Decision on Mićo Stanišić's Motion Requesting a Declaration of Mistrial and Stojan Župljanin's Motion to Vacate Trial Judgement, 2 April 2014.

reconsideration of the Decision on Mistrial and Vacation of Trial Judgement,[50] which was denied on 24 July 2014.[51]

18.	On 25 August 2014, Stanišić and Župljanin filed a motion seeking expedited adjudication of their respective additional grounds of appeal 1*bis* and six,[52] which the Appeals Chamber denied on 22 October 2014.[53]

### E.	Provisional release and request for custodial visit

19.	On 19 December 2013, the Appeals Chamber dismissed Stanišić's and Župljanin's motions for provisional release.[54] On 16 October 2015, the Appeals Chamber dismissed Župljanin's request for custodial visit on humanitarian grounds.[55]

### F.	Other decisions and orders

20.	In addition to the above, the Appeals Chamber issued 11 decisions and orders concerning evidentiary and other matters. Further, the Appeals Chamber issued 28 orders and decisions concerning applications pursuant to Rule 75 of the Rules. **[page 530]**

### G.	Status conferences

21.	In accordance with Rule 65 *bis*(B) of the Rules, status conferences were held on 4 September 2013,[56] 11 December 2013,[57] 9 April 2014,[58] 24 July 2014,[59] 12 November 2014,[60] 9 March 2015,[61] 30 June 2015,[62] 15 October 2015,[63] 10 February 2016,[64] and 25 May 2016.[65]

### H.	Appeal hearing

22.	On 30 October 2015, the Appeals Chamber issued a scheduling order for the Appeal Hearing in this case.[66] On 4 December 2015, the Appeals Chamber issued an *addendum* informing the parties of certain

---

[50]	Motion on Behalf of Mićo Stanišić Seeking Reconsideration of Decision on Stanišić's Motion for a Declaration of Mistrial and Župljanin Motion to Vacate Trial Judgement, 10 April 2014.
[51]	Decision on Mićo Stanišić's Motion Seeking Reconsideration of Decision on Stanišić's Motion for Declaration of Mistrial and Župljanin's Motion to Vacate Trial Judgement, 24 July 2014.
[52]	Joint Motion on Behalf of Mićo Stanišić and Stojan Župljanin Seeking Expedited Adjudication of Their Respective Grounds of Appeal 1*Bis* and 6, 25 August 2014.
[53]	Decision on Joint Motion on Behalf of Mićo Stanišić and Stojan Župljanin Seeking Expedited Adjudication of Their Respective Grounds of Appeal 1*Bis* and 6, 22 October 2014.
[54]	Decision on Motion on Behalf of Mićo Stanišić Seeking Provisional Release, 19 December 2013; Decision on Stojan Župljanin's Request for Provisional Release, 19 December 2013.
[55]	Decision on Stojan Župljanin's Request for Custodial Visit on Humanitarian Grounds, 16 October 2015 (confidential).
[56]	Scheduling Order, 10 July 2013; Status Conference, 4 Sep 2013, AT. 1-5.
[57]	Scheduling Order, 2 December 2013; Status Conference, 11 Dec 2013, AT. 6-13.
[58]	Scheduling Order, 10 March 2014; Status Conference, 9 Apr 2014, AT. 14-19.
[59]	Scheduling Order, 3 June 2014; Status Conference, 24 Jul 2014, AT. 20-28.
[60]	Scheduling Order, 1 October 2014; Amendment to Order Scheduling Status Conference, 17 October 2014; Status Conference, 12 Nov 2014, AT. 29-37.
[61]	Scheduling Order, 29 January 2015; Status Conference, 9 Mar 2015, AT. 38-46. See Decision on Urgent Motion on Behalf of Mićo Stanišić Seeking Rescheduling of 6th March Status Conference, 2 March 2015.
[62]	Scheduling Order, 14 May 2015; Status Conference, 30 Jun 2015, AT. 47-53.
[63]	Scheduling Order, 8 September 2015; Status Conference, 15 Oct 2015, AT. 54-60.
[64]	Scheduling Order, 11 January 2016; Status Conference, 10 Feb 2016, AT. 245-249.
[65]	Scheduling Order, 21 April 2016; Status Conference, 25 May 2016, AT. 250-254.
[66]	Scheduling Order for Appeal Hearing, 30 October 2015, p. 1.

modalities of the Appeal Hearing[67] and inviting the parties to address several specific issues.[68] The Appeal Hearing was held on 16 December 2015.[69] **[page 531]**

XII. ANNEX B – GLOSSARY

A. <u>Jurisprudence</u>

1. <u>ICTY</u>

ALEKSOVSKI

Prosecutor v. Zlatko Aleksovksi, Case No. IT-95-14/1-A, Judgement, 24 March 2000 ("*Aleksovski* Appeal Judgement")

BABIĆ

Prosecutor v. Milan Babić, Case No. IT-03-72-A, Judgement on Sentencing Appeal, 18 July 2005, ("*Babić* Sentencing Appeal Judgement")

BANOVIĆ

Prosecutor v. Predrag Banović, Case No. IT-02-65/1-S, Sentencing Judgement, 28 October 2003 ("*Banović* Sentencing Judgement")

BLAGOJEVIĆ ET AL.

Prosecutor v. Vidoje Blagojević et al., Case No. IT-02-60-PT, Decision on Blagojević's Application Pursuant to Rule 15(B), 19 March 2003

Prosecutor v. Vidoje Blagojević and Dragan Jokić, Case No. IT-02-60-T, Judgement, 17 January 2005 ("*Blagojević and Jokić* Trial Judgement")

Prosecutor v. Vidoje Blagojević and Dragan Jokić, Case No. IT-02-60-A, Judgement, 9 May 2007 ("*Blagojević and Jokić* Appeal Judgement")

BLAŠKIĆ

Prosecutor v. Tihomir Blaškić, Case No. IT-95-14-A, Judgement, 29 July 2004 ("*Blaškić* Appeal Judgement")

BOŠKOSKI AND TARČULOVSKI

Prosecutor v. Ljube Boškoski and Johan Tarčulovski, Case No. IT-04-82-A, Judgement, 19 May 2010 ("*Boškoski and Tarčulovski* Appeal Judgement")

BRALO

Prosecutor v. Miroslav Bralo, Case No. IT-95-17-A, Judgement on Sentencing Appeal, 2 April 2007 ("*Bralo* Sentencing Appeal Judgement")

---

[67] *Addendum* to Scheduling Order for Appeal Hearing, 4 December 2015, pp 1-2, setting out the timetable for the appeal hearing. On 11 December 2015, granting the Prosecution's urgent motion in part, the Appeals Chamber amended the timetable for the Appeal Hearing, by adjusting the distribution of time allocated to the parties (Decision on Prosecution Urgent Motion to Revise the Timetable for the Appeal Hearing, 11 December 2015, pp 2-3).
[68] *Addendum* to Scheduling Order for Appeal Hearing, 4 December 2015, pp 2-3.
[69] Appeal Hearing, 16 Dec 2015, AT. 61-244.

BRĐANIN AND TALIĆ

Prosecutor v. Radoslav Brđanin and Momir Talić, Case No. IT-99-36-PT, Decision on Form of Further Amended Indictment and Prosecution Application to Amend, 26 June 2001

Prosecutor v. Radoslav Brđanin, Case No. IT-99-36-AR73.10, Decision on Interlocutory Appeal, 19 March 2004 ("*Brđanin* Appeal Decision of 19 March 2004")

Prosecutor v. Radoslav Brđanin, Case No. IT-99-36-T, Judgement, 1 September 2004 ("*Brđanin* Trial Judgement")

Prosecutor v. Radoslav Brđanin, Case No. IT-99-36-A, Judgement, 3 April 2007 ("*Brđanin* Appeal Judgement") **[page 532]**

DELALIĆ ET AL. ("ČELEBIĆI")

Prosecutor v. Zejnil Delalić et al., Case No. IT-96-21-T, Decision of the Bureau on Motion to Disqualify Judges Pursuant to Rule 15 or in the Alternative that Certain Judges Recuse Themselves, 25 October 1999 ("*Delalić et al.* Disqualification and Recusal Decision")

Prosecutor v. Zejnil Delalić et al., Case No. IT-96-21-T, Judgement, 16 November 1998 ("*Čelebići* Trial Judgement")

Prosecutor v. Zejnil Delalić et al., Case No. IT-96-21-A, Judgement, 20 February 2001 ("*Čelebići* Appeal Judgement")

DELIĆ

Prosecutor v. Rasim Delić, Case No. IT-04-83-T, Judgement, 15 September 2008 ("*Delić* Trial Judgement")

DERONJIĆ

Prosecutor v. Miroslav Deronjić, Case No. IT-02-61-S, Sentencing Judgement, 30 March 2004 ("*Deronjić* Sentencing Judgement")

Prosecutor v. Miroslav Deronjić, Case No. IT-02-61-A, Judgement on Sentencing Appeal, 20 July 2005 ("*Deronjić* Sentencing Appeal Judgement")

ĐORĐEVIĆ

Prosecutor v. Vlastimir Đorđević, Case No. IT-05-87/1-A, Judgement, 27 January 2014 ("*Đorđević* Appeal Judgement")

ERDEMOVIĆ

Prosecutor v. Dra'en Erdemović, Case No. IT-96-22-Tbis, 5 March 1998 ("*Erdemović* Sentencing Judgement")

FURUNDŽIJA

Prosecutor v. Anto Furundžija, Case No. IT-95-17/1-A, Judgement, 21 July 2000 ("*Furundžija* Appeal Judgement")

GALIĆ

Prosecutor v. Stanislav Galić, Case No. IT-98-29-A, Judgement, 30 November 2006 ("*Galić* Appeal Judgement")

GOTOVINA ET AL.

Prosecutor v. Ante Gotovina et al., Case No. IT-06-90-AR73.1, Decision on Miroslav Šeparović's Interlocutory Appeal Against Trial Chamber's Decisions on Conflict of Interest and Finding of Misconduct, 4 May 2007

Prosecutor v. Ante Gotovina et al., Case No. IT-06-90-T, Judgement, 15 April 2011 (*"Gotovina et al.* Trial Judgement")

Prosecutor v. Ante Gotovina and Mladen Markač, Case No. IT-06-90-A, Judgement, 16 November 2012 (*"Gotovina and Markač* Appeal Judgement")

HADŽIHASANOVIĆ AND KUBURA

Prosecutor v. Enver Hadžihasanović and Amir Kubura, Case No. IT-01-47-T, Judgement, 15 March 2006 (*"Hadžihasanović and Kubura* Trial Judgement") **[page 533]**

Prosecutor v. Enver Hadžihasanović and Amir Kubura, Case No. IT-01-47-A, Judgement, 22 April 2008 (*"Hadžihasanović and Kubura* Appeal Judgement")

HARADINAJ ET AL.

Prosecutor v. Ramush Haradinaj et al., Case No. IT-04-84-A, Judgement, 19 July 2010 (*"Haradinaj et al.* Appeal Judgement")

Prosecutor v. Haradinaj et al., Case No. IT-04-84*bis*-T, Judgement, 29 November 2012 (*"Haradinaj et al.* Retrial Judgement")

JELISIĆ

Prosecutor v. Goran Jelisić, Case No. IT-95-10-T, Judgement, 14 December 1999 (*"Jelisić* Trial Judgement")

Prosecutor v. Goran Jelisić, Case No. IT-95-10-A, Judgement, 5 July 2001 (*"Jelisić* Appeal Judgement")

JOKIĆ

Prosecutor v. Miodrag Jokić, Case No. IT-01-42/1-S, Sentencing Judgement, 18 March 2004 (*"Jokić* Sentencing Judgement")

KARADŽIĆ

Prosecutor v. Radovan Karadžić, Case No. IT-95-5/18-PT, Decision on Six Preliminary Motions Challenging Jurisdiction, 28 April 2009

Prosecutor v. Radovan Karadžić, Case No. IT-95-05/18-PT, Decision on Motion to Disqualify Judge Picard and Report to the Vice-President Pursuant to Rule 15(B)(ii), 22 July 2009 (" *Karadžić* Disqualification Decision")

KORDIĆ AND ČERKEZ

Prosecutor v. Dario Kordić and Mario Čerkez, Case No. IT-95-14/2-T, Judgement, 26 February 2001 (*"Kordić and Čerkez* Trial Judgement")

Prosecutor v. Dario Kordić and Mario Čerkez, Case No. IT-95-14/2-A, Judgement, 17 December 2004 (*"Kordić and Čerkez* Appeal Judgement")

KRAJIŠNIK

Prosecutor v. Momčilo Krajišnik, Case No. IT-00-39-T, Decision on Prosecution's Motion for Clarification and Reconsideration of the Decision on 28 February 2008, 11 March 2008

Prosecutor v. Momčilo Krajišnik, Case No. IT-00-39-T, Judgement, 27 September 2006 (*"Krajišnik* Trial Judgement")

Prosecutor v. Momčilo Krajišnik, Case No. IT-00-39-A, Judgement, 17 March 2009 (*"Krajišnik* Appeal Judgement")

KRNOJELAC

Prosecutor v. Milorad Krnojelac, Case No. IT-97-25-T, Judgement, 15 March 2002 (*"Krnojelac* Trial Judgement")

Prosecutor v. Milorad Krnojelac, Case No. IT-97-25-A, Judgement, 17 September 2003 (*"Krnojelac* Appeal Judgement") **[page 534]**

KRSTIĆ

Prosecutor v. Radislav Krstić, Case No. IT-98-33-T, Judgement, 2 August 2001, (*"Krstić* Trial Judgement")

Prosecutor v. Radislav Krstić, Case No. IT-98-33-A, Judgement, 19 April 2004 (*"Krstić* Appeal Judgement")

KUNARAC ET AL.

Prosecutor v. Dragoljub Kunarac et al., Case Nos. IT-96-23-T & IT-96-23/1-T, 22 February 2001 (*"Kunarac et al.* Trial Judgement")

Prosecutor v. Dragoljub Kunarac et al., Case Nos. IT-96-23-A & IT-96-23/1-A, 12 June 2002 (*"Kunarac et al.* Appeal Judgement")

KUPREŠKIĆ ET AL.

Prosecutor v. Zoran Kupreškić et al., Case No. IT-95-16-A, Appeal Judgement, 23 October 2001 (*"Kupreškić et al.* Appeal Judgement")

KVOČKA ET AL.

Prosecutor v. Miroslav Kvočka et al., Case No. IT-98-30/1-T, Judgement, 2 November 2001, (*"Kvočka et al.* Trial Judgement")

Prosecutor v. Miroslav Kvočka et al., Case No. IT-98-30/1-A, 28 February 2005, (*"Kvočka et al.* Appeal Judgement")

LIMAJ ET AL.

Prosecutor v. Fatmir Limaj et al., Case No. IT-03-66-T, Judgement, 30 November 2005 (*"Limaj et al.* Trial Judgement")

Prosecutor v. Fatmir Limaj et al., Case No. IT-03-66-A, Judgement, 27 September 2007 (*"Limaj et al.* Appeal Judgement")

LUKIĆ AND LUKIĆ

Prosecutor v. Milan Lukić and Sredoje Lukić, Case No. IT-98-32/1-AR65.1, Decision on Defence Appeal Against Trial Chamber's Decision on Sredoje Lukić's Motion for Provisional Release, 16 April 2007

Prosecutor v. Milan Lukić and Sredoje Lukić, Case No. IT-98-32/1-A, Judgement, 4 December 2012 (*"Lukić and Lukić* Appeal Judgement")

MARTIĆ

Prosecutor v. Milan Martić, Case No. IT-95-11-T, Judgement, 12 June 2007 (*"Martić* Trial Judgement")

Prosecutor v. Milan Martić, Case No. IT-95-11-A, Judgement, 8 October 2008 (*"Martić* Appeal Judgement")

MILOŠEVIĆ, D.

Prosecutor v. Dragomir Milošević, Case No. IT-98-29/1-T, Judgement, 12 December 2007 (*"D. Milošević* Trial Judgement")

Prosecutor v. Dragomir Milošević, Case No. IT-98-29/1-A, Judgement, 12 November 2009 (*"D. Milošević* Appeal Judgement") **[page 535]**

MILUTINOVIĆ ET AL.

Prosecutor v. Milan Milutinović et al., Case No. IT-99-37-AR72, Decision on Dragoljub Ojdanic's Motion Challenging Jurisdiction – Joint Criminal Enterprise, 21 May 2003 (*"Milutinović et al.* Appeal Decision on Joint Criminal Enterprise of 21 May 2003)

Prosecutor v. Milan Milutinović et al., Case No. IT-05-87-T, Judgement, 26 February 2009, (*"Milutinović et al.* Trial Judgement")

MRĐA

Prosecutor v. Darko Mrđa, Case No. IT-02-59-S, Sentencing Judgement, 31 March 2004 (*"Mrđa* Sentencing Judgement")

MRKŠIĆ AND ŠLJIVANCANIN

Prosecutor v. Mile Mrkšić and Veselin Šljivančanin, Case No. IT-95-13/1-A, Judgement, 5 May 2009 (*"Mrkšić and Šljivančanin* Appeal Judgement")

NALETILIĆ AND MARTINOVIĆ

Prosecutor v. Mladen Naletilić, a.k.a. "Tuta" and Vinko Martinović, a.k.a. "Štela", Case No. 98-34-A, Judgement, 3 May 2006 (*"Naletilić and Martinović* Appeal Judgement")

NIKOLIĆ, D.

Prosecutor v. Dragan Nikolić, Case No. IT-94-2-S, Sentencing Judgement, 18 December 2003 (*"D. Nikolić* Sentencing Judgement")

Prosecutor v. Dragan Nikolić, Case No. IT-94-2-A, Judgement on Sentencing Appeal, 4 February 2005 (*"D. Nikolić* Sentencing Appeal Judgement")

NIKOLIĆ, M.

Prosecutor v. Momir Nikolić, Case No. IT-02-60/1-A, Judgement on Sentencing Appeal, 8 March 2006 (*"M. Nikolić* Sentencing Appeal Judgement")

ORIĆ

Prosecutor v. Naser Orić, Case No. IT-03-68-T, Judgement, 30 June 2006 (*"Orić* Trial Judgement")

Prosecutor v. Naser Orić, Case No. IT-03-68-A, Judgement, 3 July 2008 (*"Orić* Appeal Judgement")

PERIŠIĆ

Prosecutor v. Momčilo Perišić, Case No. IT-04-81-T, Judgement, 6 September 2011 (public with confidential annex C) (*"Perišić* Trial Judgement")

Prosecutor v. Momčilo Perišić, Case No. IT-04-81-A, Judgement, 28 February 2013 (*"Perišić* Appeal Judgement")

PLAVŠIĆ

Prosecutor v. Biljana Plavšić, Case No. IT-00-39&40/1-S, Sentencing Judgement, 27 February 2003 (*"Plavsic* Sentencing Judgement")

POPOVIĆ ET AL.

Prosecutor v. Vujadin Popović et al., Case No. IT-05-88-T, Judgement, 10 June 2010 (public redacted version) (*"Popović et al.* Trial Judgement")

Prosecutor v. Vujadin Popović et al., Case No. IT-05-88-A, Decision on Drago Nikolić Motion to Disqualify Judge Liu Daqun, 20 January 2011(*"Popović et al.* Decision") **[page 536]**

Prosecutor v. Vujadin Popović et al., Case No. IT-05-88-A, Judgement, 30 January 2015 (public redacted version) (*"Popović et al.* Appeal Judgement")

ŠAINOVIĆ ET AL.

Prosecutor v. Nikola Šainović et al., Case No. IT-05-87-A, Judgement, 23 January 2014 (*"Šainović et al.* Appeal Judgement")

ŠEŠELJ

Prosecutor v. Vojislav Šešelj, Case No. IT-03-67-R77.3, Decision on Motion by Professor Vojislav Šešelj for the Disqualification of Judges O-Gon Kwon and Kevin Parker, 19 November 2010

Prosecutor v. Vojislav Šešelj, Case No. IT-03-67-R77.4-A, Decision on Vojislav Šešelj's Motion to Disqualify Judges Arlette Ramaroson, Mehmet Güney and Andresia Vaz, 10 January 2013

Prosecutor v. Vojislav Šešelj, Case No. IT-03-67-T, Professor Vojislav Šešelj's Motion for Disqualification of Judge Frederik Harhoff, 9 July 2013

Prosecutor v. Vojislav Šešelj, Case No. IT-03-67-T, Decision on Defence Motion for Disqualification of Judge Frederik Harhoff and Report to the Vice-President, 28 August 2013 (*"Šešelj* Decision on Disqualification")

Prosecutor v. Vojislav Šešelj, Case No. IT-03-67-T, Decision on Prosecution Motion for Reconsideration of Decision on Disqualification, Requests for Clarification, and Motion on Behalf of Stanišić and Župljanin", 7 October 2013 (*"Šešelj* Reconsideration Decision")

Prosecutor v. Vojislav Šešelj, Case No. IT-03-67-T, Order Assigning a Judge Pursuant to Rule 15, 31 October 2013 (*"Šešelj* Order Replacing Judge Harhoff")

Prosecution v. Vojislav Šešelj, Case No. IT-03-67-T, Decision on Appeal Against Decision on Continuation of Proceedings, 6 June 2014

SIMIĆ ET AL.

Prosecutor v. Blagoje Simić et al., Case No. IT-95-9-T, Judgement, 17 October 2003 (*"Simić et al.* Trial Judgement")

Prosecutor v. Blagoje Simić, Case No. IT-95-9-A, Judgement, 28 November 2006 (*"Simić* Appeal Judgement")

STAKIĆ

Prosecutor v. Milomir Stakić, Case No. IT-97-24-T, Judgement, 31 July 2003 (*"Stakić* Trial Judgement")

Prosecutor v. Milomir Stakić, Case No. IT-97-24-A, Judgement, 22 March 2006 (*"Stakić* Appeal Judgement")

STANIŠIĆ AND SIMATOVIĆ

Prosecutor v. Mićo Stanišić, Case No. IT-04-79-AR65.1, Decision on Prosecution's Interlocutory Appeal of Mićo Stanišić's Provisional Release, 17 October 2005

Prosecutor v. Mićo Stanišić, Case No. IT-04-79-AR65.1, Decision on Prosecution's Interlocutory Appeal of Mićo Stanišić's Provisional Release, 17 October 2005

Prosecutor v. Jovica Stanišić and Franko Simatović, Case No. IT-03-69-T, Judgement, 30 May 2013 (*"Stanišić and Simatović* Trial Judgement") **[page 537]**

Prosecutor v. Jovića Stanišić and Franko Simatović, Case No. IT-03-69-A, Judgement, 15 December 2015 (*"Stanišić and Simatović* Appeal Judgement")

STANIŠIĆ AND ŽUPLJANIN

Prosecutor v. Mićo Stanišić and Stojan Župljanin, Case No. IT-08-91-PT, Decision on Mićo Stanišić's and Stojan Župljanin's Motions on Form of the Indictment, 19 March 2009 ("Decision on Form of the Indictment")

Prosecutor v. Mićo Stanišić and Stojan Župljanin, Case No. IT-08-91-T, Decision Granting in Part Prosecution's Motions for Judicial Notice of Adjudicated Facts Pursuant to Rule 94(B), 1 April 2010 ("Adjudicated Facts Decision")

Prosecutor v. Mićo Stanišić and Stojan Župljanin, Case No. IT-08-91-A, Supplemental Submission in Support of Mićo Stanišić's Motion to Amend Notice of Appeal, 9 September 2013

Prosecutor v. Mićo Stanišić and Stojan Župljanin, Case No. IT-08-91-A, [Ž]upljanin's Second Request to Amend His Notice of Appeal and Supplement His Appeal Brief, 9 September 2013

Prosecutor v. Mićo Stanišić and Stojan Župljanin, Case No. IT-08-91-A, Decision on Motion Requesting Recusal of Judge Liu from Adjudication of Motion to Vacate Trial Judgement, 24 February 2014

Prosecutor v. Mićo Stanišić and Stojan Župljanin, Case No. IT-08-91-A, Decision on Mićo Stanišić's Motion requesting a Declaration of Mistrial and Stojan Župljanin's Motion to Vacate Trial Judgement, 2 April 2014 ("Mistrial Decision")

Prosecutor v. Mićo Stanišić and Stojan Župljanin, Case No. IT-08-91-A, Decision on Mićo Stanišić's Motion Seeking Admission of Additional Evidence Pursuant to Rule 115, 14 April 2014 ("Rule 115 Decision")

Prosecutor v. Mićo Stanišić and Stojan Župljanin, Case No. IT-08-91-A, Decision on Mićo Stanišić's Motion Seeking Leave to Amend Notice of Appeal, 14 April 2014 ("Decision on Stanišić's Motion to Amend Notice of Appeal")

Prosecutor v. Mićo Stanišić and Stojan Župljanin, Case No. IT-08-91-A, Decision on Župljanin's Second Request to Amend His Notice of Appeal and Supplement His Appeal Brief, 14 April 2014

Prosecutor v. Mićo Stanišić and Stojan Župljanin, Case No. IT-08-91-A, Prosecution Motion to Admit Rebuttal Material, 1 May 2014

Prosecutor v. Mićo Stanišić and Stojan Župljanin, Case No. IT-08-91-A, Decision on Prosecution Motion to Admit Rebuttal Material, 11 June 2014

Prosecutor v. Mićo Stanišić and Stojan Župljanin, Case No. IT-08-91-A, Decision on Mićo Stanišić's Motion Seeking Reconsideration of Decision on Stanišic's Motion for Declaration of Mistrial and Župljanin's Motion to Vacate Trial Judgement, 24 July 2014

STRUGAR

Prosecutor v. Pavle Strugar, Case No. IT-01-42-T, Judgement, 31 January 2005 (*"Strugar* Trial Judgement")

Prosecutor v. Pavle Strugar, Case No. IT-01-42-A, Judgement, 17 July 2008 (*"Strugar* Appeal Judgement") **[page 538]**

477

TADIĆ

Prosecutor v. Dusko Tadić, Case No. IT-94-1-A, Judgement, 15 July 1999 ("*Tadić* Appeal Judgement")

Prosecutor v. Dusko Tadić, Case No. IT-94-1-A and IT-94-1-A*bis*, Judgement in Sentencing Appeals, 26 January 2000 ("*Tadić* Sentencing Appeal Judgement")

TOLIMIR

Prosecutor v. Zdravko Tolimir, Case No. IT-05-88/2-T, Judgement, 12 December 2012 ("*Tolimir* Trial Judgement")

Prosecutor v. Zdravko Tolimir, Case No. IT-05-88/2-A, Judgement, 8 April 2015 ("*Tolimir* Appeal Judgement")

VASILJEVIĆ

Prosecutor v. Mitar Vasiljević, Case No. IT-98-32-A, Judgement, 25 February 2004 ("*Vasiljević* Appeal Judgement")

ZELENOVIĆ

Prosecutor v. Dragan Zelenović, Case No. IT-96-23/2-S, Sentencing Judgement, 4 April 2007 ("*Zelenović* Sentencing Judgement")

Prosecutor v. Dragan Zelenović, Case No. IT-96-23/2-A, Judgement on Sentencing Appeal, 31 October 2007 ("*Zelenović* Sentencing Appeal Judgement")

2.   ICTR

AKAYESU

The Prosecutor v. Jean-Paul Akayesu, Case No. ICTR-96-4, Judgement, 2 Spetember 1998, ("*Akayesu* Trial Judgement")

The Prosecutor v. Jean-Paul Akayesu, Case No. ICTR-96-4-A, Judgement, 1 June 2001 ("*Akayesu* Appeal Judgement")

BAGOSORA AND NSENGIYUMVA

Theoneste Bagosora and Anatole Nsengiyumva v. The Prosecutor, Case No. ICTR-98-41-A, Judgement, 14 December 2011 ("*Bagosora and Nsengiyumva* Appeal Judgement")

BIKINDI

Simon Bikindi v. The Prosecutor, Case No. ICTR-01-72-A, Judgement, 18 March 2010 ("*Bikindi* Appeal Judgement")

BIZIMUNGU

Augustin Bizimungu v. The Prosecutor, Case No. ICTR-00-56B-A, Judgement, 30 June 2014, ("*Bizimungu* Appeal Judgement")

GACUMBITSI

Sylvestre Gacumbitsi v. The Prosecutor, Case No. ICTR-2001-64-A, Judgement, 7 July 2006 ("*Gacumbitsi* Appeal Judgement") **[page 539]**

GATETE

Jean-Baptiste Gatete v. The Prosecutor, Case No. ICTR-00-61-A, Judgement, 9 October 2012 (*"Gatete* Appeal Judgement")

HATEGEKIMANA

Ildephonse Hategekimana v. The Prosecutor, Case No. ICTR-00-55B-A, Judgement, 8 May 2012 (*"Hategekimana* Appeal Judgement")

KAJELIJELI

Juvénal Kajelijeli v. The Prosecutor, Case No. ICTR-98-44A-T, Judgement and Sentence, 1 December 2003 (*"Kajelijeli* Trial Judgement")

Juvénal Kajelijeli v. The Prosecutor, Case No. ICTR-98-44A-A, Judgement, 23 May 2005 (*"Kajelijeli* Appeal Judgement")

KAMUHANDA

Jean de Dieu Kamuhanda v. The Prosecutor, ICTR-99-54A-A, Judgement, 19 September 2005 (*"Kamuhanda* Appeal Judgement")

KAREMERA ET AL.

Édouard Karemera et al. v. The Prosecutor, Case No. ICTR-98-44-AR15bis.2, Reasons for Decision on Interlocutory Appeals Regarding the Continuation of Proceedings with a Substitute Judge and on Nzirorera's Motion for Leave to Consider New Material, 22 October 2004

The Prosecutor v. Édouar Karemera et al., Case No. ICTR-98-44-T, Decision on Joseph Nzirorera's Motion for Disqualification of Judge Byron and Stay of the Proceedings, 20 February 2009 (*"Karemera et al.* Disqualification Decision")

Édouar Karemera and Matthieu Ngirumpatse v. The Prosecutor, Case No. ICTR-98-44-A, Judgement, 29 September 2014 (*"Karemera and Ngirumpatse* Appeal Judgement")

KARERA

François Karera v. The Prosecutor, Case No. ICTR-01-74-A, Judgement, 2 February 2009 (*"Karera* Appeal Judgement")

MUGENZI AND MUGIRANEZA

Justin Mugenzi and Prosper Mugiraneza v. The Prosecutor, Case No. ICTR-99-50-A, Judgement, 4 February 2013 (*"Mugenzi and Mugiraneza* Appeal Judgement")

MUNYAKAZI

The Prosecutor v. Yussuf Munyakazi, Case No. ICTR-97-36A-A, Judgement, 28 September 2011 (*"Munyakazi* Appeal Judgement")

MUSEMA

Alfred Musema v. The Prosecutor, Case No. ICTR-96-13-A, Judgement, 16 November 2001 (*"Musema* Appeal Judgement")

NAHIMANA ET AL.

Ferdinand Nahimana et al. v. The Prosecutor, Case No. ICTR-99-52-T, Judgement and Sentence, 3 December 2003 (*"Nahimana et al.* Trial Judgement")

Ferdinand Nahimana et al. v. The Prosecutor, Case No. ICTR-99-52-A, Judgement, 28 November 2007 (*"Nahimana et al.* Appeal Judgement") **[page 540]**

NCHAMIHIGO

Siméon Nchamihigo v. The Prosecutor, Case No. ICTR-2001-63-A, Judgement, 18 March 2010 (*"Nchamihigo* Appeal Judgement")

NDAHIMANA

Grégoire Ndahimana v. The Prosecutor, Case No. ICTR-01-68-A, Judgement, 16 December 2013 (*"Ndahimana* Appeal Judgement")

NDINDILIYIMANA ET AL.

Augustin Ndindiliyimana et al. v. The Prosecutor, Case No. ICTR-00-56-A, Judgement, 11 February 2014 (public redacted) (*"Ndindiliyimana et al.* Appeal Judgement")

NIYITEGEKA

Eliézer Niyitegeka v. The Prosecutor, Case No. ICTR-96-14-A, Judgement, 9 July 2004 (*"Niyitegeka* Appeal Judgement")

NIZEYIMANA

Ildéphonse Nizeyimana v. The Prosecutor, Case No. ICTR-00-55C-A, Judgement, 29 September 2014 (*"Nizeyimana* Appeal Judgement")

NTABAKUZE

Aloys Ntabakuze v. The Prosecutor, Case No. ICTR-98-41A-A, Judgement, 8 May 2012 (*"Ntabakuze* Appeal Judgement")

NTAGERURA ET AL.

The Prosecutor v. André Ntagerura et al., Case No. ICTR-99-46-A, Judgement, 7 July 2006 (*"Ntagerura et al.* Appeal Judgement")

NTAKIRUTIMANA AND NTAKIRUTIMANA

The Prosecutor v. Elizaphan Ntakirutimana and Gerard Ntakirutimana, Case Nos. ICTR-96-10-A and ICTR-96-17-A, Judgement, 13 December 2004 (*"Ntakirutimana and Ntakirutimana* Appeal Judgement")

NYIRAMASUHUKO ET AL.

Pauline Nyiramasuhuko et al. v. The Prosecutor, Case No. ICTR-98-42-A, Judgement, 14 December 2015 (*"Nyiramasuhuko et al.* Appeal Judgement")

RENZAHO

Tharcisse Renzaho v. The Prosecutor, Case No. ICTR-97-31-A, Judgement, 1 April 2011 (*"Renzaho* Appeal Judgement")

RUTAGANDA

Géorges Anderson Nderubumwe Rutaganda v. The Prosecutor, Case No. ICTR-96-3-A, Judgement, 26 May 2003 (*"Rutaganda* Appeal Judgement")

RWAMAKUBA

André Rwamakuba v. The Prosecutor, Case No. ICTR-98-44-AR72.4, Decision on Interlocutory Appeal Regarding Application of Joint Criminal Enterprise to the Crime of Genocide, 22 October 2004 ("*Rwamakuba* Appeal Decision on Joint Criminal Enterprise of 22 October 2004")

SEMANZA

Laurent Semanza v. The Prosecutor, Case No. ICTR-97-20-A, Judgement, 20 May 2005 ("*Semanza* Appeal Judgement") **[page 541]**

SEROMBA

The Prosecutor v. Athanase Seromba, Case No. ICTR-2001-66-T, Decision on Motion for Disqualification of Judges, 25 April 2006

The Prosecutor v. Athanase Seromba, Case No. ICTR-2001-66-A, Judgement, 12 March 2008 ("*Seromba* Appeal Judgement")

SIMBA

Aloys Simba v. The Prosecutor, Case No. ICTR-01-76-A, Judgement, 27 November 2007 ("*Simba* Appeal Judgement")

ZIGIRANYIRAZO

Protais Zigiranyirazo v. The Prosecutor, Case No. ICTR-01-73-A, Judgement, 16 November 2009 ("*Zigiranyirazo* Appeal Judgement")

3. Mechanism for International Criminal Tribunals

NGIRABATWARE

Augustin Ngirabatware v. The Prosecutor, Case No. MICT-12-29-A, Judgement, 18 December 2014 ("*Ngirabatware* Appeal Judgement")

4. Decisions related to crimes committed during World War II

The United States of America, the French Republic, the United Kingdom of Great Britain and Northern Ireland, and the Union of Soviet Socialist Republics against Herman Wilhelm Goring et al., Judgement, 1 October 1946, Trial of Major War Criminals Before the International Military Tribunal Under Control Council Law No. 10, Vol. 1 (1947)

The United States of America v. Alstoetter et al., U.S. Military Tribunal, Judgement, 3-4 December 1947, Trials of War Criminals Before the Nuernberg Military Tribunals Under Control Council Law No. 10 (1951), Vol. III

The United States of America v. Greifelt et al., U.S. Military Tribunal, Judgement, 10 March 1948, Trials of War Criminals Before the Nuernberg Military Tribunals Under Control Council Law No.

10 (1951), Vol. V

5. SCSL

SESAY ET AL. ("RUF")

Prosecutor v. Issa Hassan Sesay, Case No. SCSL-2004-15-AR15, Decision on Defence Motion Seeking the Disqualification of Justice Robertson from the Appeals Chamber, 13 March 2004 ("*RUF* Decision")

Prosecutor v. Issa Hassan Sesay et al., Case No SCSL-04-15-T, Sentencing Judgement, 8 April 2009**[page 542]**

Prosecutor v. Issa Hassan Sesay et al., Case No. SCSL-04-15-A, Judgement, 26 October 2009 (*"RUF* Appeal Judgement")

TAYLOR

Prosecutor v. Charles Ghankay Taylor, Case No. SCSL-03-01-T, Judgement, 18 May 2012 (*"Taylor* Trial Judgement")

6. STL

The Prosecutor. v. Salim Jamil Ayyash et al., Case No. STL-11-01/I/AC/R176bis, Interlocutory Decision on the Applicable Law: Terrorism, Conspiracy, Homicide, Perpetration, Cumulative Charging, 16 February 2011 ("STL Decision of 16 February 2011")

7. ECCC

Ambos, Kai, Amicus Curiae Concerning Criminal Case File NO. 001/1807-ECCC/OCIJ (PTC 02), 27 October 2008 ("Kai Ambos *Amicus Curiae* Application")

Prosecutor v. Ieng Thirith et al., Case File No. 002/19-09-2007-ECCC/OCIJ (PTC38), Decision on the Appeals Against the Co-Investigative Judges Orders on Joint Criminal Enterprise (JCE), 20 May 2010, ("ECCC Decision on JCE")

Co-Prosecutors v. Guek Eav Kaing alias "Duch", Case File: 001/18-07-2007/ECCC/TC, Trial Judgement, 26 July 2010 (*"Duch* Trial Judgement")

Co-Prosecutors v. Guek Eav Kaing alias "Duch", Case File: 001/18-07-2007/ECCC/SC, Appeal Judgement, 3 February 2012

Co-Prosecutors v Chea Nuon et al., Case No. 002/19-09-2007/ECCC/TC, Decision on Ieng Sary's Application to Disqualify Judge Nil Nonn and Related Requests, 28 January 2011

8. European Court of Human Rights

Piersack v. Belgium, Application No. 8692/79, ECtHR, Judgement, 1 October 1982 (*"Piersack v. Belgium"*)

Ruotsalainen v. Finland, European Court of Human Rights, no. 13079/03, Judgement, 16 June 2009 (*"Ruotsalainen v. Finland"*)

Sergey Zolotukhin v. Russia, European Court of Human Rights, no. 14939/03, Judgement, 10 February 2009 (*"Zolotukhin v. Russia"*) **[page 543]**

9. Courts of domestic jurisdictions

(a) Australia

Gaudie v. Local Court of New South Wales and Anor [2013] NSWSC 1425

Newcastle City Council v. Lindsay [2004] NSWCA 198

(b) United Kingdom

Hoekstra v. HM Advocate (No. 2) (Scottish High Court of Justiciary), 2000 J.C. 391 (*"Hoekstra v. HM Advocate"*)

Kienapple v. The Queen, [1975] 1 S.C.R. 7829 (*"Kienapple v. The Queen"*)

(c) United States

Hatchcock v. Navistar Intern. Transp. Corp., 53 F. 3d 36, 39 (4th Cir 1995) (*"Hatchcock v. Navistar"*)

Liteky v. United States, 510 U.S. 540, 555 (1994)

Blockburger v. United States, 284 U.S. 299, 304 (1932) (*"Blockburger v. United States"*)

Ex parte Lange, 85 U.S. 163 (1873) (*"Ex parte Lange"*)

Rutledge v. United States, 517, U.S. 292 (1996) (*"Rutledge v. United States"*)

Whalen v. United States, 445 U.S. 684 (1980) (*"Whalen v. United States"*)

B. Other authorities

1. Publications

A. Cassese, "Proper Limits of Individual Responsibility Under the Doctrine of JCE", *International Criminal Justice Journal*, 5 (2007) ("Judge Cassese Article on JCE")

G. Binder, "Felony Murder and Mens Rea Default Rules: A study in Statutory Interpretation", *Buffalo Criminal Law Review*, vol. 4:399 (2000-2001) ("Binder Article")

J. D. Ohlin, *"Joint Intentions to Commit International Crimes"*, Cornell Law Faculty Publications, 169 (2011) ("Ohlin Article")

S. H. Pillsbury, *Judging Evil: Rethinking the Law of Murder and Manslaughter* (1998) ("Pillsbury Article")

2. Other documents

European Convention for the Protection of Human Rights and Fundamental Freedoms signed in Rome on 4 November 1950 ("European Convention on Human Rights") **[page 544]**

Geneva Convention Relative to the Protection of Civilian Persons in Time of War (Fourth Geneva Convention), 12 August 1949, 75 UNTS 287 ("Geneva Convention IV")

Homicide Act 1957, 5 & 6 Eliz.2, Ch. 11 (United Kingdom) ("UK Homicide Act")

International Committee of the Red Cross, Commentary on Article 42 of the Geneva Convention Relative to the Protection of Civilian Persons in Time of War (Fourth Geneva Convention), 12 August 1949, 75 UNTS 287 (1958) ("ICRC Commentary on Geneva Convention IV")

International Covenant on Civil and Political Rights, G.A. res. 2200A (XXI), 21 U.N. GAOR Supp. (No. 16) at 52, U.N. Doc. A/6316 (1966), 999 UNTS 171, entered into force 23 March 1976 ("ICCPR")

International Convention for the Suppression of Terrorist Bombing, U.N. Doc. A/RES/52/164; 37 ILM 249 (1998); 2149 UNTS 284, entered into force 23 May 2001 ("Convention for the Suppression of Terrorist Bombing")

Statute of the International Criminal Court, adopted by a Diplomatic Conference in Rome on 17 July 1998 ("ICC Statute") **[page 545]**

C.   List of Designated Terms and Abbreviations

1 April 1992 BiH-MUP Collegium	A collegium of BiH Ministry of Interior officials on 1 April 1992, following the split of the Ministry of Interior
11 February 1992 Meeting	A meeting held by Serb officials of Ministry of the Interior of the Socialist Republic of Bosnia and Herzegovina in Banja Luka on 11 February 1992, where a Serb collegium was created to prepare for establishing a Serb Ministry of Interior
11 July 1992 Collegium	The first collegium meeting of senior officials of the Ministry of Interior of *Republika Srpska* on 11 July 1992
12 May 1992 BSA Session	A session of the Bosnian Serb Assembly held on 12 May 1992
15 October 1991 SDS Meeting	A meeting of the Serbian Democratic Party held on 15 October 1991
17 April 1992 Dispatch	A dispatch from Mićo Stanišić to Security Services in Banja Luka, Bijeljina, Doboj, and Sarajevo, calling for the prosecution of perpetrators of the appropriation and plunder of real estate and public and private property committed by members in the service of the Ministry of Interior of *Republika Srpska*
17 July 1992 Report	A report on the 11 July 1992 Collegium to the President and the Prime Minister of *Republika Srpska*, dated 17 July 1992 (Exhibit P427.08)
18 March 1992 BSA Session	A session of the Bosnian Serb Assembly held on 18 March 1992
19 July 1992 Order	An order issued by Mićo Stanišić on 19 July 1992 to chiefs of the Security Services Centres requesting information on procedures for arrest, treatment of prisoners, conditions of collection camps, and Muslim prisoners detained by the army at "undefined camps" without proper documentation (Exhibit 1D76)
1st Council Meeting	The first meeting of the Council of Ministers of the Bosnian Serb Assembly on 11 January 1992
1st KK	1st Krajina Corps**[page 546]**
21 June 1992 Intercept	An intercepted conversation between Mićo Stanišić and Tomilsav Kovač on 21 June 1992 (Exhibit P1171)
22 April 1992 Instruction	The 22 April 1992 instruction from the Socialist Federal Republic of Yugoslavia
24 March 1992 BSA Session	A session of the Bosnian Serb Assembly held on 24 March 1992
25 February 1992 BSA Session	A session of the Bosnian Serb Assembly held on 25 February 1992
25 May 1992 Work Plan	Operative work plan of the Banja Luka Security Services Centre, dated 25 May 1992

27 July 1992 Meeting	A meeting on 27 July 1992 in Sokolac of leading personnel of criminology departments from the area of the Romanija-Birač Security Services Centre
29 July 1992 Session	A session of the Government of *Republika Srpska* held on 29 July 1992
30 April 1992 Dispatch	A dispatch sent on 30 April 1992 by Stojan Župljanin (Exhibit P1002)
31 July 1992 Order	An order issued by Stojan Župljanin requesting the chiefs of the Public Security Stations of the ARK to implement an ARK Crisis Staff decision that individuals leaving the ARK could take with them a maximum of 300 Deutsche Mark, to issue certificates of temporary seizure when amounts in excess of 300 Deutsche Mark were taken, and to deposit seised amounts at the Banja Luka Security Services Centre cash office (Exhibit P594)
4 July 1992 Session	A session of the Government of *Republika Srpska* held on 4 July 1992
5 October 1992 Order	An order issued by Mićo Stanišić on 5 October 1992, by letter, repeating to all Security Services Centres an earlier instruction to report on war crimes (Exhibit 1D572)
Appeals Chamber	Appeals Chamber of the Tribunal
ARK	Autonomous Region of Krajina
Arkan	An alias of Željko Ražnatović[page 547]
Arkan's Men	A paramilitary group led by Željko Ražnatović also known as the Serbian Volunteer Guard or Arkan's Tigers
ARK Municipalities	The municipalities of Banja Luka, Donji Vakuf, Ključ, Kotor Varoš, Prijedor, Sanski Most, Skender Vakuf, and Teslić
AT.	Transcript page from hearings on appeal in the present case
BiH	Bosnia and Herzegovina
BiH Assembly	Assembly of the Socialist Republic of Bosnia and Herzegovina
Bosanska Vila Meeting	A meeting at Bosanska Vila attended by Witness Milorad Davidović, Momčilo Krajišnik, Pero Mihaljović, Frenki Simatović, Mićo Stanišić, and Željko Ražnatović (alias Arkan)
BSA	Bosnian Serb Assembly
BSA and SDS Meetings	The 15 October 1991 SDS Meeting, the 25 February 1992 BSA Session, and the 18 March 1992 BSA Session, collectively
Communications Logbook	The communications logbook of the Ministry of Interior of *Republika Srpska* Headquarters and the Sarajevo Security Services Centre from 22 April 1992 to 2 January 1993 (Exhibit P1428)
CSB(s)	(Regional) Security Services Centre(s)

Cutileiro Plan	The peace plan enunciated at the conclusion of a the International Commission convened in Lisbon, in around February 1992
Daily Report of 8 July 1992	A daily report from the operative team of the Manjača detention camp to the 1st Krajina Corps Command, dated 8 July 1992 (Exhibit P486)
December 1993 BSA Session	The 36th session of the Bosnian Serb Assembly held in December 1993
December 1993 BSA Transcript	Transcript of the 36th session of the Bosnian Serb Assembly in December 1993
Đerić Letter	A letter sent by Mićo Stanišić to Branko Đerić, Prime Minister of *Republika Srpska* on 18 July 1992 (Exhibit P190) **[page 548]**
Disciplinary Rules	Rules on Disciplinary Responsibility of Employees of the Ministry of Interior of *Republika Srpska*
ECCC	Extraordinary Chambers in the Courts of Cambodia
Federal SUP	Federal Secretariat of Internal Affairs of Serbia
fn. (fns)	Footnote (footnotes)
Geneva Conventions	Geneva Conventions I-IV of 12 August 1949
Glas Article	Stojan Župljanin's interview with the *Glas* newspaper in which he stated that those claiming to be members of the Serb Defence Forces but engaged in unlawful measures and activities were not welcome in the Banja Luka Regional Security Services Centre Special Police Detachment (Exhibit P560)
Gymnasium	A detention facility at the gymnasium in the municipality of Pale
HDZ	Croatian Democratic Union
Holiday Inn Meeting	The meeting of the SDS Main and Executive Boards on 14 February 1992, in Sarajevo
ICC Statute	Statute of the International Criminal Court, adopted by a Diplomatic Conference in Rome on 17 July 1998
ICRC	International Committee of the Red Cross
ICTR	International Criminal Tribunal for the Prosecution of Persons Responsible for Genocide and Other Serious Violations of International Humanitarian Law Committed in the Territory of Rwanda and Rwandan Citizens Responsible for Genocide and Other Such Violations Committed in the Territory of Neighbouring States, between 1 January 1994 and 31 December 1994
ICTY	International Tribunal for the Prosecution of Persons Responsible for Serious Violations of International Humanitarian Law Committed in the Territory of the former Yugoslavia since 1991**[page 549]**

486

Indictment	*Prosecutor v. Mićo Stanišić and Stojan Župljanin*, Case No. IT-08-91-T, Second Amended Consolidated Indictment, 23 November 2009
Instructions	*See* Variant A and B Instructions
Interview	Mićo Stanišić's interview with the Prosecution, conducted between 16 and 21 July 2007
JCE	The joint criminal enterprise found in this case
JCE I Crimes	The crimes of deportation, and inhumane acts (forcible transfer), and persecutions through the underlying acts of forcible transfer and deportation, as crimes against humanity
JNA	Yugoslav People's Army
July 1992 Sessions	4 July 1992 Session and 29 July 1992 Session, collectively.
Karadžić's 1 July 1992 Order	An order of Radovan Karadžić to Mićo Stanišić of 1 July 1992 to transfer 60 specially trained policemen, deployed in Crepolojsko, and "place them under the military command of the SRK"[70] (Exhibit 1D99)
KT Logbooks	1992 logbooks of the Basic Prosecutor's Office in Sarajevo, Sokolac, Vlasenica, and Višegrad including criminal offences against *known* perpetrators
KTN Logbooks	1992 logbooks of the Basic Prosecutor's Office in Sarajevo, Sokolac, Vlasenica, and Višegrad including criminal offences against *unknown* perpetrators
KU Registers	Police registers of criminal cases reported to and investigated by the police in *Republika Srpska* in 1992
Law of 1990	Law on Internal Affairs of the former Socialist Republic of Bosnia and Herzegovina which was published on 29 June 1990 (Exhibit P510)
Letter	A letter written by Judge Frederik Harhoff and addressed to 56 recipients, dated 6 June 2013 (Exhibit 1DA1) **[page 550]**
LIA	Law on Internal Affairs of *Republika Srpska* (Exhibit P530)
Media Articles	Two media articles entitled "Two Puzzling Judgements in The Hague" dated 1 June 2013 and published by *The Economist* (Exhbiit PA2) and "What Happened to the Hague Tribunal?" published by *The New York Times* (Exhibit PA3) on 2 June 2013, collectively
Memorandum	A memorandum dated 8 July 2013 from Judge Frederik Harhoff to Judge Jean-Claude Antonetti, Presiding Judge in the *Šešelj* case in relation to the Letter
Mens Rea Section	The section of the Trial Judgement dedicated to Stanišić's intent pursuant to the first category of joint criminal enterprise
Miloš Group	A unit collecting intelligence for the National Security Service

---

[70] Trial Judgement, vol. 2, para. 591.

Minister of Interior	Minister of the Ministry of Interior of *Republika Srpska*
MOD	Minstry of Defence of *Republika Srpska*
MOJ	Ministry of Justice of *Republika Srpska*
Municipalities	The municipalities of Banja Luka, Bijeljina, Bileća, Bosanski Šamac, Brčko, Doboj, Donji Vakuf, Gacko, Ilijaš, Ključ, Kotor Varoš, Pale, Prijedor, Sanski Most, Skender Vakuf, Teslić, Vlasenica, Višegrad, Vogošća, and Zvornik
November 1992 BSA Session	A session of the Bosnian Serb Assembly held on 23 and 24 November 1992
NSC	National Security Council
Order of 15 April 1992	Mićo Stanišić's order of 15 April 1992 concerning the sanctioning of persons involved in criminal activities and protecting the civilian population (Exhibit 1D61)
Orders of 15 and 16 April 1992	Mićo Stanišić's orders of 15 and 16 April 1992 concerning the sanctioning of persons involved in criminal activities and protecting the civilian population (Exhibits 1D61 and 1D634)
P. (pp)	Page (pages)
Para. (paras)	Paragraph (paragraphs) **[page 551]**
Perišić Report	The report by the Chief of the Višegrad Public Security Station, Risto Perišić, dated 13 July 1992
PIP	Prijedor Intervention Platoon
Prijedor War Presidency	War Presidency of the Prijedor Municipal Assembly
Prosecution	Office of the Prosecutor of the Tribunal
Prosecution Appeal Brief	Prosecution Appeal Brief, 19 August 2013
Prosecution Consolidated Reply Brief	Consolidated Prosecution Reply to Mićo Stanišić's Respondent's Brief and Stojan Župljanin's Response to Prosecution Appeal, 11 November 2013
Prosecution Consolidated Supplemental Response Brief	Prosecution's Consolidated Supplemental Response Brief, 18 July 2014
Prosecution Final Trial Brief	*Prosecutor v. Mićo Stanišić and Stojan Župljanin*, Case No. IT-08-91-T, Prosecution's Final Trial Brief, 14 May 2012 (confidential with confidential annexes)
Prosecution Notice of Appeal	Prosecution Notice of Appeal, 13 May 2013
Prosecution Response Brief (Stanišić)	Prosecution Response to Appeal of Mićo Stanišić, 21 October 2013 (confidential, public redacted version filed on 15 November 2013)
Prosecution Response Brief (Župljanin)	Prosecution Response to Stojan Župljanin's Appeal Brief, 21 October 2013 (confidential; public redacted version filed on 25 June 2014)

Prosecutor's Logbooks	1992 logbooks of the Basic Prosecutor's Office in Sarajevo, Sokolac, Vlasenica, and Višegrad including criminal offences against *known* and *unknown* perpetrators, respectively, from the Basic Public Prosecutor's Offices in Sarajevo, Sokolac, Vlasenica, and Višegrad, the 1993 entries in the logbook from the "Sarajevo Basic Prosecutor's Office II", and prosecutor logbooks for the period 1992 to 1995, covering the Municipalities charged in the Indictment, collectively **[page 552]**
Rebuttal Material	A reference to two media articles entitled "Two Puzzling Judgments in The Hague" dated 1 June 2013 and published by *The Economist* and "What Happened to the Hague Tribunal?" dated 2 June 2013 and published by *The New York Times*, collectively as well as a memorandum dated 8 July 2013 from Judge Frederik Harhoff to Judge Jean-Claude Antonetti, Presiding Judge in the *Šešelj* case, in relation to the Letter
Red Berets	*See* SOS
RS	*Republika Srpska*, Serb Republic in Bosnia and Herzgovina
RS Government	Government of *Republika Srpska*
RS MUP	Ministry of Interior of *Republika Srpska*
RS Presidency	A small institution that consisted of the President of the *Republika Srpska* and senior members of Serbian Democratic Party, namely Nikola Koljević and Biljana Plavšić, which was expanded at some point to include more members such as Branko Đerić, former Prime Minister of the *Republika Srpska*, who was not member of the Serbian Democratic Party
Rules	Rules of Procedure and Evidence of the Tribunal
Sanski Most Incident	The incident in which 20 detainees died during their transportation from Betonirka detention camp in Sanski Most to Manjača detention camp in Banja Luka municipality by Sanski Most police officers on 7 July 1992
SCSL	Special Court for Sierra Leone
SDA	Party of Democratic Action
SDS	Serbian Democratic Party
Second Commission for Detention Facilities	The commission for detention facilities in the municipalities of Trebinje, Gacko, and Bileća
September 1992 Dispatch	A dispatch issued by Stojan Župljanin in September 1992, tasking the Prijedor police with escorting buses of non-Serb detainees to Croatia (Exhibit P1905) **[page 553]**
Serb forces	Members of the Ministry of Interior of *Republika Srpska*, the Army of *Republika Srpska*, Yugoslav People's Army, the Yugoslav Army, the Territorial Defence, Serbian Ministry of Interior, crisis staffs, Serbian and Bosnian paramilitary forces, volunteer units, local Bosnian Serbs acting under their instruction or pursuant to the direction of the aforementioned forces

Šešelj Decisions	A reference to the *Šešelj* Decision on Disqualification and *Šešelj* Reconsideration Decision, collectively
SFRY	Socialist Federal Republic of Yugoslavia
SJB(s)	Public Security Station / Public Security Service
SNB	National Security Service
Sokolac Report	A report from a meeting in Sokolac of heads of departments for criminology in the area of the Romanija-Birač Security Services Centre dated 28 July 1992 (Exhibit 1D328)
SOS	Serb Defence Forces, also known as the Red Berets, an armed formation of the Serbian Democratic Party
SPD	Special Police Detachment
Special Chamber	A chamber convened in the *Šešelj* case by the Acting President of the Tribunal[71]
SRBiH	Socialist Republic of Bosnia and Herzegovina
SRBiH MUP	Ministry of Interior of the Socialist Republic of Bosnia and Herzegovina
Stanišic's 15 May 1992 Order	An order issued by Mićo Stanišić on 15 May 1992, organising RS MUP forces into war units (Exhibit 1D46) **[page 554]**
Stanišić's 16 May 1992 Order	An order issued by Mićo Stanišić on 16 May 1992, to all five Security Services Centre Chiefs to send daily fax reports on combat activities, terrorist activities, implementation of tasks under the Law on Internal Affairs of *Republika Sprksa*, and war crimes and other serious crimes committed against Serbs (Exhibit P173)
Stanišić's 23 October 1992 Order	An order issued by Mićo Stanišić on 23 October 1992, requesting the withdrawal of active-duty police members from the frontline, make the reserve police available for the wartime assignment to the Army of *Republika Srpska*, and to inform military commands that it was not the duty of the Security Services Centres and Public Security Stations to send policemen to the frontline (Exhibit 1D49)
Stanišić's 25 April 1992 Decision	A decision issued by Mićo Stanišić on 25 April 1992, allowing Security Services Centres chiefs to take over the former Ministry of Interior of the Socialist Republic of Bosnia and Herzegovina and immediately inform him when distributing former employees in their Security Services Centres and Public Security Stations (Exhibit 1D73)
Stanišić's 27 July 1992 Order	An order issued by Mićo Stanišić on 27 July 1992 (Exhibit 1D176)
Stanišić's 6 July 1992 Request	Mićo Stanišić's request of 6 July 1992 to Radovan Karadžić that 60 Ministry of Interior of *Republika Srpska* members provided to the military be replaced by members of the army due to operational needs (Exhibit 1D100) **[page 555]**

---

[71]   See *Prosecutor v. Vojislav Šešelj*, Case No. IT-03-67-T, Order Pursuant to Rule 15, 25 July 2013.

Stanišić's JCE III Crimes	Crimes that fell outside the common purpose for which Stanišić was held responsible pursuant to the third category of the joint criminal enterprise, namely persecutions (through the underlying acts of killings, torture, cruel treatment, inhumane acts, unlawful detention, establishment and perpetuation of inhumane living conditions, plunder of property, wanton destruction of towns and villages, including destruction or willful damage done to institutions dedicated to religion and other cultural buildings, and imposition and maintenance of restrictive and discriminatory measures) as a crime against humanity (Count 1), murder, torture, and cruel treatment as violations of the laws or customs of war (Counts 4, 6, and 7, respectively) as well as murder, torture, and inhumane acts as crimes against humanity (Counts 3, 5, and 8, respectively)
Stanišić Additional Appeal Brief	Additional Appellant's Brief on behalf of Mićo Stanišić, 26 June 2014
Stanišić Additional Reply Brief	Additional Brief in Reply on behalf of Mićo Stanišić, 29 July 2014
Stanišić Appeal Brief	Appellant's Brief on behalf of Mićo Stanišić, 19 August 2013
Stanišić Final Trial Brief	*Prosecutor v. Mićo Stanišić and Stojan Župljanin*, Case No. IT-08-91-T, Mr. Mićo Stanišić's Final Written Submissions Pursuant to Rule 86, 14 May 2012 (confidential with confidential annex A)
Stanišić Notice of Appeal	Amended Notice of Appeal on behalf of Mićo Stanišić, 23 April 2014
Stanišić Reply Brief	Brief in Reply on behalf of Mićo Stanišić, 11 November 2013
Stanišić Response Brief	Respondent's Brief on behalf of Mićo Stanišić, 21 October 2013
Statute	Statute of the Tribunal
STL	Special Tribunal for Lebanon
Strategic Objectives	Six strategic objectives presented to the session of the Bosnian Serb Assembly on 12 May 1992**[page 556]**
T.	Transcript page from herings at trial in the instant case
TO	Territorial Defence
Trial Chamber	Trial Chamber II in the case of *Prosecutor v. Mićo Stanišić and Stojan Župljanin*, Case No. IT-08-91-T
Trial Judgement	*Prosecutor v. Mićo Stanišić and Stojan Župljanin*, Case No. IT-08-91-T, Judgement, 27 March 2013
Tribunal	*See* "ICTY"
Variant A and B Instructions	Instructions for the Organisation and Activities of the Organs of the Serb People in Bosnia and Herzegovina in a State of Emergency adopted by the Serbian Democratic Party Main Board on 19 December 1991

VRS	Army of *Republika Srpska*
Yellow Wasps	A Serbian paramilitary group, also known as Žućo or Repic's men
Župljanin's JCE III Crimes	Crimes that fell outside the common purpose for which Stojan Župljanin was found responsible pursuant to the third category of the joint criminal enterprise, namely (persecutions through underlying acts of killings, torture, cruel treatment, inhumane acts, unlawful detention, establishment and perpetuation of inhumane living conditions, plunder of property, wanton destruction of towns and villages, including destruction or willful damage done to institutions dedicated to religion and other cultural buildings, imposition and maintenance of restrictive and discriminatory measures) as a crime against humanity (Count 1) as well as murder, torture, and cruel treatment as violations of the laws or customs of war (Counts 4, 6, and 7, respectively) as well as extermination murder, torture, and inhumane acts as crimes against humanity (Counts 2, 3, 5, and 8, respectively)
Župljanin Additional Appeal Brief	Stojan Župljanin's Supplement to Appeal Brief (Ground Six), 26 June 2014
Župljanin Additional Reply Brief	Stojan Župljanin's Reply to Prosecution's Consolidated Supplemental Response Brief Concerning Additional Ground, 25 July 2014**[page 557]**
Župljanin Appeal Brief	Stojan [Ž]upljanin's Appeal Brief, 19 August 2013 (confidential; public redacted version filed on 23 August 2013, re-filed on 21 April 2016)
Župljanin Final Trial Brief	*Prosecutor v. Mićo Stanišić and Stojan Župljanin*, Case No. IT-08-91-T, Župljanin Defence Final Trial Brief, 14 May 2012 (confidential)
Župljanin Notice of Appeal	Župljanin's Submission of Second Amended Notice of Appeal, 22 April 2014
Župljanin Reply Brief	Stojan [Ž]upljanin's Reply to Prosecution's response Brief, 11 November 2013 (confidential; public redacted version filed on 13 November 2013)
Župljanin Response Brief	Stojan [Ž]upljanin's Response to Prosecution Appeal Brief, 21 October 2013**[page 558]**

XIII.   ANNEX C – CONFIDENTIAL ANNEX

Editor's note: Annex C has remained confidential.

Commentary

1   Overview of the main content of the decision

The Appeals Chamber of the ICTY is seized of the appeals filed by the accused and the prosecution against the judgement issued by the Trial Chamber on counts of crimes against humanity and violations of laws or customs of war committed in a specified time span, within the framework of a joint criminal enterprise (JCE) in its first and third forms as they are established in the case law of international tribunals.

Both accused challenge the trial judgement, asserting that it fails in many respects to provide a reasoned opinion in support of its findings on criminal responsibility. In particular, the challenges affect the legal standard for contribution to a JCE – and, more broadly, for identifying the component elements of this particular mode of liability – as well as the factual findings with regard to the accused's behaviour. They challenge, for instance, alleged errors of fact in assessing the accused's role within the institutional context that led to the commission of crimes, the knowledge of instructions relevant to the transmission of criminal orders, the command and control over forces committing the alleged crimes, the omission of preventing, investigating and documenting crimes, the fact that the accused shared the intent to further the common criminal purpose, and similar findings.

A specific feature of the challenges, on which the Appeals Chamber takes a very clear stance, is that they have a remarkable procedural hue which is, however, of a broad methodological significance. The accused submit that the Trial Chamber made a number of findings concerning various factors related to their behaviour, but these findings lack cross references to earlier underlying findings in the judgement or citations to evidence on the record.[1]

Basically, the accused argue that the Trial Chamber "did not make any specific findings as to whether and how [he] contributed, let alone significantly contributed, to furthering the JCE".[2] This submission has an explicit procedural limb: the failure to give a reasoned opinion for the conviction of the accused. In addition, it has an implicit, hence less evident content of a substantive nature: what kind of acts and conduct shall amount to the contribution to a JCE, a category which is highly contested in trials, among commentators, and has been abandoned by the case law of the ICC in favour of the different conceptual framework of the control-over-the-crime theory.

From a procedural point of view, the Appeals Chamber stresses that in fact the judges are "required to make findings on those facts which are essential to the determination of guilt on a particular count". Therefore, "the absence of any relevant legal findings in a trial judgement also constitutes a manifest failure to provide a reasoned opinion".[3]

After noting that the Trial Chamber actually failed to indicate the evidence relied upon or excluded in the relevant part of the judgement, and therefore failed to provide a reasoned opinion, the Appeals Chamber independently assesses the findings and relevant evidence concerning the accused's acts and conduct to determine whether a reasonable trier of fact could have concluded beyond reasonable doubt that these acts and conduct amounted to prohibited behaviour and therefore underpin criminal liability.

This commentary will deal separately with this specific aspect; however, it has to be stressed from the outset that the question of connecting relevant facts to the abstract constituent elements of criminal liability is of great importance from a methodological point of view. The narrative of facts is the bedrock of judicial activity, since it is the empirical facts that are considered and selected to become the object of legal qualifications (here, the category of JCE). Indeed, any legal evaluation of the empirical facts submits them to the value-laden judgements that any legal qualification carries out. Recalling the importance of facts could sound trivial, but it is the starting point for any subsequent question regarding the law applicable to those facts and, we should add, for the assessment as to whether those same facts are anyhow legally relevant.

---

[1]   ICTY, Judgement, *Prosecutor v. Stanišić and Župljanin*, Case No. IT-08–91-A, A. Ch., 30 June 2016, (Stanišić and Župljanin Judgement), in this volume, PAGINA, par. 131 ff.

[2]   Stanišić and Župljanin Judgement, par. 134.

[3]   Stanišić and Župljanin Judgement, par. 137.

This specification is of paramount importance in the instant case, where the judgement has been specifically and sharply criticized for having conflated a legitimate political goal – the aim of the Serbian leadership "for "Serbs to live in one state with other Serbs in the former Yugoslavia"" alongside with the territorial demarcation and the forceful assumption of control over territories – with the purpose of a common criminal enterprise.

In light of the above, one important message conveyed by the instant decision is to underline in general terms the importance of an accurate reconstruction of the facts submitted to the different schemes of value judgements that can be applied to this reconstruction.

From a substantive point of view, the main gist of the decision revolves around the objective requirements and subjective components of the first and third categories of JCE as a mode of liability. The grounds for appeal relate to both the legal standard for a contribution to a JCE, and the factual findings of the judgement – the evidence of factual aspects of the concrete participation of the accused, the actual contribution to it, the concrete knowledge of concrete aspects of the context, and the like. The merely factual aspects discussed throughout the Appeals Chamber judgement will not be dealt with in this commentary, but for their methodological implications sketched above.[4]

As to the legal evaluation of them, the judgement deals with two topics of great import.
The first of these is the distinction between a legitimate political goal and the legal concept of a common criminal purpose as a form of committing international crimes. This is tantamount to setting out the boundaries between politics and law, the most contentious task conferred upon the international criminal justice mechanisms.[5]

Secondly, the judgement deals explicitly – if not perhaps consciously – with one of the fiercest criticisms raised in international trials and by a whole slew of scholars against JCE as a mode of liability resulting in actual violation of principles of individual criminal responsibility. It is commonly held, indeed, that JCE "is a form of ... liability where you may become responsible for the acts of others"; therefore this category "really stands for 'just convict everybody'".[6] I propose a reading of the instant judgement as a (convincing) response to this objection.[7]

In turn, the prosecution challenges the trial judgements on grounds related to the imposition of inadequate sentences on the accused and the failure to enter cumulative convictions for crimes against humanity for which they were found criminally responsible. This particular topic is not dealt with in this commentary.

2   JCE: the political hue of legal categories

The category of JCE is at the core of the judgement. The Trial Chamber unanimously convicted the defendants pursuant this mode of liability (in the forms of JCE I and III). It acknowledged that "a joint criminal enterprise existed, with the objective of permanently removing Bosnian Muslims and Bosnian Croats from the territory of the planned Serbian state through the commission of JCE I crimes" such as persecutions (through the underlying acts of forcible transfer and deportation), deportation, and inhumane acts –as crimes against humanity.

The Chamber also found the accused responsible pursuant to JCE III – for crimes that fell outside the common purpose but whose commission was a natural and foreseeable consequence of the implementation of the common purpose.

The most qualifying submission of the defendants is that the Trial Chamber "erred in law by conflating the legitimate political goal for Serbs to live in one state with other Serbs in the former Yugoslavia with the

---

4   See text below, par. 6.
5   See text below, par. 2.1 and 2.2.
6   Among many: D. Guilfoyle, International Criminal Law, Cambridge U.P., Cambridge 2016, p. 339 (referring to G. Sluiter, Foreword to the Symposium quoted below); see M.E. Badar, "Just Convict Everyone!" – Joint Perpetration: From Tadić to Stakić and Back Again 6 Int'l Crim. Law Rev. 2006, p. 293). The author adds that this is a form of "conspiracy liability", but this interpretation is criticized as "misleading" by other scholars: see on this R. Cryer, D. Robinson, S. Vasiliev, An Introduction to International Criminal Law and Procedure, 4th ed., Cambridge U.P., Cambridge 2019, p. 344. See furthermore the Symposium "Guilty by association: Joint Criminal Enterprise on Trial" 5 J. Int'l Crim. Just. 2007, p. 67.
7   See text below, par. 2.3.

criminal objective of the JCE".[8] In other words, "the creation of an ethnically homogeneous state" shall be considered as an overall objective of merely political nature, "not inherently criminal".[9] Other alleged errors – such as that of having arbitrarily equated "being part of the Bosnian Serb leadership with membership in the JCE" can be considered as derivative from the first basic submission. However, I will deal with this point thereafter, following the logical order commonly used in the analysis on the component elements of JCE: a plurality of persons; the existence of a common plan; the participation of the accused in the plan.[10]

Before starting a detailed analysis on the merits, some introductory remarks on the relevance of the issues addressed in the judgement is due. What is joint criminal enterprise from a functional point of view: is it a form of collective responsibility or guilt by association, to be declined as incompatible with the principle of individual criminal responsibility?

Actually, international crimes – or, with a more sociologically nuanced label, mass atrocities – are characterized by an inherent tension between individual agency and collective responsibility, two dimensions that are not mutually exclusive and that meddle playing together within a given social, economic, political and, in broad terms, situational context. In fact, it is the context that qualifies a crime as an international one, as contrasted with 'ordinary' crimes. This situational context "is difficult to reconstruct. The very nature of violence may be at odds with conventional notions of culpability. It may be hard to translate into legal labels of responsibility".[11] As Carsten Stahn has recently put it, this principle was mainly developed in reaction to fears of collective responsibility.[12]

Consequently, there has been some reluctance to punish individuals for membership in organizations as such.[13] In turn, however, individualization of wrongdoing assumes that collective criminality can be translated into individual guilt and responsibility, which is a difficult and debatable process. "Mass criminality is often both individual and collective... a full translation of collective conduct into individual responsibility cause the complex problems in relation to the knowledge and understanding of collective criminality, causality and determination of blame. The fact that an individual takes part in collective violence does not necessarily mean that this person should be responsible for every act committed within the collective structure".[14]

It is precisely the category of JCE that, on the one side, is charged with this 'translation' task. Beyond its technical-legal content, limits, and criticisms, it is a crucial concept – maybe the most qualifying of the whole body of international criminal law's general principles – because it is the legal tool conceived of[15] to deal with the inherently collective nature of international crimes. JCE works as the legal lens through which the situational context of collective crimes is looked at and reasoned about. The intertwinement between the legal evaluation and the situational context is inevitable, but it is clear that the category is the way to frame factual findings on reality in legal terms, but is not co-extensive with that reality.

It must be welcomed that the instant judgement – through its calling for a scrupulous analysis on factual findings for the context to be carefully assessed in light of legal standards – explicitly strives to make it clear.[16] This attitude seems coherent with the proceedings recently described in vivid terms by Carsten Stahn, which deserve to be quoted at length:

> International criminal investigations must first link all the pieces of the puzzle together in order to understand the crimes and the collective nature of agency. This requires an understanding of the functioning of organizational and power structures. Then the bits and pieces must be deconstructed. It must be determined which individual forms of agency and control contributed to the collective outcome.

---

8   Stanišić and Župljanin Judgement, par.64.

9   Stanišić and Župljanin Judgement, par.65, referring to Župljanin's submission on this point. See on this the text below, par. 2.2.

10   See text below, par. 2.1.

11   C. Stahn, A Critical Introduction to International Criminal Law, Cambridge U.P., Cambridge 2019, p. 125.

12   *Ibid.*, p. 123.

13   *Ibid.*, p. 124.

14   *Ibid.*, p. 125.

15   By judicial ingenuity, perhaps, to quote E. van Sliedregt, L. van den Herik, Introduction: The STL Interlocutory Decision on the Definition of Terrorism – Judicial Ingenuity or Radicalism?, in 24 Leiden J. of Int'l Law 2011, p. 251, but also within the framework of a plain interpretation of a legal text, that of Art. 7(1) ICTY Statute.

16   As we will consider below, the difference between facts and legal evaluation is made clear by the Appeals Chamber (text below, par. 6).

This is an individualization process that involves "delicate policy choices and selectivity dilemmas".[17] In spite of a recurring criticism, JCE aims at rationalizing through a legal tool this tension between the collective nature of international crimes and the need for individualization. It is not a form of guilt by association, nor of responsibility 'by position' (i.e. automatically derived from the position held by a person, for instance, in the political context, irrespective of his contribution to the common criminal plan).

As we will see below (par. 2.1) this is made clear by the Appeals Chamber in the present case. Upholding the conclusions reached by the Trial Chamber, it stresses that the judges "did not impose collective responsibility on all members of the ... leadership, nor did it criminalise membership therein". Moreover, they "assessed and made findings on the basis of individual acts and conduct".[18] This is a sound methodological way to establish individual guilt within a collective endeavour.

At the same time, through focusing on the specific relevance of individual acts and conduct, that have to be explicitly mentioned in the judicial reasoning, the Court provides a clear response to criticisms according to which "JCE easily becomes a tool to 'just convict' them all".[19] Of course, there may be the risk of an overtly broad extension of the requirements, but this danger is implied in every judicial activity, and should not be highlighted with respect to JCE alone.

Doubts have been cast against the nature of the category as a form of commission.[20] However, it should be considered that JCE as a 'mode of liability' seems to be especially apt "to accurately capture the role of the principal architects of atrocity",[21] and to deal with the 'Hitler-as-accomplice' paradox – that is, with the question "under what circumstances an individual who is physically and structurally distant from the direct commission of a crime may be held accountable as a perpetrator for collective forms of action".[22]

If one rigorously acknowledges that ordinary concepts of domestic legal systems, and therefore the entire conceptual world crafted in relation to ordinary crimes "may have to be adjusted in the context of international crimes",[23] it must be accepted that the label "commission" in the framework of ICL hints at a concept which is dramatically different from that implied by the correspondent label in the domestic context. The concept of commission revolves primarily around the (individual) contribution to the context as the specific element that makes the 'underlying' offence an international crime.

The perpetrator of (only) an underlying offence of torture can never be the perpetrator of the international crime of torture as a crime against humanity – specifically, through the very conduct of torturing a concrete person within a general framework he did *not* create. He cannot be perpetrator in the same sense and to the same degree as the indirect perpetrator who possesses the control over the crime or participates in the common enterprise at the leadership level, thus contributing to the creation or the continuation of the contextual framework of mass violence.

On the contrary, a person taking part (only) in setting up the situational context *commits* the international crime even if he does not *commit* – i.e. is neither perpetrator (nor accomplice to) – any underlying offence. The conceptual-legal possibility to commit an international crime without committing any 'underlying' crime, far from being paradoxical, is nothing but a coherent consequence of the very structure of crimes under international law.

2.1 Plurality of persons: Political leadership v. membership in a criminal enterprise

The first component element of JCE is obviously a plurality of persons. Whenever a political leadership is involved, such as in the instant case, the legal assessment loses its seemingly neutral character and unveils

---

17   C. Stahn, A Critical Introduction to International Criminal Law, Cambridge U.P., Cambridge 2019, both quotations at p. 128.
18   Stanišić and Župljanin Judgement, par. 81–82.
19   C. Stahn, A Critical Introduction to International Criminal Law, Cambridge U.P., Cambridge 2019, p. 135 and fn. 107 for further references.
20   On the nature of JCE see, for instance, R. Cryer, D. Robinson, S. Vasiliev, An Introduction to International Criminal Law and Procedure, 4th ed., Cambridge U.P., Cambridge 2019, p. 347.
21   On the Hitler-as-accessory dilemma see, for instance, J.G. Stewart, The End of 'Modes of Liability' for International Crimes, in 25 Leiden Journal of International Law 2012, p. 165, *passim*.
22   C. Stahn, A Critical Introduction to International Criminal Law, Cambridge U.P., Cambridge 2019, p. 133.
23   *Ibid.*

the political nature of the requirement. Whilst only aggression is labelled as 'leadership crime' – a crime that can only be committed by the leadership level of a state or organization – every core crime can be a leadership crime *in concreto*; i.e. if evidence shows that the contextual element of the crime would not exist without a joint contribution by senior leaders, however various in nature and degree it could transpire.

As noted above, however, there is no necessary overlap between the legal evaluation through the lens of criminal law and the underlying facts, that is the political and institutional organization. The Appeals Chamber highlights this difference, recalling that "some members of the Bosnian Serb leadership may not have shared the goal of the majority";[24] therefore, not every member of the leadership was also a member of the JCE. This mode of liability does not, therefore, lead automatically to the criminalisation of the political leadership as such.

On a similar account, the Chamber rejects the challenge that the appellant was deemed part of the JCE solely by virtue of his ministerial position. The defendant argues that, to equate this position with the participation in the JCE would represent a presumption of guilt and an "unacceptable reversal of the right to be presumed innocent".[25] The Chamber, even though too quickly, reiterates that the accused was convicted "on the basis of his membership in the JCE, not his membership in the Bosnian Serb leadership".[26] The position was considered, according to the Appeals Chamber, "in combination with other factors including his acts and conduct" to find that he contributed to the JCE and shared the requisite intent.

Whether the Appeals Chamber's account is factually sound is beyond the scope of this commentary. Judge Afande, in his dissent, decidedly expresses a different opinion, but identifies some references that are clear in making the relevant distinction: "these findings ... unequivocally refute [the accused's] argument that collective responsibility was attributed to all solely by virtue of membership of the Bosnian Serb leadership".[27]

2.2   Common plan v. legitimate political goal

Alongside the distinction between membership of the political leadership and of the JCE, the Court considers the difference between the legitimate political goal pursued by the same leadership and the criminal purpose as the subjective component element of the JCE, its *mens rea*. This is in fact the gist of the submission that the Trial Chamber "erred in law by conflating the legitimate political goal for Serbs to live in one state with other Serbs in the former Yugoslavia with the criminal objective of the JCE".[28]

The threefold findings on the leadership for Serbs to intend to live in one state, on the intensification of the processes of territorial demarcation, and on the initiation of the process of establishing Serb municipalities, would not amount to anything other than a legitimate political goal. In other words, from the accused's perspective, the creation of an ethnically homogeneous state is a purpose that belongs to the realm of politics and is not of concern to international criminal law.

The Appeals Chamber notes that the common criminal purpose of the JCE was the permanent removal of Bosnian Muslims and Bosnian Croats through the commission of crimes against humanity and war crimes. It is this close, direct connection between the allegedly legitimate goal, on the one side, and the commission of crimes involved in the implementation of that goal, on the other, that makes the demarcation line between law and politics. In light of this direct link, the common criminal purpose was "more than the mere aspiration of an ethnically-homogeneous, planned Serb state".[29]

The account that whenever a plan or purpose, which might be *per se* not inherently criminal, involves the commission of crimes as an instrument to achieve the goal, it amounts to a criminal purpose, is firmly rooted in case law (even at domestic level) and as matter of principle this view is shared by scholars. To quote the

---

24   Evidence showed that there were conflicts between the Serb forces, the party structure, the so-called "crisis staff", and the Government: "on some occasions Serb leaders made statements that their aim was not an ethnically pure state or that international humanitarian law should be respected"; Judgement, par. 81.
25   Stanišić and Župljanin Judgement, par. 83.
26   Stanišić and Župljanin Judgement, par. 86.
27   Stanišić and Župljanin Judgement, Separate Opinion, p. 514–515, especially par. 34–35.
28   Stanišić and Župljanin Judgement, par. 64.
29   Stanišić and Župljanin Judgement, par. 69.

authoritative scholar Glanville Williams, while "common purpose complicity is usually preceded by an unlawful (criminal) joint enterprise", it is not always so. There might be situations where "the underlying joint enterprise [is] lawful".[30]

However, the reasoning of the Court appears elusive to Judge Afande, who considers "that the majority has regrettably missed the opportunity... to set out clearly the distinction between the legitimate and non-criminal political goal in existence at the time of the Indictment and the common criminal purpose of the JCE". The Judge stresses furthermore with disappointment that, since the issue "has never been addressed by the Tribunal", it would have been instructive to clarify this distinction also in light of its consequences to the broader approach of the Tribunal's jurisprudence "to a number of complex issues surrounding Joint Criminal Enterprise".[31]

The position expressed in the separate opinion runs as follows: a) the aim of the Bosnian leadership that Serbs live in one state with other Serbs "is political and not criminal by nature"; b) separate from the legitimate political goal, "a programme was devised to ethnically cleanse regions of the former Yugoslavia",[32] which is undoubtedly criminal and not merely political; c) the inference made by the Trial Chamber and Appeals Chamber that, "because crimes were committed as a means to achieve the common criminal purpose beside the political goal, then the latter was also criminal", is abusive and therefore has to be strongly rejected;[33] and d) political goals and criminal purpose ran parallel to each other, and must be kept discrete.[34]

The necessity to distinguish between legitimate political goals (as well as social, economic, cultural objectives, as the case may be) and criminal purpose underlying a joint enterprise is conceptually sound. That said, is the application of such a distinction to the present case, as required by the separate opinion, really consistent?

One might wonder whether labelling the aim of "Serbs to live in one state" as a legitimate political goal – which should rather be dubbed as a strategy, politically, institutionally, militarily devised and implemented – misrepresents the actual reality of the situation adjudicated by the Tribunal. A legitimate political goal is not an abstract concept of political philosophy. It has to be read within the larger context in which the indicted behaviour took place, even if this must be done within the bounds of a criminal trial, "which is to try a specific person for specific conduct".[35]

In the instant case, the fact that no cohabitation of non-Serb population or ethnic groups was ever envisaged[36] might suggest that the very plan of creating a "pure" Serb state cannot be structurally separated from the forcible removal. To qualify it as legitimate and only "parallel" with a common criminal purpose sounds like a beautiful soul's account, that is idealistic and in fact disconnected from evidentiary findings.

---

[30]   G. Williams, Textbook of Criminal Law, 4th ed. by D. Baker, Sweet & Maxwell, London, p. 620–621 at 17–058 (and footnote 184). The author refers to an Australian case where "A drove P around so that he could pick up girls to have *consensual* sexual intercourse with them" (italics in original). There was nothing unlawful about that. "However, A knew that P had killed a girl on one occasion and believed that P would kill again were P to form the desire to kill. The court held that A encouraged P by assisting him to do a lawful act where there was a mutual understanding that P conditionally intended to kill should the desire hit him during one of their joint escapades ... There was ample evidence to support the jury's conclusion that A approved of P's murders, because he continued to drive P around after P had killed more than once".
[31]   Stanišić and Župljanin Judgement, Separate Opinion, p. 511 at par. 27.
[32]   This is the objective to permanently remove other ethnicities from the territory of the planned Serbian State.
[33]   It is further added that the aim for all Serbs to live in one state "remained a non-criminal, political goal throughout the entirety of the conflict ... Indeed, that political goal could been achieved by having all Serbs living in one territory alongside other non-Serbs populations or ethnic groups" (Stanišić and Župljanin Judgement, Separate Opinion, par. 28).
[34]   Other criticisms raised in the Separate Opinion relate to the accuracy of the language. In particular, by qualifying the commission of "JCE I crimes" as the means to pursue the common plan, the majority risks, in the opinion of the 'dissenting' judge, to add further ambiguity to the allegedly failed distinction between political goals and criminal purposes. I am not fully convinced of the soundness of this criticism. In the quoted excerpt of the judgement (par. 63), the Chamber points to specific acts, such as the forceful assumption of control over territories through the setting up of parallel and separate Serb institutions and municipalities, that was carried out through a systematic and widespread campaign of terror and violence resulting in crimes. That amounts to a plan to remove other ethnicities, which objectively is a JCE I. In light of this context, the perhaps elliptic statement "JCE-crimes" is not as inaccurate as the Separate Opinion maintains.
[35]   R. Cryer, D. Robinson, S. Vasiliev, An Introduction to International Criminal Law and Procedure, 4th ed., Cambridge U.P., Cambridge 2019, p. 39.
[36]   This is explicitly recalled by the Separate Opinion, par. 28 at p. 512.

The fact that not all the leaders shared the common criminal purpose does not impair this conclusion. Evidence that a minority might not have envisaged, say, the violation of international humanitarian law, has rather to do with a subjective assessment – that is, with the assessment of the respective *mens rea* – rather than with the objective character and dimension of the broader political goal as had been concretely conceived.

In sum, the Separate Opinion is truly convincing only as to its methodological message: Judges must always care for the distinction between law and politics by framing a legal evaluation of the situational context as a component element of the international crimes and the modes of liability for them. Conversely, the Separate Opinion is debatable as to its conclusion on the merits.

2.3 The accused's participation: JCE and individual criminal responsibility

The instant judgement deals with one the most controversial issues that affect the concept of "participating" in a crime, and the legal standard according to which a court can be satisfied by the evidence of the accused's individual contribution.

Much of the argumentation on this topic revolves around the procedural aspect of the accused's submissions: The Trial Chamber's findings "lack cross references to earlier underlying findings in the Trial judgement or citations to evidence on the record" (on this see below, par. 6). In addition, the Chamber "did not enter any express finding as to whether [the accused's] acts and conduct furthered the common purpose ... or whether his contribution to the JCE was significant". I focus here on the substantive aspect of the topic.

The Court reiterates – in line with the firmly established case law of international tribunals – that, in the framework of a JCE, the individual contribution must, first, further the common enterprise and, secondly, be "significant" (even if not "necessary" nor "substantial").[37]

Such acts and conduct are enumerated in the re-assessment that the Court made after acknowledging the procedural errors of the Trial Chamber.[38] The precise account that summarizes the findings of the Court can be deemed sufficient,[39] at least from a pragmatic point of view, for arguing that the requirement of a significant contribution is certainly met. This is not to say that the abstract criterion is evident in and of itself. It has been observed, for instance, that the difference between "substantial" and "significant" is not entirely clear, despite being steadily repeated.[40] Some judgement seems to underplay the importance of the requirement by stressing that "[w]hat is important is that the contribution furthers the execution of the common purpose".[41]

The present judgement does not offer much more insight on the issue; but it is not the judgement that has to be blamed for that; this is one of the most controversial topics of the theory of participation in a crime. An in-depth discussion on the concept of "significant contribution" falls beyond the scope of this commentary. However, it must be recalled, at least, that some scholars push for a principled elaboration of the requirement, in light of the general principle of legal certainty and foreseeability.

It has been proposed,[42] for instance, to make resort to the concept of risk, at the core of modern theories of imputation especially within the German theoretical environment: risk "creation" and risk "increase"

---

[37]   Suffice to quote R. Cryer, D. Robinson, S. Vasiliev, An Introduction to International Criminal Law and Procedure, 4th ed., Cambridge U.P., Cambridge 2019, p. 345–346. with further references to case law.

[38]   Among the findings considered: participation in the creation of the Serbian Democratic Party; involvement in the creation of the Ministry of Interior of the Serbian Republic; acceptance of the position of Minister of Interior.

[39]   Stanišić and Župljanin Judgement, especially par. 356–364.

[40]   See, for instance, D. Guilfoyle, International Criminal Law, Cambridge U.P., Cambridge 2016, p. 342, recalling the ICTY holding in the Milutinović case (ICTY, *Prosecutor v. Milutinović et al.*, Judgement-vol. I, Case No. IT-05–87-T, T. Ch. III, 26 February 2009, Klip/ Sluiter ALC-XXXVIII-39, par. 105): "a contribution that goes to the efficiency, effectiveness and smooth running of the plan may be considered significant. Relevant factors to consider include 'the size of the enterprise, the functions performed by the accused and his efficiency in performing them, and any effort made by the accused to impede the efficient functioning of the joint criminal enterprise; ... [a]n accused's leadership status and approving silence likewise militate in favour of a finding that his participation was significant... in most situations the accused will not be someone readily replaceable". For a recent reappraisal with special focus on the ECCC jurisprudence, see C. Kenny, Jurisprudence Continues to Evolve. The ECCC's Revision of Common Purpose Liability, in 16 J. Int'l Crim. Just. 2018, p. 623 at 629–630.

[41]   ICTY, Judgement, *Prosecutor v. Popović et al.*, Case No. IT-05–88-A, A. Ch., 30 January 2015, par. 1378.

[42]   K. Ambos, Treatise on International Criminal Law, I: Foundations and General Part, Oxford U.P., Oxford 2013, p. 165, with further references to German scholars.

(*Risikoerhöhung*) as causal factors for the commission of the crime. This proposal might not be entirely convincing.[43] The risk increase could be properly assessed only *ex ante*, whereas a judgement of the effects of the indicted behaviour must be assessed *ex post* – i.e. after the conduct took place.

Otherwise, the mere attempt to participate would be punishable, but this is incompatible with the current notion of complicity in an international crime. For complicity to be punished, the crime must actually occur or at least be attempted; this is now enshrined in the ICC Statute (Art. 25).

Stressing the necessity of *kausale Risikosteigerung* leads to further complications, since it is difficult to see the difference between this concept and that of the necessary/substantial contribution, on the one side, and the pertinent logical mechanism of assessment, on the other. The added value of the risk-theory is therefore not easily discernible.

One might suggest a clearly retrospective functional assessment – that is, to evaluate whether the contribution by the accused fits functionally into the process that led to the crime (at any stage of its commission) and therefore may be deemed concretely instrumental to it. If this is the case, the contribution to the crime is proved and no room is left for speculating about the "significance" or "substantiality" of the participation, apart from for sentencing purposes. Under close scrutiny, this is the method actually followed by the Appeals Chamber in the instant case, even without formally departing from the common conceptual – or rather, linguistic – approach.

3   The required intent (JCE I)

No special question in light of the legal standard for the *mens rea* assessment arises in the framework of JCE I crimes. The Court reiterates that the accused must share, with the other participants; (a) the intent to commit the crimes that form part of the common purpose; and (b) the intent to participate in a common plan aimed at their commission.

It stresses at the same time that the intent shall be "individual" – that is, it cannot be deduced "by virtue of the mere grouping" of persons who share the common purpose. The individual intent must be ascertained on the basis of individual acts and conduct. This accurate statement as to the subjective element, parallel to the similar assessment made on the *actus reus*, can help avoid the critiques towards the category as a form of strict liability incompatible with the fundamental culpability principle.

Possible discussions as to the appropriateness of the concrete analysis on factual findings arise normally in every judicial process. As a matter of fact, all this has no bearing on the soundness of the methodological statement underlined above. Indeed, intent cannot be directly assessed, it can only be inferred from external circumstances[44] – including acts that are not criminal *per se*[45] – such as "a person's knowledge of the common criminal purpose or the crime(s) it involved, combined with his or her continuing participation in the crimes or in the implementation of the common criminal purpose ... While such intent can be inferred from circumstantial evidence, this inference must be the only reasonable inference".

4   JCE III

The accused were also convicted for crimes against humanity and war crimes falling outside the common purpose – that is, pursuant to the third category of JCE (JCE III). Even though this category is highly debated in scholarship and partly in the case law of international tribunals, the Appeals Chamber sticks to the firmly

---

[43]   The cultural background of the proposal is German scholarship. This must be underlined, since in Germany the attempt to participate in a crime is punishable. In other domestic systems this is not the case. The tendency to consider certain concepts as system-independent – or having an objectively scientific dimension, beyond the conceptualization of positive law – raises some reservations.

[44]   For instance, in the case at hand, the Court is satisfied by the evidence that the accused learned of the unlawful detention of Muslims and Croats at the relevant time, he was informed of mass arrests accompanied by intention of mistreatments ("they can beat them, they can do whatever they fucking want", he had been told), was informed of the looting of property, as well as of the commission of war crimes, Stanišić and Župljanin Judgement, par. 397–398; see also par. 404–406, 411–413;furthermore, evidence was considered as to conduct and statements in relation to policies of Serbian parties and institutions, to the close relationship with Karadžić, to the approval of (para)military operations and attacks, to presence at meetings, and to continued support for and participation in the implementation of the policies of the BS leadership (par. 573 ff.).

[45]   Stanišić and Župljanin Judgement, par. 446.

established jurisprudence of the Tribunal. This relates not only to the legitimacy of JCE III as such, but also to the compatibility of this mode of liability with special intent crimes (for example, persecution, genocide).

The accused asked the Court to depart from this jurisprudence, arguing that "cogent reasons exist" for such a *revirement*, such as the critiques by many commentators and especially the jurisprudence of other tribunals.[46] I will address the methodological limb of this topic separately (below, par. 6).

As to the substantive law, the court reiterates, first, the general features of this mode of liability: "an accused can be held responsible for a crime outside the common purpose if, under the circumstances of the case: (i) it was foreseeable to the accused that such a crime might be perpetrated by one or more of the persons used by him (or by a member of the joint criminal enterprise) in order to carry out the *actus reus* of the crimes forming part of the common purpose; and (ii) the accused willingly took the risk that such a crime might occur by joining or continuing to participate in the enterprise".[47]

Secondly, the same principles apply to all crimes, with the only qualification that the possible commission of a crime with the required special intent (for example, discriminatory intent) is foreseeable. The participant in the JCE III need not personally have that intent.

As to the general features of JCE III, of special interest in the decision lies in the fact that it deepens the legal standard for assessing the 'foreseeability' of the different crime and faces the critiques explained in the Separate Opinion of Judge Afande. This point deserves peculiar attention.

As to the conviction for crimes with special intent pursuant to a JCE III, after briefly mentioning the unanimity of scholarly critique, I will sketchily propose a tentative explanation for the tenacious position held by the Tribunal, striving to verbalise what idea of participation and 'perpetratorship' in the case of international crimes seems to be implied by that position.

4.1   Foreseeability

The foreseeability of a crime (committed outside the scope of the criminal enterprise) may be assessed following two opposite legal standards, an objective and a subjective one. In fact, the accused contends that the different crime must be objectively foreseeable, a criterion that "does not depend upon the accused's state of mind".[48] This argument would lead to a restriction of the breadth of liability pursuant to JCE III. Indeed, the only way to *objectively* assess this requirement would be to contrast the component elements of both crimes (the agreed upon, and the different one) in order to consider whether they are homogeneous or structurally different. If the constituent elements are homogeneous, the different crime can be deemed foreseeable; otherwise it is not.

This argument, however, is a double-edged sword. This view would prove useful for the defence in the instant case since, in light of the objective criterion, the actual subjective knowledge, even foresight of the different, allegedly heterogeneous crimes would have had no bearing on (the exclusion of) liability. But it might be dangerous as a matter of principle: an objectively foreseeable crime could be imputed to an accused even in the absence of the subjective foreseeability.

The Appeals Chamber argues that the distinction between objective and subjective criterion is "artificial" and confirms[49] that the subjective standard is appropriate: foreseeability "must be assessed in relation to the

---

[46]   Stanišić and Župljanin Judgement, par. 588 ff. (with references): the accused made reference to a dissent of Judge Shahabuddeen in *Stakić* Trial judgement, and to recent jurisprudence of the STL and SCSL.

[47]   Stanišić and Župljanin Judgement, par. 595. The Court specifies that responsibility pursuant JCE III presupposes that "the elements of the first category of joint criminal enterprise have been satisfied" (par. 958). The Appeals Chamber further recalls (par. 994 f.) that crimes can be committed by non-members of the JCE provided that it has been shown that the crimes could be imputed to at least one member of the JCE and that this member, when using a principal perpetrator, acted in accordance with the common plan. This link must be assessed on a case-by-case basis and can be inferred from various factors, highlighted in the case law of the Tribunal: for example, evidence that a JCE member explicitly or implicitly requested the non-JCE member to commit such a crime, or instigated, ordered, encouraged, or otherwise availed himself of the non-JCE member to commit the crime (see decisions quoted in fn. 3301). See on this, the Appeals Chamber decisions in *Popović et al* (par. 1679) and Đorđević (par. 911).

[48]   Stanišić and Župljanin Judgement, par. 619.

[49]   See decisions quoted at Stanišić and Župljanin Judgement, fn. 2104.

individual knowledge"[50] of the accused (for instance, the awareness of the criminal propensity of members of the controlled forces to commit crimes. What may be foreseeable to one person, might not be foreseeable to another.

A more specific question has been submitted by one of the accused in the instant case. He contends that the Tribunal "should adopt an additional condition" of JCE III liability in the case of violent crimes graver than those agreed upon by the members of JCE. It was submitted that "liability for foreseeable violent crimes may only arise when the accused intended the adoption of violent means to implement the common purpose".[51] This connection between the type of actually intended behaviour and the type of crime actually committed outside the common purpose, although advocated by "highly respected academics" out of concern for the "untrammelled breath of JCE III",[52] is rejected by the Court, not seeing cogent reasons to depart from its jurisprudence: JCE III can attach for any crime that falls outside of an agreed upon JCE. In fact, the accused's argument relies on the objective criterion for assessing foreseeability, which was already dismissed by the Court.

This hasty dismissal has been criticised by Judge Afande.[53] In his view, the choice between the objective and subjective approach hinges upon the specific crimes to which the liability is attached. In other words, in the case of homogeneity of the crimes, those falling outside the common purpose can be nevertheless considered as a natural and foreseeable consequence of the crimes agreed upon. More precisely, this homogeneity must encompass the subjective element of the offence definition, such as the special intent (*subjectives Tatbestandslement*).[54] Only where this objective connection cannot be established due to the heterogeneity of the abstract requirements, is it incumbent on the Judges to move to a subjective level.

4.2   Taking the risk

This subjective requirement, like foreseeability, is not directly ascertainable but must be inferred from circumstantial evidence; in particular, it "may be drawn from the fact that the accused was aware that the crime was a possible consequence of a joint criminal enterprise but nevertheless decided to join or continues to participate in that enterprise".[55]

4.3   JCE III and Special Intent

As already pointed out, the Appeals Chamber reiterates the firmly established conclusion that any crime can give rise to liability pursuant to JCE III. There is no reason for excluding special intent crimes. As is well known, this tendency has been highly criticized by scholars, and the "overwhelming academic literature is … in favour of upholding the specific intent requirement".[56]

It is outside the scope of this commentary to discuss the merits of the issue. Rather, it is interesting to consider the topic from another point of view, asking a different question that aims at delving into the judicial stance beyond what is literally verbalised. One might wonder why the position on compatibility between JCE III and special intent crimes is being held so tenaciously by the Tribunal – even though some *arrêts* leave room for hoping that the approach is not settled case law. More specifically, it could be asked whether there is a particular idea of the relationship between "commission" of and "participation" in international crimes that is not verbalised by the jurisprudence and that might explain why a special intent crime might be committed without individually having that special intent. To answer this question, some preliminary remarks are in order.

---

50   Stanišić and Župljanin Judgement, par. 644; 669.
51   Stanišić and Župljanin Judgement, par. 963.
52   Stanišić and Župljanin Judgement, par. 963, fn. 3201; par. 977, fn. 3240.
53   Stanišić and Župljanin Judgement, p. 517 f., par. 41 f.
54   For instance, "there exists a clear objective link between the common criminal purpose based on "discrimination", and the crime of persecution, which also entails "discrimination". The latter is then the objectively natural and foreseeable consequence of the former": Stanišić and Župljanin Judgement, p. 517, par. 42.
55   Stanišić and Župljanin Judgement, par. 705.
56   See, K. Ambos, Treatise on International Criminal Law, I: Foundations and General Part, Oxford U.P., Oxford 2013, p. 176.

4.3.1 *Preliminary remarks: two pillars between single v. collective authorship*

International crimes are composed of two pillars.[57] The first is that of the underlying offences, with all their objective and subjective requirements (among which is possibly the special intent); the second is the "contextual", *"chapeau"* or "international" element, which is the specific feature that makes the underlying conduct –otherwise amounting to an ordinary crime: murder, rape, ill-treatment, torture, and so on – an international crime. "The connection to this context [of organized violence] turns an ordinary crime into a crime under international law. The contextual element comes into play, depending on the crime, as either a material or a mental element of the crime".[58] In the case of genocide, for instance, it is the very subjective requirement (the genocidal intent to destroy a group in whole or in part) that makes the underlying crimes amount to genocide.

That said, it must be added that the contextual element translates into legal vocabulary the social scenario of macro-criminality – that is, situations in which crimes are actually committed by many persons.

This may be true or not as regards each underlying offence, which can in fact be committed by one (*Alleintäter*) or more persons. To be noted is the fact that the offence definition of the underlying crimes is mainly crafted through envisaging the behaviour of a single person, as is usually the case for ordinary crimes at the domestic level –rather than for *Massendelikte* and crimes that can only be committed by a plurality of persons, so-called necessary participation, *notwendige Teilnahme*. In light of this, ordinary crimes are typically – according to their basic definition – committed by one single individual; the plurality of persons, however legally relevant, is a matter of fact.

In other words, joint commission or participation may occur according to the circumstances of the case, and their legal relevance rests upon a specific provision different from the one setting out the definition of the offence.

The opposite situation arises when international crimes are at stake. Here the plurality of persons is always a matter of factual reality: they are *Massendelikte* – sociologically speaking: macro-criminality. The context can be created by perpetrators not only due to the occurrence of multiple violations relevant as underlying offences – i.e. not through merely summing up multiple ordinary offences (possibly committed by single perpetrators) – but also through the setting up of a distinctive, 'differential' element, that attracts the concern of the international community as a whole. International crimes are therefore normatively conceived of and crafted as involving a plurality of persons.

Typically – that is, according to their basic definition – they envisage a plurality of persons and therefore have collective nature. At the same time, the plurality is only reflected in the contextual element of the international crime as such, which, however, does not express by itself the rule of liability. It is only a precondition for the application of such a rule – were the situational context of mass violence not present, no issue of liability for an international crime would arise.

4.3.2 *Collective nature and individual commission of international crimes*

Since "the collective nature of crimes under international law does not absolve us of the need to determine individual responsibility", additional rules are required for: (a) "establishing individual contributions to crimes within a network of collective actions", and (b) "weighing the individual contribution to the crime".[59] As considered above, the fact, at the same time actual and normative, that these crimes can only be committed if a plurality of persons is involved, does not mean that – normatively – all components of the plurality "commit" the crime or that they carry the same degree of responsibility.

The concept of "commission" must therefore be different with respect to ordinary crimes. A person can commit an underlying offence only through "putting his hands" on the victim, without giving any further

---

[57]   On the general structure of international crimes, from a comparative perspective on selected domestic legal orders, see I. Marchuk, The Fundamental Structure of Crime in International Criminal Law, Springer, 2014, especially chapter 4 and, specifically on JCE, chapter 6.

[58]   G. Werle, F. Jessberger, Principles of International Criminal Law, 4th ed., Oxford U.P., Oxford, 2020, p. 210 nr. marg. 539.

[59]   G. Werle, F. Jessberger, Principles of International Criminal Law, 4th ed., Oxford U.P., Oxford, 2020, p. 234 nr. marg. 608.

contribution to the context. A person (only) contributing to the context is necessarily part of the context he frames or contributes to frame even though far away from the actual commission of the underlying crimes. This context is composed of a plurality of persons (not necessarily part of the common purpose), and a plurality of acts, some of which amount to underlying offences. All of these requirements – persons, acts, context – are necessary in order that all the component elements of the international crime are met.

4.3.3 *Committing without perpetrating and special intent*

This complexity of international crimes might lead to the idea that the individual commission of international crimes and collective action as their structural element are closely intertwined and thus logically compatible. Commission and collective participation are only labels appended to concepts that are different from the case of ordinary crimes. An individual can *normatively* "commit" the international crime without taking part in the perpetration of any underlying offence, therefore without meeting its constituent elements, either from an objective, or from a subjective point of view, provided that a connection between his acts and the offences amounting to the international crime(s) exists according to a pertinent mode of liability. JCE III is such a mode. However, it must be added that – in spite of the broadness of the rulings on special intent crimes – the problem has mainly arisen in cases where joint enterprise occurred at leadership level.

This is an important precondition for the reasoning of judges. My reading of the Tribunals' position is that membership in a JCE at the leadership level entails such a degree of involvement in framing and pursuing the common purpose as to influence both the situational context as well as a great deal of the concrete execution of the underlying offences.

It is the perhaps unconscious perception of this structural background, which is profoundly different from that of ordinary crimes even though "verbalised" through the same words, that roots the reiterated position of the case law on this point. Therefore, it might not seem strange that a person "committing" an international crime – in the sense explained above: as a creator of or contributor to the situational context made of a plurality of persons, acts, conduct – does not have himself the special intent required by the underlying crime.

By the same token, the only exception to the application of JCE III should be genocide, precisely because the context is co-extensive with the mental element of the offence.[60] The case law on this point deserves therefore to be reversed even whilst sticking to the application of JCE III to special intent crimes of a different nature.

5 *Commission by omission outside and inside JCE. What difference, and why?*

The judgement recognises as a matter of principle the liability for omissions, consistently with the case law of the *ad hoc* Tribunals[61] and the first ICC jurisprudence.[62] In the case law of international tribunals, it is

---

[60]   See A. Cassese, The Proper Limits of Individual Responsibility under the Doctrine of Joint Criminal Enterprise, in 5 J. Int'l Crim. Just. 2007, p. 109.

[61]   It is interesting to note, however, that the ICTY has repeatedly affirmed that the Tribunal, and especially its Appeals Chamber, has never set out the requirements for a conviction for omission in detail: see ICTY, Judgement, *Prosecutor v. Orić*, Case No. IT-03–68-A. A. Ch., 3 July 2008, Klip/ Sluiter ALC-XXXV-505, par. 43; ICTY, Judgement, *Prosecutor v. Brđanin*, Case No. IT-99-36-A, A. Ch., 3 April 2007, Klip/ Sluiter ALC-XXXIII-609, par. 274. ICTY, Judgement, *Prosecutor v. Galić*, Case No. IT-98–29-A, A. Ch., 30 November 2006, Klip/ Sluiter ALC-XXXIII-429, par. 175–177, solely affirms that the omission of an act can lead to individual criminal responsibility where there is a legal duty to act; the gist of this decision concerns a different issue, whether an omission could constitute an act of "ordering". The answer is in the negative, even if an act of ordering can be proven by taking into account omissions). ICTY, Judgement, *Prosecutor v. Blaškić*, Case No. IT-95–14-A, A. Ch., 29 July 2004, Klip/ Sluiter ALC-XX-295, par. 663, labels the commission by omission as an "exception to the general rule requiring a positive act". One instance is that of "perpetration of a crime by omission pursuant to Article 7(1), whereby a *legal duty* is imposed, inter alia as a commander, to care for the persons under the control of one's subordinates" (italics added).

[62]   For references, see G. Werle, F. Jessberger, Principles of International Criminal Law, 4th ed., Oxford U.P., Oxford, 2020, p. 309 especially fn. 653–654. The most comprehensive account in the jurisprudence of the *ad hoc* Tribunals is to be found in ICTR, Judgement, *Prosecutor v. Ntagerura and others*, T.Ch. III, Case No. ICTR-99–46-T, 25 February 2004, Klip/ Sluiter ALC-XVIII-267, par. 659, cited by *Ntagerura et al.* Appeals Judgement, par. 333: "[I]n order to hold an accused criminally responsible for an omission as a principal perpetrator, the following elements must be established: (a) the accused must have had a duty to act mandated by a rule of criminal law; (b) the accused must have had the ability to act; (c) the accused failed to act intending the criminally sanctioned consequences or with awareness and consent that the consequences would occur; and (d) the failure to act resulted in the commission

accepted in general terms that even crimes whose offence definition requires an active conduct can be committed concretely through omission (commission by omission), provided that: (a) there is a legal duty to act; (b) the accused had the capacity to fulfil the duty; (c) the accused had the opportunity to undertake the required act (capacity to act); (d) there is a link between the failure to act and the commission of a crime, so that it can be normatively said that the omission "results in the commission of the crime";[63] and (e) the accused had the knowledge of the duty.

The gist of the discussion on omissions in the instant case relates to whether omission in the framework of a JCE must meet the same legal conditions set out in the case law for liability by omission.

The appellants contended, first, that participation in a JCE through omission "can only be established when the omission arises from a legal duty to act mandated by a rule of criminal law";[64] secondly, that "reliance on a failure to fulfil domestic legal obligations constitutes a 'radical and unprecedented extension of omission liability in international criminal law'";[65] and thirdly, that the capacity to act requires an accused to exercise at least "concrete influence" over subordinate physical perpetrators.

The Tribunal responds, as to the first two contentions, that "the demonstration of a duty to act that would meet the legal conditions set out ... for commission by omission is not required in relying on an accused's failure to act in the context of a joint criminal enterprise".[66] This conclusion is grounded on the premise that a contribution to a JCE need not be in and of itself criminal, as long as the accused performs acts or fails to perform acts that in some way contribute significantly to the furtherance of the common purpose.[67]

In light of this premise, the Chamber affirms that, "when establishing an accused's participation in a joined criminal enterprise through his failure to act, the existence of a legal duty to act deriving from a rule of criminal law is not required but the nature of the accused's duty and the extent of his ability to act are simply questions of evidence and not determinative of joint criminal enterprise liability."[68] The conclusion of the Chamber may be convincing, but the argument deserves further clarification. Indeed, there is considerable confusion as to the sources of the duty to act and, correlatively, to the structure of liability for omissions in general and, as a consequence, in international criminal law.

Of course, *a* legal duty to act must exist.[69] Unfortunately, the instant judgement does not explain what the sources of such a duty are. They have been sparsely enumerated in the case law of *ad hoc* Tribunals:[70] "[O] mission can incur responsibility only if there was a duty to act in terms of preventing the prohibited result from occurring. Such a duty can, in particular, arise out of responsibility for the safety of the person concerned, derived from humanitarian law or based on a position of authority, or can result from antecedent conduct by which the person concerned has been exposed to a danger".[71]

In light of this, it is misleading to affirm that the source must be one of criminal law,[72] as the Appeals Chamber in fact makes resort to the JCE category in order to overcome this requirement. Laws and customs of war, the defendant's position of authority, domestic law, or states' obligations under general international

---

of the crime". This judgement is quoted by ICTY, Judgement, *Prosecutor v. Brđanin*, Case No. IT-99–36-A, A. Ch., 3 April 2007, Klip/ Sluiter ALC-XXXIII-609, par. 274, fn. 557.

[63]   "Normatively", omissions, from a naturalistic point of view, only consist in a failure to act – that is, they are no-conduct at all; K. Ambos, Treatise on International Criminal Law, I: Foundations and General Part, Oxford U.P., Oxford 2013, p. 180 (in quite identical terms, in the framework of a comparative inquiry, K. Ambos, Omissions, in K. Ambos, A. Duff, J. Roberts, T. Weigend, Core Concepts in Criminal Law and Criminal Justice, I, Cambridge U.P., Cambridge 2020, p. 17).

[64]   Stanišić and Župljanin Judgement, par. 106 and fn. 365, referring to *Stanišić* Appeals Brief.

[65]   Stanišić and Župljanin Judgement, par. 725 and fn. 2443.

[66]   Stanišić and Župljanin Judgement, par. 109, 110, 732.

[67]   Stanišić and Župljanin Judgement, par. 110.

[68]   Stanišić and Župljanin Judgement, par. 110, text accompanying fn. 378.

[69]   In the instant case, the Appeals Chamber stresses that the accused's failure "to discipline the RS MUP personnel who had committed crimes and to protect the civilian population, despite his duties to do so, together with his ability, as the highest authority, to investigate and punish those who had committed crimes" amounts to a contribution to the JCE (par. 111).

[70]   Summarized, for instance, by V. Lanovoy, Complicity and its Limits in the Law of International Responsibility, Hart, Oxford and Portland – Oregon 2016, p. 63.

[71]   ICTY, Judgement, *Prosecutor v. Orić*, Case No. IT-03–68-T, T. Ch. II, 30 June 2006, Klip/ Sluiter ALC-XXIX-519, par. 302.

[72]   This statement is repeatedly affirmed by international tribunals and finds acceptance in A. Cassese, Cassese's International Criminal Law, 3d ed. by P. Gaeta, Oxford U.P., Oxford 2013, chapter 10 (albeit somewhat equivocally).

law are not always assisted by criminal sanctions and nevertheless can be legitimate sources of a legal duty to act. There is no reason why all these duties could not ground liability for omission provided that all the other requirements are met.[73]

Indeed, to require a rule of *criminal law* as a source of the legal duty to act would mean conflating the concept of "omission proper" or "pure omission" (*echtes Unterlassungsdelikt*), where omission is the conduct directly prohibited and therefore described by the offence definition, and commission by omission (*unechtes Unterlassungsdelikt*),[74] which is a way of committing a crime that, by its wording, requires active conduct. Why this conflation is erroneous is a question we must more explicitly delve into.

The reason for the equivalence between positive conduct and failure to act in the latter case – where the offence definition focusses on a positive act only – lies in the very structure of the crime, beyond the way the offence definition is literally phrased. In such cases, the aim of the criminal law provision is to generally criminalise the causation of a prohibited event: the external form of the causal conduct is not decisive (*Erfolgsunwert*). If such an event has been concretely brought about through a failure to act, this failure satisfies the requirements of the offence definition.

To that purpose – i.e. setting forth the functional equivalence between action and omission – at the domestic level, a special provision on omission is often enshrined in criminal codes or statutes; in international criminal law, the liability for omissions is probably rooted in customary international law or general principles of law. Even if this latter statement is controversial, the case law on that matter is undoubtedly compatible with the legality principle as a principle of international criminal law. Commission by omission is only legitimate, first of all, when a legally relevant duty to act exists.

As for the third ground of appeal, the Court coherently affirms that, whilst outside a JCE, the objective element of commission by omission requires an "elevated degree of concrete influence".[75] In the case of JCE, this requirement cannot be applied, since it would mean to conflate that requirement with that of the "significant contribution" as the only relevant requirements in JCE cases.

6   Methodological issues

As mentioned above (par. 1), the Appeals Chamber acknowledged that the trial judgement failed to give a reasoned opinion on two important aspects, which amounts to an error of law. First, no cross-references are given to the factual findings deemed to be specifically relevant to the individual contribution of the accused and to its "significance" in reaching the threshold for affirming criminal liability in the framework of the JCE I scheme.

Secondly, the same approach of omitting cross-references to earlier findings or citations to evidence on the record, explicitly labelled as "regrettable", is taken as regards the relevant *mens rea*, the requisite intent pursuant to this mode of liability.

As regards especially the first error of law, the consequence is that the Appeals Chamber engages in a re-assessment of the whole trial judgement. Whilst recalling that "the trial judgement must be read as a whole",[76] the Chamber lists and assesses that the "findings and relevant evidence concerning [the accused's] acts and conduct to determine whether a reasonable trier of fact could have concluded beyond reasonable doubt that his acts and conduct"[77] furthered the JCE, and consequently the requisite element of a significant contribution to a common criminal plan is objectively met.

---

[73]   ICTR, Judgement, *Prosecutor v. Ntagerura and others*, T.Ch. III, Case No. ICTR-99–46-T, 25 February 2004, Klip/ Sluiter ALC-XVIII-267, par. 660.
[74]   K. Ambos, Omissions, in K. Ambos, A. Duff, J. Roberts, T. Weigend, Core Concepts in Criminal Law and Criminal Justice, I, Cambridge U.P., Cambridge 2020, especially p. 20–27.
[75]   Stanišić and Župljanin Judgement, par. 733.
[76]   Stanišić and Župljanin Judgement, par. 138. The Court adds that "there is a presumption that a trial chamber has evaluated all the evidence presented to it, as long as there is no indication that the trial chamber completely disregarded any particular piece of evidence" (text accompanying footnote 470).
[77]   Stanišić and Župljanin Judgement, par. 142.

This assessment is necessary for primarily technical-procedural reasons, since it is required by fair trial principles: procedural fairness as the outer garment of substantively "rendering justice" to the accused is part of the very legitimacy of the whole endeavour of international criminal justice.

Alongside that, the instruction to accurately connect specific factual findings to abstract requirements of criminal liability is relevant from a methodological point of view. First, the meticulous narrative of facts comes to the front stage of judicial activity. The first, elementary significance of the noun 'fact' in the legal context is that of a life occurrence requiring for whatever reasons the intervention of the law. Recalling the importance of facts could sound trivial, but it is the starting point for any subsequent question as regards the law applicable to the facts and, we should add, as regards the assessment as to whether those facts are anyhow legally relevant.

As the late US Supreme Court Judge Antonin Scalia puts it:

> Don't underestimate the importance of facts. To be sure, you will be arguing to the court about the law, but what law applies – what cases are in point, and what cases can be distinguished –depends ultimately on the facts of your case.[78]

As such, the qualification of the facts in light of abstract schemes is not neutral, since the qualification scheme carries, in turn, a value judgement. Even if the (hardly resolvable) philosophical issue of distinguishing between facts and values is far beyond the content and space limits of this commentary, one can underline in general terms the importance of an accurate reconstruction of the facts in light of the different schemes of value judgements that can be applied to the reconstruction of factual findings.

6.1   Describing the case

Given the importance of the facts as a material (as well as logical) premise for building a case, one must pay the closest attention to the details of historical occurrences. The first intellectual operation to be primarily undertaken is that of setting out with humble and patient attitude the facts of the case – i.e. the actual state of things in their strict naturalistic sense. Parties to the case and, above all, judges will then sift through evidence of facts, and look at them through the lens of the specific legal narrative.

A narrative must start from its simplest forms, as they have been dubbed by André Jolles, an influential linguist of the first half of the twentieth century: units or items of which the fact(s) are composed, and which are dissected to the point in which they appear indivisible and therefore simple (*einfache Formen*). Thereafter, facts are assessed through norms and are made 'valuable-according-to-norms'. Those norms are contrasted and – if appropriate – balanced with other norms.[79]

To sum up, it is crucial to accurately split up the concrete facts into their simplest items (forms). It is not appropriate to stop at a level of typological similarities between complex situations: rather, it ought to decompose the occurrence of life (*Lebenssachverhalt*) into its simplest components, until the maximum degree of granularity.

This activity of reducing facts to their simplest components may appear obvious, but it is especially difficult in the broad context of mass atrocities, where the individual behaviour is entangled in a broader situational context but must be nevertheless sifted out and evaluated in its singularity. It is interesting to notice that some international criminal law scholars have underlined the "holistic functioning of facts"[80] in the theoretical discourse. This expression shall mean that interpreters and adjudicators must consider the constant interaction among facts, including the so-called attendant circumstances or surrounding circumstances and their added value to the rational reading of the occurrence relevant for the law: "facts are normally assessed in a holistic way – i.e. in combination with each other".

---

[78]   A. Scalia, B.A. Garner, Making Your Case. The Art of Persuading Judges, Thomson/West, St. Paul (MN) 2008, p. 9.

[79]   A. Jolles, Einfache Formen: Legende, Sage, Mythe, Rätsel, Sprüche, Kasus, Memorabile, Märsche, Witz, Max Niemeyer Verlag, Halle 1930, p., 179 ("*Norm gegen Norm*"). An English translation by P.J. Schwartz is available (Simple Forms, Verso, London-Brooklyn 2017, with a Foreword by F. Jameson).

[80]   M. Cupido, Facing Facts in International Criminal Law. A Casuistic Model of Judicial Reasoning, in 14 J. Int'l Crim. Just. 2016, 1 at 13.

Facts, in sum, are necessarily selected and interpreted in light of their context.[81] Differences in the legal treatment of similar patterns of facts are not necessarily a synonym of incoherent reasoning, as they may be rather explained in light of the different contextual circumstances. This is a "contextual legal reasoning".

Lastly, facts are decisive in order to build a 'case' – that is, in order to meet the correct legal qualification that in turn, as a 'precedent', is the starting point for later decisions asked to confirm – or to depart from – that 'precedent'. I will briefly deal with this issue in the next section.

6.2 Cases and precedent

Recalling the importance to be conferred to the facts of the case at the interpretative stage, especially in judicial settings, leads to another important aspect of the relevance of contextual legal reasoning: how to distinguish cases. On the one side, the empirical occurrence (be it a "brute fact" or an "institutional fact" in light of Searle's theory),[82] deserves the utmost attention, and descriptive and axiological (value-laden) propositions must be kept discrete.

On the other side, the binding nature of the paradigmatic case is closely related to the specular image of the precedent – that is, the recognition of a dissonant singularity that suggests the necessity to 'distinguish' cases.

In other words, it is obvious that relying on the 'precedent' requires identifying a previous decision based upon a cluster of cases, either as a binding precedent (*stare decisis*), or as persuasive authority. However, it is crucial in this same context to establish whether the case at hand has to be differentiated from those precedents. In common law, precedents are simply a starting point for the decision to be taken.[83]

Justice Antonin Scalia has clearly maintained that:

> there is another skill...that is essential to the making of a good judge. It is the technique of what is called "distinguishing" cases... Within such a precedent-bound common-law system, it is critical for a lawyer, or the judge, to establish whether the case at hand falls within a principle that has already been decided. Hence the technique – or the art, or the game – of "distinguishing" earlier cases. It is an art or a game, rather than a science, because what constitutes the "holding" of an earlier case is not well defined and can be adjusted to suit the occasion.

With specific relation to the practical experience of international criminal tribunals, where the safeguard of coherence and consistency in applying the law is of paramount importance, Marjolein Cupido has considered that "the meaning of the law is not determined by abstract rules alone, but develops on a case-by-case basis in interplay with the questions and issues raised in individual cases".[84]

In addition, it has been recalled that international tribunals adjudicating crimes under international law "have regularly drawn up lists of factual indicators, which specify the facts that can be used to determine whether a judicial criterion applies in an individual case".[85] Indeed, courts have always kept a sphere of discretion to carve the law alongside the specific features of individual cases. All that explains why facts must be adequately evaluated and examined in light of the 'prototype' to which the rule has been enacted.

---

[81] T. Salmi-Tolonen, 'On the Balance between Invariance and Context-Dependence', in D. Kurzon, B. Kryk-Kastovsky (eds.), *Legal Pragmatics* (Amsterdam/Philadelphia: John Benjamin Publishing, 2018). The author defines the context as "a matrix that surrounds the event being examined and provides resources for its appropriate interpretation" (at 237). The context may be of a physical, linguistic, legal, socio-cultural nature.

[82] J. Searle, 'How to derive "ought" from "is"', in The Philosophical Rev., 1964, p. 43–58 (here the distinction between "brute" or "non-institutional" and "institutional" facts, especially at 55).

[83] For a specification as to the contingent character of the rule (sometimes dubbed "a legend") of *stare decisis*, which is not decisive within the common law system, see U. Mattei, Common Law. Il diritto angloamericano, Utet, Torino 1999, *passim* and especially 214 ff., 214, 247–249. An authoritative account of the common law logic has been given by the famous book of A. Kronman, The Lost Lawyer, Belknap Press, Harvard 1993.

[84] M. Cupido, Facing Facts in International Criminal Law. A Casuistic Model of Judicial Reasoning, in 14 J. Int'l Crim. Just. 2016, 1 at 2.

[85] M. Cupido, Facing Facts in International Criminal Law. A Casuistic Model of Judicial Reasoning, in 14 J. Int'l Crim. Just. 2016, 1 at 4.

6.3 *Cross-fertilization admitted in principle, refused in outcome*

As considered above (par. 4.3), the accused submits that so-called specific intent crimes are not compatible with JCE III as a mode of liability. While acknowledging that the ICTY case law allows for convictions based on this mode of liability without any restriction, the defendant argues that "cogent reasons exist to depart from this jurisprudence".[86] In support of this argument, the defendant invokes ancient (post-World War II) cases,[87] as well as recent jurisprudence of other international tribunals (STL, SCSL), alongside other international sources (ICC Statute, Convention for the Suppression of Terrorist bombings). He maintains that "no support can be found' in customary international law allowing for convictions for specific intent crimes on the basis of the third category of joint criminal enterprise".[88]

On this basis, the Chamber is requested to depart from the established case law by holding that "no conviction for specific intent crimes may be entered under the third category of joint criminal enterprise".[89] While the substantive prong of the topic has been discussed above, it is worth considering at this stage the methodological stance taken by the Court as regards the case law of other Tribunals.

The Appeals Chamber recalls that, "insofar [the accused] relies upon the jurisprudence of the STL and SCSL … it is not bound by the findings of other courts – domestic, international, or hybrid – and that, even though it will consider such jurisprudence it may nonetheless come to a different conclusion on a matter than that reached by another judicial body". It further "considers that in order to constitute a cogent reason for departing from its established jurisprudence on a matter, the party advocating a departure would need to show that a non-binding opinion of another court is correct law and demonstrate that there is a clear mistake" in the Tribunal's approach.

Judge Liu in his Declaration criticizes the merits of this interpretation of the law, holding that "it defies reason to find an accused guilty of *committing* specific intent crimes while accepting at the same time that the specific intent of that accused was not proven in court. Specific intent crimes require a particularly high standard of intent (*dolus specialis*), which cannot be satisfied, via the subjective element of JCE III, by *dolus eventualis*".[90] The contribution of the accused, "who is lacking the specific intent", deserves punishment, thus, under a different label: "this criminal behavior could be criminalized under other modes of liability, such as aiding and abetting, provided that other elements are fulfilled".[91]

A slightly different argumentative path is taken by Judge Afande in his Dissenting Opinion. His account, while tilting toward the same conclusion on the merits stressed by Judge Liu,[92] directly touches upon the methodological aspect of the discussion on compatibility between specific intent and JCE III as the relevant mode of liability. Judge Afande deplores[93] the actual absence of a full discussion on the point raised by the accused. Indeed, the argument that other jurisdictions and scholarly opinion are not direct sources of law for the Tribunal is hardly debatable, and therefore the abstract statement may appear in and of itself sound.

But it is misleading. The issue of convicting a defendant of an international crime whose offence definition requires (explicitly or impliedly) specific intent, when the person did not act with the required intent, has little to do with statutory law, nor is it only relevant within the autonomous remit of a given jurisdiction. The issue is highly, if not purely, conceptual – that is, it affects the structural tenets of criminal liability, which cannot be affected by statutory provisions nor by any reference to self-referential institutional authorities.

One might consider the issue at stake as one clear instance of the existence of certain "building stones"[94] for a theory-based international criminal justice system. In light of this, what is needed is the exploration of the

---

[86]   Stanišić and Župljanin Judgement, par. 588.
[87]   See the case law quoted at Stanišić and Župljanin Judgement, par. 590, fn. 2029.
[88]   Stanišić and Župljanin Judgement, par. 590.
[89]   Stanišić and Župljanin Judgement, par. 591.
[90]   Stanišić and Župljanin Judgement, Declaration of Judge Liu, p. 498 f., par. 2 (italics in original).
[91]   *Ibid.*, par. 3.
[92]   In a less decided way, however: "I may have some difficulty in imputing those specific intent JCE III crimes to members of a JCE, without any further convincing demonstration" (p. 516, par. 39).
[93]   In Judge Afande's opinion, the majority used "cursory and doubtful arguments … to dismiss the case law and provisions" of the recalled jurisdictions (*Ibid.*).
[94]   A. Eser, Comparative Criminal Law, Oxford U.P., Oxford 2017, marg. nr. 129.

"normative foundations and underlying conceptual and logical structures". This can be deemed a judicial task, since the clarification of such logical structures underpins judicial reasoning, confers persuasive force upon it, directs future decisions, and most importantly, contributes to providing criminal justice with legitimacy.

The topic of JCE III liability for specific intent crimes would have been a suitable test case for clarifying the method of dealing with similar foundational tenets of criminal law, according to the most conceptually advanced theorizations. Comparison, an activity involved by the instant discussion, seems not to be sufficiently developed from a methodological point of view in the case law of international tribunals. Here structural comparison in its thematical sense is especially meant – that is, a comparison which, after focusing upon a "social order problem", does not "limit the investigation to individual elements and components of the criminal law system ... rather, the various structural elements of a criminal law system are to be investigated as to their overall interaction and impact, and to be compared to one another".[95]

Undoubtedly, this is a time-consuming endeavour. The Appeals Chamber should have seized the opportunity of the appellate revision to engage in a thorough assessment of the methodological soundness of the analysis carried out by the decisions quoted by the appellant, as suggested by the dissent. I have shown elsewhere in this book series that this endeavour may have led to certain conclusions (JCE III is a mode of liability well known from a functional point of view in legal systems of the world that frame the same substantive problem in seemingly different ways), which could at the same time support the account of the majority of case law as to the merits.[96]

Alberto Di Martino

---

[95]   A. Eser, Comparative Criminal Law, Oxford U.P., Oxford 2017, marg. nr. 88.
[96]   See di Martino, Commentary, Klip/ Freeland ALC-LX-339.

UNITED
NATIONS

International Tribunal for the Prosecution of Persons Responsible for Serious Violations of International Humanitarian Law Committed in the Territory of the former Yugoslavia since 1991	Case No. IT-04-74-A Date: 29 November 2017 Original: English

IN THE APPEALS CHAMBER

Before: **Judge Carmel Agius, Presiding**
                    Judge Liu Daqun
                    Judge Fausto Pocar
                    Judge Theodor Meron
                    Judge Bakone Justice Moloto

Registrar: **Mr. John Hocking**

Judgement of: **29 November 2017**

PROSECUTOR

v.

JADRANKO PRLIĆ
BRUNO STOJIĆ
SLOBODAN PRALJAK
MILIVOJ PETKOVIĆ
VALENTIN ĆORIĆ
BERISLAV PUŠIĆ

PUBLIC WITH CONFIDENTIAL ANNEX C

JUDGEMENT
Volume I

The Office of the Prosecutor:

Mr. Douglas Stringer
Ms. Laurel Baig
Ms. Barbara Goy
Ms. Katrina Gustafson

Counsel for the Accused:

Mr. Michael G. Karnavas and Ms. Suzana Tomanović for Mr. Jadranko Prlić
Ms. Senka Nožica and Mr. Karim A. A. Khan for Mr. Bruno Stojić
Ms. Nika Pinter and Ms. Natacha Fauveau-Ivanović for Mr. Slobodan Praljak
Ms. Vesna Alaburić and Mr. Davor Lazić for Mr. Milivoj Petković
Ms. Dijana Tomašegović-Tomić and Mr. Dražen Plavec for Mr. Valentin Ćorić
Mr. Fahrudin Ibrišimović and Mr. Roger Sahota for Mr. Berislav Pušić

[page i] TABLE OF CONTENTS

529

[page 1] I. INTRODUCTION

1.   The Appeals Chamber of the International Tribunal for the Prosecution of Persons Responsible for Serious Violations of International Humanitarian Law Committed in the Territory of the former Yugoslavia since 1991 ("Appeals Chamber" and "ICTY", respectively) is seised of the appeals filed by Jadranko Prlić ("Prlić"), Bruno Stojić ("Stojić"), Slobodan Praljak ("Praljak"), Milivoj Petković ("Petković"), Valentin Ćorić («Ćorić»), and Berislav Pušić ("Pušić"), and the Office of the Prosecutor ("Prosecution") against the judgement rendered by Trial Chamber III of the Tribunal ("Trial Chamber") on 29 May 2013 in the case *Prosecutor v. Jadranko Prlić, Bruno Stojić, Slobodan Praljak, Milivoj Petković, Valentin Ćorić, and Berislav Pušić*, Case No. IT-04-74-T ("Trial Judgement").

A. Background

2.   The events giving rise to this case took place in eight municipalities and five detention camps in the territory of Bosnia and Herzegovina ("BiH") claimed as part of the Croatian Community and Republic of Herceg-Bosna ("HZ(R) H-B") between 1992 and 1994.[1] The Prosecution charged Prlić, Stojić, Praljak, Petković, Ćorić, and Pušić with: (1) grave breaches of the Geneva Conventions of 12 August 1949 ("Geneva Conventions") pursuant to Article 2 of the Statute, namely wilful killing (Count 3), inhuman treatment (sexual assault) (Count 5), unlawful deportation of a civilian (Count 7), unlawful transfer of a civilian (Count 9), unlawful confinement of a civilian (Count 11), inhuman treatment (conditions of confinement) (Count 13), inhuman treatment (Count 16), extensive destruction of property, not justified by military necessity and carried out unlawfully and wantonly (Count 19), and appropriation of property, not justified by military necessity and carried out unlawfully and wantonly (Count 22); (2) violations of the laws or customs of war pursuant to Article 3 of the Statute, namely cruel treatment (conditions of confinement) (Count 14), cruel treatment (Count 17), unlawful labour (Count 18), wanton destruction of cities, towns or villages, or devastation not justified by military necessity (Count 20), destruction or wilful damage done to institutions dedicated to religion or education (Count 21), plunder of public or private property (Count 23), unlawful attack on civilians (Mostar) (Count 24), unlawful infliction of terror on civilians (Mostar) (Count 25), and cruel treatment (Mostar siege) (Count 26); and (3) crimes against humanity pursuant to Article 5 of the Statute, namely persecution on political, racial and religious grounds (Count 1), murder (Count 2), rape (Count 4), deportation (Count 6), inhumane acts (forcible transfer) (Count 8), imprisonment (Count 10), **[page 2]** inhumane acts (conditions of confinement) (Count 12), and inhumane acts (Count 15).[2] The Indictment alleges Prlić, Stojić, Praljak, Petković, Ćorić, and Pušić to be responsible for these crimes pursuant to both Article 7(1) (committing, including through participation in a joint criminal enterprise ("JCE"), planning, instigating, ordering, or aiding and abetting) and Article 7(3) (failing to prevent or punish the crimes committed by their subordinates) of the Statute.[3]

3.   The Trial Chamber concluded that crimes occurred across the BiH municipalities of Prozor, Gornji Vakuf, Jablanica (Sovići and Doljani), Mostar, Ljubuški, Stolac, Čapljina, and Vareš as well as the five detention centres, namely, the Heliodrom Camp in Mostar Municipality ("Heliodrom"), the buildings clustered in the Vojno sector in Mostar Municipality ("Vojno Detention Centre"), the military remand prison in Ljubuški town ("Ljubuški Prison"), the Dretelj Military District Prison in Čapljina Municipality ("Dretelj Prison"), and the Gabela Military District Prison in Čapljina Municipality ("Gabela Prison") during the

---

[1]   Trial Judgement, Vol. 1, para. 1.

[2]   Indictment, para. 229. In discussing the underlying offences of rape as a crime against humanity under Article 5 of the Statute and inhuman treatment (sexual assault) as a grave breach of the Geneva Conventions under Article 2 of the Statute in the Trial Judgement, the Trial Chamber employed the phrases "sexual abuse" *("sévices sexuels")* or "sexual violence" *("violences sexuelles")* as umbrella terms to refer to those offences. See, *e.g.,* Trial Judgement, Vol. 4, paras 70, 72, 434, 437, 826, 830, 1014. Similarly, in discussing the underlying offences of appropriation of property, not justified by military necessity and carried out unlawfully and wantonly as a grave breach of the Geneva Conventions under Article 2 of the Statute and plunder of public or private property as a violation of the laws or customs of war under Article 3 of the Statute in the Trial Judgement, the Trial Chamber employed the phrase "thefts" *("vols")* as an umbrella term to refer to those offences. See, *e.g.,* Trial Judgement, Vol. 4, paras 70, 72, 445-447, 838, 840, 842, 845, 1010-1011. While it would have been preferable for the Trial Chamber to precisely refer to these offences as the crimes they constitute under the Statute, for consistency and readability, the Appeals Chamber will likewise use these umbrella terms in this Judgement.

[3]   Indictment, paras 218-228.

relevant time under the Indictment.[4] The Trial Chamber found that as early as mid-January 1993, a single JCE existed with a common criminal purpose which was the domination by the Croats of the Croatian Republic of Herceg-Bosna ("HR H-B") through ethnic cleansing of the Muslim population.[5] The Trial Chamber further found that the JCE was set up in order to create a Croatian entity in BiH reconstituting in part the borders of the Croatian Banovina, facilitating the reunification of the Croatian people.[6] The Trial Chamber concluded that Prlić, Stojić, Praljak, Petković, Ćorić, and Pušić were members of that JCE.[7] Specifically, it found that: (1) Prlić, Petković, and Ćorić contributed to the JCE from January 1993 **[page 3]** to April 1994;[8] (2) Stojić and Praljak contributed to the JCE from January 1993 to November 1993;[9] and (3) Pušić contributed to the JCE from April 1993 to April 1994.[10]

4.   Prlić was born on 10 June 1959 in Đakovo, Socialist Republic of Croatia.[11] On 14 August 1992, Prlić was appointed President of the executive organ of the Croatian Community of Herceg-Bosna ("HVO HZ H-B") and as of 28 August 1993, he exercised duties of the President of the Government of the HR H-B.[12] In June 1994, he became Vice-President of the Government and Minister of Defence of BiH and of the Federation of BiH.[13] Pursuant to Article 7(1) of the Statute, the Trial Chamber found Prlić guilty of Counts 1 to 13, 15, 16, 18, 19, and 21 to 25 of the Indictment.[14] Prlić was sentenced to a single sentence of 25 years of imprisonment.[15]

5.   Stojić was born on 8 April 1955 in the village of Hamzići, Čitluk Municipality, the Socialist Republic of Bosnia and Herzegovina ("SRBiH").[16] From July 1992 until 15 November 1993, Stojić was Head of the Department of Defence and subsequently became the Head of the HR H-B Department for the Production of Military Equipment, where he remained until 27 April 1995.[17] Pursuant to Article 7(1) of the Statute, the Trial Chamber found Stojić guilty of Counts 1 to 13, 15, 16, 18, 19, and 21 to 25 of the Indictment.[18] Stojić was sentenced to a single sentence of 20 years of imprisonment.[19]

6.   Praljak was born on 2 January 1945 in Čapljina, Čapljina Municipality, the SRBiH.[20] Between March 1992 and 15 June 1993, Praljak was Assistant Minister and later Deputy Minister of Defence of Croatia.[21] With respect to his functions in the Croatian Defence Council ("HVO"), from April 1992 to mid-May 1992, Praljak was the commander of the South-Eastern Herzegovina operations group and, following that period,

---

[4]   Trial Judgement, Vol. 3, paras 655-1741.

[5]   Trial Judgement, Vol. 4, paras 41, 65-66. Specifically, the Trial Judgement found that the members of the JCE ("implemented an entire system for deporting the Muslim population of the HR H-B consisting of the removal and placement in detention of civilians, of murders and the destruction of property during attacks, of mistreatment and devastation caused during eviction operations, of mistreatment and poor conditions of confinement as well as the widespread, nearly systematic use of detainees on the front lines for labour or even to serve as human shields, as well as murders and mistreatment related to this labour and these shields, and lastly, the removal of detainees and their families outside of the territory of the HZ(R) H-B once they were released"). Trial Judgement, Vol. 4, para. 66. See also Trial Judgement, Vol. 4, paras 44-65, 67-73.

[6]   Trial Judgement, Vol. 4, paras 24, 43-44. This Croatian territorial entity in BiH was either to be united with Croatia, or become an independent state within BiH with ties to Croatia. Trial Judgement, Vol. 4, para. 24.

[7]   Trial Judgement, Vol. 4, paras 66-67, 276, 429, 627-628, 818, 1004, 1209, 1217-1231.

[8]   Trial Judgement, Vol. 4, paras 1225, 1230.

[9]   Trial Judgement, Vol. 4, paras 1227-1228, 1230.

[10]   Trial Judgement, Vol. 4, paras 1229-1230.

[11]   Trial Judgement, Vol. 4, para. 78.

[12]   Trial Judgement, Vol. 4, para. 82.

[13]   Trial Judgement, Vol. 4, para. 83.

[14]   Trial Judgement, Vol. 4, Disposition, p. 430. See also Trial Judgement, Vol. 4, paras 278-279, 288. On the basis of the principle of cumulative convictions, the Trial Chamber did not enter a conviction for Counts 14, 17, and 20 of the Indictment. Trial Judgement, Vol. 4, Disposition, p. 430.

[15]   Trial Judgement, Vol. 4, Disposition, p. 430.

[16]   Trial Judgement, Vol. 4, para. 292.

[17]   Trial Judgement, Vol. 4, paras 293, 1227.

[18]   Trial Judgement, Vol. 4, Disposition, p. 430. See also Trial Judgement, Vol. 4, paras 431-432, 450. On the basis of the principle of cumulative convictions, the Trial Chamber did not enter a conviction for Counts 14, 17, and 20 of the Indictment. Trial Judgement, Vol. 4, Disposition, p. 430.

[19]   Trial Judgement, Vol. 4, Disposition, p. 430.

[20]   Trial Judgement, Vol. 4, para. 456 & fn. 91, referring to, *inter alia, Prosecutor v. Slobodan Praljak*, Case No. IT-04-74-I, Warrant of Arrest and Order for Surrender (confidential), 4, Mar 2004.

[21]   Trial Judgement, Vol. 4, para. 457.

he remained in BiH alongside the HVO without **[page 4]** holding official functions until 24 July 1993.[22] From 24 July 1993 until 9 November 1993, Praljak was Commander of the HVO Main Staff, before returning to Croatia to serve as advisor to the Croatian Minister of Defence.[23] Pursuant to Article 7(1) of the Statute, the Trial Chamber found Praljak guilty of Counts 1 to 3, 6 to 13, 15, 16, 18, 19, and 21 to 25 of the Indictment.[24] Praljak was acquitted of Counts 4 and 5 of the Indictment.[25] He was sentenced to a single sentence of 20 years imprisonment.[26]

7.   Petković was born on 11 October 1949 in Šibenik, Croatia.[27] Between 14 April 1992 and 23 July 1993, Petković was Chief of the HVO Main Staff and subsequently served as Deputy Commander until 26 April 1994.[28] From 26 April 1994 to 5 August 1994 he served again as Chief of the HVO Main Staff.[29] Pursuant to Article 7(1) of the Statute, the Trial Chamber found Petković guilty of Counts 1 to 13, 15, 16, 18, 19, and 21 to 25 of the Indictment.[30] Petković was sentenced to a single sentence of 20 years imprisonment.[31]

8.   Ćorić was born on 23 June 1956 in the village of Paoča, Čitluk Municipality, the SRBiH.[32] As of 24 June 1992, Ćorić was Chief of the Military Police Administration before becoming Minister of the Interior of the HR H-B in November 1993.[33] On 16 February 1994, Ćorić was appointed as a member of the Presidential Council of the HR H-B.[34] Pursuant to Article 7(1) of the Statute, the Trial Chamber found Ćorić guilty of Counts 1 to 13, 15, 16, 18, 19, and 21 to 25 of the Indictment.[35] Pursuant to Article 7(3) of the Statute, the Trial Chamber also found Ćorić guilty of Counts 15, 16, 19, and 23 of the Indictment with respect to the crimes that occurred in Prozor **[page 5]** Municipality in October 1992.[36] Ćorić was sentenced to a single sentence of 16 years of imprisonment.[37]

9.   Pušić was born on 8 June 1952 in Mostar, Mostar Municipality, the SRBiH.[38] The Trial Chamber found that between February and July 1993, Pušić occupied various positions in the HVO Military Police, and was a "control officer" within the Department of Criminal Investigations of the Military Police Administration.[39] At the same time, he also represented the Military Police Administration and the HVO in negotiations for the exchange of detainees or bodies.[40] From at least 25 May 1993, Pušić was a member of the Commission for the Exchange of Prisoners and Other Persons ("Exchange Commission") and, from 5 July 1993, he was the Head of the Service for the Exchange of Prisoners and Other Persons, ("Exchange Service"), the executive organ of the Exchange Commission.[41] Pursuant to Article 7(1) of the Statute, the Trial Chamber found Pušić guilty of Counts 1 to 3, 6 to 13, 15, 16, 18, 19, 21, 24, and 25 of the Indictment.[42] Pušić was

---

[22]   Trial Judgement, Vol. 4, para. 459.
[23]   Trial Judgement, Vol. 4, para. 459.
[24]   Trial Judgement, Vol. 4, Disposition, p. 430. See also Trial Judgement, Vol. 4, paras 630-631, 644. On the basis of the principle of cumulative convictions, the Trial Chamber did not enter a conviction for Counts 14, 17, and 20 of the Indictment. Trial Judgement, Vol. 4, Disposition, p. 430.
[25]   Trial Judgement, Vol. 4, Disposition, p. 430.
[26]   Trial Judgement, Vol. 4, Disposition, p. 430.
[27]   Trial Judgement, Vol. 4, para. 650.
[28]   Trial Judgement, Vol. 4, para. 651.
[29]   Trial Judgement, Vol. 4, para. 652.
[30]   Trial Judgement, Vol. 4, Disposition, p. 431. See also Trial Judgement, Vol. 4, paras 820-821, 853. On the basis of the principle of cumulative convictions, the Trial Chamber did not enter a conviction for Counts 14, 17, and 20 of the Indictment. Trial Judgement, Vol. 4, Disposition, p. 431.
[31]   Trial Judgement, Vol. 4, Disposition, p. 431.
[32]   Trial Judgement, Vol. 4, para. 860.
[33]   Trial Judgement, Vol. 4, para. 861.
[34]   Trial Judgement, Vol. 4, para. 861.
[35]   Trial Judgement, Vol. 4, Disposition, p. 431. See also Trial Judgement, Vol. 4, paras 1006-1007, 1021.
[36]   Trial Judgement, Vol. 4, Disposition, p. 431. See also Trial Judgement, Vol. 4, paras 1245-1251. On the basis of the principle of cumulative convictions, the Trial Chamber did not enter a conviction for Counts 14, 17, and 20 of the Indictment. Trial Judgement, Vol. 4, Disposition, p. 431.
[37]   Trial Judgement, Vol. 4, Disposition, p. 431.
[38]   Trial Judgement, Vol. 4, para. 1027.
[39]   Trial Judgement, Vol. 4, para. 1028.
[40]   Trial Judgement, Vol. 4, para. 1029.
[41]   Trial Judgement, Vol. 4, para. 1030.
[42]   Trial Judgement, Vol. 4, Disposition, p. 431. See also Trial Judgement, Vol. 4, paras 1211-1212, 1216.

acquitted of Counts 4, 5, 22, and 23 of the Indictment.[43] He was sentenced to a single sentence of ten years of imprisonment.[44]

B. The Appeals

1. Prlić's appeal

10.   Prlić advances 21 grounds of appeal.[45] Prlić requests that the Appeals Chamber reverse the convictions entered by the Trial Chamber and acquit him on all counts.[46] Alternatively, he submits that the Trial Chamber committed discernible errors in determining the sentence against him and the Appeals Chamber should therefore reduce it.[47] In response, the Prosecution submits that the **[page 6]** Appeals Chamber should dismiss Prlić's appeal, with the exception of part of his ground of appeal 20.[48]

2. Stojić's appeal

11.   Stojić presents 44 grounds of appeal.[49] Stojić requests that the Appeals Chamber overturn his convictions on all counts or, alternatively, overturn his convictions on specific counts and reduce his sentence.[50] The Prosecution responds that Stojić's appeal should be dismissed, with the exception of part of his ground of appeal.[51]

3. Praljak's appeal

12.   Praljak advances 45 grounds of appeal.[52] He requests that the Appeals Chamber acquit him of all charges or, alternatively, quash the Judgement and remand his case to the Trial Chamber for a trial *de novo*.[53] The Prosecution responds that Praljak's appeal should be dismissed with the exception of part of his ground of appeal 2.[54]

4. Petković's appeal

13.   Petković presents seven grounds of appeal.[55] Petković requests that the Appeals Chamber quash and reverse his conviction on all counts or, in the alternative, order a corresponding reduction of his sentence if

---

43   Trial Judgement, Vol. 4, Disposition, p. 431. On the basis of the principle of cumulative convictions, the Trial Chamber did not enter a conviction for Counts 14, 17, and 20 of the Indictment. Trial Judgement, Vol. 4, Disposition, p. 431.

44   Trial Judgement, Vol. 4, Disposition, p. 431.

45   The Appeals Chamber notes that, in his appeal brief, Prlić does not develop the arguments contained in his notice of appeal in sub-grounds of appeal 10.9, 10.11, and 21.3. See Prlić's Appeal Brief, pp. 96-98, 197. Accordingly, the Appeals Chamber considers that Prlić has abandoned these contentions.

46   Prlić's Notice of Appeal, para. 11; Prlić's Appeal Brief, p. 197.

47   Prlić's Appeal Brief, para. 682.

48   Prosecution's Response Brief (Prlić), paras 15, 429. In relation to Prlić's ground of appeal 20, the Prosecution requests that the Appeals Chamber either partly reverse Prlić's conviction under Count 19 and substitute it with a conviction under Count 20 or otherwise dismiss the relevant appeal. Prosecution's Response Brief (Prlić), para. 429.

49   Stojić originally advanced 57 grounds of appeal, but withdrew his grounds of appeal 9, 18-19, 22, 38, 43-44, 46, 48-49, 51-53. See Stojić's Appeal Brief, pp. 32, 48, 64, 127, 134, 136, 138-139. The Appeals Chamber also observes that Stojić withdrew his sub-ground of appeal 56.1. See Stojić's Appeal Brief, p. 147.

50   Stojić's Appeal Brief, para. 7, p. 152.

51   Prosecution's Response Brief (Stojić), paras 8, 410. In relation to Stojić's ground of appeal 55, the Prosecution requests that the Appeals Chamber either partly reverse Stojić's conviction under Count 19 or otherwise dismiss the relevant appeal. Prosecution's Response Brief (Stojić), para. 410.

52   Praljak originally advanced 58 grounds of appeal, but withdrew his grounds of appeal 16-19, 22, 29-31, 33, 52, and 56-58. See Praljak's Appeal Brief, Annex 1, pp. 4-8. The Appeals Chamber also observes that Praljak withdrew his sub-grounds of appeal 20.2 to 20.13, and 28.2. See Praljak's Appeal Brief, Annex 1, pp. 4-5; Praljak's Notice of Appeal, p. 46, sub-ground of appeal 28. 2.

53   Praljak's Appeal Brief, paras 5-6, 603-604.

54   Prosecution's Response Brief (Praljak), paras 5, 334. In relation to Praljak's ground of appeal 2, the Prosecution requests that the Appeals Chamber either partly reverse Praljak's conviction under Count 19 and substitute it with a conviction under Count 20 or dismiss it. Prosecution's Response Brief (Praljak), paras 5, 334.

55   The Appeals Chamber notes that in his appeal brief, Petković uses Roman numerals to number his grounds of appeal and Arabic numerals to number the sub-headings pertaining thereto, and that these numbers do not correspond. For example, Petković

his appeal partly succeeds.[56] In further alternative, he requests the **[page 7]** Appeals Chamber to reduce his sentence.[57] The Prosecution responds that Petković's appeal should be dismissed with the exception of part of his ground of appeal 6.[58]

5. Ćorić's appeal

14. Ćorić presents 17 grounds of appeal. Ćorić requests that the Appeals Chamber acquit him of all counts or, if any of his convictions are upheld, reduce his sentence.[59] The Prosecution responds that Ćorić's appeal should be dismissed in its entirety.[60]

6. Pušić's appeal

15. Pušić advances eight grounds of appeal.[61] Pušić requests the Appeals Chamber to reverse the Trial Judgement or, in the alternative, to reduce his sentence.[62] The Prosecution responds that the Appeals Chamber should dismiss Pušić's appeal in its entirety.[63]

7. Prosecution's appeal

16. The Prosecution advances four grounds of appeal. It argues that the Trial Chamber erred in partly acquitting Prlić, Stojić, Praljak, Petković, Ćorić, and Pušić and in failing to: (1) convict them of the crimes under the third form of joint criminal enterprise liability ("JCE III"); (2) consider and adjudicate their liability under Article 7(3) of the Statute; and (3) enter convictions for wanton destruction of cities, towns or villages, or devastation not justified by military necessity (Count 20).[64] The Prosecution also submits that the Trial Chamber erred in imposing manifestly inadequate sentences and requests that the Appeals Chamber increase them.[65] Prlić, Praljak, Petković, and Pušić respond that the Appeals Chamber should dismiss the Prosecution's appeal in its entirety.[66] Stojić submits that the Appeals Chamber should dismiss the Prosecution's appeal or, in the alternative, should the Appeals Chamber grant any of the Prosecution's grounds, decline to increase his sentence.[67] Similarly, Ćorić responds that the Appeals Chamber should dismiss the **[page 8]** Prosecution's appeal or, in the alternative, remit the case to the Trial Chamber for a new determination of the sentence.[68]

C. **Appeal Hearing**

17. The Appeals Chamber heard the oral submissions of the Parties regarding their appeals from 20 March 2017 to 28 March 2017 ("Appeal Hearing"). Having considered their written and oral submissions, the Appeals Chamber hereby renders its Judgement. **[page 9]**

---

titles one section of his appeal brief "Ground IV: Errors Pertaining to Actus Reus of JCE", but the sub-headings pertaining thereto are numbered "5.1 Errors regarding Petković's 'Powers'" through "5.3 Conclusions and Relief Sought". For ease of reference, the Appeals Chamber will adhere to the numbering of Petković's brief throughout this Judgement. In general, it will use the numbering of the sub-headings, except where it is necessary to refer to a ground of appeal in its entirety. There, the Appeals Chamber will use the pertinent Roman numeral used by Petković.

[56]   Petković's Appeal Brief, paras 470-471.
[57]   Petković's Appeal Brief, para. 472.
[58]   Prosecution's Response Brief (Petković), paras 8, 323. In relation to Petković's ground of appeal VI, the Prosecution requests that the Appeals Chamber either partly reverse Petković's conviction under Count 19 or otherwise dismiss the relevant challenge. Prosecution's Response Brief (Petković), para. 323.
[59]   Ćorić's Appeal Brief, paras 5, 340.
[60]   Prosecution's Response Brief (Ćorić), paras 6, 373.
[61]   The Appeals Chamber observes that Pušić withdrew part of his ground of appeal 3. Pušić's Appeal Brief, para. 107.
[62]   Pušić's Appeal Brief, paras 6-7.
[63]   Prosecution's Response Brief (Pušić), paras 7, 241.
[64]   Prosecution's Appeal Brief, paras 2, 420-422, 424.
[65]   Prosecution's Appeal Brief, paras 2, 424.
[66]   Prlić's Response Brief, para. 25, p. 103; Praljak's Response Brief, para. 215; Petković's Response Brief, para. 120; Pušić's Response Brief, para. 1.
[67]   Stojić's Response Brief, p. 83.
[68]   Ćorić's Response Brief, paras 4, 9, 153, p. 72.

II. STANDARD OF APPELLATE REVIEW

18.   Article 25 of the Statute states that the Appeals Chamber may affirm, reverse, or revise the decisions taken by the trial chamber. On appeal, the parties must limit their arguments to errors of law that invalidate the decision and to factual errors that result in a miscarriage of justice.[69] These criteria are set forth in Article 25 of the Statute and are well established in the jurisprudence of both the Tribunal and the International Criminal Tribunal for the Prosecution of Persons Responsible for Genocide and Other Serious Violations of International Humanitarian Law Committed in the Territory of Rwanda and Rwandan Citizens Responsible for Genocide and Other Violations Committed in the Territory of Neighbouring States between 1 January 1994 and 31 December 1994 ("ICTR").[70] In exceptional circumstances, the Appeals Chamber will also hear appeals in which a party has raised a legal issue that would not lead to the invalidation of the trial judgement, but that is nevertheless of general significance to the Tribunal's jurisprudence.[71]

19.   A party alleging an error of law must identify the alleged error, present arguments in support of its claim, and explain how the error invalidates the decision.[72] An allegation of an error of law that has no chance of changing the outcome of a decision may be rejected on that ground.[73] However, even if the party's arguments are insufficient to support the contention of an error, the Appeals Chamber may still conclude for other reasons that there is an error of law.[74] It is necessary for any appellant claiming an error of law on the basis of the lack of a reasoned opinion to identify the specific issues, factual findings, or arguments that the appellant submits the trial chamber omitted to address and to explain why this omission invalidates the decision.[75]

20.   The Appeals Chamber reviews the trial chamber's findings of law to determine whether or not they are correct.[76] Where the Appeals Chamber finds an error of law in the trial judgement arising from the application of the wrong legal standard, the Appeals Chamber will articulate the **[page 10]** correct legal standard and review the relevant factual findings of the trial chamber accordingly.[77] In so doing, the Appeals Chamber not only corrects the error of law, but, when necessary, applies the correct legal standard to the evidence contained in the trial record and determines whether it is itself convinced beyond reasonable doubt as to the factual finding challenged by an appellant before the finding is confirmed on appeal.[78] The Appeals Chamber will not review the entire trial record *de novo*. Rather, it will in principle only take into account evidence referred to by the trial chamber in the body of the judgement or in a related footnote, evidence contained in the trial record and referred to by the parties, and, where applicable, additional evidence admitted on appeal.[79]

---

[69]   *Stanišić and Župljanin* Appeal Judgement, para. 17; *Stanišić and Simatović* Appeal Judgement, para. 15; *Tolimir* Appeal Judgement, para. 8; *Vasiljević* Appeal Judgement, para. 5. See *Furundžija* Appeal Judgement, paras 35-37.

[70]   *Stanišić and Župljanin* Appeal Judgement, para. 17; *Stanišić and Simatović* Appeal Judgement, para. 15; *Popović et al.* Appeal Judgement, para. 16; *Vasiljević* Appeal Judgement, para. 5. See *Nyiramasuhuko et al.* Appeal Judgement, para. 29; *Nzabonimana* Appeal Judgement, para. 7.

[71]   *Stanišić and Župljanin* Appeal Judgement, para. 17; *Stanišić and Simatović* Appeal Judgement, para. 15; *Tolimir* Appeal Judgement, para. 8; *Kupreškić et al.* Appeal Judgement, para. 22; *Tadić* Appeal Judgement, para. 247.

[72]   *Stanišić and Župljanin* Appeal Judgement, para. 18; *Stanišić and Simatović* Appeal Judgement, para. 16; *Tolimir* Appeal Judgement, para. 9; *Krnojelac* Appeal Judgement, para. 10.

[73]   *Stanišić and Župljanin* Appeal Judgement, para. 18; *Stanišić and Simatović* Appeal Judgement, para. 16; *Tolimir* Appeal Judgement, para. 9; *Krnojelac* Appeal Judgement, para. 10.

[74]   *Stanišić and Župljanin* Appeal Judgement, para. 18; *Stanišić and Simatović* Appeal Judgement, para. 16; *Tolimir* Appeal Judgement, para. 9; *Furundžija* Appeal Judgement, para. 35.

[75]   *Stanišić and Župljanin* Appeal Judgement, para. 18; *Stanišić and Simatović* Appeal Judgement, para. 16; *Tolimir* Appeal Judgement, para. 9; *Kvočka et al.* Appeal Judgement, para. 25, referring to *Kordić and Čerkez* Appeal Judgement, para. 21.

[76]   *Stanišić and Župljanin* Appeal Judgement, para. 19; *Stanišić and Simatović* Appeal Judgement, para. 17; *Tolimir* Appeal Judgement, para. 10; *Krnojelac* Appeal Judgement, para. 10.

[77]   *Stanišić and Župljanin* Appeal Judgement, para. 19; *Stanišić and Simatović* Appeal Judgement, para. 17; *Tolimir* Appeal Judgement, para. 10; *Blaškić* Appeal Judgement, para. 15.

[78]   *Stanišić and Župljanin* Appeal Judgement, para. 19; *Stanišić and Simatović* Appeal Judgement, para. 17; *Tolimir* Appeal Judgement, para. 10; *Blaškić* Appeal Judgement, para. 15.

[79]   *Stanišić and Župljanin* Appeal Judgement, para. 19; *Stanišić and Simatović* Appeal Judgement, para. 17; *Tolimir* Appeal Judgement, para. 10; *Kordić and Čerkez* Appeal Judgement, para. 21 & fn. 12.

21.   When considering alleged errors of fact, the Appeals Chamber will apply a standard of reasonableness.[80] In reviewing the findings of the trial chamber, the Appeals Chamber will only substitute its own finding for that of the trial chamber when no reasonable trier of fact could have reached the original decision.[81] The Appeals Chamber applies the same reasonableness standard to alleged errors of fact regardless of whether the finding of fact was based on direct or circumstantial evidence.[82] Further, only an error of fact which has occasioned a miscarriage of justice will cause the Appeals Chamber to overturn a decision by the trial chamber.[83]

22.   In determining whether or not a trial chamber's finding was reasonable, the Appeals Chamber will not lightly disturb findings of fact by a trial chamber.[84] The Appeals Chamber recalls, as a general principle, that:

> Pursuant to the jurisprudence of the Tribunal, the task of hearing, assessing and weighing the evidence presented at trial is left primarily to the Trial Chamber. Thus, the Appeals Chamber must give a margin of deference to a finding of fact reached by a Trial Chamber. Only where the evidence relied on by the Trial Chamber could not have been accepted by any reasonable tribunal **[page 11]** of fact or where the evaluation of the evidence is "wholly erroneous" may the Appeals Chamber substitute its own finding for that of the Trial Chamber.[85]

23.   The same standard of reasonableness and the same deference to factual findings applies when the Prosecution appeals against an acquittal.[86] Thus, when considering an appeal by the Prosecution, the Appeals Chamber will only hold that an error of fact was committed when it determines that no reasonable trier of fact could have made the impugned finding.[87] Considering that it is the Prosecution that bears the burden at trial of proving the guilt of an accused beyond reasonable doubt, the significance of an error of fact occasioning a miscarriage of justice is somewhat different for a Prosecution appeal against acquittal from that of a defence appeal against conviction.[88] An accused must show that the trial chamber's factual errors create reasonable doubt as to his guilt.[89] The Prosecution must show that, when account is taken of the errors of fact committed by the trial chamber, all reasonable doubt of the accused's guilt has been eliminated.[90]

24.   The Appeals Chamber recalls that it has inherent discretion in selecting which submissions merit a detailed reasoned opinion in writing, and may dismiss arguments which are evidently unfounded without providing detailed reasoning.[91] Indeed, the Appeals Chamber's mandate cannot be effectively and efficiently carried out without focused contributions by the parties.[92] In order for the Appeals Chamber to assess a

[80]   *Stanišić and Župljanin* Appeal Judgement, para. 20; *Stanišić and Simatović* Appeal Judgement, para. 18; *Tolimir* Appeal Judgement, para. 11; *Popović et al.* Appeal Judgement, para. 19; *Tadić* Appeal Judgement, para. 64.
[81]   *Stanišić and Župljanin* Appeal Judgement, para. 20; *Stanišić and Simatović* Appeal Judgement, para. 18; *Tolimir* Appeal Judgement, para. 11; *Kvočka et al.* Appeal Judgement, para. 18; *Tadić* Appeal Judgement, para. 64.
[82]   *Stanišić and Župljanin* Appeal Judgement, para. 20; *Stanišić and Simatović* Appeal Judgement, para. 18; *Tolimir* Appeal Judgement, para. 11; *Galić* Appeal Judgement, para. 9 & fn. 21.
[83]   *Stanišić and Župljanin* Appeal Judgement, para. 20; *Stanišić and Simatović* Appeal Judgement, para. 18; *Tolimir* Appeal Judgement, para. 11; *Furundžija* Appeal Judgement, para. 37.
[84]   *Stanišić and Župljanin* Appeal Judgement, para. 21; *Stanišić and Simatović* Appeal Judgement, para. 19; *Tolimir* Appeal Judgement, para. 12; *Popović et al.* Appeal Judgement, para. 20; *Furundžija* Appeal Judgement, para. 37.
[85]   *Kupreškić et al.* Appeal Judgement, para. 30. See *Stanišić and Župljanin* Appeal Judgement, para. 21; *Stanišić and Simatović* Appeal Judgement, para. 19; *Tolimir* Appeal Judgement, para. 12; *Popović et al.* Appeal Judgement, para. 20. See also *Tadić* Appeal Judgement, para. 64.
[86]   *Stanišić and Župljanin* Appeal Judgement, para. 22; *Stanišić and Simatović* Appeal Judgement, para. 20; *Đorđević* Appeal Judgement, para. 18; *Limaj et al.* Appeal Judgement, para. 13; *Brđanin* Appeal Judgement, para. 14.
[87]   *Stanišić and Župljanin* Appeal Judgement, para. 22; *Stanišić and Simatović* Appeal Judgement, para. 20; *Popović et al.* Appeal Judgement, para. 21; *Brđanin* Appeal Judgement, para. 14.
[88]   *Stanišić and Župljanin* Appeal Judgement, para. 22; *Stanišić and Simatović* Appeal Judgement, para. 20; *Popović et al.* Appeal Judgement, para. 21; *Limaj et al.* Appeal Judgement, para. 13.
[89]   *Stanišić and Župljanin* Appeal Judgement, para. 22; *Stanišić and Simatović* Appeal Judgement, para. 20; *Popović et al.* Appeal Judgement, para. 21; *Limaj et al.* Appeal Judgement, para. 13.
[90]   *Stanišić and Župljanin* Appeal Judgement, para. 22; *Stanišić and Simatović* Appeal Judgement, para. 20; *Popović et al.* Appeal Judgement, para. 21; *Limaj et al.* Appeal Judgement, para. 13.
[91]   *Stanišić and Župljanin* Appeal Judgement, para. 24; *Stanišić and Simatović* Appeal Judgement, para. 21; *Tolimir* Appeal Judgement, para. 13; *Kunarac et al.* Appeal Judgement, paras 47-48.
[92]   *Stanišić and Župljanin* Appeal Judgement, para. 24; *Stanišić and Simatović* Appeal Judgement, para. 21; *Popović et al.* Appeal Judgement, para. 22; *Kunarac et al.* Appeal Judgement, para. 43.

party's arguments on appeal, the party is expected to present its case clearly, logically, and exhaustively.[93] The appealing party is also expected to provide precise references to relevant transcript pages or paragraphs in the decision or judgement to which the challenges are being made.[94] The Appeals Chamber will not consider a party's submission in detail **[page 12]** when they are obscure, contradictory, vague, or suffer from other formal and obvious insufficiencies.[95]

25.   When applying these basic principles, the Appeals Chamber recalls that it has identified the types of deficient submissions on appeal which need not be considered on the merits.[96] In particular, the Appeals Chamber will dismiss without detailed analysis: (1) arguments that fail to identify the challenged factual findings, that misrepresent the factual findings or the evidence, or that ignore other relevant factual findings; (2) mere assertions that the trial chamber must have failed to consider relevant evidence, without showing that no reasonable trier of fact, based on the evidence, could have reached the same conclusion as the trial chamber; (3) challenges to factual findings on which a conviction does not rely, and arguments that are clearly irrelevant, that lend support to, or that are not inconsistent with the challenged finding; (4) arguments that challenge a trial chamber's reliance or failure to rely on one piece of evidence, without explaining why the conviction should not stand on the basis of the remaining evidence; (5) arguments contrary to common sense; (6) challenges to factual findings where the relevance of the factual finding is unclear and has not been explained by the appealing party; (7) mere repetition of arguments that were unsuccessful at trial without any demonstration that their rejection by the trial chamber constituted an error warranting the intervention of the Appeals Chamber; (8) allegations based on material not on record; (9) mere assertions unsupported by any evidence, undeveloped assertions, or failure to articulate an error; and (10) mere assertions that the trial chamber failed to give sufficient weight to evidence or failed to interpret evidence in a particular manner.[97]
[page 13]

III.   CHALLENGES CONCERNING FAIR TRIAL AND THE INDICTMENT

A.   Applicable Law

1.   Applicable law on the Right to a Fair Trial

26.   The Appeals Chamber recalls that, where a party alleges on appeal that its right to a fair trial has been infringed, it must prove that the trial chamber violated a provision of the Statute and/or the Rules and that this caused prejudice to the alleging party, such as to amount to an error of law invalidating the trial judgement.[98] Trial chambers enjoy considerable discretion in relation to the management of the proceedings before them.[99] The Appeals Chamber will only overturn a trial chamber's discretionary decision where it is found to be: (1) based on an incorrect interpretation of governing law; (2) based on a patently incorrect conclusion of fact; or (3) so unfair or unreasonable as to constitute an abuse of the trial chamber's discretion.[100] The Appeals Chamber will also consider whether the trial chamber has given weight to extraneous or

[93]   *Stanišić and Župljanin* Appeal Judgement, para. 24; *Stanišić and Simatović* Appeal Judgement, para. 21; *Tolimir* Appeal Judgement, para. 13; *Kunarac et al.* Appeal Judgement, para. 43.
[94]   Practice Direction on Formal Requirements for Appeals from Judgement, IT/201, 7 March 2002 ("Practice Direction on Formal Requirements"), paras l(c)(iii)-(iv), 4(b)(ii). See also *Stanišić and Župljanin* Appeal Judgement, para. 24; *Stanišić and Simatović* Appeal Judgement, para. 21; *Tolimir* Appeal Judgement, para. 13; *Kunarac et al.* Appeal Judgement, para. 44.
[95]   *Stanišić and Župljanin* Appeal Judgement, para. 24; *Stanišić and Simatović* Appeal Judgement, para. 21; *Tolimir* Appeal Judgement, para. 13; *Kunarac et al.* Appeal Judgement, para. 43 & fn. 21.
[96]   *Stanišić and Župljanin* Appeal Judgement, para. 25; *Stanišić and Simatović* Appeal Judgement, para. 22; *Tolimir* Appeal Judgement, para. 14; *Krajišnik* Appeal Judgement, paras 17-27; *Brđanin* Appeal Judgement, paras 17-31.
[97]   *Stanišić and Župljanin* Appeal Judgement, para. 25; *Stanišić and Simatović* Appeal Judgement, para. 22; *Tolimir* Appeal Judgement, para. 14; *Popović et al.* Appeal Judgement, para. 23; *Krajišnik* Appeal Judgement, paras 17-27.
[98]   *Šainović et al.* Appeal Judgement, para. 29; *Haradinaj et al.* Appeal Judgement, para. 17; *Krajišnik* Appeal Judgement, para. 28, referring to *Kordić and Čerkez* Appeal Judgement, para. 119.
[99]   *Šainović et al.* Appeal Judgement, para. 29; *Lukić and Lukić* Appeal Judgement, para. 17, referring to *Krajišnik* Appeal Judgement, paras 81, 99.
[100]   *Šainović et al.* Appeal Judgement, para. 29; *Lukić and Lukić* Appeal Judgement, para. 17, referring to *Krajišnik* Appeal Judgement, para. 81.

irrelevant considerations or has failed to give weight or sufficient weight to relevant considerations in reaching its decision.[101]

2. Applicable law on the Indictment

27.   The Appeals Chamber recalls that, in accordance with Article 21(4)(a) of the Statute, an accused has the right "to be informed promptly and in detail in a language which he understands of the nature and cause of the charge against him".[102] In application of this right, Rule 47(C) of the Rules states that an indictment must set forth "a concise statement of the facts of the case and of the crime with which the suspect is charged."[103] The Appeals Chamber recalls that in determining whether an accused was adequately put on notice of the nature and cause of the charges against him, the indictment must be considered as a whole.[104] In order to provide proper notice to the accused, the Prosecution is required to plead in an indictment all of the charges and the **[page 14]** underpinning material facts with sufficient precision, but is not required to set out the evidence by which the material facts are to be proven.[105]

28.   Whether or not a fact is considered material depends on the nature of the Prosecution's case.[106] The Prosecution's characterisation of the alleged criminal conduct and the proximity of the accused to the underlying crimes are decisive factors in determining the degree of specificity with which the Prosecution must plead the material facts of its case in the indictment in order to provide the accused with adequate notice.[107] The Appeals Chamber recalls the distinction between those material facts upon which the Prosecution relies, which must be pleaded in an indictment, and the evidence by which those material facts will be proved, which need not be pleaded.[108]

29.   An indictment which fails to set forth the specific material facts underpinning the charges against the accused is defective.[109] The Appeals Chamber has held: "[a]n indictment may also be defective when the material facts are pleaded without sufficient specificity, such as, unless there are special circumstances, when the times refer to broad date ranges, the places are only generally indicated, and the victims are only generally identified."[110] The prejudicial effect of a defective indictment may only be "remedied" if the Prosecution provided the accused with clear, timely, and consistent information that resolves the ambiguity or clarifies the vagueness, thereby compensating for the failure of an indictment to give proper notice of the charges.[111] In this regard, defects concerning vagueness in an indictment can be cured in certain circumstances and through post-indictment documents such as the pre-trial briefs, Rule 65*ter* witness summaries, and witness statements.[112]

[101]   *Šainović et al.* Appeal Judgement, para. 29; *Lukić and Lukić* Appeal Judgement, para. 17, referring to *Krajišnik* Appeal Judgement, para. 81.
[102]   *Šainović et al.* Appeal Judgement, para. 213.
[103]   *Šainović et al.* Appeal Judgement, para. 213.
[104]   *Nyiramasuhuko et al.* Appeal Judgement, paras 1263, 2512; *Karemera and Ngirumpatse* Appeal Judgement, para. 370.
[105]   *Đorđević* Appeal Judgement, para. 574; *Šainović et al.* Appeal Judgement, para. 213; *Martić* Appeal Judgement para. 162; *Simić* Appeal Judgement, para. 20; *Naletilić and Martinović* Appeal Judgement, para. 23; *Kvočka et al.* Appeal Judgement, para. 27; *Kupreškić et al.* Appeal Judgement, para. 88.
[106]   *Đorđević* Appeal Judgement, para. 575; *Naletilić and Martinović* Appeal Judgement, para. 24; *Kvočka et al.* Appeal Judgement, para. 28; *Kupreškić et al.* Appeal Judgement, para. 89; *Karera* Appeal Judgement, para. 292; *Nahimana et al.* Appeal Judgement, para. 322.
[107]   *Đorđević* Appeal Judgement, para. 575; *Naletilić and Martinović* Appeal Judgement, para. 24; *Kvočka et al.* Appeal Judgement, para. 28; *Kupreškić et al.* Appeal Judgement, para. 89.
[108]   *Popović et al.* Appeal Judgement, para. 47; *Blaškić* Appeal Judgement, para. 210. See *Đorđević* Appeal Judgement, para. 331; *Šainović et al.* Appeal Judgement, para. 213; *Nzabonimana* Appeal Judgement, para. 29.
[109]   *Kvočka et al.* Appeal Judgement, para. 28; *Kupreškić et al.* Appeal Judgement, para. 114; *Renzaho* Appeal Judgement, para. 55; *Karera* Appeal Judgement, para. 293; *Ntagerura et al.* Appeal Judgement, para. 22.
[110]   *Kvočka et al.* Appeal Judgement, para. 31.
[111]   *Martić* Appeal Judgement, para. 163; *Simić* Appeal Judgement, para. 23; *Naletilić and Martinović* Appeal Judgement, para. 26; *Kvočka et al.* Appeal Judgement, para. 33; *Kupreškić et al.* Appeal Judgement, para. 114.
[112]   *Đorđević* Appeal Judgement, para. 574. See *Simić* Appeal Judgement, para. 24; *Naletilić and Martinović* Appeal Judgement, para. 27; *Kvočka et al.* Appeal Judgement, para. 33.

30. A defective indictment which has not been cured causes prejudice to the accused.[113] The defect may only be deemed harmless through a demonstration that the accused's ability to prepare **[page 15]** his or her defence was not materially impaired.[114] Where an accused has previously raised the issue of lack of notice before the Trial Chamber, the burden rests on the Prosecution to prove on appeal that the ability of the accused to prepare his defence was not materially impaired.[115] When, however, the accused raises indictment defects for the first time on appeal, the burden of proof shifts from the Prosecution to the Defence who is then required to demonstrate the existence of the said prejudice.[116]

B. Alleged Errors Concerning Reliance on Evidence Related to Franjo Tuđman (Stojić's Ground 17)

31. The Trial Chamber found that for all times relevant to the Indictment, the Ultimate Purpose of the HZ(R) H-B leaders, as well as Franjo Tuđman, was to set up a Croatian entity that reconstituted, at least in part, the borders of the Banovina of 1939, and facilitated the reunification of the Croatian people ("Ultimate Purpose").[117] It further found that a JCE was established to implement the Ultimate Purpose of the JCE from at least as early as mid-January 1993, the common criminal plan of which was "domination by the HR H-B Croats through ethnic cleansing of the Muslim population" (the "Common Criminal Plan" or "CCP").[118]

32. Stojić submits that the Trial Chamber erred in law by basing this finding almost exclusively on evidence related to Tuđman, which remained untested since he died before the proceedings in this case started.[119] Stojić further submits that his passing, as well as that of the other alleged JCE members Janko Bobetko, Gojko Šušak, and Mate Boban, rendered the trial unfair as Stojić did not have access to the critical evidence that they could have provided.[120] Stojić argues that the Trial Chamber's legal error invalidates the judgement as it "relates to" the Trial Chamber's finding on the common purpose of the alleged JCE constituting an essential component of the further **[page 16]** finding that a JCE existed, which he alleges was decisively based on evidence related to Tuđman.[121] He requests that the Appeals Chamber acquit him on all Counts.[122]

33. The Prosecution responds that the Trial Chamber reasonably relied on evidence related to Tuđman's statements and conduct.[123] The Prosecution asserts that Stojić fails to demonstrate that he was unable to challenge such evidence, which is not by definition hearsay from an absent witness.[124] The Prosecution further submits that Stojić's conviction and the finding on the Ultimate Purpose are not decisively based on evidence related to Tuđman.[125] It asserts that Stojić fails to consider other findings and supporting evidence unrelated to Tuđman's statements and conduct, which underpin the Trial Chamber's finding on the CCP.[126]

---

[113] *Popović et al.* Appeal Judgement, para. 66; *Šainović et al.* Appeal Judgement, para. 262; *Renzaho* Appeal Judgement, para. 125. See *Đorđević* Appeal Judgement, para. 576.
[114] *Popović et al.* Appeal Judgement, para. 66; *Šainović et al.* Appeal Judgement, para. 262; *Renzaho* Appeal Judgement, para. 125. See *Đorđević* Appeal Judgement, para. 576.
[115] See, *e.g.*, *Nyiramasuhuko et al.* Appeal Judgement, paras 1105, 2738; *Nzabonimana* Appeal Judgement, para. 30; *Ntabakuze* Appeal Judgement, fn. 189; *Niyitegeka* Appeal Judgement, para. 200; *Kupreškić et al.* Appeal Judgement, paras 122-123.
[116] *Đorđević* Appeal Judgement, para. 573; *Šainović et al.* Appeal Judgement, paras 223-224. See *Nyiramasuhuko et al.* Appeal Judgement, para. 2738.
[117] Trial Judgement, Vol. 4, para. 24. See Trial Judgement, Vol. 4, paras 6-23.
[118] Trial Judgement, Vol. 4, paras 41, 65-66. Specifically, the Trial Judgement found that the members of the JCE "implemented an entire system for deporting the Muslim population of the HR H-B consisting of the removal and placement in detention of civilians, of murders and the destruction of property during attacks, of mistreatment and devastation caused during eviction operations, of mistreatment and poor conditions of confinement as well as the widespread, nearly systematic use of detainees on the front lines for labour or even to serve as human shields, as well as murders and mistreatment related to this labour and these shields, and lastly, the removal of detainees and their families outside of the territory of the HZ(R) H-B once they were released". Trial Judgement, Vol. 4, para. 66. See also Trial Judgement, Vol. 4, paras 44-65, 67-73.
[119] Stojić's Appeal Brief, heading before para. 133, paras 134-138. See also Stojić's Appeal Brief, para. 133.
[120] Stojić's Appeal Brief, paras 134-136, 138 & fn. 349.
[121] Stojić's Appeal Brief, heading before para. 133, paras 137-138.
[122] Stojić's Appeal Brief, para. 138.
[123] Prosecution's Response Brief (Stojić), para. 102.
[124] Prosecution's Response Brief (Stojić), para. 102.
[125] Prosecution's Response Brief (Stojić), paras 103-104.
[126] Prosecution's Response Brief (Stojić), paras 103-104.

34.   In alleging that the Trial Chamber erred in law in basing its finding on the common purpose of the alleged JCE decisively on evidence related to Tuđman, Stojić neither refers to a single paragraph in the relevant section of the Trial Judgement,[127] nor identifies or addresses any factual findings within it that rely on untested evidence related to Tuđman. The Appeals Chamber therefore finds that Stojić has failed to demonstrate that the Trial Chamber's finding on the CCP of the JCE was decisively based on such evidence, and has failed to explain how the alleged error would invalidate the decision of the Trial Chamber.[128]

35.   With regard to Stojić's argument that he was deprived of tendering allegedly critical evidence of Tuđman, Bobetko, Šušak, and Boban, rendering the trial unfair, the Appeals Chamber notes that the authorities that Stojić cites to show unfairness deal with distinctly different issues[129] or are otherwise not pertinent to the issues at hand. Particularly, it is not alleged in this case that the conviction is solely or to a decisive degree based on *hearsay* evidence from an absent witness *(i.e.* one of the deceased persons), rendering the proceedings unfair.[130] Nor does the **[page 17]** Appeals Chamber find that the case at hand can be likened to two cases holding that fair trial may be impacted because witnesses central or crucial to the Defence fail to testify due to State interference.[131] The Appeals Chamber notes in this regard that no fair trial violation was found in either of these cases.[132] Moreover, while general evidentiary rules limit the use of hearsay emanating from absent persons,[133] there is no categorical bar to eliciting evidence *on* deceased persons. The Appeals Chamber observes that a wealth of evidence, both hearsay and non-hearsay, is examined in two voluminous chapters of the Trial Judgement on the Ultimate Purpose and the CCP, including evidence on the deceased persons.[134] In light of the foregoing, the Appeals Chamber finds that the mere possibility that the deceased persons could have tendered evidence, had they remained ahve and been charged with the same crimes as JCE members,[135] cannot render the trial unfair. In this regard, it notes in particular that the nature of the evidence that could potentially have been tendered by the deceased persons is uncertain. His allegation that the trial was unfair is therefore dismissed.

36.   Thus, the Appeals Chamber dismisses Stojić's ground of appeal 17.

C. **Alleged Errors Concerning Prlić's Right to Have Adequate Time and Facilities for the Defence (Prlić's Ground 7)**

37.   Prlić contends that the Trial Chamber erred in law and fact by systematically denying him adequate time and facilities to question witnesses, thereby invalidating the Trial Judgement and occasioning a

---

[127]   Trial Judgement, Vol. 4, paras 25-73.

[128]   In alleging that the Trial Chamber erroneously based its finding on the Ultimate Purpose almost exclusively on evidence about Tuđman, Stojić misrepresents factual findings and the evidence and ignores other relevant factual findings when he incorrectly alleges that only two findings in the Ultimate Purpose chapter are not "about Tuđman". Stojić's Appeal Brief, paras 134, 137, referring to Trial Judgement, Vol. 4, paras 18-19. *Cf., e.g.,* Trial Judgement, Vol. 4, paras 13-16, 18, 20-21 at fns 28-30, 36-40, 48-49, 58-59, 66-72. In any event, Stojić only aUeges that the Trial Chamber based its finding on the Ultimate Purpose almost exclusively on evidence *about* Tuđman, but not that this evidence consisted of hearsay evidence. See *infra,* fn. 130. The Appeals Chamber therefore dismisses this argument.

[129]   Namely with disclosure. Stojić's Appeal Brief, para. 136 & fn. 351, refering to *A. and others* Decision, para. 220.

[130]   Stojić's Appeal Brief, para. 136 & fn. 350, referring to *Prosecutor* v. *Milan Martić,* Case No. IT-95-11-AR73.2, Decision on Appeal against the Trial Chamber's Decision on the Evidence of Witness Milan Babić, 14 September 2006, para. 20, *Al-Khawaja. and Tahery* Decision, paras 117, 147. Stojić's submissions rather challenge only that the Trial Chamber relied on evidence *"relating to"* or *"about"* Tuđman and other deceased persons. Stojić's Appeal Brief, heading before para. 133, paras 134, 137-138 (emphases added). The Appeals Chamber notes that Stojić does not allege that this evidence does not include direct evidence that he had the opportunity to challenge.

[131]   Stojić's Appeal Brief, para. 136 & fn. 352, referring to *Tadić* Appeal Judgement, para. 55, *Simba* Appeal Judgement, para. 41.

[132]   *Tadić* Appeal Judgement, para. 55; *Simba* Appeal Judgement, paras 40-61.

[133]   See, *e.g.,* Rule 92 *bis* and Rule 92 *quater* of the Rules.

[134]   Trial Judgement, Vol. 4, paras 6-24 (Ultimate Purpose), 41-66 (CCP). The Appeals Chamber further finds that the case at hand is therefore distinct from the other cases that Stojić cites where a violation of fair trial due to important unavailable evidence was established in the particular circumstances of those cases. Stojić's Appeal Brief, para. 136 & fn. 353, referring to *Papageorgiou* Decision, paras 35-40, *Genie-Lacayo* Judgement, para. 76.

[135]   *Cf.* Trial Judgement, Vol. 4, para. 1231.

miscarriage of justice.[136] Specifically, referring to the *Prlić et al.* Trial Decision on Cross-Examination,[137] Prlić submits that the Trial Chamber violated his right to confront witnesses and present a defence, limiting the time for cross-examination by adopting a "mathematical *one-sixth-solution*", in which, as a rule, each Defence Counsel would have one-sixth of the time allocated to the Prosecution for direct examination.[138] Prlić argues that the Trial Chamber's **[page 18]** subsequent attempt to remedy the lack of time by allocating additional time upon the Defence's request was not appropriate, since a thorough and proper cross-examination must be prepared in advance in full knowledge of the available time.[139] Prlić contends that the Trial Chamber committed factual errors by relying on the testimony of witnesses who were not properly cross-examined.[140] Prlić requests that the Appeals Chamber acquit him on all counts of the Indictment.[141]

38.   The Prosecution responds that Prlić fails to demonstrate any error in the *Prlić et al.* Trial Decision on Cross-Examination.[142] The Prosecution argues that: (1) Prlić reiterates trial arguments which were already considered and dismissed by the Appeals Chamber; and (2) Prlić's challenge is tantamount to a request for reconsideration without showing any clear error of reasoning or that "particular circumstances" would justify reconsideration in order to avoid an injustice.[143] The Prosecution submits that, in any event, the Trial Chamber applied the one-sixth approach flexibly and repeatedly granted him additional cross-examination time.[144] According to the Prosecution, Prlić disregards instances where he did not use part of his allocated time as well as an occasion where he rejected an offer of additional time.[145] The Prosecution further submits that Prlić used significantly more than one-sixth of the time used by the Prosecution for its examination-in-chief and that, in any event, he fails to substantiate the prejudice allegedly caused.[146] The Prosecution requests that Prlić's ground of appeal 7 be dismissed.[147]

39.   At the outset, the Appeals Chamber recalls that in the *Prlić et al.* Appeal Decision on Cross-Examination, it dismissed the joint Defence interlocutory appeal against the *Prlić et al.* Trial Decision on Cross-Examination.[148] In its decision, the Appeals Chamber concluded that the Trial Chamber did not "impose rigid time limits on the cross-examination" and that it adopted a "sufficiently flexible approach", preserving the right of cross-examination by each of the Defence counsel and complying with the right to cross-examine witnesses provided under Article 21(4) of **[page 19]** the Statute.[149] In this light, the Appeals Chamber recalls that it may reconsider a previous interlocutory decision under its inherent discretionary power to do so if a clear error of reasoning has been demonstrated or if it is necessary to do so to prevent an injustice.[150] To the extent that Prlić challenges the approach upheld on appeal, the Appeals Chamber considers

[136]   Prlić's Appeal Brief, paras 213, 216.
[137]   Prosecutor v. Jadranko Prlić, Bruno Stojić, Slobodan Praljak, Milivoj Petković, Valentin Ćorić, and Berislav Pušić, Case No. IT-04-74-T, T. 1475-1476, 1485-1486 (8 May 2006) ("Prlić et al. Trial Decision on Cross-Examination").
[138]   Prlić's Appeal Brief, paras 208-209, 211, 213. See T. 1475-1476, 1485-1486 (8 May 2006). Prlić also argues that the Trial Chamber: (1) erred in law by treating him as a member of a group, not an individual as required by Rule 82(A) of the Rules; and (2) failed to provide sufficient reasons why it did not adopt a "less restrictive approach" to time management, considering that he had to defend against a different case than the other accused. Prlić's Appeal Brief, paras 212, 214. Prlić further submits that the Trial Chamber erred in law by violating his right to equality of arms, putting him at a disadvantage vis-a-vis the Prosecution. Prlić's Appeal Brief, para. 215.
[139]   Prlić's Appeal Brief, paras 210, 213.
[140]   Prlić's Appeal Brief, paras 213, 216.
[141]   Prlić's Appeal Brief, para. 217.
[142]   Prosecution's Response Brief (Prlić), para. 124.
[143]   Prosecution's Response Brief (Prlić), para. 125, referring to Prosecutor v. Jadranko Prlić, Bruno Stojić, Slobodan Praljak, Milivoj Petković, Valentin Ćorić, and Berislav Pušić, Case No. IT-04-74-AR73.2, Decision on Joint Defence Interlocutory Appeal against the Trial Chamber's Oral Decision of 8 May 2006 Relating to Cross-Examination by Defence and on Association of Defence Counsel's Request for Leave to File an Amicus Curiae Brief, 4 July 2006 ("Prlić et al. Appeal Decision on Cross-Examination"), pp. 2, 4.
[144]   Prosecution's Response Brief (Prlić), para. 126.
[145]   Prosecution's Response Brief (Prlić), para. 126. See Prosecution's Response Brief (Prlić), para. 127.
[146]   Prosecution's Response Brief (Prlić), paras 126-128.
[147]   Prosecution's Response Brief (Prlić), para. 129.
[148]   Prlić et al. Appeal Decision on Cross-Examination, pp. 1, 5.
[149]   Prlić et al. Appeal Decision on Cross-Examination, p. 4.
[150]   See, e.g., Nyiramasuhuko et al. Appeal Judgement, paras 56, 127; Prosecutor v. Jadranko Prlić et al., Case No. IT-04-74-AR73.16, Decision on Jadranko Prlić's Interlocutory Appeal Against the Decision on Prlić Defence Motion for Reconsideration of the Decision on Admission of Documentary Evidence, 3 November 2009 ("Prlić et al. Appeal Decision on Motion for Reconsideration"), para. 6; Prosecutor v. Vojislav Šešelj, Case No. IT-03-67-AR72.1, Decision on Motion for Reconsideration of the

that he provides no reason for reconsideration of that appeal decision. The Appeals Chamber therefore dismisses all arguments relating to the approach set out in the *Prlić et al.* Trial Decision on Cross-Examination.

40.   Regarding the Trial Chamber's alleged subsequent attempt to remedy the lack of time by allocating additional time upon the Defence's request, the Appeals Chamber recalls that following the *Prlić et al.* Appeal Decision on Cross-Examination, the Trial Chamber issued a decision implementing the *Prlić et al.* Trial Decision on Cross-Examination.[151] Underscoring the flexibility of its approach, the Trial Chamber allowed for the possibility of allocating additional time for cross-examination upon the Defence's request "if one or several accused are directly concerned by the testimony of a witness".[152] To this end, the Trial Chamber ordered the Prosecution to submit to the Trial Chamber and to the Defence a schedule of witnesses it intended to call for the month in question and announced that it: (1) would estimate the time to be allocated for cross-examination upon receipt of the schedule; and (2) would examine the preliminary witness statements and summaries "in order to establish to what extent one or several accused are directly concerned by the hearing of witnesses".[153] The Appeals Chamber recalls that a trial chamber enjoys considerable discretion in setting the parameters of cross-examination and in outlining the exercise of this right, as well as in allocating time to the parties for the presentation of their cases.[154] In these circumstances, there is no indication that the Trial Chamber did not act within the reasonable exercise of its discretion when adopting measures to allocate additional time for cross-examination upon the Defence's request. The Appeals Chamber therefore finds that Prlić has failed to show that the Trial Chamber's subsequent attempt to remedy the lack of time by allocating additional time upon the Defence's request was inappropriate. Finally, since Prlić has not shown any error relating **[page 20]** to cross-examination, his argument concerning factual errors also fails. Accordingly, the Appeals Chamber dismisses Prlić's ground of appeal 7.

D.   Alleged Errors Concerning the JCE Theory (Stojić's Ground 13, Petković's Sub-ground 3.1)

41.   The Indictment alleges that a joint criminal enterprise existed "[f]rom on or before 18 November 1991 to about April 1994" to "politically and militarily subjugate, permanently remove and ethnically cleanse Bosnian Muslims and other non-Croats who lived in areas on the territory of the Republic of Bosnia and Herzegovina".[155] In addressing the forms of JCE liability applicable, the Indictment specifies that the Appellants are responsible under all three forms.[156]

42.   Regarding the individual criminal responsibility of the Appellants, the Indictment alleges that each Appellant committed the crimes charged in the Indictment.[157] Specifically in relation to the first form of joint criminal enterprise liability ("JCE I"), paragraph 221 of the Indictment states that:

> The crimes charged in this indictment were part of the joint criminal enterprise described in Paragraphs 2 to 17 (including 17.1 to 17.6) and 39 and were committed in the course of the enterprise [...]. Pursuant to Article 7(1), each of the accused [Prlić, Stojić, Praljak, Petković, Ćorić, and Pušić] is criminally responsible for the crimes which were committed as part of the joint criminal enterprise, in the sense that each of the accused committed these crimes as a member of or participant in such enterprise.[158]

43.   The Indictment also alleges the second form of joint criminal enterprise liability ("JCE II") for each Appellant's: (1) participation in a system of ill-treatment involving "a network of Herceg-Bosna/HVO prisons, concentration camps and other detention facilities which were systematically used in arresting, detaining and imprisoning thousands of Bosnian Muslims [...] which amounted to or involved the commission

---

'Decision on the Interlocutory Appeal Concerning Jurisdiction' dated 31 August 2004, 15 June 2006 (*"Šešelj* Appeal Decision on Motion for Reconsideration"), para. 9.
[151]   *Prosecutor v. Jadranko Prlić, Bruno Stojić, Slobodan Praljak, Milivoj Petković, Valentin Ćorić, and Berislav Pušić*, Case No. IT-04-74-T, Decision on the Implementation of the Decision of 8 May 2006 on Time Allocated for Cross-Examination by Defence, 18 July 2006 (French original 12 July 2006) (*"Prlić et al.* Trial Decision on Implementation").
[152]   *Prlić et al.* Trial Decision on Implementation, p. 2.
[153]   *Prlić et al.* Trial Decision on Implementation, pp. 2-3.
[154]   *Šainović et al.* Appeal Judgement, paras 123, 171.
[155]   Indictment, para. 15.
[156]   Indictment, paras 221, 224-225, 227. See Indictment, para. 222.
[157]   Indictment, para. 218.
[158]   Indictment, para. 221. See Indictment, para. 222 (setting out the *mens rea*).

of crimes charged in this indictment";[159] and (2) participation in a system of ill-treatment which "deported Bosnian Muslims to other countries or transferred them to parts of Bosnia and Herzegovina not claimed or controlled by Herceg-Bosna or the HVO [...] which amounted to or involved the commission of crimes charged in this indictment".[160]

44.   With regard to the pleading of the JCE III form of responsibihty, paragraph 227 of the Indictment alleges that "[i]n addition or in the alternative, as to any crime charged in this indictment which was not within the objective or an intended part of the joint criminal enterprise, such crime **[page 21]** was the natural and foreseeable consequence of the joint criminal enterprise [...] and each accused was aware of the risk of such crime or consequence and, despite this awareness, willingly took that risk [...] and is therefore responsible for the crime charged".[161]

45.   In the Prosecution's Final Brief, the Prosecution qualified Counts 1, 6-9, and 19-20 as the "core" JCE crimes.[162] Similarly, the Prosecution qualified the "expanded" JCE crimes as: (1) Counts 10-18 as of 1 July 1993;[163] (2) Counts 22-23 as of 15 June 1993;[164] and (3) Counts 24-26 as of 1 June 1993.[165] In respect of Counts 2-5 and 21, these crimes were qualified as JCE III crimes in the Prosecution's Final Brief.[166] Moreover, the Prosecution alleged that, as of 1 July 1993, Counts 10-18 for incidents identified in paragraph 224 of the Indictment as well as Counts 6-9 for incidents identified in paragraph 225 of the Indictment were JCE II crimes.[167]

46.   The Trial Chamber, after noting that the Prosecution alleged the existence of several JCEs, considered that "the evidence demonstrate[d] that there was only one, single common criminal purpose – domination by the HR H-B Croats through ethnic cleansing of the Muslim population" from mid-January 1993 until April 1994.[168] It found that a JCE was established to accomplish the political purpose and was carried out in stages.[169]

47.   The Trial Chamber, after summarising its factual findings on the events of the JCE based on the evidence, also determined which crimes fell "within the framework of the common plan of the Form 1 JCE"; and found that these crimes included all counts with the exception of the following JCE III crimes: (1) Counts 2 and 3 (murder and wilful killing) committed during evictions or closely linked to evictions and as a result of mistreatment and poor conditions of confinement during detentions; (2) Counts 4 and 5 (rape and inhuman treatment through sexual assault); (3) Count 21 (destruction or wilful damage to institutions dedicated to religion or education) committed before June 1993; and (4) Counts 22 and 23 (appropriation of property and plunder).[170] **[page 22]** In addition, the Trial Chamber found that Counts 2 and 3 committed during attacks and by virtue of forced labour as well as Count 21 committed as of June 1993 were JCE I crimes.[171] The Trial Chamber also considered that the JCE "expanded" to include Counts 24 and 25 (unlawful attack on civilians and unlawful infliction of terror on civilians) as of June 1993.[172]

---

[159]   Indictment, para. 224.
[160]   Indictment, para. 225.
[161]   Indictment, para. 227.
[162]   Prosecution's Final Brief, paras 7-18. The Prosecution also alleged that if extensive destruction as charged in Counts 19-20 were found not to be "core" crimes, these crimes should be considered as JCE III crimes, however the Prosecution did not make a similar statement regarding Counts 1, and 6-9. Prosecution's Final Brief, para. 18. See Prosecution's Final Brief, paras 7-15.
[163]   Prosecution's Final Brief, paras 19-46. The Prosecution also alleged that Counts 10-18 committed prior to 1 July 1993 were attributable to the Appellants as JCE III crimes, and for the crimes committed as of 1 July 1993, JCE III was alleged in the alternative. Prosecution's Final Brief, paras 26-27, 33-34, 45-46.
[164]   Prosecution's Final Brief, paras 47-53. The Prosecution also alleged that Counts 22 and 23 committed prior to 15 June 1993 were attributable to the Appellants as JCE III crimes, and for the crimes committed as of 15 June 1993, JCE III was alleged in the alternative. Prosecution's Final Brief, paras 52-53.
[165]   Prosecution's Final Brief, paras 54-56.
[166]   Prosecution's Final Brief, paras 57-62, 516, 636, 850, 970, 1179, 1276.
[167]   Prosecution's Final Brief, paras 63-70. The Prosecution, however, noted that these incidents also formed part of the "larger Herceg-Bosna JCE". Prosecution's Final Brief, paras 65, 69, fn. 111.
[168]   Trial Judgement, Vol. 4, paras 41, 44, 65. See Trial Judgement, Vol. 4, paras 26-38, 66, 68.
[169]   Trial Judgement, Vol. 4, paras 44-45. See Trial Judgement, Vol. 4, paras 46-66.
[170]   Trial Judgement, Vol. 4, paras 68, 70-73, 342, 433, 1213.
[171]   Trial Judgement, Vol. 4, paras 66, 68, 342, 433, 1213.
[172]   Trial Judgement, Vol. 4, paras 59, 68.

48.   Stojić and Petković both present grounds of appeal alleging that the Trial Chamber erred by modifying the JCE theory pleaded by the Prosecution.

1.   Arguments of the Parties

49.   Stojić contends that the Trial Chamber erred in law by entering convictions based on a JCE theory which was not "pleaded by the Prosecution in the Indictment and in its Final Trial Brief, thereby impermissibly altering the charges against him.[173] Stojić submits that the Trial Chamber's characterisation of the JCE is fundamentally different from that advanced by the Prosecution, which alleged that there were at least three different JCEs.[174] He argues that as the Trial Chamber applied a different theory – the existence of a single JCE by placing all the alleged crimes under JCE I or JCE III liability – clear distinctions between the Trial Judgement and the Indictment resulted.[175] In this regard, Stojić submits that the Trial Chamber: (1) placed Counts 2, 3, and 21 within JCE I while the Prosecution alleged that Counts 2-5 and 21 fell under JCE III; and (2) found that none of the crimes fell under a JCE II form of liability.[176]

50.   Stojić further contends that the Trial Chamber violated his right to a fair trial as he was not put on notice of its re-characterisation of the JCE. Stojić argues that he suffered prejudice as had he been aware of this re-characterisation, his arguments, strategy, and evidence presented would have been different.[177] Stojić requests that the Trial Chamber's finding that a JCE existed be overturned.[178]

51.   Petković submits that the Trial Chamber rejected the Prosecution's theory of multiple JCEs and changed the starting date of the JCE to mid-January 1993 resulting in significant differences **[page 23]** between the Prosecution's case and the "Chamber's case".[179] According to Petković, these differences relate to, *inter alia,* the alleged common criminal purpose, the temporal scope, the alleged *mens rea,* the number and categories of core crimes, and the classification of certain crimes as falling under JCE I or JCE III.[180] Petković argues that he was prejudiced as he was denied a fair opportunity to prepare for, and confront at trial, the theory of a single JCE.[181] He further contends that the Trial Chamber had no power to replace the Prosecution's "failed case" and in effect transformed its adjudicative function into a prosecutorial one.[182] Petković contends that the Trial Chamber's reformulation of the Prosecution's case is impermissible and violates: (1) his right to adequate notice of charges; (2) the presumption of innocence; and (3) his right to an impartial tribunal.[183]

52.   Petković further submits that the Trial Chamber "pronounced its verdict contrary to the case as presented by the OTP in their final brief. While agreeing with the Prosecution "that [this] does not impact on the right [of the] accused to a fair trial in the sense that they were informed in a timely fashion of the counts of their indictment because the indictment did cover all the possible time modalities and types of liability",[184] Petković argues that the Trial Chamber erred as it went "beyond the framework of the [I]ndictment.[185] He

---

[173]   Stojić's Appeal Brief, heading before para. 109, paras 114, 116.
[174]   Stojić's Appeal Brief, paras 112, 114. See Appeal Hearing, AT. 253-254 (21 Mar 2017). Stojić contends that the Prosecution alleged a "Herceg-Bosna criminal enterprise which was a JCE Form I and which expanded to include additional crimes around June 1993, a JCE Form II (prisoners) which was created on 1 July 1993 and a deportation and forcible transfer JCE which came into being on 1 July 1993". Stojić's Appeal Brief, para. 112.
[175]   Stojić's Appeal Brief, paras 112-114.
[176]   Stojić's Appeal Brief, para. 112 & fn. 299.
[177]   Stojić's Appeal Brief, para. 115.
[178]   Stojić's Appeal Brief, para. 116.
[179]   Petković's Appeal Brief, paras 17-18. See Petković's Appeal Brief, paras 15-16; Appeal Hearing, AT. 487-489, 500-501 (23 Mar 2017).
[180]   Petković's Appeal Brief, paras 18-19. See Petković's Reply Brief, paras 5-6; Appeal Hearing, AT. 489 (23 Mar 2017).
[181]   Petković's Appeal Brief, para. 20. Petković also argues that he was denied the opportunity to properly litigate the inadequate pleading of the JCE in the Indictment as his request for certification to appeal a decision by the Trial Chamber was denied. Petković's Reply Brief, para. 5(iii). As Petković raises this point for the first time in his reply brief, the Appeals Chamber will not consider it any further. See Practice Direction on Formal Requirements, para. 6.
[182]   Petković's Appeal Brief, para. 21.
[183]   Petković's Appeal Brief, para. 22.
[184]   Appeal Hearing, AT. 490 (23 Mar 2017).
[185]   Appeal Hearing, AT. 490 (23 Mar 2017).

requests that the Appeals Chamber quash the Trial Chamber's JCE findings and acquit him of "the case pleaded at trial".[186]

53.   In response to contentions from both Stojić and Petković, the Prosecution argues that the Indictment provided them with sufficient notice of the relevant crimes,[187] and that the Trial Chamber did not depart from the Indictment by finding the existence of a single common criminal purpose.[188] The Prosecution argues that at no point relevant to Stojić's notice did it narrow the scope of its case from what was pleaded in the Indictment.[189] It also submits that its opening statement and Rule 98 *bis* submissions were consistent with the Indictment.[190] The Prosecution **[page 24]** submits that it is immaterial that the Trial Chamber did not adopt the allegation that there were two JCEs under JCE II liability as the Indictment alleged responsibility for all charged crimes under JCEI.[191]

54.   The Prosecution also contends that: (1) its final trial brief contains submissions on the evidence at the end of the trial and is not relevant for the preparation of an accused's case; and (2) it is irrelevant that it "took a narrower view of the core JCE I crimes" in its final trial brief than what the Trial Chamber found.[192] It also submits that it is the Indictment which sets the parameters of the case and not the Prosecution's Final Brief and that the Trial Chamber did not reformulate the charges as its findings were within the scope of the Indictment.[193] The Prosecution further responds that both Appellants fail to show any prejudice resulting from any possible lack of notice as they categorically rejected any criminal enterprise in their closing submissions at trial.[194]

2.   Analysis

55.   The Appeals Chamber recalls that "[i]n order for an accused charged with joint criminal enterprise to fully understand which acts he is allegedly responsible for, the indictment should clearly indicate which form of joint criminal enterprise is being alleged".[195] The Appeals Chamber considers that it is patent from the relevant paragraphs of the Indictment that liability under the first form of JCE was pleaded for all the crimes charged.[196] Further, the Appeals Chamber considers that the operative pleading of the crimes under JCE III is that they were "in the alternative" to falling under JCE I. The Appeals Chamber recalls that while the three forms of JCE are mutually incompatible to the extent that a defendant may not be convicted for the same criminal incident under multiple forms, an indictment may charge a defendant cumulatively with multiple forms of JCE.[197] The Appeals Chamber notes that the Prosecution may "alternatively rely on one or more legal theories, on condition that it is done clearly, early enough and, in any event, allowing enough time to enable the accused to know what exactly he is accused of and to enable him to prepare his defence accordingly".[198] In this case, the Appellants were clearly on notice that a common criminal purpose was expressly pleaded in the Indictment and that they were alleged to be responsible for crimes committed pursuant to this criminal plan under all three forms of JCE liability based on **[page 25]** alternative theories.[199]

---

[186]   Petković's Appeal Brief, para. 23.
[187]   Prosecution's Response Brief (Stojić), para. 86; Prosecution's Response Brief (Petković), para. 19. See Appeal Hearing, AT. 550 (23 Mar 2017).
[188]   Prosecution's Response Brief (Stojić), para. 87, referring to Indictment, para. 15, Trial Judgement, Vol. 4, paras 24, 41, 44, 65; Prosecution's Response Brief (Petković), para. 18.
[189]   Prosecution's Response Brief (Stojić), para. 88.
[190]   Prosecution's Response Brief (Petković), para. 19.
[191]   Prosecution's Response Brief (Stojić), para. 87.
[192]   Prosecution's Response Brief (Stojić), para. 88; Prosecution's Response Brief (Petković), para. 21.
[193]   Prosecution's Response Brief (Petković), paras 20-21.
[194]   Prosecution's Response Brief (Stojić), para. 89; Prosecution's Response Brief (Petković), para. 22.
[195]   *Ntagerura et al.* Appeal Judgement, para. 24. See *Statić* Appeal Judgement, para. 66; *Kvočka et al.* Appeal Judgement, para. 28; *Krnojelac* Appeal Judgement, paras 115-117; *Nizeyimana* Appeal Judgement, para. 315.
[196]   Indictment, para. 221. See Indictment, paras 15, 17, 39, 222. See also *supra*, paras 41-44.
[197]   *Simba* Appeal Judgement, para. 77. See also *Čelebići* Appeal Judgement, para. 400.
[198]   *Krnojelac* Appeal Judgement, para. 115. See *Krnojelac* Appeal Judgement, para. 117.
[199]   The Appeals Chamber also notes, that the Pre-Trial Chamber dismissed Prlić's challenge that the Indictment failed to specify which form of JCE liability the Prosecution was charging under Article 7(1) of the Statute. In doing so, it relied in particular on paragraphs 15, 224-225, and 227 of the Indictment, and held that they sufficiently informed the Appellants of "the nature, time frame, geographical frame, criminal objective, *form of the JCE and whether the crimes not included in the objective of the JCE could be the natural and foreseeable consequence of the alleged criminal enterprise*". *Prosecutor v. Jadranko Prlić et al.*, Case No. IT-04-74-PT,

The Appeals Chamber finds that the Trial Chamber did not exceed the scope of the Indictment in concluding that a legal theory expressly pleaded by the Prosecution in the Indictment – a common criminal plan resulting in JCE I liability, and alternatively JCE III liability for crimes ultimately found not to have fallen within the CCP – was established on the evidence.

56.   Further, the Appeals Chamber considers Petković's argument concerning the differences in the JCEs pleaded in the Indictment and the one the Trial Chamber found to have existed to be unpersuasive. In the Appeals Chamber's view, the findings of the Trial Chamber concerning the CCP, the time-frame of the JCE, the *mens rea* of the participants, and the number and categories of crimes are within allegations pleaded in the Indictment.[200] Notably, for example, paragraphs 15, 17, 39, 221, and 222 of the Indictment allege that Counts 2-3 and 21 are pleaded as JCE I crimes, and alternatively as JCE III crimes.[201] The Appeals Chamber thus finds that Stojić and Petković have not shown that the Trial Chamber exceeded the scope of the Indictment regarding the theory of the JCE and the crimes falling within the common criminal purpose as pleaded in the Indictment.

57.   As noted above,[202] the Prosecution qualified certain crimes in various circumstances as JCE I (core or expanded) crimes, JCE II crimes, or JCE III crimes in its final trial brief.[203] **[page 26]** Specifically, the Prosecution qualified Counts 2, 3, and 21 as JCE III crimes, and qualified Counts 10-18 as being part of the CCP only as of 1 July 1993 in its final trial brief. The Appeals Chamber will now address whether the Trial Chamber impermissibly transformed the Prosecution's case as alleged in the Prosecution's Final Brief.

58.   The core argument presented by Petković is that the Trial Chamber impermissibly changed the Prosecution's theory of the case as articulated *only* in the Prosecution's Final Brief. In this regard, the Appeals Chamber notes that Petković does not refer to any post-Indictment disclosure or the presentation of evidence.[204] Moreover, the Appeals Chamber recalls that "Prosecution final trial briefs are only filed at the end of a trial, after the presentation of all the evidence, and are therefore not relevant for the preparation of an accused's case".[205] In this regard, Petković and Stojić had sufficient notice that the case against them included charges of Counts 2-3, 10-18, and 21 under the JCE I form of liability[206] from the Indictment, Prosecution's

---

Decision on Defence Preliminary Motions Alleging Defects in the Form of the Indictment, 22 July 2005, paras 18-21 (emphasis added). See *Prosecutor v. Jadranko Prlić et al.*, Case No. IT-04-74-PT, Preliminary Motion to Dismiss the Defective Indictment Against Jadranko Prlić Pursuant to Rule 72(A)(ii), 15 December 2004, para. 7; *Prosecutor v. Jadranko Prlić et al.*, Case No. IT-04-74-PT, Jadranko Prlić's Reply to Prosecutor's Response to Defence Motions on the Form of the Indictment, 4 February 2005, para. 5.

[200]   The Indictment states that from on or before 18 November 1991 to about April 1994 various persons established and participated in the JCE, while the Trial Chamber found that the JCE was established "at least as early as mid-January 1993". Indictment, para. 15; Trial Judgement, Vol. 4, para. 44. For the CCP, see Indictment, paras 15-16, 23-28; Trial Judgement, Vol. 4, paras 41-44, 65. Regarding the charges and categories of crimes, see Indictment, paras 17, 39, 221, 229; Trial Judgement, Vol. 4, paras 66, 68. Concerning the *mens rea* requirements, see Indictment, para. 222; Trial Judgement, Vol. 4, paras 43, 67.

[201]   The Indictment pleads that each accused participated in the JCE in one or more ways including by organising, commanding, directing, ordering, facilitating, participating in, or operating the HVO military and police forces through which the objectives of the JCE were pursued and implemented and by which various crimes charged such as "persecutions, killing [...] and destruction of property, were committed". Indictment, para. 17(b). See Indictment, paras 17.1(n)-(o), 17.1(u) (Prlić), 17.2(j)-(k), 17.2(m) (Stojić), 17.3(h), 17.3(k) (Praljak), 17.4 (h)-(j) (Petković), 17.5(f), 17.5(i) (Ćorić), 17.6(c) (Pušić). See also Prosecution's Pre-Trial Brief, para. 17. At paragraph 39 of the Indictment, it is pleaded that all the Accused engaged in the use of force, intimidation, terror, forced labour, and destruction of property which specifically included killings during mass arrests, evictions, and forced labour as well as destruction of mosques. Indictment, para. 39(b), (c), (f). See Prosecution's Pre-Trial Brief, paras 39(b)-(c), 39(f). Lastly, the Indictment alleges that each Accused was responsible for Counts 2, 3, and 21 "punishable under Statute Articles 5(a), 7(1) and 7(3)" followed by a list of each paragraph in the Indictment which outlined the factual narrative of each incident of killing and destruction of mosques, including paragraph 39. Indictment, para. 229.

[202]   See *supra*, para. 45.

[203]   In its closing arguments, the Prosecution did not address the categorisation of Counts 2-3, 10-18, and 21 as JCE I or JCE III crimes. See, generally, Prosecution Closing Arguments, T. 51765-51873 (7 Feb 2011), 51874-51975 (8 Feb 2011), 51976-52080 (9 Feb 2011), 52081-52171 (10 Feb 2011), 52819-52898 (1 Mar 2011).

[204]   See Petković's Appeal Brief, paras 15-23; Petković's Reply Brief, paras 5-6.

[205]   *Simba* Appeal Judgement, para. 73. See *Simba* Appeal Judgement, para. 69. The ICTR Appeals Chamber concluded in the *Mugenzi and Mugiraneza* case that "closing submissions cannot constitute proper notice. Accordingly, the Appeals Chamber is not persuaded that any minor ambiguity at that stage demonstrates that the notice provided by the Prosecution Pre-Trial Brief and opening statement lacked clarity or consistency". *Mugenzi and Mugiraneza* Appeal Judgement, para. 124. See *Ntabakuze* Appeal Judgement, para. 80; *Ntawukulilyayo* Appeal Judgement, para. 202.

[206]   The Appeals Chamber will focus only on Counts 2, 3, 10-18, and 21 because these were the counts which the Trial Chamber found fell within the CCP from January 1993 contrary to the Prosecution's submission in its final brief that, in the period between

Pre-Trial Brief and throughout the presentation of the evidence.[207] Thus, as conceded by Petković,[208] the Prosecution's categorisation of these counts as falling only under JCE III liability (Counts 2, 3, and 21) and under JCE III liability prior to 1 July 1993 (Counts 10-18) in its final trial brief does not affect this notice.[209] Therefore, Petković's and Stojić's argument that they did not have adequate notice is dismissed.[210] **[page 27]**

59.   Moreover, the Appeals Chamber is of the view that the primary purpose of requiring the parties to file a final trial brief is to benefit a trial chamber as such briefs will set out the parties' factual and legal arguments.[211] Notably, the ICTR Appeals Chamber in *Semanza* stated that the purpose of a final trial brief is for each party "to express its own position regarding the charges set out in the indictment and the evidence led in the case".[212] In this context, and having reviewed the Prosecution's relevant submissions in its final brief, the Appeals Chamber, Judge Pocar dissenting, observes that in qualifying the crimes at issue as JCE III crimes rather than JCE I crimes, the Prosecution is merely putting forward what it believes can be established on the evidence beyond a reasonable doubt.[213]

60.   As the Prosecution did not expressly and formally withdraw JCE I as a form of liability that could possibly be applied to all counts,[214] the Appeals Chamber, Judge Pocar dissenting, considers that the

---

January and July 1993, they were in fact JCE III crimes. In other words, the Appeals Chamber will not consider Counts 22 and 23 for which the Trial Chamber followed the Prosecution's submission in the alternative when it found that crimes encompassed by Counts 22 and 23 were JCE III crimes throughout the relevant period.

[207]   See *supra*, para. 57. A reading of Petković's final trial brief indicates that he understood the case against him to be that all crimes charged fell under JCE I liability, with JCE III and the other modes of liability charged in the alternative. A reading of Stojić's final trial brief also leads to a similar conclusion. Petković's Final Brief, paras 513-557, 568-570, 664-665; Stojić's Final Brief, paras 548-556. See Praljak's Final Brief, paras 5, 606-610. See also Ćorić's Final Brief, paras 136-139, 772; Pušić's Final Brief, paras 27-36, 54-63.

[208]   Appeal Hearing, AT. 490 (23 Mar 2017). See *supra*, para. 52.

[209]   Similarly, the closing arguments on this issue would not affect the notice given to Petković and Stojić that the case against them included charges of Counts 2-3, 10-18, and 21 under JCE I. See Petković Closing Arguments, T. 52526-52527 (21 Feb 2011) (Petković noted in his closing arguments that the "Prosecution, in its final trial brief, stated that the crimes of murders and wilful killings were not planned by the HVO or in the context of JCE, that these crimes were not part of the criminal common plan"). Other than Petković, the Accused did not address the categorisation of Counts 2 and 3 as JCE I or JCE III crimes in the closing arguments. Further, none of the Accused addressed the categorisation of Counts 10-18, 21. At times, the Appellants briefly mentioned killings or raised other issues where the Prosecution departed from the Indictment in its final trial brief, but did not mention the mode of liability applicable. See Stojić Closing Arguments, T. 52399 (16 Feb 2011); Praljak Closing Arguments, T. 52508 (17 Feb 2011); Ćorić Closing Arguments, T. 52636 (22 Feb 2011); Pušić Closing Arguments, T. 52789-52790 (24 Feb 2011).

[210]   See *supra*, paras 50-51.

[211]   See *International Criminal Procedure: Principles and Rules,* Göran Sluiter, Håkan Friman, Suzannah Linton, Sergey Vasiliev, Salvatore Zappalà, OUP Oxford, 21 March 2013, pp. 675, 679. See also *International Criminal Trials: A Normative Theory,* Vasiliev, S. (2014), p. 830.

[212]   *Semanza* Appeal Judgement, para. 36. In the *Setako* case, the ICTR Trial Chamber first stated that the Prosecution's final trial brief contained a comprehensive list of the events on which it was seeking a conviction for a particular count. It then considered based on a number of factors, including the comprehensive list, that "although the Prosecution expressly withdrew only paragraph 62 of the Indictment", it left the strong impression that it is equally not pursuing two other events which were not referred to in its final trial brief as part of its case. It therefore decided not to address them "in detail". However, it went on to state that "it suffices to note" that the evidence presented in support of the relevant events is uncorroborated, explaining its concerns regarding the reliability of the evidence and declined to accept it in the absence of corroboration. See *Setako* Trial Judgement, paras 71-72.

[213]   See, *e.g.*, Prosecution's Final Brief, para. 516 ("The evidence proves beyond a reasonable doubt that the crimes of murder/ wilful killing, rape/inhuman treatment and destruction of religious and educational institutions, as charged in Counts 2-5. and 21, were the natural and foreseeable consequence[s] of [the] implementation of the Herceg-Bosna JCE").

[214]   The Appeals Chamber further notes that the Prosecution did not request leave to amend the indictment to withdraw Counts 2, 3, and 21 as JCE I crimes and Counts 10-18 as JCE I crimes prior to 1 July 1993 in accordance with Rule of 50 of the Rules. See, *e.g., Popović et al.* Trial Judgement, fns 1614 (noting that the Prosecution dropped allegations from the Indictment and referred to the corrigendum to the Prosecution's final trial brief where it was stated that some killings were "no longer charged" as "the Prosecution recognises that there is insufficient evidence upon this record for a finding beyond reasonable doubt" (see *Prosecutor v Vujadin Popović et al.,* Case No. IT-05-88-T, Corrigendum to the Prosecution Final Trial Brief, 1 September 2009, para. 9)), 2866 (noting that the Prosecution dropped allegations on two killings referred to in the same corrigendum where the Prosecution noted that it previously dropped these allegations in a separate filing (see *Prosecutor v Vujadin Popović et al.,* Case No. IT-05-88-T, Prosecution Submission Concerning Paragraphs 31.1b and 31.1c of the Indictment, 18 February 2008, "withdrawing" the latter charges)); *The Prosecutor v. Édouard Karemera et al.,* Case No. ICTR-98-44-AR73, Decision on Prosecutor's Interlocutory Appeal Against Trial Chamber III Decision of 8 October 2003 Denying Leave to File an Amended Indictment, 19 December 2003, paras 12, 15, 25, 27; *The Prosecutor v. Emanuel Ndindabahizi,* Case No. ICTR-2001-71-I, Decision on Prosecution Request to Amend Indictment, 30 June 2003, paras 2, 4 (the Prosecution requested leave to amend the indictment so as to withdraw charges and allegations, including superior responsibility as a mode of liability); *Prosecutor v. Stanislav Galić,* Case No. IT-98-29-AR72, Decision on Application by Defence for Leave to Appeal, 30 November 2001, paras 14-16. The Appeals Chamber recalls that Rule

557

Prosecution's Final Brief cannot be reasonably interpreted to mean that the Prosecution abandoned JCE I as a possible mode of liability for some crimes by qualifying those crimes as only **[page 28]** JCE III crimes or as JCE I crimes only as of 1 July 1993 in its final trial brief. The Appeals Chamber, Judge Pocar dissenting, is of the view that the Prosecution merely articulated its view on the more appropriate mode of liability.

61.   Moreover, the Appeals Chamber, Judge Pocar dissenting, considers that the Trial Chamber, after summarising the Prosecution's positions in its final trial brief, did not interpret the Prosecution's qualifications as reflecting a decision not to pursue the relevant crimes as JCE I crimes.[215] In this respect, the Appeals Chamber recalls the Prosecution's submission, made in response to Stojić's and Petković's arguments, that it is the Indictment that sets out the parameters of the case and not the Prosecution's Final Brief.[216] The Appeals Chamber, Judge Pocar dissenting, further notes that the Prosecution stated that the relevant section in its final trial brief "described the crimes involved in the JCEs" and that the "accused are also responsible for those crimes pursuant to other modes of liability contained in Article 7(1) and 7(3)".[217] Thus, the Appeals Chamber, Judge Pocar dissenting, considers that the Prosecution's qualification of some crimes as only JCE III crimes in its final trial brief was not binding on the Trial Chamber's assessment of the evidence. The Appeals Chamber, Judge Pocar dissenting, therefore finds that the Trial Chamber was entitled to exercise its discretion to characterise the Appellants' form of responsibility for incidents of Counts 2-3, 10-18, and 21 as JCE I liability once it was satisfied that this was the most appropriate mode of liability based on the evidence.

62.   Under these circumstances, the Appeals Chamber, Judge Pocar dissenting, finds that, for the same reasons discussed above, the Trial Chamber cannot be seen as acting partially or in a prosecutorial manner merely because its assessment of the evidence at the end of the trial led it to conclude that one of the modes of liability alleged in the Indictment is more appropriate than the one articulated in the Prosecution's Final Brief. Thus, the Appeals Chamber, Judge Pocar dissenting, dismisses as unsubstantiated Petković's arguments on the violation of his rights to the presumption of innocence and to an impartial tribunal.[218]

63.   Based on the foregoing, the Appeals Chamber, Judge Pocar dissenting, finds that Stojić and Petković have failed to demonstrate that they were not put on notice of the JCE liability allegations, that their fair trial rights were violated, or that the Trial Chamber impermissibly altered the **[page 29]** Prosecution's case.[219] The Appeals Chamber, Judge Pocar dissenting in part, dismisses Stojić's ground of appeal 13 and Petković's sub-ground of appeal 3.1.

E.   Alleged Error Concerning the Attack on the Village of Skrobućani (Petković's Sub-ground 5.2.2.1 in part)

64.   The Indictment alleges that between June and mid-August 1993, HVO forces attacked Bosnian Muslim civilians and destroyed and looted Muslim property in, *inter alia*, Skrobućani.[220] The Indictment also states that HVO forces burned down the mosque in Skrobućani.[221] After noting the time-period alleged in the Indictment and considering evidence from Witness BS, the Trial Chamber found that the attack on Skrobućani occurred "probably in May or June 1993"[222] and that the Skrobućani mosque was burned down in May or June 1993.[223]

50(A)(i)(c) of the Rules provides that after a case has been assigned to a Trial Chamber, the Prosecutor may amend an indictment with leave of that Trial Chamber or a Judge of that Chamber after having heard the parties. See *Prosecutor v. Vujadin Popović et al. and Prosecutor v. Milorad Trbić*, Case Nos. IT-05-88-PT & IT-05-88/1-PT, Decision on Further Amendments and Challenges to the Indictment, 13 July 2006, paras 6-11 ("Under Rule 50, a Trial Chamber has wide discretion to allow an indictment to be amended, even in the late stages of pre-trial proceedings, or indeed even after trial has begun. Nevertheless, [...] such leave will not be granted unless the amendment" meets various conditions (see, para. 8)).

[215]   See Trial Judgement, Vol. 4, paras 28-38.
[216]   See *supra*, para. 54.
[217]   Prosecution's Final Brief, fn. 2.
[218]   See *supra*, para. 51.
[219]   The Appeals Chamber considers that it is unnecessary to address the arguments on prejudice or remedies.
[220]   Indictment, para. 53.
[221]   Indictment, para. 53.
[222]   Trial Judgement, Vol. 2, para. 95, referring to Witness BS, T(F). 8189-8190 (closed session) (11 Oct 2006). See Trial Judgement, Vol. 2, paras 92, 96-97, Vol. 4, para. 695.
[223]   Trial Judgement, Vol. 2, para. 97, Vol. 4, para. 695.

65.   Petković argues that the Trial Chamber erroneously "modified the Prosecution case" by finding, without evidence, that the village of Skrobućani in Prozor Municipality was attacked in May.[224] He contends that the Prosecution did not allege that any HVO military action was launched, or crimes committed, in May 1993.[225]

66.   The Prosecution responds that Petković had sufficient notice and that the discrepancy between the Indictment and the Trial Chamber's findings regarding the date of the attack was immaterial.[226] It also submits that Petković presented a defence on the substance of the evidence and the timing of the attack.[227]

67.   The Appeals Chamber recalls that charges against an accused and the material facts supporting those charges must be pleaded with sufficient precision in an indictment so as to provide notice to an accused.[228] Moreover, the Appeals Chamber recalls "that, in general, minor differences **[page 30]** between the indictment and the evidence presented at trial are not such as to prevent the trial chamber from considering the indictment in light of the evidence presented at trial".[229]

68.   In the instant case, it is clear that the attack on Skrobućani referred to in the Indictment was a single, clearly identifiable event which included the destruction of property belonging to Muslims and the burning of the village mosque.[230] As to the alleged discrepancy between the material facts pleaded in the Indictment and the Trial Chamber's ultimate conclusions concerning the date of the attack, the Appeals Chamber considers that this discrepancy does not constitute a significant variation in this case. Therefore, although the Indictment and the Trial Judgement refer to different but partially overlapping date ranges, the material facts as pleaded in the Indictment were sufficient to inform Petković of the charge as ultimately found by the Trial Chamber.[231] Thus, Petković was provided with timely and clear notice of the attack on Skrobućani and approximately when it occurred, and that this event formed part of the charges against him. Moreover, the evidence adduced by the Prosecution in relation to the incident was consistent with the Indictment and Petković cross-examined the relevant witness, particularly on the date of the attack.[232] His sub-ground of appeal 5.2.2.1 is therefore dismissed in relevant part.

F.   Alleged Errors in Concluding That the Existence of a State of Occupation was Pleaded (Ćorić's Sub-ground 3.2.1)

69.   The Indictment states that at the relevant time, "a state of armed conflict, international armed conflict and partial occupation existed in Bosnia and Herzegovina [...]. All acts and omissions charged in this indictment as Grave Breaches of the Geneva Conventions of 1949, [...] occurred during and in nexus with such international armed conflict and partial occupation".[233] The Trial Chamber noted that a state of partial occupation was alleged in the Indictment before considering specific arguments from Praljak and Petković and concluding that "the Defence teams were adequately informed of the allegations brought against the Accused Praljak and Petković as commanding officers in a zone of occupation".[234] The Trial Chamber later found that the HVO occupied the villages of Duša, Hrsanica, Ždrimci, Uzričje, Sovići, Doljani, and Stupni

---

[224]   Petković's Appeal Brief, para. 218, referring to, *inter alia,* Trial Judgement, Vol. 2, paras 95-97, Vol. 3, para. 1564. See Trial Judgement, Vol. 4, para. 695. The Appeals Chamber notes that as Petković does not refer to the Indictment or the subsequent trial proceedings, it is not clear whether Petković argues that the Indictment does not plead that Skrobućani village was attacked in May 1993 or that the Trial Chamber impermissibly exceeded the scope of the Prosecution's case as presented during the trial. See Petković's Appeal Brief, para. 218. However, as the presentation of the Prosecution's case on this issue is consistent with the Indictment, the lack of clarity in Petković's argument is immaterial. See *infra,* para. 68.

[225]   Petković's Appeal Brief, para. 218.

[226]   Prosecution's Response Brief (Petković), para. 162, referring to, *inter alia,* Indictment, para. 53, Trial Judgement, Vol. 2, paras 96-97, Witness BS, T. 8189-8190, 8238-8239 (closed session) (11 Oct 2006).

[227]   Prosecution's Response Brief (Petković), para. 162, referring to Witness BS, T. 8238-8240 (closed session) (11 Oct 2006).

[228]   *Popović et al.* Appeal Judgement, para. 65; *Šainović et al.* Appeal Judgement, para. 225.

[229]   *Nyiramasuhuko et al.* Appeal Judgement, para. 478.

[230]   Indictment, para. 53. See also Prosecution's Pre-Trial Brief, para. 53 (The Prosecution referred to the attack on Skrobućani and the destruction of the mosque as occurring between June and mid-August 1993).

[231]   See *Kvočka et al.* Appeal Judgement, para. 436. *Cf. Đorđević* Appeal Judgement, paras 598, 615.

[232]   See Trial Judgement, Vol. 2, paras 95-97, and references cited therein; Ex. 2D00200, pp. 2-3 (confidential); Witness BS, T. 8192, 8209, 8238-8240 (closed session) (11 Oct 2006).

[233]   Indictment, para. 232. See Indictment, paras 235-238; Trial Judgement, Vol. 3, paras 569, 577.

[234]   Trial Judgement, Vol. 1, para. 91, referring to, *inter alia,* Indictment, paras 8, 10, 218-228. See Trial Judgement, Vol. 1, para. 90.

Do; Vareš **[page 31]** town; West Mostar; as well as the municipalities of Prozor, Ljubuški, Stolac, and Čapljina, all during different time spans.[235]

70.   Ćorić argues that the Trial Chamber erred in law and in fact by concluding that the Defence teams were adequately informed that a state of occupation was pleaded in the Indictment.[236] Ćorić contends that this conclusion is unsupported by the Trial Chamber's reliance on paragraphs 8 and 10 of the Indictment and that, unlike its reference to Petković and Praljak, the Trial Chamber was silent on allegations against Ćorić in relation to the state of occupation due to lack of notice.[237] Ćorić submits that the Trial Chamber erred by entering convictions based on what he refers to as "full occupation" when the Indictment referred only to the existence of a state of partial occupation, thereby exceeding the scope of the Indictment.[238]

71.   The Prosecution responds that Ćorić had notice that a state of occupation formed part of the case against him and that his failure to object at trial to any lack of notice amounts to waiver.[239]

72.   Ćorić replies that as the issue of occupation, which he objected to, was not clearly stated in the Prosecution's final trial brief and closing arguments, waiver is not an available argument.[240]

73.   The Appeals Chamber will first consider whether the Indictment was defective with regard to the pleading of a state of occupation. It is recalled that an indictment which fails to set forth the specific material facts underpinning the charges against the accused is defective.[241] As noted above,[242] the Indictment pleaded that at the relevant time, "a state of armed conflict, international armed conflict and partial occupation existed in Bosnia and Herzegovina".[243] The material facts supporting the allegations on the existence of a state of occupation and the relevant crimes committed in occupied territory are also clearly set out in the Indictment.[244] The Trial Chamber noted the reference to "partial occupation" in the Indictment,[245] and proceeded to enter findings – after discussing the evidence – on whether certain municipalities, towns, and villages were **[page 32]** occupied by the HVO.[246] The Appeals Chamber considers that the Indictment clearly provided notice to the Appellants that they were charged with responsibility for certain crimes committed during an international armed conflict and partial occupation.

74.   Turning to the question of whether the Trial Chamber's findings were within the scope of the Indictment, the Appeals Chamber notes that although the Trial Chamber did not use the specific term "partial" in its findings, its analysis on whether specific geographical areas within the BiH were occupied is consistent with the allegations in the Indictment. There is nothing in the Trial Judgement which suggests that the Trial Chamber considered a state of "full occupation" as argued by Ćorić.[247] The Appeals Chamber thus finds Ćorić's argument that the Trial Chamber exceeded the scope of the Indictment to be unsubstantiated and unpersuasive.[248]

75.   Further, the Appeals Chamber finds that Ćorić's contention concerning the Trial Chamber's observation that "the Defence teams were adequately informed of the allegations brought against the

---

[235]   Trial Judgement, Vol. 3, paras 577-589.
[236]   Ćorić's Appeal Brief, paras 75, 80. See Ćorić's Appeal Brief, paras 76, 79. See also Appeal Hearing, AT. 579-580 (24 Mar 2017).
[237]   Ćorić's Appeal Brief, para. 80. See Appeal Hearing, AT. 580 (24 Mar 2017).
[238]   Ćorić's Appeal Brief, para. 80. See Ćorić's Reply Brief, para. 26.
[239]   Prosecution's Response Brief (Ćorić), para. 69.
[240]   Ćorić's Reply Brief, para. 26. See Appeal Hearing, AT. 580 (24 Mar 2017). See also Appeal Hearing, AT. 609-611, 626-628 (24 Mar 2017).
[241]   *Kvočka et al.* Appeal Judgement, para. 28. See *supra*, para. 29.
[242]   See *supra*, para. 69.
[243]   Indictment, para. 232.
[244]   Indictment, paras 45-59 (Prozor Municipality), 66-72 (Duša, Hrsanica, Ždrimci, and Uzričje), 73-87 (Sovići and Doljani), 100, 105, 107, 118 (West Mostar), 150 (Ljubuški Municipality), 159, 162, 164-168 (Stolac Municipality), 175, 177, 179-180, 182-183, 185 (Čapljina Municipality), 211, 213 (Vareš Municipality). See Trial Judgement, Vol. 3, paras 577-588.
[245]   Trial Judgement, Vol. 1, para. 91. See Trial Judgement, Vol. 3, para. 569.
[246]   Trial Judgement, Vol. 3, paras 577-589.
[247]   *Contra* Ćorić's Appeal Brief, para. 80.
[248]   To the extent that it can be interpreted that Ćorić argues that there is a legal distinction between "full occupation" and partial occupation, the Appeals Chamber notes that he provides no support for this assertion and will not consider it. See Ćorić's Appeal Brief, para. 80.

Accused Praljak and Petković as commanding officers in a zone of occupation"[249] to be irrelevant to the notice given to Ćorić on the charges against him concerning the state of occupation. In this respect, the Appeals Chamber observes that the Trial Chamber did not find that there was "full occupation" as Ćorić suggests,[250] but rather made this observation in response to Petković's argument at trial that the Prosecution gave no notice of allegations that Praljak and Petković were responsible as commanding officers of an occupied territory in various municipalities in the BiH.[251]

76.   Based on the foregoing, the Appeals Chamber finds that Ćorić has failed to demonstrate that he lacked adequate notice that a state of occupation was alleged and that the Trial Chamber exceeded the scope of the Indictment. Ćorić's sub-ground of appeal 3.2.1 is thus dismissed.

G.   Alleged Errors Regarding Notice of the Protected Status of Muslim HVO Members (Ćorić's Ground 4 in part)

77.   The Trial Chamber found that HVO Muslims, detained by the HVO from 30 June 1993 onwards, had fallen into the hands of the enemy power and were thus persons protected within the meaning of Article 4 of Geneva Convention IV.[252] **[page 33]**

78.   Ćorić argues that the Trial Chamber's holding "overstepped" the Indictment, which purportedly only alleged that the HVO's Muslim members were protected under Additional Protocol I and Common Article 3 of the Geneva Conventions.[253]

79.   The Prosecution argues that the Trial Judgement did not overstep the Indictment, which gave the Appellants sufficient notice of the charges brought under Article 2 of the Statute.[254]

80.   The Appeals Chamber considers that the Indictment provided the Appellants notice of the charges against them under Article 2 of the Statute,[255] and specifically alleged that "[a]ll acts and omissions charged as crimes against persons were committed against or involved persons protected under the Geneva Conventions of 1949 (and the additional protocols thereto) and the laws and customs of war".[256] The Indictment referred clearly to the arrest and detention of "Bosnian Muslim military-aged men (including many who had served in the HVO)"[257] as part of the pattern of the HVO's actions. The Indictment also specified that during the time from 30 June 1993 until mid-July 1993, the HVO conducted mass arrests of Bosnian Muslim men, including Muslim members of the HVO, and detained many of them at Dretelj Prison.[258] Thus, the Indictment gave clear notice to the Appellants that their responsibility covered crimes committed against detained Muslim members of the HVO in contravention of the Geneva Conventions of 1949, which included Geneva Convention IV, and the Additional Protocols thereto.

81.   To the extent that Ćorić argues that the Indictment alleged that detained Muslim members of the HVO were protected only under Additional Protocol I and Common Article 3 of the Geneva Conventions, he fails to support this argument. Ćorić does not refer to any statement in the Indictment or post-Indictment documents which could indicate that allegations were limited to breaches of Additional Protocol I and Common Article 3 of the Geneva Conventions. Further, Ćorić extensively addressed the status of detained Muslim HVO members under Geneva Convention IV at trial.[259] Notably, the Trial Chamber summarised Ćorić's arguments concerning this issue, but nonetheless concluded that detained Muslim members of the

---

[249]   Trial Judgement, Vol. 1, para. 91, referring to, *inter alia*, Indictment, paras 8, 10, 218-228.
[250]   See *supra*, para. 70.
[251]   Trial Judgement, Vol. 1, para. 90.
[252]   Trial Judgement, Vol. 3, para. 611. See Trial Judgement, Vol. 3, paras 591-601.
[253]   Ćorić's Appeal Brief, para. 90. ^
[254]   Prosecution's Response Brief (Ćorić), para. 86.
[255]   Indictment, paras 229, 235-238.
[256]   Indictment, para. 236.
[257]   Indictment, para. 38. See Indictment, para. 39.
[258]   Indictment, para. 189. See Indictment, para. 197.
[259]   Ćorić's Final Brief, paras 352-368.

HVO were protected under Geneva Convention IV as they had fallen into the hands of the enemy power.[260]
[page 34]

82.   Therefore, the Appeals Chamber rejects Ćorić's assertion that the Trial Chamber's finding on the HVO Muslims' protected status under Geneva Convention IV overstepped the Indictment. Ćorić's ground of appeal 4 is dismissed in part.

H.   Alleged Errors Concerning Ćorić's Notice of Allegations Regarding His Responsibility as Minister of the Interior (Ćorić's Ground 11 in part)

83.   The Trial Chamber concluded that on 24 June 1992, at the latest, Ćorić became Chief of the Military Police Administration, where he remained until 10 November 1993, when he was appointed Minister of the Interior of the HR H-B.[261] The Trial Chamber examined Ćorić's powers throughout the Indictment period and found that as Minister of the Interior he had the: (1) ability to participate in fighting crime within the HVO; and (2) power to control the freedom of movement of people and goods in the territory of the HZ(R) H-B, including humanitarian convoys.[262] The Trial Chamber also examined whether, in the exercise of his powers in both positions, Ćorić acted or failed to act resulting in a significant contribution to the achievement of the CCP.[263] In this regard, the Trial Chamber referred to Ćorić's powers as Minister of the Interior once in relation to movement of people and convoys, but subsequently found that regarding this power he only contributed to the CCP through his actions concerning the blockade of the Muslim population of East Mostar and of humanitarian aid until April 1994.[264] The Trial Chamber found that Ćorić remained a member of the JCE after he became Minister of the Interior and continued to carry out important functions supporting the CCP until April 1994.[265] Ćorić appeals against the Trial Chamber's consideration of his powers and actions as Minister of the Interior for lack of notice.

1.   Arguments of the Parties

84.   Ćorić submits that the Trial Chamber erred by considering the exercise of his powers as Minister of the Interior from 10 November 1993 to April 1994 as contributing to the JCE since this was not charged in the Indictment.[266] Ćorić argues that the Trial Chamber erroneously found that the Prosecution could address his responsibility as Minister of the Interior in its final trial brief, as no reasonable trial chamber could conclude that he had adequate notice.[267] In this regard, Ćorić contests the Trial Chamber's interpretation of his reference in his own final trial brief to his power **[page 35]** over civilian police as Minister of the Interior since he was simply comparing a request he issued in that capacity to one he issued as Chief of the Military Police Administration.[268]

85.   Ćorić further submits that the Trial Chamber exceeded the scope of the Indictment and "impermissibly tried to cure pleading deficiencies".[269] Ćorić argues that the Indictment is defective as it failed to specify the material facts concerning allegations for the period after he was appointed Minister of the Interior. These material facts include: (1) his alleged conduct; (2) the crimes committed; and (3) how his actions in this position led to the commission of the crimes.[270] He argues that no appropriate notice was given throughout the trial which would have allowed him to. lead evidence on this issue or to rebut the allegations.[271] Ćorić

---

[260]   Trial Judgement, Vol. 3, paras 593-594, 597, 606-611, referring to, *inter alia,* Ćorić's Final Brief, paras 352-360, 373-375.
[261]   Trial Judgement, Vol. 4, para. 861.
[262]   Trial Judgement, Vol. 4, paras 863-887, 917.
[263]   Trial Judgement, Vol. 4, paras 918-1006.
[264]   Trial Judgement, Vol. 4, paras 939-945, 1003. See Trial Judgement, Vol. 4, paras 919-938, 946-1002, 1004-1005.
[265]   Trial Judgement, Vol. 4, para. 1226.
[266]   Ćorić's Appeal Brief, paras 248, 250, 258.
[267]   Ćorić's Appeal Brief, para. 250. See Ćorić's Appeal Brief, para. 253; Ćorić's Reply Brief, para. 60.
[268]   Ćorić's Appeal Brief, para. 253.
[269]   Ćorić's Appeal Brief, para. 254.
[270]   Ćorić's Appeal Brief, paras 254-255, 257-258. See Ćorić's Reply Brief, para. 57.
[271]   Ćorić's Appeal Brief, para. 256. See Ćorić's Appeal Brief, para. 258; Ćorić's Reply Brief, paras 57-59.

contends that his right to a fair trial was violated as he was hot fully informed of the charges until final briefs and closing arguments.[272]

86.   The Prosecution responds that the Indictment provided Ćorić with clear notice that charges against him encompassed crimes committed after his appointment as Minister of the Interior.[273] It argues that the Indictment specifically mentions Ćorić's position as Minister of the Interior and that, apart from one paragraph which limits his acts to his role as Chief of the Military Police Administration, all other paragraphs speaking to his actions are general and without reference to his specific position.[274] The Prosecution also contends that the Indictment pleaded the material facts, including many which arose after 10 November 1993,[275] as well as the nature of his participation in the JCE which was not limited to the time-period when Ćorić was Chief of the Military Police Administration.[276]

87.   Referring to its pre-trial brief, opening statement, and witness summaries pursuant to Rule 65*ter* of the Rules, the Prosecution submits that Ćorić suffered no prejudice as any perceived defect was cured through timely, clear, and consistent notice of the case against him.[277] The Prosecution also contends that as Ćorić never objected to evidence being led at trial concerning his role as Minister of the Interior, he must now demonstrate that his ability to prepare his defence was **[page 36]** materially impaired.[278] It argues that Ćorić fails to meet this burden as he presented a defence concerning his actions as Minister of the Interior.[279] The Prosecution further responds that the Trial Chamber did not misconstrue Ćorić's arguments in his final brief and was not seeking "to cure a pleading deficiency".[280]

88.   Ćorić replies that as soon as he had notice of the defect in the Indictment, he raised it before the Trial Chamber, which erred in its assessment of the matter. He argues, therefore, that the burden is with the Prosecution to prove that his ability to prepare his defence was not materially impaired.[281]

2.   Analysis

89.   In order to determine whether the Trial Chamber erred in considering Ćorić's powers and actions as Minister of the Interior, the Appeals Chamber will assess whether: (1) the Indictment was defective in this regard; (2) any defect was curable and, if so, whether it was cured; and (3) Ćorić suffered any prejudice.

(a) Whether the Indictment was defective

90.   The Appeals Chamber notes that at trial Ćorić submitted that the Prosecution alleged his responsibility as Minister of the Interior for the first time in its final brief and closing arguments.[282] The Trial Chamber – relying on, *inter alia,* paragraphs 12 and 17.5(b)-(n) of the Indictment – considered that the Prosecution could do so as allegations of Ćorić's responsibility in the Indictment were not limited to the time-period when he was Chief of the Military Police Administration.[283] The Appeals Chamber will first consider whether the Trial Chamber erred in its consideration of this issue.

---

[272]   Ćorić's Appeal Brief, para. 258. See Ćorić's Appeal Brief, para. 256; Ćorić's Reply Brief, para. 58.
[273]   Prosecution's Response Brief (Ćorić), paras 272, 275, 279, 285.
[274]   Prosecution's Response Brief (Ćorić), paras 276-277, referring to, *inter alia,* Indictment, paras 11-12, 15, 17.5(a)-(n).
[275]   Prosecution's Response Brief (Ćorić), paras 276-277, referring to, *inter alia,* Indictment, paras 60, 118, 135, 143, 153, 203. The Prosecution also argues that several paragraphs of the Indictment detail allegations which continued after November 1993. Prosecution's Response Brief (Ćorić), para. 277 & fn. 1044.
[276]   Prosecution's Response Brief (Ćorić), para. 278.
[277]   Prosecution's Response Brief (Ćorić), paras 272, 280.
[278]   Prosecution's Response Brief (Ćorić), paras 273, 281-283. According to the Prosecution, Ćorić's failure to object also amounts to waiver. Prosecution's Response Brief (Ćorić), para. 282.
[279]   Prosecution's Response Brief (Ćorić), para. 283.
[280]   Prosecution's Response Brief (Ćorić), para. 284.
[281]   Ćorić's Reply Brief, para. 60.
[282]   Trial Judgement, Vol. 4, para. 863, fn. 1595.
[283]   Trial Judgement, Vol. 4, para. 863, fn. 1597, referring to Indictment, paras 12, 17.5(a)-(n).

91.   The Appeals Chamber recalls that when the Prosecution alleges JCE liability in an indictment, it must plead, among other material facts, the nature of the accused's participation in the joint criminal enterprise.[284] The Appeals Chamber recalls the distinction between the material facts upon which the Prosecution relies, which must be pleaded in an indictment, and the evidence by **[page 37]** which those material facts will be proved, which need not be pleaded.[285] A decisive factor in determining the degree of specificity with which the Prosecution is required to particularise the facts of its case in the indictment is the nature of the alleged criminal conduct of the accused.[286] The Appeals Chamber further recalls that in determining whether an accused was adequately put on notice of the nature and cause of the charges against him, the indictment must be considered as a whole.[287]

92.   The Appeals Chamber considers that since a large component of the case against Ćorić concerned the exercise of his powers and functions – both in relation to JCE liability and superior responsibility[288] – facts concerning his acts and conduct after the change of an official position should have been clearly pleaded in the Indictment as material facts.[289] The Appeals Chamber will now consider whether the Indictment sufficiently pleaded Ćorić's role as Minister of the Interior as material facts.

93.   The Appeals Chamber notes that Ćorić was generally alleged to have participated in the JCE by, *inter alia,* acting through his "positions and power",[290] but the sole mention of Ćorić's position as Minister of the Interior is found in paragraph 11 of the Indictment. In this regard, paragraph 11 of the Indictment only states that "[i]n November 1993, [Ćorić] was appointed Minister of Interior in the Croatian Republic of Herceg-Bosna".[291] The Appeals Chamber also notes that the Trial Chamber relied on paragraphs 17.5(a)-(n), which set out Ćorić's acts and conduct by which he participated in the JCE, to state that his position was not specified except in paragraph 17.5(a).[292] This paragraph refers to Ćorić as Chief of the Military Police Administration.[293] Further, while the Indictment states that Ćorić was a member of the JCE, which was alleged to be in existence from on or before 18 November 1991 to about April 1994,[294] it is not apparent whether his contributions to the JCE spanned this entire time-period.[295] Thus, while the Indictment clearly alleges that Ćorić's **[page 38]** JCE acts and conduct stemmed from his position as Chief of the Military Pohce Administration, it is unclear whether his conduct as Minister of the Interior was also pleaded in this respect.

94.   Moreover, the Appeals Chamber notes that paragraph 12 of the Indictment states that "[i]n his various positions and functions, [Ćorić], *from at least April 1992 to November 1993,* played a central role in the establishment, administration and operation of the HVO Military Police",[296] before setting out his control and influence over the Military Police. The Appeals Chamber considers that this paragraph is limited to Ćorić's powers or functions as Chief of the Military Police Administration. This conclusion is based on the limited time-frame stated ("to November 1993") and the explicit mention of his role regarding the Military

---

[284]   *Popović et al.* Appeal Judgement, paras 47, 58; *Šainović et al.* Appeal Judgement, para. 214; *Simić* Appeal Judgement, para. 22; *Karemera and Ngirumpatse* Appeal Judgement, para. 105.

[285]   *Popović et al.* Appeal Judgement, para. 47; *Blaškić* Appeal Judgement, para. 210. See *Đorđević* Appeal Judgement, para. 331; *Šainović et al.* Appeal Judgement, para. 213; *Nzabonimana* Appeal Judgement, para. 29.

[286]   *Popović et al.* Appeal Judgement, para. 65; *Krnojelac* Appeal Judgement, para. 132; *Bagosora and Nsengiywnva* Appeal Judgement, para. 132. See *Đorđević* Appeal Judgement, para. 575.

[287]   See, *e.g., Nyiramasuhuko et al.* Appeal Judgement, paras 1263, 2512. See also *supra,* para. 27.

[288]   Indictment, paras 12, 17, 17.5, 218-223, 228. See Trial Judgement, Vol. 4, paras 854-855, 915-918, 1000-1006, 1247-1251.

[289]   *Cf. Šainović et al.* Appeal Judgement, paras 214-215.

[290]   Indictment, para. 17.

[291]   Indictment, para. 11.

[292]   Trial Judgement, Vol. 4, para. 863, fn. 1597, referring to Indictment, paras 12, 17.5(a)-(n).

[293]   Trial Judgement, Vol. 4, fn. 1597. While other passages in the Indictment could be interpreted as referring to bodies under Ćorić's authority as Minister of the Interior, the Appeals Chamber considers them to be vague as they relate to Ćorić's alleged responsibility for his conduct as Minister of the Interior. See Indictment, paras 17.5(b), 25. See also Trial Judgement, Vol. 1, para. 652, Vol. 4, para. 883.

[294]   Indictment, para. 15.

[295]   Indictment, paras 17, 17.5. The Indictment alleged that crimes continued to be committed after 10 November 1993 and generally state that Ćorić was responsible. The Appeals Chamber, though, notes that this is ambiguous regarding whether Ćorić's alleged responsibility arose *before* 10 November 1993 or throughout the Indictment period. See Indictment, paras 35, 37, 54, 59-60, 117-119, 128, 135-136, 143, 148, 153, 188, 194, 196, 203.

[296]   Indictment, para. 12 (emphasis added).

Police.[297] Based on the generality of the remaining relevant paragraphs of the Indictment,[298] the Appeals Chamber finds that paragraph 12 of the Indictment would lead Ćorić to understand that the Prosecution's case against him, as set out in the Indictment, based on the exercise of his powers and functions was confined to his acts and conduct as Chief of the Military Police Administration. The Appeals Chamber therefore finds that the Indictment itself did not provide clear notice to Ćorić that his alleged responsibility extended to his acts and conduct as Minister of the Interior between 10 November 1993 and April 1994.

95.   In light of the above, the Appeals Chamber finds that the ambiguous nature of the Indictment on Ćorić's alleged responsibility for crimes committed based on the exercise of his powers and functions as well as his control over the peipetrators as Minister of the Interior renders the Indictment vague and defective.[299] However, the Appeals Chamber considers that this defect is curable as the allegations of Ćorić's acts and conduct as Minister of the Interior do not constitute a new charge but fell within the broader allegations on bis authority over and use of the perpetrators of crimes. In this regard, the Appeals Chamber notes that the Prosecution's case against Ćorić primarily concerned: (1) his authority over the perpetrators of crimes; (2) his knowledge of crimes; (3) his failure to prevent crimes or punish the perpetrators as well his use of them, particularly, the Military Police; and (4) his control over checkpoints and the provision of humanitarian assistance **[page 39]** and public services.[300] These factors then formed the basis of Ćorić's responsibility as a JCE member and the crimes committed as charged under the relevant Counts of the Indictment. Notably, the Trial Chamber discussed his role and actions as Minister of the Interior in relation to his communications with the Military Police Administration,[301] his power to control the freedom of movement of people and goods, including humanitarian convoys,[302] and his ability to participate in fighting crime.[303] Thus, the material facts concerning Ćorić's acts and conduct as Minister of the Interior do not, on their own, support separate charges.[304] The Appeals Chamber will now consider whether this defect has been subsequently cured.

(b) Whether the defect in the Indictment was cured

96.   The Appeals Chamber recalls that the omission of a material fact underpinning a charge in the indictment can, in certain cases, be cured by the provision of timely, clear and consistent information detailing the factual basis underpinning the charges.[305] This can be done in post-indictment documents such as the pre-trial briefs, Rule 65*ter* witness summaries, as well as in opening statements.[306]

97.   In its pre-trial brief, the Prosecution provides no clear notice to Ćorić that his alleged responsibility extended to his acts and conduct as Minister of the Interior, as its references relate to the time-period when Ćorić was Chief of the Military Police Administration.[307] Likewise, the Prosecution's opening statement does not make it apparent that the allegations against Ćorić extended beyond 10 November 1993.[308] The Appeals Chamber also notes that the Prosecution's Rule 65*ter* witness summaries did not provide clear

---

[297]   The Appeals Chamber further considers that the phrase "his various positions", read in light of the remainder of paragraph 12 of the Indictment as well as the allegations that most of the Appellants acted in accordance with their "various positions and functions", to be at best ambiguous. See Indictment, paras 8, 10, 12, 14.
[298]   See *supra*, para. 93. Notably, the Indictment does not set out his functions and powers as Minister of the Interior. *Cf.* Indictment, para. 12.
[299]   The Appeals Chamber recalls that an indictment which fails to set forth the specific material facts underpinning the charges against the accused is defective. *Popović et al.* Appeal Judgement, para. 65; *Đorđević* Appeal Judgement, paras 574, 576; *Karemera and Ngirumpatse* Appeal Judgement, para. 371.
[300]   See Trial Judgement, Vol. 4, paras 854-855, referring to Indictment, paras 17, 17.5(a), 17.5(d), 17.5(g)-(l), 17.5(n), Prosecution's Final Brief, paras 981-1175.
[301]   Trial Judgement, Vol. 4, para. 872. See *supra*, para. 83; *infra*, para. 103
[302]   Trial Judgement, Vol. 4, paras 886-887. See *supra*, para. 83; *infra*, para. 103.
[303]   Trial Judgement, Vol. 4, para. 883. See *supra*, para. 83; *infra*, para. 103.
[304]   See *Đorđević* Appeal Judgement, para. 575; *Nyiramasuhuko et al.* Appeal Judgement, para. 2785.
[305]   *Popović et al.* Appeal Judgement, para. 66; *Šainović et al.* Appeal Judgement, para. 262; *Karemera and Ngirumpatse* Appeal Judgement, para. 371; *Bizimungu* Appeal Judgement, para. 46.
[306]   See *Đorđević* Appeal Judgement, para. 574, and references cited therein. See also *Šainović et al.* Appeal Judgement, para. 263; *Ndindiliyimana et al.* Appeal Judgement, paras 187-189.
[307]   See Prosecution's Pre-Trial Brief, paras 146.5, 189.2, 189.4, 196.2, fns 49-56, 287.
[308]   See Prosecution Opening Statement, T. 880-881 (26 Apr 2006) (The Prosecution summarised Ćorić's functions and powers as Chief of the Military Police Administration and stated that "he continued in this position until approximately the 20th of

information on this issue.[309] The Prosecution refers to the Rule 65*ter* witness summary of Marijan Biškić to support its argument that it provided notice.[310] However, the Appeals Chamber notes that while the summary of Biškić's evidence speaks **[page 40]** to events occurring between 6 November 1993 and December 1993,[311] this information did not provide Ćorić with adequate notice that his alleged responsibility also covered the period after 10 November 1993 when he was appointed Minister of the Interior.[312] Notably, any specific reference to Ćorić in the witness summaries relates to his position as Chief of the Military Police Administration.[313]

98.   The Appeals Chamber will now address Ćorić's challenge to the Trial Chamber's use of a reference in his final brief to his capacity as Minister of the Interior as support for its conclusion that his powers as Minister of the Interior could be considered.[314] In this regard, the Trial Chamber noted that Ćorić raised the issue of his power over the civilian police in his capacity as Minister of the Interior in his final brief.[315] Notably, the single reference in Ćorić's Final Brief cited by the Trial Chamber speaks to Ćorić issuing a request to the civilian police, which, he argued, showed his lack of criminal intent and genuine belief that he was participating in legitimate practices to enforce the law and prevent crimes.[316] Thus, the context of this reference does not clearly support a conclusion that Ćorić was aware that his acts and conduct as Minister of the Interior were alleged to be part of his JCE contribution. While an accused's understanding of the nature of the Prosecution's case can also be observed in their final trial briefs and closing arguments,[317] the Appeals Chamber finds that the Trial Chamber erred in considering the reference in paragraph 221 of Ćorić's Final Brief to his position as Minister of the Interior as support for its conclusion that the Prosecution could present allegations on Ćorić's responsibility in this capacity.

99.   The Appeals Chamber thus finds that the defect in the Indictment was not subsequently cured through post-Indictment disclosures. The Appeals Chamber will now consider whether Ćorić suffered any prejudice as a result.

(c) Whether Ćorić suffered any prejudice

100.   The Appeals Chamber recalls that a defective indictment which has not been cured causes prejudice to the accused. The defect may only be deemed harmless through a demonstration that the **[page 41]** accused's ability to prepare his or her defence was not materially impaired.[318] Where an accused has previously raised the issue of lack of notice before the Trial Chamber, the burden rests on the Prosecution to prove on appeal that the ability of the accused to prepare his defence was not materially impaired.[319] However, "[i]n the case of objections based on lack of notice, the Defence must challenge the admissibility of evidence of material facts not pleaded in the indictment by interposing a specific objection at the time the evidence is introduced".[320] The Appeals Chamber also recalls that "where the Trial Chamber has treated a challenge to

---

November of 1993, at which time he was appointed the minister of interior [...]"). The Prosecution did not elaborate on Ćorić's functions and powers as Minister of the Interior and all mention of Ćorić's acts relate to the time-period before this appointment.

[309]   See Prosecution's List of *Viva Voce* Witnesses; Prosecution's List of Rule 92 *bis* Witnesses.

[310]   Prosecution's Response Brief (Ćorić), para. 280.

[311]   Prosecution's List of *Viva Voce* Witnesses, pp. 38-39.

[312]   The Appeals Chamber notes that this conclusion relates to various witness summaries. See, *e.g.*, Prosecution's List of *Viva Voce* Witnesses, pp. 32-34, 255, 339-343; Prosecution's List of Rule 92 *bis* Witnesses, pp. 98-99.

[313]   See, *e.g.*, Prosecution's List of *Viva Voce* Witnesses, pp. 23-24, 49-53, 81-83, 271-272, 311-314, 331-339.

[314]   See *supra*, para. 84.

[315]   Trial Judgement, Vol. 4, para. 863, referring to Ćorić's Final Brief, para. 211.

[316]   Ćorić's Final Brief, paras 210-212.

[317]   *Kvočka et al.* Appeal Judgement, para. 53. See *Naletilić and Martinović* Appeal Judgement, para. 27 ("an accused's submissions at trial, for example the motion for judgement of acquittal, final trial brief or closing arguments, may in some instances assist in assessing to what extent the accused was put on notice of the Prosecution's case and was able to respond to the Prosecution's allegations").

[318]   *Popović et al.* Appeal Judgement, para. 66; *Šainović et al.* Appeal Judgement, para. 262; *Renzaho* Appeal Judgement, para. 125. See *Đorđević* Appeal Judgement, para. 576; *Nyiramasuhuko et al.* Appeal Judgement, para. 2738.

[319]   See, *e.g.*, *Nyiramasuhuko et al.* Appeal Judgement, paras 1105, 2738; *Nzabonimana* Appeal Judgement, para. 30; *Ntabakuze* Appeal Judgement, fn. 189; *Niyitegeka* Appeal Judgement, para. 200; *Kupreškic et al.* Appeal Judgement, paras 122, 123.

[320]   *Niyitegeka* Appeal Judgement, para. 199. See *Gacumbitsi* Appeal Judgement, para. 51; *Ndindiliyimana et al.* Appeal Judgement, paras 196, 230.

an indictment as being adequately raised, the Appeals Chamber should not invoke the waiver doctrine".[321] When, however, the accused raises indictment defects for the first time on appeal, the burden of proof shifts from the Prosecution to the Defence who is then required to demonstrate the existence of the said prejudice.[322]

101. The Appeals Chamber notes that the Trial Chamber considered that "in its Closing Arguments, the Ćorić Defence criticised the Prosecution for having raised the issue of Valentin Ćorić's responsibility as Minister of the Interior for the first time in its Final Brief and its Closing Arguments".[323] The Trial Chamber concluded that the Prosecution could do so.[324] As Ćorić raised the issue in his closing arguments and the Trial Chamber addressed his claim without considering it untimely, the Appeals Chamber considers that the burden of proof rests with the Prosecution to demonstrate Ćorić's ability to prepare his defence was not materially impaired.

102. The Prosecution argues that Ćorić never objected to the evidence it led on his role as Minister of the Interior and that Ćorić, in fact, presented a defence concerning his actions in this position.[325] The Prosecution relies on Ćorić's submission on his power over the civilian police in his capacity as Minister of the Interior in his final brief.[326] As noted above, this reference speaks to Ćorić issuing a request to the civilian police which, he argued, showed his lack of criminal intent and genuine belief that he was participating in legitimate practices to enforce the law and prevent **[page 42]** crimes.[327] In making this submission, Ćorić relied on the Prosecution's evidence – Exhibit P06837 – which the Trial Chamber also considered when discussing Prlić's powers. In this regard, the Trial Chamber noted that Ćorić informed Mate Boban, Prlić, and others on 28 November 1993 that he planned on implementing a Government decision that active police be replaced by HVO reserve units on the front lines.[328]

103. The Appeals Chamber recalls that Ćorić's only submission in his final trial brief and closing arguments at trial on his role as Minister of the Interior was limited to showing his lack of criminal intent as it concerns one issue.[329] Thus, the Appeals Chamber is not convinced that the Prosecution has shown on appeal that this trial submission is sufficient to show that Ćorić mounted a defence to allegations on his responsibility as Minister of the Interior.

104. Moreover, in its conclusions on Ćorić's JCE I and JCE III responsibilities,[330] the Trial Chamber's only express reference to the exercise of his powers as Minister of the Interior or events after 10 November 1993 concerned his power to control the freedom of movement of people and goods, including the movement of humanitarian convoys, until April 1994 – particularly by way of HVO checkpoints.[331] In this regard, the Trial

---

[321]   *Gacumbitsi* Appeal Judgement, para. 54, referring to *Ntakirutimana* Appeal Judgement, para. 23.

[322]   *Đorđević* Appeal Judgement, para. 573; *Šainović et al.* Appeal Judgement, paras 223-224. See *Nyiramasuhuko et al.* Appeal Judgement, para. 2738.

[323]   Trial Judgement, Vol. 4, para. 863, fn. 1595, referring to Ćorić› Closing Arguments, T(F). 52639-52640 (22 Feb 2011). See Ćorić› Closing Arguments, T. 52636 (22 Feb 2011).

[324]   Trial Judgement, Vol. 4, para. 863, fn. 1597, referring to Indictment, paras 12, 17.5(a)-(n).

[325]   Prosecution's Response Brief (Ćorić), paras 281, 283-285.

[326]   Prosecution's Response Brief (Ćorić), paras 283-284, referring to Ćorić's Final Brief, paras 210-211. See *supra*, para. 98.

[327]   Ćorić's Final Brief, paras 210-212, referring to Ex. P06837, p. 1. See *supra*, para. 98.

[328]   Trial Judgement, Vol. 4, para. 110, referring to Ex. P06837 (discussing Prlić's powers in military matters, but providing no indication that this evidence was considered in relation to Ćorić's responsibilities).

[329]   See *supra*, paras 98, 102.

[330]   The Appeals Chamber also notes that Ćorić's only conviction for superior responsibility stemmed from events in Prozor in October 1992, and thus, is irrelevant to this discussion. See Trial Judgement, Vol. 4, paras 1245-1251.

[331]   Trial Judgement, Vol. 4, para. 1003. See Trial Judgement, Vol. 4, paras 886-887, 1000-1002, 1004-1006, 1008-1020. Notably, in analysing Ćorić's powers, contributions, and knowledge in relation to the JCE, the Trial Chamber referred to his role and actions as Minister of the Interior after 10 November 1993 in the following circumstances by noting that he: (1) that he received daily bulletins compiled by the Military Police Administration but there was no evidence that he still retained some power over the Military Police units subordinated to the HVO (Trial Judgement, Vol. 4, para. 872, referring to Marijan Biškić, T(F). 15054-15056 (5 Mar 2007), Ex. P06722, pp. 6-7 (tendered through Marijan Biškić). See Marijan Biškić, T. 15054-15056 (5 Mar 2007)); and (2) that he had the ability to participate in fighting crimes until at least February 1994 as he participated in several meetings about the security situation in the HR H-B territory until that time, and as he was instructed to work with the Minister of Defence to improve collaboration between the civilian police and the Military Police. Trial Judgement, Vol. 4, para. 883, referring to Ex. P07850, Marijan Biškić, T(F). 15063, 15073-15074 (5 Mar 2007); See Marijan Biškić, T. 15060-15063, 15073-15074 (5 Mar 2007). The Appeals Chamber notes that in finding that Ćorić had the ability to fight crime as Minister of the Interior, the Trial Chamber relied on Prosecution Witness Marijan Biškić, who was cross-examined by the Ćorić Defence and Ćorić himself on the co-operation between

Chamber primarily considered the evidence of Defence Witness Martin Raguž, head of the Office for Displaced Persons and Refugees ("ODPR"), that he asked Ćorić on 31 January 1994 for assistance in providing an escort for a convoy transporting a field hospital to a checkpoint.[332] Notably, the Ćorić Defence did not cross-examine this witness despite this evidence.[333] The fact that Ćorić did not call any witness or make any **[page 43]** attempt at trial to refute any allegation concerning his power – as Minister of the Interior – to control the freedom of movement of people and goods, including the movement of humanitarian convoys, demonstrates his lack of preparation to address this issue. Thus, Ćorić did not mount a defence on this power as Minister of the Interior as his ability to defend against the allegations on this power was materially impaired due to a lack of notice. The exercise of this power was eventually considered to be part of Ćorić's significant contribution to the JCE, and in fact, his only explicit contribution to the JCE after 10 November 1993.[334] Therefore, Ćorić suffered prejudice in this regard.

105.   Based on the foregoing, the Appeals Chamber finds that the Prosecution has failed to demonstrate that Ćorić's defence was not materially impaired in relation to his role in the JCE as Minister of the Interior, thus, it has not met its burden on appeal. Considering the prejudice suffered by Ćorić, the Appeals Chamber grants his ground of appeal 11 in part, reverses the Trial Chamber's findings on his role in the JCE as Minister of the Interior as of 10 November 1993, and vacates his convictions in relation to his JCE responsibility as Minister of the Interior. The impact, if any, on Ćorić's sentence will be addressed in the relevant sections below.[335]

I.   Conclusion

106.   The Appeals Chamber has granted Ćorić's ground of appeal 11 in part, and dismissed all other challenges relating to the fair trial rights of the Appellants and the Indictment covered in the present chapter. **[page 44]**

IV.   ADMISSIBILITY AND WEIGHT OF THE EVIDENCE

A.   Introduction

107.   Prlić, Stojić, Praljak, and Ćorić challenge various decisions by the Trial Chamber to admit evidence (documentary and testimonial) or to deny admission of evidence. They further challenge the Trial Chamber's evaluation of the evidence, purportedly resulting in erroneous findings.

B.   The Mladić Diaries (Prlić's Ground 5, Stojić's Ground 16, Praljak's Ground 50)

1.   Introduction

108.   On 6 October 2010, the Trial Chamber, by majority, partially granted the Prosecution's request to reopen its case on the basis of the discovery of Ratko Mladić's diaries ("Mladić Diaries"), admitting eight of the 18 tendered documents, including four excerpts from the diaries.[336] On 23, 24, and 25 November 2010,

---

Military Police stations and the Ministry of the Interior. Marijan Biškić, T. 15061-15063, 15072-15074, 15256-15311, 15309-15310 (7 Mar 2007).

[332]   Trial Judgement, Vol. 4, para. 886, referring to Martin Raguž, T(F). 31339 (26 Aug 2008), Ex. 1D02182. See Trial Judgement, Vol. 1, para. 635, referring to Martin Raguž, T(F). 31353-31355 (26 Aug 2008), Exs. 1D02025, Art. 1, P05926, p. 2.

[333]   Martin Raguž, T. 31414 (26 Aug 2008). The Appeals Chamber also notes that Raguž was called as a witness by Prlić.

[334]   See Trial Judgement, Vol. 4, paras 918-1004. *Cf* Trial Judgement, Vol. 4, paras 934 (the evidence showed "that from at least mid-June 1993, Valentin Ćorić was aware that members of the HVO were committing crimes during the eviction operations in Mostar. By avoiding to take measures against those HVO members, Valentin Ćorić facilitated and encouraged the commission of crimes which continued until February 1994"), 1000 (Ćorić "as Chief of the HVO Military Police Administration [...] while having the duty to fight crime [...] knowingly turned a blind eye to crimes perpetrated by the HVO members against Muslims in West Mostar during eviction operations [...] which continued to be carried out with impunity until September 1993").

[335]   See *infra*, para. 3364.

[336]   *Prlić et al.* Trial Decision on Reopening the Prosecution's Case, para. 1, pp. 28-29 (Disposition). The Trial Chamber admitted Exhibits P11376, P11377, P11380, P11386, P11388, P11389, P11391, andP11392, of which the following are diary entries: Exhibits P11376, P11380, P11386, and P11389. *Prlić et al.* Trial Decision on Reopening the Prosecution's Case, fn. 1, p. 28 (Disposition).

the Trial Chamber denied Prlić's, Praljak's, and Stojić's requests for reopening their cases to admit evidence, and partially granted Petković's request.[337]

109.   Prlić, Stojić, and Praljak challenge the Trial Chamber's: (1) admission into evidence of extracts of the Mladić Diaries in a reopening of the Prosecution's case; (2) decisions to deny Defence requests to reopen their cases and to present evidence in rebuttal; and/or (3) assessment of the evidence from the Mladić Diaries. The Prosecution responds that their arguments should be dismissed.

2.   Arguments of the Parties

(a) Prlić's, Stojić's, and Praljak's submissions

110.   Prlić and Praljak submit that the Trial Chamber erred in admitting and relying on evidence from the Mladić Diaries, while denying them the opportunity to tender evidence in response.[338] **[page 45]**

Praljak argues that the Trial Chamber did not establish exceptional circumstances justifying the admission of the diaries and did not properly consider the prejudice to the Appellants in admitting the evidence at a late stage of the trial proceedings.[339] Praljak further argues that the Trial Chamber did not properly establish the authenticity of the diaries as it: (1) declined a graphological analysis of the diaries; (2) improperly relied on a decision of another trial chamber; and (3) did not sufficiently establish the circumstances in which the diaries were written.[340]

111.   Prlić argues that the Trial Chamber erred in finding that he was not diligent in requesting to reopen his defence case, considering that: (1) he had filed a notice of intent to reopen his case conditioned on the reopening of the Prosecution's case; (2) only once the Trial Chamber had decided on whether to grant the Prosecution's request to reopen the case could he make an informed decision about whether to reopen his own case; and (3) it is the Prosecution that bears the burden of proof.[341] Prlić argues that the Trial Chamber also erred in denying, without a reasoned opinion, admission of evidence, including additional excerpts from the Mladić Diaries, that he presented in rebuttal to the Prosecution's new evidence, even though: (1) the documents met the Trial Chamber's criteria for rebuttal; (2) they were relevant as recognised in large part by at least one of the Judges; and (3) the Prosecution had no objection to many of the tendered diary entries.[342] Specifically with regard to documents 1D03193 and 1D03194, Prlić argues that he became aware of their significance after the admission of the Prosecution's entries from the Mladić Diaries, and that the Trial Chamber admitted Prosecution documents on the same basis.[343]

---

[337]   *Prlić et al.* Trial Decision on Reopening Praljak's Case; *Prlić et al.* Trial Decision on Reopening Petković's Case; *Prlić et al.* Trial Decision on Prlić's Motion to Admit Evidence in Rebuttal; *Prlić et al.* Trial Decision on Reopening Stojić's Case. In reopening Petković's case, the Trial Chamber admitted into evidence three excerpts of the Mladić Diaries. *Prlić et al.* Trial Decision on Reopening Petković's Case, para. 1 & fn. 1, paras 22-23, p. 11 (Disposition).

[338]   Prlić's Appeal Brief, paras 160-161, 165, 168, 174-176; Prlić's Reply Brief, para. 51; Praljak's Appeal Brief, paras 545-546, 549, 559, 562, 565; Praljak's Reply Brief, para. 125; Appeal Hearing, AT. 170-171, 173 (20 Mar 2017); AT. 472-473 (22 Mar 2017); AT. 796 (28 Mar 2017). See also Stojić's Appeal Brief, heading before para. 127, para. 129. Prlić and Praljak submit in this regard that the Trial Chamber applied a double standard in the admission of evidence. Prlić's Appeal Brief, para. 174; Praljak's Reply Brief, paras 119-120. See also Prlić's Appeal Brief, para. 164; Prlić's Reply Brief, para. 51. Prlić and Praljak contend that by denying the reopening of their cases, the Trial Chamber violated their rights to equality of arms, to confrontation, to present an effective defence, and/or to a fair trial. Prlić's Appeal Brief, paras 160, 163, 174-175; Praljak's Appeal Brief, paras 548, 559-562, 565. See also Stojić's Appeal Brief, para. 129.

[339]   Praljak's Appeal Brief, para. 547; Appeal Hearing, AT. 472-473 (22 Mar 2017). See Praljak's Appeal Brief, paras 557, 565.

[340]   Praljak's Appeal Brief, paras 550-552; Appeal Hearing, AT. 472 (22 Mar 2017). Stojić alleges that the Trial Chamber did not give proper consideration to the authenticity of the Mladić Diaries. Stojić's Appeal Brief, heading before para. 127.

[341]   Prlić's Appeal Brief, paras 161-163; Prlić's Reply Brief, para. 51; Appeal Hearing, AT. 171 (20 Mar 2017). See also Prlić's Appeal Brief, para. 165. Prlić further submits that "there was a lack of clarity on a host of issues related to the Mladić Diaries". Prlić's Appeal Brief, para. 162.

[342]   Prlić's Appeal Brief, paras 160-161, 163-164, 166, 174-175; Prlić's Reply Brief, para. 51; Appeal Hearing, AT. 171 (20 Mar 2017); AT. 796 (28 Mar 2017).

[343]   Prlić's Appeal Brief, para. 164. See also Prlić's Appeal Brief, para. 166.

112.   Praljak submits that the Trial Chamber erred by denying him the opportunity to challenge entries of the Mladić Diaries that dealt with his own acts and conduct.[344] Prlić and Praljak argue that in denying Praljak's request to reopen his case, the Trial Chamber conceived of Praljak's Counsel's submissions in his final brief and closing arguments as a substitute for Praljak's *viva voce* **[page 46]** testimony, thereby wrongly conflating evidence and submissions.[345] Prlić argues that by denying Praljak's request to testify, the Trial Chamber denied Prlić his right to confront Praljak in cross-examination to test the uncorroborated hearsay statements attributed to Praljak in the Mladić Diaries.[346] Praljak argues that the Trial Chamber incorrectly found that the material he tendered aimed to refute allegations that did not fall within the scope of the motions to reopen the case, as it proceeded to use the Mladić Diaries to prove those same allegations in the Trial Judgement.[347] Finally, Stojić submits that the Trial Chamber wrongly denied his application to reopen his case, thereby depriving him of an opportunity to challenge the Mladić Diaries.[348]

113.   Praljak contends that the Trial Chamber did not apply to the Mladić Diaries the principles it announced it would apply to documentary evidence, evidence not subjected to adversarial argument in court, and hearsay evidence.[349] Praljak argues that the Trial Chamber failed to provide a reasoned opinion on the probative value of the Mladić Diaries and their impact on its findings, despite basing key findings regarding the existence of the JCE and the Appellants' role in it solely on these diaries.[350] Prlić also argues that the Trial Chamber assessed two entries from the Mladić Diaries (Exhibits P11376 and P11380) without the context of other evidence and the material that was denied admission.[351] He submits that it thereby failed to consider "alternative explanations" for these two entries and that it drew unsustainable conclusions regarding his membership and participation in a JCE.[352]

114.   Stojić submits that in finding that no later than October 1992 he knew that the implementation of the CCP would involve the Muslim population moving outside the territory of the Croatian Community of Herceg-Bosna ("HZ H-B"), the Trial Chamber erred in law and fact and **[page 47]** failed to give a reasoned opinion by failing to consider contradicting evidence and defence arguments.[353] He further submits that the Trial Chamber erred in law and violated his right to a fair trial by basing this finding solely on alleged extracts of the Mladić Diaries, which constituted uncorroborated and untested hearsay.[354] According to him,

---

[344]   Praljak's Appeal Brief, paras 548, 563; Praljak's Reply Brief, para. 119; Appeal Hearing, AT. 472-473 (22 Mar 2017). Praljak adds that the Mladić Diaries were not available when he previously testified. Praljak's Appeal Brief, para. 563; Praljak's Reply Brief, para. 119.

[345]   Prlić's Appeal Brief, para. 167; Praljak's Appeal Brief, para. 563; Appeal Hearing, AT. 171-172 (20 Mar 2017); AT. 472 (22 Mar 2017). See Prlić's Appeal Brief, para. 161; Prlić's Reply Brief, para. 51. Prlić also submits that the Trial Chamber denied without a reasoned opinion Praljak's request for certification to appeal the decision on the request to reopen his case. Prlić's Appeal Brief, para. 167. See also Prlić's Appeal Brief, para. 161.

[346]   Prlić's Appeal Brief, paras 160-161; Prlić's Reply Brief, para. 51; Appeal Hearing, AT. 172 (20 Mar 2017). See Prlić's Appeal Brief, para. 167.

[347]   Praljak's Appeal Brief, para. 564; Appeal Hearing, AT. 472-473 (22 Mar 2017).

[348]   Stojić's Appeal Brief, heading before para. 127, para. 129; Appeal Hearing, AT. 284-285 (21 Mar 2017).

[349]   Praljak's Appeal Brief, paras 553-556; Appeal Hearing, AT. 472 (22 Mar 2017).

[350]   Praljak's Appeal Brief, paras 553, 557-558; Appeal Hearing, AT. 472-473 (22 Mar 2017). Praljak argues that the Trial Chamber was obliged to provide a reasoned opinion on this because: (1) these documents were admitted at a very late stage of the trial; (2) the Accused strongly opposed their admission; and (3) they contested, *inter alia,* their authenticity. Praljak's Appeal Brief, para. 557. See also Praljak's Appeal Brief, para. 558.

[351]   Prlić's Appeal Brief, paras 160, 168, 172-174, 176; Prlić's Reply Brief, para. 51.

[352]   Prlić's Appeal Brief, paras 160, 168-174, 176; Prlić's Reply Brief, para. 51. See Prlić's Appeal Brief, para. 167. As for Exhibit P11376, Prlić claims that the meeting discussed in the diary entry was about pressing issues, such as the exchange of prisoners, the shelling of Slavonski Brod, the conflict around Jajce in BiH and implications for the electricity supply, the need for international involvement, and not about Prlić discussing the partition of BiH to re-establish the 1939 Banovina. Prlić's Appeal Brief, para. 169. According to Prlić, Exhibit P11380 records his remark at a follow-up meeting, made in light of the developments around Jajce, that he considered further discussions with the Serbian side to be futile if there was no intention to respect agreements reached, implying that the meeting was not about the division of BiH. Prlić's Appeal Brief, paras 170-176.

[353]   Stojić's Appeal Brief, heading before para. 127, paras 127, 132. See Stojić's Appeal Brief, para. 130.

[354]   Stojić's Appeal Brief, heading before para. 127, paras 127-129, 131-132; Stojić's Reply Brief, paras 33-34; Appeal Hearing, AT. 284-285 (21 Mar 2017). In connection with this argument, Stojić alleges that the Mladić Diaries were the sole evidence to support the finding that he "was linked as an individual to the JCE". Appeal Hearing, AT. 284-285 (21 Mar 2017).

in any event, the content of the diary extracts does not support the Trial Chamber's finding.[355] Prlić, Stojić, and Praljak request that the Appeals Chamber reverse all of their convictions.[356]

(b) The Prosecution's response

115.   The Prosecution responds that the Trial Chamber did not abuse its discretion in admitting into evidence two extracts from the Mladić Diaries (Exhibits P11376 and P11380).[357] It argues that the Trial Chamber thoroughly assessed multiple indicators of their authenticity, of which a decision on admission by another trial chamber was merely one, and properly determined that a graphological analysis was not necessary.[358]

116.   The Prosecution submits that the Trial Chamber provided the Appellants with the opportunity to challenge the admitted extracts, and that the Appellants fail to demonstrate that the Trial Chamber abused its discretion in denying their requests to reopen their cases.[359] Regarding Prlić's argument that he could only make an informed decision to reopen his case after a decision was taken to reopen the Prosecution's case, the Prosecution submits that his reasoning could only apply to material that would directly rebut new Prosecution evidence.[360] It points out that for such material the Trial Chamber had explicitly allowed Prlić to file a request to reopen.[361] The Prosecution also contends that Prlić's argument that his notice of intent to reopen his case was a **[page 48]** proper substitute for filing an actual motion fails to show how the Trial Chamber erred by not taking this into account in evaluating diligence.[362]

117.   The Prosecution contends that the Trial Chamber properly found that Praljak failed to substantiate his request to testify in the reopening of his case and noted that he could respond to the Prosecution evidence in his closing brief and submissions.[363] It submits that in so doing the Trial Chamber did not conflate Praljak's evidence and his Counsel's submissions.[364] The Prosecution argues that Prlić fails to explain how the Trial Chamber violated his rights by not allowing him to cross-examine Praljak on testimony he never gave.[365] In any event, the Prosecution argues that Prlić has waived the right to raise this issue on appeal, as he took no position at trial on the reopening of Praljak's case.[366]

118.   The Prosecution submits that the Trial Chamber drew straightforward, common-sense inferences from the plain words of the excerpts from the Mladić Diaries (Exhibits P11376 and P11380).[367] The Prosecution argues that there is no requirement that all hearsay evidence be corroborated, and that the extracts from the Mladić Diaries were in any event corroborated by other evidence.[368] According to the

---

[355]   Stojić's Appeal Brief, paras 130-131; Stojić's Reply Brief, para. 35.

[356]   Prlić's Appeal Brief, para. 177; Stojić's Appeal Brief, para. 132; Stojić's Reply Brief, para. 35; Praljak's Appeal Brief, para. 545; Appeal Hearing, AT. 472 (22 Mar 2017). See also Praljak's Reply Brief, para. 125.

[357]   Prosecution's Response Brief (Praljak), para. 305, referring to, *inter alia, Prlić et al.* Trial Decision on Reopening the Prosecution's Case; Appeal Hearing, AT. 478 (22 Mar 2017). See Prosecution's Response Brief (Praljak), paras 307-308.

[358]   Prosecution's Response Brief (Praljak), para. 306. See Prosecution's Response Brief (Praljak), para. 307. The Prosecution also argues that by seeking to tender other entries from the Mladić Diaries, Prlić and Praljak accepted their overall authenticity and reliability. Prosecution's Response Brief (Prlić), para. 93; Prosecution's Response Brief (Praljak), para. 306.

[359]   Prosecution's Response Brief (Prlić), paras 79, 81-83; Prosecution's Response Brief (Stojić), paras 94, 99-100; Prosecution's Response Brief (Praljak), paras 305, 309. See Prosecution's Response Brief (Praljak), paras 310-312; Appeal Hearing, AT. 478-479 (22 Mar 2017). In particular, the Prosecution argues that Prlić had the same opportunity as the Prosecution to request a reopening of his case, but failed to avail himself of that opportunity, and that he therefore fails to demonstrate any violation of his rights to an effective defence or equality of arms. Prosecution's Response Brief (Prlić), paras 79, 81-82.

[360]   Prosecution's Response Brief (Prlić), para. 83.

[361]   Prosecution's Response Brief (Prlić), para. 83. See Prosecution's Response Brief (Prlić), para. 81.

[362]   Prosecution's Response Brief (Prlić), para. 83.

[363]   Prosecution's Response Brief (Praljak), para. 312; Appeal Hearing, AT. 479 (22 Mar 2017).

[364]   Prosecution's Response Brief (Praljak), para. 312.

[365]   Prosecution's Response Brief (Prlić), para. 90. See Prosecution's Response Brief (Prlić), para. 93.

[366]   Prosecution's Response Brief (Prlić), para. 90. Further, the Prosecution argues that Prlić's silence at trial signals his implicit recognition that the decision on the reopening of Praljak's case does not affect his rights. Prosecution's Response Brief (Prlić), para. 90.

[367]   Prosecution's Response Brief (Prlić), para. 78; Prosecution's Response Brief (Stojić), paras 94-96, 98; Appeal Hearing, AT. 353-354 (21 Mar 2017). See Prosecution's Response Brief (Prlić), paras 89, 93.

[368]   Prosecution's Response Brief (Prlić), para. 93; Prosecution's Response Brief (Praljak), para. 308; Appeal Hearing, AT. 479 (22 Mar 2017). See Prosecution's Response Brief (Praljak), para. 307.

Prosecution, Prlić's "alternative explanations" for Exhibits P11376 and P11380[369] are not based on the evidence he tendered in reopening and are anyhow unsustainable.[370] The Prosecution submits that the Trial Chamber based the finding challenged by Stojić also on other evidence and that Stojić's conviction therefore does not rest solely, or in a decisive manner, on the diaries.[371] The Prosecution also contends that the Mladić Diaries support the challenged finding.[372] Finally, the Prosecution submits that Prlić and Praljak fail to demonstrate that the admission into evidence of extracts from the Mladić Diaries had any impact on the Trial Judgement, considering the wealth of other evidence on which the Trial Chamber based its conclusions.[373]
[page 49]

3. Analysis

119. The Appeals Chamber recalls the law applicable to a trial chamber's decision on whether to reopen a party's case:

> [W]hen considering an application for reopening a case to allow for the admission of fresh evidence, a Trial Chamber should first determine whether the evidence could, with reasonable diligence, have been identified and presented in the case-in-chief of the party making the application. If not, the Trial Chamber has the discretion to admit it, and should consider whether its probative value is substantially outweighed by the need to ensure a fair trial. When making this determination, the Trial Chamber should consider the stage in the trial at which the evidence is sought to be adduced and the potential delay that would be caused to the trial.[374]

The Appeals Chamber recalls that a trial chamber's decision to allow the reopening of a party's case is a discretionary decision to which the Appeals Chamber must accord deference. The Appeals Chamber's examination is therefore limited to establishing whether the trial chamber has abused its discretion in committing a "discernible error". The Appeals Chamber will only overturn a trial chamber's exercise of its discretion where it is found to be: (1) based on an incorrect interpretation of governing law; (2) based on a patently incorrect conclusion of fact; or (3) so unfair or unreasonable as to constitute an abuse of the trial chamber's discretion. The Appeals Chamber will also consider whether the Trial Chamber has given weight to extraneous or irrelevant considerations or has failed to give weight or sufficient weight to relevant considerations in reaching its decision.[375]

(a) Admission into evidence of extracts from the Mladić Diaries in the reopening of the Prosecution's case

120. The Appeals Chamber observes that Praljak, in arguing that the Trial Chamber did not establish "exceptional circumstances" justifying the admission of the diaries and did not properly consider the prejudice to the Appellants in admitting the evidence at a late stage of the trial proceedings, misrepresents the applicable law, as recalled above, which does not require "exceptional circumstances".[376] The Trial Chamber correctly articulated the law,[377] and applied it, finding that the criteria for reopening the Prosecution's case were met with regard to some of the **[page 50]** tendered exhibits.[378] Praljak fails to engage

---

[369] See *supra*, fn. 352.
[370] Prosecution's Response Brief (Prlić), paras 87-88.
[371] Prosecution's Response Brief (Stojić), para. 95; Appeal Hearing, AT. 354 (21 Mar 2017). The Prosecution submits that prior knowledge of the JCE is not a prerequisite for JCE liability. Appeal Hearing, AT. 354 (21 Mar 2017).
[372] Prosecution's Response Brief (Stojić), paras 96-97.
[373] Prosecution's Response Brief (Prlić), paras 79, 81, 84, 89; Prosecution's Response Brief (Praljak), para. 313. The Prosecution also argues that Prlić fails to explain the relevance of the evidence he tendered to the Trial Chamber's findings relating to Exhibits P11376 and P11380 or how the evidence would have affected those findings. Prosecution's Response Brief (Prlić), para. 85. See Prosecution's Response Brief (Prlić), para. 86. Similarly, the Prosecution contends that Prlić fails to show how the Trial Chamber's denial of Praljak's request to testify on the admitted extracts of the Mladić Diaries had any impact on the Trial Judgement. Prosecution's Response Brief (Prlić), paras 79, 91-92.
[374] *Gotovina et al.* Appeal Decision on Reopening, para. 23. See *Gotovina et al.* Appeal Decision on Reopening, para. 24.
[375] *Gotovina et al.* Appeal Decision on Reopening, para. 5; *Popović et al.* Appeal Decision on Reopening, para. 3.
[376] Praljak's Appeal Brief, para. 547 and references cited therein. See *supra*, para. 119.
[377] *Prlić et al.* Trial Decision on Reopening of the Prosecution's Case, paras 32-33. See also *Prlić et al.* Trial Decision on Reopening of the Prosecution's Case, paras 31, 34.
[378] *Prlić et al.* Trial Decision on Reopening of the Prosecution's Case, paras 40, 55-59, 61-63. Notably, the Trial Chamber found that the Prosecution did not have the Mladić Diaries when it closed its case and would have been unable to obtain them by then even

with the Trial Chamber's application of the law, much less demonstrate any error in it. His argument is therefore dismissed.

121. Turning to Praljak's argument that the Trial Chamber did not properly establish the authenticity of the Mladić Diaries, the Appeals Chamber observes that the Trial Chamber in its admission decision considered the issue at length, finding sufficient indicia of authenticity in: (1) the fact that another trial chamber had admitted them into evidence; (2) a witness statement recognising Mladić's handwriting in the diaries; (3) a witness statement pertaining to the chain of custody of the Mladić Diaries; and (4) documents corroborating certain facts reported in the diaries.[379] Considering these indicia on which the Trial Chamber relied, of which the admission into evidence of the diaries by another trial chamber was only one, the Appeals Chamber finds that Praljak has failed to show an error in this regard. In light of the various indicia relied upon for admission, and the fact that proving authenticity is not a separate threshold requirement for the admissibility of documentary evidence,[380] the Appeals Chamber further considers that Praljak has failed to show that the Trial Chamber erred in the exercise of its discretion by admitting the diaries into evidence without ordering a graphological analysis of them or without further information about the circumstances in which the diaries were written. Praljak's argument is therefore dismissed.[381]

(b) Denial of Defence requests to reopen their cases and present evidence in rebuttal

122. At the outset, the Appeals Chamber turns to Prlić's argument that the Trial Chamber erred in finding that he was not diligent in requesting to reopen his defence case. It recalls in this regard the pertinent procedural background as was considered by the Trial Chamber: (1) Prlić received an electronic version of the Mladić Diaries in Cyrillic script on 11 June 2010 and was informed of the contents of the specific entries tendered for admission on 9 July 2010;[382] (2) the Prosecution disclosed the translated versions of the Mladić Diaries to Prlić in the Bosnian/Croatian/Serbian language ("BCS") and English within, approximately one month between 11 June and **[page 51]** 16 July 2010;[383] (3) Prlić filed a notice on 14 July 2010, announcing his intent of submitting a future request to reopen his case should the Prosecution's request to reopen its case be granted;[384] and (4) at the time of the Trial Chamber's decision on the Prosecution's motion to reopen its case on 6 October 2010, Prlić had failed to submit a general request for reopening based on the discovery of the diaries.[385]

123. The Appeals Chamber observes that in its decision on the Prosecution's motion to reopen its case, the Trial Chamber made specific reference to the fact that Prlić had not filed a motion for reopening his case, almost four months after learning about the contents of the Mladić Diaries.[386] The Trial Chamber further held that in assessing diligence concerning Prlić's general request for reopening, it could not take into account his notice of intent of 14 July 2010, since such a notice "cannot be likened to a formal request for re-opening".[387] The Trial Chamber thus found that any general request for reopening his case based on the diaries (*i.e.* other than to refute the diary entries tendered by the Prosecution and admitted by the Trial Chamber in the Prosecution's reopened case) would fail due to lack of diligence.[388] Prlić impugns this finding.[389]

---

if it had deployed "all diligence". *Prlić et al.* Trial Decision on Reopening of the Prosecution's Case, para. 40. Further, weighing the probative value of the Mladić Diaries against the need to ensure a fair trial, the Trial Chamber decided to only admit "evidence going directly to the alleged participation of certain accused in the JCE". *Prlić et al.* Trial Decision on Reopening of the Prosecution's Case, para. 59. See *Prlić et al.* Trial Decision on Reopening of the Prosecution's Case, paras 57-58.

[379] *Prlić et al.* Trial Decision on Reopening of the Prosecution's Case, paras 46-51.

[380] See *Naletilić and Martinović* Appeal Judgement, para. 402.

[381] Stojić's allegation that the Trial Chamber did not give proper consideration to the authenticity of the Mladić Diaries is an undeveloped assertion not supported by any references to the trial record. It is therefore dismissed.

[382] *Prlić et al.* Trial Decision on Reopening the Prosecution's Case, para. 40 & fn. 110, paras 56, 64.

[383] *Prlić et al.* Trial Decision on Reopening the Prosecution's Case, paras 40, 64.

[384] *Prlić et al.* Trial Decision on Reopening the Prosecution's Case, fn. 143. See *infra*, para. 123.

[385] *Prlić et al.* Trial Decision on Reopening the Prosecution's Case, para. 64.

[386] *Prlić et al.* Trial Decision on Reopening the Prosecution's Case, para. 64.

[387] *Prlić et al.* Trial Decision on Reopening the Prosecution's Case, fn. 145. See *Prlić et al.* Trial Decision on Reopening the Prosecution's Case, fn. 143.

[388] *Prlić et al.* Trial Decision on Reopening the Prosecution's Case, para. 64. See also *Prlić et al.* Trial Decision on Reopening the Prosecution's Case, p. 29 (Disposition).

[389] See *supra*, para. 111.

124.   The Appeals Chamber first notes that the Trial Chamber's decision not to take into account Prlić's notice of intent when assessing diligence concerning his request to reopen his case was based on its established practice prior to that date concerning notices.[390] This practice would have alerted Prlić to the fact that the Trial Chamber would not entertain his notice of intent to request a reopening of his case, and would have only considered such a request by way of a motion. Prlić does not show how the Trial Chamber's decision not to consider his notice of intent when assessing **[page 52]** diligence concerning a general request for reopening constituted an abuse of discretion so as to amount to a discernible error.

125.   The Appeals Chamber next recalls that the Mladić Diaries were first disclosed to Prlić in Cyrillic script on 11 June 2010 with the translations provided throughout the period of approximately one month thereafter.[391] From this period onwards, Prlić had the opportunity to identify any material that he considered relevant to his case, and could have sought a reopening of his case at that stage. Prlić's argument that he could only make an informed decision as to whether to seek a reopening of his case if the Prosecution's request to reopen its case were granted, is not convincing. A party's request to open its case cannot be conditional upon the Trial Chamber granting the other party's respective request to do the same.

126.   Finally, the Appeals Chamber observes that with respect to any material necessitating a reopening of Prlić's case for the purpose of rebutting evidence admitted in the Prosecution's reopened case, the Trial Chamber expressly allowed Prlić this opportunity[392] and he availed himself of it.[393] Accordingly, Prlić has failed to,show any discernible error in the impugned finding.[394]

127.   The Appeals Chamber recalls that the Trial Chamber expressly allowed Prlić the opportunity to request the reopening of his case to refute entries of the Mladić Diaries admitted into evidence in the reopening of the Prosecution's case.[395] It considers that the Trial Chamber, in doing so, inherently took into consideration that the Prosecution bears the burden of proof at trial, and allowed Prlić to make an informed decision about whether to reopen his own case for that purpose. The Appeals Chamber considers that Prlić has failed to demonstrate that the Trial Chamber committed a discernible error.[396] Prlić's argument is therefore dismissed.

128.   Turning to Prlić's argument that the Trial Chamber erred in denying admission of evidence that he tendered in rebuttal to the Prosecution's new evidence, the Appeals Chamber observes that **[page 53]** Prlić merely asserts that the Trial Chamber erred and refers to his arguments at trial.[397] This amounts to a mere

---

[390]   *Prlić et al.* Trial Decision on Reopening the Prosecution's Case, fn. 145, referring to *Prosecutor v. Jadranko Prlić, Bruno Stojić, Slobodan Praljak, Milivoj Petković, Valentin Ćorić, and Berislav Pušić*, Case No. IT-04-74-T, Decision on the Prosecution Motion for Reconsideration or Certification to Appeal Concerning Ordonnance Relative a la Demande de l'Accusation de Suspendre le Délai de Dépôt de sa Demande de Réplique, 6 My 2010, p. 10 & fn. 44 (where the Trial Chamber relied on its "established practice [...] in this proceeding with respect to notices" to find that a "Notice of 27 April 2010 [simply informing the Chamber of the Prosecution's desire to file a request to reply generally after the close of the Defence cases] could not and cannot now in any way be likened to a request, [...] remind[ing] the parties that it can only be seized of a matter when a party properly and timely files a request"), T(F). 41355 (15 June 2009) (where the Trial Chamber held that: "For clarity's sake, the Chamber will recall that pursuant to the rules, it is seized of a matter only when the party concerned files it as a proper motion, which then enables the other parties to respond. Therefore, the Chamber does not consider that it is seized of the questions presented in the forms of notices or correspondence exchanged between the parties. Therefore, it invites the parties to abstain from sending such notices to the Chamber").
[391]   See *supra*, fns 382-383.
[392]   *Prlić et al.* Trial Decision on Reopening the Prosecution's Case, pp. 28-29 (Disposition).
[393]   *Prosecutor v. Jadranko Prlić, Bruno Stojić, Slobodan Praljak, Milivoj Petković, Valentin Ćorić, and Berislav Pušić*, Case No. IT-04-74-T, Jadranko Prlić's Motion to Rebut the Evidence Admitted by the Trial Chamber in the Decision on the Prosecution's Motion to Reopen its Case, 20 October 2010 (public with confidential annex); *Prosecutor v. Jadranko Prlić, Bruno Stojić, Slobodan Praljak, Milivoj Petković, Valentin Ćorić, and Berislav Pušić*, Case No. IT-04-74-T, Jadranko Prlić's Revised Motion to Rebut the Evidence Admitted by the Trial Chamber in the Decision on the Prosecution's Motion to Reopen its Case, 1 November 2010 (public with confidential annex); *Prlić et al.* Trial Decision on Prlić's Motion to Admit Evidence in Rebuttal. See also *Prlić et al.* Trial Decision on Prlić's Motion to Admit Evidence in Rebuttal, paras 19-20 (clarifying that these motions should be treated as motions for the reopening of the case noting that both referred to the applicable law for the reopening of a case, notably to the interpretation of the nature of "fresh" evidence).
[394]   See *supra*, paras 119, 123.
[395]   *Prlić et al.* Trial Decision on Reopening the Prosecution's Case, para. 64, p. 29 (Disposition).
[396]   See *supra*, para. 119. The Appeals Chamber dismisses as vague and obscure Prlić's submission that "there was a lack of clarity on a host of issues related to the Mladić Diaries".
[397]   See Prlić's Appeal Brief, paras 163-166 and references cited therein. See, in particular, Prlić's Appeal Brief, fns 384, 387-388, 392-393 and references cited therein.

repetition of arguments that were unsuccessful at trial without any demonstration that their rejection by the Trial Chamber constituted an error warranting the intervention of the Appeals Chamber.[398] In support of his contention that the Trial Chamber did not provide a reasoned opinion, Prlić refers to the Trial Chamber's finding that "none of the exhibits deal with the statement or actions of the Accused Prlić himself".[399] Prlić thereby ignores other relevant findings of the Trial Chamber and fails to demonstrate that the Trial Chamber did not provide a reasoned opinion.[400] Notably, the Trial Chamber found, in light of its previous decisions on the matter, that it could not "admit fresh evidence unless it goes to refute the alleged participation of the Accused in achieving the objectives of the JCE and, in particular, in the case of the Accused Prlić".[401] With regard to documents 1D03193 and 1D03194, Prlić asserts an error without even referring to the reasons provided by the Trial Chamber for denying their admission into evidence.[402] These undeveloped and unsupported arguments are therefore dismissed.

129.   With regard to the Trial Chamber's denial of Praljak's request to reopen his case in order to testify, the Appeals Chamber considers that Prlić and Praljak misrepresent the Trial Chamber's reasoning. First, the Appeals Chamber observes that the Trial Chamber offered Praljak an opportunity to challenge the entries of the Mladić Diaries admitted into evidence during the reopening of the Prosecution's case as he was given the opportunity to file a request to reopen his case for that purpose.[403] Second, the Trial Chamber reasoned, in relevant parts, that Praljak merely invoked the right of an accused to respond without providing facts justifying why he needed to testify *viva voce* before the Trial Chamber within the context of the reopening of his case.[404] The Trial Chamber then recalled that the Praljak Defence "could once again exercise its right to *respond* in its closing brief and closing arguments".[405] The Appeals Chamber can discern no indication that the Trial Chamber either denied Praljak the opportunity to challenge the Mladić Diaries or conflated Praljak's evidence with his Counsel's submissions. With regard to Prlić's right of confrontation, the Appeals Chamber notes that Prlić does not refute the Prosecution's submission that he took no **[page 54]** position at trial on the reopening of Praljak's case.[406] The Appeals Chamber therefore concludes that Prlić has waived his right to claim any prejudice resulting from the Trial Chamber's decision not to allow Praljak's testimony.[407] All these arguments are therefore dismissed.

130.   The Appeals Chamber turns to Praljak's argument that the Trial Chamber incorrectly found that the material he tendered aimed to refute allegations that did not fall within the scope of the motions to reopen the case, as it proceeded to use the Mladić Diaries to prove those same allegations in the Trial Judgement. The Appeals Chamber notes that Praljak misrepresents the Trial Chamber's finding. Contrary to his contentions, the Trial Chamber identified for only one document (3D03845) that the allegation to be refuted would be the intention of the Bosnian Croats, pursuant to their meetings with Serb authorities, to commit crimes in order to achieve their goal of a Herceg-Bosna dominated by Croats, which is an issue that the Trial Chamber concluded fell outside the scope of the Prosecution's reopened case.[408]

---

[398]   See *Prlić et al.* Trial Decision on Prlić's Motion to Admit Evidence in Rebuttal, paras 6-9, 15-26. In addition, the Appeals Chamber observes that the fact that a dissenting judge finds tendered documents to be relevant and that the Prosecution does not object to their admission into evidence do not suffice to demonstrate that the Trial Chamber erred by denying admission into evidence.

[399]   Prlić's Appeal Brief, paras 161, 174; Prlić Reply Brief, para. 51, referring to *Prlić et al.* Trial Decision on Prlić's Motion to Admit Evidence in Rebuttal, para. 24.

[400]   See *Prlić et al.* Trial Decision on Prlić's Motion to Admit Evidence in Rebuttal, paras 22-24.

[401]   *Prlić et al.* Trial Decision on Prlić's Motion to Admit Evidence in Rebuttal, para. 22.

[402]   See Prlić's Appeal Brief, para. 164. *Cf. Prlić et al.* Trial Decision on Prlić's Motion to Admit Evidence in Rebuttal, paras 25-26.

[403]   *Prlić et al.* Trial Decision on Reopening the Prosecution's Case, para. 64, p. 29 (Disposition).

[404]   *Prlić et al.* Trial Decision on Reopening Praljak's Case, para. 28.

[405]   *Prlić et al.* Trial Decision on Reopening Praljak's Case, para. 28 (emphasis added).

[406]   Prosecution's Response Brief (Prlić), para. 90; Prlić's Reply Brief, para. 51.

[407]   *Cf. Popović et al.* Appeal Judgement, para. 176. By implication, the Appeals Chamber also dismisses Prlić's submission that the Trial Chamber denied without a reasoned opinion Praljak's request for certification to appeal the decision on the request to reopen his case.

[408]   *Prlić et al.* Trial Decision on Reopening Praljak's Case, para. 22 & fn. 43, referring to Annex A to Supplement of Praljak's Motion, pp. 7-8 (concerning document 3D03845). The Trial Chamber identified as other allegations to be refuted by the other documents: (1) the existence of co-operation between the Army of the Serbs of Bosnia and Herzegovina ("VRS") and the ABiH (for 3D03844); and (2) the siege of Mostar (for 3D03846). *Prlić et al.* Trial Decision on Reopening Praljak's Case, para. 22 & fns 42

131.   The Appeals Chamber notes the proximity between the allegations to be rebutted by the document tendered by Praljak (namely, the intention of the Bosnian Croats, pursuant to their meetings with Serb authorities, to commit crimes in order to achieve their goal of a Herceg-Bosna dominated by Croats)[409] and those for which reopening was allowed (namely, the possible involvement of the Appellants in achieving the objectives of the JCE, *i.e.* a change in the ethnic make-up in the territories concerned through the commission of crimes under the Statute, to achieve the political goal of establishing a Croatian entity).[410] The Appeals Chamber therefore finds that no reasonable trier of fact could have found that the former allegation did not fall into the scope of the latter and of the motions to reopen the case. In this regard, the Appeals Chamber notes additionally, as correctly pointed out by Praljak, that the Trial Chamber in its judgement in fact proceeded to rely on entries of the Mladić Diaries admitted in the reopened Prosecution case to prove precisely the existence of this JCE.[411] **[page 55]**

132.   However, the Appeals Chamber considers that the Trial Chamber found that the document concerned did not qualify as "fresh" evidence and was inadmissible not only on the ground that the allegation to be rebutted did not fall within the scope of the motion to reopen the case, which was the only ground that Praljak addressed.[412] The Trial Chamber also deemed that the document in question did not qualify as "fresh" evidence and consequently was inadmissible because Praljak failed to substantiate how it would constitute "fresh" evidence and to identify which of the exhibits admitted as the Prosecution's new evidence would be refuted by it.[413] The Appeals Chamber concurs with this assessment and notes that Praljak's submissions in relation to document 3D03845 lack clarity to an extent that they do not assist in assessing whether the document was in fact "fresh".[414] In addition, the passages of the document as referred to by Praljak in his submissions have no apparent value and relevance to the allegations. to be rebutted.[415] Praljak has therefore failed to show that the Trial Chamber erred by denying admission into evidence of this document and that the error identified above occasioned a miscarriage of justice.[416] His argument is therefore dismissed.

133.   Regarding Stojić's submission that the Trial Chamber deprived him of an opportunity to challenge the Mladić Diaries by denying his application to reopen his case, the Appeals Chamber observes that the Trial Chamber gave him an opportunity to challenge the Mladić Diaries,[417] but found he did not meet the criteria for reopening his case since the tendered documents failed to qualify as "fresh" evidence for a number of reasons.[418] Stojić ignores the Trial Chamber's reasoning in this regard and has therefore failed to show any error. His submission is dismissed.

(c) The Trial Chamber's assessment of the Mladić Diaries in the Trial Judgement

134.   The Appeals Chamber finds that Praljak fails to provide support for his contention that the Trial Chamber weighed the Mladić Diaries contrary to the principles it affirmed with regard to the assessment of evidence.[419] Moreover, the Appeals Chamber observes that the challenged findings that are based on the

---

(referring to Annex A to Supplement of Praljak's Motion, pp. 6-7), 44 (referring to Annex A to Supplement of Praljak's Motion, p. 12).

[409]   *Prlić et al.* Trial Decision on Reopening Praljak's Case, para. 22.

[410]   *Prlić et al.* Trial Decision on Reopening Praljak's Case, paras 21-22, referring to, *inter alia, Prlić et al.* Trial Decision on Reopening the Prosecution's Case, paras 59, 61; Trial Judgement, Vol. 4, paras 43, 65.

[411]   Trial Judgement, Vol. 4, paras 43 (referring to, *inter alia,* Trial Judgement, Vol. 4, paras 14, 18), 65; Praljak's Appeal Brief, para. 564.

[412]   *Prlić et al.* Trial Decision on Reopening Praljak's Case, para. 22, referring to, *inter alia,* document 3D03845.

[413]   *Prlić et al.* Trial Decision on Reopening Praljak's Case, para. 22. See also *Prlić et al.* Trial Decision on Reopening Praljak's Case, para. 21.

[414]   Annex A to Supplement of Praljak's Motion, pp. 7-8.

[415]   Annex A to Supplement of Praljak's Motion, pp. 7-8.

[416]   See *supra,* para. 131.

[417]   *Prlić et al.* Trial Decision on Reopening the Prosecution's Case, para. 64, p. 29 (Disposition).

[418]   *Prlić et al.* Trial Decision on Reopening Stojić's Case, paras 21-30 (pointing out that the proposed exhibits either: (1) were not tendered with the aim to refute the exhibits admitted in the Prosecution's reopened case (para. 26); (2) did not concern the statements or behaviour of Stojić and thus did not refute these exhibits (paras 27-28); (3) failed to do so because they were irrelevant (paras 28-29); or (4) did not satisfy the diligence test as Stojić failed to show that he was unable to identify and present them during his case-in-chief (para. 29)).

[419]   *Cf.* Praljak's Appeal Brief, paras 553-556 and references cited therein.

diaries[420] are a few out of a large number of findings stretching over seven **[page 56]** pages of the Trial Judgement, based on various sources of evidence, which support the concluding finding on the Ultimate Purpose of Croatian political leaders.[421] Having examined all these findings, the Appeals Chamber sees no indication that the challenged findings were in any way decisive to the concluding finding. Praljak thus fails to show that the concluding finding arid the conviction should not stand on the basis of the remaining evidence.[422] In sum, he has failed to demonstrate that the Trial Chamber erred in its assessment of documentary evidence, evidence not subjected to adversarial argument in court, and hearsay evidence, and his contention is therefore dismissed.

135.   With regard to Praljak's argument that the Trial Chamber failed to provide a reasoned opinion on the probative value of the Mladić Diaries and their impact on its findings, the Appeals Chamber recalls:

> As a general rule, a Trial Chamber "is required only to make findings on those facts which are essential to the determination of guilt on a particular count"; it "is not required to articulate every step of its reasoning for each particular finding it makes" nor is it "required to set out in detail why it accepted or rejected a particular testimony." However, the requirements to be met by the Trial Chamber may be higher in certain cases.[423]

The Appeals Chamber recalls the aforementioned fact that the challenged findings based on the Mladić Diaries make up only a fraction of a large number of findings underlying the concluding finding of the Ultimate Purpose,[424] and that the challenged findings were in no way decisive to the concluding finding. It therefore disagrees with Praljak's characterisation of the findings based "solely on [...] these diaries" as "key findings regarding the existence of the JCE and the Accused's role in it" that would constitute special circumstances requiring a heightened standard to provide a reasoned opinion.[425] In these circumstances, the Appeals Chamber is not persuaded that the Trial Chamber failed to provide a reasoned opinion and consequently dismisses Praljak's argument.

136.   With regard to Prlić's argument that the Trial Chamber assessed Exhibits P11376 and P11380 without the context offered by other evidence and the material denied admission into evidence, the Appeals Chamber recalls that it dismissed all challenges to the Trial Chamber's **[page 57]** decisions to deny admission of evidence.[426] With regard to Prlić's challenges that are based on evidence on the record,[427] the Appeals Chamber finds that Prlić fails to show, with this evidence, that no reasonable trier of fact could have found that the partition of BiH was discussed in meetings held on 5 and 26 October 1992, in which Prlić, Stojić, Praljak, Petković, and Mladić participated.[428] To the extent Prlić contests that they met "for the specific

---

[420]   Praljak's Appeal Brief, paras 553, 555, referring to, *inter alia,* Trial Judgement, Vol. 4, para. 18 & fns 52-54.

[421]   Trial Judgement, Vol. 4, para. 24, relying on findings and evidence in Trial Judgement, Vol. 4, paras 8-23. For an overview of these many findings, see *infra,* para. 592.

[422]   See *infra,* para. 782.

[423]   *Krajišnik* Appeal Judgement, para. 139 (internal references omitted). See *Stanišić and Župljanin* Appeal Judgement, paras 378, 1063; *Popović et al.* Appeal Judgement, paras 972, 1906; *Šainović et al.* Appeal Judgement, paras 325, 378, 392, 461, 490; *Kvočka et al.* Appeal Judgement, para. 398. See also *Kvočka et al.* Appeal Judgement, para. 23. However, factual and legal findings on which the trial chamber relied to convict or acquit an accused should be set out in a clear and articulate manner. *Stanišić and Župljanin* Appeal Judgement, para. 137; *Stanišić and Simatović* Appeal Judgement, para. 78; *Popović et al.* Appeal Judgement, para. 1906; *Hadžihasanović and Kubura* Appeal Judgement, para. 13.

[424]   *Cf.* Praljak's Appeal Brief, para. 553 & fn. 1260 (referring to the findings based on the diaries in Trial Judgement, Vol. 4, para. 18 & fns 52-54). See *supra,* para. 134.

[425]   See *infra,* paras 828-973. The Appeals Chamber considers the late and contested admission into evidence of the Mladić Diaries to be irrelevant to the Trial Chamber's obligation to provide a reasoned opinion in the Trial Judgement. Regarding the authenticity of the Mladić Diaries, see *supra,* para. 121.

[426]   See *supra,* paras 122-133.

[427]   See Prlić's Appeal Brief, paras 169-170 and references cited therein. See also Prlić's Appeal Brief, para. 171.

[428]   Trial Judgement, Vol. 4, para. 18 and references cited therein. The Appeals Chamber notes in particular that one of the exhibits on which the Trial Chamber relied reports about this meeting, *inter alia:* "PRALJAK: [...] We're on a good path to compel Alija to divide Bosnia. – – We will compel Alija, partly by logistics partly by force, to sit down at the table with BOB AN and KARADŽIĆ. [...] *President TUĐMAN agreed to a meeting with KARADŽIĆ, ĆOSIĆ and BOBAN. [...] PRALJAK: – We must stop with the shooting, the Croatian state borders are obvious, but in BH, they are yet to be established." Exhibit P11380, pp. 1-2. The Appeals Chamber notes that Prlić in his submissions opts to merely focus on other topics discussed at the same meeting thereby simply denying the issue of partition. The Appeals Chamber finds that Prlić has failed to explain why these other topics and evidence he cites in support should detract from Praljak's remarks about dividing BiH. See Prlić's Appeal Brief, paras 169-170.

purpose of discussing the partition of BiH",[429] the Appeals Chamber observes that the French original version of the Trial Judgement does not convey that this was necessarily the specific purpose of the meeting.[430] Prlić's argument is therefore dismissed.

137. Turning to Stojić's arguments, the Appeals Chamber notes that he fails to identify the allegedly contradictory evidence and defence arguments he contends the Trial Chamber did not consider, and therefore dismisses this argument as an undeveloped assertion. Concerning his allegation that the Trial Chamber erred in finding that he knew at least as of October 1992 "that the implementation of the common purpose would involve the Muslim population moving outside the territory, of HZHB" solely based on the extracts of the Mladić Diaries,[431] the Appeals Chamber recalls that a conviction may not rest solely, or in a decisive manner, on the evidence of a witness whom the accused has had no opportunity to examine or to have examined either during the investigation or at trial, and that it is considered "to run counter to the principles of fairness [...] to allow a conviction based on evidence of this kind without sufficient corroboration".[432] The Appeals Chamber notes that the Trial Chamber based its finding on various other findings regarding the development of the HZ H-B and the functions, aspirations, and dealings of the main political and military actors, including Stojić, which in turn were based on extensive evidence,[433] and not **[page 58]** solely on extracts of the Mladić Diaries. In any event, Stojić fails to explain why the conviction should not stand on the basis of the remaining evidence, considering that the challenged finding predates the start of the JCE in mid-January 1993.[434] This warrants dismissal of the argument.[435] Finally, the Appeals Chamber is not persuaded that no reasonable trier of fact could have relied on the extracts of the Mladić Diaries in support of the finding. The Appeals Chamber therefore dismisses Stojić's arguments.

4. Conclusion

138. In light of the foregoing, the Appeals Chamber finds that the Appellants have failed to demonstrate any error in the Trial Chamber's: (1) admission into evidence of extracts of the Mladić Diaries in the reopening of the Prosecution's case; (2) decisions to deny Defence requests to reopen their cases and to present evidence in rebuttal; and (3) assessment of the Mladić Diaries.[436] Consequently, the Appeals Chamber dismisses Prlić's ground of appeal 5, Stojić's ground of appeal 16, and Praljak's ground of appeal 50.

C. **Admission of Evidence**

1. Denial of admission of Stojić's evidence (Stojić's Ground 5)

139. On 21 July 2009, the Trial Chamber rejected the admission of a number of documents submitted by Stojić related to the co-operation between the HVO and the ABiH.[437] Having concluded that the proposed

---

[429] Trial Judgement, Vol. 4, para. 18.

[430] "Les 5 et 26 octobre 1992, Jadranko Prlić, Bruno Stojić, Slobodan Praljak et Milivoj Petković rassemblés au sein d'une 'délégation de Croatie et de la HZ H-B' ont rencontré Ratko Mladić, général de la VRS, pour notamment discuter de la division de la BiH.» Trial Judgement (French Original), Vol. 4, para. 18 (internal references omitted).

[431] Stojić's Appeal Brief, heading before para. 127, paras 127, 132, referring to Trial Judgement, Vol. 4, para. 43 & fn. 121. The Appeals Chamber notes that Stojić misrepresents the Trial Chamber's finding insofar as he states that it found that the implementation of the *common purpose* would involve removing Muslims from the area, when in fact the Trial Chamber's finding referred to the implementation of the *Ultimate Purpose*. Trial Judgement, Vol. 4, para. 43, in particular fns 119, 121.

[432] *Popović et al.* Appeal Judgement, para. 96.

[433] Trial Judgement, Vol". 4, para. 43 & fn. 121, referring to, *inter alia,* Trial Judgement, Vol. 1, paras 426-490, Vol. 4, paras 6-24, 289-450. See also Trial Judgement, Vol. 4, fn. 120..

[434] *Cf.* Trial Judgement, Vol. 4, paras 41, 44, 65-66, 1218.

[435] Consequently, Stojić's submission that the Mladić Diaries were the sole evidence to support the finding that he "was linked as an individual to the JCE" and constituted uncorroborated hearsay evidence which the Defence had no opportunity to confront, misrepresents the factual findings and the evidence and ignores other relevant factual findings, and is therefore dismissed. See Trial Judgement, Vol. 4, paras 289-450; *infra,* para. 1401 *et seq.*

[436] Thus, the Appeals Chamber also dismisses the submissions that the Trial Chamber applied a double standard in the admission of evidence and, by denying the reopening of Defence cases, violated the Appellants' rights to equality of arms, to confrontation, to present an effective defence, and to a fair trial.

[437] *Prosecutor* v. *Jadranko Prlić et al.,* Case No. IT-04-74-T, Decision on Stojić Defence Motion for the Admission of Documentary Evidence (Cooperation between the Authorities and the Armed Forces of Herceg-Bosna and the Authorities and the

exhibits are too vague as regards the allegations in the Indictment or do not allow a relationship to be established between them and the Indictment, it refused their admission as not presenting sufficient indicia of relevance.[438] The Trial Chamber also rejected the admission of a number of documents related to crimes committed against Croatian civilians in Bosnia or to the conflict between the HVO and the ABiH. It found that these documents did not **[page 59]** contribute to disproving allegations made against the accused in the Indictment,[439] due to a lack of explanation of the geographical and temporal link with the crimes charged in the Indictment and/or with the Appellants' alleged responsibility for these crimes.[440] As such, it held that these documents similarly did not present sufficient indicia of relevance.[441]

140.   On 15 February 2010, the Trial Chamber denied Stojić's request to admit certain evidence including documents 2D01541 to 2D01561 in the context of Praljak's testimony in this case.[442] The Trial Chamber stated that Stojić had failed to establish through the testimony of Praljak that there is a sufficiently relevant link between proposed Exhibits 2D01541 to 2D01561 and the Indictment, referring back to the topics covered in the *Prlić et al.* Trial Decision on Admission of Evidence on Co-operation, concerning non-admission of documents.[443]

141.   Stojić submits that the Trial Chamber erred in law, abused its discretion, and denied him a fair trial by not admitting relevant evidence and by limiting certain lines of cross-examination, which resulted in the erroneous finding that there was a JCE to drive Muslims out of the territory of the HZ H-B.[444] Specifically, he alleges that the Trial Chamber erred by not admitting into evidence: (1) lists of HVO combatants grouped according to ethnicity, which show that Muslims also served in the ranks of the HVO;[445] (2) material on the co-operation between the HVO and the ABiH, which would be inconceivable if the JCE had existed; and (3) material on the existence of ABiH offensive operations (including Exhibit 2D00403), showing that crimes allegedly committed by the HVO were merely a reaction to ABiH offensive operations.[446] Stojić asserts that the Trial Chamber's error of law invalidates the Trial Judgement, and requests that the Appeals Chamber overturn the Trial Chamber's finding that a JCE existed, and to acquit him on all Counts.[447] **[page 60]**

142.   The Prosecution responds that Stojić fails to show that the Trial Chamber abused its discretion when declining to admit these materials into evidence, or that their admission would have impacted the finding on the CCP.[448] It submits that none of this material was geographically or otherwise connected to the Indictment,[449] and that in any event, the Trial Chamber considered that the HVO included Muslims and that there were instances of HVO-ABiH co-operation.[450] With regard to material on ABiH attacks, the Prosecution

---

Aimed Forces of the ABiH), 28 July 2009 (French original 21 July 2009) *("Prlić et al.* Trial Decision on Admission of Evidence on Co-operation"), para. 27, p. 14.
[438]   *Prlić et al.* Trial Decision on Admission of Evidence on Co-operation, para. 27. The Trial Chamber stated that the same was true for the proposed exhibits relating to medical aid provided to Bosnian Muslims by the Croatian Government, the HV, or the HVO, as well as to the existence of good relations between the HVO and the ABiH. See *Prlić et al.* Trial Decision on Admission of Evidence on Co-operation, para. 27.
[439]   *Prlić et al.* Trial Decision on Admission of Evidence on Co-operation, paras 28, 33.
[440]   *Prlić et al.* Trial Decision on Admission of Evidence on Co-operation, paras 30-31. See also *Prlić et al.* Trial Decision on Admission of Evidence on Co-operation, paras 32-33.
[441]   *Prlić et al.* Trial Decision on Admission of Evidence on Co-operation, paras 32-33.
[442]   *Prosecutor v. Jadranko Prlić et al.*, Case No. IT-04-74-T, Order to Admit Evidence Relating to the Testimony of Slobodan Praljak, 24 February 2010 (French original 15 February 2010) *("Prlić et al.* Order to Admit Evidence in relation to Praljak's Testimony"), pp. 9, 29-32. On 29 March 2010, the Trial Chamber denied Stojić's request for reconsideration or certification to appeal the Order of 15 February 2010. See *Prosecutor v. Jadranko Prlić et al.*, Case No. IT-04-74-T, Decision on the Request of the Stojić's Defence for Reconsideration, or, in the Alternative, for Certification to Appeal the Order Admitting Evidence Relating to the Testimony of Slobodan Praljak, 6 May 2010 (French original 29 March 2010).
[443]   *Prlić et al.* Order to Admit Evidence in relation to Praljak's Testimony, pp. 6, 29-32.
[444]   Stojić's Appeal Brief, headings before paras 59, 64, paras 60, 62-64, 66, 68-69; Appeal Hearing, AT. 267-268 (21 Mar 2017).
[445]   Stojić's Appeal Brief, heading before para. 61, paras 61-63.
[446]   Stojić's Appeal Brief, heading before para. 64, paras 64-69; Appeal Hearing, AT. 267, 272 (21 Mar 2017). Stojić singles out document 2D00959 as an example of the non-admitted documents addressed in his appeal brief on the topic of military materiel being provided by the HVO to the ABiH. Appeal Hearing, AT. 272 (21 Mar 2017); Stojić's Appeal Brief, para. 65 & fn. 198.
[447]   Stojić's Appeal Brief, paras 63, 69.
[448]   Prosecution's Response Brief (Stojić), paras 40-46. See also Appeal Hearing, AT. 347 (21 Mar 2017).
[449]   Prosecution's Response Brief (Stojić), paras 41, 43, 45.
[450]   Prosecution's Response Brief (Stojić), paras 42, 44.

submits that Stojić's argument concerning Exhibit 2D00403 is moot, since it was admitted by the Trial Chamber.[451]

143.   At the outset, regarding Stojić's assertion that the Trial Chamber erroneously limited certain lines of cross-examination, the Appeals Chamber notes that he does not point to any specific lines of cross-examination which were allegedly not allowed, and therefore dismisses the assertion as unsupported and undeveloped.[452] Concerning the material that the Trial Chamber did not admit into evidence, the Appeals Chamber recalls that it is well established that trial chambers exercise a broad discretion in determining the admissibility of evidence and must be accorded deference in this respect.[453] By pointing to findings in the Trial Judgement to show that the documents were relevant, Stojić falls short of demonstrating that the Trial Chamber abused its discretion in denying their admission on the basis of a lack of explanation of the geographical and temporal link with crimes charged in the Indictment and/or with the Appellants' alleged responsibility for these crimes.[454]

144.   Moreover, the Appeals Chamber notes that the Trial Chamber took into account other evidence on the presence of Muslims within the HVO, co-operation between the HVO and the ABiH, and the existence of ABiH offensives.[455] Its finding on the CCP relied on extensive evidence establishing a "clear pattern of conduct" of crimes committed by HVO forces between **[page 61]** January 1993 and April 1994.[456] Stojić has failed to demonstrate how the Trial Chamber's decision not to admit these documents impacts its finding on the CCP, and therefore how, in light of other evidence on the record, the conviction could not stand even if the referenced material had been admitted. The Appeals Chamber therefore dismisses Stojić's ground of appeal 5.

2.   Denial of admission of Praljak's evidence (Praljak's Ground 51)

145.   On 15 February 2010, in its *Prlić et al.* Order to Admit Evidence in relation to Praljak's Testimony, the Trial Chamber decided on the admission of 250 documents submitted by Praljak, specifying the reasons for their admission or non-admission in an annex thereto.[457]

146.   On 16 February 2010, the Trial Chamber rejected the admission of 155 written statements and transcripts of testimonies submitted by Praljak.[458] The Trial Chamber noted, *inter alia*, that: (1) *prima facie* the figure of 155 was "disproportionate and excessive"[459]; (2) some of the statements submitted for admission did not meet the formal requirements enumerated in Rule 92 *bis* (B) of the Rules[460]; and (3) the majority of the statements or transcripts of testimonies requested for admission dealt with character evidence relating to the "acts and conduct of the accused as charged in the Indictment" and were as such not admissible pursuant

---

[451]   Prosecution's Response Brief (Stojić), paras 45-46.

[452]   See Stojić's Appeal Brief, headings before paras 59, 64.

[453]   *Prosecutor v. Jadranko Prlić et al.*, Case No. IT-04-74-AR73.19, Decision on Jadranko Prlić's Consolidated Interlocutory Appeal Against the Trial Chamber's Orders of 6 and 9 October 2008 on Admission of Evidence, 12 January 2009 *("Prlić et al. Appeal Decision on Admission of Evidence")*, para. 5, referring to *Prosecutor v. Vujadin Popović et al.*, Case No. IT-05-88-AR73.3, Decision on Appeals Against Decision on Impeachment of a Party's Own Witness, 1 February 2008, para. 12. See also *Čelebići* Appeal Judgement, para. 533. The Appeals Chamber recalls, further, that it will only overturn a trial chamber's exercise of its discretion where it is found to be: (1) based on an incorrect interpretation of governing law; (2) based on a patently incorrect conclusion of fact; or (3) so unfair or unreasonable as to constitute an abuse of discretion. See *Prlić et al.* Appeal Decision on Admission of Evidence, para. 5, referring to *Prosecutor v. Jadranko Prlić et al.*, Case No. IT-04-74-AR73.11, Decision on Slobodan Praljak's Appeal of the Trial Chamber's Decision on the Direct Examination of Witnesses Dated 26 June 2008, 11 September 2008, para. 5 and references cited therein.

[454]   The Appeals Chamber also dismisses Stojić's argument, in relation to Exhibit 2D00403 since the document was admitted into evidence on 14 January 2010. See *Prosecutor v. Jadranko Prlić et al.*, Case No. IT-04-74-T, Order to Admit Evidence Regarding Witness 4D-AB, 3 February 2010 (French original 14 January 2010).

[455]   Trial Judgement, Vol. 1, paras 463, 774, Vol. 2, paras 524-525, Vol. 4, para. 308.

[456]   Trial Judgement, Vol. 4, paras 41-65.

[457]   *Prlić et al.* Order to Admit Evidence in relation to Praljak's Testimony, pp. 2, 11-40.

[458]   *Prosecutor v. Jadranko Prlić et al.*, Case No. IT-04-74-T, Decision on Slobodan Praljak's Motion to Admit Evidence Pursuant to Rule 92 *bis* of the Rules, 21 December 2010 (French original 16 February 2010) *("Prlić et al.* Trial Decision on Admission of Evidence Pursuant to Rule 92 *bis")*, paras 1, 48, p. 21.

[459]   *Prlić et al.* Trial Decision on Admission of Evidence Pursuant to Rule 92 *bis*, para. 32.

[460]   *Prlić et al.* Trial Decision on Admission of Evidence Pursuant to Rule 92 *bis*, para. 37.

to Rule 92 *bis* of the Rules.[461] On this basis, the Trial Chamber deemed it appropriate to send back the request for admission, inviting Praljak to proceed with a new selection, and ordering him to refile a maximum of 20 statements and transcripts.[462] On 1 July 2010, the Appeals Chamber upheld the Trial Chamber's decision of non-admission.[463]

147.   Praljak submits that the Trial Chamber abused its discretion in denying admission into evidence of Rule 92 *bis* statements and transcripts, and other documents tendered by him, thereby violating bis right to a fair trial.[464] He argues that the Trial Chamber applied a stricter standard of **[page 62]** admission to evidence tendered by him than to evidence tendered by the Prosecution.[465] He also asserts that the Trial Chamber misapplied the law on admission of evidence by assessing the documents' overall probative value and weight at the time of its decision on admissibility rather than at the close of the proceedings.[466] He submits that having applied the wrong standard, the non-admission of the statements relating to the Mujahideen in Central Bosnia led the Trial Chamber to find that the HVO and Praljak "conceived a transfer of Croats and the threat from the Mujahideen in the absence of any real danger".[467] Praljak contends, further, that the non-admission of these and other tendered documents deprived the Judges of evidence providing a complete picture and "alternative plausible explanations to the benefit of Praljak", affecting the Trial Judgement in its entirety.[468] He requests that the Trial Judgement be reversed and that he be acquitted on all Counts.[469]

148.   The Prosecution responds that the Trial Chamber did not misapply the law on admission of evidence, nor did it apply a stricter standard of admission to evidence tendered by him.[470] It avers that Praijak merely disagrees with the Trial Chamber's decisions on admission and evaluation of evidence, without showing an abuse of its discretion.[471] According to the Prosecution, the Trial Chamber properly denied admission into evidence of the Rule 92 *bis* statements and transcripts, and other documents.[472] With regard to the Rule 92 *bis* statements and transcripts specifically, the Prosecution submits that the Appeals Chamber already approved their non-admission and that Praljak has failed to show exceptional circumstances warranting reconsideration.[473] With regard to the other documents, the Prosecution submits that Praljak's mere **[page 63]**

---

[461]   *Prlić et al.* Trial Decision on Admission of Evidence Pursuant to Rule 92 *bis,* paras 42-47.

[462]   *Prlić et al.* Trial Decision on Admission of Evidence Pursuant to Rule 92 *bis,* paras 47-48.

[463]   *Prosecutor* v. *Jadranko Prlić et al.,* Case No. IT-04-74-AR73.17, Decision on Slobodan Praljak's Appeal of the Trial Chamber's Refusal to Decide upon Evidence Tendered Pursuant to Rule 92 *bis,* 1 July 2010 *("Prlić et al.* Appeal Decision on Admission of Evidence Pursuant to Rule 92 *bis"),* para. 37. It is noted that in this decision, the Appeals Chamber did find that the Trial Chamber erred in relation to restricting the number of pages per tendered Rule 92 *bis* statement, and remanded the issue to the Trial Chamber for reconsideration and clarification. See *Prlić et al.* Appeal Decision on Admission of Evidence Pursuant to Rule 92 *bis,* para. 38 and p. 24.

[464]   Praljak's Appeal Brief, paras 566-568, 573, 576; Praljak's Reply Brief, para. 120. See Praljak's Appeal Brief, paras 569-572, 574. See also Appeal Hearing, AT. 472-474 (22 Mar 2017).

[465]   Praljak's Appeal Brief, paras 566-568, 570, 572; Praljak's Reply Brief, para. 120; Appeal Hearing, AT. 472-474 (22 Mar 2017). Praljak submits in particular that, had he known before the presentation of his defence case that, unlike the Prosecution, he was allowed to tender only a maximum number of 20 Rule 92 *bis* statements not exceeding 30 pages each, he would have organised his case differently. Praljak's Appeal Brief, paras 567-568. Similarly, he submits that the Trial Chamber considered that documents tendered by the Defence lacking a stamp or signature were not authentic, while it admitted documents with identical defects tendered by the Prosecution. Praljak's Appeal Brief, para. 572.

[466]   Praljak's Appeal Brief, paras 570-571.

[467]   Appeal Hearing, AT. 474-475 (22 Mar 2017), referring to Trial Judgement, Vol. 4, paras 54-55. See also Appeal Hearing, AT. 471 (22 Mar 2017). He submits in particular that the Trial Chamber erred in finding that the tendered documents were not relevant, considering that they concerned the presence of Mujahideen in Central Bosnia and that the JCE was allegedly implemented through frightening Croats into leaving Central Bosnia based on unfounded fear of the Mujahideen. Praljak's Appeal Brief, paras 570-571, 573-575; Appeal Hearing, AT. 474-475 (22 Mar 2017).

[468]   Praljak's Appeal Brief, paras 575-576; Appeal Hearing, AT. 473-474 (22 Mar 2017). See Praljak's Appeal Brief, para. 573. Praljak submits that this "simplification and reduction of facts" resulting from the non-admission affected his conviction "with regard to the existence of the JCE, *de facto* control, [and] effective control". Appeal Hearing, AT. 473 (22 Mar 2017). He further asserts that it is impossible to assess his *mens rea* without determining a pattern of conduct, his motivations, and his actions. Appeal Hearing, AT. 474 (22 Mar 2017).

[469]   Praljak's Appeal Brief, para. 576.

[470]   Prosecution's Response Brief (Praljak), paras 318-320.

[471]   Prosecution's Response Brief (Praljak), para. 304.

[472]   Prosecution's Response Brief (Praljak), paras 304, 314-320. The Prosecution asserts that one document listed by Praljak as having erroneously been denied admission appears to not have been tendered. Prosecution's Response Brief (Praljak), fn. 1570.

[473]   Prosecution's Response Brief (Praljak), para. 315. See Prosecution's Response Brief (Praljak), paras 316-317.

assertion that, if admitted, they would have offered "alternative plausible explanations" to his benefit falls short of showing that he suffered prejudice.[474]

149.   The Appeals Chamber first notes that the Trial Chamber did not misapply the law on admission of evidence. As Praljak does not demonstrate that the Trial Chamber did, in fact, consider the overall probative value and weight of the tendered evidence at the time of admission, the Appeals Chamber dismisses this argument.[475] Concerning the general submission that the Trial Chamber applied a stricter standard to the admission of evidence tendered by him than that tendered by the Prosecution, the Appeals Chamber finds that Stojić has not sufficiently substantiated this argument.[476]

150.   Concerning Praljak's argument on the non-admission of Rule 92 *bis* statements and transcripts specifically, the Appeals Chamber observes that Praljak's contention regarding their admission is also based in part on the restriction imposed by the Trial Chamber to limit the number of Rule 92 *bis* statements and transcripts that he could tender for admission.[477] The Appeals Chamber notes that the Rule 92 *bis* statements and transcripts at issue are among those the non-admission of which the Appeals Chamber has already upheld.[478] In this decision, it found that the Trial Chamber's limitation of the number of Rule 92 *bis* statements and transcripts that Praljak could tender for admission did not amount to a denial of his right to present evidence and was within the Trial Chamber's discretion.[479] The Appeals Chamber recalls that it may reconsider a previous interlocutory decision under its inherent discretionary power to do so if a clear error of reasoning has been demonstrated or if it is necessary to do so to prevent an injustice.[480] However in this case, Praljak merely repeats arguments already addressed by the Appeals Chamber without showing a clear error of reasoning or that reconsideration is necessary to prevent an injustice.

151.   With regard to the other documents at issue, the Appeals Chamber observes that the Trial Chamber rejected their admission on the basis that Praljak failed to establish a relevant link between the documents and the Indictment, or failed to demonstrate with sufficient clarity their **[page 64]** relevance and probative value.[481] Recalling a trial chamber's broad discretion in assessing admissibility of evidence it deems relevant,[482] the Appeals Chamber finds that Stojić has not demonstrated that the Trial Chamber abused its discretion in not admitting the documents. The Appeals Chamber further observes that Praljak merely alleges in a sweeping manner that the documents, if admitted, would have offered "alternative plausible explanations" to his benefit[483] but fails to explain what these alternative plausible explanations would be or to identify any particular factual finding that is affected and to explain how the documents, if admitted, would have impacted the finding.[484]

---

[474]   Prosecution's Response Brief (Praljak), paras 314, 320.

[475]   See *Prlić et al.* Trial Decision on Admission of Evidence Pursuant to Rule 92 *bis*.

[476]   The Appeals Chamber notes that in the *Prlić et al.* Appeal Decision on Admission of Evidence concerning a challenge brought by Prlić against the alleged "'more lenient approach'" to the admission of evidence tendered by the Prosecution than to the evidence tendered by Prlić, it dismissed Prlić's allegations, recalling that the assessment of admissibility criteria must be done on a case-by-case basis with respect to each tendered document. See *Prlić et al.* Appeal Decision on Admission of Evidence, para. 25. The Appeals Chamber adopts this consideration for purposes of dismissing Praljak's similar unsubstantiated challenge at issue here.

[477]   See Praljak's Appeal Brief, paras 567-568.

[478]   *Prlić et al.* Appeal Decision on Admission of Evidence Pursuant to Rule 92 *bis*, paras 15-17; Praljak's Appeal Brief, paras 567-569, 576.

[479]   *Prlić et al.* Appeal Decision on Admission of Evidence Pursuant to Rule 92 *bis*, para. 37.

[480]   See, *e.g.*, *Nyiramasuhuko et al.* Appeal Judgement, paras 56, 127; *Prlić et al.* Appeal Decision on Motion for Reconsideration, para. 6; *Šešelj* Appeal Decision on Motion for Reconsideration, para. 9.

[481]   See *Prlić et al.* Order to Admit Evidence in Relation to Praljak's Testimony, Annex, pp. 11-40. *Cf.* Praljak's Appeal Brief, fns 1301-1302, 1307-1308. The Appeals Chamber notes that with respect to documents referred to by Praljak in paragraphs 572-573 (and cited in footnotes 1303-1306) of his appeal brief, he fails to identify with sufficient clarity the specific Trial Chamber decisions and respective reasoning which he challenges. The Appeals Chamber recalls that an appellant is expected to provide precise references to relevant paragraphs in the decision to which the challenges are being made. See *supra*, para. 24. His arguments relating to these decisions are therefore dismissed.

[482]   See *supra*, para. 143.

[483]   See *supra*, para. 147.

[484]   The Appeals Chamber recalls that an appellant is expected to provide precise references to relevant paragraphs in the judgement to which the challenges are being made. See *supra*, para. 24. Praljak does identify one challenged finding in Trial Judgement, Vol. 4, paras 54-55. See Appeal Hearing AT. 475 (22 Mar 2017); *supra*, fn. 467. The Appeals Chamber notes, however, that he ignores other relevant factual findings in the same paragraphs which in fact acknowledge that part of the Croatian population was in danger due to the clashes in Central Bosnia. His argument is dismissed.

152.   On the basis of the above, the Appeals Chamber finds that Praljak has failed to demonstrate that the Trial Chamber abused its discretion and committed a discernible error by denying admission of the Rule 92 *bis* statements and transcripts, and other documents at issue. Praljak's ground of appeal 51 is therefore dismissed.

3.   Erroneous decisions relating to evidence (Ćorić's Ground 12)

(a) Arguments of the Parties

153.   Ćorić submits that the Trial Chamber erred by admitting the evidence of a co-Appellant as well as inauthentic documents.[485] Ćorić first submits that the Trial Chamber erred in law and fact and violated his fair trial rights when it admitted and relied on a statement given by Prlić to the Prosecution in December 2001 against his co-Appellants ("Prlić's Statement").[486] Ćorić contends in particular that: (1) Prlić's rights were violated since he was not properly informed before bis questioning; (2) the other Parties did not have an opportunity to cross-examine him; (3) the admission of the statement violates requirements under Rules 92 *bis,* 92 *ter* and 92 *quater* of the Rules; (4) the statement contains answers to leading questions; and (5) it should have been excluded **[page 65]** pursuant to Rule 89 (D) of the Rules.[487] Ćorić also asserts that the Trial Chamber's error in admitting Prlić's Statements is further compounded by its error in not admitting Praljak's and Petković's respective statements, since: (1) they could have been admitted pursuant to Rule 89 of the Rules like Prlić's Statements; (2) unlike Prlić, both Praljak and Petković testified and could be cross-examined; (3) consequently, their statements did not need to be excluded pursuant to Rule 89 (D) of the Rules; and (4) the fact that they contain hearsay evidence does not pose problems since the Trial Chamber relied on other hearsay evidence[488]

154.   Ćorić further contends that the Trial Chamber erred when it admitted and relied on Exhibits P03216/P03220 and P03666 as they are forgeries.[489] Regarding Exhibit P03216/P03220,[490] Ćorić submits that the Trial Chamber erred in admitting it and in not recognising in the Trial Judgement that it was not authentic.[491] He argues that no reasonable trier of fact could have concluded that it was authentic since: (1) it is not Ćorić's signature on the document; (2) [Redacted, see Annex C – Confidential Annex] and none of the witnesses who could have been recipients confirmed receiving it; and (3) it is not recorded in the Heliodrom Prison Logbook while the Trial Chamber for other documents required verification in the Heliodrom Prison Logbook as proof of authenticity.[492] He asserts that in admitting and relying on Exhibit P03216/P03220 the Trial Chamber erred in law and fact, violated his fair trial rights, and failed to provide a reasoned opinion.[493]

155.   Regarding Exhibit P03666, Ćorić contends that the Trial Chamber erred in admitting this evidence despite his objections as it is missing the most essential indicia of authenticity and reliability.[494] He adds that the Trial Chamber erred in concluding in the Trial Judgement that Exhibit P03666 was authentic since: (1) the Trial Chamber erroneously relied on similarities between the exhibit and other documents; and (2) contrary to what the Trial Chamber found, **[page 66]** Witness BB did not confirm substantial parts of Exhibit

---

[485]   Ćorić's Appeal Brief, para. 260; Appeal Hearing, AT. 611 (24 Mar 2017). See Ćorić's Appeal Brief, heading before para. 260.
[486]   Ćorić's Appeal Brief, para. 260; Ćorić's Reply Brief, para. 62.
[487]   Ćorić's Appeal Brief, para. 260. See also Ćorić's Reply Brief, para. 62.
[488]   Ćorić's Appeal Brief, para. 261.
[489]   Ćorić's Appeal Brief, paras 262-266, 268-270; Appeal Hearing, AT. 611-616 (24 Mar 2017).
[490]   The Appeals Chamber observes that Exhibit P03216 and Exhibit P03220 are the same document. See Trial Judgement, Vol. 1, para. 913 & fn. 2234. For the sake of clarity, the Appeals Chamber will refer to this document as Exhibit P03216/P03220.
[491]   Ćorić's Appeal Brief, paras 263-264, 266-267.
[492]   Ćorić's Appeal Brief, paras 264-265, referring to, *inter alia,* Exhibit P00285 ("the Heliodrom Prison Logbook"). See Ćorić's Reply Brief, para. 63. He also contends that Witness C confirmed that people could only be released from Dretelj Prison with Colonel Neđeljko Obradović's approval which is the complete opposite to Exhibit P03216/P03220. See Ćorić's Appeal Brief, para. 264.
[493]   Ćorić's Appeal Brief, paras 262-266; Appeal Hearing, AT. 611-616 (24 Mar 2017). He also asserts that the Trial Chamber relied heavily on this exhibit in its findings on: (1) his responsibility in the alleged network of Herceg-Bosna/HVO prisons; (2) the Military Police Administration's authority to release the HVO's prisoners; and (3) Ćorić's belief that only this administration held the power to release prisoners. See Ćorić's Appeal Brief, paras 262-265; Appeal Hearing, AT. 611-613, 616-617 (24 Mar 2017). He asserts that without Exhibit P03216/P03220, his link to prisons and his alleged responsibility or membership in the alleged JCE "would not exist or would have [to be] significantly differently evaluated". Appeal Hearing, AT. 617 (24 Mar 2017).
[494]   Ćorić's Appeal Brief, paras 268-269.

P03666.[495] Ćorić requests that due to the Trial Chamber's erroneous reliance on these documents, and erroneous rulings, his convictions be vacated.[496]

156.   The Prosecution responds that the Trial Chamber acted well within its broad discretion in admitting Prlić's Statement and Exhibits P03216/P03220 and P03666, and in denying admission of Praljak's and Petković's statements.[497] With regard to Prlić's Statements, the Prosecution contends that the Appeals Chamber has already confirmed their admission in an interlocutory appeal, and that Ćorić has not shown that reconsideration of the Appeals Chamber's decision is warranted.[498] With regard to Praljak's and Petković's statements, the Prosecution asserts that Ćorić should be precluded from raising on appeal the issue of their admissibility, since he argued at trial that these statements should be denied admission, and that in any event, he fails to show any error.[499] The Prosecution submits with regard to Exhibits P03216/P03220 and P03666 that Ćorić largely repeats his trial arguments without showing any error in the Trial Chamber's consideration of their authenticity and decision to admit them.[500] In relation to Exhibit P03216/P03220 specifically, the Prosecution contends that: (1) the document bears the stamp of the chief of the Military Police Administration; (2) Ćorić misrepresents Witness E's testimony; and (3) the Trial Chamber did not require verification in the Heliodrom Prison Logbook as proof of authenticity.[501] Finally, the Prosecution submits that Ćorić fails to show how the Trial Chamber's decision to admit Prlić's Statements and Exhibit P03666 had any impact on his convictions or occasioned a miscarriage of justice.[502]

(b) Analysis

(i) Admission of Prlić's Statements

157.   On 22 August 2007, the Trial Chamber admitted Prlić's Statement essentially considering that its probative value was not substantially outweighed by the need to ensure a fair trial.[503] On 23 November 2007, the Appeals Chamber dismissed the Appellants' interlocutory appeal against **[page 67]** the *Prlić et al.* Trial Decision on Admission of Prlić's Statement.[504] The Appeals Chamber concluded that the Trial Chamber, in light of its careful balancing exercise of the probative value of Prlić's Statements and the potential prejudice to the co-Appellants resulting from their admission, had not misinterpreted or misapplied the law governing admission of evidence.[505] On 5 September 2007 and 17 October 2007, the Trial Chamber denied the Prosecution's request to admit Praljak's and Petković's prior testimonies in other cases before the Tribunal, on the basis that admitting these prior testimonies would be a serious violation of the right of the accused as Praljak and Petković had not been informed about their right to remain silent.[506]

---

[495]   Ćorić's Appeal Brief, paras 269-270.

[496]   Ćorić's Appeal Brief, para. 270; Appeal Hearing, AT. 611-612 (24 Mar 2017).

[497]   Prosecution's Response Brief (Ćorić), paras 286-292, 294-300, 302.

[498]   Prosecution's Response Brief (Ćorić), paras 286-288.

[499]   Prosecution's Response Brief (Ćorić), paras 286, 290-291.

[500]   Prosecution's Response Brief (Ćorić), paras 292, 294, 298-300. See also Prosecution's Response Brief (Ćorić), paras 197 (responding to Ćorić's ground of appeal 7), 295-297 (responding to Ćorić's ground of appeal 12), 329-332 (responding to Ćorić's ground of appeal 14). The Prosecution further submits that Ćorić's assertion that he had no power to release prisoners is proven incorrect by a wealth of evidence. Appeal Hearing, AT. 646-647, 651 (24 Mar 2017).

[501]   Prosecution's Response Brief (Ćorić), paras 294-296. The Prosecution adds that the information in the exhibit is consistent with the evidence as a whole. Prosecution's Response Brief (Ćorić), para. 297.

[502]   Prosecution's Response Brief (Ćorić), paras 289, 301.

[503]   *Prosecutor v. Jadranko Prlić et al.*, Case No. IT-04-74-T, Decision on Request for Admission of the Statement of Jadranko Prlić, 6 September 2007 (French original 22 August 2007) *("Prlić et al.* Trial Decision on Admission of Prlić's Statement"), paras 1, 31-32, p. 16. See Trial Judgement, Vol. 1, para. 391.

[504]   *Prosecutor v. Jadranko Prlić et al.*, Case No. IT-04-74-AR73.6, Decision on Appeals Against Decision Admitting Transcript of Jadranko Prlić's Questioning into Evidence, 23 November 2007 *("Prlić et al.* Appeal Decision on Admission of Prlić's Statement"), paras 1, 7, p. 20. See Trial Judgement, Vol. 1, para. 392.

[505]   *Prlić et al.* Appeal Decision on Admission of Prlić's Statements, para. 62.

[506]   *Prosecutor v. Jadranko Prlić et al.*, Case No. IT-04-74-T, Decision on the Admission into Evidence of Slobodan Praljak's Evidence in the Case of [Naletelić] and Martinović, 17 September 2007 (French original 5 September 2007) *("Pilić et al.* Trial Decision on Admission of Praljak's Prior Testimony"), para. 22, p. 11; *Prosecutor v. Jadranko Prlić et al.*, Case No. IT-04-74-T, Decision on Prosecution Motion for the Admission into Evidence of the Testimony of Milivoj Petković Given in Other Cases Before

158.   The Appeals Chamber observes that it has already addressed and dismissed the Appellants' arguments, including those of Ćorić, in the *Prlić et al.* Appeal Decision on Admission of Prlić's Statements.[507] It recalls that it may reconsider a previous interlocutory decision in exceptional cases under its inherent discretionary power to do so if a clear error of reasoning has been demonstrated or if it is necessary to do so to prevent an injustice.[508] The Appeals Chamber finds that Ćorić's arguments on appeal merely repeat arguments previously addressed by the Appeals Chamber without showing a clear error of reasoning or that reconsideration is necessary to prevent an injustice.[509] In addition, the fact that Prlić was not going to ultimately testify at trial was not known at the time of the *Prlić et al.* Appeal Decision on Admission of Prlić's Statement. Nevertheless, the possibility that he would not testify had already been expressly considered by the Appeals Chamber when it concluded that Prlić's Statement could be introduced into evidence even if his co-Appellants might not be able to cross-examine him, since as a matter of principle nothing bars the **[page 68]** admission of evidence that is not tested or might not be tested through cross-examination.[510] As such, the Appeals Chamber is not convinced that Ćorić has shown that the fact that Prlić did not testify at trial should lead the Appeals Chamber to reconsider its previous decision in order to prevent an injustice. To the extent that Ćorić also argues that the Trial Chamber erred in relying on Prlić's Statements, the Appeals Chamber observes that he does not point to any Trial Chamber findings where the Trial Chamber in fact relied on them.[511] His unsupported argument is dismissed.

159.   The Appeals Chamber also fails to see how a possible error of the Trial Chamber in not admitting Praljak's and Petković's prior testimonies in other cases at the Tribunal would assist in showing that the Trial Chamber erred in admitting Prlić's Statements. Moreover, none of Ćorić's arguments alleging errors with the *Prlić et al.* Trial Decision on Admission of Praljak's Prior Testimony and the *Prlić et al.* Trial Decision on Admission of Petković's Prior Testimony address the Trial Chamber's finding that admitting these prior testimonies would be a serious violation of the rights of the accused as they were not informed about their right to remain silent.[512]

(ii) Exhibit P03216/P03220

160.   On 27 September 2007 and 10 October 2007 respectively, the Trial Chamber admitted Exhibits P03216 and P03220.[513] In the Trial Judgement, the Trial Chamber observed that Exhibits P03216 and P03220 are the same document and noted Ćorić's objection that Exhibit P03216/P03220 was a forgery.[514] However, the Trial Chamber recalled that by admitting Exhibit P03216/P03220, it considered that it had sufficient

---

the Tribunal, 25 October 2007 (French original 17 October 2007) *("Prlić et al.* Trial Decision on Admission of Petković's Prior Testimony"), para. 20, p. 9.

[507]   *Prlić et al.* Appeal Decision on Admission of Prlić's Statement, paras 7, 31-63, p. 20.

[508]   See, *e.g., Nyiramasuhuko et al.* Appeal Judgement, para. 127; *Prosecutor v. Jadranko Prlić et al.,* Case No. IT-04-74-AR73.16, Decision on Jadranko Prlić's Interlocutory Appeal Against the *Decision on Prlić Defence Motion for Reconsideration of the Decision on Admission of Documentaiy Evidence,* 3 November 2009, para. 6; *Prosecutor v. Vojislav Šešelj,* Case No. IT-03-67-AR72.1, Decision on Motion for Reconsideration of the "Decision on the Interlocutory Appeal Concerning Jurisdiction" dated 31 August 2004, 15 June 2006, para. 9. See also *Nyiramasuhuko et al.* Appeal Judgement, para. 56.

[509]   In particular, the Appeals Chamber already dismissed arguments related to analogies with Rules 92 *bis* and 92 *quater* of the Rules, the possibility of cross-examination, and the distinction between the admission of Prlić's Statement and its evaluation in light of the whole trial record. See *Prlić et al.* Appeal Decision on Admission of Prlić's Statement, paras 31-63.

[510]   *Prlić et al.* Appeal Decision on Admission of Prlić's Statement, para. 55. See also *Prlić et al.* Appeal Decision on Admission of Prlić's Statements, paras 50-54.

[511]   See Ćorić's Appeal Brief, para. 260.

[512]   *Prlić et al.* Trial Decision on Admission of Praljak's Prior Testimony, para. 22; *Prlić et al.* Trial Decision on Admission of Petković's Prior Testimony, para. 20. In addition, the Appeals Chamber observes that Ćorić's position at trial was that the Prosecution's request to admit Praljak's and Petković's prior testimonies in other cases before the Tribunal should be rejected. See *Prlić et al.* Trial Decision on Admission of Praljak's Prior Testimony, para. 3 (incorrectly spelling Ćorić's name as "Jorić"); *Prlić et al.* Trial Decision on Admission of Petković's Prior Testimony, para. 4. Ćorić also does not show that he requested the admission at trial of Praljak's and Petković's prior testimonies in other cases at the Tribunal, or that he raised at trial the arguments he raised on appeal.

[513]   *Prosecutor v. Jadranko Prlić et al.,* Case No. IT-04-74-T, Order on Admission of Evidence Relative to Witness E, 2 November 2007 (French original 27 September 2007), pp. 2-3, 5; *Prosecutor v. Jadranko Prlić et al.,* Case No. IT-04-74-T, Order to Admit Evidence Regarding Witness C, 19 October 2007 (French original 10 October 2007), pp. 2-4.

[514]   Trial Judgement, Vol. 1, para. 913 & fn. 2231, referring to Ćorić's Final Brief, paras 699-701.

indicia of authenticity and reliability.[515] The Trial Chamber relied on Exhibit P03216/P03220 to find, *inter alia,* that the Military Police Administration had the power and authority to order the release of persons detained by the HVO.[516] **[page 69]**

161.   The Appeals Chamber observes that Exhibit P03216/P03220 bears the stamp of the Military Police Administration and the type written name of Valentin Ćorić.[517] Ćorić does not challenge these aspects but asserts that the handwritten signature was not his.[518] Ćorić further makes contradictory arguments suggesting on the one hand that it looks like his deputy Rade Lavrić's signature but on the other hand states that Witness Slobodan Božić testified that it was neither Ćorić nor Lavrić's signature but a forgery.[519] Having reviewed the relevant part of Božić's testimony, the Appeals Chamber is not convinced that the witness testified that Exhibit P03216/P03220 was a forgery, nor that he was in a position to conclusively state that the signature was not that of Rade Lavrić.[520] Even accepting that the handwritten signature on the document does not belong to Ćorić, the Appeals Chamber is not convinced that Ćorić has demonstrated that the document did not come from the Military Police Administration, or that it indeed was a forgery. Consequently, Ćorić has not shown that the Trial Chamber could not have relied on it to conclude that the Military Police Administration had the power and authority to order the release of persons detained by the HVO.[521]

162.   In addition, as pointed out by the Prosecution, even though Witness E testified that, [Redacted, see Annex C – Confidential Annex] and further testified that Ćorić had the authority to release prisoners.[522] The Appeals Chamber is further not convinced that the absence of a mention of Exhibit P03216/P03220 in the Heliodrom Prison Logbook[523] establishes that the document is not authentic. Ćorić has not demonstrated that the Trial Chamber in fact required verification in the Heliodrom Prison Logbook for a document to be considered authentic.[524] Nor does the Appeals Chamber consider that the fact that Exhibit P00316, an order from Colonel Obradović mentioned in Exhibit P03216/P03220, is recorded in the Heliodrom Prison Logbook demonstrates that Exhibit P03216/P03220 is inauthentic,[525] since the fact that other documents were entered in the Heliodrom Prison Logbook does not establish that the entries contained therein were exhaustive.[526] **[page 70]**

163.   In light of the foregoing, the Appeals Chamber is not convinced that Ćorić has shown that the Trial Chamber erred in considering that Exhibit P03216/P03220 had sufficient indicia of authenticity and reliability for the purpose of admission, and that no reasonable trier of fact could have relied on Exhibit P03216/P03220 to conclude that the Military Police Administration had the power and authority to order the release of persons detained by the HVO.[527] Consequently, the Appeals Chamber dismisses Ćorić's arguments relating to Exhibit P03216/P03220.

---

[515]   Trial Judgement, Vol. 1, para. 913.
[516]   Trial Judgement, Vol. 1, paras 913-914.
[517]   See Exs. P03216, P03220.
[518]   See *supra*, para. 154.
[519]   See Ćorić's Appeal Brief, para. 264.
[520]   See Slobodan Božić, T. 36412-36414 (4 Feb 2009), T. 36642-36644 (10 Feb 2009).
[521]   Trial Judgement, Vol. 1, paras 913-914.
[522]   Witness E, T. 22051-22053 (closed session) (10 Sept 2007). Moreover the fact that Witness C testified that people could only be released from Dretelj Prison with Colonel Nedeljko Obradović's approval does not establish that Exhibit P03216/P03220 was a forgery. Ćorić's argument in this respect is dismissed. See Ćorić's Appeal Brief, para. 264, referring to, *inter alia*, Witness C, T. 22398 (closed session) (18 Sept 2007).
[523]   See Ćorić's Appeal Brief, para. 264, referring to Ex. P00285.
[524]   Ćorić's Appeal Brief, para. 264, referring to Trial Judgement, Vol. 2, para. 1431. The Appeals Chamber notes that in this paragraph, the Trial Chamber relied on the Heliodrom Prison Logbook to reach the conclusion that the instructions of Stojić were sent to and received at the Heliodrom, but does not address specifically whether the document was authentic. See Trial Judgement, Vol. 2, para. 1431. Even if Ćorić had demonstrated that the Trial Chamber required verification in the Heliodrom Prison Logbook for a document to be considered authentic, the Appeals Chamber notes that this would not have detracted from the fact that the admissibility decision had remained in the discretion of the Trial Chamber. See *Naletilić and Martinović* Appeal Judgement, para. 402.
[525]   Ćorić's Appeal Brief, para. 265 & fn. 710, referring, *inter alia*, to Ex. P00316.
[526]   See Ex. P00285, p. 121.
[527]   The Appeals Chamber further observes that the Trial Chamber did not rely only on Exhibit P03216/P03220 to reach this conclusion but found that it was corroborated by further evidence. See Trial Judgement, Vol. 1, paras 912-913.

(iii) Exhibit P03666

164.   On 23 August 2007, the Trial Chamber admitted into evidence Exhibit P03666.[528] In the Trial Judgement, the Trial Chamber noted Ćorić's claim raised in his final trial brief that Exhibit P03666 is a forgery, but recalled the *Prlić et al.* Trial Decision on Admission of Evidence related to the Municipalities of Čapljina and Stolac whereby it admitted the exhibit.[529] The Trial Chamber further stated that Ćorić had raised no objection to the authenticity of this document until his final trial brief.[530] It then found that the document was shown to Witness BB who confirmed a substantial part of its contents and that the format of the document is entirely similar to other reports admitted and whose authenticity was not contested by Ćorić.[531] On this basis, the Trial Chamber held that Exhibit P03666 was indeed authentic.[532]

165.   The Appeals Chamber observes that Ćorić challenges both the admission into evidence of Exhibit P03666 at trial as well as the Trial Chamber's confirmation in the Trial Judgement that it considered that Exhibit P03666 was indeed authentic.[533] The Appeals Chamber recalls that if a party raises no objection to a particular issue before a trial chamber when it could have reasonably done so, in the absence of special circumstances, the Appeals Chamber will find that the party has waived his right to raise the issue on appeal.[534] Having reviewed the *Prlić ei al.* Trial Decision on Admission of Evidence related to the Municipalities of Čapljina and Stolac and the Joint Defence Response of 12 July 2007 pointed out by Ćorić to show that he had objected to the admission of Exhibit P03666,[535] the Appeals Chamber confirms the Trial Chamber's finding that he did not raise **[page 71]** specific issues with the authenticity of Exhibit P03666 at the time of its admission at trial.[536] Accordingly, Ćorić cannot claim for the first time on appeal that the Trial Chamber erred in admitting Exhibit P03666 because it was not authentic.

166.   As for Ćorić's distinguishable argument challenging the Trial Chamber's confirmation of Exhibit P03666's authenticity in the Trial Judgement,[537] the Appeals Chamber observes that he does not point to any Trial Chamber finding relying on this evidence. The Appeals Chamber notes, however, that the Prosecution points to three findings where the Trial Chamber relied on Exhibit P03666,[538] unrelated specifically to Ćorić's responsibility.[539] Nevertheless, the Appeals Chamber observes that the Trial Chamber relied on other evidence to reach these findings,[540] and that in any event, Ćorić does not explain how, even if the document was found to be inauthentic, it would affect his convictions. Accordingly, the Appeals Chamber dismisses the remainder of Ćorić's arguments related to the Trial Chamber's finding that Exhibit P03666 was authentic.

167.   Ćorić's ground of appeal 12 is therefore dismissed.

---

[528]   *Prosecutor v. Jadranko Prlić et al.*, Case No. IT-04-74-T, Decision on the Motions For Admission of Documentary Evidence (Čapljina/Stolac Municipalities), 3 September 2007 (French original 23 August 2007) *("Prlić et al.* Trial Decision on Admission of Evidence related to the Municipalities of Čapljina and Stolac"), p. 9.
[529]   Trial Judgement, Vol. 3, para. 75.
[530]   Trial Judgement, Vol. 3, para. 75.
[531]   Trial Judgement, Vol. 3, para. 75.
[532]   Trial Judgement, Vol. 3, para. 75.
[533]   Ćorić's Appeal Brief, paras 268-270.
[534]   *Popović et al.* Appeal Judgement, para. 176. See *Haradinaj et al.* Appeal Judgement, para. 112.
[535]   Ćorić's Appeal Brief, para. 269, referring to *Prosecutor v. Jadranko Prlić et al.*, Case No. IT-04-74-T, Joint Defence Response to Prosecution Motion for Admission of Documentary Evidence (Čapljina/Stolac Municipalities), 12 My 2007 ("Joint Defence Response of 12 July 2007"), Ćorić's Final Brief, para. 698. Ćorić mistakenly refers to the 2 July 2007 as the filing date of the Joint Defence Response of 12 July 2007. Ćorić's Appeal Brief, para. 269.
[536]   See *Prlić et al.* Trial Decision on Admission of Evidence related to the Municipalities of Čapljina and Stolac, Joint Defence Response of 12 July 2007. See also Joint Defence Response of 12 July 2007, Annex, Specific Objections of the Ćorić Defence (where Ćorić notes that the Prosecution had already proposed to tender proposed Exhibit P03666 into evidence through the testimony of Witness BB and that pending a decision, the Prosecution should not be allowed to push this document in through other provisions).
[537]   See Ćorić's Appeal Brief, paras 268-270. See also Trial Judgement, Vol. 3, para. 75.
[538]   See Prosecution's Response Brief (Ćorić), para. 301, referring to Trial Judgement, Vol. 3, para. 74 & fn. 180, para. 587 & fn. 1195, Vol. 4, para. 939 & fn. 1761.
[539]   The Trial Chamber relied on Exhibit P03666 to find that: (1) some prisoners were released from Dretelj Prison; (2) the HVO conducted a campaign of mass arrests of Muslim men of military age throughout Čapljina Municipality in July 1993; and (3) from June 1993 and until at least the end of February 1994, nobody could pass through the HVO checkpoints. See Trial Judgement, Vol. 3, para. 74 & fn. 180, para. 587 & fn. 1195, Vol. 4, para. 939 & fn. 1761.
[540]   See Trial Judgement, Vol. 3, para. 74.

D. **Assessment of Evidence**

1. Erroneous approach to the evaluation of evidence (Prlić's Ground 1)

(a) Arguments of the Parties

168.   Under his ground of appeal 1, Prlić submits that the Trial Chamber erred in law and fact by failing to properly assess relevant evidence on the record when making various findings in relation to the historical background to the creation, development, and structure of the HZ(R) H-B.[541] Prlić argues that such erroneous findings form the basis of findings on his JCE responsibility, which led the Trial Chamber to unreasonably conclude that the HZ(R) H-B was linked to the reconstitution of **[page 72]** the Banovina 1939 borders, in furtherance of a JCE.[542] He avers that a proper assessment of the evidence would have shown that: (1) the HZ H-B was established out of necessity; (2) he and the Executive organs/Governments of the Croatian Community and Republic of Herceg-Bosna, referred to jointly ("HVO/Government of the HZ(R) H-B") had no power over the municipalities or their presidents; (3) "the Departments, Sub-departments, Services, and Commissions" were independent and not subordinated to him or the HVO/Government of the HZ(R) H-B; and (4) the HR H-B was created as a result of the Owen-Stoltenberg Peace Plan, rather than in furtherance of the JCE.[543] Prlić requests that the Appeals Chamber overturn his convictions on all Counts.[544]

169.   The Prosecution responds that Prlić fails to explain how the alleged errors support his claim that no reasonable trier of fact would have linked the HZ(R) H-B to reconstituting the Banovina 1939 borders in furtherance of a JCE.[545] The Prosecution further argues that Prlić relies on sweeping, unexplained assertions that the supposed errors lead to erroneous conclusions regarding the existence of a JCE and Prlić's membership therein.[546] Consequently, the Prosecution submits that Prlić fails to demonstrate an error affecting the verdict.[547] It further argues that the alleged legal errors are undeveloped, because: (1) Prlić fails to identify the allegedly incorrect legal standard used to assess evidence; (2) much of the allegedly ignored evidence either was expressly considered by the Trial Chamber, is irrelevant, or supports the Trial Chamber's findings; and (3) the alleged mischaracterisations of the evidence merely reflect his disagreement with the Trial Chamber's interpretation of the evidence, without demonstrating that it was unreasonable.[548]

(b) Analysis

170.   The Appeals Chamber observes that Prlić takes issue with a number of discrete findings in three sections in Volume 1 of the Trial Judgement concerning: (1) the historical background of the proclamation of the HZ H-B;[549] (2) the events following the creation of the HZ(R) H-B;[550] and (3) the structure of the HZ(R) H-B.[551] **[page 73]**

171.   With respect to Prlić's challenges concerning the findings on the historical background to the creation of the HZ H-B,[552] the Appeals Chamber observes that in the introduction of this section, the Trial Chamber expressly stated that this analysis was "strictly historical" and did not concern any events which might have "an impact on the criminal responsibility of the Accused, particularly as to whether there was a JCE or

---

[541]   Prlić's Appeal Brief, paras 26-89 (sub-grounds of appeal 1.1-1.4). See also Appeal Hearing, AT. 128-129, 134-136, 149 (20 Mar 2017). See also Prlić's Reply Brief, paras 32-36.

[542]   Prlić's Appeal Brief, paras 27, 45, 77, 87, referring to his grounds of appeal 9-10. See also Prlić's Appeal Brief, paras 24-25, 30, 33, 36, 46.

[543]   Prlić's Appeal Brief, para. 88, referring to his grounds of appeal 9-10 and sub-grounds of appeal 11.3-11.9, 12.1.

[544]   Prlić's Appeal Brief, para. 89.

[545]   Prosecution's Response Brief (Prlić), para. 16.

[546]   Prosecution's Response Brief (Prlić), paras 16, 20, 29, 36, 40.

[547]   Prosecution's Response Brief (Prlić), paras 16, 18, 20, 29-30, 37, 40.

[548]   Prosecution's Response Brief (Prlić), paras 17, 21-27, 31, 33-35, 39, 42-43.

[549]   Trial Judgement, Vol. 1, paras 406-425 ("The Creation of Herceg-Bosna: Background").

[550]   Trial Judgement, Vol. 1, paras 426-490 ("Principal Events Following the Creation of Herceg-Bosna").

[551]   Trial Judgement, Vol. 1, paras 491-986 ("Political, Administrative, Military and Judicial Structure of the HZ(R) H-B").

[552]   Prlić's Appeal Brief, paras 27-37.

whether the Accused participated in the said enterprise".[553] Moreover, the relevant portions of Volume 4 of the Trial Judgement concerning the existence of the JCE and Prlić's contribution thereto show that in reaching its conclusions, the Trial Chamber did not refer to its analysis or any of the findings contained in the section concerned.[554] Accordingly, the Appeals Chamber finds that Prlić's convictions do not rely on the impugned factual findings on the historical background to the creation of the HZ H-B and, thus, dismisses Prlić's arguments in this respect.

172.   As to Prlić's claims concerning the findings on the events following the creation of the HZ(R) H-B and the structure of the HZ(R) H-B contained in the other two sections of Volume 1 of the Trial Judgement,[555] the Appeals Chamber notes that the Trial Chamber referred to some of the findings therein in the sections related to the Ultimate Purpose of the JCE, the CCP, and Prlić's contribution to the JCE.[556] However, other than claiming that these alleged errors resulted in a "false narrative" affecting the conclusions concerning his JCE responsibility,[557] Prlić does not attempt to explain how his challenges to the Trial Chamber's sections concerning the events following the creation of the HZ(R) H-B and its structure, even if accepted, could affect any findings material to his conviction.

173.   Further, the Appeals Chamber observes that in concluding his submissions under this ground of appeal, Prlić refers to his grounds of appeal 9, 10, 11, and 12, where he challenges the Trial Chamber's findings with respect to the Ultimate Purpose of the JCE, the CCP, and his contribution to the JCE.[558] Nevertheless, the Appeals Chamber considers that the use of the cross-references does not provide any further clarity to Prlić's arguments.

174.   On the contrary, a review of his grounds of appeal 9, 10, 11, and 12 shows that in several instances, Prlić simply asserts that he adopts "by reference" single excerpts or entire portions of his **[page 74]** submissions contained in his ground of appeal 1 without providing any explanation as to how these arguments have any merit in the context of his challenges against different Trial Chamber conclusions reached with respect to his criminal liability.[559] In this regard, a joint reading of his ground of appeal 1 and his challenges concerning the Ultimate Purpose of the JCE, the CCP, and his contribution to the JCE in light of these cross-references, reveals an incoherent and often convoluted narrative, which is decidedly unhelpful to understanding the crux of his contentions or any purported impact on his conviction. While nothing prevents a party from cross-referencing to arguments in different sections of its appeal brief, in order for the Appeals Chamber to assess a party's arguments, the party is expected to present its case clearly, logically, and exhaustively.[560] The manner and degree to which Prlić cross-references to arguments in other sections under his ground of appeal 1 renders the merits of his contentions unclear and obscure.[561]

---

[553]   Trial Judgement, Vol. 1, para. 408. The Trial Chamber added that it "considered it more appropriate to address these events in the parts concerning the responsibility of the Accused". Trial Judgement, Vol. 1, para. 408.

[554]   Trial Judgement, Vol. 4, paras 6-24 (Ultimate Purpose of the JCE), 41-73 (Existence of a Common Criminal Plan), 74-289 (Prlić's contribution to the JCE).

[555]   Prlić's Appeal Brief, paras 38-86.

[556]   See Trial Judgement, Vol. 4, paras 13, 17 (Ultimate Purpose of the JCE), 43-44 (Existence of a Common Criminal Plan) 82, 88-89, 91, 95, 99, 101, 105-106, 110, 125, 198 (Prlić's contribution to the JCE).

[557]   Prlić's Appeal Brief, paras 27, 45, 77.

[558]   See Prlić's Appeal Brief, paras 87-88, referring to his grounds of appeal 9-10 and sub-grounds of appeal 11.3-11.9, 12.1.

[559]   See Prlić's Appeal Brief, paras 234 (referring to Prlić's sub-ground of appeal 1.1, paras 27-28, 36-41), 235 (referring to Prlić's sub-grounds of appeal 1.1, para. 30, 1.2, para. 51), 240 (referring to Prlić's sub-ground of appeal 1.3, paras 80-81), 241 (referring to Prlić's sub-ground of appeal 1.3, paras 80-82), 253 (referring to Prlić's sub-ground of appeal 1.1, para. 44), 257 (referring to Prlić's sub-grounds of appeal 1.1, paras 27-40, 1.2, paras 48-49, 53, 58-59), 263 (referring to Prlić's sub-grounds of appeal 1.1, para. 36, 1.3, para. 82), 276 (referring to Prlić's sub-ground of appeal 1.3), 283 (referring to Prlić's sub-grounds of appeal 1.1, 1.3), 302 (referring to Prlić's sub-ground of appeal 1.3, para. 82), 309 (referring to Prlić's sub-grounds of appeal 1.1, 1.3), 315 (referring to Prlić's sub-ground of appeal 1.2, paras 45-47, 1.4), 318 (referring to Prlić's sub-ground of appeal 1.1), 320 (referring to Prlić's sub-ground of appeal 1.2, paras 50-51, 54-55), 324 (referring to Prlić's sub-grounds of appeal 1.2, paras 45-57, 1.4, paras 83-86), 328 (referring to Prlić's sub-ground of appeal 1.3, paras 47-57), 339 (recalling Prlić's sub-ground of appeal 1.2, para. 54), 343 (referring to Prlić's sub-ground of appeal 1.2), 344 (referring to Prlić's sub-grounds of appeal 1.2, para. 52, 1.2.4-1.2.5), 351 (referring to Prlić's sub-ground of appeal 1.2, para. 51), 354 (referring to Prlić's sub-grounds of appeal 1.2, para. 52, 1.2.4-1.2.5), 361 (recalling Prlić's sub-grounds of appeal 1.2, para. 52, 1.2.4-1.2.5), 364 (referring to Prlić's sub-grounds of appeal 1.2, para. 52, 1.2.4-1.2.5), 375 (referring to Prlić's sub-grounds of appeal 1.2, paras 54-55, 1.2.6), 401 (referring to Prlić's ground of appeal 1, paras 184-185).

[560]   See *supra*, para. 24.

[561]   In addition, the Appeals Chamber observes that Prlić's relevant arguments in grounds 9, 10, 11, and 12 are all dismissed. See *infra*, paras 592-782 (Ground of Appeal 9), 783-1014 (Ground of Appeal 10), 831, 849, 1097, 1127.

175. Moreover, Prlić's submissions are undeveloped and abstract and for this reason alone do not warrant appellate review. Specifically, Prlić's arguments are principally based on assertions: (1) that the Trial Chamber failed to consider certain evidence, yet lacking any explanation as to why no reasonable trier of fact, based on the evidence, could have reached the same conclusion;[562] and (2) reflecting mere disagreement with the Trial Chamber's assessment of the evidence.[563] In none of his challenges, under this ground of appeal, does Prlić explain why it was unreasonable for the Trial Chamber to have reached its conclusions. In combination with the lack of clarity and obscurity referred to above, the Appeals Chamber is unable to properly assess what, if any, impact Prlić's **[page 75]** challenges might have upon the verdict, when read alone or in the context of the other grounds of his appeal.

176. Based on the foregoing, the Appeals Chamber dismisses Prlić's ground of appeal 1.

2. Failure to explain assessment of documentary evidence (Prlić's Ground 3)

(a) Arguments of the Parties

177. Prlić submits that the Trial Chamber systematically failed to make specific findings on how it assessed documentary evidence, thereby erring in law by applying an incorrect legal standard and failing to provide a reasoned opinion.[564] Prlić argues that the Trial Chamber made general statements on how it assessed documentary evidence, without indicating how it applied its general approach to specific evidence.[565] Prlić asserts in this regard that the Trial Chamber's general statements do not allow for verification that it actually assessed the evidence in the manner it claims.[566] He also submits that numerous examples in the Trial Judgement indicate that the Trial Chamber did not apply its own approach when assessing documentary evidence.[567] Prlić argues that the Trial Chamber provided no analysis as to how it assessed the evidence upon which it based its findings, placing him in the dark as to which pieces of evidence the Trial Chamber actually assessed and relied upon and which ones it ignored.[568] Consequently, Prlić contends that he could not meet his burden as an appellant, which denied him his right to an effective appeal.[569] Prlić concludes that the Appeals Chamber should overturn his convictions on Counts 1-25.[570]

178. The Prosecution responds that Prlić fails to develop his assertion that the Trial Chamber applied an incorrect legal standard.[571] The Prosecution further argues that Prlić misconstrues the obligation to issue a reasoned opinion, which does not require a trial chamber to set out an item-by-item analysis of numerous pieces of evidence.[572] The Prosecution contends that Prlić's assertion that he cannot tell which pieces of evidence the Trial Chamber assessed and which ones it did not rests on the unfounded premise that it ignored evidence.[573] Finally, the Prosecution argues that Prlić fails to demonstrate any denial of his right of appeal, considering that the Trial Chamber's **[page 76]** clearly referenced factual findings gave him the opportunity to challenge the Trial Chamber's reliance or non-reliance on particular pieces of evidence in reaching those findings.[574]

---

[562] Prlić's Appeal Brief, paras 28-31, 35-40, 43, 45-64, 67-68, 70, 73-74; 79-80, 83-84.
[563] Prlić's Appeal Brief, paras 32-33, 41-42, 44, 62-64, 66, 69-72, 78, 80-82. In some cases, Prlić's arguments are only supported by cross-references to other arguments of his brief. Prlić's Appeal Brief, paras 58-61.
[564] Prlić's Appeal Brief, paras 134-136, 146. See Prlić's Appeal Brief, paras 137, 140, 142, 144.
[565] Prlić's Appeal Brief, paras 134, 137, 140, 142, 144, referring to, *inter alia*, Trial Judgement, Vol. 1, paras 287, 380-382; Prlić's Reply Brief, para. 45.
[566] Prlić's Appeal Brief, paras 134, 138, 141, 143, 145.
[567] Prlić's Appeal Brief, paras 134, 138-139, 141, 143, 145; Prlić's Reply Brief, para. 45.
[568] Prlić's Appeal Brief, paras 139, 141, 143, 145-146.
[569] Prlić's Appeal Brief, para. 146.
[570] Prlić's Appeal Brief, para. 147.
[571] Prosecution's Response Brief (Prlić), fn. 184.
[572] Prosecution's Response Brief (Prlić), paras 59-62.
[573] Prosecution's Response Brief (Prlić), para. 63.
[574] Prosecution's Response Brief (Pilić), para. 63.

(b) Analysis

179.   The Appeals Chamber notes that the Trial Chamber set out its approach to the assessment of documentary evidence in a general section of the Trial Judgement entitled "Standards Governing the Assessment of the Evidence Admitted".[575] The Trial Chamber explained that "whenever something a witness said disputed a logical sequence of documents in a manner less than persuasive", it "afforded greater weight to the documentary evidence than to his oral statements".[576] The Trial Chamber stated that, in general, it "assigned greater weight to the contents of a document convincingly explained by a witness than to documents admitted by way of written motion".[577] Nevertheless, the Trial Chamber explained that it "did assign some weight to documents not commented on by witnesses in cases where their contents were corroborated by other documents, and particularly when they belonged to a cohesive set of documentary evidence constituting a reliable whole".[578] Finally, the Trial Chamber stated that it "considered all the documentary evidence admitted by way of written motion and assessed it in the context of the other evidence admitted".[579]

180.   At the outset, the Appeals Chamber considers that Prlić does not explain why the alleged failure to make specific findings amounts to an application of an incorrect legal standard and therefore dismisses this submission as an undeveloped assertion.[580] With regard to the alleged failure to provide a reasoned opinion, the Appeals Chamber recalls that the reasoned opinion requirement relates to a trial chamber's judgement rather than to each and every submission made at trial.[581] The Appeals Chamber further recalls that the assessment of the credibility of evidence cannot be undertaken by a piecemeal approach – rather, individual documents admitted into evidence have to be analysed in the light of the entire body of evidence adduced.[582] Finally, the Appeals Chamber recalls:

> With regard to factual findings, a Trial Chamber is required only to make findings on those facts which are essential to the determination of guilt on a particular count. It is not necessary to refer to the testimony of every witness or every piece of evidence on the trial record. In short, a **[page 77]** Trial Chamber should limit itself to indicating in a clear and articulate, yet concise manner, which, among the wealth of jurisprudence available on a given issue and the myriad of facts that emerged at trial, are the legal and factual findings on the basis of which it reached the decision either to convict or acquit an individual. A reasoned opinion consistent with the guidelines provided here allows for a useful exercise of the right of appeal by the Parties and enables the Appeals Chamber to understand and review the Trial Chamber's findings as well as its evaluation of the evidence.[583]

181.   In light of this case-law, the Appeals Chamber considers that Prlić does not demonstrate any error. The Trial Chamber's general approach to the assessment of documentary evidence, as set out at the beginning of the Trial Judgement,[584] is to be read in conjunction with factual findings that reference the underlying evidence and sources throughout the Trial Judgement. The Trial Chamber was not required to explain in detail how it applied this general approach to specific evidence in every factual finding. Thus, the Appeals Chamber concludes that in setting out in general its approach to documentary evidence, the Trial Chamber did not violate its obligation to provide a reasoned opinion allowing for the useful exercise of the right of appeal.[585] As for each individual factual finding, the Trial Judgement contains references to the sources, allowing Prlić to determine on which evidence, adjudicated facts, or other factual findings the Trial Chamber

---

[575]   Trial Judgement, Vol. 1, p. 100.
[576]   Trial Judgement, Vol. 1, para. 287.
[577]   Trial Judgement, Vol. 1, para. 380.
[578]   Trial Judgement, Vol. 1, para. 381.
[579]   Trial Judgement, Vol. 1, para. 382.
[580]   The Appeals Chamber notes that Prlić neither advances specific submissions in this respect, nor points to any authority in support of his assertion. See, in particular, Prlić's Appeal Brief, paras 134, 146.
[581]   *Limaj et al.* Appeal Judgement, para. 81; *Kvočka et al.* Appeal Judgement, para. 23.
[582]   *Halilović* Appeal Judgement, para. 125.
[583]   *Hadžihasanović and Kubura* Appeal Judgement, para. 13 (internal references omitted).
[584]   See *supra*, para. 179.
[585]   *Cf. infra*, para. 189 at fn. 605 with further reference.

relied, thereby allowing him to usefully exercise his right of appeal.[586] Further, Prlić does not identify any specific factual finding lacking sufficient references.[587]

182. As for the argument that Prlić was unable to determine which pieces of evidence the Trial Chamber actually assessed and which ones it ignored, the Appeals Chamber recalls that it is to be presumed that a trial chamber evaluated all the evidence presented to it, as long as there is no indication that the trial chamber completely disregarded any particular piece of evidence.[588] In the present case, Prlić has failed to provide any indication that the Trial Chamber completely disregarded any particular piece of evidence.

183. For the foregoing reasons, the Appeals Chamber concludes that Prlić has failed to demonstrate any error of law, and dismisses his ground of appeal 3. **[page 78]**

E. Disregard of Evidence

1. Prlić's witnesses (Prlić's Ground 2)

(a) Arguments of the Parties

184. Prlić submits that the Trial Chamber erred in law by ignoring the evidence of almost all of his witnesses, thereby violating his right under Article 21(4) of the Statute to present a defence and challenge evidence.[589] Prlić further submits that the Trial Chamber erred in applying a double standard by choosing to rely on the Prosecution's evidence rather than his evidence without pointing to inconsistencies in the evidence or identifying reasons for doubting witnesses' credibility.[590] He contends that these errors amount to failures to provide a reasoned opinion and invalidate the Trial Judgement.[591]

185. Prlić also contends that the Trial Chamber disregarded relevant evidence of Defence Witnesses 1D-AA, Mile Akmadžić, Zdravko Batinić, Zoran Buntić, Milan Cvikl, Ilija Kožulj, Miroslav Palameta, Zoran Perković, Žarko Primorac, Borislav Puljić, Martin Raguž, Adalbert Rebić, Zdravko Sančević, Marinko Šimunović, Neven Tomić, Mirko Zelenika, Damir Zorić, and Miomir Žužul ("Prlić's Defence Witnesses"), who testified "on all issues related to the alleged JCE and JCE core crimes". Because of the failure to consider these witnesses' evidence, he submits, the Trial Chamber erred in fact by drawing unsustainable conclusions regarding the existence of a JCE and Prlić's powers and responsibilities, leading to a miscarriage of justice.[592] In support of his contentions, Prlić points to background information concerning the function and role of these witnesses during the period encompassed by the Indictment and refers to other sub-grounds of his appeal.[593] Prlić concludes that the Appeals Chamber should overturn his convictions on Counts 1-25.[594]

---

[586] See generally Trial Judgement, Vol. 4, paras 74-288. In his submissions under his ground of appeal 3, Prlić provides no specific references to the contrary.
[587] The Appeals Chamber observes that Prlić supports his argument that the Trial Chamber did not actually assess the evidence in the manner it claims with cross-references to arguments made under other grounds of appeal, which the Appeals Chamber dismisses elsewhere. See Prlić's Appeal Brief, para. 138, referring to (sub-)grounds of appeal 1.2, 4-6; Prlić's Reply Brief, para. 45, referring to, *inter alia*, Prlić's Appeal Brief, paras 137-140, 142, 144 (ground of appeal 3), 330-331, 333 (sub-ground of appeal 11.1), 345-347 (sub-ground of appeal 11.3), 356 (sub-ground of appeal 11.4), 372 (sub-ground of appeal 11.8), 376-378 (sub-ground of appeal 11.9), 383 (sub-ground of appeal 12.1), 425 (ground of appeal 13), 430 (ground of appeal 14), 467 (sub-ground of appeal 16.1.3), 489 (sub-grounds of appeal 16.2.3-16.2.5), 492 (sub-ground of appeal 16.2.6), 521 (sub-ground of appeal 16.4.2), 555 (sub-grounds of appeal 16.5.1-16.5.2), 562-564, 566 (sub-ground of appeal 16.6.2), 588 (sub-ground of appeal 16.7.2); Prlić's Reply Brief, para. 42 (ground of appeal 2); *infra*, paras 107-138, 168-191, 204-218, 1021-1043, 1048-1070, 1089-1096, 1099-1122, 1128-1134, 1162-1167, 1193-1204, 1225-1230, 1317, 1335-1343, 1286-1298, 1318-1333, 1335-1343, 1356-1373.
[588] *Popović et al.* Appeal Judgement, paras 306, 340, 830; *Đorđević* Appeal Judgement, fn. 2527; *Haradinaj et al.* Appeal Judgement, para. 129; *Kvočka et al.* Appeal Judgement, para. 23. See also Trial Judgement, Vol. 1, para. 382.
[589] Prlić's Appeal Brief, paras 90, 94-95, 132. See Prlić's Appeal Brief, para. 93; Prlić's Reply Brief, paras 37-38. See also Appeal Hearing, AT. 150-154, 157-159, 168-169 (20 Mar 2017).
[590] Prlić's Appeal Brief, paras 90, 132. See Prlić's Reply Brief, paras 41-44; Appeal Hearing, AT. 162-165 (20 Mar 2017) (focusing on the Trial Chamber's credibility assessments of Batinić, Buntić, and Zelenika).
[591] Prlić's Appeal Brief, paras 90, 132; Appeal Hearing, AT. 151-152, 154, 169 (20 Mar 2017). See also Prlić's Appeal Brief, paras 91-92.
[592] Prlić's Appeal Brief, paras 94-132.
[593] Prlić's Appeal Brief, paras 96-131.
[594] Prlić's Appeal Brief, para. 133.

186.   The Prosecution responds that the Trial Chamber properly considered the evidence and credibility of Prlić's Defence Witnesses, and expressly considered significant aspects of his case.[595] **[page 79]**

It further submits that much of the allegedly ignored evidence does not contradict the Trial Chamber's findings.[596]

(b) Analysis

187.   The Appeals Chamber recalls that every accused has the right to a reasoned opinion under Article 23 of the Statute and Rule 98 *ter* (C) of the Rules. However, it is not necessary to refer to the testimony of every witness or every piece of evidence on the trial record. It is to be presumed that the trial chamber evaluated all the evidence presented to it, as long as there is no indication that the trial chamber completely disregarded any particular piece of evidence. There may be an indication of disregard when evidence which is clearly relevant to the findings is not addressed by the Trial Chamber's reasoning. If the Trial Chamber did not refer to the evidence given by a witness, even if it is in contradicton to the Trial Chamber's finding, it is to be presumed that the Trial Chamber assessed and weighed the evidence, but found that the evidence did not prevent it from arriving at its actual findings.[597] The Appeals Chamber notes that, in certain cases, the requirements to be met by the trial chamber are higher.[598] But even in those cases, the trial chamber is only expected to identify the *relevant* factors, and to address the *significant* negative factors. If the Defence adduced the evidence of several other witnesses, who were unable to make any meaningful contribution to the facts of the case, even if the conviction of the accused rested on the testimony of only one witness, the trial chamber is not required to state that it found the evidence of each Defence witness irrelevant. On the contrary, it is to be presumed that the trial chamber took notice of this evidence and duly disregarded it because of its irrelevance. In general, as the *Furundžija* Appeal Judgement stated:

> The case-law that has developed under the European Convention on Human Rights establishes that a reasoned opinion is a component of the fair hearing requirement, but that "the extent to which this duty [...] applies may vary according to the nature of the decision" and "can only be determined in the light of the circumstances of the case".[599]

The Appeals Chamber therefore emphasises that it is necessary for any appellant claiming an error of law because of the lack of a reasoned opinion to identify the specific issues, factual findings, or **[page 80]** arguments which he submits the trial chamber omitted to address and to explain why this omission invalidated the decision.[600]

188.   As to Prlić's argument that the Trial Chamber failed to provide a reasoned opinion with respect to its assessment of testimonial evidence, the Appeals Chamber notes that the Trial Chamber stated that it "analysed and assessed all the evidence admitted into the record".[601] It set out its general approach to the assessment of *viva voce* witnesses, including credibility issues, and provided examples of witnesses whose testimony lacked credibility.[602] The Trial Chamber also "disregarded the testimony of witnesses whose credibility seemed doubtful throughout the session" and provided the testimony of Mirko Zelenika as an example in this regard.[603] The Appeals Chamber notes that the Trial Chamber did not further discuss in detail the credibility of each Prlić Defence Witness.

---

[595]   Prosecution's Response Brief (Prlić), paras 44, 46-52, 54-58; Appeal Hearing, AT. 194 (20 Mar 2017). See also Appeal Hearing, AT. 193 (20 Mar 2017).

[596]   Prosecution's Response Brief (Prlić), paras 44, 53; Appeal Hearing, AT. 194 (20 Mar 2017).

[597]   *Kvočka et al.* Appeal Judgement, paras 23-24. See also *Tolimir* Appeal Judgement, paras 53, 161, 299; *Popović et al.* Appeal Judgement, paras 925, 1017.

[598]   *Krajišnik* Appeal Judgement, para. 139, referring to *Kvočka et al.* Appeal Judgement, para. 24 (concerning the appraisal of witness testimony with regard to the identity of the accused). See also *Popović et al.* Appeal Judgement, para. 133.

[599]   *Kvočka et al.* Appeal Judgement, para. 24, referring to *Furundžija* Appeal Judgement, para. 69. See *Kvočka et al.* Appeal Judgement, para. 23.

[600]   *Krajišnik* Appeal Judgement, para. 139; *Kvočka et al.* Appeal Judgement, para. 25.

[601]   Trial Judgement, Vol. 1, para. 282.

[602]   Trial Judgement, Vol. 1, para. 284. See also Trial Judgement, Vol. 1, paras 285-288.

[603]   Trial Judgement, Vol. 1, para. 286.

189.   In light of the applicable law set out above,[604] and the Trial Chamber's general explanation of its approach to the assessment of witness testimony, the Appeals Chamber is not persuaded that the fact that the Trial Chamber did not address specifically and in detail its assessment of each witness's evidence shows that the Trial Chamber contravened its obligation to provide a reasoned opinion.[605] On the contrary, it was open to the Trial Chamber to rely on the evidence of certain witnesses over that of other witnesses, without necessarily referring to the testimony of each and every witness who testified on a given topic.[606] While the requirements to be met by a trial chamber may be higher in certain cases,[607] Prlić's underdeveloped arguments fail to demonstrate that the Trial Chamber had to meet a higher burden in the present case. Accordingly, the Appeals Chamber finds that Prlić has not shown that the Trial Chamber failed to provide a reasoned opinion with respect to the assessment of evidence.

190.   Turning to Prlić's arguments that the Trial Chamber failed to consider relevant evidence of Prlić's Defence Witnesses, the Appeals Chamber observes that it has already addressed and dismissed his specific allegations concerning these witnesses in the respective sub-grounds of appeal he refers to.[608] Under this ground of appeal, Prlić only provides background information about these witnesses and points to other sub-grounds of his appeal without articulating the **[page 81]** relevance of their evidence vis-a-vis a specific Trial Chamber finding.[609] As a result, the Appeals Chamber finds that Prlić has failed to rebut the presumption that the Trial Chamber duly considered the evidence of these witnesses and consequently has failed to show that the Trial Chamber disregarded relevant evidence.[610]

191.   For the foregoing reasons, Prlić fails to show that the Trial Chamber contravened its obligation to provide a reasoned opinion or that any of its conclusions were unsustainable. In light of the applicable law and Prlić's undeveloped assertions, the Appeals Chamber considers that he has failed to show any error, and consequently dismisses his ground of appeal 2.

2.   Defence expert Witness Vlado Šakić's evidence (Praljak's Ground 53)

192.   The Trial Chamber found that the objective of Defence expert Witness Vlado Šakić's report was to examine the difficulties which superiors may encounter in ensuring effective control of their troops, particularly in wartime, and apply this analysis to the conflict in BiH, concluding that it was impossible for political and military powers in BiH to establish control over various defence groups who committed crimes.[611] The Trial Chamber found that the Prosecution succeeded in casting doubt on Šakić's impartiality as an expert by revealing his ties with the Croatian Government and the Croatian Intelligence Services.[612] It further found that Šakić failed to review any document specifically addressing the BiH conflict, particularly from the HVO command, and that his report therefore addressed the issue of effective troop control from a purely theoretical perspective.[613] Finally, the Trial Chamber found that Šakić was evasive during cross-examination.[614] Based on the foregoing, the Trial Chamber concluded that it could not rely on his expert report.[615]

---

[604]   See *supra*, para. 187.
[605]   *Cf. Krajišnik* Appeal Judgement, paras 140-141, 147. See also *supra*, para. 181.
[606]   *Cf. Čelebići* Appeal Judgement, para. 481.
[607]   See *supra*, para. 187.
[608]   See, *supra*, para. 176; *infra*, paras 211, 592-782 (Ground of Appeal 9), 783-1014 (Ground of Appeal 10), 1144-1399 (Ground of Appeal 16).
[609]   See Prlić's Appeal Brief, paras 97, 99, 101, 103, 105, 107, 109, 111, 113, 115, 117, 119, 121, 123, 125, 127, 129, 131-132.
[610]   See *supra*, para. 187. The Appeals Chamber also rejects Prlić's unsupported argument that the Trial Chamber applied a double standard by choosing to rely on the Prosecution's evidence rather than his evidence since he does not refer to any specific Trial Chamber finding. To the extent that, in support of his argument, he refers to other sub-grounds of appeal (Prlić's Appeal Brief, paras 97, 99, 101, 103, 105, 107, 109, 111, 113, 115, 117, 119, 121, 123, 125, 127, 129, 131-132), the Appeals Chamber dismisses these grounds of appeal elsewhere in the Judgement. See *supra*, fn. 608. The Appeals Chamber further observes that, in his reply brief, Prlić refers to specific paragraphs of the Trial Judgement but does not identify any spepific findings. See Prlić's Reply Brief, paras 39-40.
[611]   Trial Judgement, Vol. 1, paras 358-360. See Trial Judgement, Vol. 1, para. 356.
[612]   Trial Judgement, Vol. 1, paras 377, 379.
[613]   Trial Judgement, Vol. 1, paras 378-379.
[614]   Trial Judgement, Vol. 1, para. 379.
[615]   Trial Judgement, Vol. 1, para. 379.

193.   Praljak argues that the Trial Chamber erred in setting aside the evidence of Šakić based on his irrelevant ties with Croatia and without providing a reasoned opinion.[616] In doing so, the **[page 82]** Trial Chamber purportedly treated Praljak in a biased manner vis-a-vis the Prosecution, and violated his right to a fair trial.[617] Praljak further submits that the Trial Chamber erred when it found Šakić's report to be of low probative value because the report addressed the topic of effective control from a theoretical point of view without considering specific documents.[618] Praljak argues in this regard that the Trial Chamber misunderstood the role of an expert in a criminal trial, which is not to assess the evidence in lieu of the Judges.[619] In addition, Praljak argues that the Trial Chamber misunderstood the purpose of the report which was to provide a socio-psychological view, and not that of a military analyst, on the 1991-1995 war in BiH.[620] In Praljak's submission, the report aimed to highlight: (1) that the war was "generally violent and chaotic", which was important for the "proper assessment of evidence and correct establishment of the facts"; and (2) the situation in which he found himself, which was "extremely important" to assess his responsibility properly.[621] Praljak concludes that he should be acquitted of all charges.[622]

194.   The Prosecution responds that Praljak shows no error with the Trial Chamber's decision not to rely on Šakić's expert evidence.[623] It submits that Praljak largely affirms the Trial Chamber's findings on the report in conceding that Šakić had no military background.[624] The Prosecution further submits that Praljak fails to demonstrate that the report is relevant and probative to any live issue in this case.[625] It asserts that Praljak also fails to show that the Trial Chamber abused its discretion in concluding that Šakić was biased since it carefully considered his ties to Croatia.[626] In the Prosecution's submission, the Trial Chamber's detailed analysis of Šakić's report and testimony also refutes Praljak's claim that the Trial Chamber failed to provide a reasoned opinion.[627]

195.   On that point, the Appeals Chamber notes that the Trial Chamber discussed its evaluation of Šakić's evidence and credibility in great detail, referring to his ties to Croatia among several other reasons not to rely on his expert report,[628] thus allowing Praljak to exercise his right of appeal in a meaningful manner and the Appeals Chamber to understand and review the Trial Chamber's findings as well as its evaluation of the evidence.[629] The Appeals Chamber therefore dismisses **[page 83]** Praljak's claim that the Trial Chamber violated its obligation to provide a reasoned opinion.[630] Insofar as Praljak claims a violation of fair trial in that the Trial Chamber assessed a Prosecution expert witness with ties to the Prosecution differently, the Appeals Chamber notes that Praljak has failed to show that the Trial Chamber applied the identical set of

---

[616]   Praljak's Appeal Brief, paras 577-580, 584, referring to Trial Judgement, Vol. 1, para. 377; Appeal Hearing, AT. 475-476 (22 Mar 2017). See also Praljak's Reply Brief, para. 121. Praljak argues that the obligation to provide a reasoned opinion required the Trial Chamber to explain why Šakić's ties with Croatia affected his credibility. Praljak's Appeal Brief, paras 578-580 & fn. 1311, referring to *Lukić and Lukić* Appeal Judgement, para. 62.
[617]   Praljak's Appeal Brief, paras 580, 584; Appeal Hearing, AT. 472, 475-476 (22 Mar 2017).
[618]   Praljak's Appeal Brief, para. 581, referring to Trial Judgement, Vol. 1, para. 378.
[619]   Praljak's Appeal Brief, para. 582. See also Praljak's Appeal Brief, para. 583.
[620]   Praljak's Appeal Brief, para. 581; Praljak's Reply Brief, para. 121.
[621]   Praljak's Appeal Brief, para. 583.
[622]   Praljak's Appeal Brief, para. 585.
[623]   Prosecution's Response Brief (Praljak), para. 321. See also Prosecution's Response Brief (Praljak), para. 323.
[624]   Prosecution's Response Brief (Praljak), paras 321-322.
[625]   Prosecution's Response Brief (Praljak), para. 322.
[626]   Prosecution's Response Brief (Praljak), para. 323.
[627]   Prosecution's Response Brief (Praljak), para. 323.
[628]   Trial Judgement, Vol. 1, paras 377-379. See *supra*, para. 192.
[629]   Art. 23(2) of the Statute; Rule 98 *ter(C)* of the Rules. See *Stanišić and Župljanin* Appeal Judgement, para. 137; *Popović et al.* Appeal Judgement, paras 1123 (and references cited therein), 1367, 1771.
[630]   Contrary to what Praljak alleges, the obligation to provide a reasoned opinion does not entail an obligation to provide a reasoned opinion specifically on the impact of the mentioned ties on the witness's credibility. His reliance on *Lukić and Lukić* Appeal Judgement, para. 62, is inapposite, since it deals with a situation where the trial chamber in that case had failed to address the witnesses' ties. See *Lukić and Lukić* Appeal Judgement, para. 62. *Cf. Lukić and Lukić* Appeal Judgement, para. 61. In any event, the Appeals Chamber notes that the Trial Chamber explicitly considered several factors in assessing Šakić's credibility which also play a role in the assessment of how his ties to Croatia influence his credibility, namely: (1) it recalled that experts must provide expertise that is objective, impartial, and independent, if they are to assist the Trial Chamber in ruling beyond a reasonable doubt; (2) it further recalled that Šakić's expert testimony concerns an essential issue in this case, namely superior responsibility, and found that under these circumstances a particularly close attention to his impartiality was warranted; and, above all, (3) it noted Šakić's evasive conduct during cross-examination. Trial Judgement, Vol. 1, paras 377, 379.

factors in assessing the credibility of both witnesses and nevertheless arrived at different conclusions, thereby committing an error.[631] The Appeals Chamber recalls in this regard the broad discretion of the Trial Chamber in considering relevant factors on a case-by-case basis and assessing the appropriate weight and credibility to be accorded to the testimony of a witness since it is best placed to assess these issues, and that the Appeals Chamber's review is limited to establishing whether the challenging party has demonstrated that the trial chamber has committed an error.[632]

196. The Appeals Chamber now turns to the submission that the Trial Chamber erred when it found Šakić's report to be of low probative value because the report addressed the topic of effective control from a theoretical point of view without considering specific documents. The Appeals Chamber recalls that the purpose of expert testimony is to supply specialised knowledge that might assist the trier of fact in understanding the evidence before it, and that in the ordinary case an expert witness offers a view based on specialised knowledge regarding a technical, scientific or otherwise discrete set of ideas or concepts that is expected to fall outside the lay person's ken.[633] The Appeals Chamber understands that the Trial Chamber considered that Šakić's expert report did not assist it in understanding the evidence, when it found that he failed to review any document specifically addressing the BiH conflict, particularly from the HVO command, and that his report therefore addressed the issue of effective troop control from a purely theoretical perspective.[634] In light of this, the Appeals Chamber can see no indication that the Trial Chamber considered that an expert in a criminal trial should assess the evidence in lieu of the judges, or in any other way misunderstood the role of an expert, and consequently dismisses this argument. **[page 84]**

197. Finally, the Appeals Chamber notes Praljak's argument that the Trial Chamber misunderstood the purpose of Šakić's report, which was to provide a socio-psychological view on the 1991-1995 war, highlighting the above-mentioned two aspects.[635] Praljak merely asserts that these aspects were "important" for the "proper assessment of evidence and correct establishment of facts" and "extremely important" for the proper assessment of his responsibility, without expanding on these assertions. In particular, he does not show in which regard these aspects were important for the Trial Chamber's findings and assessment of his responsibility. Thus, Praljak challenges the Trial Chamber's failure to rely on Šakić's evidence without explaining why the conviction should not stand even if the Trial Chamber had relied on it in combination with the remaining evidence. The Appeals Chamber therefore dismisses this argument.

198. For the foregoing reasons, the Appeals Chamber dismisses Praljak's ground of appeal 53.

F. Conclusion

199. The Appeals Chamber dismisses all challenges with regard to the admissibility or weight of evidence as discussed in the present chapter. **[page 85]**

V. WITNESS CREDIBILITY

A. Introduction

200. The Appeals Chamber recalls that a trial chamber is best placed to assess the credibility of a witness and reliability of the evidence adduced.[636] Therefore, trial chambers have broad discretionary power in assessing the credibility of a witness and in determining the weight to be accorded to his or her testimony.[637]

---

[631]   *Cf. supra*, fn. 630, with Praljak's Appeal Brief, para. 580 & fn. 1314, referring to William Tomljanovich, T. 5928-5929 (4 Sept 2006); Praljak's Reply Brief, para. 121. In particular, Praljak has not shown that this witness was also evasive in cross-examination. See *infra*, para. 200 *et seq.*

[632]   *Popović et al.* Appeal Judgement, paras 131-132. See *infra*, para. 200 *et seq.*

[633]   *Popović et al.* Appeal Judgement, para. 375 and references cited therein.

[634]   Trial Judgement, Vol. 1, paras 378-379.

[635]   See *supra*, para. 193 at fn. 621.

[636]   *Popović et al.* Appeal Judgement, para. 513; *Šainović et al.* Appeal Judgement, para. 464; *Nahimana et al.* Appeal Judgement, para. 949.

[637]   *Lukić and Lukić* Appeal Judgement, paras 86, 112; *Nzabonimana* Appeal Judgement, para. 45; *Ndindiliyimana et al.* Appeal Judgement, para. 331; *Kanyarukiga* Appeal Judgement, para. 121.

This assessment is based on a number of factors, including the witness's demeanour in court, his or her role in the events in question, the plausibility and clarity of the witness's testimony, whether there are contradictions or inconsistencies in his or her successive statements or between his or her testimony and other evidence, any prior examples of false testimony, any motivation to lie, and the witness's responses during cross-examination.[638] In addition, the Appeals Chamber has previously stated that it is within a trial chamber's discretion to accept or reject a witness's testimony, after seeing the witness, hearing the testimony, and observing him or her under cross examination.[639]

201. In the context of the deference accorded to the trier of fact with respect to the assessment of evidence, the jurisprudence of both the Tribunal and the ICTR has reiterated that it is within a trial chamber's discretion to, *inter alia*: (1) assess and resolve any inconsistencies that may arise within or among witnesses' testimonies, consider whether the evidence taken as a whole is reliable and credible, and to accept or reject the fundamental features of the evidence;[640] (2) decide, in the circumstances of each case, whether corroboration of evidence is necessary and to rely on uncorroborated, but otherwise credible, witness testimony;[641] (3) accept a witness's testimony, notwithstanding inconsistencies between the said testimony and his or her previous statements, as it is for the trial chamber to determine whether an alleged inconsistency is sufficient to cast doubt on the evidence of the witness concerned;[642] and (4) rely on hearsay evidence, provided that it is **[page 86]** reliable and credible.[643] The Appeals Chamber further recalls that it is not unreasonable for a trial chamber to accept the substance of a witness's evidence notwithstanding the witness's inability to recall certain details, especially when a significant amount of time has elapsed since the events to which the witness's evidence relates[644] as well as to accept some but reject other parts of a witness's testimony.[645]

202. The Appeals Chamber further recalls that a trial chamber is not required to set out in detail why it accepted or rejected a particular testimony, and that an accused's right to a reasoned opinion does not ordinarily demand a detailed analysis of the credibility of particular witnesses.[646] However, "[u]nder some circumstances, a reasoned explanation of the Trial Chamber's assessment of a particular witness's credibility *is* a crucial component of a 'reasoned opinion' – for instance, where there is a genuine and significant dispute surrounding a witness's credibility and the witness's testimony is truly central to the question whether a particular element is proven".[647]

203. Prlić, Stojić, and Praljak allege that the Trial Chamber erred in its assessment of the credibility of certain witnesses and/or failed to provide a reasoned opinion in this regard.

B. Expert Witnesses Donia, Tomljanovich, and Ribičić (Prlić's Ground 4)

204. Prlić submits that the Trial Chamber erred in law and fact by failing to properly assess the evidence and credibility of Prosecution expert Witnesses Robert Donia, William Tomljanovich, and Ciril Ribičić.[648] In particular, Prlić argues that the Trial Chamber failed to consider that: (1) the witnesses lacked qualifications

---

[638] *Nzabonimana* Appeal Judgement, para. 45; *Kanyarukiga* Appeal Judgement, para. 121; *Nchamihigo* Appeal Judgement, para. 47.

[639] *Nzabonimana* Appeal Judgement, para. 45; *Kanyarukiga* Appeal Judgement, para. 121; *Nchamihigo* Appeal Judgement, para. 210.

[640] *Popović et al.* Appeal Judgement, para. 1228; *Karemera and Ngirumpatse* Appeal Judgement, para. 467; *Nzabonimana* Appeal Judgement, para. 319.

[641] *Popović et al.* Appeal Judgement, paras 243, 1009; *Gatete* Appeal Judgement, para. 138; *Ntawukulilyayo* Appeal Judgement, para. 21.

[642] *Lukić and Lukić* Appeal Judgement, para. 234; *Hategekimana* Appeal Judgement, para. 190, referring to *Rukundo* Appeal Judgement, para. 86; *Kajelijeli* Appeal Judgement, para. 96.

[643] *Šainović and Župljanin* Appeal Judgement, para. 510; *Popović et al.* Appeal Judgement, paras 1276, 1307; *Šainović et al.* Appeal Judgement, para. 846.

[644] *Nchamihigo* Appeal Judgement, para. 149; *Kvočka et al.* Appeal Judgement, para. 591.

[645] *Popović et al.* Appeal Judgement, paras 1126, 1243; *Nizeyimana* Appeal Judgement, paras 17, 93, 108; *Šainović et al.* Appeal Judgement, paras 294, 336, 342.

[646] *Popović et al.* Appeal Judgement, para. 133 and references cited therein.

[647] *Bizimungu* Appeal Judgement, para. 64; *Kajelijeli* Appeal Judgement, para. 61.

[648] Prlić's Appeal Brief, paras 148-158. See Prlić's Reply Brief, paras 46, 48-50.

or otherwise lacked credibility as expert witnesses;[649] (2) the witnesses were employees of the Prosecution or entertained close ties with the Prosecution;[650] and (3) the reports of the witnesses contained methodological flaws and were framed to fit the **[page 87]** Prosecution's narrative.[651] Prlić argues that the Trial Chamber relied heavily on these witnesses for a series of critical findings against him.[652] Prlić contends that the Trial Chamber thereby failed to provide reasoned opinions and applied an incorrect legal standard in assessing the evidence, invalidating the Trial Judgement.[653] Prlić further submits that there was a miscarriage of justice as the Trial Chamber drew unsustainable conclusions on the existence of a JCE and Prlić's powers and responsibilities.[654] As a result, Prlić avers that the Appeals Chamber should overturn his convictions on Counts 1-25 of the Indictment.[655]

205.   The Prosecution responds that Prlić's submissions are unfounded and that he fails to articulate any error or explain why the convictions should not stand on the remainder of the evidence.[656] The Prosecution submits that the Trial Chamber properly assessed the evidence of the expert witnesses and that the factors Prlić alleges the Trial Chamber failed to consider consist of mischaracterised and irrelevant claims.[657]

206.   With respect to Prlić's challenge that the Trial Chamber failed to provide a reasoned opinion with respect to its assessment of the expert evidence, the Appeals Chamber observes that while not discussing in detail the credibility of Expert Witnesses Donia, Tomljanovich, and Ribičić, the Trial Chamber did explain in general its approach to expert evidence.[658] The Trial Chamber noted that when analysing the experts' reports it "gave consideration to the experts' field of professional expertise, their impartiality, the methodology employed in their report, the material available to the experts for conducting their analyses and the credibility of the conclusions drawn in light of these factors and the other evidence admitted".[659] In addition, the Trial Chamber determined in advance of each expert witness appearing to testify that, having given due consideration to the information and arguments submitted by the Parties, the witnesses were competent to testify as experts.[660] **[page 88]** Recalling that a trial chamber is not required to set out in detail why it accepted or rejected a particular testimony,[661] the Appeals Chamber finds that Prlić's reference to excerpts of each expert witnesses' testimony fails to show that the Trial Chamber's analysis of the reports and the testimony of the experts was insufficient to explain its assessment of their credibility and evidence. In addition, the Appeals Chamber considers that the mere fact that the Trial Chamber did not expressly

---

[649]   With respect to Witness Donia, Prlić argues that he "was not a lawyer, ethnographer, demographer, or political scientist, and his Ph.D. was constrained to BiH Muslims in the late 19th century". See Prlić's Appeal Brief, para. 152 (internal references omitted). As to Witness Tomljanovich, Prlić contends that he did not understand the role of expert witness in legal proceedings, that he is not a lawyer or political scientist and that his "Ph.D. was constrained to early modern Central European History, focusing on a 19th Century Croatian Bishop". See Prlić's Appeal Brief, para. 154 (internal references omitted). With respect to Witness Ribičić, Prlić submits that he lacked credibility as an expert, and in support refers to testimony purportedly showing that he: (1) was not aware that every municipality in the former Yugoslavia had official gazettes; (2) relied on extraneous political statements; (3) did not go beyond the documents provided by the Prosecution; and (4) did not consider "newly available evidence" against his original analysis to verify if it was correct. See Prlić's Appeal Brief, para. 156.

[650]   Prlić's Appeal Brief, paras 152, 154, 156.

[651]   Prlić's Appeal Brief, paras 152, 154, 156; Prlić's Reply Brief, paras 48-50; Appeal Hearing, AT. 165-167 (20 Mar 2017).

[652]   Prlić's Appeal Brief, paras 148-149, 153, 155, 157.

[653]   Prlić's Appeal Brief, paras 151, 158. Prlić argues that the Trial Chamber applied a double standard in which Defence witnesses closely associated with the accused were found to lack credibility, while Prosecution witnesses employed by the Office of the Prosecutor were not. Appeal Hearing, AT. 166 (20 Mar 2017). See Appeal Hearing, AT. 162, 165 (20 Mar 2017).

[654]   Prlić's Appeal Brief, paras 149, 158.

[655]   Prlić's Appeal Brief, para. 159.

[656]   Prosecution's Response Brief (Prlić), paras 65-66, 76-77.

[657]   Prosecution's Response Brief (Prlić), paras 65, 67-75.

[658]   Trial Judgement, Vol. 1, paras 291-292. See also Trial Judgement, Vol. 1, paras 289-290, 293. Moreover, the Trial Chamber provided a lengthy and detailed decision to disregard the evidence of two other expert witnesses. See Trial Judgement, Vol. 1, paras 293-379.

[659]   Trial Judgement, Vol. 1, para. 291.

[660]   Trial Judgement, Vol. 1, para. 290. With respect to Witness Ribičić, the Appeals Chamber observes that he testified in the *Kordić and Čerkez* case as an expert witness and his evidence was further admitted by the Trial Chamber pursuant to Rules 92 *bis* and 94 *bis* of the Rules. See *The Prosecutor v. Jadranko Prlić et al.*, Case No. IT-04-74-T, *Décision relative aux demandes de l'accusation aux fins du versement de comptes rendus de témoignage en application de l'article 92 bis du règlement*, 8 December 2006, paras 17-27.

[661]   *Popović et al.* Appeal Judgement, para. 133. See also *Lukić and Lukić* Appeal Judgement, para. 112.

discuss specific challenges related to the credibility of Donia, Tomljanovich, and Ribičić does not establish that the Trial Chamber failed to consider these challenges when assessing the witnesses' credibility.

207. Turning to Prlić's specific argument that the Trial Chamber erred in its assessment of the qualifications of Donia, Tomljanovich, and Ribičić as experts, the Appeals Chamber observes that the matter was addressed by the Trial Chamber in its decision to admit the relevant evidence under Rule 94 *bis* of the Rules.[662] Moreover, the Appeals Chamber finds that Prlić's argument fails to articulate any error in the Trial Chamber's assessment of their status as expert witnesses warranting appellate review.[663]

208. As to the relationships of Donia, Tomljanovich, and Ribičić with the Office of the Prosecutor, the Appeals Chamber recalls that the mere fact that an expert witness is employed or paid by a party does not disqualify him or her from testifying as an expert witness.[664] Accordingly, Prlić's assertion that the expert witnesses were employed or entertained close ties with the Office of the Prosecutor is insufficient to demonstrate that the Trial Chamber failed to consider these relationships or incorrectly assessed the witnesses' evidence.

209. With respect to Prlić's argument that the expert evidence provided by Donia, Tomljanovich, and Ribičić is affected by methodological flaws, the Appeals Chamber observes that Prlić merely refers to excerpts of their testimony without showing why it was unreasonable for the **[page 89]** Trial Chamber to rely on these witnesses and their evidence. Prlić's argument reflects mere disagreement with the Trial Chamber's assessment of the relevant evidence. Accordingly, Prlić's assertion that the Trial Chamber applied an incorrect legal standard in assessing the evidence of the expert witnesses fails to include any demonstration that the Trial Chamber strayed from its broad discretion in the assessment of witness credibility.[665]

210. In relation to Prlić's argument that the Trial Chamber heavily relied on Donia, Tomljanovich, and Ribičić for a series of critical findings against him, the Appeals Chamber considers that Prlić refers to instances where the Trial Chamber relied on the evidence of these expert witnesses, but ignores the fact that in those instances the Trial Chamber also relied on numerous other testimonial and documentary evidence.[666] Prlić fails to elaborate how the reliance by the Trial Chamber on the evidence of the three expert witnesses was inconsistent with their role in assisting the Trial Chamber in its assessment of the evidence before it or how it constituted an error by the Trial Chamber. This argument is therefore dismissed.

211. Based on the foregoing, the Appeals Chamber finds that Prlić has failed to show any error in the Trial Chamber's assessment of the evidence and credibility of Witnesses Donia, Tomljanovich, and Ribičić. Accordingly, the Appeals Chamber dismisses Prlić's ground of appeal 4.

---

[662] See T(F). 790-791 (25 Apr 2006) (Witness Donia); T(F). 3805-3806 (Witness Tomljanovich); The Prosecutor v. Jadranko Prlić et al., Case No. IT-04-74-T, Decision relative aux demandes de l'accusation aux fins du versement de comptes rendus de témoinage en application de l'article 92 bis du règlement, 8 December 2006, paras 17-27 (Witness Ribičić).

[663] Specifically, the Appeals Chamber fails to see how the fact that Donia "was not a lawyer, ethnographer, demographer, or political scientist, and his Ph.D. was constrained to BiH Muslims in the late 19th century" and that Tomljanovich's "Ph.D. was constrained to early modern Central European History, focusing on a 19th Century Croatian Bishop" would, in and of itself, undermine each witness's credibility as an expert. See Prlić's Appeal Brief, paras 152, 154 (references omitted). Similarly, the Appeals Chamber finds no merit in Prlić's speculative assertion that Witness Tomljanovich did not understand the role of an expert witness in criminal proceedings. See Prlić's Appeal Brief, para. 152. With respect to Ribičić, Prlić merely points to aspects of his testimony without showing how these excerpts would undermine the credibility of the witness or that the Trial Chamber failed to consider them. See Prlić's Appeal Brief, para. 156.

[664] *Tolimir* Appeal Judgement, para. 69; *Prosecutor v. Vujadin Popović et al.*, Case No. IT-05-88AR73.2, Decision on Joint Defence Interlocutory Appeal Concerning the Status of Richard Butler as an Expert Witness, 30 January 2008, para. 20; *Nahimana et al.* Appeal Judgement, para. 199.

[665] In support of his argument that the Trial Chamber applied a double standard in assessing the evidence of Defence witnesses who are closely associated with the accused as compared to Prosecution witnesses who are employees of the Prosecution, Prlić offers only one example – between Defence Witness Zdravko Batinić and Prosecution expert Witness William Tomljanovich. See Appeal Hearing, AT. 162, 165-166 (20 Mar 2017). The Appeals Chamber considers that this example comparing the evidentiary assessment of a lay witness with an expert witness does not assist in showing that the Trial Chamber applied a double standard. See Trial Judgement, Vol. 1, para. 407, Vol. 2, para. 308. See also *Tolimir* Appeal Judgement, para. 69.

[666] Prlić's Appeal Brief, fns 300-302, referring to Trial Judgement, Vol. 1, paras 409, 413, 420-422, 424, 426, 428-429, 432, 436, 438-440, 442, 447, Vol. 4, paras 13-14 (in respect of Donia); Vol. 1, paras 419, 421, 436-437, 452-454, 467, 483-484, 500-501, 504, 506, 511, 515, 522, 525, 528, 532, 534, 555, 640, 670, Vol. 4, paras 21, 81-82, 88, 125, 138, 158 (in respect of Tomljanovich); Vol. 1, paras 421-422, 424, 465, 480, 483-484, 493, 495-496, 498, 500-511, 515-516, 522-525, 527-528, 531, 631, 633, 638, 685, 689, 694, 698, 711, 769, Vol. 3, paras 549, 552, 556, Vol. 4, paras 11, 14-16, 18, 21, 82 (in respect of Ribičić).

599

C. Witnesses BA, BB, BC, BD, Beese, BH, DZ, Galbraith, Lane, and Manolić (Prlić's Ground 6)

1. Arguments of the Parties

212. Prlić submits that the Trial Chamber erred in law and fact by failing to properly assess the credibility and evidence of certain Prosecution witnesses upon whom it heavily relied in "drawing unsustainable conclusions regarding the existence of a JCE and [his] powers and responsibilities".[667] He proposes that a proper credibility assessment of a witness's evidence must encompass its internal consistency, its strength during cross-examination and coherence against **[page 90]** prior statements, its credibility in light of other evidence, and the possible motives of the witness.[668] According to Prlić, if the testimony of a witness "shows weakness in any of these respects", the Trial Chamber cannot rely on this evidence without corroboration.[669]

213. Specifically, Prlić submits that the Trial Chamber erred in assessing the testimonies of Prosecution Witnesses BA, BB, BC, BD, Christopher Beese, BH, DZ, Peter Galbraith, Ray Lane, and Josip Manolić.[670] He contends that the Trial Chamber failed to take into account specific aspects of these witnesses' testimonies that affect their credibility, namely: (1) alleged discrepancies within and among their testimonies; (2) the witnesses' failure to recollect the details of the events or the fact that they testified on the basis of documents shown to them; (3) their lack of knowledge of background information concerning the events they testified about; (4) the fact that some witnesses provided exculpatory or uncorroborated hearsay evidence; and (5) their bias against the Croats or possible motives in implicating him with their testimony.[671] As a result, Prlić contends that the Trial Chamber erred in relying on the evidence of these witnesses in reaching specific findings pertaining to the existence of the JCE, as well as his powers and responsibility.[672]

214. The Prosecution responds that Prlić's allegations are unfounded and that he fails to demonstrate any error or impact on the verdict.[673] The Prosecution further submits that the Trial Chamber reasonably relied upon and correctly assessed the witnesses' credibility and that the factors which Prlić claims the Trial Chamber failed to consider consist of mischaracterised trivial claims.[674]

2. Analysis

215. The Appeals Chamber dismisses Prlić's incorrect claim that corroboration of a witness's testimony is required whenever that testimony contains internal discrepancies or is inconsistent with other evidence or prior statements. It is within the discretion of a trial chamber to determine whether, in the circumstances of the case, corroboration is necessary.[675] This principle applies **[page 91]** equally to the evidence of witnesses who may have a motive to implicate the accused, provided that the trier of fact applies the appropriate caution in assessing such evidence.[676] Finally, there is no general requirement that the testimony of a witness be corroborated if deemed otherwise credible.[677] Accordingly, the Appeals Chamber rejects this argument.

---

[667] Prlić's Appeal Brief, para. 204. See Prlić's Appeal Brief, paras 178-203; Prlić's Reply Brief, para. 53.

[668] Prlić's Appeal Brief, para. 179.

[669] Prlić's Appeal Brief, para. 179.

[670] Prlić's Appeal Brief, paras 181-203.

[671] See Prlić's Appeal Brief, paras 182, 184, 187, 189, 191, 193-194, 196, 198, 200, 202. Prlić's Reply Brief, paras 54-55. In addition, Prlić avers that the Trial Chamber: (1) erred in relying on the prior statements and testimonies of Witnesses BA and DZ as during the interviewing sessions they were shown documents not referenced in their statements and the interviewing sessions were not properly recorded, thus denying Prlić the right to effective confrontation; and (2) failed to consider that the interview of Witnesses BH and Lane were not properly recorded. Prlić's Appeal Brief, paras 181-182, 184, 193, 202. See also Prlić's Reply Brief, para. 53.

[672] Prlić's Appeal Brief, paras 183, 185, 188, 190, 192, 195, 197, 199, 201, 203.

[673] Prosecution's Response Brief (Prlić), paras 94-95, 122-123.

[674] Prosecution's Response Brief (Prlić), paras 94, 101-120. The Prosecution also submits that Prlić's arguments that he was deprived of the right to confront Witnesses BA, BH, DZ, and Lane are unmeritorious and should be dismissed. Prosecution's Response Brief (Prlić), paras 96-100, 114, 121.

[675] See, e.g., *Popović et al.* Appeal Judgement, paras 243, 1009; *D. Milošević* Appeal Judgement, para. 215.

[676] *Popović et al.* Appeal Judgement, para. 135; *Šainović et al.* Appeal Judgement, para. 1101; *Nchamihigo* Appeal Judgement, para. 48.

[677] *Popović et al.* Appeal Judgement, paras 243, 1264; *D. Milošević Appeal* Judgement, para. 215. See also *Kordić and Čerkez* Appeal Judgement, para. 274.

216.   As to the specific challenges concerning Witnesses BA, BB, BC, BD, Beese, BH, DZ, Galbraith, Lane, and Manolić, the Appeals Chamber observes that Prlić lists specific features of their testimony that he claims the Trial Chamber disregarded without explaining how such aspects, whether taken individually or together, would undermine the Trial Chamber's assessment of the evidence or its impugned findings.[678] By merely arguing that the witnesses' testimonies were inconsistent, or that these witnesses failed to recollect events or lacked knowledge thereof, provided exculpatory or uncorroborated hearsay evidence, and had motives which could affect their reliability, Prlić fails to show any error in the Trial Chamber's assessment of the evidence.[679] Thus, Prlić's contentions fail.

217.   Moreover, the Appeals Chamber observes that in the portion of the Trial Judgement titled "Standards Governing the Assessment of the Evidence Admitted", the Trial Chamber discussed its general approach to assessing witness evidence in this case.[680] The Trial Chamber stated that, in assessing testimonial evidence, it took into account the demeanour of the witnesses, any discrepancies in their evidence, and their possible motives which could call into question their reliability, as well as the time that had elapsed since the events.[681] The Trial Chamber also explicitly addressed arguments that some Prosecution witnesses, *e.g.,* European Community Monitoring Mission ("ECMM") and United Nations Protection Force ("UNPROFOR") personnel, lacked first-hand local knowledge and were unable to evaluate the information received from other sources, finding that in certain cases these witnesses "had limited knowledge of the sequence of events and limited preparation for their mission in the field".[682] Recalling that a trial chamber does **[page 92]** not need to set out in detail why it accepted or rejected a particular witness's testimony,[683] the Appeals Chamber finds that the mere fact that the Trial Chamber did not expressly discuss the specific aspects noted by Prlić of the testimonies of Witnesses BA, BB, BC, BD, Beese, BH, DZ, Galbraith, Lane, and Manolić does not establish that the Trial Chamber failed to consider these aspects when assessing the witnesses' credibility. Therefore, the Appeals Chamber finds that Prlić has not shown that the Trial Chamber failed to consider some aspects of the witnesses' testimonies and erroneously assessed their evidence.

218.   Accordingly, the Appeals Chamber finds that Prlić has failed to show any error in the Trial Chamber's assessment of the evidence of Witnesses BA, BB, BC, BD, Beese, BH, DZ, Galbraith, Lane, and Manolić and, accordingly, dismisses his ground of appeal 6.

D.   Praljak's testimony (Praljak's Ground 55)

1.   Alleged denial of a reasoned opinion (Sub-ground 55.1)

219.   Praljak submits that the Trial Chamber erred by not providing a reasoned opinion with regard to the credibility assessment of his testimony.[684] Specifically, Praljak argues that the Trial Chamber failed to explain which parts of his testimony it found credible or not credible, and why.[685] Praljak further argues that the Trial Chamber should have done so given the importance and extent of his evidence.[686] Praljak concludes that the error affects the entire Trial Judgement and that he should therefore be acquitted of all charges.[687]

220.   The Prosecution responds that Praljak identifies neither any failure to address aspects of his testimony that is sufficiently prejudicial to invalidate the Trial Judgement, nor any error that would occasion a

---

[678]   See Prlić's Appeal Brief, paras 182, 184, 187, 189, 191, 193, 196, 198, 200, 202.
[679]   As to Prlić's argument that he was deprived of the fight to effectively confront Witnesses BA and DZ, the Appeals Chamber observes that Prlić cross-examined each witness on the circumstances in which their respective statements were taken. See Witness BA, T. 7328-7333 (closed session) (26 Sept 2006), T. 7395-7405 (closed session) (27 Sept 2006); Witness DZ, T. 26651-26652 (closed session) (23 Jan 2008). Further, Prlić fails to explain how the manner in which the witnesses were questioned by the Prosecution affected the reliability of their evidence. Similarly, regarding Prlić's claim that he could not properly challenge the evidence of Witnesses BH and Lane, he fails to show any resulting prejudice. Accordingly, these arguments are dismissed.
[680]   Trial Judgement, Vol. 1, paras 284-288.
[681]   Trial Judgement, Vol. 1, paras 284-287.
[682]   Trial Judgement, Vol. 1, para. 288.
[683]   See *supra*, para. 202.
[684]   Praljak's Appeal Brief, paras 592-593, 596, 599. See also Appeal Hearing, AT. 472 (22 Mar 2017).
[685]   Praljak's Appeal Brief, paras 595-596, 598.
[686]   Praljak's Appeal Brief, paras 594-595, 598-599.
[687]   Praljak's Appeal Brief, para. 592; Praljak's Reply Brief, para. 125.

miscarriage of justice.[688] In particular, the Prosecution argues that the Trial Chamber properly assessed Praljak's testimony in the context of the totality of the evidence and that it was not obliged to explain its assessment in detail.[689]

221.   The Appeals Chamber recalls that a trial chamber is not required to set out in detail why it accepted or rejected the testimony of an accused person, nor systematically justify why it rejected each part of that evidence.[690] The Trial Chamber found that Praljak's testimony was credible on certain points, and relied on his testimony in those instances, but was hardly credible on others, in **[page 93]** particular when seeking to limit his responsibility in respect of certain allegations.[691] In making this finding, the Trial Chamber does not cite to specific parts of Praljak's evidence, nor does it refer to other parts of the Trial Judgement where it discussed Praljak's testimony in more detail. However, in referring generally to the volume and importance of his evidence, Praljak does not demonstrate how the lack of a more detailed discussion of this evidence invalidates the Trial Judgement. As such, he has not met the burden of proof required for an appellant alleging an error of law on the basis of a lack of a reasoned opinion. Praljak's sub-ground of appeal 55.1 is dismissed.

2.   Alleged failure to properly assess Praljak's testimony (Sub-ground 55.2)

222.   Praljak submits that the Trial Chamber erred by failing to properly assess his testimony.[692] In particular, Praljak argues that the Trial Chamber: (1) wrongly found that his testimony contained inherent contradictions and distorted his words to suit its preconceptions; and (2) ignored some of his testimony even if it was confirmed by other evidence.[693] As a result, Praljak submits that the Trial Chamber reached erroneous conclusions affecting the entire Trial Judgement and that he should be acquitted of all charges.[694]

223.   The Prosecution responds that Praljak fails to show that the Trial Chamber abused its discretion when assessing his credibility.[695] Specifically, the Prosecution submits that Praljak's arguments should be summarily dismissed, as: (1) his contention that the Trial Chamber distorted his testimony in order to confirm its preconceptions merely repeats arguments made elsewhere; and (2) the alleged disregard of his testimony is a mere assertion that the Trial Chamber failed to interpret the evidence in a particular manner.[696]

224.   The Appeals Chamber observes that Praljak bases his arguments on cross-references to other sections of his appeal brief,[697] which the Appeals Chamber dismisses elsewhere.[698] His arguments that the Trial Chamber wrongly found that his testimony contained inherent contradictions and distorted his words to suit its preconceptions are dismissed as either **[page 94]** unsubstantiated or for lack of possible impact on the relevant findings of the Trial Chamber.[699] His argument that the Trial Chamber ignored some of his testimony even if it was confirmed by other evidence is not supported by the reference he provides to his appeal brief.[700] The Appeals Chamber considers that Praljak has failed to demonstrate that the Trial Chamber abused its discretion in assessing his testimony and reached erroneous conclusions affecting the entire Trial Judgement. The Appeals Chamber therefore dismisses Praljak's sub-ground of appeal 55.2.

---

[688]   Prosecution's Response Brief (Praljak), para. 329. See Prosecution's Response Brief (Praljak), para. 333.
[689]   Prosecution's Response Brief (Praljak), paras 330-331.
[690]   *Karera* Appeal Judgement, paras 20-21. See also *supra*, para. 202.
[691]   Trial Judgement, Vol. 1, para. 399.
[692]   Praljak's Appeal Brief, paras 592, 600-602.
[693]   Praljak's Appeal Brief, paras 600-601; Praljak's Reply Brief, para. 124.
[694]   Praljak's Appeal Brief, paras 592, 602; Praljak's Reply Brief, para. 125.
[695]   Prosecution's Response Brief (Praljak), para. 329. See Prosecution's Response Brief (Praljak), para. 333.
[696]   Prosecution's Response Brief (Praljak), para. 332.
[697]   See Praljak's Appeal Brief, para. 601, referring to, *inter alia*, Praljak's Appeal Brief, paras 378 (sub-ground of appeal 38.1), 404 (sub-ground of appeal 39.1), 437 (sub-ground of appeal 40.4), 462 (ground of appeal 42), 495 (sub-ground of appeal 45.1).
[698]   See *infra*, paras 1837, 1844-1852 (dismissing Praljak's Appeal Brief, para. 378), 1892, 1895 (dismissing Praljak's Appeal Brief, para. 437), 1912, 1914-1918 (dismissing Praljak's Appeal Brief, para. 404), 1950, 1954-1957 (dismissing Praljak's Appeal Brief, para. 462), 2038, 2042-2054 (dismissing Praljak's Appeal Brief, para. 495).
[699]   See *infra*, paras 1837, 1844-1852 (dismissing Praljak's Appeal Brief, para. 378), 1892, 1895 (dismissing Praljak's Appeal Brief, para. 437), 1912, 1914-1918 (dismissing Praljak's Appeal Brief, para. 404), 2038, 2042-2054 (dismissing Praljak's Appeal Brief, para. 495).
[700]   See Praljak's Appeal Brief, para. 601, referring to, *inter alia*, Praljak's Appeal Brief, para. 462. See also *infra*, paras 1950, 1954-1957 (dismissing Praljak's Appeal Brief, para. 462).

E. **Conclusion**

225.   The Appeals Chamber dismisses all challenges to the Trial Chamber's assessment of the credibility of witnesses. **[page 95]**

VI.   CHALLENGES TO CHAPEAU REQUIREMENTS OF ARTICLE 2 OF THE STATUTE

226.   The Trial Chamber convicted Prlić, Stojić, Praljak, Petković, Ćorić, and Pušić of various crimes as grave breaches of the Geneva Conventions under Article 2 of the Statute, namely, wilful killing, inhuman treatment, the extensive destruction of property not justified by military necessity and carried out unlawfully and wantonly, the appropriation of property not justified by military necessity and carried out unlawfully and wantonly, deportation, the unlawful transfer of civilians, and the unlawful confinement of civilians. In so doing, the Trial Chamber found that the chapeau requirements of Article 2 of the Statute were satisfied on the basis that in almost all municipalities relevant to the Indictment: (1) an armed conflict existed between the HVO and the ABiH;[701] (2) the armed conflict was international in character due to both the direct involvement of the Army of the Republic of Croatia ("HV") in the conflict, and the overall control wielded by Croatia and its military, the HV, over the HVO;[702] (3) the acts charged as crimes pursuant to Article 2 of the Statute were closely linked to that international armed conflict;[703] and (4) the relevant acts were committed against persons and property protected under the relevant Geneva Conventions.[704]

227.   Recalling that the civilian population and civilian property in occupied territory are protected and may be the subject of grave breaches of the Geneva Conventions, the Trial Chamber also held that it was necessary for it to establish the existence of an occupation when crimes were alleged under Article 2 of the Statute in places and on dates for which the Trial Chamber was unable to establish the existence of a conflict between the HVO and ABiH.[705] Accordingly the Trial Chamber analysed the evidence and found that the HVO, over which Croatia's army, the HV, wielded overall control, occupied: (1) Prozor Municipality from August to December 1993;[706] (2) the villages of Duša, Hrasnica, Ždrimci, and Uzričje in Gornji Vakuf Municipality after 18 January 1993; (3) the villages of Sovići and Doljani in Jablanica Municipality after 17 April 1993; (4) West Mostar from May 1993 to February 1994; (5) Ljubuški Municipality in August 1993; (6) Stolac Municipality in July and August 1993; (7) Čapljina Municipality from **[page 96]** July to September 1993; and (8) the town of Vareš and the village of Stupni Do in Vareš Municipality after 23 October 1993.[707]

228.   The Appellants do not contest the chapeau requirements laid down by the Trial Chamber for the application of Article 2 of the Statute,[708] but rather challenge the Trial Chamber's findings that the requirements were satisfied in this case.[709] The Appeals Chamber will address these challenges below.

A.   **Existence of an International Armed Conflict**

1.   Scope of the international armed conflict

229.   At the outset, the Appeals Chamber observes that the Trial Chamber examined whether a state of occupation existed in those municipalities where, in its view, no international armed conflict had been

---

[701]   See Trial Judgement, Vol. 3, para. 514.
[702]   See Trial Judgement, Vol. 3, paras 529-531, 543-544, 567-568.
[703]   See Trial Judgement, Vol. 3, para. 624.
[704]   See, *e.g.*, Trial Judgement, Vol. 3, paras 611, 618-619.
[705]   See Trial Judgement, Vol. 3, paras 574-575. See also Trial Judgement, Vol. 3, para. 576 (on the crime of deportation as a transfer across the boundary of occupied territory).
[706]   The Trial Chamber in particular found that the town of Prozor was occupied by the HVO from 24 to 30 October 1992 and that the village of Parcani was occupied at least during the days following the attack of 17 April 1993. See Trial Judgement, Vol. 3, para. 589.
[707]   See Trial Judgement, Vol. 3, paras 578-589.
[708]   See Trial Judgement, Vol. 1, para. 83.
[709]   Prlić's Appeal Brief, paras 652-668; Stojić's Appeal Brief, paras 406-420; Praljak's Appeal Brief, paras 7-41; Praljak's Reply Brief, paras 6-13; Petković's Appeal Brief, paras 410-429; Ćorić's Appeal Brief, paras 67-74; Pušić's Appeal Brief, paras 230-234.

proven.[710] Limiting the scope to situations where "there is resort to armed force between States or protracted armed violence between government authorities and organised armed group or between such groups within a State",[711] the Trial Chamber examined the "resort to armed force" on a municipality-by-municipality basis, concluding that an international armed conflict existed in most, but not all, of the municipalities covered by the Indictment.[712] This conclusion was reached despite all of these municipalities being part of BiH that constituted the territory of the conflict between the HVO and ABiH.

230.   The Appeals Chamber recalls that an armed conflict is not limited to the specific geographical municipalities where acts of violence and actual fighting occur, or to the specific periods of actual combat. Rather, the question of whether a situation constitutes an "armed conflict" requires a holistic evaluation of the parameters of the conflict. As the Appeals Chamber held in the *Tadić* case, "the temporal and geographical scope of both internal and international armed conflicts extends beyond the exact time and place of hostilities".[713] In the *Kordić and Čerkez* case, the Appeals Chamber upheld the Trial Chamber's conclusion that in determining the international character of a conflict "all that is required is a showing that a state of armed conflict existed in the **[page 97]** larger territory of which a given location forms a part".[714] Concerning the temporal scope, the Appeals Chamber has emphasised that:

> International humanitarian law applies from the initiation of [an armed conflict] and extends beyond the cessation of hostilities until a general conclusion of peace is reached; or, in the case of internal conflicts, a peaceful settlement is achieved. Until that moment, [it] continues to apply in the whole territory of the warring States or, in the case of internal conflicts, the whole territory under the control of a party, whether or not actual combat takes place there.[715]

231.   The Appeals Chamber recalls that the Trial Chamber held, in accordance with the Appeals Chamber's jurisprudence, that it was not necessary, for the purpose of classifying an armed conflict as international or non-international, to prove that troops were present in each of the places where crimes were committed.[716] Similarly, it noted that to prove the nexus between the crimes and the armed conflict or occupation, it was not necessary to show that fighting took place in the same municipalities where alleged crimes were committed, but only that the crimes were directly connected with the hostilities taking place in other parts of the territory.[717]

232.   The Appeals Chamber considers that while stating the law correctly, the Trial Chamber erred when applying it and in finding that crimes committed where no active combat occurred were not committed in an international armed conflict situation.[718] The Appeals Chamber is satisfied that the Trial Chamber's finding that the HVO and ABiH were engaged in hostilities amounting to an international armed conflict in specific parts of BiH territory and during specific time periods relevant to the Indictment,[719] was sufficient for the Trial Chamber to apply the "grave breaches" regime of the Geneva Conventions to all crimes committed anywhere on the entire BiH territory and at any time until the end of the armed conflict and in close

---

[710]   See Trial Judgement, Vol. 3, paras 575, 577-580, 583-585, 587-589. The Trial Chamber also examined the existence of a state of occupation where the crime of deportation was alleged. See Trial Judgement, Vol. 3, para. 576.

[711]   See Trial Judgement, Vol. 1, para. 84, referring to *Kunarac et al.* Appeal Judgement, para. 56, *Tadić* Appeal Decision on Jurisdiction, para. 70.

[712]   See Trial Judgement, Vol. 3, paras 528-544. See also Trial Judgement, Vol. 3, paras 545-568.

[713]   *Tadić* Appeal Decision on Jurisdiction, para. 67.

[714]   *Kordić and Čerkez* Appeal Judgement, para. 314. See also *Kordić and Čerkez* Appeal Judgement, para. 320, referring to *Kordić and Čerkez* Trial Judgement, para. 70 ("it would be wrong to construe the Appeals Chamber's Decision [in *Tadić*] as meaning that evidence as to whether a conflict in a particular locality has been internationalised must necessarily come from activities confined to the specific geographical area where the crimes were committed, and that evidence of activities outside that area is necessarily precluded in determining that question").

[715]   *Tadić* Appeal Decision on Jurisdiction, para. 70. The Appeals Chamber also stated that "the very nature of the [Geneva] Conventions [...] dictates their application throughout the territories of the parties to the conflict; any other construction would substantially defeat their purpose". *Tadić* Appeal Decision on Jurisdiction, para. 68. See also *Kordić and Čerkez* Appeal Judgement, para. 321 ("Once an armed conflict has become international, the Geneva Conventions apply throughout the respective territories of the warring parties.").

[716]   See Trial Judgement, Vol. 1, para. 85, Vol. 3, para. 518.

[717]   See Trial Judgement, Vol. 3, para. 623. See also Trial Judgement, Vol. 1, para. 109.

[718]   See Trial Judgement, Vol. 1, para. 85, Vol. 3, paras 514, 517-518. *Cf.* Trial Judgement, Vol. 3, para. 575 (in the context of occupation), Appeal Hearing, AT. 302-305 (21 Mar 2017).

[719]   See Trial Judgement, Vol. 3, paras 514, 517.

connection with that conflict. Article 2 of the Statute thus applies irrespective of whether such crimes were perpetrated in zones of active combat. In light of the above principles, the Trial Chamber's rigid differentiation between crimes committed in places where and while active fighting was taking place, and crimes committed in places where no active combat was taking place at the time of the commission of the **[page 98]** crimes but which were occupied by the HVO (and during that occupation)[720] was only necessary vis-à-vis crimes allegedly committed against persons or property in the context of occupied territory, as will be discussed below.[721]

233.   The Appeals Chamber, therefore, reverses as legally erroneous the Trial Chamber's conclusions that there was no international armed conflict in the places covered by the Indictment where no active combat was taking place, *i.e.* West Mostar, the municipalities of Prozor, Gornji Vakuf, Jablanica, Stolac, Ljubuški, and Čapljina, the town of Vareš, and the village of Stupni Do.[722]

2.   Alleged error of law with regard to the application of the overall control test (Praljak's Sub-ground 1.4 and Ćorić's Sub-ground 3.1 in part)

(a) Arguments of the Parties

234.   Praljak and Ćorić allege that the Trial Chamber erred in finding that the armed conflict between the HVO and ABiH was international in character on the basis of its erroneous conclusions that: (1) HV units participated directly in the conflict; and (2) the Republic of Croatia had overall control over the HVO, based on its organising, co-ordinating, or planning of military operations and its financing, training, and equipping of the HVO.[723] In this respect, the Appeals Chamber understands Praljak's argument that "global control is extremely disputed in international law and rejected by the International Court of Justice ("ICJ"), and Ćorić's related argument that the "ICJ emphasizes the concept of effective control of operations." to be that the Trial Chamber should have applied the "effective control" test, consistent with the precedent of the ICJ, and not the "overall control" test, as established by the Appeals Chamber in the *Tadić* Appeal Judgement ("Overall Control Test").[724]

235.   In his submissions, Praljak recognises that, irrespective of the similarities between the various cases tried by the Tribunal, each trial chamber of the Tribunal is to make an individual assessment as to whether the evidence before it establishes the existence of an international armed **[page 99]** conflict at a particular place and time.[725] Nevertheless, Praljak argues that the Prosecution's failure to plead an international armed conflict in three other cases before the Tribunal, involving the responsibility of ABiH officers in the same HVO-ABiH conflict,[726] casts doubt on the international character of the conflict at issue in this case.[727] Praljak argues that this inconsistent approach by the Prosecution could prejudice the Tribunal's credibility and should have prompted the Trial Chamber to consider "with particular attention" the issue and to have established beyond reasonable doubt that the conflict was international, which, he asserts, it failed to do.[728]

236.   The Prosecution responds that the Trial Chamber's application of the Overall Control Test was consistent with the jurisprudence of the Appeals Chamber.[729] It also submits that Praljak's arguments are

---

[720]   See Trial Judgement, Vol. 3, para. 575 where "the Trial Chamber was unable to establish the existence of a conflict between the ABiH and the HVO").

[721]   See Trial Judgement, Vol. 3, paras 574-576. See *infra*, paras 298-345.

[722]   See Trial Judgement, Vol. 3, paras 578-589. The Appeals Chamber notes that the related issue of whether a state of armed conflict and occupation can co-exist will be discussed below. See *infra*, para. 335.

[723]   Praljak's Appeal Brief, paras 32-41; Ćorić's Appeal Brief, paras 67-74.

[724]   Praljak's Appeal Brief, paras 33-36 (emphasis removed), referring to, *inter alia*, *Tadić* Appeal Judgement, paras 90-144, *Aleksovski* Appeal Judgement, paras 134, 145, *Bosnia Genocide* Judgement, paras 403-406; Appeal Hearing, AT. 375-377 (22 Mar 2017); Ćorić's Appeal Brief, paras 71, 73, referring, *inter alia*, to *Tadić* Appeal Judgement, paras 137-138, *Nicaragua Activities* Judgement, paras 110, 112, 115, 215-220.

[725]   Praljak's Appeal Brief, para. 37.

[726]   Praljak's Appeal Brief, para. 38, referring to *Delić* Indictment, *Hadžihasanović et al.* Indictment; *Halilović* Indictment.

[727]   Praljak's Appeal Brief, para. 38.

[728]   Praljak's Appeal Brief, paras 39-41.

[729]   Prosecution's Response Brief (Praljak), para. 13; Prosecution's Response Brief (Ćorić), para. 63.

irrelevant and unsubstantiated.[730] The Prosecution asserts that Praljak's claims contradict his own submission regarding the importance of maintaining a case-by-case approach to these determinations.[731]

(b) Analysis

237. The Trial Chamber found that the armed conflict was international in character due both to the direct involvement of the HV in the conflict pitting the HVO and ABiH against each other, and to the overall control wielded by the HV and by Croatia over the HVO.[732]

238. The Appeals Chamber recalls that the *Tadić* Appeal Judgement established the Overall Control Test to specify "what *degree of authority or control* must be wielded by a foreign State over armed forces fighting on its behalf in order to render international an armed conflict which is *prima facie* internal".[733] The Appeals Chamber notes in this regard that the ICJ refrained from taking a position on whether the Overall Control Test employed by the Appeals Chamber in the *Tadić* case was correct.[734] The Appeals Chamber considers that Praljak and Ćorić have presented no **[page 100]** cogent reason why the Appeals Chamber should depart from its well-settled precedent regarding the Overall Control Test as applied by the Trial Chamber.[735] It therefore dismisses this argument.

239. With regard to Praljak's argument that the Prosecution failed to plead an international armed conflict in other cases before the Tribunal, the Appeals Chamber recalls that Praljak himself concedes that the character of a conflict alleged in a case shall only be determined on the basis of the facts and evidence pertaining to that case.[736] It is well-settled in the Tribunal's jurisprudence that the Prosecution possesses broad discretion as to what to plead in each case.[737] Moreover, contrary to what Praljak suggests, there is no indication that the Trial Chamber did not consider the nature of the conflict with the required attention. Rather, this issue was extensively considered by the Trial Chamber.[738] The Appeals Chamber therefore dismisses this argument.

240. The Appeals Chamber therefore dismisses Praljak's sub-ground of appeal 1.4 and Ćorić's sub-ground of appeal 3.1 in part.

3. Alleged errors of fact with regard to classifying the conflict as international (Prlić's Sub-ground 19.1, Praljak's Sub-grounds 1.1 and 1.2, Petković's Sub-grounds 7.1.1 in part, 7.1.2, and 7.1.4)

(a) Arguments of the Parties

241. Petković submits that as the internal conflict was between "two equal entities in BiH", the HVO and the ABiH, and not between the HVO and the State or *de jure* government of BiH, the Trial Chamber erred

---

[730] Prosecution's Response Brief (Praljak), para. 22.
[731] Prosecution's Response Brief (Praljak), para. 22.
[732] See Trial Judgement, Vol. 3, para. 568. See also Trial Judgement, Vol. 3, paras 528-556, 559-567.
[733] *Tadić* Appeal Judgement, para. 97 (emphasis in original). See also *Tadić* Appeal Judgement, para. 145. This test has since also been applied by the ICC. See *The Prosecutor* v. *Thomas Lubanga Dyilo*, Case No. ICC-01/04-01/06, Decision on the Confirmation of Charges, 29 January 2007 *("Lubanga* Confirmation of Charges Decision"), para. 211; *Lubanga* Article 74 Judgement, para. 541.
[734] *Bosnia Genocide* Judgement, para. 404. The ICJ specifically held that, "[i]nsofar as the 'overall control' test is employed to determine whether or not an armed conflict is international, which was the sole question which the [ICTY] Appeals Chamber was called upon to decide [in the *Tadić* case], it may well be that the test is applicable and suitable." *Bosnia Genocide* Judgement, para. 404. See also *Bosnia Genocide* Judgement, paras 405-407.
[735] See *Aleksovski* Appeal Judgement, paras 107-109; *Tadić* Appeal Judgement, paras 116-123. See also *Tadić* Appeal Judgement, paras 125-144.
[736] See Praljak's Appeal Brief, para. 37 & fns 75-76. The Appeals Chamber recalls that the principle that the character of an armed conflict should be determined on a case-by-case basis has been affirmed by this Tribunal. See, *e.g., Kordić and Čerkez* Appeal Judgement, para. 320.
[737] See generally *Čelebići* Appeal Judgement, paras 601-605.
[738] See Trial Judgement, Vol. 3, paras 517-568.

by classifying the conflict as international.[739] In his view, to qualify as international, an internal conflict must necessarily involve an official or *de jure* government.[740]

242.   Prlić, Praljak, and Petković further argue that the Trial Chamber erred in finding that there was an international armed conflict in BiH because HV troops were deployed on the "southern front" which covered part of HZ(R) H-B in BiH but also neighbouring territory in Croatia, and Montenegro.[741] Prlić and Praljak submit that the Trial Chamber ignored evidence that because of **[page 101]** persistent JNA attacks from BiH territory and BiH's inability or unwillingness to stop them, Croatia had to cross into BiH to defend its own territory and that this was done in self-defence.[742]

243.   The Prosecution responds that the conflict was not between two equal entities of BiH but between the ABiH – acting under Alija Izetbegović, whose government was the legitimate authority of BiH – and the HZ(R) H-B, which was not a legitimate power.[743] The Prosecution points in this regard to the Trial Chamber's findings that the HZ(R) H-B had been declared unconstitutional by the BiH Constitutional Court in September 1992, and that the legitimate authorities of BiH had continuously rejected the HZ(R) H-B and the HVO's authority.[744]

244.   As to Prlić's, Praljak's, and Petković's arguments with regard to the location of the southern front, the Prosecution responds that the Trial Chamber reasonably concluded that the southern front included both territory in BiH and areas of southern Croatia, and submits that the Trial Chamber correctly found that HV forces were present on BiH territory during the conflict in question, thus evidencing the HV's direct involvement in BiH.[745]

(b) Analysis

245.   The Trial Chamber found that there was an international armed conflict between the HVO and the ABiH which was:

> fundamentally internal, inasmuch as it took place between two entities of the [Republic of Bosnia and Herzegovina (following independence) ("RBiH")]. In determining whether this conflict, internal as of first impression, possesses the qualification of an international armed conflict, it is necessary to prove either (1) the direct involvement of armed troops from Croatia in BiH alongside the HVO, or (2) that the HVO was either an organised hierarchically structured group over which Croatia wielded overall control, or was not an organised group, or was a group of isolated individuals, and that this group or these individuals acted as instruments of Croatia or complicifly with the Croatian authorities.[746]

246.   The Appeals Chamber notes that the Trial Chamber applied the Overall Control Test as laid down in the *Tadić* Appeal Judgement to determine when armed forces fighting in an armed conflict which is *"prima facie* internal" may be regarded as acting on behalf of a foreign Power.[747] The Appeals Chamber notes that the Trial Chamber then went on to examine the evidence adduced to **[page 102]** find that the HVO, an organised and hierarchically-structured group, was under Croatia's overall control, concluding that the conflict was therefore international.[748] The Appeals Chamber considers that Petković consequently has failed to show any error on the part of the Trial Chamber in classifying the conflict as international.

---

[739]   Petković's Appeal Brief, para. 415 (emphasis omitted); Petković's Reply Brief, para. 83.
[740]   Petković's Appeal Brief, paras 413-415, referring to, *inter alia, Tadić* Appeal Judgement, para. 84; Petković's Reply Brief, paras 83-84.
[741]   Prlić's Appeal Brief, paras 652-653; Praljak's Appeal Brief, paras 8-11; Petković's Appeal Brief, para. 418.
[742]   Prlić's Appeal Brief, paras 653-654, referring to, *inter alia*, Ivan Beneta, T. 46570-46572 (9 Nov 2009), 46697-46698 (10 Nov 2009), Radmilo Jasak, T. 48632 (20 Jan 2010); Praljak's Appeal Brief, paras 8-11, referring to, *inter alia*, Ivan Beneta, T. 46564, 46572-46573 (9 Nov 2009), 46668-46669 (10 Nov 2009), Radmilo Jasak, T. 48632 (20 Jan 2010).
[743]   Prosecution's Response Brief (Petković), para. 300.
[744]   Prosecution's Response Brief (Petković), para. 300, referring to Trial Judgement, Vol. 1, paras 426, 432-433, 457, 459, 467, Vol. 2. para. 341.
[745]   Prosecution's Response Brief (Prlić), para. 414; Prosecution's Response Brief (Praljak), paras 11-12.
[746]   Trial Judgement, Vol. 3, para. 523.
[747]   *Tadić* Appeal Judgement, paras 90, 97. See also *Tadić* Appeal Judgement, para. 120, referring to "an organised and hierarchically structured group."
[748]   See Trial Judgement, Vol. 3, paras 524-567.

247. As to his argument that an international armed conflict requires an official or *de jure* government as one of its parties, the Appeals Chamber notes that Petković ignores relevant findings of the Trial Chamber that, at the time, Izetbegović's government was recognised by the international community as the legitimate government of BiH, with the ABiH as its army.[749] Petković's argument that there was no State or *de jure* government involved in the armed conflict therefore fails. With regard to Petković's claim that the HVO and the ABiH were "equal entities of the RBiH", the Appeals Chamber observes that the Trial Chamber did not deem them to be "equal" entities but "two entities of the RBiH".[750] The Appeals Chamber therefore dismisses Petković's arguments.

248. With respect to the challenges made to the findings on the location of the southern front, the Trial Chamber found that the southern front crossed through a portion of the HZ(R) H-B and that there were HV troops on the southern front in BiH at all times relevant to the Indictment.[751] The Appeals Chamber notes that Prlić, Praljak, and Petković concede that the southern front crossed through portions of the HZ(R) H-B, and considers that even if this may have been done in self-defence, as Prlić and Praljak contend, this consideration does not undermine the Trial Chamber's impugned finding that the HV in fact crossed into BiH territory. With regard to the allegation that the Trial Chamber ignored evidence of JNA attacks in making this finding,[752] the Appeals Chamber notes that, contrary to Prlić's, Praljak's, and Petković's submissions, the Trial Chamber relied on, *inter alia,* some of the allegedly ignored evidence, including Defence Witnesses Ivan Beneta's and Radmilo Jasak's testimonies, to find that there were HV troops on the southern front in BiH at times relevant to the Indictment.[753] The Appeals Chamber thus dismisses these arguments.

249. For the foregoing reasons, the Appeals Chamber dismisses Prlić's sub-ground of appeal 19.1 in part, Praljak's sub-ground of appeal 1.1 in part, and Petković's sub-grounds 7.1.1 in part, 7.1.2, and 7.1.4 in part.
[page 103]

4. Challenges to Croatian intervention in the HVO-ABiH conflict

250. The Trial Chamber found that the HV, and thus Croatia, was directly involved alongside the HVO in the conflict between the HVO and the ABiH at all relevant times and in most of the camps and municipalities relevant to the Indictment.[754] The Trial Chamber also found that Croatia intervened indirectly and wielded overall control over the HVO.[755] Because of both the HV's and Croatia's direct and indirect involvement – the overall control wielded by the HV and Croatia – over the HVO, the Trial Chamber concluded that the armed conflict between the HVO and the ABiH was international in character.[756]

251. The Appeals Chamber will now turn to the Appellants' various challenges to the Trial Chamber's finding that the armed conflict was international in character, due to both the direct involvement of Croatia's military, the HV, in the conflict, and the overall control wielded by Croatia and the HV over the HVO.[757] It will specifically discuss the challenges made to the findings on: (1) the presence and engagement of HV soldiers in the conflict; (2) Croatia's organisation, co-ordination, and planning of the military operations of the HVO, including the alleged voluntary nature of the participation of HV troops in the HVO-ABiH conflict; and (3) the military reports shared between the HVO and the HV.

---

[749]   See Trial Judgement, Vol. 1, paras 426-427, 432-433.
[750]   See *supra,* para. 245.
[751]   See Trial Judgement, Vol. 3, paras 529-530.
[752]   See Prlić's Appeal Brief, para. 653, fns 1659, 1661 and references cited therein; Praljak's Appeal Brief, para. 8, fn. 5 and references cited therein.
[753]   See Trial Judgement, Vol. 3, paras 529-530 & fns 1100-1102, referring to Ivan Beneta, T. 46559-46560 (9 Nov 2009), 46672(10 Nov 2009), Radmilo Jasak, T. 48860 (25 Jan 2010). See also *infra,* para. 267.
[754]   Trial Judgement, Vol. 3, paras 528-543.
[755]   Trial Judgement, Vol. 3, paras 545-567.
[756]   Trial Judgement, Vol. 3, paras 544-545, 568.
[757]   See Prlić's Appeal Brief, paras 653-658, 660, 662-668; Stojić's Appeal Brief, paras 406-419; Praljak's Appeal Brief, paras 12-15, 18-20, 29-30, 35; Praljak's Reply Brief, paras 7, 9, 12; Petković's Appeal Brief, paras 418-423, 425-429; Petković's Reply Brief, paras 85-87; Ćorić's Appeal Brief, paras 67-68, 70-74; Ćorić's Reply Brief, para. 24; Pušić's Appeal Brief, paras 230, 232-233.

(a) Direct involvement of HV soldiers and units in the conflict (Prlić's Sub-grounds 19.1 in part and 19.2, Stojić's Sub-ground 54.1, Praljak's Sub-grounds 1.1 in part, 1.2 in part, 1.3 in part, and 1.4 in part, Petković's Sub-grounds 7.1.1 in part, 7.1.3 and 7.1.4 in part, Ćorić's Sub-ground 3.1 in part, and Pušić's Ground 7 in part)

(i) Arguments of the Parties

252.   Ćorić argues that there was no documentary evidence showing there was an international armed conflict between BiH and Croatia and no reasonable trier of fact could have reached such a conclusion.[758] Ćorić asserts that, in fact, there is documentary evidence to the contrary – showing that the HVO and ABiH were allies and any support given to the HVO by Croatia was support **[page 104]** given to one of the constituent parts of the ABiH and as such cannot be considered hostile to or an act of war against BiH.[759] Petković also argues that the HVO and ABiH were allies at the time.[760]

253.   Petković additionally points out that the Indictment includes allegations about the existence of an international armed conflict for the period from July 1993 and thus the Trial Chamber should not have made factual findings for the period prior to July 1993.[761] Pušić likewise notes that the Indictment only refers to Croatian involvement in the HVO-ABiH conflict in July 1993.[762] According to Petković, the two reports cited by the Trial Chamber to demonstrate the HV's participation in HVO operations were from July and November 1993 and neither of these reports nor any other evidence cited by the Trial Chamber showed the deployment of HV troops to the southern front prior to July 1993.[763]

254.   Prlić and Praljak claim that the Trial Chamber erroneously concluded that HV units participated in the conflict between the HVO and the ABiH, and that the mere presence of HV soldiers or units on BiH territory is neither sufficient nor conclusive evidence that the HV was operating at the behest of Croatia.[764] Petković submits that the Trial Chamber erred in inferring that whole HV units were present in BiH from the presence of HV members in the HVO.[765] Prlić, Stojić, and Praljak further argue that the Trial Chamber erred in concluding from the mere presence of some HV elements "in the service of the HVO" that they were there on the direct order of Croatia.[766] Prlić and Praljak contend that while individual HV *members* were permitted to volunteer for either the HVO or the ABiH, HV *units* were not permitted to join the HVO or the ABiH.[767] Praljak adds that HV officers volunteering for both the HVO and the ABiH were temporarily relieved of their duties in the HV.[768] Citing ICC and ICJ jurisprudence, as well as the *Tadić* Appeal Judgement and *Kordić and Čerkez* Appeal Judgement, Stojić contends that the mere presence of **[page 105]** foreign troops in a conflict zone is insufficient to render a conflict international and thus asserts that the Trial Chamber's relevant findings were wrong.[769] Stojić also claims that the Trial Chamber erred in finding that the HV directly participated in the conflict in Prozor and Sovići – the only two occasions when the Trial Chamber specifically found HV direct participation.[770] In this regard, Stojić argues that no reasonable trier of fact could have

---

[758]   Ćorić's Appeal Brief, paras 70-71; Appeal Hearing, AT. 581-582 (24 Mar 2017).

[759]   Ćorić's Appeal Brief, para. 70 & fns 177-185 and references cited therein; Appeal Hearing, AT. 582-583 (24 Mar 2017).

[760]   Petković's Appeal Brief, para. 418. Petković asserts that the HV was engaged in the spring and summer of 1992 until July 1992 when HV General Janko Bobetko withdrew HV troops from BiH territory. Petković's Appeal Brief, para. 418.

[761]   Petković's Appeal Brief, paras 416-417; Petković's Reply Brief, para. 84.

[762]   Pušić's Appeal Brief, para. 232.

[763]   Petković's Appeal Brief, paras 419-420.

[764]   Prlić's Appeal Brief, paras 657-658; Praljak's Appeal Brief, para. 32; Praljak's Reply Brief, para. 9.

[765]   Petković's Appeal Brief, paras 422, 425. The Appeals Chamber also considers this argument in the context of Petković's challenges to the findings on Croatia's indirect control over the HVO. See *infra*, para. 278.

[766]   Prlić's Appeal Brief, para. 659, referring to *Kordić and Čerkez* Appeal Judgement, para. 359; Stojić's Appeal Brief, para. 408, referring to *Kordić and Čerkez* Appeal Judgement, para. 359; Praljak's Reply Brief, para. 7. See also Praljak's Appeal Brief, paras 22, 32, referring to *Kordić and Čerkez* Appeal Judgement, para. 359. Stojić also argues that the Trial Chamber erroneously held that it "matters little" whether HV members participated in the BiH conflict as volunteers to determine whether they were there on Croatia's direct order. Stojić's Appeal Brief, para. 408. See *infra*, paras 277, 285.

[767]   Prlić's Appeal Brief, paras 660-661; Praljak's Appeal Brief, paras 18-19. The Appeals Chamber observes that Praljak repeats these same arguments when challenging the Trial Chamber's findings on the Overall Control Test. See *infra*, paras 277, 285.

[768]   Praljak's Appeal Brief, paras 18-19, 32.

[769]   Stojić's Appeal Brief, paras 406-407.

[770]   Stojić's Appeal Brief, paras 409-411.

found that the HV attacked Prozor on 23 October 1992 based on the inconclusive evidence cited by the Trial Chamber.[771] Similarly, Stojić argues that no reasonable trier of fact could have concluded that soldiers from the HV participated alongside the HVO in the 17 April 1993 Sovići attack, as the Trial Chamber erroneously relied on inconclusive and vague evidence.[772]

255.   Prlić and Praljak argue that in establishing the presence of HV units in the conflict zone, the Trial Chamber erroneously relied upon the uncorroborated testimonies of Prosecution Witnesses Omer Hujdur, Philip Watkins, DW, and Klaus Johann Nissen.[773] Prlić and Praljak argue that: (1) Witness DW, a member of an international organisation, only provided hearsay testimony, recanted his statement, and had no direct knowledge of the HV's presence in BiH; (2) Hujdur,'a Muslim inhabitant of Prozor, did not have actual knowledge of the HV's presence in BiH; (3) Watkins, an ECMM observer, inappropriately inferred the HV's presence solely on the basis of the weapons he saw; and (4) Nissen testified that the ECMM, of which he was a member, had no direct knowledge and had not observed HV troops in BiH.[774]

256.   To the extent that HV troops were present on BiH territory during the relevant period, Prlić and Praljak allege that this presence – and any military operations by the HV inside the territory – was justified on self-defence grounds, as the JNA was crossing into BiH territory to attack Croatia.[775] Prlić and Praljak note that because the topography of the area prevented the HV forces from properly defending Croatia against VRS/JNA attacks from within Croatian borders, the HV needed to use border regions to defend Croatia.[776] According to Prlić and Praljak, the Trial Chamber failed to take into account the Serbian aggression against Croatia in determining **[page 106]** whether the HV's presence on the southern front was on its own account or in support of the HVO.[777]

257.   The Prosecution submits that the Trial Chamber reasonably relied on evidence showing that: (1) HV officers were appointed to positions within the HVO; (2) the members of the HVO Main Staff were simultaneously HV officers; (3) HV soldiers were paid by Croatia, commanded by HV commanders, including Praljak himself, and re-subordinated to the HV upon returning to Croatia; and (4) HV units could not be sent to BiH without the order of the HV Supreme Commander, demonstrating that HV units could only enter BiH at Croatia's command.[778] The Prosecution further submits that Prlić's and Praljak's arguments that HV soldiers were incorporated into the HVO command but that HV units could not go to BiH or be incorporated into the HVO is contradictory, and fails to show an error on the part of the Trial Chamber.[779] Moreover, it notes that other evidence showing that HV units could not go to BiH without the Supreme Commander's order further supports the Trial Chamber's conclusion.[780] Further, in the Prosecution's view, evidence of HV soldiers' subordination into the HVO command chain supports rather than undermines the Trial Chamber's findings that they were there at Croatia's behest.[781] According to the Prosecution, the question of whether HV soldiers were able to voluntarily join either the HVO or the ABiH is irrelevant.[782]

258.   Responding to Ćorić's challenge that there was no armed conflict between the HVO and the ABiH, the Prosecution argues that Ćorić fails to show why the Trial Chamber's findings regarding the existence of an

---

[771]   Stojić's Appeal Brief, para. 410, referring to Exs. P09989, P09925, P09204 (confidential), P01542, P01656 (confidential), P09926, P09400, Omer Hujdur, T. 3508-3510 (20 June 2006). Stojić also submits that since the Trial Chamber found that the JCE commenced in January 1993, the HV's involvement in the earlier 17 October 1992 Prozor attack is irrelevant. Stojić's Appeal Brief, para. 410. Stojić also argues that the Trial Chamber failed to consider that, even if HV troops participated in this attack, they may have done so voluntarily. Stojić's Appeal Brief, para. 410.
[772]   Stojić's Appeal Brief, para. 411, referring to Exs. P02620, 2D00285, P09870 (confidential), Christopher Beese, T. 3222-3224 (15 June 2006). Stojić also argues that the Trial Chamber failed to consider that, even if HV soldiers participated in this attack, they may have done so voluntarily. Stojić's Appeal Brief, para. 411.
[773]   Prlić's Appeal Brief, para. 658; Praljak's Appeal Brief, paras 13-15.
[774]   Prlić's Appeal Brief, para. 658; Praljak's Appeal Brief, paras 14-15.
[775]   Prlić's Appeal Brief, paras 653-656, 659; Praljak's Appeal Brief, paras 9-11, 16; Praljak's Reply Brief, para. 8.
[776]   Prlić's Appeal Brief, para. 655; Praljak's Appeal Brief, paras 9-10, 16-17.
[777]   Prlić's Appeal Brief, paras 653-655; Praljak's Appeal Brief, paras 8-10, 16-17.
[778]   Prosecution's Response Brief (Praljak), para. 9. See also Prosecution's Response Brief (Prlić), para. 413.
[779]   Prosecution's Response Brief (Prlić), para. 413.
[780]   Prosecution's Response Brief (Prlić), para. 413, referring to Ex. 3D00300.
[781]   Prosecution's Response Brief (Petković), para. 288.
[782]   Prosecution's Response Brief (Prlić), para. 413; Prosecution's Response Brief (Praljak), para. 10.

international armed conflict are unreasonable.[783] The Prosecution submits that it is irrelevant whether the HVO and ABiH were allies before the intervention of the HV alongside the HVO against the ABiH.[784] Further, the Prosecution avers that the HVO was not, in fact, a constituent part of the ABiH.[785]

259.   With regard to Petković's contention that, based on the parameters of the Indictment, the Trial Chamber should not have made factual findings concerning the intervention of HV troops prior to July 1993, the Prosecution asserts that Petković ignores the parts of the Indictment where it **[page 107]** explicitly alleged a state of international armed conflict at all times relevant to the Indictment.[786] Moreover, the Prosecution notes that Petković ignores evidence of the presence of HV troops on the southern front from May 1992 into 1994, which was cited by the Trial Chamber.[787]

260.   As to Petković's argument that the Trial Chamber should not have inferred the presence of HV units from the mere presence of HV soldiers, the Prosecution submits that the intervention of individual soldiers is sufficient.[788] The Prosecution further argues that the Trial Chamber relied on evidence showing that entire HV units and brigades were present on the southern front and on other parts of BiH territory.[789] It argues that the Trial Chamber did not only rely on evidence of HV officers' presence in the HVO to find that Croatia appointed HV officers within the HVO but also on other evidence, including Stojić's own correspondence to Gojko Šušak, showing that members of the HVO Main Staff leadership were simultaneously HV officers.[790] The Prosecution argues that the Trial Chamber also relied on evidence that the salaries of the HV soldiers integrated in the HVO continued to be paid by Croatia.[791]

261.   The Prosecution also avers that the Trial Chamber reasonably rejected the argument that HV soldiers involved in BiH were volunteers, finding that they were only characterised as such for the express purpose of hiding Croatia's involvement.[792] The Prosecution further argues that the *Kor die and Čerkez* Appeal Judgement does not require anything more than mere presence of foreign troops in a conflict zone for the conflict to qualify as international.[793] In any case, according to the Prosecution, the Trial Chamber correctly found that the HV was directly involved, and not merely present, in the HVO-ABiH conflict.[794]

262.   Regarding the attacks on Prozor and Sovići, the Prosecution asserts that Stojić fails to demonstrate an error or show that the Trial Chamber acted unreasonably in finding that the HV participated in the Prozor attack on the side of the HVO.[795] The Prosecution notes that even if the **[page 108]** crimes in Prozor occurred before the start date of the JCE, this has no bearing on the separate question of whether the conflict was

---

[783]   Prosecution's Response Brief (Ćorić), para. 67.
[784]   Prosecution's Response Brief (Petković), para. 286. The Prosecution also points to evidence of the HVO's attack on Gornji Vakuf, the siege of East Mostar, and the HVO arrest and eviction campaign that followed the ABiH offensive of 30 June 1993, to counter the argument that Croatia was never hostile to BiH. Prosecution's Response Brief (Ćorić), para. 67.
[785]   Prosecution's Response Brief (Ćorić), para. 67, referring to Prosecution's Response Brief (Ćorić), para. 74.
[786]   Prosecution's Response Brief (Petković), para. 285.
[787]   Prosecution's Response Brief (Petković), para. 286.
[788]   Prosecution's Response Brief (Petković), para. 287.
[789]   Prosecution's Response Brief (Petković), para. 288. The Prosecution argues that Petković ignores this evidence. Prosecution's Response Brief (Petković), para. 288.
[790]   Prosecution's Response Brief (Stojić), para. 381. See also Prosecution's Response Brief (Stojić), para. 383.
[791]   Prosecution's Response Brief (Stojić), para. 381.
[792]   Prosecution's Response Brief (Stojić), para. 381; Appeal Hearing, AT. 311-313 (21 Mar 2017); Prosecution's Response Brief (Praljak), para. 9. See also Prosecution's Response Brief (Prlić), para. 413.
[793]   Prosecution's Response Brief (Stojić), para. 378 & fn. 1558.
[794]   Prosecution's Response Brief (Prlić), para. 412, referring to, *inter alia*, Trial Judgement, Vol. 3, paras 532-541; Prosecution's Response Brief (Stojić), para. 378, referring to, *inter alia*, Trial Judgement, Vol. 3, paras 543-544, 568; Prosecution's Response Brief (Praljak), para. 7, referring to, *inter alia*, Trial Judgement, Vol. 1, para. 85, Vol. 3, paras 543-544, 568; Prosecution's Response Brief (Petković), para. 286, referring to, *inter alia*, Trial Judgement, Vol. 3, paras 529-531.
[795]   Prosecution's Response Brief (Stojić), paras 379-380. In this respect, the Prosecution points to Witness DR's testimony that soldiers told him that the HV took part in the attack, as well as to various eyewitness testimonies corroborating Witness DR's account, and other testimony identifying HV troops, based on the weapons and equipment they had. Prosecution's Response Brief (Stojić), para. 379.

international.[796] Similarly, according to the Prosecution, the Trial Chamber reasonably relied upon eyewitness testimony identifying HV soldiers as participating in the Sovići attack.[797]

263. In response to challenges to the credibility of Hujdur, Watkins, and Witness DW, the Prosecution contends that Prlić and Praljak did not demonstrate how the Trial Chamber's reliance on these witnesses was unreasonable, since, contrary to Prlić's and Praljak's claims, these testimonies were corroborated.[798] With regard to Nissen, the Prosecution points to other evidence demonstrating that ECMM monitors observed HV troops in territory claimed by the HZ(R) H-B.[799]

264. The Prosecution also rejects the self-defence claims of Prlić and Praljak, arguing that the threat of Serb attacks on Croatia, and the co-ordination between the HV and ABiH in response to these attacks, by no means contradicts the finding of Croatia's intervention in the HVO-ABiH conflict.[800] The Prosecution notes that for a large part of the 1992-to-1994 period, there is no evidence of attacks by Serb forces against Croatia.[801] More specifically, the Prosecution avers that co-ordination between the HV and ABiH in late 1992 to fight the Serb forces along the Croatian border does not undermine the Trial Chamber's finding that Croatia also intervened alongside the HVO against the ABiH elsewhere, as evidenced by HV units operating in the Heliodrom.[802]

(ii) Analysis

265. With regard to Ćorić's contention that there was no documentary evidence showing there was an armed conflict which was international in character between Croatia and BiH, the Appeals Chamber considers that he ignores the evidence, including various *viva voce* testimony and documentary evidence, on which the Trial Chamber relied.[803] As to Petković's and Ćorić's related arguments that documentary evidence shows the contrary – that the HVO and ABiH were allies at the time – the Appeals Chamber notes that the Trial Chamber considered evidence of military co-operation between the HVO and ABiH at times relevant to the Indictment, and in fact, refers to **[page 109]** some of the same evidence as Ćorić.[804] Nevertheless, the Appeals Chamber considers that this did not prevent the Trial Chamber from concluding that the support given by Croatia to the HVO was a hostile act or an act of war against the BiH. Nor did it preclude it from finding that there was an armed conflict which was international in character. The Appeals Chamber accordingly dismisses these arguments.

266. With respect to Petković's and Pušić's contentions that, on the basis of the parameters of the Indictment, the Trial Chamber should not have made factual findings concerning the intervention of HV troops prior to July 1993, the Appeals Chamber observes that they ignore the parts of the Indictment where it explicitly alleged a state of international armed conflict *at all times* relevant to it and the evidence the Trial Chamber pointed to with regard to the presence of HV troops on the southern front from May 1992 into 1994.[805] This argument is therefore dismissed.

267. Turning to Prlić's, Stojić's, Praljak's, and Petković's claim that the Trial Chamber erred in concluding that HV units participated in the conflict between the HVO and ABiH, the Appeals Chamber recalls that the Trial Chamber's finding of Croatia's and the HV's intervention in the HVO-ABiH conflict was not solely

---

[796]   Prosecution's Response Brief (Stojić), para. 379.
[797]   Prosecution's Response Brief (Stojić), para. 380. The Prosecution submits that this evidence was also corroborated by other evidence. Prosecution's Response Brief (Stojić), para. 380. The Prosecution further submits that the Trial Chamber considered and reasonably rejected the argument that HV soldiers were volunteers. Prosecution's Response Brief (Stojić), para. 381.
[798]   Prosecution's Response Brief (Prlić), para. 412; Prosecution's Response Brief (Praljak), para. 8.
[799]   Prosecution's Response Brief (Prlić), para. 412; Prosecution's Response Brief (Praljak), para. 8.
[800]   Prosecution's Response Brief (Prlić), para. 414; Prosecution's Response Brief (Praljak), para. 12.
[801]   Prosecution's Response Brief (Praljak), para. 12.
[802]   Prosecution's Response Brief (Prlić), para. 414; Prosecution's Response Brief (Praljak), para. 12.
[803]   See Trial Judgement, Vol. 3, paras 514, 528-568 and references cited therein.
[804]   See Ćorić's Appeal Brief, para. 70 & fns 177-185 and references cited therein; Trial Judgement, Vol. 1, paras 440-441 & fns 1038, 1040, referring to Exs. 1D02458 and P10481, Annex, pp. 2-4. The Appeals Chamber notes that this annex is Ex. P00339, the agreement between the Republics of Croatia and BiH, dated 21 July 1992, that Ćorić refers to. The Appeals Chamber considers the other evidence referred to by Ćorić to be irrelevant to the Indictment. See Exs. 2D00439, P02155. Further, the Appeals Chamber rejects Petković's assertion in this regard as unsubstantiated.
[805]   See Indictment, para. 232. See also Trial Judgement, Vol. 3, paras 529-543.

based on the presence of HV troops in the area claimed by the HZ(R) H-B throughout the relevant period, *i.e.* in 1992, 1993, and 1994.[806] The Trial Chamber also found that HV troops actively participated in the conflict alongside the HVO between October 1992 and January 1994.[807] Relying on several exhibits and witness testimonies, the Trial Chamber found in particular that the HV participated in the fighting on the side of the HVO in the HVO's attacks on Prozor and Sovići.[808] The Appeals Chamber therefore considers that Stojić's reliance on ICC and ICJ jurisprudence to support his claim that mere presence of foreign troops within a State is insufficient to constitute foreign intervention in a conflict is inapposite.[809] **[page 110]**

268.   Moreover, the Appeals Chamber recalls that, contrary to Prlić's, Stojić's, Praljak's, and Petković's contentions, the Trial Chamber considered multiple indicators of Croatian involvement in the conflict, and not merely the presence of individual HV members or units in the ranks of the HVO. In particular, the Trial Chamber considered evidence that: (1) the Croatian government paid HV personnel; (2) an HV commander brought disciplinary proceedings against HV soldiers for refusing to follow their unit to the southern front; (3) the Croatian government and military leaders appointed HVO leadership; and (4) HV officers within the HVO structure, including Praljak and Petković, maintained their positions as members of the HV.[810] As such, the Appeals Chamber dismisses Prlić's, Stojić's, Praljak's, and Petković's arguments regarding the presence of individual HV members or units in the ranks of the HVO on BiH territory.

269.   Further, the Appeals Chamber considers that Prlić's, Stojić's, Praljak's, and Petković's submissions that the evidence only establishes the presence of individual HV soldiers in BiH are contradicted by other pieces of evidence, relied upon by the Trial Chamber, which show that entire HV units were, in fact, present on the southern front.[811] Moreover, with respect to Prlić's and Praljak's specific submissions that the Trial Chamber erred by finding that the mere presence of HV soldiers or units was sufficient and conclusive evidence that the HV was operating at the behest of Croatia, the Appeals Chamber notes that the Trial Chamber considered, as discussed above,[812] multiple indicators of Croatian involvement in the conflict, and not merely the presence of individual HV members in the ranks of the HVO. Prlić and Praljak therefore have failed to show that no reasonable trier of fact could have reached the Trial Chamber's conclusion.

270.   With regard to Praljak's argument that the Trial Chamber failed to consider that some HV members joined the HVO voluntarily, the Appeals Chamber recalls that the Trial Chamber assessed but rejected the claim that the HV officers and soldiers integrated in the HVO command were acting as mere volunteers.[813] It did so based on unchallenged evidence, showing the contrary.[814] The Appeals Chamber considers that Praljak has failed to show that no reasonable trier of fact could have reached the same conclusion as the Trial Chamber. With respect to Prlić's and Praljak's arguments that individual HV members were allowed to volunteer for both the HVO and the ABIH, **[page 111]** and Praljak's argument that HV soldiers who joined both the HVO and the ABIH continued to be paid by Croatia, and were all relieved of their duties in the HV, the Appeals Chamber considers that Prlić and Praljak have failed to show how the HV's similar treatment of

---

[806]   See Trial Judgement, Vol. 3, paras 528-544.

[807]   See Trial Judgement, Vol. 3, paras 529-544. With regard to Stojić's argument that the Trial Chamber erred in holding that "it matters little" whether HV members participated in the BiH conflict as volunteers to determine that they were there on the direct order of Croatia, the Appeals Chamber recalls that the Trial Chamber made this finding in light of other evidence showing that Croatia paid the salaries of the HV personnel deployed in BiH. In any event, the Trial Chamber had addressed the issue of volunteers earlier in that same paragraph and dismissed it because of evidence to the contrary. See Trial Judgement, Vol. 3, para. 529 & fns 1098-1099. The Appeals Chamber thus dismisses Stojić's argument misrepresenting the Trial Chamber's findings.

[808]   See Trial Judgement, Vol. 3, paras 514, 532-533, 535.

[809]   In any event, the Appeals Chamber considers that the determination that there was no international armed conflict in the ICC and ICJ jurisprudence relied upon by Stojić was based on a lack of evidence in those cases. *Prosecutor v. Jean-Pierre Bemba Gombo*, Case No. ICC-01/05-01/08, Decision Pursuant to Article 67(1)(a) of the Rome Statue on the Charges of the Prosecutor Against Jean-Pierre Bemba Gombo, 15 June 2009, paras 245-246; *Lubanga* Confirmation of Charges Decision, para. 226; *Armed Activities* Judgement, paras 174-177 (in the context of occupation).

[810]   See Trial Judgement, Vol. 3, paras 529, 546-548, 555 and evidence referred to therein.

[811]   See Trial Judgement, Vol. 3, paras 530; 539, 541 referring to, *inter alia*, Exs. P00854, pp. 3-4, P01187, para. 32, P07587, P00785 (confidential), P02738, P03990, p. 4, P07959, pp. 1-2, P07887, pp. 7-8, P07789, P07365, P02787, p. 5, P09807(confidential), pp. 5-9, P03587(confidential), p. 8, P03771 (confidential), p. 4, para. 6(a)(2) Witness DZ, T. 26541 (closed session) (22 Jan 2008), Peter Galbraith, T. 6483-6484 (12 Sept 2006), Witness CW, T. 12674 (closed session), 12689-12692 (22 Jan 2007).

[812]   See *supra*, para. 268.

[813]   See Trial Judgement, Vol. 3, para. 529.

[814]   See Trial Judgement, Vol. 3, paras 529-567 and references cited therein.

HV members who joined either the HVO or the ABiH in the two distinct conflicts Croatia was involved in at the time, precluded the Trial Chamber from finding that the HV soldiers reinforcing the HVO were sent on behalf of Croatia.[815] Moreover, the Appeals Chamber considers that Prlić has failed to show how his contention that HV members who were allowed to volunteer were not incorporated in either the HVO or the ABiH, detracts from the Trial Chamber's finding that HV soldiers reinforcing the HVO were sent on behalf of Croatia.[816] The Appeals Chamber thus dismisses these arguments.

271. Further, the Appeals Chamber notes Stojić's arguments that the Trial Chamber based its finding that the HV participated in the attacks in Prozor and Sovići on the side of the HVO, on insufficient evidence, and observes that the Trial Chamber relied on various pieces of evidence, including eyewitness accounts and a report from an international organisation.[817] The Appeals Chamber has reviewed the challenged evidence[818] and considers that Stojić has failed to show that no reasonable trier of fact could have concluded that there was direct involvement of the HV on the side of the HVO in these attacks based on this evidence, especially when assessed cumulatively.[819] The Appeals Chamber therefore dismisses these arguments.

272. Turning to Stojić's argument that since the Trial Chamber had found that the JCE was conceived in January 1993, the HV's involvement in the October 1992 Prozor attack is not relevant to the question of whether the conflict was international, the Appeals Chamber recalls the Trial Chamber's finding that it could not conclude that the crimes committed in Prozor in October 1992 formed part of the JCE.[820] The Appeals Chamber considers that this matter is separate from, and not relevant to, the question of whether an international armed conflict existed between the HVO and the ABiH even as early as October 1992. Stojić has demonstrated no reason why the Trial Chamber could not consider the October 1992 attack against Prozor and the HV's participation in it as evidence of the existence of an international armed conflict. His argument is therefore dismissed. **[page 112]**

273. As to Prlić's and Praljak's challenges to the evidence on which the Trial Chamber relied to establish the HV's involvement on BiH territory, the Appeals Chamber considers that, contrary to what they claim, the testimonies of Hujdur, Witness DW, and Watkins were, in fact, corroborated.[821] As to the challenge that Nissen, an ECMM monitor, lacked personal knowledge of the presence of HV troops on BiH territory, Prlić and Praljak have failed to show that no reasonable trier of fact could have reached the same conclusion as the Trial Chamber, based on other evidence from international organisations confirming the presence of HV troops in areas claimed by the HZ(R) H-B.[822] As a result, the Appeals Chamber dismisses these arguments.

274. With respect to Prlić's and Praljak's argument that, to the extent that HV troops were on BiH territory, this was in self-defence as the JNA was crossing into BiH territory to attack Croatia, the Appeals Chamber notes that this argument was considered and rejected by the Trial Chamber.[823] In any case, the Appeals Chamber further considers that they have failed to demonstrate that no reasonable trier of fact could have reached the same conclusion as the Trial Chamber – that there was an international armed conflict between BiH and Croatia. This finding was based on evidence of the existence of a conflict between the HVO and the ABiH and of the HV's involvement, on the side of the HVO, at all relevant times.[824] The Appeals Chamber thus dismisses this argument.

---

[815]   See Trial Judgement, Vol. 3, paras 529-531.

[816]   See Trial Judgement, Vol. 3, paras 529-531.

[817]   See Trial Judgement, Vol. 3, paras 532-533, 535 and references cited therein.

[818]   See, *e.g.*, Exs. P09989, P09925, P09204 (confidential), P01542, P01656 (confidential), P02620, P09870 (confidential), 2D00285; Omer Hujdur, T. 3508-3510 (20 June 2006); Christopher Beese, T. 3222-3224 (15 June 2006).

[819]   As to Stojić's argument that even if HV troops had participated in these attacks, the Trial Chamber failed to consider that they may have done so voluntarily, the Appeals Chamber dismisses this as misconstrued because the Trial Chamber considered but rejected this possibility. See Trial Judgement, Vol. 3, paras 529-531 and references cited therein.

[820]   See Trial Judgement, Vol. 4, para. 44. See also *infra*, para. 854.

[821]   See Trial Judgement, Vol. 3, paras 532-533, 539-540 and references cited therein. With regard to the challenges to the credibility of these Prosecution witnesses, the Appeals Chamber further recalls that "[i]n any event, there is no general requirement that the testimony of a witness be corroborated if deemed otherwise credible". *Popović et al* Appeal Judgement, paras 243, 1264; *D. Milošević* Appeal Judgement, para. 215. See also *Kordić and Čerkez* Appeal Judgement, para. 274.

[822]   See Trial Judgement, Vol. 3, paras 534-535 and references cited therein.

[823]   See Trial Judgement, Vol. 3, paras 521, 525.

[824]   See Trial Judgement, Vol. 3, paras 514, 518-544 and references cited therein.

275. In light of the foregoing, the Appeals Chamber concludes that the Appellants have failed to show that the Trial Chamber erred in finding that the HV's presence on BiH territory, in conjunction with its direct intervention in the HVO-ABiH conflict, rendered the conflict international. Thus, the Appeals Chamber dismisses Prlić's sub-grounds of appeal 19.1 in part and 19.2, Stojić's sub-ground of appeal 54.1, Praljak's sub-grounds of appeal 1.1 in part, 1.2 in part, 1.3 in part, and 1.4 in part, Petković's sub-grounds of appeal 7.1.1 in part, 7.1.3, and 7.1.4 in part, Ćorić's sub-ground of appeal 3.1 in part, and Pušić's ground of appeal 7 in part, to the extent that these grounds of appeal concern the presence of HV troops on BiH territory and their direct and voluntary participation in the conflict between the HVO and the ABiH. **[page 113]**

(b) Croatia's organisation, co-ordination, and planning of the HVO's military operations (Prlić's Sub-ground 19.3, Stojić's Sub-ground 54.2 in part, Praljak's Sub-grounds 1.3 in part and 1.4 in part, Petković's Sub-grounds 7.1.1 in part and 7.1.5 in part, Ćorić's Sub-ground 3.1 in part, and Pušić's Ground 7 in part)

(i) Arguments of the Parties

276. The Appellants challenge the Trial Chamber's finding that the HVO-ABiH conflict was international due to Croatia's overall control over the HVO as evidenced by, *inter alia,* the HV and HVO's joint organisation, co-ordination, supervision, and direction of such operations.[825] Praljak alleges that the Trial Chamber failed to specify exactly where and when Croatia participated in planning or conducting military operations and how it exercised overall control over the HVO.[826] According to Pušić, for purposes of the Overall Control Test, the Trial Chamber was required to find that the HVO's military operations were planned either by the Croatian government in Zagreb or by the HV, which the Trial Chamber did not find.[827] Pušić submits that pursuant to the evidence presented to the Trial Chamber, operational leadership on the ground remained with the HVO and the material and logistical assistance provided by the HV to the HVO fell short of the Overall Control Test.[828] To the extent that the Trial Chamber relied upon evidence of the Croatian President Franjo Tuđman's involvement in the dispute, Pušić relies on the Judge Antonetti Dissent, which allegedly points to evidence that President Tuđman was not always cognisant of the HVO's activities.[829] Pušić also contests the Trial Chamber's finding that HV officers were actively involved in the HVO's operations and asserts that evidence of the transfer of certain Croatian officers to BiH does not, *per se,* suffice to demonstrate Croatia's overall control over the HVO.[830]

277. Stojić, Praljak, and Petković argue that the mere presence of individual HV members in the ranks of the HVO is insufficient to establish that the HV was operating at the behest of Croatia.[831] Petković further submits that the Trial Chamber erred in inferring that whole HV units were present **[page 114]** in BiH from the presence of HV members in the HVO.[832] In this regard Stojić and Praljak argue that even if some HV elements were "in the service of the HVO", the Trial Chamber erred in concluding that this implied that they were there on the direct order of Croatia.[833] Further, Praljak argues that the Trial Chamber failed to consider

---

[825] Prlić's Appeal Brief, paras 662, 664-668 (also referring to his submissions in ground of appeal 15); Stojić's Appeal Brief, paras 412-413, 417-419; Praljak's Appeal Brief, para. 35; Petković's Appeal Brief, para. 429; Ćorić's Appeal Brief, paras 71, 73-74; Ćorić's Reply Brief, para. 24; Pušić's Appeal Brief, paras 232-233. Ćorić reiterates, on appeal, the argument raised in the Judge Antonetti Dissent from the Trial Judgement: that there was only one undated exhibit evidencing HV involvement in the planning of the HVO's military operations, arguing that it was insufficient to prove the HV's overall control over the HVO for the entire period covered by the Indictment. The Appeals Chamber dismisses this argument as Ćorić has failed to identify the exhibit to which he refers. See Ćorić's Appeal Brief, para. 71.
[826] Praljak's Appeal Brief, para. 31; Appeal Hearing, AT. 373-374 (22 Mar 2017).
[827] Pušić's Appeal Brief, para. 232.
[828] Pušić's Appeal Brief, paras 232-233.
[829] Pušie"s Appeal Brief, para. 232 & fn. 375.
[830] Pušić's Appeal Brief, para. 232.
[831] Stojić's Appeal Brief, para. 413; Praljak's Appeal Brief, paras 21-22, 32; Petković's Appeal Brief, paras 419, 421-423, 425; Petković's Reply Brief, paras 85-86.
[832] Petković's Appeal Brief, paras 422, 425.
[833] Stojić's Appeal Brief, para. 413, referring to *Kordić and Čerkez* Appeal Judgement, para. 359; Praljak's Appeal Brief, para. 22. In this respect, Stojić contends that the only direct evidence of Croatian involvement in HVO activities concerned the deployment by Croatia of a "logistical assistant" to the HVO, which falls short of demonstrating overall control over the HVO. Stojić's Appeal Brief, para. 413 & fn. 1040, referring to Ex. P00332.

that some HV members joined the HVO voluntarily, especially given that many of them were born on BiH territory where their families still lived.[834] While Praljak concedes that HV officers who integrated into the HVO remained HV officers and continued to receive their salaries from Croatia, he alleges that the Trial Chamber overlooked the fact that this was the same for those HV officers integrated into the ABiH and thus not indicative of Croatian control.[835] He adds that HV officers volunteering for both the HVO and the ABiH were temporarily relieved of their duties in the HV.[836]

278.   Prlić, Stojić, Praljak, and Petković further challenge the evidence on which the Trial Chamber relied to find that the HV was actively involved in the planning and conduct of the HVO's military operations.[837] In particular, they challenge as erroneous the Trial Chamber's interpretation of the testimonies of: (1) constitutional expert Witness Ciril Ribičić; (2) Witness Marijan Biškić of the HR H-B Ministry of Defence; and (3) Witness Ivan Beneta, an HV Commander.[838] Stojić, in particular, claims that whether the HV and the HVO jointly conducted military operations was beyond the scope of Ribičić's expertise.[839] Prlić and Praljak assert that the Trial Chamber erroneously rejected Biškić's claim that the Croatian Minister of Defence, Gojko Šušak, visited BiH in his personal capacity and not in his official capacity, as the Trial Chamber found.[840] Praljak adds that even if Šušak had travelled in his official capacity, such contacts between Šušak and the HVO were natural and logical, and did not prove the HV's involvement in the HVO's operational planning.[841] As to Beneta, they allege that the Trial Chamber distorted his testimony by finding that HV commanders gave orders to HVO units, when in fact Beneta testified **[page 115]** that the HV members integrated into the HVO were under HVO command.[842] Prlić and Praljak additionally contend that the Trial Chamber erroneously relied on the testimony of Witness Peter Galbraith, the United States Ambassador to Croatia during the relevant time, to find that the HV wielded overall control over the HVO.[843] Finally, Prlić and Petković challenge the Trial Chamber's reliance on adjudicated facts to find that the HV and the HVO jointly directed military operations,[844] while Stojić also argues that the Trial Chamber erred in relying on evidence of indirect political influence.[845]

279.   The Prosecution responds that the Trial Chamber correctly found that Croatia had an active role in jointly co-ordinating, planning, and conducting military operations in BiH with the HVO.[846] According to the Prosecution, the Appellants fail to show that the Trial Chamber's findings in this regard were erroneous.[847]

---

[834]   Praljak's Appeal Brief, para. 21. Similarly, Stojić contends that the Trial Chamber disregarded evidence that HV officers joined voluntarily and failed to consider whether they acted on the orders of Croatia. Stojić's Appeal Brief, para. 413.

[835]   Praljak's Appeal Brief, para. 22. See also Praljak's Reply Brief, para. 11.

[836]   Praljak's Appeal Brief, paras 21-23. See also Praljak's Reply Brief, para. 11.

[837]   Prlić's Appeal Brief, paras 664-666; Stojić's Appeal Brief, para. 414; Praljak's Appeal Brief, paras 26-28, Appeal Hearing, AT. 372-373 (22 Mar 2017); Petković's Appeal Brief, para. 426.

[838]   Prlić's Appeal Brief, paras 664-666; Stojić's Appeal Brief, para. 414; Praljak's Appeal Brief, paras 26-28; Petković's Appeal Brief, para. 426.

[839]   Stojić's Appeal Brief, para. 414.

[840]   Prlić's Appeal Brief, para. 666; Praljak's Appeal Brief, para. 28. Praljak also submits that even if Šušak was in BiH in his capacity as Defence Minister, it does not mean that the HV was involved in planning and conducting HV-HVO military operations. Praljak's Appeal Brief, para. 28, Appeal Hearing, AT. 374-375 (22 Mar 2017). See also Stojić's Appeal Brief, para. 415.

[841]   Praljak's Appeal Brief, para. 28.

[842]   Prlić's Appeal Brief, paras 664-665; Stojić's Appeal Brief, para. 414; Praljak's Appeal Brief, para. 27; Petković's Appeal Brief, para. 426.

[843]   Prlić's Appeal Brief, paras 662-663; Praljak's Appeal Brief, para. 21. Praljak also claims that the Trial Chamber exclusively relied on the testimony of Peter Galbraith. Praljak's Appeal Brief, para. 21.

[844]   Prlić's Appeal Brief, para. 663; Petković's Appeal Brief, para. 426.

[845]   Stojić's Appeal Brief, para. 418. The Appeals Chamber also notes the argument raised by Prlić, Stojić, Praljak, Petković, and Ćorić that the Trial Chamber erroneously failed to acknowledge that, in addition to the support provided to the HVO, Croatia also provided, through the HV, material and technical equipment, supplies, training, and financial assistance to the ABiH, which, in Prlić's, Stojić's, Praljak's, Petković's, and Ćorić's view, undermines the finding of overall control over the HVO. See Prlić's Appeal Brief, para. 667; Stojić's Appeal Brief, para. 417; Praljak's Appeal Brief, para. 24; Petković's Appeal Brief, para. 428; Ćorić's Appeal Brief, paras 70, 72. See also Appeal Hearing, AT. 657 (24 Mar 2017).

[846]   Prosecution's Response Brief (Prlić), paras 415-417; Prosecution's Response Brief (Stojić), paras 382-387; Appeal Hearing, AT. 308-311, 313-316, (21 Mar 2017); Prosecution's Response Brief (Praljak), paras 18-22; Prosecution's Response Brief (Petković), paras 289-295; Prosecution's Response Brief (Ćorić), para. 64; Prosecution's Response Brief (Pušić), paras 213, 215.

[847]   Prosecution's Response Brief (Prlić), paras 415-417; Prosecution's Response Brief (Stojić), paras 382-387; Prosecution's Response Brief (Praljak), paras 18-22; Prosecution's Response Brief (Petković), paras 289-295; Prosecution's Response Brief (Ćorić), para. 65; Prosecution's Response Brief (Pušić), paras 213, 215.

The Prosecution points, *inter alia,* to the Trial Chamber's findings that: (1) the Croatian government assigned HV officers to the HVO; (2) the HV and HVO jointly directed operations in BiH; and (3) HVO organs reported on their operations to Croatian/HV authorities, while HV members in BiH reported to HVO officers.[848] The Prosecution also points to evidence of Stojić's communications with Croatian Defence Minister Šušak concerning the re-assignment of HV members to the HVO, arguing that this proves that the HVO leadership was composed, in essence, of HV officers who retained their positions in the HV while posted to the HVO.[849] The Prosecution notes that, under the Overall Control Test, the Trial Chamber was not required to find that the HV or the Croatian government issued specific orders to the HVO or directed any particular relevant operations.[850] **[page 116]**

280.   The Prosecution responds that the Trial Chamber reasonably found that HV soldiers were present in BiH at the behest of Croatia.[851] It argues that the Trial Chamber did not only rely on evidence of HV officers' presence in the HVO to find that Croatia appointed HV officers within the HVO but also on other evidence, including Stojić's own correspondence to Šušak, showing that members of the HVO Main Staff leadership were simultaneously HV officers.[852] The Prosecution also avers that the Trial Chamber reasonably rejected the argument that HV soldiers involved in BiH were volunteers, finding that they were only characterised as such for the express purpose of hiding Croatia's involvement.[853] According to the Prosecution, the question of whether HV soldiers were able to voluntarily join either the HVO or the ABiH is irrelevant.[854]

281.   The Prosecution avers that Prlić, Stojić, and Petković fail to show why the Trial Chamber's reliance upon the testimony of Ribičić or the rejection of the claim that Defence Minister Šušak met with the HVO military leadership in his personal capacity, were unreasonable.[855] According to the Prosecution, the Trial Chamber correctly interpreted and relied upon Biškić's testimony and other evidence (most notably the transcripts of a meeting held on 24 April 1993 in Zagreb, between among others, President Tuđman of Croatia, President Izetbegović of BiH, Mate Boban, President of HZ(R) H-B, and Lord David Owen, Co-Chairman of the International Conference on the Former Yugoslavia ("ICFY")) to establish that the HV and the leadership of the HZ(R) H-B met to plan military operations.[856] Regarding the claim that Beneta did not testify that HV commanders issued orders to HVO units, the Prosecution points to his evidence that HV officer Luka Džanko issued an attack order for, and personally commanded, a joint HV/HVO operation, which, according to the Prosecution, the Trial Chamber considered.[857] The Prosecution also refutes the challenges to Galbraith's testimony regarding the appointment of officers, which, according to the Prosecution, was both well-corroborated and based on the witness's particular experience as United States Ambassador to Croatia.[858] Further, the Prosecution responds that Prlić's and Petković's mere **[page 117]** assertions that the Trial Chamber relied exclusively on adjudicated facts (and on Ribičić's testimony, in Prlić's case) demonstrates no error and is belied by other evidence.[859]

---

[848]   Prosecution's Response Brief (Prlić), paras 415-416; Prosecution's Response Brief (Stojić), paras 382-386; Prosecution's Response Brief (Praljak), paras 15-18; Prosecution's Response Brief (Petković), paras 289-290, 292-293; Prosecution's Response Brief (Ćorić), paras 64-65. See also Prosecution's Response Brief (Pušić), para. 215.
[849]   Prosecution's Response Brief (Stojić), para. 383.
[850]   Prosecution's Response Brief (Stojić), para. 382.
[851]   Prosecution's Response Brief (Stojić), paras 383-384; Prosecution's Response Brief (Praljak), para. 16.
[852]   Prosecution's Response Brief (Stojić), paras 383-384, referring to, *inter alia,* Trial Judgement, Vol. 3, para. 547 & fn. 1133, referring to, *inter alia,* Exs. P10336, P03957.
[853]   Prosecution's Response Brief (Praljak), para. 16.
[854]   Prosecution's Response Brief (Praljak), para. 17; Prosecution's Response (Petković), para. 293.
[855]   Prosecution's Response Brief (Prlić), para. 416; Prosecution's Response Brief (Stojić), para. 385; Prosecution's Response Brief (Petković), para. 291.
[856]   Prosecution's Response Brief (Prlić), para. 416. See also Prosecution's Response Brief (Stojić), para. 385, Appeal Hearing, AT. 205-207 (20 Mar 2017).
[857]   Prosecution's Response Brief (Prlić), para. 416; Prosecution's Response Brief (Stojić), para. 385; Prosecution's Response Brief (Praljak), para. 18. See also Prosecution's Response Brief (Petković), para. 291.
[858]   Prosecution's Response Brief (Prlić), para. 415; Prosecution's Response Brief (Praljak), para. 15. Regarding the challenge to Galbraith, the Prosecution argues that his testimony was based on his official interactions with Croatian authorities in his capacity as United States Ambassador to Croatia, and was corroborated by other evidence. Prosecution's Response Brief (Prlić), para. 415; Prosecution's Response Brief (Praljak), para. 15. See *infra,* para. 288.
[859]   Prosecution's Response Brief (Prlić), para. 416; Prosecution's Response Brief (Petković), para. 291. The Prosecution responds to Ćorić's arguments regarding Croatia also providing HV material and financial assistance to the ABiH by stating that this happened during times or in areas other than those subject of the Indictment. Appeal Hearing, AT. 657 (24 Mar 2017).

(ii) Analysis

282.   At the outset, the Appeals Chamber recalls its jurisprudence that in order for acts of a military group to be attributed to a State, the Overall Control Test requires proof that "the State wields overall control over the group, not only by equipping and financing the group, but also by co-ordinating or helping in the general planning of its military activity".[860] Indeed, the Overall Control Test "calls for an assessment of all the elements of control taken as a whole, and a determination to be made on that basis as to whether there was the required degree of control".[861]

283.   The Trial Chamber found that Croatia wielded overall control over the HVO and that such control manifested itself in several ways.[862] Specifically, the Trial Chamber relied on evidence that: (1) HV officers were placed within the HVO;[863] (2) the HV and the HVO jointly directed military operations;[864] (3) the HV sent reports on its activities to the Croatian authorities and/or the HVO;[865] (4) there was logistical support from Croatia, including financial support, dispatching of arms and materiel, and assistance in the form of training and expertise;[866] and (5) Croatia wielded political influence over the HVO and the HZ(R) H-B authorities.[867]

284.   Contrary to the Appellants' suggestions, the Trial Chamber did not need to find that the HV maintained the ultimate decision-making authority and command over each and every military operation conducted or planned by the HVO on BiH territory, or that HV troops were present and participated in every single operation undertaken by the HVO against the ABiH.[868] Nor was it necessary, as Praljak argues, for the Trial Chamber to concretely identify when and where the HV participated in the planning of specific military operations by the HVO.[869] Further, the Appeals Chamber finds that Pušić's argument, that the presence of HV troops in BiH was not **[page 118]** sufficient for overall control to be established, is not inconsistent with the challenged finding. This was only one factor considered by the Trial Chamber in reaching its finding.[870] In this regard, the Appeals Chamber considers Pušić's argument that Tuđman himself was not aware of the HVO's operations in BiH as unsubstantiated and dismisses it accordingly. For the foregoing reasons, the Appeals Chamber considers that the Appellants have failed to show that no reasonable trier of fact, based on the evidence as a whole, could have reached the same conclusion as the Trial Chamber and thus dismisses their arguments.

285.   Turning to Prlić's, Stojić's, and Praljak's reliance on the *Kordić and Čerkez* Appeal Judgement to argue that the Trial Chamber erred in inferring that the HV members were in BiH on the direct order of Croatia because of HV officers' presence there and because some HV members were in the service of the HVO, the Appeals Chamber recalls that in the *Kordić and Čerkez* case, it was merely considering the reliance on certain evidence in that case.[871] The mere reference to a conclusion in a different appeal judgement concerning an alleged error does not show that no reasonable trier of fact could have reached the same conclusion as the Trial Chamber did in the present case, based on the evidence adduced at trial. Accordingly, the Appeals Chamber dismisses this contention. Additionally, contrary to Prlić's, Stojić's, and Praljak's arguments, the Appeals Chamber recalls that the Trial Chamber in this case did not only rely on the presence of the HV personnel integrated into the HVO to find that Croatia had overall control of the HVO but on

---

[860]   *Tadić* Appeal Judgement, para. 131. See also *Tadić* Appeal Judgement, paras 130, 137-138, 145.

[861]   *Aleksovski* Appeal Judgement, para. 145. See also *Kordić and Čerkez* Appeal Judgement, para. 371 (upholding the Trial Chamber's decision to consider "a multitude of factors when making its analysis" regarding the planning, co-ordination, and organisation of the activities of the HVO).

[862]   See Trial Judgement, Vol. 3, paras 545-568.

[863]   See Trial Judgement, Vol. 3, paras 546-548 and references cited therein.

[864]   See Trial Judgement, Vol. 3, paras 549-552 and references cited therein.

[865]   See Trial Judgement, Vol. 3, para. 553 and references cited therein.

[866]   See Trial Judgement, Vol. 3, paras 554-559 and references cited therein.

[867]   See Trial Judgement, Vol. 3, paras 560-566 and references cited therein.

[868]   *Tadić* Appeal Judgement, para. 137. See Trial Judgement, Vol. 1, para. 86.

[869]   *Tadić* Appeal Judgement, para. 137. See Trial Judgement, Vol. 3, paras 545-553.

[870]   See *supra*, para. 283. See also Trial Judgement, Vol. 3, paras 545-568.

[871]   *Kordić and Čerkez* Appeal Judgement, para. 359 (referring to the content of HVO orders). In that context, the Appeals Chamber in *Kordić and Čerkez* held that "[t]he fact that members of the HV were in the service of the HVO does not imply without doubt that they were there on the direct order of Croatia". *Kordić and Čerkez* Appeal Judgement, para. 359.

various factors.[872] Specifically, the Appeals Chamber observes that the Trial Chamber considered evidence showing that: (1) high-ranking HV officers, such as Praljak and Petković, were sent by Croatia to join the ranks of the HVO; (2) the HV and HVO jointly directed military operations;[873] (3) the HVO dispatched reports concerning its activities to the Croatian authorities; (4) Croatia provided logistical support to the HVO; and (5) Croatia exercised political influence over the HVO and the HZ(R) H-B.[874] The Appeals Chamber thus dismisses this argument as a misrepresentation of the factual findings.[875] **[page 119]**

286.   Turning to Prlić's, Stojić's, Praljak's, and Petković's challenges to the Trial Chamber's assessment of the testimonies of Ribičić, Biškić, and Beneta on which the Trial Chamber relied to find that the HV and the HVO jointly directed military operations,[876] the Appeals Chamber considers their challenges amount to disagreements with the Trial Chamber's evidentiary assessments. As such the Appeals Chamber dismisses their arguments as a mere assertion that the Trial Chamber failed to interpret evidence in a particular way. Regarding Stojić's specific argument that Ribičić's testimony exceeded the scope of his expertise, the Appeals Chamber recalls its jurisprudence that "it is for the Trial Chamber to accept or reject, in whole or in part, the contribution of an expert witness" and that "a Trial Chamber's decision with respect to evaluation of evidence received pursuant to Rule 94 *bis* of the Rules is a discretionary one".[877] The Appeals Chamber observes that Stojić has failed to show that the Trial Chamber abused its discretion when relying on Ribičić, a constitutional law expert and "expert on the genesis of constitutional systems in the territory of the former Yugoslavia",[878] and his evidence on the establishment of the armed forces of HZ H-B and their relationship with neighbouring Croatia,[879] to find that the HZ(R) H-B co-ordinated its military activities with Croatia.[880] In any event, the Appeals Chamber observes that Ribičić's testimony was only one of several pieces of evidence relied upon by the Trial Chamber to find that the HV and the HVO jointly directed military operations.[881] Stojić has failed to demonstrate that the Trial Chamber erred in relying on the remaining evidence. This argument is therefore dismissed.

287.   Further, with regard to Beneta's testimony, the Appeals Chamber considers that Prlić, Stojić, Praljak, and Petković misconstrue the relevant finding. In particular, the Trial Chamber found, based on evidence other than – but consistent with – his testimony,[882] that commanding officers of the HV issued orders to the units of the HVO for *certain* military operations, implying that operational control for other HVO activities remained in the hands of the HVO.[883] It thus rejects this argument. As to Prlić's contention that the Trial Chamber erred in relying on adjudicated facts, the Appeals Chamber notes that the Trial Chamber merely referred to one **[page 120]** Adjudicated Fact as a further reference[884] and thus considers that Prlić has failed to show that no reasonable trier of fact, based on the remaining evidence,[885] could have reached the same conclusion as the Trial Chamber.

872   See *supra*, para. 283.
873   See Trial Judgement, Vol. 3, paras 549-552.
874   See Trial Judgement, Vol. 3, paras 545-567 and references cited therein. See also Trial Judgement, Vol. 3, fn. 1130, referring to, *inter alia*, Ex. P00332 (referred to by Stojić); Trial Judgement, Vol. 3, fn. 1133 referring, *inter alia*, to Exs. P10336, P03957 (correspondence from Stojić to Šušak showing that members of the HVO Main Staff leadership were simultaneously HVO officers).
875   To the extent that Stojić argues that direct evidence is required to prove Croatia's overall control of the HVO, the Appeals Chamber dismisses this argument as being based on an erroneous understanding of the jurisprudence. See *Kordić and Čerkez* Appeal Judgement, para. 308; *Čelebići* Appeal Judgement, para. 47; *Aleksovski* Appeal Judgement, paras 144-146; *Tadić* Appeal Judgement, paras 131, 137.
876   See Trial Judgement, Vol. 3, paras 549-552 & fns 1138-1140, 1145 and references cited therein.
877   *Strugar* Appeal Judgement, para. 58.
878   See Ex. P08973, p. 2; Trial Judgement, Vol. 3, fn. 1138.
879   See Trial Judgement, Vol. 3, fn. 1139, referring to Ex. P08973, p. 25 (stating that several provisions of the Decree on the Armed Forces of the HZ H-B, adopted by the Presidency of the HZ H-B on 3 July 1992, establishing the armed forces of the HZ H-B, indicated that the HZ H-B acted as an autonomous and sovereign state, separate from BiH, and with respect to the armed forces, it co-ordinated its activities with Croatia, and they formed the basis for financial, personnel, and other assistance from Croatia to the HVO).
880   See Trial Judgement, Vol. 3, para. 549 & fn. 1139.
881   See Trial Judgement, Vol. 3, paras 549-552 and references cited therein.
882   See Trial Judgement, Vol. 3, para. 550 & fn. 1140, referring to Exs. P03048, p. 3, P07055.
883   See Trial Judgement, Vol. 3, para. 550 & fn. 1140, referring to Ivan Beneta, T(F). 46632, 46634, 46639, 46656 (10 Nov 2009).
884   See Trial Judgement, Vol. 3, fn. 1139.
885   See Trial Judgement, Vol. 3, paras 549-552 and references cited therein.

288.   As to Prlić's and Praljak's arguments that the testimony of Galbraith was insufficient to find that officers from the HV were sent by Croatia to join the ranks of the HVO, and that the HV wielded overall control over the HVO, the Appeals Chamber observes that the Trial Chamber did not solely rely on Galbraith's testimony to make these findings but also on other pieces of evidence that showed the presence of HV officers on BiH territory and their integration into the HVO command structure.[886] The Appeals Chamber finds that Prlić and Praljak have failed to demonstrate that no reasonable trier of fact, based on this evidence, could have reached the same conclusion as the Trial Chamber. Further, with regard to their challenges to Galbraith's credibility and the Trial Chamber's assessment of his testimony, they have failed to show that the Trial Chamber abused its discretion.[887] Consequently, the Appeals Chamber will not disturb the Trial Chamber's assessment of that witness's credibility and the probative value of his testimony.[888] It thus dismisses their arguments.

289.   In light of the foregoing, the Appeals Chamber finds that the Appellants have failed to show an error in the Trial Chamber's conclusion that Croatia, through the HV, had overall control over the HVO through its involvement in the organisation, co-ordination, and planning of the HVO's military operations. The Appeals Chamber therefore dismisses Prlić's sub-ground of appeal 19.3, Stojić's sub-ground of appeal 54.2 in part, Praljak's sub-grounds of appeal 1.3 in part and 1.4 in part, Petković's sub-grounds 7.1.1 in part and 7.1.5 in part, Ćorić's sub-ground of appeal 3.1 in part, and Pušić's ground of appeal 7 in part.

(c) Other challenges – shared military reports (Stojić's Sub-ground 54.2, Praljak's Sub-ground 1.3, and Petković's Sub-ground 7.1.5, all in part)

(i) Arguments of the Parties

290.   Stojić, Praljak, and Petković object to the Trial Chamber's reliance on the HV's and the HVO's sharing of military reports in support of its finding of Croatia's overall control over the **[page 121]** HVO.[889] Stojić argues that the Trial Chamber failed to analyse the purpose of these reports from the HVO to the HV, which were mostly requests for logistical assistance.[890] Stojić also asserts that the military reports involved co-ordination against the common "Serbian threat", rather than the conflict with the ABiH.[891] Praljak in particular states that any exchange of communications between the HV and HVO was attributable to the geographical proximity of the two armies and the historical connection of their people.[892]

291.   Like Stojić and Praljak, Petković concedes that HVO reports were sent to the Croatian authorities, but points out that the HVO chose the topics of the shared reports, which is inconsistent with the Trial Chamber's finding concerning Croatia's control over the HVO.[893] Petković also contests the Trial Chamber's reliance on: (1) the order from the Croatian Ministry of Defence to the Head of the Defence Department of the HZ(R) H-B to provide more information;[894] (2) the internal HVO report mentioning Šušak's order for the reorganisation of HVO logistical operations;[895] as well as (3) the testimony of Witness Josip Manolić, a high-level Croatian political official.[896] This evidence, in Petković's view, does not support a finding of overall control.[897]

---

886   See Trial Judgement, Vol. 3, paras 546-548 and references cited therein.
887   See *Popović et al.* Appeal Judgement, paras 131-132. See also *supra,* paras 215-218.
888   See Trial Judgement, Vol. 3, paras 546-547 & fn. 1132. The Appeals Chamber further considers that Prlić, Stojić, Praljak, Petković, and Ćorić fail to demonstrate that the provision of HV logistical and other support to the ABiH against their common enemy, the Bosnian Serbs, undermines or is incompatible with the finding that through the HV, Croatia exercised overall control over the HVO.
889   Stojić's Appeal Brief, paras 415-416; Praljak's Appeal Brief, paras 29-30; Praljak's Reply Brief, para. 12; Petković's Appeal Brief, para. 427.
890   Stojić's Appeal Brief, para. 416.
891   Stojić's Appeal Brief, para. 416.
892   Praljak's Appeal Brief, paras 29-30.
893   Petković's Appeal Brief, para. 427.
894   Petković's Appeal Brief, para. 427, referring to Ex. P03242, Trial Judgement, Vol. 3, para. 553, fn. 1146.
895   Petković's Appeal Brief, para. 427, referring to Ex. P07135.
896   Petković's Appeal Brief, para. 427.
897   Petković's Appeal Brief, para. 427.

292.   The Prosecution responds that Praljak fails to demonstrate how the existence of historical links between Croatia and the Bosnian Croats and common enemies undermines the finding of Croatia's overall control over the HVO.[898] The Prosecution further argues that the claim that the Trial Chamber misinterpreted the documents is unsubstantiated, pointing specifically to Manolić's testimony that the HVO officers reported regularly to Šušak.[899] The Prosecution contends that Stojić does not demonstrate how the exchange of reports between the HV and HVO regarding the conflict with the Serbs undermines the proposition that Croatia and its armed forces possessed overall control over the HVO.[900] The Prosecution rejects as unfounded Stojić's claim that most reports relied upon by the Trial Chamber pertained to logistics.[901]

293.   In response to Petković, the Prosecution contends that he does not cite any evidence supporting his argument that the HVO decided independently which topics to raise in reports shared **[page 122]** with the HV, nor did he sufficiently establish why this fact could impact the Trial Chamber's conclusion.[902] The Prosecution also argues that Petković failed to demonstrate why it was unreasonable for the Trial Chamber to rely upon an instruction from the Croatian Ministry of Defence to the Head of the Defence Department of the HZ(R) H-B and on the relevant report of the HVO Chief of Staff.[903] The Prosecution notes that contrary to Petković's assertion, Manolić did, in fact, testify that HVO authorities sent reports to the HV.[904]

   (ii) Analysis

294.   The Trial Chamber concluded, based on the evidence before it, that the exchange of military reports between the HV and HVO was one of multiple indicators of Croatia's overall control over the HVO.[905] Stojić, Praljak, and Petković all contest the Trial Chamber's assessment of various exhibits and testimony relied upon by the Trial Chamber in this respect as evidence of overall control without demonstrating that the Trial Chamber erred in its assessment of the probative value of the evidence or testimony.[906] The Appeals Chamber rejects Petković's contentions concerning the sufficiency of the evidence because he has failed to submit any reason why the reports considered by the Trial Chamber, including the information from the Croatian Ministry of Defence and Manolić's testimony,[907] are not relevant to, or probative of, Croatia's overall control over the HVO.

295.   With respect to Stojić's arguments in particular, the Appeals Chamber finds that he has not demonstrated why the mere possibility that HV-HVO reporting may have also covered the common "Serbian threat" ultimately invalidates the Trial Chamber's reliance on the exchange of reports as proof of Croatia's overall control. Similarly, the Appeals Chamber considers that Praljak's argument that the long-standing historical links between Croatia and the Bosnian Croat community could explain the exchange of reports between the HV and HVO is unpersuasive. Praljak has failed to show how the impugned finding would not stand on the basis of the remaining evidence of the close interaction between the HV and HVO, and of the Croatian government's involvement in the HVO-ABiH conflict and in the governance of the HZ(R) H-B, which was relied upon by the Trial Chamber.[908] Stojić's and Praljak's arguments therefore have failed. **[page 123]**

---

[898]   Prosecution's Response Brief (Praljak), para. 19.
[899]   Prosecution's Response Brief (Praljak), para. 19.
[900]   Prosecution's Response Brief (Stojić), para. 386.
[901]   Prosecution's Response Brief (Stojić), para. 386.
[902]   Prosecution's Response Brief (Petković), para. 292.
[903]   Prosecution's Response Brief (Petković), para. 292, referring to Exs. P03242, P07135.
[904]   Prosecution's Response Brief (Petković), para. 292.
[905]   See Trial Judgement, Vol. 3, paras 545, 553, 567-568.
[906]   See Trial Judgement, Vol. 3, para. 553 and references cited therein. See also *supra*, paras 170-176, 179-183.
[907]   See Trial Judgement, Vol. 3, fns 1146-1147 and references cited therein.
[908]   See Trial Judgement, Vol. 3, paras 545-568. The Appeals Chamber has also considered Praljak's argument that if the HV possessed control over the HVO, the trial record would indicate that the HVO submitted reports to the HV and that the HV gave orders to the HVO, rather than the mutual exchange of information by two equal armies that emerges. See Praljak's Reply Brief, para. 12. The Appeals Chamber notes that a two-way exchange of information between a military group participating in an internal conflict and a foreign State's army does not *a priori* preclude the possibility that the State possesses overall control over the foreign military group. Further, the Overall Control Test does not require the existence of a hierarchical relationship between the HV and HVO, a relationship that Praljak's argument erroneously presumes. The Appeals Chamber thus dismisses this argument.

296.   In light of the above, the Appeals Chamber dismisses Stojić's sub-ground of appeal 54.2 in part, Praljak's sub-ground of appeal 1.3 in part, and Petković's sub-ground 7.1.5 in part.

5.   Conclusion

297.   For the foregoing reasons, the Appeals Chamber finds that the Trial Chamber erred in finding that a state of international armed conflict only existed in places where active combat took place and reverses this finding. The Appeals Chamber also finds that the Appellants have failed to show an error in the Trial Chamber's application of the Overall Control Test to assess the character of the armed conflict, its findings on the parties to the international armed conflict, on the location of the southern front, on the sharing of military reports, and Croatia's intervention in the HVO-ABiH conflict, both directly and indirectly.

B.   The State of Occupation

1.   Whether the inquiry into a state of occupation was necessary (Prlić's Ground 20, Stojić's Ground 55, Praljak's Ground 2, Petković's Sub-ground 7.2, and Ćorić's Sub-ground 3.2)

298.   Given that a state of international armed conflict was established throughout the whole territory of BiH during the time relevant to the Indictment,[909] the Appeals Chamber will now turn to whether the Trial Chamber properly found that a state of occupation also existed in some places where the crimes of deportation, extensive destruction and appropriation of property not justified by military necessity and carried out unlawfully and wantonly as grave breaches of the Geneva Conventions were alleged.[910]

299.   The Trial Chamber held that it was necessary to examine whether there was a state of occupation in places where the crime of unlawful deportation of a civilian as a grave breach of the Geneva Conventions was charged under Count 7 of the Indictment,[911] even where it had already found that there was an international armed conflict and for which the threshold requirement for Article 2 had already been met.[912] The Trial Chamber reasoned that the crime of unlawful **[page 124]** deportation can only occur when a person is transferred by force over a *de facto* border, *i.e.* the boundary of an occupied territory, or a *de jure* border.[913] According to the Trial Chamber, a finding of occupation was required to find that a *de facto* border existed and, consequently, for it to find that there had been a forced crossing of a *de facto* border.[914]

300.   At the outset, the Appeals Chamber recalls that Article 49 of Geneva Convention IV applies to instances of displacement across the *de facto* borders of an occupied territory.[915] In the *Stakić* case, the Appeals Chamber held that "the *actus reus* of deportation is the forced displacement of persons by expulsion or other forms of coercion from the area in which they are lawfully present, across a *de jure* state border or, in certain circumstances, a *de facto* border, without grounds permitted under international law".[916]

301.   The Appeals Chamber considers, therefore, that the Trial Chamber properly examined whether a state of occupation existed in those places in relation to which the Indictment raised allegations of deportation as a grave breach of the Geneva Conventions, *i.e.* in West Mostar and the municipalities of Prozor, Ljubuški,

---

[909]   See *supra*, para. 233.

[910]   Prlić's Appeal Brief, paras 671-676 (ground of appeal 20); Stojić's Appeal Brief, paras 421-425 (ground of appeal 55); Praljak's Appeal Brief, paras 42-56 (ground of appeal 2); Praljak's Reply Brief, paras 14-17; Petković's Appeal Brief 434-444 (sub-ground of appeal 7.2); Petković's Reply Brief, paras 88-89; Ćorić's Appeal Brief paras 75-83 (sub-ground of appeal 3.2); Ćorić's Reply Brief, paras 26-27.

[911]   See Trial Judgement, Vol. 3, para. 576.

[912]   See Trial Judgement, Vol. 3, paras 575-576.

[913]   See Trial Judgement, Vol. 1, para. 55, Vol. 3, para. 576.

[914]   See Trial Judgement, Vol. 1, para. 55, Vol. 3, para. 576.

[915]   See Geneva Convention IV, Art. 49. See also *Stakić* Appeal Judgement, para. 300 (relying on Article 49 of Geneva Convention IV to conclude that "displacement across a *de facto* border may be sufficient to amount to deportation" and that "the question whether a particular *de facto* border is sufficient for the crime of deportation should be examined on a case by case basis in light of customary international law").

[916]   *Stakić* Appeal Judgement, para. 278. See also *Stakić* Appeal Judgement, paras 296-297, 300.

Stolac, and Čapljina.[917] That inquiry involved an element of the crime of deportation itself – the crossing of a *de facto* border, *i.e.* the boundary of the occupied territory, or across a *de jure* border – which was separate and distinct from the general requirements for the application of the "grave breaches" regime under Article 2 of the Statute.

302. Turning to the crimes of extensive destruction and appropriation of property not justified by military necessity and carried out unlawfully and wantonly as grave breaches of the Geneva Conventions, the Appeals Chamber recalls that the Trial Chamber found it necessary to establish the existence of an occupation not only when it had been unable to establish the existence of a conflict between the ABiH and the HVO, based on its erroneous interpretation of an armed conflict,[918] but also because, in the Trial Chamber's view, two categories of property are protected pursuant to Article 2(d) of the Statute – property falling under the general protection of the Geneva Conventions, as well as property in occupied territory.[919] **[page 125]**

303. With respect to the grave breaches of extensive destruction and appropriation of property, the Appeals Chamber recalls that the Trial Chamber held that Article 2(d) of the Statute offers protection to certain property, *e.g.,* civilian hospitals and medical convoys, from acts of destruction wherever such property is located.[920] The Trial Chamber further held that protection is also afforded to real or personal, public or private property, if situated on occupied territory.[921] Because there were allegations of grave breaches of extensive destruction and appropriation of real or personal, public or private property in the Indictment,[922] the Appeals Chamber finds that it was necessary for the Trial Chamber to inquire into whether there was a state of occupation in the municipalities at times when such alleged grave breaches of extensive destruction and appropriation occurred.

304. The Appeals Chamber will now turn to Prlić's, Stojić's, Praljak's Petković's, and Ćorić's challenges to the Trial Chamber's finding of a state of occupation in the limited context of the relevant crimes, *i.e.* deportation and extensive destruction and appropriation of property.

2. The legal requirements of occupation (Prlić's Ground 20, Stojić's Ground 55, Praljak's Ground 2, Petković's Sub-ground 7.2 and Ćorić's Sub-ground 3.2)

(a) Arguments of the Parties

305. Prlić, Stojić, Praljak, Petković, and Ćorić argue that the Trial Chamber erred in law and in fact by finding a state of occupation in certain municipalities.[923] More specifically, Praljak contends that the Trial Chamber erroneously found that a state of armed conflict and a state of occupation co-existed in some municipalities, while Stojić and Petković argue that the Trial Chamber erred in finding that an armed conflict existed in certain municipalities that were occupied.[924] In particular, Stojić – and Petković with respect to West Mostar and Vareš – claims that the Trial Chamber therefore erred in finding a state of occupation in Gornji Vakuf, Sovići, Doljani, West Mostar, Vareš, and Stupni Do at certain times because it established the existence of an occupation before combat had ended.[925] In this regard, Stojić and Petković submit, *inter alia,*

---

917   See Trial Judgement, Vol. 3, paras 575-581, 585-588; Appeal Hearing, AT. 307 (21 Mar 2017). See also Appeal Hearing, AT. 568-567 (23 Mar 2017), AT. 682 (27 Mar 2017). *Cf.* Appeal Hearing, AT. 305 (21 Mar 2017).
918   See *supra*, para. 299.
919   See Trial Judgement, Vol. 1, paras 106-108, 122, 128-129, Vol. 3, para. 575.
920   See Trial Judgement, Vol. 1, paras 106, 108, 122 referring to, *inter alia,* Geneva Convention IV, Arts 18, 21-22. See also Geneva Convention IV, Art. 147; Commentary on Geneva Convention IV, pp. 301, 601.
921   See Trial Judgement, Vol. 1, paras 106-107, 122 referring to, *inter alia,* Geneva Convention IV, Art. 53. See also Geneva Convention IV, Art. 147; Commentary on Geneva Convention IV, pp. 301, 601.
922   See Indictment, paras 15-17.6, 39, 46, 48, 51, 53, 57, 66-68, 82-85, 99-100, 107-108, 116, 159, 162, 164-166, 175, 177, 179-180, 182, 209, 211, 213.
923   See Prlić's Appeal Brief, paras 671-676; Stojić's Appeal Brief, paras 421-425; Praljak's Appeal Brief, paras 42-56; Appeal Hearing, AT. 369, 371-372 (22 Mar 2017); Petković's Appeal Brief, paras 436-444; Petković's Reply Brief, paras 83-89; Ćorić's Appeal Brief, paras 75-83; Appeal Hearing, AT. 580 (24 Mar 2017); Ćorić's Reply Brief, paras 26-27.
924   Stojić's Appeal Brief, para. 424; Praljak's Appeal Brief, para. 50; Praljak's Reply Brief, para. 14; Petković's Appeal Brief, paras 441-442, Appeal Hearing, AT. 568 (23 Mar 2017).
925   Stojić's Appeal Brief, para. 424; Petković's Appeal Brief, paras 441-442; Appeal Hearing, AT. 568 (23 Mar 2017).

that the Trial Chamber erred in finding that the HVO occupied parts of Gornji Vakuf from 18 January 1993, because the **[page 126]** "first real lull in combat" was not until 26 or 27 January 1993, that Sovići and Doljani in Jablanica Municipality were occupied from 17 April 1993 because "mopping up" operations continued after that date, and that West Mostar was occupied from May 1993 because there were "ongoing operations affecting all of Mostar", referencing the attack by the ABiH on the HVO Tihomir Mišić Barracks in the north of Mostar town on 30 June 1993 ("Attack on the HVO Tihomir Mišić Barracks").[926] Stojić also argues that the Trial Chamber did not explain why it reached a contrary conclusion to the *Naletilić and Martinović* Trial Chamber, which had found no occupation in the areas of Sovići and Doljani in Jablanica Municipality prior to 23 April 1993.[927]

306.   Ćorić contends that a state of occupation is a transitional period that must follow an act of invasion, and that the Trial Chamber failed to find that there was an invasion which is an essential element of occupation.[928] Prlić, Stojić, Praljak, and Ćorić also argue that the HVO could not have invaded because it was a legitimate governing authority within BiH and could not be considered a foreign invading army.[929] Praljak notes further that the Trial Chamber erroneously failed to establish the start and end of the occupation which could only have happened when combat activity had ceased, a finding the Trial Chamber also failed to make.[930]

307.   According to Stojić and Praljak, the Trial Chamber erred in law in failing to find that it was Croatia, rather than the HVO, that occupied the relevant municipalities.[931] Praljak contends that the Trial Chamber did not find that the HVO occupied BiH as Croatia's agent and erred when it did not establish that the HVO acted in each municipality on behalf of Croatia and under its control.[932]

308.   Moreover, Prlić, Stojić, Praljak and Petković argue that the Trial Chamber misapplied the *Naletilić and Martinović* Trial Judgement criteria to establish the level of authority required of a power that is occupying a territory, leading to the erroneous conclusion that a state of occupation existed in BiH.[933] Stojić and Petković challenge the Trial Chamber's finding that the HV's overall control over the HVO was sufficient to establish a state of occupation by the State of Croatia in BiH **[page 127]** at the relevant time.[934] In Stojić's and Praljak's view, the mere presence of HVO troops in HZ(R) H-B, even combined with certain administrative control, is insufficient to indicate control for the purposes of occupation.[935] Petković further argues that the criteria found in the *Naletilić and Martinović* Trial Judgement are cumulative, and that the Trial Chamber erred when it found a state of occupation in some municipalities on the basis of only two criteria.[936] In this regard, Petković submits that the correct test to apply is the effective control test.[937] Stojić argues that occupation requires that the territory be "actually placed under the authority" of the occupying power, which is a "further degree of control" than overall control, and therefore that the Trial Chamber erred in finding that the municipalities were occupied by Croatia rather than by the HVO.[938]

---

[926]   Stojić's Appeal Brief, para. 424; Petković's Appeal Brief, paras 441-442; Appeal Hearing, AT. 568 (23 Mar 2017).

[927]   Stojić's Appeal Brief, para. 424.

[928]   Ćorić's Appeal Brief, para. 81; Appeal Hearing, AT. 580-581 (24 Mar 2017); Ćorić's Reply Brief, para. 27. See also Praljak's Appeal Brief, para. 49; Appeal Hearing, AT. 370 (22 Mar 2017). Praljak, referring to the Tribunal's jurisprudence that occupation is "a transitional period following invasion and preceding the agreement on the cessation of the hostilities", submits that it is important to establish that there "already was a transitional period". Praljak's Appeal Brief, para. 49.

[929]   Prlić's Appeal Brief, paras 672-673; Stojić's Appeal Brief, para. 422; Praljak's Appeal Brief, paras 55-56; Appeal Hearing, AT. 370-371 (22 Mar 2017); Ćorić's Appeal Brief, paras 81-82; Appeal Hearing, AT. 581-582 (24 Mar 2017).

[930]   Praljak's Appeal Brief, para. 49; Praljak's Reply Brief, para. 14.

[931]   Stojić's Appeal Brief, para. 422; Praljak's Reply Brief, para. 15.

[932]   Praljak's Reply Brief, para. 15.

[933]   Prlić's Appeal Brief, para. 671; Stojić's Appeal Brief, paras 422-423; Praljak's Appeal Brief, para. 45; Petković's Appeal Brief, paras 436-438.

[934]   Petković's Appeal Brief, para. 439; Appeal Hearing, AT. 569-570 (23 Mar 2017). See also Stojić's Appeal Brief, para. 422.

[935]   Stojić's Appeal Brief, para. 423; Praljak's Appeal Brief, paras 48, 51.

[936]   Petković's Appeal Brief, paras 436-437; Appeal Hearing, AT. 569 (23 Mar 2017).

[937]   Petković's Appeal Brief, para. 439, referring to *Naletilić and Martinović* Trial Judgement, para. 214.

[938]   Stojić's Appeal Brief, para. 422 referring to Hague Regulations, Art. 42, *Advisory Opinion on the Wall*, para. 90, *Naletilić and Martinović* Trial Judgement, paras 214-216.

309. Further, Prlić avers that an occupying power must completely displace the pre-existing civil government in order for the requisite degree of control to be established.[939] Praljak argues further that the relevant test which the Trial Chamber failed to consider, and which would not have been satisfied, was either whether the pre-existing authority in the allegedly occupied territory remained capable of functioning, or if a temporary administrative body had been put in its place.[940] Praljak also submits that the Trial Chamber ought to have identified which authorities were in place prior to the occupation or established that the occupied authorities in fact had continued to function.[941]

310. Lastly, Praljak argues that the principle of self-determination of peoples negates any finding that the HVO occupied territory in BiH because Croats had been living in the territory of HZ(R) H-B for centuries, possessed a right to assert their own political, economic, and cultural identity there, constituted legitimate governing authorities, compensated for the lack of government functions, and therefore did not in any way qualify as an occupying power.[942]

311. The Prosecution responds that the Trial Chamber correctly found that Croatia exercised overall control over the HVO, that the HVO had sufficient authority in the municipalities to occupy parts of BiH during the Indictment period, and that Prlić, Stojić, Praljak, Petković, and Ćorić fail to **[page 128]** demonstrate any error.[943] The Prosecution submits that areas such as West Mostar could be administered by the occupying power or its agent despite armed resistance and could therefore be occupied, including areas behind battle lines, thus allowing the HVO to set up important administrative and other offices there.[944] With regard to the Gornji Vakuf villages of Duša, Hrasnica, Ždrimci, and Uzričje, found by the Trial Chamber to have been occupied, the Prosecution avers that sporadic local resistance or combat operations in other parts of the municipality do not affect the occupied status of those villages.[945] As to Sovići and Doljani in Jablanica Municipality, the Prosecution avers that combat operations there ceased on 17 April 1993 and sporadic fighting in the hills ceased the following morning, when mopping up operations were nearly completed.[946] With regard to Stojić's argument that another trial chamber had found differently that there was no occupation in Sovići and Doljani, the Prosecution avers that another trial chamber's different conclusion based on the evidence in that case does not impact the reasonableness of the Trial Chamber's finding.[947] It argues that invasion is not a required element of occupation.[948] Further, the Prosecution submits that occupation can be established immediately once combat ceases.[949]

312. According to the Prosecution, the HVO was an agent of Croatia as the occupying power and was not a recognised authority within BiH – the legitimate authority in BiH was the BiH government with Izetbegović at its head.[950] The Prosecution also submits that the HVO's actions were not in accordance with the principle of self-determination of peoples as they did not represent the free will of the peoples concerned and they infringed upon the human rights of others.[951]

---

[939]   Prlić's Appeal Brief, para. 674, referring to *Naletilić and Martinović* Trial Judgement, para. 217, *Armed Activities* Judgement, para. 173, *Hostage* Trial Case, pp. 55-56. Praljak further argues that the fact that the individuals elected in 1990, such as in Prozor, continued to govern through 1993 ultimately signals that no change in governmental authority took place and therefore it was impossible that the HVO occupied these municipalities. Praljak's Reply Brief, para. 17.

[940]   Praljak's Appeal Brief, para. 49.

[941]   Praljak's Appeal Brief, para. 49.

[942]   Praljak's Appeal Brief, paras 52-53; Praljak's Reply Brief, para. 16. See also Prlić's Appeal Brief, paras 674-675; Petković's Appeal Brief, para. 438.

[943]   Prosecution's Response Brief (Prlić), paras 418-421; Prosecution's Response Brief (Stojić), paras 388-395; Appeal Hearing, AT. 316-323, 328 (21 Mar 2017); Prosecution's Response Brief (Praljak), paras 23-30; Appeal Hearing, AT. 418 (22 Mar 2017); Prosecution's Response Brief (Petković), paras 296-303; Prosecution's Response Brief (Ćorić), paras 68, 70-74; Appeal Hearing, AT. 656-657 (24 Mar 2017).

[944]   Prosecution's Response Brief (Stojić), para. 394; Prosecution's Response Brief (Petković), para. 301.

[945]   Prosecution's Response Brief (Stojić), para. 391. See also Prosecution's Response Brief (Praljak), para. 25.

[946]   Prosecution's Response Brief (Stojić), para. 392. See also Prosecution's Response Brief (Praljak), para. 25.

[947]   Prosecution's Response Brief (Stojić), para. 392.

[948]   Prosecution's Response Brief (Ćorić), para. 73.

[949]   Prosecution's Response Brief (Praljak), para. 25.

[950]   Prosecution's Response Brief (Prlić), para. 421; Prosecution's Response Brief (Stojić), para. 389; Appeal Hearing, AT. 319, 328 (21 Mar 2017); Prosecution's Response Brief (Praljak), para. 29; Prosecution's Response Brief (Petković), para. 300; Prosecution's Response Brief (Ćorić), para. 74; Appeal Hearing, AT. 656-657 (24 Mar 2017).

[951]   Prosecution's Response Brief (Praljak), para. 29.

313.   The Prosecution further contends that the Trial Chamber applied the correct legal test, that a foreign State may be an occupying power by agency if it exercises overall control over the armed **[page 129]** forces of a party to the armed conflict and provided that such forces have established the requisite authority over the territory.[952]

314.   The Prosecution also submits that establishing a temporary administration is an indicator of, but not necessary for, occupation.[953] As to the argument that the Trial Chamber relied only on the HVO's mere presence to establish occupation, the Prosecution rejects this as, in its view, the Trial Chamber also based its finding on evidence that the HVO issued orders to the local population and had them carried out.[954] The Prosecution submits that Praljak's argument that the HVO compensated for the "lack of governmental functions" in the municipalities supports the conclusion that the HVO was able to exercise authority instead of the local authorities.[955] In the Prosecution's view, the Trial Chamber correctly noted that the criteria found in the *Naletilić and Martinović* Trial Judgement were not cumulative, and further that it is not required that the occupying power substitute its authority for that of the occupied power, but only that it be in a position to do so.[956]

315.   Finally, after noting the Trial Chamber's findings that Vareš town and the village of Stupni Do in Vareš Municipality were occupied *after* 23 October 1993, and the evidence the Trial Chamber relied upon showing that the crimes of extensive appropriation and destruction of property by the HVO occurred *on* 23 October 1993, the Prosecution concedes that it was not proven that these places were occupied when such crimes were committed.[957] Accordingly, the Prosecution argues that the Appellants' convictions for Count 19 (extensive destruction of property not justified by military necessity and carried out unlawfully and wantonly as a grave breach of the Geneva Conventions) as to Vareš "should be vacated, and substituted with a conviction for Count 20" (wanton destruction of cities, towns, or villages, or devastation not justified by military necessity as a violation of the laws or customs of war).[958] **[page 130]**

(b) Analysis

316.   Belligerent occupation[959] forms part of the law of armed conflict. As the ICJ held with respect to Geneva Convention IV in its *Advisory Opinion on the Wall:*

> The object of the second paragraph of Article 2[960] is [...] directed simply to making it clear that, even if occupation effected during the conflict met no armed resistance, the Convention is still applicable. This interpretation reflects the intention of the drafters of the Fourth Geneva Convention to protect civilians who find themselves, in whatever way, in the hands of the occupying Power [...] [T]he Court considers that the

---

[952]   Prosecution's Response Brief (Prlić), para. 419; Prosecution's Response Brief (Stojić), para. 388; Appeal Hearing, AT. 317-319, 321 (21 Mar 2017); Prosecution's Response Brief (Praljak), para. 23; Prosecution's Response Brief (Petković), paras 297, 300; Prosecution's Response Brief (Ćorić), para. 70.
[953]   Prosecution's Response Brief (Stojić), para. 390. See also Prosecution's Response Brief (Ćorić), para. 71.
[954]   Prosecution's Response Brief (Stojić), paras 390-394; Prosecution's Response Brief (Praljak), paras 26-28; Prosecution's Response Brief (Petković), paras 299, 301-302; Prosecution's Response Brief (Ćorić), paras 71-72.
[955]   Prosecution's Response Brief (Praljak), para. 26; Appeal Hearing, AT. 320-323 (21 Mar 2017).
[956]   Prosecution's Response Brief (Petković), para. 298; Appeal Hearing, AT. 319-320, 328 (21 Mar 2017). The Prosecution also argues that the demographic make-up of the results of a 1990 election are irrelevant to determining whether Prozor was occupied during the relevant time period. Prosecution's Response Brief (Praljak), para. 27.
[957]   Prosecution's Response Brief (Prlić), fn. 1529, referring to Trial Judgement, Vol. 3, paras 401, 403, 465-466, 588, 1554, 1650; Prosecution's Response Brief (Stojić), fn. 1605; Prosecution's Response Brief (Praljak), fn. 121; Prosecution's Response Brief (Petković), fn. 1219; Prosecution's Response Brief (Ćorić), fn. 250; Prosecution's Response Brief (Pušić), fn. 414.
[958]   Prosecution's Response Brief (Prlić), fn. 1529; Prosecution's Response Brief (Stojić), fn. 1605 (also stating that the Prosecution has appealed Stojić's acquittal under Count 22 for thefts in Vareš); Prosecution's Response Brief (Praljak), fn. 121 (also stating that the Prosecution has appealed Praljak's acquittal under Count 22 for thefts in Vareš); Prosecution's Response Brief (Petković), fn. 1219 (also stating that the Prosecution has appealed Petković's acquittal under Count 22 for thefts in Vareš); Prosecution's Response Brief (Ćorić), fn. 250; Prosecution's Response Brief (Pušić), fn. 414. See also Prosecution's Appeal Brief, para. 31.
[959]   The Appeals Chamber emphasises that the discussion that follows is on *occupatio bellica* and not occupation as an original mode of acquisition of unclaimed territory by States. See Jennings and Watts, *Oppenheim's International Law*, pp. 686-687.
[960]   Article 2, second paragraph states that: "The Convention shall also apply to all cases of partial or total occupation of the territory of a High Contracting Party, even if the said occupation meets with no armed resistance."

Fourth Geneva Convention is applicable in any occupied territory in the event of an armed conflict arising between two or more High Contracting Parties.[961]

317. The Appeals Chamber notes that a definition of occupation can be found in the Hague Regulations, which constitute customary international law.[962] Article 42 of the Hague Regulations provides that "[t] erritory is considered occupied when it is actually placed under the authority of the hostile army. The occupation extends only to the territory where such authority has been established and can be exercised."[963] The Appeals Chamber considers this to be the controlling law.[964]

318. The notion of occupation is traditionally described as one State invading another State and establishing military control over part or all of its territory.[965] However, while occupation normally **[page 131]** follows invasion by a hostile armed force, this is not necessarily always the case.[966] Indeed, the ICJ has held that a non-invading State became an occupying power when its armed forces remained in another State's territory after the withdrawal of consent for their presence.[967]

319. The Appeals Chamber further notes that occupation is a question of fact and needs to be examined on a case-by-case basis.[968] Vagaries of war and the changing situation on the ground may influence the parameters of the territory under occupation.[969] The fact that a territory is occupied does not exclude the possibility that hostilities may resume.[970] If the occupying power continues to maintain control of the territory in spite of resistance and sporadic fighting, the territory is still considered occupied.[971]

320. In this regard, the Appeals Chamber considers that the following indicators of authority, as first outlined in the *Naletilić and Martinović* Trial Judgement ("Occupation Guidelines"), assist in the factual determination of whether the authority of an occupying power has been proven:

(1) the occupying power must be in a position to substitute its own authority for that of the occupied power, rendered incapable of functioning publicly from that time forward;[972] **[page 132]**

---

[961] Advisory Opinion on the Wall, paras 95, 101.

[962] *Mrkšić and Šljivančanin* Appeal Judgement, fn. 248 ("The Hague Regulations undoubtedly form part of customary international law"); *Kordić and Čerkez* Appeal Judgement, para. 92 ("Hague Convention IV is considered by the Report of the Secretary-General [Report of the Secretary-General Pursuant to Paragraph 2 of Security Council Resolution 808 (1993), S/25704, 3 May 1993] as being without doubt part of international customary law").

[963] Hague Regulations, Art. 42. See *Armed Activities* Judgement, para. 172.

[964] See *Mrkšić and Šljivančanin* Appeal Judgement, fn. 248. See also *Brđanin* Trial Judgement, para. 638; *Naletilić and Martinović* Trial Judgement, para. 216; *Kordić and Čerkez* Trial Judgement, para. 339. With regard to Stojić's and Petković's suggestions that the Trial Chamber erred in not finding that a state of occupation requires the "effective control" of the occupying power, the Appeals Chamber observes that both Stojić and Petković rely on a statement in the *Naletilić and Martinović* Trial Judgement, and that the *Naletilić and Martinović* Trial Chamber expressly endorsed the definition of occupation provided by Article 42 of the Hague Regulations. The Appeals Chamber dismisses these challenges. See *Naletilić and Martinović* Trial Judgement, para. 216. See also Stojić's Appeal Brief, para. 422 & fn. 1064; Petković's Appeal Brief, para. 439 & fn. 577. Stojić also refers to Article 42 of the Hague Regulations when he identifies "the test for the existence of an occupation". Stojić's Appeal Brief, para. 422 & fn. 1063. The Appeals Chamber will utilise the terminology of "actual authority" from the Hague Regulations, which it has recognised to form part of customary international law.

[965] ICRC, *International Humanitarian Law: A Comprehensive Introduction*, https://shop.icrc.org/e-books/international-humanitarian-law-ebook.international-humanitarian-law-a-comprehensive-introduction.html, p. 60. The Appeals Chamber distinguishes between the traditional notion of occupation relevant to this case, and the contemporary notion of transformative occupation. See, *e.g.*, ICRC, *International Humanitarian Law, A Comprehensive Introduction*, https://shop.icrc.org/e-books/international-humanitarian-law-ebook/international-humanitarian-law-a-comprehensive-introduction.html, p. 237; Carcano, *The Transformation of Occupied Territory in International Law*, pp. 70, 72-108, 436-439.

[966] See Oppenheim, *International Law, War and Neutrality*, p. 170; Dinstein, *The International Law of Belligerent Occupation*, para. 95. See also *Katanga* Article 74 Judgement, para. 1179, referring, *inter alia*, to Arai-Takahashi, *The Law of Occupation*, p. 8.

[967] See *Armed Activities* Judgement, paras 45, 47, 49-51, 53.

[968] See *Brđanin* Trial Judgement, fn. 1632; *Naletilić and Martinović* Trial Judgement, para. 211; *Kordić and Čerkez* Trial Judgement, para. 339. See also *Hostage* Trial Case, para. 55; *Armed Activities* Judgement, para. 173; Oppenheim, *International Law, War and Neutrality*, p. 171; Benvenisti, *The International Law of Occupation*, pp. 43, 51, 56.

[969] Dinstein, The International Law of Belligerent Occupation, para. 103.

[970] See *Naletilić and Martinović* Trial Judgement, para. 217 referring to, *inter alia*, 1958 UK Manual on the Law of War, para. 509, 1956 US Manual on the Law of War, para. 360; Dinstein, *The International Law of Belligerent Occupation*, para. 101.

[971] *Hostage* Trial Case, p. 56.

[972] See *Naletilić and Martinović* Trial Judgement, para. 217 & fn. 584, referring to *Prosecutor v. Ivica Rajić a/k/a Vitktor Andrić*, Review of the Indictment Pursuant to Rule 61 of the Rules of Procedure and Evidence, Case No. IT-95-12-R61, 13 September 1996 *("Rajić* Review Decision"), paras 41-42; 1956 US Manual on the Law of War, para. 355 ("Military occupation is a question of

(2) the enemy's forces have surrendered, been defeated or have withdrawn. In this respect, battle zones may not be considered as occupied territory. Despite this, the status of occupied territory remains unchallenged by sporadic local resistance, however successful;[973]

(3) the occupying power has a sufficient force present, or the capacity to send troops within a reasonable time to make the authority of the occupying power felt;[974] **[page 133]**

---

fact. It presupposes a hostile invasion, resisted or unresisted, as a result of which the invader has rendered the invaded government incapable of publicly exercising its authority, and that the invader has successfully substituted its own authority for that of the legitimate government in the territory invaded"); 1958 UK Manual on the Law of War, para. 503 ("It has been proposed as a test of occupation that two conditions should be satisfied: first, that the legitimate government should, by the act of the invader, be rendered incapable of publicly exercising its authority within the occupied territory; secondly, that the invader should be in a position to substitute his own authority for that of the legitimate government. These conditions afford in most cases a useful guide. This is so even though Hague Rules 42 stipulates distinctly that the authority of the Occupant must actually have been established. For it must always be a question of degree when the occupation is actually established. The advent of mechanised warfare and the use of airborne forces has emphasised the difference between mere invasion and occupation, but the test formulated at the beginning of this paragraph will in most cases provide an answer to the question whether the occupation is actually established"); New Zealand Defence Force, 26 Nov 1992, paras 1302.2, 1302.5; Adam Roberts, "What is a Military Occupation?", Vol. 55, British Yearbook of International Law, https://academic.oup.com/bybil/issue/55/1, pp. 249, 300.

[973] See *Naletilić and Martinović* Trial Judgement, para. 217 & fn. 585, referring to 1958 UK Manual on the Law of War, paras 502 ("Occupation must be actual and effective, that is, there must be more than a mere declaration or proclamation that possession has been taken, or that there is the intention to take possession. Occupation does not take effect merely because the main forces of the county have been defeated. On the other hand, to occupy a district it is not necessary to keep troops permanently stationed in every isolated house, village, or town. It is sufficient that the national forces should not be in possession, that the inhabitants have been disarmed, that measures have been taken to protect life and property and to secure order, and that, if necessary, troops can within a reasonable time be sent to make the authority of the occupying army felt. It does not matter by what means in what ways the authority is exercised, whether by military enclaves or mobile columns, by large or by small. The manner of occupation will usually vary with the density of the population-a thinly populated country requiring, as a rule, a smaller number of centries to be garrisoned than the one which is thickly populated. The fact that there is a defended place or zone still in possession of the national forces within an occupied district does not make the occupation of the remainder invalid, provided that such place or defended zone is surrounded and effectively cut off from the rest of the occupied district"), 506 ("The test of the commencement of occupation is the establishment of the Occupant's authority by the presence of sufficient force following on the cessation of local resistance, in consequence of the surrender, defeat, or withdrawal of the enemy's forces, and the submission of the inhabitants. In practice the moment may be difficult to determine, and considerable latitude must therefore be allowed"), 509 ("Occupation does not become invalid because some of the inhabitants are in a state of rebellion, or through occasional successes of guerrilla bands or žresistance' fighters. Even a temporarily successful rebellion is not sufficient to interrupt or terminate occupation, provided that the authority of the legitimate government is not effectively re-established and that the Occupant suppresses the rebellion at once. If, however, the power of the Occupant is effectively displaced for any length of time, his position *vis-à-vis* the inhabitants is the same as before the occupation"); 1956 US Manual on the Law of War, paras 356 ("It follows from the definition that belligerent occupation must be both actual and effective, that is, the organized resistance must have been overcome and the force in possession must have taken measures to establish its authority. It is sufficient that the occupying force can, within a reasonable time, send detachments of troops to make its authority felt within the occupied district. It is immaterial whether the authority of the occupant is maintained by fixed garrisons or flying columns, whether by small or large forces, so long as the occupation is effective. The number of troops necessary to maintain effective occupation will depend on various considerations such as the disposition of the inhabitants, the number and density of population, the nature of the terrain, and similar factors. The mere existence of a fort or defended area within the occupied district, provided the fort or defended area is under attack, does not render the occupation of the remainder of the district ineffective. Similarly, the mere existence of local resistance groups does not render the occupation ineffective"), 360 ("Occupation, to be effective, must be maintained. In case the occupant evacuates the district or is driven out by the enemy, the occupation ceases. It does not cease, however, if the occupant, after establishing its authority, moves forward against the enemy, leaving a smaller force to administer the affairs of the district. Nor does the existence of a rebellion or the activity of guerrilla or para-military units of itself cause the occupation to cease, provided the occupant could at any time it desired assume physical control of any part of the territory. If, however, the power of the occupant is effectively displaced for any length of time, its position towards the inhabitants is the same as before occupation"); 1992 German Manual on the Law of War, para. 528 ("Occupied territory does not include battle areas, *i.e.* areas which are still embattled and not subject to permanent occupation authority (area of invasion, withdrawal area). The general rules of international humanitarian law shall be applicable here."), New Zealand Defence Force, 26 Nov 1992, paras 1302.2, 1302.5.

[974] See *Naletilić and Martinović* Trial Judgement, para. 217 & fn. 586, referring to 1958 UK Manual on the Law of War, paras 502 ("Occupation must be actual and effective, that is, there must be more than a mere declaration or proclamation that possession has been taken, or that there is the intention to take possession. Occupation does not take effect merely because the main forces of the county have been defeated. On the other hand, to occupy a district it is not necessary to keep troops permanently stationed in every isolated house, village, or town. It is sufficient that the national forces should not be in possession, that the inhabitants have been disarmed, that measures have been taken to protect life and property and to secure order, and that, if necessary, troops can within a reasonable time be sent to make the authority of the occupying army felt. It does not matter by what means in what ways the authority is exercised, whether by military enclaves or mobile columns, by large or by small. The manner of occupation will usually vary with the density of the population-a thinly populated country requiring, as a rule, a smaller number of centries to be garrisoned than the one which is thickly populated. The fact that there is a defended place or zone still in possession of the national forces within

(4) a temporary administration has been established over the territory;[975]

(5) the occupying power has issued and enforced directions to the civilian population.[976]

321.   The Appeals Chamber considers that in order to make a finding as to whether a state of occupation exists in any given place, a trier of fact must look at the situation in its entirety.[977] The Appeals Chamber further considers the Occupation Guidelines to form a non-exhaustive set of indicators that can assist in this factual determination of whether actual authority has been established and can be exercised for the purposes of occupation.[978]

322.   The Appeals Chamber also considers that the occupying power need only be in a position to exercise its authority.[979] This is supported by a plain reading of the relevant article of the Hague Regulations, which states in part that "[t]he occupation extends only to the territory where such authority has been established and *can* be exercised".[980] Such authority may be exercised by proxy **[page 134]** through *de facto* organised and hierarchically structured groups.[981] The rationale behind this is that States should not be allowed to evade their obligations under the law of occupation through the use of proxies.[982] This legal position has been implicitly accepted by the ICJ and it is the position taken by this Tribunal in a number of trial judgements.[983]

---

an occupied district does not make the occupation of the remainder invalid, provided that such place or defended zone is surrounded and effectively cut off from the rest of the occupied district"), 506 ("The test of the commencement of occupation is the establishment of the Occupant's authority by the presence of sufficient force following on the cessation of local resistance, in consequence of the surrender, defeat, or withdrawal of the enemy's forces, and the submission of the inhabitants. In practice the moment may be difficult to determine, and considerable latitude must therefore be allowed"); 1956 US Manual on the Law of War, para. 356 ("It follows from the definition that belligerent occupation must be both actual and effective, that is, the organized resistance must have been overcome and the force in possession must have taken measures to establish its authority. It is sufficient that the occupying force can, within a reasonable time, send detachments of troops to make its authority felt within the occupied district. It is immaterial whether the authority of the occupant is maintained by fixed garrisons or flying columns, whether by small or large forces, so long as the occupation is effective. The number of troops necessary to maintain effective occupation will depend on various considerations such as the disposition of the inhabitants, the number and density of the population, the nature of the terrain, and similar factors. The mere existence of a fort or defended area within the occupied district, provided the fort or defended area is under attack, does not render the occupation of the remainder of the district ineffective. Similarly, the mere existence of local resistance groups does not render the occupation ineffective"); New Zealand Defence Force, 26 Nov 1992, paras 1302.2, 1302.3, 3102.5.
[975]   See *Naletilić and Martinović* Trial Judgement, para. 217 & fn. 587, referring to 1958 UK Manual on the Law of War, para. 501 ("Invasion is not necessarily occupationj although as a rule occupation will be coincident with invasion. Reconnoitring parties, patrols, commando units, and similar bodies which move on or withdraw after carrying out their special mission, cannot, however, be considered to occupy the country which they have traversed. They certainly occupy every locality of which they are in possession and where they set up a temporary administration, but such occupation ceases the moment they move on or withdraw"); Lauterpacht, *Oppenheim's International Law*, para. 167.
[976]   See *Naletilić and Martinović* Trial Judgement, para. 217 & fn. 588, referring to Hague Regulations, Art. 43 ("The authority of the legitimate power having in fact passed into the hands of the occupant, the latter shall take all the measures in his power to restore, and ensure, as far as possible, public order and safety, while respecting, unless absolutely prevented, the laws in force in the country"); 1992 German Manual on the Law of War, para. 527 ("A force invading hostile territory will not be able to substantiate its occupational authority unless it is capable of enforcing directions issued to the civilian population."); Fleck, *The Handbook of Humanitarian Law in Armed Conflicts*, para. 525.2.
[977]   See Oppenheim, International Law, War and Neutrality, pp. 171-173.
[978]   See generally Oppenheim, *International Law, War and Neutrality*, pp. 171-172.
[979]   See *Hostage* Trial Case, p. 55; *Armed Activities* Judgement, Separate Opinion of Judge Kooijmans, paras 44-49. See also Benvenisti, *The International Law of Occupation*, p. 5; Dinstein, *The International Law of Belligerent Occupation*, paras 96-100, 130; von Glahn, *The Occupation of Enemy Territory*, p. 29.
[980]   Hague Regulations, Art. 42 (emphasis added).
[981]   ICRC, *International Humanitarian Law: A Comprehensive Introduction*, https://shop.icrc.org/e-books/international-humanitarian-law-ebook/international-humanitarian-law-a-comprehensive-introduction.html, p. 60. See also Dinstein, *The International Law of Belligerent Occupation*, para. 98; Haupais, "Les Obligations de la Puissance Occupante au Regard de la Jurisprudence et de la Pratique Récentes», pp. 121-122; Benvenisti, *The International Law of Occupation*, pp. 61-62; Dinstein, *The International Law of Belligerent Occupation*, paras 98-99.
[982]   See ICRC, *International Humanitarian Law: A Comprehensive Introduction*, https://shop.icrc.org/e-books/international-humanitarian-law-ebook/international-humanitarian-law-a-comprehensive-introduction.html, p. 60.
[983]   See *Naletilić and Martinović* Trial Judgement, paras 213-214; *Blaškić* Trial Judgement, paras 149-150; *Rajić* Decision, para. 42. See also *Armed Activities* Judgement, paras 173-177; Benvenisti, *The International Law of Occupation*, p. 62; Haupais, "Les Obligations de la Puissance Occupante au Regard de la Jurisprudence et de la Pratique Récentes», pp. 121-122.

629

323.   Turning to the Trial Chamber's assessment of occupation in this case, the Appeals Chamber notes that the Trial Chamber relied on Croatia/the HV's overall control over the HVO,[984] and the Occupation Guidelines to determine that there was the level of authority required for a finding of occupation.[985]

324.   The Appeals Chamber will first examine whether the Trial Chamber found Croatia to be the occupying power. It will then address challenges concerning the level of authority that Croatia, through the HVO, wielded over the territory, and whether such level of authority met the legal threshold necessary for a finding of a state of occupation in the relevant municipalities. Finally, it will consider the other challenges made regarding the finding of occupation.

325.   Stojić and Praljak allege that the Trial Chamber failed to find that Croatia, rather than the HVO, occupied the relevant municipalities.[986] In this regard, the Appeals Chamber recalls that the Trial Chamber held that a state of occupation is established "if the Prosecution proves that the party to the armed conflict under the overall control of a foreign State fulfils the criteria for control of a territory" as set out in the Occupation Guidelines.[987] The Trial Chamber also found that "the occupation by the HVO can be established, inasmuch as Croatia/the HV wielded overall control over the HVO",[988] and that the HVO occupied the relevant parts of Prozor, Gornji Vakuf, Jablanica, West Mostar, Ljubuški, Stolac, and Čapljina.[989] With regard to Croatia's role, the Trial Chamber found that: (1) Croatia, through the HV, directly intervened alongside the HVO in the conflict **[page 135]** between the HVO and the ABiH;[990] and (2) "the authorities of Croatia and the HV wielded overall control of the HVO in the period relevant to the Indictment".[991] The Appeals Chamber considers that while it would have been preferable for the Trial Chamber to expressly state that Croatia, through the HVO, occupied the relevant municipalities in BiH, reading the Trial Chamber's findings in their entirety,[992] the Appeals Chamber considers it is clear that the Trial Chamber was considering an occupation by Croatia through the HVO.[993] Accordingly, the Appeals Chamber finds that Stojić and Praljak fail to show an error on the part of the Trial Chamber. It therefore dismisses their arguments.

326.   Turning next to Prlić's, Stojić's, Praljak's, and Petković's challenges concerning the level of authority that Croatia and/or the HVO wielded over the territory,[994] the Appeals Chamber recalls that the Trial Chamber concluded Croatia wielded overall control over the HVO based on the following findings:[995]

(1) officers from the HV were sent by Zagreb to join the ranks of the HVO;[996]

(2) the HV and the HVO jointly directed military operations;[997]

---

[984]   See Trial Judgement, Vol. 1, paras 96, 575 & fn. 1175.

[985]   See Trial Judgement, Vol. 1, para. 88, Vol. 3, paras 578-587, 589. The Appeals Chamber notes that the finding on occupation in Vareš Municipality is overturned elsewhere in the Judgement. See *infra*, para. 343.

[986]   See *supra*, para. 307.

[987]   See Trial Judgement, Vol. 1, para. 96.

[988]   See Trial Judgement, Vol. 3, fn. 1175. See also Trial Judgement, Vol. 3, para. 568.

[989]   See Trial Judgement, Vol. 3, paras 578-589. The Appeals Chamber notes that the finding on occupation in Vareš Municipality is overturned elsewhere in this Judgement. See *infra*, para.343.

[990]   See Trial Judgement, Vol. 3, paras 523-526, 528-543.

[991]   Trial Judgement, Vol. 3, para. 567. See also Trial Judgement, Vol. 3, paras 523-526, 545-567.

[992]   See Trial Judgement, Vol. 3, paras 517-518, 523-589.

[993]   See *supra*, para. 325.

[994]   See *supra*, paras 307-308.

[995]   See Trial Judgement, Vol. 3, paras 545-567. *Cf.* Trial Judgement, Vol. 3, paras 575 & fn. 1175, 578-587.

[996]   See Trial Judgement, Vol. 3, paras 546-548. The Appeals Chamber notes that the Trial Chamber found that this included persons who held the positions of the highest responsibility within the HVO, such as Petković, Praljak, and Žarko Tole – who served as Chief of the Main Staff at various times – and Ivan Kapular, Assistant Chief of the Main Staff, all of whom were contemporaneously also officers in the HV. See Trial Judgement, Vol. 3, para. 547. It also included other high-ranking HVO officers who were likewise members of the HV. For instance, Željko Šiljeg, commanding officer of the North-West OZ of the HVO, was a colonel in the HV; Vladimir Primorac, who belonged to the 145th Brigade of the HV, held the office of deputy commander of the 3rd Military Police Battalion of the HVO; Neđeljko Obradović, commanding officer of the 1st Knez Domagoj Brigade of the HVO on 21 January 1993, was also assigned to the 116th Brigade of the HV on that same date; and Stanko Šopta, a colonel in the HV, held the posts of deputy commander for the Convicts Battalion of the HVO, and commander of the 3rd Brigade of the HVO. See Trial Judgement, Vol. 3, para. 548.

[997]   See Trial Judgement, Vol. 3, paras 549-552. The Appeals Chamber notes that the Trial Chamber found that: some evidence indicated that commanding officers of the HV issued orders to the units of the HVO for certain military operations. See Trial Judgement, Vol. 3, para. 550. The Trial Chabmer further found that between November 1993 and early January 1994, Croatia's

(3) the HVO dispatched military reports concerning its activities to the Croatian authorities;[998]

(4) there was logistical support from Croatia which included financial support, dispatching of arms and materiel,[999] and assistance in the form of training and expertise;[1000] and **[page 136]**

(5) there were political aspects to the control Croatia wielded over the HVO.[1001]

327. The Appeals Chamber further notes that the Trial Chamber then applied the Occupation Guidelines to determine the authority required for occupation over the territory.[1002] As discussed above, given that the Occupation Guidelines are a non-exhaustive list of indicators of actual authority over territory, the Appeals Chamber dismisses Prlić's, Stojić's, Praljak's, and Petković's arguments that the Trial Chamber misapplied the Occupation Guidelines.[1003] Further, contrary to what Stojić and Praljak claim, the Trial Chamber did not only rely on the military presence of the HVO or on some administrative control, or on only both these factors, to find occupation in the municipalities. It considered more than one of the Occupation Guidelines, showing that in August 1993, in Prozor Municipality and Ljubuški Municipality, the HVO carried out mass arrests of Muslims without encountering any resistance from the ABiH.[1004] It found that after 18 January 1993, in Gornji Vakuf Municipality (in Duša, Hrasnica, Ždrimci, and Uzričje), after 17 April 1993, in Jablanica Municipality (in Sovići and Doljani), from May 1993 until February 1994 in West Mostar, and in July and August 1993, in Stolac Municipality, the HVO arrested and removed the Muslim population in these places.[1005] Further, it found that in July 1993, in Čapljina Municipality, the HVO conducted a campaign of mass arrests of Muslim men of military age without encountering any resistance from the ABiH and in so doing, the HVO also destroyed or stole property belonging to the Muslims there.[1006] The Trial Chamber also found that between July and September 1993, in Čapljina Municipality, the HVO forcibly removed the Muslim population.[1007] **[page 137]**

328. The Appeals Chamber recalls that the Trial Chamber reasoned that this evidence showed that the HVO's military presence was "sufficient",[1008] "strong enough",[1009] "sufficiently strong",[1010] or "to the extent needed to impose its authority",[1011] thus enabling it to give orders to the population and to have them carried

---

Minister of Defence, Gojko Šušak, visited the territory of the HR H-B four to five times to participate in unofficial meetings relating to the prevailing situation in the territory of the HR H-B with Marijan Biškić, Mate Boban, Ćorić, General Roso, Perica Jukić, the Minister of Defence, as well as the Minister's deputies and officers from the HVO Main Staff. See Trial Judgement, Vol. 3, para. 551.

[998]   See Trial Judgement, Vol. 3, para. 553.

[999]   See Trial Judgement, Vol. 3, paras 554-556. The Appeals Chamber notes that the Trial Chamber found that the salaries of some HVO soldiers were paid by Croatia, *e.g.*, Marijan Biškić's salary was paid in Croatia by the Croatian government and he never received any emoluments from the government of the RBiH. The Trial Chamber also found that the Croatian Ministry of Defence supplied arms and materiel and transferred funds to the HVO. See Trial Judgement, Vol. 3, para. 556.

[1000]   See Trial Judgement, Vol. 3, para. 559.

[1001]   See Trial Judgement, Vol. 3, paras 560-566. The Appeals Chamber notes that the Trial Chamber found that the HV Military Police assisted the HVO Military Police by providing training and helping it to structure its work, and that the Croatian MUP likewise created training programmes intended for the HVO police. See Trial Judgement, Vol. 3, para. 559. The Trial Chamber also found that the international community frequently requested the Croatian leadership, particularly President Franjo Tuđman, to use their influence with the leaders of the HZ(R) H-B to bring about the end of hostilities between the HVO and the ABiH. Trial Judgement, Vol. 3, paras 561-564. Croatian leaders, specifically Gojko Šušak, Mate Granić and Tuđman, decisively influenced decisions taken in relation to the political structure of the HR H-B and the appointment of its most senior officials – for example, at a meeting in Zagreb on 10 November 1993, Boban and Prlić agreed with Granić and Tuđman on which persons would be appointed to head certain ministries in the HR H-B. See Trial Judgement, Vol. 3, para. 565. Tuđman presented himself as the representative of the BiH Croats in the peace talks held under the auspices of the international community and he took decisions on their behalf. See Trial Judgement, Vol. 3, para. 566.

[1002]   See Trial Judgement, Vol. 1, para. 88, Vol. 3, para. 570.

[1003]   See *supra*, paras 308, 321.

[1004]   See Trial Judgement, Vol. 3, paras 578, 584.

[1005]   See Trial Judgement, Vol. 3, paras 579-581, 585.

[1006]   See Trial Judgement, Vol. 3, para. 587.

[1007]   See Trial Judgement, Vol. 3, para. 587.

[1008]   See Trial Judgement, Vol. 3, paras 578, 585, 587.

[1009]   See Trial Judgement, Vol. 3, paras 579, 584.

[1010]   See Trial Judgement, Vol. 3, para. 580.

[1011]   See Trial Judgement, Vol. 3, para. 583.

out.[1012] The Appeals Chamber considers that it was based on all of these factors, taken cumulatively, that the Trial Chamber found a state of occupation in these municipalities.[1013]

329.   The Appeals Chamber considers that it would have been preferable for the Trial Chamber to have identified with precision the findings that supported its conclusion that Croatia exercised the authority required for occupation.[1014] The Appeals Chamber recalls, however, that a trial judgement is to be read as a whole,[1015] and notes that the Trial Chamber made a number of factual findings that established Croatia's authority over the HVO, its proxy.[1016] These findings concerned: (1) the strong links between Croatia and the HVO as epitomised in the close relationship Prlić, Praljak, and Petković had with senior Croatian political, military, or administrative authorities; (2) the fact that the members of the JCE included both Croatian political, governmental, and military officials as well as officials of the HZ(R) H-B political, military, and administrative structures; and (3) HV troops directly intervening alongside the HVO in the conflict with the ABiH at the relevant time and in the relevant locations. The Appeals Chamber will address these findings in turn.

330.   Turning to the first set of findings, the Appeals Chamber recalls that the Trial Chamber held, *inter alia,* that on 5 and 26 October 1992, Prlić, Stojić, Praljak, and Petković, as members of a "delegation of Croatia and the HZ H-B", met with Ratko Mladić to discuss the division of BiH between the Serbs and the Croats.[1017] With regard to Prlić, the Trial Chamber found that between September 1992 and the end of April 1994, he attended meetings in Croatia with Tuđman and other Croatian leaders, and from 17 September 1992 onwards, he held discussions with Tuđman about the internal policy of the HZ(R) H-B.[1018] The Trial Chamber also found that Prlić was one of Tuđman's **[page 138]** principal interlocutors for discussions about the political and military strategy of the HZ(R) H-B.[1019] The Trial Chamber further held that Prlić had influence on the defence strategy and the military operations of the HVO, including the power to, *inter alia,* take decisions which had a direct impact on the course of the military operations of the HVO.[1020]

331.   As to Praljak,[1021] the Appeals Chamber recalls that the Trial Chamber held that his role in both the Croatian government and his *de facto* and/or *de jure* authority in the HVO, which he exercised simultaneously in both BiH and Croatia, demonstrated his knowledge of and willingness to implement the senior Croatian and HVO leadership's policies regarding Herceg-Bosna.[1022] It found that Praljak contributed to the CCP by serving as a conduit between Croatia and the HZ(R) H-B.[1023] The Trial Chamber also found that Praljak personally and directly contributed to posting HV members to the HVO, and on his request, the Croatian government continued paying the salaries of HV soldiers who had been authorised by the Croatian government to go to BiH to join the HVO.[1024] With respect to Petković, the Appeals Chamber observes that in April 1992, on his request, he was released from active military service in the HV "for the purpose of

---

1012	See Trial Judgement, Vol. 3, paras 578-580, 583-585, 587.
1013	The Appeals Chamber notes that the finding on occupation in Vareš Municipality is overturned elsewhere in the Judgement. See *infra,* para. 343.
1014	See *supra,* para. 325.
1015	See *Stanišić and Župljanin* Appeal Judgement, paras 1107, 1115, 1148, 1162, 1181; *Popović et al.* Appeal Judgement, para. 2006; *Mrkšić and Šljivančanin* Appeal Judgement, para. 379.
1016	See, *e.g.,* Trial Judgement, Vol. 4, paras 15-24, 106, 111, 119, 121, 520, 522-545, 651, Vol. 3, paras 529-544. The Appeals Chamber notes that the underpinning factual findings have been upheld elsewhere in the Judgement. See *supra,* paras 237-240, 245-249, 265-275, 282-289, 294-297. See also *infra,* paras 835-836, 840-842, 1138-1139, 1521-1522, 1895-1897, 1900-1902, 1904-1905, 1911, 1914-1916.
1017	See Trial Judgement, Vol. 4, para. 18.
1018	See Trial Judgement, Vol. 4, para. 119.
1019	See Trial Judgement, Vol. 4, para. 119.
1020	See Trial Judgement, Vol. 4, paras 106, 111, 121.
1021	The Trial Chamber found that from approximately March 1992 to 15 June 1993, Praljak was the Assistant Minister of Defence of Croatia and then its Deputy Minister of Defence, first at the rank of brigadier and then as major-general of the HV. See Trial Judgement, Vol. 4, para. 457.
1022	See Trial Judgement, Vol. 4, para. 545.
1023	See Trial Judgement, Vol. 4, paras 520, 522-545.
1024	See Trial Judgement, Vol. 4, paras 541-544.

632

joining the RBiH".[1025] After his stint in the HVO,[1026] in March 1993, Stojić requested Šušak to assign Petković to the rank of senior officer within the HV, in recognition of his contribution to defending a large part of HZ(R) H-B territory.[1027]

332.   These findings establish both: (1) the pivotal role played by Prlić and Praljak in facilitating the Croatian political and military support needed in HZ(R) H-B; and (2) the fact that the HVO accepted Praljak's and Petković's concurrent and subsequent membership respectively, in the HV and the HVO, at this crucial time in the conflict with the ABiH. The Appeals Chamber considers that this is indicative of the actual authority exercised by Croatia through the HVO over BiH territory.

333.   Moving on to the second set of findings, the Appeals Chamber notes the Trial Chamber's findings that members of the Croatian and the HZ(R) H-B political, governmental, and military **[page 139]** structures consulted each other to devise and implement the CCP.[1028] The Appeals Chamber considers this to be another factor that shows the actual authority exercised by Croatia over the HVO and over BiH territory. Lastly, the Appeals Chamber notes that the Trial Chamber concluded that there was direct intervention by HV troops alongside the HVO in the conflict with the ABiH.[1029]

334.   In conclusion, and in light of the foregoing, the Appeals Chamber finds that there are a number of factors that indicate that Croatia through the HVO had actual authority over the relevant municipalities. These are: (1) the overall control Croatia had over the HVO;[1030] (2) the continued presence of the HVO in the relevant municipalities after the occupation;[1031] (3) the HVO's issuance of directives to the population and having them enforced; (4) the close links Prlić, Praljak, and, to a lesser extent, Petković had with Croatia; (5) the ongoing consultations between members of the Croatian and the HZ(R) H-B political and governmental structures and the HVO, and their common membership in the JCE; and (6) the engagement of HV units with the HVO in combat in the attacks on towns and villages. Looking at all these factors and the situation in the various municipalities in its entirety, the Appeals Chamber considers that Prlić, Stojić, Praljak, and Petković have failed to show an error on the part of the Trial Chamber. The Appeals Chamber therefore dismisses all the relevant arguments.

335.   Turning next to Praljak's argument that an armed conflict and occupation cannot co-exist, the Appeals Chamber notes that a state of occupation and that of an international armed conflict are not necessarily mutually exclusive.[1032] Further, with regard to Stojić's and Petković's argument that ongoing combat and occupation cannot co-exist, the Appeals Chamber recalls that a finding of active hostilities in certain municipalities does not necessarily preclude the Trial Chamber from finding that a state of occupation existed on the ground in those municipalities. The Appeals Chamber considers that the issue is one of authority, *i.e.* whether the occupying power is able to maintain its authority over the territory in spite of some ongoing active combat.[1033] **[page 140]**

336.   The Appeals Chamber notes that the Trial Chamber found that once the HVO assumed control over the villages of Duša, Hrasnica, Ždrimci, and Uzričje on 18 January 1993, the HVO arrested and removed the

---

[1025]   See Trial Judgement, Vol. 4, fn. 1245.
[1026]   Petković was appointed chief of the HVO Main Staff by Boban on 14 April 1992 and remained in that position until 24 July 1993. See Trial Judgement, Vol. 4, para. 651.
[1027]   See Trial Judgement, Vol. 4, fn 1245.
[1028]   See Trial Judgement, Vol. 4, para. 1231, referring to Tuđman, Šušak, Bobetko, Boban, Prlić, Stojić, Praljak, Petković, Ćorić, and Pušić. See *infra*, paras 1521-1522.
[1029]   See Trial Judgement, Vol. 3, paras 529-544. See also *supra*, paras 265-275. For instance, the Trial Chamber found that a mixed unit of HVO and HV troops attacked and took over the town of Prozor on 23 October 1992, HV troops were in the Prozor area on several dates between November 1992 and January 1994, and Prozor Municipality generally was occupied by the HVO during part of that period, from August to December 1993. See Trial Judgement, Vol. 3, paras 532-533, 589. The Trial Chamber also found that in the villages of Sovići and Doljani in Jablanica Municipality – which were occupied after 17 April 1993 – HV soldiers participated alongside the HVO in the attack on Sovići on 17 April 1993, and HV troops were seen there until May 1993. See Trial Judgement, Vol. 3, paras 535, 589.
[1030]   See Trial Judgement, Vol. 3, paras 545-567 & fn. 1175.
[1031]   See Trial Judgement, Vol. 3, paras 578-580, 583-585, 587.
[1032]   See *Hostage* Trial Case, p. 56.
[1033]   See also *supra*, para. 319.

Muslim population, and destroyed and stole property belonging to the Muslims there.[1034] In so doing, the Trial Chamber found that the HVO had sufficient authority for a finding of occupation in Duša, Hrasnica, Ždrimci, and Uzričje in Gornji Vakuf Municipality.[1035] Stojić's argument that this finding cannot stand because the "first real lull in combat" was not until 26 or 27 January 1993[1036] does not take into account the establishment of the HVO's authority over the area prior to this date – a fact inferred from its strong military presence and its ability to give orders to the Muslim population and to have such orders carried out.[1037]

337. As to Stojić's argument that the Trial Chamber erred in finding that the HVO occupied Sovići and Doljani in Jablanica Municipality from 17 April 1993 because "mopping up" operations continued after this date is without merit.[1038] The Trial Chamber found that most of the fighting in Sovići and Doljani had ended late in the afternoon of 17 April 1993 following which the HVO and the MUP made the first Muslim arrests – showing that the HVO's military presence was sufficiently strong to enable it to give orders to the Muslim population and have them carried out.[1039] In fact, the Trial Chamber also found that such arrests continued between 18 and 23 April 1993, again showing the HVO still exercised control over Sovići and Doljani.[1040] With respect to Stojić's related argument that another trial chamber found differently (*i.e.* that there was no occupation in Sovići and Doljani in Jablanica Municipality at the relevant time), the Appeals Chamber recalls that the factual finding of one trial chamber is not binding upon that of another.[1041]

338. Further, in concluding that West Mostar was occupied by the HVO, the Trial Chamber took note that from May 1993 to February 1994, the HVO removed the Muslim population of West Mostar and that this attested to the fact that the HVO was present militarily to the extent needed to impose authority and was capable of giving orders to the inhabitants of West Mostar and having such orders carried out.[1042] The Appeals Chamber is not convinced by Stojić's argument that **[page 141]** the Trial Chamber's finding that the Attack on the HVO Tihomir Mišić Barracks in Mostar on 30 June 1993 undermines its finding that West Mostar was occupied by the HVO, as the HVO was still able to arrest Muslim men, including members of the ABiH and Muslim HVO soldiers *after* the Attack on the HVO Tihomir Mišić Barracks.[1043] This reasonably shows the HVO still maintained actual authority over West Mostar.[1044] For these same reasons, Petković's argument that the whole of Mostar was a combat zone and therefore could not be occupied is unpersuasive.

339. With regard to Ćorić's argument that an occupation must follow an act of invasion, the Appeals Chamber recalls its statement of the law above, and holds that invasion is not a prerequisite for the determination of a state of occupation.[1045] This argument, as well as the argument that the Trial Chamber failed to make a finding on invasion being an element of occupation, are accordingly dismissed.[1046] Moreover,

---

[1034] See Trial Judgement, Vol. 3, para. 579.

[1035] See Trial Judgement, Vol. 3, para. 579.

[1036] Stojić's Appeal Brief, para. 424, referring to Trial Judgement, Vol. 2, para. 395.

[1037] See Trial Judgement, Vol. 2, paras 369, 374, 386, 398, Vol. 3, paras 579, 589.

[1038] Stojić's Appeal Brief, para. 424, referring to Trial Judgement, Vol. 2, para. 549. The Appeals Chamber notes that the Trial Chamber found that occupation was established *after* 17 April 1993 and not *from* 17 April 1993 as argued by Stojić. See Stojić's Appeal Brief, para. 424; Trial Judgement, Vol. 3, para. 580.

[1039] See Trial Judgement, Vol. 2, paras 541, 545-548, 550, 552, 554, Vol. 3, paras 580, 589. The Appeals Chamber considers that the challenges to the finding of a state of occupation in Vareš town and Stupni Do in Vareš Municipality are moot. See *infra*, para. 343.

[1040] See Trial Judgement, Vol. 2, paras 558-564.

[1041] See *Lukić and Lukić* Appeal Judgement, para. 260. *Aleksovski* Appeal Judgement, para. 114.

[1042] See Trial Judgement, Vol. 3, paras 583, 589.

[1043] See Trial Judgement, Vol. 2, paras 878-883, 895.

[1044] See Trial Judgement, Vol. 2, paras 878-883, 895.

[1045] See *supra*, para. 318; *Armed Activities* Judgement, paras 43, 45, 51, 53, 149, 178 (Uganda was found to be the occupying power in a part of the Democratic Republic of the Congo following the expiration of Congolese consent which had allowed the presence of Ugandan troops in its territory); *Lepore* Case, pp. 354-357 (following the change of Italian government and Italy's 'declaration of war on Germany in 1943, Germany was found to be the occupying power of parts of Italy where it already had a military presence as a result of its alliance with Italy's previous government). The Appeals Chamber rejects Praljak's related argument that the Trial Chamber failed to establish there "already was a transitional period" as an undeveloped assertion. The Appeals Chamber also dismisses this argument.

[1046] See *supra*, paras 306, 318. As to Prlić's, Stojić's, Praljak's, and Ćorić's challenges that the HVO could not have invaded as it was a legitimate governing authority in BiH, the Appeals Chamber recalls that they ignore other relevant findings on the recognition of Izetbegović's government by the international community as the legitimate government of BiH, and that the HZ(R) H-B and its

contrary to Praljak's argument, the Appeals Chamber highlights that the Trial Chamber established when occupation started in each relevant town and village in each affected municipality.[1047] The Appeals Chamber also considers that the Trial Chamber properly found that occupation can be established, once combat ceases, if the occupying power has the required control.[1048]

340. The Appeals Chamber further considers unpersuasive Prlić's, Stojić's, and Praljak's arguments that the Trial Chamber should have determined that the pre-existing civil government had been displaced, and that the relevant test should have been whether either the pre-existing authority in the allegedly occupied territory remained capable of functioning, or if a temporary administration body had been put in its place.[1049] This is because they fail to demonstrate that the Trial Chamber did not find that the HVO was the authority replacing the pre-existing government, given the facts of the case.[1050] Moreover, even if the HVO was carrying out government functions **[page 142]** because of a power vacuum, the Appeals Chamber finds that the factual test of the HVO substituting its authority for that of the pre-existing legitimate government is still met.[1051] This argument is therefore also dismissed.

341. Lastly, with regard to the argument that the principle of self-determination of peoples negates any finding that the HVO occupied territory in BiH because Croats had been living in the territory of HZ(R) H-B for centuries, the Appeals Chamber considers that this is not inconsistent with the Trial Chamber's finding that the HVO occupied territory in BiH as an agent of Croatia.[1052] This is because the test for occupation is actual authority over the territory and population and not the motivation behind such an occupation. The Appeals Chamber thus rejects this argument.

342. In conclusion, Prlić, Stojić, Praljak, Petković, and Ćorić have failed to show that the Trial Chamber erred in finding that the HVO occupied: (1) the villages of Duša, Hrasnica, Ždrimci, and Uzričje in Gornji Vakuf Municipality after 18 January 1993 ;[1053] (2) the villages of Sovići and Doljani in Jablanica Municipality after 17 April 1993;[1054] and (3) West Mostar from May 1993 until February 1994.[1055]

343. Finally, the Appeals Chamber notes the Trial Chamber's findings that Vareš town and the village of Stupni Do in Vareš Municipality were occupied *after* 23 October 1993, that the crime of extensive destruction of property not justified by military necessity and carried out unlawfully and wantonly by the HVO occurred *on* 23 October 1993,[1056] as well as the Prosecution's submission that the evidence that the Trial Chamber relied upon demonstrates that the crime of extensive appropriation of property not justified by military necessity and carried out unlawfully and wantonly by the HVO also occurred *on* 23 October 1993.[1057] Taking into account these findings and evidence, the Prosecution concedes that it was not proven that these places were occupied when the crimes were committed.[1058] The Appeals Chamber considers that, based on the factual error made by the Trial Chamber, it is in the Appellants' interest and the interests of justice to vacate

---

military, the HVO, were rejected by the BiH authorities throughout the period relevant to the Indictment. Further, the Appeals Chamber notes what it held above, that the law of occupation may be applicable to cases other than foreign invading armies. See *supra*, 318. It thus dismisses this argument. See Trial Judgement, Vol. 1, paras 426-428, 432-433, 457, 459, 467, Vol. 2. paras 339, 341.

[1047]   See Trial Judgement, Vol. 3, paras 578-589.

[1048]   See Trial Judgement, Vol. 3, paras 578-589 & fn. 1175. See *supra*, paras 335-338.

[1049]   See *supra*, para. 319.

[1050]   See *supra*, paras 319-320. The Appeals Chamber also rejects the argument that some individuals elected in a 1990 election in some municipalities were still governing locally in 1993, indicating that no change in governmental authority had taken place, as Praljak fails to show that no reasonable trier of fact could have found a state of occupation in those municipalities, based on the entirety of the evidence before the Trial Chamber.

[1051]   See *supra*, paras 320-321.

[1052]   See Trial Judgement, Vol. 3, fn. 1175. See also Trial Judgement, Vol. 3, para. 568.

[1053]   See Trial Judgement, Vol. 3, paras 579, 589.

[1054]   See Trial Judgement, Vol. 3, paras 580, 589.

[1055]   See Trial Judgement, Vol. 3, paras 581, 583, 589.

[1056]   See Trial Judgement, Vol. 3, paras 588-589, 1554-1556.

[1057]   See *supra*, para. 315. The Prosecution makes this submission despite the Trial Chamber's finding that the appropriation of Muslim property in question occurred "during and after the arrests of the Muslims in the town of Vareš between 23 October and 1 November 1993 and during and after the attack on the village of Stupni Do on 23 October 1993". See Trial Judgement, Vol. 3, paras 1650-1653; *supra*, para. 315. The Appeals Chamber observes that, in fact, the Prosecution's submission is in conformity with the evidence on which the Trial Chamber relied in making these findings. See Trial Judgement, Vol. 3, paras 401, 403, 465-467 and the evidence cited therein.

[1058]   See *supra*, para. 315.

the Appellants' convictions for Count 19 (extensive destruction as a grave breach of the Geneva **[page 143]** Conventions) and Count 22 (appropriation of property as a grave breach of the Geneva Conventions) with regard to Vareš Municipality. Exercising its discretion under Article 25(2) of the Statute,[1059] the Appeals Chamber refrains from entering new convictions on appeal for Count 20 (wanton destruction as a violation of the laws or customs of war) with regard to Vareš. In so finding, the Appeals Chamber considers the interests of fairness to the Appellants, the nature of the offences, and the circumstances of this case.[1060]

(c) Conclusion

344. For the foregoing reasons, the Appeals Chamber dismisses Prlić's ground 20, Stojić's ground 55, Praljak's ground 2, Petković's sub-ground 7.2, and Ćorić's sub-ground 3.2.

345. The Appeals Chamber upholds the Trial Chamber's conclusion that it was necessary to examine whether a state of occupation existed in those municipalities where deportation (across a *de facto* border), extensive destruction and appropriation of property were alleged under the "grave breaches" regime of the Geneva Conventions and Article 2 of the Statute. It also dismisses Prlić's, Stojić's, Praljak's, Petković's, and Ćorić's arguments related to the legal requirements of occupation. Finally, the Appeals Chamber vacates the Appellants' convictions for extensive destruction and appropriation of property not justified by military necessity and carried out unlawfully and wantonly as grave breaches of the Geneva Conventions (Counts 19 and 22 respectively) for the incidents in Vareš Municipality.

C. **The Protected Persons Requirement**

346. The Appeals Chamber recalls that, to constitute grave breaches of the Geneva Conventions, the crimes enumerated under Article 2 of the Statute must be committed against persons or property protected under the provisions of the relevant Geneva Convention.[1061] Geneva Convention IV protects "those who, at a given moment and in any manner whatsoever, find themselves, in case of **[page 144]** a conflict or occupation, in the hands of a Party to the conflict or Occupying Power of which they are not nationals", excluding protected persons under other Geneva Conventions and nationals of States that have normal diplomatic representation in the detaining State.[1062]

347. The Trial Chamber separately considered the protected status of two categories of Muslim men detained by the HVO: (1) Muslim members of the HVO; and (2) military-aged Muslim men. The Appeals Chamber will address each category in turn. It will then turn to arguments that the detention of the HVO's Muslim members and the military-aged Muslim men was justified.

1.   Muslim members of the HVO (Stojić's Ground 42, Praljak's Ground 3, Petković's Sub-grounds 5.2.1.1
in part and 5.2.1.3 in part, and Ćorić's Ground 4)

348. The Trial Chamber held that the Muslim members of the HVO who were detained by the HVO were not prisoners of war ("POWs") protected under Geneva Convention III because, as members of the authority

---

[1059]   See *Stanišić and Župljanin* Appeal Judgement, para. 1096 & fn. 3625; *Đorđević* Appeal Judgement, para. 928; *Šainović et al.* Appeal Judgement, fn. 5269; *Jelisić* Appeal Judgement, para. 73.

[1060]   *Cf. Stanišić and Župljanin* Appeal Judgement, para. 1096 & fn. 3626 and references cited therein; *Jelisić* Appeal Judgement, paras 73, 77.

[1061]   *Tadić* Appeal Decision on Jurisdiction, para. 81 (holding that the reference to "persons or property protected under the provisions of the relevant Geneva Conventions" under Article 2 of the Statute "is clearly intended to indicate that the offences listed under Article 2 can only be prosecuted when perpetrated against persons or property regarded as 'protected' by the Geneva Conventions under the strict conditions set out by the Conventions themselves. This reference in Article 2 to the notion of 'protected persons or property' must perforce cover the persons mentioned in Articles 13, 24, 25 and 26 (protected persons) and 19 and 33 to 35 (protected objects) of Geneva Convention I; in Articles 13, 36, 37 (protected persons) and 22, 24, 25 and 27 (protected objects) of Convention II; in Article 4 of Convention III on prisoners of war; and in Articles 4 and 20 (protected persons) and Articles 18, 19, 21, 22, 33, 53, 57 etc. (protected property) of Convention IV on civilians. Clearly, these provisions of the Geneva Conventions apply to persons or objects protected only to the extent that they are caught up in an international armed conflict.").

[1062]   Geneva Convention IV, Art. 4. See also Commentary on Geneva Convention IV, p. 51 (explaining that the definition of protected persons under Geneva Convention IV "is a very broad one which includes members of the armed forces [...] who fall into enemy hands" to whom, "for some reason, prisoner of war status [...] [was] denied").

by which they were detained (*i.e.* the HVO), they "cannot be considered to 'have fallen into the power of the enemy'" within the meaning of that Convention.[1063] Instead, the Trial Chamber held that the HVO Muslim members were protected by Geneva Convention IV because the criterion for determining the status of protected persons is not nationality but allegiance, and from at least 30 June 1993, the HVO Muslims were perceived by the HVO as loyal to the ABiH and therefore "had fallen into the hands of the enemy power".[1064]

(a) Arguments of the Parties

349.   Stojić, Praljak, Petković, and Ćorić contend that the Trial Chamber erred by finding that Muslim members of the HVO, who were detained by the HVO, were protected persons pursuant to Article 4 of Geneva Convention IV.[1065] First, Stojić, Praljak, and Petković argue that Geneva Convention IV only protects civilians, and that the Muslim members of the HVO necessarily fall outside of its ambit.[1066] Second, Stojić, Praljak, Petković, and Ćorić assert that the HVO's Muslim members detained by the HVO were not "in the hands of a Party to the conflict or Occupying Power of which they are not nationals", as Article 4 of Geneva Convention IV requires.[1067] They **[page 145]** also argue that the Trial Chamber erred by considering the HVO's Muslim members' ethnicity[1068] and the HVO's subjective suspicions that their allegiance had changed, instead of objective criteria, to be determinative of their lack of allegiance to the HVO.[1069] Stojić, Petković, and Ćorić also argue that, in this regard, the Trial Chamber failed to take into account other factors – and according to Ćorić, also ignored evidence – showing that the HVO considered them members of the HVO itself and not of the ABiH.[1070]

350.   Stojić, Petković, and Ćorić further submit that the Trial Chamber made contradictory findings on this issue by finding, on one hand, that in the context of Geneva Convention III, the HVO's Muslim members cannot be considered to "have fallen into the power of the enemy", while also finding, in the context of Geneva Convention IV, that they had "indeed fallen into the hands of the enemy power".[1071] Moreover, Stojić, Praljak, Petković, and Ćorić argue that national law and not international humanitarian law regulates a State's treatment of its soldiers (*e.g.,* its response to mutiny and other disciplinary issues) or any crimes

---

[1063]   Trial Judgement, Vol. 3, para. 604.

[1064]   Trial Judgement, Vol. 3, paras 608-611.

[1065]   Stojić's Appeal Brief, paras 386, 391; Praljak's Appeal Brief, paras 57-63; Petković's Appeal Brief, paras 186-191; Ćorić's Appeal Brief, paras 84-94.

[1066]   Stojić's Appeal Brief, para. 387; Praljak's Appeal Brief, para. 58; Praljak's Reply Brief, para. 114; Petković's Appeal Brief, paras 188, 191, 197; Petković's Reply Brief, paras 37-38.

[1067]   Stojić's Appeal Brief, para. 388; Praljak's Appeal Brief, para. 60; Petković's Appeal Brief, para. 189; Petković's Reply Brief, para. 37; Ćorić's Appeal Brief, para. 87.

[1068]   Praljak's Appeal Brief, paras 59-60.

[1069]   Stojić's Appeal Brief, para. 389, referring to *Blaškić* Appeal Judgement, para. 172, *Čelebići* Appeal Judgement, paras 83-84. Stojić argues that while subjective suspicions of the detaining power are relevant, they are not determinative of allegiance, and refers to the *Čelebići* Trial Judgement, which found that the Bosnian authorities considered that the Bosnian Serb detainees owed them no allegiance on the basis of objective factors, including the Bosnian Serbs' declaration of independence and their subsequent receipt of arms from the Federal Republic of Yugoslavia. See Stojić's Reply Brief, para. 73, referring to *Čelebići* Trial Judgement, para. 265. Praljak also submits that, in the Tribunal's jurisprudence, the ethnically-based allegiance criterion was only applied to civilians who had never pledged allegiance to a party to the conflict. He argues that it cannot be applied to Muslim HVO members who had willingly joined the HVO. Praljak's Appeal Brief, para. 60, referring to *Čelebići* Appeal Judgement, para. 105, *Blaškić* Appeal Judgement, para. 175. Praljak further submits that the fact that they posed a threat to the security of the HVO does not invalidate in itself their allegiance to the HVO. Praljak's Appeal Brief, para. 60. See also Petković's Appeal Brief, para. 190; Ćorić's Appeal Brief, paras 87, 91.

[1070]   Stojić's Reply Brief, para. 74, referring to Trial Judgement, Vol. 2, para. 1403; Petković's Appeal Brief, paras 189-190, referring to Ex. 4D01466, Petković's Final Trial Brief, para. 256; Ćorić's Appeal Brief, paras 87, 91-92, referring to Exs. 4D01466, P04756, P00514, p. 8, P00956, p. 14, Milivoj Petković, T. 49579 (17 Feb 2010), Witness CJ, T. 10952 (closed session) (30 Nov 2006), Slobodan Božić, T. 36379-36380 (4 Feb 2009), Josip Praljak, T. 14649-14651 (26 Feb 2007). Ćorić further argues that: (1) the Muslim HVO members could only be protected persons if they owed *no* allegiance to the party to the conflict in whose hands they found themselves and of which they were nationals; (2) the HVO cannot be an "enemy power" since it was one of the constituent members of the BiH armed forces; and (3) the Tribunal's jurisprudence requires that the Muslim HVO members had to be under the control of another party to the conflict, *i.e.* the ABiH, and the Trial Chamber did not fully analyse to whom they owed allegiance. Ćorić's Appeal Brief, paras 87, 89-91, referring to *Kordić and Čerkez* Appeal Judgement, para. 330, *Tadić* Appeal Judgement, para. 166.

[1071]   Stojić's Appeal Brief, para. 390; Stojić's Reply Brief, para. 75; Petković's Appeal Brief, paras 187-189; Ćorić's Appeal Brief, paras 85-87.

committed by servicemen against their own forces.[1072] Petković, in particular, submits that the Trial Chamber failed to give a reasoned opinion as to whether service personnel within an army fall within the jurisdiction of international **[page 146]** humanitarian law.[1073] In the alternative, he argues that if the HVO's Muslim members are considered to have "fallen into the hands of the enemy power" they should be deemed POWs under international humanitarian law and protected by Geneva Convention III, rather than under Geneva Convention IV.[1074]

351.   The Prosecution responds that the Trial Chamber did not err by deeming the HVO's Muslim members protected persons under Geneva Convention IV.[1075] First, citing the Commentary on Geneva Convention IV, the Prosecution contends that as members of the HVO, these men nevertheless had protected status, because the definition of protected persons under Geneva Convention IV "is a very broad one which includes members of the armed forces" and "[e]very person in enemy hands must have some status under international law".[1076] Second, the Prosecution submits that the Trial Chamber correctly applied the governing jurisprudence, interpreting "nationality" to mean "allegiance", and finding that the HVO's Muslim members fell into enemy hands when the HVO detained them, in light of their perceived loyalty to the ABiH.[1077] Further, the Prosecution points to evidence showing their indiscriminate and *en masse* arrest by the HVO and their treatment in detention, which more closely resembled that of other Muslim detainees than that of detained Croat HVO members.[1078]

352.   The Prosecution also responds that the Trial Chamber did not contradict itself by finding that the HVO's Muslim members were not POWs under Geneva Convention III because they did not belong to the armed forces of an enemy (the ABiH) as Article 4 of that Convention requires.[1079] It avers that the non-Tribunal authorities cited by Stojić, Praljak, Petković, and Ćorić purporting to show that international humanitarian law is not applicable to a State's treatment of its own soldiers **[page 147]** do not address the situation at hand, where detained soldiers are factually in the hands of the enemy.[1080]

(b) Analysis

353.   At the outset, the Appeals Chamber will address Stojić's, Praljak's, and Petković's arguments that only civilians are entitled to protection under Geneva Convention IV.[1081] It considers that while Geneva Convention IV primarily concerns the protection of civilians, the plain language of Article 4 defines

---

[1072]   Stojić's Reply Brief, para. 76, referring to *Sesay et al.* Trial Judgement, paras 1451-1453; Praljak's Appeal Brief, paras 61-62, referring to *Sesay et al.* Trial Judgement, para. 1451, Cassese, *International Criminal Law*, p. 82; Petković's Appeal Brief, paras 182-185, 196, referring to *Sesay et al.* Trial Judgement, paras 1451-1453, Cassese, *International Criminal Law*, p. 82; Appeal Hearing, AT. 519 (23 Mar 2017); Petković's Reply Brief, para. 40; Ćorić's Appeal Brief, paras 87, 91, 93-94, referring to, *inter alia, Sesay et al.* Trial Judgement, paras 1451-1453, Cassese, *International Criminal Law*, p. 82; Ćorić's Reply Brief, paras 28-29.

[1073]   Petković's Appeal Brief, paras 181, 196.

[1074]   Petković's Appeal Brief, paras 190-191, 197; Appeal Hearing, AT. 520-521(23 Mar 2017); Petković's Reply Brief, para. 37. In this regard, Petković argues that the Trial Chamber erred by failing to first inquire whether the HVO's Muslim members detained by the HVO were denied POW status. See Petković's Reply Brief, paras 39-40. See *infra*, paras 373-374.

[1075]   Prosecution's Response Brief (Stojić), paras 353-354; Prosecution's Response Brief (Praljak), paras 277-278; Prosecution's Response Brief (Petković), para. 144; Prosecution's Response Brief (Ćorić), para. 75.

[1076]   Prosecution's Response Brief (Stojić), para. 355; Prosecution's Response Brief (Praljak), paras 279-281; Prosecution's Resjponse Brief (Petković), paras 145-147; Appeal Hearing, AT. 551, 554 (23 Mar 2017); Prosecution's Response Brief (Ćorić), paras 77-79.

[1077]   Prosecution's Response Brief (Stojić), paras 354, 356; Prosecution's Response Brief (Praljak), para. 278, referring to *Čelebići* Appeal Judgement, paras 83-84, *Tadić* Appeal Judgement, para. 166; Prosecution's Response Brief (Petković), para. 144; Prosecution's Response Brief (Ćorić), paras 76, 80. With respect to Ćorić, the Prosecution responds that he repeats the same arguments he made at trial without showing any error, which should be dismissed. Prosecution's Response Brief (Ćorić), paras 80, 82-83. See Ćorić's Appeal Brief, paras 89-90.

[1078]   Prosecution's Response Brief (Stojić), para. 356; Prosecution's Response Brief (Praljak), paras 278, 282; Prosecution's Response Brief (Petković), para. 148; Appeal Hearing, AT. 551-556 (23 Mar 2017).

[1079]   Prosecution's Response Brief (Stojić), para. 357; Prosecution's Response Brief (Praljak), paras 280-281; Prosecution's Response Brief (Petković), paras 146-147; Appeal Hearing, AT. 556-559 (23 Mar 2017); Prosecution's Response Brief (Ćorić), paras 78-80.

[1080]   Prosecution's Response Brief (Praljak), para. 282; Prosecution's Response Brief (Petković), para. 148; Prosecution's Response Brief (Ćorić), para. 85.

[1081]   See Stojić's Appeal Brief, para. 387; Praljak's Appeal Brief, para. 58; Praljak's Reply Brief, para. 114; Petković's Appeal Brief, paras 188, 191, 197; Petković's Reply Brief, paras 37-38.

protected persons more broadly, encompassing all persons – not just civilians – who fall into the hands of a party to the conflict, or occupying power of which they are not nationals, and who are not protected under the other Geneva Conventions.[1082] The Appeals Chamber thus dismisses this argument.

354.   The Appeals Chamber now turns to Stojić's, Praljak's, Petković's, and Ćorić's arguments challenging the legal standard applied by the Trial Chamber to determine the status of the HVO's Muslim members and their protection under Geneva Convention IV. It reiterates its jurisprudence that:

> depriving victims, who arguably are of the same nationality under domestic law as their captors, of the protection of the Geneva Conventions solely based on that national law would not be consistent with the object and purpose of the Conventions. Their very object could indeed be defeated if undue emphasis were placed on formal legal bonds [...]. It finds that Article 4 of Geneva Convention IV cannot be interpreted in a way that would exclude victims from the protected persons status merely on the basis of their common citizenship with a perpetrator. They are protected as long as they owe no allegiance to the Party to the conflict in whose hands they find themselves and of which they are nationals.[1083]

The Appeals Chamber also recalls that it has held that:

> already in 1949 the legal bond of nationality was not regarded as crucial and allowance was made for special cases. [In the case of World War II refugees], the lack of both allegiance to a State and diplomatic protection' by this State was regarded as more important than the formal link of nationality. In the cases provided for in Article 4(2), in addition to nationality, account was taken of the existence or non-existence of diplomatic protection: nationals of a neutral State or a co-belligerent State are not treated as "protected persons" unless they are deprived of or do not enjoy diplomatic protection. In other words, those nationals are not "protected persons" as long as they benefit from the normal diplomatic protection of their State; when they lose it or in any event do not enjoy it, the Convention automatically grants them the status of "protected persons".[1084] **[page 148]**

355.   In this respect, the Appeals Chamber further notes that the allegiance analysis "hinging on substantial relations more than on formal bonds, becomes all the more important in present-day international armed conflicts [...] [where] ethnicity rather than nationality may become the grounds for allegiance".[1085] In this case, the Trial Chamber correctly took into account the allegiance of the Muslim HVO members rather than merely considering their nationality.[1086] Moreover, to reach the conclusion that Muslim HVO members were protected by Geneva Convention IV from 30 June 1993 onwards, the Trial Chamber relied on the perceived allegiance of the Muslim HVO members by the HVO.[1087] Recalling that the detaining authority's view of the victims' allegiance has been considered a relevant factor by the Appeals Chamber,[1088] the Appeals Chamber considers that Stojić, Praljak, Petković, and Ćorić have failed to show an error on the part of the Trial Chamber.[1089]

356.   The Appeals Chamber notes Stojić's, Petković's, and Ćorić's argument that the Trial Chamber failed to take into account other factors showing that the HVO viewed its Muslim members as belonging to the HVO.[1090] Recalling the relevant Trial Chamber findings, the Appeals Chamber considers that the Trial Chamber addressed Praljak's, Petković's, and Ćorić's final briefs, and Petković's Closing Arguments at trial, where it was argued that when placed in isolation by the HVO, the HVO Muslim members "did not forfeit their status as HVO soldiers".[1091] The Appeals Chamber further observes that the Trial Chamber also noted

---

[1082]   Geneva Convention IV, Art. 4(4). See also Commentary on Geneva Convention IV, pp. 50-51.
[1083]   *Kordić and Čerkez* Appeal Judgement, para. 329 (internal references omitted). See also *Kordić and Čerkez* Appeal Judgement, para. 330.
[1084]   *Tadić* Appeal Judgement, para. 165 (internal references omitted).
[1085]   *Tadić* Appeal Judgement, para. 166. See *Čelebići* Appeal Judgement, paras 83-84.
[1086]   Trial Judgement, Vol. 3, para. 608.
[1087]   Trial Judgement, Vol. 3, paras 609-611.
[1088]   *Čelebići* Appeal Judgement, para. 98.
[1089]   Nor have they shown any cogent reason for the Appeals Chamber to depart from the allegiance analysis jurisprudence. See *Aleksovski* Appeal Judgement, paras 107-109.
[1090]   Stojić's Reply Brief, para. 74, referring to Trial Judgement, Vol. 2, para. 1403; Petković's Appeal Brief, paras 189-190, referring to Ex. 4D01466, Petković's Final Brief, para. 256; Ćorić's Appeal Brief, paras 87, 91, referring to Exs. 4D01466, P04756, Milivoj Petković, T. 49579 (17 Feb 2010), Witness CJ, T. 10952 (closed session) (30 Nov 2006).
[1091]   See Trial Judgement, Vol. 3, para. 594, referring to Praljak's Final Brief, paras 85, 96, Petković's Final Brief, paras 255-260, referring to Milivoj Petković, T. 49579 (17 Feb 2010), Ex. 4D01466, Petković Closing Arguments, T(F). 52545, 52549-52550, 52558 (21 Feb 2011), Ćorić's Final Brief, paras 352-368, referring to Exs. 4D01466, P04756.

Ćorić's argument that the HVO Muslim members, due to their membership in the HVO, owed allegiance to the authorities of the HZ(R) H-B.[1092] The Appeals Chamber therefore considers that Stojić, Petković, and Ćorić have failed to show that the Trial Chamber ignored relevant factors allegedly showing that the HVO viewed its Muslim members as belonging to the HVO.[1093]

357.   With regard to Ćorić's related argument that the Trial Chamber ignored evidence showing that the HVO considered Muslim members of the HVO to be members of the HVO itself and not of **[page 149]** the ABiH,[1094] the Appeals Chamber observes that the arguments that the Trial Chamber referred to, as just discussed, also identified supporting evidence.[1095] The Appeals Chamber notes that some of the evidence Ćorić claimed was ignored, purporting to show that the HVO distinguished between detained Muslim HVO members and POWs, was also included in the arguments the Trial Chamber referred to.[1096] In any event, the Appeals Chamber considers that Ćorić has failed to explain how this evidence showing that "military prisoners" were separated from the "enemy POWs" while in detention pertained to HVO Muslim members.[1097] It therefore dismisses Ćorić's argument.

358.   Turning to Stojić's, Praljak's, Petković's, and Ćorić's arguments relying on non-Tribunal authorities that war crimes cannot be committed by soldiers against members of their own military force, the Appeals Chamber first recalls that it is not bound by the findings of other courts – domestic, international, or hybrid.[1098] The Appeals Chamber also considers that these non-ICTY cases are inapposite to the case at hand. Although they relate to whether war crimes can be committed by service personnel against members of their own military force,[1099] none of these cases apply the allegiance criterion developed in ICTY jurisprudence to determine whether the service personnel had fallen into the hands of a party to the conflict, or occupying power of which they are not nationals, as required under Geneva Convention IV.[1100] Moreover, the Appeals Chamber finds that Stojić's, Praljak's, Petković's, and Ćorić's arguments fall short of demonstrating that there are cogent reasons for the Appeals Chamber to depart from its established jurisprudence in this regard.[1101] Accordingly, these arguments are dismissed. Further, the Appeals Chamber therefore dismisses Stojić's, Praljak's, Petković's, and Ćorić's challenges to the Trial Chamber's application of international humanitarian law in finding that the HVO's Muslim members were protected under Geneva Convention IV.[1102] **[page 150]**

359.   As to Stojić's, Petković's, and Ćorić's allegation that the Trial Chamber contradicted itself by finding that the HVO's Muslim members detained by the HVO were, on one hand, not "[m]embers of the armed forces of a Party to the conflict" who had "fallen into the power of the enemy" under Geneva Convention III, but on the other, that they had "indeed fallen into the hands of the enemy power", under Geneva Convention IV, the Appeals Chamber considers that the Trial Chamber's findings, read in context, are not contradictory. The Appeals Chamber finds that the Trial Chamber reasonably concluded that the Muslim HVO members could not be deemed POWs within the strict meaning of Geneva Convention III as they did not formally

---

[1092]   See Trial Judgement, Vol. 3, para. 593, referring to Ćorić's Final Brief, paras 352-360, referring to Exs. 4D01466, P04756.
[1093]   See Trial Judgement, Vol. 3, paras 608-611.
[1094]   See Ćorić's Appeal Brief, para. 92, referring to Exs. P00514, p. 8, P00956, p. 14, Milivoj Petković, T. 49579 (17 Feb 2010), Slobodan Božić, T. 36379-36380 (4 Feb 2009), Josip Praljak, T. 14649-14651 (26 Feb 2007).
[1095]   See Trial Judgement, Vol. 3, paras 593-594, referring to Petković's Final Brief, paras 255, 257, referring to Exs. P00514, p. 8 (Instruction for the Operation of the Central Military Prison of the Croatian Defence Council, 22 September 1992), P00956, p. 14 (Military Police Report, 26 December 1992), Milivoj Petković, T. 49579 (17 Feb 2010). See also *supra*, para. 356.
[1096]   See Exs. P00514, p. 8 (Instruction for the Operation of the Central Military Prison of the Croatian Defence Council, 22 September 1992), P00956, p. 14 (Military Police Report, 26 December 1992), Milivoj Petković, T. 49579 (17 Feb 2010).
[1097]   *Cf.* Ćorić's Appeal Brief, para. 92, referring to Exs. P00514, p. 8, P00956, p. 14, Milivoj Petković, T. 49579 (17 Feb 2010), Slobodan Božić, T. 36379-36380 (4 Feb 2009), Josip Praljak, T. 14649-14651 (26 Feb 2007); Trial Judgement, Vol. 3, paras 593-594, referring to Petković's Final Brief, paras 255, 257, referring to Exs. P00514, p. 8 (Instruction for the Operation of the Central Military Prison of the Croatian Defence Council, 22 September 1992), P00956, p. 14 (Military Police Report, 26 December 1992), Milivoj Petković, T. 49579 (17 Feb 2010).
[1098]   *Stanišić and Župljanin* Appeal Judgement, para. 598; *Popović et al.* Appeal Judgement, para. 1674. See also *Đorđević* Appeal Judgement, para. 50.
[1099]   See *Pilz* Case, p. 391; *Motosuke* Case, p. 682; *Sesay et al.* Trial Judgement, paras 1388-1396, 1451-1453 & fn. 2754. See also Cassese, *International Criminal Law*, p. 82, referring to the *Pilz* and *Motosuke* cases.
[1100]   See Geneva Convention IV, Art. 4(4). See also Commentary on Geneva Convention IV, pp. 50-51.
[1101]   See *Aleksovski* Appeal Judgement, paras 107-109.
[1102]   See also *supra*, para. 349.

belong to the ABiH, the "armed forces of a Party other than the detaining Party".[1103] They could nevertheless be protected under Geneva Convention IV because they were *in fact* in enemy hands, and "[e]very person in enemy hands must have some status under international law [...]. There is no intermediate status; nobody in enemy hands can be outside the law."[1104] For these same reasons, Petković's alternative argument that the HVO's Muslim members should be deemed POWs under Geneva Convention III is dismissed.

(c) Conclusion

360. For the foregoing reasons, the Appeals Chamber affirms the Trial Chamber's ruling that the HVO's Muslim members who were detained by the HVO were protected persons under Geneva Convention IV. Consequently, the Appeals Chamber dismisses Stojić's ground of appeal 42, Praljak's ground of appeal 3, Petković's sub-ground of appeal 5.2.1 in part, and Ćorić's ground of appeal 4.

> 2. Muslim men of military age (Praljak's Ground 4, Petković's Sub-grounds 5.2.1.1 in part, 5.2.1.2, and 5.2.1.4, Ćorić's Ground 5, and Pušić's Sub-ground 7.1)

361. The Trial Chamber held that the Muslim men of military age, even if they were part of the reserves of the armed forces of BiH under national law, did not fit the definition of members of armed forces within the meaning of the applicable international humanitarian law.[1105] It reasoned that a reservist becomes a member of the armed forces once he has been mobilised and has taken up active duty.[1106] It held that it is only then that a member of the reserves acquires the status of combatant and becomes a POW if he falls into the hands of the opposing party during an **[page 151]** international armed conflict.[1107] The Trial Chamber further reasoned that from that moment on, until he is demobilised, a member of the reserves is not a civilian.[1108] It therefore concluded that a party to an international conflict cannot justify the detention of a group of men solely on the ground that they are of military age and that, at the outbreak of war, national law required the general mobilisation of the men in this age group.[1109] According to the Trial Chamber, such a party must verify whether the person has actually mobilised and entered into active duty.[1110]

(a) Arguments of the Parties

362. Praljak, Petković, Ćorić, and Pušić submit that the Trial Chamber erred when it found that military-aged Muslim men were not members of the armed forces under international humanitarian law.[1111] Praljak, Petković, and Ćorić argue that the Trial Chamber failed to consider that: (1) BiH law regarded the reserve forces as a component of the ABiH; and (2) pursuant to a general mobilisation order,[1112] the reservists were in fact mobilised as ABiH members which meant, under international humanitarian law, that they became members of the armed forces.[1113] Petković and Ćorić contend that the Trial Chamber failed to consider that non-combatants, such as the military-aged Muslim men detained by the HVO, may nevertheless be members

[1103] See Trial Judgement, Vol. 3, paras 602-605. See also *supra,* paras 354-355; Stojić's Appeal Brief, para. 390; Stojić's Reply Brief, para. 75; Petković's Appeal Brief, paras 187-189; Ćorić's Appeal Brief, paras 85-87. The Appeals Chamber dismisses Ćorić's argument that the HVO cannot be an enemy power as it has affirmed the Trial Chamber's findings that the HVO was under the overall control of Croatia and was engaged in an international armed conflict with the ABiH. See *supra,* paras 234-240, 276-297.
[1104] Commentary on Geneva Convention IV, p. 51.
[1105] See Trial Judgement, Vol. 3, paras 616-618.
[1106] See Trial Judgement, Vol. 3, para. 619.
[1107] See Trial Judgement, Vol. 3, para. 619.
[1108] See Trial Judgement, Vol. 3, para. 619.
[1109] See Trial Judgement, Vol. 3, para. 620.
[1110] See Trial Judgement, Vol. 3, para. 620.
[1111] Praljak's Appeal Brief, paras 64-68; Appeal Hearing, AT. 472 (22 Mar 2017); Petković's Appeal Brief, paras 200-202, 211; Petković's Reply Brief, para. 43; Ćorić's Appeal Brief, paras 95-100; Pušić's Appeal Brief, paras 228-229. Pušić adopts the Judge Antonetti Dissent on this issue. See Pušić's Appeal Brief, para. 229.
[1112] See Praljak's Appeal Brief, para. 66, referring to Ex. 4D01164; Petković's Appeal Brief, para. 201, referring to Exs. 4D01030, 4D00412, 4D01731, para. 119, 4D01164; Ćorić's Appeal Brief, paras 97-98, referring to, *inter alia,* Exs. 1D00349, 4D01030, 4D00412, 4D01731, para. 64, 4D01164.
[1113] Praljak's Appeal Brief, paras 65-66; Petković's Appeal Brief, paras 200-201; Petković's Reply Brief, paras 41-42; Ćorić's Appeal Brief, paras 95-98, 100.

of the armed forces and that it was necessary to consider national legislation to determine when reservists become members of the armed forces.[1114]

363.   Praljak, Petković, and Ćorić also submit that the reservists' obligations under BiH law, in addition to other evidence that both Bosnian Muslim and HVO authorities treated the reservists as members of the ABiH, create a strong presumption of their incorporation into the ABiH and that the Trial Chamber failed to apply the proper burden of proof by not requiring the Prosecution to prove **[page 152]** that the reservists were civilians.[1115] In this regard, Petković asserts that the Trial Chamber erred by repeatedly referring to Muslim men of military age as "men who did not belong to any armed force" without applying the appropriate evidentiary standard.[1116]

364.   The Prosecution responds that the Trial Chamber properly determined that the military-aged Muslim men, even if reservists under national law, retained their civilian status.[1117] The Prosecution submits that consistent with customary international law, the Trial Chamber correctly focused on whether the men had actually been incorporated into the ABiH and found that they had not been.[1118] Finally, the Prosecution asserts that the Trial Chamber properly applied the applicable burden of proof and correctly distinguished between civilians and members of the armed forces.[1119]

(b) Analysis

365.   The Appeals Chamber notes that Praljak's, Petković's, Ćorić's, and Pušić's challenges is essentially that the Trial Chamber failed to consider that, pursuant to a general mobilisation order, Muslim men of military age were reserve members of the ABiH, and therefore members of the armed forces, protected under Geneva Convention III.

366.   At the outset, the Appeals Chamber recalls that the the Trial Chamber considered the arguments made by Petković at trial, and some of the evidence cited by him, Praljak, and Ćorić in their respective final trial briefs, purporting to show that reserve forces were part of the ABiH, and that reservists were mobilised as ABiH members.[1120] The Appeals Chamber notes that one of the pieces of evidence that Petković and Ćorić relied upon is the "Decree Law on Compulsory Military Service", published on 1 August 1992 ("Decree on Compulsory Military Service"), which states **[page 153]** that "all citizens of [BiH] who are fit to work shall

---

[1114]   Petković's Appeal Brief, paras 199-200, referring to the Hague Regulations, Art. 3, Henckaerts and Doswald-Beck, *Customary International Humanitarian Law*, p. 14. In this context, Petković argues that the Trial Chamber did not provide a reasoned opinion about the difference between combat and non-combat members of the armed forces and the right of non-combatants to be given POW status if imprisoned. Petković's Appeal Brief, para. 200; Ćorić's Appeal Brief, para. 100, referring to the Hague Regulations, Art. 3, Henckaerts and Doswald-Beck, *Customary International Humanitarian Law*, p. 13. See also Praljak's Appeal Brief, para. 65 (arguing that members of the armed forces and the TO residing in their homes remained combatants whether or not they were in combat).

[1115]   Praljak's Appeal Brief, paras 66-67; Praljak's Reply Brief, paras 115-116; Petković's Appeal Brief, paras 180, 201-203; Ćorić's Appeal Brief, paras 99-100. Petković also notes that the Trial Chamber acknowledged, when considering the HVO, that conscripts were members of the armed forces. See Petković's Appeal Brief, para. 204.

[1116]   Petković's Appeal Brief, paras 178-180. Petković raises the same argument with respect to the HVO's Muslim members, which is, however, dismissed in light of the Appeals Chamber's foregoing analysis on the status of the HVO's Muslim members. See *supra*, paras 348-360.

[1117]   Prosecution's Response Brief (Praljak), para. 284; Prosecution's Response Brief (Petković), para. 149; Prosecution's Response Brief (Ćorić), para. 87.

[1118]   Prosecution's Response Brief (Praljak), paras 284-286; Prosecution's Response Brief (Petković), paras 149-151; Prosecution's Response Brief (Ćorić), para. 88. The Prosecution contends that the HVO itself did not treat the military-aged Muslim men as POWs, as it subjected them to the same treatment as the Muslim civilian detainees. See Prosecution's Response Brief (Praljak), para. 287; Prosecution's Response Brief (Petković), para. 152; Prosecution's Response Brief (Ćorić), para. 89.

[1119]   Prosecution's Response Brief (Praljak), para. 283; Prosecution's Response Brief (Petković), paras 140-141; Prosecution's Response Brief (Ćorić), para. 92.

[1120]   See Trial Judgement, Vol. 3, para. 612, referring to the "RBIH's Presidency's Order for general mobilisation on 20 June 1992", *i.e.* Ex. 4D01164. See also Trial Judgement, Vol. 3, paras 612-614 & fns 1222-1225, referring to, *inter alia*, Petković's Final Trial Brief, paras 261-275, referring to Exs. 1D00349, 4D01030, 4D00412, 4D01731, 4D01164, Petković Closing Arguments, T. (F) 52551-52556 (21 Feb 2011), referring to, *inter alia*, Exs. 4D00412, 4D1030, 1D00349, Petković's Rejoinder, T. (F) 52929-52930 (2 Mar 2011), referring to Exs. 4D00412, 4D01164. The Appeals Chamber also notes that the Trial Chamber refers to Ex. 4D01731 in the previous sub-section of the Trial Judgement, in the context of the discussion on the status of the HVO's Muslim members. See Trial Judgement, Vol. 3, fn. 1218.

be subject to compulsory military service".[1121] It defines "compulsory military service" as "the recruitment obligation, the obligation to complete military service and the obligation to serve in the reserve forces."[1122] However, the Appeals Chamber considers that this same Decree on Compulsory Military Service also defines several categories of citizens of BiH who are, or may be, excused from military service regardless of their age.[1123] Similarly, the "Decree Law on Service in the Army of the Republic of Bosnia and Herzegovina", also published on 1 August 1992, referred to by Petković and Ćorić, states that "military personnel shall be understood to mean active military personnel, soldiers and persons in the reserve force as long as they are on military duty in the Army".[1124] In other words, even according to the evidence referred to by Petković and Ćorić, military-aged Muslim men could not be considered as a group belonging to the ABiH. The Appeals Chamber therefore considers that Praljak, Petković, Ćorić, and Pušić fail to show that in the circumstances of this case no reasonable trier of fact could have concluded that military-aged Muslim men – as a general category – did not belong to the ABiH.

367.   Further, the Appeals Chamber considers that the Trial Chamber made findings on the status of all Muslim men detained, *e.g.,* the Trial Chamber categorised the Muslims detained as elderly men, boys of 14 years of age or younger, HVO Muslim members, ABiH members, and "politicians or teachers who were not members of any armed forces".[1125] Moreover, where relevant, it also **[page 154]** considered that some of the men who were not members of the armed forces were accused of illegal activity related to the conflict.[1126] Nonetheless, the Appeals Chamber considers that even in this latter case, Praljak, Petković, Ćorić, and Pušić have not demonstrated that a reasonable trier of fact could not have concluded that the HVO failed to carry out an individual assessment of the military-aged Muslim men within a reasonable time, as required by law. In this regard, the Appeals Chamber recalls that it has previously held that:

> The detaining power has a reasonable time to determine whether a particular person is a civilian and further to determine whether there are reasonable grounds to believe that the security of the detaining power is threatened [...]. The assessment that each civilian taken into detention poses a particular risk to security of the State must be made on an individual basis. The Appeals Chamber, in the Čelebići Appeal Judgement, accepted that some reasonable time is given to the detaining power to determine, which of the detainees is a threat.[1127]

[1121]   Ex. 4D01030, Art. 2.

[1122]   Ex. 4D01030, Art. 4.

[1123]   Ex. 4D01030, Art. 25(4). See also Ex. 4D01030, Arts 5-7, 24-26. For example "a person who has graduated from the School of Internal Affairs lasting at least two years and has worked as a policemen for at least two years". Ex. 4D01030, Art. 25(4).

[1124]   Ex. 4D00412, Art. 3. The Appeals Chamber further notes that the "Order amending the Order of the War Presidency of Jablanica Municipality Assembly" refers to a general mobilisation in that municipality of all people between the ages of 15 and 65 for military units but also for labour units and civilian protection. See Ex. 1D00349. The "Order Proclaiming General Public Mobilisation in the Territory of the Republic of Bosnia and Herzegovina" of 20 June 1992 refers to the mobilisation of "military conscripts" on one hand, and the mobilisation of all "remaining citizens", both men and women, to report to the civil protection units on the other. See Ex. 4D01164, Arts 1-2. Moreover, the Appeals Chamber notes that Defence expert Witness Milan Gorjanc's Military Expert Report also states that even though "[f]rom that moment on [referring to Ex. 4D01164, dated 20 June 1992] all men became members of the armed forces of [BiH]. It is understandable that due to shortage of weapons and equipment, as well as initial problems in establishing and organising a [BiH] wartime army, not all men fit for military service and conscripts could be actively engaged in combat operations were in the reserve or performed other tasks important for the defence of the country." Ex. 4D01731, para. 119.

[1125]   See, *e.g.,* Trial Judgement, Vol. 2, paras 1511 (finding that among the detainees in the Heliodrom were people under the age of 15 and over the age of 60 and that "due to their age, they did not belong to any armed force"), 1809 (finding that in the days after 9 May 1993, many Muslim detainees, for the most part members of the ABiH or the TO, again arrived at Ljubuški Prison from Mostar), 1816 (finding that, in September 1993, many Muslim intellectuals and prominent figures were transferred to Ljubuški Prison, which had become a detention site for "persons of interest" or "of importance"), 1915-1917, 1921 (finding that in April and July 1993, in Stolac Municipality, the HVO arrested and detained HVO Muslim members, members of the ABiH, and civilians, such as an economist, teachers, and the Director of Koštana Hospital, Dr. Kapić). See also Trial Judgement, Vol. 3, paras 1020-1027 (Mostar Municipality), 1030 (Ljubuški Municipality and Ljubuški Prison), 1032 (finding that with regard to the Muslim men held at the Vitina-Otok Camp, in July and August 1993, the HVO "detained Muslim men between 20 and 60 years of age, regardless of whether or not they were members of the ABiH"), 1034-1036, 1038 (finding that "Muslim men who were members of the HVO or the ABiH, or were not members of any armed forces, were arrested by the HVO in the Municipality of Stolac and held at Koštana Hospital between May and October 1993"), 1039, 1041.

[1126]   See Trial Judgement, Vol. 2, para. 1917 (noting evidence showing that some of the prominent Muslim men detained in April 1993 had been accused of setting up barricades in Stolac in March 1992, in order to prevent the leaders of the Stolac HVO from entering the town).

[1127]   *Kordić and Čerkez* Appeal Judgement, para. 609.

368.   Moreover, the Appeals Chamber observes that the Trial Chamber made other relevant findings that demonstrate that the military-aged Muslim men were arrested *en masse* together with Muslim women, children, and the elderly, and *all* Muslims were detained and treated in the same manner, irrespective of their status.[1128] Based on the foregoing, the Appeals Chamber considers that Petković and Ćorić have failed to show an error on the part of the Trial Chamber that invalidates the conclusion that the military-aged Muslim men could not be considered as a group as members of the armed forces. It therefore dismisses their arguments.

369.   With regard to Praljak's, Petković's, and Ćorić's arguments that the Trial Chamber relieved the Prosecution from its burden of proving the civilian status of the military-aged Muslim men, the Appeals Chamber recalls that the Trial Chamber held that the Prosecution carried the burden of proving civilian status, and in the absence of such evidence, it stated that it would find, *in dubio pro reo,* that such persons are combatants.[1129] In fact, when the evidence was insufficient to show what the circumstances of the military-aged Muslim men's detention were, the Trial Chamber did not find that the HVO unlawfully imprisoned civilians, *e.g.,* in October 1992 in Prozor Municipality, and between August 1993 and January 1994 in the Vojno Detention Centre.[1130] The Appeals Chamber thus rejects Praljak's, Petković's, and Ćorić's arguments.
[page 155]

(c) Conclusion

370.   For the foregoing reasons, the Appeals Chamber finds that Praljak, Petković, Ćorić, and Pušić have failed to show that no reasonable trier of fact could have reached the same conclusion as the Trial Chamber. Consequently, the Appeals Chamber dismisses Praljak's ground of appeal 4, Petković's sub-ground of appeal 5.2.1 in part, Ćorić's ground of appeal 5, and Pušić's sub-ground of appeal 7.1, insofar as they relate to the military-aged Muslim men.

   3.   Defences to detention (Petković Sub-grounds 5.2.1.1, 5.2.1.3, 5.2.1.4, all in part)

371.   The Trial Chamber found that following the attack on the HVO Tihomir Mišić Barracks on 30 June 1993, which was executed by the ABiH in co-operation with HVO Muslim soldiers who had deserted, Petković issued an order ("30 June 1993 Order") to the South-East Herzegovina Operative Zone (HVO) ("South-East OZ"), indicating that all HVO Muslim members should be disarmed and isolated, and that all the military-aged Muslim men residing in the South-East OZ should also be isolated.[1131] The Trial Chamber further found that as a result of the 30 June 1993 Order, the HVO proceeded with a widespread and massive campaign to arrest Muslim men in and around the town, of Mostar, whether members of an armed force or not.[1132]

372.   The Trial Chamber rejected the argument that the HVO had a right to isolate all the HVO Muslims for security reasons because such limitation on the liberty "can result only from individual measures that must be determined on a case by case basis and cannot in any case be decided generally in respect to an entire segment of the population".[1133] It also rejected the argument that military-aged Muslim men could be detained as a group,[1134] and concluded that Petković "ordered the arrest of men who did not belong to any armed force".[1135]

(a) Arguments of the Parties

373.   Petković raises two arguments regarding the HVO's detention of protected persons. First, Petković argues that even if the two categories of detainees – the HVO's Muslim members and military-aged Muslim

---

[1128]   See, *e.g.,* Trial Judgement, Vol. 2, paras 894-895, 1876-1877, 1920-1921, 2082-2083, 2170-2171, 2174, Vol. 3, paras 970-972, 974-975, 980, 984, 986-987, 995, 1003-1004, 1006-1007, 1014-1016, 1020-1023, 1025-1028, 1030-1033, 1035-1036, 1038-1042, 1049-1058.
[1129]   See Trial Judgement, Vol. 3, para. 621.
[1130]   See Trial Judgement, Vol. 3, paras 1000, 1006, 1028.
[1131]   See Trial Judgement, Vol. 2, paras 881-882, 890-891, Vol. 4, para. 737, referring to Ex. P03019.
[1132]   See Trial Judgement, Vol. 2, paras 890-895, Vol. 4, paras 737-738, 757-759.
[1133]   Trial Judgement, Vol. 3, para. 599. See also Trial Judgement, Vol. 2, paras 894-895, Vol. 4, paras 737-738, 757-759.
[1134]   See Trial Judgement, Vol. 3, para. 620. See also Trial Judgement, Vol. 2, paras 894-895, Vol. 4, paras 737-738, 757-759.
[1135]   Trial Judgement, Vol. 4, para. 738.

men – were protected persons under Geneva Convention IV, evidence highlights that their detention was nevertheless necessary for security reasons and thus justified **[page 156]** under Article 42 of Geneva Convention IV.[1136] Second, Petković contends that under the Tribunal's jurisprudence, a detaining authority is permitted to hold individuals while it determines their status and risk, and that he was only responsible for the initial decision to lawfully detain the military-aged Muslim men but not for their subsequent continuous detention when it was required that a case-by-case risk assessment be carried out.[1137]

374.   The Prosecution responds that Petković's blanket order to arrest all able-bodied Muslim men was illegal and that the Trial Chamber properly rejected Petković's claim that the detention of military-aged Muslim men was a legitimate security measure.[1138] Further, in the Prosecution's view, the evidence before the Trial Chamber confirmed the critical distinction, in line with customary international law, between a general call for mobilisation and the separate act of recruitment into the ABiH, and that the military-aged Muslim men were not treated as ABiH POWs.[1139] Moreover, none of the Muslim prisoners were afforded the possibility to challenge their detention, and regardless of their status, no individualised inquiry was made to determine whether they posed a security risk.[1140]

(b) Analysis

375.   According to Article 42 of Geneva Convention IV, protected persons may be detained "only if the security of the Detaining Power makes it absolutely necessary".[1141] While protected persons may be detained when it is absolutely necessary, the Appeals Chamber recalls that such deprivation of liberty is "permissible only where there are reasonable grounds to believe that the security of the State is at risk",[1142] based on "an assessment that each civilian taken into detention poses a *particular risk* to the security of the State".[1143] As previously held by the Appeals Chamber:

> To hold the contrary would suggest that, whenever the armed forces of a State are engaged in armed conflict, the entire civilian population of that State is necessarily a threat to security and therefore may be detained. It is perfectly clear from the provisions of Geneva Convention IV referred to above that there is no such blanket power to detain the entire civilian population of a party to the conflict in such circumstances.[1144] **[page 157]**

Thus, without such assessment, an individual may not be detained solely because he or she is a national of, or aligned with, an enemy party.[1145]

376.   The Appeals Chamber recalls that the Trial Chamber found that the detention of HVO Muslim members and the military-aged Muslim men could not be justified solely on the concerns regarding the group[1146] and, therefore, concluded that Petković's order to *arrest* these groups of Muslim men was not in compliance with Article 42 of Geneva Convention IV.[1147] The Appeals Chamber therefore considers that Petković has failed to demonstrate that no reasonable trier of fact could have found that the detention of HVO Muslim members and the military-aged Muslim men following his 30 June 1993 Order was justified.

377.   The Appeals Chamber highlights that the Trial Chamber's conclusion that the arrest of Muslim men following Petković's 30 June 1993 Order was not justified by military necessity, as set forth in Article 42, is

---

[1136]   Petković's Appeal Brief, paras 192-195, 198, 205-207; Appeal Hearing, AT. 518-519 (23 Mar 2017).
[1137]   Petković's Appeal Brief, paras 208-210, referring to *Kordić and Čerkez* Appeal Judgement, paras 608-609, 615, 623; Appeal Hearing, AT. 485, 519-521 (23 Mar 2017); Petković's Reply Brief, para. 44.
[1138]   Prosecution's Response Brief (Petković), paras 149-150, 153; Appeal Hearing, AT. 535-536 (23 Mar 2017).
[1139]   Prosecution's Response Brief (Petković), paras 151-152.
[1140]   Prosecution's Response Brief (Petković), paras 152-153; Appeal Hearing, AT. 536 (23 Mar 2017).
[1141]   Geneva Convention IV, Art. 42.
[1142]   *Čelebići* Appeal Judgement, para. 321.
[1143]   *Čelebići* Appeal Judgement, para. 327 (emphasis in original).
[1144]   *Čelebići* Appeal Judgement, para. 327 (emphasis in original).
[1145]   *Čelebići* Appeal Judgement, para. 327. See Geneva Convention IV, Arts 42-43.
[1146]   See Trial Judgement, Vol. 3, para. 610.
[1147]   See Trial Judgement, Vol. 1, paras 134-135, Vol. 3, paras 599, 620. The Appeals Chamber recalls that it rejects elsewhere in the Judgement the argument that the Trial Chamber erred in finding that detention could not be justified solely on the grounds of HVO membership (in the case of the HVO's Muslim members), reservist status, or a legal obligation to mobilise (in the case of military-aged Muslim men). See *supra*, paras 360, 370; *infra*, paras 2384-2385, 2462 &fn. 8179.

also supported by its finding that boys around the age of 14 and men over the age of 60 were arrested as well.[1148] Moreover, the Trial Chamber's more general findings with regard to the arrest and detention of civilians by the HVO in the different municipalities, including Mostar, demonstrate that civilians were arrested and detained "irrespective of their status"[1149] or "without taking their civilian status into consideration",[1150] that the "HVO did not hold these civilians because they posed a threat to the security of its armed forces",[1151] and that they included women, children, the elderly,[1152] and prominent Muslims.[1153] The lack of legal basis for the arrest is reinforced by the Trial Chamber's findings that the HVO authorities did not make any individual assessment of the security reasons that could have led to their detention and that the detained Muslim civilians did not have the possibility of challenging their detention with the relevant authorities.[1154] Petković has failed to show that no reasonable trier of fact could have found that the detention of the HVO Muslim members and military-aged Muslim men was not justified.[1155] **[page 158]**

378.   The Appeals Chamber further notes that Petković's argument, that the Trial Chamber erred when it failed to distinguish between the initial and continuing detention of the HVO's Muslim members and military-aged Muslim men, is premised on an erroneous understanding of the Trial Chamber's findings. The Trial Chamber did not find that the initial detention of the protected persons was legal and, therefore, it was not necessary for it to distinguish between their initial detention and the legality of the continued detention.[1156] The Appeals Chamber thus rejects this argument.

(c) Conclusion

379.   The Appeals Chamber therefore dismisses Petković's sub-grounds of appeal 5.2.1.1, 5.2.1.3, 5.2.1.4, all in part, as far as they concern his defences to the detention of the HVO's Muslim members and military-aged Muslim men.

D.   **Conclusion**

380.   The Appeals Chamber thus rejects the Appellants' challenges that the chapeau requirements for the application of Article 2 of the Statute were not met. The Appeals Chamber is satisfied that the Trial Chamber did not err in applying Article 2 for the purposes of convicting the Appellants for wilful killing, inhuman treatment, the extensive destruction and appropriation of property not justified by military necessity and carried out unlawfully and wantonly, unlawful deportation, the unlawful transfer of civilians, and the unlawful confinement of civilians as "grave breaches" under the Geneva Conventions.

381.   Further, the Appeals Chamber vacates the Appellants' convictions under Counts 19 and 22, with respect to Vareš Municipality, for extensive destruction and appropriation of property not justified by military necessity and carried out unlawfully and wantonly as grave breaches of the Geneva Conventions. However, it declines to enter convictions under Count 20, with respect to Vareš Municipality, for wanton destruction of property and plunder as violations of the laws or customs of war. Finally, Stojić's, Praljak's, Petković's, and Ćorić's challenges to the Trial Chamber's findings on the protected status of persons under the Geneva Conventions have failed. **[page 159]**

[1148]   See Trial Judgement, Vol. 2, para. 895.
[1149]   Trial Judgement, Vol. 3, paras 1012, 1014, 1025, 1030, 1032, 1035-1036, 1039, 1041, 1050, 1054, 1057-1058.
[1150]   Trial Judgement, Vol. 3, para. 103.
[1151]   Trial Judgement, Vol. 3, para. 1007.
[1152]   Trial Judgement, Vol. 3, paras 1011, 1014, 1020, 1030.
[1153]   Trial Judgement, Vol. 3, para. 1035.
[1154]   See, *e.g.,* Trial Judgement, Vol. 3, paras 1012, 1014, 1021, 1025, 1030, 1032, 1035-1036, 1038-1039, 1041, 1050, 1054, 1057-1058.
[1155]   Petković refers to several exhibits in support of his argument that the Trial Chamber ignored all evidence that proves that HVO Muslims were disarmed and isolated for justified security reasons. Petković's Appeal Brief, para. 193. However, the Appeals Chamber considers that Petković has failed to show that the Trial Chamber ignored the evidence or that it could have affected the Trial Chamber's finding regarding the illegality of detaining the HVO Muslims based on security risks that are attached to the group rather than to the individual.
[1156]   The Appeals Chamber recalls that an initially *lawful* internment can become unlawful if the detaining party does not respect the basic procedural rights of the detained persons and does not establish an appropriate court or administrative board as prescribed in Article 43 of Geneva Convention IV. See *Čelebići* Appeal Judgement, paras 320, 328.

382.   Based on the foregoing, the Appeals Chamber dismisses: (1) Prlić's grounds of appeal 19 and 20; (2) Stojić's grounds of appeal 42, 54, and 55; (3) Praljak's grounds of appeal 1, 2, 3, and 4; (4) Petković's sub-grounds of appeal 5.2.1, 7.1, and 7.2; (5) Ćorić's grounds of appeal 3, 4, and 5; and (6) Pušić's ground of appeal 7 in part. **[page 160]**

VII.   CHALLENGES TO THE UNDERLYING CRIMES

A.   Introduction

383.   The Trial Chamber found that members of the JCE, including the Appellants, implemented an entire system for deporting the Muslim population of the HR H-B, a system which consisted of the commission of crimes by HVO forces from January 1993 to April 1994, namely: the removal and detention of civilians, murders and the destruction of property during attacks, mistreatment and devastation during evictions, mistreatment in and poor conditions of confinement, the widespread, nearly systematic use of detainees for front line labour or as human shields, murders and mistreatment related to this labour and these human shields, and the removal of detainees and their families outside of the territory of the HZ(R) H-B following their release.[1157] Prlić, Stojić, Praljak, Petković, Ćorić, and Pušić were convicted of grave breaches of the Geneva Conventions under Article 2 of the Statute, violations of the laws or customs of war under Article 3 of the Statute, and crimes against humanity under Article 5 of the Statute, committed in various municipalities and detention centres by virtue of their participation in the JCE.[1158]

384.   The Parties, including the Prosecution, present challenges to the Trial Chamber's findings regarding the underlying crimes of the JCE. These challenges relate to: (1) the Appellants' *mens rea* for crimes against humanity; (2) the Trial Chamber's alleged failure to enter convictions for wanton destruction of cities, towns, or villages, or devastation not justified by military necessity; (3) the HVO's attacks of 18 January 1993 in Gornji Vakuf Municipality and subsequent criminal events; (4) the arrest, detention, and removal of Muslims in Prozor Municipality in July and August 1993; and (5) crimes committed in Mostar Municipality, in particular relating to the siege of East Mostar.

B.   *Mens rea* for Crimes Against Humanity (Stojić's Ground 26, Praljak's Ground 48, and Petković's Sub-grounds 4.1 and 4.4 both in part)

385.   The Trial Chamber concluded that certain acts of violence committed on the territory of eight BiH municipalities from May 1992 until April 1994 constituted a widespread and systematic attack against a civilian population.[1159] It further concluded that the perpetrators of these acts – "the armed and political forces of the HVO" – had knowledge of the attack and were aware that their **[page 161]** acts were part of this attack.[1160] Stojić, Praljak, and Petković were subsequently convicted of, *inter alia,* crimes against humanity by virtue of their participation in the JCE.[1161]

1.   Arguments of the Parties

386.   Stojić, Praljak, and Petković submit that the Trial Chamber erred when it convicted them of crimes against humanity without making a finding that they knew or intended that their acts would form part of a

---

[1157]   Trial Judgement, Vol. 1, para. 26, Vol. 4, paras 65-66. See also Trial Judgement, Vol. 4, para. 68.
[1158]   Trial Judgement, Vol. 4, Disposition, pp. 430-431. See Trial Judgement, Vol. 4, paras 67-68, 278-279 (Prlić), 431-432 (Stojić), 630-631 (Praljak), 820-821 (Petković), 1006-1007 (Ćorić), 1211-1212 (Pušić).
[1159]   Trial Judgement, Vol. 3, paras 646-648. See Trial Judgement, Vol. 3, paras 638-645.
[1160]   Trial Judgement, Vol. 3, para. 651.
[1161]   Trial Judgement, Vol. 4, Disposition, pp. 430-431. See Trial Judgement, Vol. 4, paras 67-68, 431-432 (Stojić), 630-631 (Praljak), 820-821 (Petković).

647

widespread and systematic attack on a civilian population.[1162] Stojić, Praljak, and Petković therefore request that the Appeals Chamber overturn their convictions under the relevant counts.[1163]

387.   The Prosecution responds that Stojić's, Praljak's, and Petković's knowledge that HVO crimes formed part of a widespread and systematic attack was implicit in the Trial Chamber's findings that they shared and contributed to the CCP.[1164] Additionally, the Prosecution claims that in light of the finding that direct perpetrators within the HVO were aware that their crimes formed part of such an attack, the Trial Chamber was satisfied that Stojić, Praljak, and Petković, given their positions, also had the requisite knowledge.[1165]

[page 162]

388.   Praljak replies that the Prosecution attempts to fill the gaps by drawing its own conclusions from the Trial Chamber's findings and that the requisite *mens rea* cannot be implicit but must be established unequivocally.[1166]

2. Analysis

389.   The Appeals Chamber recalls that in order to satisfy the *mens rea* of crimes against humanity, the accused must have *knowledge* that there is an attack on the civilian population and that his act is part thereof.[1167]

390.   The Appeals Chamber observes that the Trial Chamber did not make express findings that the Appellants fulfilled this requirement.[1168] When reaching its conclusion that the chapeau requirements of Article 5 of the Statute were satisfied,[1169] the Trial Chamber found that, in all the municipalities, evictions were accompanied in many instances by episodes of violence that were similar in nature and directed against Muslims, including, *inter alia,* the burning of their houses, the destruction of institutions dedicated to religion, and the confiscation of property belonging to Muslims.[1170] The Trial Chamber held that such acts were carried out in an organised fashion by "the armed and political forces of the HVO" and constituted the

---

[1162]   Stojić's Appeal Brief, heading before para. 228, paras 229-230; Praljak's Appeal Brief, paras 537-538; Petković's Appeal Brief, paras 134, 136, 138. See Stojić's Appeal Brief, para. 228; Praljak's Appeal Brief, para. 535; Praljak's Reply Brief, para. 54; Petković's Appeal Brief, para. 90(i). Stojić argues that the Trial Chamber only determined whether the *mens rea* chapeau requirement of Article 5 of the Statute was satisfied with respect to direct perpetrators, and only considered his knowledge that there was an international armed conflict. Stojić's Appeal Brief, para. 229. Praljak argues that the Trial Chamber merely found that the direct perpetrators of acts constituting the widespread and systematic attack on the Muslim civilian population of HZ H-B had knowledge of the attack and were aware that their acts were part of this attack. Praljak's Appeal Brief, para. 537, referring to Trial Judgement, Vol. 3, para. 651. Petković submits that the Trial Chamber's error constituted a failure to render a reasoned opinion. Petković's Appeal Brief, paras 90(i), 134, 136. Further, Petković argues that the Trial Chamber "failed to consider or, if it did, to exclude through a reasoned opinion, evidence that contradicted its findings that [he] possessed the requisite *mens rea*", thereby rendering such findings unreasonable. Petković's Appeal Brief, para. 135. See Petković's Appeal Brief, para. 136.
[1163]   Stojić's Appeal Brief, para. 230; Praljak's Appeal Brief, para. 538; Petković's Appeal Brief, paras 138-139. See Praljak's Reply Brief, para. 55. Specifically, Stojić requests that the Appeals Chamber overturn his convictions under Counts 1, 2, 6, 8, 10, and 15. Stojić's Appeal Brief, para. 230. In addition to these counts, Praljak also requests to be acquitted of Counts 3 and 12. Praljak's Appeal Brief, para. 538.
[1164]   Prosecution's Response Brief (Stojić), paras 191-192; Prosecution's Response Brief (Praljak), paras 100, 102; Prosecution's Response Brief (Petković), paras 70-71.
[1165]   Prosecution's Response Brief (Stojić), paras 191, 193; Prosecution's Response Brief (Praljak), paras 101-102; Prosecution's Response Brief (Petković), paras 70, 72. With respect to Petković, the Prosecution argues that the Trial Judgement read as a whole supports this conclusion, notwithstanding his "self-serving testimony" denying such knowledge. Prosecution's Response Brief (Petković), para. 70.
[1166]   Praljak's Reply Brief, para. 54.
[1167]   *Popović et al.* Appeal Judgement, para. 570; *Kordić and Čerkez* Appeal Judgement, paras 99-100 and references cited therein.
[1168]   See Trial Judgement, Vol. 3, paras 630-654 ("Other General Requirements for the Application of Article 5 of the Statute: Widespread or Systematic Attack Directed Against a Civilian Population"), Vol. 4, paras 270-277 (summary of findings on Prlić's JCE I responsibility), 425-430 (summary of findings on Stojić's JCE I responsibility), 624-629 (summary of findings on Praljak's JCE I responsibility), 814-819 (summary of findings on Petković's JCE I responsibility), 1000-1005 (summary of findings on Ćorić's JCE I responsibility), 1202-1210 (summary of findings on Pušić's JCE I responsibility).'
[1169]   Trial Judgement, Vol. 3, para. 654.
[1170]   Trial Judgement, Vol. 3, paras 645-646. See also Trial Judgement, Vol. 3, paras 638-644, 648.

means used to implement the attack on the civilian population.[1171] The Trial Chamber also found that the direct perpetrators of the acts constituting the widespread and systematic attack on the Muslim civilian population of HZ H-B – who "belonged to the HVO" – had knowledge of the attack and were aware that their acts were part of this attack.[1172]

391.   When addressing the CCP, the Trial Chamber found that JCE members "implemented an entire system for deporting the Muslim population of the HR H-B" which involved the commission of numerous crimes, including those falling under Article 5 of the Statute.[1173] The Trial Chamber further found that in the vast majority of cases the crimes committed by the HVO were not random, **[page 163]** but followed a clear pattern of conduct.[1174] The Trial Chamber concluded that insofar as Stojić, Praljak, and Petković controlled the HVO and the Military Police, and contributed to their operations, they knew these crimes were being committed and intended that they be committed in furtherance of the CCP.[1175] Moreover, the Trial Chamber made numerous findings concerning the Appellants' awareness that the commission of crimes was pursuant to a plan and/or was of a widespread and systematic nature.[1176] Notably, it found that they knew of or contributed to the atmosphere of violence in which the HVO operations in various municipalities took place.[1177] In this respect, the Appeals Chamber also notes the Trial Chamber's findings that Stojić, Praljak, and Petković participated in the implementation of an ultimatum adopted by the HVO HZ-HB on 15 January 1993 envisaging, *inter alia,* the subordination of the ABiH to the HVO in Provinces 3, 8, and 10 within five days ("15 January 1993 Ultimatum"), which led to a "systematic and widespread attack in the Municipality of Gornji Vakuf".[1178]

392.   In light of the foregoing, the Appeals Chamber considers that the Trial Chamber was satisfied that Stojić, Praljak, and Petković knew that there was an attack on the civilian population and that their acts were part thereof, and as such had the requisite *mens rea* for crimes against humanity.[1179] The Appellants have not identified an error of law that invalidates the Trial Chamber's decision.[1180] Accordingly, Stojić's ground of appeal 26, Praljak's ground of appeal 48, and Petković's sub-grounds of appeal 4.1 and 4.4, in relevant part, are dismissed. **[page 164]**

[1171]   Trial Judgement, Vol. 3, para. 649. See Trial Judgement, Vol. 3, para. 646.

[1172]   Trial Judgement, Vol. 3, para. 651.

[1173]   Trial Judgement, Vol. 4, paras 66, 68 (specifically, it included the crimes against humanity of persecution (Count 1), murder (Count 2), deportation (Count 6), inhumane acts through forcible transfer (Count 8), imprisonment (Count 10), inhumane acts through conditions of confinement (Count 12), and other inhumane acts (Count 15)). See Trial Judgement, Vol. 3, paras 646-648. See also *infra,* para. 886.

[1174]   Trial Judgement, Vol. 4, para. 65.

[1175]   Trial Judgement, Vol. 4, paras 67, 426, 428-429, 624, 628, 814-818, 1232. The Appeals Chamber dismisses challenges to these findings elsewhere in the Judgement. See *infra,* paras 1806, 2083, 2468.

[1176]   See, *e.g.,* Trial Judgement, Vol. 4, paras 341, 347-348, 356-357, 362-363, 377-378 (Stojić), 561-562, 572-573, 586 (Praljak), 704, 708, 717, 732-735, 737-738, 757-758, 807-808 (Petković).

[1177]   Trial Judgement, Vol. 4, paras 439, 445-446 (Stojić), 633-638 (Praljak), 734-735, 827, 830, 834, 837, 840, 844 (Petković). See also Trial Judgement, Vol. 4, para. 72.

[1178]   Trial Judgement, Vol. 4, para. 142 (also finding that the plan for an attack on several villages in Prozor Municipality was the result of the implementation of an ultimatum adopted by the HVO HZ H-B on 3 April 1993 and published on 4 April 1993 ("4 April 1993 Ultimatum"), which was identical to the one the HVO issued in January 1993). See, *e.g.,* Trial Judgement, Vol. 4, paras 125-128, 146, 304, 475, 553, 556, 685, 702-704. See also, *e.g.,* Trial Judgement, Vol. 4, para. 138 (regarding the implementation of the 4 April 1993 Ultimatum); *infra,* paras 1579, 1588, 1824, 2177, 2210.

[1179]   *Cf. Šainović et al.* Appeal Judgement, para. 281. When submitting that the Trial Chamber "failed to consider or, if it did, to exclude through a reasoned opinion, evidence that contradicted its findings that [he] possessed the requisite *mens rea*", Petković points particularly to his own testimony to demonstrate that he was unaware of crimes being committed on a widespread or systematic basis. See Petković's Appeal Brief, para. 135, referring to Milivoj Petković, T. 50698 (9 Mar 2010). The Appeals Chamber notes that the Trial Chamber explicitly considered Petković's testimony and stated that it did not accept it on occasions when he sought to limit his responsibility in respect of certain allegations, as it found it to be hardly credible. See Trial Judgement, Vol. 1, para. 399. The Appeals Chamber recalls that trial chambers are best placed to assess the evidence and that they have broad discretion in doing so. *Stanišić and Župljanin* Appeal Judgement, para. 654 and references cited therein. Since Petković is merely asserting that the Trial Chamber failed to give sufficient weight to evidence without showing that no reasonable trier of fact could have reached the same conclusion as the Trial Chamber did, his argument is dismissed.

[1180]   See, *e.g., Kvočka et al.* Appeal Judgement, para. 25.

C. Alleged Errors Relating to Wanton Destruction Of Cities, Towns Or Villages, or Devastation Not Justifed by Military Necessity (Prosecution's Ground 3 in part, Praljak's Ground 23, and Petković's Sub-ground 5.2.2.4 in part)

1. Failure to enter convictions

393.   The Trial Chamber made findings regarding the destruction or damage of: (1) Muslim property in Prozor Municipality between May/June and July 1993;[1181] (2) Muslim property in Gornji Vakuf Municipality on 18 January 1993;[1182] (3) the Old Bridge in Mostar on 8-9 November 1993;[1183] and (4) ten mosques in East Mostar between June and December 1993 (collectively, "Four Groups of Incidents").[1184] In the "Legal Findings of the Chamber" section of the Trial Judgement, the Trial Chamber found that these incidents constituted the crime of wanton destruction of cities, towns or villages, or devastation not justified by military necessity as a violation of the laws or customs of war under Article 3 of the Statute (Count 20),[1185] but not the crime of extensive destruction of property not justified by military necessity and carried out unlawfully and wantonly as a grave breach of the Geneva Conventions under Article 2 of the Statute (Count 19), since these properties were not on an occupied territory when they were destroyed and, therefore, did not have the status of protected property within the meaning of Geneva Convention IV.[1186] Subsequently, in the section of the Trial Judgement devoted to the law on cumulative convictions, the Trial Chamber determined that the crime of wanton destruction not justified by military necessity (Count 20) does not contain a materially distinct element from the crime of extensive destruction of property not justified by military necessity (Count 19), and consequently held that cumulative convictions based on the same criminal conduct for Count 20 and Count 19 are not possible and that only a single conviction under Count 19 may be entered.[1187] However, when applying the law on cumulative convictions to the legal findings on wanton destruction not justified by military necessity (Count 20) and extensive destruction of property not justified by military necessity (Count 19), the Trial Chamber convicted Prlić, Stojić, Praljak, Petković, Ćorić, and Pušić under Count 19 only, thereby entering convictions for all incidents of criminal property destruction *except* the Four Groups of Incidents. It did not enter any convictions under Count 20, including for the Four Groups of Incidents.[1188] The Trial Chamber recalled that **[page 165]** Pušić was not prosecuted for the crimes committed in Gornji Vakuf Municipality in January 1993.[1189]

(a) Arguments of the Parties

394.   The Prosecution submits that the Trial Chamber erred in failing to convict Prlić, Stojić, Praljak, Petković, Ćorić, and Pušić with regard to the Four Groups of Incidents, for wanton destruction of property as a war crime under Count 20 (Article 3 of the Statute), with the exception of Pušić for the destruction of Muslim property in Gornji Vakuf Municipality on 18 January 1993.[1190] The Prosecution argues that the Trial Chamber declined to convict on the basis of the principle against cumulative convictions and because it "incorrectly assumed" that it had convicted the Appellants for these crimes for extensive destruction of property as a grave breach under Count 19 (Article 2 of the Statute).[1191] It submits that the convictions

---

[1181]   Trial Judgement, Vol. 2, paras 95-97, 102-105, Vol. 3, para. 1566.
[1182]   Trial Judgement, Vol. 2, paras 367-368, 373, 379, 387, Vol. 3, para. 1570.
[1183]   Trial Judgement, Vol. 2, para. 1366, Vol. 3, para. 1587.
[1184]   Trial Judgement, Vol. 2, para. 1377, Vol. 3, para. 1580.
[1185]   Trial Judgement, Vol. 3, paras 1566, 1570, 1580, 1587.
[1186]   Trial Judgement, Vol. 3, paras 1530, 1534, 1545. See Trial Judgement, Vol. 3, para. 589.
[1187]   Trial Judgement, Vol. 4, paras 1254, 1264-1266.
[1188]   Trial Judgement, Vol. 4, Disposition, pp. 430-431.
[1189]   Trial Judgement, Vol. 4, fn. 178.
[1190]   Prosecution's Appeal Brief, paras 325-326, 328-330; Prosecution's Reply Brief, para. 132; Appeal Hearing, AT. 766-768, 771, 851-852 (28 Mar 2017).
[1191]   Prosecution's Appeal Brief, para. 328. See Prosecution's Appeal Brief, paras 327, 329; Appeal Hearing, AT. 766-768, 771 (28 Mar 2017).

entered therefore do not fully reflect the criminality of the Appellants and that the Appeals Chamber should enter convictions against them under Count 20 for the Four Groups of Incidents.[1192]

395.   Prlić responds that the Trial Chamber *may* have erred in its application of the principle against cumulative convictions.[1193] Stojić concedes that the Trial Chamber erred.[1194] Prlić, Stojić, Praljak, Ćorić, and Pušić dispute, however, the findings upon which the Prosecution relies for a conviction under Count 20.[1195] Petković and Ćorić argue that the Prosecution's appeal lacks merit as the Trial Chamber did in fact convict them for wanton destruction of property under Article 3 of the Statute (Count 20) for all or some of the Four Groups of Incidents.[1196] Prlić claims that the Trial Chamber already mistakenly convicted him for extensive destruction of property under **[page 166]** Article 2 of the Statute (Count 19) despite its finding that the Four Groups of Incidents did not constitute this crime.[1197]

396.   Additionally, Stojić and Ćorić contend that any alleged error and/or consequence thereof in the application of the principle against cumulative convictions is immaterial as it would have no impact on the verdict.[1198] Further, Stojić argues that, although the principle against cumulative convictions allows for the entering of a conviction under Count 20 in addition to his conviction under Count 21 (destruction or wilful damage done to institutions dedicated to religion or education as a violation of the laws or customs of war under Article 3 of the Statute) for the destruction of the ten mosques in Mostar, doing so would not promote the interests of justice.[1199] The Appellants request that the Appeals Chamber dismiss the Prosecution's ground of appeal 3.[1200]

397.   The Prosecution replies that the Trial Judgement contradicts: (1) Petković's and Ćorić's submissions to the extent that they argue that they were convicted under Count 20; and (2) Prlić's argument that he was convicted for the Four Groups of Incidents under Count 19.[1201]

(b) Analysis

398.   The Appeals Chamber observes that the Trial Chamber found that the crimes charged in Count 20 fell within the framework of the CCP.[1202] It also found that, insofar as the Appellants committed crimes with the aim of furthering the CCP, they were responsible for all crimes that were part of the CCP.[1203] Therefore, it is clear that the Trial Chamber considered that the Appellants should be found guilty of, *inter alia,* the war crime of wanton destruction of property not justified by military necessity (Count 20) for the Four Groups of Incidents, with the exception of Pušić who was not found guilty for the destruction of Muslim property in

---

[1192]   Prosecution's Appeal Brief, paras 329-330; Prosecution's Reply Brief, paras 137, 152-153; Appeal Hearing, AT. 766, 768, 771, 851-852 (28 Mar 2017). The Prosecution submits, however, that to the extent that the Trial Chamber already considered the conduct underlying convictions under Count 20, their sentences need not be increased. Prosecution's Reply Brief, para. 153.
[1193]   Prlić's Response Brief, para. 184.
[1194]   Stojić's Response Brief, paras 145-146; Appeal Hearing, AT. 800 (28 Mar 2017).
[1195]   Prlić's Response Brief, paras 171-173, 184; Stojić's Response Brief, para. 147; Ćorić's Response Brief, para. 95. See Praljak's Response Brief, paras 145, 149-151, 153-154, 156-158; Pušić's Response Brief, para. 28. See also Prlić's Response Brief, paras 174-183; Stojić's Response Brief, headings before paras 149, 154, paras 149-163; Appeal Hearing, AT. 800 (28 Mar 2017). Stojić argues that the fact that he first addressed these errors in his response brief does not prevent the Appeals Chamber from taking them into account when assessing the Prosecution's ground of appeal. Stojić's Response Brief, para. 147, heading before para. 164, paras 164-167.
[1196]   Petković's Response Brief, paras 109-110; Ćorić's Response Brief, para. 93; Appeal Hearing, AT. 822-823 (28 Mar 2017). See also Petković's Appeal Brief, paras 277-278.
[1197]   Prlić's Response Brief, para. 173. See Prlić's Response Brief, para. 170.
[1198]   Stojić's Response Brief, para. 146; Ćorić's Response Brief, paras 94, 96. See also Stojić's Response Brief, paras 148, 170-178; Ćorić's Response Brief, para. 93; Pušić's Response Brief, para. 28.
[1199]   Stojić's Response Brief, paras 147, 169. See also Stojić's Response Brief, para. 175.
[1200]   Stojić's Response Brief, para. 178; Praljak's Response Brief, para. 159; Petković's Response Brief, para. 110; Ćorić's Response Brief, para. 96. See also Prlić's Response Brief, para. 184; Pušić's Response Brief, para. 28.
[1201]   Prosecution's Reply Brief, para. 133.
[1202]   Trial Judgement, Vol. 4, paras. 68. See also Trial Judgement, Vol. 4, para. 66 (finding that the JCE members implemented an entire system for the commission of crimes including the destruction of property during attacks).
[1203]   Trial Judgement, Vol. 4, paras 279 (Prlić), 432 (Stojić), 631 (Praljak), 821 (Petković), 1007 (Ćorić), 1212 (Pušić). See also Trial Judgement, Vol. 4, paras 66-68.

Gornji Vakuf Municipality on 18 January 1993.[1204] As mentioned above, although the Trial Chamber found that the Four Groups of Incidents constituted wanton destruction of property not justified by military necessity under Article 3 of the Statute (Count 20),[1205] the Trial Chamber found that they did not constitute **[page 167]** extensive destruction of property not justified by military necessity as a grave breach of the Geneva Conventions under Article 2 of the Statute (Count 19), as the property that was destroyed was not "protected" within the meaning of Geneva Convention IV.[1206] It is therefore clear that the Trial Chamber did not intend to convict the Appellants under Count 19 for the Four Groups of Incidents.[1207]

399. When entering convictions against the Appellants, the Trial Chamber applied the law on cumulative convictions, overlooking its previous finding that the Four Groups of Incidents did not fall under Article 2 of the Statute (Count 19).[1208] Consequently, the Trial Chamber did not enter convictions for the Four Groups of Incidents under either Count 19 or Count 20. The Appeals Chamber recalls that a trial chamber is bound to enter convictions for all distinct crimes which have been proven in order to fully reflect the criminality of the convicted person.[1209] Thus, the Appeals Chamber considers that the Trial Chamber erred by failing to enter convictions for wanton destruction of property not justified by military necessity under Article 3 of the Statute (Count 20) for the Four Groups of Incidents.

400. The Appeals Chamber recalls that pursuant to paragraph 5 of the Practice Direction on Formal Requirements, if an appellant relies on a ground of appeal to reverse an acquittal, the respondent may support the acquittal on additional grounds of appeal in the respondent's brief. The Appeals Chamber notes that some of the Appellants advance submissions in their respective responses challenging the legal and factual findings underpinning the Trial Chamber's finding that they committed wanton destruction of property under Article 3 of the Statute (Count 20) in the municipalities of Prozor, Mostar, and Gornji Vakuf. Moreover, the submissions concerning the Old Bridge of Mostar, in particular, are closely linked to those advanced separately by Praljak in his ground of appeal 23 and Petković in his sub-ground of appeal 5.2.2.4, in part.[1210] All submissions concerning the Old Bridge will be addressed together. The Appeals Chamber will now address: (1) general submissions concerning the Four Groups of Incidents and submissions related to Muslim property in Prozor Municipality and the ten mosques in Mostar Municipality; and (2) submissions concerning the Old Bridge.[1211] **[page 168]**

2. Challenges to the legal and factual findings upon which the wanton destruction findings were based

(a) General submissions concerning the Four Groups of Incidents and submissions related to Muslim property in Prozor Municipality and the ten mosques in Mostar Municipality

401. The Trial Chamber found that Prlić, Stojić, Praljak, Petković, Ćorić, and Pušić should be found guilty, under Count 20 (wanton destruction of property under Article 3 of the Statute), for the Four Groups of Incidents, with the exception of Pušić who was not found guilty for the destruction of Muslim property in Gornji Vakuf Municipality on 18 January 1993, but failed to enter convictions for Count 20.[1212]

[1204]   See Trial Judgement, Vol. 4, fn. 178 (recalling that Pušić was not prosecuted for the crimes committed in Gornji Vakuf Municipality in January 1993).

[1205]   Trial Judgement, Vol. 3, paras 1566 (Prozor Municipality), 1570 (Gornji Vakuf Municipality), 1580 (mosques in East Mostar), 1587 (Old Bridge in Mostar).

[1206]   Trial Judgement, Vol. 3, paras 1530, 1534, 1545. See also Trial Judgement, Vol. 3, para. 589.

[1207]   Prlić's submission to the contrary is therefore dismissed. See *supra*, para. 395.

[1208]   Trial Judgement, Vol. 4, Disposition, pp. 430-431.

[1209]   *Popović et al.* Appeal Judgement, para. 538; *Karemera and Ngirumpatse* Appeal Judgement, para. 711; *Gatete* Appeal Judgement, para. 261.

[1210]   See Praljak's Appeal Brief, paras 280-296; Petković's Appeal Brief, paras 277-278.

[1211]   The submissions specifically related to the wanton destruction of property in Gornji Vakuf Municipality are addressed further below. See *infra*, paras 444-453.

[1212]   See Trial Judgement, Vol. 4, fn. 178 (recalling that Pušie was not prosecuted for the crimes committed in Gornji Vakuf Municipality in January 1993), paras 68 (finding that the crimes charged in Count 20 fell within the framework of the CCP), 279, 432, 631, 821, 1007, 1212 (finding that insofar as Prlić, Stojić, Praljak, Petković, Ćorić, and Pušić committed crimes with the aim of furthering the CCP, they were responsible for all crimes that were part of the CCP). See also *supra*, paras 393, 398.

402.   Prlić and Ćorić contest their responsibility for the Four Groups of Incidents on the basis that the Trial Chamber erred in its findings as to their authority or "effective control" over HVO forces.[1213] Ćorić specifically contests his responsibility under JCE liability.[1214] Likewise, Praljak submits that the Trial Chamber did not find him liable for the destruction of property in Prozor Municipality, considering the lack of clarity of its findings on the CCP.[1215] Prlić submits that the Trial Chamber erred in its evidentiary assessments of his involvement in property destruction in Prozor and Mostar.[1216] Praljak further submits that the Trial Chamber did not establish the date of the destruction of mosques in East Mostar and erroneously concluded that the HVO destroyed them.[1217] Ćorić also contends that the Trial Chamber's findings ignore the hostilities between the HVO and ABiH.[1218]

403.   The Prosecution replies that Ćorić's arguments relate to superior responsibility and are irrelevant.[1219] Further, it contends that Praljak and Ćorić misunderstand the Trial Judgement and JCE liability, respectively.[1220] The Prosecution also argues that Ćorić fails to support or develop the contention that the Trial Chamber ignored the hostilities between the HVO and ABiH.[1221] **[page 169]**

404.   With respect to Prlić's and Ćorić's challenges regarding their authority or "effective control" over HVO forces, and insofar as these submissions appear to be premised on the notion of superior responsibility, the Appeals Chamber notes that the Trial Chamber did not find them responsible as superiors for wanton destruction of property with regard to any of the Four Groups of Incidents.[1222] Their submissions are therefore dismissed. As to the other arguments advanced by Prlić, Praljak, and Ćorić, the Appeals Chamber observes that they are based on references to other grounds of appeals, which the Appeals Chamber dismisses elsewhere.[1223] Their arguments are therefore rejected.

(b) The Old Bridge of Mostar

405.   The Trial Chamber found that throughout the day on 8 November 1993, an HVO tank fired at the Old Bridge of Mostar.[1224] The Trial Chamber found that the Old Bridge was destroyed by the evening of 8 November 1993 as it was unusable and on the verge of collapse.[1225] The Old Bridge collapsed the next morning after the tank shelling resumed and also possibly due to explosives set off by a detonating cord on the left bank of the Neretva River.[1226]

[1213]   Prlić's Response Brief, paras 171-172; Ćorić's Response Brief, para. 95.
[1214]   Ćorić's Response Brief, para. 95 & fn. 184, referring to his ground of appeal 7 regarding JCE I responsibility.
[1215]   Praljak's Response Brief, para. 145.
[1216]   Prlić's Response Brief, paras 182-183.
[1217]   Praljak's Response Brief, paras 156-158.
[1218]   Ćorić's Response Brief, para. 95.
[1219]   Prosecution's Reply Brief, para. 134.
[1220]   Prosecution's Reply Brief, paras 134, 136.
[1221]   Prosecution's Reply Brief, para. 135.
[1222]   See Trial Judgement, Vol. 4, paras 1234, 1251 (finding Ćorić guilty under Article 7(3) of the Statute only for crimes that occurred in Prozor Municipality in October 1992), Disposition, pp. 430-431. Insofar as Prlić's and Ćorić's submissions could also be interpreted to impugn the Trial Chamber's findings as to their respective contributions to the JCE, the Appeals Chamber considers that they are unsubstantiated except by cross-reference to grounds of appeal dismissed elsewhere. See *infra*, paras 1400, 2595.
[1223]   See Praljak's Response Brief, paras 145, 156-158 & fns 351, 353, 373-374, 379-380, referring to his grounds of appeal 7, 24, and 49, and alleging that the Trial Chamber: (1) was not clear in its finding that he is held responsible for all crimes forming part of the CCP; (2) failed to establish precisely the scope of the CCP; and (3) did not establish the exact date of the destruction of mosques in East Mostar and erroneously concluded that the HVO destroyed them. See *supra*, paras 211, 218, 402; *infra*, paras 569, 814, 824. See, however, *infra*, paras 2002-2003. See Prlić's Response Brief, paras 180-183 & fns 369, 377, referring to or relying upon grounds of appeal 4, 6, and 16 and submitting that the Trial Chamber erroneously: (1) relied upon, *inter alia*, uncorroborated hearsay and a mischaracterisation of evidence with respect to his intent to commit crimes in Prozor; and (2) ignored evidence demonstrating that he did not encourage the destruction of property in Mostar. See *supra*, paras 211, 218, 402; *infra*, para. 1400. See Ćorić's Response Brief, para. 95 & fn. 184, referring to his ground of appeal 7 and: (1) contesting his responsibility under JCE liability; and (2) contending that the Trial Chamber's findings ignore and fail to analyse the battles between the HVO and ABiH and the number of casualties on the HVO side. See *supra*, para. 402; *infra*, para. 2595.
[1224]   Trial Judgement, Vol. 2, paras 1315, 1366. See also Trial Judgement, Vol. 2, paras 1311-1313, 1343, 1345, Vol. 3, para. 1581.
[1225]   Trial Judgement, Vol. 2, paras 1318, 1345, 1366. See also Trial Judgement, Vol. 2, para. 1343, Vol. 3, para. 1581.
[1226]   Trial Judgement, Vol. 2, paras 1326, 1345, 1366. See also Trial Judgement, Vol. 2, paras 670, 1321, 1343.

406. The Trial Chamber found that the Old Bridge, real property normally used by civilians, was used by both the ABiH and the inhabitants of the right and left banks of the Neretva between May and November 1993.[1227] The Trial Chamber further found that the Old Bridge was essential to the ABiH for combat activities of its units on the front line, for evacuations, and for the sending of troops, food, and materiel, and that it was indeed utilised to this end.[1228] It found that the Old Bridge was a military target at the time of the attack given the HVO's military interest in destroying the **[page 170]** Old Bridge which cut off practically all possibilities for the ABiH to continue its supply operations.[1229] However, the Trial Chamber also found that the destruction of the Old Bridge put the residents of Donja Mahala in "virtually total isolation", resulting in a serious deterioration of the humanitarian situation for the population living there, and had a "very significant psychological impact" on the Muslim population of Mostar.[1230] The HVO's destruction of the Kamenica Bridge – a makeshift bridge that the ABiH constructed – a few days after the destruction of the Old Bridge definitively cut off all access across the Neretva River in Mostar.[1231] The Trial Chamber therefore found that the impact of the destruction of the Old Bridge on the Muslim civilian population of Mostar was disproportionate to the concrete and direct military advantage expected.[1232] It further found that the "destruction of the Old Bridge [...] was extensive", and that it was intended by the HVO command, thereby sapping the morale of the Muslim population.[1233] The Trial Chamber therefore concluded that by destroying the Old Bridge, the HVO committed the crime of wanton destruction of cities, towns or villages, or devastation not justified by military necessity, a violation of the laws or customs of war and a crime recognised by Article 3 of the Statute.[1234]

(i) Arguments of the Parties

407. Stojić submits that the Trial Chamber erred in law in finding that the destruction of the Old Bridge was disproportionate.[1235] With respect to the Trial Chamber's finding that the Old Bridge's destruction placed the civilian population in isolation, Stojić contends that it erroneously assessed the actual harm sustained after the subsequent destruction of the Kamenica Bridge, rather than the reasonably anticipated harm of the destruction of the Old Bridge.[1236] Further, he submits that the Trial Chamber erred in basing its finding that the destruction was disproportionate entirely on indirect effects, particularly the long-term harm through isolation and the psychological impact on the civilian population.[1237] More to this point, he submits that the Trial Chamber failed to analyse the harm caused by isolation and the psychological impact in terms of tangible injuries.[1238] Stojić also argues that the Trial Chamber should have placed more weight on its findings regarding the Old Bridge's importance to the ABiH and properly assessed the HVO's lack of alternative means to achieve the military objective of cutting off ABiH supply **[page 171]** lines.[1239] Finally, he alleges that the Trial Chamber failed to explain why the expected harm to civilians was excessive given the anticipated military advantage.[1240] Stojić submits in response to the Prosecution's request for additional convictions that the Appeals Chamber should therefore refrain from doing so in relation to the destruction of the Old Bridge.[1241]

[1227] Trial Judgement, Vol. 3, para. 1582. See Trial Judgement, Vol. 2, paras 1284-1293.
[1228] Trial Judgement, Vol. 3, para. 1582. See Trial Judgement, Vol. 2, para. 1290.
[1229] Trial Judgement, Vol. 3, para. 1582. See Trial Judgement, Vol. 2, paras 1354, 1357.
[1230] Trial Judgement, Vol. 3, para. 1583. See Trial Judgement, Vol. 2, paras 1354, 1356-1357.
[1231] Trial Judgement, Vol. 3, para. 1583. See Trial Judgement, Vol. 2, para. 1355.
[1232] Trial Judgement, Vol. 3, para. 1584.
[1233] Trial Judgement, Vol. 3, para. 1585-1586.
[1234] Trial Judgement, Vol. 3, para. 1587.
[1235] Stojić's Response Brief, heading before para. 154, paras 154, 156, 163. See Stojić's Response Brief, para. 161. Stojić also argues that no reasonable chamber could have found that the destruction of the Old Bridge was disproportionate. Stojić's Response Brief, para. 162.
[1236] Stojić's Response Brief, paras 154, 158. See also Stojić's Response Brief, paras 156, 162.
[1237] Stojić's Response Brief, para. 157. See Stojić's Response Brief, paras 154, 156, 159.
[1238] Stojić's Response Brief, paras 158-159.
[1239] Stojić's Response Brief, paras 154, 160-161. See also Stojić's Response Brief, paras 156, 162.
[1240] Stojić's Response Brief, para. 162. See also Stojić's Response Brief, para. 156.
[1241] Stojić's Response Brief, para. 163. See *supra*, para. 394.

408.   Praljak submits that the Trial Chamber erred in its conclusions pertaining to the Old Bridge, notably by finding that HVO forces were responsible for its destruction and in its analysis relating to the protection of cultural property and the principle of proportionality, and requests that the Appeals Chamber reverse his conviction under Count 1 (persecution as a crime against humanity).[1242] Petković submits that the Trial Chamber erred in law and fact in this regard, notably in relation to the elements of the crime of wanton destruction of property not justified by military necessity and in its proportionality analysis.[1243]

409.   The Prosecution replies that Stojić fails to show that the Trial Chamber erred in concluding that the destruction of the Old Bridge was wanton.[1244] The Prosecution avers that the isolation of the population of Donja Mahala was the immediate effect of the destruction of the Old Bridge.[1245] It further submits that the Trial Chamber appropriately considered the psychological harm as well as the physical impact caused by isolation as these effects were not mere incidental by-products of an attack on a military objective, but were the primary aim of the HVO as part of its campaign of terror against the civilian population.[1246] The Prosecution also argues that Stojić fails to show that the Trial Chamber did not give appropriate weight to the anticipated military advantage of the Old Bridge's destruction.[1247]

410.   The Prosecution rejects Praljak's and Petković's arguments and submits that the Trial Chamber properly concluded that the destruction of the Old Bridge amounted to the crime of wanton destruction not justified by military necessity.[1248] **[page 172]**

(ii) Analysis

411.   Turning to Stojić's and the Prosecution's submissions on the Trial Chamber's finding that the destruction of the Old Bridge was disproportionate and wanton, the Appeals Chamber notes that the Trial Chamber found that the Old Bridge, real property normally used by civilians, was used by both the ABiH and the inhabitants of the right and left banks of the Neretva between May and November 1993.[1249] The Trial Chamber further found that "the armed forces of the HVO had a military interest in destroying this structure" and, consequently, found that "at the time of the attack, the Old Bridge was a military target".[1250] The Trial Chamber, however, also found that the destruction of the bridge put the residents of Donja Mahala in virtually total isolation and that it had a very significant psychological impact on the Muslim population of Mostar.[1251] It therefore held that:

> [T]he damage to the civilian population was indisputable and substantial. It therefore holds by a majority, with Judge Antonetti dissenting, that the impact on the Muslim civilian population of Mostar was disproportionate to the concrete and direct military advantage expected by the destruction of the Old Bridge.[1252]

[1242]   Praljak's Appeal Brief, headings before paras 280, 283, 286, 290, paras 280, 283-296; Praljak's Response Brief, paras 153-154; Appeal Hearing, AT. 378 (22 Mar 2017).
[1243]   Petković's Appeal Brief, paras 277-278(i)-(iii).
[1244]   Prosecution's Reply Brief, paras 143, 145. See also Prosecution's Reply Brief, para. 151.
[1245]   Prosecution's Reply Brief, para. 148. The Prosecution argues that, in any case, the subsequent destruction of the Kamenica Bridge was harm reasonably anticipated by the HVO. Prosecution's Reply Brief, para. 149.
[1246]   Prosecution's Reply Brief, paras 147, 150. See Prosecution's Reply Brief, para. 144.
[1247]   Prosecution's Reply Brief, para. 146. See Prosecution's Reply Brief, para. 143.
[1248]   Prosecution's Response Brief (Praljak), paras 199-205, 207-210; Prosecution's Response Brief (Petković), paras 211-215. In response to the Appeals Chamber's request to discuss any impact an error regarding the Trial Chamber's legal findings on the destruction of the Old Bridge as a crime of wanton destruction would have on its findings that the destruction also constituted the crimes of persecution and unlawful infliction of terror on civilians, the Prosecution submits that the attack on the Old Bridge was unlawful because, although it was a lawful military target, it was not targeted for that reason. It argues that the bridge was instead destroyed as part of the HVO's protracted campaign of terror directed against the Muslims of Mostar. It further submits that the attack was retribution for the fall of Vareš to ABiH forces, and that because the Old Bridge was completely unusable and could be considered destroyed after the shelling attacks on 8 November 1993, it "no longer had any military value" and no military advantage was to be gained "by bringing about its complete obliteration and collapse" on the following day. On these bases, the Prosecution submits that its destruction was not justified by military necessity. Appeal Hearing, AT. 450-454 (22 Mar 2017). See Order for the Preparation of the Appeal Hearing, p. 5, para. 2.
[1249]   Trial Judgement, Vol. 3, para. 1582. See Trial Judgement, Vol. 2, paras 1284-1293.
[1250]   Trial Judgement, Vol: 3, para. 1582.
[1251]   Trial Judgement, Vol. 3, para. 1583.
[1252]   Trial Judgement, Vol. 3, para. 1584.

The Appeals Chamber recalls that the elements of wanton destruction not justified by military necessity, as a violation of the laws or customs of war, include, *inter alia,* the destruction of property that occurs on a large scale and that the destruction is not justified by military necessity.[1253] Since the Trial Chamber found that the Old Bridge was a military target at the time of the attack,[1254] and, thus, its destruction offered a definite military advantage,[1255] the Appeals Chamber, Judge Pocar dissenting, finds that it cannot be considered, in and of itself, as wanton destruction not justified by military necessity.[1256] Moreover, the Appeals Chamber, Judge Pocar dissenting, notes that when outlining the damage caused to the civilian population in its determination of whether the crime of wanton destruction had been committed, the Trial Chamber did not make any finding about other property being collaterally destroyed as a result of the attack **[page 173]** on the Old Bridge.[1257] Rather, in reaching its conclusion that the attack on the Old Bridge was disproportionate, the Trial Chamber found that the attack isolated the Muslim population in Mostar and caused a very significant psychological impact.[1258] Thus, in the absence of any destruction of property *not justified by military necessity* in the Trial Chamber's legal findings for Count 20, the Appeals Chamber, Judge Pocar dissenting, concludes that a requisite element of the crime was not satisfied. Accordingly, the Appeals Chamber, Judge Pocar dissenting, finds that the Trial Chamber erred in finding that the destruction of the Old Bridge of Mostar constituted the crime of wanton destruction not justified by military necessity as a violation of the laws or customs of war.[1259] As a result, the Appeals Chamber, Judge Pocar dissenting, dismisses the Prosecution's submissions in this regard. The Appeals Chamber declines to enter convictions on appeal for wanton destruction not justified by military necessity, as a violation of the laws or customs of war, of the Old Bridge in Mostar.

412.   In light of the preceding analysis and the Appeals Chamber's analysis, below, of its effects on the Trial Chamber's findings in relation to Count 1,[1260] the Appeals Chamber, Judge Pocar dissenting, considers that Praljak's and Petković's arguments are moot. **[page 174]**

3.   Conclusion on wanton destruction not justified by military necessity

413.   In sum, the Appeals Chamber agrees with the Prosecution's ground of appeal 3, in part, as it pertains to the Trial Chamber's failure to enter convictions under Count 20 against Prlić, Stojić, Praljak, Petković, Ćorić, and Pušić for the wanton destruction of property not justified by military necessity, as a violation of

---

[1253]   *Hadžihasanović and Kubura* Decision on Rule 98*bis*, fn. 53; *Kordić and Čerkez* Appeal Judgement, para. 74.

[1254]   Trial Judgement, Vol. 3, para. 1582.

[1255]   *Kordić and Čerkez* Appeal Judgement, para. 53. See also Trial Judgement, Vol. 2, paras 1357, 1365, Vol. 3, paras 1582, 1584.

[1256]   Cf. *Brđanin* Appeal Judgement, paras 337 ("Determining whether destruction occurred pursuant to military necessity involves a determination of what constitutes a military objective."), 341; *Kordić and Čerkez* Appeal Judgement, paras 54, 74.

[1257]   Trial Judgement, Vol. 3, paras 1583-1584. See Trial Judgement, Vol. 2, paras 1355-1357, 1365.

[1258]   See Trial Judgement, Vol. 2, paras 1355-1357, 1365, Vol. 3, paras 1583-1586. The Appeals Chamber observes that the Trial Chamber found that "the destruction of the Old Bridge by the HVO may have been justified by military necessity", and subsequently, having discussed the question of proportionality, did not enter a discrete finding that the destruction was not justified by military necessity. Trial Judgement, Vol. 3, para. 1584. See also Trial Judgement, Vol. 3, para. 1587.

[1259]   With regard to the Prosecution's submission that the attack on the Old Bridge was unlawful because, although it was a lawful military target, it was not targeted for that reason, and its argument that the bridge was instead destroyed as part of the HVO's protracted campaign of terror directed against the Muslims of Mostar, the Appeals Chamber considers that the Prosecution falls into circular reasoning. It cannot be said that destruction was not justified by military necessity because of the existence of a campaign of terror, if the fact that the bridge was a military target raises reasonable doubt as to whether its destruction was part of that campaign. Further, the argument that the destruction of the Old Bridge was retribution for the fall of Vareš to the ABiH forces deals with the question of the HVO's motive, which is irrelevant in law. *Limaj et al.* Appeal Judgement, para. 109; *Tadić* Appeal Judgement, paras 268-269; *Kanyarukiga* Appeal Judgement, para. 262. Finally, the Appeals Chamber turns to the Prosecution argument that because the Old Bridge was completely unusable and could be considered destroyed after the shelling attacks on 8 November 1993, it "no longer had any military value" and no military advantage was to be gained "by bringing about its complete obliteration and collapse" on the following day. The Trial Chamber found that the Old Bridge was or could be considered destroyed by the evening of 8 November 1993 as it was unusable and on the verge of collapse, and that it collapsed the following morning. However, it made no finding that the bridge ceased being a military target on the evening of 8 November 1993 or that the HVO knew that the ABiH could no longer use it for military purposes. Trial Judgement, Vol. 2, paras 1318, 1321, 1343, 1345, 1366. See also Trial Judgement, Vol. 2, para. 1326, Vol. 3, para. 1581. The Appeals Chamber notes in this regard that none of the evidence on which the Trial Chamber relied to find that the Old Bridge was destroyed by the evening of 8 November 1993 emanated from the HVO. See Trial Judgement, Vol. 2, paras 1316-1317. As such, the Prosecution fails to show that the HVO targeted the Old Bridge on any basis other than its status as a military target. The Appeals Chamber therefore dismisses its arguments.

[1260]   See *infra*, paras 422-423.

the laws or customs of war, in Prozor Municipality between May and early July 1993[1261] and Mostar Municipality between June and December 1993 (ten mosques).[1262] However, pursuant to its discretion under Article 25 of the Statute,[1263] the Appeals Chamber finds it appropriate to refrain from entering new convictions on appeal for wanton destruction not justified by military necessity as a violation of the laws or customs of war under Article 3 of the Statute.[1264] In so finding, the Appeals Chamber considers the interests of fairness to the Appellants balanced with considerations of the interests of justice, and taking into account the nature of the offences and the circumstances of this case.[1265]

414. With respect to the Old Bridge in Mostar, the Appeals Chamber, Judge Pocar dissenting, recalls that the Trial Chamber erred in finding that the destruction of the Old Bridge of Mostar constituted the crime of wanton destruction not justified by military necessity.[1266] The Appeals Chamber, Judge Pocar dissenting in part, therefore dismisses the relevant part of the Prosecution's ground of appeal 3 seeking a conviction for wanton destruction not justified by military necessity, as a violation of the laws or customs of war (Count 20), with respect to the Old Bridge.

4. Impact of errors in relation to the Old Bridge on the crimes of persecution and unlawful infliction of terror on civilians

415. The Trial Chamber relied on its finding on the destruction of the Old Bridge as a basis for its findings that the HVO committed both persecution as a crime against humanity (Count 1) and unlawful infliction of terror on civilians as a violation of the laws or customs of war (Count 25),[1267] and consequently convicted the Appellants for these crimes in relation to the Old Bridge.[1268] **[page 175]**

416. Specifically, when finding that persecution had been committed, the Trial Chamber considered a number of "crimes against the Muslims of the Municipality of Mostar",[1269] including the destruction of the Old Bridge, which it recalled as having "undeniable cultural, historical and symbolic value for the Muslims".[1270] The Trial Chamber found that by committing all these crimes, the HVO specifically targeted Muslims, introduced *de facto* discrimination, and violated their basic rights to "life, freedom and dignity".[1271] Thus, it was satisfied that the HVO intended to discriminate against these Muslims and violate their basic rights to "life, human dignity, freedom and property".[1272]

417. In its legal findings on the unlawful infliction of terror on civilians, the Trial Chamber also considered various acts by the HVO including the destruction of the Old Bridge.[1273] It recalled that the destruction had a major psychological impact on the morale of the population and that the HVO had to be aware of that impact, in particular because of its "great symbolic, cultural and historical value".[1274] The Trial Chamber was satisfied that the deliberate isolation of the population in East Mostar for several months, after forcibly transferring a large part of the population there, and thus the exacerbation of their distress and difficult living conditions, demonstrated the specific intention of the HVO to spread terror.[1275] The Trial Chamber concluded

---

[1261] See Trial Judgement, Vol. 3, para. 1566.

[1262] See Trial Judgement, Vol. 3, para. 1580. The Appeals Chamber notes in this regard that, for reasons set out elsewhere, this errror applies only to the destruction of three mosques between June 1993 and: (1) 15 November 1993, in relation to Stojić; (2) 9 November 1993, in relation to Praljak; and (3) 10 November 1993, in relation to Ćorić. See *supra*, para. 105; *infra*, paras 2002-2003, fn. 5395.

[1263] *Cf. Stanišić and Župljanin* Appeal Judgement, para. 1096 & fn. 3625; *Đorđević* Appeal Judgement, para. 928; *Šainović et al.* Appeal Judgement, fn. 5269; *Jelisić* Appeal Judgement, para. 73.

[1264] The Appeals Chamber notes however that insofar as the ten mosques in Mostar are concerned, the Trial Chamber also convicted the Appellants under Count 21. Trial Judgement, Vol. 3, paras 1609-1610.

[1265] *Cf. Stanišić and Župljanin* Appeal Judgement, para. 1096 & fn. 3626 and references cited therein.

[1266] See *supra*, para. 411.

[1267] Trial Judgement, Vol. 3, paras 1690-1692, 1711-1713.

[1268] See Trial Judgement, Vol. 3, paras 1690-1692, 1711-1713, Vol. 4, para. 59, Disposition, pp. 430-431.

[1269] Trial Judgement, Vol. 3, para. 1712. See Trial Judgement, Vol. 3, paras 1707-1711, 1713.

[1270] Trial Judgement, Vol. 3, para. 1711.

[1271] Trial Judgement, Vol. 3, para. 1712.

[1272] Trial Judgement, Vol. 3, paras 1712-1713.

[1273] Trial Judgement, Vol. 3, paras 1689-1692.

[1274] Trial Judgement, Vol. 3, para. 1690.

[1275] Trial Judgement, Vol. 3, para. 1691.

that the HVO committed acts of violence, "the main aim of which was to inflict terror on the population", thereby committing unlawful infliction of terror on civilians.[1276]

(a) Arguments of the Parties

418.   At the Appeal Hearing, Stojić, Praljak, and the Prosecution were asked to discuss any impact an error regarding the Trial Chamber's legal findings on the destruction of the Old Bridge as a crime of wanton destruction (Count 20) would have on its findings that the destruction also constituted the crimes of persecution (Count 1) and unlawful infliction of terror on civilians (Count 25).[1277]

419.   Stojić argues that to state that one can comply with international humanitarian law in relation to distinction and targeting but still be responsible for persecution, for example, for the [page 176] destruction of the Old Bridge, leads to massive policy implications unsupported by law or practice.[1278]

420.   Praljak argues that the Trial Chamber's errors relating to the destruction of the Old Bridge have an impact on the crimes of persecution and terror as they show that these crimes have been tried on the basis of erroneous facts.[1279] Praljak submits that although the Trial Chamber considered a number of acts in Mostar Municipality – including the destruction of the Old Bridge and mosques, sniping, "bombings", the isolation of the population, and forced transfer – when concluding that the crimes of persecution and terror had been committed, none of the facts relating to these acts had been properly established with regard to him or the HVO.[1280] In particular, Praljak challenges the underlying findings pertaining to sniping, "bombings", and the destruction of or damage to mosques and submits that the "crime[s] of persecution and spreading terror" must be reversed.[1281]

421.   The Prosecution submits that, if the Appeals Chamber were to find an error with respect to the legal findings under Count 20 on the destruction of the Old Bridge, it would have an impact on Stojić's and Praljak's convictions for persecution and the unlawful infliction of terror, but that the impact would be minimal.[1282] In this regard, it argues that a determination that the destruction was lawful would mean that it could not form part of the convictions for persecution or unlawful infliction of terror given that the attack would not have been carried out with the primary intent to inflict terror or with the intent to discriminate.[1283] The Prosecution submits, however, that since the legal findings for persecution (Count 1) and unlawful infliction of terror on civilians (Count 25) are based on the aggregation of numerous crimes and acts, Stojić's and Praljak's convictions on those counts would remain intact.[1284]

(b) Analysis

422.   Turning first to persecution as a crime against humanity under Article 5 of the Statute (Count 1), the Appeals Chamber recalls that it consists of an act or omission which:

> 1. discriminates in fact and which denies or infringes upon a fundamental right laid down in international customary or treaty law (the *actus reus*); and [page 177]
>
> 2. was carried out deliberately with the intention to discriminate on one of the listed grounds, specifically race, religion or politics (the *mens rea*).[1285]

[1276]   Trial Judgement, Vol. 3, para. 1692.
[1277]   Order for the Preparation of the Appeal Hearing, p. 5, para. 2.
[1278]   Appeal Hearing, AT. 283 (21 Mar 2017).
[1279]   Appeal Hearing, AT. 377-378 (22 Mar 2017).
[1280]   Appeal Hearing, AT. 377, 379-380 (22 Mar 2017).
[1281]   Appeal Hearing, AT. 378 (22 Mar 2017). See Appeal Hearing, AT. 379 (22 Mar 2017).
[1282]   Appeal Hearing, AT. 449 (22 Mar 2017).
[1283]   Appeal Hearing, AT. 449 (22 Mar 2017).
[1284]   Appeal Hearing, AT. 449-450 (22 Mar 2017), referring to Trial Judgement, Vol. 3, paras 1689-1692, 1694-1741.
[1285]   *Kvočka et al.* Appeal Judgement, para. 320, referring to *Krnojelac* Appeal Judgement, para. 185, *Vasiljević* Appeal Judgement, para. 113, *Blaškić* Appeal Judgement, para. 131, *Kordić and Čerkez* Appeal Judgement, para. 101. See also, *e.g.*, *Nyiramasuhuko et al.* Appeal Judgement, para. 2138, citing *Nahimana et al.* Appeal Judgement, para. 985.

Persecution as a crime against humanity requires evidence that the principal perpetrator had the specific intent to discriminate on one of these grounds.[1286] While the requisite discriminatory intent may not be inferred directly from the general discriminatory nature of an attack characterised as a crime against humanity, the "discriminatory intent may be inferred from such a context as long as, in view of the facts of the case, circumstances surrounding the commission of the alleged acts substantiate the existence of such intent".[1287] Further, the Appeals Chamber has found that the destruction of property, depending on the nature and extent of the destruction, may constitute a crime of persecution of equal gravity to other crimes listed in Article 5 of the Statute.[1288]

423.   The Appeals Chamber, Judge Pocar dissenting, recalls that the Trial Chamber erred in finding that the destruction of the Old Bridge of Mostar constituted the crime of wanton destruction not justified by military necessity as a violation of the laws or customs of war.[1289] The Appeals Chamber notes that the Trial Chamber previously found that "the armed forces of the HVO had a military interest in destroying this structure" and that "at the time of the attack, the Old Bridge was a military target".[1290] However, the Trial Chamber subsequently reached the conclusion that the destruction was carried out deliberately with the intent to discriminate against Muslims by noting that the Old Bridge "had undeniable cultural, historical and symbolic value for the Muslims".[1291] Considering the Trial Chamber's findings that the HVO had a military interest in the destruction of the Old Bridge and that it was a military target, the Appeals Chamber, Judge Pocar dissenting, finds that no reasonable trier of fact could have found, beyond reasonable doubt, that the HVO had the specific intent to discriminate. The Appeals Chamber, Judge Pocar dissenting, finds that this error occasions a miscarriage of justice that invalidates the Trial Chamber's conclusion on the crime of persecution as it concerns the destruction of the Old Bridge. **[page 178]**

424.   With respect to the war crime of unlawful infliction of terror on civilians as a violation of the laws or customs of war (Count 25),[1292] the Appeals Chamber notes that it is comprised of acts or threats of violence the primary purpose of which is to spread terror among the civilian population,[1293] and that the *mens rea* includes the specific intent to spread terror among the civilian population.[1294] Other purposes of the unlawful acts or threats may have coexisted simultaneously with the purpose of spreading terror among the civilian population, provided that the intent to spread terror among the civilian population was principal among the aims.[1295] Such intent can be inferred from the "nature, manner, timing and duration" of the acts or threats.[1296] The Appeals Chamber in the *Galić* case described the crime of terror as not being "a case in which an explosive device was planted outside of an ongoing military attack but rather a case of 'extensive trauma and psychological damage' being caused by 'attacks [which] were designed to keep the inhabitants in a constant state of terror'".[1297]

425.   The Trial Chamber considered the destruction of the Old Bridge as an "act[] of violence, the main aim of which was to inflict terror on the population".[1298] Although, as stated above, the act of destroying the Old Bridge could have simultaneously served multiple purposes, the Trial Chamber made no express mention of its previous findings that the HVO had a military interest in destroying the bridge and that it was a military target[1299] – findings that would have been essential to an assessment of the purpose of its destruction. In a

---

[1286]   *Šainović et al.* Appeal Judgement, para. 579; *Blaškić* Appeal Judgement, para. 164; *Krnojelac* Appeal Judgement, para. 184.
[1287]   *Šainović et al.* Appeal Judgement, para. 579; *Blaškić* Appeal Judgement, para. 164; *Krnojelac* Appeal Judgement para. 184.
[1288]   *Kordić and Čerkez* Appeal Judgement, para. 108; *Blaškić* Appeal Judgement, para. 149. See also *Blaškić* Appeal Judgement, para, 146.
[1289]   See *supra*, para. 411.
[1290]   Trial Judgement, Vol. 3, para. 1582. See also Trial Judgement, Vol. 2, paras 1290, 1354, 1357; *supra*, paras 406, 411.
[1291]   Trial Judgement, Vol. 3, para. 1711. See Trial Judgement, Vol. 3, paras 1712-1713.
[1292]   Judge Liu dissents from all portions of this Judgement dealing with the unlawful infliction of terror on civilians as a violation of the laws or customs of war (Count 25) since he is of the view that the Tribunal does not have jurisdiction over this crime and that the elements of this offence as set out in the present paragraph do not adequately define a criminal charge.
[1293]   *D. Milošević* Appeal Judgement, paras 32-33, 37; *Galić* Appeal Judgement, paras 69, 102.
[1294]   *D. Milošević Appeal* Judgement, para. 37; *Galić* Appeal Judgement, paras 102, 104.
[1295]   *Galić* Appeal Judgement, para. 104. See *D. Milošević* Appeal Judgement, para. 37.
[1296]   *D. Milošević* Appeal Judgement, para. 37, citing *Galić* Appeal Judgement, para. 104.
[1297]   *Galić* Appeal Judgement, para. 102 (internal references omitted).
[1298]   Trial Judgement, Vol. 3, para. 1692. See Trial Judgement, Vol. 3, para. 1690.
[1299]   See Trial Judgement, Vol. 3, para. 1582. See also Trial Judgement, Vol. 2, paras 1290, 1354, 1357; *supra*, paras 406, 411, 423.

notable contrast, the Trial Chamber expressly considered the lack of military value of ten mosques destroyed in East Mostar.[1300] The Trial Chamber instead reached its conclusion about the purpose of the destruction of the Old Bridge after recalling its factual findings on the *impact* of the destruction on the population and that the HVO had to have been aware of such impact.[1301] Considering the Trial Chamber's findings that the HVO had a military interest in the destruction of the Old Bridge and that it was a military target, the Appeals Chamber, Judge Pocar dissenting, finds that no reasonable trier of fact could have found, beyond reasonable doubt, that the HVO had the specific intent to commit terror. The Appeals Chamber, Judge Pocar dissenting, finds that this error occasions a miscarriage of justice that **[page 179]** invalidates the Trial Chamber's conclusion on the crime of unlawful infliction of terror as it concerns the destruction of the Old Bridge.

426.   In light of the foregoing, the Appeals Chamber, Judge Pocar dissenting, reverses the Trial Chamber's findings that the destruction of the Old Bridge constituted persecution as a crime against humanity (Count 1) and the unlawful infliction of terror on civilians as a violation of the laws or customs of war (Count 25) and, Judge Pocar dissenting, acquits the Appellants of these counts in relation to the Old Bridge. The Appeals Chamber, Judge Pocar dissenting, will consider below the impact of these acquittals, if any, upon the sentences of the Appellants. The Appeals Chamber further notes that the Trial Chamber considered a number of other underlying acts when holding that these crimes had been committed.[1302] Praljak's submissions challenging the underlying findings of these other acts are dismissed elsewhere.[1303] Thus, to the extent that he contends that his convictions under Counts 1 and 25 should be reversed in their entirety,[1304] the Appeals Chamber, Judge Pocar dissenting in part, dismisses his argument.

D.   Attacks of 18 January 1993 in Gornji Vakuf Municipality and Related Crimes

427.   The Trial Chamber found that on 18 January 1993, the HVO attacked the villages of Duša, Hrasnica, Uzričje, and Ždrimci in Gornji Vakuf Municipality with mortar shells, heavy machine guns, and artillery.[1305] It found that in Duša, the HVO killed seven inhabitants who had gathered in the cellar of Enver Šljivo's house and who were not taking part in the fighting,[1306] while in all four villages houses belonging to the Muslim inhabitants were destroyed by shelling during the attacks.[1307]

1.   The killing of seven civilians in Duša (Stojić's Sub-ground 45.1 arid Praljak's Ground 12)

428.   The Trial Chamber found that "the HVO attacked the village [of Duša] by using weapons – more specifically, shells – the nature of which is such that it is impossible to distinguish military from civilian targets".[1308] It further found that the HVO forces made no effort to allow the civilian population of the village to flee before the attack. Consequently, it held that the shelling of Duša was an indiscriminate attack. On this basis, it found that the HVO, by firing several shells at the village and in particular at Enver Šljivo's house, intended to cause serious bodily harm to the **[page 180]** civilians who had taken refuge there, harm that it could reasonably have foreseen could cause their deaths, thereby committing murder as a crime against humanity (Count 2) and wilful killing as a grave breach of the Geneva Conventions (Count 3) against each of these persons, crimes under Articles 5 and 2 of the Statute, respectively.[1309] The Trial Chamber subsequently relied on these findings in its analysis of persecution as a crime against humanity under Article 5 (Count 1), inhumane acts as a crime against humanity under Article 5 (Count 15), and inhuman treatment as a grave breach of the Geneva Conventions under Article 2 (Count 16).[1310]

[1300]   See Trial Judgement, Vol. 3, para. 1690.
[1301]   See Trial Judgement, Vol. 3, para. 1690 & fn. 2625.
[1302]   See Trial Judgement, Vol. 3, paras 1689-1692, 1694-1741. See also *infra*, para. 563.
[1303]   See *supra*, para. 419 & fns 1280-1281; *infra*, paras 541, 543 (sniping), 549, 554 (shelling), 567, 569 (destruction of or damage to mosques).
[1304]   See *supra*, para. 419.
[1305]   Trial Judgement, Vol. 2, paras 357-358, 369, 374, 381.
[1306]   Trial Judgement, Vol. 2, paras 366, 368.
[1307]   Trial Judgement, Vol. 2, paras 367-368, 373, 379, 387.
[1308]   Trial Judgement, Vol. 3, paras 663, 711.
[1309]   Trial Judgement, Vol. 3, paras 663, 711.
[1310]   Trial Judgement, Vol. 3, paras 1224, 1315, 1699.

(a) Arguments of the Parties

429.   Stojić and Praljak submit that the Trial Chamber erred in concluding that HVO forces indiscriminately shelled Duša and intended to cause serious bodily harm to civilians.[1311] Praljak argues that the Trial Chamber erroneously concluded that the attack was led by HVO and HV soldiers.[1312] Stojić and Praljak argue that the Trial Chamber erred in law and fact when concluding that shells are by their nature indiscriminate.[1313] Stojić submits that the Trial Chamber erred when finding that the shelling of Enver Šljivo's house, in particular, was indiscriminate, rather than an attack on a legitimate military target.[1314] Praljak argues that the Trial Chamber failed to consider that Muslim defence lines were situated in proximity to Enver Šljivo's house and that the shell that hit it was therefore aimed at a legitimate military target.[1315] In this regard, he. further submits that the Trial Chamber did not establish: (1) the probability of the shell missing its target;[1316] and (2) that the HVO knew or should have known that civilians were in the house.[1317] Stojić and Praljak contend that the Trial Chamber relied solely on its erroneous finding that the attack on Duša was indiscriminate to incorrectly conclude that the HVO intended to cause serious bodily harm to **[page 181]** civilians.[1318] Stojić and Praljak request to be acquitted of these charges under Counts 1, 2, 3, 15, and 16.[1319]

430.   The Prosecution responds that, contrary to Praljak's assertion, the Trial Chamber reasonably concluded that the HVO and HV soldiers attacked Duša.[1320] The Prosecution does not expressly dispute Stojić's and Praljak's submissions that the attack was not indiscriminate, but submits that the Trial Chamber reasonably rejected the argument that the HVO aimed at legitimate military targets.[1321] It submits that the HVO directly targeted Enver Šljivo's house with the intent to kill and cause serious bodily and mental harm to civilians, and that this conclusion is supported by the evidence.[1322]

431.   Stojić replies that there is no basis in the Trial Chamber's findings for a conclusion that the HVO directly targeted civilians.[1323] Praljak replies that the Trial Chamber's and Prosecution's analyses of events in Duša are based on the erroneous finding that the HVO attack on Gornji Vakuf was part of an overall plan to take control of the area.[1324]

[1311]   Stojić's Appeal Brief, heading before para. 393, paras 393-394; Praljak's Appeal Brief, headings before paras 186, 195, paras 194, 199; Appeal Hearing, AT. 396 (22 Mar 2017). See also Stojić's Reply Brief, para. 78.
[1312]   Praljak's Appeal Brief, para. 186, referring to, *inter alia,* Trial Judgement, Vol. 2, para. 358; Appeal Hearing, AT. 397-398 (22 Mar 2017). See also Praljak's Appeal Brief, paras 189, 195.
[1313]   Stojić's Appeal Brief, para. 394; Praljak's Appeal Brief, paras 187-188. See Appeal Hearing, AT. 278 (21 Mar 2017) (specifying that it was a legal error), 398 (22 Mar 2017). See also Stojić's Response Brief, para. 150; *infra,* para. 448. Praljak also argues that the Trial Chamber's finding that the HVO made no effort to allow the civilian population to flee before the attack is unfounded. Praljak's Appeal Brief, para. 193, referring to, *inter alia,* Exs. P01162, 4D00348, p. 3.
[1314]   Stojić's Appeal Brief, para. 395. See also Stojić's Response Brief, paras 151-152; Appeal Hearing, AT. 278-279 (21 Mar 2017); *infra,* para. 448.
[1315]   Praljak's Appeal Brief, paras 190-192, 198; Praljak's Reply Brief, para. 66. See Praljak's Appeal Brief, paras 187 (referring to, *inter alia,* Trial Judgement, Vol. 2, paras 362, 366), 189.
[1316]   Praljak's Appeal Brief, para. 198. See also Appeal Hearing, AT. 403 (22 Mar 2017).
[1317]   Praljak's Appeal Brief, paras 189, 192, 198; Praljak's Reply Brief, para. 66; Appeal Hearing, AT. 397 (22 Mar 2017). Praljak submits in this regard that Enver Šljivo was the commander of the village defence. Praljak's Appeal Brief, paras 189 (referring to, *inter alia,* Trial Judgement, Vol. 2, para. 365), 192; Praljak's Reply Brief, para. 66.
[1318]   Stojić's Appeal Brief, heading before para. 393, para. 397; Praljak's Appeal Brief, paras 197-198. See also Praljak's Appeal Brief, para. 195,.
[1319]   Stojić's Appeal Brief, paras 396-397; Stojić's Reply Brief, para. 78; Praljak's Appeal Brief, para. 185.
[1320]   Prosecution's Response Brief (Praljak), para. 130; Appeal Hearing, AT. 418-419 (22 Mar 2017). See Prosecution's Response Brief (Praljak), paras 125-126.
[1321]   Prosecution's Response Brief (Stojić), paras 360-361; Prosecution's Response Brief (Praljak), paras 127-128. See also Prosecution's Reply Brief, para. 142 & fn. 550; *infra,* para. 449. The Prosecution also argues that the Trial Chamber reasonably found, in line with the evidence, that HVO forces made no effort to allow civilians to flee before the attack. Prosecution's Response Brief (Praljak), para. 129.
[1322]   Prosecution's Response Brief (Stojić), paras 361-362; Prosecution's Response Brief (Praljak), paras 128, 131 (referring to, *inter alia,* Trial Judgement, Vol. 3, paras 663, 711); Prosecution's Reply Brief, fn. 550. See also *infra,* para. 449; Prosecution's Response Brief (Stojić), paras 359, 363. Specifically, the Prosecution refers to evidence that an HVO tank, that is, a direct-fire weapon, penetrated the wall of Enver Šljivo's basement and continued firing on the house as civilians fled. Prosecution's Response Brief (Stojić), para. 360; Prosecution's Response Brief (Praljak), para. 127; Prosecution's Reply Brief, fn. 550.
[1323]   Stojić's Reply Brief, para. 78. See also Stojić's Reply Brief, para. 77.
[1324]   Praljak's Reply Brief, para. 65.

432.   At the Appeal Hearing, the Parties were invited to discuss the basis for the Trial Chamber's finding that during the attack on Duša on 18 January 1993, HVO forces intended to cause serious bodily harm to the civilians who had taken refuge in Enver Šljivo's house, harm which they could reasonably have foreseen could cause their deaths.[1325] The Prosecution reiterates its position that the attack on Enver Šljivo's house was a deliberate attack on civilians,[1326] and refers to further evidence in this regard.[1327] It also argues, however, that when assessed overall, "the Gornji Vakuf attack" was **[page 182]** conducted with no regard for the principle of distinction, and that the Trial Chamber's conclusion that the civilians killed in Duša were victims of an indiscriminate attack was therefore correct.[1328] Finally, the Prosecution suggests that even under the Defence theory that the shelling of Enver Šljivo's house was an attack on a lawful target, the evidence discloses an indiscriminate or, at best, a "grossly disproportionate" attack.[1329] Stojić and Praljak argue that neither the Trial Chamber's findings nor the evidence referred to by the Prosecution establish that the HVO forces had the requisite intent.[1330] Stojić also impugns the Rule 92 *bis* evidence of Witness Kemal Šljivo.[1331]

(b) Analysis

433.   As a preliminary matter, the Appeals Chamber observes that the Trial Chamber's legal findings in relation to the killing of seven civilians in Duša on 18 January 1993 under Counts 1 (persecution as a crime against humanity), 15 (inhumane acts as a crime against humanity), and 16 (inhuman treatment as a grave breach of the Geneva Conventions) are substantiated solely by reference to its legal findings under Counts 2 (murder as a crime against humanity) and 3 (wilful killing as a grave breach of the Geneva Conventions).[1332] In other words, the Trial Chamber made no distinct legal findings on the killings in relation to Counts 1, 15, and 16. Insofar as Stojić's and Praljak's submissions impugn the Trial Chamber's findings under Counts 1, 15, and 16, they are premised exclusively on their challenges to findings under Counts 2 and 3. The Appeals Chamber will accordingly address the challenges to the findings through consideration of the challenges to Counts 2 and 3 before assessing any impact on the remaining counts.

434.   The Trial Chamber found that the attack on Duša was indiscriminate on the basis that: (1) the HVO attacked the village using weapons – more specifically, shells – the nature of which is such that it is impossible to distinguish military from civilian targets; and (2) the HVO made no effort to allow the civilian population to flee before the attack.[1333] It provided no references in support of the finding that "shells" are of such a nature that it is impossible to distinguish between civilian and military targets.[1334] The Appeals Chamber would have expected such a finding to be **[page 183]** based on evidence that the weapon employed in the attack, when used in its normal or designed circumstances, will inevitably be indiscriminate, in the sense that it is incapable of being directed at a specific military objective or its effects are incapable of being limited as required by law.[1335] In the absence of such an assessment, the Appeals Chamber considers that no

---

[1325]   Order for the Preparation of the Appeal Hearing, pp. 5-6, para. 3.
[1326]   Appeal Hearing, AT. 211, 214 (20 Mar 2017).
[1327]   The Prosecution refers to evidence as to: (1) the locations and positions of the defenders of the village relative to Enver Šljivo's house and each other; (2) the HVO tank's line of sight to Enver Šljivo's house; (3) the supposedly "precise" nature of direct-fire weapons; (4) the fact that the tank fired "at least two" consecutive shells, including on fleeing civilians; and (5) the HVO's knowledge that the house was a civilian object. Appeal Hearing, AT. 211-214, 216-217 (20 Mar 2017), referring to, *inter alia*, Ex. P10108, p. 3. The Prosecution also submits that a residential house is a *"prima facie* civilian object". Appeal Hearing, AT. 419 (22 Mar 2017).
[1328]   Appeal Hearing, AT. 215-216 (20 Mar 2017), referring to, *inter alia*, Trial Judgement, Vol. 2, para. 372, Vol. 4, paras 45, 48, 704.
[1329]   Appeal Hearing, AT. 217-218 (20 Mar 2017), AT. 420 (22 Mar 2017).
[1330]   Appeal Hearing, AT. 277-280 (21 Mar 2017), AT. 396-398, 400, 403 (22 Mar 2017). Ćorić also responds to the Prosecution's submissions in relation to the killing of seven civilians in Duša. Appeal Hearing, AT. 586-587 (24 Mar 2017).
[1331]   Appeal Hearing, AT. 279-280 (21 Mar 2017).
[1332]   Trial Judgement, Vol. 3, para. 1224 & fn. 1965 (Count 15, inhumane acts as a crime against humanity), para. 1315 & fn. 2116 (Count 16, inhuman treatment as a grave breach of the Geneva Conventions), para. 1699 (Count 1, persecution as a crime against humanity).
[1333]   Trial Judgement, Vol. 3, paras 663, 711.
[1334]   See Trial Judgement, Vol. 3, paras 663, 711 and references cited therein.
[1335]   See, *e.g.*, William H. Boothby, *Weapons and the Law of Armed Conflict* (1st ed., 2009), pp. 83, 226-227, referring to, *inter alia*, Steven Haines, "Weapons, Means and Methods of Warfare", *in* Elizabeth Wilmshurst and Susan Breau (eds.), *Perspectives on the ICRC Study on Customary International Humanitarian Law* (2007), p. 266.

reasonable trier of fact could have found that "shells", without further specification, are inherently indiscriminate, and accordingly reverses this finding.

435.   In light of this error, the Trial Chamber's finding that the attack on Duša was indiscriminate therefore rests exclusively on its finding that the HVO made no effort to allow the civilian population to flee before the attack.[1336] The Appeals Chamber considers that no reasonable trier of fact could have reached the conclusion that the attack on Duša was indiscriminate on this basis alone.[1337]

436.   The Appeals Chamber notes that the Trial Chamber relied on its finding that the attack on the village of Duša was indiscriminate to substantiate its finding that the HVO forces had the requisite *mens rea* for murder and wilful killing.[1338] Having reversed this finding, therefore, the Appeals Chamber now turns to the question of whether the Trial Chamber's conclusion that the HVO forces had the requisite *mens rea* for murder and wilful killing still stands on the basis of the Trial Chamber's remaining findings and evidence referred to by the Parties, in order to determine if its error of fact occasioned a miscarriage of justice.

437.   It will first address the Prosecution's argument that when assessed overall, "the Gornji Vakuf attack" was conducted with no regard for the principle of distinction, and that the Trial Chamber's conclusion that the civilians killed in Duša were victims of an indiscriminate attack is therefore correct. The Prosecution refers in support to, *inter alia,* Trial Chamber findings in relation to the attack on Hrasnica and on how the Gornji Vakuf attacks formed part of a "preconceived plan", that is, the implementation of the CCP in Gornji Vakuf.[1339] The Appeals Chamber notes, however, that the Trial Chamber's finding that the attacks on Hrasnica, Uzričje, and Ždrimci on 18 January 1993 were indiscriminate is reversed elsewhere.[1340] This argument is therefore dismissed. **[page 184]**

438.   The Prosecution's remaining arguments seek, on the basis of the evidence, to characterise the HVO attack as a deliberate attack on civilians, a "grossly disproportionate attack", or an indiscriminate attack (the latter on an alternative basis to that of the Trial Chamber's finding).[1341] The Appeals Chamber notes that the Prosecution's submissions are in effect offered as an alternative to the Trial Chamber's findings on the attack rather than in support of them, and in some instances even appear to contradict them. The crux of the Prosecution's argument, for example, is that Enver Šljivo's house was targeted by tank fire,[1342] where the Trial Chamber made no such finding, and in fact found that the HVO attacked Duša with mortar shells, heavy machine guns, and artillery.[1343]

439.   In the present case, the Trial Chamber found that there were members of the ABiH in Duša in mid-January 1993,[1344] and that prior to the attack on 18 January 1993, men from the ABiH and the village defence were "preparing to defend the village, taking up positions in particular in the forest of Duša".[1345] An HVO intelligence report dated 16 January 1993 indicated that there were 25 Muslim soldiers in Duša and that they were situated in the middle of the village "near the big house".[1346] The Appeals Chamber notes in particular that Witness BW explicitly accepted that Enver Šljivo's house was *between* the position of HVO forces which fired the shells and the Muslim defence lines,[1347] *i.e.* the house was situated in the line of fire between the HVO forces and the defenders of the village.

[1336]   Trial Judgement, Vol. 3, paras 663, 711.
[1337]   Praljak's argument with regard to the Trial Chamber's finding that the HVO made no effort to allow the civilian population to flee before the attack is therefore moot.
[1338]   Trial Judgement, Vol. 3, paras 663, 711.
[1339]   See *supra,* para. 432 & fn. 1328.
[1340]   See *infra,* para. 453.
[1341]   See *supra,* paras 430, 432.
[1342]   See *supra,* fns 1322, 1327.
[1343]   Trial Judgement, Vol. 2, para. 357. See Trial Judgement, Vol. 2, para. 358.
[1344]   Trial Judgement, Vol. 2, para. 364.
[1345]   Trial Judgement, Vol. 2, para. 362 (internal reference omitted).
[1346]   Ex. 3D00527. The "big house" appeal's to refer to the house of Enver Šljivo. See Ex. P10108, p. 3. See also Ex. IC00059 (confidential); Witness BY, T. 9076-9077 (27 Oct 2006); Witness BW, T. 8770 (closed session) (19 Oct 2006).
[1347]   Witness BW, T. 8807 (closed session) (19 Oct 2006). See also Ex. IC00059 (confidential). The Trial Chamber expressly gave credence to Witness BW's evidence. Trial Judgement, Vol. 2, para. 344.

440. The Appeals Chamber notes that Witness BY testified that there was gunfire after the civilians taking shelter left the basement,[1348] and that Kemal Šljivo stated that he heard "gun shots coming from all directions".[1349] Neither of these statements clearly establishes whether the Muslim defenders of the village returned fire at the HVO forces, nor do other relevant sections of the trial record referred to by the Parties.[1350]

441. In light of these findings and the relevant evidence considered as a whole, the Appeals Chamber finds that no reasonable trier of fact could have concluded that the HVO forces in **[page 185]** Duša possessed the requisite *mens rea* for murder and wilful killing, given the ongoing combat activity in the vicinity of the house and, in particular, the position of the defenders of the village relative to the house. As such, the Trial Chamber's factual error occasioned a miscarriage of justice insofar as it underpinned the Trial Chamber's finding that the killing of seven civilians during the attack on Duša constituted murder as a crime against humanity (Count 2) and wilful killing as a grave breach of the Geneva Conventions (Count 3).[1351] The Appeals Chamber accordingly reverses these findings.

442. Further, as the Appeals Chamber has noted above, the Trial Chamber's findings under Counts 2 and 3 provided the sole basis for its subsequent findings in relation to the killings in Duša under Counts 1, 15, and 16.[1352] As this sole basis is reversed, so too are these subsequent findings.

443. The Appeals Chamber accordingly grants Stojić's sub-ground of appeal 45.1 and Praljak's ground of appeal 12. The convictions of the Appellants under Counts 1, 2, 3, 15, and 16 with regard to the killing of seven civilians in Duša are reversed.[1353] The impact of this reversal, if any, on the Trial Chamber's findings as to the CCP, as well as on the Appellants' sentences, will be assessed below.[1354]

2. Wanton destruction of cities, towns or villages, or devastation not justified by military necessity in Gornji Vakuf Municipality (Prosecution's Ground 3 in part)

444. With regard to the destruction of houses by shelling during the attacks on Duša, Hrasnica, Uzričje, and Ždrimci, the Trial Chamber noted that the destruction was extensive.[1355] It further noted that members of the ABiH were present in the villages at the time of the HVO attacks and that some armed Muslim men were hidden inside the houses from time to time.[1356] The Trial Chamber then referred to its legal findings in relation to murder and wilful killing in Gornji Vakuf Municipality and recalled its finding that the shelling of these villages was an indiscriminate attack.[1357] It therefore found that the destruction of houses by shelling during the attacks constituted **[page 186]** wanton destruction of cities, towns or villages, or devastation not justified by military necessity as a violation of the laws or customs of war (Count 20).[1358]

(a) Arguments of the Parties

445. The Appeals Chamber recalls that the Prosecution has requested that it enter convictions against Prlić, Stojić, Praljak, Petković, and Ćorić for wanton destruction of cities, towns or villages, or devastation not

[1348] Witness BY, T. 9077 (27 Oct 2006). The Trial Chamber expressly gave credence to Witness BY's evidence. Trial Judgement, Vol. 2, para. 344.
[1349] Ex. P10108, p. 4. The Trial Chamber expressly gave credence to Kemal Šljivo's evidence. Trial Judgement, Vol. 2, para. 344.
[1350] See, *e.g.*, Witness BY, T. 9077-9078 (27 Oct 2006); Witness BW, T. 8781 (19 Oct 2006).
[1351] Trial Judgement, Vol. 3, paras 663, 711.
[1352] See *supra*, para. 433.
[1353] The Appeals Chamber recalls that Pušić was not convicted of any charges in relation to these killings as he was not a member of the JCE as of January 1993. Trial Judgement, Vol. 4, para. 1229.
[1354] See *infra*, paras 886, 3359-3365.
[1355] Trial Judgement, Vol. 3, para. 1568. See Trial Judgement, Vol. 3, paras 1569-1570. See also Trial Judgement, Vol. 2, paras 367-368 (referring to evidence that two houses in Duša had been destroyed by shelling), 373 (referring to testimony that three houses in Hrasnica were destroyed by shelling), 379 (referring to evidence that at least two houses in Uzričje were destroyed by shelling), 387 (referring to evidence that "a number" of houses in Ždrimci were destroyed by shelling).
[1356] Trial Judgement, Vol. 3, para. 1569.
[1357] Trial Judgement, Vol. 3, para. 1569 & fn. 2468.
[1358] Trial Judgement, Vol. 3, para. 1570. The Trial Chamber noted, however, that as the HVO had not yet occupied the municipality of Gornji Vakuf as of the time of the attacks, this property was not protected under the Geneva Conventions, and that these incidents therefore did not constitute extensive destruction of property not justified by military necessity and carried out unlawfully and wantonly as, a grave breach of the Geneva Conventions (Count 19). Trial Judgement, Vol. 3, para. 1534. See also *supra*, para. 398.

justified by military necessity (Count 20), a violation of the laws or customs of war and a crime punishable under Article 3 of the Statute, in relation to the destruction of houses belonging to Bosnian Muslims in the villages of Duša, Hrasnica, Uzričje, and Ždrimci in Gornji Vakuf Municipality on 18 January 1993.[1359] It further recalls that pursuant to paragraph 5 of the Practice Direction on Formal Requirements, if an appellant relies on a ground of appeal to reverse an acquittal, the respondent may support the acquittal on additional grounds of appeal in the respondent's brief.[1360]

446.   Prlić responds that he was not responsible for destruction in Gornji Vakuf and claims that the Trial Chamber relied upon a mischaracterisation of evidence and unreliable testimony when making findings regarding his participation in the attack on Gornji Vakuf and regarding his intent to commit property destruction crimes.[1361]

447.   Praljak responds that the Trial Chamber made erroneous findings with regard to "his role in Gornji Vakuf municipality" and the inclusion of the crimes committed there in the CCP.[1362] Praljak also submits that the Trial Chamber did not properly consider evidence or establish certain factual findings with respect to the destruction of houses in the Gornji Vakuf Municipality.[1363]

448.   Stojić responds that the Trial Chamber erred in law in finding that the destruction of houses on 18 January 1993 in the villages of Duša, Hrasnica, Uzričje, and Ždrimci in the Gornji Vakuf Municipality was indiscriminate and thus wanton and/or not justified by military necessity.[1364] Specifically, he submits that the Trial Chamber: (1) relied on its erroneous finding that shells are inherently indiscriminate;[1365] (2) failed to give adequate weight to the presence of **[page 187]** armed defenders in or around the property in question;[1366] (3) failed to identify exactly which houses were destroyed or where they were located in relation to the legitimate military targets;[1367] and (4) did not assess how the absence of civilian casualties in three of the villages could be consistent with an indiscriminate attack.[1368]

449.   The Prosecution replies that Stojić and Praljak fail to show that the Trial Chamber's findings on wanton destruction of property in Gornji Vakuf Municipality on 18 January 1993 were erroneous.[1369] The Prosecution submits that: (1) the Trial Chamber considered the presence of armed Muslim defenders in the villages;[1370] and (2) the evidence shows that the destruction of property was not the incidental by-product of military targeting.[1371] It argues that the HVO's intent to destroy Muslim property is in line with its preconceived plan and confirmed by subsequent events, including the burning of houses after the villages were taken by the HVO.[1372]

450.   At the Appeal Hearing, the Prosecution, Prlić, Stojić, Praljak, Petković, and Ćorić were invited to discuss the basis for the Trial Chamber's finding that the property destruction caused during the attacks on the villages of Duša, Hrasnica, Ždrimci, and Uzričje was wanton and not justified by military necessity, and whether there would be any effect, if this finding were overturned, on the finding that the property destruction caused during attacks on several localities in Gornji Vakuf Municipality was "extensive".[1373] The Prosecution submits that if the Appeals Chamber were to overturn the Trial Chamber's finding that the property destruction caused during the attacks on the four villages was wanton and not justified by military necessity,

---

[1359]   See *supra*, para. 394.
[1360]   See *supra*, para. 400.
[1361]   Prlić's Response Brief, paras 174-179. See Prlić's Response Brief, heading before para. 174.
[1362]   Praljak's Response Brief, paras 150-151.
[1363]   Praljak's Response Brief, para. 149, referring to, *inter alia*, Praljak's Appeal Brief, para. 179.
[1364]   Stojić's Response Brief, para. 147, heading before para. 149, paras 149-150, 153.
[1365]   Stojić's Response Brief, para. 150.
[1366]   Stojić's Response Brief, paras 151-152.
[1367]   Stojić's Response Brief, para. 152.
[1368]   Stojić's Response Brief, para. 152.
[1369]   Prosecution's Reply Brief, paras 138, 142. See Prosecution's Reply Brief, paras 139-141.
[1370]   Prosecution's Reply Brief, para. 141; Appeal Hearing, AT. 769 (28 Mar 2017).
[1371]   Prosecution's Reply Brief, para. 142.
[1372]   Prosecution's Reply Brief, para. 142; Appeal Hearing, AT. 655-656 (24 Mar 2017), 768-770 (28 Mar 2017). See Prosecution's Reply Brief, paras 139-140.
[1373]   Order for the Preparation of the Appeal Hearing, pp. 6-7, para. 5.

there would be no effect on the Trial Judgement as no conviction was entered.[1374] Praljak and Ćorić argue that the Trial Chamber erred in its finding that the destruction was wanton and not justified by military necessity, pointing in particular to the ongoing clashes between the defenders of the villages and the HVO.[1375] Prlić, Stojić, and Petković make no submissions on this particular matter. **[page 188]**

(b) Analysis

451.   The Appeals Chamber recalls that the Trial Chamber, after noting that it had received evidence that members of the ABiH were present in each of the locations, based its finding that the destruction of the houses belonging to the Muslim inhabitants of the villages of Duša, Hrasnica, Ždrimci, and Uzričje was wanton and not justified by military necessity on a supposed prior finding that the attacks were indiscriminate.[1376] In addressing this part of the Prosecution's ground of appeal 3, the Appeals Chamber will first assess the impact of its analysis in relation to the killing of seven civilians in Duša on the finding that the destruction of Muslim-owned houses during the attack on that village constituted wanton destruction. It will then address the Prosecution's ground of appeal 3 in relation to the remaining three villages.

452.   With regard to Duša, the Appeals Chamber recalls that it finds elsewhere that the Trial Chamber's finding of indiscriminate attack Was premised on an error of fact occasioning a miscarriage of justice, leading to its reversal.[1377] In light of the reversal of this underlying finding, the Appeals Chamber considers that no reasonable trier of fact could have reached the conclusion that the attack was wanton and not justified by military necessity, and reverses that conclusion. The Prosecution's ground of appeal 3 is accordingly dismissed with regard to Duša.

453.   With regard to the other three villages, the Appeals Chamber notes that the Trial Chamber only expressly found the attack on Duša to be indiscriminate; it made no direct findings on whether the attacks on, Hrasnica, Ždrimci, and Uzričje were indiscriminate or otherwise.[1378] The Appeals Chamber recalls, however, that a trial judgement is to be read as a whole.[1379] In this instance, the Trial Chamber found that the attacks all began on the morning of 18 January 1993, and that all the villages were attacked with mortar shells, heavy machine guns, and artillery.[1380] It further found that the HVO operations "unfolded in exactly the same way", including by firing "shells" that destroyed several houses.[1381] Having regard to these findings, it is clear that the Trial Chamber considered that the attacks on Hrasnica, Ždrimci, and Uzričje were indiscriminate on the same bases as its finding in relation to the attack on Duša: that the HVO attacked the village by using weapons – more specifically, shells – the nature of which is such that it is impossible to distinguish military from civilian targets, and that they made no effort to allow the civilian **[page 189]** population of the village to flee before the attack. Recalling that this finding is reversed in relation to Duša,[1382] the Appeals Chamber reverses it in relation to Hrasnica, Ždrimci, and Uzričje for the same reasons. In light of the fact that the Trial Chamber relied on its finding of indiscriminate attack to conclude that the destruction of the houses was wanton and not justified by military necessity,[1383] the Appeals Chamber reverses this finding also, and the. subsequent finding that the elements of the crime of wanton destruction not justified by military necessity were met.[1384] The Prosecution's ground of appeal 3 is accordingly dismissed in relevant part. Finally, insofar as the Trial Chamber appears to have found the destruction of the

---

[1374]   Appeal Hearing, AT. 770 (28 Mar 2017).
[1375]   Appeal Hearing, AT. 404-405 (22 Mar 2017), 600-603 (24 Mar 2017). In addition, Praljak argues that the Trial Chamber did not establish the perpetrators or timing of the destruction of the property, while Ćorić argues that there was no evidence as to the location of civilians relative to combatants and military objectives, or any assessment by the Trial Chamber of the margin of error of artillery shelling. Appeal Hearing, AT. 405 (22 Mar 2017), 601-603 (24 Mar 2017).
[1376]   See *supra*, para. 444; Trial Judgement, Vol. 3, paras 1569 (referring to, *inter alia*, Trial Judgement, Vol. 3, paras 663-664, 711-712), 1570.
[1377]   See *supra*, paras 435, 442.
[1378]   Trial Judgement, Vol. 3, paras 663-664, 711-712. See also Trial Judgement, Vol. 2, paras 356-388.
[1379]   See *Stanišić and Župljanin* Appeal Judgement, paras 1107, 1115, 1148, 1162, 1181; *Popović et al.* Appeal Judgement, para. 2006; *Mrkšić and Šljivančanin* Appeal Judgement, para. 379.
[1380]   Trial Judgement, Vol. 2, para. 357.
[1381]   Trial Judgement, Vol. 4, para. 561. See also Trial Judgement, Vol. 4, para. 45.
[1382]   See *supra*, paras 435, 442.
[1383]   Trial Judgement, Vol. 3, para. 1569.
[1384]   Trial Judgement, Vol. 3, para. 1570.

houses during attacks on the four villages to have constituted an underlying act of the crime of persecution,[1385] the Appeals Chamber reverses this finding and the convictions of all Appellants under Count 1 in this regard.

3.   Burning of houses in Duša and Uzričje (Praljak's Ground 11)

454.   The Trial Chamber found that, on 18 January 1993, the HVO attacked the villages of Duša and Uzričje.[1386] Thereafter, the HVO took control of Duša "after one or two days of fighting",[1387] and occupied Uzričje from 19 January 1993 onwards.[1388] The Trial Chamber further found that, after the attack and takeover of Duša, HVO soldiers set fire to houses there.[1389] In so finding, it noted, *inter alia,* that, once the fighting ended, several witnesses specifically reported houses burned down by HVO soldiers.[1390] It also found that the HVO set fire to houses belonging to the Muslims of Uzričje to prevent those who lived there from returning.[1391] Further, it considered testimony that some houses that were burned down in Duša and Uzričje bore the inscription "HOS", that is, the abbreviated name of the paramilitary wing of the Croatian Party of Rights.[1392] The Trial Chamber concluded that, since the houses were burned down once the HVO had taken control of the villages, they did not constitute a military target.[1393] It accordingly found that the destruction of property belonging to the Muslim residents of Duša and Uzričje in the days following the attack of 18 January 1993 and the takeover of the villages constituted extensive destruction of property, not justified by military necessity and carried out unlawfully and wantonly as a grave breach of the **[page 190]** Geneva Conventions (Count 19) and wanton destruction of property not justified by military necessity as a violation of the laws or customs of war (Count 20).[1394]

(a) Arguments of the Parties

455.   Praljak submits that the Trial Chamber erroneously concluded that after the HVO took over the villages of Duša and Uzričje, HVO soldiers burned down houses therein in order to prevent inhabitants from returning.[1395] Praljak argues that the Trial Chamber's finding that the houses were burned on occupied territory is legally erroneous,[1396] considering that: (1) the evidence does not support the Trial Chamber's finding that houses in Duša were burned after fighting ended;[1397] (2) the Trial Chamber did not make a finding that houses in Uzričje were burned after fighting ended;[1398] and (3) even if houses were burned after combat ended, it was unreasonable to consider that the HVO could establish authority immediately after entering the villages.[1399] Praljak contends that the Trial Chamber's conclusion that the HVO burned houses in Uzričje in order to prevent inhabitants from returning is "deprived of any foundation" and in complete disregard of relevant evidence.[1400] He further submits that the Trial Chamber could not properly establish whether the houses were military targets as it: (1) incorrectly found that houses were burned down after the end of combat; and (2) did not consider military positions – situated in and near the houses – from which Muslims opened fire on HVO soldiers.[1401] In addition, Praljak submits that the Trial Chamber concluded that

---

[1385]   See Trial Judgement, Vol. 3, para. 1699.
[1386]   Trial Judgement, Vol. 2, paras 358, 374. See also Trial Judgement, Vol. 2, paras 357, 431.
[1387]   Trial Judgement, Vol. 2, paras 365, 398.
[1388]   Trial Judgement, Vol. 2, paras 374, 431.
[1389]   Trial Judgement, Vol. 2, para. 402.
[1390]   Trial Judgement, Vol. 2, para. 398.
[1391]   Trial Judgement, Vol. 2, paras 432, 436.
[1392]   Trial Judgement, Vol. 1, para. 777, Vol. 2, paras 401, 434.
[1393]   Trial Judgement, Vol. 3, paras 1537, 1572.
[1394]   Trial Judgement, Vol. 3, paras 1539, 1574.
[1395]   Praljak's Appeal Brief, para. 184, referring to Trial Judgement, Vol. 2, paras 398, 402, 432, 436, Vol. 3, paras 1537, 1572. See Praljak's Appeal Brief, paras 180-181; Praljak's Reply Brief, para. 64.
[1396]   Praljak's Appeal Brief, para. 178.
[1397]   Praljak's Appeal Brief, paras 175-177. See also Praljak's Appeal Brief, para. 179; Praljak's Reply Brief, paras 63-64. In further support, Praljak submits that the Trial Chamber could not establish exactly when the fighting ended in Duša and did not establish that the whole Muslim resistance stopped in both villages. Praljak's Appeal Brief, paras 175, 179.
[1398]   Praljak's Appeal Brief, para. 177. See also Praljak's Appeal Brief, para. 179; Praljak's Reply Brief, paras 63-64.
[1399]   Praljak's Appeal Brief, para. 178.
[1400]   Praljak's Appeal Brief, para. 180, referring to, *inter alia,* Trial Judgement, Vol. 2, para. 432, Ex. 4D00347.
[1401]   Praljak's Appeal Brief, para. 179; Praljak's Reply Brief, paras 63-64.

houses in Uzričje and Duša were burned by HVO members on the basis of inconclusive evidence.[1402] He claims that the Trial Chamber ignored the possibility that HOS soldiers, not under HVO command, burned the houses.[1403] Praljak requests that his conviction under Count 19 (extensive destruction of property as a grave breach of the Geneva Conventions) be reversed with respect to the relevant charges.[1404]

456. The Prosecution responds that Praljak fails to demonstrate any error with respect to the Trial Chamber's findings.[1405] It submits that the Trial Chamber: (1) applied the correct legal **[page 191]** standard when determining whether the property was in occupied territory; and (2) carefully analysed the evidence concerning the timing of the burning of the houses.[1406] Regarding Praljak's challenge to the Trial Chamber's conclusion that the HVO burned houses in Uzričje to prevent the Muslim population from returning, the Prosecution submits that the evidence upon which Praljak relies is unpersuasive.[1407] The Prosecution argues that the houses were not legitimate military targets and that the evidence does not support the claim that the Trial Chamber failed to consider possible military positions.[1408] Concerning Praljak's submission that the Trial Chamber's finding that HVO soldiers were responsible for the burning of houses was based on inconclusive evidence, the Prosecution argues that: (1) Praljak merely offers his own interpretation of the evidence; and (2) the Trial Chamber's finding that some burned houses bore the inscription "HOS" does not undermine its finding that HVO soldiers set the fires.[1409]

(b) Analysis

457. Concerning Praljak's submission that the Trial Chamber's finding that the houses were burned on occupied territory is legally erroneous because the evidence does not support its finding that houses in Duša were burned after fighting ended, the Appeals Chamber notes that Praljak refers to evidence which, according to him, demonstrates that *some,* but not all, houses were or may have been destroyed prior to the end of combat.[1410] The evidence he points to is therefore not inconsistent with the Trial Chamber's finding.[1411] In further support, Praljak submits that the Trial Chamber could not establish exactly when the fighting ended in Duša or did not establish that the whole Muslim resistance stopped in both villages.[1412] The Appeals Chamber considers that Praljak fails to show how the Trial Chamber's finding that the HVO took control of Duša "after one or two days of fighting"[1413] invalidates its finding that after the attack and takeover, HVO soldiers set fire to houses.[1414] Additionally, in submitting that the Trial Chamber did not establish that the whole Muslim resistance stopped in both villages, Praljak misrepresents the Trial Judgement as he actually points to the Trial Chamber's findings that ABiH members were present *during* the attacks on Duša **[page 192]** and Uzričje, prior to their surrender and the HVO's takeover.[1415] His arguments are therefore dismissed.

458. As to his submission that the Trial Chamber failed to make a finding that houses in Uzričje were burned after fighting ended, the Appeals Chamber finds that Praljak demonstrates no error, considering that

---

[1402]   Praljak's Appeal Brief, paras 181-182. See also Appeal Hearing, AT. 398, 404-405 (22 Mar 2017).
[1403]   Praljak's Appeal Brief, para. 183; Praljak's Reply Brief, para. 62.
[1404]   Praljak's Appeal Brief, para. 184.
[1405]   Prosecution's Response Brief (Praljak), para. 118.
[1406]   Prosecution's Response Brief (Praljak), para. 122. See also Prosecution's Response Brief (Praljak), para. 123; Appeal Hearing, AT. 419 (22 Mar 2017). The Prosecution submits that if any argument of Praljak's ground of appeal 11 succeeds and the Appeals Chamber finds that the villages were not occupied, it should enter convictions under Count 20 (wanton destruction as a violation of the laws or customs of war). Prosecution's Response Brief (Praljak), para. 124 & fn. 662.
[1407]   Prosecution's Response Brief (Praljak), para. 121, referring to, *inter alia,* Trial Judgement, Vol. 2, para. 432.
[1408]   Prosecution's Response Brief (Praljak), para. 119.
[1409]   Prosecution's Response Brief (Praljak), para. 120.
[1410]   See Praljak's Appeal Brief, paras 176-177, referring to, *inter alia,* Exs. P01291, P10108, p. 4, P10109, p. 2, P10110, p. 2, Fahrudin Agić, T. 9332 (1 Nov 2006), Witness BY, T. 9065, 9090-9091, 9122 (27 Oct 2006).
[1411]   See Trial Judgement, Vol. 2, paras 398, 402, Vol. 3, paras 1535, 1537, 1539, 1571-1572, 1574.
[1412]   Praljak's Appeal Brief, paras 175, 179.
[1413]   Trial Judgement, Vol. 2, paras 365, 398.
[1414]   Trial Judgement, Vol. 2, para. 402. See also Trial Judgement, Vol. 2, para. 398 (noting that once the fighting ended, several witnesses specifically reported houses burned down by HVO soldiers).
[1415]   See Praljak's Appeal Brief, para. 179 & fn. 408, referring to Trial Judgement, Vol. 2, paras 363-364, 377; Trial Judgement, Vol. 2, paras 365, 378.

the Trial Chamber assessed evidence and made findings demonstrating that Uzričje was occupied from 19 January 1993 and that houses were burned after the attack which had occurred on the previous day.[1416] In addition, when submitting that even if houses were burned after combat ended, it was unreasonable to consider that the HVO could establish authority immediately after entering the villages, Praljak argues that this is particularly true given that combat was still ongoing in Gornji Vakuf and refers to the Trial Chamber's consideration of testimony in this regard.[1417] Praljak bases his overall contention on his sub-ground of appeal 2.1 in which he challenges the Trial Chamber's finding that a state of occupation existed by arguing, *inter alia,* that armed conflict existed at the same time.[1418] The Appeals Chamber recalls that this submission is dismissed elsewehere,[1419] and therefore rejects Praljak's argument.

459. In support of his contention that the Trial Chamber's conclusion that the HVO burned houses in Uzričje in order to prevent inhabitants from returning is "deprived of any foundation" and in complete disregard of relevant evidence, Praljak draws attention to an HVO document ordering the release of Muslim civilians "to go home freely".[1420] He does not engage, however, with the evidence on which the Trial Chamber relied.[1421] The Appeals Chamber therefore considers that Praljak asserts that the Trial Chamber must have failed to consider relevant evidence, without showing that no reasonable trier of fact could have reached the same conclusion based on the evidence upon which the Trial Chamber relied. His argument is therefore dismissed. In arguing that the Trial Chamber could not properly establish whether the houses were military targets as it incorrectly found that houses were burned down after the end of combat, Praljak relies upon his submission dismissed above.[1422] His argument is therefore dismissed. Concerning Praljak's submission that the Trial Chamber did not consider military positions from which Muslims opened **[page 193]** fire on HVO soldiers, the Appeals Chamber notes that Praljak relies upon evidence and Trial Chamber findings indicating that there was an ABiH presence prior to and during the HVO's attack.[1423] Insofar as most of the houses were burned down after the HVO's attack and the subsequent surrender of ABiH soldiers,[1424] his submission is temporally irrelevant. The Appeals Chamber considers that he merely presents an alternative explanation and fails to show that no reasonable trier of fact could have reached the Trial Chamber's conclusion.[1425] Thus, his argument is dismissed.

460. As to his argument that the Trial Chamber concluded that houses in Uzričje were burned by HVO members on the basis of inconclusive evidence, Praljak claims that a document of the BiH Ministry of the Interior and the testimony of Witness Zijada Kurbegović, on which the Trial Chamber relied, are contradictory.[1426] The Appeals Chamber notes that the document of the BiH Ministry of the Interior lists HVO soldiers allegedly responsible for burning houses and that Praljak merely claims that "Kurbegovi[ć] could not recognize any of [the] persons listed in [the] document although two [of] these persons were her neighbors".[1427] The Appeals Chamber dismisses this argument as Praljak fails to demonstrate any contradiction.

[1416] Trial Judgement, Vol. 2, paras 431-433. See also *supra,* para. 344.
[1417] Praljak's Appeal Brief, para. 178 & fn. 407, referring to Trial Judgement, Vol. 2, para. 395.
[1418] Praljak's Appeal Brief, para. 178 & fn. 406, referring to Praljak's Appeal Brief, paras 46, 49-50.
[1419] See *supra,* para. 344.
[1420] See Praljak's Appeal Brief, para. 180, referring to Ex. 4D00347.
[1421] See Trial Judgement, Vol. 2, para. 432 & fn. 1023 and references cited therein (noting that the Croat-owned houses in Uzričje were left intact, finding that the evidence indicated that "the HVO burned down houses belonging to Muslims particularly", and referring in this regard to the testimony of Andrew Williams, Zijada Kurbegović, Senada Bašić, and Fahrudin Agić).
[1422] See *supra,* paras 457-458; Praljak's Reply Brief, para. 64 & fn. 136, referring to Praljak's Appeal Brief, paras 176-177.
[1423] Praljak's Appeal Brief, para. 179, referring to, *inter alia,* Trial Judgement, Vol. 2, paras 363-364, 377, Ex. 3D00527. Praljak relies on other evidence to demonstrate that there were Muslim military positions inside houses inhabited by civilians. However, the Appeals Chamber notes that the testimony to which he points does not indicate when this allegedly occurred. See Praljak's Appeal Brief, para. 179, referring to, *inter alia,* Rudy Gerritsen, T. 19350 (30 May 2007).
[1424] See Trial Judgement, Vol. 2, paras 365, 378, 398-402, 432-436, Vol. 3, paras 1535, 1537.
[1425] See Trial Judgement, Vol. 3, para. 1537.
[1426] See Praljak's Appeal Brief, para. 181, referring to, *inter alia,* Zijada Kurbegović, T. 8981 (26 Oct 2006), Trial Judgement, Vol. 2, para. 436 & fns 1029-1030, referring to, *inter alia,* Ex. P07350 (document of the BiH Ministry of the Interior), Zijada Kurbegović, T(F). 8982, 8988 (26 Oct 2006).
[1427] Praljak's Appeal Brief, para. 181. See Ex. P07350. In this regard, Praljak misrepresents the testimony wherein Kurbegovic clearly stated that she recognised persons listed in the document and that they were her neighbours. See Zijada Kurbegović, T. 8981 (26 Oct 2006). The Appeals Chamber also considers that Praljak notes statements he alleges were made by Kurbegović while citing instead to the evidence of another witness. Praljak does not adequately develop or explain the relevance of his assertions in this

461.   With respect to Duša, Praljak claims that the Trial Chamber's finding was based on the inconclusive evidence of Kemal Šljivo and Witness BY, and further argues that although Witness BY said HVO soldiers were in Duša, "she did not describe them or their uniforms and it is very likely that all armed Croats were for her the HVO members".[1428] The Appeals Chamber notes that in the testimony to which Praljak refers, Witness BY explicitly states that the soldiers were HVO members.[1429] While the testimony does not explain how she identified them as such, Praljak's argument that "it is very likely that all armed Croats were for her the HVO members" falls short of demonstrating that no reasonable trier of fact could have relied on this evidence in the absence of a **[page 194]** specific description of their uniforms. Further, Praljak misrepresents the evidence of Šljivo who, according to Praljak, "never claimed that the HVO members burned houses in Du[š]a".[1430] The Appeals Chamber notes that Šljivo stated that HVO members burned down houses in Duša in the evidence to which Praljak cites as well as evidence ignored by Praljak and upon which the Trial Chamber relied.[1431] Thus, these arguments are dismissed.

462.   When contending that the Trial Chamber ignored the possibility that HOS soldiers burned the houses, Praljak: (1) challenges the Trial Chamber's reliance on a 1994 report to find that most of the former members of the HOS joined the ranks of the HVO, while it failed to acknowledge that the report states that former HOS soldiers were targeted by the HVO; and (2) submits that the evidence shows that some HOS members joined the ABiH ranks.[1432] With respect to the Trial Chamber's reference to this report, the Appeals Chamber recalls that a failure to discuss an inconsistency or contradiction in the evidence is not necessarily indicative of disregard; rather, "it is within the discretion of the Trial Chamber to evaluate it and to consider whether the evidence as a whole is credible, without explaining its decision in every detail".[1433] Moreover, the Appeals Chamber notes that Praljak ignores the other evidence upon which the Trial Chamber relied when finding that most of the former members of the HOS joined the ranks of the HVO, and considers that he fails to show that the Trial Chamber could not have reached its conclusion in light of this evidence.[1434] Further, Praljak fails to show how the fact that some HOS members may have joined the ABiH – which the Trial Chamber explicitly noted – is inconsistent with the Trial Chamber's finding that *most* of the former HOS members joined the HVO.[1435] Insofar as Praljak is implicitly suggesting, by this assertion, that Muslim houses may have been destroyed by the HOS members who may have joined the ABiH, he fails to provide any support for this claim.

463.   For the above reasons, the Appeals Chamber dismisses Praljak's ground of appeal 11. **[page 195]**

4.   Arrest and detention of civilians from Duša, Hrasnica, Uzričje, and Ždrimci (Praljak's Ground 13)

464.   The Trial Chamber concluded that, following the attack on 18 January 1993, the HVO unlawfully imprisoned and confined civilians from the villages of Duša, Hrasnica, Uzričje, and Ždrimci.[1436] With regard to Duša specifically, the Trial Chamber found that women, children, and the elderly were arrested after

---

regard. See Praljak's Appeal Brief, para. 181 & fns 415-417, referring to Senada Bašić, T. 8893, 8895-8896 (25 Oct 2006), Ex. P09711 (witness statement by Senada Bašić), p. 3.

[1428]   Praljak's Appeal Brief, para. 182, referring to Witness BY, T. 9089-9091 (27 Oct 2006), Exs. P09202 (confidential), pp. 21-22, P10109, p. 2, P10110, p. 2. See also Praljak's Appeal Brief, para. 181.

[1429]   Witness BY, T. 9090 (27 Oct 2006).

[1430]   Praljak's Appeal Brief, para. 182. See also Appeal Hearing, AT. 398 (22 Mar 2017).

[1431]   See Praljak's Appeal Brief, para. 182, referring to, *inter alia*, Ex. P10110, p. 2; Trial Judgement, Vol. 2, para. 399, referring to, *inter alia*, Ex. P10108, p. 4.

[1432]   Praljak's Reply Brief, para. 62, referring to, *inter alia*, Ex. 3D00331.

[1433]   *Stanišić and Župljanin* Appeal Judgement, para. 458; *Popović et al.* Appeal Judgement, para. 1151; *Kvočka et al.* Appeal Judgement, para. 23. The Appeals Chamber notes that although the Trial Chamber did not address any inconsistency in Exhibit 3D00331, it did note, in light of an order by Sefer Halilović, that "one might conceivably conclude [...] that some former members of the HOS swore allegiance to the ABiH". Trial Judgement, Vol. 1, para. 778.

[1434]   Trial Judgement, Vol. 1, para. 778 & fns 1821-1825 and references cited therein. For example, when reaching this conclusion, it relied on a number of pieces of evidence to find that HOS and HVO soldiers conducted military operations alongside each other during which some former HOS members were still allowed to display their uniforms and insignia. See Trial Judgement, Vol. 1, para. 778 & fns 1822-1825 and references cited therein.

[1435]   See Trial Judgement, Vol. 1, para. 778.

[1436]   Trial Judgement, Vol. 3, paras 962, 1013. See also Trial Judgement, Vol. 3, paras 960-961, 1011-1012.

taking refuge in Enver Šljivo's house,[1437] after which HVO soldiers ordered them to go to Paloč, where they were further detained.[1438] In respect of Hrasnica, the Trial Chamber found that the HVO separated the men of military age from the women, children, and elderly, and arrested them, thereby creating two distinct groups of detainees.[1439] The arrested women, children, and elderly were then removed and detained by the HVO at various places, including the furniture factory in Trnovača and houses in Hrasnica and Trnovača.[1440] Regarding Uzričje, the Trial Chamber found that the Muslim villagers were held by the HVO inside the village as of 19 January 1993 for about a month-and-a-half.[1441] The villagers of Uzričje were assembled in houses in the village and had to observe a curfew, despite having some freedom of movement during the day.[1442] As for Ždrimci, the Trial Chamber found that the HVO detained Muslim women and children in houses that were under guard.[1443] It based this finding, *inter alia,* on: (1) the 27 January 1993 HVO report stating that 70 Muslim "civilians" from Ždrimci were arrested and detained;[1444] (2) the testimony of Witness Muamer Trkić estimating that 40 Muslim men and a greater number of women were arrested;[1445] and (3) the testimony of Witness Đulka Brica that HVO soldiers held her and others for a period of 15 days to a month in the basement of a house in Ždrimci.[1446] The Trial Chamber held that the HVO authorities did not make any individual assessments of the security reasons which could have led to the detention of civilians from Duša, Hrasnica, Uzričje, and Ždrimci.[1447] Based on all those findings the Trial Chamber concluded that the detention of the civilians from Duša, Hrasnica, Uzričje, and Ždrimci amounted to imprisonment **[page 196]** as a crime against humanity (Count 10) and unlawful confinement of civilians as a grave breach of the Geneva Conventions (Count 11).[1448]

(a) Arguments of the Parties

465.   Praljak submits that the Trial Chamber erred in law and fact when it concluded that civilians from the villages of Duša, Hrasnica, Uzričje, and Ždrimci in Gornji Vakuf Municipality were unlawfully arrested and detained by the HVO.[1449] With respect to the arrest of Muslim civilians in Duša in particular, Praljak argues that Witness BY's testimony indicates that HVO soldiers were not in the village and that it was Muslim troops who sent the civilians to the village of Paloč.[1450] He also submits that the 27 January 1993 HVO report to which the Trial Chamber referred does not support its findings as the report: (1) states that only some of the captured Muslims were detained; (2) does not allow for a conclusion that it refers to civilians from Duša accommodated in Paloč; and (3) contradicts another HVO report specifying that civilians in Duša and Uzričje were not detained.[1451] Concerning the treatment of civilians in Ždrimci, Praljak argues that the Trial Chamber based a conviction exclusively on Brica's untested Rule 92 *bis* statement.[1452] He argues that

---

[1437]   Trial judgement, Vol. 2, para. 405. With respect to both Duša and Uzričje, the Trial Chamber considered Exhibit P01333, a 27 January 1993 HVO report, noting the arrest and detention of 40 "Muslim civilians" from the villages. Trial Judgement, Vol. 2, paras 405, 445 & fns 973, 1042.

[1438]   Trial judgement, Vol. 2, paras 406-410. The Trial Chamber considered the evidence of Witness BY when finding that HVO soldiers ordered the women, children, and the elderly to go to Paloč, where they were detained. Trial Judgement, Vol. 2, paras 406-409 and references cited therein.

[1439]   Trial Judgement, Vol. 2, para. 416.

[1440]   Trial Judgement, Vol. 2, para. 427. See Trial Judgement, Vol. 2, paras 418-426.

[1441]   Trial Judgement, Vol. 2, para. 446.

[1442]   Trial Judgement, Vol. 2, para. 446.

[1443]   Trial Judgement, Vol. 2, para. 468.

[1444]   Trial Judgement, Vol. 2, para. 462.

[1445]   Trial Judgement, Vol. 2, para. 462.

[1446]   Trial Judgement, Vol. 2, para. 463.

[1447]   Trial Judgement, Vol. 3, paras 961, 1012.

[1448]   Trial Judgement, Vol. 3, paras 962, 1013.

[1449]   Praljak's Appeal Brief, para. 214, referring to, *inter alia,* Trial Judgement, Vol. 2, paras 416, 446, 468. See Praljak's Appeal Brief, paras 200 (referring to, *inter alia,* Trial Judgement, Vol. 3, paras 960-962, 1011-1013), 201, 203, 206, 209. See also Praljak's Reply Brief, para. 67.

[1450]   Praljak's Appeal Brief, para. 200. See Trial Judgement, Vol. 2, para. 410.

[1451]   Praljak's Appeal Brief, para. 202, referring to, *inter alia,* Trial Judgement, Vol. 2, para. 405 & fn. 973, Ex. P01333. Praljak also submits, referring to Exhibit P01351, that he does not "accept the qualification of the Trial Chamber" that 23 of the people who were detained in Duša were "defenders of the village", when they were in fact ABiH soldiers. Appeal Hearing, AT. 403 (22 Mar 2017). See Appeal Hearing, AT. 402 (22 Mar 2017), referring to Ex. P01351.

[1452]   Praljak's Appeal Brief, para. 209, referring to, *inter alia,* Trial Judgement, Vol. 2, paras 463, 467.

moreover, Brica's statement was contradicted by Trkić's testimony.[1453] He further submits that the Trial Chamber misrepresented Brica's statement and Trkić's evidence and failed to consider other evidence which makes no mention of confinement or imprisonment.[1454] Praljak disputes that civilians in Duša, Hrasnica, and Uzričje were detained by pointing to evidence allegedly indicating that they could leave the houses in which they were accommodated and that, with respect to Duša and Uzričje, these houses were not under guard.[1455] He additionally relies on the Trial Chamber's acknowledgement that the Muslim population in Uzričje had some freedom of movement during the day and that some left the village.[1456] **[page 197]**

466.   Further, Praljak argues that the Trial Chamber ignored that the 27 January 1993 HVO report stated that arrested and detained civilians, in some villages, were immediately released.[1457] He alleges that the Trial Chamber therefore erroneously concluded that the HVO did not conduct any individual assessments of the security reasons which could have led to the detention.[1458] Praljak, moreover, refers to evidence allegedly demonstrating that fighting was ongoing in or near Hrasnica and Ždrimci at the relevant time.[1459] Thus, he contends that the only reasonable conclusion is that the HVO evacuated the civilian population of Hrasnica from the combat area and imposed only the restrictions necessary for the security of the population of both Ždrimci and Hrasnica.[1460] In this regard, Praljak argues that a curfew – not limited to the Muslim population and legal under international humanitarian law – was imposed already in June 1992 upon Gornji Vakuf Municipality.[1461] Praljak requests that his convictions under Counts 10 (imprisonment as a crime against humanity) and 11 (unlawful confinement as a grave breach of the Geneva Conventions) be reversed with respect to the relevant charges for Gornji Vakuf Municipality.[1462]

467.   The Prosecution responds that Praljak fails to show that the Trial Chamber erred in convicting him under Counts 10 and 11.[1463] It submits that the Trial Chamber's findings pertaining to Duša are supported by the evidence.[1464] As to Ždrimci, the Prosecution avers that the Trial Chamber's findings are not dependent on just one witness, but on several.[1465] The Prosecution further submits that the Trial Chamber's finding that HVO soldiers detained Muslim civilians in Uzričje is not undermined by the fact that they had limited freedom of movement.[1466] According to the Prosecution, the 27 January 1993 HVO report confirms the Trial Chamber's reasonable finding that the HVO failed to conduct individual security evaluations in the four villages.[1467] Finally, the Prosecution argues that Praljak's unsupported and unpersuasive assertions that civilians in Hrasnica **[page 198]** and Ždrimci were merely evacuated from the combat area and their movement restricted for their protection, respectively, must fail.[1468]

(b) Analysis

468.   In relying on Witness BY's testimony to posit that the HVO did not arrest civilians in Duša and send them to Paloč, Praljak merely disagrees with the Trial Chamber's interpretation of the testimony. In that regard, the Appeals Chamber notes that the Trial Chamber interpreted Witness BY's testimony as stating

---

[1453]   Praljak's Appeal Brief, para. 210.
[1454]   Praljak's Appeal Brief, paras 210-211.
[1455]   Praljak's Appeal Brief, paras 201, 205-207 & fns 461, 472-473, 476-477, 479-480, referring to, *inter alia,* Articles 27 and 49 of Geneva Convention IV. ,
[1456]   Praljak's Appeal Brief, para. 207, referring to, *inter alia,* Trial Judgement, Vol. 2, paras 444, 446, 451.
[1457]   Praljak's Appeal Brief, paras 202, 210, 213, referring to, *inter alia,* Trial Judgement, Vol. 3, paras 961, 1012, Ex. P01333.
[1458]   Praljak's Appeal Brief, para. 213.
[1459]   Praljak's Appeal Brief, paras 203-204, 212.
[1460]   Praljak's Appeal Brief, paras 203-205, 212, referring to, *inter alia,* Articles 27 and 49 of Geneva Convention IV. In further support of this contention, Praljak notes that: (1) the HVO told civilians that they would be able to go home after the HVO took control of Dolac; and (2) the Ždrimci villagers recovered complete freedom of movement as soon as the cease-fire was signed. Praljak's Appeal Brief, paras 204, 212.
[1461]   Praljak's Appeal Brief, para. 208.
[1462]   Praljak's Appeal Brief, para. 214. See also Praljak's Reply Brief, para. 68.
[1463]   Prosecution's Response Brief (Praljak), para. 132.
[1464]   Prosecution's Response Brief (Praljak), para. 133.
[1465]   Prosecution's Response Brief (Praljak), para. 136..
[1466]   Prosecution's Response Brief (Praljak), para. 135. The Prosecution submits in this regard that Praljak merely disagrees with the Trial Chamber's interpretation of the evidence without showing any error. Prosecution's Response Brief (Praljak), para. 135.
[1467]   Prosecution's Response Brief (Praljak), para. 137, referring to, *inter alia,* Trial Judgement. Vol. 3, paras 961, 1012.
[1468]   Prosecution's Response Brief (Praljak), paras 134, 136.

that it was the HVO that ordered the civilians to go to Paloč.[1469] The Appeals Chamber considers that a reasonable trier of fact could have adopted this interpretation.[1470] In addition, Praljak fails to explain why the conviction should not stand on the basis of the remaining evidence.[1471]

469. With respect to Praljak's assertion that the 27 January 1993 HVO report does not support the Trial Chamber's findings, he fails to demonstrate how the fact that only some captured Muslims were detained or that the report may have referred to other detained Muslims from Duša shows any error in the impugned finding that civilians from Duša and Uzričje were detained. As to Praljak's related argument that the 27 January 1993 HVO report contradicts another HVO report, issued two days later,[1472] specifying that civilians in Duša and Uzričje were not detained, the Appeals Chamber first notes that Praljak ignores that the Trial Chamber did in fact note such a contradiction.[1473] Having reviewed the 27 January 1993 HVO report, the Appeals Chamber observes that the Trial Chamber referred only to page 1 of that report, which states that civilians were arrested and detained. It made no mention of page 2 of that same report, which states that they were released immediately, suggesting that no such contradiction exists. Nevertheless, the Trial Chamber relied on other evidence, including the evidence of those detained, indicating that the civilians in all four villages were not released immediately.[1474] In any event, the two reports, and the Trial Chamber's assessment thereof, do not support Praljak's contention that civilians were not detained in the first place. Thus, the Appeals Chamber dismisses Praljak's argument.[1475] **[page 199]**

470. The Appeals Chamber now turns to Praljak's arguments concerning the treatment of civilians in Ždrimci.[1476] Regarding Praljak's argument that the Trial Chamber based a conviction exclusively on Brica's Rule 92 *bis* statement, the Appeals Chamber considers that when making its finding that Muslim women and children were detained by the HVO in guarded houses in Ždrimci, the Trial Chamber also relied on other evidence.[1477] As to the argument that Brica's evidence was contradicted by Trkić's testimony, the Appeals Chamber considers that Praljak has failed to establish any contradiction.[1478] Praljak asserts but has failed to demonstrate that the Trial Chamber misrepresented Brica's evidence.[1479] Similarly, Praljak's argument that the Trial Chamber misrepresented Trkić's evidence is a mere assertion, referenced to a part of the Trial Judgement that makes no mention of his evidence.[1480] The Appeals Chamber further rejects the argument

---

[1469] See Trial Judgement, Vol. 2, para. 406, referring to, *inter alia,* Witness BY, T(F). 9082-9083 (27 Oct 2006).

[1470] The Appeals Chamber notes that, when asked who told the civilians to go to Paloč, Witness BY testified that "they told our troops" and then said that "[o]ur troops ordered us to do this because we didn't see any HVO soldiers in the village then". The Appeals Chamber notes that Witness BY also explained that the Muslim men from the village had surrendered to the HVO before the civilians were told to go to Paloč. See Witness BY, T. 9083 (27 Oct 2006).

[1471] See Trial Judgement, Vol. 2, paras 405-407 and references cited therein.

[1472] See *infra,* fn. 3703.

[1473] Trial Judgement, Vol. 2, para. 445, referring to Exs. P01351, P01333, p. 1.

[1474] See Trial Judgement, Vol. 2, paras 409-410, 421, 426-427, 441-443, 446, 463, 467-468 and references cited therein. See also Trial Judgement, Vol. 3, paras 961, 1012.

[1475] With regard to Praljak's submission that he does not "accept the qualification of the Trial Chamber" that 23 of the people who were detained in Duša were "defenders of the village", when they were in fact ABiH soldiers, the Appeals Chamber recalls that the Trial Chamber found that the persons that the HVO arrested included women, children, and the elderly who had taken refuge in Enver Šljivo's house in Duša, that is, persons who had not defended the village. Trial Judgement, Vol. 2, para. 405. See Trial Judgement, Vol. 2, paras 406-410 & fn. 979. The argument is therefore dismissed.

[1476] See Praljak's Appeal Brief, paras 209-211 and references cited therein. The Appeals Chamber considers that it is unclear whether Praljak impugns the Trial Chamber's findings regarding whether the civilians were detained or regarding how they were treated while in detention. However, the Trial Chamber found that it did not have sufficient evidence to determine the conditions of detention in Ždrimci and how detainees were treated there. Trial Judgement, Vol. 2, para. 468. See also Trial Judgement, Vol. 2, para. 464. The Appeals Chamber therefore understands that he impugns the Trial Chamber's finding that the HVO detained Muslim women and children in guarded houses in Ždrimci. Trial Judgement, Vol. 2, para. 468.

[1477] See Trial Judgement, Vol. 2, paras 461-462, 466, 468 and references cited therein.

[1478] Praljak merely alleges that "Trkić said that the population was not forced to go anywhere, it was just told to stay in the houses". Praljak's Appeal Brief, para. 210.

[1479] See Praljak's Appeal Brief, para. 210 & fn. 487, referring to Trial Judgement, Vol. 2, para. 463, referring to, *inter alia,* Ex. P09797, paras 9, 13-14, 23. The Appeals Chamber notes that the cited evidence provides support for the Trial Chamber's findings.

[1480] See Praljak's Appeal Brief, para. 210 & fn. 487, referring to Trial Judgement, Vol. 2, para. 463. To the extent that Praljak means to challenge the Trial Chamber's consideration of Trkić's testimony in paragraph 462 of Volume 2 of the Trial Judgement, the Appeals Chamber considers that the Trial Chamber merely noted therein that Trkić "estimated the total number of Muslims arrested at 40 men and a greater number of women". In asserting that "Trki[ć] said that the population was not forced to go anywhere, it was just told to stay in the houses", Praljak does not demonstrate how the Trial Chamber's statement was a misrepresentation of the testimony. See Praljak's Appeal Brief, para. 210.

that the Trial Chamber failed to consider certain evidence, specifically a 31 January 1993 document, making no mention of confinement or imprisonment[1481] as the Trial Chamber in fact did consider this evidence.[1482] Praljak also points to witness testimony that, according to him, confirms that the situation on the ground corresponded to his interpretation of the 31 January 1993 document.[1483] The Appeals Chamber considers that, in so doing, Praljak merely asserts that the Trial Chamber must have failed to consider relevant evidence, without showing that no reasonable trier of fact, based on the evidence, could have reached the same conclusion as the Trial Chamber did. Finally, in advancing the possibility that the HVO imposed only the restrictions necessary for the security of the population of Ždrimci, Praljak merely presents his own alternative explanation of the evidence **[page 200]** without showing that no reasonable trier of fact could have reached the same conclusion as the Trial Chamber did.[1484] All these arguments are dismissed.

471. Regarding Praljak's argument that civilians in Duša, Hrasnica, and Uzričje were not detained, the Appeals Chamber recalls that unlawful confinement as a grave breach of the Geneva Conventions arises in the following two circumstances:

> (i) [...] a civilian or civilians have been detained in contravention of Article 42 of Geneva Convention IV, *i.e.* they are detained without reasonable grounds to believe that the security of the Detaining Power makes it absolutely necessary; and

> (ii) [...] the procedural safeguards required by Article 43 of Geneva Convention IV are not complied with in respect of detained civilians, even where their initial detention may have been justified.[1485]

In adopting this definition, the Appeals Chamber noted that restrictions on the rights of civilians, such as the *"deprivation of their liberty* by confinement" are subject to the safeguards in Article 42, as well as Article 5, of Geneva Convention rv.[1486] As for imprisonment as a crime against humanity, the Appeals Chamber recalls that it "should be understood as arbitrary imprisonment, that is to say, *the deprivation of liberty* of the individual without due process of law, as part of a widespread or systematic attack directed against a civilian population".[1487]

472. Thus, it is clear from the above that both crimes concern the deprivation of liberty of an individual. Further, with the exception of chapeau requirements for war crimes and crimes against humanity, imprisonment – in the context of armed conflict – and unlawful confinement of civilians overlap significantly given that the Appeals Chamber has confirmed that the legality of imprisonment and the procedural safeguards pertaining to it are to be determined based on Articles 42 and 43 of Geneva Convention IV.[1488]

473. Finally, the Appeals Chamber considers that determining whether a person has been deprived of his or her liberty will depend on the circumstances of each particular case and must take into account a range of factors, including the type, duration, effects, and the manner of implementation of the measures allegedly amounting to deprivation of liberty.[1489] In that respect, the Appeals Chamber notes that it has in the past confirmed that both imprisonment and unlawful **[page 201]** confinement of civilians can occur even in situations where the civilians are held in houses in villages, including those who are held in their own village and their own houses, without guards, and where they have some freedom of movement. In *Kordić and Čerkez*, the Appeals Chamber upheld the Trial Chamber's finding that the civilians in the village of Rotilj

---

[1481]   Praljak's Appeal Brief, para. 211 & fn. 491, referring to Ex. P01373.

[1482]   Trial Judgement, Vol. para. 466, referring to Ex. P01373, p. 2. The Appeals Chamber considers that Praljak merely asserts that the Trial Chamber failed to interpret the evidence in a particular manner.

[1483]   Praljak's Appeal Brief, para. 211 & fn. 492, referring to Jacqueline Carter, T. 3364 (19 June 2006), Zrinko Tokić, T. 45373 (29 Sept 2009).

[1484]   See Trial Judgement, Vol. 3, paras 961, 1012.

[1485]   *Kordić and Čerkez* Appeal Judgement, para. 73. See *Čelebići* Appeal Judgement, para. 322.

[1486]   *Kordić and Čerkez* Appeal Judgement, para. 72 (emphasis added). See *Čelebići* Appeal Judgement, para. 321.

[1487]   *Kordić and Čerkez* Appeal Judgement, para. 116 (emphasis added, internal reference omitted). See also *Kordić and Čerkez* Appeal Judgement, para. 1043 (listing, in the context of cumulative convictions for persecution and imprisonment, deprivation of liberty without due process of law as an element of the crime of imprisonment).

[1488]   See *Kordić and Čerkez* Appeal Judgement, paras 114-115.

[1489]   See *Nada* Decision, para. 225; *Guzzardi* Decision, para. 92. The Appeals Chamber recalls that even though the ECtHR case-law is not binding on the Tribunal, it may be instructive in cases where there is no well-established Tribunal jurisprudence, as is the case here. See, *e.g., Popović et al.* Appeal Judgement, para. 436; *Đorđević* Appeal Judgement, para. 83; *Šainović et al* Appeal Judgement, paras 1647-1648; *Čelebići* Appeal Judgement, para. 24.

were imprisoned and unlawfully confined since the village was surrounded by HVO, the civilians were not held there for their own safety, and they were prevented from leaving while at the same time were subjected to beatings, thefts, and sexual abuse.[1490] Accordingly, the mere fact that the civilians from Duša, Hrasnica, and Uzričje had some freedom of movement does not necessarily mean that they were not deprived of their liberty and thus imprisoned or unlawfully confined. The Appeals Chamber will examine the facts relied on by the Trial Chamber in relation to each of the three locations, bearing in mind the evidence Praljak puts forward for this ground of appeal.

474.   In support of his argument that civilians from Duša, Hrasnica, and Uzričje were not detained, Praljak points to evidence and testimony which, according to him, suggest that civilians were able to move within certain areas at certain times.[1491] Specifically, he argues that: (1) in Paloč, according to Witness BY, there were no guards and women could leave the house;[1492] (2) the civilian population from Hrasnica was "secured and evacuated" from the combat area in the vicinity of Hrasnica according to Article 49 of Geneva Convention IV; after one night in a "collection center", it was "released" and "accommodated" in houses in Trnovača village and, according to Witness BX, was not prevented from leaving those houses;[1493] and (3) the Muslim population in Uzričje had some freedom of movement during daytime, which was acknowledged by the Trial Chamber.[1494] **[page 202]**

475.   The Appeals Chamber notes that the Trial Chamber explicitly considered the evidence relied upon by Praljak.[1495] Thus, with respect to Paloč and Trnovača, the Trial Chamber considered and relied on the evidence of Witnesses BY and BX, as well as the evidence of other witnesses, and ultimately concluded that civilians in both locations were detained and thus imprisoned and unlawfully confined.[1496] Concerning specifically Witness BY's evidence on Paloč, while she did state that there were "no guards protecting" them and that women could leave the house, she also stated that only some women did so in order to prepare food.[1497] As for Witness BX, the relevant portion of her evidence relied on by Praljak indicates in fact that she considered herself a "prisoner" as she could not go anywhere except to get food.[1498] Indeed, the Trial Chamber found, relying on the evidence of Witness BX, that the houses in Trnovača were guarded by HVO soldiers.[1499]

476.   As for Uzričje, the Trial Chamber noted trial arguments raised by Petković that the civilians in Uzričje "were neither locked-in nor kept prisoner, but sheltered from the hostilities" and that as soon as fighting stopped, the civilians were again authorised to move about as they wished.[1500] The Trial Chamber then considered evidence that villagers held in two Muslim houses in Uzričje retained a certain freedom of movement during the day to do domestic chores, listen to news reports, or find food, and that they were

[1490]   *Kordić and Čerkez* Trial Judgement, paras 792-793 & fn. 1688, 800 (finding that despite detainees having some liberty of movement inside the village of Rotilj, their conditions, which included overcrowding and forced labour, still amounted to detention); *Kordić and Čerkez* Appeal Judgement, paras 638-640 (upholding the detention finding). See also *Simić et al.* Trial Judgement, paras 563-567, 666, 680 (finding that despite detainees having some liberty of movement inside and outside of the village of Zasavica, where certain witnesses testified that detainees were essentially "free" and living a "normal life there" in individual houses, their conditions still amounted to detention); *Blaškić* Trial Judgement, paras 684, 691, 700 (finding that despite the defence argument that Bosnian Muslims in the village of Rotilj were not detained because their freedom of movement was not limited, their conditions still amounted to detention). These Trial Chamber findings in the *Simić et al.* and *Blaškić* cases on the nature of detentions in Zasavica and Rotilj, respectively, were not an issue on appeal.
[1491]   Praljak's Appeal Brief, paras 201, 205-207 & fns 461, 472-473, 476-477, 479-480.
[1492]   Praljak's Appeal Brief, para. 201, referring to Witness BY, T. 9085 (27 Oct 2006).
[1493]   Praljak's Appeal Brief, paras 204-205, referring to Witness BX, T. 8874 (25 Oct 2006). In connection with his argument that restrictions on movement of the Hrasnica villagers were necessary for the villagers' own security, Praljak argues that these were allowed under Article 27 of Geneva Convention IV. Praljak's Appeal Brief, para. 205, referring to his ground of appeal 8.1 where he relies on the Commentary to Article 27 of Geneva Conventions IV. The Appeals Chamber dismisses this ground of appeal elsewhere. See *infra*, paras 514, 517.
[1494]   Praljak's Appeal Brief, para. 207, referring to, *inter alia*, Trial Judgement, Vol. 2, paras 444, 446, 451.
[1495]   See, *e.g.*, Trial Judgement, Vol. 2, paras 406-407, 409, 418-420, 422, 424-426, 441-442, 444 & fns 974-975, 983-984, 991-998, 1001-1002, 1004-1009, 1032-1033, 1036-1040.
[1496]   See Trial Judgement, Vol. 2, paras 406-407, 409, 418-419, 424-426 & fns 974-975, 983-984, 993-995, 997-998, 1002, 1004-1009, Vol. 3, paras 962, 1013.
[1497]   See Witness BY, T. 9085 (27 Oct 2006).
[1498]   See Witness BX, T. 8874 (25 Oct 2006).
[1499]   Trial Judgement, Vol. 2, para. 425 and references cited therein.
[1500]   Trial Judgement, Vol. 2, para. 439.

required to return by nightfall.[1501] However, the Trial Chamber also considered that after the villagers surrendered, on 19 January 1993, the HVO arrested and separated them into two main groups which were put in these two houses.[1502] It further considered witness testimony that villagers were held until March or April 1993 at one house and 45 days at another, and that HVO soldiers guarded both houses.[1503] The Trial Chamber also took into account evidence of a witness who stated that she was held under HVO guard in various houses in Uzričje until February 1993 and that although one house at which she stayed was not under HVO control, HVO soldiers armed with rifles and stationed in the neighbouring house frequently made rounds about the house.[1504] The Trial Chamber found, in view of the evidence, that the Muslim villagers were indeed held by the HVO inside the village for about a month-and-a-half, considering, in this regard, that despite having some freedom of movement during the day, they were assembled in houses and had to observe a curfew.[1505] In its legal findings, the Trial Chamber concluded that **[page 203]** these civilians, arrested by the HVO in the course of large-scale operations during which the HVO arrested and then detained all the Muslims, were imprisoned and unlawfully confined, crimes under Articles 5 and 2 of the Statute, respectively.[1506]

477.   Given the evidence and the findings outlined above, the Appeals Chamber considers that Praljak fails to demonstrate that the Trial Chamber erred in qualifying its factual findings as amounting to deprivation of liberty in relation to the civilians from Duša, Hrasnica, and Uzričje. While these civilians had some freedom of movement, that freedom consisted of individuals occasionally leaving the houses they were in, notably to obtain food.[1507] Additionally, the evidence and the factual findings outlined above indicate that armed HVO troops ordered and even moved the civilians to various locations and also were present in those locations, such that the civilians did not feel free to leave; indeed, in Trnovača and Uzričje the houses were in fact guarded by the HVO.[1508]

478.   Regarding Praljak's remaining submission on freedom of movement, the Appeals Chamber notes that in further support of his argument that the Trial Chamber acknowledged that the Muslim population in Uzričje had some such freedom,[1509] he points to, *inter alia,* a paragraph in the Trial Judgement and states that the Muslims "were not confined to the house and even not to the village as some of them left the village".[1510] The Trial Chamber indeed noted evidence according to which a number of villagers being held by the HVO in houses under guard left the village because "they were still afraid of the fighting or of what might happen to them".[1511] It proceeded to find that a witness, who was held for 45 days in a house guarded by the HVO and fled with members of her family, was "seizing the opportunity when there were no HVO guards around the house".[1512] Praljak misrepresents the Trial Judgement to the extent that he suggests that the Trial Chamber's consideration of evidence of villagers who escaped as a result of fear is demonstrative of the fact that they were not deprived of their liberty.

479.   As for Praljak's arguments relating to the lawfulness of the detentions in Hrasnica, while he argues that the civilians from Hrasnica were "evacuated" to Trnovača, relying on Article 49 of Geneva Convention IV, the Appeals Chamber notes that in referring to the removal of the population as an "evacuation" Praljak merely disagrees with the Trial Chamber's qualification of what happened to the civilians. Indeed, the Trial Chamber specifically found that this removal was **[page 204]** not an evacuation.[1513] Further, with respect to his submission that these civilians had their movement restricted for their own security, which is permitted under Article 27 of Geneva Convention IV, the Appeals Chamber notes that Article 27(4) of Geneva Convention IV is broadly worded and provides that the Parties to the conflict "may take such measures of control and security in regard to protected persons as may be necessary as a result of the war". The

---

[1501]   Trial Judgement, Vol. 2, para. 444.
[1502]   Trial Judgement, Vol. 2, paras 440-441.
[1503]   Trial Judgement, Vol. 2, paras 441-442.
[1504]   Trial Judgement, Vol. 2, para. 443.
[1505]   Trial Judgement, Vol. 2, para. 446.
[1506]   Trial Judgement, Vol. 3, paras 961-962, 1012-1013.
[1507]   See *supra,* paras 475-476.
[1508]   See *supra,* paras 464, 475-476.
[1509]   See *supra,* paras 465, 471 & fn. 1494.
[1510]   Praljak Appeal Brief, para. 207, referring to Trial Judgement, Vol. 2, para. 451.
[1511]   Trial Judgement, Vol. 2, para. 451.
[1512]   Trial Judgement, Vol. 2, para. 452.
[1513]   Trial Judgement, Vol. 3, paras 846, 902. See also *infra,* para. 482.

Commentary to Article 27 then states that while restriction of movement is one of the measures a belligerent may inflict on protected persons, internment of civilians and the placing of civilians in assigned residences are the two most severe measures that may be inflicted on protected persons under Article 27 and, as such, are subject to strict rules outlined in Articles 41-43 and 78 of Geneva Convention IV.[1514] One of these rules is that the internment or placement in assigned residence may be ordered only if the security of the detaining party makes it absolutely necessary, while another provides that an initially lawful internment or placement in assigned residence clearly becomes unlawful if the detaining party does not respect the basic procedural rights of the detained persons and does not establish an appropriate court or administrative board as prescribed in Article 43 of Geneva Convention IV.[1515] As explained earlier, the Appeals Chamber considers that the Trial Chamber did not err in concluding that the events concerning Hrasnica villagers amounted to deprivation of liberty, and thus concerned more than a mere restriction of movement.[1516] Further, using the Geneva Convention IV terminology, the Appeals Chamber considers that the Trial Chamber findings and the evidence it relied on indicate that the civilians from Hrasnica were placed by the HVO in a number of "assigned residences" in Trnovača and elsewhere.[1517] In fact, Praljak himself argues that the civilians first spent a night in a "collection centre" and then were "accommodated" in houses in Trnovača.[1518] That being the case, this placement was subject to strict rules and requirements noted above. However, there is nothing in the factual findings outlined above to indicate that these rules were followed, namely that the civilians were moved to various locations because the HVO had reasonable grounds to believe that this was absolutely necessary for reasons of security,[1519] or that **[page 205]** the HVO established an appropriate court or administrative board in line with Article 43 of Geneva Convention IV.[1520]

480.   The Appeals Chamber considers as speculative Praljak's assertion that a statement in the 27 January 1993 HVO report – that civilians arrested in some villages were released immediately – demonstrates that the HVO conducted individual assessments of the security reasons which could have led to the detention. As to his assertion that the Trial Chamber ignored this statement, Praljak disregards the Trial Chamber's reliance on other evidence indicating that the civilians in all four villages were not released immediately.[1521] As such, it is a mere assertion that the Trial Chamber must have failed to consider relevant evidence without showing that no reasonable trier of fact, based on the evidence, could have reached the same conclusion as the Trial Chamber did. With respect to his argument, in particular, that a curfew was imposed already in June 1992 upon the whole population of Gornji Vakuf Municipality, the Appeals Chamber considers that Praljak fails to demonstrate how this assertion, and the evidence upon which he relies, is temporally relevant to the impugned findings. All these arguments are dismissed.

481.   For the foregoing reasons, the Appeals Chamber dismisses Praljak's ground of appeal 13.

5.   Displacement of Muslims from Duša, Hrasnica, Uzričje, and Ždrimci (Praljak's Ground 14)

482.   The Trial Chamber found that, following the attack on 18 January 1993, the HVO forcibly removed and transferred women, children, and the elderly from the villages of Duša, Hrasnica, Uzričje, and Ždrimci.[1522]

[1514]   Commentary on Geneva Convention IV, Article 27, p. 207.
[1515]   Geneva Convention IV, Arts. 42 and 78; *Čelebići* Appeal Judgement, para. 320. See also *Čelebići* Appeal Judgement, para. 327 ("the reasonable time which is to be afforded to a detaining power to ascertain whether detained civilians pose a security risk must be the minimum time necessary to make enquiries to determine whether a view that they pose a security risk has any objective foundation such that it would found a 'definite suspicion' of the nature referred to in Article 5 of Geneva Convention IV").
[1516]   See *supra*, para. 477.
[1517]   See *Kordić and Čerkez* Trial Judgement, para. 283 (noting that, according to the Commentary on Geneva Convention IV, assigned residence consists of moving people from their domicile and forcing them to live in a locality which is generally out of the way and where supervision is more easily exercised).
[1518]   See Praljak's Appeal Brief, para. 205.
[1519]   See Trial Judgement, Vol. 3, paras 961, 1012 (concluding that the HVO made no individual assessments of security reasons which could have led to the detention of civilians).
[1520]   See Trial Judgement, Vol. 3, paras 961, 1012 (holding that the Muslim civilians had no possibility of challenging their confinement with the relevant authorities).
[1521]   See Trial Judgement, Vol. 2, paras 409-410, 421, 426-427, 441-443, 446, 463, 467-468 and references cited therein. See also Trial Judgement, Vol. 3, paras 961, 1012.
[1522]   Trial Judgement, Vol. 3, paras 845-848, 900-906.

483.   With regard to Duša, the Trial Chamber found that after the inhabitants and the defenders of the village had surrendered, the HVO ordered women, children, and the elderly to go to Paloč, where they were further held for about a fortnight.[1523] The Trial Chamber also found that, during the first half of February 1993, these civilians were then taken from Paloč to Gornji Vakuf by UNPROFOR, noting that most of them were never able to return to their homes as their houses had been destroyed by the HVO.[1524] In that context, the Trial Chamber found that, by burning the **[page 206]** houses belonging to Bosnian Muslims at the time the fighting in Duša had ceased, the HVO deliberately prevented the Duša population from returning.[1525]

484.   With respect to Hrasnica, the Trial Chamber found that after the attack on the village, and after having arrested the men of military age and separated them from the women, children, and the elderly, the HVO removed the women, children, and the elderly and detained them successively at various places: in Hrasnica, a house in the hamlet of Volari, the furniture factory in Trnovača (arriving in three buses), and eventually houses surrounding the Trnovača factory.[1526] After about three weeks in detention in those houses, the HVO released the civilians without instructing them to go to any specific place but the Trial Chamber found that UNPROFOR "had to take" some of them to Bugojno as they could not return to their houses, which had been burnt down by the HVO.[1527] Other Hrasnica civilians detained in Volari were taken by the HVO to the Trnovača School; they were released after about a fortnight and ordered by the HVO to go to ABiH-held territory.[1528] The Trial Chamber was satisfied that the removal of these civilians from Hrasnica was "on no account an evacuation carried out for security purposes" and emphasised that by destroying the houses belonging to Bosnian Muslims in Hrasnica, while in control of the village, the HVO deliberately prevented the Hrasnica population from returning.[1529]

485.   Regarding Uzričje, the Trial Chamber found that, after the attack on the village, the HVO stole property from Muslim houses, set fire to them, and detained the Muslim population of Uzričje in a number of houses in the village, for about a month-and-a-half.[1530] The Trial Chamber also found that some detained Muslims fled Uzričje in the direction of ABiH-controlled territory, in fear of what lay ahead or following pressure from HVO soldiers.[1531] In regard to the latter, the Trial Chamber considered, *inter alia,* the testimony of Witness Zijada Kurbegović, who testified that the HVO ordered some Uzričje villagers, including herself and her family, to leave.[1532] The Trial Chamber also held that by burning the Muslim houses, the HVO deliberately prevented the Muslim population of Uzričje from returning.[1533]

486.   As for Ždrimci, the Trial Chamber found that, after the attack on the village, the HVO set fire to Muslim houses, stole Muslim property, arrested the men, and detained the Muslim women **[page 207]** and children in a number of houses in the village.[1534] After about a month-and-a-half in detention, these civilians were told by the joint HVO-ABiH commission, under the auspices of UNPROFOR, that they had been released and, according to the Trial Chamber, many had no choice but to leave the village since the HVO burned down at least about 30 houses belonging to Muslim families.[1535] The Trial Chamber also found that by destroying numerous Muslim houses the HVO deliberately prevented the Muslim population of Ždrimci from returning.[1536]

487.   On the basis of all these findings, the Trial Chamber concluded that the events in Duša, Hrasnica, Uzričje, and Ždrimci constituted inhumane acts (forcible transfer) as a crime against humanity (Count 8) and an unlawful transfer of civilians as a grave breach of the Geneva Conventions (Count 9).[1537]

[1523]   Trial Judgement, Vol. 2, paras 406, 410, Vol. 3, paras 845, 899.
[1524]   Trial Judgement, Vol. 2, para. 410, Vol. 3, paras 845, 900.
[1525]   Trial Judgement, Vol. 3, paras 845, 900. See Trial Judgement, Vol. 2, paras 398-402.
[1526]   Trial Judgement, Vol. 2, paras 416, 418-424, 427, 473, Vol. 3, paras 846, 902.
[1527]   Trial Judgement, Vol. 2, paras 426-427, Vol. 3, paras 846, 902.
[1528]   Trial Judgement, Vol. 2, paras 420-421, Vol. 3, paras 846, 902. See Trial Judgement, Vol. 2, para. 421.
[1529]   Trial Judgement, Vol. 3, paras 846, 902. See Trial Judgement, Vol. 2, paras 412-415 (where the Trial Chamber found that before burning Muslim houses the HVO searched them and stole property from them).
[1530]   Trial Judgement, Vol. 2, paras 432-436, 440-443, 446.
[1531]   Trial Judgement, Vol. 2, para. 454.
[1532]   Trial Judgement, Vol. 2, para. 453.
[1533]   Trial Judgement, Vol. 3, paras 847, 904.
[1534]   Trial Judgement, Vol. 2, paras 456-468.
[1535]   Trial Judgement, Vol. 3, paras 848, 905-906. See Trial Judgement, Vol. 2, paras 466-468.
[1536]   Trial Judgement, Vol. 3, paras 848, 906.
[1537]   Trial Judgement, Vol. 3, paras 845-848, 899-906.

(a) Arguments of the Parties

488.   Praljak submits that the Trial Chamber erroneously concluded that the Muslim population was unlawfully displaced from the villages of Duša, Hrasnica, Uzričje, and Ždrimci in Gornji Vakuf Municipality.[1538] With respect to Duša, Praljak argues that Witness BY stated that Muslim troops, not the HVO, ordered civilians in Duša to go to Paloč.[1539] He also submits that Paloč is not sufficiently remote from Duša to fulfil the *actus reus* of forcible transfer.[1540] In the same vein, Praljak contends that given that some people from Ždrimci went to nearby villages where they lived with their families in a familiar environment, the Trial Chamber failed to establish that the population was uprooted from the territory and environment in which it normally lived.[1541] Regarding Hrasnica, Praljak submits that: (1) it is not clear whether the Trial Chamber considered that forcible transfer was committed when the population was removed from Hrasnica or three weeks later when some decided to go elsewhere;[1542] and (2) the finding that some people were told to go to ABiH territory was based on hearsay.[1543] With respect to Duša and Hrasnica, Praljak submits that: (1) as the populations were found to be "arrested/detained", they could not be considered to have been forcibly transferred;[1544] (2) people who left Duša and Hrasnica were **[page 208]** returning to the places from which they originally came;[1545] and (3) people were able to and did return to their homes.[1546]

489.   Praljak argues that, in any case, forcible transfer assumes force or coercion and that therefore the Trial Chamber's findings that the populations were unable to return to their homes cannot constitute a sufficient basis for the crime.[1547] Praljak further argues that while the burning of houses might sometimes constitute coercion, the Trial Chamber failed to establish: (1) the nexus between this act and the removal of the population;[1548] and (2) that those who burned houses did so with the intent to forcibly remove.[1549] He submits that the Trial Chamber did not consider that civilians may have fled out of fear for their safety following the "commencement of the armed conflict".[1550] Praljak requests that his convictions under Counts 8 (inhumane acts (forcible transfer) as a crime against humanity) and 9 (unlawful transfer as a grave breach of the Geneva Conventions) be reversed with respect to the relevant charges for Gornji Vakuf Municipality.[1551]

490.   The Prosecution responds that Praljak merely disagrees with the Trial Chamber's interpretation of evidence without showing an error.[1552] The Prosecution argues that the Trial Chamber's findings that villagers were unlawfully detained do not preclude its well-grounded findings that they were forcibly transferred or expelled.[1553] It also contends that, given that the Muslims had no choice in leaving, their

---

[1538]   Praljak's Appeal Brief, para. 230, referring to, *inter alia,* Trial Judgement, Vol. 3, paras 845-848, 900-906. See also Praljak's Reply Brief, para. 67.
[1539]   Praljak's Appeal Brief, para. 217. Praljak also submits that "[i]t seems that the [Trial Chamber] does not consider that the HVO is responsible for the subsequent removal of [the] population from the area by UNPROFOR". Praljak's Appeal Brief, para. 215.
[1540]   Praljak's Appeal Brief, para. 218.
[1541]   Praljak's Appeal Brief, para. 228, referring to, *inter alia,* Trial Judgement, Vol. 3, paras 848, 906.
[1542]   Praljak's Appeal Brief, para. 220. See Praljak's Appeal Brief, para. 224.
[1543]   Praljak's Appeal Brief, para. 221.
[1544]   Praljak's Appeal Brief, paras 216 (referring to, *inter alia,* Trial Judgement, Vol. 2, para. 405), 220.
[1545]   Praljak's Appeal Brief, paras 217, 223. See Praljak's Appeal Brief, para. 222.
[1546]   Praljak's Appeal Brief, paras 219, 222.
[1547]   Praljak's Appeal Brief, paras 222 (referring to Trial Judgement, Vol. 2, para. 427), 226, 229. With specific regard to Uzričje, Praljak also argues that the Trial Chamber's finding that the HVO forced the Muslim population to leave was based solely on Kurbegović's testimony, which was imprecise and contradicted by an ABiH document (Ex. P01226). Praljak's Appeal Brief, para. 225.
[1548]   Praljak's Appeal Brief, para. 229. Praljak submits that the Trial Chamber found, without evidence, that some Ždrimci villagers left because their houses had been destroyed. Praljak's Appeal Brief, para. 227.
[1549]   Praljak's Appeal Brief, para. 229.
[1550]   Praljak's Appeal Brief, para. 229. See Praljak's Appeal Brief, paras 221-222, 227. Praljak also argues that civilians were removed from Hrasnica during combat for their own security. Praljak's Appeal Brief, para. 221.
[1551]   Praljak's Appeal Brief, para. 231. See also Praljak's Reply Brief, para. 68.
[1552]   Prosecution's Response Brief (Praljak), para. 138. The Prosecution also submits that UNPROFOR's efforts relating to the removal of some victims does not alter the unlawfulness of the HVO's conduct. Prosecution's Response Brief (Praljak), para. 140.
[1553]   Prosecution's Response Brief (Praljak), para. 139.

transfer was unlawful, notwithstanding the type of coercion or distance.[1554] The Prosecution avers that the displacements were not intended to be temporary but to drive the Muslims from their homes.[1555] **[page 209]**

(b) Analysis

491.   The Appeals Chamber recalls that it has already dismissed Praljak's argument concerning Witness BY's evidence relating to Duša.[1556] Regarding Praljak's arguments that Paloč is not sufficiently remote from Duša and that some people from Ždrimci went to nearby villages where they lived with their families in a familiar environment, the Appeals Chamber recalls that it has found in the context of the crime against humanity of persecution through forcible displacement that:

> The prohibition against forcible displacements aims at safeguarding the right and aspiration of individuals to live in their communities and homes without outside interference. The forced character of displacement and the forced uprooting of the inhabitants of a territory entail the criminal responsibility of the perpetrator, not the destination to which these inhabitants are sent.[1557]

The Appeals Chamber considers that this rationale applies equally to the crime of unlawful transfer of a civilian as a grave breach of the Geneva Conventions and the crime against humanity of other inhumane acts through forcible transfer.

492.   The Trial Chamber found that the HVO burned down about 16 and 30 houses belonging to Muslim families in Duša and Ždrimci, respectively.[1558] The Trial Chamber considered that because it was impossible for them to return to their homes, these persons were deprived of their right to enjoy a normal social and family life.[1559] The Appeals Chamber notes that, contrary to Praljak's claim, the *actus reus* of forcible displacement does not require that the population be removed to a "location sufficiently remote from its original location".[1560] Given the findings set out above, Praljak's arguments regarding Duša and Ždrimci are dismissed.

493.   Regarding Hrasnica, the Appeals Chamber considers that Praljak misrepresents the Trial Chamber's findings when submitting that it is not clear whether the Trial Chamber considered that forcible transfer was committed when the population was removed from Hrasnica or three weeks later when some decided to go elsewhere. In that respect, the Trial Chamber concluded that the "women, children and elderly person from the village of Hrasnica were forcibly removed *from their village*" indicating that the removal started at the moment when they were forced to leave the village.[1561] This is in line with the rationale outlined above.[1562] The Appeals Chamber further notes **[page 210]** that the Trial Chamber reached this conclusion based on the totality of the events, namely that: (1) after the HVO attack on the village, the HVO took civilians to various locations where they were subsequently detained; (2) after about three weeks in detention, the HVO released them – admittedly without instructing them to go to a specific location – but UNPROFOR had to take some of them to Bugojno, since their houses had been burnt by the HVO; and (3) another group of civilians held at the Trnovača school was released after a fortnight and ordered by the HVO to go to ABiH-held territory.[1563] The Trial Chamber additionally found that by making sure that all the houses belonging to Muslim families had been destroyed, the HVO – which was in control of the village – deliberately prevented the civilian population from returning.[1564] Praljak ignores the latter finding. As to Praljak's submission that the Trial

---

[1554]   Prosecution's Response Brief (Praljak), para. 139.
[1555]   Prosecution's Response Brief (Praljak), paras 140-141. The Prosecution also submits that the Trial Chamber explicitly rejected the possibility that the Muslims were removed for their own security or for compelling military reasons. Prosecution's Response Brief (Praljak), para. 140.
[1556]   See *supra*, para. 468. The Appeals Chamber notes that Praljak's assertion that "[i]t seems that the [Trial Chamber] does not consider that the HVO is responsible for the subsequent removal of [the] population from the area by UNPROFOR" does not allege any error. Praljak's Appeal Brief, para. 215.
[1557]   *Krnojelac* Appeal Judgement, para. 218. See *Naletilić and Martinović* Appeal Judgement, para. 153.
[1558]   Trial Judgement, Vol. 3, paras 845, 848, 900, 906. See Trial Judgement, Vol. 2, paras 402, 467-468.
[1559]   Trial Judgement, Vol. 3, paras 845, 848, 900, 906.
[1560]   Praljak's Appeal Brief, para. 218. See *Krnojelac* Appeal Judgement, para. 222.
[1561]   Trial Judgement, Vol. 3, para. 902 (emphasis added).
[1562]   See *supra*, para. 491.
[1563]   Trial Judgement, Vol. 3, paras 846, 902. See Trial Judgement, Vol. 2, paras 419-427.
[1564]   Trial Judgement, Vol. 3, paras 846, 902. See Trial Judgement, Vol. 2, paras 426-427.

Chamber's finding that some people from Hrasnica were told to go to ABiH territory was based on hearsay, the Appeals Chamber recalls that the Trial Chamber is entitled to rely upon hearsay evidence, provided it is reliable and credible,[1565] and notes that Praljak provides no argument to the contrary,[1566] For the foregoing reasons, his arguments are dismissed.

494. As to Praljak's argument, pertaining to Duša and Hrasnica, that the populations found to be "arrested/detained" could not be considered to have been forcibly removed, the Appeals Chamber considers that Praljak merely makes a blanket statement and fails to show how a finding that people were detained detracts from a finding that they were forcibly transferred. In support of his contentions that people who left were returning to the places from which they originally came and that people were able to and did return to their homes, Praljak relies on evidence and a Trial Chamber finding that, at most, indicate this to be the case for *some* people.[1567] In that respect, the Appeals Chamber notes that for Duša Praljak relies on the evidence of Witness BY and Witness BW, who testified that a few people from Paloč arrived to Duša prior to the removal of the population because they felt unsafe in Paloč.[1568] The Appeals Chamber does not consider that the presence of a small number of locals from Paloč among the population of Duša undermines the impugned finding. As for Hrasnica, Praljak relies on the evidence of Witness BX who testified that she was from the village of Planinci in Bugojno and came to Hrasnica with her family in 1992.[1569] Her testimony shows that following the detention in Trnovača factory and **[page 211]** Trnovača houses she was able to go back home to Bugojno.[1570] The Appeals Chamber does not consider that the mere fact that Witness BX was ultimately able to go back home undermines the Trial Chamber's finding that the women, children, and the elderly from Hrasnica were forcibly removed and transferred. Praljak fails to show how these arguments contradict the impugned finding. These arguments are therefore dismissed.

495. Concerning Praljak's claim that forcible transfer assumes force or coercion and that the Trial Chamber's findings that the populations were unable to return to their homes therefore cannot constitute a sufficient basis for the crime, the Appeals Chamber recalls that it is the absence of genuine choice that makes displacement unlawful.[1571] Factors other than force itself may render displacement involuntary and include "the threat of force or coercion, such as that caused by fear of violence, duress, detention, psychological oppression or abuse of power [...] or by taking advantage of a coercive environment".[1572] The Appeals Chamber has previously also confirmed that creating "severe living conditions" for a certain population – which in turn makes it impossible for that population to remain in their homes – can amount to forced displacement.[1573] Finally, whether a transferred person had a genuine choice is a determination to be made within the context of a particular case.[1574] The Appeals Chamber therefore considers that Praljak has failed to show that no reasonable trier of fact could reach the conclusion that civilians in the four villages were forcibly transferred because the HVO destroyed their houses and deliberately made it impossible for them to

---

[1565] *Stanišić and Župljanin* Appeal Judgement, para. 463 & fn. 1574; *Popović et al.* Appeal Judgement, para. 1276; *Šainović et al.* Appeal Judgement, para. 846.

[1566] See Praljak's Appeal Brief, para. 221.

[1567] See Praljak's Appeal Brief, para. 217 & fn. 503 (referring to Witness BW, T. 8769 (closed session) (19 Oct 2006), Witness BY, T. 9073 (27 Oct 2006)), para. 219 & fn. 507 (referring to Witness BY, T. 9085-9086 (27 Oct 2006)), paras 222-223 & fn. 519 (referring to Ex. P09710 (confidential), pp. 2, 4, Witness BX, T. 8845 (25 Oct 2006)).

[1568] Witness BY, T. 9073 (27 Oct 2006); Witness BW, T. 8769 (closed session) (19 Oct 2006) (stating that a group of six people from Paloč came to Duša).

[1569] See Ex. P09710 (confidential), p. 2; Witness BX, T. 8845 (25 Oct 2006).

[1570] See Ex. P09710 (confidential), p. 4; Trial Judgement, Vol. 2, para. 422.

[1571] *Đorđević* Appeal Judgement, para. 727 (in the context of the crime against humanity of other inhumane acts through underlying acts of forcible transfer); *Stakić* Appeal Judgement, para. 279 (in the context of deportation as a crime against humanity); *Krnojelac* Appeal Judgement, para. 229 (in the context of the crime against humanity of persecution through underlying acts of forcible displacement).

[1572] *Đorđević* Appeal Judgement, para. 727 (in the context of the crime against humanity of other inhumane acts through underlying acts of forcible transfer); *Krajišnik* Appeal Judgement, para. 319 (in the context of deportation as a crime against humanity); *Stakić* Appeal Judgement, para. 279 (in the context of deportation as a crime against humanity); *Krnojelac* Appeal Judgement, para. 229 (in the context of the crime against humanity of persecution through underlying acts of forcible displacement).

[1573] *Krajišnik* Appeal Judgement, paras 308, 319.

[1574] *Đorđević* Appeal Judgement, para. 727 (in the context of the crime against humanity of other inhumane acts through underlying acts of forcible transfer); *Stakić* Appeal Judgement, para. 282 (in the context of deportation as a crime against humanity); *Krnojelac* Appeal Judgement, para. 229 (in the context of the crime against humanity of persecution through underlying acts of forcible displacement).

return.[1575] Praljak's argument that the Trial Chamber failed to establish the nexus between the act of burning houses and the removal of the population also fails as the Trial Chamber clearly made findings establishing that nexus in relation to all four villages.[1576] **[page 212]**

496.   As for Praljak's argument that the Trial Chamber failed to consider that civilians may have fled out of fear for their safety following "the commencement of the armed conflict",[1577] the Appeals Chamber notes that the Trial Chamber was satisfied that the removals in Duša, Hrasnica, and Uzričje occurred at a time when the HVO controlled the villages and there was no more fighting. The Trial Chamber also found that the HVO made no arrangements for the population to return and, in fact, deliberately prevented them from returning by destroying property.[1578] Further, with respect to Ždrimci, the Trial Chamber established that following the 18 January 1993 attack, numerous civilians also had no choice but to leave the village given that the HVO burned down at least about 30 houses, all of which belonged to Muslim families.[1579] In light of these findings, the Appeals Chamber dismisses Praljak's argument, as he merely disagrees with the Trial Chamber's findings without demonstrating an error. Finally, contrary to Praljak's assertion, the Trial Chamber established that those who burned the houses did so with the intent to forcibly remove.[1580]

497.   For the foregoing reasons, the Appeals Chamber dismisses Praljak's ground of appeal 14.

6.   Commission of crimes by the Bruno Bušič Regiment in Ždrimci and Uzričje (Petković's Sub-grounds 5.2.2.2 and 5.2.3.1 both in part)

498.   The Trial Chamber found that on 18 January 1993, the inhabitants of Ždrimci gradually surrendered to HVO soldiers, including soldiers from the Bruno Bušić Regiment.[1581] It further found that the arrested inhabitants included women, children, and the elderly, and that the HVO detained all Muslims irrespective of their status.[1582] With regard to the village of Uzričje, it found that members of the Bruno Bušić Regiment were among the HVO soldiers most implicated in thefts and in setting fire to houses.[1583]

499.   Petković submits that there is no evidence that members of the Bruno Bušić Regiment committed crimes in Gornji Vakuf.[1584] He challenges the Trial Chamber's reliance on the testimony of Witness Nedžad Čaušević with regard to the arrest of the inhabitants of Ždrimci, arguing that Čaušević actually stated that the HVO, including members of the Bruno Bušić Regiment, detained him and other men *who defended the village,* and that the detention of combatants is not a war **[page 213]** crime.[1585] Petković further notes that the Trial Chamber's finding that members of the Bruno Bušić Regiment were implicated in the thefts and fires in Uzričje is based on: (1) a document of the BiH intelligence service in which three soldiers allegedly belonging to the Regiment are mentioned; and (2) the testimony of Witness Zijada Kurbegović, which he contends does not mention the Regiment.[1586]

[1575]   See, *e.g.,* Trial Judgement, Vol. 3, paras 845-848, 900, 902, 904, 906. The Appeals Chamber dismisses Praljak's challenge to Kurbegović's testimony as he fails to demonstrate that no reasonable trier of fact could have concluded that the HVO forcibly transferred the Muslim population, having considered, *inter alia,* her evidence as well as Exhibit P01226. See Trial Judgement, Vol. 2, paras 451-454, Vol. 3, paras 847, 904.

[1576]   See *supra,* paras 483-486. Moreover, contrary to Praljak's related submission, the Trial Chamber did in fact rely on evidence that some Ždrimci villagers left because their houses had been destroyed. See Trial Judgement, Vol. 2, para. 467 & fn. 1071, referring to Ex. P09797, para. 23. This argument is therefore dismissed.

[1577]   Praljak's Appeal Brief, para. 229. When arguing that civilians were removed from Hrasnica during combat for their own security, Praljak relies on his ground of appeal 13 which the Appeals Chamber dismisses elsewhere. See Praljak's Appeal Brief, para. 221 & fn. 512; *supra,* paras 468-481. See also Trial Judgement, Vol. 2, paras 451-454.

[1578]   Trial Judgement, Vol. 3, paras 845-847, 900, 902, 904.

[1579]   Trial Judgement, Vol. 3, paras 848, 906.

[1580]   Trial Judgement, Vol. 3, paras 845-848, 900, 902, 904, 906.

[1581]   Trial Judgement, Vol, 2, para. 384.

[1582]   Trial Judgement, Vol. 2, para. 468.

[1583]   Trial Judgement, Vol. 2, para. 436.

[1584]   Petković's Appeal Brief, paras 234(iii), 343; Petković's Reply Brief, paras 34(ii), 35; Appeal Hearing, AT. 573-574 (23 Mar 2017). Petković also submits that "no document dating from the first half of 1993 exists indicating that the Bruno Bušić unit committed any crimes in Jablanica in April 1993". Appeal Hearing, AT. 573 (23 Mar 2017).

[1585]   Petković's Appeal Brief, paras 234(iii)(a), 343.

[1586]   Petković's Appeal Brief, paras 234(iii)(b), 343.

500.   The Prosecution responds that the villagers in Ždrimci who were detained by members of the Bruno Bušić Regiment included civilians and that the evidence leaves no doubt that it was members of the Regiment who perpetrated the crimes in Uzričje.[1587]

501.   The Appeals Chamber rejects Petković's suggestion that only combatants were detained in Ždrimci. In the testimony to which Petković refers, Čaušević stated that he and others surrendered because they "could see that the other civilians were in danger if we still tried to hide" and that those detained by the soldiers from the Bruno Bušić Regiment were "mostly older men and young boys, one was only 12 years old".[1588] As such, Petković misrepresents the evidence. With regard to Uzričje, the Appeals Chamber notes that Petković fails to articulate an error in the Trial Chamber's reliance on the report of the BiH intelligence service under reference. His argument that there is no evidence that members of the Bruno Bušić Regiment committed crimes in Gornji Vakuf is accordingly dismissed,[1589] as are his sub-grounds of appeal 5.2.2.2 and 5.2.3.1, both in relevant part.

E.   Arrest, Detention, and Displacement of Muslims in Prozor Municipality in July-August 1993

1.   Arrest and detention of civilians from Prozor (Praljak's Ground 8)

502.   The Trial Chamber concluded that, between late **July** and early August 1993, the HVO unlawfully imprisoned civilians in the Podgrađe neighbourhood of Prozor and the villages of Lapsunj and Duge, in Prozor Municipality, thereby committing imprisonment as a crime against humanity (Count 10) and unlawful confinement of civilians as a grave breach of the Geneva **[page 214]** Conventions (Count 11).[1590] Further, it found that the conditions in which the Muslims of Podgrađe, Lapsunj, and Duge were held between late July and late August 1993 were very harsh,[1591] amounting to inhumane acts (conditions of confinement) as a crime against humanity (Count 12) and inhuman treatment (conditions of confinement) as a grave breach of the Geneva Conventions (Count 13).[1592] In reaching these conclusions, the Trial Chamber found that in late July and early August 1993, following the arrests of Muslim men, the HVO rounded up and escorted a number of Muslim women, children, and elderly from Prozor Municipality to Podgrađe, Lapsunj, and Duge.[1593] Further, the Trial Chamber held that: (1) from about 19 August 1993 until 28 August 1993, at least 1,760 Muslims were being held in Podgrađe in about 100 houses;[1594] (2) the houses in Podgrađe held 20 to 70 women, children, and elderly people, and some houses held more than 80 people;[1595] (3) in August 1993, the Muslims in Lapsunj were crowded together, 20-30 per house, and had no running water or hygienic products thus contracting lice and various skin problems;[1596] and (4) on 20 August 1993, between 700 and 800 Muslims were held in the houses in Duge in overcrowded conditions, with around 30 people per house, and without sufficient food.[1597] The Trial Chamber also found that the HVO soldiers and members of the Military Police committed thefts against Muslims in all three locations and that Muslim women and girls were subjected to sexual attacks and rapes by those forces.[1598] The Trial Chamber further concluded that the objective of placing the Muslim civilians in detention was to accommodate the Croats who were arriving in

---

[1587]   Prosecution's Response Brief (Petković), para. 177. See also Prosecution's Response Brief (Petković), para. 134. The Prosecution notes that the Bruno Bušić Regiment was also present in Duša, where HVO troops also committed crimes against Muslims and their property. Prosecution's Response Brief (Petković), para. 177.
[1588]   Ex. P09201, p. 20.
[1589]   The Appeals Chamber also dismisses as an undeveloped assertion Petković's submission that "no document dating from the first half of 1993 exists indicating that the Bruno Bušić unit committed any crimes in Jablanica in April 1993". Appeal Hearing, AT. 573 (23 Mar 2017).
[1590]   Trial Judgement, Vol. 3, paras 958-959, 1009-1010. See Trial Judgement, Vol. 2, paras 225, 232. Specifically, the Trial Chamber considered that HVO soldiers – the Trial Chamber did not know to which unit they belonged – as well as Military Police officers under Ilija Franjić's command, arrested Muslim women, children, and elderly people. Trial Judgement, Vol. 2, para. 232.
[1591]   Trial Judgement, Vol. 2, paras 249, 257, 267, Vol. 3, para. 958.
[1592]   Trial Judgement, Vol. 3, paras 1059-1067, 1102-1111.
[1593]   Trial Judgement, Vol. 2, paras 225-227, 239, 254, 263.
[1594]   Trial Judgement, Vol. 2, para. 240.
[1595]   Trial Judgement, Vol. 2, para. 244. See Trial Judgement, Vol. 3, para. 1009.
[1596]   Trial Judgement, Vol. 2, paras 255-256.
[1597]   Trial Judgement, Vol. 2, paras 263, 266.
[1598]   Trial Judgement, Vol. 2, paras 250-253, 258-262, 268-272.

the municipality.[1599] It arrived at this conclusion after having found, on the basis of, *inter alia,* a report by Luka Markešić ("Luka Markešić Report"), who was in charge of the Rama Brigade of the HVO Information and Security Service ("SIS"), that the removal of the Muslim population was related to the arrival *en masse* of Croats and that the HVO authorities took properties of Muslims who had been moved to Podgrađe, Lapsunj, and Duge so that they could house these newly arrived Croats.[1600] **[page 215]**

(a) Arguments of the Parties

503.   Praljak submits that the Trial Chamber erred when concluding that civilians from Prozor were arrested and detained.[1601] He argues that the Trial Chamber "could not" establish that the HVO coercively transported Muslims to Podgrađe, Lapsunj, and Duge or placed them in houses therein.[1602] In this regard, he submits that: (1) the Trial Chamber did not consider that "a number of Muslims"[1603] might have relocated voluntarily; (2) people found and moved into houses themselves upon their arrival in Podgrađe; and (3) the Trial Chamber recognised that it did not know which HVO unit would have arrested and detained the Muslims.[1604] Further, Praljak submits that: (1) relocation was a necessary and reasonable measure taken in the interest of the population;[1605] and (2) the Trial Chamber did not consider the reasonable possibility that the HVO was concerned with the safety of all civilians in Prozor.[1606] In particular, Praljak submits that the Trial Chamber erroneously concluded, on the basis of its "free and unfounded interpretation" of the Luka Markešić Report, that Muslims were put into the three villages and detained for the purpose of accommodating Croats who were arriving in the municipality.[1607]

504.   With regard specifically to the Trial Chamber's finding that the population was detained, Praljak contends that the Trial Chamber: (1) acknowledged that people could go to Prozor and other villages; and (2) found that houses in Podgrađe were not under guard but that the population had restricted freedom of movement, which Praljak argues was lawful under the circumstances.[1608] He submits that, as the Muslims in Podgrađe, Lapsunj, and Duge were not detained, a necessary condition for a conviction for imprisonment, unlawful confinement, inhumane acts, and inhuman treatment was not satisfied.[1609] Praljak finally submits that the Trial Chamber erred in finding that living conditions in Podgrađe were very harsh, mainly on the basis of evidence of overcrowding and, specifically, in drawing a conclusion as to the number of Muslims held in houses that was **[page 216]** "mathematically impossible".[1610] Praljak requests that his convictions under Counts 10, 11, 12, and 13 with respect to Prozor be reversed.[1611]

505.   The Prosecution responds that Praljak merely disagrees with the Trial Chamber's interpretation of evidence without showing that it erred.[1612] It submits that Praljak's arguments that Muslims relocated voluntarily and that their freedom of movement was merely restricted must fail in light of the crimes

---

[1599]   Trial Judgement, Vol. 2, para. 232, Vol. 3, paras 958, 1008.

[1600]   Trial Judgement, Vol. 2, paras 227-228, referring to, *inter alia,* Ex. P04177, p. 2. The Trial Chamber also considered evidence that Mijo Jozić, President of Prozor Municipality, stated that the most important problem facing them was the massive influx of Croats and that they needed to make more room for them. Trial Judgement, Vol. 2, para. 227.

[1601]   Praljak's Appeal Brief, heading before para. 140, para. 146. See also Praljak's Appeal Brief, para. 144.

[1602]   Praljak's Appeal Brief, paras 141, 144.

[1603]   Praljak's Appeal Brief, para. 140.

[1604]   Praljak's Appeal Brief, paras 140-141.

[1605]   Praljak's Appeal Brief, para. 143. See Praljak's Appeal Brief, para. 149. Praljak also submits that many Muslims who relocated to these three villages seemingly came from other parts of the country, so they presumably had no houses in Prozor. Praljak's Appeal Brief, para. 143.

[1606]   Praljak's Appeal Brief, para. 142. See Praljak's Appeal Brief, para. 151.

[1607]   Praljak's Appeal Brief, heading before para. 149, paras 149-150, referring to Ex. P04177. Praljak contends that: (1) Markešić did not testify and could not explain what he meant when making a link between the relocation of Muslims and the arrival of Croats; and (2) the report does not indicate Markešić's source of information. Praljak's Appeal Brief, para. 150.

[1608]   Praljak's Appeal Brief, para. 144. Praljak argues that the restriction of movement was a necessary and reasonable measure given the chaotic situation prevailing in Prozor at the time. Praljak's Appeal Brief, para. 144, referring to the Commentary on Geneva Convention IV, Article 27.

[1609]   Praljak's Appeal Brief, paras 145-146, 148; Praljak's Reply Brief, para. 76. See Praljak's Appeal Brief, para. 139.

[1610]   Praljak's Appeal Brief, para. 147.

[1611]   Praljak's Appeal Brief, para. 139.

[1612]   Prosecution's Response Brief (Praljak), para. 159. See Prosecution's Response Brief (Praljak), para. 162.

committed.[1613] The Prosecution further submits that the Trial Chamber considered the argument that Muslims were held for their protection, but nonetheless reasonably established that they were: (1) unlawfully arrested and detained; and (2) removed to accommodate newly arrived Croats.[1614] Regarding Praljak's submission that the Trial Chamber failed to properly assess the conditions of confinement for the purposes of the crimes of inhumane acts and inhuman treatment, the Prosecution argues that: (1) Praljak ignores relevant findings and evidence; and (2) the Trial Chamber's conclusion concerning detention conditions in Podgrađe was not based on a mathematical calculation of civilians in detention.[1615]

(b) Analysis

506. The Appeals Chamber notes that in support of his arguments that a number of Muslims might have voluntarily relocated and that people found and moved into houses upon their arrival in Podgrađe, Praljak relies on evidence reflective of the experience of one particular witness, Witness BK, and her family.[1616] In contrast, the Trial Chamber relied upon various pieces of evidence when finding that the HVO and some Military Police officers rounded up, arrested, and relocated Muslims from Prozor Municipality[1617] and that "around 5,000 women, children and elderly people were held in Podgrađe and in the villages of Lapsunj and Duge".[1618] Accordingly, Praljak merely asserts that the Trial Chamber failed to give sufficient weight to Witness BK's testimony, without explaining why the conviction should not stand on the basis of the remaining evidence.[1619] Further, **[page 217]** with respect to Praljak's assertion that the Trial Chamber did not know which HVO unit was involved in the arrest and detention of the population, the Appeals Chamber notes that the Trial Chamber considered, in view of all the evidence, that "HVO soldiers [...] as well as some military police officers under Il[ji]a Franji[ć]'s command" arrested and detained the population.[1620] The Trial Chamber's acknowledgement that it did "not know to which unit [the HVO soldiers] belonged"[1621] does not undermine its finding that the HVO soldiers and the Military Police were involved in the arrest and detention of the population. Therefore, Praljak fails to demonstrate any error of fact and his arguments are dismissed.

507. As to Praljak's submission that the Muslims were relocated in the interest of the population, the Appeals Chamber notes that the Trial Chamber considered a statement by Mijo Jozić, the President of Prozor Municipality, that the Muslims were relocated for their own safety, but found, on the basis of the Luka Markešić Report, that Muslims were arrested in the course of a large-scale operation to make room for newly arrived Croats.[1622] The Trial Chamber also: (1) considered evidence that Jozić stated that they needed to make more room for the Croats;[1623] and (2) found that the HVO took the properties of the relocated Muslims so they could house Croats who arrived in Prozor.[1624] Praljak argues that the Trial Chamber failed to consider the reasonable possibility that the HVO was concerned with the safety of *all* civilians in Prozor, but he does not show that no reasonable trier of fact, based on the above evidence, could have reached the same conclusion as the Trial Chamber did. The Appeals Chamber further finds that Praljak merely asserts that the Trial

---

[1613]   Prosecution's Response Brief (Praljak), para. 161. See Prosecution's Response Brief (Praljak), para. 160.

[1614]   Prosecution's Response Brief (Praljak), paras 161, 163. The Prosecution also contends that Praljak's assertion that Muslims were held for their own protection is untenable in light of the crimes they suffered. Prosecution's Response Brief (Praljak), para. 161.

[1615]   Prosecution's Response Brief (Praljak), para. 162. The Prosecution argues in this regard that the Trial Chamber's conclusion that civilians lived in' a climate of terror in overcrowded houses, with restricted freedom of movement, was based on substantial evidence concerning detention conditions. Prosecution's Response Brief (Praljak), para. 162.

[1616]   See Praljak's Appeal Brief, para. 140 & fns 332-333, referring to Witness BK, T. 5496-5497, 5527-5528 (24 Aug 2006).

[1617]   See Trial Judgement, Vol. 2, paras 225 (and references cited therein), 232. See also, *e.g.*, Trial Judgement, Vol. 2, paras 229-231 and references cited therein.

[1618]   Trial Judgement, Vol. 2, para. 227 and references cited therein. See also, *e.g.*, Trial Judgement, Vol. 2, paras 231 (and references cited therein), 232.

[1619]   In this regard, the Appeals Chamber notes that the Trial Chamber considered the testimony to which Praljak points. See Trial Judgement, Vol. 2, paras 225-226 & fns 566, 569.

[1620]   Trial Judgement, Vol. 2, para. 232. See also, *e.g.*, Trial Judgement, Vol. 2, paras 225, 229-231.

[1621]   Trial Judgement, Vol. 2, para. 232.

[1622]   Trial Judgement, Vol. 2, paras 227, 232, Vol. 3, paras 958, 1008.

[1623]   Trial Judgement, Vol. 2, para. 227.

[1624]   Trial Judgement, Vol. 2, para. 228.

Chamber failed to interpret the Luka Markešić Report in a particular manner.[1625] His argument therefore warrants dismissal.[1626]

508.   Regarding Praljak's argument that the requisite element of detention of the crimes charged in Counts 10, 11, 12, and 13 had not been satisfied, the Appeals Chamber recalls its earlier finding that both unlawful confinement and imprisonment concern the deprivation of liberty of an individual.[1627] Further, with the exception of chapeau requirements for war crimes and crimes against humanity, imprisonment and unlawful confinement of civilians in the context of armed **[page 218]** conflict overlap significantly since the Appeals Chamber has confirmed that the legality of imprisonment and the procedural safeguards pertaining to it are to be determined based on Articles 42 and 43 of Geneva Convention IV.[1628]

509.   The Appeals Chamber notes that Praljak supports his contention on detention by pointing only to findings made by the Trial Chamber regarding the freedom of movement of Muslims in Podgrađe, and not referring to Lapsunj and Duge.[1629] However, given the importance of his submissions and the fact that they ultimately challenge the detention in all three locations, the Appeals Chamber will exercise its discretion and consider this issue also in relation to the Trial Chamber's findings concerning the villages of Lapsunj and Duge. The Appeals Chamber recalls that the question of whether the civilians in Podgrađe, Lapsunj, and Duge were deprived of their liberty will depend on the circumstances of each particular case and must take into account a range of factors, including the type, duration, effects, and the manner of implementation of the measures allegedly amounting to deprivation of liberty.[1630]

510.   The Trial Chamber found that between late July and the beginning of August 1993, the HVO held Muslim civilians in Podgrađe, Lapsunj, and Duge without legal justification, thereby committing the crimes of imprisonment and unlawful confinement.[1631] With respect to Podgrađe, in its factual findings on the arrests, detention, and removal of civilians in Prozor Municipality, the Trial Chamber found that "[a]lthough the Military Police were indeed present within [Podgrađe], the evidence shows that the houses themselves were not under guard and that there was some freedom of movement, with restrictions".[1632] The Trial Chamber also found that most of the Muslims did not leave Podgrađe, with the exception of, *inter alios*, probably one person per house who went to seek food at the Prozor distribution centre.[1633] Further, it found that some women left the houses at night and hid in the woods around Podgrađe out of fear of being raped by HVO soldiers.[1634] However, the Trial Chamber also found that:[1635] (1) there was only one road for **[page 219]** entering and leaving Podgrađe, which was controlled by the HVO with a barrier;[1636] (2) Muslim civilians from other Prozor villages arrived in Podgrađe by truck, under the escort of HVO members;[1637] (3) at least

---

[1625]   With respect to Praljak's arguments that Markešić did not testify and could not explain what he meant when making a link between the relocation of Muslims and the arrival of Croats and that the report does not indicate Markešić's source of information, the Appeals Chamber finds that it was within the Trial Chamber's discretion to rely on the report.

[1626]   As to Praljak's related argument that many Muslims who relocated came from other parts of the country and presumably did not have houses in Prozor, the Appeals Chamber finds that Praljak has not sufficiently explained the relevance of this argument to the impugned findings, and dismisses it as obscure.

[1627]   See *supra*, paras 471-473.

[1628]   *Kordić and Čerkez* Appeal Judgement, paras 114-115.

[1629]   See Praljak's Appeal Brief, para. 144 & fns 341-342, referring to Trial Judgement, Vol. 2, paras 241-242.

[1630]   See *Nada* Decision, para. 225; *Guzzardi* Decision, para. 92. The Appeals Chamber recalls that even though ECtHR case-law is not binding on the Tribunal, it may be instructive in cases where there is no well-established Tribunal jurisprudence, as is the case here. See, *e.g., Popović et al* Appeal Judgement, para. 436; *Đorđević* Appeal Judgement, para. 83; *Šainović et al* Appeal Judgement, paras 1647-1648; *Čelebići* Appeal Judgement, para. 24.

[1631]   Trial Judgement, Vol. 3, paras 958-959, 1008-1010.

[1632]   Trial Judgement, Vol. 2, para. 241.

[1633]   Trial Judgement, Vol. 2, para. 242.

[1634]   Trial Judgement, Vol. 2, para. 242.

[1635]   The Appeals Chamber notes that the Trial Chamber made these findings specifically when it assessed the conditions of detention in Podgrađe and not when determining whether arrest and detention actually occurred. See Trial Judgement, Vol. 2, paras 238-249. *Cf.* Trial Judgement, Vol. 2, paras 225-232. In any event, considering the margin of deference to be given to the Trial Chamber's evaluation of the evidence and findings, the Appeals Chamber is satisfied that the Trial Chamber considered the evidence underlying these findings when concluding that HVO soldiers and Military Police officers detained Muslims in Podgrađe, Lapsunj, and Duge. See Trial Judgement, Vol. 2, para. 232. See *also Aleksovski* Appeal Judgement, para. 63.

[1636]   Trial Judgement, Vol. 2, para. 238.

[1637]   Trial Judgement, Vol. 2, para. 239. See Trial Judgement, Vol. 2, paras 225-226.

1,760 Muslims were "collected into about 100 houses";[1638] (4) the Muslims were guarded by the Military Police – although houses themselves were not under guard – and most of them did not leave Podgrađe;[1639] (5) Muslim men were terrified by the Military Police presence while the women were "afraid of stepping outside the houses and being 'raped' by HVO soldiers, who entered Podgrađe freely";[1640] and (6) HVO members stole the property of the Muslims in Podgrađe, and forced Muslim women and girls there to have sexual relations under the threat of weapons and subjected them to sexual abuse.[1641]

511.   With respect to the freedom of movement in Duge, the Trial Chamber noted Witness Rudy Gerritsen's testimony that Duge village was not a "prison proper", but that the people felt imprisoned because they could not leave as they had nowhere to go.[1642] However, it also noted evidence indicating that the Military Police units came to Duge regularly to patrol that sector.[1643] Further, as with Podgrađe, the Trial Chamber also found that: (1) Muslim women, children, and elderly from Prozor and the villages surrounding Prozor were arrested and taken to Lapsunj and Duge by the HVO and Military Police;[1644] (2) both Lapsunj and Duge were overcrowded as the Muslims lived together, 20 to 30 per house, and slept on the floor;[1645] and (3) the Muslims held there were exposed to thefts and assaults by HVO soldiers and the Military Police, while Muslim women were taken away, humiliated, sexually abused, and raped.[1646] While it did not describe in detail how the freedom of movement of civilians located in Lapsunj was restricted, the Trial Chamber found that the running water in Lapsunj had been cut off and that there was no soap for washing, as a result of which the Muslims contracted lice.[1647]

512.   Finally, when reaching its findings with respect to all three locations, the Trial Chamber considered the Luka Markešić Report which indicated that the Military Police "rounded up the **[page 220]** entire Muslim population of Prozor Municipality into the three 'collection centres' in Podgrađe, Duge and Lapsunj".[1648]

513.   The Appeals Chamber recalls that it has in the past confirmed that detention amounting to imprisonment and unlawful confinement of civilians can occur even in situations where the civilians are held in houses without guards and where they have some freedom of movement. In *Kordić and Čerkez*, the Appeals Chamber confirmed the Trial Chamber's finding that the civilians in the village of Rotilj were imprisoned and unlawfully confined since the village was surrounded by HVO, the civilians were not held there for their own safety, and they were prevented from leaving while at the same time subjected to beatings, thefts, and sexual abuse.[1649] Bearing that in mind and in light of the Trial Chamber's findings outlined above,[1650] the Appeals Chamber considers that Praljak fails to demonstrate that the Trial Chamber erred in concluding that Muslims in Podgrađe, Lapsunj, and Duge were deprived of their liberty. In that respect, the

---

[1638]   Trial Judgement, Vol. 2, para. 240.

[1639]   Trial Judgement, Vol. 2, paras 241-242.

[1640]   Trial Judgement, Vol. 2, para. 242. See also Trial Judgement, Vol. 2, para. 243.

[1641]   Trial Judgement, Vol. 2, paras 252-253.

[1642]   Trial Judgement, Vol. 2, para. 264.

[1643]   Trial Judgement, Vol. 2, para. 264.

[1644]   Trial Judgement, Vol. 2, paras 254, 263 (noting that by 20 August 1993 between 700 to 800 Muslim women, children, and elderly persons were held in the village of Duge).

[1645]   Trial Judgement, Vol. 2, paras 256, 266.

[1646]   Trial Judgement, Vol. 2, paras 259-262, 269-272. In reaching these findings, the Trial Chamber relied on, among other things, the Luka Markešić Report and another HVO report dated 13 August 1993, which refer to the thefts, abuse, humiliating acts, brutality, sexual assault, forced prostitution, and rape being committed against the Muslim population in Podgrađe, Lapsunj, and Duge by the Rama Brigade members, local soldiers, and the Military Police. See Trial Judgement, Vol. 2, paras 235, 250, 258, 268, referring to Exs. P04161 (confidential), P04177.

[1647]   Trial Judgement, Vol. 2, para. 256.

[1648]   Trial Judgement, Vol. 2, para. 231. See also Trial Judgement, Vol. 2, paras 225, 227.

[1649]   *Kordić and Čerkez* Trial Judgement, paras 793, 800 (finding that despite detainees having some liberty of movement inside the village of Rotilj, their conditions, which included overcrowding and forced labour, still amounted to detention); *Kordić and Čerkez* Appeal Judgement, paras 638-640 (upholding the detention finding). See also *Simić et al.* Trial Judgement, paras 563-567, 666, 680 (finding that despite detainees having some liberty of movement inside and outside of the village of Zasavica, where certain witnesses testified that detainees were essentially "free" and living a "normal life there" in individual houses, their conditions still amounted to detention); *Blaškić Trial* Judgement, paras 684, 691, 700 (finding that despite the defence argument that Bosnian Muslims in the village of Rotilj were not detained because their freedom of movement was not limited, their conditions still amounted to detention). These Trial Chamber findings in the *Simić et al.* and *Blaškić* cases on the nature of detentions in Zasavica and Rotilj, respectively, were not an issue on appeal.

[1650]   See *supra*, paras 510-512.

Appeals Chamber notes that even though the civilians had some freedom of movement in those three locations, the factual findings outlined above show that it was limited and that the great majority of the civilians were in fact confined to the three locations in very harsh conditions, as was the case in *Kordić and Čerkez*. The freedom of movement consisted of some individuals occasionally leaving the houses they were housed in, either to obtain food or to hide from potential abuse and sexual assaults at night-time. The Appeals Chamber considers that, given the findings on the presence of HVO soldiers and Military Police in those locations and the fact that the civilians were arrested and brought there by those forces, the Trial Chamber did not err in concluding that the population could not leave Podграđe, Lapsunj, and Duge.

514. As to Praljak's contention that the events in the three locations illustrated mere restrictions of movement which were also lawful under the circumstances, the Appeals Chamber notes that he relies on the Commentary to Article 27 of Geneva Convention IV.[1651] While referring to restriction of movement as one of the measures a belligerent may inflict on protected persons under Article 27, the Commentary also elaborates that internment of civilians and the placing of civilians in assigned **[page 221]** residences are the two most severe measures that may be inflicted on protected persons under Article 27 and, as such, are subject to strict rules outlined in Articles 41-43 and 78 of Geneva Convention IV.[1652] One of these rules is that the internment or placement in assigned residence may be ordered only if the security of the detaining party makes it absolutely necessary, while another provides that an initially lawful internment or placement in assigned residence clearly becomes unlawful if the detaining party does not respect the basic procedural rights of the detained persons and does not establish an appropriate court or administrative board as prescribed in Article 43 of Geneva Convention IV.[1653]

515. As explained above, the Appeals Chamber considers that the Trial Chamber made no error when it concluded that the events in Podграđe, Lapsunj, and Duge did not constitute a mere restriction of movement as alleged by Praljak, but were more serious, amounting to deprivation of liberty and thus could amount to imprisonment and unlawful confinement.[1654] Using the Geneva Convention IV terminology, this deprivation of liberty was achieved by the HVO and the Military Police placing Muslim civilians in "assigned residences" in the three locations in question.[1655] Specifically, the Muslim population was rounded up, arrested, and then escorted by the HVO and the Military Police to those three locations.[1656] As such, this placement was subject to strict rules and requirements.[1657] However, there is nothing in the factual findings outlined above to indicate that these rules were followed, namely that the civilians were moved to the three locations because the HVO and the Military Police had reasonable grounds to believe that this was absolutely necessary for reasons of security,[1658] or that the HVO and the Military Police established an appropriate court or administrative board in line with Article 43 of Geneva Convention IV.[1659] Instead, the Trial Chamber findings indicate that Muslim civilians were taken to Podграđe, Lapsunj, **[page 222]** and Duge for the purpose of

---

[1651] See *supra*, fn. 1608. Article 27(4) of Geneva Convention IV provides that parties to a conflict may take such measures of control and security in regard to protected persons as may be necessary as a result of the war.

[1652] Commentary on Geneva Convention IV, Article 27, p. 207.

[1653] Geneva Convention IV, Arts. 42 and 78; *Čelebići* Appeal Judgement, para. 320. See also *Čelebići* Appeal Judgement, para. 327 ("the reasonable time which is to be afforded to a detaining power to ascertain whether detained civilians pose a security risk must be the minimum time necessary to make enquiries to determine whether a view that they pose a security risk has any objective foundation such that it would found a 'definite suspicion' of the nature referred to in Article 5 of Geneva Convention IV").

[1654] See *supra*, para. 513.

[1655] See *Kordić and Čerkez* Trial Judgement, para. 283 (noting that, according to the Commentary on Geneva Convention IV, assigned residence consists of moving people from their domicile and forcing them to live in a locality which is generally out of the way and where supervision is more easily exercised).

[1656] See *supra*, paras 510-511. In addition, the Appeals Chamber notes that the Luka Markešić Report, which the Trial Chamber relied on to make its findings concerning detentions in Prozor, refers to the entire Muslim population of Prozor Municipality being "rounded up" into three "collection centres" in Podграđe, Lapsunj, and Duge, See *supra*, para. 512.

[1657] See *supra*, para. 514.

[1658] See Trial Judgement, Vol. 3, paras 958, 1008 (concluding that the HVO made no individual assessments of security reasons which could have led to the detention of civilians but rather had the intention of holding the civilians without legal justification for the purpose of making room for the newly-arrived Croats).

[1659] See Trial Judgement, Vol. 3, para. 1008 (holding that the Muslim civilians had no possibility of challenging their confinement with the relevant authorities).

making space for newly-arrived Croats.[1660] Accordingly, Praljak's arguments that what transpired in Podgrađe, Lapsunj, and Duge was not detention but rather a lawful restriction of movement is dismissed.

516.   Regarding Praljak's final submission that the Trial Chamber erred in finding that living conditions in Podgrađe were very harsh, on the basis of evidence of overcrowding and, specifically, in drawing a conclusion as to the number of Muslims held in houses that was "mathematically impossible",[1661] the Appeals Chamber notes that while the Trial Chamber found that Muslims were collected into about 100 houses,[1662] each holding 20 to 70 people (some holding more),[1663] it also found that *at least* 1,760 Muslims were held in Podgrađe.[1664] This finding was clearly a minimum approximation, as further supported by the fact that the Trial Chamber noted evidence indicating that there were about 6,000 Muslims held in Podgrađe.[1665] In any event, the Trial Chamber reached its conclusion that living conditions were very harsh by also relying on its findings that the Muslims: (1) had to sleep on the ground due to lack of space;[1666] and (2) lived in fear because of the Military Police presence.[1667] The Appeals Chamber finds that Praljak has failed to demonstrate any error in the impugned finding.[1668] His argument is therefore dismissed.

517.   For the above reasons, the Appeals Chamber dismisses Praljak's ground of appeal 8.

2.   Displacement of Muslims from Prozor Municipality (Praljak's Ground 9)

518.   The Trial Chamber concluded that on 28 August 1993 the HVO forcibly transferred Muslim women, children, and elderly persons who were held in the Podgrađe neighbourhood of Prozor and in the villages of Lapsunj and Duge.[1669] The Trial Chamber found that these Muslims were moved to ABiH territory.[1670] In reaching these findings, the Trial Chamber: (1) could not determine exactly the number of Muslims from Prozor Municipality removed by the HVO on 28 August 1993, but considered that the evidence supports a finding that at least 2,500 people were removed;[1671] (2) considered the testimony of Witness CC that the removals required organization **[page 223]** and planning by the HVO;[1672] and (3) considered evidence that, on 28 August 1993, the day Muslims were removed from Prozor to Kučani and then towards ABiH territories, Praljak ordered the commander of the Rama Brigade to deploy 30 soldiers in the Kučani area between 28 and 31 August 1993.[1673] The Trial Chamber concluded that this transfer and removal, at a time when these persons were being held by HVO soldiers and there was no fighting in the area, was "on no account an evacuation carried out for security purposes nor was it justified for compelling military reasons", further demonstrated by the fact that the HVO had not made any arrangements for the population to return.[1674] The Trial Chamber concluded that these events in Podgrađe, Lapsunj, and Duge constituted inhumane acts (forcible transfer) as a crime against humanity (Count 8), unlawful transfer of civilians as a grave breach of the Geneva Conventions (Count 9), inhumane acts as a crime against humanity (Count 15), and inhuman treatment as a grave breach of the Geneva Conventions (Count 16).[1675]

[1660]   See Trial Judgement, Vol. 2, para. 227 & fn. 571 (referring to Exs. P09627, P10030, p. 8, Rudy Gerritsen, T(F). 19226, 19228 (29 May 2007)), Vol. 3, paras 958, 1008.
[1661]   See Praljak's Appeal Brief, para. 147.
[1662]   Trial Judgement, Vol. 2, para. 240.
[1663]   Trial Judgement, Vol. 2, para. 244.
[1664]   Trial Judgement, Vol. 2, para. 240.
[1665]   Trial Judgement, Vol. 2, fn. 599.
[1666]   Trial Judgement, Vol. 2, para. 244.
[1667]   Trial Judgement, Vol. 2, paras 242-243.
[1668]   See Trial Judgement, Vol. 2, para. 249.
[1669]   Trial Judgement, Vol. 3, paras 842, 896. See Trial Judgement, Vol. 2, paras 225, 280.
[1670]   Trial Judgement, Vol. 2, para. 280, Vol. 3, paras 841, 895.
[1671]   Trial Judgement, Vol. 2, para. 277 and references cited therein.
[1672]   Trial Judgement, Vol. 2, para. 278, referring to, *inter alia*, Ex. P09731 (confidential), p. 3.
[1673]   Trial Judgement, Vol. 2, para. 278, referring to, *inter alia*, Ex. 3D02448.
[1674]   Trial Judgement, Vol. 3, paras 841, 895.
[1675]   Trial Judgement, Vol. 3, paras 840-842, 894-896, 1220-1221, 1310-1311.

(a) Arguments of the Parties

519.   Praljak submits that the Trial Chamber erroneously concluded that the HVO unlawfully displaced Muslims from Prozor Municipality, who were being held in Podgrađe, Lapsunj, and Duge, and removed them to territory under ABiH control.[1676] Praljak submits that the Trial Chamber did not establish that the displaced Muslims were forced to leave, and argues in this regard that they may have had a genuine choice and wish to leave since: (1) only a portion of the population was displaced; and (2) Šiljeg, "the HVO representative in Prozor", "talked about voluntary departure".[1677] Praljak submits further that the Trial Chamber "could not" establish who displaced the Muslims, and that it referred speculatively to an order he issued, which he contends was ineffective and not executed, as evidence that the HVO planned and organised the removal.[1678] Further, Praljak claims that the Trial Chamber did not establish whether the removal of Muslims was permitted for the security of the population, imperative military reasons, and/or humanitarian reasons.[1679] He also challenges as "baseless" the Trial Chamber's explanation that the removal was not a lawful evacuation because the HVO did not make arrangements for the population to **[page 224]** return.[1680] Finally, Praljak avers that the Trial Chamber failed to consider that members of the population were not in their homes as they had already been displaced.[1681] Praljak requests that his convictions under Counts 8, 9, 15, and 16 with respect to Prozor be reversed.[1682]

520.   The Prosecution responds that Praljak ignores the totality of the Trial Chamber's findings and fails to show an error.[1683] It submits that Praljak's assertion that the Trial Chamber could not establish who moved the population must fail when considering the Trial Chamber's findings and the evidence on which it relied.[1684] The Prosecution also submits that it is irrelevant whether those expelled originated from Prozor or elsewhere.[1685] The Prosecution further argues that: (1) the fact that only some members of the population were removed does not mean they left voluntarily; and (2) the claim by Šiljeg, "the HVO's regional commander", that the Muslims left voluntarily does not impact the Trial Chamber's findings.[1686] Moreover, the Prosecution submits that the Trial Chamber properly relied on Praljak's order as corroborative of other evidence indicating that the removal required organisation and planning.[1687] Finally, the Prosecution contends that the Trial Chamber reasonably rejected the argument that the Muslims' removal from Podgrađe, Lapsunj, and Duge was for humanitarian, security, or military reasons.[1688]

(b) Analysis

521.   With regard to Praljak's assertion that the Trial Chamber did not establish that the displaced Muslims were forced to leave, the Appeals Chamber notes that, to the contrary, the Trial Chamber found that HVO soldiers used military and civilian trucks to move Muslims being held in Podgrađe, Lapsunj, and Duge and that when the Muslims reached Kučani, they were forced to walk on foot towards Ćelina, escorted by HVO soldiers.[1689] The Trial Chamber also noted evidence that HVO soldiers surrounded the village of Duge and

---

[1676]   Praljak's Appeal Brief, para. 160, referring to Trial Judgement, Vol. 2, paras 272, 280, Vol. 3, paras 841-842, 895-896; Praljak's Reply Brief, para. 77. See also Praljak's Appeal Brief, para. 152.

[1677]   Praljak's Appeal Brief, para. 154, referring to Ex. P09636, Rudy Gerritsen, T. 19235-19236 (29 May 2007). See Praljak's Appeal Brief, paras 152-153. See also Praljak's Reply Brief, para. 77.

[1678]   Praljak's Appeal Brief, paras 152, 155. Praljak also submits that, during his testimony, he was not asked whether this order was related to the removal of the population and he did not make any link between the two. Praljak's Appeal Brief, para. 155.

[1679]   Praljak's Appeal Brief, para. 156. See Praljak's Appeal Brief, paras 152, 157, 160. Praljak argues that the Trial Chamber also failed to consider that international observers considered that the "exchange of minorities" might be the best solution in the area. Praljak's Appeal Brief, para. 157.

[1680]   Praljak's Appeal Brief, para. 158.

[1681]   Praljak's Appeal Brief, para. 159. See also Praljak's Appeal Brief, para. 152; Praljak's Reply Brief, para. 77.

[1682]   Praljak's Appeal Brief, para. 161.

[1683]   Prosecution's Response Brief (Praljak), para. 164. See Prosecution's Response Brief (Praljak), para. 165.

[1684]   Prosecution's Response Brief (Praljak), paras 165-166.

[1685]   Prosecution's Response Brief (Praljak), para. 166.

[1686]   Prosecution's Response Brief (Praljak), para. 166.

[1687]   Prosecution's Response Brief (Praljak), para. 167.

[1688]   Prosecution's Response Brief (Praljak), para. 168.

[1689]   Trial Judgement, Vol. 2, paras 273, 276, 280.

fired into the air to force the Muslims to get into trucks.[1690] Moreover, Praljak fails to demonstrate how the fact that only a portion of the population in the three locations was displaced[1691] is inconsistent with the Trial Chamber's finding that Muslims were forcibly displaced. As to Praljak's argument that, **[page 225]** according to the evidence of Witness Rudy Genitsen, Šiljeg "talked about voluntary departure",[1692] the Appeals Chamber notes that Praljak ignores that, although Gerritsen stated that Šiljeg told him that the population was moved on a voluntary basis, Gerritsen did not believe this to be the case.[1693] Because Praljak merely asserts that the Trial Chamber failed to give sufficient weight to the statement attributed to Šiljeg – that the population was moved on a voluntary basis – his argument is dismissed.

522.   The Appeals Chamber now turns to Praljak's submission that the Trial Chamber could not establish who displaced the Muslims and that, in this regard, it referred speculatively to an order he issued, which he alleges was ineffective and not executed, as evidence that the HVO planned and organised the removal. The Appeals Chamber notes the impugned finding that the HVO moved women, children, and elderly persons who were held in Podgrađe, Lapsunj, and Duge to ABiH-controlled territories.[1694] In reaching this conclusion, the Trial Chamber found, *inter alia,* that on 28 August 1993, the same day Muslims were moved from Prozor to Kučani and then towards ABiH-controlled territories, Praljak ordered the commander of the Rama Brigade to deploy 30 soldiers in the Kučani area between 28 and 31 August 1993.[1695] However, the Appeals Chamber notes that the Trial Chamber relied on other evidence and findings, including that of civilians who were moved to Kučani,[1696] to find that HVO soldiers moved people being held in Podgrađe, Lapsunj, and Duge to ABiH-controlled territories.[1697] Praljak's argument ignores relevant factual findings and therefore warrants dismissal.[1698]

523.   As to Praljak's claim that the Trial Chamber did not establish whether the removal of Muslims was permitted for the security of the population and/or imperative military reasons, the Appeals Chamber notes that the Trial Chamber considered that: (1) the people in Podgrađe, Lapsunj, and Duge were being held by the HVO; (2) there was no fighting in the area at the time of the transfer; and (3) the HVO did not make arrangements for the population to return.[1699] On this basis, the Trial Chamber found that the HVO held the Muslims in Podgrađe, Lapsunj, and Duge in order to be able to remove them from their homes without the possibility of returning, and it explicitly rejected the possibility that this constituted an evacuation for security or compelling **[page 226]** military reasons.[1700] The Appeals Chamber dismisses Praljak's argument as it ignores several relevant factual findings.

524.   When challenging as "baseless" the Trial Chamber's explanation that the removal was not a lawful evacuation because the HVO did not make arrangements for the population to return, Praljak argues that Article 49(2) of Geneva Convention IV "does not require that arrangements for the population return be made at the time of evacuation".[1701] The Appeals Chamber recalls that Article 49 of Geneva Convention IV states that an evacuation is not prohibited "if the security of the population or imperative military reasons so demand" and provided that "[p]ersons thus evacuated shall be transferred back to their homes as soon as hostilities in the area in question have ceased".[1702] As noted above, when reaching its conclusion that the transfer was on no account a lawful evacuation, the Trial Chamber found that the transfer had already taken place "at a time when [...] there was no fighting in the area".[1703] The Appeals Chamber considers that the

---

[1690]   Trial Judgement, Vol. 2, para. 274.
[1691]   See Trial Judgement, Vol. 2, paras 227, 277. See also Trial Judgement, Vol. 2, paras 281-292.
[1692]   See Praljak's Appeal Brief, para. 154, referring to Ex. P09636, Rudy Gerritsen, T. 19235-19236 (29 May 2007).
[1693]   Rudy Gerritsen, T. 19235-19236 (29 May 2007). See also Ex. P10030, pp. 11-12.
[1694]   Trial Judgement, Vol. 2, para. 280.
[1695]   Trial Judgement, Vol. 2, para. 278.
[1696]   Trial Judgement, Vol. 2, paras 273-274, 276-278.
[1697]   Trial Judgement, Vol. 2, para. 280.
[1698]   For the same reasons, the Appeals Chamber dismisses Praljak's corresponding argument that he was not asked whether this order was related to the removal of the population and he did not make any link between the two.
[1699]   Trial Judgement, Vol. 3, paras 841, 895.
[1700]   Trial Judgement, Vol. 3, paras 841, 895.
[1701]   Praljak's Appeal Brief, para. 158.
[1702]   See also Trial Judgement, Vol. 1, para. 52.
[1703]   Trial Judgement, Vol. 3, paras 841, 895.

Trial Chamber could conclude on this basis alone that the transfer was unlawful. Praljak has therefore failed to show an error of law that invalidates the Trial Chamber's decision.

525. With regard to Praljak's contention that the Trial Chamber did not establish whether the removal of Muslims was permitted for humanitarian reasons, the Appeals Chamber notes that he points to the Trial Chamber's findings that conditions in Podграđe, Lapsunj, and Duge were harsh.[1704] However, displacement of a population is not justified where a humanitarian crisis that caused the displacement is the result of the accused's own unlawful activity.[1705] Praljak ignores the Trial Chamber's findings that the HVO and Military Police officers arrested Muslims from Prozor Municipality, unlawfully detained them, and imposed the harsh conditions in which they lived.[1706] His argument is therefore dismissed.[1707]

526. With respect to Praljak's submission that the Trial Chamber failed to consider that members of the population were not in their homes as they had already been displaced, the Appeals Chamber understands him to argue that the Trial Chamber should have considered that **[page 227]** they could not have been forcibly removed from a location in which they did not reside.[1708] The Appeals Chamber notes that the Trial Chamber found that Muslims were removed from their homes and detained in Podграđe, Lapsunj, and Duge.[1709] It found that the HVO subsequently moved Muslims detained in these three locations to ABiH-controlled territories.[1710] An overall reading of the relevant findings demonstrates that the Trial Chamber duly considered that the Muslims who were relocated to ABiH-controlled territories were previously relocated from their homes. Particularly, when assessing the lawfulness of the transfer, the Trial Chamber considered that "they were evicted from their homes without the possibility of returning".[1711] Praljak's argument is therefore dismissed.

527. For the above reasons, the Appeals Chamber dismisses Praljak's ground of appeal 9.

F. Crimes Committed in Mostar Municipality

1. The siege of East Mostar and related crimes

528. The Trial Chamber concluded that, from June 1993 to April 1994, East Mostar was under siege by the HVO.[1712] It found that, during that siege, the HVO: (1) intentionally inflicted serious bodily and mental harm on the inhabitants of East Mostar and caused a serious attack on their dignity;[1713] (2) intentionally subjected the civilian population of East Mostar to serious deprivation and acts of violence that led to death or caused serious injury to body or health;[1714] (3) committed acts of violence the main aim of which was to inflict terror on the population;[1715] and (4) committed crimes with the intention of discriminating against the Muslims of Mostar Municipality and violating their basic rights to life, human dignity, freedom, and property.[1716] The Trial Chamber therefore concluded that the HVO committed, *inter alia,* persecution as a crime against humanity (Count 1), inhumane acts as a crime against humanity (Count 15), inhuman treatment as a grave breach of the Geneva Conventions (Count 16), unlawful attack on civilians as a violation of the **[page 228]**

[1704] See Praljak's Appeal Brief, para. 156 & fn. 373, referring to Trial Judgement, Vol. 2, paras 249, 257, 267.
[1705] *Tolimir* Appeal Judgement, para. 158; *Krajišnik* Appeal Judgement, para. 308 & fn. 739; *Stakić* Appeal Judgement, para. 287.
[1706] Trial Judgement, Vol. 3, paras 1008-1010. See also, *e.g.*, Trial Judgement, Vol. 3, paras 958-959, 1059-1067, 1102-1111.
[1707] With regard to Praljak's argument that the Trial Chamber failed to consider that international observers considered that the exchange of minorities might be the best solution in the area, the Appeals Chamber finds that Praljak has not sufficiently explained the relevance of this argument to the impugned findings, and dismisses it as obscure.
[1708] The Appeals Chamber recalls that the "prohibition against forcible displacements aims at safeguarding the right and aspiration of individuals to live in their communities and homes without outside interference". *Krnojelac* Appeal Judgement, para. 218. See also *Krajišnik* Appeal Judgement, para. 308 ("[D]eportation and forcible transfer both entail the forcible displacement of persons from the area in which they are lawfully present, without grounds permitted under international law.").
[1709] Trial Judgement, Vol. 2, paras 227, 232.
[1710] Trial Judgement, Vol. 2, paras 273, 276, 280.
[1711] Trial Judgement, Vol. 3, para. 841. See Trial Judgement, Vol. 3, para. 895.
[1712] Trial Judgement, Vol. 2, para. 1378. See also Trial Judgement, Vol. 3, para. 1255.
[1713] Trial Judgement, Vol. 3, paras 1256, 1350.
[1714] Trial Judgement, Vol. 3, para. 1687. See Trial Judgement, Vol. 3, para. 1688.
[1715] Trial Judgement, Vol. 3, para. 1692. See Trial Judgement, Vol. 3, para. 1689.
[1716] Trial Judgement, Vol. 3, para. 1713. See Trial Judgement, Vol. 3, para. 1711. See also Trial Judgement, Vol. 3, para. 1712.

laws or customs of war (Count 24), and unlawful infliction of terror on civilians as a violation of the laws or customs of war (Count 25).[1717]

529.   The Appeals Chamber will examine the Appellants' challenges relating to: (1) the HVO keeping Muslims of East Mostar crowded in an enclave; (2) the humanitarian conditions during the siege of East Mostar; (3) the sniping campaign in Mostar; (4) the shelling of East Mostar; and (5) the destruction of or damage to mosques in East Mostar.[1718]

(a) <u>Keeping Muslims of East Mostar crowded in an enclave (Stojić's Ground 50 and Praljak's Ground 25)</u>

530.   As part of the siege of East Mostar, the Trial Chamber found that the HVO "kept the population crowded in an enclave where it was forced to remain".[1719] The Trial Chamber based this finding on, *inter alia,* the following findings: (1) from June 1993 until, at least, February 1994 the HVO blocked Muslims from East Mostar from entering West Mostar by erecting checkpoints;[1720] (2) the only possible way to cross the checkpoints was to have, first, an exit permit issued by the ABiH, and, second, an entry permit issued by the HVO;[1721] (3) there was a mountain path out of East Mostar but there was evidence indicating that it was physically difficult and dangerous to use;[1722] (4) using the M-17 main road linking East Mostar and Jablanica could be dangerous and risky because of HVO artillery shelling;[1723] and (5) certain sections of the roads out of East Mostar also came under HVO control from time to time.[1724] The finding that the HVO kept the population crowded in an enclave formed part of the basis of the Trial Chamber's conclusion that the HVO committed the crimes under Counts 1, 15, 16, 24, and 25 in East Mostar.[1725]

531.   Stojić and Praljak submit that the Trial Chamber erred by finding that the HVO kept the population of East Mostar crowded in an enclave.[1726] They argue that it was the ABiH that **[page 229]** prevented the population from leaving East Mostar.[1727] Stojić submits that since the ABiH was the "first" barrier to civilians leaving East Mostar, it was not established that the HVO caused the isolation of the Muslim population.[1728] Moreover, Stojić argues that the Trial Chamber only found that the HVO checkpoints controlled access to West Mostar and that "certain routes" out of East Mostar remained open.[1729] Praljak argues that no evidence exists indicating that the HVO interfered with the population's movement from East Mostar, and that the evidence shows that the HVO proposed free movement and guaranteed safety when doing so.[1730] Stojić submits that the Trial Chamber did not explain the basis for the inclusion of the crimes under Counts 1, 15, 16, and 24 within the CCP, despite the ABiH's "critical role" in causing civilians to

---

[1717]   Trial Judgement, Vol. 3, paras 1256, 1350, 1688, 1692, 1713.
[1718]   The Appeals Chamber addresses elsewhere the destruction of the Old Bridge of Mostar. See *supra,* paras 405-411, 415-426.
[1719]   Trial Judgement, Vol. 3, paras 1255, 1349, 1685. See Trial Judgement, Vol. 2, para. 1255, Vol. 3, para. 1711. See also Trial Judgement, Vol. 2, para. 1378.
[1720]   Trial Judgement, Vol. 2, para. 1247.
[1721]   Trial Judgement, Vol. 2, para. 1248. See also Trial Judgement, Vol. 2, paras 1249-1250.
[1722]   Trial Judgement, Vol. 2, paras 1252-1253.
[1723]   Trial Judgement, Vol. 2, para. 1254.
[1724]   Trial Judgement, Vol. 2, para. 1254.
[1725]   Trial Judgement, Vol. 3, paras 1255-1256, 1349-1350, 1685, 1688, 1691-1692, 1711, 1713.
[1726]   Stojić's Appeal Brief, para. 403; Praljak's Appeal Brief, para. 308. Stojić contends in particular that the Trial Chamber erred in finding that civilians could not leave East Mostar because of HVO checkpoints. Stojić's Appeal Brief, heading before para. 403, para. 405. He argues that the Trial Chamber's findings that the Muslim population could not leave East Mostar because of HVO checkpoints and that the HVO kept the population crowded in an enclave where it was forced to remain were erroneous in law and fact as they were inconsistent with the Trial Chamber's findings that the ABiH did not want Muslims to leave East Mostar and forced them to remain in the area by requiring that individuals obtain exit permits. Stojić's Appeal Brief, heading before para. 403, para. 403.
[1727]   Stojić's Appeal Brief, heading before para. 403, para. 403; Praljak's Appeal Brief, paras 305-307; Praljak's Reply Brief, para. 93.
[1728]   Stojić's Appeal Brief, para. 403. Further to this point, Stojić submits that there was no evidence that the HVO prevented the departure of anyone whom the ABiH would have allowed to leave. Stojić's Appeal Brief, para. 403.
[1729]   Stojić's Appeal Brief, para. 404. Stojić also argues that the Trial Chamber's finding that "[c]ertain sections of the roads out of East Mostar [...] could also come under HVO control from time to time" was "manifestly insufficient" to establish that the HVO prevented the Muslim population from leaving the area. Stojić's Appeal Brief, para. 404, referring to Trial Judgement, Vol. 2, para. 1254.
[1730]   Praljak's Appeal Brief, para. 307. Praljak further argues that: (1) the lack of evidence that the proposal was ever implemented "does not undermine the HVO willingness to allow free movement of civilians"; and (2) the fact that the proposal was made six

remain.[1731] Stojić further contends that, with the exception of Count 15, the Trial Chamber failed to address the impact of the ABiH's policy in forcing civilians to remain.[1732] Stojić and Praljak therefore request that the Appeals Chamber acquit them under Counts 1, 15, 16, and 24 of the relevant charges with respect to Mostar.[1733]

532. The Prosecution responds that the Trial Chamber's findings are reasonable and that Stojić and Praljak fail to demonstrate an error.[1734] The Prosecution argues that Stojić misrepresents the Trial Judgement when asserting that other routes out of East Mostar remained open when, in actuality, these routes were at risk of shelling by the HVO or at times under its control.[1735] Further, the Prosecution contends that the HVO's alleged proposal for the free movement of East Mostar's population does not impact the Trial Chamber's finding.[1736] Finally, the Prosecution submits that, in **[page 230]** any event, the Trial Chamber's conclusion that crimes under Counts 1, 15, 16, and 24 occurred did not depend on its finding that the HVO isolated Muslims in East Mostar.[1737]

533. The Appeals Chamber observes that the Trial Chamber extensively considered what contributed to the Muslim population being forced to remain in East Mostar.[1738] The Trial Chamber acknowledged that the ABiH did not want the population to leave[1739] and considered the ABiH's role in isolating the Muslim population in East Mostar.[1740] However, the Trial Chamber also articulated the ways in which the HVO prevented departure from the region.[1741] Specifically, it found that: (1) the HVO refused to allow Muslims in East Mostar to cross its positions and blocked them from entering West Mostar by erecting checkpoints;[1742] (2) the HVO would only issue entry permits to cross the checkpoints for humanitarian evacuations which were "laboriously negotiated between the parties under the auspices of the international officials";[1743] and (3) of the few roads open to the outside, one was dangerous because of HVO artillery shelling and others could also come under HVO control from time to time.[1744] The Trial Chamber considered that the HVO intensely shelled East Mostar and fired at civilians on a daily basis while they were obliged to remain in that sector,[1745] forcing them to live underground and in "extremely harsh living conditions".[1746] It considered that these conditions were exacerbated by the HVO's blocking or hindering of humanitarian aid and access for humanitarian organisations.[1747] On this basis, the Trial Chamber was satisfied that the HVO intended to cause serious bodily and mental harm and suffering to the Muslims of East Mostar, attack their dignity, and subject them to serious deprivations and acts of violence.[1748] Stojić and Praljak ignore these relevant factual

---

months into the siege "is without importance as the proposal was made in December 1993 and the siege would have lasted from June 1993 to April 1994". Praljak's Reply Brief, para. 92.
[1731]   Stojić's Appeal Brief, para. 405.
[1732]   Stojić's Appeal Brief, para. 403.
[1733]   Stojić's Appeal Brief, para. 405; Praljak's Appeal Brief, para. 308. See Stojić's Appeal Brief, para. 403.
[1734]   Prosecution's Response Brief (Stojić), paras 373-374, 376; Prosecution's Response Brief (Praljak), paras 217, 219-220. The Prosecution argues that there is no inconsistency between the Trial Chamber's finding that the HVO kept Muslims in East Mostar in isolation and its finding that individuals needed to obtain exit permits from the ABiH. Prosecution's Response Brief (Stojić), para. 374. The Prosecution also contends that Praljak repeats arguments that the Trial Chamber considered and rejected. Prosecution's Response Brief (Praljak), para. 217.
[1735]   Prosecution's Response Brief (Stojić), para. 374.
[1736]   Prosecution's Response Brief (Praljak), para. 221.
[1737]   Prosecution's Response Brief (Stojić), para. 375. The Prosecution argues in this regard that the Trial Chamber also considered the HVO's shelling and sniping attacks on East Mostar, its blocking of humanitarian aid, and the harsh conditions in which civilians were forced to live. Prosecution's Response Brief (Stojić), para. 375.
[1738]   See Trial Judgement, Vol. 2, paras 1247-1255.
[1739]   Trial Judgement, Vol. 2, para. 1255. See Trial Judgement, Vol. 2, para. 1250.
[1740]   Trial Judgement, Vol. 3, para. 1256. See Trial Judgement, Vol. 2, paras 1248-1249, 1255.
[1741]   See Trial Judgement, Vol. 2, paras 1247-1249, 1254-1255.
[1742]   Trial Judgement, Vol. 2, para. 1247.
[1743]   Trial Judgement, Vol. 2, para. 1249. See Trial Judgement, Vol. 2, para. 1248.
[1744]   Trial Judgement, Vol. 2, paras 1254-1255.
[1745]   Trial Judgement, Vol. 3, paras 1253-1256, 1349-1350, 1686, 1688, 1711, 1713. See Trial Judgement, Vol. 2, para. 1255.
[1746]   Trial Judgement, Vol. 3, paras 1256, 1350. See Trial Judgement, Vol. 2, para. 1255, Vol. 3, paras 1255, 1349, 1711. See also Trial Judgement, Vol. 3, paras 1685-1686.
[1747]   Trial Judgement, Vol. 3, paras 1255, 1349, 1685-1686, 1688, 1711.
[1748]   Trial Judgement, Vol. 3, paras 1256, 1350, 1688, 1711-1713 (finding that the HVO committed the crimes of inhumane acts, inhuman treatment, and unlawful attack on civilians with the intention to discriminate against Muslims and violate their basic rights to life, freedom, dignity, and property).

findings, thereby misrepresenting the Trial Chamber's analysis and overlooking the evidence relied upon for their convictions for crimes in East Mostar under Counts 1, 15, 16, and 24.

534.   Further, in submitting that the ABiH was the "first" barrier to civilians leaving East Mostar, that "certain routes" out of East Mostar remained open, and that the ABiH had a "critical role" in **[page 231]** causing civilians to remain, Stojić essentially disagrees with the Trial Chamber's interpretation of the evidence without demonstrating that no reasonable trier of fact could have found that the HVO "kept the population crowded in an enclave where it was forced to remain".[1749] As to Praljak's argument that the evidence shows that the HVO proposed free movement and guaranteed safety when doing so, he relies on a document containing a proposal signed by Prlić which was issued on 2 December 1993, approximately six months after the start of the siege.[1750] Additionally, the Trial Chamber noted that it did not have any evidence to support a finding that the proposal was ever implemented.[1751] In light of this,[1752] and considering the basis for the Trial Chamber's conclusion,[1753] Praljak has failed to demonstrate that no reasonable trial chamber could have found that the HVO kept the population crowded in an enclave where it was forced to remain. Stojić's and Praljak's arguments are therefore dismissed.

535.   In light of the foregoing, the Appeals Chamber dismisses Stojić's ground of appeal 50 and Praljak's ground of appeal 25.

(b) Humanitarian conditions during the siege of East Mostar (Praljak's Ground *26)*

536.   The Trial Chamber concluded that, from June 1993 to April 1994, East Mostar was under siege by the HVO. It considered, *inter alia,* that: (1) although the roads to the north and south of East Mostar were open, the town was the target of a prolonged military attack by the HVO that included intense constant shooting and shelling, including sniper fire, on a cramped densely-populated residential zone; (2) the population could not leave East Mostar of its own free will and had to live under extremely harsh conditions, without food, water, electricity, or appropriate medical care; and (3) the HVO hindered and at times blocked the arrival of humanitarian aid and deliberately targeted members of international organisations.[1754] **[page 232]**

537.   Praljak submits that the Trial Chamber erred in finding that the HVO held East Mostar under siege without any conclusive evidentiary basis and while ignoring relevant evidence.[1755] Specifically, he argues that the evidence: (1) does not show that the HVO targeted the town or its population but rather that it targeted ABiH military objectives within the town;[1756] and (2) does show that the "HVO" offered assistance to the East Mostar population, including providing medical treatment and food, while it was the BiH authorities who were reluctant to accept the HVO's offers.[1757] Praljak further argues that the Trial Chamber based its conclusion on various other erroneous conclusions, including wrongly attributing responsibility to the HVO for certain facts.[1758] He additionally argues that the Trial Chamber's conclusion contradicts its

---

[1749]   Trial Judgement, Vol. 3, paras 1255, 1349, 1685. See Trial Judgement, Vol. 3, para. 1711; *supra,* para. 530.

[1750]   Praljak's Appeal Brief, para. 307, referring to Ex. 1D01874, p. 2; Trial Judgement, Vol. 2, para. 1203, Vol. 4, para. 181. See Trial Judgement, Vol. 2, paras 1196, 1378 (noting that the siege took place between June 1993 and April 1994). See also Trial Judgement, Vol. 2, para. 1222.

[1751]   Trial Judgement, Vol. 2, para. 1203, Vol. 4, para. 181. See also Trial Judgement, Vol. 2, para. 1222.

[1752]   With regard to Praljak's argument in reply that the lack of evidence that the proposal was ever implemented does not undermine the HVO's willingness to allow free movement of civilians, the Appeals Chamber finds that he fails to show that no reasonable trial chamber could have come to the opposite conclusion. In addition, the Appeals Chamber considers that in arguing that it is not important that the proposal was made six months into the siege, Praljak merely advances his own preferred interpretation of the evidence. These arguments are dismissed.

[1753]   See *supra*, para. 533.

[1754]   Trial Judgement, Vol. 2, para. 1378.

[1755]   Praljak's Appeal Brief, paras 309-310, 313-314.

[1756]   Praljak's Appeal Brief, para. 309.

[1757]   Praljak's Appeal Brief, para. 313, referring to Ex. P05428, p. 5, Ex. 1D01874, p. 2 (a letter by Prlić containing such offers). Praljak replies that in any event, he cannot be held responsible for shortages of food or medical care, since the Trial Chamber could not find that he participated in or knew of the HVO hindering humanitarian aid and since he in fact personally intervened to facilitate access to such aid. Praljak's Reply Brief, para. 94.

[1758]   Praljak's Appeal Brief, para. 310. Praljak refers to the Trial Chamber's conclusions on shelling, sniping, and the destruction of the Old Bridge and mosques in Mostar. See Praljak's Appeal Brief, para. 310.

acknowledgement that: (1) the roads from East Mostar to the north and south were open;[1759] and (2) it lacked evidence as to who cut off the electricity and water supplies to East Mostar, while evidence showed HVO efforts to restore them.[1760] Praljak therefore requests that the Appeals Chamber overturn the Trial Judgement and acquit him under Counts 1, 15, 16, and 24 of the relevant charges with respect to Mostar.[1761]

538.   The Prosecution responds that Praljak shows no error in the Trial Chamber's findings and repeats arguments that the Trial Chamber considered and rejected.[1762] It argues that the Trial Chamber reasonably rejected Praljak's argument that the HVO only targeted military objectives in East Mostar and reasonably found that during the siege of East Mostar, the HVO created and aggravated the extremely harsh living conditions for the Muslim population.[1763] The Trial Chamber made reasonable and nuanced findings, the Prosecution submits, acknowledging that the HVO did not have exclusive responsibility for electricity and water shortages.[1764] The Prosecution contends that the Trial Chamber properly attributed responsibility to the HVO for food shortages.[1765] It also argues that the Trial Chamber considered evidence regarding Prlić's proposals **[page 233]** for providing food and medical care and the BiH's reluctance to accept HVO offers, but ultimately concluded that the HVO impeded evacuations by setting onerous conditions.[1766]

539.   The Appeals Chamber observes that the Trial Chamber acknowledged that it could not establish that the HVO was responsible for cutting off electricity or water supplies to East Mostar;[1767] and that the roads to the north and south were open and, therefore, East Mostar was not completely surrounded.[1768] It likewise did consider evidence of Prlić's offer of medical care and food to the East Mostar population[1769] and evidence indicating that the BiH authorities were unlikely to accept an HVO offer to medically evacuate women and children.[1770] The Appeals Chamber notes that the Trial Chamber nonetheless found that the HVO caused harsh living conditions in East Mostar, with shortages of food and medical care, by creating an influx of Muslims into the town and hindering humanitarian convoys.[1771] Praljak ignores these relevant factual findings that support the finding that the HVO besieged East Mostar.[1772] The Appeals Chamber therefore dismisses his ground of appeal 26.[1773]

(c) Sniping campaign in Mostar (Praljak's Ground 20)

540.   In concluding that East Mostar was under siege by the HVO, the Trial Chamber determined, *inter alia,* that the town was the target of a prolonged military attack by the HVO that included sniper fire.[1774] The Trial Chamber identified several shooting positions involved in sniping incidents, which included Stotina hill and other West Mostar locations.[1775] The Trial Chamber considered that the evidence "allow[ed]" for a finding that Stotina hill was controlled by the HVO.[1776] The Trial Chamber then found that the HVO controlled the hill on all of the dates of the relevant sniping incidents.[1777] It also found that the HVO "had a sufficient military presence to impose its authority in the western part of town", and therefore controlled other shooting

---

[1759]   Praljak's Appeal Brief, para. 309.
[1760]   Praljak's Appeal Brief, paras 311-312.
[1761]   Praljak's Appeal Brief, para. 314.
[1762]   Prosecution's Response Brief (Praljak), paras 217, 222.
[1763]   Prosecution's Response Brief (Praljak), para. 222.
[1764]   Prosecution's Response Brief (Praljak), para. 222.
[1765]   Prosecution's Response Brief (Praljak), para. 223.
[1766]   Prosecution's Response Brief (Praljak), para. 224, referring to Ex. P05428, p. 5.
[1767]   Trial Judgement, Vol. 2, paras 1210-1212, 1218.
[1768]   Trial Judgement, Vol. 2, para. 1378.
[1769]   Trial Judgement, Vol. 2, paras 1203, 1222, referring to, *inter alia,* Ex. 1D01874, p. 2. See also Trial Judgement, Vol. 2, para. 1244.
[1770]   Trial Judgement, Vol. 2, para. 1249 & fn. 3118, referring to Ex. P05428, p. 5.
[1771]   See Trial Judgement, Vol. 2, paras 1202, 1204, 1223, 1242, 1244, 1249, Vol. 3, paras 1255, 1349.
[1772]   Trial Judgement, Vol. 2, para. 1378, Vol. 3, paras 1255, 1349, 1685.
[1773]   The Appeals Chamber notes that it dismisses elsewhere Praljak's arguments submitted under other grounds of appeal and incorporated in Praljak's ground of appeal 26 by way of reference. Praljak's Appeal Brief, paras 309-310. See *supra,* paras 412, 533; *infra,* paras 543, 565, 569.
[1774]   Trial Judgement, Vol. 2, para. 1378.
[1775]   Trial Judgement, Vol. 2, para. 1032.
[1776]   Trial Judgement, Vol. 2, para. 1033; Trial Judgement (French original), Vol. 2, para. 1033 *("permettent").*
[1777]   Trial Judgement, Vol. 2, para. 1035. See also Trial Judgement, Vol. 2, para. 1034.

positions in West Mostar – such as the Ledera and Centar II buildings – on the dates the relevant incidents occurred.[1778] The Trial Chamber relied on the evidence of several witnesses, including Witness **[page 234]** Anthony Turco's Rule 92 *bis* statement, in finding that HVO snipers targeted women, children, and the elderly.[1779]

541.   Praljak submits that the Trial Chamber failed to apply the beyond reasonable doubt standard in evaluating evidence on a sniping campaign in Mostar, and instead made a "possible finding" without establishing that it was the only reasonable conclusion.[1780] Specifically, Praljak submits that the Trial Chamber erred in fact when it found that areas in Mostar where snipers operated were under the HVO's control.[1781] He submits that the HVO's control over Stotina is "very questionable" in light of ABiH positions above that location,[1782] and that the Trial Chamber erred in deeming that the evidence allowed the finding that the HVO was in control of Stotina, instead of making a finding beyond reasonable doubt.[1783] He further submits that even if the Trial Chamber found that sniper fire came from HVO-controlled territory in West Mostar, it does not mean that it can be attributed to the HVO as the evidence shows that the ABiH had its own people within the HVO who, although HVO members, were under ABiH orders.[1784] Praljak additionally argues that it "remains unknown" how the Trial Chamber could attribute the sniper shots to the HVO as it acknowledged that it could not verify the exact location from where the shots came, and no evidence points to HVO control over access to "concerned buildings".[1785] Finally, Praljak contends that the Trial Chamber based its conclusions on the suffering of the Muslim population in East Mostar "entirely" on Turco's Rule 92 *bis* statement, which cannot constitute in itself the basis for a conviction.[1786] Praljak therefore requests that the Appeals Chamber acquit him under Counts 1, 2, 3, 15, 16, 24, and 25 of the relevant charges with respect to Mostar.[1787]

542.   The Prosecution responds that the Trial Chamber applied the correct standard of proof, properly finding that HVO-controlled snipers in West Mostar deliberately targeted Muslim civilians, and that Praljak fails to demonstrate that the Trial Chamber erred in attributing such responsibility to the HVO.[1788] It contends that Praljak ignores the Trial Chamber's findings that the HVO controlled Stotina when its snipers were positioned there and relevant testimony that the **[page 235]** ABiH did not fire from its positions above Stotina.[1789] The Prosecution submits that Praljak's claim about HVO members under ABiH control is speculative and unsupported, and his claim regarding "concerned buildings" ignores Stojić's admission that HVO-controlled snipers were in the "Blue Bank" building at the time of the sniping incidents.[1790] Additionally, the Prosecution contends that the Trial Chamber reasonably concluded that the HVO was responsible, even without pinpointing where the shots originated, as there was no indication of firing from the ABiH or from Serb positions.[1791] Finally, the Prosecution argues that the Trial Chamber did not rely solely on Turco to find that HVO snipers targeted women, children, and the elderly.[1792]

543.   The Appeals Chamber observes that the Trial Chamber focused on establishing who was in control of the areas from where HVO snipers allegedly opened fire on Mostar, noting with specificity potential shooting

---

[1778]   Trial Judgement, Vol. 2, para. 1038. See Trial Judgement, Vol. 2, paras 1036-1037, 1041.
[1779]   Trial Judgement, Vol. 2, para. 1188. See Trial Judgement, Vol. 2, paras 1186-1187, 1194.
[1780]   Praljak's Appeal Brief, para. 254. See Praljak's Appeal Brief, para. 246; Praljak's Reply Brief, para. 85.
[1781]   Praljak's Appeal Brief, heading before para. 247; Appeal Hearing, AT. 378 (22 Mar 2017). See Praljak's Appeal Brief, para. 246.
[1782]   Praljak's Appeal Brief, para. 248. See Praljak's Appeal Brief, paras 247, 250.
[1783]   Praljak's Appeal Brief, para. 248.
[1784]   Praljak's Appeal Brief, paras 249, 253. Praljak also argues that individuals could be acting outside of any control, taking "pot shots" at anyone. Praljak's Appeal Brief, para. 249.
[1785]   Praljak's Appeal Brief, paras 249, 252; Appeal Hearing, AT. 378-379 (22 Mar 2017).
[1786]   Praljak's Appeal Brief, para. 251. Praljak also argues that Turco could not confirm that the HVO was responsible for the sniping events. Praljak's Appeal Brief, para. 251.
[1787]   Praljak's Appeal Brief, para. 246.
[1788]   Prosecution's Response Brief (Praljak), paras 185-186.
[1789]   Prosecution's Response Brief (Praljak), para. 187.
[1790]   Prosecution's Response Brief (Praljak), para. 188.
[1791]   Prosecution's Response Brief (Praljak), para. 189. The Prosecution further contends that this conclusion is confirmed by other Trial Chamber findings. Prosecution's Response Brief (Praljak), para. 189.
[1792]   Prosecution's Response Brief (Praljak), para. 190.

positions.[1793] On the basis of the evidence, the Trial Chamber then established that the HVO controlled most of these positions.[1794] Finally, the Trial Chamber examined the evidence pertaining to specific sniping incidents. When it was unable to determine the precise locations from which the shots were fired, it proceeded to examine – and eliminate – the possibility that they may have originated from the ABiH or Serbian forces.[1795] In light of these findings, which Praljak misrepresents when arguing that it "remains unknown" how the Trial Chamber could attribute the sniper shots to the HVO,[1796] the Appeals Chamber finds that he merely disagrees with the Trial Chamber's assessment of the evidence without showing that the Trial Chamber erred.

544. Further, while the Trial Chamber used the phrase "the consistency of the testimonies and the evidence collected *allow*" a finding that Stotina hill was controlled by the HVO,[1797] the Appeals Chamber notes that immediately thereafter, the Trial Chamber continued its examination of whether the HVO controlled Stotina hill, considering further evidence,[1798] rejecting Praljak's trial submissions to the contrary,[1799] and concluding that Stotina hill "was controlled by the HVO armed, forces on all of the dates of the alleged incidents".[1800] In the opinion of the Appeals Chamber, the Trial Judgement does not reflect that the Trial Chamber failed to apply the correct "beyond [page 236] reasonable doubt" standard.[1801] Rather, Praljak suggests reading out of context a finding relied upon by the Trial Chamber to reach its ultimate conclusion beyond reasonable doubt that Stotina hill was controlled by the HVO armed forces.

545. Finally, the Appeals Chamber observes that, contrary to Praljak's contention, the Trial Chamber did not base its conclusions on the suffering of the Muslim population in East Mostar "entirely" on a Rule 92 *bis* statement. In particular, the Trial Chamber stated that "[a]lthough [it] notes that the testimony of *Anthony Turco* was taken pursuant to Rule 92 *bis* of the Rules, it deems that all the evidence relating to the victims of the sniping incidents examined above corroborates what he said".[1802] In this regard, the Trial Chamber found that several witnesses "testified before the Chamber that women and children were targeted by snipers positioned in sectors controlled by the HVO".[1803] Notably, Witness Dževad Hadžizukić testified about his wife being killed by a sniper, and Witness Grant Finlayson testified about a woman and a child who were killed by sniper fire.[1804] Finally, the Trial Chamber relied on several contemporaneous documents describing incidents in which women and children were wounded or killed by snipers.[1805] Accordingly, the Appeals Chamber dismisses Praljak's ground of appeal 20.

(d) Shelling of East Mostar (Praljak's Ground 21 and Petković's Sub-ground 5.2.2.4 both in part)

546. The Trial Chamber concluded that East Mostar was subjected to intense and uninterrupted firing and shelling from the HVO between June 1993 and March 1994.[1806] In reaching this conclusion, the Trial

---

[1793] Trial Judgement, Vol. 2, para. 1032.
[1794] Trial Judgement, Vol. 2, paras. 1033-1038. See also Trial Judgement, Vol. 2, paras 1039-1041.
[1795] Trial Judgement, Vol. 2, paras 1042 *et seq.*
[1796] See Praljak's Appeal Brief, para. 252.
[1797] Trial Judgement, Vol. 2, para. 1033 (emphasis added); Trial Judgement (French original), Vol. 2, para. 1033 *("la constance des témoignages et des éléments recueillis permettent de conclure en ce sens").*
[1798] Trial Judgement, Vol. 2, para. 1033.
[1799] Trial Judgement, Vol. 2, para. 1034.
[1800] Trial Judgement, Vol. 2, para. 1035.
[1801] The Appeals Chamber further notes that the Trial Chamber set out the correct standard in a general section devoted to evidentiary standards and stated that, although it did not systematically restate the expression "beyond reasonable doubt" in each finding of fact or in respect of the criminal responsibility of the Appellants, it applied this standard throughout the Trial Judgement. Trial Judgement, Vol. 1, para. 267.
[1802] Trial Judgement, Vol. 2, para. 1188.
[1803] Trial Judgement, Vol. 2, para. 1186 (internal reference omitted).
[1804] Trial Judgement, Vol. 2, para. 1186" & fn. 2952, referring to, *inter alia*, Dževad Hadžizukić, T(F). 13343, 13350 (1 Feb 2007), Ex. P09859 (witness statement of Dževad Hadžizukić), pp. 3-4, Grant Finlayson, T(F). 18045 (7 May 2007), referring to Ex. P02751, p. 2. See also Trial Judgement, Vol. 2, para. 1186 & fns 2951-2952, referring to, *inter alia*, Jeremy Bowen, T(F). 12744-12745, 12748 (23 Jan 2007) (sniper fire over the heads of women, children, and the elderly), P10039 (witness statement by Martin Mol), para. 42 (woman wounded by sniping), fn. 2965, referring to Ratko Pejanović, T. 1329-1330 (4 May 2006) (an elderly man wounded by sniper fire), Miro Salčin, T(F). 14184 (15 Feb 2007) (women, children, and the elderly being subjected to sniper fire).
[1805] Trial Judgement, Vol. 2, para. 1186 & fns 2951-2952, referring to, *inter alia*, Exs. P06925 (confidential), pp. 2-3 (woman killed by sniper fire), P02751, p. 2 (woman and child killed by sniper fire), P02947 (confidential), pp. 4-5 (girl wounded by sniper fire).
[1806] Trial Judgement, Vol. 2, para. 1018.

Chamber noted, *inter alia,* that: (1) it received information indicating that the HVO used small aeroplanes to drop shells or bombs;[1807] (2) the ABiH chiefly had light infantry weapons and, even if the ABiH had heavy weapons, the HVO was better equipped, chiefly used **[page 237]** heavy artillery, and proceeded to shell and fire on East Mostar daily, intensely, and closely;[1808] (3) there was also shelling from the Serbian armed forces between June and December 1993 ;[1809] (4) in an UNPROFOR communique, Witness Cedric Thornberry stressed that not a single structure seemed to have been spared by the shelling;[1810] (5) the Donja Mahala neighbourhood was hit by home-made bombs in the form of tyres filled with explosives launched from Hum mountain, located in HVO-controlled territory;[1811] (6) an HVO report sent to the Main Staff mentioned that the HVO dropped two napalm bombs on the Donja Mahala neighbourhood;[1812] and (7) the HVO firing and shelling killed and injured many people in East Mostar, evidenced by, *inter alia,* the records of the East Mostar Hospital showing the number of patients treated for injuries caused by bullets or explosives.[1813]

547.   As for the targets of the HVO shelling, the Trial Chamber found that the attack was indiscriminate in light of the weapons used and how they were used, which were not suited to the destruction of military targets alone.[1814] It found, in particular, that the zone in which obvious military targets were located – such as the ABiH headquarters – was a small residential area with a high population density into which the HVO forcibly transferred Muslims from West Mostar. As a result, repeated heavy artillery attacks would have to result in civilian loss of life and injury, as well as damage to property, which was substantial and excessive in relation to the concrete and direct military advantage anticipated.[1815] The Trial Chamber found that the firing and shelling were not limited to specific targets.[1816] In reaching these findings, the Trial Chamber noted, *inter alia,* that: (1) according to Witness DV, a professional soldier, the use of heavy artillery by the HVO was not an appropriate method of combat for the type of conflict in the town of Mostar;[1817] (2) the HVO was technically able to identify its targets, notably using adjustment calculations; (3) East Mostar, overall, came under HVO shelling and fire, but certain locations were targeted more particularly by the HVO, including the Donja Mahala sector and Marshal Tito Street;[1818] (4) the evidence showed that HVO shelling and artillery fire affected all of East Mostar, made up of densely inhabited and **[page 238]** populated areas, and that many buildings were destroyed;[1819] (5) it was impossible for the HVO to precisely target with shots, shells, and tyres filled with explosives ABiH soldiers who were not assembled at a specific location in Donja Mahala;[1820] and (6) evidence indicated that the ABiH positioned mobile mortars near the East Mostar Hospital.[1821]

548.   The Trial Chamber also found that the constant and intense shelling and artillery fire had the effect of terrifying the population of East Mostar.[1822] In arriving at this finding, the Trial Chamber took into consideration evidence of the fear of the population living under the deafening sounds of HVO shelling and firing and them having to run for cover in the streets.[1823] It referred to this terrifying effect when finding that the HVO committed the crime of unlawful infliction of terror on civilians.[1824] Moreover, it relied on the

---

[1807]   Trial Judgement, Vol. 2, para. 997.
[1808]   Trial Judgement, Vol. 2, paras 996-998, 1000.
[1809]   Trial Judgement, Vol. 2, para. 1001.
[1810]   Trial Judgement, Vol. 2, para. 1004.
[1811]   Trial Judgement, Vol. 2, para. 1005.
[1812]   Trial Judgement, Vol. 2, para. 1006.
[1813]   Trial Judgement, Vol. 2, para. 1016.
[1814]   Trial Judgement, Vol. 3, paras 1686, 1689.
[1815]   Trial Judgement, Vol. 3, para. 1686. See Trial Judgement, Vol. 3, para. 1689.
[1816]   Trial Judgement, Vol. 2, para. 1018, Vol. 3, paras 1254, 1348, 1684, 1689. See Trial Judgement, Vol. 2, para. 1014.
[1817]   Trial Judgement, Vol. 2, para. 997.
[1818]   Trial Judgement, Vol. 2, para. 1003. See also Trial Judgement, Vol. 3, paras 1254, 1348, 1684. The Trial Chamber noted that Marshal Tito Street – one of the main streets in East Mostar – was the location of the headquarters of the 4th Corps of the 41st ABiH Brigade. Trial Judgement, Vol. 2, para. 1009. It also noted that, according to Witness Miro Salčin, there was no specific headquarters or fixed assembly point in Donja Mahala for the 120 ABiH soldiers who were present and armed with only light infantry weapons. Trial Judgement, Vol. 2, para. 1007.
[1819]   Trial Judgement, Vol. 2, para. 1004.
[1820]   Trial Judgement, Vol. 2, para. 1008. See also Trial Judgement, Vol. 3, paras 1254, 1348, 1684.
[1821]   Trial Judgement, Vol. 2, para. 1013.
[1822]   Trial Judgement, Vol. 2, para. 1015.
[1823]   Trial Judgement, Vol. 2, para. 1015.
[1824]   Trial Judgement, Vol. 3, paras 1689, 1692.

indiscriminate nature of the attack, taking into consideration that the HVO's shelling and firing were not limited to military targets; rather, the whole of East Mostar was subjected to daily and intense shelling and artillery fire in which heavy artillery was used.[1825] Finally, the Trial Chamber considered, *inter alia,* the HVO's deliberate shelling and destruction of ten mosques in East Mostar.[1826]

(i) Arguments of the Parties

549. Praljak submits that the Trial Chamber erred when concluding that the HVO shelled East Mostar intensively and indiscriminately and that the HVO shelling caused numerous victims.[1827] First, Praljak puts forth evidence which he alleges contradicts the following Trial Chamber findings: (1) the HVO used napalm bombs;[1828] (2) the HVO was better equipped than the ABiH and intensely shelled and fired at East Mostar between early June 1993 and early March 1994;[1829] and (3) home-made bombs, which hit the Donja Mahala neighbourhood, were attributable to the HVO, rather than the ABiH.[1830] He contends that the Trial Chamber should have **[page 239]** adopted a more careful approach to the evidence as it admitted that Serbs also shelled Mostar.[1831] Praljak further submits that particular pieces of evidence to which the Trial Chamber referred do not: (1) attribute any responsibility to the HVO for the situation in Mostar; or (2) confirm that an HVO aeroplane dropped shells.[1832] Additionally, he argues that the UNPROFOR Spanish Battalion ("SpaBat") documents do not allow for a conclusion on the number of shells fired by the HVO as they only indicate the number of incoming and outgoing shells in East Mostar, not West Mostar.[1833] Praljak alleges that there, is no evidence about the origin of the shelling and victims injured by the HVO as the Trial Chamber justified its findings on the basis of the number of victims admitted into the East Mostar Hospital.[1834]

550. Praljak avers that the Trial Chamber should have unambiguously established whether the HVO was able to target military objectives and yet intentionally targeted the civilian population or whether it was unable to do so and therefore its attacks were indiscriminate.[1835] Petković argues that the Trial Chamber did not infer that the HVO targeted civilian objects and/or the civilian population, as is required to establish the crime of unlawful attack on civilians.[1836] Praljak contends that: (1) the Trial Chamber was required to ascertain "the objective and the modalities" of the attack as to each shelling incident;[1837] and (2) the fact that shelling affected a densely populated area does not mean that civilian areas were targeted or that the attacks were indiscriminate or disproportionate.[1838] Praljak submits that the Trial Chamber had no basis to assess whether the method or means of the attack were such that it could be directed at a specific military objective.[1839] Specifically, he submits that the Trial Chamber: (1) made no effort to establish the nature of the alleged attacks – seemingly basing its finding in this regard on a distortion of Witness DV's testimony – or

---

[1825] Trial Judgement, Vol. 3, para. 1689.
[1826] Trial Judgement, Vol. 2, paras 1367-1377, Vol. 3, para. 1690.
[1827] Praljak's Appeal Brief, headings before para. 256. See also Praljak's Appeal Brief, para. 256; Praljak's Reply Brief, para. 86.
[1828] Praljak's Appeal Brief, para. 258, referring to, *inter alia,* Trial Judgement, Vol. 2, para. 1006, Vol. 3, paras 1254, 1348, 1684.
[1829] Praljak's Appeal Brief, para. 260, referring to, *inter alia,* Trial Judgement, Vol. 2, para. 1000. Praljak also submits that the Trial Chamber based its conclusions on Exhibits P05278 and P05452, which were not in evidence. Praljak's Appeal Brief, para. 260 & fn. 615.
[1830] Praljak's Appeal Brief, para. 264, referring to, *inter alia,* Trial Judgement, Vol. 2, para. 1005. Praljak further submits that it cannot be excluded that these bombs were isolated criminal acts committed by individuals who were not under anyone's control. Praljak's Appeal Brief, para. 264.
[1831] Praljak's Appeal Brief, para. 267. See Praljak's Appeal Brief, para. 262. Praljak also submits that: (1) it cannot be excluded that at least some victims and damage can be attributed to the activities of groups operating within East Mostar who did not agree with the East Mostar government; and (2) the ABiH probably tried to expel the HVO from a small pocket it held on the east side of the Neretva River, thereby causing collateral damage among its own population. Praljak's Appeal Brief, para. 267.
[1832] Praljak's Appeal Brief, paras 257, 261, referring to, *inter alia,* Trial Judgement, Vol. 2, para. 1004.
[1833] Praljak's Appeal Brief, para. 263, referring to Ex. P06554.
[1834] Praljak's Appeal Brief, para. 262, referring to, *inter alia,* Ex. P04573, Trial Judgement, Vol. 2, para. 1016; Appeal Hearing, AT. 379 (22 Mar 2017), referring to Ex. P04573.
[1835] Praljak's Appeal Brief, paras 269-270. See also Praljak's Appeal Brief, para. 256 & fn. 596.
[1836] Petković's Appeal Brief, para. 269. See also Petković's Appeal Brief, fn. 356. The Appeals Chamber notes that Petković also states, conversely, that he "does not challenge the Chamber's findings that crimes were committed by shelling". Petković's Reply Brief, para. 61.
[1837] Praljak's Appeal Brief, para. 270. See Praljak's Reply Brief, para. 87.
[1838] Praljak's Appeal Brief, para. 271. See also Praljak's Appeal Brief, paras 265-266, 270.
[1839] Praljak's Appeal Brief, para. 272.

the weapons used by the HVO;[1840] and (2) failed to consider evidence confirming that the shelling was limited and aimed at military targets.[1841] Moreover, Praljak contends that the **[page 240]** Trial Chamber's finding that the damage was excessive in relation to the anticipated military advantage was unfounded.[1842]

551.   Finally, Praljak alleges errors related to the Trial Chamber's conclusion that the HVO committed the crime of unlawful infliction of terror by shelling the population of East Mostar.[1843] He submits that, in light of the Trial Chamber's admission that the shelling was aimed at military targets, it failed to establish that the purpose of the shelling was to spread terror and that any HVO member had the specific intent to spread terror.[1844] He further submits that the Trial Chamber merely stated that the shelling terrified the population, without any conclusive evidence and without establishing the required degree of trauma and psychological damage.[1845] Praljak requests that his convictions under Counts 1, 2, 3, 16, 24, and 25 be reversed with respect to the relevant charges for Mostar.[1846] Petković requests to be acquitted on Count 24.[1847]

552.   The Prosecution responds that Praljak merely disagrees with the Trial Chamber's interpretation of evidence without showing error.[1848] It submits that, contrary to Praljak's claims: (1) the Trial Chamber's reasonable considerations regarding the nature of the attack were based on the totality of evidence; (2) the Trial Chamber did not distort Witness DV's evidence; and (3) the HVO's home-made tyre bombs were different from ABiH handheld bombs.[1849] The Prosecution submits that claims concerning alleged shelling by forces other than the HVO do not undermine the Trial Chamber's finding that the HVO "daily, intensely and closely" shelled East Mostar.[1850] In this regard, it submits that: (1) the Trial Chamber's finding that occasional Serb shelling occurred is well-grounded; and (2) the Trial Chamber properly relied on SpaBat reports confirming the HVO's responsibility for the shelling.[1851] Further, the Prosecution argues that the Trial Chamber was not required to establish the "objective and modalities" of each shelling incident.[1852] It submits, **[page 241]** moreover, that Praljak ignores the extensive evidence considered by the Trial Chamber and its explicit findings that, *inter alia*, intense and continuous shelling formed a key part of the HVO's unlawful attack on and terrorisation of the civilian population.[1853] Finally, the Prosecution argues that, contrary to Petković's claim, the Trial Chamber "explicitly found that HVO shelling targeted the civilian population and civilian property".[1854]

553.   Regarding Praljak's challenge to his conviction under Count 25 (unlawful infliction of terror on civilians as a violation of the laws or customs of war), the Prosecution argues that: (1) the Trial Chamber's findings amply demonstrate that the HVO committed acts of violence the primary purpose of which was to

---

[1840]   Praljak's Appeal Brief, paras 268, 272. See Praljak's Appeal Brief, para. 256 & fn. 597.
[1841]   Praljak's Appeal Brief, para. 272. See Praljak's Appeal Brief, para. 265 & fn. 633. Additionally, Praljak argues that the Trial Chamber accepted Witness Miro Salčin's statements although they conflicted with its own findings that: (1) the ABiH had heavy weapons, including mobile mortars near the hospital; and (2) the headquarters of the 4 Corps*of the 41st ABiH Brigade was located on Marshal Tito Street. He further alleges that the Trial Chamber failed to consider the ABiH mobile mortars when concluding that the HVO firing and shelling were not limited to specific military targets. Praljak's Appeal Brief, paras 259 (referring to, *inter alia*, Trial Judgement, Vol. 2, paras 1007, 1009), 273. See also Praljak's Appeal Brief, para. 256 & fn. 596, para. 266.
[1842]   Praljak's Appeal Brief, para. 273, referring to, *inter alia*, Trial Judgement, Vol. 3, para. 1686; Praljak's Reply Brief, para. 87.
[1843]   Praljak's Appeal Brief, headings before paras 274-275. See Praljak's Appeal Brief, paras 274, 276. See also Praljak's Appeal Brief, para. 256; Praljak's Reply Brief, paras 86, 88.
[1844]   Praljak's Appeal Brief, paras 274, 277-279; Appeal Hearing, AT. 380-381 (22 Mar 2017). Praljak also submits that HVO orders show that shelling was aimed at military targets. Praljak's Appeal Brief, para. 277.
[1845]   Praljak's Appeal Brief, paras 275-276.
[1846]   Praljak's Appeal Brief, para. 255.
[1847]   Petković's Appeal Brief, paras 251, 269, 282.
[1848]   Prosecution's Response Brief (Praljak), paras 191, 194.
[1849]   Prosecution's Response Brief (Praljak), para. 194. The Prosecution submits that Praljak's claim that these bombs were used in isolated criminal acts is unsupported and speculative. Prosecution's Response Brief (Praljak), para. 194.
[1850]   Prosecution's Response Brief (Praljak), para. 196. The Prosecution submits that the Trial Chamber cited many other supporting exhibits apart from two documents not in evidence. Prosecution's Response Brief (Praljak), para. 196.
[1851]   Prosecution's Response Brief (Praljak), para. 196.
[1852]   Prosecution's Response Brief (Praljak), para. 195.
[1853]   Prosecution's Response Brief (Praljak), paras 192-193. The Prosecution submits that the HVO intended to attack Muslim civilians and destroy Muslim civilian objects and that this was not collateral damage. Prosecution's Response Brief (Praljak), para. 192.
[1854]   Prosecution's Response Brief (Petković), para. 205.

spread terror; and (2) it applied the correct *mens rea* standard.[1855] The Prosecution argues that Praljak merely repeats his untenable claim that HVO shelling targeted military objects and not Muslims.[1856]

(ii) Analysis

554.   The Appeals Chamber will first address Praljak's arguments regarding the Trial Chamber's findings on the HVO's use of napalm bombs and home-made bombs and its findings that the HVO was better equipped than the ABiH and intensely shelled and fired at East Mostar between early June 1993 and early March 1994. With respect to Praljak's submission that the Trial Chamber erred in relying on proposed Exhibits P05278 and P05452 as they were not in evidence, the Appeals Chamber considers that Praljak ignores the voluminous amount of evidence upon which the Trial Chamber relied in addition to these exhibits.[1857] The Appeals Chamber notes that his remaining arguments are substantiated solely by reference to isolated pieces of evidence which Praljak claims support an alternative conclusion to that reached by the Trial Chamber.[1858] He does not, in these arguments, identify the evidence actually relied upon by the Trial Chamber in making the relevant findings, let alone articulate error in that reliance.[1859] As such and in each case, his arguments challenge the Trial Chamber's failure to rely on one piece of **[page 242]** evidence, without explaining why the relevant findings, and by extension the conviction, should not stand on the basis of the remaining evidence. They are accordingly dismissed.

555.   With respect to Praljak's argument that the Trial Chamber should have adopted a more careful approach to the evidence as it admitted that Serbs also shelled Mostar, he ignores that the Trial Chamber ultimately found, on the basis of the evidence, that Serbian forces only occasionally fired shells.[1860] Further, Praljak merely challenges the Trial Chamber's failure to rely on particular evidence without explaining why the conviction should not stand on the basis of the remaining evidence.[1861] In this regard, the Appeals Chamber notes that the Trial Chamber considered extensive evidence when finding that the HVO shelled and fired at East Mostar daily, intensely, and closely, thereby killing and injuring people.[1862] When arguing that evidence to which the Trial Chamber referred does not attribute any responsibility to the HVO for the situation in Mostar, Praljak points to the Trial Chamber's finding that HVO shelling and artillery fire affected all of East Mostar,[1863] and ignores the other evidence the Trial Chamber relied upon in this regard.[1864] The Appeals Chamber further rejects Praljak's allegations – that there is no evidence about the origin of the shelling and victims injured by the HVO as the Trial Chamber justified its findings on the basis of the number of victims admitted into the East Mostar Hospital – as he ignores the other evidence upon which the Trial

---

[1855]   Prosecution's Response Brief (Praljak), paras 197-198.

[1856]   Prosecution's Response Brief (Praljak), para. 198.

[1857]   See Trial Judgement, Vol. 2, para. 1000 and references cited therein. *Cf. Kordić and Čerkez* Appeal Judgement, para. 865.

[1858]   See Praljak's Appeal Brief, paras 258 (referring to, *inter alia,* Miro Salčin, T. 14219-14220 (15 Feb 2007)), 260 (referring to, *inter alia,* Cedric Thornberry, T. 26286 (15 Jan 2008), Grant Finlayson, T. 18042 (7 May 2007)), 264 (referring to, *inter alia,* Larry Forbes, T. 21288-21289 (16 Aug 2007)).

[1859]   See Trial Judgement, Vol. 2, paras 996, 1000, 1005-1006 and references cited therein. See also Trial Judgement, Vol. 2, para. 1018. As to Praljak's argument that it cannot be excluded that the home-made bombs were isolated criminal acts committed by individuals who were not under anyone's control, the Appeals Chamber finds it to be unsubstantiated and speculative.

[1860]   Trial Judgement, Vol. 2, para. 1001.

[1861]   See Praljak's Appeal Brief, para. 267 & fns 651, 653, referring to Witness CB, T. 10155 (14 Nov 2006), Grant Finlayson, T. 18224 (9 May 2007) (both referred to in Trial Judgement, Vol. 2, para. 1001).

[1862]   See, *e.g.,* Trial Judgement, Vol. 2, paras 996-997, 1000, 1003-1004, 1014, 1016, 1018 and references cited therein. The Appeals Chamber finds speculative Praljak's submissions that it cannot be excluded that at least some victims and damage can be attributed to the activities of groups operating within East Mostar and that the ABiH probably tried to expel the HVO from a small pocket it held on the east side of the Neretva River, thereby causing collateral damage among its own. population.

[1863]   Praljak's Appeal Brief, para. 261, referring to, *inter alia,* Trial Judgement, Vol. 2, para. 1004.

[1864]   See, *e.g.,* Trial Judgement, Vol. 2, para. 1004 & fns 2321, 2324-2325. When pointing to evidence contrary to the Trial Chamber's finding, Praljak merely asserts that the Trial Chamber must have failed to consider relevant evidence, without showing that no reasonable trier of fact, based on the evidence, could have reached the same conclusion as the Trial Chamber did. See Praljak's Appeal Brief, para. 261 & fns 622-623. In this regard, the Appeals Chamber recalls that the Trial Chamber found, on the basis of various pieces of evidence, that HVO shelling and artillery fire affected all of East Mostar, made up of densely inhabited and populated areas, in which homes, stores, and public buildings were destroyed. Trial Judgement, Vol. 2, para. 1004 and references cited therein.

Chamber relied when reaching its findings that the HVO shelled and fired at East Mostar and killed and injured many people, notably women, children, and the elderly.[1865] The foregoing arguments are dismissed.

556.   Regarding Praljak's claim that the evidence to which the Trial Chamber referred does not confirm that an HVO aeroplane dropped shells, the Appeals Chamber notes that the Trial Chamber merely noted that it received information indicating that the HVO had small aeroplanes with which **[page 243]** it dropped shells or bombs, notably on Donja Mahala, which is amply supported by the evidence on which it relied.[1866] Praljak fails to demonstrate any error. As to his argument that the SpaBat documents do not allow for a conclusion on the number of shells fired by the HVO and only indicate the number of incoming and outgoing shells in East Mostar, not West Mostar, the Appeals Chamber notes that Praljak refers only to a 9 November 1993 report and fails to identify the Trial Chamber finding he is challenging or cite to the other evidence to which he refers.[1867] His argument is dismissed.

557.   With regard to the argument that the Trial Chamber should have unambiguously established whether the HVO was able to target military objectives and yet intentionally targeted the civilian population or whether it was unable to do so and therefore its attacks were indiscriminate, the Appeals Chamber notes that the Trial Chamber found that the attack was indiscriminate in light of the weapons used and, most of all, how they were used.[1868] The HVO used napalm bombs and tyres filled with explosives,[1869] and although it was technically able to identify its targets using adjustment calculations, the whole of East Mostar was subjected to intense and daily firing and shelling in which heavy artillery was used.[1870] Praljak has failed to demonstrate how the question of whether the shelling and firing constituted a direct attack on civilians or an indiscriminate attack would have any bearing on the Trial Chamber's decision as to the commission of the crime of an unlawful attack.[1871] His argument is dismissed. In light of the above, the Appeals Chamber also dismisses Petković's submission that the Trial Chamber did not infer that the HVO targeted civilian objects and/or the civilian population.

558.   When contending that the Trial Chamber was required to ascertain the objectives and modalities of the attack with regard to each shelling incident, Praljak points to the *D. Milošević* Appeal Judgement.[1872] In its assessment therein, the Appeals Chamber referred to a limited number of sniping and shelling incidents.[1873] In the present case, the Trial Chamber reviewed a large volume of evidence establishing the various weapons used by the HVO, the impact on specific neighbourhoods and zones, and incidents in which locations and buildings may have been targeted **[page 244]** for military purposes.[1874] In light of the Trial Chamber's finding that intense shelling and artillery fire occurred on a daily basis over the course of nine months,[1875] and bearing in mind that a trial chamber must make its own final assessment based on the totality of the evidence before it,[1876] the Appeals Chamber is satisfied that a reasonable trier of fact could have taken such

---

[1865]   Trial Judgement, Vol. 2, paras 996-997, 1000, 1004-1006, 1009-1012, 1015-1016 & fns 2352-2354 and references cited therein. Insofar as Praljak also puts forth evidence to challenge the Trial Chamber's findings on the origin of the shelling, he is merely asserting that the Trial Chamber must have failed to consider relevant evidence without showing that no reasonable trier of fact, based on the evidence, could have reached the same conclusion as the Trial Chamber did.

[1866]   Trial Judgement, Vol. 2, para. 997, referring to, *inter alia*, Exs. P04785, p. 2 (reporting the HVO's use of aircraft to drop clusters of mortar bombs), P05091, para. 26 (noting allegations that the HVO dropped mortar grenades from two crop-duster aeroplanes), P05210 (confidential), p. 6 (reporting a flyover by a light airplane at times coinciding with the times at which, according to the ABiH, it was shelled from the air), P09834, para. 16 (stating that the HVO had a small plane which it would use to drop bombs on Donja Mahala as well as the areas of Luka and Tekija), Miro Salčin, T(F). 14276-14277 (private session) (19 Feb 2007) (confirming the HVO's use of aircraft).

[1867]   See Praljak's Appeal Brief, para. 263.

[1868]   Trial Judgement, Vol. 3, paras 1686, 1689.

[1869]   Trial Judgement, Vol. 2, paras 1005-1006, Vol. 3, paras 1254, 1348, 1451, 1684.

[1870]   Trial Judgement, Vol. 2, paras 997, 1000, 1003-1004, 1018, Vol. 3, paras 1254, 1348, 1451, 1684, 1686, 1689.

[1871]   See *Kordić and Čerkez* Appeal Judgement, para. 48 (recalling the fundamental principle of customary international law, as outlined in Article 51 of Additional Protocol I, whereby a civilian population shall not be the object of attack).

[1872]   Praljak's Appeal Brief, para. 270 & fn. 663, referring to *D. Milošević* Appeal Judgement, para. 143.

[1873]   See *D. Milošević* Appeal Judgement, paras 140-143.

[1874]   Trial Judgement, Vol. 2, paras 996-997, 1000, 1003-1014 and references cited therein.

[1875]   See, *e.g.*, Trial Judgement, Vol. 2, paras 996, 1000, 1018, Vol. 3, para. 1689.

[1876]   *Lukić and Lukić* Appeal Judgement, para. 260, referring to *Stakić* Appeal Judgement, para. 346; *Karemera and Ngirumpatse* Appeal Judgement, para. 52.

703

an approach and therefore finds that Praljak has failed to demonstrate any error. His argument is therefore dismissed.

559. When submitting that the fact that shelling affected a densely populated area does not mean that civilian areas were targeted or that the attack was indiscriminate or disproportionate, Praljak recalls that international humanitarian law does not *per se* prohibit attacks aimed at military targets when they are situated in populated areas.[1877] He presents numerous pieces of evidence to demonstrate that, *inter alia,* the ABiH placed military staff, equipment, and positions in civilian areas and used them for attacks on HVO positions.[1878] The Appeals Chamber notes that the Trial Chamber considered evidence of the locations and shelling of ABiH positions in East Mostar.[1879] Praljak merely points to evidence he prefers without showing that no reasonable trier of fact, based on the evidence, could have reached the conclusion that the firing and shelling were not limited to specific military targets.[1880] His argument is therefore dismissed.

560. In support of his submission that the Trial Chamber made no effort to establish the nature of the alleged attacks, Praljak argues that the Trial Chamber distorted Witness DV's testimony which, according to him, did not address the appropriateness of the method of combat used in East Mostar, but rather the military usefulness of the artillery in this kind of combat.[1881] The Appeals Chamber rejects this argument as Praljak merely disagrees with the Trial Chamber's interpretation of the evidence, without showing that no reasonable trier of fact could have adopted **[page 245]** it.[1882] Moreover, Praljak's claim that the Trial Chamber made no effort to establish the weapons used by the HVO is unfounded.[1883] As to his submission that the Trial Chamber failed to consider evidence confirming that the shelling was limited and aimed at military targets, the Appeals Chamber notes that Praljak repeats his submission expressly addressed, analysed at length, and rejected by the Trial Chamber, that the shelling was "selective and minimal".[1884] The Appeals Chamber considers that he merely asserts that the Trial Chamber must have failed to consider relevant evidence without showing that no reasonable trier of fact, based on the evidence, could have concluded that the HVO firing and shelling were not limited to specific military targets.[1885] Praljak's overall submission – based on the above-mentioned arguments – that the Trial Chamber had no basis to assess whether the method or means of the attack were such that it could be directed at a specific military objective is therefore dismissed;

561. With respect to the crime of unlawful attacks on civilians under Article 3 of the Statute, the Appeals Chamber recalls that although the principles of distinction and the protection of a civilian population do not

---

[1877] Praljak's Appeal Brief, para. 271.

[1878] See Praljak's Appeal Brief, paras 265-266.

[1879] Trial Judgement, Vol. 2, paras 1007-1014, noting: (1) that there was no specific headquarters or fixed assembly point in Donja Mahala for the ABiH soldiers there; (2) the presence on Marshal Tito Street of the war presidency headquarters of the Muslim political authorities, the headquarters of the 4th Corps of the 41st ABiH Brigade, the United Nations Military Observers ("UNMO") premises, the SpaBat premises, and the East Mostar Hospital; and (3) the presence of ABiH mobile mortars near the hospital.

[1880] Trial Judgement, Vol. 2, para. 1018. Particularly, with respect to ABiH positions in the vicinity of Marshal Tito Street, the Trial Chamber found that assuming those positions were the HVO's only targets, the firing and shelling inevitably affected that whole zone, which was the location of not only the East Mostar Hospital where injured people were being treated but also numerous homes and a significant proportion of the population. Trial Judgement, Vol. 2, para. 1014. See Trial Judgement, Vol. 2, paras 1009-1013.

[1881] Praljak's Appeal Brief, para. 268, referring to, *inter alia,* Trial Judgement, Vol. 2, para. 997, Witness DV, T. 23046 (2 Oct 2007).

[1882] See Witness DV, T. 23046 (2 Oct 2007) ("Mostar is a different kettle of fish. Mostar is not an open battlefield. The artillery is not as useful and perhaps it was infantry that was needed most, but I am not familiar about the preparation for the attack.").

[1883] See, *e.g.,* Trial Judgement, Vol. 2, paras 997, 1005-1006, Vol. 3, paras 1254, 1348, 1451, 1684, 1686, 1689. See also *supra,* paras 554-558.

[1884] Trial Judgement, Vol. 2, para. 1002. See Trial Judgement, Vol. 2, paras 1003-1014 (and references cited therein), 1018.

[1885] See Trial Judgement, Vol. 2, para. 1018. As to Praljak's additional argument that the Trial Chamber accepted Salčin's statements although they conflicted with its own findings that the ABiH had heavy weapons and that the headquarters of the 4th Corps of the 41st ABiH Brigade was located on Marshal Tito Street, the Appeals Chamber dismisses his submission as he: (1) ignores the Trial Chamber's finding that the ABiH chiefly had light infantry weapons; and (2) conflates its separate assessments of the situations in Donja Mahala and the zone of Marshal Tito Street. See Trial Judgement, Vol. 2, paras 998, 1007, 1009-1014. Concerning his related allegation that the Trial Chamber failed to consider the ABiH mobile mortars when concluding that the HVO firing and shelling were not limited to specific military targets, Praljak fails to demonstrate any error as the Trial Chamber considered the mobile mortars and found that the firing and shelling were not limited to specific targets, possibly military ones "such as" the headquarters of the 4th Corps and the 41st Brigade of the ABiH. Trial Judgement, Vol. 2, para. 1018. See Trial Judgement, Vol. 2, paras 1013-1014. His arguments are dismissed.

exclude the possibility of legitimate civilian casualties incidental to the conduct of military operations, those expected casualties must not be disproportionate to the concrete and direct military advantage anticipated before the attack.[1886] In support of his contention that the Trial Chamber's finding – that the damage was excessive in relation to the anticipated military advantage – was unfounded, Praljak argues that the Trial Chamber did not make any assessment of the collateral damage and comparative military advantage.[1887] The Appeals Chamber notes that the Trial Chamber found that the damage was excessive in relation to the concrete and direct military advantage anticipated,[1888] without determining this military advantage,[1889] and as **[page 246]** such erred in law by failing to provide a reasoned opinion. Nevertheless, in light of the preceding analysis,[1890] and considering the basis for the Trial Chamber's finding that the HVO committed the crime of unlawful attack on civilians,[1891] the Appeals Chamber considers that Praljak has failed to identify an error that would invalidate the Trial Chamber's decision.

562. Turning to Praljak's submissions related to the Trial Chamber's finding that the crime of unlawful infliction of terror was committed, the Appeals Chamber first recalls that the Trial Chamber was required to establish that the primary purpose of the acts or threats of violence committed in East Mostar was to spread terror among the civilian population and that the perpetrators of the crime acted with the specific intent to spread terror.[1892] The Appeals Chamber considers that Praljak ignores findings when submitting that, in light of the Trial Chamber's admission that the shelling was aimed at military targets, it failed to establish that the purpose of the shelling was to spread terror and that any HVO member had the specific intent to spread terror. Namely, the Trial Chamber found that the attack was indiscriminate as the HVO's shelling and firing were not limited to military targets; rather, the whole of East Mostar was subjected to daily and intense shelling and artillery fire in which heavy artillery was used.[1893] The indiscriminate nature of an attack was a reasonable factor for the Trial Chamber to consider in determining specific intent to spread terror.[1894] The Trial Chamber also considered, *inter alia,* the HVO's deliberate shelling and destruction of ten mosques in East Mostar.[1895] Finally, it expressly linked shelling and sniping as factors contributing to the terrorisation of the population of East Mostar.[1896] The Appeals Chamber considers that a reasonable trier of fact could conclude that HVO actions were conducted with the requisite specific intent to spread terror on these bases. Praljak fails to show that the Trial Chamber erred in this respect.[1897] His argument is dismissed.

563. The Appeals Chamber recalls that although it has previously found that the crime of unlawful infliction of terror involves cases in which "extensive trauma and psychological damage" **[page 247]** are caused by "attacks [which] were designed to keep the inhabitants in a constant state of terror",[1898] the actual terrorisation of the civilian population is not an element of the crime of unlawful infliction of terror.[1899] Thus, with respect to Praljak's assertion that the Trial Chamber merely stated that the shelling terrified the East

---

[1886] See *Galić* Appeal Judgement, paras 190-192; Article 51(5)(b) of Additional Protocol I. See *also Gotovina and Markač* Appeal Judgement, para. 82.

[1887] Praljak's Appeal Brief, para. 273; Praljak's Reply Brief, para. 87.

[1888] Trial Judgement, Vol. 3, para. 1686. See Trial Judgement, Vol. 3, para. 1689.

[1889] See Trial Judgement, Vol. 3, paras 1684-1686.

[1890] See *supra,* paras 557-560 (recalling that the Trial Chamber assessed the various weapons used by the HVO, the impact on specific neighbourhoods and zones, and incidents in which locations and buildings may have been targeted for military purposes, and that the Trial Chamber found that, in light of the weapons used and, most of all, how they were used, the attack was indiscriminate) & fn. 1871 (referring to *Kordić and Čerkez* Appeal Judgement, para. 48, recalling the fundamental principle of customary international law, as outlined in Article 51 of Additional Protocol I, whereby a civilian population shall not be the object of an attack).

[1891] See Trial Judgement, Vol. 3, para. 1688 (finding that by, *inter alia,* "shelling and firing at the civilian population of East Mostar", the HVO committed the crime of an unlawful attack on civilians).

[1892] *D. Milošević Appeal* Judgement, para. 37; *Galić* Appeal Judgement, para. 104.

[1893] Trial Judgement, Vol. 2, paras 997, 1000, 1004, 1018, Vol. 3, paras 1254, 1348, 1451, 1684, 1686, 1689. See *supra,* para. 557. In submitting that HVO orders show that shelling was aimed at military targets, Praljak points to submissions that the Appeals Chamber previously rejected. Praljak's Appeal Brief, fn. 683. See *supra,* para. 560.

[1894] See *D. Milošević* Appeal Judgement, para. 37; *Galić* Appeal Judgement, para. 102 ("The acts or threats of violence constitutive of the crime of terror shall not however be limited to direct attacks against civilians or threats thereof but may include indiscriminate or disproportionate attacks or threats thereof.").

[1895] Trial Judgement, Vol. 2, paras 1367-1377, Vol. 3, para. 1690. See *infra,* paras 566-569.

[1896] Trial Judgement, Vol. 3, para. 1689. See *supra,* paras 540-545.

[1897] See Trial Judgement, Vol. 1, paras 194-197, Vol. 3, paras 1689-1692.

[1898] *Galić* Appeal Judgement, para. 102. See *D. Milošević* Appeal Judgement, para. 35.

[1899] *D. Milošević* Appeal Judgement, para. 35, citing *Galić* Appeal Judgement, para. 104.

Mostar population, without any conclusive evidence and without establishing the "required" degree of trauma and psychological damage, the Appeals Chamber considers that the Trial Chamber was not, *stricto sensu,* required to establish such.

564.   The Appeals Chamber notes, however, that evidence of actual terrorisation may contribute to establishing other elements of the crime of terror.[1900] In the instant case, the Trial Chamber considered evidence regarding the terrifying effect on the civilian population, particularly evidence of the fear of the civilian population of East Mostar living under the deafening sound of HVO shelling and firing and them having to run for cover in the streets.[1901] It recalled this terrifying effect in its legal findings on unlawful infliction of terror on civilians,[1902] and while it did not expressly indicate why it did so, the Appeals Chamber notes that it has previously held that psychological impact on a population may satisfy the required gravity threshold of the crime.[1903] The Appeals Chamber considers that a reasonable trier of fact could rely on the evidence regarding the terrifying effect on the civilian population outlined above for this purpose. In light of the fact that this psychological impact was therefore relevant to the Trial Chamber's legal conclusion that the crime of unlawful infliction of terror had been established, the Appeals Chamber considers that Praljak fails to show that the Trial Chamber erred in law in its reasoning. In light of the foregoing, the Appeals Chamber finds that Praljak fails to show that the Trial Chamber erred. Accordingly, Praljak's allegations related to the Trial Chamber's conclusion that the HVO committed the crime of unlawful infliction of terror on the civilian population of East Mostar are dismissed.

565.   For the above reasons, the Appeals Chamber dismisses Praljak's ground of appeal 21 and Petković's sub-ground of appeal 5.2.2.4 both in relevant part.[1904] **[page 248]**

(e) Destruction of or damage to mosques in East Mostar (Praljak's Ground 24)

566.   The Trial Chamber found that the HVO's constant shooting and shelling of East Mostar destroyed or significantly damaged ten mosques between June and December 1993.[1905] It was satisfied that the HVO deliberately targeted these ten mosques.[1906] In reaching these findings, the Trial Chamber noted, *inter alia,* that: (1) eight out of the ten mosques were damaged or partially destroyed by the JNA and/or the VRS in 1992, while the remaining two mosques did not sustain damage and were still intact in January 1993, and probably until 9 May 1993;[1907] (2) each of the mosques in East Mostar was damaged or destroyed essentially by artillery fire between June and December 1993 and, in 1994, all mosques in Mostar town had been destroyed;[1908] and (3) various sources of evidence indicated that the HVO knowingly, systematically, and deliberately attacked the mosques in East Mostar.[1909]

567.   Praljak submits that the Trial Chamber erred when it concluded that the HVO deliberately targeted and destroyed or damaged ten mosques in East Mostar between June and December 1993.[1910] He submits that while the Trial Chamber noted that eight of the ten mosques had been damaged or partially destroyed by non-HVO forces in 1992, it did not establish what further damage occurred to those mosques in 1993, nor could it establish whether the two other mosques remained intact after January 1993.[1911] Praljak further

---

[1900]   *D. Milošević* Appeal Judgement, para. 35.
[1901]   Trial Judgement, Vol. 2, para. 1015 & fns 2350-2351. See also Trial Judgement, Vol. 2, para. 1016.
[1902]   Trial Judgement, Vol. 3, para. 1689. Moreover, in establishing that the HVO committed the crime of unlawful. infliction of terror on civilians, the Trial Chamber considered multiple underlying acts including the HVO's campaign of sniper fire which left the population under constant threat of being killed or wounded and prevented them from carrying out activities that were indispensable for their survival. Trial Judgement, Vol. 3, para. 1689. See Trial Judgement, Vol. 2, para. 1176, Vol. 3, paras 1690-1692.
[1903]   *D. Milošević* Appeal Judgement, para. 35.
[1904]   The Appeals Chamber observes that a review of the Trial Chamber's legal findings reveals that killings resulting from shellings were not considered under Counts 2 or 3. See *infra,* para. 2264. Therefore Praljak's request to be acquitted under those counts is moot.
[1905]   Trial Judgement, Vol. 2, para. 1377. See Trial Judgement, Vol. 2, paras 1372-1375.
[1906]   Trial Judgement, Vol. 2, para. 1377.
[1907]   Trial Judgement, Vol. 2, para. 1369. See Trial Judgement, Vol. 2, paras 1370-1371.
[1908]   Trial Judgement, Vol. 2, paras 1372-1375.
[1909]   Trial Judgement, Vol. 2, para. 1376.
[1910]   Praljak's Appeal Brief, headings before paras 298, 301, paras 299, 301.
[1911]   Praljak's Appeal Brief, paras 298, 300, referring to, *inter alia,* Trial Judgement, Vol. 2, paras 1369-1371; Appeal Hearing, AT. 379 (22 Mar 2017). See Praljak's Reply Brief, para. 91. The non-HVO forces Praljak refers to are the JNA and VRS. See Praljak's Appeal Brief, para. 298.

submits that the evidence does not allow for the Trial Chamber's finding because all but one of the mosques had been destroyed by May 1993.[1912] Additionally, Praljak submits that it was impossible for the Trial Chamber to attribute the destruction to the HVO and conclude that the HVO deliberately targeted the mosques because Exhibit P02636, on which it relied to do so, did not indicate how they were destroyed or who destroyed them.[1913] Finally, Praljak submits that with the exception of one mosque in West Mostar, there is no evidence that the HVO was involved in the destruction of any mosque in Mostar.[1914] Praljak therefore requests that the Appeals Chamber acquit him under Counts 1 (persecution as a crime against humanity) and 21 (destruction or wilful damage done to institutions **[page 249]** dedicated to religion or education as a violation of the laws or customs of war) of the relevant charges with respect to Mostar.[1915]

568.   The Prosecution responds that Praljak repeats his claims from trial, ignoring the Trial Chamber's explicit findings that the HVO subjected East Mostar to intense and uninterrupted shelling and constant shooting which damaged nearly all the buildings, as well as its analysis of evidence indicating systematic and intentional attacks on mosques.[1916] The Prosecution argues that the Trial Chamber considered evidence regarding each of the ten mosques, and properly determined that the HVO deliberately damaged and destroyed them between June and December 1993.[1917] Additionally, the Prosecution submits that the Trial Chamber considered what further damage the HVO inflicted on each mosque during the siege.[1918] Further, the Prosecution contends that Praljak's interpretation of the evidence, that all mosques in Mostar (except for one) were destroyed by May 993, is undermined by other evidence.[1919] The Prosecution contends that Praljak's argument regarding Exhibit P02636 shows no error in the Trial Chamber's finding.[1920]

569.   The Appeals Chamber observes that the Trial Chamber considered the condition of each of the ten mosques prior to June 1993, and noted with specificity which mosques were previously damaged and which mosques remained intact at the time.[1921] The Trial Chamber then systematically articulated how each mosque was either completely destroyed or sustained further damage as a result of HVO attacks between June and December 1993.[1922] In light of these findings, which Praljak misrepresents when claiming that the Trial Chamber did not establish what further damage occurred to the mosques in 1993, the Appeals Chamber dismisses his arguments regarding the extent of the damage done to the mosques in 1993. Regarding Praljak's argument that Exhibit P02636 did not indicate how the mosques were destroyed or who destroyed them, the Appeals Chamber observes that he ignores all the other evidence on which the Trial Chamber relied to attribute the destruction to the HVO and conclude that the HVO deliberately targeted the **[page 250]** mosques, and therefore finds that he fails to demonstrate that no reasonable trier of fact could have concluded as the Trial Chamber did.[1923] Similarly, in arguing that there is no evidence that the HVO was involved in the

[1912]   Praljak's Appeal Brief, para. 299; Appeal Hearing, AT. 379 (22 Mar 2017).
[1913]   Praljak's Appeal Brief, paras 302-303 & fns 736-737. Praljak further argues that attribution to the HVO is also impossible because multiple micro-wars were ongoing in East Mostar with different groups under different command. See Praljak's Appeal Brief, para. 302.
[1914]   Praljak's Appeal Brief, para. 304; Appeal Hearing, AT. 379 (22 Mar 2017). Praljak specifically refers to one mosque in West Mostar that was destroyed by an HVO member, but contends that the only evidence that the HVO ordered its destruction is unconfirmed and doubtful. Praljak's Appeal Brief, para. 304.
[1915]   Praljak's Appeal Brief, para. 297.
[1916]   Prosecution's Response Brief (Praljak), paras 211-212, 215. The Prosecution submits that even though the Trial Chamber did not need to establish the intent of perpetrators used by JCE members, it properly determined that the HVO forces did possess the required intent. Prosecution's Response Brief (Praljak), para. 215.
[1917]   Prosecution's Response Brief (Praljak), para. 213.
[1918]   Prosecution's Response Brief (Praljak), para. 213. The Prosecution also states that Praljak's argument regarding the West Mostar mosque is unpersuasive because whether or not the HVO ordered its destruction, Praljak could foresee that mosques would be destroyed for the purposes of JCE III liability. Prosecution's Response Brief (Praljak), para. 216, referring to, *inter alia*, Praljak's Appeal Brief, para. 304.
[1919]   Prosecution's Response Brief (Praljak), para. 214, referring to, *inter alia*, Praljak's Appeal Brief, para. 299. See Prosecution's Response Brief (Praljak), para. 211.
[1920]   Prosecution's Response Brief (Praljak), para. 215, referring to Trial Judgement, Vol. 2, para. 1376.
[1921]   Trial Judgement, Vol. 2, paras 1369-1371.
[1922]   Trial Judgement, Vol. 2, paras 1372-1375.
[1923]   See, *e.g.*, Trial Judgement, Vol. 2, paras 1375-1377 and references cited therein. *Cf.* Praljak's Appeal Brief, para. 302, referring to Ex. P02636, pp. 2, 4.

destruction of any mosque in East Mostar, Praljak disregards the evidence the Trial Chamber relied upon in this respect.[1924] Accordingly, the Appeals Chamber dismisses Praljak's ground of appeal 24.

2. Deaths of four Muslim men during the attack on Raštam (Praljak's Ground 27)

570. The Trial Chamber deemed "that the evidence allows finding" that on 24 August 1993, during the attack on the village of Raštani, HVO soldiers killed four Muslim men who had surrendered.[1925] It made this finding having noted, *inter alia,* that: (1) around 15 people including two Muslim families sought refuge in the house of Mirsad Žuškić, an ABiH soldier, to escape from the HVO attack;[1926] (2) a group of HVO soldiers fired at the house demanding that the occupants come out, and subsequently killed four men who had come out to surrender;[1927] and (3) according to Witness DA, only one of the men was a member of the ABiH and none of them wore a military uniform when they surrendered.[1928]

571. Praljak submits that the Trial Chamber erred in deeming "that the evidence allows finding", where there was not enough evidence for a finding beyond reasonable doubt, that in Raštani on 24 August 1993 four Muslim men (one of whom was an ABiH member) were killed by HVO soldiers after the four men had surrendered.[1929] He submits that the Trial Chamber ignored that Raštani was a place of "constant combats" between the HVO and ABiH and that the ABiH used many buildings in Raštani for military purposes, including the house where the four men were sheltered.[1930] Praljak also submits that the Trial Chamber accepted but did not critically assess the witnesses' questionable assertions that three of the four men were civilians.[1931] Further, Praljak submits that the Trial Chamber did not consider significant contradictions in the witnesses' statements, which cast doubt on their version of the event.[1932] Finally, Praljak submits that it is **[page 251]** impossible to attribute the killings to the HVO because there is no evidence about the identities of the perpetrators or the unit of which they were a part.[1933] Praljak therefore requests that the Appeals Chamber acquit him under Counts 1 (persecution as a crime against humanity), 2 (murder as a crime against humanity), and 3 (wilful killing as a grave breach of the Geneva Conventions) of the charges relating to the event in Raštani.[1934]

572. The Prosecution responds that Praljak reiterates arguments – that the HVO conducted legitimate military operations in Raštani and that the four men were not civilians – which the Trial Chamber considered but rejected as irrelevant, because the killings occurred after they surrendered, rendering their civilian or combatant status immaterial.[1935] The Prosecution submits that Praljak merely disagrees with the Trial Chamber's interpretation of evidence without showing error, and that the Trial Chamber assessed contradictions in the evidence and reasonably concluded that the house was not used for military purposes.[1936] Therefore, the Prosecution contends that Praljak's assertion that the Trial Chamber failed to apply the correct burden of proof is wrong, and further, Praljak ignores his own burden.[1937] Finally, the Prosecution argues that Praljak ignores the fact that the Trial Chamber properly attributed the killings to the HVO.[1938]

[1924] Trial Judgement, Vol. 2, paras 1372-1376 and references cited therein.
[1925] Trial Judgement, Vol. 2, para. 963. See Trial Judgement, Vol. 2, paras 955-962.
[1926] Trial Judgement, Vol. 2, para. 956.
[1927] Trial Judgement, Vol. 2, paras 957-961.
[1928] Trial Judgement, Vol. 2, para. 962.
[1929] Praljak's Appeal Brief, para. 315, referring to Trial Judgement, Vol. 2, para. 963. See Praljak's Appeal Brief, para. 322; Praljak's Reply Brief, para. 95.
[1930] Praljak's Appeal Brief, para. 316. Praljak further argues that the Trial Chamber neither explained why people gathered in the house of an ABiH soldier nor noted contradictory evidence regarding their arrival there. Praljak's Appeal Brief, para. 317.
[1931] Praljak's Appeal Brief, para. 318. Praljak admits, however, that if the events matched the witnesses' descriptions, the three men's possible ABiH affiliation would have no bearing on the Trial Chamber's finding. Praljak's Appeal Brief, para. 319.
[1932] Praljak's Appeal Brief, paras 319-320.
[1933] Praljak's Appeal Brief, para. 321.
[1934] Praljak's Appeal Brief, para. 323. See Praljak's Reply Brief, para. 96.
[1935] Prosecution's Response Brief (Praljak), paras 225-226.
[1936] Prosecution's Response Brief (Praljak), paras 225, 227. The Prosecution states that the Trial Chamber found that the house was instead used for refuge. Prosecution's Response Brief (Praljak), para. 227.
[1937] Prosecution's Response Brief (Praljak), para. 227.
[1938] Prosecution's Response Brief (Praljak), paras 225, 228.

573.   The Appeals Chamber notes that while the Trial Chamber used the phrase "the evidence allows finding",[1939] it in fact set out the correct standard in a general section on evidentiary standards and stated that although it did not systematically restate the expression "beyond reasonable doubt" in each finding of fact or in respect of the criminal responsibility of the Appellants, it applied this standard throughout the Trial Judgement.[1940] The specific language identified by Praljak must be considered in this context. Regarding Praljak's argument that the Trial Chamber did not consider significant contradictions in witness statements, the Appeals Chamber notes that the Trial Chamber referred to all of the evidence on which Praljak relies,[1941] and finds that Praljak fails to show that no reasonable trier of fact, based on the evidence, could have reached the same conclusion as the Trial Chamber did, namely that the four Muslim men were killed "even though they had surrendered".[1942] As a result, the following arguments are dismissed as irrelevant: that Raštani was a place of "constant combats" between the HVO and ABiH, that the ABiH used **[page 252]** the house where the four men were sheltered for military purposes, and that the Trial Chamber did not critically assess the witnesses' assertions that three of the four men killed were civilians. Finally, the Appeals Chamber dismisses his arguments regarding the soldiers' identities and unit affiliation, considering that the Trial Chamber was not required to establish those as a prerequisite for its finding that the perpetrators belonged to the HVO.[1943] Accordingly, the Appeals Chamber dismisses Praljak's ground of appeal 27.

3.   Commission of crimes by the Bruno Bušić Regiment at the Heliodrom (Petković's Sub-ground 5.2.3.1 in part)

574.   The Trial Chamber found that from May 1993 to mid-April 1994, members of the Military Police and "[m]embers of the HVO armed forces, including those of KB professional units and the *Bruno Bušić* Regiment as well as other individuals [...] brutally and regularly beat the Heliodrom prisoners".[1944]

575.   Petković submits that the finding that members of the HVO, including the Bruno Bušić Regiment, "regularly and brutally" beat Heliodrom detainees is incorrect and groundless.[1945] He argues that the finding is based solely on the testimony of Witness A, who was detained for several days in May 1993 and who testified that he saw members of the Regiment take prisoners out of the room where they were held in order to beat them.[1946]

576.   The Prosecution responds that the Trial Chamber reasonably found that soldiers from the Bruno Bušić Regiment regularly and brutally beat detainees at the Heliodrom in May 1993.[1947]

577.   The Appeals Chamber notes that Petković's submission is unclear as to whether he is challenging the Trial Chamber's findings on the beatings of Heliodrom detainees generally, or specifically the implication of members of the Bruno Bušić Regiment in these beatings.[1948] It considers, however, that in light of the context in which the argument is made, it relates to the latter.[1949] In this regard, the Trial Chamber found that HVO members, including from the Bruno Bušić Regiment, regularly and brutally beat the Heliodrom prisoners, referring to the evidence of **[page 253]** Witness A.[1950] The Appeals Chamber recalls that there is no general requirement that the testimony of a witness be corroborated if deemed otherwise credible.[1951] In this instance,

---

[1939]   Trial Judgement, Vol. 2, para. 963; Trial Judgement (French original), Vol. 2, para. 963 *("ces elements de preuve lui permettent de conclure").*
[1940]   Trial Judgement, Vol. 1, para. 267.
[1941]   *Cf.* Praljak's Appeal Brief, fns 784-785, 787; Trial Judgement, Vol. 2, fns 2217, 2222.
[1942]   Trial Judgement, Vol. 2, para. 963. See Trial Judgement, Vol. 2, paras 958-959, 962.
[1943]   Trial Judgement, Vol. 2, para. 963. See Trial Judgement, Vol. 2, paras 957-959, 962.
[1944]   Trial Judgement, Vol. 2, para. 1591. See Trial Judgement, Vol. 2, paras 1580-1590.
[1945]   Petković's Appeal Brief, para. 347; Petković''s Reply Brief, paras 34(vi), 35.
[1946]   Petković's Appeal Brief, para. 347.
[1947]   Prosecution's Response Brief (Petković), para. 136.
[1948]   See Petković's Appeal Brief, para. 347.
[1949]   See Petković's Appeal Brief, paras 339-351. The Appeals Chamber considers in any event that the Trial Chamber based its findings on the beatings of Heliodrom detainees on a wide range of evidence, which Petković ignores. See Trial Judgement, Vol. 2, paras 1580-1590 and references cited therein.
[1950]   Trial Judgement, Vol. 2, para. 1591. See Trial Judgement, Vol. 2, para. 1584 & fn. 3996, referring to Witness A, T(F). 14044 (closed session) (13 Feb 2007).
[1951]   *Popović et al.* Appeal Judgement, paras 243, 1264; *D. Milošević* Appeal Judgement, para. 215. See also *Kordić and Čerkez* Appeal Judgement, para. 274.

Witness A stated that soldiers who had on their left arm a Bruno Bušić patch would beat prisoners, sometimes until they could barely walk, and that this occurred "frequently".[1952] Petković has failed to show that no reasonable trier of fact could have made the impugned finding based on this evidence which was accepted by the Trial Chamber to be credible, and the credibility of which is not challenged by Petković. His argument, and sub-ground of appeal 5.2.3.1 in relevant part, is accordingly dismissed.

G. Conclusion

578.   The Appeals Chamber grants Stojić's sub-ground of appeal 45.1 and Praljak's ground of appeal 12 and consequently reverses the convictions of the Appellants[1953] under Counts 1 (persecution as a crime against humanity), 2 (murder as a crime against humanity), 3 (wilful killing as a grave breach of the Geneva Conventions), 15 (inhumane acts as a crime against humanity), and 16 (inhuman treatment as a grave breach of the Geneva Conventions) with regard to the killing of seven civilians in Duša.[1954] In addition, the Appeals Chamber reverses the Trial Chamber's finding that the shelling during attacks on the villages of Duša, Hrasnica, Uzričje, and Ždrimci was indiscriminate and amounted to wanton destruction not justified by military necessity (Count 20) and persecution (Count 1), and reverses the convictions of all Appellants under Count 1 in this regard.[1955] Finally, the Appeals Chamber reverses the Trial Chamber's finding that the destruction of the Old Bridge constituted wanton destruction not justified by military necessity (Count 20), and thus persecution as a crime against humanity (Count 1) and unlawful infliction of terror on civilians as a violation of the laws or customs of war (Count 25),[1956] and reverses the Appellants' convictions on these counts insofar as they concern the Old Bridge. The impact of these reversals, if any, on the Trial Chamber's findings as to the CCP, as well as on the Appellants' sentences, will be assessed below.[1957]

579.   The Appeals Chamber dismisses all remaining grounds of appeal regarding the underlying crimes of the JCE.

[1952]   Witness A, T. 14044-14045 (closed session) (13 Feb 2007).
[1953]   The Appeals Chamber recalls that Pušić was not convicted of any charges in relation to these killings as he was not a member of the JCE as of January 1993. Trial Judgement, Vol. 4, para. 1229.
[1954]   See *supra*, para. 442.
[1955]   See *supra*, para. 453. See also *supra*, paras 399, 413 (agreeing with the Prosecution that the Trial Chamber erred in not entering convictions for the Four Groups of Incidents under Count 20).
[1956]   See *supra*, paras 411-412, 414, 426.
[1957]   See *infra*, paras 886, 3359-3365.

[page 254] VIII.   JOINT CRIMINAL ENTERPRISE

A.   Introduction

580.   The Trial Chamber found that the Appellants were members of a JCE,[1958] the common criminal purpose of which was "domination by the HR H-B Croats through ethnic cleansing of the Muslim population",[1959] and entailed the commission of a wide range of crimes to that effect.[1960] The Trial Chamber further found that the JCE members, including the Appellants, used the political and military apparatus of the HZ(R) H-B to achieve this goal.[1961] It found that, as JCE members, the Appellants shared the intent to expel the Muslim population, from the HZ(R) H-B through the commission of various crimes and made a significant contribution to that end.[1962] It accordingly convicted them, pursuant to Article 7(1) of the Statute, of the crimes charged in Counts 1-3, 6-13, 15-16, 18-19, 21, and 24-25 of the Indictment.[1963]

581.   The Trial Chamber also found that certain established crimes did not form part of the CCP.[1964] It nevertheless concluded that Prlić, Stojić, Praljak, Petković, and Ćorić were responsible [page 255] for a number of these crimes pursuant to JCE III and entered convictions against them on thatbasis.[1965]

582.   The Appellants raise challenges in relation to the Trial Chamber's findings concerning their individual criminal responsibility under JCE I and JCE III.[1966] In addition, the Prosecution submits that the Trial

---

[1958]   Trial Judgement, Vol. 4, paras 66-67, 1231-1232.

[1959]   Trial Judgement, Vol. 4, para. 41.

[1960]   Trial Judgement, Vol. 4, paras 65-66, 68. The crimes which the Trial Chamber found formed part of the CCP were: persecution as a crime against humanity (Count 1); murder as a crime against humanity (Count 2); wilful killing as a grave breach of the Geneva Conventions (Count 3); deportation as a crime against humanity (Count 6); unlawful deportation of a civilian as a grave breach of the Geneva Conventions (Count 7); inhumane acts (forcible transfer) as a crime against humanity (Count 8); unlawful transfer of a civilian as a grave breach of the Geneva Conventions (Count 9); imprisonment as a crime against humanity (Count 10); unlawful confinement of a civilian as a grave breach of the Geneva Conventions (Count 11); inhumane acts (conditions of confinement) as a crime against humanity (Count 12); inhuman treatment (conditions of confinement) as a grave breach of the Geneva Conventions (Count 13); cruel treatment (conditions of confinement) as a violation of the laws or customs of war (Count 14); inhumane acts as a crime against humanity (Count 15); inhuman treatment as a grave breach of the Geneva Conventions (Count 16); cruel treatment as a violation of the laws or customs of war (Count 17); unlawful labour as a violation of the laws or customs of war (Count 18); extensive destruction of property, not justified by military necessity and carried out unlawfully and wantonly, as a grave breach of the Geneva Conventions (Count 19); wanton destruction of cities, towns, or villages, or devastation not justified by military necessity as a violation of the laws or customs of war (Count 20); destruction or wilful damage done to institutions dedicated to religion or education as a violation of the laws or customs of war (Count 21); unlawful attack on civilians as a violation of the laws or customs of war (Count 24); and unlawful infliction of terror on civilians as a violation of the laws or customs of war (Count 25). See Trial Judgement, Vol. 4, para. 68.

[1961]   Trial Judgement, Vol. 4, para. 41. See also Trial Judgement, Vol. 4, para. 1232.

[1962]   Trial Judgement, Vol. 4, paras 276, 428-429, 627-628, 817-818, 1004, 1208-1209.

[1963]   Trial Judgement, Vol. 4, Disposition, pp. 430-431. See also *supra,* fn. 1960. The Trial Chamber found that the following violations of the laws or customs of war also fell within the framework of the CCP, but did not enter convictions for them based on the principles relating to cumulative convictions: cruel treatment (conditions of confinement) as a violation of the laws or customs of war (Count 14); cruel treatment as a violation of the laws or customs of war (Count 17); and wanton destruction of cities, towns, or villages, or devastation not justified by military necessity (Count 20). See Trial Judgement, Vol. 4, para. 68, Disposition, pp. 430-431. See also Trial Judgement, Vol. 4, paras 1260-1266.

[1964]   These crimes are those committed during eviction operations and in detention which were found to constitute: murder as a crime against humanity (Count 2); wilful killing as a grave breach of the Geneva Conventions (Count 3); rape as a crime against humanity (Count 4); inhuman treatment (sexual assault) as a grave breach of the Geneva Convention (Count 5); extensive appropriation of property, not justified by military necessity and carried out unlawfully and wantonly, as a grave breach of the Geneva Conventions (Count 22); and plunder of public or private property as a violation of the laws or customs of war (Count 23). Trial Judgement, Vol. 4, para. 70, 72. The Trial Chamber also found that instances of destruction or wilful damage done to institutions dedicated to religion or education as a violation of the laws or customs of war (Count 21) which took place prior to June 1993 were not part of the CCP. Trial Judgement, Vol. 4, paras 342, 433, 1213-1214, 1216. See also Trial Judgement, Vol. 4, paras 71, 73.

[1965]   Trial Judgement, Vol. 4, paras 288 (finding Prlić guilty of Counts 2-5, 21-23), 450 (finding Stojić guilty of Counts 2-5, 22-23), 644 (finding Praljak guilty of Counts 22-23), 853 (finding Petković guilty of Counts 4-5, 21-23), 1021 (finding Ćorić responsible for Counts 2-5, 22-23), Disposition, pp. 430-431. The Trial Chamber did not find Pušić responsible for any crimes under JCE III. See Trial Judgement, Vol. 4, paras 1213-1216.

[1966]   Prlić's grounds of appeal 8-18; Stojić's grounds of appeal 1-4, 6-8, 10-12, 14-15, 20-21, 23-25, 27-31, 33-37, 39-41, 47; Praljak's grounds of appeal 5-7, 10, 15, 21.4 (in part), 28, 32, 34-47, 49; Petković's grounds of appeal I-V; Ćorić›s grounds of appeal 1-2, 6-8, 10-11 (in part), 13-14; Pušić's grounds of appeal 1-6.

Chamber erred in failing to convict the Appellants of certain JCE III crimes.[1967] The Appeals Chamber will address these submissions in turn. **[page 256]**

B. JCE and JCE III as Firmly Established Under Customary International Law

583. The Trial Chamber held that, in accordance with the jurisprudence of the Appeals Chamber, "JCE was a mode of responsibility firmly established under customary international law" at the time of the commission of the crimes at issue and that the "settled case-law of the Tribunal" recognises the three forms of JCE liability.[1968] On appeal, Prlić, Praljak, Ćorić, and Pušić contend that the Trial Chamber erred in so holding.[1969]

1. Arguments of the Parties

584. Prlić, Praljak, Ćorić, and Pušić argue that there are cogent reasons for the Appeals Chamber to depart from its prior jurisprudence that JCE, in all of its forms, was a mode of liability firmly established under customary international law at the time of the commission of the crimes falling under the Tribunal's jurisdiction.[1970] Relying upon the Judge Antonetti Dissent on this issue, case-law from the ICC and the Extraordinary Chambers in the Courts of Cambodia ("ECCC"), as well as the personal opinions of former Judges Shahabuddeen and Schomburg, Prlić, Praljak, Ćorić, and Pušić challenge the correctness of the *Tadić* Appeal Judgement.[1971] They argue that, contrary to the *Tadić* Appeal Judgement, JCE, and in particular JCE III, were not part of customary international law at the time of the commission of the crimes at issue and, therefore, the application of JCE as a mode of liability violates the principle of *nullum crimen sine lege.*[1972] Ćorić refutes JCE as a mode of liability completely and relies upon the Judge Antonetti Dissent and ICC case-law for support. He argues that there is no basis for JCE liability in the Tribunal's Statute and no uniform state practice on this mode of liability during the relevant time period.[1973] Specifically with respect **[page 257]** to JCE III, Prlić and Ćorić argue that this extended form of JCE liability finds no basis in the Statute, state practice, or *opinio juris,* and amounts to collective responsibility.[1974] Finally, Ćorić challenges the Trial Chamber's summary dismissal of arguments on this issue which, according to him, amounts to a lack of reasoning and an error of law under Article 23(2) of the Statute.[1975]

[1967] Prosecution's ground of appeal 1.

[1968] Trial Judgement, Vol. 1, paras 202-205, 210.

[1969] Prlić's Appeal Brief, paras 218-231; Praljak's Appeal Brief, paras 339-345; Ćorić›s Appeal Brief, paras 6-17; Pušić's Appeal Brief, paras 65-70. The Appeals Chamber notes that Stojić had raised the same issue in his Notice of Appeal, but explicitly withdrew the relevant ground in his appeal brief. See Stojić's Notice of Appeal, para. 45; Stojić's Appeal Brief, p. 127.

[1970] Prlić's Appeal Brief, paras 218, 220, 227; Praljak's Appeal Brief, para. 344; Ćorić›s Appeal Brief, paras 12, 14; Pušić's Appeal Brief, para. 67.

[1971] Prlić's Appeal Brief, paras 218, 223-224, 226-230; Praljak's Appeal Brief, paras 340-343; Ćorić›s Appeal Brief, paras 9-11, 13-15; Pušić's Appeal Brief, paras 66-70. In particular, Ćorić notes that the Judge Antonetti Dissent cites numerous Special Court for Sierra Leone ("SCSL") cases that call the JCE doctrine into question. See Ćorić›s Appeal Brief, para. 10. Prlić and Praljak, in turn, challenge the *Tadić* Appeal Judgement's reliance on the International Convention for the Suppression of Terrorist Bombings. See Prlić's Appeal Brief, para. 222; Praljak's Appeal Brief, para. 340. Concerning ECCC case-law, Prlić further argues that the *Đorđević* Appeal Judgement misstated the relevant ECCC findings and thus erred in rejecting JCE-related arguments based on the jurisprudence of the ECCC. See Prlić's Appeal Brief, paras 226-229. Prlić, finally, also points to the position expressed in an article by Judge Shahabuddeen, who presided over the *Tadić* appeal, that the *Tadić* Appeal Judgement erred in upholding the customary status of the JCE doctrine. See Prlić's Appeal Brief, paras 218, 227.

[1972] Prlić's Appeal Brief, paras 218, 220, 222, 224-225, 230; Praljak's Appeal Brief, paras 339-340, 342-345; Ćorić›s Appeal Brief, paras 6, 9-10, 13-15; Pušić's Appeal Brief, paras 67-68.

[1973] Ćorić›s Appeal Brief, paras 9-10, 13, 16. Prlić and Pušić agree with the Judge Antonetti Dissent that JCE and JCE III in particular, should be abandoned as a form of liability. Prlić's Appeal Brief, paras 230-231; Pušić's Appeal Brief, paras 69-70. Pušić further proposes that the Tribunal adopt co-perpetration in place of JCE. Pušić's Appeal Brief, para. 70.

[1974] Prlić's Appeal Brief, paras 219, 221-225; Ćorić›s Appeal Brief, para. 14. In this respect, Prlić, *inter alia,* cites a study by the Max Planck Institute purporting to show a lack of uniform state practice with respect to JCE III. Prlić's Appeal Brief, para. 221. Ćorić, in turn, refers to Judge Liu's dissent in the *Šainović et al.* Appeal Judgement concerning the application of JCE III to specific intent crimes. Ćorić›s Appeal Brief, para. 11. The Appeals Chamber, however, rejects the latter argument as irrelevant, as no Appellant in this case was convicted of a specific intent crime through the third form of the JCE mode of liability. See Trial Judgement, Vol. 4, paras 288, 450, 644, 853, 1021, 1214-1216. See also Appeal Hearing, AT. 175 (20 Mar 2017), AT. 252-253 (21 Mar 2017), AT. 583-584 (24 Mar 2017).

[1975] Ćorić›s Appeal Brief, paras 7-11. Ćorić additionally argues that the application of JCE to leadership cases inappropriately dilutes the standard for superior responsibility. Ćorić›s Appeal Brief, para. 17. The Appeals Chamber dismisses this argument as vague and undeveloped, as Ćorić fails to elaborate further upon the alleged correlation between these two modes of liability.

585.   The Prosecution responds that Prlić, Praljak, Ćorić, and Pušić have failed to provide cogent reasons for the Appeals Chamber to depart from its settled jurisprudence.[1976] The Prosecution observes that the Appeals Chamber has consistently affirmed the status of JCE, and JCE III in particular, as a mode of liability grounded in customary international law at the time of the commission of the crimes and argues that their application in this case did not violate the principle of *nullum crimen sine lege*.[1977] The Prosecution defends the analysis in the *Tadić* Appeal Judgement as sound and notes that the Appeals Chamber has previously rejected similar challenges.[1978] The Prosecution finally contends that the Trial Judgement was adequately reasoned in this respect.[1979]

2.   Analysis

586.   At the outset, the Appeals Chamber rejects Ćorić›s contention that the Trial Chamber failed to issue a reasoned opinion. The Appeals Chamber notes that the Trial Chamber methodically laid out the law on JCE as established by the Appeals Chamber and dismissed arguments to the contrary as "fail[ing] to justify calling into question the settled case-law of the Tribunal with regard to JCE".[1980] It considers that this was sufficient reasoning; the well-established case-law of the Tribunal amply justified the dismissal of these arguments.[1981] **[page 258]**

587.   The Appeals Chamber recalls that it is the settled jurisprudence of the Tribunal that the three forms of JCE, as forms of commission of a crime, have been established in customary international law since at least 1992.[1982] The Appeals Chamber has repeatedly affirmed the relevant analysis in *Tadić*, which examined post-World War II war crimes cases extensively in concluding that joint criminal enterprise as a mode of criminal responsibility is firmly established in customary international law, and has recognised three forms of this mode of liability – JCE I, JCE II, and JCE III.[1983] The Appeals Chamber has also held that "the long and consistent stream of judicial decisions, international instruments, and domestic legislation in force at the time" provided "reasonable notice that committing an international crime on the basis of participating in a JCE incurs individual criminal liability".[1984]

588.   The Appeals Chamber also recalls that it may exceptionally depart from its previous decisions if there are cogent reasons to do so.[1985] The notion of "cogent reasons" encompasses considerations that are clear and compelling.[1986] As such, cogent reasons requiring a departure from previous decisions in the interests of justice include situations where a previous decision was made "on the basis of a wrong legal principle" or given *per incuriam*, that is, "wrongly decided, usually because the judge or judges were ill informed about

---

[1976]   Prosecution's Response Brief (Prlić), para. 130; Prosecution's Response Brief (Praljak), paras 291, 294; Prosecution's Response Brief (Ćorić), paras 8-9, 11, 15, 18; Prosecution's Response Brief (Pušić), paras 58, 61.

[1977]   Prosecution's Response Brief (Prlić), paras 130, 132; Prosecution's Response Brief (Praljak), paras 291-292; Prosecution's Response Brief (Ćorić), paras 8-9, 14; Prosecution's Response Brief (Pušić), paras 56-57.

[1978]   Prosecution's Response Brief (Prlić), paras 133-135, 137; Prosecution's Response Brief (Praljak), para. 293; Prosecution's Response Brief (Ćorić), paras 11-13, 15-16; Prosecution's Response Brief (Pušić), paras 59-60.

[1979]   Prosecution's Response Brief (Ćorić), para. 10.

[1980]   Trial Judgement, Vol. 1, para. 210. See also Trial Judgement, Vol. 1, 202-205, 211-221.

[1981]   See *Aleksovski* Appeal Judgement, para. 113 (holding that "the *ratio decidendi* of [the Appeals Chamber's] decisions is binding on Trial Chambers"). Moreover, the Appeals Chamber recalls that "it is in the discretion of the Trial Chamber as to which legal arguments to address". See *Kvočka et al.* Appeal Judgement, para. 23 (explaining that "the right to a reasoned opinion under Article 23 of the Statute and Rule 98*ter*(C) of the Rules [...] relates to the Trial Chamber's Judgement; the Trial Chamber is not under the obligation to justify its findings in relation to every submission made during the trial").

[1982]   *Tadić* Appeal Judgement, paras 195-226; *Kvočka et al.* Appeal Judgement, paras 79-80; *Brđanin* Appeal Judgement, paras 363, 405, 410; *Krajišnik* Appeal Judgement, para. 662.

[1983]   See *Tadić* Appeal Judgement, paras 195-226; *Kvočka et al.* Appeal Judgement, paras 79-80, 82-83; *Brđanin* Appeal Judgement, paras 363-364; *Krajišnik* Appeal Judgement, para. 659; *Đorđević* Appeal Judgement, paras 35, 40-41, 58; *Popović et al.* Appeal Judgement, para. 1673.

[1984]   *Popović et al.* Appeal Judgement, para. 1672 (internal quotation marks omitted). The Appeals Chamber has also addressed and rejected in the past the argument that JCE III amounts to collective responsibility, holding that an accused has "done far more than merely associate with criminal persons" when all of the requirements for liability under JCE III have been met. *Brđanin* Appeal Judgement, para. 431.

[1985]   *Đorđević* Appeal Judgement, para. 23; *Krajišnik* Appeal Judgement, para. 655; *Galić* Appeal Judgement, para. 117; *Aleksovski* Appeal Judgement, para. 107. See also *Stanišić and Župljanin* Appeal Judgement, para. 596.

[1986]   *Đorđević* Appeal Judgement, para. 24.

the applicable law".[1987] It is for the party advocating a departure to demonstrate that there are cogent reasons in the interests of justice that justify such departure.[1988]

589. The Appeals Chamber finds that Prlić, Praljak, Ćorić, and Pušić have failed to make a showing that there are cogent reasons in the interests of justice that justify such departure. It notes that it has squarely addressed and rejected arguments similar to those raised in the present instance challenging the *Tadić* Appeal Judgement's reliance upon international instruments. In *Popović et al.* **[page 259]** the Appeals Chamber observed that its consideration in the *Tadić* Appeal Judgement of the International Convention for the Suppression of Terrorist Bombings and the ICC Statute was "limited to demonstrating the consistent legal view of a large number of States on the existence of a notion of a 'common criminal purpose' as such".[1989] In *Đorđević,* the Appeals Chamber also rejected the argument that it had erroneously relied, in *Tadić,* upon Article 25(3) of the ICC Statute in support of its JCE analysis.[1990] The Appeals Chamber noted that in *Tadić,* it had "relied on the ICC Statute only as evidence revealing the existence of a mode of liability based on 'a group of persons acting with a common purpose' distinct from aiding and abetting", and reasoned that ICC jurisprudence elaborating on that form of liability was "based on the [...] ICC Statute" and did not exclude or even address the existence of JCE in customary international law.[1991] Prlić, Praljak, Ćorić, and Pušić offer no new arguments to compel the Appeals Chamber to revisit and depart from these holdings.

590. Prlić's, Praljak's, and Ćorić's reliance on ECCC jurisprudence is also misplaced. In this regard, the Appeals Chamber recalls that it is not bound by the findings of other courts – domestic, international, or hybrid – and that, even though it might take them into consideration, it may, after careful consideration, come to a different conclusion on a matter than that reached by another judicial body.[1992] Moreover, they have not shown that ECCC case-law demonstrates a clear mistake in the Appeals Chamber's JCE precedent. Indeed, in *Đorđević,* the Appeals Chamber recognised that the ECCC "identified flaws in the reasoning of the *Tadić* Appeals Chamber", but remained "satisfied that the sources of law examined by the *Tadić* Appeals Chamber are reliable" and that JCE in is "well-established in both customary international law and the jurisprudence of this Tribunal".[1993] The Appeals Chamber sees no reason to depart from these holdings.

591. For the foregoing reasons, the Appeals Chamber concludes that Prlić, Praljak, Ćorić, and Pušić have failed to establish that the Trial Chamber erred in holding that JCE, including JCE III, was firmly established under customary international law at the time of the relevant events. Accordingly, the Appeals Chamber dismisses Prlić's ground of appeal 8, Praljak's ground of appeal 34, Ćorić's ground of appeal 1.A, and Pušić's ground of appeal 2 in their entirety. **[page 260]**

C.   The Ultimate Purpose of the JCE

1.   Introduction

592. The Trial Chamber found that: (1) at all times relevant under the Indictment, the ultimate purpose of the HZ(R) H-B leaders and Franjo Tuđman was to set up a Croatian entity that reconstituted, at least in part, the borders of the Banovina, thereby facilitating the reunification of the Croatian people; and (2) such entity was either supposed to be annexed to Croatia directly or to become an independent State within BiH with

---

[1987] *Đorđević* Appeal Judgement, para. 24; *Aleksovski* Appeal Judgement, para. 108. See also *Stanišić and Župljanin* Appeal Judgement, para. 596.

[1988] *Đorđević* Appeal Judgement, para. 24; *Krajišnik* Appeal Judgement, para. 655; *Galić* Appeal Judgement, para. 117. See also *Stanišić and Župljanin* Appeal Judgement, para. 596. Contrary to the Appellants' suggestions, the extrajudicial opinions expressed by former Judges of the Tribunal in scholarly articles do not constitute a cogent reason for departing from the Appeals Chamber's well-established jurisprudence. *Cf. Stanišić and Župljanin* Appeal Judgement, para. 974; *Đorđević* Appeal Judgement, para. 83.

[1989] *Popović et al.* Appeal Judgement, para. 1673.

[1990] *Đorđević* Appeal Judgement, paras 35-39.

[1991] *Đorđević* Appeal Judgement, para. 38.

[1992] *Stanišić and Župljanin* Appeal Judgement, para. 598; *Popović et al.* Appeal Judgement, para. 1674. See also *Đorđević* Appeal Judgement, para. 50 (holding that ECCC jurisprudence is not binding on the Appeals Chamber and, "as such, does not constitute a cogent reason to depart from its well-established case law").

[1993] *Đorđević* Appeal Judgement, paras 51-52.

close ties to Croatia ("Ultimate Purpose of the JCE").[1994] In reaching its conclusion on the Ultimate Purpose of the JCE, the Trial Chamber found that: (1) between 1991 and 1994, Tuđman sought to expand the borders of Croatia by incorporating the HZ(R) H-B either directly or indirectly;[1995] (2) between 1992 and 1993, the HZ(R) H-B leaders, including Prlić, Stojić, Praljak, and Petković were involved in meetings and discussions on the partition of BiH;[1996] (3) although the HZ H-B was created in the context of the "Serb aggression", it was not merely a temporary defence initiative;[1997] (4) the representatives of the "delegation of BiH Croats" accepted the principles of the Vance-Owen Peace Plan, although they were not genuinely in agreement with such principles;[1998] and (5) with the proclamation of the HR H-B, the HZ H-B leaders established a "mini-State" within BiH.[1999]

2. Alleged errors in the Trial Chamber's finding that Tuđman intended to expand the Croatian borders

593. The Trial Chamber found that Tuđman: (1) sought to expand the Croatian borders into BiH directly or indirectly; (2) participated in several meetings from 1990 to 1992, including one at Karađorđevo on 25 March 1991 to discuss the plans concerning the division of BiH ("25 March 1991 Karađorđevo Meeting"); (3) adopted a double policy, advocating in public respect for the existing BiH borders, while privately supporting the partition of BiH and sharing his desire for the reunification of the Croatian people; (4) supported the creation of the HZ H-B on 18 November 1991; (5) "continued to be pre-occupied" with the Croatian Banovina between January 1993 and March 1994; and (6) abandoned his plan to expand the Croatian borders, under the force of international pressure, only around 21 February 1994.[2000] **[page 261]**

594. Prlić, Stojić, and Praljak submit that the Trial Chamber erred in assessing evidence with respect to specific findings underlying its conclusion on Tuđman's intentions.[2001] Additionally, Prlić, Stojić, and Pušić argue that the Trial Chamber committed errors vis-à-vis its overall conclusion on Tuđman's intentions.[2002] The Prosecution responds that the Trial Chamber's findings were reasonable and the Appellants' arguments should be dismissed.[2003]

[003] The Appeals Chamber will address the arguments in turn.

(a) Challenges to underlying findings concerning Tuđman's intentions

(i) Tuđman's plan to expand the Croatian borders

595. The Trial Chamber noted the evidence of Witnesses AR and Peter Galbraith that according to Tuđman, BiH was not supposed to exist as a sovereign State and that a substantial part of it was supposed to be annexed to the territory of Croatia.[2004] It also highlighted the evidence of Witness Josip Manolić that Tuđman wanted to annex Western Herzegovina as it was "ethnically pure" and adjacent to Croatia.[2005] Lastly, it noted that Witness Herbert Okun testified that Tuđman's plan to expand the Croatian borders was supposed to be implemented either directly or by incorporating the HR H-B "in some way or other".[2006] The Trial Chamber found that in connection with this plan "Tuđman advocated dividing BiH between Croatia and Serbia,

---

[1994] Judgement, Vol. 4, para. 24. See also Trial Judgement, Vol. 4, para. 43.
[1995] Trial Judgement, Vol. 4, paras 9-15, 17-18, 22-23.
[1996] Trial Judgement, Vol. 4, paras 13, 18-19.
[1997] Trial Judgement, Vol. 4, paras 15-16.
[1998] Trial Judgement, Vol. 4, para. 20.
[1999] Trial Judgement, Vol. 4, para. 21.
[2000] Trial Judgement, Vol. 4, paras 9-12, 14-15, 17-18, 20, 22-23.
[2001] Prlić's Appeal Brief, paras 237-261; Stojić's Appeal Brief, paras 8-9, 19; Praljak's Appeal Brief, paras 70-83, 85-88, 114.
[2002] Prlić's Appeal Brief, para. 236; Stojić's Appeal Brief, paras 8-16; Pušić's Appeal Brief, paras 84-98.
[2003] Prosecution's Response Brief (Prlić), paras 139-141; Prosecution's Response Brief (Stojić), paras 9, 19; Prosecution's Response Brief (Praljak), paras 31-32, 103; Prosecution's Response Brief (Pušić), paras 62-64.
[2004] Trial Judgement, Vol. 4, para. 9.
[2005] Trial Judgement, Vol. 4, para. 9.
[2006] Trial Judgement, Vol. 4, para. 9.

incorporating part of BiH into Croatia, or at least, the existence of an autonomous Croatian territory within BiH that would enjoy close ties with Croatia."[2007]

a. Prlić's appeal (Sub-ground 9.2 in part)

596.   Prlić submits that the Trial Chamber mischaracterised and ignored Manolić's evidence in relation to "Tuđman's attitudes and actions towards BiH".[2008] Specifically, he points to Manolić's evidence that Tuđman: (1) promoted the referendum for the independence of BiH; (2) supported the sovereignty of BiH and was against changing borders; (3) accepted all peace plans and proposed the **[page 262]** deployment of UN forces on the borders; (4) was against the borders of the Banovina and supported the internationally-recognised borders; and (5) never stated that he was for the partition of BiH.[2009]

597.   The Prosecution responds that Prlić fails to show any error in the Trial Chamber's reliance on Manolić's corroborated evidence, while declining to rely on potentially conflicting testimony.[2010]

598.   With respect to the Trial Chamber's finding that Tuđman advocated the division of BiH and either its partial annexation to Croatia or the creation of an autonomous entity with close ties to Croatia, the Appeals Chamber observes that the Trial Chamber considered Manolić's evidence that Tuđman wished to annex Western Herzegovina because it was ethnically pure and adjacent to Croatia.[2011] The Appeals Chamber finds that Prlić fails to show how the Trial Chamber misrepresented Manolić's evidence and dismisses his contention. Further, in claiming that the Trial Chamber disregarded Manolić's evidence concerning Tuđman's attitudes and actions towards BiH, Prlić fails to appreciate that the Trial Chamber's reliance on Manolić's testimony was confined to only assessing Tuđman's aspiration to annex Western Herzegovina.[2012] As such, Prlić does not show that Manolić's evidence on Tuđman's support for the referendum and the international arbitration, his proposal to deploy a peacekeeping force, and his acceptance of the peace plans can affect the Trial Chamber's reliance on another portion of Manolić's testimony that Tuđman desired to annex Western Herzegovina to Croatia. Moreover, the Appeals Chamber observes that Manolić's testimony concerning Tuđman's desire to annex Western Herzegovina was largely corroborated by the evidence provided by Witness AR, Galbraith, and Okun.[2013] Based on these considerations and recalling that it is within the discretion of a trial chamber to evaluate inconsistencies in the evidence and to consider whether the evidence taken as a whole is reliable and credible,[2014] the Appeals Chamber dismisses these arguments. **[page 263]**

599.   Turning to Prlić's argument that the Trial Chamber ignored Manolić's testimony that Tuđman was against the borders of Banovina and supported the internationally-recognised borders, a review of this portion of the transcripts does not show with clarity Tuđman's position in this regard.[2015] By contrast, the

---

[2007]   Trial Judgement, Vol. 4, para. 10

[2008]   Prlić's Appeal Brief, para. 237, referring to Trial Judgement, Vol. 4, para. 9.

[2009]   Prlić's Appeal Brief, para. 237, referring to Josip Manolić, T. 4276-4277, 4282-4283, 4290-4291, 4296, 4281-4282 (3 July 2006), 4494-4495, 4585-4586, 4601-4602 (5 July 2006), 4631-4632, 4685-4686, 4707-4708 (6 July 2006). See also Appeal Hearing, AT. 147-148 (20 Mar 2017).

[2010]   Prosecution's Response Brief (Prlić), para. 146. See also Prosecution's Response Brief (Prlić), paras 142-143.

[2011]   See Trial Judgement, Vol. 4, para. 9, referring to Josip Manolić, T(F). 4323, 4325 (4 July 2006).

[2012]   Trial Judgement, Vol. 4, para. 9. See Josip Manolić, T. 4323 (4 July 2006) ("President Tudjman wanted to annex Western Herzegovina to Croatia. This was a wish. It was the request of those seven or eight municipalities, the names of which we read out yesterday. The people who lived in those areas felt that their future and their security could be found within the borders of the Republic of Croatia. However, wishes are one thing and realistic possibilities of realising your desire are something else, and there were no realistic preconditions for realising that wish. Therefore, this was in dispute between me and President Tudjman, and we never agreed on it until the very last day, until the Washington agreements were signed which put an end to this dilemma and created the federation of Croats and Muslims in that area").

[2013]   See Trial Judgement Vol. 4, para. 9.

[2014]   *Nyiramasuhuko et al.* Appeal Judgement, para. 1661; *Karemera and Ngirumpatse* Appeal Judgement, para. 467; *Hategekimana* Appeal Judgement, para. 82; *Setako* Appeal Judgement, para. 31; *Rukundo* Appeal Judgement, para. 207.

[2015]   See Josip Manolić, T. 4281-4282, 4290-4291, 4296 (3 July 2006). Specifically, the Appeals Chamber observes that from the transcript it is not clear whether Manolić is testifying about Tuđman's position concerning the Banovina borders. See Josip Manolić, T. 4283 (3 July 2006).

Appeals Chamber observes that Manolić testified that Tuđman did not agree with such borders[2016] and that his main goal was the realisation of the Banovina borders.[2017] Accordingly, this argument is dismissed.

600.   Further, the Appeals Chamber observes that in claiming that Manolić testified that Tuđman never stated that he was for the partition of BiH, Prlić refers to a portion of the trial record which does not support his argument.[2018]

601.   The Appeals Chamber therefore finds that Prlić has failed to demonstrate that the Trial Chamber erred in concluding that Tuđman advocated the division of BiH, and dismisses the relevant part of his sub-ground of appeal 9.2.

b. Praljak's appeal (Sub-grounds 5.1 and 5.2 in part)

602.   Praljak submits that the Trial Chamber's conclusion concerning Tuđman's support for the division of BiH is "contradictory *per se*" since the Trial Chamber could not find that "Tuđman supported the incorporation of a part of BiH in Croatia and left a possibility of [the] establishment of an autonomous Croatian entity within BiH", which, in Praljak's view, does not imply its division.[2019] Praljak further argues that the Trial Chamber failed to consider Tuđman's position that he was always in favour of the independence and integrity of BiH as a union of three constituent peoples.[2020] Specifically, Praljak avers that Tuđman: (1) was against the division of BiH as it ran **[page 264]** counter to Croatia's interest;[2021] and (2) maintained his position during the conflict between Croats and Muslims of BiH.[2022] Praljak further argues that, had Tuđman had the intention to annex part of BiH territory, he would not have recognised BiH's independence.[2023]

603.   The Prosecution responds that there is no contradiction in the Trial Chamber's reasonable finding that the Ultimate Purpose of the JCE could be accomplished by the HZ(R) H-B either joining Croatia or through an alliance with Croatia.[2024] The Prosecution also submits that Tuđman concealed his real intentions concerning the division of BiH while publicly supporting its independence and territorial integrity.[2025] It further argues that Praljak repeats arguments already made at trial and raises challenges without showing any error or impact.[2026]

604.   The Appeals Chamber observes that when concluding that Tuđman advocated the division of BiH between Croatia and the Republic of Serbia ("Serbia"), incorporating part of BiH into Croatia or, at least, the

---

[2016]   See Josip Manolić, T. 4275-4276 (3 July 2006) ("A. Well, essentially it was the position that Mesic and I advocated and that is that one should [...] accept the AVNOJ borders which existed between the republics in the former Yugoslavia, and that it wouldn't be realistic or wise to tamper with those borders, the AVNOJ borders. Q. And did Mr. Tudjman hold a different view as to what borders should exist? A. Well, the very fact that he talked to Milošević about the division of that particular territory, that fact alone speaks that the position was different at that point in time"). See also Josip Manolić, T. 4280-4281 (3 July 2006).

[2017]   See Josip Manolić, T. 4281 (3 July 2006).

[2018]   Prlić's Appeal Brief, para. 237, referring to Josip Manolić, T. 4602 (5 July 2006), 4631-4632 (6 July 2006).

[2019]   Praljak's Appeal Brief, para. 71, referring to Trial Judgement, Vol. 4, paras 10, 16; Appeal Hearing, AT. 385 (22 Mar 2017). See also Praljak's Appeal Brief, para. 70.

[2020]   Praljak's Appeal Brief, para. 73, referring to Exs. P00366, P00498, P01544, P00167, Josip Manolić, T. 4315, 4318 (3 July 2006). See also Praljak's Appeal Brief, para. 75, referring to Ex. P00167. According to Praljak, the failure to consider the evidence regarding Tuđman's position favouring the BiH as an independent State led the Trial Chamber to distort and erroneously assess his acts and statements, as well as conclude that Tuđman: (1) attended several meetings with Milošević in 1991 and 1992 to discuss the division of BiH, although it only identified such a meeting at Karađorđevo; and (2) supported the creation of the HZ(R) H-B in connection with his plan to expand the Croatian borders. Praljak's Appeal Brief, paras 76, 78. Praljak also submits that Tuđman's approach was entirely consistent with BiH's position and its constitution. Praljak's Appeal Brief, para. 73, referring to Exs. 1D02994, 1D01236.

[2021]   Praljak's Appeal Brief, para. 72, referring to, *inter alia*, Ex. P06454; Appeal Hearing, AT. 385 (22 Mar 2017). Praljak also argues that the division of BiH was a solution considered by the international community and that in any case Tuđman was aware that BIH depended on its decision. Praljak's Appeal Brief, para. 72, referring to Judge Antonetti Dissent, pp. 9-10, Ex. P00108; Appeal Hearing, AT. 385 (22 Mar 2017).

[2022]   Praljak's Appeal Brief, para. 74, referring to Exs. P02302, P03112, P00336, P06454, P00134; Appeal Hearing, AT. 386 (22 Mar 2017).

[2023]   Praljak's Appeal Brief, para. 75, referring to Judge Antonetti Dissent, p. 375.

[2024]   Prosecution's Response Brief (Praljak), para. 41, referring to Trial Judgement, Vol. 4, paras 10, 24. See also Prosecution's Response Brief (Praljak), para. 40; Appeal Hearing, AT. 420 (22 Mar 2017).

[2025]   Prosecution's Response Brief (Praljak), para. 37, referring to, *inter alia*, Trial Judgement, Vol. 4, paras 12, 17.

[2026]   Prosecution's Response Brief (Praljak), para. 41. See also Prosecution's Response Brief (Praljak), para. 42.

existence of an autonomous Croatian territory within BiH that would enjoy close ties with Croatia, the Trial Chamber took into account Okun's evidence that for Tuđman, the plan to expand the Croatian borders was "supposed to occur either directly or by incorporating the HR H-B into Croatia in some way or other".[2027] Praljak argues that the Trial Chamber's finding is contradictory *per se* as the creation of an autonomous Croatian entity in BiH "does not imply" its division. The Appeals Chamber considers that, contrary to Praljak's argument that the Trial Chamber made contradictory findings, it simply concluded that Tuđman envisaged two different ways to realise his plan. Thus, as long as the incorporation of part of BiH into Croatia and the creation of an autonomous Croatian entity in BiH are compatible with Tuđman's plan to expand the Croatian borders – as the Trial Chamber found – there is no contradiction in its conclusion. Accordingly, this argument is dismissed.

605.   The Appeals Chamber turns to Praljak's argument that the Trial Chamber failed to consider evidence that Tuđman was always in favour of the independence and integrity of BiH as a union of three constituent peoples. The Appeals Chamber notes that some evidence referred to by Praljak was explicitly considered by the Trial Chamber in its analysis of Tuđman's position towards BiH, **[page 265]** in particular, when finding that he publicly supported the territorial integrity of BiH while continuing to affirm his desire for reunification of the Croatian people.[2028] With respect to the remaining evidence which Praljak claims the Trial Chamber disregarded,[2029] the Appeals Chamber observes that while not expressly stated, the Trial Chamber discussed at length evidence similar in nature that shows Tuđman's support for the independence of BiH and concluded that it reflected his double policy.[2030] In light of its repetitive character, the Appeals Chamber is not persuaded that the Trial Chamber disregarded the evidence concerned, but rather that the Trial Chamber found that the evidence did not prevent it from reaching its conclusion.[2031] Therefore, the Appeals Chamber rejects this contention.

606.   Lastly, the Appeals Chamber rejects Praljak's argument that had Tuđman had expansionist intentions with regard to BiH, he would not have recognised its independence, as it falls short of showing an error in the Trial Chamber's conclusion.

607.   The Appeals Chamber therefore finds that Praljak has failed to demonstrate that the Trial Chamber erred in concluding that Tuđman advocated the division of BiH between Croatia and Serbia, incorporating part of BiH into Croatia or, at least, the existence of an autonomous Croatian territory within BiH that would enjoy close ties with Croatia. Accordingly, the Appeals Chamber dismisses Praljak's sub-grounds of appeal 5.1 and 5.2 in relevant part.

(ii) 25 March 1991 Karađorđevo Meeting

608.   Relying on the evidence of, *inter alios,* Witness AR, Manolić, Galbraith, Okun, and Ciril Ribičić, the Trial Chamber found that between 1990 and 1992, Tuđman participated in several meetings, including the 25 March 1991 Karađorđevo Meeting with Slobodan Milošević, concerning the finalisation of "plans […] to divide BiH between Croatia and Serbia".[2032] **[page 266]**

a. Prlić's appeal (Sub-ground 9.3)

i. Arguments of the Parties

609.   Prlić submits that the Trial Chamber erred in finding that during the 25 March 1991 Karađorđevo Meeting, Tuđman and Milošević planned to finalise the division of BiH.[2033] Prlić argues that: (1) Manolić

[2027]   Trial Judgement, Vol. 4, para. 9, referring to Herbert Okun, T(F). 16996 (5 Apr 2007).
[2028]   See Trial Judgement, Vol. 4, para. 17, referring to Exs. P00336, P01544, P00108, P02302, P00167. See also Trial Judgement, Vol. 4, para. 15, referring, *inter alia,* to Josip Manolić, T(F). 4313-4315, 4344, 4345 (3 July 2006), Exs. P00498, P02302, P06454, P00167.
[2029]   See Praljak's Appeal Brief, para. 72, referring to Exs. P03112, P00134, 1D01236, Josip Manolić, T. 4318 (3 July 2006).
[2030]   See Trial Judgement, Vol. 4, paras 12, 17.
[2031]   Moreover, the Appeals Chamber observes that Praljak points to Exhibits P03112, P00134, and 1D01236, without providing the precise references to information allegedly disregarded by the Trial Chamber.
[2032]   Trial Judgement, Vol. 4, para. 11.
[2033]   Prlić's Appeal Brief, paras 244-246.

denied having knowledge of the 25 March 1991 Karadorđevo Meeting or of any agreement between Milošević and Tuđman as he noted that the referendum held a year later confirmed BiH's independence and that "in 1991 Yugoslavia was still in existence and BiH was not on the agenda for discussion";[2034] (2) Witness AR's evidence indicates that Tuđman was prepared to accept an independent BiH;[2035] (3) Okun could not have known Tuđman's intentions in 1991 since he became involved in peace negotiations in September 1992;[2036] (4) Galbraith arrived in Croatia in June 1993 and did not testify about meetings between Milošević and Tuđman;[2037] and (5) Ribičić's evidence concerning Tuđman and Milošević's plan is based on a portion of the Presidential Transcripts which is "an unreliable and inappropriate source for basing legal/constitutional expertise".[2038]

610.   The Prosecution responds that the Trial Chamber reasonably found that Tuđman met Milošević during the 25 March 1991 Karadorđevo Meeting to negotiate a partition of BiH, relying on evidence reflecting "Tuđman's own admissions".[2039] It argues that the evidence of Manolić, Witness AR, and Okun in fact confirms the Trial Chamber's conclusion in this regard.[2040]

ii. Analysis

611.   The Appeals Chamber considers that Prlić misrepresents Manolić's testimony with respect to the 25 March 1991 Karadorđevo Meeting. A review of Manolić's evidence reflects that Tuđman told Manolić that he met with Milošević during the 25 March 1991 Karadorđevo Meeting and that they discussed the division of BiH.[2041] Moreover, the Appeals Chamber finds that Prlić has failed to **[page 267]** show that Manolić's testimony on the referendum on the independence of BiH or the fact that Yugoslavia was still a State in 1991 affects the Trial Chamber's finding on the meeting.[2042]

612.   Further, Prlić refers to aspects of Witness AR's testimony which do not contradict or undermine this witness's evidence that Tuđman told him that he met with Milošević in Karadorđevo in March 1991 to discuss the partition of BiH as referred to by the Trial Chamber.[2043] Accordingly, the Appeals Chamber finds that Prlić has failed to show that the Trial Chamber unreasonably assessed Witness AR's evidence and dismisses Prlić's arguments in this regard.

613.   With respect to Prlić's contention that Okun "could not have known Tuđman's intention in 1991", the Appeals Chamber observes that the Trial Chamber referred to Okun's testimony that Tuđman and Gojko Šušak discussed the division of BiH in Okun's presence in 1992.[2044] It finds that the Trial Chamber relied on Okun's testimony in relation to its overall conclusion that Tuđman participated in several meetings with Milošević to discuss the partition of BiH "from 1990 until at least 1992", rather than to support the more

---

[2034]   Prlić"'s Appeal Brief, para. 245.
[2035]   Prlić's Appeal Brief, para. 246, referring to Witness AR, Ex. P10027(confidential), T. 4703-4706, 4712-4714, 4726-4730, 4739, 4744-4746 (closed session) (8 Dec 1997).
[2036]   Prlić's Appeal Brief, para. 247, referring to Herbert Okun, T. 16653 (9 May 2006).
[2037]   Prlić's Appeal Brief, para. 248, referring to Peter Galbraith, T. 6422-6423 (12 Sept 2006).
[2038]   Prlić's Appeal Brief, para. 249, referring to Ex. 1D02036, Ciril Ribičić, T. 25549-25555 (11 Dec 2007), Milan Cvikl, T. 35384-35386 (14 Jan 2009), Prlić's ground of appeal 4.3.
[2039]   Prosecution's Response Brief (Prlić), para. 152. See also Prosecution's Response Brief (Prlić), para. 151.
[2040]   Prosecution's Response Brief (Prlić), para. 152.
[2041]   Josip Manolić, T. 4274, 4277-4278 (3 July 2006). See also Josip Manolić, T. 4672-4673 (6 July 2006). The Appeals Chamber observes that Prlić's claim that Manolić acknowledged not knowing about the 25 March 1991 Karadorđevo Meeting is unsupported by the evidence he relies on. See Prlić's Appeal Brief, para. 245, referring to Josip Manolić, T. 4726 (3 July 2006). With respect to his argument that Manolić denied knowing any agreement between Milošević and Tuđman, Prlić refers to a portion of Manolić's evidence that during the 25 March 1991 Karadorđevo Meeting, Tuđman and Milošević, rather than agreeing on the partition of BiH, discussed its division. Prlić's Appeal Brief, para. 245, referring to Josip Manolić, T. 4494 (5 July 2006). However, the Appeals Chamber finds that this reference does not show any error in the Trial Chamber's assessment of Manolić's evidence. Furthermore, the Appeals Chamber is of the view that the other portions of Manolić's evidence referred to by Prlić do not support his contention in this regard. See Prlić's Appeal Brief, para. 245, referring to Josip Manolić, T. 4473-4475 (5 July 2006), 4636, 4671-4476, 4682 (6 July 2006).
[2042]   See Prlić's Appeal Brief, para. 245, referring to Josip Manolić, T. 4274-4278 (3 July 2006), T. 4633-4635 (6 July 2006).
[2043]   Witness AR, Ex. P10027 (confidential), T. 4715 (closed session) (8 Dec 1997). See Trial Judgement, Vol. 4, para. 11.
[2044]   See Trial Judgement, Vol. 4, para. 11, referring to, *inter alia,* Herbert Okun, T(F). 16711-16713 (2 Apr 2007), Ex. P00829, p. 5.

specific finding concerning the 25 March 1991 Karađorđevo Meeting.[2045] Against this background, the Appeals Chamber fails to see how the fact that Okun did not know Tuđman's intentions in 1991 disturbs the Trial Chamber's impugned finding. Prlić's argument is therefore dismissed.

614.   Turning to Prlić's argument that Galbraith did not testify about meetings between Tuđman and Milošević, the Appeals Chamber observes that a review of the relevant trial record shows that Galbraith's evidence concerns Tuđman's aspiration to annex Bosnian territories to Croatia, rather than meetings between Tuđman and Milošević.[2046] As such, the Appeals Chamber considers that no reasonable trier of fact could have relied on this aspect of Galbraith's testimony when concluding that Tuđman and Milošević met several times in order to discuss the division of BiH. However, Prlić fails to explain how this error would impact the Trial Chamber's conclusion as well as its reliance on various others pieces of evidence, including the testimonies of Manolić, Witness AR, **[page 268]** and Okun.[2047] Accordingly, the Appeals Chamber finds that this error has no impact on the relevant finding. Moreover, the Appeals Chamber sees no merit in Prlić's undeveloped contention that Ribičić's evidence on Tuđman and Milošević's plan was based on a portion of the Presidential Transcripts.[2048] Prlić's argument therefore fails.

615.   The Appeals Chamber therefore finds that Prlić has failed to show that the Trial Chamber erroneously found that during the 25 March 1991 Karađorđevo Meeting, Tuđman and Milošević planned to finalise the division of BiH, and dismisses Prlić's sub-ground of appeal 9.3.

b. Praljak's appeal (Sub-grounds 5.1 and 5.2 in part)

616.   Praljak submits that the Trial Chamber erred in concluding that between 1990 and 1992, Tuđman and Milošević discussed the division of BiH.[2049] He specifically claims that the Trial Chamber ignored that the 25 March 1991 Karađorđevo Meeting took place "before the conception of the alleged JCE", which the Trial Chamber found was established in January 1993.[2050] He further contends that: (1) at the time of the meeting, the Socialist Federal Republic of Yugoslavia ("SFRY") still existed and thus BiH was neither an independent State nor at war;[2051] and (2) the Trial Chamber concluded that the 25 March 1991 Karađorđevo Meeting addressed the plans concerning the partition of BiH, while acknowledging that it did not receive any conclusive evidence on this plan.[2052]

617.   The Prosecution responds that the Trial Chamber correctly assessed the evidence concerning the 25 March 1991 Karađorđevo Meeting, and that Praljak repeats arguments raised at trial without demonstrating any error by the Trial Chamber.[2053]

618.   The Appeals Chamber observes that Praljak's contentions do not articulate a specific error in the Trial Chamber's finding concerning the 25 March 1991 Karađorđevo Meeting. He merely argues that the Trial Chamber did not consider the fact that the 25 March 1991 Karađorđevo Meeting occurred before the conception of the JCE, but fails to explain how this factor undermines the Trial Chamber's conclusion. Likewise, Praljak does not show how the fact that SFRY still existed and thus BiH was neither an independent State nor at war at the time of the meeting renders unreasonable the Trial Chamber's conclusion that the plans concerning the partition of BiH were **[page 269]** addressed at this meeting. With respect to Praljak's contention that the Trial Chamber did not receive details of the plans concerning the division of BiH discussed by Tuđman and Milošević, the Appeals Chamber observes that the Trial Chamber relied on corroborating evidence reflecting that during the 25 March 1991 Karađorđevo Meeting, Tuđman and

---

[2045]   See Trial Judgement, Vol. 4, para. 11.
[2046]   See Trial Judgement, Vol. 4, para. 11, referring to, *inter alia,* Peter Galbraith, T(F). 6429, 6436 (12 Sept 2006), 6580 (13 Sept 2006).
[2047]   See Trial Judgement, Vol. 4, para. 11.
[2048]   Moreover, the Appeals Chamber notes that in this context, Prlić refers to submissions in his ground of appeal 4, which the Appeals Chamber dismisses elsewhere. See *supra,* paras 206-211.
[2049]   Praljak's Appeal Brief, para. 76, referring to Trial Judgement, Vol. 4, para. 11.
[2050]   Praljak's Appeal Brief, para. 76.
[2051]   Praljak's Appeal Brief, para. 76; Appeal Hearing, AT. 386-387 (22 Mar 2017).
[2052]   Praljak's Appeal Brief, para. 77.
[2053]   Prosecution's Response Brief (Praljak), paras 39, 41.

Milošević discussed the partition of BiH.[2054] Against this background, the Appeals Chamber finds that Praljak fails to explain how the absence of the details of these plans renders the relevant finding erroneous.

619.   Accordingly, the Appeals Chamber finds that Praljak has failed to show an error in relation to the Trial Chamber's conclusion concerning the 25 March 1991 Karađorđevo Meeting and dismisses the relevant parts of his sub-grounds of appeal 5.1 and 5.2.

c. Stojić's appeal (Ground 1 in part)

620.   Stojić submits that the Trial Chamber erred in reaching its conclusion about the 25 March 1991 Karađorđevo Meeting, as it disregarded the testimony of Manolić that the agreements reached were only "stories and rumours", as well as evidence from Witness Stjepan Kljujić.[2055] Stojić concludes that no reasonable trier of fact could have relied on this meeting as evidence of the Ultimate Puipose of the JCE.[2056]

621.   The Prosecution responds that Stojić ignores Manolić's evidence which supports the existence of an agreement between Tuđman and Milošević concerning the partition of BiH.[2057] It also responds that Kljujić only testified that while he heard rumours of a "secret agreement" on partition, Tuđman did not discuss it with Kljujić.[2058]

622.   With respect to Stojić's argument regarding Manolić's evidence, the Appeals Chamber considers that Stojić mischaracterises his testimony, taking the evidence out of context. A careful review of the relevant evidence shows that Manolić did not testify that the agreements between Tuđman and Milošević were only "stories and rumours". In fact, Manolić stated that Tuđman's decision that the Croats should take part in the referendum for the independence of BiH was "in contradiction with all the stories and rumours [...] *and* the agreements that he had with Milošević about the division of [BiH]".[2059] The Appeals Chamber further observes that Manolić gave evidence about Tuđman and Milošević's negotiation concerning the division of BiH during the **[page 270]** 25 March 1991 Karađorđevo Meeting.[2060] Stojić's argument on this point is dismissed.[2061] Finally, the Appeals Chamber rejects Stojić's argument that the Trial Chamber failed to consider Kljujić's testimony since he fails to demonstrate how the evidence affects the Trial Chamber's conclusion regarding the 25 March 1991 Karađorđevo Meeting.

623.   The Appeals Chamber therefore finds that Stojić has failed to show that the Trial Chamber erroneously found that during the 25 March 1991 Karađorđevo Meeting, Tuđman and Milošević planned to finalise the division of BiH. Accordingly, the Appeals Chamber dismisses the relevant part of Stojić's ground of appeal 1.

(iii) Tuđman's double policy

624.   Relying on the evidence of Manolić and Witness AR, as well as on portions of the Presidential Transcripts concerning the presidential meetings of 27 December 1991 and 17 July 1993, the Trial Chamber found that Tuđman "spoke equivocally, advocating, on the one hand, respect for the existing borders of BiH, knowing that the international community was opposed to dividing BiH, and, on the other, the partition of BiH between the Croats and Serbs".[2062] Similarly, the Trial Chamber concluded that, in 1992, while Tuđman publicly supported BiH's independence advocating the constitutional or confederative model, he continued, with other Croatian governmental representatives, to assert his desire to reunify the Croatian people.[2063] The

---

[2054]   See Trial Judgement, Vol. 4, para. 11, fns 20-21.
[2055]   Stojić's Appeal Brief, para. 19, referring to Josip Manolić, T. 4277 (3 July 2006), Stjepan Kljujić, T. 3845-3846 (26 June 2006).
[2056]   Stojić's Appeal Brief, paras 19, 22.
[2057]   Prosecution's Response Brief (Stojić), para. 17, referring to, *inter alia,* Josip Manolić, T. 4275-4276 (3 July 2006).
[2058]   Prosecution's Response Brief (Stojić), para. 17, referring to Stjepan Kljujić, T. 3845-3846 (26 June 2006).
[2059]   See Josip Manolić, T. 4277 (3 July 2006) (emphasis added).
[2060]   See Josip Manolić, T. 4274-4276 (3 July 2006).
[2061]   In relation to Stojić's argument that the Trial Chamber found no evidence on the trial record concerning the details of the plans discussed during the 25 March 1991 Karađorđevo Meeting (Stojić's Appeal Brief, para. 19), the Appeals Chamber recalls that it has dismissed similar arguments made by Praljak. See *supra,* para. 618.
[2062]   Trial Judgement, Vol. 4, para. 12.
[2063]   Trial Judgement, Vol. 4, para. 17.

Trial Chamber observed that Tuđman repeatedly spoke of unifying the Croatian people and dividing BiH during presidential meetings held on 11 and 17 September 1992 ("11 September 1992 Presidential Meeting" and "17 September 1992 Presidential Meeting", respectively), as well as during a meeting at Brioni on 28 November 1992 ("28 November 1992 Brioni Meeting").[2064]

a. Prlić's appeal (Sub-grounds 9.2 and 9.3 in part)

i. Arguments of the Parties

625. Prlić submits that in concluding that Tuđman adopted a double policy, the Trial Chamber ignored Tuđman's assistance to BiH in accepting refugees and ABiH soldiers in Croatia and providing logistics to the ABiH and financial support.[2065] He also argues that the Trial Chamber misrepresented the relevant portions of the Presidential Transcripts, which, in his view, demonstrate **[page 271]** that Tuđman: (1) stated on 27 December 1991 that discussions with Alija Izetbegović and Radovan Karadžić must be held to find a peaceful solution, stressing that he was for a sovereign BiH; and (2) denied any agreement with Milošević on 17 July 1993.[2066] Prlić contends that "Tuđman was transparent during his meetings, never advocated carving up BiH between Croatia and Serbia and opposed BiH's division".[2067]

626. Moreover, Prlić submits that the Trial Chamber mischaracterised Tuđman's remark during the 17 September 1992 Presidential Meeting, since the Presidential Transcripts do not reflect a statement by Tuđman that the HR H-B had to be incorporated into Croatia.[2068] With respect to the 28 November 1992 Brioni Meeting, Prlić contends that the Trial Chamber ignored contradictions in Okun's evidence, arguing that Okun's contemporaneous notes do not reflect any discussions about the partition of BiH between Croats and Serbs.[2069]

627. The Prosecution responds that Prlić's contention regarding Muslims and Croats' co-operation is immaterial and, in any event, the Trial Chamber noted the co-operation in certain circumstances.[2070] With respect to Prlić's argument that Tuđman publicly denied any agreement with Milošević, the Prosecution contends that such evidence reflects his "two track policy".[2071] Concerning the 17 September 1992 Presidential Meeting, the Prosecution contends that Prlić provides an implausible interpretation of the evidence and fails to show that the Trial Chamber acted unreasonably.[2072] Lastly, the Prosecution submits that the Trial Chamber reasonably relied on Okun's description of the 28 November 1992 Brioni Meeting.[2073]

ii. Analysis

628. The Appeals Chamber observes that the Trial Chamber did not expressly refer to the evidence concerning Tuđman's co-operation with BiH which Prlić references.[2074] Yet, when discussing Tuđman's double policy, the Trial Chamber relied on Manolić's evidence that Croatia's **[page 272]** efforts to offer military and humanitarian assistance to BiH reflected Tuđman's "dual policy".[2075] Recalling that a trial

---

[2064] Trial Judgement, Vol. 4, para. 18.
[2065] Prlić's Appeal Brief, para. 250, referring to, *inter alia*, Exs. 3D03720, 3D02633; Appeal Hearing, AT. 128-129 (20 Mar 2017).
[2066] Prlić's Appeal Brief, para. 250, referring to, *inter alia*, Exs. P00089, P03517, Miomir Žužul, T. 27631 (6 May 2008). See also Appeal Hearing, AT. 127-128 (20 Mar 2017).
[2067] Prlić's Appeal Brief, para. 250 (internal references omitted). See also Prlić's Appeal Brief, para. 251, referring to Prlić's Appeal Brief, ground of appeal 19.
[2068] Prlić's Appeal Brief, para. 239, referring to Ex. P00498; Appeal Hearing, AT. 237-240 (20 Mar 2017). Prlić also submits that the HR H-B was established 11 months after that meeting, referring to sub-ground of appeal 1.3. See Prlić's Appeal Brief, para. 239.
[2069] Prlić's Appeal Brief, para. 238, referring to Herbert Okun, T. 16711-16714 (2 Apr 2007), Ex. P00829, p. 2.
[2070] Prosecution's Response Brief (Prlić), para. 149.
[2071] Prosecution's Response Brief (Prlić), para. 152.
[2072] Prosecution's Response Brief (Prlić), para. 145; Appeal Hearing, AT. 200-201 (20 Mar 2017). See also Prosecution's Response Brief (Prlić), para. 142.
[2073] Prosecution's Response Brief (Prlić), para. 148. See also Prosecution's Response Brief (Prlić), para. 142.
[2074] See Trial Judgement, Vol. 4, para. 12.
[2075] See Trial Judgement, Vol. 4, para. 12, referring to Josip Manolić, T(F). 4490-4493 (5 July 2006). Moreover, the Appeals Chamber observes that the Trial Chamber explicitly considered evidence reflecting efforts of co-operation between Croatia and BiH. See, *e.g.*, Trial Judgement, Vol. 1, paras 440-441.

chamber need not refer to every witness testimony or every piece of evidence on the record and that there is a presumption that the trial chamber evaluated all the evidence presented to it as long as there is no indication that the trial chamber completely disregarded evidence which is clearly relevant,[2076] the Appeals Chamber finds that Prlić has failed to show that the Trial Chamber disregarded the evidence he references concerning Tuđman's co-operation with BiH.

629.   The Appeals Chamber is similarly not persuaded that the Trial Chamber mischaracterised the Presidential Transcripts. A careful review of the relevant portions of the Presidential Transcripts shows that Tuđman stated that while he previously supported the sovereignty of BiH "because the greater Serbian policy raised the issue of Serbian areas in Croatia", he was in favour of the demarcation of the BiH borders even if he did not want to raise this position openly for "tactical reasons".[2077] With respect to Prlić's submission that on 17 July 1993 Tuđman denied any agreement with Milošević, the Appeals Chamber observes that Tuđman's statement merely reflects his public position and, consequently, does not affect the finding concerning his double policy.[2078]

630.   Further, the Appeals Chamber considers that in contending that "Tuđman was transparent during his meetings, never advocated carving up BiH between Croatia and Serbia and opposed BiH's division", Prlić merely disagrees with the Trial Chamber's interpretation of the evidence without identifying any error.[2079] The Appeals Chamber dismisses this challenge.

631.   The Appeals Chamber turns to Prlić's argument that the Trial Chamber misrepresented evidence by finding that during the 17 September 1992 Presidential Meeting, Tuđman envisioned incorporating the HR H-B into Croatia while the HR H-B was only established 11 months later. A review of the relevant portion of the Presidential Transcripts shows that while Tuđman does not specifically refer to the HR H-B, he argues that part of BiH should be annexed into Croatia if the interests of the Croatian people were not taken care of.[2080] As such, the Appeals Chamber does not **[page 273]** find that such a minor discrepancy – the Trial Chamber's reference to the HR H-B – could impact on the Trial Chamber's conclusion.[2081] Prlić's contention is dismissed.

632.   Prlić asserts that the Trial Chamber failed to consider contradictions between Okun's testimony and his contemporaneous notes as the latter do not provide any reference to discussions about the partition of BiH at the 28 November 1992 Brioni Meeting.[2082] By contrast, a review of the portion of Okun's notes referred to by the Trial Chamber reflects Tuđman and Šušak›s discussion concerning the partition of BiH.[2083] Accordingly, Prlić has failed to demonstrate any inconsistency between Okun's notes and his testimony on this matter. The Appeals Chamber therefore finds no error in the Trial Chamber's assessment of Okun's evidence in this respect and dismisses Prlić's argument.

633.   Accordingly, the Appeals Chamber. finds that Prlić has failed to show an error in the Trial Chamber's assessment of the evidence invalidating its conclusion on Tuđman's double policy. The Appeals Chamber therefore dismisses the relevant part of Prlić's sub-grounds of appeal 9.2 and 9.3.

[2076]   See *Kvočka et al.* Appeal Judgement, paras 23-24. See also *Tolimir* Appeal Judgement, para. 53, 161, 299; *Popović et al.* Appeal Judgement, paras 925, 1017.

[2077]   Ex. P00089, pp. 29-30.

[2078]   See Ex. P03517, p. 5.

[2079]   The Appeals chamber also notes that Prlić broadly refers to submissions in his ground of appeal 19, which the Appeals Chamber dismisses elsewhere. See *supra*, paras 249, 275, 289, 382.

[2080]   Ex. P00498, pp. 80-81 ("[t]herefore, I said, either a Bosnia that would also provide for the interests of the Croatian people, or separation, on the provision, I said, that one part went to Serbia, one part to Croatia, with perhaps a small Muslim statelet remaining in the middle [...]").

[2081]   See Trial Judgement, Vol. 4, para. 17. The Appeals Chamber also notes that Prlić refers to submissions in his sub-ground of appeal 1.3, which the Appeals Chamber dismisses elsewhere. See *supra*, paras 168-176.

[2082]   Prlić's Appeal Brief, para. 23 8.

[2083]   See Ex. P00829, p. 5 ("FT says he supports this idea for more than a decade, even wrote about it [.] GS: [The] problem is we can't do it. Looks like [a] collusion of future partition of BiH"). See also Herbert Okun, T. 16711-16712 (2 Apr 2007); Trial Judgement, Vol. 4, para. 18.

b. Praljak's appeal (Sub-grounds 5.1, 5.2, and 6.2 in part)

i. Arguments of the Parties

634.   Praljak submits that the Trial Chamber erred in finding that "Tuđman spoke equivocally", arguing that it: (1) failed to provide any example of "Tuđman['s] double language preferring to refer [to] Manolić['s] testimony";[2084] and (2) erred in assessing the testimony of Manolić since he did not testify about "double language but about [a] double policy".[2085] Praljak also avers that Tuđman consistently supported BiH's sovereignty and independence when he was in the "Croat circle".[2086]

635.   Further, Praljak contends that, contrary to the Trial Chamber's finding concerning the 11 and 17 September 1992 Presidential Meetings, BiH's independence and sovereignty was never called into question during those meetings.[2087] He avers that "the political aim of the HVO was **[page 274]** formulated as the forming and ordering of BiH in accordance with the EC principles, but Croats [...] were also permanently pursuing the goal to end the war".[2088] With respect to the 17 September 1992 Presidential Meeting, Praljak argues that the question of the division of BiH was only mentioned as a solution the international community once considered,[2089] and that Tuđman recalled that Croatia's position was in favour of organising BiH into three constituent peoples and that the Croatian people's interests could be assured in BiH.[2090]

636.   Additionally, Praljak submits that the Trial Chamber erred in concluding that during the 28 November 1992 Brioni Meeting, Tuđman repeatedly made reference to the division of BiH.[2091] He argues that Okun's testimony on which the Trial Chamber relied is contradicted by his contemporaneous notes[2092] and that the other evidence on the record shows that Tuđman had no intention to divide BiH in November 1992.[2093]

637.   The Prosecution responds that there is no merit in Praljak's argument that the Trial Chamber erred when concluding that Tuđman spoke equivocally since Manolić's and Okun's evidence supports the Trial Chamber's conclusion.[2094] Moreover, the Prosecution contends, Praljak repeats arguments already made at trial and raises challenges without demonstrating any error or impact.[2095]

ii. Analysis

638.   The Appeals Chamber sees no merit in Praljak's contention that the Trial Chamber did not provide any example of Tuđman's "double language" and preferred to refer to Manolić's testimony. When concluding that Tuđman "spoke equivocally", the Trial Chamber relied, in addition to Manolić's testimony, on various pieces of evidence which Praljak does not challenge.[2096] With respect to Praljak's claim that Manolić testified about Tuđman's "double policy" rather than "double language", the Appeals Chamber finds that the difference between the two notions is a mere question of semantics. Accordingly, his argument is dismissed.

[2084]   Praljak's Appeal Brief, para. 86.
[2085]   Praljak's Appeal Brief, para. 86.
[2086]   Praljak's Appeal Brief, para. 86, referring to, *inter alia,* Judge Antonetti Dissent, pp. 392-393, Ex. P00822. See also Praljak's Appeal Brief, para. 87.
[2087]   Praljak's Appeal Brief, para. 114.
[2088]   Praljak's Appeal Brief, para. 114, referring to Ex. P00498, pp. 28, 72.
[2089]   Praljak's Appeal Brief, para. 80, referring to Ex. P00498, pp. 80-81.
[2090]   Praljak's Appeal Brief, para. 80. Praljak also argues that Croatia recognised BiH independence and Tuđman made all possible efforts to cooperate with Muslims. Praljak's Appeal Brief, para. 81, referring to Ex. 1D00896, p. 3; Appeal Hearing, AT. 386 (22 Mar 2017).
[2091]   Praljak's Appeal Brief, para. 82, referring to, *inter alia,* Trial Judgement, Vol. 4, para. 18.
[2092]   Praljak's Appeal Brief, para. 82.
[2093]   Praljak's Appeal Brief, para. 82, referring to, *inter alia,* Exs. P00080, p. 46, P00498, pp. 80, 82, P00822, p. 52. See also Praljak's Appeal Brief, para. 83.
[2094]   Prosecution's Response Brief (Praljak), para. 38; Appeal Hearing, AT. 421 (22 Mar 2017).
[2095]   Prosecution's Response Brief (Praljak), para. 41.
[2096]   See Trial Judgement, Vol. 4, para. 12 & fn. 22, referring to Witness AR, Ex. P10027 (confidential), T(F). 4744, 4778 (closed session) (8 Dec 1997); Ex. P00089, pp. 29-30, Ex. P03517, p. 5.

639. The Appeals Chamber further rejects Praljak's contention that Tuđman consistently supported BiH's sovereignty and independence when he was in the "Croat circle". Rather than **[page 275]** identifying an error in the Trial Chamber's analysis, Praljak merely seeks to substitute bis own interpretation of the evidence for that of the Trial Chamber.[2097] His argument is dismissed.

640. Turning to Praljak's challenges to the Trial Chamber's findings on the 11 and 17 September 1992 Presidential Meetings, the Appeals Chamber observes that the Trial Chamber found that: (1) at the 11 September 1992 Presidential Meeting, Tuđman recalled his territorial ambitions for a Croatian Banovina; and (2) at the 17 September 1992 Presidential Meeting, Tuđman still envisioned incorporating the HR H-B into Croatia.[2098] The Appeals Chamber considers that when arguing that the BiH's independence and sovereignty was undisputed at the meetings and that the HVO's political aim was "formulated as the forming and ordering of BiH in accordance with the EC principles, but Croats, concerned by victims, were also permanently pursuing the goal to end the war",[2099] Praljak merely disagrees with the Trial Chamber's conclusion on Tuđman's positions expressed at these meetings and fails to show that no reasonable trier of fact could have reached the same conclusion as the Trial Chamber did. Praljak's assertion is therefore dismissed.

641. Praljak claims that during the 17 September 1992 Presidential Meeting, the division of BiH was mentioned as a solution the international community previously considered. In this respect, the Appeals Chamber notes that from the portion of the Presidential Transcripts Praljak refers to, it is unclear whether Tuđman made reference to the division of BiH in the context suggested by Praljak.[2100] However, in reaching its conclusion that Tuđman affirmed his desire for the reunification of the Croatian people in 1992, the Trial Chamber relied, in addition, upon the evidence that Tuđman spoke of the division of BiH during the 11 September 1992 Presidential Meeting and the 28 November 1992 Brioni Meeting.[2101] Thus, the Appeals Chamber finds that, by only pointing to the respective portion of the Presidential Transcripts, Praljak fails to show that the Trial Chamber was unreasonable in reaching the impugned finding based on the remaining evidence and, accordingly, dismisses his argument.

642. Finally, the Appeals Chamber rejects Praljak's challenge to the Trial Chamber's assessment of Okun's evidence regarding the 28 November 1992 Brioni Meeting. The Appeals Chamber **[page 276]** reiterates that Okun's notes confirm, rather than contradict, his evidence in court.[2102] Similarly, the Appeals Chamber finds that in arguing that "the other evidence" shows that in November 1992, Tuđman had no intention to divide BiH, Praljak simply attempts to substitute his assessment of the evidence for that of the Trial Chamber without showing an error. Accordingly, these arguments are dismissed.

643. The Appeals Chamber therefore finds that Praljak has failed to show that the Trial Chamber erroneously found that Tuđman adopted a double policy. Therefore, the Appeals Chamber dismisses the relevant parts of Praljak's sub-grounds of appeal 5.1, 5.2, and 6.2.

(iv) Tuđman's support for the creation of the HZ H-B on 18 November 1991

644. The Trial Chamber found that, in connection with the plan to expand Croatian borders, Tuđman supported the creation of the HZ H-B on 18 November 1991, which was defined as a Croatian entity protecting the rights of the Croats and defending the "ethnically and historically Croatian" territories, inspired by the territorial borders of the Banovina.[2103] The Trial Chamber also found that Tuđman, Praljak, and the founders of the HZ H-B., including Mate Boban, repeatedly mentioned the Banovina.[2104]

[2097] Appeals Chamber further observes that in support of his contention, Praljak also relies upon the Judge Antonetti Dissent. See Praljak's Appeal Brief, para. 86, referring to Judge Antonetti Dissent, pp. 392-393. In this regard, the Appeals Chamber recalls that the mere existence of a dissent does not render the majority's conclusion unreasonable. See, *e.g., Galić* Appeal Judgement, para. 226.

[2098] Trial Judgement, Vol. 4, para. 18.

[2099] Praljak's Appeal Brief, para. 114.

[2100] See Ex. P00498, p. 81.

[2101] See Trial Judgement, Vol. 4, paras 17-18.

[2102] See *supra*, para. 632.

[2103] Trial Judgement, Vol. 4, para. 14.

[2104] Trial Judgement, Vol. 4, para. 14.

a. Prlić's appeal (Sub-ground 9.5)

i. Arguments of the Parties

645. Prlić submits that the Trial Chamber erred in concluding that Tuđman supported the creation of the HZ H-B as part of the plan to expand Croatian borders since it contradicted its own previous finding in paragraph 423 of Volume 1 of the Trial Judgement.[2105] He further argues that the Trial Chamber failed to properly assess all relevant evidence.[2106] Specifically, he submits that the Trial Chamber ignored evidence showing that "HDZ[-]BiH's policy was always for BiH".[2107] Moreover, according to Prlić, "the actions of HDZ-BiH cannot [be] fully appreciated in the absence **[page 277]** of context: the Muslim policy of pursuing a unitary/Muslim dominated state, and how the [BiH] government became a Muslim government".[2108]

646. Prlić also avers that the Trial Chamber failed to consider: (1) the testimony of "Tuđman's close associates" about Tuđman's reference to the Banovina;[2109] (2) evidence concerning Tuđman's opposition to the change of the internationally recognised borders;[2110] (3) Praljak's testimony on the 17 September 1992 Presidential Meeting that "Banovina was not the goal" and the HZ H-B would cease to exist "upon solving BiH's internal organization";[2111] and (4) Prlić's remarks at the 17 September 1992 Presidential Meeting, which confirm "his understanding of an inviolable BiH of three constituent peoples".[2112]

647. The Prosecution responds that Prlić fails to show that the Trial Chamber erred in finding that the HZ H-B was created for future annexation or alliance to Croatia.[2113] The Prosecution argues that the Trial Chamber considered Defence arguments that the HZ(R) H-B served defence or administrative purposes, concluding that while it may have also served these aims, it was designed to be annexed or allied to Croatia.[2114] The Prosecution further responds that Prlić ignores the Trial Chamber's adverse credibility findings with respect to Praljak's testimony.[2115]

ii. Analysis

648. The Appeals Chamber is not persuaded that the Trial Chamber's finding that Tuđman supported the creation of the HZ H-B conflicts with its finding made elsewhere that during the 39th session of the Supreme Council of Croatia on 18 November 1991, he announced that the establishment of the HZ H-B did not constitute a decision to separate from BiH.[2116] On the contrary, a reading of the Trial Judgement as a whole suggests that the fact that Tuđman publicly advocated the respect of BiH borders while privately supporting the separation of BiH is consistent with the Trial Chamber's finding on Tuđman's double policy.[2117] This argument is thus dismissed.

[2105] Prlić's Appeal Brief, para. 255. See also Prlić's Appeal Brief, para. 255 & fn. 723, referring to Trial Judgement, Vol. 1, paras 423, 428, Vol. 4, paras 14, 17.

[2106] Prlić's Appeal Brief, paras 256, 258-261. See also Prlić's Appeal Brief, para. 257, referring to Prlić's Appeal Brief, sub-grounds of appeal 1.1-1.2; Appeal Hearing, AT. 136 (20 Mar 2017).

[2107] Prlić's Appeal Brief, para. 258. Specifically, Prlić points at evidence on the record allegedly showing that HDZ-BiH's policy was "for BiH" since HDZ-BiH: (1) reacted to the war in Croatia which was conducted in part from BiH; (2) acted because the BiH government was unable to protect BiH and Croats in BiH; (3) organised a defence with different measures, "including establishing a number of Croatian communities inside HDZ"; and (4) offered a defence to Muslims. Prlić's Appeal Brief, para. 258.

[2108] Prlić's Appeal Brief, para. 259 (internal references omitted).

[2109] See Prlić's Appeal Brief, para. 260.

[2110] Prlić's Appeal Brief, para. 260.

[2111] Prlić's Appeal Brief, para. 261.

[2112] Prlić's Appeal Brief, para. 261.

[2113] Prosecution's Response Brief (Prlić), paras 155-156.

[2114] Prosecution's Response Brief (Prlić), para. 159, referring to Trial Judgement, Vol. 4, paras 15-16.

[2115] Prosecution's Response Brief (Prlić), para. 147.

[2116] See Prlić's Appeal brief, para. 255, referring to Trial Judgement, Vol. 1, para. 423.

[2117] See Trial Judgement, Vol. 4, para. 12.

649. The Appeals Chamber now moves to Prlić's argument that the Trial Chamber failed to properly assess all relevant evidence. Insofar as he inserts by reference arguments raised in his **[page 278]** sub-grounds of appeal 1.1 and 1.2, the Appeals Chamber notes that it dismisses these arguments elsewhere.[2118]

650. With respect to Prlić's contention that the Trial Chamber failed to consider the evidence concerning the "HDZ-BiH's policy", Prlić fails to show how the evidence he cites is relevant to the Trial Chamber's conclusion on Tuđman's intentions and his support for the creation of the HZ H-B. Similarly, the Appeals Chamber dismisses as unsubstantiated Prlić's blanket argument that the actions of HDZ-BiH cannot be fully appreciated in the absence of context. Prlić's arguments thus fail.

651. Turning to Prlić's challenge that the Trial Chamber failed to consider the evidence of Tuđman's close associates regarding Tuđman's reference to the Banovina, the Appeals Chamber observes that Prlić misrepresents the testimony of Ribičić and Witness Miomir Žužul.[2119] They did not testify about the meaning of Tuđman's references to the Banovina during his speeches and utterances, but rather about the reference to the Banovina and its meaning in the preamble of the Croatian Constitution.[2120] Prlić's argument is dismissed.

652. The Appeals Chamber also rejects Prlić's contention that the Trial Chamber failed to consider evidence that Tuđman was against the change of the borders recognised by the international community as he merely claims that the Trial Chamber failed to consider the evidence without properly articulating an error. Moreover, he does not attempt to show how, based on this evidence, no reasonable trier of fact could have reached the same conclusion.[2121] Accordingly, Prlić's arguments are dismissed.

653. Similarly, the Appeals Chamber rejects Prlić's claims that the Trial Chamber failed to consider Praljak's testimony concerning the 17 September 1992 Presidential Meeting and Prlić's remarks at this meeting.[2122] The Trial Chamber explained that while it found Praljak's testimony credible on certain points, it found his evidence "hardly credible" when he attempted to limit his responsibility, and consequently did not accept it in those instances.[2123] Therefore, the Appeals Chamber finds that the Trial Chamber did not disregard Praljak's testimony, but rather considers that the Trial Chamber weighed his testimony and concluded that this evidence did not prevent it from arriving at its findings. Accordingly, this argument is dismissed. **[page 279]**

654. The Appeals Chamber therefore finds that Prlić has failed to show that the Trial Chamber erroneously found that Tuđman supported the creation of the HZ H-B on 18 November 1991 as part of the plan to expand Croatian borders, and dismisses Prlić's sub-ground of appeal 9.5.

b. Praljak's appeal (Sub-grounds 5.1 and 5.2 in part)

655. Praljak argues that the Trial Chamber erred in finding that Tuđman supported the creation of the HZ(R) H-B in connection with the plan to expand Croatian borders.[2124] Praljak asserts that: (1) Croatia was only concerned about its defence;[2125] and (2) Tuđman stated that the proclamation of the HZ(R) H-B was not a decision to establish the Community of Herceg-Bosna, but a declaration that the BiH Croats were working to establish a community without separating from BiH, which contradicts the Trial Chamber's finding on Tuđman's intentions to divide BiH.[2126]

656. Praljak also argues that after the signing of the Vance-Owen Peace Plan, Tuđman expressed his reservations about the position of some Croats who wanted to proclaim Herceg-Bosna as part of Croatia,

---

[2118] Prlić's Appeal Brief, paras 256-257, referring to Prlić's Appeal Brief, sub-grounds of appeal 1.1-1.2. See *supra*, paras 168-176.

[2119] See Prlić's Appeal Brief, para. 260, referring to, *inter alios*, Ciril Ribičić, T. 25466-25468, 25570 (10 Dec 2008), Miomir Žužul, T. 27648-27651 (7 May 2008).

[2120] Ciril Ribičić, T. 25466-25468, 25570 (10 Dec 2008), Miomir Žužul, T. 27648-27651 (7 May 2008).

[2121] See *supra*, para. 25.

[2122] See Prlić's Appeal Brief, para. 260.

[2123] Trial Judgement, Vol. 1, para. 399.

[2124] Praljak's Appeal Brief, para. 78, referring to Trial Judgement, Vol. 4, para. 14.

[2125] Praljak's Appeal Brief, para. 78, referring to Ex. P00068.

[2126] Praljak's Appeal Brief, para. 78, referring to Ex. P00080.

constantly made reference to the need for co-operation with Muslims, and supported BiH's independence.[2127]

657. The Prosecution responds that the Trial Chamber's finding was reasonable.[2128] It also argues that Praljak fails to show the impact of the alleged errors on the Trial Chamber's finding and makes unsubstantiated claims showing no error in the Trial Chamber's assessment of the evidence.[2129]

658. The Appeals Chamber notes that in support of his submission that Croatia was only concerned about its defence, Praljak refers to the evidence that a week before the creation of the HZ H-B, Tuđman told Boban that Croatia would support and co-ordinate military organs of seven municipalities, which were situated close to Croatian areas involved in the conflict.[2130] However, Praljak makes no attempt to explain how this evidence undermines the Trial Chamber's conclusion. Praljak's argument is dismissed.

659. With respect to Praljak's argument that Tuđman stated that the proclamation of the HZ(R) H-B did not constitute a decision to separate from BiH,[2131] the Appeals Chamber observes that the Trial Chamber explicitly relied upon the evidence referred to by Praljak in its analysis of **[page 280]** the proclamation of the HZ H-B.[2132] Praljak does not show how this evidence contradicts the Trial Chamber's conclusion that Tuđman supported the creation of the HZ H-B in connection with the plan to expand Croatian borders.[2133] The Appeals Chamber also rejects Praljak's contention regarding Tuđman's reservations about the position of some Croats who wanted to proclaim Herceg-Bosna as part of Croatia, as well as his contention concerning Tuđman's support for both co-operation with Muslims and BiH's independence, as he merely points to the evidence without articulating any error vis-à-vis the Trial Chamber's conclusion. In any event, the Appeals Chamber observes that in support of his contention, Praljak refers to evidence reflecting a speech of Tuđman during a meeting with Cyrus Vance, David Owen, Ambassador Martti Ahtisaari, Boban, and Izetbegović.[2134] In this regard, the Appeals Chamber does not find that this evidence could show an error in the impugned finding as it is consistent with the Trial Chamber's conclusion concerning Tuđman's double policy, namely that while Tuđman publicly supported the independence and the territorial integrity of BiH, he continued to affirm his desire to reunify the Croatian people in private with other Croatian governmental representatives.[2135] Accordingly, the Appeals Chamber dismisses this claim.

660. The Appeals Chamber therefore finds that Praljak has failed to show that the Trial Chamber erroneously found that in connection with the plan to expand the Croatian borders, Tuđman supported the creation of the HZ H-B on 18 November 1991. The Appeals Chamber dismisses the relevant parts of Praljak's sub-grounds of appeal 5.1 and 5.2.

(v) Tuđman's references to the Croatian Banovina between January 1993 and March 1994

661. The Trial Chamber concluded that between January 1993 and March 1994, Tuđman was still "pre-occupied with the borders of Croatia and by the Croatian Banovina".[2136] Specifically, the Trial Chamber found that Tuđman: (1) asserted on 20 May 1993 that "Croats surely cannot agree to lose some areas that used to be a part of the Banovina"; (2) stated on 6 July 1993 that the BiH Croats would not conquer the territories of others, but rather the lands that belonged to the Croats for centuries; (3) stated on 21 September 1993 that Stolac and the entire region of Jablanica-Konjic had formed part of the Banovina; and (4) reiterated at a presidency meeting on 6 January 1994 that his military support for Croats in BiH was to ensure that certain

---

[2127]   See Praljak's Appeal Brief, para. 85. According to Praljak, "whatever the position of HZ(R) H-B Leaders and/or Croats living in BiH might have been, Tuđman['s] and Croatia['s] position was to preserve BiH as a sovereign and independent State in its internationally recognized borders". Praljak's Appeal Brief, para. 85.
[2128]   Prosecution's Response Brief (Praljak), para. 40.
[2129]   Prosecution's Response Brief (Praljak), para. 41.
[2130]   Praljak's Appeal Brief, para. 78, referring to Ex. P00068.
[2131]   Praljak's Appeal Brief, para. 78, referring to Ex. P00080.
[2132]   Trial Judgement, Vol. 1, para. 423, referring to Ex. P00080.
[2133]   See *supra*, para. 648. See also Trial Judgement, Vol. 4, paras 12, 14.
[2134]   See Praljak's Appeal Brief, para. 85, referring to Ex. P01558, p. 45.
[2135]   Trial Judgement, Vol. 4, para. 17. See also Trial Judgement, Vol. 4, para. 12.
[2136]   Trial Judgement, Vol. 4, para. 22.

BiH territories did not fall into **[page 281]** Muslim hands, to preserve the territories considered Croatian, and to determine the future borders of the Croatian State "perhaps for centuries".[2137]

a. Prlić's appeal (Sub-ground 9.2 in part)

662. Prlić submits that the Trial Chamber erroneously found that Tuđman remained preoccupied with the Banovina borders by: (1) relying on selective portions of the Presidential Transcripts; (2) failing to consider evidence from witnesses who attended relevant meetings; and (3) ignoring "contextually relevant" events during the meetings.[2138] Specifically, he argues that "Tuđman cannot be understood without considering the [Owen-Stoltenberg Peace Plan] and the signing of a secret agreement between Tuđman and Izetbegović connecting the Muslim and Croat Republics in BiH, and a confederation with Croatia".[2139]

663. Prlić contends that the Trial Chamber mischaracterised other portions of the Presidential Transcripts which show that Tuđman: (1) supported an independent BiH and asked UNPROFOR to protect the border between BiH and Croatia;[2140] and (2) mentioned the Banovina as an argument against demographic changes in BiH or changes of the borders of Croatia.[2141] Prlić further asserts that Tuđman: (1) did not refer to the Banovina in the context of dividing or annexing BiH and the term was "merely a reference point during negotiations about the internal organization of BiH"; (2) supported the independence of BiH regardless of the audience; and (3) was consistently for a peaceful solution.[2142]

664. The Prosecution responds that the evidence to which Prlić refers demonstrates the continuing preoccupation that members of the JCE had with the Banovina, including Tuđman.[2143]

665. The Appeals Chamber observes that in arguing that the Trial Chamber relied selectively on the Presidential Transcripts, Prlić merely refers to certain evidence without explaining how the Trial Chamber unreasonably assessed it. Similarly, his submission that the Trial Chamber failed to consider evidence and contextually relevant events fails to show how, based on this evidence and events, no reasonable trier of fact could have reached the same conclusion as the Trial Chamber did. **[page 282]**

The Appeals Chamber further considers that Prlić's assertion that "Tuđman cannot be understood without considering the [Owen-Stoltenberg Peace Plan] and the signing of a secret agreement with Izetbegović connecting the Muslim and Croat Republics in BiH, and a confederation with Croatia"[2144] reflects a different interpretation of the evidence without demonstrating an error warranting appellate intervention.[2145] Accordingly, the Appeals Chamber dismisses Prlić's arguments.

666. The Appeals Chamber also finds that when claiming that the Trial Chamber mischaracterised parts of the Presidential Transcripts, Prlić merely disagrees with the Trial Chamber's assessment of evidence but fails to show how the Trial Chamber erred in such assessment. In relation to his claims that the Trial Chamber erred in assessing Tuđman's reference to the Banovina, the Appeals Chamber notes that Prlić supports this assertion by referring to evidence on the record without showing that no reasonable trier of fact could have reached the same conclusion as the Trial Chamber.[2146] Recalling that mere assertions that the Trial Chamber

---

[2137] Trial Judgement, Vol. 4, para. 22.

[2138] Prlić's Appeal Brief, para. 240. Prlić points to a portion of the Presidential Transcripts dated 5 November 1993 that the Trial Chamber cited. See Prlić's Appeal Brief, para. 240 & fn. 687, referring to, *inter alia*, Ex. P06454, pp. 1-2, Slobodan Praljak, T. 41763-41765 (22 June 2009), Trial Judgement, Vol. 4, para. 22. See also Appeal Hearing, AT. 235-236 (20 Mar 2017).

[2139] Prlić's Appeal Brief, para. 240. See also Prlić's Appeal Brief, para. 241, referring to Prlić's Appeal Brief, sub-ground of appeal 1.3.

[2140] Prlić's Appeal Brief, para. 242, referring to Exs. P04740, P03324, P02452.

[2141] Prlić's Appeal Brief, para. 242, referring to Exs. P02466, P03279.

[2142] Prlić's Appeal Brief, para. 243. See also Prlić's Appeal Brief, para. 242.

[2143] Prosecution's Response Brief (Prlić), para. 144. See also Prosecution's Response Brief (Prlić), para. 142. The Prosecution also submits that Prlić fails to show any error in the Trial Chamber's conclusion as he relies on Praljak's evidence, which the Trial Chamber deemed unreliable. Prosecution's Response Brief (Prlić), para. 147.

[2144] Prlić's Appeal Brief, para. 240.

[2145] The Appeals Chamber also notes that Prlić refers to submissions in his sub-ground of appeal 1.3, which the Appeals Chamber dismisses elsewhere in the Judgement. See *supra*, paras 168-176.

[2146] See Prlić's Appeal Brief, para. 243.

failed to give sufficient weight to evidence or failed to interpret evidence in a particular manner warrant a dismissal, the Appeals Chamber declines to consider Prlić's unsubstantiated argument.

667.   The Appeals Chamber finds that Prlić has failed to show that the Trial Chamber erroneously concluded that between January 1993 and March 1994, Tuđman continued to be preoccupied by the Banovina and with the borders of Croatia. Accordingly, the Appeals Chamber dismisses Prlić's sub-ground of appeal 9.2 in relevant part.

b. Praljak's appeal (Sub-grounds 5.1 and 5.2 in part)

668.   Praljak submits that the Trial Chamber misconstrued Tuđman's references to the Banovina, because they were historical rather than political in character.[2147] He mentions in particular the presidential meeting of 20 May 1993 ("20 May 1993 Presidential Meeting") where Tuđman refers to the Banovina in the frame of the Vance-Owen Peace Plan, which reaffirmed BiH's independence and sovereignty within its internationally recognised borders.[2148] Praljak contends that two weeks **[page 283]** later, Tuđman reaffirmed his intention to persuade BiH Croats to remain in a "confederal BiH" and informed Izetbegović that the Croats supported BiH.[2149]

669.   The Prosecution responds that Praljak's argument that Tuđman's references to the Banovina were merely historical is contradicted by Praljak's own admission that achieving the separation from BiH with borders matching the Banovina was "Croatia's policy, and Tuđman's, and Jadranko Prlić's and all of us".[2150] The Prosecution further submits that the Trial Chamber agreed with Praljak when it found that in order to achieve the Ultimate Purpose of the JCE, the JCE members forcibly seized the territories linked to the Banovina to demarcate borders based on their control over these provinces.[2151]

670.   The Appeals Chamber notes that in support of his contention that Tuđman's references to the Banovina were historical in character, Praljak relies upon the Judge Antonetti Dissent.[2152] The Appeals Chamber recalls that the mere existence of a dissent does not render the majority's conclusion unreasonable.[2153] In relation to Praljak's claim that during the 20 May 1993 Presidential Meeting, Tuđman made reference to the Banovina in the frame of the Vance-Owen Peace Plan, the Appeals Chamber observes that in reaching its conclusion that Tuđman was still concerned with the Banovina, the Trial Chamber took into account Tuđman's remarks during four different meetings, including the 20 May 1993 Presidential Meeting.[2154] The Appeals Chamber finds that Praljak challenges the Trial Chamber's reliance on the 20 May 1993 Presidential Meeting without explaining how the impugned finding could not stand on the basis of the remaining evidence. With regard to Praljak's argument that Tuđman reaffirmed his intention to persuade BiH Croats to remain in a "confederal BiH", and that Tuđman informed Izetbegović of the Croat's support for BiH, the Appeals Chamber considers that Praljak only points to excerpts of the Presidential Transcripts without showing how such evidence would disturb the impugned finding. The Appeals Chamber finds that Praljak fails to show that no reasonable trier of fact could have reached the impugned conclusion.

671.   The Appeals Chamber therefore finds that Praljak has failed to show that the Trial Chamber erroneously concluded that between 1993 and 1994, Tuđman was still "pre-occupied with the borders of Croatia and by the Croatian Banovina". Accordingly, the Appeals Chamber dismisses the relevant part of Praljak's sub-grounds of appeal 5.1 and 5.2. **[page 284]**

[2147]   Praljak's Appeal Brief, para. 79 & fn. 146, referring to Judge Antonetti Dissent, p. 391; Appeal Hearing, AT. 386-387 (22 Mar 2017).
[2148]   Praljak's Appeal Brief, para. 79, referring to, *inter alia*, Ex. P02466.
[2149]   Praljak's Appeal Brief, para. 79, referring to Exs. P02613, P02719.
[2150]   Prosecution's Response Brief (Praljak), para. 36, referring to Slobodan Praljak, T. 43370-43371 (17 Aug 2009).
[2151]   Prosecution's Response Brief (Praljak), para. 36, referring to, *inter alia*, Trial Judgement, Vol. 4, paras 18, 22.
[2152]   *See supra*, fn. 2147.
[2153]   See, *e.g.*, *Galić* Appeal Judgement, paras 226-227.
[2154]   Trial Judgement, Vol. 4, para. 22.

(b) Challenges to the overall finding that Tuđman claimed that BiH was not supposed to exist as an independent State and that part of BiH was to be annexed to Croatia

(i) Prlić's appeal (Ground 9.2 in part)

672.   Prlić submits that the Trial Chamber erroneously concluded that Tuđman claimed that BiH was not supposed to exist as an independent State and that part of BiH was to be annexed to Croatia.[2155] Specifically, he argues that the Trial Chamber relied on "selective snippets" of the evidence, including the Presidential Transcripts, and the evidence of Witness AR, Galbraith, Manolić, and Okun,[2156] and failed to consider relevant evidence from the Presidential Transcript that shows Tuđman's co-operation with the BiH government.[2157]

673.   The Prosecution responds that the Trial Chamber reasonably found that the JCE members sought to reclaim the Banovina borders and unify the Croatian people by establishing an autonomous Croat entity in BiH in preparation for future integration or alliance with Croatia.[2158] The Prosecution also contends that Prlić's argument regarding Croat-Muslim co-operation is irrelevant.[2159]

674.   The Appeals Chamber observes that Prlić provides no support for his assertion that the Trial Chamber relied on "selective snippets" of the Presidential Transcripts. Furthermore, in challenging the testimony of Witness AR, Prlić refers to Žužul's and Robert Donia's evidence without explaining how their testimony would render unreasonable the Trial Chamber's reliance on Witness AR.[2160] With respect to the testimonies of Galbraith and Manolić, Prlić simply cross-references other grounds of appeal, which the Appeals Chamber dismisses elsewhere.[2161] Lastly, as to Okun's evidence, Prlić points to portions of his testimony without providing any explanation.[2162] The Appeals Chamber finds that Prlić fails to show any error in the Trial Chamber's assessment of the evidence of Witness AR, Galbraith, Manolić, or Okun and, therefore, dismisses these arguments. **[page 285]**

675.   Turning to Prlić's argument that the Trial Chamber disregarded evidence reflecting Tuđman's co-operation with the BiH government, the Appeals Chamber reiterates that the Trial Chamber considered Tuđman's efforts to co-operate with BiH and concluded that they reflected his double policy.[2163] Against this background, Prlić merely asserts that the Trial Chamber failed to consider certain evidence without showing that, based on this evidence, no reasonable trier of fact could have reached the same conclusion as the Trial Chamber. Accordingly this argument is dismissed.

676.   The Appeals Chamber finds that Prlić has failed to show that the Trial Chamber erred in reaching its conclusion about Tuđman's intentions. Accordingly, the Appeals Chamber dismisses the relevant part of Prlić's ground of appeal 9.2.

(ii) Stojić's appeal (Ground 1 in part)

a. Arguments of the Parties

677.   Stojić submits that when concluding that Tuđman had intentions to reconstitute the Banovina, the Trial Chamber failed to consider relevant evidence.[2164] Specifically, he argues that the Trial Chamber's analysis of

---

[2155]   Prlić's Appeal Brief, para. 236, referring to Trial Judgement, Vol. 1, para. 428, Vol. 4, paras 9, 18, 22-24; Appeal Hearing, AT. 127-128 (20 Mar 2017). See also Appeal Hearing, AT. 237 (20 Mar 2017).

[2156]   Prlić's Appeal Brief, para. 236, referring to Miomir Žužul, T. 31155-31163 (22 July 2008), Robert Donia, T. 1931-1933 (11 May 2006), Prlić's Appeal Brief, sub-ground of appeal 6.2.

[2157]   Prlić's Appeal Brief, para. 236, referring to, *inter alia*, Exs. P00312, P00414, P00466.

[2158]   Prosecution's Response Brief (Prlić), para. 142; Appeal Hearing, AT. 188-190 (20 Mar 2017).

[2159]   Prosecution's Response Brief (Prlić), para. 149.

[2160]   Prlić's Appeal Brief, para. 236, referring to Miomir Žužul, T. 31155-31163 (22 July 2008), Robert Donia, T. 1931-1933 (11 May 2006).

[2161]   See Prlić's Appeal Brief, para. 236, referring to Prlić's Appeal Brief, sub-ground of appeal 6.2. See also *supra*, paras 213, 216-218.

[2162]   Prlić's Appeal Brief, para. 236, referring to Herbert Okun, T. 16653 (2 Apr 2007).

[2163]   See *supra*, para. 624. See also Trial Judgement, Vol. 1, paras 440-441, 463-464, 467, 471-472, 477, Vol. 2, paras 696-697.

[2164]   Stojić's Appeal Brief, paras 10-16.

presidential meetings is wholly inadequate as the Trial Chamber only relied on a limited part of the Presidential Transcripts, "while disregarding other relevant documents entirely", in contrast to the detailed analysis provided by Judge Antonetti in his dissent.[2165] Stojić contends that the relevant evidence from the Presidential Transcripts which the Trial Chamber disregarded is inconsistent with its conclusion on Tuđman's intentions,[2166] and shows that Tuđman: (1) advocated the independence of BiH as a confederation of three constituent peoples;[2167] and (2) placed importance on co-operation with Muslims and on "international opinion".[2168] **[page 286]**

678.   Moreover, Stojić contends that the Trial Chamber also disregarded: (1) evidence showing that Croatia agreed to a succession of peace plans;[2169] (2) evidence from Witness 4D-AB that there was no Croatian policy in the area;[2170] and (3) evidence from Manolić that Tuđman was not enthusiastic about the reconstitution of the Banovina.[2171] Finally, Stojić argues that the Trial Chamber made contradictory findings when it concluded that Tuđman supported the creation of the HZ H-B in order to expand and also to protect the borders of Croatia.[2172]

679.   The Prosecution responds that the Trial Chamber did not disregard the evidence referred to by Stojić and reasonably relied on the evidence showing the "two-track policy" of the JCE members.[2173] The Prosecution submits that: (1) the Trial Chamber reasonably gave more weight to the "overwhelming evidence from the JCE members' contemporaneous statements" supporting the Ultimate Purpose of the JCE than to the testimony of Witness 4D-AB;[2174] and (2) contrary to Stojić's submission, Manolić testified that Tuđman's main goal was the reconstitution of "the Banovina Croatia borders".[2175] Finally, the Prosecution contends that there is no inconsistency in the Trial Chamber's finding regarding Tuđman's intentions to protect and expand the Croatian borders as Tuđman stated that "the question above all others is how to preserve the Republic of Croatia, how to gain as much as possible" in BiH.[2176]

680.   Stojić replies that the Prosecution's argument concerning the double policy is contradicted by evidence which reflects that in his private statements in 1992 and 1993, Tuđman supported the independence of BiH as a "union of the three constituent peoples",[2177] and he was willing to help Bosnian Muslims.[2178]

b. Analysis

681.   With respect to Stojić's argument that the Trial Chamber failed to consider the evidence from the Presidential Transcripts indicating that Tuđman advocated for the independence of BiH and placed emphasis

---

[2165]   Stojić's Appeal Brief, para. 10, referring to Judge Antonetti Dissent, pp. 7-50; Appeal Hearing, AT. 258-262, 266-267 (21 Mar 2017). See also Stojić's Appeal Brief, para. 16.

[2166]   Stojić's Appeal Brief, paras 11, 15, referring to Trial Judgement, Vol. 4, paras 9, 14.

[2167]   Stojić's Appeal Brief, para. 11; Appeal Hearing, AT. 260-261 (21 Mar 2017), referring to, *inter alia*, Exs. P00080, P00167, P00336, P04740, P07198, P00822, P00498, P00882, P00866, P01544, P01883, P02302, P03704, P03517.

[2168]   Stojić's Appeal Brief, para. 12; Appeal Hearing, AT. 262-263, 301 (21 Mar 2017). In particular, Stojić refers to portions from the Presidential Transcripts reflecting that Tuđman: (1) insisted on co-operation with Bosnian Muslims; (2) criticised HVO leaders for fighting with Muslims; (3) reproached Boban for his remark that he did not believe in joint politics with Muslims; (4) "was concerned about what outcome would be acceptable to Europe and the world"; and (5) supported solutions "within the international order", fearing international sanctions. Stojić's Appeal Brief, para. 12, referring to Exs. P01297, P01883, P07198, P07480, P07485, P03112, P06930, P00108, P02122, P02466, Judge Antonetti Dissent, p. 51. According to Stojić, these statements were also consistent with Croatia's actions, including its invitation of international observers to its borders. Stojić's Appeal Brief, para. 12, referring to Exs. P00324, P03467, P02613.

[2169]   Stojić's Appeal Brief, para. 13, referring to Exs. 3D03720, P09276, P01391, P01038, Trial Judgement, Vol. 1, paras 438, 444, 451, 462, 482 (concerning the Cutileiro Plan, the Vance-Owen Peace Plan, and the Owen-Stoltenberg Peace Plan).

[2170]   Stojić's Appeal Brief, para. 14, referring to Witness 4D-AB, T. 47098 (23 Nov 2009).

[2171]   Stojić's Appeal Brief, para. 14, referring to Josip Manolić, T. 4282-4283 (3 July 2006).

[2172]   Stojić's Appeal Brief, para. 15, referring to Trial Judgement, Vol. 4, paras 14-15.

[2173]   Prosecution's Response Brief (Stojić), paras 10-13; Appeal Hearing, AT. 348-349 (21 Mar 2017). See also Prosecution's Response Brief (Stojić), para. 9.

[2174]   Prosecution's Response Brief (Stojić), para. 15.

[2175]   Prosecution's Response Brief (Stojić), para. 14.

[2176]   Prosecution's Response Brief (Stojić), para. 15, referring to Ex. P05237.

[2177]   Stojić's Reply Brief, para. 5, referring to Ex. P01544.

[2178]   Stojić's Reply Brief, para. 5, referring to Exs. P00822, P00866. Stojić also points to evidence showing that Tuđman encouraged co-operation and criticised the crimes committed by the HVO. Stojić's Reply Brief, para. 6, referring to Exs. P06581, P01798. See also Appeal Hearing, AT. 263-264 (21 Mar 2017).

on co-operation with Bosnian Muslims and on international opinion, the **[page 287]** Appeals Chamber notes that a review of the relevant findings shows that the Trial Chamber expressly considered most of the evidence Stojić references in its analysis concerning the Ultimate Purpose of the JCE, including in its conclusion concerning Tuđman's double policy, according to which Tuđman publicly supported BiH's existing borders, while privately advocating for its division.[2179] The Appeals Chamber therefore finds that Stojić does not show that the Trial Chamber disregarded the evidence. As regards the remaining evidence Stojić relies on,[2180] the Appeals Chamber observes that it is similar to the evidence expressly relied on by the Trial Chamber in finding that Tuđman adopted a double policy.[2181] Accordingly, the Appeals Chamber is not persuaded that the Trial Chamber disregarded this evidence, but rather that the Trial Chamber assessed it and concluded that it did not prevent it from reaching its conclusion. Stojić's arguments are therefore dismissed.

682. With respect to Stojić's contention that the Trial Chamber disregarded evidence showing that Croatia agreed to a succession of peace plans, the Appeals Chamber notes that he supports his contention by pointing to evidence which was expressly considered in relation to the international peace plans and negotiations,[2182] or by referring to the Trial Chamber's findings without explaining how these findings support his argument that it disregarded relevant evidence.[2183] Accordingly, the Appeals Chamber finds that Stojić fails to show an error in the Trial Chamber's conclusion.

683. With respect to the statements of Tuđman reflected in Exhibits P01544, P00866, and P00822, referred to by Stojić in his reply, the Appeals Chamber notes that the respective portions of Exhibits P01544 and P00866 were expressly considered by the Trial Chamber in its conclusions that Tuđman spoke equivocally when advocating for the existence and the legitimacy of the BiH.[2184] A careful review of Exhibits P01544 and P00866 suggests that, rather than advocating for the independence of BiH during these Presidential Meetings, Tuđman was simply describing his public position in this regard,[2185] or showing his doubts about the possibility of BiH remaining **[page 288]** united,[2186] Against this background, the Appeals Chamber finds that Stojić merely attempts to give a different interpretation of the evidence without articulating an error warranting appellate intervention. As to Stojić's reference to Exhibit P00822, the relevant portion of the evidence does not clearly indicate the extent to which Tuđman advocated for the independence of BiH.[2187] In any event, the Appeals Chamber finds that Stojić fails to show how this piece of evidence could impair the

---

[2179] See Trial Judgement, Vol. 4, paras 12 (referring to Exs. P03517, P00108), 15 (referring to Exs. P00167, P00036, P00498, P00866), 17 (referring to Exs. P00336, P01544, P02302, P00167), 22 (referring to Exs. P04740, P07485, P02466).

[2180] See Stojić's Appeal Brief, paras 11 (referring to Exs. P00080, P07198, P00882, P01883, P03704), 12 (referring to Exs. P01297, P01883, P07198, P07480, P03112, P06930, P02122).

[2181] See Exs. P00080, P07198, P00822, P01883, P03704, P01297, P07480, P03112, P06930, P02122. Specifically, the Appeals Chamber reiterates that the Trial Chamber noted evidence concerning Tuđman's efforts to co-operate with BiH in concluding that it reflected his double policy. See *supra*, para. 624.

[2182] See Trial Judgement, Vol. 1, paras 445-446, 451, 455 (referring to Ex. P01038), 461-462 (referring to Ex. P01391); Vol. 4, paras 14 (referring to Ex. P09276), 681 (referring to Ex. 3D03720).

[2183] See Stojić's Appeal Brief, para. 13, referring to Trial Judgement, Vol. 1, paras 438, 444, 451, 462, 482.

[2184] See Trial Judgement, Vol. 4, paras 15 (referring to Ex. P00866), 17 (referring to Ex. P01544).

[2185] See Ex. P01544, pp. 23-24 ("Gentlemen, due to both our interest in a definitive solution and international relations, because in this Croatia is in a very delicate position in relation to Europe, America and the Islamic world, because they were actually looking for a possibility to put pressure on Croatia as it apparently has no correct attitude, it apparently made [an] agreement to divide Bosnia etc. So, we must persevere in our stand that Bosnia and Herzegovina is to remain independent, but only as a union of the three constituent peoples [...]. There is something, the Bosnian Muslims are striving and partly succeeding in convincing the world that they are not fundamentalists. Fundamentalists in the Shia sense, as West looks on Iranian fundamentalists. But, gentlemen, OZAL was greeted outside the mosque Bosnia, Allah. So they are not fundamentalists in the Shia sense, but in practice they want to dominate anyway and this is manifested in reality in all areas and it is in this context that we must explain to the world what this is about").

[2186] See Ex. P00866, pp. 9-10 ("But, looking at the whole, we can say that even in this – in this sense of state, politics and strategy -we won the battle to prevent Bosnia and Herzegovina be included in a greater Serbia. And today it can be discussed that Bosnia and Herzegovina survives as/sic/, if it survives as a confederate community of three nations. So, that Croat people in Bosnia and Herzegovina have full independence in the area – to say it in this way, the Herzeg-Bosnia community, and even the international recognition, that we have the right to that part of Bosanska Posavina that was predominately inhabited by Croat population. And, between us – but please do not say it in the street -whether this is the thing that Bosnia and Herzegovina can really survive only as such confederate community, /sic/ But, to you people of responsibility in the Croatian Army, I have to make it known to you that many international signs indicate that those most responsible European and American factors alike are asking themselves about the possibility and expedience of the survival of Bosnia and Herzegovina").

[2187] Ex. P00822, p. 52.

Trial Chamber's assessment of various pieces of evidence in support of its conclusion that Tuđman adopted a double policy with respect to the integrity and independence of BiH.[2188] Accordingly, this argument is dismissed.

684. Further, considering that the Trial Chamber took into account the overwhelming evidence reflecting Tuđman's concerns for the Banovina, the Appeals Chamber sees no error in the Trial Chamber's decision not to address Witness 4D-AB's testimony that there was no Croatian policy in the area.[2189] Turning to Stojić's claim that the Trial Chamber disregarded the evidence from Manolić that Tuđman was "not enthusiastic" about reconstituting the Banovina, the Appeals Chamber considers that Stojić mischaracterises Manolić's testimony. A review of the portion of the evidence referred to by Stojić shows that Manolić testified that Tuđman was "not enthusiastic" about the situation of the borders of Istria and Baranja, rather than about the reconstitution of the Banovina.[2190] Accordingly, the Appeals Chamber finds that Stojić fails to show any error in the Trial Chamber's impugned conclusion vis-à-vis Tuđman's intentions. **[page 289]**

685. Finally, the Appeals Chamber rejects Stojić's argument that the Trial Chamber made contradictory findings in assessing Tuđman's intentions vis-à-vis his support for the creation of HZ H-B. Specifically, the Appeals Chamber is not persuaded that the intention to protect the Croatian border would negate the aim to expand it. The Appeals Chamber further observes that the Trial Chamber's conclusions in this regard are consistent with its earlier findings that "Tuđman advocated dividing BiH between Croatia and Serbia, incorporating part of BiH into Croatia, or at least, the existence of an autonomous Croatian territory within the BiH that would enjoy close ties with Croatia".[2191] Accordingly, this argument is dismissed.

686. In light of the foregoing, the Appeals Chamber finds that Stojić has failed to show that the Trial Chamber erred in its relevant findings concerning Tuđman's intentions. Accordingly, the Appeals Chamber dismisses the relevant part of Stojić's ground of appeal 1.

(iii) Pušić's appeal (Ground 3 in part)

a. Arguments of the Parties

687. Pušić submits that the Trial Chamber erred in reaching its conclusion concerning Tuđman's intentions, by failing to apply the beyond reasonable doubt standard of proof and ignoring other reasonable inferences available from the evidence.[2192] In particular, relying extensively on the Judge Antonetti Dissent, Pušić contends that the evidence on the trial record does not support: (1) the Trial Chamber's findings concerning Tuđman's intentions to divide BiH or to intervene in BiH with the aim to create a Greater Croatia;[2193] (2) the Trial Chamber's "assumption" that Tuđman controlled, the HZ(R) H-B's military activities due to "a joint

---

[2188] Trial Judgement, Vol. 4, paras 12, 15, 17.

[2189] See also Trial Judgement, Vol. 4, paras 9-12, 14-15, 17-18, 22-23.

[2190] Josip Manolić, T. 4282-4283 (3 July 2006) ("Q. Sir, can you tell us when President Tudjman came back from [Karađorđevo], did he have a view that by his agreement with Milošević the Banovina borders could be recreated in Bosnia? A. No, because President Tudjman was not very enthusiastic about those borders since a new situation had arisen. Within the Croatian Banovina, there was no Istria or Baranja at the time, and those were areas that the Croatian state wanted preserved. They didn't want these borders changed in that area. So President Tudjman did not insist on the Banovina borders of Croatia. [...] This new situation was that the borders of the Banovina of Croatia were unrealistic in the newly arisen situation where Croatia had acquired Istria after World War II and Baranja also became part of the Socialist Republic of Yugoslavia. This was too important. The historical Banovina could not be justified because of this").

[2191] See Trial Judgement, Vol. 4, para. 10. See also Trial Judgement, Vol. 4, paras 16, 24.

[2192] Pušić's Appeal Brief, paras 84-97. See also Pušić's Reply Brief, para. 23; Appeal Hearing, AT. 675, 678, 680 (27 Mar 2017).

[2193] Pušić's Appeal Brief, paras 86-91, 97(a)-(b), 98; Appeal Hearing, AT. 678 (27 Mar 2017). Specifically, Pušić argues that the Presidential Transcripts as well as other evidence on the record show that Tuđman: (1) frequently changed his position making it difficult to ascertain "his true motives"; (2) often emphasised his preference to cooperate with the international community and Muslims to find a solution to the conflict and to reach an agreeable settlement; (3) supported the idea of the Banovina only as a measure of last resort in response to Serb aggression; and (4) supported the independence of BiH and the inviolability of the BiH borders. Pušić's Appeal Brief, paras 88, 90, 91, 97(a)-(b).

command structure";[2194] and (3) the Trial Chamber's finding of Tuđman's "two-track policy".[2195] According to Pušić, another **[page 290]** reasonable inference based on the evidence is that Tuđman "harboured a desire for a Greater Croatia which he did not want to see implemented through criminal means" as this would have put Croatia's relationship with the international community at risk.[2196]

688.   Additionally, Pušić submits that in no other case concerning Croats in BiH has the Tribunal ever made findings "confirming the existence" of the Ultimate Purpose of the JCE, and that the *Gotovina et al.* Trial Judgement did not infer the existence of a JCE from Tuđman's speeches.[2197]

689.   The Prosecution responds that Pušić fails to show that no reasonable trier of fact could have reached the conclusion on the Ultimate Purpose of the JCE.[2198] The Prosecution specifically submits that the mere existence of a dissent does not render the majority's conclusion unreasonable and that a trial chamber is not obliged to discuss other inferences it considered as long as it was satisfied that the one it retained was the only one reasonable.[2199] The Prosecution also contends that ample evidence from the record supports the Trial Chamber's reasoning as to Tuđman's preoccupation with the Banovina and his desire to ensure that this territory be dominated by Croats.[2200]

b. Analysis

690.   With respect to Pušić's contentions that the evidence does not prove Tuđman's intentions to divide BiH, the Appeals Chamber observes that Pušić bases his arguments almost entirely on the Judge Antonetti Dissent.[2201] In this regard, the Appeals Chamber reiterates that the mere existence of a dissent does not render the majority's conclusion unreasonable.[2202] Accordingly, Pušić fails to **[page 291]** show any error in the Trial Chamber's assessment of the evidence. The Appeals Chamber dismisses these contentions.

691.   Turning to Pušić's contention that the evidence does not support the Trial Chamber's conclusion on the Ultimate Purpose of the JCE as it is based on the assumption that the existence of a joint command structure allowed Tuđman to control the HZ(R) H-B's military activities, the Appeals Chamber observes that in no part of the analysis concerning the Ultimate Purpose of the JCE did the Trial Chamber make such

---

[2194]   Pušić's Appeal Brief, paras 92-94; Appeal Hearing, AT. 676-679 (27 Mar 2017). Pušić argues that the Presidential Transcripts show that Tuđman: (1) only authorised the deployment of volunteers and "certain individual officers" to the HZ(R) H-B with some logistical support; and (2) denied that the HVO forces were present in BiH and did not have full knowledge of the extent of military operations. Pušić's Appeal Brief, para. 92, referring to, *inter alia,* Judge Antonetti Dissent, pp. 38-39. Pušić also highlights that there were "significant divisions of opinion" between Tuđman and the HZ(R) H-B leaders. Pušić's Appeal Brief, paras 93-94, referring to Judge Antonetti Dissent, pp. 45, 49, 376, 381, 385, 393.

[2195]   Pušić's Appeal Brief, para. 98. Pušić argues that: (1) the Prosecution's theory on Tuđman's double policy "presupposes that Tuđman was playing a highly dangerous and risky double game [...] in his communications with international negotiators" at a time when Croatia's position, as an emerging nation state, was not secured; and (2) Tuđman repeated the statements made to international representatives, and relied upon by the Trial Chamber in its conclusion of his double policy, to his closest allies as well. Pušić's Appeal Brief, para. 98, referring to Judge Antonetti Dissent, pp. 374-375, 384, 392.

[2196]   Pušić's Appeal Brief, para. 97(c), referring to Judge Antonetti Dissent, pp. 32, 385, 391. In support of his contention, Pušić argues that Tuđman could not take action to implement his aspirations for a Greater Croatia at the time because: (1) Tuđman was not elected on a "Greater Croatia platform"; (2) as Croatia was newly constituted and facing Serb aggression, Tuđman did not have the internal or international support to realise his vision; (3) the idea of "a Greater Croatian Republic project" was in contradiction to Tuđman's effort to assert Croatia's identity and security; (4) by promoting the "Greater Croatia idea" Tuđman "would *ipso facto* have to accept the Serbs['] vision of a Greater Serbia"; and (5) Croatia was not able to bear the economic burden of absorbing the population from a Croat dominated territory in BiH. Pušić's Appeal Brief, para. 97(d)(i)-(v), referring to Judge Antonetti Dissent, pp. 385, 393, 417-418.

[2197]   Pušić's Appeal Brief, paras 95-96, referring to Judge Antonetti Dissent, pp. 146, 369, 373, 377.

[2198]   Prosecution's Response Brief (Pušić), paras 72, 74-76.

[2199]   Prosecution's Response Brief (Pušić), para. 73.

[2200]   Prosecution's Response Brief (Pušić), paras 74-76. See also Prosecution's Response Brief (Pušić), paras 62-64, 66-67; Appeal Hearing, AT. 709 (27 Mar 2017).

[2201]   The Appeals Chamber observes that a close reading of Pušić's arguments shows that they are predicated on, and closely mirror, the Judge Antonetti Dissent which elaborates on and interprets evidence concerning Tuđman's intentions. Compare Pušić's Appeal Brief, paras 86-91, 97(a)-(b), 98 & fns 142-147, 162-164 with Judge Antonetti Dissent, *inter alia,* pp. 9-10, 21-25, 32-33, 50, 375-376, 383-389, 417-418. The Appeals Chamber further observes that in support of his allegations, Pušić also relies upon the Presidential Transcripts and Witness AR's evidence. Pušić's Appeal Brief, paras 90-91. The Appeals Chamber finds that Pušić simply refers to the evidence without showing that the Trial Chamber was unreasonable in reaching its conclusion.

[2202]   See *supra,* para. 670.

a finding.[2203] The Appeals Chamber also observes that in support of his contention, Pušić refers to the Trial Chamber's analysis concerning the international character of the conflict without explaining how the findings therein are relevant to the Trial Chamber's conclusion on the Ultimate Purpose of the JCE.[2204] Accordingly, Pušić's argument is dismissed.

692.   The Appeals Chamber further rejects Pušić's challenge concerning Tuđman's double policy. The Appeals Chamber observes that in support of his submission, Pušić advances unsupported and speculative assertions,[2205] and relies entirely on the Judge Antonetti Dissent without showing that no reasonable trier of fact could have reached this conclusion.[2206] Finally, the Appeals Chamber sees no merit in Pušić's comparison between this case and a trial judgement assessing the evidence in another case. The Appeals Chamber recalls in this regard that an error cannot be established by merely pointing to the fact that another trial chamber has reached a different conclusion.[2207] Pušić's argument is dismissed.

693.   The Appeals Chamber finds that Pušić has failed to show that the Trial Chamber erred in its relevant findings concerning Tuđman's intentions and therefore dismisses the relevant part of Pušić's ground of appeal 3.

3.   Alleged errors in finding that the HZ(R) H-B leaders were involved in meetings and discussions concerning the partition of BiH

694.   The Trial Chamber found that on 6 May 1992, representatives of the Croatian community of BiH, including Boban, met with representatives of the Serbian community of BiH, including Karadžić, to discuss the division of BiH in accordance with the demarcation of the Croatian **[page 292]** Banovina at Graz in Austria ("6 May 1992 Graz Meeting").[2208] It further concluded that on 5 and 26 October 1992, Prlić, Stojić, Praljak, and Petković, as part of a delegation from Croatia and the HZ H-B, met with Ratko Mladić to discuss the partition of BiH ("5 October 1992 Meeting", "26 October 1992 Meeting", and collectively, "5 and 26 October 1992 Meetings").[2209] According to the Trial Chamber, Praljak stated during these meetings that "[t]he goal is Banovina or nothing" and that "it is in our interest that the Muslims get their own canton so they have somewhere to move to".[2210] The Trial Chamber also noted the testimony of Raymond Lane that during an interview with Prlić, Prlić drew a circle dividing BiH in two parts with the Serbs on one side and the Croats on the other, without any mention of the Muslims.[2211]

(a) Prlić's appeal (Sub-grounds 9.4, 9.7, and 9.8)

695.   Prlić submits that the Trial Chamber erred in concluding that the 6 May 1992 Graz Meeting was connected to the plan to divide BiH so as to expand Croatia along the borders of the Banovina, by: (1) ignoring Witness Franjo Boras's testimony about internal administrative arrangements, rather than the division of BiH;[2212] and (2) mischaracterising the testimony of Witness Zdravko Sančević as he did not testify about the meeting.[2213] He also argues that the Trial Chamber erred in finding that he met with Mladić to discuss the partition of BiH during the 5 and 26 October 1992 Meetings.[2214] Prlić further submits that the

---

[2203]   Trial Judgement, Vol. 4, paras 9-24.
[2204]   Trial Judgement, Vol. 3, paras 526-528.
[2205]   Pušić's Appeal Brief, para. 98 (claiming that the Prosecution's theory on Tuđman's double policy "presupposes that Tuđman was playing a highly dangerous and risky double game (considering the public and the media scrutiny he was under) in his communications with international negotiators").
[2206]   Pušić's Appeal Brief, para. 98, referring to Judge Antonetti Dissent, pp. 374-375, 384, 392.
[2207]   See *Stanišić and Župljanin* Appeal Judgement, para. 652; *Đorđević* Appeal Judgement, para. 257; *Krnojelac* Appeal Judgement, para. 12.
[2208]   Trial Judgement, Vol. 4, para. 13.
[2209]   Trial Judgement, Vol. 4, para. 18.
[2210]   Trial Judgement, Vol. 4, para. 18.
[2211]   Trial Judgement, Vol. 4, para. 19.
[2212]   Prlić's Appeal Brief, paras 252-254.
[2213]   Prlić's Appeal Brief, paras 252-254, referring to Zdranko Sančević, T. 28744-28746 (28 May 2008). The Appeals Chamber notes that Prlić also refers to his sub-ground of appeal 1.1. Prlić's Appeal Brief, para. 253.
[2214]   Prlić's Appeal Brief, paras 269-270, referring to Prlić's ground of appeal 5.

Trial Chamber erred in law and fact when it concluded that during an interview with Lane, Prlić drew a circle dividing BiH between Serbs and Croats, without any evidence corroborating Lane's testimony.[2215]

696.   The Prosecution responds that the Trial Chamber reasonably relied on Boras's evidence with respect to its findings on the 6 May 1992 Graz Meeting.[2216] It also contends that Prlić fails to articulate any error in the Trial Chamber's finding that Prlić and other BiH Croat leaders met with Mladić to discuss the partition during the 5 and 26 October 1992 Meetings.[2217] Similarly, the Prosecution argues that Prlić's contention that the Trial Chamber erred in relying on the uncorroborated evidence of Lane is unsubstantiated and should be dismissed.[2218] **[page 293]**

697.   The Appeals Chamber notes that while Prlić argues that the Trial Chamber ignored Boras's evidence that the 6 May 1992 Graz Meeting was to address internal administrative arrangements, the portion of Boras's evidence Prlić refers to does not support this assertion.[2219] The Appeals Chamber further considers that Prlić has failed to substantiate his claim that the Trial Chamber mischaracterised Sančević's evidence as it is clear from the Trial Judgement that the Trial Chamber only referenced Sančević's evidence when explaining the historical and geographic background of the "Croatian Banovina".[2220] Prlić's arguments are therefore dismissed.

698.   With regard to Prlić's argument that the Trial Chamber erred in finding that he met with Mladić to discuss the partition of BiH during the 5 and 26 October 1992 Meetings, the Appeals Chamber notes that Prlić bases his argument entirely on a cross-reference to his ground of appeal 5, which the Appeals Chamber dismisses elsewhere.[2221] As regards Prlić's contention in relation to the Trial Chamber's reliance on Lane's uncorroborated evidence, the Appeals Chamber observes that during the examination by the Prosecution, Lane stated that Prlić drew a circle representing BiH divided between Croats and Serbs without any reference to Muslims.[2222] Recalling that nothing prohibits a Trial Chamber from relying on uncorroborated but otherwise credible evidence,[2223] the Appeals Chamber finds that Prlić fails to show that the Trial Chamber erred in reaching the challenged finding.[2224] His arguments are thus dismissed.

699.   In light of the above, the Appeals Chamber finds that Prlić has failed to demonstrate that the Trial Chamber erred in its findings on the 6 May 1992 Graz Meeting as well as the 5 and 26 October 1992 Meetings. The Appeals Chamber dismisses Prlić's sub-grounds of appeal 9.4, 9.7, and 9.8.

(b) Stojić's appeal (Ground 1 in part)

(i) Arguments of the Parties

700.   Relying on Boras's evidence, Stojić submits that the Trial Chamber erred by misinterpreting the 6 May 1992 Graz Meeting and failing to take into account evidence that this meeting was part **[page 294]** of the framework of the Cutileiro Plan and that there were similar negotiations underway between Bosnian Croats and Muslims.[2225] Stojić also argues that the Trial Chamber failed to consider its previous finding that

---

[2215]   Prlić's Appeal Brief, paras 271-272, referring to Prlić's Appeal Brief, paras 202-203 (sub-ground of appeal 6.2).

[2216]   Prosecution's Response Brief (Prlić), para. 153.

[2217]   Prosecution's Response Brief (Prlić), para. 154; Appeal Hearing, AT. 201-203 (20 Mar 2017).

[2218]   Prosecution's Response Brief (Prlić), para. 150.

[2219]   See Prlić's Appeal Brief, paras 252-254, referring to Franjo Boras, T. 29248 (9 June 2008). The Appeals Chamber observes that the transcript page number he cites reflects discussions on procedural matters.

[2220]   Trial Judgement, Vol. 4, para. 13 & fn. 26, referring to, *inter alia*, Zdravko Sančević, T(F). 28745 (28 May 2008).

[2221]   See *supra*, paras 136, 138.

[2222]   Raymond Lane, T. 23711-23712 (15 Oct 2007), T. 23749-23750 (16 Oct 2007). See also Raymond Lane, T. 23757-23760 (16 Oct 2007), T. 23955-23956 (17 Oct 2007); Ex. P10319, para. 47.

[2223]   See, *e.g., Popović et al.* Appeal Judgement, paras 243, 1264; *D. Milošević* Appeal Judgement, para. 215. See also *Kordić and Čerkez* Appeal Judgement, para. 274.

[2224]   The Appeals Chamber further notes that when challenging the Trial Chamber's finding based on Lane's evidence, Prlić cross-references another ground of appeal, in which he challenges the Trial Chamber's failure to consider the reliability of Lane's evidence. The Appeals Chamber dismisses this specific challenge elsewhere. See *supra*, paras 217-218.

[2225]   Stojić's Appeal Brief, para. 20, referring to Franjo Boras, T. 28952-28953 (2 June 2008).

the meeting ended without any agreement.[2226] He further contends that no evidence on the record supports the Trial Chamber's finding that the purpose of the 5 and 26 October 1992 Meetings was to discuss the division of BiH.[2227] Stojić argues that the meetings were "hardly cooperative", no agreement was reached, and the only outcome they reached was a release of prisoners.[2228] Stojić concludes that no reasonable trier of fact could have relied on these meetings as evidence of the Ultimate Purpose of the JCE.[2229]

701.   The Prosecution responds that the Trial Chamber correctly found that the JCE members' efforts to negotiate the division of BiH with the Serbs proved the Ultimate Purpose of the JCE and that this finding is supported by ample evidence.[2230] With respect to the 6 May 1992 Graz Meeting, the Prosecution contends that the Trial Chamber did not misconstrue this meeting and that it is immaterial whether the meeting was part of the framework of the Cutileiro Plan or was unsuccessful.[2231] As to Stojić's argument that similar negotiations were also underway between the Bosnian Croats and Bosnian Muslims, the Prosecution argues that they were not "equivalent" to the meetings between Croats and Serbs and that in any event, this contention is immaterial with respect to the Trial Chamber's conclusion on the Ultimate Purpose of the JCE.[2232] As to the 5 and 26 October 1992 Meetings, the Prosecution avers that, contrary to Stojić's submission, evidence confirms that these meetings took place to discuss the partition of BiH.[2233]

(ii) Analysis

702.   With respect to Stojić's contention that the Trial Chamber disregarded Boras's evidence that the 6 May 1992 Graz Meeting occurred in the framework of the Cutileiro Plan, the Appeals Chamber considers that Stojić fails to show why this evidence is relevant to the Trial Chamber's finding that during the meeting, representatives of the Croatian community of BiH discussed the division of BiH with representatives of the Serbian community of BiH. Further, the facts that similar negotiations were -underway between Bosnian Croats and Muslims and that the **[page 295]** 6 May 1992 Graz Meeting ended without signing any agreement do not call into question the Trial Chamber's finding.[2234] Stojić's arguments are thus dismissed.

703.   With respect to Stojić's challenge to the Trial Chamber's conclusion on the objectives of the 5 and 26 October 1992 Meetings, the Appeals Chamber observes that the Trial Chamber based its finding on portions of the Mladić Diaries – Exhibits P11376 and P113 80.[2235] The Trial Chamber found that Praljak stated at the 5 October 1992 Meeting that "[t]he goal is Banovina or nothing"[2236] and at the 26 October 1992 Meeting that "it is in our interest that the Muslims get their own canton so they have somewhere to move to".[2237] As such, the Appeals Chamber finds no merit in Stojić's assertion that there is no evidence supporting the Trial Chamber's conclusion. The Appeals Chamber further considers that it is immaterial to the Trial Chamber's Ultimate Purpose finding that the meetings were hostile and that no agreement was reached, Stojić's arguments therefore fail.

704.   In light of the above, the Appeals Chamber finds that Stojić has failed to demonstrate that the Trial Chamber erred in its findings concerning the 6 May 1992 Graz Meeting, as well as the 5 and 26 October 1992

[2226]   Stojić's Appeal Brief, para. 20, referring to Trial Judgement, Vol. 1, para. 439. See also Stojić's Appeal Brief, para. 22.
[2227]   Stojić's Appeal Brief, para. 21, referring to, *inter alia,* Trial Judgement, Vol. 4, para. 18, Exs. P11380, P11376. Stojić also refers to paragraph 130 of his appeal brief, which is related to his ground of appeal 16.
[2228]   Stojić's Appeal Brief, para. 21.
[2229]   Stojić's Appeal Brief, para. 19. See also Stojić's Appeal Brief, para. 22; Stojić's Reply Brief, para. 7.
[2230]   Prosecution's Response Brief (Stojić), para. 17.
[2231]   Prosecution's Response Brief (Stojić), para. 17. The Prosecution also refers to evidence on the record showing that between 1991 and 1992, discussions about the partition of BiH were ongoing between Bosnian Serbs and Bosnian Croats. See Prosecution's Response Brief (Stojić), para. 17, referring to Exs. P00089, P00108, P00185.
[2232]   Prosecution's Response Brief (Stojić), para. 17.
[2233]   Prosecution's Response Brief (Stojić), para. 17, referring to Exs. P11376, P11380.
[2234]   Trial Judgement, Vol. 1, para. 439.
[2235]   Trial Judgement, Vol. 4, para. 18, referring to Exs. P11376, p. 1, P11380, pp. 1-2. With regard to Stojić's specific challenge to these exhibits, see *supra,* paras 112, 114.
[2236]   Trial Judgement, Vol. 4, para. 18, referring to Ex. P11376, p. 1. The Appeals Chamber notes that Praljak's statement appears on page 2 of Exhibit P11376, not on page 1.
[2237]   Trial Judgement, Vol. 4, para. 18, referring to Ex. P11380, p. 3.

Meetings, and its assessment of the Mladić Diaries in relation to the latter meetings. Accordingly, the Appeals Chamber dismisses Stojić's ground of appeal 1 in relevant part.

(c) Praljak's appeal (Sub-grounds 6.1 in part and 6.4)

(i) Arguments of the Parties

705. Praljak submits that the Trial Chamber erred in finding that during the 6 May 1992 Graz Meeting, representatives of the Croatian community of BiH and their Serbian counterparts discussed the division of BiH. He argues that the Trial Chamber: (1) accorded improper weight to "hear-say evidence and media reports"; and (2) misconstrued and discarded direct evidence.[2238] Specifically regarding the first aspect of his challenge, Praljak contends that the joint statement issued by Boban and Karadžić following the meeting ("Joint Statement") does not support the Trial Chamber's findings.[2239] He also argues that the Trial Chamber erred in relying on: (1) Witness Robert Donia's testimony and his expert report, arguing that they are merely based on public **[page 296]** information;[2240] and (2) Okun's testimony, as it is based on media reports and, as acknowledged by him, he does not have direct knowledge of the 6 May 1992 Graz Meeting.[2241] As to the second aspect of his challenge, Praljak submits that, *inter alia,* the Trial Chamber failed to consider that: (1) Izetbegović suspended international negotiations after the Serbs had accepted the principles of further organisation of BiH and that the EC then suggested bilateral meetings;[2242] (2) bilateral meetings with Muslims were held at the same time;[2243] (3) there were frequent bilateral negotiations and agreements throughout the war with the international community's active involvement;[2244] and (4) the 6 May 1992 Graz Meeting was held as part of a series of meetings encouraged by the international community.[2245]

706. Praljak contends that the 5 and 26 October 1992 Meetings were not about dividing BiH, but about finding a solution to end the war or at least minimise "its disastrous consequences".[2246] Praljak further submits that the Trial Chamber erred in inferring the existence of the JCE based on events that occurred before the creation of the JCE, arguing that the Trial Chamber refers to the political meetings and negotiations in 1991 and 1992, where some of the Appellants and Croatian officials met "in [a] political environment drastically different [from] the situation in which the JCE would be created".[2247] He claims that the Trial Chamber: (1) relied on meetings and negotiations when BiH was not an independent State to demonstrate the Croatian position and intention; and (2) "presented only one side of these negotiations leaving completely aside Muslim positions and neglecting the international proposals in the frame of which Croatian officials and BiH Croats expressed their positions".[2248]

707. The Prosecution contends that the evidence shows that Praljak and other JCE members met with Mladić during the 5 and 26 October 1992 Meetings to discuss the division of BiH.[2249] It also **[page 297]**

[2238] Praljak's Appeal Brief, paras 101-106, referring to Trial Judgement, Vol. 1, para. 439, Vol. 4, para. 13.

[2239] Praljak's Appeal Brief, paras 102-103, referring to Exs. P00187, 1D00428. See also Praljak's Appeal Brief, para. 101.

[2240] Praljak's Appeal Brief, para. 104, referring to, *inter alia,* Exs. P09536, pp. 39-40, 52, 71, P00192, p. 3, Robert Donia, T. 1832 (10 May 2006).

[2241] Praljak's Appeal Brief, para. 105, referring to Herbert Okun, T. 16662-16663 (2 Apr 2007), T. 16831 (3 Apr 2007).

[2242] Praljak's Appeal Brief, para. 101, referring to Ex. P09526.

[2243] Praljak's Appeal Brief, para. 101, referring to Exs. P09526, 1D02739, Franjo Boras, T. 29149-29152 (4 June 2008).

[2244] Praljak's Appeal Brief, para. 101, referring to Exs. 1D00475, P00339, 2D00798, 1D01543, P00717, 1D02853, P01988, P02259, P02344, P02564 (confidential), 1D02404, P02726, 4D01234. Praljak also argues that the Trial Chamber's conclusion that during the period of tri-partite negotiations, the HVO negotiated with the Serbs over the partition of BiH suggests that "the HVO negotiations with Serbs were conducted secretly in parallel with tri-partite negotiations." Praljak's Appeal Brief, para. 101 referring to Trial Judgement, Vol. 1, para. 439.

[2245] Praljak's Appeal Brief, para. 101, referring to, *inter alia,* Franjo Boras, T. 28954 (2 June 2008).

[2246] Praljak's Appeal Brief, para. 114, referring to Ex. P00498, pp. 73, 76. Praljak also argues that the Trial Chamber drew an erroneous conclusion from documents which should not have been admitted and are unreliable, cross-referencing his ground of appeal 50.

[2247] Praljak's Appeal Brief, para. 125, referring to Trial Judgement, Vol. 4, paras 11, 13-15, 17-18, 43. See also Praljak's Appeal Brief, para. 126.

[2248] Praljak's Appeal Brief, para. 126, referring to Ex. 1D00896, p. 3.

[2249] Prosecution's Response Brief (Praljak), para. 39.

responds that the Trial Chamber correctly exercised its discretion in relying on "pre-JCE events" to infer the existence of the JCE, including the 6 May 1992 Graz Meeting.[2250]

(ii) Analysis

708. The Appeals Chamber observes that when examining evidence related to events following the creation of Herceg-Bosna, the Trial Chamber detailed the 6 May 1992 Graz Meeting.[2251] The Trial Chamber found that the meeting was held in the absence of Muslim representatives to discuss BiH's future. Following the meeting, Boban and Karadžić issued the Joint Statement which they described "as a 'peace agreement', which provided for the territorial division of BiH based on the 1939 borders of Croatian Banovina and called for a general cease-fire".[2252] The Trial Chamber also concluded that: (1) the proposed division did not include certain regions over which the parties wanted the EU to arbitrate their respective claims; and (2) ultimately the parties did not sign an agreement.[2253] In so finding, the Trial Chamber took into account, *inter alia,* the Joint Statement, Donia's expert report and testimony, and Okun's testimony.[2254] Although Praljak points to other parts of the Joint Statement, he fails to demonstrate that no reasonable trier of fact could have relied on this evidence to reach the Trial Chamber's conclusion. The Appeals Chamber also finds no error in the Trial Chamber's reliance on Donia's report and his testimony, as well as Okun's testimony. In this regard, the Appeals Chamber recalls that a trial chamber is best placed to assess the credibility of a witness and reliability of the evidence adduced,[2255] and therefore has broad discretion in assessing the appropriate weight and credibility to be accorded to the testimony of a witness.[2256] Praljak's arguments are thus dismissed.

709. The Appeals Chamber notes that Praljak also alleges that the Trial Chamber disregarded the surrounding contextual circumstances, including Izetbegović's suspension of international negotiations, ongoing bilateral meetings with Muslims, as well as frequent bilateral agreements and negotiations, including the 6 May 1992 Graz Meeting as being one of a series of meetings encouraged by the international community.[2257] However, Praljak fails to show how these factors and the evidence he cites demonstrate that the Trial Chamber erred in finding that the relevant **[page 298]** representatives held the 6 May 1992 Graz Meeting to discuss the division of BiH along the Banovina borders. His arguments are dismissed.

710. Turning to Praljak's contention that the purpose of the 5 and 26 October 1992 Meetings was not to discuss BiH's partition, but to find a solution to end the war or minimise its results, the Appeals Chamber notes that Praljak points to a portion of the Presidential Transcripts which has no plain and direct bearing on these meetings.[2258] The Appeals Chamber also rejects Praljak's contention that the Trial Chamber drew an erroneous conclusion from unreliable documents which should not have been admitted, as his submission is based entirely on a cross-reference to another ground of appeal, which the Appeals Chamber dismisses elsewhere.[2259] His arguments are thus dismissed.

711. Finally, the Appeals Chamber finds no merit in Praljak's contention that the Trial Chamber erred in inferring the existence of the JCE from events before its creation and considering them out of context.[2260] Specifically, the Appeals Chamber observes that the Trial Chamber relied on events which occurred before the JCE in order to infer the circumstances surrounding the formation of the JCE in January 1993 as well as

---

[2250]   Prosecution's Response Brief (Praljak), para. 39.
[2251]   Trial Judgement, Vol. 1, para. 439.
[2252]   Trial Judgement, Vol. 1, para. 439.
[2253]   Trial Judgement, Vol. 1, para. 439.
[2254]   Trial Judgement, Vol. 1, para. 439, fns 1030-1035, referring to, *inter alia,* Exs. P00187, P00192, P09536, pp. 44-45 (French translation), Robert Donia, T(F). 1833-1835 (10 May 2006), Herbert Okun, T(F). 16663-16664 (2 Apr 2007).
[2255]   See, *e.g., Tadić* Appeal Judgement, para. 64; *Šainović et al.* Appeal Judgement, paras 437, 464, 1296; *Stanišić and Župljanin* Appeal Judgement, para. 99; *Tolimir* Appeal Judgement, para. 469.
[2256]   See, *e.g., Haradinaj et al.* Appeal Judgement, para. 1291; *Stanišić and Župljanin* Appeal Judgement, para. 99; *Tolimir* Appeal Judgement, para. 76.
[2257]   Praljak's Appeal Brief, para. 101.
[2258]   See Praljak's Appeal Brief, para. 114, referring to Ex. P00498, pp. 73, 76.
[2259]   See *supra,* paras 120-121, 129-132, 134-135, 138.
[2260]   The Appeals Chamber notes that Praljak refers to Exhibit 1D00896 without articulating how this document supports his contention. See Praljak's Appeal Brief, para. 126.

its CCP.[2261] Insofar as the Trial Chamber's reliance on this evidence was not used to convict the Appellants for conduct predating his contribution to the JCE, the Appeals Chamber finds no error in such an approach. In any event, the Appeals Chamber has already considered specific arguments relating to "meetings and negotiations" that took place prior to the formation of the JCE and dismissed them elsewhere.[2262] Praljak's argument is therefore dismissed.

712.   In light of the above, the Appeals Chamber finds that Praljak has failed to demonstrate that the Trial Chamber erred in its findings on the meetings held in 1991-1992 generally, and specifically, the 6 May 1992 Graz Meeting, as well as the 5 and 26 October 1992 Meetings. The Appeals Chamber therefore dismisses Praljak's grounds of appeal 6.1 in relevant part and 6.4.

(d) Petković's appeal (Sub-grounds 2.2 and 2.3 in part)

713.   Petković submits that the Trial Chamber erred in finding that he and other HZ H-B leaders met with Mladić at the 5 and 26 October 1992 Meetings to discuss the division of BiH.[2263] Specifically, Petković contends that: (1) he was not present during the 5 October 1992 Meeting; and **[page 299]** (2) the 26 October 1992 Meeting, which he attended, did not address the partition of BiH but the "realization of the previous agreement to calm the front line near Mostar and to re-connect [the] electric power in Jajce".[2264]

714.   The Prosecution responds that the fact that Petković did not attend the meeting on 5 October 1992 is immaterial to the Trial Chamber's finding.[2265] With respect to the meeting of 26 October 1992, the Prosecution avers that Petković's argument focuses on other topics discussed during this meeting, ignoring Praljak's statement of the division of BiH.[2266]

715.   Petković replies that the Prosecution: (1) implicitly acknowledges that he did not participate in the 5 October 1992 Meeting; and (2) misinterprets Praljak's statement about the "Muslim canton" at the meeting of 26 October 1992 as referring to the division of BiH, while "the word 'canton' necessarily implies an *internal organizational unit*" within BiH.[2267]

716.   The Appeals Chamber notes that the Trial Chamber's finding implies that Petković, among others, attended both meetings in October 1992,[2268] although one of the Mladić Diaries does not explicitly indicate that Petković was part of the Croatian delegation at the 5 October 1992 Meeting.[2269] Nevertheless, the Appeals Chamber considers that Petković has failed to demonstrate that the issue of his absence at this meeting has any impact on the Trial Chamber's finding that a delegation from Croatia and the HZ H-B met with Ratko Mladić to discuss the division of BiH. Regarding Petković's challenge to the 26 October 1992 Meeting, the Appeals Chamber observes that the Trial Chamber arrived at the conclusion that the division of BiH was addressed at this meeting by taking into account Praljak's statement that "it is in our interest that the Muslims get their own canton so they have somewhere to move to".[2270] The Appeals Chamber considers that, while one of the Mladić Diaries, which Petković relies on, shows that Praljak also addressed the adherence to the agreement on the front line near Mostar and the electric power near Jajce at this meeting,[2271] this does not affect the Trial Chamber's finding on the purpose of the meeting itself.

717.   Based on the foregoing, the Appeals Chamber finds that Petković has failed to show any error in the Trial Chamber's findings on the 5 and 26 October 1992 Meetings which occasioned a miscarriage of justice. The Appeals Chamber therefore dismisses the relevant part of Petković's sub-grounds of appeal 2.2 and 2.3 in relevant part. **[page 300]**

[2261]   Trial Judgement, Vol. 4, paras 9-24, 41, 43-44.
[2262]   See *supra*, paras 608-643.
[2263]   Petković's Appeal Brief, para. 11. See also Petković's Appeal Brief, para. 14.
[2264]   Petković's Appeal Brief, para. 11, referring to Exs. P11376, P11380, pp. 1-2.
[2265]   Prosecution's Response Brief (Petković), para. 14.
[2266]   Prosecution's Response Brief (Petković), para. 14.
[2267]   Petković's Reply Brief, para. 3 (emphasis in original).
[2268]   Trial Judgement, Vol. 4, para. 18.
[2269]   Ex. P11376, p. 1.
[2270]   Trial Judgement, Vol. 4, para. 18, referring to Ex. P11380, p. 3.
[2271]   Ex. P11380, p. 1.

4. Alleged errors in finding that the creation of the HZ H-B was not merely a temporary defence initiative

718. The Trial Chamber found that, although the HZ H-B was created in response to the "Serb aggression", its establishment "was not merely a temporary defence initiative".[2272] The Trial Chamber noted: (1) Ribičić's evidence that the reference to the right to self-determination in the decision establishing the HZ H-B proved that its establishment was not just an interim defensive measure but was aimed at creating a "mini-State";[2273] and (2) Okun's testimony that the creation of the HZ H-B was designed to facilitate the annexation of the Croat-majority BiH territories to Croatia and not merely to provide self-defence.[2274] Based on the evidence of, *inter alios,* Witnesses Ole Brix-Andersen, Ribičić, Lane, and Suad Ćupina, the Trial Chamber concluded that the "autonomous territorial entity desired by the HZ H-B was to exist either within BiH by forming an alliance with Croatia, or directly as a[n] integral part of Croatia".[2275]

(a) Prlić's appeal (Sub-grounds 9.1 and 9.6)

(i) Arguments of the Parties

719. Prlić submits that the Trial Chamber erred by failing to consider whether there was a legitimate purpose for establishing the HZ(R) H-B,[2276] specifically, that it was needed to "take care of all Croats in BiH"[2277] because they received inadequate protection and governmental services.[2278] Prlić also argues that the Trial Chamber failed to properly assess all relevant evidence.[2279] He contends that the evidence shows that the HZ H-B was always part of BiH as an interim structure, and was established "to fill a vacuum left by the defunct BiH state government".[2280] He asserts that the Trial Chamber disregarded evidence showing that any BiH municipality could join the HZ H-B "debunking the notion that the HZ H-B had defined borders [as] more than 50 municipalities joined" the HZ H-B.[2281] He argues that: (1) as the HZ H-B areas had no boundaries and covered a **[page 301]** large part of BiH, the view that the HZ H-B was an attempt to reconstitute the Banovina borders was absurd;[2282] and (2) the HVO was devoted to defending BiH sovereignty.[2283]

720. Moreover, Prlić submits that, in finding that the HZ H-B was established to create a "mini-State" aligned with Croatia, the Trial Chamber erroneously relied on the evidence of Ribičić, Brix-Andersen, Lane, and Okun.[2284] According to Prlić, Ribičić testified that the HZ H-B was not a "mini-State",[2285] and his evidence that the goal of the HZ H-B was to be connected with Croatia is speculative.[2286] Prlić argues that the Trial Chamber ignored that, in his book, Ribičić explained that he changed his analysis of the HZ H-B

[2272] Trial Judgement, Vol. 4, para. 15. See Trial Judgement, Vol. 1, paras 420-425, Vol. 4, para. 14.

[2273] Trial Judgement, Vol. 4, para. 15 & fn. 39, referring to Ciril Ribičić, T(F). 25451 (10 Dec 2007), Exs. P08973, pp. 48-49, P00302, P00078, p. 1.

[2274] Trial Judgement, Vol. 4, para. 15.

[2275] Judgement, Vol. 4, para. 16 (internal references omitted).

[2276] Prlić's Appeal Brief, paras 233, 235. See Prlić's Appeal Brief, para. 232. See also Appeal Hearing, AT. 125-126, 130-131, 154-157 (20 Mar 2017).

[2277] Prlić's Appeal Brief, para. 235 & fn. 666, referring to, *inter alia,* Zdravko Sančević, T. 28605-28609, 28688-28695 (27 May 2008), 28744-28746 (28 May 2008), Radmilo Jašak, T. 48881-48882 (25 Jan 2010).

[2278] Prlić's Appeal Brief, para. 235, referring to Prlić's Appeal Brief, paras 30, 51 (sub-grounds of appeal 1.1-1.2). See also Appeal Hearing, AT. 129-130, 132 (20 Mar 2017). Prlić also argues that the Trial Chamber failed to consider evidence necessary to understanding the chronology of events. Prlić's Appeal Brief, para. 234, referring to Prlić's Appeal Brief, paras 27-28, 36-41 (sub-ground of appeal 1.1).

[2279] Prlić's Appeal Brief, para. 262.

[2280] Prlić's Appeal Brief, para. 267, referring to, *inter alia,* Mile Akmandžić, T. 29445-29448, 29625-29631 (17 June 2008).

[2281] Prlić's Appeal Brief, para. 268. See also Appeal Hearing, AT. 134 (20 Mar 2017).

[2282] Prlić's Appeal Brief, para. 268; Appeal Hearing, AT. 136 (20 Mar 2017). Prlić also argues that the HZ H-B never sought independence. Prlić's Appeal Brief, para. 268; Appeal Hearing, AT. 136 (20 Mar 2017).

[2283] Prlić's Appeal Brief, para. 268.

[2284] Prlić's Appeal Brief, para. 262, referring to Prlić's Appeal Brief, grounds of appeal 4 and 6. Prlić also adopts his submissions made in his sub-grounds of appeal 1.1 and 1.3, which the Appeals Chamber dismisses elsewhere. Prlić's Appeal Brief, para. 263, referring to Prlić's Appeal Brief, paras 36, 82 (sub-grounds of appeal 1.1 and 1.3). See *supra,* paras 168-176.

[2285] Prlić's Appeal Brief, para. 264, referring to Ciril Ribičić, T. 25462-25463 (10 Dec 2007), T. 25586-25588 (11 Dec 2007).

[2286] Prlić's Appeal Brief, para. 264, referring to Ex. P08973, p. 52, Milan Cvikl, T. 35384-35386 (14 Jan 2009).

after reading the Presidential Transcript of 27 December 1991.[2287] Prlić further contends that: (1) Brix-Andersen's evidence is speculative as he had no personal knowledge about BiH and never met with Boban, Prlić, Stojić, or Krešimir Zubak;[2288] (2) Lane was unreliable and "demonstrated a profound ignorance of the HZ H-B's structure, its leadership, BiH, and the ongoing peace plans while he was *in situ"?*[2289] and (3) Ćupina gave contradictory testimony and lacked credibility.[2290]

721.   The Prosecution responds that Prlić "identifies no authority supporting his novel 'legitimate purpose' rule",[2291] and that the Trial Chamber found that while the HZ(R) H-B may also have served defence-related purposes, it was designed to be annexed or closely allied to Croatia.[2292] The Prosecution submits that while Prlić claims that the HZ H-B never had defined borders, in June 1993 he asserted otherwise.[2293] It also contends that Prlić's assertions on Ribičić's testimony **[page 302]** are contradicted by his own evidence,[2294] and that he fails to show how the Trial Chamber unreasonably relied on the evidence of Brix-Andersen, Lane, Okun, and Ćupina.[2295]

(ii) Analysis

722.   Prlić's first argument is essentially that the conclusion that the HZ H-B was intended to facilitate the establishment of a Croatian entity, that was either to join Croatia or be an autonomous entity within BiH forming an alliance with Croatia, is not the only reasonable inference that can be drawn from the evidence.[2296] Notably, Prlić argues that the HZ H-B was necessary to "take care of all Croats in BiH", but the evidence he relies on does not call into question the Trial Chamber's assessment and findings.[2297] In this respect, the Appeals Chamber observes that the Trial Chamber did consider the "Serb aggression",[2298] assertions that the Bosnian Croats were subject to direct occupation by Serbia, and the need for protection due to the lack of action by the government,[2299] as well as evidence that the HZ H-B "was defined as being a Croatian entity that guaranteed the rights of Croats".[2300] Thus, Prlić's argument concerning the purpose for establishing the HZ H-B is dismissed.[2301]

723.   Regarding Prlić's arguments that the HZ H-B was always part of BiH and functioned as an interim structure within BiH, the Appeals Chamber considers that Prlić neither explains how these assertions would impact the Trial Chamber's findings nor shows how the evidence he refers to supports his claims. Specifically, Prlić's assertion that the HZ H-B was always part of BiH does not stand in contradiction with the Trial

---

[2287]   Prlić's Appeal Brief, para. 264, referring to Ex. 1D02036, pp. 6-7, Ciril Ribičić, T. 25554-25555, 25582-25583 (11 Dec 2007).

[2288]   Prlić's Appeal Brief, para. 265, referring to Ex. P10356, pp. 10742, 10752, 10792. Prlić argues that Brix-Andersen's evidence was that "there was never a clear agenda". Prlić's Appeal Brief, para. 265, referring to Ex.P10356, p. 10831.

[2289]   Prlić's Appeal Brief, para. 266, referring to Raymond Lane, T. 23703-23704, 23721-23733, 23739-23740, 23770-23771, 23775-23776, 23779-23781, 23789-23794 (15 Oct 2007), Prlić's Appeal Brief, paras 202-203 (sub-ground of appeal 6.2).

[2290]   Prlić's Appeal Brief, para. 266, referring to Safet Idrizović, T. 9898 (9 Nov 2006), Slobodan Praljak, T. 40391-40393 (19 May 2009), Exs. 2D00073, 2D00072, 2D00076.

[2291]   Prosecution's Response Brief (Prlić), para. 159. The Prosecution argues that Prlić fails to explain the relevance of the chronology of the events leading to the establishment of the HZ H-B and how it renders the Trial Chamber's conclusions unreasonable. Prosecution's Response Brief (Prlić), para. 160.

[2292]   Prosecution's Response Brief (Prlić), para. 159. See Prosecution's Response Brief (Prlić), para. 155. The Prosecution argues that Prlić ignores his own admission that Tuđman, Boban, and Šušak created another plan to integrate a part of BiH into Croatia. Prosecution's Response Brief (Prlić), para. 159, referring to Ex. P09078, pp. 64-66.

[2293]   Prosecution's Response Brief (Prlić), para. 160, referring to Exs. P07856, pp. 46-47, P09712 (confidential), p. 14.

[2294]   Prosecution's Response Brief (Prlić), para. 157. See also Prosecution's Response Brief (Prlić), para. 156, referring to Ex. P00498.

[2295]   Prosecution's Response Brief (Prlić), para. 158.

[2296]   See Prlić's Appeal Brief, paras 232-233, 235.

[2297]   See Zdravko Sančević, T. 28688-28695 (27 May 2008) (testimony that he, as an ambassador, was concerned with the protection of the Croatian people who were in BiH); Radmilo Jašak, T. 48881 (25 Jan 2010) (testimony that the HZ H-B was organised to help all Croats in villages where they were in the majority).

[2298]   Trial Judgement, Vol. 4, para. 15.

[2299]   Trial Judgement, Vol. 1, para, 413 & fn. 951, See Trial Judgement, Vol. 1, para. 415. See also Trial Judgement, Vol. 4, para. 7 (summary of similar arguments presented at trial by the Appellants).

[2300]   Trial Judgement, Vol. 4, para. 14.

[2301]   With regard to Prlić's argument on the chronology of the events, the Appeals Chamber notes that it is entirely based on a cross-reference to his sub-ground of appeal 1.1, which the Appeals Chamber dismisses elsewhere. See *supra*, paras 168-176.

Chamber's particular finding that "the said autonomous territorial entity desired by the HZ[ ]H-B was to exist either within BiH by forming an alliance with Croatia, or directly as a[n] integral part of Croatia".[2302]

724.   In relation to Prlić's argument that the HZ H-B had no boundaries, the Appeals Chamber observes that the Trial Chamber considered various pieces of evidence in concluding that the **[page 303]** intention was to set up a Croatian entity that reconstituted, at least in part, the borders of the Banovina.[2303] Against this background, Prlić's reference to evidence indicating that 50 municipalities joined the HZ H-B[2304] falls short of showing any error in the Trial Chamber's assessment of the relevant evidence as well as in its conclusion. The Appeals Chamber also considers Prlić's contention that the HVO defended BiH sovereignty to be unpersuasive, especially as he fails to address the Trial Chamber's consideration of evidence showing that the HVO was established "as the supreme body for the defence of the Croatian people in the HZ H-B".[2305] Thus, the Appeals Chamber finds that Prlić fails to show that no reasonable trier of fact could have arrived at the Trial Chamber's conclusions.[2306] Prlić's arguments are therefore dismissed.

725.   As regards Prlić's argument that the Trial Chamber ignored evidence of Ribičić changing his analysis on the HZ H-B after having read the Presidential Transcript of 27 December 1991, the Appeals Chamber recalls that a trial chamber need not refer to every witness testimony or every piece of evidence on the record and that there is a presumption that the trial chamber evaluated all the evidence presented to it, as long as there is no indication that the trial chamber completely disregarded evidence which is clearly relevant.[2307] The Appeals Chamber is not convinced that the Presidential Transcript of 27 December 1991, to which Prlić refers, is clearly relevant to the reasons for establishing the HZ H-B. Additionally, the Appeals Chamber finds that neither Ribičić's testimony nor his book which Prlić cites show that Ribičić "changed his legal analysis and opinion".[2308] Further, Prlić's assertion that Ribičić testified that the HZ H-B was not a "mini-State" is not supported by the section of the evidence which he cites.[2309] **[page 304]**

726.   The Appeals Chamber is also not persuaded by Prlić's argument that Ribičić and Brix-Andersen speculated about the goal of the HZ H-B.[2310] In this respect, the Appeals Chamber notes that the Trial Chamber clearly accepted Ribičić's and Brix-Andersen's statements after considering various pieces of evidence.[2311] Notably, Brix-Andersen expressed his evaluation of the situation, while expressly stating his position and sources of information.[2312] Prlić merely offers his own assessment of the evidence without showing that the Trial Chamber erred in giving weight to this contested evidence. Similarly, the Appeals Chamber dismisses

---

[2302]   Trial Judgement, Vol. 4, para. 16 (internal references omitted). See Trial Judgement, Vol. 4, para. 10. The Appeals Chamber also dismisses Prlić's argument that the HZ H-B never sought independence as the evidence he cites in support thereof is not relevant. See Miomir Žužul, T. 27696-27698 (7 May 2008).
[2303]   Trial Judgement, Vol. 4, paras 13-16, 22, 24, and references cited therein. Notably, the Trial Chamber concluded that the HZ H-B consisted of 30 municipalities. Trial Judgement, Vol. 1, para. 425, Vol. 4, para. 14.
[2304]   The Appeal chamber notes that, under his sub-ground of appeal 9.1, Prlić cites testimony concerning the HZ H-B having no borders. Prlić's Appeal Brief, para. 235. See, *e.g.*, Zdravko Sančević, T. 28745 (28 May 2008); Zoran Buntić, T. 30796-30797 (16 July 2008); Filip Filipović, T. 47762 (7 Dec 2009) (testifying that the territory of Herceg-Bosna was never defined to his knowledge). The Appeals Chamber considers that by doing so, Prlić in effect challenges the weight given by the Trial Chamber to these pieces of evidence. Recalling the broad discretion afforded to the Trial Chamber in assessing the appropriate weight to be accorded to the evidence, the Appeals Chamber finds that Prlić fails to show an error by the Trial Chamber in this regard. See *Popović et al.* Appeal Judgement, para. 131.
[2305]   Trial Judgement, Vol. 1, para. 436. See also Trial Judgement, Vol. 4, para. 15.
[2306]   See *supra*, para. 719.
[2307]   *Kvočka et al.* Appeal Judgement, paras 23-24. See also *Tolimir* Appeal Judgement, paras 53, 161, 299; *Popović et al.* Appeal Judgement, paras 925, 1017.
[2308]   See Ex. 1D02036, pp. 6-7 (a foreword in a book authored by Ribičić stating that the Presidential Transcript of 27 December 1991 "considerably influenced [his] final opinion on Herceg-Bosna and its mistakes"); Ciril Ribičić, T. 25554-25555 (in which Ribičić confirmed that he placed a high premium on the Presidential Transcript of 27 December 1991), 25582-25583 (in which the parties discussed procedure issues about Ribičić's testimony concerning the Presidential Transcript of 27 December 1991) (11 Dec 2007). See Prlić's Appeal Brief, para. 264 & fns 739-740.
[2309]   Ciril Ribičić, T. 25462-25463 (10 Dec 2007), T. 25586-25588 (11 Dec 2007).
[2310]   See Prlić's Appeal Brief, para. 264, referring to Ex. P08973, p. 52 (Ribičić's legal analysis in which he says that it did not proceed directly from certain enactments that the intention was to integrate with Croatia, "although it could have been the well concealed, ultimate goal in establishing the HZ H-B"), Milan Cvikl, T. 35384-35386 (14 Jan 2009) (expressing surprise at Ribičić's report).
[2311]   Trial Judgement, Vol. 4, para. 15 & fns 36, 39, 41-42.
[2312]   See Ex. P10356, pp. 10724-10725.

Prlić's contention that Lane was an unreliable witness, as he only seeks to replace the Trial Chamber's assessment of Lane's evidence with his own without showing an error.[2313] Finally, with regard to Cupina, the Appeals Chamber observes that the Trial Chamber considered that certain discrepancies weakened the credibility of his testimony in part,[2314] but in relation to the issue at hand, it relied on his testimony along with other evidence.[2315] Thus, the Appeals Chamber is not satisfied that the Trial Chamber erred in relying on the evidence of Ribičić, Brix-Andersen, Lane, or Okun,[2316] and dismisses Prlić's arguments accordingly.

727.   In light of the above, the Appeals Chamber dismisses Prlić's sub-grounds of appeal 9.1 and 9.6 challenging the Trial Chamber's findings that the creation of the HZ H-B was not merely a temporary defence initiative.

(b) Stojić's appeal (Ground 1 in part)

728.   Stojić submits that, in reaching its conclusion about the Ultimate Purpose of the JCE, the Trial Chamber "disregarded the context of Serbian aggression".[2317] Stojić argues that the Trial Chamber focused only on the creation of the HZ H-B in November 1991 and disregarded its own findings or clearly relevant evidence on the HVO formation, namely, that the HVO was created as a defensive response to the Serbian offensive against BiH,[2318] and to protect the **[page 305]** "Croatian people as well as other peoples".[2319] In reply, Stojić argues that the inferences drawn from the evidence were not the only reasonable ones available.[2320]

729.   The Prosecution responds that the Trial Chamber: (1) "did not disregard the context of Serb aggression" and that its conclusions were reasonable;[2321] and (2) considered the evidence Stojić cites, which states that the HVO was not established only for defence purposes.[2322]

730.   The Appeals Chamber recalls that the Trial Chamber considered the context of the "Serb aggression" in arriving at its conclusions[2323] as well as the evidence Stojić cites.[2324] In this respect, the Appeals Chamber finds that Stojić's arguments regarding HVO policies show no error in the Trial Chamber's findings. Further, insofar as Stojić argues that there is another reasonable inference that can be drawn from the evidence, the Appeals Chamber finds that he merely disagrees with the Trial Chamber's conclusion without showing an error. Therefore, the relevant parts of Stojić's ground of appeal 1 are dismissed.

(c) Praljak's appeal (Ground 6.2 in part)

(i) Arguments of the Parties

731.   Praljak submits that the Trial Chamber erred in concluding that the HZ H-B officials established a Croatian "mini-State" within BiH by failing to consider various factors.[2325] Praljak contends that, at the time

---

[2313]   The Appeals Chamber notes that it considers and dismisses Prlić's arguments concerning Lane's elsewhere. See *supra*, paras 215-218.
[2314]   See Trial Judgement, Vol. 1, para. 285 (considering Ćupina's evidence on whether there were ABiH prisoners in Mostar).
[2315]   Trial Judgement, Vol. 4, para. 15, fn. 42.
[2316]   The Appeals Chamber notes that Prlić does not present any specific arguments on the Trial Chamber's reliance on Okun's evidence.
[2317]   Stojić's Appeal Brief, para. 17. See Stojić's Appeal Brief, paras 9, 18.
[2318]   Stojić's Appeal Brief, paras 17-18, referring to Trial Judgement, Vol. 1, paras 408, 415, 434, 436, Vol. 4, paras 14-15; Appeal Hearing, AT. 264-265, 290-291 (21 Mar 2017).
[2319]   Stojić's Appeal Brief, para. 18, referring to Exs. P08973, p. 44, P00151, Arts 1-2; Appeal Hearing, AT. 265-266 (21 Mar 2017).
[2320]   Stojić's Reply Brief, para. 7.
[2321]   Prosecution's Response Brief (Stojić), para. 16, referring to Trial Judgement, Vol. 4, para. 15. The Prosecution also repeats its argument that Tuđman, Boban, and Šušak created another plan to integrate a part of BiH into Croatia. Prosecution's Response Brief (Stojić), para. 16, referring to Ex. P09078, pp. 64-66. See *supra*, fn. 2292.
[2322]   Prosecution's Response Brief (Stojić), para. 16, referring to Ex. P08973, pp. 44, 48-49, 51. The Prosecution asserts that one of the HVO's objectives was to defend "the sovereignty" of the HZ H-B. Prosecution's Response Brief (Stojić), para. 16, referring to Ex. P00151, Art. 2.
[2323]   See *supra*, paras 718, 722.
[2324]   See Trial Judgement, Vol. 1, para. 436 & fn. 1015 (referring to Ex. P00151 concerning the HVO's establishment), Vol. 4, para. 15, fn. 33 (referring to Ex. P08973, p. 44).
[2325]   Praljak's Appeal Brief, heading before para. 107. See Praljak's Appeal Brief, para. 118.

of the first meetings between the Croat leaders, BiH was not an independent State and there was a legitimate fear concerning Serb aggression.[2326] He also contends that the only conclusion that can be drawn from the HZ H-B's establishment – which was consistent with the SRBiH Constitution – is that the Croat people wished to exercise their right of self-determination.[2327] Praljak also submits that the HZ H-B's establishment was in line with international plans and agreements to strengthen the RBiH as a State of three constituent nations, **[page 306]** and that it was never intended to establish a separate State.[2328] According to Praljak, the HVO was established to protect all people in the HZ(R) H-B and was necessary in light of the Serb offensive actions in BiH.[2329] Praljak further contends that the Trial Chamber should have more carefully assessed the evidence of, *inter alios,* Okun and Galbraith, "who pursued [...] the policy of their States".[2330]

732. The Prosecution responds that Praljak ignores the Trial Chamber's findings and evidence relied on, raises irrelevant issues, and repeats his trial arguments without showing an error.[2331]

(ii) Analysis

733. The Appeals Chamber first recalls that the Trial Chamber considered that the HZ H-B was created against a backdrop of "Serb aggression"[2332] and finds that Praljak fails to show how the fact that BiH was not an independent State at the relevant time impacts on the Trial Chamber's findings. Praljak also fails to demonstrate that the alleged desire of the BiH Croats to exercise their right of self-determination is in contradiction to the Trial Chamber's conclusions.[2333] Further, by arguing that this is the only conclusion that can be drawn, Praljak merely offers his own interpretation of the evidence without showing that the Trial Chamber's conclusions were unreasonable. In this regard, the Appeals Chamber observes that the Trial Chamber specifically referred to Ribičić's evidence that the reference to the right to self-determination in the decision establishing the HZ H-B proved that its establishment was not just an interim defensive measure but was aimed at creating a "mini- State".[2334] For the same reasons, the Appeals Chamber finds Praljak's argument that the HZ H-B was never intended to be a separate State to be unconvincing and also finds that the evidence he cites does not call into question the Trial Chamber's findings.[2335] Notably, the Trial Chamber evaluated issues similar to those Praljak raises in support of his argument.[2336] Regarding Praljak's **[page 307]** argument that the HVO was created to protect all people in BiH, the Appeals Chamber notes that the Trial Chamber, relying on various pieces of evidence, including Exhibit P00152 (an 8 April 1992 decision signed by Boban on the creation of the HVO) cited by Praljak,[2337] found that the HVO was established to defend the Croatian people in the HZ H-B.[2338] Moreover, Praljak fails to show an error in the Trial Chamber's finding that the establishment of the HZ-H-B was aimed at creating a mini-State. Additionally, the Appeals Chamber considers Praljak's final argument regarding the Trial Chamber's assessment of certain witnesses' testimonies

---

[2326] Praljak's Appeal Brief, paras 107, 109, 111. Praljak argues that the Serbs had *de facto* control over a great portion of the territory when the future of BiH was uncertain. Praljak's Appeal Brief, para. 111.

[2327] Praljak's Appeal Brief, paras 108, 117. See Praljak's Appeal Brief, para. 111; Praljak's Reply Brief, para. 24. Praljak also contends that the only objective of the Croatian BiH leaders was to ensure equality of rights for the BiH Croats with the two other constituent people. Praljak's Appeal Brief, para. 116.

[2328] Praljak's Appeal Brief, paras 115-117. Praljak argues that the "BiH Croats never ceased to participate in BiH central organs and continuously made efforts [for] coordinated/joint actions". Praljak's Appeal Brief, para. 116.

[2329] Praljak's Appeal Brief, para. 113, referring to Ex. P00152. Praljak asserts that the HVO had no objective contrary to the overall BiH interests and became an integral part of the united forces of the RBiH. Praljak's Appeal Brief, para. 113.

[2330] Praljak's Appeal Brief, para. 117.

[2331] Prosecution's Response Brief (Praljak), paras 41-42. See Prosecution's Response Brief (Praljak), para. 40. The Prosecution submits that "Praljak points to no evidence showing HVO support to the ABiH [...] detrimental to the HVO's campaigns in the HZ(R) H-B". Prosecution's Response Brief (Praljak), para. 37.

[2332] See *supra,* paras 718, 722, 730.

[2333] See Trial Judgement, Vol. 4, para. 15.

[2334] Trial Judgement, Vol. 4, para. 15

[2335] See Praljak's Appeal Brief, paras 108, 112-113, 115, referring to, *inter alia,* Exs. 1D00896, 1D00892, 1D01312.

[2336] See, *e.g.,* Trial Judgement, Vol. 1, paras 423 (noting Tuđman's announcement that the HZ H-B's establishment did not constitute a decision to separate from BiH), 438 (noting that the principles of the Cutileiro Plan envisaged the continuity of BiH while nevertheless dividing the State into three, non-contiguous territorial entities), 446 (noting that the Vance-Owen Peace Plan was based on multi-ethnicity, decentralisation and democracy).

[2337] Praljak's Appeal Brief, para. 113, referring to Ex. P00152.

[2338] Trial Judgement, Vol. 1, para. 436. See *supra,* para. 724.

to be speculative and notes that he fails to provide any support for this contention. Thus, the Appeals Chamber dismisses the relevant parts of Praljak's sub-ground of appeal 6.2.

5. Alleged errors concerning the BiH Croat delegation's agreement with the Vance-Owen Peace Plan principles and Tuđman's involvement in negotiations

734. The Trial Chamber found that, during the international peace negotiations in January 1993, the constitutional principles of the Vance-Owen Peace Plan were proposed.[2339] The Trial Chamber noted Okun's testimony that the "delegation of BiH Croats", which consisted of Tuđman, Boban, Petković, and Mile Akmadžić was not genuinely in agreement with these principles, but accepted them "in order to get the Serbs to sign", while being fully aware that they would be amended later.[2340] The Trial Chamber also observed, in relying on Okun's testimony, that, while not officially the head of the BiH Croat delegation, Tuđman "was so in fact", as Boban needed his approval before taking decisions.[2341]

(a) Prlić's appeal (Sub-ground 9.9)

735. Prlić submits that the Trial Chamber, relying exclusively on Okun's uncorroborated testimony, erred in finding that Tuđman was the *de facto* head of the BiH Croatian delegation at the ICFY.[2342] Prlić argues that Tuđman was asked by the international community to participate in peace negotiations and that the Trial Chamber ignored evidence of this role.[2343] He also contends **[page 308]** that the diaries authored by Okun did not mention Tuđman as the *de facto* head of the delegation.[2344]

736. The Prosecution responds that Prlić fails to show how the impugned finding affects the verdict but that, in any event, the Trial Chamber reasonably relied on Okun's first-hand account of events.[2345]

737. The Appeals Chamber observes that by solely relying on Okun's testimony, the Trial Chamber stated that while Tuđman was not officially the head of the BiH Croat delegation, he "was so in fact".[2346] To the extent that Prlić argues that the Trial Chamber's impugned finding was supported only by Okun's uncorroborated testimony, the Appeals Chamber recalls that a trial chamber has the discretion to decide in the circumstances of each case whether corroboration is necessary or whether to rely on uncorroborated, but otherwise credible, witness testimony.[2347] It also notes that Prlić does not contest Okun's credibility in this context. The Appeals Chamber therefore finds Prlić's argument to be unpersuasive. Regarding Tuđman's role in the peace negotiations, the Appeals Chamber considers that Prlić fails to explain how this role is inconsistent with the Trial Chamber's finding that Tuđman was in fact the head of the BiH Croatian delegation.[2348] Further, whether Tuđman was asked to participate in peace negotiations is irrelevant to the issue of his authority, and the evidence that Prlić contends was ignored by the Trial Chamber does not call into question the impugned finding.[2349] His arguments are therefore dismissed.

738. In relation to the contention that Okun's diaries did not mention Tuđman as the *de facto* head of the BiH Croatian delegation, the Appeals Chamber notes that the only evidence cited by Prlić refers to the cross-

---

[2339] Trial Judgement, Vol. 1, para. 445, Vol. 4, para. 20, referring to, *inter alia,* Herbert Okun, T(F). 16731-16732 (2 Apr 2007). See Trial Judgement, Vol. 1, paras 442-444, 446-451.

[2340] Trial Judgement, Vol. 4, para. 20, referring to Herbert Okun, T(F). 16673-16674, 16735-16736 (2 Apr 2007). See Trial Judgement, Vol. 1, para. 443.

[2341] Trial Judgement, Vol. 1, para. 443, Vol. 4, para. 20, referring to Herbert Okun, T(F). 16675 (2 Apr 2007).

[2342] Prlić''s Appeal Brief, para. 273.

[2343] Prlić's Appeal Brief, paras 273-274, referring to, *inter alia,* Miomir Žužul, T. 27820-27821 (8 May 2008), T. 31137-31138 (22 July 2008).

[2344] Prlić's Appeal Brief, para. 273, referring to Herbert Okun, T. 16656-16658 (2 Apr 2007), T. 16821-16823 (3 Apr 2007), T. 16888-16889 (4 Apr 2007).

[2345] Prosecution's Response Brief (Prlić), para. 162. See also Appeal Hearing, AT. 182 (20 Mar 2017).

[2346] See *supra,* para. 734.

[2347] *Popović et al.* Appeal Judgement, paras 243, 1264; *D. Milošević* Appeal Judgement, para. 215. See also *Kordić and Čerkez* Appeal Judgement, para. 274.

[2348] See, *e.g.,* Trial Judgement, Vol. 1, para. 443, Vol. 4, para. 20.

[2349] See Miomir Žužul, T. 27820-27821 (8 May 2008) (testifying that the international community wanted Tuđman to participate in peace negotiations as it would be more efficient), T. 31137-31138 (22 July 2008) (stating that the international community asked Tuđman to use his influence in the peace negotiations and that Tuđman "had quite an influence over the Croat representatives").

examination of Okun during which he specifically clarified that his diaries indicated that Tuđman was in fact the representative of the Croat people.[2350] The Appeals Chamber observes that the Trial Chamber noted that Boban sought Tuđman's approval before taking decisions.[2351] Further, the Trial Chamber considered Okun's testimony and concluded that "Tuđman **[page 309]** also took part in the negotiations, and had influence over the BiH Croatian representatives".[2352] On this issue, the Appeals Chamber recalls that a trial chamber has broad discretion in assessing the appropriate weight and credibility to be accorded to the evidence.[2353] Thus, even if Prlić's contention is accurate, the Appeals Chamber finds that he has failed to show that the Trial Chamber erred in giving little or no weight to the alleged absence of any mention in Okun's diaries that Tuđman was in fact the head of the delegation. Prlić's argument is thus dismissed.

739.   In light of the above, the Appeals Chamber finds that Prlić has failed to show that no reasonable trier of fact could have concluded that Tuđman, although not officially the head of the BiH Croatian delegation at the ICFY, was so in fact. Prlić's sub-ground of appeal 9.9 is dismissed.

(b) Praljak's appeal (Sub-grounds 5.1 in part, 5.2 in part, and 5.3)

(i) Arguments of the Parties

740.   Praljak submits that the Trial Chamber erroneously considered Okun's speculative testimony that the BiH Croats accepted the Vance-Owen Peace Plan principles despite not being genuinely in agreement with them.[2354] Praljak argues that the Trial Chamber went "even beyond [Okun's] statement" as he was not able to ascertain that the Croats were fully aware that the principles would be amended.[2355] Praljak also argues that the Trial Chamber failed to consider Exhibit P00866, which indicates that shortly before the plan's acceptance, "Tuđman stated that it was now possible to discuss the internal organisation of BiH as a federal community of three nations".[2356]

741.   Praljak further submits that the Trial Chamber improperly assessed Okun's testimony in finding that Tuđman was the "real chief" of the BiH Croatian delegation at the ICFY and that Boban needed to obtain his approval.[2357] Specifically, he argues that Okun's testimony did not show or support a finding that: (1) Tuđman took part in the negotiations;[2358] (2) Boban stated that he needed Tuđman's approval;[2359] and (3) a conversation which Okun had with Tuđman confirmed **[page 310]** that the latter was in fact the head of the delegation.[2360] Praljak also argues that had Tuđman participated in negotiations, he would not have needed to ask Okun to keep him informed or to express his readiness to deal with the issues raised.[2361]

742.   The Prosecution responds that Praljak repeats his trial arguments without showing an error or an impact,[2362] and seeks to substitute his assessment of evidence for that of the Trial Chamber.[2363]

[2350]   Herbert Okun, T. 16821-16823 (3 Apr 2007).
[2351]   Trial Judgement, Vol. 1, para. 443, referring to Herbert Okun, T(F). 16675 (2 Apr 2007).
[2352]   Trial Judgement, Vol. 1, para. 443, In a passage cited by Prlić, Okun also testified that Tuđman "was the boss" and was "the very important person". Herbert Okun, T. 16888 (4 Apr 2007). See Prlić's Appeal Brief, para. 273.
[2353]   *Popović et al.* Appeal Judgement, para. 131.
[2354]   Praljak's Appeal Brief, para. 84.
[2355]   Praljak's Appeal Brief, para. 84, referring to Herbert Okun, T. 16735-16736 (2 Apr 2007).
[2356]   Praljak's Appeal Brief, para. 84, referring to Ex. P00866, p. 9.
[2357]   Praljak's Appeal Brief, paras 89, 92. See Praljak's Appeal Brief, paras 90-91.
[2358]   Praljak's Appeal Brief, paras 90-92, referring to Herbert Okun, T. 16673, 16675 (2 Apr 2007); Appeal Hearing, AT. 387 (22 Mar 2017).
[2359]   Praljak's Appeal Brief, paras 90, 92. According to Praljak, Okun's testimony concerning consultations between Boban and Tuđman is based on what Boban might have said to Okun in informal conversations, and is not a reflection of Boban's remarks during negotiations. Praljak's Appeal Brief, para. 90, referring to Herbert Okun, T. 16675 (2 Apr 2007).
[2360]   Praljak's Appeal Brief, paras 91-92.
[2361]   Praljak's Appeal Brief, para. 91, referring to Herbert Okun, T. 16675 (2 Apr 2007).
[2362]   Prosecution's Response Brief (Praljak), para. 41, referring to, *inter alia*, Ex. P00866, p. 9.
[2363]   Prosecution's Response Brief (Praljak), para. 34.

(ii) Analysis

743.   Regarding the acceptance of the Vance-Owen Peace Plan principles by the BiH Croatian delegation, the Appeals Chamber has reviewed the portion of Okun's evidence relied on by the Trial Chamber.[2364] Okun testified that "[the BiH Croatian delegation] did not like the principles but went along with them because they knew, again, that there would have to be, or they thought there would have to be, some adjustment in the principles if the co-chairmen were to gain Serb acceptance".[2365] Based on these considerations, Praljak fails to show that the Trial Chamber unreasonably relied upon this evidence in concluding that the BiH Croatian delegation was "fully aware that [the principles] would later be amended".[2366] Thus, Praljak's arguments on this issue are unconvincing, particularly as Okun's testimony was based on his first-hand knowledge of the events. In this regard, the Appeals Chamber finds that Praljak fails to show that the Trial Chamber improperly assessed or erroneously exercised its broad discretion in considering this evidence.[2367]

744.   Concerning Tuđman's statement reflected in Exhibit P00866 regarding his readiness to discuss the internal organisation of BiH,[2368] the Appeals Chamber notes that the Trial Chamber was aware of and considered this evidence in noting that Tuđman advocated the existence and legitimacy of the BiH Croatian people to protect the Croatian borders.[2369] Moreover, Praljak does not show any error by the Trial Chamber, particularly as Tuđman's statement is in line with the impugned finding. Praljak's argument is dismissed.
[page 311]

745.   Turning to Praljak's arguments on Tuđman's role in the negotiations, insofar as he argues that the Trial Chamber relied only on Okun's testimony, the Appeals Chamber has considered and dismissed a similar argument,[2370] and Praljak fails to present any new submissions on this point. The Appeals Chamber recalls that the Trial Chamber considered that Tuđman took part in the negotiations, had influence over the BiH Croatian representatives,[2371] and while not officially the head of the BiH Croatian delegation, was so in fact because Boban needed his approval before taking decisions.[2372] Praljak disputes these findings by citing the same evidence considered by the Trial Chamber and therefore merely offers his own interpretation of the evidence without showing an error in the Trial Chamber's assessment of the same.[2373]

746.   The Appeals Chamber also considers Praljak's remaining argument – that had Tuđman participated in negotiations, he would not have needed to ask Okun to keep him informed or to express his readiness to deal with the issues raised – to be unmeritorious.[2374] Regardless, Praljak fails to show how the argument, particularly on Tuđman's request to be informed and his willingness to deal with issues, calls the Trial Chamber's findings into question. His arguments are thus dismissed.

747.   For the foregoing reasons, the Appeals Chamber finds that Praljak has failed to demonstrate an error in the Trial Chamber's assessment of Okun's testimony regarding the Croatian delegation's acceptance of the Vance-Owen Peace Plan principles at the ICFY and Tuđman's role in the negotiations. The Appeals Chamber

---

[2364]   Trial Judgement, Vol. 4, para. 20.

[2365]   Herbert Okun, T. 16735-16736 (2 Apr 2007). Okun also testified that the Croatian delegation "could accept the Vance-Owen Plan in the secure knowledge that it would not go anywhere because of Bosnian Serb rejection". Herbert Okun, T. 16735 (2 Apr 2007).

[2366]   Trial Judgement, Vol. 4, para. 20.

[2367]   See *Popović et al.* Appeal Judgement, para. 131.

[2368]   See *supra*, para. 740.

[2369]   Trial Judgement, Vol. 4, para. 15 & fn. 35.

[2370]   See *supra*, para. 738.

[2371]   Trial Judgement, Vol. 1, para. 443. See *supra*, para. 738.

[2372]   Trial Judgement, Vol. 1, para. 443, Vol. 4, para. 20, referring to Herbert Okun, T(F). 16675 (2 Apr.2007).

[2373]   See Herbert Okun, T. 16673-16675 (2 Apr 2007). Okun testified that: (1) the principal representatives or participants of the BiH Croat party included Tuđman and Boban (see Herbert Okun, T. 16673 (2 Apr 2007)); and (2) Tuđman was not formally the head of the delegation, but that he was the *de facto* head (see Herbert Okun, T. 16675 (2 Apr 2007)). Okun also testified that ("Well, I should state at the outset that most of our dealings were with Mate Boban, but President Tudjman took a very active interest in the affairs of the conference and the conflict in Bosnia and Herzegovina, and made it plain to Mr. Vance and me that he, A, was in charge; B, wished to be kept informed, and; C, would be happy to deal with us on these issues. And also in conversation, everyday conversation, Mate Boban might say to me, 'Yes, Mr. Ambassador, I think that's possible, but I'd have to check with President Tudjman'"). See Herbert Okun, T. 16675 (2 Apr 2007).

[2374]   See *supra*, para. 741.

therefore dismisses Praljak's sub-grounds of appeal 5.1 and 5.2, both in part, as well as his sub-ground of appeal 5.3.

6. Alleged errors in finding that the HZ H-B leaders established a "mini-State" within BiH

748. The Trial Chamber found that in the months following the signing of the Vance-Owen Peace Plan by the BiH Croats and until August 1993, the HZ H-B leaders gradually established a Croatian "mini-State" within BiH, with the primary objective of preserving the so-called Croatian **[page 312]** territories claimed under the Vance-Owen Peace Plan.[2375] The Trial Chamber concluded that: (1) the proclamation of the HR H-B on 28 August 1993 formalised the creation of the "mini-State" within BiH; (2) the HR H-B was defined as a "community-state" and an integral and indivisible democratic state of the Croatian people in BiH; (3) in a statement of the HR H-B Chamber of Deputies on 8 February 1994, the HR H-B proclaimed itself the sole legitimate "government" of the BiH Croats, expressing the need to consolidate its statehood ("HR H-B Chamber of Deputies' Proclamation of 8 February 1994"); and (4) at the meeting on 13 February 1994 ("13 February 1994 Meeting"), Prlić said to several leaders, including Tuđman, that the HR H-B displayed every single attribute of a state and that it needed to obtain the widest possible borders which could be attained by military means.[2376]

(a) Prlić's appeal (Sub-ground 9.10)

(i) Arguments of the Parties

749. Prlić submits that the Trial Chamber erred in concluding that the leaders of the HZ H-B created a "mini-State" by relying on and misrepresenting Ribičić's evidence, as well as disregarding other relevant evidence.[2377] Prlić also argues that the Trial Chamber relied on two documents which do not support its conclusion that the primary objective of the HZ H-B leaders was to preserve the Croatian territories claimed under the Vance-Owen Peace Plan.[2378] In this regard, Prlić submits that: (1) Zrinko Tokić testified that Exhibit P02486, an Ante Starčević Brigade military report, expresses his own opinion;[2379] and (2) Exhibit P05391, a document from the 1st Knez Domagoj Brigade, was admitted from the bar table.[2380] He also contends that the Trial Chamber misrepresented the HR H-B Chamber of Deputies' Proclamation of 8 February 1994, which was a mere depiction of HR H-B's support for the Owen-Stoltenberg Peace Plan.[2381] Prlić further submits that the Trial Chamber mischaracterised the 13 February 1994 Meeting, arguing that he stated at the meeting that "we have created a state in Herceg Bosna with all systems [...], in accordance with the competencies of the Republic envisaged by the Union of Republics [of BiH]".[2382] **[page 313]**

750. The Prosecution responds that the Trial Chamber reasonably concluded that a Croatian "mini-State" within BiH was formalised with the proclamation of the HR H-B and that Prlić fails to show any error in the Trial Chamber's reliance on the evidence in support of its findings.[2383]

(ii) Analysis

751. The Appeals Chamber notes that Prlić's challenge to the Trial Chamber's conclusion on the creation of a "mini-State" within BiH is entirely based on cross-references to other grounds of appeal, which the

---

[2375]   Trial Judgement, Vol. 4, para. 21.
[2376]   Trial Judgement, Vol. 4, para. 21.
[2377]   Prlić's Appeal Brief, para. 275, referring to Trial Judgement, Vol. 1, paras 409-490, Vol. 4, para. 21. Prlić also refers to his sub-ground of appeal 1.3 in support of his challenge in this regard, and his sub-ground of appeal 4.3 in respect of challenges related to Ribičić. Prlić's Appeal Brief, paras 275-276.
[2378]   Prlić's Appeal Brief, para. 277, referring to Exs. P02486, P05391.
[2379]   Prlić's Appeal Brief, para. 277, referring to Ex. P02486, Zrinko Tokić, T. 45533-45537 (1 Oct 2009).
[2380]   Prlić's Appeal Brief, para. 277, referring to Ex. P05391.
[2381]   Prlić's Appeal Brief, para. 278, referring to Ex. P07825.
[2382]   Prlić's Appeal Brief, para. 278, referring to Exs. P07856, 1D02911, p. 47, P03990, p. 14, Art. 3. ^
[2383]   Prosecution's Response Brief (Prlić), para. 161.

Appeals Chamber dismisses elsewhere.[2384] With respect to Prlić's contention that the Trial Chamber erred when concluding that the HZ H-B leaders' main objective was to preserve the Croatian territories claimed under the Vance-Owen Peace Plan, the Appeals Chamber observes that in support of the impugned finding, the Trial Chamber relied on Petković's testimony that the purpose of the HVO was to "preserve as much territory inhabited by Croats as possible".[2385] The Appeals Chamber further notes that Prlić does not challenge the Trial Chamber's reliance on this evidence, which thus remains undisturbed. In addition, with regard to Exhibit P05391, the Appeals Chamber notes that by challenging the Trial Chamber's reliance on it, Prlić merely submits that the document was admitted from the bar table,[2386] conflating the issue of admissibility of the evidence with its weight. Prlić has also failed to show how his remaining challenge with regard to the Trial Chamber's reliance on Exhibit P02486 would have an impact on the impugned finding. Prlić's arguments are therefore dismissed.

752. As regards Prlić's submission that the Trial Chamber misrepresented the HR H-B Chamber of Deputies' Proclamation of 8 February 1994 as it merely shows the HR H-B's support for the Owen-Stoltenberg Peace Plan, the Appeals Chamber observes the Trial Chamber's finding that this evidence indicated that: (1) the HR H-B proclaimed itself the sole legitimate "government" of the BiH Croats and needed to work to consolidate its statehood; and (2) within the "Union of the Republics of Bosnia and Herzegovina", the HR H-B was to ensure the right of the Croatian people to self-determination and to attain a state, with respect for the rights of the other two constituent **[page 314]** nations.[2387] The Appeals Chamber considers that Prlić merely proposes an alternative interpretation of this proclamation, without showing an error in the Trial Chamber's conclusion.[2388]

753. Concerning Prlić's argument that the Trial Chamber mischaracterised the 13 February 1994 Meeting, the Appeals Chamber observes that the Trial Chamber specifically considered the transcript of the meeting. It concluded that at this meeting, Prlić said to several leaders from Croatia, including Tuđman, that the HR H-B displayed every single attribute of a state, and that this state needed to attain the widest possible borders, comprising all of Central Bosnia, which could be achieved by military means.[2389] Other than pointing to a different part of the statement that he made at the same meeting, Prlić fails to demonstrate that the Trial Chamber mischaracterised the 13 February 1994 Meeting and committed any error in its finding. His arguments are therefore dismissed.

754. In light of the above, the Appeals Chamber finds that Prlić has failed to show that no reasonable trier of fact could have concluded that the HZ H-B leaders gradually established a Croatian "mini-State" within BiH, the objective of which was the preservation of so-called Croatian territories claimed under the Vance-Owen Peace Plan. Prlić has also failed to show any error in the Trial Chamber's findings on the HR H-B's proclamation and the 13 February 1994 Meeting. Prlić's sub-ground of appeal 9.10 is therefore dismissed.

(b) Praljak's appeal (Sub-grounds 5.1 and 5.2 in part)

755. Praljak submits that the Trial Chamber erred in concluding that the HZ H-B was gradually established as a "mini-State", and argues that the Trial Chamber misunderstood political developments in BiH after the Vance-Owen Peace Plan since the HZ H-B leaders, only tried to implement the plan.[2390]

[2384]   See *supra*, paras 176, 211.
[2385]   See Trial Judgement, Vol. 4, para. 21, referring to, *inter alia*, Milivoj Petković, T(F). 49482 (16 Feb 2010). See also Milivoj Petković, T. 49483 (16 Feb 2010).
[2386]   See Prlić's Appeal Brief, para. 277. The Appeals Chamber notes that Exhibit P05391 was admitted into evidence on 11 December 2007. See *Prosecutor v. Jadranko Prlić, Bruno Stojić, Slobodan Praljak, Milivoj Petković, Valentin Ćorić, and Berislav Pušić*, Case No. IT-04-74-T, *Décision portant sur la demande d'admission d'éléments de preuve documentaire presentee par l'Accusation (Deux requêtes HVO/Herceg-Bosna)*, 11 December 2007, Annex 2.
[2387]   Trial Judgement, Vol. 4, para. 21 & fns 71-72, referring to, *inter alia*, Ex. P07825, pp. 1-2.
[2388]   The Appeals Chamber also dismisses Prlić's contention that the Trial Chamber "ignored contextual evidence" as undeveloped and unsubstantiated. See Prlić's Appeal Brief, para. 278.
[2389]   Trial Judgement, Vol. 4, para. 21 & fns 73-74, referring to Ex. P07856, pp. 46-47. The Appeals Chamber considers that Ex. 1D02911 is identical to Ex. P07856 with regard to the parts to which Prlić refers and on which the Trial Chamber relied in its findings.
[2390]   Praljak's Appeal Brief, para. 85.

756.   The Prosecution responds that Praljak's contention in this regard is unsubstantiated and shows no error in the Trial Chamber's assessment of the evidence.[2391]

757.   The Appeals Chamber finds that Praljak has failed to provide any support for his contention that the Trial Chamber misinterpreted political developments in BiH after the signing of the Vance-Owen Peace Plan because the HZ H-B leaders only attempted to carry out this plan. The **[page 315]** Trial Chamber clearly determined that, in the months that followed the signing of the Vance-Owen Peace Plan, the HZ H-B leaders gradually created a Croatian "mini-State" with a view to preserving so-called Croatian territories claimed under the Vance-Owen Peace Plan.[2392] The Appeals Chamber therefore dismisses his argument as unsubstantiated and failing to articulate any error.

758.   Accordingly, the Appeals Chamber finds that Praljak has failed to show an error in the Trial Chamber's findings in this regard. The Appeals Chamber therefore dismisses the relevant parts of Praljak's sub-grounds of appeal 5.1 and 5.2.

7.   Alleged errors concerning the Ultimate Purpose of the JCE

759.   The Trial Chamber found that:

> the ultimate purpose of the HZ(R) H-B leaders and of Franjo Tuđman at all times relevant under the Indictment was to set up a Croatian entity that reconstituted, at least in part, the borders of the Banovina of 1939, and facilitated the reunification of the Croatian people. This Croatian entity in BiH was either supposed to be joined to Croatia directly subsequent to a possible dissolution of BiH, or otherwise, to be an independent state within BiH with close ties to Croatia.[2393]

(a) Stojić's appeal (Ground 1 in part)

760.   Stojić submits that the Trial Chamber's conclusion on the Ultimate Purpose of the JCE was ambiguous, arguing that when referring to the "HZ(R) H-B leaders", the Trial Chamber failed to determine: (1) the identity of the "leaders"; and (2) whether all of the Appellants fall in this category "at all times".[2394] Stojić argues that the Trial Chamber's conclusion was based primarily on Tuđman's intentions, not his, and that given the scarcity of findings on the HZ(R) H-B leadership, the Trial Chamber failed to appropriately consider individual criminal responsibility.[2395]

761.   The Prosecution responds that the Trial Chamber identified individuals, including the Appellants, who shared the intent to achieve the ultimate purpose by criminal means, while the identity of other HZ(R) H-B leaders sharing the ultimate purpose is immaterial.[2396]

762.   The Appeals Chamber observes that an overall reading of the Trial Judgement shows that the Trial Chamber identified Stojić as among the "HZ(R) H-B leaders" sharing the Ultimate Purpose of the JCE. In the relevant analysis, the Trial Judgement specifies that as one of the participants of the 5 and 26 October 1992 Meetings, Stojić met with Mladić to discuss the division **[page 316]** of BiH.[2397] Similarly, in the sections concerning the existence of the CCP, the Trial Chamber found that no later than October 1992, Stojić knew that the implementation of the Ultimate Purpose of the JCE would involve the Muslim population moving outside the territory of the HZ H-B.[2398] Accordingly, Stojić's argument is dismissed.

763.   Therefore, the Appeals Chamber finds that Stojić has failed to show any error in the Trial Chamber's conclusion concerning the Ultimate Purpose of the JCE and rejects the relevant part of his ground of appeal 1.

[2391]   Prosecution's Response Brief (Praljak), para. 42.

[2392]   See *supra*, para. 748.

[2393]   Trial Judgement, Vol. 4, para. 24. See also Trial Judgement, Vol. 4, para. 43.

[2394]   Stojić's Appeal Brief, paras 9, 23; Appeal Hearing, AT. 257-258, 295 (21 Mar 2017).

[2395]   Appeal Hearing, AT. 258, 284 (21 Mar 2017).

[2396]   Prosecution's Response Brief (Stojić), para. 18, referring to Trial Judgement, Vol. 4, para. 1232. See also Appeal Hearing, AT. 350-351 (21 Mar 2017).

[2397]   Trial Judgement, Vol. 4, para. 18.

[2398]   Trial Judgement, Vol. 4, para. 43, referring to, *inter alia*, Trial Judgement, Vol. 1, paras 426-490, Vol. 4, paras 9-24, 326-431.

(b) <u>Praljak's appeal (Sub-ground 6.5)</u>

764. Praljak submits that the Trial Chamber erred in its conclusion vis-à-vis the Ultimate Purpose of the JCE by taking "events and evidence" out of context.[2399] He contends that the "Croatian political views, particularly those expressed before BiH became an independent State, are irrelevant for determining the criminal responsibility of the individuals".[2400] Moreover, Praljak contends that as the Trial Chamber "could not establish the CCP", it engaged in political considerations outside of its mandate.[2401]

765. The Prosecution responds that Praljak's arguments ignore the Trial Chamber's "detailed JCE analysis".[2402]

766. The Appeals Chamber considers that Praljak challenges the Trial Chamber's reliance on "events and evidence" and "political views" without providing any argument in support of his contention. The Appeals Chamber declines to address Praljak's unsubstantiated allegations of error, and dismisses them.[2403] With regard to Praljak's argument that the Trial Chamber engaged in political considerations outside of its mandate since it "could not establish the CCP", the Appeals Chamber notes that Praljak refers to his submissions in his ground of appeal 7, which the Appeals Chamber dismisses elsewhere.[2404]

767. The Appeals Chamber therefore finds that Praljak has failed to show any error in the Trial Chamber's conclusion concerning the Ultimate Purpose of the JCE and rejects his sub-ground of appeal 6.5. **[page 317]**

(c) <u>Petković's appeal (Sub-grounds 2.1, 2.2 in part, and 2.3 in part)</u>

(i) <u>Arguments of the Parties</u>

768. Petković submits that to the extent that the Trial Chamber found that he was among the HZ(R) H-B leaders sharing the Ultimate Purpose of the JCE, no evidence on the record allows for such a conclusion.[2405] Petković contends that: (1) during his testimony, he denied having discussed or shared the Ultimate Purpose of the JCE;[2406] (2) the Trial Chamber failed to provide any reasoned opinion when rejecting Petković's evidence that he did not share the Ultimate Purpose of the JCE;[2407] (3) there is no evidence on the record that shows that he supported this purpose;[2408] (4) no reasonable inference vis-à-vis his views could be drawn from his presence during meetings or views expressed by others in those meetings;[2409] and (5) there is no evidence that he knew the content of other meetings or the views expressed therein.[2410]

769. The Prosecution responds that: (1) Petković reiterates arguments rejected at trial; (2) the Trial Judgement is sufficiently clear that Petković was among the HZ(R) H-B leaders who shared the Ultimate

---

[2399] Praljak's Appeal Brief, para. 128, referring to Praljak's Appeal Brief, paras 125-126 (sub-ground of appeal 6.4).
[2400] Praljak's Appeal Brief, para. 127; Appeal Hearing, AT. 385-386 (22 Mar 2017).
[2401] Praljak's Appeal Brief, para. 127, referring to Praljak's Appeal Brief, paras 130-134 (sub-ground of appeal 7.1).
[2402] Prosecution's Response Brief (Praljak), para. 34.
[2403] The Appeals Chamber also notes that Praljak refers to his submissions in his sub-ground of appeal 6.4, which the Appeals Chamber dismisses elsewhere. See *supra*, paras 705-712.
[2404] See *infra*, paras 793-814.
[2405] Petković's Appeal Brief, paras 8, 10, 14. Furthermore, Petković submits that the Trial Chamber erred in finding that Tuđman and the HZ H-B leaders sought to create a Croatian entity in BiH through the division of BiH between Croatia and Serbia. Petković's Appeal Brief, para. 8. According to Petković, the evidence on the record proves that: (1) Herceg-Bosna was established before BiH became independent; (2) BiH became independent after the referendum; (3) "all documents of the international community [...] established the firm rule that the borders of Yugoslav republics [could not] be changed by force"; (4) the international community planned on offering a "composite" internal organisation of BiH based on the premise that BiH should be composed of three constituent people; (5) the HZ H-B leaders stated that BiH was to be organised as a composite federation; and (6) the HVO was established as an *ad hoc* wartime army and as a component of the ABiH. See Petković's Appeal Brief, para. 8.
[2406] Petković's Appeal Brief, para. 13. Petković also argues that the Prosecution did not question him or any other witness about whether Petković shared the Ultimate Purpose of the JCE. See Petković's Appeal Brief, para. 13.
[2407] Petković's Appeal Brief, paras 6-7, 13. Petković also submits that the Trial Chamber failed to identify which of the Accused shared the Ultimate Purpose of the JCE. See Petković's Appeal Brief, para. 5.
[2408] Petković's Appeal Brief, para. 13.
[2409] Petković's Appeal Brief, para. 13, referring to *Mugenzi and Mugiraneza* Appeal Judgement, paras 88, 92.
[2410] Petković's Appeal Brief, para. 13.

Purpose of the JCE; and (3) the Trial Chamber rejected his "self-serving" evidence adduced during his testimony.[2411]

770.   Petković replies that the Prosecution fails to point to "any [Trial] Chamber's *reasoning*" or any evidence supporting that he shared the Ultimate Purpose of the JCE.[2412] **[page 318]**

(ii) Analysis

771.   The Appeals Chamber recalls its previous finding that no error has been shown in the Trial Chamber's conclusion that during the 26 October 1992 Meeting, Prlić, Stojić, Praljak, and Petković, as part of a delegation from Croatia and the HZ H-B, met with Mladić to discuss the partition of BiH.[2413] Concerning Petković's contention that the Trial Chamber did not provide a reasoned opinion when rejecting his evidence that he did not share the Ultimate Purpose of the JCE, the Appeals Chamber observes that the Trial Judgement reflects Petković's closing arguments that he never mentioned "'Greater Croatia', the Banovina, the purported intent to redraw the ethnic map of BiH or any other political questions of this nature with Franjo Tuđman [...] or any other person".[2414] The Appeals Chamber recalls that a trial chamber is not required to articulate every step of its reasoning[2415] as long as it indicates clearly the legal and factual findings on the basis of which it reached the decision either to convict or acquit an individual.[2416] Moreover, Petković fails to appreciate that the Trial Chamber specifically concluded that while it accepted Petković's testimony to be credible "on certain points", it found him not credible when he attempted to limit his responsibility and consequently did not accept those portions of his evidence.[2417] Recalling that a trial judgement should be read as a whole,[2418] the Appeals Chamber finds that Petković does not demonstrate that the Trial Chamber failed to provide a reasoned opinion vis-à-vis its analysis of his evidence concerning the Ultimate Purpose of the JCE.[2419] Accordingly, this argument is dismissed.[2420]

772.   The Appeals Chamber further rejects Petković's unsubstantiated argument that no evidence shows that he expressed support for the Ultimate Purpose of the JCE. Specifically, the Appeals Chamber finds that the mere absence of evidence showing Petković's clear utterance in this regard does not prevent a reasonable trier of fact, on the basis of the totality of the evidence **[page 319]** accepted by the Trial Chamber, from finding that he nonetheless shared the Ultimate Purpose of the JCE. In any event, Petković merely repeats the arguments unsuccessfully made at trial without showing an error.[2421]

773.   As for Petković's claim that no reasonable inference regarding his intention could be drawn from his presence during meetings, the Appeals Chamber observes that in support of this contention Petković

[2411]   Prosecution's Response Brief (Petković), paras 9, 12-13. The Prosecution argues that the Trial Chamber found that all the Accused shared the Ultimate Purpose of the JCE. Prosecution's Response Brief (Petković), para. 12. In addition, the Prosecution contends that it cross-examined Petković on his awareness of the Ultimate Purpose of the JCE. See Prosecution's Response Brief (Petković), para. 13. The Prosecution further responds that Petković's claim that the Trial Chamber erred in finding that Tuđman and the HZ H-B leaders sought to create a Croatian entity in BiH has no merit. See Prosecution's Response Brief (Petković), paras 10-11.

[2412]   Petković's Reply Brief, paras 2, 4 (emphasis in original). See also Petković's Reply Brief, para. 3.

[2413]   See *supra*, paras 695-717.

[2414]   Trial Judgement, Vol. 4, para. 7, referring to Petković's Final Brief, para. 41.

[2415]   *Stanišić and Župljanin* Appeal Judgement, paras 378, 1063; *Popović et al.* Appeal Judgement, paras 972, 1906; *Šainović et al.* Appeal Judgement, paras 325, 378, 392, 461, 490; *Kvočka et al.* Appeal Judgement, para. 398. See also *Kvočka et al.* Appeal Judgement, para. 23.

[2416]   *Stanišić and Župljanin* Appeal Judgement, para. 137; *Stanišić and Simatović* Appeal Judgement, para. 78; *Popović et al.* Appeal Judgement, para. 1906; *Hadžihasanović and Kubura* Appeal Judgement, para. 13.

[2417]   Trial Judgement, Vol. 1, para. 399.

[2418]   *Stanišić and Župljanin* Appeal Judgement, para. 202; *Šainović et al.* Appeal Judgement, paras 306, 321; *Boškoski and Tarčulovski* Appeal Judgement, para. 67.

[2419]   The Appeals Chamber also recalls that when faced with competing versions of the same event, it is the prerogative of the trier of fact to decide which version it considers more credible. See, *e.g., Nyiramasuhuko et al.* Appeal Judgement;* para. 645 and references cited therein. The Appeals Chamber also fails to see the relevance of Petković's argument that the Prosecution did not question him or any other witness on the Ultimate Purpose of the JCE. In any event, a review of the trial transcripts shows that the Prosecution did in fact cross-examine him in this regard. See Milivoj Petković, T. 50466 (4 Mar 2010).

[2420]   Additionally, the Appeals Chamber rejects Petković's argument concerning the Trial Chamber's failure to identify which of the Accused shared the Ultimate Purpose of the JCE as he fails to show how this alleged error is material vis-à-vis his responsibility.

[2421]   See Petković''s Final Brief, paras 41, 537(iv), 537(ix).

merely refers to the *Mugenzi and Mugiraneza* Appeal Judgement.[2422] The mere reference to a conclusion in a different appeal judgement concerning an error of fact vis-à-vis the *mens rea* of the crime of conspiracy to commit genocide does not show that no reasonable trier of fact could have reached the same conclusion as the Trial Chamber did in the present case based on the evidence adduced at trial. In addition, the issue at hand is not pertinent to the *mens rea* of conspiracy to commit genocide. Accordingly, the Appeals Chamber dismisses this contention. Additionally, and contrary to Petković's argument, the Trial Chamber did not depend only on Petković's mere presence at meetings in support of its conclusion. Specifically, the Appeals Chamber observes that the Trial Chamber also expressly referred to Okun's evidence that during the international peace negotiations in January 1993 the "delegation of BiH Croats", which included Petković, was not genuinely in agreement with the constitutional principles of the Vance-Owen Peace Plan.[2423]

774.   Lastly, with respect to Petković's contention that there is no evidence that he knew about the views expressed in meetings in which he did not participate, the Appeals Chamber recalls that, in its analysis concerning the Ultimate Purpose of the JCE, the Trial Chamber specifically found that Petković: (1) participated as part of the delegation from Croatia and the HZ H-B in the 26 October 1992 Meeting to discuss the partition of BiH with Mladić;[2424] and (2) was part of the "delegation of BiH Croats" at international peace negotiations in January 1993 which was not genuinely in agreement with the constitutional principles of the Vance-Owen Peace Plan.[2425] Against this background, the Appeals Chamber finds that Petković fails to show that his convictions rely on the Trial Chamber's findings concerning other meetings he did not attend. Accordingly, this contention is dismissed.[2426] **[page 320]**

775.   The Appeals Chamber therefore finds that Petković has failed to show any error in the Trial Chamber's conclusion concerning the Ultimate Purpose of the JCE and rejects his sub-grounds of appeal 2.1, 2.2 in relevant part, and 2.3 in relevant part.

(d) Pušić's appeal (Ground 3 in part)

(i) Arguments of the Parties

776.   Pušić submits that the Trial Chamber's definition of the "stated aims (statements of intent, written in broad terms) contradict the objectives (specific statements which define measurable outcomes) of the JCE ultimate purpose".[2427] Pušić argues that the creation of an independent Croatian State within BiH – one of the objectives – is inconsistent with the alleged aims to reconstitute the Banovina and facilitate the reunification of the Croatian people.[2428] Pušić also argues that the Trial Chamber used vague terminology when defining the nature of the Ultimate Purpose of the JCE, arguing that the terms used "have multiple possible interpretations".[2429]

[2422]   See Petković's Appeal Brief, para. 13, referring to *Mugenzi and Mugiraneza* Appeal Judgement, paras 88, 92.
[2423]   Trial Judgement, Vol. 4, para. 20.
[2424]   See *supra*, paras 694, 713-717.
[2425]   Trial Judgement, Vol. 4, para. 20.
[2426]   With respect to Petković's arguments that the evidence on the record disproves the Trial Chamber's conclusion on the Ultimate Purpose of the JCE, the Appeals Chamber considers that his arguments reflect mere disagreement with the Trial Chamber's assessment and he simply points to the evidence on the record without showing how the Trial Chamber's conclusion is unreasonable. Accordingly, the Appeals Chamber dismisses this argument.
[2427]   Pušić's Appeal Brief, para. 77. Pušić specifically argues that the aims the Trial Chamber found consisted of multi-faceted non-criminal ingredients, namely a desire to set up a Croatian entity, reconstructing, at least in part, the borders of the Banovina to facilitate the reunification of the Croatian people. Pušić's Appeal Brief, para. 78, referring to Trial Judgement, Vol. 4, para. 24. According to Pušić, the objectives of the JCE included a Croatian entity which was either to: (1) be incorporated by Croatia after the dissolution of BiH; or (2) remain an independent state within BiH with close ties to Croatia. See Pušić's Appeal Brief, para. 79, referring to Trial Judgement, Vol. 4, para. 24.
[2428]   Pušić's Appeal Brief, para. 80. See also Pušić's Appeal Brief, para. 81.
[2429]   Pušić's Appeal Brief, para. 82 (submitting that "[w]hat is meant by the terms 'Croatian entity' and the import of the phrases with 'the aim of reconstituting, at least in part, the borders of the 1939 Banovina' in order to 'facilitate the reunification' of the 'Croatian people' is unclear").

777.   Moreover, Pušić contends that the evidence on the record demonstrates that there was "no shared ultimate purpose between the Accused" but instead "a multitude of such purposes".[2430] He further argues that the Trial Chamber erred in law, as the ultimate purpose "theory" does not reflect the complexity of the historical reality.[2431]

778.   The Prosecution responds that the Trial Chamber's conclusion on the Ultimate Purpose of the JCE was not contradictory and was supported by the evidence on the record that the JCE members considered the creation of the HZ(R) H-B as the first step towards the reunification of the Croatian people.[2432] It also argues that the Trial Chamber was not vague in terms of the **[page 321]** geographical scope or the target group of the Ultimate Purpose of the JCE, and that Pušić fails to appreciate the Trial Chamber's distinction between the JCE members' political goals – the ultimate purpose – and the criminal means.[2433] Responding to Pušić's argument that the evidence does not support a shared ultimate purpose, the Prosecution submits that Pušić fails to show any error in the Trial Chamber's analysis.[2434] It also argues that Pušić fails to show any impact on his conviction when arguing that the Trial Chamber erred in attempting to arbitrate the historical truth.[2435]

(ii) Analysis

779.   Regarding Pušić's argument that the Trial Chamber made contradictory findings on the objectives of the Ultimate Purpose of the JCE, the Appeals Chamber observes that it has already considered similar allegations of error concerning Tuđman's intention and found no contradiction in this regard.[2436] This argument is therefore dismissed. Moreover, the Appeals Chamber finds no merit in Pušić's contention concerning the ambiguity of the impugned finding. Pušić merely argues that some terms are "unclear" and "have multiple possible interpretations",[2437] failing to show how this alleged ambiguity affects the Trial Chamber's finding on the Ultimate Purpose of the JCE and, ultimately, his conviction.

780.   The Appeals Chamber further observes that, in contending that the evidence on the record demonstrates that there was no shared ultimate purpose but a multitude of purposes, Pušić entirely relies on the Judge Antonetti Dissent without further substantiating his submission.[2438] Recalling that the mere existence of a dissenting opinion does not render the majority's conclusion unreasonable,[2439] the Appeals Chamber rejects this submission.[2440] Finally, the Appeals Chamber finds that Pušić's argument that the Trial Chamber's ultimate purpose "theory" does not reflect the complexity of the historical reality fails to identify an error in the Trial Chamber's conclusion concerning the Ultimate Purpose of the JCE. His arguments are therefore dismissed.

781.   The Appeals Chamber, therefore, finds that Pušić has failed to show any error in the Trial Chamber's conclusion concerning the Ultimate Purpose of the JCE and rejects the relevant part of his ground of appeal 3. **[page 322]**

[2430]   Pušić's Appeal Brief, para. 102, referring to Judge Antonetti Dissent, p. 408. See also Appeal Hearing, AT. 678-689 (27 Mar 2017). Pušić also argues that there was no CCP. See Pušić's Appeal Brief, para. 102. See also Pušić's Appeal Brief, para. 103.

[2431]   Pušić's Appeal Brief, para. 103. Pušić submits, *inter alia,* that the Trial Chamber: (1) erred in trying "to take on the mantle of an 'arbiter[] of historical truth'"; (2) failed to strike the correct balance between "history and law or between context and act"; and (3) erred "in trying such issues 'in the context of criminal proceedings'" without input from Croatia or in the absence of Tuđman or other senior leaders. See Pušić's Appeal Brief, paras 104-105; Appeal Hearing, AT. 680-681 (27 Mar 2017).

[2432]   Prosecution's Response Brief (Pušić), para. 68. According to the Prosecution, Pušić's liability is not affected by what the JCE members were planning to do after they achieved their political aim of Croatian control. See Prosecution's Response Brief (Pušić), para. 69. See also Appeal Hearing, AT. 709 (27 Mar 2017).

[2433]   Prosecution's Response Brief (Pušić), paras 70-71.

[2434]   Prosecution's Response Brief (Pušić), para. 89.

[2435]   Prosecution's Response Brief (Pušić), para. 77.

[2436]   See *supra,* para. 604.

[2437]   Pušić's Appeal Brief, para. 82.

[2438]   Pušić's Appeal Brief, para. 102, referring to Judge Antonetti Dissent, p. 408.

[2439]   See *supra,* para. 670.

[2440]   Similarly, the Appeals Chamber dismisses as unsubstantiated Pušić's argument that there was no CCP.

8. Conclusion

782. In light of the foregoing, the Appeals Chamber dismisses all challenges to the Trial Chamber's findings related to the Ultimate Purpose of the JCE. **[page 323]**

D. **Existence of the Common Criminal Plan of the JCE**

1. Introduction

783. The Trial Chamber concluded that as of December 1991, the leaders of the HZ(R) H-B, including Boban, and leaders of Croatia, including Tuđman, believed that in order to achieve the Ultimate Purpose of the JCE, it was necessary to change the ethnic make-up of the territories claimed to form part of the HZ H-B.[2441] The Trial Chamber also found that from no later than October 1992, Prlić, Stojić, Praljak, and Petković knew that the implementation of the Ultimate Purpose of the JCE ran counter to the peace negotiations being conducted in Geneva and would involve the Muslim population moving outside the territory of the HZ H-B.[2442] The Trial Chamber then concluded that the evidence demonstrated that from mid-January 1993, the leaders of the HVO and certain Croatian leaders aimed to consolidate HVO control over Provinces 3, 8, and 10, and to eliminate all Muslim resistance within these provinces and to "ethnically cleanse" the Muslims so that the provinces would become in "majority or nearly exclusively Croatian".[2443] It thus found that a JCE was established to implement the Ultimate Purpose of the JCE from at least as early as mid-January 1993, the common criminal plan of which was "domination by the HR H-B Croats through ethnic cleansing of the Muslim population" (the "Common Criminal Plan" or "CCP").[2444]

784. The Trial Chamber found that the JCE was then implemented in "stages",[2445] by way of crimes that "tended to follow a clear pattern of conduct".[2446] In this regard, the Trial Chamber took account of: (1) crimes committed pursuant to military campaigns in the municipalities of Gornji Vakuf, Prozor, Jablanica, and Mostar between January and June 1993 ;[2447] (2) the expansion of the CCP with the siege of East Mostar from June 1993 to April 1994;[2448] (3) the organised system of deportation of Muslims introduced following the ABiH attack on 30 June 1993;[2449] (4) the relocation of Croats from June 1993 to April 1994;[2450] and (5) the events in and around Vareš in October 1993.[2451] **[page 324]**

785. The Appellants allege errors regarding: (1) the definition of the CCP;[2452] (2) the Trial Chamber's approach to its scope and expansion;[2453] (3) the Trial Chamber's findings on the stages of implementation of the CCP;[2454] and (4) a number of other findings made as part of the CCP analysis.[2455]

[2441]   Trial Judgement, Vol. 4, para. 43.
[2442]   Trial Judgement, Vol. 4, para. 43.
[2443]   Trial Judgement, Vol. 4, para. 44.
[2444]   Trial Judgement, Vol. 4, paras 41, 43-44.
[2445]   Trial Judgement, Vol. 4, para. 45.
[2446]   Trial Judgement, Vol. 4, para. 65.
[2447]   Trial Judgement, Vol. 4, paras 45-54, 56-58.
[2448]   Trial Judgement, Vol. 4, para. 59.
[2449]   Trial Judgement, Vol. 4, paras 57, 64.
[2450]   Trial Judgement, Vol. 4, paras 54-55, 60, 62-63.
[2451]   Trial Judgement, Vol. 4, paras 61-63.
[2452]   Stojić seeks acquittal on all counts as a result of this alleged error. See Stojić's Appeal Brief, paras 7, 86. See also Petković's Appeal Brief, para. 27.
[2453]   Stojić and Praljak seek acquittals on all counts as a result of this alleged error. See Stojić's Appeal Brief, paras 7, 58, 101, 108; Praljak's Appeal Brief, paras 129, 134, 138, 544; Stojić's Reply Brief, para. 31.
[2454]   The Appellants seek acquittals on some or all counts as a result of the alleged errors. See Prlić's Appeal Brief, paras 311-312; Stojić's Appeal Brief, paras 7, 94, 398, 402; Praljak's Appeal Brief, paras 100, 162, 232, 324; Petković's Appeal Brief, paras 33, 53, 58, 67, 70, 76, 80, 85.
[2455]   The Appellants seek acquittals on some or all counts as a result of the alleged errors. See Prlić's Appeal Brief, paras 311-312; Stojić's Appeal Brief, paras 7, 37, 47, 58; Petković's Appeal Brief, para. 85; Ćorić›s Appeal Brief, para. 5; Pušić's Appeal Brief, paras 108-109.

2. Alleged errors regarding the definition of the CCP (Stojić's Ground 8 and Petković's Sub-grounds 3.2.1.1 and 3.2.1.2 in part)

786. The Trial Chamber concluded that there was "only one, single [CCP] – domination by the HR H-B Croats through ethnic cleansing of the Muslim population".[2456]

(a) Arguments of the Parties

787. Stojić submits that although the Trial Chamber indicated that there was "one, single" CCP, it failed to consistently identify such a single purpose.[2457] In his view, the Trial Chamber vacillated between "five different common purposes", namely: (1) "domination" by the HR H-B Croats; (2) "reconstituting the Banovina"; (3) "modifying the ethnic composition of the territory"; (4) "expelling the Muslim population"; and (5) "ethnic cleansing".[2458] In the course of his submissions that the Trial Chamber erred in law and fact in holding that "the only reasonable inference was that the crimes were the result of the implementation of a common criminal plan",[2459] Petković asserts that the Trial Chamber referred to the CCP variously as "domination", "ethnic cleansing", and "political purpose".[2460] Stojić argues that these inconsistencies violate his right to a "reasoned decision" and invalidate the Trial Judgement.[2461] Similarly, Petković argues that the Trial Chamber failed to explain what "ethnic cleansing" meant, thus breaching his right to a **[page 325]** reasoned opinion.[2462] Further, both Stojić and Petković argue in this context that the Trial Chamber's classification of the CCP as "ethnic cleansing" did not amount to, or involve, the commission of crimes within the Statute.[2463] Petković also argues that the Trial Chamber erred in equating "the crime of deportation/forcible transfer" with ethnic cleansing since a small number of deportations and/or forcible transfers in an area cannot amount to ethnic cleansing and yet the Trial Chamber concluded that the CCP was implemented even in those locations where only a small number of civilians were deported or forcibly transferred.[2464]

788. The Prosecution responds that the Trial Chamber correctly identified a single CCP, namely to establish, by criminal means, a Croatian entity reconstituting the Banovina borders.[2465] It asserts that the Trial Chamber consistently distinguished between the political purpose and its criminal implementation,[2466] and was also consistent in describing the CCP as domination by the HR H-B Croats through "ethnic cleansing".[2467] The Prosecution also responds that the Trial Chamber enumerated the specific crimes which

---

[2456] Trial Judgement, Vol. 4, para. 41.

[2457] Stojić's Appeal Brief, heading before para. 81, paras 83, 85, referring to Trial Judgement, Vol. 4, para. 41. See also Stojić's Appeal Brief, paras 81-82.

[2458] Stojić's Appeal Brief, para. 83, referring to Trial Judgement, Vol. 4, paras 41, 43, 65, 429, 1232. See also Stojić's Appeal Brief, para. 81. Stojić also submits that the Trial Chamber oscillated between defining ethnic cleansing as the common purpose of the JCE to be achieved through the perpetration of other crimes, or as the criminal means to realise the common purpose. Stojić's Appeal Brief, para. 84, referring to Trial Judgement, Vol. 4, paras 41, 43, 65, 429, 1232. See also Stojić's Appeal Brief, para. 82.

[2459] Petković's Appeal Brief, heading 3.2.1 before para. 25.

[2460] Petković's Appeal Brief, para. 26.

[2461] Stojić's Appeal Brief, heading before para. 81, paras 81, 85-86, referring to, *inter alia, Krajišnik* Appeal Judgement, para. 724, *Limaj et al.* Appeal Judgement, para. 81.

[2462] Petković's Appeal Brief, para. 28. Petković also argues that "it could be inferred that the Trial Chamber used the term 'ethnic cleansing' as the synonym for [the] creation of [an] ethnically homogenous geographic area supposed to be [a] Croatian entity (provinces, federal or confederal unit) through [the] removal of Muslim population[s]." Petković's Appeal Brief, para. 29.

[2463] Stojić's Appeal Brief, heading before para. 81, para. 86; Petković's Appeal Brief, paras 26-27, referring to Trial Judgement, Vol. 4, paras 41, 44. Stojić raises this challenge with regard to the classification of the CCP as ethnic cleansing, in the alternative to his submission that the Trial Chamber failed to clearly identify what the CCP was. See Stojić's Appeal Brief, heading before para. 81, paras 83, 85. Stojić submits that domination by the HR H-B Croats or ethnic cleansing is not a crime proscribed by the Statute, and Petković argues that "domination", "ethnic cleansing", and "political purpose" do not amount to a crime under the Statute. See Stojić's Appeal Brief, para. 86; Petković's Appeal Brief, para. 26. See also Stojić's Appeal Brief, para. 82; Petković's Appeal Brief, para. 25; Petković's Reply Brief, paras 7-8; Appeal Hearing, AT. 287, 292-295, 299 (21 Mar 2017); AT. 483, 490-493 (23 Mar 2017).

[2464] See Petković's Appeal Brief, para. 27; Appeal Hearing, AT. 485-486, 491 (23 Mar 2017).

[2465] Prosecution's Response Brief (Stojić), para. 59. See also Prosecution's Response Brief (Petković), paras 16, 23.

[2466] Prosecution's Response Brief (Stojić), paras 59-61, 63, referring to Trial Judgement, Vol. 4, paras 24, 43-44, 65, 1232. See also Prosecution's Response Brief (Stojić), para. 62.

[2467] Prosecution's Response Brief (Stojić), para. 63, referring to Trial Judgement, Vol. 4, paras 65-66, 68, 1232. See also Prosecution's Response Brief (Stojić), para. 62; Appeal Hearing, AT. 345-346 (21 Mar 2017).

made up the CCP, and thus did not err in using the term "ethnic cleansing".[2468] It finally argues that Petković's allegation of lack of reasoned opinion should be summarily dismissed, particularly given his subsequent acknowledgment that the Trial Chamber explained what it meant by "ethnic cleansing".[2469]

(b) Analysis

789. Regarding the allegations of ambiguity in the Trial Chamber's approach to identifying the CCP, the Appeals Chamber considers that the Trial Chamber consistently identified the CCP as the ethnic cleansing of the Muslim population in pursuit of the Ultimate Purpose of the JCE.[2470] In this regard, the Appeals Chamber also notes that the Trial Chamber clearly distinguished between the **[page 326]** Ultimate Purpose of the JCE – the territorial political aspirations of the JCE members – and the criminal means by which it was implemented.[2471] In particular, no ambiguity is presented by the fact that in some cases, the Trial Chamber referred to the Ultimate Purpose of the JCE as context when discussing the CCP,[2472] while in others, it did not.[2473] The Appeals Chamber also finds that the Trial Chamber's use of different, but substantively identical, phrasing to describe the "ethnic cleansing" process does not reflect any ambiguity.[2474] Stojić's and Petković's submissions are thus dismissed in relevant part.

790. As for the allegations that the Trial Chamber erred in defining the CCP as "ethnic cleansing" which did not necessarily involve the commission of crimes, the Appeals Chamber recalls that for JCE liability to be established, the Prosecution must prove "the existence of a common plan, design or purpose which amounts to or involves the commission of a crime provided for in the Statute".[2475] In the present case, the Trial Chamber found that in pursuit of the Ultimate Purpose of the JCE, the JCE members devised a CCP to ethnically cleanse Muslims from Provinces 3, 8, and 10,[2476] and it outlined the precise crimes which were committed to implement the JCE in stages.[2477] The Appeals Chamber finds no error or inconsistency in this approach, and Stojić's and Petković's arguments on these points are rejected. Considering that the CCP was carefully particularised by the Trial Chamber so as to include various crimes through which "ethnic cleansing" was achieved, including but not limited to forcible transfer and deportation, the Appeals Chamber also finds that the Trial Chamber provided adequate reasons for its conclusion that "ethnic cleansing" occurred, and dismisses Petković's submission in this respect. As a result, the Appeals Chamber dismisses, as unsubstantiated and unsupported, Petković's arguments that the Trial Chamber equated ethnic cleansing with forcible transfer/deportation and failed to make adequate findings regarding the occurrence of "ethnic cleansing" in practice.[2478] Further, given that "ethnic cleansing" can be achieved through a number of different crimes,[2479] as indeed was found by the Trial Chamber in **[page 327]** relation to the CCP, the Appeals Chamber considers Petković's argument that a few instances of deportation and forcible transfer cannot

---

[2468] Prosecution's Response Brief (Stojić), para. 64; Prosecution's Response Brief (Petković), para. 24, referring to Trial Judgement, Vol. 4, paras 41, 43-44, 65-66, 68. See also Prosecution's Response Brief (Stojić), para. 65.

[2469] Prosecution's Response Brief (Petković), para. 27. See also Prosecution's Response Brief (Petković), paras 28-29.

[2470] See Trial Judgement, Vol. 4, paras 44, 65, 1232.

[2471] See Trial Judgement, Vol. 4, paras 2-24, 41-73.

[2472] See Trial Judgement, Vol. 4, paras 43-44, 65.

[2473] See Trial Judgement, Vol. 4, paras 429, 1232. See also Trial Judgement, Vol. 4, para. 276.

[2474] The Appeals Chamber notes that in the paragraphs referred to by Stojić the Trial Chamber refers to a plan "seeking to modify the ethnic composition of the so-called Croatian provinces" and "to ethnically cleanse the Muslim population from the territory claimed as Croatian". See Trial Judgement, Vol. 4, paras 65, 1232. See also Trial Judgement, Vol. 4, paras 41 ("there was only one, single common criminal purpose – domination by the HR H-B Croats through ethnic cleansing of the Muslim population"), 428 ("Bruno Stojić intended to expel the Muslim population from the HZ(R) H-B").

[2475] *Tadić* Appeal Judgement, para. 227(ii). See also *Šainović et al.* Appeal Judgement, paras 610-611; *Stakić* Appeal Judgement, para. 64; *Brđanin* Appeal Judgement, paras 364, 418.

[2476] See Trial Judgement, Vol. 4, paras 41, 44, 65, 1232.

[2477] Trial Judgement, Vol. 4, paras 45-68.

[2478] See Petković's Appeal Brief, para. 27.

[2479] See *Stakić* Appeal Judgement, Partly Dissenting Opinion of Judge Shahabuddeen, para. 50 (stating that ethnic cleansing "is not a crime in its own right under customary international law" but rather a "policy" the general purpose of which can be used "to draw inferences as to the existence of elements of crimes referred to in the Statute"). See also United Nations, Security Council, Final Report of the Commission of Experts established pursuant to Security Council Resolution 780 (1992), 27 May 1994, UN Doc. S/1994/674 (1994), Part III: General Studies, B. Ethnic Cleansing, para. 129, p. 33 referring to para. 55 of the Interim Report S/25274 (noting that ethnic cleansing in the region was carried out not only by means of forcible displacement and deportation but also by means of, *inter alia*, deliberate attacks on civilians, arbitrary arrest and detention, arid wanton destruction of property).

amount to ethnic cleansing to be premised on a misunderstanding of the relevant jurisprudence and accordingly rejects his argument in that respect.[2480]

791.   In light of the above, the Appeals Chamber finds that Stojić and Petković have failed to demonstrate an error in the Trial Chamber's findings on the definition of the CCP. Stojić's ground of appeal 8 and Petković's sub-grounds of appeal 3.2.1.1 and 3.2.1.2 in relevant part are therefore dismissed.

3.   Alleged errors of law regarding the scope and expansion of the CCP

792.   As noted earlier, the Trial Chamber found that the evidence demonstrated that there was one single CCP, namely, the "domination by the HR H-B Croats through ethnic cleansing of the Muslim population".[2481] The Trial Chamber also found that the JCE came into being in mid-January 1993 and was carried out "in stages".[2482] It found that between January and June 1993, the stages included military campaigns in the municipalities of Gornji Vakuf, Jablanica, Prozor, and Mostar, and relocations of Croatian civilians.[2483] The Trial Chamber also found that the CCP expanded from June 1993, with the siege of East Mostar.[2484] The Trial Chamber also held that the CCP became more efficient with the implementation of an organised system of deportation from July 1993.[2485] Finally, in its discussion of the applicable law, the Trial Chamber referred to the Appeals Chamber jurisprudence that the "criminal activities implementing the JCE may evolve over time", that a joint criminal enterprise may expand to encompass crimes other than those originally contemplated, and that in these circumstances proof of an agreement concerning its expansions is subject to the same requirements applicable to the original agreement.[2486] Further, relying on the *Krajišnik* Appeal Judgement, the Trial Chamber noted that it was "required to make findings that the members of the JCE were informed of the expansion of criminal activities, that they did nothing to prevent this and **[page 328]** persisted in implementing the expansion of the common design and determine at which precise point in time the additional crimes were integrated into the common design".[2487]

(a) Stojić's appeal (Grounds 11 and 12) and Praljak's appeal (Ground 7)

(i) Arguments of the Parties

793.   Stojić and Praljak submit that the Trial Chamber erred in law in failing to define which crimes were part of the original JCE and which were part of the expanded JCE.[2488] Specifically, Stojić argues that it is unclear whether the expanded JCE from June 1993 was limited to Counts 24-26 only, or "perhaps extend[ed] to all crimes committed after June 1993".[2489] As an example, he submits that it is unclear whether the deportations which began in June 1993 formed part of the original or the expanded JCE.[2490] Both Appellants submit that the Trial Chamber erred in law in failing to make findings showing that leading JCE members were informed of the expanded crimes or failed to prevent their recurrence.[2491]

[2480]   See also *infra*, paras 872, 894.

[2481]   Trial Judgement, Vol. 4, para. 41.

[2482]   Trial Judgement, Vol. 4, paras 44-45.

[2483]   Trial Judgement, Vol. 4, paras 45-63.

[2484]   Trial Judgement, Vol. 4, para. 59.

[2485]   Trial Judgement, Vol. 4, paras 57, 64.

[2486]   Trial Judgement, Vol. 1, para. 212 (2).

[2487]   Trial Judgement, Vol. 1, para. 212 (2).

[2488]   Stojić's Appeal Brief, paras 97, 102-103, 108; Praljak's Appeal Brief, paras 132, 134, 137. See also Stojić's Appeal Brief, paras 95-96. Praljak also raises arguments regarding the non-criminal nature of the plan and the means of identifying the CCP. Praljak's Appeal Brief, paras 130-131; Appeal Hearing, AT. 382-383 (22 Mar 2017) (arguing further that the term "ethnic cleansing" is not a legal term and is too vague to specify the alleged crimes). These arguments have been considered and dismissed above. See *supra*, paras 789-790.

[2489]   Stojić's Appeal Brief, para. 98.

[2490]   Stojić's Appeal Brief, para. 98.

[2491]   Stojić's Appeal Brief, heading before para. 102, paras 104-105; Praljak's Appeal Brief, paras 132, 136; Stojić's Reply Brief, paras 27, 31; Appeal Hearing, AT. 383 (22 Mar 2017). See also Stojić's Reply Brief, paras 28-30. Stojić also alleges that the Trial Chamber erred in fact and failed to provide a "reasoned decision". Stojić's Appeal Brief, heading before para. 102.

794. Stojić argues in addition that the Trial Chamber failed to make findings on: (1) whether the "local component" of the JCE or the Croatian leaders of the JCE had knowledge of the expanded crimes;[2492] and (2) when "leading JCE members went from being merely aware of the crime[s] to intending [them]".[2493] Stojić argues that the absence of such findings in the Trial Chamber's CCP analysis cannot be cured by reference to other sections of the Trial Judgement,[2494] or by reference to the Prosecution's trial pleadings regarding the expanded crimes, which were rejected by the Trial Chamber.[2495] Praljak also submits that the Trial Chamber particularly erred as regards him, as it had found that no evidence supported his role in criminal events in Mostar before 24 July 1993, **[page 329]** so that it is unclear when and how Praljak would have acquired knowledge about the expansion of the CCP.[2496]

795. Stojić and Praljak both argue, pointing to the alleged ambiguities, that the Appeals Chamber cannot be required to speculate on the meaning of the Trial Chamber's findings on the scope of the CCP, which is a central element of criminal responsibility.[2497] Furthermore, according to Stojić, the alleged ambiguities compromise his right to a fair trial and make it impossible for him to challenge the Trial Chamber's findings.[2498] Stojić and Praljak both submit that the alleged legal errors invalidate the Trial Chamber's findings on JCE, and request that the Trial Judgement be set aside and their convictions overturned on all counts.[2499]

796. The Prosecution responds that the Trial Judgement identified Counts 21, 24, and 25 as the crimes that were part of the expanded JCE, and that all other counts for which the Appellants were convicted under JCE I were the crimes that were part of the CCP from the beginning.[2500] It submits that the Trial Chamber made sufficient findings that all the Appellants, including Stojić and Praljak, knew about, and shared the intent for, the expanded crimes.[2501] Whether the Trial Chamber made findings that non-accused JCE members also accepted the expanded crimes, the Prosecution claims, is irrelevant.[2502] Finally, the Prosecution argues that Praljak was correctly held liable for the expanded crimes committed by other JCE members regardless of the fact that his own direct contribution to these crimes was limited to the time period from 24 July 1993 to 9 November 1993.[2503]

(ii) Analysis

797. The Appeals Chamber will first address the argument that the Trial Chamber failed to identify the crimes that formed part of the expanded CCP and will then proceed to consider whether the Trial Chamber adopted the correct legal approach in this regard. **[page 330]**

798. The Appeals Chamber recalls that a trial judgement should be read as a whole.[2504] In the present case, the Trial Chamber found that, "[f]rom June 1993, the [CCP] was expanded with the siege of East Mostar and encompassed new crimes".[2505] The Trial Chamber then proceeded to describe the crimes that took place in

---

[2492] Stojić's Appeal Brief, para. 106. See also Stojić's Reply Brief, paras 28-29, 31.

[2493] Stojić's Appeal Brief, para. 107, referring to *Krajišnik* Appeal Judgement, para. 173. See Stojić's Reply Brief, paras 28-31.

[2494] Stojić's Appeal Brief, paras 98, 106.

[2495] Stojić's Appeal Brief, para. 99. Stojić points to the fact that the Prosecution pled that the original JCE crimes were Counts 1, 6-9, and 19-20, and that the JCE was later expanded to include Counts 10-11, 12-18, and 22-26.

[2496] Praljak's Appeal Brief, para. 137; Praljak's Reply Brief, para. 28; Appeal Hearing, AT. 384-385 (22 Mar 2017). See also Stojić's Reply Brief, para. 30. Praljak also argues that there was another reasonable inference for the events in Mostar. These submissions are addressed below. See *infra*, paras 927, 941-946.

[2497] Stojić's Appeal Brief, para. 98; Praljak's Appeal Brief, para. 133, referring to *Krajišnik* Appeal Judgement, para. 176. See Stojić's Reply Brief, para. 26. Praljak argues that if the CCP is "unspecified, as it is in the present case, it is impossible to impute the responsibility for crimes to anyone except the direct perpetrator". Praljak's Appeal Brief, para. 133.

[2498] Stojić's Appeal Brief, para. 100.

[2499] Stojić's Appeal Brief, paras 101, 108; Praljak's Appeal Brief, paras 129, 134, 138.

[2500] Prosecution's Response Brief (Stojić), paras 72-76; Prosecution's Response Brief (Praljak), paras 44-45. See also Prosecution's Response Brief (Praljak), para. 49.

[2501] Prosecution's Response Brief (Stojić), paras 79, 81-83; Prosecution's Response Brief (Praljak), paras 44, 46-48.

[2502] Prosecution's Response Brief (Stojić), para. 84.

[2503] Prosecution's Response Brief (Praljak), paras 47-48.

[2504] *Stanišić and Župljanin* Appeal Judgement, para. 138; *Popović et al.* Appeal Judgement, para. 2006; *Orić* Appeal Judgement, para. 38; *Naletilić and Martinović* Appeal Judgement, para. 435; *Stakić* Appeal Judgement, para. 344.

[2505] Trial Judgement, Vol. 4, para. 59.

East Mostar, including shelling and firing at the Muslim population of East Mostar, with the consequence of killing and injuring many inhabitants, forcing them to live in very harsh conditions, impeding or blocking the passage of humanitarian aid, and deliberately targeting the members of international organisations, killing and wounding some of them.[2506] The Trial Chamber also referred to: (1) the destruction of the Old Bridge by the HVO, which caused harm to the Muslim population of East Mostar out of proportion to the legitimate military objective sought; and (2) the severe damage and/or destruction of ten East Mostar mosques.[2507] With respect to (1), the Appeals Chamber recalls that it has reversed the Trial Chamber's findings that the destruction of the Old Bridge constituted persecution as a crime against humanity (Count 1) and unlawful infliction of terror on civilians as a violation of the laws or customs of war (Count 25) and has therefore acquitted the Appellants of these charges insofar as they concern the Old Bridge.[2508] Accordingly, as the destruction of the Old Bridge is no longer part of any remaining counts in this case, the Appeals Chamber will not rely in its subsequent analysis on the Trial Chamber's findings concerning that destruction.

799.   In view of the above and contrary to Stojić's submission, the Trial Chamber did not consider that *all* the crimes committed after June 1993 were new and thus encompassed by the expanded JCE. Instead, it considered that the new crimes were the whole of Count 24 (unlawful attack on civilians – Mostar) and the whole of Count 25 (unlawful infliction of terror on civilians – Mostar),[2509] which were therefore not part of the CCP before June 1993. In addition, the destruction of or severe damage to the ten mosques in East Mostar[2510] also forms a part of Count 21 (destruction or wilful damage to institutions dedicated to religion or education).[2511] As for the other incidents forming part of that count, the Trial Chamber explained elsewhere in the Trial Judgement **[page 331]** that Count 21 was not part of the CCP before June 1993,[2512] thus making it clear that it fell within the scope of the CCP only when it expanded to include events in East Mostar, that is, from June 1993 onwards.

800.   As regards Stojić's assertion that it is unclear whether the Trial Chamber considered deportation to be an expanded crime or part of the original CCP, the Appeals Chamber recalls that the Trial Chamber was explicit in its finding that only the new crimes that took place with the siege of East Mostar in June 1993 constituted the expanded CCP.[2513] However, the Trial Chamber found no instances of deportation by the HVO of Muslims living in East Mostar. Further, the Trial Chamber found that, from mid-May 1993, the HVO forced the Muslim population from West Mostar across a *de facto* border and thus committed the crime of deportation.[2514] The Trial Chamber also found that, following the deportations in Mostar, subsequent instances of deportation occurred in other municipalities, particularly from detention centres located therein.[2515] Later, in its analysis of the existence of the CCP, the Trial Chamber recounted the events in Mostar in May 1993.[2516] It also held that subsequent to an ABiH attack on 30 June 1993 the implementation of the JCE became more efficient, with the HVO arresting and detaining Muslims and sending them to, among others, third countries,[2517] and that "at least as of 30 June 1993", the HZ(R) H-B authorities introduced "a system of deportation utilising the release of Muslim detainees from the HVO detention centres contingent upon their departure from Croatia".[2518] Thus, the Trial Chamber's findings regarding deportation show that

---

[2506]   Trial Judgement, Vol. 4, para. 59.
[2507]   Trial Judgement, Vol. 4, para. 59.
[2508]   See *supra*, para. 426. The Appeals Chamber also reversed the Trial Chamber's conclusion that the destruction of the Old Bridge constituted wanton destruction of cities, towns, or villages or devastation not justified by military necessity as a violation of the laws or customs of war. See *supra*, para. 416.
[2509]   See Trial Judgement, Vol. 3, paras 1684-1692.
[2510]   Trial Judgement, Vol. 4, para. 59.
[2511]   See Trial Judgement, Vol. 3, paras 1609-1610. The remaining part of Count 21 in relation to Mostar, as found by the Trial Chamber, concerns a crime committed prior to June 1993. See Trial Judgement, Vol. 3, para. 1608. See also Trial Judgement, Vol. 3, para. 1611.
[2512]   Trial Judgement, Vol. 4, paras 342, 433, 1213. See also Trial Judgement, Vol. 4, paras 71, 148, 718, 822; *infra*, paras 2447-2455. See also *infra*, paras 2443-2446.
[2513]   See *supra*, para. 798.
[2514]   Trial Judgement, Vol. 3, paras 783-784, 813-814. See Trial Judgement, Vol. 4, paras 56-57.
[2515]   Trial Judgement, Vol. 3, paras 786-809, 810-839.
[2516]   Trial Judgement, Vol. 4, paras 56-57.
[2517]   Trial Judgement, Vol. 4, para. 57.
[2518]   Trial Judgement, Vol. 4, para. 64.

instances of deportation began occurring in mid-May 1993 and that the JCE became "more efficient" from 30 June 1993 because a system of deportation was devised by the HZ(R) H-B authorities. Accordingly, the Appeals Chamber considers that, reading the Trial Judgement as a whole, deportation was found by the Trial Chamber to be part of the CCP before the JCE expanded in June 1993 and thus it was not deemed by the Trial Chamber as one of the expanded crimes that became part of the CCP in June 1993. The Appeals Chamber is further reinforced in this view by the fact that, in contrast to its conclusion as regards Count 21,[2519] the Trial Chamber made no findings indicating that deportation became part of the CCP only in June 1993. Accordingly, Stojić's argument regarding deportation is dismissed.

801.   As to whether the Trial Chamber made the necessary legal findings to support its conclusion that Counts 21, 24, and 25 formed the expanded crimes, the Appeals Chamber recalls that the **[page 332]** Trial Chamber held, relying on the *Krajišnik* Appeal Judgement, that it was required to determine at which point the additional crimes became integrated into the common plan and make findings that "the members of the JCE" were informed of the expansion of criminal activities but did nothing to prevent it and continued to implement the expansion.[2520]

802.   The Appeals Chamber observes that the *Krajišnik* Appeals Chamber found that, as is the case with a common criminal plan in its inception, it is not necessary for the JCE members to explicitly agree to the expansion of criminal means; instead, as with the original criminal plan, that agreement may materialise extemporaneously and be inferred from circumstantial evidence.[2521] Noting that the *Krajišnik* Trial Chamber found that expanded crimes were added to the JCE after "leading members" of that JCE were informed of them, the Appeals Chamber in *Krajišnik* stated:

> The Appeals Chamber notes that in order to impute responsibility to leading JCE members, including Krajišnik, for the expanded crimes, the Trial Chamber was therefore required to make findings as to (1) whether leading members of the JCE were informed of the crimes, (2) whether they did nothing to prevent their recurrence and persisted in the implementation of this expansion of the common objective, and (3) *when* the expanded crimes became incorporated into the common objective.[2522]

It then concluded that the *Krajišnik* Trial Chamber failed to find: (1) who the leading JCE members were, including whether Momčilo Krajišnik was one of them; (2) at which specific point in time the expanded crimes became part of the common plan; and (3) whether JCE members had any intent for those crimes.[2523] It also found that the *Krajišnik* Trial Chamber did not find when the members of the "local component" of the JCE became aware of the expanded crimes and thus when those crimes became incorporated in the common objective.[2524]

803.   As a preliminary matter, the Appeals Chamber notes that in *Krajišnik* it focused on the knowledge of "leading JCE members" primarily because the *Krajišnik* Trial Chamber did the same.[2525] However, contrary to Stojić's argument, this does not necessarily lead to the conclusion that the elements elucidated by the Appeals Chamber in *Krajišnik* require that in every case where the expansion of a JCE is an issue, *all* JCE members, including both accused and non-accused JCE members, must be found to have been informed of the expanded crimes in order to show that they had agreed to expand the JCE. Accordingly, while the knowledge of the expanded crimes on the **[page 333]** part of the "local component" of the JCE was important in the *Krajišnik* case in order to ascertain when those crimes became part of the common plan,[2526] the Appeals Chamber considers that it was not necessary in this case as the Trial Chamber inferred that the agreement to expand the JCE materialised between the Appellants in relation to the crimes in East Mostar in

---

[2519]   See Trial Judgement, Vol. 4, para. 71. See also *supra*, para. 798.
[2520]   Trial Judgement, Vol. 1, para. 212(2), referring to, *inter alia, Krajišnik* Appeal Judgement, paras 171, 175-176, 193-194. See also *supra*, para. 792.
[2521]   *Krajišnik* Appeal Judgement, para. 163.
[2522]   *Krajišnik* Appeal Judgement, paras 170-171 (emphasis in original).
[2523]   *Krajišnik* Appeal Judgement, paras 172-173 & fn. 432.
[2524]   *Krajišnik* Appeal Judgement, para. 174.
[2525]   *Krajišnik* Appeal Judgement, paras 162, 170-173. Indeed, the *Krajišnik* Trial Chamber's own analysis of how an expansion of a JCE is to be established refers to the knowledge of leading JCE members about the expanded crimes and their failure to take measures to prevent them as well as their persistence in implementing the common objective. See *Krajišnik* Appeal Judgement, para. 162, referring to *Krajišnik* Trial Judgement, para. 1098.
[2526]   *Krajišnik* Appeal Judgement, para. 174.

June 1993. As noted above,[2527] as is the case with an original common criminal plan, an expansion of criminal means may be inferred from circumstantial evidence. Determining when additional crimes became integrated into a common criminal plan will therefore be different from case to case. Accordingly, the Trial Chamber in the present case was under no obligation to conduct its expansion analysis in relation to the local component.

804. Concerning Stojić's argument that the Trial Chamber failed to make findings on the knowledge of Croatian leaders, the Appeals Chamber notes that it was necessary to consider the knowledge of "leading JCE members" in the *Krajišnik* case because it was a single-accused case in which the Trial Chamber had to establish a plurality of persons, both for the original and for the expanded JCE. However, the present case is a multi-accused case and thus, once it made findings regarding the Appellants and their membership in the original JCE, the Trial Chamber was not required to concern itself with the knowledge of the Croatian leaders, namely Tuđman, Bobetko, and Šušak. Indeed, when outlining what requirements it had to satisfy before it could attribute the new crimes to the Appellants, the Trial Chamber noted that it was required to make findings that "the members of the JCE" were informed of the expansion of criminal activities, did nothing to prevent them, and persisted in implementing the expansion of the CCP.[2528] The Trial Chamber then proceeded to do so in relation to the Appellants who were all deemed to be JCE members. Moreover, the Trial Chamber made findings that Prlić, Stojić, Praljak, and Petković were among the most important members of the JCE, and thus considered them to be "leading JCE members".[2529] As a result, and in light of the Trial Chamber's analysis outlined below regarding the Appellants' knowledge and intent in relation to East Mostar which indicates that an agreement to expand the relevant crimes materialised between them,[2530] the Appeals Chamber considers that it was not necessary for the Trial Chamber to assess whether other members of the JCE, including Tuđman, Bobetko, and Šušak, agreed to that expansion. In any event, the Trial Chamber made findings that **[page 334]** indicate that these Croatian leaders did so agree.[2531] Stojić's argument that the Trial Chamber erred in law in not addressing the knowledge of the Croatian leaders or the local component is therefore rejected.

805. In addressing whether the Trial Chamber made the necessary findings to impute criminal responsibility for the expanded crimes, the Appeals Chamber will examine the Trial Chamber's analysis concerning each of the Appellants' involvement in the events in East Mostar, as well as whether the Trial Chamber made findings it said it would, namely findings concerning the precise point at which the CCP expanded and, in that connection, found that the Appellants were informed of the expansion of the criminal activities, did nothing to prevent their occurrence, and went on to persist in implementing the expansion of the common design.[2532]

806. Starting with Prlić, the Trial Chamber found that he "knew about the HVO crimes committed during the HVO campaign of fire and shelling against East Mostar – that is, the murders and destruction of property" – and that by minimising them or attempting to deny them he accepted, encouraged, and supported these crimes and the campaign of shelling and sniping.[2533] It further found that he knew about the difficulties international humanitarian organisations had to access East Mostar and that he contributed to this by blocking the delivery of humanitarian aid there from June to at least December 1993, therefore intending to cause "great suffering" to the Mostar population.[2534] The Appeals Chamber finds that the Trial Chamber

---

[2527] See *supra*, para. 802.
[2528] See *supra*, para. 801.
[2529] Trial Judgement, Vol. 4, paras 276, 429, 628, 818.
[2530] See *infra*, paras 806-812.
[2531] Trial Judgement, Vol. 4, paras 1219, 1222-1223 (finding, *inter alia*, that there was a "continuous link" between Praljak on one side and Tuđman, Bobetko, and Šušak on the other). See also Trial Judgement, Vol. 4, paras 522-523, 529-530, 540.
[2532] See *supra*, paras 792, 802.
[2533] Trial Judgement, Vol. 4, para. 176. See Trial Judgement, Vol. 4, paras 174-175, 272 (finding that Prlić was well aware of the shelling and sniping of East Mostar, particularly against civilians and international organisations, and that he attempted to conceal the HVO's responsibility for the destruction of the Old Bridge).
[2534] Trial Judgement, Vol. 4, para. 185. See Trial Judgement, Vol. 4, paras 179-184, 272 (finding that Prlić deliberately impeded the attempts to repair the water supply system in East Mostar, did nothing to improve the living conditions in East Mostar, and on a number of occasions refused to grant authorisation for humanitarian convoys to enter East Mostar).

made the necessary findings relating to Prlić's knowledge about the expanded crimes, the fact that he did nothing to prevent their recurrence, and that he persisted in implementing the expanded JCE.[2535]

807. As for Stojić, the Trial Chamber found that he knew of the "HVO's plan of action" with regard to East Mostar, entailing "the murders and the destruction of property, including mosques, related to the shelling and the harsh living conditions of the population of [East Mostar] caused by the lack of food and water".[2536] This conclusion is supported by findings that Stojić acquired knowledge of HVO crimes in Mostar as early as May 1993,[2537] and by other findings that Stojić **[page 335]** participated in the evictions of Muslims from West Mostar as of June 199 3[2538] that led to an increased concentration of the Muslim population in East Mostar.[2539] The Trial Chamber also found that Stojić knew that HVO forces destroyed Muslim property in January 1993[2540] and mosques in particular in April 1993,[2541] which Stojić also knew occurred during the HVO's campaign in East Mostar.[2542] Further, the Trial Chamber found that Stojić controlled all HVO snipers in West Mostar and knew about and accepted that they sniped civilians and members of international organisations in East Mostar.[2543] It also found that he facilitated the hindering of access of humanitarian aid to East Mostar at times between June and December 1993.[2544] The Trial Chamber found that Stojić had knowledge of the HVO crimes in East Mostar but nevertheless continued to exercise his functions in the HVO, which it took as him accepting those crimes.[2545] The Appeals Chamber finds therefore that the Trial Chamber made the necessary findings relating to Stojić's knowledge about the expanded crimes, the fact that he did nothing to prevent their recurrence, and that he persisted in implementing the expanded JCE.

808. With regard to Praljak, the Trial Chamber found that it had no evidence to "support a finding on Slobodan Praljak's role *in the criminal events* in the Municipality of Mostar between 9 May and 24 July 1993".[2546] At the same time, the Trial Chamber found that he arrived in Mostar on 11 May 1993[2547] and "participated in directing and planning the HVO operations in the Municipality of Mostar between July and early November 1993".[2548] It then recalled, *inter alia,* the events in East Mostar, including that from early June 1993 it was subjected to intense sniping and shelling by the HVO, which resulted in many deaths and woundings and in the destruction of East Mostar mosques.[2549] The Trial Chamber then concluded that, insofar as Praljak was directing the HVO military operations which it found were "orchestrated by the HZ(R) H-B leadership" and were not random acts, he knew that *"these crimes"* would be committed during the operations in **[page 336]** Raštani and Mostar".[2550] As a consequence, it inferred that Praljak "intended to have buildings in East Mostar destroyed, including mosques" as well as that he intended "to deliberately target civilians, to have murders, wounding, physical and psychological abuse and attacks on members of international organisations committed and, lastly, to have women and children removed".[2551] In doing so, the Trial Chamber did not restrict its conclusion on Praljak's intent to post-24 July 1993. Instead, it held Praljak

---

[2535] See *infra*, paras 1276-1285.
[2536] Trial Judgement, Vol. 4, para. 363. See Trial Judgement, Vol. 4, paras 359-362.
[2537] Trial Judgement, Vol. 4, para. 359.
[2538] Trial Judgement, Vol. 4, para. 355.
[2539] Trial Judgement, Vol. 2, paras 1198-1200.
[2540] Trial Judgement, Vol. 4, paras 336-337.
[2541] Trial Judgement, Vol. 4, para. 342. See Trial Judgement, Vol. 4, para. 341.
[2542] Trial Judgement, Vol. 4, para. 363. See Trial Judgement, Vol. 4, para. 359.
[2543] Trial Judgement, Vol. 4, paras 368-370.
[2544] Trial Judgement, Vol. 4, para. 372.
[2545] Trial Judgement, Vol. 4, paras 363, 370. See Trial Judgement, Vol. 4, para. 372. See also *infra*, paras 1800-1804.
[2546] Trial Judgement, Vol. 4, para. 577 (emphasis added). See Trial Judgement, Vol. 4, para. 576.
[2547] Trial Judgement, Vol. 4, para. 576, referring to Slobodan Praljak, T(F). 41519 (16 June 2009). Other findings made by the Trial Chamber confirm that Praljak was in and around Mostar during the relevant time-period, as he was found to have been present in the municipalities of Gornji Vakuf, Ljubuški, Prozor, Jablanica, and Mostar for long periods before 24 July 1993 and was found to have participated in a meeting in the village of Međugorje near Mostar on 18 May 1993. Trial Judgement, Vol. 4, paras 470, 526.
[2548] Trial Judgement, Vol. 4, para. 581. See Trial Judgement, Vol. 4, para. 579 ("Generally speaking, Slobodan Praljak played an important role in planning and directing the military operations in the Municipality of Mostar between 24 July 1993 and 9 November 1993."). See also Trial Judgement, Vol. 4, para. 580.
[2549] Trial Judgement, Vol. 4, paras 582-583.
[2550] Trial judgement, Vol. 4, para. 586 (emphasis added). It is clear from the Trial Chamber's findings that "these crimes" included the shelling and the sniping of East Mostar starting already from early June 1993. See Trial Judgement, Vol. 4, paras 59, 582-584, 586 (referring to "the crimes described above", namely described in paragraphs 582-584).
[2551] Trial Judgement, Vol. 4, para. 586. See also Trial Judgement, Vol. 4, para. 625.

responsible under Counts 21, 24, and 25 for crimes committed in Mostar Municipality.[2552] Further, it held that "[i]nsofar as Slobodan Praljak committed these crimes with the aim of furthering the [CCP]" he was responsible not only for the crimes explicitly set out by the Trial Chamber[2553] but also for all other crimes forming part of the CCP.[2554]

809.   On the basis of the above, the Trial Chamber considered that Praljak was responsible for the expanded crimes even before 24 July 1993, as made clear in its finding that all the Appellants intended to further the CCP, including the expanded crimes.[2555] The Appeals Chamber considers that a reasonable trier of fact could have made this inference despite not having evidence to "support a finding" on Praljak's role "in the criminal events" in Mostar between 9 May and 24 July 1993,[2556] particularly as: (1) the jurisprudence is clear that a member of a JCE need not contribute to an *actus reus* of each specific crime;[2557] (2) the Trial Chamber found that in the period between autumn 1992 to 24 July 1993 Praljak had *de facto* command authority over the HVO and the Military Police, and was present in various municipalities, including in Mostar, between January and June 1993;[2558] and (3) the Trial Chamber held that Praljak planned and directed HVO military operations in Mostar between July and November 1993.[2559] The Appeals Chamber finds therefore that the Trial Chamber made the necessary findings relating to Praljak's knowledge about the expanded crimes, the fact that he did nothing to prevent their recurrence, and that he persisted in implementing the expanded JCE. Indeed, in its final analysis of Praljak's responsibility, having recalled its findings that Praljak was informed of HVO crimes through internal HVO channels, the Trial Chamber found "that the only reasonable inference it can draw from the fact that Slobodan Praljak participated in the planning of the HVO military operations" in, *inter alia*, Mostar "during **[page 337]** the summer of 1993" and that "he continued to exercise control over the armed forces while knowing that its members were committing crimes in other municipalities in BiH, is that he intended to have these crimes committed".[2560] As the Trial Chamber made findings on Praljak's knowledge and activities in the relevant period, its statement that it had no evidence to support a finding about his exact role in the "criminal events" in Mostar between 9 May and 24 July 1993 does not undermine its conclusion. Accordingly, the Appeals Chamber dismisses Praljak's argument regarding the Trial Chamber's consideration of his role in Mostar prior to 24 July 1993.[2561]

810.   As for Petković, the Trial Chamber found that he planned the shelling of East Mostar and knew that HVO forces were shelling and firing on the population of East Mostar "causing deaths, injuries and the destruction of property, including mosques".[2562] The Trial Chamber found that he knew that members of international organisations were affected by the HVO shelling, and that the Muslim population of East Mostar lived in a state of terror.[2563] It found, insofar as he ordered and contributed to planning this shelling, that Petković intended to have these crimes committed.[2564] Further, the Trial Chamber made findings that Petković was aware that HVO military operations before June 1993 involved the destruction of mosques.[2565] The Trial Chamber also found that Petković had "the power to allow humanitarian convoys to pass through and reach East Mostar" and occasionally let them through, but that, when he failed to do so, he intended to hinder the humanitarian convoys.[2566] The Appeals Chamber therefore finds that the Trial Chamber made the

---

[2552]   Trial Judgement, Vol. 4, para. 630.
[2553]   See Trial Judgement, Vol. 4, para. 630.
[2554]   Trial Judgement, Vol. 4, para. 631.
[2555]   Trial Judgement, Vol. 4, paras 67-68. See Trial Judgement, Vol. 4, para. 59.
[2556]   Trial Judgement, Vol. 4, para. 577. See Trial Judgement, Vol. 4, para. 576.
[2557]   *Krajišnik* Appeal Judgement, paras 695-696 (holding that a contribution to the JCE need not be criminal *per se* and that the accused need not physically commit or participate in the *actus reus* of a perpetrated crime, but that it is sufficient that he perform acts that are in some way directed to the furthering of the JCE).
[2558]   Trial Judgement, Vol. 4, paras 470, 472-482.
[2559]   Trial Judgement, Vol. 4, para. 581.
[2560]   Trial Judgement, Vol. 4, para. 625.
[2561]   See also *infra*, paras 1982, 2003.
[2562]   Trial Judgement, Vol. 4, paras 747, 750.
[2563]   Trial Judgement, Vol. 4, para. 750.
[2564]   Trial Judgement, Vol. 4, para. 750. See also Trial Judgement, Vol. 4, para. 815.
[2565]   Trial Judgement, Vol. 4, paras 695, 699, 729-730.
[2566]   Trial Judgement, Vol. 4, para. 755.

necessary findings relating to Petković's knowledge about the expanded crimes, the fact that he did nothing to prevent their recurrence, and that he persisted in implementing the expanded JCE.[2567]

811.   With regard to Ćorić, the Trial Chamber found that he had knowledge of the HVO campaign of fire, shelling, and sniping against the population of East Mostar and the crimes committed during that campaign.[2568] It further found that, inasmuch as he lent support to the campaigns, Ćorić intended to facilitate the crimes directly linked to the HVO military operations against East Mostar, namely, "the murders and destruction of property, including mosques, resulting from the shelling".[2569] Moreover, it found that, around January 1993, Ćorić knew that the **[page 338]** destruction of mosques formed part of the HVO military operations.[2570] The Trial Chamber also found that on 1 June 1993, in light of checkpoints he directed, Ćorić knew of the difficult humanitarian conditions that prevailed in East Mostar and nevertheless impeded the delivery of humanitarian aid, thereby contributing to the creation of unbearable living conditions for the Muslim population of East Mostar.[2571] Consequently, the Appeals Chamber finds that the Trial Chamber made the necessary findings relating to Ćorić›s awareness of the expanded crimes, the fact that he did nothing to prevent their recurrence, and that he persisted in implementing the expansion of the common design.[2572]

812.   Lastly, with regard to Pušić, the Trial Chamber found that he knew that the HVO was "intensively and continuously shelling East Mostar",[2573] and that it was being subjected to "continuous shooting and shelling as part of a siege between June 1993 and April 1994".[2574] It further found that he knew that this was causing destruction to buildings dedicated to religion and deaths among the population, and knew about the difficulties international organisations were having in gaining access to East Mostar, as well as the extremely harsh conditions the population was living in.[2575] The Trial Chamber found that Pušić worsened the living conditions in East Mostar by obstructing humanitarian evacuations.[2576] As a result, the Trial Chamber found that Pušić accepted the expanded crimes in East Mostar.[2577] Referring later to his knowledge of the living conditions in East Mostar caused by the HVO siege, the Trial Chamber concluded that the only reasonable inference was that Pušić intended the siege-related crimes.[2578] The Appeals Chamber therefore finds that the Trial Chamber made the necessary findings relating to Pušić's knowledge of the expanded crimes, the fact that he did nothing to prevent their recurrence, and that he persisted in implementing the expanded JCE.[2579]

813.   In light of the findings above, the Appeals Chamber dismisses Stojić's and Praljak's arguments that the Trial Chamber erred in law in failing to make findings on when leading members of the JCE were informed of the expanded crimes or whether they did anything to prevent their recurrence.[2580] With regard to Stojić's argument that it failed to find when leading JCE **[page 339]** members "went from being merely aware of the crime to intending it",[2581] the Appeals Chamber considers that the Trial Chamber found that when the JCE members became aware of the expanded crimes, and did not take any measures to prevent their recurrence but contributed to them and persisted in implementing the common objective, they thereby came to intend

---

[2567]   See also *infra*, paras 2226-2258, 2397-2402, 2406.

[2568]   Trial Judgement, Vol. 4, para. 938. See also Trial Judgement, Vol. 4, para. 945.

[2569]   Trial Judgement, Vol. 4, para. 938. See also Trial Judgement, Vol. 4, para. 945.

[2570]   Trial Judgement, Vol. 4, para. 923. See Trial Judgement, Vol. 4, paras 919-922.

[2571]   Trial Judgement, Vol. 4, paras 940, 944-945.

[2572]   See also *infra*, paras 2566-2569, 2580-2581.

[2573]   Trial Judgement, Vol. 4, para. 1120.

[2574]   Trial Judgement, Vol. 4, para. 1122.

[2575]   Trial Judgement, Vol. 4, para. 1122.

[2576]   Trial Judgement, Vol. 4, para. 1122.

[2577]   Trial Judgement, Vol. 4, para. 1122. See Trial Judgement, Vol. 4, para. 59.

[2578]   Trial Judgement, Vol. 4, para. 1206.

[2579]   See also *infra*, paras 2748-2753, 2800-2802, 2806.

[2580]   In reaching this conclusion, the Appeals Chamber has relied on sections of the Trial Judgement discussing the Appellants' responsibility. The Appeals Chamber considers that Stojić fails to substantiate his claim that one cannot do so. See Stojić's Appeal Brief, para. 106. In light of its conclusion, the Appeals Chamber also dismisses Stojić's claim that the Trial Chamber erred in fact and failed to provide a "reasoned decision". See *supra*, fn. 2491.

[2581]   Stojić"s Appeal Brief, para. 107.

those expanded crimes.[2582] Stojić fails to demonstrate an error in this approach.[2583] Therefore, the Appeals Chamber dismisses Stojić's argument.

814.   Reading the Trial Judgement as a whole, the Appeals Chamber considers that the Trial Chamber sufficiently understood and explained Counts 21 (in part), 24, and 25 as consisting of the crimes that were added as part of the expanded JCE, hence distinguishing them from the remaining crimes that the Trial Chamber found were part of "the CCP from the beginning. Given that the Trial Chamber identified explicitly that the expanded crimes became part of the CCP in June 1993, with the siege of East Mostar,[2584] and came to that conclusion based on the findings it made in relation to each individual Appellant as set out above, the Appeals Chamber finds that the Trial Chamber described with sufficient precision when and under what circumstances the scope of the CCP broadened. Thus, the Appeals Chamber finds that Stojić and Praljak have not demonstrated that the Trial Chamber erred in failing to define which crimes were part of the original JCE and which were part of the expanded JCE.[2585] Consequently, it dismisses Praljak's ground of appeal 7 as well as Stojić's grounds of appeal 11 and 12.

(b) Stojić's appeal (Ground 4 in part)

(i) Arguments of the Parties

815.   Referring to several Tribunal trial judgements, Stojić submits that the Trial Chamber erred in law in failing to consider whether each individual crime in each municipality and each detention centre had the objective of furthering the CCP.[2586] Specifically, he submits that the Trial Chamber erred in: (1) omitting to analyse whether crimes in Gornji Vakuf, Prozor, Mostar, Čapljina, and Stolac, as well as at the Hehodrom and Ljubuški, Dretelj, and Gabela Prisons, were part of the **[page 340]** CCP;[2587] (2) failing to address the crimes at Vojno Detention Centre in its CCP assessment;[2588] (3) "expressly declin[ing]" to determine the underlying purpose of HVO actions in Jablanica;[2589] and (4) wrongly including the Stupni Do attack in Vareš Municipality in its analysis having found that it was not ordered by "HVO leaders".[2590]

816.   The Prosecution responds that the Trial Chamber exhaustively analysed the crimes elsewhere in the Trial Judgement.[2591] In particular, it asserts that the Trial Chamber: (1) examined the HVO actions in Jablanica and concluded that these events were part of the CCP;[2592] (2) found that Vojno Detention Centre was "within the network of detention centres used to implement" the CCP, thus making it unnecessary to mention the crimes that took place there in its CCP assessment;[2593] and (3) reasonably found that the crimes in Stupni Do were committed pursuant to the CCP.[2594]

[2582]   See *supra*, paras 806-812; Trial Judgement, Vol. 4, paras 67-68 (where the Trial Chamber found that all the Appellants intended the crimes that were part of the CCP, including the expanded crimes). See also *infra*, paras 1800-1804.

[2583]   *Cf. Krajišnik* Appeal Judgement, paras 171-172.

[2584]   Trial Judgement, Vol. 4, para. 59.

[2585]   See also *infra*, paras 874-886.

[2586]   Stojić's Appeal Brief, para. 50, referring to *Tolimir* Trial Judgement, paras 1021-1024, 1028-1030, *Kupreškić et al.* Trial Judgement, paras 163-164, 336-338, *Boškoski and Tarčulovski* Trial Judgement, para. 572. See also Stojić's Appeal Brief, heading before para. 48, paras 48-49; Stojić's Reply Brief, para. 23; Appeal Hearing, AT. 276 (21 Mar 2017).

[2587]   Stojić's Appeal Brief, para. 51, referring to Trial Judgement, Vol. 2, paras 80-91, 343-488, 758-1377, 1379-1663, 1787-1878, 1879-2034, 2035-2191, Vol. 3, paras 1-274, Vol. 4, paras 45, 47, 56-59.

[2588]   Stojić's Appeal Brief, para. 52, referring to Trial Judgement, Vol. 4, paras 41-68.

[2589]   Stojić's Appeal Brief, para. 52, referring to Trial Judgement, Vol. 2, para. 526.

[2590]   Stojić's Appeal Brief, para. 52, referring to Trial Judgement, Vol. 4, para. 61. See also Stojić's Appeal Brief, para. 58.

[2591]   Prosecution's Response Brief (Stojić), para. 33, referring to Trial Judgement, Vol. 2, paras 1-2191, Vol. 3, paras 1-1741.

[2592]   Prosecution's Response Brief (Stojić), para. 37, referring to Trial Judgement, Vol. 2, paras 538-543, Vol. 4, paras 146, 341, 714, 717.

[2593]   Prosecution's Response Brief (Stojić), para. 37, referring to Trial Judgement, Vol. 4, para. 890. The Prosecution submits that for instance, Heliodrom detainees were transported to Vojno Detention Centre, held in very harsh conditions, mistreated, and even murdered while performing forced labour, and that some detainees agreed to leave for ABiH-controlled territories or other countries. See Prosecution's Response Brief (Stojić), para. 37, referring to Trial Judgement, Vol. 2, paras 1650, 1654-1655, 1662, 1694-1700, 1703-1709, 1721, 1723-1724, 1726, 1731, 1740, 1749, 1757, Vol. 4, para. 64.

[2594]   Prosecution's Response Brief (Stojić), para. 37, referring to Trial Judgement, Vol. 3, paras 492, 503, 507, 699-700, 752-753, 1294-1295, 1396-1397, 1498-1499, 1554-1556, 1596-1599, 1740-1741, Vol. 4, paras 61-63, 65-66, 68, 202, 594, 596-597, 621, 623, 626, 765, 767, 772, 775-777, 805, 815-816, 1220. The Prosecution does not expressly respond to Stojić's challenges to the Trial Chamber's

(ii) <u>Analysis</u>

817. With respect to Stojić's submission that the Trial Chamber failed to assess whether each individual crime in each municipality and each detention centre formed part of the CCP, the Appeals Chamber recalls that JCE liability requires proof of a common purpose "which amounts to or involves the commission of a crime".[2595] In this regard, the Appeals Chamber observes that the Trial Chamber found that the CCP – a common criminal plan to ethnically cleanse the provinces considered Croatian – came into being in mid-January 1993, and was implemented through various crimes that took place in a number of different municipalities and detention centres.[2596] The **[page 341]** Trial Chamber found that the CCP came into being in mid-January 1993 based on a number of factors, including the presentation of the Vance-Owen Peace Plan on 2 January 1993, and the ultimatum adopted by the HVO HZ-HB envisaging the subordination of the ABiH to the HVO ("the 15 January 1993 Ultimatum").[2597] The Trial Chamber's factual findings regarding the crimes in Gornji Vakuf, Prozor, Mostar, Čapljina, and Stolac, as well as at the Heliodrom and Ljubuški, Dretelj, and Gabela Prisons, were then expressly referenced or cross-referenced by the Trial Chamber in its CCP analysis, including by finding that the JCE was carried out in stages.[2598] Further, in the same section of the Trial Judgement, the Trial Chamber made clear that it considered that these events, among others, formed part of the CCP because they "tended to follow a clear pattern of conduct".[2599]

818. Regarding the crimes at Vojno Detention Centre, the Appeals Chamber observes that the Trial Chamber did not expressly refer to these crimes in its analysis of the CCP.[2600] However, the Trial Chamber made clear that the entire CCP analysis was underpinned by factual findings regarding, *inter alia,* the detention centres,[2601] and found that the overall system of detention centres formed an integral part of the system for deporting the Muslim population of the HR H-B.[2602] The Appeals Chamber also recalls that the Trial Judgement must be read as a whole,[2603] and observes that the Trial Chamber's analysis of Prlić's, Petković's, and Pušić's criminal responsibility made clear that the crimes at Vojno Detention Centre fell within the CCP.[2604] The Appeals Chamber finds that Stojić has failed to demonstrate an error with regard to the Trial Chamber's approach to these crimes. This submission is rejected.

819. Regarding Stojić's assertion that the Trial Chamber erred in "expressly declining]" to determine the underlying purpose of HVO actions in Jablanica, the Appeals Chamber observes that the Trial Chamber concluded that it was unable to determine the underlying reason for the clashes between the HVO and ABiH in Jablanica Municipality.[2605] The Trial Chamber, however, concluded that the events in Jablanica fell within the CCP because the crimes that were committed there **[page 342]** formed part of "a clear pattern of conduct".[2606] The explanation for the clashes between the HVO and ABiH thus forms background context, and has no direct bearing on this conclusion. Stojić fails to explain how this omission has an impact on his conviction. This argument is dismissed.

---

approach to the crimes in Gornji Vakuf, Prozor, Mostar, Čapljina, and Stolac, as well as at the Heliodrom and Ljubuški, Dretelj, and Gabela Prisons. See Prosecution's Response Brief (Stojić), para. 33.

[2595] *Tadić* Appeal Judgement, para. 227(I). See also *Šainović et al.* Appeal Judgement, para. 611; *Statić* Appeal Judgement, para. 64; *Brđanin* Appeal Judgement, paras 364, 418; *supra,* para. 790.

[2596] Trial Judgement, Vol. 4, paras 44-65. See *supra,* paras 789-790.

[2597] Trial Judgement, Vol. 1, paras 445, 451-452, Vol. 4, paras 44, 125. See also *infra,* paras 852-853.

[2598] Trial Judgement, Vol. 4, paras 45, 47-48, 57, 59, 61, 64 & fns 124 (referring to Gornji Vakuf), 126 (referring to findings on Prozor), 127-128 (referring to Jablanica and Gornji Vakuf), 154-157 (referring to Prozor, Čapljina, Stolac, the Heliodrom, and Ljubuški and Gabela Prisons), 165-167 (referring to Mostar), 169-172 (referring to Vareš), 175-177 (referring to Mostar, the Heliodrom, and Ljubuški, Dretelj, and Gabela Prisons).

[2599] Trial Judgement, Vol. 4, para. 65. See also Trial Judgement, Vol. 4, paras 45-64.

[2600] See Trial Judgement, Vol. 2, paras 1664-1716.

[2601] See Trial Judgement, Vol. 4, para. 45.

[2602] See Trial Judgement, Vol. 4, paras 66, 68, 1298. See also Trial Judgement, Vol. 4, para. 890.

[2603] *Popović et al.* Appeal Judgement, para. 2006; *Mrkšić and Šljivančanin* Appeal Judgement, para. 379. See also *Kalimanzira* Appeal Judgement, para. 227.

[2604] See Trial Judgement, Vol. 4, paras 236-239, 274, 797-798, 1186-1187, 1203. See also Trial Judgement, Vol. 4, paras 240, 287-288, 1215.

[2605] Trial Judgement, Vol. 2, para. 526 ("Whatever the underlying reasons may have been, clashes between the HVO and the ABiH did break out on 13-14 April 1993 in Jablanica Municipality.").

[2606] Trial Judgement, Vol. 4, paras 46, 48, 65.

820. As regards Stojić's challenge to the findings on the attack at Stupni Do on 23 October 1993, the Appeals Chamber observes that although the Trial Chamber found that the HVO leaders did not order the attack, it still found that the crimes committed there fell within the CCP because they formed part of the said pattern of conduct and because of the HVO leaders' attempts to conceal them.[2607] In that respect, the Trial Chamber focused on two leaders specifically, namely Praljak and Petković, and their involvement in concealment of Stupni Do crimes.[2608] Further, the Trial Chamber found that both Praljak and Petković participated in planning and directing the HVO operations in Vareš Municipality in October 1993.[2609] Similarly, the Trial Chamber found that Stojić facilitated the HVO military operations in Vareš Municipality.[2610] The Appeals Chamber discerns no issue with this approach and notes that the absence of an order by HVO leaders to attack Stupni Do does not necessarily result in a conclusion that the crimes that took place during the attack were not part of the CCP, so long as there are other factors that can be used to lead to that conclusion, such as the pattern of crimes. In that regard, the Appeals Chamber notes the reversal of some of the Vareš-Municipality-related findings concerning Petković and Praljak, namely that Petković contributed to the commission of crimes in Vareš town and Stupni Do,[2611] and that Praljak facilitated the crimes in Stupni Do by contributing to their concealment and by planning and directing the operations in Vareš Municipality.[2612] However, a number of the Trial Chamber's other findings concerning the events in Vareš Municipality remain undisturbed, including that: (1) Praljak planned and directed the HVO operations in Vareš Municipality; (2) Petković contributed to concealment of the Stupni Do crimes; (3) Stojić facilitated the HVO military operations in Vareš Municipality; (4) Stojić, Petković, and Praljak were all informed of Stupni Do crimes soon after they happened; and (5) Stojić and Petković accepted these crimes.[2613] Further, all three were found to have intended the type of crimes that took place in Stupni Do months before the Stupni Do attack and, additionally, continued to participate in the JCE following that attack.[2614] The Appeals Chamber considers that these undisturbed findings provide a sufficient link between the JCE members and the crimes that **[page 343]** took place in Stupni Do.[2615] As a result, and recalling again that the Trial Chamber considered that Stupni Do crimes were part of a clear pattern of conduct, the Appeals Chamber finds that Stojić has failed to demonstrate any error in the Trial Chamber's conclusion that Stupni Do events fell within the CCP.

821. Based on the above, the Appeals Chamber concludes that Stojić has not shown that the Trial Chamber erred in failing to specifically address whether each individual crime had the objective of furthering the CCP. Stojić's ground of appeal 4 is dismissed in relevant part.

(c) Praljak's appeal (Ground 49)

822. Praljak submits that the Trial Chamber failed to provide a reasoned opinion for its conclusions on crimes charged under JCE I and his responsibility for those crimes, thereby denying him his right to an effective appeal.[2616] Specifically, Praljak claims a lack of reasoned opinion as regards: (1) his conviction under JCE I for murders in Mostar which the Trial Chamber held not to form part of the CCP;[2617] (2) the

[2607] Trial Judgement, Vol. 4, paras 61-62, 65. See Trial Judgement, Vol. 3, paras 484-486, 492.
[2608] Trial Judgement, Vol. 4, para. 61.
[2609] Trial Judgement, Vol. 4, paras 591-594, 597, 767.
[2610] Trial Judgement, Vol. 4, paras 380, 383.
[2611] See *infra*, paras 2275-2280.
[2612] See *infra*, paras 2059-2062.
[2613] See *infra*, paras 1698, 1701-1703, 1707, 1709-1711, 2028, 2042-2047, 2050-2054, 2283-2284, 2289-2294.
[2614] See Trial Judgement, Vol. 4, paras 68, 1225, 1227-1228.
[2615] In this respect, the Appeals Chamber recalls that for JCE I liability "it is sufficient for the participant to perform acts that in some way are directed to the furthering" of the common plan or purpose. *Tadić* Appeal Judgement, para. 229. See *Popović et al.* Appeal Judgement, paras 1378, 1653; *Šainović et al.* Appeal Judgement, para. 1445; *Krajišnik* Appeal Judgement, para. 695 ("It is sufficient that the accused 'perform acts that in some way are directed to the furthering' of the JCE in the sense that he significantly contributes to the commission of the crimes involved in the JCE"). See also *Karemera and Ngirumpatse* Appeal Judgement, paras 109 ("the Trial Chamber was not required to find that he personally contributed to each criminal act, but rather that he made a significant contribution to the common purpose and that each of the criminal acts for which he was held responsible formed part of that purpose"), 153.
[2616] Praljak's Appeal Brief, paras 539-540, 543-544; Praljak's Reply Brief, paras 112-113. See Appeal Hearing, AT. 383 (22 Mar 2017).
[2617] Praljak's Appeal Brief, para. 541.

variation in crimes included in the CCP as between different municipalities;[2618] and (3) whether he was found guilty of crimes committed in Jablanica, Stolac, Ljubuški, and Čapljina.[2619]

823.   The Prosecution responds that the Trial Chamber clearly established the scope of Praljak's convictions, with sufficient reasoning, thereby allowing him to exercise his right of appeal.[2620] With regard to Mostar, the Prosecution contends that Praljak was convicted under JCE I for murders **[page 344]** other than those which the Trial Chamber considered not to form part of the CCP.[2621] The Prosecution argues that Praljak's other arguments warrant summary dismissal.[2622]

824.   With regard to Praljak's argument that the Trial Chamber failed to provide a reasoned opinion in relation to how the crimes included in the CCP could vary between different municipalities, the Appeals Chamber considers that Praljak does not explain why a criminal plan perpetrated across a wide geographical area would have to be exactly consistent in the crimes committed in different locations. With regard to Praljak's argument that the Trial Chamber failed to provide a reasoned opinion in relation to his conviction under JCE I for murders in Mostar which it held not to form part of the CCP, the Appeals Chamber notes that the Trial Chamber found that certain murders committed during the HVO's detention and eviction operations were not part of the CCP.[2623] However, the Trial Chamber also found that murders committed "during attacks", including during the HVO attacks on East Mostar and during the HVO attack on the village of Raštani in Mostar, formed part of the CCP.[2624] Praljak was accordingly convicted of those specific murders rather than murders that did not form part of the CCP. He misrepresents the Trial Chamber's findings and his argument is therefore dismissed. Finally, Praljak's argument that the Trial Chamber failed to make clear findings as regards his responsibility for the crimes committed in Jablanica, Stolac, Ljubuški, and Čapljina misrepresents the Trial Judgement. Although the Trial Chamber found that Praljak had not personally contributed to the crimes in these municipalities,[2625] it found that these crimes formed part of the CCP,[2626] and that Praljak, as a JCE member, was responsible for these crimes.[2627] The Appeals Chamber finds that Praljak has failed to show that the Trial Chamber violated his right to a reasoned opinion, and dismisses his ground of appeal 49.

(d) Petković's appeal (Sub-ground 3.2.1.3)

825.   Petković argues that the Trial Chamber was required to establish through a reasoned opinion that each underlying crime charged was a consequence of the implementation of the JCE.[2628] In the **[page 345]** present case, he submits that the Trial Chamber erred in assuming that the crimes were the result of the implementation of the CCP.[2629]

[2618]   Praljak's Appeal Brief, para. 541.

[2619]   Praljak's Appeal Brief, para. 542. Praljak also claims under this ground of appeal that the Trial Chamber failed to provide a reasoned opinion in relation to the scope of the CCP and its expansion and when concluding that crimes committed in Gornji Vakuf Municipality fell within the CCP. Praljak's Appeal Brief, paras 540, 542. However, these arguments are premised on his submissions in other grounds of appeal, which the Appeals Chamber dismisses elsewhere. See Praljak's Appeal Brief, para. 540 & fns 1238-1239 (referring to, *inter alia*, sub-grounds of appeal 7.1-7.2, 39.2), para. 542. See also *supra*, para. 814; *infra*, paras 867, 1921. Accordingly, the Appeals Chamber will not consider them here.

[2620]   Prosecution's Response Brief (Praljak), paras 272-274, 276.

[2621]   Prosecution's Response Brief (Praljak), para. 275.

[2622]   Prosecution's Response Brief (Praljak), para. 274. The Prosecution does not specifically address Praljak's submission regarding Jablanica, Stolac, Ljubuški, and Čapljina.

[2623]   Trial Judgement, Vol. 4, paras 70, 72.

[2624]   Trial Judgement, Vol. 4, paras 59, 66. See also Trial Judgement, Vol. 2, paras 948-963.

[2625]   See Trial Judgement, Vol. 4, para. 630.

[2626]   Trial Judgement, Vol. 4, paras 48, 57. See also Trial Judgement, Vol. 4, para. 63.

[2627]   Trial Judgement, Vol. 4, para. 631.

[2628]   Petković's Appeal Brief, para. 34, referring to *Zigiranyirazo* Trial Judgement, para. 418, *Limaj et al.* Trial Judgement, para. 669, *Limaj et al.* Appeal Judgement, para. 99. Petković argues in particular that jurisprudence demands this step in order to exclude the possibilities that: (1) crimes might have occurred in the absence of a specific plan, or independently thereof; or (2) the perpetrators' relationship to the JCE members was too tenuous. Petković's Appeal Brief, para. 34.

[2629]   Petković's Appeal Brief, paras 35-36. Petković submits in particular that the Trial Chamber's decision was based on unproven factual presumptions, namely that: (1) all crimes were the consequence of a plan and had no other cause; (2) the underlying crimes were the consequence of that particular plan and no other; (3) the plan was implemented in each and every location where the crimes

826. The Prosecution responds that the Trial Chamber did not assume that the crimes were part of the CCP, but engaged in a detailed analysis of the pattern of the crimes committed in various municipalities.[2630]

827. The Appeals Chamber recalls that the Trial Chamber was required to provide clear findings as to the scope of the JCE,[2631] and further recalls its finding that the Trial Chamber complied with this test in the present case.[2632] Moreover, Petković merely claims that the Trial Chamber unreasonably assumed that the crimes occurred as a result of the implementation of the CCP, without supporting the argument with any evidence. The Appeals Chamber finds that Petković fails to show an error in the inference the Trial Chamber drew, and thus dismisses bis sub-ground of appeal 3.2.1.3.

4. Alleged errors as regards the constituent events of the CCP

(a) Introduction

828. While noting that the Prosecution alleged the existence of several JCEs set up at various times and under various forms, the Trial Chamber found that there was only one, single CCP, namely "domination by the HR H-B Croats through ethnic cleansing of the Muslim population."[2633] The Trial Chamber also found that already as of December 1991, leaders of HZ(R) H-B and leaders of Croatia, including Tuđman, believed that in order to achieve the Ultimate Purpose of the JCE, it was necessary to change the ethnic make-up of the territories claimed to form part of the HZ H-B.[2634] Additionally, it found that from no later than October 1992, Prlić, Stojić, Praljak, and Petković knew that the implementation of the Ultimate Purpose of the JCE ran counter to the peace negotiations being conducted in Geneva and would involve the Muslim population moving outside the territory of the HZ H-B.[2635] The Trial Chamber found that the JCE came into being in mid-January 1993, and was carried out in stages.[2636] In particular, it referenced and cross-referenced **[page 346]** its findings that the HVO committed crimes: (1) in Gornji Vakuf Municipality between January and April 1993;[2637] (2) in Jablanica Municipality in April 1993;[2638] (3) in Prozor Municipality in April 1993;[2639] (4) in Mostar Municipality between April 1993 and April 1994;[2640] (5) following the ABiH attack on the Tihomir Mišić Barracks on 30 June 1993;[2641] and (6) in Vareš Municipality in October 1993.[2642]

(b) Alleged errors regarding the findings concerning the pre-CCP period

(i) Prlić's appeal (Sub-ground 10.1)

829. Prlić argues that the Trial Chamber erred in concluding that the CCP existed.[2643] He submits that the Trial Chamber erroneously relied on "selective evidence" in concluding that the HZ(R) H-B leaders sought to change the ethnic make-up of the territories, and that Prlić knew that the implementation of the plan ran counter to the peace negotiations being conducted in Geneva.[2644]

---

were allegedly committed; and (4) all of the Appellants partook in and shared that common plan. Petković's Appeal Brief, para. 36. See also Petković's Reply Brief, para. 12.

[2630] Prosecution's Response Brief (Petković), para. 33.

[2631] See *Krajišnik* Appeal Judgement, paras 161-178. See also *supra*, para. 817.

[2632] See also *supra*, paras 817-821, 824.

[2633] Trial Judgement, Vol. 4, para. 41.

[2634] Trial Judgement, Vol. 4, para. 43.

[2635] Trial Judgement, Vol. 4, para. 43.

[2636] Trial Judgement, Vol. 4, paras 44-45.

[2637] Trial Judgement, Vol. 4, paras 45, 48 & fns 124, 127.

[2638] Trial Judgement, Vol. 4, paras 46, 48.

[2639] Trial Judgement, Vol. 4, para. 47.

[2640] Trial Judgement, Vol. 4, paras 49, 51, 53, 56-59.

[2641] Trial Judgement, Vol. 4, paras 57, 64.

[2642] Trial Judgement, Vol. 4, paras 61-63.

[2643] Prlić's Appeal Brief, para. 281.

[2644] Prlić's Appeal Brief, para. 282, referring to Trial Judgement, Vol. 4, para. 43. Prlić also adopts by reference his sub-grounds of appeal 1.1, 1.3, 9.6, 9.7, 16.1, 16.2, and 16.3. See Prlić's Appeal Brief, para. 283. See also Appeal Hearing, AT. 141-142, 159-162,

830. The Prosecution responds that Prlić makes mere assertions unsupported by evidence[2645] with "redundant and unexplained cross-references to arguments" made elsewhere in his appeal brief.[2646] The Prosecution submits that these arguments do not warrant detailed consideration and thus should be summarily dismissed.[2647]

831. The Appeals Chamber notes that in asserting that the Trial Chamber erred in relying on "selective evidence", Prlić simply references a single paragraph of the Trial Judgement, without explaining how the Trial Chamber erred. The Appeals Chamber also observes that Prlić merely makes reference, without explaining their relevance, to a number of his sub-grounds of appeal **[page 347]** which it considers and dismisses elsewhere.[2648] The Appeals Chamber therefore rejects Prlić's sub-ground of appeal 10.1.[2649]

(ii) Praljak's appeal (Sub-ground 5.4 in part)

832. Praljak challenges the Trial Chamber's conclusion that as of December 1991, HZ(R) H-B leaders and Croatian leaders believed that in order to achieve the Ultimate Purpose of the JCE, it was necessary to change the ethnic make-up of the territories claimed to form part of HZ(R) H-B. Praljak submits that this finding contradicts other findings in which the Trial Chamber considered that "the possible aim" of the. plan was to establish an autonomous Croatian entity in BiH.[2650] Praljak also argues that the Trial Chamber confused the CCP with political aims when concluding that the JCE was established to accomplish the political purpose of establishing an autonomous Croatian entity in BiH, as this purpose was legitimate and not criminal.[2651] In addition, he contends that the Trial Chamber "recognized that Tuđman was solely led by" Croatia, which indicates that Tuđman was concerned about Croatia's interests.[2652]

833. The Prosecution responds that Praljak's semantic argument about contradiction between a Croatian entity in BiH and partition disregards the findings on partition discussions between the Croats and Serbs.[2653] The Prosecution also submits that the Trial Chamber did not confuse the CCP and the Ultimate Purpose of the JCE, but rather identified a single common criminal purpose, namely, to establish, by criminal means, a Croatian entity in BiH reconstituting at least in part the Banovina borders.[2654] It further asserts that Praljak selectively cites passages from the **[page 348]** Trial Judgement out of context and fails to read the Trial Judgement as a whole, thus ignoring the detailed JCE analysis.[2655]

---

169 (20 Mar 2017) (where he argues, *inter alia,* that the CCP did not exist and that the Croat plans about division of territory were based on various international peace plans which in turn never called for ethnic cleansing).

[2645] Prosecution's Response Brief (Prlić), para. 166, referring to *Đorđević* Appeal Judgement, para. 20(ix), *Galić* Appeal Judgement, para. 246.

[2646] Prosecution's Response Brief (Prlić), paras 166-167.

[2647] Prosecution's Response Brief (Prlić), para. 166. See also Prosecution's Response Brief (Prlić), paras 163-165. The Prosecution further submits that the evidence and the pattern of events in BiH clearly show that the goal was to change the ethnic composition of Herceg-Bosna through crimes and that this was ultimately achieved. See Appeal Hearing, AT. 180, 190-192 (20 Mar 2017).

[2648] See *supra,* paras 170-176, 697-699, 722-727. See also *infra,* paras 1146-1221.

[2649] With respect to Prlić's argument that the plans for division of territory did not call for ethnic cleansing as they were based on various international peace plans, the Appeals Chamber notes that Prlić made the same argument in his Final Brief. See Prlić's Final Brief, paras 239-262. This argument was rejected by the Trial Chamber. Prlić now repeats his arguments using his own interpretation of the evidence without showing that no reasonable trier of fact could have interpreted this evidence as the Trial Chamber did. For that reason, Prlić's argument regarding ethnic cleansing is also dismissed.

[2650] Praljak's Appeal Brief, para. 93, referring to Praljak's Appeal Brief, para. 71 (Praljak's sub-grounds of appeal 5.1-5.2), Trial Judgement, Vol. 4, paras 10, 24, 43. Praljak also takes issue with the Trial Chamber's finding that the CCP was established in January 1993, arguing that: (1) any idea Tuđman had ever had to divide BiH vanished in early 1992 with the proclamation of BiH's independence; and (2) following the proclamation, Tuđman reiterated that the Croatian people's future was within BiH. Praljak's Appeal Brief, para. 94, referring to, *inter alia,* Praljak's Appeal Brief, paras 73-75, 79-80, 82-85 (Praljak's sub-grounds of appeal 5.1-5.2).

[2651] Praljak's Appeal Brief, para. 95, referring to Trial Judgement, Vol. 4, para. 44; Appeal Hearing, AT. 382 (22 Mar 2017).

[2652] Praljak's Appeal Brief, para. 96, referring to Trial Judgement, Vol. 4, para. 15.

[2653] Prosecution's Response Brief (Praljak), para. 40.

[2654] Prosecution's Response Brief (Praljak), para. 33. See also Prosecution's Response Brief (Praljak), para. 41.

[2655] Prosecution's Response Brief (Praljak), para. 34. The Prosecution also argues that Praljak repeats trial arguments. Prosecution's Response Brief (Praljak), para. 40, referring to, *inter alia,* Trial Judgement Vol. 4, paras 432-433, Praljak's Appeal Brief, para. 94.

834.   Praljak replies that contrary to the Prosecution's assertion, the Trial Chamber did not establish a single common criminal purpose.[2656]

835.   To the extent that Praljak argues that there is a contradiction between the findings on the CCP and those on the Ultimate Purpose of the JCE, the Appeals Chamber notes that he refers to submissions in his sub-grounds of appeal 5.1 and 5.2, which are dismissed elsewhere.[2657] In any event, the Appeals Chamber observes that, contrary to Praljak's contention that the political aim was to establish an autonomous Croatian province in BiH, the Trial Chamber concluded that the Ultimate Purpose of the JCE was to set up a Croatian entity that reconstituted, at least in part, the Banovina borders and facilitated the reunification of the Croatian people and that such entity was either supposed to be joined to Croatia directly or to be an independent state within BiH with close ties to Croatia.[2658]

836.   Praljak's claim that the Trial Chamber confused the CCP with legitimate political aims also has no merit as the Trial Chamber consistently identified the CCP as the ethnic cleansing of the Muslim population in pursuit of the Ultimate Purpose of the JCE.[2659] Given that the Trial Chamber found that the ethnic cleansing was to be achieved through a number of different crimes, it clearly distinguished between the Ultimate Purpose of the JCE – the territorial political aspirations of the JCE members – and the criminal means by which it was implemented.[2660] Praljak's argument is therefore dismissed. Finally, the Appeals Chamber considers that when claiming that the Trial Chamber recognised that Tuđman was solely led by Croatia and he was mainly concerned about Croatia's interests, Praljak mischaracterises the relevant finding, namely that Tuđman was "advocating the existence and the legitimacy of the BiH Croatian people in order to protect the borders of Croatia".[2661] Praljak fails to show any error in the Trial Chamber's findings concerning the CCP. Therefore, this contention is dismissed. **[page 349]**

837.   The Appeals Chamber therefore finds that Praljak has failed to demonstrate any error in the impugned Trial Chamber's findings and dismisses Praljak's sub-ground of appeal 5.4 in relevant part.

(iii) Petković's appeal (Sub-ground 3.2.1.2 in part)

a. Arguments of the Parties

838.   Petković submits that the Trial Chamber erroneously inferred that "'ethnic cleansing' was [a] *necessary* implication of the establishment of a Croatian entity in BiH" and failed to give a reasoned opinion about this inference, or to refer to relevant evidence.[2662] In this regard, he argues that the international community envisaged BiH not as a unitary state, but as one composed of territorial units based on criteria of nationality.[2663] Petković also challenges the evidence underpinning the finding that JCE members believed that in order to achieve the Ultimate Purpose of the JCE it was necessary to change the ethnic make-up of the territories claimed to form HZ(R) H-B.[2664] In particular, he argues that neither of the two documents relied on by the Trial Chamber – Exhibits P00089 and P00021 – supports this finding.[2665]

839.   The Prosecution responds that the Trial Chamber reasonably determined that Petković and the other JCE members intended to ethnically cleanse the Muslim population in order to achieve the Ultimate Purpose

---

[2656]   Praljak's Reply Brief, para. 20.

[2657]   See *supra*, paras 602-607.

[2658]   Trial Judgement, Vol. 4, para. 24. See also Trial Judgement, Vol. 4, paras 10, 16.

[2659]   See Trial Judgement, Vol. 4, paras 44, 1232. See also Trial Judgement, Vol. 4, para. 65 (referring to modification of the ethnic composition of the Croatian provinces).

[2660]   See *supra*, para. 789.

[2661]   Trial Judgement, Vol. 4, para. 15.

[2662]   Petković's Appeal Brief, para. 30 (emphasis in original), referring to Trial Judgement, Vol. 4, para. 41. See also Petković's Appeal Brief, paras 32-33; Appeal Hearing, AT. 493 (23 Mar 2017). Petković raises this argument in the alternative to his submission that the Trial Chamber failed to provide a clear definition of the term "ethnic cleansing". See Petković's Appeal Brief, paras 28-29; *supra*, paras 787-790.

[2663]   Petković's Appeal Brief, para. 30.

[2664]   Petković's Appeal Brief, para. 31, referring to Trial Judgement, Vol. 4, para. 43.

[2665]   Petković's Appeal Brief, para. 31, referring to Trial Judgement, Vol. 4, para. 43 & fn. 120; Appeal Hearing, AT. 493 (23 Mar 2017).

of the JCE.[2666] It submits that the Trial Chamber did not rely solely on Exhibits P00089 and P00021, but on numerous well-supported findings, and argues that Exhibits P00089 and P00021 in any event provided further support for the Trial Chamber's conclusion.[2667]

b. Analysis

840.   At the outset, the Appeals Chamber considers that Petković's argument regarding the intentions of the international community for BiH is a mere assertion unsupported by evidence, and **[page 350]** dismisses this argument. The remainder of Petković's challenges relate to the exhibits cited by the Trial Chamber as support for the conclusion that as of December 1991 the leaders of the HZ(R) H-B, including Boban, and leaders of Croatia, including Tuđman, believed that changing the ethnic make-up of the provinces was necessary in order to achieve the Ultimate Purpose of the JCE,[2668] namely Exhibits P00089 and P00021.

841.   Exhibit P00089 is the Presidential Transcript of 27 December 1991, with the referenced pages containing part of a speech by Tuđman, in which the establishment of a purely Croatian community "inside the widest possible borders" is discussed.[2669] The Appeals Chamber notes that in the course of this discussion, Boban refers to "cleansing border areas".[2670] However, the relevant parts of the Presidential Transcripts do not, as a whole, reflect a clear consensus regarding a political purpose that would have ethnic cleansing as its logical corollary.[2671] Turning to Exhibit P00021, a 1991 book by Ante Valenta, entitled "Dividing Bosnia and Struggling for Its Integrity", the Appeals Chamber notes that the book discusses the relocation of Muslims to central BiH.[2672] The Appeals Chamber also notes, however, that although Valenta occupied the position of HZ(R) H-B Vice-President in 1993,[2673] his book does not support the broader proposition that JCE members held this belief in December 1991.

842.   The Appeals Chamber considers, however, that these ambiguities have no impact on the Trial Chamber's conclusions. The Trial Chamber made a number of findings elsewhere demonstrating that the HZ(R) H-B leaders and Tuđman acquired the intention to change the ethnic make-up of the territories claimed to form part of the HZ(R) H-B – namely to ethnically cleanse the Muslims from the territory claimed as Croatian – before the JCE came into being in mid-January 1993.[2674] These are not challenged by Petković in this sub-ground of appeal.[2675] In any **[page 351]** event, the Appeals Chamber observes that the Trial Chamber expressly found that the CCP came into existence only by mid-January 1993, because the evidence was insufficient to reach a finding as to its existence at an earlier stage.[2676] The Appeals Chamber

---

[2666]   Prosecution's Response Brief (Petković), para. 25.

[2667]   Prosecution's Response Brief (Petković), paras 25-26, referring to Trial Judgement, Vol. 4, paras 11-12, 18-19, 43, 45-66. In particular, the Prosecution refers to the findings that: (1) JCE members such as Prlić and Boban made statements that Muslims had to be removed from the HZ(R) H-B; (2) on 26 October 1992, Praljak made a statement that "it is in our interest that the Muslims get their own canton so they have somewhere to move to"; (3) Petković and others made efforts to divide BiH between the Croats and Serbs, leaving little or no space for Muslims; and (4) widespread ethnic cleansing by the HVO forces occurred throughout the HZ(R) H-B during the JCE time period, following a clear pattern. See also Prosecution's Response Brief (Petković), paras 16-18; Appeal Hearing, AT. 660 (24 Mar 2017).

[2668]   Trial Judgement, Vol. 4, para. 43, referring to Exs. P00021, P00089, pp. 34-35. The Appeals Chamber notes that while it could appear from footnote 120 of Volume 4 of the Trial Judgement that the Trial Chamber relied on pages 18-24 of Exhibit P00021 for this finding, page numbers 18-24 do not correspond fully to the two pages of the book that were admitted during trial under Exhibit P00021, namely pages 43 and 66 of the BCS version of the exhibit. See Philip Roger Watkins, T. 18803-18804; *Prosecutor v. Jadranko Prlić et al*, Case No. IT-04-74-T, Order to Admit Evidence Regarding Witness Philip Watkins, 30 August 2007. The Appeals Chamber notes that only page 23 of the English version corresponds to page 66 of the BCS version. The Appeals Chamber therefore considers that the reference to pp. 18-24 is a typographical error.

[2669]   Ex. P00089, pp. 34-35. The Appeals Chamber notes that there appear to be two translations of Exhibit P00089 on the judicial record and considers that the Trial Chamber's finding relates to the most recently added translation, ET 0085-0386-0085-0510.

[2670]   Ex. P00089, p. 35.

[2671]   See Trial Judgement, Vol. 4, para. 12 ("The Chamber notes that Franjo Tuđman spoke equivocally, advocating, on the one hand, respect for the existing borders of BiH, knowing that the international community was opposed to dividing BiH, and, on the other, the partition of BiH between the Croats and the Serbs"), referring to, *inter alia*, Ex. P00089, pp. 29-30.

[2672]   See Ex. P00021, p. 40; Ex. 1D01538, pp. 42-43.

[2673]   See Trial Judgement, Vol. 1, para. 524 & fn. 1281.

[2674]   See Trial Judgement, Vol. 4, paras 9-24, 44, 1232.

[2675]   See *infra*, paras 868-873.

[2676]   Trial Judgement, Vol. 4, para. 44.

considers therefore that Petković fails to demonstrate that ambiguities in the evidential basis proffered by the Trial Chamber would have any impact on his conviction.

843. The Appeals Chamber therefore finds that Petković has not demonstrated that the Trial Chamber failed to provide a reasoned opinion or failed to refer to relevant evidence when finding that ethnic cleansing was necessary in order to achieve the Ultimate Purpose of the JCE. His sub-ground of appeal 3.2.1.2 is dismissed in relevant part.

(c) Alleged errors in the findings that the JCE commenced in mid-January 1993 and that Muslim civilians were removed from villages in Gornji Vakuf Municipality

844. The Trial Chamber concluded that the JCE began to be implemented in January 1993 when, as the HZ H-B leaders were participating in peace talks, the HVO conducted military campaigns in the provinces it considered Croatian in order to consolidate its presence.[2677] In particular, the Trial Chamber found that on 18 January 1993, the HVO launched an attack on the town of Gornji Vakuf and the villages of Duša, Hrasnica, Uzričje, and Ždrimci in Gornji Vakuf Municipality,[2678] and removed members of the Muslim population.[2679]

(i) Prlić's appeal (Sub-grounds 10.2, 10.3, and 10.4 in part)

a. Arguments of the Parties

845. Prlić argues that the Trial Chamber erred in concluding that the CCP came into being in January 1993.[2680] He submits that the Trial Chamber erred in relying "solely" on the unsubstantiated evidence of international witnesses, whose lack of credibility the Trial Chamber overlooked,[2681] while ignoring other relevant evidence.[2682] Further, pointing to the evidence of Prosecution Witness Cedric Thornberry, Prlić argues that the Trial Chamber overlooked that the evidence from the international witnesses was based on "unsubstantiated perceptions".[2683] Prlić also alleges errors in the finding that the HZ H-B leaders carried out the JCE in stages, and more specifically that the **[page 352]** HVO launched an attack in Gornji Vakuf on 18 January 1993, shelled villages, took control over them, and conducted military campaigns in the provinces considered as Croatian.[2684]

846. The Prosecution responds that Prlić's challenges should be summarily dismissed as misrepresenting factual findings or evidence.[2685] Specifically, the Prosecution submits that: (1) the Trial Chamber relied on evidence other than that of international witnesses,[2686] and Prlić does not support his argument that these witnesses lacked credibility and their evidence was unsubstantiated;[2687] and (2) Prlić does not identify evidence that the Trial Chamber ignored.[2688] In relation to Prlić's challenge to the Trial Chamber's finding on the implementation of the JCE in stages, the Prosecution argues that he makes "'mere assertions unsupported by any evidence' coupled with redundant and unexplained cross-references", warranting summary dismissal.[2689]

[2677] Trial Judgement, Vol. 4, para. 45.
[2678] Trial Judgement, Vol. 4, para. 561. See also Trial Judgement, Vol. 2, paras 343-388, 396-468, Vol. 4, para. 45.
[2679] Trial Judgement, Vol. 4, para. 48.
[2680] Prlić's Appeal Brief, para. 284, referring to Trial Judgement, Vol. 1, paras 452-464, Vol. 2, paras 330-342, 503-506, 514, 521, Vol. 4; para. 44.
[2681] Prlić's Appeal Brief, para. 284, referring to Christopher Beese, T. 5328-5332 (private session) (22 Aug 2006), Ex. P02787.
[2682] Prlić's Appeal Brief, para. 284.
[2683] Prlić's Appeal Brief, para. 284, referring to Ex. P10041, para. 42 (witness statement of Witness Cedric Thornberry).
[2684] Prlić's Appeal Brief, paras 286(a)-(c), 287(a) (referring to sub-ground of appeal 16.1). The Appeals Chamber notes that Prlić also cross-references his sub-ground of appeal 16.2. See Prlić's Appeal Brief, para. 288.
[2685] Prosecution's Response Brief (Prlić), para. 168, referring to Đorđević Appeal Judgement, para. 20(i).
[2686] Prosecution's Response Brief (Prlić), para. 169, referring to Trial Judgement, Vol. 1, paras 452-464, Vol. 2, paras 330-342, 503-506, 514, 521, Vol. 4, para. 44.
[2687] Prosecution's Response Brief (Prlić), para. 170.
[2688] Prosecution's Response Brief (Prlić), para. 172.
[2689] Prosecution's Response Brief (Prlić), para. 166, referring to Đorđević Appeal Judgement, para. 20(ix), *Galić* Appeal Judgement, para. 246.

b. Analysis

847.   In respect of Prlić's argument that the Trial Chamber erred in relying solely on the uncorroborated evidence of international witnesses, the Appeals Chamber notes that contrary to his submission, the Trial Chamber's conclusion regarding the formation of the JCE was based not only on the evidence of international witnesses, but on findings made elsewhere in the Trial Judgement,[2690] which were in turn based on a range of evidence.[2691] Prlić fails to explain why the conclusion should not stand on the basis of these other findings. In addition, as for his argument regarding the lack of credibility of international witnesses, Prlić argues that the Trial Chamber "overlooked" the testimony of Witness Christopher Beese, in which Beese confirmed that the ECMM reports prepared by international witnesses were criticised by Lord David Owen for lacking **[page 353]** analysis and being irrelevant.[2692] Although the Trial Chamber did not refer to this testimony in the portions of the Trial Judgement Prlić points to,[2693] the Appeals Chamber recalls that a trial chamber need not refer to the testimony of every witness or every piece of evidence on the trial record and that there is a presumption that the trial chamber evaluated all evidence presented to it, as long as there is no indication that it completely disregarded evidence which is clearly relevant.[2694] Given that the Trial Chamber relied on Beese's evidence at various points in the Trial Judgement, including in the section discussing the formation of the JCE, it is clear that it did not disregard his evidence.[2695] Accordingly * Prlić fails to explain how no reasonable trier of fact could have reached the same conclusion as the Trial Chamber.[2696] As for Prlić's challenge in respect of Thornberry's evidence, Prlić merely refers to the paragraph of the witness's statement which he claims is an "unsubstantiated perception" without providing any support for this assertion, and thus fails to explain why the Trial Chamber erred in relying on it.[2697] The Appeals Chamber further notes that the Trial Chamber relied on a range of other evidence to corroborate Thornberry's evidence that Croats were contemplating ethnic cleansing in BiH.[2698] The Appeals Chamber also dismisses, as undeveloped, Prlić's submission that the Trial Chamber disregarded relevant evidence, as he fails to explain what evidence was disregarded or how it had any impact on the Trial Chamber's findings.[2699]

848.   As for Prlić's challenge to the Trial Chamber's findings on the HVO's military campaigns from January 1993 and in particular the attacks in Gornji Vakuf, the Appeals Chamber notes that Prlić makes his argument solely by cross-reference to his grounds of appeal 16.1 and 16.2, which the Appeals Chamber dismisses elsewhere.[2700] This argument is thus rejected.

[2690]   See Trial Judgement, Vol. 4, para. 44, referring to, *inter alia,* Trial Judgement, Vol. 1, paras 442-451 ("Negotiations within the Framework of the Vance-Owen Plan (August 1992-January 1993)"), 452-476 ("Subsequent History of the Vance-Owen Plan; Attempts to Implement the Principles of this Plan in the Field (January 1993-August 1993)").
[2691]   See Trial Judgement, Vol. 1, paras 443 (referring to, *inter alia,* Exs. 1D00288, 1D00289, p. 2, 1D02664, pp. 13-16, 1D02848, p. 2, 1D02849, p. 1, 1D02850, 1D02851, 4D00830), 445 (referring to, *inter alia,* Ex. 1D01521), 446 (referring to, *inter alia,* 3D03720), 447 (referring to, *inter alia,* Ex. 1D02935 (confidential)), 451 (referring to, *inter alia,* Ex. 1D01521), 455 (referring to, *inter alia,* Ex. 1D01195), 457 (referring to, *inter alia,* Exs. 3D01537, 1D01195, pp. 1-2), 458 (referring to, *inter alia,* Ex. 1D01521), 459 (referring to Ex. 1D01195, pp. 1-2), 460 (referring to, *inter alia,* Exs. 1D02729, 2D00206), 461 (referring to, *inter alia,* Exs. 2D00093, 4D00358), 462 (referring to, *inter alia,* Ex. 4D01235), 463 (referring to, *inter alia,* Exs. 2D01111, pp. 1-2, 2D00289), 464 (referring to, *inter alia,* Ex. 4D00557), 465 (referring to, *inter alia,* Exs. 1D02903, 1D01193, 1D01822, 1D02890), 473 (referring to, *inter alia,* Ex. 1D00817, p. 4), 476 (referring to Exs. 1D01281, 1D01388, p. 2).
[2692]   See Prlić's Appeal Brief, para. 284, referring to Christopher Beese, T. 5328-5332 (private session) (22 Aug 2006).
[2693]   See Prlić's Appeal Brief, para. 284, referring to Trial Judgement, Vol. 1, paras 452-464, Vol. 2, paras 330-342, 503-506, 514, 521, Vol. 4, para. 44.
[2694]   *Kvočka et al.* Appeal Judgement, paras 23-24. See also *Tolimir* Appeal Judgement, paras 53, 161, 299; *Popović et al.* Appeal Judgement, paras 925, 1017.
[2695]   See, *e.g.,* Trial Judgement, Vol. 4, paras 21, 45, 54-55 & fns 66, 123, 149, 152-153.
[2696]   See *Mrkšić and Šljivančanin* Appeal Judgement, para. 224.
[2697]   See Trial Judgement, Vol. 4, para. 44, referring to, *inter alia,* Ex. P10041, para. 42.
[2698]   See Trial Judgement, Vol. 4, para. 44, referring to, *inter alia,* Witness BH, T(F). 17534-17535 (closed session) (25 Apr 2007), Ole Brix-Andersen, Ex. P10356 *("Kordić and Čerkez* Case") T. 10752, 10777-10779 & T(F). 10871-10872, Ex. P01353 (confidential), p. 1, Ex. P02327 (confidential), p. 6, Ex. P02787, p. 4.
[2699]   The Appeals Chamber also notes that Prlić refers to his submissions in sub-ground of appeal 16.1, which the Appeals Chamber dismisses elsewhere. See *infra,* paras 1147-1174.
[2700]   The Appeals Chamber notes that Prlić's sub-ground of appeal 16.1 concerns his significant contribution to the the JCE in Gornji Vakuf, whereas his sub-ground of appeal 16.2 concerns his significant contribution to the JCE in Prozor, Sovići, and Doljani. See *infra,* paras 1146-1208.

849. The Appeals Chamber finds that Prlić has failed to show that the Trial Chamber erred in concluding that the JCE crystallised in mid-January 1993 and that the HZ H-B leaders carried out the JCE in stages. Prlić's sub-grounds of appeal 10.2, 10.3, and 10.4 in relevant part are therefore dismissed. **[page 354]**

(ii) Stojić's appeal (Ground 10)

a. Arguments of the Parties

850. Stojić submits that the Trial Chamber failed to provide a "reasoned decision" in entering its finding that the JCE was established "at least as early as mid-January 1993".[2701] He also submits, in the alternative, that no reasonable trial chamber could have made this finding.[2702] In support of both submissions, Stojić first argues that the Trial Chamber relied on evidence that does not support the conclusion that the JCE came into being by mid-January 1993,[2703] and that the Trial Chamber could not rely on earlier findings in the Trial Judgement because they were "strictly historical and brief".[2704] Second, Stojić argues that the Trial Chamber's finding that the JCE came into being by mid-January 1993 was inconsistent with its other findings that, at the same time, the HZ H-B leaders were participating in peace talks with the BiH Muslims and then, after 30 January 1993, attempted to co-operate with them.[2705] Third, Stojić submits that the Trial Chamber offered insufficient reasons for its finding that the military actions in Gornji Vakuf formed part of the JCE, whereas those in Prozor in 1992 did not.[2706] He posits that the Trial Chamber found that the military actions in Prozor in 1992 fell outside the JCE because they were not alleged against Pušić, but since the same was true for the military actions in Gornji Vakuf, they too must also have fallen outside the JCE.[2707] Last, Stojić argues that there was no change of circumstances in January 1993 that could lead a reasonable trial chamber to find that a JCE came into existence at this time and that, in particular, the attack on Gornji Vakuf was a result of escalating tensions that began there in September 1992.[2708]

851. The Prosecution responds that the Trial Chamber reasonably concluded that the CCP existed by mid-January 199 3[2709] and identified the evidentiary basis for its finding.[2710]. It argues that there was no inconsistency between the findings that a CCP existed and that peace talks were ongoing at **[page 355]** the same time, and that Stojić ignores the connection the Trial Chamber drew between the two.[2711] Further, the Prosecution contends that Stojić misunderstands the Trial Chamber's reason for not finding the attack in Prozor in 1992 to be part of the CCP, which was that it was not convinced beyond reasonable doubt that the JCE members were acting in concert at that time.[2712] Finally, the Prosecution argues that the preceding tensions in Gornji Vakuf did not preclude the Trial Chamber from finding that the JCE members used the 18 January 1993 attack to implement the CCP.[2713]

[2701] Stojić's Appeal Brief, paras 87-88, referring to Trial Judgement, Vol. 4, para. 44. See Stojić's Appeal Brief, para. 93.
[2702] Stojić's Appeal Brief, paras 88, 92-93.
[2703] Stojić's Appeal Brief, para. 89, referring to Cedric Thornberry, T. 26166-26168, 26173-26176 (14 Jan 2008), Witness BH, T. 17534-17535 (closed session) (25 Apr 2007), Exs. P10041, para. 42, P01353 (confidential), P10356, pp. 10752, 10777-10779, 10871-10872, P02327 (confidential), P02787.
[2704] Stojić's Appeal Brief, para. 89. See Stojić's Appeal Brief, para. 87.
[2705] Stojić's Appeal Brief, para. 90.
[2706] Stojić's Appeal Brief, para. 91, referring to Trial Judgement, Vol. 4, para. 69.
[2707] Stojić's Appeal Brief, para. 91, referring to Trial Judgement, Vol. 4, para. 69 & fn. 179. See Stojić's Appeal Brief, para. 87.
[2708] Stojić's Appeal Brief, paras 92-93.
[2709] Prosecution's Response Brief (Stojić), para. 66.
[2710] Prosecution's Response Brief (Stojić), para. 70. See Prosecution's Response Brief (Stojić), para. 68.
[2711] Prosecution's Response Brief (Stojić), para. 67. See also Prosecution's Response Brief (Stojić), para. 68; Appeal Hearing, AT. 347-348 (21 Mar 2017) (arguing that Stojić ignores the Trial Chamber's findings that the JCE members relied on their own interpretation of the Vance-Owen Peace Plan to implement the CCP).
[2712] Prosecution's Response Brief (Stojić), para. 69.
[2713] Prosecution's Response Brief (Stojić), para. 68.

b. Analysis

852.   The Trial Chamber found that the JCE was established "at least as early as mid-January 1993".[2714] The Trial Chamber explained that, from that date:

> the leaders of the HVO and certain Croatian leaders aimed to consolidate HVO control over Provinces 3, 8 and 10, which under the Vance-Owen Plan, were attributed to the BiH Croats, and, as the HVO leaders interpreted it, to eliminate all Muslim resistance within these provinces and to "ethnically cleanse" the Muslims so that the provinces would become majority or nearly exclusively Croatian.[2715]

853.   Regarding Stojić's claims that the evidence the Trial Chamber relied on cannot support these findings, the Appeals Chamber considers that the Trial Chamber reasonably relied on evidence, emanating from as early as January 1993, indicating that the HVO aimed to consolidate control over territories that it considered to be Croatian.[2716] Further, the finding that a JCE existed as of mid-January 1993 is supported by two previous sections of the Trial Judgement detailing, among other things, evidence of orders issued in mid-January 1993 to implement the 15 January 1993 Ultimatum.[2717] While Stojić claims that these previous sections may not be relied on because they were "strictly historical and brief",[2718] the Appeals Chamber considers that the Trial Chamber was not barred from relying on them to support subsequent findings. To the extent that the previous findings impact on criminal responsibility,[2719] the Trial Chamber addressed their significance in the chapter discussing the CCP and the criminal responsibility of the Appellants, which included explaining how the events in mid-January 1993 formed part of the CCP.[2720] The Appeals Chamber **[page 356]** finds no fault in this approach and dismisses Stojić's argument that the Trial Chamber's conclusion was not supported by the evidence and findings on which it relied.

854.   As to Stojić's argument that the Trial Chamber's findings are inconsistent, the Appeals Chamber finds that the establishment of a JCE by mid-January 1993 is not, in itself, contradicted by the findings that BiH Croats and Muslims participated in peace talks and attempted to co-operate after 30 January 1993.[2721] Stojić ignores relevant Trial Chamber findings, notably that the HVO conducted military campaigns in the provinces it considered Croatian while conducting peace talks and that JCE members sought "to modify the ethnic composition of the so-called Croatian provinces in light of their interpretation of the Vance-Owen Plan" according to which those provinces were to become "majority or nearly exclusively Croatian".[2722] Accordingly, the Appeals Chamber dismisses Stojić's argument.

855.   Turning to Stojić's argument regarding the Prozor attack, the Appeals Chamber notes that the Trial Chamber found that "the evidence does not support a finding that the crimes committed in Prozor in October 1992 formed part of the [CCP inasmuch as the Trial Chamber] was not in a position to establish that, at that time, the members of the JCE were acting in concert".[2723] The Appeals Chamber also observes that, in a footnote at the end of this finding, the Trial Chamber recalled that "Pušić [was] not being prosecuted for the crimes committed in Prozor in October 1992".[2724] The Appeals Chamber sees no ambiguity with the inclusion of this footnote.

856.   Moreover, the Appeals Chamber recalls that the Trial Chamber found that the CCP came into being in January. 1993 based on a number of factors, including in particular the presentation of the Vance-Owen

---

[2714]   Trial Judgement, Vol. 4, para. 44.
[2715]   Trial Judgement, Vol. 4, para. 44.
[2716]   See Trial Judgement, Vol. 4, fn. 122, referring to, *inter alia*, Ex. P01353 (confidential), p. 1. See also Trial Judgement, Vol. 4, paras 44 *et seq.* and references cited therein.
[2717]   See Trial Judgement, Vol. 4, fn. 122, referring to, *inter alia*, Trial Judgement, Vol. 1, "Negotiations within the Framework of the Vance-Owen Plan (August 1992 – January 1993)", "Subsequent History of the Vance-Owen Plan; Attempts to Implement the Principles of this Plan in the Field (January 1993 – August 1993)".
[2718]   Stojić's Appeal Brief, para. 89, citing Trial Judgement, Vol. 1, para. 408.
[2719]   See Trial Judgement, Vol. 1, para. 408.
[2720]   See Trial Judgement, Vol. 4, paras 44-45, 65. See also Trial Judgement, Vol. 4, paras 125-128.
[2721]   See also *infra*, paras 985-990.
[2722]   Trial Judgement, Vol. 4, paras 44-45, 65. See also Trial Judgement, Vol. 4, paras 46, 52, 54-55.
[2723]   Trial Judgement, Vol. 4, para. 69.
[2724]   Trial Judgement, Vol. 4, para. 69 & fn. 179.

Peace Plan on 2 January 1993 and the 15 January 1993 Ultimatum,[2725] as well as the evidence discussed above.[2726] Further, the Trial Chamber explicitly found that "many crimes committed by HVO forces from January 1993 to April 1994 tended to follow a clear pattern of conduct" and that in the vast majority of cases these crimes were not committed by chance or randomly.[2727] Accordingly, the Trial Chamber's finding on the start of the JCE was not based on the membership of the JCE alone but rather also on the pattern of events starting in January 1993. The **[page 357]** Appeals Chamber therefore considers that, reading the Trial Judgement as a whole,[2728] the Trial Chamber clearly explained why it found that the CCP came into being in January 1993 and not in October 1992.

857. As for Stojić's argument that tensions began escalating in Gornji Vakuf in September 1992, the Appeals Chamber considers that this did not preclude the Trial Chamber from finding that a JCE was established by mid-January 1993 and that the 18 January 1993 attack on Gornji Vakuf was evidence of the implementation of the CCP.[2729] Further, the Appeals Chamber considers that the Trial Chamber's findings do reflect a change of circumstances in January 1993, notably the presentation of the Vance-Owen Peace Plan on 2 January 1993 and the 15 January 1993 Ultimatum, as discussed above.[2730] Finally, the Appeals Chamber recalls that the Trial Chamber found that the JCE was established *"at least* as early as mid-January 1993".[2731] The Appeals Chamber therefore dismisses Stojić's argument.

858. In light of the above, the Appeals Chamber considers that the Trial Chamber's selection of the date of mid-January 1993 was neither arbitrary nor unreasoned.[2732] The Appeals Chamber therefore dismisses Stojić's arguments that the Trial Chamber failed to provide a reasoned opinion. Further, having dismissed all of his submissions above, the Appeals Chamber also rejects his alternative argument that no reasonable trier of fact could have found that the JCE came into being in mid-January 1993. Stojić's ground of appeal 10 is therefore dismissed.

(iii) Stojić's appeal (Ground 4 in part)

859. Stojić argues that the Trial Chamber erred in finding that the 18 January 1993 attacks in Gornji Vakuf Municipality fell within the JCE.[2733] He submits that the 18 January 1993 attacks cannot be divorced from the fighting that broke out in Gornji Vakuf Municipality on 11 January 1993, and that the Trial Chamber thus unreasonably found that the earlier episode of fighting was not part of the JCE, whereas its continuation on 18 January 1993 was.[2734]

860. The Prosecution responds that the Trial Chamber acknowledged HVO-ABiH clashes prior to 18 January 1993 in Gornji Vakuf Municipality, but reasonably found that the crimes committed **[page 358]** by the HVO during and after 18 January 1993 formed part of the CCP.[2735] In particular, the Prosecution highlights the "total similarity" in the way in which the operations and the crimes in January 1993 unfolded.[2736]

[2725] Trial Judgement, Vol. 1, paras 445, 451-452, Vol. 4, paras 44, 125. See also *supra*, paras 852-853.

[2726] See *supra*, para. 853.

[2727] Trial Judgement, Vol. 4, para. 65. The Appeals Chamber also notes in this regard that the Trial Chamber found that the operations in Gornji Vakuf villages unfolded "in exactly the same way" and that "[b]earing in mind the total similarity in the way the operations unfolded and the crimes committed in each of these villages" it was satisfied that they "corresponded to a preconceived plan". Trial Judgement, Vol. 4, para. 561. See also Trial Judgement, Vol. 4, para. 704.

[2728] *Popović et al.* Appeal Judgement, para. 2006; *Mrkšić and Šljivančanin* Appeal Judgement, para. 379. See *Kalimanzira* Appeal Judgement, para. 227.

[2729] Trial Judgement, Vol. 4, paras 44-45.

[2730] Trial Judgement, Vol. 1, paras 445, 451-452, Vol. 4, paras 44, 125. See *supra*, paras 855-856.

[2731] Trial Judgement, Vol. 4, para. 44 (emphasis added).

[2732] See Stojić's Appeal Brief, para. 93.

[2733] Stojić's Appeal Brief, para. 56, referring to Trial Judgement, Vol. 4, paras 44-45, 69.

[2734] Stojić's Appeal Brief, para. 56, referring to Trial Judgement, Vol. 2, paras 336-337. See Stojić's Reply Brief, para. 22; Appeal Hearing, AT. 276-277 (21 Mar 2017) (arguing that had there been a JCE to take over Banovina, the HVO would have taken over the whole of Gornji Vakuf Municipality but did not do so).

[2735] Prosecution's Response Brief (Stojić), para. 37.

[2736] Prosecution's Response Brief (Stojić), para. 37, referring to Trial Judgement, Vol. 4, para. 561. See also Appeal Hearing, AT. 347-348 (21 Mar 2017).

861.   The Appeals Chamber considers that Stojić mischaracterises the Trial Chamber's approach regarding the 11 and 18 January 1993 attacks. The Trial Chamber's finding that the 18 January 1993 attacks formed part of the CCP is based on findings regarding: (1) the crystallisation of the CCP by mid-January 1993, on the basis of broader geopolitical circumstances, such as the presentation of the Vance-Owen Peace Plan on 2 January 1993 and the 15 January 1993 Ultimatum;[2737] (2) the "total similarity in the way the operations unfolded and the crimes [were] committed" in particular during the HVO attacks of the villages of Duša, Hrasnica, Uzričje, and Ždrimci on 18 January 1993, which led the Trial Chamber to find that they "corresponded to a preconceived plan";[2738] and (3) the fact that these events formed part of a "pattern of conduct" with later crimes.[2739] Stojić fails to show how the clashes between the HVO and ABiH earlier in the month of January 1993 – which the Trial Chamber took into account[2740] – had any impact on the finding that the 18 January 1993 attacks formed part of the CCP. Stojić's submission is dismissed. The Appeals Chamber therefore finds that Stojić has failed to show that the Trial Chamber erred in finding that the 18 January 1993 attacks in Gornji Vakuf Municipality fell within the JCE, and rejects his ground of appeal 4 in relevant part.

(iv) Praljak's appeal (Ground 15)

a. Arguments of the Parties

862.   Praljak submits that the Trial Chamber erred when it concluded that the crimes in Gornji Vakuf in January 1993, including the killings in the village of Duša, fell within the CCP.[2741] In this regard, he submits that as fighting broke out in Gornji Vakuf Municipality on 11 January 1993, the finding that the CCP was established in mid-January 1993 is contradictory,[2742] and an alternative reasonable inference was that HVO attacks occurred in response to military operations initiated by the ABiH and that the HVO had no interest in military activities against the **[page 359]** ABiH.[2743] Praljak also argues that while a common criminal plan need not be previously arranged or formulated and may materialise extemporaneously, it must be established prior to the commission of an action or a crime,[2744] and that the Trial Chamber erred in law when it inferred the existence of a plan from the "sole commission" of the crimes in Gornji Vakuf.[2745] Finally, Praljak contends that the Trial Chamber did not give reasons why the killings in Duša should be included in the CCP.[2746] He argues that the Trial Chamber did not properly establish that all JCE members "shared [the] intent to perpetrate this crime",[2747] and "did not establish the required intent for the said crime", referring to his arguments made elsewhere challenging the Trial Chamber's findings that the HVO intended to cause serious bodily harm to civilians in Duša and thus committed murder and wilful killing in that village.[2748]

863.   The Prosecution responds that the Trial Chamber reasonably concluded that the crimes in Gornji Vakuf Municipality in the latter part of January 1993 formed part of the CCP.[2749] In particular, the Prosecution responds that: (1) there was no alternative reasonable explanation for the events in Gornji Vakuf;[2750] (2)

[2737]   Trial Judgement, Vol. 1, paras 445, 451-452, Vol. 4, paras 44, 125, 131, 142, 271.

[2738]   Trial Judgement, Vol. 4, para. 561. See also Trial Judgement, Vol. 4, paras 562, 704, 708, 922.

[2739]   Trial Judgement, Vol. 4, para. 65.

[2740]   Trial Judgement, Vol. 2, paras 336-337.

[2741]   Praljak's Appeal Brief, paras 239-245. See Appeal Hearing, AT. 399 (22 Mar 2017).

[2742]   Praljak's Appeal Brief, paras 233, 238. Praljak argues in particular that the fact that HVO activities ceased without taking over the entire Gornji Vakuf Municipality shows that the actions were not planned. See Praljak's Appeal Brief, para. 236; Appeal Hearing, AT. 402 (22 Mar 2017). See also Praljak's Appeal Brief, paras 242, 244-245.

[2743]   Praljak's Appeal Brief, paras 234-236, 243, 245. Praljak also submits that: (1) the HVO tried to calm tensions in conflicts in the municipality; (2) the HVO Main Staff instructed all HVO commands to solve the problems through talks; and (3) at the relevant time, the HVO and ABiH were allies against the VRS. See Praljak's Appeal Brief, para. 235. See also Praljak's Appeal Brief, para. 243; Appeal Hearing, AT. T. 472 (22 Mar 2017).

[2744]   Praljak's Appeal Brief, paras 237-238, referring to *Brđanin* Appeal Judgement, para. 418, *Statić* Appeal Judgement, para. 64, *Vasiljević* Appeal Judgement, para. 100, *Kvočka et al.* Appeal Judgement, para. 117, *Tadić* Appeal Judgement, para. 227.

[2745]   Praljak's Appeal Brief, para. 237, referring to Trial Judgement, Vol. 4, para. 45.

[2746]   Praljak's Appeal Brief, heading before para. 239, paras 239-241.

[2747]   Praljak's Appeal Brief, para. 240, referring to *Tadić* Appeal Judgement, para. 228, *Statić* Appeal Judgement, para. 65; Appeal Hearing, AT. 400 (22 Mar 2017).

[2748]   Praljak's Appeal Brief, para. 240, referring to Praljak's Appeal Brief, paras 196-198 (sub-ground of appeal 12.2).

[2749]   Prosecution's Response Brief (Praljak), para. 107. See also Prosecution's Response Brief (Praljak), paras 104, 106.

[2750]   Prosecution's Response Brief (Praljak), paras 107-108, 112.

Praljak repeats his failed trial arguments or merely offers an alternative interpretation of the evidence;[2751] (3) as the Trial Chamber reasonably concluded, the JCE members were actively involved in the progress of HVO operations in Gornji Vakuf, which "unfolded in exactly the same way" and "were part of an attack plan for the capture of the municipality by the HVO";[2752] and (4) the Trial Chamber's finding on the commencement of the CCP was not based "solely on" the occurrence of the crimes in Gornji Vakuf Municipality, but on broader factors including the Vance-Owen Peace Plan and the 15 January 1993 Ultimatum, as well as the similarity between the Gornji Vakuf crimes and other military operations.[2753] **[page 360]**

b. Analysis

864.   The Appeals Chamber turns first to Praljak's argument that the Trial Chamber erred in including the 18 January 1993 events within the CCP, as it failed to consider the alternative reasonable inference that these events were a defensive response to earlier clashes with the ABiH. The Appeals Chamber discerns no contradiction between the finding that clashes between the HVO and ABiH occurred on 11-12 January 1993, and that the JCE came into existence "as early as mid-January 1993".[2754] While the Trial Chamber did not specifically refer to the fighting that broke out on 11-12 January 1993 when reaching this conclusion, the Appeals Chamber recalls the Trial Chamber's finding that the 18 January 1993 Gornji Vakuf events fell within the CCP was based on a number of findings,[2755] and was not affected by the fact that conflict with the ABiH continued.[2756] For this reason, the Appeals Chamber also dismisses the assertion that the Trial Chamber based its conclusion that the CCP came into existence on the events in Gornji Vakuf alone.[2757] The Appeals Chamber finds that Praljak has not demonstrated that no reasonable trier of fact could conclude that the only reasonable inference from the evidence was that the attacks on Gornji Vakuf Municipality were part of the CCP. The Appeals Chamber finds no legal error in the Trial Chamber's finding. Praljak's argument in this regard therefore fails.

865.   Regarding Praljak's submissions that the Trial Chamber did not give reasons why the killings in Duša should be included in the CCP, the Appeals Chamber observes that the Trial Chamber did not expressly refer to those killings.[2758] However, the Trial Chamber explained, based on a number of factors, as stated earlier,[2759] that in furtherance of the CCP the HVO launched the attack on 18 January 1993 on the town of Gornji Vakuf and "several surrounding villages", including Duša.[2760] The Trial Chamber then noted that the HVO "first shelled these sites", and provided a cross-reference to its earlier findings on the crimes that occurred in this village,[2761] including that the HVO killed seven people through shelling in Duša.[2762] The Appeals Chamber therefore considers that the Trial Chamber included the killings in Duša within the scope of the **[page 361]** CCP, as illustrated also by its finding that, with the exception of Pušić, all the Appellants intended the crimes in Gornji Vakuf and possessed intent for murder at that point in time.[2763]

[2751]   Prosecution's Response Brief (Praljak), para. 107, referring to Praljak's Appeal Brief, paras 234-236, 243, Praljak's Final Trial Brief, paras 231-232, 235, 243, Praljak Closing Arguments, T. 52485 (17 Feb 2011).

[2752]   Prosecution's Response Brief (Praljak), paras 110-111, referring to, *inter alia,* Trial Judgement, Vol. 4, paras 126-127, 130-132, 330-334, 336, 561.

[2753]   Prosecution's Response Brief (Praljak), paras 108-109. The Prosecution responds in respect of Praljak's arguments with regard to Duša that the Trial Chamber: (1) properly applied the law as regards JCE liability; and (2) did not make any error with regard to its findings as to Duša, given the broader basis for the conclusion that the CCP existed. See Prosecution's Response Brief (Praljak), para. 107.

[2754]   Trial Judgement, Vol. 4, para. 44.

[2755]   See *supra,* paras 852, 858, 861.

[2756]   See Trial Judgement, Vol. 1, paras 460-461. See also Trial Judgement, Vol. 4, para. 45.

[2757]   *Cf.* Praljak's Appeal Brief, paras 237-238. The Appeals Chamber also rejects Praljak's submissions regarding alleged HVO co-operation with the ABiH on the basis that he fails to show how this would impact on the Trial Chamber's CCP findings relevant to his conviction. *Cf.* Praljak's Appeal Brief, paras 234-236, 243, 245.

[2758]   See Trial Judgement, Vol. 4, para. 45.

[2759]   See *supra,* paras 852, 858, 861.

[2760]   Trial Judgement, Vol. 4, para. 45. See Trial Judgement, Vol. 2, paras 358-368, 398-410.

[2761]   See Trial Judgement, Vol. 4, para. 45 & fn. 124 (referring to "the Chamber's factual findings with regard to the Municipality of Gornji Vakuf). See also Trial Judgement, Vol. 2, paras 358-368, 398-410.

[2762]   See Trial Judgement, Vol. 2, paras 366, 368 and references cited therein. See also Trial Judgement, Vol. 3, paras 663, 711.

[2763]   Trial Judgement, Vol. 4, paras 134, 337, 562, 710, 923. With respect to Pušić, as noted earlier, he was found to have been a member of the JCE only from April 1993. See *supra,* para. 855.

866. However, as found earlier in relation to Praljak's ground of appeal 12, the Appeals Chamber has overturned the Trial Chamber's finding that the deaths of seven civilians in Duša constituted murder and wilful killing ("Duša Reversal") and, as a result, has overturned the Appellants' convictions related to those deaths under Counts 1, 2, 3, 15, and 16.[2764] On that basis, the Appeals Chamber considers that Praljak has demonstrated that the deaths of seven civilians in Duša were not part of the CCP. Accordingly, the Appeals Chamber dismisses his remaining arguments on this issue as moot. The impact of this finding, as far as the scope of the CCP is concerned, will be examined below.[2765]

867. For the foregoing reasons, the Appeals Chamber grants Praljak's ground of appeal 15, in part, and reverses the Trial Chamber's finding that the Duša killings were part of the CCP. As for the remainder of ground 15, the Appeals Chamber finds that Praljak has failed to show that the Trial Chamber erred in finding that the crimes in Gornji Vakuf Municipality in January 1993, with the exception of the killings in Duša, fell within the CCP.[2766]

(v) Petković's appeal (Sub-ground 3.2.2.1 in part)

a. Arguments of the Parties

868. Petković argues that the evidence and findings relied upon by the Trial Chamber do not support the inference that the plan to ethnically cleanse Provinces 3, 8, and 10 had crystallised by mid-January 1993.[2767] Petković also alleges errors in the conclusion that the HVO removed the Muslim population from the villages of Duša, Hrasnica, Uzričje, and Ždrimci in Gornji Vakuf Municipality to ethnically cleanse the municipality.[2768] In this regard, he submits that with the exception of an "unknown number" of citizens from Duša and Hrasnica, the Trial Chamber's findings show that most of the villagers of Duša, Hrasnica, Uzričje, and Ždrimci stayed within **[page 362]** Gornji Vakuf Municipality.[2769] In Petković's view, given that the "ethnic map of the Municipality remained unchanged", no reasonable trier of fact could have concluded that HVO military actions in Gornji Vakuf in January 1993 fell within the CCP, or that the local Muslim population was "ethnically cleansed" from this municipahty.[2770]

869. The Prosecution responds that the Trial Chamber reasonably found that the JCE existed from at least mid-January 1993.[2771] It argues that Petković ignores the Trial Chamber's findings about the events following the 15 January 1993 Ultimatum, as well as other evidence and findings relied upon to support the conclusion that the CCP commenced by mid-January 1993.[2772] As for the crimes in Gornji Vakuf Municipality, the Prosecution submits that they were reasonably found to further the CCP, given the similarities between these

---

[2764] See *supra*, paras 441-443.

[2765] See *infra*, paras 874 *et seq.*

[2766] See also *infra*, para. 883.

[2767] Petković's Appeal Brief, para. 43, referring to, *inter alia*, Exs. P10041, para. 42, P01353 (confidential), p. 1, P02327 (confidential), p. 6, P02787, p. 4, P10356, Cedric Thornberry, T. 26166-26168, 26173-26176 (14 Jan 2008), Witness BH, T. 17478-17479 (closed session) (24 Apr 2007). See also Petković's Appeal Brief, paras 42, 44.

[2768] Petković's Appeal Brief, para. 46. See also Petković's Appeal Brief, para. 45. Petković also submits that the Appellants were not charged "with the deportation/forcible transfer of Muslims" from Gornji Vakuf. Petković Appeal Brief, para. 46.

[2769] Petković's Appeal Brief, paras 47-50, referring to Trial Judgement, Vol. 2, paras 405, 426-427, 452-454, 466-468, Vol. 3, paras 845-848, 899-900, 902, 904, 906. Petković argues that the Trial Chamber based its findings regarding the removal of Muslims from Hrasnica on Exhibits P09710 (confidential) and P10106. See Petković's Appeal Brief, para. 47. Petković also asserts that an unidentified number of civilians asked UNPROFOR to take them to the municipality of Bugojno. See Petković's Appeal Brief, para. 49.

[2770] Petković's Appeal Brief, para. 50. See also Petković's Appeal Brief, paras 44, 51; Appeal Hearing, AT. 485-486, 494-495, 524 (23 Mar 2017).

[2771] Prosecution's Response Brief (Petković), para. 38. See Prosecution's Response Brief (Petković), paras 16-18.

[2772] Prosecution's Response Brief (Petković), paras 38-39, referring to, *inter alia*, Trial Judgement, Vol. 4, fn. 122. In particular, the Prosecution argues that Petković disregards: (1) further findings elsewhere in the Trial Judgement regarding the 15 January 1993 Ultimatum; (2) Exhibit P01353 (confidential), as well as Cedric Thornberry's testimony confirming Exhibit P01353's accuracy; (3) the evidence of Ole Brix-Anderson; (4) the testimony of Witness BH; (5) Exhibit P02327 (confidential); and (6) Exhibit P02787. See Prosecution's Response Brief (Petković), para. 39, referring to, *inter alia*, Trial Judgement, Vol. 1, paras 452-454, 460, Vol. 4, para. 112, fns 1092-1093, 2449, Cedric Thornberry, T. 26175-26176 (14 Jan 2008), Ex. P10356, pp. 3, 34, Witness BH, T. 17534-17353 (closed session) (25 Apr 2007).

crimes and later ones in other municipalities.[2773] The Prosecution also argues, relying on the *Đorđević* Appeal Judgement, that the Tribunal's jurisprudence disproves Petković's claim that the ethnic composition of a region needs to change for ethnic cleansing to occur.[2774] It notes that, in any event, Petković ignores that the crime of forcible displacement occurred on a "massive scale" and thus the ethnic map was redrawn in several municipalities, including Gornji Vakuf.[2775]

870.   Petković replies that the *Đorđević* Appeals Chamber's finding confirms that at least a temporary change in ethnic balance is necessary in order to establish a common criminal plan.[2776] **[page 363]**

    b. Analysis

871.   Regarding Petković's evidential challenges in relation to the finding that the JCE came into existence as of mid-January 1993, the Appeals Chamber notes that he points to the evidence underpinning the Trial Chamber's inference that the leaders of the HVO and certain Croatian leaders aimed, by mid-January 1993, to ethnically cleanse the Muslim population in order to achieve the Ultimate Purpose of the JCE,[2777] and argues that the evidence and findings do not support the Trial Chamber's conclusion. In other words, Petković offers his own interpretation of the evidence without showing that no reasonable trier of fact could have interpreted this evidence as the Trial Chamber did. Accordingly, Petković's submissions are dismissed.

872.   As for Petković's submissions regarding the change in the ethnic composition of Gornji Vakuf Municipality, the Appeals Chamber notes that the findings pointed to by Petković indeed indicate that only some, as opposed to all, of the occupants of the villages left the municipality.[2778] However, the Appeals Chamber considers there to be no error in the Trial Chamber's conclusion that, despite this, the events in Gornji Vakuf formed part of the CCP as the Trial Chamber relied on a number of factors in addition to the removal of villagers from the municipality. For example, the Trial Chamber found that the crimes in Gornji Vakuf, as well as subsequent crimes, "tended to follow a clear pattern of conduct".[2779] The Trial Chamber also drew explicit parallels between the HVO operations in Gornji Vakuf and its subsequent operations in the municipalities of Jablanica and Prozor, showing in turn that these operations, and the resulting crimes, were part of the CCP.[2780] Further, in the present case, the Trial Chamber concluded that the removal of persons from villages in Gornji Vakuf Municipality amounted to crimes on the basis of, *inter alia,* the serious mental harm that these transfers engendered,[2781] and the deprivation of civilians' right to enjoy a normal family life.[2782] The Trial Chamber also expressly took account of the fact that the transfers affected a particular portion of the population, namely women, children, **[page 364]** and the elderly.[2783] Finally, the Appeals Chamber notes that,

---

[2773]   Prosecution's Response Brief (Petković), para. 41; Appeal Hearing, AT. 533 (23 Mar 2017). See also Prosecution's Response Brief (Petković), para. 40.

[2774]   Prosecution's Response Brief (Petković), para. 42, referring to *Đorđević* Appeal Judgement, para. 154. See Appeal Hearing, AT. 532-533 (23 Mar 2017).

[2775]   Prosecution's Response Brief (Petković), para. 43; Appeal Hearing, AT. 533, 546-550 (23 Mar 2017). The Prosecution also argues that the Trial Chamber's findings regarding the forcible removals from Hrasnica village were based on more than the exhibits (Exs. P09710 (confidential) and P10106) to which Petković refers. See Prosecution's Response Brief (Petković), para. 43. See also Prosecution's Response Brief (Petković), para. 44.

[2776]   Petković's Reply Brief, para. 14(i), referring to *Đorđević* Appeal Judgement, para. 154; Appeal Hearing, AT. 567 (23 Mar 2017).

[2777]   See Trial Judgement, Vol. 4, para. 44 & fn. 122, referring to the evidence of Witnesses Cedric Thornberry, BH, Ole Brix-Andersen, Exs. P02327 (confidential), P02787, Trial Judgement, Vol. 1, paras 441-451 ("Negotiations within the Framework of the Vance-Owen Plan (August 1992-January 1993)"), 452-456 ("Subsequent History of the Vance-Owen Plan; Attempts to Implement the Principles of this Plan in the Field (January 1993 – August 1993)").

[2778]   See Trial Judgement, Vol. 2, paras 405, 426-427, 466-468, Vol. 3, paras 845-848, 899-906. The Appeals Chamber notes that paragraphs 452-454 of Volume 2 of the Trial Judgement refer to the removal of named individual civilians in the village of Uzričje and do not directly support the conclusion that only some citizens were affected.

[2779]   Trial Judgement, Vol. 4, para. 65. In this respect, the Appeals Chamber notes that contrary to Petković's submission, the Appellants were charged with forcible transfer in Gornji Vakuf Municipality (Count 8), as well as unlawful transfer of a civilian (Count 9), and that he himself was convicted for those crimes in relation to Gornji Vakuf. Trial Judgement, Vol. 4, para. 820.

[2780]   Trial Judgement, Vol. 4, paras 45-48. See also Trial Judgement, Vol. 4, para. 142 (finding that the 4 April 1993 Ultimatum which led to crimes in Prozor was identical to the 15 January 1993 Ultimatum).

[2781]   Trial Judgement, Vol. 3, paras 845-848. See also Trial Judgement, Vol. 4, paras 94-95, 141, 197, 251, 315.

[2782]   Trial Judgement, Vol. 3, paras 899-906. See also Trial Judgement, Vol. 4, paras 94-95, 141, 197, 251, 315.

[2783]   Trial Judgement, Vol. 3, paras 845-848, 899-906.

contrary to Petković's argument, the *Đorđević* Appeal Judgement does not assist him as it holds that, as a matter of law, a common purpose need not be achieved in order for a trial chamber to conclude that a plurality of persons shared it or that crimes were committed in furtherance of a joint criminal enterprise.[2784] The Appeals Chamber thus finds that Petković fails to demonstrate any error in the Trial Chamber's conclusion that the crimes in Gornji Vakuf formed part of the CCP. Petković's argument is therefore dismissed.

873.   The Appeals Chamber finds that Petković has failed to show that the Trial Chamber erred in inferring that the plan to ethnically cleanse Provinces 3, 8, and 10 had crystallised by mid-January 1993 and that the military actions in Gornji Vakuf Municipality formed part of the CCP. Petković's sub-ground of appeal 3.2.2.1 is dismissed in relevant part.

   (vi) Impact of the Duša Reversal on the CCP

874.   Elsewhere in the Judgement, the Appeals Chamber has overturned the Trial Chamber's findings that the deaths of seven civilians in Duša in January 1993 constituted the crimes of murder and wilful killing and, as a result, has overturned the Appellants' convictions related to those killings under Counts 1, 2, 3, 15, and 16.[2785] The Appeals Chamber will now examine what impact, if any, the Duša Reversal has on the Trial Chamber's conclusions concerning the scope of the CCP and, more particularly, the crimes that formed part of it.[2786]

875.   As a preliminary matter, the Appeals Chamber notes that the Trial Chamber found that certain murders and wilful killings charged under Counts 2 and 3 formed part of the CCP, while others did not. Specifically, the Trial Chamber found that murders and wilful killings committed during attacks on villages ("attack murders") or in the context of the systematic use of detainees for labour on the front line or as human shields ("forced labour murders") formed part of the CCP (collectively, "CCP murders"), whereas murders and wilful killings committed during evictions (or closely linked thereto), or as a result of mistreatment or poor conditions of confinement during detention, did not.[2787] **[page 365]**

876.   The Trial Chamber found that the deaths of seven civilians in Duša, along with the established crimes in the Gornji Vakuf Municipality, marked the very start of the JCE. In addition, according to the Trial Chamber's findings, these deaths were, with one exception, the sole established attack murders that occurred in the period from January 1993 until June 1993,[2788] the latter date marking the expansion of the CCP with the addition of East Mostar-related crimes.[2789] This one exception is the 19 April 1993 incident in the village of Tošćanica in Prozor Municipality, where the Trial Chamber found that HVO soldiers killed two unarmed men during the HVO attack on the village.[2790] In contrast to this period, a number of attack murders was found by the Trial Chamber to have occurred from June 1993, starting with the East Mostar siege.[2791] As for

---

[2784]   See *Đorđević* Appeal Judgement, para. 154 ("The Appeals Chamber considers that this goal [of demographically modifying Kosovo] does not require a finding that the ethnic balance be changed permanently, or that all members of the JCE shared the intent to permanently remove [...]. [T]he Trial Chamber's conclusion that the common purpose was to change the ethnic balance of Kosovo to ensure Serb control over the province would still be reasonable even if the shift in ethnic balance was temporary and the purpose in fact not achieved."). *Cf.* Petković's Reply Brief, para. 14(i).

[2785]   See *supra*, paras 441-443, 866.

[2786]   See *supra*, para. 866.

[2787]   Compare Trial Judgement, Vol. 4, paras 59, 61, 66, 68, with Trial Judgement, Vol. 4, paras 70-71, 281, 433, 632, 822, 1008, 1213.

[2788]   See generally Trial Judgement, Vol. 3, paras 655-756 (containing the Trial Chamber's legal findings with respect to Counts 2 and 3 concerning murder and wilful killing, respectively).

[2789]   See *supra*, paras 792-814.

[2790]   The Appeals Chamber notes that, having found that two unarmed men were killed during an attack on the village, the Trial Chamber made legal findings under Counts 2 and 3 for those murders. See Trial Judgement, Vol. 2, para. 91, Vol. 3, paras 656-657, 705-706. However, there is no discussion of those murders in the Appellants' responsibility sections concerning their contribution and intent for crimes in Prozor Municipality. See Trial Judgement, Vol. 4, paras 141, 147 (Prlić), 329 (Stojić), 573 (Praljak), 692-693, 699 (Petković), 998 (Ćorić), 1099 (Pušić). While for Prlić the Trial Chamber appears to have found him responsible for Counts 2 and 3 in relation to Prozor Municipality, Prlić's responsibility section establishes only that, given his contribution to the events in Prozor, he accepted the commission of crimes committed against Muslims in Prozor, "namely the destruction of Muslim property and the arrests and removal of the Muslim population" and makes no mention of the Prozor killings. See Trial Judgement, Vol. 4, paras 141, 146-147. *Cf.* Trial Judgement, Vol. 4 para. 278 (listing Counts 2 and 3 under Prozor Municipality as being among the crimes for which it found Prlić guilty through his participation in a joint criminal enterprise).

[2791]   See Trial Judgement, Vol. 3, paras 672-679, 681, 683, 699-700, 721-722, 724-729, 732, 734, 752-753. The first such murder took place in East Mostar on 6 June 1993. See Trial Judgement, Vol. 2, paras 1061-1070. The Appeals Chamber also notes that the

forced labour murders, the Trial Chamber found that the Heliodrom detainees were killed during forced labour in the period between May 1993 and March 1994.[2792] However, a close analysis of the evidence relied upon for this finding shows that no forced labour murders in fact occurred before June 1993 and that the majority occurred in July 1993 and onwards.[2793] Accordingly, the Trial Chamber made an error of fact in relation to its finding that the Heliodrom killings during forced labour took place already in May 1993. The impact of this error will be considered below.[2794]

a. Arguments of the Parties

877. The incident in Duša being such a significant event in relation to the scope of the CCP, the Appeals Chamber invited the Parties to make submissions at the Appeal Hearing as to the impact a **[page 366]** potential reversal of the murder of the seven civilians in Duša would have, if any, on the CCP and on the *mens rea* of each of the Appellants.[2795]

878. While Prlić and Petković fail to address this specific issue,[2796] Praljak argues that should the Trial Chamber's findings regarding the HVO's intent for killings in Duša be overturned, "the events" in Gornji Vakuf could not be part of the CCP and should be seen as an incident between the HVO and ABiH, which did not spread to the entire area of the HZ H-B.[2797] As for the impact on his *mens rea,* Praljak refers to his ground of appeal 12 and submits that the evidence did not support the finding that he intended civilians to be killed in Duša.[2798] Ćorić makes a similar argument, namely that the events in Gornji Vakuf were an isolated local incident. He also submits that if the murders in Duša are overturned no basis would exist for the Trial Chamber's findings that there was a pattern of crimes and the resulting conclusion that he was responsible for murder and wilful killing, even in relation to the killing incidents that occurred after June 1993 in Mostar and the Heliodrom.[2799] Ćorić further argues that since murder was found to be part of the clear pattern of conduct by the Trial Chamber, it is "essential" to the finding that the CCP existed such that its removal means that Ćorić cannot be said to have had any JCE I liability and should be fully acquitted under Counts 2 and 3.[2800] Pušić acknowledges that the Duša convictions do not apply to him due to his JCE membership starting later but argues that should the Appeals Chamber reverse convictions of other Appellants under Counts 2 and 3, then the same should happen for him.[2801]

879. The Prosecution argues that even if the Duša murder findings are overturned, neither the scope of the CCP nor the *mens rea* of the Appellants as regards murder and wilful killing would be affected. According to the Prosecution, this is because the Trial Chamber included attack murders within the CCP on the ground that they were a part of the "entire system designed for deporting the Muslim population", which in turn was a finding based on the Trial Chamber's overall assessment of the pattern of crimes throughout the existence of the JCE.[2802] The Prosecution adds that this pattern of crimes was one of extreme violence, which included not only the CCP murders but also mistreatment of Muslims during evictions and cruel and inhumane

---

Trial Chamber found that East Mostar was subjected to intense and uninterrupted firing and shelling from June 1993 to March 1994. See Trial Judgement, Vol. 2, para. 1018.

[2792]   See Trial Judgement, Vol. 3, paras 674-676, 724-726 & fns 1310, 1369 (referring to the Trial Chamber's factual findings regarding the forced labour murders in the Heliodrom).

[2793]   See Trial Judgement, Vol. 2, paras 1600-1604 and references cited therein. See also Trial Judgement, Vol. 2, para. 1616 (stating that the evidence showed the use of human shields only in the months of July to September 1993), Vol. 3, paras 677-679, 727-729.

[2794]   See *infra,* paras 881-882 (& fn. 2810), 2792.

[2795]   See Order for the Preparation of the Appeal Hearing, 1 March 2017, p. 6 (question 4(a) and (b)).

[2796]   Stojić addressed the issue at the Appeal Hearing but did so only in a written submission he referred to as a "skeleton" argument. However, the Appeals Chamber will not consider the skeleton argument because it was not admitted into the judicial record. Stojić made no oral submissions on this issue during the Appeal Hearing despite being encouraged to do so. See Appeal Hearing, AT. 255-256, 301-302 (21 Mar 2017).

[2797]   Appeal Hearing, AT. 398-401 (22 Mar 2017).

[2798]   Appeal Hearing, AT. 400-401 (22 Mar 2017).

[2799]   Appeal Hearing, AT. 584-585 (24 Mar 2017).

[2800]   Appeal Hearing, AT. 585 (24 Mar 2017).

[2801]   Appeal Hearing, AT. 682-683 (27 Mar 2017). Pušić also submits that since the Trial Chamber made no findings as to his *metis rea* in relation to the Duša killings, the reversal should have no impact on his *mens rea* for JCE. Appeal Hearing, AT. 683 (27 Mar 2017).

[2802]   Appeal Hearing, AT. 219-220 (20 Mar 2017).

treatment of Muslims detained in **[page 367]** HVO detention centres.[2803] In addition, the Prosecution submits that the overall conduct of attacks in Gornji Vakuf shows that the HVO employed an extreme level of violence indicating that murder was an acceptable means of achieving the objective of ethnic cleansing, which was then confirmed by subsequent attacks in Prozor, Jablanica, East Mostar, Raštani, and Stupni Do and by use of prisoners for labour on the front line who were killed as a result.[2804]

b. Analysis

880.   As noted earlier, with the Duša Reversal, the CCP murders, bar one, started occurring only from June 1993, with the siege of East Mostar, which was some four-and-a-half months after the start of the JCE.[2805] In other words, in the period from January 1993 until June 1993 "a clear pattern of conduct" in HVO crimes found by the Trial Chamber[2806] included only one instance of CCP murders.[2807] Based on these circumstances and contrary to the Prosecution's submission, the Appeals Chamber considers that no reasonable trier of fact could conclude that there was a pattern of conduct with respect to the attack or forced labour murders such that they were a part of the "entire system designed for deporting the Muslim population" in the period from January 1993 until June 1993. Similarly, with respect to the Prosecution's argument that the Trial Chamber's findings show a pattern of violence throughout the existence of the JCE such that the Duša Reversal has no effect on its scope, the Appeals Chamber considers that such pattern of violence is not enough, on its own and with only one incident involving two murders during an attack on the village of Tošćanica in April 1993, to infer – as the only reasonable conclusion – that murder and wilful killing were part of the CCP from January 1993. This is particularly so when, with the exception of **[page 368]** Pušić,[2808] all the Trial Chamber's remaining findings relating to the Appellants' contribution to and intent for the CCP murders concern the period starting from June 1993.[2809]

881.   With respect to the Appellants' *mens rea*, the Prosecution's submission that the Appellants' intent for murder and wilful killing are not affected by the Duša Reversal suggests that all the Appellants, with the exception of Pušić who joined the JCE later, must have had the intent for murder and wilful killing months before the first proven CCP killing occurred. In this case, however, again with the exception of Pušić,[2810] the Trial Chamber's remaining findings do not establish beyond reasonable doubt that the Appellants had the intent for murder and wilful killing prior to June 1993.[2811] Further, while the Trial Chamber made its conclusions on the nature of the CCP and its commencement based on factors other than just the events in

---

[2803]   Appeal Hearing, AT. 219-220 (20 Mar 2017), AT. 648 (24 Mar 2017), AT. 731 (27 Mar 2017), AT. 762-763 (28 Mar 2017).

[2804]   Appeal Hearing, AT. 220-222 (20 Mar 2017). To illustrate this submission, the Prosecution refers to the HVO attack on Muslim civilians in Hrasnica in Gornji Vakuf Municipality in January 1993, their subsequent rounding up by the HVO, and the execution of one of the Muslim men by an HVO soldier. However, the Prosecution also acknowledges that the Trial Chamber made no findings on this incident. It further cites to the Trial Chamber's findings relating to the murder of two unarmed men during an attack on the village of Tošćanica in April 1993 in Prozor Municipality. Appeal Hearing, AT. 220-221 (20 Mar 2017). See also *supra*, fn. 2790.

[2805]   See *supra*, para. 876 & fn. 2793. While the Prosecution refers to the Hrasnica execution, the Appeals Chamber notes that the Trial Chamber made no findings relating to that killing incident and, furthermore, explicitly held that it had no evidence to find that the "death of villagers resulted from the HVO attack and artillery fire on the village of Hrasnica". See Trial Judgement, Vol. 2, paras 369-373. Accordingly, that incident will not be considered by the Appeals Chamber for the purposes of this discussion.

[2806]   See Trial Judgement, Vol. 4, para. 65.

[2807]   The Appeals Chamber notes that a number of other killings took place in that period but those were not considered by the Trial Chamber to have been part of the CCP and, as such, are not relevant to this discussion. See *supra*, para. 874.

[2808]   See *infra*, para. 881.

[2809]   See Trial Judgement, Vol. 4, paras 174, 176, 232, 237-238, 272, 274 (Prlić), 362-363, 368-370, 395, 426 (Stojić), 579-582, 585-586, 625 (Praljak), 749-750, 790-796, 798, 815 (Petković), 936-938, 964-966, 971, 1000-1004 (Ćorić), 1120-1122, 1147-1151, 1186-1187, 1206 (Pušić).

[2810]   See *supra*, para. 876 & fn. 2793. Pušić challenges this intent finding in his ground of appeal 5. See *infra*, paras 2791-2792. Ultimately, the Appeals Chamber does not consider that this intent finding is relevant for the purposes of the incorporation of murder and wilful killing in the CCP as it is not enough, on its own, to conclude that these crimes were intended by all JCE members and thus were part of the CCP before June 1993.

[2811]   See *supra*, fn. 2809. While the Prosecution cites to two killing incidents that took place in January and April 1993, the Appeals Chamber considers that these are not enough to establish intent on the part of the Appellants, particularly since: (1) the Trial Chamber made no factual findings relating to the January 1993 killing in Hrasnica and therefore did not enter any intent findings in relation thereto; and (2) as noted earlier, the Trial Chamber did not discuss the killings in Tošćanica in any of the Appellants' responsibility sections when considering their intent for the crimes in Prozor. See *supra*, para. 876 & fn. 2790.

municipalities and crimes on the ground, these factors also do not establish that the Appellants intended murder and wilful killing from January 1993.[2812]

882.   Accordingly, in light of the Trial Chamber's error regarding the civilian deaths in Duša, and considering the lack of any pattern of CCP murders or findings concerning the Appellants' intent for murder and wilful killing from January 1993 until June 1993, the Appeals Chamber considers that no reasonable trier of fact could conclude that murder and wilful killing were part of the CCP in the period from January 1993 until June 1993. The Trial Chamber's remaining findings, including the lone intent finding for Pušić regarding forced labour murders, do not establish beyond reasonable doubt that murder and wilful killing were part of the CCP from January 1993 until June 1993.

883.   On the other hand, and contrary to Praljak's and Ćorić's submissions, insofar as other crimes that took place in Gornji Vakuf are concerned, they are enough to sustain the Trial Chamber's conclusion that the events in Gornji Vakuf formed part of the CCP. This is because the other HVO crimes which the Trial Chamber considered as forming a clear pattern of **[page 369]** conduct,[2813] such as forcible transfers and imprisonment of civilians in Gornji Vakuf, remain unaffected by the Duša Reversal.[2814] Accordingly, Praljak's submission that the events in Gornji Vakuf should be removed from the CCP and Ćorić's submission that Gornji Vakuf was an isolated incident not connected to the CCP are dismissed.

884.   The Appeals Chamber will now examine whether, on the basis of the Trial Chamber's remaining findings, it remains established that murder and wilful killing were part of the CCP from June 1993.[2815] As noted above, the Trial Chamber made extensive findings concerning all of the Appellants' contribution to, knowledge of, and intent for the crimes that took place in East Mostar, including murder and wilful killing.[2816] These findings were made for the purpose of: (1) assessing whether crimes that were not already found to be part of the CCP, namely unlawful attack on civilians in East Mostar, unlawful infliction of terror on civilians in East Mostar, and destruction of religious property in East Mostar, became part of the CCP in June 1993; and (2) establishing the Appellants' responsibility for crimes committed in East Mostar that the Trial Chamber considered to be original CCP crimes.[2817] In making those findings, the Trial Chamber specifically noted the Appellants' knowledge and acceptance of killings that took place in East Mostar due to the HVO fire on the city.[2818] The Appeals Chamber is satisfied that the Trial Chamber's findings in relation to the expansion of crimes in East Mostar establish beyond reasonable doubt that murder and wilful killing were also expanded crimes, particularly since those findings show that the Trial Chamber considered: (1) that murder and wilful killing were part of the CCP in June 1993; and (2) that the Appellants were informed of murder and wilful killings but did nothing to prevent them.[2819] Further, the Trial Chamber also found that despite their knowledge of the killings in East Mostar, the Appellants continued to participate in the CCP and therefore accepted the crimes in question.[2820] **[page 370]**

885.   The Appeals Chamber also notes that, contrary to Ćorić's submission, the Trial Chamber's findings regarding the Appellants' contribution to, knowledge of, and intent for the crimes in East Mostar – including

---

[2812]   See *supra*, paras 847, 856-858, 861, 864, 872.

[2813]   See Trial Judgement, Vol. 4, para. 65.

[2814]   See *supra*, paras 468-481.

[2815]   The Appeals Chamber notes that the Trial Chamber found that the first murder in East Mostar occurred on 6 June 1993 and was a result of HVO sniper fire. See Trial Judgement, Vol. 2, paras 1061-1070.

[2816]   See *supra*, paras 792-814. With respect to Prlić, the Appeals Chamber notes that the Trial Chamber made findings regarding his intent for and contribution to both sniping and shelling, and yet did not include murder and wilful killing in its list of crimes for which Prlić was found directly responsible in relation to Mostar. See Trial Judgement, Vol. 4, paras 174-176, 272. *Cf.* Trial Judgement, Vol. 4, para. 278. Reading the Trial Judgement as a whole, however, including the above-mentioned East Mostar findings, it is clear that the Trial Chamber was satisfied that Prlić had the intent for murder and wilful killing of civilians in East Mostar and that he contributed to them. See Trial Judgement, Vol. 4, paras 174-176 ("Prlić knew about the HVO crimes committed during the HVO campaign of fire and shelling against East Mostar – that is, the murders and destruction of property … by minimising them or attempting to deny them, he accepted and encouraged them"), 272 ("Prlić supported the HVO campaign of fire and shelling against East Mostar and its impact on the civilian population … and accepted the crimes directly linked to the HVO military operations against East Mostar"). Accordingly, the Appeals Chamber considers the omission of Counts 2 and 3 from the list of crimes to have been an inadvertent omission on part of the Trial Chamber. See also *infra*, para. 1245.

[2817]   See, *e.g.*, *supra*, paras 798-799.

[2818]   See *supra*, paras 798, 805,-812.

[2819]   See *supra*, paras 806-812 and references cited therein.

[2820]   See *supra*, paras 806-812 and references cited therein.

murder and wilful killing – were not dependent on the Trial Chamber's conclusion that there was a pattern of conduct in the HVO crimes. Rather, the Trial Chamber focused on the evidence concerning the Appellants' involvement in and knowledge of the events in East Mostar.[2821] Accordingly, the Duša Reversal does not affect those findings. Further, given the small number of CCP murders found by the Trial Chamber to have been committed in the period from January 1993 until June 1993 the removal of murder and wilful killing from the CCP in that period does not impact the Trial Chamber's finding that there was a pattern of crimes or that the CCP existed, such that Ćorić should be relieved of any JCE liability or acquitted on Counts 2 and 3.

886.   Accordingly, the Appeals Chamber finds, on the basis of the Trial Chamber's remaining findings, that there is no impact on the Trial Chamber's conclusion that murder and wilful killing were part of the CCP as of June 1993, when the CCP murders started occurring more regularly and when the Appellants were all found to have had the requisite intent. As the remaining findings do not establish that murder and wilful killing were part of the CCP in April 1993, the Appeals Chamber considers that Prlić's conviction pursuant to JCE I for the murders of two unarmed men in Prozor must be reversed.[2822] Insofar as the other Appellants, as members of the JCE, were also found responsible pursuant to JCE I for these murders, the Appeals Chamber reverses their convictions as well.[2823] The impact of these findings on the Appellants' sentences, if any, will be assessed below.

(d) Alleged errors regarding events in Jablanica Municipality between February and May 1993

887.   The Trial Chamber found that in Jablanica Municipality, tensions between the HVO and ABiH mounted between the beginning of February and mid-April 1993.[2824] On 15 April 1993, the HVO commenced shelling the town of Jablanica, and on 17 April 1993, the HVO launched an attack in the Jablanica Valley, shelling the villages of Sovići and Doljani and ultimately taking control of these villages.[2825] Given the context of the broader attack in the Jablanica Valley, the Trial Chamber concluded that the attack on 17 April 1993 was not a "purely defensive" reaction to **[page 371]** the ABiH attack on the same day.[2826] The Trial Chamber also found that these military campaigns were accompanied by: (1) arrests and detentions of Muslims under harsh conditions (ABiH members and non-members alike); (2) the removal of ABiH members as well as several other men to Ljubuški Prison; and (3) the removal of the remaining Muslim population outside Jablanica Municipality.[2827]

(i) Prlić's appeal (Sub-grounds 10.3 and 10.4 in part)

888.   Prlić submits that the Trial Chamber erred in concluding that the HZ H-B leaders carried out the JCE in stages, by finding that the HVO attacked Sovići and Doljani on 17 April 1993, and in concluding that this attack was not a defensive reaction to an ABiH attack.[2828] In support of his assertions, Prlić adopts his sub-ground of appeal 16.2 by reference.[2829]

889.   The Prosecution responds that Prlić's arguments are unsupported assertions and warrant summary dismissal.[2830] In relation to Prlić's challenge to the Trial Chamber's finding on the implementation of the JCE

[2821]   See Trial Judgement, Vol. 4, paras 174-176, 179-184, 336-337, 341-342, 355, 359, 362-363, 368-370, 372, 579-582, 586, 745-756, 936, 938, 940-945, 1118-1122.

[2822]   See also *supra,* fn. 2810; *infra,* paras 2791-2792.

[2823]   As it has not been asked to do so by the Parties, the Appeals Chamber will not engage in an analysis of whether the elements of JCE III liability are met with respect to the Appellants in connection to these incidents, particularly since doing so would require the Appeals Chamber to have a comprehensive understanding of the entire trial record. See also *infra,* para. 3125.

[2824]   Trial Judgement, Vol. 4, para. 46.

[2825]   Trial Judgement, Vol. 4, para. 46. The Trial Chamber also found that on 5 May 1993, in the village of Sovići, approximately 450 women, children, and the elderly were moved by HVO soldiers from the Sovići School and the houses of Junuzovići hamlet towards Gornji Vakuf. Trial Judgement, Vol. 2, para. 609.

[2826]   Trial Judgement, Vol. 4, para. 46.

[2827]   Trial Judgement, Vol. 4, para. 48.

[2828]   Prlić's Appeal Brief, paras 286(d), 287, referring to Trial Judgement, Vol. 1, paras 452-476, Vol. 2, paras 84, 87, 89, 330-342, 346-395, 445, 465-467, 503-506, 514, 521-536, 538-549, 753, Vol. 4, paras 45-47, 668, 1220.

[2829]   Prlić's Appeal Brief, para. 288, referring to Prlić's sub-ground of appeal 16.2. Prlić submits that the Trial Chamber "mischaracterized events and actions, failed to provide reasoned opinions, and applied an incorrect legal standard in assessing the evidence". Prlić's Appeal Brief, para. 311. See also Prlić's Appeal Brief, paras 281, 312.

[2830]   Prosecution's Response Brief (Prlić), paras 166-167. The Prosecution submits that Prlić fails to explain how his arguments made under other grounds of appeal support the claims he makes in this instance. Prosecution's Response Brief (Prlić), para. 167.

in stages, the Prosecution argues that his unsupported assertions are coupled with redundant and unexplained cross-references, which also warrant summary dismissal.[2831]

890.   The Appeals Chamber notes that beyond referring to arguments made elsewhere in his appeal brief, Prlić fails to explain why the Trial Chamber erred in concluding that the HVO attacked Sovići and Doljani on 17 April 1993, and in concluding that this attack was not a purely defensive reaction to the ABiH attack on the same day. In this regard, the Appeals Chamber notes that it dismisses the submissions in Prlić's sub-ground of appeal 16.2 elsewhere.[2832] The Appeals Chamber thus finds that Prlić has failed to demonstrate an error and dismisses Prlić's sub-grounds of appeal 10.3 and 10.4 in relevant part. **[page 372]**

(ii) Petković's appeal (Sub-ground 3.2.2.1 in part)

a. Arguments of the Parties

891.   Petković submits that the evidence does not support the Trial Chamber's conclusions that: (1) 450 women, children, and the elderly were moved from Sovići on 5 May 1993 in the direction of Gornji Vakuf, causing serious mental suffering; and (2) the purpose of HVO actions in the region was to ensure that BiH Muslims were moved outside Jablanica Municipality, not to return.[2833] He asserts in this regard that the Trial Chamber disregarded evidence demonstrating that the civilians from Sovići were later transported from Gornji Vakuf to Jablanica, which, in his view, shows that the removal of citizens to Gornji Vakuf was just a temporary solution and did not result in a permanent change in the ethnic composition of Jablanica Municipality.[2834] Petković also argues that the Trial Chamber erred when concluding that the HVO attack on Sovići and Doljani was part of the CCP, given its acknowledgement that this attack was at least in part a defensive reaction to the ABiH attack on the same day.[2835]

892.   The Prosecution responds that the Trial Chamber reasonably concluded that the crimes in Jablanica Municipality formed part of the CCP, given that they were systematically committed pursuant to a well-organised and orchestrated plan.[2836] It asserts that these events formed part of the attempt to enforce the JCE members' interpretation of the Vance-Owen Peace Plan,[2837] and responds that Petković's argument that the ethnic map of Jablanica must change for the crimes to fall within the CCP runs contrary to the *Đorđević* Appeal Judgement.[2838] The Prosecution also submits that Petković's argument regarding a military justification for the attack on Jablanica should be summarily dismissed as a repetition of his trial argument without a demonstration of error, asserting that in any event, Appeals Chamber jurisprudence demonstrates that the existence of **[page 373]** a defensive element to operations "does not undermine their link to the common criminal purpose".[2839]

893.   Petković replies that the *Đorđević* Appeals Chamber finding confirms that at least a temporary change in ethnic balance is necessary in order to establish the common criminal plan.[2840]

[2831]   Prosecution's Response Brief (Prlić), para. 166, referring to *Đorđević* Appeal Judgement, para. 20(ix); *Galić* Appeal Judgement, para. 246. See also Appeal Hearing, AT. 182-183 (20 Mar 2017).

[2832]   See *infra*, paras 1177-1208.

[2833]   Petković's Appeal Brief, paras 54-56, referring to, *inter alia*, Trial Judgement, Vol. 2, paras 609, 613, Vol. 3, paras 850, 908, Vol. 4, paras 30, 48. See also Petković's Reply Brief, para. 14(iii).

[2834]   Petković's Appeal Brief, paras 55-56, referring to Trial Judgement, Vol. 2, para. 613, Ex. P02825, Nihad Kovač, T. 10311 (16 Nov 2006), Witness CA, T. 10042 (13 Nov 2006). See also Appeal Hearing, AT. 485-486, 496-497 (23 Mar 2017).

[2835]   Petković's Appeal Brief, para. 57, referring to Trial Judgement, Vol. 4, para. 46. See also Petković's Appeal Brief, para. 58.

[2836]   Prosecution's Response Brief (Petković), para. 47, referring to, *inter alia*, Trial Judgement, Vol. 4, paras 142, 146, 271, 341, 717.

[2837]   Prosecution's Response Brief (Petković), para. 47.

[2838]   Prosecution's Response Brief (Petković), para. 48, referring to, *inter alia*, Prosecution's Response Brief (Petković), para. 42, *Đorđević* Appeal Judgement, para. 154. See Appeal Hearing, AT. 532-533 (23 Mar 2017). The Prosecution argues that the Trial Chamber was aware that Witness CA returned to Jablanica in June 1993. Prosecution's Response Brief (Petković), para. 48, referring to Trial Judgement, Vol. 2, para. 612.

[2839]   Prosecution's Response Brief (Petković), para. 49, referring to Trial Judgement, Vol. 2, para. 523, *Kordić and Čerkez* Appeal Judgement, para. 812, *Tolimir* Appeal Judgement, paras 345-347.

[2840]   Petković's Reply Brief, para. 14(i), referring to *Đorđević* Appeal Judgement, para. 154; Appeal Hearing, AT. 567 (23 Mar 2017). See also Petković's Reply Brief, para. 14(iii).

b. Analysis

894.   As for Petković's challenge regarding the Trial Chamber's findings on Sovići, the Appeals Chamber notes that the Trial Chamber found that on 5 May 1993, approximately 450 villagers (women, children, and the elderly) were moved towards Gornji Vakuf.[2841] It then concluded that it did not have sufficient evidence to establish what happened next to the affected civilians.[2842] The Appeals Chamber recalls that a common criminal plan to demographically modify a certain region "does not require a finding that the ethnic balance be changed permanently".[2843] Accordingly, whether or not Petković is correct that the Trial Chamber disregarded evidence showing that the population from Sovići returned to Jablanica Municipality[2844] is irrelevant. As a result, the Appeals Chamber considers that the Trial Chamber did not err in finding that the crimes that took place in Jablanica Municipality, including the removal of the population from Sovići, fell within the CCP. Further, the Trial Chamber concluded that the removal of civilians on 5 May 1993 amounted to crimes,[2845] having taken account of, *inter alia,* a number of contemporaneous circumstances, including that the transfer was pre-planned by the HVO,[2846] caused serious mental suffering to a particularly vulnerable group of civilians,[2847] and deprived victims of the right to a normal social, family, and cultural life.[2848] Thus, the Appeals Chamber finds that Petković has failed to demonstrate an error in the Trial Chamber's finding and his submission is dismissed.

895.   Turning to Petković's assertion that the Trial Chamber erred in failing to take account of the fact that the HVO's attack on the villages of Sovići and Doljani was a defensive response to an **[page 374]** ABiH attack, the Appeals Chamber observes that the Trial Chamber stated that it could not find that the attack on Sovići and Doljani was "purely a defensive reaction to the ABiH attack on that same day",[2849] indicating that the attacks may have been, at least in part, motivated by offensive considerations. However, the Appeals Chamber recalls that "whether an attack was ordered as pre-emptive, defensive or offensive is from a legal point of view irrelevant, [...] [t]he issue at hand is whether the way the military action was carried out was criminal or not".[2850] In the present case, the Trial Chamber found that on 17 April 1993, the HVO launched an attack in the Jablanica Valley, shelling several localities, including Sovići and Doljani and committing crimes during and following the attack.[2851] Considering the evidence pertaining to the attack on the entire Jablanica Valley, the Trial Chamber found that these crimes formed part of the CCP on the basis that they occurred as part of the campaigns which were committed systematically and "had to be the result of a preconceived HVO plan".[2852] Finally, it concluded that the crimes formed part of a "clear pattern of conduct", along with other crimes that were committed by the HVO between January 1993 and April 1994.[2853] Accordingly, even if the attack on Sovići and Doljani was partly defensive, this has no bearing on the Trial Chamber's ultimate conclusion that it resulted in crimes which it reasonably found formed part of the CCP. Petković's argument is therefore dismissed.[2854]

[2841]   See Trial Judgement, Vol. 2, paras 609-615, Vol. 3, paras 849, 907.

[2842]   Trial Judgement, Vol. 2, para. 613.

[2843]   See *supra,* fn. 2784. *Cf.* Petković's Reply Brief, para. 14(i).

[2844]   See Petković's Appeal Brief, paras 55-56, referring to Ex. P02825, p. 2 (a report indicating that there were buses carrying refugees from Gornji Vakuf to Jablanica between 10 and 15 June 1993), Nihad Kovač, T. 10311 (16 Nov 2006) (noting that the witness went to Jablanica from Gornji Vakuf); Witness CA, T. 10042 (13 Nov 2006) (noting that the witness returned to Jablanica). The Appeals Chamber notes that in any event, the Trial Chamber did take account of Witness CA's testimony regarding the return to Jablanica in June 1993. See Trial Judgement, Vol. 2, para. 612.

[2845]   Trial Judgement, Vol. 3, paras 852, 910, 1703, 1706. See also Trial Judgement, Vol. 4, paras 145, 718, 723, 1103.

[2846]   See, *e.g.;* Trial Judgement, Vol. 3, paras 851, 909.

[2847]   See, *e.g.,* Trial Judgement, Vol. 3, paras 850-851. See also Trial Judgement, Vol. 3, para. 907.

[2848]   See, *e.g.,* Trial Judgement, Vol. 3, paras 850, 908.

[2849]   Trial Judgement, Vol. 4, para. 46, referring to, *inter alia,* Ex. P01915, p. 2 (indicating that the HVO attack on the village of Sovići was to start on 16 April 1993).

[2850]   *Kordić and Čerkez* Appeal Judgement, para. 812.

[2851]   Trial Judgement, Vol. 4, paras 46, 48.

[2852]   Trial Judgement, Vol. 4, para. 146.

[2853]   Trial Judgement, Vol. 4, para. 65. See Trial Judgement, Vol. 4, paras 46-48 (noting, *inter alia,* that while the attack on Sovići and Doljani was taking place, the HVO was also conducting "offensive actions" in several villages in the Municipality of Prozor).

[2854]   The Appeals Chamber recalls its reversal of the Trial Chamber's finding that murder and willful killing were part of the CCP in the period from January 1993 until June 1993. See *supra,* paras 874-886. Since the Trial Chamber found that no Jablanica killings were in fact part of the CCP, the Appeals Chamber does not consider that the change in the scope of the CCP in the period from

896. The Appeals Chamber therefore finds that Petković has failed to show that the Trial Chamber erred in its conclusion that the crimes in Jablanica Municipality fell within the CCP, and dismisses Petković's sub-ground of appeal 3.2.2.1 in relevant part.

(e) Alleged errors in the findings on HVO offensive actions in Prozor Municipality

897. The Trial Chamber found that, between 17 and 19 April 1993, the HVO was conducting "offensive actions" and took possession of several villages in Prozor Municipality, committing acts of violence such as setting fire to Muslim houses, causing the Muslim population to flee, and **[page 375]** thereby preventing any possibility of return.[2855] The Trial Chamber concluded that these actions fell within the CCP.[2856]

(i) Prlić's appeal (Sub-grounds 10.3 and 10.4 in part)

898. Prlić argues that the Trial Chamber wrongly concluded that the HZ H-B leaders carried out the JCE in stages by erroneously finding that, *inter alia,* the HVO attacked villages in Prozor Municipality between 17 and 19 April 1993, committing acts of violence and causing the Muslim population to flee.[2857] He also relies by reference on submissions made in his sub-ground of appeal 16.2.[2858]

899. The Prosecution responds that Prlić's sub-ground of appeal in relevant part consists of mere assertions unsupported by any evidence coupled with unexplained cross-references to arguments he makes elsewhere, and requests that it be summarily dismissed.[2859]

900. The Appeals Chamber dismisses Prlić's sub-grounds of appeal 10.3 and 10.4 in relevant part as undeveloped, since he fails to reference any part of the trial record in support of the mere assertion that the findings on the Prozor attacks are erroneous and fails to particularise how or why his submissions in his sub-ground of appeal 16.2 support his present contentions.

(ii) Petković's appeal (Sub-ground 3.2.2.1 in part)

901. Petković submits that the Trial Chamber erred in finding that the HVO military actions in Prozor Municipality in April 1993 that caused the Muslim population to flee were launched pursuant to the CCP.[2860] He argues that no reasonable trier of fact could conclude this because the Trial Chamber found that the crimes in relation to the removal of Muslims from Prozor Municipality (forcible transfer and unlawful transfer of civilians) were only committed on 28 August and 14 November 1993.[2861]

902. The Prosecution responds that the Trial Chamber reasonably concluded that crimes committed during the HVO operations in Prozor Municipality in April 1993 furthered the CCP.[2862] The Prosecution argues that although the Trial Chamber only found crimes of deportation and **[page 376]** forcible transfer in Prozor Municipality in August 1993,[2863] the Trial Chamber's factual findings link the April 1993 crimes to the CCP because the HVO offensive in Prozor Municipality involved violent crimes causing the Muslim population to flee and preventing their return.[2864]

January 1993 until June 1993 affects in any way the Trial Chamber's reasoning that the crimes in Jablanica which were part of the CCP followed a pattern of conduct that took place in other municipalities. See *supra,* para. 876. See also Trial Judgement, Vol. 2, paras 580-581, Vol. 4, para. 72.

[2855] Trial Judgement, Vol. 4, para. 47.

[2856] Trial Judgement, Vol. 4, paras 44-45, 47, 65-66.

[2857] Prlić''s Appeal Brief, para. 286(d). See also Prlić's Appeal Brief, para. 281.

[2858] Prlić's Appeal Brief, para. 288.

[2859] Prosecution's Response Brief (Prlić), paras 166-167. See also Appeal Hearing, AT. 183 (20 Mar 2017).

[2860] Petković's Appeal Brief, paras 52-53. See also Petković's Appeal Brief, paras 24, 42-44; Petković's Reply Brief, para. 14.

[2861] Petković's Appeal Brief, para. 52; Petković's Reply Brief, para. 14; Appeal Hearing, AT. 497-498 (23 Mar 2017).

[2862] Prosecution's Response Brief (Petković), para. 45.

[2863] Prosecution's Response Brief (Petković), para. 46. The Prosecution notes that contrary to Petković's submissions, the Trial Chamber found that crimes of forcible displacement were not established in Prozor for November 1993. Prosecution's Response Brief (Petković), para. 46 & fn. 168.

[2864] Prosecution's Response Brief (Petković), para. 46.

903.   The Appeals Chamber considers that the Trial Chamber based its conclusion on the CCP on, *inter alia,* its findings that the HVO offensive in Prozor Municipality in April 1993 involved acts of violence such as the burning of Muslim houses, "causing the Muslim population to flee, and thereby preventing any possibility of return".[2865] The finding that these violent acts, among other facts, support the conclusion on the CCP is not dependent on the findings regarding the crimes of forcible transfer and unlawful transfer of civilians.[2866] The Appeals Chamber therefore dismisses Petković's sub-ground of appeal 3.2.2.1 in relevant part.

(iii) Praljak's appeal (Ground 10)

a. Arguments of the Parties

904.   Praljak submits that the Trial Chamber erred in concluding that the crimes in Prozor Municipality formed part of the CCP.[2867] In support, he argues that the Trial Chamber: (1) did not establish the identity of the "authors" of the CCP that resulted in the commission of crimes in Prozor,[2868] or the "common action" of the JCE members, including Croatian officials;[2869] (2) did not have evidence that the Croatian officials allegedly involved in the JCE had any knowledge of the Prozor events before they occurred;[2870] (3) reached its conclusion on the basis of Exhibit P11380, which was admitted erroneously;[2871] (4) found that the Prozor crimes were not discussed among the JCE members;[2872] and (5) in basing its conclusion on circumstantial evidence only, erred in disregarding evidence providing an alternative reasonable explanation for the events in Prozor, namely that they were a consequence of ABiH military activities threatening the population.[2873] In **[page 377]** this respect, Praljak argues, *inter alia,* that the Trial Chamber erred in disregarding evidence on the great influx of Muslims into central BiH fleeing Serb-controlled territories disrupting the ethnic balance between Croats and Muslims and contributing to the outbreak of the war.[2874]

905.   The Prosecution responds that the Trial Chamber reasonably concluded that crimes committed in Prozor during HVO operations in 1993 furthered the CCP.[2875] Specifically, the Prosecution submits that: (1) Praljak's arguments regarding the identity of the authors of the CCP and the JCE members' common action ignore the Trial Chamber's clear finding that the crimes in Prozor were linked to the implementation of the 4 April 1993 Ultimatum, and followed the pattern of HVO crimes committed in other locations; (2) it is unnecessary to show that every JCE member knew precisely how the CCP would be implemented in Prozor;[2876] (3) the Trial Chamber's findings regarding the plan of ethnic cleansing in Prozor are not dependent on Exhibit P11380;[2877] (4) whether Prozor was discussed in certain meetings is irrelevant;[2878] and (5) the Prozor crimes were not a legitimate response to ABiH military activities nor solely the consequence of the existing situation in Prozor or of the instability caused by the arrival of refugees[2879] but were, rather, a part

[2865]   Trial Judgement, Vol. 4, para. 47. See Trial Judgement, Vol. 4, paras 44-45, 65-66.
[2866]   *Cf.* Trial Judgement, Vol. 3, paras 840-842, 894-896, Vol. 4, para. 47.
[2867]   Praljak's Appeal Brief, paras 163-164, 167-168, 173-174.
[2868]   Praljak's Appeal Brief, para. 163.
[2869]   Praljak's Appeal Brief, para. 168.
[2870]   Praljak's Appeal Brief, para. 168.
[2871]   Praljak's Appeal Brief, para. 165 & fn. 380. Praljak argues, relying on his ground of appeal 50, that Exhibit P11380 – one of the Mladić Diaries – was admitted erroneously because it was admitted in violation of his fundamental right to a fair trial. Praljak's Appeal Brief, para. 165 & fn. 381.
[2872]   Praljak's Appeal Brief, para. 164.
[2873]   Praljak's Appeal Brief, paras 166-167, 169-171, 173-174. In this regard, Praljak further argues that the Trial Chamber ignored evidence: (1) regarding the population in Prozor consisting of 62.2 per cent Croats (which would render any plan to change the ethnic composition in favour of Croats absurd); and (2) that Croats were seeking refuge from an ABiH offensive in central BiH in, *inter alia,* Prozor, which resulted in a chaotic situation. Praljak's Appeal Brief, paras 169, 171. See also Appeal Hearing, AT. 472 (22 Mar 2017).
[2874]   Praljak's Appeal Brief, paras 171-172.
[2875]   Prosecution's Response Brief (Praljak), para. 146.
[2876]   Prosecution's Response Brief (Praljak), para. 150.
[2877]   Prosecution's Response Brief (Praljak), para. 153.
[2878]   Prosecution's Response Brief (Praljak), para. 150. The Prosecution further submits that in any event Prozor was discussed. Prosecution's Response Brief (Praljak), para. 150.
[2879]   Prosecution's Response Brief (Praljak), paras 151-152. The Prosecution argues that Praljak's submission that the Prozor events were a consequence of an ABiH offensive merely repeats trial arguments without showing an error. Prosecution's Response

of the JCE members' CCP to consolidate HVO control over Prozor by "'ethnically cleans[ing]' the Muslims".[2880] The Prosecution argues, in particular, that the ABiH's Neretva 93 offensive was launched in September 1993 and was therefore after the Prozor crimes.[2881]

906. Praljak replies that the ABiH offensive during which Croats were expelled started well before summer 1993.[2882] **[page 378]**

b. Analysis

907. With regard to Praljak's arguments that the Trial Chamber failed to make findings as to the identity of the "authors" of the CCP that resulted in the commission of crimes in Prozor and as to the common action of the JCE members, the Appeals Chamber notes that he both fails to identify the challenged factual findings and ignores other relevant factual findings.[2883] It therefore dismisses these arguments. With respect to his claim that there was no evidence that the Croatian officials allegedly involved in the JCE had prior knowledge of the Prozor events, the Appeals Chamber notes that the Trial Chamber found that the CCP entailed consolidating HVO control over the so-called Croatian provinces under the Vance-Owen Peace Plan, which included Prozor Municipality.[2884] Further, it found that the crimes that took place in Prozor "tended to follow a clear pattern of conduct" as did the crimes that took place in other municipalities between January 1993 and April 1994.[2885] Consequently, the Trial Chamber found that the criminal plan of the JCE members, including the Croatian leaders, did encompass Prozor Municipality. The Appeals Chamber further notes that the Trial Chamber was not required to establish that a participant in the JCE knew about each specific crime committed pursuant to the JCE.[2886] Likewise, the lack of a finding that the JCE members discussed events in Prozor does not undermine the Trial Chamber's ultimate conclusion that Prozor crimes fell within the CCP. The Appeals Chamber further notes that this conclusion was based on many sources of evidence and is not dependent on Exhibit P113 80.[2887] Praljak's argument is therefore dismissed.[2888]

908. Turning finally to Praljak's argument that the Trial Chamber ignored evidence suggesting an alternative reasonable explanation for the Prozor events, namely that they were a consequence of ABiH military operations threatening the population, the Appeals Chamber notes that the **[page 379]** Trial

---

Brief (Praljak), para. 146. The Prosecution claims that, in arguing that any plan to modify the ethnic composition in Prozor would have been absurd, Praljak misunderstands the CCP, which included consolidating HVO control to make so-called Croatian provinces nearly exclusively Croatian. Prosecution's Response Brief (Praljak), para. 152. Furthermore, the Prosecution responds that the Trial Chamber did not ignore Prozor's pre-conflict demographics or evidence of Croat refugees moving from central BiH to Prozor in mid-1993. Prosecution's Response Brief (Praljak), para. 152. It also argues that the Trial Chamber reasonably found that the objective to detain Prozor's Muslim women, children, and the elderly was to accommodate the Croats arriving in Prozor Municipality. Prosecution's Response Brief (Praljak), para. 152.

[2880] Prosecution's Response Brief (Praljak), para. 151. See Prosecution's Response Brief (Praljak), paras 147-149. In this respect, the Prosecution argues that Praljak ignores key findings. Prosecution's Response Brief (Praljak), para. 146.

[2881] Prosecution's Response Brief (Praljak), para. 151.

[2882] Praljak's Reply Brief, para. 72. See also Praljak's Reply Brief, paras 69-71.

[2883] The Appeals Chamber notes that: (1) the Trial Chamber explicitly found that the attacks on the Prozor villages in April 1993 "were planned by Milivoj Petković, pursuant to an ultimatum issued by Jadranko Prlić to the ABiH" (Trial Judgement, Vol. 4, paras 1220, 1231 (internal references omitted)); and (2) the Trial Chamber made further findings as to how the JCE members, including Croatian leaders, collaborated as a plurality of persons in implementing the CCP (Trial Judgement, Vol. 4, paras 1217-1232; see, in particular, Trial Judgement, Vol. 4, paras 1219, 1222-1223, 1231).

[2884] See, *e.g.*, Trial Judgement, Vol. 1, para. 446 & fn. 1062, para. 447 & fn. 1065 (both referring to Ex. P09276, map 11), Vol. 4, paras 44, 47, 65.

[2885] Trial Judgement, Vol. 4, paras 47, 65.

[2886] *Šainović et al.* Appeal Judgement, para. 1491; *Kvočka et al.* Appeal Judgement, para. 276.

[2887] Trial Judgement, Vol. 4, paras 41-68. See, in particular, Trial Judgement, Vol. 4, para. 47 and the section of the Trial Judgement referenced therein with underlying findings and evidence. The Appeals Chamber notes that, in any event, it addresses and dismisses the arguments Praljak makes regarding the allegedly erroneous admission of Exhibit P11380 elsewhere. See *supra*, para. 121.

[2888] The Appeals Chamber recalls its reversal of the Trial Chamber's finding that murder and willful killing were part of the CCP from January 1993 until June 1993. See *supra*, paras 874-886. Ultimately, however, the Appeals Chamber does not consider that this change in the scope of the CCP in the period from January 1993 until June 1993 affects the Trial Chamber's reasoning concerning the clear pattern of conduct in relation to crimes in Prozor Municipality particularly since, as noted earlier, the Trial Chamber found that only two murders that formed part of the CCP occurred in Tošćanica, which is in contrast to June 1993 and onwards. See *supra*, para. 876 & fn. 2790. See also Trial Judgement, Vol. 4, paras 47, 65.

Chamber expressly considered evidence and reached findings on the various topics to which Praljak refers, partly relying on the same evidence he now cites.[2889] Accordingly, the relevant evidence to which Praljak refers in support of his argument was not ignored by the Trial Chamber in its reasoning.[2890] Moreover, the Appeals Chamber observes that, having considered these topics and underlying evidence, the Trial Chamber nevertheless concluded that the events in Prozor Municipality involving HVO acts of violence, including setting fire to Muslim houses, fell within the CCP to consolidate HVO control over provinces considered Croatian under the Vance-Owen Peace Plan by modifying their ethnic composition.[2891] In this regard, the Appeals Chamber notes, in particular, that ethnic tensions in Prozor Municipality caused by the influx of Muslim refugees, contrary to Praljak's submission, do not contradict this finding. The Appeals Chamber further notes that the Trial Chamber considered other evidence and findings in this respect, including in relation to the pattern of the many crimes committed and the context of enforcing the HZ(R) H-B leaders' interpretation of the Vance-Owen Peace Plan.[2892] In sum, Praljak has failed to demonstrate that no reasonable trier of fact could have reached, as the only reasonable inference, the conclusion that the crimes committed in Prozor Municipality in April 1993 fell within the CCP. The Appeals Chamber therefore dismisses Praljak's ground of appeal 10.

(f) Alleged errors in the findings on HVO actions in Mostar Municipality

909. The Trial Chamber found that: (1) on 15 April 1993 the Mostar municipal HVO adopted a decision on the rights of refugees and displaced and deported persons ("15 April 1993 Decision"), and, as a result, Muslims had no access to humanitarian aid forcing them to leave Mostar;[2893] (2) an HVO policy existed that entailed drastically reducing the Muslim population of the HZ H-B, especially in Mostar, while increasing the Croatian population there;[2894] (3) the HVO arranged removals of Croats to Provinces 8 and 10, including those not fearing real danger due to combat, either by force or voluntarily, and by so doing could have altered the balance of power in these **[page 380]** provinces so that it favoured the Croats;[2895] and (4) the HVO launched an attack on Mostar on 9 May 1993.[2896] The Trial Chamber further found that these actions fell within the CCP.[2897]

(i) Prlić's appeal (Sub-ground 10.5)

a. Arguments of the Parties

910. Prlić contends that the Trial Chamber erred in concluding that the Mostar municipal HVO adopted the 15 April 1993 Decision which led to discrimination against Muslims.[2898] He argues that the Trial Chamber erred in concluding that Croats became the majority in Mostar Municipality in May-June 1992 and that a subsequent influx of refugees again changed the demographic structure in Mostar in May 1993, this time in favour of Muslims.[2899]

[2889] The Trial Chamber considered evidence and found that: (1) the Croats constituted around 63 per cent of Prozor Municipality's population in 1991 (Trial Judgement, Vol. 2, paras 5, 8; *cf.* Praljak's Appeal Brief, para. 169); (2) some of the Croats moving from central BiH were under threat from the ABiH (Trial Judgement, Vol. 4, paras 53 (referring to, *inter alia*, Ex. 3D00837), 54-55; *cf.* Praljak's Appeal Brief, para. 171, referring to the same exhibit); and (3) many of them arrived in Prozor (Trial Judgement, Vol. 4, paras 53, 60, 63; see also Trial Judgement, Vol. 2, paras 5-6; *cf.* Praljak's Appeal Brief, para. 171).

[2890] In any event, the Appeals Chamber notes that the Trial Chamber was not required to refer to the testimony of every witness and to every piece of evidence on the record. See *Mrkšić and Šljivančanin* Appeal Judgement, para. 224.

[2891] Trial Judgement, Vol. 4, paras 44-45, 47, 55, 65-66.

[2892] See Trial Judgement, Vol. 4, paras 44, 65. See also Trial Judgement, Vol, 4, paras 45-64.

[2893] Trial Judgement, Vol. 4, para. 49.

[2894] Trial Judgement, Vol. 4, para. 51.

[2895] Trial Judgement, Vol. 4, para. 55.

[2896] Trial Judgement, Vol. 2, para. 775, Vol. 4, para. 56.

[2897] Trial Judgement, Vol. 4, paras 44-45, 49, 51, 54-56, 65-66.

[2898] Prlić's Appeal Brief, para. 289. See also Prlić's Appeal Brief, para. 281.

[2899] Prlić's Appeal Brief, para. 290. In support, Prlić argues that the Trial Chamber relied on: (1) Witness BA's unsubstantiated statement; (2) "mischaracterized documents"; and (3) the testimony of Witness CS, whose evidence, when compared with Exhibit 1D00936, is inconclusive. Furthermore, he argues that the Trial Chamber ignored evidence, *inter alia*: (1) that data from the ODPR

911.   Prlić further argues that the Trial Chamber erred in concluding that the 15 April 1993 Decision denied Muslim refugees humanitarian aid, forcing them to leave Mostar, as well as that at the beginning of May 1993, the HVO issued an ultimatum to Muslims occupying abandoned homes to leave by 9 May 1993 and that evictions started on 8 May 1993.[2900] In support of his argument, he submits that the Trial Chamber: (1) erroneously relied on adjudicated facts and Prosecution Witnesses BA's and BB's uncorroborated statements, excluding other relevant evidence such as evidence showing their lack of credibility;[2901] (2) ignored Witness BB's "demonstrated lack of knowledge" of relevant issues;[2902] (3) ignored Defence Witness Martin Raguž's testimony that the 15 April 1993 Decision was in accordance with the law on refugees, which regulated the obligations of military conscripts, and, in reality, changed nothing concerning the status of displaced persons regardless of their ethnicity;[2903] and (4) ignored Defence Witness Marinko Šimunović's testimony that: (i) similar decisions were adopted by Muslim-majority municipalities, (ii) there was no connection between the 15 April 1993 Decision and the movement of people or distribution of aid,[2904] (iii) the level of humanitarian aid went down in April 1993 in **[page 381]** part because of the 15 April 1993 Decision,[2905] (iv) contrary to international reports, no one lost refugee status due to this decision,[2906] (v) humanitarian aid was distributed transparently and without discrimination in Mostar Municipality,[2907] and (vi) the Red Cross was independent and distributed aid equally.[2908]

912.   The Prosecution responds that Prlić misrepresents the record in challenging the Trial Chamber's finding regarding the 15 April 1993 Decision denying Muslims humanitarian aid, arguing that Witnesses BA and BB corroborate each other and are corroborated by other evidence cited by the Trial Chamber.[2909] The Prosecution also claims that Prlić does not substantiate his claim that the Trial Chamber ignored Witness BB's "demonstrated lack of knowledge" and does not explain how this renders the Trial Chamber's reliance on the evidence unreasonable.[2910] It further argues that Prlić misrepresents the record with his assertion that the Trial Chamber ignored testimony from Raguž and Šimunović.[2911] Finally, the Prosecution contends that Prlić fails to show how the alleged errors could have affected the verdict.[2912]

b. Analysis

913.   Turning first to Prlić's arguments that the Trial Chamber erred in concluding that Croats became the majority in Mostar Municipality in May-June 1992, and that a subsequent influx of refugees changed the demographic structure in Mostar in May 1993 in favour of Muslims, the Appeals Chamber notes that these arguments are made within the scope of his overarching challenge under ground of appeal 10 concerning the Trial Chamber's finding that the HZ(R) H-B had a CCP to dominate the Muslim population through ethnic cleansing.[2913] The Appeals Chamber considers that the findings regarding the existence of the CCP and, consequently, Prlić's convictions,[2914] do not rely on the demographic findings challenged under his sub-ground of appeal 10.5.[2915] The Appeals Chamber therefore dismisses these arguments. **[page 382]**

---

and ICRC from May 1993 onwards related only to West Mostar; and (2) from Witness CS that by May 1992, 7,905 refugees occupied abandoned apartments in Mostar town illegally. Prlić's Appeal Brief, para. 290.

[2900]   Prlić's Appeal Brief, para. 291, referring to Trial Judgement, Vol. 2, paras 739-742, Vol. 4, paras 49, 159.

[2901]   Prlić's Appeal Brief, para. 291; Prlić's Reply Brief, para. 56.

[2902]   Prlić's Appeal Brief, para. 291.

[2903]   Prlić's Appeal Brief, para. 292. See also Prlić's Reply Brief, para. 57.

[2904]   Prlić's Appeal Brief, para. 293. See also Prlić's Reply Brief, para. 57.

[2905]   Prlić's Appeal Brief, para. 293. See also Prlić's Reply Brief, para. 57.

[2906]   Prlić's Appeal Brief, para. 293. See also Prlić's Reply Brief, para. 57.

[2907]   Prlić's Appeal Brief, para. 294. See also Prlić's Reply Brief, para. 57.

[2908]   Prlić's Appeal Brief, para. 294. See also Prlić's Reply Brief, para. 57.

[2909]   Prosecution's Response Brief (Prlić), para. 173. See also Prosecution's Response Brief (Prlić), para. 168.

[2910]   Prosecution's Response Brief (Prlić), para. 174. The Prosecution contends that, in any event, Prlić's assertions regarding Witness BB's ignorance are untrue. Prosecution's Response Brief (Prlić), para. 174.

[2911]   Prosecution's Response Brief (Prlić), para. 175. See also Prosecution's Response Brief (Prlić), para. 168.

[2912]   Prosecution's Response Brief (Prlić), para. 176.

[2913]   Prlić's Appeal Brief, para. 281.

[2914]   See, *e.g.*, Trial Judgement,. Vol. 4, para. 278.

[2915]   See Prlić's Appeal Brief, para. 290, referring to, *inter alia*, Trial Judgement, Vol. 2, paras 672-673. In this regard, the Appeals Chamber notes that Prlić fails to explain how the finding regarding the influx of mostly Muslim refugees into Mostar changing the demography there in May 1993 should have any impact on the Trial Chamber's findings regarding the existence of the

914.   The Appeals Chamber turns to Prlić's contention that the Trial Chamber erred in concluding that the 15 April 1993 Decision denied Muslim refugees humanitarian aid, forcing them to leave Mostar, as well as that at the beginning of May 1993 the HVO issued an ultimatum to Muslims occupying abandoned homes to leave by 9 May 1993 and that evictions started on 8 May 1993.[2916] With regard to his argument that Witnesses BA's and BB's statements are uncorroborated, the Appeals Chamber observes that the Trial Chamber's findings indicate that it found that these two witnesses corroborated each other,[2917] and were corroborated by other evidence and adjudicated facts.[2918] In any event, there is no general requirement that the testimony of a witness be corroborated if deemed otherwise credible.[2919] Further, Prlić's argument that the Trial Chamber excluded evidence showing Witnesses BA's and BB's lack of credibility relies on his ground of appeal 6, which the Appeals Chamber dismisses elsewhere.[2920] As for his argument that the Trial Chamber ignored Witness BB's lack of knowledge on a number of issues, Prlić fails to demonstrate how this renders the Trial Chamber's reliance on Witness BB's evidence with regard to the 15 April 1993 Decision unreasonable.

915.   With regard to Prlić's arguments that the Trial Chamber ignored the evidence of Raguž and Šimunović, the Appeals Chamber observes that Prlić challenges two sets of Trial Chamber findings: (1) that the 15 April 1993 Decision denied Muslim refugees humanitarian aid and forced them to leave Mostar;[2921] and (2) that, at the beginning of May 1993, the HVO issued an ultimatum to Muslims occupying abandoned homes to leave by 9 May 1993 and that evictions started on 8 May 1993.[2922] The Appeals Chamber considers that the evidence of Raguž and Šimunović highlighted by Prlić concerns the 15 April 1993 Decision,[2923] and is thus irrelevant to the latter finding.[2924] To the extent that the allegedly ignored evidence is relevant to the former finding,[2925] the Appeals **[page 383]** Chamber considers that Prlić fails to provide support for his claim that Raguž testified that the 15 April 1993 Decision in reality changed nothing concerning the status of displaced persons regardless of their ethnicity.[2926] He also fails to support his submission that Šimunović testified that there was no connection between that decision and the movement of people or distribution of humanitarian aid.[2927] Further, Prlić's claim that contrary to international reports no one lost refugee status based on the

---

CCP to dominate the Muslim population through ethnic cleansing. *Cf. Brđanin* Appeal Judgement, para. 22. The Appeals Chamber further notes that the finding that the Croats became the majority in Mostar Municipality in May-June 1992 relates to a period outside of the time frame of the CCP. See Trial Judgement, Vol. 4, paras 44 *et seq.*

2916   Prlić's Appeal Brief, para. 291, referring to, *inter alia*, Trial Judgement, Vol. 2, paras 739-742, Vol. 4, paras 49, 159.
2917   Trial Judgement Vol. 2, para. 739, referring to, *inter alia*, Ex. P09712 (confidential), paras 23, 26, Witness B A, T(F). 7173 (closed session) (25 Sept 2006), Witness BB, T(F). 17142, 17144 (closed session) (16 Apr 2007).
2918   Trial Judgement, Vol. 2, paras 739 (referring to, *inter alia*, Ex. P09840 (confidential), para. 5), 741-742 (referring to, *inter alia, Prosecutor* v. *Jadranko Prlić et al.*, Case No. IT-04-74-T, Decision on Prosecution Motions for Judicial Notice of Adjudicated Facts of 14 and 23 June 2006, 7 September 2006, Adjudicated Fact no. 79, Ex. P02227, p. 2). Prlić's mere assertion that the Trial Chamber erroneously relied on adjudicated facts is dismissed.
2919   *Popović et al.* Appeal Judgement, paras 243, 1264; *D. Milošević* Appeal Judgement, para. 215. See also *Kordić and Čerkez* Appeal Judgement, para. 274.
2920   See Prlić's Appeal Brief, para. 291; Prlić's Reply Brief, para. 56, referring to Prlić's Appeal Brief, paras 182-183, 189-190 (Prlić's ground of appeal 6). See *supra*, para. 218. The Appeals Chamber understands that Prlić intended to refer to Witness BB, not Witness BC. *Cf.* Prlić's Appeal Brief, para. 291; Prosecution's Response Brief (Prlić), fn. 591; Prlić's Reply Brief, para. 56). Prlić's argument that the Trial Chamber erroneously excluded "other relevant evidence" without any further specification is dismissed as a mere assertion.
2921   See Prlić's Appeal Brief, para. 291, referring to Trial Judgement, Vol. 2, paras 739-741, Vol. 4, paras 49, 159.
2922   See Prlić's Appeal Brief, para. 291, referring to Trial Judgement, Vol. 2, para. 742.
2923   See Prlić's Appeal Brief, paras 292-293, and references cited therein.
2924   See Prlić's Appeal Brief, para. 291, referring to, *inter alia*, Trial Judgement, Vol. 2, para. 742.
2925   See Prlić's Appeal Brief, para. 291, referring to, *inter alia*, Trial Judgement, Vol. 2, paras 739-741, Vol. 4, para. 49.
2926   The Appeals Chamber notes that the references to Raguž's testimony that Prlić cites in his appeal brief, fn. 809, do not support this assertion. The Appeals Chamber notes that Raguž testified that the 15 April 1993 Decision envisaged who could be granted refugee or displaced person status and that it regulated the entitlement to refugee cards and aid in Mostar Municipality. Martin Raguž, T. 31481, 31483 (27 Aug 2008). See also Martin Raguž, T. 31284 (25 Aug 2008). The Appeals Chamber fails to see how the assertion that the 15 April 1993 Decision was in accordance with the law on refugees, which regulated the obligations of military conscripts, carries any relevance to the challenged finding.
2927   The Appeals Chamber notes that the references to Šimunović's testimony that Prlić cites in his appeal brief, fn. 810, do not support this assertion. Šimunović, to the contrary, testified that he and the Red Cross had to distribute aid according to the criteria of the 15 April 1993 Decision. Marinko Šimunović, T. 33588, 33596-33597 (22 Oct 2008). The Appeals Chamber further notes that, in addition, Šimunović testified that in accordance with the 15 April 1993 Decision: (1) internally displaced persons moved to their formerly abandoned homes when they were able to do so; and (2) displaced persons accommodated in schools were to be relocated

15 April 1993 Decision is not borne out by the testimony he cites.[2928] As for the remainder of the allegedly ignored evidence, the Appeals Chamber considers that Prlić fails to explain how this evidence could impugn the challenged finding.[2929] Prlić's arguments that the Trial Chamber ignored testimony from Raguž and Šimunović are therefore dismissed.

916.   Having dismissed the arguments above, the Appeals Chamber considers that Prlić has failed to demonstrate that the Trial Chamber erred in concluding that: (1) the Mostar municipal HVO adopted the 15 April 1993 Decision, which led to discrimination against Muslims; (2) Croats became the majority in Mostar Municipality in May-June 1992, and that a new influx of refugees changed the demographic structure in Mostar in May 1993 in favour of Muslims; (3) the 15 April 1993 Decision denied Muslim refugees humanitarian aid, forcing them to leave Mostar; and (4) at the beginning of May 1993, the HVO issued an ultimatum to Muslims occupying **[page 384]** abandoned homes to leave by 9 May 1993 and that evictions started on 8 May 1993. The Appeals Chamber therefore dismisses Prlić's sub-ground of appeal 10.5.

(ii) Prlić's appeal (Sub-grounds 10.6. 10.7. and 10.8)

a. Arguments of the Parties

917.   Prlić asserts that the Trial Chamber erred in concluding that an HVO policy existed to drastically reduce the Muslim population of the HZ H-B, especially in Mostar, through removing the Muslim population and increasing the Croatian population.[2930] Prlić argues that the Trial Chamber relied on Witness BA's testimony without other supporting evidence, and disregarded all contrary evidence.[2931] Prlić also claims that the Trial Chamber erred in concluding that there was a new influx of people in Mostar around 5 May 1993, changing the demography in favour of Muslims.[2932] He further claims that the Trial Chamber erred in concluding that Prlić requested humanitarian organisations' assistance in moving Croats to areas considered to be Croatian.[2933] Lastly, Prlić submits that the Trial Chamber erred in concluding that the HVO arranged the removal of Croats to Provinces 8 and 10 to alter the balance of power.[2934] In support of his submission, Prlić argues that Prosecution Witnesses Beese's and BD's evidence was unsubstantiated, and that it "defies logic" that Croats would ethnically cleanse Croats from Province 10 to Province 8, which in 1992 was already 90 per cent Croatian.[2935]

---

to other buildings. Marinko Šimunović, T. 33444-33445 (20 Oct 2008), T. 33594 (22 Oct 2008). The Appeals Chamber fails to see how the assertion that decisions similar to the 15 April 1993 Decision were adopted in Muslim-majority municipalities is relevant to the impugned finding.

[2928]   The Appeals Chamber again notes that the references to Šimunović's testimony that Prlić cites in his appeal brief, fn. 812, do not support his assertion. To the contrary, Šimunović testified that the number of beneficiaries, in particular in the category of militarily able-bodied men, did change as a result of the 15 April 1993 Decision. Marinko Šimunović, T. 33632-33633 (22 Oct 2008).

[2929]   The Appeals Chamber fails to see how the assertion that the level of international humanitarian aid went down in April 1993 in part because of the 15 April 1993 Decision could cast doubt on the challenged finding. It further notes that the evidence that Prlić cites in support in his appeal brief, fns 813-814, does not support his assertions that the aid was distributed in Mostar Municipality in a non-discriminatory manner and that the Red Cross distributed it equally. Insofar as Marinko Šimunović testified that: (1) the Mostar Red Cross "did its job" irrespective of persons' ethnic background (Marinko Šimunović, T. 33681 (23 Oct 2008)); (2) the Mostar Red Cross operated free from the influence of the executive authorities (Marinko Šimunović, T. 33409 (20 Oct 2008)); and (3) the Muslims were receiving humanitarian aid under the same conditions as the Croats (Marinko Šimunović, T. 33527 (21 Oct 2008)), the Appeals Chamber notes that he also testified that he distributed aid according to the 15 April 1993 Decision. See *supra*, fn. 2927. The Appeals Chamber notes that the witness also stated that the Red Cross relied for the determination as to who required aid on lists of persons created by "professional services of the municipality and the Social Services on the ground". Marinko Šimunović, T. 33419 (20 Oct 2008). See Marinko Šimunović, T. 33418, 33420-33421 (20 Oct 2008). See also Marinko Šimunović, T. 33495-33496 (21 Oct 2008).

[2930]   Prlić's Appeal Brief, paras 295-296, referring to Prlić's grounds of appeal 16.5, 16.6.2, 16.6.5-16.6.6. See also Prlić's Appeal Brief, para. 281.

[2931]   Prlić's Appeal Brief, para. 295. See Prlić's Appeal Brief, para. 296.

[2932]   Prlić's Appeal Brief, para. 297.

[2933]   Prlić's Appeal Brief, para. 298. See Prlić's Appeal Brief, para. 299.

[2934]   Prlić's Appeal Brief, para. 300.

[2935]   Prlić's Appeal Brief, para. 300.

918.   The Prosecution responds that Prlić fails to show an error in arguing that Witness BA's evidence was not supported by other evidence, and that he ignores ample evidence corroborating the existence of an HVO policy of ethnic cleansing.[2936] The Prosecution argues that Prlić's claim that the Trial Chamber disregarded all evidence contrary to Witness BA's testimony is unsubstantiated, fails to identify the allegedly contrary evidence, and is contradicted by the Trial Chamber's express consideration of Prlić's case denying such a policy.[2937] Finally, the Prosecution argues that the Ultimate Purpose of the JCE is not contradicted by the Trial Chamber's finding on the HVO seeking to move Croats from Province 10 to Province 8, since the HVO lost control of Travnik (the capital of Province 10) to the ABiH in mid-June 1993.[2938] **[page 385]**

b. Analysis

919.   Turning first to Prlić's challenge to the Trial Chamber's finding on the existence of an HVO policy entailing the drastic reduction of the Muslim population while increasing the Croat population in HZ H-B, the Appeals Chamber considers that Prlić fails to articulate any error when arguing that Witness BA's evidence is not supported by other evidence, given that there is no legal requirement for corroboration.[2939] Moreover, the Appeals Chamber observes that, contrary to Prlić's assertion, the Trial Chamber considered ample corroborating evidence.[2940] The Appeals Chamber also dismisses Prlić's claim that the Trial Chamber disregarded all contrary evidence, as it is unsupported by any evidence.[2941] Further, Prlić fails to particularise how his submissions in sub-grounds of appeal 16.5, 16.6.2, 16.6.5, and 16.6.6 support his present arguments, and, therefore, they are dismissed as undeveloped.[2942]

920.   The Appeals Chamber further dismisses as undeveloped Prlić's claims that the Trial Chamber erred in concluding that: (1) there was a new influx of people in Mostar around 5 May 1993, changing the demography in favour of Muslims;[2943] and (2) Prlić requested humanitarian organisations' assistance in moving Croats to areas considered to be Croatian. In this regard, Prlić fails to particularise how his submissions in sub-ground of appeal 16.6.2 support his claims.

921.   With regard to Prlić's submission that the Trial Chamber erred in concluding that the HVO arranged removals of the Croat population to alter the balance of power, the Appeals Chamber notes that he fails to support his claim that the evidence of Beese and Witness BD is unsubstantiated. This argument is therefore dismissed as undeveloped. The Appeals Chamber further considers that Prlić's argument that it "defies logic"[2944] that Croats would ethnically cleanse other Croats from Province 10 to Province 8 (which in 1992 was already 90 per cent Croatian) is baseless, given that the Trial Chamber clearly explained how these relocations formed an integral **[page 386]** part of the project to consolidate HVO control by criminal means.[2945] Prlić simply attempts to substitute his own evaluation of this evidence for that of the Trial Chamber and, therefore, this argument is dismissed.

922.   For the foregoing reasons, the Appeals Chamber finds that Prlić has failed to show that the Trial Chamber erred in concluding that an HVO policy existed to drastically reduce the Muslim population of the

---

[2936]   Prosecution's Response Brief (Prlić), para. 177. See also Appeal Hearing, AT. 184-185 (20 Mar 2017).
[2937]   Prosecution's Response Brief (Prlić), para. 177.
[2938]   Prosecution's Response Brief (Prlić), para. 178.
[2939]   *Kor die and Čerkez* Appeal Judgement, para. 274. See *Krajišnik* Appeal Judgement, para. 21. Furthermore, Prlić's argument regarding Witness B A relies on his challenges to the witness's credibility under sub-ground of appeal 6.1, which the Appeals Chamber dismisses elsewhere. See *supra*, para. 218.
[2940]   See, *e.g.*, Trial Judgement, Vol. 4, para. 51, referring to Bo Pellnäs, T(F). 19511-19512 (5 June 2007), Witness BB, T(F). 17185, 17188 (16 April 2007) (closed session), Exs. P09593, para. 3 (confidential), P09712, paras 24-25 (confidential).
[2941]   The Appeals chamber also notes that the Trial Chamber specifically considered both of Prlić's arguments that there was no plan or any measures designed to ethnically cleanse the regions controlled by the HZ(R) H-B or the surrounding regions, and that the accusations of "reverse ethnic cleansing" were without any basis. Trial Judgement, Vol. 4, para. 39.
[2942]   The Appeals Chamber notes that, in any event, it dismisses elsewhere the submissions made under these sub-grounds. See *infra*, paras 1287-1298, 1300-1317.
[2943]   The Appeals Chamber notes that it dismisses elsewhere Prlić's sub-ground of appeal 10.5, to which he refers in this submission. See Prlić's Appeal Brief, fn. 817; *supra*, paras 910-916.
[2944]   Prlić's Appeal Brief, para. 300.
[2945]   See, *e.g.*, Trial Judgement, Vol. 4, paras 51-56, 60-64.

HZ H-B, especially in Mostar, through removing the Muslim population and increasing the Croatian population. The Appeals Chamber therefore dismisses Prlić's sub-grounds of appeal 10.6, 10.7, and 10.8.

(iii) Stojić's appeal (Ground 47)

a. Arguments of the Parties

923. Stojić submits that the Trial Chamber erred in fact and law and failed to give a "reasoned decision" in finding that the HVO launched the attack on Mostar on 9 May 1993.[2946] First, given that the Trial Chamber acknowledged that the evidence remained "very divided",[2947] Stojić argues that it was "impossible" to conclude beyond reasonable doubt that the attack was launched by the HVO.[2948] Second, Stojić argues that no witness could reliably establish that the HVO launched the attack.[2949] In particular, he contends that: (1) the local witnesses did not give evidence that adequately supported this conclusion; (2) contrary to the Trial Chamber's conclusion, most of the international witnesses were not in Mostar on 9 May 1993 ;[2950] and (3) there is another reasonable inference to be drawn from the HVO radio broadcast on the need to establish law and order which the civilian witnesses heard, namely, that the attack could have been a response to ABiH actions.[2951] Third, Stojić claims that the Trial Chamber failed to explain why it disregarded submissions and evidence suggesting that the ABiH initiated the attack, in particular that: (1) the ABiH was planning an attack on Mostar in April 1993; (2) military and technical equipment was supplied to the ABiH in Mostar in May 1993 by the HVO; (3) only five or six men were present at the relevant HVO command post just before the attack commenced; (4) none of the Appellants were in Mostar; and **[page 387]** (5) the HVO needed to call reinforcements to Mostar.[2952] Stojić contends that these errors led the Trial Chamber to find that the events in Mostar were part of the CCP, as opposed to a defensive response to the ABiH attack.[2953]

924. The Prosecution responds that the Trial Chamber, having considered the totality of the evidence, reasonably concluded that the HVO launched the attack on Mostar on 9 May 1993.[2954] It argues that the inhabitants of Mostar all gave similar accounts of the 9 May 1993 events – consistent with the evidence from the international witnesses – that the HVO attacked the town.[2955] The Prosecution further responds that Stojić misrepresents the evidence, considering that local witnesses were able to establish that the HVO started the attack.[2956] Lastly, the Prosecution argues that the Trial Chamber considered the evidence Stojić referred to, but ultimately relied, instead, on other evidence regarding the attack.[2957]

[2946]   Stojić's Appeal Brief, heading before para. 398, paras 398-402.

[2947]   Stojić's Appeal Brief, para. 399, referring to Trial Judgement, Vol. 2, para. 764.

[2948]   Stojić's Appeal Brief, paras 399-400.

[2949]   Stojić's Appeal Brief, para. 400.

[2950]   Stojić's Appeal Brief, para. 400, referring to, *inter alia*, Trial Judgement, Vol. 2, para. 775. Stojić refers here to Witnesses BF, Beese, and Klaus Johann Nissen. He further argues that Witness Grant Finlayson was in the relevant area, but was unable to explain the basis for concluding that the HVO started the attack. Stojić's Appeal Brief, para. 400.

[2951]   Stojić's Appeal Brief, para. 400, referring to Trial Judgement, Vol. 2, para. 765.

[2952]   Stojić's Appeal Brief, para. 401, referring, *inter alia*, to Exs. P01962, P01970, 3D01010, 3D01023, 3D01008, 3D01009. In support of his submission that MTS was supplied to the ABiH in Mostar in May 1993, Stojić refers to paragraph 29 and footnotes 85 and 86 of his appeal brief, under his ground of appeal 2.

[2953]   Stojić's Appeal Brief, paras 398, 402.

[2954]   Prosecution's Response Brief (Stojić), para. 364.

[2955]   Prosecution's Response Brief (Stojić), paras 365-368, 371. The Prosecution submits that it is immaterial that most of the international witnesses were not in Mostar during the attack, as they testified about reports they received from observers present in Mostar. Prosecution's Response Brief (Stojić), para. 367. It also maintains that according to inhabitants of Mostar the shelling was coming from HVO controlled areas and was directed at ABiH-controlled areas. Prosecution's Response Brief (Stojić), para. 365. The Prosecution further argues that contemporaneous reports of international observers also describe HVO shelling of ABiH positions. Prosecution's Response Brief (Stojić), para. 366.

[2956]   Prosecution's Response Brief (Stojić), para. 369. Furthermore, the Prosecution submits that the evidence of the HVO radio broadcast together with the other evidence supports the Trial Chamber's finding that the HVO launched the 9 May 1993 attack. Prosecution's Response Brief (Stojić), para. 370.

[2957]   Prosecution's Response Brief (Stojić), para. 371. See Prosecution's Response Brief (Stojić), para. 364.

b. Analysis

925. Turning first to Stojić's claim that the evidence of local witnesses failed to reliably establish that the HVO launched the attack on Mostar, the Appeals Chamber notes that contrary to Stojić's claim, evidence, including that of several local witnesses, supports the Trial Chamber's finding that the initial attack came from Hum mountain and West Mostar,[2958] which were controlled by the HVO.[2959] The Trial Chamber also took account of the fact that Mostar residents testified that at around 9:00 a.m. on 9 May 1993, the HVO broadcast an official press announcement to the effect that the HVO had undertaken a "large-scale action" to restore law and order and called on the **[page 388]** Muslims to place white flags in their windows "as a sign of their capitulation".[2960] Finally, the Appeals Chamber observes that when discussing the evidence of local witnesses, the Trial Chamber also relied on Adjudicated Fact no. 81 which states that the "HVO attacked Mostar using artillery, mortars, heavy weapons and small arms".[2961] The Appeals Chamber finds that Stojić has failed to show that, in light of the totality of this evidence, no reasonable trier of fact could have interpreted it in the way the Trial Chamber did. Accordingly, the Appeals Chamber finds no error in the conclusion that the evidence of local witnesses supported the finding that the HVO launched the attack on 9 May 1993.

926. As for Stojić's claim that "most" of the international witnesses relied upon by the Trial Chamber were not in Mostar on 9 May 1993, the Appeals Chamber observes as a preliminary matter that the Trial Chamber relied on the evidence of a large number of international witnesses in respect of the events of 9 May 1993, including the three witnesses referred to by Stojić.[2962] As Stojić points out, Beese, Nissen, and Witness BF testified that they were not in Mostar on 9 May 1993.[2963] However, when making a finding that the "observers from the international community *in Mostar on 9 May 1993* confirmed the description of the fighting on 9 May provided by the inhabitants of Mostar",[2964] the Trial Chamber did not rely on the evidence of Beese, Nissen, and Witness BF. Rather, it relied on a number of other international witnesses and documents, including relevant international reports.[2965] Thus, the Appeals Chamber finds that the Trial Chamber considered the evidence of Beese, Nissen, and Witness BF only as corroborative of its findings about the incident which were based on eyewitness testimony.[2966] The Appeals Chamber thus finds no error in the Trial Chamber's approach to the evidence of Beese, Nissen, and Witness BF, and dismisses Stojić's argument to the contrary. **[page 389]**

[2958] Trial Judgement, Vol. 2, para. 765 & fn. 1767, referring to Ex. P09805 (confidential), p. 2 (Witness CT heard that the shooting came from the upper part of the settlement formerly called Bakamluk, renamed Vatican); Ex. P10032, para. 7 (Witness Mujo Čopelj stated that he was awoken by the sounds of shelling coming from the "Western side" and from Mount Hum and Bakina Luka); Ex. P10033, para. 7 (Witness Muris Marić stated that "the HVO" launched the offensive from the "West side"); Ex. P10034 (confidential), paras 6-7 (Witness DY stated that she was told that the shelling came from Hum hill and from the Velež stadium); Ex. 3D03101, p. 4 (excerpt of a book by Ismet Haždiosmanović stating that the "HVO firing" came from the locality of Hum hill as he could clearly see from his apartment).

[2959] See Trial Judgement, Vol. 2, paras 761, 769. The Appeals Chamber notes that Stojić does not challenge these findings under the present ground of appeal.

[2960] Trial Judgement, Vol. 2, para. 766.

[2961] Trial Judgement, Vol. 2, fn. 1764. See also *Prosecutor* v. *Jadranko Prlić et al.,* Case No. IT-04-74-T, Decision on Prosecution Motions for Judicial Notice of Adjudicated Facts of 14 and 23 June 2006, 7 September 2006, p. 16.

[2962] See Trial Judgement, Vol. 2, paras 771-772, and references cited therein. See also Trial Judgement, Vol. 2, para. 764.

[2963] See Stojić's Appeal Brief, para. 400, referring to Christopher Beese, T. 3156, 3167 (14 June 2006) (Beese testified that he left Mostar on the afternoon of 8 May 1993 for Split, and was on leave from 9 May 1993), Klaus Johann Nissen, T. 20602 (27 June 2007) (Nissen was on leave on 9 May 1993), Witness BF, T. 25909 (8 Jan 2008) (closed session), T. 25959 (9 Jan 2009) (closed session). See also Trial Judgement, Vol. 2, paras 771 & fn. 1795 (referring, *inter alia,* to Klaus Johann Nissen, T(F). 20601-20601 (27 June 2007)), 772 (referring, *inter alia,* to Christopher Beese, T(F). 3167-3169 (14 June 2006), Witness BF, T(F). 25909-25910 (14 June 2006)).

[2964] Trial Judgement, Vol. 2, para. 771 (emphasis added).

[2965] Trial Judgement, Vol. 2, para. 771 & fn. 1794. The Trial Chamber also observed later in the same paragraph that some of the international observers were able to see that the HVO was shelling Mostar intensely. This finding also did not depend on the evidence of Beese, Nissen, and Witness BF. See Trial Judgement, Vol. 2, para. 771 & fn. 1796.

[2966] The Trial Chamber took account of, *inter alia,* Nissen's evidence to support the finding that the HVO had restricted the movement of international observers (see Trial Judgement, Vol. 2, para. 771 & fn. 1795), and Beese's, Nissen's, and Witness BF's evidence to support the conclusion that the HVO had started the attack on 9 May 1993 (see Trial Judgement, Vol. 2, para. 772 & fn. 1798).

927.   As regards Stojić's argument that there was an alternative reasonable inference in respect of the HVO's radio broadcast, namely, that the attack could have been a response to ABiH actions, the Appeals Chamber recalls that Mostar residents testified that around 9:00 a.m. on 9 May 1993, the HVO broadcast an official press announcement to the effect that the HVO had undertaken a large-scale action to restore law and order.[2967] The Appeals Chamber considers that Stojić merely suggests a different interpretation of the evidence without demonstrating that the Trial Chamber unreasonably concluded, based on the totality of evidence, that the attack on 9 May 1993 was launched by the HVO.

928.   As for Stojić's submission that the Trial Chamber failed to explain why it disregarded submissions and evidence suggesting that the ABiH initiated the attack, the Appeals Chamber notes that contrary to Stojić's submission, the Trial Chamber expressly considered evidence that only five or six men were present at the relevant HVO command post just before the attack commenced,[2968] that none of the Appellants were in Mostar,[2969] and that the HVO needed to call reinforcements to Mostar.[2970] Further, as regards Stojić's argument that the Trial Chamber disregarded evidence that military and technical equipment was supplied to the ABiH in Mostar in May 1993, the Appeals Chamber notes that the Trial Chamber found that the HVO and ABiH co-operated militarily from May 1992 against the JNA and VRS.[2971] It further found, considering, *inter alia,* the evidence referred to by Stojić, that in furtherance of this co-operation, the HVO supplied the ABiH with medical aid, weapons, and military equipment in 1992 and 1993.[2972] Lastly, with regard to Stojić's argument that the Trial Chamber disregarded evidence that the ABiH was planning an attack on Mostar in April 1993, the Appeals Chamber recalls that a trial judgement should be read as a whole,[2973] and notes that the Trial Chamber found that both the HVO and the ABiH seemed to be preparing for a potential attack on the eve of 9 May 1993.[2974] It also considered evidence suggesting that it was the ABiH that attacked the HVO on the morning of 9 May 1993 but nevertheless concluded that it was the HVO that launched an attack on Mostar on that day.[2975] Accordingly, the **[page 390]** Appeals Chamber finds that Stojić does not demonstrate that the Trial Chamber failed to provide a reasoned opinion by not expressly considering the evidence regarding events in April 1993.

929.   Turning finally to Stojić's claim that the Trial Chamber erred in relying on "divided evidence" when concluding that the HVO initiated the attack, the Appeals Chamber notes that the Trial Chamber observed that "the evidence remains very divided with respect to how the attack of 9 May 1993 started".[2976] The Appeals Chamber considers that there is no error, *per se,* in the Trial Chamber making a finding adverse to Stojić's submission while recognising that the evidence in respect of the attack was very divided. Moreover, Stojić fails to highlight any inconsistencies that the Trial Chamber left unresolved.[2977]

930.   In conclusion, the Appeals' Chamber finds that Stojić has not demonstrated that the Trial Chamber failed to provide a reasoned opinion, and has not succeeded in showing that no reasonable trier of fact could have concluded that the HVO launched the attack on Mostar on 9 May 1993. Stojić's ground of appeal 47 is dismissed.

[2967]   Trial Judgement, Vol. 2, para. 766.
[2968]   Trial Judgement, Vol. 2, para. 768.
[2969]   Trial Judgement, Vol. 2, para. 773.
[2970]   Trial Judgement, Vol. 2, paras 770 (referring to, *inter alia,* Exs. 3D01007, 3D01008, 3D01009, 3D01010, 3D01023), 772 (noting testimony to the effect that the HVO redeployment orders could be explained by the fact that the HVO was surprised by the ABiH's strong resistance).
[2971]   See Trial Judgement, Vol. 1, para. 440.
[2972]   See Trial Judgement, Vol. 1, para. 440 & fns 1037-1039, Vol. 2, para. 696 & fn. 1562, Vol. 4, para. 308 & fn. 732. *Cf.* Stojić's Appeal Brief, para. 29 & fns 85-86, referring to, *inter alia,* Anđelko Makar, T. 38447-38448, 38453-38456 (23 Mar 2009), Exs. 2D01107, 2D01108. See also Trial Judgement, Vol. 1, fn. 1114. *Cf.* Stojić's Appeal Brief, fn. 86, referring to, *inter alia,* Anđelko Makar, T. 38447-38448 (23 Mar 2009). See generally *infra,* paras 985-990.
[2973]   *Stanišić and Župljanin* Appeal Judgement, para. 202; *Šainović et al.* Appeal Judgement, paras 306, 321; *Boškoski and Tarčulovski* Appeal Judgement, para. 67.
[2974]   Trial Judgement, Vol. 2, para. 774.
[2975]   Trial Judgement, Vol. 2, paras 768-770, 775.
[2976]   Trial Judgement, Vol. 2, para. 764.
[2977]   See *Kupreškić et al.* Appeal Judgement, para. 31 (stating that it is "certainly" within the discretion of the trial chamber to evaluate any inconsistencies, and that it is the trial chamber that has the main responsibility to resolve any inconsistencies that may arise within and/or among witnesses' testimonies).

(iv) Praljak's appeal (Ground 28)

931.   Praljak submits that the Trial Chamber erred in concluding that the crimes in Mostar formed part of the CCP.[2978] In support, he argues that: (1) this is not the only reasonable conclusion from the evidence since the events in Mostar were a consequence of ABiH attacks and not "part of any plan";[2979] (2) the Trial Chamber did not establish the identity of the "authors" of the CCP that resulted in the commission of crimes in Mostar, nor Praljak's involvement in these crimes before 24 July 1993,[2980] nor the common action of the JCE members, including Croatian leaders, in Mostar;[2981] and (3) there is no evidence that either Praljak or the Croatian officials allegedly involved in the JCE had any knowledge of actions in Mostar before they occurred.[2982] **[page 391]**

932.   The Prosecution responds that the Trial Chamber reasonably concluded that crimes committed in Mostar formed part of the CCP.[2983] In particular, the Prosecution submits that: (1) Praljak's claim that the Mostar events were a consequence of ABiH attacks ignores several Trial Chamber findings and repeats failed trial arguments;[2984] (2) his argument regarding the identity of the authors of the CCP resulting in the Mostar crimes likewise ignores key findings;[2985] (3) the Trial Chamber's finding that Praljak did not contribute to crimes committed in Mostar before 24 July 1993 has no impact on whether such crimes formed part of the CCP, particularly in light of the Trial Chamber's findings that these crimes were part of a preconceived plan, implemented in a co-ordinated manner by other JCE members;[2986] (4) his argument regarding the JCE members' common action ignores various Trial Chamber findings;[2987] and (5) his insistence on evidence that Croatia's representatives had prior knowledge of HVO activities in Mostar is misplaced.[2988]

933.   With regard to Praljak's argument that the Mostar events were a consequence of ABiH attacks and not part of a plan, the Appeals Chamber notes that he both fails to identify the challenged factual findings and ignores other relevant factual findings.[2989] The same is the case with his arguments that the Trial Chamber omitted to make findings as to the identity of the "authors" of the CCP that resulted in the commission of the crimes in Mostar and as to the common action of the JCE members including Croatian leaders in Mostar.[2990] The Appeals Chamber therefore dismisses these submissions.

[2978]   Praljak's Appeal Brief, paras 326, 329; Praljak's Reply Brief, para. 79.
[2979]   Praljak's Appeal Brief, paras 325, 328-329; Appeal Hearing, AT. 383-384, 400 (22 Mar 2017). Praljak further contends that the ABiH attacks forced the HVO to protect itself and the Croatian population and to engage in battle in a populated urban environment; most of the resulting victims were collateral damage. Praljak's Appeal Brief, para. 328. With regard to some crimes that might have been committed by HVO members, Praljak asserts that these were isolated acts and not part of any criminal plan. Praljak's Appeal Brief, para. 328.
[2980]   Praljak's Appeal Brief, para. 326; Praljak's Reply Brief, paras 79, 81. Praljak submits that the Trial Chamber's findings show that his actions, contrary to HVO policy, aimed at assisting international organisations in bringing humanitarian aid into Mostar. Praljak's Reply Brief, para. 81.
[2981]   Praljak's Appeal Brief, para. 327.
[2982]   Praljak's Appeal Brief, para. 327; Praljak's Reply Brief, para. 80.
[2983]   Prosecution's Response Brief (Praljak), para. 173.
[2984]   Prosecution's Response Brief (Praljak), para. 175. See Prosecution's Response Brief (Praljak), para. 174. The Prosecution further submits that the HVO's crimes cannot be justified as mere collateral damage, considering that HVO shelling: (1) also targeted civilians and civilian objects; (2) included the use of indiscriminate weapons; and (3) affected the whole of East Mostar. Prosecution's Response Brief (Praljak), para. 175.
[2985]   Prosecution's Response Brief (Praljak), paras 173-174.
[2986]   Prosecution's Response Brief (Praljak), para. 176.
[2987]   Prosecution's Response Brief (Praljak), para. 176.
[2988]   Prosecution's Response Brief (Praljak), para. 176.
[2989]   Notably, Praljak ignores various findings on events in Mostar that clearly do not qualify as responses to ABiH military action, such as withholding humanitarian aid from Muslims, large-scale arrests and systematic eviction operations of civilians, and impeding or blocking humanitarian convoys. See, *e.g.*, Trial Judgement, Vol. 4, paras 49, 57-59, 64.
[2990]   See Praljak's Appeal Brief, para. 327 & fn. 792. The Appeals Chamber notes in this respect that the Trial Chamber explicitly found that the Appellants, all of whom were found to be JCE members, contributed to the crimes that took place in Mostar. See, *e.g.*, Trial Judgement, Vol. 4, paras 165, 171, 348-349, 355-357, 581, 586, 734-735, 738, 928, 933-934, 1110, 1112, 1116. The Appeals Chamber further notes that the Trial Chamber made findings as to how the JCE members, including Croatian leaders, collaborated as a plurality of persons in implementing the CCP. See Trial Judgement, Vol. 4, paras 1219, 1222-1223, 1231. See also Trial Judgement, Vol. 4, paras 1217-1218, 1220-1221, 1224-1230, 1232. To the extent Praljak argues that the JCE members were not present

934. With respect to Praljak's claim that there was no evidence that he or the Croatian officials who were allegedly involved in the JCE had prior knowledge of the actions in Mostar, the **[page 392]** Appeals Chamber notes that the Trial Chamber found that the CCP entailed consolidating HVO control over the so-called Croatian provinces under the Vance-Owen Peace Plan, which included Mostar Municipality.[2991] Further, it found that the crimes that took place in Mostar "tended to follow a clear pattern of conduct" along with the crimes that took place in other municipalities between January 1993 and April 1994.[2992] Consequently, the Trial Chamber found that the criminal plan of the JCE members, including the Croatian leaders, did encompass Mostar Municipality.[2993] The Appeals Chamber further notes that the Trial Chamber was not required to establish that a participant in the JCE knew about each specific crime committed pursuant to the JCE.[2994] Praljak's argument that the Trial Chamber did not establish his involvement in the Mostar crimes before 24 July 1993 is not determinative as to whether the crimes in Mostar formed part of the CCP.[2995] The Appeals Chamber therefore concludes that Praljak has failed to show that no reasonable trier of fact could have concluded that the crimes in Mostar formed part of the CCP. The Appeals Chamber dismisses Praljak's ground of appeal 28.

(v) Petković's appeal (Sub-ground 3.2.2.1 in part)

935. Petković submits that the Trial Chamber erred when it found that "ethnic cleansing" began in Mostar in mid-May 1993 and that Muslims were forcibly transferred from West Mostar to East Mostar on 26 May 1993.[2996] Petković argues that neither of these findings is supported by the cited evidence which was either not concerned with the second half of May or did not relate to evictions and expulsions at all.[2997] Petković further argues that the totality of the evidence shows that, in fact, the 26 May 1993 transfer was a voluntary exchange of Croats and Muslims.[2998] **[page 393]**

936. The Prosecution responds that the Trial Chamber reasonably concluded that crimes committed during HVO operations in Mostar furthered the CCP.[2999] It argues that the Trial Chamber's finding that the HVO forcibly removed Muslims from West Mostar to East Mostar in the second half of May 1993 is supported by a wide range of evidence, and that Petković fails to show that the Trial Chamber erred in this regard.[3000] The Prosecution submits that Petković wrongly asserts that there was a voluntary population exchange of Croats and Muslims.[3001]

937. Turning first to Petković's argument that the finding regarding the transfer of Muslims starting in mid-May 1993 was not supported by the evidence, the Appeals Chamber observes that he misrepresents the

---

in Mostar, the Appeals Chamber recalls that it is not necessary that a participant in a JCE be physically present at the site of the crime at the time it is committed. See *Kvočka et al.* Appeal Judgement, para. 112; *Krnojelac* Appeal Judgement, para. 81.

[2991] See, *e.g.,* Trial Judgement, Vol. 1, para. 446 & fn. 1062, para. 447 & fn. 1065 (both referring to Ex. P09276, map 11), para. 449, Vol. 4, paras 44, 49-52, 54-58, 65.

[2992] Trial Judgement, Vol. 4, paras 49, 51, 54-58, 65. The Appeals Chamber recalls its reversal of the Trial Chamber's finding that murder and willful kilhng were part of the CCP from January 1993 until June 1993. See *supra*, paras 874-886. Ultimately, however, the Appeals Chamber does not consider that this change in the scope of the CCP in that period affects the Trial Chamber's reasoning concerning the clear pattern of conduct in relation to crimes, particularly since not many instances of murders which were part of the CCP took place in that period, in contrast to June 1993 and onwards. See *supra*, para. 876 & fn. 2790.

[2993] This included the expanded crimes that took place in East Mostar from June 1993 as the Trial Chamber made findings indicating that the Croatian leaders were informed about events in BiH, including in East Mostar, mainly through Praljak but also through other Appellants. See *supra*, paras 2453, 2458, 2531.

[2994] *Šainović et al.* Appeal Judgement, para. 1491; *Kvočka et al.* Appeal Judgement, para. 276.

[2995] See, *e.g., Karemera and Ngirumpatsè* Appeal Judgement, para. 153. To the extent that Praljak challenges his own participation in the JCE, the Appeals Chamber addresses this argument below. See *infra*, paras 1975-2014.

[2996] Petković's Appeal Brief, para. 66. See Petković's Appeal Brief, paras 60, 63. See also Petković's Appeal Brief, paras 24, 42-44, 59; Petković's Reply Brief, para. 14; Appeal Hearing, AT. 498-499 (23 Mar 2017).

[2997] Petković's Appeal Brief, paras 61-62, 64, 66, referring to Exs. P02425, P09677 (confidential), P09384 (witness statement of Miro Salčin), para. 9; Petković's Reply Brief, para. 14.

[2998] Petković's Appeal Brief, paras 65-66; Petković's Reply Brief, para. 14, referring to Exs. P02512, P02524, Witness A, T. 14111 (closed session) (14 Feb 2007).

[2999] Prosecution's Response Brief (Petković), para. 50. See also Prosecution's Response Brief (Petković), paras 16-17.

[3000] Prosecution's Response Brief (Petković), paras 52, 54. See also Prosecution's Response Brief (Petković), paras 18, 51.

[3001] Prosecution's Response Brief (Petković), para. 53.

evidence on which the Trial Chamber relied,[3002] and ignores other relevant factual findings.[3003] With regard to Petković's challenge to the Trial Chamber's finding that "the HVO [moved] at least 300 Muslims from West Mostar to East Mostar on 26 May 1993 without their having the possibility of returning to West Mostar",[3004] the Appeals Chamber notes that Petković incorrectly claims that it was based on one exhibit, P09677, which does not support it.[3005] In fact, Exhibit P09677 supports the finding,[3006] which is furthermore based on a much broader spectrum of evidence and other relevant factual findings that Petković ignores.[3007] Regarding the assertion that the transfers took place on a voluntary basis, the Appeals Chamber observes that Petković points to evidence indicating that the transfer was part of an organised exchange between the HVO and ABiH, who drew up lists of "individuals who want[ed] to move from one local community to another".[3008] However, the Appeals Chamber notes that the Trial Chamber also made findings on the violent context in which these movements were occurring, including that: (1) the Muslims were forcibly expelled from their homes and transported either to the Heliodrom or directly to East Mostar; (2) in some cases, the Muslims had to move to collection centres or sleep on the streets; (3) one witness testified that he felt so unsafe in West Mostar that he signed up to be **[page 394]** moved to East Mostar; and (4) the Muslims were then prevented from returning to West Mostar.[3009] In ignoring these findings, Petković fails to demonstrate any error in the Trial Chamber's approach in this regard.

938.   The Appeals Chamber finds that Petković has failed to demonstrate any error in the Trial Chamber's conclusions as regards the transfers that began in Mostar in mid-May 1993, and dismisses Petković's sub-ground of appeal 3.2.2.1 in relevant part.

(vi) Praljak's appeal (Sub-ground 6.3) and Petković's appeal (Sub-ground 3.2.2.3)

a. Arguments of the Parties

939.   Both Praljak and Petković submit that the Trial Chamber erred in fact in finding that the HVO organised the displacement of Croats to Provinces 8 and 10 in order to alter the balance of power in favour of the Croats.[3010] Praljak argues that the Trial Chamber ignored the fact that Croats left central BiH because the ABiH and the Mujahideen threatened them,[3011] while Petković argues that since the Trial Chamber acknowledged that Croatian population movements were at least partly caused by fear of the ABiH, it was not justified "to consider that assistance of the HVO authorities to refugees of Croatian ethnicity was part of the [CCP]".[3012] Praljak also contends that, contrary to what the Trial Chamber found, the HVO requested the assistance of international organisations for moving the Croats because of their disastrous situation in

---

[3002]   Trial Judgement, Vol. 2, fn. 1899, referring to Miro Salčin, T(F). 14232, 14234 (15 Feb 2007), T(F). 14300 (19 Feb 2007), Exs. P02425 (confidential), para. 12, P09834, para. 9. The Appeals Chamber observes that much of this evidence relates to expulsions from West Mostar to East Mostar on 9 May 1993 and onwards, which would therefore include the mid-May period, and considers that Petković fails to demonstrate an error in the Trial Chamber's statement that "[a]ccording to evidence received by the Chamber, between 1,200 and 2,000 Muslim inhabitants were forced to leave West Mostar during this HVO operation". Trial Judgement, Vol. 2, para. 814.

[3003]   See Trial Judgement, Vol. 2, paras 812-813, 815. *Cf.* Petković's Appeal Brief, para. 62 (claiming that "there is no evidence that the HVO soldiers forced Muslims to leave West Mostar in the second half of May 1993").

[3004]   Trial Judgement, Vol. 2, para. 818.

[3005]   See Petković's Appeal Brief, para. 64, referring to Ex. P09677 (confidential).

[3006]   See, in particular, Ex. P09677 (confidential), para. 2 (reporting from Mostar on 26 May 1993 that "approximately 300 civilians were escorted from the West to East Bank [who] appear to have been Muslim DP/Rs or Muslim residents of the West Bank who were recently evicted from their flats").

[3007]   See Trial Judgement, Vol. 2, paras 816-817 and references cited therein.

[3008]   Ex. P02512, para. 2. See also Witness A, T. 14111 (closed session) (14 Feb 2007); Ex. P02524.

[3009]   See, *e.g.*, Trial Judgement, Vol. 2, paras 812-813, 817, Vol. 4, para. 57.

[3010]   Praljak's Appeal Brief, para. 124; Petković's Appeal Brief, paras 77, 79. See also Praljak's Appeal Brief, para. 100; Praljak's Reply Brief, para. 25; Petković's Appeal Brief, paras 24, 42-44.

[3011]   Praljak's Appeal Brief, paras 122-123. See Praljak's Appeal Brief, para. 119; Praljak's Reply Brief, para. 25.

[3012]   Petković's Appeal Brief, para. 78. See Petković's Appeal Brief, para. 77; Appeal Hearing, AT. 498 (23 Mar 2017). Petković further argues that the Trial Chamber erred by failing to distinguish between the Croats who were expelled by the ABiH and those whom the HVO allegedly removed, thereby treating the removal of all Croats as a part of the alleged CCP. Petković's Appeal Brief, para. 79.

Zenica.[3013] Praljak further argues that the Trial Chamber misunderstood the meaning of the expression "evacuation in [an] organized manner" used by the HVO authorities with regard to what to do with the expelled Croats.[3014] Praljak also points out that the Trial Chamber itself found that Croats were displaced from Travnik, "that is, from Province 8 *[sic]*".[3015] Finally, he argues that the displaced Croats were only temporarily accommodated on the territory of the HZ(R) H-B before being transferred to Croatia.[3016]
[page 395]

940.   The Prosecution responds that the Trial Chamber reasonably found that JCE members moved Croats into the HZ(R) H-B to alter the ethnic balance in favour of Croats.[3017] With respect to Praljak's arguments, the Prosecution argues that: (1) he ignores the Trial Chamber's assessment of the evidence and repeats his trial arguments without identifying any error;[3018] (2) the displacement of Croats from Travnik, located in Province 10, to Province 8 is consistent with the Ultimate Purpose of the JCE since the ABiH took control of Travnik from the HVO in mid-June 1993;[3019] and (3) the common purpose to change the ethnic balance existed even if JCE members only partially succeeded and the ethnic balance was only temporarily altered.[3020] As for Petković, the Prosecution contends that his argument regarding HVO assistance to ethnic Croats is undermined by the fact that the HVO used force and propaganda to encourage their displacement.[3021] The Prosecution also submits that, contrary to Petković's submission, the Trial Chamber did distinguish between the Croats forced to flee by the ABiH and those forced to flee by the HVO.[3022]

b. Analysis

941.   With regard to Praljak's argument that the Trial Chamber ignored the fact that Croats left central BiH because the ABiH and the Mujahideen threatened them, the Appeals Chamber first observes that the Trial Chamber noted evidence indicating that Croats from central BiH were under threat from the ABiH and the Mujahideen and that some of them fled the fighting on their own initiative, as well as evidence indicating that the HVO was stirring up fears in these Croats in order to make them leave.[3023] The Appeals Chamber consequently finds that the Trial Chamber did not ignore evidence that some Croats left central BiH under threat from the ABiH and the Mujahideen, and that Praljak merely advances his own preferred interpretation of the evidence. His argument is dismissed.

942.   In addition, and concerning Petković's argument that the Trial Chamber was not justified in considering the assistance of HVO authorities to Croatian refugees as part of the CCP given its findings on the motives for the movement of Croatian refugees, the Appeals Chamber recalls that the Trial Chamber found that the HVO was animated by a dual purpose:

> It is clear from all the evidence that the HVO arranged these removals to Provinces 8 and 10, not merely to come to the rescue of one part of the Croatian population located in combat zones, but **[page 396]** also to remove the other part of the population that did not fear any real danger, doing so either by force or voluntarily. By doing this, the HVO could alter the balance of power in these provinces so that it favoured the Croats.[3024]

[3013]   Praljak's Appeal Brief, para. 121.
[3014]   Praljak's Appeal Brief, para. 120, referring to Exs. P02142, p. 4, 1D01829, 1D01672, p. 2. Praljak argues that this expression was used by HVO authorities to show that the expelled Croats would be taken in by the HVO authorities and that their reception and accommodation would be organised. Praljak Appeal Brief, para. 120.
[3015]   Praljak's Appeal Brief, para. 124. The Appeals Chamber notes that Travnik was in Province 10. See Trial Judgement, Vol. 1, fn. 1062, referring to, *inter alia*, Ex. P09276, map 11.
[3016]   Praljak's Appeal Brief, para. 124. See Praljak's Reply Brief, para. 25.
[3017]   Prosecution's Response Brief (Praljak), para. 43; Prosecution's Response Brief (Petković), para. 28. See Prosecution's Response Brief (Petković), paras 16-17, 29-30.
[3018]   Prosecution's Response Brief (Praljak), para. 43.
[3019]   Prosecution's Response Brief (Praljak), para. 43.
[3020]   Prosecution's Response Brief (Praljak), para. 43.
[3021]   Prosecution's Response Brief (Petković), para. 31, referring to, *inter alia*, Petković's Appeal Brief, para. 78. See also Prosecution's Response Brief (Petković), para. 18.
[3022]   Prosecution's Response Brief (Petković), para. 31. See also Prosecution's Response Brief (Petković), para. 18.
[3023]   Trial Judgement, Vol. 4, paras 53-54.
[3024]   Trial Judgement, Vol. 4, para. 55 (internal references omitted).

The Appeals Chamber cannot see why the first of these purposes would undercut the second and finds that Petković has failed to articulate an error in this regard. Furthermore, with regard to Petković's argument that the Trial Chamber erred by failing to distinguish between Croats expelled by the ABiH or HVO, thereby treating the removal of all Croats as a part of the alleged CCP, the Appeals Chamber observes that the Trial Chamber did make that distinction,[3025] and that Petković merely asserts, without providing any support, that the Trial Chamber treated the removal of all Croats as a part of the CCP.

943. As for Praljak's contention that the HVO requested the assistance of international organisations for moving the Croats because of their disastrous situation in Zenica, the Trial Chamber considered evidence that the request for assistance was made due to the threat the Croats were facing in central BiH, but it nevertheless arrived at the conclusion that the HVO arranged removals of Croats to Provinces 8 and 10, including removals of those not fearing real danger.[3026] Praljak fails to demonstrate that no reasonable trier of fact could have reached the same conclusion.

944. Regarding Praljak's argument that the Trial Chamber misunderstood the meaning of the expression "evacuation in [an] organized manner" used by HVO authorities,[3027] the Appeals Chamber notes that in support of this argument Praljak does not refer to a specific part of the Trial Judgement but simply cites to three exhibits, two of which contain the relevant expression.[3028] The Appeals Chamber further notes that the relevant paragraph where the Trial Chamber analysed the reasons for the movements of Croats refers to two of those exhibits without mentioning the relevant expression; rather the Trial Chamber cited to these exhibits, among many others, while noting that certain documents, originating with the HVO, suggest that the movement of the population was due to ABiH threats.[3029] The Trial Chamber then proceeded to outline evidence to the contrary, and found that the removals were in fact organised not only to protect one part of the Croatian population but also to remove the other part that had nothing to fear, in order to alter the balance of power in Provinces 8 and 10 in favour of Croats.[3030] Accordingly, **[page 397]** Praljak fails to show that the Trial Chamber gave any particular significance to this expression. His argument is therefore dismissed. With regard to Praljak's point about Croats being displaced from Travnik, the Appeals Chamber observes that the subsequent displacement of Croats from Travnik is not inconsistent with the challenged finding.[3031] Further, the Trial Chamber found that in mid-June 1993, HVO members drove Muslims out of West Mostar, telling them that they needed to make way for Croats coming from Travnik.[3032]

945. Turning to Praljak's final argument that the displaced Croats were only temporarily accommodated on the territory of the HZ(R) H-B before being transferred to Croatia, the Appeals Chamber notes that he refers to evidence indicating that some displaced Croats transited through the territory of the HZ(R) H-B and continued on to Croatia.[3033] This is not inconsistent with the Trial Chamber's finding that the HVO arranged removals to Provinces 8 and 10 to alter the balance of power in these provinces so that it favoured the Croats.[3034] In addition, the Appeals Chamber recalls that, as a matter of law, the objective or common purpose of a JCE does not need to be achieved in order for a trial chamber to conclude that a plurality of persons shared a common purpose or that crimes were committed in furtherance of a JCE.[3035] Praljak's argument is dismissed.

[3025] See Trial Judgement, Vol. 4, paras 54-55.

[3026] Trial Judgement, Vol. 4, paras 54-55, referring to, *inter alia*, Ex. P02714, p. 2.

[3027] Praljak's Appeal Brief, para. 120.

[3028] See Praljak's Appeal Brief, para. 120, referring to Exs. P02142, 1D01829, 1D01672.

[3029] Trial Judgement, Vol. 4, paras 53-54 & fns 142, 148, referring to Exs. P02142, 1D01672. While the Trial Chamber used the phrase "in an organised manner" in a subsequent finding, that finding appears to have no relevance to Praljak's challenges here. See Trial Judgement, Vol. 4, para. 60.

[3030] Trial Judgement, Vol. 4, paras 54-55 & fns 149-153 and references cited therein.

[3031] The Appeals Chamber further observes that the Prosecution points to evidence indicating that the ABiH took control of Travnik from the HVO in mid-June 1993, which Praljak does not contest in his reply brief. *Cf.* Prosecution's Response Brief (Praljak), para. 43 & fn. 211 and references cited therein; Praljak's Reply Brief, para. 25.

[3032] Trial Judgement, Vol. 4, para. 57.

[3033] See Praljak's Appeal Brief, para. 124 & fn. 304 and references cited therein.

[3034] Trial Judgement, Vol. 4, para. 55.

[3035] *Đorđević* Appeal Judgement, para. 154.

946. For these reasons, the Appeals Chamber finds that Praljak has failed to show that the Trial Chamber erred in finding that the HVO organised the displacement of Croats to Provinces 8 and 10 in order to alter the balance of power in favour of the Croats. It therefore dismisses Praljak's sub-ground of appeal 6.3. Similarly, the Appeals Chamber finds that Petković has failed to demonstrate any error in the Trial Chamber's conclusions regarding the removal of Croats, and dismisses Petković's sub-ground of appeal 3.2.2.3.

(g) Alleged errors in the findings regarding the events before and after the attack on the HVO Tihomir Mišić Barracks in Mostar on 30 June 1993

947. The Trial Chamber found that "in the opinion of the international organisations present", the process of "ethnic cleansing", which began in Mostar and surrounding areas, appeared irreversible.[3036] In this regard, the Trial Chamber observed that, on 4 June 1993, during a meeting in **[page 398]** Divulje in Croatia ("4 June 1993 Divulje Meeting") with Prlić, Petković, and Boban, Witness DZ spoke of "ethnic cleansing" in these areas.[3037] It also found that all the participants, including Boban, denied the existence of ethnic cleansing, although Boban stated that the Muslims in BiH had to be chased out of Mostar and BiH entirely.[3038]

948. The Trial Chamber further concluded that after the ABiH attacked the HVO Tihomir Mišić Barracks in Mostar on 30 June 1993, the implementation of the JCE became "more efficient".[3039] It found that the HVO arrested Muslims from the municipalities of Mostar, Stolac, Čapljina, Ljubuški, and Prozor, detaining them in HVO detention centres or sending them to ABiH-controlled territories and to third countries via Croatia.[3040] In this regard, the Trial Chamber found that the HZ(R) H-B authorities implemented a "system of deportation utilising the release of Muslim detainees from the HVO detention centres contingent upon their departure from Croatia – often with their families – where they were supposed to stay only temporarily prior to being transferred to a third country".[3041] Moreover, the Trial Chamber found that due to the "very harsh conditions of confinement" which could lead to detainee deaths, Muslim detainees agreed to leave for ABiH-controlled territories or for another country rather than remain in confinement.[3042]

(i) Prlić's appeal (Sub-grounds 10.10 and 10.15)

a. Arguments of the Parties

949. Prlić submits that the Trial Chamber erred in concluding that the arrests and detentions of Muslims from Mostar, Stolac, Čapljina, Ljubuški, and Prozor and their forcible removal after the Attack on the HVO Tihomir Mišić Barracks were part of the JCE.[3043] Further, Prlić argues that the Trial Chamber erred when it concluded that the JCE became "more efficient" as the HZ(R) H-B authorities introduced, on 30 June 1993, a system of deportation predicated upon the release of **[page 399]** Muslims from HVO detention centres, which was contingent upon their departure to Croatia and their subsequent transfer to a third country.[3044]

950. Prlić submits that the Trial Chamber erred in finding that the process of "ethnic cleansing" was irreversible, by solely relying on Exhibit P09677, a report of Witness BB.[3045] He also contends that the Trial

---

[3036] Trial Judgement, Vol. 4, para. 58, referring to, *inter alia*, Witness BB, T(F). 17185, 17188 (closed session) (16 Apr 2007), Ex. P09677 (confidential).
[3037] Trial Judgement, Vol. 4, para. 58, referring to, *inter alia*, Witness DZ, T(F). 26469 (closed session) (22 Jan 2008), Exs. P09677 (confidential), P02652.
[3038] Trial Judgement, Vol. 4, para. 58, referring to Witness DZ, T(F). 26550, 26552-26554 (closed session) (22 Jan 2008), Ex. P10367 (confidential), para. 63.
[3039] Trial Judgement, Vol. 4, paras 57, 64.
[3040] Trial Judgement, Vol. 4, para. 57. See also Trial Judgement, Vol. 4, para. 64.
[3041] Trial Judgement, Vol. 4, para. 64.
[3042] Trial Judgement, Vol. 4, para. 64.
[3043] Prlić's Appeal Brief, para. 301, referring to Trial Judgement, Vol. 2, paras 921-923, 1642-1655, Vol. 3, paras 140-145, 264-266, 270, 272-274, Vol. 4, paras 57-58. Prlić argues in this respect that the Trial Chamber disregarded evidence that: (1) Muslim HVO members were arrested in response to the ABiH attack; (2) there were international negotiations and an agreement reached in September 1993 concerning the release of HVO and ABiH prisoners; and (3) Croats from Travnik "were not accommodated" in Mostar. Prlić's Appeal Brief, para. 302, referring to Prlić's sub-grounds of appeal 1.3, 16.3.1, 16.5.1-16.5.2.
[3044] Prlić's Appeal Brief, paras 308-309, referring to Prlić's sub-grounds of appeal 1.1, 1.3, 16.1-16.3.
[3045] Prlić's Appeal Brief, paras 303, referring to Ex. P09677 (confidential).

Chamber ignored evidence indicating that international organisations adopted "different approaches" and that "civilians from different communes were organized in agreement with the UN and ECMM with the same number crossing over from East to West Mostar".[3046] Prlić contends that the Trial Chamber mischaracterised Exhibit P02652, a report on the 4 June 1993 Divulje Meeting, as this meeting focused on: (1) the implementation of the Vance-Owen Peace Plan; (2) the establishment of the provisional government; and (3) the cessation of hostilities, specifically in the Konjic area.[3047] He further contends that "contrary to [Witness] DZ", Exhibit P02652 does not reflect Boban's remarks that "BiH Muslims had to be chased out from Mostar and BiH entirely".[3048]

951.   The Prosecution responds that Prlić's arguments have no merit as they are based on mere assertions, misrepresentations, and unexplained claims that are not inconsistent with, nor contradictory to, the Trial Chamber's finding.[3049] It also argues that Prlić relies on other sub-grounds of his appeal without explaining how they support his arguments.[3050] With respect to Prlić's allegation of error concerning the 4 June 1993 Divulje Meeting, the Prosecution contends that the Trial Chamber's finding on Boban's remarks was not based on Exhibit P02652, but rather on Witness DZ's evidence.[3051]

    b. Analysis

952.   The Appeals Chamber rejects Prlić's contentions that the Trial Chamber erred in finding that the arrests and detentions of Muslims from Mostar, Stolac, Čapljina, Ljubuški, and Prozor and their forcible removal following the Attack on the HVO Tihomir Mišić Barracks were part of the JCE and that the JCE became more efficient after the introduction of a system of deportation as of 30 June 1993. In this regard, the Appeals Chamber observes that, in support of his arguments, Prlić **[page 400]** merely cross-references his sub-grounds of appeal 1.1, 1.3, 16.1-16.3, 16.3.1, and 16.5.1-16.5.2, which the Appeals Chamber dismisses elsewhere.[3052] Accordingly, the Appeals Chamber dismisses Prlić's arguments in this regard.

953.   As to Prlić's submission that the Trial Chamber erred in finding that the process of ethnic cleansing was irreversible since it "solely" relied on Exhibit P09677, the Appeals Chamber observes that in reaching the impugned conclusion, the Trial Chamber also relied on Witness BB's testimony confirming the contents of Exhibit P09677.[3053] Prlić's argument is thus dismissed. Similarly, the Appeals Chamber rejects Prlić's undeveloped arguments that the Trial Chamber ignored evidence showing "the different approaches used by the international organizations, and that civilians from different communes were organized in agreement with the UN and ECMM with the same number crossing over from East to West Mostar"[3054] for lack of clarity.[3055] In any event, Prlić fails to explain how the cited evidence would materially impact the impugned finding. Moreover, the Appeals Chamber observes that in support of this argument Prlić refers to his submissions in sub-grounds of appeal 16.4.3-16.4.4, which it dismisses elsewhere.[3056] Accordingly, these arguments are dismissed.

954.   Further, the Appeals Chamber sees no merit in Prlić's contention that the Trial Chamber misrepresented confidential Exhibit P02652 which reported on the 4 June 1993 Divulje Meeting. Prlić simply argues that this meeting focused on the implementation of the Vance-Owen Peace Plan, the establishment of the provisional government, and the cessation of hostilities without showing any error in the Trial Chamber's finding. A

[3046]   Prlić's Appeal Brief, para. 303, referring to Witness BC, T. 18481-18484 (closed session) (15 May 2007), Klaus Johann Nissen, T. 20655-20658 (private session) (27 June 2007), Exs. P02512, P02547 (confidential), p. 7, 6D00007, 4D00496, p. 1. In this regard, Prlić adopts his submissions of sub-grounds of appeal 16.4.3-16.4.4 by reference. Prlić's Appeal Brief, para. 304.
[3047]   Prlić's Appeal Brief, para. 305, referring to Ex. P02652 (confidential), ground of appeal 6.1.
[3048]   Prlić's Appeal Brief, para. 305.
[3049]   Prosecution's Response Brief (Prlić), paras 166-167, 179-180. See also Prosecution's Response Brief (Prlić), para. 182; Appeal Hearing, AT. 185-187 (20 Mar 2017).
[3050]   Prosecution's Response Brief (Prlić), paras 166-167.
[3051]   Prosecution's Response Brief (Prlić), para. 181, referring to Trial Judgement, Vol. 4, para. 58 & fn. 164.
[3052]   See *supra*, para. 176; *infra*, paras 1146-1221, 1286-1298.
[3053]   See Trial Judgement, Vol. 4, para. 58 & fn. 161, referring to Witness BB, T(F). 17185, 17188 (closed session) (16 Apr 2007), Ex. P09677 (confidential), para. 12.
[3054]   Prlić's Appeal Brief, para. 303 (internal reference omitted).
[3055]   See *supra*, para. 24.
[3056]   See *infra*, paras 1232-1241.

review of the relevant finding shows that, rather than relying on Exhibit P02652, the Trial Chamber referred to Witness DZ's testimony as well as his Rule 92 *ter* statement, which plainly support Boban's utterance as recalled in the impugned conclusion.[3057] Accordingly, the Appeals Chamber dismisses this contention.

955.   In light of the foregoing, the Appeals Chamber finds that Prlić has failed to show that the Trial Chamber erroneously found that the arrests and detentions of Muslims from Mostar, Stolac, Čapljina, Ljubuški, and Prozor and their forcible removal were part of the JCE. He has also failed to show an error in relation to the Trial Chamber's conclusions that the process of "ethnic cleansing" appeared irreversible to the international organisations and that the JCE became more efficient after **[page 401]** the Attack on the HVO Tihomir Mišić Barracks. The Appeals Chamber therefore dismisses his sub-grounds of appeal 10.10 and 10.15.

(ii) Petković's appeal (Sub-ground 3.2.2.2)

a. Arguments of the Parties

956.   Petković submits that the Trial Chamber erred in concluding that the "HVO measures of 30 June 1993 were taken to further [the CCP] of 'ethnic cleansing in a more efficient manner'".[3058] He argues that this conclusion contradicts the Trial Chamber's factual findings on the events, namely that on 30 June 1993 the ABiH launched an offensive in co-operation with HVO soldiers of Muslim ethnicity and that, in response to this offensive, the HVO "took certain actions".[3059] Petković further argues that the Trial Chamber failed to evaluate evidence about the ABiH's offensives after April 1993 and its territorial expansion.[3060] He submits, therefore, that the evidence supports the conclusion that "the underlying reason for taking special security measures by the HVO leaders on 30 June 1993 was [in response to the] broad military offensive of the ABiH and HVO's losing control over certain areas".[3061] Petković concludes that the Trial Chamber's inferences that the HVO leaders decided to implement the JCE more efficiently and that the HVO's authorities and forces launched political and military activities to further the CCP as of 30 June 1993 should be reversed, as should his conviction for "expanded core crimes".[3062]

957.   The Prosecution responds that Petković fails to show an error in the impugned findings as he merely repeats arguments raised at trial and that his arguments should be summarily dismissed.[3063] The Prosecution also submits that Petković misconstrues the Trial Chamber's findings since its conclusion' on the increased efficiency of the implementation of the CCP has no bearing on the expanded crimes, but on the crimes which were part of the criminal means from the outset of the CCP.[3064] **[page 402]**

b. Analysis

958.   The Appeals Chamber notes that the Trial Chamber concluded that following the Attack on the HVO Tihomir Mišić Barracks, the implementation of the JCE became more efficient as HZ(R) H-B authorities introduced "a system of deportation utilising the release of Muslim detainees from the HVO detention

---

[3057]   Trial Judgement, Vol. 4, para. 58, referring to Witness DZ, T(F). 26552-26554 (closed session) (22 Jan 2008), Ex. P10367 (confidential), para. 63.
[3058]   Petković's Appeal Brief, para. 75. See Petković's Appeal Brief, para. 73, referring to Trial Judgement, Vol. 2, paras 880-886; Appeal Hearing, AT. 502 (23 Mar 2017). See also Petković's Appeal Brief, paras 71-72; Petković's Reply Brief, para. 16, referring to *Prosecutor v. Zoran Kupreškić et al.*, Case No. IT-95-16-T, Decision on Evidence of the Good Character of the Accused and the Defence of *Tu Quoque*, 17 February 1999 *("Kupreškić et al. Tu Quoque* Decision").
[3059]   Petković's Appeal Brief, para. 73, referring to Trial Judgement, Vol. 2, paras 880-886; Appeal Hearing, AT. 502-512 (23 Mar 2017).
[3060]   Petković's Appeal Brief, para. 74. By contrast, according to Petković, the Trial Chamber "indirectly acknowledged" ABiH expansion when considering the relocation of Croatians from central BiH. Petković's Appeal Brief, para. 74, referring to Trial Judgement, Vol. 3, para. 284, Vol. 4, para. 60. See also Petković's Appeal Brief, paras 71-72.
[3061]   Petković's Appeal Brief, para. 75.
[3062]   Petković's Appeal Brief, para. 76.
[3063]   Prosecution's Response Brief (Petković), paras 61-63, referring to Petković's Final Brief, para. 133.
[3064]   Prosecution's Response Brief (Petković), paras 58-60.

centres contingent upon their departure from Croatia".[3065] The Trial Chamber further found that the evidence showed the occurrence of: (1) arrests and detention of Muslims from Mostar, Stolac, Čapljina, Ljubuški, and Prozor; and (2) their transfer to ABiH-controlled territories and third countries via Croatia after their detention in HVO detention centres.[3066] The Appeals Chamber observes that in arguing that the "security measures taken by the HVO" subsequent to the Attack on the HVO Tihomir Mišić Barracks were in response to the ABiH offensives, rather than part of the CCP,[3067] Petković simply repeats unsuccessful submissions already raised at trial without demonstrating how the Trial Chamber erred in this regard.[3068] Moreover, Petković's argument that the Trial Chamber's conclusions as to the events of 30 June 1993 are contradicted by other factual findings also amounts to a further attempt to reargue his submission that these events were a defensive response to the ABiH. These submissions are dismissed.

959.   The Appeals Chamber also rejects Petković's argument that the Trial Chamber failed to consider relevant evidence about the ABiH's offensives after April 1993 and its territorial expansion as he does not identify any relevant piece of evidence in this regard.[3069] Finally, with respect to Petković's contention that his conviction for the "expanded core crimes" should be reversed, the Appeals Chamber observes that he misunderstands the relevant findings because the increased efficiency of the CCP implementation concerns the introduction of a deportation system rather than any "expanded core crimes".[3070] Accordingly, the Appeals Chamber finds no merit in Petković's submission. His argument thus fails. **[page 403]**

960.   In light of the foregoing, the Appeals Chamber finds that Petković has failed to show that the Trial Chamber unreasonably found that the JCE became more efficient following the Attack on the HVO Tihomir Mišić Barracks and dismisses his sub-ground of appeal 3.2.2.2.

(h) Alleged errors in the findings as to events in late 1993

961.   The Trial Chamber concluded that from early June 1993 until late that year, approximately 22,000 to 24,000 Croats arrived in the territory of the HZ(R) H-B, in particular in Prozor, Stolac, Čapljina, and Ljubuški.[3071] It also found that in October 1993, the HVO arrested and detained Muslim men from the town of Vareš,[3072] and conducted an attack on Stupni Do on 23 October 1993, killing part of the Muslim population.[3073] The Trial Chamber concluded that after this attack, the HVO warned the Croatian population of an imminent risk of reprisal by the ABiH and requested that they leave Vareš Municipality urgently.[3074] Some of the Croatian population were forced to leave Vareš Municipality, whereas other persons left of their own accord.[3075] While the Trial Chamber concluded that the HVO leaders did not order the attack on Stupni Do,[3076] it found that they attempted to conceal the HVO's responsibility for these crimes inasmuch as this encouraged the Croatian population to leave the Vareš region.[3077]

[3065]   Trial Judgement, Vol. 4, para. 64.

[3066]   Trial Judgement, Vol. 4, paras 57, 64. See also Trial Judgement, Vol. 3, paras 889-900. The Appeals Chamber also notes that the Trial Chamber found that the crimes against Muslims – either members of the HVO or the ABiH – who were held in detention centres formed part of the widespread and systematic attack on the Muslim civilian population. Trial Judgement, Vol. 3, para. 650.

[3067]   Petković's Appeal Brief, para. 73. See Petković's Appeal Brief, para. 75.

[3068]   See Petković's Final Brief, paras 133-151, 525-526. Moreover, the Appeals Chamber finds Petković's reliance on the *Kupreškić et al. Tu Quoque* Decision inapposite since it deals with the admission of evidence rather than its assessment. See *Kupreškić et al. Tu Quoque* Decision, pp. 2-5.

[3069]   The Appeals Chamber also fails to see how the fact that the Trial Chamber considered the "expansion of the territory under the control of the ABiH" materially affects its conclusion concerning the CCP. See Petković's Appeal Brief, para. 74.

[3070]   Trial Judgement, Vol. 4, para. 64. In addition, the Appeals Chamber recalls that it has already concluded that the expanded crimes of the JCE only encompassed those encapsulated in Counts 21 (in part), 24, and 25. See *supra*, paras 798, 814.

[3071]   Trial Judgement, Vol. 4, para. 60.

[3072]   Trial Judgement, Vol. 4, para. 61.

[3073]   Trial Judgement, Vol. 4, para. 61.

[3074]   Trial Judgement, Vol. 4, para. 61.

[3075]   Trial Judgement, Vol. 4, para. 61.

[3076]   Trial Judgement, Vol. 4, para. 61.

[3077]   Trial Judgement, Vol. 4, para. 62.

(i) Prlić's appeal (Sub-grounds 10.12, 10.13, and 10.14)

962.   Prlić submits that the Trial Chamber mischaracterised and ignored evidence when it concluded that: (1) "22,000-24,000 Croats" from Travnik, Novi Travnik, Vareš, Kiseljak, and Bugojno arrived in HZ(R) H-B territory in an organised manner; (2) in October 1993, the HVO forced Croats to leave Vareš; and (3) HVO leaders concealed events in Stupni Do in order to encourage the Croats of Vareš to move in accordance with "their plan".[3078]

963.   The Prosecution responds that Prlić's arguments should be summarily dismissed as he fails to explain how or why the Trial Chamber erred, and does not show how the referenced sub-grounds of appeal are relevant or support his contention.[3079] **[page 404]**

964.   The Appeals Chamber notes that beyond reference to arguments made elsewhere in his appeal brief, which the Appeals Chamber has dismissed,[3080] Prlić fails to particularise his allegations of error. The Appeals Chamber thus finds that Prlić has failed to demonstrate an error and dismisses Prlić's sub-grounds of appeal 10.12, 10.13, and 10.14.

(ii) Praljak's appeal (Ground 32)

a. Arguments of the Parties

965.   Praljak submits that the Trial Chamber ignored relevant evidence and made contradictory findings when concluding that the events in Vareš formed part of the CCP.[3081] He asserts that the Trial Chamber failed to consider the alternative reasonable inference that these events were a consequence of the ABiH offensive that began earlier in 1993, as well as the "chaotic situation" provoked by the consequential influx of Croats.[3082] Praljak also argues that the Trial Chamber erred in not taking into account evidence that in October 1993, the HVO tried to calm hostilities,[3083] and in ignoring the fact that the ethnic composition of Vareš Municipality was already weighted in favour of Croats.[3084] Praljak further submits that the contention that HVO leaders tried to conceal the crimes in Stupni Do is baseless, given that the attack on Stupni Do was planned by soldiers and local HVO commanders without the knowledge of HVO leaders.[3085] According to Praljak, the same applies to the conclusion that the HVO concealed events to encourage the Croatian population to leave Vareš Municipality.[3086]

966.   The Prosecution responds that the Trial Chamber reasonably concluded that the crimes committed in Vareš Municipality formed part of the CCP,[3087] and submits that Praljak simply disagrees with the Trial Chamber's findings, as opposed to showing an error.[3088] In particular, the Prosecution submits that the Trial Chamber reasonably found that: (1) the HVO crimes in Vareš followed a clear pattern of conduct, as opposed

---

[3078]   Prlić's Appeal Brief, para. 306, referring to Trial Judgement, Vol. 2, paras 227, 232, 824, 874, 1786, Vol. 3, paras 502, 508, Vol. 4, paras 60-62. Prlić adopts his sub-grounds of appeal 16.5 and 16.6 by reference. Prlić's Appeal Brief, para. 307.

[3079]   Prosecution's Response Brief (Prlić), paras 166-167. See also Appeal Hearing, AT. 187 (20 Mar 2017).

[3080]   See *infra*, paras 1287-1298, 1300-1317.

[3081]   Praljak's Appeal Brief, para. 336.

[3082]   Praljak's Appeal Brief, paras 330, 336-337, referring to, *inter alia*, Praljak's Appeal Brief, paras 170-171 (sub-ground of appeal 10.2), Ex. 3D00800. Praljak also argues that the Trial Chamber "did not take into account that [the] situation in Vare[š] was specific with many problems". Praljak's Appeal Brief, para. 331.

[3083]   Praljak's Appeal Brief, para. 331, referring to, *inter alia*, Exs. 3D00807 (confidential), 3D00809.

[3084]   Praljak's Appeal Brief, paras 332, 335, referring to, *inter alia*, Ex. P00020.

[3085]   Praljak's Appeal Brief, para. 337. Praljak submits that the HVO Main Staff had no control or authority over persons who committed crimes and that the HVO Main Staff did not even know what happened in Stupni Do. See Praljak's Appeal Brief, para. 334, referring to Exs. P06026, P06091, P06104, P06140, P06144. See also Praljak's Reply Brief, paras 97-99.

[3086]   Praljak's Appeal Brief, para. 335, referring to Trial Judgement, Vol. 3, para. 508, Vol. 4, para. 62. Praljak argues that this is contradicted by the Trial Chamber's finding that the departure of Croats was caused by the threat of ABiH attacks. See Praljak's Appeal Brief, para. 336.

[3087]   Prosecution's Response Brief (Praljak), para. 232.

[3088]   Prosecution's Response Brief (Praljak), paras 232, 237.

to defensive measures;[3089] (2) the crimes **[page 405]** encouraged the Croatian population to leave Vareš;[3090] and (3) although the evidence does not indicate that Praljak or Petković were directly involved in the decision to attack Stupni Do, the Trial Chamber reasonably found that they participated in planning and directing the HVO's operations in Vareš in October 1993, took steps to conceal HVO responsibility for the crimes, and had effective control over soldiers in the field.[3091]

b. Analysis

967. The Appeals Chamber turns first to Praljak's argument that the Trial Chamber failed to consider alternative reasonable inferences for the events in Vareš Municipality. In this regard, the Appeals Chamber notes that the Trial Chamber concluded that the events fell within the CCP because the HVO leaders attempted to conceal the HVO's responsibility for the crimes committed in Stupni Do in order to "encourage the Croatian population of the Vareš region to move in the direction of BiH, which suited their plan"[3092] and because they formed part of a pattern of conduct with other crimes.[3093] In reaching this conclusion, the Trial Chamber was well aware of the broader context of ABiH attacks, as well as the consequential relocation of Croatian civilians.[3094] Recalling that a trial chamber does not have to discuss other inferences it may have considered, as long as it is satisfied that the inference it retained was the only reasonable one,[3095] the Appeals Chamber finds that Praljak fails to demonstrate any error in the Trial Chamber's conclusion. The Appeals Chamber also considers that Praljak fails to explain how the evidence indicating that the HVO tried to calm hostilities in Vareš,[3096] or as regards the ethnic composition of Vareš,[3097] was relevant to the Trial Chamber's finding that the events in Vareš Municipality formed part of the CCP. Praljak's submissions are thus dismissed.[3098] **[page 406]**

968. Regarding Praljak's challenges to the Trial Chamber's findings in respect of the HVO's involvement in the Stupni Do crimes, the Appeals Chamber considers that he mischaracterises the Trial Chamber's findings. The Trial Chamber expressly took account of the HVO leaders not having ordered the attack and acknowledged that Ivica Rajić did not inform Petković of his decision to launch the attack on Stupni Do until it was launched on 23 October 1993.[3099] However, as stated earlier,[3100] the Trial Chamber's finding that these crimes were part of the CCP was based not only on the HVO leaders' attempts to conceal the crimes in Stupni Do, but also on the pattern of crimes it found to have existed between January 1993 and April 1994 and the links between the attack in Stupni Do and Stojić, Praljak, and Petković.[3101]

[3089]   Prosecution's Response Brief (Praljak), para. 235. See Prosecution's Response Brief (Praljak), paras 232-234.

[3090]   Prosecution's Response Brief (Praljak), paras 236, 238-240. The Prosecution also submits that: (1) the Trial Chamber did not ignore the demographic composition of Vareš, but that Praljak misunderstands the Trial Chamber's findings on this; (2) Praljak does not explain how an omission to refer to earlier ABiH fighting would affect any relevant factual findings; (3) evidence cited to support the claim that the HVO sought to prevent conduct in Vareš mainly refers to conduct unrelated to the CCP; and (4) the Trial Chamber did consider the "chaotic situation" in Vareš. See Prosecution's Response Brief (Praljak), para. 237.

[3091]   Prosecution's Response Brief (Praljak), paras 238-240.

[3092]   Trial Judgement, Vol. 4, para. 62. See also Trial Judgement, Vol. 4, para. 61.

[3093]   Trial Judgement, Vol. 4, para. 65.

[3094]   Trial Judgement, Vol. 3, paras 283-285, 502, Vol. 4, paras 57, 60-61. See also Trial Judgement, Vol. 3, paras 311-312, 411.

[3095]   See, *e.g., Đorđević* Appeal Judgement, para. 157, referring to *Krajišnik* Appeal Judgement, para. 192.

[3096]   See Ex. 3D00807 (confidential); Ex. 3D00809 (chronology of events prepared by the Bobovac Brigade Commander dated 20 October 1993 affirming that the HVO attempted to maintain peace in this area).

[3097]   See Ex. P00020 (census for BiH giving the population numbers for the different ethnicities in each municipalities, dated 1991). See also Trial Judgement, Vol. 3, para. 283, referring to, *inter alia,* Ex. P09276, p. 31 (indicating the composition of Vareš Municipality in 1991).

[3098]   The Appeals Chamber recalls its reversal of the Trial Chamber's finding that murder and willful killing were part of the CCP from January 1993 until June 1993. See *supra,* paras 874-886. Ultimately, however, the Appeals Chamber does not consider that this change in the scope of the CCP in that period affects the Trial Chamber's reasoning concerning the clear pattern of conduct, particularly since not many instances of murder as part of the CCP took place in that period, in contrast to June 1993 and onwards but before the events in Vareš. See *supra,* para. 876 & fn. 2790.

[3099]   Trial Judgement, Vol. 4, para. 61. See also Trial Judgement, Vol. 3, paras 409-412.

[3100]   See *supra,* para. 820.

[3101]   Trial Judgement, Vol. 4, paras 61-62, 65. See Trial Judgement, Vol. 3, paras 484-486, 492. See also *supra,* fn. 3098.

969.   In light of the foregoing, the Appeals Chamber finds that Praljak has failed to show that the Trial Chamber ignored relevant evidence and made contradictory findings when concluding that the events in Vareš Municipality formed part of the CCP, and dismisses Praljak's ground of appeal 32.

(iii) Petković's appeal (Sub-ground 3.2.2.1 in part)

970.   Petković submits that the Trial Chamber failed to provide a reasoned opinion by not expressly establishing that the HVO actions in Vareš and Stupni Do in October 1993 were committed to further the CCP.[3102] Further, Petković submits that the Trial Chamber erred in law and fact as "[t]here is no evidence about forcible transfer or deportation of Muslims, and the Trial Chamber did not even infer otherwise".[3103]

971.   The Prosecution responds that the Trial Chamber reasonably found that the crimes committed during the HVO operations in Vareš Municipality furthered the CCP, as did the subsequent movement of the Croatian population.[3104] It also submits that Petković's focus on the fact that forcible displacement was not established for Vareš fails to demonstrate any error as regards the other crimes committed there as part of the CCP.[3105]

972.   With reference to the assertion that the Trial Chamber did not make the findings necessary to conclude that the events in Vareš formed part of the CCP, the Appeals Chamber observes that the Trial Chamber, in its analysis of the CCP, made detailed findings with respect to the events which **[page 407]** took place in Vareš Municipality, including killings, detention, and the destruction of buildings.[3106] The Trial Chamber also found that these crimes, *inter alia,* "tended to follow a clear pattern of conduct" with the other crimes committed by HVO forces from January 1993 to April 1994.[3107] The Appeals Chamber thus considers that the Trial Chamber clearly explained the basis for its conclusion that the crimes in Vareš Municipality, including in Stupni Do, were committed in furtherance of the CCP. Petković's submission is dismissed.

973.   The Appeals Chamber therefore finds that Petković has failed to demonstrate that the Trial Chamber erred in not providing a reasoned opinion by not expressly establishing that the HVO actions in Vareš Municipality and Stupni Do in October 1993 were committed to further the CCP and dismisses Petković's sub-ground of appeal 3.2.2.1 in relevant part.

5.   Other challenges to evidence and alternative reasonable inferences

974.   The Appellants raise certain other challenges to the CCP, alleging errors as regards: (1) the conclusion regarding a pattern of the crimes and the overall existence of the CCP; and (2) the context of the conflict between the HVO and ABiH.

(a) Alleged errors regarding the pattern of the crimes and the overall existence of the CCP (Prlić's Sub-grounds 10.16 and 10.17, Stojić's Ground 4 in part, and Pušić's Ground 3 in part)

975.   The Trial Chamber concluded that the crimes committed by HVO forces from January 1993 to April 1994 tended to "follow a clear pattern of conduct" and "[i]n the vast majority of cases [...] were not committed by chance or randomly".[3108] The Trial Chamber found that the only reasonable inference was that these

---

[3102]   Petković's Appeal Brief, paras 68-69, referring to Trial Judgement, Vol. 4, paras 61-63. See also Petković's Appeal Brief, paras 24, 70, 284-286.
[3103]   Petković's Appeal Brief, para. 70; Appeal Hearing, AT. 499 (23 Mar 2017). See also Petković's Appeal Brief, para. 68; Petković's Reply Brief, para. 15.
[3104]   Prosecution's Response Brief (Petković), para. 55. See also Prosecution's Response Brief (Petković), paras 16-17.
[3105]   Prosecution's Response Brief (Petković), para. 56.
[3106]   See Trial Judgement, Vol. 4, paras 61-63. See also Trial Judgement, Vol. 3, paras 333-399 (arrest and detention in Vareš), 400-404 (thefts and sexual abuse in Vareš), 426-429 (sexual abuse in Stupni Do), 430-464 (killings and deaths in Stupni Do), 465-467 (burning and destruction of Muslim property).
[3107]   Trial Judgement, Vol. 4, para. 65. See also *supra*, fn. 3098.
[3108]   Trial Judgement, Vol. 4, para. 65.

crimes were committed as part of the CCP,[3109] and that the JCE members "lent support and co-ordination to field operations for the purpose of carrying out [...] the crimes".[3110]

(i) <u>Arguments of the Parties</u>

976.   Prlić, Stojić, and Pušić all challenge the existence of the CCP and the Trial Chamber's conclusion that there was a clear pattern of conduct with respect to the HVO activities. More specifically, Prlić submits that the Trial Chamber erred in failing to offer any supporting authority **[page 408]** for its conclusions that a clear pattern of conduct existed, and that "HZ(R)HB political and military leaders, especially Prlić" assisted in the implementation of the JCE.[3111] Similarly, Stojić argues that no reasonable trier of fact could have concluded that all the events – in Gornji Vakuf, Jablanica, Prozor, Mostar, Vareš, as well as at the Heliodrom and Ljubuški, Dretelj, and Gabela Prisons[3112] – formed part of the CCP.[3113] He asserts that had the events unfolded pursuant to a single common criminal plan, "the result would have been a consistent wave of attacks implementing that plan"[3114] but that this was not the case, because there was a three-month "hiatus" after the conflict in Gornji Vakuf,[3115] and a "further gap" between the events of June 1993 and the military activities in Vareš in October 1993.[3116] Stojić also alleges other errors, arguing that: (1) the findings that the crimes "tended to follow a clear pattern" and the "vast majority" were not committed by chance, were "erroneously unspecific";[3117] (2) the finding that crimes committed from January 1993 to March 1994 were "the result of a plan established by the leaders of the HZ(R) H-B" is erroneous, because the Trial Chamber found that the JCE also included the "leaders of Croatia";[3118] and (3) the Trial Chamber disregarded evidence showing that witnesses were not aware of a common criminal plan or did not believe that events had occurred pursuant to a single plan.[3119] Finally, Pušić submits that the Trial Chamber failed to consider that "the ethnic cleansing in BiH" was the result of the "unplanned effects of the new situation created by the influx of refugees who by their very presence upset the demographic equilibrium between the ethnicities".[3120] He submits that the Trial Chamber's failure to address this inference demonstrates a failure to provide a reasoned opinion that invalidates the Trial Judgement.[3121]

977.   The Prosecution responds that Prlić ignores the Trial Chamber's overall findings as to the events and crimes that formed part of the CCP, and asserts that his sub-grounds of appeal **[page 409]** 10.16-10.17 ought to be summarily dismissed.[3122] With respect to Stojić's arguments, the Prosecution responds that the identification of a common criminal plan is a fact-based inquiry that can turn on a number of factors, and does not require a "consistent wave of attacks".[3123] It also submits that: (1) the HVO halted its Gornji Vakuf operations in January 1993 only after having captured a number of villages;[3124] (2) the violence recurred in

---

3109   Trial Judgement, Vol. 4, para. 65.

3110   Trial Judgement, Vol. 4, para. 66.

3111   Prlić's Appeal Brief, para. 310, referring to Trial Judgement, Vol. 4, paras 65-67.

3112   Stojić's Appeal Brief, para. 48.

3113   Stojić's Appeal Brief, paras 49, 58; Appeal Hearing, AT. 275-276 (21 Mar 2017).

3114   Stojić's Appeal Brief, para. 53.

3115   Stojić's Appeal Brief, para. 53. Stojić submits that the HVO ceased actions in January 1993 without attempting to take over the whole municipality of Gornji Vakuf. See Stojić's Reply Brief, para. 20; Appeal Hearing, AT. 276-277 (21 Mar 2017).

3116   Stojić's Appeal Brief, para. 53. Stojić contends that "there were never any standing conflicts [...] only sporadic conflicts here and there". Stojić's Appeal Brief, paras 53, 58, referring to Judge Antonetti Dissent, pp. 394-395.

3117   Stojić's Appeal Brief, para. 55. See also Trial Judgement, Vol. 4, para. 44.

3118   Stojić's Appeal Brief, para. 54, referring to Trial Judgement, Vol. 4, paras 43, 65, 1222.

3119   Stojić's Appeal Brief, para. 57, referring to Kiaus Johann Nissen, T. 20649-20650 (27 June 2007), Andrew Pringle, T. 24259 (7 Nov 2007), Radmilo Jašak, T. 48682-48683 (20 Jan 2010), Dragan Ćurčić, T. 45809 (12 Oct 2009), Hamid Bahto, T. 37911-37913 (11 Mar 2009). See also Stojić's Reply Brief, para. 21.

3120   Pušić's Appeal Brief, para. 100, referring to Judge Antonetti Dissent, p. 370. Pušić argues in particular that the influx stemmed from the "ethnic cleansing by Serb forces driving Croat[s] and Muslims into central [BiH] creating overcrowding and conflict". Pušić's Appeal Brief, para. 100, referring to Judge Antonetti Dissent, pp. 369-370. See also Pušić's Appeal Brief, para. 99; Pušić's Reply Brief, para. 23; Appeal Hearing, AT. 675-678, 681 (27 Mar 2017).

3121   Pušić's Appeal Brief, para. 101.

3122   Prosecution's Response Brief (Prlić), para. 182, referring to Trial Judgement, Vol. 4, paras 41-64, 67; Appeal Hearing, AT. 180 (20 Mar 2017). The Appeals Chamber notes that the Prosecution mistakenly characterises its response paragraph as going to Prlić's sub-grounds of appeal 10.15-10.16. However it relates to sub-grounds of appeal 10.16-10.17.

3123   Prosecution's Response Brief (Stojić), para. 35.

3124   Prosecution's Response Brief (Stojić), para. 35.

April 1993 in a similar fashion; and (3) there was no gap in hostilities between June 1993 and the activities in October 1993.[3125] As for Stojić's remaining challenges, the Prosecution responds that: (1) the Trial Chamber's findings were not erroneously unspecific;[3126] (2) although the Trial Chamber "inadvertently" failed to list the Croatian leadership among those who devised the CCP in one paragraph, it made clear elsewhere – including in the next paragraph – that the JCE members included both Croatian and HVO leaders;[3127] and (3) Stojić's "general reference" to witness testimony demonstrates no error in the Trial Chamber's findings regarding the CCP.[3128] Concerning Pušić, the Prosecution responds that the Trial Chamber acknowledged that population movement occurred because of fighting in the municipalities relevant to this case and other BiH regions, but reasonably concluded both that the JCE members knew by October 1992 that achieving their territorial objectives would require moving the Muslim population from HZ(R) H-B, and that from mid-January 1993 they started implementing this plan by conducting military attacks, arrests, detentions, and evictions aimed at the Muslim population.[3129]

978.   In reply, Stojić argues that he did not submit that the CCP "requires" a consistent wave of attacks,[3130] but that the fluctuation in hostilities shows that the events of 1993 were better understood as reflective of "isolated flashpoints, rather than a unified purpose".[3131] **[page 410]**

(ii) Analysis

979.   Starting with Prlić, the Appeals Chamber finds that he misrepresents the Trial Chamber's findings. Contrary to his submission, the Trial Chamber discussed at length the evidence regarding crimes in various municipalities and detention centres throughout the Trial Judgement and then expressly cross-referenced the factual findings regarding those crimes in its CCP analysis, in order to reach the finding that there existed a pattern of crimes.[3132] Further, even though the Trial Chamber's finding that murder and wilful killing were part of the CCP in the period from January 1993 until June 1993 has been reversed,[3133] the Appeals Chamber does not consider that this change in the scope of the CCP in that period affects the Trial Chamber's reasoning concerning the clear pattern of conduct in relation to crimes forming part of the CCP, particularly since not many instances of murders which were considered to have been part of the CCP took place in that period, in contrast to the period after June 1993.[3134] Prlić fails to demonstrate any error in the Trial Chamber's approach.

980.   With regard to Stojić's claim that there was no consistent wave of attacks implementing the CCP, the Appeals Chamber notes that the Trial Chamber found that the CCP crystallised in January 1993, and was implemented in "stages", including: (1) crimes committed in Gornji Vakuf in January 1993; (2) crimes committed in Prozor and Jablanica in April 1993; and (3) crimes committed in and around Vareš in October 1993.[3135] The Appeals Chamber considers that Stojić mischaracterises the Trial Chamber's approach when considering the implementation of the CCP, as the Trial Chamber focused on the overall pattern of events from January 1993 until April 1994 when reaching its conclusions, which in turn is not affected by a hiatus

---

[3125]   Prosecution's Response Brief (Stojić), para. 36. See also Appeal Hearing, AT. 344-346 (21 Mar 2017) (arguing that the basis of the Trial Chamber's findings regarding the CCP was "the very obvious pattern of criminal activity targeted at Muslims during and after HVO operations", as well as various statements by JCE members).
[3126]   Prosecution's Response Brief (Stojić), para. 33.
[3127]   Prosecution's Response Brief (Stojić), para. 34, referring to, *inter alia,* Trial Judgement, Vol. 4, paras 44, 66, 1231.
[3128]   Prosecution's Response Brief (Stojić), para. 38.
[3129]   Prosecution's Response Brief (Pušić), para. 87, referring to Trial Judgement, Vol. 4, paras 43, 45-51, 53-54, 56-59, 61, 64, 66. The Prosecution also submits that the Trial Chamber reasonably based its conclusions regarding the CCP on, *inter alia,* the pattern of crimes, the collaboration of the political and military leadership of the HZ(R) H-B, and direct statements of intent by JCE members, all of which are ignored by Pušić. Prosecution's Response Brief (Pušić), para. 80, referring to Trial Judgement, Vol. 4, paras 51, 54, 58, 62-66, 1219; Appeal Hearing, AT. 709-710 (27 Mar 2017). See also Prosecution's Response Brief (Pušić), paras 81-85, 88.
[3130]   Stojić's Reply Brief, para. 19, referring to Prosecution's Response Brief (Stojić), para. 35.
[3131]   Stojić's Reply Brief, paras 19-20; Appeal Hearing, AT. 275-276 (21 Mar 2017).
[3132]   Trial Judgement. Vol. 4, paras 43-65 and references cited therein.
[3133]   See *supra,* paras 874-886.
[3134]   See *supra,* para. 876 & fn. 2790.
[3135]   Trial Judgement, Vol. 4, paras 45-47, 61.

in attacks.[3136] In particular, the Trial Chamber found that the events in Jablanica in April 1993 took place in the context of conflicts between the HVO and ABiH, which had been underway since the beginning of February 1993,[3137] and also found that from June 1993, the CCP expanded with the siege of East Mostar and became more efficient with the system of deportation.[3138] The Appeals Chamber finds that Stojić fails to demonstrate any error in the Trial Chamber's approach, and rejects his submission. **[page 411]**

981.   As for Stojić's argument that certain parts of the Trial Chamber's findings were "erroneously unspecific", the Appeals Chamber considers that the relevant findings evince no ambiguity,[3139] appearing as overall conclusions following a detailed and full analysis in which the Trial Chamber explained which crimes formed part of the CCP, and why.[3140] This submission is rejected. As for Stojić's argument regarding the Croatian leadership findings, the Appeals Chamber notes that in an isolated paragraph, the Trial Chamber suggested that the crimes were "the result of a plan established by the leaders of the HZ(R) H-B".[3141] However, it is clear from a broader reading of the Trial Judgement that this sentence contains an unintentional omission, as the Trial Chamber consistently held elsewhere that the JCE members also included Croatian leaders, who were involved in planning and implementing the CCP.[3142] This argument is also dismissed. Finally, in relation to Stojić's challenges to witnesses' evidence, the Appeals Chamber notes that he simply makes general allegations regarding the Trial Chamber's omission to consider the evidence of certain witnesses,[3143] without explaining why the Trial Chamber erred in reaching the conclusions it did regarding the CCP on the basis of other evidence and findings.[3144] This argument is thus also dismissed.

982.   As for Pušić's arguments, the Appeals Chamber first notes that in support of his submission, Pušić relies entirely on the Judge Antonetti Dissent without showing that no reasonable trier of fact could have inferred as the Trial Chamber did. In any event, the Majority expressly took account of the fact that some population movements were generated as a consequence of fighting, and others occurred deliberately as part of the CCP.[3145] However, after a detailed assessment of the evidence,[3146] the Majority concluded that the CCP came into existence in mid-January 1993 on the basis of broader geopolitical circumstances, such as the presentation of the Vance-Owen Peace Plan on 2 January 1993 and the 15 January 1993 Ultimatum,[3147] and that the HVO's interpretation of the Vance-Owen Peace Plan resulted in the commission of crimes which formed part of a "clear pattern of conduct".[3148]

983.   In sum, as Prlić has failed to demonstrate any error on the part of the Trial Chamber, his sub-grounds of appeal 10.16 and 10.17 are dismissed. Similarly, as Stojić has failed to show that no **[page 412]** reasonable trier of fact could have concluded that the only reasonable inference from the evidence was that all the events formed part of a single common criminal plan, Stojić's ground of appeal 4 is dismissed in relevant part. The Appeals Chamber also finds that Pušić has not demonstrated any error in the Trial Chamber's finding, including a failure by the Trial Chamber to provide a reasoned opinion. His ground of appeal 3 is therefore also dismissed in relevant part.

(b) Alleged errors regarding the context of the conflict with the ABiH

984.   In its analysis of the CCP, the Trial Chamber took account of the fact that the crimes took place in the context of conflict between the HVO and ABiH, considering, *inter alia,* that: (1) "tensions between the ABiH

[3136]   See Trial Judgement, Vol. 4, para. 65. See also Trial Judgement, Vol. 4, para. 66. As noted earlier, this pattern is also not affected by the change in the scope of the CCP in the period from January 1993 until June 1993. See *supra,* para. 979.
[3137]   Trial Judgement, Vol. 4, para. 46.
[3138]   Trial Judgement, Vol. 4, paras 57, 59, 64. See also Trial Judgement, Vol. 4, para. 66.
[3139]   See Trial Judgement, Vol. 4, para. 65 (observing that the crimes committed from January 1993 to April 1994 "tended to follow a clear pattern of conduct", and in the "vast majority of cases" were not committed by chance or randomly).
[3140]   See Trial Judgement, Vol. 4, paras 41-64. See also Trial Judgement, Vol. 4, paras 66-73.
[3141]   Trial Judgement, Vol. 4, para. 65.
[3142]   See, *e.g.,* Trial Judgement, Vol. 4, paras 44, 66, 1222, 1231.
[3143]   *See supra,* fn. 3119.
[3144]   See Trial Judgement, Vol. 4, para. 44.
[3145]   See Trial Judgement, Vol. 4, paras 43, 51, 54, 60-61.
[3146]   See Trial Judgement, Vol. 4 paras 46-64 and references cited therein.
[3147]   See Trial Judgement, Vol. 1, paras 445, 451-452, Vol. 4, paras 44, 125, 131, 142, 271.
[3148]   Trial Judgement, Vol. 4, para. 65. See also *supra,* para. 979.

and the HVO mounted" in Jablanica Municipality, "particularly between the beginning of February and mid-April 1993";[3149] (2) the JCE became more efficient with the introduction of a system of detention and deportation after the Attack on the HVO Tihomir Mišić Barracks on 30 June 1993;[3150] and (3) the events in Vareš in October 1993 took place subsequent to the attack conducted by the ABiH on the village of Kopjari.[3151] Elsewhere in the Trial Judgement, the Trial Chamber also made findings on the existence of co-operation between the HVO and ABiH in 1992 and 1993, particularly as to, *inter alia:* (1) military co-operation between the HVO and ABiH when fighting the JNA and VRS;[3152] (2) the HVO's provision of MTS and medical aid to the ABiH;[3153] (3) the creation of joint commands and commissions between the HVO and ABiH;[3154] and (4) the inclusion of Muslims within the ranks of the HVO.[3155]

(i) Stojić's appeal (Ground 2)

a. Arguments of the Parties

985.   Stojić submits that the Trial Chamber failed to give a "reasoned decision" by finding that there was a JCE without proper consideration of evidence proffered and his submissions at trial of the substantial co-operation between Croatia "and/or" the HVO and ABiH.[3156] Stojić argues that the Trial Chamber disregarded evidence and submissions – or failed to evaluate their effect on the alleged existence of the JCE[3157] – demonstrating that: (1) Croatia and the HVO delivered and/or **[page 413]** provided MTS and other forms of aid to the ABiH;[3158] (2) the HVO and ABiH engaged in close military co-operation, fighting side by side and establishing effective joint commands and commissions as common parts of the BiH armed forces;[3159] and (3) Muslims made up a substantial proportion of the HVO armed forces.[3160] Stojić asserts that: (1) the only reasonable conclusion from the evidence is that the HVO and Croatia did not regard the ABiH as their enemy;[3161] and (2) had the Trial Chamber evaluated the evidence and submissions, it could not have concluded that a JCE existed.[3162]

986.   The Prosecution responds that Stojić does not demonstrate that the Trial Chamber failed to consider co-operation between the HV/HVO and the ABiH, nor how such co-operation would render the Trial Chamber's CCP findings unreasonable.[3163] It submits that Stojić: (1) cites evidence confirming that the HV/HVO only supplied the ABiH with MTS at locations and times the ABiH was fighting Serbs[3164] and allowed only a meagre amount of humanitarian supplies through to East Mostar;[3165] and (2) fails to explain how

---

[3149]   Trial Judgement, Vol. 4, para. 46.

[3150]   Trial Judgement, Vol. 4, para. 57.

[3151]   Trial Judgement, Vol. 4, para. 61.

[3152]   Trial Judgement, Vol. 1, para. 440, Vol. 2, paras 695-697. See also Trial Judgement, Vol. 4, para. 308.

[3153]   Trial Judgement, Vol. 1, para. 440, Vol. 2, para. 696, Vol. 4, para. 308.

[3154]   Trial Judgement, Vol. 1, paras 441, 463-464. See also Trial Judgement, Vol. 1, paras 458-477.

[3155]   Trial Judgement, Vol. 1, para. 774.

[3156]   Stojić's Appeal Brief, heading before para. 25, paras 27, 37. See Stojić's Appeal Brief, paras 25-26, referring to, *inter alia,* Trial Judgement, Vol. 4, paras 9-73. See also Stojić's Reply Brief, paras 8, 13; Appeal Hearing, AT. 267-275 (21 Mar 2017).

[3157]   Stojić's Appeal Brief, paras 25-27, 37; Stojić's Reply Brief, para. 15. See also Stojić's Appeal Brief, para. 33.

[3158]   Stojić's Appeal Brief, paras 25, 28-29, 35; Stojić's Reply Brief, paras 9-11; Appeal Hearing, AT. 269-272, 356 (21 Mar 2017), AT. 812-813 (28 Mar 2017). See also Stojić's Appeal Brief, heading before para. 25. Stojić submits that the MTS was: (1) portable (thus its deployment was not controlled by the donor); and (2) provided even in areas where there was conflict between the HVO and ABiH. Stojić's Appeal Brief, para. 36. As to aid other than MTS, Stojić submits, *inter alia,* that medical supplies were sent to the ABiH, Muslim civilians and ABiH members were treated in Mostar and Croatian hospitals, humanitarian organisations operated in Croatia for the ABiH's benefit, and the ABiH operated offices in Zagreb and Split. Stojić's Appeal Brief, paras 29, 35; Appeal Hearing, AT. 272-273 (21 Mar 2017).

[3159]   Stojić's Appeal Brief, paras 30-32, 35. See also Stojić's Appeal Brief, para. 34; Appeal Hearing, AT. 272-273 (21 Mar 2017).

[3160]   Stojić's Appeal Brief, para. 33. See also Stojić's Reply Brief, para. 14; Appeal Hearing, AT. 273-274 (21 Mar 2017).

[3161]   Stojić's Appeal Brief, para. 35. See also Stojić's Reply Brief, paras 8, 11-12; Appeal Hearing, AT. 275 (21 Mar 2017).

[3162]   Stojić's Appeal Brief, para. 37. See also Stojić's Appeal Brief, paras 25-26, 35; Stojić's Reply Brief, paras 8, 11-14; Appeal Hearing, AT. 267, 274-275 (21 Mar 2017).

[3163]   Prosecution's Response Brief (Stojić), para. 20; Appeal Hearing, AT. 346-347 (21 Mar 2017). See also Prosecution's Response Brief (Stojić), para. 26.

[3164]   Prosecution's Response Brief (Stojić), para. 22. See Prosecution's Response Brief (Stojić), para. 21.

[3165]   Prosecution's Response Brief (Stojić), para. 23. The Prosecution submits that the JCE members' manipulation of humanitarian aid access supports the Trial Chamber's findings. Prosecution's Response Brief (Stojić), para. 23.

certain evidence – much of which was expressly considered or related to exhibits deemed inadmissible – invalidates or undermines the Trial Chamber's findings.[3166] The Prosecution argues that, contrary to Stojić's assertion, the Trial Chamber made express findings concerning joint HVO-ABiH commands and commissions and that Stojić, regardless, fails to demonstrate how piecemeal co-operation contradicts the "clear pattern" of HVO crimes.[3167] Finally, it submits that the evidence Stojić cites regarding Muslims in the HVO **[page 414]** demonstrates a progressive decimation that was consistent with the JCE members' goal of ethnic domination and mirrored demographic changes across the HZ(R) H-B.[3168]

b. Analysis

987.   With respect to Stojić's assertion that the Trial Chamber disregarded evidence on the existence of co-operation between Croatia "and/or" the HVO and ABiH, the Appeals Chamber recalls that a trial judgement should be read as a whole.[3169] In this respect, the Appeals Chamber notes that the Trial Chamber made factual findings on the issue of co-operation throughout the Trial Judgement, expressly considering and relying upon, *inter alia*, numerous pieces of evidence to which Stojić refers. First, the Trial Chamber found that the HVO and ABiH co-operated militarily in 1992 and 1993 when fighting the JNA and VRS and that, in particular, an independent Mostar battalion made up of Muslims and Croats was created in April 1992, co-operating closely with the HVO in the defence of Mostar.[3170] It additionally found that, in furtherance of this co-operation, the HVO supplied the ABiH with, *inter alia*, medical aid, weapons, and military equipment in 1992 and 1993.[3171] Moreover, the Trial Chamber found that: (1) on 21 July 1992, Tuđman and Izetbegović signed a treaty, proclaiming the HVO an integral part of the ABiH that was to be represented within the joint command of the Republic of Bosnia and Herzegovina ("RBiH") armed forces;[3172] and (2) the HVO itself included Muslims within its ranks in 1992 and 1993, although the evidence showed that the Muslims left the ranks of the HVO *en masse* in May and June 1993.[3173] The Trial Chamber also discussed at length peace negotiations and the creation of joint commissions and commands between the HVO and ABiH during 1993 in several municipalities in order to implement the Vance-Owen Peace Plan[3174] and noted that clashes between the HVO and ABiH broke out in the **[page 415]** municipalities during this period of co-operation.[3175] In terms of the HVO providing aid to the ABiH, the Appeals Chamber notes that the Trial Chamber found that the HVO: (1) hindered the delivery of humanitarian aid to East Mostar between June and December 1993 by restricting access of international organisations to East Mostar; and (2) provided sporadic humanitarian aid to East Mostar between June and September 1993 that was conditional on obtaining certain advantages.[3176] Accordingly, the Appeals Chamber finds that Stojić fails to demonstrate that the Trial

---

[3166]   Prosecution's Response Brief (Stojić), paras 22(4)-(5), 23. See also Prosecution's Response Brief (Stojić), para. 21.

[3167]   Prosecution's Response Brief (Stojić), para. 24. The Prosecution contends, moreover, that it was only in the context of peace negotiations and joint initiatives that the ABiH "recognised" the HVO as a constituent part of the BiH armed forces. Prosecution's Response Brief (Stojić), para. 24.

[3168]   Prosecution's Response Brief (Stojić), para. 25.

[3169]   *Popović et al.* Appeal Judgement, para. 2006; *Orić* Appeal Judgement, para. 38; *Naletilić and Martinović* Appeal Judgement, para. 435; *Stanić* Appeal Judgement, para. 344.

[3170]   Trial Judgement, Vol. 1, para. 440 & fn. 1037, Vol. 2, paras 695-697 & fns 1563-1564. *Cf.* Stojić's Appeal Brief, para. 30, referring to, *inter alia*, Exs. 3D00208, 3D00211, 4D00615, P00708. See also Trial Judgement, Vol. 4, para. 308.

[3171]   Trial Judgement, Vol. 1, para. 440 & fns 1037-1039, Vol. 2, para. 696 & fns 1559, 1561-1562, Vol. 4, para. 308 & fns 730, 732. *Cf.* Stojić's Appeal Brief, paras 26, 28-29, 35, referring to, *inter alia*, Mile Akmadžić, T. 29443 (17 June 2008), 29611-29612 (19 June 2008), Hamid Bahto, T. 37897-37911 (11 Mar 2009), Nedžad Čengić, T. 37950-37951 (11 Mar 2009), Tihomir Majić, T. 37850-37852 (9 Mar 2009), Anđelko Makar, T. 38417-38418, 38447-38448, 38453-38456 (23 Mar 2009), T. 38472 (24 Mar 2009), Slobodan Praljak, T. 40138-40140 (14 May 2009), T. 40141-40142 (private session) (14 May 2009), 41132-41134 (3 June 2009), T. 42146 (29 June 2009), Exs. 2D00320, 2D00325, 2D00502, 2D00522, 2D00809, 2D01101, 2D01111; Stojić's Reply Brief, paras 9-10 & fns 21-22, 24-25. See also Trial Judgement, Vol. 1, fn. 1114. *Cf.* Stojić's Appeal Brief, para. 28 & fn. 86, referring to, *inter alia*, Anđelko Makar, T. 38447-38448 (23 Mar 2009).

[3172]   Trial Judgement, Vol. 1, para. 441.

[3173]   Trial Judgement, Vol. 1, para. 774 & fn. 1807. *Cf.* Stojić's Appeal Brief, para. 33, referring to, *inter alia*, Ex. 2D00150. See also Trial Judgement, Vol. 1, fn. 1806.

[3174]   Trial Judgement, Vol. 1, paras 463-464 & fns 1115-1119. See Trial Judgement, Vol. 1, paras 440-441, 458-477 & fns 1037, 1133, 1140, 1144, Vol. 4, paras 45, 127 & fns 123, 368. *Cf.* Stojić's Appeal Brief, para. 32, referring to, *inter alia*, Bo Pellnäs, T. 19753 (7 June 2007), Exs. 4D01700, pp. 5, 7-8, P01238, paras 1, 3, P01467, paras 1-3, P01709, para. 8, P02016, pp. 2-4.

[3175]   See, *e.g.*, Trial Judgement, Vol. 1, paras 460, 470, 477, Vol. 4, para. 45.

[3176]   Trial Judgement, Vol. 2, paras 1243-1244 & fns 3100-3101. *Cf.* Stojić's Appeal Brief, para. 29, referring to, *inter alia*, Exs. 2D00119, 2D00120, 2D00321, 2D00322, 2D00323, 2D00333, 2D00455, 2D00504, P02703 (confidential), para. 5, P02782 (confidential), para. 3, P02929 (confidential), para. 1.

Chamber disregarded evidence on the existence of co-operation between Croatia "and/or" the HVO and the ABiH. Rather, he simply attempts to substitute his own interpretation of this evidence for that of the Trial Chamber. His argument is therefore dismissed.

988.   Concerning Stojić's submissions in relation to evidence not referred to by the Trial Chamber when making the aforementioned findings on co-operation,[3177] the Appeals Chamber notes that much, but not all, of the evidence Stojić refers to concerns co-operation in 1992 and is therefore temporally outside the scope of the JCE, which came into being in mid-January 1993.[3178] Stojić does not demonstrate how this evidence would have an impact on the impugned finding. The same applies to the evidence which Stojić argues concerns co-operation in 1993. The Appeals Chamber considers that he merely asserts that the Trial Chamber failed to consider relevant evidence, without showing that no reasonable trier of fact, based on the evidence, could have reached the same conclusion as the Trial Chamber did. Thus, his argument is dismissed.

989.   When submitting that the Trial Chamber disregarded his trial submissions concerning the co-operation, Stojić claims that the Trial Chamber "did not even mention them in its summary of the Defence arguments on the JCE".[3179] The Appeals Chamber considers that Stojić misrepresents the Trial Chamber's approach, as its brief summary of each Appellant's submissions was not **[page 416]** intended to be an exhaustive enumeration thereof.[3180] Further, the Trial Chamber was not under an obligation to justify its findings in relation to every submission made during the trial. The Appeals Chamber recalls, rather, that the Trial Chamber maintained the discretion as to which legal arguments to address.[3181] The Appeals Chamber thus sees no merit in Stojić's assertion that no reasonable trier of fact could have concluded that the JCE existed had it evaluated the evidence and submissions. His submission is dismissed.

990.   Turning to Stojić's assertion regarding the Trial Chamber's alleged failure to evaluate the effect of evidence of co-operation between Croatia "and/or" the HVO and ABiH when finding that a JCE existed, thus breaching his right to a "reasoned decision", the Appeals Chamber recalls that a trial chamber is obliged to provide a reasoned opinion ensuring that an appellant can exercise his right of appeal in a meaningful manner and that the Appeals Chamber can understand and review the trial chamber's findings as well as its evaluation of the evidence.[3182] In the present case, the Appeals Chamber notes that, in addition to the various factual findings regarding co-operation mentioned above,[3183] in its analysis of the CCP the Trial Chamber explicitly considered co-operation between the two sides only insofar as it found that the HZ H-B leaders participated in peace talks at the outset of the JCE while the HVO conducted military campaigns in the provinces it considered Croatian in order to consolidate its presence.[3184] However, the Trial Chamber nevertheless concluded that a JCE came into being in mid-January 1993 on the basis of circumstances such as the presentation of the Vance-Owen Peace Plan on 2 January 1993 and the 15 January 1993 Ultimatum,[3185] finding that the JCE was then implemented by numerous criminal acts, which took place pursuant to a "clear pattern of conduct" from January 1993 to April 1994.[3186] The Appeals Chamber considers that Stojić fails to show an error in the Trial Chamber's approach or how the existence of co-operation between Croatia "and/

[3177]   See Stojić's Appeal Brief, paras 28 (referring to, *inter alia,* Marijan Biškić, T. 15194 (6 Mar 2007), Dragutin Čehulić, T. 38700 (1 Apr 2009), Mario Miloš, T. 38656-38657, 38659-38660, 38662 (30 Mar 2009), Exs. 2D00229, 2D00311, 2D00527, 2D00955, 2D01046, 2D01048, 2D01050, 2D01068, 2D01069, 2D01070, 2D01078, 2D01086, 2D01091, 2D01093, 2D01095, 2D01097, 2D01100, 2D01107, 2D01108, 2D01110, 2D01116, 2D01243, 3D00299, 3D00314, 3D00436, 3D00437), 29 (referring to, *inter alia,* Exs. 1D01302, 2D00317, 2D00318, 2D00319, 2D00324, 2D00602, 2D00603, 3D00615, 3D00667, 3D01034, P02731 (confidential), para. 5, P02923 (confidential), para. 3), 30 (referring 'to, *inter alia,* Exs. 2D01278, 2D01279, 2D01281, 2D01283, 2D01284, 2D01285, 2D01286, 2D01287, 2D01289, 2D01290, 2D01291, 2D01292, 2D01293, 2D03057, P00492), 31-32 (referring to, *inter alia,* Filip Filipović, T. 47444 (30 Nov 2009), Witness 4D-AB, T. 47190 (24 Nov 2009), Exs. 2D00643, 4D00434 4D00554), 33 (referring to, *inter alia,* Ex. P03260, pp. 2, 4-5), 34 (referring to, *inter alia,* Ex. P01675), 36 & fns 94-97, 99-100, 111-113, 115-116, 125 and references cited therein. See also Stojić's Reply Brief, fns 20, 24, 32 and references cited therein.
[3178]   See Trial Judgement, Vol. 4, paras 44-45.
[3179]   Stojić's Appeal Brief, para. 26, referring to, *inter alia,* Trial Judgement, Vol. 4, para. 39. See Stojić's Reply Brief, para. 15.
[3180]   See Trial Judgement, Vol. 4, para. 39, referring to, *inter alia,* Stojić's Final Brief, paras 64-152.
[3181]   *Kvočka et al.* Appeal Judgement, para. 23.
[3182]   Art. 23(2) of the Statute; Rule 98 *ter(C)* of the Rules. See *Stanišić and Župljanin* Appeal Judgement, para. 137; *Popović et al.* Appeal Judgement, paras 1123 (and references cited therein), 1367, 1771.
[3183]   See *supra,* para. 987.
[3184]   Trial Judgement, Vol. 4, para. 45. See also Trial Judgement, Vol. 4, para. 46.
[3185]   Trial Judgement, Vol. 1, paras 445, 451-452, Vol. 4, paras 44, 125. See also *supra,* paras 852-858.
[3186]   Trial Judgement, Vol. 4, para. 65.

or" the HVO and ABiH necessarily invalidates these findings. Thus, his argument that the Trial Chamber failed to provide a reasoned opinion is dismissed.[3187] For similar reasons, his assertion that the only reasonable conclusion from the evidence is that the HVO and Croatia did not regard the ABiH as their enemy is dismissed.

991.   The Appeals Chamber therefore finds that Stojić has failed to show that the Trial Chamber did not provide a reasoned opinion in finding that there was a JCE without properly considering the submissions and evidence proffered at trial regarding the existence and impact of substantial **[page 417]** co-operation between Croatia "and/or" the HVO and the ABiH. Stojić's ground of appeal 2 is dismissed.

(ii) Stojić's appeal (Ground 3)

a. Arguments of the Parties

992.   Stojić submits that the Trial Chamber failed to provide a "reasoned decision" by not properly taking account of trial submissions and underlying evidence that demonstrate that the HVO military actions from January 1993 were a reaction to specific ABiH offensives.[3188] Stojić first argues that the Trial Chamber erred when it failed to determine why clashes between the HVO and ABiH broke out in April 1993, disregarding the significance of Defence evidence that the HVO action in April 1993 occurred in response to an ABiH offensive that started on 13 and 14 April 1993 and was directed at Konjic, Jablanica, and Prozor.[3189] Second, Stojić argues that the Trial Chamber: (1) failed to consider the purpose of the April 1993 attacks in Prozor; and (2) erred in concluding that the attacks on Sovići and Doljani in Jablanica Municipality were not a "defensive reaction to the ABiH attack that same day", because it failed to take account of the fact that the attack was a response to the ABiH offensive in the area rather than on that day alone.[3190] Third, Stojić argues that the Trial Chamber failed to consider evidence and submissions showing that the HVO actions following 30 June 1993 were a response to an ABiH offensive in central BiH which included the Attack on the HVO Tihomir Mišić Barracks.[3191] Stojić also avers that the Trial Chamber failed to provide a reasoned opinion in concluding that the deportation system implemented after this attack was merely a "more efficient" implementation of the CCP.[3192]

993.   The Prosecution responds that the Trial Chamber explained why the crimes committed by the HVO formed part of the CCP.[3193] In particular, it submits that: (1) the Trial Chamber specified the purpose of the HVO's April 1993 attacks in Prozor Municipality, which was to take control of **[page 418]** villages by acts of violence against the Muslim population, and the attacks were part of the implementation of the 4 April 1993 Ultimatum;[3194] (2) the existence of a "defensive component" to the HVO attacks against the villages of Sovići and Doljani does not undermine the link of these events to the CCP;[3195] and (3) the Trial Chamber

---

[3187]   Regarding the clear pattern of conduct, see also *supra*, para. 979.

[3188]   Stojić's Appeal Brief, heading before para. 38, paras 38-39; Stojić's Reply Brief, paras 16-17. See also Stojić's Appeal Brief, para. 47; Appeal Hearing, AT. 275-276, 282-282 (21 Mar 2017). Stojić also argues that HVO actions in Mostar in May 1993 were a response to an ABiH attack on 9 May 1993, referring to his ground of appeal 47. See Stojić's Appeal Brief, para. 38; *supra*, paras 923-929.

[3189]   Stojić's Appeal Brief, paras 40-41. Stojić argues that the Trial Chamber abrogated its responsibility to provide a reasoned opinion in choosing not to determine why clashes between the HVO and ABiH broke out at this time. Stojić's Appeal Brief, para. 41, referring to Trial Judgement, Vol. 2, para. 526.

[3190]   Stojić's Appeal Brief, para. 42, referring to Trial Judgement, Vol. 2, para. 543, Vol. 4, para. 46. Stojić argues that the Trial Chamber erred in finding that these events fell within the CCP. Stojić's Appeal Brief, para. 42. See also Stojić's Appeal Brief, paras 43-44.

[3191]   Stojić's Appeal Brief, paras 45-46, referring to Stojić's Final Brief, paras 141-151, Trial Judgement, Vol. 2, paras 882-895. Stojić also argues that while the Trial Chamber linked the detention of Muslim men in Mostar, Stolac, Čapljina, Ljubuški, and Prozor to the Attack on the HVO Tihomir Mišić Barracks, it failed to explain how these arrests were connected to the CCP established in January 1993. Stojić's Appeal Brief, para. 46.

[3192]   Stojić's Appeal Brief, para. 46, referring to Trial Judgement, Vol. 4, paras 57, 64.

[3193]   Prosecution's Response Brief (Stojić), para. 27. See also Prosecution's Response Brief (Stojić), para. 31.

[3194]   Prosecution's Response Brief (Stojić), para. 28.

[3195]   Prosecution's Response Brief (Stojić), para. 28.

explained how the arrests and detentions of Muslim men after 30 June 1993 formed part of the CCP, as well as how the CCP became more efficient.[3196]

b. Analysis

994.   Considering first the Trial Chamber's conclusions regarding the conflict between the HVO and ABiH in Jablanica Municipality in April 1993, the Appeals Chamber notes that the Trial Chamber concluded that "clashes between the HVO and the ABiH" broke out in the municipality on 13 and 14 April 1993.[3197] The Trial Chamber also stated that, having considered Defence evidence and submissions that HVO engagements in mid-April 1993 were intended to repel the ABiH offensive in the area,[3198] it was unable to determine the reason for the clashes.[3199] The Appeals Chamber considers that Stojić fails to demonstrate any error in the Trial Chamber's conclusion that these events fell within the CCP despite being aware of this context. As for Stojić's submission that the Trial Chamber failed to appreciate the broader context of the entire ABiH offensive in Jablanica, the Appeals Chamber observes that the Trial Chamber found, in addition to referring to the clashes on 13 and 14 April 1993, that on 15 April 1993, the HVO commenced shelling the town of Jablanica and that on 17 April 1993, the HVO launched an attack in Jablanica Valley, which was not purely defensive, shelling several localities, including Sovići and Doljani, and committing crimes during and following the attack.[3200] Thus, contrary to Stojić's submission, the Trial Chamber clearly considered the broader context of the events in Jablanica. As for Prozor, the Trial Chamber found that the HVO's "offensive actions" in Prozor Municipality in April 1993 resulted in taking possession of several villages, committing acts of violence such as setting fire to Muslim houses, causing the Muslim population to flee, and thus preventing any possibility of return.[3201] It also considered that these crimes in Jablanica and Prozor, along with others, formed **[page 419]** part of a clear "pattern of conduct".[3202] As noted earlier, the Appeals Chamber considers that this pattern of conduct, rather than the offensive or defensive nature of the operations, was the basis of the Trial Chamber's conclusions concerning the events that fell within the CCP.[3203] Stojić thus fails to show that the Trial Chamber did not provide a reasoned opinion in this regard.[3204]

995.   Turning to Stojić's challenges to the events following 30 June 1993, the Appeals Chamber notes that in its analysis of the CCP the Trial Chamber recalled that the ABiH attacked the HVO Tihomir Mišić Barracks on that day.[3205] In doing so the Trial Chamber cross-referenced its factual findings concerning this attack.[3206] The Trial Chamber nevertheless found that after this event, "the implementation of the JCE became more efficient",[3207] finding that the HVO "arrested and detained many Muslims" from a number of municipalities, before sending them to ABiH-controlled territories or to third countries via Croatia, or putting them in HVO detention centres, including the Heliodrom and Ljubuški, Gabela, and Dretelj Prisons.[3208] In light of these conclusions, the Appeals Chamber considers that, contrary to Stojić's submission, the Trial Chamber did not fail to consider evidence and submissions showing that the HVO actions following 30 June 1993 were a response to an ABiH offensive in central BiH which included the Attack on the HVO Tihomir Mišić Barracks. Rather, having considered that evidence, it came to the conclusion that the Attack on the HVO Tihomir Mišić Barracks was a catalyst that made the JCE implementation more efficient. The Appeals Chamber finds that Stojić has failed to show any error and dismisses his arguments.

[3196]   Prosecution's Response Brief (Stojić), paras 29-30.
[3197]   Trial Judgement, Vol. 2, para. 526. See also Trial Judgement, Vol. 2, paras 524-525.
[3198]   Trial Judgement, Vol. 2, paras 523-524. See also Stojić's Final Brief, paras 133-140.
[3199]   Trial Judgement Vol. 2, para. 526 ("Whatever the underlying reasons may have been, clashes between the HVO and the ABiH did break out on 13-14 April 1993 in Jablanica Municipality.").
[3200]   Trial Judgement, Vol. 4, paras 46, 48. The Trial Chamber also found that on 5 May 1993, in the village of Sovići, approximately 450 women, children, and the elderly were moved by the HVO soldiers from the Sovići School and the houses of Junuzovići hamlet towards Gornji Vakuf. See Trial Judgement, Vol. 2, para. 609. See also *supra*, paras 819, 895.
[3201]   Trial Judgement, Vol. 4, para. 47.
[3202]   Trial Judgement, Vol. 4, paras 46-48, 65. Regarding this pattern of conduct, see also *supra*, para. 979.
[3203]   See *supra*, para. 895.
[3204]   See, *e.g., Popović et al.* Appeal Judgement, paras 1367, 1402, 1771; *Kvočka et al.* Appeal Judgement, para. 25.
[3205]   Trial Judgement, Vol. 4, para. 57.
[3206]   Trial Judgement, Vol. 4, fn. 155, referring to Trial Judgement, Vol. 2, paras 878-886.
[3207]   Trial Judgement, Vol. 4, para. 57.
[3208]   Trial Judgement, Vol. 4, para. 57.

996.   As for Stojić's contention that the Trial Chamber offered no explanation for concluding that the system of deportation implemented after 30 June 1993 was simply a more efficient implementation of the "original" CCP, the Appeals Chamber notes that it has already dealt with, and dismissed, this argument.[3209]

997.   In light of the foregoing, the Appeals Chamber finds that Stojić has failed to show that the Trial Chamber did not provide a reasoned opinion and did not properly consider trial submissions and underlying evidence that demonstrate that the HVO military actions from January 1993 were a reaction to specific ABiH offensives. The Appeals Chamber dismisses his ground of appeal 3. **[page 420]**

(iii) Petković's appeal (Sub-grounds 3.2.2 and 3.2.2.4)

a. Arguments of the Parties

998.   Petković first argues that the Trial Chamber erred when it concluded that HVO military operations formed part of a plan, and that although the Trial Chamber took note of the need to "carefully distinguish between the legitimate/permissible use of military force and the commission of crimes that might accompany such instances", it failed to do so.[3210] Petković also argues, relying on evidence concerning the events in Stupni Do, that the finding that the crimes were planned by the Appellants is contradicted by "evidence of multiple reactions to these crimes, which were duly reported up the chain of command and condemned by supposed JCE-members".[3211]

999.   Second, Petković submits that the Trial Chamber erred because it concluded that there was a "clear pattern of conduct" in the crimes committed as a result of the implementation of the CCP, as opposed to a pattern of military operations.[3212] In support, he asserts that damage to civilian property is often collateral to military operations.[3213] In addition, Petković submits that the Trial Chamber "had to carefully evaluate destruction of Muslim houses on each location to establish whether the destruction was done for special, underlying purpose of 'ethnic cleansing' or not".[3214] In this regard, he asserts that no reasonable trier of fact could have concluded that the destruction of Muslim houses in Gornji Vakuf, Jablanica, and Prozor formed part of the CCP.[3215] Petković argues in particular that: (1) the demographic composition of the municipalities of Gornji Vakuf and Prozor stayed the same; and (2) crimes in the villages of Sovići and Doljani were committed as "an act of revenge of members of one HVO unit".[3216]

1000.   The Prosecution responds that the Trial Chamber reasonably relied on evidence of the pattern of crimes committed throughout the JCE period in finding that the CCP existed.[3217] In response to Petković's first challenge, the Prosecution submits that the Trial Chamber properly distinguished between legitimate aspects of military operations and the commission of crimes **[page 421]** during such operations.[3218] The Prosecution also asserts that the Trial Chamber was aware of the evidence cited by Petković as regards the reporting of crimes up the chain of command, but found that the JCE members failed to follow up on initial reports or condemnations, and denied or concealed the crimes committed.[3219] In response to Petković's second challenge, the Prosecution submits that: (1) crimes such as those at issue are never permitted, even in

---

[3209]   See *supra*, para. 800.
[3210]   Petković's Appeal Brief, paras 37-38, referring to Trial Judgement, Vol. 4, para. 39; Petković's Reply Brief, paras 12-13. Petković also argues that the Trial Chamber reasoned that because both military operations and the crimes were planned, they must have been committed pursuant to the same plan. See Petković's Appeal Brief, paras 38-40. See also Petković's Appeal Brief, para. 37.
[3211]   Petković's Appeal Brief, para. 41, referring to Exs. P02050, P02059, P02088, P02112, P09494, Milivoj Petković, T. 49438-49446, 49450-49451 (15 Feb 2010).
[3212]   Petković's Appeal Brief, paras 81-82, 84. See also Appeal Hearing, AT. 484, 575 (23 Mar 2017).
[3213]   Petković's Appeal Brief, para. 82.
[3214]   Petković's Appeal Brief, para. 83.
[3215]   Petković's Appeal Brief, para. 83.
[3216]   Petković's Appeal Brief, para. 83, referring to Trial Judgement, Vol. 2, para. 643, Vol. 3, paras 1526-1529, 1559-1563; Appeal Hearing, AT. 494-495, 497-498, 524 (23 Mar 2017).
[3217]   Prosecution's Response Brief (Petković), para. 32.
[3218]   Prosecution's Response Brief (Petković), para. 34.
[3219]   Prosecution's Response Brief (Petković), para. 35.

connection with military operations;[3220] and (2) the Trial Chamber carefully examined how the criminal destruction of property fits within the CCP.[3221]

b. Analysis

1001. The Appeals Chamber turns first to Petković's argument that the Trial Chamber failed to distinguish between legitimate use of military force and crimes that might accompany such instances. The Appeals Chamber recalls that, in the present case, crimes were charged in the context of an armed conflict.[3222] Contrary to Petković's assertion, in considering whether those crimes were committed, the Trial Chamber made findings that certain incidents did not amount to crimes because the possibility of legitimate military conduct could not be excluded.[3223] Having found that a wide range of crimes did occur, however, the Trial Chamber then concluded that the numerous criminal acts committed during military campaigns were carried out in furtherance of the CCP and formed a pattern of conduct.[3224] The Appeals Chamber finds no error in the Trial Chamber's reasoning,[3225] and therefore dismisses Petković's argument that the Trial Chamber failed to distinguish between legitimate use of military force and crimes that might accompany such instances. Further, and as a consequence, Petković's argument that the Trial Chamber failed to **[page 422]** consider that damage to civilian property may be deemed collateral damage in military campaigns is also dismissed.

1002. As for Petković's submission, relying on the events in Stupni Do, that the conclusion that the crimes were planned by the Appellants was contradicted by evidence of crimes being reported up the chain of command and JCE members' reaction to the crimes, the Appeals Chamber notes that the Trial Chamber considered this in its analysis of the CCP. It, however, found that despite not taking part in the decision to attack Stupni Do on 23 October 1993, Petković, among others, attempted to conceal the crimes and thereby furthered the CCP.[3226] The Appeals Chamber therefore finds no error in the Trial Chamber's analysis. Petković's submission is thus dismissed.

1003. The Appeals Chamber also rejects the submission that the Trial Chamber erred in concluding that there was a clear pattern of crimes as opposed to a pattern of military operations, noting that the Trial Chamber's conclusion in this regard was based on the findings that a large number of crimes were committed, in "stages", in order to implement the JCE.[3227] Accordingly, Petković's arguments are dismissed.

1004. As for Petković's argument that the Trial Chamber erred in concluding that destruction of Muslim houses in Gornji Vakuf, Jablanica, and Prozor formed part of the CCP, the Appeals Chamber recalls that it has considered, and dismissed, the submission that the absence of permanent demographic change has any

---

[3220] Prosecution's Response Brief (Petković), para. 36.

[3221] Prosecution's Response Brief (Petković), para. 37.

[3222] See, *e.g.*, Trial Judgement, Vol. 3, paras 514-589. See also Trial Judgement, Vol. 2, paras 34-299, 326-488, 520-655.

[3223] See, *e.g.*, Trial Judgement, Vol. 3, paras 655 (the Trial Chamber could not exclude the possibility that villagers were taking part in hostilities and could not find that those villagers were civilian victims of the crime of murder), 701 (the Trial Chamber could not establish whether certain individuals belonged to the village guard or were members of the ABiH, and therefore could not find that they were victims of murder), 704 (the Trial Chamber could not establish the source of shots that were fired when HVO soldiers broke down the door of a house, and could not exclude the possibility that its occupants were taking part in the hostilities, and therefore was unable to find that certain villagers were victims of wilful killing), 706 (the Trial Chamber recalled that an individual was armed and could not find that the individual was a victim of wilful killing), 950 (the Trial Chamber could not find that those who were being detained were civilians, and therefore could not find that the crime of imprisonment was committed), 1525 (the Trial Chamber could not exclude the possibility that Muslims inside the house took part in the combat activities, thus making the house a legitimate military target for the HVO soldiers), 1558 (the Trial Chamber could not exclude the possibility that the destruction of a house was justified by military necessity), 1563 (the Trial Chamber could not exclude the possibility that the destruction caused during an HVO attack was justified by military necessity).

[3224] Trial Judgement, Vol. 4, paras 45-47, 56, 59, 61, 65. Regarding this pattern of conduct, see also *supra*, para. 979.

[3225] The Appeals Chamber also considers that Petković fails to substantiate his assertion that the Trial Chamber concluded that as both military operations and criminal acts were planned, they must have formed part of the same plan. Furthermore, the Appeals Chamber notes that the Trial Chamber did not find that military operations *per se* formed part of the CCP, and considered only the crimes which – in certain incidents – accompanied such operations. This submission is also dismissed. See *supra*, fn. 3210.

[3226] See Trial Judgement, Vol. 4, paras 61-62. See also Trial Judgement, Vol. 3, paras 317-326, 411-425, 476-498, Vol. 4, paras 760-777, 846-849. See also *infra*, paras 2289-2294.

[3227] Trial Judgement, Vol. 4, para. 45. See Trial Judgement, Vol. 4, paras 46-66. See also *supra*, para. 979.

bearing on the conclusion that crimes were committed.[3228] The Appeals Chamber thus dismisses Petković's challenges insofar as they relate to Gornji Vakuf, Jablanica, and Prozor. As for the argument that the Trial Chamber erred in failing to consider that crimes committed in Sovići and Doljani in Jablanica Municipality were an act of revenge of members of one HVO unit,[3229] the Appeals Chamber finds that Petković merely suggests a different interpretation of the evidence without showing that the Trial Chamber reached an unreasonable conclusion.[3230] His arguments thus fail.

1005. The Appeals Chamber therefore finds that Petković has failed to show that the Trial Chamber erred when it concluded that: (1) HVO military operations formed part of a plan by failing to distinguish the crimes and legitimate military conduct; and (2) there was a "clear pattern **[page 423]** of conduct" in the crimes committed as a result of the implementation of the CCP. Petković's sub-grounds of appeal 3.2.2 and 3.2.2.4 are dismissed.

(iv) Ćorić's appeal (Ground 1 in part)

a. Arguments of the Parties

1006. Ćorić argues that the Trial Chamber erred in concluding that the CCP existed, having failed to take into account reasonable alternative inferences and having ignored certain evidence.[3231] He argues that "[n]o such plan was shown to exist in documents, orders and meeting notes introduced into evidence".[3232] Ćorić submits that there was "abundant evidence" showing that the acts of the HZ H-B were defensive, pointing to: (1) witness testimony;[3233] (2) documentary evidence regarding the establishment of the HZ H-B as a temporary response to aggression;[3234] (3) the HVO co-operation with the ABiH;[3235] (4) the fact that the ABiH was involved in planning attacks against the HZ H-B even whilst participating in peace negotiations;[3236] and (5) the lack of discrimination against Muslims, which was evidenced by, *inter alia,* Muslims joining the HVO.[3237] Ćorić also **[page 424]** submits that the Trial Chamber's failure to consider the totality of evidence

---

[3228] See *supra,* paras 872, 894. See also Petković's Appeal Brief, paras 27, 79.

[3229] See Trial Judgement, Vol. 2, para. 643.

[3230] See, *e.g.,* Trial Judgement, Vol. 4, para. 146.

[3231] Ćorić›s Appeal Brief, paras 18, 20, 29. See also Ćorić›s Appeal Brief, paras 19, 21.

[3232] Ćorić›s Appeal Brief, para. 22.

[3233] Ćorić›s Appeal Brief, para. 23, referring to Ex. 5D05110 (confidential) (witness statement of Prosecution Witness NO), para. 10, Zdenko Andabak, T. 50965 (15 Mar 2010), Dragan Ćurčić, T. 45809 (12 Oct 2009), Radmilo Jašak, T. 48682-48685 (20 Jan 2010), Klaus Johann Nissen, T. 20648-20650 (27 June 2007), Slobodan Praljak, T. 41832-41833 (23 June 2007), Andrew Pringle, T. 24259 (7 Nov 2007), Zvonko Vidović, T. 51462 (29 Mar 2010).

[3234] Ćorić›s Appeal Brief, paras 24-25, referring to Exs. 1D00410, 1D02147, 1D02314, 1D02441, 1D02096, 1D02908, 2D00093, P00047, P00050, P00052, P00060, P00078, P00079, P00081, P00117, P00128, P00151, P00152, P00289, P00292, P00303, P00339, P01467, P00498, P00543, P01798, P01467, P01988, P02088, Mile Akmadžić, T. 28482 (17 June 2008), Stjepan Kljuić, T. 3937-3938, (27 June 2006), T. 4216-4217 (28 June 2006), Ciril Ribičić, T. 25462-25463 (10 Dec 2007).

[3235] Ćorić›s Appeal Brief, para. 26, referring to Exs. 1D00507, 1D02147, 1D02432, 1D02441, 1D02664, 2D00147, 2D00311, 2D00522, 2D00523, 2D00630, 2D00809, 2D01177, 2D01185, 2D01253, 3D00008, 3D00437, 4D00397, 4D00410, 4D00476, 4D00478, 4D01026, 4D01048, 4D01521, P00151, P00155, P00339, P01988, P02002, P02091, Witness DE, T. 15615, 15597-15598 (closed session) (13 Mar 2007), T. 15671 (closed session) (14 Mar 2007), Stjepan Kljuić, T. 4187-4188 (27 June 2006), Robert Donia, T. 1830 (10 May 2006), Borislav Puljić, T. 32251-32252 (16 Sept 2008), Mile Akmadžić, T. 29424-29426 (17 June 2008), T. 29601, 29603-29604 (18 June 2008), Hamid Bahto, T. 37916-37918 (11 Mar 2009), Tihomir Majić, T. 37850-37851 (9 Mar 2009), Filip Filipović, T. 47778 (7 Dec 2009), Mario Miloš, T. 38651 (30 Mar 2009), Bo Pellnäs, T. 19730 (7 June 2007), Dragan Pinjuh, T. 37700 (4 Mar 2009), Mirko Zelenika, T. 33248 (15 Oct 2008), Anđelko Makar, T. 38381-38386 (23 Mar 2009).

[3236] Ćorić›s Appeal Brief, para. 27, referring to Exs. 1D01264, 1D01662, 1D01652, 1D02729, 2D00229, 2D00253, 2D01107, 3D00837, 4D00568, 4D00895, 4D00896, 4D01700, P00633, P01240, P01305, P01317, P01675, P02346, P02760, P02849, P03038, P03337, Zoran Buntić, T. 30723-30724 (15 July 2008), Filip Filipović, T. 47444 (30 Nov 2009), Dragan Jurić, T. 39308, 39345-39346 (27 Apr 2009), Witness DE, T. 15698-15699 (closed session) (14 Mar 2007). Ćorić asserts that against this backdrop, it is evident that "self-defence was the guiding principle of the HVO, not any pre-conceived plan to ethnically cleanse Muslims". Ćorić›s Appeal Brief, para. 27.

[3237] Ćorić›s Appeal Brief, paras 28-29, referring to Exs. 1D00442, 1D00669, 1D01153, 1D02001, 1D02124, 1D02381, 2D00439, 4D00455, P00128, P00672, P00824, P01097, P01264, P01439, P01511, P01536, P01563, P01627, P01652, P02059, P02091, P02155, P03673, P04008, P04111, P04699, P04735, P07279, P07674, P10220 (confidential), Witness CQ, T. 11424 (private session) (11 Dec 2006), Milivoj Petković, T. 49342 (11 Feb 2010), Zoran Buntić, T. 30724-30725 (15 July 2008), Anđelko Makar, T. 38414 (23 Mar 2009), Witness CJ, T. 10952 (closed session) (30 Nov 2006). Ćorić submits in particular that: (1) Muslims were appointed to all levels of the HZ-HB and steps were taken to oppose demographic changes; and (2) the disarming and detention of Muslim members of the

invalidates its conclusion that a JCE existed, arguing that the Trial Chamber: (1) "could not distinguish criminal events during the attacks and after"; and thus (2) could not "distinguish damage and injury that occurred as part of legitimate combat apart from those that were criminally incurred".[3238]

1007. The Prosecution responds that: (1) the majority of Ćorić's arguments warrant summary dismissal as they were made in his final brief;[3239] and (2) the evidence he refers to does not support his own claims.[3240] It points to the Trial Chamber's findings on the CCP and argues that Ćorić ignores the evidence relied on by the Trial Chamber which demonstrates that the events were part of a JCE, as opposed to a defensive reaction to the ABiH offensive.[3241] In particular, the Prosecution argues that given the "massive scope, scale, duration and similarity" of the crimes, the Trial Chamber reasonably concluded that a JCE existed despite ABiH planning of attacks during ongoing negotiations and the inclusion of Muslims in the HVO.[3242]

b. Analysis

1008. The Appeals Chamber will first address Ćorić's assertion that the Trial Chamber found that it could not distinguish between criminal events occurring during military attacks and criminal events occurring after the HVO takeover of villages. It considers that Ćorić takes this solitary finding out of context. In assessing evidence concerning the alleged destruction of Muslim houses and thefts of their property in the village of Hrasnica, the Trial Chamber referred to paragraph 67 of the Indictment which alleges that *"following* the HVO attack on Duša, Hrasnica, Uzričje and Ždrimci the HVO plundered and burned Bosnian Muslim houses and property in and around these villages"[3243] and stated that "[t]he evidence did not always facilitate distinguishing the criminal events alleged to have occurred during the actual attack of the village from the criminal events once the HVO took over the village".[3244] Noting, however, that some witnesses provided sufficient detail, the Trial Chamber concluded that HVO members committed thefts and plundered Muslim houses in Hrasnica but that it had no evidence to find that the HVO stole valuables from some Muslims **[page 425]** during their arrests in Hrasnica.[3245] Accordingly, contrary to Ćorić's submission, this conclusion by the Trial Chamber has no impact on the existence of the JCE.

1009. The remainder of Ćorić's arguments essentially go to the assertion that the Trial Chamber failed to consider evidence demonstrating that the acts of the HZ H-B were acts of self-defence as opposed to being part of the CCP.[3246] Considering first Ćorić's argument in relation to witness evidence, the Appeals Chamber notes that Ćorić argues that the Trial Chamber disregarded the evidence of a number of witnesses to the effect that they did not know of or participate in a criminal plan, as well as other testimony which, in his view, supports the hypothesis that the acts of the HZ H-B were defensive. The Appeals Chamber notes that contrary to Ćorić's submission, the Trial Chamber considered much of the testimonial evidence he points to at various junctures in the Trial Judgement.[3247] Further, the Appeals Chamber considers that Ćorić fails to explain how the conclusion that the CCP existed – made on the basis of other evidence and findings, which

---

HVO was a military necessity which came about following the Attack on the HVO Tihomir Mišić Barracks on 30 June 1993. See Ćorić's Appeal Brief, paras 28-29. See also Ćorić's Appeal Brief, para. 27.

[3238] Ćorić's Appeal Brief, para. 29, referring to Trial Judgement, Vol. 2, para. 412.
[3239] Prosecution's Response Brief (Ćorić), para. 19.
[3240] Prosecution's Response Brief (Ćorić), para. 24.
[3241] Prosecution's Response Brief (Ćorić), paras 20-24.
[3242] Prosecution's Response Brief (Ćorić), para. 26. The Prosecution argues in particular that: (1) the fact that the HVO was "careful enough" to avoid explicit reference to the CCP in documentation is irrelevant; (2) arguments regarding efforts to oppose demographic changes are undermined by the HVO's active role in the displacement of Muslims; and (3) regardless of whether disarming and detentions of Muslims became a military necessity following June 1993, it did not justify the crimes which occurred. Prosecution's Response Brief (Ćorić), paras 21, 25-26; Appeal Hearing, AT. 659-660 (24 Mar 2017).
[3243] Indictment, para. 67 (emphasis added); Trial Judgement, Vol. 2, para. 413. See also Trial Judgement, Vol. 2, para. 411.
[3244] See Trial Judgement, Vol. 2, para. 412.
[3245] See Trial Judgement, Vol. 2, paras 413, 415. See also Trial Judgement, Vol. 2, para. 414.
[3246] The Appeals Chamber has considered, and dismissed, a number of arguments in this regard above. See *supra*, paras 861, 864, 895, 908, 928, 958, 967, 979, 982.
[3247] See, *e.g.*, Trial Judgement, Vol. 1, para. 946 & fn. 2344 (referring to Ex. 5D05110 (confidential)), Vol. 2, paras 40 (referring to Zdenko Andabak, T(F). 50965 (15 Mar 2010)), 513, 524, 880-881 (referring to, *inter alia*, Radmilo Jašak, T(F). 48684-48685 (20 Jan 2010)).

Ćorić does not challenge[3248] – is affected by this evidence. Ćorić simply attempts to substitute his own interpretation of the evidence for that of the Trial Chamber, often repeating submissions made at trial without showing an error by the Trial Chamber.[3249] His argument is thus dismissed.

1010. The Appeals Chamber turns next to Ćorić›s argument that the Trial Chamber failed to consider evidence demonstrating that the HZ H-B was established as a temporary response to aggression. The Appeals Chamber recalls that it has considered, and dismissed, identical challenges to this finding above.[3250] The Appeals Chamber also notes that the Trial Chamber found, based on a range of evidence, including the evidence referenced by Ćorić, that the HZ H-B was created against a backdrop of war in response to Serbian aggression, but was not solely an "interim defensive measure to counter aggression but was instead sought to create a 'mini-state' separate from the RBiH".[3251] Similarly, with respect to Ćorić›s argument that the Trial Chamber failed to take account of the fact that the ABiH was planning attacks against the HZ H-B, the Appeals Chamber notes that the Trial Chamber took account of the fact that clashes between the HVO and ABiH broke out in the municipalities during the period of co-operation in 1993.[3252] It also took account, in its analysis of the CCP, of a number of specific ABiH attacks, including the Attack on the HVO Tihomir Mišić **[page 426]** Barracks.[3253] Further, the majority of evidence Ćorić refers to in this respect was considered by the Trial Chamber throughout the Trial Judgement, and used to make findings on co-operation between the two sides during which clashes erupted between them.[3254] Accordingly, the Appeals Chamber again finds that Ćorić simply attempts to substitute his own evaluation of the evidence for that of the Trial Chamber, repeating submissions made at trial,[3255] without showing an error by the Trial Chamber.

1011. Regarding Ćorić›s challenges concerning the question of HVO co-operation with the ABiH, the Appeals Chamber recalls that the Trial Chamber did not expressly consider this issue in its analysis of the CCP, apart from referring to the HZ H-B leaders' participation in peace talks.[3256] However, as stated earlier, the Trial Chamber made a number of findings on the issue throughout the Trial Judgement.[3257] The Appeals Chamber also recalls that it has found that the Trial Chamber's findings on co-operation did not impact on the conclusion that the CCP came into being in mid-January 1993.[3258] For the same reasons, the Appeals Chamber finds that the further evidence of co-operation that Ćorić pointed to – the vast majority of which was again considered in the Trial Judgement and used to make findings on co-operation between the two sides[3259] – fails to demonstrate any error in the Trial Chamber's conclusion. This argument is also rejected.

1012. The Appeals Chamber also rejects Ćorić›s submissions regarding the Trial Chamber's approach to evidence with respect to the alleged lack of discriminatory intent against Muslims. The Appeals Chamber notes that the Trial Judgement is replete with findings concerning attacks on Muslims and crimes committed

---

[3248]   See Trial Judgement, Vol. 4, paras 44-73.
[3249]   See, *e.g.*, Ćorić›s Final Brief, paras 153-155, 160.
[3250]   See *supra*, paras 728-733.
[3251]   Trial Judgement, Vol. 4, para. 14 & fn. 31 (referring to Ex. P00078), para. 15 & fns 34, 39 (referring to Exs. P00052, P00078).
[3252]   See, *e.g.*, Trial Judgement, Vol. 1, paras 460, 470, 477, Vol. 4, para. 45.
[3253]   See Trial Judgement, Vol. 4, paras 46, 57, 61.
[3254]   Trial Judgement, Vol. 1, para. 440 & fn. 1037 (referring to Ex. 4D01700), para. 460 & fn. 1105 (referring to Ex. 1D02729), para. 462 & fns 1110-1111 (referring to Ex. P01240), para. 754 & fn. 1762 (referring to Ex. P00633), Vol. 2, para. 1896 & fn. 4729 (referring to Ex. 4D00568), Vol. 3, para. 284 & fns 636-637 (referring to Ex. 1D01264), Vol. 4, para. 53 (referring to Exs. 3D00837, P02760). Other evidence cited to by Ćorić was also analysed and considered by the Trial Chamber, albeit in contexts other than co-operation and clashes between the two sides. See Trial Judgement, Vol. 1, para. 740 & fns 1738, 1740 (referring to Exs. 4D00895, P03337, 4D00896), Vol. 4, para. 88 & fn. 235 (referring to Ex. P01317). The Appeals Chamber recalls that it is to be presumed that the Trial Chamber evaluated all the evidence presented to it as long as there is no indication that the Trial Chamber completely disregarded any particular piece of evidence. See *Popović et al.* Appeal Judgement, para. 306; *Đorđević* Appeal Judgement, fn. 2527. Given that the Trial Chamber was aware of Exhibits 4D00895, P03337, 4D00896, and P01317, Ćorić fails to demonstrate that the Trial Chamber erred in not expressly referring to these exhibits in relation to the issue of discrimination against the Muslims.
[3255]   See, *e.g.*, Ćorić›s Final Brief, paras 153-155, 160.
[3256]   See *supra*, para. 990.
[3257]   See *supra*, para. 987.
[3258]   See *supra*, paras 987-991. See also *supra*, para. 861.
[3259]   Trial Judgement, Vol. 1, para. 440 & fns 1037-1038 (referring to Exs. 4D00478, 4D01026, 4D01048, 4D01521, Mile Akmadžić, T(F). 29443, 29602-29606 (17 June 2008)), para. 443 & fn. 1054 (referring to Ex. 1D02664), para. 472 & fns 1145-1147 (referring to Ex. P02091), para. 754 & fn. 1762 (referring to Ex. P02002), Vol. 2, paras 696-697 & fns 1559-1564 (referring to Exs. 2D00523, 2D00522).

against them,[3260] including the conclusion that "in all the municipalities the evictions were accompanied in many instances by episodes of violence directed **[page 427]** against Muslims".[3261] Furthermore, the Trial Chamber found that while the HVO included Muslims within its ranks in 1992 and 1993, the evidence showed that the Muslims left the ranks of the HVO *en masse* in May and June 1993.[3262] It also noted in the context of the CCP that the 15 April 1993 Decision denied some 16,000 to 20,000 people, "primarily Muslims", the status of displaced persons, as a result of which Muslims had no access to humanitarian aid.[3263] The Trial Chamber also observed that following the ABiH attack on 30 June 1993, the implementation of the CCP became "more efficient" with, *inter alia,* the arrests and detentions of a number of Muslims.[3264] In light of these findings, the Appeals Chamber finds that Ćorić fails to show how the evidence he cites to – much of which was considered elsewhere in the Trial Judgement to make various findings[3265] – would have an impact on the Trial Chamber's finding that the CCP existed.

1013. In sum, the Appeals Chamber finds that Ćorić has failed to demonstrate that no reasonable trier of fact could have found that the existence of the CCP was the only reasonable inference. Ćorić›s ground of appeal 1 is therefore dismissed in relevant part.

6. Conclusion

1014. The Appeals Chamber recalls that it has granted Praljak's ground of appeal 15 in part and reversed the Trial Chamber's finding that the deaths of seven civilians in Duša were part of the CCP. As a consequence, the Appeals Chamber has also: (1) reversed the Trial Chamber's finding that murder and wilful killing were part of the CCP from January 1993; (2) found that the remaining findings establish that murder and wilful killing were part of the CCP from June 1993; and (3) reversed the Appellants' convictions for murder and wilful killing in relation to two killings in Prozor. The impact of the reversal of these findings on sentencing, if any, will be addressed **[page 428]** below.[3266] The Appeals Chamber further recalls that it has dismissed the Appellants' remaining challenges with respect to the CCP. **[page 429]**

E. Alleged Errors in Relation to Jadranko Prlić's Participation in the JCE

1. Introduction

1015. Starting on 14 August 1992, Prlić served as the President of the HVO HZ H-B and after the establishment of the HR H-B on 28 August 1993, as the President of the Government of HR H-B.[3267] On

---

3260   See Trial Judgement, Vol. 2, paras 1-2191, Vol. 3, paras 1-1741.
3261   Trial Judgement, Vol. 3, para. 645.
3262   Trial Judgement, Vol. 1, para. 774 & fn. 1807.
3263   Trial Judgement, Vol. 4, para. 49.
3264   Trial Judgement, Vol. 4, para. 57.
3265   Some of the evidence cited by Ćorić was used by the Trial Chamber to make findings on topics indirectly relevant to the issue of discrimination against Muslims, including for example the co-operation between the two sides through the establishment of a joint command, desertion of Muslims from the HVO, the establishment of a commission to deal with war crimes allegations, and appointments of judges and prosecutors to the civil and military courts. See Trial Judgement, Vol. 1, para. 472 & fn. 1145 (referring to Ex. P02091), para. 522 & fn. 1275 (referring to Exs. P00824, P01652), para. 548 & fn. 1330 (referring to Ex. P01511), para. 649 & fn. 1533 (referring to Ex. P01536), Vol. 2, para. 882 & fn. 2066 (referring to Ex. P04699), para. 1552 & fn. 3911 (referring to Ex. P03673), Vol. 4, para. 52 & fn. 141 (referring to Ex. P02059), para. 158 & fn. 428 (referring to Ex. P00672). Much of the evidence now cited by Ćorić was also considered and used by the Trial Chamber, but in another context. See Trial Judgement, Vol. 1, para. 519 & fn. 1268 (referring to Ex. P00128), para. 537 & fn. 1311 (referring to Ex. P07674), para. 544 & fn. 1327 (referring to Ex. P01097), para. 777 & fn. 1816 (referring to Ex. P10220 (confidential)), para. 978 & fn. 2461 (referring to Ex. 1D02124), Vol. 4, para. 88 & fns 235, 252 (referring to Exs. P01264, P04111, P07279, P01439). The Appeals Chamber recalls that it is to be presumed that the Trial Chamber evaluated all the evidence presented to it, as long as there is no indication that the Trial Chamber completely disregarded any particular piece of evidence. See *Popović et al.* Appeal Judgement, para. 306; *Đorđević* Appeal Judgement, fn. 2527. Given that the Trial Chamber was aware of much of the evidence now cited by Ćorić and given that it analysed it throughout the Trial Judgement, Ćorić fails to demonstrate that the Trial Chamber erred in not expressly considering it when making its findings concerning discrimination against Muslims.
3266   See *infra,* paras 3359-3365.
3267   Trial Judgement, Vol. 4, para. 82. See Trial Judgement, Vol. 1, paras 483, 516, 524, 534.

16 February 1994, Prlić also became a member of the Presidential Council of the HR H-B.[3268] The Trial Chamber found that Prlić had significant *de jure* and *de facto* powers in co-ordinating and directing the work of the HVO/Government of the HZ(R) H-B. It found in particular that he chaired high-level meetings, in which decisions on the political and military strategy in the HZ(R) H-B were taken collectively, could issue military decisions that were sent through the military chain of command, played a key role in the relations of the HVO/Government of the HZ(R) H-B with the Government of Croatia, and had powers over detention centres.[3269]

1016. Further, the Trial Chamber found that Prlić was a principal member of the JCE and significantly contributed to it from January 1993 to April 1994.[3270] In particular, the Trial Chamber found that he contributed to the JCE in the municipalities of Gornji Vakuf, Jablanica, Prozor,[3271] and Mostar,[3272] and through his involvement in blocking the delivery of humanitarian aid,[3273] the campaign of mass arrest of Muslims,[3274] the movement of the population,[3275] and the concealment of crimes.[3276] Finally, the Trial Chamber found that Prlić intended to implement the CCP and shared with the other members of the JCE the discriminatory intent to expel the Muslim population from the HZ(R) H-B.[3277] The Trial Chamber convicted Prlić under Article 7(1) of the Statute of committing, pursuant to JCE I liability, various crimes amounting to grave breaches of the Geneva Conventions, violations of the laws or customs of war, and/or crimes against humanity under Articles 2, 3, and 5 of the Statute, respectively.[3278] Prlić was sentenced to a single sentence of 25 years of imprisonment.[3279] **[page 430]**

1017. Prlić challenges these and related findings of the Trial Chamber with regard to his JCE contribution and *mens rea*.[3280] These challenges will be addressed in the following sections.

2. Prlić's role as President of the HVO/Government of the HZ(R) H-B

1018. In the present section, the Appeals Chamber will address Prlić's challenges to the Trial Chamber's findings regarding his: (1) powers in civilian matters; (2) powers in military matters; (3) powers pertaining to humanitarian aid; and (4) role in the relations between HZ(R) H-B and Croatia.

[3268] Trial Judgement, Vol. 4, para. 82. See Trial Judgement, Vol. 1, para. 497.
[3269] Trial Judgement, Vol. 4, para. 270.
[3270] Trial Judgement, Vol. 4, paras 276, 1225, 1230.
[3271] Trial Judgement, Vol. 4, para. 271.
[3272] Trial Judgement, Vol. 4, para. 272.
[3273] Trial Judgement, Vol. 4, para. 272.
[3274] Trial Judgement, Vol. 4, para. 272. See Trial Judgement, Vol. 4, para. 155.
[3275] Trial Judgement, Vol. 4, para. 275.
[3276] Trial Judgement, Vol. 4, paras 273-274.
[3277] Trial Judgement, Vol. 4, para. 276.
[3278] Trial Judgement, Vol. 4, paras 68, 278, Disposition, p. 430. These crimes are: persecution as a crime against humanity (Count 1); murder as a crime against humanity (Count 2); wilful killing as a grave breach of the Geneva Conventions (Count 3); deportation as a crime against humanity (Count 6); unlawful deportation of a civilian as a grave breach of the Geneva Conventions (Count 7); inhumane acts (forcible transfer) as a crime against humanity (Count 8); unlawful transfer of a civilian as a grave breach of the Geneva Conventions (Count 9); imprisonment as a crime against humanity (Count 10); unlawful confinement of a civilian as a grave breach of the Geneva Conventions (Count 11); inhumane acts (conditions of confinement) as a crime against humanity (Count 12); inhuman treatment (conditions of confinement) as a grave breach of the Geneva Conventions (Count 13); inhumane acts as a crime against humanity (Count 15); inhuman treatment as a grave breach of the Geneva Conventions (Count 16); unlawful labour as a violation of the laws or customs of war (Count 18); extensive destruction of property, not justified by military necessity and carried out unlawfully and wantonly, as a grave breach of the Geneva Conventions (Count 19); destruction or wilful damage done to institutions dedicated to religion or education as a violation of the laws or customs of war (Count 21); unlawful attack on civilians as a violation of the laws or customs of war (Count 24); and unlawful infliction of terror on civilians as a violation of the laws or customs of war (Count 25). The Trial Chamber found that the following crimes also fell within the framework of the JCE, meaning Prlić was also responsible for them, but did not enter convictions for them based on the principles relating to cumulative convictions: cruel treatment (conditions of confinement) as a violation of the laws or customs of war (Count 14); cruel treatment as a violation of the laws or customs of war (Count 17); and wanton destruction of cities, towns, or villages, or devastation not justified by military necessity as a violation of the laws or customs of war (Count 20). See Trial Judgement, Vol. 4, para. 68, Disposition, p. 430. See also Trial Judgement, Vol. 4, paras 1260-1266. The Appeals Chamber discusses Prlić's convictions pursuant to JCE III below. See *infra*, para. 2833 *et seq.*
[3279] Trial Judgement, Vol. 4, Disposition, p. 430.
[3280] Prlić's Appeal Brief, paras 313-629, 642-651. See also Appeal Hearing, AT. 173, 177-178, 233-234, 245-246 (20 Mar 2017).

(a) Alleged errors related to Prlić's functions and responsibilities in civilian matters

1019. The Trial Chamber found that Prlić, as President of the HVO/Government of the HZ(R) H-B, had various powers in civilian matters.[3281] Prlić submits that the Trial Chamber erred in law and fact by finding that he had significant *de jure* and *de facto* powers in co-ordinating and directing the work of the HVO/Government of the HZ(R) H-B.[3282] As a result, Prlić submits that he should be acquitted on all Counts.[3283] The Prosecution responds that Prlić's submissions should be dismissed.[3284]

1020. The Appeals Chamber will examine Prlić's challenges relating to: (1) his decision-making powers; (2) the expansion of Government powers; and (3) his powers over various official bodies, namely the Departments/Ministries of Defence, the Interior, and Justice, as well as fiscal organs of **[page 431]** the Government, the Office for Displaced Persons and Refugees ("ODPR"), the Exchange Service, and municipal governments.

(i) Prlić's decision-making powers (Prlić's Sub-ground 11.1)

1021. The Trial Chamber found that Prlić: (1) participated in the HVO/Government of the HZ(R) H-B meetings and was informed of the situation in the territory of the HZ(R) H-B; (2) contributed to the adoption of decisions taken collectively, which comprised HVO policy, by taking an active part in drawing them up, including decisions relating to the appointment and dismissal of some members of the HVO; and (3) signed laws, decisions, and decrees adopted by the HVO/Government of the HZ(R) H-B.[3285]

a. Prlić's powers vis-a-vis other organs and officials

i. Arguments of the Parties

1022. Prlić submits that the Trial Chamber erroneously assessed the functions and responsibilities of the HZ H-B President, the HR H-B President, the HZ H-B Presidency, the HR H-B House of Representatives, the HVO HZ H-B President, and the President of the HR H-B Government.[3286] He further submits that the Trial Chamber erred by not distinguishing the HVO HZ H-B from the HR H-B Government.[3287] He argues that the Trial Chamber ignored evidence that: (1) HDZ-BiH played a significant role in the division of powers in BiH and the HZ H-B;[3288] and (2) Mate Boban was the supreme authority in the HZ H-B.[3289] Prlić also submits that the Trial Chamber failed to assess the powers of the HR H-B President and that it wrongly found that it was Boban who appointed him to the Presidential Council.[3290] He argues that the Trial Chamber erroneously assessed his powers by ignoring that HVO HZ H-B Vice-President Krešimir Zubak's powers were much greater than his.[3291] Finally, Prlić argues that the Trial Chamber ignored evidence showing the differences in

---

[3281] Trial Judgement, Vol. 4, paras 88-105.

[3282] Prlić's Appeal Brief, paras 313, 379. Similarly, Prlić contends that the Trial Chamber repeatedly erred in its assessment of his *de jure* and *de facto* powers by repeating that he was "involved in the supervision and activities" of all HVO HZ H-B departments, sub-departments, and offices. Prlić's Appeal Brief, para. 341. The Appeals Chamber deals with those allegations below. See *infra*, paras 1048-1092.

[3283] Prlić's Appeal Brief, para. 380.

[3284] Prosecution's Response Brief (Prlić), para. 186. See Prosecution's Response Brief (Prlić), paras 183-185; Appeal Hearing, AT. 195 (20 Mar 2017).

[3285] Trial Judgement, Vol. 4, para. 90. See Trial Judgement, Vol. 4, paras 88-89.

[3286] Prlić's Appeal Brief, para. 314. See Prlić's Appeal Brief, para. 315, referring to Prlić's Appeal Brief, paras 45-76 (sub-ground of appeal 1.2), sub-ground of appeal 1.4.

[3287] Prlić's Appeal Brief, para. 316.

[3288] Prlić's Appeal Brief, para. 317. See Prlić's Appeal Brief, para. 318, referring to Prlić's Appeal Brief, sub-ground of appeal 1.1.

[3289] Prlić's Appeal Brief, para. 319. See Prlić's Appeal Brief, para. 320, referring to Prlić's Appeal Brief, paras 50-51, 54-55 (sub-ground of appeal 1.2).

[3290] Prlić's Appeal Brief, para. 321.

[3291] Prlić's Appeal Brief, para. 322. See also Appeal Hearing, AT. 139 (20 Mar 2017).

the functioning of the HZ H-B and the HVO HZ H-B executive, the HR H-B, and the HR H-B Government and municipalities during different periods of war in 1991-1994.[3292] **[page 432]**

1023. The Prosecution responds that Prlić fails to explain the relevance of the evidence on the HDZ-BiH's role.[3293] The Prosecution argues that the Trial Chamber addressed Boban's authority in his various functions, that Prlić fails to explain how evidence of Boban's authority as HZ H-B President renders unreasonable the Trial Chamber's findings on Prlić's authority as President of its Government, and that Prlić's claim that Boban made decisions that had to be implemented by the HVO HZ H-B is not supported by the evidence he cites.[3294] The Prosecution further argues that it is irrelevant who appointed Prlić to the Presidential Council and that, in any event, Prlić fails to show that the Trial Chamber unreasonably relied on Boban's decision appointing him.[3295] It contends that Prlić's claim that Vice-President Zubak's powers exceeded those of Prlić is not supported by the cited evidence.[3296] Finally, the Prosecution argues that Prlić fails to connect to any findings the evidence the Trial Chamber allegedly ignored on the differences in the functioning of various organs.[3297]

ii. Analysis

1024. With respect to Prlić's argument that the Trial Chamber erroneously assessed the functions and responsibilities of the HZ H-B President, the HR H-B President, the HZ H-B Presidency, the HR H-B House of Representatives, the HVO HZ H-B President, and the President of the HR H-B Government, the Appeals Chamber observes that Prlić only references a section of the Trial Judgement in which the Trial Chamber reached some conclusions on Prlić's actions as President of the HVO/Government of the HZ(R) H-B, without explaining how the Trial Chamber erred or showing that no reasonable trier of fact, based on the evidence, could have reached the same conclusion.[3298] The Appeals Chamber therefore dismisses Prlić's argument.

1025. Regarding the alleged error in not distinguishing the HVO HZ H-B from the Government of the HR H-B,[3299] the Appeals Chamber observes that Prlić does not explain how this alleged failure resulted in the Trial Chamber making any specific erroneous finding. The Appeals Chamber further considers that Prlić does not explain how the evidence regarding the role played by the HDZ-BiH, which the Trial Chamber allegedly ignored, demonstrates that the Trial Chamber's findings were **[page 433]** unreasonable.[3300] Finally, regarding the Trial Chamber's alleged disregard for evidence showing that Boban was the supreme authority in HZ H-B, the Appeals Chamber observes that the Trial Chamber examined Boban's powers and various positions,[3301] and that Prlić has failed to show that the allegedly ignored evidence would have had any impact on the Trial Chamber's findings.[3302] These arguments are dismissed.

1026. The Appeals Chamber further dismisses Prlić's submission that the Trial Chamber wrongly found that Boban appointed him to the Presidential Council, as the Trial Chamber's finding is supported by the

---

[3292] Prlić's Appeal Brief, para. 323. See Prlić's Appeal Brief, para. 324, referring to Prlić's Appeal Brief, paras 45-57 (sub-ground of appeal 1.2), 83-86 (sub-ground of appeal 1.4).

[3293] Prosecution's Response Brief (Prlić), para. 193.

[3294] Prosecution's Response Brief (Prlić), para. 192.

[3295] Prosecution's Response Brief (Prlić), para. 196.

[3296] Prosecution's Response Brief (Prlić), para. 194. The Prosecution also argues that Prlić fails to explain how the Presidential Council, of which he was a member, undermined his powers as Government President. Prosecution's Response Brief (Prlić), para. 195.

[3297] Prosecution's Response Brief (Prlić), para. 197.

[3298] See Prlić's Appeal Brief, para. 314, referring to Trial Judgement, Vol. 4, paras 88-90. The Appeals Chamber also notes that Prlić refers to his submissions in sub-grounds of appeal 1.2 and 1.4, which it dismisses elsewhere in the Judgement. See *supra*, paras 168-176.

[3299] The Appeals Chamber notes that the Trial Chamber made this distinction. See, *e.g.*, Trial Judgement, Vol. 1, paras 515-521, Vol. 4, para. 82. See also *infra*, paras 1034-1039.

[3300] The Appeals Chamber also notes that Prlić refers to his submissions in sub-ground of appeal 1.1, which it dismisses elsewhere in the Judgement. See *supra*, paras 168-176.

[3301] Trial Judgement, Vol. 1, paras 493-510, 691-708. See also Trial Judgement, Vol. 1, para. 511.

[3302] The Appeals Chamber also notes that Prlić refers to his submissions in sub-ground of appeal 1.2, which it dismisses elsewhere in the Judgement. See *supra*, paras 168-176.

referenced evidence,[3303] while Prlić's submission is not.[3304] With regard to the Trial Chamber's alleged disregard for HVO HZ H-B Vice-President Zubak's powers, the Appeals Chamber considers that Prlić merely points to evidence of Zubak taking certain actions, without demonstrating that Zubak's powers "far exceeded"[3305] his own. The argument is therefore dismissed.

1027. Turning lastly to Prlić's argument that the Trial Chamber ignored evidence showing the differences in the functioning of the HZ H-B and the HVO HZ H-B executive, the HR H-B, and the HR H-B Government and municipalities during different periods of war in 1991-1994, the Appeals Chamber observes that this argument is based on a reference to vast portions of an expert report and fails to identify any specific challenged findings.[3306] Prlić has failed to demonstrate any error and his argument is dismissed.

b. Prlić's statutory powers and role within the HVO/Government of the HZ(R) H-B

i. Arguments of the Parties

1028. Prlić submits that the Trial Chamber erroneously concluded that as HVO HZ H-B President, he played a significant role within the HVO HZ H-B because he signed official documents, directed debates about adopting decisions, organised votes, and sometimes proposed revisions to "texts".[3307] He submits that the Trial Chamber based this conclusion on: (1) documentary evidence introduced **[page 434]** through a bar table motion;[3308] (2) a misinformed interpretation of the "Statutory Decision of 3 July 1993" *[sic]*;[3309] (3) Witness Davor Marijan's biased and discredited testimony; and (4) Witness Zoran Perković's accurate testimony.[3310] Prlić further argues that the HVO HZ H-B departments never submitted programs to the HVO HZ H-B, despite his requests.[3311] Prlić also claims that, in assessing his responsibilities, the Trial Chamber ignored changes in legislation after Boban relinquished his position to Prlić.[3312] Finally, he contends that the Trial Chamber ignored evidence when reaching conclusions on the decision-making process in the HVO HZ H-B and argues that he had a vote equal to others but no power to appoint anyone.[3313]

1029. The Prosecution responds that Prlić's interpretation of the Statutory Decision of 3 July 1992 is not supported by the evidence he cites.[3314] It argues that Prlić's assertion that HVO HZ H-B departments never submitted work programs' to the HVO HZ H-B does not undermine Prlić's statutory powers and is contradicted by evidence on one such program.[3315] The Prosecution also argues that Prlić fails to address evidence on which the Trial Chamber relied and which shows him exercising his statutory powers,[3316] and

---

[3303]   Trial Judgement, Vol. 1, para. 497, referring to, *inter alia*, Ex. P07876.

[3304]   See Prlić's Appeal Brief, para. 321 & fns 851, 853 and references cited therein.

[3305]   Prlić's Appeal Brief, para. 322. '

[3306]   See Prlić's Appeal Brief, para. 323 & fn. 859. The Appeals Chamber also notes that Prlić refers to his submissions in sub-grounds of appeal 1.2 and 1.4, which it dismisses elsewhere in the Judgement. See *supra*, paras 168-176.

[3307]   Prlić's Appeal Brief, para. 325; Appeal Hearing, AT. 137 (20 Mar 2017).

[3308]   Prlić's Appeal Brief, para. 325.

[3309]   Prlić's Appeal Brief, paras 325-326, referring to Prlić's Appeal Brief, sub-grounds of appeal 1.2.4 and 1.2.5. Prlić claims in this regard that the Trial Chamber "ignored evidence showing, *de facto*, that Article 9 [of the Statutory Decision of 3 July 1992] could not be implemented after Prlić replaced Boban on 14 August 1992, ignoring the Decree on the Organization and Responsibilities of Departments and Commissions of the HVOHZHB". He submits that Article 5 of this Decree required the HVO HZ H-B departments and commissions to execute policies and apply regulations and other acts of the HZ H-B Presidency, and thus department heads and commissions were directly responsible to the HZ H-B Presidency and not to the HVO HZ H-B President. Prlić's Appeal Brief, para. 326.

[3310]   Prlić's Appeal Brief, para. 325.

[3311]   Prlić's Appeal Brief, para. 327.

[3312]   Prlić's Appeal Brief, para. 328, referring to Prlić's Appeal Brief, paras 47-57 (sub-ground of appeal 1.2). Prlić further argues that the Trial Chamber mischaracterised his words regarding how the power of the HVO HZ H-B President was reduced by the changes in legislature after Boban ceased to be its President, leaving Prlić unable to make any decisions independently. Prlić's Appeal Brief, para. 337.

[3313]   Prlić's Appeal Brief, para. 336; Appeal Hearing, AT. 137, 234 (20 Mar 2017). Prlić further argues that he "signed all decisions even though in theory he could have been against them". Appeal Hearing, AT. 137 (20 Mar 2017).

[3314]   Prosecution's Response Brief (Prlić), para. 188. See Prosecution's Response Brief (Prlić), para. 187.

[3315]   Prosecution's Response Brief (Prlić), para. 188 & fn. 648.

[3316]   Prosecution's Response Brief (Prlić), para. 189.

furthermore relies on evidence that affirms the findings he challenges.[3317] Finally, it argues that Prlić fails to identify the alleged changes in legislation after Boban relinquished his position to Prlić or to explain how they impacted his authority.[3318]

ii. Analysis

1030. The Trial Chamber found that:

> [...] the President of the HVO played a more significant role within the Government of the HVO than the Prlić Defence suggests. In fact, under the Statutory Decision of 3 July 1992, the President of the HVO was in charge of and responsible for the activities of the HVO. The President signed the official HVO documents, such as decrees and decisions, including certain decisions to appoint. Article 9 of the said Decision also indicates that the President of the HVO was supposed to ensure **[page 435]** unity of political and administrative action within the HVO and to cooperate with the other organs of the HZ H-B. In legislative affairs, Jadranko Prlić, as President of the [...] HVO, directed debates during discussions over adopting a statute or a decree, organised votes and sometimes even proposed revisions to the texts.[3319]

1031. The Appeals Chamber considers that in arguing that the Trial Chamber relied on documentary evidence introduced through a bar table motion, Prlić fails to articulate an error.[3320] Further, the Appeals Chamber considers that in attempting to demonstrate that the Trial Chamber misinterpreted the Statutory Decision of 3 July 1992, Prlić advances arguments that are unsupported[3321] or disconnected from any specific impugned findings.[3322] The Appeals Chamber also observes that while Prlić impugns the credibility of Marijan alleging that he "could not grasp basic legal issues relevant to understanding the collective decision-making process of the HVOHZHB",[3323] the Trial Chamber relied on his testimony merely to find that the President of the HVO signed certain decisions to appoint,[3324] a fact that Prlić concedes.[3325] The Appeals Chamber finds that Prlić has failed to demonstrate that the Trial Chamber's assessment of Marijan's evidence was wholly erroneous.[3326] Finally, the Appeals Chamber observes that Perković's testimony, which Prlić submits was accurate, confirms in part the impugned finding.[3327] All these arguments are therefore dismissed.

1032. The Appeals Chamber further observes that Prlić's argument that the HVO HZ H-B departments never submitted programs to the HVO HZ H-B fails to articulate an error in the Trial Chamber's findings and dismisses it on this basis. The Appeals Chamber also notes that Prlić's claim that the Trial Chamber ignored changes in legislation after Boban relinquished his **[page 436]** position to Prlić is entirely based on a cross-reference to his sub-ground of appeal 1.2, which the Appeals Chamber dismisses elsewhere.[3328]

[3317] Prosecution's Response Brief (Prlić), para. 190; Appeal Hearing, AT. 195-196 (20 Mar 2017).

[3318] Prosecution's Response Brief (Prlić), para. 191.

[3319] Trial Judgement, Vol. 1, para. 536 (internal references omitted). See also Trial Judgement, Vol. 4, paras 88-90.

[3320] The Appeals Chamber notes in particular its standing jurisprudence that the admission of documents from the bar table is permissible. See, *e.g.*, *Prosecutor v. Sefer Halilović*, Case No. IT-01-48-AR73.2, Decision on Interlocutory Appeal Concerning Admission of Record of Interview of the Accused from the Bar Table, 19 August 2005, paras 16-17.

[3321] Specifically, the Appeals Chamber observes that Prlić fails to provide support for his claim that "Article 9 [of the Statutory Decision of 3 July 1992] could not be implemented after Prlić replaced Boban on 14 August 1992". Prlić's Appeal Brief, para. 326.

[3322] Specifically, the Appeals Chamber considers that Prlić's submission that department heads and commissions were directly responsible to the HZ H-B Presidency fails to demonstrate that the Trial Chamber reached any specific erroneous findings by ignoring the Decree on the Organisation and Responsibilities of Departments and Commissions of the HVO HZ H-B. See Prlić's Appeal Brief, para. 326. Prlić points to the findings that he signed official documents, directed debates about adopting decisions, organised votes, and sometimes proposed revisions to texts. See Prlić's Appeal Brief, para. 325, referring to, *inter alia*, Trial Judgement, Vol. 1, para. 536. The Appeals Chamber considers that Prlić's argument is not inconsistent with these challenged findings. The Appeals Chamber also notes that Prlić refers to his submissions in sub-grounds of appeal 1.2.4 and 1.2.5, which it dismisses elsewhere in the Judgement. See *supra*, paras 168-176.

[3323] See Prlić's Appeal Brief, para. 325 & fn. 862, referring to Davor Marijan, T. 35716-35728 (21 Jan 2009).

[3324] Trial Judgement, Vol. 1, para. 536 & fn. 1307, referring to Davor Marijan, T(F). 35717, 35721 (21 Jan 2009).

[3325] See Prlić's Appeal Brief, para. 336.

[3326] See *Popović et al.* Appeal Judgement, para. 131, referring to, *inter alia*, *Kupreškić et al.* Appeal Judgement, paras 30, 41, 130, 225.

[3327] See, in particular, Zoran Perković, T. 31726-31727 (2 Sept 2008).

[3328] See *supra*, paras 168-176. The Appeals Chamber further dismisses Prlić's argument that the Trial Chamber mischaracterised his words as it is not supported by his references to the trial record.

1033. Regarding Prlić's contention that the Trial Chamber ignored evidence when reaching conclusions on the decision-making process in the HVO HZ H-B, the Appeals Chamber observes that the evidence Prlić claims the Trial Chamber ignored, allegedly indicating that he had a vote equal to others but no power to appoint anyone, is not inconsistent with the Trial Chamber's findings on the HVO HZ H-B decision-making process to which he points.[3329] This argument is therefore dismissed.

c. Distinction between the HZ H-B and the HR H-B

i. Arguments of the Parties

1034. Prlić submits that the Trial Chamber erroneously assessed his *de jure* decision-making powers between August 1992 and April 1994 by not distinguishing between the HZ H-B and the HR H-B at all relevant times and in all relevant circumstances.[3330] Prlić argues that the Trial Chamber erroneously concluded that he presided over "cabinet" meetings of the HR H-B Government, which had the power to make urgent decisions on defence and security, relying exclusively on documentary evidence introduced through a bar table motion, whereas there is no evidence that "cabinet" meetings ever took place.[3331] Prlić further argues that the Trial Chamber erroneously concluded that at the recommendation of the President of the HR H-B Government, the Government appointed and removed heads and deputy heads of the "cabinet", relying exclusively on irrelevant documentary evidence introduced through a bar table motion.[3332] Finally, Prlić argues that the Trial Chamber, by relying on irrelevant evidence, erred in finding that Ćorić, as Chief of the Military Police Administration, attended HVO HZ H-B sessions, whereas there is no evidence that he ever did so.[3333]

1035. The Prosecution responds that Prlić's claim that the Trial Chamber erred in conflating his powers as President of the HVO HZ H-B and President of the Government of the HR H-B ignores the finding that the Law on the Government of the HR H-B granted Prlić similar powers in both **[page 437]** positions.[3334] As for Prlić's claim that the Trial Chamber erred with regard to "cabinet" meetings, the Prosecution argues that he fails to demonstrate that any such error would have any impact since the Government regularly met and discussed and decided matters of defence and security.[3335] The Prosecution further contends that Prlić's argument regarding the appointment and removal of heads and deputy heads of the "cabinet" has no impact on the verdict.[3336] Finally, the Prosecution argues that it is irrelevant whether Ćorić attended Government sessions as Chief of the Military Police Administration and that the Trial Chamber properly relied on minutes of Government meetings showing Ćorić in attendance.[3337]

ii. Analysis

1036. Regarding Prlić's argument that the Trial Chamber erroneously concluded that he presided over "cabinet" meetings of the HR H-B Government, the Appeals Chamber recalls the Trial Chamber's finding that "between August 1992 and April 1994, Jadranko Prlić organised and presided over many meetings of the HVO/Government of the HZ(R) H-B, which met at least once a week, as well as those of the 'cabinet' of the Government of the HR H-B, which had the authority to make urgent decisions on defence and security when the circumstances did not allow for a meeting of the government to be held".[3338] The Appeals Chamber

---

[3329]   See Prlić's Appeal Brief, fn. 883, referring to Trial Judgement, Vol. 1, para. 536, Vol. 4, paras 89-90. Similarly, Prlić's argument that he signed all decisions whether or not he agreed with them is not inconsistent with these findings.
[3330]   Prlić's Appeal Brief, para. 329.
[3331]   Prlić's Appeal Brief, para. 330, referring to, *inter alia*, Prlić's Appeal Brief, ground of appeal 3.
[3332]   Prlić's Appeal Brief, para. 331, referring to, *inter alia*, Prlić's Appeal Brief, ground of appeal 3. Prlić submits that the evidence "came into effect" during a period outside the Indictment period, was not relevant to the HR H-B, and/or concerned the appointments and dismissals of "head of offices" rather than the heads of the "cabinet". Prlić's Appeal Brief, para. 331.
[3333]   Prlić's Appeal Brief, para. 330.
[3334]   Prosecution's Response Brief (Prlić), para. 198.
[3335]   Prosecution's Response Brief (Prlić), para. 199.
[3336]   Prosecution's Response Brief (Prlić), para. 201.
[3337]   Prosecution's Response Brief (Prlić), para. 200.
[3338]   Trial Judgement, Vol. 4, para. 88 (internal references omitted). See also Trial Judgement, Vol. 1, para. 527.

notes that none of the evidence on which the Trial Chamber relied with regard to the "cabinet" supports that Prlić actually presided over such "cabinet" meetings,[3339] as the cabinet is defined by the Law on Government of the HR H-B: "Government shall have a close cabinet which shall be comprised of president, vice presidents and ministers of defence and internal affairs."[3340] The Appeals Chamber therefore finds that no reasonable trier of fact could have made this finding based on the evidence on which the Trial Chamber relied. As such, the Trial Chamber erred in fact. However, the Appeals Chamber notes that the Trial Chamber found that Prlić presided over many meetings of the HVO/Government of the HZ(R) H-B,[3341] and sees no indication that the Trial Chamber relied specifically on Prlić presiding over "cabinet" meetings to make any adverse findings against **[page 438]** him.[3342] Consequently, the Appeals Chamber finds that Prlić has not demonstrated that this error resulted in a miscarriage of justice, and consequently dismisses his argument.

1037. The Appeals Chamber turns to Prlić's argument that the Trial Chamber erroneously concluded that at the recommendation of the President of the Government, the Government appointed and removed the heads and deputy heads of the "cabinet", relying exclusively on irrelevant documentary evidence introduced through a bar table motion. In making this finding,[3343] the Trial Chamber relied on evidence that does not appear to concern the "cabinet".[3344] To this extent, it erred in fact. However, the Appeals Chamber sees no indication that the Trial Chamber relied specifically on this erroneous finding to make any adverse findings against Prlić.[3345] The Appeals Chamber therefore finds that this error did not result in a miscarriage of justice and dismisses his argument.

1038. Prlić's argument that the Trial Chamber relied on irrelevant evidence in finding that Ćorić, as Chief of the Military Police Administration, attended HVO HZ H-B sessions, appears to be based on a misreading of the Trial Judgement. The Trial Chamber relied on the evidence in question to find that Ćorić was the Chief of the Military Police Administration, not that he attended HVO HZ H-B sessions.[3346] Further, the Trial Chamber found that a number of persons, including Ćorić, attended meetings of "the HVO/Government of the HZ(R) H-B", *i.e.* either the HVO HZ H-B or the HR H-B Government, and referred in support to examples of evidence indicating Ćorić's presence at HR H-B Government meetings, but not at HVO HZ H-B meetings.[3347] In light of the broad scope of the finding, covering the meetings of both bodies, this does not amount to an error of fact. In any event, Prlić has not demonstrated any miscarriage of justice based on the alleged absence of evidence that Ćorić ever attended any HVO HZ H-B sessions. The Appeals Chamber therefore dismisses Prlić's argument.

1039. The Appeals Chamber dismisses above all arguments advanced by Prlić in support of his contention that the Trial Chamber erroneously assessed his *de jure* decision-making powers between August 1992 and April 1994 by not distinguishing between the HZ H-B and the HR H-B at all relevant times and in all relevant circumstances. In addition, the Appeals Chamber observes that Prlić has failed to explain why the Trial Chamber was required to make this distinction, considering **[page 439]** the Trial Chamber's finding, which Prlić ignores, that his powers as President of the HVO HZ H-B and as President of the Government of the HR H-B were similar.[3348] Thus, Prlić's contention is dismissed.

d. Government discussions

1040. Prlić submits that the Trial Chamber erroneously concluded that from August 1992 to April 1994 the "HVO/Government of the HZ(R)H-B" discussed: (1) measures to ensure the observance of the code of war,

---

[3339] See Trial Judgement, Vol. 4, para. 88 & fn. 236, referring to Exs. P05517, p. 2, P06667, P07279, P07310, P08092. See also Prosecution's Response Brief (Prlić), para. 199.
[3340] Ex. P05517, p. 2 (Article 9).
[3341] Trial Judgement, Vol. 4, para. 88.
[3342] See, in particular, Trial Judgement, Vol. 4, para. 90.
[3343] Trial Judgement, Vol. 1, para. 537.
[3344] See Trial Judgement, Vol. 1, fn. 1312, referring to Exs. 1D01402, Art. 27, p. 10, P06817, P07461. The Appeals Chamber considers that, although Exhibit 1D01402 appears on its face to have entered into force in June 1994, Prlić fails to demonstrate that the evidence was not relevant to the HR H-B or "came into effect" during a period outside the Indictment period. See Ex. 1D01402, pp. 2, 16.
[3345] See, in particular, Trial Judgement, Vol. 1, paras 536-537, Vol. 4, paras 89-90. ,
[3346] Compare Prlić's Appeal Brief, para. 330 & fn. 875, with Trial Judgement, Vol. 4, para. 88 & fn. 242.
[3347] See Trial Judgement, Vol. 4, para. 88 & fn. 241, referring to, *e.g.*, Exs. P06667, P07082, P07514.
[3348] Trial Judgement, Vol. 537. See Trial Judgement, Vol. 1, para. 536.

as it relied on unsupportive evidence;[3349] (2) the budget of the "HZ(R)HB", as it relied on unsupportive evidence and ignored other relevant evidence;[3350] and (3) the location, detention conditions, and exchange of "prisoners of war" with the ABiH, as it wrongly assessed the evidence.[3351]

1041. The Prosecution responds that Prlić fails to demonstrate any error in the Trial Chamber's findings that the Government discussed the above topics.[3352]

1042. As a preliminary matter, the Appeals Chamber understands that the Trial Chamber's expression "HVO/Government of the HZ(R) H-B" covers all forms of the Government between August 1992 and April 1994.[3353] Regarding Prlić's challenge to the Trial Chamber's finding that during this time period the Government discussed measures to ensure the observance of the "codes of war",[3354] the Appeals Chamber considers that Prlić has failed to establish that no reasonable trier of fact could have made this finding based on the evidence on which the Trial Chamber relied, **[page 440]** which included an exhibit containing information about Prlić, President of the Government, discussing measures to ensure the observance of the "Codes of War" in November 1993.[3355] The Appeals Chamber further observes that the Trial Chamber's finding that the budget of the HZ(R) H-B was discussed at Government meetings between August 1992 and April 1994, is supported by the evidence the Trial Chamber relied on, such as minutes of meetings held in October 1992, January 1993, and March 1994.[3356] The Appeals Chamber finds that Prlić has failed to demonstrate any error in this regard.[3357] Finally, the Trial Chamber's finding that the location, detention conditions, and exchange of "prisoners of war" with the ABiH were discussed, is supported by evidence,[3358] which Prlić fails to challenge in any convincing manner.[3359] All these submissions are therefore dismissed.

[3349] Prlić's Appeal Brief, para. 332. Specifically, Prlić argues that the Trial Chamber relied on Witness Philip Roger Watkins's testimony and report (Exhibit P06687 (confidential)), which cannot be used to assess Prlić's responsibilities as HVO HZ H-B President, as the HVO HZ H-B did not exist at the time of the report. He also argues that the report contains nothing about the HR H-B Government discussing measures to be taken for ensuring the observance of the code of war. Prlić's Appeal Brief, para. 332.

[3350] Prlić's Appeal Brief, para. 333, referring to, *inter alia*, Prlić's Appeal Brief, ground of appeal 3. See also Prlić's Reply Brief, para. 58. Specifically, Prlić argues that the Trial Chamber erroneously relied on Exhibit 2D01262, which concerned the HZ H-B Presidency rather than the HVO HZ H-B, and Exhibit P01097, which was admitted into evidence through the bar table. He further argues that the Trial Chamber ignored Witness Neven Tomić's testimony that: (1) on 28 August 1993 the HZ H-B Presidency ceded its competency over the budget to the House of Representatives of the HR H-B; (2) the HZ H-B budget was never enacted; and (3) the first law on the budget was proposed and enacted in 1994 by the House of Representatives of the HR H-B. Finally, Prlić submits that Exhibit P08092, admitted into evidence through the bar table, concerns the HR H-B and therefore does not show that the HVO HZ H-B had a budget. Prlić's Appeal Brief, para. 333; Prlić's Reply Brief, para. 58.

[3351] Prlić's Appeal Brief, para. 334. See Prlić's Appeal Brief, para. 335, referring to Prlić's Appeal Brief, ground of appeal 13. Specifically, Prlić argues that the HVO HZ H-B never discussed the exchange of prisoners of war. In support, he submits that: (1) Exhibit P01439 concerns a proposal of the Exchange Commission to exchange 30 civilians from Glamoč (controlled by Serb forces) and Livno (controlled by HVO forces); (2) Exhibit P02679 concerns military prisons, which were not for detaining prisoners of war; and (3) Exhibit P03560 concerns an emergency situation when the issue of accommodation of prisoners of war was discussed based on a request of the municipal HVO Čapljina. Prlić's Appeal Brief, para. 334.

[3352] Prosecution's Response Brief (Prlić), paras 202-204. See also Prosecution's Response Brief (Prlić), para. 205.

[3353] See Trial Judgement, Vol. 4, para. 88. See also *supra*, para. 1015.

[3354] Prlić's Appeal Brief, para. 332, referring to Trial Judgement, Vol. 4, para. 88.

[3355] Trial Judgement, Vol. 4, para. 88 & fn. 249, referring to Ex. P06687 (confidential), p. 2; Philip Roger Watkins, T(F). 18798-18799 (21 May 2007). Since the Trial Chamber's finding covers all incarnations of the Government between August 1992 and April 1994, the Appeals Chamber considers that Prlić's assertion that the HVO HZ H-B did not exist at the time of confidential Exhibit P06687 shows no error.

[3356] Trial Judgement, Vol. 4, para. 88 & fn. 250, referring to, *e.g.*, Exs. 2D01262 (minutes of a HZ H-B Presidency meeting of 17 October 1992), P01097 (minutes of an HVO HZ H-B working meeting on 11 January 1993), p. 3, P08092 (minutes of an HR H-B Government meeting on 19 March 1994). Regarding Exhibits P01097 and P08092, the Appeals Chamber recalls that the Trial Chamber's finding covered all incarnations of the Government between August 1992 and April 1994, and considers that Prlić has failed to articulate an error in alleging that the Trial Chamber relied on evidence admitted from the bar table. Regarding Exhibit 2D01262, the Appeals Chamber considers that while it is the minutes of an HZ H-B Presidency meeting rather than a Government meeting, several members of the Government were present at that meeting, and in any event the Trial Chamber's finding remains supported by Exhibits P01097 and P08092. Finally, the Appeals Chamber considers that Tomić's testimony, as Prlić's represents it, is not inconsistent with the finding that the Government discussed the budget, regardless of who had competency over it and when the first budget was actually enacted.

[3357] The Appeals Chamber also notes that Prlić refers to his submissions in ground of appeal 3, which it dismisses elsewhere in the Judgement. See *supra*, paras 177-183.

[3358] Trial Judgement, Vol. 4, para. 88 & fn. 252, referring to, *e.g.*, Exs. P01439, P02679, P03560, item 7, P04841, conclusion 1.

[3359] Prlić misunderstands on which part of Exhibit P01439 the Trial Chamber relied. See Ex. P01439, p. 5, third dash ("The meeting [of the "International Red Cross"] will be held on 11 and 12 February 1993 in Geneva and it will pertain to the exchange of

e. Conclusion

1043. For the foregoing reasons, the Appeals Chamber dismisses Prlić's sub-ground of appeal 11.1.
[page 441]

(ii) Expansion of Government powers (Prlić's Sub-ground 11.2)

1044. The Trial Chamber found that despite being subordinated to the Presidency of the HZ H-B, the HVO HZ H-B gradually arrogated to itself all executive, administrative, and some legislative power, without effective oversight by the Presidency of the HZ H-B.[3360]

1045. Prlić submits that the Trial Chamber erred in concluding that the HVO HZ H-B progressively appropriated all executive and administrative powers including legislative functions because the Presidency of the HZ H-B met infrequently and lacked oversight.[3361] Prlić argues that the Trial Chamber mischaracterised Witnesses Neven Tomić's and Zoran Buntić's testimonies.[3362] Prlić further points to evidence allegedly contrary to the Trial Chamber's finding.[3363]

1046. The Prosecution responds that the Trial Chamber's finding was based on evidence about events happening at the time and that Prlić – relying primarily on evidence regarding the *de jure* relationship between the Presidency of the HZ H-B and the HVO HZ H-B – fails to show that it was unreasonable.[3364]

1047. The Appeals Chamber observes that the impugned finding is based in part on the testimonies of Tomić and Buntić.[3365] Having examined these in relevant parts,[3366] the Appeals Chamber finds no indication that the Trial Chamber mischaracterised them, and observes that the witnesses testified about the transfer of powers from the Presidency of the HZ H-B to the HVO HZ H-B, which exercised considerable powers. The Appeals Chamber further observes that the allegedly contrary evidence indicates, notably, that the HVO HZ H-B exercised substantial *de facto* powers as the Presidency of the HZ H-B ceased to convene.[3367] As such, Prlić fails to **[page 442]** demonstrate that no reasonable trier of fact could have made the impugned finding.[3368] Consequently, the Appeals Chamber dismisses Prlić's sub-ground of appeal 11.2.

---

prisoners."). *Cf.* Prlić's Appeal Brief, para. 334, referring to Ex. P01439, p. 5, second dash ("The proposal submitted by the Commission for the exchange of prisoners on the exchange of 30 civilians from Glamoč and Livno is accepted."). See also Prosecution's Response Brief (Prlić), para. 204. With regard to Exhibit P02679, Prlić fails to provide any support for his assertion that military prisons were not for detaining prisoners of war. See Prlić's Appeal Brief, para. 334. Prlić's submission regarding Exhibit P03560 – that it concerns an emergency situation when the issue of accommodation of prisoners of war was discussed based on a request of the municipal HVO Čapljina – fails to articulate any error. Finally, Prlić does not challenge Exhibit P04841, which provides further support for the Trial Chamber's finding. See Trial Judgement, Vol. 4, para. 88 & fn. 252. The Appeals Chamber also notes that Prlić refers to his submissions in ground of appeal 13, which it dismisses elsewhere in the Judgement. See *infra*, paras 1318-1333, 1335-1343, 1356-1373.
[3360]   Trial Judgement, Vol. 1, para. 522, referring to, *inter alia*, Trial Judgement, Vol. 1, para. 511.
[3361]   Prlić's Appeal Brief, para. 338.
[3362]   Prlić's Appeal Brief, paras 338-339, referring to Prlić's Appeal Brief, para. 54 (sub-ground of appeal 1.2).
[3363]   Prlić's Appeal Brief, paras 338, 340. Prlić claims that expert Witness Ciril Ribičić "acknowledged that the HVOHZHB adopted decrees on an interim basis in emergency situations and exceptional circumstances to be confirmed by the HZHB Presidency; a common practice permitting the HZHB Presidency (the Presidents of municipal HVOs) to retain power." Prlić's Appeal Brief, para. 338. He further claims: "Articles 38-43 of the Rules of Procedures of the HZHB Presidency (P00596) show that the HZHB Presidency was superior to the HVOHZHB. As the supreme administrative body, the HZHB Presidency was kept fully informed. The changes to Article 18 of the Statutory Decision enabled the HVOHZHB to pass pressing decrees for immediate enactment until determined otherwise by the HZHB Presidency. The HVOHZHB urged the HZHB Presidency to meet. Similar measures in emergency situations were prescribed in the BiH legal system (All People's Defence system)." Prlić's Appeal Brief, para. 340 (internal references omitted).
[3364]   Prosecution's Response Brief (Prlić), paras 206-207.
[3365]   See Trial Judgement, Vol. 1, para. 511 & fn. 1246, para. 522 & fn. 1274, referring to, *inter alia*, Zoran Buntić, T(F). 30761-30762 (15 July 2008), 30889-30890 (17 July 2008), Neven Tomić, T(F). 34145-34146 (3 Nov 2008).
[3366]   Zoran Buntić, T(F). 30761-30762 (15 July 2008), 30889-30890 (17 July 2008), Neven Tomić, T(F). 34145-34146 (3 Nov 2008).
[3367]   See Prlić's Appeal Brief, paras 338, 340 and references cited therein.
[3368]   The Appeals Chamber also notes that Prlić refers to his submissions in sub-ground of appeal 1.2, which it dismisses elsewhere in the Judgement. See *supra*, paras 168-176.

(iii) Department/Ministry of Defence (Prlić's Sub-ground 11.3)

1048. The Trial Chamber found that Prlić was involved in the supervision and activities of the Department/ Ministry of Defence of the HZ(R) H-B.[3369]

a. Arguments of the Parties

1049. Prlić challenges this finding, submitting that the Trial Chamber ignored contrary evidence.[3370] Prlić argues in particular that the HZ H-B Presidency established the Defence Department, which enjoyed a certain independence,[3371] and that neither the HVO HZ H-B nor he could issue orders to the Head of the Defence Department.[3372] Prlić further submits that the Trial Chamber erroneously concluded, on the basis of insufficient evidence, that he participated in setting up the military and defence program and structures of the HZ(R) H-B.[3373] He also submits that the Trial Chamber wrongly concluded on the evidence that he approved the methodology for adopting defence plans and participated in the adoption of the decision on the control of HZ(R) H-B airspace.[3374] In addition, Prlić submits that the Trial Chamber, by ignoring relevant evidence, erroneously concluded that Stojić regularly reported to "his President" on defence matters including the military situation on the ground.[3375] Prlić contends that the Trial Chamber erroneously concluded that the "HVO agreed" that he would organise a special working meeting with the collegiums of the Departments of Defence and the Interior, by misinterpreting evidence and ignoring evidence to the contrary.[3376] Prlić also submits that the Trial Chamber erroneously concluded, by mischaracterising evidence, that he appointed Biškić as a Deputy Defence Minister.[3377] Moreover, Prlić contends that the Trial Chamber "erred regarding Jukić's appointment".[3378] Finally, he contends that the Trial Chamber erred by ignoring evidence showing the differences between the HVO HZ H-B and the HR H-B Government.[3379] **[page 443]**

1050. The Prosecution responds that clear evidence supports the Trial Chamber's finding that Prlić participated in the supervision and activities of the Department/Ministry of Defence, and that Prlić fails to demonstrate any errors in the impugned findings.[3380]

b. Analysis

1051. With regard to Prlić's submission that the Trial Chamber ignored evidence contrary to the finding that he was involved in the supervision and activities of the Department/Ministry of Defence of the HZ(R) H-B, the Appeals Chamber considers that neither of his assertions in this regard – that the HZ H-B Presidency established the Department of Defence, which enjoyed a certain independence, and that the HVO HZ H-B and he could not issue orders to the Head of the Defence Department – are inconsistent with the impugned finding. To the extent that Prlić argues that the Department/Ministry of Defence was so independent that there was no room for him to be involved in its supervision and activities, the Appeals Chamber considers that his claims are not borne out by the evidence on which he relies.[3381] For these reasons, Prlić's submission is dismissed.

[3369]   Trial Judgement, Vol. 4, para. 92. See Trial Judgement, Vol. 4, para. 91.
[3370]   Prlić's Appeal Brief, paras 341-343; Appeal Hearing, AT. 137 (20 Mar 2017). See Prlić's Appeal Brief, para. 344, referring to Prlić's Appeal Brief, para. 52 (sub-ground of appeal 1.2), (sub-)grounds of appeal 1.2.4, 1.2.5, 12.
[3371]   Prlić's Appeal Brief, para. 343; Appeal Hearing, AT. 137-138 (20 Mar 2017).
[3372]   Prlić's Appeal Brief, para. 342.
[3373]   Prlić's Appeal Brief, para. 345, referring to, *inter alia*, Prlić's Appeal Brief, ground of appeal 3.
[3374]   Prlić's Appeal Brief, para. 346, referring to, *inter alia*, Prlić's Appeal Brief, grounds of appeal 3, 12.
[3375]   Prlić's Appeal Brief, para. 347, referring to, *inter alia*, Prlić's Appeal Brief, ground of appeal 3.
[3376]   Prlić's Appeal Brief, para. 348.
[3377]   Prlić's Appeal Brief, para. 349, referring to, *inter alia*, Prlić's Appeal Brief, sub-ground of appeal 11.1.
[3378]   Prlić's Appeal Brief, para. 350.
[3379]   Prlić's Appeal Brief, para. 351, referring to, *inter alia*, Prlić's Appeal Brief, para. 51 (sub-ground of appeal 1.2).
[3380]   Prosecution's Response Brief (Prlić), paras 208-215. See Appeal Hearing, AT. 208-209 (20 Mar 2017).
[3381]   See Appeal Hearing, AT. 137 (20 Mar 2017), referring to Exs. P00303, Arts 2-22, 1D00001, Arts 2-7, P00434 (not admitted into evidence), 1D00010, 1D00171, 1D00173, 1D00174; Prlić's Appeal Brief, para. 343 & fns 903, 907 and references cited therein (testimony of Witnesses Neven Tomić, Slobodan Božić, and "I", as well as Ex. P00588, Art. 170). The Appeals Chamber notes that, for example, Exhibits 1D00010 and 1D00171, decisions on the appointment of heads of the Department of Education, Culture, and Sport and the Department of Economic Affairs, do not show that the Department/Ministry of Defence was so independent that there

1052. Regarding Prlić's challenge to the Trial Chamber's finding that "Prlić participated in particular in setting up the military and defence programme and structures of the HZ(R) H-B",[3382] the Appeals Chamber finds that a reasonable trier of fact could have made this finding based on the evidence on which the Trial Chamber relied.[3383] The Appeals Chamber notes in this regard that Exhibit P00518 sets out that "The Service Regulations of the Armed Forces and the Decision on the Basic Organisation of the Defence Department have been drafted and will be signed by the President of the HZ H-B", and that Exhibit P00988, a 1993 "Decision on the Internal Organisation of Defence Offices and Administrations within the Croatian Community of Herceg-Bosna", bears Prlić's name.[3384] Prlić has failed to demonstrate an error.[3385] His challenge is dismissed.

1053. The Appeals Chamber turns to Prlić's challenge to the Trial Chamber's findings that he "approved the methodology for adopting defence plans" and "participated in the adoption of the **[page 444]** decision on the control of HZ(R) H-B airspace".[3386] In making these findings, the Trial Chamber relied on minutes of Government meetings, where Prlić was present and in which the participants unanimously adopted a decision on the methodology for making defence plans[3387] and a decision to control the airspace of the HR H-B.[3388] The Appeals Chamber considers that Prlić has failed to show any error in the Trial Chamber's findings.[3389] His challenge is dismissed.

1054. With respect to Prlić's challenge to the Trial Chamber's finding that "Stojić regularly reported to his President on defence matters, including the military situation on the ground",[3390] the Appeals Chamber observes that this finding was based on minutes of Government meetings, over which Prlić presided and at which Stojić reported on such matters.[3391] Prlić contends that the Trial Chamber ignored relevant evidence, namely the minutes of another Government meeting which state: "[i]t was recommended that in the future the Department of Defence should issue timely reports about the situation at the front line to the public and to the members of leading bodies of the HVO of the HZHB".[3392] The Appeals Chamber considers that this evidence is not inconsistent with the challenged finding, and consequently dismisses Prlić's argument.[3393]

1055. The Appeals Chamber understands that Prlić challenges the Trial Chamber's finding that "on 29 July 1993, because of the overall military situation in the territory of the HZ H-B, especially in the Mostar area, the HVO [HZ H-B] agreed that Jadranko Prlić would organise special working meetings with the collegiums of the departments of defence and the interior".[3394] The Appeals Chamber observes that this narrowly tailored finding is based on verbatim support in the minutes of the HVO HZ H-B meeting held on 29 July 1993,[3395] and considers that it is unclear how any of Prlić's factual assertions could undermine the finding.[3396] His challenge in this regard is therefore dismissed.

---

was no room for Prlić to be involved in its supervision and activities. The Appeals Chamber also notes that Prlić refers to his submissions in (sub-)grounds of appeal 1.2, 1.2.4, 1.2.5, and 12, which it dismisses elsewhere in the Judgement. See *infra*, paras 168-176, 1098-1127.

[3382]   Trial Judgement, Vol. 4, para. 91.
[3383]   Trial Judgement, Vol. 4, fns 262-263, referring to Exs. P00518, p. 3, P00988. See also *supra*, paras 1044-1047.
[3384]   Exhibits P00518, p. 3, P00988.
[3385]   The Appeals Chamber also notes that Prlić refers to his submissions in ground of appeal 3, which it dismisses elsewhere in the Judgement. See *supra*, paras 177-183.
[3386]   Trial Judgement, Vol. 4, para. 91.
[3387]   Ex. P00767, pp. 1, 3-4; Trial Judgement, Vol. 4, para. 91 & fn. 264.
[3388]   Ex. P07310, pp. 1, 7; Trial Judgement, Vol. 4, para. 91 & fn. 265.
[3389]   The Appeals Chamber also notes that Prlić refers to his submissions in grounds of appeal 3 and 12, which it dismisses elsewhere in the Judgement. See *infra*, paras 177-183, 1098-1127.
[3390]   Trial Judgement, Vol. 4, para. 91.
[3391]   Trial Judgement, Vol. 4, para. 91 & fn. 267, referring in particular to Exs. P01324, pp. 2-3, 1D02179.
[3392]   Prlić's Appeal Brief, para. 347, referring to, *inter alia*, Ex. P03796, p. 5.
[3393]   Prlić's Appeals Chamber also notes that Prlić refers to his submissions in ground of appeal 3, which it dismisses elsewhere in the Judgement. See *supra*, paras 177-183.
[3394]   Trial Judgement, Vol. 4, para. 91.
[3395]   Trial Judgement, Vol. 4, para. 91, referring to Ex. P03796, p. 5.
[3396]   See Prlić's Appeal Brief, para. 348. In particular, Prlić's assertion that he "could not independently organize working meetings with the department, but only with the approval of the collective body/HVOHZHB" is not inconsistent with the challenged finding. Prlić's Appeal Brief, para. 348.

1056. Next, Prlić challenges the Trial Chamber's finding that Prlić "made some appointments, for example, Marijan Biškić who on 1 December 1993 was appointed Deputy Minister responsible for **[page 445]** security in the Ministry of Defence of the HR H-B",[3397] with reference to evidence that indicates that the appointment was a collective decision.[3398] Nevertheless, considering that the Trial Chamber relied on evidence showing Prlić's involvement in the appointment of Biškić,[3399] as the President of the Government of HR H-B who signed the decision of appointment,[3400] the Appeals Chamber finds that Prlić has failed to show that no reasonable trial chamber could have made the impugned finding. His challenge is therefore dismissed.[3401]

1057. Regarding Prlić's contention that the Trial Chamber "erred regarding Jukić's appointment", the Appeals Chamber notes that he does not explain how the Trial Chamber erred. Since he fails to articulate an error, his argument is dismissed. Finally, concerning Prlić's contention that the Trial Chamber erred by ignoring evidence showing the differences between the HVO HZ H-B and the HR H-B Government, the Appeals Chamber is unable to discern which findings he challenges. Consequently, it dismisses his argument on the basis that he has failed to identify the challenged findings.[3402]

1058. For the foregoing reasons, the Appeals Chamber dismisses Prlić's sub-ground of appeal 11.3.

(iv) Department/Ministry of the Interior (Prlić's Sub-ground 11.4)

1059. The Trial Chamber found that Prlić was involved in the supervision and activities of the Department/Ministry of the Interior of the HZ(R) H-B.[3403] **[page 446]**

a. Arguments of the Parties

1060. Prlić challenges this finding,[3404] arguing that the Trial Chamber erroneously relied on evidence that he signed appointments to conclude that he had power over the other members of the HVO HZ H-B, while ignoring evidence that he only signed collectively adopted decisions.[3405]

1061. Prlić contends that the fact that he presided over meetings of the HVO/Government of the HZ(R) H-B, during which decisions about the Ministry of the Interior and its activities were adopted, does not prove that he was involved in the supervision and activities of the Ministry of the Interior.[3406] He argues in this regard that the Trial Chamber relied on exhibits admitted through a bar table motion that: (1) do not concern the Indictment period; (2) do not mention his presence at meetings; (3) do not mention decisions about the Ministry of the Interior; or – in one case – (4) concern a decision the implementation of which is not supported by any evidence.[3407]

1062. Prlić also submits that the Trial Chamber erroneously concluded that: (1) the HVO HZ H-B agreed that he would organise special working meetings with the collegiums of the Departments of Defence and the Interior;[3408] and (2) he, rather than Boban, proposed to Tuđman that Ćorić be appointed Minister of the Interior of the HR H-B.[3409]

[3397] Trial Judgement, Vol. 4, para. 91.

[3398] See Prlić's Appeal Brief, para. 349 & fn. 919 and references cited therein.

[3399] Trial Judgement, Vol. 4, para. 91, referring to, *inter alia*, Trial Judgement, Vol. 1, para. 608, referring to, *inter alia*, Ex. P06994, Marijan Biškić, T(F). 15039, 15048-15049 (5 Mar 2007). *Cf.* Trial Judgement, Vol. 4, para. 92.

[3400] Trial Judgement, Vol. 4, para. 92; Ex. P06994.

[3401] The Appeals Chamber also notes that Prlić refers to his submissions in sub-ground of appeal 11.1, which the Appeals Chamber dismisses above. See *supra*, paras 1022-1043.

[3402] In addition, the Appeals Chamber notes that Prlić's challenge is entirely based on a cross-reference to his sub-ground of appeal 1.2, which it dismisses elsewhere in the Judgement. See *supra*, paras 168-176.

[3403] Trial Judgement, Vol. 4, para. 94. See Trial Judgement, Vol. 4, para. 93.

[3404] Prlić's Appeal Brief, para. 352; Appeal Hearing, AT. 137 (20 Mar 2017).

[3405] Prlić's Appeal Brief, para. 353. See Prlić's Appeal Brief, para. 354, referring to Prlić's Appeal Brief, para. 52 (sub-ground of appeal 1.2), sub-grounds of appeal 1.2.4 and 1.2.5, para. 350 (sub-ground of appeal 11.3); Appeal Hearing, AT. 137 (20 Mar 2017).

[3406] Prlić's Appeal Brief, para. 356.

[3407] Prlić's Appeal Brief, para. 356, referring to, *inter alia*, Prlić's Appeal Brief, ground of appeal 3.

[3408] Prlić's Appeal Brief, para. 355, referring to, *inter alia*, Prlić's Appeal Brief, sub-ground of appeal 11.3.

[3409] Prlić's Appeal Brief, para. 357. Specifically, Prlić argues that the Trial Chamber erred in relying on Exhibit P06581 in finding that he proposed to Tuđman that Ćorić be appointed Minister of the Interior of the HR H-B. Prlić's Appeal Brief, para. 357.

1063. Finally, Prlić submits that, in assessing the "supervision" over the Department/Ministry of the Interior, the Trial Chamber ignored evidence that the Departments/Ministries of Defence and the Interior independently decided about the engagement of police forces.[3410] By contrast, Prlić argues, there is no evidence that he issued orders to the Department of the Interior.[3411]

1064. The Prosecution responds that Prlić's assertion that the Government's collective decision-making process absolves him of responsibility for its powers and decisions is unfounded.[3412] It argues that Prlić fails to explain how no reasonable trial chamber could have found, based on explicit evidence, that he would organise special meetings with the collegiums of the Departments of Defence and the Interior.[3413] With regard to Prlić presiding over Government **[page 447]** meetings during which decisions about the Ministry of the Interior and its activities were adopted, the Prosecution submits that he repeatedly misrepresents the evidence supporting the Trial Chamber's findings, while ignoring other evidence that supports them.[3414] It also argues that Prlić fails to demonstrate that the Trial Chamber unreasonably concluded, despite clear evidence in support, that he proposed the appointment of Ćorić as Minister of the Interior.[3415] Finally, the Prosecution argues that the evidence of the Interior and/or Defence Department and/or military authorities issuing orders relating to deployment of police forces does not undermine the Trial Chamber's finding on Prlić's supervisory role.[3416]

b. Analysis

1065. In arguing that the Trial Chamber erroneously relied on evidence – specifically Exhibits P03791 and 1D00190[3417] – that he signed appointments to conclude that he had power over the other members of the HVO HZ H-B, Prlić misrepresents the Trial Chamber's findings.[3418] The Trial Chamber did not conclude on the basis of this evidence that he had power over the other members of the HVO HZ H-B, but rather concluded, based on this and other evidence,[3419] that he "was involved in the supervision and activities of the Department/Ministry of the Interior of the HZ(R) H-B".[3420] Prlić has failed to demonstrate how the Trial Chamber erred in relying on the evidence he cites in reaching this conclusion and his argument is therefore dismissed.[3421]

1066. As for Prlić's argument that the fact that he presided over Government meetings during which decisions about the Ministry of the Interior and its activities were adopted, does not prove that he was involved in the supervision and activities of the Ministry of the Interior, the Appeals Chamber first notes that this was only one consideration – among many others – supporting the impugned finding.[3422] Further, the Appeals Chamber considers that a reasonable trier of fact could have found the fact that Prlić presided over Government meetings, during which **[page 448]** decisions about the Ministry of the Interior and its activities were adopted, to be an indicator of his involvement in the supervision and activities of the Ministry of the interior. With regard to Prlić's challenge to the Trial Chamber's reliance on exhibits admitted through a bar

---

[3410] Prlić's Appeal Brief, paras 358-359; Appeal Hearing, AT. 137 (20 Mar 2017).
[3411] Prlić's Appeal Brief, para. 359.
[3412] Prosecution's Response Brief (Prlić), para. 216.
[3413] Prosecution's Response Brief (Prlić), para. 217.
[3414] Prosecution's Response Brief (Prlić), para. 218, referring to, *inter alia*, Prlić's Appeal Brief, para. 356.
[3415] Prosecution's Response Brief (Prlić), para. 221.
[3416] Prosecution's Response Brief (Prlić), para. 219. The Prosecution adds that, in any event, Prlić and the Government could, and did, make decisions directly impacting the deployment of police forces. Prosecution's Response Brief (Prlić), para. 219. See also Prosecution's Response Brief (Prlić), para. 220.
[3417] See Prlić's Appeal Brief, para. 353, referring to, *inter alia*, Exs. P03791, 1D00190 (decisions relating to the Department of the Interior, bearing Prlić's name and published in the official gazette of the HZ H-B).
[3418] See Prlić's Appeal Brief, paras 352 (referring to Trial Judgement, Vol. 4, paras 93-94), 353 (which appears to relate to the first two sentences in Trial Judgement, Vol. 4, para. 93).
[3419] See Trial Judgement, Vol. 4, para. 93 and references cited therein.
[3420] Trial Judgement, Vol. 4, para. 94, To the extent that Prlić argues that the Department/Ministry of the Interior was so independent that there was no room for him to be involved in its supervision and activities, the Appeals Chamber considers that his claims are not borne out by the evidence on which he relies. See Appeal Hearing, AT. 137 (20 Mar 2017), referring to Exs. P00303, Arts 2-22, 1D00001, Arts 2-7, P00434 (not admitted into evidence), 1D00010, 1D00171, 1D00173, 1D00174. See also *supra*, para. 1051 & fn. 3381.
[3421] The Appeals Chamber also notes that Prlić refers to his submissions in sub-grounds of appeal 1.2, 1.2.4, 1.2.5, and 11.3, which it dismisses elsewhere in the Judgement. See *supra*, paras 168-176, 1048-1058.
[3422] See Trial Judgement, Vol. 4, paras 93-94.

table motion, the Appeals Chamber finds that he repeatedly misrepresents the evidence on which the Trial Chamber based its finding.[3423] This evidence includes minutes of Government meetings, dated within the Indictment period, which indicate that Prlić was present and that decisions about the Ministry of the Interior were made.[3424] The existence of evidence as to whether one of the adopted decisions was implemented or not has no impact on the impugned finding, which does not deal with the question of implementation. Consequently, the Appeals Chamber dismisses Prlić's argument.[3425]

1067. Regarding Prlić's challenge to the Trial Chamber's finding that the HVO HZ H-B agreed that he would organise special working meetings with the collegiums of the Departments of Defence and the Interior,[3426] the Appeals Chamber recalls that it has previously dismissed a challenge to a similar finding supported by the same evidence.[3427] Prlić does not add any discernible argument under the present sub-ground of appeal, and his challenge is consequently dismissed.

1068. With regard to Prlić's submission that the Trial Chamber erroneously concluded that he, rather than Boban, proposed to Tuđman that Ćorić be appointed Minister of the Interior of the HR H-B, the Appeals Chamber notes that he ignores evidence on which the Trial Chamber based its finding, which explicitly supports this finding.[3428] His argument is therefore dismissed.

1069. Finally, with respect to Prlić's submission that the Trial Chamber ignored evidence that the Departments/Ministries of Defence and the Interior independently decided about the engagement of police forces, the Appeals Chamber observes that this alleged fact is not inconsistent with the impugned finding.[3429] Therefore, the Appeals Chamber dismisses the argument.

1070. For the foregoing reasons, the Appeals Chamber dismisses Prlić's sub-ground of appeal 11.4. **[page 449]**

(v) Department/Ministry of Justice and General Administration (Prlić's Sub-ground 11.5)

1071. The Trial Chamber found that Prlić was involved in the supervision and activities of the Department/ Ministry of Justice and General Administration of the HZ(R) H-B.[3430]

1072. Prlić challenges this finding, submitting that it was based on the fact that he presided over HVO/ Government of the HZ(R) H-B meetings and signed some appointments.[3431] He argues in this regard that presiding over these meetings did not give him the power to supervise those bodies,[3432] and that the Trial Chamber ignored evidence that the HVO HZ H-B was responsible for judicial appointments.[3433]

1073. The Prosecution responds that Prlić cites no evidence to support his claim that his presiding role gave him no power of supervision.[3434] The Prosecution also argues that the Trial Chamber did rely on the allegedly ignored evidence, which furthermore supports the impugned finding.[3435]

[3423] See Trial Judgement, Vol. 4, para. 93 & fns 271-272 and references cited therein. *Cf.* Prlić's Appeal Brief, para. 356.

[3424] Exs. P01403, pp. 1, 3-4; P06667, pp. 1, 4; P07354, pp. 1-3.

[3425] The Appeals Chamber also notes that Prlić refers to his submissions in ground of appeal 3, which it dismisses elsewhere in the Judgement. See *supra*, paras 177-183.

[3426] Trial Judgement, Vol. 4, para. 93.

[3427] See *supra*, para. 1055. See also Prlić's Appeal Brief, para. 355, referring to, *inter alia*, Prlić's Appeal Brief, para. 348 (sub-ground of appeal 11.3).

[3428] Trial Judgement, Vol. 4, para. 93 & fn. 274, referring to, *inter alia*, Ex. P06583 ("[T]he President of the Croatian Republic of Herceg-Bosna, Mr. Mate Boban, has appointed Dr. Jadranko Prlić Prime Minister. At the Prime Minister's suggestion, the following people were appointed members of the government: [...] Valentin Corid – interior minister".) Prlić fails to explain why the Trial Chamber's conclusion could not stand on the basis of this evidence. As such, the Appeals Chamber dismisses his argument that the Trial Chamber erred in relying on Exhibit P06581, among other evidence, in finding that he proposed to Tuđman that Ćorid be appointed Minister of the Interior of the HR H-B.

[3429] See also *supra*, para. 1051 & fn. 3381.

[3430] Trial Judgement, Vol. 4, para. 96. See Trial Judgement, Vol. 4, para. 95.

[3431] Prlić's Appeal Brief, para. 360.

[3432] Prlić's Appeal Brief, para. 360; Appeal Hearing, AT. 137 (20 Mar 2017). See Prlić's Appeal Brief, para. 361, referring to Prlić's Appeal Brief, para. 52 (sub-ground of appeal 1.2), sub-grounds of appeal 1.2.4-1.2.5.

[3433] Prlić's Appeal Brief, para. 362.

[3434] Prosecution's Response Brief (Prlić), para. 222.

[3435] Prosecution's Response Brief (Prlić), para. 222.

1074. The Appeals Chamber dismisses Prlić's argument that he had no power of supervision as it is not borne out by the evidence on which he relies.[3436] The Appeals Chamber further dismisses the argument that the Trial Chamber ignored evidence that the HVO HZ H-B was responsible for judicial appointments, as this alleged fact is not inconsistent with the impugned finding. Thus, the Appeals Chamber dismisses Prlić's sub-ground of appeal 11.5.[3437]

(vi) Fiscal organs of the Government (Prlić's Sub-ground 11.6)

1075. The Trial Chamber found that Prlić directed and controlled the fiscal organs of the HVO/Government of the HZ(R) H-B and its budget.[3438]

a. Arguments of the Parties

1076. Prlić submits that this finding was erroneous, as the Trial Chamber relied on documents covering the period when the Ministry of Finance did not function and mischaracterised the **[page 450]** testimony of Witness Miroslav Rupčić,[3439] whereas Prlić argues that he could only act with authorisation from the HVO HZ H-B.[3440] Prlić further challenges the Trial Chamber's underlying findings that he: (1) directed, supported, and facilitated raising or collecting funds, arguing that no decrees proposed by the Department of Finance and enacted by the HVO HZ H-B gave him such power, and Rupčić's evidence does not support the Trial Chamber's conclusions;[3441] and (2) drew up, supervised, and controlled the budget of the HVO/Government of the HZ(R) H-B, which Prlić argues was based on a mischaracterisation of the evidence.[3442]

1077. The Prosecution responds that Prlić: (1) neither provides support for his claim that the Ministry of Finance did not function during unspecified dates, nor explains how that would undermine the Trial Chamber's findings on his powers;[3443] (2) ignores that he himself signed the decrees on which he relies,[3444] and fails to explain how the Trial Chamber erred in relying on the evidence of Rupčić;[3445] and (3) fails to substantiate his claim that the Trial Chamber mischaracterised evidence that squarely supports its finding that he drew up, supervised, and controlled the budget.[3446]

b. Analysis

1078. Turning first to Prlić's challenge to the Trial Chamber's conclusion that he directed and controlled the fiscal and financial organs of the HVO/Government of the HZ(R) H-B and its budget, the Appeals Chamber notes that Prlić provides no support for his assertions that the Ministry of Finance did not function during a certain period and that he could only act with authorisation from the HVO HZ H-B. He furthermore fails to

---

[3436] See Appeal Hearing, AT. 137 (20 Mar 2017), referring to Exs. P00303, Arts 2-22, 1D00001, Arts 2-7, P00434 (not admitted into evidence), 1D00010, 1D00171, 1D00173, 1D00174. See also *supra*, para. 1051 &fn. 3381.
[3437] The Appeals Chamber also notes that Prlić refers to his submissions in sub-grounds of appeal 1.2, 1.2.4, and 1.2.5, which it dismisses elsewhere in the Judgement. See *supra*, paras 168-176.
[3438] Trial Judgement, Vol. 4, para. 98. See Trial Judgement, Vol. 4, para. 97.
[3439] The Appeals Chamber understands that the witness Prlić describes as "Witness I" is Rupčić.
[3440] Prlić's Appeal Brief, para. 363. See Prlić's Appeal Brief, para. 364, referring to Prlić's Appeal Brief, para. 52 (sub-ground of appeal 1.2), sub-grounds of appeal 1.2.4-1.2.5, 11.1. See also Appeal Hearing, AT. 133 (20 Mar 2017).
[3441] Prlić's Appeal Brief, para. 365.
[3442] Prlić's Appeal Brief, para. 366. Specifically, Prlić submits that: (1) in Exhibits 1D02135 and 1D02136 the HVO HZ H-B is reminding the Finance Department of its obligations – pursuant to HVO HZ H-B decrees – to estimate the inflow of funds in the budget; (2) the House of Representatives was in charge of the HR H-B budget, as found by the Trial Chamber; (3) the Head of the Finance Department of the HVO HZ H-B was vested with the executive authority to implement the budget without any authorisation from the HVO HZ H-B President; and (4) in 1992 and 1993 expenditures were made pursuant to HVO HZ H-B decisions and only in 1994 was the first HR H-B budget adopted. Prlić's Appeal Brief, para. 366. See Appeal Hearing, AT. 133 (20 Mar 2017).
[3443] Prosecution's Response Brief (Prlić), para. 223.
[3444] Prosecution's Response Brief (Prlić), para. 223.
[3445] Prosecution's Response Brief (Prlić), para. 223. See Prosecution's Response Brief (Prlić), fn. 749.
[3446] Prosecution's Response Brief (Prlić), para. 224.

demonstrate that the Trial Chamber mischaracterised the testimony of Rupčić.[3447] Prlić's challenge amounts to a mere assertion and is dismissed as such.[3448] **[page 451]**

1079. Regarding Prlić's challenge to the Trial Chamber's finding that he directed, supported, and facilitated raising or collecting funds,[3449] the Appeals Chamber notes that this finding is supported by official publications of HVO HZ H-B decrees, bearing Prlić's name, concerning the raising or collection of funds.[3450] Prlić has failed to demonstrate that no reasonable trier of fact could have made this finding. His arguments in this regard are therefore dismissed.

1080. Finally, concerning Prlić's challenge to the Trial Chamber's finding that he drew up, supervised, and controlled the budget of the HVO/Government of the HZ(R) H-B,[3451] the Appeals Chamber notes that this finding is supported by evidence showing his role in this regard.[3452] Prlić either ignores this evidence[3453] or fails to show that the Trial Chamber mischaracterised it.[3454] His challenge is therefore dismissed.

1081. For the foregoing reasons, the Appeals Chamber dismisses Prlić's sub-ground of appeal 11.6.

(vii) Office for Displaced Persons and Refugees (Prlić's Sub-ground 11.7)

1082. The Trial Chamber found that Prlić was involved in directing and organising the activities of the ODPR and had the power to direct and control it.[3455]

a. Arguments of the Parties

1083. Prlić challenges this finding, submitting that it contradicts another finding that the ODPR was accountable to the HVO HZ H-B and not to Prlić.[3456] He argues in this regard that the **[page 452]** Trial Chamber erred by basing its conclusion on HVO HZ H-B decisions signed by him and by mischaracterising Witness Martin Raguž's testimony.[3457] Prlić further submits that the Trial Chamber erred in finding that he "instructed" the ODPR to assist with regard to a visit by experts from the Croatian ODPR, when in fact he was just pleading on behalf of the HVO HZ H-B.[3458] Finally, Prlić submits that the Trial Chamber wrongly found, based on a single exhibit, that he participated in a meeting attended by Zubak and Tadić, during which they allegedly "informed an international organization of their plan to negotiate with the Croatian ODPR for

---

[3447] See Trial Judgement, Vol. 4, paras 97-98, referring to, *inter alia*, Exs. P00102, P01097, p. 1, 1D00036, Art. 2, Miroslav Rupčić, T(F). 23448-23451 (9 Oct 2007).

[3448] The Appeals Chamber notes that Prlić refers to his submissions in sub-grounds of appeal 1.2, 1.2.4, 1.2.5, and 11.1, which it dismisses elsewhere in the Judgement. See *supra*, paras 168-176, 1021-1043.

[3449] Trial Judgement, Vol. 4, para. 97.

[3450] See Trial Judgement, Vol. 4, para. 97, referring to, *inter alia*, Exs. P00102, P00408/1D00013, 1D00025, 1D00028, 1D00030, 1D00034.

[3451] Trial Judgement, Vol. 4, para. 97.

[3452] Trial Judgement, Vol. 4, para. 97, referring to Exs. P00412, P00511, P01403, pp. 3-4, P06189, p. 2, P07628, 1D02135, 1D02136, Miroslav Rupčić, T(F). 23342-23343 (8 Oct 2007).

[3453] Compare Prlić's Appeal Brief, para. 366, with Trial Judgement, Vol. 4, fn. 283.

[3454] Regarding Prlić's submission that in Exhibits 1D02135 and 1D02136 the HVO HZ H-B is reminding the Finance Department of its obligations – pursuant to HVO HZ H-B decrees – to estimate the inflow of funds in the budget, the Appeals Chamber considers that both exhibits relate to the Government of the HR H-B and support the impugned finding. Concerning Prlić's submission that the House of Representatives was in charge of the HR H-B budget, the Appeals Chamber observes that the Trial Chamber found that the House of Representatives of the HR H-B, established on 28 August 1993, was charged with *adopting* the budget of the HR H-B. Trial Judgement, Vol. 1, para. 508 (emphasis added). Prlić fails to demonstrate that this finding (or the evidence to which he refers in support) is inconsistent with the impugned finding. See Prlić Appeal Brief, fns 944-945 and references cited therein. With regard to Prlić's submission that the Head of the Finance Department of the HVO HZ H-B was vested with the executive authority to implement the budget without any authorisation from the HVO HZ H-B President, the Appeals Chamber observes that he cites to a single exhibit discussing a draft decree yet to be adopted. See Prlić's Appeal Brief, fn. 946, referring to Ex. P00578, p. 2. Finally, the Appeals Chamber fails to see how Prlić's last submission – that in 1992 and 1993 expenditures were made pursuant to HVO HZ H-B decisions and only in 1994 was the first HR H-B budget adopted – shows any error in the impugned finding.

[3455] Trial Judgement, Vol. 4, para. 100. See Trial Judgement, Vol. 4, para. 99.

[3456] Prlić's Appeal Brief, para. 367.

[3457] Prlić's Appeal Brief, para. 367 & fn. 952, referring to Martin Raguž, T. 31310-31316 (25 Aug 2008).

[3458] Prlić's Appeal Brief, para. 368.

transit visas for Muslims".[3459] Prlić argues in this regard that nothing supports the conclusion that he ever directed or controlled the ODPR.[3460]

1084. The Prosecution responds that the Trial Chamber reasonably found that Prlić had the power to direct and control the ODPR and that he was involved in directing and organising its activities.[3461] It argues that Prlić fails to establish the alleged contradiction in the Trial Chamber's findings,[3462] and has not explained how the Trial Chamber erred in relying on, or in interpreting, certain evidence.[3463]

  b. Analysis

1085. With regard to Prlić's argument that the impugned finding is contradicted by the Trial Chamber's finding that the ODPR was accountable to the HVO HZ H-B and not to Prlić, the Appeals Chamber notes that in the section discussing Prlić's powers with respect to the ODPR, the Trial Chamber first recalled "its findings that, at the organisational level, the ODPR was accountable to the HVO HZ H-B and not to its president personally".[3464] The Trial Chamber then considered documentary and witness evidence indicating that Prlić was personally involved in the activities of the ODPR and its management, on the basis of which it reached the impugned finding.[3465] The Appeals Chamber therefore considers that Prlić does not demonstrate any contradiction in the Trial Chamber's findings. The Appeals Chamber further considers that Prlić's argument that the Trial Chamber erred by basing its conclusion on HVO HZ H-B decisions signed by him is an undeveloped assertion that also ignores other evidence on which the Trial Chamber **[page 453]** relied.[3466] Finally, the Appeals Chamber finds that Prlić merely asserts that the Trial Chamber mischaracterised the testimony of Raguž without demonstrating an error.[3467] Prlić's arguments are therefore dismissed.

1086. Turning to Prlić's submission that the Trial Chamber erroneously concluded that he "instructed" the ODPR to assist with regard to a visit by experts from the Croatian ODPR when he was just pleading on behalf of the HVO HZ H-B, the Appeals Chamber notes that the Trial Chamber based this finding on Exhibit 1D02141,[3468] a letter signed by Prlić which reads: "We ask that you provide".[3469] The Appeals Chamber finds that a reasonable trier of fact could have found that this amounted to an instruction, notwithstanding the irrelevant evidence on which Prlić relies to argue that he was pleading rather than instructing.[3470] Prlić's submission is therefore dismissed.

1087. Turning at last to Prlić's challenge to the Trial Chamber's conclusion that he participated in a meeting attended by Zubak and Tadić, during which they informed an international organisation of their plan to negotiate with the Croatian ODPR for transit visas for approximately 10,000 Muslims "wishing to leave",[3471] the Appeals Chamber notes that the Trial Chamber's finding is explicitly supported by the exhibit on which it relied,[3472] and that Prlić fails to develop why the Trial Chamber would have erred in basing this finding on

---

[3459] Prlić's Appeal Brief, para. 369.
[3460] Prlić's Appeal Brief, paras 369. See Prlić's Appeal Brief, para. 370, referring to Prlić's Appeal Brief, sub-grounds of appeal 16.6.3-16.6.4. Prlić also submits that: "[t]he Headquarters for refugees was formed due to the gravity of the humanitarian situation at the time, for activities usually performed by the municipalities. Zubak headed the Headquarters and was authorized to make autonomous decisions in the Headquarters' area of responsibility, with the ODPR becoming more autonomous." Prlić's Appeal Brief, para. 371 (internal references omitted).
[3461] Prosecution's Response Brief (Prlić), para. 225.
[3462] Prosecution's Response Brief (Prlić), para. 226.
[3463] Prosecution's Response Brief (Prlić), para. 226.
[3464] Trial Judgement, Vol. 4, para. 99, referring to Trial Judgement, Vol. 1, paras 629-631.
[3465] Trial Judgement, Vol. 4, paras 99-100.
[3466] Compare Prlić's Appeal Brief, para. 367 & fns 951-952 and references cited therein, with Trial Judgement, Vol. 4, paras 99-100 and references cited therein.
[3467] The Appeals Chamber notes that the part of Raguž's testimony cited by Prlić squarely supports the Trial Chamber's finding that "[o]n 31 May 1993, [Prlić] proposed to the HVO HZ H-B that Martin Raguž be appointed Deputy Head of the ODPR and signed the decision to that effect". Trial Judgement, Vol. 4, para. 99 & fn. 287, referring to, *inter alia*, Martin Raguž, T(F). 31310-31316 (25 Aug 2008).
[3468] Trial Judgement, Vol. 4, para. 99 & fn. 297.
[3469] Ex. 1D02141.
[3470] See Prlić's Appeal Brief, para. 368 & fn. 953 and references cited therein.
[3471] Trial Judgement, Vol. 4, para. 99.
[3472] Trial Judgement, Vol. 4, fn. 296, referring to Ex. P09679 (confidential), p. 1.

a single piece of evidence. In light of the fact that the finding is explicitly supported by the evidence, and that the Trial Chamber also relied on other evidence to find that Prlić was involved in directing and organising the activities of the ODPR and had the power to direct and control it,[3473] the Appeals Chamber also dismisses Prlić's final submission that nothing supports the conclusion that he ever directed or controlled the ODPR.[3474]
[page 454]

1088. For the foregoing reasons, the Appeals Chamber dismisses Prlić's sub-ground of appeal 11.7.

    (viii) <u>Exchange Service (Prlić's Sub-ground 11.8)</u>

1089. The Trial Chamber found that Prlić exercised direct authority over the Exchange Service by supervising its establishment, organisation, and activities and by being kept informed of its activities.[3475]

1090. Prlić submits that the Trial Chamber erroneously concluded that he exercised direct power over the Exchange Service, in particular by supervising its establishment, organization, and activities and by being kept informed of its activities.[3476] Prlić argues that the Trial Chamber erroneously relied on: (1) Exhibit P03796, introduced through a bar table motion;[3477] (2) Exhibit P07102, which allegedly bears no indicia of reliability – specifically no signature or stamp – and is not corroborated by any evidence indicating that it is genuine and was ever sent to or received by the HR H-B Government or Prlić;[3478] and (3) three "uncorroborated" "reports" not identified by exhibit numbers, in disregard of other evidence showing that the Service was: (a) an autonomous body communicating directly with other entities; and (b) not accountable to the HVO HZ H-B, as shown by the fact that it is not referenced in Government reports.[3479]

1091. The Prosecution responds that the Trial Chamber reasonably found that Prlić exercised direct authority over the Exchange Service.[3480] The Prosecution argues that Prlić misidentifies the evidence on which the Trial Chamber relied, makes misleading, irrelevant, incorrect, and unsupported claims, and fails to demonstrate how the Trial Chamber erred in its assessment of evidence.[3481]

1092. The Appeals Chamber notes that in arguing that the Trial Chamber erroneously relied on Exhibit P03796, Prlić has failed to articulate any error and dismisses the argument on this basis.[3482] With regard to Exhibit P07102, the Appeals Chamber observes that while the document is not signed or stamped, the Trial Chamber accepted its authenticity in light of other evidence on the **[page 455]** record.[3483] In this regard, the Appeals Chamber recalls that the final assessment of a piece of evidence is based on the totality of the evidence in a given case.[3484] As such, the Appeals Chamber finds that Prlić has failed to establish that no reasonable trier of fact could have considered it to be authentic or could have relied on it.[3485] Concerning the three reports on which the Trial Chamber relied, the Appeals Chamber notes that the Trial Chamber

[3473] See *supra*, paras 1085-1086; Trial Judgement, Vol. 4, paras 99-100.
[3474] See Prlić's Appeal Brief, para. 369. The Appeals Chamber also notes that Prlić refers to his submissions in sub-grounds of appeal 16.6.3 and 16.6.4, which it dismisses elsewhere in the Judgement. See *infra*, paras 1300, 1304-1306, 1308-1309, 1315, 1317. Prlić's submissions regarding the "Headquarters for refugees" and Zubak's role in that regard are not inconsistent with the impugned finding.
[3475] Trial Judgement, Vol. 4, para. 104. See Trial Judgement, Vol. 4, paras 101-103.
[3476] Prlić's Appeal Brief, para. 372.
[3477] Prlić's Appeal Brief, para. 372, referring to Ex. P03796, Prlić's Appeal Brief, ground of appeal 3.
[3478] Prlić's Appeal Brief, para. 372.
[3479] Prlić's Appeal Brief, para. 373 & fn. 962, referring to Exs. P07178, P07246, P07468.
[3480] Prosecution's Response Brief (Prlić), para. 227.
[3481] Prosecution's Response Brief (Prlić), para. 228. The Prosecution further argues that Prlić improperly raises for the first time on appeal a challenge to the authenticity of Exhibit P07102, which moreover bears indicia of reliability. Prosecution's Response Brief (Prlić), para. 228 & fn. 779.
[3482] *Cf.* Judgement, Vol. 4, para. 102, referring to Ex. P03796. The Appeals Chamber notes that Prlić also refers to his submissions in ground of appeal 3, which it dismisses elsewhere in the Judgement. See *supra*, paras 177-183.
[3483] See Trial Judgement, Vol. 4, paras 1062, 1089, 1092, 1127 *et seq.*, referring to, *inter alia*, Ex. P07102. The Appeals Chamber notes that these portions of the Trial Judgement relate to Pušić's liability and that Pušić does not challenge the authenticity of Exhibit P07102.
[3484] See *Lukić and Lukić* Appeal Judgement, para. 261.
[3485] The Appeals Chamber observes that the impugned finding makes no mention of Exhibit P07102 being sent to or received by the HR H-B Government or Prlić. Trial Judgement, Vol. 4, para. 103 ("Moreover, in a letter dated 10 December 1993, Berislav Pušić proposed to Jadranko Prlić, among other things, that a body other than the [Exchange Service] be entrusted with the classification of

described them and referenced them with sufficient specificity,[3486] allowing Prlić to identify them.[3487] The Appeals Chamber further notes that the aforementioned reports all concern information on the release of prisoners transmitted by Pušić, the head of the Exchange Service,[3488] to the Government of the HR H-B and thus corroborate each other insofar as they show that Prlić was kept informed of the service's activities, and are in any event corroborated by other evidence on the record[3489] supporting the concluding finding that Prlić was kept informed.[3490] Prlić therefore establishes no error in this regard. Finally, with respect to the allegedly disregarded evidence that the Exchange Service was an autonomous body not accountable to the HVO HZ H-B, the Appeals Chamber considers that Prlić's submissions that this body communicated directly with various entities and is not referenced in Government reports are not inconsistent with the challenged finding.[3491] For these reasons, the Appeals Chamber dismisses Prlić's sub-ground of appeal 11.8. **[page 456]**

(ix) <u>Municipal governments (Prlić's Sub-ground 11.9)</u>

1093.   The Trial Chamber found that Prlić directed and supervised the work of the HVO municipal authorities, considering that the Government: (1) co-ordinated the work of the municipal administrative bodies; (2) could dissolve the municipal HVOs, annul their enactments, and appoint and dismiss their members; and (3) could abrogate the decisions of the municipal HVOs that contravened the regulations in force.[3492]

1094.   Prlić challenges this finding,[3493] arguing that the Trial Chamber erroneously found, based on unsupportive documents admitted from the bar table, that he: (1) participated in the dissolution of the municipal HVOs that did not conform to HZ(R) H-B policies; (2) received reports from the municipal HVOs; and (3) participated in the appointment of members of various municipal HVO councils.[3494]

1095.   The Prosecution responds that the Trial Chamber's findings are reasonable and that Prlić fails to explain his claims to the contrary.[3495]

1096.   Regarding Prlić's submissions that the Trial Chamber erred in making findings based on unsupportive bar table documents, the Appeals Chamber finds that the impugned findings are supported by the exhibits on which the Trial Chamber relied,[3496] and dismisses Prlić's submissions as they misrepresent the evidence.[3497] The Appeals Chamber dismisses Prlić's sub-ground of appeal 11.9. **[page 457]**

---

prisoners and that the Government of the HR H-B, whose President was Jadranko Prlić, approve a list of 'persons [civilians] who voluntarily want to leave the part of the HR H-B' drawn up by the Service for the Exchange of Prisoners and Other Persons.").
[3486]   Trial Judgement, Vol. 4, para. 103 & fn. 302 and references cited therein.
[3487]   See Prlić's Appeal Brief, fn. 962, referring to Exs. P07178, P07246, P07468.
[3488]   Trial Judgement, Vol. 4, para. 101 & fn. 299.
[3489]   Trial Judgement, Vol. 4, para. 103 & fn. 301 and reference cited therein.
[3490]   Trial Judgement, Vol. 4, para. 104.
[3491]   See Prlić's Appeal Brief, para. 373 & fns 963-964 and references cited therein.
[3492]   Trial Judgement, Vol. 4, para. 105.
[3493]   Prlić's Appeal Brief, para. 374. See Prlić's Appeal Brief, para. 375, referring to Prlić's Appeal Brief, paras 54-55 (sub-ground of appeal 1.2), sub-ground of appeal 1.2.6.
[3494]   Prlić's Appeal Brief, paras 376-378; Prlić's Reply Brief, para. 59, referring to, *inter alia*, Prlić's Appeal Brief, ground of appeal 3.
[3495]   Prosecution's Response Brief (Prlić), paras 229-230.
[3496]   See Trial Judgement, Vol. 4, para. 105 and references cited therein. Specifically, the finding that Prlić "participated in the decision of 22 March 1993 on the dissolution of the municipal HVOs which did not conform to the policies in force in the HZ(R) H B, for example the Ljubuški HVO because of the difficulties linked to the mobilisation of conscripts in that municipality" is supported by Exhibits P01781 ("By the decision of Jadranko Prlić, President of the HVO HZ H-B, which was adopted on 22 March 1993, the Ljubuški HVO was dismissed") and P01700 (Prlić's decision dated 22 March 1993, referring to "the difficulties to mobilise conscripts" in Ljubuški Municipality). The finding that Prlić "received reports from the municipal HVOs" is supported by Exhibits P01853 (a report of the Travnik HVO addressed to, *inter alios*, Prlić), P06292 (a report on the work of the Vitez Defence Office addressed to, *inter alios*, Prlić), and 2D00852 (containing a request – adopted by the HVO HZ H-B with Prlić in attendance – for all municipal HVOs to submit detailed reports). Finally, the finding that "Prlić participated in the appointment of members of various municipal HVO councils, among others, those of the municipalities of Vareš, Jablanica and Ljubuški" is supported by Exhibits P05805 (a letter from the President of the Ljubuški municipal HVO to Prlić, requesting a decision on the appointment of the Ljubuški municipal HVO) and P08239 (Minutes of a session of the Government of the HR H-B, at which Prlić was present, setting out appointments to, *inter alia*, the Vareš and Jablanica municipal councils).
[3497]   The Appeals Chamber notes that Prlić refers to his submissions in (sub-)grounds of appeal 1.2, 1.2.6, and 3, which it dismisses elsewhere in the Judgement. See *supra*, paras 168-176, 177-183.

847

(x) Conclusion

1097. The Appeals Chamber dismisses Prlić's ground of appeal 11 in its entirety.

(b) Alleged errors regarding powers in military matters (Prlić's Ground 12)

(i) Introduction

1098. Prlić submits that the Trial Chamber erred in law and fact in finding that he and the Government had power in military matters (sub-ground of appeal 12.1) and that reports on HVO combat activities were routinely sent to the Government (sub-ground of appeal 12.2),[3498] undermining his JCE convictions,[3499] and warranting his acquittal on Counts 1-25.[3500] The Prosecution responds that Prlić's submissions should be dismissed.[3501]

(ii) The Government's and Prlić's powers in military matters (Prlić's Sub-ground 12.1)

1099. The Trial Chamber found that the HVO/Government of the HZ(R) H-B had the power and responsibility to control, in general and particularly in terms of the military strategy, the HVO.[3502] The Trial Chamber also found that, as President of the HVO/Government of the HZ(R) H-B, Prlić had an influence on the defence strategy and the military operations of the HVO.[3503] It found that he specifically had the power to: (1) preside over and participate in meetings at which decisions on the strategy and the military situation in the HZ(R) H-B were taken; (2) adopt decisions and decrees on such matters; (3) be informed about the military situation; and (4) if necessary, "take decisions directly which had a direct impact" on the course of the military operations of the HVO.[3504]

1100. The Appeals Chamber will address in turn Prlić's challenges to the Trial Chamber's findings on the Government's powers in military matters and his own powers in that regard. **[page 458]**

a. The Government's powers in military matters

i. Arguments of the Parties

1101. Prlić first argues that the Trial Chamber erred in finding that the HVO HZ H-B played a role in military matters.[3505] He submits that the Trial Chamber based this finding exclusively on the Amended 3 July 1992 Decree on the Armed Forces (Exhibit P00588) ("3 July 1992 Decree on the Armed Forces"),[3506] which requires the production of defence plans, while ignoring other evidence indicating that such plans had "nothing to do with the usage of military forces".[3507]

1102. Prlić argues that the Trial Chamber mischaracterised Petković's evidence when claiming that he acknowledged that the HVO HZ H-B – as the civilian authority in the HZ H-B – exercised control over the

---

[3498] Prlić's Appeal Brief, paras 382, 403, 408. Specifically, Prlić alleges that by ignoring evidence, the Trial Chamber failed to provide reasoned opinions and applied an incorrect legal standard in assessing the evidence, amounting to an error of law. Prlić's Appeal Brief, para. 408.
[3499] Prlić's Appeal Brief, paras 381, 408.
[3500] Prlić's Appeal Brief, para. 409.
[3501] Prosecution's Response Brief (Prlić), para. 233. See Prosecution's Response Brief (Prlić), paras 231-232.
[3502] Trial Judgement, Vol. 4, para. 106, referring to Trial Judgement, Vol. 1, paras 517-521.
[3503] Trial Judgement, Vol. 4, para. 106.
[3504] Trial Judgement, Vol. 4, para. 111. See Trial Judgement, Vol. 4, paras 106-110.
[3505] Prlić's Appeal Brief, paras 382-383; Appeal Hearing, AT. 137 (20 Mar 2017).
[3506] The decree was amended on 17 October 1992. Exhibit P00588, a decree issued by Mate Boban on 17 October 1992 on the armed forces of the Croatian Community of Herceg Bosna (edited version) ("Amended 3 July 1992 Decree on the Armed Forces"), p. 1.
[3507] Prlić's Appeal Brief, para. 383, referring to, *inter alia*, Prlić's Appeal Brief, ground of appeal 3. See Prlić's Reply Brief, paras 60-61. Prlić also submits that there is no evidence of any HVO HZ H-B defence plans. Prlić's Appeal Brief, para. 383; Appeal Hearing, AT. 138 (20 Mar 2017).

HVO/military authorities.[3508] In addition, Prlić argues that the Trial Chamber erroneously relied on Petković's Final Brief, which has no legal authority.[3509]

1103. Prlić also submits that the Trial Chamber misinterpreted Petković's testimony when claiming he acknowledged that the civilian authorities of the HVO HZ H-B were asked to set the "overall strategy" of the HZ H-B, and based this finding on evidence that could not sustain a finding beyond reasonable doubt.[3510] He contends that the Trial Chamber also erroneously relied on the 3 July 1992 Decree on the Armed Forces (Exhibit P00289), which was only in effect before Mate Boban relinquished his executive authority within the HVO HZ H-B.[3511] Finally, Prlić contends that the Trial Chamber relied on a HVO HZ H-B report (Exhibit P00128), which does not show that the HVO HZ H-B made political or "overall strategy" decisions.[3512]

1104. Prlić challenges the Trial Chamber's finding that "[t]he government was allowed to make proposals and form conclusions concerning issues of a military nature, which the Ministry of Defence could then forward to the Senior Main Staff or to the principal commanding officers, but **[page 459]** lacked authority to give orders of a military nature",[3513] as it mischaracterised Petković's testimony.[3514]

1105. Finally, Prlić contends that the Trial Chamber misrepresented Marijan's testimony – and ignored other evidence – when concluding that he stated that the "Government of the HVO" adopted reports and decisions concerning issues related to defence and as a consequence provided instructions for their enforcement.[3515]

1106. The Prosecution responds that the Trial Chamber did not base its finding that the HVO HZ H-B played a role in military matters exclusively on the Amended 3 July 1992 Decree on the Armed Forces and that Prlić fails to explain the relevance of his argument regarding defence plans.[3516] The Prosecution also argues that the Trial Chamber did not mischaracterise Petković's evidence,[3517] that the Trial Chamber's reference to Petković's Final Brief is irrelevant,[3518] and that the Trial Chamber did not err in relying on the 3 July 1992 Decree on the Armed Forces.[3519] Finally, it argues that Prlić does not demonstrate that the Trial Chamber misrepresented Marijan's evidence and that the other evidence he refers to fails to show any error in the Trial Chamber's findings.[3520]

ii. Analysis

1107. The Appeals Chamber observes that the Trial Chamber did not base its finding that the HVO HZ H-B played a role in military matters exclusively on the Amended 3 July 1992 Decree on the Armed Forces. Rather, the Trial Chamber assessed "the Prlić Defence's theory that reforms in the Decree on the Armed

---

[3508] Prlić's Appeal Brief, para.'384.

[3509] Prlić's Appeal Brief, para. 385, referring to, *inter alia*, Prlić's Appeal Brief, para. 161 (ground of appeal 5).

[3510] Prlić's Appeal Brief, para. 386, referring to, *inter alia*, Prlić's Appeal Brief, paras 455-459 (sub-ground of appeal 16.1.1).

[3511] Prlić's Appeal Brief, para. 387. In this regard, Prlić also argues that: (1) the 3 July 1992 Decree on the Armed Forces was then amended, stripping the HVO HZ H-B and its President of any power over the HVO; (2) Witness Davor Marijan "carelessly" analysed the 3 July 1992 Decree on the Armed Forces although "this blunder was exposed when he testified"; and (3) the Amended 3 July 1992 Decree on the Armed Forces provides an accurate account of the HVO HZ H-B's actual powers or lack thereof over the HVO. Prlić's Appeal Brief, para. 387; Appeal Hearing, AT. 137-138 (20 Mar 2017).

[3512] Prlić's Appeal Brief, para. 388 & fn. 982.

[3513] Trial Judgement, Vol. 1, para. 519. See Prlić's Appeal Brief, para. 389, referring to, *inter alia*, Trial Judgement, Vol. 1, para. 519; Appeal Hearing, AT. 234 (20 Mar 2017).

[3514] Prlić's Appeal Brief, paras 389-390. Prlić also submits that: (1) Praljak, the second Chief of the Main Staff, testified that neither Prlić nor the' HVO HZ H-B could give him orders and that the HVO was only obliged to implement Boban's orders; and (2) the Trial Chamber found that the Chief of the Main Staff was directly accountable to the Supreme Commander with regard to strategic planning and the use of the HVO. Prlić's Appeal Brief, para. 391.

[3515] Prlić's Appeal Brief, para. 392, referring to, *inter alia*, Trial Judgement, Vol. 1, para. 519. The quote is from the Trial Judgement.

[3516] Prosecution's Response Brief (Prlić), para. 234.

[3517] Prosecution's Response Brief (Prlić), paras 235-238.

[3518] Prosecution's Response Brief (Prlić), para. 236.

[3519] Prosecution's Response Brief (Prlić), para. 234. The Prosecution further argues that Prlić repeats his trial argument that the amendment of the 3 July 1992 Decree on the Armed Forces stripped the Government of power over the HVO, without showing that the Trial Chamber erred in rejecting this argument. Prosecution's Response Brief (Prlić), para. 234.

[3520] Prosecution's Response Brief (Prlić), paras 239-240.

Forces of 3 July 1992 stripped the HVO of its role in military matters",[3521] **[page 460]** and reviewed a number of pieces of evidence before reaching its conclusions to the contrary.[3522] Prlić misrepresents the factual findings and his argument is therefore dismissed.

1108. With regard to Prlić's argument that the Trial Chamber mischaracterised Petković's evidence when claiming that he acknowledged that the HVO HZ H-B exercised control over the HVO, the Appeals Chamber considers that the evidence cited by the Trial Chamber supports its summary of Petković's testimony and that Prlić has failed to demonstrate any error in this regard.[3523] As the Trial Chamber's assessment of this evidence is supported by the record, the Appeals Chamber considers that the Trial Chamber's additional reference to Petković's Final Brief is inconsequential.[3524] Prlić's arguments are therefore dismissed.

1109. Turning to Prlić's argument that the Trial Chamber erred in claiming that Petković acknowledged that the civilian authorities of the HVO HZ H-B were asked to set the "overall strategy" of the HZ H-B, the Appeals Chamber again considers that the evidence cited by the Trial Chamber supports the Trial Chamber's summary of Petković's testimony and that Prlić has failed to demonstrate any error in this regard.[3525] The Appeals Chamber further dismisses Prlić's arguments regarding the Trial Chamber's reliance on the 3 July 1992 Decree on the Armed Forces (Exhibit P00289) and HVO HZ H-B report (Exhibit P00128), as he has failed to demonstrate that no reasonable trier of fact could have found as the Trial Chamber did, based on the other evidence on which it relied.[3526]

1110. As for Prlić's challenge to the Trial Chamber's finding that "[t]he government was allowed to make proposals and form conclusions concerning issues of a military nature, which the Ministry of Defence could then forward to the Senior Main Staff or to the principal commanding officers, but lacked authority to give orders of a military nature",[3527] the Appeals Chamber considers that he merely makes factual assertions that either are not supported by the evidence to which he refers,[3528] **[page 461]** or are not inconsistent with the challenged finding.[3529] Thus, Prlić has failed to demonstrate that no reasonable trier of fact could have made this finding and his arguments are therefore dismissed.

1111. Regarding Prlić's contention that the Trial Chamber misrepresented Marijan's testimony, the Appeals Chamber notes that, according to the Trial Chamber, *"Davor Marijan* stated that although the Government of the HVO did not form part of the chain of command of the armed forces, during its sittings, it adopted reports and decisions concerning issues related to defence, and as a consequence, provided instructions for their enforcement".[3530] The Appeals Chamber considers that the evidence cited by the Trial Chamber supports its summary of Marijan's testimony, although there is no explicit reference to enforcement. This, however, has no discernible impact on any ensuing finding of the Trial Chamber and therefore does not

---

[3521] Trial Judgement, Vol. 1, para. 518.
[3522] Trial Judgement, Vol. 1, paras 518-521. The Appeals Chamber also notes that Prlić refers to his submissions in ground of appeal 3, which it dismisses elsewhere in the Judgement. See *supra*, paras 177-183.
[3523] See Trial Judgement, Vol. 1, para. 519 & fn. 1264, referring to, *inter alia*, Milivoj Petković, T(F). 50014-50015 (25 Feb 2010), 50342 (3 Mar 2010). Regarding Prlić"s submissions that: (1) Praljak testified that neither Prlić nor the HVO HZ H-B could give him orders and that the HVO was only obliged to implement Boban's orders; and (2) the Trial Chamber found that the Chief of the Main Staff was directly accountable to the Supreme Commander with regard to strategic planning and the use of the HVO, the Appeals Chamber considers that Prlić has failed to articulate an error.
[3524] See Trial Judgement, Vol. 1, para. 519 & fn. 1264, referring to, *inter alia*, Petković's Final Brief, paras 55, 64(ii). The Appeals Chamber also notes that Prlić refers to his submissions in ground of appeal 5, which it dismisses elsewhere in the Judgement. See *supra*, paras 107-138.
[3525] See Trial Judgement, Vol. 1, para. 519 & fn. 1265 and references cited therein. See, in particular, Milivoj Petković, T. 50350 (3 Mar 2010). The Appeals Chamber also notes that Prlić refers to his submissions in sub-ground of appeal 16.1.1, which it dismisses elsewhere in the Judgement. See *infra*, paras 1146-1153.
[3526] See Trial Judgement, Vol. 1, para. 519 at fns 1265, 1268 and references cited therein.
[3527] Trial Judgement, Vol. 1, para. 519.
[3528] See Prlić's Appeal Brief, para. 390 & fns 985-986, referring to Milivoj Petković, T. 49771 (22 Feb 2010), 50186-50188 (1 Mar 2010). The Appeals Chamber considers that the evidence relied on by Prlić does not support his assertions that only the Supreme Commander and the Main Staff could decide on military matters and that the HVO HZ H-B was not part of the military. The first citation appears to be an error. The second citation makes no mention of the HVO HZ H-B and only relates to the Supreme Commander's and the Main Staff's position in the command structure of the combat component of the HVO without asserting that they had exclusive authority in military matters.
[3529] See Prlić's Appeal Brief, paras 389-391 at fns 984, 987-991.
[3530] Trial Judgement, Vol. 1, para. 519 (internal references omitted), referring to, *inter alia*, Ex. 2D02000, pp. 11-12, para. 13.

occasion any miscarriage of justice.[3531] With regard to the allegedly ignored evidence, the Appeals Chamber considers that Prlić merely makes factual assertions that are either not supported by the evidence to which he refers,[3532] or are not inconsistent with the challenged finding.[3533] These arguments are dismissed,

b. Prlić's powers in military matters

i. Arguments of the Parties

1112. Prlić contends that the Trial Chamber erroneously concluded that the Government, with his participation, discussed the HVO's military strategy and adopted regulations concerning the mobilisation of military personnel, in contradiction to: (1) its previous finding that "areas related to mobilization and appointment constituted some of the stated powers wielded directly by Mate Boban"; and (2) evidence that only Boban was authorised to proclaim mobilisation, with the Defence Department having the obligation to prepare and execute mobilisation.[3534]

1113. Prlić further submits that the Trial Chamber incorrectly found that Petković testified that Prlić could issue operative orders to the armed forces through the Defence Department, in contradiction to: (1) Petković's explicit testimony to the contrary; and (2) other findings of the **[page 462]** Trial Chamber.[3535] Moreover, he contends that the Trial Chamber erroneously concluded that he issued decisions that had a direct impact on military operations, based on evidence that does not support the conclusion.[3536] In this regard, Prlić argues that the Trial Chamber mischaracterised Exhibit P02967, which is not signed by Boban and does not relate to military issues.[3537]

1114. Prlić also contends that the Trial Chamber placed undue weight on the statements of representatives of the international community that he appeared to be very well-informed about the situation on the ground, whereas "[o]ther documents in support of this statement actually show" that he had neither knowledge nor power in military affairs.[3538] He submits that the Trial Chamber erroneously concluded that he played a key role in a series of ceasefire negotiations in Gornji Vakuf and Mostar, whereas there is no credible evidence supporting this conclusion.[3539] Finally, Prlić contends that the Trial Chamber erroneously found, based on unsupportive evidence and contradicting itself, that he had the power to co-ordinate the deployment of civilian police units that were under the direct power of the Ministry of the Interior.[3540]

1115. The Prosecution responds that Prlić fails to explain how the Trial Chamber erroneously concluded that the Government, with his participation, discussed military matters, or how the Trial Chamber allegedly contradicted itself.[3541] It further argues that Petković did testify that Prlić could issue operative orders to the armed forces through the Defence Department, and that Prlić ignores relevant evidence.[3542] The Prosecution contends that Prlić shows no error in the Trial Chamber's finding that he could issue decisions that had a direct impact on military operations.[3543] The Prosecution further argues that Prlić fails to articulate an error

---

[3531]   Namely, the concluding findings on the powers of Prlić and the HVO/Government of the HZ(R) H-B in military matters. See Trial Judgement, Vol. 1, paras 518-521, Vol. 4, paras 106-111.

[3532]   See Prlić's Appeal Brief, para. 392 & fn. 997.

[3533]   See Prlić's Appeal Brief, para. 392 at fns 993-996.

[3534]   Prlić's Appeal Brief, para. 393, referring to, *inter alia*, Trial Judgement, Vol. 4, para. 106. See Prlić's Appeal Brief, para. 394, referring to, *inter alia*, Prlić's Appeal Brief, sub-grounds of appeal 16.1-16.2; Appeal Hearing, AT. 137 (20 Mar 2017).

[3535]   Prlić's Appeal Brief, para. 395.

[3536]   Prlić's Appeal Brief, paras 396-397. See Prlić's Appeal Brief, para. 399, referring to, *inter alia*, Prlić's Appeal Brief, sub-ground of appeal 16.3.

[3537]   Prlić's Appeal Brief, para. 398.

[3538]   Prlić's Appeal Brief, para. 400.

[3539]   Prlić's Appeal Brief, para. 401, referring to, *inter alia*, Prlić's Appeal Brief, paras 184-185 (sub-ground of appeal 6.1), 202-203 (sub-ground of appeal 6.2). Prlić argues that Witness DZ was not in a position to comment on ceasefire agreements, since he admitted to having no business in military matters. Prlić's Appeal Brief, para. 401.

[3540]   Prlić's Appeal Brief, para. 402, referring to, *inter alia*, Trial Judgement, Vol. 4, para. 110; Prlić's Reply Brief, para. 62.

[3541]   Prosecution's Response Brief (Prlić), para. 241: See also Prosecution's Response Brief (Prlić), para. 245.

[3542]   Prosecution's Response Brief (Prlić), para. 237.

[3543]   Prosecution's Response Brief (Prlić), paras 243-245. See Appeal Hearing, AT. 208-209 (20 Mar 2017). The Prosecution argues in this regard that Prlić is correct that the order with exhibit number P02967 is not signed by Boban, but this only supports

when contending that the Trial Chamber placed undue weight on the statements of representatives of the international community that he appeared to be very well-informed about the situation on the ground.[3544] It also argues that, contrary to Prlić's claim, there is credible evidence supporting the Trial Chamber's **[page 463]** finding that he played a key role in ceasefire negotiations.[3545] Finally, the Prosecution submits that the Trial Chamber's finding that he had the power to co-ordinate the deployment of civilian police units is well-supported by the evidence.[3546]

ii. Analysis

1116.   Turning first to Prlić's contention that the Trial Chamber erroneously concluded that the Government discussed, with his participation, the HVO's military strategy and adopted regulations concerning the mobilisation of military personnel, the Appeals Chamber considers that Prlić has failed to demonstrate any contradiction between these findings[3547] and the finding that the areas related to mobilisation and appointment constituted some of the stated powers wielded directly by Boban.[3548] Specifically, Prlić has not demonstrated that either the Government or Boban had exclusive power in the area of mobilisation. To the contrary, he points to evidence allegedly showing that only Boban was authorised to proclaim mobilisation, with the Defence Department having the obligation to prepare and execute mobilisation. These assertions are not inconsistent with the challenged finding that the Government *adopted regulations* concerning mobilisation.[3549] The Appeals Chamber consequently dismisses Prlić's arguments in this regard.

1117.   Regarding Prlić's submission that the Trial Chamber incorrectly found that Petković testified that Prlić could issue operative orders to the armed forces through the Defence Department, the Appeals Chamber has reviewed the evidence relied on by the Trial Chamber and the evidence cited by Prlić. The Appeals Chamber considers that he has failed to demonstrate that no reasonable trier of fact could have made the challenged finding.[3550] In this regard, the Appeals Chamber considers that Prlić has failed to demonstrate the alleged contradictions.[3551] It considers in particular that Petković's testimony, cited in relation to the challenged finding that Prlić could issue operative orders to the armed forces through the Defence Department, squarely supports that finding.[3552] The Appeals Chamber further notes that the citations by Prlić, in support of his contention that Petković explicitly testified that Prlić could not issue operative orders to the military, are about other **[page 464]** matters[3553] or only state that nobody outside the chain of command (namely Mate Boban and Stojić) issued orders to Petković or the army.[3554] His arguments are dismissed.

1118.   With regard to Prlić's challenge to the Trial Chamber's finding that he "issued decisions which had a direct impact on the course of the military operations",[3555] the Appeals Chamber notes that the Trial Chamber based its finding on documents, signed by Prlić, relating to military matters.[3556] While the impugned finding

---

the Trial Chamber's finding on Prlić's power by demonstrating that Boban's signature was not required. Prosecution's Response Brief (Prlić), para. 244.

[3544]   Prosecution's Response Brief (Prlić), para. 242.

[3545]   Prosecution's Response Brief (Prlić), para. 246.

[3546]   Prosecution's Response Brief (Prlić), para. 247.

[3547]   See Trial Judgement, Vol. 4, para. 106.

[3548]   Trial Judgement, Vol. 1, para. 704 & fn. 1651, referring to Ex. P00289, Arts 29, 34, Ex. P00588, Arts 29, 34.

[3549]   The Appeals Chamber also notes that Prlić refers to his submissions in sub-grounds of appeal 16.1 and 16.2, which it dismisses elsewhere in the Judgement. See *infra*, paras 1146-1208.

[3550]   Trial Judgement, Vol. 4, para. 107 & fn. 321 and references cited therein.

[3551]   The alleged contradiction at Prlić's Appeal Brief, fn. 1003, is not supported by the references to the evidence. The alleged contradiction at Prlić's Appeal Brief, fn. 1004, is not inconsistent with the challenged finding. The alleged contradiction at Prlić's Appeal Brief, fn. 1005, is obscure and vague.

[3552]   Trial Judgement, Vol. 4, para. 107 & fn. 321, referring to Milivoj Petković, T(F). 50009-50010 (25 Feb 2010), 50342-50343 (3 Mar 2010).

[3553]   This includes, for exampie; Petković's description of his first time encounter with Prlić in July 1992 and the need for a decision made at the political level expressed at an HVO-ABiH meeting to remodel the command structure to improve efficiency. Prlić's Appeal Brief, para. 395 & fn. 1003, referring to, *inter alia*, Milivoj Petković, T. 49762-49764 (22 Feb 2010), 50775-50777 (10 Mar 2010).

[3554]   Prlić's Appeal Brief, para. 395 & fn. 1003, referring to, *inter alia*, Milivoj Petković, T. 50361-50362 (3 Mar 2010).

[3555]   Trial Judgement, Vol. 4, para. 107.

[3556]   See Trial Judgement, Vol. 4, para. 107 & fns 322-324, referring to, *inter alia*, Exs. P01184, P02967, P03038, p. 1, 1D01588. The Appeals Chamber dismisses Prlić's claim that Exhibit P02967 does not relate to military issues, considering that the exhibit

does not refer to any evidence concerning the direct impact of these documents on the course of the military operations of the HVO, the Appeals Chamber recalls that a trial judgement must be read as a whole.[3557] Since the Trial Chamber made findings elsewhere in the Trial Judgement regarding the direct impact of these decisions,[3558] and Prlić does not demonstrate any error in those findings,[3559] the Appeals Chamber concludes that Prlić has failed to show that no reasonable trier of fact could have made the impugned finding.

1119. Prlić's contention that the Trial Chamber placed undue weight on the statements of representatives of the international community that he appeared to be very well-informed of the situation on the ground,[3560] does not adequately address the broad range of evidence on which the Trial Chamber relied,[3561] offering only an unsupported claim about one allegedly contradictory piece of evidence.[3562] Thus, the contention is dismissed as a mere assertion that the Trial Chamber must have failed to consider relevant evidence, without showing that no reasonable trier of fact, based on the evidence, could have reached the same conclusion as the Trial Chamber.

1120. With regard to Prlić's submission that the Trial Chamber erroneously concluded that he played a key role in a series of ceasefire negotiations in Gornji Vakuf and Mostar, the Appeals Chamber considers that the Trial Chamber's findings in this regard are based on clearly supportive evidence. For instance, the Trial Chamber relied on Ray Lane who testified to a meeting **[page 465]** attended, *inter alios,* by Prlić that aimed at terminating the hostility in Gornji Vakuf, and on Exhibit 1D0218, a report on a meeting to find an interim arrangement for Mostar which, *inter alios,* Prlić attended.[3563] Prlić bases his challenge to the credibility of this evidence on cross-references to his ground of appeal 6, which the Appeals Chamber dismisses elsewhere.[3564] As such, he fails to demonstrate that the evidence lacks credibility. Further, he makes factual assertions that are not inconsistent with the impugned conclusions.[3565] Thus, he has failed to show that no reasonable trier of fact could have made those findings. His submission is dismissed.

1121. Turning finally to Prlić's challenge to the Trial Chamber's finding that he had the power to co-ordinate the deployment of civilian police units that were under the direct authority of the Ministry of the Interior,[3566] the Appeals Chamber considers that this finding was based on evidence on the basis of which a reasonable trier of fact could have made the impugned finding[3567] and that Prlić has failed to point to evidence to the contrary.[3568] The Trial Chamber relied, namely, on a letter from the Ministry of the Interior to, *inter alios,* Prlić, referring to a prior agreement on the governmental level as reflected in a statement by Prlić, that the civilian police be withdrawn from the front line, and the decision dated 20 October 1993 of the government

---

contains an explicit order to military authorities. Further, the Appeals Chamber considers that even on the assumption that the Trial Chamber erred in finding that Exhibit P02967 was co-signed by Boban, Prlić fails to demonstrate that this would lead to any miscarriage of justice. See Trial Judgement, Vol. 4, para. 107 & fn. 323.

[3557] *Šainović et al.* Appeal Judgement, paras 306, 321 and references cited therein.
[3558] See, *e.g.,* Trial Judgement, Vol. 2, paras 884-885 (referring to, *inter alia,* Ex. P03038, p. 1), Vol. 4, paras 126-127 (referring to, *inter alia,* Ex. P01184), 151-154 (referring to, *inter alia,* Ex. P03038), 265-267 (referring to, *inter alia,* Exs. P01184, P03038). See *infra,* paras 1149-1152, 1159-1160, 1165, 1171.
[3559] See, *e.g., infra,* para. 1160 & fn. 3679 (referring to Ex. P01184), para. 1218 & fns 3820-3821 (referring to, *inter alia,* Ex. P03038).
[3560] Trial Judgement, Vol. 4, para. 108.
[3561] See Trial Judgement, Vol. 4, fn. 325.
[3562] See Prlić's Appeal Brief, para. 400 & fns 1015-1016.
[3563] See Trial Judgement, Vol. 4, para. 109, referring to, *e.g.,* Raymond Lane, T(F). 23687-23688 (15 Oct 2007), Ex. 1D02189 (confidential), p. 1.
[3564] See *supra,* paras 212-218. Further, the Appeals Chamber fails to see why Witness DZ's statement that "the military conflict was not part of my business" (Witness DZ, T. 26494 (closed session) (22 Jan 2008)) would prevent him from providing credible evidence about Prlić's involvement in the ceasefire negotiations. See Trial Judgement, Vol. 4, para. 109 & fn. 327.
[3565] Prlić's Appeal Brief, para. 401 at fns 1018 ("Petković and Pašalić signed the Order to stop the fighting in Gornji Vakuf after Petković received Boban's order."), 1019 ("P01215 confirms that Petković and Pašalić agreed that a joint order by the ABiH and HVO high commands be sent to the local commanders in Gornji Vakuf to ease tensions."), 1022 ("Boban was directly involved in ceasefire negotiations in relation to Mostar through his proposal for an interim agreement, although the Muslims did not accept it because they wanted Prlić to be the leader of both sides."). None of these assertions are inconsistent with the impugned Trial Chamber conclusions that Prlić played a key role in a series of ceasefire negotiations in Gornji Vakuf in January 1993 and in Mostar in December 1993 and around January 1994. Trial Chamber, Vol. 4, para. 109.
[3566] Trial Judgement, Vol. 4, para. 110.
[3567] See Trial Judgement, Vol. 4, para. 110, referring to Exs. P05963, P06837.
[3568] See Prlić's Appeal Brief, para. 402 & fn. 1025 and references cited therein.

of the HR H-B, signed by Prlić, on the same issue.[3569] Prlić has also failed to demonstrate that the Trial Chamber contradicted itself when it found that he had the power to co-ordinate the deployment of these civilian police, and that his direct authority over HZ(R) H-B civilian police was not proven beyond a reasonable doubt, as these two findings are not mutually exclusive.[3570] Prlić's challenge is therefore dismissed. **[page 466]**

c. Conclusion

1122. For the foregoing reasons, the Appeals Chamber concludes that Prlić has failed to demonstrate that the Trial Chamber erred in concluding that he had power in military matters and that the HVO/Government of the HZ(R) H-B had the power and responsibility to control the HVO. As a result, the Appeals Chamber dismisses Prlić's sub-ground of appeal 12.1.

(iii) Prlić's knowledge of combat activities (Prlić's Sub-ground 12.2)

1123. The Trial Chamber found that reports on the HVO's combat activities were compiled by the Main Staff and routinely sent to the President of the HZ H-B, the Government, and the Head of the Department of Defence.[3571]

1124. Prlić submits that the Trial Chamber erred in concluding that reports on combat activities of the HVO were routinely sent to the Government,[3572] arguing that the cited documents are not reports on combat activities[3573] and that the Trial Chamber ignored relevant evidence.[3574]

1125. The Prosecution responds that Prlić ignores other findings demonstrating that he and his Government were well-informed of the military situation and, in any event, fails to show how the impugned finding, even if erroneous, could have impacted the verdict.[3575]

1126. The Appeals Chamber notes that the impugned finding was based, in part, on reports that included information on HVO combat activities,[3576] and therefore dismisses Prlić's argument to the contrary. Regarding the allegedly ignored evidence, the Appeals Chamber considers that Prlić's factual assertions are not inconsistent with the impugned finding, as they do not deal with whether information on HVO combat activities was sent to the Government,[3577] and therefore dismisses his argument in this regard. In any event, Prlić ignores other factual findings which further support the impugned finding.[3578] For these reasons, the Appeals Chamber considers that Prlić has failed to establish that no reasonable trier of fact could have reached the Trial Chamber's conclusion.[3579] Prlić's sub-ground of appeal 12.2 is dismissed. **[page 467]**

(iv) Conclusion

1127. Having dismissed Prlić's sub-grounds of appeal 12.1 and 12.2, the Appeals Chamber finds that he has failed to demonstrate any error regarding his JCE convictions under his ground of appeal 12, which is consequently dismissed in its entirety.

[3569] Exs. P05963, P06837.

[3570] Trial Judgement, Vol. 1, para. 655. The Appeals Chamber notes that the Trial Chamber expressly recalled this finding in Trial Judgement, Vol. 4, para. 110.

[3571] Trial Judgement, Vol. 1, paras 767. See Trial Judgement, Vol. 1, paras 766, 768.

[3572] Prlić''s Appeal Brief, para. 403; Appeal Hearing, AT. 138 (20 Mar 2017).

[3573] Prlić's Appeal Brief, paras 403, 405.

[3574] Prlić's Appeal Brief, paras 404, 406. See Prlić's Appeal Brief, para. 407, referring to Prlić's Appeal Brief, sub-ground of appeal 11.3.

[3575] Prosecution's Response Brief (Prlić), para. 248. See Prosecution's Response Brief (Prlić), para. 232.

[3576] See Trial Judgement, Vol. 1, para. 767 & fn. 1786, referring to, *inter alia*, Exs. P07302, pp. 2-4, 4D00830, pp. 1-2.

[3577] See Prlić's Appeal Brief, paras 404, 406.

[3578] See Trial Judgement, Vol. 1, paras 767-768.

[3579] The Appeals Chamber also notes that Prlić refers to his submissions in sub-ground of appeal 11.3, which it dismisses elsewhere in the Judgement. See *supra*, paras 1048-1058.

(c) Alleged errors regarding Prlić's powers pertaining to humanitarian aid (Prlić's Ground 14)

1128. The Trial Chamber found that Prlić held the power to negotiate and authorise the delivery of humanitarian aid in the territory of the HZ(R) H-B and in BiH.[3580] This finding was based on, *inter alia,* the finding that in June to August 1993, Prlić participated in many meetings with representatives of international organisations negotiating free access for humanitarian convoys to the HZ(R) H-B.[3581]

(i) Arguments of the Parties

1129. Prlić submits that the Trial Chamber erred in law and fact in concluding that he, as President of the HVO/Government of the HZ(R) H-B, had the power to negotiate and authorise the delivery of humanitarian aid in the territory of the HZ(R) H-B and BiH.[3582] Prlić argues that the Trial Chamber erroneously relied on: (1) Exhibit 1D00898, which does not grant authorisation to negotiate and authorise delivery of humanitarian aid;[3583] (2) Witness Klaus Johann Nissen's speculative testimony;[3584] and (3) the testimony of Witness BA who was not responsible for convoys and lacked credibility.[3585]

1130. Prlić further contends that the Trial Chamber erroneously concluded that from June to August 1993 he participated in many meetings between representatives of international organisations and the HVO negotiating free access for humanitarian convoys, as none of the **[page 468]** evidence it relied on refers to "negotiations of free access of humanitarian aid" with him.[3586] Finally, Prlić claims that the Trial Chamber ignored evidence relevant to the agreement made on 10 July 1993 between the ABiH and the HVO on the free passage of humanitarian convoys, ("Makarska Agreement"),[3587] as well as evidence that other persons had the power to approve the passage of humanitarian aid, whereas there is no evidence that he had any such power.[3588] As a result, Prlić argues that he should be acquitted of Count 25.[3589]

1131. The Prosecution responds that Prlić misrepresents the factual findings and the evidence, fails to substantiate his claims that the Trial Chamber improperly assessed or ignored evidence, and fails to demonstrate that no reasonable trial chamber could have made the challenged findings.[3590]

(ii) Analysis

1132. Turning first to Prlić's challenge based on Exhibit 1D00898, the Appeals Chamber observes that the Trial Chamber relied on this exhibit to find that "on 17 November 1992, Mile Akmadžić, President of the Government of the RBiH, appointed Jadranko Prlić as the representative of the BiH Government, in particular, for co-operation with the logistics centres of the Republic of Croatia in the distribution of humanitarian aid to the inhabitants of BiH",[3591] a finding supported by that exhibit and relevant to the

---

[3580]   Trial Judgement, Vol. 4, para. 118.

[3581]   Trial Judgement, Vol. 4, para. 117. See Trial Judgement, Vol. 4, paras 115-116, 118.

[3582]   Prlić's Appeal Brief, paras 428, 437; Appeal Hearing, AT. 145 (20 Mar 2017). Specifically, Prlić alleges that by attaching undue weight to certain evidence, and ignoring other evidence, the Trial Chamber failed to provide a reasoned opinion and applied an incorrect standard in the assessment of evidence, amounting to an error of law. Prlić's Appeal Brief, para. 437.

[3583]   Prlić's Appeal Brief, para. 435, referring to Ex. 1D00898 (a decision appointing Prlić member of the RBiH Government Staff for the Collection of Items to Help the RBiH Population Survive). See Prlić's Appeal Brief, para. 436, referring to Prlić's Appeal Brief, sub-ground of appeal 16.4.7.

[3584]   Prlić's Appeal Brief, para. 428.

[3585]   Prlić's Appeal Brief, para. 429, referring to, *inter alia,* Prlić's Appeal Brief, paras 182-183 (sub-ground of appeal 6.2). See Prlić's Reply Brief, paras 66-67. Prlić further argues that the Trial Chamber inferred from a bar table document the conclusion, which was speculative and not the only plausible one, that since the UNHCR reported an incident to Prlić in February 1993 and Ćorić responded to that report, Prlić must have entrusted Ćorić with the matter. Prlić's Appeal Brief, para. 430, referring to, *inter alia,* Prlić's Appeal Brief, ground of appeal 3.

[3586]   Prlić's Appeal Brief, para. 431. See Prlić's Appeal Brief, para. 432, referring to Prlić's Appeal Brief, sub-ground of appeal 16.4.

[3587]   Prlić's Appeal Brief, para. 433.

[3588]   Prlić's Appeal Brief, para. 434.

[3589]   Prlić's Appeal Brief, para. 438. See also Prlić's Reply Brief, para. 65.

[3590]   Prosecution's Response Brief (Prlić), paras 261-268.

[3591]   Trial Judgement, Vol. 4, para. 115, referring to Ex. 1D00898.

impugned finding.[3592] The Appeals Chamber further observes that in the part of Nissen's testimony on which the Trial Chamber relied, he appears to infer Prlić's authority regarding humanitarian convoys from Prlić's position.[3593] The Appeals Chamber considers that Prlić has failed to demonstrate that no reasonable trier of fact could have relied on this evidence, in combination with other evidence, to reach the impugned finding.[3594] Further, the Appeals Chamber considers that Prlić has failed to demonstrate that Witness BA lacked credibility or, considering **[page 469]** his/her background, that no reasonable trier of fact could have relied on his/her evidence because the witness was not responsible for convoys.[3595] These arguments are dismissed.

1133. Turning to Prlić's challenge to the Trial Chamber's finding that from June to August 1993 he participated in many meetings with representatives of international organisations negotiating free access for humanitarian convoys, the Appeals Chamber observes that in making this finding the Trial Chamber recalled a series of factual findings pertaining to Prlić's participation in contemporaneous meetings concerning freedom of access for humanitarian convoys.[3596] Regarding Prlić's argument that none of the evidence the Trial Chamber relied on refers to "negotiations of free access of humanitarian aid" with him, the Appeals Chamber considers that the Trial Chamber relied on evidence of several meetings dealing with access of humanitarian convoys in which Prlić participated,[3597] and that Prlić has failed to demonstrate that no reasonable trier of fact could have relied on that evidence to make the impugned finding.[3598] As to Prlić's argument that the Trial Chamber ignored evidence relevant to the Makarska Agreement, the Appeals Chamber considers that he has failed to explain why his assertions in this regard are inconsistent with the challenged finding.[3599] Finally, the Appeals Chamber considers that Prlić is wrong when he states that there is no evidence that he had any power to approve the passage of humanitarian aid.[3600] As such, his assertion that other persons had that power is not inconsistent with the impugned finding. These arguments are dismissed.

1134. In light of the foregoing, the Appeals Chamber dismisses Prlić's ground of appeal 14. **[page 470]**

[3592] Prlić's Appeals Chamber observes that the cited exhibit refers to Prlić being a representative of, and supporting the distribution of humanitarian aid to the inhabitants of, the "RBiH" rather than "BiH", but considers this difference to be immaterial in the context of the Trial Chamber's assessment of Prlić's powers pertaining to humanitarian aid. The Appeals Chamber also notes that Prlić refers to his submissions in sub-ground of appeal 16.4.7, which it dismisses elsewhere in the Judgement. See *infra*, paras 1262-1285.

[3593] Klaus Johann Nissen, T. 20467-20468 (25 June 2007) ("Q. We see in – in this document on the third page there's a list of people who attended – there's a list of people who attended the meeting. It says: 'For the Croatian Defence Council, Dr. Jadranko Prli[ć].' Are you in a position to comment on his authority regarding matters such as these, humanitarian convoys, to conclude such an agreement? A. I think he was authorised to conclude such an agreement, because he was the head, as I might call him, of the HVO, and it concerned the HVO as a whole, politically and militarily, to agree to such convoys to the north, to middle Bosnia").

[3594] See Trial Judgement, Vol. 4, paras 115-118. The Appeals Chamber also notes that Prlić's assertions regarding Nissen's whereabouts, knowledge, and testimony are not supported by his references to the trial record. See Prlić's Appeal Brief, para. 428 at fns 1108-1110.

[3595] See Trial Judgement, Vol. 4, para. 116 & fn. 344 and references cited therein. The Appeals Chamber notes in this regard that Prlić refers to his submissions in sub-ground of appeal 6.2, which it dismisses elsewhere in the Judgement. See *supra*, paras 212-218. With regard to the alleged error in interpreting a bar table document, the Appeals Chamber considers that Prlić fails to demonstrate that no reasonable trial chamber could have drawn the inference that Prlić must have entrusted Ćorić with the matter, in light of Witness BA's evidence on Prlić's role with regard to the passage of humanitarian convoys. See Trial Judgement, Vol. 4, para. 116 & fn. 344. The Appeals Chamber also notes that Prlić refers to his submissions in ground of appeal 3, which it dismisses elsewhere in the Judgement. See *supra*, paras 177-183.

[3596] Trial Judgement, Vol. 4, para. 117, referring to, *inter alia*, Trial Judgement, Vol. 2, paras 1230, 1238-1239.

[3597] Trial Judgement, Vol. 2, paras 1230 (referring to, *inter alia*, Ex. P09712 (confidential), para. 64), 1238 (referring to, *inter alia*, Witness BC, T(F). 18360-18365 (closed session) (14 May 2007), Ex. P09999 (confidential)), 1239 (referring to, *inter alia*, Exs. P10367 (confidential), para. 79, P04027 (confidential), pp. 1-2). For context, see Exs. P09712 (confidential), paras 62-63, 65, P10367 (confidential), paras 80-81. See also Trial Judgement, Vol.4, para. 117, referring to, *inter alia*, Ex. P10264.

[3598] The Appeals Chamber notes that Prlić makes factual assertions that are not inconsistent with the challenged finding. See Prlić's Appeal Brief, para. 431 at fns 1117-1118. The Appeals Chamber also notes that Prlić refers to his submissions in sub-ground of appeal 16.4, which it dismisses elsewhere in the Judgement. See *infra*, paras 1222-1285.

[3599] See Prlić's Appeal Brief, para. 433. *Cf.* Prlić's Appeal Brief, paras 428, 431; Trial Judgement, Vol. 4, para. 117. The Appeals Chamber notes that Prlić does not challenge in his ground of appeal 14 any findings on his *mens rea*.

[3600] See *supra*, para. 1132.

(d) Alleged errors regarding Prlić's role in the relations between HZ(R) H-B and Croatia

(i) Prlić's ties with leaders of Croatia (Prlić's Ground 15)

1135. The Trial Chamber found that between September 1992 and the end of April 1994, Prlić attended five meetings in Croatia with Franjo Tuđman, President of Croatia, and other Croatian leaders.[3601] The Trial Chamber also found that Prlić worked on economic co-operation between the HZ(R) H-B and Croatia and co-operated with the Croatian ODPR in organising the departure of Muslims "wishing to leave" the HZ H-B for Croatia or third countries.[3602]

1136. Prlić submits that the Trial Chamber erred in law and fact by finding that he, as President of the HVO/Government of the HZ(R) H-B, played a key role in the relations of the HVO/Government of the HZ(R) H-B with the Government of Croatia.[3603] Prlić first challenges the finding that from September 1992 to April 1994 he attended five meetings in Croatia with Tuđman and other Croatian leaders, arguing that the evidence shows that after the first meeting on 17 September 1992 he did not meet with Tuđman again until 5 November 1993.[3604] Second, Prlić submits that the Trial Chamber erroneously concluded that he worked on economic co-operation between HZ(R) H-B and Croatia, when in fact no economic issue or co-operation was discussed.[3605] Finally, Prlić submits that the Trial Chamber erroneously found that he co-operated with the Croatian ODPR in organising the departure of Muslims, relying on one document from Witness BA and one bar table document.[3606] As a result, Prlić argues that the Trial Chamber's findings on his JCE membership and significant contribution to the JCE are erroneous and that he should be acquitted on Counts 1-25.[3607]

1137. The Prosecution responds that the Trial Chamber's findings are reasonable and that Prlić fails to show otherwise, instead making unsubstantiated or irrelevant assertions and offering alternative explanations of the evidence.[3608] In addition, the Prosecution argues that Prlić fails to **[page 471]** show how his arguments, even if accepted, would warrant reversing his convictions on Counts 1-25.[3609]

1138. The Appeals Chamber observes that Prlić's argument that, after the first meeting on 17 September 1992, he did not meet Tuđman again until 5 November 1993 is not inconsistent with the impugned finding that they met five times between September 1992 and the end of April 1994. Further, the evidence on which the Trial Chamber relied supports the fact that Prlić met with Tuđman five times within this time period.[3610] The Appeals Chamber therefore dismisses this argument. The Appeals Chamber further considers that Prlić has failed to show that no reasonable trier of fact could have concluded that he worked on economic co-operation between HZ(R) H-B and Croatia, as the two exhibits on which the Trial Chamber relied support its finding.[3611] His submission in this regard is therefore dismissed. Finally, the Appeals Chamber considers

[3601] Trial Judgement, Vol. 4, para. 119.
[3602] Trial Judgement, Vol. 4, para. 120.
[3603] Prlić's Appeal Brief, paras 439, 447. Specifically, Prlić alleges that by attaching undue weight to certain evidence, and ignoring other evidence, the Trial Chamber failed to provide a reasoned opinion and applied an incorrect standard in the assessment of evidence, amounting to an error of law. Prlić's Appeal Brief, para. 447.
[3604] Prlić's Appeal Brief, para. 439. See Prlić's Appeal Brief, para. 440, referring to Prlić's Appeal Brief, ground of appeal 18. See also Prlić's Appeal Brief, para. 441. Prlić also argues that the Trial Chamber erred in relying on the Mladić Diaries. Prlić's Appeal Brief, para. 442. See Prlić's Appeal Brief, para. 443, referring to Prlić's Appeal Brief, ground of appeal 5.
[3605] Prlić's Appeal Brief, para. 444; Prlić's Reply Brief, para. 68.
[3606] Prlić's Appeal Brief, para. 445. See Prlić's Appeal Brief, para. 446, referring to Prlić's Appeal Brief, sub-grounds of appeal 16.6.3-16.6.4.
[3607] Prlić's Appeal Brief, paras 439, 448.
[3608] Prosecution's Response Brief (Prlić), paras 269-273, 275; Appeal Hearing, AT. 196-200, 203-205 (20 Mar 2017).
[3609] Prosecution's Response Brief (Prlić), paras 270, 274.
[3610] Trial Judgement, Vol. 4, para. 119 & fn. 348, referring to Exs. P00498, P06454, P06581, P07570, P07856. The Appeals Chamber also notes that Prlić refers to his submissions in ground of appeal 18, which it dismisses elsewhere in the Judgement. See *infra*, paras 1391-1399. In addition, the Appeals Chamber dismisses as irrelevant the factual submissions made in Prlić's Appeal Brief, para. 441. With regard to Prlić's claim that the Trial Chamber erred in relying on the Mladic Diaries, the Appeals Chamber notes that it is entirely based on a cross-reference to his ground of appeal 5, which it dismisses elsewhere in the Judgement. See *supra*, paras 107-138.
[3611] See Trial Judgement, Vol. 4, para. 120 & fn. 353, referring to Exs. P00498, p. 30 (referring to discussions on customs), P06454, pp. 37-39. The Appeals Chambers observes that the latter reference does not directly concern economic co-operation with Croatia. As pointed out by the Prosecution, other parts of Exhibit P06454 provide support for the relevant factual finding. See

that the Trial Chamber's finding that Prlić co-operated with the Croatian ODPR in organising the departure of Muslims is supported by the evidence on which the Trial Chamber relied[3612] and dismisses Prlić's submission accordingly.[3613]

1139. For the foregoing reasons, the Appeals Chamber dismisses Prlić's ground of appeal 15.

(ii) Prlić's knowledge of an international armed conflict involving Croatia (Prlić's Sub-ground 16.16)

1140. The Trial Chamber found that Prlić knew that an international armed conflict between the HVO/HV and the ABiH was taking place while he held the posts of "HVO President" and President of the Government of the HR H-B, as he: (1) was informed of the HVO military operations against the ABiH; and (2) knew about the participation of Croatia in this conflict, and facilitated it.[3614] **[page 472]** 1141. Prlić submits that the Trial Chamber erroneously concluded that he facilitated Croatia's participation in the armed conflict and knew that it was international in character.[3615] Prlić argues in this regard that: (1) there was no international armed conflict; and (2) Witness Ray Lane's evidence that he was informed of the HVO military operations against the ABiH is unsubstantiated.[3616]

1142. The Prosecution responds that the Trial Chamber reasonably found that Prlić was aware of the international character of the armed conflict and his submissions should be summarily dismissed.[3617]

1143. The Appeals Chamber notes that Prlić provides no support for his argument that there was no international armed conflict; rather, he refers to the Trial Chamber's finding that there *was* an international conflict.[3618] The Appeals Chamber therefore dismisses this argument as a mere assertion unsupported by any evidence. With regard to Prlić's challenge to Lane's evidence, the Appeals Chamber notes that the Trial Chamber based the impugned finding only in part on the evidence of Lane. Prlić ignores the remaining evidentiary basis of the finding[3619] without explaining why the conviction should not stand on the basis of the remaining evidence.[3620] The Appeals Chamber therefore dismisses this argument. For these reasons, the Appeals Chamber dismisses Prlić's sub-ground of appeal 16.16.

3. Alleged errors in relation to Prlić's significant contribution to the CCP and his intent

1144. The Trial Chamber found that Prlić, by his acts or failures to act in exercising his functions, was a principal member of the JCE, significantly contributed to it, and intended to implement the CCP, an intention he shared with the other JCE members.[3621]

1145. In the present section, the Appeals Chamber will address Prlić's challenges to the Trial Chamber's findings regarding his: (1) contribution to the JCE in the municipalities of Gornji Vakuf, Prozor, Jablanica, Mostar, and Vareš; (2) involvement in the arrest and detention of Muslims, the movement of population, and the concealment of crimes; and (3) *mens rea* and *actus reus* of commission through a JCE. **[page 473]**

Prosecution's Response Brief (Prlić), fn. 935, referring to, *inter alia*, Ex. P06454, pp. 31, 34. Noting that the Trial Chamber relied on these pages elsewhere in the relevant section of the Trial Judgement, the Appeals Chamber finds that Prlić does not demonstrate a factual error resulting in a miscarriage of justice. See Trial Judgement, Vol. 4, para. 119 & fn. 349, referring to, *inter alia*, Ex. P06454, pp. 30-39 (referring to, *inter alia*: (1) co-operation between the respective ministries of finance; and (2) potential Croatian investments).

[3612]   See Trial Judgement, Vol. 4, para. 120 & fn. 355, referring to Exs. P07019, P09679 (confidential), p. 1.
[3613]   The Appeals Chamber also notes that Prlić refers to his submissions in sub-grounds of appeal 16.6.3 and 16.6.4, which it dismisses elsewhere in the Judgement. See *infra*, paras 1300, 1304-1306, 1308-1309, 1315, 1317.
[3614]   Trial Judgement, Vol. 4, para. 277.
[3615]   Prlić's Appeal Brief, paras 624-625.
[3616]   Prlić's Appeal Brief, para. 624. See Prlić's Appeal Brief, para. 626, referring to Prlić's Appeal Brief, paras 202-203 (sub-ground of appeal 6.2), ground of appeal 15, para. 649 (ground of appeal 18).
[3617]   Prosecution's Response Brief (Prlić), para. 398.
[3618]   See Prlić's Appeal Brief, para. 624 & fn. 1598, referring to Trial Judgement, Vol. 4, para. 277.
[3619]   See Trial Judgement, Vol. 4, para. 277, referring to Ray Lane, T(F). 23681-23684, 23687-23688, 23691, 23697 (15 Oct 2007), Exs. P01215, P03038, Trial Judgement, Vol. 4, paras 119-120.
[3620]   The Appeals Chamber also notes that Prlić refers to his submissions in (sub-)grounds of appeal 6.2, 15, and 18, which it dismisses elsewhere in the Judgement. See *supra*, paras 212-218, 1135-1139; *infra*, paras 1391-1399.
[3621]   See Trial Judgement, Vol. 4, paras 122-276.

(a) Gornji Vakuf Municipality (Prlić's Sub-ground 16.1)

(i) The 15 January 1993 Ultimatum (Prlić's Sub-ground 16.1.1)

1146. The Trial Chamber found that on 15 January 1993, Prlić signed a decision, adopted at an HVO session that same day, whereby all ABiH units stationed in the so-called Croatian provinces 3, 8, and 10 were to submit themselves to the command of the HVO Main Staff within five days ("15 January 1993 Ultimatum").[3622] It further found that by drafting, *inter alia,* this ultimatum, Prlić significantly contributed to the implementation of the JCE in Gornji Vakuf Municipality.[3623]

a. Arguments of the Parties

1147. Prlić submits that the Trial Chamber erred in making these findings by mischaracterising evidence and disregarding relevant evidence.[3624] He asserts in particular that: (1) the 15 January 1993 Ultimatum and "orders by Stojić and Petković" did not represent an "ultimatum" to the ABiH;[3625] (2) the Trial Chamber ignored evidence that Alija Izetbegović signed the constitutional principles of the Vance-Owen Plan, and that its Annex VII provided for a withdrawal of all formations into provinces where the ethnic group of their affiliation represented the majority until complete demilitarisation was reached;[3626] (3) the 15 January 1993 Ultimatum implemented the agreement reached in Zagreb on the same day;[3627] and (4) after Izetbegović reneged on this agreement, Mate Boban accordingly issued an order to withdraw the 15 January 1993 Ultimatum, with which the HVO HZ H-B complied.[3628] Finally, Prlić argues that the Trial Chamber erred in **[page 474]** finding that HVO Colonel Miro Andrić issued two orders for subordination, on 14 and 16 January 1993 considering: (1) that an order issued on 14 January 1993 could not have been based on the 15 January 1993 Ultimatum; and (2) the lack of corroborating evidence that there was any other "decision" or "subordination order".[3629]

1148. The Prosecution responds that the Trial Chamber's findings on the 15 January 1993 Ultimatum are reasonable.[3630] It contends further that in claiming that there was no ultimatum, Prlić makes irrelevant and erroneous assertions.[3631] The Prosecution argues that the Trial Chamber considered evidence "that

---

[3622]   Trial Judgement, Vol. 4, paras 125, 127.

[3623]   Trial Judgement, Vol. 4, para. 271.

[3624]   Prlić's Appeal Brief, para. 451. See Appeal Hearing, AT. 139-142, 162 (20 Mar 2017). Prlić also argues that the Trial Chamber erred in relying on Witness William Tomljanovich. Prlić's Appeal Brief, para. 451, referring to Prlić's ground of appeal 4.2. See also Prlić's Appeal Brief, paras 449-450, 627-629.

[3625]   Prlić's Appeal Brief, para. 452; Appeal Hearing, AT. 139-142, 160-162 169-170, 243 (20 Mar 2017). See Prlić's Appeal Brief, para. 451. See also Appeal Hearing, AT. 244 (20 Mar 2017). In this regard, Prlić further argues, *inter alia,* that: (1) the decision and orders called for reciprocity in re-subordination, the establishment of an ABiH-HVO joint command, and HVO commanders to initiate talks with ABiH commanders on the best way of setting up joint commands; (2) the decision and orders prescribed no measures for lack of compliance (referring to Witness Christopher Beese's evidence); (3) weapons flowed freely from the HZ H-B to the ABiH at that time, including the area of Gornji Vakuf; and (4) the HVO HZ H-B resolved to provide help to HVO units in Provinces 1, 5, and 9 according to the Vance-Owen Peace Plan which were to be subordinated to the ABiH. Prlić's Appeal Brief, para. 452; Appeal Hearing, AT. 139-140 (20 Mar 2017).

[3626]   See Prlić's Appeal Brief, para. 455; Appeal Hearing, AT. 159-160, 243 (20 Mar 2017). See also Appeal Brief, para. 454. In this regard, Prlić further contends that the ICFY's co-chairmen concurred that it was up to the ABiH and HVO to make arrangements concerning this withdrawal. Prlić's Appeal Brief, para. 455.

[3627]   Prlić's Appeal Brief, paras 456-459; Appeal Hearing, AT. 160-162, 170, 243 (20 Mar 2017). See Appeal Hearing, AT. 140 (20 Mar 2017). Prlić submits that this agreement had to be implemented swiftly due to the tensions erupting in Gornji Vakuf. Appeal Hearing, AT. 160-162, 169-170, 241-244 (20 Mar 2017). In particular, Prlić contends that the Trial Chamber disregarded its own finding that on 18 January 1993, Mate Boban and Mile Akmadžić sent a letter to Alija Izetbegović explaining that the 15 January 1993 Ultimatum was "in accordance with the Geneva Conference". Prlić's Appeal Brief, para. 457; Appeal Hearing, AT. 140 (20 Mar 2017). See also Prlić's Appeal Brief, para. 456.

[3628]   Prlić's Appeal Brief, para. 459; Appeal Hearing, AT. 141, 160-161, 243 (20 Mar 2017). See also Appeal Hearing, AT. 133-134 (20 Mar 2017).

[3629]   Prlić's Appeal Brief, para. 453, referring to, *inter alia,* Trial Judgement, Vol. 4, para. 125.

[3630]   Prosecution's Response Brief (Prlić), paras 280-282; Appeal Hearing, AT. 181, 192, 208-210 (20 Mar 2017). See also Prosecution's Response Brief (Prlić), paras 276-279.

[3631]   Prosecution's Response Brief (Prlić), para. 281. See Appeal Hearing, AT. 181 (20 Mar 2017).

Izetbegović signed the constitutional principles" since it found that the Muslims accepted those principles.[3632] It contends that Prlić mischaracterises the evidence and the Trial Judgement by suggesting that the 15 January 1993 Ultimatum was in accordance with the Vance-Owen Peace Plan.[3633] The Prosecution further submits that Prlić's claim of a Zagreb agreement relies almost entirely on the self-serving claims of Praljak, who even conceded that Izetbegović never signed the document containing the alleged agreement.[3634] The Prosecution contends that: (1) Prlić's claim that Boban "withdrew" the 15 January 1993 Ultimatum is not supported by the evidence cited;[3635] and (2) he erroneously claims that the Trial Chamber found that two "subordination orders" existed.[3636]

b. Analysis

1149. The Appeals Chamber turns first to Prlić's submission that the Trial Chamber mischaracterised the evidence and disregarded relevant evidence.[3637] With regard to Prlić's argument that the 15 January 1993 Ultimatum and orders by Stojić and Petković did not represent an "ultimatum" to the ABiH, the Appeals Chamber considers that a reasonable trier of fact could have reached the conclusion of the Trial Chamber,[3638] based on, notably, the findings, supported by ample evidence, that: (1) the 15 January 1993 Ultimatum contained an order to all ABiH units in **[page 475]** the so-called Croatian provinces under the Vance-Owen Peace Plan to subordinate themselves to the HVO within five days;[3639] (2) Stojić's order down the chain of command of the same day, implementing the decision, prescribed measures in case of failure to comply;[3640] and (3) Stojić's order was restated in substance in the order of the same day sent down the chain of command by Petković.[3641]

1150. The evidence that Prlić refers to in support of his argument that the decision and orders at issue do not represent an ultimatum[3642] does not show that no reasonable trier of fact could have reached the findings of the Trial Chamber.[3643] Prlić's submissions in this regard amount to a mere disagreement with the Trial Chamber's interpretation of the evidence. In particular, contrary to his assertions,[3644] the evidence he refers to supports the Trial Chamber's findings that the 15 January 1993 Ultimatum as implemented by the orders down the HVO chain of command foresaw measures for lack of compliance.[3645] This argument is dismissed.

[3632] Prosecution's Response Brief (Prlić), para. 282.

[3633] Prosecution's Response Brief (Prlić), para. 282; Appeal Hearing, AT. 182 (20 Mar 2017).

[3634] Prosecution's Response Brief (Prlić), para. 283. It asserts that Prlić fails to demonstrate that the Trial Chamber acted unreasonably when it declined to credit Slobodan Praljak's testimony, which is contradicted by contemporaneous records. Prosecution's Response Brief (Prlić), para. 283.

[3635] Prosecution's Response Brief (Prlić), para. 284. The Prosecution further contends that Prlić fails to explain how the Trial Chamber disregarded its finding on the 18 January 1993 letter. Prosecution's Response Brief (Prlić), para. 283.

[3636] Prosecution's Response Brief (Prlić), para. 285.

[3637] With regard to Prlić's argument that the Trial Chamber erred in relying on Tomljanovich, the Appeals Chamber notes that it is entirely based on a cross-reference to his sub-ground of appeal 4.2, which it dismisses elsewhere in the Judgement. See *supra*, paras 204-211.

[3638] See, in particular, Exs. P01139, nos 4, 8, P01140, nos 2-3, 7, P01146/P01155, nos 1, 4-5. The Appeals Chamber understands Prlić to refer for the finding of an "ultimatum" to the challenged findings in Trial Judgement, Vol. 4, paras 127, 271, which in turn are based on challenged findings in Trial Judgement, Vol. 4, para. 125, and underlying findings.

[3639] Trial Judgement, Vol. 4, para. 125, referring to, *inter alia*, Trial Judgement, Vol. 1, para. 452.

[3640] Trial Judgement, Vol. 4, para. 125, referring to, *inter alia*, Trial Judgement, Vol. 1, para. 453.

[3641] Trial Judgement, Vol. 4, para. 125, referring to, *inter alia*, Trial Judgement, Vol. 1, para. 454.

[3642] Prlić's Appeal Brief, para. 452 & fn. 1145.

[3643] Further, the Appeals Chamber notes that the referenced evidence does not provide support for Prlić's assertions that the 15 January 1993 Ultimatum and the two orders down the chain of command did not contain an ultimatum since (as Prlić appears to assert by way of referencing evidence to this effect) an agreement on a joint command was allegedly reached in Zagreb. See *infra*, fn. 3648. Other evidence that Prlić refers to supports the Trial Chamber's findings of an ultimatum (see, *e.g.*, Exs. P01139 nos 4, 8, P01140, nos 2-3, 7, P01146/P01155, nos 1, 4-5) or is irrelevant (see, *e.g.*, Exs. P01032, p. 16 (referring to an HVO order in relation to Travnik, Mostar, and Posavina only), P03642, pp. 1-2). The Appeals Chamber notes in particular that Prlić's assertions regarding reciprocal subordination and an ABiH-HVO joint command are not inconsistent with the finding of the 15 January 1993 decision's and the orders' nature as an ultimatum. See also Trial Judgement, Vol. 1, para. 399.

[3644] Prlić's Appeal Brief, para. 452 & fn. 1148.

[3645] Exs. P01139, nos 4, 8, P01140, nos 2-3, 7, P01146/P01155, nos 4-6. Beese's lack of knowledge of such measures is of no assistance to Prlić's argument. Christopher Beese, T. 5205-5206 (21 Aug 2006). Further, the Appeals Chamber considers that Prlić's assertions on the free flow of weapons into Gornji Vakuf and the resolve of the HVO HZ H-B to assist HVO units in Provinces 1, 5, and 9 are irrelevant to his challenge to the characterisation as an "ultimatum" of the 15 January 1993 decision and the two orders.

1151. The Appeals Chamber notes that the Trial Chamber explicitly found that the Muslims accepted the constitutional principles of the Vance-Owen Peace Plan[3646] and therefore dismisses Prlić's claim that the Trial Chamber ignored evidence to this effect. Insofar as Prlić calls into question the findings on the character of the decision and the orders as an ultimatum by referring to Annex VII of the Vance-Owen Peace Plan providing for a withdrawal of all units into their ethnic majority provinces until complete demilitarisation, the Appeals Chamber considers that Prlić has failed to demonstrate that an agreement concerning withdrawal had been reached.[3647] Similarly, **[page 476]** Prlić has failed to demonstrate the existence of a "Zagreb agreement".[3648] The Appeals Chamber therefore dismisses these arguments.[3649]

1152. As for Prlić's argument that Izetbegović reneged on the alleged Zagreb agreement, and that as a result, Boban issued an order to withdraw the 15 January 1993 Ultimatum, which was complied with, the Appeals Chamber has examined the evidence that Prlić cites in support of this argument.[3650] At the outset, the Appeals Chamber observes that since Prlić has failed to demonstrate the existence of a "Zagreb agreement",[3651] it follows that he fails to show that Izetbegović reneged on it. In this regard, the Appeals Chamber further observes that Exhibit P01158 does not confirm that he reneged on the alleged agreement – rather, Gojko Šušak, speaking to Izetbegović, refers to a "gentleman's agreement that you *would work on this*"[3652] and the exhibit contains no answer from Izetbegović confirming that he was distancing himself from any such agreement. With regard to Praljak's testimony on the matter,[3653] the Appeals Chamber recalls that the Trial Chamber found parts of Praljak's testimony "hardly credible".[3654] Finally, concerning the alleged withdrawal of the 15 January 1993 Ultimatum, the Appeals Chamber notes that the evidence on which Prlić relies concerns a change of the deadline of the 15 January 1993 Ultimatum, not its withdrawal.[3655] For these reasons, the Appeals Chamber dismisses Prlić's argument.

1153. With regard to Prlić's argument that the Trial Chamber erred in finding that two orders for subordination by Andrić existed, dated 14 and 16 January 1993, the Appeals Chamber notes that he essentially only advances arguments militating against the existence of and concerning the finding on the earlier order.[3656] The Appeals Chamber recalls the Trial Chamber's findings that: **[page 477]**

> On 16 January 1993, implementing an HVO decision adopted the same day, Miro Andrić, a colonel in the HVO Main Staff, passed on the general order on subordination issued by Milivoj Petković on 15 January 1993 to the representatives of the ABiH in Gornji Vakuf and again demanded that all the ABiH forces subordinate themselves to the HVO forces. The Chamber recalls that, according to *Fahrudin Agić,* on 14 January 1993 Miro Andrić had demanded the subordination of all the ABiH forces to the HVO forces in the Municipality of Gornji Vakuf. *Fahrudin Agić* also stated that Miro Andrić issued the order on the basis

---

[3646]   Trial Judgement, Vol. 1, para. 451.

[3647]   See Prlić's Appeal Brief, para. 455. Prlić makes submissions and refers to evidence suggesting that agreement on this matter had yet to be reached. See *supra*, fn. 3626. See also Trial Judgement, Vol. 1, para. 451.

[3648]   The Appeals Chamber has examined the evidence Prlić cites in support and finds it unclear and unconvincing in this regard. See Prlić's Appeal Brief, paras. 456-459 and references cited therein. In addition, with regard to Praljak's testimony, the Appeals Chamber recalls that the Trial Chamber found parts of it "hardly credible". Trial Judgement, Vol. 1, para. 399. In these circumstances, the Appeals Chamber considers that Prlić has failed to demonstrate that the Trial Chamber erred in its assessment of the evidence relating to the alleged "Zagreb agreement".

[3649]   The Appeals Chamber considers that Prlić fails to show that the Trial Chamber disregarded its own finding that in the letter addressed to Alija Izetbegović on 18 January 1993, Mate Boban and Mile Akmadzić recalled that the 15 January 1993 Ultimatum was "in accordance with the 'Geneva Conference'", since the finding on the content of the letter is not a finding on the truth of the matter asserted therein and that, in any event, this does not show that an agreement was reached as asserted by Prlić. See Trial Judgement, Vol. 1, para. 458.

[3650]   See Prlić's Appeal Brief, para. 459, referring to Slobodan Praljak, T. 40572-40576 (21 May 2009). 40617-40622 (25 May 2009), 41959-41962, 41975-41976 (24 June 2009), Exs. P01158, P01240, pp. 5-19, P01267, 1D00820, 1D00821; Appeal Hearing, AT. 141 (20 Mar 2017), referring to Exs. P01267, P02046/1D01655, 1D00820, 1D00821.

[3651]   See *supra*, para. 1151.

[3652]   Ex. P01158, p. 51 (emphasis added).

[3653]   See Prlić's Appeal Brief, fn. 1177 and references cited therein. See also Prlić's Appeal Brief, fn. 1178 and references cited therein.

[3654]   Trial Judgement, Vol. 1, para. 399.

[3655]   See Prlić's Appeal Brief, fns 1179-1180, referring to Exs. 1D00820, 1D00821, P01267. *Cf.* Ex. P01146/P01155, no 5.

[3656]   Prlić's Appeal Brief, para. 453, referring to, *inter alia,* Trial Judgement, Vol. 4, para. 125. Prlić's reference to Trial Judgement, Vol. 2, para. 330 appears to be mistaken.

of documents signed by Jadranko Prlić. On 16 and 17 January 1993, the ABiH rejected Miro Andrić's orders to subordinate.[3657]

The Appeals Chamber observes, first, that the Trial Chamber did not claim that the order issued on 14 January 1993 was based on the 15 January 1993 Ultimatum.[3658] Further, the Appeals Chamber considers that the Trial Chamber based its finding that Andrić issued a subordination order on 14 January 1993 on the testimony of Witness Fahrudin Agić[3659] and that there is no general requirement that the testimony of a witness be corroborated if deemed otherwise credible.[3660] Even assuming that no reasonable trier of fact could have found that Andrić issued two separate subordination orders, the Appeals Chamber sees no indication that the Trial Chamber relied specifically on the existence of *two* such orders to make any adverse findings against Prlić.[3661] Consequently, the Appeals Chamber finds that any such error would not have resulted in a miscarriage of justice. The Appeals Chamber consequently dismisses this argument. Sub-ground of appeal 16.1.1 is dismissed.

(ii) Military operations following the 15 January 1993 Ultimatum (Prlić's Sub-ground 16.1.2)

1154. The Trial Chamber found that the 15 January 1993 Ultimatum was followed by systematic and widespread military operations undertaken through the chain of command of the HVO, including in Gornji Vakuf in January 1993, which involved the commission of many crimes against the Muslim population as part of a single preconceived plan.[3662] The Trial Chamber further found, as one of many findings on which it based the aforementioned conclusion, that on 18 January 1993, Colonel Miro Andrić ordered HVO troops in Gornji Vakuf to use force to compel the ABiH to implement the ceasefire agreement of 13 January 1993 and to capture the village of Uzričje in order to open a route to Gornji Vakuf, in accordance with an order sent by his "superiors".[3663] Another such underlying finding was that Prlić sent a letter on 18 January 1993 to the Gornji Vakuf municipal HVO and its Croatian population, assuring them of the support of his government which **[page 478]** would not leave them "at the mercy of the Muslim extremists", promising assistance by the HVO as necessary.[3664]

a. Arguments of the Parties

1155. Prlić submits that the Trial Chamber erred in finding that the 15 January 1993 Ultimatum was followed by military operations in Gornji Vakuf by contradicting its own findings and by mischaracterising and ignoring evidence.[3665] In particular, Prlić submits that the Trial Chamber: (1) ignored testimony by Witness Milan Gorjanc that Petković's orders (Exhibits P01135 and P01139) did not represent orders to attack the ABiH, and that the latter order on the contrary obliged operative zone commanders to initiate talks with ABiH commanders in order to establish joint commands;[3666] (2) mischaracterised Andrić's report of 27 January 1993, arguing that Andrić's actions were unrelated to the 15 January 1993 Ultimatum;[3667] and (3) mischaracterised the HVO HZ H-B letter dated 18 January 1993 addressed to Gornji Vakuf and erroneously referred to it as "Prlić's letter".[3668]

3657   Trial Judgement, Vol. 4, para. 125 (internal references omitted). See also Trial Judgement, Vol. 4, fns 362, 364.

3658   See Trial Judgement, Vol. 4, para. 125 & fn. 364.

3659   Trial Judgement, Vol. 4, para. 125 & fn. 363, referring to, *inter alia*, Fahrudin Agić, T(F). 9285-9288 (31 Oct 2006).

3660   *Popović et al.* Appeal Judgement, paras 243, 1264; *D. Milošević* Appeal Judgement, para. 215. See also *Kordić and Čerkez* Appeal Judgement, para. 274; Trial Judgement, Vol. 4, fn. 362.

3661   See Trial Judgement, Vol. 4, paras 125-135.

3662   Trial Judgement, Vol. 4, para. 271. See Trial Judgement, Vol. 1, para. 460.

3663   Trial Judgement, Vol. 4, para. 126. See Trial Judgement, Vol. 4, para. 127.

3664   Trial Judgement, Vol. 4, para. 126.

3665   Prlić's Appeal Brief, para. 460. See Prlić's Appeal Brief, paras 461-463.

3666   Prlić's Appeal Brief, para. 461; Appeal Hearing, AT. 141 (20 Mar 2017). See Appeal Hearing, AT. 149-150 (20 Mar 2017).

3667   Prlić's Appeal Brief, para. 462; Prlić's Reply Brief, para. 69; Appeal Hearing, AT. 140-141 (20 Mar 2017). Prlić' further submits that the Trial Chamber ignored testimony by Praljak and Witness Zrinko Tokić and Exhibit 4D00356 when finding that military operations in Gornji Vakuf followed the 15 January 1993 Ultimatum. Prlić's Appeal Brief, para. 460 & fn. 1182. Prlić also argues that the Trial Chamber relied on an erroneous translation of Andrić's report of 27 January 1993 (Ex. 3D03065/4D00348), which correctly reads in relevant parts "following a higher order" instead of "following an order from [their] superiors", resulting in erroneous findings. Prlić's Reply Brief, para. 69, referring to, *inter alia*, Prlić's Response Brief, para. 177 (Prosecution's ground 3).

3668   Prlić's Appeal Brief, para. 463.

1156. The Prosecution responds that Prlić fails to show that no reasonable trial chamber could have found that the 15 January 1993 Ultimatum resulted in HVO attacks on Gornji Vakuf involving crimes against the Muslim population forming part of the CCP.[3669] In particular, it submits that Prlić fails to show any error in his attempts to "recharacterise" Petković's order as unrelated to the 15 January 1993 Ultimatum.[3670] It further contends that the Trial Chamber reasonably interpreted Andrić's report and that the evidence Prlić cites does not support that the Gornji Vakuf attacks were unrelated to the 15 January 1993 Ultimatum.[3671] The Prosecution further submits that Prlić fails to explain how the Trial Chamber mischaracterised his 18 January 1993 letter.[3672] **[page 479]**

b. Analysis

1157. The Appeals Chamber turns first to Prlić's claim that the Trial Chamber, in reaching the challenged findings that the 15 January 1993 Ultimatum was followed by military operations in Gornji Vakuf, contradicted its own findings. The Appeals Chamber notes that the portion of the Trial Judgement that Prlić references as containing the findings that are allegedly contradicted is irrelevant to the findings on military operations in Gornji Vakuf in January 1993 that he challenges.[3673] The Appeals Chamber dismisses this undeveloped assertion.

1158. Turning to Prlić's argument concerning Petković's orders, the Appeals Chamber notes that Gorjanc, in his testimony referenced by Prlić, asserted that he could not glean from one of Petković's orders (Exhibit P01135) that it contained an order for military operations against the ABiH. However, he confirmed the HVO's heightened readiness to resort to armed force in Gornji Vakuf, which supports rather than undermines the challenged findings on military operations in Gornji Vakuf following the 15 January 1993 Ultimatum.[3674] The HVO's heightened readiness is also evident from Exhibit P01135 itself and other evidence Prlić refers to.[3675] In light of this, Prlić's reliance on the instruction contained in Petković's other order (Exhibit P01139) to HVO commanders to initiate talks with ABiH commanders on joint commands, in support of his challenge to the Trial Chamber's findings, also fails. Prlić's arguments do not show that no reasonable trier of fact could have reached the impugned findings and are therefore dismissed.

1159. Further, having reviewed the relevant Trial Chamber findings and supporting evidence, the Appeals Chamber finds no merit in Prlić's assertion that the Trial Chamber mischaracterised Andrić's 27 January 1993 report.[3676] Turning to Prlić's assertion that "Andrić's actions", which the Appeals Chamber understands to refer to his 18 January 1993 order to the HVO to attack the ABiH, were unrelated to the 15 January 1993 Ultimatum, the Appeals Chamber notes that none of the **[page 480]** references Prlić cites support his

---

[3669]   Prosecution's Response Brief (Prlić), para. 286; Appeal Hearing, AT. 182 (20 Mar 2017). See also Prosecution's Response Brief (Prlić), para. 288; Appeal Hearing, AT. 192, 210-211 (20 Mar 2017).

[3670]   Prosecution's Response Brief (Prlić), para. 287.

[3671]   Prosecution's Response Brief (Prlić), para. 288; Appeal Hearing, AT. 208-210 (20 Mar 2017).

[3672]   Prosecution's Response Brief (Prlić), para. 289.

[3673]   Prlić's Appeal Brief, para. 460, referring to, *inter alia*, Trial Judgement, Vol. 1, paras 336-337, which pertain to findings on changes in the ethnic composition in "Herceg-Bosna" in the period 1991-1994.

[3674]   Milan Gorjanc, T. 46380-46382 (2 Nov 2009).

[3675]   See Prlić's Appeal Brief, para. 461, referring to, *e.g.*, Ex. P01163, pp. 2-4 (report dated 16 January 1993 on an HVO general's message to the ABiH in Gornji Vakuf to subordinate and abide by further conditions while pointing to the presence of two HVO brigades, artillery, and tanks in Prozor, which would be ready to advance on Gornji Vakuf should the HVO demands not be met by the following day).

[3676]   The Trial Chamber found, *inter alia*, based on the report, that "[o]n 18 January 1993, Colonel Miro Andrić ordered the HVO troops in Gornji Vakuf to use force to compel the ABiH to implement the terms of the ceasefire agreement of 13 January 1993 and to capture the village of Uzričje in order to open a route to Gornji Vakuf, in accordance with the order sent by his 'superiors'". Trial Judgement, Vol. 4, para. 126, referring to Ex. 3D03065/4D00348. Prlić asserts, based on the report, that "on 18 January [1993] Andrić ordered the implementation of the 13 January 1993 [ceasefire] Agreement". Prlić's Appeal Brief, para. 462. The Appeals Chamber fails to see any inconsistency between the two statements. Insofar as Prlić challenges the finding that Andrić's actions were "in accordance with the order sent by his 'superiors'", the Appeals Chamber can see no relevant material difference between this formulation and the alternative translation "following a higher order". See also *supra*, paras 177-183, *infra*, fn. 5050. Prlić merely offers an alternative interpretation of the evidence without showing that no reasonable trier of fact could have made the impugned findings.

assertion.[3677] On the contrary, many referenced exhibits indicate that the use of force on 18 January 1993 was a reaction to the ABiH not bowing to the conditions of the 15 January 1993 Decision.[3678] Prlić therefore has failed to show that no reasonable trier of fact could have reached the impugned findings and the Appeals Chamber dismisses his arguments.

1160.   Turning to Prlić's argument concerning the HVO HZ H-B letter dated 18 January 1993, the Appeals Chamber considers that the text of the letter supports the impugned finding and that Prlić has failed to show that no reasonable trier of fact could have made this finding or characterised the letter – bearing his typed name – as Prlić's.[3679] Further, he has failed to explain the relevance of his remaining assertions regarding the letter to his challenge to the Trial Chamber's finding on the letter.[3680]

1161.   In light of the above, sub-ground of appeal 16.1.2 is dismissed.[3681]

(iii) <u>Various findings concerning the January 1993 attacks on Gornji Vakuf (Prlić's Sub-ground 16.1.3)</u>

1162.   The Trial Chamber found that: (1) Prlić was directly involved in planning the attack on Gornji Vakuf, the 15 January 1993 Ultimatum signed by him, and its implementation on the ground until the ceasefire when he ordered the cessation of HVO attacks on 25 January 1993;[3682] (2) on 19 January 1993, Prlić attended ceasefire negotiations in Mostar concerning Gornji Vakuf Municipality;[3683] (3) Colonel Miro Andrić stated that his "superiors" had ordered him to use force in Gornji Vakuf, and that Prlić was one of his "superiors";[3684] and (4) Prlić said at a meeting on **[page 481]** 25 January 1993 with an ECMM representative in Mostar that he had ordered the HVO commander in Gornji Vakuf to stop all attacks immediately.[3685]

a. Arguments of the Parties

1163.   Prlić submits that the Trial Chamber erred in concluding that: (1) he was involved in planning the attack on Gornji Vakuf; (2) on 19 January 1993, he attended ceasefire negotiations, considering that Witness Ray Lane's evidence was not reliable;[3686] (3) Prlić was one of Andrić's superiors, by relying solely on one

---

[3677]   The same applies to the testimony of Praljak and Tokić and Exhibit 4D00356 to which Prlić refers as allegedly ignored by the Trial Chamber in reaching the impugned finding that military operations in Gornji Vakuf followed the 15 January 1993 Ultimatum. For Slobodan Praljak, T. 44073-44074, 44085 (31 Aug 2009), the Appeals Chamber also recalls that the Trial Chamber found Praljak's evidence "hardly credible" on certain points. Trial Judgement, Vol. 1, para. 399. This argument is dismissed.

[3678]   Exs. P01163; P01174; P01182; P01185, p. 4; P01226; P01236, pp. 3-4; 1D00816. See also Exs. P01227, p. 1; 3D03065/4D00348, pp. 2-3. Regarding Slobodan Praljak, T.' 40578-40581 (21 May 2009), 40591-40594 (25 May 2009), the Appeals Chamber again recalls that the Trial Chamber found Praljak's evidence "hardly credible" on certain points. Trial Judgement, Vol. 1, para. 399.

[3679]   Ex. P01184.

[3680]   See Prlić's Appeal Brief, para. 463.

[3681]   The Appeals Chamber recalls that it has overturned the Trial Chamber's findings regarding the deaths of seven civilians in Duša and that murder and wilful killing were part of the CCP in the period from January until June 1993. See *supra*, paras 441-443, 882. The Appeals Chamber does not consider that these changes affect the Trial Chamber's finding that is challenged under this ground insofar as it concerns the remaining crimes, namely that the HVO operations following the 15 January 1993 Ultimatum, including those in Gornji Vakuf, involved the commission of many crimes against the Muslim population as part of a single preconceived plan. This is in particular since the Duša killings were the only killings among those crimes. See *supra*, para. 876.

[3682]   Trial Judgement, Vol. 4, para. 131. See also Trial Judgement, Vol. 4, paras 126-127, 132, 134.

[3683]   Trial Judgement, Vol. 4, para. 127.

[3684]   Trial Judgement, Vol. 4, paras 126-127, 133.

[3685]   Trial Judgement, Vol. 4, para. 129.

[3686]   Prlić's Appeal Brief, para. 464; Prlić's Reply Brief, paras 70-73, referring to Prlić's Appeal Brief, paras 202-203 (sub-ground of appeal 6.2). See also Prlić's Appeal Brief, para. 466. With regard to the finding on negotiations, Prlić submits in particular that Lane was a poor witness who did not recall the meeting's location and what was discussed, and that he speculated about Prlić's powers. He further argues that Lane was discredited by Exhibit P01215, p. 1, which suggests that Petković, Arif Pašalić, and Prlić met separately. Prlić's Appeal Brief, para. 464; Prlić's Reply Brief, paras 70-73. Further, he submits that the Trial Chamber erred in concluding that the 20 January 1993 order by Petković and Pašalić to abort all combat activities in Gornji Vakuf was based on a meeting of these two persons with Prlić and Jean-Jacques Beaussou. This contradicts, in Prlić's submission, another finding that the order by Petković and Pašalić rather "concurred" with an order by Mate Boban, as corroborated by other evidence. Prlić's Appeal Brief, para. 465.

sentence in one exhibit;[3687] (4) he stated on 25 January 1993 that he had ordered the HVO in Gornji Vakuf to stop all attacks;[3688] and (5) Željko Šiljeg's reports on Gornji Vakuf were "particularly" sent to the HVO HZ H-B.[3689]

1164. The Prosecution responds that Prlić fails to show that no reasonable trial chamber could have found that he was directly involved in planning the attack on Gornji Vakuf, the 15 January 1993 Ultimatum, and its implementation on the ground.[3690] Notably, it argues that the Trial Chamber's findings are supported by the evidence and that Prlić fails to explain how the Trial Chamber acted unreasonably and how his submissions impact the challenged findings.[3691]

b. Analysis

1165. The Appeals Chamber will first address Prlić's challenge to the finding that he was one of Andrić's "superiors". It notes that Prlić reproduces the findings he claims contradict the challenged **[page 482]** finding in an incomplete manner and misrepresents them.[3692] Prlić alleges that the Trial Chamber found that he was not in the military chain of command, but omits that the Trial Chamber qualified this finding by determining that: (1) as President of the Government he had influence on the defence strategy and military operations of the HVO; (2) the HVO/Government of HZ(R) H-B, as a civilian authority, had the power and responsibility to control, in general and particularly in terms of military strategy, the HVO; (3) that during meetings between August 1992 and April 1994, in which Prlić participated as President of the Government, the situation and military strategy of the HVO in the territory claimed to be part of the HZ(R) H-B were discussed and the Government adopted various regulations, concerning, for instance, mobilisation of military personnel and the supply of weapons.[3693] Notably, the Trial Chamber considered in this respect the 15 January 1993 Ultimatum.[3694] In light of these findings, the Appeals Chamber concludes that Prlić has failed to show that no reasonable trier of fact could have found that Andrić stated that his "superiors" had ordered him to use force in Gornji Vakuf, and that Prlić was one of his "superiors".[3695]

1166. Prlić further claims that the Trial Chamber erred in concluding that he was involved in planning the attack on Gornji Vakuf, but offers no arguments in support of this assertion. Insofar as Prlić's argument that he was not Andrić's superior could be interpreted as a submission in support of this assertion, this argument has been dismissed above.[3696] Consequently, the Appeals Chamber dismisses as undeveloped Prlić's challenge to the Trial Chamber's finding that he was involved in planning the attack on Gornji Vakuf. Prlić has failed to show that no reasonable trier of fact could have found, relying on Lane, that he attended the 19 January 1993 ceasefire negotiations.[3697] The Appeals Chamber further finds that Prlić has failed to

---

[3687]   Prlić's Appeal Brief, para. 466, referring to Ex. 3D03065/4D00348, p. 2. In particular, Prlić submits that there is no evidence that the HVO HZ H-B or Prlić had any power to issue orders to the military, that no such orders exist, and that the Trial Chamber correctly concluded that Prlić was outside the chain of command. Prlić's Appeal Brief, para. 466.

[3688]   Prlić's Appeal Brief, para. 468. In particular, Prlić argues that the Trial Chamber ignored evidence indicating that Prlić merely said that an order had been given, not that he himself had issued the order. In this regard, Prlić submits that: (1) another report, Exhibit P01309, which reported that Prlić himself had issued the order to stop the fighting, faultily reproduced Exhibit P01303; and (2) Šiljeg's 24 January 1993 order to respect the ceasefire (Ex. P01300) was issued pursuant to an HVO Main Staff order (Ex. 4D00048 (confidential)). Prlić's Appeal Brief, para. 468 and references cited therein.

[3689]   Prlić's Appeal Brief, para. 467. In particular, Prlić submits that these reports were sent to the HZ H-B presidency, the Defence Department, the HVO Main Staff, and the North-West OZ. Prlić's Appeal Brief, para. 467, referring to, *inter alia,* Prlić's ground of appeal 3.

[3690]   Prosecution's Response Brief (Prlić), para. 290.

[3691]   Prosecution's Response Brief (Prlić), paras 290-294.

[3692]   Prlić's Appeal Brief, para. 466, referring to, *inter alia,* Trial Judgement, Vol. 1, paras 708, 743-768, Vol. 4, para. 106.

[3693]   Trial Judgement, Vol. 4, para. 106.

[3694]   Trial Judgement, Vol. 4, para. 106.

[3695]   Trial Judgement, Vol. 4, paras 126-127, 133 (quotation marks in original). These findings also rebut Prlić's assertions that there is no evidence that the HVO HZ H-B or Prlić had any power to issue orders to the military, and that no such orders exist. See *supra,* paras 1098-1127; *infra,* paras 1212, 1214, 1219.

[3696]   See *supra,* para. 1165.

[3697]   Trial Judgement, Vol. 4, para. 127. The Appeals Chamber notes that with regard to his claims of Lane's poor memory, Prlić refers to his submissions in his sub-ground of appeal 6.2, which it dismisses elsewhere in the Judgement. See *supra,* paras 212-218. Prlić fails to explain in which regard his assertion that Lane speculated about his powers is relevant to the impugned finding on his attendance at the 19 January 1993 negotiations. This argument is therefore dismissed. With regard to Prlić's assertion that Exhibit

demonstrate that no reasonable trier of fact could have found that he said at a meeting on 25 January 1993 with an ECMM representative in **[page 483]** Mostar that he had ordered the HVO commander in Gornji Vakuf to stop all attacks immediately.[3698] Finally, with regard to Prlić's argument that the Trial Chamber erred in finding that Šiljeg's reports on Gornji Vakuf were "particularly" sent to the HVO HZ H-B, the Appeals Chamber notes that this argument is entirely based on a cross-reference to his ground of appeal 3, which it dismisses elsewhere.[3699]

1167. For all of the reasons set out above, sub-ground of appeal 16.1.3 is dismissed.

(iv) Prlić's intent concerning crimes in Gornji Vakuf (Prlić's Sub-ground 16.1.4)

1168. The Trial Chamber found that since Prlić participated in planning the attack on Gornji Vakuf, knew about the course of operations and the crimes committed, and continued to exercise his functions in the HVO/Government of the HZ(R) H-B, he intended that those crimes be committed, namely the destruction of Muslim houses, the murder and detention of Muslims who did not belong to any armed force, and the removal of the region's inhabitants to Gornji Vakuf by the HVO in January 1993.[3700] The Trial Chamber based this finding on, *inter alia,* its finding that between 19 and 30 January 1993, Željko Šiljeg, Commander of the North-West OZ, sent several reports particularly to the HVO HZ H-B on the situation in Gornji Vakuf, reporting, *inter alia,* that: (1) several buildings were on fire in Gornji Vakuf town and in the villages of Uzričje and Duša; (2) most buildings in Donja Hrsanica had been burnt down or demolished; (3) no civilian population remained in Donja Hrsanica and Gornja Hrsanica; and (4) a number of Muslim houses had been torched and items stolen in Uzričje, Duša, and Trnovača, and seven Muslim "civilians" had been killed during the HVO shelling of Duša.[3701] **[page 484]**

a. Arguments of the Parties

1169. Prlić claims that the Trial Chamber erred in concluding that he intended the crimes in Gornji Vakuf.[3702] He argues that Šiljeg's reports dated 19, 29, and 30 January 1993 were sent to the HZ H-B Presidency, the HVO HZ H-B Defence Department, the HVO Main Staff, and the North-West OZ, and do not show that he

---

P01215, p. 1, suggests that Petković, Pašalić, and Prlić met separately, the Appeals Chamber has examined the exhibit in its entirety and finds that a reasonable trial chamber could have found that there was only one meeting. See Ex. P01215, pp. 1-3. See also Ray Lane, T. 23681-23685 (15 October 2007). Prlić fails to identify any challenged factual finding by way of reference to a paragraph of the Trial Judgement with regard to his assertion that the Trial Chamber erred in finding that the 20 January 1993 order by Petković and Pašalić to abort all fighting in Gornji Vakuf was based on a meeting of Petković, Pašalić, Prlić, and Beaussou. Since it is unclear which is the challenged finding, this argument is dismissed. See Practice Direction on Formal Requirements, para. 4(b)(ii). To the extent that Prlić intended to challenge with these submissions any of the other findings that he challenges under this ground, he fails to explain how these submissions impact any of these other findings.

[3698] With regard to Prlić's argument that the Trial Chamber ignored evidence indicating that he merely said that an order had been given, not that he himself had issued the order, the Appeals Chamber notes that he points to a report dated 25 January 1993 stating that Prlić said that an order had been given "on Saturday" to Colonel Šiljeg to stop immediately any attack. Prlić"s Appeal Brief, para. 468, referring to Ex. P01303 (confidential). However, the Appeals Chamber considers that none of the evidence that Prlić cites to supports his assertion that another report, Exhibit P01309, which stated that Prlić himself had issued the order to stop the fighting, faultily reproduced Exhibit P01303. Lane was not present at the meeting which is documented in the two reports and was in no position to comment. Ray Lane, T. 23784-23786 (16 Oct 2007). Likewise, the other evidence Prlić cites as allegedly having been ignored does not support his claim that it indicates that he merely said that an order had been given, not that he himself had issued the order. Witness Christopher Beese could not comment on the version of events that Prlić's counsel put to him ("It's quite difficult to respond to this. [...] I am not in a position really to comment on how this was addressed [...] I can only offer explanations I don't know"). Christopher Beese, T. 5314-5315 (private session) (22 Aug 2006). Lastly, Prlić's submission that Šiljeg's 24 January 1993 order to respect the ceasefire (Ex. P01300) was issued pursuant to an HVO Main Staff order (Ex. 4D00048 (confidential)), suggesting that this was the order referred to in Exhibits P01303 and P01309, fails to acknowledge that Šiljeg's order contained in Exhibit P01300 in fact dates from 25 January 1993 and refers to Main Staff orders dated 20 and 24 January 1993 (see also Exs. P01238/1D00819, P01293), whereas in Exhibit P01303 (confidential), Prlić is reported to have stated that the order was given "on Saturday", which would have been 23 January 1993. These arguments are dismissed.

[3699] See *supra,* paras 177-183.

[3700] Trial Judgement, Vol. 4, para. 134.

[3701] Trial Judgement, Vol. 4, paras 127, 130.

[3702] Prlić's Appeal Brief, para. 469. See Prlić's Appeal Brief, para. 470, referring to Prlić's sub-ground of appeal 16.1.3.

or the HVO HZ H-B were aware of developments in the field on 15 to 25 January 1993.[3703] Prlić submits further that no such awareness can be gleaned from the minutes of HVO HZ H-B meetings.[3704] Finally, Prlić claims that the Trial Chamber ignored evidence showing that neither he nor the HVO HZ H-B had any involvement in the Gornji Vakuf military operations, pointing to various orders calling for the identification of the persons responsible for clashes and to evidence that the military commanders executed these orders.[3705]

1170. The Prosecution responds that the Trial Chamber's finding on Prlić's intention concerning crimes in Gornji Vakuf is based on extensive evidence.[3706] It submits that Prlić fails to show that the Trial Chamber acted unreasonably in concluding that he was informed of the contents of Šiljeg's January 1993 reports.[3707] The Prosecution submits that: (1) these reports expressly state that they were sent to the Government, as Prlić admitted at trial; and (2) the minutes of Government meetings over which Prlić presided clearly show his interest in the developments in Gornji Vakuf.[3708] The Prosecution further submits that the evidence Prlić cites does not support his claim that neither he nor his Government were involved in any way in the Gornji Vakuf military operations.[3709] It argues, finally, that Prlić's powers in military matters were amply demonstrated.[3710]

b. Analysis

1171. At the outset, the Appeals Chamber recalls that it has overturned the Trial Chamber's finding that the deaths of seven civilians in Duša in January 1993 constituted murder and wilful killing, and that as a result, it has vacated Prlić's convictions under Counts 1, 2, 3, 15, and 16 with **[page 485]** regard to these killings.[3711] Consequently, the Appeals Chamber dismisses as moot Prlić's submissions under this sub-ground to the extent that they challenge the finding that he intended that murders be committed in Gornji Vakuf in January 1993.

1172. The Appeals Chamber notes that all three of Šiljeg's reports to which Prlić refers are addressed to the HVO HZ H-B,[3712] a fact which Prlić ignores when he lists the recipients. It therefore finds that Prlić misrepresents the evidence and fails to show that no reasonable trier of fact could have found that the reports were sent, or particularly sent, to the HVO HZ H-B.[3713] The evidence Prlić cites does not support his claim that his awareness of the developments in Gornji Vakuf cannot be gleaned from minutes of HVO HZ H-B meetings, which, on the contrary, show that the situation in Gornji Vakuf was discussed.[3714] These arguments are dismissed.[3715]

1173. With respect to Prlić's argument that the Trial Chamber ignored evidence that neither he nor the HVO HZ H-B had any involvement in the Gornji Vakuf military operations, the Appeals Chamber recalls that the

---

[3703] Prlić's Appeal Brief, para. 471, referring to, *inter alia*, Exs. P01206, P01351, P01357. The Appeals Chamber notes that the date of one of Šiljeg's reports (Exhibit P01351) is illegible as it reads "2/?/January 1993" but that its contents concern the situation in Gornji Vakuf on 28 January 1993. Ex. P01351. The Appeals Chamber also notes that the Trial Chamber referred to the date of this report at times as 29 January 1993 and at times as 28 January 1993. See Trial Judgement, Vol. 2, para. 445, Vol. 4, paras 333, 705 (referring to the date as 28 January 1993); Trial Judgement, Vol. 2, paras 367, 398, Vol. 4, paras 130, 333 (referring to the date as 29 January 1993). Given that there is no dispute between the Parties on the date of this report and that the Trial Chamber relied on it as evidence of some Appellants' knowledge of crimes, the Appeals Chamber adopts the Trial Chamber's determination of the date of this report as 29 January 1993, which is to the benefit of the Appellants.

[3704] Prlić's Appeal Brief, para. 471.

[3705] Prlić's Appeal Brief, para. 472.

[3706] Prosecution's Response Brief (Prlić), para. 295.

[3707] Prosecution's Response Brief (Prlić), para. 296.

[3708] Prosecution's Response Brief (Prlić), para. 296.

[3709] Prosecution's Response Brief (Prlić), para. 297.

[3710] Prosecution's Response Brief (Prlić), para. 297.

[3711] See *supra*, para. 441-443.

[3712] Exs. P01206, p. 1.P01351, p. 1, P01357, p. 1.

[3713] Trial Judgement, Vol. 4, paras 127, 130. Counsel for Prlić at trial conceded that the period following 15 January 1993 was the only period when the HVO HZ H-B emerged as one of the addressees when information was submitted on the situation that unfolded in Gornji Vakuf. Jadranko Prlić, T. 27572 (6 May 2008). The Appeals Chamber also notes that Prlić refers to bis submissions in sub-ground of appeal 16.1.3, which it dismisses elsewhere in the Judgement. See *supra*, paras 1162-1167.

[3714] Exs. P01227, P01324, pp. 1-3, P01403, p. 3.

[3715] See also *infra*, para. 3052 & fn. 10012.

Trial Chamber's conclusion that Prlić participated in planning the attack on Gornji Vakuf is based on, *inter alia,* the findings that he: (1) signed the 15 January 1993 Ultimatum ordering the subordination of ABiH units to HVO command; (2) assured the municipal HVO and the population of Gornji Vakuf of his Government's support on the day of the attack on 18 January 1993; and (3) attended ceasefire negotiations on 19 January 1993 for Gornji Vakuf, at which he stated that in order to show his "good will" the HVO would not enact by force "the decision [...] whose deadline was 20 January 1993".[3716] In addition, the Trial Chamber found that the facts that: (1) the attacks on Gornji Vakuf's villages followed the same pattern; and (2) Šiljeg's reports failed to refer to the unlawful nature of destruction and appropriation of property in these villages, support the conclusion that the capture of these villages and ensuing crimes were part of the attack plan for the capture of the municipality by the HVO.[3717] In light of these underlying findings, neither Prlić's claims that various orders called for identifying the persons responsible for clashes and that these orders were executed, nor the evidence he cites in support, show that no **[page 486]** reasonable trier of fact could have found that he participated in planning the attack on Gornji Vakuf. Prlić's arguments are dismissed.

1174. Having dismissed all of Prlić's arguments pertaining to the basis for the Trial Chamber's finding on his intent,[3718] the Appeals Chamber concludes that he has failed to demonstrate that the Trial Chamber erred in concluding that he intended the crimes in Gornji Vakuf, excluding the crimes of murder and wilful killing as discussed above.[3719] Thus, Prlić's sub-ground of appeal 16.1.4 fails.

(b) The municipalities of Prozor and Jablanica (Prlić's Sub-ground 16.2)

(i) The 4 April 1993 Ultimatum (Prlić's Sub-grounds 16.2.1 and 16.2.2)

1175. The Trial Chamber found that on 3 April 1993, the HVO HZ H-B adopted an ultimatum, published on 4 April 1993 – that is, the 4 April 1993 Ultimatum –, envisaging that, if the Muslim authorities refused to sign a statement on the subordination of the ABiH to the HVO in Provinces 3, 8, and 10 by 15 April 1993, the HVO would apply it unilaterally, including by military means.[3720] Based on, *inter alia,* that finding, the Trial Chamber concluded that in April 1993 the HVO planned an attack on villages in the municipalities of Prozor and Jablanica (located in Province 8[3721]) to implement the 4 April 1993 Ultimatum by force, and that by drafting this ultimatum, Prlić significantly contributed to the implementation of the JCE in these municipalities.[3722]

1176. The Trial Chamber further found that on 15 April 1993 and the days that followed, orders were given to the HVO aiming to consolidate the HVO's positions and to enforce subordination of the ABiH forces.[3723]

a. Arguments of the Parties

1177. Prlić argues that the Trial Chamber erred in making the above findings on the 4 April 1993 Ultimatum by: (1) mischaracterising evidence; (2) erroneously relying on Witness William Tomljanovich, Witness DZ, and uncorroborated hearsay news reports;[3724] and (3) ignoring **[page 487]** reliable evidence that no ultimatum

---

[3716] Trial Judgement, Vol. 4, paras 125-127.
[3717] Trial Judgement, Vol. 4, para. 131. The Appeals Chamber recalls that it has overturned the Trial Chamber's findings regarding the deaths of seven civilians in Duša and that murder and wilful killing were part of the CCP in the period from January until June 1993. See *supra,* paras 441-443, 882. The Appeals Chamber does not consider that these changes affect the Trial Chamber's reasoning and conclusion, insofar as it concerns the remaining crimes, that the capture of these villages and ensuing crimes were part of the attack plan for the capture of the municipality by the HVO, particularly since the Duša killings were the only killings among those crimes. See *supra,* para. 876.
[3718] See *supra,* para. 1168.
[3719] See *supra,* para. 1171.
[3720] Trial Judgement, Vol. 1, paras 467-468, Vol. 4, paras 138-140.
[3721] See Trial Judgement, Vol. 1, para. 446 & fn. 1062, referring, in particular, to Ex. P09276, map 11.
[3722] See Trial Judgement, Vol. 4, paras 138-147, 271. See also Trial Judgement, Vol. 1, paras 465-476, Vol. 2, para. 89, Vol. 4, para. 1220.
[3723] Trial Judgement, Vol. 1, para. 469.
[3724] Prlić's Appeal Brief, paras 473-474, 479, 486. For his submissions on Tomljanovich, see Prlić's Appeal Brief, fn. 1219, referring to Prlić's sub-ground of appeal 4.2. With respect to Witness DZ, Prlić submits that he was not competent to testify on the 4 April 1993 Ultimatum, since he: (1) relied on a January 1993 document and newspaper articles; (2) [Redacted, see Annex C –

was issued, showing that the media reports were incorrect.[3725] Prlić asserts in particular that the Trial Chamber ignored evidence, which, he submits, is essential to understanding the 3 April 1993 conclusions of the HVO HZ H-B, namely evidence that: (1) Alija Izetbegović undertook efforts to restructure the BiH by forming new districts, which Prlić claims was unconstitutional and contrary to the Vance-Owen Peace Plan and a 3 March 1993 agreement between Muslims and Croats;[3726] (2) on 13 March 1993, the BiH Presidency dismissed the legally elected presidents of the municipal assemblies in Konjic and Jablanica; (3) on 20 March 1993, Safet Ćibo was illegally appointed "to the 4th Corps of ABiH" and to the regional board of the SDA for Herzegovina; and (4) the HVO HZ H-B had doubts about the sincerity of the Muslim leadership, in particular that of Izetbegović.[3727]

1178. Prlić further challenges the findings on the 4 April 1993 Ultimatum by pointing to allegedly ignored evidence on: (1) Izetbegović's and Mate Boban's agreement to implement the Vance-Owen Peace Plan;[3728] (2) Lord David Owen's statement that after their "bilateral agreement" on the Vance-Owen Peace Plan on 25 March 1993 it was decided that both sides would try to reach an agreement on controversial issues;[3729] (3) the proposed Izetbegović-Boban joint statement's compliance with the terms of the Vance-Owen Peace Plan;[3730] (4) the minutes of the 3 April 1993 HVO HZ H-B meeting showing that Boban made arrangements for the Vance-Owen Peace Plan's implementation with regard to interim provincial governments;[3731] and (5) the 25 April 1993 joint statement on the establishment of a co-ordinating body to implement the Vance-Owen Peace Plan and a joint command.[3732]

1179. Prlić also submits that a reasonable trial chamber would have concluded that the 4 April 1993 Ultimatum was not linked to a JCE, pointing to a number of documents.[3733] Finally, in arguing that the Trial Chamber erred in finding that on 15 April 1993 and the days that followed, **[page 488]** the HVO was ordered to enforce the ABiH's subordination, Prlić alleges that the Trial Chamber disregarded several orders issued as of March 1993 aimed at "ensuring] greater performance of assignments in operational zones" of directly subordinated units and preventing misunderstandings between the HVO and ABiH.[3734]

1180. The Prosecution responds that Prlić fails to show that the findings concerning the 4 April 1993 Ultimatum are unreasonable.[3735] The Prosecution argues in particular that: (1) he fails to explain the relevance of the alleged unilateral acts by the SDA/ABiH in March 1993 and how they would render the Trial Chamber's findings unreasonable; (2) Prlić's claim that Izetbegović had signed the entire Vance-Owen Peace Plan on 25 March 1993 is irrelevant, since the plan expressly stated that the question of subordination was to be resolved in future negotiations;[3736] (3) Prlić wrongly submits that the "proposed Boban-Izetbegović 'Joint Statement'" of 2 April 1993 complied with the terms of the Vance-Owen Peace Plan in light of the unilateral

---

Confidential Annex]; (3) never referred to the Vance-Owen Peace Plan in his statement; (4) was not involved in its implementation; and (5) was ignorant of its provisions. Prlić's Appeal Brief, para. 486.

[3725] Prlić''s Appeal Brief, paras 478-479, 482; Appeal Hearing, AT. 142 (20 Mar 2017).

[3726] Prlić's Appeal Brief, paras 475-478; Appeal Hearing, AT. 143 (20 Mar 2017).

[3727] Prlić's Appeal Brief, para. 478. See Appeal Hearing, AT. 132, 142-143 (20 Mar 2017).

[3728] Prlić's Appeal Brief, para. 480. Prlić submits that the Trial Chamber found that both sides had signed the entire Vance-Owen Peace Plan on 25 March 1993. Prlić's Appeal Brief, para. 480.

[3729] Prlić's Appeal Brief, para. 482; Appeal Hearing, AT. 142 (20 Mar 2017). Prlić submits that Owen stated that the command/ control of "the two military forces" remained a controversial issue between the parties, and that "[i]t was then decided that both sides would try, as much as they could, to reach an agreement and if an agreement was not reached within 14 days, the two Co-Chairmen would offer their good services". Prlić's Appeal Brief, para. 482.

[3730] Prlić's Appeal Brief, para. 483.

[3731] Prlić's Appeal Brief, para. 481, referring to, *inter alia*, Ex. P01798.

[3732] Prlić's Appeal Brief, para. 484; Appeal Hearing, AT. 143 (20 Mar 2017). Prlić submits further that the Trial Chamber ignored its own findings and that an isolated view on these documents and events presents a distorted picture, but when viewed in context the documents allow for the only reasonable conclusion that no JCE existed. Prlić's Appeal Brief, para. 484, referring to, *inter alia*, Trial Judgement, Vol. 1, para. 472.

[3733] Prlić''s Appeal Brief, para. 487.

[3734] Prlić's Appeal Brief, para. 485. In particular, he submits that these orders were unrelated to the 3 April 1993 HVO HZ H-B meeting and that during that time, weapons flowed freely from the HZ H-B to the ABiH. Prlić's Appeal Brief, para. 485.

[3735] Prosecution's Response Brief (Prlić), paras 298-299; Appeal Hearing, AT. 182 (20 Mar 2017). See Appeal Hearing, AT. 192 (20 Mar 2017). The Prosecution asserts that he instead makes irrelevant and/or erroneous assertions and denies that the HVO's threat of unilateral implementation represented an "ultimatum". Prosecution's Response Brief (Prlić), para. 299.

[3736] Prosecution's Response Brief (Prlić), paras 298-299.

demand for subordination, which had not been settled under the plan;[3737] and (4) to the extent that Prlić submits that the unilateral demand for subordination under threat of military force was meant to implement a "peace plan", this assertion is untenable.[3738]

1181. The Prosecution contends that in arguing that the 4 April 1993 Ultimatum was unrelated to the JCE, Prlić only refers to evidence unrelated to subordination or dating from late April and fails to explain how it renders the Trial Chamber's findings unreasonable.[3739] It further submits that he fails to show that no reasonable trier of fact could have concluded that commencing on 15 April 1993, the HVO was enforcing the ABiH's subordination, and fails to explain the relevance of the March 1993 orders he cites.[3740]

1182. The Prosecution asserts that Prlić fails to show an error in the Trial Chamber's reliance on multiple media reports[3741] and Witness DZ's corroborated evidence[3742] when making its findings on **[page 489]** the 4 April 1993 Ultimatum.[3743] The Prosecution further submits that Prlić fails to demonstrate that the Trial Chamber acted unreasonably in not crediting his public denial in late April 1993, given the wealth of contrary evidence, including his own concession shortly after issuing the 4 April 1993 Ultimatum that it could "lead to bloodshed".[3744]

1183. Prlić replies that the Prosecution wrongly claims that he conceded shortly after the 4 April 1993 Ultimatum that it could "lead to bloodshed".[3745]

b. Analysis

1184. With regard to Prlić's argument that the Trial Chamber erred in relying on the evidence of Tomljanovich, the Appeals Chamber notes that this argument is entirely based on a cross-reference to his sub-ground of appeal 4.2, which it dismisses elsewhere.[3746] The Appeals Chamber notes further that in making the impugned findings on the 4 April 1993 Ultimatum,[3747] the Trial Chamber relied on Witness DZ's evidence in combination with ample other evidence.[3748] Prlić has failed to show any error in this regard,[3749] and his argument concerning Witness DZ is dismissed.

1185. With regard to Prlić's argument that the Trial Chamber erroneously relied on "uncorroborated" media reports in its findings on the 4 April 1993 Ultimatum, the Appeals Chamber notes that the challenged

---

[3737] Prosecution's Response Brief (Prlić), paras 298-299.
[3738] Prosecution's Response Brief (Prlić), para. 299.
[3739] Prosecution's Response Brief (Prlić), para. 303.
[3740] Prosecution's Response Brief (Prlić), para. 301. The Prosecution submits further that the evidence of weapons transport Prlić cites to is unrelated to the area in question and only shows that the HVO allowed such transports to ABiH regions where it was fighting the Serbs jointly with the ABiH, an uncontested fact. Prosecution's Response Brief (Prlić), para. 301.
[3741] Prosecution's Response Brief (Prlić), para. 300. The Prosecution submits in particular that Prlić fails to explain how no reasonable trier of fact could have preferred the Defence Department's spokesperson's (Veso Vegar's) contemporaneous statement to the press that "[i]t is definitely an ultimatum" over his implausible later assertion that he "did not give any statements" during this period. Prosecution's Response Brief (Prlić), para. 300. See also Prosecution's Response Brief (Prlić), para. 298.
[3742] Prosecution's Response Brief (Prlić), para. 302.
[3743] Prosecution's Response Brief (Prlić), para. 300.
[3744] Prosecution's Response Brief (Prlić), para. 300.
[3745] Prlić's Reply Brief, para. 74.
[3746] See *supra*, paras 204-211.
[3747] Trial Judgement, Vol. 4, para. 140.
[3748] Trial Judgement, Vol. 4, paras 138-139.
[3749] Trial Judgement, Vol. 4, para 139 With regard to Prlić's claim that Witness DZ relied on newspaper articles and a document from January 1993, the Appeals Chamber observes that the transcript pages that Prlić cites indicate that the witness relied on various first-hand sources. Witness DZ, T. 26483-26485 (closed session) (22 Jan 2008). The Appeals Chamber notes further that the witness [Redacted, see Annex C – Confidential Annex]. Witness DZ, T. 26473-26475, 26480 (closed session) (22 Jan 2008); Ex. P10367 (confidential), paras 4-7. Noting that the witness testified on the Vance-Owen Peace Plan in his viva *voce* testimony, the Appeals Chamber sees no merit in Prlić's submission that his written statement does not contain any reference to this plan. Witness DZ, T. 26480, 26483-26485 (closed session) (22 Jan 2008). Prlić's claim that the witness was not involved in the peace plan's implementation is irrelevant for the reliability of his testimony on the plan. Prlić's claim that the witness was ignorant of the plan's provisions is not supported by the cited testimony, which deals with a separate document. Witness DZ, T. 26729-26730 (closed session) (24 Jan 2008). On the contrary, he testified that as soon as he arrived in the region he carefully reviewed the Vance-Owen Peace Plan, which he considered to be the very basis of all initiatives taking place in the region at the time. Witness DZ, T. 26480-26481 (closed session) (22 Jan 2008).

findings are based not only on the media reports, but also on other corroborating evidence, notably the very minutes of the HVO HZ H-B meeting at which the ultimatum was adopted, Exhibit P01798.[3750] With regard to Prlić's submissions that the **[page 490]** Trial Chamber ignored reliable evidence showing that the media reports were incorrect and that no ultimatum was issued, the Appeals Chamber has considered the evidence he refers to and finds that Prlić has failed to show that no reasonable trier of fact could have reached the impugned findings.[3751] Specifically, the Appeals Chamber considers that: (1) Prlić fails to demonstrate that no reasonable trier of fact could have preferred the evidence on which the Trial Chamber based the impugned findings to the testimony of Witness Veso Vegar; and (2) Exhibit P09519 and the testimony of Witness Neven Tomić are not inconsistent with the impugned findings, notwithstanding Tomić's understanding of the word "ultimatum". Prlić has also failed to show that the Trial Chamber, in making the impugned findings, mischaracterised evidence.[3752] These arguments are dismissed.

1186. The Appeals Chamber fails to see how Prlić's assertions on Izetbegović's unilateral efforts to restructure BiH's districts, the BiH Presidency's dismissal of legally elected presidents of municipal assemblies, Safet Ćibo's illegal appointment to the ABiH's 4th Corps and the regional board of the Herzegovina SDA, and the HVO HZ H-B's mistrust towards the Muslim leadership are relevant to and could have impacted the challenged findings that the HVO HZ H-B adopted an ultimatum on 3 April 1993 for the Muslim authorities to subordinate the ABiH to the HVO.[3753] Prlić merely asserts that this evidence is "essential to understanding the 3 April 1993 HVOHZHB conclusions"[3754] but does not elaborate on – and therefore fails to clarify – the alleged connection between these issues and the challenged findings. As such, the Appeals Chamber concludes that he has failed to show that no reasonable trier of fact, based on the evidence, could have reached the conclusions of the Trial Chamber. To the extent that Prlić argues that these alleged facts provide ulterior motives for the HVO HZ H-B's ultimatum, negating any link to the JCE, the Appeals Chamber considers, in light of his deficient and unclear submissions, that he has failed to demonstrate that no reasonable trier of fact could have found a link to the JCE. These arguments are dismissed. **[page 491]**

1187. With regard to Prlić's submission that the Trial Chamber ignored evidence on the agreement between Izetbegović and Boban regarding the implementation of the Vance-Owen Peace Plan, the Appeals Chamber finds that this agreement is irrelevant to the challenged findings, since the plan expressly foresaw further negotiations and agreement between the two sides with regard to the deployment of ABiH and HVO forces in Provinces 5, 8, 9, and 10.[3755] This submission is therefore dismissed.

1188. With regard to Prlić's claim that the proposed Izetbegović-Boban joint statement complied with the terms of the Vance-Owen Peace Plan, the Appeals Chamber notes that the proposed joint statement foresaw

---

[3750] The Appeals Chamber understands Prlić's argument to refer to the findings in Trial Judgement, Vol. 1, para. 468 at fns 1131-1134, Vol. 4, para. 139 at fn. 396. Other evidence corroborating the media reports in question (Exs. P01804, P01808, P10675) includes Witness DZ, T(F). 26482-26483 (closed session) (22 Jan 2008) and Exhibits P02045, pp. 1-2 and P09545, pp. 83-85. To the extent that Prlić also intends to challenge the reliance on the media reports for the findings in Trial Judgement, Vol. 4, para. 138 at fns 392-393, the Appeals Chamber notes that the reports provide direct evidence for the findings that the 4 April 1993 Ultimatum was released to the press on 4 April 1993 and that several newspaper articles referred to it as an "ultimatum" with a deadline of 15April 1993. Prlić has failed to show any error.

[3751] See Prlić's Appeal Brief, para. 479, referring to Veso Vegar, T. 37071-37075 (17 Feb 2009), 37083-37088, 37150-37152 (18 Feb 2009), Ex. P09519, Neven Tomić, T. 34710-34714 (17 Nov 2008). See also Appeal Hearing, AT. 142 (20 Mar 2017), referring to Exs. P01883, P02059, P03642, 1D02159, 2D00689, 2D00891.

[3752] Prlić claims that the Trial Chamber mischaracterised Exhibits P01798 and P02046/1D01655. See Prlić's Appeal Brief, para. 474 & fn. 1221, para. 482 & fn. 1241. With regard to Exhibit P01798, the Appeals Chamber understands that Prlić challenges the Trial Chamber's findings in Trial Judgement, Vol. 1, para. 468 at fns 1130-1131, 1133-1135, Vol. 4, para. 138 at fns 388-389, 391. With regard to Exhibit P02046/1D01655, the Appeals Chamber understands that Prlić challenges the Trial Chamber's finding in Trial Judgement, Vol. 1, para. 468 at fn. 1133, Vol. 4, para. 138 at fn. 394. The Appeals Chamber can see no indication that the Trial Chamber mischaracterised either exhibit in these findings.

[3753] See *supra*, para. 1175. See also *supra*, para. 1176.

[3754] Prlić's Appeal Brief, para. 478.

[3755] Ex. P01398, p. 30, heading E. This is further supported by the quote of Lord Owen that the issue of command/control of the two military forces remained controversial between the Croatian and the Muslim sides after their agreement to the Vance-Owen Peace Plan, and that "[i]t was then decided that both sides would try, as much as they could, to reach an agreement" on this issue within a fortnight. Ex. P02059, p. 2. Prlić's argument that the Trial Chamber ignored this statement by Lord Owen setting out the next steps expected of the Croat and Muslim sides after their "bilateral agreement" on the Vance-Owen Peace Plan on 25 March 1993 is therefore dismissed. See also Herbert Okun, T. 16798 (3 Apr 2007). As a result, Prlić also fails to demonstrate the relevance of his submission that the Trial Chamber found that both sides had signed the entire Vance-Owen Peace Plan on 25 March 1993.

a three-day deadline for the withdrawal of outside forces from the designated provinces and the subordination of HVO forces in Provinces 1, 5, and 9 to ABiH command, and of ABiH forces in Provinces 3, 8, and 10 to HVO command.[3756] The Vance-Owen Peace Plan, however, did not envisage this.[3757] The Appeals Chamber therefore finds that Prlić has failed to show that the proposed Izetbegović-Boban joint statement complied with the terms of the Vance-Owen Peace Plan, and dismisses his submission. Turning to Prlić's claim that the minutes of the 3 April 1993 HVO HZ H-B meeting show that Boban made arrangements for the Vance-Owen Peace Plan's implementation with regard to interim provincial governments, the Appeals Chamber notes that any steps taken towards implementation of the plan concerning such government institutions bear no relevance to the challenged findings that the HVO HZ H-B at that meeting adopted an ultimatum to the ABiH for subordination in certain provinces. It therefore dismisses this claim.

1189. The Appeals Chamber notes that the 25 April 1993 Croatian and Muslim joint statement on the establishment of a co-ordinating body to implement the Vance-Owen Peace Plan and a joint command, to which Prlić points and which the Trial Chamber considered, postdates the 4 April 1993 Ultimatum.[3758] The Appeals Chamber fails to see why this evidence should render the **[page 492]** impugned findings unreasonable.[3759] Prlić's submission regarding the 25 April 1993 joint statement is therefore dismissed.

1190. The Appeals Chamber notes that the documents which Prlić cites in support of his claim that a reasonable trial chamber would have concluded that the 4 April 1993 Ultimatum was not linked to a JCE, relate to a different time frame and/or subject matter than the subordination of ABiH units to HVO command in certain provinces as envisaged in the 4 April 1993 Ultimatum. As such, these documents fail to show that no reasonable trier of fact could have concluded that by drafting this ultimatum, Prlić significantly contributed to the implementation of the JCE in the municipalities of Prozor and Jablanica.[3760] Prlić's claim regarding the link to a JCE is therefore dismissed.

1191. Finally, with regard to the orders issued as of March 1993, the Appeals Chamber fails to see their relevance to Prlić's challenge to the finding that, on 15 April 1993 and the days that followed, the HVO was ordered to enforce the ABiH's subordination.[3761] The Appeals Chamber therefore dismisses this challenge.

1192. For the foregoing reasons, Prlić's sub-grounds of appeal 16.2.1 and 16.2.2 fail.

(ii) Military operations following the 4 April 1993 Ultimatum (Prlić's Sub-grounds 16.2.3, 16.2.4, and 16.2.5)

1193. The Trial Chamber found that the HVO operations in the municipalities of Prozor and Jablanica in April 1993 resulted from a preconceived HVO plan to implement the 4 April 1993 Ultimatum by force.[3762] As part of this implementation, on 16 April 1993, Željko Šiljeg, Commander of the North-West OZ, drew up

---

[3756] Ex. P01798, pp. 2-3. The proposed joint statement was not even signed by the Muslim side, a fact that Prlić does not challenge. Trial Judgement, Vol. 1, paras 467-468; Ex. P01798, pp. 2-4; Prlić's Appeal Brief, para. 483.

[3757] See *supra*, fn. 3755. See also Ex. 1D02908, p. 12, heading E.

[3758] Prlić's Appeal Brief, para. 484, referring to, *inter alia*, Exs. P02078, P02088. The Trial Chamber expressly considered the 25 April 1993 joint statement in Trial Judgement, Vol. 1, para. 472. The Appeals Chamber therefore dismisses Prlić's allegation that the Trial Chamber ignored this finding. Prlić also refers, without any explanation as to why it should impact the impugned finding on the 4 April 1993 Ultimatum, to Exhibit P02054 (confidential), the relevance of which is unclear to the Appeals Chamber.

[3759] The Appeals Chamber also fails to see how the documents and events to which Prlić refers, when viewed in a broader context, demonstrate that the Trial Chamber erred in concluding that a JCE existed, and therefore dismisses Prlić's submission that an isolated view of these documents and events presents a distorted picture.

[3760] See also Trial Judgement, Vol. 1, paras 464-473, referring to, *inter alia*, Exs. P01983, P02078, 1D02903, 3D00320; Trial Judgement, Vol. 4, paras 45-46. *Cf.* Prlić's Appeal Brief, para. 487 and references cited therein.

[3761] The Appeals Chamber further observes that in reaching this finding the Trial Chamber relied upon some of the orders that Prlić alleges it disregarded, but those orders in fact date from April 1993. See Trial Judgement, Vol. 1, para. 469, referring to, *inter alia*, Exs. P01900, P01913. *Cf.* Prlić's Appeal Brief, para. 485 and references cited therein. Likewise, the Appeals Chamber fails to see in which way his reference to evidence on the transport of weapons to the ABiH from the HZ H-B is relevant to the impugned finding, considering that the evidence pertains to March 1993. See Prlić's Appeal Brief, para. 485 and references cited therein.

[3762] Trial Judgement, Vol. 4, para. 146. See Trial Judgement, Vol. 4, paras 138-145. In paragraph 146, Volume 4, of the Trial Judgement, the Trial Chamber inadvertently referred to "the ultimatum of 15 April 1993". However, it is clear from the context of the Trial Judgement that the Trial Chamber meant to refer to the 4 April 1993 Ultimatum, which set the deadline on 15 April 1993. See Trial Judgement, Vol. 4, paras 138-140, 142.

a "plan" for an attack on several villages in Prozor Municipality, including the village of Parcani, and sent it to the Main Staff.[3763] **[page 493]**

a. Arguments of the Parties

1194. Prlić submits that the Trial Chamber erroneously concluded that the 4 April 1993 Ultimatum caused clashes around Jablanica Municipality (in particular in Sovići and Doljani) and was followed by systematic and widespread HVO military operations around Prozor.[3764] He contends that the Trial Chamber erred in finding that, following this ultimatum, a plan to attack villages in Prozor Municipality was drawn up, as it relied on exhibits introduced through a bar table motion and ignored Witness Radmilo Jašak's testimony that no plan for attack existed and that the HVO action was a reaction to an ABiH offensive that had commenced on 13 April 1993.[3765] Prlić further alleges that the Trial Chamber made contradictory findings in concluding on the one hand that the HVO started shelling the town of Jablanica on 15 April 1993, and on the other hand that clashes between the HVO and the ABiH started on 13-14 April 1993.[3766] Finally, Prlić argues that the Trial Chamber disregarded evidence showing that the HVO did not plan to take control of Jablanica and was rather defending against an ABiH offensive that began on 23 March 1993.[3767]

1195. The Prosecution responds that the Trial Chamber reasonably concluded, based on various findings and evidence, that: (1) the HVO operations in the municipalities of Prozor and Jablanica resulted from the HVO's plan to implement the 4 April 1993 Ultimatum by force;[3768] and (2) the HVO drew up a plan of attack on Prozor.[3769]

b. Analysis

1196. Turning to Prlić's contention that the Trial Chamber erred in finding that following the 4 April 1993 Ultimatum, a plan to attack villages in Prozor Municipality was drawn up, the Appeals Chamber finds that Prlić's submission that the Trial Chamber relied upon exhibits admitted by decision on a bar table motion fails to show that no reasonable trier of fact could have reached the impugned finding based on the evidence before it.[3770] Concerning Jašak's testimony, the **[page 494]** Appeals Chamber notes that he testified that there was no plan *at the level of the Main Staff* whereas the Trial Chamber found that the plan for attack was drawn up by Šiljeg, Commander of the North-West OZ, and sent to the Main Staff; Jašak's testimony is therefore not inconsistent with the impugned finding.[3771] Further, the Appeals Chamber recalls that where a trial chamber does not refer to evidence it is to be presumed that it assessed and weighed the evidence, provided

---

[3763] Trial Judgement, Vol. 4, paras 141-142.

[3764] Prlić's Appeal Brief, para. 488.

[3765] Prlić's Appeal Brief, para. 489, referring to, *inter alia,* Prlić's Appeal Brief, ground of appeal 3. See also Appeal Hearing, AT. 144 (20 Mar 2017).

[3766] Prlić's Appeal Brief, para. 490.

[3767] Prlić's Appeal Brief, para. 491. See also Appeal Hearing, AT. 142-143 (20 Mar 2017).

[3768] Prosecution's Response Brief (Prlić), paras 304, 306. The Prosecution submits in particular that to the extent that Prlić relies on Petković's "self-serving'statement that the HVO never planned to take control of Jablanica to show that it did not plan to attack Sovići and Doljani, this claim is contradicted by several contemporaneous reports to Petković. Prosecution's Response Brief (Prlić), para. 306. The Prosecution further argues that there is no contradiction between the Trial Chamber's findings that: (1) HVO-ABiH clashes broke out in Jablanica Municipality on 13-14 April 1993, with the HVO surrounding the town of Jablanica; and (2) the HVO commenced shelling the town of Jablanica on 15 April 1993. Prosecution's Response Brief (Prlić), para. 306.

[3769] Prosecution's Response Brief (Prlić), para. 305. The Prosecution submits further that Prlić fails to demonstrate how the Trial Chamber acted unreasonably in favouring the plain words of contemporaneous reports over Jašak's self-serving testimony. Prosecution's Response Brief (Prlić), para. 305.

[3770] The Appeals Chamber notes in particular that the Trial Chamber in reaching the impugned finding relied on HVO reports setting out the plan on raiding, *inter alia,* Parcani in Prozor Municipality, implementing the plan, and reporting thereon. Trial Judgement, Vol. 4, para. 141, referring to, *inter alia,* Exs. P01909, P01917, P01936, P01952. Further, the Appeals Chamber notes that in making this argument, Prlić refers to his submissions under ground of appeal 3, which it dismisses elsewhere in the Judgement. See *supra,* paras 177-183.

[3771] Radmilo Jašak, T. 48951 (26 Jan 2010); Trial Judgement, Vol. 4, para. 141. Moreover, the possibility that the HVO action may have been a reaction to an ABiH offensive that had commenced on 13 April 1993, allegedly suggested in Jašak's testimony, is not inconsistent with the impugned finding that the "plan" for an attack on several villages in Prozor Municipality was drawn up as part of the implementation of the 4 April 1993 Ultimatum.

that there is no indication that the trial chamber completely disregarded evidence which is clearly relevant.[3772] In the present case, the Appeals Chamber considers that Prlić has failed to rebut the presumption that the Trial Chamber assessed the evidence. These arguments are therefore dismissed.

1197. The Appeals Chamber further sees no contradiction between the Trial Chamber's findings that the HVO commenced shelling Jablanica town on 15 April 1993, and that clashes between the HVO and the ABiH broke out on 13-14 April 1993 in Jablanica Municipality.[3773] The argument is dismissed.

1198. With regard to Prlić's argument that the Trial Chamber disregarded evidence showing that the HVO did not plan to take control of Jablanica and was rather defending against an ABiH offensive that began on 23 March 1993, the Appeals Chamber first notes that Prlić does not point to any finding that the HVO *planned* to take control of Jablanica but rather to a finding concerning the capture of two villages in Jablanica Municipality.[3774] The Appeals Chamber further notes that his assertions that the HVO action constituted a defence against an ABiH offensive do not detract from and are not inconsistent with the finding that the HVO eventually captured the villages. To the extent that Prlić suggests that these submissions are inconsistent with the Trial Chamber's finding that the HVO military operations in the municipalities of Jablanica and Prozor resulted from an HVO plan to implement by force the 4 April 1993 Ultimatum,[3775] the Appeals Chamber fails to see how ABiH military operations that began on 23 March 1993 could show that no reasonable trier of fact could have found that HVO military operations in April 1993 were carried out pursuant to the 4 April 1993 Ultimatum. **[page 495]**

1199. Having dismissed all arguments under the present sub-grounds of appeal, the Appeals Chamber considers that Prlić has failed to demonstrate that the Trial Chamber erroneously concluded that the 4 April 1993 Ultimatum caused clashes around Jablanica Municipality and was followed by systematic and widespread HVO military operations around Prozor.[3776]

1200. For the foregoing reasons, Prlić's sub-grounds of appeal 16.2.3, 16.2.4, and 16.2.5 fail.

(iii) Removal of Muslims from Doljani and Sovići (Prlić's Sub-ground 16.2.6)

1201. The Trial Chamber found that on 5 May 1993, the President of the Gornji Vakuf HVO, Ivan Šarić, wrote to Prlić informing him that the HVO had removed approximately 300 Muslims from Doljani and Sovići, and that Prlić did nothing to protect them.[3777]

1202. Prlić submits that the Trial Chamber erred in finding, solely relying on Exhibit P02191, that he was personally informed of the removal of these civilians and did nothing to protect them, while no evidence supports a finding that he received this document or was informed of its content.[3778] He claims that the Trial Chamber found no involvement of the HVO HZ H-B or Prlić in the evacuation of civilians.[3779]

1203. The Prosecution responds that Prlić fails to show that the impugned finding was unreasonable, since it is based on a 5 May 1993 report addressed directly to him and bearing a stamp confirming receipt on the same day.[3780] It submits that his remaining assertions are irrelevant.[3781]

[3772] *Tolimir* Appeal Judgement, para. 53; *Popović et al.* Appeal Judgement, paras 925, 1017; *Kvočka et al.* Appeal Judgement, para. 23.

[3773] See Trial Judgement, Vol. 2, paras 526, 528, Vol. 4, para. 143. The Appeals Chamber observes in addition that all references to Trial Chamber findings contained in Prlić's Appeal Brief, para. 490, are erroneous, and recalls that an appellant is expected to provide precise reference to relevant paragraphs in the trial judgement to which the challenges are being made. See *supra*, para. 24.

[3774] See Prlić's Appeal Brief, para. 491, referring to, *inter alia*, Trial Judgement, Vol. 4, para. 144.

[3775] Trial Judgement, Vol. 4, para. 146. See *supra*, fn. 3762.

[3776] Prlić's Appeal Brief, para. 488. The Appeals Chamber notes that Prlić fails to identify the impugned finding by way of reference to the Trial Judgement, but understands his challenges to refer to the finding in the first sentence in Trial Judgement, Vol. 4, para. 146, recalled *supra*, para. 1193 at fn. 3762.

[3777] Trial Judgement, Vol. 2, para. 613, Vol. 4, paras 145-146.

[3778] Prlić's Appeal Brief, para. 492, referring to, *inter alia*, Prlić's ground of appeal 3.

[3779] Prlić's Appeal Brief, para. 493.

[3780] Prosecution's Response Brief (Prlić), para. 307.

[3781] Prosecution's Response Brief (Prlić), para. 307.

1204. The Appeals Chamber notes that the Trial Chamber found that the report (Exhibit P02191) was received by the HVO Main Staff in Mostar on the same day that it was sent, and was addressed to the President of the HVO HZ H-B in Mostar.[3782] It finds that Prlić has failed to show that no reasonable trier of fact could have found, relying on this exhibit, that he was personally informed of the removal of civilians from Sovići and Doljani.[3783] Regarding Prlić's submission that the Trial Chamber found no involvement of the HVO HZ H-B or Prlić in the evacuation of civilians, **[page 496]** the Appeals Chamber fails to see its relevance to the impugned finding. Prlić's sub-ground of appeal 16.2.6 is dismissed.

(iv) *Mens rea* (Prlić's Sub-ground 16.2.7)

1205. The Trial Chamber found that, being aware of the HVO crimes committed against the Muslim population in the wake of the 15 January 1993 Ultimatum, Prlić had reason to know that the similar 4 April 1993 Ultimatum would have the same outcome, namely the commission of crimes by the HVO against the Muslim population, and that he intended this to happen.[3784] Thus, the Trial Chamber found that by participating in drafting the latter ultimatum, Prlić accepted the destruction of Muslim property and the arrests and removal of the Muslim population in the municipalities of Jablanica and Prozor in mid-April 1993.[3785]

1206. Prlić submits that the Trial Chamber erred in concluding that by participating in drafting the 4 April 1993 Ultimatum he intended that crimes be committed against Muslims in the municipalities of Prozor and Jablanica, as it ignored evidence that the alleged crimes were investigated and that it was Boban, rather than Prlić or the HVO HZ H-B, who was involved in the investigations.[3786]

1207. The Prosecution responds that: (1) the impugned finding is reasonable; (2) the alleged investigations were in fact only preliminary inquiries that were never followed through and which the Trial Chamber did not ignore; and (3) Prlić fails to explain how his lack of involvement in this regard demonstrates that he did not intend the crimes.[3787]

1208. The Appeals Chamber notes that Prlić relies on Petković's evidence that there were investigations into crimes committed by the Convicts' Battalion in the second half of April 1993 in Sovići and Doljani in Jablanica Municipality.[3788] Contrary to Prlić's assertion, the Trial Chamber did not ignore Petković's evidence on this topic.[3789] The Trial Chamber found in this regard that: "It is clear from all the evidence that not only were no measures taken, but moreover, these units, which were known since 1993 to be violent and dangerous, took part in HVO numerous military operations during which many crimes were committed."[3790] As for the submission that it was Boban who was involved, the Appeals Chamber notes that Prlić refers to some evidence indicating that **[page 497]** Boban had some involvement in investigations into crimes.[3791] However, the Appeals Chamber finds that the mere fact that someone else may have been involved in the investigation rather than Prlić cannot show an error in the Trial Chamber's finding on his *mens rea*[3792] His sub-ground of appeal 16.2.7 is therefore dismissed.

[3782] Trial Judgement, Vol. 2, para. 613, Vol. 4, para. 145.

[3783] Prlić's Appeal Brief, para. 492, referring to, *inter alia*, Trial Judgement, Vol. 2, para. 613, Vol. 4, paras 145-146. The Appeals Chamber notes that Prlić also refers to his submissions in ground of appeal 3, which it dismisses elsewhere in the Judgement. See *supra*, paras 177-183.

[3784] Trial Judgement, Vol. 4, paras 146-147. See *supra*, fn. 3762.

[3785] Trial Judgement, Vol. 4, paras 146-147.

[3786] Prlić's Appeal Brief, para. 494, referring to, *inter alia*, Trial Judgement, Vol. 4, paras 146-147; Ex. 2D00089; Ex. P02088, Milivoj Petković, T. 49439-49442 (15 Feb 2010).

[3787] Prosecution's Response Brief (Prlić), para. 308.

[3788] See Prlić's Appeal Brief, para. 494 & fn. 1281 and references cited therein.

[3789] See Trial Judgement, Vol. 4, para. 806 & fn. 1522.

[3790] Trial Judgement, Vol. 4, para. 806. See *infra*, paras 2338-2349.

[3791] Prlić's Appeal Brief, para. 494, referring to, *inter alia*, Ex. 2D00089, Ex. P02088, Milivoj Petković, T. 49439-49442 (15 Feb 2010).

[3792] The Appeals Chamber recalls that it has overturned the Trial Chamber's findings regarding the deaths of seven civilians in Duša and Prlić's convictions for the 19 April 1993 killings in the village of Tošćanica in Prozor Municipality. See *supra*, paras 441-443, 876 & fn. 886. The Appeals Chamber does not consider that these changes affect the Trial Chamber's finding that is challenged under this ground, insofar as it concerns the remaining crimes, *i.e.* that Prlić, being aware of the HVO crimes committed against the Muslim population in the wake of the 15 January 1993 Ultimatum, had reason to know that the similar 4 April 1993

(c) Prlić's involvement in the campaign of mass arrest of Muslims beginning on 30 June 1993 in several municipalities (Prlić's Sub-ground 16.3)

1209. The Trial Chamber found that on 30 June 1993, following an ABiH attack on HVO positions, Prlić and Stojić issued a joint proclamation ("30 June 1993 Joint Proclamation"), containing a call to arms to the Croatian people in BiH to defend themselves against the Muslim aggression.[3793] Despite the fact that the 30 June 1993 Joint Proclamation did not, *per se,* call for the mass arrest of Muslims, the Trial Chamber concluded that Prlić accepted, knew, and intended to have Muslim men arrested indiscriminately and *en masse,* and placed in detention.[3794] In reaching this conclusion, the Trial Chamber considered that the "chronological account of the events that occurred after the [30 June 1993 Joint Proclamation] attests to the implementation of a preconceived plan",[3795] including the actions undertaken by the military authorities after the 30 June 1993 Joint Proclamation.[3796] In this regard, the Trial Chamber found that: (1) the military chain of command perceived the 30 June 1993 Joint Proclamation, which Stojić was charged with implementing,[3797] "in the same way it did" the 15 January 1993 Ultimatum and the 4 April 1993 Ultimatum; and (2) based on the testimony of Petković, the military authorities could not have **[page 498]** made arrests without the approval of the civilian authorities, including the consent of President Prlić.[3798]

(i) Arguments of the Parties

1210. Prlić challenges the Trial Chamber's findings regarding his involvement in the campaign of arrests and mass detention of Muslims beginning on 30 June 1993 in several municipalities.[3799] First, Prlić argues that the Trial Chamber ignored evidence of a Muslim offensive starting on 30 June 1993 and made contradictory findings when concluding that Prlić and Stojić called on the Croats to arm themselves against the Muslims in the 30 June 1993 Joint Proclamation,[3800] rather than accepting this proclamation as an act of defence.[3801] Second, Prlić claims that the Trial Chamber erred in concluding that the 30 June 1993 Joint Proclamation was linked to a JCE, while it ignored evidence that the HVO: (1) was surprised by the ABiH attack; (2) had not taken any preventive measures; and (3) had made no preparations for the arrests resulting from the ABiH attack and killings of HVO Croats by HVO Muslims.[3802]

1211. Prlić also submits that the Trial Chamber erred in concluding that the military chain of command perceived the 30 June 1993 Joint Proclamation in the same way as it perceived the 15 January 1993 Ultimatum and the 4 April 1993 Ultimatum.[3803] He specifically submits that the evidence does not support the Trial Chamber's finding that Stojić was tasked with implementing this proclamation.[3804] **[page 499]**

Ultimatum would have the same outcome, namely the commission of crimes by the HVO against the Muslim population, and that he intended this to happen. See Trial Judgement, Vol. 4, para. 146; *supra,* fn. 3762. This is in particular so since not many instances of murder took place in that period. See *supra,* para. 876.

[3793]   Trial Judgement, Vol. 4, paras 151, 154.

[3794]   Trial Judgement, Vol. 4, paras 154-155.

[3795]   Trial Judgement, Vol. 4, paras 154.

[3796]   Trial Judgement, Vol. 4, paras 151 (the Commander of the North-West OZ, Željko Šiljeg, requested "instructions for work" from Petković and Stojić on the basis of the 30 June 1993 Joint Proclamation and forwarded "the order of the Defence Department and the HVO HZ H-B" to the Rama Brigade and the 2ⁿᵈ Military Police Battalion, among others), 152 (Radoslav Lavrić sent an order, pursuant to the 30 June 1993 Joint Proclamation, to all the departments and sections of the Military Police Administration and to all Military Police battalions demanding, *inter alia,* the arrest of all conscripts who had not regulated their status).

[3797]   Trial Judgement, Vol. 4, para. 151.

[3798]   Trial Judgement, Vol. 4, para. 154.

[3799]   Prlić's Appeal Brief, para. 495. See Prlić's Appeal Brief, para. 503. See also Prlić's Appeal Brief, para. 449.

[3800]   Prlić''s Appeal Brief, paras 496-497; Appeal Hearing, AT. 144-145 (20 Mar 2017).

[3801]   Prlić's Appeal Brief, para. 498. See Prlić's Appeal Brief, paras 496-497. Prlić specifically argues that the attack on 30 June 1993 was an act of treason by Muslim HVO soldiers and that he himself issued no orders to military units and made no inflammatory remarks demonising Muslims or the ABiH. Prlić's Appeal Brief, paras 497-498.

[3802]   Prlić's Appeal Brief, para. 499. See Prlić's Appeal Brief, para. 500, referring to Witness Klaus Johann Nissen's and Witness Božo Pavlović's testimonies; Appeal Hearing, AT. 144-145 (20 Mar 2017).

[3803]   Prlić's Appeal Brief, para. 503. See Prlić's Appeal Brief, para. 504, referring to Prlić's sub-grounds of appeal 16.1-16.2.

[3804]   Prlić's Appeal Brief, paras 505-506. Prlić submits that the Trial Chamber erred in finding that the 30 June 1993 Joint Proclamation was the basis for the following acts: (1) Šiljeg's request, Exhibit P03026, for "instructions for work"; and (2) Lavrić's order to the Military Police, Exhibit P03077, demanding, *inter alia,* the arrest of all conscripts who had not regulated their status. Prlić's Appeal Brief, paras 507-508. Prlić contends that the 30 June 1993 Joint Proclamation was never sent to the HVO Main Staff

1212. In addition, Prlić claims that the Trial Chamber erred in concluding that the military authorities could not have made arrests without the approval of the civilian authorities, including Prlić, as it mischaracterised Petković's testimony.[3805]

1213. Finally, regarding his knowledge and intent, Prlić submits that the Trial Chamber erred in concluding that he knew of "the plan" and intended to have Muslim men arrested indiscriminately and *en masse,* and placed in detention.[3806] Prlić argues that the Trial Chamber ignored evidence of his attempts to reduce tension and improve the situation by: (1) informing the "internationals" about the arrests as soon as he became aware; and (2) appealing to all sides in BiH not to use humanitarian operations as a weapon in the conflict.[3807]

1214. The Prosecution responds that Prlić fails to show an error in the Trial Chamber's findings.[3808] It submits that the Trial Chamber specifically considered the attack launched by the ABiH forces and that it is irrelevant whether this attack came as a surprise or not.[3809] The Prosecution also argues that Prlić's attempts to distance himself from Stojić's "mobilisation order" are unfounded.[3810] Further, it claims that Prlić failed to demonstrate an error in the Trial Chamber's conclusion that the 30 June 1993 Joint Proclamation and Petković's order caused orders to be issued down the military chain of command.[3811] With respect to Petković's testimony, the Prosecution argues that Prlić fails to explain how the Trial Chamber erred in relying on his evidence that the HVO was structured for the civilian authorities to "exert control over the military".[3812] **[page 500]**

1215. Finally, the Prosecution submits that Prlić's knowledge and intent are amply demonstrated by his attempt to justify the mass detentions and arrests, and that his submissions to the contrary are unfounded.[3813]

(ii) Analysis

1216. The Appeals Chamber turns first to Prlić's argument that the Trial Chamber ignored evidence of a Muslim offensive starting on 30 June 1993 and made contradictory findings when concluding that the 30 June 1993 Joint Proclamation called on the Croats to arm themselves against the Muslims. The Appeals Chamber recalls that the Trial Chamber concluded that early on 30 June 1993, the ABiH launched an offensive on the HVO Tihomir Mišić Barracks, located in the north of the town of Mostar, and that following this and other attacks that took place during the course of several days, the ABiH succeeded in taking control of the north zone of East Mostar.[3814] The Trial Chamber also found that the 30 June 1993 Joint Proclamation called for the Croatian people in BiH to defend themselves against the Muslim aggression.[3815] Considering these findings, the Appeals Chamber finds that Prlić fails to show that the Trial Chamber ignored evidence

---

or any military structure. Prlić's Appeal Brief, para. 507. Prlić also submits that the Trial Chamber contradicted itself regarding who ordered the mobilisation and ignored the following evidence: (1) Lavrić's order "conformed" to Stojić's order; (2) the arrests were based on HVO Main Staff orders; and (3) Petković's order of 30 June 1993 was based on an authorisation from Boban and did not refer to the 30 June 1993 Joint Proclamation. Prlić's Appeal Brief, paras 507-509.

[3805] Prlić's Appeal Brief, para. 501. See Prlić's Appeal Brief, para. 502, referring to Prlić's sub-ground of appeal 12.1.

[3806] Prlić's Appeal Brief, para. 510. See Prlić's Appeal Brief, para. 511, referring to Prlić's sub-grounds of appeal 16.3.1-16.3.2.

[3807] Prlić's Appeal Brief, para. 512, referring to, *inter alia,* Prlić's Appeal Brief, para. 433 (Prlić's ground of appeal 14).

[3808] Prosecution's Response Brief (Prlić), paras 309-310. See Appeal Hearing, AT. 192 (20 Mar 2017).

[3809] Prosecution's Response Brief (Prlić), para. 312. The Prosecution notes that in any event, Prlić relies on evidence indicating that the HVO had envisaged that the situation in Mostar could escalate. Prosecution's Response Brief (Prlić), para. 312.

[3810] Prosecution's Response Brief (Prlić), para. 311.

[3811] Prosecution's Response Brief (Prlić), para. 313. See also Prosecution's Response Brief (Prlić), para. 315. The Prosecution further submits that the 30 June , 1993 Joint Proclamation was indeed forwarded to military units. Prosecution's Response Brief (Prlić), para. 313. In addition, the Prosecution argues that Prlić fails to explain how the Trial Chamber erred in relying on Petković's testimony to find that the military authorities could not have carried out the mass arrests without the approval of the civilian authorities, including Prlić. Prosecution's Response Brief (Prlić), para. 314.

[3812] Prosecution's Response Brief (Prlić), para. 314. See Prosecution's Response Brief (Prlić), fn. 1101. The Prosecution submits further that it is beside the point whether Petković's order was based on authority from Boban. Prosecution's Response Brief (Prlić), para. 315.

[3813] Prosecution's Response Brief (Prlić), para. 316. The Prosecution also submits that Prlić's appeal of 6 July 1993 not to use humanitarian operations as a weapon is irrelevant to the arrest campaign and only highlights his failure to take action in that regard. Prosecution's Response Brief (Prlić), para. 317.

[3814] Trial Judgement, Vol. 2, paras 880-881. See also Trial Judgement, Vol. 4, paras 57, 64.

[3815] Trial Judgement, Vol. 4, para. 151.

of a Muslim offensive starting on 30 June 1993, and is merely offering his own interpretation of the evidence.[3816] Further, Prlić fails to explain how the Trial Chamber contradicted itself.[3817] Consequently, the Appeals Chamber dismisses his argument.

1217. Concerning Prlić's second challenge that this proclamation was not linked to the JCE, the Appeals Chamber finds that the allegedly ignored evidence does not provide clear support for Prlić's assertions that the HVO was surprised, had not taken any preventive measures with regard to the ABiH attack, and had made no preparations for the arrests.[3818] In any event, Prlić fails to explain why the mass arrest of. Muslims could not be linked to the JCE if it had not been planned prior to the ABiH attack.[3819] The Appeals Chamber dismisses his argument accordingly.

1218. With respect to Prlić's challenge that the Trial Chamber erred in finding that the military chain of command perceived the 30 June 1993 Joint Proclamation in the same way as it did the **[page 501]** 15 January 1993 Ultimatum and the 4 April 1993 Ultimatum, the Appeals Chamber finds, having reviewed the Trial Chamber's findings regarding the issuance and chain of command in respect of the 30 June 1993 Joint Proclamation and the supporting evidence, that Prlić has failed to articulate an error that would invalidate the Trial Chamber's conclusion in this respect. The Appeals Chamber notes in particular that the Trial Chamber's findings on how the military chain of command perceived the 30 June 1993 Joint Proclamation find explicit support in the evidence on which it relied.[3820] The Appeals Chamber further considers that a reasonable trier of fact could have found, based on the 30 June 1993 Joint Proclamation and events that followed, that Stojić was tasked with implementing this proclamation.[3821] Bearing in mind the Trial Chamber's findings with respect to, and in particular the chronology of events following the signing of, the 15 January 1993 Ultimatum and the 4 April 1993 Ultimatum,[3822] the Appeals Chamber finds that a reasonable trier of fact could have made the impugned finding. The Appeals Chamber therefore dismisses Prlić's challenge.

1219. Concerning Prlić's challenge to the Trial Chamber's conclusion that the military authorities could not have made arrests without the approval of the civilian authorities, the Appeals Chamber considers that Prlić fails to explain how Petković's statement that Prlić's influence was limited by the decree on armed forces would show that the Trial Chamber mischaracterised his testimony. The Appeals Chamber observes that the Trial Chamber specifically considered Petković's testimony that Prlić could only issue operative orders to the armed forces through the Department of Defence, but also noted that he, as President of the HVO Government, issued decisions that had a direct impact on the course of military operations of the HVO.[3823] Against this

---

[3816] See Prlić"s Appeal Brief, para. 497.

[3817] See Prlić's Appeal Brief, para. 496 & fn. 1287, referring to Trial Judgement, Vol. 2, paras 879-884.

[3818] See Prlić's Appeal Brief, para. 499, referring to, *inter alia*, Ex. 4D00702, Radmilo Jašak, T. 48700-48701 (20 Jan 2010), Milivoj Petković, T. 49585, 49589 (17 Feb 2010).

[3819] The Appeals Chamber further finds no merit in Prlić's reference to Nissen's evidence, in which he speculated about, but acknowledged having no personal knowledge of, any plan or preparations for mass arrests of Muslims, and to Pavlović's testimony, in which he said that he did not recall the 30 June 1993 Joint Proclamation. See Prlić's Appeal Brief, para. 500 and references cited therein.

[3820] See Trial Judgement, Vol. 4, paras 151-152, referring to Exs. P03026, P03038, P03039, P03077. Notably, Šiljeg's order, Exhibit P03026, specifically states that it is based on, *inter alia*, "the command issued by the Head of Defence Department and the President of the HVO HB HZB". Exhibit P03077 similarly indicates that it was issued "[p]ursuant to the order by the Head of the Defence Department, Mr Bruno Stojić, and the HZ H-B HVO President, Dr. J. Prlić". In addition, the Appeals Chamber finds that Prlić has failed to demonstrate that the 30 June 1993 Joint Proclamation "was never sent to the HVO Main Staff or to any military structure". Prlić's Appeal Brief, para. 507. See Ex. P03039 (forwarding the 30 June 1993 Joint Proclamation to, *inter alia*, all HVO representatives in municipalities, all Defence Offices in municipalities, and Military Police command). The Appeals Chamber also finds no contradiction in the Trial Chamber's findings regarding who ordered the mobilisation. Compare Trial Judgement, Vol. 2, para. 884, with Trial Judgement, Vol.4, paras 151-152. Finally, the Appeals Chamber considers that Prlić fails to show that the allegedly ignored evidence is relevant to or impacts the impugned finding.

[3821] See Trial Judgement, Vol. 4, para. 151, referring to, *inter alia*, Ex. P03038. The Appeals Chamber considers that Prlić fails to point to any evidence that would show an error in this regard. See Prlić's Appeal Brief, para. 506. The Appeals Chamber also notes that Prlić refers to his submissions in sub-grounds of appeal 16.1 and 16.2, which it dismisses elsewhere in the Judgement. See *supra*, paras 1146-1208.

[3822] Trial Judgement, Vol. 4, paras 125, 138-140. See *supra*, paras 1149-1152, 1184-1189.

[3823] Trial Judgement, Vol. 4, para. 107. See also Trial Judgement, Vol. 4, para. 106; *supra*, para. 1118.

background, the Appeals Chamber finds that Prlić merely disagrees with the Trial Chamber's finding without showing an error and dismisses his argument.[3824] **[page 502]**

1220. Finally, turning to Prlić's arguments concerning his intent and knowledge of the plan to have Muslim men arrested indiscriminately and *en masse,* and placed in detention, the Appeals Chamber notes that these challenges are based in part on mere cross-reference to arguments that were considered and dismissed above.[3825] Regarding the argument that the Trial Chamber ignored evidence of his attempts to reduce tension and improve the situation by informing the "internationals" about the arrests, the Appeals Chamber notes that the Trial Chamber specifically found, *inter alia,* that Prlić informed representatives of an international organisation of the 6,000 Muslim military-aged men whom the HVO had arrested for security reasons and placed in detention.[3826] The Appeals Chamber thus dismisses his argument as he ignores relevant findings. In relation to the argument that the Trial Chamber ignored evidence of Prlić's appeal to all sides in BiH not to use humanitarian operations as a weapon, the Appeals Chamber finds that Prlić has failed to show how such evidence demonstrates that the Trial Chamber's findings regarding the campaign of arrests and mass detention of Muslims are unreasonable and dismisses his argument accordingly.[3827]

1221. In light of the above, the Appeals Chamber finds that Prlić has failed to show any error in the impugned findings and dismisses his sub-ground of appeal 16.3.

(d) Mostar Municipality (Prlić's Sub-ground 16.4)

(i) West Mostar

a. Alleged error in concluding that the Croatian culture was introduced (Prlić's Sub-ground 16.4.1)

1222. Prlić submits that the Trial Chamber erred in finding, by relying on the testimony of Tomljanovich, while ignoring other evidence, that he approved the introduction of a Croatian culture in HZ(R) H-B through the use of the Croatian language and Dinar and the HZ H-B coat of arms and flag.[3828] **[page 503]**

1223. The Prosecution responds that Prlić's conviction does not rely on the findings made on his involvement in "Croatisation" and as such his arguments should be summarily dismissed.[3829]

1224. The Appeals Chamber notes that while the Trial Chamber found that Prlić did debate and sign regulations approving the introduction of a Croatian culture, it did not find that Prlić promoted the municipal HVO's policy of discrimination against Muslims, thus encouraging their departure from Mostar.[3830] It also did not find that he was informed of such a policy.[3831] As Prlić challenges factual findings on which his conviction does not rely,[3832] the Appeals Chamber dismisses his sub-ground of appeal 16.4.1.

[3824] The Appeals Chamber also notes that Prlić refers to his submissions in sub-ground of appeal 12.1, which it dismisses elsewhere in the Judgement. See *supra,* paras 1099-1122.

[3825] Specifically, Prlić refers to his challenges in sub-grounds of appeal 16.3.1 and 16.3.2 (Prlić's Appeal Brief, paras 496-500), which concern the 30 June 1993 Joint Proclamation. See Prlić's Appeal Brief, para. 511; *supra,* paras 1210, 1216-1217.

[3826] Trial Judgement, Vol. 2, para. 894 & fn. 2091, specifically noting the testimony of Petković that "the HVO had never tried to conceal the isolation measures against HVO Muslim soldiers and Muslims fit for combat from the international observers", referring to, *inter alia,* Milivoj Petković, T(F). 49581-49584 (17 Feb 2010). See also Trial Judgement, Vol. 2, para. 895, Vol. 4, para. 153.

[3827] The Appeals Chamber also notes that Prlić refers to his submissions in ground of appeal 14, which it dismisses elsewhere in the Judgement. See *supra,* paras 1128-1134.

[3828] Prlić's Appeal Brief, paras 514-520.

[3829] Prosecution's Response Brief (Prlić), para. 319.

[3830] Trial Judgement, Vol. 4, para. 158.

[3831] Trial Judgement, Vol. 4, para. 160.

[3832] *Cf.* Trial Judgement, Vol. 4, paras 270-276. See *supra,* paras 1149-1152, 1157-1159, & fn. 3677, para. 1190; *infra,* paras 1314, 1317 & fns 4077, 4092.

b. Alleged error regarding Prlić's acceptance of the arrest of Muslims that took place around 9 May 1993 (Prlić's Sub-ground 16.4.2)

1225. The Trial Chamber found that the situation in Mostar was discussed during the 38th session of the HVO on 17 May 1993, and that:

> [...] The HVO expressed its support for the relocation of civilians to the Heliodrom and said that the women, children and elderly people had been released. The Chamber considers that by participating in the meeting and raising no objections while continuing to exercise his functions at the head of the HVO, Jadranko Prlić accepted the arrests of Muslim men of Mostar who did not belong to any armed forces carried out around 9 May 1993.[3833]

i. Arguments of the Parties

1226. Prlić challenges the above finding arguing that the Trial Chamber misconstrued Exhibit 1D01666 (minutes of the 38th HVO meeting), the single document on which it based its conclusion.[3834] According to Prlić, the HVO HZ H-B did not express its support for the relocation of civilians to the Heliodrom but for the activities of the ODPR.[3835] Prlić submits that the Trial Chamber ignored evidence and its own findings that the ODPR did not participate in the relocation of civilians.[3836] Further, he submits that nothing suggests that only Muslims were relocated.[3837] He also submits that the Trial Chamber ignored evidence that he and the HVO HZ H-B were not involved in any "activities or agreements during this period".[3838] **[page 504]**

1227. The Prosecution responds that Prlić fails to show that no reasonable trial chamber could have relied on the plain words of the minutes of the 38th HVO meeting to reach its conclusions.[3839] According to the Prosecution, these minutes clearly demonstrate that the Government expressed support for the ODPR's activities in the context of its moving civilians from Mostar to the Heliodrom.[3840] The Prosecution argues that the Trial Chamber's findings and the evidence show that only Muslims were relocated.[3841] Lastly, the Prosecution submits that Prlić ignores contrary evidence as to his and the Government's involvement in "activities" at this time.[3842]

ii. Analysis

1228. The Appeals Chamber notes that the impugned finding was based on the minutes of the 38th HVO meeting, held on 17 May 1993, which state that:

> [...] Support was expressed for the activities of the [ODPR] which has been active since the first day civilians were relocated from Mostar to the former Military Gymnasium and Heliodrom, after the commencement of combat activities in Mostar. [...] The HVO HZ H-B was informed that all elderly persons, women and children have already been sent back to their homes, and that some of them have been sent, at their own request, to the part of town on the left bank of the river Neretva.[3843]

The Appeals Chamber considers with regard to Prlić's argument that the HVO HZ H-B did not express its support for the relocation of civilians to the Heliodrom but rather for the activities of the ODPR, that based on a contextual reading of the minutes of the 38th HVO meeting, a reasonable trier of fact could have concluded that the HVO HZ H-B expressed its support for such relocation of civilians.[3844] The Appeals Chamber therefore dismisses Prlić's argument.

[3833] Trial Judgement, Vol. 4, para. 165.
[3834] Prlić's Appeal Brief, para. 521, referring to Prlić's Appeal Brief, ground of appeal 3.
[3835] Prlić's Appeal Brief, para. 522.
[3836] Prlić's Appeal Brief, para. 522.
[3837] Prlić's Appeal Brief, paras 523-524.
[3838] Prlić's Appeal Brief, para. 524.
[3839] Prosecution's Response Brief (Prlić), para. 320.
[3840] Prosecution's Response Brief (Prlić), para. 320.
[3841] Prosecution's Response Brief (Prlić), para. 321.
[3842] Prosecution's Response Brief (Prlić), para. 321.
[3843] Ex. 1D01666, pp. 1-2.
[3844] Having dismissed the argument that the Trial Chamber misconstrued Exhibit 1D01666 (the minutes of the 38th HVO meeting), the Appeals Chamber notes that Prlić does not clearly articulate any error in the Trial Chamber's reliance on "a single

1229. As to Prlić's submission that the Trial Chamber ignored evidence and its own findings that the ODPR did not participate in the relocation of civilians, the Appeals Chamber considers that this submission is not supported by the references on which Prlić relies.[3845] For instance, he refers to Petković's testimony on an agreement between him and Sefer Halilović concerning, *inter alia,* displaced persons and the fact that Petković was informed of civilians being released from the Heliodrom,[3846] which the Appeals Chamber does not consider demonstrates that the ODPR did not participate in relocating civilians. The Appeals Chamber thus dismisses Prlić's argument as a mere **[page 505]** assertion and misrepresentation of the evidence. The Appeals Chamber further dismisses Prlić's claim that the evidence does not indicate that only Muslims were relocated, as he ignores other relevant findings of the Trial Chamber.[3847] Lastly, Prlić's argument that neither he nor the HVO HZ H-B participated in "activities or agreements during this period" is vague and irrelevant to the challenged factual finding and is dismissed on this basis.

1230. For the foregoing reasons, the Appeals Chamber dismisses Prlić's sub-ground of appeal 16.4.2.

    c. Alleged errors regarding Prlić's contribution to the eviction process (Prlić's Sub-grounds 16.4.3 and 16.4.4)

1231. The Trial Chamber found that on 6 July 1993, Prlić signed a decree on the use of apartments abandoned by the tenants ("Decree of 6 July 1993"),[3848] and that he thereby accepted the HVO HZ H-B's practice of appropriating the apartments of Muslims expelled from West Mostar and contributed to their eviction because once the Muslims were deprived of their apartments, their return to Mostar became unrealistic.[3849] It also found that from at least June 1993, Prlić was repeatedly alerted to the forcible evictions of Muslims, which continued until February 1994.[3850] By failing to act, by validating the loss of apartments belonging to Muslims in Mostar, and by remaining in power while fully aware of the crimes committed against Muslims, Prlić contributed to the climate of violence and accepted the commission of acts of violence linked to the eviction campaign.[3851]

    i. Arguments of the Parties

1232. Prlić challenges these findings.[3852] Specifically, Prlić claims that there is no evidence that the HVO HZ H-B appropriated the apartments of expelled Muslims from West Mostar or allocated apartments of expelled Muslims to soldiers and Croatian families, and that the Trial Chamber made findings supporting this view.[3853] **[page 506]**

1233. Prlić further argues that the Trial Chamber mischaracterised the Decree of 6 July 1993, which was similar to a 1992 BiH law on abandoned apartments.[3854] He also claims that the Trial Chamber ignored evidence showing: (1) the "chaotic" use of socially-owned abandoned apartments; (2) efforts made by municipal authorities to introduce order in the use of apartments; (3) that the aim of the Decree of 6 July 1993 was to standardise legislation in all municipalities; (4) that this decree was more in line with human rights than the 1992 BiH law; and (5) that the majority of abandoned apartments were allotted to Muslims and ABiH soldiers.[3855]

---

document". In this regard, the Appeals Chamber also notes that Prlić refers to his submissions in ground of appeal 3, which it dismisses elsewhere in the Judgement. See *supra,* paras 177-183.

[3845]   See Prlić's Appeal Brief, fns 1343-1344 and references cited therein.
[3846]   Prlić's Appeal Brief, fn. 1344, referring to, *inter alia,* Milivoj Petković, T. 49552-49553 (16 Feb 2010), 49555 (24 Feb 2010).
[3847]   The Trial Chamber found that between 9 and 11 May 1993 Muslims were arrested and transported to the Heliodrom and, following that, only Muslims were detained in the Heliodrom. Trial Judgement, Vol. 2, paras 805, 1495, 1497-1498.
[3848]   Trial Judgement, Vol. 4, para. 169; Ex. P03089.
[3849]   Trial Judgement, Vol. 4, para. 170.
[3850]   Trial Judgement, Vol. 4, para. 171. See Trial Judgement, Vol. 4, para. 170.
[3851]   Trial Judgement, Vol. 4, para. 171.
[3852]   Prlić's Appeal Brief, para. 525.
[3853]   Prlić's Appeal Brief, para. 526.
[3854]   Prlić's Appeal Brief, para. 527. See Appeal Hearing, AT. 148 (20 Mar 2017).
[3855]   Prlić's Appeal Brief, para. 528; Appeal Hearing, AT. 148 (20 Mar 2017).

1234. Prlić also challenges the Trial Chamber's conclusion that when Muslims were deprived of their apartments "their return became unrealistic" as, according to him, the Trial Chamber ignored evidence that the HVO HZ H-B adopted measures to protect private property and to preserve the demographic structure by decreeing that refugees and displaced persons retain their places of domicile in the places of residence as of 1 April 1992.[3856]

1235. The Prosecution responds that Prlić shows no error in the Trial Chamber's conclusions and that the Trial Chamber reasonably found that he endorsed the practice of evicting Muslims and appropriating their apartments.[3857] According to the Prosecution, Prlić ignores relevant evidence[3858] and does not explain how the similarities between the Decree of 6 July 1993 and the 1992 BiH law render the Trial Chamber's findings unreasonable.[3859] The Prosecution further avers that Prlić fails to explain how the "chaotic use" of abandoned apartments, efforts made by municipal authorities to introduce order in the use of apartments, and assertions that the Decree of 6 July 1993 aimed to standardise municipal legislation and was more in line with human rights than the 1992 BiH law on abandoned apartments, are relevant to the impugned finding.[3860] Finally, the Prosecution submits that Prlić fails to support his claim that the majority of abandoned apartments were allotted to Muslims and ABiH soldiers.[3861]

1236. With regard to Prlić's challenge to the Trial Chamber's finding that once Muslims were deprived of their apartments, their return became unrealistic, the Prosecution submits that Prlić ignores the plain language of the Decree of 6 July 1993 – giving the previous tenant only seven days after a declaration of cessation of imminent threat of war to retake occupancy.[3862] The **[page 507]** Prosecution submits that Prlić also fails to explain how alleged Government measures to protect property and restrict property transactions facilitated the return of Muslim tenants to their apartments.[3863] Further, the Prosecution claims that, in light of the ongoing violent HVO ethnic cleansing campaign, Prlić's suggestion that the aim of a decree that refugees and displaced persons were to maintain their registered domicile as of 1 April 1992 was to prevent demographic change, is untenable.[3864]

ii. Analysis

1237. The Appeals Chamber will first address Prlić's argument that there is no evidence that the HVO HZ H-B appropriated the apartments of expelled Muslims from West Mostar or that it allocated apartments of expelled Muslims to soldiers and Croatian families. The Appeals Chamber recalls that the Trial Chamber found that it was HVO forces who evicted Muslims from their apartments and allocated them to HVO soldiers and Croatian families.[3865] The Appeals Chamber also recalls that the Trial Chamber found that by signing the Decree of 6 July 1993, issued by the HVO HZ H-B itself,[3866] Prlić accepted the HVO HZ H-B practice of appropriating the apartments of the Muslims expelled from West Mostar and knew about it as of June 1993.[3867] In these circumstances, the Appeals Chamber considers that Prlić has failed to show that no reasonable trier of fact could have made the impugned finding. The Appeals Chamber further considers that the fact that the Trial Chamber was unable to find that in July and August 1993, apartments from which Muslims had been evicted were allocated to Bosnian Croat *civilians* is not inconsistent with the impugned finding.[3868] For these reasons, Prlić's argument is dismissed.

[3856] Prlić's Appeal Brief, para. 529; Appeal Hearing, AT. 149 (20 Mar 2017). See Appeal Hearing, AT. 148 (20 Mar 2017). See also Prlić's Appeal Brief, para. 530, referring to Prlić's Appeal Brief, sub-ground of appeal 10.5.

[3857] Prosecution's Response Brief (Prlić), paras 322-323.

[3858] Prosecution's Response Brief (Prlić), para. 324.

[3859] Prosecution's Response Brief (Prlić), para. 324.

[3860] Prosecution's Response Brief (Prlić), para. 325.

[3861] Prosecution's Response Brief (Prlić), para. 325.

[3862] Prosecution's Response Brief (Prlić), para. 326.

[3863] Prosecution's Response Brief (Prlić), para. 326.

[3864] Prosecution's Response Brief (Prlić), para. 327.

[3865] See Trial Judgement, Vol. 2, paras 824, 827, 864-866, 872-874, 919-920, 930, 937.

[3866] See Ex. P03089.

[3867] See Trial Judgement, Vol. 4, para. 170.

[3868] See Trial Judgement, Vol. 2, para. 938.

1238. With regard to Prlić's claim that the Trial Chamber mischaracterised the Decree of 6 July 1993, the Appeals Chamber considers that he selectively refers to articles of the Decree of 6 July 1993 that purportedly support his claim, without demonstrating that the Trial Chamber misinterpreted them or other relevant articles.[3869] Specifically, the Appeals Chamber considers that Prlić ignores Articles 7 and 12 of the Decree of 6 July 1993 stating that an abandoned apartment, except for the HZ H-B's own military apartments, "may be allocated for temporary use to HVO members or other active participants in the struggle against the enemy or to persons who have been deprived of a dwelling place because of the war". It also recalls that Article 10, to which Prlić refers, only gives seven days' time, after a proclamation of a "cessation of imminent danger of war" **[page 508]** for a tenant to reclaim occupancy of an apartment, otherwise "the apartment shall be considered to have been permanently vacated".[3870] Prlić's claim is therefore dismissed. The Appeals Chamber considers that Prlić has not explained how any similarities to a 1992 BiH law on abandoned apartments render the Trial Chamber's findings erroneous and dismisses this contention as irrelevant.

1239. The Appeals Chamber notes that Prlić's argument that the Trial Chamber ignored evidence showing the "chaotic" use of abandoned apartments is not supported by any reference to the trial record. Thus, it is a mere assertion unsupported by any evidence and the Appeals Chamber dismisses it as such. Regarding Prlić's argument that the Trial Chamber ignored evidence showing the efforts made by municipal authorities to introduce order in the use of apartments and that the Decree of 6 July 1993 was meant to standardise the legislation in all municipalities and was more in line with human rights than the 1992 BiH law on abandoned apartments, the Appeals Chamber fails to see its relevance to the impugned finding and notes that Prlić provides no explanation in this regard. The Appeals Chamber therefore dismisses the argument as irrelevant. As to Prlić's argument that the Trial Chamber ignored evidence showing that the majority of abandoned apartments were allotted to Muslims and ABiH soldiers, the Appeals Chamber considers that Prlić points to evidence which is not specific to the relevant time period, and dismisses his argument as temporally irrelevant.[3871]

1240. With regard to Prlić's argument that the Trial Chamber erroneously concluded, because it ignored evidence, that when Muslims were deprived of their apartments "their return to Mostar became unrealistic",[3872] the Appeals Chamber notes that the Trial Chamber relied on the wording of the Decree of 6 July 1993, which stated that "[w]hen cessation of imminent danger of war is proclaimed and the holder of tenancy rights […] fails to take up occupancy of the apartment within seven days, the apartment shall be considered to have been permanently vacated".[3873] The Appeals Chamber considers that Prlić has failed to show that no reasonable trier of fact, based on **[page 509]** this evidence, and notwithstanding the allegedly ignored evidence,[3874] could have reached the same conclusion as the Trial Chamber.[3875]

1241. For the foregoing reasons, the Appeals Chamber dismisses Prlić's sub-grounds of appeal 16.4.3 and 16.4.4.

   (ii) East Mostar

     a. The HVO campaign of fire and shelling of East Mostar (Prlić's Sub-ground 16.4.5)

1242. The Trial Chamber found that Prlić knew about the HVO crimes committed during the HVO campaign of fire and shelling against East Mostar – namely the murders and destruction of property, including mosques

---

[3869]   See Prlić's Appeal Brief, para. 527, referring to, *inter alia*, Ex. P03089, Arts 1-3, 9-11.

[3870]   Ex. P03089, Arts 7, 10, 12. See Trial Judgement, Vol. 4, para. 169 & fn. 454.

[3871]   See Prlić's Appeal Brief, para. 528(e), referring to Exs. 3D01027 (dated September 1992), 1D00641 (dated September 1992), 3D00734 (dated October 1992), Borislav Puljić, T. 32291-32292 (17 Sept 2008) (on Ex. 3D01027), Veso Vegar, T. 37054-37058 (17 Feb 2007) (on Ex. 3D01027). *Cf.* Trial Judgement, Vol. 4, paras 169-171, fn. 455 (referring to May/June 1993 and onwards). With regard to the HVO member Jašak's testimony that in August 1993 there was no available housing for him, the Appeals Chamber considers this evidence not to be inconsistent with the impugned finding. See Prlić's Appeal Brief, fn. 1361, referring to Radmilo Jašak, T. 48802-48804 (25 Jan 2010). Finally, the Appeals Chamber considers Prlić's reference to "Puljić […] 32309/21-32210/3" to be defective. Prlić's Appeal Brief, fn. 1360.

[3872]   See Trial Judgement, Vol. 4, para. 170.

[3873]   Trial Judgement, Vol. 4, para. 169 & fn. 454, referring to, *inter alia*, Ex. P03089, Art. 10.

[3874]   See Prlić's Appeal Brief, para. 529 and references cited therein.

[3875]   The Appeals Chamber also notes that Prlić refers to his submissions in sub-ground of appeal 10.5, which it dismisses elsewhere in the Judgement. See *supra*, paras 910-916.

and the Old Bridge – and that by minimising or attempting to deny them, he accepted and encouraged them.[3876] The Trial Chamber concluded on this basis that Prlić supported the HVO campaign of fire and shelling against East Mostar as well as its impact on the population of East Mostar.[3877]

i. Arguments of the Parties

1243. Prlić challenges these findings.[3878] He claims there is no evidence that he in any way encouraged the murders and destruction in East Mostar.[3879] Prlić also argues that in finding that he minimised or concealed the HVO's responsibility in the destruction of the Old Bridge, the Trial Chamber misinterpreted his comments at a meeting with Franjo Tuđman and in a BBC interview and ignored evidence that from 7 to 11 November 1993 he was not in Mostar.[3880]

1244. The Prosecution responds that Prlić incorrectly claims that there is no evidence that he encouraged crimes that accompanied the HVO campaign of firing and shelling against East Mostar.[3881] In the Prosecution's view, Prlić misrepresents his comments in his meeting with Tuđman and to the BBC, which in fact support the Trial Chamber's finding that he sought to **[page 510]** conceal or minimise HVO responsibility in the destruction of the Old Bridge.[3882] Finally, the Prosecution submits that his argument that he was not in Mostar from 7 to 11 November 1993 is irrelevant.[3883]

ii. Analysis

1245. The Appeals Chamber recalls that the Trial Chamber found, based on supporting evidence,[3884] that Prlić accepted and encouraged the murders and destruction of property in Mostar by *minimising or attempting to deny* these crimes that he knew had been committed.[3885] This included evidence relating specifically to East Mostar.[3886] The Appeals Chamber thus dismisses Prlić's assertion that there is no evidence that he in any way encouraged the murders and destruction in East Mostar.[3887]

1246. Turning to the Old Bridge, the Appeals Chamber recalls that it has reversed the Trial Chamber's findings that the destruction of the Old Bridge constituted persecution as a crime against humanity (Count 1) and unlawful infliction of terror on civilians as a violation of the laws or customs of war (Count 25) and has therefore acquitted the Appellants of these charges insofar as they concern the Old Bridge.[3888] In its analysis of Prlić's contribution to the JCE, the Trial Chamber referred to its finding that the destruction of the Old Bridge amounted to wanton destruction not justified by military necessity[3889] and found that Prlić knew about the *crime* of the destruction of the Old Bridge by the HVO.[3890] Thus, the Appeals Chamber considers that the Trial Chamber's findings on Prlić's contribution to the JCE, as far as the Old Bridge is concerned, are premised on the destruction of the Old Bridge being a crime. Consequently, the Appeals Chamber reverses the Trial Chamber's finding – insofar as it concerns the Old Bridge – that Prlić knew about the HVO crimes committed during the HVO campaign of fire and shelling against East Mostar and that by minimising

---

[3876] Trial Judgement, Vol. 4, para. 176. See Trial Judgement, Vol. 4, paras 173-175, referring to, *inter alia,* Trial Judgement, Vol. 2, paras 1347-1351.

[3877] Trial Judgement, Vol. 4, para. 176.

[3878] Prlić's Appeal Brief, para. 531.

[3879] Prlić's Appeal Brief, para. 531.

[3880] Prlić's Appeal Brief, paras 531-533. With regard to the BBC interview, Prlić points specifically to his comments that the destruction of the Old Bridge "is terrible", that there was no political or military reason to destroy it, and that he still hoped that Muslims, Croats, and Serbs could live harmoniously in the region. Prlić's Appeal Brief, para. 533.

[3881] Prosecution's Response Brief (Prlić), para. 328. See Appeal Hearing, AT. 192-193 (20 Mar 2017).

[3882] Prosecution's Response Brief (Prlić), para. 329.

[3883] Prosecution's Response Brief (Prlić), para. 329.

[3884] See Trial Judgement, Vol. 2, paras 1347-1351, Vol. 4, paras 174-176 and references cited therein.

[3885] Trial Judgement, Vol. 4, para. 176.

[3886] See Trial Judgement, Vol. 4, para. 174.

[3887] See *supra,* fn. 2816.

[3888] See *supra,* para. 426. The Appeals Chamber also reversed the Trial Chamber's conclusion that the destruction of the Old Bridge constituted wanton destruction not justified by military necessity as a violation of the laws or customs of war (Count 20). See *supra,* para. 414.

[3889] Trial Judgement, Vol. 4, para. 175 & fn. 469.

[3890] Trial Judgement, Vol. 4, para. 176.

or attempting to deny them, he accepted and encouraged them.[3891] As a result, Prlić's submissions with regard to the Old Bridge are moot.

1247. For the foregoing reasons, the Appeals Chamber dismisses Prlić's sub-ground of appeal 16.4.5. **[page 511]**

b. The living conditions in East Mostar (Prlić's Sub-ground 16.4.6)

1248. The Trial Chamber found that in June 1993, the HVO hindered repair works on the water supply system in East Mostar proposed by the THW Company.[3892] The Trial Chamber accepted Witnesses BA's and BC's evidence that despite Prlić's assurances that there would be no obstacles to repairing the water supply system and that he would permit repair work to go ahead, the HVO constantly raised bureaucratic obstacles to prevent the repair.[3893] The Trial Chamber considered the only possible explanation to be that Prlić deliberately impeded the attempts to repair the water supply system by placing bureaucratic obstacles in the way.[3894] The Trial Chamber nevertheless noted that between July and November 1993, the HVO attempted to repair the hydraulic system.[3895] The Trial Chamber also noted Prlić's proposals of 2 December 1993 to alleviate the suffering of the population of East Mostar, but found no evidence that the proposals were ever implemented.[3896] The Trial Chamber found that Prlić knew of the bad living conditions of the population of East Mostar, in particular the lack of food and water, and had the power to intervene but failed to act to improve such conditions.[3897]

i. Arguments of the Parties

1249. Prlić submits that the Trial Chamber erroneously concluded that, having had the power to intervene, he failed to act to improve the living conditions of the population of East Mostar.[3898] He argues that the Trial Chamber disregarded evidence showing his efforts to facilitate the flow of humanitarian aid and his negotiation efforts at the end of 1993 to find a solution for Mostar.[3899]

1250. Prlić also claims the Trial Chamber erred in concluding, based on selective evidence and uncorroborated hearsay, that in June 1993 the HVO hindered repair on the water supply in East Mostar,[3900] and that, by creating "bureaucratic obstacles", he deliberately impeded the THW Company's attempts to have it repaired.[3901] Prlić further submits that the Trial Chamber mischaracterised some evidence and ignored other evidence which demonstrates that there were **[page 512]** other reasons why the water supply system had not been repaired, such as security reasons, that West Mostar also lacked water, that the Mostar municipal authority controlled the water supply, and that bridges had to be repaired before the water supply could be fixed.[3902] He submits that it is "illogical" for the Trial Chamber to conclude that the HVO obstructed the repairs on the water supply in June 1993 when it found that from July until November 1993, the HVO attempted to manage the water supply issues in Mostar and performed the necessary repairs.[3903]

1251. Prlić further argues that the Trial Chamber erroneously concluded that his proposals to alleviate the suffering of the population of East Mostar were not followed through, implying his non-commitment or

---

[3891]   Trial Judgement, Vol. 4, para. 176.
[3892]   Trial Judgement, Vol. 2, paras 1213, 1218, Vol. 4, para. 179.
[3893]   Trial Judgement, Vol. 2, para. 1213, Vol. 4, paras 179-180.
[3894]   Trial Judgement, Vol. 4, para. 180.
[3895]   Trial Judgement, Vol. 2, paras 1215, 1218, Vol. 4, para. 179.
[3896]   Trial Judgement, Vol. 2, paras 1203, 1222, Vol. 4, para. 181.
[3897]   Trial Judgement, Vol. 4, para. 182.
[3898]   Prlić's Appeal Brief, para. 534.
[3899]   Prlić's Appeal Brief, para. 534, referring to, *inter alia*, Prlić's Appeal Brief, paras 397 (ground of appeal 12), 433 (ground of appeal 14), 544, 546 (sub-ground of appeal 16.4.7).
[3900]   Prlić's Appeal Brief, para. 535.
[3901]   Prlić's Appeal Brief, para. 535, referring to, *inter alia*, Prlić's Appeal Brief, paras 179-180 (ground of appeal 6), 186-187 (sub-ground of appeal 6.2). Prlić claims in this regard that Witness BA offered no specifics for his claims that the HVO constantly raised "bureaucratic obstacles". Prlić's Appeal Brief, para. 535.
[3902]   Prlić's Appeal Brief, para. 536.
[3903]   Prlić's Appeal Brief, para. 536.

obstruction, while ignoring its own finding that there was a front line separating Mostar and evidence that the ABiH rejected all offers for help from West Mostar and that the possibilities to help were limited.[3904] Finally, Prlić submits that the Trial Chamber ignored evidence that the peace proposal after the inauguration of the HR H-B Government reaffirmed previous efforts to provide necessary utilities and healthcare for all inhabitants of Mostar, that the new government, having more powers, played a more prominent role in humanitarian issues, and that Prlić sincerely tried to find solutions for all of Mostar and its inhabitants.[3905]

1252. The Prosecution responds that Prlić shows no error in the Trial Chamber's conclusion that he failed to intervene to improve living conditions in East Mostar.[3906] It argues that the Trial Chamber relied on corroborated evidence to conclude that he deliberately impeded repairs to the water system[3907] and that it did not mischaracterise the evidence supporting its finding that the HVO impeded repairs on the water system.[3908] According to the Prosecution, the Trial Chamber considered evidence, analogous to the evidence Prlić claims it ignored, of objective obstacles and ABiH non-co-operation.[3909] Finally, the Prosecution submits that none of the other evidence Prlić refers to undermines the Trial Chamber's findings.[3910] **[page 513]**

ii. Analysis

1253. The Appeals Chamber notes that the Trial Chamber considered evidence showing Prlić's negotiation efforts at the end of 1993 to find a solution for Mostar, at times even the specific evidence that Prlić claims it ignored, and accordingly dismisses Prlić's claims to the contrary.[3911] Further, Prlić's argument that the Trial Chamber disregarded evidence of his efforts to facilitate the flow of humanitarian aid is based on a cross-reference to his (sub-)grounds of appeal 12, 14, and 16.4.7, which the Appeals Chamber dismisses elsewhere.[3912]

1254. With respect to Prlić's argument that the Trial Chamber relied on selective evidence and uncorroborated hearsay to find that he and the HVO hindered repair on the water supply in East Mostar in June 1993,[3913] the Appeals Chamber notes that the Trial Chamber relied on several pieces of mutually corroborating evidence to reach this finding.[3914] Prlić's argument is therefore dismissed.

1255. With regard to Prlić's claim that the Trial Chamber mischaracterised evidence that showed that there were other reasons for the non-repair of the water supply in East Mostar, the Appeals Chamber considers that the Trial Chamber characterised this evidence in a manner similar to that of Prlić.[3915] In particular the Trial Chamber found that:

[3904]   Prlić's Appeal Brief, para. 537.

[3905]   Prlić's Appeal Brief, para. 538.

[3906]   Prosecution's Response Brief (Prlić), para. 330.

[3907]   Prosecution's Response Brief (Prlić), para. 331.

[3908]   Prosecution's Response Brief (Prlić), para. 332.

[3909]   Prosecution's Response Brief (Prlić), para. 333.

[3910]   Prosecution's Response Brief (Prlić), paras 333-335. As to the evidence Prlić cites to argue that the HR H-B Government sought to provide utilities and healthcare for all inhabitants of Mostar, the Prosecution notes that he only refers to one such effort: the establishment of a soup kitchen in West Mostar. Further, the Prosecution argues that Prlić's suggestion that it was only with the creation of the HR H-B that the Government had the necessary power to intervene with respect to humanitarian issues ignores the Trial Chamber's findings on the Government's consistent authority throughout the relevant period. Prosecution's Response Brief (Prlić), para. 335.

[3911]   See Trial Judgement, Vol. 4, paras 109 (referring to, *inter alia*, the testimony of Witness DZ and Ex. 1D02189 (confidential)), 181 (referring to, *inter alia*, Exs. 1D01874, P07008). See also Trial Judgement, Vol. 2, para. 1203 and references cited therein. *Cf.* Prlić's Appeal Brief, para. 534 & fn. 1375; *supra*, para. 1120.

[3912]   See *supra*, paras 1098-1134; *infra*, paras 1262-1285.

[3913]   Trial Judgement, Vol. 2, para. 1218, Vol. 4, paras 179-180, 182.

[3914]   See Trial Judgement, Vol. 2, para. 1213 & fns 3035-3037, referring to, *inter alia*, Exs. P09712 (confidential), paras 43, 65, P09842 (confidential), p. 3, Witness BC, T(F). 18331-18332 (closed session) (14 May 2007). As to Prlić's claim that Witness BA offered no specifics for his claims that the HVO constantly raised "bureaucratic obstacles", the Appeals Chamber considers that it fails to demonstrate that no reasonable trial chamber could have found that the HVO created bureaucratic obstacles to prevent the repair works in June 1993, based on the evidence of Witnesses BA and BC. Trial Judgement, Vol. 2, para. 1213, Vol. 4, paras 179-180. The Appeals Chamber also notes that Prlić refers to his submissions within ground of appeal 6, which it dismisses elsewhere in the Judgement. See *supra*, paras 212-218.

[3915]   See Prlić's Appeal Brief, para. 536 at fns 1379-1380.

THW ultimately broke off its activities at the end of June 1993, but the evidence shows that this was for security reasons linked to the escalating combat in Mostar. [...] Furthermore, since one part of the infrastructure was located on HVO-controlled territory and the other on ABiH-controlled territory, repairs to water pipes could be done only when the respective troops of the HVO and the ABiH withdrew from the zone where the infrastructure was located. However, neither the HVO nor the ABiH co-operated fully and withdrew their troops so the pipes could be repaired.[3916] **[page 514]**

Neither the evidence supporting this finding nor the allegedly ignored evidence[3917] is inconsistent with the challenged conclusion. The Appeals Chamber therefore dismisses Prlić's arguments in this regard.

1256. The Appeals Chamber further considers that Prlić fails to explain how the Trial Chamber's finding that, between July and November 1993, the HVO had attempted to manage the water supply issues in Mostar and perform the necessary repairs,[3918] but that in June 1993 it had not,[3919] was "illogical", as one finding does not preclude the other. The Appeals Chamber therefore dismisses the argument.

1257. Turning to Prlić's argument that the Trial Chamber erroneously found that his proposals to help the population of East Mostar were not followed through,[3920] the Appeals Chamber first considers that Prlić has failed to show how the factual finding that there was a front line dividing Mostar[3921] is inconsistent with the impugned findings. The Appeals Chamber further considers that Prlić's claim that the Trial Chamber ignored evidence showing that the ABiH rejected all offers to help mainly relies on the testimony of Witness Ivan B agaric who testified that, at the time, he thought that the Muslim leadership was refusing offers of medical help as a political tactic.[3922] The Appeals Chamber notes that the other evidence Prlić refers to is similar to that which the Trial Chamber considered.[3923] The Appeals Chamber considers that the Trial Chamber thus duly considered evidence of a similar nature, but nevertheless concluded that the evidence did not demonstrate that such offers were ever implemented.[3924] Prlić has failed to demonstrate that no reasonable trier of fact could have reached the same conclusion as the Trial Chamber. These arguments are dismissed.

1258. As to Prlić's related argument that there were limited possibilities to help East Mostar, the evidence to which he refers only indicates that the ABiH allowed inhabitants of East Mostar permission to leave it in extreme medical cases.[3925] Prlić has failed to show how this evidence is **[page 515]** inconsistent with the impugned findings.[3926] The Appeals Chamber therefore dismisses the argument.

1259. With respect to Prlić's argument that the Trial Chamber ignored evidence that the peace proposal after the inauguration of the HR H-B Government reaffirmed previous efforts to provide utilities and healthcare for all inhabitants of Mostar, the Appeals Chamber considers that the evidence Prlić relies upon amounts to one effort to set up a soup kitchen in West Mostar.[3927] It finds that Prlić has failed to show that no reasonable trier of fact could have reached the impugned finding in light of this evidence and dismisses his argument.[3928] With regard to his argument that the new government had more powers to play a more prominent role in humanitarian issues, Prlić relies on two letters he sent at the end of November and beginning of December

---

[3916]   Trial Judgement, Vol. 2, paras 1214 (referring to, *inter alia*, Klaus Johann Nissen, T(F). 20511 (26 June 2007)), 1217 (internal references omitted) (referring to, *inter alia*, Ex. P02598, Grant Finlayson, T(F). 18151-18156 (8 May 2007)). The Appeals Chamber notes that Prlić also refers to document 2D00156, which was not admitted into evidence. *Cf.* Prlić's Appeal Brief, fns 1379-1380.
[3917]   See Prlić's Appeal Brief, para. 536 at fns 1381-1384.
[3918]   See Trial Judgement, Vol. 2, paras 1215-1218, Vol. 4, para. 179.
[3919]   See Trial Judgement, Vol. 2, paras 1213, 1218, Vol. 4, para. 179.
[3920]   See Trial Judgement, Vol. 2, paras 1203, 1222, Vol. 4, para. 181.
[3921]   See Trial Judgement, Vol. 2, para. 992. The Appeals Chamber considers that Prlić's reference to Vol. 1 of the Trial Judgement is erroneous and was meant to refer to Vol. 2. See Prlić's Appeal Brief, para. 537 & fn. 1387.
[3922]   See Ivan Bagarić, T. 39161-39166 (22 Apr 2009), 39176-39177 (23 Apr 2009).
[3923]   See Ex. P02923 (confidential) (a report on which Bagarić testified); Ivan Bagarić, T. 38973-38974 (21 Apr 2009), 39213-39216, (23 Apr 2009); Witness BD, T. 20951-20952 (closed session) (5 July 2007); Trial Judgement, Vol. 2, para. 1222 and references cited therein. *Cf.* Prlić's Appeal Brief, fn. 1388.
[3924]   The Appeals Chamber observes moreover that the Trial Chamber merely found that there was no evidence to support a finding that such proposals were ever implemented, rather than finding that such proposals were not implemented as Prlić asserts. See Trial Judgement, Vol. 4, para. 181; Prlić's Appeal Brief, para. 537.
[3925]   See Witness BC, T. 18486-18487 (closed session) (15 May 2007).
[3926]   See also Trial Judgement, Vol. 2, para. 1217.
[3927]   Marinko Šimunović, T. 33519-33521 (21 Oct 2008); Exs. 1D02764, 1D02765, 1D02766, 1D02767. See Prlić's Appeal Brief, fn. 1390.
[3928]   See Trial Judgement, Vol. 2, para. 1203, Vol. 4, paras 181-182.

1993 to the commander of UNPROFOR and one witness's interpretation of these letters, stating Prlić's *intentions* to improve the humanitarian situation.[3929] Again, the Appeals Chamber considers that Prlić fails to show that, in light of this evidence, no reasonable trier of fact could have reached the impugned findings that there was "no evidence to support a finding that the proposals [to improve the suffering of the population of East Mostar] were ever implemented",[3930] or that, "even though he was aware of the appalling overall situation of the inhabitants of East Mostar and had the power to intervene, Jadranko Prlić failed to act to improve the living conditions of the population of East Mostar".[3931] Consequently, the Appeals Chamber dismisses this argument.

1260. Similarly, with regard to Prlić's final argument that the Trial Chamber ignored evidence that he sincerely tried to find solutions for all of Mostar, and its inhabitants, the Appeals Chamber has considered the evidence he points to,[3932] which at most indicates that Prlić made some efforts in this regard, namely, that he mentioned at a meeting with internationals "his own initiatives [...] referring to the [...] provision of public kitchens for Muslims [and] provision of hospital facilities for Muslims".[3933] The Appeals Chamber finds that Prlić has failed to show that no reasonable trier of fact could have reached the impugned findings based on the remaining evidence.[3934] The argument is therefore dismissed. **[page 516]**

1261. For the foregoing reasons, the Appeals Chamber dismisses Prlić's sub-ground of appeal 16.4.6.

c. Prlić's contribution to blocking humanitarian aid to East Mostar (Prlić's Sub-ground 16.4.7)

1262. The Trial Chamber found that by contributing to blocking the delivery of humanitarian aid to East Mostar, from June to at least December 1993, Prlić must have foreseen that it would cause serious bodily harm to the inhabitants of East Mostar and would constitute a serious attack on their human dignity, and therefore he intended to cause great suffering to the Mostar population.[3935] The Trial Chamber also found that in a meeting on 10 June 1993, Prlić and other HVO officials informed Witness BA that the ODPR had laid down stricter administrative requirements for the movement of humanitarian aid convoys, requiring that each convoy be individually approved by the HVO.[3936]

1263. Further, the Trial Chamber found that Prlić was one of the HVO officials with the authority to grant passage to the international and humanitarian organisations to deliver humanitarian aid to East Mostar.[3937] It also found that the HVO impeded the regular delivery of humanitarian aid, at least between June and December 1993, by restricting access to East Mostar for international organisations, in particular through administrative restrictions, and that the HVO completely blocked access for humanitarian convoys for almost two months in the summer of 1993 and in December 1993.[3938] The Trial Chamber found that Prlić knew of the difficulties the international organisations, particularly humanitarian ones, had regarding access to East Mostar, that he had the power to grant them access, and that between June and at least December 1993, he created numerous administrative barriers in order to restrict the delivery of humanitarian aid to East Mostar.[3939]

1264. The Trial Chamber further found that the frequent meetings between representatives of the international organisations and the HVO in July and August 1993 held to negotiate free access for humanitarian convoys to East Mostar, including the meeting held on 8 August 1993 in Makarska, attested to

---

[3929] Zoran Perković, T. 31799-31800 (2 Sept 2008); Exs. 1D01873, 1D01912. See Prlić's Appeal Brief, fn. 1391.
[3930] Trial Judgement, Vol. 4, para. 181. See Trial Judgement, Vol. 2, paras 1203, 1222.
[3931] Trial Judgement, Vol. 4, para. 182.
[3932] See Prlić's Appeal Brief, fn. 1392 and references cited therein. Witness DZ talks favourably about Prlić's role in the December 1993 negotiations and that the ABiH wanted him as a negotiating partner. Witness DZ, T. 26689 (23 Jan 2008), 26701-26704, 26716 (closed session) (24 Jan 2008).
[3933] Ex. 1D02189, p. 2.
[3934] See Trial Judgement, Vol. 2, paras 1203, 1222, Vol. 4, paras 181-182 and references cited therein.
[3935] Trial Judgement, Vol. 4, para. 185.
[3936] Trial Judgement, Vol. 2, para. 1230, Vol. 4, para. 184.
[3937] Trial Judgement, Vol. 2, para. 1231, Vol. 4, para. 183.
[3938] Trial Judgement, Vol. 2, para. 1244, Vol. 4, para. 183. See also Trial Judgement, Vol. 2, paras 1227, 1237-1242.
[3939] Trial Judgement, Vol. 4, para. 185.

the difficulties faced by the international organisations in obtaining permission for the delivery of humanitarian aid.[3940] **[page 517]**

i. Arguments of the Parties

1265. Prlić submits that the Trial Chamber erroneously concluded that he foresaw and intended the suffering and attack on human dignity of East Mostar inhabitants by contributing to the blocking of humanitarian aid delivery to East Mostar from June to at least the end of December 1993.[3941]

1266. According to Prlić, the Trial Chamber erroneously concluded, based on Witness BA's uncorroborated evidence, that in a meeting held on 10 June 1993, international organisations were informed that the ODPR had decided to set administrative requirements for the movement of humanitarian aid convoys.[3942] Prlić submits in this regard that Witness BA [Redacted, see Annex C – Confidential Annex].[3943]

1267. Prlić also submits that the Trial Chamber erred in finding that he had the power to grant passage to organisations delivering humanitarian aid.[3944] He argues that he needed the permission of the HVO to move about.[3945]

1268. Prlić contends further that the Trial Chamber erroneously concluded, by mischaracterising Witness BC's evidence, that in July 1993, he refused to authorise access for international organisations to East Mostar.[3946] Prlić argues that the Trial Chamber ignored evidence that just after the Makarska Agreement and when a joint Muslim-Croat convoy was ready for departure from Croatia, the ABiH attacked the municipalities of Stolac and Čapljina on 12 July 1993, thereby preventing any movement from the south.[3947] Prlić argues that this is an alternative plausible explanation for the blocking of delivery of humanitarian aid.[3948]

1269. Prlić also argues that the Trial Chamber's findings that "during some periods [he] blocked all access to the area" were unsubstantiated by the evidence and also contradicted by the evidence on the "milk convoy" and evidence that it was Boban, not Prlić, who decided on the movement of representatives of international organisations in July 1993.[3949]

1270. Prlić claims the Trial Chamber erroneously concluded, relying on mischaracterised and irrelevant evidence, that the meeting held on 8 August 1993 in Makarska attests to difficulties faced by international organisations in obtaining permission to deliver humanitarian aid to the inhabitants **[page 518]** of East Mostar, when the Makarska Agreement was in fact organised to eliminate obstacles in the delivery of humanitarian aid.[3950]

1271. Prlić also argues that the Trial Chamber ignored evidence that some administrative procedures were necessary, and that all convoys were approved and reached their destinations.[3951] Similarly, according to Prlić, the Trial Chamber ignored evidence on the "Joint Commission" initiated by him and the "Protocol", instructions on the passage of humanitarian convoys,[3952] which ensured the unhindered passage of humanitarian convoys in BiH from June to December 1993, as confirmed by the UNHCR.[3953] Finally, Prlić contends that the Trial Chamber ignored evidence that, despite his limited powers, he endeavoured to ensure

---

[3940]   Trial Judgement, Vol. 2, para. 1239, Vol. 4, para. 184.
[3941]   Prlić's Appeal Brief, para. 539.
[3942]   Prlić's Appeal Brief, para. 540.
[3943]   Prlić's Appeal Brief, para. 540, referring to Prlić's Appeal Brief, paras 179-180 (ground of appeal 6).
[3944]   Prlić's Appeal Brief, para. 541.
[3945]   Prlić's Appeal Brief, para. 541. See also Prlić's Appeal Brief, para. 542, referring to Prlić's Appeal Brief, ground of appeal 14.
[3946]   Prlić's Appeal Brief, para. 543 and references cited therein.
[3947]   Prlić's Appeal Brief, para. 543 and references cited therein.
[3948]   Prlić's Appeal Brief, para. 543.
[3949]   Prlić's Appeal Brief, para. 544.
[3950]   Prlić's Appeal Brief, para. 545. See Prlić's Appeal Brief, para. 546.
[3951]   Prlić's Appeal Brief, para. 546.
[3952]   See Prlić's Appeal Brief, fn. 1412, referring to, *inter alia*, Exs. 1D01855, 1D02024, 1D02025.
[3953]   Prlić's Appeal Brief, para. 546.

the free flow of humanitarian aid, as shown by his request to Praljak to use his influence to persuade protesters to allow convoys to enter East Mostar in late August 1993.[3954]

1272. The Prosecution responds that Prlić demonstrates no error in the Trial Chamber's finding that he deliberately participated in blocking humanitarian aid to East Mostar, intending to cause great suffering to the population.[3955] It submits that Prlić misrepresents the record when claiming that the Trial Chamber erred by relying on the evidence of Witness BA[3956] and ignores contrary evidence to challenge the Trial Chamber's finding that he could approve the passage of humanitarian aid.[3957] The Prosecution argues that Prlić misconstrues the evidence in his attempt to show that no movement from the south was possible for security reasons due to an ABiH attack on 12 July 1993.[3958]

1273. In the Prosecution's view, the Trial Chamber's conclusion that Prlić blocked all access to Mostar during certain periods is not "unsubstantiated".[3959] The Prosecution also claims that Prlić mischaracterises the Trial Judgement when he suggests that the Trial Chamber relied solely on the meeting held on 8 August 1993 in Makarska to conclude that international organisations encountered difficulties in negotiating humanitarian convoy access.[3960] **[page 519]**

1274. Further, the Prosecution argues that Prlić's claim that some administrative procedures were necessary cannot explain the deliberate nature of the obstruction to access for humanitarian convoys.[3961] Moreover, according to the Prosecution, Prlić's claim that all convoys were approved and reached their destination ignores clear contrary evidence.[3962] In the Prosecution's view, Prlić's assertion that the UNHCR "confirmed" a Joint Commission had ensured the unhindered passage of humanitarian convoys in BiH between June and December 1993, relies solely on one piece of evidence which is vague and unsubstantiated.[3963]

1275. The Prosecution also submits that Prlić's contention that he endeavoured to ensure the free flow of humanitarian aid is not supported by the evidence he cites and that he ignores other relevant evidence.[3964] Lastly, the Prosecution avers that Prlić fails to explain how his request for Praljak to intervene to allow a convoy to enter Mostar renders the Trial Chamber's overall conclusion unreasonable.[3965]

ii. Analysis

1276. At the outset, the Appeals Chamber observes that the Trial Chamber relied on the evidence of Witness BA to find that, in a 10 June 1993 meeting, Prlić and other HVO officials informed Witness BA that the ODPR had laid down stricter administrative requirements for the movement of humanitarian aid convoys.[3966] With regard to Witness BA's testimony allegedly being uncorroborated, the Appeals Chamber recalls that there is no general requirement that the testimony of a witness be corroborated if deemed otherwise credible.[3967] The other reasons Prlić proffers for not crediting Witness BA's evidence –[Redacted, see Annex

---

[3954] Prlić''s Appeal Brief, para. 547.
[3955] Prosecution's Response Brief (Prlić), para. 336.
[3956] Prosecution's Response Brief (Prlić), para. 337.
[3957] Prosecution's Response Brief (Prlić), para. 338.
[3958] Prosecution's Response Brief (Prlić), para. 339. The Prosecution further argues that the fact that a humanitarian convoy was cancelled due to fighting does not undermine the Trial Chamber's conclusion that Prlić contributed to the blocking of humanitarian aid. Prosecution's Response Brief (Prlić), para. 340.
[3959] Prosecution's Response Brief (Prlić), para. 341. According to the Prosecution, Prlić misleadingly refers to the "milk convoy" in My 1993, which did not go through. Prosecution's Response Brief (Prlić), para. 341.
[3960] Prosecution's Response Brief (Prlić), para. 342.
[3961] Prosecution's Response Brief (Prlić), para. 343.
[3962] Prosecution's Response Brief (Prlić), para. 343.
[3963] Prosecution's Response Brief (Prlić), para. 343. Moreover, the Prosecution submits that Prlić contradicts his own claim by citing evidence showing that this Joint Commission was only formed following a 17 October 1993 meeting. Prosecution's Response Brief (Prlić), para. 343.
[3964] Prosecution's Response Brief (Prlić), para. 344.
[3965] Prosecution's Response Brief (Prlić), para. 345.
[3966] Trial Judgement, Vol. 2, para. 1230 & fn. 3066, Vol. 4, para. 184 & fn. 481, referring to Ex. P09712 (confidential), para. 64.
[3967] *Popović et al.* Appeal Judgement, paras 243, 1264; *D. Milošević* Appeal Judgement, para. 215. See also *Kordić and Čerkez* Appeal Judgement, para. 274.

C – Confidential Annex]– are not, in the Appeals Chamber's opinion, sufficient to affect the credibility of Witness BA.[3968] The Appeals Chamber thus rejects this argument.

1277. The Appeals Chamber further notes that Prlić's argument that he himself needed permission from the HVO to move about is not inconsistent with the challenged finding that he had the **[page 520]** authority to grant passage to organisations to deliver humanitarian aid to East Mostar.[3969] This argument is therefore dismissed.

1278. With regard to Prlić's challenge to the allegedly mischaracterised evidence of Witness BC, which the Trial Chamber relied upon to find that, in July 1993, Prlić refused international organisations access to East Mostar, the Appeals Chamber notes that the Trial Chamber based its finding on the testimony of Witness BC *and* Prlić's letter dated 14 July 1993.[3970] Witness BC testified that in a meeting with Prlić and others, held some time between 10 and 15 July 1993, Prlić linked "humanitarian access to East Mostar [...] to the military situation on the ground".[3971] This link recurs in Prlić's letter dated 14 July 1993:

> By this letter we would like to warn both the addressee and the public of the unpredictable and immeasurable consequences of [the Muslim party's] violations of the Makarska Agreement [...] [aimed at procuring free passage for humanitarian convoys]. HVO will have to reconsider its duties and obligations concerning the implementation of this agreement unless B-H Army stops their offensive in the Neretva valley at once.[3972]

Witness BC further testified that Prlić "said as long as the military situation continues as it is, [...] referring to the events [...] at the north barracks, then [the Bosnian Croat leadership] would not be in a position to grant humanitarian access to East Mostar".[3973] The Appeals Chamber considers that Prlić has failed to demonstrate that no reasonable trier of fact, based on this evidence, could have reached the impugned finding.

1279. With respect to Prlić's argument that the Trial Chamber ignored evidence that the ABiH's attack on 12 July 1993 on the municipalities of Stolac and Čapljina (located to the south of Mostar) had prevented any movement from the south, and that this was an alternative plausible explanation for the blocking of the delivery of humanitarian aid, the Appeals Chamber recalls that a trial chamber need not refer to every witness testimony or every piece of evidence on the record and that there is a presumption that the trial chamber evaluated all evidence presented to it, as long as there is no indication that the trial chamber completely disregarded evidence which is clearly relevant.[3974] The Appeals Chamber notes that the Trial Chamber did not refer to this particular ABiH attack in the context of considering the blocking of humanitarian aid.[3975] The Appeals Chamber has **[page 521]** considered the evidence Prlić points to and notes that it indicates that an ABiH attack had taken place and as a result a humanitarian convoy destined for the Heliodrom in Mostar Municipality could not go through.[3976] The Appeals Chamber also considers that Prlić relies on evidence which indicates that the same humanitarian convoy could not go through because of fighting *and* because "access was prevented".[3977] The Appeals Chamber therefore finds that Prlić has failed to demonstrate that the allegedly ignored evidence was so clearly relevant that the Trial Chamber's lack of reference to the 12 July 1993 attack amounts to disregard. Therefore, the Appeals Chamber finds that Prlić has failed to show that no reasonable trier of fact could have reached the same conclusion as the Trial Chamber: that in July 1993, Prlić refused to authorise access to East Mostar for representatives of international organisations.[3978]

[3968]   The Appeals Chamber notes that Prlić also refers to his submissions in ground of appeal 6, which it dismisses elsewhere in the Judgement. See *supra*, paras 212-218.
[3969]   Trial Judgement, Vol. 2, para. 1231, Vol. 4, para. 183. The Appeals Chamber also notes that Prlić refers to his submission in ground of appeal 14, which it dismisses elsewhere in the Judgement. See *supra*, paras 1128-1134.
[3970]   Trial Judgement, Vol. 2, para. 1238, Vol. 4, para. 184, referring to Witness BC, T(F). 18360-18365 (closed session) (14 May 2007), Ex. P09999 (confidential).
[3971]   Witness BC, T. 18362 (closed session) (14 May 2007). See Witness BC, T. 18360-18361 (closed session) (14 May 2007).
[3972]   Ex. P09999 (confidential).
[3973]   Witness BC, T. 18362 (closed session) (14 May 2007).
[3974]   *Kvočka et al.* Appeal Judgement, paras 23-24. See also *Tolimir* Appeal Judgement, paras 53, 161, 229; *Popović et al.* Appeal Judgement, paras 925, 1017.
[3975]   See Trial Judgement, Vol. 2, para. 1233, Vol. 4, para. 184.
[3976]   See Prlić's Appeal Brief, para. 543 & fns 1400-1404 and references cited therein. See also Trial Judgement, Vol. 2, para. 1233, Vol. 4, para. 184 and references cited therein.
[3977]   Klaus Johann Nissen, T. 20564 (26 June 2007). See also Klaus Johann Nissen, T. 20564 (26 June 2007) (testifying that, contrary to what happened in July 1993, a humanitarian convoy had entered East Mostar in June 1993, in spite of ongoing sniping).
[3978]   See Trial Judgement, Vol. 1, para. 1238, Vol. 4, para. 184.

1280. Turning to Prlić's challenges to the Trial Chamber's finding that during some periods he blocked all access to the area, the Appeals Chamber first observes that Prlić's argument regarding the "milk convoy" disregards relevant evidence that the convoy did not go through.[3979] The Appeals Chamber also considers that Prlić has failed to show how Boban's authority to grant international organisations access to East Mostar precludes the Trial Chamber from finding on the evidence that he also had such authority.[3980] The Appeals Chamber considers that Prlić has failed to show, based on the evidence relied upon by the Trial Chamber, that no reasonable trier of fact could have reached the same conclusion as the Trial Chamber: that, at times, Prlić blocked all access of humanitarian aid to the area.[3981] The Appeals Chamber thus rejects Prlić's challenges.

1281. As to his argument that the Trial Chamber mischaracterised evidence and relied upon irrelevant evidence to erroneously conclude that the meeting held on 8 August 1993 in Makarska attested to difficulties faced by international organisations in obtaining permission to deliver humanitarian aid to the population of East Mostar, the Appeals Chamber notes that Prlić misrepresents the factual finding.[3982] It reads as follows:

> *The frequent meetings held bet M'een July and August 1993* between the representatives of the international organisations and the HVO – like the one on 8 August 1993 in Makarska [...] to negotiate unobstructed access for humanitarian convoys to East Mostar *attest to the difficulties* **[page 522]** *faced by the international organisations* in obtaining permission to deliver humanitarian aid to the population of East Mostar [...].[3983]

Prlić's allegations that the Trial Chamber relied on mischaracterised and irrelevant evidence misconstrue how and why it relied on this evidence.[3984] The Appeals Chamber considers that Prlić has failed to demonstrate any error and dismisses his argument.

1282. As to Prlić's submission that the Trial Chamber ignored evidence that some administrative procedures were necessary, the Appeals Chamber notes that the Trial Chamber did not explicitly refer to this evidence when considering the blocking of access to East Mostar of members of international organisations and humanitarian aid.[3985] The Appeals Chamber has reviewed the evidence Prlić relies upon, which indicates that checkpoints were necessary, for example, to combat criminal activities, and has in particular considered the evidence indicating that some humanitarian convoys had been found to carry weapons and ammunition destined for Muslims.[3986] The Appeals Chamber however considers that Prlić has failed to show how this evidence is inconsistent with the impugned findings[3987] or would justify blocking – as opposed to placing more stringent control measures on – the delivery of humanitarian aid to East Mostar. As such, he has also failed to demonstrate that the Trial Chamber disregarded clearly relevant evidence.[3988] Prlić's submission is therefore dismissed.

1283. With regard to Prlić's argument that all convoys were approved and reached their destinations, the Appeals Chamber considers that Prlić misconstrues the evidence[3989] and ignores other relevant contrary evidence on which the Trial Chamber relied to find that this was not always the case.[3990] Similarly, as to his

---

[3979] Ex. P10367 (confidential), para. 73. See also Witness BD, T. 20720, 20729 (closed session) (3 July 2007), Ex. P03530 (confidential).
[3980] See Trial Judgement, Vol. 2, para. 1231, Vol. 4, paras 183-184, referring to, *inter alia,* Witness BD, T(F). 20700 (closed session) (3 July 2007).
[3981] See Trial Judgement, Vol. 4, paras 183-185, referring to, *inter alia,* Witness BC, T(F). 18360-18365 (closed session) (14 May 2007), Exs. P09712 (confidential), para. 64, P09999 (confidential).
[3982] Trial Judgement, Vol. 2, para. 1239. See also Trial Judgement, Vol. 4, para. 184.
[3983] Trial Judgement, Vol. 2, para. 1239 (emphasis added; internal references omitted).
[3984] See Trial Judgement, Vol. 2, para. 1239, referring to, *inter alia,* Exs. P04027 (confidential), pp. 1-2, P04420 (confidential), p. 1, Witness BD, T(F). 20719-20720 (closed session) (3 July 2007). *Cf.* Prlić's Appeal Brief, para. 545, referring to Trial Judgement, Vol. 2, para. 1239, Vol. 4, para. 184, Exs. P04027 (confidential), P04420 (confidential), Witness BD, T. 20720-20721 (closed session) (3 July 2007). The evidence referenced in Prlić's Appeal Brief, fn. 1411, also fails to demonstrate any error in this regard.
[3985] Compare Prlić's Appeal Brief, para. 546 & fn. 1410 and references cited therein, with Trial Judgement, Vol. 2, paras 1224-1244, Vol. 4, paras 183-185 and references cited therein.
[3986] See Prlić's Appeal Brief, para. 546 & fn. 1410 and references cited therein.
[3987] See *supra,* fn. 3985. See, *e.g., supra,* paras 1265, 1269.
[3988] See *supra,* para. 1279.
[3989] The Appeals Chamber considers that Witness Martin Raguž testified that every request that was submitted by an international organisation for safe passage for a humanitarian convoy that followed the Protocol was approved. He also testified, however, that it was "another matter whether some convoys were stopped and whether they had problems en route". Martin Raguž, T. 31357-31358 (26 Aug 2008).
[3990] See Trial Judgement, Vol. 2, paras 1233, 1238-1242, Vol. 4, paras 183-184 and references cited therein.

argument that the Trial Chamber ignored evidence that the Joint Commission and the Protocol ensured unhindered passage of humanitarian convoys in BiH from June to December 1993, the Appeals Chamber considers that Prlić has failed to provide evidence **[page 523]** that humanitarian convoys passed unhindered to East Mostar during this time period,[3991] and as such fails to demonstrate an error in any impugned finding. The Appeals Chamber therefore rejects Prlić's arguments.

1284. With regard to Prlić's claim that the Trial Chamber ignored evidence that he had endeavoured to ensure the free flow of humanitarian aid, the Appeals Chamber notes that the Trial Chamber did rely on evidence similar to that which Prlić points to with regard to Praljak's involvement.[3992] In fact, the Trial Chamber found that, on 21 and 25 August 1993, humanitarian convoys were able to get into East Mostar, supplies were air dropped, and that Praljak intervened to ensure the security of the convoy on 25 August 1993.[3993] The Appeals Chamber further recalls that the Trial Chamber also found that between June and September 1993, the HVO itself provided humanitarian aid, albeit sporadically, to East Mostar but that such sporadic aid was conditional on obtaining certain advantages,[3994] and did "not cast doubt on the observation that the HVO obstructed the delivery of the humanitarian aid to East Mostar".[3995] The Appeals Chamber further considers that while the Trial Chamber did not expressly refer to evidence indicating that Prlić, at times, spoke in favour of allowing humanitarian aid to pass,[3996] Prlić fails to show that no reasonable trier of fact, based on the evidence on which the Trial Chamber relied,[3997] could have reached the same conclusion as the Trial Chamber. The Appeals Chamber thus rejects this claim.

1285. Having dismissed all of Prlić's arguments, the Appeals Chamber finds that he has failed to demonstrate that the Trial Chamber erroneously concluded that he foresaw and intended the suffering and attack on human dignity of East Mostar inhabitants by contributing to the blocking of humanitarian aid delivery to East Mostar from June to at least the end of December 1993. Thus, the Appeals Chamber dismisses Prlić's sub-ground of appeal 16.4.7.

(e) Displacement of Croats from Vareš Municipality (Prlić's Sub-ground 16.5)

1286. The Trial Chamber found that: (1) Vareš Municipality was not included in Provinces 3, 8, and 10 of the Vance-Owen Peace Plan; (2) in June 1993, between 10,000 and 15,000 BiH Croats from Kakanj arrived in Vareš town; and (3) after 23 October 1993 and the events in Stupni Do, the **[page 524]** HVO political authorities called on the Croatian population to leave this municipality because of the risk of a response by the ABiH.[3998] The Trial Chamber also found that Prlić contributed to the organisation of the removal of the Croats from the municipalities of Kakanj and Vareš and their rehousing in the HZ(R) H-B in August 1993, considering, *inter alia*, that he communicated on 18 August 1993 a decision to evacuate Croats from Vareš Municipality to western Herzegovina.[3999] The Trial Chamber further found that in October 1993 Prlić was concerned about the arrival of Croatian refugees and that he attended the HR H-B Government meeting on 4 November 1993 where it was decided that the ODPR would take care of the receipt and accommodation of the Croatian "refugees".[4000] Based on these and other facts, the Trial Chamber then concluded that:

> Prlić knew that some HZ(R) H-B officials did not wish that municipality to be included in the area of BiH considered "Croatian". Inasmuch as he contributed to the movement of the Croatian population in the

---

[3991]   See Prlić''s Appeal Brief, para. 546 & fns 1412-1414 and references cited therein. The Appeals Chamber notes further that the Protocol on which Prlić relies dates to 1994 and is therefore not relevant to the time-frame in question. See Prlić's Appeal Brief, para. 546, referring to, *inter alia*, Exs. 1D01855, 1D02024, 1D02025.

[3992]   See Prlić's Appeal Brief, para. 547 & fn. 1418, referring to Trial Judgement, Vol. 2, para. 1240 and references cited therein.

[3993]   Trial Judgement, Vol. 2, para. 1240.

[3994]   Trial Judgement, Vol. 2, para. 1243.

[3995]   Trial Judgement, Vol. 2, para. 1244. See also Trial Judgement, Vol. 2, para. 1241.

[3996]   See, *e.g.*, Exs. P03673, 1D01529, 1D02070; Slobodan Praljak, T. 44394-44395 (3 Sept 2009).

[3997]   See Trial Judgement, Vol. 2, paras 1230, 1238-1239, Vol. 4, paras 184-185, referring to, *inter alia*, Witness BC, T(F). 18360-18365 (closed session) (14 May 2007), Exs. P09999 (confidential), P04420 (confidential), Witness BD, T(F). 20719-20720 (closed session) (3 July 2007).

[3998]   See Trial Judgement, Vol. 4, paras 198-199, 202, referring to, *inter alia*, Trial Judgement, Vol. 3, para. 284.

[3999]   Trial Judgement, Vol. 4, para. 200.

[4000]   Trial Judgement, Vol. 4, paras 200-203.

territories of the HZ(R) H-B and continued to exercise his functions in the HVO/Government of the HZ(R) H-B, the Chamber finds that he shared that wish.[4001]

(i) Arguments of the Parties

1287. Prlić submits that the Trial Chamber erred in finding that he was involved in the displacement of Croats from Vareš to territories claimed to be part of the HZ H-B.[4002] He first contends that the Trial Chamber erred in concluding that this displacement occurred because some HZ(R) H-B officials did not wish Vareš Municipality to be included in the "area of BiH considered Croatian", arguing that there was no evidence to support this conclusion.[4003]

1288. Prlić also contends that the Trial Chamber erred in finding that he contributed to organising the removal of the Croats from the municipalities of Kakanj and Vareš and their rehousing in the HZ(R) H-B in August 1993, arguing that the Trial Chamber ignored evidence that in June 1993 between 10,000 and 15,000 Bosnian Croats arrived in Vareš town, escaping from ABiH attacks, and that his 18 August 1993 letter did not communicate to the Mostar Municipal HVO a decision to **[page 525]** evacuate Kakanj Croats, but was addressed to the Vareš Municipal HVO in response to repeated requests for evacuation.[4004]

1289. Prlić further contends that the Trial Chamber erred in finding that the HVO political authorities called on Croats to leave Vareš Municipality after the events in Stupni Do, as it relied on "one document of unsubstantiated hearsay" (Exhibit P02980), which did not identify the authorities.[4005]

1290. Further, challenging the findings that the HR H-B Government decided on 4 November 1993 that the ODPR would receive and accommodate refugees and that Vareš town fell to the ABiH on 5 November 1993, Prlić argues that the Trial Chamber ignored evidence that: (1) the town actually fell on 3 November 1993; (2) the citizens left it early on 3 November 1993; (3) the HVO Main Staff then asked UNPROFOR to pull out the civilians from the battle zone; and (4) on 4 November 1993 the HR H-B Government was reacting to this humanitarian catastrophe.[4006]

1291. Finally, Prlić contends that the Trial Chamber erred in concluding that he shared the wish to displace Croats from Vareš Municipality because it was not considered to be Croatian, considering that his October 1993 letter shows that neither he nor the HVO HZ H-B expected the arrival of Vareš Croats in November 1993.[4007]

1292. The Prosecution responds that there is clear support in the evidence for the Trial Chamber's finding that Prlić and other HZ(R) H-B officials wished to exclude Vareš Municipality from the territories considered Croatian.[4008] Further, the Prosecution submits that Prlić does not contest his role in removing Kakanj Croats,

---

[4001]   Trial Judgement, Vol. 4, para. 204.
[4002]   Prlić's Appeal Brief, paras 548-549.
[4003]   Prlić's Appeal Brief, paras 549-550. See Prlić's Appeal Brief, para. 557. Prlić also argues that the HZ H-B never had defined borders and was established to protect all BiH Croats, and that Vareš was always part of the HZ H-B. Prlić's Appeal Brief, para. 550; Appeal Hearing, AT. 136 (20 Mar 2017). Prlić further claims that the Trial Chamber ignored evidence that Croats were expelled from Travnik, Bugojno, Fojnica, and Konjic, areas designated by international negotiators as part of Croat-majority provinces, yet Croats did not leave from Kiseljak and Kreševo, areas that were not designated as Croat-majority provinces. See Prlić's Appeal Brief, para. 551.
[4004]   Prlić's Appeal Brief, para. 552. Prlić further challenges the Trial Chamber's finding regarding his direct power over the ODPR and argues that the Trial Chamber ignored evidence that all Croats displaced from Vareš ended up in Croatia. Prlić's Appeal Brief, paras 553-554. See Appeal Hearing, AT. 235 (20 Mar 2017).
[4005]   Prlić's Appeal Brief, para. 555, referring to, *inter alia*, Prlić's Appeal Brief, ground of appeal 3. In addition, Prlić argues that the arrival of 5,000 refugees in Herzegovina "had nothing to do with the alleged call of 'the HVO political authorities' to the Croats to leave Vareš". Prlić's Appeal Brief, para. 555.
[4006]   Prlić's Appeal Brief, paras 556. See Appeal Hearing, AT. 148-149 (20 Mar 2017).
[4007]   Prlić's Appeal Brief, paras 549, 557.
[4008]   Prosecution's Response Brief (Prlić), paras 346-347. The Prosecution further submits that Prlić's submission that the HZ(R) H-B "never had defined borders" is contradicted by, *inter alia*, his own stated goal of "rounding off territories" that were believed to be "Croatian". Prosecution's Response Brief (Prlić), para. 348. It submits that it is irrelevant whether Vareš was always part of the HZ H-B as it was not part of the historic Banovina, and HZ(R) H-B leaders accepted its exclusion from the so-called Croatian provinces under the Vance-Owen Peace Plan. Prosecution's Response Brief (Prlić), para. 349.

but merely argues that he responded to a request for evacuation.[4009] Concerning Prlić's challenge that the Trial Chamber relied on one unsubstantiated hearsay document to find that the HVO political authorities called on Croats to leave Vareš Municipality after the events in Stupni Do, the Prosecution submits that: (1) Prlić ignores UNPROFOR's first-**[page 526]**hand account of the events; and (2) the document in question was authenticated and corroborated.[4010] It further submits that the evidence cited by Prlić with respect to the date when Vareš town fell is consistent with the Trial Chamber's finding in this regard.[4011] The Prosecution also contends that the evidence refutes Prlić's submission that the Government was merely reacting to a "humanitarian catastrophe".[4012]

    (ii) Analysis

1293. Turning to Prlić's challenge that there is no evidence supporting the Trial Chamber's finding that the HZ(R) H-B officials did not "wish" to include Vareš Municipality in areas they considered Croatian, the Appeals Chamber observes that the Trial Chamber considered that, *inter alia,* Praljak indicated in April 1993 that Vareš Municipality would not be included in the territory of the HZ H-B.[4013] The Trial Chamber also noted Prlić's remark during a meeting on 5 November 1993, in the context of the fall of Vareš town:

> We must move closer to rounding off territories. As a government, last spring we defined both the proposals and the conclusions, even with regard to moving certain brigades from some areas, which would include moving the population from those areas and concentrating it in certain directions that we think could become and remain Croatian areas.[4014]

Finally, the Trial Chamber considered the fact that Vareš Municipality was not placed in a province under Croatian control, in accordance with the Vance-Owen Peace Plan.[4015] Against this background, the Appeals Chamber finds that Prlić ignores relevant factual findings, as well as the evidence underlying them. The Appeals Chamber therefore dismisses his argument.[4016]

1294. With respect to Prlić's argument that the Trial Chamber ignored evidence indicating that several thousands of BiH Croats arrived in Vareš in June 1993, escaping from ABiH attacks, the Appeals Chamber observes that the Trial Chamber specifically noted that in June 1993, "between 10,000 and 15,000 BiH Croats arrived in the town of Vareš",[4017] in addition to noting that this **[page 527]** happened "[f]ollowing an ABiH attack" on Kakanj Municipality.[4018] His argument is thus dismissed. Regarding Prlić's challenge raised with respect to his letter dated 18 August 1993, the Appeals Chamber agrees that the letter was addressed to the Vareš Municipal HVO.[4019] However, it finds that this does not undermine the Trial Chamber's finding that Prlić contributed to the organisation of the removal of Croats from the municipality and their resettlement in HZ(R) H-B territory. On the contrary, the letter supports the Trial Chamber's finding, as it is signed by Prlić and states that "we have decided to secure the evacuation [of Kakanj Croats exiled from

---

[4009]   Prosecution's Response Brief (Prlić), para. 350. The Prosecution submits that only 1,770 out of the 5,500 Croats from Vareš moved to Croatia, while the rest stayed in Čapljina. Prosecution's Response Brief (Prlić), para. 354.

[4010]   Prosecution's Response Brief (Prlić), para. 352, referring to, *inter alia,* Prlić's Appeal Brief, para. 555.

[4011]   Prosecution's Response Brief (Prlić), para. 353.

[4012]   Prosecution's Response Brief (Prlić), para. 351.

[4013]   Trial Judgement, Vol. 4, para. 198.

[4014]   Trial Judgement, Vol. 4, para. 214. See Trial Judgement, Vol. 4, para. 191. See also *infra,* para. 1316.

[4015]   Trial Judgement, Vol. 4, para. 198.

[4016]   Similarly, considering the Trial Chamber's findings recalled above, the Appeals Chamber dismisses Prlić's arguments that the HZ H-B never had defined borders and was established to protect all BiH Croats, and that Vareš was always part of the HZ H-B, as they fail to demonstrate any error in the impugned finding. See *supra,* paras 719-723. Further, regarding Prlić's submission that Croats were expelled from Travnik, Bugojno, Fojnica, and Konjic, areas designated by international negotiators as part of Croat-majority provinces, yet Croats did not leave from Kiseljak and Kreševo, which were not designated as a Croat-majority provinces, the Appeals Chamber finds that Prlić has failed to show the relevance of his argument to the impugned finding, which concerns HZ(R) H-B officials' intentions with regard to Vareš Municipality. This argument is also dismissed.

[4017]   Trial Judgement, Vol. 4, para. 199. See Trial Judgement, Vol. 3, paras 284, 502.

[4018]   Trial Judgement, Vol. 3, para. 284.

[4019]   See Trial Judgement, Vol. 4, para. 200 & fn. 515, referring to Ex. P04282. Prlić incorrectly cites to Exhibit P04248. See Prlić's Appeal Brief, para. 522 & fn. 1431.

Vareš Municipality who are children, women, sick, or elderly] in the region of Western Herzegovina".[4020] The Appeals Chamber therefore dismisses his argument.[4021]

1295. Concerning the Trial Chamber's finding that the HVO political authorities called on the Croatian population to leave Vareš Municipality because of the risk of a response by the ABiH,[4022] and noting Prlić's challenge related to the Trial Chamber's reliance on Exhibit P02980,[4023] an UNPROFOR diary, the Appeals Chamber observes that the finding is referenced to a single excerpt of this diary, covering events in Vareš Municipality on 29-30 October 1993.[4024] The most relevant part reads as follows: "We came by information indicating that the HVO were encouraging people to flee by spreading rumours about Muslim atrocities and by making transportation possibilities available."[4025] The Appeals Chamber observes that this evidence neither specifically indicates that the HVO *political authorities* called on them to leave nor reveals the source of the quoted information. Regardless, the Appeals Chamber considers that the Trial Chamber's conclusion[4026] is sufficiently supported by the Trial Chamber's other findings,[4027] and therefore finds that Prlić has failed to demonstrate an error of fact which has occasioned a miscarriage of justice. The Appeals Chamber therefore dismisses his argument. **[page 528]**

1296. Turning to Prlić's challenges to the Trial Chamber's findings that the HR H-B Government decided on 4 November 1993 that the ODPR would receive and accommodate refugees, and that Vareš town fell on 5 November 1993, the Appeals Chamber observes that the Trial Chamber took into account the state of affairs in Vareš Municipality, including the ongoing battle between the HVO and ABiH,[4028] the Government's actions,[4029] as well as the departure of Croats.[4030] With regard to Prlić's claim that Vareš town fell already on 3 November 1993, the Appeals Chamber recalls that the Trial Chamber found that Vareš town fell *into ABiH hands* on 5 November 1993,[4031] which is consistent with all of the evidence to which he refers.[4032] As a result, the Appeals Chamber finds that Prlić has failed to demonstrate that any of the other allegedly ignored evidence shows an error in the impugned findings and dismisses his arguments accordingly.

1297. Finally, regarding Prlić's challenge, based on his letter from October 1993, to the Trial Chamber's conclusion that he shared the wish that Vareš Municipality not be included in the area of BiH considered "Croatian", the Appeals Chamber first observes that the Trial Chamber relied on several findings before reaching its conclusion.[4033] In support of his claim that this letter affirms that he and the HVO HZ H-B did not expect the arrival of Vareš Croats in November 1993, Prlić cites the following portion: "if there is no new aggression on the territories inhabited with Croatian population, by the winter period all of the displaced

---

[4020] Ex. P04282.

[4021] Regarding Prlić's challenge to the Trial Chamber's finding related to his direct power over the ODPR, the Appeals Chamber notes that his challenges to his powers in relation to ODPR and Croatia are addressed and dismissed above. See *supra*, para. 1085. Concerning his challenge that the Trial Chamber ignored that displaced Croats ended up in Croatia, the Appeals Chamber finds that Prlić in essence relies on one document that supports the Trial Chamber's finding and thus dismisses his argument. Compare Ex. 1D00927 with Trial Judgement, Vol. 4, para. 199.

[4022] Trial Judgement, Vol. 3, para. 503, Vol. 4, para. 202.

[4023] The Appeals Chamber also notes that Prlić refers to his submissions in ground of appeal 3, which it dismisses elsewhere in the Judgement. See *supra*, paras 177-183.

[4024] Trial Judgement, Vol. 3, para. 503 & fn. 1071, Vol. 4, para. 202 & fn. 520, referring to Ex. P02980, p. 21.

[4025] Ex. P02980, p. 21.

[4026] See *supra*, para. 1286.

[4027] See Trial Judgement, Vol. 4, paras 198-203; *supra*, para. 1293. With regard to Prlić's argument that the arrival of 5,000 refugees in Herzegovina had nothing to do with the alleged call of the HVO political authorities to the Croats to leave Vareš, the Appeals Chamber considers that Prlić fails to demonstrate that the Trial Chamber made any such connection and therefore dismisses his argument. See Trial Judgement, Vol. 4, para. 202.

[4028] Trial Judgement, Vol. 3, para. 503, Vol. 4, para. 203.

[4029] Trial Judgement, Vol. 4, paras 203, 214.

[4030] Trial Judgement, Vol. 3, paras 504-506.

[4031] Trial Judgement, Vol. 3, para. 507, Vol. 4, para. 203.

[4032] See Prlić's Appeal Brief, para. 556 & fn. 1441, referring to Exs. 3D00971, 3D00984, 4D00519, p. 11, Milivoj Petković, T. 49610-49611 (17 Feb 2010). Exhibit 4D00519 (confirmed by Petković in his testimony), p. 11, states that Vareš fell on 3 November 1993, but only describes the HVO leaving that day, not the ABiH coming. Exhibit 3D00971, dated 3 November 1993, refers to intense ongoing battle in and around Vareš but not to its fall. Exhibit 3D00984, dated 4 November 1993, suggests that Vareš was not yet in ABiH hands.

[4033] Trial Judgement, Vol. 4, paras 198-204.

persons will be taken care of, in the adequate and to human needs appropriate way."[4034] The first part of this sentence reads as a hypothetical qualifying the assertion in the second part of the sentence. As such, the Appeals Chamber can draw no inference from this sentence as to Prlić's or the HVO HZ H-B's actual expectations with regard to the arrival of Vareš Croats in November 1993. In any event, Prlić's argument is not inconsistent with the challenged finding. For these reasons, the Appeals Chamber dismisses this argument.

1298. In light of the above, the Appeals Chamber finds that Prlić has failed to show that the Trial Chamber erred in finding that he was involved in the displacement of Croats from Vareš and dismisses his sub-ground of appeal 16.5. **[page 529]**

(f) <u>Prlić's contribution to a policy of population movement (Prlić's Sub-ground 16.6)</u>

1299. The Trial Chamber found that Prlić supported the policy of moving Muslim detainees and their families outside the HZ(R) H-B and planned and facilitated the movement of the Croatian population to the areas claimed to belong to the HZ(R) H-B.[4035] It further found that even though the latter movement could be partly justified by the ongoing fighting, it was also prompted by the HVO and constituted part of a policy by the HZ(R) H-B leadership.[4036]

    (i) <u>Arguments of the Parties</u>

1300. Prlić submits that the Trial Chamber erred in reaching these conclusions,[4037] by challenging a number of findings on which the Trial Chamber relied. First, he submits that the Trial Chamber erred in finding that on 1 February 1993, the HVO HZ H-B established the Commission for the Question of the Migration of Population by relying on one document introduced through a bar table motion, although there is no evidence that this commission ever existed.[4038] He also challenges the finding that at a meeting on 5 May 1993, Prlić advocated a population and property exchange program, giving the example that a Muslim in Mostar and a Croat in Zenica could exchange their flats, arguing that the Trial Chamber erred in relying on Witness BA's testimony and excluding other relevant evidence.[4039]

1301. Prlić further challenges the Trial Chamber's finding that according to a 13 June 1993 ECMM report, the HVO was conducting a large-scale propaganda campaign to provoke a mass exodus of the Croatian population from Travnik Municipality to the north, claiming that the Trial Chamber erroneously gave weight to ECMM reports and Witness Christopher Beese's testimony.[4040] Prlić also contends that in finding that the HVO HZ H-B organised the anticipated **[page 530]** relocation of many Croats from central Bosnia, the Trial

---

[4034] See Prlić's Appeal Brief, para. 557, referring to Ex. 1D00927, p. 2.

[4035] Trial Judgement, Vol. 4, paras 215, 275.

[4036] Trial Judgement, Vol. 4, para. 215.

[4037] Prlić's Appeal Brief, paras 558-559, 561, 575-577, 583. See Prlić's Appeal Brief, para. 560, referring to Prlić's sub-grounds of appeal 16.4.3, 16.9-16.10.

[4038] Prlić's Appeal Brief, para. 562, referring to, *inter alia,* Prlić's ground of appeal 3.

[4039] Prlić's Appeal Brief, para. 563, referring to, *inter alia,* Trial Judgement, Vol. 4, para. 208. Prlić specifically argues, pointing to evidence in support, that: (1) Witness BA was not informed about Zenica in the spring of 1993; (2) Croats wished to escape Zenica as they were under attack; (3) there was no resettlement policy of Croats from Zenica; (4) Boban's 7 May 1993 letter to the UN sought the protection of Croats "to enable the free movement of Croats entering and leaving the areas of Zenica, Konjic and Jablanica"; (5) the Croatian exodus was due to ABiH attacks (referring to Prlić's Appeal Brief, paras 497 (sub-ground of appeal 16.3.1), 499 (sub-ground of appeal 16.3.2), 566 (sub-ground of appeal 16.6.2), 582 (sub-grounds of appeal 16.6.3 and 16.6.4)); (6) evacuation was requested for the wounded; and (7) the Mujahideen were "real and frightening". He further submits that there is no evidence on any property exchange, "forbidden by the HVOHZHB". Prlić's Appeal Brief, para. 563, referring to, *inter alia,* Trial Judgement, Vol. 4, para. 208.

[4040] Prlić's Appeal Brief, para. 564 & fn. 1459, referring to, *inter alia,* Trial Judgement, Vol. 4, para. 209, Prlić's Appeal Brief, paras 200-201 (sub-ground of appeal 6.2). Prlić also points to evidence in support of his claim. See Prlić's Appeal Brief, para. 564. See also Prlić's Appeal Brief, para. 565, referring to Prlić's Appeal Brief, sub-ground of appeal 16.5. Prlić argues in particular that Beese's testimony that the movement was an effort to change the voting pattern is unsustainable in light of evidence that the HVO HZ H-B took measures to the contrary and that his testimony that the danger from the Mujahideen was propaganda was not credible. Prlić submits further that it "defies logic to suggest that the HZHB/HVOHZHB would pursue a reverse ethnic cleansing policy to resettle Croats from a designated Croat-majority province", submitting that Travnik was the capital of one of the Croat-majority provinces according to the Vance-Owen Peace Plan. Prlić's Appeal Brief, para. 564.

Chamber misinterpreted two documents and ignored evidence.[4041] In particular, Prlić argues that the Trial Chamber ignored evidence on: (1) ABiH attacks in the Travnik area where civilians had to be evacuated to Serb-controlled territory; (2) the HVO HZ H-B's proposals, in light of the information about the imminent threat to central Bosnian Croats, to the HZ(R) H-B Presidency to take action; and (3) the expulsion of 30,000 Croats from central Bosnia when the ABiH captured Travnik on 9 June 1993 and Kakanj on 13 June 1993.[4042]

1302. Prlić further claims that the Trial Chamber erroneously found that Muslims were forced to leave West Mostar in order to accommodate the arriving Croats, in light of contrary evidence and a lack of evidence on a policy to forcibly remove Muslims and settle Croats in Mostar or Herzegovina.[4043]

1303. Referring to the Trial Chamber's finding that on 21 June 1993 Prlić signed a decision creating a staff for organising and co-ordinating efforts concerning expelled persons and refugees, Prlić argues that the HVO HZ H-B created this staff to deal with the high number of displaced persons arriving in HZ H-B territories in June 1993 due to the ABiH offensive in central Bosnia.[4044] Further, Prlić challenges the Trial Chamber's reliance on Witness DZ's evidence that during a meeting on 23 June 1993, Vladislav Pogarčić, Boban's Chief of Staff, expressed, *inter alia*, Prlić's wish to gather the Croatian population in one Croatian entity, claiming that there is no evidence linking Pogarčić to Prlić, or that Witness DZ "reported this claim".[4045]

1304. Prlić also claims that the Trial Chamber erred in finding that at a meeting on 16 July 1993 he stated that 10,000 Muslims wished to leave Mostar for third countries and that he negotiated with Croatia for transit visas for Muslims to go through its territory.[4046] He argues that the Trial Chamber erroneously relied on Witness BA[4047] and ignored and mischaracterised evidence indicating, notably, that transit visas were not intended for Muslims alone.[4048] Prlić also submits that the **[page 531]** Trial Chamber erred in finding that he directed or participated in expelling Muslims from HZ(R) H-B territories, as it ignored evidence that Muslim refugees returned to HVO-controlled areas.[4049]

1305. Finally, Prlić claims that the Trial Chamber erred: (1) in finding that he participated in organising and facilitating the departure of the Croatian population of central Bosnia to Herzegovina between August and November 1993;[4050] (2) in finding that the ODPR sent him a letter on 3 November 1993;[4051] (3) by ignoring the context of his statement, made at a meeting held on 5 November 1993, about population movements into areas that "could become and remain Croatian";[4052] and (4) in finding that the HVO exerted pressure on Croats to leave Vareš, implying that some Croats from Vareš were removed as part of the JCE.[4053]

[4041] Prlić's Appeal Brief, para. 566 & fn. 1464, referring to Trial Judgement, Vol. 4, para. 209, Prlić's Appeal Brief, ground of appeal 3.
[4042] Prlić's Appeal Brief, paras 566-567.
[4043] Prlić's Appeal Brief, para. 568.
[4044] Prlić's Appeal Brief, para. 569 & fn. 1476, referring to Trial Judgement, Vol. 4, para. 210.
[4045] Prlić's Appeal Brief, para. 570 & fn. 1479, referring to Trial Judgement, Vol. 4, para. 211.
[4046] Prlić's Appeal Brief, para. 577, referring to, *inter alia*, Trial Judgement, Vol. 4, para. 212.
[4047] Prlić's Appeal Brief, para. 578. Prlić submits in particular that contrary to Witness BA's testimony, confidential Exhibit 6D00577 does not mention his presence at the meeting. Prlić's Appeal Brief, para. 578.
[4048] Prlić's Appeal Brief, paras 577-581, referring to, *inter alia*, Prlić's Appeal Brief, paras 182-183 (sub-ground of appeal 6.1).
[4049] Prlić's Appeal Brief, para. 583. See also Prlić's Appeal Brief, para. 584, referring to Prlić's sub-grounds of appeal 16.6.2, 16.6.3-16.6.4.
[4050] Prlić's Appeal Brief, para. 571. Prlić argues that the Trial Chamber erred in relying on its finding that at a 29 July 1993 meeting of the HVO HZ H-B, the organisation and logistics concerning the anticipated arrival of 10,000 Croats from central Bosnia were discussed. Prlić's Appeal Brief, paras 571, 582. Prlić further submits that the Trial Chamber ignored evidence showing why 10,000 Croats fled from central Bosnia and why they ultimately arrived in Croatia. Prlić's Appeal Brief, para. 571. See also Prlić's Appeal Brief, fn. 1482, referring to, *inter alia*, Prlić's sub-ground of appeal 16.6.2. He also submits that the Trial Chamber ignored evidence concerning the 29 July 1993 meeting, showing that the ODPR had no goal of ethnically cleansing territory of Muslims. Prlić's Appeal Brief, para. 582.
[4051] Prlić's Appeal Brief, para. 572. Prlić argues in particular that the letter was sent to the Presidents of the municipal HVOs. Prlić's Appeal Brief, para. 572.
[4052] Prlić's Appeal Brief, para. 573, referring to, *inter alia*, Trial Judgement, Vol. 4, para. 214, Prlić's Appeal Brief, para. 240 (sub-ground of appeal 9.2). Prlić submits that he stated that Herzegovina could not accommodate Croats from Vareš and that Croatia should accommodate them. Prlić's Appeal Brief, para. 573.
[4053] Prlić's Appeal Brief, para. 574; Appeal Hearing, AT. 148-149 (20 Mar 2017). Prlić argues in particular that this contradicts the Trial Chamber's finding that even if the HVO exerted this pressure "the threat of attacks by the ABiH and the fact that they did

1306. The Prosecution responds that Prlić fails to demonstrate an error in the Trial Chamber's conclusion that he played a key role in removing the Muslim population from territory claimed by the HZ(R) H-B and simultaneously settling Croats from central Bosnia there.[4054] It submits that Prlić ignores the bulk of the findings and evidence supporting the Trial Chamber's conclusion regarding his contribution and intent to remove Muslims from the HZ(R) H-B.[4055] Regarding the allegation that there is no evidence of moving Muslims out of West Mostar and the resettling of Croats in Mostar or Herzegovina, the Prosecution contends that Prlić himself cites evidence demonstrating the resettlement of Croats throughout Herzegovina, and that he ignores extensive evidence in support of the impugned finding.[4056] Similarly, regarding the claim that no Muslims **[page 532]** were expelled, the Prosecution argues that Prlić ignores many underlying findings and his own prior admission.[4057]

1307. With respect to Prlić's challenge to the Trial Chamber's finding regarding his conduct at the meeting on 5 May 1993, the Prosecution argues that Prlić fails to explain how the evidence he cites renders the Trial Chamber's finding unreasonable.[4058] With regard to the challenged finding concerning a 13 June 1993 ECMM report on an HVO campaign to provoke a mass exodus of the population in Travnik, the Prosecution submits that Prlić misrepresents Beese's testimony and shows no error in the Trial Chamber's reliance on this witness's evidence.[4059]

1308. The Prosecution also submits that Prlić fails to show that the Trial Chamber acted unreasonably in crediting Witness DZ's testimony, considering that any lack of connection between Pogarčić and Prlić is beside the point and Witness DZ's evidence is corroborated.[4060] With respect to the Trial Chamber's findings regarding Prlić's statements at the 16 July 1993 meeting, the Prosecution submits that Prlić fails to demonstrate that no reasonable trial chamber could have relied on Witness BA's first-hand and corroborated testimony.[4061]

1309. The Prosecution submits that the Trial Chamber reasonably concluded that Prlić planned and facilitated the movement of Central Bosnian Croats into territory claimed by the HZ(R) H-B as part of a policy.[4062] It contends that he incorrectly argues, that the Trial Chamber ignored evidence that Croats were fleeing ABiH attacks.[4063] It further argues that Prlić's claims concerning the 3 November 1993 letter are irrelevant since the Government echoed its content at a meeting on the following day.[4064] In the Prosecution's submission, Prlić's challenges to findings concerning HVO **[page 533]** pressure on Vareš Croats and his statement on 5 November 1993 about population movements are likewise without merit.[4065]

---

happen were sufficient to bring about the departure of Croats from the municipality", and that there was no policy to relocate Croats from central Bosnia to HZ(R) H-B territories. Prlić's Appeal Brief, para. 574; Appeal Hearing, AT. 148-149 (20 Mar 2017).

[4054]   Prosecution's Response (Prlić), para. 355. See Appeal Hearing, AT. 228 (20 Mar 2017).

[4055]   Prosecution's Response (Prlić), paras 356-357.

[4056]   Prosecution's Response (Prlić), para. 359.

[4057]   Prosecution's Response (Prlić), para. 358. The Prosecution submits that Prlić ignores evidence showing that the return of some expelled Muslims, if any, to HVO-controlled territory was contrary to the JCE members' intentions. Prosecution's Response Brief (Prlić), para. 358.

[4058]   Prosecution's Response Brief (Prlić), para. 367. The Prosecution argues further that Prlić's claims regarding events in Zenica ignore that Zenica was mentioned in the impugned finding only as an illustrative example of a possible exchange. Prosecution's Response Brief (Prlić), para. 367.

[4059]   Prosecution's Response Brief (Prlić), para. 364, referring to, *inter alia*, Prlić's Appeal Brief, para. 564, Trial Judgement, Vol. 4, para. 209. The Prosecution further argues that the evidence Prlić cites does not support his claim. With regard to Prlić's argument that it defies logic that the HVO would remove Croats from Travnik in Province 10, the Prosecution claims that Prlić ignores the fact that the HVO lost control of this area in mid-June 1993, which explains the relocation of Croats from Travnik. Prosecution's Response Brief (Prlić), para. 364.

[4060]   Prosecution's Response Brief (Prlić), para. 368.

[4061]   Prosecution's Response Brief (Prlić), para. 360. The Prosecution further submits that Prlić relies on evidence that relates to a different meeting. Prosecution's Response Brief (Prlić), para. 360. See also Prosecution's Response Brief (Prlić), para. 361.

[4062]   Prosecution's Response Brief (Prlić), para. 362. The Prosecution further argues that Prlić's attempts to attribute this influx solely to external factors is at odds with the evidence. Prosecution's Response Brief (Prlić), para. 362.

[4063]   Prosecution's Response Brief (Prlić), para. 363.

[4064]   Prosecution's Response Brief (Prlić), para. 366.

[4065]   Prosecution's Response Brief (Prlić), para. 365, referring to, *inter alia,* Prlić's Appeal Brief, para. 573. In particular, with regard to the former finding, the Prosecution submits that Prlić fails to identify any contradiction. Prosecution's Response Brief (Prlić), para. 365. See also Prosecution's Response Brief (Prlić), para. 366. With regard to the latter finding, the Prosecution argues that Prlić's claims are not supported by the evidence he cites. Prosecution's Response Brief (Prlić), para. 365.

(ii) Analysis

1310. With regard to Prlić's argument that the Trial Chamber erred in finding that on 1 February 1993 the HVO HZ H-B established the Commission for the Question of the Migration of Population, the Appeals Chamber considers that a reasonable trier of fact could have made this finding based on the documentary evidence relied on by the Trial Chamber.[4066] It is irrelevant for the challenged finding whether there was evidence on the commission's existence after its establishment.[4067] Prlić's argument is therefore dismissed.

1311. Turning to Prlić's challenge to the Trial Chamber's finding that during a meeting on 5 May 1993, he advocated a population and property exchange programme whereby, for example, a Muslim in Mostar could exchange his flat for a flat occupied by a Croat in Zenica, the Appeals Chamber finds that Prlić fails to demonstrate that the Trial Chamber erred by relying on Witness BA's evidence, which directly supports the impugned finding.[4068] The Appeals Chamber further finds that the evidence which Prlić alleges the Trial Chamber ignored was either considered by the Trial Chamber,[4069] or does not show that the impugned finding was unreasonable.[4070] Thus, this challenge fails.

1312. Concerning Prlić's challenge to the Trial Chamber's finding that according to an ECMM report dated 13 June 1993, the HVO was conducting a large-scale propaganda campaign to provoke **[page 534]** a mass exodus of the Croatian population from Travnik Municipality,[4071] the Appeals Chamber considers that the evidence Prlić points to fails to demonstrate that the Trial Chamber erred in the weight it gave to the ECMM reports and Beese's testimony that support the impugned finding[4072] This argument is therefore dismissed. Further, regarding Prlić's contention that the Trial Chamber misinterpreted two documents in reaching its finding that the HVO HZ H-B organised the anticipated relocation of many Croats from central Bosnia, the Appeals Chamber finds that the finding is well supported by the contents of the documents and that Prlić has failed to show any error in this respect.[4073] Concerning Prlić's argument that the Trial Chamber ignored

---

[4066]   Trial Judgement, Vol. 4, para. 207, referring to Ex. P01388, point 6, p. 2.

[4067]   The Appeals Chamber also notes that Prlić refers to his submissions in ground of appeal 3, which it dismisses elsewhere in the Judgement. See *supra*, paras 177-183.

[4068]   Trial Judgement, Vol. 4, para. 208, referring to Ex. P09712 (confidential), para. 38. For context, see Ex. P09712 (confidential), para. 37.

[4069]   The Appeals Chamber notes that the Trial Chamber specifically considered that one part of the Croatian population of central Bosnia was actually fleeing the fighting between the ABiH and HVO. See, *e.g.*, Trial Judgement, Vol. 4, paras 53-55, 215. The Appeals Chamber also notes that Prlić refers in this respect to his submissions in sub-grounds of appeal 16.3.1 and 16.3.2, which it dismisses elsewhere in the Judgement. See *supra*, paras 1209-1211, 1213-1218, 1220-1221.

[4070]   The Appeals Chamber finds Prlić's arguments concerning Zenica unpersuasive since the reference to Zenica in the impugned finding provides just an example to illustrate how the programme would operate. It further considers that Boban's 7 May 1993 letter to the UN seeking the free movement of Croats entering and leaving the areas of Zenica, Konjic, and Jablanica is not inconsistent with the impugned finding. Compare Ex. P09606, p. 2, with Trial Judgement, Vol. 4, para. 208. Finally, the Appeals Chamber considers that the evidence that Prlić cites does not support his claim that property exchange was forbidden by the HVO HZ H-B. See Prlić's Appeal Brief, fn. 1455 and references cited therein.

[4071]   Trial Judgement, Vol. 4, para. 209 & fn. 533 and references cited therein.

[4072]   With regard to Prlić's argument that Beese's testimony that the movement was an effort to change the voting pattern is unsustainable, the Appeals Chamber notes that the Trial Chamber did not specifically rely on this part of Beese's testimony for the impugned finding, and dismisses Prlić's argument accordingly. See Trial Judgement, Vol. 4, para. 209 & fn. 533 and references cited therein. The Appeals Chamber further observes that Prlić's claim that Beese "incredibly" noted that the danger from the Mujahideen was propaganda is not supported by the cited evidence. See Prlić's Appeal Brief, para. 564 & fn. 1463, referring to Christopher Beese, T. 5442-5443 (23 Aug 2006). Prlić's submission that Travnik was part of a designated Croat-majority province and that it would therefore defy logic to resettle Croats from there fails to account for Prlić's own statement that the ABiH took control of Travnik on 9 June 1993. See Prlić's Appeal Brief, para. 566. The Appeals Chamber also notes that Prlić refers to his submissions in sub-grounds of appeal 6.2 and 16.5, which it dismisses elsewhere in the Judgement. See *supra*, paras 212-218, 1286-1298.

[4073]   Trial Judgement, Vol. 4, para. 209 & fn. 534, referring to Exs. 1D01668, conclusion 3 (Minutes of an HVO HZ H-B meeting held on 15 June 1993, which Prlić chaired, recording the following conclusion: "A proposal was made to the Presidency of the HZ H-B and the HVO Supreme Commander to adopt a decision to pull out all military units from areas outside the designated Croatian provinces, together with the Croatian inhabitants living there. To this effect, demand cooperation and assistance from UNPROFOR and UNHCR"), P03413, p. 1 (Letter from Prlić to the President of the HZ H-B dated 13 July 1993, referring to the conclusion reached by the HVO HZ H-B on 15 June 1993 as follows: "A proposal has been put to the Presidency of the HZ H-B and the Supreme Commander of the HVO to reach the decision to withdraw all military units together with the local Croatian population from the areas outside of the defined Croat provinces. For that purpose an assistance of UNPROFOR and UNHCR needs to be requested in a form of an ultimatum."). The Appeals Chamber also notes that Prlić refers to his submissions in ground of appeal 3, which it dismisses elsewhere in the Judgement. See *supra*, paras 177-183.

evidence, the Appeals Chamber observes that, contrary to Prlić's submissions, the Trial Chamber specifically considered that one part of the Croatian population of central Bosnia, including Travnik Municipality, was fleeing the fighting between the ABiH and HVO.[4074] Similarly, contrary to Prlić's suggestions, the Trial Chamber considered evidence regarding the HVO HZ H-B's proposals to the Presidency to take action after having been informed of the imminent threat to central Bosnian Croats.[4075] The Appeals Chamber considers that Prlić merely asserts that the Trial Chamber has failed to interpret the evidence in a particular manner. Consequently, the Appeals Chamber dismisses all these arguments.

1313. The Appeals Chamber further considers that Prlić has failed to show that no reasonable trier of fact could have found that between 400 and 650 Muslims were forced to leave their homes in West Mostar in order to accommodate the Croats from other areas in BiH and in particular from **[page 535]** Travnik. In particular, it dismisses Prlić's challenge that there is no evidence on a policy that Muslims were forced to leave Mostar or Herzegovina in order to accommodate Croats, since the Trial Chamber's finding to the contrary is based on ample evidence, which Prlić fails to address.[4076]

1314. With respect to Prlić's challenge to the finding that on 21 June 1993, he signed a decision creating a staff for organising and co-ordinating the effort to accommodate and provide for expelled people and refugees, the Appeals Chamber considers that Prlić's submission that the staff aimed to deal with the humanitarian crisis fails to articulate an error. Further, Prlić's argument is irrelevant to the impugned finding, which concerns the staff's creation, and does not demonstrate an error in the Trial Chamber's overarching conclusion.[4077] This argument is therefore dismissed. Next, concerning the Trial Chamber's reliance on Witness DZ's evidence that during a meeting on 23 June 1993, Pogarčić, speaking on behalf of, *inter alios,* Prlić, expressed Prlić's wish to gather the Croatian population in one Croatian entity, the Appeals Chamber considers that evidence of a specific link between Pogarčić and Prlić is not required for the finding that, according to Witness DZ, the former reported about the latter's wishes.[4078] Similarly, the Appeals Chamber considers that a reasonable trier of fact could have made this finding, based on the evidence relied on by the Trial Chamber, even in the absence of further evidence that Witness DZ "reported this claim".[4079] In this regard, the Appeals Chamber notes Witness DZ's evidence stating that, during the 23 June 1993 meeting, "Pogarčić was voicing the idea expressed by [...] Prlić, [...] that they would absorb the Croat population from other areas of [BiH] into a Croat entity".[4080] Prlić's arguments are dismissed.

1315. As regards Prlić's challenges to the findings that in a meeting held on 16 July 1993 Prlić stated that 10,000 Muslims wished to leave Mostar for third countries, and that he negotiated with Croatia for transit visas to be granted to the Muslims wishing to go to third countries,[4081] the Appeals Chamber first considers that Prlić fails to show that confidential Exhibit 6D00577, which he alleges the Trial Chamber ignored, concerns that specific meeting.[4082] Regarding Prlić's argument that the Trial Chamber ignored and mischaracterised evidence indicating, notably, that transit visas were not intended for Muslims alone, the Appeals Chamber finds that Prlić has failed to demonstrate that no reasonable trier of fact could have reached the relevant conclusions of the **[page 536]** Trial Chamber in light of the evidence on which it relied,[4083] notwithstanding the evidence to which Prlić refers.[4084] Finally, the Appeals Chamber finds that in submitting that the Trial Chamber ignored

---

[4074] See *supra*, fn. 4069. The Appeals Chamber therefore sees no merit in Prlić's assertion that the Trial Chamber ignored evidence on the expulsion of 30,000 Croats from central Bosnia when the ABiH captured Travnik on 9 June1993 and Kakanj on 13 June 1993. Prlić's Appeal Brief, para. 566.

[4075] Trial Judgement, Vol. 4, para. 209 & fn. 534 and references cited therein. *Cf.* Prlić's Appeal Brief, paras 566-567 & fns 1466-1467, 1469-1470 and references cited therein.

[4076] Trial Judgement, Vol. 4, para. 209 & fn. 535, referring to Trial Judgement, Vol. 2, paras 860-876. See, in particular, Trial Judgement, Vol. 2, paras 874-876.

[4077] See *supra*, para. 1299.

[4078] Trial Judgement, Vol. 4, para. 211.

[4079] Trial Judgement, Vol. 4, para. 211, referring to Ex. P10367 (confidential), para. 70; Witness DZ, T(F). 26564 (closed session) (22 Jan 2008), 26577 (closed session) (23 Jan 2008).

[4080] Ex. P10367 (confidential), para. 70. See also Witness DZ, T(F). 26577 (closed session) (23 Jan 2008).

[4081] Trial Judgement, Vol. 4, para. 212.

[4082] See Trial Judgement, Vol. 4, para. 212, referring to, *inter alia*, Ex. P09679 (confidential), para. 1.

[4083] See Trial Judgement, Vol. 4, paras, 212, 275 & fns 538-539. See also Trial Judgement, Vol. 2, para. 1446, Vol. 4, paras 64, 969.

[4084] See Prlić's Appeal Brief, paras 578-581 & fns 1495-1503 and references cited therein. The Appeals Chamber also notes that Prlić refers to his submissions in sub-ground of appeal 6.1, which it dismisses elsewhere in the Judgement. See *supra*, paras 212-218.

evidence that Muslim refugees returned to, *inter alia,* HVO-controlled areas, indicating they were not expelled, Prlić ignores many of the Trial Chamber's factual findings in support of the impugned finding that there existed a policy of moving Muslim detainees and their families outside the HZ(R) H-B.[4085] In light of this, Prlić's assertion that Muslims later returned is of no consequence. Prlić's arguments are therefore dismissed.

1316. Regarding Prlić's challenge to the finding that he participated in organising and facilitating the departure of the Croatian population of central Bosnia to Herzegovina between August and November 1993, the Appeals Chamber considers that he misrepresents the basis of the finding,[4086] and fails to show that no reasonable trier of fact could have reached this conclusion.[4087] As regards Prlić's challenge to the finding that the ODPR sent him a letter on 3 November 1993, the Appeals Chamber notes that the letter indicates that it was sent to the "President, personally".[4088] In light of this, the Appeals Chamber finds that a reasonable trier of fact could have reached this finding.[4089] Finally, the Appeals Chamber finds that Prlić has failed to demonstrate, on the basis of the evidence he cites, any error in how the Trial Chamber interpreted the transcript of the meeting held on 5 November 1993, containing Prlić's statement on the population movements into Croatian areas,[4090] or in its finding that the HVO exerted pressure on the Croats to leave Vareš.[4091] All these arguments are dismissed. **[page 537]**

1317. Having dismissed the supporting arguments, the Appeals Chamber therefore also dismisses Prlić's challenges to the Trial Chamber's concluding findings.[4092] Thus, the Appeals Chamber dismisses Prlić's sub-ground of appeal 16.6.

(g) Prlić's authority over detention centres

(i) Prlić's general powers over detention centres (Prlić's Ground 13 in part)

1318. The Trial Chamber found that Prlić had authority over detention facilities, particularly to open and close them.[4093] It also found that he had the power to grant international organisations access thereto.[4094]

[4085] See, *e.g.,* Trial Judgement, Vol. 2, paras 814, 876, 2101-2104, 2115, 2131, 2161. In any event, Prlić fails to show that no reasonable trial chamber could have made the impugned finding.
[4086] See Trial Judgement, Vol. 4, para. 213 & fn. 541, referring to Trial Judgement, Vol. 4, paras 196-204 ("Jadranko Prlić's Involvement in Moving Croats from Vareš"). *Cf.* Prlić's Appeal Brief, para. 571 (Prlić incorrectly claims that the Trial Chamber, in reaching the impugned finding, relied on its finding contained in Trial Judgement, Vol. 4, para. 212, that at a 29 July 1993 meeting of the HVO HZ H-B, the organisation and logistics concerning the anticipated arrival of 10,000 Croats from central Bosnia were discussed).
[4087] Prlić's Appeals Chamber notes that Prlić fails to explain in which regard the allegedly ignored evidence on the reasons why the 10,000 Croats fled central Bosnia and why they ended up in Croatia and not in Herzegovina undermines the impugned finding. In any event, the Trial Chamber considered that one part of the Croatian population of central Bosnia was actually fleeing the fighting. See *supra,* fn. 4069. See also Trial Judgement, Vol. 4, para. 209 & fn. 534, referring to Exs. 1D01668, conclusion 3, P03413, p. 1. In light of the above, the Appeals Chamber considers that Prlić has failed to explain how the allegedly ignored evidence concerning the 29 July 1993 meeting, relating to the goal of the ODPR, would show an error in the relevant conclusions of the Trial Chamber regarding Prlić. Compare Trial Judgement, Vol. 4, para. 212, with Prlić's Appeal Brief, para. 582. See also *supra,* para. 1299.
[4088] Trial Judgement, Vol. 4, para. 213 & fn. 542, referring to, *inter alia,* Ex. 1D01354.
[4089] The Appeals Chamber also considers that Prlić's claims are in any event inconsequential in light of the finding that the Government meeting on the following day, 4 November 1993, which Prlić attended, dealt with the same issues as those addressed in the letter. Trial Judgement, Vol. 4, para. 213.
[4090] Trial Judgement, Vol. 4, para. 214. See also *supra,* para. 1293. *Cf.* Ex. P06454, pp. 36, 38. Prlić's submission that he stated that Herzegovina could not accommodate Croats from Vareš and that Croatia should accommodate them is not supported by the evidence to which he refers. See Prlić's Appeal Brief, para. 573 & fn. 1487, referring to Ex. P06454, p. 38. The Appeals Chamber also notes that Prlić refers to his submissions in sub-ground of appeal 9.2, which it dismisses elsewhere in the Judgement. See *supra,* paras 595-601, 625-633, 661-667, 672-676.
[4091] Trial Judgement, Vol. 4, para. 214. See also *supra,* paras 1293-1296. Prlić fails to show any contradiction between this finding and the Trial Chamber's finding that "even if the HVO forces exerted pressure on the Croats to leave Vareš, the threat of attacks by the ABiH and the fact that they did happen were sufficient to bring about the departure of Croats from the municipality". Trial Judgement Vol. 3, para. 508. Further, the Appeals Chamber fails to see how Prlić's argument that expelled Croats mainly ended up in Croatia is inconsistent with the challenged finding that HVO forces exerted pressure on Croats to leave Vareš.
[4092] See *supra,* paras 1299-1300 & fn. 4037. The Appeals Chamber notes that in challenging the Trial Chamber's concluding findings, Prlić refers to bis submissions in sub-grounds of appeal 16.4.3, 16.9, and 16.10, which it dismisses elsewhere in the Judgement. See *supra,* paras 1231-1241; *infra,* paras 1360-1367, 1374-1376.
[4093] Trial Judgement, Vol. 4, paras 112, 114, 218, 270.
[4094] Trial Judgement, Vol. 4, paras 113-114.

1319. The Trial Chamber further found that Prlić knew of the harsh conditions under which the Muslims arrested by the HVO were being detained at the prisons in Dretelj, Gabela, and the Heliodrom, yet justified such detentions, denied that the situation was bad, and on occasion took some measures which were insufficient to address the situation.[4095]

1320. The Trial Chamber held that Prlić accepted and encouraged the extremely precarious conditions and the mistreatment of the detainees in the prisons in Dretelj, Gabela, and the Heliodrom.[4096] It concluded on the basis of this and other findings that Prlić's contribution to the JCE was significant and showed his intention to implement the CCP to expel the Muslim population from the HZ(R) H-B.[4097]

a. Arguments of the Parties

1321. Prlić claims that the Trial Chamber erred in law and fact in concluding that he was a member of a JCE and made a significant contribution to it, having power over the detention centres **[page 538]** of the HZ(R) H-B.[4098] Prlić submits that there is no evidence connecting him or the HVO HZ H-B to the 17 detention centres identified by the Trial Chamber.[4099] In particular, Prlić submits that the Trial Chamber ignored evidence on the differences between detention centres – for POWs – and civilian or military prisons – for persons subject to criminal proceedings.[4100]

1322. Further, Prlić argues that the municipal HVO had authority over Dretelj and Gabela military facilities.[4101] Prlić also contends that contrary to the Trial Chamber's findings, the HVO HZ H-B did not approve any request from the HVO Čapljina to move detainees elsewhere, and that HVO HZ H-B officials were not tasked with finding space for prisoners in other detention centres, but in other municipalities.[4102] He also asserts that the HVO HZ H-B had no power to force the municipal HVOs to accommodate detainees to help the HVO Čapljina.[4103]

1323. Prlić submits that the Trial Chamber erroneously concluded, based on selective evidence, that he could close detention centres.[4104] He argues that his alleged representation that "it was his intention to close POW camps" is not proof of his *de jure* or *de facto* powers over detention centres.[4105] Prlić also argues that the Trial Chamber ignored evidence that, *inter alia,* Mate Boban had begun closing detention centres in July 1993 and asserts that based on a joint declaration of 14 September 1993, signed by Franjo Tuđman and Alija Izetbegović ("Tuđman-Izetbegović Declaration"), Boban decided to close all detention centres by 10 December 1993.[4106] Prlić further argues that the Trial Chamber misconstrued the letters he sent in December 1993 on behalf of the HR H-B Government.[4107]

1324. Finally, Prlić contends that the Trial Chamber erroneously concluded that he had the power to grant international organisations access to detention centres by relying on one uncorroborated piece of evidence, which was also hearsay.[4108] He also argues that the Trial Chamber ignored **[page 539]** evidence that

---

[4095] Trial Judgement, Vol. 4, para. 273.
[4096] Trial Judgement, Vol. 4, para. 273.
[4097] Trial Judgement, Vol. 4, para. 276.
[4098] Prlić's Appeal Brief, paras 410, 426. Specifically, Prlić alleges that by mischaracterising evidence, attaching undue weight to certain evidence, and failing to consider alternatives, the Trial Chamber applied an incorrect legal standard in assessing the evidence, amounting to an error of law. Prlić's Appeal Brief, para. 426.
[4099] Prlić's Appeal Brief, para. 414. Nor is there evidence, according to Prlić, that: (1) information was exchanged between the detention centres and him or the HVO HZ H-B; or (2) the latter budgeted for or financed the detention centres. Prlić's Appeal Brief, para. 415.
[4100] Prlić's Appeal Brief, paras 412-413; Appeal Hearing, AT. 147 (20 Mar 2017). See Prlić's Reply Brief, paras 63-64.
[4101] Prlić's Appeal Brief, paras 416-417. See Appeal Hearing, AT. 145 (20 Mar 2017).
[4102] Prlić's Appeal Brief, para. 417, referring to, *inter alia,* Trial Judgement, Vol. 3, para. 211.
[4103] Prlić's Appeal Brief, para. 417. See also Prlić's Appeal Brief, para. 418, referring to Prlić's Appeal Brief, sub-grounds of appeal 1.2.6, 11.9.
[4104] Prlić's Appeal Brief, para. 421; Appeal Hearing, AT. 145 (20 Mar 2017). Prlić further submits that district prisons are different from detention centres. Prlić's Appeal Brief, para. 421, referring to Prlić's Appeal Brief, paras "413-416".
[4105] Prlić's Appeal Brief, para. 421, referring to, *inter alia,* Prlić's Appeal Brief, paras 181-182 (sub-ground of appeal 6.1).
[4106] Prlić's Appeal Brief, paras 422-423. See also Prlić's Appeal Brief, para. 606 (under Prlić's sub-ground of appeal 16.9).
[4107] Prlić's Appeal Brief, para. 424.
[4108] Prlić's Appeal Brief, para. 425, referring to, *inter alia,* Prlić's Appeal Brief, ground of appeal 3.

international organisations regularly visited the Heliodrom in May to July 1993, without seeking his authorisation.[4109] Prlić concludes that he should be acquitted on Counts 1-3 and 6-18.[4110]

1325. The Prosecution responds that the impugned findings are reasonable and that Prlić fails to show otherwise.[4111] The Prosecution avers that the Trial Chamber reasonably relied on evidence to find that Prlić opened and closed Gabela Prison and that he fails to explain the relevance in this regard of any distinction between prisons for persons subject to criminal proceedings and detention centres for POWs.[4112] The Prosecution contends that there is ample evidence demonstrating Prlić's and the Government's authority over detention facilities.[4113] Further, the Prosecution argues that Prlić fails to show that the Trial Chamber unreasonably relied on his statements and letters as evidence of his authority.[4114] In the Prosecution's view, Prlić misconstrues and ignores evidence showing that he had authority to grant humanitarian access to detention centres.[4115] Finally, the Prosecution submits that evidence of international organisations visiting the Heliodrom without his permission does not undermine the Trial Chamber's conclusion on his authority.[4116]

b. Analysis

1326. The Appeals Chamber observes at the outset that the Trial Chamber's finding that Prlić had authority over detention centres is substantiated by several pieces of evidence.[4117] In particular, the Appeals Chamber considers that in making this finding the Trial Chamber relied on evidence that Prlić signed decisions to, or presided over meetings of the HVO HZ H-B in which decisions were taken to, *inter alia:* (1) open and appoint a director of Gabela Prison and to then close it;[4118] (2) set up a working group to visit Čapljina Municipality, inspect the detention sites, and propose measures to improve the conditions of confinement;[4119] and (3) establish the Exchange Service with Pušić as its head.[4120] The Trial Chamber specifically addressed in more detail Prlić's participation in the **[page 540]** crimes committed in the Heliodrom, Vojno Detention Centre, and Dretelj and Gabela Prisons.[4121] Further, the Appeals Chamber considers that Prlić himself points to evidence that indicates the Government's responsibility for detention facilities and prisoners.[4122] Based on the foregoing, the Appeals Chamber considers that Prlić has failed to show an error and thus dismisses the argument that there is no evidence connecting him or the HVO HZ H-B to the detention centres.[4123]

1327. As to Prlić's claim that the Trial Chamber ignored evidence as to a distinction between detention centres – for POWs – and prisons – for persons subject to criminal proceedings – Prlić fails to explain how evidence that there was such a distinction would impact the impugned finding in light of the Trial Chamber's finding that no distinction was in practice made at Gabela Prison between detainees based on their status.[4124] Based on the above, the Appeals Chamber considers that Prlić has failed to show that no reasonable trier of fact could have reached the impugned finding.

[4109]   Prlić's Appeal Brief, para. 425.
[4110]   Prlić's Appeal Brief, para. 427.
[4111]   Prosecution's Response Brief (Prlić), paras 249-250. See Appeal Hearing, AT. 193, 226-231 (20 Mar 2017).
[4112]   Prosecution's Response Brief (Prlić), paras 254-256. In any case, the Prosecution submits that the distinction is irrelevant as no differentiation was made in fact among Gabela Prison detainees who included Muslim members of the HVO, ABiH members, and Muslim civilians, some of whom were subject to criminal proceedings. Prosecution's Response Brief (Prlić), para. 255.
[4113]   Prosecution's Response Brief (Prlić), paras 252-253. See Appeal Hearing, AT. 232 (20 Mar 2017).
[4114]   Prosecution's Response Brief (Prlić), paras 257-258.
[4115]   Prosecution's Response Brief (Prlić), para. 259.
[4116]   Prosecution's Response Brief (Prlić), para. 260.
[4117]   See Trial Judgement, Vol. 4, paras 112-114, 218-219 and references cited therein.
[4118]   See Trial Judgement, Vol. 3, para. 154 & fns 359 (referring to Exs. P02679, P03350, p. 3), 360 (referring to Exs. P02674, P03350, p. 3), para. 155 & fn. 364 (referring to Ex. P07668), para. 156. See also *infra*, paras 1368-1373.
[4119]   See Trial Judgement, Vol. 3, paras 59, 211 & fns 117, 483, referring to, *inter alia*, Ex, P03560.
[4120]   See Trial Judgement, Vol. 4, para. 101 & fn. 299. See also Trial Judgement, Vol. 4, paras 102-104.
[4121]   See Trial Judgement, Vol. 4, para. 220 *et seq.*
[4122]   See Prlić's Appeal Brief, para. 412, referring to, *inter alia*, Ex. P00292, Zoran Buntić, T. 30655 (14 July 2008), Zoran Perković, T. 31982 (4 Sept 2008).
[4123]   The Appeals Chamber also considers that Prlić has failed to explain how the alleged absence of evidence on exchanges of information between the detention centres and Prlić or the HVO HZ H-B, or on the latter's budgeting for or financing of detention centres, affect the impugned finding, given the remaining evidence the Trial Chamber relied upon. The Appeals Chamber thus dismisses these arguments.
[4124]   See Trial Judgement, Vol. 3, paras 200, 203-204. See also Trial Judgement, Vol. 3, paras 194-195.

1328. With regard to his argument that the municipal HVO had authority over Dretelj and Gabela military facilities, the Appeals Chamber considers that Prlić misrepresents the Trial Chamber's finding.[4125] In any event, even assuming that Prlić had demonstrated that the local HVO had some authority over detention centres,[4126] he has failed to show that no reasonable trier of fact could have reached the same conclusion as the Trial Chamber, based on the remaining evidence,[4127] that Prlić had authority over detention centres. The Appeals Chamber thus dismisses his argument.

1329. Turning to Prlić's challenge to the Trial Chamber's findings that the HVO HZ H-B approved the request from the HVO Čapljina to move detainees and tasked certain persons with finding alternative accommodation for detainees in other detention facilities, the Appeals Chamber considers that these findings are amply supported by the evidence on which they are based,[4128] and **[page 541]** finds that Prlić has failed to show that no reasonable trier of fact could have reached these findings. As to his argument that the HVO HZ H-B could not force the municipal HVOs to help the HVO Čapljina in accommodating detainees, the Appeals Chamber considers that even if no municipality was willing to help the Čapljina Municipality by taking in a number of detainees, as the evidence Prlić points to indicates,[4129] Prlić has failed to show that this is inconsistent with the challenged finding that he had power over detention centres. The Appeals Chamber thus dismisses it accordingly.[4130]

1330. With regard to the challenge to the finding that Prlić had the power to close detention centres, the Appeals Chamber considers that a reasonable trier of fact could have made this finding based on the evidence on which the Trial Chamber relied.[4131] Further, the Appeals Chamber observes that the Trial Chamber considered Boban's decision of 10 December 1993 to close detention centres, to which Prlić refers,[4132] and found that Boban, among others, had power over them.[4133] As to the Trial Chamber's reliance on letters sent by Prlić in December 1993, in which he discussed the process of closing detention facilities, the Appeals Chamber considers that Prlić has failed to show that no reasonable trier of fact could have inferred Prlić's authority over detention centres from these letters, which Prlić sent in his official capacity.[4134] Accordingly, the Appeals Chamber dismisses all these arguments.

1331. Turning to Prlić's contention that the Trial Chamber erroneously concluded that he had the power to grant international organisations access to detention centres by relying on one uncorroborated document containing hearsay, the Appeals Chamber recalls that in assessing the probative value of hearsay evidence, the surrounding circumstances must be considered.[4135] In the circumstances of this case, the Appeals Chamber considers that the author of the document relied upon by the Trial Chamber, a report by an

---

[4125] See Trial Judgement, Vol. 2, para. 2081 (finding that Stojić issued an order on 3 July 1993 transferring the management of detention of Muslim men of military age in Čapljina Municipality to the local HVO but also finding that it had no evidence showing that the local HVO took responsibility for the detention of the Muslim men arrested).

[4126] Prlić's Appeal Brief, para. 416, referring to, *inter alia*, Exs. 1D01105, 2D01019; Zoran Buntić, T. 30499-30500, 30502-30503 (9 July 2008).

[4127] See *supra*, para. 1326.

[4128] See Trial Judgement, Vol. 3, para. 211 & fns 481, 486, referring to, *inter alia*, Exs. P03560, pp. 1, 4 ("After a discussion of the request by the HVO of Čapljina municipality to relocate prisoners [...] unanimous approval was given to [...] designate new sites and transfer prisoners of war"), 5, P03573 (An HVO HZ H-B work group "has visited Čapljina municipality and assessed the existing conditions concerning [...] the accommodation of prisoners of war and isolated individuals [and] proposes the relocation of the part of the detained individuals from Čapljina [...]. The following individuals are assigned [...] to explore possibilities to accommodate a certain number of detained individuals from Čapljina»), Zoran Buntić, T(F). 30585 (10 My 2008) (regarding other municipalities' lack of willingness to accommodate detainees from Čapljina in their own facilities).

[4129] See Zoran Buntić, T. 30582-30586 (10 July 2008).

[4130] The Appeals Chamber also notes that Prlić refers to his submissions in sub-grounds of appeal 1.2.6 and 11.9, which it dismisses elsewhere in the Judgement. See *supra*, paras 168-176, 1093-1096.

[4131] See Trial Judgement, Vol. 3, para. 158, Vol. 4, paras 112, 254, referring to, *inter alia*, Exs. P06965 (UN report of 30 November 1993 referring to Prlić's statement that he intended to close POW camps), para. 6, P07668 (HR H-B decree dated 23 December 1993 closing Gabela Prison and bearing Prlić's name). Prlić's submission that district prisons are different from detention centres is dismissed elsewhere. See *supra*, para. 1326. The Appeals Chamber also notes that Prlić refers to his submissions in sub-ground of appeal 6.1, which it dismisses elsewhere in the Judgement. See *supra*, paras 212-218.

[4132] See Prlić's Appeal Brief, para. 423. See also *infra*, para. 1366.

[4133] Trial Judgement, Vol. 2, para. 1441, Vol. 3, para. 191. See also Trial Judgement, Vol. 3, para. 158, to which Prlić refers. See Prlić's Appeal Brief, fn. 1099; *infra*, para. 1372.

[4134] See Trial Judgement, Vol. 4, para. 112 & fns 335-336 and references cited therein.

[4135] *Lukić and Lukić* Appeal Judgement, para. 303. See also *Popović et al.* Appeal Judgement, paras 1276, 1307.

international organisation, wrote what Prlić had said to him in person in a meeting the night before and considers that a reasonable trier of fact could have **[page 542]** relied upon it.[4136] Further, the Appeals Chamber notes that there is evidence on the record confirming that this meeting took place and was reported in the document in question,[4137] as well as evidence corroborating Prlić's power to grant international organisations access to detention centres.[4138] The Appeals Chamber therefore dismisses Prlić's argument.

1332. With respect to Prlić's allegation that the Trial Chamber ignored evidence that international organisations regularly visited the Heliodrom in May to July 1993 without seeking his authorisation, the Appeals Chamber recalls that the Trial Chamber found that Prlić was one of several persons who regulated access to the Heliodrom for representatives of international organisations,[4139] and finds that Prlić's argument is not inconsistent with the challenged finding that Prlić also had the power to grant international organisations access to detention centres. The Appeals Chamber thus dismisses this argument.

1333. Having dismissed the arguments above, the Appeals Chamber finds that Prlić has failed to demonstrate that no reasonable trier of fact could have found that he had power over detention centres,[4140] or power to grant international organisations access to them. The Appeals Chamber therefore dismisses Prlić's ground 13 in part.

(ii) The Heliodrom

a. Prlić's power over the Heliodrom (Prlić's Sub-grounds 16.7.1 and 16.7.3)

1334. Prlić submits that the Trial Chamber erroneously concluded that he had power over the Heliodrom and that he was involved in and/or had the power to grant representatives of international organisations access to it.[4141] The Prosecution responds that Prlić's mere assertions should be summarily dismissed.[4142] The Appeals Chamber considers that Prlić's submissions are **[page 543]** entirely based on cross-references to his ground of appeal 13, which it dismisses elsewhere in this Judgement.[4143] Prlić's sub-grounds of appeal 16.7.1 and 16.7.3 are dismissed.

b. Prlić's facilitation of and support for the detention of civilians in the Heliodrom (Prlić's Ground 13 in part and Sub-ground 16.7.2)

1335. The Trial Chamber held that at the 38th session of the HVO on 17 May 1993, attended, *inter alios,* by Prlić, the HVO expressed its support for the relocation of civilians from Mostar to the Heliodrom, stating that the women, children, and the elderly had been released.[4144] The Trial Chamber found that at several meetings of the HVO/Government of the HZ(R) H-B attended by Prlić, particularly those held on 19 and 20 July 1993, the situation of the detainees in the detention centres was raised, and the Government conceded that efforts had to be made to improve the detention conditions but did not consider itself responsible for that.[4145]

[4136]   See Trial Judgement, Vol. 2, para. 1437 (referring to Ex. P09846 (confidential)), Vol. 4, para. 113. The Appeals Chamber considers in particular that a reasonable trial chamber could have understood the statement in the report in question – "I was offered a visit to Rodoc" – to refer to the Heliodrom. See, *e.g.,* Philip Roger Watkins, T. 18868 (22 May 2007) ("Rodoc is also sometimes referred to as the Heliodrom"). The Appeals Chamber also notes that Prlić refers to his submissions in ground of appeal 3, which it dismisses elsewhere in the Judgement. See *supra,* paras 177-183.

[4137]   Witness BB, T. 17284-17285 (closed session) (17 Apr 2007).

[4138]   Ex. P03573 (Minutes of the 47th session of the HVO HZ H-B held on 20 July 1993 over which Prlić presided and at which the following conclusion was reached: "The access is allowed to the International Red Cross and other international organizations in order to inspect the conditions in the facilities where detained individuals are accommodated."). The Appeals Chamber notes that the Trial Chamber relied on this exhibit to find, notably, that the Government discussed the situation of the detainees in the detention centres and possible actions in that regard. See Trial Judgement, Vol. 4, para. 219 & fn. 558, para. 224 & fn. 569.

[4139]   See Trial Judgement, Vol. 2, para. 1441.

[4140]   The Appeals Chamber addresses Prlić's specific challenges with regard to the Heliodrom, Vojno Detention Centre, Dretelj Prison, and Gabela Prison elsewhere in the Judgement. See *infra,* paras 1334-1373.

[4141]   Prlić's Appeal Brief, paras 586-587, 592-593, referring to Prlić's Appeal Brief, ground of appeal 13.

[4142]   Prosecution's Response Brief (Prlić), para. 369.

[4143]   See *supra,* paras 1318-1333; *infra,* paras 1335-1343, 1356-1373.

[4144]   Trial Judgement, Vol. 4, para. 222.

[4145]   Trial Judgement, Vol. 4, para. 224.

1336. The Trial Chamber also found that Prlić was informed at the meetings on 19 and 20 July 1993 of the precarious situation of the detained Muslims at the detention centres.[4146] The Trial Chamber held that by issuing the press release on 23 July 1993 – stating that the detainees in all the detention centres, including the Heliodrom, were men of military age, that the women, children, and elderly had been released from there, and that medical checks had been carried out on all the detainees and those with any medical problems were released regardless of age – Prlić imparted information about the detention of Muslims which he knew was inaccurate.[4147]

1337. The Trial Chamber considered that the fact that Prlić took measures to improve the detention conditions of the detainees, but did not deem himself responsible for their implementation, did not exonerate him.[4148] The Trial Chamber further found that Prlić ought to have ensured the actual implementation of the decision of 19 July 1993 but that, instead, on 23 July 1993, Prlić publicly justified the detention of Muslims at the Heliodrom and denied that their situation was bad.[4149] The Trial Chamber thus found that Prlić facilitated the detention of civilians and the bad conditions in which the detainees were living.[4150] **[page 544]**

i. Arguments of the Parties

1338. Prlić submits that the Trial Chamber erroneously concluded, by "effectively" relying on one document, the minutes of the 38th session of the HVO HZ-HB meeting held on 17 May 1993, that he and the HVO HZ-HB facilitated and supported the detention of civilians and the bad conditions in the Heliodrom.[4151]

1339. Prlić further submits that the Trial Chamber erroneously concluded that the HVO HZ H-B "conceded that efforts had to be made to improve the detention conditions" and that by issuing the press release on 23 July 1993, having been previously informed of the bad situation of the detained Muslims on 19 and 20 July 1993, publicly denying such bad conditions, he knowingly gave inaccurate information.[4152] Prlić contends that the 19 and 20 July 1993 meetings related to the Čapljina prisons, not the Heliodrom.[4153] Prlić argues further that the Trial Chamber ignored contextual evidence when assessing the press release.[4154]

1340. The Prosecution responds that Prlić's claim that the Trial Chamber relied on one document to conclude that he facilitated and supported the detention of civilians and the bad conditions in the Heliodrom is incorrect, articulates no error, and fails to show that the Trial Chamber unreasonably interpreted that document.[4155] The Prosecution avers that Prlić fails to show that no reasonable trial chamber could have concluded that he knowingly imparted inaccurate information through the 23 July 1993 press release, and argues that while the Government meetings of 19 and 20 July 1993 focused on the conditions in Čapljina prisons, the minutes reflect an awareness of generally poor detention conditions.[4156] **[page 545]**

[4146] Trial Judgement, Vol. 4, paras 224-225.

[4147] Trial Judgement, Vol. 4, paras 223 (referring to Ex. P03673, p. 2), 225.

[4148] Trial Judgement, Vol. 4, para. 225.

[4149] Trial Judgement, Vol. 4, para. 225.

[4150] Trial Judgement, Vol. 4, para. 225.

[4151] Prlić's Appeal Brief, paras 588-589, referring to, *inter alia*, Ex. 1D01666, Prlić's Appeal Brief, ground of appeal 3 and sub-ground of appeal 16.4.2. See also Prlić's Appeal Brief, para. 414(g).

[4152] Prlić's Appeal Brief, para. 590.

[4153] Prlić's Appeal Brief, para. 590, referring to Prlić's Appeal Brief, para. 417 (ground of appeal 13).

[4154] Specifically, Prlić argues that: (1) he issued the press release in response to Mate Granić's appeal to address the deteriorating humanitarian situation in BiH at the time; (2) the information in the press release came from the authorities in charge of the detention centres; (3) there is no evidence that those in charge of the Heliodrom were obliged to send information to him or the HR H-B Government, or that any such information was exchanged; (4) he had no *de jure* power over any of the detention centres, including the Heliodrom; (5) there is no evidence that he "exceeded his legitimate powers"; and (6) he could not implement any measures in the Heliodrom. Prlić's Appeal Brief, para. 590. See Prlić's Appeal Brief, para. 591, referring to Prlić's Appeal Brief, ground of appeal 13.

[4155] Prosecution's Response Brief (Prlić), para. 370.

[4156] Prosecution's Response Brief (Prlić), para. 371. See Appeal Hearing, AT. 228-229 (20 Mar 2017). The Prosecution also refers to other findings and supporting evidence, which it argues show that Prlić lied on 23 July 1993. Prosecution's Response Brief (Prlić), para. 371. In the Prosecution's view, it was irrelevant that the press release was in response to Granić's appeal. Prosecution's Response Brief (Prlić), para. 371. Finally, the Prosecution argues that Prlić's claim that the information in the press release came from the authorities in charge of detention centres ignores information which he actually had. Prosecution's Response Brief (Prlić), para. 372.

ii. Analysis

1341. At the outset, the Appeals Chamber considers that Prlić misrepresents the challenged factual finding when he claims that the Trial Chamber effectively relied on one document. The Appeals Chamber considers that the Trial Chamber reached the impugned finding after a discussion of various pieces of evidence, including the minutes of the 38th session of the HVO HZ H-B on 17 May 1993, a press release dated 23 July 1993, minutes of the HVO HZ H-B sessions held on 19 and 20 July 1993, as well as other findings.[4157] As Prlić has failed to demonstrate any error in the Trial Chamber's finding, the Appeals Chamber dismisses this argument.

1342. The Appeals Chamber now turns to the impugned findings that the HVO HZ H-B conceded that efforts were needed to improve detention conditions and that Prlić, despite knowing about these bad conditions, publicly denied them and thus knowingly gave inaccurate information. With regard to Prlić's argument that the 19 and 20 July 1993 meetings related to the Čapljina prisons, not the Heliodrom, the Appeals Chamber has reviewed the underlying evidence and considers that, based on this evidence, a reasonable trier of fact could have found that the discussion revolved around all detention centres and not just Čapljina prisons.[4158] With regard to Prlić's argument that the Trial Chamber ignored contextual evidence when assessing the press release, the Appeals Chamber considers that he has failed to explain how the evidence he submits the Trial Chamber ignored is inconsistent with the challenged findings.[4159] It thus dismisses all these arguments.

1343. The Appeals Chamber therefore dismisses Prlić's ground of appeal 13 in part, as well as his sub-ground of appeal 16.7.2. **[page 546]**

c. Prlić's facilitation and acceptance of the use of Heliodrom detainees for front line labour (Prlić's Sub-ground 16.7.4)

1344. The Trial Chamber found that Prlić was one of the HZ(R) H-B officials who were informed of incidents during the work at the front line of detainees from the Heliodrom and elsewhere.[4160] The Trial Chamber found that Prlić, once notified of these incidents, had the power to intervene and put an end to the practice and by failing to act, he both facilitated the use of detainees from the Heliodrom for work at the front line and as human shields and accepted their abuse and the death of some of them.[4161]

i. Arguments of the Parties

1345. Prlić submits that the Trial Chamber erred in finding that he facilitated the use of the detainees from the Heliodrom for work at the front line and as human shields, that he had the power to intervene, and that he accepted their abuse and the death of some of them.[4162] Prlić argues that he had no power over the military or over those authorised at the Heliodrom to assign detainees to forced labour.[4163] He submits that the HVO

[4157] See Trial Judgement, Vol. 4, paras 222-224, referring to, *inter alia*, Exs. P03560, P03573, P03673, 1D01666. The Appeals Chamber also notes that Prlić refers to his submissions in ground of appeal 3 and sub-ground of appeal 16.4.2, which it dismisses elsewhere in the Judgement. See *supra*, paras 177-183, 1225-1230.

[4158] Trial Judgement, Vol. 4, para. 224 & fn. 569, referring to Exs. P03560, p. 4, P03573. The Appeals Chamber notes in particular that Exhibit P03560, minutes of the 46th session of the HVO HZ H-B held on 19 July 1993, states that: "[a]fter a discussion of the request by the HVO of Čapljina municipality to relocate prisoners *and a discussion of the status and accommodation conditions of prisoners and persons in isolation*, with the aim of improving their accommodation conditions and overcoming the newly-arisen situation, unanimous approval was given to adopt the following [c]onclusions [...] [s]ecure accommodation conditions, material and medical support for prisoners of war in accordance with the Geneva Convention relative to the Treatment of Prisoners of War." Ex. P03560, p. 4 (emphasis added). The Appeals Chamber also notes that Prlić refers to his submissions in ground of appeal 13, which it dismisses elsewhere in the Judgement. See *supra*, paras 1318-1333, *infra*, paras 1356-1373.

[4159] See *supra*, fn. 4154. The Appeals Chamber also notes that Prlić refers to his submissions in ground of appeal 13, which it dismisses elsewhere in the Judgement. See *supra*, paras 1318-1333; *infra*, paras 1356-1373.

[4160] Trial Judgement, Vol. 2, paras 1481, 1492, Vol. 4, para. 229.

[4161] Trial Judgement, Vol. 4, para. 232. See Trial Judgement, Vol. 4, para. 274.

[4162] Prlić's Appeal Brief, para. 594. See Prlić's Appeal Brief, para. 595, referring to Prlić's Appeal Brief, grounds of appeal 12-13.

[4163] Prlić's Appeal Brief, para. 596.

Main Staff had authority over such matters and prohibited the taking of prisoners for labour in dangerous zones, and that the Defence Minister issued orders to prevent such practices.[4164]

1346. Prlić submits that the Trial Chamber erroneously concluded, by relying on selective evidence, including letters from the ICRC on which he was copied, that he was informed of the forced labour carried out by detainees.[4165] He argues that there is no evidence that he received these letters and even if he did, they were not proof of his *de jure* and *de facto* powers, let alone that he "acquiesced by dereliction".[4166] Prlić also argues that the Trial Chamber ignored evidence that the ICRC sent a report in November 1993 on the issue of forced labour to Boban and Pogarčić, who – unlike Prlić – were responsible, that Marijan Biškić received the ICRC's letters, that the Military Police as the competent authority and the SIS responded to each letter, and that measures were taken to investigate the allegations made in the ICRC's letters.[4167]

1347. The Prosecution responds that Prlić shows no error in the impugned finding that he facilitated the use of detainees for work on the front line since he was aware of the practice and **[page 547]** failed to intervene.[4168] It argues that he ignores the Trial Chamber's findings on his authority over the military and the Department of Defence whose officials were found to have authority over the use of Heliodrom detainees for forced labour.[4169] It also avers that there is evidence that he was personally informed of the use of Heliodrom detainees for front line labour.[4170] In the Prosecution's view, evidence that the Military Police and SIS "reacted" to this issue does not undermine the Trial Chamber's findings on Prlić's failure to intervene.[4171] In any case, the Prosecution argues that Prlić points to no evidence reflecting actual prevention or punishment, or evidence otherwise undermining the Trial Chamber's finding that no HVO member was ever sanctioned for using Heliodrom prisoners for forced labour.[4172]

ii. Analysis

1348. Concerning Prlić's argument that he had no power over the military or over those authorised at the Heliodrom to assign detainees to forced labour, the Appeals Chamber recalls that it dismisses elsewhere Prlić's general challenges to his powers in military matters and over detention centres.[4173] The Trial Chamber listed several persons, not including Prlić, who had power to authorise the use of Heliodrom detainees for forced labour, but included him among the persons who were informed of the incidents during forced labour performed by Heliodrom detainees.[4174] The Trial Chamber found that Prlić had the power to intervene and end the practice based on his position of authority.[4175] In light of the above, the Appeals Chamber considers that Prlić's arguments concerning the HVO Main Staff's authority and the Defence Minister's orders are not inconsistent with the impugned finding that Prlić facilitated the use of detainees from the Heliodrom for work at the front line and as human shields, and accepted their abuse and the death of some of them.[4176] The Appeals Chamber thus dismisses these arguments.

1349. With regard to Prlić's argument that the Trial Chamber erroneously relied on selective evidence – *i.e.* a report of an international organisation on a meeting with him, dated 17 August 1993, and two letters dated 18 February and 16 March 1994 by an international organisation – to conclude that he was informed of the work of the detainees,[4177] the **[page 548]** Appeals Chamber observes that the 17 August 1993 document reported on a personal meeting with Prlić the previous evening where he "brushed over" ICRC allegations

---

[4164]   Prlić's Appeal Brief, para. 596.
[4165]   Prlić's Appeal Brief, para. 597.
[4166]   Prlić's Appeal Brief, para. 597.
[4167]   Prlić's Appeal Brief, para. 597; Prlić's Reply Brief, para. 75.
[4168]   Prosecution's Response Brief (Prlić), para. 373; Appeal Hearing, AT. 229 (20 Mar 2017).
[4169]   Prosecution's Response Brief (Prlić), para. 374.
[4170]   Prosecution's Response Brief (Prlić), para. 375.
[4171]   Prosecution's Response Brief (Prlić), para. 376.
[4172]   Prosecution's Response Brief (Prlić), para. 376.
[4173]   *See supra*, paras 1098-1127, 1318-1333.
[4174]   Trial Judgement, Vol. 2, para. 1492.
[4175]   Trial Judgement, Vol. 4, para. 232.
[4176]   See Prlić's Appeal Brief, para. 594, referring to Trial Judgement, Vol. 4, para. 232.
[4177]   See Trial Judgement, Vol. 2, para. 1481 & fn. 3749, Vol. 4, para. 229 & fn. 575, referring to Exs. P07895, p. 1, P08079 (confidential), p. 2, P09846 (confidential).

on the use of prisoners from the Heliodrom and elsewhere to work on the front line.[4178] The Appeals Chamber also considers that Prlić was copied on the 18 February and 16 March 1994 letters, and that based on these three documents, a reasonable trier of fact could have made the impugned finding. Further, the Appeals Chamber considers that the Trial Chamber did not find that Prlić had the power to intervene to stop detainees from the Heliodrom being used to work on the front fine, nor that he "acquiesced by dereliction", based on the two letters.[4179] The Appeals Chamber thus dismisses these arguments.

1350. As to Prlić's final argument that the Trial Chamber ignored evidence that other officials received a report and letters from the ICRC on this issue, that the Military Police and SIS responded to each letter, and that measures were taken to investigate the allegations made, the Appeals Chamber considers that, regardless of the allegedly ignored evidence,[4180] Prlić has failed to show that the conclusion of the Trial Chamber could not stand on the basis of the above-mentioned evidence that Prlić was also informed of the use of detainees for work on the front line.[4181] The Appeals Chamber therefore dismisses this argument.

1351. For the foregoing reasons, the Appeals Chamber rejects Prlić's sub-ground of appeal 16.7.4.

     d. Prlić's planning and facilitation of the organisation of the departure of about 2,500 detainees from the Heliodrom to Croatia (Prlić's Sub-ground 16.7.5)

1352. The Trial Chamber found that, at least on one occasion in July 1993, Prlić planned and facilitated the organisation of the departure of about 2,500 detainees from the Heliodrom to Croatia, although he knew that an international organisation had called the plan "ethnic cleansing".[4182]

1353. Prlić submits that the Trial Chamber erred in making this finding, relying on limited and uncorroborated evidence.[4183] He argues that there is no evidence that he was involved in releasing persons from the Heliodrom.[4184] In Prlić's view, the Trial Chamber ignored evidence making no mention of 10,000 persons wishing to leave Mostar and that only 71 persons, of the 502 who **[page 549]** applied for transit visas to Croatia for family, security, employment, or health-related reasons, were from Mostar.[4185]

1354. The Prosecution responds that Prlić misrepresents the evidence the Trial Chamber relied upon.[4186] The Prosecution argues that Prlić ignores evidence showing his central role in organising the displacement of prisoners, and that the fact that others had authority to release detainees does not undermine the Trial Chamber's conclusion that Prlić "planned and facilitated" the departure of Heliodrom detainees.[4187] It also argues that even if some of the 2,500 persons had applied for transit visas this does not undermine the Trial Chamber's finding that the departure was involuntary.[4188]

1355. With regard to the argument that the Trial Chamber relied on limited and uncorroborated evidence, the Appeals Chamber observes that Prlić misrepresents in both regards the Trial Chamber's findings, which were based on several pieces of mutually corroborating evidence.[4189] As to Prlić's challenge that there is no evidence that he was involved in releasing persons from the Heliodrom, the Appeals Chambers considers that the Trial Chamber's finding that the Military Police and other HVO authorities – not listing Prlić – had

---

[4178] See Ex. P09846 (confidential).
[4179] See Trial Judgement, Vol. 4, para. 232 ("Given his position of authority"). See also *supra*, paras 1021-1127, 1318-1333.
[4180] See Prlić's Appeal Brief, para. 597, referring to, *inter alia*, Ex. P00284 and the testimony of Marijan Biškić.
[4181] See *supra*, paras 1348-1349.
[4182] See Trial Judgement, Vol. 4, para. 235.
[4183] Prlić's Appeal Brief, para. 598.
[4184] Prlić's Appeal Brief, para. 598. See Prlić's Appeal Brief, para. 599, referring to Prlić's Appeal Brief, sub-grounds 16.6.3-16.6.4.
[4185] Prlić's Appeal Brief, para. 600.
[4186] Prosecution's Response Brief (Prlić), para. 377.
[4187] Prosecution's Response Brief (Prlić), para. 379.
[4188] Prosecution's Response Brief (Prlić), para. 378. The Prosecution also submits that Prlić refers to scant or irrelevant evidence and ignores relevant findings of the Trial Chamber. Prosecution's Response Brief (Prlić), para. 378.
[4189] See Trial Judgement, Vol. 4, paras 234-235 & fns 588-591 and references cited therein. *Cf.* Prlić's Appeal Brief, para. 598 & fn. 1533. In any event, there is no general requirement that the testimony of a witness be corroborated if deemed otherwise credible. *Popović et al.* Appeal Judgement, paras 243, 1264; *D. Milošević* Appeal Judgement, para. 215. See also *Kordić and Čerkez* Appeal Judgement, para. 274.

the power to release detainees,[4190] does not preclude it from making the impugned finding, which is supported by evidence.[4191] Similarly, the Appeals Chamber considers that Prlić has failed to explain how the allegedly ignored evidence undermines the impugned finding.[4192] For these reasons, the Appeals Chamber dismisses all of Prlić's arguments, as well as Prlić's sub-ground of appeal 16.7.5.

(iii) Vojno Detention Centre (Prlić's Ground 13 in part and Sub-ground 16.8)

1356. The Trial Chamber found that, as of 20 January 1994, Prlić was informed that detainees from Vojno Detention Centre were being used to work at the front line and that several had been mistreated, wounded, and killed during such work.[4193] The Trial Chamber also found that by continuing to exercise his functions, and because he took no measures to stop the crimes which **[page 550]** continued until the end of January 1994, Prlić accepted the use of detainees at the front line and their consequent death and wounding.[4194]

1357. Prlić submits that the Trial Chamber erroneously concluded that he had power over Vojno Detention Centre and its detainees.[4195] Prlić further asserts that the Trial Chamber erroneously concluded that he accepted the use of detainees at the front line and their death and wounding based on letters sent by the ICRC to others, on which he was copied.[4196]

1358. The Prosecution responds that the Trial Chamber's findings were reasonable and that Prlić's arguments should be summarily dismissed.[4197]

1359. At the outset, the Appeals Chamber recalls that it dismisses Prlić's challenge to his overall authority over detention centres in another part of the Judgement,[4198] and considers that he fails to demonstrate any error specifically with regard to his authority over Vojno Detention Centre.[4199] With regard to Prlić's claim that the Trial Chamber erroneously concluded that he accepted the use of detainees at the front line and the death and wounding of some of them based on letters sent by the ICRC, on which he was copied,[4200] the Appeals Chamber considers that a reasonable trier of fact could have found that he was informed on the basis of this evidence[4201] and therefore finds that Prlić has failed to show that the Trial Chamber erred. It. further considers that Prlić misrepresents the impugned finding. The Appeals Chamber notes that while the Trial

---

[4190]   See Trial Judgement, Vol. 2, paras 1445-1452.

[4191]   See Trial Judgement, Vol. 4, paras 234-235 and references cited therein. The Appeals Chamber also notes that Prlić refers to his submissions in sub-grounds of appeal 16.6.3 and 16.6.4, which it dismisses elsewhere in the Judgement. See *supra*, paras 1300, 1304-1306, 1308-1309, 1315, 1317.

[4192]   See Prlić's Appeal Brief, para. 600, referring to Exs. P03554 (confidential), P09682 (confidential), pp. 3-4, Adalbert Rebić, T. 28462-28465 (partly private session) (22 May 2008). *Cf.* Ex. P09679 (confidential).

[4193]   Trial Judgement, Vol. 4, paras 238, 274. See Trial Judgement, Vol. 4, paras 236-237. See also Trial Judgement, Vol. 2, paras 1685-1686.

[4194]   Trial Judgement, Vol. 4, paras 238, 274.

[4195]   Prlić's Appeal Brief, paras 414(h), 601.

[4196]   Prlić's Appeal Brief, para. 601. See Prlić's Appeal Brief, para. 602, referring to Prlić's Appeal Brief, (sub-)grounds of appeal 12.1, 13, 16.7.4.

[4197]   Prosecution's Response Brief (Prlić), para. 380.

[4198]   See *supra*, paras 1318-1333.

[4199]   The Appeals Chamber notes in particular that Prlić partly relies on the Trial Chamber's findings that other persons and bodies had authority over Vojno Detention Centre, but considers that this does not preclude the Trial Chamber from finding that Prlić had a general authority over detention facilities, particularly to open and close them. See Prlić's Appeal Brief, para. 414(h), referring to Trial Judgement, Vol. 2, paras 1669-1682. See also *supra*, paras 1318, 1326. The Appeals Chamber further considers that Prlić fails to demonstrate that the Trial Chamber relied on him being copied on letters sent by the ICRC to conclude that he had power over Vojno Detention Centre and its detainees. See Prlić's Appeal Brief, para. 601 & fn. 1537, referring to Trial Judgement, Vol. 2, paras 1685, 1694, 1711, 1729.

[4200]   See Trial Judgement, Vol. 2, para. 1620 & fn. 4107, Vol. 4, paras 236-237 & fns 592-594, referring to, *inter alia*, Exs. P07636, p. 1, P07660, P08079 (confidential), p. 1.

[4201]   See Exs. P07636 (ICRC letter dated 20 January 1994), p. 1 ("The majority of the prisoners were wounded by shelling or rifle fire, while working on the frontline, in Mostar, Vojno or Vrdi; they either died on the spot or during the transfer to the hospital. In August and September [1993], during military offensives, a large number[] of prisoners were made to work on the frontline in Mostar."); P07660 (ICRC letter dated 24 January 1994) ("[P]risoners are again being used for work on the front line [...] a large number of detainees are still held under working obligation in front line areas like Vo[j]no, Hum, Mostar and Vrdi [...] the detainees held in these places are used for work of military character, such as building fortifications, and [...] several of them have been injured."); P08079 (confidential) (ICRC letter dated 16 March 1994), p. 1 ("On the 8th of November [1993], 75 prisoners were transferred from Rodoc to Vojno. They worked everyday on the frontline, starting at 6 am.") The letter proceeds to describe in detail

Chamber inferred his knowledge of the use of detainees at the front line and their ensuing death and wounding from the **[page 551]** ICRC letters,[4202] his knowledge of such crimes being committed was only one of the considerations leading the Trial Chamber to conclude that he accepted such crimes – the other two were his continued exercise of his functions and the fact that he took no measures to stop the commission of such crimes.[4203] The Appeals Chamber therefore rejects this argument. For the foregoing reasons, the Appeals Chamber dismisses Prlić's ground of appeal 13 in part, as well as his sub-ground of appeal 16.8.

(iv) Dretelj Prison (Prlić's Ground 13 in part and Sub-ground 16.9)

1360. The Trial Chamber found that in July 1993, in meetings of the HVO/Government of the HZ(R) H-B in which Prlić participated, decisions were taken to improve the conditions of detention of detainees.[4204] These decisions did not bring about the expected improvements, however, because at the end of September 1993, the conditions were still as bad.[4205] The Trial Chamber found that, while exercising his functions in the HVO/ Government of HZ(R) H-B, Prlić continued to be informed of the bad conditions of detention and the mistreatment of detainees.[4206] It also found that instead of having the detainees released, they were moved to other detention centres or to third countries via Croatia.[4207] The Trial Chamber concluded therefore that Prlić accepted the extremely precarious conditions and the mistreatment of detainees in Dretelj Prison and "even facilitated them by not releasing the detainees", and facilitated their departure to foreign countries through his failure to act.[4208]

a. Arguments of the Parties

1361. Prlić submits that the Trial Chamber erroneously concluded that he had power over Dretelj Prison and its detainees and that he accepted the precarious conditions and mistreatment of detainees.[4209] He challenges the Trial Chamber's reliance on the minutes of two HVO HZ H-B meetings to find that the decision taken in July 1993 to improve the conditions of detention "did not bring about the expected improvements because in September 1993 the detention conditions were still just as bad".[4210] In his submission, the HVO HZ H-B's holding discussions to find solutions for **[page 552]** problems outside its responsibility and powers, and to which it did not contribute, "does not impute *de jure* or *de facto* responsibility".[4211]

1362. Prlić further asserts that the Trial Chamber erred, by ignoring relevant evidence regarding the 20 September 1993 meeting with international organisations, in concluding that he moved prisoners from Dretelj Prison to other locations.[4212] Referring to the joint Tuđman-Izetbegović Declaration, which provided for the disbanding of detention camps and the release of detainees, Prlić argues that Mate Granić and Haris Silajdžić, charged with implementing this agreement, took measures to abolish Dretelj Prison and release detainees from this facility, in co-operation with international organisations and based on the free will of the detainees.[4213] Prlić claims that neither the HVO HZ H-B nor he were "involved in these matters".[4214]

---

the alleged mistreatment and wounding of the prisoners by the soldiers guarding them. See also Ex. P08079 (confidential), p. 2 (regarding detainees killed on the front line).

[4202] See also Trial Judgement, Vol. 2, para. 1685 & fn. 4237, referring to, *inter alia*, Ex. P07895 regarding his knowledge of similar events that were occurring in the Heliodrom.

[4203] See Trial Judgement, Vol. 4, para. 238. The Appeals Chamber also notes that Prlić refers to his submissions in (sub-)grounds of appeal 12.1, 13, and 16.7.4, which it dismisses elsewhere in the Judgement. See *supra*, paras 1099-1122, 1318-1333, 1335-1351; *infra*, paras 1360-1373.

[4204] Trial Judgement, Vol. 4, para. 248.

[4205] Trial Judgement, Vol. 4, para. 248.

[4206] Trial Judgement, Vol. 4, para. 249.

[4207] Trial Judgement, Vol. 4, para. 249.

[4208] Trial Judgement, Vol. 4, para. 249.

[4209] Prlić's Appeal Brief, paras 414(1), 603. See Prlić's Appeal Brief, paras 604 (referring to Prlić's (sub-)grounds of appeal 12.1, 13, 16.7.4), 606 & fn. 1556 (referring to Prlić's Appeal Brief, ground of appeal 13).

[4210] Prlić's Appeal Brief, para. 605.

[4211] Prlić's Appeal Brief, para. 605, referring to, *inter alia*, Prlić's Appeal Brief, (sub-)grounds of appeal 3, 16.7.

[4212] Prlić's Appeal Brief, para. 606.

[4213] Prlić's Appeal Brief, para. 606. See Prlić Appeal Brief, para. 423 (under Prlić's ground of appeal 13).

[4214] Prlić's Appeal Brief, para. 606 & fn. 1556, referring to Prlić's Appeal Brief, ground of appeal 13.

1363. The Prosecution responds that there is ample evidence to show that Prlić accepted and facilitated the precarious conditions and mistreatment of detainees in Dretelj Prison.[4215] It avers that the Trial Chamber logically inferred that Prlić facilitated the movement of prisoners from Dretelj Prison to other detention centres or to third countries by failing to take genuine steps to improve detention conditions and/or release detainees.[4216] The Prosecution notes that the evidence on which Prlić relies to show his purported non-involvement in fact underscores his and his Government's failure to use their authority to take appropriate steps to release prisoners.[4217]

1364. The Prosecution also argues that the Trial Chamber did not ignore relevant evidence and took note of evidence of: (1) the 20 September 1993 meeting attended by Prlić relating to the implementation of the joint Tuđman-Izetbegović Declaration; and (2) the ICRC transferring a certain number of detainees following this meeting.[4218] In the Prosecution's view, neither of these pieces of evidence undermines the impugned finding.[4219] It also argues that Prlić cites irrelevant evidence in claiming that Dretelj Prison detainees were transferred based on their "free will" and that, in any case, this argument cannot account for clear contrary evidence.[4220] **[page 553]**

      b. Analysis

1365. At the outset, the Appeals Chamber recalls that it dismisses elsewhere Prlić's general challenges to his overall authority over detention centres.[4221] It therefore turns to Prlić's specific claim that the Trial Chamber erred in finding that the HVO/Government's decision in July 1993 to take measures to improve conditions of detention did not bring about the expected improvements and that detention conditions remained as bad in September 1993. The Appeals Chamber notes that in support of this finding, the Trial Chamber relied on the minutes of HVO HZ(R) H-B meetings held in July and September 1993, the latter of which recorded a conclusion that detention conditions were still bad in September.[4222] It also referred to other evidence in this regard.[4223] Prlić's argument makes no attempt to explain how the Trial Chamber erred in relying on the minutes, ignores the other evidence, and as such amounts to mere assertion.[4224] It is dismissed as such. Further, the Appeals Chamber notes that, contrary to what Prlić suggests, the Trial Chamber did not "impute *de jure* or *de facto* responsibility"[4225] to the HVO/Government of the HZ(R) H-B on the basis of these minutes.[4226] This claim is therefore also dismissed.

1366. With respect to Prlić's claim that the Trial Chamber ignored evidence relevant to the 20 September 1993 meeting in finding that he moved prisoners from Dretelj Prison to other locations, the Appeals Chamber considers that he misrepresents the challenged finding, which is limited to him facilitating their departure to foreign countries through his failure to act.[4227] Further, while the Trial Chamber did not refer to the joint Tuđman-Izetbegović Declaration *per se*,[4228] it relied extensively on a report of the 20 September 1993 meeting of an international organisation, which cited the start of the implementation of this joint Tuđman-Izetbegović Declaration as the reason for such meeting.[4229] Moreover, the Appeals Chamber considers that

---

[4215] Prosecution's Response Brief (Prlić), para. 381. See also Prosecution's Response Brief (Prlić), para. 382; Appeal Hearing, AT. 229-230 (20 Mar 2017).

[4216] Prosecution's Response Brief (Prlić), para. 383. See Appeal Hearing, AT. 228 (20 Mar 2017).

[4217] Prosecution's Response Brief (Prlić), para. 383.

[4218] Prosecution's Response Brief (Prlić), paras 384-385.

[4219] Prosecution's Response Brief (Prlić), paras 384-385.

[4220] Prosecution's Response Brief (Prlić), para. 385.

[4221] See *supra*, paras 1318-1333.

[4222] See Trial Judgement, Vol. 4, paras 241, 244 & fns 598, 603, referring to, *inter alia*, Exs. P03573, P04841, pp. 1-2.

[4223] See Trial Judgement, Vol. 4, paras 241, 244 & fns 598, 603, referring to, *inter alia*, Zoran Buntić, T(F). 30585 (10 July 2008), Andrew Pringle, T(F). 24145-24151, 24155 (6 Nov 2007), Ex. P04863 (confidential). See also Trial Judgement, Vol. 4, para. 245 & fns 605-606, referring to, *inter alia*, Ex. P05219 (confidential).

[4224] Prlić's Appeal Brief, para. 605.

[4225] Prlić's Appeal Brief, para. 605.

[4226] See Trial Judgement, Vol. 4, paras 248-249. The Appeals Chamber also notes that Prlić refers to his submissions in (sub-) grounds of appeal 3 and 16.7, which it dismisses elsewhere in the Judgement. See *supra*, paras 177-183, 1334-1355.

[4227] See Trial Judgement, Vol. 4, para. 249.

[4228] See Ex. P05051.

[4229] See Trial Judgement, Vol. 4, para. 245 & fns 605-608, 610, referring to, *inter alia*, Ex. P05219 (confidential), pp. 1-2.

the Trial Chamber in fact relied on some of the same evidence that Prlić claims was ignored.[4230] The Appeals Chamber also notes that the evidence referred to by Prlić does not support his contention that detainees were **[page 554]** transferred from Dretelj Prison based on their "free will"; in particular, none of the evidence speaks to their consent to being transferred.[4231] Moreover, even if there is some evidence that the ICRC confirmed the release of 516 detainees from Dretelj Prison on medical grounds in September 199 3[4232] and that some were treated as refugees while in transit in Croatia,[4233] Prlić fails to show how this detracts from the challenged finding. Similarly, as to Prlić's claim that neither the HVO HZ-HB nor he were involved "in these matters", the Appeals Chamber recalls that the Trial Chamber found that he facilitated their departure by *failing to act*.[4234] These arguments are dismissed.

1367. For the foregoing reasons, the Appeals Chamber considers that Prlić has failed to demonstrate that the Trial Chamber erroneously concluded that he had power over Dretelj Prison and its detainees and that he accepted the precarious conditions and mistreatment of the detainees.[4235] The Appeals Chamber therefore dismisses Prlić's ground of appeal 13 in part, as well as his sub-ground of appeal 16.9.

(v) Gabela Prison (Prlić's Ground 13 in part and Sub-ground 16.11)

1368. The Trial Chamber found that on 8 June 1993, Prlić, as President of the HVO HZ H-B, officially established Gabela Prison and appointed its warden, and that on 22 December 1993, when he was President of the HR H-B, he officially closed the prison.[4236]

a. Arguments of the Parties

1369. Prlić submits that the Trial Chamber erroneously concluded that he and/or the HVO HZ H-B had power over Gabela Prison and established and closed it.[4237] He contends that the Trial Chamber erroneously concluded that Gabela Prison was established on 8 June 1993 pursuant to his decision, by relying on the HVO HZ H-B decision to set up a County Military Prison and County Prison in Gabela and by ignoring evidence on the difference between detention centres and civilian or military prisons.[4238] He also argues that there is no evidence that the decision **[page 555]** establishing Gabela Prison was in force given that it had not been officially published.[4239] Prlić further submits that the Trial Chamber's conclusion that he or the HVO HZ-HB established and closed Gabela Prison is contrary to its findings that Gabela Prison functioned within the military structure as of April 1993, and that the Gabela authorities implemented Boban's order to close all detention centres by releasing prisoners.[4240] Lastly, Prlić asserts that reports on and information about Gabela Prison were sent to the Office of the HR H-B President and not to him or the Government.[4241]

1370. The Prosecution responds that Prlić fails to show any error in the Trial Chamber's conclusion that he opened and closed Gabela Prison.[4242] With respect to Prlić's argument that his orders did not relate to Gabela Prison, the Prosecution submits that Prlić ignores the testimony of former detainees who identified the

---

[4230] See Trial Judgement, Vol. 4, para. 245 & fns 604 (referring to Ex. P04863 (confidential)), 606-608 (referring to, *inter alia*, Zdravko Sančević, T(F). 28815-28818 (29 May 2008), Adalbert Rebić, T(F). 28312-28313 (20 May 2008), Ex. 1D01936, p. 1).
[4231] See Prlić's Appeal Brief, fn. 1553 and references cited therein.
[4232] See Ex. P05304.
[4233] See Adalbert Rebić, T. 28317 (20 May 2008), 28501-28502 (22 May 2008); Ex. 1D02735.
[4234] See Trial Judgement, Vol. 4, para. 249.
[4235] The Appeals Chamber notes that Prlić refers to his submissions under (sub-)grounds of appeal 12.1, 13, and 16.7.4, which the Appeals Chamber dismisses, in relevant part, elsewhere in the Judgement. See *supra*, paras 1099-1122, 1318-1333, 1344-1351.
[4236] Trial Judgement, Vol. 3, paras 154-158, Vol. 4, para. 251. See also Trial Judgement, Vol. 4, para. 112.
[4237] Prlić's Appeal Brief, paras 414(m), 609.
[4238] Prlić's Appeal Brief, para. 411. See Prlić's Appeal Brief, paras 412-413; Prlić's Reply, para. 64. Prlić adds that the decision was not his and he did not set up a detention centre. Prlić's Appeal Brief, para. 411. Prlić also argues that there is no evidence indicating that Gabela Prison was referred to as the "County Military Prison". Prlić's Appeal Brief, para. 419.
[4239] Prlić's Appeal Brief, para. 419.
[4240] Prlić's Appeal Brief, para. 420. See Prlić's Appeal Brief, para. 416.
[4241] Prlić's Appeal Brief, paras 420, 609. See Prlić's Appeal Brief, para. 610, referring to Prlić's Appeal Brief, (sub-)grounds of appeal 12.1, 13, 16.7, 16.9.
[4242] Prosecution's Response Brief (Prlić), paras 254, 387. See Appeal Hearing, AT. 227 (20 Mar 2017).

warden, whom he had appointed, as the warden of Gabela Prison.[4243] The Prosecution submits that Prlić fails to show that no reasonable trial chamber could conclude that both Boban and Prlić had and exercised the power to close detention facilities.[4244] Further, the Prosecution avers that the facts that Gabela Prison took in detainees as of April 1993, and that Gabela Prison authorities began implementing Boban's order of 10 December 1993 to close all detention centres, do not contradict the Trial Chamber's findings that Prlić officially established Gabela Prison on 8 June 1993 and that he officially closed it on 22 December 1993.[4245] Finally, the Prosecution argues that Prlić's claim that reports relating to Gabela Prison were sent to Boban but not to Prlić or the Government is undercut by his reliance on material generated by his own Government.[4246]

b. Analysis

1371. The Appeals Chamber first turns to Prlić's contention that the Trial Chamber erroneously concluded that Gabela Prison was established on 8 June 1993 pursuant to his decision. First, the Appeals Chamber considers that Prlić has failed to show that no reasonable trier of fact could have relied on, for the impugned finding, the HVO HZ H-B decision, signed by Prlić, to set up a County Military Prison and County Prison in Gabela.[4247] Concerning the allegedly ignored evidence, the **[page 556]** Appeals Chamber recalls that it dismisses elsewhere Prlić's submissions on the difference between detention centres and civilian or military prisons.[4248] Finally, the Appeals Chamber considers that Prlić fails to demonstrate that no reasonable trier of fact could have reasoned that his decision of 22 December 1993 overturning the decisions of 8 June 1993 – establishing Gabela Prison and appointing its warden – indicated, among other evidence, that the 8 June 1993 decision had entered into force.[4249] His arguments are therefore dismissed.

1372. Regarding Prlić's argument that the Trial Chamber's findings on who opened and closed Gabela Prison are contradicted by other findings, the Appeals Chamber considers that neither the findings that Gabela Prison had already begun operating in April 1993 and functioned within the military structure,[4250] nor the finding that the Gabela Prison authorities implemented Boban's order to close all detention centres by releasing prisoners,[4251] detract from the impugned findings that he or the HVO HZ H-B officially established Gabela Prison on 8 June 1993 and officially closed it on 22 December 1993.[4252] His argument is therefore dismissed. Finally, the Appeals Chamber considers that Prlić's claim that reports of and information about Gabela Prison were sent to the Office of the HR H-B President, not to him or the Government, is not inconsistent with his or the Government's specific authority over Gabela Prison as set out in the challenged finding.[4253] His argument in this regard also fails.

1373. For the foregoing reasons, the Appeals Chamber dismisses Prlić's ground of appeal 13 in part, as well as his sub-ground of appeal 16.11.

[4243]   Prosecution's Response Brief (Prlić), para. 255.

[4244]   Prosecution's Response Brief (Prlić), para. 256.

[4245]   Prosecution's Response Brief (Prlić), para. 256.

[4246]   Prosecution's Response Brief (Prlić), para. 387.

[4247]   See Trial Judgement, Vol. 3, para. 154, Vol. 4, para. 251, referring to, *inter alia*, Ex. P02679. With respect to Prlić's claim that there is no evidence that Gabela Prison was referred to as the "County Military Prison", the Appeals Chamber notes that Prlić has failed to demonstrate that no reasonable trier of fact, based on the testimonies of former Gabela Prison detainees who recognised the warden of Gabela Prison, Boško Previšić, Prlić's appointee, could have concluded that the evidence related to Gabela Prison. His argument is therefore dismissed. See Trial Judgement, Vol. 3, paras 236-237, 251, Vol. 4, para. 251 and references cited therein.

[4248]   See *supra*, paras 1321, 1325, 1327.

[4249]   See Trial Judgement, Vol. 3, para. 155. See also Exs. P02674, P02679, P07668.

[4250]   See Trial Judgement, Vol. 3, paras 157, 165-166.

[4251]   See Trial Judgement, Vol. 3, paras 264-265. See also Trial Judgement, Vol. 3, para. 158.

[4252]   See Trial Judgement, Vol. 3, paras 154-158, Vol. 4, para. 251. See also Trial Judgement, Vol. 4, para. 112.

[4253]   See Trial Judgement, Vol. 3, paras 154-158, Vol. 4, para. 251. See also Trial Judgement, Vol. 4, para. 112. The Appeals Chamber notes that Prlić refers to his submissions in (sub-)grounds of appeal 12.1, 13, 16.7, and 16.9, which it dismisses elsewhere in the Judgement. See *supra*, paras 1099-1122, 1318-1367.

(vi) <u>Prlić's facilitation of the departure of detainees to foreign countries via Croatia (Prlić's Sub-ground 16.10)</u>

1374. Prlić claims that the Trial Chamber erroneously concluded that he facilitated the departure of detainees to foreign countries via Croatia.[4254] In this regard, he argues that the Trial Chamber **[page 557]** ignored evidence that under the authority of the ICRC, detainees "voluntarily chose where to be released" to.[4255]

1375. The Prosecution responds that Prlić's reliance on evidence regarding the ICRC does not support the suggestion that he participated in genuinely voluntary departures and that Prlić ignores that detainees had no genuine choice given the extremely harsh conditions of detention to which he contributed.[4256]

1376. The Appeals Chamber has reviewed the evidence Prlić claims the Trial Chamber ignored,[4257] and notes that the Trial Chamber explicitly considered some of it.[4258] The Appeals Chamber therefore dismisses Prlić's argument insofar as this evidence is concerned. As to the remaining evidence, the Appeals Chamber recalls that when a trial chamber does not refer to certain evidence, it is to be presumed that the trial chamber evaluated all the evidence presented to it, as long as there is no indication that the trial chamber completely disregarded evidence which is clearly relevant.[4259] The Appeals Chamber considers that Prlić does not rebut this presumption as he fails to show how the evidence to which he refers undermines the impugned finding.[4260] Thus, the Appeals Chamber finds that he has failed to demonstrate that no reasonable trier of fact could have reached the same conclusion as the Trial Chamber based on the other evidence before it.[4261] Prlić also ignores other relevant factual findings that detainees did not exercise a real choice when they departed to third countries, given their other option was to remain in harsh conditions of detention.[4262] In light of all of the above, Prlić's argument fails, and the Appeals Chamber dismisses his sub-ground of appeal 16.10. **[page 558]**

(h) <u>Denial concealment, and encouragement of crimes and failure to prevent or punish crimes (Prlić's Sub-grounds 16.12, 16.13, 16.14, and 16.15)</u>

1377. The Trial Chamber found that Prlić knowingly sought to minimise or conceal the crimes committed by the HVO in order to facilitate the implementation of the JCE.[4263] The Trial Chamber also found that Prlić through his official and public statements engendered fear, mistrust, and hatred of Bosnian Muslims among Bosnian Croats and exacerbated nationalist sentiments, thus he contributed to the realisation of the JCE.[4264] The Trial Chamber concluded that Prlić denied, concealed, and encouraged the crimes against Muslims and took no appropriate measures to prevent the crimes or punish the perpetrators.[4265] With respect to his ability to do so, the Trial Chamber found that Prlić had the authority and power to intervene within the hierarchy of

---

[4254] Prlić"s Appeal Brief, para. 607.

[4255] Prlić's Appeal Brief, para. 607. See Prlić's Appeal Brief, para. 608, referring to Prlić's Appeal Brief, sub-grounds of appeal 16.4.3, 16.9.

[4256] Prosecution's Response Brief (Prlić), para. 386. The Prosecution further contends that, in any event, the evidence cited by Prlić post-dates the findings of the Trial Chamber and much of it says nothing about detainees exercising any choice with respect to the terms of their departure. Prosecution's Response Brief (Prlić), para. 386.

[4257] See Prlić's Appeal Brief, fn. 1558 and references cited therein. See *infra*, fns 4258-4260.

[4258] See Trial Judgement, Vol. 2, para. 1647, referring to Exs. 1D00938 (ICRC letter dated 7 October 1993), 1D02213 (Official Note Defence Ministry HR H-B dated 7 March 1994).

[4259] See *Tolimir* Appeal Judgement, para. 53; *Kvočka et al.* Appeal Judgement, para. 23.

[4260] The Appeals Chamber notes that the evidence includes a list of detainees wishing to move to third countries (Ex. P07371), Witness Marijan Biškić's testimony that the ICRC representatives were involved in the implementation of the decision to release detainees (Marijan Biškić, T. 15319-15322 (8 Mar 2007)), internal official documents discussing where detainees should go (Exs. P07148, P07149, 6D00499), and an UNPROFOR document reporting Prlić as saying that the wishes of the detainees with regard to their destination on release "including third countries [...] must be strictly honored" (Ex. P06965, p. 3).

[4261] See Trial Judgement, Vol. 4, paras 64, 233-234 and references cited therein. See also Trial Judgement, Vol. 4, para. 249.

[4262] See Trial Judgement, Vol. 3, paras 787, 805, 817, 835, Vol. 4, paras 64, 233 and references cited therein. The Appeals Chamber notes that Prlić refers to his submissions in sub-grounds of appeal 16.4.3 and 16.9, which it dismisses elsewhere in the Judgement. See *supra*, paras 1231-1241, 1360-1367.

[4263] Trial Judgement, Vol. 4, para. 263.

[4264] Trial Judgement, Vol. 4, para. 267.

[4265] Trial Judgement, Vol. 4, para. 269.

the HVO and HR H-B, particularly in relation to the other Appellants, and thus change the course of events.[4266]

(i) Arguments of the Parties

1378. With respect to the Trial Chamber's finding that he knowingly sought to minimise or conceal crimes committed by the HVO, Prlić argues that the Trial Chamber erred by relying only on the testimony of Witness BA, which it mischaracterised.[4267] Prlić further refers to evidence showing his views that evictions were not an official policy, were carried out by "gangster elements", and were contrary to Croat interests.[4268] He also contends that the Trial Chamber ignored evidence that there were "random evictions", which were carried out by irregular forces, and that the Military Police regularly reported these crimes.[4269] Prlić also submits that the Trial Chamber relied on unsubstantiated evidence in concluding that in August 1993 he informed an international representative that Muslims from Ljubuški were being interned for their own safety.[4270]

1379. Prlić further contends that the Trial Chamber erroneously concluded that through his official and public statements, he engendered fear, mistrust, and hatred of Bosnian Muslims among Bosnian Croats and exacerbated nationalist sentiments, and thus contributed to the realisation of the JCE.[4271] Prlić submits in this regard that the Trial Chamber erroneously concluded that a letter of **[page 559]** 18 January 1993 and a proclamation of 30 June 1993 were issued at crucial times and influenced an HVO attack and a campaign of mass arrests of Muslims.[4272] Prlić also contends that the Trial Chamber ignored all of his other statements against population movement and the war.[4273]

1380. Finally, Prlić contends that the Trial Chamber erroneously concluded that despite having the hierarchical power to intervene with respect to members of the JCE he did nothing to prevent crimes and to punish perpetrators.[4274] In this regard he argues that the Trial Chamber failed to establish that he had power over the perpetrators of crimes and that he had the power to intervene within the hierarchy of the HVO and the HZ(R) H-B.[4275] Prlić further argues that the Trial Chamber ignored evidence which was contrary to its conclusion that he did not sincerely condemn crimes, as well as evidence of efforts to prosecute and combat crimes.[4276]

1381. The Prosecution responds that Prlić fails to demonstrate any error.[4277] It argues that the Trial Chamber neither mischaracterised nor relied exclusively on Witness BA's evidence in reaching its conclusion that Prlić denied and concealed crimes against Muslims.[4278] It submits that Prlić cites no relevant evidence in arguing that the Trial Chamber ignored evidence of "random evictions" by "irregular forces" and fails to address the Trial Chamber's findings on systematic eviction operations carried out by the HVO and Prlić's knowledge thereof.[4279] The Prosecution also argues that Prlić fails to show that no reasonable trial chamber could have

[4266] Trial Judgement, Vol. 4, para. 268.
[4267] Prlić's Appeal Brief, para. 612, referring to Prlić's Appeal Brief, sub-ground of appeal 6.1. See also Prlić's Appeal Brief, paras 449, 627-629.
[4268] Prlić's Appeal Brief, para. 612.
[4269] Prlić's Appeal Brief, para. 612.
[4270] Prlić's Appeal Brief, para. 613, referring to, *inter alia*, Prlić's Appeal Brief, paras 187-188 (ground of appeal 6.2). Prlić adds that, even if he did make these remarks, considering the ongoing events, "they were not beyond the ken". Prlić's Appeal Brief, para. 613. See also Prlić's Appeal Brief, para. 614, referring to Prlić's Appeal Brief, (sub-)grounds of appeal 13, 16.7.
[4271] Prlić's Appeal Brief, para. 615. See Prlić's Appeal Brief, para. 616, referring to Prlić's Appeal Brief, sub-grounds of appeal 16.1.2, 16.3.1.
[4272] Prlić's Appeal Brief, para. 617.
[4273] Prlić's Appeal Brief, para. 618. See also Appeal Hearing, AT. 133-134 (20 Mar 2017).
[4274] Prlić's Appeal Brief, paras 611, 619.
[4275] Prlić's Appeal Brief, para. 619. Prlić also argues that the evidence contradicts the Trial Chamber's assumption that he had such powers. Prlić's Appeal Brief, paras 619-620, referring to Prlić's Appeal Brief, grounds of appeal 11-13.
[4276] Prlić's Appeal Brief, paras 621-623. See Appeal Hearing, AT. 145-147 (20 Mar 2017).
[4277] Prosecution's Response Brief (Prlić), para. 389. See Prosecution's Response Brief (Prlić), paras 390-397. See also Prosecution's Response Brief (Prlić), paras 276-279.
[4278] Prosecution's Response Brief (Prlić), para. 390.
[4279] Prosecution's Response Brief (Prlić), para. 391. The Prosecution also submits that Prlić's argument in this regard is contradicted by his prior admission that the evictions were carried out by military authorities with the backing of politicians.

relied on specific evidence that Prlić informed an international representative that Muslims were being interned for their own safety.[4280]

1382. The Prosecution further submits that Prlić fails to articulate any error in the Trial Chamber's conclusion that he publicly incited fear, mistrust, and hatred of Bosnian Muslims among Croats and **[page 560]** that he fails to explain why the evidence he referred to rendered the Trial Chamber's findings unreasonable.[4281]

1383. The Prosecution also submits that Prlić incorrectly claims that the Trial Chamber failed to establish that he had hierarchical powers to prevent and punish crimes, given its detailed findings in this regard.[4282] Finally, the Prosecution argues that Prlić's statements condemning crimes are consistent with the Trial Chamber's finding that, in the majority of cases, he did not sincerely condemn crimes committed by the HVO, and that the evidence he cites does not undermine the Trial Chamber's findings on his failure to take appropriate steps to prevent or punish the mass crimes committed against Muslims.[4283]

   (ii) Analysis

1384. Turning to Prlić's challenge to the Trial Chamber's finding that he knowingly sought to minimise or conceal crimes committed by the HVO, the Appeals Chamber notes that, contrary to Prlić's submission, the Trial Chamber neither mischaracterised[4284] nor relied exclusively on Witness BA's evidence in reaching its conclusion.[4285] The evidence referred to by Prlić, in which he represented that evictions were not an official policy, were carried out by "gangster elements", and were contrary to Croat interests, is not inconsistent with the challenged finding.[4286] His arguments in this regard are therefore dismissed.

1385. Regarding Prlić's challenge that the Trial Chamber ignored evidence that there were "random evictions" which were carried out by irregular forces, the Appeals Chamber notes that he ignores the Trial Chamber findings on the involvement of the HVO in eviction operations and his knowledge of such operations.[4287] Further, with respect to Prlić's submission that the Trial Chamber failed to consider evidence that the Military Police regularly reported the acts allegedly carried out by irregular forces, he has failed to show how his submission is in any way inconsistent with the challenged finding, which concerns crimes carried out by the HVO. His argument is therefore dismissed. **[page 561]**

1386. In addition, Prlić has failed to show that no reasonable trier of fact could have concluded that he informed an international representative in August 1993 that Muslims from Ljubuški were being interned for their own safety. Contrary to his submission, the Appeals Chamber can see no indication that the evidence on which the Trial Chamber relied in reaching this conclusion was unsubstantiated.[4288] His argument is therefore dismissed.

1387. The Appeals Chamber now turns to Prlić's contention that the Trial Chamber erroneously concluded that through his official and public statements, he engendered fear, mistrust, and hatred 0/*-of Bosnian

---

Further, it argues that Prlić mischaracterises the content of reports to imply that evictions were punished and ignores the contrary findings of the Trial Chamber in this regard. Prosecution's Response Brief (Prlić), para. 391.

[4280]   Prosecution's Response Brief (Prlić), para. 392. The Prosecution submits that he also ignores that HVO authorities conducted no case-by-case evaluation of possible safety reasons for detention. Prosecution's Response Brief (Prlić), para. 392.

[4281]   Prosecution's Response Brief (Prlić), para. 393.

[4282]   Prosecution's Response Brief (Prlić), para. 394. The Prosecution contends that Prlić cites evidence that does not undermine his authority and ignores evidence in which he confirmed it to international representatives. Prosecution's Response Brief (Prlić), para. 395.

[4283]   Prosecution's Response Brief (Prlić), paras 396-397.

[4284]   See Trial Judgement, Vol. 4, para. 259 & fn. 633 and references cited therein. The Appeals Chamber also notes that Prlić refers to his submissions in sub-ground of appeal 6.1, which it dismisses elsewhere in the Judgement. See *supra*, paras 212-218.

[4285]   Trial Judgement, Vol. 4, paras 259-263 and references cited therein.

[4286]   Prlić's Appeal Brief, para. 612, referring to, *inter alia*, Exs. P09712 (confidential), para. 73, P09846 (confidential).

[4287]   See Trial Judgement, Vol. 2, paras 815, 822-823, 876, 900, 919-920, 985-987, Vol. 4, paras 166-171, 259. *See supra*, paras 1231-1241.

[4288]   See Trial Judgement, Vol. 4, para. 260, referring to, *inter alia*, Ex. P09846 (confidential), Witness BB, T(F). 17284-17286 (closed session) (17 Apr 2007). The Appeals Chamber dismisses as obscure Prlić's argument that these remarks "were not beyond the ken". The Appeals Chamber also notes that Prlić refers to his submissions in (sub-)grounds of appeal 6.2, 13, and 16.7, which it dismisses elsewhere in the Judgement. See *supra*, paras 212-218, 1318-1373.

Muslims among Bosnian Croats and exacerbated nationalist sentiments, and thus contributed to the realisation of the JCE.[4289] Considering the letter of 18 January 1993 and the proclamation of 30 June 1993 referred to by Prlić, the Appeals Chamber notes that he merely asserts that the Trial Chamber erroneously reached a conclusion as to the meaning and effect of this evidence, but fails to articulate an error in this regard. Regarding Prlić's contention that the Trial Chamber ignored his statements against population movement and the war, the Appeals Chamber notes that it is clear from the Trial Judgement that the Trial Chamber expressly considered some of the evidence to which Prlić refers.[4290] With respect to other evidence, Prlić merely asserts that the Trial Chamber must have failed to consider it, but fails to show any relevance of this evidence[4291] or that the Trial Chamber did not consider it. In this regard, the Appeals Chamber recalls that the Trial Chamber need not refer to every witness testimony or every piece of evidence on the record and that there is a presumption that the trial chamber evaluated all evidence presented to it, as long as there is no indication that the Trial Chamber completely disregarded evidence which is clearly relevant.[4292] The Appeals Chamber finds that this is not the case here, noting that the Trial Chamber considered similar evidence.[4293] His argument is therefore dismissed. **[page 562]**

1388. With respect to Prlić's submission that the Trial Chamber erroneously concluded that despite having the hierarchical power to intervene with respect to members of the JCE, he did nothing to prevent crimes and to punish perpetrators, the Appeals Chamber notes that the Trial Chamber made general findings on Prlić's powers, to which it referred, and which support its conclusion that he had such hierarchical powers.[4294] Prlić merely asserts that the Trial Chamber did not establish these hierarchical powers, but fails to show that no reasonable trier of fact, based on the evidence, could have reached the same conclusion.[4295] His argument therefore fails.

1389. While Prlić refers to evidence in which he condemned crimes,[4296] the Appeals Chamber notes that this evidence is not inconsistent with the Trial Chamber's conclusion that in the majority of cases he did not sincerely condemn the crimes committed by the HVO.[4297] In addition, Prlić fails to show how the evidence he cites, which refers to some measures taken to prosecute and combat crimes,[4298] undermines the Trial Chamber's conclusion that *he* took no appropriate measures to prevent crimes or punish the perpetrators of those crimes.[4299] The Appeals Chamber notes that Prlić does not identify any such appropriate measures that he took and recalls that it has upheld the Trial Chamber's finding that he had the authority and power to intervene within the hierarchy of the HVO and HR H-B and thus change the course of events.[4300] Prlić has failed to show that no reasonable trier of fact, based on the evidence, could have reached the conclusion that he took no appropriate measures to prevent crimes or punish the perpetrators of those crimes. In light of the above; the Appeals Chamber dismisses the argument that the Trial Chamber ignored evidence which was contrary to its conclusion that he did not sincerely condemn crimes, as well as evidence of efforts to prosecute and combat crimes.

[4289] The Appeals Chamber notes that Prlić refers to his submissions in sub-grounds of appeal 16.1.2 and 16.3.1, which it dismisses elsewhere in the Judgement. *See supra*, paras 1154-1161, 1209-1210, 1214, 1216, 1221.

[4290] See, *e.g.*, Prlić's Appeal Brief, fns 1576-1581, referring to, *inter alia*, Exs. P01015, P01215, 1D01655, 1D02189. See also Trial Judgement, Vol. 1, fn. 1073, Vol. 2, fns 944, 3410, Vol. 3, fn. 463, Vol. 4, paras 15, 109 & fns 37, 200, 325-328, 368, 393-394.

[4291] See, *e.g.*, Prlić's Appeal Brief, fns 1577-1578, 1580-1581, referring to, *inter alia*, Exs. P00672, P02046, P02124.

[4292] *Kvočka et al.* Appeal Judgement, paras 23-24, See also *Tolimir* Appeal Judgement, paras 53, 161, 299; *Popović et al.* Appeal Judgement, paras 925, 1017.

[4293] See Prlić's Appeal Brief, fns 1576-1581, referring to, *inter alia*, Exs. P00578, P00921, P01317, P02021, P06510, 1D00190, 1D00193, 1D00818, 1D02076, 1D02078, 1D02123, 1D02124, 1D02149, 1D02225, 1D02379, Belinda Giles, T. 2061-2062, 2064-2073 (15 May 2006), Witness DZ, T. 26689 (23 Jan 2008), T. 26701-26704, 26716 (24 Jan 2008), Prlić's Opening Statement, T. 27555 (6 May 2008), Borislav Puljić, T. 32126-32131 (15 Sept 2008), T. 32238-32241 (16 Sept 2008), Miroslav Palameta, T. 32789-32790 (2? Sept 2008), Neven Tomić, T. 34677-34688 (17 Nov 2008).

[4294] Trial Judgement, Vol. 4, para. 268 & fn. 654, referring to Trial Judgement, Vol. 4, paras 84-121.

[4295] Prlić's Appeal Brief, paras 619-620. The Appeals Chamber notes that Prlić refers to his submissions in grounds of appeal 11, 12, and 13, which it dismisses elsewhere in the Judgement. See *supra*, paras 1021-1127, 1318-1333, 1335-1343, 1356-1373.

[4296] See Prlić's Appeal Brief, fns 1585-1588, 1595 and references cited therein.

[4297] Trial Judgement, Vol. 4, para. 268.

[4298] See Prlić's Appeal Brief, fns 1589-1594, 1596 and references cited therein. See also Appeal Hearing, AT. 146 (20 Mar 2017), referring to, *inter alia*, Exs. 5D05024, 5D05027.

[4299] Trial Judgement, Vol. 4, paras 268-269 and references cited therein.

[4300] See *supra*, paras 1377, 1388.

1390. For the foregoing reasons, the Appeals Chamber dismisses Prlić's sub-grounds of appeal 16.12, 16.13, 16.14, and 16.15.

(i) *Mens rea* and *actus reus* of commission through a JCE (Prlić's Ground 18)

1391. The Trial Chamber found that: (1) Prlić made a significant contribution to, and was one of the "principal members" of, the JCE; (2) his contribution showed his intention to implement the **[page 563]** CCP; and (3) he shared with the other members of the JCE a discriminatory intent to expel the Muslim population from the HZ(R) H-B ,[4301]

(i) Arguments of the Parties

1392. Prlić submits that the Trial Chamber erred in law and fact in concluding that he possessed the requisite *mens rea* for membership in the JCE and that he carried out the *actus reus* of the JCE.[4302] He asserts that an omission may only constitute a contribution to a JCE if it is combined with a duty to act and authority over the perpetrators.[4303] Prlić argues that the Trial Chamber "essentially applied a strict liability standard", finding him responsible by virtue of his position and the continued exercise of his functions.[4304] Prlić further submits that the Trial Chamber erroneously interpreted "legislative decisions in light of subsequent events" and found that by participating in drafting those decisions, he intended the crimes.[4305] Prlić refers to a number of conclusions reached by the Trial Chamber relating to his *mens rea*, which in his submission are "premised on erroneous inferences from selective evidence, ignoring other relevant evidence and alternative plausible explanations".[4306] Prlić further submits that the Trial Chamber failed to consider evidence regarding his mental state and ignored several relevant factors, namely his: (1) Government service in BiH from 1989 to 2003 based on free democratic elections; (2) understanding of the HZ H-B as forming part of a tri-national BiH; (3) negotiation efforts at the end of 1993 to find a solution for Mostar; (4) ideas for the future of BiH; (5) aims for the HVO HZ H-B; (6) efforts to prevent crimes and punish perpetrators; and (7) non-membership in the Croatian Democratic Union during the Indictment period.[4307] Prlić concludes that he should be acquitted on Counts 1-25.[4308]

1393. The Prosecution responds that the Trial Chamber did not apply a strict liability standard or find Prlić responsible simply by virtue of his position and the continued exercise of his **[page 564]** functions.[4309] The Prosecution avers that the Trial Chamber found that Prlić made active contributions to each of the assessed crime bases and that his contributions through omissions complemented his active conduct.[4310] It further contends that Prlić's suggestion that his omissions could not constitute contributions to the CCP is based on

---

[4301] Trial Judgement, Vol. 4, para. 276.

[4302] Prlić's Appeal Brief, paras 642, 646, 650. Specifically, Prlić alleges that by ignoring evidence and alternative plausible explanations, the Trial Chamber failed to provide reasoned opinions and applied an incorrect legal standard in assessing the evidence, amounting to an error of law invalidating the Trial Judgement. Prlić's Appeal Brief, para. 650. Prlić also contends that no reasonable trier of fact would find that he assumed the risk of reasonably foreseeable crimes being committed outside the alleged JCE. Prlić's Appeal Brief, para. 650.

[4303] Prlić's Appeal Brief, para. 643. See Prlić's Appeal Brief, para. 648.

[4304] Prlić's Appeal Brief, para. 646; Prlić Reply Brief, para. 76. See also Prlić's Appeal Brief, paras 643-645.

[4305] Prlić's Appeal Brief, para. 646-647, referring to, *inter alia, Gotovina and Markač* Appeal Judgement, paras 93-98; Prlić Reply Brief, para. 76.

[4306] Prlić's Appeal Brief, para. 648, referring to, *inter alia,* Prlić's Appeal Brief, (sub-)grounds of appeal 6.1, 10, 11, 16.1-16.15, 17.

[4307] Prlić's Appeal Brief, para. 649, referring to, *inter alia,* Prlić's Appeal Brief, sub-grounds of appeal 16.12-16.15; Appeal Hearing, AT. 135-136, 138 (20 Mar 2017). See also Appeal Hearing, AT. 134, 139 (20 Mar 2017). Prlić argues that the Trial Chamber failed to take into account that he took measures in order to set up effective organs of authority in BiH "with the intent of applying international plan of construction of a normal Bosnia-Herzegovina, attempting to include third parties in this". Appeal Hearing, AT. 138 (20 Mar 2017).

[4308] Prlić's Appeal Brief, para. 651. See also Appeal Hearing, AT. 173, 177-178 (20 Mar 2017).

[4309] Prosecution's Response Brief (Prlić), paras 400-401. It contends that Prlić fails to demonstrate that no reasonable trial chamber could have relied on his continued exercise of his functions as a relevant factor in inferring intent or as a fact relevant to his failure to use his authority to intervene. Prosecution's Response Brief (Prlić), para. 401.

[4310] Prosecution's Response Brief (Prlić), paras 400, 407.

an erroneous premise that he did not have actual powers which would trigger a duty to act.[4311] The Prosecution argues that Prlić's mere assertion that the Trial Chamber interpreted legislative decisions in light of subsequent events should be summarily dismissed.[4312] The Prosecution also submits that Prlić wrongly claims that the Trial Chamber found that he intended crimes based only on his participation in drafting legislative decisions.[4313] Lastly, the Prosecution avers that Prlić did not establish that the Trial Chamber failed to consider any evidence which was relevant to his mental state, instead listing factors that: (1) he fails to explain; (2) bear no apparent relevance to his *mens rea;* and/or (3) the Trial Chamber did consider.[4314]

(ii) Analysis

1394. The Appeals Chamber interprets Prlić's statement that an omission may only constitute a contribution to a JCE if it is combined with a duty to act and authority over the perpetrators as an allegation that the Trial Chamber erred in law in this regard. The Appeals Chamber recalls that "when establishing an accused's participation in a joint criminal enterprise through his failure to act, the existence of a legal duty to act deriving from a rule of criminal law is not required".[4315] The Appeals Chamber further recalls that a failure to act has been taken into account in assessing an accused's contribution to a joint criminal enterprise and intent, where the accused had some power and influence or authority over the perpetrators to prevent or halt the abuses, but failed to exercise such powers.[4316] The existence of such influence or authority is a factual matter to be determined on a case-by-case basis.[4317] The Appeals Chamber notes that Prlić advances no factual challenge to his **[page 565]** authority over the perpetrators under the present ground of appeal.[4318] The Appeals Chamber concludes that Prlić has failed to establish an error of law and dismisses his argument.

1395. Regarding Prlić's argument that the Trial Chamber erred by essentially applying a "strict liability" standard, finding him responsible by virtue of bis position and the continued exercise of his functions, the Appeals Chamber notes that the Trial Chamber properly articulated the requisite *mens rea* for JCE I liability, which is "the intent to commit a specific crime, an intent that must be shared by all the co-participants".[4319] Applying this standard, the Trial Chamber found that Prlić shared with the other members of the JCE a discriminatory intent to expel the Muslim population from the HZ(R) H-B.[4320] Prlić's position and continued exercise of his functions were only two of several factors assessed by the Trial Chamber which led it to conclude that he significantly contributed to, and shared the intent of, the JCE.[4321] Other factors included his actions, his contemporaneous knowledge of crimes committed, his attempts at minimising or concealing such crimes, and his failure to stop or prevent such crimes when he had the *de jure* and/or *de facto* power to do so.[4322] Further, the Appeals Chamber finds that Prlić fails to demonstrate that no reasonable trier of fact could have relied on the relevant factors of his position and continued exercise of his functions in its

---

[4311] Prosecution's Response Brief (Prlić), para. 408. In this regard, the Prosecution notes that the Trial Chamber found that his failure to prevent and punish crimes was a culpable omission given bis hierarchical authority and power to intervene and that Prlić's duties were grounded in international law and in HZ(R) H-B legislation. Prosecution's Response Brief (Prlić), paras 408-409.

[4312] Prosecution's Response Brief (Prlić), para. 402.

[4313] Prosecution's Response Brief (Prlić), para. 403. The Prosecution further submits that having mischaracterised the Trial Chamber's method of analysis, Prlić's attempt to draw an analogy to the method used by the *Gotovina et al.* trial chamber should be summarily dismissed. Prosecution's Response Brief (Prlić), para. 404.

[4314] Prosecution's Response Brief (Prlić), paras 400, 405-406.

[4315] *Stanišić and Župljanin* Appeal Judgement, para. 110. See *Popović et al.* Appeal Judgement, para. 1653; *Šainović et al.* Appeal Judgement, para. 985; *Krajišnik* Appeal Judgement, paras 215, 695-696; *Brđanin* Appeal Judgement, para. 427; *Stakić* Appeal Judgement, para. 64; *Kvočka et al.* Appeal Judgement, para. 99; *Tadić* Appeal Judgement, para. 227.

[4316] *Stanišić and Župljanin* Appeal Judgement, para. 752.

[4317] *Stanišić and Župljanin* Appeal Judgement, para. 752.

[4318] See, in particular, Prlić's Appeal Brief, paras 648-649. See also *infra,* paras 1397-1398.

[4319] Trial Judgement, Vol. 1, para. 214, referring to, *inter alia, Vasiljević* Appeal Judgement, para. 101, *Tadić* Appeal Judgement, paras 196, 228.

[4320] Trial Judgement, Vol. 4, para. 276.

[4321] Regarding Prlić's position and continued exercise of his functions, see Trial Judgement, Vol. 4, paras 134, 147, 165, 168, 174, 204, 232, 238, 249, 270-276.

[4322] See Trial Judgement, Vol. 4, paras 121, 134, 147, 165, 168, 174, 185, 204, 232, 238, 249, 263, 269-275. Insofar as the Trial Chamber relied on Prlić's contemporaneous knowledge of crimes committed (see Trial Judgement, Vol. 4, paras 134, 147, referring to January and April 1993), the Appeals Chamber recalls that it has overturned the Trial Chamber's findings regarding the deaths of seven civilians in Duša. See *supra,* paras 441-443. The Appeals Chamber does not consider that these changes affect the Trial Chamber's reasoning and conclusion, insofar as it concerns the remaining crimes, that he significantly contributed to, and shared the

assessment. In this respect, the Appeals Chamber also recalls that the fact that the participation of an accused amounted to no more than his or her routine duties will not exculpate the accused – what matters is whether the act in question furthered the CCP and whether it was carried out with the requisite intent.[4323] Prlić's argument is therefore dismissed.

1396. Regarding Prlić's submission that the Trial Chamber erred in interpreting "legislative decisions in light of subsequent events", the Appeals Chamber considers Prlić's reliance on the *Gotovina and Markač* Appeal Judgement to be inapposite, as the majority of the Appeals Chamber in that case did not find that the trial chamber erred by interpreting evidence in light of subsequent events; rather, having reversed the trial chamber's findings with regard to those subsequent events, the Majority found that the trial chamber's interpretation of the evidence in question was no longer **[page 566]** the only reasonable one.[4324] The Appeals Chamber also considers that in the present case the Trial Chamber inferred Prlić's *mens rea* from his contribution after assessing the totality of the evidence, not merely from "legislative decisions".[4325] His submission is therefore dismissed.

1397. With regard to Prlić's claim that the Trial Chamber's findings on his *mens rea* were premised on erroneous inferences from selective evidence, ignoring other relevant evidence and alternative plausible explanations, the Appeals Chamber notes that this claim is entirely based on cross-references to his (sub-) grounds of appeal 6.1, 10, 11, 16.1-16.15, and 17, which it dismisses elsewhere.[4326]

1398. With respect to Prlić's submission that the Trial Chamber failed to consider evidence regarding his mental state, the Appeals Chamber observes that the Trial Chamber in fact relied on some of the evidence Prlić indicates,[4327] and considers that he fails to substantiate the relevance of the factors which he lists.[4328] The submission is dismissed.

1399. Having rejected the arguments above, the Appeals Chamber considers that Prlić has failed to demonstrate that the Trial Chamber erred in concluding that he possessed the requisite *mens rea* for membership in the JCE and that he carried out the *actus reus* of the JCE.[4329] The Appeals Chamber therefore dismisses Prlić's ground of appeal 18.

4. Conclusion

1400. In light of the foregoing, the Appeals Chamber dismisses all challenges to the Trial Chamber's findings related to Prlić's contribution to, and his *mens rea* for, the JCE. The Appeals Chamber recalls, however, that it reverses above the Trial Chamber's finding – insofar as it **[page 567]** concerns the Old Bridge – that Prlić knew about the HVO crimes committed during the HVO campaign of fire and shelling

---

intent of, the JCE, based on, *inter alia*, this contemporaneous knowledge, particularly since not many instances of murder took place in that period. See *supra*, para. 876.

[4323] *Stanišić and Župljanin* Appeal Judgement, para. 154. See also *Stanišić and Župljanin* Appeal Judgement, paras 182, 244.

[4324] *Gotovina and Markač* Appeal Judgement, para. 93. See *Gotovina and Markač* Appeal Judgement, paras 91-92, 94-98.

[4325] See Trial Judgement, Vol. 4, paras 122-276.

[4326] See *supra*, paras 212-218, 1021-1097, 1146-1317, 1334-1390, 2837-2848.

[4327] See Trial Judgement, Vol. 4, paras 109 (concerning Prlić's role in ceasefire negotiations in Mostar), 932 (regarding Prlić's efforts to fight crime). See also Trial Judgement, Vol. 4, para. 75. *Cf.* Prlić's Appeal Brief, para. 649.

[4328] With regard to Prlić's submission that he took measures in order to set up effective organs of authority in BiH "with the intent of applying international plan of construction of a normal Bosnia-Herzegovina, attempting to include third parties in this", the Appeals Chamber notes that the Trial Chamber considered similar submissions at trial. See Trial Judgement, Vol. 4, para. 75 & fn. 186, referring to Prlić's Final Brief, paras 316, 332. The Appeals Chamber finds that this explanation of the relevance to his intent does not demonstrate an error in the Trial Chamber's finding on his *mens rea*, based on its detailed analysis of his position, actions, contemporaneous knowledge of crimes committed (see also *supra*, fn. 4322), attempts at minimising or concealing such crimes, failure to stop or prevent such crimes when he had the power to do so, and continued exercise of his functions. See, in particular, *supra*, paras 1391, 1395 & fns 4321-4322 and references cited therein; *infra*, para. 1400. With regard to the remaining factors advanced, Prlić does not even attempt to explain their relevance. See *supra*, para. 1392 & fn. 4307, referring to, *inter alia*, Prlić's Appeal Brief, para. 649. The Appeals Chamber also notes that Prlić refers to his submissions in sub-grounds of appeal 16.12, 16.13, 16.14, and 16.15, which it dismisses elsewhere in the Judgement. See *supra*, paras 1377-1390.

[4329] Regarding Prlić's contention that no reasonable trier of fact would find that he assumed the risk of reasonably foreseeable crimes being committed outside the alleged JCE, see 2837-2848.

against East Mostar and that by minimising or attempting to deny them, he accepted and encouraged them.[4330] **[page 568]**

F.   Alleged Errors in Relation to Bruno Stojić's Participation in the JCE

1.   Introduction

1401.   Bruno Stojić was appointed the Head of the Department of Defence within the HZ(R) H-B Government on 3 July 1992 and exercised the functions of the position until 15 November 1993, after which he was the head of the department for the production of military equipment.[4331] The Trial Chamber found that Stojić contributed to the JCE from January 1993 to 15 November 1993,[4332] and concluded that his contribution was significant.[4333] The Trial Chamber concluded that Stojić was one of the most important JCE members as he controlled the HVO and the Military Police, and served as the link between the HVO and the Government.[4334] The Trial Chamber also found that Stojić used the HVO, including the Military Police to commit crimes that formed part of the CCP.[4335] It made several findings concerning Stojić's contributions to the JCE including, *inter alia*, that: (1) he had significant *de jure* and *de facto* powers over most components of the HVO and the Military Police, which he exercised by taking decisions related to military operations and having those decisions implemented through the armed forces' chain of command, forwarding Government decisions down the armed forces' chain of command, and making proposals to the Government about military matters which were approved;[4336] (2) he continued to exercise effective control knowing that HVO members had committed crimes;[4337] (3) he made no serious efforts to stop the HVO and the Military Police from committing crimes;[4338] and (4) he participated in some HVO military operations in the municipalities.[4339]

1402.   The Trial Chamber convicted Stojić under Article 7(1) of the Statute of committing, pursuant to JCE I liability, various crimes amounting to grave breaches of the Geneva Conventions, violations of the laws or customs of war, and/or crimes against humanity under Articles 2, 3, and 5 of the Statute, respectively.[4340] Stojić was sentenced to a single sentence of 20 years of imprisonment.[4341] **[page 569]**

[4330]   See *supra*, para. 1246.

[4331]   Trial Judgement, Vol. 1, paras 555-557, Vol. 4, paras 293, 325, 425, 1227. See Trial Judgement, Vol. 1, paras 539-554, 558-584.

[4332]   Trial Judgement, Vol. 4, paras 1227, 1230.

[4333]   Trial Judgement, Vol. 4, para. 429.

[4334]   Trial Judgement, Vol. 4, paras 425, 429.

[4335]   Trial Judgement, Vol. 4, paras 429, 1232.

[4336]   Trial Judgement, Vol. 4, paras 304, 312, 425. The Appeals Chamber interprets that where the Trial Chamber stated that Stojić "forwarded HVO decisions down the chain of command and made proposals to the HVO about military matters which were then approved by that collective body" (see Trial Judgement, Vol. 4, para. 425), it referred to the political component of the HVO, *i.e.* the "Government".

[4337]   Trial Judgement, Vol. 4, paras 425-426. See Trial Judgement, Vol. 4, para. 429.

[4338]   Trial Judgement, Vol. 4, para. 427.

[4339]   Trial Judgement, Vol. 4, paras 426, 430.

[4340]   Trial Judgement, Vol. 4, paras 431-432, Disposition, p. 430. These crimes are: persecution as a crime against humanity (Count 1); murder as a crime against humanity (Count 2); wilful killing as a grave breach of the Geneva Conventions (Count 3); deportation as a crime against humanity (Count 6); unlawful deportation of civilians as a grave breach of the Geneva Conventions (Count 7); inhumane acts (forcible transfer) as a crime against humanity (Count 8); unlawful transfer of a civilian as a grave breach of the Geneva Conventions (Count 9); imprisonment as a crime against humanity (Count 10); unlawful confinement of a civilian as a grave breach of the Geneva Conventions (Count 11); inhumane acts (conditions of confinement) as a crime against humanity (Count 12); inhuman treatment (conditions of confinement) as a grave breach of the Geneva Conventions (Count 13); inhumane acts as a crime against humanity (Count 15); inhuman treatment as a grave breach of the Geneva Conventions (Count 16); unlawful labour as a violation of the laws or customs of war (Count 18); extensive destruction of property, not justified by military necessity and carried out unlawfully and wantonly, as a grave breach of the Geneva Conventions (Count 19); destruction or wilful damage done to institutions dedicated to religion or education as a violation of the laws or customs of war (Count 21); unlawful attack on civilians as a violation of the laws or customs of war (Count 24); and unlawful infliction of terror on civilians as a violation of the laws or customs of war (Count 25). The Trial Chamber found that the following crimes also fell within the framework of the JCE, meaning Stojić was also responsible for them, but did not enter convictions for them based on the principles relating to cumulative convictions: cruel treatment (conditions of confinement) as a violation of the laws or customs of war (Count 14); cruel treatment as a violation of the laws or customs of war (Count 17); and wanton destruction of cities, towns, or villages, or devastation not justified by military necessity (Count 20). See Trial Judgement, Vol. 4, para. 68, Disposition, p. 430. See also Trial Judgement, Vol. 4, paras 1260-1266. The Appeals Chamber discusses Stojić's convictions pursuant to JCE III *infra*, paras 2833-2834, 2849-2880.

[4341]   Trial Judgement, Vol. 4, Disposition, p. 430.

1403. Regarding Stojić's *mens rea* under JCE I liability, the Trial Chamber concluded that he: (1) intended the crimes committed in the various municipalities,[4342] at times inferring his intent from his failure to make any serious efforts to stop the HVO and the Military Police from committing crimes;[4343] (2) shared the intent to expel the Muslim population from the territory of Herceg-Bosna with other JCE members;[4344] and (3) intended to discriminate against Muslims in order to facilitate their eviction from the territory of Herceg-Bosna.[4345]

1404. Stojić challenges several findings of the Trial Chamber with regard to his contribution to the JCE and his *mens rea*.[4346] These challenges will be addressed below.

2. Alleged errors in finding that Stojić commanded and had "effective control" over the HVO (Stojić's Ground 20)

1405. The Trial Chamber was satisfied beyond reasonable doubt that Stojić, as Head of the Department of Defence, commanded and had "effective control" over the HVO.[4347] In coming to this conclusion, the Trial Chamber considered that Stojić: (1) played a fundamental role in the establishment and organisation of the HVO;[4348] (2) was regularly informed of the military operations conducted by the HVO;[4349] (3) was the member of the HZ(R) H-B Government in charge of informing it about the military operations;[4350] (4) had the authority to send military-related **[page 570]** Government decisions through the military chain of command and used that authority;[4351] (5) had the authority to issue orders directly to the HVO and to ensure that they were carried out, which he used;[4352] (6) received reports from the HVO Military Intelligence Service ("VOS") on a daily basis;[4353] (7) was responsible for all the logistical and financial aspects as well as the human resources of the HVO;[4354] and (8) had the authority to designate representatives of the HVO in peace negotiations.[4355] The Trial Chamber also found that Stojić made proposals about defence which were then adopted by the Government.[4356]

1406. Stojić contends that the Trial Chamber erred by finding that he commanded and had effective control over the HVO.[4357] Specifically, he: (1) asserts that the Trial Chamber erroneously inferred that he had "effective operational authority" over the HVO from evidence that he had "limited administrative competences"; and (2) further challenges some of the underlying findings.[4358]

(a) Stojić's administrative and logistical roles in the HVO

1407. Stojić argues that the Trial Chamber erroneously inferred that he had "effective operational authority" over the HVO from evidence that he had "limited administrative competences" or logistical functions.[4359]

[4342]   Trial Judgement, Vol. 4, para. 426.
[4343]   Trial Judgement, Vol. 4, para. 427.
[4344]   Trial Judgement, Vol. 4, para. 428.
[4345]   Trial Judgement, Vol. 4, para. 429.
[4346]   Stojić's Appeal Brief, paras 122-126, 139-369.
[4347]   Trial Judgement, Vol. 4, para. 312. See Trial Judgement, Vol. 4, paras 425-429.
[4348]   Trial Judgement, Vol. 4, paras 299, 312.
[4349]   Trial Judgement, Vol. 4, paras 300, 302, 312.
[4350]   Trial Judgement, Vol. 4, paras 300, 312, 425.
[4351]   Trial Judgement, Vol. 4, paras 304-305, 312, 425.
[4352]   Trial Judgement, Vol. 4, paras 306, 312, 425.
[4353]   Trial Judgement, Vol. 4, paras 301, 312.
[4354]   Trial Judgement, Vol. 4, paras 308-310, 312.
[4355]   Trial Judgement, Vol. 4, paras 311-312.
[4356]   Trial Judgement, Vol. 4, paras 300, 425. The Appeals Chamber interprets the Trial Chamber's finding that Stojić "made proposals about defence which were then adopted by the HVO" (see Trial Judgement, Vol. 4, para. 300), as a reference to the political component of the HVO or, in other words, the Government.
[4357]   Stojić's Appeal Brief, paras 139-140, 146, 166. Stojić avers that this finding is the basis for the Trial Chamber's findings that he had the necessary intent and that he significantly contributed to the JCE. Stojić's Appeal Brief, paras 139, 166.
[4358]   Stojić's Appeal Brief, paras 139-140, 146, 166. The Appeals Chamber notes that Stojić does not directly challenge, under this ground of appeal, the Trial Chamber's finding that he was regularly informed of the military operations conducted by the HVO or that he received reports from the VOS on a daily basis.
[4359]   Stojić's Appeal Brief, paras 140-141, 145.

Specifically, Stojić contends that the Trial Chamber failed to properly distinguish the functions of a civilian administrator from the command of combat operations.[4360] He asserts that the Trial Chamber "entirely disregarded" his qualifications and experience, which did not include combat experience.[4361] Stojić also argues that the functions of the Department of Defence were limited to administrative and logistical matters, which is demonstrated by the Trial Chamber's findings and the fact that no operational order was signed by him alone.[4362] He also submits that the Trial Chamber, disregarding its previous conclusions, failed to distinguish between **[page 571]** substantive and administrative competences in relation to his power of appointment as he merely administered appointments initiated by others.[4363] Stojić further argues that "only operational command can justify the vital conclusions that [he] directly participated in specific operations and 'used' the armed forces to commit crimes".[4364]

1408. The Prosecution responds that Stojić fails to show an error, and argues that the Trial Chamber considered and rejected his argument that he was a mere civilian administrator.[4365] It submits that Stojić's "logistical and administrative competencies as [Department of Defence] Head strengthened his control over the HVO armed forces by giving him authority over, *inter alia*, arming, financing and human resource matters, all factors indicative of his effective control".[4366]

1409. The Appeals Chamber will first address Stojić's more specific challenges. Regarding Stojić's qualifications and experience, the Appeals Chamber notes that the Trial Chamber did summarise bis background leading up to his appointment as Head of the Department of Defence.[4367] Regardless, Stojić fails to show that his alleged lack of operational experience was so relevant to the Trial Chamber's determination of his role and conduct during the JCE period that a consideration of the same would have had an impact on any of the Trial Chamber's findings. Further, the Trial Chamber considered Stojić's arguments at trial that his role in appointments was purely administrative,[4368] but still found that the Head of the Department of Defence: (1) appointed, and removed from office, brigade commanders and high-ranking officers;[4369] (2) had the power to appoint officers within the HVO brigades up to and including the rank of Deputy Brigade Commander;[4370] and (3) appointed deputy commanders for security in the OZs and in the brigades on the advice of the deputy chief for security of the Department of Defence.[4371] Stojić relies on the latter finding to argue that his role was purely administrative,[4372] but fails to provide any further **[page 572]** support. The Appeals Chamber finds that Stojić fails to call into question the Trial Chamber's findings on his power to make appointments. His arguments are dismissed.

1410. The Appeals Chamber now turns to Stojić's overarching challenge that "effective operational authority" cannot be inferred from administrative and logistical functions. The Appeals Chamber first notes that the Trial Chamber did not find that Stojić had "effective operational authority".[4373] Rather, it found that

---

[4360]   Stojić's Appeal Brief, para. 141. See Stojić's Appeal Brief, paras 142-145; Stojić's Reply Brief, para. 37.
[4361]   Stojić's Appeal Brief, para. 142. Stojić submits that it is "inconceivable that a man with no operational experience could have the authority to issue operational orders". Stojić's Appeal Brief, para. 142.
[4362]   Stojić's Appeal Brief, para. 143, referring to Trial Judgement, Vol. 1, paras 544, 565, Vol. 4, paras 304-305, 308-310, 312, *Orić* Trial Judgement, para. 312.
[4363]   Stojić's Appeal Brief, para. 144, referring to Trial Judgement, Vol. 1, paras 571-575, 577-578, Vol. 4, para. 303.
[4364]   Stojić's Reply Brief, para. 37 (internal references omitted).
[4365]   Prosecution's Response Brief (Stojić), para. 106, referring to, *inter alia*, Trial Judgement, Vol. 1, para. 557, Vol. 4, paras 295, 409. The Prosecution also asserts that the fact that Stojić made some appointments on the advice of others does not undermine the Trial Chamber's finding that he exercised the power to appoint officers in the HVO brigades, or suggests that his role was "purely administrative". Prosecution's Response Brief (Stojić), para. 126.
[4366]   Prosecution's Response Brief (Stojić), para. 106 (internal references omitted), referring to *Nahimana et al.* Appeal Judgement, para. 606, *Blaškić* Trial Judgement, para. 522, *Musema* Trial Judgement, para. 880.
[4367]   Trial Judgement, Vol. 4, para. 293.
[4368]   Trial Judgement, Vol. 1, para. 568.
[4369]   Trial Judgement, Vol. 1, para. 571.
[4370]   Trial Judgement, Vol. 1, para. 573, Vol. 4, para. 303.
[4371]   Trial Judgement, Vol. 1, para. 575, Vol. 4, para. 303.
[4372]   In arguing that the Trial Chamber found that "he only made appointments on the advice of others, his role was appointing or 'consenting] to' appointments" (see Stojić's Appeal Brief, para. 144), Stojić refers to findings on his involvement in appointing staff within the SIS and the Military Police Administration, the Deputy Chief of the Main Staff as well as its assistant chiefs, and the heads of Defence administration in the municipalities. See Trial Judgement, Vol. 1, paras 574-575, 577-578. The Appeals Chamber finds that Stojić fails to show that this involvement is inconsistent with the Trial Chamber's finding on his power to make appointments.
[4373]   *Contra* Stojić's Appeal Brief, para. 140.

Stojić "commanded and had effective control over the HVO armed forces".[4374] Moreover, the Trial Chamber was not required to find that Stojić had "effective operational authority".[4375] The Appeals Chamber recalls that the *actus reus* for liability under JCE I is the participation of the accused in the common criminal plan which may take the form of assistance in, or contribution to, the execution of this plan,[4376] and that this contribution to the crimes is significant.[4377] Whether an accused significantly contributed to a JCE is a matter of evidence.[4378] Thus, conduct pursuant to an "administrative" or "logistical" function can be a factor in determining whether Stojić's contribution to the JCE was significant.[4379] Stojić provides no support for his argument that only "operational command", which he does not define, can justify the conclusion that he participated in operations and used the HVO and the Military Police to commit crimes and thus significantly contributed to the JCE.[4380]

1411. Moreover, the Appeals Chamber rejects Stojić's contention that his functions were limited to "administrative" and "logistical" matters. To the contrary, the Trial Chamber considered that Stojić, *inter alia:* (1) ordered the mobilisation of Croatian conscripts and imposed a curfew in the HZ H-B;[4381] (2) issued an order to units in charge of the Military Police checkpoints in Mostar **[page 573]** instructing them to check all vehicles leaving the town;[4382] (3) issued orders directly to the HVO, particularly with regard to ceasefires, the detention centres, the freedom of movement of humanitarian or international organisations, and the mobilisation and reinforcement of HVO troops;[4383] (4) ordered a commanding officer to allow the passage of UNPROFOR convoys in the Central Bosnia Operating Zone ("Central Bosnia OZ") on 23 February 1993;[4384] and (5) ordered Miro Andrić, a colonel in the Main Staff, to capture the Gornji Vakuf area by the use of force, which resulted in crimes.[4385]

1412. Further, the Appeals Chamber considers that Stojić interprets the Trial Chamber's finding that he "commanded and had effective control" over the HVO as a finding that he had "effective operational authority" or "effective operational control".[4386] On this issue, the Appeals Chamber considers that "commanded" necessarily means that Stojić had sufficient influence and authority over the HVO so as to be able to control its members effectively.[4387] Thus, Stojić does not demonstrate that the influence and authority

---

[4374] See *supra*, para. 1405. See also Trial Judgement, Vol. 4, paras 326 ("Stojić had effective control over the activities of the components of the HZ(R) H-B armed forces"), 426 (Stojić "continued to exercise effective control over the armed forces"). Stojić challenges the underlying findings that the Trial Chamber relied on in coming to this conclusion, and the Appeals Chamber dismisses these challenges below. See *infra*, paras 1414-1415, 1418-1419, 1422-1423, 1427-1435, 1441-1453, 1456.

[4375] See also *infra*, paras 1528-1530.

[4376] *Popović et al.* Appeal Judgement, para. 1615; *Krajišnik* Appeal Judgement, para. 695; *Stakić* Appeal Judgement, para. 64; *Tadić* Appeal Judgement, para. 227(iii).

[4377] *Popović et al.* Appeal Judgement, para. 1378; *Krajišnik* Appeal Judgement, para. 706; *Brđanin* Appeal Judgement, para. 430. See *Popović et al.* Appeal Judgement, para. 1653; *Šainović et al.* Appeal Judgement, para. 1445; *Krajišnik* Appeal Judgement, para. 695 ("It is sufficient that the accused 'perform acts that in some way are directed to the furthering' of the JCE in the sense that he significantly contributes to the commission of the crimes involved in the JCE" (internal references omitted)).

[4378] See *Krajišnik* Appeal Judgement, para. 696 ("Beyond that, the law does not foresee specific types of conduct which *per se* could not be considered a contribution to the common purpose. Within these legal confines, the question of whether the accused contributed to a JCE is a question of fact to be determined on a case-by-case basis").

[4379] See *Popović et al.* Appeal Judgement, paras 1544-1545 (in considering Radivoje Miletić's "technical" role in the UNPROFOR convoy notification procedure, the Appeals Chamber concluded that "[w]hether an act is 'technical' does not *per se* preclude it from being a contribution to a JCE").

[4380] Stojić's Appeal Brief, paras 139-141, 145, 166; Stojić's Reply Brief, para. 37.

[4381] Trial Judgement, Vol. 4, para. 305, referring to Ex. P03038. See *infra*, para. 1422.

[4382] Trial Judgement, Vol. 4, para. 316, referring to Ex. P02578.

[4383] Trial Judgement, Vol. 4, para. 306, referring to Exs. P00610, P00619, P05232, P05235, 4D00461. See also Trial Judgement, Vol. 1, para. 795, referring to Ex. P01316. See *infra*, para. 1429.

[4384] Trial Judgement, Vol. 1, para. 562, referring to Ex. 2D00984.

[4385] Trial Judgement, Vol. 4, paras 330, 334, referring to Ex. 4D00348. See *infra*, paras 1565-1569. In addition, the Trial Chamber found, *inter alia*, that Stojić: (1) ordered all the HZ H-B MUP military units in Mostar to be re-subordinated on 2 July 1993 (see Trial Judgement, Vol. 2, para. 703); and (2) issued orders directly to the HVO, including for the immediate halt of offensive operations against the ABiH in April 1993 (see Trial Judgement, Vol. 1, para. 562, referring to Ex. P02093).

[4386] See Trial Judgement, Vol. 4, para. 312; Stojić's Appeal Brief, paras 140-141.

[4387] See *Stanišić and Župljanin* Appeal Judgement, paras 111, 734 (a failure to intervene to prevent recurrence of crimes or to halt abuses has been taken into account in assessing an accused's contribution to a joint criminal enterprise and his intent "where the accused had some power and influence or authority over the perpetrators sufficient to prevent or halt the abuses but failed to exercise such power").

he obtained by his direct control over the human, financial, and logistical resources of the HVO[4388] cannot be considered as a factor in determining his command authority.[4389] Notably, Stojić's command authority was not based only on his administrative and logistical functions.[4390] Stojić's argument that the Trial Chamber erroneously inferred his command authority from, *inter alia,* his administrative or logistical functions is dismissed.

(b) Stojić's role in the establishment and organisation of the HVO

1413.   Stojić submits that the Trial Chamber's finding that he played a fundamental role in the establishment and organisation of the HVO is unsupported by the evidence, *i.e.* Exhibit P00646, **[page 574]** and contradicted by the fact that the Main Staff and the HVO existed prior to his appointment.[4391] The Prosecution responds that the Trial Chamber's finding is supported by Exhibit P00646,[4392] and that Stojić's role in creating the Main Staff as well as evidence on its organisation was considered.[4393]

1414.   The Appeals Chamber first notes that the Trial Chamber was aware that the HVO and the Main Staff existed as of April 1992,[4394] whereas Stojić was appointed as the Head of the Department of Defence on 3 July 1992.[4395] However, the Trial Chamber considered that while there was a chief of the Main Staff as early as April 1992, "the structure of the Main Staff was not officially introduced until September 1992"[4396] and that it was not until the "close of 1992" that the HVO developed its structure.[4397] Consistent with these observations, the Trial Chamber noted that on 15 September 1992, Mate Boban issued a decision establishing the overall structure of the Main Staff,[4398] and that on 18 September 1992, Stojić announced its provisional establishment.[4399] Moreover, the Trial Chamber considered that between September 1992 and November 1993, Stojić participated in approximately 40 Government sessions and meetings at which legislation including, *inter alia,* the amended decree on the HVO, was adopted.[4400] The Appeals Chamber therefore considers that Stojić fails to show how the fact that the Main Staff and the HVO existed before his appointment could have impacted on the Trial Chamber's findings on his role in their establishment and organisation.

1415.   Additionally, in making its finding, the Trial Chamber considered that on 24 October 1992 Stojić prepared an operations programme for the HVO which "explained the structure of the various components of the armed forces, including the Military Police, and set the objectives and the work plan for each of them".[4401] The Trial Chamber relied on Exhibit P00646 in which the operations programme for the Military Police was set out and it was noted that the operations programme for **[page 575]** the Main Staff was attached.[4402] Thus, considering the above,[4403] the Appeals Chamber is not convinced by Stojić's contention

---

[4388]   Trial Judgement, Vol. 4, paras 308, 312. See *infra,* paras 1414-1415, 1418, 1422-1423, 1427-1435, 1441-1453, 1456.

[4389]   See *Nahimana et al.* Appeal Judgement, para. 606. See also *Blaškić* Trial Judgement, para. 522; *Musema* Trial Judgement, para. 880.

[4390]   See *supra,* para. 1410.

[4391]   Stojić's Appeal Brief, para. 147; Stojić's Reply Brief, para. 39. Stojić contends that the only evidence relied on by the Trial Chamber – Exhibit P00646 – contains no targets, objectives, or work plans, and is irrelevant to the establishment of the armed forces. Stojić's Appeal Brief, para. 147; Stojić's Reply Brief, para. 39.

[4392]   Prosecution's Response Brief (Stojić), paras 107-108.

[4393]   Prosecution's Response Brief (Stojić), para. 109, referring to, *inter alia,* Trial Judgement, Vol. 1, paras 711-712, fn. 1668. The Prosecution also submits that the Trial Chamber was aware that the Main Staff was in existence prior to the issuance of Exhibit P00646. Prosecution's Response Brief (Stojić), para. 109.

[4394]   The Trial Chamber noted that Petković became Chief of the Main Staff in April 1992 and that the "HVO armed forces spontaneously organised on the territory of the HZ H-B" during the first half of 1992. Trial Judgement, Vol. 1, paras 715, 780, Vol. 4, para. 651. These dates are consistent with the evidence cited by Stojić to support his contention that the Main Staff and HVO existed prior to his appointment. Stojić's Appeal Brief, fn. 373; Ex. 1D02716; Ex. P00154.

[4395]   Trial Judgement, Vol. 4, para. 293.

[4396]   Trial Judgement, Vol. 1, para. 715.

[4397]   Trial Judgement, Vol. 1, para. 780.

[4398]   Trial Judgement, Vol. 1, para. 711.

[4399]   Trial Judgement, Vol. 1, para. 712.

[4400]   Trial Judgement, Vol. 4, para. 297. See *infra,* paras 1509-1513.

[4401]   Trial Judgement, Vol. 4, para. 299, referring to Ex. P00646.

[4402]   Ex. P00646, pp. 1-2. Exhibit P00646 also states that the operations programme for the SIS "was specially developed and as such [would] be presented by the chief of the Defence Department". Ex. P00646, p. 1.

[4403]   See *supra,* paras 1414-1415.

that the Trial Chamber's finding was unsupported. Stojić fails to show that no reasonable trier of fact could have concluded, on the basis of this evidence and the Trial Chamber's findings, that he played a fundamental role in the establishment and organisation of the HVO. His arguments are dismissed.

(c) Stojić's responsibility to inform the HZ(R) H-B Government of military operations and to make proposals which were adopted

1416. Stojić asserts that there is no basis for the Trial Chamber's finding that he informed the Government about the military situation and made proposals about defence which were adopted.[4404] He argues that the evidence the Trial Chamber analysed – concerning the events in Gornji Vakuf in January 1993 and in Vareš in October 1993 – merely shows that he reported on issues that were already well-known and that no decisions resulted from his reports.[4405] Specifically, he asserts that: (1) his 19 January 1993 report on the situation in Gornji Vakuf repeated the contents of reports that had already been received by the Government;[4406] and (2) a 4 November 1993 decision by the Government that the ODPR would be responsible for refugees from Vareš was based on information sent by the ODPR that it was already working on refugee services in the area, rather than on information provided by Stojić.[4407] Stojić contends that any instructions issued in the remaining evidence cited related to "purely administrative matters".[4408]

1417. The Prosecution responds that, in addition to reports on the Gornji Vakuf and Vareš events, the minutes of other Government meetings show that Stojić regularly informed the Government of the military and security situation, and that decisions were made based on those briefings.[4409] **[page 576]**

1418. The Appeals Chamber notes that in finding that Stojić "informed the [Government] – both through reports and during [Government] sessions – about the military and security situation on the ground and made proposals about defence which were then adopted by the [Government]",[4409] the Trial Chamber not only analysed Stojić's reports of events in Gornji Vakuf and Vareš,[4410] but also relied on the minutes of numerous meetings at which Stojić briefed the Government on military and security situations.[4411] Turning to Stojić's specific challenges, the Appeals Chamber notes that the Trial Chamber relied on Exhibit 1D02179 which is the minutes of the 4 November 1993 meeting at which the Government took a decision to continue

---

[4404] Stojić's Appeal Brief, para. 148, referring to Trial Judgement, Vol. 4, para. 300. The Appeals Chamber interprets that where the Trial Chamber stated that Stojić "informed the HVO – both through reports and during HVO sessions – about the military and security situation on the ground and made proposals about defence which were then adopted by the HVO", (see Trial Judgement, Vol. 4, para. 300), it was referring to the political component of the HVO, *i.e.* the Government.

[4405] Stojić's Appeal Brief, paras 148-149, referring to, *inter alia*, Exs. P01227, P01206, P01197, p. 4, 1D01354; Stojić's Reply Brief, para. 42.

[4406] Stojić's Appeal Brief, para. 148, referring to Trial Judgement, Vol. 4, para. 300, Exs. P01227, P01206, P01197, p. 4.

[4407] Stojić's Appeal Brief, para. 149, referring to Trial Judgement, Vol. 4, para. 300, Ex. 1D02179.

[4408] Stojić's Appeal Brief, para. 149, referring to Exs. 1D01609, P01197, 1D01667, 1D01610, 1D01608, P00518, 2D00851, 4D00508, P05799, P05769.

[4409] Trial Judgement, Vol. 4, para. 300. See Trial Judgement, Vol. 4, paras 312, 425. The Appeals Chamber interprets that where the Trial Chamber stated that Stojić "informed the HVO – both through reports and during HVO sessions – about the military and security situation on the ground and made proposals about defence which were then adopted by the HVO" (Trial Judgement, Vol. 4, para. 300), it is referring to the political component of the HVO, which is referred to as the Government by the Appeals Chamber.

[4410] Trial Judgement, Vol. 4, para. 300.

[4411] Trial Judgement, Vol. 4, fn. 707, citing Exs. P01197, p. 4 (the Government sent encouragement to the HVO and Croatian population in Gornji Vakuf on the basis of a report on the military situation submitted by the Department of Defence during a meeting attended by Stojić), P01227, pp. 1-2 (Stojić reported on the situation in Gornji Vakuf and that Muslim forces were being depicted in a positive light and proposed that measures be taken to counter misinformation in the media), 1D01609, pp. 1-2 (Government decisions were made after Stojić's involvement in discussions on the implementation of the Vance-Owen Plan, recruitment, and materiel shortages), 1D01667, p. 2 (Stojić reported about the military and security situation in the HZ H-B), 1D01610, pp. 1-2 (a draft decision on troop mobilisation submitted by the Department of Defence was adopted, and Stojić reported on the military and security situation in Central Bosnia), 1D01608, pp. 1-3 (Stojić reported about the current military and security situation in the HZ H-B), 4D00508, p. 1, P05769/P05799, p. 2 (Stojić, along with Praljak and Petković, submitted a report on the military and security situation and warned of the harmful consequences of inconsistent implementation of regulations on the combat readiness and morale of the soldiers, after which the Government issued a decision for consistent implementation), 2D00851, pp. 1, 3 (Stojić gave a report on the military situation highlighting the shortage of materiel and technical equipment and made proposals which were upheld by the Government), P00518 (report from Stojić on Department of Defence activities including, *inter alia*: (1) drafting documents for the functioning of the department such as the Decree on the Treatment of Persons Captured in Armed Conflicts in the HZ H-B and Regulations on Military Discipline; (2) dividing the military into OZs; (3) forming brigades; and (4) establishing training centres).

measures to protect displaced Croats after a briefing of the military situation in Vareš given by Stojić.[4412] Stojić's assertion that the ODPR had previously reported to the Government that it was working with refugees in Vareš does not call into question the Trial Chamber's reliance on this exhibit to support its finding, in particular that Stojić informed the Government about the military and security situation on the ground.[4413] Moreover, Stojić's assertion that he "merely reported on issues that were already well-known"[4414] does not undermine the Trial Chamber's finding that he was the member of the Government responsible for informing it of military operations, and in fact did so. His argument in relation to the Trial Chamber's reliance on his 19 January 1993 report on the situation in Gornji Vakuf is therefore also dismissed.

1419. Moreover, the Appeals Chamber notes, in particular, that the Trial Chamber relied on Exhibit 2D00851, the minutes of a 15 June 1993 Government meeting, at which Stojić gave a report on the military situation in the territory of the HZ H-B highlighting the shortage of materiel and **[page 577]** technical equipment. Notably, at this meeting Stojić made proposals which were upheld by the Government.[4415] Stojić's assertion that there is no basis for the Trial Chamber's finding that he made proposals about defence which were adopted is, therefore, dismissed. To the extent that Stojić argues that his reports and proposals concerned "purely administrative issues", the Appeals Chamber recalls its finding that he has not shown that an administrative role cannot evidence command authority.[4416] Thus, Stojić fails to show an error and the Appeals Chamber dismisses his arguments.

(d) Stojić's authority to send military-related Government decisions through the military chain of command

1420. Stojić challenges the Trial Chamber's reliance on him forwarding Government decisions to the Main Staff,[4417] as the three orders it cited show that he forwarded them within his administrative competence.[4418] Specifically, Stojić submits that he forwarded one order only as an "administrative conduit"[4419] and that the other two orders were co-signed by him because they contained administrative or logistical matters.[4420] He argues that forwarding decisions made by others does not amount to effective control.[4421] Stojić asserts that reliance on orders that he merely co-signed was misplaced as they do not prove that he, as opposed to the other signatory, had effective control.[4422]

1421. The Prosecution responds that the Trial Chamber reasonably relied on evidence showing that Stojić did not just "forward decisions", but also enforced military-related Government decisions on matters beyond administration and logistics.[4423] **[page 578]**

1422. The Trial Chamber, in analysing Stojić's role within the military chain of command, recalled that "as Head of the Department of Defence, Bruno Stojić forwarded [the] decisions of the Government of the HZ

[4412] Trial Judgement, Vol. 4, fn. 707, citing Ex. 1D02179, pp. 1-2.
[4413] Trial Judgement, Vol. 4, para. 312.
[4414] Stojić's Appeal Brief, para. 148.
[4415] Ex. 2D00851, pp. 1, 3.
[4416] See *supra*, paras 1410-1412. See also *supra*, para. 1401.
[4417] Stojić's Appeal Brief, paras 143, 150, referring to Trial Judgement, Vol. 4, paras 304-305.
[4418] Stojić's Appeal Brief, paras 143, 150, referring to Exs. P01140, P03038, P03128; Stojić's Reply Brief, para. 40. Stojić argues that he was unable to issue operational orders. Stojić's Appeal Brief, para. 150.
[4419] Stojić's Appeal Brief, para. 150, referring to Ex. P01140.
[4420] Stojić's Appeal Brief, para. 150, referring to Exs. P03038, P03128.
[4421] Stojić's Appeal Brief, paras 143, 150.
[4422] Stojić's Reply Brief, para. 38.
[4423] Prosecution's Response Brief (Stojić), paras 110-113. The Prosecution submits, as examples, that: (1) Stojić implemented the 15 January 1993 Ultimatum by ordering ABiH units to subordinate to the HVO, and rather than merely acting as an "administrative conduit", he instructed that he personally receive reports every eight hours (Prosecution's Response Brief (Stojić), para. 111, referring to Trial Judgement, Vol. 4, para. 304, Exs. P01140, P01146); (2) in June 1993, Stojić implemented the 30 June 1993 Joint Proclamation by ordering mobilisation and imposing a curfew (Prosecution's Response Brief (Stojić), para. 112, referring to Trial Judgement, Vol. 4, para. 305, Ex. P03038); and (3) in July 1993, Stojić and Petković ordered HVO units to carry out tasks "with the aim of eliminating" Muslim troops in the South-East OZ, and there is no indication that Stojić signed the order strictly due to logistical tasks within it (Prosecution's Response Brief (Stojić), para. 113, citing Ex. P03128). The Prosecution argues that Exhibits P01140 and P03128 are combat orders that exemplify Stojić's authority over military operations. Prosecution's Response Brief (Stojić), para. 114.

H-B to the HVO Main Staff which then forwarded them to the commanders of the units deployed on the ground to implement them."[4424] In this regard, the Trial Chamber considered a chain of orders in which Stojić was instructed to implement a decision issued by Prlić that certain ABiH units subordinate themselves to the HVO, Stojić ordered the Main Staff and the Military Police Administration to carry out Prlić's decision, and Petković forwarded Stojić's order to the commanders of the OZs.[4425] The Trial Chamber further noted that following the 30 June 1993 Joint Proclamation from Prlić and Stojić in relation to defending against ABiH attacks: (1) Stojić, as Head of the Department of Defence, ordered the mobilisation of Croatian conscripts and imposed a curfew in the HZ H-B, after which Ćorić issued a further implementation order;[4426] and (2) Stojić and Petković co-signed an order on 2 July 1993 to all HVO units in the South-East OZ to "eliminate" the Muslim troops in the area.[4427] Thus, the Appeals Chamber is not convinced by Stojić's contention that he merely forwarded Government decisions as an "administrative conduit".[4428] Notably, in Stojić's order for the implementation of Prlić's decision, he also ordered that chiefs of the Main Staff and the Military Police Administration would be responsible to him regarding the implementation of his order.[4429] The Appeals Chamber considers that a reasonable trier of fact could have concluded that these orders cited by the Trial Chamber show that Stojić not only forwarded them, but also implemented and enforced Government orders.[4430]

1423. The Appeals Chamber is also not convinced by Stojić's submission that he merely co-signed some of the orders as he does not show that any authority his co-signatories had precludes him from also having authority.[4431] Moreover, the Appeals Chamber dismisses elsewhere Stojić's argument that an administrative role cannot evidence command authority.[4432] Therefore, Stojić fails to demonstrate that the Trial Chamber unreasonably considered his role in forwarding and implementing Government decisions as a relevant factor in determining his command authority over the HVO. His arguments are dismissed. **[page 579]**

(e) Stojić's authority to issue orders directly to the HVO and to ensure that they were carried out

(i) Arguments of the Parties

1424. Stojić argues that the Trial Chamber unreasonably found that he could issue operational orders to the HVO and ensure they were carried out.[4433] Stojić submits that the Trial Chamber erred by disregarding previous relevant conclusions to the contrary, including its findings that: (1) the Head of the Department of Defence was not *de jure* part of the military chain of command;[4434] (2) only "administrative and technical tasks" were assigned to the Department of Defence;[4435] (3) the "classic" chain of command proceeded through the Main Staff;[4436] (4) the "few occasions" on which Stojić issued orders did not "upset the proper functioning of the military chain of command";[4437] (5) the Main Staff was the pivotal link in the chain of command;[4438] and (6) key parts of the armed forces – the VOS and the Anti-Terrorist Groups ("ATGs") – were not *de jure* within the Department of Defence.[4439] He also asserts that the orders cited by the Trial

---

[4424]   Trial Judgement, Vol. 4, para. 304.
[4425]   Trial Judgement, Vol. 4, para. 304, referring to, *inter alia*, Exs. P01146, P01140, P01139.
[4426]   Trial Judgement, Vol. 4, para. 305, referring to Exs. P03038, P03077.
[4427]   Trial Judgement, Vol. 4, para. 305, referring to Ex. P03128.
[4428]   Stojić's Appeal Brief, para. 150.
[4429]   Ex. P01140, pp. 1-2.
[4430]   See Trial Judgement, Vol. 4, para. 425 ("Stojić took decisions related to military operations and had them implemented through the armed forces' chain of command", and "forwarded HVO decisions down the chain of command".).
[4431]   See Ex. P03038 (co-signed by Prlić); Ex. P03128 (co-signed by Petković).
[4432]   See *supra*, para. 1412. See also *supra*, para. 1401.
[4433]   Stojić's Appeal Brief, para. 151.
[4434]   Stojić's Appeal Brief, para. 152, referring to Trial Judgement, Vol. 4, para. 306.
[4435]   Stojić's Appeal Brief, para, 152, referring to Trial Judgement, Vol. 1, para. 559.
[4436]   Stojić's Appeal Brief, para. 152, referring to Trial Judgement, Vol. 1, para. 791.
[4437]   Stojić's Appeal Brief, para. 152, referring to Trial Judgement, Vol. 1, para. 796.
[4438]   Stojić's Appeal Brief, para. 152, referring to Trial Judgement, Vol. 1, para. 708.
[4439]   Stojić's Appeal Brief, para. 152, referring to Trial Judgement, Vol. 4, paras 301, 307; Stojić's Reply Brief, para. 40. Stojić also asserts that the SIS did not send regular reports to the Department of Defence. Stojić's Appeal Brief, para. 152, referring to Trial Judgement, Vol. 4, para. 302.

Chamber were confined to mostly logistical matters, were not combat orders, and do not demonstrate that he had overall authority.[4440]

1425. Stojić further contends that the conclusion that he issued orders on specified topics is unsupported by the evidence cited.[4441] He specifically asserts that: (1) Exhibit P00610 is a report sent by Ćorić to the HVO generally without referring to any order issued by Stojić and was not addressed to him; (2) of the orders relating to mobilisation, namely Exhibits P05232 and P05235, only one was signed by him but was corrected and signed by Praljak; (3) Exhibit P00582 is an order to withdraw stamps which is an administrative activity; (4) Exhibit 4D00461 is "inauthentic and unreliable"; and (5) Exhibits P02292 and P03026 were merely requests for instructions addressed to Stojić and Petković without any evidence that Stojić responded.[4442] Stojić also argues that the Trial Chamber erroneously relied on Article 30 of the Amended Decree Regarding the Armed Forces of 17 October 1992 ("Amended 3 July 1992 Decree on the Armed Forces"), which indicates that certain command responsibilities could be delegated to the Head of the Department of Defence, **[page 580]** because no such delegation occurred.[4443] He further contends that no evidence was cited to support the finding that he could ensure that his orders were carried out[4444] and that the Trial Chamber disregarded its own conclusions that orders he issued were not followed.[4445]

1426. The Prosecution responds that Stojić issued orders to the HVO and could ensure their compliance. It argues that: (1) the Trial Chamber found that Stojić issued orders on a range of matters;[4446] (2) Stojić's challenges to the Trial Chamber's reliance on certain orders issued by him are unpersuasive;[4447] and (3) regardless of whether Boban formally delegated command responsibilities under Article 30 of the Amended 3 July 1992 Decree on the Armed Forces, Stojić did issue orders directly to the HVO, thus demonstrating his command authority.[4448] The Prosecution contends that Stojić merely offers his own interpretation of the evidence without showing an error.[4449]

(ii) Analysis

1427. The Trial Chamber was satisfied that the "evidence showed that even though the Head of the Department of Defence was not *de jure* part of the military chain of command, Bruno Stojić, as head of that department, did issue orders directly to the HZ(R) H-B armed forces".[4450] Stojić challenges this conclusion by asserting that the Trial Chamber disregarded its own previous relevant conclusions.[4451] In this respect, the Appeals Chamber first notes that Stojić is overly broad in asserting that the Trial Chamber found that *"only* 'administrative and technical tasks' were assigned to the [Department of Defence]".[4452] In fact, the Trial Chamber merely observed that "administrative and logistical tasks" were assigned to the Department of Defence by Article 10 of the Amended 3 July 1992 Decree on the Armed Forces, but did not suggest that these were the "only" tasks performed by the Department of Defence.[4453] Stojić ignores the Trial Chamber's subsequent analysis which considered the authority held by the Head of the Department of Defence beyond Article 10 of the Amended 3 July 1992 Decree on the Armed Forces. In particular, it considered that, theoretically, the President of the HZ H-B could delegate certain command responsibilities to the Head of the Department of Defence and that several orders from Stojić **[page 581]** addressed directly to the HVO had

---

[4440]   Stojić's Appeal Brief, para. 153; Stojić's Reply Brief, para. 41.
[4441]   Stojić's Appeal Brief, paras 153-154, referring to Trial Judgement, Vol. 4, para. 306 ("Stojić [...] did issue orders [...] particularly with regard to the ceasefires, the detention centres, the troop movements, the reorganisation of the military units, the assignment of the troops as reinforcements for other units, freedom of movement of humanitarian or international organisations and the mobilisation of HVO troops").
[4442]   Stojić's Appeal Brief, para. 154.
[4443]   Stojić's Appeal Brief, para. 157, referring to Trial Judgement, Vol. 1, para. 562, Vol. 4, para. 306.
[4444]   Stojić's Appeal Brief, para. 155, referring to Trial Judgement, Vol. 2, para. 2081, Vol. 4, para. 1039.
[4445]   Stojić's Appeal Brief, para. 155, referring to Trial Judgement, Vol. 2, para. 2081, Vol. 4, paras 480, 1039.
[4446]   Prosecution's Response Brief (Stojić), paras 115-117.
[4447]   Prosecution's Response Brief (Stojić), paras 118-119, referring to Stojić's Appeal Brief, para. 154.
[4448]   Prosecution's Response Brief (Stojić), para. 120.
[4449]   Prosecution's Response Brief (Stojić), paras 142-143.
[4450]   Trial Judgement, Vol. 4, para. 306. See Trial Judgement, Vol. 1, para. 565.
[4451]   Stojić's Appeal Brief, paras 151-152.
[4452]   Stojić's Appeal Brief, para. 152 (emphasis added).
[4453]   Trial Judgement, Vol. 1, para. 559, referring to Ex. P00588, Art. 10, p. 3.

been admitted into evidence.[4454] Thus, Stojić fails to show that the Trial Chamber later disregarded this observation, and his argument is dismissed. Moreover, the Appeals Chamber has already found that Stojić has not demonstrated that an administrative or logistical role cannot evidence command authority.[4455] Therefore, Stojić does not show that the Trial Chamber erroneously considered his orders on logistical matters as an indicator of his control authority. Stojić's argument is dismissed.

1428. Turning to Stojić's submissions in relation to the Trial Chamber's findings on the functioning of the HVO's chain of command,[4456] the Appeals Chamber notes that while the Trial Chamber held that "the classic chain of command of the armed forces proceeded from the Main Staff, which was in direct contact with the OZs, which directed the HVO brigades",[4457] it specifically found that exceptions occurred whereby Stojić issued orders directly to the OZs and brigade commanders.[4458] Further, Stojić takes the Trial Chamber's finding that it Was "incontrovertible that orders intended for the armed forces customarily flowed through the chain of command, whose pivotal link was the Main Staff"[4459] out of context. In making this finding, the Trial Chamber was addressing an assertion that Boban "bypassed" the Main Staff "when it suited him" to issue orders directly to the HVO.[4460] In this context, the Trial Chamber again noted that while orders "customarily flowed" through the Main Staff, there were exceptions whereby orders were transmitted directly to the HVO without going through the Main Staff.[4461] The Appeals Chamber therefore considers that Stojić fails to show how the Trial Chamber's finding that the Main Staff was the pivotal link within the military chain of command undermines the Trial Chamber's finding that Stojić had the authority to issue orders directly to the HVO. Moreover, Stojić does not substantiate his assertion that the Trial Chamber's findings that the VOS and ATGs were not within the hierarchy of the Department of Defence and that the SIS did not send regular reports to the Department of Defence are inconsistent with the finding that Stojić issued orders to the HVO.[4462] Stojić's arguments are thus dismissed.

1429. The Appeals Chamber will now turn to Stojić's challenges to the Trial Chamber's reliance on certain evidence in finding that he issued orders directly to the HVO, "particularly with regard to the ceasefires, the detention centres, the troop movements, the reorganisation of the military units, the assignment of the troops as reinforcements for other units, freedom of movement of **[page 582]** humanitarian or international organisations and the mobilisation of HVO troops".[4463] The Appeals Chamber notes that Exhibit P00610, a report by Ćorić to the HVO, indicates that troop movements had been implemented "[b]y order from the head of the Defence Department".[4464] The Appeals Chamber further notes that Exhibit P05232 is an order signed by Stojić not only for immediate mobilisation of forces "following the incursion of MOS /Muslim armed forces/ terrorist groups", but also for the mobilised forces to be used to "eliminate the infiltrated terrorist groups without compromise".[4465] The content of this order signed by Stojić is almost identical to that of Exhibit P05235 issued on the same day by Praljak.[4466] In challenging the Trial Chamber's reliance on this order, Stojić asserts that Exhibit P05235 shows that it was Praljak, not him, who had operational command.[4467] However, the Appeals Chamber notes that not only does Praljak's order state that it was being issued "with regard to the Order from the Head of the Defence Department",[4468] but also that Praljak testified that he issued his order "immediately pursuant" to Stojić's order.[4469] Praljak's testimony that he made a correction

---

[4454] Trial Judgement, Vol. 1, paras 560-565. See *infra*, para. 1433.
[4455] See *supra*, para. 1412. See also *supra*, para. 1401.
[4456] See *supra*, para. 1424.
[4457] Trial Judgement, Vol. 1, para. 791.
[4458] Trial Judgement, Vol. 1, para. 795. See Trial Judgement, Vol. 1, paras 562, 565, Vol. 4, para. 306.
[4459] Trial Judgement, Vol. 1, para. 708.
[4460] Trial Judgement, Vol. 1, paras 701, 704, 708.
[4461] Trial Judgement, Vol. 1, para. 708.
[4462] See Stojić"s Appeal Brief, para. 152.
[4463] Trial Judgement, Vol. 4, para. 306. See Stojić's Appeal Brief, para. 154.
[4464] Ex. P00610, p. 1. *Contra* Stojić's Appeal Brief, para. 154.
[4465] Ex. P05232, p. 1.
[4466] Ex. P05235 (stating that the mobilised forces are to be used to "destroy, in an uncompromising manner, the MOS terrorist groups that have infiltrated /the area/").
[4467] Stojić's Appeal Brief, para. 154.
[4468] Ex. P05235, p. 1.
[4469] Slobodan Praljak, T. 42081 (25 June 2009).

to Stojić's original order[4470] does not undermine the Trial Chamber's finding in relation to Stojić's authority to issue such orders.[4471]

1430. The Appeals Chamber further notes that in Exhibit P00582, Zdravko Šagolj, commander of the Herceg Stjepan Brigade, noted that he had acted "[i]n line with orders issued verbally by Mr. Bruno STOJIĆ".[4472] Stojić's assertion that this order is "a clear example of administrative activity",[4473] does not satisfy the Appeals Chamber that the Trial Chamber erred in relying on it to find that Stojić issued orders directly to the HVO.[4474] Finally, by only cross-referencing another ground of appeal, Stojić does not show that the Trial Chamber erred in relying on Exhibit 4D00461.[4475] Thus, considering the above, Stojić fails to show that no reasonable trier of fact could have concluded on the basis of the evidence discussed, as well as other relevant evidence cited by the Trial Chamber,[4476] that he issued orders directly to the HVO on the specified topics. **[page 583]**

1431. Moreover, the Appeals Chamber notes that the Trial Chamber did not disregard its finding that Stojić was not *de jure* part of the military chain of command, as Stojić asserts.[4477] Rather the Trial Chamber specifically considered this argument before it found that the above described orders[4478] provided evidence that "even if the Head of the Department of Defence did not fit *de jure* into the chain of military command, Bruno Stojić, as Head of the Department of Defence, did dispatch orders directly to [the HVO]".[4479] Stojić fails to show an error and his argument is dismissed.

1432. In addition to concluding that Stojić issued orders to the HVO, the Trial Chamber also considered, on the basis of Exhibits P02292 and P03026, that "on at least two occasions, the commander of the forward command post of the South-East OZ requested instructions from both Bruno Stojić and Milivoj Petković about the conduct of the military operations in central Bosnia and Herzegovina".[4480] The Appeals Chamber notes that the Trial Chamber assessed these requests in the context of the evidence cited above and considers that Stojić has not shown that it erred in considering that they support its finding on his ability to issue operational orders.[4481] Stojić's assertion that there is no evidence that he responded to these requests is irrelevant. Thus, his argument is dismissed.

1433. Furthermore, Stojić has not demonstrated that the Trial Chamber erred by relying on Article 30 of the Amended 3 July 1992 Decree on the Armed Forces to find that Boban, as Supreme Commander of the Armed Forces, could delegate certain command responsibilities to the Head of the Department of Defence.[4482] Contrary to Stojić's assertion that no such delegation occurred,[4483] the Trial Chamber made no finding on this issue, but rather, only noted that it had no evidence referring to a transfer of authority from Boban to Stojić.[4484] It then considered that it had received "several orders" from Stojić addressed directly to the HVO.[4485] Within this context, Stojić has not shown that no reasonable trier of fact could have concluded that Article 30 of the Amended 3 July 1992 Decree on the Armed Forces provided some support for a finding that Stojić issued orders directly to the HVO.[4486] **[page 584]**

[4470]   Praljak testified that Stojić's order mistakenly referred to "Mostar" and that he corrected it to "Ljubuski" and clarified that he "signed it to indicate that [he] had made the correction". Slobodan Praljak, T. 42081-42082 (25 June 2009).

[4471]   *Contra* Stojić's Appeal Brief, para. 154.

[4472]   Ex. P00582.

[4473]   Stojić's Appeal Brief, para. 154.

[4474]   See *supra*, para. 1412. See also *supra*, para. 1401.

[4475]   See *infra*, paras 1676, 1681-1684 (finding that the Trial Chamber reasonably considered Exhibit 4D00461 as reliable).

[4476]   See Trial Judgement, Vol. 1, fns 1362-1364, Vol. 4, fn. 725.

[4477]   See Stojić's Appeal Brief, para. 152, referring to Trial Judgement, Vol. 4, para. 306.

[4478]   See *supra*, paras 1428-1429.

[4479]   Trial Judgement, Vol. 1, para. 565. See Trial Judgement, Vol. 1, paras 560-564, Vol. 4, para. 306. See also *supra*, para. 1429.

[4480]   Trial Judgement, Vol. 4, para. 306, referring to Exs. P02292, P03026.

[4481]   See Stojić's Appeal Brief, para. 154.

[4482]   Trial Judgement, Vol. 1, para. 560, referring to, *inter alia*, Ex. P00588, p. 10.

[4483]   Stojić's Appeal Brief, para. 157.

[4484]   Trial Judgement, Vol. 1, para. 562.

[4485]   Trial Judgement, Vol. 1, para. 562.

[4486]   See Trial Judgement, Vol. 4, para. 306 & fn. 725, referring to, *inter alia*, Ex. P00588.

1434. Finally, the Appeals Chamber notes that the Trial Chamber did not make a general conclusion that Stojić's orders were not followed.[4487] Rather, in the findings referenced by Stojić the Trial Chamber noted that: (1) it had no evidence that the HVO took responsibility for the detention of Muslim men following an order from Stojić transferring the management of their detention from the 1st Knez Domagoj Brigade to the local HVO;[4488] (2) Praljak intervened when an HVO unit blocked the passage of an UNPROFOR convoy that had an authorisation for passage issued by Stojić;[4489] and (3) it had no evidence that the Detention Commission which was created on the order of Stojić,[4490] accomplished the tasks assigned to it.[4491] The Appeals Chamber is not convinced this undermines the Trial Chamber's finding that Stojić had the authority to ensure that his orders were carried out. The Appeals Chamber dismisses elsewhere a similar challenge by Stojić that the Trial Chamber disregarded instances where his orders were disobeyed and where he relies on the same sections of the Trial Judgement.[4492] Additionally, as the above evidence demonstrates,[4493] Stojić's orders were regularly followed.[4494] Stojić has not shown that the Trial Chamber erred in finding that he had the authority to not only issue orders, but also to ensure that they were followed.

1435. For the above reasons, the Appeals Chamber dismisses Stojić's contention that the Trial Chamber erred in finding that he had the authority to issue orders directly to the HVO and to ensure that they were carried out.

(f) Stojić's responsibility for the human, financial, and logistical resources of the HVO

(i) Arguments of the Parties

1436. Stojić challenges the Trial Chamber's finding that he "directly controlled" the human, financial, and logistical resources of the HVO.[4495] He contends that the evidence relied on by the Trial Chamber does not support a finding that he had direct control over finances as: (1) Exhibit 2D01443 predates the JCE; (2) Exhibit P04399/3D01206 is a request that Stojić be informed of financial problems but does not show that he had the power to resolve those problems; **[page 585]** (3) Exhibit 2D01246 demonstrates that technical resources for the care of the wounded were provided by the municipal HVOs, rather than by him; (4) Exhibit P06807 relates to the administrative redistribution of telephone lines; and (5) Exhibit P00970 is a report on Military Police activities, which is irrelevant, and it was not proven that it was sent to Stojić.[4496]

1437. In relation to logistics, Stojić contends that the evidence of Witness Christopher Beese, which the Trial Chamber relied on to conclude that Stojić bought arms for the HVO from German arms dealers, was uncorroborated and speculative.[4497] He also argues that a finding that he was authorised to request weapons and materiels from the HV is unsupported as Exhibits P01164 and 2D00809 are irrelevant, and Exhibit P03998, is but one request, "made in a state of emergency".[4498] Stojić similarly submits that the Trial Chamber's finding that he organised the purchase of weapons from the VRS is not supported as the evidence

---

[4487] *Contra* Stojić's Appeal Brief, para. 155.

[4488] Trial Judgement, Vol. 2, para. 2081.

[4489] Trial Judgement, Vol. 4, para. 480.

[4490] Trial Judgement, Vol. 1, para. 622. The Commission for Prisons and Detention Centres was a commission created on 6 August 1993 by the Department of Defence to take charge of all detention units and prisons in which POWs and military detainees were held, and which began its work as of 10 August 1993 ("Detention Commission"). Trial Judgement, Vol. 1, paras 622, 624, referring to, *inter alia*, Ex. P03995.

[4491] Trial Judgement, Vol. 4, para. 1039.

[4492] See *infra*, para. 1487 & fn. 4743. See Stojić's Appeal Brief, para. 155, referring to Trial Judgement, Vol. 1, para. 772, Vol. 2, para. 2081, Vol. 4, paras 480, 1039.

[4493] See *supra*, para. 1429.

[4494] See, *e.g.*, Trial Judgement, Vol. 4, paras 304-305, 330, 334, 354-355.

[4495] Stojić's Appeal Brief, para. 158, referring to Trial Judgement, Vol. 4, paras 308-310. See Stojić's Appeal Brief, para. 143.

[4496] Stojić's Appeal Brief, para. 160.

[4497] Stojić's Appeal Brief, para. 161, referring to Christopher Beese, T. 5386 (23 Aug 2006). Stojić asserts that none of the other evidence cited by the Trial Chamber – namely the evidence of Witnesses Stipo Buljan, BF, and Davor Korać – corroborates Beese's evidence. Stojić's Appeal Brief, para. 161 & fn. 431.

[4498] Stojić's Appeal Brief, para. 162. Stojić asserts that Exhibit P03998 does not prove that he regularly sent requests to the HV or generally had the authority to do so. Stojić's Appeal Brief, para. 162.

only establishes that he was aware of the purchase of weapons and occasionally relayed information about pricing.[4499]

1438. Stojić further argues that the Trial Chamber's underlying finding that he directly financed the HVO disregards "clearly relevant" evidence and findings which established that the pertinent funding came from the Department of Finance or the municipalities.[4500] Specifically, he contends that the Trial Chamber disregarded: (1) Exhibits 1D01609, 1D01934, P06689, and P08118, all of which indicate that by default the Department of Finance controlled the finances of the armed forces; (2) 25 exhibits, including Exhibit 1D03036, which all indicate that the HVO was financed by the municipalities; and (3) his trial submissions as well as Witness Petković's testimony.[4501] Stojić further challenges the Trial Chamber's underlying findings that: (1) he was responsible for preparing the budget of the Department of Defence, asserting that the Trial Chamber relied on one paragraph in Exhibit 2D02000 but disregarded the following paragraph which indicated that no budget was prepared, and that Exhibit P08118 "confirms that the lack of a budget contributed to a significant lack of clarity on the financing of the HVO";[4502] (2) he contacted the Croatian Department of Defence for the payment of wages, arguing that Exhibits P10291, P00910, and **[page 586]** P10290 were not signed by him and Exhibits P00098 and P00910, as well as the testimony of Witness Miroslav Rupčić, do not relate to loan requests from Croatia;[4503] and (3) he could authorise others to withdraw money from HVO bank accounts.[4504]

1439. Finally, Stojić asserts that the Trial Chamber's finding that he was responsible for financing the training centres and mobilising the HVO is unsupported by the evidence it relied on.[4505] He argues that: (1) Exhibits P00907, P00965, P04074, 2D01459, and P01350 provide no support; and (2) Exhibit 3D01460, a request sent to both Stojić and Petković for changes to the military recruitment and admissions process, illustrates a mere administrative competence.[4506] Moreover, Stojić asserts that the Trial Chamber misrepresented Witness Praljak's testimony. He argues that when Praljak said that the Government, through Stojić, looked after the army's training, food, and mobilisation, his point was that Stojić did not possess operational authority. Stojić adds that Praljak clearly did not believe that he was under Stojić's command.[4507]

1440. The Prosecution responds that the Trial Chamber reasonably found that Stojić directly controlled the human, financial, and logistical aspects of the HVO.[4508] It argues that the Trial Chamber did not find that Stojić "bought arms for the HVO from German arms dealers", but rather that he "had to see to the logistical needs, in material and weapons, of the HVO", a matter, it adds, that Stojić conceded at trial.[4509] The Prosecution further argues that: (1) Stojić's role in the procurement of weapons was supported by the evidence;[4510] (2) the Trial Chamber relied on various pieces of evidence to find that Stojić was authorised to request weapons and materiels from the HV;[4511] and (3) the evidence relied on by the Trial Chamber shows

---

[4499]   Stojić's Appeal Brief, para. 162; Stojić's Reply Brief, para. 43. Stojić suggests that the cited evidence of Witness Radmilo Jasak was not relevant to weapons procurement. Stojić's Appeal Brief, para. 162, fn. 434, referring to Radmilo Jasak, T. 49026 (27 Jan 2010).

[4500]   Stojić's Appeal Brief, para. 159, referring to Trial Judgement, Vol. 1, paras 675, 679, 681; Stojić's Reply Brief, para. 43.

[4501]   Stojić's Appeal Brief, para. 159.

[4502]   Stojić's Appeal Brief, para. 163, referring to Trial Judgement, Vol. 4, para. 309; Stojić's Reply Brief, para. 43. Stojić argues that "[n]o relevant budget was admitted into evidence". Stojić's Appeal Brief, para. 163.

[4503]   Stojić's Appeal Brief, para. 164. Stojić submits that the testimony of Witness Davor Marijan also does not relate to loan requests from Croatia. Stojić's Appeal Brief, para. 164.

[4504]   Stojić's Appeal Brief, para. 164. Stojić asserts that: (1) Exhibit 2D01352, an HVO payroll he signed, simply lists the employees of the Office of the Head of the Department of Defence; (2) Exhibit P10301 and the testimony of Rupčić evidences a single incident in which Stojić requested a cash withdrawal, which was authorised by Rupčić, and does not, on its own, establish general authority; and (3) Exhibit P00098 only establishes that he was one of five individuals authorised to sign payment orders. Stojić's Appeal Brief, para. 164.

[4505]   Stojić's Appeal Brief, para. 165, referring to Trial Judgement, Vol. 4, para. 310.

[4506]   Stojić's Appeal Brief, para. 165.

[4507]   Stojić's Appeal Brief, para. 165.

[4508]   Prosecution's Response Brief (Stojić), para's 127, 132, 139.

[4509]   Prosecution's Response Brief (Stojić), para. 127, referring to Stojić's Final Brief, para. 254.

[4510]   Prosecution's Response Brief (Stojić), paras 127-128. The Prosecution further submits that Stojić's challenges to the evidence cited by the Trial Chamber in footnote 729 of Volume 4 of the Trial Judgement "misapprehend[] the Judgement". Prosecution's Response Brief (Stojić), para. 138.

[4511]   Prosecution's Response Brief (Stojić), para. 129, referring to Exs. P03998, P01164, P00098.

that Stojić was heavily involved in organising weapons purchases from the VRS.[4512] It asserts that as the Trial Chamber was mindful of Stojić's trial arguments regarding the funding of the HVO and the evidence cited supports the **[page 587]** Trial Chamber's finding, Stojić fails to show any error.[4513] Moreover, the Prosecution submits that Stojić ignores Exhibit P01521 which further supports' the Trial Chamber's finding that he was responsible for the HVO's finances.[4514] It also submits that Stojić fails to show any error regarding the remaining Trial Chamber findings that he challenges in this regard.[4515]

(ii) <u>Analysis</u>

a. <u>The logistical needs of the HVO</u>

1441. In finding that Stojić was "responsible for all the logistical and financial aspects and for the human resources of the armed forces"[4516] the Trial Chamber first considered that "Stojić had to see to the logistical needs, in materiel and weapons, of the HVO armed forces."[4517] The Trial Chamber based this conclusion, in part, on Exhibit 2D01443,[4518] the minutes of a Department of Defence meeting held on 24 November 1992, at which Stojić issued an order so that the costs of barracks reconstruction could be examined.[4519] While this meeting predates the JCE and his contribution to the CCP,[4520] Stojić does not substantiate his assertion that the Trial Chamber erred in relying on it to determine his responsibilities as Head of the Department of Defence as his conduct pursuant to these responsibilities extended into the JCE period.[4521] The Trial Chamber also relied on Exhibit P04399 in which the assistant commander of the Information and Propaganda Department asked that Stojić be informed of problems in relation to the supply of newspapers to soldiers and a shortage in workspace, specifically "with the aim of improving the conditions of work and life".[4522] The Appeals Chamber rejects Stojić's assertion that this does not support that he had the power to resolve such problems.[4523] Thus, Stojić fails to show how the Trial Chamber erred in considering Exhibit P04399 as evidence that he saw "to the logistical needs" of the HVO.[4524] Similarly, the Appeals Chamber also rejects Stojić's contentions that: (1) Exhibit 2D01246, an order from Stojić **[page 588]** to OZ commanders that they provide business space and technical resources, "in cooperation with the president of municipal HVO[s]"[4525] shows that he did not provide such resources;[4526] (2) the Trial Chamber unreasonably relied on Exhibit P06807, which relates to the administrative redistribution of telephone lines for the HVO;[4527] and (3) Exhibit P00970, which reports that military equipment was allowed to be transported to Central Bosnia "with the approval of Mr. STOJIĆ",[4528] is irrelevant.

[4512] Prosecution's Response Brief (Stojić), para. 130.
[4513] Prosecution's Response Brief (Stojić), para. 136.
[4514] Prosecution's Response Brief (Stojić), para. 137.
[4515] Prosecution's Response Brief (Stojić), paras 133-135, 139-141.
[4516] Trial Judgement, Vol. 4, para. 312.
[4517] Trial Judgement, Vol. 4, para. 308.
[4518] Trial Judgement, Vol. 4, para. 308. The Appeals Chamber notes that Stojić challenges the Trial Chamber's reliance on Exhibit 2D01443, as well as certain other evidence, by arguing that it does not establish that he "had direct control over finances". Stojić's Appeal Brief, para. 160, referring to Exs. 2D01443, P04399/3D01206, 2D01246, P06807, P00970. This argument misinterprets the Trial Chamber's reliance on this evidence: the Trial Chamber relied on it to support its finding that "Stojić had to see to the logistical needs, in materiel and weapons, of the HVO armed forces." Trial Judgement, Vol. 4, para. 308, fn. 729. The Appeals Chamber will consider whether a reasonable trial chamber could have relied on this evidence to conclude that Stojić was responsible for logistical resources.
[4519] Ex. 2D01443, p. 2.
[4520] Trial Judgement, Vol. 4, para. 1230.
[4521] See *Šainović et al.* Appeal Judgement, fn. 3858 ("certain conduct of a JCE member which started prior to, and continued during, the period when a common purpose of a JCE was found to have existed could constitute an act in furtherance of the common purpose by virtue of the continuation of this conduct"). See *infra*, para. 1891.
[4522] Ex. P04399, pp. 3-4.
[4523] *Contra* Stojić's Appeal Brief, para. 160. See *supra*, para. 1436.
[4524] See Trial Judgement. Vol. 4, para. 308.
[4525] Ex. 2D01246, p. 1. See also Stipo Buljan, T. 36753 (11 Feb 2009).
[4526] *Contra* Stojić's Appeal Brief, para. 160.
[4527] Ex. P06807. *Contra* Stojić's Appeal Brief, para. 160.
[4528] Ex. P00970, p. 7. The Appeals Chamber also considers that it is immaterial whether this report was sent to Stojić. *Contra* Stojić's Appeal Brief, para. 160.

1442. The Appeals Chamber further notes that the Trial Chamber also relied on the evidence of Witness Christopher Beese to support its conclusion that Stojić was responsible for the HVO's logistical needs.[4529] Beese testified, and stated in a contemporaneous report, that on multiple occasions he saw persons in Stojić's office – whom he was later told were German arms salesmen – with what Beese recognised as munitions boxes.[4530] [Redacted, see Annex C – Confidential Annex][4531] [Redacted, see Annex C – Confidential Annex][4532] Thus, Stojić does not show that Beese's evidence was uncorroborated or so speculative that the Trial Chamber erred in relying on it.[4533] Stojić does not show that no reasonable trier of fact could have relied on this evidence in concluding that he was responsible for the HVO's logistical needs, in materiel and weapons.

1443. The Trial Chamber further considered that in order to see to the logistical needs of the HVO, Stojić was authorised to send requests for materiel and weapons directly to the HV.[4534] In reaching this finding, the Trial Chamber relied on: (1) Exhibit P01164, a Military Police order, issued pursuant to the order by the Head of the Department of Defence among others, which stipulates, *inter alia,* that "documentation for arms, military equipment, and ammunition imported from the Republic of Croatia or another country that needs to cross over checkpoints [...] should be signed by the head of the defense department of HZ HB, Bruno '/last name illegible, probably STOJIĆ/'";[4535] (2) Exhibit 2D00809, minutes of a meeting attended by Stojić at which an **[page 589]** agreement was reached for the transport of supplies to produce ammunition;[4536] and (3) Exhibit P03998, a request from Stojić to the HV for weapons.[4537] The Appeals Chamber considers that Stojić's arguments concerning Exhibits P01164 and P03998 are unpersuasive.[4538] As Exhibit 2D00809 does not specifically speak to the HV's involvement in the supply of materiel and weapons, the Trial Chamber erred in relying on this exhibit. However, Stojić fails to show that no reasonable trier of fact could have arrived at the impugned finding on the basis of the remaining evidence. Moreover, Stojić ignores the Trial Chamber's reliance on Exhibit P00098, a request from Boban to open a bank account "for the purpose of performing financial transactions with the Republic of Croatia", which lists Stojić as one individual authorised to sign payment orders.[4539] In sum, Stojić merely offers his own interpretation of the evidence without showing that no reasonable trier of fact could have interpreted this evidence as the Trial Chamber did.

1444. The Trial Chamber also considered that Stojić, on behalf of the HVO, organised the purchase of weapons from the VRS.[4540] In doing so, it relied on a series of communications in June 1993 between Stojić and Ivica Rajić, an HVO commander,[4541] discussing the negotiation for and transfer of weapons from the VRS to the HVO.[4542] Notably, in one communication Rajić relays that he asked his VRS contact to negotiate the price of weapons with Stojić and that he was awaiting Stojić's instructions on how to proceed.[4543] The Trial Chamber also relied on subsequent communications which included: (1) a report sent from Rajić to Stojić, "as per request", listing the weapons and ammunition received from the VRS;[4544] (2) a proposed price

---

[4529]   Trial Judgement, Vol. 4, para. 308, fn. 729.

[4530]   Christopher Beese, T. 5385-5387 (23 Aug 2006). Beese further testified that he recognised the boxes from his experience as a British army officer. Christopher Beese, T. 5387-5388 (23 Aug 2006). See Ex. P02620, p. 2.

[4531]   Witness BF, T. 25835 (closed session) (8 Jan 2008).

[4532]   Witness BF, T. 25835-25836 (closed session) (8 Jan 2008).

[4533]   The Appeals Chamber notes that Stojić argues that the evidence of Witnesses Stipo Buljan and Davor Korać does not corroborate Witness Beese's evidence. See *supra,* fn. 4498. The Appeals Chamber notes, however, that the evidence of Witnesses Buljan and Korać was not cited by the Trial Chamber to corroborate the evidence of Witness Beese and has no bearing on the reliability of Witness Beese's testimony.

[4534]   Trial Judgement, Vol. 4, para. 308. The Trial Chamber also found that Stojić was authorised to make payments from HVO accounts, but Stojić does not challenge this consideration. Trial Judgement, Vol. 4, para. 308.

[4535]   Ex. P01164, p. 1.

[4536]   Ex. 2D00809.

[4537]   Ex. P03998.

[4538]   See *supra,* para. 1436, fn. 4499.

[4539]   Ex. P00098. See Miroslav Rupčić, T. 23338-23339 (8 Oct 2007).

[4540]   Trial Judgement, Vol. 4, para. 308.

[4541]   See Trial Judgement, Vol. 1, fn. 1650.

[4542]   Ex. P09820; Ex. P02934; Ex. P02966. The testimony of Radmilo Jasak supports the interpretation that references in these documents to "the XY side" refer to Serbia. Radmilo Jasak, T. 49024-49028 (27 Jan 2010).

[4543]   Ex. P02966.

[4544]   Ex. P06364.

list for armaments in which Rajić requests that Stojić confirm that the criteria will be "sorted out at the Government level";[4545] and (3) a request from Rajić, addressed to Boban, Petković, and Stojić, in which he requests that they reach "an urgent agreement" with the VRS for the use of "heavy and armoured equipment".[4546] In arguing that this evidence "establishes only that Stojić was aware of the purchase of weapons from the VRS and that on occasions he relayed information about pricing agreements",[4547] but that it "does not establish any personal involvement in the purchases **[page 590]** themselves",[4548] Stojić merely offers his own interpretation of the evidence without showing an error on the part of the Trial Chamber. Stojić's arguments are therefore dismissed.

b. The finances of the HVO

1445. Turning to the Trial Chamber's finding that Stojić "was responsible for the finances of the armed forces of the HZ(R) H-B",[4549] the Trial Chamber relied exclusively on Exhibit 2D02000 to find that Stojić "prepared the budget of the Department of Defence".[4550] Exhibit 2D02000 indicates that when Stojić took over as Head of the Department of Defence, preparing its budget was one of 12 "priority tasks".[4551] Contrary to Stojić's assertion,[4552] Exhibit 2D02000 merely notes that "some" of the listed tasks were not completed, but makes no reference to the budget and, therefore, does not indicate that no budget was prepared.[4553] Moreover, Exhibit P08118 does not confirm that "the lack of a budget contributed to a significant lack of clarity on the financing of the HVO",[4554] rather the concerns it raised revolve around a lack of funds.[4555] The Appeals Chamber considers that the evidence cited by the Trial Chamber establishes only that Stojić was responsible for preparing the budget and that no reasonable trial chamber could have relied on it to find that Stojić did, in fact, prepare one. However, considering the discussion below,[4556] the Appeals Chamber finds that Stojić fails to show how this error could have an impact on the Trial Chamber's overall conclusion that he was responsible for the finances of the HVO.

1446. The Trial Chamber also found that Stojić was "responsible for the payment of salaries to the members of the armed forces as he was authorised to withdraw funds from the HVO bank accounts" and that he "contacted the Department of Defence of Croatia for money to pay the salaries."[4557] In relation to the latter, the Trial Chamber relied on Exhibits P10291, P00910, and P10290, requests from Stojić to the Croatian Department of Defence to transfer money to an HVO bank account for the payment of salaries.[4558] The Trial Chamber accepted that while the requests are not personally signed by Stojić, they are signed on his behalf.[4559] The Trial Chamber further relied on: (1) Exhibit P00910, an order from Gojko Šušak that the HVO be given a loan for the **[page 591]** payment of HVO salaries;[4560] (2) Exhibit P00098, a request from Boban to open a bank account "for the purpose of performing financial transactions with the Republic of Croatia" which lists Stojić as one individual authorised to sign payment orders;[4561] and (3) the testimony of Rupčić addressing paperwork used in transactions for the payment of HVO salaries, including Exhibits P10290 and P10291, by the Department of Defence of Croatia.[4562] The Appeals Chamber is not convinced that, as argued

---

[4545] Ex. P09967, p. 3.
[4546] Ex. P03403, p. 1.
[4547] Stojić's Appeal Brief, para. 162.
[4548] Stojić's Appeal Brief, para. 162.
[4549] Trial Judgement, Vol. 4, para. 309.
[4550] Trial Judgement, Vol. 4, para. 309, referring to Ex. 2D02000.
[4551] Ex. 2D02000, para. 94.
[4552] Stojić's Appeal Brief, para. 163.
[4553] Ex. 2D02000, para. 95.
[4554] Stojić's Appeal Brief, para. 163.
[4555] Ex. P08118, p. 4.
[4556] See *infra*, paras 1446-1450.
[4557] Trial Judgement, Vol. 4, para. 309.
[4558] Trial Judgement, Vol. 4, para. 309, referring to Exs. P10291, P10290, P00910.
[4559] See Trial Judgement, Vol. 4, para. 309, referring to, *inter alia*, Davor Marijan, T(F). 35736 (21 Jan 2009). In the questioning of Witness Marijan, it was suggested that when "za" appeared on a BCS document this signified that the document was being signed on behalf of someone, which was not denied by the witness. Davor Marijan, T. 35736-34737 (21 Jan 2009).
[4560] Trial Judgement, Vol. 4, para. 309, referring to Ex. P00910.
[4561] Trial Judgement, Vol. 4, para. 309, referring to Ex. P00098.
[4562] Trial Judgement, Vol. 4, para. 309, referring to Miroslav Rupčić, T(F). 23366-23369, 23387 (8 Oct 2007).

by Stojić, this evidence does "not actually relate to requests for loans from Croatia" for the payment of HVO salaries.[4563] Stojić fails to show an error by the Trial Chamber.[4564]

1447. The Trial Chamber also found that "[a]s the person in charge of the finances of the Department of Defence, Bruno Stojić could authorise other people to withdraw funds from the HVO bank accounts".[4565] The Trial Chamber relied on, *inter alia*, Exhibit P10301, a bank slip that indicates that money was withdrawn by Rupčić "based on the request for cash withdrawal issued by Bruno STOJIĆ".[4566] Stojić does not substantiate his assertion that a single incident cannot demonstrate that he had the authority to authorise others to withdraw funds and therefore he fails to show an error by the Trial Chamber in this respect. Moreover, the Trial Chamber also relied on Exhibit P01521,[4567] an order from Stojić in which he designated individuals within the HVO with "authority to deal with material and financial /?/supplies"[4568] and detailed instructions on the procedure. Stojić does not challenge the Trial Chamber's reliance on this document.

1448. Stojić further asserts that the Trial Chamber unreasonably found that he "directly financed the armed forces" because it disregarded evidence and findings that relevant funding came from the Department of Finance or the municipalities.[4569] The Appeals Chamber first considers that at trial, Stojić raised similar arguments.[4570] The Appeals Chamber also notes that the Trial Chamber did not find that Stojić "directly financed the armed forces", but rather found that he "directly controlled" and "was responsible" for HVO finances.[4571] Further, the Trial Chamber considered the role of the **[page 592]** Department of Finance and noted that it was responsible for collecting taxes and duties, establishing a customs system, and deciding a Government budget.[4572] The Trial Chamber also noted evidence that "the HVO initiated the implementation of a centralised system of taxation for the purpose of financing the HZ H-B".[4573] Regarding the municipalities, the Trial Chamber noted evidence that they financed the military units.[4574] It also reviewed "evidence indicating that the municipalities used their own' resources to finance their municipal defences"[4575] and that municipalities were forced to collect revenue on their own.[4576] While those findings were not made in the section of the Trial Judgement discussing Stojić's responsibility, the Appeals Chamber observes that the Trial Chamber considered some of the same evidence Stojić now cites.[4577] Thus, the Trial Chamber was cognisant of the involvement of the Department of Finance and the municipalities in financing the municipalities' defences.

1449. Additionally, although Exhibit 1D01609 – the minutes of a 26 May 1993 Government meeting – indicates that the Department of Finance was in charge of implementing measures to ensure continuous payment of soldiers' salaries, to fulfil contracts for the production of materiel and technical equipment, and the payment of taxes, the relevant decisions were taken after Stojić briefed the Government on problems with recruitment and shortages in materiel and technical equipment.[4578] The Appeals Chamber also notes that Stojić points to Exhibit P06689, a letter from Prlić indicating the need for a unified financial system and that any payments outside of the budget to, *inter alios,* soldiers would be considered illegal, and calling for the

---

[4563]   *Contra* Stojić's Appeal Brief, para. 164.
[4564]   See *supra*, para. 1438.
[4565]   Trial Judgement, Vol. 4, para. 309.
[4566]   Ex. P10301. See Miroslav Rupčić, T. 23387-23388 (8 Oct 2007). The Trial Chamber also relied on Exhibit 2D01352, a payroll signed by Stojić. The Appeals Chamber does not consider that this supports the Trial Chamber's conclusion that Stojić could authorise others to withdraw funds, however this has no impact on the Trial Chamber's finding. Ex. 2D01352, p. 3.
[4567]   Trial Judgement, Vol. 4, fn. 734.
[4568]   Ex. P01521, p. 1.
[4569]   Stojić's Appeal Brief, para. 159.
[4570]   Stojić's Final Brief, paras 315, 359-361.
[4571]   Trial Judgement, Vol. 4, paras 308, 309, 312.
[4572]   Trial Judgement, Vol. 1, paras 640-644.
[4573]   Trial Judgement, Vol. 1, para. 643.
[4574]   Trial Judgement, Vol. 1, para. 679.
[4575]   Trial Judgement, Vol. 1, para. 679.
[4576]   Trial Judgement, Vol. 1, para. 681.
[4577]   Trial Judgement, Vol. 1, fns 1595 (referring to, *inter alia*, Exs. 1D01771, 2D00538, 1D01759, 1D00307), 1598 (referring to, *inter alia*, Exs. 1D00559, 1D00561). See Stojić's Appeal Brief, para. 159 & fn. 419, referring to, *inter alia*, Exs. 1D01771, 2D00538, 1D01759, 1D00307, 1D00559, 1D00561.
[4578]   Ex. 1D01609, p. 2.

Ministry of Defence and the Ministry of Finance, among others, to undertake the legal steps.[4579] However, this exhibit does not provide direct support for Stojić's contention that the Department of Finance controlled the finances of the armed forces by default. Similarly, the Appeals Chamber is not convinced by Stojić's reliance on Exhibit P08118, a Defence Department Annual Report, which does not suggest that the Department of Finance controlled the finances of the armed forces, as asserted by Stojić.[4580] Further, the Appeals Chamber notes that the Trial Chamber expressly considered that Witness Petković testified that "Stojić was to contact the Government of the HZ H-B for material and **[page 593]** financial resources for the HVO armed forces", but found that the evidence showed that Stojić "directly controlled the human and financial resources of the HVO armed forces".[4581] The Appeals Chamber finds that, by only asserting that the Trial Chamber "discarded without explanation" Witness Petković's evidence and "disregarded" his trial submissions, Stojić ignores the Trial Chamber's relevant findings and evidence relied upon and fails to show an error.[4582]

1450. Moreover, as found above, the Trial Chamber reasonably concluded that Stojić: (1) was responsible for the payment of salaries to the members of the HVO; (2) was authorised to withdraw funds from HVO bank accounts; (3) was authorised to request funds from Croatia to pay salaries; and (4) could authorise others to withdraw funds from HVO bank accounts.[4583] Stojić does not demonstrate that any alleged role that either the Department of Finance or the municipalities played in the funding of the HVO calls into question the Trial Chamber's finding that Stojić, as Head of the Department of Defence, was responsible for its finances. Stojić's arguments are dismissed.

1451. For the foregoing reasons, the Appeals Chamber dismisses Stojić's contention that the Trial Chamber erred in finding that he was responsible for the finances of the HVO.

c. Human resources

1452. Regarding the management of HVO human resources, the Trial Chamber found that Stojić was responsible for "ensuring the financing of the training centres and the mobilisation of the members of the HZ(R) H-B armed forces."[4584] In reaching this conclusion, the Trial Chamber relied on: (1) Exhibit P00907, a report from Petković to Stojić which describes the military situation and addresses problems associated with mobilisation;[4585] (2) Exhibit P00965, a report from the Assistant Chief of the Main Staff for Professional Units, Ivica Primorac, to Stojić and Petković describing the composition and capabilities of professional units within the HVO;[4586] (3) Exhibit P04074, an order from Praljak, "[p]ursuant to the order of the Defence Department [...] regarding the training of recruits";[4587] (4) Exhibit 2D01459, an order issued by Stojić appointing the "chief of Administration for military obligation and mobilization";[4588] (5) Exhibit 2D01350,[4589] a request from Primorac to **[page 594]** Stojić and Petković for the resolution of a personnel dispute about the transfer of soldiers to the professional units;[4590] (6) Exhibit 3D01460, a "Request to resolve a problem"

[4579] Ex. P06689. See Ex. 1D01934 (a report from the Head of the Department of Finance outlining its decisions to prevent potential consequences of implementing a functioning financial system).

[4580] Specifically, the articles cited by Stojić indicate that the Defence Department was limited in its ability to provide logistical support for the HVO due to: (1) "[t]he lack of a uniform finance system"; (2) "[t]he self-financing of HVO units through municipal bodies"; (3) "[t]he lack of regulations governing salaries of individuals financed through the budget"; and (4) "[t]he lack of a single market". Ex. P08118, p. 4.

[4581] Trial Judgement, Vol. 4, para. 308, referring to Milivoj Petković, T(F). 50344-50345 (3 Mar 2010).

[4582] Stojić's Appeal Brief, para. 159. See *Popović et al.* Appeal Judgement, para. 131 (the Trial Chamber has "broad discretion in assessing the appropriate weight and credibility to be accorded to the testimony of a witness"); *Kvočka et al.* Appeal Judgement, para. 23 ("the Trial Chamber is not under the obligation to justify its findings in relation to every submission made during the trial").

[4583] See *supra*, paras 1446-1447, fn. 4535.

[4584] Trial Judgement, Vol. 4, para. 310.

[4585] Ex. P00907, p. 6.

[4586] Ex. P00965.

[4587] Ex. P04074, p. 1.

[4588] Ex. 2D01459.

[4589] The Appeals Chamber notes that Stojić challenges the Trial Chamber's reliance on Exhibit P01350, however, the Appeals Chamber considers this to be an editorial mistake as the Trial Chamber cited Exhibit 2D01350, not Exhibit P01350. See *supra*, para. 1439; Trial Judgement, Vol. 4, fn. 737.

[4590] Ex. 2D01350, p. 1.

addressed to Stojić and Petković, in which Željko Šiljeg outlines problems related to mobilisation and requests certain action to remedy the situation;[4591] and (7) Praljak's testimony that the Government, through Stojić, was competent to ensure that mobilisation was in place for the HVO.[4592]

1453. From the outset, the Appeals Chamber notes that while Exhibit P04074 suggests that the Department of Defence, and therefore Stojić, had the authority to issue orders in relation to the training of recruits, nothing in the evidence cited by the Trial Chamber supports its specific finding that Stojić "was responsible for ensuring the financing of the training centres".[4593] However, Stojić has not shown that the cited evidence does not support the Trial Chamber's finding that he was responsible for the mobilisation of members of the HVO. Specifically in relation to Exhibit 3D01460, the fact that Šiljeg addressed his request to both Stojić and Petković does not demonstrate that it was Petković, and not Stojić, who had the authority to resolve the problem, particularly within the context of the other cited evidence demonstrating Stojić's role in relation to mobilisation. Further, while Praljak testified that he did not consider himself to be under Stojić's command,[4594] he also clearly stated that Stojić did have the competency to ensure that "mobilisation was in place".[4595] Therefore, Stojić's assertion that the Trial Chamber's finding that he was responsible for the mobilisation of the HVO is not supported by the evidence is dismissed. Moreover, while the Trial Chamber erred in considering that Stojić was responsible for the financing of the training centres, in light of the above analysis upholding the Trial Chamber's finding that Stojić was responsible for HVO finances,[4596] Stojić has not shown how this error impacts the Trial Chamber's overall finding that he was responsible for "all the logistical and **[page 595]** financial aspects and for the human resources of the armed forces" or that he had command authority over the HVO.[4597] His arguments are dismissed.

(g) Stojić's authority to designate representatives of the HVO in ceasefire negotiations

1454. Stojić disputes that he had the authority to designate representatives of the HVO in ceasefire negotiations,[4598] as: (1) Petković was found to be in charge of negotiations;[4599] (2) the only reasonable inference from the orders cited by the Trial Chamber was that Stojić communicated authority already possessed by Petković;[4600] and (3) there is no evidence that Stojić himself had the power to represent the HVO in ceasefire negotiations.[4601]

1455. The Prosecution responds that Stojić merely offers his own interpretation of the evidence without showing an error on the part of the Trial Chamber.[4602]

1456. The Trial Chamber relied on two documents to support its finding that Stojić had the authority to designate individuals to represent the HVO in ceasefire negotiations: (1) Exhibit P00811, an appointment of Dario Kordić as Petković's deputy at tripartite negotiations, signed by Stojić and dated 26 November

---

[4591]   Ex. 3D01460.

[4592]   Slobodan Praljak, T. 40422-40423 (20 May 2009).

[4593]   Trial Judgement, Vol. 4, para. 3lo, referring to Exs. P04074 (an order dated 10 August 1993 from Praljak, pursuant to an order from the Department of Defence, in relation to the assignment of recruits to further training), 3D01460, p. 1 (a communication dated 24 July 1993 from Željko Šiljeg to Stojić requesting that he resolve problems associated with recruitment), 2D01459 (an order dated 9 June 1993 by Stojić appointing the Chief of Administration for military obligation and mobilisation), 2D01350 (communication dated 31 July 1993 from Ivica Primorac to Stojić requesting that he resolve an issue associated with the assignment of volunteers to certain units), P00907 (a report dated 15 December 1992 from Petković to the Main Staff noting, *inter alia*, the difficulty in mobilising HVO units due to differing requirements in the municipalities).

[4594]   Slobodan Praljak, T. 40421-40422 (20 May 2009).

[4595]   Slobodan Praljak, T. 40422-40423 (20 May 2009).

[4596]   See *supra*, paras 1445-1451.

[4597]   Trial Judgement, Vol. 4, para. 312.

[4598]   Stojić's Appeal Brief, para. 156, referring to Trial Judgement, Vol. 4, para. 311.

[4599]   Stojić's Reply Brief, para. 44, citing Trial Judgement, Vol. 4, para. 680. See Stojić's Appeal Brief, para. 156.

[4600]   Stojić's Appeal Brief, para. 156; Stojić's Reply Brief, para. 44. Stojić submits that Exhibit P00811 indicates that Dario Kordić had been appointed as deputy for one meeting whereas Exhibit P00812, which was disregarded by the Trial Chamber, shows that this delegation of authority was actually made by Petković. He asserts that Exhibit P03922 is merely an explanation he provided on the existing command structure. Stojić's Appeal Brief, para. 156.

[4601]   Stojić's Appeal Brief, para. 156.

[4602]   Prosecution's Response Brief (Stojić), paras 142-143.

1992;[4603] and (2) Exhibit P03922, a communication dated 3 August 1993 from Stojić to UNPROFOR indicating that Petković, "as Chief of the HVO Main Staff, commands all HVO forces, and as the sole such / individual/ has full authority in negotiations".[4604] In relation to Exhibit P00811, the Appeals Chamber considers that a plain reading of the document, in particular the language that "KORDIĆ is hereby appointed",[4605] belies Stojić's assertion that it was merely paperwork indicating an appointment made by Petković. Moreover, in support of his argument, Stojić cites Exhibit P00812 which is an order dated 26 November 1992 from both Stojić and Petković directing Kordić to attend the negotiations.[4606] Thus, this exhibit does not demonstrate that it was Petković, and not Stojić, who had the authority to make such an appointment. Regarding Exhibit P03922, the Appeals Chamber is not convinced by Stojić's argument as this exhibit supports the Trial Chamber's finding that Stojić designated persons. Even if he was only communicating that Petković had pre-existing authority, the Appeals Chamber **[page 596]** considers that Stojić fails to show how this would preclude a finding that he had the authority to designate persons to represent the HVO, especially since the Trial Chamber's finding is supported by other evidence.[4607] Further, the Trial Chamber's finding that Petković, as Deputy Commander of the Main Staff, was able to negotiate with the international community on behalf of the HVO[4608] is not inconsistent with the impugned finding. Stojić merely offers his own interpretation of the evidence without showing an error. His arguments are thus dismissed.

(h) Conclusion

1457.   On the basis of the foregoing, the Appeals Chamber finds that Stojić has failed to demonstrate that the Trial Chamber erred by finding that he commanded and had "effective control" over the HVO. The Appeals Chamber dismisses Stojić's ground of appeal 20.

   3.   Alleged errors in finding that Stojić commanded and had "effective control" over the Military Police (Stojić's Ground 21)

1458.   The Trial Chamber concluded that it was satisfied beyond reasonable doubt that Stojić, as Head of the Department of Defence, commanded and had "effective control" over the Military Police.[4609] In reaching this finding, the Trial Chamber considered that Stojić: (1) issued instructions for the reorganisation of the Military Police units;[4610] (2) appointed its most senior officers with the exception of the Chief of the Military Police Administration;[4611] (3) was regularly informed about its activities;[4612] (4) had the authority to issue orders to the Chief of the Military Police Administration, including those directly linked to operations on the ground such as resubordination;[4613] and (5) was responsible for all aspects of logistics and staffing.[4614]

(a) Arguments of the Parties

1459.   Stojić contends that the Trial Chamber arrived at the unreasonable conclusion that he commanded and had effective control over the Military Police on the basis of his "limited administrative competences".[4615] In addition to arguing that he was not involved in the appointment of the Chief of the Military Police Administration, Stojić submits that he was not a decision-maker **[page 597]** and merely administered

---

[4603]   Trial Judgement, Vol. 4, para. 311, referring to Ex. P00811.

[4604]   Ex. P03922, p. 1. See Trial Judgement, Vol. 4, para. 311, referring to Ex. P03922.

[4605]   Ex. P00811.

[4606]   Ex. P00812. See *supra*, fn. 4601.

[4607]   Ex. P00811; Ex. P00812.

[4608]   Trial Judgement, Vol. 1, para. 748.

[4609]   Trial Judgement, Vol. 4, para. 320. See Trial Judgement, Vol. 4, paras 293, 425.

[4610]   Trial Judgement, Vol. 4, paras 319-320.

[4611]   Trial Judgement, Vol. 1, para. 859, Vol. 4, paras 313, 320.

[4612]   Trial Judgement, Vol. 4, paras 318, 320.

[4613]   Trial Judgement, Vol. 4, paras 314-316, 320.

[4614]   Trial Judgement, Vol. 4, paras 317, 320.

[4615]   Stojić's Appeal Brief, paras 168, 176. See Stojić's Appeal Brief, para. 167; Stojić's Reply Brief, paras 45, 53. Stojić avers that this finding was critical to the Trial Chamber's findings that he had the necessary intent and that he significantly contributed to the JCE. Stojić's Appeal Brief, para. 177.

appointments initiated by others.[4616] He also submits that his administrative roles in logistics, staffing, and the re-organisation of the Military Police units do not evidence effective control or command authority.[4617] Stojić argues that, even if he was hierarchically superior to the Chief of the Military Police Administration, this did not mean that he exercised effective control over the Military Police as: (1) the powers of the Chief of the Military Police Administration were administrative and diminished over time;[4618] and (2) the Military Police had a "fuzzy" chain of command creating reasonable doubt about the operative chain of command.[4619]

1460. Regarding the orders he issued, Stojić contends that the Trial Chamber failed to consider whether issuing only nine orders throughout the Indictment period suggested effective control, and argues that these orders were administrative or logistical.[4620] He submits that the Trial Chamber disregarded its previous conclusion that it was not persuaded that he issued a substantial number of orders to the Military Police units.[4621] Stojić also submits that none of the evidence relied on by the Trial Chamber supported its finding that he issued orders consistent with operational command and that he could ensure that the orders were implemented.[4622] Stojić avers that the orders: (1) demonstrated that command authority resided in the Main Staff; (2) were not addressed to, or issued by, him alone and thus do not prove that he exercised command authority as opposed to the other signatories or addressees; and (3) were administrative and related to internal discipline.[4623]

1461. Stojić further contends that the Trial Chamber erroneously concluded that he received regular reports about the activities of the Military Police as the evidence showed that he received only a limited number of reports on specific occasions.[4624] Particularly, Stojić submits that the evidence relied on by the Trial Chamber: (1) showed that reporting was sporadic; (2) included two requests for reports which indicated *ad hoc* reporting; or (3) was irrelevant to the reporting procedure. Stojić also argues that the Trial Chamber failed to establish that various Military Police **[page 598]** reports were actually received by him.[4625] Stojić avers that the "simple receipt of reports, in the absence of evidence that [he] actually acted on their contents, does not prove effective control".[4626]

1462. The Prosecution responds that the Trial Chamber's findings were reasonable and the evidence correctly considered.[4627] The Prosecution submits that Stojić possessed and exercised his power to make appointments within the Military Police.[4628] It also argues that an accused's power to control finances or organise troops is relevant to establishing effective control.[4629] The Prosecution submits that Stojić repeats his trial arguments that the powers of the Chief of the Military Police Administration were administrative without showing an error.[4630] It argues that: (1) confusion in the dual chain of command of the Military Police, does not mean that the Military Police Administration lacked effective control;[4631] and (2) Stojić ignores his effective control over the Military Police along the HVO chain of command.[4632]

[4616] Stojić's Appeal Brief, para. 169.
[4617] Stojić's Appeal Brief, paras 173-174.
[4618] Stojić's Appeal Brief, para. 170; Stojić's Reply Brief, paras 46, 48.
[4619] Stojić's Appeal Brief, para. 170; Stojić's Reply Brief, para. 47.
[4620] Stojić's Appeal Brief, para. 171. See Stojić's Reply Brief, para. 49.
[4621] Stojić's Appeal Brief, para. 171.
[4622] Stojić's Appeal Brief, para. 172.
[4623] Stojić's Appeal Brief, para. 172; Stojić's Reply Brief, para. 50. Stojić replies that the orders for subordination to the armed forces, for redeployment, and in relation to checkpoints were exclusively administrative or logistical. Stojić's Reply Brief, para. 49.
[4624] Stojić's Appeal Brief, para. 175. See Stojić's Reply Brief, para. 51.
[4625] Stojić's Appeal Brief, para. 175, referring to Exs. P01053, P03314 (confidential), P02863.
[4626] Stojić's Appeal Brief, para. 175.
[4627] Prosecution's Response Brief (Stojić), paras 145-146, 152, 158, 160. See also Prosecution's Response Brief (Stojić), para. 161. See also Appeal Hearing, AT. 325-327 (21 Mar 2017).
[4628] Prosecution's Response Brief (Stojić), paras 158-159. The Prosecution argues that Stojić, as the most senior officer in the Department of Defence, could appoint senior Military Police leaders and denies that he merely administered appointments initiated by others. Prosecution's Response Brief (Stojić), para. 159.
[4629] Prosecution's Response Brief (Stojić), para. 160, referring to, *inter alia, Nahimana et al.* Appeal Judgement, para. 606.
[4630] Prosecution's Response Brief (Stojić), para. 147. The Prosecution submits that the Trial Chamber did not disregard its previous findings and that it found that Ćorić›s authority was not purely administrative. Prosecution's Response Brief (Stojić), para. 147, referring to Trial Judgement, Vol. 1, para. 971.
[4631] Prosecution's Response Brief (Stojić), para. 148.
[4632] Prosecution's Response Brief (Stojić), para. 148, referring to Trial Judgement, Vol. 4, para. 312.

1463. The Prosecution also submits that the Trial Chamber's finding that Stojić did not issue a substantial number of orders directly to the Military Police units did not include orders to the Chief of the Military Police Administration.[4633] It further submits that Stojić also issued orders that were directly linked to operations on the ground,[4634] and that his challenges to the evidence relied on by the Trial Chamber are undeveloped.[4635] The Prosecution also responds that Stojić fails to show that the Trial Chamber's finding that he received regular reports is undermined,[4636] and that the receipt of reports is relevant for assessing effective control.[4637] **[page 599]**

1464. Stojić replies that the Prosecution fails to address the regularity of the reports he received, and that this limited flow of information is inconsistent with effective control.[4638]

(b) Analysis

(i) Stojić's involvement in appointments within the Military Police and his administrative roles

1465. Stojić first disputes the Trial Chamber's finding that he "appointed the people who would hold the most senior posts within the [Military Police] units and the Military Police Administration".[4639] Notably, the Trial Chamber expressly considered that the Chief of the Military Police Administration was an exception,[4640] but observed that he was appointed on the advice of the Head of the Department of Defence.[4641] In this regard, the Appeals Chamber considers that Stojić fails to show that he "had no involvement at all in the appointment of the most senior person in the department"[4642] and, regardless, he does not demonstrate how his contention would have had an impact on the Trial Chamber's finding.

1466. The Appeals Chamber is also not persuaded by Stojić's argument that he was not the decision-maker but merely administered appointments. Referring to various pieces of evidence, the Trial Chamber found that Stojić appointed, *inter alios,* the deputy chief and the Assistant Chief of the Military Police Administration, the heads of department and the chiefs of section as well as the commanders and the deputy commanders of the Military Police battalions "on the advice of the Chief of the Military Police and with the approval of the assistant, chief for Security of the Department of Defence".[4643] Stojić relies only on the latter part of this Trial Chamber finding[4644] without showing how taking advice or obtaining approval from others affected his decision-making powers. Thus, Stojić fails to show that no reasonable trier of fact could have considered his involvement in the appointment of senior staff within the Military Police as a relevant indicator that he had "effective control" and command authority over the Military Police.[4645] Stojić's arguments are dismissed. **[page 600]**

1467. Stojić also challenges the Trial Chamber's consideration of his responsibility for "the logistical and staffing needs of the Military Police, including the payment of salaries to its members and mobilisation",[4646]

[4633] Prosecution's Response Brief (Stojić), para. 149. The Prosecution argues that the fact that Stojić could issue orders directly to the Military Police units when needed supports the conclusion that he had effective control. Prosecution's Response Brief (Stojić), para. 149.

[4634] Prosecution's Response Brief (Stojić), para. 150, referring to Trial Judgement, Vol. 1, para. 965, Vol. 4, paras 304, 315, 320.

[4635] Prosecution's Response Brief (Stojić), para. 151.

[4636] Prosecution's Response Brief (Stojić), paras 153-156. The Prosecution also argues that Stojić received and requested regular reports about Military Police activities and was kept apprised of related activities. Prosecution's Response Brief (Stojić), para. 152.

[4637] Prosecution's Response Brief (Stojić), para. 157, referring to, *inter alia, Popović et al.* Appeal Judgement, para. 1861, *Popović et al.* Trial Judgement, para. 2024.

[4638] Stojić's Reply Brief, para. 51. Stojić argues that the evidence shows, at its highest, that he received 13 reports in 16 months of office. Stojić's Reply Brief, para. 51. Stojić also submits that Exhibit P08548, a history of the Military Police from 1992 to 1995, does not mention him thus proving his lack of authority. Stojić's Reply Brief, para. 52.

[4639] Trial Judgement, Vol. 4, para. 313. See Trial Judgement, Vol. 1, para. 859.

[4640] Trial Judgement, Vol. 1, para. 859, Vol. 4, para. 313.

[4641] Trial Judgement, Vol. 1, fn. 2029, referring to Ex. P00837, p. 4. See Ex. P00837, p. 4 ("At the proposal of the head of the Defence Department, the HVO HZ HB appoints the chief of administration of the military police.").

[4642] Stojić's Appeal Brief, para. 169.

[4643] Trial Judgement, Vol. 1, para. 575. See Trial Judgement, Vol. 1, paras 858-859, 954.

[4644] See Stojić's Appeal Brief, para. 169.

[4645] See *supra*, para. 1412. See also *supra*, para. 1401.

[4646] Trial Judgement, Vol. 4, para. 317.

and the instructions he gave for the reorganisation of the Military Police units.[4647] The Appeals Chamber notes that Stojić only contends that these matters "cannot support a finding of, or "do[] not evidence", "effective control" and operational command over the Military Police.[4648] Stojić merely offers his own conclusions without showing that the Trial Chamber erroneously considered his role in logistics, staffing, and the reorganisation of units as an indicator of authority. To the extent that Stojić argues that his roles concerned "purely administrative matters", he does not support his argument that an administrative role cannot be a factor to consider as evidence of command authority,[4649] and more broadly, that such a role cannot contribute to the implementation of a JCE.[4650] Moreover, Stojić does not show that any alleged error by the Trial Chamber in this regard would affect the overall finding that he exercised "effective control" and command authority, which was based on several other factors.[4651] The Appeals Chamber therefore dismisses Stojić's argument.

(ii) The authority of the Military Police Administration

1468. Regarding Stojić's arguments concerning the authority of the Military Police Administration,[4652] the Appeals Chamber notes that the Trial Chamber considered numerous orders issued by Ćorić with regard to the establishment of checkpoints, the freedom of movement, and unit deployment. In so doing, the Trial Chamber rejected arguments made at trial by Stojić that the role of the Military Police Administration was "purely administrative".[4653] The Appeals Chamber further notes that Stojić merely relies on the Trial Chamber's observation that witnesses stated that the Military Police Administration had jurisdiction over the Military Police units in an administrative and logistical sense.[4654] However, the Trial Chamber then observed that "it seems that the Military Police Administration occasionally acted in order [...] to issue orders to the Military Police which went beyond the administrative and logistical framework and that it could in fact [...] order their resubordination"[4655] before addressing evidence of these orders and power of **[page 601]** resubordination.[4656] Thus Stojić repeats his unsuccessful trial arguments and fails to show an error by the Trial Chamber.

1469. Furthermore, the Trial Chamber also found that: (1) Ćorić, as Chief of the Military Police Administration, had command and control power over the Military Police units;[4657] (2) the Military Police Administration gradually relinquished its power to exercise direct command over the Military Police units but that this did not lead to a complete renunciation of its command;[4658] and (3) the Military Police had a dual chain of command which led to confusion.[4659] The Trial Chamber therefore was aware of, and made findings on, the same factors which, according to Stojić, show that he did not necessarily have "effective control" and command authority over the Military Police units by virtue of being Ćorić›s hierarchical superior. While those findings were not made in the section of the Trial Judgement discussing Stojić's responsibility, the

---

[4647] Trial Judgement, Vol. 4, para. 319. See Ex, P00957; Ex. P00960.

[4648] See Stojić"s Appeal Brief, paras 173-174.

[4649] See *supra*, para. 1412, referring to *Nahimana et al.* Appeal Judgement, para. 606. See also *Blaškić* Trial Judgement, para. 522; *Musema* Trial Judgement, para. 880.

[4650] See *Popović et al.* Appeal Judgement, paras 1544-1545 (in considering Radivoje Miletić's "technical" role in the UNPROFOR convoy notification procedure, the Appeals Chamber concluded that "[w]hether an act is 'technical' does not *per se* preclude it from being a contribution to a JCE"); *supra*, para. 1401.

[4651] See *supra*, para. 1458.

[4652] See *supra*, para. 1459.

[4653] Trial Judgement, Vol. 1, para. 971. See Trial Judgement, Vol. 4, paras 871, 887, 915.

[4654] Trial Judgement, Vol. 1, para. 953. See Stojić's Appeal Brief, para. 170.

[4655] Trial Judgement, Vol. 1, para. 953.

[4656] Trial Judgement, Vol. 1, paras 959-974.

[4657] Trial Judgement, Vol. 4, para. 1000. See Trial Judgement, Vol. 4, paras 871, 887, 915.

[4658] Trial Judgement, Vol. 1, paras 963-964. Similarly, the Trial Chamber found that Ćorić's power of command over the Military Police units weakened as of July 1993 but "did not disappear completely". Trial Judgement, Vol. 4, para. 868.

[4659] Trial Judgement, Vol. 1, paras 971, 974. Regarding the Military Police's dual chain of command, the Appeals Chamber further notes that Stojić had *de facto* powers over the HVO through the HVO military chain of command, which included the Military Police units embedded in the HVO brigades, thus any confusion on the ground on where orders emanated from would not necessarily affect Stojić's command authority. See Trial Judgement, Vol. 1, paras 961, 971, 974, Vol. 4, paras 306, 312, 425. See also *supra*, para. 1457.

Appeals Chamber recalls that the Trial Judgement is to be read as a whole.[4660] Stojić thus fails to show that the Trial Chamber "overlooked" its other findings;[4661] especially as these other findings are not inconsistent with Stojić having command authority over the Military Police units through his ability to give orders to Ćorić regarding various areas.[4662] Stojić's arguments are thus dismissed.[4663]

(iii) Stojić's issuance of orders to the Military Police

1470. In relation to the Trial Chamber's consideration of the orders he issued to the Military Police, Stojić's argument suggesting that issuing only nine orders throughout the Indictment period is not indicative of "effective control" is unpersuasive.[4664] First, Stojić's argument is premised on the Trial Chamber's alleged reliance on "only" nine orders in finding that he could issue orders to the Chief of the Military Police Administration.[4665] However, the Trial Chamber referred to additional evidence – some of which the Appeals Chamber will address below – in concluding that **[page 602]** Stojić did issue orders to the Military Police and that these orders were implemented.[4666] Moreover, the Appeals Chamber considers that Stojić's argument that the issuance of nine orders is insufficient to show that he had "effective control" or command authority is inapposite as the Trial Chamber's consideration of his ability to issue orders to the Military Police does not relate to his responsibility as a commander pursuant to Article 7(3) of the Statute. The Appeals Chamber recalls that the *actus reus* for liability under JCE I is the participation of the accused in the common criminal plan which may take the form of assistance in, or contribution to, the execution of this plan,[4667] and that this contribution to the crimes is significant.[4668] As such, in and of itself, the number of orders Stojić issued to the Military Police has no bearing on the Trial Chamber's conclusion that he contributed to the furtherance of the JCE through their issuance. Thus, Stojić's argument is dismissed.

1471. In addition, Stojić's contention that the Trial Chamber disregarded its earlier finding that it was not persuaded that Stojić issued "a substantial number of orders" directly to Military Police units[4669] ignores the context of this observation. The Trial Chamber continued to say that it was not persuaded that the number of orders issued directly to the Military Police units implied that Stojić was circumventing the Military Police Administration's authority.[4670] Stojić's contention is thus dismissed.

1472. Stojić also argues that the orders relied on by the Trial Chamber do not substantiate its findings. Regarding his first contention in support,[4671] while Exhibits P00875, 5D02002, and 5D00548 indicate that the Main Staff had authority over the Military Police units resubordinated to the HVO command,[4672] Stojić does not show that this precludes his authority over the same units. In this regard,.the Appeals Chamber

---

[4660] *Stanišić and Župljanin* Appeal Judgement, paras 138, 376, 705; *Popović et al.* Appeal Judgement, para. 2006; *Mrkšić and Šljivančanin* Appeal Judgement, para. 379. See *Kalimanzira* Appeal Judgement, para. 227.

[4661] See Stojić's Appeal Brief, para. 170.

[4662] Trial Judgement, Vol. 4, para. 314.

[4663] Regarding Stojić's argument on Exhibit P08548, the Appeals Chamber notes that this publication does not list the entire chain of command over the Military Police and that thus does not call into question the Trial Chamber's finding regarding Stojić's authority. See Stojić's Reply Brief, para. 52.

[4664] See Stojić's Appeal Brief, para. 171.

[4665] Stojić's Appeal Brief, para. 171, referring to Trial Judgement, Vol. 4, para. 314.

[4666] Trial Judgement, Vol. 4, paras 315-316. In addition to the evidence Stojić challenges and which is addressed below (see *infra*, para. 1472), the Trial Chamber referred to other testimony and exhibits showing that Stojić issued orders to the Military Police, which were implemented. Trial Judgement, Vol. 4, paras 315-316, fns 741-745. These orders, *inter alia*: (1) concerned the movement of people and goods in Jablanica; (2) prohibited the carrying of long barrel weapons by civilians and members of military units as well as restricted the carrying of short barrel weapons, and instructed checkpoints to implement the order; (3) concerned the prevention of banned movement of goods and weapons; (4) concerned the detention of trucks with trailers; (5) increased control of exit and entry points in Mostar; and (6) concerned inspection of all persons and motor vehicles leaving Mostar due to increased number of thefts of both public and private property. See Trial Judgement, Vol.4, paras 315-316, referring to, *inter alia*, Exs. P01164, p. 1, P01121, pp. 1-4, P01517, P03327 (confidential), p. 5, P01868, p. 1, P02578.

[4667] *Popović et al.* Appeal Judgement, para. 1615; *Krajišnik* Appeal Judgement, para. 695; *Stakić* Appeal Judgement, para. 64; *Tadić* Appeal Judgement, para. 227(iii).

[4668] *Popović et al.* Appeal Judgement, para. 1378; *Krajišnik* Appeal Judgement, para. 706; *Brđanin* Appeal Judgement, para. 430.

[4669] Trial Judgement, Vol. 1, para. 965. See Stojić's Appeal Brief, para. 171.

[4670] Trial Judgement, Vol. 1, para. 965.

[4671] See. *supra*, para. 1460.

[4672] See Trial Judgement, Vol. 4, para. 315 & fns 741-742, 744, referring to Exs. P00875, 5D02002, 5D00548.

considers that authority over a unit can be exercised by various **[page 603]** persons within the chain of command.[4673] Notably, Stojić as Head of the Department of Defence had authority over the Main Staff and, in fact, two of the exhibits cited by Stojić were signed by him.[4674] Similarly, Stojić's contention that his command authority was not proven from the cited evidence as the orders or requests did not come to or from him alone is unconvincing and insufficient to show an error by the Trial Chamber. In this respect, Stojić does not substantiate the assertion that he could not exercise authority on his own accord or that it was the other signatories that had command authority. Thus, Stojić fails to show that no reasonable trier of fact could have concluded that he had command authority over the Military Police after assessing the evidence cited by the Trial Chamber. Likewise, the Appeals Chamber dismisses elsewhere Stojić's argument as far as it concerns the administrative or logistical nature of his involvement as evidence of command authority, which necessarily includes the orders he issued.[4675] Notably, Stojić had the authority to issue orders to the Chief of the Military Police Administration, including those directly linked to operations on the ground such as release of detainees, resubordination of Military Police units, and the engagement of Military Police forces.[4676] Furthermore, his references to two exhibits being "purely administrative orders relating to internal discipline"[4677] and a confidential exhibit cited by the Trial Chamber among other various pieces of evidence[4678] fail to demonstrate an error by the Trial Chamber in its assessment of the evidence. Thus, Stojić's arguments are dismissed.

(iv) <u>Stojić's receipt of reports on Military Police activities</u>

1473. Stojić also contests the Trial Chamber's finding that he regularly received reports about the activities of the Military Police,[4679] by arguing that the reports were sporadic.[4680] Notably, the Trial Chamber cited various pieces of evidence to support its finding,[4681] but Stojić only challenges the reliance on one exhibit and states that other reports prepared by the author of that exhibit were not sent to him.[4682] The Appeals Chamber is unconvinced by this argument as Stojić fails to show how any alleged "sporadic" reporting from one individual affects the Trial Chamber's finding that he received regular reports which did clearly emanate from various sources.[4683] Stojić also argues that **[page 604]** as Exhibits P03274 and P00518 were requests for reports, this showed *ad hoc* reporting.[4684] The Appeals Chamber notes that Exhibit P00518 is not a request for reports but a report sent by Stojić, on 22 September 1992, to the HVO and the Government, reporting, *inter alia*, on the activities of the Military Police, including how many reports it had filed by that point[4685] As such, it indicates that Stojić and the Department of Defence were aware of the activities of the Military Police.

1474. With respect to Exhibit P03274, the Appeals Chamber notes that it is Stojić's request, directed to *all* HVO bodies, in which he asks for an "assessment of the current situation in your area" in order for the Department of Defence to be able to submit its own report to the Government for the period January 1993 to July 1993. Stojić does not explain how this request calls into question the Trial Chamber's finding that he received regular reports about the activities of the Military Police,[4686] particularly given the other documents cited by the Trial Chamber in support of its finding, including an "interim report" sent by Ćorić to Stojić

[4673] See *Popović et al.* Appeal Judgement, para. 1892 ("the exercise of effective control by one commander does not necessarily exclude effective control being exercised by a different commander").

[4674] See Ex. P00875; Ex. 5D02002.

[4675] See *supra*, paras 1412, 1467. See also *supra*, para. 1401.

[4676] Trial Judgement, Vol. 4, paras 314-316, 320.

[4677] Stojić's Appeal Brief, para. 172, referring to Exs. P01121, P01098.

[4678] See Stojić's Appeal Brief, para. 172, referring to Ex. P03327 (confidential); Trial Judgement, Vol. 4, para. 315 & fn. 741, referring to, *inter alia*, Ex. P03327 (confidential).

[4679] Trial Judgement, Vol. 4, para. 318. See Trial Judgement, Vol. 4, para. 320.

[4680] Stojić's Appeal Brief, para. 175. See *supra*, para. 1460.

[4681] Trial Judgement, Vol. 4, para. 318 & fns 747-749.

[4682] See Stojić's Appeal Brief, para. 175, referring to Ex. P03314 (confidential).

[4683] See Trial Judgement, Vol. 4, para. 318, referring to, *inter alia*, Exs. P03274 (order from Stojić that various personnel including the Chief of the Military Police Administration submit reports to the Department of Defence), P01053 (report to Stojić personally from Ćorić), P02863 (report to, *inter alios*, Stojić personally from the Deputy Commander of the Rama Brigade).

[4684] See *supra*, para. 1460.

[4685] Ex. P00518, pp. 4, 6.

[4686] See Stojić's Appeal Brief, para. 175.

personally informing him of the Military Police units' activities in Gornji Vakuf in early January 1993.[4687] Furthermore, given that this request was directed to all HVO bodies and that Stojić asked for the "assessment of the current situation", his assertion that if he had regular reports from the Military Police he would not have needed to request them is speculative. Accordingly, he fails to show an error.

1475.   As it concerns Stojić's submission that two of the exhibits cited by the Trial Chamber are irrelevant to the reporting procedure, the Appeals Chamber notes that although Exhibits 2D02000 and P01409 do not directly speak to Stojić receiving reports, they concern activities of the Military Police and clearly indicate that he would have been informed of these activities.[4688] In this regard, the Appeals Chamber notes that Exhibit 2D02000 lists one of Stojić's priority tasks as ensuring that the Military Police submit reports to the military courts,[4689] while Exhibit PO1409 is an order issued by Stojić on 3 February 1993 regarding the mobilisation of the Military Police.[4690] Thus, Stojić fails to show that there are reasonable inferences that can be drawn from these exhibits other than that he was kept informed of Military Police activities. A reasonable trier of fact could have considered these exhibits as evidence of a reporting procedure and Stojić's arguments are thus dismissed. **[page 605]** Consequently, Stojić's argument that the "limited flow of information" is inconsistent with "effective control"[4691] is also dismissed, since he fails to demonstrate the irregularity of reports.

1476.   With regard to Stojić's argument that the Trial Chamber failed to establish that he actually received three Military Police reports,[4692] the Appeals Chamber notes that the Trial Chamber found that he regularly received reports about Military Police activities and cited these three reports as support.[4693] Considering that the three reports in question were addressed to Stojić personally,[4694] and the Trial Chamber made numerous findings on the reporting procedure involving Stojić, he does not demonstrate that the Trial Chamber failed to find that he received these three reports. In this regard, the Trial Chamber found that Stojić had ordered all heads of units, including the Military Police Administration, to submit reports on their activities to him.[4695] In addition, the Trial Chamber found that Stojić received reports from other organs and exercised a reporting function in relation to the Government; reports which would include the activities of Military Police units embedded in the HVO brigades.[4696] Thus, the Trial Chamber found, *inter alia,* that: (1) Stojić received reports on the situation in BiH, in particular the military situation, sent by the Main Staff;[4697] and (2) Stojić, in turn, informed the HZ(R) H-B Government, both through reports and during Government sessions, about the military and security situation on the ground.[4698]

1477.   Further, the Trial Chamber, in discussing Stojić's authority over the HVO, relied on evidence[4699] which also shows that he ordered several units, including the Military Police Administration, to provide him with written reports every eight hours on the implementation of the 15 January 1993 Ultimatum.[4700] The Appeals Chamber also notes that some of the reports relied on by the Trial Chamber were addressed to Stojić or the Department of Defence,[4701] and considers that he does not present any arguments demonstrating that the flow of information was interrupted in those instances thus preventing his receipt of the reports.

[4687]   See Ex. P01053. Although Exhibit P01053 predates the JCE, the Appeals Chamber is of the view that the Trial Chamber reasonably considered it as supporting the finding that Stojić was regularly informed of the Military Police units' activities. See also Exs. P02863 (report from the deputy commander of the Military Police units in Prozor informing Stojić and Ćorić of the activities of Tuta's men in Prozor Municipality), P03314 (confidential) (report from the commander of the Military Police units in Prozor informing Stojić and Ćorić of the influx of civilians and soldiers in Prozor Municipality).
[4688]   See Ex. 2D02000, para. 94(7); Ex. P01409.
[4689]   Ex. 2D02000, para. 94(7).
[4690]   Ex. P01409.
[4691]   Stojić's Reply Brief, para. 51.
[4692]   See Stojić's Appeal Brief, para. 175, referring to Exs. P01053, P03314 (confidential), P02863.
[4693]   Trial Judgement, Vol. 4, para. 318, referring to, *inter alia,* Exs. P01053, P03314 (confidential), P02863. See *supra,* para. 1473.
[4694]   Ex. P01053; Ex. P03314 (confidential); Ex. P02863.
[4695]   Trial Judgement, Vol. 4, para. 318.
[4696]   See *supra,* paras 1418-1419.
[4697]   Trial Judgement, Vol. 4, para. 300. See Trial Judgement, Vol. 1, paras 767-768.
[4698]   Trial Judgement, Vol. 4, para. 300.
[4699]   Trial Judgement, Vol. 4, para. 304, referring to, *inter alia,* Ex. P01140. See Trial Judgement, Vol. 1, paras 453, 562.
[4700]   Ex. P01140, para. 9. See Ex. P01053 (Interim Report sent by Ćorić to Stojić on 5 January 1993). See also Prosecution's Response Brief (Stojić), para. 153.
[4701]   Ex. P01053; Ex. P02863; Ex. P03314 (confidential); Ex. P04224. See Trial Judgement, Vol. 4, para. 318 & fns 747-749.

Therefore, in light of the reporting function Stojić was found to have exercised on the basis of various reports sent to him, the Appeals Chamber concludes that Stojić fails to show that no reasonable trier of fact could have concluded **[page 606]** that the Military Police reports addressed and sent to him, particularly the three reports he challenges on appeal, were also received by him.

1478. Stojić further argues that "effective control" is not proven by the receipt of reports unless he acted on their contents.[4702] The Appeals Chamber first considers that the receipt of information and regular reports on the activities of the Military Police, as part of the information flow, can be a relevant indicator in determining Stojić's authority over the Military Police.[4703] Moreover, the Appeals Chamber notes that acting on the contents of a report is not a necessary requirement in determining command authority.[4704] As Stojić fails to show the contrary, his arguments are dismissed.

(c) Conclusion

1479. In sum, the Appeals Chamber finds that Stojić has failed to demonstrate that the Trial Chamber erred by finding that he commanded and had "effective control" over the Military Police. Stojić's ground of appeal 21 is dismissed.

4. Alleged errors concerning Stojić's failure to prevent and punish crimes committed by the HVO and the Military Police (Stojić's Ground *23)*

1480. The Trial Chamber found that "Stojić did not intend to prevent or punish the crimes by the HVO armed forces, including the Military Police, whereas he had the *de facto* power to do so".[4705] It concluded that "if [Stojić] did not issue orders to prevent or punish crimes or if those orders were not obeyed, it was because he knowingly did not want to take those measures".[4706] The Trial Chamber also found that Stojić was informed about the serious discipline problems within the KB unit under the command of Mladen Naletilić, alias "Tuta", and their crimes. It concluded that, although Stojić had the power to prevent or punish the crimes committed by Naletilić's men, he had no intention of doing so and in fact accepted and encouraged the crimes by praising the unit.[4707]

1481. Stojić challenges these findings of the Trial Chamber, and argues that it erroneously: (1) found that he had the power to prevent and punish crimes committed by the HVO, including the Military Police, and Naletilić's troops and deliberately failed to do so;[4708] and (2) relied on his **[page 607]** failure to prevent and punish crimes as a basis for its conclusion that he significantly contributed to the JCE and shared the intent of other JCE members.[4709]

(a) Stojić's *de facto* power to prevent and punish crimes (Stojić's Sub-ground 23.1)

(i) Arguments of the Parties

1482. Stojić submits that the Trial Chamber erred by failing to provide a reasoned "decision" regarding its finding that he had the *de facto* power to prevent and punish crimes.[4710] Specifically, Stojić argues that the Trial Chamber failed to identify any *de jure* or *de facto* power he possessed or any mechanism he could have used to prevent and punish crimes.[4711] He avers that the "vague reference to 'operative orders' is insufficient"

4702 Stojić's Appeal Brief, para. 175.
4703 *Cf. Popović et al.* Appeal Judgement, para. 1861.
4704 *Cf. Popović et al.* Appeal Judgement, para. 1860.
4705 Trial Judgement, Vol. 4, para. 423. See Trial Judgement, Vol. 4, paras 410-415, 421-422, 427.
4706 Trial Judgement, Vol. 4, para. 415. See Trial Judgement, Vol. 4, paras 410-414, 427.
4707 Trial Judgement, Vol. 4, para. 420. See Trial Judgement, Vol. 4, paras 416-419, 427.
4708 Stojić's Appeal Brief, paras 178-188.
4709 Stojić's Appeal Brief, para. 189. Stojić argues that these errors invalidate the Trial Judgement and his convictions on all counts should be overturned. Stojić's Appeal Brief, para. 189.
4710 Stojić's Appeal Brief, para. 178.
4711 Stojić's Appeal Brief, para. 179.

as it failed to explain how such orders could prevent or punish crimes.[4712] Stojić also submits that the Trial Chamber's conclusion is inconsistent with, and opposite to, an earlier finding that he did not have the *de jure* obligation to prevent or punish crimes.[4713] He contends that having found that he had no obligation to punish crimes, the Trial Chamber "should not have relied on any omission to prevent or punish crimes as a way of establishing his culpability".[4714] Stojić also submits that the Trial Chamber disregarded: (1) its earlier finding that crimes could not be effectively opposed;[4715] and (2) clearly relevant Defence submissions and cited evidence that the Department of Justice and Administration ("DoJA") was responsible for setting up and administering the military judiciary.[4716]

1483. The Prosecution responds that the Trial Chamber specified how Stojić could have taken measures to prevent and punish crimes on the basis of bis power to issue and enforce orders to the HVO, including the Military Police and identified two types of operative orders he issued as examples.[4717] The Prosecution further argues that Stojić: (1) issued other orders which demonstrate his effective control, such as orders relating to, *inter alia,* manpower, the formation and dissolution **[page 608]** of units, and the tasking and removal of military personnel;[4718] and (2) "could have spoken out against crimes".[4719] It further responds that the Trial Chamber found that Stojić had *de facto* power to prevent and punish through his orders.[4720] The Prosecution submits that the Trial Chamber did not base its findings on whether Stojić could refer matters to the military courts,[4721] and that the Defence submissions at trial on the DoJA "have no bearing on measures Stojić could have taken to suppress crimes".[4722]

1484. Stojić replies that as "effective control" requires the material ability to prevent or punish crimes all factors which might impede this material ability must be taken into account,[4723] and thus argues that the Trial Chamber should have considered the non-compliance with his orders.[4724]

    (ii) Analysis

1485. Regarding Stojić's contention that the Trial Chamber failed to identify the powers he possessed or any mechanism he could have used to prevent or punish crimes, the Appeals Chamber recalls that the Trial Chamber found that the evidence did "not support a finding that Bruno Stojić had the *de jure* obligation to apply [his] instructions to punish the members of the HVO armed forces and the Military Police who had committed a crime".[4725] Thus, the relevant issue is the *de facto* powers which the Trial Chamber found Stojić

[4712] Stojić's Appeal Brief, para. 179, referring to Trial Judgement, Vol. 4, para. 414. See also Appeal Hearing, AT. 291 (21 Mar 2017).
[4713] Stojić's Appeal Brief, para. 180, referring to Trial Judgement, Vol. 4, para. 413. In this regard, Stojić highlights the Trial Chamber's findings that the Military Police had a dual chain of command which resulted in a "fuzzy" chain of command and that the Military Police Administration's control diminished over time. Stojić's Appeal Brief, para. 180, referring to Trial Judgement, Vol. 1, paras 949-950, 964, 971, 974.
[4714] Stojić's Appeal Brief, para. 180. See also Appeal Hearing, AT. 291 (21 Mar 2017).
[4715] Stojić's Appeal Brief, para. 181, referring to Trial Judgement, Vol. 1, paras 972, 986; Stojić's Reply Brief, para. 56.
[4716] Stojić's Appeal Brief, para. 182, referring to Stojić's Final Brief, para. 406, referring to Exs. P03350, 1D01974, P01536, P01652, 1D01179, P00559. Stojić argues that the Trial Chamber only considered that the DoJA *de facto* proposed military judicial appointments and disregarded the remainder of the Defence submissions. Stojić's Appeal Brief, para. 182.
[4717] Prosecution's Response Brief (Stojić), para. 164, referring to Trial Judgement, Vol. 4, paras 312, 320, 410, 413-415.
[4718] Prosecution's Response Brief (Stojić), para. 164 & fns 629-636, referring to, *inter alia,* Ex. P01098. As part of its response to Stojić's ground of appeal 21, the Prosecution submits that Exhibit P01098 demonstrates Stojić's ability to punish military personnel without authorisation through the Chief of the Military Police Administration. See Prosecution's Response Brief (Stojić), para. 151.
[4719] Prosecution's Response Brief (Stojić), para. 164. See also Appeal Hearing, AT. 333-334 (21 Mar 2017).
[4720] Prosecution's Response Brief (Stojić), para. 166. See also Appeal Hearing, AT. 333 (21 Mar 2017).
[4721] Prosecution's Response Brief (Stojić), para. 167. See also Appeal Hearing, AT. 339 (21 Mar 2017).
[4722] Prosecution's Response Brief (Stojić), para. 168.
[4723] Stojić's Reply Brief, para. 55. Stojić replies that Exhibit P01098, which the Prosecution argues shows his ability to punish military personnel, actually "shows that his authority was limited to requesting a 'report to the competent court'". Stojić's Reply Brief, para. 59.
[4724] Stojić's Reply Brief, para. 57. Stojić replies that there was no evidence that he could ensure that his orders were carried out, and that his material ability to prevent or punish was negated by the inability of the Military Police to function. Stojić's Reply Brief, paras 56-57.
[4725] Trial Judgement, Vol. 4, paras. 413. See *supra,* para. 1428. The Appeals Chamber also notes that the Trial Chamber similarly found that the Head of the Department of Defence was not *de jure* part of the military chain of command. Trial Judgement, Vol. 1, para. 565, Vol. 4, para. 306.

possessed.[4726] In this regard, the Appeals Chamber observes that the Trial Chamber made various findings, including that Stojić: (1) had "the power to issue operative orders to [the HVO and the Military Police] as well as the power to have his orders forwarded through the chain of command of the HVO armed forces, including the Military Police";[4727] (2) had the power to issue orders directly to the HVO and the Military Police and to ensure they were carried out and used that authority;[4728] (3) issued orders directly to the **[page 609]** HVO, particularly with regard to ceasefires, detention centres, troop movements, reorganisation of military units, assignments and mobilisation of troops, and freedom of movement of humanitarian or international organisations;[4729] and (4) had the authority to issue orders to the Chief of the Military Police Administration, including those directly linked to operations on the ground, such as resubordination.[4730] The Appeals Chamber recalls that it dismisses elsewhere Stojić's challenges to these findings on his powers and the evidence the Trial Chamber relied on in concluding that he could issue various orders.[4731] Stojić's contention is dismissed.

1486. Concerning whether the Trial Chamber was required to explain how the orders, which Stojić had the power to issue, could have been used to prevent or punish crimes, the Appeals Chamber finds this argument to be unpersuasive for the following reasons. Among the findings noted above,[4732] the Trial Chamber considered that Stojić issued orders to conduct autopsies whenever the commission of a war crime was suspected and for HVO commanders to respect international humanitarian law.[4733] The Trial Chamber also observed that Stojić: (1) had the power to issue instructions about matters of discipline in the HVO;[4734] (2) had the power to have his orders forwarded through the chain of command;[4735] and (3) was hierarchically superior to Ćorić.[4736] Moreover, the Trial Chamber noted that the Main Staff was an integral part of the Department of Defence.[4737] The Trial Chamber then concluded that in light of these powers, Stojić's failure to issue orders to prevent or punish crimes, and any failure to obey the orders he did issue, was the result of him making no serious effort to prevent or punish crimes.[4738] In light of this analysis, the Appeals Chamber finds that it was unnecessary for the Trial Chamber to expand on or discuss further how Stojić's orders could have prevented or punished crimes. The Appeals Chamber therefore dismisses Stojić's argument.

1487. Stojić also argues, in reply, that he did not have the "material ability" to prevent or punish crimes and that the Trial Chamber should have considered the non-compliance with his orders as an impediment to his ability to prevent and punish.[4739] In this regard, the Appeals Chamber notes that the Trial Chamber was not required to establish that Stojić had a "material ability" to prevent or **[page 610]** punish crimes given that it conducted its analysis in the context of Stojić's JCE I liability.[4740] However, the Appeals Chamber also notes that a failure to intervene to prevent recurrence of crimes or to halt abuses has been taken into account in assessing an accused's contribution to a joint criminal enterprise and his intent "where the accused had some power and influence or authority over the perpetrators sufficient to prevent or halt the abuses but failed to exercise such power".[4741] Nonetheless, Stojić refers only to four instances in the Trial Judgement which do not clearly speak to his direct orders being disobeyed.[4742] He also does not address the fact that the Trial

---

[4726]   Trial Judgement, Vol. 4, para. 423.
[4727]   Trial Judgement, Vol. 4, para. 414. See *supra*, paras 1427-1435, 1470-1472.
[4728]   Trial Judgement, Vol. 4, paras 312, 410. See Trial Judgement, Vol. 4, paras 304-311, 325-326, 423. See also *supra*, paras 1427-1435, 1470-1472.
[4729]   Trial Judgement, Vol. 1, paras 562, 564-565, 795, Vol. 4, para. 306. See Trial Judgement, Vol. 4, para. 413. See also *supra*, paras 1427-1435, 1470-1472.
[4730]   Trial Judgement, Vol. 4, paras 314, 320. See *supra*, paras 1458, 1472.
[4731]   See *supra*, paras 1424-1435, 1470-1472.
[4732]   See *supra*, para. 1485.
[4733]   Trial Judgement, Vol. 4, paras 412, 414.
[4734]   Trial Judgement, Vol. 4, para. 413.
[4735]   Trial Judgement, Vol. 4, paras 414-415.
[4736]   Trial Judgement, Vol. 1, paras 854, 862, Vol. 4, para. 314.
[4737]   Trial Judgement, Vol. 4, para. 306.
[4738]   Trial Judgement, Vol. 4, paras 415, 423, 427.
[4739]   Stojić's Reply Brief, para. 57, referring to *Strugar* Appeal Judgement, paras 256-257. See *supra*, para. 1484.
[4740]   See *supra*, para. 1410.
[4741]   *Stanišić and Župljanin* Appeal Judgement, paras 111, 734.
[4742]   Trial Judgement, Vol. 4, para. 772 ("Although the evidence shows that mobilisation was a challenging process, particularly due to the lack of response to the call to arms and due to desertion [...] the armed forces of the HVO in late 1992 already numbered 45,000 men"), Vol. 2, para. 2081 (the Trial Chamber's finding that it had no evidence that one order Stojić issued on 3 July 1993 – to

Chamber did note that "if [his] orders were not obeyed, it was because he knowingly did not want to take those measures".[4743] Thus, Stojić fails to show that his orders were not complied with to such an extent that any alleged failure by the Trial Chamber to consider this factor was an error. He fails to demonstrate that these four instances cited could have impacted the Trial Chamber's findings on his ability to issue orders.

1488. Stojić also argues that the Trial Chamber's conclusions that he had no *de jure* obligation to prevent and punish crimes and that he had the *de facto* power to prevent and punish crimes are inconsistent.[4744] Stojić, however, fails to substantiate his argument and does not address the distinguishing features between *de jure* and *de facto* powers, in that, having *de facto* powers does not necessarily mean that *de jure* powers must also exist.[4745] In this respect, the Appeals Chamber recalls that Stojić was found to have had command authority and "effective control" over most of the HVO and the Military Police through his *de facto* powers.[4746] Thus, Stojić does not show an inconsistency in the Trial Chamber's findings and his argument is dismissed. For the same reasons, the Appeals Chamber dismisses Stojić's remaining assertion – that the Trial Chamber erred in relying on his failure to prevent and punish crimes – as the basis of his culpable omission stems from his *de facto* powers.[4747] In any event, provided the accused shares the intent to implement the common purpose by criminal means, the Appeals Chamber recalls that "when establishing an **[page 611]** accused's participation in a joint criminal enterprise through his failure to act, the existence of a legal duty to act deriving from a rule of criminal law is not required".[4748] In addition, any alleged error in this regard does not impact on the Trial Chamber's consideration of whether Stojić used his authority to undertake measures which could have prevented or punished crimes as a factor in inferring his JCE I intent.[4749]

1489. Stojić also contends that the Trial Chamber disregarded his trial submissions on the role of the DoJA in prosecuting crimes;[4750] however, he does not explain how these trial submissions could have impacted on the Trial Chamber's findings. In particular, the Appeals Chamber notes that the Trial Chamber did discuss that the DoJA "was tasked with establishing effective judicial authority".[4751] Recalling that the Trial Chamber is not under the obligation to justify its findings in relation to every submission made during the trial,[4752] Stojić's contention is dismissed.

1490. Regarding Stojić's argument that the Trial Chamber disregarded its earlier finding that crimes could not be effectively opposed, the Appeals Chamber takes note of the Trial Chamber's discussion on the difficulties experienced by organs involved in taking criminal action against the HVO, and in particular, its finding that because the Military Police was forced to devote major parts of its force to combat operations, "crime within the ranks of the HVO armed forces – including the Military Police – [...] could not, for example, be effectively opposed, especially inasmuch as the civilian police forces and the military tribunals failed to operate in satisfactory fashion".[4753] Nonetheless, even if the organs involved in investigating and prosecuting crimes experienced difficulties, the Appeals Chamber considers that this did not preclude the

---

transfer the management of the detention of Muslim men of military age arrested in Čapljina Municipality from the 1st Knez Domagoj Brigade to the local HVO – was implemented), Vol. 4, paras 480 (the Trial Chamber observed that Praljak intervened when an HVO unit blocked the passage of an UNPROFOR convoy authorised by Stojić, allowing for the convoy to pass through), 1039 (the Trial Chamber's finding that it was not aware of evidence showing that the Detention Commission – under the authority of the Department of Defence – accomplished its tasks).

4743 Trial Judgement, Vol. 4, para. 415. See also *infra*, para. 1494.

4744 See Trial Judgement, Vol. 4, paras 413, 423.

4745 The Appeals Chamber has made this clear in the context of its discussions regarding Article 7(3) responsibility. See *Čelebici* Appeal Judgement, para. 193 ("The power or authority to prevent or to punish does not solely arise from *de jure* authority conferred through official appointment"). See also *Nahimana et al.* Appeal Judgement, para. 625; *Kayishema and Ruzindana* Appeal Judgement, para. 294, quoting *Čelebici* Appeal Judgement, para. 192.

4746 Trial Judgement, Vol. 4, paras 306, 312, 320, 326. See also *supra*, para. 1457.

4747 See *supra*, para. 1482.

4748 *Stanišić and Župljanin* Appeal Judgement, para. 110. See *Stanišić and Župljanin* Appeal Judgement, para. 111.

4749 Trial Judgement, Vol. 4, paras 423, 427-428. See also *Šainović et al.* Appeal Judgement, para. 1045. See also *Popović et al.* Appeal Judgement, paras 1368-1369; *infra*, para. 2081 ("For the purposes of establishing the *mens rea* element of commission through participation in a JCE [...], it was within the Trial Chamber's discretion to consider, among other factors, whether Praljak used his command authority to undertake measures which could have prevented or punished the commission of crimes.").

4750 Stojić's Appeal Brief, para. 182, referring to Stojić's Final Brief, para. 406. See *supra*, para. 1482.

4751 Trial Judgement, Vol. 1, para. 646. See Trial Judgement, Vol. 1, paras 645, 647-650.

4752 *Kvočka et al.* Appeal Judgement, para. 23. See *Popović et al.* Appeal Judgement, paras 305, 1841.

4753 Trial Judgement, Vol. 1, para. 972. See also Trial Judgement, Vol. 4, para. 411.

Trial Chamber from finding that Stojić had command authority and "effective control" over the HVO and the Military Police as he had other avenues available to prevent and punish crimes.[4754] Stojić's *de facto* powers gave him sufficient power or influence to deal with crimes, which he has not shown was hindered in such a way that he could not at least make inquiries, initiate investigations, or report the perpetrators to the competent authorities. For example, as noted by the Trial Chamber, on 6 February 1993 Stojić ordered the brigades of the North-West OZ to conduct autopsies whenever there were suspicions of a war crime; further, on 23 April 1993, having heard of the killings and **[page 612]** torching of houses in Jablanica, he issued a joint order with Petković instructing the HVO commanders to respect international humanitarian law.[4755] Stojić's argument is dismissed as he fails to show that no reasonable trier of fact, after finding that some organs involved in opposing crime were not operating in a satisfactory fashion, could have concluded that he had the *de facto* power to prevent or punish crimes.

1491. In sum, the Appeals Chamber finds that Stojić has failed to demonstrate that the Trial Chamber erred in finding that he had the *de facto* power to prevent and punish crimes committed by the HVO and the Military Police. Stojić's sub-ground of appeal 23.1 is dismissed.

(b) Whether Stojić did not intend to prevent or punish crimes (Stojić's Sub-ground 23.3)

1492. Stojić submits that no reasonable trier of fact could have concluded that he "did not intend to prevent or punish the crimes".[4756] In this regard, Stojić argues that he issued instructions encouraging the investigation of crimes, ordered commanders to respect international humanitarian law, and promulgated regulations for the treatment of POWs.[4757] Stojić also contends that the Trial Chamber failed to explain its conclusion that he "knowingly did not want to take measures", especially in light of its findings that the judicial system was "seriously limited" and that crime could not be effectively opposed.[4758] Stojić argues that alternative reasonable inferences include that he did not have the power to ensure that his instructions were carried out.[4759]

1493. The Prosecution responds that Stojić fails to show that no reasonable trier of fact could have found that he did not intend to prevent or punish crimes.[4760] It argues that the Trial Chamber was cognisant of the unenforced orders Stojić issued, was mindful of difficulties in the judicial system, and reasonably concluded that he made "no serious effort" to prevent or punish crimes.[4761] **[page 613]**

1494. Stojić challenges the Trial Chamber's conclusion that "he knowingly did not want to take" measures to prevent or punish crimes.[4762] In this regard, the Appeals Chamber recalls that a Trial Judgement must be read as a whole,[4763] and notes that the Trial Chamber made numerous findings which put the impugned conclusion into context. In addition to Stojić's ability to issue orders to punish and prevent crimes,[4764] the Trial Chamber also found that he: (1) participated in or planned HVO military operations and knew of crimes being committed

---

[4754] See Trial Judgement, Vol. 4, paras 312, 320, 410, 415, 425-427.

[4755] See Trial Judgement, Vol. 4, paras 340, 342, 412, 414. In addition, while Stojić submits, referring to Exhibit P01098, that "his authority was limited to requesting a 'report to the competent court'", the Appeals Chamber considers that this was nevertheless an authority he had and could exercise. See Stojić's Reply Brief, para. 59. Furthermore, in the Appeals Chamber's view, Exhibit P01098 demonstrates that Stojić could in fact initiate criminal proceedings against military personnel through the Chief of the Military Police Administration. See Ex. P01098, p. 2 (where Stojić instructs that "[a]ny person who opens fire in an inhabited area without authorisation shall be immediately arrested and detained, and a report submitted to the competent organ".).

[4756] Stojić's Appeal Brief, paras 186-187, referring to Trial Judgement, Vol. 4, para. 423.

[4757] Stojić's Appeal Brief, para. 187, referring to Exs. P02578, p. 1, P02050, P01474.

[4758] Stojić's Appeal Brief, para. 188, referring to Trial Judgement, Vol. 1, paras 972, 986.

[4759] Stojić's Appeal Brief, para. 188; Stojić's Reply Brief, para. 58. See Stojić's Reply Brief, para. 57.

[4760] Prosecution's Response Brief (Stojić), para. 165. See Prosecution's Response Brief (Stojić), para. 163. The Prosecution submits that Stojić instead concealed crimes and commended and secured promotions for perpetrators he knew had participated in crimes. Prosecution's Response Brief (Stojić), para. 165.

[4761] Prosecution's Response Brief (Stojić), paras 165, 167. See Prosecution's Response Brief (Stojić), para. 163. See also Appeal Hearing, AT. 333-337, 339 (21 Mar 2017).

[4762] Trial Judgement, Vol. 4, para. 415.

[4763] *Stanišić and Župljanin* Appeal Judgement, paras 138, 376, 705; *Popović et al.* Appeal Judgement, para. 2006; *Mrkšić and Šljivančanin* Appeal Judgement, para. 379. See *Kalimanzira* Appeal Judgement, para. 227.

[4764] See *supra*, paras 1485-1486.

and thus intended to have those crimes committed;[4765] (2) encouraged crimes committed by Naletilić's troops and commended Naletilić;[4766] (3) requested and obtained a promotion for Ivica Rajić knowing that he committed crimes;[4767] and (4) denied to international representatives that the evictions of Muslims from West Mostar were being carried out by the HVO which proved that the HVO authorities did not genuinely intend to prevent crimes.[4768] The Trial Chamber also considered evidence that Stojić wished to punish offences but could not do so in practice because of the situation in BiH at the time, including that the military courts were not functioning,[4769] as well as his trial submissions that he was not in a position to prevent or punish crimes.[4770] It is on the basis of these findings and considerations that the Trial Chamber concluded that Stojić "did not intend to prevent or punish the crimes"[4771] and that "he knowingly did not want to take" such measures.[4772] The Appeals Chamber finds that Stojić fails to demonstrate that the Trial Chamber erred in concluding that his intention not to prevent or punish crimes was the only reasonable inference available from the evidence. The Appeals Chamber also dismisses Stojić's assertions on crimes not being effectively opposed, the limitation of the judicial system, and his lack of power to ensure compliance with his orders.[4773]

1495. Further, the Trial Chamber was aware of, and considered, Stojić's: (1) order on 23 April 1993 to the commanders of all OZs to treat civilians and detainees in accordance with international law;[4774] (2) promulgation of regulations on 11 February 1993 for the treatment of POWs imprisoned in detention centres;[4775] and (3) order for vehicles exiting the town of Mostar to **[page 614]** be checked in an attempt to combat thefts.[4776] Stojić fails to show how these actions call into question the Trial Chamber's conclusion that he "made no serious effort to prevent or punish the crimes" based on its findings discussed above.[4777] Stojić's sub-ground of appeal 23.3 is therefore dismissed.

(c) Stojić's power to prevent or punish the crimes committed by Naletilić's troops (Stojić's Sub-ground 23.2)

1496. Stojić submits that the Trial Chamber's finding that he had the power to prevent or punish the crimes committed by Naletilić's troops was unreasonable and inconsistent with earlier findings.[4778] Stojić argues that the Trial Chamber found elsewhere that the ATGs reported directly to the Main Staff and that he was not in their chain of command.[4779] He also submits that no evidence was presented showing that he had command authority over the KB and its ATGs.[4780]

1497. The Prosecution responds that the Trial Chamber reasonably found that Stojić had the power to prevent or punish crimes committed by the KB and its ATGs.[4781] The Prosecution avers that this finding is unaffected by the fact that the Trial Chamber could not find that Stojić exercised a power of command over the KB and its ATGs under Naletilić's command.[4782] It argues that the findings show that Stojić accepted and encouraged crimes committed by the KB and its ATGs.[4783]

[4765]   Trial Judgement, Vol. 4, para. 426. See also *infra*, paras 1534-1537, 1541-1542, 1545-1550.

[4766]   Trial Judgement, Vol. 4, paras 423, 427. See Trial Judgement, Vol. 4, paras 416-420. See also *infra*, paras 1498-1499.

[4767]   Trial Judgement, Vol. 4, para. 427. See Trial Judgement, Vol. 4, paras 380-383. See also *infra*, para. 1707 (limiting consideration that Stojić requested and obtained a promotion for Ivica Rajić knowing that he committed crimes in Vareš town, and not Stupni Do).

[4768]   Trial Judgement, Vol. 4, paras 421-422, 427. See *infra*, paras 1625-1630.

[4769]   Trial Judgement, Vol. 4, para. 411. See Trial Judgement, Vol. 1, paras 972, 980-986. See also *supra*, para. 1489.

[4770]   Trial Judgement, Vol. 4, para..409.

[4771]   Trial Judgement, Vol. 4, para. 423.

[4772]   Trial Judgement, Vol. 4, para. 415.

[4773]   See *supra*, paras 1486-1489, 1492.

[4774]   Trial Judgement, Vol. 4, para. 340, referring to Ex. P02050.

[4775]   Trial Judgement, Vol. 4, para. 386, referring to, *inter alia*, Ex. P01474. See Trial Judgement, Vol. 4, para. 387.

[4776]   Trial Judgement, Vol. 4, para. 446, referring to Ex. P02578, p. 1.

[4777]   Trial Judgement, Vol. 4, para. 423. See Stojić's Appeal Brief, para. 187, referring to Exs. P02578, p. 1, P02050, P01474.

[4778]   Stojić's Appeal Brief, paras 183, 185; Stojić's Reply Brief, para. 60.

[4779]   Stojić's Appeal Brief, para. 184, referring to Trial Judgement, Vol. 1, paras 565, 708, 791, 795-796, 829, 835.

[4780]   Stojić's Appeal Brief, para. 184; Stojić's Reply Brief, para. 60, referring to Trial Judgement, Vol. 1, para. 835.

[4781]   Prosecution's Response Brief (Stojić), para. 170.

[4782]   Prosecution's Response Brief (Stojić), para. 170, referring to Trial Judgement, Vol. 1, para. 835, Vol. 4, paras 307, 420. The Prosecution argues that the Main Staff was an integral part of the Department of Defence, and that the absence of direct orders from Stojić to the KB or the ATGs does not exclude his effective control over them. Prosecution's Response Brief (Stojić), para. 170.

[4783]   Prosecution's Response Brief (Stojić), para. 171, referring to Trial Judgement, Vol. 4, paras 416-418, Exs. P02770, P04401 (confidential), pp. 4-5, P03928 (0300-3205). See Appeal Hearing, AT. 337-338 (21 Mar 2017).

1498. The Trial Chamber found that, although "there were structural and operational ties between Bruno Stojić and Mladen Naletilić and his ATGs",[4784] it had "no evidence supporting a finding that the Department of Defence exercised a power of command over the KB and its ATGs under Mladen Naletilić's command".[4785] The Trial Chamber also concluded that "Stojić had effective control over the activities of the components of the HZ(R) H-B armed forces – save the KB – and over the Military Police".[4786] Stojić argues that the former finding is contradictory to the holding by the Trial Chamber that he had the power to prevent or punish crimes committed by "Tuta's men" **[page 615]** but had no intention of doing so.[4787] However, in arriving at this impugned finding, the Trial Chamber also: (1) considered evidence that Stojić was asked "to use his authority and influence" to put an end to a situation involving "Tuta's men" and their "severe discipline problems";[4788] (2) observed various instances where Stojić stated that he had confidence in "Tuta" and commended the KB and its commander "Tuta";[4789] and (3) found that there were structural and operational ties between Stojić and Naletilić and his ATGs.[4790]

1499. Moreover, Stojić fails to take into consideration that the Trial Chamber also found that: (1) the Main Staff was an integral part of the Department of Defence;[4791] (2) he had the power to have his orders forwarded through the chain of command;[4792] (3) he had the *de facto* power to prevent and punish crimes by the HVO;[4793] and (4) the KB and its ATGs, under Naletilić's command, were integrated into the overall HVO chain of command and reported directly to the Main Staff.[4794] Thus, Stojić would have been able to issue orders to, or could have used his position and influence over, the Main Staff, and more specifically Petković and then subsequently Praljak as Chief/Commander of the Main Staff, regarding the prevention or punishment of crimes committed by the units under Naletilić's command. Considering the authority that Stojić could have exercised over the Main Staff as well as the "structural and operational ties" between him and Naletilić, the Appeals Chamber is not persuaded by his argument that the Trial Chamber's findings were inconsistent or contradictory.[4795] Stojić's sub-ground of appeal 23.2 is therefore dismissed.

(d) Conclusion

1500. In sum, Stojić has failed to demonstrate that the Trial Chamber erred in: (1) finding that he had the power to prevent and punish crimes committed by the HVO, including the Military Police, and Naletilić's troops and deliberately failed to do so; and (2) relying on his failure to prevent and punish crimes as a basis for its conclusion that he significantly contributed to the JCE and shared the intent of other JCE members. Stojić's ground of appeal 23 is dismissed. **[page 616]**

5.   Alleged errors concerning Stojić's powers and responsibilities (Stojić's Ground 24)

(a) Whether Stojić represented the Government in peace negotiations (Stojić's Sub-ground 24.1)

1501. Stojić submits that the Trial Chamber erred in finding that he represented "the HVO" in peace negotiations at the highest level based on the three meetings it relied on.[4796] Stojić argues that: (1) the meeting

---

[4784]   Trial Judgement, Vol. 4, para. 307. See Trial Judgement, Vol. 1, paras 832-835.
[4785]   Trial Judgement, Vol. 4, para. 307. See Trial Judgement, Vol. 1, para. 835.
[4786]   Trial Judgement, Vol. 4, para. 326.
[4787]   Trial Judgement, Vol. 4, para. 420.
[4788]   Trial Judgement, Vol. 4, para. 419.
[4789]   Trial Judgement, Vol. 1, para. 834, Vol. 4, paras 418, 420, 427.
[4790]   Trial Judgement, Vol. 4, para. 307. See Trial Judgement, Vol. 1, paras 832-835.
[4791]   Trial Judgement, Vol. 4, para. 306.
[4792]   Trial Judgement, Vol. 4, para. 414.
[4793]   Trial Judgement, Vol. 4, para. 423. See Trial Judgement, Vol. 4, paras 410-415, 421-422, 427.
[4794]   Trial Judgement, Vol. 1, para. 829.
[4795]   The Appeals Chamber further finds that Stojić's remaining arguments highlight the Trial Chamber's findings, which he does not challenge, and thus he fails to show how these arguments would impact on the conclusions of the Trial Chamber. See Stojić's Appeal Brief, para. 184; *supra*, para. 1496.
[4796]   Stojić's Appeal Brief, para. 190, referring to Trial Judgement, Vol. 4, paras 321-324. The Appeals Chamber notes that Stojić refers to the "HVO" in this sub-ground of appeal without clarifying whether this refers to the HVO armed forces or the HVO Government. Given that he is challenging the Trial Chamber's findings in paragraphs 321 to 324 of Volume 4 of the Trial Judgement,

on 25 March 1993 merely concerned an attempt to resolve a specific issue in the Konjic area;[4797] (2) he did not attend the 18 April 1993 meeting as he "interrupted" this meeting with news about an ABiH offensive causing the meeting to be postponed;[4798] and (3) the only evidence on his involvement in the 2 June 1993 meeting is not that he attended the negotiation but that he later ratified the resulting agreement.[4799] He asserts that the evidence, at most, shows that he participated in local meetings on isolated occasions, and that there is no evidence that he attended any high-level or international negotiation.[4800]

1502. The Prosecution responds that the Trial Chamber's finding was reasonable.[4801] It argues that Stojić: (1) minimises the importance of the 25 March 1993 meeting;[4802] (2) ignores the evidence of ECMM monitor, Klaus Johann Nissen, that Stojić represented the HZ(R) H-B at the 18 April 1993 meeting concerning, *inter alia,* a ceasefire and withdrawal of troops, and his late attendance does not undermine the finding;[4803] and (3) misrepresents the evidence on the 2 June 1993 meeting regarding joint HVO-ABiH Mostar patrols.[4804]

1503. The Appeals Chamber notes that the Trial Chamber found that Stojić was "one of the HVO HZ H-B officials authorised to represent that body in peace negotiations at the highest level".[4805] In doing so, it considered evidence showing that Stojić participated in meetings aimed at resolving the conflicts between the HVO and the ABiH, as well as evidence of an agreement he signed setting up **[page 617]** a joint patrol of HVO and ABiH soldiers.[4806] In challenging the Trial Chamber's reliance on this evidence, Stojić contends that the 25 March 1993 meeting was aimed at resolving a specific issue but cites evidence which the Trial Chamber took into account.[4807] The Appeals Chamber considers that Stojić fails to demonstrate that this evidence or his assertion is inconsistent with the Trial Chamber's finding that this meeting was aimed at resolving the conflicts between the HVO and the ABiH in the municipalities of Konjic and Jablanica.[4808] In any event, as Stojić does not challenge that he participated in these negotiations as one of the representatives of the HVO HZ H-B, he fails to show how his assertion could affect the Trial Chamber's overall finding.

1504. Regarding the 18 April 1993 meeting, the Appeals Chamber observes that the Trial Chamber found that Prlić, Stojić, and Petković attended this meeting on behalf of the HVO.[4809] In support of this finding, the Trial Chamber relied solely on the evidence of the ECMM monitor Klaus Johann Nissen who testified that Stojić was one of the participants in the meeting along with Prlić and Petković on the "HVO side".[4810] The Appeals Chamber notes, however, that Exhibit P01950 indicates that Stojić interrupted the meeting and reported on a large scale offensive of the ABiH in central Bosnia.[4811] [Redacted, see Annex C – Confidential Annex].[4812] The Trial Chamber did not refer to this evidence. The Appeals Chamber considers that Stojić's alleged late arrival to and interruption of the 18 April 1993 meeting is not consistent with Nissen's evidence that he was a participant in this meeting.[4813] Nonetheless, given the limited scope of the Trial Chamber's finding of Stojić's attendance at this meeting on behalf of the HVO, the Appeals Chamber does not consider

---

which in turn concern Stojić's representation of the Government, the Appeals Chamber interprets Stojić's use of the term "HVO" in this particular sub-ground of appeal as a reference to the HVO Government.

[4797]   Stojić's Appeal Brief, para. 190, referring to Ex. 2D00643.

[4798]   Stojić's Appeal Brief, para. 190, referring to Ex. P01950 (confidential), para. 4, [Redacted, see Annex C – Confidential Annex]

[4799]   Stojić's Appeal Brief, para. 190, referring to Exs. P02652 (confidential), p. 1, P10367 (confidential), para. 58.

[4800]   Stojić's Appeal Brief, para. 191.

[4801]   Prosecution's Response Brief (Stojić), para. 174. See Prosecution's Response Brief (Stojić), para. 173. See also Appeal Hearing, AT. 325 (21 Mar 2017).

[4802]   Prosecution's Response Brief (Stojić), para. 174.

[4803]   Prosecution's Response Brief (Stojić), para. 174, referring to, *inter alia,* Trial Judgement, Vol. 4, para. 322, Klaus Johann Nissen, T. 20417 (25 June 2007).

[4804]   Prosecution's Response Brief (Stojić), para. 174.

[4805]   Trial Judgement, Vol. 4, para. 324.

[4806]   Trial Judgement, Vol. 4, paras 321-323.

[4807]   See Stojić's Appeal Brief, para. 190, referring to Ex. 2D00643; Trial Judgement, Vol. 4, para. 321, referring to, *inter alia,* Ex. 2D00643.

[4808]   Trial Judgement, Vol. 4, para. 321.

[4809]   Trial Judgement, Vol. 4, para. 322.

[4810]   Trial Judgement, Vol. 4, para. 322, referring to Klaus Johann Nissen, T(F). 20416-20417 (25 June 2007).

[4811]   Ex. P01950 (confidential), para. 4.

[4812]   [Redacted, see Annex C – Confidential Annex]

[4813]   Klaus Johann Nissen, T. 20417 (25 June 2007).

that this inconsistency impugns its overall finding that he represented "the HVO" in peace negotiations at the highest level.

1505. Regarding the 2 June 1993 "meeting", the Trial Chamber in fact considered that on 2 June 1993, Boban, Stojić, and Petković signed an agreement on setting up joint HVO and ABiH patrols, and not that they attended a meeting on that date.[4814] Stojić's argument that he did not attend a negotiation around that date[4815] therefore shows a misunderstanding of the Trial Chamber's reliance on the relevant evidence. The Appeals Chamber considers that the Trial Chamber considered the agreement as evidence that Stojić was authorised to sign agreements concerning the **[page 618]** HVO.[4816] Furthermore, Stojić does not dispute that he was one of the competent authorities empowered to sign agreements resulting from peace negotiations. Thus, his argument is dismissed.

1506. The Appeals Chamber also dismisses Stojić's argument that there is no evidence that he attended any high-level or international negotiation. Notably, the 25 March 1993 and 18 April 1993 meetings, as well as the agreement signed on 2 June 1993, all concern resolutions discussed between senior representatives of the HVO HZ H-B and the SDA/ABiH/HDZ, and thus Stojić fails to show that the Trial Chamber erred in considering these meetings to be held at "the highest level".[4817] The Appeals Chamber therefore finds that Stojić fails to demonstrate that no reasonable trier of fact could have concluded that he was one of the officials within the HVO HZ H-B authorised to represent that body in peace negotiations at the highest level. Stojić's sub-ground of appeal 24.1 is dismissed.

(b) Whether Stojić took part in formulating the defence policy of the HZ(R) H-B Government (Stojić's Sub-ground 24.2)

1507. Stojić submits that the Trial Chamber erred in finding that he took part in the formulation of the HZ(R) H-B Government's defence policy based on his participation in meetings of the Government.[4818] Stojić argues that mere attendance at a meeting only establishes that he knew about the subject-matter under discussion, and that the Trial Chamber failed to assess what contributions he made to the meetings.[4819] In particular, Stojić contends that the cited evidence shows no direct or relevant contribution by him,[4820] pre-dates the JCE,[4821] or does not establish that his contributions related to the formulation of defence policy.[4822] Stojić further contends that the Trial Chamber erred in finding that defence policy was formulated during the Government meetings as: (1) the military situation was discussed in two meetings but no decisions were made;[4823] and (2) the detention **[page 619]** centres and technical rules relating to military service were discussed at one Government session.[4824]

1508. The Prosecution responds that the Trial Chamber's finding was reasonable,[4825] and contends that Stojić's arguments fail to show an error.[4826] It argues that even if Stojić did not voice his opinion during the

---

[4814]   Trial Judgement, Vol. 4, para. 323.

[4815]   See Stojić's Appeal Brief, para. 190.

[4816]   Trial Judgement, Vol. 4, para. 323; Ex. P10367 (confidential), para. 58; Ex. P02652 (confidential), p. 2.

[4817]   Trial Judgement, Vol. 4, para. 324.

[4818]   Stojić's Appeal Brief, paras 192, 194, 196. While Stojić refers to "meetings of the HVO" in his submissions relating to this ground of appeal, the Appeals Chamber notes that he challenges a finding of the Trial Chamber which concerns Stojić's attendance at Government meetings. See Trial Judgement, Vol. 4, heading before para. 297.

[4819]   Stojić's Appeal Brief, paras 193-194, referring to *Krstić* Appeal Judgement, para. 87, *Milutinović et al.* Trial Judgement, Vol. 3, para. 143. Stojić submits that the evidence only establishes that he attended Government meetings during which various topics were discussed and does not show that he played a leading role in these meetings. Stojić's Appeal Brief, para. 196.

[4820]   Stojić's Appeal Brief, para. 194, referring to Exs. P00559, p. 3, 1D01666, P05955. See Stojić's Appeal Brief, para. 196.

[4821]   Stojić's Appeal Brief, para. 194, referring to Exs. P00578, p. 5, P00672, pp. 4, 6. According to Stojić, the evidence which pre-dates the JCE has no relevance to the formulation of defence policy during the JCE period. See Stojić's Appeal Brief, para. 194.

[4822]   Stojić's Appeal Brief, para. 194. Stojić argues that in the meeting of 6 September 1993 he spoke on administrative issues and not the establishment of detention centres, and that during a meeting on 4 November 1993 he only provided an update on the situation in Vareš. Stojić's Appeal Brief, para. 194, referring to Exs. P04841, pp. 3-4, 1D01354.

[4823]   Stojić''s Appeal Brief, para. 195, referring to Exs. 1D02179, 1D01666.

[4824]   Stojić's Appeal Brief, para. 195, referring to Ex. P04841. See Stojić's Appeal Brief, para. 196.

[4825]   Prosecution's Response Brief (Stojić), para. 175. See Prosecution's Response Brief (Stojić), para. 173.

[4826]   Prosecution's Response Brief (Stojić), para. 178.

Government meetings, he participated by exercising his vote.[4827] The Prosecution submits that Stojić: (1) disseminated information and made defence-related proposals to the Government;[4828] and (2) participated in meetings where discussions took place, and proposals were adopted, concerning, *inter alia,* the armed forces' organisational structure, the mobilisation of forces, the detention and treatment of POWs, the detention centres, and the military and security situation.[4829]

1509. The Appeals Chamber notes that the Trial Chamber found that Stojić participated in many Government meetings in his capacity as Head of the Department of Defence, and "in that context took part in formulating defence policy of the HZ(R) H-B".[4830] The Trial Chamber considered that decisions were taken at these meetings on various subjects including: (1) the status of refugees and displaced persons; (2) the amended decree on the armed forces; (3) the decree imposing the war tax in the territory of the HZ H-B; (4) the military situation on the ground; (5) the mobilisation of the HVO; and (6) the situation in the HVO detention centres.[4831] Notably, the evidence relied on by the Trial Chamber shows that a majority of proposals were unanimously adopted during these meetings, and Stojić does not argue that he abstained or voted against any of the proposals or decisions.[4832] Further, there is evidence of Stojić actively participating in some meetings by making proposals and providing reports and updates on the military situation.[4833] Thus, a reasonable trier of fact could have concluded that Stojić participated in these meetings by providing reports as well as by voting on the proposals discussed and adopted. **[page 620]**

1510. The Appeals Chamber is also not convinced by Stojić's argument that a finding on his personal contributions to the meetings was required in order to conclude, as the Trial Chamber did, that he took part in formulating the defence policy of the HZ(R) H-B by virtue of his participation.[4834] Considering that the case-law cited by Stojić is distinguishable from his case,[4835] the Appeals Chamber also finds his argument to be unsupported. His arguments are thus dismissed.

1511. Further, the Appeals Chamber is not convinced by Stojić's contentions that no defence policies were formulated during the meetings and that some meetings cited as evidence by the Trial Chamber pre-date the JCE.[4836] The evidence relied on by the Trial Chamber shows that various issues affecting the defence policy were discussed and formulated at these meetings, including the military situation on the ground and the mobilisation of the HVO.[4837] Stojić only supports his argument by asserting that evidence of discussions on the military situation and the detention centres in three meetings is insufficient to support the Trial Chamber's finding.[4838] The Appeals Chamber recalls that it is to be presumed that the Trial Chamber evaluated all the evidence presented to it as long as there is no indication that the Trial Chamber completely disregarded any

---

[4827] Prosecution's Response Brief (Stojić), para. 175.
[4828] Prosecution's Response Brief (Stojić), para. 175.
[4829] Prosecution's Response Brief (Stojić), paras 176-178. The Prosecution argues that the pre-JCE Government meetings demonstrated Stojić's role in formulating defence policy. Prosecution's Response Brief (Stojić), para. 178. See also Appeal Hearing, AT. 325 (21 Mar 2017).
[4830] Trial Judgement, Vol. 4, para. 298. See *supra,* para. 1418.
[4831] Trial Judgement, Vol. 4, para. 297, referring to, *inter alia,* Exs. P00559, p. 7, P00578, p. 5, P00672, p. 3, P01097, P05955, 1D01666, 1D02179, P04841.
[4832] Trial Judgement, Vol. 4, para. 297, referring to, *inter alia,* Exs. P00559, p. 7, P00578, p. 5, P00672, p. 3, P01097, P04841, P05955, 1D02179. See Ex. P00543, p. 7; Ex. P00921; Ex. P01227; Ex. P01324; Ex. P02606, p. 2; Ex. P05610, p. 2; Ex. 1D01181,pp. 3-5; Ex. 1D01669.
[4833] Ex. P05799; Ex. 1D01608, pp. 2-3; Ex. 1D01668; Ex. 1D01275, pp. 2-3. See Trial Judgement, Vol. 4, paras 300 & fns 235, 247
[4834] See *Šainović et al.* Appeal Judgement, para. 925 (The Appeals Chamber considered that, apart from being present at a meeting, Nikola Šainović did not issue any instructions or make any statements and thus did not exert any influence; it considered though that his presence showed his continuous involvement with the issues).
[4835] See *Krstić* Appeal Judgement, paras 85-87 (The Appeals Chamber considered that Radislav Krstić's presence at two meetings could at most establish his knowledge of decisions taken and that there is no evidence suggesting that he was aware of any genocidai intent of Ratko Mladić as it was highly unlikely that Mladić would have discussed this in front of UNPROFOR leaders or the foreign media present); *Milutinović et al.* Trial Judgement, Vol. 3, paras 132, 142-143 (In discussing the Prosecution's argument that Milan Milutinović's presence at meetings conferred legitimacy to the decisions taken, it was considered that Milutinović only attended a limited number of meetings and that he did not play a significant role in them).
[4836] Stojić's Appeal Brief, paras 194-195. See *supra,* para. 1418.
[4837] See *supra,* fn. 4833.
[4838] Stojić's Appeal Brief, para. 195.

evidence which is clearly relevant.[4839] In this regard, the Trial Chamber specifically referred to over 40 Government sessions and meetings that Stojić attended when making its findings thus indicating that the evidence on the ten meetings it cited to explicitly did not encompass all the evidence it considered.[4840] Since Stojić fails to address the other evidence on the record,[4841] the Appeals Chamber is not convinced that he has shown an error in the Trial Chamber's reasoning and the ultimate finding.

1512. Finally, as the Trial Chamber took account of various meetings held between January and November 1993, the Appeals Chamber finds that Stojić fails to show how any alleged error in the Trial Chamber's consideration of, *inter alia*, the evidence on meetings which pre-date the JCE **[page 621]** could have affected its finding that he participated in the formulation of the defence policy of the HZ(R) H-B both before and after the JCE came into effect.[4842]

1513. In light of the above, the Appeals Chamber finds that Stojić has failed to demonstrate that no reasonable trier of fact could have concluded that by providing reports, taking part in, and voting in the Government sessions and meetings Stojić participated in the formulation of the defence policy of HZ(R) H-B. Stojić's sub-ground of appeal 24.2 is thus dismissed.

(c) Whether Stojić exercised the functions of the Head of the Department of Defence until 15 November 1993 (Stojić's Sub-ground 24.3)

1514. Stojić submits that no reasonable trier of fact could have concluded that he left the office of the Head of the Department of Defence on 15 November 1993.[4843] Stojić argues that his successor was appointed on 10 November 1993 and that he took up his new position at the Department for the Production of Military Equipment on the same day.[4844] He also argues that there is no evidence that he performed any function related to the Department of Defence after 10 November 1993.[4845]

1515. The Prosecution responds that the Trial Chamber's finding was reasonable, and that Stojić ignores Exhibit 2D00416, a transfer of duties he signed on 15 November 1993.[4846]

1516. The Appeals Chamber notes that the Trial Chamber found that by a declaration of 10 November 1993, Boban appointed Perica Jukić as Minister of Defence[4847] and that Stojić exercised his functions as Head of the Department of Defence until 15 November 1993.[4848] Stojić does not address Exhibit 2D00416, the evidence relied on by the Trial Chamber in concluding that the transfer of responsibilities from Stojić to Jukić was made official on 15 November 1993.[4849] Thus, Stojić fails to demonstrate that no reasonable trier of fact could have concluded based on the evidence that he exercised the functions of the Head of the Department of Defence until 15 November 1993. Moreover, Stojić fails to explain how any alleged error in this regard would have an impact on his convictions. His arguments in his sub-ground of appeal 24.3 are dismissed. **[page 622]**

(d) Conclusion

1517. In sum, Stojić's ground of appeal 24 is dismissed.[4850]

[4839]   *Tolimir* Appeal Judgement, para. 53; *Popović et al.* Appeal Judgement, paras 925, 1017; *Kvočka et al.* Appeal Judgement, para. 23.

[4840]   Trial Judgement, Vol. 4, para. 297.

[4841]   See *supra*, fns 4833-4834.

[4842]   See *supra*, para. 1441 & fn. 4522.

[4843]   Stojić's Appeal Brief, para. 197.

[4844]   Stojić's Appeal Brief, para. 197, referring to Trial Judgement, Vol. 4, para. 293, Exs. P06583, 2D03001.

[4845]   Stojić's Appeal Brief, para. 197.

[4846]   Prosecution's Response Brief (Stojić), para. 179, referring to Ex. 2D00416. See Prosecution's Response Brief (Stojić), para. 173.

[4847]   Trial Judgement, Vol. 1, para. 556, referring to, *inter alia*, Ex. P06583.

[4848]   Trial Judgement, Vol. 4, para. 293.

[4849]   Trial Judgement, Vol. 1, para. 556, Vol. 4, fn. 687, referring to Ex. 2D00416.

[4850]   Given that the Appeals Chamber dismisses all three sub-grounds of appeal under ground of appeal 24, it does not need to address Stojić's argument that these three alleged errors of fact cumulatively occasion a miscarriage of justice. See Stojić's Appeal Brief, para. 198.

6. Alleged errors in identifying the members of the JCE (Stojić's Ground 7)

1518. Stojić contends that the Trial Chamber erred in law by failing to identify the members of the JCE with sufficient specificity.[4851] He asserts that the Trial Chamber's finding that the JCE included "notably commanders of the HVO armed forces, political and administrative officials of the HVO/government and municipal HVOs"[4852] fails to identify whether all or only some of the individuals encompassed in these groups were JCE members.[4853] Stojić contends that the impugned finding is extraordinarily broad and vague as, *inter alia*, it has no temporal or geographic limitation.[4854] Stojić asserts that the Trial Chamber's failure to unambiguously identify the JCE members, "which is an essential precursor to a finding that there was a JCE at all",[4855] necessitates a reversal of its finding that a JCE existed, and that his convictions must be set aside.[4856]

1519. The Prosecution responds that the Trial Chamber exceeded the requirement of identifying JCE members by groups or categories when it named ten members, including the Appellants.[4857] It asserts that as the crimes were attributable to Stojić, either directly or via the other Appellants, the fact that additional JCE members were not identified in detail has no impact on his convictions.[4858]

1520. Stojić replies that the Trial Chamber's "failure to define the JCE membership precisely is not remedied by its blanket finding that all crimes perpetrated by non-members are attributable to JCE-members,"[4859] as a link must be established between the perpetrator and a JCE member.[4860]

1521. The Appeals Chamber first notes that the Trial Chamber correctly stated the law on the element of "plurality of persons" in relation to the *actus reus* of JCE participation.[4861] After a **[page 623]** detailed analysis of how the CCP was implemented through a joint and concerted action, including the means by which the Appellants contributed to it,[4862] the Trial Chamber concluded that "a plurality of persons consulted each other to devise and implement the [CCP]."[4863] It found that "[t]he group included Franjo Tuđman, Gojko Šušak, Janko Bobetko, Mate Boban, Jadranko Prlić, Bruno Stojić, Slobodan Praljak, Milivoj Petković, Valentin Ćorić and Berislav Pušić."[4864] In identifying these individuals, the Appeals Chamber considers that the Trial Chamber fulfilled the requirement of establishing that a plurality of persons shared the CCP.[4865] In this ground of appeal, Stojić does not dispute the Trial Chamber's findings as far as they concern the plurality of persons and the named individuals, but challenges the identification of the remaining JCE members.

1522. In this regard, the Appeals Chamber recalls that "[t]he plurality of persons can be sufficiently identified by referring to 'categories or groups of persons', and it is not necessary to name each of the individuals involved".[4866] The Appeals Chamber also notes that the Trial Chamber made detailed findings on the timing

---

[4851]   Stojić's Appeal Brief, paras 79-80. See Stojić's Appeal Brief, paras 76-77.

[4852]   Stojić's Appeal Brief, para. 78, referring to Trial Judgement, Vol. 4, para. 1231.

[4853]   Stojić's Appeal Brief, paras 77-79, referring to *Krajišnik* Appeal Judgement, para. 157.

[4854]   Stojić's Appeal Brief, para. 79. Stojić also argues that by using the word "notably", the Trial Chamber signalled that it "thought that there were other entirely unidentified members beyond even the vague categories identified". Stojić's Appeal Brief, para. 79.

[4855]   Stojić's Appeal Brief, para. 80.

[4856]   Stojić's Appeal Brief, para. 80. See also Appeal Hearing, AT. 256-257 (21 Mar 2017).

[4857]   Prosecution's Response Brief (Stojić), para. 57, referring to Trial Judgement, Vol. 4, para. 1231. See also Prosecution's Response Brief (Stojić), para. 58.

[4858]   Prosecution's Response Brief (Stojić), para. 57.

[4859]   Stojić's Reply Brief, para. 24.

[4860]   Stojić's Reply Brief, para. 24. Stojić submits, by way of example, that there is no basis for a finding that a JCE member used the perpetrators to commit crimes in Stupni Do and that "[t]he *assumption* that all crimes are imputable to a JCE-member is thus insufficient." Stojić's Reply Brief, para. 25 (emphasis in the original).

[4861]   Trial Judgement, Vol. 1, para. 212, Vol. 4, para. 1217.

[4862]   Trial Judgement, Vol. 4, paras 1217-1230.

[4863]   Trial Judgement, Vol. 4, para. 1231.

[4864]   Trial Judgement, Vol. 4, para. 1231.

[4865]   See *Popović et al.* Appeal Judgement, para. 1409; *Đorđević* Appeal Judgement, para. 141; *Brđanin* Appeal Judgement, para. 364; *Tadić* Appeal Judgement, para. 227. See also *Gatete* Appeal Judgement, para. 239.

[4866]   *Đorđević* Appeal Judgement, para. 141, referring to *Krajišnik* Appeal Judgement, para. 156. See *Brđanin* Appeal Judgement, para. 430; *Karemera and Ngirumpatse* Appeal Judgement, para. 150.

and geographical scope of the JCE.[4867] Considering the above, the Appeals Chamber is not convinced by Stojić's submission that the Trial Chamber's description of the plurality of persons belonging to the JCE had "extraordinary breadth and vagueness"[4868] or that it was required in this case to find whether all or only some of the individuals from these groups were JCE members.[4869] Furthermore, the Appeals Chamber finds that Stojić fails to show how any alleged ambiguity regarding the unidentified JCE members would affect the Trial Chamber's findings that the named individuals were JCE members,[4870] and that a JCE existed. Additionally, his allegations, if any, that the Trial Chamber incorrectly attributed crimes to members of the JCE will be considered when addressing Stojić's related challenges.[4871] **[page 624]**

1523. In light of the foregoing, the Appeals Chamber finds that Stojić has not demonstrated that the Trial Chamber erred in law in the manner in which it identified the members of the JCE. Stojić's ground of appeal 7 is thus dismissed.

7. Alleged errors in finding that Stojić made a significant contribution to the JCE in general (Stojić's Ground 27)

1524. In concluding that Stojić made a significant contribution to the implementation of the CCP,[4872] the Trial Chamber found, *inter alia,* that he: (1) commanded, controlled, and had "effective control" over most of the HVO and the Military Police;[4873] (2) was the link between the HZ(R) H-B Government and the HVO and the Military Police;[4874] (3) controlled the human and financial resources of the HVO and their logistics;[4875] and (4) was in charge of the logistical and staffing needs of the Military Police.[4876] Furthermore, the Trial Chamber found that Stojić "used the armed forces and the Military Police to commit crimes that were part of the common criminal purpose"[4877] and that their actions were attributable to him.[4878] Stojić submits that the Trial Chamber erred in finding that he significantly contributed to the CCP in general.[4879]

(a) Alleged legal errors in the application of JCE liability (Stojić's Sub-ground 27.1, in part)

1525. Stojić contends that the Trial Chamber erroneously based its findings that he significantly contributed to the JCE on a finding that he had "effective control" over the HVO and the Military Police.[4880] He argues that "effective control" is not directly relevant for an analysis of his contribution, and thus the Trial Chamber blurred the tests for superior responsibility and JCE liability.[4881] He avers that this resulted in a "lower threshold" by establishing his criminal responsibility without considering whether he significantly contributed to the crimes or had control over specific perpetrators.[4882]

[4867]   See, *e.g.,* Trial Judgement, Vol. 4, paras 41-66, 1218-1230. See also *supra,* paras 783-784, 813-814.
[4868]   Stojić's Appeal Brief, para. 79.
[4869]   See *Tolimir* Appeal Judgement, para. 436 (referring to *Tolimir* Trial Judgement, para. 1071: "[The Trial Chamber] is convinced that this plan was carried out by a plurality of persons, including numerous high-ranking VRS officers and their subordinates, and members of the Bosnian Serb MUP"); *Popović et al.* Appeal Judgement, para. 1409 (finding that the "plurality of persons" requirement was met with the identification of categories or groups and the naming of the appellants as participants in the JCE); *Karemera and Ngirumpatse* Appeal Judgement, para. 150 (finding no error in the description that the JCE members were "'political leaders', 'persons of authority within the military, the *Interahamwe,* and the territorial administration', and 'influential businessmen'" as some members of these groups were identified by name in other findings). *Contra Krajišnik* Appeal Judgement, para. 157.
[4870]   See *Krajišnik* Appeal Judgement, para. 231.
[4871]   See *Popović et al.* Appeal Judgement, para. 1410.
[4872]   Trial Judgement, Vol. 4, para. 429. See *supra,* para. 568.
[4873]   Trial Judgement, Vol. 4, paras 312, 320, 425, 429.
[4874]   Trial Judgement, Vol. 4, paras 425, 429.
[4875]   Trial Judgement, Vol. 4, paras 308, 312.
[4876]   Trial Judgement, Vol. 4, paras 317, 320.
[4877]   Trial Judgement, Vol. 4, para. 429.
[4878]   Trial Judgement, Vol. 4, para. 429.
[4879]   Stojić's Appeal Brief, paras 231-232.
[4880]   Stojić's Appeal Brief, para. 236.
[4881]   Stojić's Appeal Brief, para. 236.
[4882]   Stojić's Appeal Brief, para. 236.

1526. The Prosecution responds that the Trial Chamber did not blur the tests for superior responsibility and JCE or consider effective control at the expense of determining Stojić's **[page 625]** significant contribution,[4883] and avers that it was unnecessary for the Trial Chamber to decide whether he controlled specific perpetrators.[4884]

1527. The Trial Chamber found that Stojić commanded and had "effective control" over the HVO and Military Police.[4885] After making this determination, the Trial Chamber proceeded to analyse the extent to which Stojić contributed to the commission of the crimes perpetrated by the HVO and the Military Police in the various municipalities and detention centres,[4886] as well as his denial of crimes and his failure to prevent crimes and punish the perpetrators.[4887] The Trial Chamber, in its conclusions, considered that Stojić: (1) had powers over the HVO and the Military Police, which he exercised;[4888] (2) continued to exercise "effective control" after being informed of crimes;[4889] and (3) made no serious effort to stop the commission of crimes.[4890]

1528. The Appeals Chamber first considers that nothing prevented the Trial Chamber from considering Stojić's "effective control" over most of the HVO and the Military Police as a factor in determining whether his contribution to the JCE was significant.[4891] In this regard, the Appeals Chamber recalls that although authority or control over principal perpetrators "is not a necessary element to establish JCE liability", it is "one of the various factors that a chamber *may* take into account in determining whether crimes of principal perpetrators were linked with the accused".[4892] Notably, the Trial Chamber considered that Stojić "controlled the HVO armed forces and the Military Police" and "used the armed forces and the Military Police to commit crimes that were part of the common criminal purpose",[4893] before concluding that the actions of the HVO and the Military Police were attributable to him.[4894] Thus, the Appeals Chamber dismisses Stojić's contention that "effective control" is not directly relevant to a finding on his significant contribution.

1529. Further, in addition to his role in linking the HZ(R) H-B Government with its military component and his participation in military operations,[4895] the Trial Chamber considered that Stojić's intent and significant contribution stemmed from the fact that he made no serious efforts to **[page 626]** stop the commission of crimes despite having power over the HVO and the Military Police.[4896] In this regard, an accused's shared intent and contribution to a JCE can be inferred from his control and command authority over the perpetrators and his failure to intervene in order to stop or punish the crimes committed pursuant to the CCP.[4897] Thus, the Appeals Chamber finds that Stojić fails to show that the Trial Chamber "blurred the tests for command responsibility and JCE"[4898] or erred by considering his command authority and powers over the HVO and the Military Police as factors establishing his significant contribution.

1530. To the extent that Stojić argues that the Trial Chamber relied on his "effective control" in assessing his significant contribution without first determining his control over specific perpetrators and thus his ability to prevent or punish their crimes,[4899] the Appeals Chamber recalls that "JCE liability does not require, as a constitutive element, the failure of an accused to punish subordinates' crimes despite his knowledge

---

[4883]   Prosecution's Response Brief (Stojić), para. 197.
[4884]   Prosecution's Response Brief (Stojić), paras 197-198.
[4885]   Trial Judgement, Vol. 4, paras 312, 320.
[4886]   Trial Judgement, Vol. 4, paras 326-407.
[4887]   Trial Judgement, Vol. 4, paras 408-423.
[4888]   Trial Judgement, Vol. 4, para. 425.
[4889]   Trial Judgement, Vol. 4, para. 426.
[4890]   Trial Judgement, Vol. 4, para. 427.
[4891]   See, *e.g.*, *Đorđević* Appeal Judgement, para. 264. See also *supra*, para. 1410.
[4892]   *Šainović et al.* Appeal Judgement, para. 1520 (emphasis in original).
[4893]   Trial Judgement, Vol. 4, para. 429.
[4894]   Trial Judgement, Vol. 4, para. 429.
[4895]   Trial Judgement, Vol. 4, paras 425-426.
[4896]   See Trial Judgement, Vol. 4, paras 425, 427-429.
[4897]   *Šainović et al.* Appeal Judgement, para. 1242. See *Šainović et al.* Appeal Judgement, paras 1233, 1237.
[4898]   Stojić's Appeal Brief, para. 236.
[4899]   See Stojić's Appeal Brief, para. 236. The Appeals Chamber will consider Stojić's challenges regarding his significant contribution to specific crimes below. See *infra*, paras 1551-1748.

thereof".[4900] Since the Trial Chamber convicted Stojić as a participant in a JCE and not as a superior pursuant to Article 7(3) of the Statute, all it had to establish was his significant contribution to the JCE. However, the Appeals Chamber also notes that a failure to intervene to prevent recurrence of crimes or to halt abuses has been taken into account in assessing an accused's contribution to a joint criminal enterprise and his intent "where the accused had some power and influence or authority over the perpetrators sufficient to prevent or halt the abuses but failed to exercise such power".[4901] Accordingly, once it established that Stojić had command authority over the HVO and the Military Police in general and assessed that his failure to use it to prevent or punish crimes in general amounted, along with other factors, to a significant contribution to the JCE, it was unnecessary also to find that he controlled the specific perpetrators of specific crimes such that he was able to punish them or prevent their crimes.[4902] Therefore, Stojić fails to show that the Trial Chamber applied a "lower threshold" in considering his significant contribution.

1531. Based on the foregoing, the Appeals Chamber dismisses Stojić's sub-ground of appeal 27.1 as it relates to the Trial Chamber's consideration of his command authority over the HVO and the Military Police in determining his significant contribution to the JCE. **[page 627]**

(b) <u>Whether Stojić's assistance to military operations contributed to the JCE (Stojić's Sub-ground 27.1 in part)</u>

(i) <u>Arguments of the Parties</u>

1532. Stojić contends that the Trial Chamber erred by considering the "general assistance" he provided to the military as significant contribution because such assistance had no direct link to the individual crimes and was not necessarily directed at furthering a JCE.[4903] Specifically, Stojić argues that the Trial Chamber failed to assess whether any of his orders contributed to the crimes, and that his logistical support cannot amount to a contribution to the commission of specific crimes.[4904] Stojić also submits that logistical assistance and arranging finance for the armed forces are too equivocal and remote to find that he furthered a JCE.[4905]

1533. The Prosecution responds that the Trial Chamber's findings on Stojić's significant contribution were reasonable, and that his conduct was not "general assistance".[4906] It argues that the Trial Chamber considered Stojić's control of finances and logistical resources in addition to other factors, such as the orders he issued.[4907]

(ii) <u>Analysis</u>

1534. Stojić argues that his "general assistance" to the military did not further the JCE. The Appeals Chamber notes that the Trial Chamber analysed Stojić's conduct in detail,[4908] and did not classify his activities as only "general assistance", but rather concluded that he, *inter alia*: (1) played a fundamental role

---

[4900] *Šainović et al.* Appeal Judgement, para. 1237. See *Šainović et al.* Appeal Judgement, para. 1233.

[4901] *Stanišić and Župljanin* Appeal Judgement, paras 111, 734.

[4902] See *Šainović et al.* Appeal Judgement, paras 1256-1257 ("Close cooperation between a principal perpetrator and a JCE member, including the accused, is but one of various factors from which a chamber may infer that a crime formed part of the common purpose and is thus imputable to JCE members" and "it is not a prerequisite for imputing the crime to JCE members"). *Cf. Šainović et al.* Appeal Judgement, para. 1237 (considering Nebojša Pavković's argument that his knowledge of specific crimes was not established and finding that his general knowledge of crimes and failure to intervene etc., were correctly considered as evidence of his intent and contribution to a JCE).

[4903] Stojić's Appeal Brief, paras 233-234, referring to Trial Judgement, Vol. 4, para. 429. See also Stojić's Appeal Brief, paras 231, 242.

[4904] Stojić's Appeal Brief, para. 235. See also Stojić's Reply Brief, para. 68.

[4905] Stojić's Reply Brief, para. 68.

[4906] Prosecution's Response Brief (Stojić), para. 196. See Prosecution's Response Brief (Stojić), para. 195. The Prosecution lists, as examples, Stojić's planning and/or facilitating of HVO operations, his hindrance of the delivery of humanitarian aid to the civilian population of East Mostar, and his encouragement to perpetrators to continue committing crimes. Prosecution's Response Brief (Stojić), para. 196. See also Appeal Hearing, AT. 324-325 (21 Mar 2017).

[4907] Prosecution's Response Brief (Stojić), para. 197. See also Appeal Hearing, AT. 325-327 (21 Mar 2017).

[4908] See, *e.g.*, Trial Judgement, Vol. 4, paras 298, 305, 312, 320, 324, 337, 348-349, 355, 357, 372, 380, 415-418, 420, 423, 425-427, 429, 1220.

in the establishment and the organisation of the HVO and took part in formulating the defence policy;[4909] (2) was regularly informed about the HVO military operations and Military Police activities and was in charge of keeping the Government informed;[4910] (3) issued orders directly to the HVO[4911] and had the authority to issue orders to the Chief of the Military Police Administration, including orders directly linked to operations on the ground, such as orders **[page 628]** on resubordination;[4912] (4) had the authority to designate persons to represent the HVO in ceasefire negotiations, and personally represented the Government in peace negotiations;[4913] (5) reorganised the Military Police and appointed its most senior officers;[4914] and (6) planned or facilitated the HVO military operations in Gornji Vakuf, Mostar, and Vareš,[4915] and was involved in organising and conducting the eviction campaigns in West Mostar.[4916] Further, in arriving at its findings, the Trial Chamber considered, and rejected, Stojić's arguments at trial that his role was solely administrative and logistical, and that he had no command or control authority over the armed forces.[4917] Thus, the Appeals Chamber is not convinced by Stojić's mischaracterisation of his contribution, which is merely an attempt to minimise his involvement with the HVO and the Military Police. Nonetheless, the Appeals Chamber recalls that the administrative and logistical roles played by Stojić were considered, among others, by the Trial Chamber in its determination of whether he commanded and had "effective control" over the HVO and the Military Police.[4918]

1535. Further, with respect to Stojić's submission that his logistical assistance did not have a direct link to individual crimes, the Appeals Chamber notes that the jurisprudence of the Tribunal does not require a direct link between an accused's contribution and crimes as the accused does not have to contribute to a specific crime in order to be held responsible for it[4919] and because a contribution to a JCE may take the form of contribution to the execution of a common criminal purpose.[4920] Therefore, Stojić fails to demonstrate an error regarding whether his "general assistance" was directly linked to crimes as this is unnecessary for JCE liability. His arguments are dismissed.

1536. Regarding Stojić's argument that the Trial Chamber failed to evaluate whether his orders contributed to the crimes, the Appeals Chamber notes that Stojić had *de facto* command over the HVO and the Military Police which extended beyond financial and logistical powers.[4921] In support of his argument, Stojić relies on the Trial Chamber's findings that he issued orders on "mobilisations, troop movements, reorganisation of units, assignment of reinforcements, free **[page 629]** movement of convoys and ceasefires".[4922] However, while some of Stojić's orders may be considered logistical, the Trial Chamber also found that he issued operational orders, such as those concerning the detention centres,[4923] Military Police checkpoints,[4924] and the redeployment and resubordination of Military Police units.[4925] Specifically, the Appeals Chamber notes, as examples, that Stojić ordered: (1) all HVO units in the South-East OZ to "eliminate" the Muslim troops in the area;[4926] (2) a commanding officer to allow the passage of UNPROFOR convoys in Central Bosnia OZ on 23 February 1993;[4927] and (3) Miro Andrić, a colonel in the Main Staff, to capture the Gornji Vakuf area by

---

[4909] Trial Judgement, Vol. 4, paras 298-299, 312. See *supra*, paras 1509-1513.

[4910] Trial Judgement, Vol. 4, paras 300, 312, 318, 320. See *supra*, paras 1418, 1473-1478.

[4911] Trial Judgement, Vol. 4, paras 306, 312. See *supra*, paras 1427-1435.

[4912] Trial Judgement, Vol. 4, paras 314-315, 320. See *supra*, paras 1470-1472.

[4913] Trial Judgement, Vol. 4, paras 311-312, 324. See *supra*, paras 1456, 1503-1506.

[4914] Trial Judgement, Vol. 4, paras 319-320. See *supra*, paras 1465-1467.

[4915] Trial Judgement, Vol. 4, paras 334-335, 337, 348, 380-381. See *infra*, paras 1579-1580, 1605, 1611, 1598, 1654-1625, 1703.

[4916] Trial Judgement, Vol. 4, paras 355, 357. See *infra*, paras 1617-1653.

[4917] Trial Judgement, Vol. 1, paras 557, 563, 565, Vol. 4, paras 295, 312, 320. See *supra*, paras 1401-1412.

[4918] See *supra*, paras 1409-1412.

[4919] See *Kvočka et al.* Appeal Judgement, para. 263; *Karemera and Ngirumpatse* Appeal Judgement, paras 109, 153.

[4920] *Krajišnik* Appeal Judgement, para. 695 (internal references omitted). See *Popović et al.* Appeal Judgement, para. 1378; *Šainović et al.* Appeal Judgement, para. 987.

[4921] See *supra*, paras 1429-1432, 1457, 1468-1472, 1479. *Cf.* Stojić's Appeal Brief, para. 235, referring to Trial Judgement, Vol. 4, paras 306, 314.

[4922] Stojić's Appeal Brief, para. 235, referring to Trial Judgement, Vol. 4, paras 306, 314.

[4923] Trial Judgement, Vol. 4, para. 306.

[4924] Trial Judgement, Vol. 4, para. 316.

[4925] Trial Judgement, Vol. 1, para. 965, Vol. 4, paras 315, 320.

[4926] Trial Judgement, Vol. 4, para. 305.

[4927] Trial Judgement, Vol. 1, para. 562. See also Trial Judgement, Vol. 1, para. 795.

the use of force, which resulted in crimes.[4928] The Appeals Chamber is therefore satisfied that the Trial Chamber implicitly considered that Stojić's orders, whether logistical or operational, contributed to the commission of the crimes. Thus, Stojić's *de facto* command over the HVO and the Military Police was not based only on the logistical or financial orders that he issued.[4929] Regardless, considering the above,[4930] Stojić does not demonstrate that his "logistical support cannot amount to a contribution to the commission of specific crimes",[4931] or that this assistance was "too remote".[4932] The Appeals Chamber therefore dismisses Stojić's arguments in this regard.

1537. Based on the foregoing, the Appeals Chamber finds that Stojić has failed to demonstrate that the Trial Chamber erred in considering his logistical assistance to the military operations as a factor establishing his significant contribution. The Appeals Chamber therefore dismisses Stojić's sub-ground of appeal 27.1 in part. **[page 630]**

(c) Whether Stojić's role as a link between the armed forces and the Government contributed to the JCE (Stojić's Sub-ground 27.2 in part)

1538. Stojić submits that the Trial Chamber's finding that he formed a link between the HVO and the Government could not "in itself establish that he made a significant contribution to crimes", since this link was "not inherently unlawful".[4933] Stojić also contends that linking the civilian government with the military is too equivocal and remote to support a finding that he furthered a JCE.[4934]

1539. The Prosecution responds that Stojić translated Government decisions into ground-level action[4935] and thus used his link between HVO and the Government to plan the crimes.[4936]

1540. The Trial Chamber found that Stojić was the link between the civilian government of the HZ(R) H-B and the HVO military component.[4937] It considered that "Stojić took decisions related to military operations and had them implemented through the armed forces' chain of command, forwarded HVO [Government] decisions down the chain of command and made proposals to the HVO [Government] about military matters which were then approved by that collective body".[4938]

1541. Regarding Stojić's submission that the link itself cannot amount to significant contribution, the Appeals Chamber notes that the Trial Chamber analysed evidence on how Stojić used his role as a "link" to further the JCE. These activities included his participation in approximately 40 HVO Government sessions and meetings, which involved discussions and decision-making on the military situation on the ground, the

---

[4928] Trial Judgement, Vol. 4, paras 330, 334, referring to Ex. 4D00348. In addition, the Trial Chamber found, *inter alia,* that Stojić: (1) ordered a general mobilisation and imposed a curfew in all municipalities of HZ H-B (see Trial Judgement, Vol. 2, para. 884); (2) ordered all the HZ H-B MUP military units in Mostar to be re-subordinated on 2 July 1993 (see Trial Judgement, Vol. 2, para. 703); and (3) issued orders directly to the HVO, including for the immediate halt of offensive operations against the ABiH in April 1993 (see Trial Judgement, Vol. 1, para. 562, referring to Ex. P02093). See *infra,* paras 1562-1569.

[4929] See *supra,* paras 1414-1415, 1418, 1422-1423, 1456-1457, 1468, 1473-1479. Stojić: (1) was involved in military operations in central BiH (see Trial Judgement, Vol. 4, para. 306); (2) was regularly informed of the military operations conducted by the armed forces and in turn informed the Government accordingly (see Trial Judgement, Vol. 4, para. 306); and (3) sent military-related Government decisions through the military chain of command (see Trial Judgement, Vol. 4, para. 312).

[4930] See *supra,* paras 1534-1536.

[4931] Stojić's Appeal Brief, para. 235. See *supra,* paras 1401-1412.

[4932] See *supra,* paras 1532.

[4933] Stojić's Appeal Brief, para. 238. See Stojić's Appeal Brief, para. 237. See also Stojić's Appeal Brief, paras 231, 242; Stojić's Reply Brief, para. 68.

[4934] Stojić's Reply Brief, para. 68.

[4935] Prosecution's Response Brief (Stojić), para. 199. The Prosecution lists several of Stojić's activities, such as his enforcement of the 15 January 1993 Ultimatum and his participation in the planning of indiscriminate arrests of Muslim males. Prosecution's Response Brief (Stojić), para. 199.

[4936] Prosecution's Response Brief (Stojić), para. 200. The Prosecution argues that "it makes no difference whether Stojić's link between the Government and armed forces/MP was 'inherently unlawful'". Prosecution's Response Brief (Stojić), para. 200. See Prosecution's Response Brief (Stojić), para. 195.

[4937] Trial Judgement, Vol. 4, paras 425, 429.

[4938] Trial Judgement, Vol. 4, para. 425. See Trial. Judgement, Vol. 4, paras 297, 300, 304, 312. See also *supra,* paras 1418-1419, 1422-1423.

mobilisation of the HVO, and the situation in the detention centres.[4939] Stojić also received reports on the military operations and informed the Government about the situation on the ground thus facilitating the decision-making process.[4940] These decisions were then forwarded by Stojić to the Main Staff and the Military Police for implementation.[4941] Furthermore, the Trial Chamber also found that Stojić played a fundamental role in the **[page 631]** establishment and organisation of the HVO,[4942] and had the authority to make appointments in HVO brigades up to the level of deputy brigade commanders and assistant commanders for security.[4943] Thus, the Appeals Chamber finds that Stojić fails to demonstrate that no reasonable trier of fact could have concluded that he used his role to ensure that Government decisions were communicated to the HVO and Military Police and implemented, thus furthering the JCE. Likewise, Stojić fails to show that his role as a link between the Government and the HVO military component was "too remote".

1542. In light of the above, Stojić's sub-ground of appeal 27.2 is dismissed in part.

(d) Whether Stojić used the HVO and Military Police to commit crimes (Stojić's Sub-grounds 27.2 (in part) and 27.3)

(i) Arguments of the Parties

1543. Stojić contends that the Trial Chamber erred by finding that he used the HVO and the Military Police to commit crimes that were part of the CCP.[4944] Stojić asserts that the Trial Chamber erred by finding that all the actions of the HVO and Military Police were attributable to him as it failed to articulate a legal basis for its conclusion.[4945] He argues that the Trial Chamber thus imposed a form of superior responsibility without establishing that he controlled the direct perpetrators of any specific crimes.[4946] According to Stojić, the Trial Chamber did not cite any evidence in support nor explain how he used these forces to commit crimes.[4947] He also argues that the Trial Chamber's finding was inconsistent with other findings that he was not in the military chain of command and only issued logistical orders.[4948] Stojić further avers that the Trial Chamber failed to analyse each Appellant's significant contribution individually as it used identical language in relation to him, Praljak, and Petković without distinguishing between the functions and powers of civilian leaders and military generals.[4949]

1544. The Prosecution responds that the Trial Chamber's finding was reasonable, and refers to findings on Stojić's involvement in HVO operations.[4950] The Prosecution submits that it was irrelevant that Stojić Was not *de jure* within the military chain of command because of his ability to **[page 632]** issue orders to the HVO and Military Police beyond logistical matters and his "effective control" over them.[4951] It also submits that the crimes were correctly attributed to Stojić because he used the HVO and the Military Police to commit crimes within the CCP.[4952] The Prosecution argues that the Trial Chamber did not impose a form of superior responsibility, and that authority or control over the principal perpetrators is not a necessary element of JCE liability.[4953] It argues that the Trial Chamber's findings on Praljak and Petković show that Stojić and "his fellow JCE members" worked together to further the CCP.[4954]

[4939]   Trial Judgement, Vol. 4, para. 297. See *supra*, paras 1418, 1509-1513.
[4940]   Trial Judgement, Vol. 4, para. 300. Notably, Stojić informed the Government about the consequences of the implementation of the 15 January 1993 Ultimatum as well as the military situation in Vareš on 4 November 1993. Trial Judgement, Vol. 4, para. 300. See *supra*, paras 1418, 1422-1423.
[4941]   Trial Judgement, Vol. 4, para. 304. See *supra*, paras 1422-1423.
[4942]   Trial Judgement, Vol. 4, para. 299. See *supra*, paras 1414-1415.
[4943]   Trial Judgement, Vol. 4, para. 303. See *supra*, paras 1409, 1465-1467.
[4944]   Stojić's Appeal Brief, para. 240, referring to Trial Judgement, Vol. 4, para. 429. See also Stojić's Appeal Brief, paras 231, 242.
[4945]   Stojić''s Appeal Brief, para. 239.
[4946]   Stojić's Appeal Brief, para. 239.
[4947]   Stojić's Appeal Brief, para. 240.
[4948]   Stojić's Appeal Brief, para. 240, referring to Trial Judgement, Vol. 1, para. 565, Vol. 4, para. 306.
[4949]   Stojić's Appeal Brief, para. 241.
[4950]   Prosecution's Response Brief (Stojić), para. 202. See Prosecution's Response Brief (Stojić), para. 195.
[4951]   Prosecution's Response Brief (Stojić), para. 202.
[4952]   Prosecution's Response Brief (Stojić), para. 201.
[4953]   Prosecution's Response Brief (Stojić), para. 201, referring to *Šainović et al.* Appeal Judgement, para. 1520.
[4954]   Prosecution's Response Brief (Stojić), para. 203.

(ii) Analysis

1545. In relation to Stojić's submission that the Trial Chamber erroneously attributed all actions of the HVO and the Military Police to him,[4955] the Appeals Chamber observes that Stojić does not address the Trial Chamber's relevant findings. Notably, the Trial Chamber found that Stojić: (1) commanded and had "effective control" over most of the HVO and the Military Police;[4956] (2) planned or facilitated various military operations involving these armed forces;[4957] and (3) made no serious effort to prevent or punish the commission of crimes by these armed forces.[4958] The Trial Chamber also concluded that Stojić and other JCE members used the HVO and the Military Police to commit crimes forming part of the CCP.[4959] The Appeals Chamber recalls that under JCE liability, once it is established that an accused participated in a JCE,[4960] "he is appropriately held liable also for those actions of other JCE members, or individuals used by them, that further the common criminal purpose (first category of JCE) [...], or that are a natural and foreseeable consequence of the carrying out of this crime (third category of JCE)".[4961] Further, as the Trial Chamber did correctly set out the law on the *actus reus* for participation in a JCE,[4962] Stojić's assertion that the Trial Chamber failed to articulate a legal basis for attributing to him the actions of the HVO and the Military Police is without merit.[4963] Therefore, Stojić fails to demonstrate that the **[page 633]** Trial Chamber erred in law by concluding that the actions of the HVO and the Military Police were attributable to him. His arguments are dismissed.

1546. Regarding Stojić's assertion that there is no evidentiary basis for the Trial Chamber's finding that he used the HVO and the Military Police to commit crimes that were part of the CCP,[4964] the Appeals Chamber notes that the Trial Chamber made numerous findings establishing his role and power in relation to these armed forces. Specifically, the Trial Chamber found that, *inter alia*, Stojić: (1) planned and facilitated the HVO military operations, and was informed of the crimes committed, in Gornji Vakuf,[4965] Mostar,[4966] West Mostar,[4967] Čapljina,[4968] and Vareš;[4969] (2) facilitated the hindering of the delivery of humanitarian aid to the civilian population in East Mostar;[4970] (3) praised the direct perpetrators of crimes thus accepting and encouraging the crimes;[4971] and (4) allowed perpetrators within the HVO and the Military Police to continue committing crimes by failing to punish them.[4972] The Appeals Chamber considers that, on the basis of these findings, a reasonable trier of fact could conclude that Stojić used both the HVO and the Military Police under his control to commit the crimes that were part of the CCP. The Appeals Chamber

---

[4955] See *supra*, para. 1543.
[4956] Trial Judgement, Vol. 4, paras 312, 320, 425. See *supra*, paras 1457, 1479.
[4957] Trial Judgement, Vol. 4, paras 337, 357, 378, 383, 426, 1220.
[4958] Trial Judgement, Vol. 4, paras 423, 427. See *supra,* paras 1480, 1491, 1494-1495, 1498-1499.
[4959] Trial Judgement, Vol. 4, paras 429, 1232.
[4960] See *Brđanin* Appeal Judgement, paras 429-430; *Stakić* Appeal Judgement, para. 64; *Tadić* Appeal Judgement, para. 227.
[4961] *Martić* Appeal Judgement, para. 172. See *Šainović et al.* Appeal Judgement, para. 1520; *Brđanin* Appeal Judgement, para. 431.
[4962] Trial Judgement, Vol. 1, para. 212. The Trial Chamber specifically noted that "for a participant in a JCE to be held responsible for a crime committed by a person outside of the JCE, it is necessary to prove that the crime may be imputed to one of the members of the JCE" and that "such person – utilising the direct perpetrator of the crime – acted in furtherance of the common plan". Trial Judgement, Vol. 1, para. 212(1).
[4963] See *supra,* para. 1543.
[4964] See *supra*, para. 1543.
[4965] Trial Judgement, Vol. 4, para. 337. See Trial Judgement, Vol. 4, paras 330, 334-335, referring to, *inter alia*, Exs. 4D00348, P01206, P01357, P01351, Slobodan Praljak, T(F). 40689-40690 (26 May 2009). See *infra*, paras 1561, 1565-1569, 1572-1575, 1578-1579.
[4966] Trial Judgement, Vol. 4, paras 344.349, referring to, *inter alia*, Witness A, T(F). 14009 (closed session) (13 Feb 2007), Exs. P01868, P04238 (44:22-44:52). See *infra*, paras 1598, 1601-1605, 1608-1611, 1614-1598.
[4967] Trial Judgement, Vol. 4, paras 354-355, referring to Ex. P10367 (confidential), paras 33, 69. See *infra*, paras 1617, 1621-1625, 1628-1631, 1633-1637, 1646-1649, 1652, 1654-1655, 1658-1661, 1664-1667.
[4968] Trial Judgement, Vol. 4, para. 375. See *infra*, paras 1681-1688, 1691-1696.
[4969] Trial Judgement, Vol. 4, paras 380-383, referring to Exs. P06219, P06267, P06307, P06328, P06339, P06362. See *infra*, paras 1701-1703, 1707-1711.
[4970] Trial Judgement, Vol. 2, paras 1227-1244, Vol. 4, para. 372, referring to, *inter alia*, Exs. P09712 (confidential), para. 64, P03900 (confidential), p. 2, Klaus Johann Nissen, T(F). 20453-20454, 20457 (25 June 2007). See *infra*, paras 1670-1674.
[4971] Trial Judgement, Vol. 4, paras 416-420 (referring to Exs. P02770, P04401 (confidential), pp. 4-5, P05303) 423. See *supra*, paras 1480, 1485-1491, 1494-1495, 1498-1500.
[4972] Trial Judgement, Vol. 4, paras 410-415. See *infra*, paras 1628-1625.

also observes that, in making these findings, the Trial Chamber referred extensively to evidence, both exhibits and witness testimony.[4973] Recalling that a Trial Judgement must be read as whole,[4974] the fact that the Trial Chamber did not cite evidence in its conclusion,[4975] which is based on its prior analysis, is not indicative of an error.

1547. Notably, Stojić does not challenge the Trial Chamber's findings on the principal perpetrators of the crimes in this ground of appeal, but disputes his "use" of them. Specifically, in arguing that the Trial Chamber erred by finding that all the actions of the HVO and the Military Police were attributable to him, Stojić ignores that the crimes falling within the JCE are attributable **[page 634]** to him once it is proven that he or other JCE members used the principal perpetrators to commit these crimes.[4976] In this regard, the Appeals Chamber notes that, for each of the crime sites, the Trial Chamber identified a link between the specific group or unit of the HVO and Military Police involved in crimes and at least one JCE member,[4977] and at times, Stojić himself.[4978] The Appeals Chamber recalls that the link between the underlying crime or physical perpetrator in question and a JCE member can be inferred from various factors, including "evidence that the JCE member explicitly or implicitly requested the non-JCE member to commit such a crime or instigated, ordered, encouraged, or otherwise availed himself of the non-JCE member to commit the crime".[4979] Considering the above,[4980] Stojić fails to show that the Trial Chamber's finding that he, and other JCE members, used the HVO and the Military Police to commit crimes has no evidentiary basis. Similarly, Stojić's contention that the Trial Chamber imposed a form of superior responsibility without establishing that he controlled the direct perpetrators is dismissed,[4981] as his control over the perpetrators is not a requirement under JCE liability.

1548. Concerning Stojić's assertion that the Trial Chamber's findings are inconsistent,[4982] the Appeals Chamber notes that, although the Trial Chamber found that Stojić was not *de jure* part of the military chain of command,[4983] he nevertheless had command and "effective control" over the HVO and the Military Police based on his *de facto* powers.[4984] Further, the Appeals Chamber dismisses elsewhere Stojić's arguments concerning the logistical nature of his orders.[4985] Thus, Stojić fails to demonstrate that there is any inconsistency concerning the Trial Chamber's findings. Regarding Stojić's submission that the Trial Chamber used identical language in its findings on Praljak's and Petković's significant contribution, the Appeals Chamber notes that similar language was used in the concluding paragraphs.[4986] However, the Appeals Chamber observes that the **[page 635]** relevant distinctions were made in the detailed analysis on each Appellant's participation in the JCE and their responsibility under JCE liability,[4987] particularly with regard to their functions and powers.[4988] Stojić's argument is thus dismissed as unmeritorious.

[4973] See *supra,* fns 4966-4971.

[4974] *Stanišić and Župljanin* Appeal Judgement, paras 138, 376, 705; *Popović et al.* Appeal Judgement, para. 2006; *Mrkšić and Sljivančanin* Appeal Judgement, para. 379. See *Kalimanzira* Appeal Judgement, para. 227.

[4975] Trial Judgement, Vol. 4, para. 429. See Stojić's Appeal Brief, para. 240.

[4976] See *supra,* para. 1545.

[4977] See, *e.g.,* Trial Judgement, Vol. 4, paras' 558, 562 (Praljak in Gornji Vakuf), 694, 699 (Petković in Prozor), 711-724 (Petković in Jablanica), 928 (Ćorić in West Mostar), 1147, 1151 (Pušić in relation to the Heliodrom), 1220 (the Appellants' involvement in planning, facilitating, or conducting military operations).

[4978] See, *e.g.,* Trial Judgement, Vol. 4, paras 334-337 (Gornji Vakuf), 354-355, 357 (West Mostar), 363, 368-370, 372 (East Mostar), 378 (Čapljina), 380-383 (Vareš), 395 (the Heliodrom), 396 (Ljubuški Prison), 407 (Dretelj Prison and Gabela Prison). For example, the Trial Chamber found that Stojić: (1) ordered Miro Andrić, a colonel in the Main Staff, to capture the Gornji Vakuf area by the use of force, and crimes were committed during this operation (see Trial Judgement, Vol. 4, paras 330, 334; *infra,* paras 1565-1569); (2) was actively involved in eviction campaigns in West Mostar, with evidence that he ordered that "people" be evicted from their homes and their houses burned by HVO members (see Trial Judgement, Vol. 4, paras 354-357; *infra,* paras 1621-1618); and (3) controlled the HVO snipers in East Mostar (see Trial Judgement, Vol. 4, paras 368-370; *infra,* paras 1664-1667).

[4979] *Popović et al.* Appeal Judgement, para. 1050, quoting *Krajišnik* Appeal Judgement, para. 226. See *Šainović et al.* Appeal Judgement, paras 1257, 1259.

[4980] See *supra,* paras 1545-1547, fns 4978-4979.

[4981] See *supra,* para. 1543.

[4982] See *supra,* para. 1543.

[4983] Trial Judgement, Vol. 1, para. 565, Vol. 4, para. 306.

[4984] Trial Judgement, Vol. 4, paras 312, 320. See *supra,* paras 1427-1428, 1457, 1479.

[4985] See *supra,* paras 1409-1412, 1419, 1423, 1427, 1467, 1534, 1536.

[4986] See Trial Judgement, Vol. 4, paras 427. 429, 626, 628, 816, 818.

[4987] See Trial Judgement, Vol. 4, paras 299-424, 469-623, 657-813.

[4988] See Trial Judgement, Vol. 4, paras 299-325, 469-511, 657-686.

1549. In sum, the Appeals Chamber finds that Stojić fails to show that no reasonable trier of fact could have concluded on the basis of the evidence that he, and other JCE members, used the HVO and Military Police to commit crimes pursuant to the CCP, and that the actions of these armed forces are attributable to him. Stojić's sub-grounds of appeal 27.2, in part, and 27.3 are dismissed.

(e) Conclusion

1550. Based on the foregoing, Stojić's ground of appeal 27 is dismissed.

8. Alleged errors concerning Stojić's involvement in crimes committed in the municipalities and detention centres

(a) Prozor Municipality and Ljubuški Prison (Stojić's Ground 28)

1551. The Trial Chamber found that Stojić was informed on 13 July 1993 that detained men, including prisoners of war, but also men who did not belong to any armed force, were relocated from Prozor Secondary School to Ljubuški Prison. It further found that since Stojić continued to exercise his functions, the only reasonable inference was that he accepted the detention of men not belonging to any armed force at Ljubuški Prison in July 1993.[4989] Notably, in reaching this conclusion the Trial Chamber relied on one report from Željko Šiljeg to Stojić and Petković on 13 July 1993 ("Šiljeg's Report of 13 July 1993").[4990]

(i) Arguments of the Parties

1552. Stojić submits that no reasonable trier of fact could have arrived at the Trial Chamber's finding on his knowledge on the basis of Šiljeg's Report of 13 July 1993.[4991] He asserts that because this report was found to be insufficient to establish Petković's knowledge of the detentions, it was equally insufficient regarding his own knowledge of those detentions.[4992] Stojić also argues that the only relevant paragraph in Šiljeg's Report of 13 July 1993 does not support the inference that he **[page 636]** knew about the detention of civilians.[4993] Furthermore, Stojić asserts that the Trial Chamber erred by inferring that he accepted the detention of civilians at Ljubuški Prison because, *inter alia,* he had no personal responsibility for this detention centre.[4994] He also contends that he did not have the authority to intervene which is shown by the fact that Petković responded to Šiljeg without copying Stojić[4995] Stojić avers that "the receipt of a single report relating to detentions at a facility outside of [his] control, which was being addressed by [the] Main Staff, cannot amount to a significant contribution to the relevant crime.[4996]

1553. The Prosecution responds that the Trial Chamber's findings were reasonable,[4997] and that it correctly classified the "men who did not belong to any armed force" as civilians.[4998] The Prosecution submits that given Stojić's role in planning the indiscriminate arrests, he knew that Muslim men who did not belong to

---

[4989]   Trial Judgement, Vol. 4, paras 329, 396.

[4990]   Trial Judgement, Vol. 4, paras 329, 396, referring to Ex. P03418, p. 4. See Trial Judgement, Vol. 2, para. 149.

[4991]   Stojić's Appeal Brief, para. 244. See Stojić's Appeal Brief, paras 243, 248. See also Stojić's Reply Brief, para. 70.

[4992]   Stojić's Appeal Brief, para. 244, referring to Trial Judgement, Vol. 4, para. 799. See Appeal Hearing, AT. 361-362 (21 Mar 2017). Stojić asserts that the Trial Chamber concluded the opposite with regard to Petković and that its inconsistency is "unjustifiable". Stojić's Appeal Brief, para. 244.

[4993]   Stojić's Appeal Brief, para. 245, referring to Ex. P03418, para. 13. Stojić also submits that Šiljeg's Report of 13 July 1993 did not inform him that individuals were detained at Ljubuški Prison, but indicated that their accommodation was "unclear". Stojić's Appeal Brief, para. 246.

[4994]   Stojić's Appeal Brief, para. 247. See Stojić's Appeal Brief, para. 248. See also Stojić's Reply Brief, para. 70.

[4995]   Stojić's Appeal Brief, para. 247, referring to Ex. P03455, para. 12.

[4996]   Stojić's Appeal Brief, para. 248. See Stojić's Appeal Brief, para. 249. Stojić replies that it was not established that he saw Šiljeg's Report of 13 July 1993. Stojić's Reply Brief, para. 70.

[4997]   Prosecution's Response Brief (Stojić), paras 206-207, 209.

[4998]   Prosecution's Response Brief (Stojić), para. 207, referring to, *inter alia,* Trial Judgement, Vol. 3, paras 951-952, 1001-1002, Vol. 4, para. 329, Exs. P03380, P03971.

any armed force had been arrested.[4999] It argues that it is irrelevant that Petković did not copy Stojić in his response to Šiljeg,[5000] and that the. Trial Chamber's inconsistent finding on Petković's knowledge based on Šiljeg's Report of 13 July 1993 does not impact on Stojić's conviction.[5001]

(ii) Analysis

1554. Regarding Stojić's argument that Šiljeg's Report of 13 July 1993 does not support the inference that he knew about the detention of civilians, the Appeals Chamber notes that the Trial Chamber considered that, through Šiljeg's Report of 13 July 1993, Stojić and Petković were informed that Šiljeg "had relocated detainees – mostly prisoners of war, but also some 'civilians'" from Prozor Secondary School to Ljubuški Prison.[5002] Notably, this report states only that Šiljeg had requested a reply "regarding relocating Muslims v/o /liable for military service/ from Rama to **[page 637]** Herzegovina",[5003] and that "there was no reply until we had, on our own initiative, driven them into Ljubuški".[5004] On reviewing the exhibit, the Appeals Chamber considers that Šiljeg's Report of 13 July 1993, neither includes an explicit reference to civilians, nor sufficient information about the detainees to conclude that Stojić knew that Šiljeg was referring to the relocation of "civilians". In addition, there is no reference in the report to the Prozor Secondary School, but only the statement that the persons referred to were transported from Rama to Herzegovina.[5005] The Appeals Chamber notes, however, that the Trial Chamber considered that Prozor Municipality was also called "Rama".[5006] Considering the above, the exhibit – on its face – only speaks to the relocation of Muslims "liable for military service" from Prozor Municipality to Ljubuški.[5007]

1555. The Appeals Chamber takes particular note of the fact that the Trial Chamber made no finding that the phrase "Muslims liable for military service" necessarily denoted "men who did not belong to any armed force". Thus, the phrase is not sufficient – by itself – to conclude that at least some of these men and boys did not belong to any armed force.[5008] Therefore, the Appeals Chamber finds that no reasonable trier of fact could have concluded from Šiljeg's Report of 13 July 1993 alone that the only reasonable inference was that Stojić had been informed about the detention of "civilians" or "men and boys who did not belong to any armed force" in Prozor Municipality or Ljubuški Prison.[5009]

1556. On whether Šiljeg's Report of 13 July 1993 read together with the Trial Chamber's other findings could support the inference that Stojić knew of detentions, the Appeals Chamber notes that the Trial Chamber also referred to its previous factual findings when arriving at its conclusion on Stojić's knowledge.[5010] The section of the Trial Judgement on Prozor Secondary School outlines evidence that: (1) in the summer of 1993, between 400 and 500 people were held at Prozor Secondary School;[5011] (2) most of the detainees were

---

[4999] Prosecution's Response Brief (Stojić), paras 206-207, referring to, *inter alia*, Trial Judgement, Vol. 4, paras 57, 151-155, 953, 973, 984, 996, 1220. The Prosecution also argues that the Trial Chamber reasonably found from Šiljeg's Report of 13 July 1993 that detainees were taken to Ljubuški Prison and then sent to Dretefj Prison. Prosecution's Response Brief (Stojić), para. 209.

[5000] Prosecution's Response Brief (Stojić), para. 210. The Prosecution further submits that the HVO and the Military Police operating in Ljubuški Prison were under Stojić's control and that he was found to have issued detention-related orders. Prosecution's Response Brief (Stojić), para. 211, referring to Trial Judgement, Vol. 4, paras 312, 320. The Prosecution also asserts that, regardless of his authority over Ljubuški Prison, Stojić planned the arrests of Muslims detained there. Prosecution's Response Brief (Stojić), para. 212.

[5001] Prosecution's Response Brief (Stojić), para. 208.

[5002] Trial Judgement, Vol. 4, paras 329, 396, referring to Ex. P03418, p. 4. See Trial Judgement, Vol. 2, para. 149.

[5003] Ex. P03418, para. 13, p. 4.

[5004] Ex. P03418, para. 13, p. 4.

[5005] Ex. P03418, para. 13, p. 4.

[5006] Trial Judgement, Vol. 2, para. 5 ("Prozor, which means 'window' and is also called *Rama*, is the entry point from Herzegovina into Central Bosnia"). The Appeals Chamber also notes that the "Military Prison of the *Rama* Brigade" was "[t]he official name of the [Prozor] Secondary School as a detention facility". Trial Judgement, Vol. 2, para. 138.

[5007] See Ex. P03227 (an order from Šiljeg referring to the Prozor area as "Rama").

[5008] See Trial Judgement, Vol. 2, para. 146, Vol. 4, para. 799.

[5009] See *infra*, paras 2150, 2154-2156 (discussing Šiljeg's Report of 13 July 1993, the Appeals Chamber found that "it is not satisfied that a reasonable trier of fact could have concluded, as the only reasonable inference, that Petković knew that men who did not belong to any armed force were being detained at the Prozor Secondary School and were transferred to Ljubuški Prison in July 1993", see *infra*, para. 2155).

[5010] Trial Judgement, Vol. 4, paras 329, 396 & fns 764, 857, referring to Trial Judgement, Vol. 2, paras 145-156, 1800-1818.

[5011] Trial Judgement, Vol. 2, para. 145.

Muslim men who were members of the TO/ABiH and between 16 and 60 years of age;[5012] (3) there were seven detainees under 16 years of **[page 638]** age and 40 detainees over 60 years of age, "who did not belong to any armed force";[5013] and (4) 237 detainees, described as "not prisoners of war", were moved to Ljubuški Prison.[5014] However, the Appeals Chamber observes that the evidence cited by the Trial Chamber in its discussion only shows that there were men who did not belong to any armed force detained at Prozor Secondary School, but not that Stojić had been informed of this detention, and particularly, that civilians or men and boys who did not belong to any armed force were detained and relocated.[5015]

1557. Furthermore, in the Trial Chamber's analysis of the evidence on the arrival and transfer of detainees of Ljubuški Prison no mention is made of Stojić or his knowledge of events in the factual findings or in the evidence cited.[5016] On a broader scale, the Trial Chamber did not refer to any involvement by Stojić in the events taking place in Ljubuški Municipality or Ljubuški Prison.[5017] Considering the above,[5018] the Appeals Chamber finds that even when reading the Trial Chamber's findings on the detention of civilians at Prozor Secondary School and Ljubuški Prison in conjunction with Šiljeg's Report of 13 July 1993, no reasonable trier of fact could have concluded that the only reasonable inference was that Stojić was informed of the detention and relocation of civilians or men and boys who did not belong to any armed force in Prozor Municipality and at Ljubuški Prison in July 1993.

1558. Moreover, the Appeals Chamber notes that Stojić was involved in planning some of the HVO's military operations, and more relevantly, planned and was informed of the campaign of arrests and mass detentions of Muslims who did not belong to any armed force in Čapljina.[5019] Elsewhere, the Appeals Chamber has noted the Trial Chamber's finding that following the 30 June 1993 Joint Proclamation issued by Stojić and Prlić "the chain of command was set in **[page 639]** motion in order to arrest Muslims" in the municipalities of Mostar, Stolac, Čapljina, and Prozor.[5020] However, the Trial Chamber made no findings on Stojić's involvement in the July 1993 events in Prozor and Ljubuški, other than the receipt of Šiljeg's Report of 13 July 1993.[5021] Absent a determination that Stojić participated in planning, directing, or facilitating the July 1993 operations in Prozor and Ljubuški, the Appeals Chamber is not satisfied that a reasonable trier of fact could have concluded that the only reasonable inference was that Stojić was informed and knew of the detention of civilians or men and boys who did not belong to any armed force in Prozor Municipality and Ljubuški Prison.

1559. In light of the above, the Trial Chamber also erred in concluding, as the only reasonable inference, that Stojić accepted the detention of men who did not belong to any armed forces at Ljubuški Prison.[5022] Stojić's argument on the Trial Chamber's erroneous reliance on Šiljeg's Report of 13 July 1993 is granted. Thus, the

---

[5012]   Trial Judgement, Vol. 2, para. 146, referring to, *inter alia*, Exs. P09731 (confidential), pp. 4-5, P09197, p. 11, P03266, P09925, p. 3.
[5013]   Trial Judgement, Vol. 2, para. 146, referring to, *inter alia*, Exs. P09685, P09699, p. 2, P09722, p. 2, Witness BL, T(F). 5856-5857, 5859-5860 (31 Aug 2006).
[5014]   Trial Judgement, Vol. 2, para. 148, referring to, *inter alia*, Exs. P03380, P09989, p. 5, P09925, p. 3, P03418.
[5015]   See Trial Judgement, Vol. 2, paras 145-156, fns 351-378, and evidence cited therein. Notably, the Trial Chamber referred to two reports of Luka Markešić from the SIS which state that "civilians" were among the detainees, but these reports were not sent to Stojić or the Department of Defence. Thus, neither of Markešić's reports establish that Stojić was informed of the detention of men and boys who did not belong to any armed force at Prozor Secondary School. See Trial Judgement, Vol. 2, paras 148 (referring to Ex. P03380, p. 1), 152 (referring to Ex. P03971).
[5016]   See Trial Judgement, Vol. 2, paras 1800-1818, and evidence cited therein. Specifically on the transfer of detainees from Prozor Municipality to Ljubuški Prison in July 1993, the evidence cited by the Trial Chamber does not give any indication that Stojić, or the Department of Defence, was informed of the detention and relocation of civilians or men and boys who did not belong to any armed force from Prozor Municipality. Trial Judgement, Vol. 2, para. 1813, and evidence cited therein.
[5017]   Trial Judgement, Vol. 2, paras 1765-1878. See Trial Judgement, Vol. 2, paras 1768, 1774. *Cf.* Trial Judgement, Vol. 2, para. 1789 (the Prosecution argued at trial that Stojić, *inter alios*, was responsible for running Ljubuški Prison, however, the Trial Chamber made no finding on this issue).
[5018]   See *supra*, paras 1554-1557, fns 5016-5017.
[5019]   Trial Judgement, Vol. 4, paras 373-375, 1220 & fn. 2283. See Trial Judgement, Vol. 4, paras 151-152, 154, 341-342, 388-389, 397-398, 406-407, 953. See also *infra*, paras 1687-1688, 1696.
[5020]   See *infra*, para. 1687.
[5021]   Trial Judgement, Vol. 4, paras 329, 396. *Cf. infra*, para. 1586 (noting Stojić's knowledge of a preconceived plan regarding events in Prozor in April 1993 following the 4 April 1993 Ultimatum).
[5022]   See Trial Judgement, Vol. 4, paras 329, 396.

Appeals Chamber finds that it is unnecessary to deal with Stojić's remaining arguments in this regard, which are moot.

(iii) Conclusion

1560. Based on the foregoing, the Appeals Chamber grants Stojić's ground of appeal 28 in part, and reverses the Trial Chamber's findings that Stojić was informed of the detention of civilians in Prozor and Ljubuški Prison based on Šiljeg's Report of 13 July 1993, and that he accepted the detention of men who did not belong to any armed forces at Ljubuški Prison. The impact of this reversal of findings on Stojić's contribution to the JCE, *mens rea,* and convictions, if any, will be discussed in the relevant sections below.[5023]

(b) Gornji Vakuf Municipality (Stojić's Ground 29)

1561. The Trial Chamber found that, on 18 January 1993, the HVO and the Military Police attacked Gornji Vakuf Municipality, which resulted in the destruction of Muslim houses, the murder and detention of Muslims who did not belong to any armed force, and the removal of women, children and the elderly from the area.[5024] The Trial Chamber considered that, as Stojić sent Colonel Miro Andrić to Gornji Vakuf who then reported to Stojić on the situation in Gornji Vakuf **[page 640]** and Prozor in a report dated 27 January 1993 ("Andrić's Report"), the only reasonable inference it could draw was that Stojić was one of Andrić's superiors who ordered him to capture the Gornji Vakuf area by force.[5025] It also found that Stojić facilitated and closely followed the HVO operations in the area.[5026] The Trial Chamber further found that Stojić was aware of the reports sent by Željko Šiljeg about the situation in Gornji Vakuf and was thus informed of the destruction of Muslim houses, the murder and detention of Muslim civilians, and the removal of inhabitants of the area by the HVO.[5027] The Trial Chamber concluded that "inasmuch as Bruno Stojić planned and facilitated the HVO military operations in Gornji Vakuf in January 1993 and was informed of the crimes committed during the operations, he intended to commit those crimes".[5028]

(i) Whether Stojić ordered Miro Andrić to capture Gornji Vakuf by force (Stojić's Sub-ground 29.1)

1562. Stojić submits that the Trial Chamber erred in finding that he was one of the superiors who ordered Andrić to use force in Gornji Vakuf, and that this inference is not supported by Andrić's Report.[5029] He contends that this report shows that he ordered Andrić to resolve the situation peacefully.[5030] Further, Stojić submits that Andrić's Report is addressed to him personally, and as it uses his name when referring to his orders, "[i]t is inconceivable that later in the same document Andrić would have referred to an order from Stojić as an order 'from our superiors' without identifying him by name".[5031] Stojić also contends that Andrić

[5023] See *infra,* paras 1806-1807.

[5024] Trial Judgement, Vol. 2, paras 344-345, 347, 358, 368-369, 374, 381, Vol. 4, para. 331. The Appeals Chamber recalls that it has reversed the Trial Chamber's finding that the killing of the seven civilians in Duša amounted to murder and wilful killing, and thus has overturned the findings on these crimes in Gornji Vakuf Municipality and Stojić's conviction thereof. On the same basis, the Appeals Chamber considers elsewhere that no reasonable trier of fact could conclude that murder and wilful killing were part of the CCP from January 1993 until June 1993. Thus, the following section will only focus on the remaining crimes committed in Gornji Vakuf. See *supra,* paras 441-443, 882.

[5025] Trial Judgement, Vol. 4, para. 334. See Trial Judgement, Vol. 2, para. 338, Vol. 4, para. 330. The Appeals Chamber notes that the Trial Chamber found that Andrić's Report was sent to Stojić on 22 January 1993. Trial Judgement, Vol. 4, paras 330, 334. However, it is clear from the signature page of Andrić's Report that it was signed by Andrić on 27 January 1993. See Ex. 4D00348/3D03065, p. 3.

[5026] Trial Judgement, Vol. 4, para. 335.

[5027] Trial Judgement, Vol. 4, para. 336. See Trial Judgement, Vol. 4, paras 331-333.

[5028] Trial Judgement, Vol. 4, para. 337.

[5029] Stojić's Appeal Brief, paras 251-252, 255, referring to Trial Judgement, Vol. 4, para. 334, Ex. 4D00348/3D03065, pp. 1-2. See Appeal Hearing, AT. 356-358 (21 Mar 2017).

[5030] Stojić's Appeal Brief, para. 252, referring to Ex. 4D00348/3D03065, p. 1. See Appeal Hearing, AT. 356-357 (21 Mar 2017).

[5031] Stojić's Appeal Brief, para. 252, referring to Ex. 4D00348/3D03065, p. 1. Stojić argues that there was a mistranslation as the order actually says "following a higher order" instead of "following an order from our superiors" which further distances him from the order. Stojić's Appeal Brief, fn. 637. See Appeal Hearing, AT. 358 (21 Mar 2017).

sending the report nine days after the attack, on 27 January 1993, would be "astonishing" if he was one of Andrić's superiors.[5032]

1563. Stojić also submits that the Trial Chamber's finding is inconsistent with its findings on the military chain of command.[5033] He contends that he was not part of the military chain of command **[page 641]** and that he did not send direct combat orders.[5034] Stojić argues that the usual chain of command, which went through the Main Staff, was operational in Gornji Vakuf at the time.[5035] In this regard, he contends that: (1) Andrić was in the Main Staff and thus his reference to "our superiors" could not relate to Stojić;[5036] (2) Praljak consulted with Andrić on 15 or 16 January 1993 after Andrić's last evidenced contact with Stojić;[5037] (3) on 16 January 1993, Praljak told the ABiH that they would be annihilated if they did not comply with the 15 January 1993 Ultimatum;[5038] (4) on 18 January 1993, Praljak ordered that weapons be sent to Gornji Vakuf;[5039] and (5) the order to cease combat operations came from Boban and was transmitted by Petković.[5040]

1564. The Prosecution responds that the evidence relied on by the Trial Chamber demonstrates that Andrić acted under the authority of Stojić,[5041] and argues that Andrić: (1) managed the situation in Gornji Vakuf following a verbal order from Stojić;[5042] (2) transmitted the order containing the 15 January 1993 Ultimatum from Petković, which was issued pursuant to an order from Stojić;[5043] and (3) reported to Stojić on the capture of Gornji Vakuf Municipality after the ABiH rejected the 15 January 1993 Ultimatum.[5044] It argues that, although Andric indicated that he was sent on 12 January 1993 to resolve the situation peacefully, "this is not inconsistent with the interpretation that Stojić later ordered Andrić to use force after the HVO's demands had not been met".[5045] It further argues that Stojić's argument that Andrić's Report identifies him by name whenever referencing him is flawed.[5046] The Prosecution contends that it is immaterial whether Stojić was in the *de jure* military chain of command and whether this chain of command functioned in Gornji Vakuf.[5047]

[page 642]

1565. The Appeals Chamber notes that the Trial Chamber, relying on Andrić's Report, found that: (1) further to an oral order of 12 January 1993 from Stojić, Andrić went to Prozor on 13 January 1993 in order to calm down the situation in Gornji Vakuf Municipality;[5048] and (2) on 18 January 1993, Andrić ordered the HVO forces in Gornji Vakuf to use force to ensure that the ABiH honoured the ceasefire agreement concluded on 13 January 1993 and that the HVO take Uzričje village so as to open a route to Gornji Vakuf.[5049] The Appeals Chamber notes that in Andrić's Report, he stated that he arrived "in Prozor in the early morning

[5032] Stojić's Appeal Brief, para. 252, referring to Ex. 4D00348/3D03065, p. 3.
[5033] Stojić's Appeal Brief, para. 253.
[5034] Stojić's Appeal Brief, para. 253, referring to Trial Judgement, Vol. 1, paras 565, 791-796, Vol. 4, para. 306.
[5035] Stojić's Appeal Brief, paras 253-254.
[5036] Stojić's Appeal Brief, para. 253, referring to Trial Judgement, Vol. 2, para. 338.
[5037] Stojić's Appeal Brief, para. 254, referring to Ex. P01174.
[5038] Stojić's Appeal Brief, para. 254, referring to Ex. P01162.
[5039] Stojić's Appeal Brief, para. 254, referring to Ex. P01202.
[5040] Stojić's Appeal Brief, para. 254, referring to Exs. 1D00472, P01238, P01286. Stojić argues that a similar order was sent by Boban on 27 January 1993, and transmitted by Petković. Stojić's Appeal Brief, para. 254, referring to Exs. P01329, P01322.
[5041] Prosecution's Response Brief (Stojić), para. 215.
[5042] Prosecution's Response Brief (Stojić), para. 215, referring to Trial Judgement, Vol. 2, para. 338, Vol. 4, paras 330, 334-335.
[5043] Prosecution's Response Brief (Stojić), para. 215, referring to Trial Judgement, Vol. 4, para. 304.
[5044] Prosecution's Response Brief (Stojić), para. 215, referring to Trial Judgement, Vol. 2, paras 341, 345, Vol. 4, paras 45, 330, 334. See also Appeal Hearing, AT. 327-328 (21 Mar 2017).
[5045] Prosecution's Response Brief (Stojić), para. 216, referring to Ex. 4D00348/3D03065, p. 1, Trial Judgement, Vol. 4, para. 334.
[5046] Prosecution's Response Brief (Stojić), para. 217.
[5047] Prosecution's Response Brief (Stojić), para. 218. The Prosecution asserts that Praljak was also not *de jure* within the military chain of command in January 1993. Prosecution's Response Brief (Stojić), para. 218. It also argues that Stojić ordered that the 15 January 1993 Ultimatum be executed, sent Andrić to manage the situation in Gornji Vakuf, and received and relayed reports on the situation to the Government. Prosecution's Response Brief (Stojić), para. 218, referring to, *inter alia*, Trial Judgement, Vol. 2, para. 338, Vol. 4, paras 127, 304, 334-336.
[5048] Trial Judgement, Vol. 2, paras 337-338, Vol. 4, para. 330.
[5049] Trial Judgement, Vol. 4, paras 330, 334, referring to Ex. 4D00348/3D03065, p. 2 ("On 18 January 1993, following a higher order, it was decided to use force to exert pressure on the [ABiH] and to force them to honour what they had agreed, while the simultaneous taking of Uzričje would open a route to Gornji Vakuf."). See Trial Judgement, Vol. 4, paras 124, 126. The Appeals Chamber notes that the authoritative translation of the exhibit reads as "following a higher order" instead of the phrase which was considered by the Trial Chamber, *i.e.* "following an order from our superiors". See Decision on Prlić's Motion to Replace Translation of Exhibits 4D00348 and 3D03065, 11 March 2015, p. 2.

hours of 13 January", familiarised himself with the situation, saw that the situation was tense and clashes were likely, and scheduled a meeting with representatives of the OS BH at the camp of UNPROFOR in Gornji Vakuf.[5050] Andrić then reports that he arrived in Gornji Vakuf, that negotiations were very difficult,[5051] and that "[d]uring the entire time between 13 January and 17 January 1993 we met several times in the UN camp and appealed to the OS BH".[5052]

1566. The Appeals Chamber further recalls the Trial Chamber's finding that on 16 January 1993, at a meeting between representatives of the HVO and the ABiH, Andrić transmitted the general subordination order issued by Petković the previous day – pursuant to the orders of Prlić and Stojić[5053] – to the ABiH representatives, insisting on the subordination of all ABiH forces to the HVO.[5054] The Trial Chamber found that on 16 and 17 January 1993, the ABiH rejected these subordination orders.[5055] Moreover, following the HVO attack in Gornji Vakuf on 18 January 1993, Andrić reported to Stojić on the operations. Based on this sequence of events and the related Trial Chamber findings, the Appeals Chamber considers that Stojić fails to show that the Trial Chamber's inference – that he was one of Andrić's "superiors" who ordered the use of force – was not the only **[page 643]** reasonable one. Additionally, Stojić does not demonstrate how the references in Andrić's Report to the instructions Andrić received to resolve differences peacefully[5056] would have an impact on the Trial Chamber's finding in this regard.

1567. With regard to Stojić's argument that, because of the contents of the report, it is "inconceivable" that he was one of the superiors who ordered the use of force, the Appeals Chamber considers this argument to be speculative and merely his own interpretation of the evidence without him showing an error.[5057] The Appeals Chamber is also not convinced by Stojić's contention that a report on events sent nine days after those events occurred indicates that he was not one of the "superiors".[5058] Stojić's arguments are dismissed.

1568. The Appeals Chamber notes that Stojić's argument that he was not part of the military chain of command ignores the Trial Chamber's findings that the Main Staff was an integral part of the Department of Defence and that, although the Head of the Department of Defence was not *de jure* part of the military chain of command, Stojić commanded and had "effective control" over the HVO and the Military Police by, *inter alia*, issuing orders directly to the HVO.[5059] Thus, the Main Staff's involvement, and particularly that of Praljak and Petković, does not call into question the conclusion that Stojić was one of Andrić's "superiors". Stojić's arguments are dismissed.

[5050] Ex. 4D00348/3D03065, p. 1.
[5051] Ex. 4D00348/3D03065, p. 1.
[5052] Ex. 4D00348/3D03065, p. 2. The Appeals Chamber notes that in the section dealing with Stojić's responsibility, the Trial Chamber also found – recalling a factual finding in a previous section of the Trial Judgement related to Gornji Vakuf Municipality – that it was Stojić who had sent Andrić to Gornji Vakuf. See Trial Judgement, Vol. 2, para. 334 ("In the part relating to the structure of the Municipality of Gornji Vakuf, the Chamber notes that it was Bruno Stojić who had sent Colonel Miro Andrić to Gornji Vakuf"). Upon review of the factual finding relied upon by the Trial Chamber to make this finding, the Appeals Chamber notes, however, that this earlier finding relates to Stojić dispatching Andrić, on 12 January 1993, "to manage the situation in Gornji Vakuf, and not to go to Gornji Vakuf. See Trial Judgement, Vol. 2, para. 338. In reading this finding together with paragraph 330 of Volume 4 of the Trial Judgement, it is evident that Stojić dispatched Andrić to Prozor to attend meetings relating to the situation in Gornji Vakuf. As such, the Trial Chamber erred when finding that Stojić sent Andrić to Gornji Vakuf. However, the Appeals Chamber does not consider the issue of whether Stojić physically sent Andrić to Gornji Vakuf to be determinative of the issue at hand, namely, whether Stojić was one of the superiors who ordered Andrić to use force.
[5053] Trial Judgement, Vol. 2, fn. 816.
[5054] Trial Judgement, Vol. 2, para. 339.
[5055] Trial Judgement, Vol. 2, para. 341.
[5056] See Ex. 4D00348/3D03065, p. 1. See also Trial Judgement, Vol. 4, paras 126, 334.
[5057] The Appeals Chamber also not convinced that any alleged error in the translation of Exhibit 4D00348 would have an impact on the Trial Chamber's findings. See *supra*, fns 5032, 5050.
[5058] The Appeals Chamber recalls that the Trial Chamber erroneously found that Exhibit 4D00348 was sent to Stojić on 22 January 1993 as the exhibit is dated 27 January 1993. See *supra*, fn. 5026. However, this error has no impact, particularly as Andrić recounts in his report that he was wounded on 22 January 1993 and thus had to dictate this report from his hospital bed. See Ex. 4D00348/3D03065, p. 3.
[5059] Trial Judgement, Vol. 4, paras 303-306, 312, 320. See *supra*, paras 1435, 1457, 1470-1472, 1479 (dismissing Stojić's challenges to the findings that he commanded the HVO and the Military Police).

1569. In light of the above, Stojić fails to demonstrate that the Trial Chamber erred in finding that he was one of Andrić's superiors who ordered him to capture the Gornji Vakuf area by force. Stojić's sub-ground of appeal 29.1 is dismissed.

(ii) Whether Stojić was aware of the commission of crimes based on reports from Željko Šiljeg (Stojić's Sub-ground 29.2)

1570. Stojić submits that the Trial Chamber erred in finding that he was aware of the crimes committed in Gornji Vakuf through the reports from Šiljeg.[5060] He contends that the Trial Chamber failed to analyse the reliability of one of these reports, Exhibit P01357, which he argues is a compilation of documents with different dates and recipients and the authenticity of which cannot **[page 644]** be established.[5061] Stojić argues that there is no evidence that he received these reports.[5062] He also submits that Šiljeg's reports were addressed "simply" to the Department of Defence, that the Trial Chamber relied on its "flawed" inference that he ordered the use of force, and that it cannot be inferred that he was aware of all subsequent reports from Gornji Vakuf Municipality.[5063] Stojić contends that, even if he had read the reports, their contents do not support an inference that he was aware of the destruction of Muslim homes, the detention and removal of civilians, or the murders.[5064] He argues that the reports state that properties were on fire or destroyed and record the number of civilian casualties, but maintains that this was in the context of the ongoing hostilities.[5065] He submits that nothing in the reports refers to civilian detentions,[5066] the HVO's responsibility, or the occurrence of crimes.[5067]

1571. The Prosecution responds that Stojić's late challenge to the authenticity of Exhibit P01357 should be dismissed.[5068] The Prosecution also responds that, in addition to its inference that Stojić ordered the use of force, the Trial Chamber relied on Stojić's overall control over the HVO and the Military Police as well as his "deep" involvement in the Gornji Vakuf operations.[5069] It submits that Šiljeg's reports were sent to the Department of Defence, received by Stojić, and confirmed that HVO forces committed crimes in Gornji Vakuf.[5070] The Prosecution contends that the Trial Chamber correctly assessed the totality of the evidence, namely Šiljeg's reports and Stojić's knowledge of the military operations.[5071] It further submits that Stojić incorrectly asserts that no report mentions the detention of civilians and refers to a report dated 30 January 1993 from Šiljeg which alerted Stojić to the fact that there were civilian detainees.[5072] **[page 645]**

1572. Regarding Stojić's knowledge of the Gornji Vakuf crimes, the Appeals Chamber notes that the Trial Chamber relied on Exhibit P01357 as well as other reports from Šiljeg to find that Stojić was aware of the

---

[5060] Stojić's Appeal Brief, paras 256-257, referring to Trial Judgement, Vol. 4, para. 336. See Stojić's Appeal Brief, para. 260.

[5061] Stojić's Appeal Brief, para. 257, referring to Ex. P01357.

[5062] Stojić's Appeal Brief, para. 257. See Appeal Hearing, AT. 280 (21 Mar 2017), 804-806 (28 Mar 2017).

[5063] Stojić's Appeal Brief, para. 258, referring to Exs. P01206, p. 1, P01357, p. 1, P01351, p. 1. See also Appeal Hearing, AT. 280 (21 Mar 2017), 804-806 (28 Mar 2017).

[5064] Stojić's Appeal Brief, para. 259.

[5065] Stojić's Appeal Brief, para. 259, referring to Exs. P01206, P01357, P01351.

[5066] Stojić's Appeal Brief, para. 259. Stojić argues that Exhibit P01351 confirms that there were detainees but that they were all members of the ABiH. Stojić's Appeal Brief, para. 259, referring to Ex. P01351.

[5067] Stojić's Appeal Brief, para. 259. Stojić submits the Trial Chamber erroneously concluded, from a report stating that "there [was] no civilian population left", that the HVO removed the inhabitants of the area as this conclusion cannot follow from a reading of this report. Stojić's Appeal Brief, para. 259, referring to Ex. 01357, p. 6, Trial Judgement, Vol. 4, para. 336.

[5068] Prosecution's Response Brief (Stojić), para. 223, referring to @@*Šainović et al.* Appeal Judgement, paras 532-533. The Prosecution further argues that Stojić mischaracterises the exhibit as it is a single report in which several orders and reports are reproduced and referenced. Prosecution's Response Brief (Stojić), para. 223, referring to Ex. P01357.

[5069] Prosecution's Response Brief (Stojić), para. 220, referring to Trial Judgement, Vol. 4, paras 300, 312, 334-336.

[5070] Prosecution's Response Brief (Stojić), paras 220-221, referring to, *inter alia,* Trial Judgement, Vol. 4, para. 334, Exs. P01206, p. 1, P01357, p. 1, P01351, p. 1.

[5071] Prosecution's Response Brief (Stojić), para. 221, referring to Trial Judgement, Vol. 4, paras 131, 561. The Prosecution contends that Stojić knew that the references in Šiljeg's reports documented HVO crimes. Prosecution's Response Brief (Stojić), para. 221. See also Appeal Hearing, AT. 328-330 (21 Mar 2017).

[5072] Prosecution's Response Brief (Stojić), para. 222, referring to Ex. P01357. The Prosecution argues that this 30 January 1993 report indicated that no civilian population was left in Gornja and Donja Hrasnica and that "some of the population were taken prisoner […] and taken to Trnovača". Prosecution's Response Brief (Stojić), para. 222, referring to Ex. P01357, pp. 6-7. It also asserts that Stojić learned of allegations of mistreatment in Trnovača through an earlier report. Prosecution's Response Brief (Stojić), para. 222, referring to Ex. P01351, p. 4.

crimes committed there.[5073] The Appeals Chamber notes that Stojić challenged the authenticity or reliability of Exhibit P01357 during trial by arguing that the original document was partly illegible, and that information contained therein could not be admitted based only on a draft translation.[5074] The Trial Chamber rejected this argument and concluded that the exhibit had sufficient indicia of reliability, relevance and probative value.[5075] By only submitting that the Trial Chamber "failed to analyse the reliability" of Exhibit P01357 as "[i]ts authenticity cannot be established",[5076] Stojić fails to show that the Trial Chamber erred in exercising its broad discretion regarding the admissibility or reliability of this exhibit.[5077]

1573. On the issue of whether Stojić received or was aware of Šiljeg's reports, Exhibits P01357, P01206, and P01351 were all addressed to the Department of Defence.[5078] However, in the Appeals Chamber's view, the fact that the reports were not addressed to Stojić personally does not undermine the Trial Chamber's finding that he, as Head of the Department of Defence, was aware of these reports due to his: (1) involvement in the Gornji Vakuf operations; and (2) position as the member of the Government who was "responsible for the armed forces".[5079] With respect to the latter, the Appeals Chamber recalls that Stojić was found to have exercised a reporting function visa-vis the Government and would receive various reports from different military organs in order to be able to exercise that function.[5080] Accordingly, in light of the reporting function Stojić was found to have exercised and taking into account the Trial Chamber's findings as to his involvement in the Gornji Vakuf operations, the Appeals Chamber concludes that Stojić fails to show that no reasonable trier of fact could have concluded that he received Šiljeg's reports concerning the operations in Gornji Vakuf.
[page 646]

1574. Regarding Stojić's argument that it cannot be inferred from Šiljeg's reports that he knew of the crimes committed, the Appeals Chamber notes that: (1) Exhibit P01206 states that several facilities were on fire;[5081] (2) Exhibit P01351 mentions persons, including "civilians" as being killed and the destruction of houses through torching and shelling;[5082] and (3) Exhibit P01357 states that most buildings in Donja Hrasnica were burned down or demolished, that there "[was] no civilian population left in Gornja Hrsanica and Donja Hrasnica", and that "some of the population were taken prisoners [...] and some fled".[5083] In this regard, the Appeals Chamber finds that although the reports, by themselves, do not expressly state that the HVO were committing the relevant crimes, Stojić's awareness of the crimes stems from the reports read in conjunction with his overall role in and knowledge of the operations. Notably, in considering these exhibits, the Trial Chamber recalled its previous findings that the Gornji Vakuf operations involved the HVO burning down and destroying buildings and houses, forcibly removing the women, children and the elderly, and detaining people.[5084] Considering the Trial Chamber's findings and the evidence cited above, as well as the finding that Stojić facilitated and closely followed the Gornji Vakuf operations, the Appeals Chamber finds that Stojić fails to demonstrate that the Trial Chamber erred in concluding that he was aware of the destruction of

---

[5073] Trial Judgement, Vol. 4, paras 331-333, 336, referring to Exs. P01206, P01357, P01351.

[5074] *Prosecutor v. Jadranko Prlić et al.*, Case No. IT-04-74-T, Joint Defence Response to Prosecution Motion for Admission of Documentary Evidence, 8 October 2007 (confidential) ("Joint Response"), p. 12. For other exhibits, Stojić specifically objected to the lack of authenticity, the lack of probative value, and the lack of relevance. Joint Response, pp. 11-15.

[5075] See *Prosecutor v. Jadranko Prlić et al.*, Case No. IT-04-74-T, Decision on the Prosecution Motion for Admission of Documentary Evidence (Two Motions: HVO and Herceg-Bosna), 24 January 2008 (French original filed on 11 December 2007), para. 32, p. 9, Annex 1, p. 4 (admitting document with Rule 65 *ter* number 01357, which later became Ex. P01357, into evidence).

[5076] Stojić's Appeal Brief, para. 257.

[5077] See *Stanišić and Župljanin* Appeal Judgement, paras 99, 470 ("the Appeals Chamber recalls that a trial chamber is best placed to assess the credibility of a witness and reliability of the evidence adduced"). See also *Popović et al.* Appeal Judgement, paras 74, 131.

[5078] Ex. P01357, p. 1; Ex. P01206, p. 1; Ex. P01351, p. 1. See *supra*, fn. 3703.

[5079] See Trial Judgement, Vol. 4, para. 336.

[5080] See *supra*, paras 1418-1419, 1476.

[5081] Ex. P01206, p. 1.

[5082] Ex. P01351, pp. 2-4. See *supra*, fn. 3703. The Appeals Chamber recalls that it has reversed the Trial Chamber's finding that the killing of the seven civilians in Duša amounted to murder and wilful killing, and thus has overturned the findings on these crimes in Gornji Vakuf Municipality and Stojić's conviction thereof. Moreover, the Appeals Chamber has overturned the Trial Chamber's finding that the destruction of Muslim houses in Duša resulting from shelling was wanton and not justified by military necessity. See *supra*, paras 435, 441-443, 452.

[5083] Ex. P01357, pp. 6-7. Šiljeg also recounts a conversation with "BIJEDIĆ", from the Muslim delegation, who told Šiljeg that he could raze Gornji Vakuf to the ground but he could not kill every single person. Ex. P01357, pp. 1-2.

[5084] Trial Judgement, Vol. 4, paras 331-333.

Muslim houses, detention of Muslims who did not belong to any armed force, and the removal of the inhabitants of the area through Šiljeg's reports.[5085] Stojić's argument is thus dismissed.

1575. Based on the foregoing, the Appeals Chamber finds that Stojić has failed to demonstrate that no reasonable trier of fact could have found that he was aware of the crimes committed during the Gornji Vakuf operations. Stojić's sub-ground of appeal 29.2 is dismissed.

> (iii) Whether Stojić facilitated and closely followed the military operations in Gornji Vakuf and intended the crimes to be committed (Stojić's Sub-ground 29.3)

1576. Stojić submits that the Trial Chamber's finding that he facilitated and closely followed the operations in Gornji Vakuf is "a remarkable construction".[5086] He contends that the Trial Chamber **[page 647]** made several inferences based on other inferences, and specifically that he facilitated and closely followed the military operations, then as a result he must have been aware of the reports sent by Šiljeg, before concluding that he planned and intended the commission of crimes in Gornji Vakuf.[5087] Stojić argues that the only direct evidence is that he sent Andrić to Gornji Vakuf on 12 January 1993 "to calm the situation" and Andrić's Report.[5088] He asserts that this evidence cannot lead to the inference that he planned or facilitated the HVO military operations.[5089] Further, Stojić submits that his receipt of a report nine days after the attack does not amount to "'closely following' events" and thus the first inference cannot be sustained.[5090]

1577. The Prosecution responds that the Trial Chamber's findings were reasonable.[5091] The Prosecution submits that Stojić incorrectly argues that the only direct evidence relied on was Andrić's Report[5092] and ignores the evidence which shows his involvement in implementing the 15 January 1993 Ultimatum,[5093] and that he received Šiljeg's reports.[5094] It also submits that the Trial Chamber's finding that Stojić intended the crimes is supported by the findings that he planned the operations, failed to punish the perpetrators, and continued contributing to the CCP.[5095]

1578. The Appeals Chamber notes that the Trial Chamber's finding that Stojić closely followed and facilitated the military operations in Gornji Vakuf is based on the fact that: (1) he ordered Andrić to become involved in negotiations in order to calm down the situation in Gornji Vakuf; (2) Andrić then ordered the HVO to use force in Gornji Vakuf to ensure that the ABiH honoured the ceasefire agreement concluded on 13 January 1993; and (3) Andrić subsequently informed Stojić about the results of the military operations and the negotiations with the ABiH.[5096] Other than asserting that the Trial Chamber's reliance on Andrić's Report "cannot support an inference" that **[page 648]** he planned and facilitated the operations, Stojić does

---

[5085]   See Trial Judgement, Vol. 4, para. 336. The Appeals Chamber recalls that it has reversed the Trial Chamber's finding that the killing of the seven civilians in Duša amounted to murder and wilful killing, and thus has overturned the findings on these crimes in Gornji Vakuf Municipality and Stojić's conviction thereof. On the same basis, the Appeals Chamber considers elsewhere that no reasonable trier of fact could conclude that murder and wilful killing were part of the CCP from January 1993 until June 1993. See *supra*, paras 441-443, 882.

[5086]   Stojić's Appeal Brief, para. 261, referring to Trial Judgement, Vol. 4, paras 335-337.

[5087]   Stojić's Appeal Brief, para. 261, referring to Trial Judgement, Vol. 4, paras 335-337. See Stojić's Appeal Brief, paras 250, 262-263.

[5088]   Stojić's Appeal Brief, para. 262, referring to Ex. 4D00348/3D03065.

[5089]   Stojić's Appeal Brief, para. 262.

[5090]   Stojić's Appeal Brief, para. 262.

[5091]   Prosecution's Response Brief (Stojić), para. 224, referring to Trial Judgement, Vol. 4, para. 337. See Prosecution's Response Brief (Stojić), para. 214.

[5092]   Prosecution's Response Brief (Stojić), para. 225.

[5093]   Prosecution's Response Brief (Stojić), para. 225, referring to Trial Judgement, Vol. 4, paras 125, 127, 304, 919. See also Appeal Hearing, AT. 327-328 (21 Mar 2017).

[5094]   Prosecution's Response Brief (Stojić), para. 225, referring to Trial Judgement, Vol. 4, paras 331-333, 336. See also Appeal Hearing, AT. 328-330 (21 Mar 2017).

[5095]   Prosecution's Response Brief (Stojić), para. 226, referring to Trial Judgement, Vol. 4, paras 337, 415, 423, 426. See also Appeal Hearing, AT. 327-328 (21 Mar 2017).

[5096]   Trial Judgement, Vol. 4, para. 335. See *supra*, paras 1565-1566. The Appeals Chamber notes the Trial Chamber's findings made elsewhere that: (1) Stojić was responsible for the implementation of the 15 January 1993 Ultimatum; (2) he ordered the HVO and the Military Police to implement the 15 January 1993 Ultimatum; and (3) he analysed the implementation during a meeting chaired by Prlić on 19 January 1993 where he also stated that the situation in Gornji Vakuf had finally calmed down thus showing that he was aware of the events in Gornji Vakuf even prior to receiving Andrić's Report on 27 January 1993. Trial Judgement, Vol.

not offer any other reasonable inferences that can be drawn from the evidence. Similarly, Stojić's argument on his belated receipt of Andrić's Report is unpersuasive.[5097] For both arguments, Stojić merely provides his own interpretation of the evidence without showing an error. Accordingly, Stojić's arguments are dismissed. As the remainder of Stojić's contentions are based on his challenge to the inference that he planned and facilitated the Gornji Vakuf operations, and he only asserts that the Trial Chamber erroneously used this inference to make further inferences on his knowledge and intention, these contentions are also dismissed.

1579. Based on the above, Stojić has failed to show that the Trial Chamber erroneously found that he planned and facilitated the Gornji Vakuf operations and intended the crimes committed during these operations. Stojić's sub-ground of appeal 29.3 is dismissed.

(iv) Conclusion

1580. In sum, the Appeals Chamber finds that Stojić has failed to demonstrate that the Trial Chamber erred in determining his contribution and intent regarding the crimes committed in Gornji Vakuf Municipality.[5098] Stojić's ground of appeal 29 is therefore dismissed.

(c) Jablanica Municipality (Stojić's Ground 30)

1581. The Trial Chamber found that on 17 April 1993 the HVO launched an attack on the Jablanica area, shelling the villages of Sovići and Doljani.[5099] The Trial Chamber held that the HVO operations in Jablanica Municipality followed a preconceived plan of which Stojić "must have been informed".[5100] It also found that Stojić must have been aware of the crimes committed by the HVO in Sovići and Doljani, that is, the destruction of buildings and mosques as well as the arrest of people not belonging to any armed forces.[5101] It further found that Stojić must have been aware of these crimes, especially as on 23 April 1993 he – along with Petković – ordered the commanders of all the OZs to respect international law ("23 April 1993 Order").[5102] In arriving at its findings, the Trial Chamber also considered that Stojić was informed of: (1) the military operations in Jablanica through a report dated 23 April 1993 from Ivica Primorac, Assistant Chief of the Main Staff **[page 649]** ("Primorac's Report of 23 April 1993");[5103] and (2) crimes committed by the HVO through an ICRC report dated 20 April 1993 ("ICRC Report of 20 April 1993").[5104] It concluded that Stojić knew about the crimes, continued to exercise his functions, making no "apparent efforts" to ensure that the 23 April 1993 Order was respected, and thus accepted these crimes.[5105]

(i) Whether Stojić must have been aware of the plan in relation to the HVO military operations in Jablanica Municipality (Stojić's Sub-ground 30.2)

a. Arguments of the Parties

1582. Stojić submits that the Trial Chamber erred in inferring that he knew about the HVO military operations in Jablanica before they took place and that the events followed a preconceived plan.[5106] Specifically, Stojić argues that: (1) the only report cited – Primorac's Report of 23 April 1993 – was a general

4, paras 125, 127, 304. See Trial Judgement, Vol. 4, paras 142, 146 (noting that the HVO committed crimes in Gornji Vakuf Municipality following the 15 January 1993 Ultimatum).
[5097] See also *supra*, fn. 5059.
[5098] See *supra*, fns 5025, 5086 (excluding murder and wilful killing (Counts 2 and 3)).
[5099] Trial Judgement, Vol. 4, para. 338.
[5100] Trial Judgement, Vol. 4, para. 341.
[5101] Trial Judgement, Vol. 4, para. 341. The Trial Chamber excluded the destruction of mosques in Jablanica Municipality from the CCP and therefore considered the related crimes within the framework of JCE III liability. Trial Judgement, Vol. 4, paras 73, 342, 449.
[5102] Trial Judgement, Vol. 4, paras 340-341, referring to Ex. P02050.
[5103] Trial Judgement, Vol. 4, paras 339, 341, referring to Ex. 4D01034.
[5104] Trial Judgement, Vol. 4, paras 340-341, referring to Ex. P01989.
[5105] Trial Judgement, Vol. 4, para. 342.
[5106] Stojić's Appeal Brief, paras 269-273.

update on various locations six days after the attack;[5107] (2) the attack in Jablanica was directed by the "usual military chain of command", and since he was not in the military chain of command, the orders the Trial Chamber referred to do not mention him, and thus it was unreasonable to infer that he was aware of the operations in advance;[5108] and (3) his knowledge could not be established as the only reasonable inference from Primorac's Report of 23 April 1993, which stated that the HVO had conquered Sovići and Doljani, and from the ICRC Report of 20 April 1993.[5109] Stojić asserts that "evidence of such meagre involvement cannot support a finding that [he] significantly contributed to those crimes".[5110]

1583. The Prosecution responds that the Trial Chamber reasonably concluded that Stojić knew of the plan to attack Jablanica Municipality. According to the Prosecution, Stojić was aware that the 4 April 1993 Ultimatum would be enforced through crimes in Jablanica Municipality the same way as the 15 January 1993 Ultimatum was enforced in Gornji Vakuf.[5111] It also submits that Stojić: **[page 650]** (1) commanded and had "effective control" over the HVO and was informed of military operations;[5112] and (2) was informed of the progress of the operations by Primorac's Report of 23 April 1993.[5113]

b. Analysis

1584. Regarding Stojić's argument that no evidence was cited by the Trial Chamber that he knew of the HVO military operations in Jablanica "before" they happened,[5114] the Appeals Chamber notes that this does not correspond with the Trial Chamber's finding. Notably, the Trial Chamber found that "Stojić must have been informed of that plan" and that he "must have been aware of the crimes committed by the HVO troops in Sovići and Doljani".[5115] The Appeals Chamber finds that the Trial Chamber did not infer that Stojić was necessarily informed *in advance* of the military operations, but relied on, *inter alia,* the ICRC Report of 20 April 1993, Primorac's Report of 23 April 1993, and a report submitted by Marko Rozić to Slobodan Božić on 23 April 1993 ("Rozić's Report of 23 April 1993")[5116] to conclude that he must have been informed of the plan and the crimes.[5117] Further, Stojić's knowledge of the plan *before* the operations occurred is not a necessary factor in determining his participation in those operations. Therefore, Stojić's argument is dismissed as it concerns his knowledge of the plan before the operations took place.

[5107]   Stojić's Appeal Brief, para. 270, referring to Ex. 4D01034.
[5108]   Stojić's Appeal Brief, para. 271, referring to, *inter alia,* Trial Judgement, Vol. 1, paras 565, 791-796, Vol. 4, para. 306, Exs. P01896, P01915, p. 2, P01932, P02037, p. 1.
[5109]   Stojić's Appeal Brief, para. 272.
[5110]   Stojić's Appeal Brief, para. 272.
[5111]   Prosecution's Response Brief (Stojić), para. 229. The Appeals Chamber recalls that the Trial Chamber found that on 3 April 1993 the HZ(R) H-B Government held a session in which it was decided that if the subordination of the ABiH armed forces to the HVO in provinces 3, 8, and 10, and the establishment of a joint HVO/ABiH command in other provinces by 15 April 1993 was refused, then the HVO would apply it unilaterally, including by military means, and this statement (the 4 April 1993 Ultimatum) was released on 4 April 1993. Trial Judgement, Vol. 4, para. 138. Referring to the 4 April 1993 Ultimatum, the Prosecution submits that Stojić: (1) was present at the Government session held on 3 April 1993; (2) was in charge of implementing the 15 January 1993 Ultimatum; (3) planned the violent operations in Gornji Vakuf; and (3) received reports documenting violent crimes against Muslims in Gornji Vakuf operations. Prosecution's Response Brief (Stojić), para. 229. See also Prosecution's Response Brief (Stojić), para. 228.
[5112]   Prosecution's Response Brief (Stojić), para. 230. The Prosecution points to one exhibit, a report from Šiljeg, concerning preparations for the Jablanica operations which was sent to the Department of Defence. Prosecution's Response Brief (Stojić), para. 230, referring to Ex. P01915.
[5113]   Prosecution's Response Brief (Stojić), para. 231.
[5114]   Stojić's Appeal Brief, paras 270, 272.
[5115]   Trial Judgement, Vol. 4, para. 341.
[5116]   The Appeals Chamber considers that the Trial Chamber mistakenly cited Primorac's Report of 23 April 1993 in the second sentence of paragraph 341 in Volume 4 of the Trial Judgement as it is Rozić's Report of 23 April 1993 which speaks to the destruction of houses and mosques pursuant to superior orders. Thus, the Appeals Chamber finds that the Trial Chamber was in fact referring to Rozić's Report of 23 April 1993. See Trial Judgement, Vol. 4, paras 338, 341, Ex. P02063. *Cf.* Ex. 4D01034. See also Prosecution's Response Brief (Stojić), fn. 955; *infra,* fn. 5150. Marko Rozić was the HVO Defence Bureau Chief in Jablanica (see Trial Judgement, Vol. 2, para. 649), and his report stated that "[w]hen the conflict had ceased, by order of the senior commanders, all Muslim houses were burnt down and two mosques were demolished" and sought instructions on the further treatment of "the prisoners". Ex. P02063.
[5117]   Trial Judgement, Vol. 4, paras 338-341.

1585. In any event, the Appeals Chamber is not convinced by Stojić's challenges to the Trial Chamber's findings. Concerning Stojić's submission that the Trial Chamber erred by inferring that events in Jablanica followed a preconceived plan, the Appeals Chamber observes that the existence of a preconceived plan was not "entirely unexplained".[5118] The Appeals Chamber notes that elsewhere in the Trial Judgement, the Trial Chamber found that the HVO operations in Jablanica and Prozor followed a "systematic course of action",[5119] and that the 4 April 1993 Ultimatum resulted in a "plan" for an attack on several villages in Prozor before discussing a similar attack in **[page 651]** Jablanica.[5120] The Trial Chamber reasonably considered the above as evidence of a preconceived plan. The Trial Chamber also noted Rozić's Report of 23 April 1993, which refers to orders from superior HVO commanders to set fire to Muslim houses and mosques, in this respect.[5121] Further, the Trial Chamber made other findings from which a preconceived plan regarding Jablanica could be reasonably inferred, including that: (1) Petković ordered on 15 April 1993 that combat readiness be raised in the Jablanica area;[5122] (2) Zdravko Sagolj, the Herceg Stjepan Brigade commander, requested reinforcements on 15 April 1993 from the Main Staff and various OZs and for them to "act IMMEDIATELY in accordance with our previous agreement";[5123] and (3) on 16 April 1993, heavy artillery batteries and assault tanks had already taken up positions around Sovići, HVO soldiers were kept in reserve in case they were needed, and "coordination" with "Tuta" was planned.[5124] Thus, Stojić fails to show that the Trial Chamber erred in considering that a preconceived plan existed.

1586. Stojić further contests the Trial Chamber's finding that he must have been aware of the preconceived plan by arguing that the attack in Jablanica was directed by the "usual military chain of command" and that Stojić was not part of this chain of command.[5125] In support of this argument, he cites to a number of reports from Šiljeg and orders given by Petković relating to the HVO's operations in Jablanica that do not refer to Stojić by name.[5126] The Appeals Chamber first notes that the Trial Chamber did not rely on these reports or orders to find that Stojić must have been aware of the preconceived plan.[5127] Moreover, one of the reports – the report sent by Šiljeg on 16 April 1993 to the Department of Defence – stated that "[w]e continue to work according to plan".[5128] Regarding Stojić's role in the military chain of command, the Appeals Chamber recalls that the Trial Chamber reasonably found that he: (1) commanded and had "effective control" over the HVO and the Military Police;[5129] (2) was informed about their military actions;[5130] (3) informed the HZ(R) H-B Government, both through reports and during Government sessions, about the military and security situation on the ground;[5131] and (4) was not *de jure* part of the military chain of **[page 652]** command but had *de facto* powers.[5132] Thus, Stojić fails to show that his position in the military chain of command calls into question the Trial Chamber's findings.

1587. Further, the Trial Chamber established that the 4 April 1993 Ultimatum was developed during the 3 April 1993 meeting which Stojić attended.[5133] Additionally, Stojić facilitated and closely followed the operations in Gornji Vakuf which implemented the 15 January 1993 Ultimatum.[5134] Notably, the Trial Chamber found that the attack on Prozor in April 1993 was a result of the implementation of the 4 April 1993

[5118]   Stojić's Appeal Brief, para. 271.
[5119]   Trial Judgement, Vol. 4, paras 146, 341. See Trial Judgement, Vol. 4, para. 717 ("the HVO operations in Jablanica were part of a well-organised and orchestrated plan by the HVO leadership").
[5120]   Trial Judgement, Vol. 4, paras 142-146.
[5121]   Trial Judgement, Vol. 4, para. 341. See *supra*, fn. 5117.
[5122]   Trial Judgement, Vol. 4, paras 712-713.
[5123]   Trial Judgement, Vol. 2, para. 533, quoting Ex. 4D00453.
[5124]   Trial Judgement, Vol. 2, para. 534.
[5125]   Stojić"s Appeal Brief, para. 271.
[5126]   Stojić's Appeal Brief, para. 271. See also Stojić's Appeal Brief, fn. 688.
[5127]   Trial Judgement, Vol. 4, para. 341.
[5128]   Ex. P01915, p. 3. See Trial Judgement, Vol. 4, para. 46 & fn. 125, referring to Ex. P01915.
[5129]   Trial Judgement, Vol. 4, paras 312, 320. See *supra*, paras 1457, 1479.
[5130]   Trial Judgement, Vol. 4, paras 300-301, 312, 318, 320. See *supra*, paras 1418, 1473-1476.
[5131]   Trial Judgement, Vol. 4, para. 300. See *supra*, para. 1476.
[5132]   Trial Judgement, Vol. 1, para. 565, Vol. 4, paras 304, 306, 423. The Appeals Chamber dismisses elsewhere Stojić's challenges to the findings on his command authority. See *supra*, paras 1457, 1479.
[5133]   Trial Judgement, Vol. 4, para. 138.
[5134]   Trial Judgement, Vol. 4, paras 331-333, 336. See *supra*, paras 1578-1579.

Ultimatum which was "identical" to the 15 January 1993 Ultimatum.[5135] It also found that "the HVO operations in the municipalities of Prozor and Jablanica followed a systematic course of action and therefore had to be the result of a preconceived HVO plan to implement the ultimatum of 15 April 1993 by force".[5136] Thus, in addition to the Trial Chamber's reliance on Primorac's Report of 23 April 1993,[5137] the Appeals Chamber considers that similarities in the military operations could also be reasonably used to infer Stojić's knowledge of the plan in relation to Jablanica. The Appeals Chamber finds that Stojić fails to show that no reasonable trier of fact could have inferred, as the only reasonable inference, that he was aware of the preconceived plan. His arguments are dismissed.[5138]

1588. Based on the foregoing, the Appeals Chamber finds that Stojić has failed to demonstrate that the Trial Chamber erred by finding that he must have been aware of the plan concerning the HVO operations in Jablanica.[5139] Stojić's sub-ground of appeal 30.2 is thus dismissed. **[page 653]**

    (ii) Whether Stojić must have been aware of the crimes committed in Sovići and Doljani (Stojić's Sub-ground 30.1)

      a. Arguments of the Parties

1589. Stojić submits that the Trial Chamber erred in its conclusion that he knew about the crimes committed in Sovići and Doljani, as there was no evidence in support.[5140] He argues that the ICRC Report of 20 April 1993 does not identify these villages as places where crimes were committed, but only mentions Doljani as a location "cut-off by the fighting" and disconnected from humanitarian aid.[5141] Further, Stojić contends that the Trial Chamber unreasonably found that the ICRC Report of 20 April 1993 informed him of the destruction of mosques and the detention of civilians, since these crimes were not mentioned in the report.[5142] Stojić also avers that the Trial Chamber erred by concluding that the 23 April 1993 Order was linked to Sovići and Doljani as: (1) the order was sent to all commanders and soldiers; (2) there is no indication that the order was precipitated by events in any particular location or by the ICRC Report of 20 April 1993, which did not refer to these two villages, but to all "HVO/BiH controlled areas".[5143] Stojić further contends that it was unreasonable to conclude from the term "cleansing" in Primorac's Report of 23 April 1993 that he had knowledge about the crimes, because this term is ambiguous and could also refer to lawful clean-up operations following military actions.[5144]

1590. The Prosecution responds that the Trial Chamber reasonably relied on the ICRC Report of 20 April 1993 to establish Stojić's awareness of HVO crimes.[5145] It argues that as Stojić knew that Sovići and Doljani would be attacked and the Muslims removed,[5146] upon receipt of the ICRC Report of 20 April 1993 he knew

---

[5135]   Trial Judgement, Vol. 4, para. 142.
[5136]   Trial Judgement, Vol. 4, para. 146. The Trial Chamber found that the ultimatum was released to the press on 4 April 1993 with a deadline of 15 April 1993, thus the Appeals Chamber considers that the Trial Chamber was in fact referring to the 4 April 1993 Ultimatum. Trial Judgement, Vol. 4, paras 138, 140.
[5137]   Trial Judgement, Vol. 4, para. 341.
[5138]   The Appeals. Chamber will address Stojić's submissions concerning the ICRC Report of 20 April 1993 and Primorac's Report of 23 April 1993 in the section below. See *infra*, paras 1591-1595.
[5139]   To the extent that the "preconceived" plan included a pattern of conduct regarding murder and wilful killing, the Appeals Chamber recalls that no reasonable trier of fact could conclude that murder and wilful killing were part of the CCP from January 1993 until June 1993 due to the Duša reversal and the lack of any pattern of CCP murders. See *supra*, para. 882. However, given that no killings that formed part of the CCP were found to have occurred in Jablanica, this change in the scope of the CCP has no impact on the Trial Chamber's findings above concerning Stojić's responsibility for the events in Jablanica. See *supra*, para. 876.
[5140]   Stojić's Appeal Brief, para. 265. See Stojić's Appeal Brief, para. 264. See also Stojić's Reply Brief, para. 70.
[5141]   Stojić's Appeal Brief, para. 265, referring to Ex. P01989, p. 1.
[5142]   Stojić's Appeal Brief, para. 266, referring to Ex. P01989, p. 1.
[5143]   Stojić's Appeal Brief, para. 267.
[5144]   Stojić's Appeal Brief, para. 268, referring to Trial Judgement, Vol. 2, paras 558, 561, *Kordić and Čerkez* Appeal Judgement, para. 403. Stojić also contends that there is no evidence that he received this report. Stojić's Appeal Brief, fn. 679.
[5145]   Prosecution's Response Brief (Stojić), para. 233. The Prosecution also responds that Stojić received information that the HVO had committed crimes in Jablanica Municipality but did not enforce the 23 April 1993 Order. Prosecution's Response Brief (Stojić), para. 232.
[5146]   Prosecution's Response Brief (Stojić), para. 233, referring to Prosecution's Response Brief (Stojić), paras 229-231. See also *supra*, para. 1583.

that crimes were committed there.[5147] The Prosecution submits that Rozić alerted Stojić to HVO crimes in Sovići and Doljani.[5148] In addition, it contends that the **[page 654]** Trial Chamber did not rely on Primorac's Report of 23 April 1993 to establish Stojić's knowledge of crimes in Sovići and Doljani, but rather his awareness of the military operations in these villages.[5149]

 b. Analysis

1591. The Trial Chamber relied on the ICRC Report of 20 April 1993 to conclude that "since the ICRC informed Bruno Stojić of the crimes committed by the HVO armed forces in [Jablanica Municipality], he must have been aware of the crimes committed [...] in Sovići and Doljani during the operations".[5150] The Trial Chamber considered that the ICRC Report of 20 April 1993 informed Stojić that: (1) since 15 April 1993, people had been killed and "civilian" houses regularly torched in the areas under the HVO control, including Jablanica; and (2) the security situation was so difficult that the ICRC delegates had to be evacuated from that municipality.[5151] Regarding Stojić's challenges to the Trial Chamber's reliance on the ICRC Report of 20 April 1993, the Appeals Chamber observes that the ICRC reported that "the situation in HVO/BiH controlled areas ha[d] greatly deteriorated since April 15th"[5152] and specifically noted that "[s]ummary executions, hostage-taking, indiscriminate shelling such as that on Zenica market [...], and the deliberate destruction of numerous homes have resulted in the flight of hundreds of terrorized civilians."[5153] Further, the ICRC informed that: (1) "[s]everal villages and municipalities, such as Doljani, Jablanica [...], Zenica and Tuzla ha[d] been cut-off by the fighting";[5154] and (2) "[f]or security reasons, the ICRC delegates in Jablanica had to be evacuated temporarily".[5155]

1592. Although Stojić argues that only the crimes committed in Zenica were mentioned in the ICRC Report of 20 April 1993,[5156] the Appeals Chamber notes that the report also lists crimes committed in HVO/BiH controlled areas since 15 April 1993 and uses an incident of indiscriminate shelling on the Zenica market as an example. Further, the report refers in this context to several villages and municipalities "such as" Doljani and Jablanica, which were "cut-off by the fighting".[5157] Sovići is a part of Jablanica Municipality and is not excluded from the listed **[page 655]** places.[5158] Therefore, the Appeals Chamber finds that the Trial Chamber reasonably concluded that Stojić was informed through the ICRC Report of 20 April 1993 that crimes were committed in Jablanica Municipality. Thus, Stojić's argument that the ICRC Report of 20 April 1993 does not identify Doljani and Sovići as crime sites is dismissed.

1593. Concerning Stojić's submission that the Trial Chamber unreasonably found that the ICRC Report of 20 April 1993 informed him of the destruction of mosques and the detention of civilians, the Appeals Chamber considers that Stojić misinterprets the Trial Judgement. As noted above, the Trial Chamber found that Stojić was informed by the ICRC Report of 20 April 1993 that people had been killed and civilian houses

[5147] Prosecution's Response Brief (Stojić), para. 233. In addition, the Prosecution submits that the ICRC Report of 20 April 1993 urged for the proper treatment of captured combatants and civilians. Prosecution's Response Brief (Stojić), para. 233, referring to Ex. P01989, p. 3.
[5148] Prosecution's Response Brief (Stojić), para. 234, referring to Ex. P02063 (referenced in Trial Judgement, Vol. 2, paras 641, 648). The Prosecution submits that Rozić's Report of 23 April 1993 was addressed to Stojić's immediate subordinate, Slobodan Božić, who would have alerted Stojić to the report, due to its contents. Prosecution's Response Brief (Stojić), para. 234. Slobodan Božić was the assistant to the Head of the Department of Defence from mid-January 1993 to November 1993. Trial Judgement, Vol. 2, para. 649.
[5149] Prosecution's Response Brief (Stojić), para. 235. The Prosecution asserts that the Trial Chamber incorrectly stated that Primorac's Report of 23 April 1993, rather than Rozić's Report of 23 April 1993, indicated that houses and mosques were destroyed. Prosecution's Response Brief (Stojić), fn. 955. See *supra*, fn. 5117.
[5150] Trial Judgement, Vol. 4, para. 341.
[5151] Trial Judgement, Vol. 4, para. 340, referring to Ex. P01989.
[5152] Ex. P01989, p. 2.
[5153] Ex. P01989, p. 2.
[5154] Ex. P01989, p. 2. The ICRC Report of 20 April 1993 also states that "[t]he ICRC has neither been able to provide relief and medical assistance, nor protection to those in need". Ex. P01989, p. 3.
[5155] Ex. P01989, p. 3.
[5156] Stojić's Appeal Brief, para. 265.
[5157] Ex. P01989, p. 2.
[5158] See Trial Judgement, Vol. 2, para. 538, Vol. 4, para. 338.

regularly torched in the areas under HVO control, including Jablanica.[5159] The Appeals Chamber considers that the Trial Chamber then inferred that Stojić must have been aware of the crimes committed by the HVO in Sovići and Doljani, having also taken into account that: (1) the operations in Jablanica Municipality were a result of a preconceived plan of which Stojić must have been informed;[5160] (2) the houses and mosques in Sovići and Doljani had been destroyed pursuant to an order by superior HVO officials in the execution of that preconceived plan;[5161] (3) Primorac's Report of 23 April 1993, sent to Stojić, referred to the "cleansing" of Doljani on 19 April 1993;[5162] and (4) after he was informed of the commission of crimes, including killings and the deliberate destruction of houses, by the ICRC Report of 20 April 1993, Stojić issued the 23 April 1993 Order for HVO commanders to "treat the civilians and detainees in accordance with international law".[5163] Therefore, the Appeals Chamber considers that Stojić fails to demonstrate that the Trial Chamber unreasonably inferred that Stojić must have been aware of the crimes committed by the HVO in Sovići and Doljani, that is, the destruction of buildings, including mosques, and the arrests of people who did not belong to any armed force. Stojić's argument is dismissed.

1594. In relation to Primorac's Report of 23 April 1993, the Trial Chamber noted that the report referred to the "cleansing" of Doljani on 19 April 1993.[5164] The Appeals Chamber is not convinced by Stojić's argument that, since the term "cleansing" is ambiguous, it was unreasonable for the Trial Chamber to rely on this term to find that he must have been aware of the crimes.[5165] Stojić refers to **[page 656]** evidence that the term meant the "taking of an area" during military actions[5166] in arguing that the term referred to lawful clean-up operations,[5167] but fails to show that the Trial Chamber did not take this evidence into account. Notably, in addition to the reference to "cleansing" in Primorac's Report of 23 April 1993, the Trial Chamber considered several pieces of evidence that the women, children, and the elderly residing in Doljani after the attack were arrested.[5168] Thus, the Appeals Chamber finds that Stojić fails to show an error in the Trial Chamber's approach of considering, *inter alia,* Primorac's Report of 23 April 1993 as evidence that Stojić must have been aware of the crimes. His argument is thus dismissed.

1595. With regard to Stojić's argument that the Trial Chamber erred by linking the 23 April 1993 Order to the operations in Sovići and Doljani,[5169] the Appeals Chamber notes that the Trial Chamber found that "Stojić must have been aware of the crimes committed by the HVO troops in Sovići and Doljani especially as he then ordered the commanders of all the OZs to respect international law".[5170] In the Appeals Chamber's view, such an order, especially since the HVO operations were regularly conducted in a similar way,[5171] was relevant to all military staff involved in military operations. Notably, the Trial Chamber also considered this issue by taking account of the fact that the 23 April 1993 Order was sent "to the commanders of all OZs".[5172] Stojić therefore fails to demonstrate how the fact that the order was not addressed only to the HVO in Sovići and Doljani calls into question the Trial Chamber's finding that he must have been aware of the crimes committed in Sovići and Doljani especially as he then issued the 23 April 1993 Order.[5173] Further, as the 23 April 1993 Order addressed what was requested in the ICRC Report of 20 April 1993 – the medical assistance and behaviour in accordance with international law[5174] – a reasonable trier of fact could have

---

[5159] See *supra*, para. 1591.
[5160] Trial Judgement, Vol. 4, para. 341.
[5161] Trial Judgement, Vol. 4, paras 338, 341, referring to, *inter alia,* Ex. P02063.
[5162] Trial Judgement, Vol. 4, paras 339, 341. See *infra*, para. 1594.
[5163] Trial Judgement, Vol. 4, para. 340, referring to Ex. P02050. See Trial Judgement, Vol. 4, para. 341.
[5164] Trial Judgement, Vol. 2, para. 563, Vol. 4, para. 339, referring to Ex. 4D01034.
[5165] Stojić's Appeal Brief, para. 268. See *supra*, para. 1589. The Appeals Chamber dismisses Stojić's argument that there is no evidence establishing that he received this report, as the report is addressed to him and he does not submit any further arguments on why he would not have received it. See Stojić's Appeal Brief, fn. 679.
[5166] Witness 4D-AA, T. 49217 (closed session) (9 Feb 2010).
[5167] Stojić's Appeal Brief, para. 268, referring to Witness 4D-AA, T. 49217 (closed session) (9 Feb 2010).
[5168] Trial Judgement, Vol. 2, paras 562-563.
[5169] Stojić's Appeal Brief, para. 267. See *supra*, para. 1589.
[5170] Trial Judgement, Vol. 4, para. 341.
[5171] Trial Judgement, Vol. 4, paras 142-144, 146. See *supra*, para. 1586.
[5172] Trial Judgement, Vol. 4, para. 340.
[5173] Trial Judgement, Vol. 4, para. 341.
[5174] Ex. P02050; Ex. P01989, p. 3.

concluded, as the only reasonable inference, that this order had been triggered by the ICRC Report of 20 April 1993. Thus, Stojić's arguments are dismissed.

1596. The Appeals Chamber finds that Stojić has failed to demonstrate that the Trial Chamber erroneously inferred that he knew about the crimes committed in Sovići and Doljani and his sub-ground of appeal 30.1 is dismissed. In light of the above,[5175] Stojić's general argument that no **[page 657]** reasonable trier of fact "could have constructed the further inference that he accepted" the crimes committed in Sovići and Doljani[5176] is also dismissed,

(iii) Conclusion

1597. Based on the foregoing, Stojić's ground of appeal 30 is dismissed.

(d) The May 1993 operations in Mostar town (Stojić's Ground 31)

1598. The Trial Chamber found that the HVO attacked Mostar town on 9 May 1993,[5177] resulting in crimes against its Muslim inhabitants.[5178] The Trial Chamber found that the only inference it could draw was that Stojić participated in planning these Mostar military operations,[5179] and that "he also participated in planning the acts of violence which accompanied the operations".[5180] The Trial Chamber considered as evidence a British Broadcasting Corporation interview with Stojić after 9 May 1993 ("BBC Video"), in which he explained that "the HVO could clear its part of the town in several hours".[5181] The Trial Chamber concluded that, in the BBC Video, Stojić presented himself as an HVO military chief who had control over West Mostar in May 1993.[5182] In arriving at this conclusion, the Trial Chamber rejected the evidence of Defence expert Witness Davor Marijan, that the BBC Video did not prove that Stojić was in charge of the May 1993 operations in Mostar, on the basis that he, *inter alia,* was biased in favour of Stojić and the HVO.[5183] The Trial Chamber also found that Stojić "participated in the preparation of the HVO troops in Mostar in the days preceding the attack of 9 May 1993" and "knew of the troops' plans, of their ability and of their plan of action".[5184]

(i) Stojić's participation in preparing the troops and planning the HVO operations in Mostar (Stojić's Sub-ground 31.1)

1599. Stojić submits that no reasonable trial chamber could have inferred that he participated in preparing the troops and planning the HVO military operations on the basis of the BBC Video.[5185] In particular, he argues that the inference is not supported as: (1) the interview occurred after **[page 658]** 9 May 1993;[5186] (2) the only words directly attributed to him were not clear enough as they were voiced over by the journalist, no plan was mentioned,[5187] and the Trial Chamber failed to consider whether the statement that the troops could clear their part of the city in five hours was realistic given that the conflict continued for months;[5188]

[5175]   See *supra,* paras 1584-1588, 1591-1595.
[5176]   Stojić's Appeal Brief, para. 272.
[5177]   Trial Judgement, Vol. 2, para. 775.
[5178]   Trial Judgement, Vol. 2, paras 822-824, 826-827, 1494-1498, Vol. 4, para. 347. See also Trial Judgement, Vol. 2, paras 797-806, 812-818.
[5179]   Trial Judgement, Vol. 4, para. 348.
[5180]   Trial Judgement, Vol. 4, para. 349.
[5181]   Trial Judgement, Vol. 4, para. 344, referring to Ex. P04238, 44:22-44:52. The Appeals Chamber refers to the video clip corresponding to Exhibit P04238, 43:22-44:33 as the BBC Video. Notably, the partial transcript of this video clip is provided under the same exhibit number, Exhibit P04238. See Ex. P04238, p. 3.
[5182]   Trial Judgement, Vol. 4, para. 346.
[5183]   Trial Judgement, Vol. 4, paras 345-346.
[5184]   Trial Judgement, Vol. 4, para. 348.
[5185]   Stojić's Appeal Brief, paras 276, 279. See also Stojić's Appeal Brief, para. 274.
[5186]   Stojić's Appeal Brief, para. 276.
[5187]   Stojić's Appeal Brief, para. 277. See Stojić's Appeal Brief, para. 275. Stojić argues that these words could not support the finding that he knew of the troops' plan. Stojić's Appeal Brief, para. 277.
[5188]   Stojić's Appeal Brief, para. 277, referring to Trial Judgement, Vol. 2, paras 1184, 1196. Stojić argues that these words did not support the finding that he knew of the troops' ability. Stojić's Appeal Brief, para. 277.

and (3) the Trial Chamber failed to consider the context surrounding the relevant statement, which was only a snippet of an interview and did not address the 9 May 1993 attack or the eviction operations.[5189] Stojić contends that the Trial Chamber failed to consider other inferences, such as whether "an individual might want to present an image of strength or control which was not the situation on the ground."[5190]

1600. The Prosecution responds that the Trial Chamber reasonably relied on Stojić's comment in the BBC Video,[5191] and that it is immaterial that the interview was recorded after 9 May 1993.[5192] It also argues that Stojić presents no basis to question the accuracy of the words attributed to him.[5193] The Prosecution argues that Stojić's comment on clearing Mostar in five hours showed that he knew of his troops' plans and ability to execute them, and was consistent with the conduct of HVO operations.[5194] It further submits that it is irrelevant that Stojić did not specifically refer to the 9 May 1993 attack or the evictions as his comments came in the midst of the HVO operations in May 1993.[5195]

1601. Regarding Stojić's first argument, the Appeals Chamber considers that he fails to explain why the Trial Chamber could not rely on the BBC Video to infer his participation in the operations merely because the interview was recorded after the 9 May 1993 attack began.[5196] The Appeals Chamber notes that there is no requirement that such evidence must refer to conduct that occurred at the same time as, or before, the military operations. In any event, it is clear from the context that this interview was recorded contemporaneously with the events in Mostar town in May 1993.[5197] With regard to Stojić's contention that the relevant statement in the BBC Video was voiced over by a journalist, the Appeals Chamber notes that he merely repeats his argument at trial without **[page 659]** demonstrating how its rejection by the Trial Chamber constituted an error.[5198] Nonetheless, Stojić fails to show how the Trial Chamber erred in relying on the journalist's account of Stojić's words, given that it had the discretion to rely on hearsay evidence.[5199] Stojić's arguments are thus dismissed.

1602. As for Stojić's argument that no plan was mentioned in the BBC Video, the Appeals Chamber considers that the statement attributed to Stojić – that the HVO troops could clear its part of Mostar – plainly indicates his awareness of the events on the ground and thus any plan being executed.[5200] Moreover, this statement is consistent with the actions of the troops that took place, which was to engage "in a campaign aimed at evicting the Muslims of West Mostar from their flats" shortly following the 9 May 1993 attack.[5201] The Trial Chamber considered that these operations were conducted in "waves and in an orchestrated manner" involving recurring acts of violence that indicated that they were part of a "preconceived plan".[5202] Additionally, the Trial Chamber also considered that Stojić knew that the HVO implemented a plan aimed at intensifying control over the town of Mostar by placing HVO forces, including the Military Police, on alert since 14 April 1993, which further supports the conclusion that he knew of a plan regarding Mostar.[5203] Stojić

[5189]   Stojić's Appeal Brief, para. 278.

[5190]   Stojić's Appeal Brief, para. 278.

[5191]   Prosecution's Response Brief (Stojić), para. 238. See Prosecution's Response Brief (Stojić), para. 237. The Prosecution argues that the Trial Chamber reasonably found that how Stojić presented himself in the BBC Video was consistent with his actual role. Prosecution's Response Brief (Stojić), para. 242, referring to Trial Judgement, Vol. 4, para. 346. See also Appeal Hearing, AT. 330-331 (21 Mar 2017).

[5192]   Prosecution's Response Brief (Stojić), para. 239.

[5193]   Prosecution's Response Brief (Stojić), para. 240.

[5194]   Prosecution's Response Brief (Stojić), para. 240, referring to Trial Judgement, Vol. 2, paras 805, 812-815, 826-828, Vol. 4, paras 347-348.

[5195]   Prosecution's Response Brief (Stojić), para. 241.

[5196]   See Trial Judgement, Vol. 4, para. 344.

[5197]   See Trial Judgement, Vol. 4, paras 344-347.

[5198]   Compare Stojić's Appeal Brief, para. 277 with Stojić Closing Arguments, T. 52380 (16 Feb 2011). See Trial Judgement, Vol. 4, paras 344-346.

[5199]   *Stanišić and Župljanin* Appeal Judgement, para. 510; *Popović et al.* Appeal Judgement, paras 1276, 1307; *Šainović et al.* Appeal Judgement, para. 846.

[5200]   The Appeals Chamber notes that the transcript of the BBC Video states the following: "the Minister says his forces could clear their part of the city in five hours". Ex. P04238, p. 3. In the BBC Video, however, the words actually used were: "the Minister says his forces could clear their *half* of the city in five hours" (emphasis added). Ex. P04238, 43:58-44:03.

[5201]   Trial Judgement, Vol. 4, para. 347. See also Trial Judgement, Vol. 2, paras 797-806, 812-818, 822-824, 826-827, 1494-1498.

[5202]   Trial Judgement, Vol. 4, para. 347.

[5203]   Trial Judgement, Vol. 4, para. 344, referring to, *inter alia*, Ex. P01868.

thus fails to show that no reasonable trier of fact could have found that he "knew of the troops' plans" simply on the basis that no plan was mentioned in the BBC Video.[5204]

1603. Further, Stojić fails to show how the estimate given in the BBC Video that this "clearing" could be done in five hours is inconsistent with the finding that he knew of the troops' ability.[5205] Stojić argues that this estimate "bore no resemblance to reality", asserting that "the conflict in Mostar continued for months rather than hours".[5206] In supporting the assertion that the conflict continued for months, Stojić refers to findings relating to the campaign of sniping and the siege of East Mostar beginning in June 1993, and not findings on the May 1993 operations in West Mostar discussed in the BBC Video.[5207] The Appeals Chamber notes the Trial Chamber's finding that the **[page 660]** initial eviction operations in West Mostar, in fact, took place between 9 and 11 May 1993,[5208] which is relatively consistent with the estimate provided in the BBC Video. Stojić's arguments that the statement attributed to him was not clear enough to support the finding that he participated in planning the Mostar operations[5209] are therefore dismissed.

1604. The Appeals Chamber further considers that the Trial Chamber's findings are not undermined by the absence of express references to the 9 May 1993 attack or eviction operations in the BBC Video, particularly considering the above analysis.[5210] Stojić fails to show that no reasonable trier of fact could have reached its findings in light of the evidence it considered.[5211] With regard to Stojić's argument that the Trial Chamber failed to consider other inferences that could be drawn from the BBC Video, the Appeals Chamber notes that the Trial Chamber considered that the BBC Video "speaks for itself";[5212] namely, that "Stojić presented] himself as an HVO military chief who had control over West Mostar in May 1993."[5213] Stojić provides no evidentiary support for his alternative inference that he "may" have been trying to "present an image of strength or control which was not the situation on the ground",[5214] and does not show how this inference would impact the impugned finding, which was based on various other factors.[5215] His arguments are thus dismissed.

1605. In light of the above, the Appeals Chamber finds that Stojić has failed to demonstrate, in his sub-ground of appeal 31.1, that the Trial Chamber erred in relying on the BBC Video to conclude that he participated in preparing the troops and planning the Mostar military operations. His sub-ground of appeal 31.1 is dismissed.

(ii) Alleged errors in the assessment of and reliance on Expert Witness Davor Marijan's evidence (Stojić's Sub-ground 31.2)

1606. Stojić submits that the Trial Chamber erred in rejecting certain aspects of Witness Marijan's evidence while relying on other parts.[5216] Stojić argues that the Trial Chamber's finding that Marijan was biased in favour of him and the HVO was inconsistent with its reliance on Marijan's evidence, which it "routinely accepted" throughout the Trial Judgement, including that Stojić did **[page 661]** not issue any "combat orders".[5217] He further argues that the Trial Chamber erred in rejecting Marijan's evidence on the basis that he "merely offered hypotheses"[5218] since, as an expert witness, Marijan was entitled to offer opinions within

---

[5204]   Trial Judgement, Vol. 4, para. 348.
[5205]   Trial Judgement, Vol. 4, para. 348.
[5206]   Stojić's Appeal Brief, para. 277.
[5207]   See Stojić's Appeal Brief, para. 277, referring to Trial Judgement, Vol. 2, paras 1184, 1196.
[5208]   Trial Judgement, Vol. 2, paras 805 (the round-up and detention of Muslim inhabitants of West Mostar between 9 and 11 May 1993), 812-815 (Muslims were expelled from their homes and made to cross the front line towards East Mostar or placed in the Heliodrom in the second half of May 1993), 816-818 (at least 300 Muslims were moved from West Mostar to East Mostar on 26 May 1993).
[5209]   See *supra*, para. 1599.
[5210]   See *supra*, paras 657, 1601-1602, fn. 5197.
[5211]   Trial Judgement, Vol. 4, paras 344, 346-349, and evidence cited therein.
[5212]   Trial Judgement, Vol. 4, para. 346.
[5213]   Trial Judgement, Vol. 4, para. 346.
[5214]   See *supra*, para. 1599.
[5215]   See *supra*, para. 1598.
[5216]   Stojić's Appeal Brief, para. 281.
[5217]   Stojić's Appeal Brief, para. 281, referring to, *inter alia*, Trial Judgement, Vol. 1, paras 559, 565.
[5218]   Stojić's Appeal Brief, para. 282, referring to Trial Judgement, Vol. 4, para. 346.

his expertise which do not have to be based on firsthand knowledge.[5219] Stojić also contends that the Trial Chamber failed to give sufficient reasons for rejecting Marijan's conclusions, arguing that it did not consider: (1) whether the maps and the office shown in the BBC Video were of a military nature; (2) the absence of documentary evidence that he directed military operations in Mostar; and (3) Witness Slobodan Božić's corroborative testimony that everyone wore uniforms at that time.[5220] Stojić submits that had Marijan's evidence been taken into account, the Trial Chamber could not have inferred from the BBC Video that he participated in planning the military operations in Mostar.[5221]

1607. The Prosecution responds that the Trial Chamber reasonably rejected Marijan's evidence concerning the BBC Video, and that its decision was reasoned.[5222] It submits that the Trial Chamber was not inconsistent in its approach regarding Marijan's evidence, relying on it only when uncontroversial and corroborated.[5223] The Prosecution argues that Stojić mischaracterises or misconceives the Trial Chamber's approach to Marijan's entire testimony.[5224] It contends that the Trial Chamber rejected Marijan's evidence on the BBC Video because it was found to be unconvincing.[5225] The Prosecution further contends that Stojić fails to show how Božić's testimony – whose credibility was "extremely weak"[5226] – undermines the Trial Chamber's finding.[5227]

1608. The Appeals Chamber notes that the Trial Chamber held that, after having heard his entire testimony, Marijan "had a bias in favour of Bruno Stojić and the HVO".[5228] It considered that Marijan was a former HVO soldier and that, throughout his testimony and expert report, he sought to exonerate Stojić instead of providing objective answers as an expert.[5229] Regarding Stojić's argument that the Trial Chamber treated Marijan's evidence inconsistently, the Appeals Chamber **[page 662]** first recalls that "it is for the Trial Chamber to accept or reject, in whole or in part, the contribution of an expert witness".[5230] The Appeals Chamber further observes that, with regard to the BBC Video, the Trial Chamber provided specific reasons for rejecting Marijan's conclusion, namely that it found his answers unconvincing, that he was not in the office at the time of the interview, and that his hypotheses were "uncorroborated by the evidence."[5231] In the other parts of the Trial Judgement where Marijan's evidence was accepted, the Appeals Chamber observes that it was generally corroborated by other evidence.[5232] Further, the Trial Chamber did not "routinely" accept Marijan's evidence, and notably, it found that Stojić issued operational orders directly to the HVO[5233] contrary to the evidence Marijan gave that the Head of the Department of Defence did not issue orders related to combat activities.[5234] Therefore, the Appeals Chamber finds that Stojić has failed to show that the Trial Chamber's reliance on Marijan's evidence was inconsistent throughout the Trial Judgement or demonstrated a discernible error.[5235] His arguments are dismissed.

[5219] Stojić's Appeal Brief, para. 282, referring to *Prosecutor v. Vujadin Popović et al.*, Case No. IT-05-88-AR73.2, Decision on Joint Defence Interlocutory Appeal Concerning the Status of Richard Butler as an Expert Witness, 30 January 2008, para. 27 *("Popović et al.* Decision of 30 January 2008"), *Semanza* Appeal Judgement, para. 303.
[5220] Stojić's Appeal Brief, para. 283, referring to Slobodan Božić, T. 36315 (private session) (3 Feb 2009).
[5221] Stojić"s Appeal Brief, para. 284.
[5222] Prosecution's Response Brief (Stojić), para. 243.
[5223] Prosecution's Response Brief (Stojić), para. 244. The Prosecution argues that Stojić ignores instances where the Trial Chamber noted inconsistencies within Marijan's evidence or with other evidence. Prosecution's Response Brief (Stojić), para. 244, referring to Trial Judgement, Vol. 1, paras 561, 867.
[5224] Prosecution's Response Brief (Stojić), paras 244-245, referring to Trial Judgement, Vol. 1, paras 559, 565, Vol. 4, para. 312.
[5225] Prosecution's Response Brief (Stojić), para. 246.
[5226] Prosecution's Response Brief (Stojić), para. 247, referring to Trial Judgement, Vol. 1, para. 551.
[5227] Prosecution's Response Brief (Stojić), para. 247.
[5228] Trial Judgement, Vol. 4, para. 346.
[5229] Trial Judgement, Vol. 4, para. 346.
[5230] *Strugar* Appeal Judgement, para. 58. See *Popović et al.* Appeal Judgement, para. 132 ("a trial chamber can reasonably accept certain parts of a witness's testimony and reject others.").
[5231] Trial Judgement, Vol. 4, para. 346.
[5232] See, *e.g.,* Trial Judgement, Vol. 1, paras 495, 505, 544, 600, 640, 676, 679, 694, 702, 767, 772, 855, 924, 946. The Appeals Chamber notes that on one occasion, the Trial Chamber rejected Marijan's evidence for being contradictory. Trial Judgement, Vol. 1, para. 561.
[5233] Trial Judgement, Vol. 1, para. 565. See *supra,* paras 1427-1435.
[5234] See Trial Judgement, Vol. 1, para. 559, referring to, *inter alia,* Davor Marijan, T(F). 35693 (20 Jan 2009), 36073-36074 (27 Jan 2009), Ex. 2D02000, para. 86.
[5235] See *Popović et al.* Appeal Judgement, para. 131.

1609. With regard to Stojić's argument that the Trial Chamber erroneously rejected Marijan's evidence because he offered hypotheses, the Appeals Chamber notes that the views of expert witnesses need not be based upon firsthand knowledge or experience.[5236] However, the Appeals Chamber recalls that, just as for any other evidence presented, trial chambers have the discretion to assess the reliability and probative value of expert reports and testimony.[5237] Bearing in mind the reasons given by the Trial Chamber for rejecting Marijan's evidence,[5238] and as Stojić has failed to show that the Trial Chamber rejected Marijan's evidence solely on the basis that he offered hypotheses or provided evidence that was not firsthand, the Appeals Chamber dismisses Stojić's argument.

1610. As for Stojić's argument that the Trial Chamber failed to provide sufficient reasons for rejecting Marijan's conclusion, the Appeals Chamber recalls that a trial chamber is not "required to set out in detail why it accepted or rejected a particular testimony".[5239] In this regard, the Appeals Chamber is not persuaded that the deficiencies Stojić alleges concerning the maps, the office, or the **[page 663]** lack of documentary evidence undermine the Trial Chamber's reasoning, especially as the Trial Chamber expressly noted these issues.[5240] In relation to Witness Božić's evidence, the Appeals Chamber considers that there is no indication that the Trial Chamber relied only on the fact that Stojić was wearing a uniform in the BBC Video to arrive at its findings, having also taken into account his conduct and words in concluding that he presented himself as an HVO military chief who had control over West Mostar in May 1993.[5241] Thus, Stojić has failed to show that any disregard of this evidence would impact on the Trial Chamber's findings. Stojić's arguments are dismissed.

1611. Based on the foregoing, the Appeals Chamber finds that Stojić has failed to demonstrate that the Trial Chamber erred in rejecting Marijan's evidence concerning the BBC Video and thus inferring from this video that he participated in planning the Mostar operations. Stojić's sub-ground of appeal 31.2 is dismissed.

(iii) <u>Stojić's participation in planning the acts of violence which accompanied the HVO operations in Mostar (Stojić's Sub-ground 31.3)</u>

1612. Stojić submits that the Trial Chamber erroneously inferred, from his participation in planning the military operations in Mostar, that he participated in planning the acts of violence, and that it gave no explanation for this inference.[5242] Specifically, he argues that he did not participate in planning the military operations and that, even if he did, it does not follow that he participated in planning the acts of violence, given that there are other reasonable inferences available from the evidence. Stojić also contends that there was no evidence that he was involved in planning the details of how the operations were to be carried out.[5243]

1613. The Prosecution responds that the Trial Chamber's conclusion was reasonable.[5244] It argues that the Trial Chamber did not merely rely on its conclusion that Stojić planned the operations, but found that acts of violence were an intrinsic part of those operations.[5245]

1614. The Appeals Chamber notes that it has dismissed Stojić's arguments challenging his participation in planning the Mostar military operations above.[5246] Regarding Stojić's argument that **[page 664]** the Trial Chamber gave no explanation for inferring that he participated in planning the acts of violence, the Appeals Chamber notes that the Trial Chamber found that as Stojić participated in, among other things, planning the

---

[5236] *Popović et al.* Decision of 30 January 2008, para. 27, citing *Nahimana et al.* Appeal Judgement, para. 198, *Semanza* Appeal Judgement, para. 303.
[5237] *Tolimir* Appeal Judgement, para. 69. See *Popović et al.* Appeal Judgement, paras 131-132.
[5238] See *supra*, para. 1608.
[5239] *Popović et al.* Appeal Judgement, para. 133; *Krajišnik* Appeal Judgement, para. 139.
[5240] Trial Judgement, Vol. 4, para. 345.
[5241] Trial Judgement, Vol. 4, paras 344, 346. See *infra*, para. 1621.
[5242] Stojić's Appeal Brief, para. 285. See also Stojić's Appeal Brief, para. 286; Stojić's Reply Brief, paras 70-71.
[5243] Stojić's Appeal Brief, para. 285.
[5244] Prosecution's Response Brief (Stojić), para. 248.
[5245] Prosecution's Response Brief (Stojić), para. 249, referring to Trial Judgement, Vol. 4, para. 349. See Prosecution's Response Brief (Stojić), para. 250. The Prosecution also argues that the Trial Chamber's findings show that the HVO "systematically and violently evicted Muslims." Prosecution's Response Brief (Stojić), para. 249, referring to Trial Judgement, Vol. 4, para. 356.
[5246] See *supra*, paras 1601-1605, 1611.

HVO operations in Mostar on 9 May 1993 and continued to exercise control over the HVO and Military Police knowing that they were committing crimes in other municipalities, he intended them.[5247] It also found that, during the days that followed the attack of 9 May 1993, the HVO engaged in a campaign aimed at evicting Muslims of West Mostar from their flats and detaining between 1,500 and 2,500 Muslims in an orchestrated manner.[5248] This orchestrated campaign was accompanied by acts of violence on a scale that indicated that these crimes "were part of a preconceived plan and were in no way the acts of a few undisciplined individuals."[5249] Thus, the Appeals Chamber considers that it was unnecessary for the Trial Chamber to give further reasons having already found that: (1) the crimes and violent acts committed during the operations were done in pursuance of "an orchestrated and organised plan";[5250] and (2) Stojić participated in planning those operations.[5251] Stojić fails to support his contention that an inference that he participated in planning the violent acts does not follow from these previous findings. Similarly, the Appeals Chamber finds that Stojić fails to show that this inference was one that no reasonable trier of fact could have drawn, particularly as he offers no other reasonable inference. His arguments are dismissed.

1615. In light of the above, the Appeals Chamber finds that Stojić has failed to demonstrate that the Trial Chamber erred in concluding that he participated in planning the acts of violence accompanying the Mostar military operations. His sub-ground of appeal 31.3 is dismissed.

(iv) Conclusion

1616. In sum, Stojić's ground of appeal 31 is dismissed.

(e) The eviction of the Muslim population from West Mostar (Stojić's Grounds 32 and 33)

1617. The Trial Chamber found that, beginning in June 1993, the HVO expelled many Muslims from West Mostar, evicting them from their homes and committing crimes against them.[5252] It **[page 665]** concluded that Stojić was not only informed of the evictions but was also "actively involved in organising and conducting the eviction campaigns",[5253] and intended to have the acts of violence linked to the eviction campaigns committed.[5254] In this respect, the Trial Chamber considered that: (1) Stojić received a report from Dragan Ćurčić dated 2 June 1993 ("Ćurčić's Report of 2 June 1993")[5255] informing him of the occupancy of vacant flats in Čapljina and Mostar assigned to members of the HVO; (2) a Main Staff report dated 14 June 1993 ("CED Report"), informing him of the evictions of Muslims from West Mostar;[5256] and (3) Stojan Vrlić's report dated 5 July 1993 ("Vrlić's Report of 5 July 1993"), containing a list of Muslim homes to be raided that evening.[5257] The Trial Chamber also considered that: (1) as of 16 June 1993, international representatives alerted, *inter alios,* Stojić to the evictions of Muslims from West Mostar to East Mostar based on, *inter alia,* Exhibits P03804 and P09712;[5258] (2) Stojić told international representatives at a dinner on 17 July 1993 that "the loss of territory in some areas was part of a preconceived strategy Of the HVO whose objective was to exert maximum pressure on the southern part of the town of Mostar", expressed his "concern" for the

---

[5247] Trial Judgement, Vol. 4, para. 426.

[5248] Trial Judgement, Vol. 4, para. 347. See also Trial Judgement, Vol. 2, paras 823, 827, 866, 868, 872, 876, 924, 928, 930-931, 934, 937, 980-987, Vol. 4, para. 356.

[5249] Trial Judgement, Vol. 4, para. 347. See also Trial Judgement, Vol. 2, paras 823, 827, 866, 868, 872, 876, 924, 928, 930-931, 934, 937, 980-987, Vol. 4, para. 356. To the extent that the "preconceived" plan included a pattern of conduct regarding murder and wilful killing, the Appeals Chamber recalls that no reasonable trier of fact could conclude that murder and wilful killing were part of the CCP from January 1993 until June 1993 due to the Duša reversal and the lack of any pattern of CCP murders. See *supra,* para. 882.

[5250] Trial Judgement, Vol. 4, para. 349. See Trial Judgement, Vol. 2, paras 797-806, 812-818, 822-824, 826-827, 1494-1498, Vol. 4, para. 347.

[5251] Trial Judgement, Vol. 4, paras 344, 346, 348-349, 426.

[5252] Trial Judgement, Vol. 2, paras 876, 900, 914, 920, 934-935, Vol. 4, paras 57, 356.

[5253] Trial Judgement, Vol. 4, para. 355.

[5254] Trial Judgement, Vol. 4, para. 357.

[5255] Ex. P02608. See Trial Judgement, Vol. 4, para. 351, referring to, *inter alia,* Ex. P02608.

[5256] Trial Judgement, Vol. 4, para. 351, referring to, *inter alia,* Ex. P02770.

[5257] Ex. P03181. See Trial Judgement, Vol. 4, para. 352, referring to, *inter alia,* Ex. P03181.

[5258] Trial Judgement, Vol. 4, para. 350, referring to, *inter alia,* Exs. P02806 (confidential), P03804 (confidential), P09712 (confidential).

Muslim civilians living in the ABiH-controlled areas in East Mostar, suggested that the largest possible number of these civilians should be evacuated and offered his assistance, and estimated that the conflict between the Muslims and Croats in Mostar would be resolved in 20 days;[5259] and (3) Witness DZ was told that Stojić was in charge of implementing the plan to cleanse Mostar town, and heard HVO members say that Stojić ordered evictions and destruction of homes.[5260]

(i) Whether Stojić received reports concerning the evictions of Muslims and crimes against them, and was involved in organising and conducting the eviction campaigns (Stojić's Sub-ground 33.1)

1618. Stojić submits that the Trial Chamber erroneously disregarded clearly relevant evidence in reaching its conclusions.[5261] Referring to his trial arguments, Stojić contends that the Trial Chamber disregarded the evidence of Witness Slobodan Božić,[5262] who testified that any documents received by the Department of Defence were stamped, registered, and signed by Stojić.[5263] As the CED **[page 666]** Report and Vrlić's Report of 5 July 1993 were neither stamped nor signed by him, Stojić submits that the Trial Chamber erred in concluding that they were received.[5264] He argues that elsewhere the Trial Chamber disregarded another document because it lacked a signature, stamp, and seal.[5265] Stojić avers that the intake register indicating whether the documents were received was not entered into evidence.[5266] He also argues that Ćurčić's Report of 2 June 1993 is irrelevant because he had no role in the distribution of flats,[5267] and that Exhibits P03804 and P09712 do not relate to him.[5268] Stojić contends that no reasonable trier of fact could have found, based on the single report that international representatives alerted him to evictions on 16 June 1993, that the only reasonable inference was his active involvement in organising and conducting the evictions.[5269]

1619. The Prosecution responds that the Trial Chamber reasonably concluded that Stojić knew of evictions of Muslims in West Mostar, having received the relevant reports.[5270] It submits that the Trial Chamber considered Slobodan Božić's credibility to be "extremely weak",[5271] and that Stojić's lack of involvement in the distribution of flats is irrelevant to his knowledge of the contents of Ćurčić's Report of 2 June 1993.[5272] It also argues that Exhibits P03804 and P09712 show that Stojić and other JCE members acted together to further the expulsion campaign, and that the Trial Chamber reasonably relied on them.[5273] The Prosecution further asserts that it was "impossible" for Stojić, who was based in West Mostar at the time of the crimes, to be unaware of their occurrence.[5274]

1620. Stojić replies that demonstrating that a document was sent to the Department of Defence in general does not establish beyond reasonable doubt that he saw it.[5275] **[page 667]**

[5259] Trial Judgement, Vol. 4, para. 353.
[5260] Trial Judgement, Vol. 4, para. 354.
[5261] Stojić's Appeal Brief, para. 295.
[5262] Stojić's Appeal Brief, para. 295, referring to Stojić's Final Brief, para. 482, Stojić Closing Arguments, T. 52399 (16 Feb 2011).
[5263] Stojić's Appeal Brief, para. 295, referring to Slobodan Božić, T. 36246-36247 (3 Feb 2009).
[5264] Stojić's Appeal Brief, para. 295. Stojić asserts that the name "Bruno" handwritten on the CED Report (Exhibit P02770) casts further doubt that it was seen by him, and that Vrlić's Report of 5 July 1993 (Exhibit P03181) bears the stamp of the Military Police, showing that the latter received it. Stojić's Appeal Brief, para. 295.
[5265] Stojić's Appeal Brief, para. 295, referring to Trial Judgement, Vol. 3, para. 117.
[5266] Stojić's Appeal Brief, para. 295, referring to Ex. 2D01399.
[5267] Stojić's Appeal Brief, para. 295, referring to Trial Judgement, Vol. 2, paras 730-733.
[5268] Stojić's Appeal Brief, para. 295.
[5269] Stojić's Appeal Brief, para. 296.
[5270] Prosecution's Response Brief (Stojić), para. 257, referring to, *inter alia*, Trial Judgement, Vol. 4, paras 351-352, 355. The Prosecution specifies that Stojić: (1) ignores that Vrlić's Report of 5 July 1993 (Exhibit P03181) was personally addressed to him and has Department of Defence stamps on it; (2) incorrectly refers to the stamp as one from the Military Police as it is a Department of Defence stamp with the Military Police abbreviation, "MP", written on it; and (3) acknowledges that his first name "Bruno" is written on the CED Report (Exhibit P02770) but his argument is illogical. Prosecution's Response Brief (Stojić), para. 258. See also Appeal Hearing, AT. 330-332, 336-337 (21 Mar 2017). Moreover, regarding the CED Report, the Prosecution argues that witnesses "confirmed that Stojić received reports generated by the HVO Main Staff's electronic operations centre, the CED". Appeal Hearing, AT. 336 (21 Mar 2017), referring to Trial Judgement, Vol. 1, para. 736, Vol. 2, para. 870.
[5271] Prosecution's Response Brief (Stojić), para. 258, referring to Trial Judgement, Vol. 1, para. 551.
[5272] Prosecution's Response Brief (Stojić), para. 259.
[5273] Prosecution's Response Brief (Stojić), para. 260.
[5274] Prosecution's Response Brief (Stojić), para. 261.
[5275] Stojić's Reply Brief, para. 70.

1621. The Appeals Chamber recalls that it is to be presumed that the Trial Chamber evaluated all the evidence presented to it as long as there is no indication that the Trial Chamber completely disregarded any evidence which is clearly relevant.[5276] Concerning Slobodan Božić's testimony, the Appeals Chamber notes that this witness testified as to "how documents were received and processed" by the Department of Defence, namely that they would receive a reception stamp, and Stojić would sign them and indicate where they were to be forwarded for processing.[5277] The Trial Chamber did not expressly take account of this witness's evidence when reaching its conclusions about the reports received by Stojić in relation to West Mostar.[5278] However, the Appeals Chamber also notes that, earlier in the Trial Judgement, the Trial Chamber held that it had "heard and analysed [Slobodan Božić's] entire testimony", but found his credibility to be "extremely weak" on one issue,[5279] recalled that "it assigned very little credibility to [Slobodan Božić]",[5280] and concluded that, "[throughout his testimony, Slobodan Božić remained extremely vague in respect of any question regarding [the] possible responsibility of the Accused Stojić".[5281] The Appeals Chamber is therefore satisfied that the Trial Chamber did not disregard Slobodan Božić's evidence on the receipt of reports by the Department of Defence but rather considered his evidence with caution, generally relying on his testimony when it was corroborated by other evidence.[5282] Recalling that a trial chamber can reasonably accept certain parts of a witness's testimony and reject others,[5283] Stojić fails to demonstrate that the Trial Chamber erred in not expressly considering Slobodan Božić's evidence in its discussion of the reports concerning the evictions of the West Mostar Muslims. This argument is thus dismissed.

1622. Regarding the exhibits themselves, the Appeals Chamber notes that the CED Report has "Bruno" handwritten on it, while Ćurčić's Report of 2 June 1993 and Vrlić's Report of 5 July 1993 were both personally addressed to Stojić, which a reasonable trier of fact could have concluded meant that they were in fact brought to his attention.[5284] The Appeals Chamber also rejects the **[page 668]** assertion that the Trial Chamber disregarded another piece of evidence from a different department on the basis that it was not stamped or signed as the Trial Chamber doubted the authenticity of that document on other bases.[5285] With regard to the intake registry, as Stojić acknowledges,[5286] the document was not admitted into evidence.[5287] Thus, the Trial Chamber could not be expected to consider the intake registry in its determinations. As for Exhibits P03804 and P09712, the Appeals Chamber notes that the Trial Chamber did not rely on these documents on the basis that Stojić had received them and knew of their contents.[5288] In light of the above, the Appeals Chamber finds that Stojić fails to show that the Trial Chamber erroneously considered Ćurčić's Report of 2 June 1993, Vrlić's Report of 5 July 1993, and the CED Report on the basis that he did not receive them.[5289]

1623. In relation to Ćurčić's Report of 2 June 1993, the Appeals Chamber notes that the Trial Chamber relied on Stojić's knowledge of vacant flats, in addition to other evidence, to demonstrate that he was aware that

---

[5276] *Tolimir* Appeal Judgement, para. 53; *Popović et al.* Appeal Judgement, paras 925, 1017; *Kvočka et al.* Appeal Judgement, para. 23.

[5277] Slobodan Božić, T. 36246-36247 (3 Feb 2009).

[5278] Trial Judgement, Vol. 4, paras 351-352, 355.

[5279] Trial Judgement, Vol. 1, para. 551 (discussing the powers assigned to the Department of Defence Collegium).

[5280] Trial Judgement, Vol. 1, para. 573.

[5281] Trial Judgement, Vol. 1, para. 551.

[5282] See, *e.g.*, Trial Judgement, Vol. 1, paras 472, 495, 556, 573 (the Trial Chamber explained that, although it assigned very little credibility to Slobodan Božić, other evidence nevertheless supported his evidence concerning the appointment of power of the President of the HZ H-B and the Head of the Department of Defence), 583, 675, 834, Vol. 2, paras 765, 768, 784, 1231, 1455, 1496, Vol. 3, paras 16, 57, Vol. 4, paras 82, 293, 300, 325 (the Trial Chamber found that, as of 15 November 1993, Stojić no longer had any control over the armed forces and the Military Police in view of: (1) Slobodan Božić's testimony that after November 1993 Stojić never again came to the Department of Defence; and (2) the absence of other evidence).

[5283] *Popović et al.* Appeal Judgement, para. 132.

[5284] Ex. P02770, p. 1; Ex. P02608, p. 2; Ex. P03181, p. 2. The Appeals Chamber also considers that Stojić fails to explain why Exhibit P03181 should be disregarded as it features a stamp showing that it was received by the Department of Defence. See Ex. P03181, p. 2.

[5285] Trial Judgement, Vol. 3, paras 116-117.

[5286] Stojić's Appeal Brief, para. 295.

[5287] See Ex. 2D01399 (letter from the Croatian Ministry of Justice stating that it had no archive material from the Department of Defence).

[5288] See Trial Judgement, Vol. 4, para. 350. See also *supra*, para. 1617.

[5289] See Trial Judgement, Vol. 4, paras 351-352.

evictions were occurring, and not to find that he had a role in the distribution of such flats.[5290] Thus, Stojić's submission on this issue is rejected. Regarding Exhibits P03804 and P09712, although they do not specifically mention Stojić, the Appeals Chamber notes that the Trial Chamber relied on other evidence explicitly stating that he told international representatives on 16 June 1993 that the evictions were carried out by criminals not under HVO control.[5291] Thus, Stojić fails to demonstrate that the finding could not stand on the basis of the remaining evidence. In this respect, Stojić also fails to substantiate his argument that no reasonable trier of fact could have reached its conclusion on the basis of the report of 16 June 1993, particularly as he offers no other reasonable inference. Stojić's arguments are dismissed.

1624. For the above reasons, the Appeals Chamber finds that Stojić has failed to demonstrate that the Trial Chamber erred in finding that he received reports concerning the eviction of Muslims and crimes against them in Mostar beginning in June 1993 and was also actively involved in organising and conducting the eviction campaigns. His sub-ground of appeal 33.1 is dismissed. **[page 669]**

(ii) Whether Stojić and the HVO authorities genuinely intended to punish crimes against Muslims in Mostar (Stojić's Sub-ground 33.2)

1625. The Trial Chamber considered evidence that on 2 June 1993, Stojić informed the HVO of measures taken to prevent thefts in flats,[5292] along with further evidence that on 16 June 1993, when representatives of the international community informed Ćorić, Pušić, Stojić, and Prlić that evictions were occurring, they responded that the evictions were carried out by "criminals who were not under HVO control".[5293] The Trial Chamber thus concluded that the HVO authorities did not genuinely intend to prevent crimes against Muslims.[5294] The Trial Chamber also held that in light of the evidence, as well as the fact that the HVO continued to commit crimes throughout the Indictment period and that Stojić encouraged the commission of the crimes by Naletilić's troops, he did not intend to prevent or punish the crimes committed by the HVO, including the Military Police, despite having the *de facto* power to do so.[5295]

1626. Stojić submits that no reasonable trier of fact could have concluded that the only reasonable inference was that he did not intend to punish crimes against Muslims.[5296] He argues that the Trial Chamber: (1) disregarded evidence of the minutes of an HZ(R) H-B meeting on 31 May 1993 ("Minutes of 31 May 1993"),[5297] requiring that appropriate measures be taken for the prevention of crimes in Mostar;[5298] (2) failed to properly consider his order of the same day ("Stojić's Order of 31 May 1993"),[5299] ordering a curfew, vehicle checks, and arrests;[5300] and (3) ignored other evidence showing the steps taken to combat crime in Mostar.[5301] Stojić argues that his statement to the representatives of the international community that the evictions were carried out by "criminals who were not under HVO control" supports the conclusion that he took steps to prevent crimes.[5302]

1627. The Prosecution responds that the Trial Chamber's conclusion was reasonable and is not undermined by Stojić's order of 31 May 1993 and the other evidence he cites.[5303] **[page 670]**

[5290] Trial Judgement, Vol. 4, paras 351, 355.
[5291] Trial Judgement, Vol. 4, fn. 788, referring to Antoon van der Grinten, T(F). 21046, 21048 (10 July 2007), Ex. P02806 (confidential), p. 2. See Antoon van der Grinten, T. 21046-21050 (10 July 2007).
[5292] Trial Judgement, Vol. 4, para. 422.
[5293] Trial Judgement, Vol. 4, para. 422. See Trial Judgement, Vol. 4, para. 350.
[5294] Trial Judgement, Vol. 4, para. 422.
[5295] Trial Judgement, Vol. 4, para. 423. See Trial Judgement, Vol. 4, para. 320.
[5296] Stojić's Appeal Brief, paras 297-298, referring to Trial Judgement, Vol. 4, paras 422-423.
[5297] Ex. P02575. See Stojić's Appeal Brief, para. 298, referring to Ex. P02575.
[5298] Stojić''s Appeal Brief, para. 298, referring to Ex. P02575, pp. 1-2.
[5299] Ex. P02578. See Stojić's Appeal Brief, para. 298, referring to Ex. P02578.
[5300] Stojić''s Appeal Brief, para. 298, referring to Ex. P02578, p. 1.
[5301] Stojić's Appeal Brief, para. 298, referring to Exs. P04111, 2D00854, P06730, P07035.
[5302] Stojić's Appeal Brief, para. 298, referring to Ex. P02806 (confidential).
[5303] Prosecution's Response Brief (Stojić), para. 262. See also Prosecution's Response Brief (Stojić), para. 256. The Prosecution further points to the ongoing campaign of mass and systematic HVO crimes against Muslims and underscores the Trial Chamber's findings on Stojić's failure to prevent or punish such crimes. Prosecution's Response Brief (Stojić), para. 263, referring to Trial Judgement, Vol. 4, paras 415, 423, 427, Ex. P07035, pp. 4, 6, 11.

1628. In relation to crime-fighting measures taken on 31 May 1993, the Appeals Chamber notes that the Minutes of 31 May 1993 refer, *inter alia,* to the need to ensure that "all appropriate measures are taken for the prevention of crime, especially the looting of private property from apartments in the territory of the Mostar Municipality,"[5304] while Stojić's Order of 31 May 1993 instructs all Military Police and civilian police at checkpoints around Mostar to enforce a curfew and mandatory vehicle checks, as well as to arrest persons with goods of unidentified origin in Mostar.[5305] The Appeals Chamber notes that the Trial Chamber did not expressly consider the Minutes of 31 May 1993, but carefully assessed Stojić's Order of 31 May 1993, and in particular took account of the fact that Stojić and Branko Kvesić, Head of the Department of the Interior, had issued that order so as to combat thefts.[5306]

1629. Moreover, the Appeals Chamber recalls that the conclusion that Stojić did not intend to prevent or punish the crimes was also based on other findings and considerations,[5307] including that: (1) the HVO continued to commit crimes throughout the relevant time period;[5308] (2) Stojić participated in or planned HVO military operations throughout this period, knew of crimes being committed, and thus intended to have those crimes committed;[5309] and (3) he encouraged the commission of the crimes by Naletilić's troops by commending them on several occasions while knowing that they were committing crimes.[5310] In light of this, the Appeals Chamber considers the evidence cited by Stojić – which further underlines that he knew that crimes were occurring, and failed to take adequate measures to address this – fails to demonstrate any error in the Trial Chamber's findings. The Appeals Chamber also dismisses, for the same reasons, the assertions that the Trial Chamber erred in disregarding other evidence showing Stojić's involvement in crime-fighting, some of which occurred after his JCE membership ended in November 1993,[5311] or in its assessment of his statement to the representatives of the international community. Stojić fails to show how this evidence could call into question the relevant Trial Chamber finding. These arguments are rejected.
[page 671]

1630. The Appeals Chamber therefore finds that Stojić has failed to demonstrate that the Trial Chamber erred in finding that he and the HVO authorities did not genuinely intend to punish the crimes against Muslims. His sub-ground of appeal 33.2 is dismissed.

    (iii) <u>Alleged errors in the assessment of Stojić's comments made on 17 July 1993 (Stojić's Sub-ground 33.3)</u>

1631. Stojić submits that no reasonable trier of fact could have concluded, based on his statements made at the dinner on 17 July 1993, that the only reasonable inference was that he was actively involved in organising and conducting the Mostar eviction campaigns.[5312] In particular, Stojić argues that: (1) the statements refer to military pressure on the ABiH as opposed to the evictions of civilians;[5313] (2) none of the comments attributed to him "reflect the way in which events subsequently unfolded",[5314] in that the conflict in Mostar was not resolved within 20 days and that the next HVO attack occurred on 24 August 1993;[5315] (3) he expressed concern for the civilians and offered his assistance in evacuating them, which is inconsistent with

---

[5304]   Ex. P02575, p. 2 (emphasis omitted).

[5305]   Ex. P02578, p. 1.

[5306]   Trial Judgement, Vol. 4, para. 446, referring to Ex. P02578.

[5307]   See *supra*, paras 1491-1492, 1494-1495.

[5308]   Trial Judgement, Vol. 4, para. 423.

[5309]   Trial Judgement, Vol. 4, para. 426. See *supra*, para. 1494.

[5310]   Trial Judgement, Vol. 4, paras 420, 423. See *supra*, paras 1498-1499.

[5311]   See Exs. P04111 (minutes of an HZ(R) H-B meeting on 11 August 1993 calling for crime prevention measures in general), 2D00854 (minutes of a meeting on 17 September 1993 discussing steps to establish a judicial system and fight crime), P06730 (a police report of 18 November 1993 detailing criminal investigation in connection with evictions), P07035 (a report of 4 December 1993 to the Croatian Information Service detailing findings on crimes).

[5312]   Stojić's Appeal Brief, para. 306. See Stojić's Appeal Brief, paras 299-300.

[5313]   Stojić's Appeal Brief, para. 301, referring to, *inter alia,* Exs. P03545 (confidential), p. 9, P03547, p. 3.

[5314]   Stojić's Appeal Brief, para. 302.

[5315]   Stojić's Appeal Brief, para. 302, referring to Trial Judgement, Vol. 2, paras 945-972, Exs. P10217 (confidential), para. 125, P03530 (confidential), para. 3.

the Trial Chamber's inference;[5316] (4) the Trial Chamber failed to consider that it was "hardly likely" that he would have made incriminating statements at an informal dinner with international representatives;[5317] and (5) the Trial Chamber disregarded the alternative reasonable inference that he was trying to present a confident and powerful position to international observers in the face of military difficulty.[5318]

1632. The Prosecution responds that: (1) Stojić ignores that the international representatives surmised from his comments that the HVO military pressure would drive Muslim civilians out of East Mostar;[5319] (2) East Mostar was the target of a prolonged HVO military attack;[5320] (3) the Trial Chamber was correct not to accept his professed concern for civilians as genuine;[5321] (4) Stojić's argument that he would not likely have said anything incriminatory shows no error;[5322] and (5) even if he was trying to present a confident and powerful position, this does not show that the Trial Chamber unreasonably relied on his comments.[5323] The Prosecution also submits that the Trial **[page 672]** Chamber's reasonable conclusion is further supported by other evidence of Stojić's role and involvement in the Mostar events.[5324]

1633. As a preliminary matter, the Appeals Chamber notes that the Trial Chamber did not reach the conclusion that Stojić was actively involved in the eviction campaigns in Mostar on the basis of the statements he made at the dinner of 17 July 1993 alone, but also on the basis of other evidence and findings.[5325] To the extent to which Stojić alleges the contrary,[5326] this submission is dismissed.

1634. With regard to Stojić's argument that the comments attributed to him related not to the evictions of civilians but to applying military pressure on the ABiH, the Appeals Chamber notes that, in the section on his knowledge of the East Mostar crimes, the Trial Chamber observed that Stojić commented that the HVO strategy was to place "maximum pressure on the southern part of the town of Mostar while leaving one route open [...] to allow the ABiH to escape".[5327] It also took account of the fact that the analysis of the situation from members of the international organisations indicated that: (1) Stojić seemed convinced of his troops' ability to achieve a definitive military solution to the "Muslim problem" in Mostar town;[5328] and (2) the HVO military pressure, in tandem with the shelling and isolation of East Mostar, would lead to shortages of food and water thus driving out the civilians.[5329] Therefore, the Appeals Chamber notes that the Trial Chamber did consider Stojić's statement related to the HVO's military strategy concerning the ABiH. However, the Trial Chamber also considered the effect such a strategy would have had on the civilian population and concluded that "the plan of action to which Bruno Stojić referred was necessarily directed against the entire population of East Mostar *and not only against the ABiH*".[5330] Stojić does not argue, much less demonstrate, that these goals of the HVO strategy were mutually exclusive. Moreover, the Trial Chamber also found that Stojić knew of the shelling of East Mostar, the attacks on representatives of international organisations in that part of town, and the shortages of food and water suffered by the Muslim population.[5331] The Appeals Chamber therefore finds that Stojić only asserts one interpretation of his statements which was acknowledged by the Trial Chamber. In light of the above, the Appeals Chamber finds that Stojić fails to show that the Trial Chamber erred in considering his statements on the basis that his comment concerned applying pressure on the ABiH. Stojić's argument is dismissed. **[page 673]**

[5316] Stojić's Appeal Brief, para. 303. Further, Stojić argues that the Trial Chamber failed to address the "significant inconsistency" between Witness DZ's witness statement and his oral testimony. Stojić's Appeal Brief, para. 303, referring to Witness DZ, T. 26791 (closed session) (24 Jan 2008); Ex. P10367 (confidential), para. 34.

[5317] Stojić's Appeal Brief, para. 304, referring to *Krstić* Appeal Judgement, para. 87.

[5318] Stojić's Appeal Brief, para. 305, referring to Exs. P03545 (confidential), p. 8, P03530 (confidential), p. 5.

[5319] Prosecution's Response Brief (Stojić), para. 265, referring to Trial Judgement, Vol. 4, para. 361.

[5320] Prosecution's Response Brief (Stojić), para. 265, referring to Trial Judgement, Vol. 2, paras 1018, 1378.

[5321] Prosecution's Response Brief (Stojić), para. 265.

[5322] Prosecution's Response Brief (Stojić), para. 265.

[5323] Prosecution's Response Brief (Stojić), para. 265. See also Appeal Hearing, AT. 330-331 (21 Mar 2017).

[5324] Prosecution's Response Brief (Stojić), para. 264, and evidence cited therein.

[5325] See Trial Judgement, Vol. 4, paras 350-352, 354. See *supra*, para. 1617.

[5326] See Stojić's Appeal Brief, para. 299.

[5327] Trial Judgement, Vol. 4, para. 361, referring to Ex. P03545 (confidential), p. 8. See also Ex. P03547, p. 3; Trial Judgement, Vol. 4, para. 353.

[5328] Trial Judgement, Vol. 4, para. 361, referring to Ex. P03545 (confidential), p. 9. See also Ex. P03547, p. 3.

[5329] Trial Judgement, Vol. 4, paras 361-362.

[5330] Trial Judgement, Vol. 4, para. 362 (emphasis added).

[5331] Trial Judgement, Vol. 4, para. 362.

1635. Turning to Stojić's argument that his comments are inconsistent with the fact that there was no HVO attack until 24 August 1993, the Appeals Chamber considers that Stojić misrepresents the Trial Chamber's findings. The Trial Chamber did conclude that there was an HVO attack in Mostar which began on 23 August 1993 in the section of the Trial Judgement pointed to by Stojić,[5332] but also found that "the HVO forces carried out a new round of operations in mid-July 1993 in which they expelled Muslims from West Mostar, including the women, children and the elderly" and that these operations "continued throughout the second half of July and in August 1993".[5333] These attacks occurred contemporaneously with Stojić's comments, and thus his argument to the contrary is rejected. As to Stojić's argument on his estimation of the duration of the conflict, the Appeals Chamber is not persuaded that his statement that the conflict would be resolved within 20 days was necessarily inconsistent with his appraisal of the situation on 17 July 1993. Stojić therefore fails to demonstrate that no reasonable trier of fact could have relied on the evidence. Regardless, Stojić does not show how this alleged inconsistency could impact on the impugned finding which was based on various other factors.[5334] This argument is rejected.

1636. As for Stojić's argument that the Trial Chamber's reliance on these statements is inconsistent with his concern for, and offer to help, the civilian population, the Appeals Chamber notes that the Trial Chamber explicitly considered evidence that Stojić "expressed his 'concern'" and "suggested that the largest possible number of these civilians be evacuated and offered his assistance".[5335] Nevertheless, the Trial Chamber concluded, on the basis of the evidence as a whole, that Stojić participated in organising and conducting the eviction campaigns.[5336] Thus, the Appeals Chamber finds that the Trial Chamber gave Stojić's concern and offer to help little or no weight and did not accept these statements as genuine. Stojić simply seeks to substitute bis own interpretation of the evidence for that of the Trial Chamber, and fails to demonstrate that no reasonable trier of fact could have reached this conclusion. His argument is dismissed.[5337] Further, the Appeals Chamber dismisses Stojić's argument that it was "hardly likely" that he would have made **[page 674]** incriminating statements at the dinner as unconvincing.[5338] Regarding Stojić's contention that the Trial Chamber failed to take account of another reasonable inference, *i.e.* that he was simply trying to present a confident and powerful position, the Trial Chamber considered the evidence he now cites in its discussion on his participation in events.[5339] Moreover, the Appeals Chamber considers that Stojić fails to show how this possible inference is inconsistent with the Trial Chamber's conclusion that he was actively involved in organising and conducting the eviction campaigns in Mostar. Stojić's argument is dismissed.

1637. Based on the foregoing, the Appeals Chamber finds that Stojić fails to demonstrate that the Trial Chamber erred in relying on statements attributed to him at a dinner on 17 July 1993 to support its finding that he was actively involved in organising and conducting the eviction campaigns. His sub-ground of appeal 33.3 is dismissed.

[5332] See Trial Judgement, Vol. 2, paras 947-972.
[5333] Trial Judgement, Vol. 2, para. 920. See Trial Judgement, Vol. 2, para. 919, referring to Ex. P10038, para. 24 ("[o]n 22 July 1993, six HVO soldiers came to the flat belonging to *Jasmina Čišić* and took her and her family to Semovac, north of Mostar; once there, the soldiers told them that they were 'allowed to leave the West area'.") (internal references omitted).
[5334] See *supra*, paras 1617, 1633.
[5335] Trial Judgement, Vol. 4, para. 353, referring to Witness DV, T(F). 22895-22896 (private session) (1 Oct 2007), Exs. P10217 (confidential), para. 124, P03545 (confidential), p. 9. See also Trial Judgement, Vol. 4, para. 361, referring to Ex. P03545 (confidential), p. 9.
[5336] Trial Judgement, Vol. 4, para. 355. See *supra*, paras 1598, 1601-1604, 1610-1611, 1614-1615, 1617, 1621-1624.
[5337] The Appeals Chamber also rejects Stojić's argument that the Trial Chamber failed to address the inconsistency between Witness DZ's witness statement and testimony, given that the content of the witness's testimony was considered by the Trial Chamber. Therefore, Stojić does not establish that evidence of a similar nature could have had an impact on the Trial Chamber's conclusions. Trial Judgement, Vol. 4, paras 353, 355. See Witness DZ, T. 26791 (closed session) (24 Jan 2008); Ex. P10367 (confidential), para. 34. See *infra*, paras 1641-1643.
[5338] The Appeals Chamber considers that the case-law cited by Stojić in support is legally and factually distinguishable from his case. See *Krstić* Appeal Judgement, para. 87 (the Appeals Chamber considered that Radislav Krstić's presence at three meetings did not suggest that he was aware of any genocidai intent of Ratko Mladić as it was unlikely that Mladić would have discussed this in front of UNPROFOR leaders or the foreign media present).
[5339] Trial Judgement, Vol. 4, fns 796 (referring to Exhibit P03545), 797 (referring to Exhibits P03545 and P03530).

(iv) <u>Alleged errors regarding Witness DZ's credibility and evidence (Stojić's Grounds 32 and 33.4)</u>

1638. The Trial Chamber relied on the evidence of Witness DZ in various instances when addressing Stojić's responsibility. Specifically, Witness DZ's evidence was used, with other evidence, to conclude that Stojić represented the HVO in peace negotiations.[5340] Further, in concluding that Stojić participated in planning the operations to evict Muslims from West Mostar and thus intended acts of violence linked to these operations,[5341] the Trial Chamber considered, *inter alia,* that Witness DZ: (1) was told by Vladislav Pogarčić that Stojić was in charge of implementing the plan to cleanse Mostar town; and (2) heard HVO members say that Stojić ordered people to be evicted from their homes and their houses burned in Mostar.[5342] The Trial Chamber also considered Witness DZ's evidence as well as other evidence in finding that Stojić knew of crimes in East Mostar such as shelling and attacks on representatives of the international community.[5343] **[page 675]**

a. <u>Alleged errors regarding the credibility of Witness DZ (Stojić's Ground 32)</u>

1639. Stojić argues that the Trial Chamber erred in law and/or fact by failing to assess and/or give a "reasoned decision" on Witness DZ's reliability and credibility.[5344] Specifically, Stojić submits that the Trial Chamber erred in law by disregarding the Defence submission that the witness was not credible, making no express findings on his credibility, failing to address inconsistencies in his evidence, and relying on his written evidence while disregarding his oral evidence.[5345] Stojić argues that no reasonable trial chamber could have found Witness DZ credible and relied on his evidence since: (1) he failed to explain, and was evasive about, why none of his contemporaneous reports contain the allegations he made against Stojić at trial; (2) he distorted the facts at trial, deliberately painting a negative picture of Stojić, thereby showing his bias; (3) his working relationships were persistently bad; and (4) he lacked background knowledge.[5346] Stojić concludes that this undermines the findings that he participated in planning eviction operations in West Mostar and knew about attacks on international organisations in East Mostar, since they are primarily based on the evidence of Witness DZ, and therefore calls for setting aside his convictions on Counts 1-3, 6-11, 15-17, 20, and 22-25.[5347]

1640. The Prosecution responds that Stojić fails to demonstrate that the Trial Chamber erred when assessing Witness DZ's credibility.[5348] The Prosecution argues that the right to a reasoned opinion does not require an explicit analysis of Witness DZ's credibility and that large parts of his evidence were well corroborated.[5349] With regard to Stojić's factual allegations, the Prosecution contends that: (1) Witness DZ's reports were not all available and did not cover all topics; (2) the witness was not biased against Stojić and did not distort the facts; (3) Stojić fails to demonstrate how being disliked by peers impacts on the witness's credibility; and (4) his alleged lack of background knowledge is irrelevant to the assessment of his credibility.[5350]

1641. The Appeals Chamber turns first to Stojić's assertion that the impugned findings are "primarily" based on Witness DZ's evidence. It notes that the Trial Chamber's finding that Stojić was "actively involved in organising and conducting the eviction campaigns" against Muslims from West Mostar is based on a variety of other testimonial and documentary evidence.[5351] Equally, the **[page 676]** Trial Chamber's finding

---

[5340]   Trial Judgement, Vol. 4, para. 323, referring to Witness DZ, T(F). 26546 (closed session) (22 Jan 2008), Ex. P10367 (confidential), para. 58.

[5341]   See *supra,* para. 1617.

[5342]   Trial Judgement, Vol. 4, para. 354, referring to Ex. P10367 (confidential), paras 33, 69. The Trial Chamber also relied on Witness DZ's evidence, in combination with other evidence, to conclude that Stojić estimated that the conflict between Muslims and Croats in Mostar could be resolved in 20 days. Trial Judgement, Vol. 4, para. 353 & fn. 797. See *supra,* paras 1631-1636, fn. 5338.

[5343]   Trial Judgement, Vol. 4, para. 359 & fn. 801.

[5344]   Stojić's Appeal Brief, heading before para. 287, paras 288-289. See Stojić's Reply Brief, paras 67-68, 70-71.

[5345]   Stojić's Appeal Brief, heading before para. 287, para. 288.

[5346]   Stojić's Appeal Brief, heading before para. 287, paras 289-293.

[5347]   Stojić's Appeal Brief, paras 287-288, 293.

[5348]   Prosecution's Response Brief (Stojić), paras 252, 255.

[5349]   Prosecution's Response Brief (Stojić), paras 252-254.

[5350]   Prosecution's Response Brief (Stojić), para. 254.

[5351]   Trial Judgement, Vol. 4, para. 355. See Trial Judgement, Vol. 4, paras 352-353, referring to, *inter alia,* Antoon van der Grinten, T(F). 21079-21080 (10 July 2007), Witness DV, T(F). 22895-22896, 22899 (closed session) (1 Oct 2007), Ex. P03181, Ex. P03547, p. 3, Ex. P10217 (confidential), paras 122-125.

regarding Stojić's knowledge of the targeting of international organisations by the HVO is based on extensive other evidence.[5352] Thus, Stojić has failed to show that the impugned findings are "primarily" based on Witness DZ's evidence or that it was the principal evidence on which the Trial Chamber relied to convict him.[5353] Moreover, the Appeals Chamber recalls that a trial chamber has broad discretion in assessing the appropriate weight and credibility to be accorded to the testimony of a witness,[5354] and thus Stojić must demonstrate a discernible error.[5355]

1642. Although the Trial Chamber did not explicitly address Stojić's trial arguments challenging the credibility of Witness DZ, it stated that to "rule on the alleged acts [in Mostar Municipality], the Chamber assessed a great amount of evidence" including the evidence of Witness DZ.[5356] The Trial Chamber then proceeded to rely on both Witness DZ's *viva voce* testimony and his/her witness statement in numerous instances, alongside other evidence, when determining the factual narrative of events in Mostar.[5357] Thus, the Trial Chamber clearly considered Witness DZ to be credible despite Stojić's trial arguments to the contrary. In this regard, the Appeals Chamber recalls that "an accused's right to a reasoned opinion does not ordinarily demand a detailed analysis of the credibility of particular witnesses",[5358] however, a trial chamber must provide reasons for accepting testimony despite alleged or material inconsistencies when it is the principal evidence relied upon to convict an accused.[5359] Having determined that Witness DZ's evidence was not the principal evidence relied upon to convict Stojić for events in Mostar, the Appeals Chamber considers that Stojić has not identified any material inconsistencies in Witness DZ's evidence that the Trial Chamber was required to address.[5360] Therefore, Stojić fails to demonstrate that the Trial Chamber committed a discernible error by not providing an explicit analysis on Witness DZ's credibility. **[page 677]**

1643. Moreover, in arguing that no reasonable trier of fact could have found Witness DZ credible and relied on his evidence, Stojić repeats his arguments that were unsuccessful at trial[5361] without demonstrating that their rejection constituted a discernible error. Accordingly, the Appeals Chamber dismisses his ground of appeal 32.

b. Alleged errors in relation to Witness DZ's hearsay evidence (Stojić's Sub-ground 33.4)

1644. Stojić submits that the Trial Chamber erred in according any weight to Witness DZ's hearsay evidence.[5362] In particular, he asserts that: (1) Witness DZ's evidence is uncorroborated;[5363] (2) one of the statements is "multiple hearsay" from unidentified HVO soldiers on unspecified occasions, which was translated by an unidentified interpreter;[5364] (3) the Trial Chamber disregarded Witness DZ's failure to record "important" statements in any contemporaneous report;[5365] and (4) Witness DZ was unable to recall the dates of conversations and who translated them for him.[5366]

[5352] Trial Judgement, Vol. 4, paras 359, 362, 367, referring to, *inter alia*, Antoon van der Grinten, T(F). 21046, 21076-21078 (10 July 2007), 21186-21187 (11 July 2007), Witness DW, T(F). 23087 (3 Oct 2007), Ex. P02806 (confidential), Ex. P03162 (confidential), p. 1, Ex. P03184 (confidential), p. 2, Ex. P10287 (confidential), para. 30.

[5353] See *supra*, para. 1639.

[5354] *Popović et al.* Appeal Judgement, para. 131; *Đorđević* Appeal Judgement, paras 781, 797, 819; *Lukić and Lukić* Appeal Judgement, paras 86, 235, 363, 375.

[5355] *Popović et al.* Appeal Judgement, para. 131. See *Popović et al.* Appeal Judgement, para. 131 ("In such cases the Appeals Chamber will deem that the witness evidence relied on by the Trial Chamber could not have been accepted by any reasonable tribunal of fact or that the evaluation of the evidence was 'wholly erroneous'", and proceed to substitute its own finding for that of the Trial Chamber).

[5356] Trial Judgement, Vol. 2, para. 667.

[5357] See Trial Judgement, Vol. 2, paras 1228, 1235, 1239, 1259-1260, 1263, 1266.

[5358] *Popović et al.* Appeal Judgement, para. 133; *Kajelijeli* Appeal Judgement, para. 60.

[5359] *Popović et al.* Appeal Judgement, para. 133; *Haradinaj et al.* Appeal Judgement, paras 129, 134, 252; *Kupreškić et al.* Appeal Judgement, paras 135, 202.

[5360] See Stojić's Appeal Brief, paras 288-290 (arguing that Witness DZ's contemporary reports of events did not contain any allegations against him, and referring to evidence on the release of UN interpreters – an event which was not considered in the Trial Judgement).

[5361] Compare Stojić Closing Arguments, T. 52322-52337 (15 Feb 2011) with Stojić's Appeal Brief, paras 288-292.

[5362] Stojić's Appeal Brief, paras 309, 311. See also Stojić's Appeal Brief, paras 307-308.

[5363] Stojić's Appeal Brief, para. 309.

[5364] Stojić's Appeal Brief, para. 309, referring to Ex. P10367 (confidential), para. 33.

[5365] Stojić's Appeal Brief, para. 310, referring to Witness DZ, T. 26781-26782 (closed session) (24 Jan 2008), Ex. P02930.

[5366] Stojić's Appeal Brief, para. 310, referring to Witness DZ, T. 26778 (closed session) (24 Jan 2008).

1645. The Prosecution responds that the Trial Chamber properly relied on Witness DZ's evidence,[5367] as: (1) it was corroborated;[5368] (2) it was based on what he learnt directly from Pogarčić in English;[5369] and (3) his contemporaneous reports were only a summary such that the parts of it which are on the record do not represent all of his communications with Pogarčić.[5370]

1646. The Appeals Chamber recalls that a trial chamber may rely on evidence, including hearsay evidence, provided that it is reliable and credible.[5371] The Appeals Chamber also recalls that a trial **[page 678]** chamber has wide discretion as to the assessment of the weight and probative value of hearsay evidence, but must proceed with caution in the assessment of such evidence.[5372]

1647. With regard to Stojić's argument that Witness DZ's hearsay evidence is uncorroborated, the Appeals Chamber recalls that two pieces of *prima facie* credible evidence are corroborative when they are compatible with one another regarding the same fact or a sequence of linked facts.[5373] In this regard, the Appeals Chamber considers that Witness DZ's evidence regarding Stojić's role in the implementation of the evictions is corroborated by evidence showing that Stojić: (1) presented himself as "an HVO military chief who had control over West Mostar in May 1993";[5374] (2) received reports from HVO officials regarding events that occurred during the course of the eviction campaigns;[5375] and (3) hosted a dinner at his house attended by international representatives, during which he informed them of HVO strategies and objectives regarding Mostar.[5376] In relation to Witness DZ's evidence that Stojić ordered homes to be burned, the Appeals Chamber notes that the evidence was not relied on to establish his responsibility for the burning of houses, but to establish that Stojić was actively involved in organising and conducting the eviction campaign,[5377] which, as discussed above, is corroborated to some extent by other evidence. Thus, Stojić's argument on the lack of corroboration of Witness DZ's evidence is dismissed.

1648. As to the assertion that Witness DZ's statements relied on hearsay from unidentified HVO soldiers on unspecified occasions, which was translated by an unidentified interpreter,[5378] the Appeals Chamber notes that the source of the information is one of the factors that should be considered when assessing the weight and probative value of hearsay evidence.[5379] In this case, the source of the information has been identified as HVO soldiers whose discussions Witness DZ heard and understood.[5380] The Appeals Chamber considers that more specific identification of the source of the information was not necessary under the circumstances, and finds that Stojić does not demonstrate an error in the Trial Chamber's decision to find Witness DZ's evidence reliable, taking **[page 679]** into account the evidence as a whole. Finally, as to Stojić's argument that Witness DZ's evidence should have been less reliable as the witness did not record this evidence in contemporary

---

[5367]   Prosecution's Response Brief (Stojić), para. 266. See also Appeal Hearing, AT. 332-333 (21 Mar 2017).

[5368]   Prosecution's Response Brief (Stojić), para. 266, referring to Trial Judgement, Vol. 4, para. 350, Prosecution's Response Brief (Stojić), paras 237-242, 257-259, 264-265. The Prosecution also asserts that Stojić ignores that Witness DZ's evidence is compatible with other reliable evidence. Prosecution's Response Brief (Stojić), para. 269. See Prosecution's Response Brief (Stojić), para. 267.

[5369]   Prosecution's Response Brief (Stojić), para. 268, referring to Witness DZ, T. 26554, 26572-26573 (closed session) (22 Jan 2008), Ex. P10367 (confidential), paras 25-26, 69.

[5370]   Prosecution's Response Brief (Stojić), para. 269, referring to Witness DZ, T. 26763-26764, 26864 (closed session) (24 Jan 2008).

[5371]   *Popović et al.* Appeal Judgement, para. 1276. See *Šainović et al.* Appeal Judgement, para. 846.

[5372]   *Lukić and Lukić* Appeal Judgement, para. 577. See *Popović et al.* Appeal Judgement, para. 1307 ("It is settled that the weight and probative value to be afforded to hearsay evidence will ultimately depend upon 'the infinitely variable circumstances which surround hearsay evidence'.").

[5373]   *Gatete* Appeal Judgement, para. 125; *Nahimana et al.* Appeal Judgement, para. 428. See *Popović et al.* Appeal Judgement, paras 243 (a trial chamber has the discretion to decide in the circumstances of each case whether corroboration is necessary or whether to rely on uncorroborated, but otherwise credible, witness testimony"), 1264; *D. Milošević* Appeal Judgement, para. 215.

[5374]   Trial Judgement, Vol. 4, para. 346. See Trial Judgement, Vol. 4, para. 344, referring to Ex. P04238. See also *supra*, paras 1598, 1601-1604, 1610-1611, 1614-1615, 1617, 1621-1624.

[5375]   Trial Judgement, Vol. 4, paras 351-352, referring to, *inter alia*, Exs. P02608, P02770, P03181. See *supra*, paras 1617, 1621-1624.

[5376]   Trial Judgement, Vol. 4, para. 353, and references cited therein. See *supra*, para. 1617.

[5377]   Trial Judgement, Vol. 4, para. 355.

[5378]   Stojić's Appeal Brief, para. 309, referring to Ex. P10367 (confidential), para. 33.

[5379]   *Lukić and Lukić* Appeal Judgement, para. 577.

[5380]   Ex. P10367 (confidential), para. 33.

reports, the Appeals Chamber considers that there is no requirement for a witness to do so before his or her evidence can be relied on by a trial chamber. This argument is dismissed.

1649. In sum, the Appeals Chamber finds that Stojić has failed to show that the Trial Chamber erred in relying on Witness DZ's evidence in establishing that Stojić was actively involved in organising and conducting the eviction campaigns. Stojić's sub-ground of appeal 33.4 is dismissed.

(v) Stojić's intention that mistreatment be committed against Muslims during the eviction campaigns (Stojić's Sub-ground 33.5)

1650. Stojić submits that no reasonable trier of fact could have concluded, as the only reasonable inference, that he intended that the mistreatment linked to the eviction campaigns be committed.[5381] Specifically, he argues that this conclusion was not based on any evidence and is inconsistent with the evidence that he expressed concern about civilians and sought the evacuation of children.[5382] Stojić also asserts that there is no evidence that he intended the acts of violence.[5383]

1651. The Prosecution responds that the Trial Chamber reasonably concluded that Stojić intended the acts of violence that occurred during the expulsion campaign.[5384] It submits that there was evidence that acts of violence were committed systematically to expel Muslims,[5385] and that the Trial Chamber "was right not to accept that Stojić genuinely cared about East Mostar civilians".[5386]

1652. With regard to Stojić's argument that the Trial Chamber failed to explain the evidential basis for its conclusion that he intended acts of violence, the Appeals Chamber notes that the paragraph of the Trial Judgement referred to by Stojić does not cite evidence.[5387] However, the Appeals Chamber finds no error in this regard, as the contested paragraph clearly contains the conclusion, summarising the findings made previously in that section.[5388] The Appeals Chamber dismisses elsewhere his challenges to those findings – including challenges on the basis of Stojić's expressed concern about civilians.[5389] This challenge is also dismissed. In respect of the alleged lack of evidence of his intention, the Appeals Chamber recalls that the Trial Chamber permissibly **[page 680]** based its inference not on direct evidence but on its other findings that the acts of violence were part of a preconceived plan and that Stojić participated in planning the operations resulting in these violent acts.[5390] Stojić merely makes an assertion without pointing to any other reasonable inference that could be drawn from the evidence. Thus, the Appeals Chamber finds that Stojić has failed to demonstrate that the Trial Chamber erred in concluding, as the only reasonable inference, that he intended that Muslims be mistreated during the course of the eviction campaigns beginning in Mostar in June 1993. His sub-ground of appeal 33.5 is dismissed.

(vi) Conclusion

1653. In sum, Stojić's grounds of appeal 32 and 33 are dismissed.

(f) The siege of East Mostar (Stojić's Ground 34)

1654. The Trial Chamber found that, between June 1993 and April 1994, the HVO laid siege to East Mostar and committed crimes.[5391] It found, *inter alia*, that: (1) the town was the target of a prolonged military attack by the HVO that included intense constant shooting and shelling, including sniper fire, that resulted in many

---

[5381] Stojić's Appeal Brief, paras 312-313, referring to Trial Judgement, Vol. 4, para. 357.
[5382] Stojić's Appeal Brief, para. 313.
[5383] Stojić's Appeal Brief, para. 313. See Stojić's Appeal Brief, para. 314.
[5384] Prosecution's Response Brief (Stojić), para. 270.
[5385] Prosecution's Response Brief (Stojić), para. 271, referring to Trial Judgement, Vol. 2, paras 827, 866, 868, 872, 876, 924, 928, 930, 934, 981-987, Vol. 4, paras 356-357.
[5386] Prosecution's Response Brief (Stojić), para. 272.
[5387] Stojić's Appeal Brief, para. 313, referring to Trial Judgement, Vol. 4, para. 357.
[5388] Trial Judgement, Vol. 4, paras 350-356.
[5389] See *supra*, paras 1621-1624, 1628-1630, 1633-1637, 1646-1649.
[5390] Trial Judgement, Vol. 4, para. 357.
[5391] Trial Judgement, Vol. 2, para. 1378. See Trial Judgement, Vol. 2, paras 992-1377; Vol. 4, para. 59.

inhabitants being injured or killed; (2) the population could not leave East Mostar of its own free will and had to live under extremely harsh conditions, without food, water, electricity and appropriate medical care; and (3) the HVO hindered and, at times, completely blocked the arrival of humanitarian aid and deliberately targeted the members of the international organisations, killing and wounding some of them.[5392]

1655. The Trial Chamber found that Stojić knew about the HVO's plan of action to exert pressure on East Mostar to force the ABiH to leave the sector and the impact it had on civilians.[5393] It concluded that, inasmuch as he continued to exercise his functions in the HVO/Government of the HR H-B, he "accepted the crimes directly linked to the HVO military operations against East Mostar, that is, the murders and the destruction of property, including mosques, related to the shelling and the harsh living conditions of the population of that part of the town caused by the lack of food and water".[5394] In reaching this conclusion it relied on, *inter alia:* (1) its earlier finding that **[page 681]** Stojić was kept informed by the representatives of the international community about the crimes committed by HVO members in Mostar, such as the shelling and the incidents when representatives of the international community were targeted by the HVO;[5395] (2) Stojić being informed through a report on 21 August 1993 that there were shortages of food, water, and electricity in East Mostar;[5396] and (3) Stojić's statement to international representatives on 17 July 1993 that the HVO's plan of action was to put pressure on East Mostar in order to force the ABiH to leave the sector, which, as found by the Trial Chamber, was necessarily directed against the entire population of East Mostar and not only against the ABiH.[5397] In relation to the sniping campaign, the Trial Chamber considered, *inter alia,* that Stojić told Witness Antoon van der Grinten that certain snipers were under his control,[5398] before concluding that Stojić must have controlled all HVO snipers in West Mostar since their actions always followed the same *modus operandi.*[5399] The Trial Chamber concluded, based on this finding and other considerations, including the testimony of Witness DZ, that Stojić must have known that the snipers in West Mostar were targeting civilians and members of international organisations in East Mostar.[5400] It also concluded that inasmuch as Stojić did nothing to remove the obstacles hindering access to humanitarian aid though he had the power and the obligation to do so, he facilitated that obstruction.[5401]

    (i) Stojić's knowledge and acceptance of the harsh living conditions of the population in East Mostar (Stojić's Sub-ground 34.1)

1656. Stojić submits that the Trial Chamber erred in finding that he knew about and accepted the harsh living conditions of the population in East Mostar.[5402] He argues that the Trial Chamber disregarded clearly relevant evidence showing that the Department of Defence took steps to supply medicine and medical

---

[5392] Trial Judgement, Vol. 2, para. 1378. See Trial Judgement, Vol. 2, paras 992-1377; Vol. 4, para. 59.

[5393] Trial Judgement, Vol. 4, para. 363. See Trial Judgement, Vol. 4, paras 361-362.

[5394] Trial Judgement, Vol. 4, para. 363. The Appeals Chamber notes that the Trial Chamber concluded that: (1) Stojić's JCE membership ended on 15 November 1993 (see *supra,* paras 1401, 1516; Trial Judgement, Vol. 4, para. 1227); and (2) sniping incidents 13 and 14 occurred in 1994 (see *infra,* para. 1995). Moreover, the Appeals Chamber finds that for seven of the ten mosques destroyed or severely damaged in Mostar, "no reasonable trier of fact could have concluded beyond reasonable doubt that they were severely damaged or destroyed before 9 November 1993, and thus before Praljak's membership in the JCE ended". See *infra,* para. 2002). Based on the same reasoning detailed in Praljak's section below (see *infra,* paras 1984-1985, 2000-2003), the Appeals Chamber finds *proprio motu* that – to the extent the Trial Chamber so found – Stojić cannot be held responsible for crimes occurring after 15 November 1993, including sniping incidents 13 and 14 as well as the destruction of or severe damage to seven mosques in Mostar as it relates to Count 21. The impact of this finding on sentencing, if any, will be addressed below. See *infra,* para. 3361.

[5395] Trial Judgement, Vol. 4, para. 359, referring to, *inter alia,* Witness DZ, T(F). 26472-26473, 26484-26485 (closed session) (22 Jan 2008). See also Trial Judgement, Vol. 2, para. 1266, referring to, *inter alia,* Witness DZ, T(F). 26484-26485, 26489-26490 (closed session) (22 Jan 2008).

[5396] Trial Judgement, Vol. 4, para. 360, referring to Ex. P04403.

[5397] Trial Judgement, Vol. 4, para. 362. See *supra,* paras 1633-1637.

[5398] Trial Judgement, Vol. 4, para. 365, referring to Antoon van der Grinten, T(F). 21046-21048, 21051, 21248 (10 July 2007), Ex. P02806 (confidential), p. 2.

[5399] Trial Judgement, Vol. 4, paras 368-369.

[5400] Trial Judgement, Vol. 4, para. 369. See Trial Judgement, Vol. 2, para. 1266 (referring to Witness DZ, T(F). 26484-26485, 26489-26490 (closed session) (22 Jan 2008), Ex. P10367 (confidential), para. 21), Vol. 4, paras 359 (and references cited therein), 364-365 (referring to, *inter alia,* Exs. 2D00116, 2D00117).

[5401] Trial Judgement, Vol. 4, para. 372. See Trial Judgement, Vol. 2, para. 1244.

[5402] Stojić's Appeal Brief, paras 315-316, 319. See Stojić's Appeal Brief, para. 331; Stojić's Reply Brief, para. 71.

equipment to Muslim civilians and the ABiH,[5403] namely the evidence: (1) of **[page 682]** Witness Ivan Bagarić;[5404] (2) that the HVO offered unconditional help with supplying medical aid, facilitated by UNPROFOR;[5405] (3) that the HVO offered to accommodate wounded Muslim civilians and ABiH soldiers at hospitals, with equal treatment;[5406] and (4) that Muslim civilians were evacuated for medical treatment.[5407] Further, Stojić asserts that the Trial Chamber erroneously found that he accepted shortages of food and water without finding that he had the power to improve the situation, and that there was no evidence that he had such control.[5408] He also contends that the Trial Chamber's finding that the HVO "attempted to manage the problem of water and electricity supplies" is inconsistent with its finding that he accepted the harsh living conditions.[5409] Stojić also argues that the Trial Chamber drew unreasonable inferences from his statements at the dinner on 17 July 1993, given that "no plan [he referred] to at that meeting actually materialised".[5410]

1657. The Prosecution responds that the Trial Chamber's conclusion was reasonable[5411] and that Stojić knew of the shelling and sniping attacks and appeared "well-informed" of events.[5412] It also contends that the Trial Chamber considered the HVO's sporadic aid but reasonably found that this did not undermine its conclusion.[5413] The Prosecution argues that it is immaterial that the Trial Chamber did not expressly find that Stojić had the power to improve the situation in Mostar given that he aggravated that situation.[5414] It further asserts that Stojić's comments on 17 July 1993 confirmed his knowledge and involvement in the HVO's plan in East Mostar.[5415]

1658. The Appeals Chamber first notes that, in disputing the Trial Chamber's finding that he accepted the shortages of food and water suffered by the Muslim population in East Mostar,[5416] Stojić does not explicitly challenge the finding that he knew of these shortages.[5417] Moreover, Stojić's argument concerning his statements at the 17 July 1993 dinner is only supported by a cross-**[page 683]**reference to arguments he made elsewhere which have already been considered and dismissed.[5418] This argument is therefore also dismissed.

1659. Stojić, though, does argue that the Trial Chamber disregarded evidence that the HVO supplied medical aid to Muslim civilians and the ABiH. However, the Appeals Chamber notes that the Trial Chamber's finding which Stojić challenges was limited to his acceptance of the "crimes directly linked to the HVO military operations against East Mostar, that is, the murders and the destruction of property, including mosques, related to the shelling and *the harsh living conditions of the population* [...] *caused by the lack of food and water*"[5419] Thus, the Appeals Chamber is not convinced that any evidence on the supply of medical aid would have an impact on the Trial Chamber's finding challenged under this sub-ground of appeal. Nonetheless, the Appeals Chamber also notes that the Trial Chamber made factual findings on the issue, in support of which it expressly considered and relied on, *inter alia,* some of the evidence that Stojić cites. Specifically, the Trial Chamber found that between June and September 1993, the HVO provided sporadic humanitarian aid to East

---

[5403] Stojić's Appeal Brief, para. 316, referring to Stojić's Appeal Brief, fn. 92. Stojić also argues that the Trial Chamber's conclusion is inconsistent with its finding that, between June and September 1993, the HVO provided humanitarian aid to East Mostar. Stojić's Appeal Brief, fn. 782, referring to Trial Judgement, Vol. 2, para. 1243.

[5404] Stojić's Appeal Brief, para. 316, referring to Ivan Bagarić, T. 38880, 38937, 38946-38948, 38962 (20 Apr 2009).

[5405] Stojić's Appeal Brief, para. 316, referring to Antoon van der Grinten, T. 21164 (11 My 2007), Exs. P02731 (confidential), P02782 (confidential), 2D00119, 2D00321, 2D00504.

[5406] Stojić's Appeal Brief, para. 316, referring to Exs. P02923 (confidential), 2D00123, 2D00455.

[5407] Stojić's Appeal Brief, para. 316, referring to Exs. 3D00615, 3D01034.

[5408] Stojić's Appeal Brief, para. 317.

[5409] Stojić's Appeal Brief, para. 317, referring to Trial Judgement, Vol. 2, para. 1218.

[5410] Stojić's Appeal Brief, para. 318, referring to Stojić's Appeal Brief, para. 302 (Stojić's Ground 33.3).

[5411] Prosecution's Response Brief (Stojić), para. 275. See Prosecution's Response Brief (Stojić), para. 274.

[5412] Prosecution's Response Brief (Stojić), para. 276, referring to, *inter alia,* Antoon van der Grinten, T. 21076 (10 July 2007). The Prosecution submits that Stojić knew of the dire situation facing Muslim civilians, given "his false concern" offering to evacuate civilians from East Mostar. Prosecution's Response Brief (Stojić), para. 276.

[5413] Prosecution's Response Brief (Stojić), para. 278. The Prosecution argues that the evidence, at best, shows that the HVO only provided limited medical supplies on three occasions. Prosecution's Response Brief (Stojić), para. 278.

[5414] Prosecution's Response Brief (Stojić), para. 279. The Prosecution asserts that any attempt by the HVO to manage the water and electricity situation is undermined by its crimes. Prosecution's Response Brief (Stojić), para, 279.

[5415] Prosecution's Response Brief (Stojić), para. 277, and evidence cited therein.

[5416] See *supra,* para. 1656.

[5417] See Trial Judgement, Vol. 4, para. 362.

[5418] See *supra,* paras 1634-1637.

[5419] Trial Judgement, Vol. 4, para. 363 (emphasis added). See Trial Judgement, Vol. 4, para. 362.

Mostar, conditional on the HVO obtaining certain advantages, which did not bring into question the finding that the HVO impeded the delivery of humanitarian aid.[5420] Stojić thus fails to demonstrate that the Trial Chamber disregarded relevant evidence and fails to show how this evidence could undermine the conclusion that he accepted the East Mostar crimes. His argument is dismissed.

1660. The Appeals Chamber turns to Stojić's argument that the Trial Chamber was inconsistent in finding that the HVO attempted to manage the water and electricity problems in East Mostar and that he accepted the harsh living conditions there. The Appeals Chamber notes that the Trial Chamber found that the HVO hindered proposed water supply repairs in June 1993 but also concluded that the HVO – namely, its municipal office for reconstruction in Mostar[5421] – did indeed attempt to manage the water and electricity shortages from July 1993 until at least November 1993 by performing necessary repairs and thus it could not find that the HVO willingly refused to restore water supplies.[5422] The Appeals Chamber therefore considers that the Trial Chamber erred in considering, as a part of his responsibility, that Stojić accepted the water shortage as a component of the harsh living conditions endured by the East Mostar population.[5423] However, the Appeals Chamber considers that this error has no impact on Stojić's conviction, given that the Trial **[page 684]** Chamber also reached its conclusion on the basis that he knew of and accepted the food shortage suffered by the Muslim population.[5424] Although Stojić also challenges this aspect of the finding by arguing that he had no control over the food supply, the Appeals Chamber notes the Trial Chamber's finding that the food shortage was due to the large number of people in East Mostar, the confinement of this part of the town, and the obstruction of humanitarian aid,[5425] which were causes that were all attributed to the HVO.[5426] Taking into account the Trial Chamber's findings concerning Stojić's contribution to the appalling living conditions of Muslim inhabitants in East Mostar, and specifically by hindering the regular arrival of humanitarian aid which included food convoys,[5427] the Appeals Chamber considers that he fails to show that the Trial Chamber's finding that he knew of and accepted the food shortage suffered by the Muslim population is undermined by any lack of evidence regarding his control over the food supply.[5428] This argument is dismissed.

1661. For the above reasons, the Appeals Chamber finds that Stojić has failed to demonstrate that the Trial Chamber erred in finding that Stojić accepted the harsh living conditions of the population in East Mostar caused by the lack of food. Stojić's sub-ground of appeal 34.1 is dismissed.

(ii) Stojić's control over HVO snipers in West Mostar and knowledge of sniper attacks in East Mostar (Stojić's Sub-grounds 34.2, 34.3, and 34.4)

1662. Stojić submits that no reasonable trier of fact could have found that he controlled all the HVO snipers in Mostar,[5429] as Witness van der Grinten clarified his testimony that Stojić controlled all the snipers as meaning that they were "under HVO control".[5430] He argues that this interpretation is consistent with Exhibit P02806 and findings on his limited powers since he was not in the military chain of command.[5431] Further, Stojić asserts that there was no evidential basis for the Trial Chamber's finding that he knew about HVO

[5420] Trial Judgement, Vol. 2, para. 1243 & fns 3100-3101, referring to, *inter alia*, Exs. 2D00119, 2D00504, 2D00321, 2D00123, 2D00455, P02782 (confidential), Antoon van der Grinten, T. 21164 (11 July 2007). See *supra*, fns 5406-5407. See also Trial Judgement, Vol. 4, para. 372.
[5421] See Trial Judgement, Vol. 2, para. 1215.
[5422] Trial Judgement, Vol. 2, para. 1218. See Trial Judgement, Vol. 2, paras 1212-1215.
[5423] Trial Judgement, Vol. 4, paras 362-363.
[5424] Trial Judgement, Vol. 4, paras 362-363.
[5425] Trial Judgement, Vol. 2, para. 1202.
[5426] See Trial Judgement, Vol. 2, paras 1198-1200, 1244, 1255.
[5427] See Trial Judgement, Vol. 2, para. 1202, Vol. 4, paras 361-363, 372. See *infra*, paras 1670-1674.
[5428] See *infra*, paras 1670-1672.
[5429] Stojić's Appeal Brief, paras 320-323. Stojić also argues that the finding that he controlled all HVO snipers in West Mostar went beyond the allegations in the Indictment. See Stojić's Appeal Brief, heading before para. 322. See also Stojić's Appeal Brief, para. 331; Stojić's Reply Brief, para. 71.
[5430] Stojić's Appeal Brief, para. 323, referring to Antoon van der Grinten, T. 21050-21051 (10 July 2007). See also Appeal Hearing, AT. 359-360 (21 Mar 2017).
[5431] Stojić's Appeal Brief, para. 323, referring to Trial Judgement, Vol. 1, paras 565, 708, 796, Ex. P02806 (confidential), para. 5.

attacks on international organisations,[5432] and that: (1) Witness DZ, who was generally unreliable,[5433] was unsure whether he raised the issue of sniping attacks with Stojić or unable to specify whether he received a response from Stojić;[5434] and (2) the **[page 685]** HVO's investigation on the death of a SpaBat lieutenant, which found that the HVO was not responsible, was based on inaccurate information from that battalion.[5435] In addition, Stojić submits that the Trial Chamber's finding that he must have known that HVO snipers were targeting civilians and international organisations is unsustainable, as it is based on the impugned finding that he controlled all HVO snipers.[5436]

1663. The Prosecution responds that the Trial Chamber reasonably found that Stojić controlled all HVO snipers in West Mostar, and knew about HVO attacks on internationals and Muslim civilians in East Mostar.[5437] The Prosecution argues that all the HVO snipers shared the same *modus operandi* as the snipers Stojić admitted were under his control, and that he exercised command and "effective control" over the armed forces.[5438] It further contends that Witness van der Grinten's evidence shows that he considered HVO control over snipers to be synonymous, with Stojić's control, which is consistent with the evidence.[5439] As for the targeting of international organisations and civilians, it asserts that Witness DZ's evidence and the incorrect information Stojić received regarding the SpaBat lieutenant's death shows no error in the Trial Chamber's finding.[5440]

1664. Turning first to Stojić's argument regarding his control over all HVO snipers in West Mostar, the Appeals Chamber notes that the Trial Chamber arrived at its inference after considering: (1) the testimony of Witness van der Grinten that Stojić admitted to controlling the snipers in two locations, which was supported by documentary evidence;[5441] (2) that all the sniping in West Mostar had the same targets and followed the same *modus operandi*;[5442] and (3) that Stojić controlled most of the HVO.[5443] Having already dismissed Stojić's challenges regarding the Trial Chamber's finding that he commanded the HVO,[5444] the Appeals Chamber is not convinced that the alleged clarification made by Witness van der Grinten calls into question the Trial Chamber's conclusion.[5445] Stojić merely seeks to substitute his own interpretation of the evidence for that of **[page 686]** the Trial Chamber without demonstrating that its evaluation was erroneous.[5446] His argument is dismissed.[5447]

1665. With regard to Stojić's argument that there was no evidential basis for the Trial Chamber's conclusion that he knew about HVO attacks on international organisations, the Appeals Chamber recalls that its dismissal of Stojić's arguments on Witness DZ's general reliability.[5448] Furthermore, the Appeals Chamber observes that, in the portions of testimony highlighted by the parties, Witness DZ testified that he told Stojić

[5432] Stojić's Appeal Brief, paras 320-321.
[5433] Stojić's Appeal Brief, para. 321, referring to Stojić's Ground 32.
[5434] Stojić's Appeal Brief, para. 321, referring Witness DZ, T. 26486-26487, 26497-26498 (closed session) (22 Jan 2008), Ex. P10367 (confidential), para. 21.
[5435] Stojić's Appeal Brief, para. 321, referring to Trial Judgement, Vol. 4, paras 364, 369, Exs. 2D00116, 2D00117.
[5436] Stojić's Appeal Brief, para. 324.
[5437] Prosecution's Response Brief (Stojić), paras 280, 283. In reaching the findings on Stojić's knowledge on East Mostar crimes, the Prosecution submits that the Trial Chamber also relied on his knowledge of the HVO's East Mostar plan and consistent witness evidence. Prosecution's Response Brief (Stojić), para. 280, and evidence cited therein. See also Appeal Hearing, AT. 335 (21 Mar 2017).
[5438] Prosecution's Response Brief (Stojić), para. 283. See Prosecution's Response Brief (Stojić), para. 284.
[5439] Prosecution's Response Brief (Stojić), para. 284, referring to Antoon van der Grinten, T. 21051 (10 July 2007), Ex. P02806 (confidential), p. 2.
[5440] Prosecution's Response Brief (Stojić), paras 281-282.
[5441] Trial Judgement, Vol. 4, paras 365, 368.
[5442] Trial Judgement, Vol. 4, para. 368.
[5443] Trial Judgement, Vol. 4, para. 368.
[5444] See *supra*, para. 1457.
[5445] See Antoon van der Grinten, T. 21050-21051 (10 July 2007) (evidence that Stojić said that "he had all snipers under control", and the witness agreeing with a question from the Bench that the snipers were under HVO control).
[5446] See Stojić"s Appeal Brief, para. 323.
[5447] Regarding Stojić's argument that the Trial Chamber's finding that he controlled all the HVO snipers in West Mostar went beyond the allegations in the Indictment, the Appeals Chamber finds that as he fails to develop or provide support for this assertion, it is dismissed. See *supra*, fn. 5430.
[5448] See *supra*, paras 1641-1643.

about the shelling and sniping directed at international organisations,[5449] and he later stated that Stojić had "no particular response" and that the matter was left "in the air".[5450] The Appeals Chamber considers that Stojić fails to demonstrate that no reasonable trier of fact could have relied on this testimony in reaching its findings that he was informed about those crimes.[5451] Moreover, the Appeals Chamber notes that the Trial Chamber, in reaching this finding, also relied on other evidence to conclude that Stojić knew that international organisations were being targeted by the HVO.[5452] As for Stojić's argument that an HVO investigation found that the HVO was not responsible for a SpaBat lieutenant's death, the Appeals Chamber notes that the Trial Chamber relied on Stojić's control of the snipers in West Mostar and his statement that the snipers had not fired on the day the lieutenant died – not the findings of the HVO investigation or his involvement in it – to find that he knew that the snipers were targeting civilians and members of international organisations.[5453] Therefore, Stojić fails to show how the incorrect information provided by SpaBat, which was acknowledged by the Trial Chamber,[5454] has an impact on the relevant findings.

1666. The Appeals Chamber now turns to Stojić's argument that the Trial Chamber erred in finding that he must have known that HVO snipers were targeting civilians and international organisations, which he argues is unsustainable solely because the Trial Chamber erred in finding that he controlled all of the snipers in Mostar.[5455] However, the Appeals Chamber notes the finding that he knew about HVO attacks on international organisations and in particular Witness DZ's **[page 687]** evidence.[5456] Specifically regarding the targeting of civilians, the Trial Chamber inferred that Stojić "must have known" of this sniping as: (1) Stojić controlled all the snipers in West Mostar; (2) the actions of the snipers followed the same pattern; and (3) civilians were regularly targeted by snipers.[5457] Having dismissed his arguments against the finding that he controlled the snipers above,[5458] the Appeals Chamber also dismisses his challenge against the finding that he must have known that HVO snipers were targeting civilians and members of international organisations as Stojić provides no additional argumentation to support his challenge.[5459] In particular, Stojić has not shown that the Trial Chamber's conclusion was not the only reasonable inference available from the factors and evidence it considered.

1667. In sum, the Appeals Chamber finds that Stojić has failed to demonstrate that the Trial Chamber erred in finding that he controlled all the HVO snipers in West Mostar, and that he was aware that the HVO was targeting civilians and members of international organisations in East Mostar. Stojić's sub-grounds of appeal 34.2, 34.3, and 34.4 are dismissed.

(iii) Whether Stojić facilitated the hindering of humanitarian aid access (Stojić's Sub-ground 34.5)

a. Arguments of the Parties

1668. Stojić submits that: (1) no reasonable trier of fact could have found that he facilitated the hindering of humanitarian aid access to Mostar or that his contribution in this regard was significant;[5460] and (2) the Trial Chamber did not sufficiently explain its conclusion by failing to cite the evidence it relied on.[5461] Stojić contends that his power to grant access could not be established from Exhibit P03900, given that the

---

[5449] Witness DZ, T. 26486-26487 (closed session) (22 Jan 2008). See Trial Judgement, Vol. 2, para. 1266, referring to, *inter alia*, Ex. P10367 (confidential), para. 21.

[5450] Witness DZ, T. 26497-26498 (closed session) (22 Jan 2008).

[5451] Trial Judgement, Vol. 2, para. 1266, Vol. 4, paras 359, 362, 367, 369.

[5452] Trial Judgement, Vol. 4, paras 359, 362, 367, referring to, *inter alia*, Antoon van der Grinten T(F). 21046, 21076-21078 (10 July 2007), 21186-21187 (11 July 2007), Witness DW, T(F). 23087 (3 Oct 2007), Exs. P02806 (confidential), P03162 (confidential), p. 1, P03184 (confidential), p. 2, P10287 (confidential), para. 30. See *supra*, paras 1641-1643.

[5453] Trial Judgement, Vol. 4, paras 365, 369. See Trial Judgement, Vol. 4, para. 364.

[5454] Trial Judgement, Vol. 4, para. 364.

[5455] See *supra*, para. 1662.

[5456] See *supra*, para. 1665.

[5457] Trial Judgement, Vol. 4, paras 366, 369.

[5458] See *supra*, para. 1664.

[5459] See Stojić's Appeal Brief, para. 324; *supra*, para. 1662.

[5460] Stojić's Appeal Brief, para. 330.

[5461] Stojić's Appeal Brief, para. 326. See also Stojić's Appeal Brief, para. 331; Stojić's Reply Brief, para. 71.

document suggests that the HVO – and not Stojić personally – approved access, and that the Trial Chamber failed to consider that there is no evidence that Prlić raised the issue with him.[5462] Further, Stojić argues that the Trial Chamber disregarded clearly relevant evidence and submissions that matters concerning the access of humanitarian organisations were ordinarily addressed by Prlić, the ODPR, or the Main Staff.[5463] Stojić also asserts that the Trial Chamber erred in finding that international representatives refuted **[page 688]** security justifications for refusing access to Mostar as the only witness relied on, Witness Klaus Johann Nissen, agreed with the security justifications.[5464]

1669. The Prosecution responds that the Trial Chamber reasonably concluded that Stojić obstructed humanitarian aid delivery to East Mostar.[5465] The Prosecution contends that Exhibit P03900 indicates that Stojić had the authority to grant international organisations access to East Mostar,[5466] which is consistent with other evidence confirming Stojić's authority to regulate humanitarian aid delivery.[5467] It further submits that international observers rejected Stojić's security considerations justifying the blockade, and that Witness Nissen only agreed on the justification in diplomatic terms.[5468] The Prosecution also argues that the Trial Chamber did not ignore Stojić's submissions that others controlled the flow of humanitarian aid.[5469]

b. Analysis

1670. With regard to Stojić's argument that the Trial Chamber failed to cite evidence in support of its finding that he hindered the access of humanitarian aid to East Mostar, the Appeals Chamber notes that, in the paragraph in question, the Trial Chamber cited to its earlier findings in the Trial Judgement.[5470] These earlier findings, which are supported by ample evidence, include that: (1) the power and authority for the distribution of humanitarian aid were conferred on the Department of Defence, and that Stojić in particular had the authority to issue passes to local humanitarian organisations;[5471] (2) the Head of the Department of Defence could give orders to the Chief of the Military Police Administration on the freedom of movement of convoys (including humanitarian convoys);[5472] (3) Stojić had the legal authority to authorise the passage of humanitarian convoys, and did in fact issue orders allowing the passage of UNPROFOR convoys;[5473] (4) the decision whether to grant access to international organisations could be taken by Stojić, among others;[5474] **[page 689]** and (5) the HVO hindered the regular delivery of humanitarian aid to East Mostar between June and December 1993 through, *inter alia*, erecting administrative obstacles and completely blocking entry by humanitarian convoys for two months in the summer of 1993 and during December 1993.[5475] Stojić's argument that the Trial Chamber failed to cite supporting evidence thus fails.

[5462] Stojić's Appeal Brief, para. 327.

[5463] Stojić's Appeal Brief, para. 328, referring to Stojić's Final Brief, paras 447-459, Martin Raguž, T. 31353-31354 (26 Aug 2008), Exs. P03346 (confidential), P03895, P04027 (confidential), P04358, P05138, P09846 (confidential).

[5464] Stojić's Appeal Brief, para. 329, referring to Trial Judgement, Vol. 2, para. 1236, Klaus Johann Nissen, T. 20456-20457 (25 June 2007).

[5465] Prosecution's Response Brief (Stojić), para. 285.

[5466] Prosecution's Response Brief (Stojić), paras 286-288, referring to Trial Judgement, Vol. 2, para. 1231, Ex. P03900 (confidential).

[5467] Prosecution's Response Brief (Stojić), paras 286, 288, referring, *inter alia*, to Exs. P02291, P02419 (confidential), p. 1, Witness DV, T. 22903-22904 (1 Oct 2007), Trial Judgement, Vol. 4, paras 372, 753.

[5468] Prosecution's Response Brief (Stojić), para. 286, referring to, *inter alia*, Trial Judgement, Vol. 2, para. 1236, Vol. 4, para. 372, Ex. P03196, Klaus Johann Nissen, T. 20455-20457 (25 June 2007).

[5469] Prosecution's Response Brief (Stojić), para. 289.

[5470] Trial Judgement, Vol. 4, para. 372 & fn. 819.

[5471] Trial Judgement, Vol. 1, para. 554, referring to Exs. 1D01609, pp. 1-2, 2D00552, 2D00553, 2D00555, 2D00556, 2D00557, 2D00986.

[5472] Trial Judgement, Vol. 1, para. 862, Vol. 4, para. 314, referring to Exs. P01316, P00864. The Appeals Chamber also notes the Trial Chamber's findings that the Military Police was tasked with preventing unauthorised persons, including unauthorised convoys, from entering into areas where military operations were ongoing. Trial Judgement, Vol. 1, paras 928, 930-937.

[5473] Trial Judgement, Vol. 1, paras 562, 635, 795.

[5474] Trial Judgement, Vol. 2, para. 1231, referring to Ex. P03900 (confidential), p. 2.

[5475] Trial Judgement, Vol. 2, para. 1244. See also Trial Judgement, Vol. 2, paras 1227-1243, and evidence cited therein. The Appeals Chamber notes the Trial Chamber's finding that the sporadic aid that the HVO brought in, which was conditional on obtaining certain advantages, did not cast doubt on the finding that the HVO obstructed the delivery of humanitarian aid to East Mostar. Trial Judgement, Vol. 2, para. 1244.

1671. In challenging the Trial Chamber's reliance on Exhibit P03900, the Appeals Chamber observes that this exhibit supports the Trial Chamber's finding that Stojić had the power to grant access to East Mostar to the international organisations.[5476] In any event, Stojić ignores that the Trial Chamber also relied on other evidence to arrive at this finding.[5477] In particular, the Trial Chamber also relied on evidence that Stojić issued passes to members of humanitarian organisations granting them freedom of movement or transport on the territory of HZ H-B,[5478] and made findings that Stojić dispatched orders directly to the HVO on the freedom of movement of humanitarian or international organisations.[5479] The Appeals Chamber considers that Stojić fails to explain how the finding should not stand on the basis of this other evidence. His argument is dismissed.

1672. As for Stojić's argument that the Trial Chamber disregarded relevant submissions, the Appeals Chamber recalls that a trial chamber is "not under the obligation to justify its findings in relation to every submission made during the trial".[5480] Stojić fails to show that the Trial Chamber erred in explicitly referring to only a part of his trial submissions. The Appeals Chamber is also not persuaded by Stojić's argument that the Trial Chamber disregarded evidence that access of humanitarian organisations was ordinarily addressed by others, and notes that the Trial Chamber expressly considered most of the evidence Stojić refers to in finding that, *inter alios*, Prlić,[5481] the ODPR,[5482] and the Main Staff,[5483] could grant such access. The Appeals Chamber considers that the remainder of the evidence Stojić points to, which was not expressly considered, was substantively addressed by the Trial Chamber's findings noted above.[5484] Stojić's argument that the Trial **[page 690]** Chamber disregarded relevant evidence thus fails. Moreover, he fails to show how the involvement of others precludes his authority and ability to grant access. His arguments are dismissed.

1673. Turning to Stojić's argument challenging the finding that international representatives rejected the security issues he raised, the Appeals Chamber notes that the Trial Chamber relied on, *inter alia*, the testimony of Witness Nissen on the issue.[5485] Although the witness testified that Stojić's justification that the ECMM's security could not be guaranteed was correct "in diplomatic terms",[5486] the witness also testified that he tried to persuade Stojić to grant them access with an armoured vehicle with "no success".[5487] The Appeals Chamber finds no error in the Trial Chamber's evaluation that the international representatives rejected security issues raised by Stojić[5488] given that the witness viewed his attempt to negotiate access with Stojić as unsuccessful. Stojić merely seeks to offer his own interpretation of the evidence without showing an error. His argument is dismissed.

1674. Based on the foregoing, the Appeals Chamber finds that Stojić fails to demonstrate that the Trial Chamber erred in finding that he had the power to grant access to East Mostar to the international organisations, and did nothing to remove the obstacles hindering access of humanitarian aid, having, in fact, facilitated them. Stojić's sub-ground of appeal 34.5 is dismissed.

(iv) Conclusion

1675. In sum, Stojić's ground of appeal 34 is dismissed.

[5476] Ex. P03900 (confidential), p. 2. See Trial Judgement, Vol. 4, para. 372.
[5477] See *supra*, para. 1670.
[5478] Trial Judgement, Vol. 1, paras 554, 562, referring to, *inter alia*, Exs. 2D00552, 2D00553, 2D00555, 2D00556, 2D00557, 2D00986.
[5479] Trial Judgement, Vol. 1, para. 565, Vol. 4, para. 306.
[5480] *Kvočka et al.* Appeal Judgement, para. 23.
[5481] Trial Judgement, Vol. 2, para. 1437 & fn. 3595, Vol. 4, paras 116-118 & fn. 345. See Trial Judgement, Vol. 2, para. 1231, Vol. 4, paras 183, 185. *Cf.* Stojić's Appeal Brief, para. 328, referring to, *inter alia*, Exs. P04027 (confidential), P04358, P09846 (confidential).
[5482] Trial Judgement, Vol. 1, paras 635-636 & fn. 1504, Vol. 2, para. 1230. *Cf.* Stojić's Appeal Brief, para. 328.
[5483] Trial Judgement, Vol. 1, para. 752 & fn. 1758. See also Trial Judgement, Vol. 1, para. 936. *Cf.* Stojić's Appeal Brief, para. 328, referring to, *inter alia*, Ex. P03895.
[5484] See *supra*, fns 5482-5484.
[5485] Trial Judgement, Vol. 2, para. 1236, referring to, *inter alia*, Klaus Johann Nissen, T(F). 20453-20455, 20457 (25 June 2007), Ex. P03196 (confidential), p. 1.
[5486] Klaus Johann Nissen, T. 20456-20457 (25 June 2007).
[5487] Klaus Johann Nissen, T. 20456-20457 (25 June 2007).
[5488] Trial Judgement, Vol. 2, para. 1236.

(g) Čapljina Municipality (Stojić's Ground 35)

1676. The Trial Chamber found that, in July 1993, Stojić knew of and facilitated the detention of men who did not belong to any armed force in Čapljina.[5489] In reaching this conclusion it referred to Exhibit 4D00461 – an order from Stojić dated 3 July 1993 – through which he transferred the "management of the detention of the Muslim men of military age arrested in the Municipality of Čapljina from the 1st *Knez Domagoj* Brigade to the local HVO" ("Stojić's Order of 3 July 1993").[5490] The Trial Chamber also found that Stojić was informed about the allegations of evictions in Čapljina from at least 20 July 1993.[5491] In this respect, the Trial Chamber referred to Exhibit P03573, namely the minutes of the 47th session of Government held on 20 July 1993 **[page 691]** attended by Stojić ("Minutes of the 47th Government Session").[5492] The Trial Chamber found that it was noted during this Government session that a working group visit to Čapljina Municipality established that the media reports concerning alleged expulsions of Muslims from that municipality were not true.[5493] The Trial Chamber further found that the operations were carried out according to a preconceived plan and concluded that as Stojić had "effective control" over most of the HVO and the Military Police who carried out the Čapljina evictions and "since he himself contributed to planning the evictions following the same plan as in West Mostar, it [could] only find that he was also informed about the evictions in Čapljina and the manner in which they were carried out."[5494] It then concluded that the only inference it could reasonably draw was that Stojić also intended to have Muslim property destroyed.[5495]

1677. Stojić argues that the Trial Chamber made a number of errors which "take away the foundation for the finding that [he] significantly contributed to the commission of crimes in Čapljina and intended to have Muslim property destroyed."[5496] The Prosecution responds that Stojić's involvement in the Čapljina operations furthered the CCP.[5497]

(i) Whether Stojić was aware of and facilitated the detention of men who did not belong to any armed force (Stojić's Sub-ground 35.1)

a. Arguments of the Parties

1678. Stojić submits that the Trial Chamber erred by failing to properly assess the weight to be attached to Stojić's Order of 3 July 1993 – the only evidence cited as support for the finding that he knew of and facilitated the Čapljina detentions. According to Stojić, because he had challenged the authenticity of this order during trial, the Trial Chamber was obliged to provide a reasoned assessment of its weight, including its authenticity.[5498] Stojić contends that the Trial Chamber failed to do so and, instead: (1) relied on its earlier assessment that Stojić's Order of 3 July 1993 was sufficiently reliable for admission into evidence confusing the test for admissibility with weight;[5499] (2) considered only three Defence submissions relating to the reliability of the order and ignored the **[page 692]** remaining submissions;[5500] and (3) gave insufficient reasons for relying on Stojić's Order of 3 July 1993, such as noting the evidence of Witness CG – who could not assist on authenticity – and merely stating that the order was similar to other orders.[5501]

[5489] Trial Judgement, Vol. 4, para. 375.
[5490] Trial Judgement, Vol. 4, para. 373. See Trial Judgement, Vol. 2, para. 2081, fn. 5087.
[5491] Trial Judgement, Vol. 4, para. 378.
[5492] Trial Judgement, Vol. 4, para. 376.
[5493] Trial Judgement, Vol. 4, para. 376.
[5494] Trial Judgement, Vol. 4, para. 378. See Trial Judgement, Vol. 4, para. 377.
[5495] Trial Judgement, Vol. 4, para. 378.
[5496] Stojić's Appeal Brief, para. 345. See Stojić's Reply Brief, para. 71. Stojić therefore submits that the Appeals Chamber should overturn his convictions on Counts 1, 6-11, and 19-21. Stojić's Appeal Brief, para. 345.
[5497] Prosecution's Response Brief (Stojić), para. 291. The Prosecution responds that Stojić's assertion that his convictions on Counts 1, 6-11, and 19-21 should be vacated if an error is found is incorrect in law. Prosecution's Response Brief (Stojić), para. 302 & fn. 1262.
[5498] Stojić's Appeal Brief, para. 333.
[5499] Stojić's Appeal Brief, para. 334, referring to Trial Judgement, Vol. 2, para. 2081, fn. 5087.
[5500] Stojić's Appeal Brief, para. 335, referring to Trial Judgement, Vol. 2, para. 2081, fn. 5087, Stojić's Final Brief, paras 545-547.
[5501] Stojić's Appeal Brief, para. 336, referring to Trial Judgement, Vol. 2, para. 2081, fn. 5087, Witness CG, T. 10843-10844 (28 Nov 2006).

1679. Stojić also contends that the Trial Chamber failed to: (1) assess Stojić's Order of 3 July 1993 in light of the whole trial record which shows that the 1ˢᵗ Knez Domagoj Brigade continued to be in charge of the detainees contrary to Stojić's Order of 3 July 1993 and that there was no reason for him to issue this order since he was not a member of the working group concerned with these individuals nor was he in charge of the relevant detention centres;[5502] and (2) scrutinise Stojić's Order of 3 July 1993 "with particular vigour" given that it was the only document relied upon to establish that he facilitated the detention of civilians in Čapljina.[5503] In addition, Stojić claims that even if authentic, Stojić's Order of 3 July 1993 was not followed and therefore had no causal effect on the detentions.[5504]

1680. The Prosecution responds that the Trial Chamber provided a reasoned assessment for relying on Stojić's Order of 3 July 1993 and did not disregard Stojić's trial arguments.[5505] It also contends that: (1) the Trial Chamber reasonably observed that Witness CG confirmed the Čapljina detentions; (2) it is immaterial that the Trial Chamber did not receive any evidence of the implementation of Stojić's Order of 3 July 1993; and (3) the Trial Chamber reasonably relied on the order's form and appearance when finding it similar to Stojić's other orders.[5506] Further, according to the Prosecution, there is no need to show a causal connection between Stojić's Order of 3 July 1993 and the unlawful detentions as JCE liability requires a significant contribution to the common criminal purpose rather than to specific crimes.[5507] The Prosecution claims that, in any event, Stojić's Order of 3 July 1993 Order is not the only evidence demonstrating Stojić's knowledge of and role in the detention of Muslim males in Čapljina.[5508] The Prosecution also responds that Stojić ignores the Trial Chamber's findings on his authority over the relevant detention centres and argues that it is irrelevant that Stojić was not a member of the working group that assessed conditions within those centres.[5509]
[page 693]

b. Analysis

1681. Addressing Stojić's submissions regarding the Trial Chamber's assessment of Stojić's Order of 3 July 1993 first, the Appeals Chamber recalls at the outset that a trial chamber has a broad discretion when deciding the weight to be accorded to an exhibit.[5510] In any event, the Appeals Chamber is satisfied that the Trial Chamber did in fact provide a reasoned assessment of the reliability and weight of Stojić's Order of 3 July 1993. Contrary to Stojić's submission, the Trial Chamber did not ignore his arguments in relation to the authenticity of the order, as evidenced by the fact that it cited all the relevant challenges he had made in his Final Brief.[5511] While the Trial Chamber then chose to outline three of those challenges in the Trial Judgement,[5512] the Appeals Chamber considers that Stojić's remaining challenges on the matter were closely related to and, in fact, subsumed within those three, such that there was no need to explicitly discuss them as well.[5513] Stojić fails to demonstrate that the Trial Chamber erred.

1682. Further, in its analysis of the *authenticity* of Stojić's Order of 3 July 1993 the Trial Chamber recalled its earlier finding that it "offered indicia of reliability, relevance and probative value *sufficient for admission into evidence.*"[5514] Thus, contrary to Stojić's argument, it is clear that the Trial Chamber was mindful of the fact that its earlier assessment was made for the purpose of admitting Stojić's Order of 3 July 1993 into evidence. Stojić fails to show how the Trial Chamber confused the test for the admissibility of evidence with

---

[5502]   Stojić's Appeal Brief, para. 337, referring to, *inter alia,* Exs. P03197, P03216, P03442, P03573, P05133.
[5503]   Stojić's Appeal Brief, para. 338.
[5504]   Stojić's Appeal Brief, para. 339.
[5505]   Prosecution's Response Brief (Stojić), para. 292.
[5506]   Prosecution's Response Brief (Stojić), paras 293-294.
[5507]   Prosecution's Response Brief (Stojić), para. 295.
[5508]   Prosecution's Response Brief (Stojić), para. 295, referring to, *inter alia,* Trial Judgement, Vol. 4, para. 154.
[5509]   Prosecution's Response Brief (Stojić), paras 296-297.
[5510]   See *Stanišić and Župljanin* Appeal Judgement, para. 470; *Popović et al.* Appeal Judgement, para. 131 (the Trial Chamber has "broad discretion in assessing the appropriate weight and credibility to be accorded to the testimony of a witness"); *Kvočka et al.* Appeal Judgement, para. 23.
[5511]   Trial Judgement, Vol. 2, fn. 5087, referring to Stojić's Final Brief, paras 544-547.
[5512]   Trial Judgement, Vol. 2, fn. 5087.
[5513]   See *Kvočka et al.* Appeal Judgement, para. 23 ("the Trial Chamber is not under the obligation to justify its findings in relation to every submission made during the trial").
[5514]   Trial Judgement, Vol. 2, fn. 5087 (emphasis added).

the weight to be accorded to that evidence once admitted. Similarly, it is also clear from the way in which the Trial Chamber's analysis is structured that this was merely one of the factors listed in support of the conclusion that Stojić's Order of 3 July 1993 was authentic and reliable.[5515]

1683. With respect to Stojić's claim that the Trial Chamber gave insufficient reasons for relying on Stojić's Order of 3 July 1993, the Appeals Chamber notes that Witness CG partially confirmed the content of the order, namely that the Muslim men referred to therein were indeed detained in Čapljina.[5516] Thus, the Appeals Chamber considers that it was not unreasonable for the Trial Chamber to use this evidence to infer the authenticity of Stojić's Order of 3 July 1993, particularly **[page 694]** as it was coupled with other factors.[5517] Indeed, the Trial Chamber also noted that Stojić's Order of 3 July 1993 was similar to other orders signed by Stojić and admitted into evidence during the trial.[5518] While the Trial Chamber did not at that point provide a list of such orders, only several pages earlier the Trial Chamber discussed Stojić's ability to issue orders to the HVO, including with respect to detention centres, and listed a number of his orders in support, one of which concerned Čapljina and was similar to Stojić's Order of 3 July 1993 in form and appearance.[5519] Thus, Stojić fails to show an error by the Trial Chamber on these issues.

1684. Additionally, the Trial Chamber's reference to similar orders also indicates that it considered Stojić's Order of 3 July 1993 in light of all the evidence in the case, contrary to Stojić's submission. The fact that Stojić was not a member of the working group concerned with conditions of detention in Čapljina or that he may not have been in charge of the relevant Čapljina detention centres, namely Dretelj Prison and Gabela Prison, does not in any way affect the Trial Chamber's findings that he was able to issue orders such as Stojić's Order of 3 July 1993, particularly bearing in mind his position and his authority over the HVO and the Military Police.[5520] Furthermore, Stojić ignores the Trial Chamber's explicit findings demonstrating that Dretelj Prison and Gabela Prison "fell within [his] responsibility" and that he was able to issue orders relevant to the Muslim men detained there.[5521] Finally, the fact that the Trial Chamber noted that it had no evidence that Stojić's Order of 3 July 1993 was ever complied with[5522] also does not call into question its authenticity or the reasoning behind the issuance of such an order. Based on the above, the Appeals Chamber dismisses Stojić's arguments concerning the authenticity of Stojić's Order of 3 July 1993 and the Trial Chamber's assessment of its weight.[5523]

1685. Turning to the Trial Chamber's use of Stojić's Order of 3 July 1993, the Appeals Chamber notes that, contrary to his submission, the Trial Chamber's finding that Stojić knew of and facilitated the detention of Muslim men who did not belong to any armed force in Čapljina was not based solely on Stojić's Order of 3 July 1993. In this regard, the Trial Chamber also recalled its earlier findings that the arrests of Muslim men in Čapljina were undertaken between 30 June 1993 **[page 695]** and mid-July 1993 by the 1st Knez Domagoj Brigade, the 3rd Company of the 3rd Military Police Battalion, the Čapljina MUP, and members of the HVO.[5524] As noted earlier, Stojić was found to have exercised "effective control" over the HVO and the Military Police[5525] as well as a reporting function vis-a-vis the Government, regarding military matters.[5526]

[5515]   The other factors considered by the Trial Chamber were: (1) its rejection of the admission into evidence of Exhibit 2D0388, tendered by Stojić to call into question Stojić's Order of 3 July 1993; (2) Witness CG's testimony when shown Stojić's Order of 3 July 1993; and (3) the fact that Stojić's Order of 3 July 1993 was similar to other orders Stojić had issued. See Trial Judgement, Vol. 2, fn. 5087.

[5516]   Witness CG, T. 10843-10844 (28 Nov 2006).

[5517]   See Trial Judgement, Vol. 2, fn. 5087.

[5518]   Trial Judgement, Vol. 2, fn. 5087: See also *supra*, fn. 5516.

[5519]   Trial Judgement, Vol. 4, paras 304-306, 312, fn. 725 (referring to, *inter alia*, Ex. P05232). See *supra*, para. 1429. See also Trial Judgement, Vol. 1, paras 562-565. Additionally, the Prosecution cited a number of orders similar in appearance, namely Exhibits 2D00985, P03146, P03163, which were also relied on by the Trial Chamber. See Prosecution's Response Brief (Stojić), para. 294 & fn. 1227; Trial Judgement, Vol. 1, paras 795, 965, fn. 1383.

[5520]   See Trial Judgement, Vol. 4, paras 397-407. In relation to Stojić's challenges regarding the Trial Chamber's findings on his authority over Dretelj Prison and Gabela Prison, see *infra*, paras 1736-1748.

[5521]   Trial Judgement, Vol. 4, paras 399, 406-407. See Trial Judgement, Vol. 4, paras 306, 312, 320.

[5522]   Trial Judgement, Vol. 2, para. 2081.

[5523]   Accordingly, Stojić's argument that the Trial Chamber was obliged to scrutinise Stojić's Order of 3 July 1993 with "particular vigour" is therefore dismissed as moot.

[5524]   Trial Judgement, Vol. 4, paras 373-374.

[5525]   See *supra*, paras 1405, 1457-1458, 1479-1480, 1485-1491.

[5526]   See *supra*, paras 1418-1419, 1476, 1572.

The Trial Chamber then referred to the fact that Stojić continued to exercise his functions "in the HVO/ Government of the HR H-B" and thus inferred that he accepted the detention of Muslim men who did not belong to any armed force.[5527] Further, the Trial Chamber was cognisant of the 30 June 1993 Joint Proclamation in which Stojić and Prlić called on all Croats in BiH to take up arms against the Muslims and which, the Trial Chamber found, was the catalyst for the arrests of Muslim men in Čapljina and other municipalities.[5528] The Trial Chamber also considered that "the military authorities could not have made arrests without the approval of the civilian authorities".[5529]

1686. The Appeals Chamber acknowledges that the Trial Chamber did not explicitly refer to the 30 June 1993 Joint Proclamation in the part of the Trial Judgement dealing with Stojić's responsibility for the arrests in Čapljina,[5530] or in the factual narrative outlining those arrests.[5531] However, the Trial Chamber noted the proclamation in the section dealing with Stojić's control over the HVO, only several pages prior to embarking on the discussion of his responsibility regarding the events in Čapljina.[5532] Further, the Trial Chamber discussed the 30 June 1993 Joint Proclamation in various other parts of the Trial Judgement including in the sections concerning: (1) the factual narrative surrounding the Attack on the HVO Tihomir Mišić Barracks on 30 June 1993;[5533] (2) Prlić's responsibility, since Prlić was a co-signatory of the proclamation;[5534] and (3) Ćorić›s responsibility because, on 1 July 1993, Radoslav Lavrić, on behalf of Ćorić, issued an order invoking the 30 June 1993 Joint Proclamation and demanding the arrest of "all conscripts who had not 'regulated their status'".[5535] Accordingly, the Appeals Chamber is satisfied that, when discussing Stojić's responsibility, the Trial Chamber was fully cognisant of the existence of the 30 June 1993 Joint Proclamation and its significance as a catalyst for the arrests of Muslim men in Čapljina. In addition, as it will become clear from the analysis below,[5536] the Trial Chamber was **[page 696]** also aware of Stojić's authority and position within the Government, insofar as it concerned detention of Muslim men in the detention centres in Čapljina.

1687. With respect to Stojić's claim that the Trial Chamber erred in law when concluding that he facilitated or significantly contributed to the commission of crimes because Stojić's Order of 3 July 1993 was not followed, the Appeals Chamber notes that this argument is premised on the view that the order was the only evidence relied upon by the Trial Chamber. However, as explained in the preceding paragraphs,[5537] this was not the case. The Appeals Chamber notes that, even if Stojić's Order of 3 July 1993 was ultimately not implemented,[5538] the Trial Chamber, in the section dealing with Prlić's responsibility, referred to the 30 June 1993 Joint Proclamation, noted that it was followed up by Lavrić's order of 1 July 1993, and then found that following the 30 June 1993 Joint Proclamation, "the chain of command was set in motion in order to arrest Muslims" in the municipalities of Mostar, Stolac, Čapljina, and Prozor.[5539] The Appeals Chamber therefore considers that a reasonable trier of fact could have concluded that Stojić both facilitated and knew of the arrests in Čapljina. In other words, this finding by the Trial Chamber is not affected by its statement that it received no evidence of the implementation of Stojić's Order of 3 July 1993 on the ground.

1688. Based on the foregoing, the Appeals Chamber considers that Stojić has failed to show that no reasonable trier of fact could have relied on Stojić's Order of 3 July 1993 or concluded that he knew of and facilitated the detention of Muslim men who did not belong to any armed forces in Čapljina. Stojić›s sub-ground of appeal 35.1 is therefore dismissed.

[5527]   Trial Judgement, Vol. 4, para. 375.
[5528]   Trial Judgement, Vol. 4, paras 151-154, 305. See Trial Judgement, Vol. 4, paras 953, 973, 984, 996, 1220. See also *supra*, para. 1422.
[5529]   Trial Judgement, Vol. 4, para. 154.
[5530]   See Trial Judgement, Vol. 4, paras 373-378.
[5531]   See Trial Judgement, Vol. 2, paras 2078-2083.
[5532]   Trial Judgement, Vol. 4, para. 305.
[5533]   See Trial Judgement, Vol. 2, para. 884.
[5534]   See Trial Judgement, Vol. 4, para. 151.
[5535]   See Trial Judgement, Vol. 4, para. 953; Ex. P03077.
[5536]   See *infra*, para. 1692.
[5537]   See *supra*, paras 1685-1686.
[5538]   Rather than concluding that Exhibit 4D00461 was not followed, the Trial Chamber noted that it received no evidence that the local HVO took responsibility for the detention of the Muslim men. Trial Judgement, Vol. 2, para. 2081. See *supra*, paras 1434, 1486.
[5539]   Trial Judgement, Vol. 4, paras 151-154. See also *supra*, para. 1422.

(ii) Whether Stojić was informed of evictions in Čapljina and the manner in which they were carried out (Stojić's Sub-grounds 35.2 and 35.3)

1689. Stojić argues that no reasonable chamber could have concluded that he was informed of the Čapljina evictions on the basis of the Minutes of the 47th Government Session, given that it was reported during that session that the allegations of expulsions were not true.[5540] Stojić further argues that the finding relating to his contribution to the planning of the evictions is ambiguous because it is unclear whether he planned the evictions in Čapljina which followed the same plan as those in West Mostar or whether he was informed of evictions in Čapljina because he had planned similar **[page 697]** evictions in West Mostar.[5541] According to Stojić, neither interpretation withstands scrutiny because: (1) there is no evidence that he planned the evictions in Čapljina, particularly since the Trial Chamber later stated that he only found out about the evictions after they had taken place;[5542] and (2) no reasonable trial chamber could have found that the only reasonable inference from an earlier finding that he planned the evictions in West Mostar was that he was also informed about the operations in Čapljina.[5543]

1690. The Prosecution responds that the Trial Chamber reasonably relied on the Minutes of the 47th Government Session since Stojić would have known, in light of: (1) his role in the planning of expulsions in Čapljina and other municipalities; (2) his authority over the perpetrators; and (3) his knowledge of HVO crimes across the BiH, that the allegations discussed in the session were well-founded.[5544] The Prosecution also responds that the finding that Stojić planned the evictions in Čapljina Municipality is neither ambiguous nor unreasonable when his role in the indiscriminate arrests of Muslim males, particularly those in West Mostar, is considered.[5545] The Prosecution further contends that the Trial Chamber's finding – made in the context of JCE III liability – that Stojić learned of the Čapljina evictions after they had taken place is not inconsistent with his role in planning them.[5546]

1691. The Appeals Chamber notes that the Trial Chamber's conclusion relating to Stojić's responsibility for the evictions in Čapljina was based on four different but related findings, namely that: (1) Stojić was informed about the allegations of evictions from at least 20 July 1993 as shown by the Minutes of the 47th Government Session;[5547] (2) the nature of evictions in Čapljina carried out by the HVO, which was in line with the *modus operandi* employed in other municipalities, demonstrated that it followed a preconceived plan to evict Muslims;[5548] (3) Stojić had "effective control" over most of the HVO and the Military Police;[5549] and (4) Stojić had, in fact, personally contributed to planning the evictions.[5550] **[page 698]**

1692. With respect to Stojić's argument that no reasonable trier of fact could have relied on the Minutes of the 47th Government Session to establish that he was informed about the evictions, the Appeals Chamber notes that the Trial Chamber found that Stojić knew of the *allegations* of such evictions from that exhibit, not of the evictions themselves.[5551] In reaching this conclusion, the Trial Chamber was fully aware that the working group reported to Stojić and others that these allegations were not true, but this did not affect its finding that he was aware of the allegations.[5552] In that respect, the Minutes of the 47th Government Session show that the working group did not deny that expulsions were taking place in Čapljina at the time, but rather

---

[5540]   Stojić's Appeal Brief, para. 344. See Stojić's Appeal Brief, para. 343.
[5541]   Stojić's Appeal Brief, para. 341. See Stojić's Appeal Brief, para. 340, referring to Trial Judgement, Vol. 4, para. 378.
[5542]   Stojić's Appeal Brief, para. 342, referring to Trial Judgement, Vol. 4, para. 448.
[5543]   Stojić's Appeal Brief, para. 342. See also Stojić's Reply Brief, para. 70. Stojić asserts that planning one specific operation cannot support a finding that an individual was informed of an entirely separate operation. Stojić's Appeal Brief, para. 342.
[5544]   Prosecution's Response Brief (Stojić), para. 301.
[5545]   Prosecution's Response Brief (Stojić), paras 298-299. The Prosecution submits that findings concerning the arrest and eviction operations demonstrate that the arrests of Muslim men occurred in conjunction with evictions of Muslim women, children, and the elderly, and that Stojić's involvement in planning and supporting the former provided a reasonable basis from which to infer that he also planned the latter. Prosecution's Response Brief (Stojić), para. 298.
[5546]   Prosecution's Response Brief (Stojić), para. 300.
[5547]   Trial Judgement, Vol. 4, paras 376, 378.
[5548]   Trial Judgement, Vol. 4, paras 377-378.
[5549]   Trial Judgement, Vol. 4, para. 378.
[5550]   Trial Judgement, Vol. 4, para. 378.
[5551]   Trial Judgement, Vol. 4, para. 378. See Trial Judgement, Vol. 4, para. 376.
[5552]   Trial Judgement, Vol. 4, para. 376.

denied that *all* Čapljina Muslims had been expelled.[5553] The minutes also show that following the debate on the working group's report, including the information that at least 2000 Muslims were accommodated in various locations in Čapljina, Stojić and others agreed to: (1) support the opening of a "transit centre" in Ljubuški for those who "want to leave the war affected areas and depart to third countries"; and (2) assign certain individuals, including Prlić himself, to "explore possibilities" of accommodating a number of "detained individuals" away from Čapljina in order to "create conditions in Čapljina in compliance with international standards".[5554]

1693. Before making its ultimate finding that Stojić was in fact aware of the expulsions, the Trial Chamber, as mentioned above, referred also to Stojić's authority over most of the HVO and the Military Police, as well as the fact that the HVO conducted the campaign of evictions in Čapljina based on a preconceived plan.[5555] Further, the Trial Chamber made multiple findings on Stojić's involvement in planning the expulsions in West Mostar and other municipalities[5556] and on his knowledge that the HVO conducted evictions across the BiH.[5557] The Appeals Chamber therefore considers that the Trial Chamber reasonably relied on the Minutes of the 47th Government Session to conclude that Stojić knew of the allegations of expulsions – and that this knowledge was one of several factors it used to infer that he was in fact informed about the evictions in Čapljina. Thus, Stojić does not demonstrate an error by the Trial Chamber in its reliance on the Minutes of the 47th Government Session. **[page 699]**

1694. In relation to Stojić's argument that the Trial Chamber's finding that since he "contributed to planning the evictions following the same plan as in West Mostar, it can only find that he was also informed about the evictions in Čapljina» is ambiguous, the Appeals Chamber acknowledges that it is not immediately clear from the Trial Chamber's language whether it was referring to the planning of Čapljina evictions specifically.[5558] However, this is ultimately irrelevant as the Appeals Chamber considers that it was not unreasonable of the Trial Chamber to rely on Stojić's involvement in planning the evictions in West Mostar, as one of several factors going to the finding that he was informed of the Čapljina evictions, particularly as the operations followed "the same plan" and began within a month of each other.[5559] Whether an inference that the planning of one specific operation by an individual can support a finding that the individual was informed of a different operation can be made will ultimately depend on the context, including the similarities between the operations, as well as the position of the individual in question. In this particular case, the Trial Chamber found that the operations were similar and that Stojić had "effective control" over most of the HVO and over the Military Police who carried out both operations.[5560]

1695. Moreover, as stated above, the similarities between the eviction campaigns in West Mostar and Čapljina was just one of the factors that the Trial Chamber considered in reaching the conclusion that Stojić was informed about evictions in Čapljina – the other factors being: (1) the Minutes of the 47th Government Session; (2) the fact that the evictions conducted by the HVO followed a preconceived plan; and (3) the findings relating to Stojić's "effective control" over most of the HVO and Military Police. The Appeals Chamber thus finds that Stojić fails to demonstrate that no reasonable trier of fact could have concluded that the only reasonable inference was that he was informed of the Čapljina evictions after considering the combination of these factors.[5561]

[5553] Ex. P03573, pp. 1-2 ("Work[ing] group has ascertained that the reports in some media concerning the alleged expulsion of all Muslims from Čapljina Municipality were not true. Namely it was established that Čapljina Student Centre and holiday homes in Počitefj polje, Ševać polje, Bivolje brdo and Višići accommodate more than two thousand Muslims mainly [from] Eastern Herzegovina.").

[5554] Ex. P03573, p. 2.

[5555] Trial Judgement, Vol. 4, para. 378.

[5556] See, *e.g.*, Trial Judgement, Vol. 4, paras 335-337, 347-349, 355. See also Trial Judgement, Vol. 4, para. 1220.

[5557] See, *e.g.*, Trial Judgement, Vol. 4, paras 331-335, 350-352, 355, 357, 416-417. See also *supra*, paras 1561, 1575, 1580, 1617, 1653.

[5558] The Appeals Chamber notes that the Trial Chamber's analysis relating to Stojić's responsibility for theft under JCE III suggests that it did not find that Stojić planned the Čapljina evictions *per se* but rather that he was merely informed of them from at least 20 July 1993. Trial Judgement, Vol. 4, para. 448 (Stojić "learned of the operations to evict Muslims from the Municipality of Čapljina on 20 July 1993, that is, after they had taken place").

[5559] See Trial Judgement, Vol. 4, paras 355-357, 377-378.

[5560] See Trial Judgement, Vol. 4, para. 378.

[5561] See Trial Judgement, Vol. 4, paras 423, 426-427.

1696. Accordingly, the Appeals Chamber considers that Stojić has failed to show that no reasonable trier of fact could have concluded that he knew of the evictions in Čapljina, and the manner in which they were carried out. Based on the foregoing, the Appeals Chamber dismisses Stojić's sub-grounds of appeal 35.2 and 35.3. **[page 700]**

(iii) Conclusion

1697. In sum, the Appeals Chamber dismisses Stojić's ground of appeal 35.[5562]

(h) Vareš Municipality (Stojić's Ground 36)

1698. The Trial Chamber found that the HVO military operations in Vareš Municipality beginning in October 1993 resulted in the commission of crimes.[5563] Specifically, these operations included: (1) the arrests, detention, and mistreatment of Muslim civilians and ABiH members in the town of Vareš between 23 October 1993 and 3-4 November 1993;[5564] and (2) the attack on the village of Stupni Do on 23 October 1993 which resulted in deaths and destruction of property.[5565] The Trial Chamber found that: (1) "in view of the fact" that the Government officials Boban and Prlić, and "those in charge of the Main Staff Petković and Praljak knew about the murders and destruction committed by Rajić's troopsin Stupni Do; (2) that Stojić was the Government member in charge of the HVO, facilitated the HVO military operations in Vareš in October 1993 and considered them to be carried out satisfactorily, the only reasonable inference it could draw was that Stojić was also informed about the deaths of Muslims, both members of the ABiH and non-members, and the destruction of their property as of 4 November 1993.[5566] It also found that, by continuing to exercise his functions while knowing of the crimes and by obtaining a promotion for Ivica Rajić, Stojić accepted the murders and destruction of property.[5567]

(i) Stojić's facilitation of the military operations in Vareš (Stojić's Sub-ground 36.2)

1699. Stojić argues that the Trial Chamber erroneously concluded that he facilitated the military operations in Vareš based on communications between Rajić and himself.[5568] Stojić submits that the Trial Chamber misunderstood these communications[5569] and that it "cannot be assumed" that his contact with Rajić on 30 October 1993 was in response to Rajić's request on 29 October 1993.[5570] Stojić argues that these communications cannot be reasonably linked to the Vareš crimes as: **[page 701]** (1) they concern the movement of HVO troops along the Berkovići-Konjic route which was unrelated to Vareš since HVO convoys needed this route in order to reach an HVO enclave near Konjic;[5571] (2) the attack on Stupni Do ended on 26 October 1993, the communications post-date the operations;[5572] and (3) the usual military chain of command – which did not include him – functioned during the operations, and that the relevant orders passed through the Main Staff to Rajić and the HVO.[5573]

[5562] Accordingly, Stojić's assertion that his convictions on Counts 1, 6-11, and 19-21 should be vacated is also dismissed.

[5563] Trial Judgement, Vol. 4, para. 61. See Trial Judgement, Vol. 3, paras 303-508.

[5564] Trial Judgement, Vol. 3, paras 339-340, 342-348, 352-399. The Trial Chamber also found that thefts and sexual abuse occurred during the operations in Vareš town. Trial Judgement, Vol. 3, paras 401-404.

[5565] Trial Judgement, Vol. 3, paras 417, 421-422, 464, 466-467. The Trial Chamber also found that thefts and sexual abuse occurred during the operations in Stupni Do. Trial Judgement, Vol. 3, paras 429, 465, 467.

[5566] Trial Judgement, Vol. 4, para. 383. See Trial Judgement, Vol. 4, paras 380-382. See *supra*, para. 820.

[5567] Trial Judgement, Vol. 4, para. 383. See Trial Judgement, Vol. 4, paras 380-382.

[5568] Stojić's Appeal Brief, paras 349, 353. See Stojić's Appeal Brief, para. 355.

[5569] Stojić's Appeal Brief, para. 349. Stojić asserts that, on 29 October 1993, Rajić asked him to establish contact with "Kovačević" in relation to the movement of men to and from Vareš, and then on 30 October 1993, he contacted Rajić with instructions regarding the movement of a convoy "along the Berkovići-Nevesinje-Borci-Konjic route". Stojić's Appeal Brief, para. 349, referring to Exs. P06219, P06267.

[5570] Stojić's Appeal Brief, para. 349. Stojić asserts that in the later communication he asked Rajić to issue an approval to be sent to "Kovačević", while Rajić's request was that he contact "Kovačević". Stojić's Appeal Brief, para. 349.

[5571] Stojić's Appeal Brief, para. 350, referring to Exs. P07622 (confidential), para. 1.1, P09276, Dragan Jurić, T. 39331-39332 (27 Apr 2009). Stojić contends that Vareš is 100km away from Konjic. Stojić's Appeal Brief, para. 350, referring to Ex. P09276.

[5572] Stojić's Appeal Brief, para. 351.

[5573] Stojić's Appeal Brief, para. 352, referring to Trial Judgement, Vol. 3, paras 313-330. Stojić asserts that none of the relevant orders on the Vareš operations mentioned him. Stojić's Appeal Brief, para. 352.

1700. The Prosecution responds that the Trial Chamber reasonably relied on Stojić's communications with Rajić to find that Stojić facilitated the military operations in Vareš.[5574]

1701. In assessing the evidence, the Trial Chamber considered that: (1) on 29 October 1993, Rajić informed Stojić, Praljak, and Petković that the VRS were not allowing his troops through to Vareš, contrary to an agreement;[5575] (2) on the following day, Stojić informed Rajić that an agreement had been reached with the VRS for the passage of an HVO convoy along the Berkovići-Nevesinje-Borci-Konjic route and ordered him to send relevant documents to "Minister Kovačević";[5576] and (3) on 31 October 1993, Rajić confirmed with Stojić that the VRS was implementing the original agreement.[5577] The Trial Chamber concluded that these communications showed that Stojić facilitated the military operations in Vareš in October 1993.[5578] Having considered the evidence cited by Stojić, which is the same evidence relied on by the Trial Chamber,[5579] the Appeals Chamber is not convinced that the Trial Chamber "misunderstood" these communications. In this regard: (1) Exhibit P06219, a communication from Rajić to Stojić and others dated 29 October 1993, states that the "XY" side was not implementing an agreement, and that it was "necessary to urgently establish contact between Mr. STOJIĆ and Mr. KOVAČEVIĆ in order to get this going so that assistance can be provided to Vareš";[5580] (2) Exhibit P06267, a communication from Stojić to Rajić dated 30 October 1993, states that pursuant to agreements reached, Rajić was to send an approval for the passage of convoys to Minister Kovačević;[5581] and (3) Exhibit P06307, a communication from Rajić to Stojić dated 31 October 1993, states that "the realisation of the **[page 702]** agreement between General PETKOVIĆ and General MILOVANOVIĆ is under way".[5582] Thus, the Appeals Chamber considers that this evidence is consistent with the Trial Chamber's underlying findings noted above[5583] and reasonably supports the conclusion that Stojić facilitated the Vareš military operations in October 1993. Further, Stojić merely argues that it "cannot be assumed" that the communications relate to each other and thus only offers his own interpretation of the evidence without showing an error. His argument on the Trial Chamber's interpretation of the evidence is dismissed.

1702. Regarding Stojić's argument contesting the link between the communications and the crimes committed during the Vareš military operations, the Appeals Chamber first dismisses his contention that the communications post-date the attack on Stupni Do.[5584] On this issue, the Appeals Chamber considers that the Trial Chamber's conclusion that Stojić facilitated the Vareš military operations, during which the crimes were committed, was not limited to the attack on Stupni Do but extended to events in Vareš Municipality, and more specifically, the operations in Vareš town.[5585] The Appeals Chamber recalls that operations in the town of Vareš began on 23 October 1993 and ended around 3 or 4 November 1993.[5586] Concerning Stojić's place in the military chain of command, the Appeals Chamber recalls that he was correctly found to have had *de facto* powers over most of the HVO and the Military Police.[5587] Moreover, even if none of the orders leading up to, or in the beginning of, the Vareš operations mentioned Stojić or were sent to him,[5588] the Appeals Chamber is satisfied that this does not impact on the Trial Chamber's finding that Stojić *facilitated* those operations, particularly as the Trial Chamber did not find that he planned or directed the operations.[5589]

[5574] Prosecution's Response Brief (Stojić), para. 306. The Prosecution asserts that the operations in Vareš were ongoing when Stojić facilitated the movement of Rajić's troops, and that the HVO withdrew from Vareš Municipality around 3 November 1993. Prosecution's Response Brief (Stojić), para. 307.

[5575] Trial Judgement, Vol. 4, para. 380, referring to Ex. P06219.

[5576] Trial Judgement, Vol. 4, para. 380, referring to Ex. P06267.

[5577] Trial Judgement, Vol. 4, para. 380, referring to Ex. P06307.

[5578] Trial Judgement, Vol. 4, para. 380. See *supra*, para. 820.

[5579] Compare Stojić's Appeal Brief, para. 349 with Trial Judgement, Vol. 4, para. 380 & fns 830-832.

[5580] Ex. P06219, p. 2.

[5581] Ex. P06267.

[5582] Ex. P06307.

[5583] See *supra*, para. 1701.

[5584] The Appeals Chamber notes that, contrary to Stojić's assertion, the attack on Stupni Do only occurred on 23 October 1993. Trial Judgement, Vol. 3, paras 417-422, 465-466.

[5585] See Trial Judgement, Vol. 4, para. 380. See also *supra*, para. 820.

[5586] Trial Judgement, Vol. 3, paras 339-340, 342-348, 352-399.

[5587] See *supra*, paras 1457, 1479, 1491.

[5588] The Appeals Chamber notes that Stojić only refers to paragraphs 313 to 330 of Volume 3 of the Trial Judgement which addresses the events between 22 and 26 October 1993 and not specifically the attack on Vareš town and Stupni Do. See Stojić's Appeal Brief, para. 352.

[5589] See Trial Judgement, Vol. 4, paras 380-381, 383.

Stojić also argues that the movement of troops addressed by the communications was unrelated to events in Vareš. However, the evidence he cites does not call into question the Trial Chamber's assessment of this issue.[5590] Notably, in Exhibit P06219, the communication dated 29 October 1993, Rajić stated that because the VRS was not implementing the agreement "for two days now they have not been allowing me to transfer my men to Vareš and to bring back the ones who have already been there for seven days" and that Stojić was to urgently **[page 703]** contact Kovačević "in order to get this going so that assistance can be provided to Vareš".[5591] Thus, Stojić fails to show that the movement of troops referenced in the communications was unrelated to the events in Vareš. Stojić's arguments are dismissed.

1703. In sum, the Appeals Chamber finds that Stojić has failed to demonstrate that the Trial Chamber erred in concluding that he facilitated the military operations in Vareš in October 1993. Stojić's sub-ground of appeal 36.2 is therefore dismissed.

    (ii) <u>Stojić's knowledge and acceptance of crimes in Vareš Municipality (Stojić's Sub-grounds 36.1 and 36.3)</u>

        a. <u>Arguments of the Parties</u>

1704. Stojić argues that the Trial Chamber erroneously inferred that he knew of murders and destruction of property in Vareš as there is no evidentiary basis for such an inference.[5592] Specifically, he contends that: (1) there is no evidence that any report on the crimes was sent to him or circulated within the Department of Defence;[5593] (2) he did not attend a meeting on 4 November 1993 during which the crimes were discussed;[5594] and (3) no witness testified about his awareness of the crimes.[5595] Stojić also submits that, even if he knew of the crimes, there was no basis for finding that he accepted them. He argues that, as he was appointed to a different post by 10 November 1993, "he did not continue in office",[5596] and that "he did not obtain the promotion of Rajić *after* allegedly learning of his crimes".[5597] On the latter point, Stojić contends that he requested Rajić's promotion on 1 November 1993 but the Trial Chamber found that he knew of the crimes as of 4 November 1993. He argues that as the Trial Chamber did not establish that he knew of the crimes before requesting the promotion, it erred in finding that he approved of or accepted the crimes.[5598]

1705. The Prosecution responds that Stojić "must have known" that Rajić's troops had committed crimes in Vareš, at the very latest, by the end of October 1993.[5599] Specifically, it asserts that Stojić's knowledge was based on reports that reached his superiors, immediate subordinates, and **[page 704]** the local HVO leaders.[5600] The Prosecution also argues that, even if Stojić only learned of the crimes on 4 November 1993, he did nothing to reverse the promotion or sanction Rajić which demonstrates his acceptance of the crimes.[5601]

1706. Stojić replies that the Prosecution: (1) argues that he knew of crimes prior to 4 November 1993 without having appealed the Trial Chamber's finding;[5602] and (2) ignores that Stupni Do investigations appeared to be underway while failing to identify any power he had to reverse a promotion.[5603]

[5590] See Ex. P07622 (confidential), para. 1.1.
[5591] Ex. P06219, p. 2.
[5592] Stojić's Appeal Brief, para. 347. See Stojić's Appeal Brief, paras 346, 355. Stojić suggests that the Trial Chamber's finding on his knowledge was based only on his official role. Stojić's Appeal Brief, para. 347.
[5593] Stojić's Appeal Brief, para. 347.
[5594] Stojić's Appeal Brief, para. 347, referring to Ex. P06454. See *infra*, fns 5608-5609 (clarifying that the relevant meeting occurred on 5 November 1993).
[5595] Stojić"s Appeal Brief, para. 347.
[5596] Stojić's Appeal Brief, para. 348, referring to Trial Judgement, Vol. 4, para. 1227.
[5597] Stojić's Appeal Brief, para. 348 (emphasis in original).
[5598] Stojić's Appeal Brief, para. 354.
[5599] Prosecution's Response Brief (Stojić), paras 304-305, 309.
[5600] Prosecution's Response Brief (Stojić), paras 304-305.
[5601] Prosecution's Response Brief (Stojić), para. 309. The Prosecution asserts that, by requesting and obtaining Rajić's promotion, Stojić showed that he shared the CCP. Prosecution's Response Brief (Stojić), paras 303, 308.
[5602] Stojić's Reply Brief, para. 70.
[5603] Stojić's Reply Brief, para. 70, referring to Trial Judgement, Vol. 3, paras 487-491, 494-495, Vol. 4, para. 381.

b. Analysis

1707. The Appeals Chamber will first address the challenges to Stojić's knowledge of crimes in Vareš prior to 4 November 1993. The Appeals Chamber notes that the Trial Chamber concluded that Stojić requested and obtained Rajić's promotion although he knew that Rajić had committed crimes.[5604] The Trial Chamber's conclusion is supported by its findings that Stojić: (1) communicated with Rajić between 29 and 31 October 1993 concerning the military operations in Vareš and facilitated those operations which he thought had been carried out satisfactorily;[5605] (2) requested Rajić's promotion on 1 November 1993;[5606] and (3) informed the Government about the military situation in the Vareš area during a meeting on 4 November 1993.[5607] However, the Trial Chamber's finding on Stojić's knowledge of crimes as of 4 November 1993 specifically concerned the crimes committed in Stupni Do.[5608] Notably, in the impugned finding, the Trial Chamber referred to Stojić being informed of "the deaths" and "the destruction of property" as of 4 November 1993.[5609] Those crimes occurred in Stupni Do.[5610] Thus, the Appeals Chamber **[page 705]** considers that the Trial Chamber found that Stojić: (1) facilitated the military operations of Rajić's troops in Vareš in October 1993, and considered that the operations were satisfactorily carried out justifying Rajić's promotion; and (2) was informed of the crimes in Stupni Do as of 4 or 5 November 1993.[5611]

1708. In light of the above, Stojić's involvement in Rajić's promotion therefore predates his awareness of the Stupni Do crimes. Notably, Rajić's promotion was granted by Boban on the same day that Stojić requested it, *i.e.* on 1 November 1993.[5612] The Appeals Chamber also notes that neither the Trial Chamber nor the Parties refer to any evidence on Stojić's ability to reverse a promotion granted by Boban. The Appeals Chamber finds that, to the extent that the Trial Chamber relied on Stojić's involvement in Rajić's promotion to find that he accepted the murders and destruction of property in Stupni Do,[5613] the Trial Chamber erred. The impact of this error, if any, will be addressed below.[5614] However, the Appeals Chamber is satisfied that Stojić's involvement in Rajić's promotion reasonably supports the Trial Chamber's conclusion that Stojić facilitated the Vareš military operations carried out by Rajić's troops and considered that these operations were carried out satisfactorily.[5615]

1709. Stojić further disputes the Trial Chamber's inference that he was informed of the murders and destruction of property in Stupni Do as of 4 November 1993 by arguing a lack of evidence. The Appeals Chamber reiterates that a trial chamber may rely on either direct or circumstantial evidence to underpin its

---

[5604] Trial Judgement, Vol. 4, paras 383, 427.
[5605] Trial Judgement, Vol. 4, paras 380-381.
[5606] Trial Judgement, Vol. 4, para. 381.
[5607] Trial Judgement, Vol. 4, para. 300, referring to Ex. 1D02179. Notably, Exhibit 1D02179 is the minutes of a Government meeting held on 4 November 1993, and attended by Prlić, Stojić and others, which discussed the military and security situation in the Vareš area. Ex. 1D02179.
[5608] Trial Judgement, Vol. 4, paras 383, 443. The Trial Chamber seemed to have based the finding that Stojić knew of the deaths and destruction of property on its earlier finding that, on 4 November 1993, key members of the Government, including Prlić, Praljak, and Boban attended a meeting which analysed the ramifications of the Stupni Do events as well as the involvement of Rajić and his troops in the area which had become public knowledge. Trial Judgement, Vol. 4, paras 382-383, referring to Ex. P06454, pp. 57-60, 72-73. Notably, the minutes of that meeting are dated 5 November 1993 (see Ex. P06454, p. 1) and elsewhere the Trial Chamber referred to this meeting being held on 5 November 1993 (see Trial Judgement, Vol. 4, paras 203, 595). Thus, the Appeals Chamber considers that the Trial Chamber mistakenly referred to this meeting as being held on 4 November 1993 in paragraphs 382 and 761 of the Trial Judgement. However, whether Stojić had the relevant knowledge as of 4 or 5 November 1993, and considering that Stojić did in fact attend another Government meeting on 4 November 1993 in which he briefed the attendees on the Vareš situation, the Trial Chamber's mistake has no impact. See Trial Judgement, Vol. 4, paras 203, 300.
[5609] Trial Judgement, Vol. 4, para. 383.
[5610] Trial Judgement, Vol. 3, paras 699-703, 752-756, 1554-1556, 1596-1599. See *supra*, para. 1698. See also Trial Judgement, Vol. 4, paras 763, 767.
[5611] See *supra*, fn. 5609.
[5612] Trial Judgement, Vol. 4, para. 381, referring to Exs. P06328, P06339, P06362. The Appeals Chamber notes that Exhibit P06362 is a document issued by Stojić on 2 November 1993 stating that Rajić was promoted by a decree from Boban. Ex. P06362.
[5613] See Trial Judgement, Vol. 4, para. 383 ("Moreover, insofar as he [...] requested and obtained Ivica Rajić's promotion, the [Trial] Chamber holds that the only reasonable inference it can draw is that Bruno Stojić accepted the murders and the destruction").
[5614] See *infra*, paras 1710-1712.
[5615] Trial Judgement, Vol. 4, paras 380-381, 383.

findings.[5616] Specifically, a trial chamber may draw inferences to establish a fact on which a conviction relies based on circumstantial evidence as long as it is the only reasonable inference that could be drawn from the evidence presented.[5617] Regarding Stojić's awareness of these crimes, the Trial Chamber considered that: (1) Government officials – Boban and Prlić – as well as those in charge of the Main Staff – Praljak and Petković – knew of these crimes in Stupni Do which had become public knowledge and were discussed during a meeting on **[page 706]** 5 November 1993;[5618] (2) Stojić was the Government member in charge of the armed forces; and (3) Stojić facilitated the Vareš military operations and considered them to have been carried out satisfactorily.[5619] Notably, Stojić has not challenged the first of these considerations, and the Appeals Chamber dismisses elsewhere his submissions disputing his control over the HVO and the Military Police,[5620] as well as his facilitation of the Vareš military operations.[5621] The Trial Chamber also found that Stojić briefed the HZ(R) H-B Government about the military and security situation in the Vareš area during another meeting on 4 November 1993.[5622] Thus, despite a lack of direct evidence that he was informed of the Stupni Do crimes,[5623] Stojić fails to show that no reasonable trier of fact could have arrived at the Trial Chamber's conclusion that the only reasonable inference was that by 4 November 1993,[5624] he was so informed. Stojić's argument is therefore dismissed.

1710. In addition to considering Stojić's role in Rajić's promotion, the Trial Chamber also took account of his continued exercise of his functions while knowing of the crimes in concluding that he accepted those crimes.[5625] Notably, the Trial Chamber concluded that the HVO informed the international community that investigations into the Stupni Do crimes were underway but that this was intended to deceive the international community.[5626] The Appeals Chamber notes in this regard that the Trial Chamber did not make any finding on this issue as it concerns Stojić, nor does Stojić point to any evidence that he was informed of an investigation of the crimes. Thus, Stojić's assertion that Stupni Do investigations "appeared to be underway" does not impact on the Trial Chamber's finding that he accepted the crimes. In this regard, the Appeals Chamber recalls that the Trial Chamber found that Stojić exercised his functions as Head of the Department of Defence until 15 November 1993,[5627] thus he had approximately ten days in which he could have taken some action after learning of the Stupni Do crimes.[5628] Further, the Trial Chamber found that despite Stojić's power and authority over the HVO and the Military Police,[5629] he made no serious **[page 707]** effort to stop the commission of crimes by their members.[5630] By failing to do so, even with the short time-frame available,[5631] the Appeals Chamber finds that the Trial Chamber reasonably concluded, as the only available

---

[5616]   *Stanišić and Župljanin* Appeal Judgement, para. 172; *Popović et al.* Appeal Judgement, para. 971; *Stakić* Appeal Judgement, para. 219.

[5617]   *Stanišić and Župljanin* Appeal Judgement, para. 375; *Popović et al.* Appeal Judgement, para. 1278; *Stakić* Appeal Judgement, para. 219.

[5618]   Trial Judgement, Vol. 4, paras 382-383, referring to Ex. P06454, pp. 57-60, 72-73. See *supra*, fn. 5608 (clarifying that the relevant meeting occurred on 5 November 1993).

[5619]   Trial Judgement, Vol. 4, para. 383. See Trial Judgement, Vol. 4, paras 380-382. The Trial Chamber also found elsewhere that Stojić briefed the HZ(R) H-B Government about the military and security situation in the Vareš area during another meeting on 4 November 1993. Trial Judgement, Vol. 4, paras 203, 300, referring to Ex. 1D02179.

[5620]   See *supra*, paras 1457, 1479, 1491.

[5621]   See *supra*, para. 1703. The Appeals Chamber also rejects Stojić's assertion that the Trial Chamber relied only on his official role to conclude that he had knowledge of the crimes. See *supra*, fn. 5593.

[5622]   Trial Judgement, Vol. 4, paras 203, 300, referring to Ex. 1D02179.

[5623]   See *supra*, para. 1704.

[5624]   See *supra*, fn. 5609.

[5625]   Trial Judgement, Vol. 4, para. 383.

[5626]   Trial Judgement, Vol. 3, paras 480, 484, 488-492.

[5627]   Trial Judgement, Vol. 4, para. 293. See *supra*, para. 1516.

[5628]   See *supra*, para. 1490.

[5629]   See *supra*, paras 1405, 1457-1458, 1479-1480, 1500.

[5630]   Trial Judgement, Vol. 4, para. 427.

[5631]   *Cf. Popović et al.* Appeal Judgment, para. 1898 & fn. 5324 (considering that Vinko Pandurević had about 30 hours to prevent his subordinates from committing crimes and finding that while he "would have indeed needed to act quickly, issuing orders requires little time and responsibility for this could have been delegated if necessary."); paras 1914 (finding that Pandurević had a few hours in which he might have made the relevant inquiries or issued orders in relation to preventing his subordinates from committing crimes), 1915 (finding that Pandurević had less than 24 hours but had ample time and opportunity to initiate action to prevent his subordinates from participating in persecution).

inference from the evidence, that Stojić accepted the murders and destruction of property. Stojić's arguments on this point are dismissed.

1711. Moreover, based on the above,[5632] the Appeals Chamber finds that the Trial Chamber's error in relying on Rajić's promotion to find that Stojić accepted the murders and destruction of property in Stupni Do does not impact its overall conclusion on his acceptance of the crimes. Further, Stojić's continued participation in the JCE after being aware of the events in Vareš Municipality – albeit for a short time frame – was also reasonably used to infer Ms shared intent. Stojić's sub-grounds of appeal 36.1 and 36.3 are dismissed.

(iii) Conclusion

1712. In sum, Stojić's ground of appeal 36 is dismissed as he has failed to demonstrate an error by the Trial Chamber that impacts on its consideration of his participation in the JCE based on his involvement in the military operations in Vareš Municipality.

(i) Detention Centres (Stojić's Ground 37)

(i) Whether Stojić was responsible for the detention centres (Stojić's Sub-ground 37.1, in part)

1713. In discussing Stojić's responsibility for the detention centres, the Trial Chamber found that on 6 August 1993 Stojić ordered that the "procedures for interrogation and release of detainees in the HZ H-B detention centres be better organised".[5633] The Trial Chamber also noted that during a 6 September 1993 meeting attended by Stojić, the Government took decisions to bring the detention centres for "prisoners of war" in line with the standards of international law and tasked the DoJA as well as the Department of Defence with overseeing the implementation of these decisions.[5634] Furthermore, the Trial Chamber found that Boban ordered the Department of Defence and the Main **[page 708]** Staff to comply with international law in the treatment of POWs.[5635] It pointed out that the regulations for the treatment of POWs in the detention centres, promulgated by Stojić on 11 February 1993, were still in force in November 1993 and provided for, *inter alia,* the sanitary, dietary, and working conditions.[5636] The Trial Chamber inferred from this evidence that Stojić was informed of the detention of Muslims and that this detention was not in conformity with international law.[5637] It also concluded that even if Stojić "did seek to improve the detention conditions and the treatment of detainees – as the [Trial] Chamber found in the parts relating to the various detention centres – the conditions and treatment remained poor until the day the centres were closed down."[5638]

a. Arguments of the Parties

1714. According to Stojić, the Trial Chamber erred in inferring that he was responsible for the conditions at detention centres from the measures which were promulgated to improve those conditions and which were ultimately ineffective.[5639] Stojić submits that the Trial Chamber failed to articulate a basis for finding that he was responsible for detained civilians as they were under the responsibility of the ODPR or the DoJA.[5640] He argues that it was the ODPR that was tasked with improving conditions concerning accommodation and diet during the Government meeting of 6 September 1993,[5641] and that Exhibits P04841, the minutes of the

---

[5632]   See *supra,* para. 1710.
[5633]   Trial Judgement, Vol. 4, para. 384, referring to Ex. P04002, p. 1.
[5634]   Trial Judgement, Vol. 4, para. 385, referring to Ex. P04841.
[5635]   Trial Judgement, Vol. 4, para. 385, referring to Ex. P05104.
[5636]   Trial Judgement, Vol. 4, para. 386.
[5637]   Trial Judgement, Vol. 4, para. 387.
[5638]   Trial Judgement, Vol. 4, para. 387.
[5639]   Stojić's Appeal Brief, para. 366, referring to Trial Judgement, Vol. 4, paras 384-386, 395, 407. Stojić refers to the Detention Commission that he attempted to establish in August 1993 for improving the prison conditions and notes that the Trial Chamber found no evidence that it carried out its functions. Stojić's Appeal Brief, para. 366, referring to Ex. P03995; Trial Judgement, Vol. 1, para. 625. Stojić replies that his acceptance of unlawful detentions is not the only reasonable inference available from the fact that Gabela Prison detainees were not categorised. Stojić's Reply Brief, para. 69.
[5640]   Stojić's Appeal Brief, para. 359, referring to, *inter alia,* Exs. P03995, 1D01666, 5D01004, 4D01105, P02925, P02915.
[5641]   Stojić's Appeal Brief, para. 359, referring to Ex. P04841.

Government working meeting of 6 September 1993, and P05104, Boban's follow up order of 15 September 1993, did not place additional responsibilities on the Department of Defence.[5642] In the same vein, Stojić contends that the order that Boban issued after this Government meeting contained only action for the Main Staff to process.[5643] Similarly, Stojić argues that the fact that the requests of the Health Section of the Department of Defence for improvement in conditions were not implemented does not mean that he accepted or was responsible for the poor conditions. Stojić contends that another alternative inference is that he failed to improve the conditions because he lacked the power to do so,[5644] and **[page 709]** submits in that regard that there was no evidence that the Health Section had *de jure* powers to order improvements.[5645] He also claims that there is no evidence that the rules he issued in February 1993, before POWs were detained, were followed, arguing that the Heliodrom operated according to the rules issued by Ćorić in September 1992.[5646]

1715.   The Prosecution responds that the Trial Chamber reasonably concluded that Stojić exercised authority over the Heliodrom, Dretelj Prison, and Gabela Prison and that he had authority to improve the detention conditions.[5647] The Prosecution also contends that Stojić ignores the role he and the authorities under his control played in operating these detention centres.[5648] According to the Prosecution, the evidence Stojić cites does not show that the ODPR or the DoJA displaced his authority over detained civilians.[5649] It further argues that the Trial Chamber, reasonably relied on Stojić's 11 February 1993 instructions regulating the treatment of POWs and that the fact that these instructions were not followed shows that he took no steps to ensure compliance.[5650] The Prosecution also submits that the Health Section of the Department of Defence could issue orders concerning health-care provisions at Dretelj Prison, Gabela Prison, and the Heliodrom and yet no such care was provided in the first two, while some detainees received no medical care in the Heliodrom.[5651] In that regard, the Prosecution submits that Stojić misrepresents the Trial Judgement by claiming that the Trial Chamber found there was no evidence of the Health Section's *de jure* powers to order improvements.[5652] **[page 710]**

b. Analysis

1716.   The Appeals Chamber recalls that a trial judgement must be read as a whole,[5653] and that the subsection dealing with Stojić's responsibility for detention centres should be read together with the other parts of the Trial Judgement. Bearing this in mind, the Appeals Chamber considers that the Trial Chamber did not err in

---

[5642]   Stojić's Appeal Brief, para. 359.

[5643]   Stojić's Appeal Brief, para. 359, referring to Exs. P05104, P05199, P05188.

[5644]   Stojić's Appeal Brief, para. 366, referring to, *inter alia,* Exs. P04145, 2D00412, P05503, 2D02000, para. 70. 2D00717, Trial Judgement, Vol. 4, para. 405.

[5645]   Stojić's Appeal Brief, para. 366, referring to Trial Judgement, Vol. 1, para. 619.

[5646]   Stojić's Appeal Brief, para. 366, referring to Trial Judgement, Vol. 2, paras 1407, 1415, 1458, Vol. 4, para. 386, Exs. P01474, P00352, p. 14. The Appeals Chamber notes that Stojić mistakenly dates Ćorić›s instructions as September 1993 and considers this to be a typographical error.

[5647]   Prosecution's Response Brief (Stojić), paras 313 (referring to, *inter alia,* Trial Judgement, Vol. 4, paras 312, 320, 384-386, 388, 390-395, 398-407, 423, 427, Ex. P03995), 332. According to the Prosecution, a decree of 3 July 1992 concerning the treatment of persons captured during combat in the HZ H-B signed by Mate Boban placed the Department of Defence in charge of HVO detention centres. Prosecution's Response Brief (Stojić), para. 313, referring to Ex. P00292. See Trial Judgement, Vol. 1, para. 648.

[5648]   Prosecution's Response Brief (Stojić), para. 328. The Prosecution avers that Stojić recognised his responsibility for detained civilians as he formed the Detention Commission and that he accepted unlawful detentions as nothing was done to categorise Gabela Prison detainees. Prosecution's Response Brief (Stojić), para. 329, referring to Trial Judgement, Vol. 3, paras 202-204, Vol. 4, para. 407, Ex. P03995.

[5649]   Prosecution's Response Brief (Stojić), para. 330. The Prosecution asserts that: (1) Stojić relies on the 6 September 1993 meeting but ignores the fact that the Department of Defence was tasked at that meeting with improving detention conditions; and (2) Stojić cites evidence showing that the Military Police – which was found to have been under his command and effective control – allowed Heliodrom detainees to be taken to work. Prosecution's Response Brief (Stojić), para. 330, referring to Trial Judgement, Vol. 4, para. 320, Exs. P02915, P04841, pp. 1-3.

[5650]   Prosecution's Response Brief (Stojić), para. 331, referring to Trial Judgement, Vol. 2, para. 1431, Vol. 4, paras 386, 395, 397-399.

[5651]   Prosecution's Response Brief (Stojić), para. 332, referring to, *inter alia,* Trial Judgement, Vol. 2, paras 1461-1463, Vol. 3, paras 30, 177, 180.

[5652]   Prosecution's Response Brief (Stojić), para. 332, referring to Trial Judgement, Vol. 1, para. 619.

[5653]   *Stanišić and Župljanin* Appeal Judgement, paras 138, 376, 705; *Popović et al.* Appeal Judgement, para. 2006; *Mrkšić and Šljivančanin* Appeal Judgement, para. 379.

inferring that Stojić was responsible for the conditions in detention centres on the basis that the promulgated measures were ineffective as submitted by Stojić.[5654] The implication of Stojić's submission here is that the Trial Chamber relied solely on these unsuccessful measures in order to infer his responsibility for those conditions, which is not the case. Notably, the Trial Chamber made findings on the identity of the personnel that operated those detention centres including the armed forces deployed to these centres,[5655] and found that Stojić commanded and had "effective control" over most of these armed forces and was hierarchically superior to Ćorić.[5656] Moreover, the Trial Chamber concluded that Stojić could issue orders directly to the HVO regarding the detention centres and to Ćorić on the release of detainees.[5657] The Trial Chamber also made findings relating to Stojić's personal involvement with respect to the Heliodrom's security arrangements, access by international organisations and journalists, and release of detainees.[5658]

1717. Further, in the introductory paragraphs of the subsection titled "Detention Centres", the Trial Chamber, in reaching its conclusion about Stojić's knowledge of conditions of detention in detention centres, discussed the level of authority Stojić had regarding those conditions based on the tasks given to the Department of Defence in relation thereto, and based on certain actions Stojić took in 1993, in accordance with that authority.[5659] Thus, the Trial Chamber found that the Department of Defence was tasked by the Government and Boban to ensure compliance with standards of international law in relation to the detention centres and treatment of prisoners.[5660] In respect of Exhibit P05104, namely Boban's order of 15 September 1993 for conditions of detention and treatment of POWs to be improved in compliance with the Geneva Conventions, the Appeals Chamber rejects Stojić's argument that Boban's order contained only action that was to be implemented by the Main Staff as this order was clearly addressed to both the Main Staff and the **[page 711]** Department of Defence.[5661] In the Appeals Chamber's view, a reasonable trier of fact could have interpreted the fact that the order was sent to both organs as indicating that the Department of Defence was to ensure that the Main Staff and the HVO complied with the order and implemented it on the ground.[5662] As such, the Trial Chamber's finding that Boban ordered both the Department of Defence and the Main Staff to ensure compliance with international law in combat and treatment of prisoners is not contradicted.[5663] Accordingly, Stojić fails to show that the Trial Chamber could not rely on Exhibit P05104 to reach its conclusions.

1718. Moreover, in the Appeals Chamber's view, the fact that some documents show that the ODPR or the DoJA dealt with civilians detained in detention centres[5664] does not impact on the fact that the Department of Defence was tasked with improving conditions of detention. In this respect, Stojić fails to demonstrate that any authority exercised by the ODPR or the DoJA precludes him from also exercising authority over the detention centres. Contrary to Stojić's submission, the minutes of the Government's working group meeting of 6 September 1993 clearly show that the Department of Defence was tasked with, *inter alia,* improving conditions in detention centres and that it was given a deadline of 15 days to do so.[5665] Stojić does not show how the fact that the ODPR was required to improve the accommodation and diet of the detainees or that the

---

[5654]   *See supra,* para. 1714.
[5655]   See Trial Judgement, Vol. 2, paras 1400-1405, 1407-1412, 1415-1416, 1428, 1441, 1452, 1456, 1464, 1472-1473, 1476, 1492 (the Heliodrom), Vol. 3, paras 17-21, 25-28, 30, 32-36 (Dretelj Prison), 165, 168-169, 171, 173-175, 180, 187-192 (Gabela Prison), Vol. 4, paras 955, 959, 964, 968, 988, 991 (Ćoric"s involvement in the detention centres).
[5656]   See Trial Judgement, Vol. 4, paras 302, 312, 314, 320, 326.
[5657]   Trial Judgement, Vol. 4, paras 306, 314. See Trial Judgement, Vol. 1, para. 915.
[5658]   Trial Judgement, Vol. 2, paras 1410, 1429, 1431-1432, 1441, 1450, 1452.
[5659]   Trial Judgement, Vol. 4, paaras. 384-386. Stojić's other actions and omissions were discussed in the sections on the specific detention centres. See Trial Judgement, Vol. 4, paras 388-395, 397-407.
[5660]   See Trial Judgement, Vol. 4, para. 385; *supra,* para. 1713.
[5661]   See Ex. P05104.
[5662]   In that regard, the Appeals Chamber recalls that the Trial Chamber found that the Main Staff was accountable to the Department of Defence with regards to a number of matters and that the HVO brigade commanders were subordinated to, *inter alia,* the Head of the Department of Defence. See Trial Judgement, Vol. 1, para. 564. See also *supra,* paras' 1409-1410, 1422-1423, 1427-1435.
[5663]   See Trial Judgement, Vol. 4, para. 385.
[5664]   See Exs. 1D01666, 5D01004, P02925. While Stojić also relies on Exhibit P02915 to show that the DoJA had authority over detained civilians in the Heliodrom, the Appeals Chamber notes that this exhibit makes no reference to the DoJA and instead shows that the Military Police was allowed to take detainees from the Heliodrom to work. Furthermore, the exhibit also bears the stamp of the Department of Defence. Ex. P02915.
[5665]   Ex. P04841, pp. 2-3.

DoJA was tasked jointly with the Department of Defence to adopt regulations pertaining to the procedure towards detained persons affects the Trial Chamber's finding. Accordingly, the Appeals Chamber considers that it was reasonable for the Trial Chamber to rely on Exhibit P04841 to reach its conclusions. Similarly, the Appeals Chamber also considers that Stojić's submission that his regulations of 11 February 1993 were never followed is unpersuasive and he does not show how this affects the Trial Chamber's findings. In the Appeals Chamber's view, a reasonable trier of fact could have relied on these regulations to arrive at the conclusions the Trial Chamber reached regarding Stojić's knowledge and therefore consider them a relevant factor in determining his authority and responsibility over detained civilians.[5666]

1719. Stojić also challenges the Trial Chamber's consideration of information given to him that preventive measures recommended by the Health Section of the Department of Defence for Gabela **[page 712]** Prison were not implemented.[5667] The fact that these recommendations were ultimately not implemented, despite the specific mandate of the Department of Defence in relation to conditions of detention, was referred to by the Trial Chamber in its conclusion that even if Stojić "did seek to improve the detention conditions and the treatment of detainees – as the [Trial] Chamber found in the parts relating to the various detention centres – the conditions and treatment remained poor until the day the centres were closed down".[5668] It was also referred to later in the discussion on Dretelj Prison and Gabela Prison when the Trial Chamber found that Stojić – even though informed of the continued bad conditions and the lack of compliance with the Health Section's recommendations – did nothing, leading to the conclusion that he "accepted the extremely precarious conditions and the mistreatment in the prisons of Dretelj and Gabela".[5669]

1720. In arguing that there is no evidence that the Health Section had *de jure* powers to make requests for improvement of conditions, Stojić relies on the Trial Chamber's finding that it had no evidence regarding the "full complement of powers" given to the Health Section.[5670] However, he ignores the Trial Chamber's finding only two paragraphs later, that the Health Section was tasked with visiting HVO detention centres, of which it informed Stojić.[5671] The Trial Chamber then proceeded to find later in the Trial Judgement that the Health Section was directly involved with the provision of medical care at the Heliodrom, Dretelj Prison, and Gabela Prison.[5672] Thus, Stojić's argument, to the extent it concerns any lack of authority of the Health Section, is dismissed. Moreover, Stojić ignores the fact that the finding that he accepted the poor detention conditions was not based only on the non-implementation of the Health Section's recommendations.[5673]

1721. Based on the above, the Appeals Chamber considers that the Trial Chamber did not only consider the ineffective promulgated measures but a multitude of other factors, most importantly, the role that Stojić, and the authorities he controlled, played in operating, assessing, and improving those detention centres, as well as his knowledge about the conditions therein. Therefore, Stojić has not shown that the Trial Chamber erred with regard to his authority over, and responsibility for the conditions at, the detention centres. Moreover, Stojić has not demonstrated that the Trial Chamber erred in considering the ineffective measures taken to improve detention conditions as a factor in determining Stojić's responsibility. His arguments to the contrary are dismissed. **[page 713]**

(ii) <u>Stojić's involvement in the Heliodrom and awareness of detention conditions (Stojić's Sub-grounds 37.1, in part, and 37.2)</u>

1722. Having made its finding about Stojić's knowledge of conditions of detention in the detention centres generally,[5674] the Trial Chamber turned to Stojić's involvement with the Heliodrom. The Trial Chamber first

---

[5666]   See Trial Judgement, Vol. 4, paras 386-387.
[5667]   See Trial Judgement, Vol. 4, para. 405.
[5668]   Trial Judgement, Vol. 4, para. 387.
[5669]   Trial Judgement, Vol. 4, para. 407. See Trial Judgement, Vol. 4, paras 405-406.
[5670]   Trial Judgement, Vol. 1, para. 619. See Stojić's Appeal Brief, para. 366.
[5671]   Trial Judgement, Vol. 1, para. 621.
[5672]   Trial Judgement, Vol. 2, paras 1461-1464, Vol. 3, paras 30, 177-180. See Trial Judgement, Vol. 4, paras 392, 404-405.
[5673]   The Appeals Chamber also does not see how Stojić's arguments regarding the fact that the Detention Commission did not carry out its function assists him. If anything, it affirms the Trial Chamber's findings that he made no genuine efforts to improve the situation in the detention centres. His argument is dismissed.
[5674]   Trial Judgement, Vol. 4, paras 384-387.

recalled its findings about the harsh conditions of detention that existed there.[5675] It also found that various officials, including the Heliodrom wardens, informed Stojić on several occasions about the conditions of detention there and about the detainees' work on the front line which resulted in the death and wounding of some detainees.[5676] The Trial Chamber determined that Stojić took no measures to rectify those conditions and found that "[i]nasmuch as he continued to exercise his functions in the [Government], [...] Stojić accepted the bad detention conditions at the Heliodrom".[5677]

a. Whether Stojić was responsible for crimes committed at the Heliodrom (Stojić's Sub-ground 37.1, in part)

i. Arguments of the Parties

1723. Stojić argues that the Trial Chamber erred in finding that he failed to rectify the detention conditions at the Heliodrom without making "an unequivocal preliminary finding that he had the power to do so"[5678] which, he claims, was inconsistent with the approach the Trial Chamber used in relation to other detention centres.[5679] Stojić also claims that no reasonable chamber could have found that he was responsible for conditions at the Heliodrom as: (1) he was not found to have had any role in establishing it; (2) he merely formalised Mile Pušić's appointment as the warden of the Heliodrom, as ordered by Ćorić; (3) the logistics, access to the Heliodrom, and the release of the detainees were controlled by the military chain of command; and (4) there is no evidence that he issued orders to the Heliodrom wardens or was involved in its daily activities.[5680] Stojić avers that he was only one of several recipients of reports about the detention conditions – most of which he did not receive, and that the only remaining report he received from the Health Section, namely **[page 714]** Exhibit P05503, does not establish that he was responsible for medical care or security at the Heliodrom.[5681]

1724. The Prosecution responds that the Trial Chamber reasonably concluded that Stojić exercised authority over the Heliodrom and its detention conditions,[5682] and argues that any lack of findings regarding other detention centres is irrelevant.[5683] Specifically, regarding the Heliodrom, the Prosecution argues that: (1) it was established by Ćorić who was under Stojić's control;[5684] (2) the Trial Chamber acknowledged Stojić's decision of 3 September 1992 to establish a central military prison at its site, and his appointment of Mile Pušić on that day;[5685] and (3) Stojić was not involved in its administration simply because he did not want to be involved.[5686] With respect to the Health Section report, the Prosecution responds that ultimately Boban

---

[5675] Trial Judgement, Vol. 4, para. 394, recalling Trial Judgement, Vol. 2, paras 1517-1545, 1552-1565, 1594-1605.
[5676] Trial Judgement, Vol. 4, paras 388-392, 395, relying on Exs. P04186, P04352, P05812, P05503.
[5677] Trial Judgement, Vol. 4, para. 395.
[5678] Stojić's Appeal Brief, para. 357. See Stojić's Appeal Brief, para. 356.
[5679] Stojić's Appeal Brief, paras 357 (referring to Trial Judgement, Vol. 2, paras 1379-1663, Vol. 4, paras 388-395), 367. According to Stojić, the Trial Chamber made no findings that he was responsible for Vojno Detention Centre, Ljubuški Prison, and Vitina-Otok Camp and thus made no findings that he failed to rectify the conditions there. Stojić's Appeal Brief, para. 357, referring to Trial Judgement, Vol. 2, paras 1675-1686, 1789-1799, 1852-1857.
[5680] Stojić's Appeal Brief, para. 358, referring to, *inter alia*, Trial Judgement, Vol. 2, paras 1395, 1416, 1428, 1445-1456, Exs. P00452, p. 1, P00352, pp. 12-13. Stojić avers that the order for detention of HVO Muslims at the Heliodrom came from Petković and was then passed through the military chain of command. Stojić's Appeal Brief, para. 359, referring to, *inter alia*, Exs. P03019, P04745.
[5681] Stojić's Appeal Brief, para. 360, referring to Trial Judgement, Vol. 2, paras 1408, 1460, Ex. P05503. See *infra*, para. 1732. Stojić asserts that Exhibit P05503 was produced in response to Boban's order to the Main Staff that the conditions be improved. Stojić's Appeal Brief, para; 360, referring to Ex. P05104.
[5682] Prosecution's Response Brief (Stojić), para. 313, referring to, *inter alia*, Trial Judgement, Vol. 4, paras 390-392, 395, 399-407, 423, 427. See also Appeal Hearing, AT. 334-335 (21 Mar 2017).
[5683] Prosecution's Response Brief (Stojić), para. 314.
[5684] Prosecution's Response Brief (Stojić), para. 315, referring to Trial Judgement, Vol. 2, para. 1395, Vol. 4, para. 320.
[5685] Prosecution's Response Brief (Stojić), para. 315, referring to Trial Judgement, Vol. 2, paras 1391, 1395. The Prosecution also submits that: (1) Ćorić acknowledged that Stojić's decision of 3 September 1992 was taken following the request of the Military Police Administration; and (2) Ćorić›s subsequent order regarding Mile Pušić's appointment demonstrated Stojić's control over Ćorić. Prosecution's Response Brief (Stojić), para. 315, referring to Trial Judgement, Vol. 2, para. 1394.
[5686] Prosecution's Response Brief (Stojić), para. 316. The Prosecution also argues that while authorities reported problems in the Heliodrom to Stojić and requested that he solve them, he did nothing. It further avers that Stojić's intervention would not have been

directed his order to both the Main Staff and the Department of Defence.[5687] It also argues that Stojić misrepresents the Trial Judgement by asserting that he was not responsible for medical care or security at the Heliodrom since he had control over: (1) the Military Police that secured the Heliodrom, and the units of the armed forces that provided medical supplies and supervised medical treatment;[5688] and (2) the personnel from the HVO, Military Police, and the SIS who dealt with logistics, prison access, and prisoner release.[5689] **[page 715]**

1725. Stojić replies that the Prosecution concedes that no explicit findings were made on his authority over the Heliodrom. He argues that "[a] reasoned decision requires an express finding on such a critical issue", and that any implicit finding is untenable given the lack of evidence.[5690]

ii. Analysis

1726. The Trial Chamber found that Stojić took no measures to rectify the detention conditions in the Heliodrom and concluded that "[i]nasmuch as he continued to exercise his functions in the [Government], [...] Stojić accepted the bad detention conditions at the Heliodrom and the use of detainees for work on the front line".[5691] Concerning Stojić's argument that the Trial Chamber failed to make an unequivocal finding that he had the power to improve the conditions in the Heliodrom, the Appeals Chamber accepts that it would have been preferable for the Trial Chamber to expressly find that Stojić had the authority over the Heliodrom, as it did with Gabela Prison and Dretelj Prison, and that by not doing so the Trial Chamber failed to provide a reasoned opinion. However, as noted above,[5692] the Trial Chamber did find that the Department of Defence was tasked with improving the conditions of detention of POWs and that Stojić had "effective control" over most of the HVO and Military Police deployed to the detention centres, including the Heliodrom. Thus, it is clear that the evidence outlined in the introductory paragraphs was used by the Trial Chamber to show the mandate Stojić had to improve the conditions of detention in the detention centres generally and thus in the Heliodrom.

1727. Moreover, the Trial Chamber: (1) heard evidence that Stojić was responsible for resolving issues likely to arise in detention centres and could take the decision to close those centres;[5693] (2) found that Stojić had authority over the release of detainees;[5694] (3) found that Stojić participated in Government meetings and took decisions on the situation in the detention centres;[5695] and (4) observed that Stojić issued orders concerning the detention centres.[5696] As indicated earlier, the Trial Chamber also made findings relating to Stojić's personal involvement with respect to the Heliodrom's security arrangements, access by international organisations and journalists, and release of detainees.[5697] The Appeals Chamber notes that Stojić does not challenge most of these **[page 716]** findings.[5698] Considering all this, the Appeals Chamber is satisfied that the Trial Chamber made sufficient factual findings to show that Stojić had authority over the Heliodrom. Accordingly, the Appeals Chamber finds that a reasonable trier of fact could have found that Stojić had

---

requested if he was powerless. Prosecution's Response Brief (Stojić), paras 316 (referring to, *inter alia,* Trial Judgement, Vol. 4, paras 393, 395, 423, 427, Josip Praljak, T. 14734 (27 Feb 2007), Exs. P03209, P04186, P04352, P05812), 319.

[5687] Prosecution's Response Brief (Stojić), para. 317, referring to Trial Judgement, Vol. 4, para. 385.

[5688] Prosecution's Response Brief (Stojić), para. 318, referring to, *inter alia,* Trial Judgement, Vol. 2, paras 1405, 1407-1409, 1412, 1464, Vol. 4, paras 312, 320. The Prosecution argues that the provision of medical supplies was initially the Department of Defence's responsibility and the Health Section was directly involved in the provision of health treatment at the Heliodrom. Prosecution's Response Brief (Stojić), para. 318.

[5689] Prosecution's Response Brief (Stojić), para. 319, referring to Trial Judgement, Vol. 2, paras 1416, 1428, 1441, 1452, 1456, Vol. 4, paras 302, 312, 320. The Prosecution further submits that it is irrelevant that the Muslim HVO members were detained at the Heliodrom pursuant to Petković's order. Prosecution's Response Brief (Stojić), para. 320.

[5690] Stojić's Reply Brief, para. 69, citing *Haradinaj et al.* Appeal Judgement, para. 128, *Krajišnik* Appeal Judgement, para. 139.

[5691] Trial Judgement, Vol. 4, para. 395.

[5692] See *supra,* paras 1713, 1716-1718.

[5693] Trial Judgement, Vol. 1, para. 542.

[5694] Trial Judgement, Vol. 1, paras 862, 915.

[5695] Trial Judgement, Vol. 4, para. 297.

[5696] Trial Judgement, Vol. 4, para. 306.

[5697] See *supra,* para. 1716.

[5698] While Stojić challenges the finding that he had authority over the release of detainees and that he could issue orders to the Heliodrom wardens, the Appeals Chamber dismisses this challenge elsewhere. See *supra,* para. 1723, *infra,* para. 1728.

authority over the detention centres, including the Heliodrom, and thus could have taken measures to improve the detention conditions.[5699]

1728. The Appeals Chamber now turns to Stojić's more specific arguments. First, the Appeals Chamber notes that, in finding that Stojić received continuous reports on the Heliodrom,[5700] the Trial Chamber considered a report from Stanko Božić, the Heliodrom warden, on logistical problems concerning lack of food and space at the Heliodrom and requesting that Stojić find a solution.[5701] It also considered that various officials, including the Heliodrom wardens, informed Stojić on several occasions about the conditions of detention and the detainees' work on the front line which resulted in the death and wounding of some detainees.[5702] The Appeals Chamber is satisfied that a reasonable trier of fact could have concluded that the reports sent to Stojić by the Heliodrom wardens show that he was viewed as someone who could improve the detention conditions. Stojić's assertion that he was only one of many recipients of these reports is insufficient to show an error.

1729. Moreover, the Trial Chamber reasonably relied on these reports to find that Stojić knew of the detention conditions.[5703] Other than challenging his receipt of these reports, Stojić argues that Exhibit P05503, that is, the report from the Health Section addressed to him personally, does not establish his responsibility for medical care or security. In this respect, the Trial Chamber considered this report – which described the various problems at the Heliodrom such as insufficient guards, overcrowding, and disastrous hygienic conditions – as evidence that Stojić was informed of **[page 717]** the detention conditions.[5704] Thus, Stojić misinterprets the Trial Chamber's reliance on the report from the Health Section. Furthermore, as noted earlier, the Trial Chamber also made findings relating to Stojić's personal involvement with respect to the Heliodrom's security arrangements and the release of detainees, as well as with regard to the personnel operating in the Heliodrom, all of whom were found to be under Stojić's control.[5705] Thus, Stojić's argument that Exhibit P05503 does not establish his responsibility is dismissed as unpersuasive.

1730. Likewise, the Appeals Chamber dismisses Stojić's remaining contentions on his alleged lack of involvement in the establishment of the Heliodrom and its daily activities, and the control exercised through the military chain of command. In light of the above considerations and his "effective control" over most of the HVO and the Military Police deployed to detention centres,[5706] Stojić fails to show how these contentions could call into question the Trial Chamber's findings. Notably, while the Trial Chamber held that it could not draw any conclusions as to the "precise role" Stojić played in establishing the Heliodrom, it was ultimately satisfied that Ćorić, whom it found to be under Stojić's control in some respects, ordered its establishment.[5707]

[5699] In addition, the Appeals Chamber considers that Stojić's arguments relating to Vojno Detention Centre, Ljubuški Prison, and Vitina-Otok Camp, are speculative and dismisses them as such. The Appeals Chamber notes that Stojić merely speculates that the Trial Chamber did not discuss Vojno Detention Centre and Vitina-Otok Camp in relation to his JCE responsibility due to his lack of authority over them but does not present convincing arguments or address the lack of evidence as to his direct involvement in those centres. As for Ljubuški Prison, while correct that the Trial Chamber did not conclude that Stojić failed to rectify conditions in Ljubuški and made no explicit findings on his authority over it, he was nevertheless convicted for the crimes that took place there on the basis that he had notice of and accepted the crimes committed there. Trial Judgement, Vol. 4, para. 396. See *supra*, para. 1560 (reversing the findings on Stojić's knowledge and acceptance of the detention of Muslim men who did not belong to any armed forces at Ljubuški Prison).

[5700] Trial Judgement, Vol. 4, para. 395.

[5701] Trial Judgement, Vol. 4, para. 388, referring to Ex. P04186.

[5702] Trial Judgement., Vol. 4, paras 388-391, referring to Exs. P04352 (noting that an ICRC representative who visited the Heliodrom complained that the conditions of detention, specifically the inadequate food, the use of detainees for work, and the isolation cells, contravened the Geneva Conventions and informing Stojić that the number of wounded and killed detainees was increasing by the day), P05812 (informing Stojić, among other things, that detainees were beaten while at work and expressing concern about the large numbers of severely wounded and suffering detainees).

[5703] The Appeals Chamber dismisses Stojić's challenges to his receipt of reports elsewhere. See *infra*, para. 1734.

[5704] Trial Judgement, Vol. 4, paras 392, 395.

[5705] See *supra*, para. 1716, fns 5656 & 5657. The Appeals Chamber also finds that the sections of the Trial Judgement cited by Stojić as support for his contention that it was expressly found that he was not responsible for medical care or security at the Heliodrom (see Stojić's Appeal Brief, para. 360 & fn. 885) in fact do not speak to Stojić or make any such finding. See Trial Judgement, Vol. 2, paras 1408, 1460.

[5706] See *supra*, paras 1716, 1726-1728.

[5707] Trial Judgement, Vol. 2, para. 1395. See Trial Judgement, Vol. 4, paras 314, 320. The Appeals Chamber notes that the Trial Chamber also referred to Stojić's decision of 3 September 1992 to establish a central military prison at the Heliodrom site and to appoint Mile Pušić as its warden. Trial Judgement, Vol. 2, para. 1391, referring to Ex. P00452, p. 1.

1731. Therefore, on the basis of the foregoing, the Appeals Chamber considers that Stojić has failed to show that the Trial Chamber erred in concluding that he took no measures to rectify the bad detention conditions at the Heliodrom.

b. Whether Stojić was aware of the conditions at the Heliodrom (Stojić's Sub-ground 37.2)

1732. Stojić submits that the Trial Chamber erred in finding that he knew about the conditions at the Heliodrom through reports and letters because there is no evidence that he actually received or read any of these reports.[5708] Stojić contends that reports received by the Department of Defence were marked with a "receipt stamp", recorded in an intake register, and then signed by him.[5709] He argues that none of the documents were stamped or signed by him,[5710] and that the intake register **[page 718]** was not entered into evidence.[5711] According to Stojić, Stanko Božić, who wrote several of the reports, "did not give evidence".[5712] Stojić also submits that the fact that he did not visit the Heliodrom shows that he was not aware of the conditions there.[5713] He asserts that the Trial Chamber's finding that he failed to improve conditions at the Heliodrom is contingent on his knowledge of the conditions.[5714]

1733. The Prosecution responds that the Trial Chamber reasonably found that Stojić was aware of the conditions at the Heliodrom,[5715] and reasonably relied on the reports from Stanko Božić.[5716] It also responds that Stojić received other information concerning the detention conditions at the Heliodrom.[5717] According to the Prosecution, Stojić's failure to visit the Heliodrom does not show that he had no knowledge of the situation there but instead shows that he accepted the crimes.[5718]

1734. With regard to Stojić's argument that there is no evidence that he actually received and read the reports related to the conditions in the Heliodrom,[5719] the Appeals Chamber notes that his only support for this argument is the evidence of Slobodan Božić and the intake registry. As the Appeals Chamber dismisses elsewhere the same arguments concerning this evidence and document, Stojić's argument under this ground of appeal is likewise dismissed.[5720] Moreover, the fact that the author of several of these reports, Stanko Božić, did not testify does not take away from the fact that they were written and sent to the Department of Defence and were addressed to Stojić personally.[5721] Having been personally addressed to Stojić, the Appeals Chamber finds that Stojić does not present any arguments demonstrating that the flow of information was interrupted in those instances thus preventing Iris receipt of the reports. Additionally, the Appeals Chamber notes that Stojić conceded to having received the report of 30 September 1993 from the Health Section which addressed the conditions in the Heliodrom and which was considered by the Trial Chamber in determining that he knew of the detention conditions.[5722] The Appeals Chamber also considers that Stojić's argument **[page 719]** that his failure to visit the Heliodrom shows that he was unaware of the situation is unconvincing, particularly as he merely offers his own interpretation of the evidence. In this respect, the Trial Chamber

---

[5708]   Stojić's Appeal Brief, para. 368, referring to Trial Judgement, Vol. 4, paras 388-392. See Stojić's Reply Brief, para. 70.
[5709]   Stojić's Appeal Brief, para. 368, referring to Slobodan Božić, T. 36246-36247 (3 Feb 2009).
[5710]   Stojić's Appeal Brief, para. 368, referring to Exs. P04352, P05812, P04186.
[5711]   Stojić's Appeal Brief, para. 368, referring to Ex. 2D01399.
[5712]   Stojić's Appeal Brief, para. 368, referring to Trial Judgement, Vol. 4, paras 388, 390-391.
[5713]   Stojić's Appeal Brief, para. 368, referring to Trial Judgement, Vol. 4, para. 393. See Stojić's Reply Brief, para. 69.
[5714]   Stojić's Appeal Brief, para. 369.
[5715]   Prosecution's Response Brief (Stojić), para. 333, referring to Trial Judgement, Vol. 2, para. 1566, Vol. 4, para. 395, Prosecution's Response Brief (Stojić), paras 316-317. See also Appeal Hearing, AT. 334-335 (21 Mar 2017).
[5716]   Prosecution's Response Brief (Stojić), para. 333, referring to Exs. P04186, P04352, P05812. The Prosecution contends that Stojić's arguments are based on the absence of the intake register which could not be located and the evidence of Slobodan Božić, whose credibility the Trial Chamber found "extremely weak". Prosecution's Response Brief (Stojić), para. 333, referring to Trial Judgement, Vol. 1, para. 551. See also Appeal Hearing, AT. 334-335 (21 Mar 2017).
[5717]   Prosecution's Response Brief (Stojić), para. 334, referring to, *inter alia*, Exs. P04841, pp. 1-2, P06167, p. 2, P05503.
[5718]   Prosecution's Response Brief (Stojić), para. 335.
[5719]   Notably, Stojić only identifies three of the reports for which he claims that there is no evidence that he received them. See Stojić's Appeal Brief, para. 368, referring to Exs. P04352, P05812, P04186.
[5720]   See *supra*, paras 1618, 1621. See also *supra*, para. 1622.
[5721]   See Ex. P04352; Ex. P05812; Ex. P04186.
[5722]   See Stojić's Appeal Brief, para. 360; Trial Judgement, Vol. 4, para. 392, referring to Ex. P05503.

expressly considered Stojić's failure to visit the Heliodrom in its discussion on his failure to take measures to rectify the detention conditions at that location.[5723]

1735. For the above reasons, the Appeals Chamber finds that Stojić fails to demonstrate that the Trial Chamber erred in finding that he knew about the detention conditions at the Heliodrom and that he failed to rectify them thereby accepting the crimes. Stojić's sub-ground of appeal 37.2 is dismissed.

(iii) Stojić's involvement in Dretelj Prison and Gabela Prison (Stojić's Sub-ground 37.1, in part)

1736. The Trial Chamber found that Dretelj Prison and Gabela Prison were within the remit of the South-East OZ, were effectively military prisons, and fell within Stojić's responsibility.[5724] In reaching these conclusions, the Trial Chamber relied on: (1) Petković's order to the South-East OZ, dated 30 June 1993, according to which the military authorities were to isolate the combat-aged Muslim men from villages in their zone of responsibility;[5725] and (2) its earlier finding that combat-aged Muslim men were indeed detained in Dretelj Prison and Gabela Prison.[5726] According to the Trial Chamber, this meant that they were effectively military prisons, despite Stojić's statement to the contrary during the Department of Defence meeting on 2 September 1993.[5727] Further, in considering Stojić's responsibility for these prisons, the Trial Chamber noted the fact that it was decided at that Department of Defence meeting on 2 September 1993 that the SIS, the Military Police Administration, and the Health Section would submit reports to Stojić on Dretelj Prison and Gabela Prison by 8 September 1993.[5728]

1737. The Trial Chamber also found that Stojić knew of and accepted the "extremely precarious conditions" in which the Muslims, some of whom did not belong to the ABiH, were detained in Dretelj Prison and Gabela Prison.[5729] It considered a number of meetings which Stojić attended, namely: (1) a Government session on 20 July 1993 where a proposal was made by a working group that visited Čapljina to resolve the problem of overcrowding in Dretelj Prison and Gabela **[page 720]** Prison;[5730] (2) a Government meeting on 6 September 1993 where the discussion concerned bad conditions of detention in various prisons which "could harm the interests of the HR H-B";[5731] and (3) a meeting Stojić, Prlić, Pušić, and others had with an ICRC representative on 20 September 1993 who said that he had seen about 20 Dretelj detainees showing signs of malnutrition.[5732] The Trial Chamber also noted that Stojić received a report dated 29 September 1993 from the head of the infectious diseases services of the Department of Defence stating that the number of detainees at Gabela Prison significantly exceeded the prison's capacities, increasing the risk of an epidemic, and that several detainees were malnourished.[5733]

i. Arguments of the Parties

1738. Stojić submits that the Trial Chamber's finding that he was responsible for Dretelj Prison and Gabela Prison is "manifestly inconsistent with earlier factual findings" because: (1) there is no finding that he was

---

[5723]   Trial Judgement, Vol. 4, paras 393, 395.

[5724]   Trial Judgement, Vol. 4, paras 397, 399.

[5725]   Trial Judgement, Vol. 4, para. 397, referring to Ex. P03019, Andrew Pringle, T(F). 24144-24145 (6 Nov 2007). See Andrew Pringle, T. 24141-24143 (6 Nov 2007).

[5726]   Trial Judgement, Vol. 4, para. 397.

[5727]   Trial Judgement, Vol. 4, para. 397; Ex. P04756, p. 4 ("My opinion is that we have two military prisons *Heliodrom* and the military prison at Ljubuški. As for the other places where detainees are held (Gabela and Dretelj), I do not consider them as military facilities and refuse to personally endorse the work of these institutions.").

[5728]   Trial Judgement, Vol. 4, para. 398.

[5729]   Trial Judgement, Vol. 4, paras 400, 406-407.

[5730]   Trial Judgement, Vol. 4, para. 401, referring to Ex. P03573, Zoran Buntić, T(F). 30585 (10 July 2008).

[5731]   Trial Judgement, Vol. 4, para. 402, referring to Ex. P04841, pp. 1-2 (noting, with respect to conditions of detention, that "the situation was declared unsatisfactory and harmful to the reputation and interests of the Croatian Republic of Herceg-Bosna" and making various conclusions regarding improvements in detention centres) Andrew Pringle, T(F). 24145-24151, 24155 (6 Nov 2007). The Trial Chamber further noted that the minutes of this meeting indicated that "the situation was not considered to fall under the Government's responsibility". Trial Judgement, Vol. 4, para. 402.

[5732]   Trial Judgement, Vol. 4, para. 403, referring to Ex. P05219 (confidential).

[5733]   Trial Judgement, Vol. 4, para. 404, referring to Ex. P05485, pp. 2-3. The Trial Chamber also noted that, on 27 October 1993, Stojić was informed by the Health Section that the measures it recommended for Gabela Prison had not yet been implemented. Trial Judgement, Vol. 4, para. 405, referring to Ex. P06167, p. 2.

involved in the establishment of the two prisons; and (2) the conditions of detention in both were controlled "wholly and exclusively" by the Commander of the 1st Knez Domagoj Brigade Colonel Nedjeljko Obradović, while the wardens were appointed by Boban and Prlić.[5734] Stojić argues that the conclusion that he was responsible for Dretelj Prison and Gabela Prison because they fell under the remit of South-East OZ and reports on their conditions were to be submitted to him is unreasonable as the Main Staff commanded the South-East OZ and he was not part of the "classic military chain of command".[5735]

1739. Stojić also claims that the Trial Chamber erred in its assessment of the 2 September 1993 meeting because it failed to consider that his statement regarding the status of the two prisons was not challenged by anyone present.[5736] According to Stojić, the Trial Chamber disregarded evidence that: (1) Dretelj Prison was a municipal prison within the remit of Čapljina Municipality and the Department of Defence had to request authorisation in order to visit;[5737] (2) no representative of the **[page 721]** Department of Defence was assigned to the working group established on 29 July 1993 to relocate Dretelj and Gabela detainees;[5738] (3) he left the 20 September 1993 meeting with the ICRC immediately after it started;[5739] and (4) the reports on the two detention centres which were supposed to be submitted by 8 September 1993 were not sent to him but directly to Boban.[5740]

1740. The Prosecution responds that the Trial Chamber reasonably concluded that Stojić exercised authority over Dretelj Prison and Gabela Prison and could have improved their detention conditions.[5741] The Prosecution argues that Stojić's arguments are contradictory * and unclear because he first argues that Dretelj Prison and Gabela Prison were controlled by Obradović, but then he claims that they were not military prisons as evidenced by his refusal to recognise them as such during the 2 September 1993 meeting.[5742] The Prosecution further argues that any control exercised by Obradović does not undermine Stojić's power since the latter commanded and exercised "effective control" over the armed forces, including the 1st Knez Domagoj Brigade, as well as the Military Police and the SIS who also played a role in operating those prisons.[5743]

1741. The Prosecution further contends that the fact that Prlić and Boban appointed the wardens and that Dretelj Prison was under municipal control does not show an error in the Trial Chamber's determination on Stojić's authority and power.[5744] The Prosecution also submits that the evidence cited by Stojić shows that the Department of Defence was involved in running Dretelj Prison and Gabela Prison,[5745] and given that role, it is irrelevant that none of its members were assigned to explore the relocation of detainees or that Stojić left the 20 September 1993 meeting.[5746] Further, it argues that the Trial Chamber reasonably relied on the 2 September 1993 meeting and that Stojić's argument that the reports were not sent to him but directly to Boban is unsupported.[5747] **[page 722]**

[5734] Stojić's Appeal Brief, para. 361, referring to Trial Judgement, Vol. 3, paras 16, 25-35, 156-157, 169-192, Exs. P07341, P05133, 5D01064, P03462, P03197, P03161.
[5735] Stojić's Appeal Brief, para. 362, referring to Trial Judgement, Vol. 1, paras 595, 708, 747, 755, 781, 791, 795-796, Vol. 4, para. 306.
[5736] Stojić's Appeal Brief, para. 363, referring to Trial Judgement, Vol. 4, para. 397, Ex. P04756, p. 4.
[5737] Stojić's Appeal Brief, para. 364, referring to Zoran Buntic, T. 30578, 30580 (10 July 2008), Ex. P05133.
[5738] Stojić's Appeal Brief, para. 364, referring to Trial Judgement, Vol. 4, para. 401, Ex. P03573.
[5739] Stojić's Appeal Brief, para. 364, referring to Trial Judgement, Vol. 4, para. 403, Ex. P05219 (confidential), p. 2.
[5740] Stojić's Appeal Brief, para. 365, referring to Trial Judgement, Vol. 4, para. 398, Exs. 2D00926, P05222, P05225, Slobodan Božić, T. 36283-36284 (3 Feb 2009).
[5741] Prosecution's Response Brief (Stojić), para. 313, referring to, *inter alia,* Trial Judgement, Vol. 4, paras 390-392, 395, 399-407, 423, 427.
[5742] Prosecution's Response Brief (Stojić), paras 321, 323-324.
[5743] Prosecution's Response Brief (Stojić), para. 323, referring to, *inter alia,* Trial Judgement, Vol. 3, paras 20, 25-28, 36, 192, Vol. 4, paras 302, 306, 312, 320.
[5744] Prosecution's Response Brief (Stojić), paras 322, 324.
[5745] Prosecution's Response Brief (Stojić), para. 325, referring to Ex. P05133. The Prosecution argues that SIS members played an important role in interrogating detainees. Prosecution's Response Brief (Stojić), para. 325, referring to Trial Judgement, Vol. 3, paras 33, 36, 190, 192, Ex. P05647, p. 3.
[5746] Prosecution's Response Brief (Stojić), para. 326.
[5747] Prosecution's Response Brief (Stojić), para. 327. According to the Prosecution, although the reports were sent to Boban by Stojić's immediate subordinate Ivica Lučić, Slobodan Božić's testimony did not exclude that Stojić received these reports and his credibility was considered to be "extremely weak". Prosecution's Response Brief (Stojić), para. 327, referring to, *inter alia,* Slobodan Božić, T. 36283 (3 Feb 2009), Trial Judgement, Vol. 1, para. 551.

1742. Stojić replies that his submission that the Trial Chamber's findings did not "prove" his responsibility for Dretelj Prison and Gabela Prison was not inconsistent with his submission that they were not military prisons.[5748]

ii. Analysis

1743. First, in light of the foregoing discussion, the Appeals Chamber considers that whether or not Dretelj Prison and Gabela Prison were strictly military facilities and thus fell within the responsibility of Stojić on that basis does not ultimately affect the Trial Chamber's findings that he nevertheless had certain authority over them. As noted earlier, Stojić was tasked with improving the conditions of detention in the detention centres which held "prisoners of war", as distinct from institutions that held persons subject to criminal proceedings.[5749] Given that military-aged Muslim men in Čapljina Municipality were found by the Trial Chamber to have been isolated and detained by the "military authorities" and then placed in Dretelj Prison and Gabela Prison, the Appeals Chamber considers that the Trial Chamber reasonably concluded that they were effectively military prisons.[5750]

1744. In any event, the Appeals Chamber considers that a reasonable trier of fact could have concluded that the fact that these prisons were run by Colonel Obradović, an HVO commander, shows that they were military facilities and thus also within Stojić's remit.[5751] Further, Stojić's own statement during the 2 September 1993 meeting regarding the status of these two prisons was duly considered by the Trial Chamber and rejected.[5752] The Appeals Chamber concludes that the fact that the Trial Chamber did not explicitly refer to the lack of objections to Stojić's statement does not mean that the reactions at the meeting were not considered by the Trial Chamber. Thus, Stojić fails to show how the lack of objections could have an impact on the Trial Chamber finding.[5753] Furthermore, Stojić's challenge to the Trial Chamber's consideration of the fact that Dretelj Prison and Gabela Prison fell under the remit of the South-East OZ because that operational zone was controlled by the Main Staff is wholly unpersuasive. In this regard, the Appeals Chamber recalls **[page 723]** that Stojić was found to have had "effective control" over most of the HVO and the Military Police deployed in detention centres although he was not *de jure* within the military chain of command.[5754] Thus, Stojić fails to show that the Trial Chamber's finding was unreasonable on this issue.[5755]

1745. Moreover, other findings made by the Trial Chamber, such as: (1) Stojić's command authority over forces involved in the operation of these prisons and his ability to issue order directly to the HVO regarding detention centres; and (2) the fact that it was agreed during the 2 September 1993 meeting that Stojić would receive reports about the conditions of detention in Dretelj Prison and Gabela Prison by 8 September 1993, from, among others, the personnel that operated in the two prisons,[5756] support its conclusion that Stojić had certain authority over Dretelj Prison and Gabela Prison.[5757] The Appeals Chamber therefore considers that

---

[5748] Stojić's Reply Brief, para. 69.
[5749] See *supra*, paras 1713, 1716-1717.
[5750] Trial Judgement, Vol. 4, para. 397.
[5751] On a related point, the control that Obradović exercised over Dretelj Prison and Gabela Prison does not, in the Appeals Chamber's view, undermine Stojić's authority over those prisons since he commanded and exercised "effective control" over most of the armed forces, including the 1st Knez Domagoj Brigade and the Military Police, and had authority over the SIS, all of whom played a role in operating the prisons. *Cf. Popović et al.* Appeal Judgement, para. 1892 ("the exercise of effective control by one commander does not necessarily exclude effective control being exercised by a different commander"). See *Nizeyimana* Appeal Judgement, para. 201. See also *supra*, para. 1716 & fns 5656-5657.
[5752] Trial Judgement, Vol. 4, paras 397-399, 406.
[5753] Indeed, the Appeals Chamber notes that, contrary to Stojić's claim, the minutes of the meeting show that Ivica Lučić responded to Stojić, stating that "we cannot just pass over the problem of the Gabela and Dretelj prisons like that" as it could "cause us a lot of harm". Ex. P04756, p. 5.
[5754] Trial Judgement, Vol, 4, paras 306, 312, 320.
[5755] See Stojić's Appeal Brief, para. 362.
[5756] See Trial Judgement, Vol. 4, para. 398. The Appeals Chamber notes that the Trial Chamber did not determine whether Stojić ultimately received these reports and thus did not use it in its discussion as to the notice he had in relation to the conditions of detention in Dretelj Prison and Gabela Prison. Accordingly, Stojić's argument in relation to the receipt of these reports is irrelevant. See Trial Judgement, Vol. 4, paras 398-407.
[5757] See *supra*, para. 1716, and references cited therein.

the Trial Chamber could rely on these factors to conclude that Stojić had authority over Dretelj Prison and Gabela Prison and particularly the conditions of detention that existed there. Accordingly, the fact that Stojić did not participate in the establishment of Dretelj Prison and Gabela Prison, that Prlić and Boban appointed the wardens in those prisons, and that no Department of Defence representative was assigned to the working group established on 29 July 1993 does not undermine the Trial Chamber's findings that Stojić had authority over the two prisons including insofar as their conditions of detention were concerned.

1746. Similarly, the fact that Dretelj Prison may have fallen under the remit of Čapljina Municipality does not affect the finding that Stojić and the Department of Defence had authority over it, given the evidence discussed by the Trial Chamber. Specifically, the Appeals Chamber considers that the evidence cited by Stojić does not call into question the Trial Chamber's finding. Witness Zoran Buntić testified that Dretelj Prison was established as a municipal prison by virtue of a decision by the municipal council of Čapljina Municipality and was under the municipality's remit.[5758] However, the Appeals Chamber notes that, on this issue, Stojić repeats his trial argument and the same evidence he cited at trial which was expressly noted by the Trial Chamber,[5759] before it nonetheless found that Dretelj Prison fell under Stojić's responsibility.[5760] By simply repeating his argument, Stojić fails to show an error in the Trial Chamber's consideration of this evidence and its **[page 724]** ultimate conclusion on his authority. Furthermore, Exhibit P05133 does not assist Stojić. While this exhibit shows that the Department of Defence requested access to Dretelj Prison for SIS operatives, this does not necessarily mean that Stojić lacked authority. The Trial Chamber clearly assessed this exhibit and referred to it in noting evidence that "agents of the SIS were able to request authorisation to go to the collection centres or the prisons [...] in order to collect information".[5761] Notably, SIS operatives were found by the Trial Chamber to have been involved in the interrogation and release of the detainees in Dretelj Prison.[5762] Thus, Stojić's arguments contesting that Dretelj Prison and Gabela Prison fell within his responsibility are dismissed.

1747. Having considered the notice that he had with respect to the harsh conditions of detention and the mistreatment of detainees, the Trial Chamber concluded that Stojić accepted these conditions and mistreatment, as well as the fact that Muslims not belonging to any armed force were detained in these locations.[5763] In doing so, the Trial Chamber relied on, among other things, a report of a meeting with an ICRC representative on 20 September 1993 during which conditions in Dretelj Prison and Gabela Prison were discussed.[5764] However, the Appeals Chamber notes that Stojić is recorded as having left the meeting before it started.[5765] Accordingly, the Appeals Chamber considers that the Trial Chamber erred in its reliance on this report. However, given the other evidence relied on by the Trial Chamber to conclude that Stojić was on notice of the conditions of detention in Dretelj Prison and Gabela Prison, in particular the meeting of 6 September 1993 where it was noted that the situation in the detention centres could harm the interests of the Government,[5766] the Appeals Chamber considers that the Trial Chamber's finding is sufficiently supported and thus this error has no impact on the ultimate conclusion.

(iv) Conclusion

1748. In sum, the Appeals Chamber finds that, in reaching its conclusions on Stojić's responsibility for detention centres, the Trial Chamber was cognisant not only of his specific actions and omissions in relation thereto, but also of: (1) the level of authority he had with respect to those detention centres, including the personnel working there; and (2) his mandate in relation to the improvement of conditions of detention.

[5758]   Zoran Buntić, T. 30575-30580 (10 July 2008). See Ex. P03573.
[5759]   Trial Judgement, Vol. 3, para. 38, referring to Stojić's Final Brief, para. 512 (citing Zoran Buntić, T. 30578, 30580 (10 July 2008)).
[5760]   Trial Judgement, Vol. 4, para. 399.
[5761]   Trial Judgement, Vol. 1, para. 614, referring to, *inter alia,* Ivan Bandić, T(F). 38084-38085, 38091 (17 Mar 2009), 38248-38251 (18 Mar 2009), Ex. P05133.
[5762]   Trial Judgement, Vol. 3, paras 26 (referring to, *inter alia,* Ex. P05133), 33, 36.
[5763]   Trial Judgement, Vol. 4, para. 407.
[5764]   See *supra,* para. 1737.
[5765]   Ex. P05219 (confidential), p. R020-9291 (Registry pagination) (noting that Stojić "left immediately [after] the meeting started – presumably he was called away on urgent business").
[5766]   Trial Judgement, Vol. 4, paras 401-402, 404-405. See *supra,* para. 1737.

Stojić has not demonstrated that the Trial Chamber's conclusions on his authority and powers, or his knowledge, concerning the detention conditions at **[page 725]** the Heliodrom, Dretelj Prison, and Gabela Prison were erroneous. Stojić has therefore failed to show that no reasonable trier of fact could have concluded that the only reasonable inference was that he accepted the crimes that took place in the Heliodrom, Dretelj Prison, and Gabela Prison. Stojić's ground of appeal 37 is therefore dismissed.

9. Alleged errors regarding Stojić's *mens rea* and related challenges

(a) Alleged errors in finding that Tuđman and others directly collaborated in, and shared the intent for, the JCE (Stojić's Grounds 6 and 14)

1749. Under his ground of appeal 14, Stojić contends that the Trial Chamber erred in finding that Tuđman, Šušak, and Bobetko directly collaborated with HVO leaders and authorities in order to further the JCE.[5767] He submits that the Trial Chamber relied on evidence that "shows only general discussions [...] but not direct collaboration in either the JCE or the commission of crimes",[5768] and disregarded evidence.[5769] He asserts that without the conclusion that Tuđman and others directly collaborated in the JCE, the Trial Chamber could not have found that Tuđman, Šušak, and Bobetko were JCE members, and its conclusions on the JCE would "unravel".[5770] Stojić further contends, under his ground of appeal 6, that the Trial Chamber erred in finding that Tuđman, Šušak, Bobetko, Boban, and other unnamed JCE members shared the intent for the JCE, without making the necessary findings that they intended the commission of specific crimes, and that the evidence would not support such findings.[5771] He submits that "in order to find a JCE, it is necessary to find that *all* the participants intended the indictment crimes to be committed",[5772] thus, inadequate findings on the shared intent of all participants invalidate the finding that there was a JCE.[5773]

1750. The Prosecution responds that the Trial Chamber reasonably found that Tuđman, Šušak, and Bobetko collaborated with HVO leaders to further the CCP[5774] and relied on this to establish their **[page 726]** shared intent.[5775] It asserts that the JCE crimes can be attributed to Stojić either directly or via the other Appellants, and that the Trial Chamber's JCE conclusions are not dependent on its findings in relation to Tuđman, Šušak, Bobetko, Boban, or unnamed JCE members.[5776]

1751. Stojić challenges the Trial Chamber's conclusion that "[t]he evidence [...] shows that Croatian leaders Franjo Tuđman, Gojko Šušak and Janko Bobetko directly collaborated with the HVO leaders and authorities to further the JCE."[5777] While Stojić asserts that a reversal of this finding would negate the Trial Chamber's

---

[5767] Stojić's Appeal Brief, paras 117, 121, referring to Trial Judgement, Vol. 4, paras 1222-1223.
[5768] Stojić's Appeal Brief, para. 121. See Stojić's Appeal Brief, para. 117. Stojić asserts that the Trial Chamber: (1) failed to identify a link between the discussions documented in the cited evidence and a JCE or the commission of crimes; and (2) unreasonably relied on transcripts of meetings about Stupni Do and Mostar Old Bridge as evidence of direct collaboration when they "actually show the absence of any shared intent". Stojić's Appeal Brief, paras 118-119.
[5769] Stojić's Appeal Brief, para. 120.
[5770] Stojić's Appeal Brief, para. 121. See also Appeal Hearing, AT. 294 (21 Mar 2017).
[5771] Stojić's Appeal Brief, paras 70-75. Stojić asserts that: (1) the finding that Tuđman, Šušak, Bobetko, and Boban '"devise[d] and implement[ed]' the common purpose or that their ultimate purpose was to reconstitute the Banovina is insufficient" (Stojić's Appeal Brief, para. 72, referring to Trial Judgement, Vol. 4, para. 1231); (2) the Trial Chamber cited no evidence about the intent of Šušak or Bobetko (Stojić's Appeal Brief, para. 73); and (3) the Trial Chamber erred in fact in finding that Tuđman intended the Indictment crimes (Stojić's Appeal Brief, para. 74). See also Appeal Hearing, AT. 275, 284, 294-295, 297-298 (21 Mar 2017).
[5772] Stojić's Appeal Brief, para. 71 (emphasis in original).
[5773] Stojić's Appeal Brief, para. 75. See Stojić's Appeal Brief, para. 74; Appeal Hearing, AT. 294-295 (21 Mar 2017).
[5774] Prosecution's Response Brief (Stojić), paras 48, 50-52. See Appeal Hearing, AT. 349 (21 Mar 2017). The Prosecution asserts, *inter alia*, that: (1) Tuđman, Šušak, and Bobetko provided the HVO with military support and participated in planning HVO military operations to implement the CCP; (2) In November 1993, Prlić conferred with Tuđman about the plan to move BiH Croats into HZ(R) H-B territories they thought "could become and remain Croatian"; and (3) Tuđman, Šušak, and Bobetko maintained a privileged and continuous link with Praljak on BiH-related issues and discussed Croatia's policy in BiH "with a view to furthering the common criminal purpose". Prosecution's Response Brief (Stojić), para. 50.
[5775] Prosecution's Response Brief (Stojić), paras 48, 50, 53. See Prosecution's Response Brief (Stojić), para. 54. The Prosecution also asserts that the evidence supports the Trial Chamber's finding that Tuđman, Šušak, and Bobetko intended the crimes. Prosecution's Response Brief (Stojić), paras 51-52; Appeal Hearing, AT. 349-356 (21 Mar 2017).
[5776] Prosecution's Response Brief (Stojić), para. 55. See Appeal Hearing, AT. 349 (21 Mar 2017).
[5777] Trial Judgement, Vol. 4, para. 1222.

conclusion that these three individuals were JCE members, he does not show that it would also negate the Trial Chamber's finding that the remaining JCE members, including Stojić and the other Appellants, formed a plurality of persons who consulted with each other to devise and implement the CCP.[5778] In this respect, the Appeals Chamber notes that the Trial Chamber provided a detailed analysis of how Stojić and the other Appellants collaborated with each other in order to implement the CCP, independent of the involvement of Tuđman, Šušak, and Bobetko.[5779] Further, the Appeals Chamber rejects Stojić's assertion that any alleged inadequacies in the findings on the shared intent of Tuđman, Šušak, Bobetko, Boban, and unnamed JCE members invalidate its finding that there was a JCE. To the contrary, the Appeals Chamber recalls that it is not required, as a matter of law, that a trial chamber make a separate finding on the intent of each member of a JCE.[5780] After a detailed discussion,[5781] the Trial Chamber found that Stojić shared the intent with the other members of the JCE: (1) to expel the Muslim population from the HZ(R) H-B territories;[5782] and (2) that the JCE I crimes be committed in order to further the CCP.[5783] Thus, it was not required to examine the individual actions or scrutinise the intent of each JCE member who was not an accused in this case. **[page 727]**

1752. Therefore, considering also that none of the crimes committed in furtherance of the CCP were attributed to the JCE through Tuđman, Šušak, Bobetko, Boban, or the unnamed members of the JCE,[5784] Stojić fails to show that any alleged error by the Trial Chamber in concluding that they directly collaborated with the HVO leaders and authorities to further the JCE and shared the common criminal intent, would have an impact on his convictions. Stojić's grounds of appeal 6 and 14 are thus dismissed.

(b) Alleged errors concerning Stojić's knowledge of the JCE and its common criminal purpose (Stojić's Ground 15)

1753. Stojić argues that the Trial Chamber erroneously found that he was a member of the JCE as it made no finding that he knew of the JCE and its CCP.[5785] According to Stojić, to the extent that the Trial Chamber made any such finding, it failed to provide a reasoned opinion.[5786] He submits that throughout its discussion of the CCP, the Trial Chamber used the generic term "leaders of the HZ(R) H-B", which did not necessarily include him.[5787] Stojić further contends that the sole relevant finding is on his knowledge in October 1992, but as the JCE was only established in mid-January 1993, this finding could only relate to his knowledge of a long-term political purpose.[5788] Stojić also submits that his knowledge could not be inferred simply from his position, and contends that many important findings pre-date his appointment as Head of the Department of Defence and that he did not attend any of the presidential meetings with Tuđman.[5789]

1754. The Prosecution responds that the Trial Chamber reasonably concluded, based on a thorough analysis, that Stojić was a JCE member from mid-January 1993 to 15 November 1993.[5790] It argues that "[i]t is inherent

---

[5778] Trial Judgement, Vol. 4, para. 1231.

[5779] Trial Judgement, Vol. 4, paras 1219-1221.

[5780] *Đorđević* Appeal Judgement, para. 141 ("[I]n order to conclude that persons identified as joint criminal enterprise members acted in furtherance of the joint criminal enterprise, a trial chamber is required to identify the plurality of persons belonging to the joint criminal enterprise and establish that they shared a common criminal purpose", and it "is therefore not required, as a matter of law, that a trial chamber make a separate finding on the individual actions and the intent of each member of a joint criminal enterprise to establish that a plurality of persons acted together in implementing the common purpose.").

[5781] Trial Judgement, Vol. 4, paras 43-68.

[5782] Trial Judgement, Vol. 4, para. 428. See *infra*, paras 1759-1760.

[5783] Trial Judgement, Vol. 4, paras 67-68, 426. See *infra*, paras 1770, 1773.

[5784] See Trial Judgement, Vol. 4, para. 1232.

[5785] Stojić's Appeal Brief, paras 122-124, 126. Stojić avers that the Trial Chamber's finding that he was a member of the JCE should be overturned. Stojić's Appeal Brief, para. 126.

[5786] Stojić's Appeal Brief, paras 122, 124.

[5787] Stojić's Appeal Brief, para. 123, referring to Trial Judgement, Vol. 4, paras 24, 43.

[5788] Stojić's Appeal Brief, para. 124, referring to Trial Judgement, Vol. 4, paras 43-44.

[5789] Stojić's Appeal Brief, para. 125. See also Appeal Hearing, AT. 360-361 (21 Mar 2017). Stojić submits that he was not involved in the creation of the HZ H-B and that his primary contribution to the meetings on 5 and 26 October 1992 concerned the release of prisoners. Stojić's Appeal Brief, para. 125, referring to Trial Judgement, Vol. 4, paras 14-15, 18, 24, Ex. P11380, p. 3.

[5790] Prosecution's Response Brief (Stojić), para. 91.

in the [Trial] Chamber's shared intent finding that Stojić was aware of the common criminal purpose",[5791] thus an express finding on this issue was unnecessary.[5792]

1755. The Trial Chamber found that "the only possible inference it [could] reasonably draw [from all the evidence was] that Bruno Stojić intended to expel the Muslim population from the HZ(R) H-**[page 728]**B", and that he shared this intention with other JCE members.[5793] It also found that: (1) "Stojić knew that crimes were being committed against the Muslims with the sole purpose of forcing them to leave the territory of BiH";[5794] (2) a plurality of persons, including Stojić, consulted with one another to devise and implement the CCP;[5795] and (3) Stojić and other JCE members used the HVO and the Military Police to commit the crimes that were part of the CCP.[5796] The Appeals Chamber considers that Stojić ignores these relevant findings and focuses only on the findings made in the general section discussing the establishment of the JCE and its CCP. In this regard, the Appeals Chamber recalls that "the *mens rea* required for liability under the first category of joint criminal enterprise is that the accused shares the intent with the other participants to carry out the crimes forming part of the common purpose".[5797] The Trial Chamber found that Stojić shared the required intent and thus it is evident that he knew of the common criminal purpose of the JCE.[5798] Stojić's argument that the Trial Chamber failed to make a finding that he knew of the JCE and its common criminal purpose is unmeritorious and is therefore dismissed. Similarly, the Appeals Chamber dismisses Stojić's argument that the Trial Chamber failed to provide a reasoned opinion.[5799]

1756. To the extent Stojić argues that no reasonable trier of fact could have concluded that he knew of the CCP and the Ultimate Purpose of the JCE, the Appeals Chamber notes that Stojić again fails to address the Trial Chamber's detailed discussion on his involvement in the relevant events,[5800] which led to findings that he knew of and intended the crimes being committed and shared the necessary intent. Specifically, the Trial Chamber found, *inter alia*, that: (1) during meetings between September 1992 and November 1993, Stojić discussed and took decisions on the military situation on the ground, the mobilisation of the HVO, and the situation in the HVO detention centres;[5801] (2) Stojić was informed of HVO military operations;[5802] (3) Stojić facilitated and closely followed all HVO operations in Gornji Vakuf;[5803] (4) Stojić participated in planning the HVO military operations, and the accompanying acts of violence, in Mostar that began on 9 May 1993;[5804] (4) Stojić was not only informed of the evictions of Muslims from West Mostar as of June 1993, but was also actively involved in organising and conducting the eviction **[page 729]** campaigns;[5805] and (5) Stojić knew of the HVO's plan of action against East Mostar and the impact it had on the civilian population and accepted the crimes directly linked to this military operation.[5806] The Appeals Chamber thus considers that Stojić misunderstands the basis of the Trial Chamber's findings on his knowledge when he argues that this knowledge cannot be inferred from "simply" his position. This argument is dismissed. Further, recalling the *mens rea* requirement for JCE I,[5807] Stojić's contentions that many of the findings concerning the formation of HZ H-B and the Ultimate Purpose to set up a Croatian entity pre-date his involvement[5808] are irrelevant

---

[5791]   Prosecution's Response Brief (Stojić), para. 92. See Prosecution's Response Brief (Stojić), para. 91.
[5792]   Prosecution's Response Brief (Stojić), para. 92, referring to *Đorđević* Appeal Judgement, para. 468, *Krajišnik* Appeal Judgement, paras 706-707.
[5793]   Trial Judgement, Vol. 4, para. 428. See *infra*, paras 1759-1760.
[5794]   Trial Judgement, Vol. 4, para. 429.
[5795]   Trial Judgement, Vol. 4, para. 1231.
[5796]   Trial Judgement, Vol. 4, para. 1232.
[5797]   *Đorđević* Appeal Judgement, para. 468, referring to *Tadić* Appeal Judgement, paras 220, 228, *Krajišnik* Appeal Judgement, para. 707. See *Popović et al.* Appeal Judgement, para. 1652.
[5798]   See *infra*, paras 1759-1760.
[5799]   See *supra*, para. 19.
[5800]   See Trial Judgement, Vol. 4, paras 297-430, 1220-1221, 1227, 1230-1232.
[5801]   Trial Judgement, Vol. 4, paras 297-298. See *supra*, paras 1509-1513.
[5802]   See, *e.g.*, Trial Judgement, Vol. 4, para. 312.
[5803]   Trial Judgement, Vol. 4, paras 335, 337. See *supra*, paras 1578-1579.
[5804]   Trial Judgement, Vol. 4, paras 348-349. See *supra*, paras 1601-1605, 1608-1611, 1614-1615.
[5805]   Trial Judgement, Vol. 4, para. 355. See *supra*, paras 1621-1624, 1633-1637, 1646-1649, 1652.
[5806]   Trial Judgement, Vol. 4, para. 363. See *supra*, paras 1658-1661, 1664-1667, 1670-1674.
[5807]   See *supra*, para. 1755.
[5808]   See Stojić's Appeal Brief, para. 125, referring to Trial Judgement, Vol. 4, paras 14-15, 18, 24.

and he fails to show how any alleged error would impact on his membership in the JCE. These contentions and Stojić's ground of appeal 15 are dismissed.

(c) <u>Alleged errors in finding that Stojić had the shared intent of the JCE (Stojić's Sub-ground 25.1)</u>

1757. Stojić argues that the Trial Chamber erred in law in finding that he possessed the shared intent of the JCE.[5809] Specifically, Stojić submits that the Trial Chamber's finding on his intent "does not mirror", and is narrower than, the finding on the "shared criminal purpose".[5810] In this respect, he compares the finding that he intended to expel the Muslim population from the HZ(R) H-B territory[5811] with the finding that the CCP of the JCE was the domination of the HR H-B Croats through the ethnic cleansing of the Muslim population.[5812] Stojić asserts that conduct such as murder and destruction of property encompassed within the CCP does "not necessarily" fall within the intent to expel the Muslim population.[5813]

1758. The Prosecution responds that the Trial Chamber's findings are not inconsistent and that Stojić fails to read the finding on his intent in conjunction with an earlier finding specifying the types of crimes through which the CCP was achieved.[5814]

1759. The Appeals Chamber notes that the Trial Chamber concluded that Stojić intended to expel the Muslim population from the HZ(R) H-B territory and shared this intention with the other JCE members.[5815] Earlier in the Trial Judgement, the Trial Chamber found that the CCP was the domination by the HR H-B Croats through the ethnic cleansing of the Muslim population, and that **[page 730]** to accomplish this purpose, the JCE members, including the Appellants, made use of the political and military apparatus of the HZ(R) H-B.[5816] In this regard, the Trial Chamber found that JCE members "implemented an entire system for deporting the Muslim population of the HR H-B" which included the removal and placement in detention of civilians; murders and the destruction of property during attacks; mistreatment and devastation caused during evictions operations; mistreatment and poor conditions of confinement and the widespread use of detainees on the front lines for labour or as human shields, as well as murders and mistreatment related thereto; and the removal of detainees and their families outside of the territory of the BiH once they were released.[5817] The Trial Chamber also found that Stojić and the other Appellants, as JCE members, intended that the relevant crimes be committed in order to further the CCP.[5818]

1760. Therefore, the Appeals Chamber considers that, in concluding that "Stojić intended to expel the Muslim population" and that he "shared that intention with other members of the JCE",[5819] the Trial Chamber was referring to the shared intent for the JCE – which it found earlier in the Trial Judgement to have existed – to be perpetuated. Reading the Trial Judgement as a whole,[5820] the Appeals Chamber considers that the Trial Chamber's finding that Stojić shared the intent to expel the Muslim population from the HZ(R) H-B territory is indistinguishable from its finding that he had the intent to ethnically cleanse the Muslim population through an "entire system for deporting the Muslim population of the HR H-B", effectuated

---

[5809] Stojić's Appeal Brief, para. 202. See Stojić's Appeal Brief, paras 200-201. See also Appeal Hearing, AT. 282-283 (21 Mar 2017). Stojić argues that the Trial Chamber's legal error invalidates the Trial Judgement and that all his convictions should be overturned. Stojić's Appeal Brief, para. 202.

[5810] Stojić's Appeal Brief, para. 202. See Stojić's Reply Brief, paras 61, 63.

[5811] Stojić's Appeal Brief, paras 200, 202, referring to Trial Judgement, Vol. 4, para. 428.

[5812] Stojić's Appeal Brief, paras 200, 202, referring to Trial Judgement, Vol. 4, para. 41.

[5813] Stojić's Appeal Brief, para. 202. See Stojić's Reply Brief, para. 62.

[5814] Prosecution's Response Brief (Stojić), para. 182, referring to Trial Judgement, Vol. 4, paras 67-68. See Prosecution's Response Brief (Stojić), para. 181.

[5815] Trial Judgement, Vol. 4, para. 428.

[5816] Trial Judgement, Vol. 4, paras 41, 43-44. See *supra*, paras 786, 789-790; Trial Judgement, Vol. 4, para. 1232.

[5817] Trial Judgement, Vol. 4, para. 66. The Appeals Chamber recalls its finding that no reasonable trier of fact could conclude that murder and wilful killing were part of the CCP from January 1993 until June 1993. See *supra*, para. 882. While this means that Stojić did not have the intent for murder and wilful killing from January 1993 until June 1993, it does not affect the Trial Chamber's remaining findings concerning his contributions and intent for various crimes – including murder and wilful killing from June 1993 – particularly as only a few murders forming part of the CCP were found to have occurred prior to June 1993. See *supra*, para. 876.

[5818] Trial Judgement, Vol. 4, paras 67, 426, 429. See Trial Judgement, Vol. 4, paras 66, 68.

[5819] Trial Judgement, Vol. 4, para. 428.

[5820] *Stanišić and Župljanin* Appeal Judgement, paras 138, 376, 705; *Popović et al.* Appeal Judgement, para. 2006; *Mrkšić and Šljivančanin* Appeal Judgement, para. 379.

through a range of crimes under the Statute.[5821] In this regard, Stojić does not show that the finding on his shared intent is "narrower" than the finding on the purpose of the JCE. Moreover, it is clear that conduct such as murder and destruction of property[5822] – found to have been a part of the system for deporting the Muslim population – fell within the Trial Chamber's findings that Stojić intended to expel the Muslim population and intended the relevant crimes. In light of the above, the Appeals Chamber finds that Stojić has failed to demonstrate a legal error on the part of the Trial Chamber in determining his shared intent to perpetuate the JCE and further its CCP. Stojić's sub-ground of appeal 25.1 is thus dismissed. **[page 731]**

(d) Alleged error in law in failing to make a specific finding on Stojić's intent to participate in the JCE (Stojić's Sub-ground 25.2)

1761. Stojić submits that the Trial Chamber did not make an express finding concerning his intent to participate in the JCE.[5823] He argues that this defect cannot be remedied by inferring his intent from other findings as: (1) the Trial Chamber's "failure to address an element of a crime is too serious to be lightly remedied";[5824] and (2) the existing findings regarding his intent "do not *inevitably* lead to the inference that [he] intended to participate in a JCE".[5825]

1762. The Prosecution responds that it was unnecessary for the Trial Chamber to separately find that Stojić intended to participate in the JCE as this is inherent in its finding on his shared intent.[5826]

1763. The Appeals Chamber notes that the Trial Judgement does not contain a finding which explicitly states that Stojić "intended to participate in the JCE". However, the Appeals Chamber considers that the Trial Chamber found that Stojić had the shared intent with the other JCE members to expel the Muslim population from the HZ(R) H-B territory,[5827] and that he intended the crimes committed in furtherance of the CCP.[5828] The Appeals Chamber observes that the *mens rea* requirement in the Tribunal's jurisprudence at times has been phrased differently, such as: (1) "the *mens rea* required for liability under the first category of joint criminal enterprise is that the accused shares the intent with the other participants to carry out the crimes forming part of the common purpose";[5829] and (2) "the accused must share both the intent to commit the crimes that form part of the common purpose of the JCE and the intent to participate in a common plan aimed at their commission".[5830] Despite the differences, these formulations are substantively consistent. Although the Trial Chamber did not use the terminology "intended, to participate in the JCE", its findings are consistent with the jurisprudence outlined above. **[page 732]**

1764. Thus, the Appeals Chamber finds that the Trial Chamber – having determined that Stojić possessed the required shared intent[5831] – did not also have to find that he intended to participate in the JCE. Moreover, Stojić's intent to participate in the JCE, as the only reasonable inference, is clearly evident from the findings

---

[5821]   Trial Judgement, Vol. 4, para. 66.
[5822]   See Trial Judgement, Vol. 4, para. 70 (excluding murders committed during expulsion campaigns in certain municipalities and in the detention centres from the CCP).
[5823]   Stojić's Appeal Brief, para. 204, referring to Trial Judgement, Vol. 4, paras 425-431. See Stojić's Appeal Brief, para. 203, referring to *Brđanin* Appeal Judgement, paras 365, 429, *Krajišnik* Appeal Judgement, para. 685. See also Appeal Hearing, AT. 282 (21 Mar 2017).
[5824]   Stojić's Appeal Brief, para. 205.
[5825]   Stojić's Appeal Brief, para. 205 (emphasis in original), referring to Trial Judgement, Vol. 4, paras 337, 357, 428-429. Furthermore, Stojić contends that the intent to participate in a JCE "is a discreet issue which connects the intent to commit specific crimes with contribution to the common purpose". Stojić's Appeal Brief, para.205.
[5826]   Prosecution's Response Brief (Stojić), para. 183, referring to *Popović et al.* Appeal Judgement, paras 1369, 1652, 1654, *Đorđević* Appeal Judgement, para. 468, *Brđanin* Appeal Judgement, paras 364-365, Trial Judgement, Vol. 4, para. 428.
[5827]   Trial Judgement, Vol. 4, para. 428. See *supra,* paras 1759-1760.
[5828]   Trial Judgement, Vol. 4, paras 67-68. See *infra,* paras 1770, 1772, 1800-1804.
[5829]   *Đorđević* Appeal Judgement, para. 468, referring to *Tadić* Appeal Judgement, paras 220, 228, *Krajišnik* Appeal Judgement, para. 707. See *Stanišić and Simatović* Appeal Judgement, para. 77 ("The *mens rea* element for the first category of JCE liability is the intent to perpetrate a certain crime (this being the shared intent on the part of all co-perpetrators)"); *Šainović et al.* Appeal Judgement, paras 996 ("The Trial Chamber correctly articulated the requisite *mens rea* for the first category of JCE, explaining that it had to be proved 'that the accused shared with the other joint criminal enterprise members the intent to commit the crime or underlying offence.'"), 1286, 1470.
[5830]   *Popović et al.* Appeal Judgement, paras 1369, 1652; *Brđanin* Appeal Judgement, para. 365. See *Stanišić and Župljanin* Appeal Judgement, paras 915, 917.
[5831]   See *supra,* paras 1759-1760.

that he shared the intent of the JCE and to commit the JCE I crimes, and that he significantly contributed to the JCE.[5832] By merely asserting that the Trial Chamber's findings "do not inevitably" lead to this inference, when in fact they do, Stojić fails to present any persuasive argument to the contrary. Stojić's sub-ground of appeal 25.2 is dismissed.

(e) Alleged errors in inferring Stojić's intent from his general logistical assistance (Stojić's Sub-ground 25.3)

1765. Stojić argues that insofar as the Trial Chamber inferred his intent to commit the relevant crimes from the general logistical support that he provided to the military operations, including the financing of the armed forces, it erred.[5833] He submits that there "is no necessary connection between [his] general logistical acts, lawful in themselves, and the commission of crimes".[5834] Stojić also avers that the Trial Chamber's statement that his intent was based on "all the evidence analysed above" made it "impossible" to understand which evidence was relied on.[5835]

1766. The Prosecution responds that the Trial Chamber's analysis of Stojić's intent was neither unclear nor based on his general logistical support to the armed forces.[5836]

1767. The Trial Chamber concluded that "[i]n view of all the evidence analysed above, [...] the only possible inference it [could] reasonably draw [was] that Bruno Stojić intended to expel the Muslim population from the HZ(R) H-B."[5837] This conclusion was made in the final section of the Trial Judgement section addressing Stojić's responsibility after the Trial Chamber summarised its findings, made in the preceding sub-sections, regarding Stojić's contribution to the JCE and his intent.[5838] The Appeals Chamber considers that, while it would have been preferable for the Trial Chamber to have provided cross-references to the evidence and findings it relied on, it was not "impossible" for Stojić to ascertain on what basis the Trial Chamber inferred his intent. On his more specific argument, the Appeals Chamber finds that it is evident that the Trial Chamber did not rely **[page 733]** on Stojić's administrative or logistical assistance to the armed forces and the military operations to infer his intent. Rather, the Appeals Chamber recalls that this assistance was explicitly considered by the Trial Chamber in determining Stojić's command authority and "effective control" over the HVO and the Military Police[5839] as well as his significant contribution to the JCE.[5840] Thus, Stojić's arguments and sub-ground of appeal 25.3 are dismissed.[5841]

(f) Alleged errors concerning Stojić's intent to commit certain crimes (Stojić's Sub-ground 25.4)

(i) Arguments of the Parties

1768. Stojić submits that the Trial Chamber failed to make clear and reasoned findings that he had the requisite intent for certain crimes.[5842] Although the convictions in the *Đorđević* case were upheld despite the failure to make precise findings on intent for each crime, Stojić contends that the crimes in the present case are less connected to the CCP and more complex, thus requiring the Trial Chamber to make individual intent

---

[5832] Trial Judgement, Vol. 4, paras 426, 428-429.
[5833] Stojić's Appeal Brief, para. 207, heading before para. 206. See Stojić's Appeal Brief, para. 206.
[5834] Stojić's Appeal Brief, para. 207. Stojić also asserts that the Trial Chamber failed to consider the absence of evidence that he ordered the commission of any crime. Stojić's Appeal Brief, heading before para. 206.
[5835] Stojić's Appeal Brief, paras 206-207, referring to Trial Judgement, Vol. 4, para. 428.
[5836] Prosecution's Response Brief (Stojić), para. 187.
[5837] Trial Judgement, Vol. 4, para. 428.
[5838] Trial Judgement, Vol. 4, paras 425-427. See *infra*, para. 1792.
[5839] See *supra*, paras 1409-1412, 1441-1453, 1470-1472.
[5840] See *supra*, paras 1534-1537.
[5841] The Appeals Chamber also dismisses Stojić's assertion – found only in a heading – on his alleged lack of orders as he fails to develop this argument or explain how evidence of an order is required in order to infer his intent.
[5842] Stojić's Appeal Brief, heading before para. 208, paras 210, 215. See Stojić's Appeal Brief, para. 208; Stojić's Reply Brief, paras 61, 64, referring to, *inter alia, Brđanin* Appeal Judgement, para. 365, *Krajišnik* Appeal Judgement, para. 200. See also Appeal Hearing, AT. 282-284 (21 Mar 2017).

findings.[5843] In this regard, he argues that the Trial Chamber failed to find that he intended to: (1) cause death or grievous bodily harm to victims (Counts 2 and 3) in any municipality;[5844] (2) destroy property or had reckless disregard to the likelihood of such destruction (Counts 19 and 20) in Jablanica, Mostar, or Vareš;[5845] (3) destroy protected property (Count 21) in Mostar;[5846] or (4) spread terror among the civilian population (Count 25).[5847] Further, Stojić argues that any finding that he intended the murders in Mostar is inconsistent with an earlier finding that those murders did not fall within the CCP because there was a "lack of common **[page 734]** intent".[5848] He also contends that the Trial Chamber's approach was inconsistent, making particular findings on his intent regarding crimes in some municipalities while failing to do so for others.[5849]

1769.   The Prosecution responds that it was sufficient for the Trial Chamber to have clearly set out the types of crimes within the CCP and determine that Stojić shared the intent with the other JCE members to commit those crimes.[5850] It argues that, in any event, the Trial Chamber made exact findings that Stojić intended the commission of particular crimes in specific locations, including the destruction of property and mosques.[5851] According to the Prosecution, the Trial Chamber's findings are consistent as it was the murders committed during evictions and in detention centres which the Trial Chamber found were not JCE I crimes,[5852]

(ii) Analysis

a. Alleged errors regarding Stojić's intent to commit crimes under Counts 2, 3, 19, 20, and 21 of the Indictment

1770.   The Appeals Chamber recalls the Trial Chamber's finding that Stojić shared the intent to expel the Muslim population from the HZ(R) H-B territory, and that this finding is indistinguishable from the Trial Chamber's finding that Stojić had the intent to ethnically cleanse the Muslim population through an "entire system for deporting the Muslim population of the HR H-B", effectuated through a range of crimes under the Statute.[5853] It also found that Stojić and the other Appellants, as JCE members, intended that the relevant crimes be committed in order to further the CCP, and then proceeded to list these crimes.[5854] Notably, the crimes enumerated by the Trial Chamber as falling within the CCP included murder (Count 2),[5855] wilful killing (Count 3), extensive destruction of property not justified by military necessity and carried out unlawfully and wantonly (Count 19), wanton destruction of cities, towns, or villages or devastation not justified by military necessity (Count 20), destruction or wilful damage done to institutions dedicated to religion **[page 735]** or education (Count 21), and unlawful infliction of terror on civilians in Mostar (Count

---

[5843]   Stojić's Appeal Brief, para. 209 (referring to *Đorđević* Appeal Judgement, para. 930); Stojić's Reply Brief, paras 62-63 (referring to *Đorđević* Appeal Judgement, paras 468, 470); Appeal Hearing, AT. 283-284 (21 Mar 2017). Stojić replies that as it only found that he intended to expel the Muslim population, the Trial Chamber should have made separate findings that he intended each diverse crime and that this is essential. Stojić's Reply Brief, paras 62-63; Appeal Hearing, AT. 284 (21 Mar 2017).

[5844]   Stojić's Appeal Brief, para. 211, referring to Trial Judgement, Vol. 4, paras 330-337, 343-372, 379-383, 388-395, *Kvočka et al.* Appeal Judgement, para. 259, *Kordić and Čerkez* Appeal Judgement, paras 36-38.

[5845]   Stojić's Appeal Brief, para. 212, referring to Trial Judgement, Vol. 4, paras 342, 363, 370, 383, *Kordić and Čerkez* Appeal Judgement, para. 74. Stojić also argues that the Trial Chamber was ambiguous in finding that he intended to commit "those crimes" in Gornji Vakuf without specifying which crimes or what *mens rea* standard it applied. Stojić's Appeal Brief, para. 212, referring to Trial Judgement, Vol. 4, para. 337.

[5846]   Stojić's Appeal Brief, para. 213, referring to Trial Judgement, Vol. 1, para. 176, Vol. 4, para. 363.

[5847]   Stojić's Appeal Brief, para. 214, referring to Trial Judgement, Vol. 1, para. 197, Vol. 4, paras 343-372, *Galić* Appeal Judgement, para. 104.

[5848]   Stojić's Appeal Brief, para. 211, referring to Trial Judgement, Vol. 4; para. 70.

[5849]   Stojić's Appeal Brief, paras 199, 213; Stojić's Reply Brief, para. 61.

[5850]   Prosecution's Response Brief (Stojić), para. 184, referring to Trial Judgement, Vol. 4, paras 67-68, 428, *Đorđević* Appeal Judgement, paras 468, 470. See Prosecution's Response Brief (Stojić), paras 181, 183.

[5851]   Prosecution's Reponse Brief (Stojić), para. 185, referring to Trial Judgement, Vol. 4, paras 336-337, 349, 355-357, 378.

[5852]   Prosecution's Response Brief (Stojić), para. 186, referring to Trial Judgement, Vol. 4, paras 65-66, 70.

[5853]   See *supra*, paras 1759-1760.

[5854]   Trial Judgement, Vol. 4, paras 67-68, 426. See Trial Judgement, Vol. 4, para. 66.

[5855]   See *infra*, para. 1773. The Appeals Chamber recalls its finding that no reasonable trier of fact could conclude that murder and wilful killing were part of the CCP from January 1993 until June 1993. See *supra*, para. 882. While this means that Stojić did not have the intent for murder and wilful killing from January 1993 until June 1993, this does not affect the Trial Chamber's remaining findings concerning his contributions and intent for various crimes – including murder and wilful killing from June 1993 – particularly since only a few murders forming part of the CCP were found to have occurred prior to June 1993. See *supra*, para. 876.

25).[5856] The Trial Chamber elaborated on these findings by determining that Stojić planned, intended, and accepted the crimes discussed in relation to the various municipalities,[5857] and concluded that the only inference it could reasonably draw was that he intended to have those crimes committed.[5858] Moreover, the Appeals Chamber recalls that the Trial Chamber explicitly found that Stojić encouraged crimes and did not intend to prevent or punish crimes committed by the HVO and the Military Police, which it later considered in inferring his intent.[5859] Before analysing whether these findings were sufficient, the Appeals Chamber will first consider Stojić's arguments on what the Trial Chamber was required to find with respect to his intent.

1771. Stojić argues that the Trial Chamber was required to make findings on the underlying elements of *mens rea* in relation to each crime, such as – in the case of murder and wilful killing – the intent to cause death or grievous bodily harm which he reasonably must have known might have lead to death.[5860] The Appeals Chamber notes, however, that none of the authorities Stojić cites support this proposition, and his attempt at distinguishing the *Đorđević* Appeal Judgement is not convincing. In the *Đorđević* case, the Appeals Chamber found no error in the approach of identifying the crimes that were part of the JCE in that case and then finding that Vlastimir Đorđević "shared the requisite intent for these crimes".[5861] While the CCP in this case involves various types of crimes, the Trial Chamber clearly identified the crimes which it found all the Appellants shared the intent to commit.[5862] Moreover, in discussing the specific intent required for persecution under JCE I liability, it was noted in the *Đorđević* Appeal Judgement that it would be preferable for a trial chamber to make "separate findings on [the accused's] intent in relation to each of the crimes that were within the JCE", but nonetheless no error was found as the essence of the JCE was clearly discriminatory.[5863] **[page 736]**

1772. Furthermore, the Appeals Chamber considers that the Trial Chamber made the requisite findings in respect of the crimes challenged by Stojić. Of particular note is the fact that the Trial Chamber set out correctly the applicable law on the various crimes and JCE liability.[5864] Importantly, the Trial Chamber also made extensive findings on the required *actus reus* and *mens rea* of the physical perpetrators for all crimes which it found were the means through which the CCP was achieved.[5865] Specifically, for the crimes of murder and wilful killing,[5866] the Appeals Chamber notes the Trial Chamber's findings that Stojić knew of, accepted, and intended: (1) the murders and wounding of Muslim civilians in East Mostar during the siege of that part of the town;[5867] (2) the murders in Stupni Do;[5868] and (3) the wounding and death of some of the detainees at the Heliodrom used for work on the front line.[5869] In relation to the crimes of extensive destruction of property and wanton destruction or devastation of cities, towns, or villages in Jablanica, Mostar, and Vareš, and destruction or wilful damage to institutions dedicated to religion or education in Mostar, the Trial Chamber found that Stojić knew of, accepted, and intended: (1) the destruction of property, including

---

[5856]   Trial Judgement, Vol. 4, para. 68. See *supra*, fn. 5856

[5857]   See Trial Judgement, Vol. 4, paras 337, 342, 349, 357, 363, 370, 378, 383, 389, 395, 407. See *infra*, paras 1800-1804. The Appeals Chamber recalls here its finding overturning Stojić's convictions for murder and wilful killing in relation to the deaths of civilians in Duša, Gornji Vakuf Municipality, and in relation to two killings in Tošćanica, Prozor Municipality. See *supra*, paras 441-443, 880-882.

[5858]   Trial Judgement, Vol. 4, para. 426.

[5859]   Trial Judgement, Vol. 4, paras 423, 427.

[5860]   See *supra*, para. 1768.

[5861]   *Đorđević* Appeal Judgement, para. 468. See also *Šainović et al.* Appeal Judgement, para. 996 (the Appeals Chamber found that there was no error in the Trial Chamber's approach regarding *mens rea* by concluding that the common purpose of the JCE was to be achieved through forcibly displacing the Kosovo Albanian population, and subsequently finding that Šainović "shared the intent to forcibly displace part of the Kosovo Albanian population"); *Karemera and Ngirumpatse* Appeal Judgement, paras 137, 154 (the trial chamber did not err in finding that the accused acted with the requisite *mens rea* when it considered that the JCE members acted with the intent to destroy the Tutsi population after expressly considering the massive scale of the killings, systematically and publicly targeting Tutsi civilians).

[5862]   See *supra*, paras 1759-1760, 1770.

[5863]   *Đorđević* Appeal Judgement, para. 470.

[5864]   Trial Judgement, Vol. 1, paras 31-221.

[5865]   Trial Judgement, Vol. 3, paras 509-1741, Vol. 4, para. 68.

[5866]   The Appeals Chamber recalls its finding that no reasonable trier of fact could conclude that murder and wilful killing were part of the CCP from January 1993 until June 1993. See *supra*, para. 882.

[5867]   Trial Judgement, Vol. 4, paras.369-370. See *infra*, paras 1773, 1800-1804.

[5868]   Trial Judgement, Vol. 4, para. 383.

[5869]   Trial Judgement, Vol. 4, para. 395. See *infra*, paras 1773, 1800-1804.

mosques, in Jablanica;[5870] (2) the destruction of property, including mosques, related to the shelling and harsh living conditions of the population of East Mostar;[5871] and (3) the destruction of property in Stupni Do.[5872] In light of these findings, the Appeals Chamber considers that the Trial Chamber made separate findings on Stojić's intent in relation to each of the crimes as required. Thus, Stojić fails to demonstrate that the requisite intent findings were not made or that they were unclear. His arguments discussed above are dismissed.

1773. The Appeals Chamber now turns to Stojić's argument that the Trial Chamber was inconsistent in its findings concerning the murders in Mostar. The Appeals Chamber notes that the Trial Chamber excluded certain murders in Mostar from the CCP, to the extent that they occurred specifically "during the HVO campaigns to expel the Muslims or while they were in detention".[5873] The Trial Chamber thus appropriately made no findings on Stojić's intent for any murders in West Mostar,[5874] although it did find that he intended murders in East Mostar in respect of the crimes connected with the siege there.[5875] Thus, the Appeals Chamber considers that the Trial Chamber's **[page 737]** findings were consistent in this respect. With regard to Stojić's argument that the Trial Chamber's approach was inconsistent in finding that he intended crimes in particular municipalities while making no such findings in others, the Appeals Chamber considers that he misinterprets' the Trial Chamber's findings. The Appeals Chamber recalls that JCE I intent can be inferred from circumstantial evidence, such as a person's knowledge of the common criminal purpose or the crime(s) involved, combined with his continuing participation in the crimes or in the implementation of the common criminal purpose, if this is the only reasonable inference available on the evidence.[5876] In the paragraphs where Stojić alleges no intent finding was made,[5877] the Trial Chamber found that he: (1) participated in planning the crimes;[5878] or (2) knew about the relevant crimes, but continued to participate in the JCE, and thus "accepted" those crimes.[5879] The Trial Chamber then concluded that the only inference it could reasonably draw was that he intended to have those crimes committed.[5880] The Appeals Chamber considers that Stojić fails to demonstrate any error or inconsistency in the Trial Chamber's approach. Stojić's arguments on inconsistencies are dismissed.

b. Alleged errors regarding Stojić's specific intent to commit the crime of unlawful infliction of terror on civilians

1774. The Appeals Chamber next turns to Stojić's argument that the Trial Chamber failed to find that he possessed the intent required for the crime of unlawful infliction of terror on civilians under Article 3 of the Statute. The Appeals Chamber recalls that the *mens rea* for this crime requires the general intent to make the civilian population or individual civilians not taking direct part in hostilities the object of the acts of violence or threats thereof and the "specific intent to spread terror among the civilian population".[5881] While spreading terror must be the primary purpose of the acts or threats of violence, it need not be the only one and can be inferred from the "nature, manner, timing, and duration" of the acts or threats.[5882] **[page 738]**

[5870]   Trial Judgement, Vol. 4, para. 342. See *infra*, paras 1773, 1800-1804. The Trial Chamber considered the destruction of mosques committed in Jablanica under Count 21 as a JCE III crime. Trial Judgement, Vol. 4, para. 342.

[5871]   Trial Judgement, Vol. 4, para. 363. See *infra*, paras 1773, 1800-1804.

[5872]   Trial Judgement, Vol. 4, para. 383.

[5873]   Trial Judgement, Vol. 4, para. 70. See Trial Judgement, Vol. 4, paras 56-58, 348-349, 357.

[5874]   Trial Judgement, Vol. 4, paras 347-349, 357.

[5875]   Trial Judgement, Vol. 4, paras 363, 369-370.

[5876]   *Stanišić and Simatović* Appeal Judgement, para. 81; *Popović et al.* Appeal Judgement, paras 1369, 1652. See *Stanišić and Župljanin* Appeal Judgement, para. 393.

[5877]   Stojić's Appeal Brief, fn. 541.

[5878]   Trial Judgement, Vol. 4, para. 349.

[5879]   Trial Judgement, Vol. 4, paras 342, 363, 369-370, 383. See *infra*, paras 1800-1804.

[5880]   Trial Judgement, Vol. 4, para. 426.

[5881]   *D. Milošević* Appeal Judgement, para. 37; *Galić* Appeal Judgement, para. 104. The *actus reus* of the crime of unlawful infliction of terror consists of "[a]cts or threats of violence directed against the civilian population or individual civilians not taking direct part in hostilities causing death or serious injury to body or health within the civilian population". *D. Milošević Appeal* Judgement, para. 31. See *Galić* Appeal Judgement, para. 100.

[5882]   *D. Milošević Appeal* Judgement, para. 37; *Galić* Appeal Judgement, para. 104. See *infra*, para. 2017.

1775. In response to Stojić's argument that the Trial Chamber failed to find that he intended to spread terror among the civilian population,[5883] the Prosecution concedes that the Trial Chamber made no explicit finding on Stojić's specific intent to commit terror.[5884] Nonetheless, the Prosecution argues that the only reasonable reading of the Trial Judgement as a whole results in the inherent conclusion that Stojić possessed the specific intent to commit terror.[5885] It avers that this conclusion is inherent from the Trial Chamber's findings on Stojić's heavy involvement in the Mostar operations, his knowledge of the same, and his shared intent for the CCP.[5886] The Prosecution also contends that "when the [Trial] Chamber found that the HVO possessed the specific intent to spread terror [...], one of the people within the HVO that the [Trial] Chamber must have been referring to was Stojić".[5887] It concludes that the Trial Chamber "had clearly satisfied itself that Stojić possessed the specific intent to spread terror".[5888] The Prosecution also responds that, if there was a failure to provide a reasoned opinion on this issue, the findings and the evidence leads to "the same inescapable conclusion".[5889]

1776. Stojić replies that the evidence is incompatible with a finding that he intended to spread terror, referring to: (1) his statements at the 17 July 1993 dinner indicating that the HVO's primary purpose in East Mostar was to gain a military advantage and that he offered to assist evacuations;[5890] (2) evidence that he provided medical supplies to Muslim civilians and the ABiH in Mostar;[5891] and (3) a Trial Chamber finding that, between July and November 1993, the HVO attempted to manage the electricity and water supply problem in Mostar.[5892] Stojić also submits that a finding on his specific intent to commit terror is such a fundamental and basic finding, that its absence from the Trial Judgement can only result in the reversal of his conviction, particularly as it relates to an expanded JCE crime and requires speculation.[5893]

1777. The Appeals Chamber recalls that, in the section on Stojić's individual responsibility pursuant to JCE I, the Trial Chamber found that Stojić "accepted the crimes directly linked to the HVO military operations against East Mostar, that is, the murders and the destruction of property, including mosques, related to shelling and the harsh living conditions of the population of that part **[page 739]** of the town caused by the lack of food and water".[5894] The Trial Chamber also found that Stojić "must have known that the snipers in West Mostar were targeting civilians and members of international organisations in East Mostar"[5895] and "accepted the murders and wounding of Muslim civilians in East Mostar during the siege of that part of the town".[5896] It also found that he facilitated the hindering of access of humanitarian aid to East Mostar.[5897] Furthermore, the Trial Chamber found that Stojić intended to expel the Muslim population from HZ(R) H-B, and that he shared this intent with other JCE members.[5898] The Trial Chamber then found Stojić responsible for committing the crime of unlawful infliction of terror on civilians in Mostar Municipality.[5899]

1778. The Appeals Chamber concludes that, in making the intent findings above[5900] and holding Stojić responsible for the crime of unlawful infliction of terror on civilians, the Trial Chamber considered that he had the required *mens rea* for this crime. However, the Appeals Chamber finds that the Trial Chamber's

---

[5883]   Stojić's Appeal Brief, para. 214, referring to Trial Judgement, Vol. 1, para. 197, Vol. 4, paras 343-372, *Galić* Appeal Judgement, para. 104. See *supra*, para. 1768.
[5884]   Appeal Hearing, AT. 339-340 (21 Mar 2017).
[5885]   Appeal Hearing, AT. 340, 342-343 (21 Mar 2017).
[5886]   Appeal Hearing, AT. 340-342 (21 Mar 2017), referring to Trial Judgement, Vol. 2, paras 1231, 1246, Vol. 4, paras 359, 362, 372.
[5887]   Appeal Hearing, AT. 340 (21 Mar 2017), referring to Trial Judgement, Vol. 3, para. 1692. See Appeal Hearing, AT. 341-342 (21 Mar 2017).
[5888]   Appeal Hearing, AT. 340 (21 Mar 2017), referring to Trial Judgement, Vol. 4, paras 428, 431.
[5889]   Appeal Hearing, AT. 342 (21 Mar 2017). See Appeal Hearing, AT. 343-344 (21 Mar 2017).
[5890]   Appeal Hearing, AT. 362-363 (21 Mar 2017), referring to Trial Judgement, Vol. 4, para. 361.
[5891]   Appeal Hearing, AT. 363 (21 Mar 2017), referring to Stojić's Appeal Brief, para. 316.
[5892]   Appeal Hearing, AT. 362-363 (21 Mar 2017), referring to Trial Judgement, Vol. 2, para. 1218.
[5893]   Appeal Hearing, AT. 362-363 (21 Mar 2017).
[5894]   Trial Judgement, Vol. 4, para. 363. See *supra*, para. 1661, fn. 5395.
[5895]   Trial Judgement, Vol. 4, para. 369. See *supra*, para. 1667.
[5896]   Trial Judgement, Vol. 4, para. 370.
[5897]   Trial Judgement, Vol. 4, para. 372. See *supra*, para. 1674.
[5898]   Trial Judgement, Vol. 4, para. 428. See Trial Judgement, Vol. 4, para. 429. See also *supra*, para. 1760.
[5899]   Trial Judgement, Vol. 4, para. 431. See Trial Judgement, Vol. 3, paras 1689-1692.
[5900]   See *supra*, para. 1777.

approach falls short of what is required under its obligation under Article 23(2) of the Statute, translated into Rule 98 *ter*(C) of the Rules, to give a reasoned opinion in writing, meaning that "all the constituent elements of a crime have to be discussed and supporting evidence has to be assessed by the Trial Chamber".[5901] Although the Appeals Chamber considers that the intent findings for Stojić provided by the Trial Chamber satisfy the general intent requirement that he intended to make the civilian population or individual civilians not taking direct part in hostilities the object of the acts of violence, they do not satisfy the specific intent requirement, namely, whether he committed the offence with the primary purpose of spreading terror among the civilian population.[5902] In this regard, the Appeals Chamber notes that, in the section outlining its legal findings, the Trial Chamber explicitly found that the HVO had "the specific intention [...] to spread terror among the civilian population of East Mostar"[5903] and "committed acts of violence, the main aim of which was to inflict terror on the population".[5904] However, no similar findings were made in the individual criminal responsibility section to clarify whether Stojić shared this specific intent.[5905] **[page 740]**

1779. In these circumstances, the Appeals Chamber finds that the Trial Chamber failed to provide a reasoned opinion, by neglecting to set out in a clear and articulate manner the factual and legal *mens rea* findings on the basis of which it reached the decision to convict Stojić for the crime of unlawful infliction of terror.[5906] The Appeals Chamber will therefore determine whether this error of law invalidates the Trial Chamber's decision to convict Stojić for this crime. In so doing, the Appeals Chamber will assess, on the basis of the Trial Chamber's findings, as well as evidence referred to by the Trial Chamber, whether a reasonable trier of fact could be satisfied beyond reasonable doubt – and as the only reasonable inference available – that Stojić intended that the acts of violence be committed with the primary purpose of spreading terror among the civilian population.[5907]

1780. The Appeals Chamber notes that, in the portion of the Trial Judgement relating to the legal findings on the crime of unlawful infliction of terror, the Trial Chamber, having described the "appalling living conditions" in East Mostar, found that:

> The [Trial] Chamber is satisfied that the deliberate isolation of a population in an area as small as East Mostar for several months – and doing so after forcibly transferring a large part of the population there – and thus the exacerbation of their distress and difficult living conditions is part of the same plan and demonstrates the specific intention of the HVO to spread terror among the civilian population of East Mostar.[5908]

1781. It reached this conclusion, having considered, *inter alia*, that: (1) between June 1993 and March 1994, the HVO subjected the civilian population of East Mostar to intense, daily, and frequent shelling and firing which resulted in the death and injury of a large number of Muslim civilians;[5909] (2) these attacks were indiscriminate particularly as they were intense and uninterrupted over a period of nine months, they were not limited to specific targets;[5910] (3) the civilian inhabitants of East Mostar were subjected to a campaign of HVO sniper fire involving the targeting of women, children, and elderly people who were going about their daily business, including firemen aiding and assisting the population;[5911] (4) the constant and intense shelling and fire – including sniper fire – had the effect of terrifying the population of East Mostar;[5912] (5) between June 1993 and December 1993, the HVO deliberately destroyed ten mosques in East Mostar, which had no military value, as well as the Old Bridge of Mostar on 8 November 1993, the destruction of which had a major psychological impact on the morale of the population and the **[page 741]** HVO had to be aware of that impact,

---

[5901]   *Kordić and Čerkez* Appeal Judgement, para. 383. See also *Kordić and Čerkez* Appeal Judgement, para. 385.
[5902]   See *supra*, para. 1774.
[5903]   Trial Judgement, Vol. 3, para. 1691. See *supra*, paras 546-565.
[5904]   Trial Judgement, Vol. 3, para. 1692. See *supra*, paras 546-565.
[5905]   See *infra*, para. 2019.
[5906]   See *Bizimungu* Appeal Judgement, para. 18, referring to *Hadžihasanović and Kubura* Appeal Judgement, para. 13.
[5907]   See *Stanišić and Župljanin* Appeal Judgement, para. 356, referring to *Kordić and Čerkez* Appeal Judgement, paras 383-388, *Nyiramasuhuko et al.* Appeal Judgement, para. 977, *Bizimungu* Appeal Judgement, para. 23, *Ndindiliyimana et al.* Appeal Judgement, para. 293. See also *supra*, para. 20; *infra*, para. 2020.
[5908]   Trial Judgement, Vol. 3, para. 1691. See also *infra*, para. 2021.
[5909]   Trial Judgement, Vol. 3, para. 1689. See *supra*, paras 546-565.
[5910]   Trial Judgement, Vol. 3, para. 1689. See *supra*, paras 546-565.
[5911]   Trial Judgement, Vol. 3, para. 1689. See *supra*, paras 540-545.
[5912]   Trial Judgement, Vol. 3, para. 1689. See *supra*, paras 546-565.

in light of the great symbolic, cultural, and historical value the mosques and the Old Bridge had;[5913] and (6) the HVO aggravated the appalling living conditions to which the Muslim inhabitants of East Mostar were subjected by blocking or hindering the regular provision of humanitarian aid or access of the international organisations to East Mostar, including by deliberately attacking the members of the international organisations, and by deliberately keeping the civilian population in the small and overcrowded enclave of East Mostar from June 1993 to April 1994.[5914] The Appeals Chamber recalls, in this regard, that the challenges presented to the Trial Chamber's finding that the HVO committed the crime of unlawful infliction of terror on the population of East Mostar have been considered and dismissed, with the exception of the challenges to the Old Bridge. Specifically, the Appeals Chamber recalls that it has found the Trial Chamber's conclusion that the destruction of the Old Bridge was unlawful to be erroneous.[5915] Thus, the Trial Chamber's findings on the Old Bridge will not be considered in determining whether Stojić had the specific intent to terrorise.

1782. The Appeals Chamber considers that, to the extent that Stojić had knowledge of and contributed to the appalling living conditions in East Mostar caused by the HVO, the Trial Chamber's reasoning outlined above is relevant for the assessment of Stojić's own specific intent for the crime of unlawful infliction of terror. Thus, in relation to his involvement in the crimes, the Appeals Chamber recalls the Trial Chamber's findings that Stojić "commanded and had effective control over the HVO armed forces" from 3 July 1992 to 15 November 1993.[5916] The Trial Chamber found, in particular, that Stojić had the power to "send military-related government decisions through the military chain of command and used that authority [and] that he had the authority to issue orders directly to the armed forces and to ensure they were carried out and used that authority".[5917]

1783. In relation to how Stojić exercised this authority in Mostar Municipality, the Appeals Chamber observes that the Trial Chamber noted Stojić's admission that he controlled the snipers positioned in the glass-walled bank building and the secondary school in Mostar.[5918] The Trial Chamber found that, inasmuch as Stojić controlled most of the HVO armed forces and as all the **[page 742]** sniping in West Mostar had the same targets and followed the same *modus operandi*, the Only inference it could draw was that Stojić controlled all the snipers in West Mostar.[5919] The Appeals Chamber notes here the Trial Chamber's findings that the HVO snipers in West Mostar subjected the civilian population of East Mostar to a campaign of sniper fire, involving the targeting of women, children, and elderly people who were going about their daily business, including firemen aiding and assisting the population,[5920] and that this sniper fire terrified the population of East Mostar.[5921] The Appeals Chamber recalls also the Trial Chamber's findings that Stojić knew that the snipers in West Mostar were targeting civilians and members of international organisations and thereby accepted the murders and wounding of Muslim civilians in East Mostar during the siege.[5922]

1784. The Appeals Chamber further notes that the Trial Chamber made findings regarding Stojić's involvement in the shelling of East Mostar and the harsh living conditions endured by the population of that part of the town. In this respect, the Trial Chamber noted evidence that on 17 July 1993, Stojić told members of international organisations that the HVO plan of action was to put pressure on East Mostar to force the ABiH to leave the sector, which the Trial Chamber considered was necessarily directed against the entire

---

[5913] Trial Judgement, Vol. 3, para. 1690. See *supra*, paras 405-426.

[5914] Trial Judgement, Vol. 3, para. 1691. See *supra*, paras 536-539.

[5915] The Appeals Chamber recalls that it has reversed the Trial Chamber's conclusion that the destruction of the Old Bridge constituted wanton destruction of cities, towns or villages or devastation not justified by military necessity as a violation of the laws or customs of war. The Appeals Chamber has also reversed the Trial Chamber's findings that the destruction of the Old Bridge constituted persecution as a crime against humanity (Count 1) and unlawful infliction of terror on civilians as a violation of the laws or customs of war (Count 25) and has therefore acquitted the Appellants of these charges insofar as they concern the Old Bridge. See *supra*, paras 411-414, 426, 548-565. See also *infra*, para. 2021.

[5916] Trial Judgement, Vol. 4, para. 312. See *supra*, paras 1405, 1457-1458, 1479.

[5917] Trial Judgement, Vol. 4, para. 312. See *supra*, paras 1422-1423, 1435, 1457.

[5918] Trial Judgement, Vol. 4, para. 368.

[5919] Trial Judgement, Vol. 4, para. 368. See *supra*, para. 1667.

[5920] Trial Judgement, Vol. 3, para. 1689, Vol. 4, paras 369-370. See *supra*, paras 540-545.

[5921] Trial Judgement, Vol. 3, para. 1689. See also Trial Judgement, Vol. 2, para. 1015.

[5922] Trial Judgement, Vol. 4, paras 369-370. See *supra*, para. 1667.

population of East Mostar and not only against the ABiH.[5923] In this regard, the Appeals Chamber dismisses elsewhere Stojić's arguments on his statements made on 17 July 1993.[5924]

1785. Additionally, the Trial Chamber considered evidence that: (1) Stojić was kept informed by representatives of the international community about crimes committed by HVO members in Mostar, such as the shelling and incidents when representatives of the international community were targeted by the HVO;[5925] and (2) Branko Kvesić, Head of the Department of the Interior of the HZ H-B, informed Stojić that there was no water or electricity in East Mostar and that there was less and less food and medical equipment there.[5926] The Trial Chamber found, in view of this evidence, that Stojić knew of the shelling of East Mostar, the attacks on representatives of international organisations, and the shortages of food and water suffered by the Muslim population.[5927] In this regard, the Appeals Chamber dismisses elsewhere Stojić's arguments concerning the medical assistance given by the HVO.[5928] However, the Appeals Chamber has granted Stojić's contentions regarding the HVO's attempts at managing the water supply and **[page 743]** concluded that the Trial Chamber erred in considering that he accepted the water shortage as a component of the harsh living conditions endured by the civilian population.[5929] However, the Trial Chamber's finding that Stojić accepted the harsh living condition caused by the lack of food is maintained, thus any error in relation to the water shortage would not impact on Stojić's knowledge and intent, particularly in light of the various other findings supporting the conclusion that he knew of and accepted the harsh living conditions.

1786. The Appeals Chamber also recalls the Trial Chamber's findings that the shelling was indiscriminate,[5930] and also had the effect of terrifying the population.[5931] The Trial Chamber concluded that Stojić knew of the HVO's plan of action and the impact it had on the civilian population of East Mostar and that, inasmuch as he continued to exercise his functions in the HVO/Government of the HR H-B, he "accepted the crimes directly linked to the HVO military operations against East Mostar, that is, the murders and the destruction of property, including mosques, related to the shelling and the harsh living conditions of the population of that part of the town caused by the lack of food".[5932]

1787. The Appeals Chamber also recalls the Trial Chamber's finding that the HVO had to be aware of the major psychological impact that the destruction of the mosques, which had no military value, had on the morale of the population.[5933] The Trial Chamber found that Stojić accepted the destruction of the mosques related to the shelling of East Mostar.[5934] In light of this, the Appeals Chamber considers that a reasonable trier of fact could conclude that Stojić must have been aware that the destruction of the mosques would have a psychological impact on the morale of the population.[5935] Furthermore, the Appeals Chamber notes the Trial Chamber's finding that, inasmuch as Stojić did nothing to remove the obstacles hindering access of humanitarian aid to East Mostar even though he had the power and obligation to do so, he in fact facilitated them.[5936]

1788. In light of all of the above, the Appeals Chamber observes that, despite not explicitly finding that Stojić had the specific intent to spread terror, the Trial Chamber considered that Stojić had extensive knowledge of, and accepted nearly all, the underlying acts that the Trial Chamber earlier considered demonstrated the HVO's specific intent to spread terror.[5937] Accordingly, the **[page 744]** Appeals Chamber

---

[5923] Trial Judgement, Vol. 4, paras 361-362. See *supra*, para. 1658.
[5924] See *supra*, paras 1631, 1634, 1636.
[5925] Trial Judgement, Vol. 4, para. 359.
[5926] Trial Judgement, Vol. 4, para. 360. See *supra*, paras 1658-1660.
[5927] Trial Judgement, Vol. 4, para. 362. See *supra*, para. 1658.
[5928] See *supra*, paras 1656, 1658.
[5929] See *supra*, paras 1656, 1660.
[5930] Trial Judgement, Vol. 3, para. 1689. See Trial Judgement, Vol. 2, para. 1008; *supra*, paras 546-565.
[5931] Trial Judgement, Vol. 3, para. 1689. See Trial Judgement, Vol. 2, para. 1015; *supra*, paras 546-565.
[5932] Trial Judgement, Vol. 3, para. 363. See Trial Judgement, Vol. 4, para. 362. See also *supra*, para. 1661.
[5933] Trial Judgement, Vol. 3, para. 1690.
[5934] Trial Judgement, Vol. 4, para. 363. See *supra*, fn. 5395.
[5935] The Appeals Chamber is of the view that the finding that Stojić is responsible for the destruction of only three of the ten mosques does not have an impact on this conclusion. See *supra*, fn. 5395. See also *infra*, para. 2023 & fn. 6911.
[5936] Trial Judgement, Vol. 4, para. 372. See *supra*, para. 1674.
[5937] See *supra*, paras 1780-1781.

concludes in the specific circumstances of this case, and given Stojić's command authority over the HVO,[5938] that a reasonable trier of fact could be satisfied beyond reasonable doubt – and as the only reasonable inference available – that Stojić intended that the acts of violence be committed with the primary purpose of spreading terror among the civilian population. Therefore, Stojić fails to show that the Trial Chamber's failure to provide a reasoned opinion invalidates his conviction for the crimes of unlawful infliction of terror on civilians. Stojić's argument is dismissed.[5939]

(iii) Conclusion

1789. In sum, the Appeals Chamber finds that the Trial Chamber erred in failing to provide a reasoned opinion on Stojić's intent for the crime of unlawful infliction of terror on civilians under Article 3 of the Statute but concludes that Stojić fails to show how this error invalidates his conviction for the crime. Additionally, Stojić has failed to demonstrate any other error in the Trial Chamber's findings with respect to his intent to commit the JCE I crimes. Thus, Stojić's sub-ground of appeal 25.4 is dismissed.

(g) Alleged errors concerning Stojić's specific intent to discriminate against the Muslim population (Stojić's Sub-ground 25.5)

1790. Stojić argues that the Trial Chamber failed to provide a reasoned "decision" when it found that, based on "all the evidence analysed above", he knew that crimes were being committed against the Muslims with the sole puipose of forcing them to leave the territory of BiH.[5940] According to Stojić, the Trial Chamber failed to sufficiently explain the basis for its finding that the crimes were committed solely for that purpose, or that he knew that the crimes were committed solely for that purpose.[5941] Further, Stojić claims that the Trial Chamber failed to identify the evidence on which it relied and that the generic reference to "all the evidence analysed above" does not allow him to understand the finding and prejudices his ability to challenge it on appeal.[5942] He also avers that the Trial Chamber failed to explain its conclusion that mere participation in the JCE was sufficient to conclude that he had the specific intent to discriminate.[5943] Stojić submits that in finding that he had discriminatory intent, the Trial Chamber disregarded clearly relevant evidence about his general **[page 745]** attitude to Muslims[5944] such as: (1) witness testimony that he helped Muslims and did not express any prejudiced views;[5945] and (2) its own findings that Stojić himself supplied materiel and technical equipment to the ABiH and that the Department of Defence provided humanitarian aid to East Mostar.[5946] Stojić asserts that since the Trial Chamber failed to give a reasoned "decision" on a required element of the crime of persecution, the Appeals Chamber should reverse the finding that he intended to discriminate against Muslims and overturn his conviction on Count 1.[5947]

1791. The Prosecution responds that the Trial Chamber reasonably concluded that Stojić possessed discriminatory intent since the CCP he shared entailed the ethnic cleansing of Muslims and thus was clearly discriminatory.[5948] It argues that the Trial Chamber reasonably relied on its factual findings regarding

---

[5938] See *supra*, paras 1457, 1782.

[5939] See *infra*, para. 2024.

[5940] Stojić's Appeal Brief, paras 216, 218, referring to Trial Judgement, Vol. 4, para. 429.

[5941] Stojić's Appeal Brief, para. 218.

[5942] Stojić's Appeal Brief, para. 218.

[5943] Stojić's Appeal Brief, para. 218.

[5944] Stojić's Appeal Brief, para. 219. Stojić argues in reply that there is no discussion of evidence suggesting that he did not intend crimes or share the CCP anywhere in the Trial Judgement's section on his responsibility. Stojić's Reply Brief, para. 65, referring to Trial Judgement, Vol. 4, paras 425-431.

[5945] Stojić's Appeal Brief, para. 219, referring to Hamid Bahto, T. 37937 (11 Mar 2009), Nedžad Čengić, T. 37943-37944 (11 Mar 2009), Antoon van der Grinten, T. 21023-21024 (10 July 2007), Davor Korać, T. 38827, 38829-38330 (7 Apr 2009), Tomislav Krešić, T. 38736 (2 Apr 2009), Stipo Buljan, T. 36751-36752, 36766, 36768 (11 Feb 2009), Ivan Bagarić, T. 38879-38880, 38947-38948 (20 Apr 2009).

[5946] Stojić's Appeal Brief, para. 219, referring to Trial Judgement, Vol. 2, para. 1243, Vol. 4, para. 308. See also Stojić's Appeal Brief, para. 217, Stojić also submits that the Trial Chamber's misunderstanding of this evidence is demonstrated, by the fact that it was only used in the context of mitigation whereas he submitted that this evidence went to his intent. Stojić's Appeal Brief, para. 219, referring to Trial Judgement, Vol. 4, para. 1334, Stojić Closing Arguments, T. 52302-52303 (15 Feb 2011).

[5947] Stojić's Appeal Brief, para. 220.

[5948] Prosecution's Response Brief (Stojić), para. 188, referring to Trial Judgement, Vol. 4, paras 41, 65, 429, 1232.

Stojić's JCE participation in this regard[5949] and did not disregard evidence favourable to him.[5950] The Prosecution also submits that Stojić was not impaired in challenging this finding due to a lack of reasoned opinion.[5951]

1792. The Appeals Chamber notes that in making its findings in relation to Stojić's responsibility under JCE I, the Trial Chamber found that Stojić had *de facto* and *de jure* powers over most of the components of the HVO and the Military Police, that he was the link between the Government and the HVO,[5952] and he made no serious effort to stop the commission of crimes.[5953] Notably, the Trial Chamber made numerous findings on Stojić's knowledge or participation in the planning of the crimes in, *inter alia,* Gornji Vakuf, Mostar, and Čapljina, which targeted the Muslim population.[5954] **[page 746]** Having found that he shared the intent to expel the Muslim population from the HZ(R) H-B territory,[5955] the Trial Chamber then concluded that "all the evidence analysed above" shows that Stojić knew that crimes were being committed with the sole purpose of forcing Muslims to leave BiH and that, by participating in the JCE, Stojić intended to discriminate against the Muslims in order to facilitate their eviction from BiH.[5956]

1793. The Appeals Chamber sees no issue with the Trial Chamber's analysis. As found by the Trial Chamber, the CCP: (1) was the ethnic cleansing of the Muslim population which entailed the expulsion of the Muslim population from the HZ(R) H-B territory through the commission of a range of crimes under the Statute;[5957] (2) was accomplished by the JCE members, including Stojić, through the "use of the political and military apparatus of the HZ(R) H-B";[5958] and (3) was intended by Stojić who shared that intent with the other JCE members.[5959] Additionally, as recalled above, the Trial Chamber made numerous findings on Stojić's knowledge or participation in the planning of the crimes against Muslims.[5960] Further, the Trial Chamber found that Stojić knew of the crimes being committed against the Bosnian Muslims, and continued to

---

[5949] Prosecution's Response Brief (Stojić), para. 188, referring to *Đorđević* Appeal Judgement, para. 470.

[5950] Prosecution's Response Brief (Stojić), para. 188, referring to *Krajišnik* Appeal Judgement, paras 139, 141, *Kvočka et al.* Appeal Judgement, paras 23-24.

[5951] Prosecution's Response Brief (Stojić), para. 188, referring to, *inter alia, Haradinaj et al.* Appeal Judgement, para. 128, *Krajišnik* Appeal Judgement, para. 139. *Limoj et al.* Appeal Judgement, para. 81.

[5952] Trial Judgement, Vol. 4, para. 425.

[5953] Trial Judgement, Vol. 4, para. 427. See also *supra,* paras 1494-1495

[5954] Trial Judgement, Vol. 4, para. 336 (Stojić was aware of the destruction of Muslim houses and detention of Muslims in Gornji Vakuf), 349 (Stojić participated in planning the operations and acts of violence against Muslims in Mostar town and during eviction campaigns in West Mostar), 362-363 (Stojić knew of HVO's plan of action for the siege of East Mostar and knew of the shortages of food and water suffered by the Muslim population), 378 (Stojić knew of the evictions of the Muslim population from Čapljina and the manner in which they were carried out), 406-407 (Stojić knew of the detention of Muslims in extremely precarious conditions in Dretelj Prison and Gabela Prison and their mistreatment), 426. See Trial Judgement, Vol. 3, paras 1694-1741 (findings on the various HVO crimes which specifically targeted Muslims and thereby the underlying crimes of persecution under Count 1).

[5955] Trial Judgement, Vol. 4, para. 428. The Trial Chamber defined the CCP as the domination of the HR H-B Croats through the ethnic cleansing of the Muslim population. Trial Judgement, Vol. 4, para. 41. As noted above, the Appeals Chamber is of the view that the Trial Chamber's finding that Stojić shared the intent to expel the Muslim population from the HZ(R) H-B territory is one and the same as the one that he had the intent to ethnically cleanse the Muslim population through a "system for deporting the Muslim population of the HR H-B". See *supra,* paraš 1759-1760.

[5956] Trial Judgement, Vol. 4, para. 429.

[5957] Trial Judgement, Vol. 4, paras 41, 66, 428.

[5958] Trial Judgement, Vol. 4, para. 41. See *supra,* paras 786, 789-790.

[5959] Trial Judgement, Vol. 4, para. 428. See *supra,* paras 1755-1756, 1759-1760.

[5960] See *supra,* para. 1792. The Appeals Chamber notes the following: (1) the Trial Chamber found that the recurrence and scale of acts of violence against Muslims during the eviction campaigns in Mostar following the attack of 9 May 1993 and during the summer of 1993 were part of a preconceived plan and that Stojić participated in planning these acts of violence following the attack of 9 May 1993 and intended those acts during the summer of 1993 (see Trial Judgement, Vol. 4, paras 347, 349, 357; *supra,* paras 1598, 1612-1615, 1617, 1652); (2) in its factual narrative of the expulsion of Muslims families from West Mostar after the Attack on the HVO Tihomir Mišić Barracks, the Trial Chamber considered Vrlić's Report of 5 July 1993, which was personally sent to Stojić and provided a list of Muslim families who had a member in the ABiH – which Vrlić called a *"balija* unit" – that included the address of each family mentioned indicating that a raid would be carried out in the course of the evening (see Trial Judgement, Vol. 2, para. 897, Vol. 4, para. 352, referring to Ex. P03181; *supra,* paras 1617, 1622); and (3) Stojić's statement to international representatives on 17 July 1993 that the HVO's plan of action was to put pressure on East Mostar in order to force the ABiH to leave the sector, which, as found by the Trial Chamber, was necessarily directed against the entire population of East Mostar and not only against the ABiH (in so finding the Trial Chamber considered evidence from members of international organisations that Stojić seemed convinced of his troops' ability to achieve a military solution to what the HVO considered was a "Muslim problem" in Mostar town (see Trial Judgement, Vol. 2, para. 1246, Vol. 4, paras 361-362, referring to Ex. P03545; *supra,* paras 1634-1637, 1655, 1658).

participate in the JCE until November 1993.[5961] Bearing in mind, moreover, that the essence of the JCE was inherently discriminatory as it consisted of the expulsion of the Muslim population from the HZ(R) H-B territory through a range of crimes under the Statute, the Appeals Chamber is of the view that the Trial Chamber did not err in its approach in concluding that Stojić possessed the specific intent to discriminate against the Muslim population. **[page 747]**

1794. The Appeals Chamber also finds that Stojić fails to show an error regarding the Trial Chamber's reference to "all the evidence analysed above". It is clear from the structure of its analysis what evidence the Trial Chamber relied on to determine that Stojić knew of crimes being committed against Muslims with the sole purpose of forcing them to leave BiH. Indeed, in the section titled "Bruno Stojić's Responsibility under JCE I", the Trial Chamber systematically outlined, under various subsections, the evidence showing Stojić's knowledge of crimes against the Muslims in the municipalities and detention centres, including his knowledge of evictions of Muslims, and made relevant findings.[5962] Following that analysis, the Trial Chamber arrived at a number of conclusions, including the conclusion as to Stojić's knowledge, consistently referring to the evidence it outlined in the section as a whole.[5963] Stojić's argument that he is prejudiced by the Trial Chamber's reference to "all the evidence analysed above" is therefore not persuasive.[5964]

1795. As for Stojić's submission that the Trial Chamber disregarded evidence favourable to him when considering his discriminatory intent, the Appeals Chamber notes that the Trial Chamber did not refer to this evidence when concluding on Stojić's discriminatory intent.[5965] However, the Appeals Chamber recalls that a trial chamber is not under an obligation to refer to the testimony of every witness and that it is to be presumed that it evaluated all the evidence presented to it, as long as there is no indication that it completely disregarded any evidence which is clearly relevant.[5966] A trial chamber is also not required to set out in detail why it accepted or rejected a particular testimony.[5967] However, a trial chamber must provide reasons for accepting testimony despite alleged or material inconsistencies when it is the principal evidence relied upon to convict an accused.[5968] Additionally, the Appeals Chamber recalls that if a trial chamber failed to refer to the evidence given by a witness, even if it is in contradiction to its finding, it is to be presumed that the **[page 748]** trial chamber assessed and weighed that evidence, but found that it did not prevent it from making its findings.[5969]

1796. The Appeals Chamber notes that, in the context of his control over the HVO and in sentencing, the Trial Chamber discussed some of the evidence Stojić relies on here going to his relationships with the Muslim side and to his good character,[5970] which indicates that it was cognisant of and assessed this evidence but found that it did not prevent it from reaching its conclusions on Stojić's discriminatory intent. With respect to other evidence raised by Stojić,[5971] the Appeals Chamber, having analysed that evidence,[5972] finds

[5961]   See *supra*, fn. 5955.

[5962]   See Trial Judgement, Vol. 4, paras 326-424. See also *supra*, para. 1792 & fn. 5955. For example, the Trial Chamber found that Stojić knew of the evictions of Muslims in Čapljina and participated in organising the eviction of Muslims in West Mostar. Trial Judgement, Vol. 4, paras 350-357, 373-378. It also found that he knew of the harsh conditions the Muslim detainees suffered in the Heliodrom, Dretelj Prison, and Gabela Prison. Trial Judgement, Vol. 4, paras 384-395, 397-407.

[5963]   See Trial Judgement, Vol. 4, paras 426 ("As it established above"), 428 ("In view of all the evidence analysed above"), 429 ("all the evidence analysed above").

[5964]   See *supra*, para. 1767.

[5965]   See Trial Judgement, Vol. 4, para. 429.

[5966]   *Tolimir* Appeal Judgement, para. 53; *Popović et al.* Appeal Judgement, paras 925, 1017; *Kvočka et al.* Appeal Judgement, para. 23.

[5967]   *Popović et al.* Appeal Judgement, para. 133; *Krajišnik* Appeal Judgement, para. 139.

[5968]   *Popović et al.* Appeal Judgement, para. 133; *Haradinaj et al.* Appeal Judgement, paras 129, 134, 252; *Kupreškić et al.* Appeal Judgement, paras 135, 202.

[5969]   *Kvočka et al.* Appeal Judgement, para. 23.

[5970]   Trial Judgement, Vol. 4, paras 308, 1334 & fns 732, 2481, referring to Hamid Bahto, T(F). 37900 (11 Mar 2009), Nedžad Čengić, T(F). 37943-37945, 37951 (11 Mar 2009). The Appeals Chamber observes that the Trial Chamber noted that Witness Nedžad Čengić and Stojić were friends. Trial Judgement, Vol. 4, fn. 2481.

[5971]   Stojić's Appeal Brief, para. 219 (referring to the evidence of Witnesses Antoon van der Grinten, Davor Korać, Tomislav Krešić, Stipo Buljan, and Ivan Bagarić).

[5972]   Antoon van der Grinten, T. 21023-21024 (10 July 2007) (stating that the Appellants, including Stojić, expressed no derogatory views concerning Muslims); Davor Korać, T. 38827, 38829-38830 (7 Apr 2009) (stating that Stojić, while serving as the Assistant Minister of the Interior of BiH prior to the conflict, did not have any issues with different ethnicities working at that ministry); Tomislav Krešić, T. 38736 (2 Apr 2009) (stating that some of Stojić's best friends before the conflict were Muslims and Serbs); Stipo

that Stojić does not show that it calls into question the findings of the Trial Chamber, particularly as he knew of the crimes targeting Muslims and continued to participate in the JCE. Thus, it was reasonable for the Trial Chamber not to refer to that evidence when discussing Stojić's discriminatory intent. Similarly, the fact that the Trial Chamber found that Stojić supplied materiel and technical equipment to ABiH and that the Department of Defence provided humanitarian aid to East Mostar, shows that despite being cognisant of these facts, the Trial Chamber did not consider them important enough to affect its finding on Stojić's discriminatory intent. Indeed, with respect to the supply of humanitarian aid to East Mostar, the Trial Chamber also noted that it was sporadic and conditional on securing "gains" in negotiations with ABiH.[5973] In any event, even if these findings were considered to be favourable to Stojić, the evidence of limited and selective assistance towards a few individuals does not preclude a trier of fact from reasonably finding that the requisite intent to discriminate existed.[5974]

1797. Accordingly, for all the reasons outlined above, Stojić has failed to demonstrate that the Trial Chamber erred in concluding that he possessed discriminatory intent. Stojić's sub-ground of appeal 25.5 is therefore dismissed. **[page 749]**

(h) Alleged errors concerning Stojić's intent to commit the crimes in Prozor, Jablanica, East Mostar, Čapljina, Vareš, and the detention centres (Stojić's Sub-ground 25.6)

1798. Stojić submits that the Trial Chamber failed to expressly find that he intended the crimes committed in Prozor, Jablanica, East Mostar, Čapljina, Vareš, and the detention centres, as it simply inferred that he "accepted" the crimes because he knew they had been committed and yet continued to exercise his official functions.[5975] According to Stojić, the Trial Chamber erred in law in inferring his intent in this way since intent must be assessed at the time the crime is committed whereas his knowledge of crimes was usually obtained from reports, after the crimes took place.[5976] He further asserts that in inferring his intent in this way, the Trial Chamber eradicated the distinction between JCE I and JCE III as knowledge and acceptance of crimes are intrinsic elements of the latter, not the former.[5977] Stojić also claims that intent is not the only reasonable inference from his continuation in office as that can be motivated by many factors, including "general support for the HZHB".[5978] Finally, Stojić submits that no reasonable chamber could have concluded that he knew that crimes had been committed in the five municipalities and the detention centres.[5979]

1799. The Prosecution responds that the Trial Chamber reasonably relied on Stojić's knowledge of crimes and his continuation in office when finding that he had the shared intent since, by remaining as Head of the Department of Defence, he continued to contribute to the CCP.[5980] It further submits that the Trial Chamber's approach did not confuse JCE I and JCE III liability.[5981]

Buljan, T. 36751-36752, 36766, 36768 (11 Feb 2009) (stating that Stojić made an effort to look after all HVO members regardless of their ethnicity); Ivan Bagarić, T. 38879-38880, 38947-38948 (20 Apr 2009) (stating that the Health Section of the Department of Defence looked after anyone who needed medical care, regardless of their ethnicity, and that it also employed experts regardless of their ethnicity).

[5973]   Trial Judgement, Vol. 2, para. 1243. The Trial Chamber also dismissed the supply of MTS as a factor that would demonstrate good character on behalf of Stojić. Trial Judgement, Vol. 4, para. 1334.

[5974]   See *Ndahimana* Appeal Judgement, para. 195; *Muhimana* Appeal Judgement, para. 32; *Rutaganda* Appeal Judgement, para. 537. See also *Kvočka et al.* Appeal Judgement, para. 233 (finding that evidence that Miroslav Kvočka was a tolerant and politically moderate man who was close to the Muslim community did not preclude a conclusion that he intended to further a joint criminal enterprise whose purpose was to persecute non-Serbs).

[5975]   Stojić's Appeal Brief, para. 221, referring to, *inter alia,* Trial Judgement, Vol. 4, paras 329, 342, 363, 370, 378, 383, 395-396, 407. See also Stojić's Appeal Brief, para. 222. Stojić contends that his convictions pertaining to these locations should be overturned and that the Trial Chamber's errors "fatally undermine" his responsibility under JCE I liability. Stojić's Appeal Brief, para. 227.

[5976]   Stojić's Appeal Brief, para. 223, referring to Trial Judgement, Vol. 4, paras 338-339.

[5977]   Stojić's Appeal Brief, para. 224, referring to *Stanišić and Simatović* Trial Judgement, Vol. 2, paras 2326, 2412-2415.

[5978]   Stojić's Appeal Brief, para. 225. Stojić also contends that "mere continuation in office is an insufficient foundation for an inference of intent because there is no nexus between continuation in office and specific crimes". Stojić's Appeal Brief, para. 225.

[5979]   Stojić's Appeal Brief, para. 226 (referring to his submissions in his grounds of appeal 28, 29.2, 30, 33.1, 33.3, 34.1, 34.4, 35, 36.1, 36.3, 37.2, and 40). See also Stojić's Reply Brief, para. 66.

[5980]   Prosecution's Response Brief (Stojić), para. 189, referring to Trial Judgement, Vol. 4, para. 426, *Đorđević* Appeal Judgement, paras 512-513, *Krajišnik* Appeal Judgement, para. 697. The Prosecution submits that Stojić's continuation in office was not the only factor relied on to find that he had the shared intent. Prosecution's Response Brief (Stojić), para. 189.

[5981]   Prosecution's Response Brief (Stojić), para. 189.

1800. As noted above, the Trial Chamber inferred Stojić's intent for the crimes that took place in the municipalities and detention centres from his participation in the HVO military operations in Mostar and Vareš, and from his continued exercise of control over the armed forces while knowing of the crimes they committed in other municipalities.[5982] Thus, the fact that he was found to have known of and accepted the crimes in Prozor, Jablanica, East Mostar, Čapljina, Vareš, and detention **[page 750]** centres was merely one of the factors used by the Trial Chamber to find his intent for all the crimes that formed part of the CCP. The Appeals Chamber recalls here that the requisite *mens rea* for a conviction under JCE I can be inferred from a person's knowledge of the common plan, combined with his continuous participation in the JCE, if this is the only reasonable inference available on the evidence.[5983] In this case, the Trial Chamber considered that Stojić was the link between the Government and the HVO military component and that he continued exercising his official functions despite having knowledge of the crimes committed by that military component.[5984] It also found that he shared the intent to further the CCP together with the other JCE members[5985] and that his contribution to the JCE was significant.[5986] Stojić fails to show an error in the Trial Chamber's reasoning in this respect.

1801. While Stojić submits that there was another reasonable inference to be drawn from his continuation in office, he also claims that "[i]n the absence of other evidence or findings, mere continuation in office" is insufficient to infer intent.[5987] However, the Appeals Chamber reiterates that Stojić's continuation in office, and thereby his continued control over the armed forces perpetrating the crimes, was not the only factor used in the Trial Chamber's conclusion. Rather, as outlined above,[5988] the Trial Chamber also relied on other factors such as his planning of the HVO military operations in Mostar and his involvement in evictions in West Mostar. In light of those activities, considered together with the Trial Chamber's findings that Stojić continued in office despite knowing of crimes and that he failed to stop or punish those crimes,[5989] Stojić fails to show that the Trial Chamber erred in concluding that the only reasonable inference it could draw was that he intended those crimes.

1802. Moreover, the Appeals Chamber is not convinced by Stojić's submission that knowledge of crimes typically obtained from reports after the fact cannot support an inference that he possessed the requisite intent to commit the crimes in question. Importantly, the Trial Chamber found that Stojić, with the other JCE members, intended the crimes falling within the CCP, *i.e.* Counts 1, 6-9, 10-20, 24-25,[5990] based on his participation in military operations, knowledge and acceptance of crimes, and his failure to act coupled with his continued participation in the JCE.[5991] Notably, the Trial Chamber made clear findings that Stojić planned, facilitated, and knew of the crimes **[page 751]** committed in Gornji Vakuf in January 1993.[5992] It then found that Stojić knew of the crimes that were being committed later during the JCE period, including in Jablanica, East Mostar, Čapljina, Vareš, and the detention centres, and yet continued to participate in the JCE.[5993] In this regard, the Appeals Chamber recalls that it is not necessary for a participant in a JCE to know of each specific crime committed in order to be criminally liable for it.[5994] Rather, it suffices that a JCE member

---

[5982] See *supra*, para. 1792.
[5983] *Popović et al.* Appeal Judgement, para. 1652, referring to, *inter alia, Đorđević* Appeal Judgement, para. 512, *Krajišnik* Appeal Judgement, paras 202, 204, 697, *Brđanin* Appeal Judgement, paras 428-429.
[5984] Trial Judgement, Vol. 4, paras 425-426, 429. See Trial Judgement, Vol. 4, paras 1227, 1230.
[5985] Trial Judgement, Vol. 4, para. 428. See also *supra*, paras 1759-1760.
[5986] Trial Judgement, Vol. 4, para. 429.
[5987] Stojić's Appeal Brief, para. 225.
[5988] See *supra*, paras 1792, 1800.
[5989] See Trial Judgement, Vol. 4, paras 415, 423, 427.
[5990] Trial Judgement, Vol. 4, paras 68, 426, 428-429.
[5991] See *supra*, para. 1800.
[5992] See *supra*, paras 1561, 1569, 1575, 1579.
[5993] Trial Judgement, Vol. 4, paras 342, 363, 378, 426. The Appeals Chamber recalls that it has reversed the findings that Stojić knew of and accepted the detention of men who did not belong to any armed forces in Prozor and Ljubuški Prison. *See, supra*, paras 1560, 1710, 1712.
[5994] *Tolimir* Appeal Judgement, para. 474; *Kvočka et al.* Appeal Judgement, para. 276. See *Šainović et al.* Appeal Judgement, para. 1491 (where the Appeals Chamber concluded that as a participant in the joint criminal enterprise, Sreten Lukić need not have known of each specific crime committed in order to be criminally liable. It concluded that it sufficed "that he shared the intent for the commission of these crimes and acted in furtherance of the common purpose". Therefore, the Appeals Chamber found that Lukić's submission that he lacked specific knowledge of the crimes committed in Prizren municipality to be inapposite).

knows that crimes are being committed according to a common plan and knowingly participates in that plan in a way that facilitates the commission of a crime or which allows the criminal enterprise to function effectively or efficiently.[5995] Therefore, it was not a requirement for the Trial Chamber to find, as an example, that Stojić knew the specific evictions in Čapljina at the time they occurred as he was found to have intended evictions as part of the CCP from January 1993. Stojić thus fails to show any error in the Trial Chamber's reasoning, even if he received reports on some criminal incidents committed in certain locations after they occurred.

1803. Further, the Appeals Chamber rejects Stojić's argument that, by using knowledge and acceptance of crimes to infer intent for those crimes, the Trial Chamber eradicated the distinction between the requirements of JCE I and JCE III.[5996] The crimes forming part of the CCP, including the crimes in Prozor, Jablanica, East Mostar, Čapljina, Vareš, and detention centres, were specifically intended by Stojić and the other JCE members.[5997] Further, contrary to Stojić's submission, knowledge and acceptance of crimes by continued participation are not "intrinsic elements" of JCE III. Rather, liability under JCE III arises when crimes are committed which, while not part of the common criminal plan, were foreseeable to the accused and he willingly took that risk.[5998] As such, this form of liability does not necessarily require knowledge and/or acceptance of **[page 752]** deviatory crimes but rather the knowledge that they were a natural and foreseeable consequence of the common criminal purpose.[5999]

1804. Based on the foregoing, Stojić fails to show that no reasonable trier of fact could have concluded that he had the intent to commit the JCE I crimes in Prozor, Jablanica, East Mostar, Čapljina, Vareš, and the detention centres. His sub-ground of appeal 25.6 is therefore dismissed.[6000]

(i) Conclusion

1805. In sum, the Appeals Chamber has dismissed all of Stojić's challenges to his *mens rea* under his sub-ground of appeal 25.

10. Conclusion

1806. Based on the above sections addressing his challenges to the findings on his JCE contribution and *mens rea,* the Appeals Chamber concludes that Stojić has failed to demonstrate any error which has an impact on the Trial Chamber's findings that: (1) a plurality of persons, including Stojić, consulted with each other to devise and implement the CCP; (2) Stojić continuously contributed to the JCE between January 1993 and 15 November 1993; (3) Stojić's contribution, which included the use of the HVO and the Military Police to commit crimes, was significant and furthered the CCP; (4) Stojić shared the intent to expel the Muslim population from the territory of Herceg-Bosna with other JCE members; (5) Stojić shared the intent to carry out the crimes forming part of the CCP; and (6) Stojić intended to discriminate against Muslims in order to facilitate their eviction from the territory of Herceg-Bosna.[6001] Therefore, the Appeals Chamber upholds the majority of Stojić's convictions under JCE I for the various crimes forming part of the CCP and committed prior to the end of his JCE membership on 15 November 1993.

[5995] *Tolimir* Appeal Judgement, para. 474. See *Šainović et al.* Appeal Judgement, para. 1491 ("It suffices that he shared the intent for the commission of [the] crimes and acted in furtherance of the common purpose").

[5996] Stojić's Appeal Brief, para. 224.

[5997] The Appeals Chamber recalls its finding that no reasonable trier of fact could conclude that murder and wilful killing were part of the CCP from January 1993 until June 1993. See *supra,* para. 882. This means that Stojić did not have the intent for murder and wilful killing from January 1993 until June 1993. In that respect, the Appeals Chamber recalls its finding overturning his convictions for murder and wilful killing in relation to two killings in Tošćanica, Prozor Municipality. See *supra,* paras 880-882.

[5998] *Stanišić and Župljanin* Appeal Judgement, para. 967; *Popović et al.* Appeal Judgement, para. 1431, quoting *Brđanin* Appeal Judgement, para. 365. See *Tolimir* Appeal Judgement, para. 514 (requiring that the possibility be "reasonably foreseeable to the accused"); *Šainović et al.* Appeal Judgement, paras 1078, 1538, 1575.

[5999] See *Kvočka et al.* Appeal Judgement, paras 83, 86.

[6000] With respect to Stojić's argument that no reasonable trial chamber could have concluded that he knew that the crimes had been committed in Prozor, Jablanica, East Mostar, Čapljina, Vareš, and the detention centres, the Appeals Chamber notes that it has dismissed most of his challenges in that respect. This argument is therefore moot. See *supra,* paras 1551-1748.

[6001] Trial Judgement, Vol. 4, paras 425-430, 1220, 1227, 1230-1232.

1807. Furthermore, the Appeals Chamber recalls that it has reversed the findings that Stojić knew of and accepted the detention of men who did not belong to any armed forces in Prozor and Ljubuški Prison.[6002] However, it also recalls that the crimes resulting from the detention of civilians – except for murder in Prozor Municipality – were crimes forming part of the CCP which were intended by Stojić to be committed. Thus, the reversal of a finding that he knew of and accepted specific criminal incidents does not affect his conviction for those crimes under JCE I liability. **[page 753]** Lastly, the impact, if any, on sentencing with regard to the finding that Stojić cannot be held responsible for crimes occurring after 15 November 1993, including certain incidents of sniping and destruction of mosques in Mostar under Count 21, will be addressed below.[6003]

Editor's note: The second part of this judgement will be published in volume 70. In that volume the commentary written by Luke Moffett is published.

[6002] See *supra*, para. 1560.
[6003] See *supra*, fn. 5395. See *infra*, para. 3361.

CONTRIBUTORS AND EDITORS

Peta-Louise Bagott is a barrister at Doughty Street Chambers, London. She obtained her LL.B. from Durham University and her LL.M. (Adv.) from Leiden University. She was called to the Bar in 2011 and specialises in domestic and international crime. Her international practice includes defending in numerous high-profile cases, as well as filing submissions as *amicus curiae*.

Enikő Deák obtained her LL.B. in European Law from Maastricht University, where she mainly focused on criminal law and human rights. She also holds an MA in Translation has been a Trainee at the European Parliament. She has a decade of experience in project management. She is also the assistant-editor for the Annotated Leading Cases of International Criminal Tribunals.

Alberto Di Martino is Professor of Criminal Law at the Sant'Anna School of Advanced Studies, Pisa, Italy. He also lectured in International and Comparative Criminal Law at the University of Pisa. He was member of Italian delegations to the OECD Working Group of Bribery in International Business Transactions, member of Law Commissions at the Ministry of Justice, Municipal Guarantor of Prisoners' Rights – City of Pisa. Among several publications, he is author of books on rules of extraterritorial criminal jurisdiction ("La frontiera e il diritto penale. Natura e contesto delle norme di diritto penale transnazionale", 2006 [The Frontier and The Criminal Law. Nature and Context of Rules on Transnational Criminal Law]), on labour exploitation ("Sfruttamento del lavoro. Il valore del contesto nella definzione del reato", 2019), editor of the Italian translation of the professor Werle's book "Völkerstrafrecht", co-editor of the book "The Court of Justice and European Criminal Law. Leading Cases in a Contextual Analysis", 2019 (with V. Mitsilegas and L. Mancano).

Steven Freeland is Emeritus Professor of International Law at Western Sydney University, where he was previously Dean of the School of Law, and Professorial Fellow at Bond University. He also holds Visiting or Adjunct positions at various other Universities/Institutes in Copenhagen, Vienna, Toulouse, Hong Kong, Montreal, Kuala Lumpur and London. Prior to becoming an academic, he had a 20-year career as an international commercial lawyer and an investment banker. He is a Member of the Advisory Group of the Australian Space Agency and has been an advisor to the Australian, New Zealand, Norwegian and several other Governments on issues relating to national space legislative frameworks and policy. He has represented the Australian Government at the Committee on the Peaceful Uses of Outer Space (UNCOPUOS) and has also been appointed by UNCOPUOS to co-chair multilateral discussions on the exploration, exploitation and utilisation of space resources. He has also been a Visiting Professional within the Appeals Chamber at the International Criminal Court, and a Special Advisor to the Danish Foreign Ministry in matters related to the International Criminal Court. He is a Co-Principal of specialised space law firm Azimuth Advisory and also a Director of the International Institute of Space Law, and a Member of the Space Law Committee of the International Law Association and of the Space Law and War Crimes Committees of the International Bar Association. In addition to co-Editing the *Annotated Leading Cases of International Criminal Tribunals* book series, he also sits on the Editorial Board / Advisory Board of a number of internationally recognised academic journals.

André Klip (1965) is Professor of Criminal Law, Criminal Procedure and the Transnational Aspects of Criminal Law at Maastricht University. Since 2016, he is a member of the Royal Netherlands Academy of Arts and Sciences. He conducted research at the Yale Law School, New Haven and the Max Planck Institute in Freiburg im Breisgau. He is a member of the Board of Directors of the International Association of Penal Law. He is author of European Criminal Law. An integrative Approach (Intersentia Cambridge, 4th edition 2021). Throughout his career, professor Klip has been frequently involved in national and international legal practice. Both as an academic and as a practitioner he is very much engaged in international cooperation. As a member of the Maastricht Institute for Criminal Sciences he heads an interdisciplinary research group which is frequently invited to conduct studies on crime, perpetrators and how to combat it. He is a Judge at the 's-Hertogenbosch Court of Appeal (criminal division) in the Netherlands.

Marnie Lloydd (BA/LLB(Hons) *Wellington*, MA *Bochum*, LLM *Geneva*, PhD *Melbourne*) is Lecturer at Victoria University of Wellington – Te Herenga Waka, Faculty of Law, New Zealand. She researches and teaches in the areas of international law related to armed conflict, migration and refugee law, counter-terrorism and humanitarianism. Prior to joining academia, she worked as Legal Advisor with the International Committee of the Red Cross and with the UNHCR.

Milton Keynes UK
Ingram Content Group UK Ltd.
UKHW050152230424
441576UK00009B/588

9 781839 702021